THE
MOTION PICTURE
GUIDE

★ ★ ★ ★ ★ ★ ★ ★ ★ ★ ★ ★ ★ ★ ★ ★ ★ ★ ★

1996 ANNUAL

THE MOTION PICTURE GUIDE

★ ★ ★ ★ ★ ★ ★ ★ ★ ★ ★ ★ ★ ★ ★ ★ ★ ★ ★ ★

1996 ANNUAL
(THE FILMS OF 1995)

Editorial Director : James Pallot

Editor : Jacob Levich

Associate Editors : Ken Fox

Maitland McDonagh

Contributing Editors : Shampa Banerjee

Charles Cassady Jr.

Penny Perkins

Gavin Smith

CineBooks

Published by CineBooks, a division of News America Publishing Incorporated,
620 Avenue of the Americas, 6th Floor, New York, NY 10011

© 1996, News America Publishing Incorporated.
First Edition
Printed in the United States
1 2 3 4 5 6 7 8 9 10

Library of Congress Catalog Number 8571145

ISBN: 0-933997-00-0 THE MOTION PICTURE GUIDE (10 Vols.)
ISBN: 0-933997-11-6 THE MOTION PICTURE GUIDE INDEX (2 Vols.)
ISBN: 0-933997-37-X THE MOTION PICTURE GUIDE 1996 ANNUAL
                    (THE FILMS OF 1995)

TABLE OF CONTENTS

FOREWORD

The 1996 *Motion Picture Guide Annual*, covering films released in the US during 1995, is the eleventh supplement to the original, 12-volume *Motion Picture Guide*. Our scope continues to broaden, particularly in the documentary area, even as we maintain the depth and accuracy of coverage that *Motion Picture Guide* readers have come to expect. In addition, this year's volume presents cast and credit information in more detail and with greater precision than ever before. This is entirely due to the extraordinary dedication and energy of our new Associate Editor, Ken Fox. Our other Associate Editor, Maitland McDonagh, has shouldered a greater editorial burden this year, and her singular wit and judgment are evident throughout this volume.

Thanks are also due to our staff of contributing editors, as distinguished and shrewd a group of cinephiles as any reference editor could desire, and to our ever-expanding roster of reviewers. We're also grateful to Frank Lovece, for whom this year's obituary section was a true labor of love; and to Noel Harrington, who annually performs the small miracle of transforming a mass of electronic data into a real book. As always, we welcome your comments, which should be sent to us at the address on the copyright page.

<table>
<tr><td>James Pallot</td><td>Jo Imeson</td><td>Jacob Levich</td></tr>
<tr><td>Editorial Director</td><td>Business Director</td><td>Editor</td></tr>
</table>

The Year in Review

While social scientists make sense of the world with reference to facts and figures, editors tend to measure the zeitgeist by clichés. Every year, it seems, a distinct set of buzzwords magically emerges from the pens and PCs of film critics nationwide. These briefly fashionable formulations may not represent the accumulated wisdom of mankind, but they are intriguing verbal snapshots of a culture that refuses to hold still long enough for us to take its true measure.

To the diverse and far-flung bunch who write *The Motion Picture Guide*, 1995 marked the resurgence of "the kind of movie they don't make anymore." The year after *Pulp Fiction*, which was supposed to usher in a new era of hip, jaundiced "alternative" cinema, was dominated by old-fashioned dramas of square-jawed men in peril (*Apollo 13*, *Crimson Tide*); lavishly appointed costume pictures (*Braveheart*, *Rob Roy*, *Restoration*); a campy reinvention of a 1930s comic book (*Batman Forever*); and the relentlessly traditional Disney formula (*Pocahontas*, *Toy Story*). We poor drudges who edit film books may not have any special wisdom to impart to the world, but we're in a good position to spot trends: after reading 10 or 12 reviews of "the kind of movie they don't make anymore," it's hard not to conclude that, yes, they *do* make that kind of movie, over and over again. Perhaps they never really stopped.

Very few of these backward-looking mainstream productions were real stinkers—not even *The Perez Family* sent audiences screaming for the exits—and indeed, the technical qualities, performances, and narrative competence of the average Hollywood film may have been higher in 1995 than at any time since the heyday of the studio system. But something intangible—call it inspiration—seemed to have been left out of the equation. The much-discussed explosion of interest in cult video—e.g., Hong Kong cheapies, Italian horror, even industrial documentaries—probably had less to do with the actual virtues of such fare than with the frustrating sameness of big-time corporate product.

The independent scene, sometimes considered the wellspring of aesthetic innovation and topical daring, offered little relief to jaded moviegoers. In 1995, the quintessential indie success story was *The Brothers McMullen*, a blandly pleasant, thoroughly conventional family drama that charmed the Sundance jury and went on to become, percentage-wise, the most profitable film of the year; needless to say, it won its 27-year-old director a lucrative Hollywood contract. While many welcomed the return of "family values" and "solid entertainment" to the indie screen, others grumbled that Sundance had become less a showcase for the cutting edge than a convenient site for industry moguls to audition and assimilate new talent.

Meanwhile, what promised to be the year's most scandalous independent, Larry Clark's *Kids*, emerged as little more than *Reefer Madness* for the age of AIDS. Disney had sought to hide its financial interest in *Kids* by forcing its subsidiary, Miramax, to release the film under a corporate pseudonym, but it needn't have bothered. Clark cleverly seeded his titillating subject matter—teen sex and drug abuse—with enough fear, loathing, and cautionary finger-wagging to keep the most reactionary would-be censors at bay. Movie-goers with a yen for truly perverse Disney fare would have to wait for *James and the Giant Peach*.

But if there was little on screen in 1995 that was actually startling or entirely fresh, many of the year's most satisfying movies were those which managed to wring some measure of novelty from familiar forms. These were not, for the most part, supercilious "postmodern" recyclings of the cultural past *à la* Tarantino, but intelligently self-conscious films that showed real respect and affection for the movie traditions within which they operated.

In *Devil in a Blue Dress*, for instance, Carl Franklin found disturbing new meanings in the classic private eye narrative by talking as his protagonist an African-American in racist Los Angeles. Rarely has a detective's conventional status as an "outsider" carried so much cultural weight and historical significance. Another LA-based crime picture, Michael Mann's *Heat*, reexamined the Hawksian themes of professionalism and masculine honor in the context of a market-driven society that has little use for either.

A more benign, if no less rigid, set of Southern California rituals was dissected in *Clueless*, a good-natured high school comedy that effortlessly transcended its genre. Director-writer Amy Heckerling based her story on Jane Austen's *Emma*, but the film's real triumph—the invention of a whole new dialect to go with its fanciful milieu—inspired comparisons with P.G. Wodehouse and Anthony Burgess.

1995's crop of neo-noirs was even more transgressive (if arguably less substantial) than those of the past several years—the best of these blended noir with horror (*Seven*) or sci-fi (*Twelve Monkeys*). But the honors for the year's most audacious genre-bending must go to

Todd Haynes, whose chilling satire of recovery culture, *Safe*, was inspired by disease-of-the-week telefilms like *The Boy in the Plastic Bubble*. The story of a woman who becomes allergic to life itself, *Safe* brilliantly politicized the personal, rendering a miniature portrait of a society in crisis that was far more persuasive than many avowedly "political" films—e.g., the ambitious, wildly flawed *Strange Days* or the ploddingly liberal *Dead Man Walking*.

Of course, viewers with a taste for political cinema have long since learned not to expect much from Hollywood; in 1995, as usual, they were far better served by foreign-language films. Milcho Manchevski's *Before the Rain*, billed as the first feature made in Macedonia, was a glossy, mystical, ultimately pessimistic take on the worldwide ripples caused by Balkan genocide. Less elliptical but even more haunting was Gianni Amelio's *Lamerica*, a sprawling, passionately realized canvas of Albania in the wake of Communist collapse and capitalist "reform." Even André Téchiné's exquisite coming-of-age story, *Wild Reeds*, was not the nostalgic reverie many viewers anticipated. This small-scale melodrama, set in the France of 1962, was chiefly concerned with charting the effects of extraordinary events—foreign wars, imperialist adventures, ideological crises—on ordinary lives.

To many, discovering the extraordinary essence of ordinary things—seeing the world in a grain of sand, as Blake famously put it—is still the hallmark, and indeed the very purpose, of artistic endeavor. If this sort of insight was getting hard to find on US screens in 1995, it would have been much rarer but for the nationwide rerelease of nine of Satyajit Ray's finest films. This, perhaps, was the year's most important cinematic event. To a generation of movie-lovers who discovered *Pather Panchali*, *Charulata*, and *The Music Room* for the first time, the Ray series was stark testimony to the revelatory potential and sheer sensual beauty of cinema at its best—quite literally, though in a very different sense, the kind of movies they don't make anymore.

Jacob Levich
New York City
May 1996

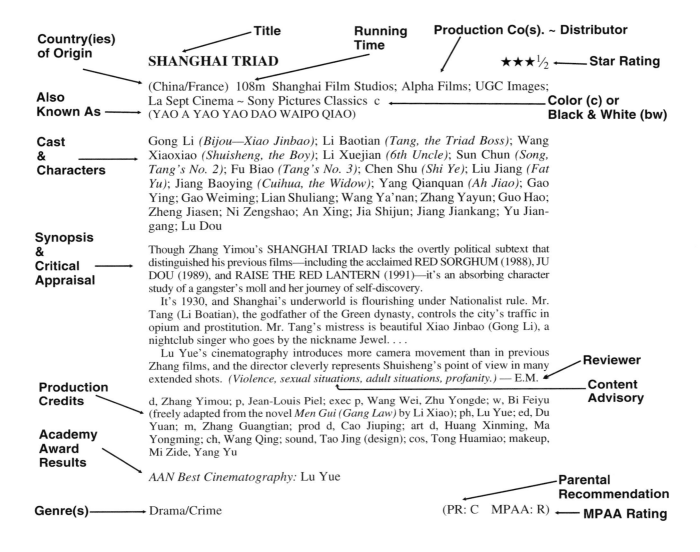

Country(ies) of Origin → SHANGHAI TRIAD ← **Title**

Running Time

Production Co(s). ~ Distributor

★★★½ ← **Star Rating**

(China/France) 108m Shanghai Film Studios; Alpha Films; UGC Images;
La Sept Cinema ~ Sony Pictures Classics c ← **Color (c) or Black & White (bw)**

Also Known As → (YAO A YAO YAO DAO WAIPO QIAO)

Cast & Characters —

Gong Li *(Bijou—Xiao Jinbao)*; Li Baotian *(Tang, the Triad Boss)*; Wang Xiaoxiao *(Shuisheng, the Boy)*; Li Xuejian *(6th Uncle)*; Sun Chun *(Song, Tang's No. 2)*; Fu Biao *(Tang's No. 3)*; Chen Shu *(Shi Ye)*; Liu Jiang *(Fat Yu)*; Jiang Baoying *(Cuihua, the Widow)*; Yang Qianquan *(Ah Jiao)*; Gao Ying; Gao Weiming; Lian Shuliang; Wang Ya'nan; Zhang Yayun; Guo Hao; Zheng Jiasen; Ni Zengshao; An Xing; Jia Shijun; Jiang Jiankang; Yu Jian-gang; Lu Dou

Synopsis & Critical Appraisal →

Though Zhang Yimou's SHANGHAI TRIAD lacks the overtly political subtext that distinguished his previous films—including the acclaimed RED SORGHUM (1988), JU DOU (1989), and RAISE THE RED LANTERN (1991)—it's an absorbing character study of a gangster's moll and her journey of self-discovery.

It's 1930, and Shanghai's underworld is flourishing under Nationalist rule. Mr. Tang (Li Boatian), the godfather of the Green dynasty, controls the city's traffic in opium and prostitution. Mr. Tang's mistress is beautiful Xiao Jinbao (Gong Li), a nightclub singer who goes by the nickname Jewel. . . .

Lu Yue's cinematography introduces more camera movement than in previous Zhang films, and the director cleverly represents Shuisheng's point of view in many extended shots. *(Violence, sexual situations, adult situations, profanity.)* — E.M. ← **Reviewer** / **Content Advisory**

Production Credits —

d, Zhang Yimou; p, Jean-Louis Piel; exec p, Wang Wei, Zhu Yongde; w, Bi Feiyu (freely adapted from the novel *Men Gui (Gang Law)* by Li Xiao); ph, Lu Yue; ed, Du Yuan; m, Zhang Guangtian; prod d, Cao Jiuping; art d, Huang Xinming, Ma Yongming; ch, Wang Qing; sound, Tao Jing (design); cos, Tong Huamiao; makeup, Mi Zide, Yang Yu

Academy Award Results —

AAN Best Cinematography: Lu Yue

Parental Recommendation

Genre(s) → Drama/Crime

(PR: C   MPAA: R) ← **MPAA Rating**

INFORMATION KEY

Titles

All entries are arranged alphabetically by title, with articles (A, AN, THE) appearing after the main title.

International Productions

When a film has been produced by a country or countries other than the US, these are noted in parentheses on the first line following the title.

Production Companies/Distributor

The film's production company or companies are listed first, with a tilde (~) separating them from the distributor.

Production Credits

The credits for the creative and technical personnel of a film include: d (director); p (producer); exp (exec. producer); asp (assoc. producer); cop (co-producer); w (writer); ph (cinematographer); ed (editor); m (music composer); md (music director); prod d (production designer); art d (art director); set d (set decorator); anim (animation); chor (choreography); sound; fx (special effects); casting; cos (costumes); makeup; stunts; tech (technical adviser).

Academy Award Results

Academy Award information is preceded by *AA,* for a winner, or *AAN,* for a nominee, followed by the category and the name of the recipient, where appropriate.

Genres

Each film is classified by up to three genres drawn from the following list: Action, Adventure, Animated, Biography, Children's, Comedy, Crime, Dance, Disaster, Docudrama, Documentary, Drama, Erotic, Fantasy, Historical, Horror, Martial Arts, Musical, Mystery, Opera, Political, Prison, Religious, Romance, Science Fiction, Sports, Spy, Thriller, War, Western.

Parental Recommendations

The parental recommendation (PR) provides parents with an indication of the film's suitability for children. The recommendations are as follows: AA – good for children; A – acceptable for children; C – cautionary, some scenes my be objectionable for children; O – objectionable for children.

Film Reviews

ABDUCTED 2: THE REUNION

(U.S.) 91m Melenny Productions; Arrow Entertainment; Reunion Productions ~ Bullseye Video c

Dan Haggerty *(Joe Evans)*; Jan-Michael Vincent *(Brad Allen)*; Raquel Bianca *(Maria Marcolini)*; Debbie Rochon *(Sharon Baker)*; Donna Jason *(Ingrid Weinhard)*; Nicholas Buchart *(Jack Webster)*; Jim Leard *(Harry)*; Jody Andrews *(Harry's Mother)*; Kenneth Kantymir *(Hunter)*; Marcus James *(Italian Lover)*; Lawrence King *(Vern)*

The original ABDUCTED was a quickie cranked out to cash in on a bizarre actual incident in which a young female athlete was briefly held hostage as a potential mate by forest-dwelling father-and-son recluses. Heavily embellishing the facts (for true-crime freaks there was a namesake TV movie ABDUCTED: THE KARI SWENSON STORY) 1986's ABDUCTED ended with the psycho suitor Vern apparently killed, but that didn't dissuade this schlock sequel by the same filmmakers.

Three women—divorcee Sharon (Debbie Rochon), Italian emigre Maria (Raquel Bianca), and Amazonian Ingrid (Donna Jason)—choose an off-season campsite for their slumber party. Nearly forced off the road by sleazeball Brad Allen (Jan-Michael Vincent), who's paying big bucks to stalk endangered species under the tutelage of Joe Evans (Dan Haggerty), the trio soon experience more serious man trouble. Creature-masked hillbilly Vern (Lawrence King), alive after all, trusses up the trio and drags them off as bridal material. Kickboxer Ingrid pretends to start a striptease, then beats the tar out of Vern before backward-somersaulting to freedom. Going into full Rambo/survivalist mode, she smudges mud on her face, liberates Sharon, and insists they stay to free Vern's sole connubial candidate Maria. At the climax Vern slaughters Allen while taunting guide Evans, Vern's long-estranged father. Ingrid, Maria and Sharon team up to send the villainous virgin over the edge of a cliff.

Haggerty and King (formerly Lawrence King Phillips) reprise their roles from the original. Is their tarnished marquee value really worth the damage? More appalling is the feminist nightmare in the center ring; this tacky movie's *raison d'etre* is to titillate male viewers with a series of thwarted rapes; although much time is spent intercutting between Evans and Allen arguing about The Environment, and impotent Vern and Maria making small talk (she: "You just need a friend"). The script changes its tune about whether Vern is an addled child-man, alfresco rapist, or Jason Vorhees freak, though King's lurid overacting cultivates zero sympathy. ABDUCTED 2 barely takes advantage of thriller possibilities in the "weaker" sex outsmarting and out-muscling a goony groom, instead offering flashbacks of Maria having intercourse back in civilization. One doesn't yearn for Vern's return. *(Graphic violence, extreme profanity, extensive nudity, sexual situations.)* — R.P.

d, Boon Collins; p, Boon Collins, Richard Goudreau; exec p, David Gil, Benjamin Gruberg; assoc p, Kenneth Kantymir, Louie Edward Lawless; w, Boon Collins, Lindsay Bourne; ph, Danny Nowak; ed, Rick Martin; m, Ronald J. Weiss; prod d, Ellen Bennett; fx, Doug Perry; casting, Maria Greco, Tony Greco; makeup, Tone Rorvik; stunts, Shishir Inocalla

Action   **(PR: O   MPAA: R)**

A

ACCUMULATOR 1   ★★★

(Czechoslovakia) 102m Heureka Film; Telexport Prague ~ Film Bridge International c
(AKUMULATOR 1)

Petr Forman *(Olda)*; Edita Brychta *(Anna)*; Zdenek Sverak *(Fisarek)*; Boleslav Povik *(Slezak)*; Jiri Kodet *(Vasek Mikulik)*; Daniela Kolarova; Marian Labuda; Marketa Frosslova; Tereza Pergnerova

This flawed but irresistible absurdist sci-fi ranks as one of the most expensive homegrown productions for the former Czecholsovakia, with a $1.5 million budget. Its eccentric mix of Kafka and Rod Serling also makes the most effective slam against TV since POLTERGEIST.

Olda (Petr Forman), an everyman surveyor, suffers bouts of fatigue that put him in the hospital, diagnosed with "a total loss of energy." There he meets Fisarek (Zkenek Sverak), an alternative healer who rehabilitates Olda by teaching him how to absorb, conserve and channel excess energy from other people. Yet deadly attacks of exhaustion continue, until Olda realizes that his life is draining away into the glass orbs of switched-on televisions. It seems that when a person is televised, his/her image survives in a riotous parallel universe behind the screens, where broadcast cowboy stars, porn performers, the Seven Dwarfs, and man-on-the-street interviewees party hearty off the energy of their human templates . . . until the hosts die. Olda clowned for a news camera; now his video *doppelganger* thrives whenever the surveyor approaches a hungry TV.

ACCUMULATOR ONE's terrific premise is hobbled by a lengthy romantic subplot that's played for offbeat tenderness but just can't compete with the main attraction, as Olda falls for a pretty dentist Anna (Edita Brychta), daughter of a previous TV victim. Olda tries to maintain their affair while avoiding any active picture tube, but Anna interprets his evasions as cold feet because she's got a kid. When not mired in the domestic pathos (or a pointless sidebar about a psycho co-worker), ACCUMULATOR ONE cooks, as Olda plans to hit the vampire dimension with more power than it can handle. Waving his arms over crowds at operas, soccer matches, and train stations, Olda accumulates and stores an apocalyptic charge of energy, then aims it at a distant TV. At the last instant Olda reconsiders and instead vents the blast skyward—saving a plummeting airliner with Fisarek aboard. Olda's energy-starved alter ego climbs into reality and merges with the triumphant hero. How this can happen is one of the maddening gaps in the picture's loopy logic that makes one wish more time had been spent in Olda II's strange netherworld than with Olda I's love life.

Yet there are immortal moments in ACCUMULATOR 1, especially the surveyor's swashbuckling remote-control duel with cathode-blue beams reaching out voraciously from the wares in an electronics-shop showcase. Except for the endangered plane (a campy miniature tossed amid cotton clouds), special effects are accomplished and inventive. Initially puzzling inserts plunge the viewer into outsized mockups of Olda's pulsating viscera, a churning car engine or a drilled tooth; all emphasizing the coexistence of microcosmos and macrocosmos, while a splendid Bernard Herrmann-esque orchestral score adds menace with tongue in cheek. The stylistic and financial gamble paid off for 29-year-old director Jan Sverak, as ACCUMULATOR 1 was its native country's top-grossing feature for 1994, but exhibition in the West was sparse. *(Adult situations, sexual situations, nudity, violence.)* — C.C.

d, Jan Sverak; p, Petr Soukup; exec p, Premysl Prazasky; w, Jan Sverak, Zdenek Sverak, Jan Slovak; ph, F.A. Brabec; ed, Alois

Fisarek; m, Ondrej Soukup, Jiri Svoboda; prod d, Premysl Prazsky; art d, Milos Kohout; sound, Zbynek Mikulik; cos, Jaroslava Pecharova

Science Fiction/Comedy/Fantasy   (PR: O   MPAA: NR)

ACE VENTURA: WHEN NATURE CALLS   ★★★
(U.S.) 105m Morgan Creek International ~ Warner Bros. c

Jim Carrey *(Ace Ventura)*; Ian McNeice *(Fulton Greenwall)*; Simon Callow *(Vincent Cadby)*; Maynard Eziashi *(Ouda)*; Bob Gunton *(Burton Quinn)*; Sophie Okonedo *(Princess)*; Tommy Davidson *(The Tiny Warrior)*; Adewale *(Hitu)*; Danny D. Daniels *(Wachootoo Witch Doctor)*; Sam Motoana Phillips *(Wachootoo Chief)*; Damon Standifer *(Wachati Chief)*; Andrew Steel *(Mick Katie)*; Bruce Spence *(Gahjii)*; Thomas Grunke *(Derrick McCane)*; Arsenio "Sonny" Trinidad *(Ashram Monk)*; Kristen Norton *(Pompous Woman)*; Michael Reid MacKay *(Skinny Husband)*; Kayla Allen *(Airplane Stewardess)*; Ken Kirzinger *(Helicopter Pilot)*; Dev Kennedy *(Dad Tourist)*; Patti Tippo *(Mom Tourist)*; Sabrinah Christie *(Girl Tourist)*; Warren Sroka *(Boy Tourist)*; Noel De Souza *(Elephant Trainer)*; Gene Williams *(Polestander)*; Leif Tilden *(Gorilla Performer)*

ACE VENTURA: WHEN NATURE CALLS is the rare sequel that actually improves on the original film. This resolutely low-brow comedy is funnier than 1994's ACE VENTURA: PET DETECTIVE and quite entertaining in its own right, at least until the nutty slapstick wears out its welcome during the last half hour.

Jim Carrey reprises the role of Ace Ventura, now a renowned pet detective. Ace has secluded himself in a Himalayan monastery after failing to save the life of a raccoon trapped on a mountainside some time earlier. Ace's spiritual quest is curtailed by Fulton Greenwall (Ian McNeice), a British emissary who asks him to help recover a white bat that has been stolen from Vincent Cadby (Simon Callow), a wealthy Englishman living in Africa.

Who would steal a bat? Ace travels to Africa, and tries to find out who would most benefit from owning the creature. Ace's suspects include the leaders of two hostile African tribes—one of which holds the bat sacred—and safari park owner Burton Quinn (Bob Gunton). Ace finally figures out that Cadby hired thugs to steal the bat to provoke war between the two tribes, leaving the way open for him to control the local bat guano industry. Ace retrieves the bat, solves the caper and saves the day.

Unlike ACE VENTURA: PET DETECTIVE, which was not written with Jim Carrey in mind, ACE VENTURA: WHEN NATURE CALLS was tailored specifically to his talents. Writer-director Steve Oedekerk exalts Carrey's goofball brand of cocky cynicism, setting it against the sort of exotic locales normally associated with colonialist action-adventure films of the TARZAN-KING SOLOMON'S MINES-INDIANA JONES type. Through tasteless bathroom humor and satiric references to pop culture, Oedekerk and Carrey subvert the genre's conventions with glee: One could still call the film racist, but the whole enterprise is just so silly it's hard to complain. In addition, the *pro forma* mystery plot provides more genuine suspense than that of the first film.

ACE is endlessly self-referential in the scattershot style of the AIRPLANE! comedies, including an on-the-money parody of CLIFFHANGER (1993) and a slew of up-to-the-minute in-jokes unlikely to mean much to the film's target audience, rowdy adolescent boys. Ian McNeice, who plays Hugh Grant's sidekick in THE ENGLISHMAN WHO WENT UP A HILL BUT CAME DOWN A MOUNTAIN (1995), plays virtually the same role here, while Simon Callow perfectly fills out the oily bad guy role of Vincent Cadby, a tweak at the ego of *New York Times* critic,

Vincent Canby. Carrey also does some merciless—if all-too-brief—impersonations, including one of Charlton Heston. Overall, adult audiences would probably prefer more satire and less scatology: The apparently unending stream of body fluid jokes is repulsive without being funny.

For all Carrey's obvious abilities, the indefatigable superstar could still learn a thing or two about comic timing. Even Jerry Lewis at his most manic knew when to pause between routines, but Carrey seems determined to be on at all times. By the film's final third, he's just exhausting to watch. If he's not careful, audiences may soon start grumbling that a little Jim Carrey can go a long way. *(Violence, sexual situations, profanity.)* — E.M.

d, Steve Oedekerk; p, James G. Robinson; exec p, Gary Barber; co-p, Andrew G. La Marca; w, Steve Oederkerk; ph, Donald E. Thorin; ed, Malcolm Campbell; m, Robert Folk; prod d, Stephen J. Lineweaver; art d, Christopher Nowak; set d, Derek Hill; sound, Stacy Brownrigg (mixer); fx, Mike Vezina, Peter Montgomery, Carolyn Soper; casting, Ferne Cassel; cos, Elsa Zamparelli; makeup, Sheryl Leigh Ptak, W.M. Creations, Inc.; stunts, Rich Barker, J.J. Makaro

Comedy/Adventure/Crime   (PR: C   MPAA: PG-13)

ACROSS THE MOON   ★★
(U.S.) 88m Airstream Films; Hemdale Communications ~ Hemdale Home Video c

Elizabeth Pena *(Carmen)*; Christina Applegate *(Kathy)*; Peter Berg *(Lyle)*; Michael McKean *(Frank)*; James Remar *(Rattlesnake Jim)*; Burgess Meredith *(Barney)*; Robert Fieldsted *(Dentist 1)*; Robert Lesser *(Dentist 2)*; Mowava Pryor *(Public Defender)*; Richard Portnow *(Roy)*; Jack Nance *(Old Cowboy)*; Michael Aniel Nundra *(Paco)*; Tony Fields *(Richie)*; Henry Harris *(Prison Guard 1)*; Sandra Gee *(Prison Guard 2)*; Gloria Gifford *(Prison Visitor)*; Jeff Doucette *(Mean Guard)*; Merle Kennedy *(Shoplifter)*; John Apicella *(Grocery Manager)*; Jack Kehler *(ATV Pop)*; T.J. Evans *(Kid)*; Stephen Schneck *(Prison Chaplain)*; Ken White *(Warden)*; Scott Burkholder *(First Gunman)*; Paul Lieber *(Second Gunman)*

Sometimes a ramshackle flick has everything going against it but still succeeds to a degree. Sabotaged by a script that stretches implausibility beyond breaking-point, ACROSS THE MOON rebounds due to the love-hate relationship of a female odd couple and sparkling performances of the lead actresses.

Barrio survivor Carmen (Elizabeth Pena) and spoiled Beverly Hills refugee Kathy (Christina Applegate) meet under strained circumstances; Carmen's old man Richie (Tony Fields) and Kathy's main squeeze Lyle (Peter Berg) are netted by a police drug sting. Their bumbling boyfriends behind bars, the antagonistic women sojourn closer to the desert-area penitentiary to set up housekeeping, along with Carmen's son Paco (Michael Aniel Nundra), in a rickety trailer owned by Lyle's scumbag lawyer Roy (Richard Portnow). Scrambling to make ends met, the two fumble a madcap whirl at prostitution before a volunteer fireman Jim (James Remar) points them toward gainful employment in bartending and supermarket checkouts. Meanwhile, truant Paco befriends down-on-his-luck Frank (Michael McKean) a former movie-animal trainer eking out a meager existence with his menagerie. As Carmen's fidelity to Richie melts under Jim's manly gaze, Kathy solidifies her bond by marrying Lyle in jail despite a later foul-up in conjugal visitation rights. An eccentric dying prospector (Burgess Meredith) wills Paco the map to his claim, but hot-tempered Jim wrecks the gold mine's landmark when he deliberately blows up an area frequented by hated tourists' all-terrain vehicles. Then lion-tamer Frank murders a cattle rancher (ERASERHEAD's Jack Nance) in a dispute over livestock Frank stole to feed his starving big cats. Abiding as ever, Kathy and Carmen visit their criminal lovers in a prison that now holds Roy the shyster, Frank the former movie-animal-star manager, and Jim the anti-ATV terrorist.

The point behind this female-directed production is that women must endlessly clean up the messes left by their lesser halves. While it's no stretch to swallow the proposition that many men spend their adult years in second childhood, this fanciful examination of that immaturity is artificial and more affected than effective. Out of what delirious imagination do the crotchety prospector and the homicidally-protective trainer spring? They aren't real people but cutesy concoctions to fluff up the material with unconvincing quirkiness. During the least contrived moments, ACROSS THE MOON is most engaging. There's enough outre appeal in the central relationship of a former Vida Loca girl and Rodeo Drive brat. Despite a screenplay that sugarcoats the pall under which inmates and their loved ones persevere, the viewer remains a willing ringside spectator at the sparring of the women from different worlds. Applegate, typed on TV by her role as a scatterbrain/slut in the sitcom "Married—With Children," gets the chance to exhibit some range. Even juicier is Pena's succulent bitchy dialogue, and she makes her frustration over fatherless Paco's delinquency seem gut-wrenchingly real. Pena and Applegate enable us to overlook this film's sunstroked whimsy, and laugh and cry along with these women-without-men. In a movie that sometimes mainlines adorableness, that is no mean achievement. *(Violence, extreme profanity, nudity, substance abuse, sexual situations, adult situations.)* — R.P.

d, Lisa Gottlieb; p, Robert Mickelson; w, Stephen Schneck; ph, Andrzej Sekula; ed, Daniel Lowenthal; m, Christopher Tyng, Exene Cervenka; prod d, Ivo Cristante; art d, Ken Larson; set d, Tim Colahan; sound, William Fiege; fx, Marty Bresin; casting, Cathy Henderson Blake, Tom McSweeney; cos, Giovanna Ottobre Melton; makeup, Felicity Bowring; stunts, Bud Davis

Comedy/Drama/Prison   (PR: O   MPAA: R)

ACROSS THE SEA OF TIME: NEW YORK 3D   ★★
(U.S.) 51m Columbia; Sony New Technologies ~
Sony Pictures Classics c

Peter Reznik *(Tomas)*; John McDonough *(Freighter Chief)*; Avi Hoffman *(Seaman/Bow)*; Victor Steinbach *(Seaman/Pilot)*; Peter Boyden *(Con Ed Worker)*; Philip Levy *(Hot Dog Vendor)*; Nick Muglia *(Policeman)*; Abby Lewis *(Julia Minton)*; Matt Malloy *(Wall Street Businessman)*; Luigi Petrozza *(Pizza Pie Man)*; Bernard Ferstenberg *(Pickle Vendor)*; Robert Buckley *(Socialite)*; Donald Trump *(Himself)*; Patrick Flynn *(Bartender)*

IMAX, the latest and most innovative 3D film viewing process, is the real star of ACROSS THE SEA OF TIME, a dreary, sentimental story of a young Russian stowaway searching for his family in New York.

Tomas Minton (Peter Reznik) stows away on a freighter heading for New York City, where he plans to find his relatives, who had emigrated many years earlier. He arrives in New York harbor with only some old photos and his stereopticon (a device for viewing 3D photos) to help him with his search. Unfamiliar with the city and knowing little English, Tomas has difficulty locating the house shown in one particular photo, where he believes his relatives still live.

After an exhausting but exhilarating day, which includes a ride on a subway train and a trip to Coney Island, Tomas ends up in Central Park, where some youths steal his photos and break his stereopticon. Just as Tomas almost gives up his quest, however, he notices a duplicate photo of his relatives' house on the wall of a saloon. A Russian bartender tells him where the house stands.

Eventually, Tomas finds the place and lets himself inside, where he meets his grandmother, Julia Minton (Abby Lewis), who then introduces Tomas to his large extended family.

ACROSS THE SEA OF TIME is the longest IMAX film to date, and only the second to incorporate a narrative (the first was Jean-Jacques Annaud's WINGS OF COURAGE). The use of 3D is impressive at times, but, clearly, Sony Pictures Classics has put nowhere near as much effort into the film as it has into the 3D system.

The only way to enjoy ACROSS THE SEA OF TIME is in a Sony IMAX theater, where the screen is several times larger than normal, and special goggles are required to view the images. The 3D camerawork (by Andrew Kitzanuk) is marvelously effective during the subway and Coney Island roller coaster sequences (and during one extended aerial shot), but the process also highlights what is wrong with the film: whenever the action stops, there is nothing to hold the viewer's attention.

The largely unknown cast is barely competent in performing the excessively mawkish script by Andrew Gellis. Director Stephen Low's view of New York is so clean and idealized that the film often feels like a Mayor's Office promotional short. ACROSS THE SEA OF TIME is an attraction best suited to undiscriminating Big Apple tourists. Next time, hopefully, Sony will assemble a better vehicle for its rising technological star. — E.M.

d, Stephen Low; p, Stephen Low; exec p, Andrew Gellis; assoc p, Carol Cuddy; w, Andrew Gellis; ph, Andrew Kitzanuk; ed, James Lahti; m, John Barry; prod d, Charley Beal; sound, Peter Thillaye (design); casting, Avy Kaufman; cos, Cynthia Flynt

Docudrama/Children's/Adventure   (PR: AA   MPAA: G)

ADDICTION, THE   ★★★½
(U.S.) 82m Fast Films ~ October Films bw

Lili Taylor *(Kathleen Conklin)*; Christopher Walken *(Peina)*; Annabella Sciorra *(Casanova)*; Edie Falco *(Jean)*; Paul Calderon *(The Professor)*; Fredro Starr *(Black)*; Kathryne Erbe *(Anthropology Student)*; Michael Imperioli *(Missionary)*; Jamel "Redrum" Simmons *(Black's Friend)*; Father Robert Castle *(Priest/Narrator)*; Michael Fella *(Cop)*; Dr. Louis A. Katz *(Doctor)*; Leroy Johnson *(Homeless Victim)*; Fred Williams *(Homeless Victim)*; Avron Coleman *(Cellist)*; Lisa Casillo *(Lisa)*; Frank (Butchy the Hat) Aquilino *(Delivery Man)*; Nicholas Decegli *(Cabby)*; Jay Julien *(Dean)*; Chuck Jeffries *(Bartender)*; Ed Conna *(Waiter)*; Nancy Ellen Anzalone *(Dress Victim)*; Heather Bracken *(Nurse)*; Susan Mitchell; Mary Ann Hannon; John Vincent McEvily; Bianca Pratt; Christina Campenella; Anthony Giangrando; Kevin Scullin *(Victims)*

A morose vampire film that wears its philosophical underpinnings on its ragged sleeve, THE ADDICTION is ambitious, strikingly beautiful, and occasionally very funny, but falls short of being an unqualified success.

Photographed in shimmering black-and-white, THE ADDICTION revolves around NYU student Kathleen Conklin (Lili Taylor), who's about to graduate with her doctorate in philosophy. Frumpy and serious, Kathleen and her best friend Jean (Edie Falco) are consumed by the usual questions, particularly those relating to the nature of evil and the burden of personal responsibility.

While walking through her Lower East Side neighborhood, Kathleen is attacked by a chicly dressed woman, Casanova (Annabella Sciorra), who drags her into an alley and bites her throat. Casanova's bite transforms Kathleen into a vampire, a fact she is reluctant to accept even after she discovers that she can't eat or tolerate sunlight, and craves human blood. Kathleen attempts to deal with her condition through sheer force of intellect, examining it as the embodiment of the clash between individual will and responsibility to society as a whole. But in the end she gives in to bloodlust, feeding first on a junkie who puts up even less fight than she did, then victimizing fellow students, would-be lovers, one of her professors (Paul Calderon), and various street people she finds huddled in neighborhood doorways. In between attacks, she and Edie attend atrocity exhibitions and continue their philosophical discussions.

Vampirism transforms Kathleen physically, giving her the pallid, scraped-to-the-bone beauty of a young Patti Smith. But her smug conviction in her own growing superiority over the teeming masses of ordinary people is shattered by the gauntly handsome Peina (Christopher Walken), an experienced blood-sucker who makes no secret of his disgust at her intemperate addiction to blood and soul-murder. He also tells her that there's no reason she has to live the vampire life, that she can—as he has—control her lust for blood and resume a life that's almost human. Kathleen's journey into darkness culminates in the party she gives to celebrate the conferral of her doctoral degree. She invites both her victims—who are by now all vampires them-selves—and her academic colleagues. The result is a bloody orgy that's both blackly funny and truly horrifying, NIGHT OF THE LIVING DEAD meets KICKING AND SCREAMING. Sick-ened, she renounces her parasitic existence and, in the film's closing scene, walks by her own grave in the midday sun, reborn as human flesh.

In a year of dueling black-and-white art-house vampire pic-tures, director Abel Ferrara and longtime writing partner Nicho-las St. John managed to make the more ambitious and less likable of the two. If Michael Almereyda's dreamy, sumptuous NADJA has the air of a feature-length perfume ad, it's nonetheless a seductive and agreeable night at the movies. THE ADDICTION, like BAD LIEUTENANT is, by contrast, a bit of an ordeal. Lili Taylor makes an extraordinary vampire, less beautiful and other-worldly than Elina Lowensohn but far more convincingly preda-tory. She and Walken are flawless Downtown ghouls, the true last word in night crawlers.

But THE ADDICTION never really adds up to more than a clever idea, executed with some flair—one expects no less from Ferrara—but never fully brought to life. In the end, what is Ferrara and St. John's point about vampirism? That it's an addic-tion, like alcoholism? That nasty, stupid people who hang around dark alleys deserve what they get? That the world's a cesspool and vampires are its great white sharks? For all the philosophiz-ing, nothing much gets said. *(Violence, profanity, adult situ-ations, substance abuse.)* — M.M.

d, Abel Ferrara; p, Denis Hann, Fernando Sulichin; exec p, Russell Simmons, Preston Holmes; assoc p, Antony Blinken, Marla Hanson; w, Nicholas St. John; ph, Ken Kelsch; ed, Mayin Lo; m, Joe Delia; prod d, Charles Lagola; art d, Beth Curtis; sound, Robert Taz; cos, Melinda Eshelman

Horror/Drama   **(PR: O   MPAA: NR)**

ADVENTURES OF MATT THE GOOSEBOY, THE ★
(Hungary) 80m Budapest Hungarofilm ~
Just For Kids Home Video c

A true Hungarian goulash, this low-grade, dispiritingly-ani-mated kiddie "treat" was dubbed into English and unleashed onto home-video in 1995.

Ruling the peasantry through firepower, Lord Blackheart hunts for sport. When he takes aim at the beloved pet of Matt the Gooseboy, the bullying noble is outraged that the lad objects, and dismisses Matt's claims of ownership with 25 lashes. Ridiculing

the rebellious boy's vow to return and avenge himself threefold, the despot supervises the halting construction of his palace. An Italian architect convinces Blackheart to order his troops away for sturdier timber. Then, tying the unguarded ruler to a tree, Matt the Gooseboy whips off his Italian camouflage and admin-isters his first pay-back with a bumbershoot. Dismayed by the limitations of court quacks tending his wounds, Blackheart de-mands the services of a country doctor. Sending the potentate's soldiers on a wild *goose* chase for curative herbs, the rural medic reveals himself to be Matt, who now scores two out of three. On Fair Day, castle minions are alerted to check for impostors rather than an actual gooseboy. With the aid of a sympathetic lord, Matt employs a look-alike to decoy away the royal horsemen, then whacks the easily-duped Blackheart for a third time. A boy and his goose beat the tyrannical system.

Why should squirming, media-wise youngsters be plunked down in front of what amounts to a sub-Hanna Barbera fairy tale with a foreign accent? Gilded with heavy-handed strains of classical music, this lugubrious morality play boasts an exotic coloring style and deliberately spare cel technique in service of a fable that may as well have been presented in Budapest dialect. Lumpen and unamusing, the GOOSEBOY experience will seem primitive to kids weaned on Disney, and may send xenophobic grade-schoolers right back to the familiar company of Aladdin, Simba, Bart Simpson and the Flintstones. Whether to broaden the American child's multicultural horizons or simply to crank out kidvid at minimal cost, certain video distributors released various unheralded East European and Japanese cartoon features in the 1980s and 90s, unflatteringly reminiscent of those sup-posed-to-be-good-for-you dubbed kidflicks that low-budget en-trepeneurs like K. Gordon Murray would import from Mexico or Lower Slobovia for yesteryear's movie-house matinees. THE ADVENTURES OF MATT THE GOOSEBOY has the same hollow ambiance. — R.P.

d, Attila Dargay, Luis Elmar; w, Jozsef Nepp, Jozsef Romhan, Attila Dargay (based on the poem by Mihaly Fazekas); ph, Iren Henrik; ed, Magda Happ; m, Franz Cis; anim, Marcell Jank-ovics, Joszef Nepp; sound, Peter Barsony

Animated/Children's/Adventure   **(PR: A   MPAA: NR)**

AI CITY   ★★½
(Japan) 86m Toho Co.; K.K. Movic; Ashi Productions ~
Right Stuf International c

VOICES OF: Yuki Ueda *(Ai)*; Hirotaka Suzuoki *(Kei)*; Nachi Nozawa *(Raiden)*; Fumi Koyama *(K2)*; Kiyoshi Kobayashi *(Lee)*; Ichirou Nagai *(Lai Lo Ching)*; Takeshi Watanabe *(Alloy)*; Shigeru Yanami *(T (Cat))*; Yoshitake Horiuchi *(Mr. J.)*; Kazuhiro Ginga *(E)*

Another spectacular animated science fiction feature from Japan, AI CITY plunges viewers into a surreal future world in which a young girl, in whom all human biodata has been encoded, is hunted by a variety of forces against a background of "biopollu-tion" run amuck.

In a future New York, the shadowy FRAUD organization oversees genetic experiments and monitors levels of biopollution caused years earlier by the discovery of Genetic Alloy during an unregulated cloning experiment. FRAUD agents seek to recover a young girl, Ai (Yuki Ueda), a clone who contains the future of mankind in her genes and can act as a trigger to reactivate human biodata memory cells. Having escaped the FRAUD laboratory with a young man, a rejected clone named Kei (Hirotaka Suzuoki), Ai allies herself with defector K2 (Fumi Koyama) and private investigator Raiden (Nachi Nozawa).

FRAUD's director, Mr. Lee (Kiyoshi Kobayashi), is engaged in a power struggle over Ai with his onetime assistant Lai Lo Chong (Ichirou Nagai). Lee succeeds in recapturing her and enables her to recall the password, "Ai City," which will activate her power. Chong is revealed to be the living embodiment of the Genetic Alloy which, upon hearing the password, seeks to expand by absorbing the DNA of all human beings around him. He becomes a biological monster enveloping the city. Only Ai has the power to overcome the threat; she causes the Alloy to consume itself.

Japanese animation typically contains spectacular effects and visuals, and AI CITY practically tops them all. The action flies fast, furious, and violent as superpowered beings pursue Ai, their battles in and around a fragile New York cityscape rending and shattering the fabric of time and space.

Unfortunately, the welter of technical and biological details and the stubbornly bizarre plotline tend to be bewildering and repeat viewings are needed in order to grasp certain important plot points. The key revelation, that the accidental discovery of Genetic Alloy jeopardized the future of the world, comes an hour into the film. A subsequent flashback explaining "the fake civilization of imitations" is too brief to provide a sufficient description of the conditions in this future society. While the concept is fascinating and the animation breathtaking, the ultimate point is unclear. However, fans of apocalyptic, futuristic *anime* in the vein of AKIRA and LEGEND OF THE OVERFIEND should not miss this one. *(Graphic violence.)* — B.C.

d, Koichi Mashimo; p, Hiroshi Kato; w, Hideki Sonoda (from a story by Shuho Itahashi); m, Shiro Sagisu; art d, Torao Arai; anim, Chuichi Iguchi

Animated/Science Fiction (PR: C MPAA: NR)

AILSA ★★★
(Ireland/France/Germany) 78m Temple Films; Radio Telefis Eireann; Westdeutscher Rundfunk; ARTE ~ Cine Electra C (AKA: ELSA)

Brendan Coyle *(Miles Butler)*; Andrea Irvine *(Sara Butler)*; Juliette Gruber *(Campbell Rourke)*; Brendan Cauldwell *(Hugh Maloney)*; Darragh Kelly *(Sean)*; Gary Lydon *(Jack)*; Blanaid Irvine *(Vera)*; Des Spillane *(Old Mrs. Johnson)*; Anne McGeown *(Mrs. Foley)*; Paddy Ashe *(Man in Post Office)*; Frankie McCafferty *(Post Office Assistant)*; Ned McLoughlin *(Postman)*; Anne Kent *(Woman in Cafe)*; Caroline Gray *(Waitress)*; Darren O'Toole *(Post Boy)*; O.Z. Whitehead *(American Tourist)*; Diane O'Kelly *(Girl on Train)*; Brendan Conroy *(Mr. Johnson, Jr.)*; Padraig O'Neill *(Taxi Driver)*; Sean Keane *(Security Guard)*; Neill O'Brien *(The Counselor)*; Choir of the Guardian Angel National School *(Carol Singers)*; Georgia Mullen *(Ailsa)*

Irish writer Joseph O'Connor adapted his own enigmatic short story for this dirge-like psychodrama of romantic obsession, uncluttered by any aspirations to ape FATAL ATTRACTION.

Narrator Miles Butler (Brendan Coyle), a young husband in a Dublin suburb, is practically lost the instant he glimpses the new tenant downstairs, a pretty American named Campbell Rourke (Juliette Gruber), who has returned to the Auld Sod to discover her roots. Even though he barely acknowledges her during their few face-to-face encounters, Miles broods constantly over Campbell. He shares her tram car to work and methodically intercepts and reads her mail, from which he learns she has an estranged boyfriend. Typing as Campbell, Miles sends the lover a note rejecting him; that and his habit of paying her bills reveal his madness to authorities. Despite a restraining order, therapy, and ultimatums from his long-suffering wife, Miles secretly hopes for some form of communion with Campbell. Then he

hears that Campbell, reunited with her boyfriend, is pregnant. Miles kills himself.

The title is Gaelic for "Elsa," a name Campbell gives her unborn daughter, perhaps a bleak joke on Miles's perpetual problems with women. AILSA offers no terrifically profound insight into the nature of obsession. Instead, it's a compact mood piece that takes the viewer into the closed universe of a stalker/voyeur. Though not a traditional thriller, the feature is endowed with a tangible menace, the tone set by Cian de Buitlear's somber cinematography. Definitely not a picture for all tastes, AILSA was originally produced for television but had scattered theatrical showings in Europe and the United States. *(Adult situations, profanity, nudity.)* — C.C.

d, Paddy Breathnach; p, Ed Guiney; exec p, Rod Stoneman; co-p, Stephen Bradley, Kathryn Lennon; w, Joseph O'Connor (based on his short story); ph, Cian de Buitlear; ed, Enar Reynolds; m, Dario Marinelli; prod d, Ed McLoughlin; art d, Padraig O'Neill; sound, Simon J. Wells (mixer); fx, Maurice Foley; cos, Marie Tierney; makeup, Linda Ni Mhaonaigh

Drama (PR: O MPAA: NR)

ALMOST DEAD ★★½
(U.S.) 92m Delta Entertainment; Zuban Productions ~ Monarch c

Shannen Doherty *(Katherine Roshak)*; Costas Mandylor *(Dominic Delaserra)*; John Diehl *(Eddie Herbek)*; Billy Moses *(Dr. Jim Schneider)*; Steve Inwood *(Police Chief)*; Eric Christmas *(Father Ambrose)*; Penelope Branning *(Mrs. Roshak)*; David Schuelke; Jimmy Schuelke *(Effenbeck Twins)*; Roy Brocksmith *(Kuranda)*; Wren Brown *(Bednarek)*; William Allen Young *(Henzes)*; George Wallace *(Caretaker)*; John Di Santi *(Brescia)*; Michael Keys Hall *(Braithwaite)*; Jack Jozefson *(Workman)*; Rachel Bovino *(Hooker)*; Joan Kelly *(Housekeeper)*

Although ALMOST DEAD is a sort of *papier mache* knock-off of a sophisticated thriller, it generates cheesy fun in its junior Grand Guignol way. Filled with collapsed gravesites, apparitions, and premature burials, this chiller is also intriguing in that the walking dead disport themselves with more animation than the film's nominal stars, Shannon Doherty and Costas Mandylor.

After being killed in an apartment explosion, supposed suicide Mrs. Roshak (Penelope Branning) seems reluctant to relinquish earthly bonds to guilt-ridden daughter Katherine (Doherty). Mama's posthumous visits compel Katherine to postpone her psychiatric research (involving twins) to visit the family cemetery in her hometown. She finds an ally in Officer Dominic Delaserra (Mandylor), bereaved by his own wife's demise. Despite police department resistance to opening Mrs. Roshak's grave, a mysteriously trashed car and torched bathroom indicates that Katherine's mother is not resting in peace, and the heroine turns to Dominic, who deposits her with his pal Eddie (John Diehl), a hunchback who freaks out Katherine with homicide fantasies. Could the motherly haunting have something to do with Katherine's inheritance from a long-lost father? When Dominic is jailed, accused of shooting Eddie, vulnerable Katherine receives aid and comfort from Father Ambrose (Eric Christmas). Ultimately, Katherine overhears that two of her twin patients, the Effenbeck siblings (David and Jimmy Schuelke) concocted the elaborate hoax about her mother to bilk Katherine out of her estate. After she fatally stabs one Effenbeck, the other twin suffers the wound in transference (like Dumas' famous Corsican Brothers) and both perish. What can't be rationally explained is how Katherine was advised by Father Ambrose, who was already dead!

ALMOST DEAD is one of those funhouse flicks in which necking couples can pretend to be scared for an excuse for propinquity. Still, this script is ingenious enough to cloud the double-trouble key to its mystery and ignites enough false climaxes (like Dominic's ordeal interred alive in a tomb) to distract one from the real scam. What gives this minor shocker a kick is how the shrink's subjects exploit their doctor's psyche for their own perverted purposes. Although photography is only serviceable, this low-budget affair benefits from a music score that nicely coaxes jolts, and crafty camera maneuvers (particularly during the twins' crypt-ic assaults) with a genuine flair for the macabre; there's also a superb trick shot that travels through a keyhole. Directorial assurance papers over the plethora of plot holes. Given the irritations wrought by these holidays from logic, ALMOST DEAD does a fairly savvy job of misleading its audience down blind alleys. *(Violence, profanity, adult situations.)* — R.P.

d, Ruben Preuss; p, Ruben Preuss, Ron Rothstein; exec p, Werner Preuss, Jerald Bovino, Miguel Tejada-Flores; w, Miguel Tejada-Flores (based on the novel *Resurrection* by William Valtos); ph, Zoran Hochstatter; ed, John Currin; m, James Donnellan; art d, Phil Brandes, Jack Jennings; sound, John Colwell (design); fx, Perpetual Motion Pictures; cos, Robyn Reicher; makeup, Karen Iverson

Thriller (PR: C MPAA: NR)

AMATEUR ★★★
(U.S./U.K./France) 105m Union Generale du Cinematographique; True Fiction Pictures; Zenith Productions; American Playhouse; Theatrical Films; Channel Four Films; La Sept Cinema ~ Sony Pictures Classics c

Isabelle Huppert *(Isabelle)*; Martin Donovan *(Thomas)*; Elina Lowensohn *(Sofia)*; Damian Young *(Edward)*; Chuck Montgomery *(Jan)*; David Simonds *(Kurt)*; Pamela Stewart *(Officer Melville)*; Erica Gimpel *(Irate Woman)*; Jan Leslie Harding *(Waitress)*; Terry Alexander *(Frank the Cook)*; Holt McCallany *(Usher)*; Hugh Palmer *(Warren)*; Michael Imperioli *(Doorman at Club)*; Angel Caban *(Detective)*; Emmanuel Xuereb *(Bartender)*; Lennie Loftin *(Taxi Driver)*; David Greenspan *(George the Photographer)*; Adria Tennor *(Kid Reading The Odyssey)*; Parker Posey *(Girl Squatter)*; Dwight Ewell *(Boy Squatter)*; Currie Graham *(Video Store Clerk)*; Jamie Harrold *(Pizza Guy)*; Patricia Scanlon *(Young Irate Mother)*; James McCauley *(Policeman)*; Benny Nieves *(Policeman)*; David Troup *(Guard)*; Tim Blake Nelson *(Young Detective)*; Marissa Copeland *(Sister at Door)*; Dael Orlandersmith *(Mother Superior)*; Michael Gaston *(Sharpshooter)*; Paul Schulze *(Cop Who Shoots Thomas)*

The talented Hal Hartley strikes a false note with AMATEUR, a hip homage to old-fashioned crime dramas. But even a weak Hartley film has its compensations: the film contains flashes of wit and substance, but they're all too rare.

Isabelle (Isabelle Huppert) is an ex-nun living in modern-day Manhattan, where she tries to earn a living writing pornographic short stories. Thomas (Martin Donovan), an amnesiac, stumbles into the coffee shop where she is composing her latest bit of erotica. Isabelle feels sorry for the lost Thomas and brings him back to her apartment.

Isabelle discovers that Thomas's past is perhaps better forgotten. It includes his wife Sofia (Elina Lowensohn), a pornographic film actress who pushed Thomas from a SoHo window, precipitating his memory loss. Isabelle also learns that Sofia tried to kill Thomas because he coerced her into appearing in dirty movies, and threatened her when she said she intended to leave him and the smut business. While Isabelle pursues Sofia, whom

she now feels she must rescue, Sofia seeks refuge with Edward, Thomas's former partner.

Edward meets Sofia at Grand Central Station and tells her he's being chased by thugs who are after some top-secret information about high-level government corruption. He asks Sofia to take two floppy disks containing the data and hide out in a house in the suburbs. Sofia agrees, but accidentally tips off the thugs, Jan and Kurt, to Edward's whereabouts. Jan and Kurt kidnap Edward and torture him. Though he escapes, the experience unhinges him. Jan and Kurt then wait for Sofia to return to her apartment, knowing she'll come looking for Edward. Fortunately for Sofia, Isabelle and Thomas are also waiting for her. They kill Kurt, and Jan flees.

Isabelle, Thomas and Sofia head for the country house together, despite Sofia's residual anger toward Thomas, who still doesn't remember her. Edward kills a police officer, then rushes to the country hideout to help Sofia. But he arrives too late. Jan shoots Sophia, Edward kills Jan, then Edward, Isabelle and Thomas take the dying Sofia to Isabelle's former convent, so she can receive last rites. Sofia dies, and the police shoot Thomas. Isabelle, bereft, is left to wonder what it all means.

In AMATEUR, Hal Hartley takes the conventions of the Hollywood crime thriller and dresses them up with New York attitude and neo-Godardian style. The result is a pretentious film that doesn't work dramatically or intellectually. Jean-Luc Godard was always a conspicuous influence on Hartley's work, though he wore Godard's inspiration far more lightly than, say, Gregg Araki (THE LIVING END). In his earlier films, including PROOF and TRUST, Hartley used similar postmodern elements to create a unique, oddball world. But those films rarely seem like imitations or homages, establishing their own identities as original reworkings of styles and forms from different periods and places.

What AMATEUR lacks is the sure, light touch that made Hartley's shorts, particularly 1991's SURVIVING DESIRE, and features so engaging. Its balletic fight scenes, plot absurdities, literary references, and mannered, deadpan exchanges between characters all feel strained and trite. Even Hartley's attempt to be sacrilegious by casting Huppert as a nymphomaniac ex-nun sounds better—and funnier—than it plays. Ultimately, AMATEUR isn't so much a bad film as one that will disappoint Hartley fans and perplex newcomers to his work. *(Violence, sexual situations, adult situations, extreme profanity.)* — E.M.

d, Hal Hartley; p, Ted Hope, Hal Hartley; exec p, Scott Meek, Jerome Brownstein, Lindsay Law, Yves Marmion; w, Hal Hartley; ph, Michael Spiller; ed, Steve Hamilton; m, Jeff Taylor; prod d, Steve Rosenzweig; art d, Ginger Tougas; set d, Jennifer Baime, Amy Tapper; sound, Jeff Pullman (mixer); fx, Drew Jiritano; casting, Billy Hopkins, Suzanne Smith; cos, Alexander Welker; makeup, Judy Chin; stunts, Phil Nielson

Drama/Thriller/Crime (PR: C MPAA: R)

AMAZING PANDA ADVENTURE, THE ★★
(U.S.) 84m Lee Rich Productions; Beijing Film Studios ~ Warner Bros. c

Stephen Lang *(Dr. Michael Tyler)*; Ryan Slater *(Ryan Tyler)*; Yi Ding *(Ling)*; Wang Fei *(Chu)*

This formulaic kids-in-peril tale treads familiar territory (think of FREE WILLY with fur). Predicted to be a hit with families, it fell flat at the box office. Children may find it mildly diverting, but it holds little interest for adults.

Ten-year old Ryan (Ryan Slater) travels to China to visit his father Michael (Stephen Lang), whom he has not seen since his parents divorced. Michael, a naturalist who runs a Giant Panda preserve, is so absorbed in his work that he has forgotten about his son's visit. Ryan makes his way to the preserve by himself, only to have his father dash out minutes later on a rescue mission. Refusing to be left alone, Ryan insists on tagging along. Joining them on the mission are Ling (Yi Ding), a young Chinese girl who works at the preserve, and her grandfather, Chu (Wang Fei).

While rescuing a trapped mother panda, Michael is shot by poachers who abduct the panda's baby. Ryan and Ling rescue the baby and become separated from the others when they fall from a rope-and-plank bridge and plunge into a raging river. They are carried far from the preserve and must find their way back through the rugged wilderness with their precious cargo. With some narrow escapes, they manage to elude the poachers and return the baby panda to the preserve.

This is a well-intentioned film with an important message about the endangered status of the Giant Panda (there are less than 1,000 of the exotic creatures surviving in the wild). Otherwise, there is little to recommend it. Children may not detect its credibility lapses and continuity glitches, but even the youngest and least movie savvy viewers will be able to predict the outcome.

Slater (actor Christian Slater's younger brother) is an unappealing lead, resentful of his father's devotion to the preserve and initially an unwilling participant in the rescue of the baby panda. But even after the panda wins his heart, he remains unlikable and petulant. Yi Ding is more engaging, but her character is unrealistically dependent on Ryan. Ling has been working at the preserve for years and is familiar with the mountainous surroundings. Yet when they are thrust into the wilderness, she becomes a damsel-in-distress, whose constant refrain of "Help me, Ryan!" quickly becomes irritating. The screenplay forces an attraction between the two preteens, which does not come across well. Lang is barely adequate as the naturalist.

The actors are upstaged by both the locations and the pandas. Filmed on location in the Sichuan province of China, on the edge of the Himalayan mountains, the picture features spectacular scenery never before filmed for a Hollywood production. The pandas are a mix of real and animatronic, and the difference is usually indiscernible. Scenes of pandas being trapped and otherwise imperiled may be upsetting to some children. *(Violence, profanity.)* — B.R.

d, Chris Cain; p, Lee Rich, John Wilcox, Gary Foster, Dylan Sellers; exec p, Gabriella Martinelli; assoc p, Josie Rosen; w, Jeff Rothberg, Laurice Elehwany (from a story by John Wilcox and Steven Alldredge); ph, Jack N. Green; ed, Jack Hofstra; m, William Ross; prod d, John Willett; art d, Willie Heslup; set d, Doug Carnegie; sound, Andy Wiskes; casting, Marion Dougherty; cos, Marjorie Chan

Adventure/Children's   **(PR: AA   MPAA: PG)**

AMERICA'S DEADLIEST HOME VIDEO   ★★
(U.S.) 84m Randum Film Group; Video Vigilantes ~ Randum Films and Entertainment c

Danny Bonaduce *(Dougie)*; Mick Wynhoff *(Clint)*; Mollena Williams *(Vezna)*; Melora Walters *(Gloria)*; Gretchen Bonaduce *(Debbie)*; Michael S. Thompson *(Frank)*; Steven Diller *(Debbie's Lover)*; Lori Brooks *(Girl on Street)*; Thomas Hunt *(Boyfriend)*; Mark Rauscher *(Kissing Man)*; Kathi Crawford *(Kissing Woman)*; Mark Hoffman *(Dead Cop)*; Danny Renteria *(Family Member)*; Carrie Renteria *(Family Member)*; Justin Renteria *(Family Member)*; Addison Grant Kerr *(Station Attendant)*; Chris Montana *(Jet Ski Guy)*; Dan Heather *(Redneck #1)*; Chris Heather *(Redneck #2)*; Lauren Campedelli *(Cashier)*; Clyde Okita *(Gun Club Man)*; Patsy Okita *(Gun Club Woman)*; Chuck

Miles *(Eagle Scout)*; Robert Russell *(Businessman)*; John Krupas *(Liquor Store Owner)*; Brenda Schaff *(Video Store Girl)*; Karen Severenson *(Video Store Lady)*; Lou Wynhoff *(Security Guard)*; Richard Scott Blades *(Video Store Owner)*; Lora Schaff *(Body Double)*; Larry Heather *(Dead Homeowner)*; Eva Scott-Perry *(Newswoman)*; Tom Simons *(Police Officer)*; Colin Campbell *(Real Lawmen Soundman)*

Toplining former "Partridge Family" moppet and broadcast personality Danny Bonaduce in an unkinder, ungentler mode, this deadpan thriller turns the shot-on-tape format to its advantage.

Seasoned viewers might notice a suspicious resemblance to the Belgian gallows satire MAN BITES DOG, as the narrative is presented from the POV of a camcorder owned by Dougie (Danny Bonaduce), who tapes everything he does, to the annoyance of wife Debbie (the star's real-life spouse Gretchen Bonaduce). After finding Debbie cheating on him, Dougie hits the road, intending to create a "video diary," and accidentally tapes a criminal trio led by Clint Dryer (Mick Wynhoff). They catch him, and though hot-tempered Vezna (Mollena Williams) wants to kill the natural born voyeur, Clint decides Dougie should join them and document their rampage of small-town robbery and murder on video—or else.

Clint soon insists Dougie take part in the robberies, but his first target turns out to be armed also. After a video store holdup becomes a bloodbath, the group holes up at a house, killing the owner. Meanwhile, Dougie has struck up a friendship with Clint's reluctant girlfriend Gloria (Melora Walters). Their escape attempt and Clint's suspicions finally lead to a shootout that leaves bodies lying all over—the whole incident captured by cameras from the TV show "Real Lawmen."

While the flat, cheap look of video ill befits dramatic storytelling, DEADLIEST writer-director Jack Perez legitimizes the shot-on-tape medium that gives events a scary verisimilitude, as when the camera turns away from a robbery victim as gunfire breaks out, and pans back to find her lying dead. The approach allows Perez to throw some well-aimed barbs at the video age. As amateur videotape of one of the gang's robberies airs on the news, Clint haughtily puts it down, knowing *his* footage is better. When Clint brings the camera and Gloria into a motel room for a videotaped bondage session, the battery dies just as things are getting hot. Having true-crime videorazzi on hand to cover the violent climax is beautifully ironic and works well on a dramatic level. The only problem is. . . that too parallels a subplot in MAN BITES DOG. At least the (even more viscerally brutal) Belgian pic can't claim to have Danny Partridge packing heat, but the sense of *deja vu* raises issues over whence Perez' true inspiration sprang. At least AMERICA'S DEADLIEST HOME VIDEO, primarily released to the small screen, works uncommonly well on VCR playback. *(Graphic violence, nudity, sexual situations, substance abuse, extreme profanity.)* — M.G.

d, Jack Perez; p, Michael L. Wynhoff; exec p, Maripat Ridge, Jonathan Furie; co-p, Steven Diller; w, Jack Perez; ph, Bill Francesco; ed, Jack Perez; m, James Edward Garcia, Isaac Ersoff, John Zehren; sound, Colin Campbell; fx, Jeffrey Lyle Segal, Addison Grant Kerr

Thriller/Crime   **(PR: O   MPAA: NR)**

AMERICAN COP   ★★
(U.S.) 91m Infinite Productions; Heatherwood Film Productions ~ A-Pix Entertainment c
(AKA: AMERIKAN COP)

William Katt *(Dr. Dell Davis)*; Wayne Crawford *(Elmo Le Grange)*; Daniel Quinn *(Franco)*; Vlad Shpoudeiko *(Vasily)*; Nickolai Nedovodin *(Nickolai)*; Ashley Laurence *(Gina)*; Olga

Vodin *(Katerina)*; Sergey Pankratiev *(Police Officer)*; Alexander Kushch *(Thug 1)*; Sveta Kochin *(Party Girl 1)*; Dina Antonenko *(Party Girl 2)*; Nickolai Baklan *(Thug 2)*; Valentin Myslivyi *(Bad Finger)*; Anatoli Lukyanenko *(Thug 3)*; Stas Baklan *(Thug 4)*; Helen Childress *(Deborah George)*; Eugene Shakh *(Ivan)*; Arthur Payne *(Embassy Clerk)*; Carlos Brooks *(Agent Michaels)*; Ivan Paitina *(Alyosha)*; Victor Grabosky *(Auto Mechanic)*; Viacheslavvornin *(Bogdanoff)*

Released directly to home video in the US, this cloak 'n' dagger travelogue reprises the amusing dogface character created by B-movie auteur Wayne Crawford in his 1991 Hong Kong fracas CRIME LORDS.

En route to a Greek vacation, lowly American cop Elmo LaGrange (Wayne Crawford) learns to regret his plane's stopover in Moscow. First ragamuffin Nickolai (Nickolai Nedovodin) steals Elmo's passport to guarantee his unofficial guardianship. Then Elmo is mistaken for a CIA ace by the Russian mob. He befriends Gina (Ashley Laurence), a gal claiming to be an American doctoral candidate abroad; Elmo doesn't realize that she's a double agent duping a transplanted Mafia chief, Franco (Daniel Quinn), whose latest order is for her to terminate Elmo. Warned by Nickolai, Elmo flees without deducing that Gina simply wants to use LaGrange's mistaken identity to cover her own lawful mission. Nickolai's sister Katerina (Olga Vodin), who hides young street crooks under a hockey stadium, talks fugitive Elmo into flying to St. Petersburg for a passport, but Franco's missiles force them to parachute down to a village. Captured Elmo is set free by Gina, but she seals her doom by confessing CIA affiliation in a bugged automobile. A Franco henchman takes the street urchins hostage, forcing Elmo to join a rescue effort led by local partisans. The proletarian guerillas bust up the Russian-American crime confederation and save the children, while Elmo gets to duel against Franco, outdrawing the villain with a bazooka. His passport returned by Nickolai, Elmo heads home but vows to lock lips with Katerina in the future.

Confront AMERICAN COP with expectations lowered, and one won't be turned off by its amateurish acting, impenetrable accents, offhand screenwriting, and one-take direction. This low-budget action retread tickles its audience with an air of *bonhomie*, an agreeably scruffy leading man, and the kick of watching American gangster cliches spelled out in Cyrillic. Unconventionally sexy (and middle-aged) hero-by-default LaGrange is the glue holding all the happenstance together. Without his mutt act, the assembly-line sadism scattered throughout the standard secret agent storyline might be curdling experience. All modest escapism needs to accomplish is invite viewers to the mayhem party, spin the punchy protagonist around a few times, and then let him remove his blindfold in time to pin the tail on a few shooters. The plot details can be stale as long as the cast behaves as if the violent circumstances are news to them. Sensibly treating the international carnage as a lark, AMERICAN COP parcels out thrills, disguises its redundancies, and ensures goodwill by calling attention to the out-of-shape hero's limitations. Although buffs could have written this script in one sitting, the pointedly non-serious flick lets viewers derive some pleasure from a droll stroll through familiar setups. *(Graphic violence, profanity.)* — R.P.

d, Wayne Crawford; p, Gregory Small; exec p, Joel Levine; assoc p, Christine Perakis, Barrie Saint Clair, Breaker Furches; w, Carlos Brooks; ph, Nicholas Von Sternberg; ed, Wayne Lines; m, Julian Laxton; prod d, Wesley Tabayoyong, II; art d, Daniel Grobler; sound, Shaun Murdoch; casting, Gino Havens; makeup, Vladimir Panchuk

Action/Spy/Romance   (PR: C   MPAA: PG-13)

AMERICAN PRESIDENT, THE   ★★½
(U.S.) 115m Castle Rock; Wildwood Enterprises, Inc.; Universal ~ Columbia c

Michael Douglas *(Andrew Shepherd)*; Annette Bening *(Sydney Ellen Wade)*; Martin Sheen *(A.J. MacInerney)*; Michael J. Fox *(Lewis Rothschild)*; Anna Deavere Smith *(Robin McCall)*; Samantha Mathis *(Janie Basdin)*; Shawna Waldron *(Lucy Shepherd)*; David Paymer *(Leon Kodak)*; Anne Haney *(Mrs. Chapil)*; Richard Dreyfuss *(Senator Rumson)*; Nina Siemaszko *(Beth Wade)*; Wendie Malick *(Susan Sloan)*; Beau Billingslea *(Agent Cooper)*; Gail Strickland *(Esther MacInerney)*; Joshua Malina *(David)*; Clement Von Franckenstein *(President D'Astier)*; Efrat Lavie *(Madame D'Astier)*; John Mahoney *(Leo Solomon)*; Taylor Nichols *(Stu)*; John Mahon *(Chairman of the Joint Chiefs)*; Tom Dahlgren *(Defense Secretary)*; Ralph Meyering, Jr. *(General)*; Kurt A. Boesen *(Security Advisor)*; Joseph Latimore *(Secret Service Agent)*; Darryl Alan Reed *(Secret Service Agent)*; Andrew Steel *(Secret Service Agent)*; Jordan Lund *(Carl)*; Richard F. McGonagle *(Rumson Staffer)*; Frank Cavestani *(Rumson Staffer)*; Richard Stahl *(Rumson Staffer)*; Alice Kushida *(Carol)*; Renee Phillips *(Lisa)*; Beans Morocco *(Doorkeeper)*; Kathryn Ish *(Education Secretary)*; Kamilah Martin *(Flower Girl)*; Augie Blunt *(Groundskeeper)*; Thom Barry *(Guard)*; Steven Gonzalez *(Hud Secretary)*; Gabriel Jarret *(Jeff)*; Karen Maruyama *(Leo's Secretary)*; Nancy Kandal *(Leslie)*; George Murdock *(Congressman)*; Bernie McInerney *(Congressman Millman)*; Jack Gilroy *(Congressman Pennybaker)*; Matthew Saks *(Congressional Staffer)*; Googy Gress *(Gil)*; Ron Canada *(Reporter Lloyd)*; Brian Pietro *(Reporter)*; Rick Garcia *(Reporter)*; Aaron Sorkin *(Aide in Bar)*; Kymberly S. Newberry *(Sally)*; Greg Poland *(Mark)*; Leslie Rae Bega *(White House Staffer Laura)*; Jennifer Crystal *(White House Staffer Maria)*; Arthur Senzy *(Deputy)*; Nick Toth *(White House Aide)*; Jorge Noa *(White House Aide)*; Maud Winchester *(White House Aide)*; Jeffrey Anderson *(TV News Anchorman)*; Suzanne Michaels *(TV News Anchorwoman)*; Mark Thompson *(Kenneth Michaels)*; David Drew Gallagher *(New Guy)*; Todd Odom *(Uniformed Secret Service Agent)*; Michael G. Alexander *(Color Guard Officer)*

THE AMERICAN PRESIDENT aspires to the liberal populism of Frank Capra films with a contemporary spin. Though apparently meant to be a romantic comedy, it more closely resembles an attenuated, if well-packaged, campaign ad from the Clinton Administration.

President Andrew Shepherd (Michael Douglas), a popular Democrat, is gearing up for his 1996 re-election campaign. A widower, Andrew falls in love with environmental lobbyist Sydney Wade (Annette Bening). Sydney at first tries to keep their relationship on a business level, enlisting the President's support for an anti-global warming bill and resisting his requests for a date. She eventually accepts his invitation to attend a White House dinner, and the word is out.

The President's girlfriend causes concern among his inner circle, including his Chief of Staff (Martin Sheen), Domestic Policy Advisor (Michael J. Fox), White House Pollster (David Paymer), Press Secretary (Anna Deavere Smith) and Personal Aide (Samantha Mathis). They are particularly alarmed after Senator Bob Rumsen (Richard Dreyfuss), the president's Republican nemesis, casts aspersions on Sydney's character. As his popularity wanes, the President cuts a deal with Congress, compromising on the environmental bill in order to get a tough crime bill passed. Sydney—feeling betrayed both personally and ideologically—leaves Andrew, who's forced to reevaluate his priorities. In a televised press conference, Andrew finally speaks out against his Republican opponents, signals his support for the original environmental bill and declares his love for Sydney.

THE AMERICAN PRESIDENT is light years away from director Rob Reiner's irreverent 1984 THIS IS SPINAL TAP, completely free of the mocking elements that could undermine what is essentially a tepid bedroom comedy whose male lead happens to be the President of the United States. The reverential tone is a pleasant change from today's knee-jerk political cynicism, but it also makes the comedy lofty and dull.

Reiner and screenwriter Aaron Sorkin, with whom he also worked on A FEW GOOD MEN, were apparently not content with making a romantic comedy with political underpinnings. THE AMERICAN PRESIDENT seems designed as a thinly disguised fable about the Clinton White House, in which all the revelations are good.

President Shepherd is surrounded by a staff resembling Clinton's (from Michael J. Fox's George Stephanopoulos-like Lewis Rothschild to Martin Sheen's "Mac" McLarty-*manque* A.J. MacInerney), has a teenage daughter (Shawna Waldron), a 1996 election opponent in the Republican Senator from Kansas *a la* Bob Dole, and image problems. Michael Douglas doesn't look, act or sound anything like President Bill Clinton, but that isn't necessarily a bad thing. Douglas' President is a tough, moral, quick-thinking *liberal* man who cares so little for image that he's furious when someone calls his retaliatory bombing of Libya "presidential." It's not presidential, he retorts, simply necessary. Andrew's one sacrifice of principle for expediency is quickly corrected.

As a $30 million re-election ad, THE AMERICAN PRESIDENT isn't bad. As entertainment, it's agreeable fluff. The production is polished, and if Michael Douglas is too serious for farce, his stiffness befits his role. Annette Bening brings off her modern Doris Day part well enough. Everyone else, however, fades quickly from memory. As political satire, it's toothless. That only the bad guys—aka the Republicans—see anything wrong with the President bedding down a lobbyist of any kind cheapens the argument about access to politicians, and obscures the fact that Sydney has become, essentially, a high-priced prostitute. The whole thing is so blandly proficient that one half hopes Jim Carrey will show up as an animal-rights lobbyist, and throw this staid White House into a real tailspin. (*Sexual situations, profanity.*) — E.M.

d, Rob Reiner; p, Rob Reiner; exec p, Charles Newirth, Jeffrey Stott; assoc p, Barbara Maltby; w, Aaron Sorkin; ph, John Seale; ed, Robert Leighton; m, Marc Shaiman; prod d, Lilly Kilvert; art d, John Warnke; set d, Karen O'Hara; sound, Robert Eber (mixer); fx, Clay Pinney, Ken Ralston, Industrial Light & Magic; casting, Jane Jenkins, Janet Hirshenson; cos, Gloria Gresham; makeup, Daniel C. Striepeke

AAN Best Musical or Comedy Score: Marc Shaiman

Romance/Comedy/Drama   **(PR: A MPAA: PG-13)**

ANDROID AFFAIR, THE   ★★
(U.S.) 90m MCA Television Entertainment; Chanticleer Films ~ MCA/Universal Home Video c

Harley Jane Kozak (*Dr. Karen Garret*); Griffin Dunne (*William—Teach 905*); Ossie Davis (*Dr. Fredrich Winston*); Saul Rubinek (*Fiedler*); Paul Outerbridge (*Thomas Benti*); Natalie Radford (*Rachel Tyler*); Chandra Galasso (*Alexx*); David Campbell (*Gunther*); Ron Hartman (*Palmer*); Michelle Moffett (*Teach 1*); Joseph Scorsiani (*Dr. Bonner*); Heidi Hatashita (*Nurse Gridley*); Wendy Murphy (*Allen*); Diana Zimmer (*Visitor No. 1*); Desmond Campbell (*Peter*); Anne Ritchie (*Reporter*); Peter

Pownall (*Security Guard*); Bryan Renfro (*Guard*); Robert Hollinger (*Cop No. 1*); T.W. Schroeder (*Cop No. 2*)

Made for cable TV, THE ANDROID AFFAIR gets asterisked as an indirect Hollywood contribution from science-fiction legend Isaac Asimov (FANTASTIC VOYAGE). Asimov's actual involvement was mere shared story credit for the short subject "Teach 109," which filmmaker Richard Kletter expanded into this mediocre programmer.

Though Asimov codified a virtual Bill of Rights for machines in his many robot stories, the tone here leans toward a very lightweight BLADE RUNNER. In the future, manlike robots are near enough to *Homo sapiens* for cruel medical experiments; these guinea pigs feel no pain and can describe their status during surgery. Rising physician Karen Garrett (Harley Jane Kozak), assigned to perfect a dicey heart procedure, is introduced to Teach 905 (Griffin Dunne), an advanced android with a mischievous personality and rebellious attitude that bristles at Karen's cold bedside manner. Among his demands is that she call him William and smuggle him out of the research lab for day trips so he can interact in everyday human society.

Eventually Karen feels genuine romantic attraction for the (anatomically correct) artificial man, but their bispecies love affair detours up various conspiratorial alleys, as William unmasks another 900-Series android already living full-time in the city, then investigates why every member of the 900 design team dropped dead except for Karen's boss, Dr. Winston (Ossie Davis). Asking too many questions sends the pair fleeing from Winston's various hirelings (including Chandra Galassa, doing Pam Grier's old bit as a baadasssss action chick). Finally the fugitives are caught and taken back to the lab, where Winston greets Karen with "Haven't you figured it out yet?" The problem is, most viewers probably have. Winston is himself an android replica of the main designer, who was stricken by the same heart ailment Karen is supposed to remedy. But android Winston pulled the plug on the real Winston's life-support and now wants the cure strictly for himself. When she resists doing the surgery he keels over, doomed. Even though William/Teach 905 was privy to the deception, Karen heads off into the sunset with him anyway—maybe male androids are *more* than anatomically correct.

The ingratiatingly casual Dunne (AFTER HOURS) is nicely cast against type as the synthetic being, as are Davis and a wildly neurotic Saul Rubinek. But a flailing, buggy story line soon crashes THE ANDROID AFFAIR. Though the feature's production design of Winston's lab complex is appropriately ominous tech noir, the outside world turns out to be a blandly generic Toronto, backdrop to many a TV-movie chase scene virtually identical to those here. Isaac Asimov is better served by his posthumously published collaboration with Harlan Ellison, *I, Robot: The Illustrated Screenplay*, written for a unrealized 1970s motion picture project but packaged in book form in 1994. (*Violence, sexual situations.*) — C.C.

d, Richard Kletter; p, Joan Carson; exec p, Thom Colwell, Jana Sue Memel; w, Richard Kletter (based on the short film "Teach 109" by Richard Kletter, from a story by Richard Kletter and Isaac Asimov); ph, Bernard Salzmann; ed, Lisa Bromwell; m, Simon Boswell; prod d, Carmi Gallo; art d, Allen Crawley; sound, Stuart French (mixer); fx, Dan Krech, Laird McMurray Film Services; casting, Leslee Dennis; cos, Luis Sequeira; makeup, Marilyn O'Quinn, Randy McInally; stunts, John Stoneham, Stoneham

Science Fiction   **(PR: C MPAA: PG-13)**

ANGUS ★★½
(U.S.) 87m Turner Pictures Worldwide;
Atlas Entertainment ~ New Line c

Kathy Bates (Meg); George C. Scott (Ivan); Charles Talbert (Angus Bethune); Ariana Richards (Melissa Lefevre); Chris Owen (Troy Wedberg); James Van Der Beek (Rick Sandford); Rita Moreno (Madame Rulenska); Lawrence Pressman (Principal Metcalf); Anna Thompson (April Thomas); Robert Curtis-Brown (Alexander); Kevin Connolly (Andy); Tony Denman (Tony); Yvette Freeman (Science Teacher); Salim Grant (Mike); Epatha Harris (Ellen); Steven Hartman (Rick—Age 11); Robin Lynn Heath (Jody Cole); Grant Hoover (Angus—Age 8); Evan Kaufman (Alex Immergluch); Perry Anzilotti (Tuxedo Salesman); James Keane (Coach); Irvin Kershner (Mr. Stoff); Michael McLeod (Rick—Age 8); Wesley Mann (Mr. Kessler); Monty O'Grady (Minister); Bob Pepper (Wedding Photographer); Tanner Lee Prairie (Rick—Age 5); Lindsay Price (Recycling Girl); Christopher Ragsdale (Boy Playing Football); Bethany Richards (Melissa—Age 11); Cameron Royds (Baby Angus); Aaron Siefers (Angus—Age 11); Eric E. Thomas, II (Kid at Birthday Party); Bryan Warloe (Troy—8 Years Old); Michael Wesley (Angus—Age 5)

ANGUS is a mild-mannered comedy about a brainy, overweight high school boy who has an opportunity to turn a night of humiliation into the night of his dreams.

Ever since he was a little boy, Angus (Charles Talbert) has been picked on by other kids, especially Rick Sanford (James Van Der Beek), the most popular boy in school. By the time the boys reach high school, Rick is quarterback of the football team, and Angus is a defensive lineman. Angus causes a fumble that helps his team win the big game, but since Rick picks up the ball and scores a touchdown, he becomes the hero. This is typical of Angus's life. He feels he has to do all work, while other people get the credit. To make matters worse, Rick is dating Melissa Lefevre (Ariana Richards), and Angus has been infatuated with her all of his young life.

As a joke, Rick arranges for Angus to be elected king of the Winter Ball, where Melissa will be queen. Angus's mother Meg (Kathy Bates) and grandfather Ivan (George C. Scott), both encourage him to go to the dance. When Ivan dies on the day of his wedding to a much younger woman, Angus decides to attend the dance in his memory. At the dance, Rick shows a video of Angus dancing with a blow-up doll. Angus runs away in shame, and Melissa too leaves, disgusted with Rick. She talks to Angus and even shares a secret with him. They return to the dance and have a great time. Rick is suspended from school. Melissa kisses Angus good night.

Angus is a likable character, but the film offers nothing we have not seen before. Rick's attempts to humiliate the helpless Angus are unrealistically extreme. Angus's final triumph is devalued by the fact that Rick is not a particularly intelligent or worthy foe.

ANGUS brings to mind LUCAS, a much better film with a similar theme, which explores complex emotions and in the process makes its happy ending more potent. In ANGUS, the ending is obvious, and inspires merely a fleeting feeling of comfort.

Bates and Scott give wonderful performances in their smaller roles, elevating the film. There are a few funny moments, though unfortunately most are at the expense of Angus. The attempts at symbolism (such as Angus toppling over a chess king when Ivan dies) are heavy-handed and fatuous. The presence of Ivan and Meg continually reminds the viewer that someday Angus will grow up and all of the troubles he now experiences will pass.

That simple message, however, is obscured by silly jokes and one-dimensional characterizations. (Profanity.) — A.M.

d, Patrick Read Johnson; p, Dawn Steel; exec p, Robert Cavallo, Susan Landau, Gary Levinsohn; w, Jill Gordon (based on the short story by Chris Crutcher); ph, Alexander Gruszynski; ed, Janice Hampton; m, Green Day; prod d, Lawrence Miller; art d, Jeff Knipp; set d, Claudia Rebar; sound, Bob Anderson, Jr. (mixer); fx, Tom Bellissimo; casting, Ronnie Yeskel; cos, Jill Ohanneson; makeup, Michael Tomasino; stunts, Dick Butler

Children's/Comedy   (PR: A   MPAA: PG-13)

APOLLO 13 ★★★½
(U.S.) 140m Imagine Entertainment ~ Universal c

Tom Hanks (Jim Lovell); Bill Paxton (Fred W. Haise); Kevin Bacon (John L. Swigart); Gary Sinise (Ken Mattingly); Ed Harris (Gene Kranz); Kathleen Quinlan (Marilyn Lovell); Mary Kate Schellhardt (Barbara Lovell); Emily Ann Lloyd (Susan Lovell); Miko Hughes (Jeffrey Lovell); Max Elliott Slade (Jay Lovell); Jean Speagle Howard (Blanch Lovell); Tracy Reiner (Mary Haise); David Andrews (Pete Conrad); Michelle Little (Jane Conrad); Chris Ellis (Deke Slayton); Joe Spano (NASA Director); Xander Berkeley (Henry Hurt); Marc McClure (Glynn Lunney); Ben Marley (John Young); Clint Howard (EECOM White); Loren Dean (EECOM Arthur); Tom Wood (EECOM Gold); Googy Gress (RETRO White); Patrick Mickler (RETRO Gold); Ray McKinnon (FIDO White); Max Grodenchik (FIDO Gold); Christian Clemenson (Dr. Chuck); Brett Cullen (CAPCOM 1); Ned Vaughn (CAPCOM 2); Andy Milder (GUIDO White); Geoffrey Blake (GUIDO Gold); Wayne Duvall (LEM Controller White); Jim Meskimen (TELMU White); Joseph Culp (TELMU Gold); John Short (INCO White); Ben Bode (INCO Gold); Todd Louiso (FAO White); Gabriel Jarret (GNC White); Christopher John Fields (Booster White); Kenneth White (Grumman Rep); Jim Ritz (Ted); Andrew Lipshultz (Launch Director); Mark Wheeler (Neil Armstrong); Larry Williams (Buzz Aldrin); Endre Hules (Guenter Wendt); Karen Martin (Tracey); Maureen Hanley (Woman); Meadow Williams (Kim); Walter Von Huene (Technician); Brian Markinson (Pad Rat); Steve Rankin (Pad Rat); Austin O'Brien (Whiz Kid); Louisa Marie (Whiz Kid Mom); Thom Barry (Orderly); Arthur Senzy (SIM Tech); Carl Gabriel Yorke (SIM Tech); Ryan Holihan (SIM Tech); Rance Howard (Reverend); J.J. Chaback (Neighbor); Todd Hallowell (Noisy Civilian); Matthew Goodall (Stephen Haise); Taylor Goodall (Fred Haise Jr.); Misty Dickinson (Margaret Haise); Roger Corman (Congressman); Lee Anne Matusek (Loud Reporter); Mark D. Newman (Loud Reporter); Mark McKeel (Suit Room Assistant); Patty Raya (Patty); Jack Conley (Science Reporter); Jeffrey S. Kluger (Science Reporter); Bruce Wright (Anchor); Ivan Allen (Anchor); Jon Bruno (Anchor); Reed Rudy (Roger Chaffee); Steve Bernie (Virgil Grisson); Steven Ruge (Edward White)

An enormous commercial success despite its complete lack of sex, violence, and trendy irony, APOLLO 13 is a meticulous, stunning drama about the moon mission that almost didn't get back.

We first see veteran astronaut Jim Lovell (Tom Hanks) watching Neil Armstrong's historic landing on TV. Eager for an opportunity to walk on the moon, he gets his chance, along with rookie Fred Haise, Jr. (Bill Paxton) and perfectionist pilot Ken Mattingly (Gary Sinise), aboard the third lunar mission, scheduled for April, 1970. Bad omens abound: Jim's car stalls, wife Marilyn (Kathleen Quinlan) loses her wedding ring, and Lovell is forced to replace Mattingly, who has been exposed to measles, with cocky backup pilot Jack Swigert (Kevin Bacon). As the rocket lifts off, public interest in the space program is on the wane, and the networks won't even preempt "I Dream of Jeannie" for live broadcasts from space. But then an oxygen tank explodes, draining the service module of most of its power and forcing shutdown of the command capsule. The landing is aborted, but that's the least of NASA's problems: they have to find a way to get the crew back home using less electricity than a coffee pot.

Flight controller Gene Kranz (Ed Harris) leads Mission Control in plotting new trajectories while Mattingly works with programmers in the simulators to solve the power supply problem. The crew is dejected, tense and miserable; Haise is physically sick (a kidney infection), Swigert fears being blamed, and Lovell is crushed by the loss of his dream. But once they pass the intended landing site he snaps out of it and takes command. Freezing in a cabin temperature of 38 degrees, choking on their own carbon dioxide, and manually adjusting their course to achieve the precise angle needed for re-entry, the crew manages to salvage something like victory from this titanic failure, while Houston technicians, NASA press officers, and the crew's families sweat out the arduous wait. The landing is successful and the astronauts are greeted as heroes.

The *real* heroes of Ron Howard's film aren't so much the astronauts (whose bravery is a matter of enduring a horrific experience without going to pieces) but the pudgy, bespectacled techno-nerds of NASA, who are charged with improvising a spectacular rescue with the tools at hand—mostly slide rules and their own brains. Their role is made comprehensible through Howard's detailed recreation of the space program's technical milieu: the use and accuracy of the simulators, the computer "that fits in a single room," the tedious vector math, and the mundane necessities of working and living in space. Howard's quest for verisimilitude went so far as to subject cast and crew to near-freezing sets, as well as his much-publicized filming aboard the KC-135 jet—a.k.a. the "Vomit Comet"—which can simulate zero-gravity for 23-second intervals. Not one frame of NASA stock footage was used; even the lift-off of the Saturn V rocket was specially recreated, giving it a surprising visceral charge. Howard's attention to minutiae adds tremendous visual depth, creating a truly immersive experience.

However, this experience is largely without context or emotional force. Despite and uncredited rewrite by John Sayles, the characters, including Lovell, are poorly drawn, and the script fails to provide any serious insight or commentary on the story. Although intelligently avoiding melodramatic interpersonal agonies, the dialogue reveals too little about these men, leaving the enormously talented cast—especially Paxton and Quinlan—without much to do.

APOLLO 13 nonetheless shows Howard to be, technically speaking, at the absolute peak of his form. And there is something sufficiently compelling, not to say indelible, in the image of that tiny tin can, spinning wildly as it hurtles toward the moon. (Look for cameos by director Howard and B-movie producer Roger Corman.) *(Profanity.)* — R.S.

d, Ron Howard; p, Brian Grazer; exec p, Todd Hallowell; assoc p, Aldric Porter, Michael Bostick; w, William Broyles, Jr., Al Reinert, John Sayles (uncredited); ph, Dean Cundey; ed, Daniel Hanley, Michael Hill; m, James Horner; prod d, Michael Corenblith; art d, David Bomba, Bruce Allan Miller; set d, Meredith Boswell; sound, David MacMillan (mixer), Kevin Patterson; fx, Matt Sweeney, Robert Legato, Digital Domain; casting, Jane Jenkins, Janet Hirshenson; cos, Rita Ryack; makeup, Daniel Striepeke; stunts, Mickey Gilbert, Jim Halty

AAN Best Picture; AAN Best Supporting Actor: Ed Harris; *AAN Best Supporting Actress:* Kathleen Quinlan; *AAN Best Adapted Screenplay:* William Broyles Jr., Al Reinert; *AAN Best Art Direction:* Eugenio Zanetti; *AA Best Editing:* Mike Hill, Dan Hanley; *AAN Best Dramatic Score:* James Horner; *AA Best Sound:* Rick Dior, Steve Pederson, Scott Millan, David MacMillan; *AAN Best Visual Effects:* Robert Legato, Michael Kanfer, Leslie Ekker, Matt Sweeney

Drama/Historical   **(PR: A   MPAA: PG)**

ARABIAN KNIGHT   ★★★½
(U.K.) 81m Allied Filmmakers ~ Miramax c

VOICES OF: Vincent Price *(Zigzag)*; Matthew Broderick *(Tack the Cobbler)*; Jennifer Beals *(Princess Yum Yum)*; Bobbi Page *(Singing Voice of Princess Yum Yum)*; Eric Bogosian *(Phido)*; Toni Collette *(Nurse/Good Witch)*; Jonathan Winters *(The Thief)*; Clive Revill *(King Nod)*; Kevin Dorsey *(One-Eye)*; Donald Pleasence; Mona Marshall

Unjustly and unceremoniously dumped into theaters for a too-brief theatrical release, the animated feature ARABIAN KNIGHT drew deserved raves from critics—who were practically the only ones to see it. Its toss-and-shrug fate is all the more calamitous since ARABIAN KNIGHT is one of the most stunning, phantasmagorical visions ever put to film—YELLOW SUBMARINE by way of M.C. Escher.

Based on the genie-less fable "The Thief of Baghdad," ARABIAN KNIGHT was developed under the working title of "The Thief and the Cobbler." The latter is Tack (voice of Matthew Broderick), a poor but honest young man in old Baghdad, a gold-hearted innocent who says almost nothing. An accident earns him the enmity of sorcerer Zigzag (Vincent Price), who has a sarcastic bird-servant, Phido (Eric Bogosian), and uses his magic to keep the sleepy King Nod (Clive Revill) from being bothersome. Fortunately for Tack, the smart and gutsy Princess Yum Yum (Jennifer Beals) takes a fancy to him and intercedes on his behalf. In a parallel story, a muttering, comically slinking thief (Jonathan Winters) swipes three golden balls from a minaret. Their absence foretells the city's fall, which Zigzag is busy actively arranging with the terrifying desert warlord One-Eye (Kevin Dorsey). The princess, no wimp, meanwhile enlists a tribe of desert brigands to defend her city. Together with Tack, who has a prophecy of his own to fulfill, and the inadvertent help of the thief, Baghdad is saved.

Begun at least 27 years prior as the dream project of fabled animator Richard Williams (director of animation on WHO FRAMED ROGER RABBIT), ARABIAN KNIGHT suffered from superficial comparisons to Disney's ALADDIN (1992). It might also have suffered from distributor Miramax's concurrent acquisition by Disney, which had no incentive to promote animation other than its own.

The story behind this orphan feature is an *Arabian Nights* tale in itself. Williams, a longtime commercial and movie title-sequence animator who won a 1972 Oscar for his short "A Christmas Carol" and shared a 1982-83 Emmy for "Ziggy's Gift," began devising the feature as early as 1968. Twenty years later, he had personally animated 15 minutes of film and pushed for financing on the strength of ROGER RABBIT. A Paris-based executive producer, Jake Eberts, eventually arranged financing after Saudi sources fell through. Williams, working in a North London studio with a team including old-hand animators from Disney and Warner Bros., labored nearly three years on the final production, completing it in December 1992. It sat on the shelf for two more years until Miramax acquired it for North American distribution. The original vocal cast was then overhauled, with the major exception of Price.

The story may be standard Disney fare, but ARABIAN KNIGHT's impressionistic visuals, crammed with an eye-popping panoply of details, are simply extraordinary. With its shifting, shimmering light-sources, strikingly rich colors, expanses of white that turn the desert into a Salvador Dali landscape, it's like a storybook come to life. The medium is fully utilized: perspectives and planes shift gloriously and unexpectedly, and the spectacular climax is a fever-pitch mechanical ballet of a literal war machine collapsing in near-miss synchronization around the deadpan thief—a marvel of timing and infinite variations. Virtually unseen at the time of its release, ARABIAN KNIGHT is a buried cinematic treasure. — F.L.

d, Richard Williams; p, Imogen Sutton, Richard Williams; exec p, Jake Eberts; co-p, Fred Calverts, Bette L. Smith; w, Richard Williams, Margaret French; ph, John Leatherbarrow; ed, Peter Bond; m, Robert Folk, Norman Gimbel; art d, Roy Naisbitt; anim, Ken Harris, Art Babbitt, Emery Hawkins, Richard Williams, Neil Boyle, David Byers-Brown, Ramon Guillaumet, Margaret Grieve, Alyson Hamilton, Brent Odell, Paul Bolger, Fred Calvert; fx, Malcolm Burns

Animated/Children's/Fantasy   **(PR: AA   MPAA: G)**

ARIZONA DREAM   ★★★½
(U.S.) 142m Union Generale Cinematographique; Constellation; Hachette Premiere; Arrowtooth Productions ~ Kit Parker Films c

Johnny Depp (*Axel Blackmar*); Jerry Lewis (*Leo Sweetie*); Faye Dunaway (*Elaine Stalker*); Lili Taylor (*Grace Stalker*); Paulina Porizkova (*Millie*); Vincent Gallo (*Paul Backmar*); Michael J. Pollard (*Fabian*); Candyce Mason (*Blanche*); Alexia Rena (*Angie*); Polly Noonan (*Betty*); Ann Schulman (*Carla*); Patricia O'Grady (*MC/Announcer*); James R. Wilson (*Lawyer*); Eric Polczwartek (*Man With Door*); Kim Keo (*Mechanical Doll*); Sal Jenco (*Man at the Phone*); James P. Marshall (*Boatman*); Vincent Tocktuo (*Eskimo Man*); Santos Romero; David Rodriguez; Juan Urrea; Jose Luis Avila; Sergio Hlarmendaris; Frank Turley; Manuel Ruiz; Narcisco Dominguez; Benjamin S. Gonzales; Serafino Flores; Miguel Moreno; Raphael Salcido; Chanaia Rodriguez (*Mariachi Band Members*)

An offbeat and whimsical fantasy, ARIZONA DREAM is a lovingly crafted film that features yet another quietly intense performance by Johnny Depp.

Depp plays Axel, a young man who works for the Department of Fish and Game, tagging fish in New York harbor and waxing philosophical about the honesty of fish and the importance of dreams. (He himself dreams of a halibut-toting Eskimo saved from frozen death by loyal sled dogs.) Cousin Paul (Vincent Gallo) has been sent by Axel's uncle, Leo (Jerry Lewis), an incredibly wealthy Arizona car dealer with a penchant for talking in metaphor, to bring Axel home. Leo, who feels responsible for his orphaned nephew, wants him to attend his wedding to Millie, his "Polish Cupcake," who is half his age and subject to crying jags. When Leo pressures Axel to work for him as a car salesman, he at first resists, agreeing only in order to humor his uncle until the wedding. He then meets resentful, suicidal copper heiress Grace (Lili Taylor) and her flirty, flaky stepmother Elaine (Faye Dunaway). Axel and Grace debate the inevitability of their respective inheritances.

At dinner, Paul and Axel, competing for Elaine's attention, get caught in a literal tug-of-war between her and Grace. Axel becomes involved with Elaine and builds man-powered flying machines for her, but someone keeps smashing them. Accordion-wielding, turtle-nurturing Grace is his prime suspect, but it might be a giant halibut swimming in the Arizona breeze. Grace and Axel have a confrontation involving Russian roulette that culminates in a passionate embrace. Leo dies suddenly, instructing Axel on his deathbed to go back to New York; instead, he goes back to Elaine. Grace has given Elaine a single-seat aircraft for her birthday (which allows aspiring actor Paul to live out his dream/nightmare: Cary Grant's chase scene from NORTH BY NORTHWEST), and Axel is now more drawn to Grace. But she shoots herself in a thunderstorm, shattering Axel's illusions about love and himself.

This independently-produced 1992 film, the first in English by Bosnian director Emir Kusturica (TIME OF THE GYPSIES), is beautifully photographed by Vilko Filao. Its dreamy, dazzling texture enhances and explicates a bizarre, non-linear story that often slides gracefully into surreal images. While the ambling plot and quirky dialogue sag in places, the richly detailed sets and deeply layered visuals are constantly entertaining; every moment is filled to bursting with things to look at and listen to. The opening Eskimo adventure sequence is very much in the European art film tradition, around which Kusturica has wound a very American story exploring personal freedom and responsibility in unusual ways.

Some characters and events, like Paul's constant recitation of film dialogue and Grace's farcical suicide attempts, wobble unsteadily between parody and self-parody. Still, the characters are original and fascinating, and the actors embrace their roles with energy and intelligence. Lewis is only a little awful, and he and Depp have a nice rapport. Dunaway gives a particularly juicy performance, and Taylor is simply amazing, seemingly able to transform herself physically for every role she plays.

In spite of a positive reception at festivals, ARIZONA DREAM was unable to find a US distributor until Warners released an edited version on video in 1994. That's a shame, because the cinematographic splendor of Kusturica's work cries out for the large screen. In addition, the video deletes several delightful moments of magic realism, including a hysterical tribute to RAGING BULL, and some dialogue that helps to make sense of Axel's relationship with Elaine (curiously, it also adds subtitles to the final "Eskimo" scene, which is spoken in gibberish). A "director's cut" received limited screenings in the US in 1995. (*Profanity, sexual situations, adult situations*) — R.S.

d, Emir Kusturica; p, Claudie Ossard, Cedomir Kolar, Yves Marmion; exec p, Paul R. Gurian; co-p, Richard Brick; w, Emir Kusturica, David Atkins; ph, Vilko Filac; ed, Andrlja Zasranovic; m, Goran Bregovic; prod d, Miljen Kljakovic; art d, Jan Pascale; set d, Jan Pascale; sound, Vincent Arnardi; fx, Greg Landerer, Kenny Estes, Max W. Anderson; casting, Pennie DuPont; cos, Jill M. Ohanneson; makeup, Patti York, Charles Balazs, Cheryl Voss; stunts, Everett L. Creach

Comedy/Drama   **(PR: A   MPAA: NR)**

ARMAGEDDON: THE FINAL CHALLENGE
(U.S.) 85m Garciafilm ~ York Home Video c

Todd Jensen (*Michael Throne*); Graham Clarke (*Plato*); Joanna Rowlands (*Voyou*); Toni Caprari (*Geiring*)

ARMAGEDDON: THE FINAL CHALLENGE is indeed the ultimate challenge to credulity. It is a chaotic recipe for an equally chaotic world after WWIII, where science and fantasy are whipped together with a spoonful of politics, a dash of religion and a pinch of romance, to create unpalatable cinema.

It is a future with a Big Brotherish, totalitarian government, where killer android-clones eliminate rebellious thinkers. One night, pilot Michael Throne (Todd Jensen) returns to the abandoned theater he lives in, plugs into "the net" to buy a new sex droid, and discovers his credit has been wiped out. Computer error or conspiracy? Then, he finds the mysterious Voyou (Joanna Rowlands) unconscious on his doorstep. He takes her in, gives her a Euro-trash outfit and *a lot* of make-up, and falls in love. Days pass. Michael has several dreams about doing battle — hand to hand, a swordfight, chess — with the evil Geiring (Toni Caprari). Voyou's father, Plato (Graham Clarke), shows up. He is a rebel and prophet come to enlist Michael's assistance in announcing The Second Coming (Michael used to be a famous DJ). Geiring kills Voyou, but it turns out she was a clone. Michael broadcasts the message of Christ's return to the world, and goes to meet the real Voyou. He finally fights and kills Geiring, and as the ships carrying Christ's armies, "in all their marmoreal majesty," descend on Earth, Michael and Voyou go off together.

It is hard to believe that anybody could seriously make a film like ARMAGEDDON. The action is not just illogical, but incoherent; the special effects are amateurish and crude; and the plot is nonexistent. This one is strictly for late-night laughs. *(Violence, sexual situations.)* — P.R.

d, Michael Garcia; exec p, Mark Bruno; assoc p, Arthur Schoenberg; co-p, Elmo DeWitt; w, George Garcia, Michael Garcia; ph, Buster Reynolds; ed, Gerrie Van Wyk, Donovan Marsh; m, Johan Laas; prod d, Gary Wilson; fx, Eugene Snyman, Real Life Creatures; casting, Paula Verster; cos, Pierre Viennings

Science Fiction (PR: O MPAA: NR)

ART FOR TEACHERS OF CHILDREN ★★★
(U.S.) 82m ~ Zeitgeist Films bw

Caitlin Grace McDonnell *(Jennifer)*; Duncan Hannah *(John)*; Coles Burroughs *(Molly)*; Bryan Keane *(Counselor)*; Jennifer Williams *(Alex)*; Lisa Anomaiprasert *(Naomi)*; Tom Carey *(FBI Agent)*; Ruth S. Montgomery *(Mother's Voice)*; Peter Hutton *(Father's Voice)*; Jennifer Montgomery *(Narration)*; Eve Heller *(Margaret)*; Craig Peterson *(Nasty Student)*; Moyra Davey *(Person Looking at "Naked" Pix)*; Michael Wacks *(Preppy)*; Eileen Myles; Dave McGuinness; Amy Sillman; Michael Gitlin; Adolfas Mekas; Peggy Ahwesh; Roy Lumadue; Bill Slowick; Jamie Patten; Rick Rock *(Art Colonists)*; Northfield Mount Hermon Gymnastics Team *(Themselves)*

Jennifer Montgomery's semi-autobiographical look at underage sex and child pornography has proved controversial for both its subject matter and its filmmaking style. Inspired by the director's boarding school affair with well-known photographer Jock Sturges, ART FOR TEACHERS OF CHILDREN challenges notions of censorship and the age of consent.

In 1990, Jock Sturges's studio was ransacked and much of his work was confiscated by the FBI after a lab technician reported finding portraits of nude children. The FBI contacted Jennifer Montgomery, seeking her testimony as one of the children photographed. Jennifer refused to cooperate with the FBI, and Sturges was never charged with child pornography.

Set mainly in the mid-1970s, ART FOR TEACHERS OF CHILDREN is a narrative expose of the relationship between 14-year-old Jennifer (Caitlin Grace McDonnell) and her married dorm counselor and photography teacher, John (Duncan Hannah). Impressionable Jennifer is keen to endear herself to the teacher who is nearly twice her age, and is flattered when he asks to photograph her. Soon she develops romantic feelings for him and asks him to sleep with her. Although he feigns resistance—citing his worry about being sent to jail if anyone found out—he is soon having sex with her in his darkroom. When the affair is discovered, John loses his job and his wife. Jennifer continues to visit John, until one day she finds out that he has also been sleeping with one of her classmates. Disappointed and disillusioned, she abandons the relationship. More than a decade

after she stops seeing John, she is contacted by the FBI. She is now a photographer herself.

ART FOR TEACHERS OF CHILDREN presents a refreshingly original angle on underage sex and child pornography. Montgomery does not deny that the relationship with Sturges affected her, but she does not blame him for making use of her. The film cleverly portrays the complexity of seduction—who seduced whom in this relationship? It also disrupts preconceived notions about power, censorship and the age of consent. As such, it is an extension of some of the ideas explored in Montgomery's superb short films, HOME AVENUE and AGE 12: LOVE WITH A LITTLE L.

As writer, director, photographer and editor of ART FOR TEACHERS OF CHILDREN, Montgomery deliberately chooses a deadpan style of filmmaking. The performances are characterized by a flatness of delivery and much of the film is shot in the middle distance (undercutting the potentially pornographic nature of the material). While this effectively allows Montgomery to separate herself from both the subject and the character of Jennifer, it also keeps the audience at a distance, retaining the film's cerebral quality, despite the controversial nature of its theme. *(Sexual situations, adult situations, extensive nudity.)* — J.S.

d, Jennifer Montgomery; p, Jennifer Montgomery; w, Jennifer Montgomery; ph, Jennifer Montgomery; ed, Jennifer Montgomery; sound, Crosby McCloy

Docudrama/Drama (PR: O MPAA: NR)

ASCENT, THE ★★½
(U.S.) 96m RHI Entertainment; Cabin Fever Entertainment ~ Cabin Fever Entertainment c

Rachel Ward *(Patricia)*; Vincent Spano *(Franco)*; Ben Cross *(Major Farrell)*; Tony Lo Bianco *(Aldo)*; Mark Ingall *(Sergeant Thomas)*; John DeVeillers *(Major Quinn)*

Respected Canadian director Donald Shebib—auteur of GOIN' DOWN THE ROAD (1970), the Canadian EASY RIDER—tries his hand at big, old-fashioned adventure. With its ultra-traditional narrative, easy masculine camaraderie, and uncomplicated wartime bonding, THE ASCENT feels like an artifact of simpler, less cynical times.

Near the end of WWII, in a POW camp in British east Africa, a plucky band of Italians and the odd German are waiting out the inevitable in the care of a stiff-lipped British commander, Major Farrell (Ben Cross). Farrell's chief obsession is to climb nearby Mt. Kenya; his nemesis Franco (Vincent Spano), a prisoner, is a world-class climber who spends all his downtime trying to escape. During one breakout attempt, Franco stops to fix a truck and is apprehended by its occupants, Patricia (Rachel Ward) and her industrialist father. Franco is drawn to Patricia, little knowing that she's the object of Major Farrell's unrequited love. Meanwhile, Franco's friend Aldo (Tony LoBianco), struggling with demoralization, devises a way to regain the prisoners' dignity: a select band of them will escape, climb the elusive Mt. Kenya, plant the Italian flag at its summit, and then escape back into camp, humiliating their captors. The linchpin is Franco, who agrees with the proviso that he will escape down the other side, even though his chances of success are minimal. Climbing gear is supplied by camp artisans, including Kist, a German (Bavarian by birth), who trades his compass for a place on the three-man climbing team. Franco is prevailed upon to repair the industrialist's antiquated sawmill and simultaneously manages a quick liaison with Patricia in the hayloft. Farrell, suspecting the worst, confronts first Franco and then Patricia; his impotent rage only precipitates the plan to take the mountain.

Once over the wire, Kist betrays the others and heads for freedom. He's quickly captured, however, and reveals the climbers' plans to Farrell, setting up a mountainside chase. When oxygen sickness leaves Aldo alternately breathless and hysterical, Franco proceeds alone, with Major Farrell hot on his trail. By day, they catch fleeting glimpses of each other across the canyons; by night, their shouted banter takes on sexual overtones, as "she"—the mountain—comes to stand for Patricia, as well as other, less tangible, aspirations. At the summit, Farrell draws a bead on Franco and implores him to halt. Franco buries the flag but then surrenders, returning to camp as a hero to the men.

In both its CinemaScope dimensions and gaudy Technicolor palette, THE ASCENT wants desperately to recall those great POW epics of the past; e.g., THE GREAT ESCAPE or THE BRIDGE ON THE RIVER KWAI. Efficiently directed and often gorgeous to look at, it's a reasonable simulation of what passed for Hollywood high adventure in the days before BONNIE AND CLYDE and THE WILD BUNCH. But contemporary American audiences—conditioned by post-Vietnam cynicism and a slew of ultra-violent action pics—no longer have much patience with this type of muscular, relatively innocent, wartime adventure. What the producers no doubt had in mind was a mass entertainment combining old-fashioned "good movie" values with the high-wire dynamics of a CLIFFHANGER—but without the latter film's sadistic villains, flashy technology, high body count, or comic-book irreverence toward its subject matter. What they come up with is a movie anachronism. (*Violence, profanity.*)

d, Donald Shebib; p, Njeri Karago; exec p, Jeff Lawenda, Robert Halmi, Jr., Thomas Molito, Robert Bantle; assoc p, Tim Harbert; w, David Wiltse; ph, David Connell; ed, Ron Wisman; m, Irwin Fisch; prod d, Michael Baugh; set d, Colin Athanasius; sound, Walter P. Anderson (mixer); casting, Lynn Kressel; cos, Elizabeth Ryrie; makeup, Suzanne Belcher, Brent Lavett

Adventure/War/Prison   **(PR: A   MPAA: PG)**

ASHES OF TIME   ★★★½
(Hong Kong) 90m Scholar Films Co.; Jet Tone Productions; Beijing Film Studio; Pony Canyon c
(DONG XIE XI DU)

Leslie Cheung *(Ouyang Feng)*; Tony Leung *Kar-fai (Huang Yaoshi)*; Tony Leung Chiu-Wai *(Blind Swordsman)*; Brigitte Lin *(Murong Yin/Murong Yang)*; Maggie Cheung *(The Woman)*; Jacky Cheung *(Hong Qi)*; Carina Liu *(Peach Blossom)*; Charlie Young *(Waiting Woman)*; Bai Li *(Hung Chi's Wife)*; Ni King; Su Tak-Fu

With his use of highly elliptical narrative and ornate imagery that are both stunningly beautiful and self-consciously arty, filmmaker Wong Kar-Wai fashions his work as a singular meditation on romantic regret and emotional isolation, embodied by a handful of heroic swordsmen.

Ouyang Feng (Leslie Cheung) is an expert swordsman who specializes in solving problems by dispatching killers for hire from his desert outpost. Feng leads an isolated existence, looking forward to the annual visit of his friend Huang Yaoshi (Tony Leung Kar-fai). After Yaoshi leaves abruptly one year, Feng receives a customer named Murong Yang (Brigitte Lin), who wants to hire Feng to kill Yaoshi, as Yaoshi had promised to marry Yang's sister and failed to do so. Soon after, Feng is visited by Yang's sister Yin (also played by Lin), who wants Feng to kill her brother instead of Yaoshi. Undecided, Feng hesitates until he discovers that Yin and Yang are indeed the same person, two identities hiding within a wounded soul.

Feng's next customer (Charlie Young) wants him to avenge her younger brother's death, but can offer only meager payment.

Feng refuses, but she chooses to wait on his premises until a potential hero comes along.

Soon Feng plays host to a swordsman (Tony Leung Chiu-Wai) who is going blind. He wants Feng to help him defend his village against horse thieves. When the horse thieves descend on Feng's outpost, the swordsman faces them, but is killed when distracted during combat by the waiting woman.

Feng is then visited by Hong Qi (Jacky Cheung), a barefoot swordsman who goes to work for him. Qi disposes of the remaining horse thieves, but loses a finger when he attempts to avenge the waiting woman. Once recovered, Qi leaves Feng's employ in search of fame. Rainy weather causes Feng to think about his lost love (Maggie Cheung), who married his elder brother after feeling neglected by Feng. Feng now realizes that Yaoshi's annual visits were a pretext for carrying news about Feng back to the woman. He waits in vain for a visit from the friend who will never come.

In an undeniably ambitious work, Wong assembles an illustrious cast of Hong Kong stars, but with the exception of Leslie Cheung and Maggie Cheung (no relation), the performers aren't given the opportunity to transcend their characters' purely symbolic nature. The exotic atmosphere is the real star of this production. Wong and cinematographer Christopher Doyle tirelessly craft a world occupied by shifting surfaces: shadows that obscure true identities, landscapes that dwarf their inhabitants, and man-made objects, like a glaringly metaphorical spinning cage in Feng's living quarters, that mirror the characters' spiritual selves.

The most impressively stylized interludes, though, are the action sequences in which Wong uses the technique of step-printing (put to an evocative use in his CHUNGKING EXPRESS), an enhanced form of slow motion which underscores the brutal nature of the violent acts being depicted.

The film is a success, despite its occasionally perplexing narrative which serves to obscure its straightforward message, that (as Yaoshi puts it) "memory is the fount of worry." (*Violence.*) — E.G.

d, Wong Kar-Wai; p, Tsai Sung-Lin, Cheng Zhigu; exec p, Jeff Lau; w, Wong Kar-Wai (based on the novel *The Eagle Shooting Heroes* by Louis Cha); ph, Christopher Doyle; ed, Patrick Tam, William Chang, Hai Kit-Wai, Kwong Chi-Leung; m, Frankie Chan, Roel A. Garcia; prod d, William Chang; art d, Yang Zhanjia; cos, Luk Ha-Fong

Drama/Martial Arts   **(PR: C   MPAA: NR)**

ASSASSINS   ★★
(U.S.) 132m Donner-Shuler/Donner Productions; Silver Pictures ~ Warner Bros. c

Sylvester Stallone *(Robert Rath)*; Antonio Banderas *(Miguel Bain)*; Julianne Moore *(Electra)*; Anatoly Davydov *(Nicolai)*; Muse Watson *(Ketcham)*; Stephen Kahan *(Alan Branch)*; Kelly Rowan *(Jennifer)*; Reed Diamond *(Bob)*; Kai Wuluff *(Remy)*; Kerry Skalsky *(Buyer #2)*; James Douglas Haskins *(Buyer #3)*; Stephen Liska *(Cop #1)*; John Harms *(Cop #2)*; Edward J. Rosen *(Cemetery Caretaker)*; Christina Orchid *(Dowager)*; Bruce R. Orchid *(Cabbie #1)*; James Louis Oliver *(Customs Officer)*; Sue Carolyn Wise *(Obnoxious Woman)*; Ron Ben Jarrett *(Maintenance Man)*; Marian Collier *(Pet Shop Lady)*; Dave Young *(Male Guard)*; Ragna Sigrun *(Female Guard)*; Mark Woodford *(Room Service Waiter)*; Anibal O. Leras *(Cabbie)*; Marta Labatut *(Cemetery Woman #1)*; Choco Orta *(Cemetery Woman #2)*; Ivonne Piazza *(Bank Teller)*; Angel Vazquez *(Bank Official)*; Axel Anderson *(Bank President)*; David Dollase *(Bodyguard #1)*; Jim Graham *(Bodyguard #2)*; Wally Dalton *(Priest)*; Paul

Tuerpe *(Reporter #1)*; John Procaccino *(Reporter #2)*; Nerissa E. Williams *(Reporter #3)*; Juan Manuel Lebron *(Puerto Rican Cafe Waiter)*; Eddie Bellaflores *(Fruit Vendor)*; Thomas Helgeland *(Soloist)*; James W. Gavin *(Police Helicopter Pilot)*; Scott Stuber *(Parking Attendant)*; Richard Blum *(Watcher)*; Michael DeCourcey *(Cabby #3)*; Whitey Shapiro *(Cop #6)*; Stefan Enriquez *(Cop #7)*; Fulvio Cecere *(Cop #8)*; Shirley Oliver *(Cop #9)*; Eric Sather *(Cab Customer)*; Wally Gudgell *(Upset Passenger)*; J. Mills Goodloe *(Newlywed Man)*; Peter Sebastian Lackaff *(Singer)*; John Lamar *(Money Hungry Man)*; Ernie Hall *(Cop #10)*; Calli Medved *(Cop #11)*; Robert Sanders *(Monorail Driver)*; Rhonda J. Osborne *(Police Dispatcher)*; Christina Herrera *(Pro Choice Woman)*; Cary Sanchez *(Bank Receptionist)*; Frankie R. Jimenez, Jr. *(Towel Boy)*; Jeff King *(Helicopter Pilot #3)*; David Shark *(Buyer #4)*; Bob Minor *(Cop #3)*; Barbara Anne Klein *(Cop #4)*

A big disappointment at the domestic box office, ASSASSINS is the fourth in a string of big-budget Sylvester Stallone action pictures that places his status as a major star in the hands of foreign moviegoers. In the film, an informal remake of the 1972 Charles Bronson film THE MECHANIC, Stallone and Antonio Banderas play duelling hit men.

Robert Rath (Sylvester Stallone) is the world's foremost professional killer; a mantle he assumed 15 years ago when he eliminated his mentor and friend, Nicolai (Anatoly Davydov). Now Rath is ready to retire, but another hit man, Miguel Bain (Antonio Banderas), wants to get to the top the same way Rath did.

The two men are a study in contrasts. Rath's hits are precise, surgical strikes. Bain treats jobs like kamikaze missions, in which he happily kills innocent bystanders. They butt heads a couple of times before finding themselves on the trail of a computer expert code-named Electra (Julianne Moore), who has a disc full of top secret information. Rath gets to Electra first, and takes her into a sort of protective custody. He figures to sell the disc back to his employers for a $20 million pension, so long as he can stay a step ahead of Bain. The action leads them to a bank in the Caribbean—the same bank in front of which Rath shot Nicolai—and Rath knows Bain won't pass up the chance to repeat history.

With Electra's help, Rath plans to outmaneuver Bain, but it turns out they've all been maneuvered there by Nicolai, who's not dead and wants both revenge and the money. After a stand-off and shoot-out, Bain and Nicolai lie dead, and Rath and Electra go off together.

Producer Joel Silver and director Richard Donner's names are synonymous with action extravaganzas, in which credulity is thrown through a plate glass window, and audiences just hang on for the ride. And though its tone is more subdued and serious than the DIE HARD and LETHAL WEAPON films, ASSASSINS starts out with enough killing and car chases to qualify as good, action entertainment. Unfortunately, ASSASSINS also has pretensions. The battle between Rath and Bain is supposed to be one of wits, and the metaphor the film persistently proposes is a chess game. But it's more like a game of Parcheesi with frequent bursts of gunfire.

A successful psychological thriller requires a depth of characterization this script never provides. The preposterous narrative rests on roles so shallowly written that they're more like shorthand than actual characterizations. Stallone is serious and marble calm. Banderas is jittery as jello. Stallone and Moore never get the chance to display any chemistry because their characters' budding romance is indicated only by their being frequently in the same room. Banderas, hot off DESPERADO, brings charisma and a comic edge to the screen, but that can only carry a

film so far. After about an hour, the action peters out, and the movie runs for over another hour, including an interminable, final 40 minutes that, instead of heightening the tension, wrings any interest in the outcome right out of the viewer. *(Violence, profanity.)* — P.R.

d, Richard Donner; p, Richard Donner, Joel Silver, Bruce A. Evans, Raynold Gideon, Andrew Lazar, James Van Wyck; exec p, Lauren Shuler-Donner, Dino De Laurentiis, assoc p, Ilyse A. Reutlinger, Cynthia L. Neber, J. Mills Goodloe, Tony Munafo, Karyn Fields, Julie Durk; co-p, Richard Solomon, Alexander Collett, Dan Cracchiolo; w, Larry Wachowski, Andy Wachowski, Brian Helgeland (from a story by Larry Wachowski and Andy Wachowski); ph, Vilmos Zsigmond; ed, Richard Marks; m, Mark Mancina; prod d, Tom Sanders; art d, Daniel T. Dorrance; set d, Lisa Dean; sound, Petur Hliddal (mixer); fx, Jon Belyeu; casting, Marion Dougherty; cos, Elizabeth McBride; makeup, Lee Harman; stunts, Conrad Palmisano, Dick Hancock

Action/Thriller (PR: C MPAA: R)

ATTACK OF THE 5'2" WOMEN
(SEE: NATIONAL LAMPOON'S ATTACK OF THE 5'2" WOMEN)

ATTACK OF THE 60-FOOT CENTERFOLD ★½
(U.S.) 84m Concorde-New Horizons; American Independent ~ New Horizons Home Video c

J.J. North *(Angel Grace)*; Raelyn Saalman *(Inga)*; Tammy Parks *(Betty)*; Ted Monte *(Wilson)*; Tim Abell *(Mark)*; Jay Richardson *(Bob Gordon)*; John LaZar *(Dr. Paul Lindstrom)*; Michelle Bauer *(Dr. Joyce Mann)*; George Stover *(Dr. Eric Kramer)*; Nikki Fritz *(Rosita)*; G. Gordon Baer *(Vic Stryker)*; Russ Tamblyn *(Gas Attendant)*; Ross Hagen *(Truck Driver)*; Tommy Kirk *(Passenger)*; Stanley Livingston *(Glenn Manning)*; Debra Dare *(Nurse Williams)*; Tony Franco *(Ray the Editor)*; Jennifer New *(Counter Girl)*; Jeff Murray *(Drunk)*; Jennifer Steven *(Receptionist)*; Tony Clay *(Invisible Man)*; Ted Newsom *(Guard #1)*; James Williams *(Guard #2)*; Claire Polan *(Grocery Lady #1)*; Shari Hicks *(Grocery Lady #2)*; Alan Baker *(Detective)*; Steve Barkett *(Police Officer)*; Tony Lorea *(Bogie)*; Forrest J. Ackerman *(Dracula)*; Jim Wynorski *(Guy Who Can't Believe His Eyes)*; Brad Linaweaver *(Running Guy)*

The title is the most entertaining part of this Fred Olen Ray production, a harmless but inconsequential direct-to-video B movie about two overly large female antagonists.

Mr. Gordon (Jay Richardson), publisher of *Plaything* magazine, is about to choose the Centerfold of the Year, and invites the three contestants, Angel (J.J. North), Inga (Raelyn Saalman), and the bitchy Betty (Tammy Parks), to his mansion to determine the winner. Insecure about how she will size up, Angel has been secretly taking a formula created by Dr. Paul Lindstrom (John LaZar) to improve her measurements and, on the eve of the contest, drinks an overdose of it. The next morning, she is 60 feet tall, and Mr. Gordon quickly determines she will be "the biggest centerfold ever."

Jealous that Angel has beaten her, Betty drinks some of the formula herself, and soon there is a monstrous catfight underway on the streets of Los Angeles. Dr. Lindstrom, alerted by the photographer's assistant Wilson (Ted Monte), arrives with an antidote, reducing Angel and Betty back to normal size and restoring Angel to Wilson's arms.

With the original ATTACK OF THE 50 FOOT WOMAN having been remade as a cable production with Daryl Hannah in 1993, it was only a matter of time before some enterprising second grade filmmaker undertook this variation. It is also no surprise that the one who did so was Ray, whose productions often evince an appreciation of 50s genre films. But beyond the basic story variation, there is little in the way of imagination in evidence here. In its own way, it conforms as much to the standards of its time as the original 50 FOOT WOMAN did in its own—only here the humor is intentional.

Ray and writer Steve Armogida drop in a few mild in-jokes and a couple of moments of Zucker Brothers-style wackiness, with plenty of topless nudity from the attractive female cast but little real action. The result is a film that is neither especially daring nor unduly restrained, neither slavishly formula-bound nor particularly creative, neither grossly prurient nor genuinely arousing. *(Extensive nudity, sexual situations, profanity.)* — M.G.

d, Fred Olen Ray; p, Fred Olen Ray; exec p, Mike Elliott; w, Steve Armogida; ph, Gary Graver; ed, Peter Miller; m, Jeffrey Walton; prod d, Candi Guterres; sound, Alan Samuels; fx, Steve Barkett, Fred Olen Ray, The Post Group; cos, Gwen Lavery; makeup, Heidi Grotsky

Comedy/Erotic/Science Fiction   (PR: O   MPAA: R)

AUGUSTIN   ★★★
(France) 61m Sepia; Cinea ~ Kino International c

Jean-Chretien Sibertin-Blanc *(Augustin)*; Stephanie Zhang *(Caroline)*; Nora Habib *(Shula)*; Thierry Lhermitte; Guy Casabonne; Claude Pecher; James Lord; Jacqueline Vimpierre; Rahim Mazioud; Rene Boulet

AUGUSTIN is a slice-of-life portrait of a social misfit. This entertaining but slight film showcases the comic talents of Jean-Chretien Sibertin-Blanc, who is in his element as the amusing title character.

Augustin Dos Santos is a stuttering, bumbling, and hyperactive guy, but people seem to embrace his good-hearted and warm nature. He works part time at an insurance company, but his aim is to be an actor. He visits a casting agent who tells him about the role of a hotel room service man in a new film.

Augustin takes all of his work very seriously, and after a productive morning at the office, he convinces a fancy hotel to let him spend one day as a temporary employee, researching for the movie role. He brings breakfast to an English guest, and trails a chambermaid as she prepares a room. He becomes enamored of her, but she declines his offer of a date.

He auditions for the movie role. Despite his misplaced seriousness and obsession with insignificant details, his nervous nature gives the part the comic edge the director wants. Augustin is offered the role, but because the day of filming conflicts with another obligation, he turns it down. Instead, he spends the day shooting a public service commercial for rabbit innoculations.

AUGUSTIN, a surprise audience favorite at several 1995 film festivals, including Cannes and New York, is unconventional in many ways. It is 61 minutes long, contains only two experienced actors, and rambles along with no real plot. The style suits the subject matter, as AUGUSTIN is a character sketch rather than a story. The film's humor comes from the protagonist's unique personality, and the overreaching literalness that makes him miss many of the realities of the world around him.

The film is entertaining, but not without flaws. While some scenes are quite funny, others merely ramble. During the rabbit commercial, for example, Augustin cannot stop laughing—inconsistent behavior for someone who previously played a comic role as if it were totally serious. The brevity works in the film's favor, allowing the meandering "plot" to be simply a comic vehicle for the main character.

Not surprisingly, Sibertin-Blanc is perfect in this role, since his sister Anne Fontaine, the film's director, tailor-made the part for his talents. Though the structure of the film is scripted, most of the dialogue is improvised. This, and the use of nonprofessional actors playing themselves, gives the film a natural, unpredictable feeling. *(Profanity.)* — A.M.

d, Anne Fontaine; p, Philippe Jacquier, Brigitte Faure; co-p, Philippe Carcassonne; w, Anne Fontaine, Jean-Chretien Sibertin-Blanc; ph, Marie Dreujou; ed, Sylvie Gadmer; sound, Francois DeMorant, Jean-Pierre LaForce

Comedy   (PR: C   MPAA: NR)

AVENGING ANGEL   ★★
(U.S.) 99m First Corps Endeavors; Curtis/Lowe Productions; Esparza-Katz Productions ~ Turner Home Entertainment c

Tom Berenger *(Miles Utley)*; Fay Masterson *(Miranda Young)*; Kevin Tighe *(Elder Rigby)*; Charlton Heston *(Brigham Young)*; James Coburn *(Porter Rockwell)*; Leslie Hope *(Eliza Rigby)*; Jeffrey Jones *(Milton Long)*; Daniel Quinn *(Alpheus Young)*; Andrew Prine *(Andrew Pike)*; Tom Bower *(Bill Hickman)*; Patrick Gorman *(Jonathan Parker)*; Rebecca Heaton *(Lisa Banes)*; Will Heaton *(Drew Snyder)*; Miles Fuelner *(Josh Heaton)*; T.J. Lowther *(Miles—Age 10)*; Bill Osborn *(Tall Easterner)*; David Kirk Chambers *(Stocky Easterner)*; Richard Jewkes *(Sheriff Randall)*; Chelsea Berenger *(Amanda Heaton)*; Chloe Berenger *(Emma Heaton)*; Wayne Brennan *(1st Prospector)*; Bus Riley *(2nd Prospector)*; Dave Jensen *(3rd Prospector)*; Craig Baxley, Jr. *(Teenaged Miles)*; Mary Christine Schaub *(Rachel Rigby)*; Sarah Schaub *(Annie Rigby)*; Jeremy Hanks *(Parker Boy #1)*

In a period vein largely untapped by Hollywood since 1940's BRIGHAM YOUNG—FRONTIERSMAN, producer/star Tom Berenger and a cast of familiar faces recreate a relatively obscure anecdote about the muscle behind the early Mormon Church. Although the scheme to eliminate founder Brigham Young, and the extreme protective measures favored by the Danite faction make fascinating research, this TV feature, originally done for Ted Turner's history-hungry cable network, handles the facts at dry face value, and the material's potential gets squelched.

By 1872 Young's Utah-based church, after much persecution back East, felt secure enough to distance itself from its Bible-thumping, holster-slapping militia, the Danites. But as resentment over Young (Charlton Heston) and his ban on gold-mining fester, high church dissidents hire outside hit men. They botch an attempt on Young's life but leave zealous Danite defender Miles Utley (Berenger) gravely injured. Utley heals in the settlement outskirts through the ministrations of Eliza (Leslie Hope), one of several battered wives of Elder Rigby (Kevin Tighe). Former mentor Porter Rockwell (James Coburn, concealed behind a Karl Marx beard) later saves Miles from Brigham's son Alpheus (Daniel Quinn), and Utley is shocked to learn how even he was co-opted for a conspiracy, coup and coverup masterminded by Elder Rigby and Elder Long (Jeffrey Jones), Miles' trusted confidant. After a frameup, gun battles and a hunt by a Mormon posse, the Danite cowboy elicits Rockwell's help in preventing Brigham Young's assassination at his St. George retreat. Armed with incriminating journals and no longer the Elders' fall guy, Miles uses Brigham's gun to shoot Long, and arrests Rigby after vowing to hang up his revolvers.

For all the skullduggery, you may as well be watching an instructional video personally supervised by a Salt Lake City temple. Given the intricacies of the intrigue and the resonance of the historical scandal to modern audiences in the era of Oliver Stone's JFK, AVENGING ANGEL is one slow gallop through holy ground. Skirting criticism of the newborn sect and its attendant polygamy, the filmmakers reserve godly reverence for Young, suitably embodied by all-purpose nobility icon Heston. They also vitiate action thrills by cross-cutting between narrow-squeak escapes and mushrooming chicanery in geriatric fashion, turning a stampede of Wild West justice into jumbled waxworks. Never once does Berenger's growth from born militant to remorseful peacekeeper accrete to the biographical data about the Mormon Church's maturity pangs. Most of the story strands never connect, despite quality acting and production values. AVENGING ANGEL gets externals right but mediocre direction makes it an unfulfilled promise. *(Graphic violence, adult situations, sexual situations.)* — R.P.

d, Craig Baxley; p, Heather Lowe, Patrick Curtis, Jay Benson; exec p, Moctesuma Esparza, Robert Katz; assoc p, Leann Martin; co-p, Tom Berenger; w, Dennis Nemec (based on the novel by Gary Stewart); ph, Mark Irwin; ed, Mark Helfrich; m, Gary Chang; prod d, Phil Leonard; set d, Larry Leonard; sound, Jonathan "Earl" Stein (mixer); fx, Russ Hessey; casting, Karen Rea; cos, Elsa Zamparelli; makeup, Cheryl Voss; stunts, Paul Baxley

Western/Historical   **(PR: C MPAA: NR)**

AWFULLY BIG ADVENTURE, AN   ★★½
(U.K./Ireland) 113m Portman Productions; BBC Films; Wolfhound Films ~ Fine Line c

Hugh Grant *(Meredith Potter)*; Alan Rickman *(P.L. O'Hara)*; Georgina Cates *(Stella)*; Alun Armstrong *(Uncle Vernon)*; Peter Firth *(Bunny)*; Prunella Scales *(Rose)*; Rita Tushingham *(Aunt Lily)*; Alan Cox *(Geoffrey)*; Edward Petherbridge *(St. Ives)*; Nicola Pagett *(Dotty Blundell)*; Carol Drinkwater *(Dawn Allenby)*; Clive Merrison *(Desmond Farichild)*; Gerard McSorely *(George)*; Ruth McCabe *(Grace Bird)*; James Frain *(John Harbour)*; Pat Laffan *(Mr. Harcourt)*; Patti Love *(Mary Deare)*; Hilary Reynolds *(Babs Osborn)*; Tom Hickey *(Freddie Reynolds)*; Robbie Doolin *(Reporter)*; Brendan Conroy *(Disley)*; Larry Murphy *(Inspector)*; Vicky Curtis *(Ellen)*; Brian McGrath *(Vicar)*; Padraig O'Raghallaigh *(GPO Clerk)*; Nick Grennel *(Actor)*; Willie Smith *(Empire Stage Manager)*; Katy O'Donnell *(Young Stella)*; Earl Gill; John Drummond; Chris Kenevey; Jack Bayle; Rolf Kholman *(Band)*; Horace Hessey; Betty Casey *(Singers)*; Paddy Casey *(Pianist)*

In light of director Mike Newell's finer achievements—the gossamer ENCHANTED APRIL and mesmerizing DANCE WITH A STRANGER—AN AWFULLY BIG ADVENTURE is a bitter disappointment. The tone is uneven and the narrative stretched to breaking point in this ironically titled escapade, an exercise in curdled period romanticism which may well leave viewers puzzled as to the point of it all.

Liverpool, 1947: Despite her working class accent and lack of social graces, Stella (Georgia Cates) has the ox-like hide of a born actress. She's so thrilled by her apprenticeship with a third rate theatrical repertory company that no backstage chore is too menial, and no role too small. The theater is her refuge from an unhappy home life with her uncle and aunt, and her persistent sadness at having been abandoned by her mother. She confides her inner longings to her missing mother through imaginary telephone calls.

The naive Stella falls head over heels in love with the company's bisexual director, Meredith Potter (Hugh Grant), and indulges the antics of the troupe's temperamental actors, blissfully ignorant of their limitations. Rose (Prunella Scales), who owns the company and has already weathered crises ranging from alcoholic outbursts to petty in-fighting, averts financial disaster by persuading an old friend, O'Hara (Alan Rickman), to rescue their season by starring in "Peter Pan," a surefire hit. Stella, virginal but calculating, turns a blind eye to Meredith's callous treatment of the aspiring actors he beds and bullies, and allows the smitten O'Hara to seduce her. She regards the affair as a warm-up for her conquest of her unworthy idol. But O'Hara makes a shocking discovery: Stella is his daughter.

Reeling from the implications of this incestuous liaison, O'Hara stumbles off a dockside ramp and accidentally drowns. Stage manager Bunny (Peter Firth) finds O'Hara's letter of confession and destroys it. Stella has trouble coming to grips with O'Hara's death, but the show goes on, with Potter playing O'Hara's role, Captain Hook. As the curtain comes down on the troupe's season, Stella has gained maturity but still knows nothing of her mother's past.

The Beryl Bainbridge novel from which this film is adapted is rich in theatrical bitchery and filled with juicy characters. But it hovers over this dank drama like the Ghost-of-Movies-that-Might-Have-Been. It's hard to see what drew Newell to the material: He seems to have no sympathy for these shallow, frustrated hams and his grim dissection of their self-destructive psychology is entirely uninformed by affection or understanding.

That said, Potter is a triumph for Grant, whose career has been defined by far too many lovable-twits-with-inexplicable-sex-appeal, notably his starring role in Newell's FOUR WEDDINGS AND A FUNERAL. Liberated from his bumbling mannerisms, Grant makes Potter the sort of failure who makes it his mission to crucify anyone who might still have hopes of succeeding. But he's one of the film's few pleasures, supported by finely tuned performances from such stalwarts as Scales and Petherbridge. Leading lady Cates—an established actress named Clare Woodgate, who auditioned as a 16-year-old unknown from Liverpool—has little screen presence. Perhaps she reserved her best efforts for that try-out, because in the film she plows ahead grimly, never revealing the stage-struck spark that defines Stella's existence. A film about acting can get by without a big budget or famous stars if it understands the promise of magic that drives struggling actors to persevere. This downer only overstates the obvious lessons about the misery of failure. *(Extreme profanity; extensive nudity; adult situations; substance abuse.)* — R.P.

d, Mike Newell; p, Hilary Heath, Philip Hinchcliffe; exec p, John Kelleher, Mark Shivas, John Sivers; assoc p, Andrew Warren; co-p, Victor Glynn, Conor Harrington; w, Charles Wood (based on the novel by Beryl Bainbridge); ph, Dick Pope; ed, Jon Gregory; m, Richard Hartley; prod d, Mark Geraghty; art d, Dave Wilson; sound, Peter Sutton (mixer); fx, Film Engineering Services Ltd.; casting, Susie Figgis; cos, Joan Bergin; makeup, Ann Buchanan; stunts, Martin Grace

Drama   **(PR: C MPAA: R)**

BABE ★★★½

(Australia) 94m Kennedy Miller Productions
~ Universal c
(AKA: BABE, THE GALLANT PIG)

Christine Cavanaugh *(Voice of Babe)*; James Cromwell *(Arthur Hoggett)*; Miriam Margolyes *(Voice of Fly)*; Hugo Weaving *(Voice of Rex)*; Danny Mann *(Voice of Ferdinand)*; Miriam Flynn *(Voice of Maa)*; Evelyn Krape *(Voice of Old Ewe)*; Russie Taylor *(Voice of Cat)*; Michael Edward-Stevens *(Voice of Horse)*; Charles Bartlett *(Voice of Cow)*; Paul Livingston *(Voice of Rooster)*; Magda Szubanski *(Esme Hoggett)*; Zoe Burton *(Daughter)*; Paul Goddard *(Son-in-law)*; Wade Hayward *(Grandson)*; Britany Byrnes *(Granddaughter)*; Mary Acres *(Valda)*; Roscoe Lee Brown *(Narrator)*; Janet Foye *(Country Woman)*; Pamela Hawken *(Country Woman)*; Karen Gough *(Country Woman)*; David Webb *(The Vet)*; Marshall Napier *(Chairman of Judges)*; Hec MacMillian *(Lion's Club Man)*; Ken Gregory *(Lion's Club Man)*; Nicholas Lidstone *(Sheep Rustler)*; Trevor Read *(Electrical Linesman)*; Nicholas Blake *(Electrical Linesman)*; Matthew Long *(Sheepdog Trial Officer)*; John Doyle *(TV Commentator)*; Mike Harris *(TV Commentator)*; VOICES OF: Ross Bagley; Gemini Barnett; Rachel Davey; Debi Derryberry; Jazzmine Dillingham; Courtland Mead; Kevin Woods *(Puppies)*; Jane Alden; Kimberly Bailey; Patrika Darbo; Michelle Davison; Julie Forsythe; Maeve Germaine; Rosanna Huffman; Carlyle King; Tina Lifford; Genni Nevinson; Linda Phillips; Paige Pollack; Kerry Walker *(Sheep)*

With no Hollywood stars, a low-key ad campaign and even a look-alike competitor (GORDY) that bombed commercially a few months earlier, BABE beat the odds to become a summer sleeper hit in 1995. Audiences knew a good thing when they saw it: it's a clever family film that brings surprising freshness to the timeworn premise of talking barnyard animals.

The title character (voice of Christine Cavanaugh) is a piglet raised for slaughter in a terrifying assembly-line breeding pen. Trucked to a county fair, Babe is won and taken home by taciturn but kind-hearted Farmer Hoggett (James Cromwell). (At the Hoggett sheep ranch, all animals speak, but mainly to their own species.) Newcomer Babe, lonely and ignorant of the rules and prejudices, unconditionally befriends all beasts, from the sheepdog bitch Fly (voice of Miriam Margolyes), who becomes Babe's surrogate mother, to the aged ewe Maa (voice of Miriam Flynn). However, the sheep hate the dogs—who in turn despise the sheep—and the two groups barely communicate.

Babe soon realizes that the only way to avoid being meat for humans is to make himself useful on the farm. Following the example of a desperate duck who strives to pass himself off as a rooster by crowing at dawn, Babe tries to herd the sheep. But yelling or charging at the bemused flock doesn't work for the piglet, so on Maa's advice Babe addresses the herd politely, requesting them to move in any desired formation. They do.

Farmer Hoggett is delighted at the antics of his "sheep-pig," and postpones his family's plans to butcher him for dinner. There's a scare when wild dogs attack the flock, fatally mauling Maa, and Babe is nearly shot as a sheep-killer. But Fly speaks respectfully to the ewes (for the first time ever) to learn the truth, and helps save Babe. Now Farmer Hoggett feels confident enough to enter Babe in a prestigious sheepdog contest. But an unfamiliar flock won't react to Babe unless he recites a password poem first, and the Hoggett sheep break with tradition to entrust the secret words to Fly. She and her mate relay the verse to Babe, who maneuvers the sheep faultlessly through an obstacle course before dumbfounded judges.

"A humorous look at the limitations and lunacy of a preordained society," was Universal's drily accurate press-kit summation of BABE, which treads a careful path between G-rated fun and didacticism. True, there's a heavy animal-rights undertone in early scenes of Babe's harsh babe-hood, and a soapy subplot about Rex, a dysfunctional dog with a dark secret, is almost too much. But a sense of whimsy prevails, the tone set by an irresistible chorus of Muppet mice who shrilly announce the story's successive chapters (". . . A Tragic Day!").

The voice-over cast, refreshingly devoid of big-name Hollywood stars, is perfect, and the animatronics, done by the Jim Henson Creature Factory (plus an Aussie outfit specializing in robot sheep!), blends neatly with about 500 separate live animal performers. Of the humans, Magda Szubanski, one of Australia's best-known comic actors, made her screen debut here as the bustling Mrs. Hoggett, but it's tall, laconic James Cromwell who must get credit for creating a gentle, three-dimensional personality out of mostly mute reaction shots. Best known for a supporting role as Archie Bunker's buddy Stretch on "All in the Family," the pinch-faced Cromwell here could pass for a lifelong Yorkshire crofter straight out of James Herriot, though a mid-summer Christmas betrays BABE's archetypal agrarian setting as Australia. Producer and co-writer George Miller is not the namesake Disney regular behind THE MAN FROM SNOWY RIVER and other Down Under family fare, but the free-ranging George Miller of MAD MAX, THE WITCHES OF EASTWICK, and LORENZO'S OIL. He had long admired the book *The Sheep-Pig* by British children's author Dick King-Smith, and delegated directing chores to Chris Noonan, a television director making his feature-film debut. At no time, according to Miller, was animation *a la* CHARLOTTE'S WEB an option. "The animal characters are so real that I felt we could best serve the story by using live animals." It was also decided to keep the title character's gender unspecified, though an actress dubbed Babe's waifish tones.

So unexpected was the $25 million pic's pork-power at the box office that toy manufacturers, fast-food joints and other customary avenues of exploitation had failed to license BABE tie-ins by the time it premiered, and quickly scrambled to fill the void—nobody noticing that it was solid film sense, not merchandising, selling all the tickets. — C.C.

d, Chris Noonan; p, George Miller, Doug Mitchell, Bill Miller; w, George Miller, Chris Noonan (based on the novel *The Sheep-Pig* by Dick King-Smith); ph, Andrew Lesnie; ed, Marcus D'Arcy, Jay Friedkin; m, Nigel Westlake; prod d, Roger Ford; art d, Colin Gibson; set d, Kerrie Brown; anim, Rhythm & Hues; sound, Ben Osmo (recordist); fx, Dave Roberts, Charles Gibson, John Stephenson, Jim Henson's Creature Shop, Rhythm & Hues; casting, Liz Mullinar, Valerie McCaffrey; cos, Roger Ford; makeup, Carolyn Tyrer

AAN Best Picture; AAN Best Supporting Actor: James Cromwell; *AAN Best Director:* Chris Noonan; *AAN Best Adapted Screenplay:* George Miller, Chris Noonan; *AAN Best Art Direction:* Roger Ford (Art Direction), Kerrie Brown (set decoration); *AAN Best Editing:* Marcus D'Arcy; *AA Best Visual Effects:* Scott E. Anderson, Charles Gibson, Neal Scanlan, John Cox

Fantasy/Children's/Comedy   (PR: A   MPAA: G)

BABY-SITTERS CLUB, THE ★★½

(U.S.) 85m Scholastic Productions; Beacon Pictures ~ Columbia c

Schuyler Fisk *(Kristy)*; Bre Blair *(Stacey)*; Rachael Leigh Cook *(Mary Anne)*; Larisa Oleynik *(Dawn)*; Tricia Joe *(Claudia)*; Stacey Linn Ramsower *(Mallory)*; Zelda Harris *(Jessi)*; Vanessa Zima *(Rosie Wilder)*; Christian Oliver *(Luca)*; Brooke Adams *(Elizabeth Thomas Brewer)*; Bruce Davison *(Watson)*; Jessica Needham *(Karen)*; Ellen Burstyn *(Mrs. Haberman)*; Peter Horton *(Patrick)*; Colleen Camp *(Maureen McGill)*; Harris Yulin *(Harold)*; Asher Metchik *(Jackie Rodowsky)*; Austin O'Brien *(Logan Bruno)*; Marla Sokoloff *(Cokie Mason)*; Ashlee Turner *(Bebe)*; Natanya Ross *(Grace)*; Katie Earle *(Nina Marshall)*; Scarlett Pomers *(Suzi Barrett)*; Kyla Pratt *(Becca)*; Anne Costner *(Anne)*; Lily Costner *(Lily)*; David Quittman *(Buddy Barrett)*; Jonah Bliss *(Nicky)*; Josh Berman *(Ricky)*; Emmy Yu *(Emmy/Camper)*; E.J. de la Pena *(Jonas)*; Madison Fisk *(Beth)*; Cleo Brock-Abraham *(Cleo)*; Lance O'Reilly *(Matt)*; Bridget Kate Geraghty *(Vanessa)*; Erica Hess *(Margie Klinger)*; Samantha Alanis *(Charlotte Johannson)*; Aaron Metchik *(Alan)*; Jeffrey Quittman *(Jamie Newton)*; Teddy Dale *(David Michael)*; Robin Swid *(Brookes)*; Richard Guiton *(Mark)*; Peter Gregory *(Bouncer)*; Candy Trabucco *(Cabbie)*; Aixa Clemente *(Louise)*; Nancy Mette *(Sheila)*

Ann M. Martin's best-selling book series hits the big screen with this minor but occasionally winning children's film.

In suburban Connecticut, seven young teen girls have formed the Baby-Sitters Club, headed by Kristy (Schuyler Fisk), who lives with her divorced mother, Elizabeth (Brooke Adams). One summer, the group opens a kids' camp in one of their backyards, leading to conflict with neighboring Mrs. Haberman (Ellen Burstyn). Meanwhile, Claudia (Tricia Joe), who hosts club meetings in her house, may have to quit the group if she doesn't pass a summer science class, and the girls begin to refurbish an abandoned greenhouse as a new gathering place; Stacey (Bre Blair) starts dating 17-year-old Luca (Christian Oliver), but is afraid to tell him her age; and Kristy is visited by her itinerant father, Patrick (Peter Horton), who makes her promise not to tell Elizabeth that he's in town.

She keeps the promise and spends many happy afternoons with Patrick, who vows to come clean to Elizabeth, but Kristy's unexplained absence from club activities upsets the others. Luca drops Stacey when he finds out she's only 13, while Claudia, with the help of the others' tutoring, passes her science final. On her birthday, Kristy forgoes her friends' party to meet Patrick at an amusement park, but he never shows; Luca (having made up with Stacey) takes the others to pick her up, and the friends are reconciled. The departed Patrick leaves behind a letter to Kristy, and Elizabeth helps her come to terms with her father's irresponsibility; the girls finish their work on the greenhouse, and decide to turn it over to Mrs. Haberman.

There's little about THE BABY-SITTERS CLUB to set it above or apart from previous direct-to-video incarnations, nor to skew it beyond its youthful target audience. The movie takes place in a fantasy world: one in which these suburban teenagers have no difficulty in securing all kinds of fancy equipment to set up their camp for littler kids, and where the 13-year-old Stacey can go on an unescorted date with 17-year-old Luca into New York City at night (and where a teenaged boy nobly refuses to date this stunning nymphet when he finds out she's only 13). The story development meanders, taking pains to establish various small crises for each girl and adding a trio of nasty girls as comic relief.

It is, however, brightly played, with likable, naturalistic performances by its young leads, and condescends neither to its characters nor its audience. And the key subplot, involving Kristy's surreptitious meetings with her father, gives the story a stronger-than-expected dramatic center. It's also refreshing to see a kids' film in which the central character is the least conventionally attractive, though Fisk (the daughter of Sissy Spacek and Jack Fisk) is a spunky, charming presence nonetheless. *(Adult situations.)* — M.G.

d, Melanie Mayron; p, Jane Startz, Peter O. Almond; exec p, Martin Keltz, Deborah Forte, Marc Abraham, Thomas A. Bliss, Armyan Bernstein; assoc p, Eileen Cowel, Maria Gillen; co-p, Tina Stern; w, Dalene Young (based on the book series by Ann M. Martin); ph, Willy Kurant; ed, Christopher Greenbury; m, David Michael Frank; prod d, Larry Fulton; art d, Charles Collum; set d, Douglas Mowat; sound, David Ronne (mixer); fx, Josh Hakian; casting, Mary Gail Artz, Barbara Cohen; cos, Susie DeSanto; makeup, Kathryn Kelly; stunts, Patrick Romano

Children's/Drama/Comedy   (PR: A   MPAA: PG)

BABYSITTER, THE   ★★½
(U.S.) 90m Spelling Films International;
Joel Shumacher Productions; Steve Perry Productions ~
Spelling Films International c

Alicia Silverstone *(The Babysitter)*; Jeremy London *(Jack)*; J.T. Walsh *(Harry Tucker)*; Lee Garlington *(Dolly Tucker)*; Nicky Katt *(Mark)*; Lois Chiles *(Bernice Holsten)*; George Segal *(Bill Holsten)*; Ryan Slater *(Jimmy)*; Brittany English Stephens *(Bitsy)*; Tuesday Knight *(Waitress)*; Erick Menyuk *(Joe)*; Matthew Kimbrough; Jane Alden *(Wilma)*; Noel Evangelisti *(Audrey)*; Michael Chieffo *(Young Man)*; Fort Atkinson, III *(Police Detective)*; Monty Silverstone *(British Party Guest)*; Cameron Corwin Fuller *(Tucker Baby)*

Though it aspires to function on two levels—as both a critique of direct-to-video erotic thriller conventions and as a film that will satisfy fans of the popular genre—THE BABYSITTER errs on the side of salaciousness. Originally released straight to the videocassette market, THE BABYSITTER later enjoyed a token theatrical run, largely by virtue of a pre-stardom performance by Alicia Silverstone.

A virginal high school student, Jennifer (Silverstone), babysits for the children of the affluent Tuckers. Alcoholic father Harry Tucker (J.T. Walsh) lusts after Jennifer; his wife Dolly (Lee Garlington), is unsatisfied with her marriage and nurses jealous resentment toward the nubile adolescent. Dolly and Harry attend a party, where he fantasizes about Jennifer, while an increasingly inebriated Dolly flirts with host Bill (George Segal), whose son Mark (Nicky Katt) is the virtuous girl's poisonous, manipulative classmate.

Mark suggests to Jennifer's jock boyfriend, Jack (Jeremy London), that she's fooling around with him. Plying Jack with liquor supplied by his indulgent parents and encouraging him to think the worst, Mark indulges in cruel mind games. He plants the idea that Jack could seduce the unchaperoned Jennifer if they were to drop by the Tucker house. The boys do so, scaring one of the children, Jimmy (Ryan Slater), so badly that he dials 911. The suavely vicious Mark claims he's there to protect Jennifer from the insistent Jack. Stalling for time after she's calmed the children down, Jennifer frets and Jack slowly realizes that Mark has set him up.

Mark knocks out Jack and chases the frightened Jennifer, who runs outside the house just as the Tuckers are returning home. Mr. Tucker swerves to avoid the girl and kills Mark.

THE BABYSITTER plays an awkward game of confounding the viewer's perceptions, shifting from tension-filled reality to bubbling fantasies of repressed lust. Too often, it comes off just like the sleazy, scopophilic sex films that it purports to critique. There's a distinct disjunction between the film's apparent intentions—it's based on an experimental short story by acclaimed novelist Robert Coover—and its achievements: it pretends to criticize the hypocrisy of parents who dream about dirty doings while denying their children's sexuality, but titillates viewers with carefully executed fantasies about raping an innocent, sweet-natured sweater girl. *(Violence, nudity, extreme profanity, sexual situations, substance abuse.)*

d, Guy Ferland; p, Kevin J. Messick, Steve Perry; exec p, Joel Schumacher; assoc p, Matt Hinkley; co-p, Spencer Franklin; w, Guy Ferland (based on the short story by Robert Coover); ph, Rick Bota; ed, Jim Prior; m, Loek Dikker; prod d, Phil Leonard; set d, Larry Leonard; sound, Geoffrey Patterson (mixer); casting, Emily Schweber, Megan McConnell; cos, Ingrid Ferrin; makeup, Melanie Hughes; stunts, Charles Picerni

Drama/Erotic/Thriller　　　　　**(PR: O　MPAA: R)**

BAD BLOOD　　　　　★★½
(U.S.) 90m Pomerance Corporation ~ LIVE Entertainment c

Lorenzo Lamas *(Travis Blackstone)*; Frankie Thorn *(Rhonda)*; Hank Cheyne *(Franklin Blackstone)*; Joe Son *(Chang)*; Kimberley Kates *(Lindee)*; John T. Ryan *(John Blackstone)*; Sigal Diamant *(Kimm)*; Cole McCay *(Baggy)*; Stanley Yale *(Preacher)*; Beau Starr *(Bo)*; Tony Peck *(Kovacs)*; Chuck Zito *(Toots)*; Warren Stevens *(Ponytail)*; Tom Bloom *(Mohawk Thug)*; Vinnie J. Curto *(Will Sharp)*; Simon Rhee *(Thug Lee)*; Kurt Bryant *(Sacs)*; Sabrina Weiner *(Lisa Alvarez)*; Gladys Jimenez *(Maria Alvarez)*; Albert Garcia *(Ricardo Alvarez)*; Gloria LeRoy *(Elderly Bank Lady)*; Jennifer MacDonald *(Ray Ann)*; Daniel Gusman *(Little League Player)*; William Washington *(Snake)*; Kim Dawson *(Chang's Girl)*; Jerry Spicer *(Security Guard)*; Robert LaVetta *(Security Guard)*

Skilled in acrobatics and kickboxing, Lorenzo Lamas is an impressive direct-to-video action star with aloof presence to burn. Boasting at least three smashing martial arts free-for-alls and a John Woo-style climax, BAD BLOOD packs the wallop of a streetfighting demo, if nothing more.

Already stung by doing prison time for his ne'er-do-well brother Franklin (Hank Cheyne), ex-cop Travis Blackstone (Lorenzo Lamas) reluctantly agrees to broker the return of $100,000 his sibling lifted from a money-laundering bank controlled by Mr. Chang (Joe Son). Travis learns that Franklin actually ripped off five million and invested it in a real estate scam. While Travis' turncoat girlfriend leads Chang to the Blackburns, Travis forcibly retrieves the loot. After a shootout at Travis' hotel hideout, Franklin stashes the moolah in the trash at an abandoned building, then is kidnapped and tortured by cartel hoodlums. Homeless people unknowingly burn the cash. At a negotiating session with Chang, Travis levels the field of hired goons, but his ex-lover Rhonda (Frankie Thorn), who had left him for Franklin, joins her weasel beau in captivity. Travis keeps a rendezvous for a showdown at Sun Valley Salvage. As numerous soldiers-of-fortune kickbox, stab, and machine gun him, Rhonda and Franklin scurry for cover. Improvising with available auto-factory equipment, unbowed Travis wipes out the enforcers and kung-fus Chang into an acid vat. Travis exits with Rhonda and his scapegrace brother.

Viscerally exciting (Although the staging of the numerous fight sequences varies in quality), this hopped-up celebration of muscle power can't override one crucial plot flaw: the unlikable, manipulative character that leading-man Lamas risks life and limb for isn't worth his or the audience's time. Since motivation takes a back seat to carnage in action pics, this won't prevent aficionados from enjoying the well-placed kicks, both literal and figurative. Since BAD BLOOD moves along in an action cyclone, viewers won't have much breathing space to ponder its

illogic. *(Graphic violence, profanity, extensive nudity, adult situations.)* — R.P.

d, Tibor Takacs; p, Alan Amiel; exec p, Tibor Takacs; assoc p, Brian Irving; w, Neil Ruttenberg; ph, Bernard Salzmann; ed, Fima Noveck; m, Joel Goldsmith, Alex Wilkinson; prod d, Devin Meadows; art d, Tom Cortese; casting, Michelle Guillermin; cos, Lisa Cacavas; makeup, Dee Mansano, Stacy Sanders

Action/Crime/Martial Arts　　　　　**(PR: O　MPAA: R)**

BAD BOYS　　　　　★★½
(U.S.) 126m Simpson-Bruckheimer Films ~ Columbia c

Martin Lawrence *(Marcus Burnett)*; Will Smith *(Mike Lowrey)*; Tea Leoni *(Julie Mott)*; Theresa Randall *(Theresa Burnett)*; Tcheky Karyo *(Fouchet)*; Marg Helgenberger *(Alison Sinclair)*; Nestor Serrano *(Detective Sanchez)*; Julio Oscar Mechoso *(Detective Ruiz)*; Saverio Guerra *(Chet the Doorman)*; Anna Thomson *(Francine)*; Kevin Corrigan *(Elliot)*; Michael Imperioli *(Jojo)*; Joe Pantoliano *(Captain Howard Eddie)*; Lisa Boyle *(Girl Decoy)*; Michael Talifero *(Carjacker)*; Emmanuel Xuereb *(Eddie Dominquez)*; Marc Macaulay *(Noah Trafficante)*; Ralph Gonzalez *(Kuni)*; Vic Manni *(Ferguson)*; Frank John Hughes *(Casper)*; Mike Kirton *(Andy)*; Will Knickerbocker *(Officer Bill O'Fee)*; Tiffany Samuels *(Megan Burnett)*; Cory Hodges *(James Burnett)*; Scott Cumberbatch *(Quincy Barnett)*; Joey Romano *(Detective)*; Sam Ayers *(Detective)*; Karen Alexander *(Max Logan)*; Fawn Reed *(Woman at Boxing Gym)*; Heather Davis *(Lois Fields)*; Maureen Gallagher *(Yvette)*; Juan Cejas *(Ether Van Driver)*; Ed Amatrudo *(Ether Van Boss)*; Jimmy Franzo *(Club Bartender)*; Tony Bolano *(Drunk Guy at Urinal)*; Shaun Toub *(Store Clerk)*; Marty McSorley *(Henchman)*; Norman Max Maxwell *(Henchman)*; Buddy Bolton *(Wally)*; Stan Miller *(News Anchor)*; Dug Jones *(Man No. 1)*; John Spider Salley *(Hacker "Fletcher")*; Dana Mark *(Police Technician)*; Mario Ernesto Sanchez *(Drug Buyer)*

TV comedy stars Martin Lawrence and Will Smith ("Fresh Prince") play loose-cannon cops in this derivative and formulaic buddy film from the Action Blockbusters 'R' Us producing team of Simpson-Bruckheimer.

Rich kid Mike Lowery (Will Smith) is a high-living, smooth-talking lady's man. Marcus Burnett (Martin Lawrence) is a hen-pecked family man. Together, they are Miami's best narcotics detectives, and magnets for violence and mayhem. When $100 million worth of heroin is stolen from their department's evidence vault, this odd couple is put on the case. Unfortunately, their first lead comes with the murder of Lowery's body-building, prostitute girlfriend, Max Logan (Karen Alexander). Max's friend, Julie Mott (Tea Leoni), comes forward as a witness, but will only deal with Lowery. Happenstance requires Burnett to impersonate his partner, continuing the role-switching ruse until the case is solved. This doesn't sit well with Burnett, who's unhinged by Julie's come-ons and the thought of Lowery staying with his wife.

Burnett and Lowery's version of protective custody includes taking Julie on stakeouts and involving her in shoot-outs and dangerous chases, where—finally—the proverbial bad guy, Fouchet (Tcheky Karyo), kidnaps her. Now the "bad boys" get serious. Their investigation leads them to an airplane hangar, where Fouchet is selling the stolen heroin. Burnett and Lowery kill Fouchet's goons, rescue Julie, and blow everything up, but not before the villain escapes. After yet another high-speed chase, they capture and kill Fouchet, too.

Producers Don Simpson and Jerry Bruckheimer (BEVERLY HILLS COP, TOP GUN, CRIMSON TIDE) are veterans of the action-adventure form, and for aficionados of that genre, BAD

BOYS would be a treat—if only the characters didn't speak. The film is brimming with helicopter and tracking shots, as well as slow-motion body rolls where the actors come up shooting; and the Miami presented is all elaborate art deco, sepia-washed by day and neon-bathed by night. Unfortunately, the characters *are* given some dialogue—and the most interesting exchanges are quotes from old TV commercials. Moreover, the plot is inconsequential to the point of being dispensable. Anyone who has seen 48 HOURS and its offspring, particularly the LETHAL WEAPON series, will be bored by the formulaic mix of bickering and bonding, fiery explosions and shattering glass.

At heart, BAD BOYS is a screwball farce—albeit one with a lot of killing—whose comedy impulses are mostly squashed by its determination to be an action extravaganza. Lawrence is a naturally charismatic comedian who, unfortunately, is stymied by Smith's action-hero posturing and "I'm a serious cop, man!" speeches. The film could have benefited from a more modest production that more fully explored its comic possibilities. *(Violence, profanity, sexual situations.)* — P.R.

d, Michael Bay; p, Jerry Bruckheimer, Don Simpson; exec p, Lucas Foster, Bruce S. Pustin; w, Michael Barrie, Jim Mulholland, Doug Richardson (from a story by George Gallo); ph, Howard Atherton; ed, Christian Wagner; m, Mark Mancina; prod d, John Vallone; art d, Peter Politanoff; set d, Kate Sullivan; sound, Peter Devlin (mixer); fx, Richard Lee Jones; casting, Francine Maisler, Lynn Kressel; cos, Bobbie Read; makeup, Laini Thompson; stunts, Ken Bates

Action/Crime/Comedy   **(PR: O   MPAA: R)**

BAD COMPANY   ★★½
(U.S.) 108m Touchstone; Tool Shed Productions ~ Buena Vista c

Ellen Barkin *(Margaret Wells)*; Laurence Fishburne *(Nelson Crowe)*; Frank Langella *(Vic Grimes)*; Spalding Gray *(Walter Curl)*; Michael Beach *(Tod Stapp)*; Gia Carides *(Julie Ames)*; David Ogden Stiers *(Judge Beach)*; Daniel Hugh Kelly *(Les Goodwin)*; Spalding Gray *(Walter Curl)*; Tegan West *(Al)*; James Hong *(Bobby Birdsong)*; Fred Henderson *(John Cartwain)*; Michelle Beaudoin *(Wanda)*; Sherry Bie *(Mrs. Beach)*; Alan Robertson *(Phil)*; L. Harvey Gold *(Doctor)*; Alan C. Peterson *(Cleaners Clerk)*; Larry Musser *(Detective Harrison)*; Brian Drummond *(Ed the Doorman)*; Sook Yin Lee *(Waitress)*; Marcus Youssef *(Concierge)*; Nicholas Lea *(Jake)*; Jill Teed *(Jane)*

Originally slated for release in 1994, and released for an eyeblink in early 1995, this espionage thriller with a complex plot runs out of steam halfway through, and coasts to an unimaginative conclusion.

Former CIA operative Nelson Crowe (Laurence Fishburne) is hired by former CIA operative Vic Grimes (Frank Langella) to work in the Toolshed, a private espionage firm that spies, blackmails, and kills for its corporate clients. Crowe is quickly taken under the wing and sheets of Grimes's second-in-command, Margaret Wells (Ellen Barkin), who enlists him in her plot to stage a *coup d'etat* against Grimes. Meanwhile, Crowe has been assigned to bribe a judge (David Ogden Stiers) to rule a case in favor of a company that poisoned a town's water. Crowe is also being blackmailed by Smitty (an uncredited Michael Murphy), a current CIA agent, to assist him in taking over the Toolshed. The judge takes the million dollars, sends his mistress, Julie Ames (Gia Carides), off to the Bahamas with the money to await him, and then commits suicide. That same weekend, Crowe and Wells murder Grimes.

Much to Crowe's dismay, Wells as the new boss is an icy, no-nonsense bitch, who orders Crowe to tie up loose ends by

killing Ames. Soon Smitty moves in, takes control of the Toolshed, and orders Wells to terminate Crowe. Meanwhile, Ames decides to seek vengeance for her lover's death by killing Crowe herself. All three meet in Crowe's apartment, and after a gun battle, only Ames is left standing. She collects the evidence Crowe had gathered about the Toolshed and Smitty, and mails it to the U.S. Attorney General, before heading off to enjoy her wealth.

BAD COMPANY displays many of the familiar trappings of classic film noir. The characters speak in hushed voices, infusing the dialogue with sexual and violent overtones. The plot is heavy with double crosses and hidden agendas. All this works to hold a viewer's interest in the first half of the film, until it becomes apparent after Grimes's murder that the narrative is out of control. The supporting cast are all very good, including a deliciously twisted Spalding Gray. The problem lies in the leads: Barkin and Fishburne have no chemistry, and her overplaying and his underplaying only bespeak mutual boredom with their roles. Damian Harris's oddly paced direction (quite possibly reflecting a cutting-room salvage job) does not help matters, and his truly remarkable use of the widescreen frame—which made BAD COMPANY a rare visual treat during its brief theatrical run—is completely wasted on video. *(Profanity, sexual situations, graphic violence.)* — P.R.

d, Damian Harris; p, Amedeo Ursini, Jeffrey Chernov; assoc p, Warren Carr; w, Ross Thomas; ph, Jack N. Green; ed, Stuart Pappe; m, Carter Burwell; prod d, Andrew McAlpine; art d, William Heslup; set d, Elizabeth Wilcox; sound, Larry Sutton (mixer); fx, Randy Shymkiw; casting, Deborah Aquila; cos, Richard Shissler, Charles DeCaro; makeup, Victoria Down, Howard Berger, Wayne Toth, Kertzman, Nicotero & Berger EFX Group; stunts, Ernie Jackson

Spy/Thriller/Drama   **(PR: O   MPAA: R)**

BALLET   ★★★
(U.S.) 170m Zipporah Films ~ Zipporah Films c

Agnes DeMille; Irina Kolpakova; David Richardson; Michael Somes; Alessandra Ferri; Cynthia Harvey; Susan Jaffe; Christine Dunham; Julio Bocca; Wes Chapman

At some three hours in length, this *cinema verite* documentary is precisely as interesting as its subject. Potentially fascinating for balletomanes and dance students, it may hold little interest for general viewers.

Directed by Frederick Wiseman, the dean of American documentarists, BALLET follows the members of American Ballet Theatre as they prepare for and undertake their 1992 European tour. One of the largest and most prestigious ballet companies in the US, American Ballet Theatre is based in New York City, and the film's first 90 minutes take place in the troupe's lower Manhattan studios. Wiseman's dispassionate camera captures the grace and discipline of the dancers, as well as the endless repetition of class and the sweat, concentration, and frustration of rehearsals. The contrast between the careless enthusiasm of the younger dancers and the careful dedication of the more senior dancers—for whom an injury is more likely to be career threatening—is also clear.

We watch as wheelchair-bound choreographer Agnes DeMille—one of the grande dames of American dance—coaches a dancer young enough to be her granddaughter, using verbal metaphors and eloquent hand gestures to convey the essence of her choreographic vision. Ballerina Georgina Parkinson, trained in the traditions of England's Royal Ballet, polishes a variation from the 19th-century classic *Raymonda*. Modern dancer and choreographer Ulysses Dove teaches his *Serious*

Pleasures. Ballet masters David Richardson (formerly of the New York City Ballet), Irina Kolpakova (of Russia's Kirov Ballet), and Michael Somes—who died before the film was released—carefully coach a new generation of dancers in the intricacies of choreographic traditions that stretch back into the 19th Century. ABT stars—including Susan Jaffee, Cynthia Harvey, Julio Bocca, Wes Chapman, and Alessandra Ferri—are glimpsed in rehearsal and in performance.

Wiseman's footage also includes sequences featuring the company's executives, notably the famously abrasive Jane Herrman, one of two administrators (the other was Oliver Smith) who had recently replaced dance superstar Mikhail Baryshnikov as the company's head. Also glimpsed are costumers, physical therapists, and other key behind-the-scenes personnel. In keeping with Wiseman's hands-off style, only two people—DeMille and Kolpakova—sit for interviews, and no one is identified on screen.

BALLET, Wiseman's 27th feature, differs markedly from his best-known earlier work. It isn't a deadpan expose like TITICUT FOLLIES (1967), nor does it chronicle an institution with which the average viewer is familiar, like HIGH SCHOOL (1968), HIGH SCHOOL II (1994), BASIC TRAINING (1971) or THE STORE (1983). BALLET doesn't work (nor is it intended) as an introduction to the art of classical dancing: there isn't enough performance footage to convert anyone who isn't already familiar with ballet, and there's no opportunity for viewers to get to know individuals and be drawn into their rarefied environment by the human interest factor. Its only potential audience consists of classical dancers and hard-core ballet fans—specifically, those familiar enough with the contemporary dance scene to recognize the featured personalities. For them, needless to say, it's a must-see. — M.M.

d, Frederick Wiseman; p, Frederick Wiseman; ph, Frederick Wiseman; ed, Frederick Wiseman

Docudrama   **(PR: A   MPAA: NR)**

BALLISTIC   ★★
(U.S.) 96m Swical Productions ~ Imperial Entertainment c

Marjean Holden *(Det. Jesse Galvin)*; Joel Beeson *(Ray Sterling)*; Sam Jones *(Nick Braden)*; Richard Roundtree *(Harold Galvin)*; James Lew *(Woo)*; Cory Everson *(Claudia)*; Charles Napier *(Capt. Underwood)*; Julie St. Clair; Deke Anderson; Michael Earl Reid; Vincent Klyn; Ben Reed; Jeff Rector; Michael White

A martial-arts also-ran that merely flirts with distinction, the direct-to-video BALLISTIC offered rising supporting actress Marjean Holden (THE PHILADELPHIA EXPERIMENT 2) a showcase as hard-kicking action star. It's no great leap for the cause of African-American women in cinema, however; the credits aren't even over before our shapely heroine has done a shower scene and donned a tight hooker outfit to patrol the mean streets of LA as undercover police detective Jesse Galvin.

Jesse's determined to nail high-profile druglord Nick Braden (a smirking Sam Jones) and prove that her cop daddy (Richard Roundtree) was framed for corruption. But all remaining LAPD males are, naturally, chauvinist thugs on Braden's payroll who arrange for Jesse to be disgraced and suspected of murder. Undeterred, she and karate instructor-lover Ray (Joel Beeson) dig up evidence that gets Galvin *pere* freed from prison. The trio converge on Braden's warehouse, conveniently filled with rocket-propelled grenades that Jesse uses to blow away the baddies.

It's nice to see Roundtree, an underrated performer too often relegated to second-banana roles, in a take-charge mode here, even if the bulk of his dialogue is devoted to disparaging Ray as

a "skinny-assed white boy." Holden is nice to watch also, for more reasons than the obvious ones. A capable actress, she wrings as much conviction as she can out of a largely one-dimensional script, and romantic interest Beeson also makes an agreeably fresh impression. While there are enough "relationship" scenes to establish Holden as a kinder, gentler death-dealer, BALLISTIC doesn't spare the usual cliches about kung-fu bloodmatches and trusted, paternal authority figures who turn traitor (and are customarily played by Charles Napier). The narrative's biggest surprise is a sardonic jab at THE KARATE KID during its mayhem-filled climax. *(Graphic violence, sexual situations, nudity, substance abuse, profanity.)* — C.C.

d, Kim Bass; p, Peter Maris; exec p, Brian Shuster; assoc p, Joleen Deatherage; w, Donald Lamoureaux; ph, Gerald Wolfe; ed, Mark Melnick; m, Tyler Bates; art d, Patricia Elias; cos, Judi Jensen; stunts, James Lew

Martial Arts/Action/Thriller   **(PR: O   MPAA: R)**

BALLOT MEASURE 9   ★★
(U.S.) 75m Oregon Tape Project ~ Zeitgeist Films c

Donna Red Wing; Kathleen Saadat; Scott Seibert; Jim Self; Elise Self; Cindy Patterson; Ann Sweet; Tom Potter; Lon Mabon; Bonnie Mabon; Scott Lively; Oren Camenish

BALLOT MEASURE 9 is a passionate, intelligent chronicle of the bitter political campaigns fought over Oregon's 1992 antigay ballot initiative. Winner of the Best Documentary Audience Award at the Sundance Film Festival, Heather Macdonald's documentary reaches beyond its immediate subject of gay rights to expose the crisis of the American political process in the 1990s.

Ballot Measure 9 was an initiative, sponsored by the Oregon Citizen's Alliance (OCA), to amend Oregon's constitution so that laws which protect gays and lesbians from discrimination would be revoked or prohibited. The referendum also sought a mandate for all government departments and schools to "recognize homosexuality, pedophilia, sadism and masochism as abnormal, wrong, unnatural, and perverse."

BALLOT MEASURE 9 allows equal time to both OCA Chair Lon Mabon and gay activists, as it follows the twists and turns of the heated debate during an eight-month period from April until the November elections. The opposition campaign became a struggle to persuade floating voters that gays and lesbians sought no special rights, merely the preservation of the same rights afforded anybody else. After an increasingly violent battle, Measure 9 lost by a 57-43% margin. Although this was a victory for opponents of the ballot, some alarming statistics emerged. The largest group voting "yes" were citizens aged 30-44, a group most likely to have children of school age, who apparently feared that "homosexuality might be taught and transmitted" in school. People over 60, who lived through WWII, saw it as an issue of discrimination and were the largest group voting "no." Also, in the year that Measure 9 was on the Oregon ballot, there were more cases of antigay violence in Portland, Oregon, than in Chicago, Detroit, San Francisco, or New York City.

While BALLOT MEASURE 9 doesn't pretend to be evenhanded, it is more than simply a plea for gay rights. Dispensing with voice-over, the film shows the political battle evolving through both the stories of key participants and interviews with members of the general community, revealing a high level of fear and hostility on both sides. The film effectively exposes the tactics of the religious right, and contextualizes their actions in Oregon within a national agenda. It shows how rhetoric and semantics are used to confuse issues — particularly with respect to concepts of "family values" and "special rights" — and how homophobia and racism are reinforced through language. BAL-LOT MEASURE 9 also shows how unprepared the opponents of Measure 9 were for the OCA's sophisticated, highly organized attack, and witnesses the courage these men and women displayed as they stood their ground in an increasingly violent atmosphere. BALLOT MEASURE 9 is at turns inspiring and horrifying, showing how human rights and cultural diversity are taking a backseat to hate politics and divisiveness. *(Profanity.)* — J.S.

d, Heather McDonald; p, Heather McDonald; exec p, David Meieran; assoc p, B.B. Jorissen, Esther Cassidy; ph, Ellen Hansen, Linda Kliewer, Heather MacDonald, Alicia Weber, Spence Palermo, Elaine Velazquez; ed, Heather MacDonald, B.B. Jorissen; m, Julian Dylan Russell, Sunny McHale Skyedancer, Linda and the Family Values

Documentary   **(PR: A   MPAA: NR)**

BALTO   ★★
(U.S.) 74m Amblimation; Universal ~ Universal c

VOICES OF: Kevin Bacon *(Balto)*; Bob Hoskins *(Boris)*; Bridget Fonda *(Jenna)*; Jim Cummings *(Steele)*; Phil Collins *(Muk/Luk)*; Jack Angel *(Nikki)*; Danny Mann *(Kaltag)*; Robbie Rist *(Star)*; Juliette Brewer *(Rosy)*; Sandra Searles Dickinson *(Sylvie/Dixie/Rosy's Mother)*; Donald Sinden *(Doc)*; William Roberts *(Rosy's Father)*; Garrick Hagon *(Telegraph Operator)*; Bill Bailey *(Butcher)*; Big Al *(Town Dog)*; LIVE ACTION: Miriam Margolyes *(Grandma Rosy)*; Lola Bates-Campbell *(Granddaughter)*

A babysitter video item, BALTO represents Universal Studios' and co-producer Steven Spielberg's modest effort to lure children away from Disney's more spectacular animated feature monopoly.

In a current-day live-action opening, Grandma Rosy (Miriam Margolyes) tells her granddaughter (Lola Bates-Campbell) the story of Balto, a dog that helped save her life when she was a little girl growing up in Nome, Alaska, in 1925. In an animated flashback, Rosy (the voice of Juliette Brewer) recounts the time she was sick with diphtheria in her parents' home in an isolated Alaskan hamlet. When the doctor (the voice of Donald Sinden) proclaims that Rosy and other residents can only be saved by an antitoxin from a faraway town, a local driver puts together a team of sleigh dogs, including the outcast mutt, Balto (the voice of Kevin Bacon).

Balto fights during the journey with his rival, the menacing Steele (the voice of Jim Cummings). The other dogs side with Steele after each confrontation, but Balto is comforted by his oddball friends, including Boris, a snow goose (the voice of Bob Hoskins), and Muk and Luk, two polar bears (both the voice of Phil Collins).

On the way back after getting the medicine, the driver nearly dies in an accident. Balto then wins a brutal battle against Steele to lead the dog team the rest of the way home. When Steele arrives in Nome first, the residents assume the mission was unsuccessful. While Steele boasts about how hard he tried to bring back the medicine, Balto shows up with it. The other dogs desert Steele and cheer Balto for saving Rosy and the village.

BALTO is based on a true story about a courageous sleigh dog, but the filmmakers have added many animal characters to the tale, as well as the live-action framework set in New York's Central Park.

Unfortunately, the quality of both the storytelling and the animation bears little evidence of any technological advancement since the days of 101 DALMATIANS (1961). The crisp but flat, uninventive drawings are more reminiscent of Saturday morning television cartoons than the commercial artistry of, say, Disney's seminal dog story, LADY AND THE TRAMP (1955). Some parents may appreciate BALTO's lack of ostentation next to the recent Disney features, and BALTO may be preferable to watching the live talking dogs in LOOK WHO'S TALKING NOW (1993), but it hardly qualifies as a significant or enlightened piece of animated entertainment. — E.M.

d, Simon Wells; p, Steve Hickner; exec p, Steven Spielberg, Kathleen Kennedy, Bonne Radford; assoc p, Rich Arons; w, Cliff Ruby, Elana Lesser, David Steven Cohen, Roger S.H. Schulman (from a story by Cliff Ruby and Elana Lesser); ed, Nick Fletcher, Sim Evan-Jones; m, James Horner; prod d, Hans Bacher; anim, Jeffrey J. Varab, Dick Zondag, Kristof Serrand, Rob Stevenhagen, Sahin Ersoz, Rodolphe Guenoden, Nicolas Marlet, William Salazar, David Bowers, Patrick Mate, Daniel Jeannette, Erik Schmidt; casting, Patsy Pollock, Bob Litvak, Ellen Parks

Children's/Animated/Adventure   **(PR: AA   MPAA: G)**

BANDIT QUEEN   ★★★½
(India/U.K.) 129m Film Four International; Kaleidoscope ~ Arrow c

Seema Biswas *(Phoolan Devi)*; Nirmal Pandey *(Vikram Mallah)*; Manoj Bajpai *(Man Singh)*; Rajesh Vivek *(Mustaquim)*; Raghuvir Yadav *(Madho)*; Govind Namdeo *(Sriram)*; Saurabh Shukla *(Kailash)*; Aditya Srivastava *(Puttilal)*; Agesh Markam *(Mad Woman)*; Anirudh Agarwal *(Babu Gujjar)*; Anil Sahu; Chotelal Siraswal; Nazim Patel; Nazim Hussain; Pawan Gupta; Pradeep Gupta; Vibanshu Vaibhav; Vinod Tiwari *(Vikram Gang Members)*; Anupam Shyam *(Ganshyam)*; Ajai Rohilla *(Behmai Man)*; Surendra Kora *(Behmai Man)*; Aseem Bajaj; Basant Rawat; Ddhawal Gwaliori; Lakshmi Narayan; Puran Bhatt; Rakesh Raekwar; Sanjeev Kuwaar; Yogesh Gupta *(Phoolan/Man Singh Gang)*; Ashok Bulani *(D.S.P.)*; Ashok Sharma *(Ashokchand Servant)*; Avinash Nemade *(Doctor)*; Deepak Chibber *(S.P. Bhind)*; Deepak Soni *(Miandad)*; Dilip Raghuvanshi *(Commander Yadav)*; Gajraj Rao *(Ashokchand)*; G.B. Dixit *(Ala Singer)*; Girish Solanki *(Tarika's Partner)*; Guddi *(Munni)*; Gyan Shivpuri *(Phool Singh)*; Harish *(Tarika)*; Hemant Mishra *(Policeman)*; Hemant Pandey *(Ashokchand's Friend)*; Jeetendra Shastri *(Bharat)*; Kamla Bhatt *(Rukhmani—Age 11)*; K.D. Segan *(A.D.C.)*; Khunni Lal Maina *(Pundit)*; Mahesh Chandra *(Chief Minister)*; Malabai Sonwani *(Mother-in-law)*; Mandakini Goswami *(Kailash's Wife)*; Pallavi Bharti *(Little Girl)*; Paritosh Sand *(Devendra Singh)*; Ram Charan Nirmalker *(Devideen)*; Ranjit Chaudhry *(Shiv Narain)*; Raj Kumar Kamle *(Thakur Gang)*; Ravi Sangde *(Messenger)*; Savitri Raekwar *(Moola)*; Sitaram Panchal *(Lalaram)*; Sunil Gaekwad *(Rattan Chand)*; Sunita Bhatt *(Little Phoolan)*; Uma Vaish *(Rukhmani)*; Vijay Shukla *(Ashokchand's Friend)*

BANDIT QUEEN, a masterful Indian epic based on the life of a latter-day woman warrior, makes few concessions to art-house taste, and viewers whose notions of India have been shaped by decorous Merchant/Ivory productions may shrink from its confrontational style and vernacular sensibility. But this harrowing, willfully controversial film has the narrative sweep and visual energy of the best Indian commercial cinema.

BANDIT QUEEN tells the story of Phoolan Devi (Seema Biswas), the near-legendary leader of a band of *dacoits*—brigands—who terrorized north central India during the late 1970s and early 1980s. The film opens in rural Uttar Pradesh in 1968, as 11-year-old Phoolan (Sunita Bhatt) is married off to a grown man (Aditya Srivastava). When Phoolan resists his sexual demands, he rapes and later abandons her. She returns to her village a social outcast.

The grown Phoolan (Biswas) runs into trouble after she fends off an attempted rape by an upper-caste villager. Accused of various crimes by the village headmen, she lands in jail, where she is beaten and raped by police and guards. Later, her upper-caste enemies sell her off to a local bandit chieftain (Anirudh Agarwal), who treats her with similar brutality until he is killed by his young lieutenant, Vikram Mallah (Nirmal Pandey). Phoolan is attracted to the handsome Vikram, the first man who has ever treated her with respect and affection. The two become lovers and co-leaders of a small but resourceful bandit gang and conduct daring raids on upper-caste landowners, sometimes distributing the proceeds among lower-caste tenant farmers. Phoolan becomes an immensely popular figure among poor villagers throughout Uttar Pradesh.

The gang's original leader, a brutal upper-caste crime boss named Sriram (Govind Namdeo), is released from prison and rejoins the gang. Soon after, he murders Vikram and arranges a gruesome punishment for Phoolan: she is gang-raped by most of men in the village of Behmai, Uttar Pradesh, and frog-marched through the village naked, bruised, and bleeding. Afterwards, she forms a gang of her own and eventually takes her revenge, presiding over a massacre that leaves 20 villagers dead. This is too much for state authorities, who organize an intensive search for the outlaws. At bay and without resources, Phoolan eventually surrenders to the government. But moral victory is hers: greeted at the prison by a cheering crowd of thousands, she defiantly brandishes her gun before submitting to arrest.

Financed in part by Britain's Channel Four, BANDIT QUEEN is an Indian film intended primarily for Western audiences. However, unlike the handful of South Asian movies that have drawn international attention over the past decade—e.g., SPICES (1985) and SALAAM BOMBAY! (1988), both directed by filmmakers then associated with the high-minded, often arty, "parallel cinema"—BANDIT QUEEN is decidedly popular art, reflecting the Bollywood background of its formidably talented director, Shekhar Kapur.

Despite the opening title—"This is a true story"—Kapur's film is less a literal biography than an explication of the popular mythology surrounding Phoolan Devi. As electrically portrayed by Biswas, she's a furious embodiment of *shakti*—feminine power—and a figure of affronted womanhood that inevitably recalls the abundant rape-revenge subgenre of Indian commercial melodrama (it's no accident that examples of the colossal hoardings used to promote Bollywood movies are prominently visible during the Behmai massacre sequence). Production values are first-rate throughout, notably the mournful score by Nusrat Fateh Ali Khan and cinematographer Ashok Mehta's dazzling use of the unearthly ravine country of Chambral Valley.

As Kapur no doubt intended, BANDIT QUEEN provoked scandal, both in India and internationally. Scenes of nudity and extremely graphic violence—not to mention depictions of lawless brutality on the part of police and government ministers—made the film unreleasable in India. (With extensive cuts, it was eventually released to a few urban art houses.) Phoolan Devi herself, an erratic figure and occasional pawn of Indian politicos, claimed that Kapur had misrepresented her story and briefly threatened legal action. She then reversed herself and embraced the film, reportedly after accepting a sizable sum from the filmmakers. But her initial disavowals damaged the film's reputation, particularly among American and European feminists—many of whom dismissed BANDIT QUEEN, sight unseen, as another example of affluent male artists presuming to speak for subaltern women. (*Graphic violence, extensive nudity, sexual situations, adult situations, extreme profanity.*) — J.L.

d, Shekhar Kapur; p, Sundeep Singh Bedi; assoc p, Varsha Bedi; w, Mala Sen; ph, Ashok Mehta; ed, Renu Saluja; m, Nusrat Fateh Ali Khan; prod d, Eve Mavrakis; art d, Ashok Bhagat; set d, Sujata Sharma; sound, Robert Taylor (mixer); casting, Tigmanshu Dhulia; cos, Dolly Ahluwalia; makeup, Edwin Williams, Mohd Iqbal Sheikh; stunts, Alan Amin

Drama/Biography/Political   (PR: O   MPAA: NR)

BAR GIRLS   ★★
(U.S.) 95m Lavender Circle Mob Productions ~
Orion Classics c

Nancy Allison Wolfe (*Loretta*); Liza D'Agostino (*Rachel*); Camila Griggs (*JR*); Michael Harris (*Noah*); Justine Slater (*Veronica*); Lisa Parker (*Annie*); Pam Raines (*Celia*); Paula Sorge (*Tracy*); Cece Tsou (*Sandy*); Caitlan Stansbury (*Kimba*); Patti Sheehan (*Destiny*); Lee Everett (*Lee*); Betsy Burke (*Cafe Waitress*); Laurie Jones (*Laurie*); Chastity Bono (*Scorp'*); T.J. McCall; Kathy Forrest; Chris Delaney; Kristin Klein; Monica Watford; Kindra Marra; Wendy Hoffman; Debra McKenna; Victoria Vaughn; Colleen Broderich; Helena Donovan; Lauren Hansen; Nicole Dion; Penelope Lindeman; Maria Elias; Lisa Podosin; Angela Emery; Tanya Blood Hinkle; Alexandra Fluga; Gayle Gibson; Gloria Joyce; Tory Minovich; Dennis Peterson; Maribel Velasquez; Jason Morris; Anna Streczyn; Donna Marie Costanza; Mary C. Howard; Libia Sambrano; Carla Ponzio; Jennifer Fisher; Ann Listenbee; Tiffany Bailey; Abbie Travis; Julie Jensen (*Barflies*)

BAR GIRLS is the debut directing effort of Marita Giovanni, with a script adapted from her own stage play by Lauran Hoffman. A romantic comedy about a group of women whose lives intersect at a Los Angeles bar, it could have been a "Cheers" for lesbians, but for the cliched characters and script which make it a film with little appeal, even for its target audience.

Stood up by Annie, Loretta is about to leave the Girl Bar, when she spots Rachel walking in. Loretta bets her friend that within ten minutes she will have lured Rachel into her white sports car. Her come-on works, but at Loretta's house the two nervous women soon realize that neither is completely free to start a new involvement. Loretta is still attached to Annie, who is now attracted to an unavailable heterosexual woman. For her part, Rachel confides that she has a husband, although the marriage is disintegrating and she is now seeing Sandy. Nevertheless, Loretta and Rachel do get involved, move in together, and vow monogamy and eternal love. Former attachments turn out to be unresolved and new players (particularly a butch cop called J.R.) appear determined to position themselves between the lovers.

The past few years has seen an increasing number of feature films made about lesbians. Starved for images of themselves on screen, lesbians flocked to theatrical documentaries like FORBIDDEN LOVE and mediocre melodramas like CLAIRE OF THE MOON. The demonstrated market for such works led to a rash of films, some of which are stylistically innovative and immensely enjoyable, such as GO FISH and THE INCREDIBLY TRUE ADVENTURE OF TWO GIRLS IN LOVE, while others rely far too heavily on the novelty of their subject matter to save them from oblivion.

BAR GIRLS unfortunately falls in the latter category. The story is populated by characters representing the worst cliches and stereotypes about lesbians (the butch who drives the Harley, the sporty-type in the track suit, the flannel clones playing pool). It is also filled with dramatic cliches and unspeakably clunky dialogue ("I love you enough to fill the hole in the ozone layer"). Flashbacks are inserted in an obvious manner; attempts at humor are forced. Perhaps the most interesting curiosity in the film is a cameo appearance by

Chastity Bono, Sonny and Cher's daughter. Try a margarita, instead. *(Adult situations, sexual situations.)* — J.S.

d, Marita Giovanni; p, Lauran Hoffman, Marita Giovanni; co-p, Doug Lindeman; w, Lauran Hoffman (based on her play); ph, Michael Ferris; ed, Cater DeHaven; art d, Darryl Fong, Keith Brunsmann; set d, Lia Niskanen, Andrew Rosen; sound, Jesse Bender (mixer); cos, Houston Sams; makeup, Beverly Anderson

Drama/Romance (PR: C MPAA: R)

BAREFOOT GEN ★★½
(Japan) 83m ~ Streamline Enterprises c

VOICES OF: Catherine Battistone; Iona Morris; Brianne Siddal; Barbara Goodson; Kurk Thornton; Dan Woven; Wendee Lee; Ardwight Chamberlain; Amike McConnohie; Joyce Kurtz; Mike Reynolds

A richly affecting piece of Japanese animation, BAREFOOT GEN adapts a highly regarded graphic novel based on the author's experiences as a boy in Hiroshima, before, during, and after the city's atomic bombing.

On August 6th, 1945, a U.S. plane drops a single atomic bomb and devastates the city of Hiroshima. Gen, a ten-year-old boy, survives the blast, as does his pregnant mother, Kimie, but he loses his father, older sister, and younger brother. Kimie soon gives birth to a little girl, but her breast milk dries up and the baby is threatened with starvation. Gen scours the city looking for food and milk and discovers some rice in a bombed-out storehouse. During this time, all of the boy's hair falls out.

Gen and Kimie set up house in an abandoned shack and are soon joined by Ryuta Kando, a little orphan boy who resembles Gen's dead brother, Shinji. Gen and Ryuta join forces and are hired to tend to Seijo, the badly injured brother of a wealthy man. After spending several days with Seijo, nursing him and encouraging him to resume his painting despite his injuries, the boys are paid a hundred yen, which they use to buy a large supply of powdered milk. When they return home, however, they find the baby has died.

Within weeks, wheat appears to be sprouting in the fields again and hair seems to be growing again on Gen's head. Recalling a promise he'd made to his brother Shinji, Gen carves a ship out of wood and sends it floating down the river, bearing a paper lantern.

Originally released in Japan in 1983, and only now available in the US in an English-dubbed version, BAREFOOT GEN is unusual for Japanese animation (or any animation for that matter) in that it deals with real historical events and human drama rather than the more typical superhero and science-fiction subjects. Based on artist Keiji Nakazawa's own experiences and adapted from his *manga* (comic book) of the same title, the film's detailed rendering of the land and cityscape is matched by explicit imagery of the devastation to people and property caused by the atomic blast.

An otherwise absorbing drama, it suffers in comparison to GRAVE OF THE FIREFLIES, a 1988 *anime* feature focusing on two children orphaned by American firebombing, which offered a more poetic texture, an insistently gloomy tone, and a rigorous attention to detail. BAREFOOT GEN offers a surprisingly upbeat ending, considering the lasting effects of Hiroshima's devastation, and is burdened with frequent and intrusive narration full of statistics and historical details. Still, it manages to tell a powerful and wrenching story which offers Americans a vivid dramatization of how the other side suffered during this catastrophic event. *(Graphic violence.)* — B.C.

d, Mamoru Shinzaki; p, Takanori Yoshimoto, Yasuteru Iwase, Keiji Nakazawa, Carl Macek; w, Keiji Nakazawa (based on his graphic novel), Ardwight Chamberlain; ph, Kinichi Ishikawa; m, Kentaro Hada; art d, Kazuo Oga; anim, Kazuo Tomisawa

Animated/Drama (PR: C MPAA: NR)

BASKETBALL DIARIES, THE ★★½
(U.S.) 102m BD Pictures; Palm Pictures; Island Pictures ~ New Line c

Leonardo DiCaprio *(Jim Carroll)*; Bruno Kirby *(Swifty)*; Lorraine Bracco *(Jim's Mother)*; Ernie Hudson *(Reggie Porter)*; Patrick McGaw *(Neutron)*; James Madio *(Pedro)*; Mark Wahlberg *(Mickey)*; Barton Heyman *(Confessional Priest)*; Roy Cooper *(Father McNulty)*; Josh Mostel *(Counterman)*; Juliette Lewis *(Diane Moody)*; Michael Rapaport *(Skinhead)*; Michael Imperioli *(Bobby)*; Marilyn Sokol *(Chanting Woman)*; Vinnie Patore *(Construction Worker)*; Jimmy Papiris *(Iggy)*; Alexander Gaberman *(Bobo)*; Ben Jorgensen *(Tommy)*; Michael Imperioli *(Bobby)*; Akiko Ashley *(Stripper)*; Manny Alfaro *(Manny)*; Cynthia Daniel *(Winkie)*; Eric Betts *(Drug Dealer)*; Joyce R. Korbin *(Mugging Victim)*; Barton Heyman *(Confessional Priest)*; Nick Gaetani *(Referee No. 1)*; Lawrence Barth *(Referee No. 2)*; Gary Iorio *(Policeman)*; Toby Huss *(Kenny)*; Jim Carroll *(Frankie Pinewater)*; William Webb *(JuJu Johnson)*; John Vennema *(Mr. Rubin)*; Doc Dougherty *(Policeman)*; John Hoyt *(Billy the Bartender)*

Based on the 1978 memoir of the same name by Jim Carroll, THE BASKETBALL DIARIES tell the story of a wild adolescent from the Lower East Side.

The youthful hijinks of Soulful Carroll (Leonardo DiCaprio) are about to land him in real trouble. With an artist's conviction, he transforms that trouble into feverish scribblings, a diary of his descent from playing basketball for his high school team and hanging with his best buddies to stealing, scamming, and hustling in his quest for the next high.

Carroll and his friends Neutron (Patrick McGaw), Mickey (Mark Wahlberg), and Pedro (James Madio) attend St. Vitus Catholic High School, and play on its basketball team, though the game's appeal is less teamwork and good, clean fun than the opportunities it affords to steal stuff from other teams' lockers. When they are not in court, the boys get high, hang out, and horse around, a term which covers everything from skinny dipping in the East River, to vomiting on a fellow passenger's head on the Staten Island Ferry, and teasing strung-out junkie prostitute Diane (Juliette Lewis). Gradually the drugs matter more and more, and Carroll progresses from popping pills, smoking the occasional joint and snorting coke with licentious Upper East Side twins to full-blown heroin addiction and tricking in Times Square.

Carroll's friends drift away, and his long-suffering mother (Lorraine Bracco) kicks him out, but he continues to write. After crawling to his mother's apartment to beg for money—which she tearfully refuses to give him, hiding from his misery behind a closed door—Carroll decides to clean up his act, and the film ends with him on-stage somewhere, mesmerizing the audience with his tales of degradation and gutter enlightenment.

What brings new readers to Carroll's book year after year—even as the New York of the 1960s and 1970s in which he came of age fades into the fog of memory—is the strength, clarity, and occasional beauty of his voice, which crackles with invulnerable optimism. The film, however, is clearly a misguided labor of love. Part of the trouble is that, although it is very much a story of its time, the filmmakers set it in a vague present that never feels right—an early scene involving corporal punishment at school is totally unconvincing if the setting is New York of the 1990s. Carroll and his friends also seem oddly naive for 1990s kids, and more like kids of an earlier, less sophisticated era.

As Carroll, Leonardo DiCaprio gives the kind of bravura performance that is hugely admirable but not altogether convincing. Its greatest weakness, though, is not of his making. The fact is, Carroll is only interesting because of his writing. *The Basketball Diaries* reminds readers of what redeems the hero and why they should not dismiss this unpleasant young man from their minds. On the screen, he is abrasive and disgusting, and there is nothing that tells viewers why they should care whether or not he dies in a gutter. *(Violence, nudity, sexual situations, adult situations, substance abuse, extreme profanity.)* — M.M.

d, Scott Kalvert; p, Liz Heller, John Bard Manulis; exec p, Chris Blackwell, Dan Genetti; w, Bryan Goluboff (based on the book by Jim Carroll); ph, David Phillips; ed, Dana Congdon; m, Graeme Revell; prod d, Christopher Nowak; set d, Harriet Zucker; sound, William Sarokin (mixer), Victor Iorillo (designer), Larry Hoki (recordist); fx, Steve Kirshoff; casting, Avy Kaufman; cos, David C. Robinson; makeup, Dianne Hammond; stunts, Edgard Mourino

Drama (PR: C   MPAA: R)

BATMAN FOREVER ★★½
(U.S.) 121m Warner Bros. ~ Warner Bros. c

Val Kilmer *(Batman/Bruce Wayne)*; Tommy Lee Jones *(Harvey Two-Face/Harvey Dent)*; Jim Carrey *(The Riddler/Edward Nygma)*; Nicole Kidman *(Dr. Chase Meridian)*; Chris O'Donnell *(Robin/Dick Grayson)*; Michael Gough *(Alfred Pennyworth)*; Pat Hingle *(Police Commissioner James Gordon)*; Debi Mazar *(Spice)*; Drew Barrymore *(Sugar)*; Ed Begley, Jr. *(Fred Stickley)*; Elizabeth Sanders *(Gossip Gerty)*; Rene Auberjonois *(Dr. Burton)*; Joe Grifasi *(Bank Guard)*; Philip Moon *(Newscaster)*; Jessica Tuck *(Newscaster)*; Dennis Paladino *(Crime Boss Moroni)*; Kimberly Scott *(Margaret)*; Michael Paul Chan *(Executive)*; Jon Favreau *(Assistant)*; Greg Lauren *(Aide)*; Ramsey Ellis *(Young Bruce Wayne)*; Michael Scranton *(Thomas Wayne)*; Eileen Seeley *(Martha Wayne)*; David U. Hodges *(Shooter)*; Jack Betts *(Fisherman)*; Tim Jackson *(Municipal Police Guard)*; Daniel Reichert *(Ringmaster)*; Glory Fioramonti *(Mom Grayson)*; Larry A. Lee *(Dad Grayson)*; Bruce Roberts *(Handsome Reporter)*; George Wallace *(Mayor)*; Bob Zmuda *(Electronic Store Owner)*; Rebecca Budig *(Teenage Girl)*; Don "The Dragon" Wilson *(Gang Leader)*; Sydney D. Minckler *(Teen Gang Member)*; Maxine Jones; Terry Ellis; Cindy Herron; Dawn Robinson *(Girls on Corner)*; Gary Kasper *(Pilot)*; Amanda Trees *(Paparazzi Reporter)*; Andrea Fletcher *(Reporter)*; Ria Coyne *(Socialite)*; Jed Curtis *(Chubby Businessman)*; William Mesnik *(Bald Guy)*; Marga Gomez *(Journalist)*; Kelly Vaughn *(Showgirl)*; John Fink *(Deputy)*; Noby Arden; Marlene Bologna; Danny Castle; Troy S. Wolf *(Trapeze Act)*

The third entry in the wildly popular BATMAN cycle boasts a new Batman, new costumes, a revamped Batmobile, and several new characters—including Robin, two super-villains, and yet another blonde love interest. Holy overkill!

Harvey Two-Face (Tommy Lee Jones) has an old score to settle with the Batman (Val Kilmer): The DA-turned-master-criminal blames the masked crimefighter for the courtroom attack that disfigured half his face and bifurcated his personality. The film opens with Batman foiling an elaborate hostage situation Two-Face has designed to snare him.

A specialist in abnormal psychology and multiple personalities, Dr. Chase Meridian (Nicole Kidman) is intrigued by both Batman and his alterego, billionaire industrialist Bruce Wayne.

The attraction is mutual. Wayne is also admired by the brilliant but unstable Edward Nygma—E. Nygma, geddit?—(Jim Carrey), who approaches him with an invention—a device that transfers other people's brainwaves into the wearer's mind. Wayne rejects the invention as unethical, but Nygma secretly continues his work and tests it on his hapless supervisor (Ed Begley, Jr.). The transfer boosts Nygma's intelligence but further unhinges him. Nygma vows vengeance on his former idol.

Wayne and Meridian attend a benefit circus performance featuring an acrobatic family act called The Flying Graysons. Two-Face and his thugs disrupt the event, and in the ensuing melee, three of the Graysons are killed. Only the youngest, Dick (Chris O'Donnell), survives. He becomes Wayne's ward and when he discovers Wayne's secret identity, asks to be his partner in battling Two-Face. Wayne refuses, but Grayson persists in his efforts, devising a name—Robin—and a costume for himself.

Meanwhile, Nygma—now calling himself the Riddler—joins Two-Face in a plot to destroy Batman and suck dry the minds of Gotham City. Nygma markets his device as a kind of super-TV and invites Wayne and Meridian to his launch party, where he goads the playboy into having his mind sucked. The Riddler and Two-Face view Wayne's memories and discover his secret identity; they invade Wayne mansion on Halloween, just as Wayne is revealing his identity to Meridian. The Riddler blows up the Batcave and Meridian is abducted.

Grayson and Batman team up to make Gotham City safe again. Two-Face takes a fatal fall and the Riddler goes totally mad from a brainpower overdose. The gibbering Nygma is committed to Arkham Asylum, where he raves that he is the Batman.

In a gambit designed to keep a profitable franchise alive—Tim Burton's dark BATMAN RETURNS was merely a solid success—Warners hired Joel Schumacher (THE CLIENT, THE LOST BOYS) to direct a lighter and more McDonald's tie-in friendly BATMAN movie. Schumacher served up a boldly campy and colorful variation that recalls both the 1960s TV show (complete with canted angles) and the brighter-hued "Batman" comic books that preceded the Gothic innovations of Frank Miller's "The Dark Knight Returns." BATMAN FOREVER doesn't shy away from Batman's murky psychology, but all the noise and color does seem designed to divert audience attention from the film's true story of twisted passion.

Most of its characters are obsessed with one another: Two-Face is obsessed with Batman, Grayson with Two-Face, Nygma with Wayne, Meridian with Wayne/Batman, and Wayne/Batman with criminals generally, as a result of his parents' murder. Several of the characters feel forced to lead double lives, and the film is surprisingly daring as it playfully posits all identity as a construct ("We all wear masks" observes Wayne). Moreover, its insistent verbal allusions to fetishism (rubber, leather, vinyl), sadomasochism (whips, spanking) and other sexual signifiers all but equate living "in the closet" with having special powers and knowledge. Not the typical stuff of comic book movies, this film's success is as powerful a sign of the mainstreaming of camp sensibilities as the recent spate of cross-dressing movies.

While ambitious in conception, the film falters a bit in execution. Schumacher brings a distinctive sensibility to the project, but seems flummoxed by the demands of cramming so much new material into one film. The star attraction is, of course, red-hot Jim Carrey, and if his stylized clowning makes little sense when he's playing Nygma, it's perfectly in synch with the Riddler persona, manic, lewd and more than a little threatening. *(Violence, adult situations.)* — K.G.

d, Joel Schumacher; p, Tim Burton, Peter MacGregor-Scott; exec p, Benjamin Melniker, Michael E. Uslan; assoc p, Mitchell

Dauterive; w, Lee Batchler, Janet Scott Batchler, Akiva Goldsman (from a story by Lee Batchler and Janet Scott Batchler based on characters created by Bob Kane); ph, Stephen Goldblatt; ed, Dennis Virkler; m, Elliot Goldenthal; prod d, Barbara Ling; art d, Chris Burian-Mohr, Joseph P. Lucky; set d, Elise "Cricket" Rowland; sound, Lance Brown (design), Frank Kniest (design), Roland Thai (design), Petur Hliddal (mixer); fx, Tommy L. Fisher, John Dykstra, Illusion Arts; casting, Mali Finn; cos, Bob Ringwood, Ingrid Ferrin; makeup, Ve Neill, Rick Baker; stunts, Conrad R. Palmisano, Jeff Gibson

AAN Best Cinematography: Stephen Goldblatt; *AAN Best Sound:* Donald O. Mitchell, Frank A. Montano, Michael Herbick, Petur Hliddal; *AAN Best Sound Effects:* John Leveque, Bruce Stambler

Adventure/Action   **(PR: C   MPAA: PG-13)**

BED YOU SLEEP IN, THE   ★★★½
(U.S.) 117m Complex Corporation ~ FilmHaus Releasing c

Tom Blair *(Ray Weiss)*; Ellen McLaughlin *(Jean Weiss)*; Kathryn Sannella; Marshall Gaddis; Thomas Morris; Brad Shelton

This is not the first time director Jon Jost has made a close study of the repressed underlayers of the American consciousness, and in particular of the working class male; SURE FIRE (1994) and JON JOST'S FRAMEUP (1995) covered similar volatile terrain. THE BED YOU SLEEP IN has much in common with Jost's previous work—the stylized realism; the documentary-like mise-en-scene; the slow, analytic study of American life; and the shocking and tragic conclusion.

Centered in a small logging town in the Pacific Northwest, the film follows Ray (Tom Blair), a perfect specimen of the ordinary, through several weeks of life. Ray's logging business is failing due to Japanese competition and the actions of environmentalists protecting an endangered owl. Ray also has a typical private life: his wife Jean (Ellen McLaughlin), and his love of fly-fishing. In contrast to the objective discourse of the men, the unhappy wives in Ray's community share dark secrets and despairs in the quiet of their failing homes, revealing their painful vulnerability, intimacy, and friendship.

The boredom of this rural lifestyle is shattered by a tragic plot twist. The Blairs' daughter, away at college, sends Jean a letter in which she confesses to having been molested by her father in her teens. Ray denies the claim and refuses to let his grieving wife visit their troubled child. One day at work he receives a phone call from his daughter's boyfriend. He listens quietly and with cold disbelief to what the boy has to say, then jumps into his truck and heads home. A flashback juxtaposed over the passing landscape reveals the face of the boyfriend as he cries into the telephone the news that the daughter has committed suicide.

When Ray arrives home, he finds his wife lying motionless on the kitchen floor. He flees to the lake and splashes his face with water, holds a rifle to his head, and fires. The camera lingers on the corpse, the bleeding head, the impassive silence of the natural surrounding.

As in his previous works, Jost highlights a moral concern for the relationship between the personal and the social; the danger of the hidden and the repressed; and the ability of a lie to undermine entire lives and social orders.

The most riveting quality of Jost's work is the primary role that form plays in establishing the force of somewhat random events. The camera spends an unusual amount of time absorbing details—each inorganic item in the local diner is observed in depth, from the salt shakers to the curves of the counter. Jost films rural America like a road surveyor, setting up a static camera on any intersection and letting the film roll as cars motor

past and children ride by on bikes. Then he moves it somewhere else. Gradually, what emerges is a tapestry of images that forces the spectator to examine the depths of meaning hidden in commonplace, day-to-day existence. *(Adult Situations.)* — R.C.

d, Jon Jost; p, Henry S. Rosenthal; w, Jon Jost; ph, Jon Jost; ed, Jon Jost; m, Erling Wold; prod d, Jon Jost; sound, John Murphey

Drama   **(PR: C   MPAA: NR)**

BEFORE SUNRISE   ★★★½
(U.S.) 101m Detour Film; Filmhaus; Castle Rock Entertainment ~ Columbia c

Ethan Hawke *(Jesse)*; Julie Delpy *(Celine)*; Andrea Eckert *(Wife on Train)*; Hanno Poschl *(Husband on Train)*; Karl Bruckschwaiger *(Guy on Bridge)*; Tex Rubinowitz *(Guy on Bridge)*; Erni Mangold *(Palm Reader)*; Dominik Castell *(Street Poet)*; Haymon Maria Buttinger *(Bartender)*; Harold Waiglein *(Guitarist in Club)*; Bilge Jeschim *(Belly Dancer)*; Kurti *(Percussionist)*; Hans Weingartner; Liese Lyon; Peter Ily Huemer; Otto Reiter; Hubert Fabian Kulterer; Branko Andric; Constanze Schweiger; John Sloss; Alexandra Seibel; Georg Schollhammer; Christian Ankowitsch; Wilbirg Reiter *(Cafe Patrons)*; Barbara Klebel *(Musician on Boat)*; Wolfgang Staribacher *(Musician on Boat)*; Wolfgang Gluxam *(Harpsichord Player)*

Director Richard Linklater's third feature, BEFORE SUNRISE, is a wry, winning portrait of a brief encounter between two young people who meet on a train, spend the night in Vienna and then part, defying Hollywood conventions of character and story development to charming effect.

BEFORE SUNRISE has little plot in the mainstream sense of that term. Jesse (Ethan Hawke), a young American man, meets Celine (Julie Delpy), a French college student, on a train heading to Austria. The two begin to talk, and do little else for the next 101 minutes. Jessie is going to catch his flight back to the US from Vienna, but has 24 hours to kill between the time the train pulls in and the time he must be at the airport. At the station stop in Vienna, Jesse suggests to Julie that they spend the time together. Julie agrees to his sudden proposition, interrupting her journey back to France from her grandmother's house.

In Vienna, Jesse and Julie talk incessantly, touching on matters philosophical and mundane. They also meet several people who play small roles in their growing attraction to one another. Two actors (Karl Bruckschwaiger, Tex Rubinowitz) invite them to a show, a palm reader (Erni Mangold) tells Julie's fortune, and a homeless street poet (Dominik Castell) dedicates one of his poems to the couple.

During the night, Jesse and Julie sleep together in a park. They wonder whether or not they should have sex, and finally decide they should. The next morning, Julie accompanies Jesse to the train station, where they pledge their love. Before saying their final good-byes, they agree to meet again on the platform.

Richard Linklater surprised many viewers by making an unapologetically romantic movie after the less conventionally sentimental SLACKER and DAZED AND CONFUSED. But BEFORE SUNRISE is a logical extension of Linklater's interests, particularly intertextual cultural references and rambling philosophical prattle.

Written by Linklater and Kim Krizan, BEFORE SUNRISE includes homages to Alfred Hitchcock's STRANGERS ON A TRAIN (the initial encounter on the train), Carol Reed's THE THIRD MAN (the Vienna setting, specifically the city's famous Ferris wheel) and Vittorio De Sica's INDISCRETION OF AN AMERICAN WIFE (the use of "real time" to tell the short story, particularly in the train station denouement, which also alludes to David Lean's BRIEF ENCOUNTER). Above all, BEFORE

SUNRISE feels like an American Eric Rohmer movie (imagine both the best and the worst that implies), defined by intimate yet heated conversations about life, art, love, religion, sex and politics.

BEFORE SUNRISE leans heavily on the appeal of its leads, who are in virtually every shot and helped develop the dialogue during the improvisational rehearsal period. Ethan Hawke rises to the occasion, delivering a relaxed, engaging performance as Jesse. Julie Delpy (of KILLING ZOE and THREE COLORS: WHITE) is a revelation as Celine. She even devised one of the film's best scenes: while sitting in a bar, Celine and Jesse talk about each other in imaginary phone calls to their best friends. Another charming scene is set in a record shop, where Jesse and Celine try to look at each other without being caught.

The film's only real flaw is its failure to address the viewer's nagging feeling that in real life, the sweetly grave Celine would quickly tire of the rather callow Jessie, whose immaturity shows in his angry reaction to the fortune teller's comments, cheery recounting of a friend's cruel practical joke on a homeless man and various other telling scenes. Still, it's encouraging to see a major Hollywood studio—Columbia Pictures—release a film that allows these characters to take center stage and keep it. *(Sexual situations, profanity.)* — E.M.

d, Richard Linklater; p, Anne Walker-McBay; exec p, John Sloss; assoc p, Gregory Jacobs; co-p, Ellen Winn Wendl, Gernot Schaffler, Wolfgang Ramml; w, Richard Linklater, Kim Krizan; ph, Lee Daniel; ed, Sandra Adair; prod d, Florian Reichmann; sound, Thomas Szabolcs (mixer); casting, Judy Henderson, Alycia Aumuller; cos, Florentina Welley; makeup, Karen Dunst

Romance/Comedy/Drama   **(PR: C   MPAA: R)**

BEFORE THE RAIN   ★★★★
(Macedonia/U.K./France) 115m Vardar Film; Aim Productions; Noe Productions ~ Gramercy c
(PO DEZJU)

Katrin Cartlidge *(Anne)*; Rade Serbedzija *(Aleksandar)*; Gregoire Colin *(Kiril)*; Labina Mitevska *(Zamira)*; Jay Villiers *(Nick)*; Silvija Stojanovska *(Hana)*; Phyllida Law *(Anne's Mother)*; Josif Josifovski *(Father Marko)*; Boris Delcevski *(Petre)*; Dejan Velkov *(Mate)*; Kiril Ristoski *(Father Damjan)*; Mladen Krstevski *(Trifun)*; Dzemail Maksut *(Kuzman)*; Milica Stojanova *(Aunt Cveta)*; Mile Jovanovski *(Priest Singing at Funeral)*; Petar Mircevski *(Zdrave)*; Ljupco Bresliski *(Mitre)*; Igor Madzirov *(Stojan)*; Metodi Psaltirov *(Tome)*; Ilko Stefanovski *(Bojan)*; Blagoja Spirkovski-Dzumerko *(Gang Leader)*; Sando Monev *(Blagoj)*; Suzana Kirandziska *(Neda)*; Katerina Kocevska *(Kate)*; Vladimir Endrovski *(Trajce)*; Abdurahman Salja *(Zekir)*; Vladimir Jacev *(Alija)*; Arben Kastrati *(Ramiz)*; Danny Newman *(Ian)*; Gabrielle Hamilton *(Woman in Cab)*; Moni Damevski *(George)*; Ljupco Todorovski *(Kizo)*; Peter Needham *(Maitre d')*; Melissa Wilkes *(Retarded Child)*; Joe Gould *(Redhead Waiter)*; Rod Woodruff *(Waiter in Fight)*; Aleksander Mikic *(Atanas)*; Meto Jovanovski *(Dr. Saso)*; Cvetko Mareski *(Boy with Gun)*; Goran *(Goran)*; Nino Levi *(Mailman)*; Lence Delova; Jordan Vitanov *(Policeman)*

The first film made in the newly declared republic of Macedonia (part of the former Yugoslavia), BEFORE THE RAIN won the Golden Lion (Best Picture) award at the 1994 Venice Film Festival and was nominated for that year's best foreign-language film Oscar. Released theatrically in the US in 1995, it enjoyed wide critical acclaim and was sometimes compared to another Oscar nominee, PULP FICTION, which employed a similarly unconventional structure.

BEFORE THE RAIN focuses on the volatile political climate in the Balkan states, particularly Macedonia, where tense relations between Orthodox Macedonians and Albanian Moslems threaten to erupt into civil war. At the time of the film's release, Macedonia remained peaceful. BEFORE THE RAIN is not a documentary, but an impassioned outcry for peace. Through this grim picture of his homeland's present and possible future, Macedonian screenwriter/director Milcho Manchevski sends a powerful message to both sides in the crisis.

Manchevski tells his story in three parts, each focusing on an individual facing a life-altering decision. "Words" is set in a Macedonian monastery, where Kiril (Gregoire Colin), a young monk, has taken a vow of silence. Returning to his cell one evening, he discovers that a frightened Albanian girl, Zamira (Labina Mitevski), has taken refuge there. Though his first instinct is to turn her in, Kiril is drawn to the girl and shelters her. The monastery is soon searched by gunmen who claim that Zamira killed their brother. Kiril escapes with Zamira, but the young couple is soon intercepted by Zamira's family. Her brother shoots and kills Zamira to prevent her from running off with a Christian.

The second tale, "Faces," is set in London. Photo editor Anne (Katrin Cartlidge) discovers she is pregnant. The baby's father is not her staid husband, Nick (Jay Villiers), but her glamorous lover, Aleksandar (Rade Serbedzija), a war photographer. Aleksandar wants her to return with him to his homeland of Macedonia, but she refuses due to the region's instability. Over dinner at a restaurant, Anne tells her husband she wants a divorce. Moments later, an argument between a patron and a waiter escalates into a shooting spree, and Nick is killed.

"Pictures" finds Aleksandar returning to Macedonia alone. In the sixteen years since his last visit, his village has changed radically. Religious and ethnic hatred have torn neighbor from neighbor. Aleksandar's childhood sweetheart, Hana (Silvija Stojanovska), is now considered an enemy because she is Albanian. Nonetheless, she turns to Aleksandar for help when her daughter Zamira is accused of killing Aleksandar's cousin. As his relatives take up arms to seek revenge, Aleksandar helps Zamira escape. Aleksandar is shot and killed by his cousins, as Zamira flees in the direction of a monastery.

BEFORE THE RAIN was filmed entirely on location in Macedonia and London, using a multi-national cast and crew. Two-thirds of the dialogue is Macedonian, with the London segment spoken in English. The trio of leads give compelling performances. Though Serbedzija has the meatiest role, Colin's wide-eyed monk makes the most indelible impression. Kiril is horrified when confronted with the violence that exists outside of the sanctuary of his monastery, and it is through his unusually expressive eyes that we see the pain of war's victims.

Comparisons to the blockbuster PULP FICTION bolstered BEFORE THE RAIN's box office draw. Though the two films are completely divergent in theme and subject matter, both tell their stories out of chronological order. The circular structure of BEFORE THE RAIN adds to its impact. Near the end of the third segment, the viewer realizes that the three seemingly separate stories are interconnected, and that events are racing toward an inevitable, tragic conclusion.

Technically superior in every department, BEFORE THE RAIN features achingly beautiful Macedonian landscapes, lovingly exploited by cinematographer Manuel Teran. The visually stunning, vibrantly colorful Macedonian segments stand in stark contrast to the harsh, gray London settings. This disparity reiterates one of the film's messages: war in one region affects another, no matter how far removed geographically or culturally. *(Violence, nudity, sexual situations, adult situations, profanity.)* — B.R.

d, Milcho Manchevski; p, Judy Counihan, Cedomir Kolar, Sam Taylor, Cat Villiers; assoc p, Sheila Fraser Milne, David Redman; co-p, Frederique Dumas-Zajdela, Marc Baschet, Gorjan Tozija; w, Milcho Manchevski; ph, Manuel Teran; ed, Nicolas Gaster; m, Anastasia; prod d, Sharon Lamofsky, David Munns; sound, Aidan Hobbs (recordist); fx, Valentin Lozey, John Fontana, Vasil Dikov; casting, Moni Damevski, Liora Reich; cos, Caroline Harris, Sue Yelland; makeup, Morag Ross, Joan Hills; stunts, Parvan Parvnov, Rob Woodruff

Drama/War/Political   **(PR: C   MPAA: NR)**

BETRAYAL   ★★½
(Sweden/U.K./Denmark) 58m Charon Film; Channel Four; Swedish Film Institute; National Film Board of Denmark; Nordic Film & TV Fund ~ SVT International c
(FORRADERI)

Sascha Anderson; Bjorn Cederberg (*Interviewer*); John Hurt (*Narrator*)

BETRAYAL tells an interesting and disturbing story of an East German artist who appears to have been a spy for the former Communist government. While this documentary is unpersuasive as an investigation, it touches on some of the larger issues related to East German history.

Secret government files have been made public to the unified Germany of the early 1990s. Bjorn Cederberg, a Swedish reporter, travels to Germany to meet with Sascha Anderson, a dissident artist accused of being an informer for Stasi, the East German secret police. Anderson denies the charges against him in a series of interviews with Cederberg, but the reporter also meets with many of Anderson's former colleagues, his ex-wife, and a former girlfriend, who confronts Anderson during a luncheon set up by Cederberg. Despite the evidence against him, Anderson remains an elusive character. Cederberg travels back to Sweden feeling he has not been told the whole story.

The research presented to the viewer regarding Anderson's alleged guilt is disturbingly scanty: one former colleague views the now-public Stasi files, but the audience never gets to see them. Thus the filmmakers leave themselves wide open to the charge that they, like the Stasi, are only too eager to substitute innuendo for truth when it suits them. BETRAYAL is better when it deals with larger themes; e.g., the complicity of others (especially the government) in Anderson's crime, or the historical oppression in Germany that set the stage for many betrayals.

The mostly unseen reporter investigating the mysterious figure is a trope borrowed from CITIZEN KANE, and it works well in the context of this film (the Stasi archive even resembles the Kane mansion). Krusenstjerna and Cederberg also evoke Orson Welles's last completed project, F FOR FAKE, by showing the lengths to which, it seems, Anderson has gone to cover up and lie about his crimes. Shots of an idyllic-looking modern-day Germany are inserted between the interviews, presenting an unsettling contrast between the place and the people. Also, a haunting musical theme is used sparingly but to good effect. The film illuminates an important piece of history with an artistic and political awareness that the subject demands. — E.M.

d, Fredrik von Krusenstjerna, Bjorn Cederberg; p, Fredrick von Krusenstjerna; ph, Jan Roed; ed, Niels Pagh Andersen

Documentary   **(PR: A   MPAA: NR)**

BETTER OFF DEAD   ★★½
(U.S.) 91m Heller/Steinem Productions; Lifetime Television; Viacom Productions ~ Turner Home Entertainment c

Mare Winningham (*Katherine "Kit" Kellner*); Tyra Ferrell (*Cutter Dubuque*); Kevin Tighe (*John Byron*); Don Harvey (*Del Collins*); Reed McCant (*Sam*); Marilyn Coleman (*Rene Dubuque*); Michael MacRae (*Frank Kellner*); Robert Nadir (*Davis*); Jan D'Arcy (*Kit's Mother*); Peter Lohnes (*Andy Riley*); Claire Brown (*Jean Kellner*); William Earl Ray, I (*Jack Rollins*); Diane Caldwell (*Judge Judith Brooks*); Tom Spiller (*Val*); Krisha Fairchild (*Lurline*); Landon Wine (*Victor Marquez*); Victor Morris (*Nathan Webster*); Bonnie Banks (*Nancy*); Moultrie Patten (*Judge Peter Lindsey*); Don Hohenstein (*Ben*); Brynna Jourden (*Young Kit*); David MacIntyre (*Warden*); Ryan Van Arnam (*Roy*); Robert James White (*Dave*); Stephen West (*Governor's Servant*); Ruth Walsh (*Reporter #1*); Drake Collier (*Reporter #2*); Don Creery (*Prison Guard #1*); Randall Lee Kenyon (*Prison Guard #2*); Allan Barlow (*Gas Chamber Guard*)

Originally produced by feminist figurehead Gloria Steinem for the Lifetime Cable TV network in 1993, this powerful 1995 home video release delivers on the considerable dramatic challenge of matching up to a legacy of bigscreen death-penalty dramas from 1958's I WANT TO LIVE! to 1995's DEAD MAN WALKING.

After her boyfriend is shot by a cop they were trying to hustle, Kit Kellner (Mare Winningham) returns fire and kills the officer. Assistant D.A. Cutter Dubuque (Tyra Ferrell) prosecutes the case against the girl, who displays no remorse, and argues that Kit is beyond rehabilitation. The sentence: death by asphyxiation. Seven years later she's still on death row. Cutter, who resigned as District Attorney, comes to realize that she was driven by ambition rather than justice in her prosecution. She takes Kit's appeal, but finds that the plaintiff wants to be executed. Cutter probes Kit's nightmare upbringing and begins to believe she doesn't belong in prison. But Kit is now pregnant from an affair with guard Andy (Peter Lohnes). She wants an abortion, but the state refuses her the right. Cutter petitions the courts and wins—but by that point Kit has decided to marry Andy and keep the baby. A new family and support system changes Kit's outlook on life, but the Supreme Court rejects her appeal, and the governor refuses to hear Cutter's impassioned pleas. Kit is executed.

BETTER OFF DEAD is jam-packed with issues—capital punishment, abortion, racism in the courts, politics versus justice—and amazingly, none of them gets short shrift. Marlane X. Meyer's script is taut and unpredictable, while director Neema Barnette keeps the energy high and elicits strong performances all around. Winningham is sensational as she transforms an initially hateful character into a sympathetic one, endowing Kit with strength and dignity, yet never inviting pity, even when being led to the gas chamber. Ferrell is her equal as the conflicted attorney, and the supporting cast members provide excellent backup. (*Violence, adult situations, profanity*) — B.R.

d, M. Neema Barnette; p, Rosilyn Heller; exec p, Rosilyn Heller, Gloria Steinem; co-p, Randy C. Baer, Grazia Caroselli; w, Marlane X. Meyer (from a story by Randy C. Baer); ph, Ueli Steiger; ed, David Beatty; m, John Barnes; prod d, Keith Burns; set d, Rondi Tucker; sound, Robert Anderson, Jr. (mixer); casting, Beth Klein; cos, Carol Oditz; makeup, Gigi Williams

Prison/Drama   **(PR: O   MPAA: NR)**

BEYOND RANGOON   ★★★
(U.S.) 99m Castle Rock; Pleskow/Spikings Productions ~ Columbia c

Patricia Arquette (*Laura Bowman*); U Aung Ko (*U Aung Ko*); Frances McDormand (*Andy*); Spalding Gray (*Jeremy Watt*); Tiara Jacquelina (*Desk Clerk*); Kuswadinath Bujang (*Colonel*); Vicor Slezak (*Mr. Scott*); Jit Murad (*Sein Htoo*); Ye Myint (*Zaw*

Win); Cho Cho Myint *(Zabai)*; Johnny Cheah *(Min Han)*; Haji Mahod Rajoli *(Karen Father)*; Azmi Assan *(Older Karen Boy)*; Ahmad Fithi *(Younger Karen Boy)*; Adelle Lutz *(Aung San Suu Kyi)*; Mohd Wan Nazri; Roslee Mansor; Zaidi Omar *(Check Point Soldiers at Train)*; Michael Pickells *(Laura's Husband)*; Enzo Rossi *(Laura's Son)*; Rudzuan Hashim *(Officer Min)*; Samko *(Birdman)*; Ramona Sanchez-Waggoner *(Woman Tourist)*; Norlela Ismail *(Young Woman (Sula))*; Nyak Osman *(Village Headman)*; Yusof Abdul Hamid *(River Trader)*; Lutang Anyie *(Karen Leader)*; Ali Fiji *(Fuel Vendor)*; Dion Abu Bakar *(Rapist)*; Yeoh Keat Chye *(BLK Beret Major)*; Johari Ismail *(BLK Beret Sergeant)*; Rashidi Mohd *(Secret Police Officer)*; William Saw *(Bandana Man)*; Anna Howard *(Australian Doctor)*; Manisah Mandin *(Aung Ko's Daughter)*; Charley Boorman *(Photographer)*; Hani Mohsin Hanafi *(Young Monk/Soldier)*; Ismail Din *(Burmese Official)*; Jamaludin Rejah *(Cig Soldier)*; Aung *(Cig Soldier)*; Peter Win *(Aung Ko's Helper)*; John Mindy *(Burmese Soldier)*; U Kyaw Win *(Sule Aide/Buddah Monk)*; Gael d'Oliviera *(French Boy)*; Pascale d'Oliviera *(French Mother)*; Gilles d'Oliviera *(French Father)*; Asmi Wahah *(Sula Commander)*; Albert Thaw *(Sule Officer)*; Mansell Rivers-Bland *(Hotel Guest)*; Siti Abdullah *(Village Woman)*; Satish Chand Bhandari *(Aung Ko's Friend)*

BEYOND RANGOON demonstrates both the strengths and weaknesses of contemporary liberal Hollywood's approach to overtly political subjects in a foreign setting. Beautifully crafted by a distinctive auteur, the film offers significant sensual and emotional pleasures but neglects to provide any historical context that might enlighten uninformed audiences.

Still reeling from the murders of her husband and son stateside, Dr. Laura Bowman (Patricia Arquette) has joined her sister, Andy (Frances McDormand) on a tour of southeast Asia. August 1988 finds them in Burma, a military dictatorship undergoing domestic unrest. Waking from a nightmare, she breaks curfew to witness a demonstration in which pro-democracy leader Aung San Suu Kyi (Adelle Lutz) peacefully defies armed soldiers. Returning to her hotel, Laura meets and confronts the Colonel (Kuswadinath Bujang) about the soldiers' brutality. Andy and American tour guide Jeremy Watt (Spalding Gray) defuse the situation but are powerless the next day when Laura discovers the theft of her passport. The group and her sister must proceed to Thailand while Laura obtains a new passport from the American embassy.

On the streets of Rangoon, Laura meets U Aung Ko (U Aung Ko), an unofficial tour guide who drives her into the countryside, where his car breaks down. They are sheltered by pro-democracy activists, U Aung's students before he was dismissed from his professorship for political reasons. The next day, Laura is delivered to the train station. She is about to board a train for Rangoon when U Aung is beaten by a soldier, who kills one of the students. Laura rescues U Aung in the car. They drive into a river and elude their pursuers. However, U Aung has received a bullet wound in the chest and Laura has lost her new passport.

Laura persuades a bamboo seller and his boys to float them to Rangoon on his raft. Killing a soldier in self-defense, she obtains medicines to treat U Aung's wounds during a brief village stopover. Laura successfully operates on U Aung but the two find danger again upon their arrival. On the Colonel's orders, she is detained upon trying to enter the American embassy. The soldiers demand U Aung, but pro-democracy activists rescue them both as soldiers mow down their ranks. The pair join a truckload of dissidents heading for the Thai border. They cross the bridge to Thailand on foot under heavy mortar fire, incurring substantial casualties. U Aung is reunited with his family while Laura goes to work helping the other doctors at a Red Cross hospital.

It's easy to see why director John Boorman (DELIVERANCE, EXCALIBUR, THE EMERALD FOREST) was drawn to this project. Boorman favors vaguely mystical voyages of self-discovery wherein the protagonist is transformed by experience, often in physically harsh surroundings. Also, like a Werner Herzog with studio backing, he seems to thrive on difficult location shooting.

BEYOND RANGOON vividly depicts Laura's journey from traumatized tourist to passionate partisan healer. However, though we see the process, we never really feel it, due partly to Arquette's somnambulistic performance and partly to her underwritten role. Only marginally less a cipher than the Burmese around her, Laura's function is to illustrate Buddhist principles of suffering leading to compassion, loving kindness and transcendence through service.

The politics of Burma, renamed Myanmar in the summer of 1989 (a year after the events of the film), remain annoyingly murky. The bad guys are just reluctant or sadistic lackeys of an evil government while the heroes are blankly virtuous democracy lovers. U Aung Ko's character underwent similar experiences to the actor's but his authenticity does nothing to enliven his performance. He's just a less animated Yoda. Aung San Suu Kyi, as portrayed by Adelle Lutz, is more iconic than ideological. She's beloved by The People but we are given no clue about her ideas. Even non-political types in the audience may come away wondering if US policy in the region is nearly as benign and disinterested as Laura is supposed to be. As is typical in modern Hollywood, BEYOND RANGOON eschews dangerous political ground, opting instead for a universal human melodrama.

On this level, the film is fairly successful. John Seale's cinematography does wonders with the exigencies of light and weather. Hans Zimmer's score is alternately stirring and dreamy. On the filmmaking level, BEYOND RANGOON delivers the goods, but it could have been much more. *(Graphic violence, adult situations.)* — K.G.

d, John Boorman; p, Barry Spikings, Eric Pleskow, John Boorman; exec p, Sean Ryerson; assoc p, Mark Egerton, Walter Donohue; co-p, Alex Lasker, Bill Rubenstein; w, Alex Lasker, Bill Rubenstein; ph, John Seale; ed, Ron Davis; m, Hans Zimmer; prod d, Anthony Pratt; art d, Errol Kelly; set d, Eddie Fowlie; sound, Gary Wilkins (mixer); fx, John Evans; casting, Mary Gail Artz, Barbara Cohen; cos, Deborah La Gorce, Kramer; makeup, Felicity Bowring; stunts, William Ong

Drama/Political/Adventure   **(PR: C   MPAA: R)**

BIG GREEN, THE   ★★
(U.S.) 100m Kick-It Productions; Walt Disney Pictures; Caravan Pictures ~ Buena Vista c

Steve Guttenberg *(Sheriff Tom Palmer)*; Olivia d'Abo *(Anna Montgomery)*; Jay O. Sanders *(Jay Huffer)*; John Terry *(Edwin V. Douglas)*; Chauncey Leopardi *(Evan Schiff)*; Yareli Arizmendi *(Marbelly Morales)*; Bug Hall *(Newt Shaw)*; Patrick Renna *(Larry Musgrove)*; Jessie Robertson *(Kate Douglas)*; Billy L. Sullivan *(Jeffrey Luttrell)*; Anthony Esquival *(Juan Morales)*; Jordan Brower *(Nick Anderssen)*; Hayley Kolb *(Sophia Covertino)*; Haley Miller *(Polly Neilson)*; Ashley Welch *(Lou Gates)*; Ariel Welch *(Sue Gates)*; Jimmy Higa *(Tak Yamato)*; Gil Glasgow *(Cookie Musgrove)*; Libby Villari *(Brenda Neilson)*; Louanne Stephens *(Bomma Cole)*; John Bourg *(Jay Huffer, Jr.)*; Tyler Bishop *(Second Knight)*; Casey Lee *(Third Knight)*; Milt Oberman *(Referee)*; Nik Hagler *(Chief Bishop)*; Stephen Parr *(Stadium Announcer)*

In this light inspirational fare served up by Disney, a group of junior high ne'er-do-wells surprises everyone (except the viewer) when they become the unlikely soccer champions of the Lone Star State.

In a prologue, four Texas lads ride their bikes to an overgrown field next to their school, lie down in the tall grass, and spread a bag of cheese puffs all over themselves. Soon the pigeons of Elma, Texas, arrive to eat their weekly snack off the boys' bodies: this is what passes for entertainment in Elma. The story really begins when the new schoolteacher, Anna Montgomery (Olivia d'Abo), comes to town from her native England and discovers a small group of self-described "losers." Their answers to her question "What makes you special?" range from asthma to burping the alphabet. She soon gets them engaged—if not in learning, at least in life—through soccer. Through practice, teamwork, and believing in themselves (supplemented by encouragement from Montgomery), the team, now known as The Big Green, rise above their lack of coordination and athletic prowess to become the state soccer champions.

There are also some subplots along the way: immigration problems with the team's only real soccer athlete, Juan Morales (Anthony Esquival); a would-be relationship between Montgomery and Sheriff Tom Palmer (Steve Guttenberg) that quickly and unconvincingly gets sublimated into coaching; a rift between tough-girl Kate Douglas (Jessie Robertson) and her divorced, unemployed, heavy-drinking dad; and a budding crush between Juan and Kate. Throughout, these additional would-be dramatic elements take a back seat to much footage of uncoordinated adolescents kicking soccer balls.

Relentlessly upbeat and achingly predictable in its small-town, underdog heroics, THE BIG GREEN—written and directed by Holly Goldberg Sloan, who also wrote ANGELS IN THE OUTFIELD—becomes wearing before long. It feels churlish to criticize a children's sports comedy that is so earnestly, doggedly good-natured, but this movie simply tries to please too many people too much of the time. That's not to say that one isn't rooting for the misfit kids as they (of course) defeat the better-trained opposing soccer team; it's that you just can't get that gnawing sense of "yeah, right" cynicism out of your heart as all wrongs are made right in a sunny, saccharine way—perhaps best symbolized by the losing bad-guy coach (Jay O. Sanders) kissing the mascot goat of The Big Green as his just deserts.

Although THE BIG GREEN does try to incorporate some serious social realities (economic recession, the emotional effects of divorce on children, alcoholism, immigration injustices, and cutthroat high school competition), the Disney whitewashing of these issues almost makes you sorry Goldberg Sloan brought them up. The good news is that boys and girls work together (and practically as equals) and the emphasis of the game is on teamwork and letting everyone play. In the final analysis, THE BIG GREEN makes for (mostly) harmless inspirational entertainment for the kids, while adults are warned to put their reality checkers on hold. *(Substance abuse.)* — P.P.

d, Holly Goldberg Sloan; p, Roger Birnbaum; exec p, Dennis Bishop; w, Holly Goldberg Sloan; ph, Ralf D. Bode; ed, John Link; m, Randy Edelman; prod d, Evelyn Sakash; art d, Harry Darrow; set d, Helen Britten; sound, Robert Alan Wald (mixer); fx, Randy E. Moore, Margaret Johnson; casting, Dan Parada, Rick Montgomery; cos, Rondi Hillstrom Davis; makeup, Carla Palmer

Sports/Children's/Comedy (PR: A MPAA: PG)

BIGFOOT: THE UNFORGETTABLE ENCOUNTER ★★
(U.S.) 86m Merhi/Pepin Productions ~ Republic Pictures Home Video c

Matt McCoy *(Nick Clifton)*; Zachery Ty Bryan *(Cody)*; David Rasche *(Chaz Frederick)*; Clint Howard *(Gary)*; Jojo Adams *(Ben)*; Crystal Chappell *(Samantha)*; Rance Howard *(Todd Brandell)*; Neal Maturazzo *(Sheldon)*; Janice Lynde *(Betty)*; Dennis Singletary *(Booker)*; Alan Wilder *(Vern)*; Clay Lilley *(Vester)*; Tohuru Masamune *(Ling)*; Ingo Neuhaus *(Boris)*; Robert Orrison *(Joe Perkins)*; David Rowden *(Dubow)*; Russell Solberg *(Stringer)*; Michael Buice *(Hal)*; George O'Mara *(Lee)*; Neil Summers *(Delbert)*; Douglas Bennett *(Walter)*; Rif Hutton *(Jess)*; Mark Kriski *(Newsman)*; John Cade *(Newscaster)*; Jerry Spicer *(Reporter #4)*; Debbie James *(Misty Vales)*; Darrell Mapson *(Ranger Voss)*; Brian Avery *(Zachery)*; Gary Maloncon *(Bigfoot)*

Family audiences (or, more accurately, filmmakers desperately pandering to them) can't get enough of movies about the bonding of children and critters, whether shaggy mutt, extraterrestrial, killer whale, or unclassified hairy biped. The son of game-show host Bob Eubanks directed this intended treat for young Sasquatch watchers and for parents who don't want their kids' recreation hours marred by thinking, BIGFOOT. . . is the ideal indoor diversion.

Multiple sightings pinpoint the legend's location in one area of the Pacific Northwest. Evil tycoon Chaz Frederick (David Rasche) orders his minions to get him that Bigfoot! Although the venal collector wishes to mount a dead Sasquatch for exhibition, comely anthropologist Samantha (Crystal Chapell), prefers to study the beast in captivity. Meanwhile vacationing boy Cody (Zachery Ty Bryan, of the TV sitcom "Home Improvement") winds up lost, caught in a bear trap, menaced by a grizzly, and rescued by benevolent Bigfoot. Sam claims the creature after locating and tranquilizing it. Regretting his part in leading his half-human savior into confinement, Cody and a younger brother free the big guy. The chase is on as Sam must recapture Bigfoot before Frederick's men do. After Sasquatch saves her life, she concedes to Ranger Nick Clifton (Matt McCoy) that Bigfoot should relocate to a wildlife sanctuary and acquire federal endangered-species status. Bigfoot and his protectors are nearly run off the highway by Frederick and his mercenaries, but the freak of the forest reaches safety and bids tearful adieu to Cody. Frederick is arrested for violating government policy on officially protected animals.

Little pathos is actually registered in this movie's key relationship between colorless Cody and his large pet. Despite the mildly scary prologue in which a soused hunter is dragged away (by some other mountain animal, it turns out), BIGFOOT: THE UNFORGETTABLE ENCOUNTER is not interested in conflicting viewer responses, it simply churns out pure, homogenized uplift that's at least inoffensive until the plot summons up its heavy-handed villain. Rasche's blowhard act is a crashing bore that overloads the bad-guy deck. The script half-heartedly dishes up a contentious courtship between manly forest ranger Nick and starchy anthro-babe Sam; it's tiresome to wait as all these stock characters learn life-lessons about animal rights, pantheism in the forest, and the side-effects of clearcutting. The animatronic apeman costume is okay but doesn't touch the screen's Bigfoot-to-beat, Rick Baker's Oscar-winning creation for the Spielberg production (and subsequent short-lived TV series) HARRY AND THE HENDERSONS. *(Violence.)* — R.P.

d, Corey Michael Eubanks; p, Joseph Merhi, Richard Pepin; w, Corey Michael Eubanks; ph, Ken Blakey; ed, Geraint Bell, Howard Flaer; m, Louis Febre; prod d, Ken Lucas; art d, Ken Lucas; sound, Mike Hall; fx, Don Powers; casting, Adriana Michel; cos, Eric Berg, Amy Wetherbee; makeup, Jori Jenae; stunts, Allan Wyatt, Wyatt

Children's/Adventure/Science Fiction (PR: AA MPAA: PG)

BIKINI BISTRO
(U.S.) 84m Private Screenings ~ Bullseye Video c

Marilyn Chambers *(Marilyn)*; Amy Lynn Baxter *(Judy)*; Isabella Fortea *(Donna)*; Joan Gerardi *(LuAnne)*; John Altamura *(Ron)*; Paul Borghese *(Mr. Rank)*; Bill Bresnan *(Collin)*; David LaScala *(Russel)*; Joseph Pallister *(David)*; Pamela Safaraba *(Bettina)*; Salvatore Thomas *(Floyd)*; Tom Russ *(Clint)*

Former porn star Marilyn Chambers plays a former porn star named Marilyn Chambers who finds that directing porn videos is too demanding in this negligible skin flick.

Marilyn is approached by former porn actress Judy (Amy Lynn Baxter), whose vegetarian cafe, "Gentle Nibbles," can't buy a customer. Faced with eviction in four days by dial-a-villain Rank (Paul Borghese), Judy's cousin Ron (John Altamura) suggests using Marilyn's sex-industry connections to revamp the cafe's image. Marilyn's redesign is a matter of moving tables around and hanging a large banner over the door bearing the subtle legend "BIKINI Bistro." Oh, and making the girls strip and squeeze into tiny shreds of mylar. She herself dresses somewhat more demurely. Thank God.

And *voila*, we have the titular establishment, where skimpily-clad waitresses toss salads on customers' heads, spill soups *du jour* in laps, and bring large, rare steaks to militant vegetarians. Marilyn guarantees the restaurants' success by schmoozing food critic Colin de la Pez (Bill Bresnan, who sounds like a Brooklyn cabbie on Quaaludes) in her own inimitable way just as the local repressive guardians of morality arrive with picket signs and horny sons. Happy endings are assured when Floyd the Bartender (Salvatore Thomas), who hides the take from the till in his pants, is exposed, and the greasy Mr. Rank falls in love with a protester.

The cast consists of moonlighting adult-film denizens and a few slobs who couldn't hope to rise to that level of emotive excellence. The script has two or three genuine jokes, lobbed like flat tennis balls by the performers. In addition to copious display of artificially-enhanced breasts, some full-frontal female nudity and a few sex scenes occur, but the film is so ineptly lit and shot that they lack the erotic appeal of the average beer ad. *(Extensive nudity, sexual situations, profanity.)* — R.S.

d, Ernest G. Sauer; p, Gary P. Conner; exec p, Ernest G. Sauer; assoc p, Brian Zadiko, Paul Borghese; w, Matt Unger (from a story by Gary P. Conner and Matt Unger); ph, Spike Marker; ed, John Rogers; m, Joey Mennonna; art d, D. Gary Phelps; casting, Paul Borghese, Ken Miceli

Erotic/Comedy   **(PR: O   MPAA: NR)**

BILLY MADISON   ★
(U.S.) 89m Billy Madison Productions ~ Universal c

Adam Sandler *(Billy Madison)*; Darren McGavin *(Brian Madison)*; Bridgette Wilson *(Veronica)*; Bradley Whitford *(Eric Gordon)*; Josh Mostel *(Max Anderson)*; Norm MacDonald *(Frank)*; Mark Beltzman *(Jack)*; Larry Hankin *(Carl Alphonse)*; Theresa Merritt *(Juanita)*; Dina Platias *(Miss Lippy)*; Hrant Alianak *(Pete)*; Vincent Marino *(Cook)*; Jack Mather *(Clemens)*; Christopher Kelk *(Janitor)*; Marc Donato *(Nodding 1st Grader)*; Keith Cole *(Penguin)*; Chris Mei *(Penguin)*; Conor Devitt *(O'Doyle—Grade 1)*; Jared Durand *(Scotty—Grade 1)*; Jessica Nakamura *(Tricia—Grade 1)*; Helen Hughes *(2nd Grade Teacher)*; Jacelyn Holmes *(2nd Grader)*; Claire Cellucci *(Attractive Lady)*; Shane Faberman *(Clown)*; Al Maini *(Chauffer)*; Jared Cook *(Ernie—Grade 3)*; Christian Matheson *(O'Doyle—Grade 3)*; Austin Pool *(Dan—Grade 3)*; Stacey Wheal *(Jennifer—Grade 3)*; Shanna Bresse *(Susan—Grade 3)*; Kyle Bailey *(Kyle)*; Vernon Chapman *(Butler)*; Mandy Watts *(Maid)*; Gladys O'Connor *(Tour Guide)*; Marcia Bennett *(4th Grade Teacher)*; Diane Douglas *(Nurse)*; Tim Herlihy *(Architect)*; Frank Nakashima *(Architect)*; Joyce Gordon *(Architect)*; Jordan Lerner-Ellis *(Pothead)*; Daniel Lerner-Ellis *(Pothead)*; Robert Smigel *(Mr. Oblaski)*; Melissa Korzenko *(Nancy Connors)*; Colin Smith *(O'Doyle—Grade 9)*; Jeff Moser *(Paul)*; Amos Crawley *(Rod)*; Tex Konig *(Crazy Person)*; Eduardo Gomez; Tanya Grout *(Eric's Secretary)*; Benjamin Barrett *(Tenth Grader)*; Matthew Ferguson *(Tenth Grader)*; Sean Lett *(O'Doyle—Grade 12)*; Michael Ayoub *(Drama Teacher)*; Lawrence Nakumara *(Lawn Guy)*; Gino Veltri *(Rock Singer)*; James Downey *(Principal)*; Bob Rodgers *(Mr. O'Doyle)*; Margo Wladyka *(Mrs. O'Doyle)*; Allison Robinson *(Newswoman)*; Marcel Jean Gilles *(Haitian Gardener)*; Suzanna Shebib *(High School Girl)*

BILLY MADISON is an unfunny farce about a slacker who repeats all 12 school grades to prove he is worthy of taking over the family business.

Billy Madison (Adam Sandler) is a spoiled rich kid in his mid-20s who whiles away his days getting drunk by the pool, perusing porn, and chasing an imaginary giant penguin. When his father (Darren McGavin) announces his intention to turn over control of the family's Fortune 500 hotel chain to company VP Eric Gordon (Bradley Whitford), Madison junior protests. He hates and distrusts Gordon, but the father knows his son is a fool. To prove him wrong, Madison agrees to repeat grades 1 to 12 in six months. If successful, he gets the business.

Madison goes through the first two grades easily, but meets his first obstacle in the third grade in the person of Veronica Vaughn (Bridgette Wilson), a gorgeous teacher of Madison's age, who has no patience for his antics. Madison eventually wins her over, then sails through grades 4 to 8 in a montage. When he reaches high school, Gordon, nervous about losing the company, blackmails the principal (Josh Mostel) into claiming that Madison paid him to pass him. Madison's father calls off the deal; but urged on by Vaughn's unfailing faith, Madison decides to challenge Gordon to an academic decathlon. The winner gets the company. Madison wins, and at his graduation announces how much he now values education, and that he plans to attend college and turn the hotel business over to a deserving, long-time employee.

In his stand-up work and on "Saturday Night Live," Adam Sandler has a mischievous, "look at me" performance quality that bespeaks his self-image as a glorified class clown. So this role would seem the perfect vehicle for him to display his talents, and he brings to it his full arsenal of weird voices and goony faces. Except, class clowns are always only sporadically funny and their prolonged antics pall easily.

BILLY MADISON has its moments, mostly courtesy of TOMMY BOY star Chris Farley's cameos as the demented bus driver, but these are few and far between. The film should have featured more absurd and nonsensical elements. Certainly the plot is ridiculous, and so completely illogical that to see it fall by the wayside in favor of some inspired lunacy would not have been a loss. The movie does have a production number, and it could have used a few more of the goofy songs that are Sandler's trademark. *(Profanity.)* — P.R.

d, Tamra Davis; p, Robert Simonds; exec p, Fitch Cady; assoc p, Jack Giarraputo; w, Tim Herlihy, Adam Sandler; ph, Victor Hammer; ed, Jeffrey Wolf; m, Randy Edelman; prod d, Perry Blake; art d, Gordon Barnes; set d, Enrico Campana; sound, Allan Byer (mixer); casting, Jaki Brown-Karman, Todd Thaler, Deidre Bowen; cos, Marie-Bylvie Deveau; makeup, Edelgarde K. Pfluegl; stunts, Ted Hanlan

Comedy   **(PR: C   MPAA: PG-13)**

BITTER VENGEANCE ★★
(U.S.) 90m Wilshire Court Productions; Fast Track Films ~ Paramount Home Video c

Virginia Madsen *(Annie Westford)*; Bruce Greenwood *(Jack Westford)*; Kristen Hocking *(Isabella Martens)*; Teresa Truesdale *(Kate)*; Eddie Velez *(Harry Carver)*; Tim Russ *(Lt. James)*; Jack Verell *(Det. Davis)*; Gordon Jump *(Arnold Fulmer)*; Carlos Gomez *(Ray Partana)*; Vince Melocchi *(Joseph)*; Peter Moore *(Gordon)*; Mary Ingersoll *(Debra)*; Rick Zorner *(Guard No. 1)*; Michael White *(Guard No. 2)*; Virginia Hawkins *(Mrs. Martens)*; Erin Chandler *(Dorothy Calloway)*; J.D. Smith *(Eddie)*; Sonya Hensley *(Forensics Woman)*; J. Michael Ross *(Prosecutor)*; Rhonda Reznick *(Female Warden)*; William Alejandro Virchis *(Jose)*; Rudy Quintanilla *(Bellboy)*; Robert Gant *(Bookstore Customer)*; Elizabeth Alvarez *(Hooker)*; Tom Huse *(Jeweler)*; Jack Banning *(Hotel Clerk)*

Cranked out for cable TV, BITTER VENGEANCE is about as generic as its title, with a good cast trapped in uninspired skullduggery.

The reliable Bruce Greenwood plays sour ex-cop Jack Westford, tired of both his dead-end job as a security guard and his flawlessly beautiful blond wife Annie (Virginia Madsen). When he commences an affair with flawlessly beautiful redhead (go figure) bank clerk Isabella Martins (Kristen Hocking), Jack hatches a scheme to steal a weekend $3 million cash shipment, flee with Isabella to Mexico, and pin the crime on oblivious Annie. The lawless lawman leaves Annie drugged and smeared with his blood on a rented yacht (called "No Illusions"), and, exactly as planned, authorities suspect her of bumping off Jack after assisting in the heist.

Late in the action, the bank's shady insurance investigator, Harry Carver (Eddie Velez), slithers promisingly into the picture and looks like he'll be a truly offbeat hero of the piece, but then Annie suddenly turns Nancy Drew to track down Jack at his south-of-the-border villa, where he's already murdered the restless Isabella. Annie alone survives a final confrontation and shootout between her husband-from-hell and Carver.

Greenwood has some strong moments as a Jekyll-and-Hyde type whose villainy knows no limits once he decides to "go bad," as his wife wistfully puts it, though since the viewer never sees him any other way, Jack's fall from grace carries little dramatic impact, and the rest of the tale connects the dots in largely routine fashion. First shown on the USA Cable network in 1994, BITTER VENGEANCE went to home video the next year. *(Violence, sexual situations.)* — C.C.

d, Stuart Cooper; p, Christopher Griffin; co-p, Stuart Cooper; w, Pablo Fenjves; ph, Frank Byers; ed, Cari Coughlin; m, David Michael Frank; prod d, Gary Griffin Constable; set d, Donna Stamps; sound, Mark Ulano (mixer); fx, Ultimate Effects; casting, Dan Shaner; cos, Robert Moore; makeup, Carme Tenuta; stunts, Ernie Orsatti

Thriller   (PR: C   MPAA: R)

BLACK FOX ★★
(U.S.) 90m Black Fox Productions; Western International Communications; Cabin Fever Entertainment ~ Cabin Fever Entertainment c
(AKA: BLACK FOX: THE PRICE OF PEACE; BLACK FOX: BLOOD HORSE; BLACK FOX: GOOD MEN AND BAD)

Christopher Reeve *(Alan Johnson)*; Tony Todd *(Britt Johnson)*; Raoul Trujillo *(Running Dog)*; Chris Wiggins *(Ralph Holtz)*; Kim Coates *(Natchez John Dunn)*; Kelly Rowan *(Hallie Russell)*; Janet Bailey *(Mary Johnson)*; Nancy Sorel *(Sarah Johnson)*; Chris Benson *(Tom Fitzpatrick)*; Cyndy Preston *(Delores Holtz)*; Michael Rhoades *(Dwayne Holtz)*; Luc Corbeil *(Ethan Holtz)*; Lawrence Dane *(Colonel McKensie)*; Dale Wilson *(Buck Barry)*; Rainbow Francks *(Frank Johnson)*; David Fox *(Carl Glenn)*; Alan Shearman *(Jason Ilicks)*; John Blackwood *(Elisha Thorne)*; Graham McPherson *(Sheriff William Morgan)*; Beverly Elliot *(Pussycat Nell)*; Alan Vansprang *(Longbaugh)*; Leon Goodstriker *(Little Buffalo)*; Morningstar Mecredi *(Talking Raven)*; Billy Morton *(Jake Wilson)*; Joel Phage-Wright *(Frank)*; Don S. Davis *(Sergeant Dills)*; Byron Chiefmoon *(Standing Bear)*; Ronald Carothers *(Smith)*; John Dodds *(Sharps)*; Buffalo Child *(Red Hawk)*; Denis LaCroix *(Lone Wolf)*

A sturdy but not truly outstanding sagebrush miniseries, THE BLACK FOX consists of three chapters: "The Black Fox", "Blood Horse", (AKA: "The Price of Peace") and "Good Men and Bad".

In the opener, ex-Virginian Alan Johnson (Christopher Reeve) and his African-American bloodbrother Britt (Tony Todd) settle on the 1861 frontier, where they face racial slurs from crackers like Ralph Holtz (Chris Wiggins) and Indian raids which proliferate once the military pulls out due to Civil War commitments. Instead of hightailing it to the fort, Alan and Britt track down their families captured by Kiowa and Commanches. Winning the respect of Running Dog (Raol Trujillo), Britt engages in hand-to-hand combat with Standing Bear (Byron Chiefmoon) and negotiates the release of all white hostages except for abused Delores Holtz (Cyndy Preston) who prefers to remain Running Dog's squaw, rather than return to Ralph, who threatens reprisals.

In "Blood Horse," ornery Ralph Holtz stirs up anti-Injun talk and secures the services of a preacher who doubles as an arms dealer. Selling the Kiowa faulty flintlocks through his middleman, Holtz primes prairie racists for what promises to be a massacre. Since most settlers adopt a neutrality policy, Alan and Britt save the day by stealing the preacher's Gatling gun and sending Holtz's brigade running for cover.

In "Good Men and Bad," Britt reluctantly accepts a federal marshall's post while Alan turns outlaw after a desperado Carl Glenn (David Fox) guns down his wife and wounds him. While hunting the killer, Alan slowly wins the trust of notorious bandit Nantchez John Dunn (Kim Coates), a compadre of Glenn's. During a stagecoach robbery, the gang captures Hallie Russell (Kelly Rowan) who, to stay alive, claims to be the ransomable wife of a tycoon. In the climactic shootout, Hallie gets Dunn with a concealed weapon, while Alan captures Glenn for a date with the hangman. Revenge satisfied, Alan returns to the right side of the Law.

As the episodes lose sight of an overarching brotherhood theme, they grow progressively less interesting. In the opening, anti-Indian and anti-Negro sentiments are paralleled in a tale that sympathizes with the plight of the uprooted and enslaved. With sturdy story construction and no-frills direction, "The Black Fox" concludes satisfyingly with Mrs. Holtz's "I Will Go Back To My Husband No More Forever" stance. "Blood Horse," continues its consideration of Indian affairs (hitching mainstream religion with bigotry as the traveling man of God turns out to be a munitions peddler with a hate agenda). Repetition mars this episode as rotter Holtz keeps regrouping his vigilantes and the Kiowa keep reiterating their noble sentiments to fight like men. Since the Native American exodus gives the triptych its unique underpinnings, the third and most conventional installment, "Good Men and Bad" is the least gripping, allowing Reeve to ride out this standard revenge tale with movie star aplomb (shortly before THE BLACK FOX premiered on cable TV,

Reeve was paralyzed by a fall from horseback; scenes showcasing his athletic equestrian prowess are unsettling). Most arresting here is the subtle performance of Rowan as her character plays a shell game with the badmen.

All in all, THE BLACK FOX trilogy lets aficionados saddle up for considerable adventure even if their ride could have sheared off a few hundred miles of here and there. Admirable for its decision to craft a straightforward saga with serious undertones, this canters, but does not gallop, down a trail of Wild West formulas. *(Violence, profanity, sexual situations, adult situations.)* — R.P.

d, Steven H. Stern; p, Les Kimber; exec p, Norman S. Powell, Robert Halmi, Jr., Tony Allard; w, Jeb Rosebrook, Joe Byrne, John Binder, Michael Michaelian (from stories by John Binder, based on the novel and characters by Matt Braun); ph, Frank Tidy; ed, Ron Wisman; m, Eric N. Robertson; prod d, John Blackie; set d, Jan Blackie-Goodine; sound, Robert (Abbott); fx, Maurice Routly; casting, Bette Chadwick, Lynn Kressel; cos, Wendy Partridge; makeup, Connie Parker; stunts, Tom Erickson

Western (PR: C MPAA: NR)

BLACK IS ... BLACK AIN'T ★★★★
(U.S.) 87m California Newsreel ~ Tara Releasing c

Angela Davis; Essex Hemphill; bell hooks; Maulana Karenga; Barbara Smith; Michele Wallace; Cornel West; Bill T. Jones; Marlon Riggs; Linda Tillery; Yvette Flunder; Djola Bernard Branner; Eric Gupton; Wayne T. Corbitt; Andrea Woods; Larry Duckette; Wayson R. Jones *(Performers)*

Watching this dazzling string of intellectual fireworks go off underscores the tragic loss of writer-documentary filmmaker Marlon T. Riggs to complications from AIDS in April, 1994, at the age of 37. BLACK IS ... BLACK AIN'T was completed by associates and released posthumously, a final statement by a man who had much left to say.

Riggs's earlier nonfiction films COLOR ADJUSTMENT and ETHNIC NOTIONS weighed depictions of blacks in popular culture. His NO REGRETS, ANTHEM, and TONGUES UNTIED took on the autobiographical subject of life as an African-American gay man. Subtitled "A Personal Journey Through Black Identity," BLACK IS ... BLACK AIN'T puts all the pieces together, asking the fundamental query: what does it mean to be black in America?

Riggs explores his subject using a collage of voice-overs, images, music and brief interviews deftly edited together, turning sound bites into succinct flashes of insight. Angela Davis recalls when being called a "black African" was a venomous insult, while modern youth answer only to the description "African-American." Adds a bemused elder, "When I came along it was 'Negro.' They went and changed it to 'black,' 'Afro-American.' I don't know what we're gonna change to next; but we be changing so fast I don't think we know what we are ourselves." Riggs's quest for genuine ethnic identity gathers input from the deep-blues clubs of Mississippi to the isolated Gullah people of the Carolina coast; from "Oyutunji," an African village recreated in Buford County, South Carolina, to the filmmaker's own roots in his Texas family.

The rapid juxtaposition of people, places and opinions, often ironic, sometimes quietly caustic, bears out an early quote: "There are as many kinds of black people as there are white people." The filmmaker concludes by comparing black society to his mother's gumbo: diverse ingredients create the flavor.

Riggs insinuates himself into the film, first as a naked figure groping through a wilderness, then later, weakened on his hospital bed, discussing work on BLACK IS ... BLACK AIN'T with a collaborator. If the former image makes a heavy-handed meta-phor, the latter adds special poignancy to segments about gender inequalities in the black community. Eddie Murphy and Louis Farrakhan crack up their respective audiences with spiteful, misogynistic remarks about women (the comparison of a super-star stand-up comic with a demagogue is priceless); then Ice Cube offers his wisdom on homosexuality, "True niggers ain't faggots!" followed by a traditional preacher man saying much the same thing. As tonic, the camera turns to articulate black feminists and a too-brief visit with Unity Fellowship, a largely black gay and lesbian church that is one of the most openly joyous religious groups shown on screen in quite a while.

These and just about any other detail from BLACK IS ... BLACK AIN'T could inspire feature documentaries all by themselves, and the viewer is always aware of Riggs's attempt to encompass a wide range of interests in what scant time he had left. The filmmaker died leaving the film in rough-cut form and severely underfunded. Co-producer Nicole Atkinson turned to public contributions to complete what the *Oakland Tribune* labelled "the film that doesn't want to be made." But the finished product is a smoothly-flowing visual document that makes its myriad points eloquently and effectively. *(Adult situations, nudity, profanity.)* — C.C.

d, Marlon Riggs, Christiane Badgely; p, Marlon Riggs; assoc p, Jasmine Dellal; co-p, Nicole Atkinson; ph, Robert Shepard; ed, Christiane Badgely, Bob Paris; m, Mary Watkins; sound, Sekou Shepard (recordist)

Documentary/Docudrama (PR: C MPAA: NR)

BLESSING ★★½
(U.S.) 94m Starr Valley Films ~ Starr Valley Films c

Melora Griffis *(Randi)*; Carlin Glynn *(Arlene)*; Guy Griffis *(Jack)*; Clovis Siemon *(Clovis)*; Gareth Williams *(Lyle)*; Randy Sue Latimer *(Fran)*; Tom Carey *(Snuff)*; Frank Taylor *(Early)*

A young woman seeks a better life for herself in BLESSING, a well-meaning but curiously flat farm melodrama.

On a Minnesota cow farm that she will someday inherit, 23-year-old Randi (Melora Griffis) tends to her daily chores with her younger brother Clovis (Clovis Siemon). All is not well within Randi's home: since their eldest son, Tommy, ran away to join the Navy, Randi's father, Jack (Guy Griffis), has been a surly alcoholic, and her mother, Arlene (Carlin Glynn), an emotional wreck. Arlene also mistakenly suspects her husband of spying on Fran (Randy Sue Latimer), the local roadhouse owner, from atop their farm silo. Tired of her parents' fights, Randi is glad to be working part-time as a waitress at Fran's roadhouse, but she feels her life is at a dead end.

When an astrologer, Lyle (Gareth Williams), enters the roadhouse one day, Randi at first dismisses his flirtations. Later, however, he helps her during one of her parents' fights, and she convinces her father to hire him as a milkman. Eventually, Randi and Lyle fall in love and make plans to move away. This news upsets Jack, who, during a drunken rage, beats one of their cows, which he is then forced to kill. Following the outburst, Randi decides she must stay on at the farm to help her troubled family, but later realizes that she must confront her parents about the past and make a clean break with Lyle for a better future.

BLESSING crosses the 1980s farm movie (COUNTRY, THE RIVER) with the plays of Horton Foote. Generational conflicts, clashing values, and the death of the small farm all factor into the wrenching family melodrama at the surface. Paul Zeher's first feature as director exhibits the stately pace of a veteran filmmaker's work, building scene after scene (with slow fades to black after each one) to reveal the depth of the characters' anguish. The treatment is sometimes overly earnest, but the situations are quite credible.

BLESSING's failure, then, stems from the problems that typically beset low-budget, first-time movie ventures. Zeher's characters are well developed, but his dialogue includes too many cliches (e.g. Fran comforts Randi by telling her, "Sometimes we can't see the forest for the trees," and Jack warns, "Don't take any wooden nickels," in his goodbye scene with his daughter). The performances are generally good, but Carlin Glynn's amateurish overacting in the pivotal role of Randi's mother lessens the impact of several scenes (as does too much postdubbing throughout). Finally, there are a few too many montages of farm work set to music, and those fades to black eventually get excessive and pretentious.

Thus, Zeher, BLESSING's director, writer, coproducer and coeditor, has not done justice to his own best instincts. Perhaps next time, the hyphenate-talent should delegate more of his work. *(Violence, adult situations, profanity.)* — E.M.

d, Paul Zehrer; p, Melissa Powell, Paul Zehrer; exec p, Christopher A. Cuddihy; w, Paul Zherer; ph, Stephen Kazmierski; ed, Paul Zherer, Andrew Morreale; m, Joseph S. DeBeasi; prod d, Steve Rosenzweig; sound, Derek Felska (recordist); casting, Sheila Jaffe, Cassandra Han; cos, Janie Bryant; makeup, Janie Bryant, Lori Tooker

Drama (PR: C MPAA: NR)

BLUE IN THE FACE ★★½
(U.S.) 90m Peter Newman Productions ~ Miramax c

Harvey Keitel *(Auggie Wren)*; Lou Reed *(Himself)*; Michael J. Fox *(Peter)*; Roseanne *(Dot)*; Mel Gorham *(Violet)*; Jim Jarmusch *(Himself)*; Lily Tomlin *(Belgian Waffle Man)*; Jared Harris *(Jimmy Rose)*; Malik Yoba *(The Creeper)*; Giancarlo Esposito *(Tommy—No. 1 OTB Guy)*; Jose Zuniga *(Jerry—No. 2 OTB Guy)*; Stephen Gevedon *(Dennis—No. 3 OTB Guy)*; Victor Argo *(Vinnie)*; Keith David *(Jackie)*; Mira Sorvino *(Blonde Woman)*; Madonna *(Singing Telegram Girl)*; Sharif Rashed; Peggy Gormley; RuPaul; The John Lurie National Orchestra

While filming SMOKE, novelist Paul Auster was so fascinated and amused watching Harvey Keitel and Giancarlo Esposito improvising dialogue in character that he decided to make a second film, shot in the same Brooklyn neighborhood with many of same actors. He and director Wayne Wang shot this messy experimental film in about a week, using a combination of improvisation and roughly sketched scenes involving Auggie Wren (Keitel) and the colorful patrons of his cigar store.

The threadbare plot, about Auggie and his girlfriend Violet (Mel Gorham), is an excuse for a slapdash filmic treatise on what makes Brooklyn so special. Somehow word spread that Wang and Auster were doing something cool, and all manner of celebrities showed up to add themselves to the local color. Some of the cameos are bizarre; e.g., an unrecognizable Lily Tomlin as the "Waffle Man." Some are funny: Michael J. Fox as a researcher with a scatological bent. Some are surprisingly dull: Madonna as a singing telegram girl. And some are more embarrassing than words can express: Rosanne as a Vegas-obsessed *hausfrau*.

Amidst the clutter are a few pieces worth saving, much as there would be in an above-average student film, but the overall effect is lost in the deluge of painfully obvious bits of "found" comedy and actors trying too hard to be spontaneously clever. Improv works best when the actors lose themselves in the moment, but the performers here seem all too self-conscious, especially Keitel, who practically winks at the camera every time he puts on his knowing grin.

Thrown into this mulligan stew are some old-fashioned documentary-style talking heads, including filmmaker Jim Jarmusch, who talks about movie cliches he loves to hate, and Lou Reed, whose reminiscences about New York and observations on his own experience are wonderful, wise, funny, and memorable ("New York doesn't scare me—I get scared in places like Sweden"). Reed becomes the real star of the film, and one longs for more of him and less of everyone else.

Those who enjoyed SMOKE will find some pleasure in seeing some of the actors in that film playing theater games, but the rest will probably find this film mystifying, if not downright annoying. Auster took the director's chair for much of the shooting, and has reportedly decided to remain a writer, which is the right decision. Although Auster the novelist has been fascinated by contingency and accident, creating a coherent film out of randomly mixed ingredients is not something a neophyte can be expected to pull off. *(Profanity, adult situations.)* — R.S.

d, Wayne Wang, Paul Auster; p, Greg Johnson, Peter Newman, Diana Phillips; exec p, Harvey Keitel, Bob Weinstein, Harvey Weinstein; co-p, Hisami Kuroiwa; w, Wayne Wang, Paul Auster (in collaboration with the actors); ph, Adam Holender; ed, Christopher Tellefsen; m, John Lurie, Calvin Weston, Billy Martin; prod d, Kalina Ivanov; art d, Jeff McDonald; set d, Karin Wiesel; sound, Andrew P. Kunin, John Hurst; casting, Heidi Levitt; cos, Claudia Brown

Comedy/Drama (PR: A MPAA: R)

BLUE TIGER ★★½
(U.S.) 88m Neo Motion Pictures; First Look Pictures; Ozla Pictures ~ Columbia TriStar Home Video c

Virginia Madsen *(Gina Hayes)*; Dean Hallo *(Henry Soames)*; Toru Nakamura *(Seiji)*; Ryo Ishibashi *(Gan)*; Sal Lopez *(Luis)*; Chris DeRose *(Detective)*; Yuji Okumoto *(Sakagami)*; Harry Dean Stanton *(Smith)*; Brenda Varda *(Emily)*; Henry Mortensen *(Darin)*; Francois Chau *(Soya)*; Claudia Templeton *(Nun)*; Toshiro Obata *(Kunimatsu)*; John Hammil *(Pharmacist)*; Thomas "Doc" Boguski *(Coroner)*; Chery Frey *(Sherry)*; Dan Bradley *(Turk)*

Steeped in film noir atmosphere, BLUE TIGER is a fatalistic revenge drama embroidered with elements of forbidden desire. Shorn of some of its metaphysical nonsense about destiny and simplistic Yin/Yang attractions, this "rub-'em-out" adventure would have been less cluttered and more gripping.

In a seedy Los Angeles, a Yakuza clan try capturing a piece of the tour bus industry monopolized by unethical Henry Soames (Dean Hallo). Although a hit on Soames fails, a Yakuza inadvertently murders an innocent bystander, Darin (Henry Mortensen), the young son of Gina Hayes (Virginia Madsen). Remembering a tattoo sported by Darin's masked assassin, Gina saunters into a tattoo parlor run by philosopher Smith (Harry Dean Stanton), who explains the magnetic attraction her own Tiger tattoo would have on a potential soulmate. While the Yakuza clan continues their turf war against Soames by killing his best friend Luis (Sal Lopez), warrior-in-training Gina becomes fluent enough in Japanese to penetrate their crimeworld. In a game of seduction, she lures Yakuza Gan (Ryo Ishibashi) into revealing himself as her son's murderer, but the veteran hit man turns the tables and soon has her at his mercy; it is only the timely interferences of Gan's sensitive brother, Seiji (Toru Nakamura) that saves her temporarily. Realizing that Gina is not a Soames operative but the dead boy's mom, the Yakuza elders direct conflicted Seiji to murder the woman for whom he's developed a passionate longing. While the police chastise Gina for her Mata Hari routine, Seiji barely escapes death in an explosion at the Yakuza home base ordered by Soames. While making love to the sole surviving Yakuza, Gina discovers in horror that tattooed Seiji, not his brother Gan, is her son's killer. After apprehension by and escape from the police, a still-handcuffed Seiji massacres everyone at the Soames Bus Company, then awaits his fate at the hands of Gina. No longer vacillating, instrument-of-justice Gina blasts her beloved right through his regretful heart.

Superficially exciting, BLUE TIGER makes Gina's maternal commando mission comprehensible if not dramatically engaging. While this neo-noir thriller captures the smoky midnight blue ambiance of crime and passion among the LA mob set, it founders in over-emphasizing the yin and yang tattoo legend that is applied to the central figures' romance. Intended to dress up a skimpy plot, the Harry Dean Stanton segments about red and blue tiger destinies interrupt the storyline more than they illustrate it. What is most striking, however, is this mongrel movie's depiction of the cesspool through which the grimly-determined mother wanders—since neither Soames nor the Yakuza clan have any redeeming qualities, Gina's mission takes on an almost mystical purity. This aside, BLUE TIGER serves up expertly-staged lethal liquidations all in the name of mother love, making a tasty chop suey out of a mix of soap opera melodrama and traditional action fare. *(Graphic violence, extreme profanity, nudity, sexual situations.)* — R.P.

d, Norberto Barba; p, Michael Leahy, Aki Komine; exec p, Taka Ichise, W.K. Border, Joel Soisson; assoc p, Alicia E. Oleszczuk; co-p, Don Phillips; w, Joel Soisson (from a story by Taka Ichise); ph, Christopher Walling; ed, Caroline Ross; md, David C. Williams; prod d, Markus Canter; art d, Anthony Stabley; sound, Larry Scharf; fx, Larry Fioritto, Bruce Mattox, Steve De Lollis; casting, Don Phillips; cos, Kathryn Shemanek; makeup, Lisa Buono

Thriller/Crime/Action   (PR: O MPAA: R)

BLUE VILLA, THE   ★★★
(Belgium/France/Switzerland) 100m Nomad Films; Euripide Films; La Sept Cinema; CAB Productions; RTBF Telefilms ~ Films Transit International c
(UN BRUIT QUI REND FOU)

Fred Ward *(Frank)*; Arielle Dombasle *(Sarah-la-Blonde)*; Charles Tordjman *(Edouard Nordmann)*; Sandrine Le Berre *(Santa)*; Dimitri Poulikakos *(Thieu)*; Christian Maillet *(The Father)*; Muriel Jacobs *(Kim)*; Michalis Maniatis *(Mars)*; Pandeas Scaramanga; Cai Jiguang; Lee Chong-Lin; Li Lai; Shi Kuifan; Qiu Lin; Giorgos Grouezas; Panaiotis Kodoulis; Antonios Vazeos; Yuriko Nakama

Conflicting perspectives emerge in the recounting of a supposed murder on a small Mediterranean island in THE BLUE VILLA, co-directed by Dimitri de Clercq and acclaimed French novelist and filmmaker Alain Robbes-Grillet. Known as the father of *le nouveau roman* (the "New Novel"), Robbes-Grillet first challenged the traditional goal of the novel to convey the interior depths of the individual with the publication of *Les Gommes* (*The Erasers*) in 1953. This book provided a phenomenological account of the surface appearance of objects, and in many respects created a novel resembling the visual logic of cinema.

THE BLUE VILLA opens with a travel-weary, sinister ship with torn red sails arriving empty into the harbor of a sleepy Mediterranean island to the sound of the local whorehouse madam, Sarah-la-Blonde (Arielle Dombasle), singing the tale from Wagner's opera, *The Flying Dutchman*. Word begins to spread throughout the village that Frank (Fred Ward) is back, and a narrator recounts the legend in which a pale mariner, guilty of killing his beloved, his ship's sails soaked with her blood, is

forced to return to port annually to repeat his crime. His soul can only be redeemed upon winning the heart of a virtuous prostitute and resting with her in a grave.

The early narration is provided by the disgruntled Edouard Nordmann (Charles Tordjman) speaking the text of his screenplay into a tape recorder. Nordmann's screenplay serves as a testimonial meant to exonerate himself, a fictional work he hopes to publish, in which he is supposedly giving a true account of the drama that occurred on this island. From his account, which he is constantly revising as he speaks, we learn that his beloved daughter, Santa (Sandrine Le Berre), was murdered by her lover Frank, who then took his own life. The local investigator, Thieu (Dimitri Poulikakos), reopens the case and confiscates Nordmann's tape as evidence, reminding him that Santa was merely his despised stepdaughter. Nordmann's drunken hallucinations of visitations from both Frank and Santa further diminishes the credibility of his version.

Meanwhile, Frank wanders the island, ragged and unkempt, frightening the villagers who believe he is a ghost. At the Blue Villa, the local casino and whorehouse, the clattering sound of ivory chips hitting the table in a perpetual game of chance establishes the eternal negotiation of forces. Upstairs, locked away like a princess in her tower, is the waiflike Lotus Blossom, who receives opera lessons and caresses from the beautiful house madam. We gradually learn that Lotus Blossom is actually Santa, and that there was no murder. She is being hidden to protect her from Nordmann, who abused her sexually and was supposedly on the verge of killing her for her inheritance.

Though loosely resembling a detective story, THE BLUE VILLA is about the incompleteness of knowledge and the insufficiency of interpretation, particularly in storytelling. In the final scene Frank and Santa are seen sailing past the island. The red sails of Frank's ship are now bright white and undamaged. A multitude of questions go unanswered. Unlike a traditional narrative, this story never seeks to draw the viewer in. We remain cool, disinterested observers, wandering from one image to the next, making associations which are later discarded in favor of new ones. *(Adult situations, sexual situations.)*

d, Alain Robbe-Grillet, Dimitri de Clercq; p, Jacques de Clercq; assoc p, Stephen Beckner; co-p, Jerome Paillard, Jacqueline Pierreux, Gerard Ruey; w, Alain Robbe-Grillet, Dimitri de Clercq; ph, Hans Meier; ed, Hans Duez; m, Nikos Kypourgos; art d, Alain Chennaux; sound, Francois Musy; cos, Bernadette Corstens

Drama   (PR: C MPAA: NR)

BOCA   ★
(U.S./Brazil) 91m Zalman King Company; JN Producoes Culturales ~ Republic Pictures Home Video c

Rae Dawn Chong *(J.J.)*; Martin Kemp *(Reb)*; Tarcisio Meira *(Boca)*; Martin Sheen *(Jesse James Montgomery)*; Carlos Dolabella *(Fonseca)*; Jose Lewgoy *(Quintella)*; Denise Milfont *(Moema)*; Patrick De Oliveira *(Tomaz)*; Nelson Xavier *(Father Silva)*; Ruth De Souza *(Mrs. Esteban)*; Anselmo Vascansellos *(Sgt. Trebe)*; Luma De Oliveira *(Celeste)*; Maria Padilha *(Maria Luiza)*; Betty Gofman *(College Friend)*; Marcia Conto *(College Friend)*; Selma *(Pamba Gira)*; Norma Surly *(Boca's Mother)*; Maria Dulce *(White Novice)*

Technically proficient to a fault, BOCA purports to be a serious political docudrama examination of the genocide of Brazilian street kids. However, given that this film was made by sexploitation maven Zalman King, it is more of an exercise in exploiting the death squads of Brazil as a backdrop for a profusion of orgasmic sex scenes.

Ace US reporter Jennifer "J.J." James (Rae Dawn Chong), scours Brazil for the story of a lifetime under the keen eye of shutterbug and former lover Reb (Martin Kemp). After befriending a shoeshine boy, Tomaz (Patrick De Oliveira), bleeding-heart liberal J.J. feels compelled to expose the government-approved conspiracy of silence against the slaughter of these homeless outcasts. The key to J.J.'s scoop is slum king Boca (Tarcisio Meira). Soulless killer with a finger in every crime pie, Boca acts as armed guardian angel for the urchins, whom merchants pay soldiers to eliminate in order to ease the economy and promote tourism. Foolishly trusting Boca, J.J. allows him to convince her to lure away the front man for the merchants' association, and then coolly informs her she must kill this go-between (Carlos Dolabella) or die herself—that's Boca's ingenious method for keeping people in his pocket. By the time J.J. learns that Boca killed Tomaz in order to ensure her worked-up complicity in his retaliation against the merchants, Reb arrives to sacrifice himself in a bloody shoot-out. After stabbing Boca to death, a shattered J.J. realizes the futility of her good Samaritan acts. Sweet-talked into handing over a video of the sanctioned child-killings by CIA agent Jesse James Montgomer (Martin Sheen), J.J. heads back to America as Brazilian leaders continue espousing their official story while the genocide continues unchecked.

Fever-pitched in the atmosphere of Rio carnival frenzy, BOCA heavy-breathes its way into a cinematic hall of shame. Far from being a South American UNDER FIRE, this thriller (full of literal climaxes) uses an international disgrace for sexy local-color value. To Zalman King and his associates, drag queens high-heeling it on parade and blindfolded tykes being machine-gunned are grist for the same cheap thrills mill. Potential audiences should be forewarned that King doesn't stop at the merely tasteless: The corpses of street kids are scattered throughout the storyline as part of a sex-and-death arousal schema. When he's not tugging at the viewers' genitals with too much fervor, King is boring the audience with a Joseph Conradian tale of the Brazilian criminal elite. Although Meira as Boca makes a despot evil enough to make one's skin crawl, one effective theatrical turn cannot compensate for so many other dismal performances. Worse than lame characterizations, however, is the film's rhythmic use of flashbacks and flashforwards. Repeating itself visually and thematically, BOCA seems to be edited with out-takes of the same scene. The upshot of the film's "political" message to North American audiences? "Let's screw and be glad that we aren't street kids in Rio." Hardly a sophisticated political science documentary, BOCA is so morally tacky that it fails as an erotic thriller as well. (*Graphic violence, extreme profanity, extensive nudity, substance abuse, sexual situations, adult situations.*) — R.P.

d, Walter Avancini, Sandra Werneck; p, Jeff Young, Jofre Rodrigues; exec p, Zalman King; assoc p, Caique Martin Ferreira, Linda Clark; w, Ed Silverstein; ph, Pedro Farkas; ed, Andy Horvitch; m, Richard Feldman, Midge Ure, Adam Gargoni; prod d, Annie Young; art d, Wilma Garcia, Claudia Medesto, Gioconda Coelho; sound, Juarez Dagaberto; casting, Denise Del Queto; cos, Reynaldo Elias; makeup, Tyler Colton

Erotic/Political/Drama (PR: O MPAA: R)

BODILY HARM ★★
(U.S.) 91m Naked Suspicion Productions; Rysher Entertainment ~ WarnerVision c

Linda Fiorentino (*Rita Cates*); Daniel Baldwin (*Sam McKeon*); Gregg Henry (*J.D. Prejon*); Bill Smitrovich (*Lt. Darryl Stewart*); Troy Evans (*Oscar Simpson*); Joe Regalbuto (*Stan Geffen*); Millie Perkins (*Dr. Spencer*); Shannon Kenny (*Krystal Lynn/Jacy*

Barclay); Todd Susman (*Jerry Roth*); William Utay (*Frangipani*); Ken Lerner (*Alex Shaw*); Casey Biggs (*Michael Cates*); Castulo Guerra (*Dr. Vasquez*); Lou Bonacki (*Judge Bellamenti*); Mari Morrow (*Diana*); Merri Contino (*Carrie*); Debra Rae (*Ginger*); Christi Fiara (*Shelly Randall*); Lauren Stark (*Young Jacy*)

Linda Fiorentino stars as a Las Vegas cop in this generic serial-killer mystery.

The bodies are piling up for police detective Rita Cates (Fiorentino). First is a Cheetah Club stripper, soon followed by a lady psychiatrist. The D.A.'s office thinks the culprit is obvious: Sam McKeon (Daniel Baldwin), an ex-cop, now wealthy casino executive and the ex-boyfriend of the two dead women—and, coincidentally, also of Rita, whose husband committed suicide over the affair. But only a witness to the first murder, B-girl Krystal (Shannon Kenny) can place McKeon on the scene. Despite possible danger and definite conflict of interest, Rita re-ignites her torrid affair with McKeon, and eventually finds a pair of bloody gloves in his house. Though this seems to clinch his guilt, the case is upset when a similar MO (the killer scrawls "Ojos de Dios" at each murder site) is recalled from one of McKeon's earlier cases, in which one Otis Barclay killed his wife. He was later slain in prison, but his young daughter Jacy grew up to be vengeful Krystal. She now menaces Rita, who kills her. Police are satisfied that Jacy/Krystal did the murders to frame McKeon to avenge her father. Following the advice of her psychiatrist Rita finally dumps McKeon. The final scene has McKeon opening his car glove compartment for his sunglasses, revealing a knife like that used in the murders.

Lightning didn't strike twice for Linda Fiorentino, whose explosive performance in THE LAST SEDUCTION can be paired with BODILY HARM to demonstrate what a difference skilled filmmaking makes with medium-budgeted neo-film noir. While BODILY HARM's plot is serviceable, the screenplay is hard put to flesh out the cliches, looping off into red herrings (especially sleazy women and strip bars), the not-fooling-anyone plot twist, and cynical "surprise" ending. B-film director James Lemmo (RELENTLESS 3, TRIPWIRE) is unable to inject much interest in the proceedings. A most glaring problem is an absolute lack of chemistry between Fiorentino and Daniel Baldwin, here lacking the magnetism of his thespian brothers Alec, Stephen and William. Fiorentino's predatory good looks have been put to better use elsewhere; now unflatteringly photographed, she's the scrawniest, unhealthiest-looking femme fatale/sexpot to hit the screen in ages. She also mistakes an actorly nervous edginess for a tortured, full characterization. Veteran Millie Perkins (DIARY OF ANNE FRANK) has a pair of brief, extraneous scenes as Rita's shrink. Produced by the veteran exploitation producer Bruce Cohn Curtis (JOYRIDE, HELL NIGHT, FEAR CITY), BODILY HARM, shot entirely in Las Vegas, including at the Riviera Hotel and Casino, and premiered at the Houston Film Festival before landing in video stores and pay-cable TV. (*Violence, nudity, sexual situations, adult situations, profanity.*) — D.B.

d, James Lemmo; p, Bruce Cohn Curtis; exec p, Keith Samples; w, Joseph Whaley, Ronda Barendse, James Lemmo; ph, Doyle Smith; ed, Carl Kress; m, Robert Sprayberry; prod d, Alfred Sole; art d, Dennis Gibbens; set d, Erica Frazier, Rafael Tapia; sound, Adam Joseph, Thomas Varga; casting, Denise Chamian; cos, Barbara Palmer; stunts, Greg Anderson

Crime/Thriller (PR: O MPAA: R)

BODY CHEMISTRY 4: FULL EXPOSURE ★★
(U.S.) 89m Sunset Films International; Concorde-New Horizons ~ New Horizons Home Video c

Shannon Tweed *(Claire Archer)*; Larry Poindexter *(Simon Mitchell)*; Andrew Stevens *(Alan Clay)*; Chick Vennera *(Freddie Summers)*; Larry Manetti *(Derrick Richmond)*; Stella Stevens *(Fran Sibley)*; Fred Holiday *(Bob Sibley)*; Marta Martin *(Lane Goodwin)*; Elaine Giftos *(Charlotte Sanders)*; Leslie Ryan *(Ami Mitchell)*; Michael Paul Chan *(Judge Hakama)*; Perla Walters *(Faye Guetierez)*; Brad Blaisdell *(Hugh Miner)*; Jim Wynorski *(Hanging Judge)*; Melissa Brasselle *(Sandra)*; Barbara K. Hill *(Jury Foreman)*; Merrifield Reed *(Bailiff)*; Kimberly Roberts *(Court Reporter)*

Playbody model-turned-actress Shannon Tweed tackles a villainous role in this rubber-stamped sequel.

Claiming she's falsely accused of an ex-lover's slaying, controversial sex-therapist Claire Archer (Tweed, the latest in a line of fleshy femmes to take the Glenn-Close-inspired part) inveigles married attorney Simon Mitchell (Larry Poindexter) into defending her personally. The depths to which Claire will go to disprove the charges include adultery with her lawyer. Spotting the Jezebel's true nature, Simon's assistant Lane (Martie Martins) who has difficulty hiding her Della Streetish yen for her boss, snoops for enough dirt to open his eyes, only to seem an obsessed stalker herself. Claire really is the killer, and the multiple murderess has reeled in Simon by videotaping their intimate moments to ensure his loyalty no matter what incriminating evidence surfaces. When Simon shows some backbone, Claire gives him one of her deadly kiss-offs, since no man ever leaves her. Having planted suspicions about Lane, Claire walks off scot-free as the lovestruck legal assistant gets both the rap and a lethal bullet fired by Simon's widow.

BODY CHEMISTRY 4 stands on its own mediocre merits; the good news is you need not view the preceding three installments in the series, riffs on the subject of a philandering fella ruled by urges he can't turn on and off. Once the camera ogles Tweed's curves, the screenplay can take a nap; viewers take one look and understand immediately what the expression "a body to die for" means. Although Tweed is an asset to any harem fantasy and effectively blunt as the conquering Lorelei, Poindexter is a colorless ball of handsomeness. Of course this flick's target audience isn't watching to see how well the chump role is handled. The mystery is guessable, and gives just a cosmetic dusting to courtroom antics. The real subject is a yummy celebration of underwear-stripping, body-rubbing sexotica, with the principals' physiques fitting together as easily as wood-block puzzles with a handful of pieces. Producer Andrew Stevens, often himself an actor in this sleazy genre, takes an in-joke role early on as the antiheroine's victim. *(Sexual situations, extreme profanity, extensive nudity, violence.)* — R.P.

d, Jim Wynorski; p, Andrew Stevens; exec p, Roger Corman; co-p, Raimond Reynolds; w, Karen Kelly; ph, Zoran Hochstatter; ed, Vanice Moradian; m, Paul Di Franco; prod d, Dave Blass; art d, Andre Sowards; sound, Dan Monihan (mixer), James Einolf (mixer); casting, Noble Henry; cos, Nadine Haders; makeup, Shauna Griesbrect

Erotic/Thriller (PR: O MPAA: R)

BODY SHOT ★★½
(U.S.) 98m Eternity Pictures; Connexion Films ~ Triboro Entertainment Group c

Robert Patrick *(Mickey Dane)*; Michelle Johnson *(Danielle Wilder/Chelsea)*; Ray Wise *(Dwight Frye)*; Jonathan Banks *(Simon Deverau/Blake Donner)*; Kim Miyori *(Christine Wyler)*; Peter Koch *(Elmer Hatch)*; William Steis *(Curt Lomann)*; J.J. Johnston *(Magruder)*; Charles Napier *(Leon)*; Kenneth Tobey *(Arthur)*; Barbara Patrick *(Candy)*; Viveka Davis *(Rita)*; Zaid Farid *(Charlie)*; Bruce Wright *(Juice)*; John Lupton *(Noah Goodman)*; C. Jack Robinson *(Detective Boyd)*; Liz Torres *(Judge Fernandez)*; Robert Le Brun *(Muscleman in Tux)*; Jon Cedar *(Senator Branford Holliday)*; Ritchie Montgomery *(Young Guard)*; John Diab *(Burly Guard)*; Peter Spellos *(Security Guard)*; Christopher Mankiewicz *(Detective Manella)*; Tony Mamet *(Bozo)*; "Poorman" Jim Trenton *(Emcee)*; J.B. McGrath *(Ambulance Technician)*; Joan Pirkle *(Middle-Aged Woman)*; David Michael O'Neill *(Yuppie)*; F. Daniel Somrack *(Bartender)*; Frederick Bailey *(Detective)*; Gene Pietragallo *(Crooner)*

Even after winding and rewinding some sequences, viewers may scratch their heads at leading lady Michelle Johnson's many incarnations and reanimations in BODY SHOT, a complicated direct-to-video thriller.

Los Angeles paparazzi photographer Mickey Dane (Robert Patrick) can't keep his lens off media sensation Chelsea Savage (Johnson). The pop diva cherishes her privacy because a tour bus crash killed her sister and several band members. Whether clicking candids over her back fence or rifling through Chelsea's garbage, Mickey can't control his one-sided *affair de Nikon*. A Chelsea-lookalike, Danielle Wilde (Johnson) undulates temptingly in Mickey's office; her story is that her husband Simon Deveraux (Jonathan Banks) requires his services for a coffee table book homage to the reclusive star. Ruled by his glands, Mickey foolhardily snaps bondage photos of the ersatz Chelsea tied to bedposts. When a woman is found stabbed to death, Mickey's fingerprints are on the knife he used to cut his photo model loose. Hornswoggled, Mickey doesn't realize that Simon is really struggling musician Blake Donner hired by Chelsea's manager Dwight Frye (Ray Wise) as part of a plot to control Chelsea's millions. Hint: remember the sister who allegedly perished in that bus crash? Mickey ends up scrutinizing his secret Chelsea snapshots for clues to piece the scheme together and vindicate himself, but the big winner is duplicitous Danielle, who scoots off scot-free with a fortune.

Because this labyrinth is maneuvered with devilish abandon by the cast, all the happenstance which might stick in the audience's throat is easier to swallow. Whether viewers will catch the finer points of the con, they still enjoy a surfeit of surprises like Banks' flaming demise and automaton actor Robert Patrick (TERMINATOR 2: JUDGMENT DAY) more animated than ever before here, bringing some panache to his seedy hero. Utilizing the development of photos to keep the narrative gliding smoothly, BODY SHOT may not be a worthy successor to BLOWUP but it does creatively incorporate viewfinder voyeurism into the tale. Dmitri Logothetis' surprisingly snappy direction cancels out occasional embarrassments like a death-threatened couple taking a sex break at Griffith Park observatory, or the plot convenience positing Chelsea not only having a twin but a *third* reasonable facsimile. Still, as femme fatales go, Johnson (BLAME IT ON RIO, GENUINE RISK) is a luscious double-crosser whom men probably wouldn't mind stopping a few bullets for. BODY SHOT sorely needs her sex appeal to convince us, as so many other of its brethren fail to do, that a lovestruck patsy might let his lust organs override his cerebral cortex. *(Graphic violence, extreme profanity, nudity, sexual situations, substance abuse.)* — R.P.

d, Dimitri Logothetis; p, Dimitri Logothetis, Gene Margoluis; exec p, David Korda, Ortwin Freyermuth; assoc p, Frederick Bailey; w, Robert Ian Strauss; ph, Nicholas Von Sternberg; ed, Mort Fallick; m, Clif Magness; prod d, Don Day; art d, Phil Brandes; set d, Shirley Starks; sound, Senator Mike Michaels;

casting, Rosemary Welden; cos, Susan Bertram; makeup, Cynthia F. Adams; stunts, Phil Adams

Crime/Thriller/Erotic (PR: O MPAA: R)

BODY STROKES ★
(U.S.) 99m Axis Films ~ A-Pix Entertainment c

Bobby Johnston *(Leo)*; Dixie Beck *(Karen)*; Kristen Knittle *(Beth)*; Catherine Weber *(Claire)*; Robert L. Newman *(Mark)*; Edward Holzman *(Mr. Sands)*; Seigel Sky *(Lois)*; Kelly Cook *(Aqua)*; Teresa Langley *(Rachel)*; Chet Tripp *(G.I.)*; Michael Simmons *(David)*; Daniel Anderson *(Mr. Roberts)*; Blake Adams *(James)*; Michael Jay *(Eric)*

Sort of a softcore reduction of the themes of LA BELLE NOISEUSE, this rather discursive heavy-breather seems to run as long as Rivette's esoteric four-hour opus.

Successful painter-hunk Leo (Bobby Johnston) and his ambitious *arriviste* wife Karen (Dixie Beck) squabble over integrity, sexual dysfunction, and the husband's artist's block. Feeling underappreciated, Karen goes to the Big Apple, leaving Leo to sulk about the future after he's dropped by a trendy art dealer. He hopes to put life in his brushstroke by hiring two fresh models, somewhat puritanical art student Beth (Kristen Knittle) whose self-esteem has been smothered by her lover, and Claire (Catherine Weber) financially strapped by a custody battle for her daughter. Over the course of a few days *avec* babes, the artist feels his painterly juices simmering until Karen unexpectedly returns and smells a *menage a trois*. Actually, this non-sexual arrangement works to everyone's advantage as (1) Leo's work revives, (2) Beth stands up for self-determination and uncorsets her libido, (3) Claire uses her modeling fee to get out of debt, (4) Karen overcomes jealousy and re-attracts her mate's ardor, and (5) Leo stops resenting Karen's management of his career. Karen and Leo become *amants* once more, the return of his creative potency accomplished without any actual adultery.

The filmmakers seem bent on tasteful sexual release and purifying the usual low-down onanistic atmosphere of titillation with their own idea of decorative smut. But those in need of video stimulus to put bounce in their mattress springs require more than the endless sex prattle here. Conceived in 1990s psychobabble, BODY STROKES boasts the kind of attractive players who only seem to exist in the pages of *Playgirl* and *Playboy*; however, audience horniness is never satisfied due to the dull self-absorption of these perfect specimens, no aphrodisiac in or out of bed. If these pretty people weren't so delectable in their ongoing nudity, viewers would shun them for the cocktail-party bores they really are. Photographed with eye-catching dexterity and drenched in the colors of a Frederick's of Hollywood catalogue, BODY STROKES is burdened by both vapid fantasy sequences and its own encounter-group mentality. Using this film to get aroused is tantamount to hiring Mother Teresa as your sex surrogate. *(Extensive nudity, sexual situations, extreme profanity, adult situations.)* — R.P.

d, Edward Holzman; p, Andrew Garroni; exec p, Walter Gernert; co-p, Edward Holzman; w, April Moscowitz; ph, Kim Haun; ed, Albert Larsen; m, Richard Bronskill; prod d, Michael Pearce; set d, Jon Barris; sound, Bill Reinhardt (mixer), Jason Johnston (mixer); casting, Lori Cobe; cos, Merrie Lawson; makeup, Tyla Guiliano

Erotic/Fantasy (PR: O MPAA: NR)

BORN TO BE WILD ★★
(U.S.) 94m Outlaw Productions; In-Law Entertainment; Fuji Entertainment ~ Warner Bros. c

Wil Horneff *(Rick Heller)*; Helen Shaver *(Margaret Heller)*; John C. McGinley *(Max Carr)*; Peter Boyle *(Gus Charnley)*; Jean Marie Barnwell *(Lacey Carr)*; Marvin J. McIntyre *(Bob—Paramedic)*; Gregory Itzin *(Walter Mallinson)*; Titus Welliver *(Sergeant Markle)*; Tom Wilson *(Det. Lou Greenberg)*; Alan Ruck *(Dan Woodley)*; Janet Carroll *(Judge Billings)*; John Procaccino *(Ed Price)*; Obba Babatunde *(Interpreter)*; David Wingert *(Gary James)*; John Pleshette *(Donald Carr)*; Keith Swift *(Dino)*; Michael MacRae *(Country Store Cop)*; Bruce Wright *(Jack Graham)*; David MacIntyre *(Charnley's Guard No. 1)*; Rob Cea *(Charnley's Guard No. 2)*; John Billingsly *(Daryl)*; Sarah Brooke *(Lacey's Mom)*; Jordan Michelman *(Lacey's Brother)*; Burton Gilliam *(Dwayne)*; Troy Evans *(Farmer)*; Sandra Lee Dejong *(Farmer's Wife)*; Larry Albert *(Plain Clothes Officer)*; Amy Scott *(Burger Girl)*; Chad Lindberg *(Burger Boss)*; Drake Collier *(Anchorman)*; Monica Hart *(Anchorwoman)*

Boy meets gorilla, FREE WILLY-style, in this predictable children's film which features commendable performances from its human leads. BORN TO BE WILD grossed a paltry $3.7 million in its theatrical release, but its video release became one of the surprise rental hits of the summer.

Behavioral researcher Margaret Heller (Helen Shaver) disciplines her rebellious son Rick (Wil Horneff) by putting him to work at her lab, cleaning animal cages. Rick's surly attitude changes after he makes friends with Katie, a 3-year-old gorilla who has been taught to communicate using sign language. Their bond is threatened when Katie's real owner, flea market proprietor Gus Charnley (Peter Boyle) cancels the lab's lease and reclaims Katie as a sideshow attraction. Rick cannot bear to see Katie caged, chained and miserable, so he rescues her from the flea market. They hit the road in a stolen van, headed for Canada, where Rick believes Katie will be free from extradition. When the law catches up with them, just short of the Canadian border, Rick is arrested. During Rick's trial, his attorney puts Katie on the witness stand. Through sign language, Katie describes Charnley's abuse and Rick's friendship. Rick is sentenced to community service for his actions, but he is awarded custody of Katie.

BORN TO BE WILD has two things going for it—Wil Horneff and Helen Shaver. They are so likable, they make the viewer really want to believe that they're making all this fuss over a real gorilla instead of a guy in a monkey suit. But Katie is one of the least convincing animatronic creations ever seen on film, a fact which makes it very difficult to suspend disbelief long enough to get any enjoyment out of this film. Katie's slapstick antics will keep tiny tots distracted, but older children and adults will quickly tire of the monkey business being foisted on them by the filmmakers. Several scenes depict roughhousing between Rick and Katie, with the gorilla wrestling with or jumping on Rick, actions which would surely cause severe bodily injury to the boy in real life.

The film tries to take itself seriously, and the courtroom climax comes close to eliciting real emotion, but juxtaposed with snippets of sincerity are too-goony-to-be-true supporting characters, and logic-defying plot developments. *(Violence.)* — B.R.

d, John Gray; p, Robert Newmyer, Jeffery Silver; exec p, Brian Reilly; assoc p, Jennifer Graham Billings, Susan E. Novick; w, Paul Young, John Bunzel (from a story by Paul Young); ph, Donald M. Morgan; ed, Maryann Brandon; m, Mark Snow; prod d, Roy Forge Smith; art d, Gilbert Wong; set d, Jan Pascale; sound, John Patrick Pritchett (mixer), Leslie Shatz (design); fx, Robbie Knott, Peter Abrahamson, Alterian Studios; casting,

Debi Manwiller; cos, Ingrid Ferrin; makeup, Katharina Hirsch-Smith; stunts, Joe Dunne

Comedy/Adventure/Children's (PR: A MPAA: PG)

BOULEVARD ★
(Canada/U.S.) 96m Norstar Entertainment ~ LIVE Home Video c

Rae Dawn Chong (Ola); Kari Wuhrer (Jennefer); Lou Diamond Phillips (Hassan); Lance Henriksen (McClaren); Joel Bissonnette (J-Rod); Judith Scott (Sheila); Amber Lea Weston (Debi); Greg Campbell (Coco); Kerman Malicki-Sanchez (Sister); Katie Griffin (Lorraine); Marcia Bennett (Mrs. Braverly); Michael Kramer (Doctor)

A gutter tale in more ways than one, BOULEVARD's highly questionable intentions are overshadowed by violent interludes that leave a nasty aftertaste.

After putting her newborn up for adoption, small-town girl Jennefer (Kari Wuhrer) decides to leave abusive boyfriend J-Rod (Joel Bissonnette) and travel to Toronto. She lives on the street until Ola (Rae Dawn Chong), a jaded prostitute, takes her in as a roommate. The pair slowly warm to each other, but their fortunes change when Ola witnesses sadistic pimp Hassan (Lou Diamond Phillips) killing one of his hookers. Ola is repeatedly threatened by Hassan, while Jennefer eventually succumbs to streetwalking. With Ola's sage advice, Jennefer gains the gumption to deal with the reappearance of vindictive J-Rod, whom she fatally shoots. Meanwhile Ola heads for a confrontation with Hassan, which results in her brutal beating and hospitalization. Jennefer seeks out and kills Hassan. Ola dies in the hospital, and Jennefer boards the next bus heading back to her small town.

The cast gamely plod through their paces, imbuing the cardboard characters with stone-faced conviction. The sole exception is Phillips, who goes willfully over the top as Hassan, an eccentric villain who relaxes after tormenting his hookers by practicing his golf swing. There's no chance, though, that the picture can simply be written off as mere sexploitation. The filmmakers attempt to emphasize the feminist bonding of Ola and Jennefer (with a lesbian liaison tossed in for good measure), but this thoroughly unpleasant straight-to-video sleaze's sudden, cruel acts of brutality disqualify it from being the evocative portrait of street life it pretends to be. Meanwhile BOULEVARD's half-baked melodramatics will alienate fans of the "streetwalkers in jeopardy" movies that flourished in the 1980s with the VICE SQUAD and ANGEL series. (Graphic violence, extensive profanity, sexual situations, adult situations.) — E.G.

d, Penelope Buitenhuis; p, Peter Simpson, Ray Sager; exec p, Ilana Frank, Peer Oppenheimer; w, Rae Dawn Chong; ph, David Frazee; ed, Nick Rotundo; m, Ian Thomas; prod d, Jasna Stefanovic; cos, Joyce Schuve

Drama (PR: O MPAA: R)

BOYS ON THE SIDE ★★★
(U.S.) 117m Le Studio Canal Plus; Regency Enterprises; Alcor Films; New Regency; Hera Productions ~ Warner Bros. c

Whoopi Goldberg (Jane DeLuca); Mary-Louise Parker (Robin Nickerson); Drew Barrymore (Holly); Matthew McConaughey (Abe Lincoln); James Remar (Alex); Billy Wirth (Nick); Anita Gillette (Elaine); Dennis Boutsikaris (Massarelli); Estelle Parsons (Louise); Amy Aquino (Anna); Stan Egi (Henry); Stephen Gevedon (Johnny Figgis); Amy Ray; Emily Saliers (Indigo Girls); Jude Ciccelella (Jerry); Gede Watanabe (Steve); Jonathan

Seda (Pete); Mimi Toro (Carrie); Lori Alan (Girl with Attitude); Mary Ann McGarry (Dr. Newbauer); Michael Storm (Tommy); Danielle Shuman (Young Robin); Julian Neil (Nightclub Owner); Niecy Nash (Woman at Diner); Ted Zerkowski (Drug Buyer); Jill Klein (Waitress); Marnie Cressen (Nurse); Aaron Lustig (Judge); Terri White (Guard); George Georgiadis (Cab Driver); Cheryl A. Kelly (Hotel Clerk); Adria Contreras (Mary Todd—5 Months Old); Malika Edwards (Mary Todd—10 Months Old); Pablo Espinosa (New Mexico Policeman); Kevin LaPresle (New Mexico Policeman); John F. Manfredonia (Obstetrician); James Shuffield (Gynecologist); Thomas Kevin Danaher (Tuscon Policeman); Richard Loewll McDole (Tuscon Policeman); Don Hewitt (Tow Truck Driver); Andy Duppin (Tow Truck Driver); Alan Mirikitami; Joe Pyles; Worthy Davis; Stephen Gevedon (Jane's Band); Josh Segal; Breta La Von; Patrice Jones; Tito Larriva; Gary Montemer (Indigo Girls' Band); Vernon Francisco; Fidelis Manuel; Sylvester Oliver; Benedict Martinez (Desert Suns Band); New Kiva Motions Puppet Theater (Day of the Dead Dancers/Puppeteers); Ballet Folklorica Azteca (Folkloric Dancers)

Excellent performances enhance this awkwardly structured film about the friendship between three very different women. BOYS ON THE SIDE starts out as a road movie, then incorporates elements of the three-hankie melodrama, disease-of-the-week picture and courtroom drama. Though BOYS ON THE SIDE recalls THELMA & LOUISE, FRIED GREEN TOMATOES, TERMS OF ENDEARMENT and STEEL MAGNOLIAS, it has a heart all its own.

Struggling rock singer Jane DeLuca (Whoopi Goldberg) wants to leave Manhattan for brighter career prospects in Los Angeles. Robin (Mary-Louise Parker), a yuppie real estate agent, is heading for a new start in San Diego and advertises for someone to share the ride. They agree to make the trip together despite their differences in background, attitude, musical taste, and sexual orientation. ("Jane is a black lesbian!" Robin's mother later gasps in horror.)

They make a stop in Pittsburgh to visit Jane's friend Holly (Drew Barrymore), arriving just as her drug-dealing boyfriend Nick (Billy Wirth) is beating her up. Nick turns on Jane and Holly beans him with a baseball bat. Leaving Nick tied to a chair—but very much alive—Holly joins Jane and Robin on the road. When the women learn that Nick is dead and Holly is wanted for his murder, they decide to continue as though they never found out. The trip ends unexpectedly in Tucson when Robin is suddenly taken ill: She has been hiding the fact that she has AIDS.

Three months later, the women are sharing a house in Tucson. Jane sings at a local gay bar. Robin, her health stabilized, enjoys a dalliance with bartender Alex (James Remar), which causes a rift in her relationship with Jane. Pregnant Holly, now a waitress, is dating a cop named Abraham Lincoln (Matthew McConaughey) to whom she divulges her past. Abe loves Holly and wants to marry her, but also feels it's his duty to turn her in. Jane and Robin rally to help Holly, who receives a light sentence thanks to Robin's heartfelt testimony. She returns home with her husband and newborn daughter, in time to share Robin's final days.

Director Herbert Ross's credits include two other films focusing on female relationships, THE TURNING POINT and STEEL MAGNOLIAS. Like them, BOYS ON THE SIDE gives all the choice roles to the women and relegates men to the sidelines. Powerhouse performer Goldberg could have dominated the proceedings, but shares the screen gracefully with her two co-stars. Her scenes with Mary-Louise Parker are the film's most compelling. Jane and Robin start out as odd couple traveling companions, bickering and grating on each other's nerves, and end up family, inextricably linked by shared experience. The actresses play off one another beautifully, their scenes together charged with an unexpressed undercurrent of love and longing. Parker, who starved herself to shocking thinness for the film's later sequences, displays an amazing versatility and depth. The film's biggest surprise is Drew Barrymore, not because of the saucy flesh she bares but because she shows real acting weight. Flighty, flirty and forthright, Holly is the perfect counterweight to her serious-minded friends.

Don Roos's screenplay is loaded with melodrama, but a healthy dose of humor helps lighten the load. The film's occasional jarring shifts in tone are a liability, but not a fatal one: It's a character-driven piece and the beautifully-crafted characters mask the narrative flaws. *(Violence, nudity, sexual situations, adult situations, profanity.)* — B.R.

d, Herbert Ross; p, Arnon Milchan, Steven Reuther, Herbert Ross; exec p, Don Roos, Patricia Karlan; assoc p, Russ Kavanaugh; co-p, Patrick McCormick; w, Don Roos; ph, Donald E. Thorin; ed, Michael R. Miller; m, David Newman; prod d, Ken Adam; art d, William F. O'Brien; set d, Rick Simpson; sound, Jim Webb (mixer); fx, Dale L. Martin, Conrad Brink; casting, Hank McCann; cos, Gloria Gresham; makeup, Michael Germain, Fern Buchner; stunts, Phil Neilson

Drama/Comedy   **(PR: C   MPAA: R)**

BRADY BUNCH MOVIE, THE   ★★★
(U.S.) 95m Paramount ~ Paramount c

Shelley Long *(Carol Brady)*; Gary Cole *(Mike Brady)*; Christopher Daniel Barnes *(Greg Brady)*; Christine Taylor *(Marcia Brady)*; Paul Sutera *(Peter Brady)*; Jennifer Elise Cox *(Jan Brady)*; Jesse Lee *(Bobby Brady)*; Olivia Hack *(Cindy Brady)*; Henriette Mantel *(Alice)*; David Graf *(Sam)*; Jack Noseworthy *(Eric)*; Megan Ward *(Donna)*; Jean Smart *(Mrs. Dittmeyer)*; Michael McKean *(Mr. Dittmeyer)*; RuPaul *(Mrs. Cummings)*; Moriah Snyder *(Missy)*; Alanna Ubach *(Noreen)*; Shane Conrad *(Doug)*; Marissa Ribisi *(Holly)*; R.D. Robb *(Charlie)*; Steven Gilborn *(Mr. Phillips)*; Alexander Pourtash *(Mr. Amir)*; Keone Young *(Mr. Watanabe)*; James Avery *(Mr. Yeager)*; Robert Rothwell *(Mr. Simmons)*; Elisa Pensler Gabrielli *(Miss Lynley)*; David Proval *(Electrician)*; Arnold Turner *(Officer Axelrod)*; Darion Basco *(Eddie)*; Gaura Vani Buchwald *(Leon)*; Shannah Laumeister *(Molly)*; David Leisure *(Jason)*; Archie Hahn *(Mr. Swanson)*; Barry Williams *(Music Producer)*; Beverly Archer *(Mrs. Whitfield)*; Tammy Townsend *(Danielle)*; Patrick Thomas O'Brien *(Auctioneer)*; Ann B. Davis *(Trucker)*; Eric Nies *(Hip MC)*; Davy Jones; Micky Dolenz; Peter Tork *(Themselves)*; Tully Jensen *(Model)*; Jennifer Blanc *(Valley Girl)*; Julie Payne *(Mrs. Simmons)*; Tamara Mello *(Stacy)*; Christopher Knight *(Coach)*; Selma Archerd *(Neighbor)*; James Randall White *(Limo Driver)*; Lisa Sutton *(Hooker)*; Dan Lipe *(Angry Neighbor)*; John R. Fors *(Angry Neighbor)*; Kim Hasse *(Student)*

THE BRADY BUNCH MOVIE is a funny, savvy, camp yet family-friendly look at the Generation-X TV icons. As if they had been freeze dried in 1974—complete with perms and garish polyester print outfits—"The Brady Bunch" have been reconstituted to face the 1990s.

Wicked real estate developer Mr. Dittmeyer (Michael McKean) wants to buy the Brady home. When they won't sell, he steals a $20,000 property tax bill from their mail, hoping that when they fail to pay up they'll be evicted.

With only a few days left before the bill comes due, Dittmeyer springs the bad news on the Bradys. Dad Mike (Gary Cole) assures mom Carol (Shelley Long) that she needn't worry about

the money, since all he has to do is sell one of his architectural designs. Unfortunately, they're all on a par with his design for his own home, which has only one bathroom for six kids.

Thanks to Cindy the tattletale (Olivia Hack), the kids find out about the financial crisis and set out to raise the money. Marcia (Christine Taylor) figures teen modeling will be lucrative, but an errant football pass breaks her nose. Greg (Christopher Daniel Barnes) plans to work as rock star Johnny Bravo, but his song—"Clowns never laughed before/beanstalks never grew"—makes David Cassidy sound funky. Meanwhile, sibling rivalry rears its ugly head: Jan (Jennifer Elise Cox) feels overshadowed by always-perfect Marcia. A guidance counselor (RuPaul) suggests Jan still her inner voices by stressing her individuality. At the big school dance, "the new Jan Brady" shows up in a huge Afro wig. Marcia upstages her by arriving with Monkee Davy Jones. Jan runs away from home, and is coaxed back by sound advice from a sympathetic truck driver (Ann B. Davis).

At the eleventh hour, the kids decide to enter the school talent contest. In their fringed and beaded day-glo jumpsuits, they perform a feel-good pop confection and win. The prize money saves the homestead, and everyone learns important lessons about honesty, self-esteem and family loyalty.

When TV's "The Brady Bunch" debuted in 1969, it was just another sitcom in which the kids got into laughably innocent trouble, realized the error of their ways and were counseled by their firm yet understanding, Dad. By series' end at the height of the Watergate era, the Bradys were already an anachronism: an artificial island of bland normality in a sea of dysfunction. As the show lived on in reruns and American families became ever more fragmented, the Bradys emerged as icons. A generation—the one that knows the words to the "Brady Bunch" theme song, but not the national anthem—simultaneously mocked their goofy innocence and secretly wished they had a family just like that.

The talents responsible for THE BRADY BUNCH MOVIE know exactly what was funny about the original TV show: nothing. The Bradys were utterly banal, and unfailingly cheerful and the film's one big joke is the juxtaposition of their "sunshine day" optimism and the smoggy cynicism of modern day LA. It recreates the show's most trivial details (the tilt of Carol's head, the Astroturf lawn, the macrame vests) with loving care, viewing it all with sly derision. Under Betty Thomas' direction, the cast makes imitation the sincerest form of mockery. Cindy's lisp makes her almost unintelligible. Peter's (Paul Sutera) changing voice is the tip of a pubescent iceberg. Tres cool Greg litters his speech with "groovy" and "far out" the way Mamet's characters curse. Gary Cole eerily mimics the late Robert Reed, but this new Mike's homilies are just confusing babble. Just beneath THE BRADY BUNCH MOVIE's nostalgic surface lies a dark truth about the myth of American family life, there for anyone who wants to see it. — P.R.

d, Betty Thomas; p, Sherwood Schwartz, Lloyd J. Schwartz, David Kirkpatrick; exec p, Alan Ladd, Jr.; co-p, Barry Berg, Jenno Topping; w, Laurice Elehwany, Rick Copp, Bonnie Turner, Terry Turner (based on characters created by Sherwood Schwartz); ph, Mac Ahlberg; ed, Peter Teschner; m, Guy Moon; prod d, Steven Jordan; art d, William J. Durrell, Jr., Nanci B. Roberts; set d, Lynn Wolverton-Parker; sound, Russell Williams, II (mixer); fx, Peter Albiez, Terry W. King, Gene Warren, Jr.; casting, Deborah Aquila, Jane Shannon; cos, Rosanna Norton; makeup, Alan "Doc" Friedman, Dina Defazio, Todd McIntosh; stunts, Pat Romano

Comedy   **(PR: A   MPAA: PG-13)**

BRAVEHEART   ★★★
(U.S.) 177m Icon Productions; The Ladd Co.; Marquis Film;
Paramount ~ Paramount c

Mel Gibson (William Wallace); Sophie Marceau (Princess Isabelle); Patrick McGoohan (Longshanks—King Edward I); Catherine McCormack (Murron); Brendan Gleeson (Hamish); James Cosmo (Campbell); David O'Hara (Stephen); Angus McFadyen (Robert the Bruce); Ian Bannen (The Leper); Peter Hanly (Prince Edward); James Robinson (Young William); Sean Lawlor (Malcolm Wallace); Sandy Nelson (John Wallace); Sean McGinley (MacClannough); Mhairi Calvey (Young Murron); Brian Cox (Argyle Wallace); Stephen Billington (Phillip); Barry McGovern (King's Advisor); John Kavanagh (Craig); Alun Armstrong (Mornay); Tommy Flanagan (Morrison); Julie Austin (Mrs. Morrison); Alex Norton (Bride's Father); Joanne Bett (Toothless Girl); Rupert Vansittart (Lord Bottoms); Michael Byrne (Smythe); Ralph Riach (Priest No. 1); Robert Paterson (Priest No. 2); Malcolm Tierney (Magistrate); William Masson (Corporal); Dean Lopata (Madbaker/Flagman); Tam White (MacGregor); Donal Gibson (Stewart); Jeanne Marine (Nicolette); Martin Dunne (Lord Dolecroft); Fred Chiverton (Leper's Caretaker); Jimmy Chisholm (Faudron); John Murtagh (Lochlan); David McKay (Young Soldier); Peter Mullan (Veteran); Martin Murphy (Lord Talmadge); Gerard McSorley (Cheltham); Bernard Horsfall (Balliol); Richard Leaf (Governor of York); Daniel Coli (York Captain); Niall O'Brien (English General); Liam Carney (Sean); Bill Murdoch (Villager); Phil Kelly (Farmer); Martin Dempsey (Drinker No. 1); Jimmy Keogh (Drinker No. 2); Joe Savino (Chief Assassin); David Gant (Royal Magistrate); Mal Whyte (Jailor); Paul Tucker (English Commander)

A massive, sweaty, sloppy and extremely heavy-handed epic, BRAVEHEART won Mel Gibson a Best Directing Oscar and delivers enough visceral excitement to make it an ideal rainy afternoon matinee.

As a boy, Scottish hero-to-be Sir William Wallace (Mel Gibson) witnesses the vicious treachery of King Edward I—known as Longshanks—when he slaughters a group of unarmed landowners. Wallace soon loses his father and brother in a bloody rebellion. Educated abroad, Wallace returns as an adult to the tiny hamlet of Ellerslie to raise crops and children. He marries his boyhood sweetheart, Murron (Catherine McCormack), and defends her from English rapists. As a result, Wallace is forced to flee and Murron is publicly executed. Wallace leads the locals in a bloody revolt that's soon joined by other clans.

Wallace finds an ally in the cause of Scottish independence in Robert the Bruce (Angus Macfayden), whose leprous father (Ian Bannen) is secretly plotting to advance his son's claim to the vacant Scottish crown. Wallace leads his army against the superior English forces at Stirling, beating them through cunning and bravery, and is declared "Guardian of Scotland." He takes his army into England, capturing the city of York. The king sends his daughter-in-law, Princess Isabelle (Sophie Marceau), to negotiate, but secretly plans to kill Wallace. Isabelle is estranged from her homosexual husband, Prince Edward (Peter Hanley), and half in love with the romantic image of Wallace. She finds the man himself irresistible and warns him of the danger.

Wallace returns north and is betrayed by Robert the Bruce and the Scottish nobles. Wallace and Isabelle meet once again and become lovers, and he begins avenging himself on his betrayers. Betrayed once again, he is delivered into English hands. Wallace defends himself against the charge of treason by declaring that he has never sworn fealty to the King and is not subject to him. Despite Isabelle's intercession, he is drawn and quartered. The dying Longshanks' triumph is short-lived: A bitter but wiser Robert the Bruce, who realizes that his loyalty should lie with his

countrymen, leads the Scots to independence at Bannockburn with "Wallace" as their battle cry.

Although BRAVEHEART's scale is impressive, Gibson's attempt to create an old fashioned epic a la EL CID or SPARTACUS is not entirely successful. The pace is uneven and Gibson's abuse of slow motion reduces many dramatic scenes to tedium, though John Toll's gorgeous cinematography and Tom Sanders' detailed, thoroughly authentic production design help overcome the film's sluggishness. And the fight sequences are truly outstanding: bloody, visceral, amazingly brutal and efficiently edited, creating a compelling sense of the way it must have felt to be in the thick of brutal battle.

The script deals honestly with the issues of class and ethnicity that muddled Scotland's quest for independence, but otherwise its fidelity to historical fact leaves something to be desired. Not only does writer Randall Wallace (no apparent relation) simplify Wallace's motivations, but he seriously misrepresents the two royal Edwards. Edward Longshanks—the brilliant diplomat who gave England its modern Parliamentary system—is played for a lunatic, and Prince Edward—later the tyrannical Edward II—as a simpering nancy boy. In a particularly miscalculated attempt at humor, Longshanks hurls Edward's lover from a window to his death. The ludicrous romance between Isabelle and Wallace concludes with the baseless suggestion that Wallace sired Edward III, who was in reality born six years after Wallace's death.

Though BRAVEHEART purports to value intelligence over brute strength, the only onscreen evidence of its reverence for brains is the quantity of them splattered about during the battle scenes. (Extreme violence, nudity, profanity, adult situations.) — R.S.

d, Mel Gibson; p, Mel Gibson, Alan Ladd, Jr., Bruce Davey; exec p, Stephen McEveety; assoc p, Dean Lopata, Elizabeth Robinson; w, Randall Wallace; ph, John Toll; ed, Steven Rosenblum; m, James Horner; prod d, Tom Sanders; art d, Dan Dorrance; set d, Peter Howitt; sound, Brian Simmons (mixer), John Pitt; fx, Nick Allder; casting, Patsy Pollock; cos, Charles Knode; makeup, Peter Frampton; stunts, Mic Rodgers, Simon Crane

AA Best Picture; AA Best Director: Mel Gibson; AAN Best Original Screenplay: Randall Wallace; AA Best Cinematography: John Toll; AAN Best Costume Design: Charles Knode; AAN Best Editing: Steven Rosenblum; AA Best Makeup: Peter Frampton, Paul Pattison, Lois Burwell; AAN Best Dramatic Score: James Horner; AAN Best Sound: Andy Nelson, Scott Millan, Anna Behlmer, Brian Simmons; AA Best Sound Effects: Lon Bender, Per Hallberg

Historical/Drama/Adventure   (PR: O   MPAA: R)

BREACH OF CONDUCT   ★★½
(U.S.) 93m Finnegan/Pinchuk Company; MCA Television
Entertainment ~ MCA/Universal Home Video c
(AKA: TOUR OF DUTY)

Peter Coyote (Colonel Andrew Chase); Courtney Thorne-Smith (Helen Lutz); Tom Verica (Lieutenant Ted Lutz); Keith Amos (Corporal Reed); Beth Toussant (Paula White); Thom Vernon (Corporal Weingart); Tom Mason (Major Matthew James); Todd McKee (Lieutenant Keith Waite); Drew Snyder (Sheriff); Thom McFadden (Deputy Sheriff); John Walcutt (Gate Guard Harper); Gregg Daniel (Police Station MP); Bill Harper (Military Police Officer); Roger Hewlett (Gatehouse Guard); Sharon Mendel (Gatehouse MP); Larry Nash (Squad Leader); Michael Raysses (Soldier in Truck); Tudi Roche (Enlisted Woman); Stan Foster (Army Clerk); Gina St. John (Nurse); Joe Camareno (Waiter); Shayne Adamson (Corpsman)

They're called "from Hell" movies, a subgenre of lookalike psychothrillers that bred like rabbits in the 1990s, all modelled on FATAL ATTRACTION (speaking of rabbits). FATAL ATTRACTION with a teenage girl = THE CRUSH; FATAL ATTRACTION with a nanny = THE HAND THAT ROCKS THE CRADLE; FATAL ATTRACTION with roommate = SINGLE WHITE FEMALE—respectively, the Nymphet, the Nanny, and the Roomie from Hell. Such scripts pretty much pen themselves, making these easy exercises for uninspired filmmakers.

Directed by actor-producer Tim Matheson, BREACH OF CONDUCT (the Commanding Officer from Hell) follows in lockstep, despite some real potential. Posted to a remote US installation in Nevada, military wife Helen Lutz (Courtney Thorne-Smith) is very nearly seduced by a dashing guy in uniform before her husband Ted (Tom Verica) arrives. When Lt. Lutz introduces Helen to his new CO, who should it be but that smooth suitor, Col. Andrew Case (Peter Coyote). With clueless Ted happily sent on assignments by Case, Helen alone must fight the latter's escalating sexual advances. He restricts her to base and cuts off her communications to the outside, and Helen realizes she's not his first victim; married neighbor Paula (Beth Toussant) set up Mrs. Lutz in trade for her own freedom. Case reveals his bachelor pad, a disused armory/fallout shelter redecorated as a love nest. Because Helen once sought therapy for depression, her frantic complaints to other army personnel are dismissed as delusions.

Neat suspense in BREACH OF CONDUCT arises from inherent paranoia in the setting. On a military base, declares Case, the commander's word is law, and he has mustered all resources under his authority to keep a succession of young, terrified army wives as mistresses. But the lame predictability of the "from Hell" routine never goes away until after standard escape attempts and standard setbacks, when Helen and Paula seize the fallout shelter and demand federal intervention. There's a giddy moment when it looks like one FATAL ATTRACTION clone might actually go nuclear, but a convenient Caine Mutiny of enlisted men against Case triggers his breakdown and suicide instead.

A similar plot concept with less hyperbole served the cause of drama in Tony Richardson's BLUE SKY (Powers Boothe as the ruthless colonel lusting after Jessica Lange). If anyone emerges from a "from Hell" looking good, it's the heavy, and Peter Coyote stands tall as the cracked Case, a deskbound career soldier who sublimates his battlefield ambitions into private strategies to divide and conquer individuals rather than armies. Other actors follow preordained paths, right down to the hint that Helen deserves what she gets for almost succumbing to temptation. Keith Amos suffers the standard character of the nonwhite—hence expendable—corporal who suspects the truth and gets killed. BREACH OF CONDUCT premiered on cable TV in 1994, marching to videocassette the next year. *(Violence, adult situations.)* — C.C.

d, Tim Matheson; p, Lori-Etta Taub; exec p, Sheldon Pinchuk, Tim Matheson; co-p, David Chisolm; w, Scott Abbott; ph, Gideon Porath; ed, Christopher Rouse; m, Terry Plumeri; prod d, David Ensley; set d, Cindy E. Downes; sound, Walt Martin (mixer); fx, Bellissimo/Belardinelli; casting, Karen Rea; cos, Victoria Auth; makeup, Zoe; stunts, Charlie Croughwell

Thriller (PR: C MPAA: PG-13)

BREAK, THE ★★
(U.S.) 105m Autumn Winds Productions ~ Vidmark Entertainment c

Vincent Van Patten *(Nick Irons)*; Ben Jorgensen *(Joel Robbins)*; Rae Dawn Chong *(Jennifer Hudson)*; Martin Sheen *(Gil Robbins)*; Gerrit Graham *(Bill Cowens)*; John E. Schneider *(Brock Hainie)*; Valerie Perrine *(Delores Smith)*; Daryl Anderson *(Dale Farley)*; Betsy Russell *(Candy)*; Trevor Goddard *(Nails)*; Dick Van Patten *(Mr. Tennis)*; Fred Stolle *(Himself)*; Cliff Drysdale *(Himself)*; Vitas Gerulaitas *(Himself)*; Justin Page Buck; Nels Van Patten; Pat Van Patten

Pro tennis provides many classic sports moments, but the few tennis-oriented movies (PLAYERS, SPRING FEVER, RACQUET) were badly strung sex 'n' jocks cliches. Real-life net pro Vincent Van Patten, actor son of longtime screen performer Dick Van Patten, decided it was time to do the BULL DURHAM of the courts, based on his own impressions of the game. For seven years he worked on THE BREAK, writing, producing, and starring in the filmed-in-Florida feature. But this is a weak serve.

Van Patten portrays washed-up former US Open superstar Nick Irons. Crushed with gambling debts, Irons accepts a deal from wealthy bookie Robbins (Martin Sheen) to coach his teen son Joel (Ben Jorgenson) as the gangling youth tries to qualify on a satellite tennis circuit. Nice touch: Robbins doesn't want Joel to triumph, but rather thinks the example of sullen, has-been Irons will cure the kid of his ambitions. Irons does treat Joel scornfully, even when he wins a few. But on tour Irons sheepishly reunites with old friends, foes, and sex-crazed tennis groupies; the latter group encompasses betrayed girlfriend Jennifer (Rae Dawn Chong), who delivers The Big Speech (in its entirety): "You used to be a guy who stood for something. You cared. But look at you. It's such a waste."). Thus admonished, Irons mentors Joel seriously—cue the standard KARATE KID montage of grueling practice rituals. Events predictably lead to Joel's showdown with a tennis bully coached by Irons's old enemy (Gerrit Graham in a thankless role), which is refereed by a pedophile official blackmailed into ruling against Joel. Nonetheless, the underdog scores the game point (sure enough, in slow motion), and Irons's epilogue narration boasts how he coached Joel all the way to the US Open—where the kid acquired lots of sex-crazed tennis groupies. Thrill of victory indeed.

If this is the best a tennis insider can do, perhaps it's time to default. Van Patten goes through the melodramatics with the assurance and fluidity that make one wish he had a better writer. Newcomer Jorgensen is convincingly dorky as the enthusiastic hacker, but director Lee H. Katzin displays little faith in the actors, resorting to hokey voice-overs during matches so the viewer knows what everyone down to the peanut vendor is thinking. Real-life announcers Fred Stolle and Cliff Drysdale play themselves in comic fashion, possibly under the misconception that they're in a MAJOR LEAGUE sequel. Tennis ace Vitas Gerulaitas also cameos. In 1995, Gerulitas, who battled drug and alcohol addiction following his tournament days, was found dead, reportedly due to carbon monoxide leak from an air conditioner. End credits eulogize the fallen athlete as "A great champion and a great friend," but it's a reminder of how trite THE BREAK seems compared with actual events. After a regional theatrical release, the feature was lobbed onto home video. *(Sexual situations, profanity, adult situations.)* — C.C.

d, Lee H. Katzin; p, Vincent Van Patten; exec p, Sid Craig; assoc p, Nels Van Patten; co-p, James Van Patten; w, Vincent Van Patten, Stephanie Warren, Dan Jenkins; ph, Frank P. Flynn; ed, Doug Ibold; m, Kim Bullard; prod d, Tim Duffy; art d, William Tabor; set d, Clare Papetti Duane; sound, Joe Foglia; casting, Alan Berger; cos, Denise Walsh

Sports/Drama (PR: C MPAA: PG-13)

BRIAN WILSON: I JUST WASN'T MADE FOR THESE TIMES ★★★

(U.S.) 69m Polomar Pictures; Cro-Magnon Films ~
Palomar Pictures c

(AKA: I JUST WASN'T MADE FOR THESE TIMES)

Brian Wilson; Tom Petty; Lindsey Buckingham; Thurston Moore; David Crosby; Graham Nash; Linda Ronstadt; David Anderle; Randy Newman; Tony Asher; Hal Blaine; John Cale; Daniel Harrison; David Leaf; Melinda Ledbetter; Danny Hutton; Andy Paley; Van Dyke Parks; Lenny Waronker; Audree Wilson; Carl Wilson; Carnie Wilson; Marilyn Wilson; Wendy Wilson

This documentary on chief Beach Boy Brian Wilson (shown on the Disney Channel and briefly in theaters) was directed by noted record producer Don Was and gives an overview of Wilson's triumphant but troubled past.

The film includes interviews with Wilson, his former and current wives, daughters Carnie and Wendy (members of the pop group Wilson Phillips), and commentary from admirers ranging from Tom Petty and Linda Ronstadt to Sonic Youth's Thurston Moore. Wilson also performs songs from the Beach Boys albums and his solo effort, concluding with "Do It Again," in which the girls join their long-estranged father.

Wilson could be considered the archetypal "tortured artist," a shy, sensitive kid, bullied and abused by his monster of a father (briefly mentioned here but more graphically portrayed in Wilson's autobiography *Wouldn't It Be Nice*), creating his own complex odes to cars, girls, and teen fun. The Beach Boys' enormous success is eventually tempered by the growing schism between Wilson and the group: he wants to branch out and they want to keep singing about girls and the beach. According to the film, the failure of the *Pet Sounds* album and the abandoning of the ambitious *Smile* LP only worsened Wilson's mental problems, already exacerbated by drugs, and he soon went into a deep depression, virtually spending several years in bed.

BRIAN WILSON: I JUST WASN'T MADE FOR THESE TIMES (the title comes from a *Pet Sounds* song) is a good beginner's guide to Wilson's achievements and influence, but it does not tell the whole story. Brother Carl is the only Beach Boy who agreed to be interviewed, and there is no mention (by name, anyway) of Dr. Eugene Landy, the controversial therapist who exerted enormous control over Brian for some years and succeeded in getting him back to recording. (In fairness to Was, both omissions may have been for legal reasons.) It is also ironic, and inexplicable, that given the colorful, sun-filled quality of the Beach Boys' music, Was chose to film in black and white.

Although it is full of great music and insight into what led to that music, a melancholy tone colors the film. Wilson is in better shape than he was in the 1970s, but he still does not seem fully recovered. The viewers remain unsure whether his childlike demeanor is genuine or the result of decades of chemical and mental abuse. Perhaps the most compelling aspect of Wilson's story is not his inability to produce anything substantial after *Smile*, but that, given the nightmares of his childhood and adulthood, he was able to create as much as he did. *(Profanity.)*

d, Don Was; p, Don Was, Larry Shapiro, David Passick, Ken Kushnick; exec p, Anne-Marie Mackay, Jonathon Ker; ph, Wyatt Troll; ed, Helen Lowe; m, Brian Wilson; art d, Justin Bailey; sound, Bob Dreebin, Gary Gossett, Mike Fredriksz; makeup, Kerry Malouf

Documentary/Musical   (PR: A   MPAA: NR)

BRIDGES OF MADISON COUNTY, THE ★★★

(U.S.) 135m Amblin/Malpaso Productions ~
Warner Bros. c

Clint Eastwood *(Robert Kincaid)*; Meryl Streep *(Francesca Johnson)*; Annie Corley *(Carolyn Johnson)*; Victor Slezak *(Michael Johnson)*; Jim Haynie *(Richard Johnson)*; Sarah Kathryn Schmitt *(Young Carolyn)*; Christopher Kroon *(Young Michael)*; Phyllis Lyons *(Betty)*; Michelle Benes *(Lucy Redfield)*; Alison Wiegert *(Child)*; Brandon Bobst *(Child)*; Pearl Faessler *(Wife)*; R.E. "Stick" Faessler *(Husband)*; Tania Mishler *(Waitress)*; Billie McNabb *(Waitress)*; Art Breese *(Cashier)*; Lana Schwab *(Saleswoman)*; Larry Loury *(UPS Driver)*; James Rivers; Mark A. Brooks; Peter Cho; Eddie Dejean, Sr.; Jason C. Brewer; Kyle Eastwood *(James Rivers Band)*; George Orrison; Ken Billeter; Judy Trask; David Trask; Edna Dolson; Dennis McCool; Michael C. Pommier; Jana Corkrean; M. Jane Seymour; Karla Jo Soper *(Cafe Patrons)*

Adapted from the best-selling and much-mocked novel, THE BRIDGES OF MADISON COUNTY is a tearjerker, pure and simple, but its warmth, humor, and charm make it an immensely satisfying one. And it's a rare example of a mainstream American romance in which two mature adults move from attraction to flirtation to love and passion.

Present day: After their mother's death, Carolyn and Michael Johnson (Annie Corley and Victor Slezak)—both in the throes of personal crises—discover mementos of a four-day love affair of which they were completely unaware, including detailed journals.

Iowa, 1965. Her family off at the State Fair, Francesca Johnson (Meryl Streep)—an Italian woman married to a Midwesterner—looks forward to a week of splendid solitude. Her plans change when Robert Kincaid (Clint Eastwood) pulls into her driveway. He's a *National Geographic* photographer on assignment to shoot some of Madison County's historic covered bridges, and he's lost. The attraction between them is immediate. Unlike her husband, a quiet, undemonstrative man—"clean," she calls him—Robert is a romantic. He picks Francesca flowers, and peppers his conversation with poetry. That night, they dine together. She's enthralled by his stories of adventures in far-off places like Africa, and her native Italy. The next night, she invites him over again, and they make love.

They spend a perfect day together, and then another perfect night. The morning after, as Robert prepares to leave, Francesca angrily confronts him. She's fallen in love, and now he's off to seduce some other lonely woman on the other side of the world. He says she is, in fact, his one true love, and asks her to come away with him. She packs, but realizes she can't abandon her family.

When Richard (Jim Haynie) and the kids return, Francesca falls back into her "life of details," busy with laundry and meals. Days later in town, Robert makes a final, silent invitation. Though tempted, Francesca declines. She returns to the farm and her family, dedicating the rest of her life to them.

After finishing the story, Michael and Carolyn take to heart Francesca's admonition that "a woman needs to be known for all she is." Both address their own marital troubles, and realize that they have underestimated their mother.

Robert Waller's *The Bridges of Madison County* was a publishing phenomenon, a best-selling brew of naive poetry, fuzzy philosophizing and over-ripe prose that was absolutely impervious to critical brickbats. To his credit, director and star Clint Eastwood managed to make a silk purse from it: his film has more in common with BRIEF ENCOUNTER than AN AFFAIR TO REMEMBER.

Screenwriter Richard LaGravenese (THE FISHER KING, A LITTLE PRINCESS) stripped the story down, and then improved it with the addition of the flashback structure. The modern day scenes provide humor—most of it at Victor Slezak's expense; he's the stereotypical mother-worshipping son who can't believe what his beloved Mom got up to—but also add a layer of meaning to what is otherwise just a tragic anecdote. Telling the story from Francesca's point of view is a smart change: her womanly wisdom—even in intrusive voice-over—is far more appealing than Kincaid's slippery New Age nonsense. Eastwood's direction is straightforward and classically simple, and cinematographer Jack Green turns the farmhouse kitchen into a magical stage on which Streep and Eastwood peform.

Eastwood brings an air of easy, romantic charm to Kincaid, but BRIDGES is Streep's film. She completely inhabits Francesca, bringing to life both the character's superficial frumpiness and a grace and natural elegance she has almost forgotten she has. Eastwood reportedly wanted the best actress of the appropriate age for the coveted role, and Streep more than lives up to his expectations. *(Sexual situations.)* — P.R.

d, Clint Eastwood; p, Clint Eastwood, Kathleen Kennedy; assoc p, Tom Rooker, Michael Maurer; w, Richard LaGravenese (based on the novel by Robert James Waller); ph, Jack N. Green; ed, Joel Cox; m, Lennie Niehaus; prod d, Jeannine Oppewall; art d, William Arnold; set d, Jay R. Hart; sound, Willie D. Burton (mixer); fx, Steve Riley, John Frazier; casting, Ellen Chenoweth; cos, Colleen Kelsall; makeup, J. Roy Helland, Michael Hancock

AAN Best Actress: Meryl Streep

Romance/Drama   (PR: C   MPAA: PG-13)

BROKEN TRUST   ★★½
(U.S.) 96m Fonda/Bonfiglio Films ~ Turner Home Entertainment c

Tom Selleck *(Tim Nash)*; Elizabeth McGovern *(Janice Diller)*; William Atherton *(Neil Roemer)*; Marsha Mason *(Ruth Fraser)*; Charles Haid *(Harold Ashley)*; Stanley DeSantis *(Vince Escobar)*; Rob LaBelle *(Louis Dale)*; Cynthia Martells *(Cyndy Duryea)*; Fritz Weaver *(Lional Nash)*; John Milford *(Frank Wister)*; Nicholas Pryor *(Paul Cleary)*; Brent Stait *(Evan Soika)*; Lorena Gale *(Carole Benisek)*; Kevin McNulty *(Judge Peatling)*; Meredith Woodward *(Suzanna Jardine)*; Jon Cuthbert *(Detective Mancuso)*; Julian Christopher *(Detective Garvey)*; Jay Sterrenberg *(Benjamin Nash)*; Rodney Turner *(Bailiff)*; L. Harvey Gold *(Carl Breck)*; Philip Granger *(Agent Sanchez)*; Robin Mossley *(Agent Testa)*; Scott Swanson *(Judge Potter)*; Maxine Miller *(Hillary Nash)*; P. Lynn Johnson *(Beth Nash)*; Tonia Usher *(Store Clerk)*; Howard Storey *(Floyd)*; Robert Thurston *(Photographer)*; Mikal Dughi *(Witness)*; Greg Thirloway *(Lawyer)*; Alan C. Peterson *(Highland)*; Helen Honeywell *(Mrs. Beller)*; Wren Roberts *(Bouncer)*; Alf Humphreys *(Officer)*

This muted courtroom drama is reasonably intelligent and cynically observant, but overall impact is constipated. With the pedigree of a John Gregory Dunne and Joan Didion script, one expects knockout. Instead, this judicial expose lets ethical issues roll around tantalizingly but independent of the plot mechanics.

A proponent of a strict judicial code, third-generation judge Tim Nash (Tom Selleck) upholds a family tradition of moral rectitude. Approached by ruthless Federal agents, Neil Roemer (William Atherton) and his second-in-command Janice Diller (Elizabeth McGovern), Nash reluctantly takes part in a bribery-sting operation to nail corrupt associates. Roemer initiates a test operation involving Judge Harry Ashley (Charles Haid) but this veteran crook is too sly to fall for a sweet deal involving police snitch Louis Dale (Rob LaBelle). By the time Nash suffers second and third thoughts, lawyers in Nash's ongoing homicide case smell a rat in Louis Dale and sense possible leverage against Nash's impending ruling. Meanwhile Roemer tries to keep the

rebellious Nash in line by showing him certifiable proof that his upstanding father Lionel (Fritz Weaver) benefitted financially from a 1964 zoning verdict. Before long, Nash is setting up lifelong friends like Ruthie Fraser (Marsha Mason), for feds whose methods are more repellent than the greased-palm court officers. After Ruthie shoots herself in front of Nash, Agent Diller provides Nash, now her lover, with dirt on Roemer that will free Nash from his duties and promote her at her boss's expense. Nash maintains his family image but is shunned as a pariah by the other judges. The government victory against influence-peddlers seems Pyrrhic.

What distinguishes BROKEN TRUST is its pessimistic ambiance. What's-in-it-for-me relationships prevail in a moral vacuum where honor is an anachronism. In this worldview, the definition of right and wrong is written on shifting sands. Although officials like Ruthie break the law, their motives—like easing divorce settlement payments—are understandably human ones. Without condoning such acts, BROKEN TRUST assumes an ambiguous position regarding how much good is accomplished by wrecking distinguished careers. Not only will other questionable officials take their place, but the worst offenders like Ashley never get caught. The movie does unequivocally smear government agents like Roemer who blindside others not out of conviction but for their own career advancement. But BROKEN TRUST has problems compressing these complexities and then addressing them through the give-and-take dialogue and the distraction of a canned thriller subplot about Dale's fatal wrangle with a sleazy attorney threatening to blow his cover. Designated hot topics stick out like lumps of oatmeal in a screenplay which relies more on mouthpieces than fully-drawn characters. The cast seems at half-mast here as if burdened by weighty themes. As in his other demanding dramatic appearances, Selleck offers muffled intensity; his one-note thesping fails to chart his character's rising inner turmoil. Adroitly produced and reverentially directed, BROKEN TRUST was made for cable TV and should engross fans of legal melodramas. What it wants to do—but never does—is stir passions. *(Violence, profanity, substance abuse, adult situations, sexual situations.)* — R.P.

d, Geoffrey Sax; p, Steve McGlothen; exec p, Lois Bonfiglio; assoc p, Ari Sloane; w, Joan Didion, John Gregory Dunne (based on the novel *Court of Honor* by William P. Wood); ph, Ron Orieux; ed, Glenn Farr; m, Richard Horowitz; prod d, Brent Thomas; art d, Randy Chodak; set d, Peter Lando; sound, Mark Holden (mixer), Joe Zappala (design); fx, Dave Gauthier; casting, Iris Grossman; cos, Trish Keating; makeup, Rosalina DaSilva; stunts, Scott Ateah

Drama/Crime   (PR: C   MPAA: NR)

BROTHERS MCMULLEN, THE   ★★★
(U.S.) 97m Marlboro Road Gang Productions; Videography Productions; Good Machine ~ Fox Searchlight Pictures c

Jack Mulcahy *(Jack)*; Connie Britton *(Molly)*; Edward Burns *(Barry)*; Mike McGlone *(Patrick)*; Shari Albert *(Susan)*; Maxine Bahns *(Audry)*; Catharine Bolz *(Mrs. McMullen)*; Peter Johansen *(Marty)*; Jennifer Jostyn *(Leslie)*; Elizabeth P. McKay *(Ann)*

Writer-director Edward Burns's entertaining, *very* low-budget debut follows the lives and loves of three Irish-Catholic brothers in New York. Though afflicted by the typical technical weaknesses of underfinanced productions, the film's great warmth and ragged charm more than offset them.

Before the ground around her husband's grave is cold, Mother McMullen races back to Ireland and the arms of her one true love. Now her sons must sort things out for themselves. Among their concerns: love and commitment, the meaning of manhood, the legacy of their abusive father, and the dictates of their faith. Fortunately, they're sharing the family home on Long Island, so it's easy to get together for soul-searching conversations.

Aspiring filmmaker Barry (Burns) has turned his back on Catholicism and love. His confirmed bachelorhood is tested when he meets Audry (Maxine Bahns), the first woman ever to resist his roguish charm. Eldest brother Jack (Jack Mulcahy) begins an ill-considered affair when his wife Molly (Connie Britton) begins to pressure him about having children; the illicit relationship soon puts a terrible strain on his marriage. The youngest and most religious brother, Patrick (Mike McGlone), is engaged to a Jewish woman named Susan (Shari Albert), and plans to work for her father in the garment business. He's getting cold feet about the whole thing, but it's still a shock when she dumps him because she's pregnant and intends to have an abortion.

Months pass as the brothers stew over their situations, stubbornly procrastinating and constructing elaborate justifications for their behavior, rather than actually doing anything about their lives. Susan decides she wants Patrick back: if he accepts, he'll have a wife, a job and a home without having to do anything more than say "yes." But he's fallen in love with tomboyish neighbor Leslie (Jennifer Jostyn), and the two of them pack up and leave for California. Molly confronts Jack about his affair, forcing him to face his responsibilities. Finally, Barry faces an ultimatum from Audry about their relationship, and makes a commitment to her.

The 27-year-old Burns filmed THE BROTHERS MCMULLEN on weekends over the course of eight months, while supporting himself as an "Entertainment Tonight" production assistant. He also borrowed equipment and crew members from the show. The semi-professional cast worked for free (Bahns is Burns' longtime girlfriend), and most of the interiors were shot in Burns's family home. Final cost: about $20,000. THE BROTHERS MCMULLEN won the Dramatic Grand Jury Prize at the Sundance Film Festival, and was the first film released by Fox Searchlight, a boutique distribution arm of Twentieth Century Fox.

THE BROTHERS MCMULLEN is such a scrappy and heartfelt picture that it's hard not to be won over. The homey interiors are poorly lit, but you can just make out Burns's film books and personal mementos in the background. The exteriors were shot on the streets of New York without permits and look it, but their hurried air just lends a refreshing feeling of spontaneity. Though the title suggests that THE BROTHERS MCMULLEN is a movie about guys, the film's women come off much better. The men are uniformly immature cowards, while the women make decisions, stand by their choices and accept the consequences.

Burns wears Woody Allen's cinematic influence like a badge of honor. He cites ANNIE HALL as a favorite, and seems to have been quite taken with the shot of Alvy's mother vigorously grating a carrot: Burns repeats the image twice in THE BROTHERS MCMULLEN—once with a cucumber, the second time with a hot dog. Barry delivers an Allen-esque monologue about the ways women emasculate men while methodically cutting up a banana. THE BROTHERS MCMULLEN may not be as insightful or accomplished as Allen's HANNAH AND HER SISTERS and CRIMES AND MISDEMEANORS, but it's an eminently promising first film.*(Adult situations, sexual situations, profanity.)* — P.R.

d, Edward Burns; p, Edward Burns, Dick Fisher; exec p, Edward J. Burns, Ted Hope, James Schamus; assoc p, Bill Baldwin, Anthony Bregman, Judy Richter, Mary Jane Sklaski; w, Edward Burns; ph, Dick Fisher; ed, Dick Fisher; m, Seamus Egan; sound,

Mario Porporino (mixer), Mike Marson (mixer), Andrew Yarme (mixer), Stefan Springman (mixer)

Drama/Comedy/Romance   **(PR: C   MPAA: R)**

BRUTE FORCE
(SEE: EXPERT, THE)

BUDDY FACTOR, THE
(SEE: SWIMMING WITH SHARKS)

BUFFALO GIRLS   ★★★
(U.S.) 180m DePasse Entertainment; CBS Entertainment Productions ~ Cabin Fever Entertainment c

Anjelica Huston *(Calamity Jane)*; Melanie Griffith *(Dora Du-Fran)*; Sam Elliott *(Wild Bill Hickok)*; Gabriel Byrne *(Teddy Blue)*; Jack Palance *(Bartle Bone)*; Peter Coyote *(Buffalo Bill Cody)*; Tracey Walter *(Jim Ragg)*; Floyd Red Crow Westerman *(No Ears)*; Reba McEntire *(Annie Oakley)*; Russell Means *(Sitting Bull)*; Liev Schreiber *(Ogden)*; Charlayne Woodard *(Doosie)*; Andrew Bicknell *(Captain James O'Neill)*; John Diehl *(General George Custer)*; Paul Lazar *(Doc Rames)*; Geoffrey Bateman *(Prince of Wales)*; Julie Bevan *(Duchess of Warwick)*; Peter Birch *(Lord Windhouvern)*; Michael Eiland *(Harry)*; David Garver *(Restless Frank)*; Jane Goold *(Skeedle)*; Robert Harnesberger *(Preacher)*; Jerry King *(Jack McCall)*; Daphne Neville *(Maid)*; Robin Nicholas *(Clerk)*; J. Michael Olivia *(Blacksmith)*; Richard Simpson *(Club Manager)*; Hanley Smith *(Mr. Fortescue)*; Boots Southerland *(Sergeant)*; Hannah Taylor-Gordon *(Janey)*

While this CBS-TV miniseries from the novel by Larry McMurtry lacks the classical simplicity of his *Lonesome Dove* adaptation, it is nonetheless a sensitively-directed feminist oater that commands attention despite slow patches. The production often whisks through essentials only to dawdle over sidebars or scenery.

As the Wild West grows tame enough to be a fit subject for mythologizing by Buffalo Bill Cody (Peter Coyote), a few weather-beaten survivors yearn for the rough-and-tumble past. Flanked by her querulous trapper buddies Bartle Bone (Jack Palance) and Jim Ragg (Tracey Walter) and Indian shaman pal No Ears (Floyd Red Crow Westerman), Calamity Jane (Anjelica Huston) frees herself fortuitously from a job commitment to General Custer, right before his famous Last Stand. Surrendering to her ardor for smoothie Wild Bill Hickock (Sam Elliot, onscreen only briefly), Calamity not only becomes pregnant but bereaved when Hickock is gunned down. Befriended by madame Dora (Melanie Griffith), who keeps her rancher beau Teddy Blue (Gabriel Byrne) at arm's length, Calamity relinquishes her illegitimate daughter to childless aristocrats, who later move back to England. During the Indian migrations, as civilization encroaches on all the rowdy frontiersmen, Teddy Blue runs out of patience and gets hitched to a chief's daughter—but continues to see Dora on the side. Bartle Bone and Jim Ragg forsake stubborn pride to join Buffalo Bill's London-bound Wild West Show, and Calamity signs on in hopes of reclaiming her daughter from the now-widowed, now-antagonistic stepfather. Frustrated Calamity persuades Bill Cody's star attraction Annie Oakley (Reba McEntire) to hold a clay-pigeon shooting match to raise funds for a custody fight. But after meeting and befriending the happy child, Jane decides to return home alone, without even telling her of her true parentage—except in long letters, which have comprised the saga's voiceover narration. Meanwhile Dora expires in childbirth after an impulsive marriage to a young husband (that did little to prevent regular trysts with Blue). Calamity Jane pours her unfulfilled maternal feelings into helping raise Dora's baby daughter.

Buttressed by sturdy production values and performances that invest legendary figures with human dimensions, BUFFALO GIRLS cast a long shadow as it traipses through a cavalcade of familiar historical events. In this teleplay's E.L. Doctorow approach, history seems to exist merely to provide a backdrop for tragic love affairs and yearning for Days Gone By. Given this superficial streak, an oft-syrupy musical score, and the awkward narrative device of (undelivered?) missives to an oblivious daughter (a Calamity Jane TV biopic starring Jane Alexander used a similar framework device to better effect), BUFFALO GIRLS still captures a bygone piece of Americana and even tempts the tear ducts to let loose on occasion.

Though her accent varies, Huston makes a magnificent heroine, limning both Jane's sheltered heart, tomboy looks and adventurous spirit. Palance and Walter overemphasize comic patter at the expense of their grizzled squabblers' pathos (and suffer an eco-correct subplot about the Dakota territory's dwindled beaver populace), but Griffith and Byrne are exceptionally moving as romantics who pine longingly for each other but never maritally connect; these two need to be at the top their form because the script never fortifies their rather skimpy aversions to wedlock. Although BUFFALO GIRLS is designed too insistently as an elegy to a vanished epoch, it commendably portrays Native American culture without condescension (Russell Means' Sitting Bull is actually a bad guy, bucking Hollywood's penchant for trendy revisionism). It also creams off the essence of the rhinestone splendor of Cody's carnival. The Wild West Show doesn't rip off its aging heroes but admiringly gussies them up for a final bow at glory. Even though the screenplay might have more deeply penetrated its characters' inner lives, BUFFALO GIRLS gets credit for insisting its female protagonists ride the range without side saddles. Calam, Dora, and Annie aren't victims mortified by sagebrush soap opera, but architects of their own destinies who refuse to be backed into any corners of a Man's World. *(Violence, profanity, sexual situations, adult situations, substance abuse.)* — R.P.

d, Rod Hardy; p, Sandra Saxon Brice, Suzanne Coston; exec p, Suzanne DePasse; w, Cynthia Whitcomb (based on the novel by Larry McMurtry); ph, David Connell; ed, Richard Bracken; m, Lee Holdridge; prod d, Cary White; art d, Michael Sullivan; set d, Barbara Haberecht; sound, David Brownlow (mixer); fx, Randy Freiling, Craig Weiss, CBS Animation Group; casting, Francine Maisler; cos, Van Broughton Ramsey; makeup, Gerald Quist

Western (PR: C   MPAA: NR)

BULLETPROOF HEART ★★★
(U.S.) 100m Republic Pictures; Keystone Pictures; Worldvision Enterprises ~ Keystone Pictures c
(GB: KILLER)

Anthony LaPaglia *(Mick)*; Mimi Rogers *(Fiona)*; Matt Craven *(Archie)*; Peter Boyle *(George)*; Monika Schnarre *(Laura)*; Joseph Maher *(Dr. Alstricht)*; Mark Acheson *(Hellbig)*; Philip Hayes; Christopher Mark Pinhey *(Partygoer)*; Claudio de Victor *(Partygoer)*; Justine Priestly *(Masseuse)*

Writer-director Mark Malone's offbeat noir fantasy is the sort of small-scale film that has largely disappeared from the theatrical marketplace, but manages to thrive on video.

Mick (Anthony LaPaglia) is an alienated, existential hit man with a secret romantic streak. He's troubled by questions about the meaning of life, and confesses to mob kingpin George (Peter Boyle) that he idly considered murdering the call-girl George sent him because she failed to excite him. George offers to set Mick up with a prominent psychiatrist if he will take a contract on an upscale lady who has stolen money from the mob. The catch: the hit must be carried out immediately.

Mick's pal Archie (Matt Craven) wants to come along. Mick is reluctant to let him, because Archie's cowardice in a previous hit nearly cost George and Mick their lives. Archie begs—he wants to prove himself, so Mick reluctantly agrees, explaining that his profession demands the kind of man who "doesn't talk, doesn't show, doesn't feel."

Much to his surprise, Mick finds that his intended victim, the elegant Fiona (Mimi Rogers), is expecting him. She's giving a swank party, but ushers out her remaining guests so she and Mick can be alone. She asks him detailed and personal questions about his work, and her cool, sophisticated manner literally disarms Mick. Soon she has him tied to the bed. The sex is playfully sadistic, and the pain arouses him intensely. But Fiona cuttingly dismisses Mick's performance as they dress and head downstairs, where Archie is waiting.

The more Mick learns about Fiona, the more ambivalent he becomes about killing her. Finally, he calls George to debate the need for this hit, leaving Archie alone with Fiona. Archie finds himself confiding in Fiona about the job he botched, and the way it has damaged his relationship with Mick. Mick returns from his conversation with George determined to go through with the job, but in no hurry to do so. At Fiona's suggestion, they pick up Chinese food and have a midnight picnic in Idlewood cemetery. But Fiona experiences a psychotic episode, and falls into a catatonic state.

Mick rushes her to the famous shrink (Joseph Maher) mentioned earlier. He reluctantly confides that Fiona has an incurable mental illness that will progressively destroy her mind. Utterly torn, Mick takes Fiona to the dockside warehouse where he is to kill her, but can't bring himself to do it. George arrives, and while he and Mick argue, Fiona goads Archie—who's been left to guard her—into killing her. Mick is shattered.

Though BULLETPROOF HEART's screenplay was credited to "Gordon Melbourne," it was in fact written by first-time director Mark Malone, whose previous screenwriting credits include DEAD OF WINTER and SIGNS OF LIFE. Neither suggested the skill and wit he brings to BULLETPROOF HEART, which twits noir conventions, Martin Scorsese, Robert De Niro and the cult of pharmaceutical therapy, without ever lapsing into self-referential smugness.

The film's performances are dense and subtle—though Craven hams it up a bit as Archie—and Malone is a confident and inventive director whose use of lighting and sound is smoothly impressive. He also pulls off a couple of flashy maneuvers, including a twice-interrupted flashback and a post-credits coda. But unlike many first-time directors, Malone never upstages his actors. BULLETPROOF HEART was well received by critics, but failed to find an audience until it was released on video. *(Violence, nudity, sexual situations, profanity.)* — R.S.

d, Mark Malone; p, Robert Vince, William Vince; exec p, Robert Sigman, Gary Delfiner, Michael Strange; assoc p, Kelsey T. Howard, Abra Edelman; w, Gordon Melbourne; ph, Tobias Schliessler; ed, Robin Russell; m, Graeme Coleman; prod d, Lynne Stopkewich; art d, Eric McNab; set d, Elizabeth Patrick; sound, Kerry Uchida, David Husby (mixer); fx, Michael S. Vincent, Al Benjamin; casting, Abra Edelman, Elisa Goodman, Marcia Shulman; cos, Maxine Baker; makeup, Pamela M. Athayde, Suzanne Willet; stunts, Marc Akerstream

Drama/Crime/Thriller (PR: C   MPAA: NR)

BURNING SEASON, THE ★★★

(U.S.) 127m HBO Pictures; Enigma Productions;
J.N. Filmes ~ Warner Home Video c
(AKA: LIFE AND DEATH OF CHICO MENDES, THE)

Raul Julia *(Chico Mendes)*; Sonia Braga *(Regina)*; Carmen Argenziamo *(Alfredo Sezero)*; Nigel Havers *(Steven Kaye)*; Luis Guzman *(Estate Boss)*; Tomas Milian *(Darli Alves)*; Edward James Olmos *(Wilson Pinheiro)*; Tony Plana *(Orlavo Galvao)*; Kamala Dawson *(Ilzamar)*; Briana Romero *(Elenira Mendes)*; Gerardo Albarran *(Darci Alves)*; Esai Morales *(Jair)*; Jorge Zepeda *(Santos)*; Jonathan Carrasco *(Genesio)*; Jose Perez *(Moacir)*; Jeffrey Licon *(Young Chico Mendes)*; Tony Perez *(Francisco Mendes)*; Jorge Viteri *(Father Ceppi)*; Valentin Santana *(Oloci Alves)*; Alberto Isaac *(Jose)*; Lolo Navarro *(Dona)*; Calos Ramono *(Partenza)*; Enrique Novi *(Nilo Sergio)*; Mario Arevado *(Gunman)*; Angel Casarin *(Union Man)*; Rene Perevra *(Disc Jockey)*; Roger Cudney *(Reporter)*; Carl Mergenthaler *(German Banker)*; Gabriel Eduardo Castanon *(Young Boy)*; Joaquin Garrido *(Joao)*; Jose Antonio Estrada *(Condemned Tapper)*; Josefina Echanove *(Town Woman)*; Julian Bucio *(Military Lieutenant)*; Alfredo Gutierrez *(Forest Worker)*; Javier Lambert *(Platoon Commander)*; Gustavo Campos *(Cutter)*; Marco Rodriguez *(Tavora)*; Carlos Carrasco *(Helio)*

A biopic of Brazilian labor/environmental activist Chico Mendes, this was produced for HBO cable television, with all the attendant flaws and virtues of a nobility-juiced feature.

As a child Mendes witnessed his father and fellow rubber-tappers stand by as a union organizer burned to death at the hands of federal soldiers. Determined to make a better future for his people, adult Chico (Raul Julia) works closely with labor leader Wilson Pinheiro (Edward James Olmos), whose advocacy of workers' rights makes enemies in high places. Business execs, cattlemen like Darli Alves (Tomas Milian) and bent politician Orlavo Galvao (Tony Plana) form a consortium to clear Amazon forests for a lucrative road project to benefit ranch and military transport. The impact on rubber-tapping would be calamitous, and Pinheiro is assassinated for his opposition. Chico assumes leadership amid a crackdown on the outraged peasants, and adopts a strictly nonviolent approach to stop the hacking and burning; he launches legal challenges to forest ownership and sit-ins to block the bulldozers. The Gandhi approach doesn't save Mendes from kidnapping and torture, while an aide's arm is severed—offscreen—via chainsaw. Documentary filmmaker Steve Kaye (Nigel Havers), on a worldwide ecological crusade, shows up and records Chico's unsuccessful run for government office. Chico loses the campaign (opponents buy votes with free chainsaws) but, thanks to Kaye, becomes an international celebrity and "Green" icon. The media spotlight eventually forces Galvao to backpedal over the issue of defoliation and swallow his losses. Unwilling to bend with shifting political winds like the power-brokers who used him, Alves orders Chico's death. Refusing to flee, Chico is fatally gunned down by Alves's son. Part of Brazil's rain forests become a protected sanctuary in Mendes's memory, while systematic denuding of land continues in other areas along the Amazon.

Like so many earnest TV productions, THE BURNING SEASON is strictiy on the side of the angels with no let-up or room for disagreement. One can wholeheartedly endorse saving the trees and still wish that not everyone on the opposing side were characterized in agitprop terms. Don't ranchers need to make a living too? Alves, according to Andrew Revkin's source book, was a thug who considered himself beyond the law, but director Frankenheimer grants him the full Emperor Nero treatment in a gratuitous orgy sequence.

What enables THE BURNING SEASON to surmount its cliches and shorthand characterizations is Julia's incendiary performance, the last before his early death. Although it's painful to observe this robust actor in visibly terminal straits, he burns up the screen, fleshing out the martyred hero beyond the dimensions of a script which sometimes seem to have an agenda at variance to the facts. THE BURNING SEASON's most scorching moment, in fact, is Mendes's blowup at Kaye (a character based on the real-life Adrian Cowell) at a gaudy Miami fundraiser; he senses himself co-opted by trendy tree-huggers wholly ignorant about peasant rubber-tappers and their welfare. Thus the pic's concluding, heavy-handed voiceover recitation of rain-forest holocausts ill befits the more complex, politicized Mendes glimpsed earlier.

At its best, THE BURNING SEASON overwhelms us with the David-vs-Goliath dimensions of its hero's apparently hopeless struggle to defang a monster called Big Business that swallows forests whole. *(Violence, profanity, nudity, sexual situations, adult situations.)* — R.P.

d, John Frankenheimer; p, Thomas M. Hammel, John Frankenheimer; exec p, David Putnam; co-p, Diane Smith; w, William Mastrosimone, Michael Tolkin, Ron Hutchinson (from a story by William Mastrosimone, based upon the books *The Burning Season* by Andrew Revkin and *Decade of Destruction* by Adrian Cowell); ph, John R. Leonetti; ed, Paul Rubell, Francoise Bonnot; m, Gary Chang; prod d, Michael Z. Hanan; art d, Charles Lagola, Theresa Wachter; sound, Glen Trew; casting, Owens Hill, Junie Lowry-Johnson; cos, Ray Summers

Drama/Biography/Political (PR: C MPAA: NR)

BURNT BY THE SUN ★★★

(Russia/France) 134m Studio Trite; Camera One;
Canal Plus ~ Sony Pictures Classics c
(UTOMLENNYE SOLNTSEM)

Nikita Mikhalkov *(Serguei Petrovitch Kotov)*; Oleg Menchikov *(Dimitri (Mitia))*; Ingeborga Dapkunaite *(Maroussia)*; Nadia Mikhalkov *(Nadia)*; Andre Umansky *(Philippe)*; Viacheslav Tikhonov *(Vsevolod Konstantinovich)*; Svetlana Kriuchkova *(Mokhova)*; Vladimir Ilyin *(Kirik)*; Alla Kazanskaia; Nina Arkhipova *(Elena Mikhailovna)*; Avangard Leontiev *(Driver)*; Inna Ulianova *(Olga Nikolaevna)*; Liubov Rudneva *(Liuba)*; Vladimir Riabov *(NKVD Officer)*; Vladimir Belousov *(NKVD Man)*; Aleksei Pokatilov *(NKVD Man)*; Evgenii Mironov *(Lieutenant)*

Joseph Stalin's purges, which claimed the lives of hundreds of thousands of Russians—including countless loyal Communist Party members—form the backdrop for BURNT BY THE SUN, which won the 1994 Academy Award for Best Foreign Language Film.

Set in 1936, it examines one fateful day in the life of aging war hero Colonel Serguei Petrovich Kotov (Nikita Mikhalkov). The bear-like Kotov lives in the country dacha of his adoring and much younger wife Maroussia's (Ingeborga Dapkounaite) family, and wields considerable local power. Though a staunch Communist party member, Kotov's loyalty is tempered by human decency and common sense. He doesn't hesitate to halt military maneuvers that threaten the village's crops, and his in-laws include elderly survivors of the old regime whose lack of familiarity with the lore and slogans of the new Russia he treats with benign tolerance. Kotov also dotes on his small daughter, Nadia (Nadia Mikhalkov). The day is disrupted by the unexpected arrival of Mitia (Oleg Menchikov), an old friend of the family. Slowly we learn the details of Mitia's past: He was Maroussia's fiance—she attempted suicide after he disappeared—and studied music with her father. Kotov welcomes him, and Mitia joins the family for an idyllic day at the lake.

Later, back at the house, Mitia blurts out a terrible secret to a drunken guest: He's working for Stalin's political police. Mitia then laughs off the revelation as a joke, but a shot of a big, black Packard waiting on a country lane assures the viewer that it isn't

We learn that Mitia supported the White Russians in the Revolution of 1917, and that Kotov was instrumental in forcing him to leave Russia after the Bolsheviks took power—the lovable Kotov was not above using his political power to solve his personal problems. Kotov confronts Mitia in private, and Mitia admits that he was an agent for the secret police in Paris and helped betray former Czarist generals. He has finally been allowed to return to Russia, but the price is Kotov's betrayal. Kotov realizes that he is doomed, and says his veiled farewells to Maroussia and Nadia, who have no idea that they are spending their last hours with him. The Packard pulls up and Kotov climbs in. Nadia clamors to be allowed to ride with her father, who gently sends her back to her mother. After the car has pulled away, Kotov is brutally beaten and executed. Mitia returns home and commits suicide. A printed epilogue informs us that Maroussia and Nadia were later arrested and imprisoned.

The title alludes to the "burning sun" of the Russian Revolution, and Mikhalov's film deals with a wide range of characters whose lives are damaged or destroyed by it. BURNT BY THE SUN is clearly a very personal project: He co-produced, played the lead and cast his own six-year-old daughter—a first-time actress with astonishingly unforced charm—as Kotov's little girl. But it is not a subtle film, and ultimately has very little to say beyond that people do terrible things for petty reasons and life is awfully unfair.

BURNT BY THE SUN is deliberately slow moving, and the contrast between the languorous day of meals, boating at the lake and conversation with friends and relatives and the brutal suddenness with which Kotov is snatched away and murdered is chilling. The idyllic, lushly photographed setting provides a bluntly ironic contrast to the vicious treachery committed by Mitia and, by extension, the Stalinist government that ruthlessly mowed down so many of its citizens in the name of progress and political expediency. Perhaps the most interesting thing about BURNT BY THE SUN is that Kotov is a genuine hero of the Revolution, and his faith in communist ideals is never really undermined: The trouble with communism, Mikhalov implies, is communists like Stalin, who perverted the ideals of the Revolution to their own personal ends. *(Adult situations, profanity, sexual situations, nudity, violence.)* — L.R.

d, Nikita Mikhalkov; p, Nikita Mikhalkov, Michel Seydoux; exec p, Leonid Vereshchagin, Jean-Louis Piel, Vladimir Sedov; assoc p, Nikita Mikhalkov, Michel Seydoux; co-p, Nicole Cann, Jean-Louis Piel, Vladimir Sedov; w, Nikita Mikhalkov, Rustam Ibragimbekov (from a story by Nikita Mikhalkov); ph, Vilen Kaliuta; ed, Enzo Meniconi; m, Eduard Artemiev; art d, Vladimir Aronin, Alexandre Samulekine; sound, Jean Umansky, Andre Rigaut, Vincent Arnardi (mixer), Thierry Lebon (mixer); casting, Tamara Odintsova; cos, Natalia Ivanova; makeup, Larissa Avdiushko

Drama/Historical/Political   (PR: C   MPAA: R)

BUSHWHACKED   ★
(U.S.) 90m 20th Century Fox ~ 20th Century Fox c
(AKA: TENDERFOOT, THE)

Daniel Stern (*Max Grabelski*); Jon Polito (*Agent Palmer*); Brad Sullivan (*Jack Erickson*); Ann Dowd (*Mrs. Patterson*); Anthony Heald (*Bragdon*); Tom Wood (*Agent McMurrey*); Blake Bashoff (*Gordy*); Corey Carrier (*Ralph*); Michael Galeota (*Dana*); Max Goldblatt (*Barnhill*); Ari Greenberg (*Fishman*); Janna Michaels

(*Kelsey Jordan*); Natalie West (*Mrs. Fishman*); Michael P. Byrne (*Mr. Fishman*); Michael O'Neill (*Jon Jordan*); Jane Morris (*Beth Jordan*); Christopher Curry (*Trooper*); Kenneth Johnson (*State Patrolman*); Robert Donley (*Proprietor*); Sue Kwon (*TV Newscaster*); Reed Clark Means (*Kid*); Harley Kelsey (*Forest Ranger*); Cesarina Vaughn (*Business Woman*); Cory Buck (*Tricycle Kid*); Theodor Scott Owens (*Business Man*)

A fish-out-of-water kiddie comedy that dumps former CITY SLICKER Daniel Stern into the great outdoors and dares him to find a gag that hasn't yet been done to death, BUSHWHACKED is predictable, crude and sentimental all at once.

Max Grabalski (Stern), a dim-witted and boorish driver for an express delivery company, carries a box full of money to a banker's home. There, a rogue FBI agent (Jon Polito) frames him for murder. Mistaken for the Scout leader whose Land Rover he has stolen, he is compelled to take a gang of motley "Ranger Scouts" on a camp-out; the kids interpret his every attempt to lose them as challenges to their Scouting ability.

The kids are familiar types: the Den Mother's Son (Blake Bashoff), the Fat Kid (Max Goldblatt), the Wise Ass (Corey Carrier), the Little Guy (Michael Galeota), the Smart Kid Who Keeps Quoting the Guide Book (Ari Greenberg) and, this being the '90s, the Girl (Janna Michaels). Along the trail, Max gets mauled by a bear and attacked by bees, also finding time to drink a bottle of bug repellent and abuse the kids in various ways. On the plus side, he teaches them to urinate in unison and sing songs with naughty words. The camping trip turns into a predictably twisty chase, with the kids first catching Max, then rescuing him when they discover he's merely a dupe. Max himself foils the bad guys, rescues the Den Mother (Ann Dowd) and then her son.

Although the screenplay, based on a story by co-writers John Jordan and Danny Byers, was doctored by the respected team of Tommy Swerdlow and Michael Goldberg (LITTLE GIANTS, COOL RUNNINGS), it remains singularly vulgar and unfunny. A typical laugh line has a three-year-old announcing, "I gotta make a dookie." Kids are not likely to find this film entertaining, and adults who willingly let them watch it should be reprimanded and sent to bed without supper. *(Profanity.)*

d, Greg Beeman; p, Charles B. Wessler, Paul Schiff; exec p, Daniel Stern; co-p, David Wisnievitz; w, John Jordan, Danny Byers, Tommy Swerdlow, Michael Goldberg (from a story by John Jordan and Danny Byers); ph, Theo Van de Sande; ed, Ross Albert; m, Bill Conti; prod d, Mark W. Mansbridge, Sandy Veneziano; art d, Bruce Crone; set d, Joe Mitchell; sound, Tim Cooney (mixer); fx, John Richardson, Mat Beck, Chris Evans; casting, Linda Lowy, John Brace; cos, Mary Zophres; makeup, Angela Moos

Comedy   (PR: A   MPAA: PG-13)

BUSINESS AFFAIR, A   ★★½
(France/U.K./Germany/Spain) 101m Osby Films; Film & General Prods.; Connexion Films; Cartel Films ~ Castle Hill c
(D'UNE FEMME A L'AUTRE)

Christopher Walken (*Vanni Corso*); Carole Bouquet (*Kate Swallow*); Jonathan Pryce (*Alec Bolton*); Sheila Hancock (*Judith*); Anna Manahan (*Bianca*); Fernando Guillen Guervo (*Angel*); Tom Wilkinson (*Bob*); Marisa Benlloch (*Carmen*); Paul Bentall (*Drunken Man*); Bhasker (*Jaboul*); Roger Brierly (*Barrister*); Allan Corduner (*Dinner Guest*); Marian McLoughlin (*Dinner Guest*); Miguel DeAngel (*Spanish Taxi Driver*); Christopher Driscoll (*Policeman*); Beth Goddard (*Student*); Fergus O'Donnell (*Student*); Richard Hampton (*Doctor*); Togo Igawa (*Japanese Golfer*); Susan Kyd (*Fawn*); Annabel Leventon (*Literary Guest*); Patti Love (*Prostitute*); Simon McBurney (*Salesman*);

Usha Patel *(Indian Woman)*; Natalie Sherman *(Indian Woman)*; Geraldine Somerville *(Saleswoman)*; William Stadiem *(William King)*; Robert Swann *(Maitre d')*; Peter Van Dissel *(Boat Guest)*; Jerome Willis *(Moderator)*; Alfonso Galan *(Bullfighter)*

A BUSINESS AFFAIR is a love triangle melodrama masquerading as a Continental comedy.

The events in the film take place in contemporary London, where Kate Swallow (Carole Bouquet) and her husband, Alec Bolton (Jonathan Pryce), live and work, he on his "great novel," and she as a model at Harrods department store. Bolton becomes jealous when Swallow quits her job to write her own novel, completes her book before he finishes his, and secures a contract from his agent, Vanni Corso (Christopher Walken), a visiting American. Meanwhile, Corso, who has more amorous than literary interest in Swallow, plots an all-out campaign to win her over, despite his inevitable loss of Bolton as a top client.

In a move to derail both her writing career and her love affair, Bolton proposes that Swallow bear a child. Swallow agrees happily, but loses the baby some months later. When she eventually figures out what had motivated Bolton to start a family, she divorces him and commences her affair with Corso. Corso then publishes Swallow's book and proposes marriage; but for Swallow the new relationship too turns sour when she realizes that Corso, jealous of her writing talent, has deliberately prevented her follow-up novel from being published. When Corso accuses Swallow of secretly dating Bolton, Swallow moves out of Corso's house to her own apartment, and finds a new publisher. Soon, her most recent work is published to great acclaim, and Bolton tries to win her back. Swallow indicates that she may after all reunite with her ex-husband.

Carole Bouquet's cool beauty has been well employed in a handful of off-beat films over the years, in addition to her more recent commercials for Chanel perfume. Luis Bunuel used her best as one-half of the temptress character in THAT OBSCURE OBJECT OF DESIRE, Bouquet's 1977 debut, and she was also just the right choice for the ice queen bride in Bertrand Blier's TOO BEAUTIFUL FOR YOU in 1990. In A BUSINESS AFFAIR, however, Bouquet is elegantly gowned but poorly cast as a naive, even masochistic woman. Her fierce, quiet intelligence never meshes well with the part of a woman who would get involved with two obnoxious men so obviously beneath her station in life.

The casting of Christopher Walken is also a problem. It is hard to believe that this crass, selfish, businessman would willingly sabotage his career for a woman. Only Pryce seems right as the arrogant husband, but Pryce is so good at being despicable that his performance highlights the main problem with the film: why did a smart, gifted woman ever marry such a man in the first place?

A BUSINESS AFFAIR is a cross between a Joan Crawford soap opera and a remake of the 1963 comedy, CRITIC'S CHOICE, which also pitted a professional author husband against his amateur author wife. But A BUSINESS AFFAIR is neither funny nor moving: it suffers from slow pacing, awkward editing, and dark, natural lighting, which both mutes the farcical elements and accentuates all unrealistic twists and turns. Fortunately, it is too minor a film to disappoint anyone greatly. *(Nudity, sexual situations, adult situations, profanity.)* — E.M.

d, Charlotte Brandstrom; p, Xavier Larere, Clive Parsons, Davina Belling; exec p, Martha Wansbrough, Willi Baer; assoc p, Diana Costes Brook; w, William Stadiem (from a story by William Stadiem and Charlotte Brandstrom, inspired by the books *Tears Before Bedtime* and *Weep No More* by Barbara Skelton); ph, Willy Kurant; ed, Laurence Mery-Clark; m, Didier Vasseur; prod d, Sophie Becher; art d, Kave Naylor; sound, Chris Munro

(mixer); casting, Simone Reynolds; cos, Tom Rand; makeup, Morag Ross

Comedy/Drama/Romance   **(PR: C   MPAA: NR)**

BYE BYE, LOVE   ★★½
(U.S.) 106m 20th Century Fox ~ 20th Century Fox c

Matthew Modine *(Dave)*; Randy Quaid *(Vic)*; Paul Reiser *(Donny)*; Janeane Garofalo *(Lucille)*; Amy Brenneman *(Susan)*; Eliza Dushku *(Emma)*; Ed Flanders *(Walter)*; Rob Reiner *(Dr. David Townsend)*; Maria Pitillo *(Kim)*; Lindsay Crouse *(Grace)*; Ross Malinger *(Ben)*; Johnny Whitworth *(Max)*; Wendell Pierce *(Hector)*; Cameron Boyd *(Jed)*; Mae Whitman *(Michele)*; Jayne Brooke *(Claire)*; Dana Wheeler-Nicholson *(Heidi)*; Amber Benson *(Meg)*; Pamela Dillman *(Sheila)*; Brad Hall *(Phil)*; Danny Masterson *(Mikey)*; James Arone *(Waiter in Italian Restaurant)*; Karlie M. Gavino Brown *(Lindsay)*; Kirstie R. Gavino Brown *(Lindsay)*; Marguerite Weisman *(Sarah)*; Max Ryan Ornstein *(Ring Bearer at Wedding)*; Dean Williams *(Wedding Photographer)*; Caroline Lagerfelt *(Mother No. 1 at McDonald's)*; Christopher Curry *(Father No. 1 at McDonald's)*; Daniel Weisman *(Boy at McDonald's)*; Stephanie Shroyer *(Mother No. 2 at McDonald's)*; Michael Bofshever *(Dad No. 2 at McDonald's)*; Christina Massari *(Girl at McDonald's)*; Brian Frank *(Screener)*; Shang Forbes *(Engineer)*; T.K. Meehan *(T-Ball Coach)*; Mina Kolb *(Dorothy)*; Geoffrey Woodhall *(Gerald)*; Michael Spound *(Mike)*; Joe Basile *(Father No. 1 Dad's Day Out)*; Dennis Bowen *(Father No. 2 Dad's Day Out)*; Donald Bishop *(Grandfather)*; Kate Williamson *(Grandmother)*; Nicholas Davey *(Heidi's Son)*; Justin Garms *(Sheila's Son)*; Lauren Kopit *(Sheila's Daughter)*; Jack Black *(DJ at Party)*; Keaton Simons *(Party Dude)*; Juney Smith *(Security Guard)*

A trio of divorced fathers with weekend custody of their kids inhabit this amiable comedy which offers plenty of laughs and even a few points to ponder. Many of the complications the men encounter are universal, but each has a different outlook on his situation: Vic (Randy Quaid) is the mad dad; Donny (Paul Reiser) is the sad dad; and Dave (Matthew Modine) is dad the cad.

The action takes place over the course of one weekend, and begins with the ritual exchange of kids on neutral territory: McDonald's. Dave's weekend is off to a bumpy start when his girlfriend Kim (Maria Pitillo) shows up at the exchange, inciting the wrath of his ex-wife Susan (Amy Brenneman). Vic's dealings with his ex, Grace (Lindsay Crouse), are invariably hostile. In contrast to his buddies, Donny enjoys a congenial relationship with his ex-wife Claire (Jayne Brook), for whom he evidently still pines. However, Donny's relationship with his 14-year-old daughter Emma (Eliza Dushku) is less harmonious. Emma would rather spend the weekend with her friends than her Dad, from whom she has grown distant.

The weekend begins benignly enough with group outings, recipe exchanges, and Little League games. By night number two, though, the tensions brewing between the fathers, kids, ex-wives, and girlfriends simultaneously erupt. Donny spends a lonely evening spying on his remarried ex-wife, despairing over his strained relationship with Emma, and commiserating with Dave's ex-wife, Susan. When his relationship with Susan takes a romantic turn, he races to Dave to ask his buddy's advice. Vic's interminable blind date with Lucille (Janeane Garofalo), a neurotic feminist, also leads him to Dave's doorstep, where a romantic evening between Dave and Kim has turned disastrous because of the separate arrival of two attractive divorcees, armed with kids and casseroles.

Interspersed between the episodes of the fathers, kids, and ex-wives are subplots involving the relationship between Walter, an elderly McDonald's employee (Ed Flanders, in his last screen role), and his teenaged boss, Max (Johnny Whitworth), and words of questionable wisdom from radio psychologist Dr. David Townsend (Rob Reiner). However, the best advice comes from the Dads themselves, who have learned that the best way to cope is to "love your kids and keep going."

With a huge cast of characters, BYE BYE, LOVE explores divorce and shared custody from several different viewpoints, much like the 1989 comedy PARENTHOOD tackled its subject. A good film, BYE BYE, LOVE would have made a better sitcom. In addition to star Reiser's small screen success ("Mad About You"), the film boasts a creative team with top flight television credits. Gary David Goldberg, creator and producer of "Family Ties" and "Brooklyn Bridge," co-produced BYE BYE, LOVE with his "Brooklyn Bridge" alumni Sam Weisman and Brad Hall. Goldberg and Hall co-wrote the script, which was inspired by an actual McDonald's which became a mecca for divorced parents to exchange weekend custody of their children. Building on this premise, Goldberg and Hall have included a wealth of anecdotes about divorce, American style. Its undeniable sitcom-like style may explain why BYE BYE, LOVE said bye-bye at the box office sooner than it deserved. With admission prices escalating, filmgoers tend to avoid films which resemble the television fare they may watch for free.

Reiser gives the most multi-dimensional performance. Donny's longing for his former life and former wife, his struggles with a resentful daughter, and his conflicting feelings of loyalty to his best friend and desire for the friend's ex-wife give the movie its heart. It's a winning performance that adds a new dimension to Reiser's popularity. Quaid scores the best punchlines, but his character's explosive anger becomes tiresome. Modine's playboy doesn't earn much sympathy, but may inspire the jealousy of bachelors less successful at playing the field. Of the gaggle of kids, Eliza Dushku (TRUE LIES) has the largest role, but gives the weakest performance. Her character's sudden change of heart at the film's climax is unconvincing and leaves Reiser with little to play against. The sub-plot involving Flanders and Whitworth is superfluous and only serves to keep the action from straying too far from those inspirational golden arches of McDonalds. *(Sexual situations, profanity.)* — B.R.

d, Sam Weisman; p, Gary David Goldberg, Brad Hall, Sam Weisman; assoc p, Jimmy Simons; co-p, Michael MacDonald; w, Gary David Goldberg, Brad Hall; ph, Kenneth Zunder; ed, Roger Bondelli; m, J.A.C. Redford; prod d, Linda DeScenna; art d, Greg Papalia; set d, Ric McElvin; sound, Robert L. Sephton (supervising mixer), David Kelson (mixer); makeup, Steve Abrums; stunts, James M. Halty

Comedy/Romance (PR: A MPAA: PG-13)

CAGED HEARTS

(U.S.) 90m c

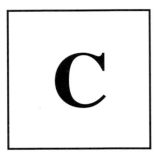

Carrie Genzel *(Kate Paris)*; Tane McClure *(Sharon O'Neal)*; Taylor Leigh *(Warden McBride)*; Nick Wilder *(Steve)*; Dink O'Neal *(George)*; Brent Keast *(Judge Winters)*; Tony Sorensen *(Stuart)*; Doug Traer *(Lt. Hill)*; Trisha Berdot *(Lisa)*; Lenny Rose *(Captain Rey)*; Chloe Cross *(Christine)*; Deborah Holness *(Nina)*

Lock out this women-in-prison specimen.

Realtor/actress Kate (Carrie Genzel) and simulated blonde Sharon (Tane McClure) follow their aerobics class with incarceration when they are accosted by a drunken ex-boyfriend and accidentally shoot him. They are convicted of premeditated murder, due mainly to their court-appointed lawyer's eagerness to join The Shield, a secret society that manipulates the judicial system to stock its own private brothel. This is, of course, Bimbo State Correctional facility, where inmates wear skimpy denim minidresses and $150 sneakers—that is when they're not sitting around naked being "examined" by male guards or assaulting each other in the shower (how do they get tan lines in the hoosegow?). Dominatrix/Warden McBride (Taylor Leigh) tries to soften Karen and Sharon up for The Hotel by putting them in The Pit, a cinderblock dorm ruled by the throaty Lisa (Trisha Berdot). Our suffering heroines end up turning tricks, the first of which is none other than their former lawyer. They manage to convince him of their innocence, and with the absurd intervention of Eurohunk kickboxer Stuart (Tonny Sorensen), the Shield is cracked, the girls rescued, and they Dancercise happily ever after.

Idiotic plotting and cinematic ineptitude aside, CAGED HEARTS commits the cardinal sin of sexploitation: it's dull. A somnambulistic pace and leaden acting create long stretches of utter boredom; one longs for some prurience just to relieve the monotony. But the ensuing soft-core orgies of viciousness have no sense of fun, so steeped are they in cruelty. The genre's ever-reliable catfights feature closed-fisted slugging, and sex scenes verge on rape. This trivialization of brutality is disturbing. Most embarrassing is the inexplicable appearance of Sorensen, who comes off as a sort of Jean Claude van Darn. Those looking for cheap thrills will find this direct-to-video turkey inadequate. Those looking for anything else will be looking elsewhere in the first place. *(Extensive nudity, profanity, sexual situations.)* — R.S.

d, Henri Charr; p, Jess Mancilla; exec p, Henri Charr; w, Taesung Yim (from a story by Henri Charr and Jess Mancilla); ph, Helga Gerull; ed, Henri Charr, Jess Mancilla; m, Larry Wolf; prod d, Frank Kia; casting, Taylor Leigh; cos, Joan Francis

Erotic/Prison (PR: O MPAA: NR)

CAGED HEAT 3000

(U.S.) 84m Concorde-New Horizons Corp. ~ New Horizons Home Video c

Cassandra Leigh *(Kira Murphy)*; Kena Land *(Daly)*; Debra Beatty *(Billie)*; Charles Moore

CAGED HEAT 3000 transplants the standard elements of a women-in-prison picture to the year 3000 AD, when a huge women's prison has been constructed underground on an uninhabitable asteroid 45 million light years from Earth. Despite the possibilities that could be teased out of such an absurd variation on the genre, CAGED HEAT 3000 never rises above humorless exploitation.

Kira Murphy (Cassandra Leigh) makes up for having been wrongly imprisoned by brutally murdering an inmate who dealt drugs to other prisoners and allowed guards to rape and kill a young friend of hers. Hoping to exploit racial tension and Kira's violent temper, prison officials transfer her to high security where she shares a cell with Daly (Kena Land), a Black activist lawyer who is loathed by the officials.

White inmates led by Billie (Debra Beatty) try to befriend Kira, but she refuses to join their racist gang, and inflicts some serious casualties when she takes them on single-handedly in the prison gym. In retaliation, Billie forms an alliance with the Black gang and plots a killing spree designed to end in Kira's death. Daly makes a last ditch effort to convince both gangs to end the violence, and barely escapes with her life. Prison administrators, distracted by visiting journalists, are unable to control the ensuing riot. In the chaos, inmates are able to tell the press about conditions at the prison. When Daly is released, Kira promises to stay out of trouble for the remainder of her sentence, and it is announced that prison officials have been indicted for mistreatment of prisoners.

Except for languid showers enjoyed by the inmates, most of the intended eroticism of the film is undermined by rape and torture scenes that not even the sadistic guards seem to enjoy. The acting is largely amateurish and the action indifferently blocked (many of the fight scenes take place in clumsy silhouette). Only the brightly-hued sets—which forego realism for a slick, if hokey, futurism—provide small respite from the mean-spiritedness of CAGED HEAT 3000. If only the story—and the acting, for that matter—had likewise been able to do so much with so little. *(Violence, extensive nudity, sexual situations, profanity.)* — C.Ch.

d, Cirio Santiago; exec p, Mike Elliot; w, Paul Ziller

Prison/Science Fiction/Erotic (PR: O MPAA: R)

CANADIAN BACON ★★

(U.S.) 90m PolyGram; Propaganda Films; Maverick Picture Company ~ Gramercy c

Alan Alda *(President of the United States)*; John Candy *(Bud B. Boomer)*; Rhea Perlman *(Deputy Honey)*; Kevin Pollak *(Stu Smiley)*; Rip Torn *(General Dick Panzer)*; Kevin J. O'Connor *(Roy Boy)*; Bill Nunn *(Kabral)*; G.D. Spradlin *(R.J. Hacker)*; Steven Wright *(Niagara Mountie)*; James Belushi *(Charles Jackal)*; Brad Sullivan *(Gus)*; Stanley Anderson *(Edwin S. Simon)*; Richard Council *(Russian President)*; Michael Copeman *(Panzer's Aide)*; Bruce Hunter *(President's Aide)*; Beth Amos *(Ruthie)*; Jack Mather *(Pops)*; Kenner Ames *(Mountie Sergeant)*; Roger Dunn *(Mountie Major)*; Natalie Rose *(Toronto Kid)*; Michael Woods *(State Trooper #1)*; Matt Cooke *(State Trooper #2)*; Barbara Schroeder *(Newswoman)*; Tara Meyer *(Candy Striper #1)*; Fab Filippo *(Candy Striper #2)*; Carlton Watson *(Clarence Thomason)*; Stan Coles *(Secretary of State)*; Adrian Hough *(Russian Aide)*; Bryan Armstrong *(Auctioneer)*; Kelsey Binder Moore *(Ice Cream Girl #1)*; Leah Binder Moore *(Ice Cream Girl #2)*; Wally Bolland *(Special Ops Soldier)*; Marcos Parilo *(Omega Force Leader)*; Jim Czarnecki *(Snake)*; Tony Proffer *(Dell)*; Ben Hamper *(Redneck Guy #1)*; Michael Moore *(Redneck Guy #2)*; Linda Genovesi *(Polite Canadian Woman)*; Sheila Gray *(Voice of Hacker Hellstorm)*; Dana Brooks *(Paulette Kalin)*

Some say it was politics that kept Michael Moore's first fiction feature on the shelf for several years; others insist it was purely a matter of the film's dubious commercial appeal. It would be gratifying to report that CANADIAN BACON, released at last in 1995, turned out to be a neglected classic, but it's a misconceived jumble, brightened intermittently by moments of politcal insight and a few successful gags.

The people of Niagara Falls, NY are unhappy about the closing of a local defense plant, thanks to the end of the Cold War. When the President (Alan Alda) arrives in town to speak at the plant, his security advisor Stu Smiley (Kevin Pollak) is admonished by the plant's owner, R.J. Hacker (G.D. Spradlin), to come up with a new enemy—or else. To boost the President's sagging popularity, Smiley recommends a war, or at least some sort of conflict with a foreign country. Soon after, Niagara Falls Sheriff Bud Boomer (John Candy) starts a brawl at a hockey game when he makes a disparaging comment about Canadian beer. This gives the President and his staff a brainstorm: Canada will become the new threat to US security.

In an act of patriotic aggression, Boomer and his deputy, Honey (Rhea Perlman), sneak across the border to dump garbage, but Honey is accidentally left behind and captured by Canadian authorities. Anti-Canadian frenzy is whipped up by the President, the angry Niagara locals, and the media, who dub the new hostility "Operation Canadian Bacon: A Line in the Snow." When Hacker begins to plan an all-out war, the PR gimmick threatens to become Armageddon, but the apocalypse is averted thanks to Honey and Boomer.

CANADIAN BACON's premise is rife with comic possibilities, but it's too choppy and unfocused to succeed as political satire. To put it mildly, it's no DR. STRANGELOVE (which it emulates shamelessly); it's not even BOB ROBERTS. Its broad approach works toward the beginning, as the plant auctions off its unused warheads and missiles to civilians, and there are some genuinely funny bits playing off the media's gung-ho war coverage and the politeness of the Canadians: at one point, Boomer's truck is pulled over by a Canadian cop (Dan Aykroyd) who informs him the anti-Canadian graffiti on his truck should be rendered bilingually.

But most of the satire is thuddingly obvious (it was also badly dated by the time the film hit theaters; the Gulf War references felt like ancient history in 1995). Moreover, there isn't much character development, which hinders the plot; we're never sure whether the President is a nice guy caught in an out-of-control situation, or a total boob led around by his advisors. The film certainly doesn't look like esteemed cinematographer Haskell Wexler had anything to do with it, and seems thrown together, especially in its last half-hour. One wonders what Moore (ROGER & ME) might have done with some help from outside writers and a tighter script. (Profanity.)

d, Michael Moore; p, Michael Moore, David Brown, Ron Rotholz, Steve Golin; exec p, Freddy De Mann, Sigurjon Sighvatsson; assoc p, Terry Miller; co-p, Kathleen Glynn; w, Michael Moore; ph, Haskell Wexler; ed, Wendy Stanzler; m, Elmer Bernstein, Peter Bernstein; prod d, Carol Spier; art d, Tamara Deverell; set d, Carol Lavoie; sound, Douglas Ganton (mixer), Keith Cultherbert (recordist), Ted Clark (recordist), Harry Higgins (recordist); fx, Bob Hall, Arthur Langevin, Trans Image Special Effects; casting, Lynn Kressell; cos, Kathleen Glynn; makeup, Katherine Southern; stunts, Branko Racki

Political/Comedy   **(PR: A   MPAA: PG)**

CANDYMAN: FAREWELL TO THE FLESH   ★½
(U.S.) 94m Propaganda Films ~ Gramercy Pictures c

Tony Todd (*Candyman/Daniel Robitaille*); Kelly Rowan (*Annie Tarrant*); Timothy Carhart (*Paul McKeever*); Veronica Cartwright (*Octavia Tarrant*); William O'Leary (*Ethan Tarrant*); Fay Hauser (*Pam Carver*); Bill Nunn (*Reverend Ellis*); Matt Clark (*Honore Thibideaux*); David Gianopoulos (*Det. Ray Levesque*);

Joshua Gibran Mayweather (*Matthew Ellis*); Caroline Barclay (*Caroline Sullivan*); Michael Bergeron (*Coleman Tarrant*); Brianna Blanchard (*Young Caroline*); George Lemore (*Drew*); Margaret Howell (*Clara*); Ralph Joseph (*Mr. Jeffries*); Clotiel Bordeltier (*Liz*); Michael Culkin (*Phillip Purcell*); Randy Oglesby (*Heyward Sullivan*); Erin Labranche (*Little Girl Doctor*); Carl Leblanc (*Little Boy King*); Maria Mason (*Befuddled Teacher*); Brian Joseph Moore (*Thug #1*); Stephen Dunn (*Thug #2*); Glen Gomez (*Kingfish*); Russell Buchanan (*Voice of Kingfish*); Steven Hartman (*Young Boy*); Carl N. Ciafalio (*Bartender*); Eric Pierson (*Ben the Busboy*); Terrence Rosemore (*Suspicious Man at Matthew's House*); Carol Sutton (*Angry Woman at Matthew's House*); Amy Ryder (*Hostile Woman at Cabrini Green*); Hunt Scarritt (*Scraggly Vagrant*); Eric Cadora (*Man in Bookstore*); Sandy Bird (*1st Woman in Bookstore*); Patricia Sansone (*2nd Woman in Bookstore*); Steve Picerni (*Police Guard*); Daniel Dupont (*Reporter #1*); Nate Bynum (*Reporter #2*); Monica L. Monica (*Reporter #3*)

This lackluster sequel forgoes everything that made the original a superior horror film in favor of simplistic genre cliches.

After a confrontation with New Orleans local Ethan Tarrant (William O'Leary), history professor Phillip Purcell (Michael Culkin) is murdered by Candyman (Tony Todd), a deadly spirit about whom Purcell has lectured. Ethan's father fell victim to a similar death, and Ethan is charged with the crime; his sister, schoolteacher Annie (Kelly Rowan), is unnerved when one of her students, Matthew (Joshua Gibran Mayweather), begins repeatedly drawing Candyman. In order to reassure her kids that Candyman is only a legend, she repeats his name five times into a mirror—the manner, according to legend, by which he can be summoned. Nothing happens at first, but that night Candyman butchers Annie's husband, Paul (Timothy Carhart), and entices her to join him in his legend.

She refuses, and begins to seek the truth about Candyman's past. From Honore Thibideaux (Matt Clark), an expert on local history, and her own mother, Octavia (Veronica Cartwright), Annie learns that Candyman is the spirit of a slave who was murdered for conducting a forbidden affair with a white woman; that woman was Annie's great-grandmother. Candyman slaughters Thibideaux, Ethan, and Octavia, and Annie goes to her family's ancestral home in the midst of a torrential storm to seek the mirror that contains Candyman's spirit. She finds it, and the killer appears, again attempting to seduce her into joining him. But before he can, Matthew and several schoolmates arrive to help her. Annie smashes the glass, destroying Candyman. Four years later, her little daughter looks into a mirror and begins to repeat Candyman's name.

One of the key elements that separated Bernard Rose's original CANDYMAN (1992) from most run-of-the-mill slasher movies was its unique and well-developed mythology (derived from Clive Barker's story "The Forbidden"). That film's Candyman was a being who lived in legend, and appeared in the real world only to strike down those who would deny his reality and attack the superstitious belief that allowed him to "live." CANDYMAN: FAREWELL TO THE FELSH dispenses with this intriguing idea to make him just another vengeful phantom, haunting the young heroine who, in a tired and predictable plot twist, turns out to be his descendant. The story on the whole is unsurprising and schematic, making it abundantly easy to guess who will fall victim to Candyman's hook and when.

As opposed to the gutsy, driven researcher played by the first film's Virginia Madsen, Annie is a wan and unremarkable protagonist both as written and as played by Rowan. Although director Bill Condon manages a genuinely exciting climax, his attempts to goose up the movie's first half with an endless series of cheap false scares make matters worse, provoking more annoyance than suspense. (Some reviewers also criticized his reliance on the sudden appearances by black men, who are mistaken for Candyman, for these jolts.) Philip Glass's music, such an integral element of the original's ethereal mood, seems out of place backing such schlocky material. (Graphic violence, profanity.) — M.G.

d, Bill Condon; p, Joni Sighvatsson, Steve Golin, Gregg D. Feinberg; exec p, Clive Barker; assoc p, Anna C. Miller; w, Rand Ravich, Mark Kruger (from a story by Clive Barker); ph, Tobias Schliesser; ed, Virginia Katz; m, Philip Glass; prod d, Barry Robison; art d, Dawn Snyder Stebler; set d, Suzette Sheets; sound, Walter Hoylman (mixer), Ben Wilkins (design); fx, John Hartigan, Ultimate Effects; casting, Carol Lewis; cos, Bruce Finlayson; makeup, Sheri P. Short, Makeup Effects Lab; stunts, William Washington

Horror　　　　　　　　　　　　**(PR: O　MPAA: R)**

CARMEN MIRANDA: BANANAS IS　　★★★½
MY BUSINESS

(U.S./Brazil) 90m International Cinema; Corporation for Public Broadcasting; Channel Four; National Latino Communications Center; Radio Televisao Portuguesa ~ International Cinema c

Helena Solberg (Narrator); Cynthia Adler (Luella Hopper); Erick Barreto (Carmen Miranda—fantasy sequences); Leticia Monte (Carmen Miranda as a Teenager); Roger Baker ; Tania Cypriano; Athos Gontijo; Cesar Valentin; David Weir (Voices)

CARMEN MIRANDA: BANANAS IS MY BUSINESS uses film clips, archival material, extensive interviews, and reenactments to investigate the real Carmen Miranda half a century after she became one of the highest paid female entertainers in the United States.

Miranda, a beloved camp icon thanks to the long memories of film buffs and the eternal life of Warner Bros. cartoon parodies, was hailed as the greatest interpreter of Brazilian popular music in the mid-1940s. In the U.S. she was best known for her flamboyant appearances on stage, screen, and radio with her broken English, outrageously exotic costumes, and fruit-festooned turbans.

The film opens with a melodramatic fantasy presentation of Miranda's death in Hollywood. Archival footage of her funeral in Rio follows while the narrator (filmmaker Helena Solberg) ponders the complex relationship between Brazil and its most famous export. Solberg dreams of Miranda escaping from a museum exhibit and traveling back to Brazil. The funeral is reenacted. Miranda's shadow looms on a little church. Her spirit is sighted on a hilltop.

Miranda's cousin reveals that she was actually born in Portugal and has no Brazilian blood. Miranda's sister Aurora remembers their youth. An aged boyfriend shares his reflections as Carmen attempts different fashion statements. Cutting her first record, she enters the male-dominated world of show business. Broadway impresario Lee Shubert "discovers" her in Rio and signs her on to appear in a Broadway musical. Miranda heads north to the US and international fame. Returning to Brazil a year and a half later, she is condemned by high society as "too Americanized." Playing before a popular Brazilian audience, Miranda dazzles with a humorous musical retort to her critics. Nonetheless, vowing to never again perform in Brazil, she leaves for Hollywood.

WWII looms as US President Roosevelt and President Vargas of Mexico decide that Miranda will embody the Good Neighbor Policy between the two allies. Now molded by Fox's Darryl Zanuck, she appears in a series of frothy musicals with synthetic Latin-American settings, distortions which cause Brazilians to become ambivalent toward their once beloved star.

The production of movies with "Latin" themes declines as WWII wanes. Miranda buys out her contract in 1947 and attempts to retool her image as an independent, but the press and public resist. She marries the abusive American film producer David Sebastian and descends into self-parody and creative frustration. She maintains a busy schedule of concerts and personal appearances with the help of pills and alcohol until her nervous breakdown in 1954. Returning to the road to honor earlier contracts, on August 12, 1955, Miranda collapses on-camera during a taping of a TV program and dies later that night of a heart attack, at age 46. Her body is returned to Brazil where she is given the biggest funeral in the country's history.

In an unconventional documentary portrait, New York-based Brazilian filmmaker Solberg draws upon the lessons of feminism and multiculturalism to inform her lively, personal, yet toughminded analysis of the complexities that shaped a once beloved Hollywood icon. Rather than pretend to some spurious notion of objectivity, Solberg embraces and examines her own subjectivity while exploring the role that fantasy plays in our perception of stars.

The film eloquently illustrates how a talented young woman was exploited and molded by powerful men with their own agendas. However, it avoids painting Miranda as a passive victim. Rather, she is initially an all-too-willing participant in the process of image-making until the fantasy consumes her aspirations, happiness, and ultimately her life. The film also touches upon the issue of her ethnicity. By adopting Brazilian culture as her own, the light-skinned Portuguese helped put a useful white face on the Black African roots of her music. Robbed of an accurate cultural context, Miranda became a colorful eccentric to whom charmed Americans could condescend. — K.G.

d, Helena Solberg; p, David Meyer, Helena Solberg; exec p, Paulo Tavares, Carlos d'Oliveira; assoc p, Paulo Jose Cardoso dos Santos, Carlos Salgado; ph, Tomasz Magierski; ed, David Meyer, Amanda Zinoman; sound, Mario Garcia, Firmino Antunes, John Jordan, Juana Sapire, Pawel Wdowczak, Alan Barker, Albee Gordon, Russel Fager, Heron Alencar, Cristiano Maciel; makeup, Debra Phillips, Sabrina Fiomi, Joette, Luiz Ferriera

Documentary/Biography　　　　**(PR: A　MPAA: NR)**

CARRINGTON　　　　　　　　　　★★★

(U.K./France) 122m PolyGram; Freeway Productions; Shedlo Productions; Dora Productions Ltd.; Cinea & Orsans; Le Studio Canal Plus; Euston Films Ltd.; European Co-production Fund ~ Gramercy c

Emma Thompson (Dora Carrington); Jonathan Pryce (Lytton Strachey); Steven Waddington (Ralph Partridge); Samuel West (Gerald Brenan); Rufus Sewell (Mark Gertler); Penelope Wilton (Lady Ottoline Morrell); Janet McTeer (Vanessa Bell); Peter Blythe (Phillip Morrell); Jeremy Northam (Beacus Penrose); Alex Kingston (Frances Partridge); Sebastian Harcombe (Rober Senhouse); Richard Clifford (Clive Bell); David Ryall (Mayor); Stephen Boxer (Military Rep); Annabel Mullion (Mary Hutchinson); Gary Turner (Duncan Grant); Georgiana Dacombe (Marjorie Gertler); Helen Blatch (Nurse); Neville Phillips (Court Usher); Christopher Birch (Dr. Starkey Smith); Daniel Betts (Porter); Simon Bye (Fly Driver); Marzio Idoni (Gondolier)

Oscar-winning screenwriter Christopher Hampton (DANGEROUS LIAISONS) makes an unsteady directorial debut in this ambitious but ultimately disappointing biopic of two eccentric members of the Bloomsbury group.

Dora Carrington (Emma Thompson) is a young painter of "great promise" who attracts the attention of flamboyant writer Lytton Strachey (Jonathan Pryce) when he initially mistakes her for a "ravishing boy." She is initially repulsed by the brilliant but scruffy homosexual, but comes to respect him as an outspoken conscientious objector during WWI. When her sexually frustrated fiancee, Mark Gertler (Rufus Sewell), encourages Strachey to befriend Carrington, the two become extremely close, forming a relationship that stops just short of sexual consummation. She yields to Gertler's sexual entreaties unhappily, but decides to leave him for the sexless passion offered by Strachey. After Mark explodes with jealous rage, Carrington and Strachey decide to set up house together, living very much like a traditional heterosexual couple.

When Reginald Partridge (Stephen Waddington), a handsome WWI vet, arrives for dinner, Strachey flirts with him shamelessly. Soon a new arrangement comes about, with Carrington bedding Partridge (who has changed his name to Ralph at Strachey's urging) in London and sharing him with Strachey in the country. Partridge uses Strachey's fondness for him to dominate the triad, even convincing them to move to a larger home (called "Ham Spray House"). When Carrington's passion for Partridge cools, she takes up with his best friend, Gerald Brenan (Samuel West), only to break his heart and provoke a jealous rage in Partridge. Inevitably, she returns to the comfort of Strachey's chaste bed.

But Strachey's desires lie elsewhere, and when he takes rooms in town to be near his latest young man, life at Ham Spray House becomes tedious for Carrington. She finds diversion below decks with yachtsman Beacus Penrose (Jeremy Northam), who cruelly reveals that he doesn't really find her sexually attractive. Strachey is likewise dumped and returns crestfallen to Carrington's doting care. She nurses him through a long illness and to his last breath, in which he confesses that he should have married her long ago. Distraught, Carrington tries to kill herself, but is rescued by Rex. Left to herself, she sleepwalks through the empty house until she finally destroys her brushes and easels and calmly shoots herself with a rabbit gun.

The film's opening states explicitly that the film is about Carrington, although the title of the book on which it is based, Michael Holroyd's classic biography *Lytton Strachey* , points to the story's true center. Pryce is clearly having a lovely time, and makes every moment of his presence entertaining, if not always illuminating. His Strachey is a soft-spoken, shabby pixie with a vicious tongue and a peculiar talent for self loathing. He dominates the film just as the writer did the painter's life, leaving Thompson stranded in an unrewarding role. Thompson looks oddly vulnerable in the pageboy haircuts and costumes she wears in the first half of the film, then settles into wan despair until she resorts to some almost comic twitching in the final reel. It's an atypical role for her—it isn't very verbal—and the urge to over-physicalize proves overwhelming. A stronger director would have reigned her in.

Hampton's direction is bogged down by stagy tableaux, lingering dolly shots and a disinclination to cut off a scene after it's ended. His screenplay is mostly leaden, exposition-heavy dialogue, punctuated by devastatingly witty asides, mostly by Strachey (and mostly from the source material). Carrington's unselfish love is unmotivated, unexplored, and unexplained (whereas we can easily understand Strachey's adoration for his devoted acolyte). We never see how Carrington derives anything from the relationship; nor do we gain any meaningful insight into her work. Ultimately, Hampton fails to do justice to to his extraordinary subjects. *(Nudity, sexual situations, profanity.)* — R.S.

d, Christopher Hampton; p, Ronald Shedlo, John McGrath; exec p, Francis Boespflug, Philippe Carcassonne, Fabienne Vonier; assoc p, Chris Thompson; w, Christopher Hampton (based on the book *Lytton Strachey* by Michael Holroyd); ph, Denis Lenoir; ed, George Akers; m, Michael Nyman; prod d, Caroline Amies; art d, Frank Walsh; sound, Peter Lindsay (mixer); casting, Fothergill & Lunn Casting; cos, Penny Rose; makeup, Chrissie Beveridge

Biography/Historical/Romance   (PR: O MPAA: R)

CASINO   ★★★
(U.S.) 182m Syalis D.A.; Legende Enterprises; Universal ~ Universal c

Robert De Niro *(Sam "Ace" Rothstein)*; Sharon Stone *(Ginger McKenna)*; Joe Pesci *(Nicky Santoro)*; James Woods *(Lester Diamond)*; Don Rickles *(Billy Sherbert)*; Alan King *(Andy Stone)*; Kevin Pollak *(Phillip Green)*; L.Q. Jones *(Pat Webb)*; Dick Smothers *(Senator)*; Frank Vincent *(Frank Marino)*; John Bloom *(Don Ward)*; Pasquale Cajano *(Remo Gaggi)*; Melissa Prophet *(Jennifer Santoro)*; Bill Allison *(John Nance)*; Vinny Vella *(Artie Piscano)*; Oscar Goodman *(Himself)*; Catherine Scorsese *(Piscano's Mother)*; Phillip Suriano *(Dominick Santoro)*; Erika Von Tagen *(Older Amy)*; Frankie Avalon; Steve Allen; Jayne Meadows; Jerry Vale *(Themselves)*; Joseph Rigano *(Vincent Borelli)*; Gene Ruffini *(Vinny Forlano)*; Dominick Grieco *(Americo Capelli)*; Richard Amalfitano *(Casino Executive)*; Richard F. Strafella *(Casino Executive)*; Casper Molee *(Counter)*; David Leavitt *(Counter)*; Peter Conti *(Arthur Capp)*; Catherine T. Scorsese *(Piscano's Daughter)*; Steve Vignari *(Beeper)*; Rick Crachy *(Chastised Dealer)*; Larry E. Nadler *(Lucky Larry)*; Paul Herman *(Gambler in Phone Booth)*; Salvatore Petrillo *(Old Man Capo)*; Joey De Pinto *(Stabbed Gambler)*; Heidi Keller *(Blonde at Bar)*; Millicent Sheridan *(Senator's Hooker)*; Nobu Matsuhisa *(Ichikawa)*; Toru Nagai *(Ichikawa's Associate)*; Barbara Spanjers *(Ticket Agent)*; Dom Angelo *(Craps Dealer)*; Joe Molinaro *(Shift Manager)*; Ali Pirouzkar *(High Roller)*; Frankie Allison *(Craps Dealer)*; Jeff Scott Anderson *(Parking Valet)*; Jennifer M. Abbott *(Cashier)*; Frank Washko, Jr. *(Parking Valet)*; Christian A. Azzinaro *(Little Nicky—7 Years)*; Robert C. Tetzlaff *(Customs Agent)*; Anthony Russell *(Bookie)*; Carol Wilson *(Classroom Nun)*; Joe Lacoco *(Detective Bob Johnson)*; John Manca *(Wiseguy Eddy)*; Ronald Maccone *(Wiseguy Jerry)*; Buck Stephens *(Credit Clerk)*; Joseph Reidy *(Winner)*; Joe La Due *(Signaller)*; Fred Smith *(Security Guard)*; Sonny D'Angelo *(Security Guard)*; Greg Anderson *(Security Guard)*; Stuart Nisbet *(LA Banker)*; Tommy DeVito *(Crooked Poker Dealer)*; Frank Adonis *(Rocky)*; Joseph Bono *(Moosh)*; Craig Vincent *(Cowboy)*; Daniel P. Conte *(Doctor Dan)*; Paul Dottore *(Slim)*; Richard T. Smith *(Security Guard/Cowboy)*; David Rose *(David)*; Jonathan Kraft *(Jonathan)*

Martin Scorsese returns to the gangster milieu of GOODFELLAS, and the result is an accomplished film that carries with it the unshakable feeling that we've seen it all before.

Ace Rothstein (Robert De Niro) leaves his opulent Las Vegas home, walks to his car and turns on the ignition. The car explodes in a ball of flames, and the credits run over the grimly fanciful image of Ace's body tumbling through fiery space. The story unfolds in flashback.

Ace is a scientific gambler. Looking to get their piece of booming 1960s Las Vegas, the Kansas City Mafia installs him as manager of the Tangiers, where he lives up to his respectful but unaffectionate nickname, "The Golden Jew." The film's first third is a celebration of pre-theme park Vegas, the money-making machine and morality car wash, where the cash flow never dries up and acts that would be criminal anywhere else are not only okay—they're the coin of the realm.

Ace runs a relatively clean casino, but the serpent in this tawdry Garden of Eden soon slithers into glitter gulch in the form of Ace's old friend Nicky Santoro (Joe Pesci), who begins busting heads and drawing unwanted attention to the Mafia's pervasive presence. The third point of the inevitable triangle is Ginger McKenna (Sharon Stone) a hooker with a heart of, well . . . stone. We first glimpse Ginger on a casino security monitor, hustling a wealthy foreigner. Where a less calculating man might see a gold-digging bitch, Ace sees a soulmate: he proposes marriage in the form of a promise of lifelong financial security.

Once Ginger and Nicky are in place, the stage is set for Ace's downfall and, by extension, the end of the Mafia's hold on Las Vegas. Unhappy with her hollow marriage and unable to sever her ties with her first pimp, perpetual lowlife Lester Diamond (James Woods), Ginger drinks and drugs and spends. Flamboyant Nicky comes under investigation by the FBI, gets himself banned from the casinos and begins a clandestine affair with the increasingly out-of-control Ginger.

In the end, it all comes tumbling down. Ace escapes to make book another day—quite a surprise, given the opening—but Nicky is beaten to death with a baseball bat, and Ginger lurches off to a rendezvous with sordid, drug-related death. Las Vegas falls into the hands of wholesome businessmen who pervert its larcenous purity and dress it up in the guise of a family theme park.

There's nothing really wrong with CASINO. In fact, there are lots of things right with it: the city in the desert has seldom looked so thrillingly sleazy (the riotous grotesquerie of '70s fashions is a delightfully horrifying bonus), and two of the three leads—Robert De Niro and Sharon Stone—do fine work, De Niro of the kind audiences have come to expect, Stone surprisingly so. The weak link is Joe Pesci, who rehashes his GOODFELLAS performance as volatile Tommy DeVito and grows tiresome long before he meets his appointed end.

The story is compelling, a morality tale in which the old-fashioned moral (you reap what you sow) is delivered with such delirious viciousness that you almost forget what a dreary cliche it is. The score, a wall-to-wall compendium of popular songs, lounge standards, and snippets of classical music, is awesomely dense and, more often than not, breathtakingly apt. As one expects from Scorsese, CASINO is beautifully staged. It's also evocatively photographed by Robert Richardson and sharply edited by Scorsese's longtime associate Thelma Schoonmacher.

But after that's been said, there's not much more to say. CASINO feels attenuated and disturbingly predictable, a meticulous and coldly proficient going-over of familiar ground. It's not just that Scorsese himself has already made MEAN STREETS and GOODFELLAS, examinations of Mafia mores and morals from without and within. The trouble is more that the metaphor of gangster-as-businessman taken to his viciously logical extremes has been wrung pretty dry. Three GODFATHER films and countless imitators down the road, there's no thrill of the transgressive in the idea that the mob-run gambling industry and its tawdry Oz, the glittering and seductive Las Vegas, is a microcosm of American capitalism at its most rapacious. We know. *(Graphic violence, nudity, sexual situations, adult situations, substance abuse, extreme profanity.)* — M.M.

d, Martin Scorsese; p, Barbara De Fina; assoc p, Joseph Reidy; w, Nicholas Pileggi, Martin Scorsese (based on the book by Nicholas Pileggi); ph, Robert Richardson; ed, Thelma Schoonmaker; prod d, Dante Ferretti; art d, Jack G. Taylor, Jr.; set d, Rick Simpson; sound, Charles M. Wilborn (mixer); fx, Paul

Lombardi, Craig Barron, The Effects House, NY, Matte World Digital; casting, Ellen Lewis; cos, Rita Ryack, John Dunn; makeup, Jo-Anne Smith-Ojeil, K.N.B. EFX Group, Inc.; stunts, Doug Coleman, Daniel W. Barringer

AAN Best Actress: Sharon Stone

Drama/Crime (PR: O MPAA: R)

CASPER ★★★
(U.S.) 100m Amblin Entertainment; Harvey Entertainment Co. ~ Universal c

Christina Ricci *(Kat Harvey)*; Bill Pullman *(Dr. James Harvey)*; Cathy Moriarty *(Carrigan Crittenden)*; Eric Idle *(Dibs)*; Malachi Pearson *(Voice of Casper)*; Joe Nipote *(Voice of Stretch)*; Joe Alaskey *(Voice of Stinkie)*; Brad Garrett *(Voice of Fatso)*; Garette Ratliff Henson *(Vic)*; Jessica Wesson *(Amber)*; Amy Brenneman *(Amelia)*; Chauncey Leopardi *(Nicky)*; Spencer Vrooman *(Andreas)*; Ben Stein *(Rugg)*; Don Novello *(Father Guido Sarducci)*; Terry Murphy *(Herself)*; Ernestine Mercer *(Woman Being Interviewed)*; Douglas J.O. Bruckner *(Voice of Reporter)*; John Kassir *(Voice of the Crypt Keeper)*; Wesley Thompson *(Mr. Curtis)*; Michael Dubrow *(Student No. 1)*; J.J. Anderson *(Student No. 2)*; Jess Harnell *(Voice of Arnold)*; Michael McCarty *(Drunk in Bar)*; Micah Winkelspecht *(Student)*; Mike Simmrin *(Phantom)*; Devon Sawa *(Casper on Screen)*; Rodney Dangerfield; Mr. Rogers; Mel Gibson; Dan Aykroyd; Clint Eastwood *(Themselves)*

This very profitable resurrection of an antiquated cartoon character should reinforce the recent trend for repackaging baby-boomer nostalgia as kiddie entertainment. Surprisingly, though, CASPER is an engaging and often clever distraction for both kids and adults.

Kat (Christina Ricci), a lonely pre-teen, has followed her nomadic father around the country ever since the death of her mother Amelia. Her dad, Dr. James Harvey (Bill Pullman), is a ghost psychiatrist, or "therapist for the living impaired." When evil heiress Carrigan Crittenden (Cathy Moriarty) and her lawyer, Dibs (Eric Idle), hire Dr. Harvey to exorcise a haunted mansion—they're hoping to find treasure hidden inside—Kat is dragged to Friendship, Maine.

On arrival at dilapidated Whipstaff Manor, Kat meets Casper (voiced by Malachi Pearson), a cuddly, translucent white ghost with big blue eyes, who just wants a friend. Dr. Harvey, on the other hand, has his hands full with Casper's three uncles, who are not so cute or friendly. As Kat and Casper become friends, they set out to reconstruct his life, the facts of which he has forgotten. They discover that Casper's father invented a one-time-only method to bring the dead back to life, a machine which Casper intends to use.

Before Casper can live gain, however, they'll need to get rid of Crittenden, who has died and become a ghost in order to further her greedy scheme. Then Dr. Harvey, who has also died, shows up as a ghost. For Kat's sake, Casper lets the doctor use the machine in his stead. That night (which is Halloween), Kat hosts a party at the manor for her new classmates. Her mother Amelia (Amy Brenneman), now a beautiful angel, visits Casper and rewards his unselfishness with one night of life. Amelia and Dr. Harvey share a final good-bye, while live Casper (Devon Sawa) and Kat share a dance and a kiss before he again becomes an animated ghost.

CASPER draws inspiration from seemingly every movie ever made, but especially Disney's animated musical hits of the previous several years. The ghost uncles morph, bicker, and wisecrack like refugees from ALADDIN or THE LION KING, sprinkling their rat-a-tat dialogue with topical jokes and celebrity imitations. The film contains homages to live-action movies ranging from APOCALYPSE NOW to THE WIZARD OF OZ, and animated Disney classics from PINOCCHIO to SNOW WHITE. Even GHOSTBUSTER Dan Ackroyd shows up in a funny cameo.

Where the production design and the special effects take over, the movie is technically dazzling but hollow. The effects (courtesy of Industrial Light and Magic) are the kind of seamless technical work that can easily be taken for granted—unless, of course, you stay to see the endless list of names on the credits. The story, however, is like a house of cards that threatens to collapse from its convolutions. Even so, there are two fine performances in CASPER, and one character to care about. Bill Pullman proves adept at physical comedy, and talented Christina Ricci brings surprising tenderness and emotional plausibility to Kat. Her monologue about her late mother conveys something of the pain of death in a film that otherwise plays fast and loose with the subject. Without Kat's (and Ricci's) humanity, CASPER would be little more than a very elaborate cartoon. (Violence.) — P.R.

d, Brad Silberling; p, Colin Wilson; exec p, Steven Spielberg, Gerald R. Molen, Jeffrey A. Montgomery; assoc p, Paul Deason; co-p, Jeffrey Franklin, Steve Waterman; w, Sherri Stoner, Deanna Oliver (based on the character "Casper, the Friendly Ghost," created by Joseph Oriolo in the story by Joseph Oriolo and Seymour Reit); ph, Dean Cundey; ed, Michael Kahn; m, James Horner; prod d, Leslie Dilley; art d, Ed Verreaux, Daniel Maltese; set d, Rosemary Brandenburg; anim, Eric Armstrong, Phil Nibbelink; sound, Gary Rydstrom (design), Charlie Wilborn (mixer); fx, Michael Lantieri, Industrial Light & Magic; casting, Nancy Nayor; cos, Rosanna Norton; makeup, Christina Smith; stunts, Gary M. Hymes

Children's/Comedy/Fantasy **(PR: A MPAA: PG)**

CASTLE FREAK ★★
(U.S.) 95m Full Moon Entertainment ~
Full Moon Home Entertainment c

Jeffrey Combs (*John Reilly*); Barbara Crampton (*Susan Reilly*); Jessica Dollarhide (*Rebecca Reilly*); Jonathan Fuller (*Giorgio D'Orsino*); Massimo Sarchielli (*Giannetti*); Elisabeth Kaza (*Agnese*); Luca Zingaretti (*Forte*); Helen Stirling (*Duchess D'Orsino*); Alessandro Sebastian Satta (*J.J.*); Raffaella Offidani (*Sylvana*); Marco Steffanelli (*Benedetti*); Tunny Piras (*Grimaldi*); Rolando Cortegiani (*Tonio*); Carolyn Gordon; Suzanna Gordon; Jillian Gordon; Margaret Gordon (*The Gelato People*)

While it lacks the wry, subversive humor of his most popular films, Stuart Gordon's CASTLE FREAK is a scary and satisfying exercise in straightforward horror.

After the death of the Duchess D'Orsino (Helen Stirling), her closest living relative, American John Reilly (Jeffrey Combs), brings his wife Susan (Barbara Crampton) and daughter Rebecca (Jessica Dollarhide) to stay at the Italian castle he has inherited. John and Susan have been at odds ever since John's drunkenness caused a car accident which killed the couple's young son and left Rebecca blind. Unbeknownst to the family, the Duchess's son Giorgio (Jonathan Fuller), who supposedly died at a young age, was actually kept as a tortured prisoner in the castle's cellar. Now a deformed freak, Giorgio breaks free and stalks the house. At first only Rebecca is aware of his presence.

As his relationship with his wife deteriorates, John goes into town, picks up prostitute Sylvana (Raffaella Offidani) and brings her back to the castle. While John is absent, Giorgio kills Sylvana and housekeeper Agnese (Elisabeth Kaza). The police arrive, discover the mutilated bodies, and arrest John, who has figured out what's happening. That night, Giorgio kills the cops who are guarding Susan and Rebecca and attacks the mother and

daughter; John escapes from the police station and confronts the human monster on the castle's roof. In the ensuing struggle, both John and Giorgio plunge to their deaths.

Like director Gordon's 1987 film DOLLS (also filmed in Italy), CASTLE FREAK deals with a family, already beset by internal conflict, that comes under attack from a horrific outside force. But while DOLL's scenario of uncaring parents getting their just deserts was simple, CASTLE FREAK takes a more complicated approach to family-based horror. Parent-child dynamics underly all of the characters' motivations, from the police chief who takes a special interest in Sylvana's fate because she's borne his child to John's guilt over the death of his son, exacerbated by the resemblance between a portrait of the supposedly dead Giorgio and the deceased boy. Given this, it's disappointing that more is not made of the potential emotional connection between John and Giorgio, particularly since they are, after all, blood relatives.

On a more basic, genre level, CASTLE FREAK succeeds quite well, especially in the unrated video version (an R-rated cut was also released) which contains some extremely disturbing gore. Eschewing the brash outrageousness that made their collaboration on RE-ANIMATOR a cult success, Gordon and writer Dennis Paoli have nonetheless whipped up a horror film that is better thought-out than most, and the cast (including RE-ANIMATOR veterans Combs and Crampton) achieves a general level of performance that's well above the usual low-budget level. Under some very grotesquely convincing special makeup, Fuller even manages to evoke a little pathos for his tormented, murderous title character. (*Graphic violence, extensive nudity, sexual situations, adult situations, substance abuse, profanity.*) — M.G.

d, Stuart Gordon; p, Maurizio Maggi; exec p, Charles Band, Albert Band; w, Dennis Paoli (from a story by Stuart Gordon and Dennis Paoli, based on an original idea by Charles Band); ph, Mario Vulpiani; ed, Bert Glatstein; m, Richard Band; art d, Richard Band; sound, Patrick M. Griffith; fx, John Vulich, Mike Measmer; casting, Robert MacDonald, Perry Bullington; cos, Tiziana Mancini; makeup, Pietro Tenoglio, Optic Nerve

Horror **(PR: O MPAA: R)**

CENTURY ★★½
(U.K.) 112m BBC Films; Beambright ~
PolyGram Video c

Charles Dance (*Professor Mandry*); Clive Owen (*Paul Reisner*); Miranda Richardson (*Clara*); Robert Stephens (*Mr. Reisner*); Joan Hickson (*Mrs. Whitweather*); Lena Heady (*Miriam*); Neil Stuke (*Felix*); Liza Walker (*Katie*); Joseph Bennett (*Edwin*); Carlton Chance (*James*); Graham Loughridge (*Theo*); Alexis Daniel (*Thomas*); Ian Shaw (*Meredith*); Bruce Alexander (*Interrogator*); Mark Strong (*Policeman*); Dail Sullivan (*Theo's Girl*); Mark Hadfield (*Club Performer*); Geoffrey Beevers (*Lecturer*); Trevor Cooper (*Posse Man*); David Barras (*Posse Man*); David Roderick (*Young Boy at Front Door*); Michael Burrell (*Doctor Makin*); Allie Byrne (*1st Girl in Basement*); Nicholas Gleaves (*Daniel*); Anna Chancellor (*Woman in Police Station*); Katherine Best (*Sick Girl*); Dorothea Phillips (*Lady at Party*)

This turn-of-the-century medical drama with sociopolitical underpinnings pays attention to period detail, but bogs down in a slow pace and bland characters.

CENTURY begins on New Year's Eve, 1899. Paul Reisner (Clive Owen), a doctor and son of Jewish immigrants, leaves Scotland for a position in a new medical research institute in London. Paul's dedication to medicine is established early on, as he argues over discredited treatments and quickly becomes the most highly-regarded researcher at the institute. However, after he disagrees with Professor Mandry (Charles Dance), head of the institute, over a friend's new discovery—insulin—Dr. Reisner is suspended. Paul turns for help to Clara (Miranda Richardson), a lab worker he has been seeing. They begin an affair as he tries to get back his position. Paul soon discovers that Mandry has been sterilizing poor women in order to control the population and sets out to expose this unauthorized exercise in eugenics. As a result the institute is closed. The film ends on New Year's Eve, 1900 with Mandry disgraced and Paul about to open his own practice with Clara.

CENTURY looks good. Much effort went into making the period-accurate sets, but similar care should have been spent paring down the verbose script by playwright-turned-filmmaker Stephen Poliakoff (CLOSE MY EYES). While the actors attempt to breathe life into it, there are too many solemn lectures about medical breakthroughs and the wonders the future will bring. Much of the surgical jargon comes across as too technical for mainstream audiences (the description of insulin is so convoluted that a voiceover tries to clear it up).

Of the actors, Charles Dance stands out in his portrayal of Mandry, a man who even at his worst inspires admiration in Paul. Clive Owen, on the other hand, takes the script's solemnity to heart and his portrayal of a second-generation-immigrant maverick healer never stands out from the turgid material. *(Nudity, sexual situations.)* — K.F.

d, Stephen Poliakoff; p, Therese Pickard; exec p, Mark Shivas, Ruth Caleb; assoc p, Ralph Wilton; w, Stephen Poliakoff; ph, Witold Stok; ed, Michael Parkinson; m, Michael Gibbs; prod d, Michael Pickwood; art d, Henry Harris; sound, Peter Edwards; casting, Joyce Gallie; cos, Anushia Nieradzik, Daphne Dare; makeup, Dorka Nieradzik

Drama/Historical (PR: C   MPAA: R)

CHARULATA ★★★★★
(India) 117m RDB & Co. ~ Sony Pictures Classics bw
(AKA: LONELY WIFE, THE)

Soumitra Chatterjee *(Amal)*; Madhabi Mukherjee *(Charulata)*; Sailen Mukherjee *(Bhupati)*; Syamal Ghosal *(Umapada)*; Gitali Roy *(Mandakini)*; Bholanath Koyal *(Braja)*; Suku Mukherjee *(Nisikanta)*; Dilip Bose *(Sasanka)*; Subrata Sen Sharma *(Motilal)*; Joydeb *(Nilatpal Dey)*; Bankim Ghosh *(Jagannath)*

Satyajit Ray's fascination with Rabindranath Tagore culminated in CHARULATA, his twelfth film, shot in 1964 and commercially released in the US 31 years later. Based on a short story by Tagore, it is a surprisingly modern tale of love, lust, fidelity, and a woman's growing self-awareness against the backdrop of the Bengal Renaissance, a vibrant intellectual awakening in 19th-century India.

It is 1879, a time when liberal Western philosophies are breaking into the stronghold of Hindu feudal orthodoxy. Charulata (Madhabi Mukherjee), the childless wife of a wealthy Bengali intellectual, lives in seclusion in her spacious and ornate home in Calcutta, while winds of change are blowing away the cobwebs outside. Her husband, Bhupati (Sailen Mukherjee), inspired by Mill and Bentham, spends his inherited wealth in the pursuit of freedom and equality, by editing an English language liberal political weekly called *The Sentinel*. But he has no time for Charu, who has little to do in a home run like a well-oiled machine by a fleet of old retainers. Sensing her boredom, Bhupati invites Charu's elder brother Umapada (Syamal Ghosal) and wife Mandakini (Gitali Roy) to live with them.

Umapada helps with the daily running of the magazine and the printing press, but Manda with her foolish chatter is no company for the sensitive and intelligent Charu. At this point arrives Amal (Soumitra Chatterjee), Bhupati's dynamic young cousin. With Bhupati's encouragement, a close friendship grows between Amal and Charu based on their common interest in literature. Their intellectual sparring, however, hides a deeper attachment and a need which initially neither is fully aware of, and one which society will never sanction.

Umapada embezzles funds put at his disposal for running the press. The upright Bhupati confesses his hurt to Amal, admitting that Amal is the only man left he can trust. Amal, now aware of the nuances of his relationship with Charu, feels guilty. He also feels discomfited by Charu's obvious intellectual superiority which he himself has helped to nurture. Taking the easy way out, he leaves unannounced. Charu hides her disappointment until, shocked by the news of Amal's decision to marry and go away to England, she gives in to her grief. Accidentally entering the room, Bhupati finally realizes the truth about Charu's feelings. Bewildered, he roams aimlessly in his carriage in the streets of the city. When he returns, they both make a hesitant effort to reach out to each other. But their extended hands remain frozen in a gesture of unfinished compromise.

For an Indian audience, the ambiguity of Charu's relationship with Amal is easily comprehensible. In the traditional Indian home, where the younger brother of the husband is often closer by age and accessibility to the wife (an Indian family makes no distinction between a cousin and a brother), the relationship between the two has always been an ambiguous one: an easy friendship tinged with the possibility of an uneasy and illicit emotion which lends piquancy. Tagore's story is a gentle reflection of his own traumatic friendship with an older brother's wife, who committed suicide at an early age. With her the youthful Tagore had shared the same interests that bring Amal and Charu together.

With its beauty, structural perfection and conceptual purity, CHARULATA remains a triumph of Ray's craftsmanship and cinematic vision. The exquisite interiors created by art director Bansi Chandragupta were among the best of his work, as were the subtle use of lights and the sensitivity of Subrata Mitra's camera. The costumes, the faces, the detailed structuring of the film created a superbly colourful piece of monochrome cinema. CHARULATA has the quality of a miniature painting, where minute details are revealed by a stroke of the finest brush, and the unspoken is made visual by a mere suggestion.

Critic Chidananda Dasgupta has written of the characters who enact the drama of CHARULATA: "Their lack of conscious knowledge of what is happening inside them gives them a certain nobility of innocence; it is in their awakening that their tragedy lies. Amal, the younger man, is the first to realize the truth; for Charu it is an imperceptible movement from the unconscious to the conscious in which it is difficult to mark out the stages; for the husband, it is a sudden, stark, unbelievable revelation of truth. All three wake up, as it were, into the 20th century, the age of self-consciousness. The rhythm of the unfolding is so gentle and true, that there is no sense of shock even for the conservative Indian, although Ray's film is as daring for the wider audience as Tagore's story was for the intelligentsia of its day." — S.B.

d, Satyajit Ray; p, R.D. Bansal; w, Satyajit Ray (based on the novella *Nastanirh* by Rabindranath Tagore); ph, Subrata Mitra; ed, Dulal Dutta; m, Satyajit Ray; art d, Bansi Chandragupta; sound, Nripen Paul, Atul Chatterjee, Sujit Sarkar

Drama (PR: A   MPAA: NR)

CHILDREN OF THE CORN III: ★★
URBAN HARVEST
(U.S.) 98m Park Avenue Productions;
Trans Atlantic Pictures ~ Dimension c

Daniel Cerny *(Eli)*; Ron Melendez *(Joshua)*; Jim Metzler *(William Porter)*; Nancy Lee Grahn *(Alice Porter)*; Jon Clair *(Malcolm)*; Mari Morrow *(Maria)*; Michael Ensign *(Father Frank)*; Duke Stroud *(Earl)*; Rif Hutton *(Arnold)*; Garvin Funches *(T-Loc)*; Johnny Legend *(Derelict)*; Gina St. John *(Diane)*; Yvette Freeman *(Samantha)*; Terrence Matthews *(Dwayne)*; James O'Sullivan *(Charles)*; Kelly Nelson *(Teacher)*; Ed Goudy *(Dr. Appleby)*; Nicholas Brendon *(Baseball Player #1)*; Brian Peck *(Jake)*; Rance Howard *(Employer)*

Against the odds, this horror series (initially based on a Stephen King short story) has actually improved over time to the point where this third installment is a creditable if far-fetched chiller.

After their father's death, teenaged brothers Eli (Daniel Cerny) and Joshua (Ron Melendez) travel from their small farming hometown to Chicago to stay with foster parents William and Alice Porter (Jim Metzler and Nancy Lee Grahn). What only Eli knows is that their dad was killed by an evil cornfield spirit called "He Who Walks Behind the Rows," which Eli worships. The boy has brought some tainted corn with him, and secretly plants it in an abandoned lot and warehouse near his new home. While Joshua adjusts to his new life and finds a girlfriend, Maria (Mari Morrow), Eli begins recruiting their classmates to his cult, and anyone who crosses him or his corn meets a horrible fate.

William discovers Eli's cornfield and, realizing the financial potential of this especially hardy strain, proceeds with plans to market it and reap the financial rewards. Meanwhile, Joshua has become suspicious of Eli, travels back to their hometown, and discovers the supernatural truth. He races home as Eli is gathering his teenaged followers at the warehouse—where "He Who Walks Behind the Rows" erupts from the floor as a huge, hideous monster. Joshua arrives just in time to rescue Maria, and puts a stop to the creature and its demonic influence.

After the laughable 1984 original and the slightly improved but muddled 1993 sequel, CHILDREN OF THE CORN III proves a pleasant surprise (and, ironically, is the first of the series to go direct to video). While hardly groundbreaking and resolutely an exploitation film, it's put together confidently and is certainly more entertaining than, for example, the same year's "official" King film, THE MANGLER. The script works some entertaining urban variations on the previously rural-set story, with William's attempts to financially exploit Eli's crop of super-corn a nice touch. Director James Hickox—brother of HELLRAISER III director Anthony, who served as this movie's executive producer—keeps the film moving swiftly past its implausibilities and holds at bay the feeling that its existence is rather gratuitous in the first place.

The actors are generally decent, with Cerny (who also played a nasty kid in DEMONIC TOYS) possessing a creepy presence as the instigator of the mayhem. The special effects vary wildly; the opening death-by-corn is especially strong, but when "He Who Walks Behind the Rows" makes his grand appearance at the end, he proves to be a combination of effective full-size props, grainy opticals and some unconvincing miniatures. On balance, CHILDREN OF THE CORN III is a superior example of the video-sequel trend; inevitably, a CHILDREN OF THE CORN IV was already in the can by the end of 1995. *(Graphic violence, profanity.)* — M.G.

d, James D.R. Hickox; p, Gary DePew, Brad Southwick; exec p, Anthony L.V. Hickox; assoc p, Thomas C. Rainone, Donald Paul Pemrick; w, Dode B. Levenson (based on the story "Children of the Corn" by Stephen King); ph, Gerry Lively; ed, Chris Peppe; m, Daniel Licht; prod d, Blair A. Martin; set d, Susanna Buono; sound, Jonathan Miller; fx, Thomas C. Rainone, Screaming Mad George, Kevin Yagher, Anthony Doublin; casting, Donald Paul Pemrick; cos, Mark Bridges; makeup, Lisa Buono, Randy Westgate

Horror (PR: O   MPAA: R)

CHILDREN OF THE DUST
(SEE: GOOD DAY TO DIE, A)

CHINA: MOVING THE MOUNTAIN
(SEE: MOVING THE MOUNTAIN)

CHRONICLE OF THE WARSAW GHETTO ★★★½
UPRISING ACCORDING TO MAREK EDELMAN
(Poland) 72m Documentary and Features Polish Films bw
(KRONIKA TOWSTANIA W GETCIE WARSZAWSKAM WEDLUG MARKA EDELMANA)

Using radically refashioned archival footage of the Warsaw ghetto, this interview with Marek Edelman is an evocative memoir of his role in the rebellion that held back the Nazis for almost a month in 1943.

The film begins with the growing list of prohibitions and regulations leading to the virtual imprisonment of about half-a-million Polish Jews in an old slum district of Warsaw with inadequate space and plumbing. An overhead tracking shot shows the number of people assembled in the first months of the relocation. The daily struggle against hunger and disease, especially among the dispossessed arrivals seen in their pitful rags, is aggravated by the German demands for "deportations to the east" that many begin to suspect are camouflaged mass murders.

By the close of 1942, people living in the ghetto realize they are doomed, and the rudiments of resistance are planned by a handful of the young, including Edelman. Following some sporadic, spontaneous fighting at the ghetto railhead, the *Umschlagplatz*, in January, led by Moredecai Anielewicz, the scene is set for the more famous and prolonged battle that will begin on 19 April 1943. In the intervening time, many of the ghetto residents construct hidden shelters or bunkers in the basements and cellars of the buildings, often with tunnels leading to other buildings. The handful of fighters who have weapons take to these shelters, giving the uprising the advantage of defensive positions.

Edelman recalls the cruel irony of a section of Warsaw battling the Germans for its survival, while the non-Jewish population of the city enjoys a sunny spring. He names various comrades whose acts of valor are obscured by time. Finally, the SS and police troops under the command of a newly appointed Jurgen Stroop adopted street fighting tactics, burnt buildings and used teargas grenades to reduce the ghetto to a smoking ruin. Edelman escaped to take part in the Warsaw city uprising 15 months later. The same year that witnessed the ghetto uprising saw a number of revolts, mass escapes and sabotage in various extermination camps, for which the Warsaw ghetto uprising was the inspiration.

Most of the footage used here, which was never shown publicly in wartime Germany, is slowed down to painfully reinforce the horrors of the situation. A column of deportees passes out of the frame, towards oblivion. Two children, a boy and a girl, frantic with fear as they try to get aboard a truck, glance backward at the camera, probably at a uniformed German cameraman. Many of the images used in the film are extremely painful: an elderly woman whose face is forced towards the camera lens by a riding crop in the hands of a uniformed German whose own face we cannot see; an impoverished family whose rags barely hide their skeletal children; two older, traditionally garbed Jews being "escorted" by a helmeted and rifle-toting SS man behind them. It is through these haunting images of the violation of the human spirit that director Jolanta Dylewska and her editor

Wanda Zeman have successfully recreated an impressionistic portait of Jewish Warsaw in its death throes. *(Violence, adult situations.)* — L.R.

d, Jolanta Dylewska; w, Jolanta Dylewska; ph, Jolanta Dylewska; ed, Wanda Zeman; m, Arthur Brauner; sound, Piotr Strzelecki; fx, Pyzsard Kujawski

Docudrama/Historical/War (PR: C MPAA: NR)

CIRCLE OF FRIENDS ★★½
(U.S./Ireland) 96m Price Entertainment; Lantana Productions; Savoy Pictures; Good Girls Productions ~ Savoy Pictures c

Chris O'Donnell *(Jack)*; Minnie Driver *(Benny)*; Geraldine O'Rawe *(Eve)*; Saffron Burrows *(Nan)*; Alan Cumming *(Sean)*; Colin Firth *(Simon Westward)*; Aidan Gillen *(Aidan)*; Mick Lally *(Dan Hogan)*; Britta Smith *(Mrs. Hogan)*; John Kavanagh *(Brian Mahon)*; Ruth McCabe *(Emily Mahon)*; Ciaran Hinds *(Professor Flynn)*; Tony Doyle *(Dr. Foley)*; Marie Mullen *(Mrs. Foley)*; Marie Conmee *(Mrs. Healy)*; Gerry Walsh *(Mr. Flood)*; Sean McGinley *(Mr. Duggan)*; Tom Hickey *(Professor Maclure)*; Seamus Forde *(Parish Priest)*; Ingrid Craigie *(Celia Westward)*; Major Lambert *(Major Westward)*; Pauline Delany *(Big House Maid)*; Jason Barry *(Nasey Mahon)*; Edward Manning *(Paul Mahon)*; Phil Kelly *(Hibernian Waiter)*; Gwynne McElveen *(Rosemary)*; Marguerite Drea *(Sheila)*; Stephen Rooney *(Bill Dunne)*; Cathy Belton *(Moaning Girl)*; Elizabeth Keller *(Sobbing Girl)*; Tanya Cawley *(Rugby Girl)*; Niamh O'Byrne *(Dancing Girl)*; Dervla O'Farrell *(Benny—10 Years Old)*; Pamela Cardillo *(Nan—10 Years Old)*; Louise Maher *(Eve—10 Years Old)*; Karen O'Neill *(1st Little Girl)*; Elaine Dunphy *(2nd Little Girl)*; Emma Lannon *(3rd Little Girl)*; Margaret O'Neill *(1st Nun)*; Maureen Lyster *(2nd Nun)*; Eliza Dear *(3rd Nun)*; Brendan Conroy *(Priest)*

CIRCLE OF FRIENDS is an old-fashioned romantic melodrama for sensitive teenaged girls, as well as grown women who are sentimental about their teen years (if there are any of either sort left these days).

In 1957, three close girlfriends are entering university in Dublin. Benny (Minnie Driver) is slightly overweight, jolly, and romantic. Nan (Saffron Burrows) is the beauty of the bunch, supremely self-confident and used to getting her way. Eve (Geraldine O'Rawe), an orphan, is a quiet shadow in the background. On the first day of classes, Benny meets Jack (Chris O'Donnell), a handsome rugby player, and is instantly smitten. Jack's no egotistical jock, and he is drawn to Benny's earthy charm. But the relationship is stymied by Benny's having to commute home each night to her small village of Knockglen. Nan becomes involved with Simon Westward (Colin Firth), an older landed aristocrat, who gets her pregnant and then blithely tosses her aside. She connives to get Jack drunk, seduces him and claims him as the father of her child. Benny, meanwhile, is at wit's end, contending with the lecherous advances of Sean (Alan Cummings), her father's sleazy shop assistant. She is forced to put on a brave face when she encounters Nan and Jack at a party, but watchful Eve catches Nan out and reveals her treachery. More evil doings are revealed when Benny discovers that slimy Sean has been bilking money out of the business. She and Jack are reunited to share their young love.

This unashamedly old-fashioned coming-of-age story is nothing new, but remains highly watchable nevertheless. Based on a novel by the popular Irish writer Maeve Binche, it has a good feel for character and the guilt-ridden atmosphere of Catholic sexual repression which conventionally stifles youthful passion. The direction is sensible and straightforward, if not daringly cine-matic, and gives full due to welling emotions. Period and place are lovingly recreated and handsomely photographed by Ken MacMillan's lens.

Driver, who delivers a piercingly subjective performance, is the linchpin of the film's quiet appeal. When told by Jack that he likes "solid girls," she quickly replies: "That's me: beef to the heels, like an Iyangar heifer." Her honesty can be almost painful: you tremble for her when she dons a too-revealing party frock (at bitchy Nan's behest) and die with her when an insensitive Jack seems to ignore her. In all, it's a wish-fulfillment triumph for every plain Jane who's ever desired a prince (a role in which the manly O'Donnell is perfectly cast). *(Adult situations, sexual situations, profanity.)* — D.N.

d, Pat O'Connor; p, Arlene Sellers, Alex Winitsky, Frank Price; exec p, Terence Clegg, Rod Stoneman; co-p, Kenith Trodd; w, Andrew Davies (based on the novel by Maeve Binchy); ph, Ken MacMillan; ed, John Jympson; m, Michael Kamen; prod d, Jim Clay; art d, Chris Seagers; set d, Judy Farr; sound, Brian Simmons (recordist); casting, Mary Selway, Simone Ireland; cos, Anushia Nierdazik; makeup, Dorka Nieradzik; stunts, Martin Grace

Romance/Drama (PR: C MPAA: PG-13)

CIRCUMSTANCES UNKNOWN ★★½
(Canada) 85m Shooting Star Entertainment; Wilshire Court Productions ~ Paramount Home Video c

Judd Nelson *(Paul Kinsey)*; Isabel Glasser *(Deena Reuschel)*; William R. Moses *(Tim Reuschel)*; Rhys Huber *(John Reuschel)*; Phillip Mackenzie *(Martin Trayne)*; William B. Davis *(Gene Reuschel)*; Sheila Moore *(Barbara Reuschel)*; Garry Chalk *(Mike Kinsey)*; Duncan Fraser *(Sheriff Frank Hall)*; Suki Kaiser *(Leah Kinsey)*; Dorothy Fehr *(Jenny Trayne)*; Pat Armstrong *(Mimi Trakas)*; Mikal Dughi *(Arlene Trakas)*; Lorena Gale *(Dakota Peal)*; Guillermo Verdecchia *(Tony Azana)*; Suzy Joachim *(Carmen Ruuz)*; Brennan Leo Kotowich *(Paul Kinsey—Age 5)*; Shane Palfenier *(Paul Kinsey—Age 8)*; Stuart Davidson *(Paul Kinsey—Age 12)*; Norma Wick *(TV Newsperson)*; Peter Hanlon *(Clerk)*; Aurelio DiNunzio *(Maitre d')*; Nantino Bellantoni *(Waiter)*; Tom Pickett *(Bob Warner)*

CIRCUMSTANCES UNKNOWN is a made-for-TV movie about a serial killer who drowns his victims and leaves flowers at their funerals. It expounds on the well-worn thesis that psychotics do the darndest things for the silliest reasons, but breaks no new ground.

Paul Kinsey (Judd Nelson) drowns a woman swimmer in Cold Creek Lake. He attends her funeral, since he is both a friend of her brother, Martin (Phillip Mackenzie), and her fiance, Tim Reuschel (William R. Moses), and deposits a bouquet of irises on the coffin. Her death is considered accidental.

Ten years later, Paul is a jeweler in Vancouver. All three men are still friends, and Tim buys an iris-patterned ring for his wife, Deena (Isabel Glasser), from Paul. Paul sells another iris ring to a young couple, then he drowns the woman in her bathtub. When Tim, Deena, and their young son John (Rhys Huber) leave to vacation at the lake, Paul follows surruptitiously and stalks them. John spots him, but is ignored when he tells Tim and Deena. Rafting on Cold Creek, Tim leaves his family to scout the rapids ahead; Paul drowns him. Mimi Trakas (Pat Armstrong), a stroke victim who lives with her grownup daughter, Arlene (Mikal Dughi), sees the killing, but she can't talk. Deena is sure Tim was murdered and starts looking for proof. Paul shows up to thwart her efforts. He steals photos which show someone hiding in the bushes. He smooth talks John. When Deena meets the Trakases, he kills Mimi, before she can reveal his guilt. When his father accuses him, he throws him downstairs. Finally, under suspicion, he kidnaps Deena and rows around the lake with her until a vision of his mother, whom he also drowned, calls him to a watery grave.

Adapted from a novel by Jonellen Heckler, CIRCUM-STANCES UNKNOWN is full of loose ends. Martin does almost nothing, Tim is killed too early, John disappears before the finale and Paul is apropriately lugubrious, but lacks intensity. The bit players fare better: Tom Pickett's town sheriff is a good drunken ignoramus, the photo clerk (Peter Hanlon) is dapper and fey, and Mimi Trakas briefly steals the show, screaming inarticulately and ringing her little bell.

Each time Paul kills, the film cuts to flashbacks of his childhood, in which his father abuses him and steals his mother's affection. In the final flashback, a 12 year-old Paul drowns his mom in a swimming pool. In the film's only interesting touch, Blue iris, Mom's favorite flower, remain colored in the otherwise black and white flashbacks. But this homage to RUMBLEFISH is crudely symbolic (blue equals water, flowers equal Mom, etc.) and the flashbacks themselves don't reveal any traumas suffcent to provide a psychological explanation for Paul's behaviour and his iris obsession: why does he kill his *mom*? Why does he keep killing?

CIRCUMSTANCES UNKNOWN's score and cinematography are unexceptional. Its acting is competent, not inspired. It sinks into the video pool, trailing bubbles. *(Violence.)* — C.M.

d, Robert Lewis; p, Mary Eilts; w, Emily Shoemaker, Thomas Hood (based on the novel by Jonellen Heckler); ph, Bruce Worrall; ed, Claudia Finkle; md, Joseph Conlan; prod d, Guy Lalande; art d, Maya Ishiura; set d, Nick Richardson; sound, Roger Stafeckis (mixer); fx, Dave Paller; casting, Sis Kozak, Lindsey Walker; cos, Cynthia Summers; makeup, Anais Browski; stunts, Scott Ateah

Crime/Thriller (PR: C MPAA: R)

CITIZEN X ★★★½
(U.S./Hungary) 120m HBO Pictures; Asylum Films; Citadel Entertainment; Budapest Films ~ HBO Home Video c

Stephen Rea *(Burakov)*; Donald Sutherland *(Fetisov)*; Max von Sydow *(Bukhanovsky)*; Jeffrey DeMunn *(Chikatilo)*; Joss Ackland *(Bondarchuk)*; John Wood *(Gorbunov)*; Radu Amzuliscu *(Federenko)*; Imelda Staunton *(Mrs. Burakova)*; Andras Balint *(Ignatiev)*; Geza Balkay *(Proturator)*; Laszlo Varadi Balogh *(Peasant)*; Zsolt Biro *(Older Gay Man)*; Ion Caramitru *(Tatevsky)*; Balazs Csapo *(Gay Partner)*; Imre Csuja *(Front Detective)*; Zoltan Dozsa *(Execution Guard)*; Jozsa Elek *(Burakov's Daughter)*; Marton Elek *(Burakov's Son)*; Murray Ewan *(Office Manager)*; Klara Falvay *(Peasant)*; Erika Fenyes *(Vague Looking Girl)*; Zoltan Galbacs *(Train Track Boy)*; Balazs Galko *(Station Drunk)*; Zoltan Gera *(Doctor)*; Jono Gero *(Plainclothesman)*; Chris Gerolmo *(Militiaman)*; Simon Gevai *(Hanging Boy)*; Czeslaw Grocholski *(Ivanov)*; Istvan Hunyadkurthy *(Drunk Father)*; Attila Kiraly *(Wall-eyed Boy)*; Karoly Korognai *(Desk Cop)*; Kati Koti *(Peasant Mother)*; Ferenc Lengyel *(Young Announcer)*; Katalin Lestyan *(Peasant)*; Gyorgy Miklosy *(Constable)*; Ralph Nossek *(Dunenkov)*; Anna Orosz *(Announcer)*; Wojciech Piekarski *(Scruffy Man)*; Tamas Puskas *(Young Attendant)*; Mari Rajna *(Slow Woman)*; Tusse Silberg *(Mrs. Chikatilo)*; Eva Toth Siman *(Drunken Woman)*; Laszlo Stier *(Man in Robe)*; Mihaly Szabados *(Kid Militiaman)*; Petra Szabo *(Beautiful Blonde Girl)*; B. Miklos Szekely *(Older Partner)*; Tibor Szervet *(Detective)*; Balazs Tardi *(Eating Soldier #1)*; Sandor Teri *(Gypsy)*; Denes Ujlaky *(Farmer)*; Katalin Varnagy *(Wizened Peasant Woman)*; Zoltan Vekony *(Eating Soldier #2)*

Fine performances by both Stephen Rea and Donald Sutherland propel this excellent direct-to-video drama, based on a true story, of how two Red Army officers hunt down a serial killer responsible for the murders of 52 people, 35 of whom were 16 years old or younger.

In 1982, newly-appointed forensic expert Burakov (Rea) investigates a body found in the woods of rural Russia—only to discover seven more clumsily-hidden corpses, all similarly murdered and disfigured, apparently after being sexually molested. Searching through his predecessor's files, Burakov discovers evidence of eight previous murders, indicating the work of a serial killer. However, when Burakov presents this evidence to his supervising committee, headed by regional secretary Bondarchuk (Joss Ackland), he is told that "there are no serial killers in the Soviet state," and that such a thing is purely "a western phenomenon." Appalled by the secretary's myopic stance, Burakov continues his investigations; he is aided only by a single committee member, Colonel Fetisov (Sutherland), who is determined to straddle the fence between legal and moral justice and loyalty to the Communist party.

For eight years, Burakov searches for the killer with Fetisov's help, although requests for publicity and manpower are routinely denied. At one point, Burakov decides to enlist the aid of a psychiatrist—an unprecedented act in Russian criminology—and convinces one professor, Bukhanovsky (Max von Sydow), to create a psychological profile of the killer. Only when the grip of the Communist party loosens in 1990 does Burakov finally get the resources he so desperately needs; in November of that year, he and his men pinpoint the killer, Andre Chikatilo (Jeffrey DeMunn), a factory worker who preys upon young vagrants and runaways in train stations. With the help of psychiatrist Bukhanovsky, the authorities extract a confession from Chikatilo, who is found guilty and executed.

Writer-director Chris Gerolmo gives us a solid crime docudrama that compares favorably to such fictional predecessors as SILENCE OF THE LAMBS. Burakov, played with convincing passion by Rea, struggles with equal valor against both the killer and the Communist party's roadblocks. (For example, at one point in 1984, Chikatilo is actually arrested by Burakov, but because his blood type does not match semen found on the bodies, he is released. It is now suspected that, because Chikatilo was a Party member, the test results were doctored in Moscow to facilitate his release). The only disappointment is that, while we see the killer's grisly methods, we're not given much insight into his motivations until almost the very last scene, when Bukhanovsky reads aloud the killer's psychological profile. Still, CITIZEN X stands as yet another example of the high-quality motion pictures being showcased by HBO Films. *(Graphic violence, sexual situations, adult situations, profanity.)* — B.T.

d, Chris Geralmo; p, Timothy Marx; exec p, Matthew Chapman, Laura Bickford, David R. Ginsburg; co-p, Webster Stone, Robert Stone; w, Chris Geralmo (based on the book *The Killer Department* by Robert Cullen); ph, Robert Fraisse; ed, William Goldenberg; m, Randy Edelman; prod d, Jozsef Romvari; art d, Lorand Javor; set d, Istvan Toth; sound, Alan Byer (mixer); fx, Ferenc Ormos; casting, Joyce Nettles; cos, Maria Hruby; makeup, Charles Balazs, Katalin Jakots, Greg Nicotero, Gino B. Crognale, K.N.B. EFX Group

Crime/Docudrama/Thriller (PR: C MPAA: NR)

CITY OF LOST CHILDREN, THE ★★★½
(France/Spain/Germany) 112m Claudie Ossard Productions; Constellation Productions; Lumiere; Le Studio Canal Plus; France 3 Cinema; Elias Querejeta; Tele Munchin; Centre

National de la Cinematographie; Cofimage 4/Cofimage 5; Studio Image ~ Sony Pictures Classics c
(LA CITE DES ENFANTS PERDUS)

Ron Perlman *(One)*; Daniel Emilfork *(Krank)*; Judith Vittet *(Miette)*; Dominique Pinon *(Diver/Clones/Stocle)*; Jean-Claude Dreyfus *(Marcello, Flea Tamer)*; Genevieve Brunet; Odile Mallet *(Octopus)*; Mireille Mosse *(Mademoiselle Bismuth)*; Serge Merlin *(Leader of the Cyclopes)*; Francois Hadji-Lazaro *(Killer)*; Rufus *(Peeler)*; Ticky Holgado *(Ex-acrobat)*; Jean-Louis Trintignant *(Voice of Irvin)*; Dominique Bettenfeld *(Bogdan)*; Lotfi Yahyajedidi; Thierry Gibault *(Brutus)*; Marc Caro *(Brother Ange-Joseph)*; Mapi Galan *(Lune)*; Briac Barthelemy *(Bottle)*; Alexis Pivot *(Tadpole)*; Leo Rubion *(Jeannot)*; Pierre-Quentin Faesch *(Pipo)*; Joseph Lucien *(Denree)*; Guillaume Billod-Morel *(Child)*; Ham-Chau Luong *(Tattoo Artist)*; Hong-Mai Thomas *(Tattoo Artist's Wife)*; Daniel Adric *(Cyclops)*; Frankie Pain *(Barmaid)*; Enrique Villanueva *(Spainard)*; Chris Huerta *(Father Christmas)*; Lorella Cravotta *(Woman at Her Window)*; Rene Marquant *(Captain)*; Bezak *(Helmsman)*; Philippe Beautier; Marc Amyot; Jean-Philippe Labadie; Cyril Aubin; Bruno Journee *(Double Clones)*; Dominique Chevallier *(Tied-up Guard)*; Rene Pivot *(Glazier)*; Michel Smolianoff *(Awake Tramp)*; Christophe Salengro *(Soldier)*; Eric Houzelot *(Soldier)*; Angelique Philibert; Antoinette Dias; Zak Russomanno; Djamila Bouda; Lauren Geoffrey *(Strippers)*; Lili Cognard *(Winner)*; Raphaele Bouchard *(Meitte, Age 15)*; Babeth Etienne *(Miette, Age 37)*; Rachel Boulenger *(Miette, Age 43)*; Nane Germon *(Miette, Age 82)*; Buster Verbraeken *(Krank, Age 4)*; Jeremie Freund *(Krank, Age 12)*; Joris Geneste *(Krank, Age 36)*; Michel Motu *(Krank, Age 45)*; Eglantine Blanckaert; Gaetan Bouyala; Mickael Bussinger; Jonathan Gatinois; Joshka Kaufmann; Morgan Mariac; Caroline Marsily; Geoffroy Morange; Sebastien Thaissart *(Schoolchildren)*; Charlotte Bienfait; Camille Dufeu; Robinson Fouille; Alysia Hoffeurt; Sandy Kontargyris; Andrew Laupen; Theo Madueno; Arthur Mazet; Fackry M'Saidie; Gabriel Pierre; Berangere Pivot; Charlotte Ribaud-Chevrey; Laura Robert; Caroline Rochand; Carolane Yvan *(Babies)*

Awash in visual imagination, this second feature from the makers of 1991's DELICATESSEN also finds a heart to support its fanciful visions.

In a bizarre harbor metropolis, a warped, aged scientist, Krank (Daniel Emilfork), lives in a platform out at sea where he experiments with children to steal their dreams, as he is unable to have his own. The youngsters are procured for him by the Cyclopes, an underground organization of one-eyed men, who kidnap Denree (Joseph Lucien), the young adopted brother of strongman One (Ron Perlman). Searching for Denree, One falls in with a band of orphan children under the thumb of female Siamese twins collectively known as the Octopus (Genevieve Brunet, Odile Mallet), who employ them as thieves. One ends up teaming with a young girl named Miette (Judith Vittet), who is searching for some missing friends who have also been taken by the Cyclopes.

The pair are captured by the Cyclopes and left to drown; One escapes and believes Miette dead when in fact she has been rescued from the harbor bed by a deep-sea diver (Dominique Pinon) who once provided the basis for a sextet of clones who serve Krank. After overcoming both the Octopus and the flea trainer Marcello (Jean-Claude Dreyfus), whose tainted insects inject his victims with mind-altering poisons and briefly turn One violently against Miette, the two head out to Krank's fortress. Miette is captured by Krank and briefly subjected to his dream-snatching device before One rescues her and the other children. At the same time, the diver has arrived and ringed the

sea platform with explosives, which destroy Krank's stronghold as One, Miette, Denree and the others row away.

While it doesn't have the consistently exhilarating comic invention of DELICATESSEN, THE CITY OF LOST CHILDREN is a more ambitious undertaking that ultimately succeeds quite well on its own terms. As in their previous movie, filmmakers Jean-Pierre Jeunet and Marc Caro pack their film with off-the-wall characters, but here they tone down the humor in favor of a heroic quest story. And while the movie takes some time to find its focus, it becomes engrossing and even touching once it narrows down to One and Miette's adventures together and the growing bond between them. Throughout, there is always plenty to engage the eye, and Jeunet and Caro's penchant for Rube Goldberg-esque comic set pieces is again very much in evidence.

Despite the slapstick and the presence of several youthful characters, this is a decidedly adult fairy tale. It plays on childhood fears in a manner that would no doubt terrify younger viewers, particularly in a striking opening dream scene involving multiple malevolent Santas and in a disturbing, fairly gratuitous moment when One, under the influence of a flea bite, goes crazy and slaps Miette around. Jeunet and Caro have put together a cast and technical crew who are right on their unique wavelength, with remarkable production design and makeup, stunning special effects (most notably those that flawlessly turn Pinon into the six screen-sharing clones) and fine performances. Perlman, whose unusual features usually relegate him to villainous roles, is just right as the sympathetic One, while Vittet is spunky and charming, and Brunet and Mallet perform their Siamese twin act with hilarious precision.

THE CITY OF LOST CHILDREN was a high-profile box office failure in France, where local audiences apparently prefer smaller-scale native product. But it could certainly teach a thing or two to some American filmmakers about how to make screen fantasies that are about more than just the virtuosity of their visual effects. *(Violence, nudity, adult situations.)* — M.G.

d, Jean-Pierre Jeunet, Marc Caro; p, Claudie Ossard ; w, Gilles Adrien, Jean-Pierre Jeunet, Marc Caro; ph, Darius Khondji; ed, Herve Schneid; m, Angelo Badalamenti; art d, Marc Caro; set d, Aline Bonetto; sound, Pierre Excoffier, Gerard Hardy, Vincent Arnardi (mixer), Thierry Lebon (mixer); fx, Yves Domenjoud, Olivier Gleyze, Jean-Baptiste Bonetto, Jean-Christophe Spadaccini, Emmanuelle Soupa; casting, Pierre-Jacques Benichou; cos, Jean-Paul Gaultier; makeup, Nathalie Tissier, Benoit Lestang; stunts, Patrick Cauderlier

Fantasy   **(PR: C   MPAA: R)**

CITY UNPLUGGED   ★★★
(Finland/U.S./Sweden) 99m Filmzolfo; Upstream Pictures; Hank Blumenthal; Filmteknik; Exitfilm ~ Filmhaus c
(AKA: DARKNESS IN TALLINN)

Ivo Uukkivi *(Toivo)*; Milena Gulbe *(Maria)*; Monika Mager *(Terje)*; Enn Klooren *(Mihhail)*; Vaino Laes *(Andres)*; Peeter Oja *(Dmitri)*; Juri Jarvet *(Anton)*; Villem Indrikson *(Officer Kallas)*; Andres Raag *(Kallas' Partner)*; Tonu Kark *(Stub)*; Ain Lutsepp *(Ernst)*

With CITY UNPLUGGED, Finnish director Ilkka Jarvilaturi has fashioned a minimalist alternative to Quentin Tarantino's now famous, glossy, robust, hypergregarious, and violent RESERVOIR DOGS. The film is set in Tallinn, Estonia, in 1991, and like many noir crime thrillers, it follows the plotting and unfolding of a crime through unexpected twists and turns to its disastrous conclusion.

In Tallin, the Russian Mafia plot to steal a billion dollars in gold stolen by the Nazis during WWII. The loot is now in transit to Estonia by way of France. The gangsters plan to cut off the city's electrical supply at night and attack the treasury under cover of darkness. They intend to melt the gold and repackage it in cigarette boxes at a local factory, finally shipping it out of the country the following morning. Vital to their success is an electrician from outside the organization, a young Estonian named Toivo (Ivo Uukkivi), who takes the job to make money for his pregnant wife Maria (Milena Gulbe).

Members of the gang's inner circle adopt pseudonyms: Earth, Smoke, Fire, and so on. Toivo joins Earth and Smoke, and manages to befriend Smoke. Meanwhile, Maria goes into premature labor, and miraculously makes it to the hospital with the help of a young neighbor named Terje (Monika Mager). Terje also tries to warn Toivo, but is driven away by Earth. When Toivo shuts down the power, all hell breaks loose.

First the Mafia attack the treasury, then rioting and looting erupt throughout Tallinn. Smoke eventually shoots Earth and tells Toivo that his wife is at the hospital. Toivo rushes to the hospital where the doctors are struggling in the dark to save his wife and child. He returns to the plant to reestablish power and winds up in a desperate car chase and shootout between the Mafia and the police. The gangsters either die or are captured, with Fire, the gang's boss, abandoning the scheme on learning that his son, Earth, is dead.

Next to Hollywood's post-Tarantino crop of ulta-violent films, Jarvilaturi's moralism and quaint provincialism might appear heavy-handed. The film carries strong Russian undertones (the gangsters, planning to to rob poor Estonia of its wealth and jeopardize its economic recovery, are unmistakable figures of Russia's political strongmen).

The cinematography is superb, providing a bleak and eerie backdrop to the events in Tallinn. Shot in high contrast, the city often is a harsh landscape divided between darkness and light. But most of the film is shot indoors, lending a claustrophobic reality to the nightmarish events. (*Violence, nudity, adult situations, profanity.*) — M.F.

d, Ilkka Jarvilaturi; p, Lasse Saarinen; exec p, Ilkka Jarvilaturi; co-p, Borje Hansson; w, Paul Kolsby; ph, Rein Kotov; ed, Christopher Tellefsen; m, Mader; sound, J. Sergio Vantanen (design)

Crime/Drama/Thriller (PR: C MPAA: NR)

CLASS OF '61 ★★½
(U.S.) 95m Pendragon; Universal Television; Amblin Television ~ MCA/Universal Home Video c

Dan Futterman *(Shelby Peyton)*; Clive Owen *(Devin O'Neil)*; Len Cariou *(Dr. Leland Peyton)*; Andre Braugher *(Lucius)*; Penny Johnson *(Lavinia)*; Joshua Lucas *(George Armstrong Custer)*; Dana Ivey *(Mrs. Julia Peyton)*; Sophie Ward *(Shannen O'Neil)*; Barry Cullison *(Sergeant Yancy)*; Scott Burkholder *(Garrett St. Clair)*; Christien Anholt *(Terry O'Neil)*; Sue-Ann Leeds *(Rose Greenhow)*; Laura Linney *(Lily Magraw)*; Niall O'Brien *(James Dugan "Da" O'Neil)*; Mark Pellegrino *(Skinner)*; Lorraine Toussaint *(Sarah)*; Robert Newman *(Captain Wyckoff)*; Rus Blackwell *(Yelling Cadet)*; Laura Carney *(Mrs. H. Vann Stratton)*; Michael Genevie *(William Avery)*; Rae'ven Kelly *(Statie)*; James Moyle *(Pierce Cadet)*; John P. Navin, Jr. *(Burmett)*; Tom Nowicki *(Major Palmer)*; Jim Peck *(Chaplain French)*; Tim Powell *(Confederate Chaplain)*; Mary Nell Santacroce *(Washington Matron)*; Andrew Stahl *(Major Harry)*; Alex Van *(Toway)*; Jordan Williams *(Provost Officer)*; Paul Guilfoyle; Frederick Rolf; Tim Scott; Ed Wiley; Peter Murnik

"A plot divided against itself cannot stand." That's how Abe Lincoln might have summed up CLASS OF '61, an ambitious but ultimately disappointing TV feature from Steven Spielberg's company.

Taking more than a little inspiration from Ken Burns' popular PBS documentary series "The Civil War" (and utilizing input from Burns's star historian Shelby Foote), CLASS OF '61 purports to span the diary entries of Shelby Peyton (Dan Futterman), a West Point cadet from 1860s Virginia. When cannon fire at Fort Sumter signals open hostility between the Union and Confederate states, Shelby and other Southern cadets enlist with the Rebel army. Yet he maintains a close friendship with West Point comrade Devin O'Neil (Clive Owen), a proud Union lieutenant whose sister Shannen (Sophie Ward) is Shelby's fiancee. There's greater division in O'Neil's Baltimore household. While father is a firm Union supporter, his other son sees in Washington all the hallmarks of tyranny his family faced back in Ireland; he agitates for the Confederate cause as an act of protest and eventually dies in battle carrying the flag of Dixie.

Meanwhile, back in Virginia, Shelby Peyton has another boyhood friend, favored family slave Lucius (Andre Braugher), whose wife is about to give birth. To celebrate, the Peytons grant Lucius his freedom, but, having just killed a white slave-hunter, that's not enough protection for Lucius. He heads north via the Underground Railroad. Shelby and Devin finally meet again at the first Battle of Bull Run, where Confederate cunning leads overconfident Union troops into a trap. When Shelby recognizes his West Point classmates among the defenders, however, he gives an order to cease fire, sparing their lives—temporarily, anyway. An abrupt epilogue states that Devin and Shelby both perished later at Gettysburg, leaving behind Shannen and her baby, Shelby's out-of-wedlock son.

The suddenness of that curtain close effectively cuts CLASS OF '61 off at the knees, just when the viewer has begun to really care for these people after spending the first hour or so trying to sort them out. The truncated tale seems uncertain whether it wants to be a mighty family saga or history lesson, never fully satisfying in either mode. Dialogue is especially academic, with one flirty Southern belle riposting, "Any man who would suspend habeas corpus without the consent of Congress is not only an enemy of the people but of the Constitution as well!" The names of Matthew Brady and George Armstrong Custer are frequently dropped, and to keep transitions and establishing shots cheap, director Gregory Hoblit inserts monochrome stock footage, drawings, and maps, all contributing to the classroom-filmstrip flavor and a low-budget ambiance. Uniformly fine acting and glowing cinematography by Janusz Kaminski (SCHINDLER'S LIST) can't wholly offset these faults.

The feature scores points in delineating the dilemma of first-generation Irish-Americans, an oppressed minority now ordered to take up arms and defend their adopted home. CLASS OF '61 does a more compelling job than did Ron Howard's epic FAR AND AWAY with similar material, even if the O'Neil trait of speaking in Celtic aphorisms ("Poetry . . . piss and vinegar is the trinity of the Irish soul") grows wearisome. In defiance of 1990s political correctness, CLASS OF '61 depicts the slavery issue with an even hand, asserting that some Southern blacks preferred the security of plantation servitude to a life as wage slaves among Northerners, who could preach equality and tolerance yet lynch any freedmen who violated the color barrier. Lucius himself proves to be no mere token character but a member of the class of '61 in his own right; the ex-slave survives the Civil War in the 54th Massachusetts, the all-black Union regiment dramatized in the theatrical film GLORY.

Despite its pedigree, CLASS OF '61 premiered to indifferent critical notice on cable TV in 1993, and graduated to the home video class of '95. (*Violence.*) — C.C.

d, Gregory Hoblit; p, Gregg Fienberg; exec p, Steven Spielberg, Jonas McCord; assoc p, Tim Harbert; w, Jonas McCord; ph, Janusz Kaminski; ed, David Rosenbloom; m, John Debney; prod d, Richard B. Lewis; art d, Guy Tuttle; set d, Laurie Scott; sound, Peter Bentley (mixer); casting, Hank McGann; cos, Mike Boyd; makeup, Harriette Landau; stunts, Troy Gilbert

Historical/War/Drama   **(PR: C   MPAA: NR)**

CLEAN, SHAVEN   ★★★
(U.S.) 80m DSM III Films ~ Strand Releasing c

Peter Greene (*Peter Winter*); Molly Castelloe (*Melinda Frayne*); Megan Owen (*Mrs. Winter*); Robert Albert (*Jack McNally*); Jennifer MacDonald (*Nicole Frayne*); Alice Levitt (*Girl with Ball*); Jill Chamberlain (*Teenager at Motel*); Agathe Leclerc (*Murdered Girl*); Roget Joly (*Police Photographer*); Rene Beaudin (*Boy on Bicycle*); J. Dixon Byrne (*Dr. Michaels*); Eliot Rockett (*Man on Ladder*); Angela Vibert (*Girl in Rain*); Karen MacDonald (*Girl in Rain*); Lee Kayman (*Bartender*); Peter Lucas (*Drunk*); Rob Benevides (*Robber*); Ismael Ramirez (*Psychotic Derelict*); Marty Clinis (*Library Patron*); Ruth Gottheimer (*Library Patron*); June Kelly (*Librarian*); Grace Vibert (*Schoolteacher*); James Hance (*Man in Adoption Agency*); Marti Wilkerson (*Adoption Agent*); Michael Benson (*Man in Jeep*); Eliot Rockett (*Man in Jeep*); Cathleen Biro (*Drunk*); Harlan Hamilton (*Drunk*)

Deserving more attention than it received during its brief 1995 release, CLEAN, SHAVEN provides a novel, searing presentation of schizophrenia in this low-budget feature about a disturbed young man searching for his daughter.

Against the bleak suburban landscape of Miscou Island in New Brunswick, Canada, Peter Winter (Peter Greene) begins a search for his daughter, Nicole (Jennifer MacDonald), who had been taken from him by his ex-wife, Melinda (Molly Castelloe), following his mental breakdown some years earlier. During Peter's journey, a detective, Jack McNally (Robert Albert), trails after Peter, who has become the prime suspect in a series of murders involving young girls.

Peter's road trip includes a visit to his mother, Mrs. Winter (Megan Owen), which only reminds him of his troubled past, and a stop at a motel, where Peter becomes increasingly tormented by the sounds he hears in his head. When Peter finally arrives at the town where he and his family used to live, he tracks down and kidnaps Nicole. He then takes her to a playground where he tries to explain why he has been missing from her life. Detective McNally, who has been closely following Peter and fears for Nicole's safety, shoots and kills Peter. Soon after, however, the detective discovers that he may have shot an innocent man.

Mental illness is difficult to represent dramatically. Over the years, mainstream cinema has seen fit to sensationalize and/or simplify the complexities of psychological disturbances. For instance, note how laughable such Hollywood "classics" as THE SNAKE PIT (1949) and THREE FACES OF EVE (1957) seem today. Even the one film on which Sigmund Freud himself consulted, G.W. Pabst's SECRETS OF THE SOUL (1926), feels limited conceptually, if not artistically. Perhaps only the avant-garde (e.g. in the Japanese classic PAGE OF MADNESS [1936]) has been able to adequately approximate emotional distress by refusing to straight-jacket the subject into the conventions of melodrama.

Lodge Kerrigan's directorial debut, CLEAN, SHAVEN, is unique because it combines both melodramatic narrative and avant-garde style. The first few reels of the film, in fact, are told almost exclusively from Peter's point of view, allowing the

viewer to share his fragmented, hallucinatory world, which is neither glamorized nor romanticized. Kerrigan uses negative screen space and an eerie guitar score to further establish the melancholy atmosphere, and the film's low budget works in favor of the barren mise-en-scene.

Thematically, too, CLEAN, SHAVEN expands upon the typical model used in other cinematic portraits of the mentally ill. The pathetic scene between Peter and his mother shows a dysfunctional family element at work, but refrains from using it to cast direct and exclusive blame on Peter's condition (*a la* the PRINCE OF TIDES [1991] flashbacks). The trick ending also forces viewers to question both their own assumptions about the mentally ill and the societal stigmas that would lead to such attitudes. If anything, it is the detective who is more dangerous by the end of the story, and Kerrigan's use of a Doppelganger effect between Peter and Jack underlines the point.

By telling the story from Peter's perspective, CLEAN, SHAVEN presents one unavoidable problem that may frustrate viewers. The ellipses created by the distorted point of view leave some unanswered questions and, at one early point, strongly suggest that Peter is indeed a violent individual. This bit of "cheating" jeopardizes both viewer empathy with the character's plight, as well as a basic understanding of story events. (The grimly humorous self-wounding scenes of Peter digging at his scalp and finger creates another severe distancing element.)

Thus, CLEAN, SHAVEN's major strength also becomes its major weakness, but it is still a film well worth seeing—if only because it is different. (*Graphic violence, nudity, sexual situations, adult situations, profanity.*) — E.M.

d, Lodge H. Kerrigan; p, Lodge H. Kerrigan; exec p, J. Dixon Byrne; assoc p, Melissa Painter; w, Lodge H. Kerrigan; ph, Teodoro Maniaci; ed, Jay Rabinowitz; m, Hahn Rowe; prod d, Tania Ferrier; sound, Michael Parsons (sound design), John Kelsey (mixer), Matthew Perry (mixer), Tony Martinez; makeup, Rob Benevides

Drama/Crime   **(PR: O   MPAA: R)**

CLIVE BARKER'S LORD OF ILLUSIONS
(SEE: LORD OF ILLUSIONS)

CLOCKERS   ★★½
(U.S.) 128m 40 Acres and a Mule Filmworks; All That and a Bag of Chips Inc.; Longview Entertainment; Universal ~ Universal c

Harvey Keitel (*Rocco Klein*); John Turturro (*Larry Mazilli*); Delroy Lindo (*Rodney*); Mekhi Phifer (*Strike*); Isaiah Washington (*Victor*); Keith David (*Andre the Giant*); Pee Wee Love (*Tyrone*); Regina Taylor (*Iris Jeeter*); Tom Byrd (*Errol Barnes*); Sticky Fingaz (*Scientific*); Fredro (*Go*); E.O. Nolasco (*Horace*); Lawrence B. Adisa (*Stan*); Hassan Johnson (*Skills*); Frances Foster (*Gloria*); Michael Imperioli (*Jo-Jo*); Lisa Arrindell Anderson (*Sharon*); Paul Calderon (*Jesus at Hambones*); Brendan Kelly (*Big Chief*); Mike Starr (*Thumper*); Graham Brown (*Mr. Herman Brown*); Steve White (*Darryl Adams*); Spike Lee (*Chucky*); Shawn McLean (*Solo*); Arthur Nascarella (*Bartucci*); Harry Lennix (*Bill Walker*); Bray Poor (*Detective #1*); Craig McNulty (*Detective #2*); Christopher Wynkoop (*Detective #3*); Paul Schulze (*Detective #4*); Lt. Donald Stephenson (*Detective #5*); John Fletcher (*Al the Medic*); J.C. MacKenzie (*Frank the Medic*); David Evanson (*Smart Mike*); Norman Matlock (*Reverend Paul*); Isaac Fowler (*Charles*); Leonard Thomas (*Onion the Bar Patron*); Maurice Sneed (*Davis the Bartender*); Calvin Hart (*Guard #1*); Ginny Yang (*Kiki*); Michael Badalucco (*Cop #1*); Ricky Aiello (*Cop #2*); Scot Anthony Robinson (*Earl*); Richard

Ziman *(Moe)*; David Batiste *(T)*; Mar'qus Sample *(Ivan)*; Mar'rece Sample *(Mark)*; Ron Brice *(Dead Man Begging)*; Ken Garito *(Louie)*; Anthony Nacerino *(Teen #1)*; Brian Konowal *(Teen #2)*; Michael McGruther *(Teen #3)*; Carlo Vogel *(Teen #4)*; Harvey Williams *("Pick Me Up" Kid)*; Michael Cullen *(Narc #1)*; Tim Kelleher *(Narc #2)*; Skipp Dudduth *(Narc #3)*; Larry Mullane *(Larry the Narc)*

Perhaps responding to persistent criticism that his films about ghetto life have shied away from the issue of drugs, Spike Lee has directed this stylish adaptation of Richard Price's novel about the drug trade. Though it's slickly made—the jerky camerawork, stuttering montage, and murky cinematography are calculated effects—CLOCKERS is such an arduous trudge over cliched ground that it's hard to imagine why he bothered.

Sixteen-year-old Strike (Mekhi Phifer) is a clocker—a low level drug dealer—in a crime-ridden Brooklyn housing project. He works for Rodney Little (Delroy Lindo), a genial but ruthless pusher, who asks him to kill Darryl, a neighborhood lowlife.

The day after Darryl is murdered, Strike's brother Victor (Isaiah Washington)—a model citizen who lives with his mother, holds down two jobs, and has a pretty wife and two small sons—turns himself in, claiming that he's the murderer. Detective Rocco Klein (Harvey Keitel) doesn't believe him: he thinks that Victor is protecting Strike, and makes it his mission to nail the young dealer. Strike feels everyone is after him: Klein, his mother, local cop Andre the Giant (Keith David)—who bullies Strike into donating goods to a neighborhood youth project Andre runs—Rodney, and even Tyrone (Pee Wee Love), a 12-year-old who idolizes him. Strike's attempt to be nice to the fatherless Tyrone has already backfired: after taking the boy to get a hip haircut, he's accosted by Tyrone's angry mother, who tells him to stay away from her impressionable son. Rocco decides to put pressure on Strike by arresting Rodney and implying that Strike betrayed him. Strike realizes that he has no choice but to get out of town: before he goes, he gives bail money to Victor's wife. He also realizes that his gun is missing.

Rodney's favorite hit man, the demented Errol Barnes (Tom Byrd) comes gunning for Strike, but Tyrone—who has "borrowed" Strike's gun—kills him. Andre beats Strike up for messing with the boy's life, and Klein helps Tyrone fake a statement that will get him the minimum possible sentence. Still trying to leave town, Strike spots Rodney and flees to the police station, where Klein tries to pressure him into admitting that he killed Darryl. But Strike's mother appears and confesses that on the night of the murder, Victor came home "acting crazy." Klein realizes that Victor really is guilty, and drops Strike off in Manhattan, where he gets on a train heading west.

Lee moved the setting of Price's novel from a housing project in New Jersey to a housing project in Brooklyn, but this matters very little. What *does* matter is that Price's complicated novel, crammed with people and places and driven by thoughtful character dynamics, has been reduced to its most formulaic elements. The not-so-bad guy who wants to get out of his life of crime but doesn't know how, the rotten cops, the criminal kingpin, the decent family, the corrupting neighborhood and the innocent victims: they're familiar from scores of movies and second-rate novels, new and old. The result is crude and hectoring (this is in contrast to most of Lee's other films, which are glossy and hectoring).

The film hits its peak in the opening credits sequence, as names appear over carefully recreated crime scenes. The apparently endless parade of starkly flash-lit shots of black men and women lying in bloody heaps says more about urban violence than most people want to hear. The story that follows is just a variation on the standard-issue "hood" story, precisely the sort of thing Lee has often claimed he's tired of seeing.

Mekhi Phifer turns in a remarkably naturalistic performance as Strike, while Harvey Keitel and John Turturro—who plays another detective—are mannered and irritating. Cinematographer Malik Sayeed shoots different portions of the film on different film stocks, and while the result is interesting, it doesn't seem to mean anything in particular. Lee's visual style may never recover from the loss of his original cameraman, Ernest Dickerson. *(Violence, extreme profanity, sexual situations, adult situations, substance abuse.)* — M.M.

d, Spike Lee; p, Martin Scorsese, Spike Lee, Jon Kilik; exec p, Rosalie Swedin, Monty Ross; co-p, Richard Price; w, Richard Price, Spike Lee (based on the novel by Richard Price); ph, Malik Hassan Sayeed; ed, Sam Pollard; m, Terence Blanchard; prod d, Andrew McAlpine; art d, Ina Mayhew; set d, Debra Schutt; sound, Skip Lievsay (design), Tod A. Maitland (mixer); fx, Steve Kirshoff; casting, Robi Reed-Humes; cos, Ruth Carter; makeup, Diane Hammond; stunts, Jeff Ward

Drama/Crime (PR: O MPAA: R)

CLUELESS ★★★★
(U.S.) 97m Robert Lawrence Productions;
Paramount ~ Paramount c

Alicia Silverstone *(Cher Horowitz)*; Stacey Dash *(Dionne)*; Brittany Murphy *(Tai)*; Paul Rudd *(Josh)*; Dan Hedaya *(Mel Hamilton)*; Donald Faison *(Murray)*; Elisa Donovan *(Amber)*; Breckin Meyer *(Travis Birkenstock)*; Jeremy Sisto *(Elton)*; Aida Linares *(Lucy)*; Wallace Shawn *(Mr. Wendell Hall)*; Twink Caplan *(Miss Toby Geist)*; Justin Walker *(Christian)*; Sabastian Rashidi *(Paroudasm)*; Herb Hall *(Principal)*; Julie Brown *(Ms. Stoeger)*; Susan Mohun *(Heather)*; Nicole Bilderback *(Summer)*; Ron Orbach *(DMV Tester)*; Sean Holland *(Lawrence)*; Roger Kabler *(College Guy)*; Jace Alexander *(Robber)*; Josh Lozoff *(Logan)*; Carl Gottlieb *(Priest)*; Joseph D. Reitman *(Student)*; Anthony Beninati *(Bartender)*; Micki Duran; Greg Russell; Jermaine Montell; Daniella Eckert *(Dancers)*

Just beneath the bubbly, candy-colored surface of this good-natured fluff about privileged California teens lies a sharply observed comedy of manners with a good deal more to say about family, romance, and friendship in the '90s than mainstream audiences have any right to expect. Like its effortlessly adorable protagonist Cher, CLUELESS is anything but.

Pretty, impeccably groomed Cher Hamilton (Alicia Silverstone) is the most popular girl at Bronson Alcott High School (Beverly Hills High in all but name). Her father (Dan Hedaya) is a successful lawyer who indulges her every whim (her mom died during routine liposuction surgery), and her best friend Dionne (Stacey Dash) shares her preoccupations: music, fitness, and fashion. Cher's perfect life is only slightly disrupted when her ex-step-brother Josh (Paul Rudd)—a *terribly* serious college student—comes to stay.

Stung by Josh's exhortations that she's frivolous and should try to do some good in the world, Cher starts small, playing secret matchmaker for two awkward, brainy teachers—Mr. Hall and Miss Geist (Wallace Shawn and Twink Caplan)—too preoccupied to see they're made for one another. To her delight, the match takes. Cher then persuades Dionne to join her in rescuing new girl Tai (Brittany Murphy) from a life of social exile. Together they make Tai over, advising her on clothes, hair, make-up and other essentials of teen life. Cher tries to fix Tai up with Elton (Jeremy Sisto), the most popular boy in school, but Elton comes on to Cher instead. She rebuffs him, and for her trouble is abandoned in a strip mall at night, where she's mugged. Josh comes to her rescue.

Cher falls for the flawlessly turned-out Christian (Dustin Walker) and plans to lose her virginity to him. Unfortunately for this plan, Christian is gay. But it's all okay, because he and Cher become best friends. Tai—who is fast becoming Cher's rival for the honor of being most popular girl at school—in turn sets her sights on Josh, whose approval has become increasingly important to Cher.

She sets about improving herself further by volunteering for charity work and assisting with one of her father's complicated legal projects. Though increasingly well-intentioned, Cher is still a bit of an airhead, and when she makes a major error in her work for her father, she's convinced that Josh will never speak to her again. Instead, he confesses that he's fallen in love with her. They attend the wedding of Mr. Hall and Miss Geist, and Cher catches the bride's bouquet.

Amy Heckerling's screenplay is a delightful variation on Jane Austen's 1815 *Emma*, a biting novel about well-intentioned social meddling by the pampered daughter of an indulgent, widowed father. To be sure, CLUELESS is a one-joke film: capricious, benignly materialistic control-freak Cher thinks she can put everyone else's business in order, but doesn't have a clue as to what to do about her own life. She gets herself into a string of harmless messes and extricates herself by virtue of her effervescent charm and fundamental decency, then finds that the love she's been searching for has been under her pretty little nose all along. But Heckerling, who also directs, gives the apparently trifling material an astringent bite of which Austen would most likely have approved. That the film's happy ending is a short step away from incest is a brilliant last word.

Cher is a beautifully packaged bundle of contradictions: superficially sophisticated but deeply ignorant, kind but oblivious, controlling but generous. She's clever without being smart, instinctively perceptive without the discipline that would tell her what to do with her insights. That Heckerling and Silverstone make Cher entirely lovable without glossing over her substantial deficiencies is one of the film's greatest triumphs. The other is its deft use of language. Cher and her friends speak a sleek, allusive patois that's almost Asian in its sensitivity to inflection and poetic in its reliance on convoluted metaphor. *(Profanity, adult situations.)* — M.M.

d, Amy Heckerling; p, Robert Lawrence, Scott Rudin; assoc p, Twink Caplan; co-p, Adam Schroeder, Barry Berg; w, Amy Heckerling; ph, Bill Pope; ed, Debra Chiate; m, David Kitay; prod d, Steve Jordan; art d, William Hiney; set d, Amy Wells; ch, Patrick Romano; sound, David Ronne (mixer); casting, Marcia S. Ross; cos, Mona May; makeup, Alan "Doc" Friedman; stunts, Patrick Romano

Comedy/Romance (PR: C MPAA: PG-13)

COLDBLOODED ★★½
(U.S.) 91m Polygram; Motion Picture Corporation of America; Snowback Productions; Propaganda Films ~ IRS Media c

Jason Priestly (*Cosmo*); Kimberly Williams (*Jasmine*); Peter Riegert (*Steve*); Robert Loggia (*Gordon*); Jay Kogen (*John*); Janeane Garofalo (*Honey*); Josh Charles (*Randy*); David Anthony Higgins (*Lance*); Doris Grau (*Rose*); Ann Carol (*Receptionist*); Buck McDancer (*Fleeing Man*); Marcos A. Ferraez (*Man with Uzi*); Gilbert Rosales (*Man with Briefcase*); Jim Turner (*Doctor*); Michael J. Fox (*Tim Alexander*); Talia Balsam (*Jean Alexander*); Marc Wolodarsky (*Creepy Guy*); Kay O'Connell (*Yoga Woman*); Cecile Krevoy (*Waitress*)

A modest little black comedy about a reluctant hit man, COLDBLOODED has enough wit and blood to find a ready audience in the fans of PULP FICTION.

Cosmo (Jason Priestley), a mob bookie, resides in the basement of a retirement home, where he sits staring at the TV, awaiting visits from Honey (Janeane Garofalo), a hooker whom he considers his girlfriend. When Gordon (Robert Loggia) takes over "the company," he promotes Cosmo to hit man. Cosmo goes under the tutelage of Steve (Peter Riegert), a seasoned professional, and it is quickly apparent that Cosmo is a natural born killer. But despite the calm with which he pulls the trigger, murdering makes Cosmo uneasy, so he starts going to yoga classes to help him relax. He begins dating his yoga instructor, Jasmine (Kimberly Williams), and soon falls in love.

Cosmo becomes more and more comfortable with killing. After Steve is wounded by some drug dealers, Cosmo "flies solo," and his poise really impresses Gordon. Gordon orders Cosmo to eliminate Steve and take over the work entirely, but Cosmo wants out so he can be with Jasmine. He kills Steve, then Gordon, and he is free. But Jasmine, now aware of his occupation, wants nothing to do with him. Crestfallen, Cosmo declares he cannot live without Jasmine, but he cannot bring himself to commit suicide either, so he decides to kill her. At this point, Jasmine realizes that they can probably work through their problems after all.

First-time writer-director M. Wallace Wolodarsky previously worked on "The Simpsons," and COLDBLOODED shares that TV series' black comic sensibility. In a style recalling Jim Jarmusch, Wolodarksy's scenes are deliberately paced and quiet, with unexpected resolutions. For example, when Cosmo goes on his first hit without Steve, he surprises a husband and wife accounting team (Michael J. Fox and Talia Balsam) by showing up at their house for breakfast. Cosmo luxuriates over a cup of coffee, while the nervous couple answer his questions about dating and their secrets for a lasting relationship. When pressed for the reason for his visit, Cosmo stands up, pulls his gun, and matter-of-factly sprays their brains all over the wall.

Like Jules and Vincent discussing Big Macs and foot massage at the beginning of PULP FICTION, Steve and Cosmo bide their time between hits mulling over car interiors and the rudiments of gun safety. COLDBLOODED doesn't have any of the razzle-dazzle that made PULP FICTION so deliciously funny, but it offers enough perverse delight to deserve more of Tarantino's audience. *(Graphic violence, extreme profanity, adult situations.)* — P.R.

d, M. Wallace Wolodarsky; p, Michael J. Fox, Matt Tolmach, Brad Krevoy, Steve Stabler, Brad Jenkel; exec p, Larry Estes; w, M. Wallace Wolodarsky; ph, Robert Yeoman; ed, Craig Bassett; m, Steve Bartek; prod d, Rae Fox; set d, Tim Colohan; sound, Giovanni DiSimone; cos, Matthew Jacobson

Crime (PR: O MPAA: R)

COLORADO COWBOY: ★★★
THE BRUCE FORD STORY
(U.S.) 78m Arthur Elgort Productions c/bw

Bruce Ford

Arthur Elgort, long a successful fashion photographer for *Vogue*, embarked upon a rather quixotic-sounding project for the 1990s, a series of documentary features celebrating unsung American heroes. Elgort's first entry, TEXAS TENOR: THE ILLINOIS JACQUET STORY, concerned a tenor sax jazz musician hugely admired in music circles but hardly a household word for the general public. COLORADO COWBOY introduces the viewer to Bruce Ford, one of the West's true remaining professional cowboys, as he tours the rodeo circuit competing for purses ranging from $400 to $500,000.

Shooting in sepia tones reminiscent of antique frontier prints, the camera follows Ford in his careful, almost ritualistic preparations for a ride. Soft-spoken, down-to-earth, but unmistakably something of a showman, Ford describes the need to change his riggings every 125 horses, his gloves every 50 or so. Without bluster, the 39-year-old Ford gives the impression of a Frederick Remington figure come to life, whether he's teaching tenderfeet the basics of horsemanship on his ranch, or lashing through the air in slow-motion astride a bucking bronco, at rodeos ranging from Cheyenne, Wyoming, to Madison Square Garden.

In the quieter moments, Elgort displays Ford's proud family—two golden-haired children, a son and daughter, both seem ready to follow in his bootprints—his Christian faith, the tragic early loss of a father and brother (old home movies comprise the only color sequences), and the sense of heritage that spurs him on. Only late in COLORADO COWBOY do the filmmakers let slip that Bruce Ford is officially ranked as one of the top 15 professional cowboys in the world. A more commonplace, star-struck profile might have stated that bald fact up front, but Elgort allows audiences the privilege of getting to know and like Ford a lot before revealing the scope of his honors and achievements. In the end, Bruce Ford participates in the National Finals of rodeo riding and finishes scant points short of winning the million-dollar first prize. But he takes the loss like a gentleman, and one doesn't doubt that he'll be back.

Elgort's background in still photography is evident: tightly focused on its subject, with nearly no outside interviews, factoids, or statistics to put Bruce Ford in a larger context, COLORADO COWBOY is reminiscent of vintage *Life* magazine pictorials (like W. Eugene Smith's "A Country Doctor"). One could argue that some of Elgort's techniques are better suited to the printed page, but his survey of overlooked "American heroes" is a welcome antidote to an era of tabloid sensations and notoriety. — C.C.

d, Arthur Elgort; p, Ronit Avneri; exec p, Arthur Elgort; w, Arthur Elgort; ph, Morton Sandtroen; ed, Paula Heredia

Documentary/Biography   (PR: AA   MPAA: NR)

COMPANION, THE   ★★½
(U.S.) 94m Windy City ~ MCA/Universal Home Video c

Kathryn Harrold (*Gillian*); Bruce Greenwood (*Geoffrey*); Talia Balsam (*Charlene*); Brion James (*Ron Cocheran*); Joely Fisher (*Stacy*); Bryan Cranston (*Alan*); James Karen (*Peter Franklin*); Brenda Leigh (*Ellen*); Earl Boen (*Marty Bailin*); Julian Brams (*Technician*); Courtney Taylor (*Shelley*); Stacey Randall (*Saleswoman*); Tracey Walter (*Leo Mirita*)

As straightforward suspense thriller, THE COMPANION evinces an edgy elan. But this made-for-cable-TV feature fails to attain a balance between erotic undertones and the underlying sci-fi riffs about things (wo)men were not meant to tamper with.

Although a successful romance novelist in the 21st century, Gillian (Kathryn Harrold) has less luck with her own philandering boyfriend. For a planned working holiday in a woodland cabin best pal Charlene (Talia Balsam) engages an alternative companion for her: a lifelike male robot from Personal Electronics. Skeptical at first, Gillian comes to rely on Jeffrey (Bruce Greenwood), her perfect "man" about the house. While progressing with the latest bodice-ripper, Gillian programs Jeffrey to be less robotic and more conversational. Gradually upgrading his duties (with a few notable exceptions, like swimming ability) to ultimately sexual pleasure and a simulcrum of love, Gillian counts her blessings—until the increasingly possessive Jeffrey

starts calling the shots. When visiting Charlene arrives and questions Jeffrey's independence, the companion kills her. The next would-be rescuer to go is a neighbor, priggish, macho sculptor Ron (Brion James, who did the android bit himself in BLADE RUNNER). After escape attempts fail, Gillian sweet-talks her mechanical swain into a lakeside picnic, where she fakes drowning. Crestfallen Jeffrey tries to self-destruct but runs amok instead. With Ron's projectile-firing sculpting tool (introduced so portentously early on that one intuitively knows it will be used as a weapon), Gillian obliterates her obsessed lover/appliance.

Rapport between Harrold's lonelyhearts romantic and Greenwood's synthetic Romeo is so appealing that viewers may root for them to find happiness in this bizarre mixed marriage. But in opting to scare us with Gillian's mechanical misalliance, the screenplay botches the opportunity to present the sci-fi dilemma tragically. Instead of building on each succeeding jittery episode and portraying a dangerous erotic vortex, THE COMPANION turns into a standard stalker flick. Much too wordy for a chiller, the awkward screenplay should have donned a darkly comic mantle as Gillian and her honeymoon machine parody human relationships and all the attendant jealousy that comes with newly-ignited passion (Jeffrey takes his cues and attitudes directly from the romance author's purple prose). After Gillian's swim for liberty, the movie exhibits FRIDAY THE 13TH syndrome as disfigured Jeffrey rages about and crushes a concept that had promised to skewer the ambiguities that plague romantic entanglements. THE COMPANION winds up a *Consumer Reports* fright flick about a defective purchase. (*Violence, sexual situations, adult situations.*) — R.P.

d, Gary Fleder; p, Richard Brams; exec p, Michael Phillips; co-p, Valerie Bennett, Rona Edwards; w, Ian Seeberg; ph, Rick Bota; ed, John Carnochan; m, David Shire; prod d, Laurence Bennett; art d, Charles L. Parker, III; fx, Gary D'Amico; casting, Melissa Skoff; cos, Betsy Cox

Science Fiction/Romance/Thriller   (PR: C   MPAA: NR)

CONGO   ★★
(U.S.) 109m Kennedy/Marshall Company; Paramount ~ Paramount C

Dylan Walsh (*Peter Elliot*); Laura Linney (*Karen Ross*); Ernie Hudson (*Monroe Kelly*); Joe Don Baker (*R.B. Travis*); Tim Curry (*Herkermer Homolka*); Taylor Nichols (*Jeffrey Weems*); Grant Heslov (*Richard*); Bruce Campbell (*Charles Travis*); Lorene Noh (*Amy*); Misty Rosas (*Amy*); Mary Ellen Trainor (*Moira*); Stuart Pankin (*Boyd*); Adewale (*Kahega*); Carolyn Seymour (*Eleanor Romy*); Romy Roseman (*Eleanor Romy's Assistant*); James Karen (*College President*); Bill Pugin (*William*); Lawrence T. Wrentz (*Arliss Wender*); Robert Almodovar (*Rudy*); Kathleen Connors (*Sally*); Joel Weiss (*Travicom Employee*); John Hawkes (*Bob Driscoll*); Peter Jason (*Mr. Janus*); Jimmy Buffett (*727 Pilot*); James R. Paradise (*Transport Worker No. 1*); William John Murphy (*Transport Worker No. 2*); Thom Barry (*Samahani*); Ayo Ade Jugbe (*African Airport Guard*); Kahara Muhoro (*Roadblock Soldier*); Kevin Grevioux (*Hospital Officer/Roadblock Officer*); M. Darnell Suttles (*Hospital Interrogator*); Michael Chinyamurindi (*Claude*); Willie Amakye (*Lead Porter*); Malang; Jay Speed Forney; Shelton Mack; David Mungai; Anthony Mutune; Sylvester Mwangi; Les Robinson; Nelson Shalita (*Porters*); Jackson Gitonga (*Mizumu Tribesman*); Andrew Kamuyu (*Mizumu Tribesman*); Fidel Bateke (*Witch Doctor*); Shayna Fox (*Amy's Voice*); David Anthony; Brian La Rosa; Jay Caputo; David St. Pierre; Nicholas Kadi; John Cameron; Garon Michael; Eldon Jackson; Christopher "Critter" Antonucci; John Alexander Lowe; Peter Elliot; Philip Tan (*Gorillas*)

Novelist Michael Crichton seems to have parlayed the colossal success of JURASSIC PARK into a screen-rights-binge on his earlier, unfilmed books. One result: CONGO, a second-rate jungle adventure that delivers far less than it promises.

Via video satellite link from a volcano in deepest, darkest Africa, Dr. Karen Ross (Laura Linney) and tycoon R.B. Travis (Joe Don Baker) watch his son and her former fiance Charles (Bruce Campbell) test a new super-laser using a mammoth diamond. Suddenly, the encampment is attacked by wild gorillas, and though it appears that everyone has been killed, Charles's body is nowhere to be seen. Karen wants to find him, while Travis is more concerned with recovering the laser weapon.

Meanwhile primate specialist Peter Elliot (Dylan Walsh) is coping with his own problems. Amy—a gorilla he has taught to use sign language and fitted with a device that converts her hand movements into digitized speech—is pining for Africa. Elliot wants to take her back, and hopes she'll teach other apes to sign, allowing researchers to learn more about their lives in the wild. Mysterious, self-proclaimed Romanian philanthropist Herkermer Homolka (Tim Curry) offers to pay for the expedition, on the condition that he can come along. Ross buys her way in at the last minute, using the scientific expedition as cover for her own, less high-minded agenda.

Ross and Elliot spar, then grow to respect and like one another. Once in Africa, they team up with Monroe Kelly (Ernie Hudson), a Great White Hunter who just happens to be Black. Kelly bribes their way through the Zaire border, but their plane is attacked by Zairean rebels and they're forced to bail out some distance from their destination.

Ross makes contact with her employers and learns that the volcano is going to erupt soon. But Amy playfully wrecks the receiver and the rains wash out the rest of the nifty high-tech gear, so they're on their own as they proceed deeper into the jungle. They finally locate the destroyed campsite of the first expedition. Homolka admits he's looking for the lost city of Zinj, home to King Solomon's fabled mines, they do indeed find Zinj. The group is attacked by savage white gorillas of exceptional intelligence and strength that were bred to guard the mines. Greedy Homolka is torn to pieces, and Ross and Elliot find Charles' corpse—and the experimental laser—atop a massive pile of human bones. Amy tries to rescue her human friends by talking to the mutant apes, but the laser weapon proves far more helpful. A simultaneous earthquake and volcanic eruption seal off the egress to Zinj. Elliot and Ross release Amy, and Ross destroys the laser gun.

Congo, written in 1980, is not one of Crichton's better novels. CONGO, adapted by John Patrick Shanley and directed by Stephen Spielberg protege Frank Marshall, is not one of the better silly action pictures set in gratuitously fake jungles and featuring nefarious foreigners, threatening natives, and talking gorillas. Marshall clearly does not share Crichton's obsession with technology: His attitude is summed up by Ross's reply to a question about her handheld satellite tracking device—"Well, ya know, it's a gadget; it has features"—and evident in the often laughable quality of the film's many special effects. Marshall appears to have envisioned CONGO as a sort of '90s version of a 1940s jungle movie (Paramount is rumored to have bought the book with an eye to developing it as an INDIANA JONES movie), but its nostalgic charms were lost on an audience brought up on the high-tech likes of, well, JURASSIC PARK. *(Profanity, graphic violence.)* — R.S.

d, Frank Marshall; p, Kathleen Kennedy, Sam Mercer; exec p, Frank Yablans; assoc p, Michael Backes, Paul Deason; w, John Patrick Shanley (based on the novel by Michael Crichton); ph, Allen Daviau; ed, Anne V. Coates; m, Jerry Goldsmith; prod d,

J. Michael Riva; art d, Richard Holland; set d, Lisa Fischer; sound, Ronald Judkins (mixer); fx, Michael Lantieri, Tom C. Peitzman, Scott Farrar, Ned Gorman, Industrial Light & Magic, Sandra Ford Karpman; casting, Mike Fenton, Allison Cowitt; cos, Marilyn Matthews; makeup, Christina Smith, Matthew W. Mungle, John E. Jackson, Stan Winston; stunts, M. James Arnett

Adventure   (PR: A   MPAA: PG-13)

CONGRESS OF PENGUINS, THE   ★★★½
(Switzerland) 91m Ariane Film; Zuerich; Swiss Television; ARTE ~ Christa Saredi World Sales c
(DER KONGRESS DER PINGUINE)

Peter Schweiger

This odd and often moving film from Switzerland depicts the past abuse of the creatures of Antarctica, as well as the apparently benevolent research by contemporary scientists and technicians. Directed and co-scripted by Hans-Ulrich Schlumpf, the first half of the film, as one wag observed, is a cross beween NIGHT AND FOG and a PBS National Geographic special.

The unseen narrator recalls a dream in which he is alone on an expanse of snow, with a horizon broken only by mesas of solid ice. Soon, the sound of animals is heard, followed by a procession of penguins who march single file towards the open sea. As the narrator listens to them, the seemingly nonsensical word, Grytviken, is all he can make out. We soon discover, however that Grytviken is a place in the South Georgia Islands. Seen today, it is a rusted and derelict factory with a harbor occupied by listing hulks. A 1930 newsreel shows the town at its productive height, as a whaling station, where the hunted mammals were skinned, butchered, and processed. Schlumpf uses older footage to explain the grim purposes of rusty cables and weatherbeaten chutes, bulky boilers and rotten slipways. The German newsreel declaims in stentorian tone the many uses of the "docile colossi" whose oil can be used for explosives, perfume and machine-guns. But there is one more distasteful horror Schlumpf has reserved for his audience: penguins, whose sleek downy fur and fat protect them from the cold and give them their characteristic look, were perfect for stoking the furnances that rendered the whale blubber.

On his knees before the assembled penguins, the narrator begs for forgiveness. Their grim verdict is interrupted with scenes of scientific activity and equipment both aboard an oceanographic icebreaker from Germany and at a base where the atmosphere and ice samples are studied. The researchers and technicians seem a far cry from the Norwegian sailors and harpooners shown teasing the animals in the shallows off Grytviken, but Schlumpf suggests there is not so great a disparity. They leave behind mountains of rubbish, not to mention abandoned housing, and there is one highly ironic shot of people cavorting on internalcombustion-powered vehicles. At the same time, their work focuses on the ozone layer and the effects of pollution. The assembled penguins, Schlumpf's narrator tells us, have already reached *their* decision.

The three species of penguins shown also provide comic relief as they waddle or slide on their bellies towards their gathering, play along the water's edge and literally fly out of the sea. Both the unsurpassable beauty and the danger of this world are featured in the film, including a visual reference to the 1948 Ealing feature, SCOTT OF THE ANTARCTIC. The film's criticism of today's human visitors is strained, but its first half remains a remarkable example of surreal strength. *(Adult situations.)* — L.R.

d, Hans-Ulrich Shlumpf; w, Hans-Ulrich Shlumpf, Franz Hohler; ph, Pio Corradi, Patrick Lindenmaier, Luc Jacquet; ed, Fee

Liechti; m, Bruno Spoerri; sound, Dieter Meyer, Dieter Lengacher, Florian Eidenbenz, Hans Kuenzi

Docudrama/Fantasy/Historical   **(PR: C   MPAA: NR)**

CONVENT, THE   ★★½
(France/Portugal) 90m Madragoa Filmes; Gemini Films;
La Sept-Cinema ~ Strand Releasing c
(O CONVENTO)

Catherine Deneuve *(Helene)*; John Malkovich *(Michael Padovic)*; Luis Miguel Cintra *(Baltar)*; Leonor Silveira *(Piedade)*; Duarte D'Almeida *(Baltazar)*; Heloisa Miranda *(Berta)*; Gilberto Goncalves *(Pescador)*

THE CONVENT tells a classic story of tangled relationships and confrontations between good and evil. For a framework, the film uses the adventures of an estranged couple who visit an ancient Portuguese convent, meet a strange gathering of characters, and eventually unite before disappearing inexplicably.

Michael (John Malkovich), an American professor, comes to Portugal with his distant and bitter wife, Helene (Catherine Deneuve), to explore the possibly Sephardic Jewish heritage of William Shakespeare. Michael plans to do his primary research in the archives of an old convent, which no longer operates but still houses a small staff, including Baltar (Luis Miguel Cintra), the dark and mysterious caretaker who takes a special interest in Helene; Piedade (Leonor Silveira), the young, beautiful librarian who helps Michael; Baltazar (Duarte D'Almeida), Baltar's elderly assistant; and Berta (Heloisa Miranda), a psychic housekeeper.

During their stay, Michael and Helene grow even further apart. Michael busies himself with work in the library, while Helene strikes up an odd friendship with Baltar, who, it is suggested, might be the Devil himself in human guise. Meanwhile, Helene becomes increasingly jealous of the time Michael spends with Piedade, and she asks Baltar to destroy the young women. Baltar obliges by seducing Piedade and taking her to a forest where, he claims, his charms will be irresistible to even the purest of hearts. In the end, we learn from a local fisherman that Michael and Helene have reunited but have also mysteriously vanished, while Baltar and Piedade have been killed in a fire.

The 1995 critical reception of THE CONVENT was overly polite, perhaps in deference to celebrated octogenarian filmmaker, Manoel de Oliveira (THE SATIN SLIPPER, VALLEY OF ABRAHAM). But THE CONVENT is not only bad Oliveira, it is bad art-house anything.

Reworking a plot used in films as diverse as Rossellini's STRANGERS (1954) and Bertolucci's SHELTERING SKY (1990), Oliveira incorporates heavy-going religious symbolism into a story about the reconciliation of an estranged married couple on a sabbatical. Oliveira's screenplay, based on an "original" idea by Agustina Bessa-Luis, begins with a fascinating premise—the professor's attempt to determine Shakespeare's religious origins—but drops it almost immediately in favor of the good versus evil plot that comprises the rest of the film.

Of course, THE CONVENT never pretends to be a traditional narrative, but the sluggish pace would be more forgivable if the many Biblical references served to illuminate the story. In one sequence, for example, Baltar, like the Devil in the Bible, takes Michael, like Christ in the Bible, to a mountain top, but, other than replicating the incident, the scene provides no new insights. It is possible that Portuguese audiences would find greater meaning in some of the specific artifacts in and around the convent, but, for many other viewers, the film will seem pretentious, and the many allusions to history, art, literature, religion and science

(including astrology) will not disguise the emptiness of the observations.

Cintra's performance as Baltar is hammy and theatrical, and his maniacal laugh is hopelessly out of place in the tranquil mise-en-scene, ruining the few potentially interesting scenes, such as Baltar's cat-and-mouse seduction of Helene, set in a catacomb. The always classy Deneuve, however, emerges unscathed, although she is not utilized to her best dramatic or physical advantage. *(Adult situations.)* — E.M.

d, Manoel de Oliveira; p, Paulo Branco; w, Manoel de Oliveira (from a story Agustina Bessa-Luis); ph, Mario Barroso; ed, Manoel de Oliveira, Valerie Loiseleux; art d, Ze Branco, Ana Vaz da Silva; sound, Jean-Paul Mugel; cos, Isabel Branco

Drama/Religious/Mystery   **(PR: C   MPAA: NR)**

CONVICT COWBOY   ★★½
(U.S.) 98m Showtime; MGM Television ~
MGM/UA Home Video c

Jon Voight *(Ry Weston)*; Kyle Chandler *(Clay Treyton)*; Marcia Gay Harden *(Maggie Sinclair)*; Glenn Plummer *(Jimmy Latrell)*; Ben Gazzara *(Warden Ferguson)*; Stephen McHattie *(Jagges Neff)*; Brent Woolsey *(Cody Stavert)*; Michael Tiernan *(Luke Cutter)*; Dean Wray *(Earl)*; Jim Baker *(Billy)*; Tom Heaton *(Lon)*; Bill Croft *(Bishop)*; Zook Matthews *(Savoy)*; Josiah Rise *(Load)*; Fred Perron *(Jitters)*; Willie Goepen *(Stoker)*; Eric Chasse *(Dax)*; Tyrone Benskin *(Curtis Sykes)*; Nathaniel Deveaux *(Otis)*; Blu Mankuma *(Warden Bill Renner)*; Jerry Ratchford *(Bob)*; David Polusen *(Announcer)*; Ryan Byrns *(Bull Fighter 1)*; Bruck Parkhouse *(Goodhew)*; Phillip Jarrett *(Ballard)*; Bryan Fustakian *(Livestock Wrangler)*; Shaun Johnston *(Cop 1)*; Ernie Jackson *(Cop 2)*; Truman Hoszouski *(Checkpoint Guard)*; Chris Nannarone *(Inmate)*; Brian Jensen *(Prison Official)*; Alex Bruhanski *(Doctor)*; Dave Leader *(Bull Fighter 2)*

Graced with a supple performance by Jon Voight, CONVICT COWBOY is a grim melodrama about how a code of ethics can survive even in a penitentiary. Ultimate uplift prevails despite the wealth of jailhouse cliches and a doomed romance unnecessarily sandwiched into a central redemptive storyline.

Cowpoke Clay Treyton (Kyle Chandler) drunkenly smashes a store window and resists arrest, landing him a severe stretch up the river. Welcomed by old pal Jimmy Letrall (Glenn Plummer), Clay gets a cold shoulder from ex-rodeo star Ryan Weston (Voight). In charge of a convict-run ranch, taciturn loner Weston recognizes in Clay's wild streak the same qualities that caused him to trash his own career years before by fatally shooting a bouncer. Once he eagerly signs up for Weston's spread, tenderfoot Clay gets the most backbreaking chores. Worse yet, the newcomer must smuggle in drugs for con kingpin Jagges Neff (Stephen McHattie) even though Weston stands against substance abuse. Encouraging his boss's untenable romance with lady vet Maggie Sinclair (Marcia Gay Harden), Clay comes to idolize Weston and is unable to escape the narcotics biz when Neff threatens to kill the rodeo champ. Clay tries outsmarting the dealer by withholding the goods, a ploy that results in Letrall's demise. During a showdown, Clay and Weston rumble with various low-lifes and leave Neff holding the dope and the shank that killed Letrall. Going to bat for his protege, Weston pleads leniency for Clay. Upon Clay's prison release, he awards the ex-con with his prized bronco saddle, thus confirming that the young man can succeed on the outside.

The film doesn't cop out with a clearly-defined happy ending but allows a lifer, who'll never taste freedom again, to gain peace of mind from the knowledge that he's saved someone else from his fate. As this loner determined to survive by suffocating his emotions, Voight sinks his teeth into his first worthy screen character in years. Without him CONVICT COWBOY would take too many tumbles, despite sturdy support from Chandler, totally convincing as the braggart who metaphorically shoots from the hip. Jailhouse drug trafficking gets outlined in luminescent magic marker colors, although the film's approximation of life in the pen is unsettling enough to stifle criticism. What sits less easily is the script's aim to humanize Weston further via his hankering for the lady animal doctor. Their scenes together could have been lifted from an old Warner Brothers B-movie. Instead the film's heart lies in Weston's resistance to the rowdy younger man's insistence on a relationship; the lone wolf's struggle to deny a kinship fuels the drama. CONVICT COWBOY premiered in 1995 on the Showtime cable TV network. *(Violence, extreme profanity, substance abuse, adult situations.)* — R.P.

d, Rod Holcomb; p, Norman S. Powell; exec p, Paul Frederick Schneier; co-p, Diane Schneier; w, Rick Way, Jim Lindsay; ph, James L. Carter; ed, Christopher Nelson; m, David Bell; art d, Terry Gunvordahl; set d, Jackie Blackie-Goodine; sound, Giovanni DiSimone (mixer); fx, Lee Routly; casting, Beth Klein; cos, Wendy Partridge; makeup, Gail Kennedy; stunts, Brent Woolsey

Drama/Action (PR: C MPAA: R)

COPYCAT ★★★
(U.S.) 123m Regency Enterprises ~ Warner Bros. c

Sigourney Weaver *(Helen Hudson)*; Holly Hunter *(M.J. Monahan)*; Dermot Mulroney *(Ruben Goetz)*; William McNamara *(Peter Foley)*; Harry Connick, Jr. *(Daryll Lee Cullum)*; J.E. Freeman *(Lt. Quinn)*; Will Patton *(Nicoletti)*; John Rothman *(Andy)*; Shannon O'Hurley *(Susan Schiffer)*; Bob Greene *(Pachulski)*; Tony Haney *(Kerby)*; Danny Kovacs *(Kostas)*; Tahmus Rounds *(Landis)*; Scott DeVenney *(Cop 1)*; David Michael Silverman *(Mike)*; Diane Amos *(Gigi)*; Richard Conti *(Harvey)*; Nick Scoggin *(Conrad)*; Bert Kinyon *(Burt)*; Dennis Richmond *(KXBU Anchorman)*; Rob Nilsson *(SWAT Commander)*; Kenny Kwong *(Chinese Kid)*; Charles Branklyn *(Doc)*; Kelly De Martino *(Festival Girl)*; Rebecca Jane Klingler *(Peter's Wife)*; Terry Brown *(Cop 2)*; Corie Henninger *(Jogger)*; Bill Bonham *(Photographer)*; Kathleen Stefano *(Peter's Mother)*; Chris Beale *(Tech Guy 1)*; Hansford Prince *(Fred)*; Don West *(Attorney)*; Jay Jacobus *(Judge)*; John Charles Morris *(Young Peter)*; Keith Phillips *(Felix Mendoza)*; Johnetta Shearer *(Paramedic)*; Ron Kaell *(Mac)*; Kelvin Han Yee *(Chinese Detective)*; James Cunningham *(Hal)*; Victor Talmadge *(Head Waiter)*; Brian Russell *(Coroner's Man)*; Damon Lawner *(Festival Dude)*; Russ Christoff *(Commissioner Petrillo)*; Doug Morrisson *(SWAT 1)*; Edith Bryson *(Landlady)*; Jeni Chua *(Michelle)*; William Oates *(Man in Corridor)*; Lee Kopp *(Haircut Man)*; Thomas J. Fieweger *(Bodger the Cop)*; Floyd Gale Holland *(L. Bottemy)*; Anthony Moore *(Uniformed Policeman)*; Stephanie Smith *(Disturbed Tenant 1)*; S.J. Spinali *(Disturbed Tenant 2)*; Katherine Fitzhugh *(Disturbed Tenant 3)*; Robert Benscoter *(Disturbed Tenant 4)*; Arlon G. Greene *(Male Jogger)*; Stuart W. Yee *(Thug)*; Vincenetta Gunn *(Screaming Woman)*; David Ferguson *(Dock On-Looker)*; Eleva Singleton *(Paramedic)*; Gena Bingham *(Victim in Car at Gas Station)*

A serial killer movie in which two women—a cop and a psychiatrist—bring down a murderer who's emulating other famous killers, COPYCAT is mean spirited but clever.

Dr. Helen Hudson (Sigourney Weaver), who's famous for her writings about serial murderers, is nearly killed by one of her subjects. Following a lecture, Hudson finds herself trapped in the toilet with Daryll Lee Cullum (Harry Connick Jr.), an escaped

lunatic who is obsessed with her. He kills her police escort and nearly kills her before he's captured and taken back to jail.

The experience leaves Helen agoraphobic, and she retreats into her fortress-like San Francisco apartment, where she drinks too much. A series of bizarre murders attracts her attention, and she calls the police with advice. Coolly efficient Detective M.J. Monahan (Holly Hunter) and her assistant Ruben (Dermot Mulroney), who have been unable to catch the killer (William McNamara), reluctantly join forces with Helen.

Helen thinks that the killer—whose crimes all differ so greatly that she and Monahan are pretty much alone in thinking they're the work of one man—is a copycat: That he's recreating murders by such famous killers as The Boston Strangler, Ted Bundy, Son of Sam and the Hillside Stranglers. What Helen doesn't realize is that he's corresponding with Cullum, who's encouraging him to torment Helen. When she first notices odd things out of place in her apartment, she thinks she's having a nervous breakdown. In fact, the killer is deliberately harassing her, showing that he can come into her apartment anytime he wants, and that the police can't stop him.

The killer picks up Helen's secretary, Andy (John Rothmen), in a bar and murders him, and Ruben is killed in a random act of violence at the precinct house. Nursing their twin sorrows, the women suddenly see the pattern in the murders: Helen recited a list of serial killers at her last lecture, and the killer is imitating them, in order. He kidnaps Helen, planning to finish his reign of terror by murdering her as Cullum intended. Instead, M.J. kills him.

COPYCAT is, at heart, a clever low-budget slasher movie tarted up with top of the line cinematography, special effects and performances, particularly from Hunter and Weaver. Weaver's Helen is equal parts bitchy frustration and impotent rage at her own psychological helplessness, while pint-sized fireball Hunter opts for the controlled surface of a workaholic. While we're meant to be impressed by the complex relationship between the two women, their characters are merely pawns in a high-concept storyline; it's clear that the bogeyman's busywork is the real draw, not their seamless teamwork.

Director John Amiel fiddles some genuine suspense out of Helen's vulnerability, but generally seems more interested in the gruesome copycat killings. COPYCAT pretends to be about female camaraderie, but all its stars and budget can't camouflage the film's inherent worshipful interest in America's favorite male-dominated spectator sport: murder by numbers. *(Graphic violence, extreme profanity, sexual situations, adult situations.)* — R.P.

d, John Amiel; p, Arnon Milchan, Mark Tarlov; exec p, Michael Nathanson, John Fiedler; co-p, Joseph M. Caracciolo, Jr.; w, Ann Biderman, David Madsen; ph, Laszlo Kovacs; ed, Alan Heim, Jim Clark; m, Christopher Young; prod d, Jim Clay; art d, Chris Seagers; set d, Catherine Davis; sound, Chris Newman (mixer); fx, R. Bruce Steinheimer; casting, Billy Hopkins, Suzanne Smith, Kerry Barden; cos, Claudia Brown; makeup, Stephen Dupuis, Mark Walas; stunts, Tim A. Davison

Thriller/Crime (PR: O MPAA: R)

COSMIC SLOP ★½
(U.S.) 86m Hudlin Bros.; HBO Pictures ~
HBO Home Video c

George Clinton *(Host)*; SPACE TRADERS: Robert Guillaume *(Gleason Golightly)*; Michele Lamar Richards *(Gail Golightly)*; Jason Bernard *(Bernard Shields)*; Edward Edwards *(Chief of Staff)*; George Wallace *(Piggy)*; Brian Reddy *(V.P.)*; Larry Anderson *(Stryker O'Rourke)*; Brock Peters *(Minister Coombs)*; Ebonie Smith *(Jennifer)*; Craig Kirkwood *(Lenny)*; Liz Larou

(Ute); Jaye Koch *(Alien Press Secretary)*; Tom Williams *(Education Secretary)*; Marte Boyle Slout *(Helen Hipmeyer)*; Joseph G. Medalis *(Defense Secretary)*; James Noah *(Interior Secretary)*; Roger Marks *(Rabbi Spector)*; Arthur Burghardt *(Justin Jasper)*; Roger Guenveur Smith *(Dr. Erik Fanon)*; Lamont Johnson *(Civil Rights Leader)*; Bertice Berry *(Herself)*; Casey Kasem *(Himself)*; Franklin Cover *(Himself)*; Roxie Roker *(Herself)*; Tom Finnegan *(General Wright)*; Robert Gunton *(President)*; TANG: Chi McBride; Paula Jai Parker; Reno Wilson; THE FIRST COMMANDMENT: Efrain Figueroa; Nicholas Turturro; Richard Herd; Bob Wisdom; J. Kenneth Campbell; Daryl Mitchell; Eugene Allen; Noelle Balfour; Marcus Salgado; George Logan; Kelly Jo Minter; Ana Mercedes; John Witherspoon; Chino Eats Williams; Lou Bowlegged; Peter Vogt; Roma Alvarez; Paul Anthony; B-Fine; Irma Williams

This made-for-cable omnibus features three stories focusing on the African-American and Hispanic experience. Occasionally funny but never as shockingly provocative as the creators intend, these mini-movies confuse soapboxing with sincerity and spew out a portrait of white people that compares with John Ford and C.B. De Mille's depiction of Native Americans.

In "Space Traders," a sagging US economy is given a potential boost when extra-terrestrial aliens offer a deal: unlimited wealth and resources in exchange for all the Black populace which they value for the melanin content in their skin. As the sole colored power broker in the presidential cabinet, Gleason Golightly (Robert Guillaume) suffers the Uncle Tom label but he's assured that the official program won't affect his loved ones. Collaborationism backfires as Golightly is betrayed by Caucasian capitalists, and his family members are beamed aboard the spacecrafts. Destination: Unknown.

In "The First Commandment", Puerto Rican priest Father Carlos (Nicholas Turturro) initially decries the white hierarchy of his Church for deciding to profit by selling a statue of the Madonna prized by a poor parish. After Santeria cultists protest the new location, the actual Blessed Virgin begins appearing in crackhouses and performing miracles much to the displeasure of the presiding cardinal (Richard Herd). In the third story, the title character of Tang (Paula Jai Parker), a woman suffering from low self-esteem finally defies her abusive lover by refusing to participate in another pharmaceutical trial. He is unprepared for Tang's gunpowdered response, echoed throughout the ghetto by all the other Afro-American women dealing with sexist oppressors.

Aiming for hipness, this sloppily-conceived anthology is really "In Living Color" with a burdensome social conscience. Shoddily executed, this tripartite urban nightmare wriggles under damaging shifts of tone and can't make up its mind whether it's party-crashing HOUSE PARTY or poised to DO THE RIGHT THING. In its most promising segment, "Space Traders," a wealth of satiric possibilities are sacrificed for a glum diatribe about a ruling class of Simon Legrees. Despite traces of inventiveness, direction weighs a ton, and the performers lack bounce. Of interest for its background info on religious cults, "The First Commandment" succeeds neither as a scary exploration of a minority sect nor as an irreverent parody of multiple Marian sightings. The most egregiously written and acted of the bunch, "Tang" is a socioeconomic horror story about battered women, yet it's socked across in a broad fashion, devoid of surprise or even the smidgen of sophistication present in its companion pieces. "Tang" vulgarizes what should be rousing affirmation of freedom through violence. Advocating revolution at every turn, COSMIC SLOP only proves that, unlike freedom fighting, filmmaking does require discipline as opposed to bulldozing force. If the creators wanted to pillory an entire race (Caucasians, of course, the new stereotype of evil incarnate),

they should at least have done so with wicked invention. Revolutionary comedy demands a fresh arsenal of insults, but this film uses rusty old weapons and the parodists' anger backfires. *(Graphic violence, extreme profanity, adult situations, substance abuse.)* — R.P.

d, Reginald Hudlin, Kevin Rodney Sullivan, Warrington Hudlin; p, Michael Jay Hill, Ernest Johnson; exec p, Reginald Hudlin, Warrington Hudlin; w, Warrington Hudlin, Trey Ellis, Kyle Baker (based on the short stories "Faces at the Bottom of the Well" by Derrick Bell and "Tang" by Chester Himes); ph, Peter Deming; ed, Richard Candib, Richard Hiltzik, Howard Scott Stein, Stephen Semel, Victor DuBois; m, John Barnes, George Clinton, Bernard Worrell; prod d, Bryan Jones; art d, Steve Karman; sound, David Chronow; fx, Bruce Long, Scott Enyart; casting, Eileen Mack Knight; cos, Shirlene Williams, Violette Jones-Faison; makeup, Judy Murdock

Comedy   **(PR: O MPAA: R)**

COUNTRY LIFE   ★★★
(Australia) 117m Dalton Films; Australian Film
Finance Corp. ~ Miramax c

Sam Neill *(Dr. Max Askey)*; Greta Scacchi *(Deborah Voysey)*; John Hargreaves *(Jack Dickens)*; Kerry Fox *(Sally Voysey)*; Michael Blakemore *(Alexander Voysey)*; Googie Withers *(Hannah)*; Patricia Kennedy *(Maude Dickens)*; Ron Blanchard *(Wally Wells)*; Robyn Cruze *(Violet)*; Maurie Fields *(Fred Livingstone)*; Bryan Marshall *(Mr. Pettinger)*; Tony Barry *(Logger)*; Terry Brady *(Logger)*; Tom Long *(Billy Livingstone)*; Rob Steele *(James)*; Ian Bliss *(David Archdale)*; Colin Taylor *(Mr. Wilson)*; Ian Cockburn *(Mr. Archdale)*; Reg Cribb *(Vicar)*; Derani Scarr *(Woman in Crowd)*; Owen Buik *(Stationhand)*

Highly inventive stage director Michael Blakemore experiments with *Uncle Vanya*, with energetic, albeit mixed, results. Spicing up Chekhov, Blakemore captures the humor often lacking in overly reverent stage productions of the classic play, but he misses out on the original's wistful melancholy.

An Australian country estate is buzzing with the impending arrival of native son Alex Voysey (Michael Blakemore) and his refined wife Deborah (Greta Scacchi). Eager to refasten family ties, Voysey's daughter Sally (Kerry Fox), whom he abandoned to pursue a career as a theater critic in England, and his brother-in-law Jack (John Hargreaves), who uncomplainingly sent him an estate allowance each week while he remained stuck on the sheep ranch, initially comply with bossy Voysey's every whim. Altogether more skeptical about Voysey's finicky demands are the family retainer Hannah (Googie Withers) and doctor-on-horseback Max Askey (Sam Neill), whose wryly detached view of his patients is exacerbated by a drinking habit.

From the outset, snooty Alex upsets traditional routine, pokes his nose into the estate books, and upsets Jack by asking him to boot out boarder Wally Wells (Ron Blanchard). Not quite as fastidious as her husband, city-bred Deborah has difficulty adjusting to country life despite an affinity for Dr. Askey who pointedly ignores the romantic signals sent his way by Sally. Though bored with her marriage, Deborah ignores Jack's obvious crush and cannot quite take the adulterous plunge with Askey. Meanwhile, after failing to force his lustful attentions on a young maid, Voysey finally goes too far when he summons a developer and offers the ranch for sale.

Pushed to paroxysms of frustration over the unavailable Deborah and to a resentful rage because Voysey has squandered opportunities denied him, a drunken Jack attempts shooting the interfering snob. Quickly packing their bags, Voysey and Deborah depart, but their stay has forced Sally and Jack to confront their own submerged desires. Realizing they are bound to the family land, each bids good-bye to unrequited loves that seem emblematic of their deeper failures of will. As Dr. Askey rides off alone, they vow to make the best of their home instead of devaluing it for not being something else.

Charmingly played, prettily photographed, and breezily scored, this bush country version of *Uncle Vanya* is an enjoyably sunny romantic romp. In some respects, director-star Blakemore tears apart the seams of the original and discovers *The Man Who Came to Dinner* lying underneath. With much fresh dialogue and newly invented comic business, the talented Blakemore (perfectly cast as Voysey) builds a rollicking environment in which mismatched souls approach each other from all directions and fail to connect. Although forcing the play to emigrate to Australia is liberating and adds to the good humor, it takes something else away: only in that final scene of Jack and Sally's resignation does the movie shimmer with any emotional resonance.

Best approached as a roguish tilt of the hat in Chekhov's direction, COUNTRY LIFE energetically allows its attractive principal players to make fools of themselves for love. The performances are memorable: Withers as the sarcastic housekeeper is as splendid, as is Fox as the solemnly beautiful wallflower doomed to be overlooked by men, and Hargreaves as the blustering Jack, whose emotions spill over volcanically. And Neill, as Askey, adds another memorably flawed character to his gallery of complex souls. *(Extreme profanity, nudity, violence, sexual situations, substance abuse.)* — R.P.

d, Michael Blakemore; p, Robin Dalton; w, Michael Blakemore (based on the play *Uncle Vanya* by Anton Chekhov); ph, Stephen Windon; ed, Nicholas Beauman; m, Peter Best; prod d, Laurence Eastwood; set d, Donna Brown; sound, Ben Osmo (recordist), Phil Judd (mixer); casting, Alison Barrett; cos, Wendy Chuck; makeup, Lesley Rouvray

Drama/Comedy/Romance   **(PR: C   MPAA: PG-13)**

COVER ME   ★½
(U.S.) 94m Motion Picture Corporation of America; Playboy Entertainment ~ Paramount Home Video c

Courtney Taylor *(Holly Jacobs)*; Rick Rossovich *(Sgt. Bobby Colter)*; Paul Sorvino *(Det. J.J. David)*; Steven Nichols *(Dmitri/Demi)*; Elliott Gould *(Capt. Richards)*; Betsy Monroe *(Lakey Snow)*; Karen Kim *(Brandi)*; Corbin Bernsen; Rob Steinberg; Hillary Matthews; Shae Marks; Frank Medrano; Peter Conti; Collin Bersen

COVER ME aspired to historical distinction by announcing itself as the first movie produced under the auspices of Playboy Enterprises, although, in fact, the company had previously backed both Polanski's MACBETH and the anthropological oddity THE NAKED APE. COVER ME did inaugurate a set of steamy *Playboy* features, released directly to video in 1995 via Paramount, but it ultimately amounts to yet another "erotic thriller" that probably would have happened anyway, even without the legendary bunny logo in the credits.

A serial strangler is stalking pinup girls, and investigating Sgt. Colter (Rick Rossovich) hatches the plot device that has been popular since Angie Dickinson did her "Police Woman" role for network TV: send a female officer undercover to pose, literally, as bait for the psycho. The voluptuous vixen volunteer is Colter's LAPD partner in and out of bed, Holly Jacobs (Courtney Taylor), suspended after a public uproar for shooting a depraved child-killer who happened to be black. (The intrusion of such a real-world detail clashes with the pandering plot themes borrowed from SHOWGIRLS, STRIPPED TO KILL, ULTIMATE DE-SIRES, and even lesser films in which the hardworking heroine

gets a charge out of being slobbered over as a sex object.) Holly indulges in nude photo sessions, exotic dancing, body doubling, and even a little lesbianism, all beyond the call of duty. The filmmakers toss in constant reminders of the murderer still at large, tranvestite Dmitri or Demi (Steven Nichols), mad because his mother used to dress him like a girl. Demi captures Holly and, in a climax that seems to go on forever, she keeps him gabbing and weeping until Colter can burst in to save the day.

Somehow it comes as no surprise that COVER ME was coproduced by DUMB AND DUMBER moguls Brad Krevoy and Steven Stabler. COVER ME is talky and depressing, the former to allow performers like Sorvino, Gould, and newcomer Taylor to do serious speechifying and lend the production a patina of acting talent. The latter quality is harder to square with *Playboy*'s oft-declared devotion to "the good life"; why dwell on the sordid slaughter of beautiful women? The Hefner philosphy would seem better served by many other auteurs in the erotic-video biz (like Andy and Arlene Sidaris, Chuck Vincent, or Zalman King), than by Paul Bartel associate Michael Schroeder (OUT OF THE DARK) and this stale noir wannabe. COVER ME certainly does not lack uncovered flesh. One cutie, after a strip-club shift under the faucets as a "shower dancer," goes home to soak in a bath. *(Violence, sexual situations, nudity, profanity, adult situations, substance abuse.)* — C.C.

d, Michael Schroeder; p, Brad Krevoy, Steven Stabler; assoc p, Jeanette Draper, Jeremy Kramer; w, Steve Johnson; ph, Jacek Laskus; ed, John Lafferty; m, Markus Barone; art d, Rob Shepps, David K. Huang; set d, Katterina Keith; cos, Kristin Anaker

Erotic/Thriller   **(PR: O   MPAA: R)**

COVER STORY
(U.S.) 93m Arrow Entertainment ~ Arrow Home Video c

Christopher McDonald *(Sam Sparks)*; William Wallace *(Matt)*; Tuesday Knight *(Reen/Tracy)*; Leland Orser *(Julian)*; Dale Dye *(Jack)*; William Jimmy Kennedy *(Donnell)*; Ram Luv *(Anthony)*; Robert Forster *(Therapist)*; William Winkler *(Paul)*; Steve Parrish *(Steven)*; Alfie Hill *(Shotgun)*; Randy Lubas *(Anselm)*; Marissa Cody *(Allison)*; Diana Angelina *(Serina)*; Peter Pfeiffer *(Mark)*; Chris Schmidt *(Lennie)*; Oliver Sain *(Odell)*; Kendrick Kendall *(Charles)*; Jamie Sheffield *(Mallman)*; Robert Bonner *(Mover)*; John Wallace *(Wally)*; Tom Aylward *(Tom)*; Mark Johnson *(Black)*; Stephen Dalton *(Tyrone)*; Nikki Smith *(Waitress)*; Patrica Corrigan *(Sales Clerk)*; Laura Bagby *(Stripper)*; Grace Collins *(Alice)*; Robin Rosenthal *(Adna)*

Execrably scripted and turgidly directed, this direct-to-video thriller is an audience cheat that rips off VERTIGO, LAURA and others while leering over softcore beddings and contempo-music sequences.

Grieving over his wife's suicide, alleged writer Matt (William Wallace) pours his heart out to an ostensible therapist (Robert Forster). Starting over in a rather funky neighborhood, Matt inherits the apartment of departed club habituee Reen (Tuesday Knight). On the prowl for drugs she pilfered, assorted thugs invade Matt's flat. Prying into Reen's involvement in the criminal underworld of gay gangster narcotics-smugglers, Matt grows enamored with notions of Reen's ballsy bravado, to the chagrin of mousy neighbor Tracy (Knight again) who moons over him. Tracy really is rip-off artist Reen, now disguised and planning to cash in on stolen stash. Matt endures even testicle-crushing torture to protect her interests, but unbeknownst to the bella-donna babe, Matt is a DEA agent who's tipped off the cops. As the police bust Reen's big score, she fires a clip into Matt before dying in a hail of bullets. Recovered, Matt still reveres the memory of his bitch goddess. Even if one forgives the cheap trick duping viewers into believing Matt is a distraught mourner pouring out his heart to a shrink instead of his DEA boss, the film's list of other offenses would cover volumes.

Ludicrously transplanting a Madonna Ciccone figure into the glamorous niche once reserved for Kim Novak in VERTIGO, COVER STORY stomps credibility in stiletto heels, giving Reen's vendetta against the male underworld hierarchy mythic stature. Reen is a punk Phyllis Dietrichson in a steel-tipped bra or a slamdancing Cora Smith wearing a nose ring. Unfortunately, the dubiously-monikered Tuesday Knight has even less oomph than the average music-video vamp, and she's not alone in the thespian mud-wrestling that passes for acting. Every scene runs too long. Each anti-climax seems to have a false bottom. The movie further fouls up by replacing effeminate gay character traits with nouveau S&M stereotypes *a la* Friedkin's CRUIS-ING. With its Neanderthal dialogue, awkward flashbacks, and eyesore of a sex object, COVER STORY deserves nothing but contempt. *(Graphic violence, extreme profanity, extensive nudity, sexual situations, substance abuse.)* — R.P.

d, Gregg Smith; p, William Wallace, Gregg Smith; exec p, Dennis Friedland; assoc p, Benjamin Gruberg, Roberta Friedman; w, Gregg Smith; ph, Gregg Smith; ed, Gregg Smith; m, Anthony Cannella; sound, Steve McGrath (recordist); casting, Suzie Sharp Kane, Jeremy Ritzer; cos, John Centuri; makeup, Patty Deak

Crime/Thriller   **(PR: O   MPAA: NR)**

COW, THE   ★★★
(Czechoslovakia) 86m Czech Television; Telexport Prague; Mirage ~ Cinema Parallel c
(KRAVA)

Radek Holub *(Adam)*; Alena Mihulova *(Rosa)*; Valerie Zawadska; Viktorie Knotkova; Antonin Molcik; Zenek Dusek

Director Karel Kachyna, whose career has spanned the volatile political terrain of Czechoslovakia since 1954, offers a remarkable achievement in THE COW, a folkloric tale revealing the circularity of life's labors and drives, and the perseverance and hope that sustain their rhythm. Based on the novel by Jan Prochazka, this film was made for Czech television.

It is the turn of the century in rural Czechoslovakia. Adam (Radek Holub), son of a local whore, has led an impoverished life in a cabin situated at the highest point in a mountain village. His childhood is suggested through flashbacks: his mother disports drunkenly with men; Adam throws himself from a cliff in despair and permanently damages his body; the boy begs his mother to wipe the lipstick from her lips. Adam's mother is now on her deathbed and suffering greatly. One day, he leads their cow, the family's only valuable possession, down the steep hill to exchange it for a vial of morphine. In his absence, the dying woman staggers to her feet and sees her wasted reflection in the mirror. When he returns with the morphine, she is dead, her face caked with white powder, her lips smeared with red lipstick.

After his mother's death, Adam is alone on his hill. When Rosa (Alena Mihulova), a peasant girl who shares his mother's sensuality, falls in love with him, he cruelly spurns her advances. Rosa persists, and one day Adam returns home to find his clothes drying on the line. In a rage he attacks and rapes her. But when she starts to leave, he asks her to stay.

A bond of love and friendship develops as they work side by side on the land and bathe their weary bodies in the stream. Their dream is to buy a cow, and thus lighten their burden, and when that day arrives, they are intoxicated with happiness. They treat the beast with care and gentleness, wrapping flowers around its

horns and giving it their sweaters in the rain. The cow is their savior, embodying all their hopes and desires.

Adam and Rosa marry and have a baby, and when Rosa falls ill, Adam repeats the gestures and sacrifices he made during his mother's illness—selling the coveted cow and returning too late with the morphine. After Rosa's death, Adam is left alone to care for the infant until the arrival of a homely peasant woman who offers to keep house and care for the baby. There is a terrible silence between them, interrupted by a single violent outburst. Time passes, and Adam returns one day with a new cow, then gestures to the enormous mound of dirt that he and Rosa had transported up the hill bucket by bucket, explaining that it will make a good field.

Kachyna uses simple metaphors and images to tell his melancholy story. The casting is impeccable, with the leads exhibiting a relentless stoicism that takes on a kind of beauty, suggesting the eternal cycle of toil, desire, and satiety. The cinematography by Petr Hojda is stunning, creating a mysterious world of fog and damp green hills, gray mornings and weary evenings. *(Violence, nudity, adult situations.)* — R.C.

d, Karel Kachyna; p, Karel Skorpik, Helena Sykorova; w, Karel Kachyna, Karel Cabradek (from the novel by Jan Prochazka); ph, Petr Hojda; ed, Jan Svoboda; m, Petr Hapka; prod d, Jiri Zavrel; sound, Jaroslav Novak; cos, Jana Smetanova

Drama   **(PR: C   MPAA: NR)**

CRACKERJACK   ★★
(Canada) 93m North American Pictures; Excalibur Pictures ~ Republic Pictures Home Video c

Thomas Ian Griffith *(Jack Wild)*; Nastassja Kinski *(K.C.)*; Christopher Plummer *(Ivan Getz)*; George Touliatos *(Sonny LaRosso)*; Lisa Bunting *(Annie Wild)*; Richard Sali *(Mike Wild)*; William Taylor *(Morey)*; Frank Cassini *(Mario Bracco)*; Frank Turner *(Oliver Green)*; Duncan Fraser *(Colonel Hardy)*

Action fans not burned out on the familiar DIE HARD formula will judge this variation at a mountain lodge passable. Others will just want to pass.

Ever since the mob murdered his wife and children, aptly-named cop Jack Wild (Thomas Ian Griffith) has turned every case into a kamikaze mission. Forced to take a vacation at a mountain resort, he finds himself right back in the fire. Don LaRosso (George Touliatos), a mafioso on his way to the Vatican to buy absolution from the Pope, is also a guest. So is former East German secret policeman Ivan Getz (Christopher Plummer), whose plans to steal the Don's fortune to finance his neo-Nazi terrorist army puts the resort under siege. With the help of a new love interest (Nastassja Kinski), Wild becomes a one-man anti-terrorist force, and the revelation that Getz is the man who killed Wild's family makes it personal. When he learns Getz plans to wipe the lodge off the mountainside, Wild helps evacuate the hostages. Getz dies, hard, with a vengeance, and Wild prepares for a new life.

CRACKERJACK is so derivative of DIE HARD that the actors should be making that quotation mark gesture with their fingers in most scenes. Still, it's no less entertaining than many other action flicks that have been copying the formula. Under Michael Mazo's direction, this carbon copy is well paced, with some good visuals and action sequences, but bland Griffith, and Plummer's comical imitation of Alan Rickman will never get this confused with the real McCoy, or more precisely, McClane. In the US the feature went direct-to-video. *(Violence, profanity, sexual situations, nudity.)* — P.R.

d, Michael Mazo; p, Lloyd A. Simandl; exec p, Lloyd A. Simandl, A. William Smyth, James R. Westwell, Robert W. Sigman, Gary Delfiner; w, Jonas Quastrel, Michael Bafaro; ph, Danny Nowak; ed, Richard Benwick; m, Peter Allen; prod d, Andrew Wilson; art d, Garth Fleming; set d, Kevin Brown; sound, David Cyr (mixer); fx, Terry Sonderhoff, Magic Camera Company; casting, Anne Anderson, Carmen Ruis-Laza; cos, Tracey Boulton, Caroline Cranstoun; makeup, Lisa Love; stunts, Mark Akerstream

Action/Thriller (PR: O MPAA: R)

CRAZYSITTER, THE ★½
(U.S.) 89m Pacific Trust; Concorde-New Horizons Corp. ~ New Horizons Home Video c

Beverly D'Angelo (Edie); Brady Bluhm (Jason Van Arsdale); Rachel Duncan (Bea Van Arsdale); Ed Begley, Jr. (Paul Van Arsdale); Carol Kane (Treva Van Arsdale); Eric Allen Kramer (Elliot); William Schilling (Dr. Wiles); Sean Whalen (Carl); Lisa Kudrow; Phil Hartman; Nell Carter; Tim Bagley; Sheila Traviss; Steve Landesberg; Mink Stole; Christopher Darga; Ted Davis; Lynne Stewart

Beverly D'Angelo brings some juice to this weak family comedy.

The wealthy Van Arsdales can't keep a steady nanny because their two blond, bland, angelic-looking fraternal twins (Brady Bluhm and Rachel Duncan, who would look at home in VILLAGE OF THE DAMNED) are incorrigible troublemakers. By chance the kids' hand-scrawled want ad for a fresh caretaker attracts Edie (D'Angelo), a hard-drinking recent parolee. Impressed by her streetwise and libertine demeanor, the youngsters trick their clueless parents (Ed Begley Jr. and Carol Kane) into hiring Edie, who schemes to sell the brats on the underground adoption black market while the elder Van Arsdales are abroad. The twins' mischief ruins one deal after another until exasperated Edie demands to know why the two terrors are so unruly. Get this: they only want good old-fashioned discipline, and after a few scenes of ordering them to clean up the house, the nanny and her charges are best pals. There's still about 40 minutes of screen time left, so Edie has to rescue the tots from her final customer, lamely villainous Dr. Wiles (William Schilling), who inflicts new diseases and inexplicable tortures on children at the behest of offscreen Evil Businessmen. Even watching D'Angelo in a thankless martial-arts brawl, one is impressed by her game spirit and energy. A competent actor can shine in a great part, but it takes a real trouper to persevere in thin, direct-to-video filler like this.

THE CRAZYSITTER was another of Roger Corman's attempts to hop the 1990s family-values bandwagon. A spokesman for Corman's fertile but oft-lowbrow production company, perceiving a booming-market for kiddie pics, pledged to crank out "the kind of movies Disney used to make but doesn't anymore." Indeed, the latter's '70s string of banal, dud features cast such a pall over the Magic Kingdom that at one point Disney management seriously considered eliminating their film division altogether. In which case THE CRAZYSITTER falls right in line. (Profanity, substance abuse.) — C.C.

d, Michael James McDonald; p, Mike Elliott; exec p, Roger Corman, Lance H. Robbins; assoc p, Paul DiFranco; co-p, Mike Upton; w, Michael James McDonald; ph, Christopher Baffa, Michael Mickens; ed, Robert Barrere; m, David Wurst, Eric Wurst; prod d, Reiko Kobayashi; art d, Michael Mosselli; cos, Maria Sundeen

Children's/Comedy (PR: A MPAA: PG-13)

CREATION OF ADAM ★★★
(Russia) 93m D. Kamandar Studio; Borchaly Film Studios ~ Water Bearer Films c
(COTBOPEHNE AGAMA)

Alexander Strizhenov (Andrei); Serghei Vinogradov (Phillip); Irina Metlitskaya (Nina); Anzhelika Nevolina (Natasha); Yury Ovsyanko (Director of Institute); Ilya Shakunov (The Double); Alexei Palchek (Pritsker)

This weird, transcendalist feature employs homosexuality as a metaphor for liberation of the spirit. As religious symbols crowd the viewer's perceptions, CREATION OF ADAM holds one in thrall despite its obfuscatory mysticism.

Forever at loggerheads with his wife Nina (Irina Melitskaya), Andrei (Alexander Strizhenov), head of a design group, contemplates a marital split while tending to endless bureaucratic details. He's ill-prepared for a flashy visiting official Phillip (Serghei Vinogradov) who hints at an extremely intimate interest in Andrei's work and his person. Uptight about homosexuality but teased by the creative leeway Phillip proposes, Andrei interrupts a gay-bashing attack on his way home and regrets his kindness when Nina misconstrues the reason a young man is showering in their flat. Subsequently Phillip reveals that his mission is not career overhaul but the remolding of Andrei's soul. At a bizarre dinner party, it becomes evident that flighty Phillip is a divine emissary sent to open Andrei's eyes to "possibilities". After hearing Phillip's tales of androgynes—dual-sexed creatures split in half—Andrei dazedly walks the streets and encounters a woman who begs him to run away with her, plus the roving homophobes from earlier. Andrei cleanses his wounds from the latters' latest assault, then returns to Nina. Not only is the wife now pregnant, she's adopted a non-judgmental attitude toward sexuality. Alert to the richness of all human experience, the couple face their future securely.

One can race through this oddity in a sort of metaphorical supermarket sweepstakes and toss as many Creation symbols as possible into the critical shopping cart, but a lesser approach may reap greater benefits. While scenes between Andrei and Phillip shimmer with homoeroticism, the movie is really about the creative process and everyone's undeniable need to express themselves and their sexuality. By suppressing his bisexuality, Andrei denies his own life-force. What's a bit murkier is the nagging question of whether the filmmaker camouflages a paean to gay love with religious gift-wrapping to make it more palatable to heterosexuals; or does this mean to portray queerness as part of a wedge toward self-actualization, a natural fact everyone must concede? In this perverse subtext, God is a divine answering machine, and Phillip makes one cockamamie kind of cruising seraphim. Blessedly, the angelic scout is both sexy and empowered, not the mincing stereotype of Hollywood cliches. Imitating Fellini and Tarkovsky by turns, the director's visual acumen isn't up to the ambition of his philosophies, but he has the makings of a true original. Mystifying but rewarding, CREATION OF ADAM may ultimately disappoint gays since the result of Andrei's coming-out party is straight domestic bliss, but the view of bisexuality as a spiritual corrective comes across clearly. Here God's greatest revelation is tolerance, earned only after self-acceptance of one's truest nature. One imagines the eyebrows this material would have raised at censorship board meetings in the former USSR—or, for that matter, the US. (Sexual situations, adult situations, violence.) — R.P.

d, Yuri Pavlov; p, Dzhavabshir Kamandar, Anatoli Kasimov; exec p, Oliga Naidenova; w, Vladimir Maslov, Vitaly Moskalenko; ph, Serghei Machilsky; ed, Raisa Lissova; m, Andrei

Sighle; prod d, Mikhail Suzdalov; sound, Alexander Birshadsky; cos, Andzhela Sapunova

Drama (PR: C MPAA: NR)

CREEP ★
(U.S.) 84m Twisted Illusions, Inc.; Panther Productions; MDM Productions ~ Twisted Illusions, Inc. c

Patricia Paul *(Jackie Ketchum)*; Joel D. Wynkoop *(Angus Lynch)*; Kathy Willets *(Kascha Lords)*; Tom Karr *(David Ketchum)*; Dika Newlin *(Baby Food Killer)*; Asbestos Felt *(Tom Russo)*; Michelle Ashton *(Danielle)*; Dan "Rattlehead" Cleveland *(Rapist)*; Lenny Blythe, Jr. *(Donny Lords)*; Pawn Boy *(Pawn Boy)*

This shot-on-video bloodbath has an accurate title, describing both the majority of its characters and its pace. Nightmares about the murder of her mother by a masked man torment lady cop Jackie Ketchum (Patricia Paul). Her father, Police Captain David Ketchum (Tom Karr), urges her not to take out her frustrations on the job. Meanwhile, psycho killer Angus Lynch (Joel D. Wynkoop) has escaped, hooks up with sister Kascha (Kathy Willets), and the two go on a killing spree. While trying to deal with the bad dreams and her own cheating spouse, Jackie retreats to her dad's cabin in the woods. There Capt. Ketchum bushwhacks and ties her up. The father reveals that he in fact killed Mrs. Ketchum, and has arranged for Angus' bust-out so the madman could bump off Jackie before her returning memories divulge his guilt. Angus does appear, but slays the police captain instead. Jackie trails the maniac to a hotel, where she sets off explosives strapped to her body and blows them both to kingdom come.

The movie's use of *verite* demolition footage in its final shot to represent the hotel's destruction demonstrates some low-budget chutzpah, and the climactic revelations and action are staged with more conviction than what has gone before. Otherwise this is cheap and unrewarding shock schlock, with a vain attempt to mask chintziness through lighting and editing tricks. Willets achieved brief tabloid notoriety in 1991 when, as wife of a Florida deputy, she taped sexual trysts with local officials and defended herself from charges of prostitution on the grounds of nymphomania (a case that inspired the softcore direct-to-video feature ANIMAL INSTINCTS); her casting is clearly intended to give CREEP some exploitation cachet. But the defendant/supporting actress's physical attributes and acting are, to put it kindly, uncompelling. *(Graphic violence, extensive nudity, sexual situations, substance abuse, extreme profanity.)* — M.G.

d, Tim Ritter; p, Michael Ornelas; exec p, Tony Granims; assoc p, Michael D. Moore, Tom Karr; w, Tim Ritter; ph, Richard Hertz, Michael Ornelas; ed, Steve McNaughton, Michael Ornelas, Tim Ritter; m, Alucarda; sound, James Moores; fx, Thomas "T.J." Mihill, Bill Cassinelli; casting, 13th Dimensional Asssociates; cos, Vicki Miller; makeup, Kathleen Ritter

Horror (PR: O MPAA: NR)

CREW, THE
(U.S.) 100m Cineville International ~ LIVE Entertainment c

Viggo Mortensen *(Phillip)*; Donal Logue *(Bill)*; Pamela Gidley *(Jennifer)*; Jeremy Sisto *(Timothy)*; Laura del Sol *(Camilla)*; Grace Zabriskie *(Gloria)*; John Philbin *(Alex)*; Sam Jenkins *(Catherine)*; Ray Wise *(Charles Pierce)*; John Archie *(Bahamian Officer)*

A situational cross between Hitchcock's LIFEBOAT and Polanski's KNIFE IN THE WATER, THE CREW is an ineffective and pointless exercise in tedium.

Writer Bill (Donal Logue) and wife Jennifer (Pam Gidley), join her brother Phillip (Viggo Mortensen), a lawyer, on his yacht for a day trip in the Caribbean. Also aboard are rock-musician Alex (John Philbin) and medical-student Catherine (Sam Jenkins). On the open sea, they rescue two people from a burning boat—transsexual Timothy (Jeremy Sisto) and the woman he is smuggling into the country, Camilla (Laura del Sol). Timothy quickly commandeers the vessel, and deposits his hostages on an island beach while he waits for help from his lover. Oddly, Bill is sympathetic toward his captor, and helps Timothy thwart Phillip's efforts to retake the yacht, but Phillip does succeed in disabling it. When it's obvious Timothy's lover has spurned him, Bill tries to prevent the jilted sex-change from committing suicide, but Phillip shoots and kills him anyway. Then Bill and Camilla take off in the life raft, leaving the others behind.

It's hard to believe someone could write a script with basically only seven characters and fail to give any one of them any personality. Potentially explosive revelations like Jennifer and Alex being lovers, Catherine's prostitution career, and Phillip's involvement with drug dealers aren't even interesting, much less meaningful in any way. The conflict between Bill, Phillip, and Timothy is supposed to parallel Bill's failure to stop his mother (Grace Zabriskie) from committing suicide in the film's prologue, viewers will likely not care about any of this. THE CREW is, simply, stupefyingly boring. *(Profanity, violence, adult situations.)* — P.R.

d, Carl-Jan Colpaert; p, Adam Stern, Dan Ireland, Daniel Hassid; exec p, Christoph Henkel, Jim Steele, Ronna Wallace; w, Carl-Jan Colpaert, Lance Smith; ph, Geza Sinkovics; ed, Emma E. Hickox; m, Alex Wurman; prod d, Vigil Sanchez; sound, Leonard Marcel; casting, Andrea Stone Guttfreund, Laurel Smith; cos, Jacqueline de la Fontaine, Leonard Pollack

Drama/Thriller (PR: C MPAA: R)

CRIMSON TIDE ★★★½
(U.S.) 116m Simpson-Bruckheimer Productions; Hollywood Pictures ~ Buena Vista c

Denzel Washington *(Lt. Commander Jim Hunter)*; Gene Hackman *(Captain Ramsey)*; George Dzundza *(Cob)*; Viggo Mortensen *(Lt. Peter Ince)*; Matt Craven *(Lt. Roy Zimmer)*; James Gandolfini *(Lt. Bobby Dougherty)*; Rocky Carroll *(Lt. Darik Westergaurd)*; Jaime Gomez *(Ood Mahoney)*; Lillo Brancato, Jr. *(Russell Vossler)*; Michael Milhoan *(Hunsicker)*; Rick Shroder *(Lt. Paul Hellerman)*; Danny Nucci *(Danny Rivetti)*; Steve Zahn *(Williama Barnes)*; Vanessa Bell Calloway *(Julia Hunter)*; Michael Milhoan *(Hunsicker)*; Scott Burkholder *(TSO Billy Linkletter)*; Eric Bruskotter *(Bennenfield)*; Marcello Thedford *(Lawson)*; R.J. Knoll *(Marty Sotille)*; Billy Devlin *(Navigator)*; Matt Barry *(Planesman)*; Christopher Birt *(Helmsman)*; Jim Boyce *(Diving Officer)*; Jacob Vargas *(Sonarman)*; Kai Lennox *(Sonarman)*; Michael Weatherred *(Radioman)*; Tommy Bush *(Admiral Williams)*; Earl Billings *(Rick Marichek)*; Mark Christopher Lawrence *(Head Cook Rono)*; Michael Chieffo *(Chief Kline)*; Ashley Smock *(Guard No. 1)*; James Lesure *(Guard No. 2)*; Trevor St. John *(Launcher)*; Dennis Garber *(Fire Control Technician)*; Daniel Von Bargen *(Vladimir Radchenko)*; Richard Valeriani *(Richard Valeriani)*; Warren Olney *(Anchorman)*; Rad Daly *(Lt. Commander Nelson)*; Sean O'Bryan *(Phone Talker No. 1)*; Brent Michael Goldberg *(Phone Talker No. 2)*; Victor Togunde *(Sailor With Oba)*; Troy A. Cephers *(Sailor)*; Armand Watson *(Seaman Davis)*; Scott Grimes *(Petty Officer Hilaire)*; Ryan Phillippe *(Seaman Grattam)*; Dale Andre Lee Everett *(Firing Key Runner)*; Angela Tortu *(Ramsey Aide)*; Ronald Ramessar *(Westergaurd Dad)*; Robin Faraday *(Westergaurd Mom)*; Henry

Mortensen *(Henry Ince)*; Bob Stone *(Bob the Magician)*; Chris Ellis *(Additional Magician)*

The testosterone really swims when Denzel Washington and Gene Hackman go toe-to-toe in this bombastic, well-acted submarine thriller from the producers and director of TOP GUN.

Nationalist rebels in the former Soviet Union have seized a Russian nuclear missile base and are threatening the United States. Aboard the *USS Alabama*, the executive officer, Ron Hunter (Denzel Washington), is at odds with Captain Frank Ramsey (Gene Hackman). The grizzled skipper believes in giving his men kicks in the butt, not pats on the back, and he shows no compassion when a crewman dies in a galley fire. Hunter, a graduate of Annapolis and Harvard, is the Navy's rising star; Ramsey is a cigar-chomping, combat-seasoned Cold Warrior. Over dinner, they debate the ethics of war in the nuclear age: Hunter believes that war itself is the ultimate enemy; Ramsey knows exactly who his enemy is.

Just as the *Alabama* receives orders to launch its nuclear missiles, the ship encounter a Russian sub. They battle, and in the midst of receiving a follow-up emergency message, communications are knocked out. When Ramsey attempts to proceed with the launch, Hunter relieves him of command, insisting that they wait until they can confirm their orders. Hunter then helms the *Alabama* through another battle with the Russian sub, and is victorious.

With the aid of the other senior officers, Ramsey forcibly retakes command. With Hunter under arrest, preparations for launch begin. Hunter escapes and sets out to stop the launch. With the countdown to the expected attack against the US continuing, two opposing factions roam the sub. The final stand-off takes place on the bridge. Hunter and Ramsey again argue their positions, but Hunter, who has the weapons key, will not yield. As time runs out for them to launch a pre-emptive strike, communications are restored. The previous order to launch has been canceled, the rebels have surrendered.

Of all the submarine movies that CRIMSON TIDE deliberately recalls, RUN SILENT, RUN DEEP is its chief inspiration. But the Burt Lancaster/Clark Gable drama lavished attention on its characters, while CRIMSON TIDE sails through its action at a breakneck pace. The direction, by Tony Scott (TOP GUN, TRUE ROMANCE) is slick, and admirably so. He effectively uses the claustrophobic confines of the sub to keep the tension high. Screenwriter Michael Schiffer has loaded the movie with enough jargony babble to make Tom Clancy fans happy. Reportedly, the characters' idiosyncratic interests—exotic horses and "Star Trek"—and the philosophical debates were the result of Quentin Tarantino's and Robert Towne's respective passes at the script. All these elements come together to make CRIMSON TIDE an engaging, if inconsequential, thriller.

All the narrative rigmarole is meant to distract viewers from the ultimate question—to which, of course, the ultimate answer is obvious. It's a foregone conclusion the film won't end with the start of WWIII and, whatever the geopolitical situation above the water, it's the war between Hunter and Ramsey that's really at issue. Thus the weight of CRIMSON TIDE rests squarely on the shoulders of the two leads, and they carry it with verve and professionalism However, the two Oscar winners aren't playing characters so much as ideologies making speeches at each other. In the end, when Ramsey retires and Hunter is promoted, it's meant to be emblematic of the Cold War generation passing the baton to a kinder, gentler era. But it's meaningless on a personal level, and therefore unmoving. *(Profanity, violence.)* — P.R.

d, Tony Scott; p, Don Simpson, Jerry Bruckheimer; exec p, Bill Unger, Lucas Foster, Mike Moder; assoc p, James W. Skotchdopole; w, Michael Schiffer (from a story by Michael Schiffer and Richard P. Henrick); ph, Dariusz Wolski; ed, Chris Lebenzon; m, Hans Zimmer; prod d, Michael White; art d, James J. Murakami, Dianne Wagner; set d, Mickey S. Michaels; sound, William B. Kaplan (mixer); fx, Alfred A. DiSarro, Jr., Hoyt Yeatman, Dream Quest Images; casting, Victoria Thomas; cos, George Little; makeup, Ellen Wong; stunts, Steve Picerni

AAN Best Editing: Chris Lebenzon; *AAN Best Sound:* Kevin O'Connell, Rick Kline, Gregory H. Watkins, William B. Kaplan; *AAN Best Sound Effects:* George Watters II

War/Thriller/Action **(PR: C MPAA: R)**

CRIMSON WOLF ★★½
(Japan) 60m Toshiba EMI; A.P.P.P. Co. Ltd. ~ Streamline Enterprises c

VOICES OF: Bob Bergen; Barbara Goodson; Daniel Woven; Mike Reynolds; Jeff Winkless; Kirk Thornton

A superior entry in the Japanese sex/violence/apocalypse animation genre, CRIMSON WOLF offers fans plenty of each in a tale of three young warriors chosen to battle an evil force arising in modern Asia. Archaeologists in Mongolia uncover the remains of Genghis Khan and his warriors. As an earthquake erupts to cover the tomb, the voice of Khan is heard warning the crew that a new "yellow peril" will destroy the West and usher in the "wrath of heaven." Only by locating and eliminating three warriors bearing the scars of an arrow's wound, can the destruction be averted.

Assassins set out to identify and locate the three *Hong Lang* (crimson wolves). One by one the trio emerge and unite. They are Kai, a martial artist in Beijing; Mizubo, a young female computer operator from Tokyo; and Rukodan, Chinese smuggler and black marketeer. They learn that, contrary to the Khan's words, the mission of the *Hong Lang* is to stop the world conquest, which is being prepared by the Goku, a giant rocket-shaped computer embodying the spirits of the three great kings, or *daiyo*, of Chinese history—Emperor T'ai-tsu, Genghis Khan and Mao Tse-Tung. In a battle royal, Kai, Mizubo and Rukodan take on the armies of the three *daiyo* as well as their dragon incarnations. The Goku is destroyed but not before promising to wreak havoc when called again by future generations.

Fast-paced and full of action, CRIMSON WOLF offers a controversial variation on the theme of global apocalypse so common to Japanese animation; demonizing three of the most important Chinese leaders of the past one thousand years may raise hackles in some quarters, particularly in light of continuing tensions between China and Japan.

A storyline of this scope demands a much greater running time than one hour and suffers from the speed with which the heroes arrive at the climactic battle. Perhaps a sequel or two is in the offing. Even so, the film offers three interesting, attractive and compelling characters, plenty of fights, one memorable love scene between Kai and Mizubo, and a spectacular final combat that ranks with some of the best showdowns in *anime*. Sex and violence, while skillfully done and not unwelcome to genre audiences, hinder the film's reach to younger males in the West who would enjoy the mayhem and fantasy. Japanese youngsters, one is often assured, are quite accustomed to the rough stuff. *(Graphic violence, nudity, sexual situations.)* — B.C.

d, Shoichi Masuo, Carl Macek; p, Kiyoshi Sugiyama, Kazufumi Nomuva, Carl Macek; exec p, Hiroshi Takao; w, Shoichi Masuo, Ardwight Chamberlain, Carl Macek (based on the graphic novel by Masahiko Takajo and Kenji Okamura); ph, Hideo Okazaki;

m, Kan Ogasawara; prod d, Yasumitsu Suetake, Isamu Imakaki; art d, Hiroshi Sasaki; anim, Mitsutoshi Koboyashi

Animated/Action/Fantasy (PR: O MPAA: NR)

CROSSING GUARD, THE ★★★
(U.S.) 117m Miramax ~ Miramax c

Jack Nicholson *(Freddy Gale)*; David Morse *(John Booth)*; Anjelica Huston *(Mary)*; Robin Wright *(JoJo)*; Piper Laurie *(Helen Booth)*; Richard Bradford *(Stuart Booth)*; Priscilla Barnes *(Verna)*; David Baerwald *(Peter)*; Robbie Robertson *(Roger)*; John Savage *(Bobby)*; Kari Wuhrer *(Mia)*; Jennifer Leigh Warren *(Jennifer)*; Kellita Smith *(Tanya)*; Richard Sarafian *(Sunny Ventura)*; Bobby Cooper *(Coop)*; Jeff Morris *(Silas)*; Buddy Anderson *(Buddy)*; Dr. Edward L. Katz *(Eddie)*; Joe Viterelli *(Joe at Bar)*; Eileen Ryan *(Woman in Shop)*; Ryo Ishabashi *(Jefferey)*; Dennis Fanning *(Cop #1)*; Lisa Crawford *(Cop #2)*; Jay Koiwai *(Asian Man)*; Elizabeth Gilliam *(Little Asian Girl)*; Michael Ryan *(Boy)*; Matthew Ryan *(Boy)*; Penny Allen *(Woman on Bus)*; Nicky Blair *(Herself)*; Gene Kirkwood *(Swinger)*; Jason Kristofer *(Bus Passenger #1)*; Randy Meadoff *(Bus Passenger's Mother)*; Leo Penn *(Hank)*; Michael Abelar *(Bum)*; Daysi Moreno *(Freddy's Chicana)*; Christel Ehde; Kamala Petty; Millicent Sheridan; Joi Travers *(Dancers)*; Erin Dignam *(Peter's Guest #1)*; Jeremiah Wayne Birkett *(Jefferey's Boyfriend)*; Hadda Brooks *(Piano Player)*; Ruby McKoy *(Deputy Sheriff)*; Hanna Newmaster *(Little Girl)*; Dr. William Dignam *(The Crossing Guard)*

In the second film written and directed by Sean Penn, Jack Nicholson stars as a father seeking revenge against the drunk driver who killed his daughter. Penn's moody visuals and the powerful performances of his cast offset the deficiencies in his script, which depicts, but doesn't examine, his characters' anguish.

Five years ago, Emily, the young daughter of Freddy Gale (Jack Nicholson), was killed at a school crossing by a drunk driver. Ever since, Gale has been waiting for the man responsible, John Booth (David Morse), to be released from prison, so he can kill him. In the interim, Gale's life has unraveled. His wife, Mary (Anjelica Huston), left him (unlike Gale, she sought counseling and was able to deal with her grief and move ahead). She has since remarried. Now, Gale is an alcoholic who spends his nights in strip joints and seedy sexual liaisons. When The Day arrives, Gale goes to Booth's home, but can't kill him—because he forgot to load his gun. Ironically, Booth seems to have been expecting him, and doesn't flinch from Gale's retribution. He tells Gale to take three days to decide if he really wants to commit murder; if so, Booth will be waiting for him, ready to die.

In the ensuing three days, Gale drinks heavily, gets in a bar fight, and spends a night in jail. Meanwhile, Booth finds a job, meets a woman (Robin Wright), and begins to fall in love, but nothing is enough to relieve his overwhelming guilt. On the appointed night, on his way to Booth's with a loaded gun, Gale is pulled over for driving drunk. He runs from the police and reaches his destination, but then Booth runs from him. It's obvious Booth is not trying to escape, but is leading Gale somewhere. They end up at Emily's gravesite, which Gale has never visited. There, the two men kneel down, join hands, and cry.

It's apparent from THE CROSSING GUARD and 1991's THE INDIAN RUNNER that Sean Penn has an affinity for stories of "real men"—hard-boiled types who aren't much for talking about their feelings. Unlike action heroes, who do violence with impunity in black-and-white moral universes, Penn's men (the brothers of THE INDIAN RUNNER, Gale and Booth here) are two sides of the same coin, connected by violence, victimized by it, and living in reaction to it on gray moral planes. Penn wants to explore the souls of such men, but he seems unable to construct a screenplay that will serve as a plausible vehicle for his insights.

If killing John Booth is Freddy Gale's obsession, why would he be willing to put it off for three days? Why is Gale willing to abandon his living sons rather than let go of his late daughter? There must be more eating at this man than grief and anger, but over those three days we don't find out what that is. When a stripper (Kari Wuhrer) dresses up as a little girl and performs to "The Good Ship Lollipop," Gale gleefully joins her onstage. Gale has a dream in which he's the drunk driver, and Booth is the crossing guard protecting Emily. Is Penn dropping hints?

The sorrow of losing a child is a pain anyone, parent or not, can understand, but Penn incorrectly assumes that this identification will extend to Gale's anger. With the exception of a great diner scene between Nicholson and Huston, in which Nicholson lets us glimpse the morass of frustrated rage that consumes his character, Gale is a cipher, and we're disconnected from him emotionally.

The strengths of THE CROSSING GUARD are Penn's as a director: his ability to create an atmosphere, sustain a mood, and elicit excellent performances. Nicholson is terrific, as is Huston, but the revelation is David Morse (of THE INDIAN RUNNER and TV's "St. Elsewhere"). It would be praise enough to say Morse is Nicholson's equal, but he's often his better, presenting a more complex characterization in less screen time. Morse and Penn have a great synergistic relationship, so that one looks forward to their next collaboration; one for which Penn might be advised to use an adapted screenplay. *(Profanity, nudity, sexual situations, violence, substance abuse.)* — P.R.

d, Sean Penn; p, David S. Hamburger, Sean Penn; exec p, Bob Weinstein, Harvey Weinstein, Richard Gladstein; w, Sean Penn; ph, Vilmos Zsigmond; ed, Jay Cassidy; m, Jack Nitzsche; prod d, Michael Haller; set d, Derek R. Hill; sound, Tommy Causey (mixer), Per Hallberg; fx, Eddie E. Surkin; casting, Don Phillips; cos, Jill Ohanneson; makeup, Stephen Abrums; stunts, Chuck Waters

Drama (PR: O MPAA: R)

CRUDE OASIS, THE ★★½
(U.S.) 80m Bluestem Films ~ Miramax c

Jennifer Taylor *(Karen Webb)*; Aaron Shields *(Harley)*; Robert Peterson *(Jim)*; Mussef Sibay *(Earp)*; Lynn Bieler *(Stone)*; Roberta Eaton *(Cheri)*

THE CRUDE OASIS is a surprisingly chilling low-budget film that follows a suicidally depressed middle-class housewife as she pursues a mysterious figure from a disturbing, recurrent dream. Alex Graves wrote, directed, edited, and produced the film and shot it in 16-mm in just 14 days.

Karen Webb (Jennifer Taylor) lives in sterile suburbia with her husband Jim (Robert Peterson), who works at the oil refinery that dominates their small town. Karen's marriage is as empty as her clean, bright, sparsely furnished home.

Karen's days are marked by a paralyzing boredom. Every morning, she drives to the same gas station and makes the same purchase: the precise amount of gasoline she will need for that day. During each of these trips, the news on the car radio airs the same, ominous report: a housewife is missing.

Every night, Karen is startled awake from the same dream. In the dream, she sees a young, working-class man (Aaron Shields) wading through a swamp overhung with tangled branches. At first the man's head is turned down, but finally he looks up and Karen sees his face.

One day, overwhelmed with despair, Karen breaks her morning routine; returning home, she attempts to use her day's gasoline supply to commit suicide by carbon monoxide poisoning. The attempt is aborted when she discovers that her tiny gas ration won't run the engine long enough to kill her, and she returns to the station to fill the tank. When the gas station attendant lowers the hood, she recognizes him as the man she has seen in her dreams.

Karen becomes obsessed with the man from the gas station, following him to a seedy bar (the Crude Oasis); watching as he conducts some sort of shady, backroom business; observing with shock as he engages in a meeting with her husband. She continues to follow the young man into the same tangled swamp he inhabits in her dreams, and she watches as he drags something heavy out of the water by a muddy rope. Suddenly the man realizes he is being watched. He drops the rope and tackles her.

Covered with dried mud, Karen awakens in a trailer, looking at her dream man, who is sitting on the toilet eating a nauseatingly sloppy plate of spaghetti. The man's name, she discovers, is Harley Underwood. He is coarse, dirty, and threatening, but Karen is attracted to him.

A clean and passionless suburban existence has almost killed her; Harley's filth and rage seem to give her the will to live. Ultimately, Karen does not stay with her nightmarish dream lover, but neither does she return to the emptiness of her former life.

The film is unremittingly tense. Half-developed subplots, never quite resolved, add to an air of anticipatory dread. Relief is promised but never delivered; even Karen's fate remains a mystery as the film ends. Graves takes the simplest of objects — water, appliances, clocks, keys — and recasts them as terrifying portents of events that don't happen. The effect is striking and somewhat disorienting.

THE CRUDE OASIS also includes a hard look at modern society and class distinctions. As Karen becomes more and more involved with Harley, she undergoes a visible transformation, gradually discarding the elements of her middle-class lifestyle, replacing them with working-class dress and mannerisms. Throughout the film, leaking oil is used to represent the messiness of real life, in contrast to the disturbingly clean surface appearance of Karen's suburban home and marriage. *(Adult situations.)* — R.C.

d, Alex Graves; p, Alex Graves; w, Alex Graves; ph, Steven Quale; ed, Alex Graves; m, Steven Bramson; prod d, Tom Mittlestadt; sound, Peter Rea (mixer)

Drama (PR: C MPAA: R)

CRUMB ★★★★
(U.S.) 120m Superior Pictures ~ Sony Pictures Classics c

Robert Crumb (*Himself*); Alice Kominsky (*Herself—Robert's Wife*); Charles Crumb (*Himself—Robert's Older Brother*); Max Crumb (*Himself—Robert's Younger Brother*); Robert Hughes (*Himself—Time Magazine Art Critic*); Martin Muller (*Himself—Owner of Modernism Gallery*); Don Donahue (*Himself—Former Zap Comix Publisher*); Dana Crumb (*Herself—Robert's First Wife*); Trina Robbins (*Herself—Cartoonist*); Spain Rodriguez (*Himself—Cartoonist*); Bill Griffith (*Himself—Cartoonist*); Deirdre English (*Herself—Former Editor Mother Jones Magazine*); Peggy Orenstein (*Herself—Journalist*); Beatrice Crumb (*Herself—Robert's Mother*); Kathy Goodell (*Herself—Ex-girlfriend*); Dian Hanson (*Herself—Leg Show Magazine Editor & Ex-girlfriend*); Sophie Crumb (*Herself—Robert & Elaine's Daughter*); Jesse Crumb (*Himself—Robert & Dana's Son*)

In examining the life and work of cult cartoonist Robert Crumb, director Terry Zwigoff—whose friendship with Crumb helped him get closer to his subject than might otherwise have been possible—probes the dark underbelly of the American family. CRUMB is an enlightening documentary about a difficult and widely misunderstood artist.

CRUMB reveals a great deal about the man behind the famous images—notable Fritz the Cat, the Janis Joplin-Big Brother and the Holding Company album, and the "Keep On Trucking" logo—and the family behind the man. Robert Crumb grew up in a middle-class Philadelphia household during the 1940s and '50s. He had a natural talent for drawing, and his erotic interest in such disparate pop icons as Bugs Bunny and Sheena, Queen of the Jungle led Crumb to create his own sexually explicit cartoons. Crumb's high school years were miserable. Girls rejected him and his father—a former military officer—got a look at his work and stopped talking to him.

Everything changed in the '60s. Crumb found success in underground comic books and he married for the first time. He was later divorced and married another cartoonist. By the 1970s and '80s, Crumb was widely regarded as a major artist.

In addition to following Crumb over a six-year period, director Zwigoff interviewed Crumb's first wife and Jesse, his son from that marriage; former girlfriends Kathy Goodell and Dian Hanson, who edits porno magazines; second wife Aline Kominsky and their daughter, Sophie; his mother, Beatrice; and his two brothers, Charles and Max. Zwigoff claimed that Crumb's two sisters—Sandra, a lesbian feminist, and Carol, a nurse—refused to appear in the film, though Carol later claimed she'd never really been asked. Zwigoff also includes interviews about Crumb's work with *Time* art critic Robert Hughes; former *Mother Jones* editor Diane English; gallery owner Martin Muller and former *Zap Comix* publisher Don Donahue.

Like Crumb's work—and Crumb himself—CRUMB is simultaneously funny and horrifying. Zwigoff depicts both Crumb's work—much of which blurs the line between the provocative and the offensive in a deliberate and aggressive way—and dysfunctional family in a candid yet matter-of-fact way that sometimes begs directorial comment. Brother Max, for example, mentions in an aside his penchant for molesting women, not an assertion that should go unremarked. But certain issues are tackled head-on and still remain unresolved: The question of whether Crumb's work is sexist and racist, for example, is vigorously debated but never brought to any conclusion.

The suicide of Crumb's talented but mentally unbalanced older brother Charles gives CRUMB a jolt that reminds viewers that his family is more than eccentric: All three brothers are disturbed, and Robert is the only one who seems to have managed to find some balance in his life. Zwigoff's film is both enthralling—in part because it's structured like a mystery—and touching, and despite Crumb's complaints that too much had been revealed, it evokes real sympathy for a man who makes it very hard to like him. And few recent documentaries have said so much about the relationship between a particular artist's background and the ways in which it shaped his aesthetic. *(Sexual situations, adult situations, profanity.)* — E.M.

d, Terry Zwigoff; p, Lynn O'Donnell, Terry Zwigoff; exec p, Lawrence Wilkinson, Albert Berger, Lianne Halfon; co-p, Neal Halfon; ph, Maryse Alberti; ed, Victor Livingston; m, David Boeddinghaus; sound, Scott Breindel

Documentary/Biography (PR: C MPAA: R)

CRY, THE BELOVED COUNTRY ★★½
(U.S.) 111m Distant Horizons; Alpine Films Ltd.;
Videovision Entertainment; Investec Bank Ltd. ~ Miramax c

James Earl Jones *(Rev. Stephen Kumalo)*; Richard Harris *(James Jarvis)*; Charles S. Dutton *(John Kumalo)*; Vusi Kunene *(Priest Msimangu)*; Leleti Khumalo *(Katie)*; Dambisa Kente *(Gertrude Kumalo)*; Eric Miyeni *(Absalom Kumalo)*; Dolly Rathebe *(Mrs. Kumalo)*; Themba Ndaba *(Matthew Kumalo)*; Anne Curteis *(Mrs. Jarvis)*; Jack Robinson *(Ian Jarvis)*; Jennifer Steyn *(Mary Jarvis)*; Ramolao Makhene *(Mpanza)*; Sam Ngakane *(Mafolo)*; Ron Smerczak *(Captain van Jaarsveld)*; Tobias Sikwayo *(Thomas)*; Abigail Kubeka *(Mrs. Mkize)*; Ian Roberts *(Evans)*; Jonathan Rands *(Glyn Henderson)*; Shirley Johnston *(Barbara Henderson)*; John Whiteley *(Father Vincent)*; Lillian Dube *(Mrs. Lithebe)*; Sydney Chama *(Dubula)*; Moses Rakharebe *(Tomlinson)*; Robert Whithead *(Carmichael)*; Patrick Shai *(Robert Ndela)*; Themba Ndaba *(Matthew Kumalo)*; Louis Seboko *(Johannes Pafuri)*; Temise Times *(Shebeen Queen)*; Jerry Mofokeng *(Hlabeni—Taxi Driver)*

CRY, THE BELOVED COUNTRY, a worthy if uninspired adaptation of Alan Paton's 1948 novel, is set in South Africa during the worst days of apartheid. In the tradition of melodrama, it seeks to convey political experience through the story of families in conflict.

After receiving written news of a sister's illness, Reverend Stephen Kumalo (James Earl Jones) travels by train from his home in rural Natal Province to Johannesburg in search of his lost family. He's generously hosted by clergymen but finds his brother, John (Charles S. Dutton), an activist and spokesman for black liberation, indifferent to his arrival, his sister (Dambisa Kente) working as a prostitute, and his son, Absalom (Eric Miyeni), living with a pregnant girlfriend in the city's worst slum and stealing to get by.

Mr. James Jarvis (Richard Harris) is home at his estate in Natal Province with his wife, daughter-in-law and grandson, when he learns that his son Arthur has been shot and killed in a robbery. Mr. Jarvis and his family travel to Johannesburg where he identifies his son's body at the morgue and witnesses his burial. Police, suspecting black South Africans of the crime, raid the slums and quickly find three young men—Absalom and two of his friends—and bring them to trial.

Mr. Jarvis is embittered by the fact that his son fought for democracy and racial equality but was robbed and murdered by blacks. He's also disturbed by evidence revealing that Arthur abhorred his parent's racism and bogus Christianity and believed he'd learned nothing about his country from them.

Both Rev. Kumalo and Mr. Jarvis attend Absalom's trial, but only Kumalo knows their connection. The men meet for the first time outside the Johannesburg home of Mr. Jarvis' in-laws, where Kumalo is overcome with grief and guilt. Mr. Jarvis is polite, then sympathetic to Kumalo's pain; he's surprised but not angry when he learns the reason for it.

Absalom is found guilty and sentenced to hang. Kumalo feels responsible for Absalom's pregnant girlfriend and persuades the two to marry so he can bring the woman and child into his family. Kumalo then returns to Natal Province and waits, hoping the court will have mercy on his son. Absalom dictates a letter to his parents telling them he regrets leaving home. The film concludes with Absalom's death, followed by sweeping, panoramic images of Kumalo on his knees, praying in the mountains of his beautiful homeland.

CRY, THE BELOVED COUNTRY, like all films that mean well and are unapologetically sentimental, both attracts and repels. The film succeeds in many ways: it's well shot and often striking, especially where the lush, spring-green valley of Natal Province forms the backdrop; there's excellent acting by Jones and Harris; the minimal dialogue and highly ritualistic gestures of South African greetings and leave-takings are effective and illuminating.

But the film also fails in many ways. The families' tragedies symbolize suffering and conflicts in South Africa and, more generally, in industrial cultures. The film pushes for the decency and nobility of two men of differing race and culture who believe in the integrity of the family and Christianity—and who, as a result, are on the verge of becoming out-of-synch with the times. Because the film focuses on the experience of these men instead of the complexities of their changing society, it is nostalgic—even elegiac—in tone, and tends to endorse its character's suspect beliefs. In the end, the film takes the conservative side of the ongoing public debate about the disintegration of the family and the moral lassitude of modern urban culture. *(Adult situations.)* — M.F.

d, Darrell James Roodt; p, Anant Singh; exec p, Harry Allan Towers, Sudhir Pragjee, Sanjeev Singh; assoc p, Helena Spring; w, Ronald Harwood; ph, Paul Gilpin; ed, David Heitner; m, John Barry; prod d, David Barkham; art d, Roland Hunter; set d, Gavin Mey; sound, Richard Sprawson (mixer); fx, Donnine Livingston, Mark Dornfeld, Buena Vista Imaging; casting, Marina Van Tonder; cos, Ruy Filipe; makeup, Gabriella Molnar, Colin Polson; stunts, Gavin Mey

Drama   (PR: A   MPAA: PG)

CURE, THE   ★★★
(U.S.) 95m Island Pictures ~ Universal c

Joseph Mazzello *(Dexter)*; Brad Renfro *(Erik)*; Bruce Davison *(Dr. Stevens)*; Annabella Sciorra *(Linda)*; Diana Scarwid *(Gail)*; Nicky Katt *(Pony)*; Craig Gierl *(Jim)*; Renee Humphrey *(Angle)*; Laurie A. Sinclair *(Cheryl)*; Aeryk Egan *(Tyler)*; Delphine French *(Tyler's Girlfriend)*; Andrew Broder *(Tyler's Buddy)*; Jeremy Howard *(Tyler's Buddy)*; Rosemary Corman *(Elderly Woman in Street)*; T. Mychael Rambo *(Garbage Man No. 1)*; David Alan Smith *(Garbage Man No. 2)*; Delia Jurek *(Angry Woman)*; Fran Korba *(Elderly Woman in Market)*; John Lynch *(Skipper No. 1)*; John Beasley *(Skipper No. 2)*; Raymond Nelson *(Skipper No. 3)*; Scott Stockton *(Skipper No. 4)*; Dale Handevidt *(Skipper No. 5)*; Stephen D'Ambrose *(Bus Station Clerk)*; Shriley Venard *(Nurse Snyder)*; Mary McCusker *(Nurse Murphy)*; Peter Moore *(Male Nurse)*; Rodney W. England *(Final Doctor)*; Bill Schoppert *(Funeral Director)*; Samantha Lemole *(Funeral Attendant)*

A preadolescent buddy movie that packs an emotional wallop, THE CURE is set in rural Minnesota, the plot centering on the friendship between two 11-year-old boys.

A southern-accented new arrival, Erik (Brad Renfro) is tormented by his schoolmates. Even so, when Dexter (Joseph Mazzello), "the AIDS boy," moves next door, Erik shares in his schoolmates' fear and scorn of Dexter, who was infected through a blood transfusion. But after talking to the disarmingly candid boy over the fence which separates their yards, Erik defies his mother's warnings and befriends Dexter. At Dexter's house, Erik finds the affection he does not get at home. Dexter's mother Linda (Annabella Sciorra) welcomes Erik into the family and is heartened to see how his friendship has brightened Dexter's life.

Erik thinks of ways to cure Dexter's illness and concludes that since the health food diet he is on has not cured him, he should try candy. Next, inspired by the film MEDICINE MAN, they try to find the cure among foliage they gather in the woods. After one of the herbal remedies Erik concocts for Dexter proves poisonous, the boys' friendship is brought to the attention of Erik's mother Gail (Diana Scarwid), who makes arrangements to send Erik away to camp to keep him away from Dexter. Determined not to be torn apart, Erik and Dexter run away together, taking a raft down the Mississippi towards New Orleans where, according to a supermarket tabloid, a doctor has found the cure for AIDS.

At first a grand adventure, the trip soon becomes difficult and dangerous. When Dexter falls ill, the boys return home by bus. Dexter is hospitalized, and Erik, constantly at his bedside, enlivens his friend's days with stories, games and practical jokes. When Dexter dies, Erik feels he has let his friend down by not finding the cure, but Linda teaches him that his friendship did heal the pain of Dexter's loneliness.

The directorial debut of actor Peter Horton, THE CURE has been criticized for glossing over the AIDS crisis. It is true that the film does not delve into the social ramifications of AIDS, as do LONGTIME COMPANION, PHILADELPHIA, or AND THE BAND PLAYED ON. Instead it looks at the disease through the eyes of two children, who approach it, and the need for a cure, as though it were a science project.

Horton elicits exquisite performances from his cast, most notably from Renfro, whose performance is all the more remarkable considering this is only his second film. Mazzello, whose credits include SHADOWLANDS, THE RIVER WILD and JURASSIC PARK, turns in a beautifully restrained performance as the precocious Dexter. Sciorra convincingly conveys her character's courage, vulnerability and anguish at losing a child. In a scantily developed character, Scarwid plays Erik's ignorant, alcoholic mother with undisguised venom.

Kuhn's script features some wonderfully tender, touching and comic moments, as well as the tearjerker conclusion, but it leaves many questions unanswered, particularly those relating to the characters' backgrounds. The script's biggest deficiency is the boys' highly improbable *Tom Sawyer*-style river adventure. But the film's overall power is only mildly muted by the loose ends in the narrative. THE CURE was critically well-received and given a wide release by Universal, only to suffer from poor box office receipts due to its depressing subject matter. *(Adult situations, profanity.)* — B.R.

d, Peter Horton; p, Mark Burg, Eric Eisner; exec p, Todd Baker, Bill Borden; w, Robert Kuhn; ph, Andrew Dintenfass; ed, Anthony Sherin; m, Dave Grusin; prod d, Armin Ganz; art d, Troy Sizemore; set d, Claire Bowin; sound, Matthew Quast (mixer); fx, Paul Murphy; casting, Mali Finn; cos, Louise Frogley; makeup, Darcy Knight

Drama   (PR: C   MPAA: PG-13)

CURSE OF THE STARVING CLASS   ★★½
(U.S.) 102m August Entertainment; Banque Paribas; Media Entertainment; Breakheart Films; Trimark Pictures ~ Vidmark Entertainment c

James Woods *(Weston Tate)*; Kathy Bates *(Ella Tate)*; Henry Thomas *(Wesley Tate)*; Kristen Fiorella *(Emma Tate)*; Randy Quaid *(Taylor)*; Louis Gossett, Jr. *(Ellis)*; James Fitzpatrick *(Emerson)*; Joel Anderson *(Slater)*; Lauren Abels *(Taylor's Assistant)*; John Cannon Nichols *(Des)*; Jerry Biggs *(Policeman)*; David McDavid *(Will)*; Gary Carter *(Weston's Buddy No. 1)*; Peyton Park *(Weston's Buddy No. 2)*; Del Roy *(Ellis' Buddy)*; Stacie McDavid *(Alibi Witness No. 1)*; Kimberly Gardener *(Alibi Witness No. 2)*; Sue Shelley *(Town Gossip)*; Michele Cochran *(Hotel Waitress)*; Choua Moua *(Vietnamese Woman)*

Adapted from a Sam Shepard play, CURSE OF THE STARVING CLASS depicts the final days in the decline of an unhappy farm family.

Weston Tate (James Wood) is strung out on alcohol, hounded by creditors, estranged from wife Ella (Kathy Bates), and ruined by bad investments. Ella dreams of selling the farm out from under him for a profit and fleeing to Paris. Their two children Wesley (Henry Thomas) and Emma (Kristen Fiorella), nearing maturity, are troubled by the loss of childhood the dissolution of the farm represents. Each family member claims to live outside the starving class, making references to the full refrigerator and those who are truly hungry. Yet the parents' neglect of basic domestic gestures—fixing a door and buying the groceries—points to inconsolable depression and want. In an act of desperation Ella has a one-night stand with a shyster Realtor, the same who conned her husband into buying a worthless plot of land in the middle of the desert. Returning home she learns that Westin has sold the farm for a loss, and is passed out cold in the barn.

Westin awakens in a delirium and stumbles about in the rain. He finds a sick lamb collapsed in the mud and believes himself to have been saved by this symbol of redemption. He nurses the lamb, bathes, dresses in clean clothes, repairs the house, does the laundry, and feels that he can right all the wrongs. Young Wesley, however, has no illusions left. He slaughters the lamb and then fishes his father's old stinking clothes out of the garbage and puts them on, affirming mother's conviction that there is a curse handed down from one generation to the next. Westin's family coaxes him to flee before his creditors kill them all. Emma departs next, leaving son and mother in a house of sighs and silence, the noise of a freeway in the distance.

The story focuses on themes common to Shepard's works—economic and spiritual bankruptcy in rural America, failed ambitions, and the complexities of family dynamics—but the translation from stage to screen is a difficult one, despite the screenplay by producer Beresford who did an Oscar-winning job of transmuting "Driving Miss Daisy" to celluloid. But this film moves in rhythm to the ennui and despair of the drama, and is tedious and slow. The unquestionably first-rate cast never lets you forget they are acting. Several theatrical gestures, (such as a nude scene with the ever-so-significant lamb), fail to convince and instead become absurd. The downbeat CURSE OF THE STARVING CLASS can perhaps best be "enjoyed" for its literary ambitions, but otherwise indicates that some properties are best left on the boards of Off-Broadway. *(Substance abuse, nudity, sexual situations, adult situations, profanity.)* — R.C.

d, J. Michael McClary; p, William S. Gilmore, Harel Goldstein; exec p, Bruce Beresford, David Goldstein, Mark Amin, William B. O'Boyle; assoc p, Bruce Weiss, Fran Roy, Evi Quaid; w, Bruce Beresford (based on the play by Sam Shepard); ph, Dick Quinlan; ed, Dean Goodhill; m, John Bryant, Frank Homes; prod d, Ladislav Wilheim; set d, J. Grey Smith; sound, Robert Wald (mixer); fx, Randy Moore, Margaret Johnson; casting, Shari Rhodes, Joseph Middleton; cos, Kathryn Morrison; makeup, Tina K. Roesler, Andre Blaise; stunts, Russell Towery

Drama   (PR: C   MPAA: NR)

CUTTHROAT ISLAND   ★★½
(U.S.) 123m Carolco; Forge Productions; Laurence Mark Productions; Beckner/Gorman Productions ~ MGM/UA c

Geena Davis *(Morgan Adams)*; Matthew Modine *(William Shaw)*; Frank Langella *(Dawg Brown)*; Maury Chaykin *(John Reed)*; Patrick Malahide *(Ainslee)*; Stan Shaw *(Glasspoole)*; Harris Yulin *(Black Harry)*; Rex Linn *(Mr. Blair)*; Paul Dillon *(Snelgrave)*; Chris Masterson *(Bowen)*; Jimmie F. Skaggs *(Scully)*; Carl Chase *(Bishop)*; Peter Geeves *(Fiddler Pirate)*; Angus Wright *(Captain Trotter)*; Ken Bones *(Toussant)*; Mary Pegler *(Mandy Rickets)*; Mary Peach *(Lady)*; Lucinda Aurel

(Lady); Thomas Lockyer *(Lieutenant)*; Roger Booth *(Auction-eer)*; George Murcell *(Mordachai Fingers)*; Simon Atherton *(Bartender)*; Dickey Beer *(Executioner)*; Christopher Halliday *(Hastings)*; Chris Johnston *(Helmsman)*; Richard Leaf *(Snake the Lookout)*; Tam White *(Fleming)*; Shayna the Monkey *(King Charles)*; Rupert Vansittart *(Captain Perkins)*; Nick Bartlett; David Bailie; Kwame Kwei-Armah; Ramon Tikaram; Chris Adamson *(Dawg's Pirates)*

One of its year's major commercial disasters, Renny Harlin's big, chaotic pirate flick is best understood as an attempt to revive the waning career of his wife, Geena Davis, but he's done her no great favor. Poor Geena gets lost in a hectic scenario that's little more than an excuse for a series of thunderous explosions, clanky sword battles and run-of-the-mill spectacular stunts.

In the buccaneer-infested waters of the 18th-century Caribbean, crusty pirate captain Black Harry (Harris Yulin) has one-third of a map leading to the fabled treasure of Cutthroat Island. When he's killed by his own brother, ruthless rival pirate Dawg Brown (Frank Langella), Black Harry's dying wish is that his tomboy daughter Morgan (Geena Davis) take over his ship, the Morning Star, and go in quest of the treasure. She gamely removes his piece of the map, which has been tattooed onto his scalp, only to discover that it is written in Latin. She learns of one William Shaw (Matthew Modine), a Latin-literate rogue, who is about to be auctioned off as a slave for his thieving ways. She buys him, then a second piece of the map, and sets sail for Cutthroat Island. Dawg Brown, who has the last piece, follows in hot pursuit.

Though storms and other travails beset the vessels, they finally reach their destination and commence a mad dash for the loot. Also on board the Morning Star are Ainslee (Patrick Malahide), the gold-hungry colonial British governor; John Reed (Maury Chaikin), an anachronistic adventure novelist in search of material; Blair (Rex Linn), a dimwitted, tattooed behemoth of a first mate, and King Charles, Morgan's adorable, camera-friendly pet monkey. Morgan duels her dastardly uncle and falls into the arms of Shaw.

Although flawed, CUTTHROAT ISLAND is not the WATER-WORLD-sized debacle that its well-publicized casting and production problems promised. It is a big, leaky galleon of a movie that manages to deliver a fitfully amusing ride. Although it was committee-written—six screenwriters are credited—the screenplay is reasonably engaging and winningly detailed. There's a kind of dogmatic, compulsive fascination to it, akin to following a silly murder mystery. This makes it a bit easier to swallow the annoying anachronisms and cartoonishly outlined characters. Director Harlin betrays his action-genre roots in the mindless explosions and frenetic chase sequences. (The actual fight scenes are ponderous, however, slowed down by cumbersome weapons and an obvious lack of fencing skill.) Harlin's sense of humor is puerile: smarmy wisecracks, gross-out effects with rotting corpses and snakes, and the endlessly lensed antics of the monkey, who seems to get more closeups than anyone else.

That the film remains watchable is largely due to the ingratiatingly goofy Davis. She's unflatteringly photographed and wholly unbelievable as a period lass, but she's unfailingly likable. It's fun to see her begrimed and butch, swinging a sword and punching out big, sweaty brutes. *(Sexual situations, adult situations, violence.)* — D.N.

d, Renny Harlin; p, Renny Harlin, Joel B. Michaels, Laurence Mark, James Gorman; exec p, Mario Kassar; assoc p, Jane Barteleme; co-p, John Baldecchi, Lynwood Spinks; w, Robert King, Marc Norman (from a story by Michael Frost Beckner, James Gorman, Bruce A. Evans, and Raynold Gideon); ph, Peter Levy; ed, Frank J. Urioste, Ralph E. Winters; m, John Debney;

prod d, Norman Garwood; art d, Roger Cain, Keith Pain; set d, Maggie Gray; sound, Ivan Sharrock (mixer); fx, Allen Hall, Mario Cassar, Jeffrey A. Okun; casting, Mindy Marin; cos, Enrico Sabbatini; makeup, Paul Engelen; stunts, Vic Armstrong

Adventure/Action/Romance   **(PR: A   MPAA: PG-13)**

CYBER BANDITS   ★½
(U.S.) 86m IRS Media; Lumiere Pictures; Cyberfilm Productions ~ Columbia TriStar Home Video c

Martin Kemp *(Jack)*; Alexandra Paul *(Rebecca)*; Adam Ant *(Manny)*; James Wong *(Tojo)*; Robert Hays *(Morgan Wells)*; Henry Gibson *(Dr.K)*; Grace Jones *(Masako)*; Nils Allen Stewart *(Morgan's Head Thug)*; Christopher Weeks *(Marcel)*; Catherine Dao *(Hotel Clerk)*; Kalique Asharri *(Morgan Thug)*; Barbara Moore *(Hope)*; Ron Devon *(Rebel Leader)*; Julie Carmen *(Olive)*; Jason Stuart *(Street Vendor)*; James Burns *(Bouncer)*

CYBER BANDITS is a high-tech hardware thriller that sputters like a wet firecracker, (or "cyberfirecracker," in deference to the trend-begging title). Unmistakable mediocrity overwhelms all surface distractions.

When sailor Jack (Martin Kemp) signs to crew for mogul Morgan Wells (Robert Hays), he finds it's risky work if you've the nerve to rub suntan oil on Morgan's chick Rebecca (Alexandra Paul). Below deck, Morgan schemes for his operatives to secure a secret weapon in the form of a CD-ROM disc that would make him the world's most powerful hombre. Rash Rebecca pilfers the disc and Jack accompanies her through a sewer to safety. The fugitives drop by a tattoo parlor where Tojo (James Hong) disguises the circuit diagram by digitally transferring it into skin art on Jack's back. Morgan eventually recovers the disc but learns the data is missing. Fortunately for Jack's epidermis, a non-lethal operation is performed which sucks up the CD-ROM data for a voice-activated indestructible handgun that Morgan schemes to sell to the highest bidder. Trapped on the pleasure cruiser, Jack and Rebecca figure out how to use the potent pistol against the merciless arms merchant. After dispatching a surprised Morgan, Rebecca tosses the superweapon into the ocean.

Only John Waters could have assembled such a motley gang of pop-music flotsam and celebrity jetsam and give them so little to do. Imagine Adam Ant (as Jack's shipmate buddy), Grace Jones (as a rogue agent after Morgan), and "Laugh-In" regular Henry Gibson in one movie! None of them pep up the script appreciably, despite much arm-waving hysteria. Aside from the nifty business of stamping the McGuffin right onto the hero's flesh, the scenario settles for *deja vu* chase sequences, comic-book villainy, and expository sidebars that postpone the inevitable without building suspense. Attractive mannequins Kemp and Paul provide soothing eyewash for oglers, but generate the combined magnetism of schoolkids bundling for a first kiss. CYBER BANDITS has just enough oomph to tread water before it drowns in overplotting, travelogue, and fussy direction. *(Graphic violence, extensive nudity, profanity, substance abuse.)* — R.P.

d, Erik Fleming; p, Paul Colichman, Lilli Rouleau; exec p, Lila Cazes, Miles Copeland, III; co-p, Albert Dickerson, III; w, Winston Beard, James Robinson (from a story by James Robinson); ph, Denis Mahoney; ed, Rebecca Ross; m, Steve Hunter; prod d, Brian Kasch; set d, Jeff Bell; sound, Bill Robbins (mixer); fx, Beverly Hartigan, Steven Robiner, Ultimate Effects; casting, Donald Paul Pemrick; cos, P. Zjene Libby; makeup, Elizabeth Barczewska; stunts, Patrick Statham

Science Fiction/Adventure   **(PR: O   MPAA: R)**

DALLAS DOLL ★★★

(Australia) 104m Dallas Doll Productions ~
Artistic License Films c

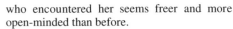

Sandra Bernhard *(Dallas Adair)*; Victoria
Longley *(Rosalind Sommers)*; Frank Gallacher
(Stephen Sommers); Jack Blundell *(Charlie
Sommers)*; Rose Byrne *(Rastus Sommers)*;
Jonathon Leahy *(Eddy)*; Douglas Hedge *(Mayor
Tonkin)*; Melissa Thomas *(Margaret)*; Elaine
Lee *(Mrs. Winthrop)*; Walter Sullivan *(Elderly
Councillor)*; William Usic *(Minister)*; Alethea
McGrath *(Aunt Mary)*; Roy Billing *(Dave Harry)*; John Frawly
(Mr. Fellows); Ken Senga *(Mr. Kurowsawa)*; Kuni Hashimoto
(Mr. Ozu); Denis Mackay *(Farmer)*; Laura Bentley *(Stewardess)*;
Sally Cahill *(Mother)*; Hannah O'Brien *(Little Girl)*; John Hinde
(Uncle Henry); Roseann McDonald *(Shop Assistant)*; Eva Di
Cesare *(Vet)*; Margie McCrae *(Thelma Tonkin)*; Phillip Adams
(Radio Announcer); Margaret Throsby *(Radio Announcer)*;
Robert Lee *(Radio Announcer)*; Luke Carroll *(Boy)*; Alan Camp-
bell *(Boy)*; David Ngoombujarra *(Storyteller)*; Bob Lovett *(Deaf
Interpreter)*; Yukari Tanimura *(Japanese Translator)*; Yumiko
Iwanaga *(Mrs. Ozu)*; Celia Ireland *(Policewoman)*; Claire Gow;
Joan Baker; Tanya McMillan; Mary Lindsay *(City Clinic
Women)*

DALLAS DOLL, made and released in Australia in 1994, and
released in the US in 1995, is an amusing, unpredictable comedy
about an American golf pro who moves to Australia, seduces a
family, and wins over a town.

Teenager Charlie Sommers (Jake Blundell), returning to Australia from a trip to New York, meets vivacious Dallas (Sandra
Bernhard) on the plane. When Charlie arrives home, he discovers
that Dallas has been hired as pro for the local golf club. His
mother Rosalind (Victoria Longley) asks Dallas home for dinner,
and Dallas manages to get invited to stay with the family indefi-
nitely. Even though she does not seem too reliable, she works her
way into the hearts of Rosalind, her husband Stephen (Frank
Gallacher), and Charlie. Only Rosalind's daughter, Rastus (Rose
Byrne), and the family dog fail to be charmed by Dallas.

Dallas's presence disturbs the family equilibrium completely.
When she motivates Rosalind into buying a farm she had always
dreamed of, Charlie and Rastus are sent off to boarding school.
Dallas also seduces Charlie, who falls in love with her and
decides to leave school. When he trys to tell his parents, he
discovers Dallas in bed with his father. In shock, he runs away.

Meanwhile, Dallas gains popularity in town, and quickly
becomes mayor. She plans to expand the golf club and begins to
attract Japanese investors. Rosalind also falls in love with Dallas,
and when she tells Stephen, he suggests that the three live
together as lovers. The idea disgusts her, and she is further
appalled when she finds Dallas making love to Charlie. She
closes the golf club and sends Dallas away.

As Dallas is leaving, Rastus discovers a huge hole left by a
UFO. Dallas falls into the hole and is stampeded by roaming
cattle. The town mourns Dallas's death. Rosalind leaves Stephen
but keeps the farm, her one true love.

DALLAS DOLL's plot is an exercise in absurdity. While it
has a precedent in Pasolini's TEOREMA, the whimsical nature
of the film and Bernhard's performance make its serious elements take a back seat to satire and farce. At one level, the film
is an allegory that indicts the seductive nature of an American
lifestyle. Dallas is as dishonest and corrupting as she is charming. But despite the damage she does, Dallas is not all bad. She
brings excitement and pleasure into the lives of the Sommers
family and much of the town, and even after she dies, everyone
who encountered her seems freer and more
open-minded than before.

The film is often hilarious. It contains several
bizarre dream sequences, and a completely unexpected and surreal ending. The miniature golf
scenes are priceless, with the supposedly prim
Rosalind dancing wildly in garters and a bra.
The performances are uniformly excellent.
Bernhard is the perfect choice for Dallas, unconventionally sexy, with a dry, clever wit, and an
untamed spirit. Longley is equally good as
Rosalind, effortlessly transformed from suburban housewife to
necklace-stealing sexpot. DALLAS DOLL did not receive much
exposure in the United States, but is a highly entertaining film.
(Extensive nudity, sexual situations, profanity.) — A.M.

d, Ann Turner; p, Ross Matthews; exec p, Peggy Chapman,
George Faber; assoc p, Ray Brown, Sue Masters; co-p, Ann
Turner, Tatiana Kennedy; w, Ann Turner; ph, Paul Murphy; ed,
Mike Honey; m, David Hirschfelder; prod d, Marcus North; art
d, Kerrie Reay; sound, Gethin Creagh (mixer), Peter Purcell
(mixer), Nicholas Wood; fx, Chris Murray, Ray Towler; casting,
Liz Mullinar; cos, Rosalea Hood; makeup, Chiara Tripodi, Bob
McCarron; stunts, Zef Eletheriou, Rocky McDonald

Comedy   **(PR: O   MPAA: NR)**

DANCE ME OUTSIDE ★★

(U.S./Canada) 87m Rez Films Ltd.; Shadow Shows, Inc.;
Yorktown Productions ~ A-Pix Entertainment c

Ryan Rajendra Black *(Silas Crow)*; Adam Beach *(Frank Fence-
post)*; Jennifer Podemski *(Sadie Maracle)*; Michael Greyeyes
(Gooch); Lisa LaCroix *(Illiana)*; Kevin Hicks *(Robert McVay)*;
Rose Marie Trudeau *(Ma Crow)*; Gloria May Eshkibok *(Mad
Etta)*; Selim Running Bear Sandoval *(Robert Coyote)*; Sandrine
Holt *(Poppy)*; Tamara Podemski *(Little Margaret)*; Herbie Bar-
nes *(Joseph)*; Hugh Dillon *(Clarence Gaskill)*; Vince Manitow-
abi *(Hobart Thunder)*; Robert Frank Pegahmagabow *(Wendel)*;
Joel King *(Pete)*; Namir Khan *(Bartender)*; David Webb *(Fed 1)*;
John Dondertman *(Fed 2)*; Wendy King *(Lucy)*; Johnny Askwith
(Bill); Brian Clancy *(Clerk)*; Steve Van Denzen *(Mean Cop)*;
Bruno Bryniarski *(Bald Cop)*; Peter Miskimmin *(Weird Cop)*;
Leslie Tabobondung *(Clifton)*

Good intentions pave the way to Message Movie Limbo. Heartfelt and sometimes trenchant, DANCE ME OUTSIDE is a rare
coming-of-age film celebrating Native American culture, too
bland in visual technique and overstated in its writing to score.

Although the perimeters of their Kidabanessee Reservation
are narrowly defined by years of White American oppression,
teens Silas Crow (Ryan Black) and Frank Fencepost (Adam
Beach) look forward to admittance to a mechanics' school.
Concerned about getting trapped in the usual early marriage
cycle, Sila's girlfriend Sadie (Jennifer Podemski) calls a halt to
their relationship so she can devote herself to Indian activism.
Meanwhile her sister Illiana (Lisa Lacroix) visits from the big
city with her infertile Caucasian hubby Robert (Kevin Hicks), a
lawyer who receives a joshing reception from his new in-laws.
Tension mounts when Illiana's ex-lover Gooch (Michael
Greyeyes) is released from jail and can't relinquish hopes of
reconciling with her.

Then a friend, Little Margaret (Tamara Podemski) is slain by
drugged-up white racist Clarence (Hugh Dillon), whose crime
nets him only a manslaughter sentence. This slap on the wrist
galvanizes many of the tribe into plans for revenge. In conjunction with a medicine woman, Silas arranges for Illiana's one-
night reunion with Gooch so that their mother can have a

grandchild. Although Silas and his buddies keep Robert occupied with fake rituals, the outsider-initiate gains their respect before the night is over. When skinhead Clarence is finally released, the Indian teens plan to execute him, but are thwarted by their women-folk. Silas and Frank don't carry out vigilante vengeance, but Gooch is suspected when Clarence is found with a slashed throat. Avoiding suspicion, Sadie and Poppy (Sandrine Holt) avenged Little Margaret's slaying and are never charged. Frank and Silas both get accepted into technical school, which will provide them with a way out of the tribal abyss of poverty.

From the start DANCE ME OUTSIDE is devalued by an over-explicit narration that does more harm than good, the type of omniscient voice that always works better in novels (in this case, W.P. Kinsella's source anthology). Though Silas's off-camera thoughts flavor the film with a native authenticity, they stolidly deliver dramatic information that the director could have better provided visually. In general the mise en scene is undistinguished, with individual scenes standing out solely due to their high-pitched emoting. No thread of connective tension causes these cathartic moments to build and swell, however.

Furthermore, although one understands the Indians' bitter payback plan for Clarence, the screenwriter evinces a stridently moralistic stance that assumes viewers must root for blood or be branded racist. Also irksome is the treatment of Illiana's heart-on-his-sleeve husband Robert by the tribal teens. Their comical humiliation of him says less about misguided Whites attempting to fit in than it does about their own biases. The film doesn't condemn their cruelty as it does the Caucasian contingent who needle Silas's crowd with Tonto jokes, sacrificing honesty to political correctness.

The film never draws us deeply into its characters' interior lives. Their unique longings are filtered through a soap-opera sensibility, and the cliches of melodrama seem even flimsier against the worthy ethnic backdrop. *(Extreme profanity, violence, substance abuse, sexual situations, adult situations.)* — R.P.

d, Bruce McDonald; p, Bruce McDonald, Brian Dennis; exec p, Norman Jewison, Sarah Hayward; assoc p, Duke Redbird, David Nancoff; w, Bruce McDonald, Don McKellar, John Frizell (based on the book by W.P. Kinsella); ph, Miroslaw Baszak; ed, Michael Pacek; m, Mychael Danna; prod d, John Dondertman; set d, Maureen Sless; sound, Daniel Pellern (mixer), Peter Kelly (mixer), Keith Elliot (mixer); fx, John Laforet; casting, Clare Walker; cos, Beth Pasternak; makeup, Lynda McCormack; stunts, Jamie Jones

Drama/Adventure　　　　　**(PR: C　MPAA: NR)**

DANCER, THE　　　　　　★★
(Sweden) 100m Svenska Filminstitutet; Sveriges TV2; Feuer Productions ~ Svenska Filminstitutet c
(DANSAREN)

Katja Bjorner; Erland Josephson; Anneli Alhanko; Clint Farha; Robert Cohan; Rudi van Dantzig; Valentina Savina; Michael Messerer; Aleksander Khmelnitski

Donya Feuer's THE DANCER looks at the life of a teenage dancer in a Swedish ballet company. Compared to Frederick Wiseman's BALLET, Feuer's documentary is both romantic and dull. More surprisingly, the film does not even provide adequate coverage of the dancing itself.

Like BALLET, THE DANCER observes the backstage story of a season with a ballet company. Whereas Wiseman chose the American Ballet Theater (ABT), Feuer selects the National Ballet of Clint Farha in Sweden. Feuer focuses on the rehearsals and performances of one particular dancer—young, beautiful Katja Bjorner—tracing her relationships with, inter alia, an older fe-

male dancer in the group, Anneli Alhanko; an elderly admirer who watches her during rehearsals (played by Erland Josephson); and the various ballet masters, especially Valentina Savina, her most devoted teacher. Bjorner is seen performing in such classics as *Romeo and Juliet*, *Giselle*, and *Sleeping Beauty*; she also has ample opportunity to express her thoughts and feelings. The film ends with Bjorner's triumphant work with her company in *Swan Lake*.

THE DANCER covers the same territory as Wiseman's BALLET (also released in 1995) in half the running time, but fails in almost every way to enlighten and entertain. If BALLET cleverly deconstructed the high-art form of the ballet, THE DANCER heavy-handedly *reconstructs* it. BALLET featured Wiseman's customary fly-on-the-wall observations, recording the ABT's daily operation from rehearsals to auditions to performances to sales negotiations to after-hours nightclubbing. THE DANCER stays clear of everything but the dancer's performance, shown in the most glamorous light possible. While BALLET observes the dancers in long takes without the mediating influences of music, voice-overs, or flashy editing, THE DANCER creates high-toned music videos in the rehearsal sequences.

Other "traditional" documentary film techniques are even more disturbing. During a lengthy sequence in which the viewer watches a ballet shoe being made, a narrator explains what a black shoemaker is doing. Thus, the only person of color in the entire film is without a voice (while other characters always speak for themselves). Just as unpleasant is the intrusion of Erland Josephson's character. His presence is poorly explained, and he appears to be playing Humbert Humbert to Bjorner's Lolita (the camera tilts and pans so much over her body that the effect is almost pornographic).

Perhaps the worst thing about the film is that Gunnar Kallstrom's cinematography poorly captures the dancer's graceful movements, using close-ups and mid-shots when full-body long-shots would be far more appropriate. Sadly, except for a few pretty shots of Bjorner reflected in mirrors, there is nothing here to recommend the film. If Wiseman documented tedium in BALLET, Feuer *creates* tedium in THE DANCER. — E.M.

d, Donya Feuer; p, Lisabeth Gabrielsson; w, Donya Feuer; ph, Gunnar Kallstrom, Per Kallberg, Lisa Hagstrand; ed, Kerstin Eriksdotter; sound, Lasse Summanen, Zsa-Zsa Tibblin

Documentary　　　　　　**(PR: A　MPAA: NR)**

DANGER OF LOVE　　　　　★
(U.S.) 95m Lois Luger Productions; Citadel Pictures ~ Vidmark Entertainment c

Joe Penny *(Michael Carlin)*; Jenny Robertson *(Carolyn Warmus)*; Deborah Benson *(Mary Ann Carlin)*; Joseph Bologna *(Detective John Pollina)*; Fairuza Balk *(Lisa Carlin)*; Richard Lewis *(Edward Sanders)*; Dee Dee Van Zyl *(Cheryl Sanders)*; Sydney Walsh *(Nikki)*; Robert Nadir *(Detective Oliver Harris)*; Michael MacRae *(Carolyn's Attorney)*; Gregg Loughridge *(Wes Larson)*; Krisha Fairchild *(Teri)*; William DeYoung *(Mr. Harlan)*; David L Wasman *(Billy Bianco)*; Evelyn Perdue *(Mrs. Barstow)*; Claire Brown *(Lois Wilson)*; Jan D'Arcy *(Psychiatrist)*; Bonnie Banks *(Policewoman)*; James Chestnutt *(1st Detective)*; Ben DiGregorio *(Detective in Car)*; Michael A. Jackson *(Desk Sergeant)*; James Monitor *(Medical Examiner)*; Stephen Godwin *(Mr. Robertson)*; Victoria Otto *(Mrs. Robertson)*; Taryn Lee *(Susan Robertson)*; John X. Deveney *(Jack)*; Liz Denison *(Jeannette)*; Woody Eney *(Family Friend)*; Dan Mahar *(Detective William Lowell)*; Joanne Klein *(Telephone Operator)*; Bill Ter Kuile *(Hotel Desk Clerk)*; Paul Mitri *(Photographer)*

When a 1989 crime of passion in Westchester County, NY, got dubbed "the FATAL ATTRACTION murder case," media exploitation cranked into high gear. One of the results was this throwaway TV docudrama, released to home video in 1995.

Michael Carlin (Joe Penny), a schoolteacher in a passionless marriage to zombified Mary Ann (Denorah Benson), becomes the prime suspect when she's found shot to death. After all, Michael was cheating on his wife with sexy young computer instructor Carolyn Warmus (Jenny Robertson). Though cops try to nail Michael, his alibi holds. Carolyn is a different story. A flaky femme with a rap sheet for harassing a succession of ex-lovers, she proceeds to hound merry widower Michael even as he tries to put his life back together (i.e., date other women). It turns out he broke off his fling with Carolyn just before the killing, and she obtained a gun with a silencer. Her wealthy family gives Carolyn the best legal defense money can buy, but after her first trial ends in a hung jury, the second sentences her to 25 years to life for murdering Mary Ann in a lethal fit of jealousy.

The performances here are so listless and glum one would surmise that cast and crew had been sentenced to life as well. Only the flashback slaughter of Mary Ann, her life snipped away *pop* by *pop* by Carolyn's silenced pistol, lingers in mind—as does the pic's unsympathetic depiction of the real-life victim, Betty Jeanne Solomon, as a much-disliked and faithless spouse herself.

Even before the verdict, three books and two TV movies germinated. DANGER OF LOVE, based on the real husband's version of events, was to have been an HBO feature via their production subsidiary Citadel. But the cable network balked over the hack script (sample Warmus dialogue: "I want to be your baby. I want to have your baby!") and, rather than spend any time on rewrites, sent the movie to CBS. Score one point for the cable industry. And thus DANGER OF LOVE premiered in October, 1993, but still lost the broadcast race to ABC's own quickie A MURDEROUS AFFAIR: THE CAROLYN WARMUS STORY, starring Virginia Madsen in the title role, which had aired about a month earlier.

By 1995, the ashes of the case had cooled, and DANGER OF LOVE's video release was packaged like a typical direct-to-video erotic thriller. One wonders if the commercial failure of Gus Van Sant's acclaimed tabloid satire TO DIE FOR that same year could be blamed on audiences benumbed by countless tacky true-crime TV schlockers like this. *(Sexual situations, violence.)* — C.C.

d, Joyce Chopra; p, Michael O. Gallant; exec p, Lois Luger, David R. Ginsburg; assoc p, Fran Bell; w, Ara Watson, Sam Blackwell; ph, Bobby Byrne; ed, Sidney Wolinsky, Martin Nicholson; m, Mark Snow; prod d, Linda Allen; set d, Tim Kirkpatrick; sound, Robert L. King, II (mixer); casting, Barbara Claman, Patti Carns Kalles; cos, Louise Frogley; makeup, Francesca Lacagnina; stunts, Chris Doyle

Thriller/Docudrama (PR: C MPAA: R)

DANGEROUS MINDS ★★
(U.S.) 99m Hollywood Pictures; Via Rosa Productions; Simpson-Bruckheimer Productions ~ Buena Vista c

Michelle Pfeiffer *(LouAnne Johnson)*; George Dzundza *(Hal Griffith)*; Courtney B. Vance *(Mr. George Grandey)*; Robin Bartlett *(Ms. Carla Nichols)*; Bruklin Harris *(Callie Roberts)*; Renoly Santiago *(Raul Sanchero)*; Wade Dominguez *(Emilio Ramirez)*; Beatrice Winde *(Mary Benton)*; Lorraine Toussaint *(Irene Roberts)*; John Neville *(Waiter)*; Marcello Thedford *(Cornelius Bates)*; Roberto Alvarez *(Gusmaro Rivera)*; Richard Grant *(Durrell Benton)*; Marisela Gonzalez *(Angela)*; Toni Nichelle Buzhardt *(Nikki)*; Norris Young *(Kareem)*; Rahman Ibraheem *(Big "G")*; Desire Galvez *(Taiwana)*; Wilson Limpo *(Roderick)*; Raymond Grant *(Lionel Benton)*; Veronica Robles *(Stephanie)*; Michael Archuleta *(Oso)*; Deshanda Carter *(Tanyekia)*; Ebony Jerido *(Deanne)*; Brandi Younger *(Grip)*; Asia Minor *(Pam)*; Karina Arroyave *(Josy)*; Paula Garces *(Alvina)*; Ivan Sergei *(Huero)*; Mark Prince Edwards *(P.J.)*; Ismael Archuleta *(Lalo)*; Skye Basset *(Jody)*; Gaura Buchwald *(Warlock)*; Cynthia Avila *(Mrs. Sanchero)*; Roman J. Cisneros *(Mr. Sanchero)*; Camille Winbush *(Tyeisha Roberts)*; Al Israel *(Mr. Santiago)*; Brian Anthony *(Joey)*; Jason Gutman *(Adam)*; Lara Spotts *(Dianna)*

Call it "Def Poets Society": Powered by a rap and hip-hop soundtrack, DANGEROUS MINDS is a movie desperately seeking street credibility, while offering enough changes in the true story of LouAnne Johnson to appeal to mainstream, white audiences. The result is a formulaic story of a teacher enlightening inner-city toughs that should come with the warning: "Sanitized For Your Protection."

Michelle Pfeiffer plays Johnson, a recently divorced and discharged Marine, who takes a job teaching English to an unruly mob masquerading as students. The first day, the predominantly black and Latino class laughs their white bread instructor right out of the room. The next day, Johnson gets their attention with an impromptu karate demonstration. She quickly dispenses with grammar drills, and starts talking to the kids about things they can understand—death, anger, pride, frustration—and the way poetry addresses these themes. Analyzing the lyrics of Bob Dylan songs (the real Johnson used rap lyrics) lights a fire in the students' bellies, and, Johnson hopes, opens their minds to new possibilities for their futures.

Her unorthodox teaching methods draw criticism from the principal and some parents, but Johnson is resolute. She scores a victory when she befriends Raul (Renoly Santiago) and persuades him that school, not crime, is the answer. She counts a loss when her best and brightest student, Callie (Bruklin Harris), gets pregnant and drops out. Defeat's sting is greatest after she reaches out to the violent Emilio (Wade Dominguez), only to see him murdered by a rival drug dealer.

At the end of the term, Johnson announces that she will not be returning next year. However, after heartfelt testimony from Raul and the other students about the difference she's made in their lives, and Callie's return to school, Johnson changes her mind.

Ever since Lulu serenaded Sidney Poitier, inspirational teacher stories have followed a formula: The new teacher faces resistance, gains acceptance, meddles, succeeds, and finally receives pledges of devotion. The resulting movie can be schmaltzy, like DEAD POETS SOCIETY (1989), or terrific like STAND AND DELIVER (1987). Even a ham-fisted use of the formula like LEAN ON ME (1989) can be effective. But the modifications to the story Johnson chronicles in her book *My Posse Don't Do Homework*—like substituting Dylan for Dr. Dre—make DANGEROUS MINDS ring false, and its failure to convey a sense of purpose makes it feel hollow.

Johnson's noble goal—she just wants the kids to *think*—is undermined by methods: Bribing students with candy bars, trips to an amusement park, and free meals every step of the way. And why does she care so much, put herself at risk, and spend all that money? Because she chooses to, she explains. True or not, that's a pretty uncompelling reason, and that she accidentally fell into the job doesn't exactly make her a Marine with a mission. Pfieffer does a pretty good job of convincing us that someone so beautiful would even be caught dead in this school, though a romantic sub-plot with Andy Garcia that was excised after test screenings may have offered insight into her character's motivations. DANGEROUS MINDS proved a surprise commercial success, partly due to Coolio's hit theme song, "Gangsta's Paradise." *(Profanity, violence.)* — P.R.

d, John N. Smith; p, Don Simpson, Jerry Bruckheimer; exec p, Sandra Rabins, Lucas Foster; w, Ronald Bass (based on the book *My Posse Don't Do Homework* by LouAnne Johnson), Elaine May (uncredited); ph, Pierre Letarte; ed, Tom Rolf; m, Wendy & Lisa; prod d, Donald Graham Burt; art d, Nancy Patton; set d, Catherine Mann; sound, David Ronne (mixer); fx, Darrell D. Pritchett; casting, Bonnie Timmermann; cos, Bobbie Read; makeup, Marietta Carter Narcisse; stunts, Bernie Pock

Drama **(PR: C MPAA: R)**

DANGEROUS, THE ★★½
(U.S.) 96m West Side Studios; Sun Lion
Productions ~ Orion Home Video c

Robert Davi *(Davalos)*; Michael Pare *(Random)*; Paula Barbieri *(Paula)*; John Savage *(Emile Lautrec)*; Elliot Gould *(Levine)*; Joel Grey *(Flea)*; Cary Hiroyuki-Tagawa *(Kon Seki)*; Layton Martens *(Pardee)*; Takayo Fisher *(Mrs. Seki)*; Marco St. John *(Polk)*; Monte Bain *(Pulaski)*; June Saruwatari *(Midori)*; Fred Lewis *(Moss)*; Mario Opinato *(Vittorio)*; Sherlyn Leonard *(Diane)*; Juan Fernandez *(Tito)*; Ron Hyatt *(Director)*; Malika Kinison *(Garland)*; Garrett E. Soto *(Ryo)*; Sven Ole Thorsen *(Sven)*; Robin Hancock *(Gordon)*; Gary Beal *(Anthony)*; Sergio Gomez *(Cesar)*; Walter Breaux, Jr. *(Marsh)*; Desiree Gaudet *(Clerk)*; Saemi Nakamura *(Akiko Seki)*

Immortalized as the starring debut of O.J. Simpson's former girlfriend-for-life, Paula Barbieri, this East-Meets-West actioner is actually more notable for its pervasive brutality and nihilistic edge. Despite its side dish of the Oriental art of revenge, a la carte violence is clearly the biggest attraction on this flick's menu.

After a Japanese reporter is buried alive in cement by publicity-paranoid drug king Tito (Juan Fernandez), her ninja brother, Kon Seki (Cary Hiroyuki-Tagawa), and sister, Akiko Seki (Saemi Nakamura), vow revenge. New Orleans police chief Polk (Marco St. John) strong-arms a former soldier of fortune, Davalos (Robert Davi), to ease mounting tensions between the drug gang and the police when Tito mistakenly suspects cops for the wave of attacks on his men by the ninja siblings. In a city where everyone seems bent, Davalos is teamed with honest cop Random (Michael Pare), but their track down is complicated by the machinations of two insane cousins hired by the mob to carve out a deadly message on policemen. Despite their success as cop-terminators, the assassins fall prey to the ninja duo at a movie theater, saving the lives of Random and Davalos. After Tito's sometime-chick Paula (Paula Barbieri) gets kidnapped due to her former ties to Davalos, the good guys invade a porn studio and, in the ensuing fight, the ninjas again come to their aid, killing Tito. Officially ordered to tidy up the case by disposing of Davalos and the ninja warriors, Random allows his targets to slip away, but the tradition-driven ninjas willingly sacrifice themselves. Davalos and Paula leave New Orleans for a fresh start.

While there's nothing wrong with jazzing up the action movie arena with a melange of cops and Rising Sun warriors, this violence-as-an-alternative-lifestyle flick could have dispensed with some of the nobility-of-slaughter nonsense. At times, the film seems like a crash course in Ninja Theory 101. *(Graphic violence, extreme profanity, extensive nudity, substance abuse, sexual situations.)* — R.P.

d, Maria Dante, Rod Hewitt; p, David Winters, Diane Daou; exec p, Tony Vincent; w, Rod Hewitt; ph, Chris Walling, Irv Goodnoff; ed, Adrian Carr, Jonathan Alvor; m, Don Peake; prod d, Dawn

Dedaux; art d, Quenby Tilley; sound, Jeffrey Wintcher (design), Chuck Bush; casting, Patricia Rose; cos, Morgan Clevenger; makeup, Amanda Poulsen-Wells

Action/Crime/Martial Arts **(PR: O MPAA: NR)**

DARK DEALER ★
(U.S.) 85m Aries Productions Inc.;
A2Z Productions ~ Aries c

Richard Hull, Jr. *(Ray)*; Kim Frazier *(Denise)*; Jeff English *(Cracker)*; Mark Fickert *(The Dealer)*; Rocky Patterson *(Pete)*; Vincent Gaskins *(Samson Burke)*; Gordon Fox *(Nickodemus)*; Kevin Walker *(Phillip Barton)*; Deborah Nunez *(Anne Taylor)*; Mark Liberato *(Kozinski)*; Charles Carroll *(Fred)*; Gene Mann *(Jack)*; John Colwell *(Harry)*; Aarron Carroll *(Dave)*; Carl Merrit *(Hotel Manager)*; Kasey Olsen Fallo *(Tanya)*; Martha Hatcher *(Donna)*; Jim Blumetti *(Bob Johnson)*

DARK DEALER is a stodgily executed, low-budget film shot entirely in Texas (and mostly indoors) and intended for video release. It features a trio of stories centered around a blackjack game, presumably taking place in purgatory, run by The Dealer (Mark Fickert). The players are three recently deceased men: Pete (Rocky Patterson); Samson Burke (Vincent Gaskins); and the newly arrived Ray (Richard Hull, Jr.), who's been chased into the "game room" in an empty office building by an airborne fireball. In "Cellar Space," hoodlums Pete and Fred (Charles Carroll) kill Jack (Gene Mann) over a gambling debt and hide from the cops in the basement apartment of nebbish scientist-alchemist Nikodemus (Gordon Fox), who, when hassled by the pair, transforms himself into a demon and slays them. In "Blues in the Night," successful entertainment lawyer and frustrated songwriter Phillip Barton (Kevin Walker) takes credit for recordings composed by an obscure, dead bluesman, Samson Burke, who takes possession of Phillip's body in revenge, leaving Phillip imprisoned in Samson's body at the Dealer's table while the singer enjoys his new life. The final (untitled) story has Ray attempting to pay girlfriend Denise's (Kim Frazier) drug debt to Cracker (Jeff English) by sneaking them into the pharmaceuticals laboratory where Ray's father works. Cracker takes an experimental drug and explodes, taking Denise with him, and turns into the fiery ball of the film's opening. Unlike Pete and Phillip/Burke, Ray wins his hand with the Dealer and finds himself once again being chased by the ball of fire, which he now destroys with a pail of water, freeing Denise. Cracker, however, enters the now empty game room for the Dealer's next round.

The omnibus film has a long history, from Griffith (INTOLERANCE) and Keaton (THE THREE AGES) to IF I HAD A MILLION, DEAD OF NIGHT, and LETTER TO THREE WIVES. For the last few decades, though, the format has been used mainly in horror fare, from AIP/Corman (TALES OF TERROR) in the 1960s and Amicus (TALES FROM THE CRYPT) in the 1970s to George Romero (CREEPSHOW) and others in the 1980s. Inferior to all of the above, DARK DEALER's episodes are like padded "Twilight Zone" episodes, but not original, scary or funny (as occasionally intended). The film's extremely low budget effectively limits anything beyond rudimentary special effects and camera technique, and the acting is ardent but mostly amateurish; only Rocky Patterson has previous experience in exploitation films (ARMED FOR ACTION, NAIL GUN MASSACRE). "Blues" is, by default, the best of the bunch, benefitting from a handful of Deltalike blues tunes by Ted D'Avi. *(Violence, nudity, sexual situations, substance abuse.)* — D.B.

d, Tom Alexander, Wynn Winberg; p, Wynn Winberg; exec p, Ted N. Winberg; w, Tom Alexander, Wynn Winberg; ph, Steve Dunning, Ian C. Wagner; ed, Jim Curtis; m, Ron DiIulio, John A.

Davis, Keith Alcorn, Ted D'Avi; art d, Jack Marty, Gretchen Goetz; set d, Tana Bishop; sound, Bonnie Bradford, Mark Negrete, Ron DiIulio (design); fx, Lawrence A. Aeschlimann; cos, Tanela Lednicky; makeup, Dovi Green, Marvella Spann, Wanda Thurston; stunts, Randy Fife, Wade Enloe, Chris Sykes

Horror (PR: O   MPAA: PG)

DARK SIDE OF GENIUS, THE ★★½
(U.S./Australia) 88m Pacific Shore Pictures ~
Paramount Home Video c

Finola Hughes *(Jennifer Cole)*; Brent Fraser *(Julian Jons)*; Seymour Cassel *(Samuel Rourke)*; Glenn Shadix *(Leon Bennini)*; Tina Cote *(Anna/Kristie)*; Moon Zappa *(Carrie)*; Patrick Bauchau *(Sherman McPhee)*; Gina Mari *(Naomi)*; John Barnard *(Patrick Richwood)*; D.J. Harder *(Pascal)*

This lurid US-Australian production, which premiered in the States on home video, manages to hoist itself out of the erotic thriller ghetto, but doesn't venture quite far enough therefrom.

Years ago unstable Soho artist Julian Jons strangled a model, completing the canvas with her blood. After a hiatus in the asylum, Jons (Brent Fraser) resurfaces in LA as a shadowy figure working on a gallery exhibition. Hard-driving art critic Jennifer Cole (Finola Hughes) tracks down the reclusive Jons and becomes his lover in spite of the guy's lethal past and wobbly sanity. When wealthy new patron Samuel Rourke (Seymour Cassel) commissions a portrait of Kristie—a lookalike for Julian's long-ago victim (both roles played by newcomer Tina Cote)—facing the girl each day triggers flashbacks in which the tormented Jons relives the murder he committed—or did he? Jennifer determines that this nutcase is actually a guilt-ridden colleague of the deceased Julian Jons. He compulsively assumed the real madman's identity and brush technique, and, in order to seal the value of the Jons forgeries, Rourke is scheming to kill both the imposter and Jennifer in a mock mental relapse. But like most bad guys in B movies, he's so busy chortling over his own cleverness that he drops the gun and gets shot down himself.

Fraser is more moody than scary, and a frilly nightgown he wears while working hardly enhances his supposed aura of menace. Hughes takes a more rewarding risk with her character, coming across as unsympathetic and more than a little perverse, getting a sexual turn-on through her proximity to a legendary psycho.

Misogynistic themes are apparent in the works of, inter alia, de Kooning, Picasso, and Dali, and THE DARK SIDE OF GENIUS hints at this issue, but ultimately sticks to familiar suspense-thriller territory. Mercifully, director-cinematographer Papamichael keeps gore stylized or offscreen. Frank Zappa's daughter Moon registers well in the thankless part of Jennifer's tart-tongued best pal. The Edvard Munch-style Julian Jons paintings were actually executed by William J. Quigley. *(Violence, nudity, sexual situations, adult situations, substance abuse, profanity.)* — C.C.

d, Phedon Papamichael; p, Ray Haboush; exec p, Richard Sheng, Lucus E. Devenn; w, Fredrick J. Stroppel; ph, Phedon Papamicheal; ed, Britton J. Petrucelli; m, Tom Hiel; prod d, Jon Gary Steele; set d, Nancy Arnold; sound, Leonard Marcel; casting, Cathy Henderson, Tom McSweeney; cos, Julie Rae Engelsman

Thriller (PR: O   MPAA: R)

DARKMAN 2: THE RETURN OF DURANT ★★
(U.S./Canada) 93m Renaissance Pictures; Universal Productions Canada ~ MCA/Universal Home Video c
(AKA: DARKMAN II: THE RETURN OF DURANT)

Arnold Vosloo *(Dr. Peyton Westlake/Darkman)*; Larry Drake *(Robert G. Durant)*; Kim Delaney *(Jill Randall)*; Renee O'Connor *(Laurie Brinkman)*; Lawrence Dane *(Dr. Hathaway)*; Jesse Collins *(Dr. David Brinkman)*; Rod Wilson *(Ivan Druganov)*; Jack Langedijk *(Rollo Latham)*; James Millington *(Perkins)*; David Ferry *(Eddie)*; Sten Eirik; Phillip Jarrett; Graham Rowatt; Adam Bramble

This direct-to-video sequel to 1990's DARKMAN, like its eponymous character, doesn't stand strong scrutiny in the light.

Essentially an action-hero reinvention of those scarred monsters typically played by Vincent Price (and Lon Chaney before him) in B movies, Darkman is Dr. Peyton Westlake, noble biochemist horrifically burned by gangsters and left for dead. However, lurking in a secret subterranean lab (serviced by his own private subway!), Darkman survives, venturing into public view for brief periods thanks to synthetic skin that lasts 99 minutes in UV light, to fight for . . . what? The original Sam Raimi production, in between stunts, hinted that Darkman's heroic deeds were basically the mindless vengeance of a mutilated madman. Resemblance to BATMAN was more than coincidental, from the booming Danny Elfman theme music right down to the inescapable comic-book level of the material.

DARKMAN 2, with nothing to add but that subway, just reruns the formula. Earlier played by a pre-SCHINDLER'S LIST Liam Neeson, Darkman is now essayed by Arnold Vosloo (HARD TARGET). Westlake meets another noble biochemist working on artificial skin implants and, on the verge of a breakthrough that will permanently restore his face, sees his new pal tortured and murdered—just as in the first movie. It turns out that sadistic crime lord Robert G. Durant (Larry Drake), a workaday secondary villain in DARKMAN, survived that picture's helicopter crash and now intends to prosper as a manufacturer of high-tech ray guns. But his desired factory location happens to be the property of a certain noble biochemist and, latterly, the noble biochemist's bereaved sister Laurie (Renee O'Connor).

Durant cajoles Laurie to sell him the real estate. Using his false flesh to impersonate assorted Durant henchmen, Darkman torments his erstwhile foe in some fun but increasingly familiar situations, until Durant kidnaps Laurie to force a showdown. Ultimately, Durant is locked in an armored car that blows up—but then again, so did the helicopter. That DARKMAN 3 had already been announced by Universal Pictures did not bode well for any noble biochemists still left around.

In fact, DARKMAN 2's milestone was Universal's boast that it was their first live-action feature done expressly for the direct-to-video market (not counting a handful of Canadian kung-fu pics and unreleasable bilge like MONOLITH). The original DARKMAN grossed $30 million domestically, cueing a small-screen follow-up done for a fraction of its forebear's $18 million budget. DARKMAN 2 was thus lensed on the cheap in Toronto under the guidance of TV director Bradford May, who does the job competently but without the hyperbolic style of Raimi. Lacking the latter's sustained visual dazzle—here supplied mainly in flashbacks—Darkman, well, pales. South African actor Vosloo (Neeson's Celtic accent was never explained either) plods acceptably through the part, as do the rest of the cast. In any case, thespian talent was never vital to this franchise, and thanks to the skull-like makeup, just about anyone can do the Darkman. That still doesn't excuse the pointless waste of Kim Delaney as a TV reporter who discovers the secret of Darkman (no great feat; Westlake visits his post office box regularly with no disguise over his hideous visage) and gets conveniently killed soon there-after. *(Violence, profanity.)* — C.C.

d, Bradford May; p, David Roessell; exec p, Sam Raimi, Robert Tapert; assoc p, Bernadette Joyce; w, Steve McKay, Chuck Pfarrer (from a story by Robert Eisele and Lawrence Hertzog, based on characters created by Sam Raimi); ph, Bradford May; ed, Daniel Cahn; m, Randy Miller, Danny Elfman; art d, Ian Brock; cos, Noreen Landry; makeup, Robert Kurtzman, Gregory Nicotero, Howard Berger, K.N.B. EFX Group; stunts, Steve Lucescu

Action/Horror (PR: C MPAA: R)

DARKNESS IN TALLINN
(SEE: CITY UNPLUGGED)

DAY THE SUN TURNED COLD, THE ★★★½
(Hong Kong) 99m Pineeast Pictures Ltd. ~
Kino International c
(TIANGUO NIEZI)

Tao Chung-Hua *(The Son)*; Siqin Gaowa *(The Mother)*; Ma Jingwu *(The Father)*; Wei Zhi *(The Lover)*; Shu Zhong *(The Son as a child)*; Li Hu *(The Captain)*

THE DAY THE SUN TURNED COLD is a gripping account of murder and culpability. In 1990, Guan Jin (Tuo Chung-Hua), a young Chinese worker, accuses his own mother of the murder of his father ten years earlier. In flashback, he recounts the grim tale of the unhappy marriage of his parents.

His mother (Siqin Gaowa) is a simple, uneducated woman who ekes out a living selling bean curd in the village market, while his father (Ma Jingwu) is the stern headmaster of the local school. "We're like two grindstones, grinding each other to smoothness with our anger," he tells his wife in an apt description of their home life. She had actually tried to run away in the first year of marriage but, as few things in China are as shameful as divorce, was soon returned to him by her relatives. As a boy, Guan Jin (Shu Zhong) is the frequent recipient of paternal beatings for playing hooky and lying. One day, he and his mother get caught in a snowstorm and are rescued by a woodsman (Wei Zhi), who before long becomes the mother's lover. The village gossips take due notice of the affair. When the father accuses her, she resolutely refuses to answer him. A predictable beating ensues. Shortly thereafter, the father falls horribly ill from a meal she serves him, and dies. His mother's suspicious behavior during this time plants the seed of doubt in little Guan Jin, which is only exacerbated by her hasty marriage to the woodsman.

A decade later, Guan Jin returns to the village with a detective to get to the bottom of things. His father's corpse is exhumed and investigated for evidence of poisoning. His mother remains noncommittal, even in the face of her obvious guilt, and as judgment day dawns for her, Guan Jin's feelings towards her reach a crisis of conflict.

Director-writer Yim has produced a cracking good yarn through the means of deliberate understatement. The mother is far from any Gong Li-like temptress; the father is merely a humorless petty tyrant. The few moments of fun are mostly provided by the children, Guan Jin and his younger brother and sister, with their simple playtime and effusive gratefulness for a delicious, special hot meal courtesy of the woodcutter. Yim Ho shrewdly times his occasional directorial flourishes for maximum effect. There is a sleigh ride, which Guan Jin later remembers as the happiest day of his life, when he had been given his new shoes, shared the treat of an orange with his mother, and played a harmless practical joke on the woodsman. Later, as his mother rides off with her new husband, her forgotten children

confront her at a mountain pass and the scene ends heartrendingly with Guan Jin dragging his wailing, siblings away.

Characters in this film do not act in prescribed or predictable ways: the woodsman is at first welcoming of his stepchildren; a few scenes later, he resents his wife's attempt to bring them food. Likewise, the mother seems at different points devoted and then dismissive of her progeny. She, her lover, and her grown son all share full-featured, sensuous faces that seldom reveal their true feelings. What is captured fully is the often bewildering perversity of familial relationships.

Although it would have benefited from more information about the adult Guan Jin and the psychological effect the family drama has upon him, the film is a moving experience, superlatively photographed by Hou Young and with an affecting, if somewhat repetitive, musical score. *(Adult situations, violence, sexual situations.)* — D.N.

d, Yim Ho; p, Ann Hui, Yim Ho; w, Yim Ho, Wong Hing-Dong; ph, Hou Young; ed, Chao Ying-Wu, Wong Yi-Sun; m, Yoshihide Ototmo; art d, Jessinta Lin; cos, Ann Hui

Drama (PR: A MPAA: NR)

DAY TO REMEMBER, A
(SEE: TWO BITS)

DEAD FUNNY ★
(U.S./U.K.) 91m Avondale Pictures; Film
Four International ~ Cinepix c

Elizabeth Pena *(Vivian Saunders)*; Andrew McCarthy *(Reggie Barker)*; Paige Turco *(Louise)*; Blanche Baker *(Barbara)*; Allison Janney *(Jennifer)*; Adelle Lutz *(Mari)*; Lisa Jane Persky *(Sarah)*; Michael Mantell *(Harold)*; Novela Nelson *(Frances)*; Kristen Wilson *(Cards)*; Lianna Pai *(Knives)*; Jorjan Fox *(Threads)*; Tanya Berezin *(Mrs. Hause)*; Ken Kensei *(Yoshi)*; Patty Scanlon *(Carmen)*; Bal Ling *(Norriko)*; Carol Schneider *(Clare)*; Edward Seamon *(Viv's Father)*; Michel Mastrototaro *(Man With Carriage)*; Samuel Baird *(Know-It-All Man)*

DEAD FUNNY is more dead than funny: a mirthless comedy about a practical joker who does not die laughing, it is black comedy disguised as a whodunit wrapped in intricate flashbacks that cloud a simple solution to the crime.

When hungover Vivian (Elizabeth Pena) discovers her secretive boyfriend Reggie (Andrew McCarthy) skewered to her kitchen table with a valuable samurai sword, she racks her fogged brain to recall what happened. She relives their volatile relationship in flashbacks, remembering painful and happy times they shared and the constant teasing between them.

The attempt to piece together the puzzle of her lover's final hours gets complicated by the intrusion of her feminist support group, whose members fuss over her, and by Vivian's suspicions about her married pal Harold (Michael Mantell) as a possible jealous suspect. As her memory revives, she remembers an irate girl busting up their party the night before with the declaration that she too was Reggie's girlfriend. When the girl (Patty Scanlon) drops by to inquire whether Vivian enjoyed Reggie's practical joke about two-timing her, the news doesn't tickle Vivian's funny bone. Coming out of shock at last, Vivian realizes that she accidentally killed Reggie during an argument about his cheating. Reggie's last practical joke was a real killer.

It is an accomplishment to wring not an ounce of merriment from a scenario about a bozo loverboy knocked out by his own punchline, but the meandering DEAD FUNNY manages it. The viewers are made to take a painstaking journey through Vivian's memory, all the time feeling trapped inside a singularly dull brain. Shedding no light on the couple's bond, the movie flashes back and forth, lingering on Reggie and Vivian's practical jokes, as if their immature tricks were amusing enough to sustain the zigzagging present-past structure the film employs.

Beyond the sheer irritation of postponing Vivian's guilt as a trumped-up suspense-manufacturer, DEAD FUNNY is weighted down with numbing repetitiveness, feeble parodying (like the take-off on the support group which seems to have been edited from a Henry Jaglom film), and a barrenness of repartee. Only the vivid color photography and the unflappable Pena make DEAD FUNNY bearable. *(Violence, extreme profanity, substance abuse, sexual situations.)* — R.P.

d, John Feldman; p, Richard Abramowitz, David Hannay; exec p, Robert Maruc, David Marlow, James M. Gold, Paul L. Newman; assoc p, Jean Russo Gould; co-p, Adam Brightman, Robert Marcus; w, John Feldman, Cindy Oswin; ph, Todd Crockett; ed, Einar Westerlund; m, Sheila Silver; prod d, Michael Shaw; art d, Daniel Goldfield; set d, Kara Cressman; sound, Melanie Johnson (mixer); fx, Timothy Considine; casting, Susan Shopmaker; cos, Sara Slotnick; makeup, Barri Scinto; stunts, Janet Paparazzo

Comedy/Mystery   **(PR: O   MPAA: R)**

DEAD MAN WALKING   ★★★
(U.S.) 120m Working Title Films; Havoc Productions; Polygram ~ Gramercy c

Susan Sarandon *(Sister Helen Prejean)*; Sean Penn *(Matthew Poncelet)*; Robert Prosky *(Hilton Barber)*; Raymond J. Barry *(Earl Delacroix)*; R. Lee Ermey *(Clyde Percy)*; Celia Weston *(Mary Beth Percy)*; Lois Smith *(Helen's Mother)*; Scott Wilson *(Chaplain Farley)*; Roberta Maxwell *(Lucille Poncelet)*; Margo Martindale *(Sister Colleen)*; Barton Heyman *(Captain Beliveau)*; Steve Boles *(Sgt. Neal Trapp)*; Nesbitt Blaisdell *(Warden Hartman)*; Ray Aranha *(Luis Montoya)*; Larry Pine *(Guy Gilardi)*; Gil Robbins *(Bishop Norwich)*; Kevin Cooney *(Governor Benedict)*; Clancy Brown *(State Trooper)*; Adele Robbins *(Nurse)*; Michael Cullen *(Carl Vitello)*; Peter Sarsgaard *(Walter Delacroix)*; Missy Yager *(Hope Percy)*; Jenny Krochmal *(Emily Percy)*; Jack Black *(Craig Poncelet)*; Jon Abrahams *(Sonny Poncelet)*; Arthur Bridgers *(Troy Poncelet)*; Steve Carlisle *(Helen's Brother)*; Helen Hester *(Helen's Sister)*; Eva Amurri *(Nine-year-old Helen)*; Jack Henry Robbins *(Opossum Kid #1)*; Gary "Buddy" Boe *(Opossum Kid #2)*; Amy Long *(Opossum Kid #3)*; Dennis F. Neal *(Henry)*; Molly Bryant *(Nellie)*; Pamela Garmon *(Mirabeau)*; Adrian Colon *(Reporter)*; John D. Wilmot *(Supporter)*; Margaret Lane *(Reporter #1)*; Sally Ann Roberts *(Reporter #2)*; Alec Gifford *(Reporter #3)*; John Hurlbutt *(Reporter #4)*; Mike Longman *(News Anchor)*; Pete Burris *(Parent #1)*; Joan Glover *(Parent #2)*; Florrie Hathorn *(Parent #3)*; Lenore Banks *(Parent #4)*; Idella Cassamier *(Idella)*; Marlon Horton *(Herbie)*; Kenitra Singleton *(Kenitra)*; Palmer Jackson *(Palmer)*; Johnathan Thomas *(Johnathan)*; Walter Breaux, Jr. *(Guard #1)*; Scott Sowers *(Guard #2)*; Cortez Nance, Jr. *(Guard #3)*; Adam Nelson *(Guard #4)*; Dalvin Ford *(Guard #5)*; Derek Steeley *(Guard #6)*; Jeremy Knaster *(Guard #7)*; Mary Robbins *(Aide to Governor Benedict)*; Miles Guthrie Robbins *(Boy in Church)*; Donald R. Smith and the Golden Voices Gospel Choir of St. Francis De Sales Catholic Church

DEAD MAN WALKING is an extraordinarily well-made message movie that punks out at the eleventh hour. Tim Robbins's film about the death penalty wants to be perceived as painstakingly balanced and fair to both sides; ultimately, however, it's just unresolved.

Sister Helen (Susan Sarandon), a nun who's abandoned her privileged background to live and work with the poor of New Orleans, is asked to write to a man on death row. Her pen pal, Matthew Poncelet (Sean Penn), asks her to help him file an appeal of his sentence. Though he was convicted of taking part in the rape and murder of a young couple—his partner in crime received a life sentence, apparently for no better reason than that he had a sharper lawyer—Poncelet says he's innocent.

Sister Helen is drawn into Poncelet's cause, step by fateful step. She writes to him because she believes nobody should be as utterly alone as he seems, and helps him file an appeal because no one else will. In addition, he points out that there are no rich men on death row, a populist sentiment that speaks to her own experiences. She stands by him because he's universally reviled, and she can't believe anyone is wholly bad. Through Poncelet, Sister Helen meets the victim's families, torn apart by grief and anger. She gradually becomes involved with them as well. The girl's family rejects her when they realize she won't take their side and call for Poncelet's death, while the boy's family—specifically his father (Raymond J. Barry)—listens to her message of forgiveness without being entirely convinced.

Poncelet's appeal fails, and his execution date is set. As the days slip away, Sister Helen becomes his spiritual adviser, getting to know his mother and brothers and persuading him to tell her more and more about the crimes and his involvement. Poncelet is not, after all, an innocent man, and Sister Helen takes on her final mission: to get Poncelet to admit to his guilt and regret his actions before he dies. She succeeds, and his execution is a deeply emotional moment for the Poncelet family, the families of the victims and Sister Helen herself.

Based closely on the memoirs of Sister Helen Prejean, a New Orleans nun whose ministry took her to the heart of Death Row, DEAD MAN WALKING avoids most of the histrionics that mar movies about issues, even as it adopts the mainstream conventional strategy of embodying the issues in individuals. DEAD MAN WALKING was released by Gramercy, a small distributor, and financed independently. Though it has the gloss of a Hollywood film—courtesy of stars Sarandon and Penn, director Robbins and a top-flight technical crew—it's a far more complex and courageous film than one can imagine being green-lighted by any major studio in the '90s.

Much has been made of the fact that supporters of the death penalty come out of DEAD MAN WALKING angry because it seems to reject state-sanctioned execution, while opponents of the death penalty dislike it because it seems to come down in favor of capital punishment. It's been taken as evidence of the film's even-handed treatment of the issue, but in fact it's proof that DEAD MAN WALKING doesn't treat the issue at all. It's a message movie without a message. The topical movies of Abby Mann or Stanley Kramer have often been assailed as simplistic or crudely moralistic, but at least they had the courage of their makers' convictions.

This ideologically muddled construction rests on a pair of phenomenal performances. Sarandon's Sister Helen is so relentlessly decent, tolerant, and committed to good works that even her flaws are virtues in disguise. Her confusion is born of the attempt to understand things that are entirely alien, and her righteousness of the desire to stand up for everyone's rights, not just those of the people she likes. Her blundering is a function of her sincerity and guilelessness, and her holier-than-thou air the reflection of real piety, a quality so rare that it's bound to seem false. In the hands of a lesser actress, Sister Helen would be absolutely intolerable, but Sarandon gives her a simple decency and conviction. She deservedly won an Oscar for the role.

Penn's Matthew Poncelet is a riveting study in Mephistophelian facial hair and white-trash attitude. Aloof and prickly, Penn eschews the villain-with-a-heart-of-gold stereotype in favor of something far tougher: Poncelet is a genuinely bad guy, but a very individuated bad guy. Hateful though Poncelet may be, his is a distinctly human face. *(Violence, profanity, adult situations.)* — M.M.

d, Tim Robbins; p, Jon Kilik, Tim Robbins, Rudd Simmons; exec p, Tim Bevan, Eric Fellner; assoc p, Allan Nicholls; w, Tim Robbins (based on the book by Sister Helen Prejean, C.S.J.); ph, Roger A. Deakins; ed, Lisa Zeno Churgin; m, David Robbins; prod d, Richard Hoover; art d, Tom Warren; sound, Tod A. Maitland (mixer), Joel Holland (recordist); casting, Douglas Aibel; cos, Renee Ehrlich Kalfus; makeup, Michal Bigger

Drama (PR: C MPAA: R)

DEAD PRESIDENTS ★★½
(U.S.) 119m Dead Presidents Inc.;
Underworld Entertainment; Hollywood Pictures;
Caravan Pictures ~ Buena Vista c

Larenz Tate *(Anthony Curtis)*; Keith David *(Kirby)*; Chris Tucker *(Skip)*; Freddy Rodriguez *(Jose)*; Rose Jackson *(Juanita Benson)*; N'Bushe Wright *(Delilah Benson)*; Alvaletah Guess *(Mrs. Benson)*; James Pickens, Jr. *(Mr. Curtis)*; Jenifer Lewis *(Mrs. Curtis)*; Clifton Powell *(Cutty)*; Elizabeth Rodriguez *(Marisol)*; Terrence Howard *(Cowboy)*; Ryan Williams *(Young Revolutionary)*; Larry McCoy *(Nicky)*; Rodney Winfield *(Mr. Warren)*; Cheryl Freeman *(Mrs. Barton)*; Sticky Fingaz *(Martin)*; Bokeem Woodbine *(Cleon)*; David Barry Gray *(Devaughn)*; Michael Imperioli *(D'Ambrosio)*; Jaimz Woolvett *(Lt. Dugan)*; Quynh Phann *(Skivvie Girl #1)*; Clifton Gonzalez Gonzalez *(Betancourt)*; Jean Claude La Marre *(Ramsuer)*; Daniel Kruse *(Corporal Rob)*; Robert Smith *(Helicopter Pilot)*; Bernard Telsey *(Protester #1)*; Rik Colitti *(Cabbie)*; Heather B. *(Peaches)*; Carlton Wilborn *(Spyder)*; Frank Albanese *(Mr. Gianetti)*; Monti Sharp *(Officer Brown)*; Tony Sirico *(Officer Spinelli)*; Robert Lupone *(Attorney Salvatore Rizzo)*; Joelle Hernandez; Jordan Hernandez *(Sarah—Juanita's Child)*; Tim Zay *(Protester #2)*; Charles E. Lesene *(Numbers Taker)*; Cuc Dinh *(Madame Minh)*; Yen Chin Grow *(Skivvie Girl #2)*

Though it contains some powerful moments, DEAD PRESIDENTS is a disappointing follow-up to the Hughes brothers' debut film, MENACE II SOCIETY. The film addresses a neglected aspect of an important film genre—the African-American veteran's experience of the Vietnam War—but shifts focus in its final act to a far less interesting armored-car heist.

Anthony Curtis (Larenz Tate) graduates from a Bronx high school in 1968, a bright young man determined to make his mark in the world. His upstanding family has started him off on firm moral ground, but Anthony also knows the mean streets of the city. He has a job delivering milk, but also runs numbers for avuncular neighborhood tough guy Kirby (Keith David), and hustles pool. Against his parent's advice, Anthony decides to enlist in the Marines rather than attend college. After a tender but awkward first sexual encounter with his girlfriend, Juanita (Rose Jackson), Anthony ships off to the maelstrom of ground combat in Vietnam.

During his two tours of duty with a reconnaissance outfit, he and his Bronx buddies, Skip (Chris Tucker) and Jose (Freddy Rodriguez), see the worst of the war's bloody fighting and gruesome atrocities. In 1973, he comes home to the Vietnam syndrome: decorated by his country for his heroic service, shunned by society for helping fight an unpopular war. For the black veteran, the conflict is intensified by the Black Power movement's opposition to the "white man's war" and economic deterioration in the black community. Caught in the bitter crossfire, Anthony becomes increasingly frustrated and desperate. He can't support Juanita and their daughter, and risks losing them to

Cutty (Clifton Powell), a neighborhood pimp. The only work he finds is as a part-time butcher. Spurred on by Juanita's militant sister Deliah (N'Bushe Wright), Anthony takes desperate action.

With Kirby, Deliah, Jose, Skip and, surprisingly, his straight-and-narrow brother Cleon (Bokeem Woodbine), Anthony plans the robbery of an armored car carrying thousands of "dead presidents" (money the US treasury is preparing to take out of circulation). The crime goes bloodily awry, ending with a 'Nam-like gun battle. Anthony is caught, tried and sent to prison.

At age 24, filmmaking twins Albert and Allen Hughes set out to make a movie about the turbulent period that coincided with their birth. The results are mixed. DEAD PRESIDENTS has some of the strengths of MENACE II SOCIETY: Deft ensemble acting, a sympathetic understanding of daily life on the margins of economic survival, and a thoughtfully motivated use of hyper-violent action. But this time around the Hugheses have taken on more than one movie can reasonably handle. Both MENACE and DEAD PRESIDENTS are anti-heroic tragedies about young black men turned into criminals by overwhelming social forces. But DEAD PRESIDENTS aims to examine the larger social forces—politics, war, race, coming-of-age, history, sex, family, urban decay—as well as the angry young men, and the Hugheses lose their focus early on. The thematic weight overwhelms the narrative, and when the film becomes preoccupied with the anticlimactic robbery, DEAD PRESIDENTS dies in its tracks.

Despite the film's ultimate let-down, there is still much to commend it. Though the disturbing scenes of gory battlefield killing are nothing new for the Vietnam genre, they pack a visceral punch and go a long way to explaining the depth of Anthony's alienation from peacetime society. Larenz Tate's performance is the standout in a fine ensemble. He transforms himself completely from the eerily psychotic trigger man O-Dog of MENACE II SOCIETY into the sympathetic Anthony.

The Hugheses make good use of songs by Sly and the Family Stone, Curtis Mayfield, Al Green, and Marvin Gaye to establish period atmosphere and comment on the action. Though not generally thought of as topical, these soul hits tap into the urban grit, cultural mood, and social change of the early '70s, when race, war, politics, crime, and the feelings they engendered were indeed bound up together. *(Graphic violence, profanity, adult situations, sexual situations.)* — D.S.

d, Allen Hughes, Albert Hughes; p, Allen Hughes, Albert Hughes; exec p, Darryl Porter; co-p, Michael Bennett; w, Michael Henry Brown (from a story by Allen Hughes, Albert Hughes, and Michael Henry Brown); ph, Lisa Rinzler; ed, Dan Lebental; m, Danny Elfman; prod d, David Brisbin; art d, Kenneth A. Hardy; set d, Karin Wiesel; sound, Frank Stettner (mixer); fx, Steve Kirshoff, Jon Farhat, R/Greenberg Associates West, Inc.; casting, Risa Bramon Garcia, Mary Vernieu; cos, Paul A. Simmons; makeup, Ellie Winslow, Lance Anderson; stunts, Jeff Ward

Drama/Crime/War (PR: O MPAA: R)

DEAD TIRED
(SEE: GROSSE FATIGUE)

DEADLY MARIA ★★½
(Germany) 107m Liebesfilm Produktion ~
Jane Balfour Films c
(DIE TODLICHE MARIA)

Nina Petri *(Maria Jakobs)*; Josef Bierbichler *(Dieter Pohlmann)*; Peter Franke *(Heinz)*; Joachim Krol *(Mr. Jakobs)*; Katya Studt *(Maria—Age 16)*; Juliane Heinemann; Jean L Maeser ; Rolf Peter Kahl; Renate Usko; Georg Winterfeld; Tom Spiess; Andreas Petri; Nada Daniels; Ortwin Spieler; Peter Hommen; Wal-friede Schmitt; Astrid Vonhoff; Heidi Klotz; Andre Von Champorcin; Peter Lichtefeld

It's accurate to call DEADLY MARIA too good of a bad thing. A cheaper, grittier (perhaps black-and-white) look would have better suited this darkly intimate Teutonic psychodrama, graced with elaborate visuals and production values suitable for a movie of much larger scope.

Maria (Nina Petri) dwells in joyless marital servitude to much older Heinz (Peter Franke). Their family unit is completed by her father Jakobs (Joachim Krol), a demanding, incontinent invalid. Flashbacks gradually fill in Maria's miserable history: after her mother's death, Maria was raised by Herr Jakobs in a virtual prison environment, with overtones of incest. When Jakobs one day glimpsed his teenaged daughter kissed by a boy, he suffered his crippling stroke. Subsequently, he arranged the union between Maria and Heinz, a drinking buddy with a similiar custo-dial attitude toward women. Maria's most treasured memories are those of a brief school acquaintance with an exchange student; now she secretly hides her getaway money in an Oriental figurine, a parting gift from that long-lost friend.

Then another man enters Maria's small orbit. Dieter (Josef Bierbichler) rents the flat overlooked by Maria's window, and there, surrounded by stacks of old newspapers, he compiles dry reference books. Monkish as he is, Dieter is still the most pleasant and exciting man in Maria's life. But while she's visiting him, Heinz locates and confiscates her cache of cash. This crushing defeat finally ignites rebellion, and Maria fatally impales Heinz with the rapier-thin figurine and lets her father perish from neglect. She then tries a suicidal plunge out the window but unintentionally lands right on top of Dieter. In the final shot the wounded couple reach out to each other.

"Don't you pretend to be harmless!" scolds Jakobs at the mousy, retiring daughter who brings disaster to all the men she meets. It's as difficult to be unmoved by this domestic horror story as it is impossible to enjoy it, with point-blank performances by the cast and a potent arsenal of camera tricks from 29-year-old first-time filmmaker Tom Tykwer, who uses jagged screen wipes to accompany the tearing open of a letter, a color-coded narrative chronology (cold tones for flashbacks, warm hues for the present), and enough morbid juxtapositions and angles to suggest an ancestral link with Polanski's REPULSION. Lead actress Petri's agonized screen presence holds true (even during a misconceived metaphorical scene in which the childless heroine suddenly swells and messily gives birth to herself). DEADLY MARIA is seldom subtle and demonstrably overdone, but it makes its points about patriarchal oppression with polish and visual finesse. (Violence, adult situations, sexual situations.) — C.C.

d, Tom Tykwer; p, Stefan Arndt, Tom Tykwer; w, Tom Tykwer; ph, Frank Griebe; ed, Katja Dringenberg; m, Klaus Garternicht, Tom Tykwer; prod d, Sybille Kelber, Attila Saygel; cos, Monica Jacobs

Drama   **(PR: O   MPAA: NR)**

DEATH IN BRUNSWICK   ★★
(Australia) 106m Meridian Films; Film Victoria; Australian Film Finance Corp. ~ Columbia Tristar Home Video c
(AKA: NOTHING TO LOSE)

Sam Neill (Carl Fitzgerald); Zoe Carides (Sophie Papafagos); John Clarke (Dave); Yvonne Lawley (Mrs. Fitzgerald); Nico Lathouris (Mustafa); Nicholas Papademetriou (Yanni Voulgaris); Deborah Kennedy (June); Boris Berkic (Laurie); Doris Younane (Carmel); Denis Moore (Catholic Priest); Kris Karahisarus

(Aris); Huriye Balkaya (Mustafa's Wife); Orhan Akkus (Aslan); Daniel Kadamani (Cousin Con); Sakis Dragonas (Mr. Papafagos); Senol Mat (Turk); Haydar Akar (Turk); Ekrem Kuloglu (Turk); Lachlan Jeffrey (Delinquent); Maria Beck (Maria); Marz Lupiere (Despina); Stephen Hutchison (Tony); David Hoflin (Dave's Boy); Glen Torrens (Dave's Boy); Anthony DeFazio (Junkie); Daniel Pollock (Junkie); Bradley Pilato (Child in Cinema); Orion Erickson (Child in Cinema); Jordan Mills (Child in Cinema); Benjamin Menzies (Dave's Baby); Dino Nicolosi (Man in Church); Con Babnoitis (Taxi Driver); George Prataris (Taxi Driver); Christos Linou (Man in Alley); Ali Ammouchi (Island Cooler Youth); Knight (Band in Club); Vortex (Band in Club)

This self-anointed black comedy never establishes or adheres to any playable comic tone. Eddying everyday catastrophes fill out a screenplay notable for its ingrained despair, about a short-order cook scrambling to stay alive in an environment where human beings get tossed out with the garbage.

Contending with a kvetching invalid mother (Yvonne Lawley), Carl Fitzgerald (Sam Neill) ekes out a meager existence as cook in a dive of a dance club while pickling his inferiority complex in alcohol. In his new post as master of a roach-filled kitchen, Carl looks the other way when his helper Mustafa (Nico Lathouris) deals drugs on the sly. Carl quickly falls for a sympathetic barmaid Sophie (Zoe Carides) whom he begins dating. Although their May-December romance blossoms, Carl never behaves responsibly enough to fully win her over. When evil club enforcer Laurie (Boris Brkic) leads Mustafa to believe that Carl has informed on him, the chef kills the furious pusher in self-defense, disposing of the body in someone else's coffin at the cemetery. Mustafa's irate relatives threaten Carl, but he in turn implicates Laurie, who is summarily slain. Reconciling, Carl weds Sophie with the grudging approval of her strict, security-conscious family.

Despite an ingratiating turn by the enchanting Carides and complex thesping by Neill as the weak-willed murderer, DEATH IN BRUNSWICK is a trawling of the lower depths with a splintered identity. Although the monotony of the chef's tormented universe is naturalistically conveyed, his persecutors are cartoonish, unrealistic clay targets for spleen. One can't accuse the film of veering in tone because this (literal) kitchen-sink opus never finds a tone to begin with. Alternately, it's a love story, drunkard drama, crime thriller, cemetery caper, and mother-love satire without once signaling its audience how they should respond to the protagonist's stake in his collapsing world. Although Neill expressively fills in Carl's nooks and crannies the movie never capitalizes on that expert characterization or how he came to hit bottom. As a result, DEATH IN BRUNSWICK is one long, dismally dysfunctional mantra uttered from Carl's gutless soul; one can only surmise that the original novel found a narrative way to bring Carl's crises to a bitterly funny boil.

In the last reel, the script throws caution to the wind and plays an overblown wedding climax with ZORBA THE GREEK merriment because Carl still registers as a vacillating child-man. A film this bleak cannot shift gears without preparing us, either with clear growth in the hero's psychology or hints that earlier decrepitude, homicide, and grave desecration are meant to be taken lightly. DEATH IN BRUNSWICK never earns our leap of faith. This is no black comedy; it's a study in stasis that tries to bluff its way to a slaphappy conclusion. (Violence, extreme profanity, substance abuse, sexual situations, adult situations.) — R.P.

d, John Ruane; p, Timothy White; exec p, Bryce Menzies; assoc p, Lynda House; w, John Ruane, Boyd Oxlade (based on the novel by Boyd Oxlade); ph, Ellery Ryan; ed, Neil Thumpston; m, Philip Judd; prod d, Chris Kennedy; sound, Roger Savage (mixer), Lloyd Carrick; fx, Peter Stubbs; casting, Greg Apps, Liz Mullinar; cos, Vicki Friedman; makeup, Noriko Watanabe; stunts, Glenn Ruehland

Comedy/Drama (PR: C MPAA: R)

DEATH MACHINE ★★★
(U.K.) 99m Fugitive Features ~ Vidmark Entertainment c

Brad Dourif *(Jack Dante)*; Ely Pouget *(Hayden Cale)*; William Hootkins *(John Carpenter)*; John Sharian *(Sam Raimi)*; Martin MacDougall *(Yutani)*; Andreas Wisniewski *(Weyland)*; Richard Brake *(Scott Ridley)*; Alex Brooks *(Sheriff Dickson)*; Stuart St. Paul *(Glitching Hardman)*; Paul Randall *(Duty Sergeant Bateman)*; Jackie Sawiris *(Waitress)*; Colleen Passard *(Anchor Man/Woman)*; Anne Marie Zola *(Demonstrator Outside Chaank Facility)*; William Marsh *(System Analyst)*; Rachel Weisz *(A.N. Other Personnel Manager)*; Robert Jezek *(A.N. Other Media Controller)*; Dominic Hawksley *(A.N. Other Sycophant)*; Nicola Van Damme *(A.N. Other Cale's PA)*

This British production may be derivative, but like its villain, it recycles spare parts into something swift and effective.

In the near future, the Chaank Corporation faces public protest because of its weapons program, which includes the "Hardman" suit, designed to transform its wearer into a fearless warrior but plagued by technical malfunctions. New executive Hayden Cale (Ely Pouget) advocates public disclosure and the ousting of psychopathic designer Jack Dante (Brad Dourif), which makes her unpopular with others in the company. But Dante has been tinkering with his own creation, a monstrous, robotic "frontline morale destroyer" called the Warbeast, and one night after hours he sics it on Cale and the other execs in the Chaank building. At the same time, a small group of protesters has broken in to take them hostage, but all are soon fleeing the metal monster, which senses and tracks them by their fear.

As the group is decimated, one of the protesters, Sam Raimi (John Sharian), dons a Hardman suit to fight the Warbeast. But he is unable to defeat the monster, which pursues him and Cale even after they make it out into the street. Fleeing back into the building, Cale lures the Warbeast into a long chase and eventually traps it in a room with Dante and an explosive that vaporizes both creator and creation.

DEATH MACHINE's story is admittedly simplistic and certainly derivative, combining the basic plot of ALIEN with the futuristic technology and wry satiric bent of ROBOCOP. But on these terms, the film succeeds quite admirably, with special effects man turned writer-director Stephen Norrington keeping the story racing along. His previous technical experience allows him to give the movie a handsome technical sheen on a low budget, and his handling of pacing and tension is expert, particularly in the Warbeast attacks. The mechanical monster is a striking creation, a hulking but fast-moving contraption with slashing claws and snapping jaws that remains a plausible and frightening menace throughout.

Norrington knows how to indulge genre fans: several characters are named after well-known genre directors, two others after the Weyland-Yutani corporation from ALIEN. But the director is also successful in translating his own fannish enthusiasm into on-screen energy. He is also well-served by an above-average cast that makes its characters vivid and believable, with Dourif doing his patented psycho act to a tee and Pouget becoming an engaging warrior woman in the Sigourney Weaver mold. *(Graphic violence, profanity.)* — M.G.

d, Stephen Norrington; p, Dominic Anciano; exec p, Jim Beach; assoc p, Heidi Lester, Stephen Norrington; co-p, Ray Burdis; w, Stephen Norrington; ph, John de Borman; ed, Paul Endacott; m,

Crispin Merrell; prod d, Chris Edwards; art d, Susan Whitaker; sound, Rudi Buckle (recordist); fx, Peter Hutchinson; casting, Beth Charkham; cos, Stephanie Collie; makeup, Lisa Boni, David Elsey, Alan Hedgcock, Cliff Wallace, Brendan Lonergan; stunts, Stuart St. Paul

Science Fiction/Horror (PR: O MPAA: R)

DECONSTRUCTING SARAH ★½
(U.S.) 92m Best Shot Productions; Carla Singer Productions; MCA Television Entertainment ~ MCA/Universal Home Video c

Rachel Ticotin *(Elizabeth Davis)*; Sheila Kelley *(Sarah Vincent)*; A. Martinez *(Kenny)*; David Andrews *(Paul Davis)*; Jennifer Lewis *(Betty)*; Dwier Brown *(Mitch)*; Peter Jason *(Cliff)*; Clyde Kusatsu *(Officer Okawa)*; John Vickery *(Swanson)*; Caroline Williams *(Dottie)*; Tony Abatemarco *(Restaurant Owner)*; Jack Andreozzi *(Frank Menghini)*; James Arone *(Desk Sergeant)*; Camilla Belle *(Young Elizabeth)*; Hank Cheyne *(Car Rental Clerk)*; Wanda Lee Evans *(Matty)*; Tess Fontana *(Young Sarah)*; Alex Knapp *(Receptionist)*; Ingrid Konupek *(Aerobics Instructor)*; Kristin Baxley *(Hostess)*; Jack Lange *(Waiter)*; Toshiyuki Nishi *(Sushi Chef)*; Brett Stimely *(Robert Swerdlow)*; Sandee Van Dyke *(Hannah)*; Don Amendolia *(Male Client)*

Deconstructing a contemporary women's film by infusing it with a noirish aura, DECONSTRUCTING SARAH never blends its two personalities and ends up immobilized by its polarities, much like its crisis-state heroine.

In the corporate world, executive Sarah Vincent (Sheila Kelley) is a finely-tailored ad agency workaholic who after work tones up with her best buddy, homemaker Elizabeth (Rachel Ticotin), in aerobics classes and dotes on Elizabeth's young daughter. After sunset, however, Sarah changes into a new slinky wardrobe and a new name, Ruth, to become the sexual aggressor in singles clubs and bars. The pressures of competing like a man by day and playing like one by night propel Sarah/Ruth into some dangerous beds, particularly one with her own private "Mr. Goodbar," Kenny (A. Martinez). Although Sarah calls the libertine shots, ex-con Kenny senses a meal ticket and jockeys to blackmail his lover at her place of work. When dependable Sarah fails to materialize for a sleep-over, suspicious Elizabeth alerts the nonchalant cops and then assumes her own late-night investigation into Kenny's activities—which includes his beating up of his passive girlfriend Dottie (Caroline Williams). Undercover as a sex worker, Elizabeth finds Sarah's corpse and Kenny—who appears the guilty party—sadistically orders Elizabeth to quit playing amateur sleuth. At Sarah's apartment, Elizabeth's husband Paul (David Andrews) races to her rescue, but not before Elizabeth knocks Kenny out the window. Having already heard taped confirmation of needy Sarah's dalliance with Paul, however, Elizabeth realizes that Paul murdered Sarah to hush up their inconvenient affair; his wife decides not to shield him from the law.

Considering the devastating impact of the film's last-minute revelation, Ticotin's character seems unusually nonplussed. This lack of satisfying emotional closure to the storyline may also be the failure of both the script and the performances of the actresses; neither portrays a believable friendship between two dissimilar women. There seems to be as little connection between these best friends as there is between Calvinist Sarah and her slutty alter ego Ruth—but at least the latter dynamic thrusts the plot forward. Despite trying to toss out a few likely candidates for Sarah's executioner and despite Martinez's sexually-charged performance, seasoned mystery buffs will quickly sense they're being led down blind alleys; the upright husband is easily guessed as the murderer. What is missing here (in addition to the lack of authenticity in the Elizabeth-Sarah bond) is the sense that Elizabeth is driven to solve her friend's murder as if her own identity depended on it. More in-depth script structuring would have been required to place the film's psychological issues into sharper relief. Unable to pull the wool over viewers' eyes, the mildly tantalizing DECONSTRUCTING SARAH say less about undying friendship than it does about how little we know our friends.

Finally, the film purports to explore feminist issues within the context of a fatalistic thriller, and the movie's direction is sleek and crafty enough to distract viewers into thinking that it is doing just that. However, getting maximum erotic tension out of its bar pick-up segments, the film works best as a reactionary tale about the dangers awaiting women who dare to challenge directly the male sexual ego. *(Violence, profanity, sexual situations.)* — R.P.

d, Craig R. Baxley; p, Sally Young; exec p, Lee Rose; w, Lee Rose; ph, Joao Fernandes; ed, Jeff Freeman; m, Tom Scott; prod d, Garreth Stover; art d, Chris Cornwell; set d, Larry Dias; sound, Mark McNabb (mixer); fx, Russ Hessey; casting, Marsha Kleinman; cos, Lynn Bernay; makeup, Jill Bennett, Patty Androff; stunts, Paul Baxley

Thriller/Erotic   **(PR: O MPAA: R)**

DECOY   ★★½
(U.S.) 98m FYDOE Films; Northwest Pictures; Mind's Eye Pictures; Prism Pictures ~ Turner Home Entertainment c

Peter Weller *(Baxter)*; Robert Patrick *(Travis)*; Charlotte Lewis *(Katya)*; Darlene Vogel *(Diana)*; Peter Breck *(Wellington)*; Scott Hylands *(Jensen)*; Vladimir Kulich *(Daniel)*; Zoltan Buday *(Gunther)*; Patricia Drake *(Madelaine)*; Phil Hayes *(Mick)*; Joe Wu *(Chinese Businessman)*; Wilfred Dube *(English Businessman)*; Brad Heck *(European Businessman)*; Richard Yoshida *(Japanese Businessman)*; Brian Ludwig *(Archer)*; Gerard Lang *(Thug 1)*; Calvert Chiefcalf *(Thug 2)*; Tom Charles *(Tracker 1)*; Victor Baptiste *(Tracker 2)*; Wayne Folk *(Large Man)*; Muriel Ross *(Cree Woman)*; Blaine Hart *(Spence)*

Mercifully, this sadistic exercise in macho gruffness grunts and groans by so rapidly that viewers can ignore the confusing plot curves and simply keep track of the fatalities. Better acted than most routine bonebusters, DECOY gets less mileage out of its central trumped-up plot reversal than it does out of the bloodbrother relationship of principals Peter Weller and Robert Patrick.

Jack Travis (Patrick), a Secret Service veteran, is hired by millionaire predator John Wellington (Peter Breck) to protect his daughter Diana (Darlene Vogel) from the machinations of a business rival, Jensen (Scott Hylands), who is still smarting because Wellington stole a computer chip from him. Travis insists his trusted former sidekick turned mercenary, Baxter (Weller), be hired also, despite his oddball ways. Travis and Baxter are introduced to Diana, but en route to a safe house, they are attacked by Jensen's hit lady, Katya (Charlotte Lewis), and commandeer a school bus to escape annihilation. Soon the bodyguards realize that the woman they're guarding is a decoy; she tells them about the computer chip theft and Baxter realizes he and his buddy have been set up—because Baxter once had an affair with Wellington's late wife. After several close calls and the kidnapping of the decoy by Jensen's thugs, Travis and Baxter confront Wellington at his compound. Meanwhile, a furious Jensen refuses to pay Katya after he discovers that she's nabbed an impersonator (the real Diana Wellington is actually a schoolgirl), having used his business feud as a cover for his desire to get Baxter's child. Baxter saves the decoy Diana and spares Katya's life but is fatally shot by Jensen, whom Travis then

dispatches. The dying Baxter requests that Travis and the actress spare no effort in locating his little girl.

Failing to exploit Wellington's deception for maximum suspense, DECOY wastes two fine performances in yet another direct-to-video revenge hunt. On the plus side, the rugged action is spiced with lots of save-your-ass sequences and a dazzling array of high-tech weaponry fit for an arms trade show. More essentially, this action sprawl is given a degree of humanity by Baxter and Travis's forged-in-misery rapport. Like mercenary vaudevillians, they use fancy footwork to rescue each other as they soft-shoe around explosives and assassins. If their circumstantial intimacy with the impostor posing as Diana lacks the required sexual-romantic dynamic, at least their comrades-in-arms bond provides a foundation of human interest. *(Graphic violence, extreme profanity.)* — R.P.

d, Victor Rambaldi; p, Gary Kaufman, Antonio Cortese; exec p, Carlo Rambaldi, Kevin DeWalt, Barry Collier; assoc p, Lloyd Martell, Vincent Di Paolo; co-p, Rob King; w, Robert Sarno; ph, John Kranhouse; ed, Jay Miracle, Frank Irvine; m, Mark Adler; prod d, Andrew Deskin; art d, Jim Phillips; set d, Mark Webb; sound, William Butler (mixer); fx, Randy Shymkiw; casting, Fern Orenstein; cos, Derek Baskerville; makeup, Tracy Lynn George

Action/Adventure/Martial Arts   **(PR: C MPAA: R)**

DEMON KNIGHT
(SEE: TALES FROM THE CRYPT: DEMON KNIGHT)

DESPERADO   ★★★
(U.S.) 106m Los Hooligans Productions; Columbia ~ Columbia c

Antonio Banderas *(El Mariachi)*; Salma Hayek *(Carolina)*; Joaquim de Almeida *(Bucho)*; Cheech Marin *(Short Bartender)*; Steve Buscemi *(Buscemi)*; Carlos Gomez *(Right Hand)*; Quentin Tarantino *(Pick-up Guy)*; Tito Larriva *(Tavo)*; Angel Aviles *(Zamira)*; Danny Trejo *(Navajas)*; Abraham Verduzco *(Nino)*; Carlos Gallardo *(Campa)*; Albert Michel, Jr. *(Quino)*; David Alvarado *(Buddy)*; Angela Lanza *(Tourist Girl)*; Mike Moroff *(Shrug)*; Robert Arevalo *(Opponent)*; Gerardo Moscoso *(Priest)*; Peter Marquardt *(Moco)*; Consuelo Gomez *(Domino)*; Jaime De Hoyos *(Bigoton)*; Cristos *(Cristos)*; Richie Gaona *(Case Opener)*; Mark Dalton *(Fighting Barfly)*; Tommy Nix *(Fighting Barfly)*; Patricia Vonne *(Bar Girl)*; Elizabeth Rodriguez *(Mariachi Fan)*

In 1991, with just $7,000 and a handful of friends acting as his crew, Robert Rodriguez created EL MARIACHI, aimed at the Spanish-language direct-to-video market. But the film's mixture of charm and gritty, stylish action pleased viewers and critics alike. DESPERADO is the putative sequel to EL MARIACHI, though it might better be described as a big-budget remake.

In EL MARIACHI, a traveling musician is caught in a nightmare of mistaken identity when he accidentally swaps his guitar for a case full of weapons. In the end, the local drug kingpin kills the woman he loves and puts a bullet through his left hand, ending his life as a musician. He still has the guitar case full of guns, though, and sets off looking for vengeance. DESPERADO finds the nameless mariachi (Antonio Banderas) near the end of his quest. He has wandered along the Texas-Mexico border, leaving a trail of dead drug lords in his wake, and now there is only one left, a man called Bucho (Joaquim de Almeida). Accompanied by his sole friend, Steve Buscemi (his character is never named, but is referred to in the credits as "Buscemi"), he tracks Bucho down to a dusty and lethargic little town whose residents have been intimidated into acting as drug runners and money launderers. After turning the local hellhole bar into an abattoir, El Mariachi narrowly escapes death at the hand of a knife-throwing mob assassin, and is sheltered by Carolina (Salma Hayek), the proprietor of the town's much-ignored book store.

Carolina shares her home and bed with him, but the mariachi suspects he may be outmatched by Bucho and his henchmen. He reluctantly calls upon Campa (Carlos Gallardo, star of EL MARIACHI) and Quino (Albert Michel, Jr.), a pair of maniacal musicians whose guitar cases conceal machine guns and rocket launchers. After a fiery battle in the streets, the mariachi is forced to deal with Bucho at his compound, *mano a mano*. Though he learns that the drug lord is actually his older brother, the mariachi exacts his final vengeance, leaving town with Carolina in one hand and his guitar case in the other.

Armed with a much larger budget than he had for EL MARIACHI, Rodriguez obviously set out to make an over-the-top, both guns blasting action picture. And DESPERADO delivers the goods: Though awesomely gory, the film displays Rodriguez's skill at crafting action sequences full of tricky gunplay, precise camera movement and intricate choreography, all showcased in loving slow motion. At its bloodiest, DESPERADO is never less than slick and stylish—a testament not only to Rodriguez's direction, but also his talents as editor and occasional cameraman. Because of its focus on action, DESPERADO was taken to task by many critics as lacking the kind of story and character development that made EL MARIACHI so refreshing. While unquestionably formulaic, DESPERADO is mercifully free of the flat dialogue and arch one-liners that undermine so many action films. And while it lacks the naive charm of EL MARIACHI, DESPERADO is far funnier than its predecessor.

1995 was a big year for Spanish actor Antonio Banderas, who appeared in MIAMI RHAPSODY, ASSASSINS, NEVER TALK TO STRANGERS, and FOUR ROOMS (in which he was directed by Rodriguez). But DESPERADO was probably the most effective showcase for his talents and smoldering, leading-man good looks. Banderas plays the mariachi as smooth, cool, and oozing sex appeal; he's positively feline—slinking stealthily through back alleys one moment, pouncing on a roomful of villains the next, and always landing gracefully on his feet. The stunning Hayek is more than his equal.

Rodriguez specially created smaller roles for friends Buscemi, Cheech Marin, and Quentin Tarantino, who plays a visiting drug buyer and tells a tediously scatological joke. It's a shame that Rodriguez disposes of them so quickly: They're some of the film's most interesting and humorous characters. Marin turns in a surprisingly strong performance as the local bartender, and their hasty executions leave a comedic hole in the film's latter half. *(Graphic violence, nudity, profanity.)* — B.T.

d, Robert Rodriguez; p, Robert Rodriguez, Bill Borden; co-p, Elizabeth Avellan, Carlos Gallardo; w, Robert Rodriguez; ph, Guillermo Navarro; ed, Robert Rodriguez; m, Los Lobos; prod d, Cecilia Montiel; art d, Felipe Fernandez del Paso; sound, Mark Ulano (mixer); fx, Bob Shelley; casting, Reuben Cannon; cos, Graciela Mazon; makeup, Douglas White, Ermahn Ospina; stunts, Steve M. Davison

Action/Crime/Drama   **(PR: C   MPAA: R)**

DESPERATE PREY   ★
(Australia) 106m Roxy Films ~ A-Pix Entertainment c
(AKA: REDHEADS)

Claudia Karvan *(Lucy Darling)*; Catherine McClements *(Diana Ferraro)*; Alexander Petersons *(Simon)*; Sally McKenzie *(War-*

den Zelda); Anthony Phelan *(Detective Quigley)*; Iain Gardiner *(Jack McCoy)*; Mark Hembrow *(Brewster)*; Jennifer Flowers *(Carolyn)*; Michael Adams *(Grundy)*; Charlie Barry *(Fireman)*; Peter Grose *(Officer O'Sullivan)*; Craig Cronin *(Junior Constable)*; Alex Sweetman *(Constable)*; Errol O'Neill *(Magistrate)*; Suzie McKenzie *(Whore)*; Malcolm Cork *(TV Reporter)*; David Wildman *(Newsreader)*; Larissa Chen *(Kim Lee)*; Josie Vendramini *(Jill)*; Bella Vendramini *(Belinda)*; Anthony Heffeman *(Lawyer)*; Jacek Koman *(Lawyer)*; Christopher *(Betts)*

If writer-director Danny Vendramini had invested his script with the same thought that he gives to his camera setups, DESPERATE PREY might have been at least interesting, instead of absurdly pointless.

This Australian film concerns the emotional bond formed between juvenile delinquent Lucy (Claudia Karvan) and her idealistic public defender Diana (Catherine McClements). After videotaping the murder of Brewster (Mark Hembrow)—her lover and Diana's boss—at the hands of a mysterious biker in black, Lucy hides out in a low security detention center. But, when the biker tracks her down, the spunky punk is forced to confide in her attorney. Diana searches for the tape, which will reveal the killer's identity. The path leads them to a criminal conspiracy involving police and lawyers, including Diana's slimy boyfriend Simon (Alexander Petersons). Diana goes public with the charges of corruption in her department, which puts her and Lucy at even greater risk. Eventually Diana finds the tape and reaches the detention center just in time to save Lucy from the killer, Warden Zelda (Sally McKenzie), who committed the murder because she was jealous of the "attention" Brewster paid her young charges.

Initially DESPERATE PREY promises to be an atmospheric, genre-bending actioner—MAD MAX with a sexy Bridget Fonda-type. When the *slow* story reaches the unsatisfying denouement, and the killer is revealed to be somebody unconnected to the plot, the effort required to cope with the accents, follow the scattershot story and care about the characters proves wasted. *(Violence, profanity, sexual situations.)* — P.R.

d, Danny Vendramini; p, Richard Mason; exec p, Danny Vendramini; w, Danny Vendramini (based on the play "Say Thank You to the Lady" by Rosie Scott); ph, Steve Mason; ed, Marc Van Buren; m, Felicity Foxx; prod d, Ross Wallace; art d, Julianne White; sound, Max Bowring (recordist); cos, Ross Wallace; makeup, April Harvey; stunts, Bob Hicks

Thriller/Drama   **(PR: O   MPAA: R)**

DESTINY TURNS ON THE RADIO   ★★
(U.S.) 102m Rysher Entertainment ~ Savoy Pictures c

James LeGros *(Thoreau)*; Dylan McDermott *(Julian)*; Quentin Tarantino *(Destiny)*; Nancy Travis *(Lucille)*; James Belushi *(Tuerto)*; Janet Carroll *(Escabel)*; David Cross *(Ralph Dellaposa)*; Richard Edson *(Gage)*; Bobcat Goldthwait *(Mr. Smith)*; Barry "Shabaka" Henley *(Dravec)*; Lisa Jane Persky *(Katrina)*; Sarah Trigger *(Francine)*; Tracey Walter *(Pappy)*; Allen Garfield *(Vinnie Vidivici)*; Ralph Brannen *(Henchman #1)*; Robert Sparks *(Henchman #2)*; Gordon Michaels *(Motorist)*; Che Lujan *(Jose)*

DESTINY TURNS ON THE RADIO, the directing debut of former executive producer Jack Baran, is the kind of film that gives hip a bad name. All laid-back attitude, with virtually no substance and precious little humor, this is a sad, aimless comedy that signals its desperate need to be loved from the opening reel.

Quentin Tarantino plays Johnny Destiny, an enigmatic gambling deity who answers the prayers of Las Vegas denizens. Conjured up by Julian (Dylan McDermott), a hot-tempered escaped con, Destiny provides a ride into town, dropping Julian off at the seedy Marilyn Motel, run by Harry Thoreau (James Le-Gros). The latter is Julian's ex-partner, who held up a bank with him three years earlier. Julian wants his share of the loot, plus his ex-girlfriend Lucille (Nancy Travis), now living with casino boss Tuerto (James Belushi) and pursuing a career as a lounge singer. She's looking forward to her big break, a performance to be attended by music mogul Vinnie Vidivici (Allen Garfield).

After Julian reignites his romance with Lucille, they run off together and get married, but Tuerto's men kidnap the woman and return her to the casino. The police insist that Lucille go ahead with her performance, knowing that it will lure Julian. Although her singing wows Vidivici, she decides her destiny lies with Julian, and the pair manage to escape together. They hook up with Thoreau by the motel swimming pool. Destiny appears, offering spiritual advice and urging the couple to jump into the mysteriously luminous pool. When the police arrive, they do so, while Thoreau makes off with the loot.

Released in the wake of PULP FICTION, no doubt with hopes of capitalizing on Tarantino's cameo, DESTINY TURNS ON THE RADIO did little to further Tarantino's acting career and exited quickly from theaters to video. The screenplay, credited to Robert Ramsey and Matthew Stone, appears to be aiming for some kind of post-beatnik mysticism too arch and unfathomable for its own good. McDermott, who is called upon to brood handsomely and have several temper tantrums, seems uneasy with more subdued aspects of his character. LeGros, a skillful character actor, takes a good stab at the dialogue he's been given, but winds up sounding less cool than dimwitted. Travis, who doesn't do her own singing, very nearly doesn't do her own acting, proving too colorless to be taken seriously as a sultry lounge singer.

Tarantino, billed third although he doesn't have much to do, is — let's be kind here — an embarrassment. His preening performance hangs entirely on his cult-figure reputation, which was earned principally by his writing and directing—day jobs he would be wise not to quit. (*Violence, adult situations, profanity.*) — E.K.

d, Jack Baran; p, Gloria Zimmerman; exec p, Keith Samples, Peter Martin Nelson; co-p, Robert Ramsey, Matthew Stone, Raquel Carreras; w, Robert Ramsey, Matthew Stone; ph, James Carter; ed, Raul Davalos; m, Steve Soles; art d, Easton Michael Smith, Dominic Wymark; set d, Lisa R. Deutsch; sound, Steuart P. Pierce; fx, David Wayne, Larry Hoki; casting, Nicole Arbusto, Joy Dickson; cos, Beverly Klein; makeup, Julie Purcell; stunts, Webster Whinery

Crime/Comedy/Fantasy   **(PR: C   MPAA: R)**

DEVIL IN A BLUE DRESS   ★★★★
(U.S.) 102m Clinica Estetico; Mundy
Lane Entertainment ~ TriStar c

Denzel Washington (*Easy Rawlins*); Tom Sizemore (*Dewitt Albright*); Jennifer Beals (*Daphne Monet*); Don Cheadle (*Mouse*); Maury Chaykin (*Matthew Terell*); Terry Kinney (*Todd Carter*); Mel Winkler (*Joppy*); Albert Hall (*Odell*); Lisa Nicole Carson (*Coretta James*); Jernard Burks (*Dupree Brouchard*); David Wolos-Fonteno (*Junior Fornay*); John Roselius (*Mason*); Beau Starr (*Miller*); Steven Randazzo (*Benny Giacomo*); Scott Lincoln (*Richard McGee*); L. Scott Caldwell (*Hattie Parsons*); Barry Shabanka Henley (*Woodcutter*); Nicky Corello (*Shariff*); Kenny Endoso (*Manny*); Joseph Latimore (*Frank Green*); Renee Humphrey (*Barbara*); Robert J. Knoll (*Herman*); Kai Lennox (*Football*); Poppy Montgomery (*Barbara's Sister*); Brendan Kelly (*Terell's Chauffeur*); Peggy Rea (*Carter's Secretary*);

Vinny Argiro (*Baxter*); Deborah Lacey (*Sophie*); Brazylia Kotere (*Neighborhood Woman*); Jeris Lee Poindexter (*Alphonso Jenkins*); Frank Davis (*Butcher*); Matt Barry (*Cop in Car*); Mark Cotone (*Cop in Station*); Brian E. O'Neal (*John's Band/Singer*); G. Smokey Campbell (*Nightclub Owner*); Alan Craig Schwartz (*Johnny*); Steve Sekely (*Abe*); J.D. Smith (*Pool Hall Owner*); Nigel Gibbs (*Bootlegger*)

DEVIL IN A BLUE DRESS is a mystery of sorts, complete with sexy lady with a secret, bad guys with guns, the threat of political scandal and the pervasive whiff of corruption: it's all very CHINATOWN. But it isn't much of a mystery—Ezekial "Easy" Rawlins (Denzel Washington) has barely started sniffing at the trail of shady lady Daphne Monet (Jennifer Beals) when she calls him up and invites him over. And her deep dark secret doesn't come as much of a surprise—it's quite literally written on her face. Rawlins isn't so much solving a puzzle as wading through a sewer and hoping he can find his way out without picking up too much muck in the process.

Los Angeles, 1948. Decorated WWII veteran Rawlins has lost his job at the airplane factory and the bills are piling up. What scares him most is the thought that the bank might repossess his little bungalow-style piece of the American Dream. So when gruff bar man Joppy sends a little work his way, Rawlins ignores the voice in his head that tells him he's about to make a big mistake. Smiling, blue-eyed reptile DeWitt Albright (Tom Sizemore) wants Rawlins to find a white woman, Daphne, who consorts with Negroes. Her fiance, rich mayoral candidate Todd Carter (Terry Kinney), wants her back, says Albright. Rawlins is no detective, but he doesn't have to be: All he has to do is show his face in some colored dives, ask some questions, and report back.

Rawlins runs into an old friend, fun-loving Coretta (Lisa Nicole Carson), who knows Daphne and lets slip that she's been keeping company with a black bootlegger named Frank Green. When Coretta is brutally murdered, Rawlins becomes the number one suspect. He's roughed up by the police, then propositioned by Carter's opponent in the upcoming mayoral race, a sleazy pervert named Matthew Terrell (Maury Chakin). And that's when Daphne calls. Rawlins meets with her and stays long enough to become a bit infatuated, drives her to a friend's house and accompanies her to the door. The friend—a pimp and blackmailer named Richard (Scott Lincoln)—is on the floor, dead.

Rawlins keeps turning up dirt, and it all leads to Daphne. Rawlins enlists the aid of an old hometown buddy, smiling psychopath Mouse (Don Cheadle), and the bodies pile up until Albright kidnaps Daphne, and Rawlins and Mouse have to get her back. Her troublesome secret is finally revealed: Daphne isn't a white girl at all. She's colored—her brother is the bootlegger—and the whole convoluted business is about political blackmail. Rawlins and Mouse rescue Daphne, who promptly disappears. Rawlins is left a sadder man with a new profession: Detective.

Director Carl Franklin, who adapted the DEVIL WITH A BLUE DRESS screenplay from Walter Mosley's novel, resists the temptation to slavishly translate the cliches of Mosley's prose into the cliches of noir filmmaking. Unlike a generation of directors who've grown up secure in the conviction that the important thing about film noir is that it looks so cool, Franklin is more interested in the faces behind the swirling cigarette smoke than the hypnotic shadows of ceiling fan blades against fashionable stark walls.

DEVIL IN A BLUE DRESS starts out looking like a skillfully straightforward recreation of genre conventions with a series of small, clever twists, the greatest and least of them being that the protagonist is black. DEVIL IN A BLUE DRESS isn't WHITE

MAN'S BURDEN, a reductive exercise in "wouldn't it be cool if. . . " race reversal. It's a subtle and unsettling character study, very like Franklin's first critical success, the low-budget ONE FALSE MOVE. And, not incidentally, it examines the racial realities of a Los Angeles in which no one even pretends to be surprised that policemen use the word nigger, never making them the story's focus, but never letting them slip out of sight or mind. The film rests on the shoulders of star Denzel Washington, an actor of demonstrable depth and seriousness who's always in danger of descending into prigdom. Washington can be a curious liability, a glum quagmire at a film's center, but here his stoic demeanor eminently suits his character. Unlike the archetypal noir detective, the ruined romantic who wallows in the horrors of a world that exists solely to disappoint him, Rawlins has stolidly ordinary aspirations, and Washington—free of the feral edge most contemporary actors cultivate—is eminently believable as a resolutely seemly guy. Unlike many neo-noir narratives, DEVIL IN A BLUE DRESS really is a moral journey: Rawlins starts out an innocent man, and ends up a compromised one. When he announces his plan to forget about the airplane factory, where he has to suck up to bigoted know-nothings, and become a detective, it's a rather sad moment. He's destined to develop a cynical skin and a knowing manner, doomed to become a more conventional character than he is. *(Violence, nudity, sexual situations, adult situations, profanity.)* — M.M.

d, Carl Franklin; p, Jesse Beaton, Gary Goetzman; exec p, Jonathan Demme, Edward Saxon; assoc p, Walter Mosley, Donna Gigliotti, Thomas A. Imperato; w, Carl Franklin (based on the novel by Walter Mosley); ph, Tak Fujimoto; ed, Carole Kravetz; m, Elmer Bernstein; prod d, Gary Frutkoff; art d, Dan Webster; set d, Kathryn Peters; sound, Ken Segal (mixer); fx, Tom Ward; casting, Victoria Thomas; cos, Sharen Davis; makeup, Edna Sheen; stunts, Tony Brubaker

Crime/Mystery/Drama　　　　　(PR: C　MPAA: R)

DIE HARD WITH A VENGEANCE　　　★★½
(U.S.) 128m Cinergi Productions; 20th Century Fox ~
20th Century Fox c

Bruce Willis *(John McClane)*; Jeremy Irons *(Simon)*; Samuel L. Jackson *(Zeus)*; Graham Greene *(Joe Lambert)*; Colleen Camp *(Connie Kowalski)*; Larry Bryggman *(Arthur Cobb)*; Anthony Peck *(Ricky Walsh)*; Nick Wyman *(Targo)*; Sam Phillips *(Katya)*; Kevin Chamberlin *(Charles Weiss)*; Sharon Washington *(Officer Jane)*; Stephen Pearlman *(Dr. Schiller)*; Michael Alexander Jackson *(Dexter)*; Aldis Hodge *(Raymond)*; Mischa Hausserman *(Mischa)*; Edwin Hodge *(Dexter's Friend)*; Rob Sedgwick *(Rolf)*; Tony Halme *(Roman)*; Bill Christ *(Ivan)*; Anthony Thomas; Glenn Herman; Kent Faulcon; Akili Prince; Ardie Fuqua; Mike Jefferson; Frank Andre Ware *(Gang Members)*; Michael Lee Merrins *(Van Driver)*; Birdie M. Hale *(Harlem Woman)*; Daryl Edwards *(Livery Driver)*; Barbara Hipkiss *(Phone Woman)*; Aasif Mandvi *(Arab Cabbie)*; Bill Kux *(Business Guy—Taxi)*; Scott Nicholson *(Transit Cop)*; Ralph Buckley *(Businessman—Station)*; Charles Dumas *(Cross)*; Michael Cristofer *(Jarvis)*; Phyllis Yvonne Stickney *(Wanda Shepard)*; J.R. Horne *(Sgt. John Turley)*; Michael Tadross *(Greek Deli Proprietor)*; Elvis Duran *(Radio D.J.)*; John McTiernan, Sr. *(Fisherman)*; Greg A. Skoric *(Kurt)*; Sven Toorvald *(Karl)*; Todd A. Langenfeld *(Berndt)*; Timothy Adams *(Gunther)*; John C. Vennema *(Felix Little)*; Gerrit Vooren *(Nils)*; Willis Sparks *(Klaus)*; Tony Travis *(Marshal #1)*; Danny Dutton *(Mashal #2)*; James Saito *(Korean Proprietor)*; Patrick Borriello *(Kid #1)*; Victor Rojas *(Kid #2)*; Jeffrey Dreisbach *(Yuppie Stockbroker)*; Joe Zaloom *(Jerry Parks)*; John Doman *(Foreman)*; Patricia Mauceri

(Miss Thomas); Franchelle Stewart Dorn *(Principal Martinez)*; Kharisma *(Little Tina)*; Gerry Becker *(Larry Griffith)*; Richard Council *(Otto)*; John Robert Tillotson *(Second Broker)*; Ray Arahna *(Janitor)*; Phil Theis *(Erik)*; Flip *(Subway Man)*; Dory Binyon *(Reporter)*; David Vitt *(Kid at Gas Station)*; John Glenn Hoyt *(Federal Reserve Guard #1)*; Bray Poor *(Federal Reserve Guard #2)*; David P. Martin *(Federal Reserve Guard #3)*; Shari-Lyn Safir *(Secretary)*; Ivan Skoric *(Villain A)*; Faisal Hassan *(FBI Agent)*; Richard Russell Ramos *(FBI Chief)*; Angela Amato *(Cop #1)*; Shirley J. Hatcher *(Cop #2)*; Richard V. Allen *(Chief Allen)*; James Patrick Whalen, Sr. *(Fat Larry Lumis)*; Paul Simon *(Man in Precinct)*; Carl Brewer *(Helicopter Villain)*

The third film in the DIE HARD series stretches a worn concept to breaking point. It supplies the requisite thrills, but lacks an interesting visual style and suffers from the kind racial humor that pretends to be hip, but is really more racist than ironic.

During the hot New York summer of 1995, a mysterious, German-accented bomber named Simon (Jeremy Irons) blows up a department store, then threatens to do more damage around the city unless suspended officer John McClane (Bruce Willis) is assigned to meet his demands. In his telephone calls to the police department, Simon promises to detonate new bombs unless John performs daring stunts at prescribed city locations. During one dangerous mission in Harlem, John teams up with Zeus (Samuel L. Jackson), a shopkeeper with black nationalist views, who subsequently becomes his partner in other Simon-engineered gambits. Eventually, John and the police realize that Simon is the brother of Hans Gruber, the criminal mastermind/terrorist John killed in DIE HARD. What's more, Simon's revenge provides cover for him and his army of thugs to break into a Treasury building that houses a fortune in gold bullion.

John and Zeus figure out Simon's scheme after he has absconded with the gold. They track Simon and his gang down to a ship, on which they try to stop him from fleeing the country. But Simon outsmarts the duo and leaves them chained together on the craft, which he plans to blow up. Miraculously, John and Zeus escape and pursue Simon. They successfully foil his escape, killing him in a helicopter crash.

The third DIE HARD film is easily the most spectacular, featuring an exploding subway train and a manic car chase through the congested streets of New York that rivals THE FRENCH CONNECTION. Indeed, for the first hour or so—as long as the action is confined to sweltering Manhattan—the film's inexorable action-pic logic is nearly as compelling as SPEED's. Unfortunately, as soon as the Blofeld-like villain makes his appearance, the whole thing turns into an overblown Bond film with a working-class hero (Bruce Willis)—if that's not a contradiction in terms.

The film is less a sequel to John McTiernan's DIE HARD (1988) and Renny Harlin's DIE HARD 2: DIE HARDER (1990), than yet another *mea culpa* from star Bruce Willis for his twin mega-bombs, THE BONFIRE OF THE VANITIES (1990) and HUDSON HAWK (1991). As in nearly all his films since those box-office disasters, Willis plays the role of a down-and-out cop who must prove his abilities all over again while fighting evil forces. Thus DIE HARD WITH A VENGEANCE tries too hard to place viewers on Willis's side in a set-up that is both familiar and offensive.

Screenwriter Jonathan Hensleigh's most obvious way of making John McClane sympathetic comes at the expense of the African-American character, Zeus, played by Samuel L. Jackson. Zeus is shoehorned into the narrative as sidekick, presumably to ameliorate some of the nastier connotations of the DIE HARD series' violent appeal to white male resentment. Initially, Zeus is seen telling two children not to accept help from white guys in a speech reminiscent of the "Black is Beautiful" rap favored by the Black Panthers. But as soon as Zeus becomes John's second banana, he is won over by his ostensible charm, eventually performing in a number of Huck-and-Jim routines that undermine his integrity. Zeus chauffeurs John around so much, in fact, the film might as well be titled DRIVING MR. WILLIS. And when Zeus and John discover the leftover gold in the Treasury, it is Zeus who stoops to stealing a bar for himself.

Perhaps if DIE HARD WITH A VENGEANCE had some visual flair, the film would suffice as an action-adventure. But while some sequences manage a fun, rollercoaster momentum, others are contrived and poorly shot. The camera actually slips during one shot in the opening montage, and John and Zeus's bungee-style jump from a bridge to the deck of a ship undermines the suspension of disbelief in even the most devoted fan (the characters emerge completely unscathed). At least this DIE HARD tones down the cartoon-style violence of the previous installment. (*Violence, adult situations, extreme profanity.*) — E.M.

d, John McTiernan; p, John McTiernan, Michael Tadross; exec p, Andrew G. Vajna, Buzz Feitshans, Robert Lawrence; assoc p, Robert H. Lemer; co-p, David Willis, Carmine Zozzora; w, Jonathan Hensleigh (based on characters created by Roderick Thorp); ph, Peter Menzies; ed, John Wright; m, Michael Kamen; prod d, Jackson DeGovia; art d, John R. Jensen, Woods Mackintosh; set d, Leslie Bloom; sound, Dennis Maitland, Sr. (mixer), Kim Maitland (recordist); fx, Phil Cory, Conrad F. Brink, John E. Sullivan, Mass. Illusion; casting, Pat McCorkle; cos, Joseph G. Aulisi; makeup, Marylin Peoples; stunts, Terry J. Leonard

Action/Adventure/Crime   (PR: C   MPAA: R)

DIGGER   ★★½
(U.S./Canada) 92m Westcom Entertainment Group; Western International Communications; Circle Northward Productions ~ Paramount Home Video c

Adam Hann-Byrd (*Digger*); Joshua Jackson (*Billy*); Timothy Bottoms (*Sam Corlett*); Barbara Williams (*Anna Corlett*); Olympia Dukakis (*Bea*); Leslie Nielsen (*Arthur*); Gabrielle Miller (*Rosemary*); P. Lynn Johnson (*Mrs. Jackson*); Danielle Fraser (*Melissa Jackson*); Lochlyn Munro (*Mark*); Andrew B. Parker (*Neville Jackson*); Colette Aubin (*Young Woman*)

Sweet-natured in temperament and muted in execution, DIGGER is a childhood friendship saga not about facing reality but about discovering another way to perceive it. One of the least plot-driven films since THE WHALES OF AUGUST, this mood piece is a paean to the therapeutic value of fantasy.

Sent to visit his Uncle Sam (Timothy Bottoms) and Aunt Anna (Barbara Williams) so that his recently-divorced mom can enjoy a breather, maladroit Digger (Adam Hann-Byrd) initially views his vacation as a prison stretch. Sensing his vinegary Aunt is uncomfortable around him (since she's grieving for her dead child), Digger resorts to his favorite mode of escape: excavating tunnels in the direction of exotic locales. Homesick, the boy's only other source of comfort is Grandma Bea (Olympia Dukakais) whose new beau Arthur (Leslie Nielsen) is willing to include Digger on their dates. What ultimately penetrates the withdrawn child's shell is his friendship with Billy (Joshua Jackson), a terminally-ill youngster whose heart has been weakened by radiation treatments. Sharing his secret world with Digger, Billy teaches his shy pal how to escape unpleasantness through the power of the mind. During their jaunts, Billy teaches Digger how to eavesdrop on the songs of the timber trees, while Digger encourages his buddy's crush on teenage beauty Rosemary (Gabrielle Miller). Living intensely because he senses his mortality, Billy introduces his pragmatic pal to the joys of Jules

Verne and draws parallels between them and the two captains in *Mysterious Island*. By the time Aunt Anna confronts her grief and forges a bond with her nephew, Digger has already become a convert to Billy's flights of fancy. When Billy's heart finally gives way, grief-stricken Digger overcomes his devastation and allow his playmate to live on by exercising his imagination when necessary. Living out his comrade's philosophy, Digger refuses to view Billy's death as a final goodbye.

Although DIGGER takes far too long to unfold a simple fish-out-of-water yarn, it could be argued that its leisurely pace accounts for some of the movie's magnetic pull. What this bittersweet bonding drama offers in place of a tight narrative or tear-jerking dexterity is a knack for facing the psychological dilemmas of childhood squarely without treating the participants as mini-adults. The boys' sidestep with divorce, abandonment trauma, and death isn't glossed over with cuteness, nor are the young actors cursed with the practiced sugary demeanor of Hollywood professionals. Without resorting to melodramatic massaging, DIGGER coaxes our sympathy despite its failure to better integrate Digger's impasse with his Aunt's emotional paralysis into the storyline. In the end, Billy isn't assumed into Heaven like Little Eva—his death is treated as the expected calamity it is. Perhaps the real reason for this movie's modest success is its refusal to portray the kids' fantasies too literally—events are doctored by the childrens' imagination. In movies as disparate as LAST ACTION HERO, THE RIVER PIRATES, and HEAVENLY CREATURES, filmmakers unleash adolescent fantasies that shed less light on the characters than they do on the directors' need to show off. Unassuming DIGGER doesn't push its Bad Things Happen to Good People ideology too far. And as a P.R. campaign for the rewards of reading, this gentle bubblegum opera succeeds far better than the over-emphatic PAGEMASTER. (*Adult situations.*) — R.P.

d, Robert Turner; p, Robert K. MacLean; exec p, Dale A. Andrews, Chris Boswell; co-p, Alexandra Lexton; w, Rodney Gibbons, Michael Chandler; ph, Michael Buckley; ed, Michael Chandler; m, Todd Boekelheide; prod d, Mark S. Freeborn; art d, Yvonne J. Hurst; set d, Rose Marie McSherry, Ann Marie Corbett; sound, Jay Boekelheide (design), Frank Griffiths; fx, John Thomas; casting, Georgianne Walker, Trish Robinson; cos, Susan DeLaval; makeup, Tom Brumberger; stunts, Jacob Rupp

Children's/Drama/Fantasy   (PR: AA   MPAA: PG)

DILLINGER   ★★
(U.S.) 95m Elliot Friedgen & Company; Wolper Organization; Bernard Sofronksi Productions; Warner Bros. Television ~ Warner Home Video c
(AKA: LAST DAYS OF JOHN DILLINGER, THE)

Mark Harmon (*Dillinger*); Sherilyn Fenn (*Billie Frechette*); Vince Edwards (*J. Edgar Hoover*); Will Patton (*Melvin Purvis*); Bruce Abbott (*Harry Pierpont*); Tom Bower (*Capt. Matt Leach*); John Philbin (*Hamilton*); Yvonne Suhor (*Jacqueline*); Patricia Arquette (*Polly Hamilton*); Larry Gittelson (*Emil Wanatka*); David Neidorf (*Clark*); Amy Yasbeck (*Elaine*); Lawrence Tierney (*Sheriff Sarber*); Joe Guzaldo (*Sam Cowley*); Michael Krawic (*Eddie Green*); Xander Berkeley (*Copeland*); Ramsay Midwood (*Charles Makley*); Ralph Foody (*Dillinger's Dad*); Tom White (*Homer Van Meter*); Malcolm Rothman (*Lou Piguett*); Kurt Naeberg (*Baby Face Nelson*); Rod Sell (*Robert Estill*); Peggy Roeder (*Sheriff Lillian Haley*); Lucy Childs (*Anna Sage*); Joe Greco (*Zarkovich*); Will Zahrn (*Gross*); Larry Brandenberg (*Pfauhl*); Tim Grimm (*Reporter #1*); Laurel Cronin (*Mrs. Sarber*); Mike McKune (*Alvin*); Bob O'Donnell (*Dr.*

May); Greg Kinnear *(Arizona Lawman)*; Mariann Mayberry *(Bank Teller)*; Rebecca Borter *(Mrs. Wanatka)*

Aesthetically pointed but cinematically pointless, DILLINGER, a 1991 made-for-television film released to home video in 1995, seems to exist only so an attractive cast can play mobster dress-up. Sadly, nothing in this crime biopic is as dramatic as the fashions, and if any tears are shed at all, it is not for the machine-gunned protagonists but for their blood-soiled overcoats.

After nine years in prison for robbery, seasoned con John Dillinger (Mark Harmon) nurses two ambitions; (1) to never serve time again and (2) to maintain a high-rolling lifestyle illegally. While his partner Copeland (Xander Berkeley) complains about spacing their heists for optimum impact, Dillinger plots to rescue jail buddy Harry Pierpont (Bruce Abbott). Instead, Dillinger gets recaptured and then sprung from jail himself by recently-escaped Harry, who raises the stakes by slaying a local sheriff (Lawrence Tierney) in the process. As Harry's gang attracts the attention of the Feds, Dillinger tricks his way out of extradition from Tucson to Indiana after another capture by using a fake gun. Sporting a flashy new female companion, Billie (Sherilyn Fenn), Dillinger encourages his crime consortium to take a vacation in Florida, but their retreat is cut short by an FBI raid that winds up killing more innocent bystanders than hoodlums. While J. Edgar Hoover (Vince Edwards) steps up pressure to capture him, nine-lives Dillinger eludes manhunts even after tight-lipped Billie gets jailed. Forcing the cooperation of the landlady of Dillinger's new girlfriend, the Feds intimidate her into identifying Dillinger (who has had plastic surgery) outside a movie theater showing the mobster flick MANHATTAN MELODRAMA. At last John Dillinger receives an inevitable machine-gun reception from the Feds, which ends his crime spree.

Trading in cheap ironies (e.g., the cops are "schlubs"; J. Edgar Hoover is more of a publicity hound than a crimefighter), DILLINGER dresses up an old folk hero in contemporary drag. Accompanied by an excruciating jazz score that fits neither the time period nor a mobster movie atmosphere, DILLINGER is strictly for young videoholic moderns who don't know that much about the anti-hero of yesteryear. Whether ripping off the homecoming scene from BONNIE AND CLYDE or presenting an interchangeable gallery of handsome hoods, nothing about this gleaming gansterama feels right. No sense of depression era verisimilitude ever surfaces, and the criminals' eat-drink-and-be-merry philosophizing rings hollow. More re-enactment than re-envisioning, this noisy but somewhat anesthetized action binge pumps some young acting blood into pickled corpses. Suitably cast as a soul-dead killer, aging pretty boy Harmon doesn't have the panache to embody a thrill-seeking mediaholic. Best advice: skip this film and catch the earlier Dillinger biopics with Warren Oates (1973), or Lawrence Tierney (1945), seen here in a tiny role. *(Graphic violence, profanity, sexual situations, adult situations, substance abuse.)* — R.P.

d, Rupert Wainwright; p, Mark Wolper; exec p, David Wolper, Bernard Sofronski; assoc p, Art Levinson; w, Paul F. Edwards; ph, Donald M. Morgan; ed, Stanford C. Allen; m, David McHugh; prod d, James Allen; set d, Olivia Peters; sound, Jim Pilcher; fx, Eddie Surkin; casting, Susan Bluestein; cos, Helen Butler; makeup, Jimi White

Crime/Biography/Historical   **(PR: O   MPAA: NR)**

DILLINGER AND CAPONE   ★★
(U.S.) 95m Concorde-New Horizons; Hillwood Entertainment ~ New Horizons Home Video c

Martin Sheen *(John Dalton/Dillinger)*; F. Murray Abraham *(Al Capone)*; Stephen Davies *(Cecil)*; Catherine Hicks *(Abigail Dal-*

ton); Don Stroud *(George)*; Sasha Jenson *(Billy)*; Michael Oliver *(Sam Dalton)*; Jeffrey Combs *(Gilroy)*; Michael C. Gwynne *(Frank Perkins)*; Anthony Crivello *(Lou Gazzo)*; Time Winters *(Eli)*; Joe Estevez *(Roy)*; Clint Howard *(Bobo)*; Bert Remsen *(Wheezy)*; Maria Ford *(Businesswoman)*; Christopher Kriesa *(Melvin Purvis)*; Debi A. Monahan *(Lady in Red)*

Yet another low-budget Roger Corman crime drama exploiting legendary criminal figures, DILLINGER AND CAPONE contrives the fanciful team-up of the famed bank robber and the retired Capone in a caper involving the Mob kingpin's secret money stash.

After watching as his brother is killed instead of him, bank robber John Dillinger (Martin Sheen) goes into hiding in California under the name of John Dalton. In 1940 he is summoned by onetime Chicago Mob boss Al Capone (F. Murray Abraham), newly released from a federal prison and retired to Florida. Holding Dillinger's wife Abigail (Catherine Hicks) and son Sam (Michael Oliver) hostage, Capone persuades Dillinger to return to Chicago to retrieve $15 million in cash hidden in a hotel basement now unwittingly occupied by Capone's Mob rival, Lou Gazzo (Anthony Crivello). Accompanied by Capone's English butler, Cecil (Stephen Davies), Dillinger arrives in Chicago and enlists the help of his former robbery partner George (Don Stroud) and George's nephew Billy (Sasha Jenson). After knocking out the building's electricity, Dillinger and crew enter the hotel posing as repairmen and gain access to the basement on the pretext of restoring power. To recover the money, they must drill through a wall to a secret room. The caper unfolds as planned until George is killed and Billy wounded in a machine gun battle with Gazzo and his men.

At their church hideout, Dillinger and Billy divide up their share of the money, Cecil having departed on his own, but are interrupted by two ex-federal agents, Gilroy (Jeffrey Combs) and Frank (Michael C. Gwynne), who have had them under surveillance. In the ensuing fight, Billy and Frank are killed, the money is burnt, and Dillinger flees. Back in Florida, Dillinger saves his wife and son from a deranged, syphillitic Capone, calming him by pretending to be Cecil, and escapes with his family.

Producer Roger Corman's long attraction to Depression-era crime figures, from MACHINE GUN KELLY (1958) to BIG BAD MAMA II (1987), has spiraled downward to a new low with DILLINGER AND CAPONE, which takes bold dramatic license to exploit both Geraldo Rivera's live TV opening of Capone's empty vaults and a widely-disputed theory that a double for Dillinger was killed by the feds, as elaborated in the book *Dillinger is Dead* by crime historian (and cocreator of *The Motion Picture Guide*) Jay Robert Nash. However, the film's intriguing pairing of the leading figures from the two poles of Depression-era crime—small town banditry and big city rackets—is so mishandled that it pales next to the sound dramatic sense and keen commercial instincts of such earlier, well-remembered combinations as FRANKENSTEIN MEETS THE WOLF MAN and BILLY THE KID VS. DRACULA.

Shot on a handful of elegant if claustrophobic location interiors, the film never achieves the intensity or keen insight into power and violence which previously distinguished Corman's own directorial efforts in this genre. Abraham shamelessly overacts as the unstable, megalomaniacal, Capone while Sheen (looking here more like Jack Palance than Dillinger) walks through his part rather too good-naturedly. Of the rest of the cast, only genre regulars Jeffrey Combs, as an overzealous ex-fed, and Don Stroud, as Dillinger's onetime partner, lend some dramatic weight to the proceedings. *(Violence.)* — B.C.

d, Jon Purdy; p, Mike Elliott; exec p, Roger Corman, Chris Peschken, Chris Naumann; w, Michael B. Druxman; ph, John

Aronson; ed, Norma Buckley; m, David Wurst, Eric Wurst; prod d, Robert de Vico; casting, Jan Glaser

Crime/Historical (PR: C MPAA: R)

DIRTY MONEY ★
(U.S.) 82m Bruce/Deane ~
Northern Arts Entertainment c

Frederick Deane *(Sam Reed)*; Timothy Patrick Cavanaugh *(Frank)*; Biff Yeager *(Tommy)*; Dagmar Stansova *(Maria)*; Charmagne Eckert *(Detective Walker)*; David Jean Thomas *(Detective Stone)*; Jorge "Maromero" Paez *(Jorge)*; Delaune Michele *(Cece)*; Taylor Nichols *(Herb)*; Larned Fowler *(Jerry)*; Jennifer Fowler *(Carol)*; Lizzie Fowler *(Lizzie/Girl on Tricycle)*; Christian Faber *(Gunstore Red Neck)*; Josephine Wallace *(Hooker in Black Mustang)*; Melissa Smith *(Tough Girl on Train)*; Martin Slusser *(Television Reporter)*; Popeye *(Homeless Man in Park)*; Cesar Garcia *(Bartender)*; John Luessenhop *(Man in White Mustang)*; James Bruce *(Beatnik in Train Station)*; David Syner *(Hotel Receptionist)*; Arturo Gonzales *(Detective Perez)*; Jorge Alberto *(Officer Fuentes)*; Enio Mejia *(Kid Outside Circus)*; Sergio Lino *(Illegal Immigrant)*; Israel Moran *(Illegal Immigrant)*; Brian Cooper *(Guard at Robbery)*; Veanne Cox *(Bus Stop Woman)*; Wendelin Slusser *(Drunk Surfer Girl)*; Romney Latko *(Drunk Surfer Girl)*; Kevin Williamson *(Surfer Dude)*; Jerry Rector *(Cop Outside Sam's House)*; Nancy Reed *(Waitress)*; Dick Sharpe *(Police Captain)*; Antonio Farre *(San Diego Policeman at Train)*; Jorge Ruiz *(Mexican Waiter)*; Shannon Wafford *(Knocked-Down Bystander)*; Circo Maromero *(Circus Performers)*

A film about blood, death, and destruction, DIRTY MONEY attempts to walk the increasingly well-trodden path taken by filmmakers like Quentin Tarantino, but is more likely to remain in late-night cable-TV obscurity.

Would-be Good Samaritan Sam Reade (Frederick Deane) makes the mistake of offering assistance to a carload of payroll robbers including psychopath Frank (Timothy Patrick Cavanaugh). He loses his car for his troubles but unknowingly gains a key to a money-filled locker. Frank kills a double-crossing colleague while Reade makes up with his estranged wife. Frank follows and murders her, framing Reade in the process. The wronged man hits the road to prove his innocence. Frank and the police pursue their quarry from Los Angeles to San Diego to Mexico, leaving a trail of bodies in their wake. By the time he seeks refuge with Maria (Dagmar Stansova), a lovely young acrobat with a traveling circus, Reade has gained an undeserved reputation as a desperate criminal. All the principals meet in a bloody showdown south of the border. Reade is one of the few left standing by the end.

DIRTY MONEY serves up the hoariest of cliches as if they still had something new to say. The film could have been salvaged either by an intriguing reinterpretation of its generic material or by employing a striking sense of style. Unfortunately, it seems content with getting its tired story told with a minimum of fuss. The characters are ciphers and even the best performances are barely adequate.

Cobbled together over 18 months of weekends by filmmakers affiliated with Fox-TV's "America's Most Wanted", the film has the sleazy casual violence of one of that show's dramatic reenactments. Some insanely charitable reviewers placed DIRTY MONEY in the nobly ragged tradition of ultra-low-budget film noir like DETOUR and PHENIX CITY STORY. Those well-made films found expressive qualities in their threadbare mise-en-scene. By contrast, DIRTY MONEY is just a waste of time. *(Nudity, violence, profanity, adult situations, sexual situations.)* — K.G.

d, James Bruce; p, James Bruce; co-p, Frederick Deane; w, Frederick Deane; ph, Christian Faber, Rick DiGregorio, Michael Mayers; ed, James Bruce, Robert Barrere; m, Paul Barrere; sound, Rick Schexnayder (mixer), Vladimir Tukan (mixer), Luis Alvarez (mixer); fx, Sergio Lino, Reelistic FX; cos, Alexandra Welker; makeup, David Syner; stunts, Ray Lykins, Dick Sharpe, Shannon Wafford

Crime/Adventure/Drama (PR: O MPAA: NR)

DR. JEKYLL & MS. HYDE ★½
(U.S.) 95m Rastar ~ Savoy Pictures c

Sean Young *(Helen Hyde)*; Tim Daly *(Richard Jacks)*; Lysette Anthony *(Sarah Carver)*; Stephen Tobolowsky *(Oliver Mintz)*; Harvey Fierstein *(Yves DuBois)*; Thea Vidale *(Valerie)*; Jeremy Piven *(Pete)*; Polly Bergen *(Mrs. Unterveldt)*; Stephen Shellen *(Larry)*; Sheena Larkin *(Mrs. Mintz)*; John Franklyn-Robbins *(Professor Manning)*; Aron Tager *(Lawyer)*; Jane Connell *(Aunt Agatha)*; Julie Cobb *(Dubois' Psychiatrist)*; Kim Morgan Greene *(Paparazzi Lady/Party Lady)*; Victor Knight *(Bill)*; Mark Camacho *(Waiter)*; Robert Wuhl *(Man With Lighter)*; Susan Trustman *(Cocktail Party Woman)*; Manon Deschenes *(Gorgeous Female Model)*; Jean-Claude Page *(Gorgeous Male Model)*; Maria Stanton *(Dress Admirer 1 & 2)*; Donna Barnes *(Young Woman)*; Rachel Bertrand *(Pneumatic Young Woman)*; Marie-Helene Pierre *(Helen Body Double)*; Herb Goldstein *(Nose #1)*; Michael Rudder *(Nose #2)*; Susan Glover *(Nose #3)*; Kate Asner *(Female Admirer)*; Liz Larson *(Carson)*; Mike Hodge *(Eagleton)*; Stephane Lefebvre *(Bus Boy)*; Don Jordan *(Driver)*; Donna Sarrasin *(Mintz's Secretary)*

DR. JEKYLL AND MS. HYDE aspires to be a comedic take on Robert Louis Stevenson's classic tale of good and evil, updating the Jekyll-Hyde story to the "post-feminist" American workplace. David Price's film is eager to please, but reduces Stevenson's classic to the cinematic equivalent of a whoopee cushion.

Richard (Tim Daly) is a fragrance developer for a perfume company who discovers that he is the great-grandson of Dr. Henry Jekyll. Unable to resist experimenting with his ancestor's scientific formula, which he obtains as a family legacy, Richard metamorphoses into Helen Hyde (Sean Young), a seductive, high-powered woman who will stop at nothing to advance up the corporate ladder. The changeover creates difficulties for Richard's fiancee Sarah (Lysette Anthony), who, of course, has no idea that the new female executive at Omage Perfumes is the man she's planning to marry. (No one seems to notice that this woman has come out of nowhere and that she is never around when Richard is present, but never mind.) Almost as confused are Richard's boss (Stephen Tobolowsky), who can't seem to resist Helen, and gay co-worker Yves DuBois (Harvey Fierstein), who has never been attracted to a woman before, but is now wavering.

In the hands of a sophisticated, or more discriminating, filmmaker, a gender-bending Jekyll-and-Hyde comedy lampooning office politics might have been fun, but the accent here is on pre-adolescent humor devoid of subtlety. Price tries to keep things moving, but he mistakes "activity" for action. Far worse is the film's view of women, who seem to be defined almost exclusively by large breasts, long fingernails, and black lingerie. DR. JEKYLL AND MS. HYDE can't overcome its leering, sputtering script, penned by four writers working from Price's original story. "Who would have thought," muses Richard, "that if another woman came between me and Sarah, it would be me?"—and that's probably the wittiest line in the movie. The cast is a game bunch, but the two principals, Young and Daly, were evidently directed to avoid nuance or believability under penalty of death. Anthony, the skilled British actress who enlivened Woody Allen's HUSBANDS AND WIVES, has some choice moments as the bewildered Sarah, and Fierstein's presence is welcome, even if only to remind us of better performances in the past, when this gifted comic actor had a real character to play. *(Profanity, sexual situations.)* — E.K.

d, David Price; p, Robert Shapiro, Jerry Leider; exec p, John Morrissey; co-p, Frank K. Isaac; w, Tim John, Oliver Butcher, William Davies, William Osborne (from a story by David Price suggested by the novel *The Strange Case of Dr. Jekyll and Mr. Hyde* by Robert Louis Stevenson); ph, Tom Priestley; ed, Tony Lombardo; m, Mark McKenzie; prod d, Gregory Melton; art d, Guy Lalande; set d, Francine Danis, Paul Hotte, Michele Nolet, Ginette Robitaille; sound, David Lewis Yewdall (designer); fx, Louis Criag, L'Intrigue, Tim Landry, Dream Quest Images, Video Image; casting, Mike Fenton, Allison Cowitt; cos, Molly Maginnis; makeup, Diane Simard, Kevin Yagher; stunts, Minor Mustain

Comedy/Horror   **(PR: C   MPAA: PG)**

DOLORES CLAIBORNE   ★★★
(U.S.) 131m Needful Productions; Castle Rock ~ Columbia c

Kathy Bates *(Dolores Claiborne)*; Jennifer Jason Leigh *(Selena St. George)*; Judy Parfitt *(Vera Donovan)*; Christopher Plummer *(Detective John Mackey)*; David Strathairn *(Joe St. George)*; Eric Bogosian *(Peter)*; John C. Reilly *(Constable Frank Stamshaw)*; Ellen Muth *(Young Selena)*; Bob Gunton *(Mr. Pease)*; Roy Cooper *(Magistrate)*; Wayne Robson *(Sammy Merchant)*; Ruth Marshall *(Secretary)*; Weldon Allen *(Bartender)*; Tom Gallant *(Searcher)*; Kelly Burnett *(Jack Donovan)*; Matt Appleby *(Kid on Street)*; Thomas Skinner *(Kid on Street)*; Vernon Steele *(Ferry Vendor)*; Taffara Jessica *(Selena—Age 5)*; Stella Murray *(Selena—Age 5)*; Susan Lane *(Crying Girl)*; Frank Adamson *(Detective Supervisor)*; Ed Rubin *(Detective Supervisor)*; Sandy MacDonald *(Sheriff)*; Dean Eilertson *(Moving Man)*

This adaptation of Stephen King's bestseller will further confuse anyone who still thinks of King as a horror specialist. Despite the centrality of two possible murders to its plot, this meticulously produced melodrama owes far more to 1950s Women's Pictures than to contemporary thrillers.

In the Maine resort community of Little Tall Island, elderly former socialite Vera Donovan (Judy Parfitt) takes a fatal fall and her longtime live-in housekeeper Dolores Claiborne (Kathy Bates) is arrested for murder. Dolores's long-estranged daughter, Selena St. John (Jennifer Jason Leigh), a successful and stressed-out Manhattan journalist, returns home to investigate. Years earlier, Dolores had been cleared of killing her husband Joe (David Strathairn), despite the best efforts of Detective John Mackey (Christopher Plummer).

Out on bail, Dolores returns with Selena to their long-disused house. In flashbacks, we learn that Joe was an alcoholic who brutalized Dolores when their daughter was out of earshot. Selena, herself now an embittered substance abuser, disbelieves her mother's stories. Visiting the Donovan house to collect Dolores's things, mother and daughter meet Mackie, who reveals that Vera had willed her valuable estate to Dolores eight years earlier. This supplies an apparent motive, and Mackie also has eyewitness accounts of Dolores's threatening to murder her strict employer. However, a flashback reveals that Vera's fall was a suicide. The frail old woman even requested Dolores's assistance in ending her misery, but died before she could comply.

In flashback, Dolores learns that Joe has been abusing Selena (who subsequently repressed the memory). Furthermore, Joe has embezzled her life savings, with which she had hoped to escape

with Selena someday. Dolores breaks down and tells her story to Vera, who calmly counsels murder. Years before, she had murdered her own straying husband. Dolores follows Vera's advice during a solar eclipse, making the murder look like an accidental fall into a disused well.

Back in the present, Selena leaves town while listening to her mother's taped confession to the first murder. She recovers the repressed memory of her father's sexual abuse and turns back. She arrives at the inquest, pleads her mother's case, and reveals Mackey's personal stake in the matter. The case is dismissed and mother and daughter are somewhat reconciled.

This film marks another classy King adaptation from Castle Rock Entertainment, whose success with STAND BY ME cleared the way for MISERY and THE SHAWSHANK REDEMPTION. An old-fashioned entertainment, DOLORES CLAIBORNE is a safe bet for mature target audiences: it's a dignified adaptation of a story told almost entirely in first-person by an irrepressibly vulgar narrator.

The novel represented one of King's ongoing attempts to embrace feminist themes and female protagonists. While retaining the empathy for the difficulty of women's work and the tyranny of patriarchy, the film jettisons the narration, eliminates one of the St. George children (a son), and makes the adult Selena a major character. (The last decision was most problematic, since the film is best whenever Leigh isn't around.)

Bates's earthy performance is quite effective, and her oddball vulgarities and put-downs provide most of the film's laughs. English character player Parfitt dazzles as the younger Vera; her tight-lipped smile and large luminous eyes suggest depths of intelligence and calculation. During their best scenes together, Bates and Donovan crackle with the crazy energy of two grande dames.

Director Taylor Hackford manages to keep up with the ladies for much of the picture. All the flashbacks are introduced with deliciously slick transitions and the vibrant cinematography bolsters the emotional content. With the eerie lighting of the eclipse sequence, the film reaches a visual crescendo that would have impressed a 1950s melodrama maestro like Douglas Sirk. The denouement, however, is a major disappointment. Perhaps fearing that audiences would find the cranky Selena too unpleasant, the filmmakers gave Leigh a big heroic wrap-up scene in which she "saves" her mother while needlessly explicating all the unspoken themes of the film. Thus the wonderfully expressive Dolores is rendered mute for the film's ostensible climax! This miscalculation nearly destroys the substantial pleasures of what came before. *(Violence, adult situations, sexual situations, profanity.)* — K.G.

d, Taylor Hackford; p, Taylor Hackford, Charles Mulvehill; assoc p, Gina Blumenfeld; w, Tony Gilroy (based on the novel by Stephen King); ph, Gabriel Beristain; ed, Mark Warner; m, Mark Warner; prod d, Bruno Rubeo; art d, Dan Yarhi; set d, Steve Shewchuk; sound, Glen Gauthier (mixer), Denise Bell (recordist), Susan McLean (recordist), Andy Bass (recordist), David Marquette (recordist); fx, Tedd Ross, Janek Sirrs, The Computer Film Company; casting, Nancy Klopper; cos, Shay Cunliffe; makeup, Luigi Rocchetti; stunts, Gary Davis

Drama/Mystery   **(PR: C   MPAA: R)**

DON JUAN DEMARCO   ★★½
(U.S.) 97m American Zoetrope; New Line ~ New Line c

Johnny Depp *(Don Juan DeMarco)*; Marlon Brando *(Dr. Jack Luchsinger)*; Faye Dunaway *(Marilyn Mickler)*; Geraldine Pailhas *(Dona Ana)*; Bob Dishy *(Dr. Paul Showalter)*; Rachel Ticotin *(Dona Inez)*; Talisa Soto *(Dona Julia)*; Marita Geraghty *(Woman in Restaurant)*; Richard Sarafian *(Detective Sy Tobias)*; Tresa Hughes *(Grandmother DeMarco)*; Stephen Singer *(Dr. Bill Dunsmore)*; Franc Luz *(Don Antonio)*; Carmen Argenziano *(Don Alfonzo)*; Jo Champa *(Sultana Gulbeyaz)*; Esther Scott *(Nurse Alvira)*; Nada Despotovich *(Nurse Gloria)*; Gilbert Lewis *(Judge Ryland)*; Tom "Tiny" Lister, Jr. *(Rocco Compton)*; Tom Mardirosian *(Baba the Eunuch)*; Al Corley *(Woman's Date)*; Nick LaTour *(Nicholas the Doorman)*; Bill Capizzi *(Sultan)*; Patricia Mauceri *(Dona Querida)*; Cliff Weissman *(Delivery Man No. 1)*; Michael Malota *(Young Don Juan)*; Renee Sicignano *(Flower Girl)*; Trevor Long *(Waiter)*; Sanjay *(Auctioneer)*; Diane Lee *(Night Duty Nurse)*; Joni Kramer *(Nurse No. 1)*; Shirlee Reed *(Nurse No. 2)*; Ken Gutstein *(Doctor No. 1)*; Adriana Jardini *(Social Worker)*; Robert Polanco Rodriguez *(Priest)*; Roberta Danza; Bridget Mariano; Christine Wolfe; Jose Hernandez *(Nuns)*; Selena Perez *(Singer)*; Rosendo Casillas; Esperanza DonLucas; Ramirez Filberto; Santiago Garcia; Ernesto V. Molina; Fernando C. Moreno *(Mariachi Band)*

The directing debut of novelist Jeremy Leven, DON JUAN DEMARCO is a light romantic comedy of the Adorable-Crazy-Person-Cures-Caregivers-of-their-Harmful-Sanity variety.

A loony youth (Johnny Depp) has reinvented himself as Byron's Don Juan. He dresses like Zorro, speaks with a Ricky Ricardo accent and comports himself in the manner of Errol Flynn. He has vowed to kill himself because though he has been with more than a thousand women, the one he truly loves has rejected him. Psychiatrist Jack Mickler (Marlon Brando)—who's about to retire from practice—persuades the *faux* Don Juan not to throw himself from a Hollywood billboard by playing along with his delusions. Mickler's by-the-book boss, Dr. Showalter (Bob Dishy), gives Mickler ten days to present the boy for a disposition hearing, but Mickler becomes enchanted with DeMarco's "beautiful world" and fights to keep him off the medication Showalter is anxious to dispense.

Through extended flashbacks, DeMarco recounts his invented life. Raised in a Mexican village, DeMarco has a blissful affair with the young wife of wicked Don Alphonso. Alphonso kills DeMarco's father, and he retaliates in kind. Forced to flee, DeMarco is sold into slavery by pirates, ends up in a harem of 1500 women and learns from them the secrets of love. He later ends up on the Island of Eros, where he finds his one true love, Dona Ana (Geraldine Pailhas). When he tells her of his passionate past, she leaves him and he is inconsolable.

DeMarco's story is alternately punctured by his grandmother—who gives a much more prosaic account of his origins—and ambiguously confirmed by his mother, Dona Inez (Rachel Ticotin). Now a nun, Dona Inez evades many of Mickler's questions, citing her vows. DeMarco's romantic idealism rubs off on Mickler, revitalizing his marriage to Marilyn (Faye Dunaway), and Mickler coaches DeMarco for his hearing. When the fateful day arrives, DeMarco recites the official story: He was born in Phoenix, became obsessed with a magazine model (Talisa Soto) after his father's death, and knows he is not Don Juan. DeMarco is released, and accompanies the Micklers on their second honeymoon to the Island of Eros, where Dona Ana awaits him.

It's as pointless to point out that the original Don Juan was not merely a seducer of women but a cynical, amoral reprobate as it is to observe that delusional schizophrenics are rarely cured in a week. DON JUAN DEMARCO is aggressively fluffy, a celebration of dreamy romanticism, built on a feel-good fantasy of Don Juan and the idealistic notion that lunatics are people too good for this ugly, brutally pragmatic world.

Depp's considerable personal charm is the movie's greatest asset. The story is painfully insubstantial, and Dunaway is sadly

wasted in the shallow, predictable role of a woman whose barren life blossoms under her husband's renewed attention. But Brando is the film's weakest element: bloated and pale, his performance is as dry, limp, and lifeless as his ghastly toupee.

To Leven's credit, the fantasy sequences are beautifully filmed (by Ralf Bode), the narration amusingly overblown, and the pacing crisp. *(Nudity, sexual situations, profanity.)* — R.S.

d, Jeremy Leven; p, Francis Ford Coppola, Fred Fuchs, Patrick Palmer; exec p, Ruth Vitale, Michael De Luca; w, Jeremy Leven; ph, Ralf Bode; ed, Tony Gibbs; m, Michael Kamen; prod d, Sharon Seymour; art d, Jeff Knipp; set d, Maggie Martin; sound, Richard Lightstone (mixer); fx, James Fredburg; casting, Lynn Kressel; cos, Kirsten Everberg, Fred Lloyd; makeup, Ron Berkeley; stunts, Victor Paul

AAN Best Original Song: Michael Kamen, Bryan Adams, Robert John "Mutt" Lange "Have You Ever Really Loved a Woman?"

Romance/Comedy/Drama   (PR: C   MPAA: PG-13)

DOOM GENERATION, THE   ★★½
(U.S.) 84m UGC; Teen Angst Movie Co.; Desperate Pictures; Blurco; Why Not Productions ~ Samuel Goldwyn Company c

James Duval *(Jordan White)*; Rose McGowan *(Amy Blue)*; Johnathon Schaech *(Xavier Red)*; Cress Williams *(Peanut)*; Skinny Puppy *(Gang of Goons)*; Dustin Nguyen *(Quickiemart Clerk)*; Margaret Cho *(Clerk's Wife)*; Lauren Tewes *(TV Anchorwoman)*; Christopher Knight *(TV Anchorman)*; Nicky Katt *(Carnoburger Cashier)*; Johanna Went *(Carnoburger Co-worker)*; Perry Farrell *(Stop'n'Go Clerk)*; Amanda Bearse *(Barmaid)*; Parker Posey *(Brandi)*; Salvator Xuereb *(Biker)*; Heidi Fleiss *(Liquorstore Clerk)*; Don Galloway *(FBI Guy)*; Dewey Weber *(George)*; Christofor Rossianov *(Dan)*; Paul Fow *(Pat)*

A twisted teen road movie, Gregg Araki's THE DOOM GENERATION has a stunningly bold visual style, a nihilistically romantic spirit, and a witty reverence for pop culture. It's definitely not for everyone, but DOOM GENERATION is further evidence of the unique vision Araki demonstrated in his earlier films.

Amy Blue (Rose McGowan) is a tough-talking teen angel, a speed freak with a jet black bob, alabaster skin and cherry red lips. Her boyfriend, virginal Jordan White (James Duval), is sweet, a bit goofy, and thinks he's in love. While cruising in Amy's car in search of some late-night action, they meet Xavier Red (Johnathan Schaech), a sexy drifter. His cool ambivalence both offends and excites them. After an argument, Amy kicks Xavier out of the car.

Amy and Jordan make a junk food pit stop at the local Quickie Mart, whose gun-toting Asian manager accuses them of shoplifting. Unexpectedly, Xavier steps back into the picture and blows off the store manager's head. The three of them escape unharmed and go on the lam together. They explore the hyperreal landscape of Los Angeles' shopping malls, fast food joints and cheesy motels, and end up killing more people. At the same time, their relationships with each other become more complex. Jordan finally loses his virginity to Amy, and his mind to the world of love and sex. Amy is also sleeping with Xavier, a much more calculating and exciting sexual partner. Xavier has lustful designs on Jordan, and they eventually indulge in a sexual threesome in an abandoned warehouse. A gang of skinheads bursts in, intending to rape Amy. But when they see Xavier and Jordan lying together, they go ballistic with homophobic rage. After a series of rapes on an American flag, the skinheads castrate Jordan with a huge pair of shears. Amy slaughters the skinheads, and only she and Xavier survive.

A self-proclaimed "Heterosexual Movie" from one of the pioneer directors of the New Queer Cinema—his previous credits are THREE BEWILDERED PEOPLE IN THE NIGHT (1987), THE LONG WEEKEND (O'DESPAIR) (1989), THE LIVING END (1992) and TOTALLY F***ED UP (1993)—THE DOOM GENERATION shows only heterosexual sex, but evokes an amazingly intense homoerotic attraction between Xavier and Jordan. It's saturated with the ultra-bright colors of pop culture and propelled by the music of Jesus and Mary Chain, Nine Inch Nails, Porno for Pyros and other Gen-X idols. Though THE DOOM GENERATION at first appears an affectionate lampoon of an American junk culture fueled by Doritos, slurpies, TV, alienation and fashionable anomie, it quickly takes on the air of a bad acid trip, careening along on its own nightmarish trajectory. Cameos by Hollywood madam Heidi Fleiss, "The Love Boat"'s Lauren Tewes, "The Brady Bunch"'s Christopher Knight, and "Married . . . With Children"'s Amanda Bearse heighten the surreal effect.

THE DOOM GENERATION has been compared to Oliver Stone's NATURAL BORN KILLERS for its apocalyptic anomie, grotesquely graphic violence and undercurrent of very black comedy. And while most of THE DOOM GENERATION's violence is played for Hong Kong action-style laughs, the final scene at the warehouse is as vicious, gruesome and sobering as any scene in Stone's atrocity show. Sharply focused and intensely stylized, THE DOOM GENERATION leaves viewers simultaneously spent and wired. (Graphic violence, extensive nudity, sexual situations, substance abuse, extreme profanity.) — J.S.

d, Gregg Araki; p, Andrea Sperling, Gregg Araki; exec p, Nicole Arbib, Pascal Caucheteux, Gregoire Sorlat; assoc p, Jim Stark, Shelley Surpin; co-p, Yves Marmion; w, Gregg Araki; ph, Jim Fealy; ed, Gregg Araki; m, Don Gallo; prod d, Therese Deprez; art d, Michael Krantz; set d, Jennifer Gentile; sound, Mark Deren (mixer); fx, Kevin Hudson, Chris Mabil; casting, Joseph Middleton; cos, Catherine Cooper-Thoman; makeup, Jason Rail; stunts, Ignacio Alvarez

Drama/Comedy/Crime   **(PR: O   MPAA: NR)**

DOOMSDAY GUN   ★★
(U.S.) 107m Griffin Productions; HBO Showcase ~
HBO Home Video c

Frank Langella (*Gerald Bull*); Alan Arkin (*Yossi*); Kevin Spacey (*Price*); Michael Kitchen (*Chris*); Francesca Annis (*Sophie*); Aharon Ipale (*Hussein's Commander*); Zia Mohyeddin (*Hashim*); Tony Goldwyn (*Duvall*); James Fox (*Whittington*); Rupert Graves (*Jones*); Clive Owen (*Duv*); Murray Melvin (*Shop Manager*); Marianne Denicourt (*Monique*); Alexandra Vandernoot (*Maria*); Roger Hammond (*Mockler*); Georgia Reece (*Brigit*); Richard Garnett (*Bobby*); David Healy (*Judge*); Drew Schofield (*Paul*); Edward Highmore (*Claude*); Nigel Hastings (*Matthew*)

DOOMSDAY GUN features a scientist with a genius for producing the ultimate weapon of destruction at the center of a complicated story of international espionage and betrayal.

Dr. Gerald Bull (Frank Langella) once invented wonderful weapons for Uncle Sam until a downsizing Pentagon withdrew its funding. Without the means of perfecting his armament dreams, Bull's shipment of war materials to South Africa lands him in prison. The disillusioned Bull now decides to sell to the highest bidder, and with his right-hand man Chris (Michael Kitchen) and a think-tank staff, he begins building a great gun with a 1000 mile range for Sadaam Hussein. While an international situation develops over the making of the gun, Bull blindly

soldiers on unaware of the impending treachery of his employers, stepping up production on his brainchild in 26 different sections, and solving its firing stress problems.

The US short-sightedly does nothing to squash the project, fearing the Iranians more than the Iraqis. Hussein's commanders murder Chris and pressure Bull to make a smaller version of the super gun fully operational. Caught in the hair-trigger sights of a monster of his own making, Bull is assassinated when the weapon is only eight segments from completion; his records disappear and his murder remains unsolved.

Although the direction is competent without being eye-openingly fresh, it cannot override flaws in the script which make the film a dull experience. To truly frighten us with Bull's scientific megalomania, the movie needed a riskier way of disseminating the basics of its cautionary tale. Played in a low-key manner by Langella, Bull registers not as a man who might have plunged the world into chaos but as a grousing science teacher frustrated with lab cutbacks. If he had been a messianic madman, the film could have worked. If the film had showcased his mistreatment by the democratic nations, then his repayment of their dirty deals would have had some impact. But Bull is portrayed as neither hero nor villain, just a self-centered absent-minded professor who got in over his head with Hussein's military machine. Played straight, DOOMSDAY GUN does not scare or stir a debate; instead, it fades into insignificance as it relates the story of an overgrown child who wanted a bigger weapon-building allowance and threw a potentially deadly tantrum when he did not get it. (*Extreme profanity, violence, adult situations.*) — R.P.

d, Robert Young; p, Adam Clapham; exec p, Michael Deakin, Colin Callender; assoc p, Michael Baker; co-p, Elaine Sperber; w, Walter Bernstein, Lionel Chetwynd; ph, Ian Wilson; ed, Tariq Anwar; m, Richard Harvey; prod d, Terry Ackland-Snow; art d, Fred Hole, Pauline Griffiths, Alan Cassie; set d, Peter Young; sound, Colin Charles; fx, Ian Wingrove; casting, Mary Coloquhoun; cos, Tiny Nicholls; makeup, Lois Burwell

Docudrama/Thriller/Spy   **(PR: C   MPAA: NR)**

DOUBLE, DOUBLE, TOIL AND TROUBLE   ★★
(U.S.) 93m Dualstar Productions;
Green-Epstein Productions; Warner Bros. Television ~
Warner Home Video c

Mary-Kate Olsen (*Kelly Farmer*); Ashley Olsen (*Lynn Farmer*); Cloris Leachman (*Aunt Agatha/Aunt Sophia*); Phil Fundacaro (*Oscar*); Eric McCormack (*Don Farmer*); Kelli Fox (*Christine Farmer*); Wayne Robson (*Gravedigger*); Matthew Walker (*George*); Meshach Taylor (*Mr. "N" Nofziger*); Denalda Williams (*Hostess*); Gary Jones (*Bernard Brewster*); Babz Chula (*Madame Lulu*); Bill Meiler (*Chairperson*); Nora McLellan (*Female Cop*); Alex Green (*Pumpkin Driver*); Claire Caplan (*Witch 1*); Karin Konoval (*Witch 2*); Glynis Leyshon (*Witch 3*); Mitch Kosterman (*Cop*); Gerry McAteer (*Fred*); Eliza Centenara (*Girl 1*); Christopher Anderson (*Boy 1*); Lynda Boyd (*Singer*); Ian Brags (*Fat Man*); Freda Perry (*Girl's Mother*)

This is another tame adventure aimed at the legions of nondiscriminating "Full House" fans. Recommended for parents contemplating pushing their own plain-Jane youngsters into show biz, this seasonal star vehicle is acceptable trick-or-treat fare for the junior pajama party set.

Preparations for a traditional jack-o-lantern Halloween get skewed when Oscar (Phil Fundacaro), a dwarf clown, awards twins Kelly (Mary-Kate Olsen) and Lynn Farmer (Ashley Olsen) a magic wand that turns out to be real. While visiting their truculent Aunt Agatha (Cloris Leachman) with their financially strapped parents (Kelli Fox and Eric McCormack), the girls shudder at the creepy tales of a roving grave digger (Wayne Robson), who fills them in on nasty Agatha's contentious relationship with her twin sister, Sophia (Cloris Leachman). Legend has it that witchy Agatha rubbed a moonstone to capture amiable Sophia's soul in a mirror. Unless Kelly and Lynn can chant the proper incantations at midnight, Sophia will be permanently imprisoned under glass. While trick or treating, Kelly and Lynn persuade two cooperative pals to take their places, unbeknownst to the sisters' mom and dad. En route to Aunt Agatha's mystery mansion, the Farmer girls meet a good-hearted con man, Mr. "N" (Meshach Taylor), and Oscar, who accompany them to Agatha's witches' coven conclave. Disguising themselves as a sorcerer with the power to double Agatha's powers, Mr. "N" and the diminutive party clown trick Agatha out of her magical bauble. Separated during a chase by black arts conventioneers, Lynn and the moonstone escape, but Kelly is nabbed and Mr. "N" is transformed into a crow. Before the twins wised-up parents can rescue them, Kelly and Lynn outwit Agatha with the help of Oscar, the grave digger, and Mr. "N" who, still in crow form, flies off with the powerful gemstone. Breaking the spell, Kelly and Lynn free Sophia, who is reunited with her boyfriend George (Matthew Walker), who had been forced to serve as Agatha's butler. With nasty Agatha safely mirrored up, Mr. "N" is released from feathery bewitchment, and Mom and Dad can save their home with the aid of beneficent Aunt Sophia.

As made-for-TV comedies go, this offshoot of the inexplicably popular "Full House" series is mezza-mezza family fare. A somewhat hokey kidflick, it explores twin psychology, the pitfalls of being physically different, and ultimate sibling rivalry. While none of the benign escapades is inspiringly conceived or executed, the plotline is developed adequately. Looming large over this harmlessly diverting project is Leachman, whose brio provides humor even during her most heinous moments, and whose presence enhances the telefilm's watchability. As for the pint-sized stars, they are an acquired taste best left unsampled by nonfans. With a uniquely offbeat comic delivery, they coil their cuteness around dialogue until innocent echoes take on surreal subtext. Everything about these TV properties bespeaks the average and homely, yet they are unmistakably stars and carefully packaged commodities whose appeal incredibly never wanes; it's as if the Baby Snooks child parody had been brought to life and then duplicated. (*Violence.*) — R.P.

d, Stuart Margolin; p, Mark Bacino, Adria Later; exec p, Jim Green, Allen Epstein; w, Jurgen Wolff; ph, Richard Leiterman; ed, George Appleby; m, Richard Bellis; prod d, David Fischer; set d, Shirley Inget; sound, Rick Patton (mixer), Jim Troutman; fx, Rory Cutler, Fantasy II; casting, Victoria Burrows; cos, Jane Still; makeup, Jayne Dancose; stunts, Ken Kirzinger

Children's/Comedy/Fantasy (PR: AA MPAA: NR)

DOUBLE HAPPINESS ★★★

(Canada) 96m First Generation Films ~ Fine Line c

Sandra Oh (*Jade Li*); Stephen Chang (*Dad Li*); Alannah Ong (*Mom Li*); Frances You (*Pearl Li*); Johnny Mah (*Andrew Chau*); Callum Rennie (*Mark*); Donald Fong (*Sau Wan Chin*); Claudette Carracedo (*Lisa Chan*); Barbara Tse (*Mrs. Mar*); Nathan Fong (*Robert Chu*); Lesley Ewen (*Carmen*); So Yee Shum (*Auntie Bing*); Greg Chen (*Uncle Bing*)

After decades of virtual invisibility in mainstream movies, Asian-American women became a hot topic in the early 1990s in features like THE JOY LUCK CLUB, PICTURE BRIDE, and A THOUSAND PIECES OF GOLD. A low-budget but worthy Canadian entry, DOUBLE HAPPINESS concerns a Hong Kong family in modern Vancouver's Chinatown, with debuting film-maker Mina Shum bringing a fresh point-of-view to a familiar account of clashing cultures.

In voice-over, Jade Li (Sandra Oh) recalls that she "grew up wondering why we could never be the Brady Bunch." Though she and younger sister Pearl (Frances You) are assimilated Chinese-Canadians, their parents remain devoted to ancient customs and rituals. The sitcom atmosphere of this lively household is tempered by the portentous memory of absent number-one son Winston, utterly disowned by father Quo Li (Stephen Chang) for straying too far from ancestral ways. Quo regards Jade's ambition to become an actress as a passing phase, while her mom (Alannah Ong) tries to match her with a succession of nice Chinese boys. The choicest catch, a young doctor, turns out to be a closet homosexual who shares Jade's amusement at their families' outmoded attitudes. They maintain a ruse of steady dating so he can cruise in secret; meanwhile Jade starts seeing Mark (Callum Rennie), a likeable Anglo.

Her thespian career is rocky. A major audition, to do Cantonese-language motion pictures for an Asian producer, fails because Jade can't read the Chinese writing in the untranslated scripts. Things finally boil over when Quo Li finds out about Mark. His daughter's relationship with a "white ghost" outrages the patriarch, and, like Winston before her, Jade is disowned and expelled. Mark now wants a serious commitment, but Jade refuses to be tied to him either, and strikes out alone, uncertain but independent.

Mina Shum and Sandra Oh, who met when both auditioned for a Canadian TV movie, drew heavily from their own lives for this bittersweet narrative. Generation gaps and tradition-bound elders are basic formulas in immigrant sagas, and it's occasionally hard to escape some sense of *deja vu*. Shum skillfully employs an overused cinematic technique—interludes in which the characters address the camera directly, explaining themselves to viewers, often more clearly than they do with each other. Mom Li recounts her carefully-controlled childhood and marriage, and the dire fates of those who dared disobey. Quo Li describes how he abandoned his dream of being an architect to raise his daughters. The script's observant sense of humor make the rigid father into a likeable, even jovial authority figure, and all the more poignant when he rejects his offspring.

Jade, in her private fantasy, is shown playing Blanche DuBois from *A Streetcar Named Desire* in full Peking Opera regalia, melding the best of East and West. Then she loses a succession of stage and screen opportunities because she's either too Chinese or not Chinese enough. Ironically, bits of DOUBLE HAPPINESS were judged by the distributor to be "too Chinese" for American audiences and some scenes were trimmed for the US release. Made on a $1 million budget, DOUBLE HAPPINESS won awards in Berlin and Torino and earned Sandra Oh Canada's Genie Award for Best Actress. (*Profanity, sexual situations.*) — C.C.

d, Mina Shum; p, Stephen Hegyes, Rose Lam Waddell; w, Mina Shum; ph, Peter Wunstorf; ed, Alison Grace; m, Shadowy Men on a Shadowy Planet; prod d, Michael Bjornson; art d, Candice Dickens, Jill Haras; set d, Francois Milly; sound, Tim Richardson; casting, Anne Anderson, Carmen Ruiz-Laza; cos, Cynthia Summers; makeup, Anya Ellis

Comedy (PR: C MPAA: PG-13)

DRACULA: DEAD AND LOVING IT ★

(U.S.) 90m Castle Rock; Brooksfilms ~ Columbia c

Leslie Nielsen (*Dracula*); Peter MacNicol (*Renfield*); Steven Weber (*Harker*); Amy Yasbeck (*Mina*); Lysette Anthony (*Lucy*); Harvey Korman (*Dr. Seward*); Mel Brooks (*Professor Van*

Helsing); Mark Blankfield *(Martin)*; Megan Cavanagh *(Essie)*; Clive Revill *(Sykes)*; Chuck McCann *(Innkeeper)*; Avery Schreiber *(Peasant in Coach)*; Cherie Franklin *(Peasant in Coach)*; Ezio Greggio *(Coach Driver)*; Leslie Sachs *(Usherette)*; Matthew Porretta *(Handsome Lieutenant at Ball)*; Rudy De Luca *(Guard)*; Jennifer Crystal *(Nurse)*; Darla Haun *(Brunette Vampire)*; Karen Roe *(Blond Vampire)*; Charlie Callas *(Man in Straight Jacket)*; Phillip Connery *(Ship Captain)*; Tony Griffin *(Crewman)*; Casey King *(Crewman)*; Nick Rempel *(Crewman)*; Zale Kessler *(Orchestra Leader)*; Barbaree Earl; Maura Nielsen; Thea Nielsen; Robin Shepard; Elaine Ballace; Maude Winchester *(Ballroom Guests)*; Lisa Cordray *(Hat Check Girl)*; Cindy Marshall-Day *(Young Lover at Picnic)*; Benjamin Livingston *(Young Lover at Picnic)*; Gregg Binkley *(Woodbridge)*; Anne Bancroft *(Gypsy Woman)*; David DeLuise; Tommy Koenig; Grinnell Morris; Vince Grant; Johnny Cocktails; Ric Coy; Michael Connors; Stephen Wolfe Smith; Richard Alan Stewart *(Interns)*; Carol Arthur; Sonje Fortag; Henry Kaiser; Loraine Shields; Derek Mark Lochran; Ira Miller; Kathleen Kane *(Villagers)*; David Savoy *(Specialty Dancer)*; Sharon Savoy *(Specialty Dancer)*

Leslie Nielsen, star of THE NAKED GUN movies, takes on the title role in Mel Brooks's lifeless and toothless parody of various Dracula flicks, especially Tod Browning's 1931 DRACULA.

In 1893, Count Dracula (Nielsen) travels from his Transylvanian castle to London, where he takes up residence next door to the asylum where Renfield (Peter MacNicol), his bug-eating minion, is confined. The asylum is run by Dr. Seward (Harvey Korman), who believes enemas are the key to good mental health. At the opera, Dracula meets Seward and his daughter, Mina (Amy Yasbeck), as well as her fiance, John Harker (Steven Weber), and Mina's friend, Lucy (Lysette Anthony). After strange bite marks appear on Lucy's unusually pale neck, Seward calls for the help of Dr. Van Helsing (Mel Brooks), a vampire expert. When Lucy becomes a vampire, Van Helsing compels Harker to drive a wooden stake into her heart. Then Dracula sets his sights on Mina. At a gala ball, Dracula is revealed to be a vampire, but he escapes and kidnaps Mina. Harker, Van Helsing, and Seward pursue and do battle with Dracula, but before he can make Mina his eternal bride, the Count is turned to dust when Renfield accidentally exposes him to sunlight.

A few effective gags emerge from this hectic concoction of unfunny pratfalls, juvenile mugging, and tedious enema jokes, but it's hard to believe that director Mel Brooks was also the man behind YOUNG FRANKENSTEIN, a coarse but frequently hilarious send-up of horror conventions. Here, the storytelling is awkward, the jokes recycled, the slapstick ineptly executed. For the most part, the cast just stands around smirking, apparently amused by their own accents. Even the title is a 30-year-old catch-phrase from Brooks's TV sitcom "Get Smart!" There was faint hope that the infusion of Nielsen's talent, along with a return to the horror milieu of the great YOUNG FRANKENSTEIN, might resurrect Brooks' reputation. Instead, DRACULA: DEAD AND LOVING IT might just be the final nail in his comedic coffin. *(Profanity.)* — P.R.

d, Mel Brooks; p, Mel Brooks; exec p, Peter Schindler; assoc p, Robert Latham Brown, Leah Zappy; w, Mel Brooks, Rudy De Luca, Steve Haberman (from a story by Rudy De Luca and Steve Haberman, based on characters created by Bram Stoker); ph, Michael D. O'Shea; ed, Adam Weiss; m, Hummie Mann; prod d, Roy Forge Smith; art d, Bruce Robert Hill; set d, Jan Pascale; ch, Alan Johnson; sound, Jeff Wexler, Don Coufal, Gary Holland; fx, Richard Ratliff, Mike Shea, Dream Quest Images; casting,

Lindsay D. Chag, Bill Shepard; cos, Dodie Shepard; makeup, Alan "Doc" Friedman; stunts, Gary Combs

Comedy/Horror (PR: C MPAA: PG-13)

DREAM A LITTLE DREAM 2 ★★
(U.S.) 91m Dreamsquared Productions ~
Columbia TriStar Home Video c

Corey Haim *(Dinger Holfield)*; Corey Feldman *(Bobby Keller)*; Stacie Randall *(Lena Drago)*; Michael Nicolosi *(Hanke)*; Robyn Lively *(Rachel Holfield)*

Corey Feldman and Corey Haim are together again in this over-plotted, straight-to-video sequel to DREAM A LITTLE DREAM, their 1989 B-movie hit.

Since their last outing, Dinger Holfield (Haim) and Bobby Keller (Feldman) have moved, with Bobby's sister Rachel (Robyn Lively), from Cleveland to Hollywood, where Dinger aspires to live a middle-class lifestyle by selling suits in a men's shop. Dinger, meanwhile, pursues a more spiritual existence, while working at a condom store. One day, Dinger and Bobby receive a package from a deceased friend containing two pairs of sunglasses. The friends quickly discover that the glasses have magical powers, compelling the wearer of one pair to carry out the wishes of the wearer of the second pair. The seductive Lena Drago (Stacie Randall) steals the glasses and Bobby is arrested for the theft. Thanks to a seance Bobby holds in his jail cell, Dinger and Rachel recover the glasses before Lena can sell them to a wealthy dealer, kill the bad guys, and discover that they have always loved each other. When Bobby is finally released from jail, he and Dinger throw away the glasses, which have only caused them trouble.

Did the world really need a sequel to 1989's DREAM A LITTLE DREAM, a belated carbon copy of the once-fashionable body-switching formula (e.g. LIKE FATHER, LIKE SON, 1987)? This time, the emphasis is on the teenagers, but the crime plot seems like a rehash of a USA cable-TV movie with voguish New Age elements and would-be arty dream sequences thrown in for good measure.

The real interest in DREAM A LITTLE DREAM 2 should have been the reteaming of the Coreys, Feldman and Haim, but the real-life friends spend little on-screen time together, and the comic potential of the Felix-and-Oscar role reversal caused by the magic glasses is almost completely thrown away. (And just why is it that the less charismatic Feldman always gets the bigger part in the Corey-Corey oeuvre?) Fans of the pair will have to return to the more suspenseful LOST BOYS (1987) or the more cheerfully screwball LICENSE TO DRIVE (1988) for a better "Corey" picture. *(Violence, sexual situations, profanity.)* — E.M.

d, James Lemmo; p, Paul Hertzberg; exec p, Christopher J. Black; w, David Weissman, Susan Forman

Comedy/Thriller/Crime (PR: C MPAA: PG-13)

DREAMING OF RITA ★★½
(Sweden) 108m FilmLance International ~
First Run Features c
(DROEMMEN OM RITA)

Marika Lagercrantz *(Rita)*; Per Oscarsson *(Bob)*; Philip Zanden *(Steff)*; Patrik Ersgard *(Erik)*; Yaba Holst *(Sandra)*; Adam Blanning *(Adam)*; Lise Ringheim; Gertt Fylking; Tomas Norstrom; Mikael Segerstrom

Alternately wistful and whimsical, DREAMING OF RITA revolves around a romance that's straitlaced even by the standards of Hollywood's golden age. But it contains several interesting characters, including one who's obsessed with Rita Hayworth.

DREAMING OF RITA is set in modern day Sweden. As a young man, cinematographer Bob (Per Oscarsson) was so enamored of Hayworth that he named his daughter after her. Now the elderly Bob seems more interested in watching Rita Hayworth movies than attending his wife's funeral. The adult Rita (Marika Lagercrantz), a musician, tries to hold her own family together while mourning her mother's death. Husband Steff (Philip Zanden) is preoccupied with his business, and Rita alone looks after their new-born, Adam (Adam Blanning), and restless teenage daughter Sandra (Yaba Holst).

After the funeral, Bob's Hayworth fixation prompts him to search for Sabine, the beautiful woman he loved before he met his wife. Rita, with Adam in tow, follows Bob as he travels by train to the hotel that Sabine used to manage. At a station, Rita persuades Bob to join her in her car and agrees to bring Erik (Patrik Ersgard), Bob's new-found traveling companion, along.

As Rita, Bob, Erik and the baby make their way toward the hotel, Steff tries to find his wife. Rita and the free-spirited Erik have a brief affair, and Erik then goes his own way. At Sabine's old hotel they learn she's no longer an employee, but the concierge suggests that they try the Hotel Cansino (Hayworth's real name) by the seashore.

Meanwhile, Steff happens to meet Erik on the road, and gets the same tip about the Hotel Cansino. Unaware that Erik has been Rita's lover, Steff invites him to come along. Bob finally finds Sabine, who doesn't remember him. Rita draws Sabine aside and asks her to pretend; she obliges by dressing up in 1940s garb and spending the night with the old man. Steff arrives the next morning and pleads with Rita to return to him. But when Steff finds out about Erik, the two men begin to duke it out. The battle is interrupted by Sabine's announcement that Bob died during the night. Erik walks away, leaving the family to pull itself together.

DREAMING OF RITA aspires to quirky originality in the manner of films by Lasse Hallstrom and Emir Kusturica. But it's really telling a resolutely old-fashioned story in a surprisingly traditional way. Staffan Erstam's screenplay not only incorporates references to GILDA—the 1946 Hayworth picture Bob so admires—but (consciously or not) duplicates the sort of melodramatic love triangle in which Hayworth was so often enmeshed. The Swedish Rita has an uncaring husband who wants to own her and a boyfriend who's less socially powerful, but more worthy of her. In a twist that makes those older films seem more progressive than the new one, DREAMING OF RITA ends with Rita returning to her spouse. Steff's journey to find Rita supposedly loosens up his character—he's wearing a leather jacket and riding a motorcycle by the time he meets up with Rita at the Hotel—but he continues to say things like,"I hate those modern feminist husbands," and there's no reason to disbelieve him.

Director Jon Lindstrom occasionally manages to make DREAMING OF RITA seem less conventional than it really is, and odd moments mix with touching ones in a pleasant way. The best of the picture's sentimental interludes include a father-daughter scene between Bob and Rita in the hotel, and Sabine's wistful recollections of the past: "They all loved Gilda, but they woke up with me," she tells Rita, in a paraphrase of Hayworth's famous lament. *(Violence, nudity, sexual situations, profanity.)* — E.M.

d, Jon Lindstrom; p, Borje Hansson; w, Jon Lindstrom, Rita Holst; ph, Khell Lagerroos; prod d, Staffan Erstam; sound, Jan Brodin, Gail Brodin; cos, Lenamari Wallstrom

Drama/Adventure/Romance   **(PR: AA   MPAA: NR)**

ECLIPSE ★★½
(Canada/Germany) 95m Fire Dog Films;
TiMe Medienvertieb ~ Strand Releasing c/bw

Von Flores *(Henry)*; John Gilbert *(Brian)*; Pascale Montpetit *(Sylvie)*; Manuel Aranguiz *(Gabriel)*; Maria Del Mar *(Sarah)*; Greg Ellwand *(Norman)*; Matthew Ferguson *(Angelo)*; Earl Pastko *(Michael)*; Daniel MacIvor *(Jim)*; Kirsten Johnson *(Carlotta)*

ECLIPSE is a gorgeously photographed but dramatically muddled study of several characters who experience sexual and spiritual crises on the eve of a solar eclipse.

Angelo (Matthew Ferguson) is documenting Toronto's carnivalesque atmosphere for a school video project two weeks prior to the much-anticipated eclipse. Over the next few days, Angelo and nine other characters form discreet sexual liaisons with one another. First, Brian (John Gilbert), a married businessman, pays Henry (Von Flores), an Asian prostitute, for sex, before returning home, where he resumes an affair with Sylvie (Pascale Montpetit), his Quebecois housekeeper. Later, Sylvie seduces Gabriel (Manuel Aranguiz), a Central American refugee, at their Second Language school. Gabriel then keeps a rendezvous with Sarah (Maria Del Mar), the Venezuelan wife of his immigration lawyer, Norman (Greg Ellwand).

That night, Sarah and Norman reaffirm their commitment to one another, but, the next day, Norman picks up Angelo, the student-documentarian, and has sex with him in a hotel room. Angelo then meets Michael (Earl Pastko), an artist, who uses him for strictly physical intimacy. Michael later visits his best friend, Jim (Daniel MacIvor), an actor, but their casual sexual union ends with Jim's admission that he has loved Michael for many years. That night in a gay disco, Jim is accosted by Carlotta (Kirsten Johnson), a wild bar girl, who forces Jim into making love. The following morning, Carlotta wakes up in Henry's bed. As darkness descends upon the city, all the film's characters view the eclipse in isolation, reflecting on the previous connections they have made.

Not to be confused with the concurrent release, TOTAL ECLIPSE, ECLIPSE represents the latest 1990s update on Arthur Schnitzler's 1890s play, *La Ronde*, which introduced the clever, circular narrative device where character A meets character B, character B meets character C, until the story comes back to character A. In 1993, there was the abysmal CIRCLE OF DESIRE, and earlier in 1995, the pretentious, overrated KIDS. Now, with ECLIPSE, director Jeremy Podeswa (in his debut feature) contributes another film that should provide amusement and pathos, but winds up creating frustration and boredom (Max Ophuls, this ain't).

The main problem is that the *La Ronde* format gives the many sketchily-drawn characters only a few minutes each to convince the audience they are worth caring about. When they break down to cry or give confessional speeches, the moments seem forced, evoking unintended titters more than sympathy. Matters are not helped by the often amateurish acting by most in the ensemble.

Even so, the sexually-charged circular character links keep one watching almost voyeuristically, and the scheme of putting each sequence in a difference monochrome color (yellow ochre, icy blue, et al.) is at least initially intriguing, even if it ultimately means nothing. However, the cinematography by Miroslaw Baszak is exquisite. Also, the documentary footage of Toronto residents during the eclipse (the only scenes in full color) breaks up the story segments by making a startling contrast, texturally and tonally. *(Nudity, sexual situations, adult situations, substance abuse, profanity.)* — E.M.

d, Jeremy Podeswa; p, Camelia Frieberg, Jeremy Podeswa; exec p, Wolfram Tichy; assoc p, Regine Schmid; co-p, Jeremy Podeswa; w, Jeremy Podeswa; ph, Miroslaw Baszak; ed, Susan Maggi; m, Ernie Tollar; art d, Tamara Deverell; set d, Michael McShane; sound, David Horton (mixer); cos, Aline Gilmore; makeup, Sylvain Cournoyer

Drama/Erotic   (PR: O   MPAA: NR)

ELSA
(SEE: AILSA)

EMBRACE OF THE VAMPIRE ★★
(U.S.) 93m General Media Entertainment;
Moving Pictures I; Ministry of Film ~
New Line Home Video c

Alyssa Milano *(Charlotte)*; Martin Kemp *(Vampire)*; Harrison Pruett *(Chris)*; Jordan Ladd *(Eliza)*; Rachel True *(Nicole)*; Charlotte Lewis *(Sarah)*; Jennifer Tilly *(Marika)*; Robbin Julien *(Rob)*; David Portlock *(Peter)*; Gregg Vance *(Jonathan)*; John Riedlinger *(Milo)*; Ladd Vance *(Mark)*; Lynn Philip Siebel *(Professor)*; Rebecca Ferratti *(Princess)*; Glori Gold *(Nymph #1)*; Shawna Ryan *(Nymph #2)*; Sabrina Allen *(Nymph #3)*; Christopher Utesch *(Guy in Hallway)*

More concerned with the soft-core than the supernatural, this is a tepid tale of bloodsucker eros.

Charlotte (Alyssa Milano) is a college student who was raised by nuns after her father died, which helps explain why she won't sleep with her boyfriend Chris (Harrison Pruett) until she turns 18. Three nights before her birthday, she begins receiving nocturnal visits from another suitor—a vampire (Martin Kemp) who was once a nobleman and needs her virgin blood to keep from falling into "eternal sleep." He begins to seduce Charlotte in what she at first believes are dreams, kills her friend Nicole (Rachel True) after a party, and attempts to plant seeds of doubt in Chris's mind.

Charlotte begins to have increasingly erotic dreams and hallucinations, and nearly gives in to a seduction by her dorm neighbor Sarah (Charlotte Lewis). The vampire transforms himself into a woman named Marika (Jennifer Tilly) to tempt Chris into straying, while Charlotte ends up biting Sarah's tongue when Sarah comes to apologize. The vampire kills the bitchy Eliza (Jordan Ladd) and impels Charlotte to come to the campus clock tower that night to give herself over to him. Chris follows her, however, and when Charlotte calls out his name, the vampire realizes that her heart truly belongs to Chris, and vanishes.

EMBRACE OF THE VAMPIRE marks the feature directing debut of Anne Goursaud, whose most pertinent previous credit would appear to be her work as an editor on BRAM STOKER'S DRACULA. But the movie has a lot more in common with her stint at the helm of one of Zalman King's RED SHOE DIARIES cable series. Goursaud and the writers forego any attempts at true horror, making their vampire a sexual predator who inspires Charlotte to dream, not of blood and death, but of hedonism and orgies. The sex scenes are occasionally effective (particularly Sarah's attempted seduction of Charlotte), but the languid pace and lack of truly interesting twists in the story prevent it from building tension or holding much interest beyond the prurient.

EMBRACE OF THE VAMPIRE was notable for marking former "Who's the Boss?" star Milano's transition into more "adult" roles—meaning that she takes her clothes off an awful lot (especially in the unrated cassette version). She and her other young co-stars are relatively convincing, and certainly look good in their various states of undress. Kemp, however, proves to be a rather dramatically ineffective vampire. He spends entirely too much time bemoaning his plight, and even announces to Charlotte up front that he won't harm Chris because that would break her heart. It doesn't make him the most compelling menace. *(Violence, extensive nudity, sexual situations, substance abuse, profanity.)* — M.G.

d, Anne Goursaud; p, Marylin Vance, Alan Mruvka; exec p, Ladd Vance, Matt Ferro; assoc p, Rick Filon; w, Halle Eaton, Nicole Coady, Rick Bitzelberger; ph, Suki Medencevic; ed, Terilyn A. Shropshire; m, Joseph Williams; prod d, Peter Stolz; art d, Fontaine Beauchamp Hebb; set d, Don Diers; sound, Serge Popovic (recordist); casting, Shana Landsburg; cos, Dana R. Woods; makeup, Donna Cicatelli-Lewis

Erotic/Horror (PR: O MPAA: NR)

EMPIRE RECORDS ★★
(U.S.) 100m New Regency Productions ~ Warner Bros. c

Anthony LaPaglia *(Joe)*; Maxwell Caulfield *(Rex Manning)*; Debi Mazar *(Jane)*; Rory Cochrane *(Lucas)*; Johnny Whitworth *(A.J.)*; Liv Tyler *(Corey)*; Robin Tunney *(Debra)*; Renee Zellweger *(Gina)*; Ethan Randall *(Mark)*; Coyote Shivers *(Berko)*; Brendan Sexton *(Warren)*; James "Kimo" Wills *(Eddie)*; Ben Bode *(Mitchell)*; Gary Bolen *(Croupier)*; Kimber Monroe *(Woman at Craps Table)*; Tony Zaar *(High Roller)*; Patt Noday *(Reporter)*; Julia Howard *(Kathy)*; Kessia Randall *(Autograph Girl)*; Michele Seidman *(Cop #1)*; Diana Taylor *(Cop #2)*; Bernard Granger *(Cop #3)*; Mike Harding *(Cop #4)*; Oderus Urungus *(Lead Singer)*; Gwar *(Band in Mark's Daydream)*; Kawan Rojanatavorn *(Flower Delivery Guy)*; Corey Joshua Taylor *(Roulette Table Man)*; Melissa Caulfield *(Ballet Dancer)*; Lara Travis *(Veronica)*; Dianna Miranda *(Lilly)*; Rico Fleming *(Couch Kid #1)*; Brandon Crawford *(Couch Kid #2)*; Elizabeth Grapentien *("Say No More" Woman)*; Pandora J. Nousianen *(CD Customer)*; Nello Tare *(Mello)*; Kelley Carruth *(Girl on Couch)*; Mark Menchhofer *(Clapton Customer)*; Toby Maguire *(Andre)*; Anthony Hemingway *(Boom Box Kid)*; Paizhe Pressley *(Girl #1)*; Joanna Canton *(Girl #2)*; Lee Etta Sutton *(Button Customer)*; Craig Edwards *(Male Rex Manning Fan)*; Jesse Bechtel *(Customer #1)*; Karen Brigman *(Customer #2)*; David Myers Gray *(Customer #3)*; Bob Sayer *(Customer #4)*; David Lenthall *(Meg Ryan Customer)*; Andrea Powell *(Mariah Carey Customer)*

This effort from director Allan Moyle is not the anthem to disaffected Gen-Xers that his first film, PUMP UP THE VOLUME, was (though he may have hoped it would be). However, EMPIRE RECORDS does have enough energy and entertaining moments to be a pleasant diversion for the same audience.

Welcome to Empire Records, an independent record store open since 1959, and open every night till midnight. Let's meet the employees. There's Joe (Anthony LaPaglia), the good guy manager; Lucas (Rory Cochrane), the beatnik Buddha; Gina (Renee Zellweger), the slut; Corey (Liv Tyler),"Little Miss Perfect"; Debra (Robin Tunney), the troubled rebel; A.J. (Johnny Whitworth), the sensitive artist; and Mark (Ethan Randall), the stoner-punk. Today is going to be a big day at Empire—not just because pop music's lamest and cheesiest video-lothario, Rex Manning (Maxwell Caulfield), is coming to sign autographs, but also because a lot of dramas are going to play out.

Joe will have to stop the store's owner, Mitchell Beck (Ben Bode), who *hates* music, from turning Empire into a corporate controlled chain store. Lucas will have to come up with the $9,104 in store receipts that he gambled away in Atlantic City

last night. Debra will shave her head and admit to a recent suicide attempt. A.J. will finally tell Corey that he loves her. Corey, though, has eyes for Rex and will offer him her virginity, but back down when he accepts. Gina will offer herself to Rex, and not back down when he accepts. A boy dubbed "Warren" (Brendan Sexton), will be caught shoplifting and later return with a gun, but his anger will be quelled when Joe offers him a job. At a mock funeral for Debra, everyone will reveal their secrets, their ambitions, and their fears. They will realize that despite their surface differences, they're all the same underneath—terrified about the future. And it will become apparent that with Joe in charge, Empire is a haven for a variety of "damaged," though stereotypically categorized, kids. When it looks like they're all going to end up on the street, they will throw a big party and get their customers to "donate" the money to keep Empire out of the hands of "The Man." And Corey will finally admit that she loves A.J. too.

If EMPIRE RECORDS was intended to combine the poignant, though simplistic, insights of THE BREAKFAST CLUB with a milder version of CLERKS's "slackers on the job" humor, it falls short on both counts. With the attractive assemblage of Empire employees spending a lot of time dancing with the music cranked, and spending a lot more time on the big couch in the back room talking, the movie plays like an extended intermixture of the TV shows "Friends" and "Hullabaloo." EMPIRE RECORDS does feature 50 *(fifty!)* songs mixmastered and played over its 90-minute running time, and what with all the montages of activity in place of actual scenes, viewers accustomed to channel-surfing and MTV won't have the chance to get bored before they figure out the movie is just a long commercial for the soundtrack album. *(Profanity, sexual situations.)* — P.R.

d, Allan Moyle; p, Arnon Milchan, Michael Nathanson, Tony Ludwig, Alan Riche; co-p, Paul Kurta; w, Carol Heikkinen; ph, Walt Lloyd; ed, Michael Chandler; prod d, Peter Jamison; art d, John Huke; set d, Linda Spheeris; sound, Douglas Axtell (mixer); fx, Greg Hull; casting, Gail Levin; cos, Susan Lyall; makeup, Jeff Goodwin; stunts, Jery Hewitt

Comedy/Drama (PR: C MPAA: PG-13)

ENEMY WITHIN, THE ★★½
(U.S.) 90m Vincent Pictures Productions; HBO Pictures ~ HBO Home Video c

Forest Whitaker *(Colonel MacCasey)*; Sam Waterston *(President William Foster)*; Dana Delany *(Chief of Staff Betsy Corcoran)*; Jason Robards *(General Lloyd)*; Josef Sommer *(Secretary of Defense Potter)*; Lisa Summerour *(Jean Casey)*; Willie Norwood, Jr. *(Todd Casey)*; George Dzundza *(Jake)*; Isabelle Glasser *(Sarah)*; Dakin Matthews *(Vice President Walter Kelly)*; William O'Leary *(Billy)*; Rory Aylward; Greg Brickman; David Combs; Patricia Donaldson; Denise Dowse; Yolanda Gaskins; Jayne Hess; Chuck Hicks; Leonard Kelly-Young; Archie Lang; Barry Lynch; Ryan MacDonald; Anthony Peck; Lawrence Pressman *(Attorney General Art Daniels)*; George Marshall Ruge; Steven Ruge; Michael Buchman Silver

Paranoia about the US government is a time-honored Hollywood tradition that has produced masterworks like THE PARALLAX VIEW, cult films like WINTER KILLS, sturdy thrillers like SEVEN DAYS IN MAY (which this cable production remakes), and assembly-line feather-rufflers like THE ENEMY WITHIN. Once again, the Pentagon brass and a flock of Benedict Arnolds serve as easy targets so one rugged individualist can save democracy single-handedly.

Career officer Col. MacCasey (Forest Whitaker) has a hard time shaking off his sneer of cold command when he comes home to his wife Jean (Lisa Summerour) and son Todd (Willie Norwood, Jr.). Meanwhile, President William Foster (Sam Waterston) infuriates militaristic General Lloyd (Jason Robards) when he announces defense cuts. Casey accesses a gambling pool in Lloyd's computer, but he doesn't realize that Lloyd and Defense Secretary Potter (Josef Sommer) are plotting to force the President's resignation, and that the Pentagon computer carries a top secret code for a domestic invasion masterminded by them. Upcoming weekend maneuvers will in fact provide a cover for a military coup deploying 100,000 troops. Attempting to embarrass great white liberal Foster out of office, the takeover, financed by millionaire businessmen, heralds a military-backed oligarchy. So determined are the right-wingers that they murder squeamish Attorney General Art Daniels (Lawrence Pressman) at a crowded party with a chemical agent that causes a heart attack. Secretly coached by KGB operative Jake (George Dzundza), who does not relish a hawklike US regime, Casey outlines the conspiracy to the skeptical President and Chief of Staff Betsy Corcoran (Dana Delaney) and interrogates the late Daniels's secretary Sarah (Isabel Glasser), a Russian double agent. By planting an incriminating document in Lloyd's files, Casey forestalls the plot to declare the President incompetent. Snatching victory from the jaws of defeat, President Foster forcibly retires Lloyd and bides his time before reckoning with Potter, 22 generals, and treacherous Vice President Walter Kelly (Dakin Matthews). Willing to sacrifice his own career by linking himself falsely with the proposed junta, Casey patriotically ensures the sanctity of the Oval Office.

Two top screenwriters, Darryl (THE LAST DETAIL) Ponsican and Ron (RAIN MAN) Bass, stub their toes on this HBO update of the classic SEVEN DAYS IN MAY. Thrillers about power-lusting politicos and crazed Pentagonians need to scare the bejeezus out of viewers if they are to have any point at all. Reasonably engrossing, THE ENEMY WITHIN is neither realistically frightening nor far-fetchedly suspenseful. It simply runs its course through the usual red herrings and obfuscatory obstacles; we seem to be one step ahead of Casey as he deciphers the Machiavellian meanings buried in Lloyd's computer database. Without the Soviets as a Cold War scapegoat, action films have been forced to scramble for villains: multinational terrorists lack the eclat of Soviet bogeymen so the government nogoodnik is a safe standby. But this kind of material requires razor-sharp timing and sweeping cinematic handling to override the inherent implausibility of the conspiracy scenario. Professional to its finger tips and adroitly acted as it is, THE ENEMY WITHIN's TV movie-of-the-week treatment is prosaic and unstylish. Frittering away precious running time on Casey's domestic shortcomings and failing to give credibility to Casey's rather quick-sprouting suspicions, the film peters out without a crescendo. (Graphic violence, profanity, adult situations.) — R.P.

d, Jonathan Darby; p, Robert A. Papazian; exec p, Peter Douglas; w, Ron Bass, Darryl Ponicsan (based on the 1964 screenplay "Seven Days in May" by Rod Serling, based on the novel by Fletcher Knebel and Charles Waldo Bailey, II); ph, Kees Van Oostrum; ed, Peter Zimmer; m, Joe Delia; prod d, Donald Light-Harris; sound, Itzhak Magal

Thriller/Political (PR: C MPAA: NR)

ENGLISHMAN WHO WENT UP A HILL ★★½
BUT CAME DOWN A MOUNTAIN, THE
(U.K.) 99m Parallax Pictures ~ Miramax c

Hugh Grant (*Reginald Anson*); Tara Fitzgerald (*Betty of Cardiff*); Colm Meaney (*Morgan the Goat*); Ian Hart (*Johnny Shell-shocked*); Kenneth Griffith (*Reverend Jones*); Ian McNiece

(*George Garrad*); Robert Blythe (*Ivor the Grocer*); Robert Pugh (*Williams the Petroleum*); Lisa Palfrey (*Blod*); Garfield Morgan (*Davies the School*); Jack Walters (*Grandfather*); Howell Evans (*Thomas the Trains*); Tudor Vaughan (*Thomas Twp*); Hugh Vaughan (*Thomas Twp, Too*); David Lloyd Meredith (*Jones the JP*); Dafydd Wyn Roberts (*Tommy Twostrokes*); Iuean Rhys (*Sergeant Thomas*); Anwen Williams (*Mavis*); Harry Kretchmer (*Young Boy*); Maisie McNeice (*Girl in Classroom*); Fraser Cains (*Evans the End of the World*)

A charming and oh-so-British curio, this LOCAL HERO variation set in Wales is hobbled by its deference to marquee attraction Hugh Grant.

A Sunday in 1917. Army map-makers Reginald Anson (Grant) and George Garrad (Ian McNiece) arrive in the tiny Welsh village of Ffynnon Garw to measure the local peak. Mid-week, they shock the villagers assembled at Morgan the Goat's (Colm Meaney's) tavern by announcing that the hill is 984 feet high, 16 feet short of the 1000 that counts for a mountain on the Queen's maps. This is quite a blow to local pride, and at the joint urging of Morgan and the Reverend Jones (Kenneth Griffith)—who otherwise have no use for each other—the people of Ffynnon Garw set out to add the necessary height to the hill. They spend a day trudging up and down the hillside, carrying dirt from their gardens in buckets by hand. The opportunistic Morgan sets up a refreshment stand along the trail, and the two cartographers find themselves stranded by mysteriously car trouble.

The job takes longer than expected, so Morgan brings in pretty, flirtatious Betty (Tara Fitzgerald) to keep Anson occupied. While the townspeople work, Betty and Reggie fall in love. The 82-year-old Reverend collapses during his labors, and with his dying breath asks to be buried at the top of "the mountain." All through the night, the people—and Anson—work. Monday morning, Anson comes down from the summit with news: Ffynnon Garw Mountain is 1002 feet high, and he wants to marry Betty.

First time writer-director Christopher Monger could be accused of making a mountain out of a molehill, but he'd doubtless take it as a compliment. The tale of THE ENGLISHMAN WHO WENT UP A HILL BUT CAME DOWN A MOUNTAIN was told to a very young Monger by his grandfather, and his sincere affection for the subject is clear. But an anecdote does not a movie make.

First, there's no real conflict—only time and the weather stand in the townspeople's way. Anson and Garrad seem only peripherally involved in the story. The story's slightness isn't an insurmountable problem, but Monger's script doesn't contain the touches of irony, absurdity, or fantasy that would flesh it out. Grant and Fitzgerald brought a playful naturalness to the roles of a minister and his wife in SIRENS, but their pairing here feels forced, and their romance seems to be occurring in another movie. The excessive screen time give to Grant—still riding the wave of FOUR WEDDINGS AND A FUNERAL—detracts from the film's real stars: Kenneth Griffith and Colm Meaney (THE SNAPPER and TV's "Star Trek: The Next Generation"). They're both wonderful, and THE ENGLISHMAN. . . would have benefited from more time spent with them and the other endearing eccentrics of Ffynnon Garw.

The character of Johnny Shellshock (Ian Hart) introduces a poignant and evocative subtext into this otherwise light-hearted affair. In 1917, British boys were dying in trenches on the continent, far from sleepy villages like Ffynnon Garw. The villagers' quest to keep their mountain suggests a larger emotional need to mount a defense against the unwelcome changes being forced on them by a heretofore unknown outside world. More honest emotion and less artificial romance would have gone a long way towards making THE ENGLISHMAN WHO WENT UP A HILL BUT CAME DOWN A MOUNTAIN a better film. — P.R.

d, Chris Monger; p, Sara Curtis; exec p, Sally Hibbin, Robert Jones, Bob Weinstein, Harvey Weinstein; assoc p, Paul Sarony; w, Chris Monger (from a story by Ifor David Monger and Ivor Monger); ph, Vernon Layton; ed, David Martin; m, Stephen Endelman; prod d, Charles Garrad; art d, Chris Lowe; set d, Tina Jones; sound, George Richards (mixer); fx, Mervyn Loynes, First Effects, Cinesite Europe Ltd.; casting, Michelle Guish; cos, Janty Yates; makeup, Kezia De Winne, Joceline Andrews

Comedy/Romance　　　　　　　　　**(PR: A　MPAA: PG)**

ERMO　　　　　　　　　　　　　　　★★★½
(Hong Kong/China) 95m Ocean Film Company; Shanghai Film Studio ~ Arrow c

Alia *(Ermo)*; Liu Peiqi *(Xiazi—Blindman)*; Ge Zhijun *(Village Chief—Ermo's Husband)*; Zhang Haiyan *(Fatwoman—Xiazi's Wife)*; Yan Zhenguo *(Huzi—Ermo's Son)*; Yang Xiao *(Xiu'er—Xiazi's Daughter)*; Yang Shenxia; Zhi Yanyan; Shen Enshen; Chen Baochang; Wu Jun; Du Hui; Li Yong'gui; Gao Songhai; Yang Wenming; Yue Guizhi; Ren Fengwu; Wang Wenzhi; Wang Shiling; Wang Jinbao; Zhang Guizhi; Li Guiming; Zhang Xiaoyan; Zhang Yiying; Yang Xiaoxia; Guo Shuguang

For its 1995 US theatrical release, this 1994 Chinese film was promoted as a serious comedy, but there aren't many laughs to be found in this otherwise wonderful story about a woman's struggle to rise in economic and social position by acquiring the largest color television in town.

Ermo (Alia) is a young, ambitious woman who must support her older, enfeebled husband (Ge Zhijun) and their son. Her husband was once chief of the village and the locals still refer to him by title, but in an affectionate, mocking tone. A competitive rivalry develops between Ermo and her neighbor Fatwoman (Zhang Haiyan). Ermo wishes she had a television and a useful husband, and Fatwoman wishes she had a son. Fatwoman's husband Blindman (Liu Peiqi) drives a truck and provides well for his wife, who sits at home stuffing her face and watching television. This television makes them popular in town, particularly with the young children, and every evening, after selling her twisted noodles on the street, Ermo must drag her son out of Fatwoman's house. Ermo believes the only escape from her rage and jealousy is to buy a color television larger than Fatwoman's.

Ermo works herself ragged making noodles, often waking in the night and pounding the dough with her feet for hours, and then pushing it through the press until her arms tremble. Blindman admires her ambition and offers to drive her to town every day. He soon falls in love with her and in an effort to help her achieve her goal gets her a job making noodles in a restaurant and secretly subsidizes her wages. One day on the way home the truck breaks down and he tries to rape her. She fends him off but then offers her body of her own free will. They become lovers, but when she discovers that he has been padding her wages she returns the money to him, ends the affair, and returns to selling noodles on the street.

When Ermo finally earns enough money to purchase the television, she discovers she can find no appropriate place for it in her home. She and her husband move it from one spot to the next and in exasperation decide to keep it on the bed. All the children in town converge on the house and bring their stools. The film ends with Ermo and her family sleeping on the floor amongst the clutter of empty stools. Ermo awakes late at night after the programming has ended and peers solemnly at the blank screen of white noise.

Underlying this plot is a strong criticism of China's movement toward capitalist values, as well as a portrait of the emerging independence of women and the bankruptcy of fetishistic desires. Ermo's husband wants to spend the extra money on a new house, but he is powerless to Ermo's will. Using a traditional metaphor to describe their new reality, he warns that a "house is a hen but a television is only an egg," and in the end his words are validated when they must sacrifice Ermo's work spoon to secure the antenna to the roof.

Ermo's longing for the luxury of a traditional female role like Fatwoman's, with a higher social status and the freedom to stay home with her child, is fetishized onto the desire for a television—paradoxically a vessel embodying dreams of a new modern society in which women have power and where hard work is rewarded by financial gain. She stubbornly insists on independence and yet secretly longs for the rewards of servitude. Similarly, Blindman hates his wife's sloth and admires Ermo, but in an effort to help Ermo he makes the traditional gestures that enslave and belittle.

Although its conclusions are rather conservative ideologically, the film interestingly compares gender conflict to the political conflict of a communist society moving to an open market—depicting the tension and ambivalent desires of a changing society emerging under the shadow of Western economic and political dominance. The cultural incongruity of this movement is exemplified by a bloated color television depicting glamorous blonde women speaking Chinese. *(Violence, sexual situations, adult situations.)* — R.C.

d, Zhou Xiaowen; p, Chen Kunming, Jimmy Tan; exec p, Li Ran; w, Lang Yun (based on the novella by Xu Baoqi); ph, Lu Gengxin; ed, Zhong Furong; m, Zhou Xiaowen; art d, Zhang Daqian; sound, Hong Yi (recordist); cos, Liu Qingli; makeup, Lu Yingchun

Comedy/Drama　　　　　　　　　**(PR: A　MPAA: NR)**

EROTIQUE　　　　　　　　　　　　★★½
(U.S./Germany) 91m Group 1 Films; Trigon; Tedpoly Films ~ Group One Distribution c

Kamala Lopez-Dawson *(Rosie)*; Bryan Cranston *(Dr. Robert Stern)*; Ron Orbach *(Nikki)*; Ray Oriel *(Eddie)*; Liane Curtis *(Officer Murphy)*; Vincent Cook; Hardy R. Franklin; Buckley Norris; Kal Clarke; Janet Haley; Tairrie B.; Dianna Miranda; Wade Dominguez; Kayla Allen; Sunshine Bainbridge; Ron Ray; Robert Kotecki; Michelle Clunie; Priscilla Barnes *(Claire)*; Camilla Soeberg *(Julia)*; Michael Carr *(Victor)*; Marianne Sagebrecht *(Hilde)*; Peter Kern *(Franz)*; Tanita Tikaram *(Azian)*; Peter Lohmeyer; Christoph Schlingensief; Christoph Eichhorn; Armin Dellapiccola; Thomas Tielsch; Alex Farfan; Frank Moller; Tim Lounibos *(Adrian)*; Hayley Man *(Ann)*; Choi Hark-kin *(The Uncle)*

EROTIQUE is a trio of short films all directed by women and marketed as a kaleidoscopic overview of female sexual fantasies.

Lizzie Borden's LET'S TALK ABOUT SEX is about a Latino actress turned phone sex operator (Kamala Lopez-Dawson), who is fed up with the same old racist, predictable lesbian fantasies of her male clientele. In danger of losing her job when she tells off one freak with a predilection for undepilated genitalia ("Call back in two weeks, it'll grow back"), she strikes up an on-line relationship with a caller (Bryan Cranston) who sounds different. Together, they verbally explore hitherto uncharted sexual territory and eventually meet in person. Borden's take on the highly profitable phone-sex biz is amusingly wry, and she and co-scriptwriter Susie Bright have filled their piece with mordant, snappy lines. Lopez-Dawson is appealingly spunky, but at times overdoes that attitudinous head-weave that is becoming as much of a behavioral stereotype for ethnics as chewing gum once was for chorus girls.

TABOO PARLOR is unmitigated Eurotrash, courtesy Monika Treut, about a pair of naughty lesbians who wreak havoc on an unsuspecting, would-be stud they meet in a Hamburg bar. They determine to show up his swaggering male effrontery in a variety of predictably teasing, belittling ways. The ladies have a waxy, mannequin-like quality that will probably appeal to some men; but their machinations are puerile, out of some high school primer on "divine decadence." The film achieves a tacky apex when the three principals writhe and groan on a public bus to the consternation and frustration of the all-male commuters.

WON TON SOUP, the final entry, is by far the most rewarding. Clara Law's film is at once funny, sexy, and poetic. It takes place in Hong Kong and centers around the love affair of Ann (Hayley Man), a fairly typical Chinese girl, and Adrian (Tim Lounibos), an Australian-Chinese student. With the looming Chinese takeover adding a note of hysteria to the already frenetic ambiance of this teeming city, their relationship is floundering. Ann is convinced that she is unable to take the too-Westernized Adrian seriously. Completely besotted by her, he enlists the help of his traditionally inclined brother (Choi Hark-kin) to win her over. He learns to cook traditional dishes packed with aphrodisiacs and pores over an ancient "pillow" book which illustrates the 33 classical positions of lovemaking. With the determination of the romantically obsessed, he puts these to actual use with a stunned Ann (the "wheelbarrow" is a special highlight). His efforts result in a lot of hysterical laughter (as well as pulled muscles), and by film's end, the two have achieved a bittersweet rapprochement. The film is visually quite beautiful: Law's keen eye records the hectic, hothouse ambiance of Hong Kong with its skyscrapers and bustling ferries contrasted with the coolly placid blue-and-orange layout of the lovers' pied-a-terre. There is a dazzling love scene in a car with a summer storm pouring rain over the windshield. Man is amusing and alluring, but it is Lounibos who proves the acting standout of EROTIQUE. Cast in the part at the last minute to replace Law's own brother when their mother protested over the script's raunchiness, he is one of the exciting new breed of Asian-American actors out to smash all lingering, malodorous ethnic stereotypes of the meek-and-mild or inscrutable-and-menacing. He comes up with an amusingly dead-on Aussie accent and uses his hunk's body to hilariously elastic effect. *(Nudity, sexual situations, adult situations, profanity.)* — D.N.

d, Lizzie Borden, Monika Treut, Clara Law; p, Christopher Wood, Vicky Herman, Monika Treut, Michael Sombetzki, Teddie Robin Kwan, Eddie Fong; exec p, Marianne Chase; w, Lizzie Borden ("Let's Talk About Sex"), Susie Bright ("Let's Talk About Sex"), Monika Treut ("Taboo Parlor"), Eddie Fong ("Wonton Soup"); ph, Larry Banks, Elfi Mikesch, Arthur Wong; ed, Richard Fields, Steve Brown, Jill Bilcock; m, Andrew Belling, Tats Lau; prod d, Jane Ann Stewart, Petra Korink, Eddie Mok; art d, Patrice Begovich; set d, Carla Weber; sound, James Thornton (production sound), Wolfgang Schukrafft (engineer), Gary Wilkins (recordist), Mike Schremp (coordinator), Darren Barnett (recordist), Tom Betz (design), Al Pecker (design), Mark Korra (design); fx, Martin Schirmacher; casting, Jerold Franks; cos, Jolie Jimenez, Susann Klindtwordt; makeup, Raqueli Dahan, Fe Ferber, Evelyn Grobe, William Lygratte

Erotic/Comedy/Drama　　　　　**(PR: O　MPAA: NR)**

ETERNITY　　　　　★★★
(Australia) 56m Vivid Productions Party Limited c/bw

Les Foxcroft *(Arthur Stace)*; Dorothy Hewett; Martin Sharp; George Gittoes; Colin Anderson; Ruth Ridley *(Witnesses)*

Lawrence Johnston's ETERNITY uses the urban myth of "Mr. Eternity" to paint an unusual portrait of Sydney, Australia. An unlikely blend of solemnity and spirit, elegance and quirkiness, fact and fantasy, this ambitious documentary is surprisingly successful.

For 40 years, the word "Eternity" would appear on the streets and sidewalks of Sydney, written in chalk in elegant copperplate script. Always written under cover of darkness, the word would last for days, weeks or months, depending on the weather. Eventually it was washed away by the rain, or blown away by the wind, but its memory lingered in the minds of people all over Sydney. It was a common experience that bound the city's citizens together. But who wrote it, and what did it mean? In 1956, 20 years after "Eternity" first began mysteriously appearing all over the city, the writer was discovered. His name was Arthur Stace, but he was immediately christened "Mr. Eternity." Some saw him as a great writer or the original graffiti artist, while others denounced him as simply an eccentric. He had lived a life of poverty, drunkenness and degradation before his conversion to Christianity. One evening, in utter despair, he decided to go to church. The Reverend's words rang clearly in his head: "I wish I could shout eternity through the streets of Sydney." As Stace left the church, he began to cry and felt a powerful call to write "Eternity." He could barely write his own name but, by the time of his death in 1967 at age 83, he had written "Eternity" on the streets of Sydney half a million times.

ETERNITY transcends the traditional form of a portrait documentary, combining interviews with witnesses, archival film clips and poetic re-creations of Stace's life. In the dramatic segments—shot in sublimely beautiful black and white—Arthur Stace (Les Foxcroft) walks through the film like a ghost, just as he walked through the lives of Sydney's inhabitants. ETERNITY tries to unlock both the mystery of Arthur Stace's life project and its impact on the city. While the character of Stace remains as elusive as ever, Johnston's ETERNITY does successfully portray Sydney as a city with an eerie, surreal, dark beauty; a view counter to its stereotypical image as bright, light, and easygoing. — J.S.

d, Lawrence Johnston; p, Susan MacKinnon; w, Lawrence Johnston; ph, Dion Beebe; ed, Annette Davey; m, Ross Edwards; art d, Tony Campbell; sound, Liam Egan

Docudrama/Biography　　　　　**(PR: A　MPAA: NR)**

EVOLVER　　　　　★★
(U.S.) 92m Blue Rider Pictures; Trimark Pictures ~ Vidmark Entertainment c

Ethan Randall *(Kyle Baxter)*; Cassidy Rae *(Jamie Saunders)*; Nicola Nassira *(Ali Baxter)*; Chance Quinn *(Zach Renzetti)*; Cindy Pickett *(Melanie Baxter)*; John De Lancie *(Russell Bennett)*; Paul Dooley *(Jerry Briggs)*; Tim Griffin *(Dwight)*; Eugene Williams *(Tiny)*; Jamie Marsh *(Ace)*; Eric Fleeks *(Cop at Zach's)*; Ian Gregory *(Cop on TV)*; Mary Gordon Murray *(Mrs. Renzetti)*; Lisa Passero *(Secretary)*; Jack Kenny *(Technician)*; Heath McLaughlin *(Cop at Crash)*; Tahitia *(Locker-Room Girl)*; Brad Blaisdell *(Criminal)*; Michael Champion *(Squad Leader)*; William H. Macy *(Voice of Evolver)*

A partial reinvention of the youth-in-peril subgenre, EVOLVER applies updated technology to familiar teen thriller material.

Just as teenaged Kyle Baxter (Ethan Randall) is about to land the top score on the Evolver virtual reality arcade game—and thus win a home version of the game's robot—an equally accomplished player, Jamie Saunders (Cassidy Rae), joins in and distracts Kyle so much that he loses. Kyle's friend Zach (Chance Quinn) convinces him to hack into the scoring computer to alter the numbers, and Kyle soon receives the Evolver robot, which engages players in progressively more difficult "war games" and can learn about and adapt to its surroundings. The early games are harmless, but when Kyle and Zach sneak the robot into school, it gets away from them and, unseen, kills bullying jock Dwight (Tim Griffin).

Kyle and Jamie, whom he has befriended, suspect Evolver might have been responsible; their suspicions are confirmed when it gravely injures Zach, and Kyle discovers that it is a modification of a discontinued war machine project. After he rescues his sister, Ali (Nicola Nassira), from the malevolent robot and disables it, Evolver's creator, Bennett (John De Lancie), arrives to take it away. But when he starts to work on it during the trip back to his lab, the robot crashes his van and heads back to Kyle's house, where it traps Ali and their mother, Melanie (Cindy Pickett), inside a laser grid. With Jamie's help, Kyle manages to outwit Evolver and blow it to pieces.

EVOLVER was written and directed by Mark Rosman, who made his film directing debut with the above-average slasher film THE HOUSE ON SORORITY ROW (1982). As in that film, he here tries to put a new spin on timeworn youth-horror standards; in HOUSE he applied touches of surrealism, while here he adopts elements of the recent computer-as-threat vogue in film plots. While EVOLVER is a better example as such than the likes of the previous year's ARCADE (which also featured John De Lancie), it doesn't transcend the subgenre either. For every intriguing idea or scene (such as Evolver getting in touch with its violent roots by watching TV news), there's a dumb, formulaic one, as when Kyle and Zach sneak the robot into school so that it can take pictures in the girls' locker room.

The Evolver itself is a well-realized creation, with fine mechanical effects by Steve Johnson, and Rosman orchestrates its mayhem with panache. The actors are appealing even if their characters are formula-bound, and the technical credits suggest a theatrical release (which it was originally intended to be) instead of the direct-to-video product it became. (Violence, nudity, profanity.) — M.G.

d, Mark Rosman; p, Jeff Geoffray, Walter Josten, Henry Seggerman; exec p, Mark Amin; co-p, Andrew Hersh; w, Mark Rosman, Manny Coto; ph, Jacques Haitkin; ed, Brent Schoenfeld; m, Christopher Tyng; prod d, Ken Aichele; art d, Candi Guterres; set d, Daniel J. Vivanco; sound, Mary Jo Devenney (mixer), David Lewis Yewdall (designer); fx, Steve Johnson, Rob Vaupel, Rich Thorne; casting, Jeffery Passero; makeup, Suzanne Sanders; stunts, John Stewart

Science Fiction/Horror　　　　　(PR: O　MPAA: R)

EXECUTIONERS　　　　　　　　　★★★
(Hong Kong) 97m c
(AKA: HEROIC TRIO 2: EXECUTIONERS;
YIN DOI HO HAP JUEN)

Anita Mui (Tung); Michelle Yeoh (Chat); Maggie Cheung (Ching); Anthony Wong (Mr. Kim); Lau Ching-Wan; Damian Lau; Takeshi Kaneshiro

Although less of an audience-pleaser than its colorful predecessor, this darker, more ambitious sequel to the superheroine saga THE HEROIC TRIO (1992) has a better grasp of its characters, and a grim, futuristic atmosphere that justifies the principal characters' superpowers. Besides supplying wonderfully sympathetic and noble roles for its three leads, the film's scenario also provides a fascinating reflection of Hong Kong's anxiety over the country's 1997 reunification with mainland China.

In a postnuclear future, radiation has contaminated the water supply. An evil genius, Mr. Kim (Anthony Wong), has developed a purification system that supplies the public, at exorbitant prices, with clean water. Kim covertly influences government activities with the aid of a high-ranking colonel, while also manipulating public opinion with a handpicked spiritual leader named Chong Hong, who is beginning to take his role as a savior quite seriously. In the meantime, the superheroines from the first film, Tung (Anita Mui), Ching (Maggie Cheung), and Chat (Michelle Yeoh), each pursuing separate destinies, enjoy a brief, happy Christmas Eve reunion. After a public appearance by Chong Hong ends in a riot, Tung's police commissioner husband, Lau, receives orders from the colonel to assassinate Hong. His efforts fail, but Hong is later killed by a gunman during a peace conference with the president. The colonel blames Lau for the murder, and Lau is eventually gunned down while trying to flee on the last train scheduled to leave the country. As she tries to rendezvous with him, Tung is arrested and imprisoned for being a rioter.

A military coup d'etat puts the colonel in power. Ching leads rebel forces who hide the president as they prepare to do battle, while Chat, a government agent named Tak, and Tung's small daughter Cindy, set out to discover the clean headwaters blocked from the populace by the colonel and Kim. Despite her vow to forsake her superpowers, Tung breaks out of prison, resumes her role as a masked avenger, and kills the colonel. She rejoins Ching and Chat for their showdown with Kim, which takes place in an empty church. Ching kills herself while exploding a bomb meant to stop Kim, and the bloody battle ends when Chat blows Kim to pieces with a grenade. Having ensured that clean water will reach the public and the President will resume his post, Chat and Tung walk into the distance with the precocious Cindy.

Unlike most standard action-movie sequels, EXECUTIONERS doesn't merely rehash its predecessor's plotline. Instead, it resurrects the central characters and places them in a more desperate setting, offering challenges that hinge more on politics than the supernatural. Most likely for budgetary as much as artistic reasons, directors Johnny To and Ching Siu-Tung, and scripter Susanne Chan, take a low-key approach toward the science-fiction aspects of the story, setting most of the action indoors. This stresses the dogged determination of the heroines and avoids cliched high-tech futuristic trappings. Certain absurd elements do pop up—like Ching's menacing hunchbacked sidekick—but the film's somber, somewhat fatalistic mood (summed up decisively in Ching's heroic but seemingly pointless death) effectively sweeps them to the sidelines. As in the first film, Wong overacts to his heart's content as the scarred, superstrong Kim (no relation to the character he played in HEROIC). The lead actresses get ample opportunity to present the human, emotional sides of their comic-book roles, with Mui once again receiving the lion's share of the melodrama as a loyal wife and mother forced back into crime-fighting. (Violence.) — E.G.

d, To Kei-Fung, Ching Siu-Tung; p, Johnny To, Ching Siu-Tung; w, Susanne Chan (from a story by Sandy Shaw); ph, Poon Hang Sang; m, Cacine Wong; prod d, Catherine Hun, Chan Pui Wah; art d, Bruce Yu; set d, Raymond Chan

Fantasy/Martial Arts　　　　　(PR: C　MPAA: NR)

EXOTICA　　　　　　　　　　　★★½
(Canada) 104m Alliance; Communication Corp.; Ego Films; Telefilm Canada; Ontario Film Development Corp. ~ Miramax c

Bruce Greenwood (Francis); Mia Kirshner (Christina); Don McKellar (Thomas); Arsinee Khanjian (Zoe); Elias Koteas

(Eric); Sarah Polley *(Tracey)*; Victor Garber *(Harold)*; Calvin Green *(Customs Officer)*; David Hemblen *(Customs Inspector)*; Peter Krantz *(Man in Taxi)*; Damon D'Oliveira *(Man at Opera)*; Billy Merasty *(Man at Opera)*; Jack Blum *(Scalper)*; Ken McDougall *(Doorman)*

Richly photographed and promising naughty sex, EXOTICA is a frustrating—and deliberate—tease. Its characters are lost in the usual Atom Egoyan territory, alienated from one another and themselves, bedeviled by longings they're afraid to indulge, tormented by memories they're unwilling to forget, and given to cryptic pronouncements delivered in affected monotones. It's the Egoyan movie for people who feel faintly guilty about never having seen one—at least most of it takes place in a strip club, even if it's an awfully portentous one.

Pet shop owner Thomas (Don McKellar), who is smuggling exotic macaw eggs into Canada, arrives at the airport and is watched carefully by customs inspectors. He takes a cab home, sharing it with a stranger who gives him ballet tickets in lieu of half the fare. The stranger gets off at Exotica, an upscale girlie club with a wildly artificial jungle motif and a high-tech sound system that blasts disco versions of Urdu *ghazals*. Its star stripper is Christina (Mia Kirshner), who exploits the pedophilic allure of her youthful face and figure by dressing in a schoolgirl's uniform. Two men are obsessed with her: longhaired DJ Eric (Elias Koteas) and tax auditor Francis (Bruce Greenwood), who regularly pays to have Christina do table dances for him. Zoe (Arsinee Khanjian), the hugely pregnant owner of Exotica, has befriended the troubled Christina; she's also entered into a business arrangement with Eric, having paid him to father her child. Finally, all the principal characters are drawn together when Francis begins an audit of Thomas's pet store.

Eric, who harbors some deep-seated hostility towards Francis, persuades him to touch Christina during a table dance, then has him thrown out of the club for violating the rules. Francis in turn blackmails Thomas—who's conducting an illegal trade in exotic pets—into entering the club and talking to Christina on his behalf. We finally learn what has drawn Eric, Christina, and Francis into their current tortured relationship.

They all come from the same suburban neighborhood, and unhappy teenager Christina used to babysit for Francis's daughter. The child was abducted and murdered, and Eric and Christina met when they volunteered to help search for her corpse, which Eric discovered. Francis's wife, who was having an affair with his brother, died a few months later in a car accident. The accident also crippled Francis's brother. The film ends on a note of reconciliation: Eric and Francis embrace, and when Francis puts his hand on Christina's leg, she removes it slowly and without rancor.

EXOTICA sounds terrifically lurid and interesting, but like most Egoyan films, it's far more interesting in the telling than in the watching. Egoyan no doubt prides himself on being a filmmaker of *ideas*, but it wouldn't hurt him to be tainted by some conventional notions of storytelling and character development. The filmmaker he most resembles is Woody Allen, who's great at assembling a bunch of clever bits and pieces but not so good at assimilating them into something greater than the sum of its parts.

It's easy to defend Egoyan as a serious and provocative filmmaker, since all his liabilities can be made to sound like the results of his rigorous intellectual defiance of mainstream norms. His characters are opaque because they're meant to defy bourgeois psychological conventions. His plots are unconvincing because they explore modes of storytelling that challenge received notions of good narrative structure. His movies are boring because he rejects the audience's Pavlovian desire for familiar

scene structure and easy narrative resolution. Egoyan is a phenomenally successful filmmaker on his own terms. But he's still a pretentious bore. *(Nudity, sexual situations, adult situations.)* — M.M.

d, Atom Egoyan; p, Atom Egoyan, Camelia Frieberg; assoc p, David Webb; w, Atom Egoyan; ph, Paul Sarossy; ed, Susan Shipton; m, Mychael Danna; prod d, Linda del Rosario, Richard Paris; ch, Claudia Moore; sound, Steve Munro (design), Ross Redfern (recordist); fx, Michael Kavonaugh; cos, Linda Muir; makeup, Nicole Demers; stunts, Ted Hanlon

Mystery/Drama   **(PR: O   MPAA: R)**

EXPERT, THE   ★★★
(U.S.) 92m Axis Films International; Arch Stanton Pictures; Davis Films; BFNC Venture ~ Orion Home Video c
(AKA: BRUTE FORCE)

Jeff Speakman *(John Lomax)*; James Brolin *(Warden Munsey)*; Michael Shaner *(Martin Kagan)*; Alex Datcher *(Dr. Alice Barnes)*; Wolfgang Bodison *(Dan Mason)*; Elizabeth Gracen *(Liz Pierce)*; Norm Woodel *(Bill Loomis)*; Jim Varney *(Snake)*; Michelle Nagy *(Jenny Lomax)*; Red West *(Judge)*; William Barry Scott *(Captain)*; Japhery Brown *(Himes)*; Robby Robinson *(Tex)*; Ramon Estevez *(Tomas)*; Dan Chandler *(Governor)*; Karen Bowden *(Lieutenant Weisser)*; Trent Walker *(Bobby Lee)*; Richard Epper *(Joe)*; Buck McDanger *(Buck)*; Joni Avery *(Bobby Sue)*; Stuart Greer *(Ritchie)*; David Compton *(Prison Chaplain)*; A. Finnigan *(Receptionist)*; Ramonale Baron *(Maria)*; Matthew Tyson *(Kyle Loomis)*; Mark Cabus *(Tower Guard)*; Rick Schulman *(Forensics Expert)*; Nicholas Barbaro *(Power Plant Guard)*; Amy Olsen *(Cocktail Waitress)*; Ronnie Allen *(Bouncer)*

Flexing brain power as well as biceps, THE EXPERT is an action flick anomaly. The movie examines every aspect of the capital punishment controversy, while still delivering enough explosive action to satisfy genre buffs.

When his college-age sister Jenny (Michelle Nagy) is sexually assaulted and slain by sociopath Martin Kagan (Michael Shaner), SWAT team instructor John Lomax (Jeff Speakman) wrongly assumes that justice will prevail at the trial, unaware that Kagan will use his keen legal knowledge to manipulate the system to his advantage. Despite Kagan's record of juvenile violence, liberal prison psychologist Dr. Alice Barnes (Alex Datcher) lobbies to have his death sentence commuted to confinement in a mental facility. Seemingly recovered from the shock of his sister's murder, as well as from an assault by crazed trailer trash trying to spring their death row sibling Bobby Lee (Trent Walker), Lomax worries his reporter girlfriend Liz Pierce (Elizabeth Gracen) and fellow officer Dan Mason (Wolfgang Bodison) when he hatches a plan to break into the jail holding Kagan, which is due for closure, and kill him. While Lomax arms up for his mission, Warden Munsey (James Brolin) is removed from office for publicly lauding capital punishment. His temporary replacement is Alice Barnes. Simultaneously, Kagan sets in motion an escape plan: revealing to his next-cell neighbor Bill Loomis (Norm Woodel), serving a sentence for killing his wife, that he commited the murder, he incites Loomis to stab him with a shiv. In the ensuing chaos, Kagan takes Barnes hostage and guns down execution junkie Munsey. All hell breaks loose as the death row inmates are about to be transferred to a new prison. Although Kagan uses the guards for lethal target practice and sics the cons on intruder Lomax, a bout between judge-and-jury Lomax and Nietzschean criminal Kagan ends when Kagan gets a savage beating and plunges to a poetically just electrocution on the penitentiary roof.

While adhering to basic action movie formulae, THE EX-PERT forces viewers to contemplate the capital punishment quandary. How often do action flicks provoke debate as half-time entertainment in between kung fu tournies? Without prose-lytizing, THE EXPERT spotlights the complexities of both the pro and con stances. Although the outwardly fawning Kagan sniffles about childhood abuse to beat a deserved rap, framed Loomis really is an innocent man awaiting execution. And if Brolin's Warden is a violencemonger, his position ultimately proves more viable than that of importunate Dr. Barnes, who revictimizes the slain to aid defendants because of her own history of incestuous child abuse. In the midst of all this food for thought, THE EXPERT invigorates its audience with a series of power-packed fight scenes, ferociously choreographed and per-formed for the camera. Loose ends remain untied (Barnes's conversion to vigilante utterances is too abrupt, wouldn't Kagan have an easier time escaping from a mental institute?), but this action pic moves forcefully enough to make such points moot.

The production values and performances are top of the line, particularly the convincingly vicious Shaner. A star whenever he fights, the sleepy-eyed Speakman looks like an Elvis impersona-tor when he acts, but he certainly exercises better script judgment than almost any other martial arts headliner. Challenging specta-tors to think during their roller-coaster ride, THE EXPERT is a prescription for proscription that wrestles equally well with both crazed assailants and moral dilemmas. *(Graphic violence, ex-treme profanity, sexual situations, adult situations.)* — R.P.

d, Rick Avery; p, Andre Garroni, Nicholas Barbaro; exec p, Samuel Hadida, Walter Gernert; assoc p, Craig Thurman Suttle; co-p, Victor Hadida; w, Max Allan Collins (from a story by Jill Gatsy); ph, Levie Isaacks; ed, Bob Murawski; m, Ashley Irwin; prod d, Clay Callaway; set d, Ty Lewis; fx, Ken Estes; casting, Rosemary Welden; cos, Emily Jane Kitos; makeup, Bill Miller-Jones; stunts, Rick Avery

Martial Arts/Prison/Action   **(PR: O   MPAA: R)**

FACES OF WOMEN ★★★
(Ivory Coast) 103m Films de la Lagune;
French Ministry of Foreign Affairs ~
New Yorker Video c
(VISAGES DES FEMMES)

Eugenie Cisse Roland *(Bernadette—Fish Seller)*; Sidiki Bakaba *(Kouassi)*; Albertine N'Guessan *(N'Guessan)*; Kouadio Brou *(Brou)*; Veronique Mahile *(Affoue)*; Carmen Levry; Anny Brigitte; Alexis Leatche; Fatou Sall; Desire Bama; Adioukrou People of Lopou Village

FACES OF WOMEN is a provocative and informative film on the domestic and business conflicts women face in today's Ivory Coast. The film was not distributed in the United States until 10 years after its production in 1985.

The film tells two stories. In the first a married couple is visited by the man's younger brother. While they work he remains idle, watches the woman, and gradually seduces her. The husband tells his wife that she is his property, and he tells his younger brother, "What is mine is yours." But, when he suspects his wife has betrayed him, he beats her.

In the second story, a middle-aged businesswoman introduces her youngest daughter to her fish-smoking business, and encourages all three of her daughters to empower themselves. The girls do not worry about their future because they believe that their mother will support them, and that their beauty will enable them to manipulate men into giving the women whatever they want. When the mother fails to secure a bank loan to increase and diversify her business, two daughters go back to the bank representative and persuade him to change his mind, offering him hope that they will return to visit him. The mother then loans a van to her younger brother on the agreement that he use it to transport goods, make money, and repay her in installments. Instead, he uses it to travel among his three wives, and asks for money to repair the van when it breaks down. When he visits, he addresses his father-in-law and not his sister.

Both stories illustrate this society's double standard—in the first, we see how men treat women as property and practice polygamy, yet punish women for expressing their desires; in the second, a hard-working woman does not receive the respect she deserves from her family or from the financial community. The film opens with scenes from a village festival and a message, "In the beginning was the festival." It concludes with another festival and a new message, "In the end the festival becomes a refuge." Director Desire Ecare depicts injustices against women to inspire them to enrich their lives, go beyond their traditional roles, and express their suffering directly.

This low-budget film was made over twelve years. The first story was shot with a handheld camera, and with characters often set in the background; the camera's perspective suggests that of a villager witnessing real events. The young woman plays a passive role, always responding to the actions of the two men. Her story emerges through her husband's suspicion and brutality and her lover's desire. The second story is urban, set inside the woman's business and home, and presented in close-ups. Camera technique, composition, and story sequence all dramatize the contrasting experiences of these women and demonstrate director Ecare's vision of a broader social activism. *(Extensive nudity, adult situations.)* — M.F.

d, Desire Ecare; p, Desire Ecare; w, Desire Ecare; ph, Francois Migeat, Dominique Gentil; ed, Giselle Miski, Madame Dje-Dje, Nicholas Barrachin; sound, Jean-Pierre Kaba

Drama (PR: C MPAA: NR)

FAIR GAME ★★
(U.S.) 91m Silver Pictures ~
Warner Bros. c

William Baldwin *(Max)*; Cindy Crawford *(Kate)*; Steven Berkoff *(Kazak)*; Christopher McDonald *(Meyerson)*; Miguel Sandoval *(Juan Toreno)*; Johann Carlo *(Jodi)*; Salma Hayek *(Rita)*; John Bedford Lloyd *(Louis)*; Olek Krupa *(Patch)*; Jenette Goldstein *(Rosa)*; Marc Macaulay *(Navigator)*; Sonny Carl Davis *(Baker)*; Frank Medrano *(Guaybera)*; Don Yesso *(Beanpole)*; Paul Dillon *(Hacker)*; Gustav Vintas *(Stefan)*; Christian Bodegaard *(Farm Boy)*; Gary Francis Hope *(Smiler)*; Hank Stone *(Ratso)*; Ski Zawaski *(Bail Bondsman)*; Nancy Nahra *(Forensics)*; Anthony Giaimo *(Cafe Romano Manager)*; Carmen Lopez *(Angry Mother)*; Erika Navarro *(Four-year-old Girl)*; Pamela Berrard *(Hotel Desk Clerk)*; Mark Wheatle *(Stop & Shop Clerk)*; Bubba Baker *(Hog Truck Driver)*; Scott Michael Campbell *(Adam)*; Ruben Rabasa *(Computer Store Manager)*; Jim Greene *(Tow Truck Driver)*; Antoni Corone *(Codebreaker)*

FAIR GAME isn't bad enough to be good, and it isn't good enough, thankfully, to launch supermodel Cindy Crawford on a movie career. This vigorous, pinheaded action flick asks us to accept Cindy as a lawyer — a *fabulous* lawyer, mind you — on the run from the Russian Mafia, currently the heavies of choice for every blocked screenwriter in Hollywood.

While jogging one day along Miami's trendy Ocean Drive, attorney Kate McQuean (Crawford) slams right into a deadly KGB operation. As part of a client's divorce settlement, she has made the mistake of repossessing a ship belonging to one of the agents, and now becomes their unwitting target. Detective Max Kirkpatrick (William Baldwin), who has just been dumped by his girlfriend, comes to her aid. After Kate nearly dies in an explosion that destroys her apartment, the two are pursued all over Florida by their enemies. At the KGB's fingertips are all the latest in surveillance, tracking and terminating devices with which to stalk and kill their prey. They are a tough bunch to shake, but McQuean and Kirkpatrick are in prime physical condition. The pair's peregrinations take them first aboard a speeding train (where they overcome their mutual distaste for each other and do what is expected of them) and then onto the ship in question for the ultimate confrontation.

As a thriller, FAIR GAME is old hat and can be easily ignored, but Crawford's film debut makes a certain kind of statement about today's presentation of female icons. Super models who have preceded her to the big screen include Suzy Parker, Twiggy and Paulina Porizkhova, who were all given the velvet glove treatment, glamorously lit and made-up for maximum allure. However, in the 1990s, action rules. Our star is called upon to be sweaty, oily and tousle-haired. Instead of twirling about in lovely frocks, she delivers a mean right to the substantial jaw of her leading man; and between near-brushes with death, she arranges herself faceup on any bed handy, the better to show off her most salient charms.

Baldwin is adequate, as always, not seeming to coast too much on his veering-on-goofy, hangdog good looks. Steve Berkoff as the lead villain appears to be doing an imitation of a malevolent Patrick Stewart, with a shaky Russian accent. *(Violence, profanity, adult situations.)* — D.N.

d, Andrew Sipes; p, Joel Silver; exec p, Thomas M. Hammel; assoc p, Alan Schecter; w, Charlie Fletcher (based on the novel by Paula Gosling); ph, Richard Bowen; ed, David Finfer, Christian Wagner, Steven Kemper; m, Marc Mancina; prod d, James Spencer; art d, William F. Matthews; set d, Don K. Ivey; sound, Peter Devlin (mixer), Dick Church (mixer); fx, Bruno Van Zeebroeck, Brad Kuehn; casting, Jackie Burch; cos, Louise Frogley

Action/Thriller/Romance   **(PR: C   MPAA: R)**

FAR FROM HOME: THE ADVENTURES   ★★★
OF YELLOW DOG
(U.S.) 80m 20th Century Fox ~ 20th Century Fox c

Mimi Rogers *(Katherine McCormick)*; Bruce Davison *(John McCormick)*; Jesse Bradford *(Angus McCormick)*; Tom Bower *(John Gale)*; Joel Palmer *(Silas McCormick)*; Josh Wannamaker *(David Finlay)*; Margot Finley *(Sara)*; Matt Bennett *(Ron Willick)*; St. Clair McColl *(Himself)*; Jennifer Weissenborn *(Labrador Helicopter Pilot)*; Gordon Neave *(Flight Engineer)*; Karen Kruper *(Nurse)*; Dean Lockwood *(Sartech)*; John LeClair *(Sartech)*; Brent Stalt *(Sartech)*

FAR FROM HOME: THE ADVENTURES OF YELLOW DOG is a boy-and-dog tale that combines good, wholesome family entertainment with lessons on surviving in the wilderness.

A yellow dog appears one day at the McCormick home in rural British Columbia, Canada. Fourteen-year-old Angus (Jesse Bradford) quickly forms a bond with the dog, which he names Yellow. When Angus accompanies his father John (Bruce Davison) on a 200-mile boat trip to pick up supplies, Yellow tags along. Father and son encounter a storm at sea and their boat capsizes. John is soon rescued, but searchers find no sign of Angus or Yellow, who have washed ashore on a rocky, unpopulated island. The resourceful teenager uses the survival skills his father has taught him to build shelter, find food, and start a signal fire. After nine days pass, Angus decides to move on. Angus and Yellow encounter much difficulty in traversing the dense forests of the Pacific Northwest. They resort to eating insects, foliage, and rodents to survive. Hungry, exhausted, and injured, Angus is beginning to lose hope when he is finally spotted by search planes while crossing a log bridge. Rescuers retrieve Angus, but Yellow slips from the log and plunges into the rushing water far below. After three weeks, the search for Yellow is abandoned. Angus is dejected, but never gives up hope. He hangs flyers around the countryside and uses his dog whistle to summon Yellow. Eventually, Yellow finds his way back to the McCormick home, and boy and dog are reunited.

While aimed at children, this heartwarming film offers ample entertainment for adults as well. The story treads familiar territory, and the outcome is predictable, but Angus's difficult—and often dangerous—trek through the wilderness provides moments of heartrending suspense. Unlike typical family-oriented films, FAR FROM HOME favors realism over fantasy, and the well-chosen cast refrains from playing it cute. Bradford, who previously starred as a Depression-era youth in KING OF THE HILL (1993), turns in another winning performance as the practical, serious-minded Angus, while Mimi Rogers and Bruce Davison evoke sympathy as Angus's concerned parents. Davison, in particular, deserves plaudits for crafting a memorable character out of a role mainly employed in cutaways from the real action. But in terms of physical acting, it seems that Yellow had the most strenuous time: credits list four stunt doubles for canine star Dakotah. FAR FROM HOME was filmed on location in Canada. *(Adult situations.)* — B.R.

d, Phillip Borsos; p, Peter O'Brian; w, Phillip Borsos; ph, James Gardner; ed, Sidney Wolinsky; m, John Scott; prod d, Mark S. Freeborn; art d, Yvonne J. Hurst; set d, Peter Louis Lando, Marianne Kaplan; sound, Bruce Nyznik (design), Michael McGee (mixer); fx, John Thomas, Dean Lockwood, Dan Krech, Ted Rogers; casting, Linda Phillips Palo; cos, Antonia Bardon; makeup, Stan Edmonds; stunts, Betty Thomas

Adventure/Children's/Drama   **(PR: A   MPAA: PG)**

FARINELLI   ★★½
(Belgium/France/Italy) 111m Stephan Films; Alinea Films; Le Studio Canal Plus; Union Generale du Cinematographique Images; France 2 Cinema; Studio Images; RTL; TV1; MG Srl; K2 Productions; Italian International Film Srl Production ~ Sony Pictures Classics c
(FARINELLI IL CASTRATO)

Stefano Dionisi *(Carlo Broschi/Farinelli)*; Enrico Lo Verso *(Riccardo Broschi)*; Elsa Zylberstein *(Alexandra)*; Caroline Cellier *(Margaret Hunter)*; Marianne Basler *(Countess Mauer)*; Jacques Boudet *(Philippe V)*; Graham Valentine *(The Prince of Wales)*; Pier Paolo Capponi *(The Father)*; Delphine Zentout *(The Young Admirer)*; Omero Antounutti *(Porpora)*; Jeroen Krabbe *(Handel)*; Renaud du Peloux de Saint Romain; Richard Reeves; Jonathan Fox; Josef Betzing; Karl-Heinz Dickman; Stefan Mazel; Wolfgang Grindemann; Hubert Burczek; Harald Gotz; Andreas Ulich; Alfonso Asenjo

The story of Farinelli, born Carlo Broschi (Stefano Dionisi)—the castrato opera singer with a three-octave vocal range, who held all Europe in his thrall in the 18th century—is an inherently fascinating one. As imagined by director Gerard Corbiau, however, it quickly degenerates into soft-core soap opera.

Carlo and his brother, Riccardo (Enrico Lo Verso), travel Europe together. Riccardo is a mediocre composer, but Carlo's bravura vocalizing enchants audiences large and small. They are also an offstage team: women swoon for Carlo, but he requires Riccardo's assistance to satisfy their lustful advances. Carlo's vague feelings of dissatisfaction with these arrangements are brought to a head when he meets the composer Handel (Jeroen Krabbe), who hears him sing in Naples and proposes that he come with him to London, leaving his brother behind. Riccardo, who realizes he's nothing without Carlo, manages to thwart the deal.

Thirteen years later, Handel reappears with an entreaty from the King of England himself, who wants to hear the now-legendary Farinelli. Though this momentous proposal so terrifies Carlo that he temporarily loses his voice, the brothers decide to go to London. They are engaged by Margaret Hunter (Caroline Cellier), who runs the one theater with enough clout to rival Covent Garden, which is ruled by the all-powerful Handel. Margaret's daughter Alexandra (Elsa Zylberstein) falls in love with Carlo and, in an effort to make peace, steals Handel's latest musical scores for him. The already strained relations between the brothers reach a breaking point when Carlo decides to sing Handel's music rather than Riccardo's.

The crafty Handel befriends Riccardo and learns the secret of Farinelli's castration. On the night of the premiere, Handel denounces the singer and high-handedly challenges him to perform the aria. An amazingly calm Carlo does so with such miraculous beauty that Handel faints. This is the great Farinelli's last public performance. He becomes attached to the court of King Philip V of Spain, singing exclusively for the melancholy monarch. Riccardo appears once more, but this time to make peace and leave his brother with the ultimate gift, a child he has sired for him with the ever-accommodating Alexandra.

FARINELLI is breathtakingly photographed by Walther Vanden Ende, who captures Gianni Quaranta's production design and the rococo costumes of Olga Berluti and Anne de Laugardiere in all their extravagant splendor. It's unfortunate that the mounting is so much more impressive than the content. Farinelli's story could have made a great film, but FARINELLI is the usual Hollywood-style mix of sex and culture: neurotic harpsichords and violins jangle and scrape as bodices heave and breeches bulge. Although Corbiau is uncharacteristically coy in his depiction of the dire genital wounding that preserves Farinelli's boyish voice, he misses nothing when it comes to the sexual hijinks of the brothers Broschi, for whom sex is quite literally a family affair.

The film's purportedly serious sections are equally cliched. Kindly old music teacher Porpora is always on hand to lend advice, the bitchy partisans of the contentious artistic salons snipe and gossip, and Jeroen Krabbe—promoted from composer's sidekick, his IMMORTAL BELOVED berth—delivers a stereotypical "Great Genius" performance as Handel. FARINELLI's sole moment of genuine artistry involves Handel's radiant aria from *Rinaldo*: even delivered in an eerie, metallic, hybrid voice—created by digitally meshing the voices of a mezzo-soprano (Ewa Mallas Godlewska) and a countertenor (Derek Lee Ragin)—retains its power to uplift the listener.

Dionisi is singularly unappealing as Farinelli: his wolverine look is better suited to the lead singer of a lesser heavy metal band, and the synthetic voice that issues from his painted lips seems patently false. Corbiau might have done better to cast a singer, particularly since Dionisi is an actor of conspicuously limited gifts. Though he looks like a Pasolini satyr, the stormy Lo Verso is little better. Only Cellier seems at home in the period, and wears the lavish costumes with great aplomb. *(Nudity, profanity, substance abuse, adult situations, sexual situations, violence.)* — D.N.

d, Gerard Corbiau; p, Vera Belmont; exec p, Linda Guttenberg, Aldo Lado, Dominique Janne, Stephane Thenoz; w, Andree Corbiau, Gerard Corbiau (based on an adaptation by Andree Corbiau, Gerard Corbiau, and Marcel Beaulieu, from a synopsis by Teff Erhat and Michel Fessler); ph, Walther Vanden Ende; ed, Joelle Hache; prod d, Gianni Quaranta; sound, Richard Schorr (designer), Jean-Paul Mugel (engineer), Dominique Hennequin (mixer), Laurent Boudaud (recordist); fx, Kuno Schlegelmilch; casting, Gerard Moulevrier, Jose Villaverde; cos, Olga Berlutti, Anne de Laugardiere; makeup, Paul le Marinel, Kuno Schlegelmilch

Drama/Musical/Biography   **(PR: O   MPAA: R)**

FATHER AND SCOUT   ★★
(U.S.) 92m New Line Television ~ Turner Home Entertainment c
(AKA: FATHER & SCOUT)

Bob Saget *(Spenser Paley)*; Brian Bonsall *(Michael Paley)*; Troy Evans *(Scoutmaster)*; Stuart Pankin *(Aaron)*; David Graf *(Chet)*; Heidi Swedberg *(Donna Paley)*; Kimberly Scott *(Francine)*; Brian Levinson *(Brent)*; Denver Pyle *(George Rosebrock)*; ChaChi Pittman *(Chip)*; Ryan Holihan *(Nolan)*; Lucy Butler *(Married Woman)*; Robert Egan *(Father/Coach)*; Hassan Nicholas *(Camper)*; Steven Kavner *(Spenser's Dad)*; John Petlock *(Doctor)*; William Mesnick *(Father #1)*; Jonathan Emerson *(Father #2)*; Jason Azikiwe *(Father #3)*

A calamitous camping trip brings a father and son closer together in FATHER AND SCOUT, a 1994 made-for-television movie released to home video in 1995.

Spenser Paley (Bob Saget) reluctantly accompanies his son Michael (Brian Bonsall) on a "Dad and Lad" camping trip to Catalina Island. The unathletic Spenser is out of his element in the great outdoors. He sinks a canoe, steps on a jellyfish, and faints in a cave. Michael is embarrassed by his father's sour attitude and recurrent ineptitude. With his incessant whining, complaining, and sarcastic put-downs, Spenser riles the other campers, particularly Chet (David Graf). Chet and his son use underhanded tactics to try to beat the Paleys in the father-son pentathlon. But when the group is trapped in a mine shaft, Spenser and Chet work together to save their sons. Spenser and Michael win the contest, and return home closer than ever.

FATHER AND SCOUT is satisfactory family entertainment. The script has little to offer in the way of originality, but it is innocuous fun. Standouts among the cast are Troy Evans as the scoutmaster and Heidi Swedberg as Mrs. Paley. Bonsall has outgrown his "Family Ties" cutesiness and is developing into a competent actor. Saget, one of the executive producers, is the film's only downer. His unhappy camper demeanor is far too disagreeable for far too much of the program. Moreover, many of his lines come off like a bad stand-up routine. By the time his attitude is adjusted, it is too late to care, especially after his pointless and unamusing public ridicule of a scoutmaster. *(Violence.)* — B.R.

d, Richard Michaels; p, Cindy Hornickel; exec p, Bob Saget, Sasha Emerson, Laura Gerson, Peter Morgan, Melissa Goddard; w, Sheldon Bull, Hoyt Hilsman; ph, Isidore Mankofsky; ed, Michael Brown, Casey Brown; m, David Kitay; prod d, C.J. Strawn; art d, James R. Barrows; set d, Irina Rivera; sound, Steve Nelson (mixer); fx, Robert Calvert, John Carlucci; casting, Sally Stiner; cos, Seok Halley Yoon; makeup, Kathleen Hagen; stunts, Jake Crawford

Comedy/Children's   **(PR: AA   MPAA: PG)**

FATHER OF THE BRIDE PART II   ★★
(U.S.) 106m Sandollar Productions; Touchstone ~ Buena Vista c

Steve Martin *(George Banks)*; Diane Keaton *(Nina Banks)*; Martin Short *(Franck Eggelhoffer)*; Kimberly Williams *(Annie Banks-MacKenzie)*; George Newbern *(Bryan MacKenzie)*; Kieran Culkin *(Matty Banks)*; B.D. Wong *(Howard Weinstein)*; Peter Michael Goetz *(John MacKenzie)*; Kate McGregor-Stewart *(Joanna MacKenzie)*; Jane Adams *(Dr. Megan Eisenberg)*; Eugene Levy *(Mr. Habib)*; Rebecca Chambers *(Young Woman at Gym)*; April Ortiz *(Olivia)*; Dulcy Rogers *(Ava—the Beautician)*; Kathy Anthony *(Beautician No. 2)*; Adrian Canzoneri *(Justin)*; Lori Alan *(Mrs. Habib)*; Stephanie Miller *(Annie—Age 4)*; Hallie Meyers-Shyer *(Annie—Age 7)*; Jay Wolpert *(Dr. Brooks)*; Ann Walker *(Dr. Brooks' Nurse)*; Sandra Silvestri *(Jogging Mom)*; William Akey *(Frantic Father No. 1)*; Seth Kaplan *(Wild Four-Year-Old)*; Jonathan Emerson *(Frantic Father No. 2)*; Joshua Preston *(Tantrum Toddler)*; K.C. Colwell *(Father Heading Off to Work)*; Chase Colwell *(Adorable Toddler)*; Tony Simotes *(Construction Foreman)*; Annie Meyers-Shyer *(Shower Guest)*; Linda DeScenna *(Shower Guest)*; Heidi Averill *(Shower Guest)*; Chelsea Lynn *(Matty's Friend)*; Sue Colwell *(Nina's Customer)*; Rodriego Botero *(Gang Kid)*; Vince Lozano *(Gang Kid)*; Caroline Lagerfelt *(Check-in Nurse)*; Ilene Waterstone *(Check-in Nurse)*; Wendy Worthington *(Prostate Nurse)*; Dorian Spencer *(ER Nurse)*; Harris Laskawy *(Prostate Doctor)*; Roxanne Beckford *(Nina's Nurse)*; Valerie Hemmerich *(Nina's Nurse)*; Peter Spears *(Dr. Wagner)*; Susan Beaubian *(Annie's Nurse)*; Mychael Bates *(Hospital Orderly)*; Jerri Rose White; Shannon Kennedy *(Baby Megan)*; Casey Boersma; Dylan Boersma *(Baby George)*;

Katie Pierce *(Two-month-old Megan)*; Jonathan Selstad; Thomas Selstad *(Two-month-old George)*

Dripping with sentiment and padded with subplots, FATHER OF THE BRIDE PART II deviates radically from FATHER'S LITTLE DIVIDEND (1951), the original sequel to the 1950 FATHER OF THE BRIDE. Fans of the Spencer Tracy originals will shudder, but even those who enjoyed the 1991 FATHER OF THE BRIDE will be disappointed by this lame farce.

George Banks (Steve Martin) explains to the audience how his middle-class life in the suburbs of Los Angeles has been thrown topsy-turvy by recent family events. First, his newly-married daughter, Annie (Kimberly Williams), surprises George and his wife, Nina (Diane Keaton), by announcing that she is pregnant. While Nina delights in the news, George reacts with fear at the prospect of being a grandfather. In a panic, George gets a youthful makeover and sells the family home—without the family's consent—to a Middle Eastern businessman, Mr. Habib (Eugene Levy).

While looking for a new home, George and Nina stay with their wealthy in-laws, the Mackenzies (Peter Michael Goetz, Kate McGregor Stewart), but, after hearing that Mr. Habib plans to demolish the old house, George changes his mind and buys back his property. Meanwhile, Annie and her husband, Bryan (George Newbern) disagree over whether to move out of their home: Annie wants to take a job promotion in Boston after the birth of their child. George ends their fight, however, by giving his consent to the move.

Next, Nina surprises everyone by announcing that she, too, is pregnant. The families receive assistance throughout the double pregnancies from Franck (Martin Short) and Howard (B.D. Wong), two interior decorators who have been hired by George to build a lavish nursery for Annie and Bryan's baby. Finally, after many false alarms in her ninth month, Annie goes into labor just as Nina does, and the women give birth to their babies on the same night. Later, the sight of his newborn baby girl eases George's pain as he watches his grown daughter move out of town.

Writer-producer Nancy Meyers and writer-director Charles Shyer (the team behind I LOVE TROUBLE and the 1991 FATHER OF THE BRIDE) consistently pander to viewers by alternating silly slapstick with sugary sentiment. A cute little 82-minute comedy (with a little drama) has been remade as a bloated, aimless drama (with a little comedy), clocking in at 106 minutes.

Presuming new audiences would be bored with the mundane matters that had preoccupied the Banks family of the 1950s, Meyers and Shyer have added the subplots about moving out of the old house, the threat of Annie's move to Boston, and the double pregnancy/double delivery scenarios that seem lifted from an equally uninspired 1995 comedy, NINE MONTHS. What had worked so well in the original—e.g. the in-laws squabbling over the baby's name, the brilliant climax during which George loses the baby in a park—have been either shortened or left out altogether.

Most of the new material has been added either to make the story more touching (it isn't, despite many, many moist moments) or to bring Martin Short into the action, even during the delivery scenes. While Short's effeminate caricature of an interior decorator may be politically incorrect, he's nevertheless the most energetic and inventive performer in the cast. That includes the once-reliable Steve Martin and Diane Keaton, who are almost as dull and conventional here as their characters, making their predecessors, Spencer Tracy and Joan Bennett, seem almost hip by comparison. (Meanwhile, Short's ex-SCTV costar, Eugene

Levy, falls flat with his racist burlesque of the predatory Middle Eastern businessman.)

Since the film aims to be more dramatic than funny, at least it might have explored the family dynamics with a bit more depth, acknowledging the unstated rivalry between pregnant mother and daughter or George's nearly incestuous jealousy over his son-in-law's affection for Kimberly. But this is a Disney film, so these topics are glossed over, as is Annie's allowing her father to determine her future job move (so much for a feminist updating!). FATHER II valorizes bourgeois values where a good comedy would demolish them. *(Sexual situations, profanity.)* — E.M.

d, Charles Shyer; p, Nancy Meyers; exec p, Sandy Gallin, Carol Baum; assoc p, Julie B. Crane; co-p, Cindy Williams, Bruce A. Block; w, Nancy Meyers, Charles Shyer (adapted from the 1951 screenplay *Father's Little Dividend* by Albert Hackett and Francis Goodrich, based on characters created by Edward Streeter); ph, William A. Fraker; ed, Stephen A. Rotter; m, Alan Silvestri; prod d, Linda DeScenna; art d, Greg Papalia; set d, Ric McElvin; sound, Richard B. Goodman (mixer); fx, Dennis Dion; casting, Jeff Greenberg, Sheila Guthrie; cos, Enid Harris; makeup, Karen Blynder

Comedy/Drama   **(PR: A   MPAA: PG)**

FATHERLAND   ★★½
(U.S.) 110m HBO Pictures ~ Warner Home Video c

Rutger Hauer *(Xavier March)*; Miranda Richardson *(Charlie Maguire)*; Michael Kitchen *(Max Jaeger)*; Jean Marsh *(Anna Von Hagen)*; Peter Vaughn *(Nebe)*; John Shrapnel *(General Globus)*; Clive Russell *(Krebs)*; John Woodvine *(Luther)*; Clare Higgins *(Klara)*; Pavel Andel *(Man in Dark Coat)*; Patronella Q. Barker *(Guide Helga)*; Sarah Berger *(Leni Halder)*; Jan Bidlas *(Bellboy)*; Stuart Bunce *(Blind Soldier)*; Charles De'Ath *(Fake Porter)*; Neil Dudgeon *(Sex Crimes Cop)*; Rudolph Fleischer *(Hitler)*; Garrick Hagon *(Elliot)*; David Hatton *(Short Man)*; Rupert Penry Jones *(Jost)*; Jan Kohout *(US President)*; Rory Jennings; Bob Mason *(Coroner Eisler)*; David McAllister *(Party Official Anchor)*; Petr Meissel *(Young Policeman)*; Patrick Opaterny *(Heinz)*; David Ryall *(Administrator Kroger)*; Zdena Seifertova *(Jaeger's Wife)*; Michael J. Shannon *(US Ambassador)*; Milan Simacek *(SS Man at Press Compound)*; Marek Vasut *(SS Cadet Instructor)*; Jan Vlasak *(1st SS Man)*

A made-for-cable film adapted from Robert Harris's novel, this tale of government conspiracy begins with a compelling premise: What if Germany had won the war in Europe and, furthermore, had successfully suppressed evidence of the Holocaust for nearly thirty years?

It is 1964, three decades after the German army turned back the D-Day invasion at Normandy, and the superpower now known as Germania is on the brink of an historic moment: detente between Germania and the United States, to be symbolized by a meeting of US President Joseph Kennedy Sr. and the seventy-five-year-old Fuhrer, Adolf Hitler. Just days before the summit, a Germanian police officer, Major March (Rutger Hauer), is called to investigate a series of murders, possibly linked; at the same time, American journalist Charlie Maguire (Miranda Richardson) is called away from her press junket by a former German military official hoping to defect to the US. Together, March and Maguire unfold Germania's horrible secret: the systematic slaughter of nearly six million Jews during WWII. With only hours remaining before the US-Germania summit, they race against the Gestapo to get evidence of the Holocaust to the US ambassador.

Capably-directed and well-acted, FATHERLAND would make a superb suspense thriller if not for one rather glaring fact: the audience already knows the solution to the puzzle (the Holocaust), even if March and Maguire do not. If written better, the story could lend itself easily to Hitchcock's classic "bomb under the chair" scenario, with the detectives inching closer and closer to the answer, assembling the pieces one by one until the last one slips satisfyingly into place. However, the detectives in FATHERLAND approach the mystery in such an elliptical fashion there seems to be no chance of them even stumbling upon the answer, let alone working it out themselves—in other words, the bomb in this scenario is under a chair in another room of a completely different house. In the end, the evidence for the Holocaust is dropped abruptly in their laps by a single informant, making the protagonists look like rather poor detectives indeed. Most likely, the luxury of well-paced revelation (which may have also answered such begged questions as "How did Joseph Kennedy become president?") was lost in the novel-to-screenplay translation. *(Violence, nudity, adult situations.)* — B.T.

d, Christopher Menaul; p, Frederick Muller, Ilene Khan; assoc p, Leonid Zisman; w, Stanley Weiser, Ron Hutchinson (based on the novel *Fatherland* by Robert Harris); ph, Peter Sova; ed, Tariq Anwar; m, Gary Chang; prod d, Veronica Hadfield; art d, Martin Maly; sound, Jacob Goldstein (mixer); fx, Jaroslav Stolba, Syd Dutton, Bill Taylor, Robert Stromberg, Illusion Arts; casting, Kathleen Mackie; cos, Barbara Lane; makeup, Eileen Kastner-Delago; stunts, Ladislav Lahoda

Thriller/Political   **(PR: C   MPAA: NR)**

FEAR, THE   ★★½
(U.S.) 93m Devin Entertainment ~ A-Pix Entertainment c

Eddie Bowz *(Richard)*; Heather Medway *(Ashley)*; Ann Turkel *(Leslie)*; Vince Edwards *(Uncle Pete)*; Darin Heames *(Troy)*; Anna Karin *(Tanya)*; Antonio Todd *(Gerald)*; Leland Hayward *(Vance)*; Monique Mannen *(Mindy)*; Erick Weiss *(Morty)*; Wes Craven *(Dr. Arnold)*; Hunter Bedrosian *(Young Richard)*; Rebecca Baldwin *(Rose)*; Greg Littman *(Claude)*; Stacy Edwards *(Becky)*; Tom Challis *(Detective #1)*; Bill Wallace *(Detective #2)*; Daniel Franklin *(Father)*; Lisa Iannini *(Mother)*; Corey Wilson *(Son)*; Bill Winkler *(Real Estate Agent)*; Ron Ford *(Security Guard)*; Greg "B.D." Roszyk *(Young Pete)*

Filmed as MORTY (after its chief agent of menace), THE FEAR is a long-winded but ultimately satisfying exercise in chills.

Psychology student Richard (Eddie Bowz), who has been troubled by scary dreams relating to his childhood, gets approval from his professor, Dr. Arnold (Wes Craven), to hold an encounter session/retreat at his boyhood home in the nearby woods. He brings his girlfriend Ashley (Heather Medway) and a group of other troubled students to the house, where they discover a carved wooden figure nicknamed Morty in a cabinet. Richard encourages the participants to reveal their deepest fears to Morty as part of their therapy. Richard's uncle Pete (Vince Edwards) shows up unexpectedly, and the group takes a break to visit a closed amusement park nearby. Soon the group members begin to fall victim to the things they each fear most, with Morty apparently the agent of their deaths; he eventually comes to life to attack them. In the midst of the mayhem, Richard comes to realize that his dreams are connected to guilt over having discovered his mother having an affair and telling his father, who killed her. Richard also discovers that Pete was his mother's lover, and Morty shoots Pete before taking off after Richard and Ashley. But by confronting and overcoming the fears that have been plaguing him, Richard is able to fend Morty off, and the wooden man walks into a lake and vanishes.

THE FEAR is refreshingly straight-faced for a modern low-budget horror film, though it borders on taking itself too seriously. While the young cast is good, their characters spend too much time declaiming their problems and dealing with their individual angsts, and the story takes its time getting up to speed. There are also some questionable psychological gimmicks in Ron Ford's screenplay, such as the word "diametric" being spoken repeatedly by masked figures in Richard's dream because it's an anagram of "matricide."

Once the horrors begin however, director Vincent Robert is able to pour on the atmosphere, with fine, shadowy photography by Bernd Heinl. Morty's evolution from inanimate totem to ambulatory menace is handled well, with convincing makeup effects by John Carl Buechler, and the fates of the various characters evoke the necessary chills. The soundtrack of rap and reggae manages to be incongruous and effective at the same time, and horror fans will get an extra kick from veteran genre director Craven's low-key appearance as Dr. Arnold in the film's opening and closing scenes. *(Violence, nudity, sexual situations, profanity.)* — M.G.

d, Vincent Robert; p, Richard Brandes; exec p, Robert Baruc; assoc p, Adam Levy; co-p, Jacob Wellington; w, Ron Ford (from a story by Greg H. Sims and Ron Ford); ph, Bernd Heinl; ed, Nancy Forner; m, Robert O. Ragland; prod d, Brian McCabe; art d, Andrew Sowards; sound, Paul Coogan, Maryjo Devenney, Jack Lindauer; fx, John Buechler, MMI; casting, Linda Berger; cos, Reve Richards; stunts, Gary Wayton

Horror   **(PR: O   MPAA: R)**

FEAST OF JULY   ★★½
(U.S.) 118m Merchant Ivory; Peregrine Productions; Touchstone ~ Buena Vista c

Embeth Davidtz *(Bella Ford)*; Tom Bell *(Ben Wainwright)*; Gemma Jones *(Mrs. Wainwright)*; James Purefoy *(Jedd Wainwright)*; Ben Chaplin *(Con Wainwright)*; Kenneth Anderson *(Matty Wainwright)*; Greg Wise *(Arch Wilson)*; David Neal *(Mitchy Mitchell)*; Daphne Neville *(Mrs. Mitchell)*; Mark Heal *(Clerk at Shoe Factory)*; Julian Protheroe *(Bowler-Hatted Man)*; Tim Preece *(Preacher)*; Charles De'ath *(Billy Swaine)*; Colin Prockter *(Man in Pub)*; Richard Hope *(Squire Wyman)*; Kate Hamblyn *(Harvest Girl)*; Paddy Ward *(Tom)*; Alan Perrin *(Ticket Clerk)*; Dominic Gover *(First Rowing Youth)*; Richard Hicks *(Second Rowing Youth)*; Arthur Kelly *(Game Keeper)*; Colin Mayes *(Seaman)*; Mark Bazeley *(Man in Restaurant)*; Stephen Frost *(Tubby Man)*; David Belcher *(Second Man)*; Frederick Warder *(Captain Rogers)*; Tim Perrin *(Hangman)*; Mark Whelehan *(Assistant Hangman)*; Rupert Bates *(Prison Warder)*; Tom Marshall *(Prison Warder)*

Produced by Merchant/Ivory, FEAST OF JULY has all the lush visual elements we've come to expect from that team. However, this Victorian tragedy of a beautiful woman's spiral into infamy is little more than a feast for the eyes, without so much as a morsel for the filmgoer's body or soul.

The film—adapted from an H.E. Bates novel—opens with a turn-of-the-century woman taking refuge in an abandoned shack on a windswept English plain and giving birth to a stillborn child. After burying the child, Bella Ford (Embeth Davidtz) stumbles into town in search of the man who deceived her into her present condition. Befriended by a kindly lamplighter, Mr. Wainwright (Tom Bell), and his family, Bella is a guest who quickly becomes a replacement for the only daughter who died, and then becomes the object of desire for the three Wainwright sons—cobbler Jedd (James Purefoy), soldier Matty (Kenneth Anderson), and poet Con (Ben Chaplin).

With each son vying for her attentions and affections, the close-knit Wainwright family begins to fall apart. During the annual Feast of July harvest, family sexual tensions explode, and two of the brothers almost kill each other. In the aftermath, Bella surprisingly chooses sensitive Con, and the two are married.

Their happiness is brief. During a Sunday afternoon rowboat excursion, Bella and Con encounter Arch (Greg Wise), the married man who impregnated Bella. Arch recognizes Bella and taunts the couple and her honor. In a blind rage, Con kills Arch. Then the newlyweds—horrified at what has just happened—escape to a sea town, intending to sail to America. However, Con's conscience won't let him run away from his deeds. Against Bella's wishes, he confesses to the murder. He is hanged, and the Wainwright family throw their curses on Bella when they pass her at the prison. The movie ends with a pregnant Bella sailing toward America and a new life.

Pictured as a beautiful and mysterious young woman thrust into a family with three handsome sons, Bella clearly captures the hearts and loins of the trio—though the reasons for this are, frankly, difficult to decipher. With a minimum of dialogue and character development—especially of its main character—and a maximum of foreboding, dimly lit images, this glacially paced feature might be described as a psychological film without psychology. The film tells us nothing of who Bella is, psychologically or socially. In essence, she is a ghost, albeit a very beautiful one. It is impossible to relate to her or the story that unfolds around her. (Adult situations, violence, sexual situations.) — P.P.

d, Chris Menaul; p, Henry Herbert, Christopher Neame; exec p, Ismail Merchant, Paul Bradley; assoc p, Jane Cussons, Donald Rosenfeld; w, Christopher Neame (based on the novel by H.E. Bates); ph, Peter Sova; ed, Chris Wimble; m, Zbigniew Preisner; prod d, Christopher Robilliard; art d, Roy Stannard, Caroline Smith, Sonja Klaus; set d, Jill Quertier; sound, Stuart Moser (recordist), Mike Shoring (recordist); fx, Stuart Brisdon; casting, Kathleen Mackie; cos, Phoebe de Gaye; makeup, Tina Earnshaw, Susie Adams

Drama/Romance (PR: C MPAA: R)

FIRST DEGREE ★★
(U.S./Canada) 98m Westcom Entertainment;
Lowry Entertainment ~ PolyGram Video c

Rob Lowe (Rick Mallory); Leslie Hope (Hadley Pyne); Tom McCamus (Amos Turou); Joseph Griffin (Rico Perrini); Nadia Capone (Tina Jerrigan); Brett Halsey (Alonzo Esterro); Peter Boret (Jacob Sarner); Dov Francks (Lou Matlin); Brian Renfro (Andrew Pyne); Pierre Kenneth Cross (Henri); Patricia Gage (Margaret Pyne); David B. Nicols (Jason); Falconer Abraham (Ed Gronic); Gayle Ackroyd (P.I. Secretary); Carlo Rota (Joe Esterro); Tony Perri (Carmen); Francois Klanfer (Albert Moliere); Graham Harley (Kurt); R.D. Reid (Nick); Silvio Olivero (Tony Fab); John Boylan (Peter Wollner); Kay Tremelay (Estelle Sarner)

FIRST DEGREE is a somber, plodding murder mystery for undemanding fans of Rob Lowe.

New York City detectives Rick Mallory (Rob Lowe), Amos Turou (Tom McCamus), and Rico Perrini (Joseph Griffin), investigate the murder of rich socialite Andrew Pyne (Brian Renfro), whose mother (Patricia Gage) believes he was killed by his beautiful wife Hadley (Leslie Hope). Led by Mallory, the cops, however, settle on gangster Joe Esterro (Carlo Rota), whose mobster uncle, Alonzo Esterro (Brett Halsey), believes he is innocent and hires Perrini, who has just quit the force to become a private detective, to find the real culprit.

Counseled by his friend, a coffee-shop philosopher-novelist, Jacob Sarner (Peter Boret), and enticing Hadley to fall in love with him, the obsessed Mallory soon estranges himself from the rest of the police by his erratic behavior. Even his pal Turou begins to suspect Mallory of the killing, which is, in fact, what happened. Meanwhile, Perrini brings in street hood Tony Fab (Silvio Olivero), who implicates Hadley. Fab's false confession is assured by Esterro kidnapping Fab's girlfriend's diabetic daughter. Mallory, however, springs Hadley, who maintains Fab was blackmailing her because her novelist friend Lou Matlin (Dov Francks) had discussed hiring Fab for Hadley to kill her abusive husband. Mallory and Turou rescue the kidnapped child in a warehouse shoot-out in which Turou and Esterro are slain. Mallory, who has got away with Pyne's murder, and Hadley, who now knows about it, leave New York, but Mallory gets involved in a gas station hold-up. When Mallory fires at the fleeing bandit, a stray bullet from his gun hits Hadley right between the eyes.

FIRST DEGREE suffers from a far-fetched, convoluted, loose-ends-galore plot by screenwriter Ron Base. The film does try to be more than just another routine police story, and first-time Canadian director Jeff Woolnough downplays the police procedural details and expected violence, adds a pretentious novelist-as-conscience character (Sarner, who is working on a novel about Mallory, called First Degree), and centers the film on Mallory's moral conflict and sexual obsession. Unfortunately, Rob Lowe is just not up to it; his inner turmoil comes off mostly as ennui, and he gives no indication of the cleverness needed to bring off the "investigate your own murder" caper. Nor is much heat generated by his and Leslie Hope's "steamy" coupling. Given Woolnough's plodding direction—even the shoot-out finale lacks suspense—FIRST DEGREE is tired, confusing stuff, despite a sturdy supporting cast. Handsomely shot in Toronto, the film was released direct-to-video and pay-cable TV. (Violence, nudity, sexual situations, profanity.) — D.B.

d, Jeff Woolnough; p, Richard O. Lowry; exec p, Terrence Turner; co-p, Ray Sager, David Korchok, Ron Base; w, Ron Base; ph, Glenn MacPherson; ed, Roushell Goldstein; m, Bruce Fowler; prod d, Elaine Smith; art d, Jasna Stefanovic; set d, Jim Lamore; sound, Dan Daniels; casting, Pamela Rack-Guest, Jon Comerford; cos, Resa McConaghy; makeup, Lisa Crown, David Scott; stunts, Shane Cardwell

Crime/Drama/Mystery (PR: O MPAA: R)

FIRST KNIGHT ★★½
(U.S.) 132m Zucker Brothers Productions;
Columbia ~ Columbia c

Sean Connery (King Arthur); Richard Gere (Lancelot); Julia Ormond (Lady Guinevere); Ben Cross (Malagant); Liam Cunningham (Sir Agravaine); Chris Villiers (Sir Kay); Valentine Pelka (Sir Patrise); Colin McCormack (Sir Mador); Ralph Ineson (Ralf); John Gielgud (Oswald); Stuart Bunce (Peter); Jane Robbins (Elise); Jean Marie Coffey (Petronella); Paul Kynman (Mark); Tom Lucy (Sir Sagramore); John Blakey (Sir Tor); Robert Gwyn Davin (Sir Gawaine); Sean Blowers (Sir Carados); Alexis Denisof (Sir Gaheris); Daniel Naprous (Sir Amant); Jonathan Cake (Sir Gareth); Paul Bentall (Jacob); Jonty Miller (Gauntlet Man); Rose Keegan (Mark's Wife); Mark Ryan (Challenger); Jeffery Dench (First Elder); Neville Phillips (Second Elder); Oliver Lewis (First Marauder); Wolf Christian (Second Marauder); Angus Wright (Third Marauder); Jonathan Jaynes (First Guard); Eric Stone (Second Guard); Ryan Todd (Young Lancelot); Albie Woodington (Scout); Richard Claxton (Child); Dido Miles (Grateful Woman); Michael Hodgson (Young Man in Crowd); Susannah Corbett (Young Woman in Crowd); Susan

Breslau *(Wedding Guest)*; Kate Zucker *(Flower Girl)*; Bob Zucker *(Little Boy With Birds)*; Charlotte Zucker *(Bread Vendor)*; Burt Zucker *(Bread Vendor)*

FIRST KNIGHT is a respectable, middlebrow rendering of the classic story of the romantic triangle of King Arthur, Queen Guinevere and Sir Lancelot. It boasts some expert performances, elegant production design and attractive Welsh locations.

An era of peace in medieval England is shattered by the aggression of Sir Malagant (Ben Cross), a former knight of Camelot who has broken with King Arthur (Sean Connery) and has designs on Arthur's idyllic kingdom. Malagant's men attempt to kidnap Arthur's intended bride, Guinevere (Julia Ormond), but are stopped by wandering swordsman Lancelot (Richard Gere), who boldly kisses the lady and disappears into the forest.

Guinevere reaches Camelot safely, but once there is abducted by Malagant's men, who take her to Malagant's lair in a cave beneath a ruined castle. Lancelot rescues her, and Arthur offers him Malagant's vacant seat at the Round Table. After much soul-searching, Lancelot accepts. Arthur and Guinevere are married in an elaborate ceremony. Malagant's army invades Lyonesse, Guinevere's homeland, and Arthur rallies his army and marches into battle. In a spectacular nighttime confrontation, Arthur's forces rout Malagant's army. Lancelot's valor in battle impresses the other knights, who were reluctant to accept his sudden entrance into their privileged circle.

Back at Camelot, Lancelot—torn by his love for Guinevere—decides to leave and bids the Queen goodbye. Arthur witnesses their passionate farewell kiss, and demands a public trial for both of them. At the trial, Lancelot affirms Guinevere's innocence and his own undying loyalty to Arthur and the Round Table. Suddenly, the trial is interrupted by a bold attack by Malagant. In the pitched battle that ensues, Arthur is mortally wounded and Lancelot duels Malagant to the death. On his deathbed, Arthur gives his blessings to both Lancelot and Guinevere.

The legends of King Arthur of Camelot have inspired many films, including KNIGHTS OF THE ROUND TABLE (1954), SWORD OF LANCELOT (1963), EXCALIBUR (1981), THE SWORD IN THE STONE (1963) and, of course, CAMELOT (1967). FIRST KNIGHT most resembles the glossy romance KNIGHTS OF THE ROUND TABLE, and aspires to be a treatise on honor, service, duty and love. The romance between Lancelot and Guinevere is a chaste one in which both characters subordinate their passions to social responsibility and their mutual respect and love for Arthur. The film's focus is Lancelot and his gradual growth from a footloose, masterless swordsman—on the order of Akira Kurosawa's YOJIMBO—into a loyal, duty-bound member of the Round Table. While the film is sometimes slow and talky, the action sequences involving the renegade knight Malagant and his snarling, lowlife henchmen are appropriately rousing. One expertly mounted nighttime battle scene almost elevates the film from romantic drama to epic status.

Sean Connery slips easily into the role of the wise, benevolent monarch who is genuinely trusted and loved by those in his court. Julia Ormond, in only her third major film, makes a feisty, earthy, willful Guinevere, possibly the most memorable of all screen Guineveres. The weak link in the casting is the much-criticized Richard Gere, who is a bit too callow for the role of Lancelot. That said, the same criticism can be leveled against such earlier Lancelots as Robert Taylor, Cornel Wilde, Franco Nero and Nicholas Clay. Gere works hard, is sincere, and handles the extensive swordplay with skillful glee.

FIRST KNIGHT eschews the fantastic elements that are an integral part of the Arthurian legend—Merlin and Excalibur are particularly conspicuous by their absence—in favor of a low-key realism and narrative clarity that are unusual in current historical dramas, which tend to rely on ostentatious effects. The authentic-looking Camelot—built at London's Pinewood Studios—and the use of Welsh locations and actual cathedrals all contribute to creating a believable context for the story's intricate romantic and moral interplay. *(Violence.)* — B.C.

d, Jerry Zucker; p, Hunt Lowry; exec p, Gil Netter, Eric Rattray, Janet Zucker; assoc p, Kathryn J. McDermott; w, William Nicholson (from a story by William Nicholson, Lorne Cameron, and David Hostelton); ph, Adam Greenberg; ed, Walter Murch; m, Jerry Goldsmith; prod d, John Box; art d, Bob Laing, Michael White; set d, Malcolm Stone; sound, Colin Charles (mixer); fx, George Gibbs, John Evans, Dennis Lowe; casting, Mary Selway; cos, Nana Cecchi; makeup, Peter Robb-King; stunts, Greg Powell, Dinny Powell

Romance/Drama/Adventure　　　**(PR: A　MPAA: PG-13)**

FLUKE　　　　　　　　　　　　　　　　　　★★½
(U.S.) 95m Rocket Pictures; MGM ~ MGM/UA c

Matthew Modine *(Thomas Johnson/Voice of Fluke)*; Nancy Travis *(Carol Johnson)*; Eric Stoltz *(Jeff Newman)*; Max Pomeranc *(Brian Johnson)*; Samuel L. Jackson *(Voice of Rumbo)*; Ron Perlman *(Sylvester)*; Jon Polito *(Boss)*; Bill Cobbs *(Bert)*; Collin Wilcox Paxton *(Bella)*; Federico Pacifici *(Professor Santini)*; Clarinda Ross *(Tom's Secretary)*; Adrian Roberts *(Night Guard)*; Bart Hansard *(Day Guard)*; Deborah Hobart *(Dog Pound Vet)*; Libby Whittemore *(Housekeeper)*; Dominique Milton *(Schoolboy)*; Mary Anne Hagan *(Woman No. 1)*; Yolanda King *(Woman No. 2)*; Brian Katz *(Paramedic No. 1)*; Mary Holloway *(Paramedic No. 2)*; David Dwyer *(News Stand Man)*; Michael H. Moss *(Policeman No. 1)*; Duke Steinemann *(Policeman No. 2)*; Georgia Allen *(Rose)*; John Lawhorn *(Farmer)*; Calvin Miller *(Skeptical Man)*; Harry Pritchett *(Priest)*; Duong Bl *(Asian Dishwasher)*; Diego La Rosa *(Security Guard)*; Angie Rene *(Delivery Boy)*; Sam Gifaldi *(Voice of Young Fluke)*

Though it has many of the trappings of a traditional family dog movie on the order of BENJI, FLUKE aspires to be taken seriously as human drama about reincarnation, karma, and self-discovery.

Tom (Mathew Modine, also Fluke's voice) dies in a car crash that appears to have been caused by his business partner, Jeff (Eric Stoltz). He is reincarnated as a dog, one of a litter of puppies born to a stray living behind a Chinese restaurant. The dogs are captured by Animal Control, and the puppy escapes certain death at the pound. He's befriended by a homeless woman, who names him Fluke because of his uncanny ability to play the shell game. She dies suddenly, and a worldly stray named Rumbo (voice of Samuel L. Jackson) takes Fluke under his paw and teaches him how to communicate telepathically with other dogs.

Fluke is plagued by what he first thinks are dreams, but grows to recognize as flashbacks; they involve his human life, his wife Carol (Nancy Travis), his son Brian (Max Pomeranc), and his own death. He sees Jeff's photo on the cover of a magazine, and becomes obsessed with the thought of returning home to set things right. Fluke is nabbed by an animal hating goon (Ron Perlman) for use in a cosmetic company's research lab, and subjected to hideous tests. But Rumbo bursts in through a plate glass window and releases all the captive animals. The goon shoots Rumbo, who guides Fluke—who's temporarily blinded—into the woods, then dies.

Fluke makes his way back to Hopewell, finds Brian and ingratiates his way into the house. He does things he did as a human, such as steal Brian's toys and wear Tom's golf hat. When Jeff visits, Fluke attacks him, prompting a call to Animal Control. Brian hides Fluke and pleads to keep him, allowing Fluke to overhear Carol and Jeff exchange intimacies. Fluke sneaks in to his old office and recalls violent arguments with Jeff, then hides in the car when Jeff heads back to help find Brian, who has disappeared searching for Fluke. Fluke attacks Jeff at the fateful corner, causing a car crash that sends him flying through the windshield. Near death, he has one final, devastating flashback: he recalls that he was a jerk, while Jeff was a fundamentally loyal and decent guy, and that he's largely responsible for the accident in which he died. The injured Fluke revives Jeff and finds Brian, whom he keeps warm in a snow storm until Carol can rescue the boy.

Based on a book by English horror novelist James Herbert, FLUKE is poised awkwardly between the conventions of talking animal comedies and moralistic kiddie fare like LOOK WHO'S TALKING NOW, OH HEAVENLY DOG, THE INCREDIBLE JOURNEY and MILO AND OTIS, and its own grimly serious ambitions. The preponderance of urination gags, the truly horrifying sequence in the cosmetics lab and the deaths of one sympathetic character after another—including Fluke's canine mother and siblings—make this an inappropriate film for younger children, and the plot hinges on emotional issues of loss and regret likely to bore older kids. FLUKE is not an entirely successful film, despite the depth of the original material, but it is far more ambitous than most films in its genre. (Violence, profanity, adult situations.) — R.S.

d, Carlo Carlei; p, Paul Maslansky, Lata Ryan; exec p, Jon Turtle, Tom Coleman; assoc p, Terri Ferraro; w, Carlo Carlei, James Carrington (based on the novel by James Herbert); ph, Raffaele Mertes; ed, Mark Conte; m, Carlo Siliotto; prod d, Hilda Stark; art d, Richard Fojo; set d, Dayna Lee; sound, Mark Mangini (design); fx, Gene Grigg, Paolo Zeccara; casting, Lynn Stalmaster; cos, Elisabetta Beraldo; makeup, Lynn Barber; stunts, M. James Arnett

Fantasy/Drama   (PR: A   MPAA: PG)

FOOL AND HIS MONEY, A   ★
(U.S.) 84m Chronicle Films ~ Vidmark Entertainment c

Jonathan Penner (Morris Codman); Gerald Orange (Dr. Ian Clarity, Ph.D.); Sandra Bullock (Debby Cosgrove); George Plimpton (God); Wendy Adams (Peggy); Chuck Pfieffer (Brenda Collins); Earl Hagan, Jr. (Rev. Billy Bob McElroy); Maggie Wagner (Sam); Michael Mandell (Joe French); Marcia Amron (Mrs. Codman); Jerzy Kosinski (The Beggar); Tama Janowitz (TV Host); Jose Torres (Himself)

The title might well describe anyone lured into renting this video release by the cassette's false promise of a romantic comedy starring Sandra Bullock.

Filmed in 1989, six years before Bullock became a box-office draw on the basis of SPEED and WHILE YOU WERE SLEEPING, this really stars Jonathan Penner as ad man Morris Codman who, after receiving a message from God (George Plimpton), tries to cash in by starting a new religion. He incorporates The Preferent Church, and hires janitor-philosopher Ian Clarity (Gerald Orange) as a figurehead. The church espouses a lifestyle of conscience-free, personal selfishness, and is a big hit with amoral businesspeople. This is too much for Codman's idealistic girlfriend Debby (Bullock), so she dumps him. The new religion is a success, and Codman and Clarity get rich, but there's still something missing from their lives. After Clarity is seen giving money to a beggar—a Preferent sin— and Debby is mugged by a disciple, Codman decides to give it all up. He comes clean

before the press, gives his fortune to the poor, and reunites with Debby.

Bullock has only a small role in this clunker, and she's fine. A FOOL AND HIS MONEY basically expands on Michael Douglas' "Greed is Good" motto from WALL STREET, but the production is too shabby-looking to approach the level of satire. Even as straightforward whimsy it fails. As if the FOOL AND HIS MONEY experience wasn't made unpleasant enough by the charisma-free team of Penner and Orange, sound quality is harsh and tinny, and the music is lousy. "Preferent" is spelled four different ways in the film, if that's indication of anything. In addition to Plimpton, literati Jerzy Kosinski and Tama Janowitz join Bullock in the cameo parade. (Profanity.) — P.R.

d, Daniel Adams; p, Michael Mailer; exec p, Laura Pensa, Emanuel Goldberg, Daniel Adams; assoc p, Simon Brook, Bill Snowden; w, Daniel Adams, Michael Mailer (from a story by Daniel Adams); ph, John Drake; ed, Thomas R. Rondinella; m, Kip Martin; prod d, Paola Ridolfi; casting, Robin Monroe

Comedy   (PR: A   MPAA: R)

FOR GOD AND COUNTRY   ★★★
(Austria) 115m Dor Film ~ Dor Film c
(AKA: I PR0MISE; ICH GELOBE)

Christoph Dostal (Private Berger); Andreas Lust (Rumpler); Andreas Simma (Moser); Marcus J. Carney (Kernstock); Leopold Altenburg (Tomschitz); Albert Weilguny (Sergeant Pfister); Johannes Kollmann (Sergeant Ernst); Robert Taurer (Lieutenant Ressl); Peter Max Januschke (Spiess Ohler); Josef Kuderna (Chaplain); Hans Sigl (Platoon Leader); Markus Schleinzer (Schwarzrot); Reinhold Moritz (Zaritsch); Sahin Ali Haydar (Karall); Josef Selzer (Wegscheider); Gerd Eichler (Knipfer); Horst Eder (Father); Herta Schell (Mother); Maria Tritremmel (Grandmother); Udo Kholmann (Stone); Rudolf Neumayr (Guitarist); Gerhard Leutgeb (Drummer); Pia Baresch (Veronika); Monika Praxmarer (Silvia); Sabine Waibel (Gerlinde); Elisabeth Lanz (Susi); Thirry Van Wervike (Ferri); Janine Wegener (Frau Leitgeb)

Many books and films have depicted the horrors of war, but few have captured the absurdities of the military in peacetime as well as FOR GOD AND COUNTRY. What sounds like a drab look at army life turns out to be affecting and surprisingly entertaining.

At an army barracks located on the Austro-Hungarian border in 1980, the Communist threat from the East is still taken seriously. The 18-year-old Private Berger (Christoph Dostal) breaks up the monotony of his cruel, rigorous daily routine by counting his remaining days in the Austrian army, daydreaming about sex with voluptuous women, and escaping periodically to a secret bathroom stall where he draws Hieronymus Bosch-like cartoons of his experiences. In the evenings Berger and his soldier friends drive recklessly through the streets, hopping from bar to bar.

Berger becomes increasingly disgusted with military philosophy. In one exercise, he and his comrades are forced to capture and kill chickens for their dinner, but all he feels is despair at the animals' deaths. He seeks comfort and sympathy from his visiting girlfriend, Veronika (Pia Baresch), but their relationship remains tentative. Berger later becomes deeply upset when one of his friends dies in a car crash following an evening of carousing. Soon after the funeral, an army sergeant discovers Berger's drawings in the bathroom and orders them removed. Finally, discharged from the army, Berger hopes for a better future.

FOR GOD AND COUNTRY begins and ends with surreal dream sequences. In between, the film depicts the irrelevance of an army without a war to fight and the grim ironies of the military institution. In some ways, FOR GOD AND COUNTRY is on par with, or even superior to, such dark-humored army tale classics as STALAG 17 (1953), M*A*S*H (1970), CATCH-22 (1970), BASIC TRAINING (1971), and FULL METAL JACKET (1987). Moreover, the film is highly cognizant of its forebears: in one scene, the soldiers watch APOCALYPSE NOW in a theatre; in the next scene, the "Ride of the Valkyries" theme music from the Coppola film overlaps with a montage of the soldiers' own grueling training session.

Director Wolfang Murnberger displays command over his medium. The stylish, erotic dream sequences provide a counterpoint to Berger's stark daily reality. The fast cutting in the club-hopping montage creates a humorous shorthand for the empty thrill-seeking the soldiers pursue in lieu of true freedom. In another montage, which depicts different types of soldiers in the army (knighted soldiers, toy soldiers, et al.) Berger's point of view expands into an impressionistic essay. And, through moments of symbolism and quietly effective narration, FOR GOD AND COUNTRY also questions or confronts such issues as patriotism, patriarchy, gender roles, "Christian" attitudes, and even Austria's stifled Nazi past. (*Violence, nudity, sexual situations, adult situations, substance abuse, profanity.*) — E.M.

d, Wolfgang Murnberger; p, Danny Krausz, Milan Dor; w, Wolfgang Murnberger; ph, Fabian Eder; ed, Maria Homolkova; m, Robert Stiegler, Mischa Krausz; art d, Renate Martin, Andreas Donhauser; sound, Reinhold Kaiser; cos, Thomas Olah; makeup, Karin Schon

Drama/War/Fantasy (PR: C MPAA: NR)

FORGET PARIS ★★½
(U.S.) 101m Castle Rock; Face Productions ~ Columbia c

Billy Crystal (*Mickey*); Debra Winger (*Ellen*); Joe Mantegna (*Andy*); Cynthia Stevenson (*Liz*); Richard Masur (*Craig*); Julie Kavner (*Lucy*); William Hickey (*Arthur*); Robert Costanzo (*Waiter*); John Spencer (*Jack*); Tom Wright (*Tommy*); Cathy Moriarty (*Lois*); Johnny Williams (*Lou*); Marv Albert; Bill Walton; Charles Barkley; David Robinson; Dan Majerle; Kevin Johnson; Paul Westphal; Sean Elliott; Patrick Ewing; Tim Hardaway; Kareem Abdul-Jabbar; Bill Laimbeer; Reggie Miller; Charles Oakley; Kurt Rambis; John Starks; Isiah Thomas; Spud Webb; Marcus Johnson; Rush Limbaugh; David Sandorn (*Themselves*); Bert Copello (*Airline Employee*); Ron Ross (*Insolent Official*); Andy Flaster (*Airline Official No. 1*); David St. James (*Airline Official No. 2*); Gregory Paul Jackson (*Airline Official No. 3*); Andreas Tessi (*Airline Official No. 4*); Chris Shaver (*Laker Girl*); Mary Oedy (*Knicks City Dancer*); Joie Shettler (*Spurs Silverdancer*); Andrea Toste (*Sonics Dancer*); Lisa Gannon (*Attractive Woman*); Richard Assad (*Suitcase Man*); Lisa Rieffel (*Receptionist*); Emmy Smith (*Woman in Porsche*); Margaret Nagle (*Marylin*); Janette Caldwell (*Andy's Date*); Tim Halligan (*Doctor*); Tim Ahern (*Fertility Doctor*); Judyann Elder (*Ivy*); Deb Lacusta (*Nurse*); Tom Ohmer (*Policeman*); E.E. Bell; Marty Brinton; Jo Farkas; Ken Johnson; Patrick Thomas O'Brien; Jay Rusumny (*Angry Fans in Crowd*); Robert Hunter, Jr. (*Detroit Fan*); Marty McSorley (*Detroit Fan*); Richard Haje (*Dangerous Man*); Clint Howard (*Exterminator*); Beverly Piper (*Organist*); Charlotte Etienne (*Girl—Age 3*); Zacharay Eginton (*Boy—Age 5*); Jennifer Mickelson (*Girl—Age 7*); Allan Kolman (*French Waiter*); Hedwige de Mouroux (*Distinguished Business Woman*); Roberto Bonanni (*Distinguished Frenchman*); Jean Shum (*Waitress*); Andre Rosey Brown (*Huge Bodyguard*); Rick Gunderson (*Motorcycle Cop No. 1*); Liz Sheridan (*Motorcycle Cop No. 2*); Irving Wasserman (*Man in Car*); Genelle Lee Baumgardner (*Veronique*); Safe-T-Man (*Himself*); Scooter

Barry; Nathaniel Bellany, Jr.; Robert M. Betts; Bernard Brown; Sam Crawford; Greg Forbes; Keith Gibbs; Anthony C. Hall; Kevin L. Hildreth; Al Joseph; Brian Kilian; Gary Maloncon; Paul McCracken; Mike McGee; Nigel Miguel; Kevin Morris; Rich Porter; Cliff Reed; Charles Rochelin; Dawan Scott; Larry Spriggs; Reggie Theus; Charles Wahlheim; Marc Wilson; Dennis Wyatt (*Basketball Team*); Suren Arzoumanian; Jim Gasso; Barry Sousa; Harvey E. Tidwell; J. Greg Willard (*Referees*); Diane Alexander; Eleni Calevas; Dana Cuartero-Giordano; Sannye Jones; Blythe Matsui; Jodie McDonald; Shauna Morrison; Janet Payne; Gloria Rodriquez; Kris Storsberg (*Dancers*)

Billy Crystal serves as producer, director, co-screenwriter, and leading man of this romantic comedy. Even Woody Allen, the filmmaker to whom Crystal is inevitably likened, hasn't dared to take on those four jobs on a single picture. So perhaps it's not surprising that, with FORGET PARIS, Crystal's reach exceeds his grasp.

Crystal plays Mickey, a National Basketball Association referee who goes to Paris for his father's burial and falls in love with Ellen (Debra Winger), an American living abroad. After a whirlwind Parisian courtship, Mickey and Ellen get married. She quits her airline PR post to be with Mickey in the States. There, reality sets in. Ellen can't find a comparable job in LA and Mickey's constant traveling with the NBA—while allowing for cameos by Charles Barkley, Kareem Abdul-Jabbar and other hoop stars—leaves little time for newlywed bliss. Mickey and Ellen argue, break up, get back together, argue, break up, etc. All this is told in flashback, tag-team style, by a quintet of friends—including affable sportswriter Andy (Joe Mantegna), male chauvinist Jack (John Spencer), and fussy dieter Lucy (Julie Kavner)—who, four years after the wedding, are waiting for Mickey, and maybe Ellen, to join them for dinner.

Crystal's 1992 directing debut, MR. SATURDAY NIGHT, compressed the unpleasant life of a fictional Borscht Belt comedian into two unwieldy hours. This time out, working again as co-writer with Lowell Ganz and Babaloo Mandel, Crystal seems less disposed to mine the darker side of his characters. But while this results in a more cheerful film, it also pushes FORGET PARIS into a strangely manic area where the conventions of romantic comedy are sporadically undermined by bursts of black comedy verging on the macabre. That the movie reaches its high points during two such sequences—one in which Ellen is relentlessly attacked by a pigeon, the other a grimly hilarious view of old age and its peculiarities—suggests that, for all his determination to create something audience-friendly, the filmmaker is drawn to, and more accomplished at, celebrating the comically grotesque.

It's ironic, if a little daring, that a movie so obviously fashioned as an ode to marriage should be at its most charming in depicting the sheer fun of Mickey and Ellen's pre-marital fling. Paris in autumn, captured ravishingly by cinematographer Don Burgess, serves as the visual equivalent of new romance all right, but it's a tough first act to follow. Once FORGET PARIS shifts to prosaic California locations, the bloom is off the rose. The drabness of the restaurant where the storytellers convene gives these interludes an oddly somber tone, which is compounded by the one-note characters involved. These friends of the main couple are defined in the broadest of strokes. Meanwhile, the ongoing saga of Mickey and Ellen, meant to be legendary, just grows tiresome.

Occupying center stage, albeit in flashback, Crystal and Winger don't exactly generate sparks together. Crystal gets off the requisite number of wisecracks in his CITY SLICKERS persona, basically a cuddly, less neurotic Woody Allen. Ever the technician, Winger does have her "sticky pigeon" routine, a tour-de-force bit of physical comedy that had theater audiences practically on the floor laughing. In years to come, if anyone remembers FORGET PARIS, it will be for this inspired touch of comic artistry, rivaled only by William Hickey's gravel-voiced evocation of Ellen's senile father, for whom the "You asked for it, you got it" Toyota jingle has taken on the gravity of a mantra. *(Profanity, adult situations.)* — E.K.

d, Billy Crystal; p, Billy Crystal; exec p, Peter Schindler; co-p, Kelly Van Horn; w, Billy Crystal, Lowell Ganz, Babaloo Mandel; ph, Don Burgess; ed, Kent Beyda; m, Marc Shaiman; prod d, Terence Marsh; art d, William Cruse; set d, William Seirton; sound, Jeff Wexler, Don Coufal, Gary Holland; casting, Pam Dixon Mickelson; cos, Judy Ruskin; makeup, Peter Montagna; stunts, Mickey Gilbert

Comedy/Romance   **(PR: A   MPAA: PG-13)**

FOUR ROOMS   ★½
(U.S.) 102m A Band Apart Productions ~ Miramax c

Tim Roth *(Ted the Bellhop)*; Marisa Tomei *(Margaret)*; THE MISSING INGREDIENT: Ione Skye *(Eva)*; Valeria Golino *(Athena)*; Alicia Witt *(Kiva)*; Lili Taylor *(Raven)*; Ione Skye *(Eva)*; Sammi Davis *(Jezebel)*; Amanda de Cadenet *(Diana)*; THE WRONG MAN: Jennifer Beals *(Angela)*; Kathy Griffin *(Betty)*; David Proval *(Sigfried)*; Lawrence Bender *(Long Hair Yuppie Scum)*; Quinn Thomas Hellerman *(Baby Bellhop)*; Unruly Julie McClean *(Left Redhead)*; Laura Rush *(Right Redhead)*; Paul Skemp *(Real Theodore)*; THE MISBEHAVERS: Antonio Banderas *(Man)*; Lana McKissack *(Sarah)*; Patricia Vonne Rodriguez *(Corpse)*; Tamlyn Tomita *(Wife)*; Danny Verduzco *(Juancho)*; Salma Hayek *(TV Dancing Girl)*; THE MAN FROM HOLLYWOOD: Bruce Willis *(Leo)*; Quentin Tarantino *(Chester)*; Jennifer Beals *(Angela)*; Paul Calderon *(Norman)*

The disastrous FOUR ROOMS follows the adventures of a hapless bellboy working the late shift at a decadent Hollywood hotel on New Year's Eve. A violent, art-film variation on films like HOTEL PARADISO and BLAME IT ON THE BELLBOY, FOUR ROOMS squanders considerable talent both in front of and behind the camera.

New bellhop Ted (Tim Roth) begins his bizarre night with a lecture on his responsibilities, delivered by his elderly predecessor.

In "The Missing Ingredient," Ted helps a group of women check into the honeymoon suite, not realizing that they're witches who plan to resurrect their goddess, Diana, who was turned into a stone on her wedding night. All the witches, including Elspeth (Madonna), Athena (Valeria Golino) and Raven (Lili Taylor), contribute a bodily fluid to the magic brew they're cooking up. Novice Eva (Ione Skye) has failed to bring the semen she was delegated to contribute, and Ted becomes her unwitting back-up plan. With all the ingredients in place, the coven brings Diana (Amanda De Cadenet) back to life.

Next, Ted becomes "The Wrong Man" when he stumbles into the wrong room to deliver a bucket of ice. Ted is held captive by Sigfried (David Proval), a jealous and violent gangster who has bound and gagged his wife, Angela (Jennifer Beals), and mistakenly believes that Ted is his wife's lover. After many skirmishes, Ted escapes the sadistic hoodlum.

Later, Ted is coerced by yet another gangster (Antonio Banderas) to babysit for his children (Lana McKissick and Danny Verduzco). Ted is unprepared for the havoc the "The Misbehavers" wreak on their hotel suite, and fails to keep the kids in line. By the time their parents return, the children have spent the evening smoking, drinking and watching the nudie channel, Ted has been stabbed with a hypodermic needle, the corpse of a

prostitute has been found hidden under the mattress and the room is on fire.

Finally, Ted is shanghaied to the penthouse suite by "The Man from Hollywood," where a pretentious director named Chester Rush (Quentin Tarantino) and his entourage have been watching "The Man From Rio" episode of "Alfred Hitchcock Presents" on TV. Chester and his pal Norman (Paul Calderon) are inspired to make a similar wager: Chester's vintage car against Norman's little finger that Norman's lighter will light ten times in a row. But Chester isn't sure he'll have the nerve to chop off Norman's pinkie, so he bribes Ted to do it. Norman's lighter fails on the first go, Ted chops off his finger, and the gamblers rush off to the hospital, leaving Ted a richer man than he was at the beginning of the night.

FOUR ROOMS is a compendium film in which four hot young independent filmmakers have each contributed a segment. Though meant to echo such all-star, multi-story Hollywood epics as TALES OF MANHATTAN and O'HENRY'S FULL HOUSE, the result is a nearly unmitigated disaster. Robert Rodriguez's "The Misbehavers" is the least objectionable episode, though that isn't saying much. The worst stories—Alexandre Rockwell's "The Wrong Man" and Quentin Tarantino's "The Man from Hollywood"—seem more like directorial stunts made up of the worst excesses from Tarantino's mini-oeuvre, and Allison Anders' "The Missing Ingredient" is a very weak and mannered piece.

Tim Roth's put-upon bellboy—supposedly patterned after Jerry Lewis—may be the only character to appear throughout, but all four stories suffer from awkward pacing, movie-star posturing from Madonna, Bruce Willis, et al., and overall pointlessness. *(Graphic violence, sexual situations, adult situations, substance abuse, extreme profanity.)* — E.M.

d, Allison Anders, Alexandre Rockwell, Robert Rodriguez, Quentin Tarantino; p, Lawrence Bender; exec p, Alexandre Rockwell, Quentin Tarantino; co-p, Paul Hellerman, Heidi Vogel, Scott Lambert; w, Allison Anders, Alexandre Rockwell, Robert Rodriguez, Quentin Tarantino; ph, Rodrigo Garcia, Guillermo Navarro, Phil Parmet, Andrzej Sekula; ed, Margie Goodspeed, Elena Maganini, Sally Menke, Robert Rodriguez; m, Combustible Edison; prod d, Gary Frutkoff; art d, Mayne Schuyler Berke; set d, Sara Andrews; anim, Bob Kurtz; sound, Pawel Wdowczak (mixer); fx, Jay Mark Johnson, Bertya Garcia, Robert Stromberg, David S. Williams, Jr., Joe Gareri, Patrick Phillips; casting, Russell Gray; cos, Susan L. Bertram, Mary Claire Hannan; makeup, Ermahn Ospina, Cristina Bartolucci, Lizbeth Williamson, K.N.B. EFX Group, Inc.; stunts, Kane Hodder, Alan Marcus, Charles Belardinelli, Tom Bellissimo

Comedy/Drama   **(PR: O   MPAA: R)**

FRAMEUP   ★★★½
(U.S.) 91m Complex Corporation ~ World Artists Home Video c/bw
(AKA: JON JOST'S FRAMEUP)

Howard Swain *(Ricky Lee Gruber)*; Nancy Carlin *(Beth-Ann Bolet)*; Kathryn Sannella

Jon Jost's FRAMEUP is an excellent, extremely formalist treatment of the American road film. It retraces the lives of an ex-con and his lover as they travel through the Pacific Northwest into California, before they are caught in an aborted robbery and killed by lethal injection for their crimes.

The film opens with a prologue of long single-take or still-camera landscape shots, accompanied by music and natural sounds, and brief bursts of speech. Then, a twelve-part narrative on the lives of Rickey Lee Gruber (Howard Swain) and Beth-

Ann Bolet (Nancy Carlin) begins. The characters are introduced separately: Rickey Lee is framed in a split screen, resembling a live mug shot, illustrating the two dominant aspects of his personality, one angry and violent, the other bored, unvaried, and vulgar. Beth-Ann is introduced inside a picture frame speaking about her high school loves while personal items from her girlhood, such as makeup, nail polish, and earrings, are inserted and removed from the frame.

Beth-Ann narrates her first sight of Ricky, at the diner in Idaho where she is a waitress, and their first night in a motel. Rickey Lee has stolen a small pickup truck and, with it, they travel first to coastal Washington and Oregon and then down into northern California. They sightsee, drive through the Redwoods, and eventually rob a convenience store, where Rickey Lee commits three murders. Rickey Lee and Beth-Ann are both sentenced to death. During their executions, as the injections are administered, Rickey Lee rages and Beth-Ann whimpers, and then both quickly lose consciousness. A narrator describes the lethal injection process in a dispassionate voice as the camera gazes at a group of spectators watching from behind glass. The film concludes with Beth-Ann commenting on her experience of death as the image of her face is gradually obscured by the nothingness of a blank screen.

Jost uses formalist techniques to express his characters' despair, isolation, and spiritual depravity, and implies the existence of such despair, naivete, and alienation in American culture. He regularly frames his characters alone, in odd compositions, or moving partially in and out of frame. There is little dialogue between characters, and when they speak they seem to speak to themselves or to an exterior or unfamiliar spectator.

The self-referentiality of the project is suggested in the opening scenes, when the words FILM, WRITE, DIRECT, EDIT, JOST, and FRAMEUP overlap with images. Later, after Rickey Lee botches the robbery, the film breaks to a news-style interview with a woman describing her experience when held up at gunpoint.

Jost's self-reflexive formal devices force the spectator to question both what he is observing and the distinction between film and reality, breaking the traditional cathartic identification of narrative cinema. The film's pacing reflects the lives of the characters, two people who lack any purpose. Rickey Lee is nervous and excited when he steals and angry and violent when things do not go his way, but he is otherwise bored and lethargic. Beth-Ann is completely uninspired, and only mildly excited by the possibility of love, romance novels, and sex. Highlights include Rickey Lee's description of a typical romance novel, Rickey Lee and Beth-Ann having sex while exchanging words associated with California, and an uncommon and humorous scene of male frontal nudity. *(Violence, extensive nudity, adult situations, extreme profanity.)* — M.F.

d, Jon Jost; p, Henry S. Rosenthal; w, Jon Jost; ph, Jon Jost; ed, Jon Jost; m, Jon A. English; sound, Ann-Marie Miguel

Drama (PR: C MPAA: NR)

FRANK & JESSE ★★½
(U.S.) 99m Cassian Elwes Productions; Elliott Kasner Productions; Trimark Pictures ~ Vidmark Entertainment c

Rob Lowe *(Jesse James)*; Bill Paxton *(Frank James)*; Randy Travis *(Cole Younger)*; William Atherton *(Allan Pinkerton)*; Dana Wheeler-Nicholson *(Annie)*; Maria Pitillo *(Zee James)*; Luke Askew *(Railroad Agent)*; Sean Patrick Flanery *(Zack Murphy)*; Alexis Arquette *(Charlie Ford)*; Todd Field *(Bob Younger)*; John Pyper Ferguson *(Clell Miller)*; Nick Sadler *(Arch Clements)*; Jim Flowers *(Bob Ford)*; Tom Chick *(Whicher)*; Mary

Neff *(Widow Miller)*; Richard Maynard *(Sheets)*; Dennis Letts *(Buchanan—Railroad CEO)*; Mari Askew; William Michael Evans; Lyle Armstrong; Cole McKay; John Stiritz; Micah Dyer; Jackie Stewart; Chad Linley; Rhed Khilling; Jerry Saunders; D.C. "Dash" Goff; Robert Moniot; Norman Hawley; Jeffrey Paul Johnson; Bryce Anthony Thomason; John Paxton; Elizabeth Hatcher-Travis; Sudie Henson

Yet another variation on the oft-told story of bank and train robbers Frank and Jesse James, the made-for-cable FRANK & JESSE tells their story concisely and with some new twists, but adds little to the previous body of film lore devoted to the famed outlaws.

When a railroad agent burns out their family's farmhouse, brothers Frank (Bill Paxton) and Jesse James (Rob Lowe), former raiders in Captain Quantrill's confederate guerrilla band, round up their old riding partners, including Cole Younger (Randy Travis) and his brother Bob (Todd Field), to form a gang to rob banks and trains controlled by the Rock Central Railroad of Chicago.

Hired by the railroad, Allan Pinkerton (William Atherton) and his agents set out to apprehend the band but are thwarted by the bandits' strong support among the populace of Missouri. Pinkerton's first break comes when captured gang member Charlie Ford (Alexis Arquette) agrees to report on the James gang's activities.

When the band journeys far afield, to rob a bank in Northfield, Minnesota, they find Pinkerton agents and townsmen lying in wait for them. The resulting shootout leaves most of the gang captured or dead. Only Frank and Jesse escape.

Cooperating with Pinkerton, Charlie Ford and his brother Bob (Jim Flowers) track down Jesse, living under an assumed name in St. Joseph, Missouri, and pay him an ostensibly friendly visit at home. When he gets the opportunity, Bob Ford shoots Jesse in the back. Frank James gives himself up to the Governor of Missouri and eventually wins his freedom after three acquittals.

As is true of most previous Jesse James films, FRANK & JESSE follows the general arc of the James' careers fairly accurately but distorts or falsifies most of the individual details. Visually, it owes a lot to Walter Hill's THE LONG RIDERS (1980), from the drab southern exteriors (in this case, Arkansas) to the murky photographic look that has too often passed for realism in westerns of the past 20 years.

The film digs a little deeper than previous films into the relationship between the doubt-ridden, Shakespeare-and-Bible-spouting Frank and the hot-headed, trigger-happy Jesse, going so far as to fabricate Frank's guilt over having instigated Jesse's life of killing by bringing the boy along on guerrilla Captain Quantrill's murderous 1863 raid on Lawrence, Kansas. (The historical record shows that Jesse did not participate in the raid on Lawrence, but went on other, equally bloody forays without Frank.)

The always dependable Bill Paxton turns in a solid performance as farmer-turned-outlaw and ultimate survivor Frank, while Rob Lowe makes an energetic, if determinedly shallow and short-lived, Jesse. Of the rest of the cast, country singer Randy Travis acquits himself well as the stubborn Cole Younger (who narrates the film) and William Atherton makes a suitably imperious and relentless Pinkerton. *(Violence, profanity.)* — B.C.

d, Robert Boris; p, Cassian Elwes, Elliot Kastner; exec p, Mark Amin; co-p, Rob Lowe, Andrew Hersh; w, Robert Boris; ph, Walt Lloyd; ed, Christopher Greenbury; m, Mark McKenzie; prod d, Michael T. Perry; art d, Scott Plauche; sound, David Chornow; casting, Ed Mitchell, Robyn Ray; cos, Betty Pecha Madden

Historical/Western (PR: C MPAA: R)

FRANK AND OLLIE   ★★★
(U.S.) 90m Walt Disney Pictures ~ Buena Vista c
(AKA: FRANK & OLLIE)

Frank Thomas; Ollie Johnston; Sylvia Roemer; John Canemaker; John Culhane; Marie E. Johnston; Jeanette A. Thomas;
Glen Keane; Andy Gaskill

FRANK AND OLLIE celebrates Frank Thomas and Ollie
Johnston, two of the unsung stars of the original Disney troupe.
Filmmaker Theodore Thomas was more than privy to their efforts; he is Frank Thomas's son, and made this as a personal
seven-year project (it premiered on the Disney Channel in 1995
before its brief regional theatrical run).

   The opening follows the two nice old gentlemen, best friends
and neighbors since the 1930s, through their amusingly mirrored
morning routine. When the pair finally sit down and talk about
their careers, one realizes how key they have been to entertainment's finest moments. Thomas and Johnston are "character
animators," masters of an arcane discipline that breathed individual life and personality into Mickey Mouse, the Seven Dwarfs,
and Captain Hook through minutely subtle details in facial expressions and gestures. Thomas and Johnston display their old
sketches and play-act segments from BAMBI, LADY AND THE
TRAMP and THE JUNGLE BOOK. Then the director runs the
finished scenes from those productions, and the newly-informed
viewer observes familiar cartoon classics with a fresh eye for
every nuance. So wonderfully lifelike are the Thomas and
Johnston creations that one could easily forget how each line and
curve, tic and wink, was painstakingly planned and painted in.

   Part home movie, part behind-the-scenes documentary,
FRANK AND OLLIE at first glance seems to go over very
familiar territory. Hasn't the work of the Disney animation studios been explored enough? Not really. Certainly there were
in-house promotional pieces made, and Walt Disney himself
joined humorist Robert Benchley for a whimsical 1941 on-
screen tour of his company that played at theaters as a supplement to THE RELUCTANT DRAGON. But Disney's looming
public image long overshadowed a talented animation team that
included Ward Kimball, Grim Natwick, Wolfgang "Woolie" Re-
itherman, and Norman Ferguson—names well-known to only
animation buffs.

   Thomas and Johnston sardonically recall Disney as a driven
man whose sheer nervous energy suggested a neurological disorder, like "one of those British kings they never talk about." As
a studio history, however, FRANK AND OLLIE is decidedly
patchy, and only hints at what life was like for young Theodore
growing up in an environment in which a boy could assume that
everyone's dad drew Pluto for a living. At the end of the film, the
viewer is left with newfound appreciation for Thomas and
Johnston, and a certainty that more tales from within the fortifi-
cations of the Magic Kingdom deserve to be told. — C.C.

d, Theodore Thomas; p, Kuniko Okubo, Theodore Thomas; w,
Theodore Thomas; ph, Erik Daarstad; ed, Kathryn Camp; m,
John Reynolds; sound, Ken King (mixer); makeup, Oona Lind,
Cindy Costello

Documentary   **(PR: AA   MPAA: PG)**

FRANKIE STARLIGHT   ★★½
(U.K./France/Ireland) 100m Ferndale Films;
Channel Four Films ~ Fine Line c

Anne Parillaud (*Bernadette Bois*); Matt Dillon (*Terry Klout*);
Gabriel Byrne (*Jack Kelly*); Rudi Davies (*Emma Kelly*); Geor-
gina Cates (*Young Emma*); Corban Walker (*Frank Bois*); Alan
Pentony (*Young Frank*); Niall Toibin (*Handy Paige*); Dearbhla

Molloy (*Effa Kelly*); Jean Claude Frissung (*Albert Bois*); Victoria
Begeja (*Anne Marie Bois*); Barbara Alyn Woods (*Marcia*); John
Davies (*Tobin*); Amber Hibler (*Charleen*); Ulrich Funke (*Lisa*);
Guy Verama (*Interpreter*); Julian Negulesco (*Bernadette's Un-
cle*); Corinne Blue (*Bernadette's Aunt*); Sage Allen (*Bar Pro-
prietress*); Ann Weakley (*Midwife*); Elizabeth Keller (*TV
Interviewer*); David Parnell (*Photographer*); Aidan Grennell
(*Bookshop Manager*); Tristin Gribbin (*Bookshop Assistant*);
Christopher Casson (*Bookshop Gentleman*); Owen Roe (*Senior
Customs Officer*); Aisling Leyne (*Girl in Gallery*); Pauline
Cadell (*Prostitute*); Alan Devine (*Bernadette's Friend on Beach
No. 1*); Edward Naessens (*Bernadette's Friend on Beach No. 2*);
Laurent Mellet (*Bernadette's Friend on Beach No. 3*); Christine
Keane (*Mother of Scabious Child*); Darren Monks (*Young Man
in Cinema*); Kit Kincannon (*Man in Bar*); Martin Murphy (*Guest
at Wedding*); Martin Dunne (*Friend at Wedding No. 1*); Derry
Power (*Friend at Wedding No. 2*)

FRANKIE STARLIGHT is an adaptation of Chet Raymo's
novel, *The Dork of Cork*, and though it's a charming film, one
can't help but feel that reading the book is a prerequisite to
appreciating it fully.

   Frank Bois (Corban Walker), a dwarf, has written a book that
combines personal memoir, astronomical observations, and a
biography of his mother, Bernadette.

   Born in Normandy, Bernadette Bois (Anne Parillaud) loses
her parents during the D-Day invasion, and at the end of WWII
stows away on an American troop ship. She becomes pregnant
and is put off in Ireland, where married Irish emigration officer
Jack Kelly (Gabriel Byrne) falls in love with her. He secretly
provides for Bernadette and her newborn son. Through the
improbable generosity of Jack's wife, Bernadette and the baby
are taken in the Kelly home, an action that deeply alienates
religious daughter Emma (Georgina Cates).

   Jack teaches young Frankie (Alan Pentony) about astronomy
and—despite his own deformity—Frankie develops a keen appreciation of beauty and becomes enamored of Emma. Eventually though, Emma must be sent to a sanitarium, and the Kellys
move away. Shortly after, Texan Terry Klout (Matt Dillon) shows
up on Bernadette's doorstep. He was on the troop ship—though
he's not Frankie's father—and never forgot her. Terry takes
Bernadette and Frankie to the States. When Terry reconciles with
his wife, Bernadette turns tricks for the money she needs to get
herself and Frankie home to Ireland, where she discovers she's
pregnant again. Bernadette commits suicide.

   Frank's book *Nightstalk* is a big success, in part because a
dwarf author is such a novelty. At a book signing, he's reunited with Emma (Rudi Davies), now an artist. They fall in
love and marry.

   The greatest pleasure of this peculiar story is that you're
never quite sure where it's headed. Parillaud (LA FEMME
NIKITA, INNOCENT BLOOD) is captivating as the sad,
mysterious Bernadette. But while she dominates the *story*, the
focus of the *film* is Frankie, and though newcomers Pentony
and Walker give fine performances as the young and adult
Frankies, the film never lets the viewer connect emotionally
with its unusual protagonist.

   In *The Dork of Cork*, Frankie explains that his story is full of
love by virtue of its total absence—an interesting philosophical
notion that doesn't play on the screen. It's hard to figure out what
he feels about the unusual circumstances of his life, and while
you could argue that Frankie always had his eyes on a bigger
picture, he's too obviously lonely and angry for us to believe he
shrugged everything off. This is a film that might actually have
benefited from extensive voice-over narration, which could
have given voice to Frankie's presumably rich inner life. As it

stands, FRANKIE STARLIGHT is a frustrating film, one that could and should have been much better than it actually is. *(Sexual situations, adult situations.)* — P.R.

d, Michael Lindsay-Hogg; p, Noel Pearson; w, Chet Raymo, Ronan O'Leary (based on the novel *The Dork of Cork* by Chet Raymo); ph, Paul Laufer; ed, Ruth Foster; m, Elmer Bernstein; prod d, Frank Conway; sound, Nick Adams, Kieran Horgan; casting, Nuala Moiselle; cos, Joan Bergin; makeup, Marie O'Sullivan

Romance/Drama/Comedy   **(PR: A   MPAA: R)**

FREE WILLY 2: THE ADVENTURE HOME   ★★½
(U.S.) 96m Le Studio Canal Plus; Regency Enterprises; Alcor Films; Warner Bros. ~ Warner Bros. c
(GB: FREE WILLY 2)

Jason James Richter *(Jesse)*; August Schellenberg *(Randolph Johnson)*; Michael Madsen *(Glenn Greenwood)*; Jayne Atkinson *(Annie Greenwood)*; Mary Kate Schellhardt *(Nadine)*; Francis Capra *(Elvis)*; Jon Tenney *(John Milner)*; Elizabeth Pena *(Dr. Kate Haley)*; M. Emmet Walsh *(Wilcox)*; Mykelti Williamson *(Dwight Mercer)*; John Considine *(Commander Blake)*; Paul Tuerpe *(Milner's Assistant)*; Steve Kahan *(Captain Nilson)*; Neal Matarazzo *(Helmsman Kelly)*; Al Sapienza *(Engineer)*; Wally Dalton *(Engineer)*; Cliff Fetters *(Engineer)*; Julie Inouye *(Reporter)*; Basil Wallace *(Reporter)*; Janet Wu *(Reporter)*; June Christopher *(Veterinarian)*; Doug Ballard *(Veterinarian)*; Marguerite Moreau *(Julie)*; Christina Orchid *(Donut Shop Lady)*; Edward J. Rosen *(Environmental Man)*; Isaac T. Arnett, Jr. *(Camper)*; Scott Stuber *(Policeman)*; Chanel Capra *(Teenage Girl at Ferry)*; Laura Gary *(Whale Spotter)*; John Harms *(Protester)*; Susan Brooks *(Protester)*; Jeff Brooks *(Protester)*; Joan Lunden *(Herself)*

More or less repeating the trajectory of the first boy-and-his-enormous-pet saga, FREE WILLY 2 offers more lavish special effects and more stunt-filled action, with teen actor Jason James Richter as Jesse looking a little long in the tooth to go joy riding on ocean mammals.

Eager to hook up with Native American whaleographer Rudolph (August Schellenberg), Jesse is less favorably inclined to a summer visit from a half-brother, Elvis (Francis Capra), whom he has never met. Jesse is soon at loggerheads with the boastful, city-dweller brother. But that does not stop him from making cow eyes at Rudolph's young assistant Nadine (Mary Kate Schellhardt), and splashily rekindling his relationship with Willy Whale, who is traveling with his mom and siblings.

Willy's family encounters a crisis when an oil tanker has an accident due to its captain's rashness and an outmoded hull. When Willy's sister runs aground and almost perishes, Willy remembers previous bad experiences with humans and refuses to let medical experts help the beached mammal.

Unbeknownst to the whale family's network of advocates, a not-so-repentant oil company executive plans to sell them to a millionaire promoter under the guise of having them transported for emergency aid. Saving the day after he runs away and eavesdrops on the bad guys' double-cross, Elvis tips off Willy's fans. Defying the unscrupulous investors, Jesse, Elvis, and Nadine get trapped in an oil fire that breaks out on the ocean during their rescue mission. A copter picks up Nadine and Elvis from the flaming sea, and Willy bravely transports Jesse under the ocean surface fire to safety. Having reinforced their unique ties, Willy and Jesse bid farewell to each other as Willy directs his family away from the ravages of the spill and Jesse appreciates the value of having a little brother.

Sometimes heart-stopping in its depiction of mega-Sea World exploits and often touching in its melodramatics about patching up broken family relations, FREE WILLY 2 offers plenty to the family values crowd. Those less easily seduced by animal films may take mild umbrage at the movie's unconcealed commercialism. With its 800 number about saving whales flashing across the screen, the movie can make everyone feel good about donating to a worthy cause. In any event, this second installment of oceanic corn sails along smoothly and sends everyone home in an upbeat mood. — R.P.

d, Dwight Little; p, Lauren Shuler-Donner, Jennie Lew Tugend; exec p, Richard Donner, Arnon Milchan, Jim Van Wyck; assoc p, Mark Marshall, Douglas C. Merrifield, Sherry Fadely; co-p, Richard Solomon; w, Karen Janszen, Corey Blechman, John Mattson (based on characters created by Keith A. Walker); ph, Laszlo Kovacs; ed, Robert Brown, Dallas Puett; m, Basil Poudouris; prod d, Paul Sylbert; art d, Gregory Bolton; set d, Casey Hallenbeck; sound, Robert Janiger; fx, John Belyeu, Michael McAlister, Kimberly K. Nelson, Walt Conti, Edge Innovations; casting, Judy Taylor, Lynda Gordon; cos, Erica Edell Phillips; makeup, Pamela Westmore, Whitney James; stunts, Conrad E. Palmisano, Jeff Imada

Children's/Adventure   **(PR: AA   MPAA: PG)**

FRENCH KISS   ★★★
(U.S.) 111m Working Title; Prufrock Pictures ~ 20th Century Fox c

Meg Ryan *(Kate)*; Kevin Kline *(Luc)*; Timothy Hutton *(Charlie)*; Jean Reno *(Jean-Paul)*; Francois Cluzet *(Bob)*; Susan Anbeh *(Juliette)*; Renee Humphrey *(Lilly)*; Michael Riley *(Campbell)*; Laurent Spiel Vogel *(Concierge)*; Victor Garrivier *(Octave)*; Elizabeth Commelin *(Claire)*; Julie Leibowitch *(Olivia)*; Miquel Brown *(Sergeant Patton)*; Louise Deschamps *(Jean-Paul's Girl)*; Olivier Curdy *(Jean-Paul's Boy)*; Claudio Todeschini *(Antoine)*; Jerry Harte *(Herb)*; Thomasine Heiner *(Mom)*; Joanna Pavlis *(Monotonous Voiced Woman)*; Florence Soyez *(Flight Attendant)*; Barbara Schulz *(Pouting Girl)*; Clement Sibony *(Pouting Boy)*; Adam Brooks *(Perfect Passenger)*; Marianne Anska *(Cop No. 1)*; Phillippe Garnier *(Cop No. 2)*; Frederick Therisod *(Cop No. 3)*; Patrice Juiff *(French Customs Official)*; Jean Corso *(Desk Clerk)*; Francois Xavier Tilmant *(Hotel Waiter)*; Williams Diols *(Beach Waiter)*; Mike Johns *(Lucien)*; Marie Christine Adam *(Juliette's Mother)*; Jean-Paul Jaupart *(Juliette's Father)*; Fausto Costantino *(Beefy Doorman)*; Jean-Claude Braquet *(Stolen Moto Owner)*; Dominique Regnier *(Attractive Passport Woman)*; Ghislaine Juillot *(Jean-Paul's Wife)*; Inge Offerman; Nicholas Hawtrey; Wolfgang Pissors; Nikola Obermann *(German Family)*; Alain Frerot *(Old Man)*; Dorothee Picard *(Mrs. Cowen)*; Jean Allain *(Mr. Cowen)*

Meg Ryan, the perpetually perky star of WHEN HARRY MET SALLY and SLEEPLESS IN SEATTLE, makes a game attempt but fails to score a hat trick of romantic comedy blockbusters. FRENCH KISS isn't bad, it just suffers in comparison to those paragons of the genre. It is light, fluffy entertainment loaded with charm and devoid of meaning.

Marriage-minded Kate (Meg Ryan) is devastated when her fiance Charlie (Timothy Hutton) calls from France to break off their engagement. Despite an overwhelming fear of flying, she boards a plane to Paris to win Charlie back from Juliette (Susan Anbeh), the French beauty who stole his heart. En route, she meets Luc (Kevin Kline), a Frenchman whom she dislikes on sight. Luc, a petty thief, stashes a stolen necklace in Kate's bag, accurately predicting that she won't be stopped at customs.

Kate faints at the sight of Charlie kissing Juliette, and her bags are stolen, along with Luc's loot. Claiming purely altruistic motives, Luc helps Kate reclaim her bags. By the time he recovers the necklace, Luc is smitten. He offers to help Kate win back her fiance, teaching her to be self-assured and aloof. When Charlie finally encounters the transformed Kate, he drops Juliette like a hot potato and begs Kate's forgiveness. But she realizes she has developed feelings for Luc.

Luc's nemesis and friend, Inspector Jean-Paul (Jean Reno) informs Kate that Luc stole the diamond necklace, but if she can convince him to return it, no charges will be filed. Luc plans to sell the necklace and use the money to realize his dream of starting his own vineyard. Kate persuades Luc to let her handle the sale. She has her nest egg wired from her bank, gives the check to Luc, and returns the necklace to the authorities. Kate and Luc part without revealing their feelings for one another. Kate boards a flight back home, but is whisked off the plane at the last moment by Luc, who has learned of her actions from Jean-Paul.

FRENCH KISS is frivolous fun, best enjoyed when not closely scrutinized. Adam Brooks's screenplay includes some jarring credibility lapses—are we really expected to believe Kate would hand over her life savings to a man she thought she would never see again?—but what it lacks in authenticity, it makes up for in charm. Ryan is at once wacky and winsome, and her mastery at broad physical comedy calls to mind that queen of screwball comedy, Lucille Ball. Kate's disdain for all things French and her quest for Canadian citizenship provide sideline laughs. However, a scene involving lactose intolerance, clearly meant to lampoon the famous orgasm scene from WHEN HARRY MET SALLY, doesn't quite hit the target. With a scruffy facade and a *tres authentique* French accent, Kline is devilishly appealing as the redeemable rogue. But while both performers are charismatic on their own, the pairing doesn't quite click. Despite a sexy title (the film's original title, PARIS MATCH, was changed after Billy Crystal objected to its similarity to his film FORGET PARIS, which was registered with the Writers Guild first), FRENCH KISS has all the passion of a peck on the cheek. Still, filmed on location in the City of Lights, FRENCH KISS features beautiful scenery and superb cinematography, including some imaginative shots of the Eiffel Tower. (*Sexual situations, profanity.*) — B.R.

d, Lawrence Kasdan; p, Tim Bevan, Eric Fellner, Meg Ryan, Kathryn F. Galan; exec p, Charles Okun; assoc p, Liza Chasin; w, Adam Brooks; ph, Owen Roizman; ed, Joe Hutshing; m, James Newton Howard; prod d, Jon Hutman; art d, Gerard Viard; set d, Kara Lindstrom; sound, John Pritchett; casting, Francoise Combadiere, Jennifer Schull; cos, Joanna Johnston

Comedy/Romance   **(PR: A   MPAA: PG-13)**

FRIDAY   ★★★
(U.S.) 90m Priority Films; New Line ~ New Line c

Ice Cube (*Craig Jones*); Paula Jai Parker (*Joi*); Chris Tucker (*Smokey*); Bernie Mac (*Pastor Cleaver*); John Witherspoon (*Craig's Father*); Regina King (*Dana*); Nia Long (*Debbie*); Anna Maria Horsford (*Craig's Mother*); Faizon Love (*Big Worm*); Tiny "Zeus" Lister, Jr. (*Deebo*); D.J. Pooh (*Red*); Angela Means (*Felisha*); Vickilyn Reynolds (*Joann*); Ronn Riser (*Stanley*); Kathleen Bradley (*Mrs. Parker*); Tony Cox (*Mr. Parker*); Anthony Johnson (*Ezal*); Demetrius Navarro (*Hector*); Jason Bose Smith (*Lil Chris*); Justin Revoner (*Kid No. 1*); Meagan Good (*Kid No. 2*); Lawanda Page (*Old Lady*); Terry J. Vaughn (*China*); F. Gary Gray (*Black Man at Store*); Yvette Wilson (*Rita*); William L. Calhoun, Jr. (*Shooter*); Renaldo Rey (*Red's Father*)

A star vehicle for rapper Ice Cube (who also cowrote and coproduced), FRIDAY is a lighthearted, comedic presentation of the realities chronicled in dramas like BOYZ N THE HOOD. Though funny, FRIDAY cannot sustain its humorous tone to the end because it ultimately has to confront those same realities.

It is Friday, but because he just lost his job, Craig Jones (Ice Cube) does not have anywhere to go but his front stoop. From this vantage point, Jones and his pot-smoking friend "Smokey" (Chris Tucker) observe the comings and goings of the peculiar people in this particular 'hood. These include a dwarf on the outs with his sexy wife, an irritating beggar, a snooty neighbor, a not-so-righteous reverend, Jones's jealous girlfriend, Smokey's better left unseen blind date, and Jones's dog-obsessed father (a hilarious John Witherspoon). Not even a couple of run-ins with Deebo (Tiny "Zeus" Lister Jr.), a hulking thug who takes whatever he wants, can ruin their day. That is, until "Big Worm" (Faizon Love), the neighborhood drug dealer and ice cream vendor, comes by to collect the $200 Smokey owes him. He gives Smokey and Jones the rest of the day to come up with the money, and when they do not, they are targeted in a drive-by shooting. They survive, but now when Deebo lays hands on Debbie (Nia Long), a sweet girl Jones has a crush on, Jones goes after Deebo with a gun. His father stops him, advising him to fight Deebo "like a man"—with his fists. Jones topples the Goliath and receives the promise of romance from Debbie.

It is just a typical summer day on a residential street kids are playing, lawns are being watered. There is a lot going on, but not much happens, and that is exactly the point. Scriptwriters Ice Cube, DJ Pooh, and director F. Gary Gray find as much humor in well-observed detail as in the oddities of the film's world. There are slapstick gags, bathroom humor (both figuratively and literally), a lot of jokes about hairstyles, and juxtapositions (huge Deebo rides a little bike, for instance). All the inaction is set to a terrific, evocative soundtrack that mixes 1960s soul and Motown classics, Rose Royce's "I Wanna Get Next to You" from CAR WASH, rap from Cypress Hill and Cube, and Dr. Dre's hit "Keep Their Heads Ringin'." (*Profanity, violence, substance abuse.*) — P.R.

d, F. Gary Gray; p, Ice Cube, Patricia Charbonnet; exec p, Ice Cube, Bryan Turner; assoc p, Andre Robinson, Jr., DJ Pooh, James Tripp-Haith; co-p, W.E. Baker; w, Ice Cube, D.J. Pooh; ph, Gerry Lively; ed, John Carter; m, Hidden Faces; prod d, Bruce Bellamy; art d, Maria Baker; set d, Michele Harding Hollie; sound, Robert Davenport (mixer), Leonard Marcel (designer); fx, Robert Loftin; casting, Jaki Brown-Karman, Kim Hardin; cos, Shawn Barton; makeup, Cassi Mari, Rea Ann Silva; stunts, Julius LeFlore

Comedy   **(PR: C   MPAA: R)**

FRIENDS   ★★½
(U.K./France/South Africa) 109m Friends Productions; British Screen; Channel Four; Chrysalide Films; Rio S.A. ~ First Run Features c

Kerry Fox (*Sophie*); Dambisa Kente (*Thoko*); Michele Burgers (*Aninka*); Tertius Meintjes (*Jeremy*); Marius Weyers (*Johan*); Dolly Rathebe (*Innocentia*); Wilma Stockenstroom (*Iris*); Carel Trichardt (*Reinhart*); Anne Curteis (*Sophie's Mother*); Ralph Draper (*Sophie's Father*); Mary Twala (*Grace*); Maphiki Mabohi (*Daphne*); Joe Kubatsi (*Mzwandile*); Vanessa Cooke (*Prison Warder*); Jerry Mofokeng (*Thami*); Trevie Jean LePere (*Jeremy's Girl*); Neil McCarthy (*Young Man in Cafe*); Motshabi Tyelele (*Thembi*); Archie Mgwenya (*Gift*); Vusi Kunene (*Chippa*); Sithole; Macbeth Khumalo; Noaxie Mabuya (*Co-Accused*); Lizzy Keketse (*Cleaning Lady*); Andre Lombard (*Airport Sol-

dier); Wilmien Roussouw *(Lizelle)*; Lindsey Stroh *(Young Sophie)*; Louisa Twala *(Young Grace)*; Pat Pellay *(1st Attorney—Indian)*; Robyn Slovo *(2nd Attorney—White Woman)*; Innocentia Tshoaedo *(Regina Mtali)*; David Phetoe *(Priest)*; Emmanuel Mohlamme *(Brother of Detainee)*; Susan Pam-Grant *(Hettie)*; Charles Vermeulen *(Hannes)*; Letitia Eilers *(Fat Woman in Turkish Baths)*; Albert Maritz *(Young Drunk Man at Wedding)*; Louis Seboko *(Sipiwe)*; Peter Kubeke *(Old Man in Park)*; Washington Xisolo *(Hostel Guard)*; Frik Bezuidenhout *(Policeman)*; Dean Stewardson *(Police Chief)*; Gustav Geldenhuys *(Policeman)*; Gideon Moegi *(Newspaper Seller)*; Mia Mpute *(Newspaper Seller)*; Andre Stoltz *(Magistrate)*

FRIENDS tells a hopeful story of a changing South Africa through the lives of three young female friends who oppose the racial prejudices of their families and the structural racism of South African society. The women must choose between the future and the past when one of them turns herself in and faces trial for an act of terrorism.

In Johannesburg in the mid and late 1980s, three women, only a few years out of college, respond differently to the poverty, injustice, and violence upsetting the country. Sophie (Kerry Fox), the daughter of a white, middle-class, English-speaking family, works in a library and is a terrorist, estranged from her family, class, and husband; Aninka (Michele Burgers), the daughter of Boer farmers, is an archeologist; Thoko (Dambisa Kente), a black South African, teaches literature in a township. The three women share a house, even after Aninka marries and returns from her honeymoon with her husband. Sophie plants bombs in public institutions for an unnamed organization, first in a school, then at Johannesburg airport. The airport blast unexpectedly kills two people. Suspecting black militants, the police and white militias retaliate against black communities. Police raid the school at which Thoko teaches and whites attack and firebomb a township housing complex. Sophie's act, her fear, and her desperation, isolate her from her friends and drive her back to her alcoholic husband. She eventually meets with fellow terrorists and narrowly escapes a police raid that results in several deaths. She returns home and confesses her part in the bombings to Thoko and then to the authorities.

Besides Sophie's imprisonment, notoriety, and trial, the film focuses on Aninka and Thoko, who represent young, nonpolitical South Africans, white and black. Both women are shaken by Sophie's secret history and forced to face the country's worsening crisis. Thoko withdraws into depression, quits her teaching position, and spends her days in the township picking and selling fruit. Aninka visits Sophie in jail, argues with her husband about her responsibility to the country's future, and eventually, after hearing her father's white supremacist rhetoric at a picnic, seeks out Thoko. Sophie is suddenly released following a pardon of political prisoners enacted to ease racial tensions. She's met kindly by her parents (Anne Curteis and Ralph Draper), but when she asks about her friends, and if they'll drive her to Thoko's township, her mother slaps her. Sophie, committed to the destruction of racism and apartheid, leaves and rejoins her two friends.

First-time writer-director Elaine Proctor's film focuses on white South African confusion about what to do in a changing and violent society, reflecting the recent history of this country and, to some extent, justifying all the different positions and acts portrayed. Proctor's film remains optimistic, and there's never any doubt that the three women in this story will be reconciled. Their reunion at the township market dramatizes the necessity of understanding and commitment, just as their revolutionary power during chaotic and violent times demonstrates the way in which personal experience fuels political consciousness. Proc-

tor's dramatization of racial problems through iconoclastic use of familiar stereotypes is comparable to the polemical work of Spike Lee, though Proctor's work is less bombastic and provocative. *(Violence, nudity, sexual and adult situations.)* — M.F.

d, Elaine Proctor; p, Judith Hunt; w, Elaine Proctor; ph, Dominique Chapuis; ed, Tony Lawson; m, Rachel Portman; prod d, Carmel Collins; art d, Mark Wilby; sound, Robin Harris (mixer); fx, Massimo Vico; cos, Moira Meyer; makeup, Annie Bartels; stunts, Gavin Mey

Drama   **(PR: C   MPAA: NR)**

FROM NINE TO FIVE
(SEE: TWENTY SOMETHING)

FUN   ★★½
(Canada/U.S.) 104m Prerogative Productions; Lighthouse Entertainment; Neo-Modern Entertainment ~ August Entertainment c

Alicia Witt *(Bonnie)*; Renee Humphrey *(Hillary)*; William R. Moses *(John)*; Leslie Hope *(Jane)*; Ania Suli *(Mrs. Farmer)*; James J. Howard, Jr. *(Male Prison Guard)*; Frederick B. Adams *(Male Prison Guard)*; Mary Ann Norment; Sabrina Ortega; Patrice F. Battle; Carmina Rubalcava; Malquele Garcia *(Female Prison Guards)*; Cindie Northrup *(Prison Librarian)*; Denise Fischer; Sharon Ben-Tal; Amy Bateman; Dena J. Pacitti; Cynthia Farris; Leah Kourtne Ballantine; Amanda Blackholly; Kimberly Ann Ross; Dana Maria Thomas; Ashley Michael Lauren *(Inmates)*; Rochelle Roderick *(Mrs. Farmer's Neighbor)*; Steven Givens *(Mrs. Farmer's Neighbor)*; Gregory Steven Ferret *(Mrs. Farmer's Neighbor)*; Steve Adelson *(Gas Station Attendant)*; Alan Shapiro *(Record Store Manager)*; Victoria Radu *(Nurse)*; Jonathan Lightstone; Gillian Lightstone; Alexander Hecht; Elizabeth Hecht; James Youngman; Jaime Anderson; Chris Gillett *(Kids)*

A pretentious look at juvenile crime and media manipulation, FUN features complex performances by leads Rene Humphrey and Alicia Witt (both of whom received Special Recognition for Acting awards at the 1994 Sundance Film Festival) but is ultimately undone by its own affectations.

Psychologist Jane (Leslie Hope) and journalist John (William P. Moses), who writes for sensationalistic *Tomorrow* magazine, meet at a grim juvenile facility to interview two 15-year-old girls, Hillary (Humphrey) and Bonnie (Witt). The teens, who are incarcerated separately, have just been convicted of the thrill-kill murder of a kindly old woman, Mrs. Farmer (Ania Suli). They met each other only a day before committing the crime, and steadfastly declare that they did it for fun. The story unfolds in a series of color flashbacks, alternating with black-and-white footage in which the girls are interviewed by Jane and John.

Both in flashback and in present-time footage, it's apparent that the differences between the girls go beyond their looks. Dark-haired, heavily made-up Hillary is angry and defensive, a loner and a compulsive diarist whose friendship with Bonnie is the most important thing in her life. The red-haired, slightly plump Bonnie is hyperactive, extroverted, and given to wild flights of fancy. When Hillary reveals that she was raped by her father at the age of 10, Bonnie tells her that she was sexually assaulted by her brother. We later learn that Bonnie has no brother and is a virgin.

In flashbacks, we learn what happened on the fateful day. The girls meet at a suburban bus stop. During the long walk home, they throw pennies off an overpass at the cars below, mess around in strip malls and video game emporiums, shoplift lipstick, and talk. They play a mean-spirited game, ringing people's doors and saying they need help, then insulting the potential good Samaritans and running off, laughing. They decide to run away together, and Hillary suggests robbing one of the houses. Pretending to be sisters and claiming that Bonnie is sick, they gain entry to Mrs. Farmer's house. Bonnie finds a knife and stabs Mrs. Farmer to death. The girls flee, pausing at a gas station to wash the blood off Bonnie's face and out of her hair. They return to Hillary's house and snuggle up in bed together, where they're found by the police.

During the interviews, John tries to ingratiate himself with Hillary. He suggests publishing some of her diary entries in the magazine, and tells her he'll try to persuade the authorities to let her see Bonnie. John also reveals to Hillary that Bonnie—who confessed to the crime before she was even asked about it—had lied to her repeatedly. Jane sympathizes with Bonnie, suspecting incorrectly that Hillary instigated the crime. She later reveals to Hillary her own abusive background, but fails to form a bond with the girl.

John leaves, having collected enough material for his story. Hillary is transferred to another institution, and Bonnie throws herself off the roof. John calls Hillary for her reaction, and she says: "No comment." She's taken to the exercise yard, where the other inmates give her a wide berth. For the first time, color bleeds into the present-day footage.

Adapted by James Bosley from his own play and directed by Rafal Zielinski—who's best known for such exploitation fare as SCREWBALLS (1984), VALET GIRLS (1987), and UNDER SURVEILLANCE (1991)—FUN tackles a complex subject about which it has nothing new to say. Despite the strong performances of the two girls, the teens are ciphers. By framing the story with interviews, Zielinski and Bosley lead viewers to believe that the film will be a search for the truth behind the sensationalistic story, but it's not. The relationship between the two interviewers, who crudely represent the exploitative media and psychiatric establishments, is stilted, and John and Jane never emerge as characters: they're only mouthpieces for cliched positions. The use of color and B&W footage is also obvious: the day of fun is in color because it was the high point of the girls' lives, while the grim present is drearily monochromatic.

Though laudably serious in intent, FUN is woefully hackneyed in execution. (*Violence, profanity, adult situations.*) — M.M.

d, Rafal Zielinsky; p, Rafal Zielinsky; exec p, Rana Joy Glickman, Jeff Kirshbaum; assoc p, Jeff Sackman, Monika Lightstone; co-p, Damian Lee; w, James Bosley (based on his play); ph, Jens Sturup; ed, Monika Lightstone; m, Marc Tschanz; prod d, Vally Mestroni; sound, Nancy Tracy (design), Dave Nelson (design), Arnold Brown (mixer), Laurent Wassmer (mixer), Andy Koyama; fx, Denise Fischer; casting, Cathy Brown, Marki Costello; cos, Renee Johnston; makeup, Denise Fischer

Crime/Drama   **(PR: C   MPAA: NR)**

FUNNY BONES   ★★★★
(U.K.) 128m Sun Trust Ltd.; Hollywood Pictures ~ Buena Vista c

Oliver Platt (*Tommy Fawkes*); Jerry Lewis (*George Fawkes*); Lee Evans (*Jack Parker*); Leslie Caron (*Katie Parker*); Richard Griffiths (*Jim Minty*); Oliver Reed (*Dolly Hopkins*); George Carl (*Thomas Parker*); Freddie Davis (*Bruno Parker*); Ian McNeice (*Stanley Sharkey*); Christopher Greet (*Lawrence Berger*); Peter Gunn (*Nicky*); Gavin Millar (*Steve Campbell*); William Hootkins (*Al*); Terence Rigby (*Billy Mann*); Ruta Lee (*Laura Fawkes*); Peter Pamela Rose (*Jenny*); Ticky Holgado (*Battison*); Olivier Py

(*Barre*); Mouss (*Poquelin*); Peter McNamara (*Canavan*); Richard Platt (*Bellows*); Francois Domange (*Pirard*); Harold Nicholas (*Hal Dalzell*); George Khan (*Francesco*); Ian Rowe (*Ringmaster*); Phil Atkinson (*Policeman*); Nick Coppin (*Policeman*); Jona Jones (*Security Guard*); Tony Barton (*Comedian*); Mike Newman (*Comedian*); Ruth Kettlewell (*Camilla Powell*); Peter Morgan (*Gofor*); Fred Evans (*Mr. Pearce*); George Raistrick (*Club Owner*); Mickey Baker (*Mayor*); Reg Griffiths; Duggie Chapman; Tony Peers; Andy Rashleigh (*Reporters*); Phil Kelly; Dave Flame & the Barbarians; Lee Jellyhead & the Ballet Hooligans; Bobbie Roberts & Elephants (*Themselves*); Andy Thompson; Peter Brande (*Leo the Leprechaun*); Frank Harvey (*Backward Talking Man*); Anthony Irvine (*Iceman*); Eileen Bell (*Doggyduo*); Rusty Goffe (*Bagpipe Playing Dwarf*); Terri Carol (*Paper Tearer*); Sadie Corre (*Poodle Woman*); Freddie Cox; Frank Cox (*Cox Twins*); Shane Robinson (*Bastard Son of Louis XIV*); Benji Ming (*Plastic Cup Smasher*); Zipporah Simon (*Puppeteer*); Maudie Blake (*Musical Saw Player*); Andras Banlaki (*Ring Boy*); Laci Endresz, Jr. (*Juggler*); Brian Webb (*Little Firewater*); Peter Martin (*Skipper*); Chloe Treend; Andrea Bretherick; Lisa Henson; Rebecca Metcalfe; Camilla Simson; Tina Yoxall (*Tropicana Dancers*); Amir Fawzi (*Little Tommy*); "Sniff" (*Toast*); Mr. Mark Raffles; Mrs. Mark Raffles (*The Wychwoods*)

Unceremoniously dumped by Hollywood Pictures, which couldn't devise a strategy to market this eccentric, exhilarating film, FUNNY BONES is a postmodern tragicomedy. It's a mesmerizing exploration of the dangerous essence of comedy; at the same time, it's an adventure film about smuggling, a heartbreaker about children and their parents' expectations, a backhanded fable about immortality, and a bracingly hilarious take on the desperation of performance.

Aging Beverly Hills brat Tommy Fawkes (Oliver Platt) is the son of America's undisputed King of Comedy, George Fawkes (Jerry Lewis). Tommy dies in his Vegas debut when he antagonizes a middle-aged audience with a daring Denis Leary-style routine. Refusing to admit he hasn't inherited his dad's "funny bones," Tommy characteristically misses the point of his failure, flies to Blackpool, England (the scene of his famous dad's early triumphs), and attempts to purchase bits of physical comedy he can import for an act in the States.

Meanwhile, troubled young performer Jack Parker (Lee Evans), who lives a distorted inversion of Tommy's privileged existence, is a convenient fall-guy for bent Police Chief Stanley Sharkey (Ian McNeice). Sharkey needs a patsy for the illegal activities of a group of French adventurers who are selling stolen life-extending power nestled inside golden eggs. When one of the smugglers gets dismembered in a ship's propeller, Jack swims for his life after retrieving one of the eggs underwater. While Tommy's plane circles Blackpool, terrified Jack is being talked down from Blackpool tower by his divorced mother Katie (Leslie Caron) and returned to the custody of his eccentric father Bruno Parker (Freddie Davies) and non-communicative uncle Thomas (George Carl), two former headliners reduced to scaring people at a funhouse. As the limbs of the murdered powder-exporter start washing ashore, Tommy sifts through the repertoire of ex-vaudevillians and discovers that the act he loves most is Jack's.

Tommy learns that his father George Fawkes not only stole the comic act of the Parker Brothers but that Jack is the love child Katie bore him while still married to Bruno. George returns to Blackpool to face the music. At a climactic performance, as the aggrieved Frenchmen close in on Jack, the Parker Brothers are rejuvenated by the magic powder and recapture their former on-stage glory. With the conjuring assistance of Katie's Egyptian vanishing act, the smugglers make Sharkey disappear. Jack, pursued by cops, loses control and climbs an acrobat's sway pole. Ultimately, he saves the life of his half-brother Tommy, who has shimmied upward after him.

In FUNNY BONES, reality mirrors theater art in the most deliriously invigorating way since CABARET. Screenwriters Peter Chelsom and Peter Flannery inventively explore what makes some lost souls hilarious while other wannabees toil at comedy like day-laborers. Each Pirandellian element rings true, enhanced by some visual correlative in Chelsom's stunning direction. A genius at transitions, Chelsom shifts from the haunting over-the-credits rendition of *La Mer* to the Americanized, toe-tapping version by Harold Nicholas, on the very stage where Tommy will commit career hari-kiri. Chelsom packs every frame with symbolic resonance and uses a dizzying resourcefulness to revitalize show-biz cliches ("I died on stage" takes on new meaning).

Consummately performed, this idiosyncratic spectacle salutes the comedian's art by contrasting the styles of polished jokemeisters like George Fawkes with the raw talent of exhibitionists like Jack, meanwhile subjecting the viewer to a hilariously awful assemblage of amateur-hour acts. In a movie rich with peripheral pleasures, this sequence of Tommy's bargain-shopping for gags is a classic, and song-and-dance man Fred Evans (so delightful in BBC-TV's "Jeeves and Wooster") dazzles as a game-for-anything trouper who tap-dances with biscuit tins on his feet. The principals, especially Evans, are superb.

Drawing on silent film comedy and the British music hall tradition, this trenchant fable extracts raucous laughter from psychic wounds. In its delirious best moments, it restores the moviegoer's belief in the revelatory power of the camera. *(Graphic violence, extreme profanity, adult situations).* — R.P.

d, Peter Chelsom; p, Simon Fields, Peter Chelsom; exec p, Nicholas Frye; assoc p, Peter McMillan; co-p, Laurie Borg; w, Peter Chelsom, Peter Flannery; ph, Eduardo Serra; ed, Martin Walsh; m, John Altman; prod d, Caroline Hanania; art d, Andrew Munro; set d, Tracey Gallacher; sound, Peter Lindsay (mixer), Mervyn Moore; fx, Tom Harris; casting, Mary Gail Artz, Barbara Cohen; cos, Lindy Hemming; makeup, Pat Hay; stunts, Simon Cran

Comedy/Drama (PR: C MPAA: R)

GALAXIS ★

(U.S.) 91m Interlight Pictures; Osmosis
Pictures ~ Turner Home Entertainment c

Brigitte Neilsen *(Ladera)*; Richard Moll *(Kyla)*;
John H. Brennan *(Jed Sanders)*; Craig Fairbrass
(Tarkin); Fred Asparagus *(Victor)*; John Romaldi
(Soldier 1); Sam Raimi *(Nervous Official)*; Russ
Fuega *(Official)*; Kristin Bauer *(Commander)*;
Steve Garrett *(Soldier)*; Arthur Mesa *(Robot
Child)*; Russ Fega *(Official)*; Louisa Moritz *(Bar
Lady)*; Michael Paul Chan *(Manny)*; Jane Clark
(Rape Victim); Joey Gaynor *(Stavros)*; Jeff Rector *(Tray)*; Chris
Doyle *(Seth)*; Roger Aaron Brown *(Carter)*; Cindy Morgan
(Kelly); Richard Narita *(Raymond)*; Nathan Jung *(Doorman)*;
George Kee Cheung *(Eddie)*; Alan Fudge *(Chief)*; Brent Pfoff
(Policeman)

A great deal of this film's miniscule budget went into dressing
up its special effects and dressing down Ms. Nielsen. Since set
models resemble a futuristic Lionel Train station, GALAXIS
wisely focuses on Brigitte's statuesque physique wrapped in
tight leather. Some screen spectacles are purely the provenance
of Mother Nature.

In a STAR WARS-wannabe opener, planet Centauri is besieged by vile tyrant Kyla (Richard Moll) who covets the inhabitants' powerful "Sacred Crystal." Slaying noble leader Tarkin
(Craig Fairbass) and palming the gem, Kyla must pit himself
against Tarkin's tough sister Ladera (Brigitte Nielsen) for a
second crystal, which has been in the custody of the Incas on
Earth. The mayhem moves, economically, to 1990s Earth, where
a poor man's Indiana Jones named Jed (John H. Brennan) has
entrusted the collectible crystal to a pal who soon gets fried by
Kyla. Jed must stay one step ahead of Kyla, investigating cops,
and Victor (Fred Asparagus) a cartoony gangster outraged that
Jed has rescinded their Inca antique deal. Teaming with Ladera,
Jed escapes Kyla's zapping long enough to trace the missing
thingamabob to the Chinese mob. Ladera and Jed escape with
their hot property, but face showdowns with Victor and Kyla in
one of those vast, abandoned steelworks so common to Z-action
movies. Though defeated almost simultaneously, the dual villains after the same artifact never do meet each other, oddly
enough; perhaps their bloodcurdling overacting combined
would chew up not only the cardboard scenery but entire distant
galaxies.

As sci-fi spacehunts go, this is a cumbersome rumble with
average demolition effects on earth, and less impressive eye-daz-
zlers in space; the disappointing visuals were overseen by debuting director William Mesa, acclaimed for his effects work on
THE FUGITIVE and UNDER SIEGE. Up on Centauri the extras
look as if they just wandered in from the set of BECKETT. Why
do art directors and costumers think the future is going to be
overrun with 12th century revivalists? A bigger question is why
anyone would endure this tedious World Wrestling Federation
bout between Amazonian Nielsen and hambone Moll. Neither
Kyla's nor Ladera's superpowers are clearly delineated. One
moment they're firing death rays through their fingers, the next
they're slugging it out. Despite her robotic emoting, Nielsen
gives space-cadet viewers something to look at as they deal with
their arrested development. She enables one to sexualize and
replay Commander Cody fantasies of boyhood. There should be
a Brigitte on every spacecraft. *(Violence, profanity, substance
abuse.)* — R.P.

d, William Mesa; p, Nile Niami, Patrick Choi; exec p, Paul L.
Newman, Barry Collier, Eung Pyo Choi; assoc p, Nick Davis;
co-p, William Mesa; w, Nick Davis; ph, Robert C. New; ed,

Patrick Lussier, Gregory Hobson; m, Christo-
pher Stone; prod d, Charles Wood; art d, Claire
Kaufman; sound, Phillip Seretti; fx, William
Mesa, Ultimate Effects; casting, Amy Elisabeth
Sabel; cos, Sharon Rosenberg, Robert Miller;
makeup, Suzanne Rodier; stunts, Christopher
Doyle

Science Fiction/Action   (PR: C   MPAA: R)

GEORGIA ★★★½

(U.S./France) 117m Georgia Film Corporation;
CiBy 2000; Miramax ~ Miramax c

Jennifer Jason Leigh *(Sadie)*; Mare Winningham *(Georgia)*; Ted
Levine *(Jake)*; Max Perlich *(Axel)*; John Doe *(Bobby)*; John C.
Reilly *(Herman)*; Jimmy Witherspoon *(Trucker)*; Jason Carter
(Chasman); Tom Bower *(Erwin Flood)*; Smokey Hormel
(Leland); Jimmy Z. *(Clay)*; Tony Marisco *(Paul)*; Jamian Briar
(Andrew); Rachel Rasco *(Mish)*; Nicole Donahoo *(Young Sadie)*;
Aisleagh Jackson *(Young Georgia)*; Coleen O'Hara *(Ticket
Agent)*; Bruce Wirth *(Dan Ferguson)*; Thomas Kuhn *(Bartender
at Larry's)*; Bill Johns *(Promoter)*; Mina Badie *(Girl with
Bobby)*; Chris Carlson *(Reporters at Larry's)*; Shawn Cox *(17-
year-old Boy)*; Jeff Steitzer *(Drunk)*; Michael Shapiro *(Brian)*;
Barbara Deering *(Nurse)*; Stephanie Shine *(Nurse #2)*; Jay Keye
(Gate Agent); Jo Miller *(Herself)*; Gary Lanz *(Backupsinger)*;
C.W. Huston *(Drunk in Crowd)*

A downbeat look at two sisters, set against a backdrop of the
Seattle music scene, GEORGIA is a moody, frequently disturbing film redeemed by its performances.

From the moment we first glimpse Sadie Flood (Jennifer
Jason Leigh), we know she's trouble, from her black
eyeshadow—which gives her the look of a drunken raccoon—and slurred speech to her general recklessness, she's an
accident waiting to happen. Her older sister Georgia (Mare
Winningham), on the other hand, is a successful country singer
who has adoring fans and a stable family life that includes
husband/manager Jake (Ted Levine). After briefly shacking up
with a bluesman (blues singer Jimmy Witherspoon) who proves
as unstable as she is, Sadie escapes to Georgia's farmhouse in the
Washington state countryside, where the sisters grew up. Georgia, who's as rational and reserved as Sadie is wild and passionate, tolerates her sister, even though it's clear she's been dealing
with Sadie's problems for a long time. Jake—who clearly genuinely likes his sister-in-law—is more sympathetic. Sadie's passionate determination to sing is far stronger than her voice, but
she soon hooks up with old friend Bobby (John Doe, of L.A.'s
pioneering punk band X), who agrees to let her sing back-up in
his band if she doesn't screw up as she has in the past. Of course
she does, nodding out during a Jewish wedding gig after one too
many swigs of Nyquil.

Sadie's temporary salvation arrives in the form of a naive,
sweet-natured delivery boy (Max Perlich). Overwhelmed by
Sadie's aura of doomed glamour, he moves in and eventually
marries her. When he realizes how damaged Sadie actually is he
leaves her, and Sadie falls back on her heroin habit for solace.
Georgia runs to the airport to bring her scraggly, near-death sister
to the hospital and a detox center, helping to nurse her back to
health. But her compassion finally gives out during a talk with
Sadie one night at the farm, when she tells her she really can't
sing. The last scenes are of Georgia and Sadie on stage at
different venues, each performing the same song in their sharply
different styles.

Although Sadie is the film's main character, director Ulu Grosbard claims he called his film GEORGIA because Sadie longs to be like her sister. But does she? We're never quite sure whether Sadie is just selfish and irresponsible by nature, or whether her sister's apparently effortless success drove Sadie to drink and drugs. At one point Georgia implies that Sadie was always like this, and if that's the case it's amazing Georgia has put up with her for so long. The film's most affecting scene—which is also the scene many viewers find intolerable—is Leigh's startling, painful and brave eight-minute rendition of Van Morrison's "Take Me Back," a song whose longing for the past is made sharper by Leigh's alternately angry and sad delivery. It appears to have been done in one bravura take, and it says more about Sadie than the rest of the film.

Written by Leigh's mother, veteran screen and TV writer Barbara Turner, and based to some degree on the troubled life of Leigh's sister (the subject of FREEDOM, a 1981 made-for-TV film written by Turner and starring Winningham as the sister), GEORGIA is a dark, meandering character study of the kind that rarely makes it to the American screen. Winningham is entirely convincing as the "good" sister, and Leigh goes full-out—as always—in the role of the alcoholic Sadie. That said, her drunken mutterings quickly become grating, which may be why Winningham was nominated for a Best Supporting Actress Oscar, while Leigh was conspicuously overlooked.

In the end, GEORGIA is an ambitious, noble failure. (*Nudity, sexual situations, adult situations, substance abuse, profanity.*)

d, Ulu Grosbard; p, Ulu Grosbard, Barbara Turner, Jennifer Jason Leigh; exec p, Ben Barenholtz; w, Barbara Turner; ph, Jan Kiesser; ed, Elizabeth Kling; prod d, Lester Cohen; sound, Mark Weingarten (mixer); fx, Don Dumas; casting, Renee Rousselot; cos, Carol Oditz; makeup, Micheline Trepanier

Drama/Musical   (PR: C   MPAA: R)

GET SHORTY   ★★★
(U.S.) 105m Jersey Films; MGM ~ MGM/UA c

John Travolta (*Chili Palmer*); Gene Hackman (*Harry Zimm*); Rene Russo (*Karen Flores*); Danny DeVito (*Martin Weir*); Dennis Farina (*Ray "Bones" Barboni*); Delroy Lindo (*Bo Catlett*); James Gandolfini (*Bear*); Jon Gries (*Ronnie Wingate*); Renee Props (*Nicki*); David Paymer (*Leo Devoe*); Martin Ferrero (*Tommy Carlo*); Miguel Sandoval (*Mr. Escobar*); Jacob Vargas (*Yayo Portillo*); Linda Hart (*Fay Devoe*); Bobby Slayton (*Dick Allen*); Ron Karabatsos (*Momo*); Alison Waddell (*Bear's Daughter*); Amber Waddell (*Bear's Daughter*); John Cothran, Jr. (*Agent Curtis*); Jack Conley (*Agent Dunbar*); Bernard Hocke (*Agent Morgan*); Big Daddy Wayne (*Ray Barboni's Bodyguard*); Xavier Montalvo (*Big Guy with Escobar*); Carlease Burke (*Rental Car Attendant*); Vito Scotti (*Manager at Vesuvio's*); Rino Piccolo (*Waiter at Vesuvio's*); Alfred Dennis (*Ed the Barber*); Ralph Manza (*Fred the Barber*); Zed Frizzelle (*Kid at Lockers*); Harry Victor (*Limo Driver with Sign*); Patrick Breen (*Resident Doctor*); Barry Sonnenfeld (*Doorman*); Donna W. Scott (*Screaming Woman*); Zack Phifer (*Ivy Restaurant Maitre d'*); Gregory B. Goossen (*Duke, Man at the Ivy*); Stephanie Kemp (*Ivy Restaurant Waitress*); Rebeca Arthur (*Las Vegas Waitress*); Jeffrey J. Stephan (*Bones' Buddy*); Ernest "Chili" Palmer (*Bones' Buddy #2*); Harvey Keitel (*Himself—uncredited*); Penny Marshall (*Herself—uncredited*)

Coming in the wake of Quentin Tarantino's PULP FICTION, which helped reshape John Travolta's image, GET SHORTY proved that Travolta is indeed a cooler actor than most people had imagined.

Chili Palmer (Travolta), a Miami-based loan collector with mafia connections and a thing for movies, finds himself in Hollywood collecting an outstanding debt from washed-up schlock film producer Harry Zimm (Gene Hackman). Chili quickly becomes intrigued with the film business—a business whose posing and power plays bear a striking resemblance to the world of loansharking and organized crime—and offers to help Zimm produce a script called "Mr. Lovejoy," to star the ultra-hot Martin Weir (Danny DeVito). The problem: Harry is hip deep in debt to Bo Catlett (Delroy Lindo), a slick drug dealer who sees Harry as his ticket into the producing business, where "the real money" is. With the help of former B-movie queen—and the former Mrs. Martin Weir—Karen Flores (Rene Russo), Chili settles comfortably into the Hollywood scene, expertly pitching a movie idea to Weir—not "Mr. Lovejoy," but Chili's own tale-in-progress of a Miami shylock's adventures in Hollywood.

Despite Chili's smooth transition from mob heavy to movie producer, forces are conspiring against him: Catlett, eager to get a piece of Zimm productions, schemes to saddle Chili with half a million dollars of Columbian drug money and get him arrested for trafficking and murder. Meanwhile, Miami wise guy Ray "Bones" Barboni (Dennis Farina)—who has a bone to pick with Chili—flies into LA looking for the outstanding debt Chili was supposed to have been collecting. Although Harry messes up at every turn, Chili executes a cool two-step that allows him to dispose of Catlett, frame Ray Bones for drug dealing and murder, and ultimately make his movie.

As the story goes, Travolta initially turned down the role of Chili Palmer, fearing the dreaded typecasting, but friend Quentin Tarantino urged him to reconsider. With its expertly executed mixture of smart, snappy dialogue, dark humor, and first rate performances, GET SHORTY is a tremendously entertaining film. While several of them are playing variations on roles they've played before, every major performer—Travolta, Hackman, Russo, DeVito, Farina, and Lindo—turns in an absolutely perfect performance. Travolta is especially impressive, imbuing Chili Palmer with enough likable accessibility to win over those moviegoers who may have been put off by PULP FICTION's smack-shooting Vincent Vega.

Much of GET SHORTY's success can be credited to director and executive producer Barry Sonnenfeld (THE ADDAMS FAMILY, THROW MOMMA FROM THE TRAIN). Using quirky camera moves and angles to survey the wiseguys, Sonnenfeld never allows the tone to become too heavy—even when the characters are doing things that are downright despicable. The slinky jazz soundtrack by John Lurie and others helps put just the right amount of spring in GET SHORTY's step.

Many of Elmore Leonard's sharp, distinctive crime novels have been adapted into mediocre films—STICK and TV's GLITZ spring immediately to mind—but screenwriter Scott Frank (DEAD AGAIN, LITTLE MAN TATE) skillfully translated Leonard's twisty plot into a smooth yet satisfyingly unpredictable story. Frank also left Leonard's streetwise and very funny dialogue essentially untouched. Leonard spent a good piece of his early career writing screenplays in Hollywood. That familiarity with the sleazy underbelly of the movie business informs GET SHORTY, which—without being as mean-spirited as THE PLAYER—manages to skewer producers, actors and screenwriters alike. (*Violence, sexual situations, profanity.*) — B.T.

d, Barry Sonnenfeld; p, Danny DeVito, Michael Shamberg, Stacey Sher; exec p, Barry Sonnenfeld; assoc p, Susan Ringo; co-p, Graham Place; w, Scott Frank (based on the novel by Elmore Leonard); ph, Don Peterman; ed, Jim Miller; m, John Lurie; prod d, Peter Larkin; art d, Steve Arnold; set d, Leslie E. Rollins; sound, Jeff Wexler, Don Coufal, Gary Holland; fx,

Danny Gill, Gary Bierend, Michael McAlister; casting, David Rubin, Debra Zane; cos, Betsy Heimann; makeup, Ellen Wong; stunts, Brian Smrz

Comedy/Crime   **(PR: C   MPAA: R)**

GETTING OUT   ★★½
(U.S.) 92m Dorothea G. Petrie Productions;
Signboard Hill Productions; RHI Entertainment ~
Hallmark Home Entertainment c

Rebecca DeMornay *(Arlene "Arlie" Holsclaw)*; Ellen Brustyn *(Arlie's Mother)*; Carol Mitchell-Leon *(Ruby)*; Robert Knepper *(Carl)*; Richard Jenkins *(The Chaplain)*; Tandy Cronyn *(Placement Worker)*; Norm Skaggs *(Brian Craig)*; Sue Bugden *(Parole Agent)*; Kevin Dewey *(Driver in Pickup)*; Sean Sweeney *(Boy in Pickup)*; Jack Swanson *(Arlie's Father)*; Amy Dott *(Young Arlie)*; Bruce Evers *(Prison Guard)*; Linda Pierce *(Shopkeeper)*; Suzi Bass *(Processor)*; Rosemary Newcott *(Job Counselor)*; David Dwyer *(Paraplegic)*

Despite sporadic melodramatic excess, GETTING OUT is a moving, made-for-TV transcription of Marsha Norman's Off-Broadway play.

Busted out of prison to give birth outside the Cage, headstrong Arlie (Rebecca DeMornay) stretches her sentence to eight years after shooting a man during a gas station holdup. Upon release, Arlie is determined to regain her son from foster care but has difficulty acclimatizing herself to liberty. With career options limited to minimum-wage work, Arlie foolishly blows her savings on a cosmetics-sales con. Although encouraged by an understanding ex-con neighbor Ruby (Carol Mitchell-Leon), Arlie finds it hard to resist old habits, particularly offers of easy cash from erstwhile pimp Carl (Robert Knepper). The loss of her dream job after a visit from her parole officer pales in comparison with the shocking realization that Arlie's son was legally adopted thanks to the maneuvers of her unfeeling mother (Ellen Burstyn). As memories of an incest-plagued childhood and monstrous parents continue gushing into her consciousness, Arlie suffers a breakdown, and stabs herself with a fork as a cry for help. With the demons of her father's sex abuse released, Arlie restarts her life from the bottom and peacefully assures Ruby that she will wait to see her child when he comes of age, secure in the knowledge that he's in a loving home.

By holding the reins in on this heartbreaking case study, GETTING OUT doubles its impact. In fact, its least effective moments arise from DeMornay's climactic nervous collapse, too artsily-filmed and over-emphatically-acted to mesh with the rest of the sparingly-directed exploration of emotional battering. This suggest that jail release doesn't break the bars that convicts feel around their wounded psyches, and playwright Norman theorizes that the crime spiral starts in childhood where victimized children shape their guilty, self-destructive sexuality. That "getting out" is near impossible is driven home by Arlie's impasse with her neurotically insecure mother, who provided parental basics while jealously denying her daughter essential support. That crippling relationship is brought to agonized life by DeMornay and Burstyn, free from stagebound theatrics. Filmed on location in Atlanta, Georgia, the teleplay is carefully guided toward its resolution by director John Korty (AUTOBIOGRAPHY OF MISS JANE PITTMAN) who has largely spent his career on network dramas for the oft-denounced idiot box; in fact, theatrical motion pictures (and direct-to-video releases) long ago consigned the women's-prison genre to campy drive-in schlock and sadistic, cheap babes-behind-bars thrills. Only television, it seems, can still do justice to material that seriously explores pent-up psychosexual needs for clues to how women

drift into lives of crime, and why they can't avoid recidivism when the rare second chance presents itself. *(Violence, profanity, adult situations, sexual situations, substance abuse.)* — R.P.

d, John Korty; p, Dorothea G. Petrie; exec p, Robert Halmi, Sr., Richard Welsh; co-p, Brent Shields; w, Eugene Corr, Ruth Shapiro (based on the play by Marsha Norman); ph, William Wages; ed, Jim Oliver; m, Mason Daring; art d, Jan Scott; set d, Joseph Litsch; sound, Kenneth B. Ross (mixer), Stephen Grubbs; casting, Lynn Barber; cos, Marjorie Bowers; makeup, Lynn Barber; stunts, Lonnie Smith

Drama/Prison   **(PR: C   MPAA: NR)**

GHOST BRIGADE   ★½
(U.S.) 93m Motion Picture Corporation of America;
Krevoy/Stabler ~ Turner Home Entertainment c

Adrian Pasdar *(Capt. John Harling)*; Corbin Bernsen *(Col. Nehemiah Strayn)*; Cynda Williams *(Rebecca)*; Ray Wise *(Col. George Thalman)*; Martin Sheen *(General Haworth)*; Roger Wilson *(Major Josiah Elkins)*; Jefferson Mays *(Martin Bradley)*; Allison A.J. Langer *(Thomas)*; Alexis Arquette *(Corporal Dawson)*; Billy Bob Thornton *(Langston)*; Dean Cameron *(Borne)*; David Arquette *(Murphy)*; Mark Dawson *(Corporal)*; Jon Beatty *(Lieutenant)*; Matt LeBlanc *(Terhune)*; Josh Evans *(Lt. Regis)*; Steve Price *(Capt. Donnelly)*; Oliver Muirhead *(Richard Bradley)*; Jed Grodin *(Private)*; Jerry Heilbron *(Valet)*; George Hickenlooper *(Painter)*; Art Gambill *(Cellist)*; Peter Sherayo *(Union Captain)*; Chuck Aronberg *(Union Soldier)*; Brian Currie *(Cannoneer)*; Jason Workman *(Union Soldier #2)*; Joy Hooper *(Slave Prisoner)*; David Wade Battle *(Shaver)*; Carl Clink *(Trooper Clink)*; John Enbom *(Armless Man)*

The South doesn't rise again, but its dead troops do in GHOST BRIGADE.

Rebel zombies result after a Union platoon opens fire on surrendering members of the Confederate 51st. After reports surface of crucified Yankee soldiers, General Matthew Haworth (Martin Sheen) orders Capt. John Harling (Adrian Pasdar) on a search-and-destroy mission. Prevailing upon the jailed leader of the 51st, Colonel Nehemiah Strayn (Corbin Bernsen), Harling mistakenly seeks live marauders. Meanwhile the undead Confederates are busy slaughtering fellow Southerners and slaves—excluding the mute Rebecca (Cynda Williams) whose voodoo powers spare her. Psychically communicating with the bigoted Strayn, Rebecca leads the reconnaissance squad toward the truth: hundreds of years ago a great evil was uprooted from Africa and transported to America by slave traders. Dormant due to slave magic, the curse was reactivated by the ambush of the 51st and can only be curtailed by silver bullets, running water, and fire. Melting down silver items into ammo and surrounding their entrenchment with a makeshift irrigation canal, Strayn and Harling combat the army of darkness and live to distinguish themselves on opposing sides of the Civil War. Sacrificing herself, Rebecca forces Ghost Brigade leader Josiah Elkins (Roger Wilson) to shoot her with an anti-phantom projectile that passes through his body and hers.

GHOST BRIGADE offers 50% folk legend exposition to 50% narrative action. The film wastes so much time filling in details of the cadaver squadron it seems longer than the Battle of Gettysburg. Trying for the hallucinatory atmosphere of the film version of Ambrose Bierce's OCCURRENCE AT OWL CREEK BRIDGE, this unusual chiller falls prey to mundane scripting, combat-booted direction, and inferior sound mixing. When dialogue, SFX and music seem to assail the ears from different parallel universes, is it any wonder that the victims' screams ring hollow? This also fails to capitalize on the fascinating symbolic concept that the demonic forces of slavery inspired the Civil War. GHOST BRIGADE is certainly off-beat enough to hook genre buffs, but it doesn't trudge the extra mile. Despite the presence of Sheen, a player in numerous War-Between-the-States flicks, cast members seem decidedly out of place in the historical period. As for the terrifying Ghost Brigade and their white warpaint makeup, they register as zombie minstrels from an 1860s touring carnival. *(Graphic violence, profanity.)* — R.P.

d, George Hickenlooper; p, Brad Krevoy, Steve Stabler; exec p, Fred Kuehnert, Mick Strawn; co-p, Brad Jenkel; w, Matt Greenberg; ph, Kent Wakeford; ed, Monte Hellman, Esther P. Russell; m, John D'Andrea, Cory Lerios; prod d, C.J. Strawn; art d, Brad Johnson; sound, Peter Meiselmann (design); fx, Ultimate Effects; casting, Ed Mitchell, Robyn Ray; cos, Matthew Jacobsen; makeup, Rene Dashiell

Horror/Western　　　　　　　　**(PR: C　MPAA: R)**

GIRL IN THE CADILLAC　　　　　　　　★★
(U.S.) 89m Steinhardt Baer Pictures Company; Cadillac Productions ~ Turner Home Entertainment c

Erika Eleniak *(Mandy)*; William McNamara *(Rick)*; Bud Cort *(Bud)*; Valerie Perrine *(Tilly)*; Michael Lerner *(Pal)*; Ed Lauter *(Wilmer)*; William Shockley *(Lamar)*; Leland Orser *(Used Car Salesman)*; Mark Voland *(Mr. Warrick)*; Meredith Salenger *(Salesgirl)*; Ed Bernard *(Judge Horton)*; Dink O'Neal *(Desk Clerk)*; Doug Cox *(Bank Manager)*; Jeanette O'Connor *(Waitress)*; Scott Vance *(Gas Station Attendant)*

Based a lesser James M. Cain novel that was published posthumously, THE GIRL IN THE CADILLAC is disappointingly softboiled. Voluptuous teen Mandy (Erika Eleniak), bummed by flighty mama Tilly (Valerie Perrine) and her taste for lustful live-in boyfriends, dreams of finding her real father and becoming part of a functional household. But the road to reunion with that super dad is full of wolves in sheeps' clothing, like good-ol'-boyish Rick Davis (William McNamara) and his shifty cohorts Pal (Michael Lerner) and Bud (Bud Cort). Planning a minimal-risk bank heist, the trio invites runaway Mandy aboard as getaway driver; to reel her in, they point out she can use her share to buy new frocks with which to impress her papa. During the botched robbery that leaves guards wounded and their partners behind, Rick and Mandy impulsively skedaddle with all the loot. Not slick enough to cover their tracks as they sample the high life, Rick and Mandy peel out on the highway in a status-symbol red Cadillac. Mandy drops in on the man she believed to be her parent, but she's stunned to discover that her mother fantasized this father figure to give Mandy the illusion of legitimacy. After conscience-stricken Mandy abandons Rick to return the money, Rick's former associates catch up and severely beat him, then try to intercept Mandy at Tilly's new home with her latest soulmate Wilmer (Ed Lauter). Replaying THE DESPERATE HOURS, the crooks force their way inside, hold the family at gunpoint, and search for the cash. Rick fortuitously arrives and kills Bud. When Pal takes aim at Rick outside Wilmer's, Mandy runs him down with that shiny Cadillac. The next day she bids farewell to prison-bound Rick, and thanks God she has found stability in nice-guy Wilmer.

As interpreted by Eleniak, Mandy lacks the vital vulnerability needed to shift this CADILLAC out of first gear. You can't believe a tough gal like her would rob a bank just to purchase clothes for a face-to-face with her fancied father. Though supporting actors, especially Lerner, give their performances some octane, the plot is one terribly predictable ride. This screenplay should race by at a pace that sticks out its tongue at speed limits; instead GIRL IN THE CADILLAC chugs along like an overcau-

tious student driver, and gives action buffs too many opportunities to simply pass it by. One nice custom detailing: the zingy musical score by Anton Sanko. *(Violence, extreme profanity, sexual situations, nudity.)* — R.P.

d, Lucas Platt; p, Thomas Baer; exec p, John Warren, Michael Steinhardt; w, John Warren (based on the novel *The Enchanted Isle* by James M. Cain); ph, Nancy Schreiber; ed, Norman D. Hollyn; m, Anton Sanko; prod d, Pamela Marcotte; set d, James Adams; sound, John Halaby (mixer); fx, Dale Newkirk; casting, Kathy Smith; cos, Cathryn Wagner; makeup, Linda Hardy; stunts, Gary Wayton

Crime/Romance　　　　　　　　**(PR: C　MPAA: R)**

GLASS SHIELD, THE　　　　　　　　★★★½
(U.S./France) 109m The Glass Shield Productions; CiBy 2000 ~ Miramax c

Michael Boatman *(Deputy J.J. Johnson)*; Lori Petty *(Deputy Deborah Fields)*; Ice Cube *(Teddy Woods)*; Elliot Gould *(Greenspan)*; Richard Anderson *(Watch Commander Clarence Massey)*; Don Harvey *(Deputy Jack Bono)*; Michael Ironside *(Detective Gene Baker)*; Michael Gregory *(Deputy Roy Bush)*; Bernie Casey *(Locket)*; M. Emmet Walsh *(Detective Jesse Hall)*; Sy Richardson *(Mr. Taylor)*; Natalija Nogulich *(Judge Helen Lewis)*; Erich Anderson *(District Attorney Ira Kern)*; Wanda De Jesus *(Carmen Munoz)*; Victoria Dillard *(Barbara Simms)*; Tommy Hicks *(Reverend Banks)*; Gary Wood *(Sergeant Chuck Gilmore)*; Linden Chiles *(Sergeant Berry Foster)*; Corbin Timbrook *(Deputy Kurt Smith)*; James Fitzpatrick *(Deputy Jim Ryan)*; David McKnight *(Mr. Harold Johnson)*; Thomas W. Babson *(U.S. Marshall)*; Monty Bane *(Coroner)*; Ernie Lee Banks *(Mr. Woods)*; Jean Hubbard-Boone *(Mrs. Woods)*; James Boyce *(Paramedic #1)*; Gaye Shannon-Burnett *(Woman Driver)*; Janet Claire *(Juror)*; Victor Contreras *(Mr. Cruz)*; Bill Dearth *(Guard)*; Marcia Del Mar *(Mrs. Cruz)*; Mkeba W. Dunn *(Teddy Woods' Girlfriend)*; Leigh Dupree *(Court Clerk)*; Eric Fleeks *(Bailiff)*; Patricia Forte *(Mrs. Marshall)*; Jim Hardie *(Insurance Investigator Robert Hill)*; Arthur L. Horst *(Deputy)*; James Ingersoll *(Jury Foreman)*; Kyle-Scott Jackson *(Mr. Marshall)*; Kimble Jemison *(Buddy Johnson)*; Richard Kuss *(Judge Speck)*; Michael R. Larson *(Arraignment Lawyer)*; Joanne K. Liebeler *(Jane Baker)*; David Lodge *(Reporter #2)*; Rod McFall *(Cyclist)*; Christine McGraw *(Reporter #1)*; Julio Oscar Mechoso *(Assistant D.A.)*; Dino Parks *(Deputy)*; Al Rodrigo *(Jose Rosario (Interpreter Castro)*; Ed Ruffalo *(Sheriff Sergeant)*; Lee Ryan *(Insurance Investigator George Beaten)*; Jason Saffran *(The Punk)*; Greta Sesheta *(Joyce)*; Drew Snyder *(Sheriff Sergeant)*; Joseph Walsh *(Councilman Ross)*; Donnice Wilson *(Mrs. Johnson)*; Biff Yeager *(Investigating Officer)*

Misleadingly marketed as a violent "gangsta" flick through ads that exploited the iconic presence of actor-rapper Ice Cube, THE GLASS SHIELD is no standard tale of "Boyz N Blue N the Hood." This is a humane and savvy drama with police-story trappings, and it may disappoint genre adherents. While flawed, the film reveals the hand of a thoughtful artist at its helm.

John Eddie "J J" Johnson (Michael Boatman) is assigned to become the first and only African-American deputy at a sheriff's station in the LA suburbs. Raised on comic books, the rookie has a clear-cut view of good and evil. Johnson tries to ignore the hostility and condescension of his fellow cops, including Chief Massey (Richard Anderson). He even loyally avoids family friend Reverend Banks (Tommy Hicks), a community activist who has become involved in the case of a Ernie Marshall, a black youth who died under suspicious circumstances in police custody. Johnson becomes friendly with his lone female (and Jewish) co-worker, Deputy Deborah Fields (Lori Petty), who is also belittled at work and on the street. Black activist attorney Locket (Bernie Casey) advises the Marshalls, who are enduring police harassment. Jesse Hall (M. Emmett Walsh), an aging veteran detective, informs his friend Detective Baker (Michael Ironside) that he has advanced cancer and wants to leave some security for his family. A high-profile arrest would end his career nicely.

Arriving at a crime scene, Fields finds the corpse of a woman slumped in the passenger seat of her car. The vicim's husband, Mr. Greenspan (Elliott Gould), has told the police that a black man shot his wife, but Fields doubts his claim. Baker and Hall laugh her off. Later, Deputy Bono (Don Harvey) stops Teddy Woods (Ice Cube) at a gas station. Johnson pulls up as Woods admits to having a stolen pistol in his car. Johnson finds the gun and Woods is arrested. After reading the incident report, Hall and Baker decide to pin the Greenspan murder on Woods, who is now represented by Locket. Bono persuades Johnson to back up his false claim that he stopped Woods for a traffic violation. Johnson subsequently discovers that his arrest report was altered; the weapon's serial number has been changed. He admits his lie to Fields and the pair begin a covert investigation, unaware they are being monitored by Massey and his cronies.

Johnson leaks information to Locket that helps Woods' case. Greenspan disappears with insurance investigators on his tail and an unidentifiable male corpse is discovered. Johnson and Fields gradually uncover an intricate web of corruption, blackmail, and cover-ups involving the upper echelons of the Sheriff's Office and the City Council. They are nearly killed for their efforts: Johnson's bulletproof vest saves him from an unidentified assailant, while Fields lands in the hospital badly beaten, presumably by disguised cops from Baker's gung-ho "Rough Riders" team. Hall dies on duty in Baker's arms. Bono cuts a deal and gives up Johnson, who is subpoenaed for perjury when the Attorney General's office swoops down on the corrupt cops. Baker is arrested; Massey is forced to retire; and a disillusioned Johnson cuts his own deal and ends up leaving the force. The other corrupt cops are merely reassigned.

While African-American writer-director Charles Burnett has amassed numerous awards, fellowships and accolades over the last two decades, his small but impressive body of work has not found the audience it merits. A topical crime drama could have been a safe bet for mainstream exposure, but Burnett confounds genre expectations in this modest French-financed production.

THE GLASS SHIELD is a cop movie without sex, profanity, high-speed chases, or graphic violence. Standard shortcuts to realism (e.g., handheld camera) are avoided in favor of saturated colors, striking angles, and bold lighting. The opening titles appear against the panels of a comic strip depicting a hyperbolic and upbeat variation of the plot, foregrounding the simplistic worldview that Johnson will be forced to abandon by the film's end. Based on a true account, THE GLASS SHIELD critiques the actions and mindset of the police without bashing policemen; even the worst are portrayed as human beings with families and motivations.

The film veers off-track when depicting the unfolding of a bewildering conspiracy. We get lost in detail and lose the thread of the revelations. Dramatically slack, the courtroom scenes drone on and diminish the impact of earlier scenes. All in all, THE GLASS SHIELD is a noble failure—it might have benefited from a little Sam Fuller-esque narrative savvy—but it's a must-see for thoughtful, empathetic viewers. (Violence.) — K.G.

d, Charles Burnett; p, Thomas Byrnes, Carolyn Schroeder; exec p, Chet Walker; assoc p, Michael D. Aglion, Robert A. Merrill; w, Charles Burnett (based in part on the screenplay "One of Us" by Ned Walsh); ph, Elliot Davis; ed, Curtiss Clayton; m, Stephen

James Taylor; prod d, Penny Barrett; art d, Joel Carter; set d, Lisa Boutillier; sound, Veda Campbell (mixer); fx, John Hartigan, Ultimate Effects; casting, Monica Swann; cos, Gaye Shannon-Burnett; makeup, Kim Davis; stunts, Bufort McClerkins, McClerkins

Drama/Crime (PR: C   MPAA: PG-13)

GLORY BOYS, THE ★★
(U.K.) 78m Yorkshire Television ~ BFS Video c

Rod Steiger *(Sokarev)*; Anthony Perkins *(Jimmy)*; Aaron Harris *(McCoy)*; Gary Brown *(Famy)*; Salleyanne Law *(Norah)*

Made for British television, THE GLORY BOYS shoots itself in the foot by relying too much on convoluted plot twists and not enough on character development.

Arab terrorist Famy (Gary Brown) is bent on killing famed Israeli nuclear scientist Dr. David Sokarev (Rod Steiger). In London he joins with Kirin McCoy (Aaron Harris) a thrill-seeking IRA terrorist who shares an interest in Sokarev's assassination. In Washington D.C., Sokarev, informed of the conspiracy, tries to cancel his itinerary, but the government refuses, believing it will send a message of capitulation to terrorism. He reluctantly proceeds to his London engagement under the protection of veteran security agent Jimmy (Anthony Perkins), an alcoholic with a maverick streak. The terrorists botch their hit and split up. Wounded McCoy stays at the suburban home of Norah (Salleyanne Law), a local girl who inexplicably loves the brutal killer. Police catch McCoy, and Jimmy pries out of him Famy's next plan: to kill Sokarev at Heathrow Airport. Jimmy leads his men in a race against time and manage to collar the Arab. Driven by vague, private motivations or perhaps just a violent impulse, Jimmy executes Famy right there on the tarmac. On the plane ride back home, Sokarev suffers a heart attack and dies. Jimmy, now unemployed and back to his business of full-time drinking, hears the news, and the picture ends with him drunkenly laughing at the irony.

Gerald Seymour's script, based on his own novel, is certainly full of fast-paced action, but primary motivations of the characters are unclear. We never learn Jimmy's true reason for killing or drinking; he just does both with no reflection. More political analysis right from the beginning would also have shored up the story's foundation. Racing between too many locales, THE GLORY BOYS has three editors, and it looks as if they each made their own cut and then haphazardly spliced them together. Performances are generally solid. Making the most of a rare good-guy lead, Perkins' Jimmy is quirky and fun to watch, Steiger's resigned Sokarev suitably moving. But when protagonists seem to so randomly choose death over life, we are left with no glory. *(Violence, adult situations.)* — J.D.

d, Michael Ferguson; p, Michael Glynn; exec p, David Cunliffe, Alan Landsburg; ph, Allan Pyrah; ed, Tim Ritson, Allen Jewhurst, Steve Gannon; m, Alan Parker; prod d, David Crozier; sound, Dan Atkinson; makeup, Pam Fox

Political/Spy/Thriller (PR: C   MPAA: NR)

GOD'S ARMY
(SEE: PROPHECY, THE)

GOLD DIGGERS: THE SECRET OF ★★½
BEAR MOUNTAIN
(U.S.) 92m Universal ~ Universal c

Christina Ricci *(Beth Easton)*; Anna Chlumsky *(Jody Salerno)*; Polly Draper *(Kate Easton)*; Brian Kerwin *(Matt Hollinger)*;

Diana Scarwid *(Lynette Salerno)*; David Keith *(Ray Karnisak)*; Gillian Barber *(Grace Briggs)*; Ashleigh Aston Moore *(Tracy Briggs)*; Jewel Staite *(Samantha)*; Amy Kirk *(Molly Morgan)*; Dwight McFee *(Sgt. Weller)*; Andrew Wheeler *(Hank)*; Roger R. Cross *(Paramedic)*; Kimberley Warnat *(Girl)*; Jesse Moss *(Adam)*; Scott Augustine *(Doug)*; Steve Makaj *(Deputy Ted)*; Betty Phillips *(Mysterious Woman)*; Jay Brazeau *(Everett Graham)*; Dustin Brooks *(Fight Boy)*; Philip Josef *(Fight Boy)*; Carren Learning *(Voice of Adult Beth)*

A rare adventure film for girls, GOLD DIGGERS: THE SECRET OF BEAR MOUNTAIN follows two pre-teens on a search for a secret gold mine in rural Washington state. The contrived storyline benefits from excellent location work in British Columbia and energetic performances by two of the best of the current crop of young actresses, Christina Ricci and Anna Chlumsky.

Twelve-year-old Beth Easton (Christina Ricci) and her widowed mother Kate (Polly Draper) travel from California to spend the summer of 1980 in Wheaton, Wash. A bored city girl, Beth makes fast friends with tomboy Jody Salerno (Anna Chlumsky), an outcast who frequently flees the home of an alcoholic mother (Diana Scarwid) and her abusive boyfriend, Ray (David Keith). Inspired by the legend of Molly Morgan, a female miner who reportedly found a hidden vein of gold in nearby Bear Mountain in the 1920s, Jody has outfitted an old boat to enter the caves of the mountain which are accessible only by water. She persuades Beth to journey there on the day of the summer solstice because legend holds that the sun at high noon on that day will reveal the location of the hidden mine by its reflection on the mountain.

A boat accident inside the mountain cave results in a rockslide which pins down Beth. Jody swims out of the cave, hikes through the forest to the nearest highway, and flags down a county patrol car. A rescue team is sent and frees Beth just before the tide engulfs her.

Angry at Jody's recklessness, Kate forbids Beth from seeing her. Beth reveals Jody's accounts of abuse at the hands of her mother's boyfriend, Ray, but neither Kate nor Sheriff Matt Hollinger (Brian Kerwin) believe her. However, when Ray and Jody disappear, Beth convinces the sheriff that Ray has taken Jody to Bear Mountain to force her to locate the hidden gold mine. Beth joins the sheriff in a search of the mountain and locates Jody, but Ray tries to stop them. An old woman—Molly Morgan?—appears, knocks Ray unconscious and then disappears. The sheriff arrives and arrests Ray. A few days later, an anonymous benefactor sends both Beth and Jody each a sack of gold nuggets.

With its elements of river boating, child abuse, treasure hunting, and cave adventures, GOLD DIGGERS offers distinct echoes of Mark Twain's Tom Sawyer and Huck Finn stories. The tales have been updated to showcase wisecracking, self-assured, smartaleck 1990s girls (in a 1980 setting) in order to draw out the young female audience which several recent films have targetted (THE BABYSITTERS CLUB, A LITTLE PRINCESS, NOW AND THEN).

The storyline careens all over the map, from a tale of summer friendship to one of treasure-seeking to one of near-drowning and rescue to one of an abused child seeking help. Since the girls never actually find the gold, the long-awaited climactic thrill of discovery never arrives. They reap the rewards, however, in a *deus ex machina* ending. The film's appeal, however, is consistently sustained by the central performances of Ricci and Chlumsky, whose energy, earnestness, and glowing screen presence overcome the frequently stilted, girls' literature-style scripting. — B.C.

d, Kevin James Dobson; p, Martin Bregman, Rolf Deyhle, Michael S. Bregman; exec p, Louis A. Stroller; assoc p, Allan

Wertheim; w, Barry Glasser; ph, Ross Berryman; ed, Stephen W. Butler; m, Joel McNeely; prod d, Michael Bolton; art d, Eric A. Fraser; set d, Elizabeth Wilcox; sound, Ralph Parker (mixer), Harry E. Snodgrass (designer); fx, Mike Vezina, Lynda Lemon, Michael Lessa, Buena Vista Visual Effects; casting, Mary Gail Artz, Barbara Cohen; cos, Mary McLeod; makeup, Connie Parker; stunts, Betty Thomas

Children's/Adventure   (PR: A   MPAA: PG)

GOLDENEYE   ★★★
(U.S.) 130m Eon Productions Ltd.; Danjaq Inc.; United Artists ~ MGM/UA c

Pierce Brosnan *(James Bond)*; Sean Bean *(Alec Trevelyan)*; Izabella Scorupco *(Natalya Simonova)*; Famke Janssen *(Xenia Onatopp)*; Joe Don Baker *(Jack Wade)*; Judi Dench *(M)*; Robbie Coltrane *(Valentin Zukovsky)*; Tcheky Karyo *(Dmitiri Mishkin)*; Gottfried John *(General Ourumov)*; Alan Cumming *(Boris Grishenko)*; Desmond Llewelyn *(Q)*; Samantha Bond *(Moneypenny)*; Michael Kitchen *(Bill Tanner)*; Serena Gordon *(Caroline)*; Simon Kunz *(Severnaya Duty Officer)*; Pavel Douglas *(French Warship Captain)*; Cmdt. Olivier Lajous *(French Warship Officer)*; Billy J. Mitchell *(Admiral Chuck Farrel)*; Constantine Gregory *(Computer Store Manager)*; Minnie Driver *(Irina)*; Michelle Arthur *(Anna)*; Ravil Isyanov *(MIG Pilot)*; Vladimir Milanovich *(Croupier)*; Trevor Byfield *(Train Driver)*; Peter Majer *(Valentin's Bodyguard)*

The 17th installment in the James Bond series and the first starring Pierce Brosnan as 007 stacks up well, despite some awkward and superficial attempts to update the post-Cold War Bond-film canon. For the most part, GOLDENEYE supplies the thrills, *bon mots*, and beautiful babes fans expect.

British superspy Bond's new superior, M (Judi Dench), gives him his latest orders: he must deter a group of Russian gangsters, the Janus Syndicate, who have stolen a space-based laser weapons system. Bond is joined in his investigation by a Russian computer expert, Natalya Simonova (Izabella Scorupco), who alone survived the annihilation of the research center which controlled the weapon system and can identify those responsible: Ourumov (Gottfried John), a highly regarded Russian general, and Xenia Onatopp (Famke Janssen), a sexy sociopath who can crush men between her thighs.

Bond's pursuit of the criminals leads him to Alec Trevelyan (Sean Bean)—his former friend and fellow agent—who confesses that he defected to the Janus Syndicate out of anger at the West for lamely accepting the former Soviet Union as an ally after the end of the Cold War. In the film's climax, Natalya thwarts Alec's elaborate plan to steal from all the banks in the western hemisphere by reprogramming his computer system, and James destroys the satellite dish controlling the laser weapon. Finally, James and Natalya are rescued from the traitor's exploding headquarters by the American forces.

Pierce Brosnan is the sixth actor to play James Bond—excluding the star parade of the parodic CASINO ROYALE (1967)—replacing Timothy Dalton, whose two earnest, dour attempts were not a hit with most fans. Brosnan may lack the earthy charm of original Bond Sean Connery, but he's just as charismatic as Roger Moore (Connery's second replacement after the ineffectual George Lazenby) and a more convincing action hero. In the same way, GOLDENEYE may not be the best Bond film, but it's far better than many recent entries in the series.

GOLDENEYE's best quality is its refusal to take itself seriously. Bond's opening, pre-title escape from a crashing airplane is his most absurd and unrealistic to date, and director Martin

Campbell (CRIMINAL LAW, NO ESCAPE) has fun throughout mounting large-scale stunts and action set pieces, cut to old Bond music themes. Brosnan, too, has a good time with the requisite 007-isms. Desmond Llewelyn reprises his role as gadget-designer Q, and while Georgian villainess Onatopp is little more than a cartoon-like *vagina dentata*, heroine Natalya supplies more than mere decoration: She actually helps save the world with her computer know-how.

Some of the film's other revisionist elements are less successful and suggest that GOLDENEYE wants to have it both ways: as a nostalgic, classic Bond romp and an updated, politically correct action picture. The clever gender-shift in the character of M—Dame Judi Dench replaces the late Bernard Lee—is almost ruined in a single overemphatic exchange, in which she calls Bond "a sexist, misogynist dinosaur." The replacement of long-time Miss Moneypenny Lois Maxwell with the younger and more beautiful Samantha Bond—now half-heartedly complaining about sexual harassment—is unfortunate: Moneypenny's unrequited crush on Bond added a poignant note to earlier films. And Natalya's bravery and ingenuity are undercut by the many shots of her cowering from fisticuffs and falling structures.

The film's oddest revision, however, is its nostalgia for the halcyon days of the Cold War. It's as though the filmmakers were as stuck in the past as the film's villain. At least the underrated LICENSE TO KILL (1989) turned to a Columbian drug cartel instead of SPECTRE for bad guys.

Perhaps there's no way to make a truly palatable James Bond film in the 1990s. But if the Broccoli bunch—longtime Bond producer "Cubby" and his daughter, Barbara—are prepared to continue with Brosnan in the lead, they may as well remodel their sexist, misogynist dinosaur without making such an issue of political correctness: let's face it, James Bond will never be P.C. *(Violence, nudity, sexual situations, profanity.)* — E.M.

d, Martin Campbell; p, Michael G. Wilson, Barbara Broccoli; exec p, Tom Pevsner; assoc p, Anthony Waye; w, Jeffrey Caine, Bruce Feirstein (from a story by Michael France, based on characters created by Ian Fleming); ph, Phil Meheux; ed, Terry Rawlings; m, Eric Serra; prod d, Peter Lamont; art d, Neil Lamont; set d, Michael Ford; sound, David John (recordist); fx, Chris Corbould, Mara Bryan, Derek Meddings; casting, Debbie McWilliams; cos, Lindy Hemming; makeup, Linda Devetta; stunts, Simon Crane

Action/Spy/Thriller (PR: C MPAA: PG-13)

GOOD DAY TO DIE, A ★★½
(U.S.) 120m Konigsberg Company ~
Vidmark Entertainment c
(AKA: CHILDREN OF THE DUST)

Sidney Poitier *(Gypsy Smith)*; Michael Moriarty *(John Maxwell)*; Billy Wirth *(Corby White)*; Regina Taylor *(Drusilla)*; Farrah Fawcett *(Nora Maxwell)*; Hart Bochner *(Shelby Hornbeck)*; Robert Guillaume *(Jolson Mossburger)*; Joanna Going *(Rachel Maxwell Hornbeck)*; Shirley Knight *(Aunt Bertha)*; James Caviezel *(Dexter)*; Grace Zabriskie *(Rose Maddox)*; Basil Wallace *(Fulton)*; John Pyper Ferguson *(Sonny Boy)*; Byron Chief-Moon *(Chief Walks-the-Clouds)*; Kevin McNulty *(Sheriff Harriman)*; Katherine Isobel *(Young Rachel)*; Mitchell LaPlante *(Young Corby)*; Zachary Savard *(Young Dexter)*; Jesse Lipscombe *(Clarence)*; Wilma Pelly *(Nita)*; Lindsey Campbell *(Miranda)*; Brent Stait *(Ballenger)*; Charles Andre *(Nez)*; Eric Keenlyside *(Boss Beeson)*; Jack Ackroyd *(Farmer Tully)*; Tom Schanley *(Cavalry Officer)*; Brian Jensen *(Lieutenant)*; Dale Wilson *(Renfro)*; Michael Elias *(Reporter)*; Crystal Verge *(Mrs. Tibbens)*; Donna Belleville *(Mrs. Clarksdale)*; Michelle Thrush

(Rainbow Woman); Edward C.K. Richardson, III *(Charlie)*; Joshua Myers *(Rachel's Child)*

Overlong and striving too obviously for epic stature, A GOOD DAY TO DIE corrals the comparative novelty of Black homesteaders, in a fatalistic potpourri of oppression, miscegenation, and the taming of the bigoted West.

Hired gun Gypsy Smith (Sidney Poitier) marshalls a regiment at a peaceful Indian village, and is horrified by the massacre that ensues at the hands of US cavalrymen. Rescuing the chief's young son, Gypsy entrusts the boy to Indian agent John Maxwell (Michael Moriarty). Although given the foster name Corby, the former Little Raven (Billy Wirth) grows up uncomfortably aware that he doesn't fit into the White Man's world, particularly when he begins a passionate affair with adoptive sister Rachel (Joanna Going). Meanwhile Gypsy assumes the role of sheriff for his jurisdiction, but resists the domestic impulses he feels for schoolmarm Druscilla (Regina Taylor). Rachel returns from college and, despite her unquenched passion for Corby, attracts the eye of wealthy racist Shelby Hornbeck (Hart Bochner). When two black youths are hanged by the KKK, Gypsy's intervention leads to his castration at the hands of the whites. The embittered lawman withdraws from society and eventually goes on a revenge spree against the hateful crackers. After wedding Shelby, Rachel discovers to her horror that he's the president of the local white supremacist lodge and personally responsible for Gypsy's gelding. When Corby is apprehended while visiting her, Rachel shoots her spouse and goes on the lam with her Indian lover, abetted by Gypsy. Pregnant Rachel is persuaded to rejoin her father Maxwell after the three fugitives are surrounded by a posse. Gypsy goes down in a blaze of glory, and a cannon blasts Corby out of his cave. In honor of their fallen men, Rachel and Druscilla continue to Do the Right Thing on the frontier.

Unable to coherently compress the main events in its source material, "Children of the Dust," this TV miniseries hits the high spots and emerges as a prairie soap opera with a bitter tang. For all the high-toned condemnation of racism, the film only reaches the level of barnstorming melodrama, with over-the-top flourishes of castration, a woman driven mad by the same symbolic wilderness that unhinged Lillian Gish in THE WIND (Farrah Fawcett limns Maxwell's suicidal wife), and a hot sex scene in which the heroine shreds her bridal gown during lovemaking with a beau who is not her fiancee. The film's insurmountable problem lies in giving equal weight to converging storylines about Gypsy's odyssey toward redemption and the star-crossed Rachel/Corby romance. The teleplay adjusts to character crises instead of fashioning the major confrontations around a carefully-mapped scenario. Some characters come and go confusingly, others are given more weight than they should have, and dispensable plot threads end up repeating exposition.

Since the piecework screenplay and uninspired direction don't strangle the actors' hadworking histrionics, the wilder moments play better than the intimate ones that fade due to the rush of happenings. Best enjoyed as a series of violent tableaux with a Message, this proves moderately effective in spite of itself. *(Graphic violence, nudity, profanity, sexual situations, adult situations.)* — R.P.

d, David Greeen; p, Harold Tichenor; exec p, Frank Konigsberg, Joyce Eliason; w, Joyce Eliason (based on the novel *Children of the Dust* by Clancy Carlile); ph, Ron Orieux; ed, Tod Feuerman; m, Mark Snow; prod d, Trevor Williams; art d, Bruce J. Sinski; set d, Robin Swiderski; sound, David Husby (mixer); fx, Digital Magic; casting, Susan Bluestein, Donna Ekholdt; cos, Wendy Partridge; makeup, Pamel Athayde; stunts, Tom Glass

Western (PR: C MPAA: R)

GOOD GIRLS DON'T
(U.S.) 85m Leo Films c

Renee Estevez *(Jeannie)*; Julia Parton *(Bettina)*; Christopher Knight *(Montana)*; Mary Woronov *(Whilhmina)*; Dan Wildman *(Cody)*

Concocted by VICE ACADEMY auteur Rick Sloane, GOOD GIRLS DON'T is cut-rate sexploitation comedy about girls on the run.

Jeannie (Renee Estevez), is a naive, feminist secretary. Bettina (Julia Parton) is a tough, worldly stripper, hired by Jeannie's sexist boss to impress a client. He propositions Jeannie. She objects, and he fires her. Bettina performs, but the boss stiffs her for her fee. Stamping out, she mistakenly grabs a bag containing $500,000. Jeannie and Bettina, now bosom buddies, decide to split with the loot. When Jeannie's slimeball cop boyfriend Montana (Christopher Knight) discovers the boss strangled with a garter, he accuses the girls. Pursued by Montana and the real murderers, a gang of crooks led by Wilhemina (Mary Woronov), Jeannie and Bettina kidnap winsome cop Cody (Dan Wildman). He saves them from the bad guys and convinces them to surrender. They go to prison, get released, are snatched by Wilhemina, saved by Cody, save Cody etc. In the end Cody and Jeannie ride into the sunset, and Bettina gets to sing the Blues, her life ambition. Viewers will be singing the blues from the start.

GOOD GIRLS DON'T is a self-conciously bad pastiche of B-movie homages and corny gags but lacks the cheesy energy of the genres it tries to parody. Bob Hayes' videography is painful, the editing drags, and Alan Dermarderosian's unimaginative score sounds muddy. Nobody acts in GOOD GIRLS DON'T; the script doesn't permit it. Gags are relentless, but unfunny, the few that actually work a welcome relief (after girls and gangsters have a huge, harmless shootout, Cody explodes the villains' car with one shot). Perpetual profanity and a clinical examination of Bettina's breasts best exemplify the level of the humor. GOOD GIRLS DON'T is supposed to spoof THELMA AND LOUISE but it's a joyless joke. As a parody of crud in general, it's indistinguishable from the real thing. *(Extensive nudity, profanity.)* — C.M.

d, Rick Sloane; p, Rick Sloane; w, Rick Sloane; ph, Bob Hayes; m, Alan Dermarderosian; art d, Scott Buckwald

Action/Comedy (PR: O MPAA: NR)

GOOFY MOVIE, A ★★½
(U.S.) 76m Walt Disney ~ Buena Vista c

VOICES OF: Bill Farmer *(Goofy)*; Jason Marsden *(Max)*; Jim Cummings *(Pete)*; Kellie Martin *(Roxanne)*; Rob Paulsen *(P.J.)*; Wallace Shawn *(Principal Mazur)*; Jenna Van Oy *(Stacey)*; Frank Welker *(Bigfoot)*; Kevin Lima *(Lester)*; Jo Anne Worley *(Miss Marples)*; Brittany Alyse Smith *(Photo Studio Girl)*; Robyn Richards *(Lester's Grinning Girl)*; Julie Brown *(Lisa)*; Klee Bragger *(Tourist Kid)*; Joey Lawrence *(Chad)*; Pat Butrum *(Possum Park Emcee)*; Wayne Allwine *(Mickey Mouse)*; Herschel Sparber *(Security Guard)*; Dante Basco; Pat Carroll; Sheryl Bernstein; Steve Moore; E.G. Daily; Brian Pimental; Corey Burton; Carol Holliday; Jason Willinger *(Additional Voices)*

The Walt Disney Studio takes one of its old formulas—Goofy's bungled attempts to bond with his son—and successfully updates it for a new, young audience. While it eschews the spectacle of the studio's more expensive animated features and lacks the charm and wit of its older cartoon shorts, A GOOFY MOVIE remains a breezy, entertaining musical feature that will keep the kids happy.

Goofy (voice of Bill Farmer), a baby photographer, is eager to spend "quality time" with his son Max (voice of Jason Marsden) and plans a cross-country trip to his favorite childhood fishing spot at Lake Destiny. This upsets Max's plans to take classmate Roxanne (voice of Kellie Martin) to the class president's party, at which all the kids plan to watch pop star Power Line in concert on pay-per-view. Before he leaves, Max lies to Roxanne, telling her that his father is an old buddy of Power Line's and that he and his father are going to Los Angeles and will share the stage with the rocker.

Max alters the planned route on Goofy's map so that they'll end up in LA instead of Lake Destiny. Max begins to feel guilty after Goofy appoints him the trip's navigator and entrusts him with the map. When Goofy learns of Max's deception, it forces him to have a heart-to-heart talk with his son and he eventually determines to get them to LA to share the stage with Power Line.

At the concert, they sneak backstage, elude security guards, and wind up dancing with Power Line. They are seen by the pay-per-view cameras, impressing Roxanne and all the high school kids back home.

The determinedly middle-class Goofy on display here is not enough like the perennially dimwitted Goofy of old (voiced by the great Pinto Colvig half a century ago) to satisfy adult cartoon buffs, so the filmmakers wisely shifted the focus to Goofy's modern, rock- and girl-crazy son, Max, and his constant frustrations with his clueless, befuddled, old-fashioned dad. The use of pop star Tevin Campbell as the voice of rocker Power Line only adds to the film's appeal to the adolescent and younger sets.

The animation, executed in France, Canada, Australia, and the US, is competent, recreating a wide variety of American landscapes, and includes one spectacular action sequence at a massive waterfall in the great southwest. While the songs sung by Goofy and Max are fairly sappy, the dance and pop performances are savvy and cleverly executed, with the appropriate high-tech flash and bursts of color and movement. — B.C.

d, Kevin Lima; p, Dan Rounds; assoc p, Patrick Reagan; w, Jymn Magon, Chris Matheson, Brian Pimental (from a story by Jymn Magon); ed, Gregory Perler; m, Carter Burwell; prod d, Fred Warter; art d, Wendell Luebbe, Lawrence Leker; anim, Carole Holliday, Sergio Pablos, William Finn, Alex Mann, Bob Scott, Bruce Smith; sound, Mike Boudry (recordist); casting, Jamie Thomason

Children's/Animated (PR: AA MPAA: G)

GORDY ★½
(U.S.) 89m Robson Entertainment; Ras Entertainment Ltd. ~ Miramax c

Michael Roescher *(Hanky Royce)*; Doug Stone *(Luke MacAllister)*; Kristy Young *(Jinnie Sue MacAllister)*; Deborah Hobart *(Jessica Royce)*; Tom Lester *(Cousin Jake)*; Tom Key *(Brinks)*; Ted Manson *(Henry Royce)*; Justin Garms *(Voice of Gordy)*; James Donadio *(Gilbert Sipes)*; Roy Clark; Moe Brandy; Mickey Gilley; Jim Stafford; Boxcar Willie; Buck Trent; Cristy Lane *(Themselves)*

GORDY is the story of a barnyard pig in search of his porcine family, who are on their way to the slaughterhouse. Before the last-minute rescue can take place, Gordy has many adventures, including inheriting a fortune with a rich little human partner.

An impoverished farm sells its herd of Yorkshire hogs to be trucked up north and ground into sausage. Accidentally left behind, piglet Gordy hits the road, vowing to find his beloved sow, sire and siblings. Because "the pure in heart" can comprehend what he says, Gordy gets adopted by wholesome, travelling country music performer Luke MacAllister (Doug Stone) and his perky daughter Jinnie Sue (Kristy Young). They are playing at the mansion of the millionaire Royce dynasty when poor little rich boy Hanky Royce (Michael Roescher) falls into the swimming pool and is rescued by Gordy in front of assembled media. Nicknamed "Hero Pig," the animal not only becomes the Royce industries' mascot, he and Hanky inherit the whole business empire when Grandpa Royce expires.

This rankles the heir apparent, Hanky's divorced, neglectful mother Jessica (Deborah Hobart), a wannabe fashion model, but it is her conniving yuppie suitor Gilbert Sipes (James Donadio) who sends bumbling thugs to assassinate Gordy at a country music jamboree. Sipes also hides the fact that a Royce subsidiary in Nebraska has Gordy's relatives headed straight for the slaughterhouse, setting the stage for a hackneyed race-against-time finale.

Worthier of comment is the pictures's promotion of C&W music as the path to spiritual redemption and traditional values. Under the influence of line dancing (not to mention tuneful cameos by Roy Clark, Jim Stafford, Mickey Gilley and Box Car Willie) selfish Jessica transforms into a good ol' gal and country wife for widowed Luke, dumping Sipes. Old Glory is waved mercilessly, and the film concludes with many tight close-ups of piggies, cowsies, kitties and squirrelies.

A labored entry in the best of times, GORDY looked especially bad in 1995 when BABE, a bright, inventive all-ages Australian comedy also about a talking pig, premiered scant months later to universal acclaim.

GORDY's director is Australian-born Mark Lewis, creator of the 1988 cult documentary CANE TOADS: AN UNNATURAL HISTORY, which approached its amphibious subjects with none of the cornpone sentiment of this pig tale. Though the animal trainers serve up some diverting stunts, GORDY opened to dismissive reviews, and failed to connect even with easy-to-please family audiences during a nationwide release. In an unusual response, producer Sybil Robson, a former TV hostess, personally appealed to the American public with an emotional prime-time network commercial. That weekend the number one movie was the R-rated DIE HARD WITH A VENGEANCE. — C.C.

d, Mark Lewis; p, Sybil Robson, Fred Brost; exec p, Leslie Stevens; w, Leslie Stevens (from a story by Jay Sommers and Dick Chevillat); ph, Richard Michalak; ed, Lindsay Frazer; m, Charles Fox; prod d, Philip Messina; sound, Mary Ellis; casting, Shari Rhodes; cos, Barcie Waite

Children's/Fantasy/Comedy (PR: AA MPAA: G)

GORILLA BATHES AT NOON ★★★
(Germany/Yugoslavia) 83m Alert Film; Extaza; Von Vietinghoff Filmproduktion ~ Jane Balfour Films c

Svetozar Cvetkovic (*Victor Borisovich*); Anita Mancic (*Miki-Miki/Lenin*); Alexandra Rohmig (*German Girl*); Petar Bozovic (*Trandafil*); Andreas Lucius (*Policeman*); Eva Ras (*Mother*); Suleyman Boyraz (*Turk*); Natasa Babic-Zoric (*Frau Schmidt*); Aleksander Davic (*Dealer*)

GORILLA BATHES AT NOON describes the adventures of Victor Borisovich (Svetozar Cvetkovic), a Soviet Army Major who is homeless in today's Berlin. The ironies of his situation are played for humor in this first film in five years from Dusan Makavejev. Written and directed by Makavejev, the film includes clips from the 1949 Soviet production, THE FALL OF BERLIN, with its patent studio reconstructions of battle and glorification of Stalin.

As Borisovich scurries in civilian clothes through the streets of united Berlin, his ignoble progress is ironically intercut with staged heroic scenes of the Red Army's real and final victory.

Sleeping atop a Berlin rooftop, he is approached by a friendly cop who allows him to get into his dress uniform before escorting him to the station house. Given a one-way Aeroflot ticket to Russia, Borisovich tries to sell it on the streets of the once and future German capital. He even lives with an odd assortment of people in what looks like an old wartime, war-torn basement whose furnishings include an enamelled sign warning people that they are leaving the western zone of the once divided city.

Having discovered that his wife in Moscow has forsaken him, he decides to remain in Berlin, going about in his uniform on a bicycle adorned with the old Bolshevik hammer-and-sickle flag. In the eastern section of the city, he sees a huge statue of Lenin desecrated, so he hoists himself atop it to clean Vladimir Illych's head of paint. And he starts to dream of him, as impersonated by his fellow basement-dweller, Miki-Miki (Anita Mancic). Although a "paper soldier", Borisovich indulges in the bloodthirsty rhetoric of Bolshevism's younger days in his erotic dreams of Comrade Lenin.

The statue itself becomes the focus of a three-sided German debate among Leftists who want to keep it, a group that wants to use it as a target for artistic protest, and others who want to dismantle it. These sequences, and the final procedures of the dismantling, form the documentary core of this film. Borisovich has his own confrontation with the Germans. Not only does he manage to save an infant from a fiery death, but he also has a brief affair with a tap-dancing flutist (Alexandra Rohmig), who has a Turkish boyfriend.

Makavejev has larded his film with a number of visual jokes: while German POWs are shown in a long-distance overhead shot from the 1949 film, the soundtrack is the rollcall of German provinces from Riefenstahl's TRIUMPH OF THE WILL. Besides his old uniform, Borisovich wears a T-shirt with the symbols of both East and West Germany, while the rescued baby is swathed in a torn banner of the old Communist state. There are constant hints of the current moral morass as well: a young German who buys ammo from Borisovich, and a sinister dealer (Aleksander Dovic) who offers to hire Borisovich as an assassin and to buy the infant. At the film's close, Borisovich strips off his uniform to offer it for sale. An oddly elegiac comedy, the film seems to lament the end of a system which, no matter how grossly debased, did after all defeat the Nazis. (*Profanity, adult situations, sexual situations.*) — L.R.

d, Dusan Makavejev; p, Alfred Hurmer, Bojana Marijan, Joachim Von Vietinghoff; w, Dusan Makavejev; ph, Aleksander Petkovic, Miodrag Milosevic; ed, Vuksan Lukovac; m, Brynmor Llewellyn-Jones; prod d, Veljko Despotovic; sound, Uros Kovacevic; fx, Srba Kabadajic; cos, Marina Vukasovic-Madenica

Comedy/Political/Docudrama (PR: C MPAA: NR)

GRANNY, THE ★★
(U.S.) 85m Tapestry Films ~ WarnerVision c

Stella Stevens (*Anastasia Gorgoli*); Shannon Whirry (*Kelly*); Luca Bercovici (*Namon Ami*); Brent Van Hoffman (*David*); Sandy Helberg (*Albert*); Pat Sturges (*Andrea*); Heather Elizabeth Parkhurst (*Antoinette*); Ryan Bollman (*Junior*); Samantha Hendricks (*Amy*); Joseph Bernard (*Mr. Sadler*); Teresa Ganzel (*Leanne*); Dan Woren (*Lenny*); Kedrick Wolf (*Dr. Hardy*); Tyrus (*Himself*); Anthony Hickox (*Frederick*); Lynn Tufield (*Franny*); Patrick Kilpatrick (*Father*); Ester Richman (*Mother*); Janelle Pardee (*Maggie*); Don Freeman (*Detective*)

A promisingly nasty chiller-comedy, THE GRANNY becomes less effective the farther it ventures into horror genre territory.

Bitter old Anastasia Gorgoli (Stella Stevens) has borne three children, but only Kelly (Shannon Whirry) cares for her and thanklessly tends to her. The rest of the clan are cretins, and during a Sunday dinner, they poison Anastasia's soup so they can get their hands on their inheritances. What they don't know is that she has taken a potion, given her by the mysterious Namon Ami (Luca Bercovici), intended to grant her eternal youth; what she doesn't know is that it has been exposed to sunlight, which corrupts its effects. After Anastasia's death, her will (which has been altered to cut Kelly out) is read and the family holds a reception in Anastasia's house. But Anatasia returns as a zombie with supernatural powers, and proceeds to knock off her greedy children, grandchildren, and in-laws. Albert (Sandy Helberg) is hacked to death; Andrea (Pat Sturges) is devoured by furs come to life; David (Brent Van Hoffman) is castrated; wrestler grandson Junior (Ryan Bollman) is pulverized; Antoinette (Heather Elizabeth Parkhurst) is possessed and attacks Kelly, but is dispatched by the arriving Namon Ami. He in turn is stabbed by little granddaughter Amy (Samantha Hendricks), now under the control of Anastasia, who then attacks Kelly. Kelly lets the rays of the rising sun in, destroying Anastasia. But Amy remains under the old woman's spell.

Up until its title character's return from the dead, THE GRANNY has a nicely wicked edge, playing like a horrific variation on GREEDY as Anastasia's loathsome brood bicker, snipe at, and cheat on each other. Writer-director Luca (GHOULIES) Bercovici plays these scenes with the right venomous spirit, and keeps things just exaggerated enough that the proceedings don't become distasteful. Unfortunately, the characters are so hateful that once they become victims in the second half, there's no way to sympathize with them and thus there are no real scares. Instead, Bercovici plays the mayhem for gruesome, but also silly and forced, humor.

Stevens (made up to look almost as bad before her zombification as after) appears to be having fun, and Whirry's sympathetic performance gives the story what gravity it has. But the fact that Kelly is the only relative with any true feeling for Anastasia is ignored, as she becomes just another target of the ghoulish old woman's wrath. Moreover most B-movie fans will be aware of Whirry's association with erotic thrillers, and know that it's just a matter of time before her glasses will come off, her hair will come down, and she'll become a lithe woman of action. *(Graphic violence, nudity, sexual situations, extreme profanity.)* — M.G.

d, Luca Bercovici; p, Natan Zahavi, Sam Bernard; w, Luca Bercovici (from a story by Sam Bernard and Luca Bercovici); ph, Wally Pfister; ed, Sherwood Jones; m, Kendall Schmidt; prod d, Claire Kaufman; art d, Dominic Wymark; sound, Jack Lindauer; fx, Christoper Nelson, Bruce K. Long; casting, Cathy Henderson; cos, Camila Fakhry-Smith; makeup, Patty Beigel, Christopher Nelson

Horror   **(PR: O   MPAA: R)**

GREAT DAY IN HARLEM, A   ★★★
(U.S.) 60m Jean Bach Productions ~
Castle Hill c

Dizzy Gillespie; Art Blakey; Art Farmer; Chubby Jackson; Paula Morris; Marian McPartland; Eddie Locke; Ernie Wilkins; Mona Hinton; Robert Benton; Sonny Rollins; Hank Jones; Johnny Griffin; Scoville Browne; Taft Jordan, Jr.; Bud Freeman; Gerry Mulligan; Elaine Lorillard; Robert Altschuler; Steve Frankfurt; Buck Clayton; Horace Silver; Milt Hinton; Felix Maxwell; Everard Powell; Max Kaminsky; Benny Golson; Nat Hentoff; Mike Lipskin

A GREAT DAY IN HARLEM is an engaging hour-long documentary recalling a 1950s photo session which assembled and immortalized some great names in jazz.

One summer morning in 1958, magazine art director Art Kane invited several dozen legendary musical friends to pose for a group photograph on a sidewalk in Harlem. Among those present were Dizzy Gillespie, Charles Mingus, Thelonious Monk, Marian McPartland, Art Blakey, Sonny Rollins, Coleman Hawkins and Lester Young, all of whom are seen in this affectionate documentary created by producers Jean Bach and Matthew Seig, and editor Susan Peehl. The film reminisces about that 10 a.m. photo shoot (Kane's assistant notes that, previously, some of the night-owl musicians "didn't realize there were two 10 o'clocks in the same day"), juxtaposing 8mm movie footage taken by bassist Milt Hinton and his wife Mona with recent interviews of those who were on hand for that historic occasion. For Gillespie, Blakey, Bud Freeman, Buck Clayton and Max Kaminsky, all of whom died soon after the interviews, these were reportedly their last on-camera appearances.

A GREAT DAY IN HARLEM is least effective when it explores behind-the-scenes aspects of the shoot, with commentary by Kane, his aides and various music business observers. The real story here is not the photograph or how it got taken, but the warmth and humor of the jazz artists, both in the Hintons' footage and in newly-shot recollections. What Kane's camera captured that long-ago July morning was not a bunch of musicians standing in front of a building, but a community of artists to rival the Symbolist authors or the Impressionist painters. Imagine a filmed record of Monet, Cezanne and Renoir trading stories about their exploits. Such a record might not be too different from this movie's visit with Sonny Rollins, who observes that saxophonist Lester Young came from another planet and "was here just for a short visit;" or Bud Freeman paying tribute to Count Basie, who "never said a disparaging word about anyone." A GREAT DAY IN HARLEM will resonate most with dedicated jazz buffs, but even casual fans should appreciate the film's genuine admiration for these great artists, whose lives were interwoven with their creativity and who changed the face of 20th-century music. — E.K.

d, Jean Bach; p, Jean Bach; assoc p, Stuart Samuels; co-p, Matthew Seig; w, Jean Bach, Susan Peehl, Matthew Seig; ph, Steve Petropoulos; ed, Susan Peehl; sound, Steven Hertzog (recordist), Judy Benjamin (recordist), Neil Gettinger (recordist)

Documentary/Musical   **(PR: AA   MPAA: NR)**

GREAT ELEPHANT ESCAPE, THE   ★★½
(U.S.) 93m Signboard Hill Productions; Hallmark Entertainment ~ Cabin Fever Entertainment c

Stephanie Zimbalist *(Beverly Cunningham)*; Joseph Gordon-Levitt *(Matt Cunningham)*; Julian Sands *(Clive Potter)*; Leo Burmester *(Harlo Etheridge)*; Frederick M'Cormac *(Jomo Batiany)*; David Mulwa *(Lenana Batiany)*; Rolf Schmit *(Vilias)*; Lenny Juma *(Juba)*; Edwin Nyutho *(Constable Ioki)*

Despite some predictability, THE GREAT ELEPHANT ESCAPE succeeds as a tale of cross-cultural friendship. Filmed on location in Nairobi, Kenya, it is also visually rewarding.

Shortly after we witness an elephant being slaughtered by poachers, Beverly and Matt Cunningham (Stephanie Zimbalist and Joseph Gordon-Levitt), a divorced mother and her son, arrive in Kenya from Los Angeles. They arrive at a ranch run by Clive Potter (Julian Sands) that also serves as a shelter for orphaned animals. Matt befriends Jomo (Frederick M'Cormac), a local boy responsible for feeding Ellie, a baby elephant. Meanwhile, Clive begins to pay considerable attention to Beverly.

Upsetting this situation is Etheridge (Leo Burmester), an obnoxious American who buys Ellie as a gift for his wife. After seeing Etheridge mistreat the elephant, the two boys set her free and run off to find a herd for her to join. With both Etheridge and Beverly going after them, the boys get into various scrapes. They are chased by a lion, frightened by hyenas, and arrested after Ellie goes on a destructive run through a village. Ellie breaks them out of jail, and together they find a herd. Etheridge finds them but his car goes over a small cliff. Matt frees him just before the car explodes. In gratitude, Etheridge gives back the elephant and donates a vehicle to the ranch. As the film closes, Ellie joins the new herd while Beverly and Matt make plans to return to Kenya the next summer.

As with many children's films, this made-for-TV project is not subtle. The outcome of every scene can be guessed beforehand, and the characters are all one-dimensional (Etheridge is practically a caricature). On the other hand, THE GREAT ELEPHANT ESCAPE does not strive for deep emotion, so who cares if it is a bit heavy-handed? The character of Matt is the strongest, and Gordon-Levitt is appealing, though his broad style and exaggerated facial movements are better suited to his sitcom work on "Roseanne" than to drama. The film benefits from its scenery and natural lighting, as well as from good African music. The animals are the real highlight of the film; they are shown as real and sometimes dangerous, and not cute and cuddly. — K.F.

d, George Miller; p, Njeri Karago; exec p, Richard Welsh; w, John Sweet, Christopher Canaan; ph, Ronald Lautore; ed, Ron Wisman; m, Bruce Rowland; prod d, Leslie Binns; art d, Peter Kendall; set d, Collins Athanasius; sound, Walter Anderson (mixer); fx, Shanni Chagger; casting, Lynn Kressel; cos, Fred Long; makeup, Myke Michaels

Children's/Adventure   **(PR: AA   MPAA: NR)**

GROSS MISCONDUCT   ★★½
(Australia/U.S.) 96m PRO Film Productions;
R.A. Becker & Co. ~ PRO/REP c

Jimmy Smits (*Justin Thorne*); Naomi Watts (*Jennifer Carter*); Sarah Chadwick; Adrian Wright (*Kenneth Carter*); Ross Williams (*David Guilderman*); Paul Sonkkila (*Rowland Curtis*); Alan Fletcher (*Henry Landers*); Leverne McDonnell (*Miriam McMahaon*); Beverly Dunn (*Judge Barlow*); Nicholas Bell (*Detective Matthews*); Fiona Corke (*Detective Cook*); Brendon Suhr (*Terry MacKnight*)

A 1993 Australian production (released in Europe the next year and in US video/cable markets in 1995), GROSS MISCONDUCT is a sex-harassment tale with a twist. The premise is nothing new, but Gothic atmosphere and a surprise ending compensate for cliches.

Justin Thorne (Jimmy Smits), an American hired to teach at an Australian university, is a family man with a sensual, flirtatious side that makes him extremely popular with students, and co-ed Jennifer Carter (Naomi Watts), develops a strong crush. She baby-sits for Justin's family, and attempts, unsuccessfully, to seduce him. Despite her failure, she pens her fantasies in a diary her father later finds and reads. When confronted, Jennifer claims she was coerced into sex with Mr. Thorne. As rumors fly about the pair, Justin advises Jennifer to transfer to another class and stop baby-sitting his kids. She throws a fit, and while trying to calm her down, he succumbs to temptation and makes love to the student. Later police find Jennifer alone and freezing on the streets; she says she can't remember what happened. Her father's lawyers convince even Jennifer that she has been raped, and a formal accusation is filed against the teacher.

Under oath Jennifer admits some of her diary is fiction. Nonetheless, Justin is found guilty. Jennifer, shaken, goes home with her father. He fondles her as she bathes, revealing their incestuous relationship. This time she refuses his advances, and in self-defense stabs and kills him. Her blood-covered visit to the Thorne house clears Justin's name. For its first 90 minutes, GROSS MISCONDUCT is average melodrama. The initial plot, in which Smits is the victim in a case of sexual harassment, continues a '90s gender-paranoia trend (DISCLOSURE, THE CRUSH, OLEANNA, DREAM LOVER, and the Italian film LA CONDANNA/THE CONVICTION all portray men as victims of conniving, evil women), and Justin gets a thoroughgoing sympathetic treatment despite his one transgression. The final twist succeeds because it is a surprise, and because it forces one to reevaluate the narrative in light of who the real villain is—a man, but not the defendant.

While Smits is excellent as the wrongly-accused, other performances lag, especially Sarah Chadwick's uneven turn as Justin's long-suffering wife. GROSS MISCONDUCT's standout quality is atmosphere. Protagonists live in huge, extravagant homes. Lighting, clothes, and decorations are dark. Fires are always burning, and there is an omnipresent sense of mystery and foreboding. Ambiance is much like a Gothic novel, and the concluding bloodshed, though unexpected, fits the fatal mood. (*Extensive nudity, sexual situations, graphic violence, profanity.*) — A.M.

d, George Miller; p, David Hannay, Richard Sheffield-Mac-Clure; exec p, Richard Becker; assoc p, Rocky Bester; co-p, Gerard Maguire, Lance Peters; w, Gerard Maguire, Lance Peters (based on the play *Assault With a Deadly Weapon* by Lance Peters); ph, David Connell; ed, Henry Dangar; m, Bruce Rowland; prod d, Jon Dowding; art d, Ken Hazelwood; set d, Georgina Campbell; sound, Andrew Ramage; cos, Aphrodite Kondos; makeup, Amanda Rowbottom

Drama   **(PR: O   MPAA: R)**

GROSSE FATIGUE   ★★★
(France) 87m Gaumont; TF1 Films Production ~ Miramax c
(AKA: DEAD TIRED)

Michel Blanc (*Himself/Patrick Olivier*); Carole Bouquet (*Herself*); Philippe DeJanerand (*The Inspector*); Dominique Besnehard (*Blanc's Agent*); Jean-Louis Richard (*The Psychiatrist*); Anne-Marie Jabraud (*Madame Olivier*); Philippe Noiret; Roman Polanski; Josiane Balasko; Charlotte Gainsbourg; Mathilda May; Regine; Gilles Jacob; Thierry Lhermitte; David Halliday (*Themselves*); Estelle Halliday; Marie Ann Chazel; Christian Clavier; Guillaume Durand; Gerard Jugnot; Dominique Lavanant

Writer-director-actor Michel Blanc examines the price of fame while poking fun at his own image in this inventive French comedy featuring many French film stars as themselves.

Movie star Michel Blanc (Blanc), exhausted from a busy TV and film schedule, is confounded by a series of odd events. He is accused of stiffing a prostitute for her fee, frequenting sordid nightspots, and a number of other indiscretions, all of which he denies. The normally mild-mannered Blanc appears to display another side to his personality in Cannes, where he attempts to seduce actresses Mathilda May and Charlotte Gainsborough, stealing money from the latter.

After he is jailed for raping his frequent co-star, actress Josiane Balasko, Blanc wonders if he is losing his mind. His friend, actress Carole Bouquet, whisks him off to her country home in Provence to relax and sort things out. While there, they stumble upon the explanation for Blanc's predicament: He has a double, Patrick Olivier (Blanc), who has been passing himself off as Blanc and sullying his reputation.

When confronted by Blanc, Olivier claims that his life has been ruined by being mistaken for the star, and he feels it's his turn to take advantage of the perks of fame. Olivier proposes that they share Blanc's identity, a scheme which would allow Blanc some much-needed down time. Blanc finds the idea preposterous until Olivier suggests that it's a common practice. Blanc agrees, and takes a long vacation while Olivier fills his shoes.

When Blanc returns, refreshed and ready to work again, Olivier refuses to return his identity. Blanc's friends believe that the real Blanc is the impostor; even Carole doesn't recognize him. In desperation, Blanc goes on a crime spree, hoping to implicate Olivier and ruin their shared reputation. Blanc is sent to prison. After his release, he tries to find acting work, even applying for work as a Michel Blanc double. He encounters Philippe Noiret's double (Philippe Noiret), who reveals that he is actually Noiret and the same thing happened to him. The two displaced stars are hired as extras in a Roman Polanski movie.

Familiarity with the French film world makes GROSSE FATIGUE's in-jokes funnier, but even the unversed will find plenty to savor. Blanc's Kafkaesque tale has a universal message: fame is both restrictive and addictive, simultaneously a curse and a blessing. The diminutive, balding Blanc is frequently referred to as the French Woody Allen, and GROSSE FATIGUE has drawn comparisons to Allen's STARDUST MEMORIES, which also concerns the perils of fame. But Blanc pushes the envelope a bit further and concocts a premise at once wildly preposterous and frighteningly plausible. His sharp, incisive screenplay won an award at the 1994 Cannes Film Festival. Blanc's handles his dual roles with aplomb, and controls the director's reins with equal skill, constructing a fast-paced, rollicking farce.

Playing herself, the beautiful Bouquet displays charm and sass as Blanc's glamorous sidekick. Their sparring scenes are the film's funniest. Of the other real personalities who pop in for cameos, Noiret has the choicest bit, which includes a diatribe against the invasion of French cinema by Hollywood. His assertion that "we'll all end up mice in their amusement parks," along with the irreverent implication that all the major French actors have been replaced by less-talented doubles, provide two of the film's more intriguing notions.

Blanc's film may seem on the surface a grim indictment of the French cinema. But his tongue is firmly planted in cheek, and it is readily apparent that he loves the industry he skewers, and that while fame comes with a price tag, he is glad to pay it. *(Violence, extensive nudity, sexual situations, adult situations, profanity.)* — B.R.

d, Michel Blanc; p, Patrice Ledoux, Jerome Chalon; w, Michel Blanc (from an idea by Bertrand Blier); ph, Eduardo Serra; ed, Maryline Monthieux; m, Rene Mark Bini; prod d, Carlos Conti; sound, Pierre Befve, Dominique Hennequin; cos, Elizabeth Tavernier

Comedy   **(PR: C   MPAA: R)**

GRUMPIER OLD MEN   ★★½
(U.S.) 101m Davis Entertainment; Lancaster Gate ~ Warner Bros. c

Jack Lemmon *(John Gustafson)*; Walter Matthau *(Max Goldman)*; Ann-Margret *(Ariel Gustafson)*; Sophia Loren *(Maria Ragetti)*; Burgess Meredith *(Grandpa Gustafson)*; Daryl Hannah *(Melanie Gustafson)*; Kevin Pollak *(Jacob Goldman)*; Katie Sagona *(Allie)*; Ann Guilbert *(Mama)*; James Andelin *(Sven)*; Marcus Klemp *(Assistant Manager Eddie)*; Max Wright *(Health

Inspector); Cheryl Hawker *(Lena)*; Wayne A. Evenson *(Handsome Hans)*; Allison Levine *(Dog Pound Assistant)*; John Patrick Martin *(Reverend)*; Adam Ward *(Skeleton)*; Ryan Waldoch *(Power Ranger No. 1)*; James Cada *(Husband Shopper)*; Jaclyn Ross *(Wife Shopper)*; Kyle Christopherson *(Stockboy)*; Jeffrey L. Smith *(The Frugal Gourmet)*; Geraldo Rivera *(Himself)*; Warren Schueneman *(Old Man No. 1)*; Jack Mitsch *(Old Man No. 2)*; Sterling Robson *(Old Man No. 3)*; Gregory Schuneman *(Pizza Kid)*; Michelle Johnston *(Chicken Polka Girl)*; Denny Schusted *(Limo Driver)*; Wallace Olson; Carl Johnson; Eugene Karels; Lawrence Grivna *(Polka Musicians)*

The not unexpected sequel to surprise hit GRUMPY OLD MEN, GRUMPIER OLD MEN serves up the same mixture of foolish slapstick, crude sexual innuendo, and unabashed sentiment. Despite its resemblance to an episode of "Three's Company"—retooled for the geriatric set—GRUMPIER OLD MEN at least features the delightful Sophia Loren, who gives the proceedings some much needed class.

GRUMPIER OLD MEN picks up six months after the end of the first film, as John Gustafson (Jack Lemmon)—now married to Ariel (Ann-Margret), whom he courted in GRUMPY OLD MEN—and Max Goldberg (Walter Matthau) continue their feuding, fussing and fighting. This time the elderly but childish men compete to catch a large catfish in their Wabasha, Minnesota lake. The dueling friends also team up to help John's daughter, Melanie (Darryl Hannah), and Max's son, Jacob (Kevin Pollak), with their marriage plans. The only hitch in their relatively peaceful lives comes when Maria Ragetti (Sophia Loren) and her mother Francesca (Ann Guilbert) turn the boys' favorite bait shop into an Italian restaurant.

John begins helping Max undermine Maria's new operation, and Ariel moves out in protest. Meanwhile, despite their rivalry, Max falls for Maria, while John's father, Grandpa Gustafson (Burgess Meredith), falls for Francesca. The mirth subsides, however, when Grandpa Gustafson dies suddenly, and Jacob and Melanie get cold feet and cancel their wedding plans. Max and John join forces to reunite their children, who decide to elope, and Max weds Maria—after helping John catch the coveted Wabasha catfish.

In GRUMPIER OLD MEN, Sophia Loren has been added to the previous outing's ensemble, giving her special brand of earthy charisma to a vehicle that hardly deserves it. Jack Lemmon and Walter Matthau perform the same low comedy shtick as before, but trade blessedly fewer puerile insults. They make a likable team even in substandard material. One happy surprise is that Burgess Meredith (at age 93) is much funnier this time around as Lemmon's oversexed father. Regrettably, his character dies half-way through the film.

Poor Ann-Margret gets little opportunity to shine, since plot developments relegate her to the cliched jealous wife role, and Darryl Hannah and Kevin Pollak regularly stop the film cold with their dreary scenes of pre-marital disharmony. Ultimately, most of GRUMPIER OLD MEN is keyed to the performance of former sitcom actor Ann Guilbert, who wildly overplays the role of Maria's fiery Italian mother. *(Profanity, sexual situations, violence.)* — E.M.

d, Howard Deutch; p, John A. Davis, Richard C. Berman; assoc p, Elena Spiotta; co-p, George Folsey, John J. Smith; w, Mark Steven Johnson (based on his original characters); ph, Tak Fujimoto; ed, Billy Weber, Seth Flaum, Maryann Brandon; m, Alan Silvestri; prod d, Gary Frutkoff; art d, Bill Rea; set d, Peg Cummings; sound, Edward Tise (mixer); fx, Jan Aaris; casting,

Sharon Howard-Field; cos, Lisa Jensen; makeup, Rick Sharp; stunts, Freddie Hice, Charlie Brewer

Comedy/Romance (PR: A MPAA: PG-13)

GUMBY: THE MOVIE ★★½
(U.S.) 90m Premavision Productions ~
Arrow Entertainment c

VOICES OF: Charles Farrington *(Gumby/Claybert/Fatbuckle/Kapp)*; Art Clokey *(Pokey/Prickle/Gumbo)*; Gloria Clokey *(Goo)*; Manny LaCarruba *(Thinbuckle)*; Alice Young *(Ginger)*; Janet MacDuff *(Gumba)*; Patti Morse *(Tara)*; Bonnie Randolph *(Lowbelly/Farm Lady)*; Ozzie Ahlers *(Radio Announcer)*

The familiar little green character leads his rainbow-hued cohorts into his pleasant if innocuous first feature film.

Landing on Gumbasia from outer space, Gumby (voiced by Charles Farrington) and his horse pal Pokey (Art Clokey), pop in and out of various books for some adventurous research, then join Thinbuckle (Manny LaCarruba), Nobuckle, and Fatbuckle (Farrington) in the Clayboys rock group for a park concert, which prompts agent Claybert (Farrington) to offer them a recording contract. But Gumby's dog Lowbelly (Bonnie Randolph) with his curious habit of weeping during the performance, with the tears hitting the ground as valuable pearls, catches the attention of the evil Blockheads G and J (Clokey), who kidnap him and substitute a robot. The cloning process is soon repeated for Gumby and the band, since Lowbelly's pearl trick works only for live music, not recordings.

With the help of his friends, Gumby eventually foils the villains and destroys the doppelganger robots, although he must first do lengthy battle with his cloned self in a series of settings from King Arthur's court to a spaceship. Reunited, the Clayboys put on a benefit concert for some soon-to-be-foreclosed-on farmers and make a knockout music video "Gumbymania" for Claybert, before Gumby and Pokey head back into outer space, presumably for more adventures.

The sweetly innocent Gumby has survived the years in fine shape, like his baby-boomer audience (who are introducing their children to his adventures, especially with this new film's release). Gumby is himself a boomer, born in 1956 as a segment of the "Howdy Doody" TV show, before moving on to his own NBC show in 1957, with further episodes produced for syndication in 1966 and 1988. Since then, Gumby has prospered, with an authorized biography, an LP, some dozen video compilations of the TV episodes, and various merchandizing schemes.

Gumby has changed little over the decades, like his creator Art Clokey, who continues to work in his Sausalito studio, like a 19th century artisan, laboriously animating his characters frame-by-frame. Not surprisingly, the movie's animation is rougher than the work of technology-aided filmmakers. The story brewed up by Clokey and his wife Gloria does not hop fast enough over some imponderables (why does Gumby's rock music inspire tears, even if they are pearls, from Lowbelly?). The humor is, as expected, childlike, but Clokey has injected some witty 1990s business here. When Gumby and Pokey arrive in Gumbasia (which is a nod to Clokey's initial film short, in 1953, made while he was studying with the legendary montage theorist Slavko Vorkapich), the Dina Toy Store has a Gumby figure set on the shelf. When the Blockheads construct their robots, they start with a steel armature-skeleton, much like Clokey does. And for the first time, Gumby and his pals jump into not only books but VHS cassettes, giving Clokey the opportunity to parody STAR WARS, THE ADVENTURES OF ROBIN HOOD, and KNIGHTS OF THE ROUND TABLE, although for legal reasons these movies are given generic titles. Unlike Clokey's figures, which are simplicity itself, the sets are occasionally richly detailed, and the character voicings are effective. The movie was briefly released to theaters late in 1995 before hitting the video stores, with each cassette complete with a rubber Gumby figure under the shrink-wrap. — D.B.

d, Art Clokey; p, Art Clokey, Gloria Clokey; assoc p, Kevin Reher; w, Art Clokey, Gloria Clokey (based on characters from the original television series "The Gumby Show" created by Art Clokey); ph, Art Clokey; ed, Lynn Stevenson; m, Jerry Gerber, Marco Ambrosio; prod d, Gloria Clokey, Holly Harman; anim, Stephen Buckley, Tony Laudati, Dan Mason, Ken Willard, Mike Belzer, Art Clokey, Angie Glocka, Kurt Hanson, Peter Kleinow, Harry Walton; sound, James Allen

Children's/Animated/Fantasy (PR: AA MPAA: G)

HACKERS ★★½
(U.S.) 104m United Artists ~
MGM/UA c

Jonny Lee Miller *(Dade)*; Angelina Jolie *(Kate)*;
Fisher Stevens *(The Plague)*; Jesse Bradford
(Joey); Matthew Lillard *(Cereal Killer)*;
Laurence Mason *(Lord Nikon)*; Renoly Santiago
(Phantom Phreak); Wendell Pierce *(Agent Dick
Gill)*; Alberta Watson *(Lauren Murphy)*; Lor-
raine Bracco *(Margo)*; Darren Lee *(Razor)*; Pe-
ter Y. Kim *(Blade)*; Ethan Browne *(Curtis)*; Penn
Jillette *(Hal)*; Michael Gaston *(Agent Bob)*; Marc Anthony
(Agent Ray); Liza Walker *(Laura)*; Bob Sessions *(Mr. Ellingson)*;
Blake Willett *(S.S. Agent, Seattle)*; Max Ligosh *(Young Dade)*;
Felicity Huffman *(Attorney)*; Paul Klementowicz *(Michael Mur-
phy)*; Richard Ziman *(Judge)*; Bill Maul *(Norm)*; William De-
Meo *(Jock)*; Denise George *(Denise)*; Jeb Handwerger *(Fresh-
man on the Roof)*; Mitchell Nguyen-McCormick *(Fresh-
man on the Roof)*; Gary Klar *(Mr. Simpson)*; Terry Porter *(Joey's
Mom)*; Johnny Myers *(1st Sysops Technician)*; Kevin Brewerton
(2nd Sysops Technician); Sam Douglas *(English Teacher)*; Kal
Weber *(1st V.P.)*; Jeff Harding *(2nd V.P.)*; Tom Hill *(2nd S.S.
Agent)*; Jennifer Rice *(Reporter)*; Douglas W. Iles *(Addict Hank)*;
Annemarie Zola *(Addict Vickie)*; Michael Potts *(Tow Truck
Driver)*; Nancy Ticotin *(Phreak's Mom)*; Mike Cicchetti *(Elling-
son Guard)*; Mick O'Rourke *(Phone Repairman)*; Dave Stewart
(London Hacker); Naoko Mori *(Tokyo Hacker)*; Roberta Gotti
(Italian Hacker); Ravil Isyanov *(Russian Hacker)*; Olegario Fe-
doro *(Russian Hacker)*; Eric Loren *(News Technician)*; Kristin
Moreu *(Flight Attendant)*; Ricco Ross *(Second Reporter)*; Tony
Sibbald *(Jail Guard)*; Richard Purro *(Talkshow Host)*; Enzo
Junior *(Da Vinci Virus)*; Yoshinori Yamamoto *(3rd V.P.)*; Ralph
Winter *(4th V.P.)*; Kimbra Standish *(Receptionist)*; Steven
Angiolini *(Rollerblader)*

Guaranteed to intimidate the cyber-phobic, Iain Softley's glossy
techno-thriller is a celebration of adolescence in cyberspace, the
computer-generated brave new world of HACKERS, where
numbers swirl and shimmy like fireflies, images flicker and
transform, and identities are infinitely mutable.

Having crashed a record 1,507 computers as a child, Dade
Murphy (Jonny Lee Miller) has been sentenced to abstain from
hacking until age 18. Murphy's long-suffering mother (Alberta
Watson) moves to New York City, where Murphy takes a new
name—Crash Override—and hooks up with a like-minded gang
of pranksters, only to find himself in the middle of a corporate
conspiracy masterminded by snotty turncoat, the Plague (Fisher
Stevens). The Plague—real name: Eugene Belford—heads computer security at Ellingson Mineral Corp., where he is embezzling millions electronically. Murphy's friend Joey (Jesse
Bradford) downloads part of the Plague's secret program and
gets himself and his friends in big trouble. In the midst of the
turmoil, Murphy falls in love with girl geek Acid Burn (Angelina
Jolie, Jon Voight's daughter), aka Kate Libby, who treats him
with thinly veiled contempt.

Belford puts the FBI on the trail of the young hackers. The
inexperienced Joey is the first to fall, while Belford tries various
tactics to get Murphy to lay off and convince his friends to do the
same. But Murphy and the gang dedicate themselves first to
figuring out what is on the disk—it turns out to be a program that
transfers small amounts of money off every transaction that
comes through Ellingson's computer system to Belford's Swiss
bank account—then to stopping Belford's evil plan.

Working together, the hackers figure out how to make sure
that Belford gets his comeuppance. And, unsurprisingly, Libby
warms up to Murphy's advances, allowing it all to end on a note

of adolescent ecstasy as the two of them go out
on their first real date.

HACKERS articulates the hackers' vision of
the world as a massive, candy-colored computer
system just waiting to be invaded. The Manhattan skyline is transformed into a glowing circuit
board; buildings metamorphose into lustrous
high-tech obelisks; and the sun rises and sets
with furious speed. It is an absolutely glorious
conception, perfectly supported by a mesmerizing score.

The movie's notion of the real world is a bit iffier. Keyboard
cowboys (and cowgirls) inhabit a techno-cocoon in which they
are free to spend their nights hacking and clubbing, and their
days plotting ever cooler computer conquests. Still more peculiar
is the movie's sexual worldview, which is simultaneously infan-
tile and fetishist. Boys wear rubber, lipstick, and spandex, but do
not seem to have a sexual bone in their unmuscled bodies. Have
these kids truly sublimated all their hormonal urges into massaging their keyboards? In the teen-movie tradition of girls imbued
with wisdom beyond their years, only Libby seems aware of her
own sexuality. Lorraine Bracco has the film's most thankless
role, playing an abrasive corporate publicist who is not smart
enough to handle a multiline phone system, let alone appreciate
the potential of Belford's scheme. She is only there to ask stupid
questions so the viewer does not have to. *(Sexual situations,
profanity.)* — M.M.

d, Iain Softley; p, Michael Peyser, Ralph Winter; exec p, Iain
Softley; assoc p, Selwyn Roberts; co-p, Janet Graham; w, Rafael
Moreu; ph, Andrzej Sekula; ed, Christopher Blunden, Martin
Walsh; m, Simon Boswell; prod d, John Beard; art d, John
Frankish; set d, Joanne Woollard; sound, Peter Lindsay (mixer),
Mervyn Moore; fx, Peter Chiang, Tim Field; casting, Dianne
Crittendon; cos, Roger Burton; makeup, Christine Blundell, Liz
Daxauer; stunts, Jery Hewit

Thriller/Science Fiction   **(PR: C   MPAA: PG-13)**

HALLOWEEN: THE CURSE OF ★
MICHAEL MYERS
(U.S.) 88m Halloween Six Productions ~ Dimension c

Donald Pleasence *(Dr. Loomis)*; Mitch Ryan *(Dr. Wynn)*; Mari-
anne Hagan *(Kara Strode)*; Paul Rudd *(Tommy Doyle)*; Mariah
O'Brien *(Beth)*; Keith Bogart *(Tim Strode)*; Devin Gardner
(Danny Strode); Kim Darby *(Debra Strode)*; Bradford English
(John Strode); George P. Wilbur *(Mike Myers)*; Leo Geter *(Barry
Simms)*; Susan Swift *(Mary)*

An incompetent addition to the exhausted franchise begun by
John Carpenter's 1978 classic, this entry only cheapens the
mythology it aspires to enrich. Six years ago, Jamie Lloyd (J.C.
Brandy) and supernatural killer Michael Myers, her uncle, van-
ished. As the film opens, Jamie escapes with her newborn baby
from the cult that has imprisoned her and controls the killer. She
makes a frantic call to Dr. Sam Loomis (Donald Pleasence),
Michael's old nemesis, and hides her baby before Michael
(George Wilbur) kills her. The infant is found by Tommy Doyle
(Paul Stephen Rudd), a survivor of Michael's first rampage still
living in Haddonfield, which is just now allowing itself the first
Halloween celebration since the killer's last massacre.

Pursuing Jamie's child, Michael kills several townspeople,
including the parents of Kara Strode (Marianne Hagan), another
distant relative of Michael whose family now lives in his old
house. She teams with Tommy, who reveals that Michael's evil
is rooted in ancient Druid mythology, and Dr. Loomis to protect
the baby and her little brother, Danny (Devin Gardner), from

Michael and the cult. Their leader, a mysterious man in black, proves to be Dr. Wynn (Mitchell Ryan), an old associate of Loomis who spirits the infant off to the sanitarium where the cult is based. Tommy and Kara rescue the baby while Michael slaughters the doctors; Michael is then apparently killed by Tommy. But after he and Kara leave with the baby, Dr. Loomis goes back into the sanitarium and discovers that Michael is very much alive.

Advertised as "the final confrontation with evil," yet clearly contrived as a rebirth of the series under new distributor Miramax/Dimension, the sixth HALLOWEEN film contradicts itself and the previous movies. Daniel Farrands's script, which crams in as many old characters and half-baked "revelations" as possible, quickly loses any sense of plausibility. The audience is supposed to believe, for example, that the Strodes have lived in the old Myers house for years without ever knowing of its frightening history, and that a Druid cult has long operated out of the sanitarium without anybody noticing.

Joe Chappelle apes Carpenter's style to little avail, and the film suffers from obvious post-production doctoring that renders a good deal of the story incoherent. The final insult is the lame open-ended finale (hastily reshot when Pleasence's death ruled out the possibility of Loomis's return in future sequels) that crassly promises yet another installment. "Curse" is right. *(Graphic violence, nudity, sexual situations.)* — M.G.

d, Joe Chappelle; p, Paul Freeman; exec p, Moustapha Akkad; assoc p, Malek Akkad; w, Daniel Farrands; ph, Billy Dickson; ed, Randy Bricker; m, Alan Howarth, John Carpenter; prod d, Bryan Ryman; art d, T.K. Kirkpatrick; sound, Mark Hopkins McNabb; fx, Larry Fioritto; casting, Ross Brown, Mary West; cos, Anne Lambert; makeup, John Buechler; stunts, Fred Lerner

Horror (PR: O   MPAA: R)

HARLEM DIARY: NINE VOICES OF RESILIENCE ★★½
(U.S.) 96m Discovery Channel; Gabriel Films ~ Discovery Communications c

Jermaine Ashwood; Amir Williams-Foster; Barr "Star Dragon" Elliot; Nikki Matos; Kahlil Hicks; Christina Head; Damon Williams; Rasheem Swindell; Akida Bailey; Michael Cousins; Kass Kalanzo; Salaim Shabazz; Diarra Cummings; Errol Kenya James

A documentary about the lives of nine young people who live in Harlem, this film has as a recurring, inescapable theme the violence and drug use that dominate existence in this neighborhood.

Nikki Matos, an eighteen-year-old African American mother describes her son as one of an "endangered species." She uses the video equipment made available to her by the filmmakers to make a movie about a friend who was killed in a random shooting. When taking leave of each other, young black men embrace and make sure never to say "Goodbye," but "See you later." A mother of nine worries about her children every time they leave the house. Hope springs eternal, however, even in the most mired of worlds. These kids' determination to make something of their lives, regardless, amounts to something very much like heroism. Jermaine Ashwood is the first in his family to go to college, having served from childhood as a father figure to his younger siblings (and mother). Twelve-year-old Amir Williams-Foster is lucky enough to star in the TV soap opera, "All My Children", but is nonetheless ever mindful of the privileges he enjoys, surrounded as he is by "the nabe," which his canny mother makes sure he remains fully a part of. Rasheem Swindell wants to escape the temptations of the street through boxing. Likewise, seventeen-year-old Barr Elliot has his hip-hop talents

to lift him up, and stands tough even in the face of the most brutally dismissive of audiences. Kahlil Hicks comes out of jail, a writer who explores the streets in new, creative ways *vide* his writing. He introduces us to a whole world of transient people living hidden away in the darkest recesses of New York City's subway. Akida Bailey talks about his experience working at a brokerage firm in midtown Manhattan. Savvy Christina Head is half-Greek, half-African American and one of the lucky few who gets to travel outside of New York City (to attend a family wedding), where she confronts her own fears about racism.

Producer-director Jonathan Stack was inspired by author Terry Williams's work with a writers' group composed of Harlem kids who documented their lives in journals. Having himself lived in Harlem, Stack wanted to record some of the more positive aspects of the community. Stack acknowledges the tenaciously-held dreams and awesome resiliency of the youngsters but maintains a welcome objectivity and avoids idealizing his subjects, showing some of them screwing up or getting sidetracked by the chaos in their lives. He also never flinches from revealing their world at its darkest: the harrowing sight of a twenty-year-old woman, Damon Williams's drug-addicted mother, ravaged by and soon dead of AIDS; the interior of a crack house, which shows up Spike Lee's speciously bravura treatment of same in JUNGLE FEVER. But the sudden, odd moment of beauty is captured, as well: a bunch of kids joyously dancing on the street to a man singing the blues; the lushly vibrant hues of a wall of graffiti created to memorialize the needlessly fallen. At times, the narration is redundant and pontifical, particularly given the simple power of the images ("Our youth walk a narrow line between hope and despair with constant reminders of life's fragility"). There is, however, no denying the film's effectiveness; viewers will come away deeply impressed by all these individuals, and with a real understanding of their environment. *(Adult situations.)* — D.N.

d, Jonathan Stack; p, Jonathan Stack; exec p, Steve Burns; assoc p, Kahlil Hicks; co-p, Terry Williams, Mary Beth Mann; w, Terry Williams (based on his book *The Uptown Kids: Struggle and Hope in the Projects*); ph, Maryse Alberti, Samuel Henriques; ed, Susanne Szabo Rostock; m, John Hicks; sound, Stuart Deutsch

Documentary (PR: A   MPAA: NR)

HARRISON BERGERON
(SEE: KURT VONNEGUT'S HARRISON BERGERON)

HEAT ★★★★
(U.S.) 160m Forward Pass Productions; New Regency Productions ~ Warner Bros. c

Al Pacino *(Vincent Hanna)*; Robert De Niro *(Neil McCauley)*; Val Kilmer *(Chris Shiherlis)*; Jon Voight *(Nate)*; Tom Sizemore *(Michael Cheritto)*; Diane Venora *(Justine)*; Amy Brenneman *(Eady)*; Ashley Judd *(Charlene)*; Mykelti Williamson *(Drucker)*; Wes Studi *(Casals)*; Ted Levine *(Bosko)*; Dennis Haysbert *(Breedan)*; William Fichtner *(Van Zant)*; Natalie Portman *(Lauren)*; Tom Noonan *(Kelson)*; Kevin Gage *(Waingro)*; Hank Azaria *(Marciano)*; Susan Traylor *(Elaine Cheritto)*; Kim Staunton *(Lillian)*; Danny Trejo *(Trejo)*; Henry Rollins *(Hugh Benny)*; Jeremy Piven *(Dr. Bob)*; Xander Berkeley *(Ralph)*; Jerry Trimble *(Schwartz)*; Marty Ferrero *(Construction Clerk)*; Ricky Harris *(Albert Torena)*; Tone Loc *(Richard Torena)*; Begonya Plaza *(Anna Trejo)*; Hazelle Goodman *(Hooker's Mother)*; Ray Buktenica *(Timmons)*; Bill McIntosh *(Armored Guard #1)*; Rick Avery *(Armored Guard #2)*; Brad Baldridge *(Children's Hospital Doctor)*; Andrew Camuccio *(Dominick)*; Brian Camuccio

(Dominick); Max Daniels *(Shooter at Drive-In)*; Vince Deadrick, Jr. *(Driver at Drive-In)*; Charles Duke *(Cop #5)*; Thomas Elfmont *(Desk Clerk Cop)*; Kenny Endoso *(Bartender)*; Kimberly Flynn *(Casals' Date)*; Steven Ford *(Officer Bruce)*; Farrah Forke *(Claudia)*; Hannes Fritsch *(Miracle Mile Bartender)*; Amanda Graves *(Linda Cheritto)*; Emily Graves *(Anita Cheritto)*; Niki Harris *(Marcia Drucker)*; Daniel O'Haco *(Detective #1)*; Ted Harvey *(Detective #2)*; Patricia Healy *(Bosko's Date)*; Paul Herman *(Sgt. Heinz)*; Cindy Katz *(Rachel)*; Brian Libby *(Captain Jackson)*; Dan Martin *(Harry Dieter)*; Rick Marzan *(Basketball Player)*; Terry Miller *(Children's Hospital Nurse)*; Paul Moyer *(News Anchorman)*; Mario Roberts *(Bank Guard #1)*; Phillip Robinson *(Alphonse)*; Thomas Rosales, Jr. *(Armored Truck Driver)*; Rainell Saunders *(Dead Hooker)*; Kai Soremekun *(Prostitute)*; Rey Verdugo *(Vegas Cop)*; Wendy L. Walsh *(News Anchorwoman)*; Yvonne Zima *(Hostage Girl)*

Writer-director Michael Mann stirs the urban crime drama from its postmodern repose by infusing the thematic elements of a classic Western into a generic, cops-and-robbers tale. Starring Al Pacino (as the cop) and Robert De Niro (as the robber), HEAT is so overloaded with ambitions it's often in danger of being crushed under its own weight, but it's packed with enough talent to carry it to the end.

Neil McCauley (De Niro) is the cautious leader of a gang that specializes in meticulously planned, high-stakes heists like the explosive robbery of an armored car that opens the film. His gang includes Chris (Val Kilmer), who is struggling to save his marriage to Charlene (Ashley Judd), and family man Michael (Tom Sizemore), apparently the sanest of the bunch. Vincent Hanna (Pacino) is a volatile LAPD detective with a special gift for tracking down bad guys and driving away wives—he's on his third marriage. Hanna's charged with bringing McCauley and company to justice, and so begins a game of cat-and-mouse between these two outsized personalities. Hanna is too busy to spend time with his wife, Justine (Diane Venora), and his troubled stepdaughter, Lauren (Natalie Portman). Meanwhile, McCauley, an ascetic loner, suddenly feels compelled to pursue a romance with a bookstore clerk, Eady (Amy Brenneman).

The battle of wits and one-upmanship, including a face-to-face where McCauley and Hanna size each other up, goes a few rounds before things come to a very violent head. McCauley's gang pulls a daring, daytime bank robbery, but a psychotic former accomplice, Waingro (Kevin Gage), double-crosses them and tips off the police. When the law arrives, the street becomes a war zone. Michael is killed and Chris is seriously wounded.

McCauley escapes. Now all he has to do is collect Eady and hop on a plane to New Zealand. The informant Waingro is holed up in a hotel, and Hanna thinks McCauley may go after him, but he's resigned to losing his quarry. When Hanna goes home, he finds that Lauren has attempted suicide and rushes her to the hospital. McCauley can't set aside the masculine code that requires him to seek revenge, and when he makes his move against Waingro, Hanna is waiting. The two men shoot it out in a field near LAX. Only Hanna walks away.

In HEAT, as in a Howard Hawks genre film, the men are dedicated professionals who thrive on action and honor; the women are forced to live with the consequences. Director-writer Mann weaves action into an elaborate tapestry of a story, as richly detailed and complex as one of McCauley's schemes. HEAT features a host of supporting characters, each integral to the complicated plot, and Mann has marshaled perhaps the most impressive array of talent in any 1995 movie to fill those roles. Chief among these are Kilmer and Judd, both of whom give excellent, nuanced performances. Their relationship effectively dramatizes men's contradictory feelings about domesticity, and

the price women must pay. Unfortunately, Brenneman's and Venora's characters are given short shrift, and as a result, the film lacks emotional impact.

The pairing of Pacino and De Niro (the first time they've shared a bill since THE GODFATHER, PART II in 1974) is HEAT's drawing card, but the real star of a Michael Mann film is always the visuals. HEAT has style to burn. Again working with the brilliant cinematographer Dante Spinotti, Mann turns the city itself into HEAT's major player. A shot of McCauley and Eady with a night cityscape as the backdrop recalls MY DARLING CLEMENTINE, but where John Ford viewed the open spaces of the Old West with optimistism, Mann presents the urban wasteland as the realization of a cynical, soulless culture. Tellingly, he sets one of his violent set pieces in the void of an abandoned drive-in.

It's on this stage that Hanna must strut and fret while his existential drama is played out. He need never meet McCauley (in fact, their mano-a-mano plays like a superfluous pissing contest). The shot of Hanna watching McCauley on an infrared video monitor, seeing the ghostly image of his doppelganger staring back at him, says everything we need to know about their fated connection. *(Profanity, graphic violence, adult situations.)* — P.R.

d, Michael Mann; p, Art Linson, Michael Mann; exec p, Arnon Milchan, Pieter Jan Brugge; assoc p, Gusmano Cesaretti, Kathleen M. Shea; w, Michael Mann; ph, Dante Spinotti; ed, Dov Hoenig, Pasquale Buba, William Goldenberg, Tom Rolf; m, Elliot Goldenthal; prod d, Neil Spisak; art d, Margie Stone McShirley; set d, Anne H. Ahrens; sound, Lee Orloff (mixer); fx, Terry D. Frazee, Neil Krepela; casting, Bonnie Timmermann; cos, Deborah L. Scott; makeup, John Caglione, Jr.; stunts, Joel Kramer

Crime/Drama (PR: O MPAA: R)

HEAVEN'S A DRAG ★★
(U.K.) 96m Victor Film Company; TDF;
London Lighthouse ~ First Run Features c
(AKA: TO DIE FOR)

Thomas Arklie *(Simon)*; Ian Williams *(Mark)*; Tony Slattery *(Terry)*; Dillie Keane *(Siobhan)*; Jean Boht *(Mrs. Downs)*; John Altman *(Dogger)*; Caroline Munro *(Mrs. Pignon)*; Gordon Milne *(Drop Dead Gorgeous)*; Nicholas Harrison *(Siobhan's First Lover)*; Ian McKellen *(Quilt Documentary Narrator)*; Sinitta *(Quilt Documentary Narrator)*; Paul Cottingham *(1st Poxy Shirt Lifter)*; Lloyd Williams *(Bodybuilder)*; Robert Sturtz *(Chris)*; Benjamin Sterz *(Man in Gym)*; Brian Carter *(Leather Man)*; Mark Hutchinson *(Hospital Visitor)*; Janet Allen *(Ward Sister)*; Nigel Fairs *(Mark Lookalike)*; Robert Whitson *(Man in Cruise Bar)*; Philip Curr *(Skinhead)*; James Greaves *(Man in Lavatory)*; Brian Ross *(Nick)*; Tony London *(Yob)*; Richard Cope *(Yob)*; Dick Bradnum *(Yob)*; Ken Kennedy *(Mr. Willoughby)*; Andrew Kennedy *(Steve)*; Alan Lowe *(Young Man in Club)*; Will Pollet *(Young Mark)*; Wayne Amiel *(Go-Go Dancer)*; Heilo *(Go-Go Dancer)*; Henrique DaSilva *(Go-Go Dancer)*; John Cannon *(Jessie Biscuit)*; Brian Carter *(Jessie's Man)*; Mike Shear *(Jessie's Man)*; David Ingram *(Archangel)*; Mark Ardell; Andy Spur; Carl Robinson; Tony MacDonald; Paul Kevin; Zeus; Danny Boy; Dark Angel; The Bronze *(Angels)*

HEAVEN'S A DRAG (aka TO DIE FOR) is a gay comedy about a man who dies from AIDS-related diseases and comes back as a ghost to haunt his lover. Comedy and AIDS is a tough combination to pull off, and this British low-budget movie appears to be an awkward hybrid of GHOST and LONGTIME COMPANION.

Simon (Thomas Arklie) and Mark (Ian Williams) have an open relationship. Mark is an HIV-positive drag performer who goes straight home after his shows to sew his own panel for the AIDS Memorial Quilt. Simon, on the other hand, spends every night cruising the London club scene. When Mark dies, Simon shuts out his grief and puts away all traces of his lover's existence including Mark's unfinished quilt panel. Soon Simon is back out cruising. But the first time he tries to bring a man home, Mark's ghost makes an unexpected appearance. Mark is back to stay—unwilling and unable to enter heaven unless Simon confronts his true feelings and mourns his lover properly.

Director Peter Mackenzie Litten tries a new angle on the AIDS story, focusing not so much on Mark's struggle with the disease as Simon's life after his lover's death. He also tries to use comedy to promote an optimistic attitude towards surviving in the face of AIDS. But while John Greyson's AIDS musical ZERO PATIENCE effectively achieved a sense of levity without sacrificing complexity, HEAVEN'S A DRAG unfortunately sinks into a sad world of empty cliches. The drag queen is big and bitchy and the butch leather boy is an emotional cripple; the heterosexual neighbors are well-meaning, overcompensating liberal "do-gooders." Although it has had a small-scale art-house release, HEAVEN'S A DRAG is unlikely to go far beyond its mixed reception at gay and lesbian film festivals. (*Sexual situations.*) — J.S.

d, Peter Mackenzie Litten; p, Gary Fitzpatrick; exec p, Stephen Garbutta; w, Johnny Byrne (from a story by Paul McEnvoy and Pater Litten); ph, John Ward; ed, Jeffrey Arsenault; m, Roger Bolton; art d, Geoff Sharp; fx, Andrew McDonald, Dave Hughs, Richard Pirkis; makeup, Victoria Wright, Darren Phillips, Helen Lennox

Drama/Comedy/Romance (PR: C MPAA: NR)

HEAVYWEIGHTS ★
(U.S.) 98m Heavy Weight Inc.; Walt Disney;
Caravan ~ Buena Vista c

Tom McGowan (*Pat*); Aaron Schwartz (*Gerry*); Shaun Weiss (*Josh*); Tom Hodges (*Lars*); Leah Lail (*Julie*); Paul Feig (*Tim*); Kenan Thompson (*Roy*); David Bowe (*Chris Donelly*); Max Goldblatt (*Phillip*); Robert Zalkind (*Simms*); Patrick LaBrecque (*Dawson*); Jeffrey Tambor (*Maury Garner*); Jerry Stiller (*Harvey Bushkin*); Anne Meara (*Alice Bushkin*); Ben Stiller (*Tony Perkis Jr./Tony Perkis Sr.*); David Goldman (*Nicholas*); Joseph Wayne Miller (*Sam*); Cody Burger (*Cody*); Allen Covert (*Kenny*); Tim Blake Nelson (*Camp Hope Salesman*); Nancy Ringham (*Mrs. Garner*); Seth St. Laurent (*Camp MVP Racer*); Bobby Fain (*Camp MVP Pitcher*); Robert E. Spencer, III (*Soccer Goalie*); Dustin Greer (*Blob Master*); Matthew R. Zboyovski (*Hope Wall Climber*); J.T. Alessi (*Balloon Shaver*); Chris Snyder (*Baseball Scorekeeper*); Jonathan Clark (*Gerry's Double*); Aubrey Dollar (*Camp Magnolia Girl*); Mary Holt Fickes (*Camp Magnolia Girl*); Jamie Olson (*Camp Magnolia Girl*); Lauren Hill (*Angelic Girl*); Landry M. Constantino (*Kissing Girl*); Lois Yaroshefsky (*Camp Magnolia Counselor*); Matthew Bradley King (*Gerry's School Buddy*); Deena Dill (*Stewardess*); Tom Kelley (*Man on Plane*); Lars Clarke (*Jack Gamer*); Judd Apatow (*Homer*)

In this summer camp story from Disney, weight-challenged boys overcome the forces of cliched adversity to win a trophy and learn some lessons about self-respect.

Spending the summer at "fat camp" is an unappealing prospect for Gerry (Aaron Schwartz), until he discovers that the easygoing, overweight head counselor, Pat (Tom McGowan), only expects his portly charges to have fun cannonballing and

go-cart racing. Then, suddenly, Camp Hope is taken over by new-age, motivational guru Tony Perkis (Ben Stiller), who is clearly insane. He is determined to make all the boys lose weight as part of his "Perkisizing" scheme. Under the fascist direction of the new, teutonic head counselor, Lars (Tom Hodges), Gerry and his friends are put on a regimen of humiliation, starvation, and abuse. The boys secretly feed their junk food habit and refuse to lose weight, much to Perkis's consternation. Punished to the limit, they finally rebel, lock Perkis up in an electrified cage, and put Pat and his love interest, a pretty nurse named Julie (Leah Lail), in charge of the camp. On a program of sensible meals, moderate exercise, and positive reinforcement, they prepare for the end-of-the-summer "Apache Relays" against the superjocks from rival Camp MVP. Thanks to brains, teamwork, and some heroics from Gerry, the Hopes defeat the MVPs. While Pat collects a victory kiss from Julie, the fat kids cheer because for the first time in their lives they are winners.

Despite its requisite feel-good ending, awash in cheers and hugs, HEAVYWEIGHTS is actually a pretty cynical movie. It reinforces the notion that brains and brawn exist exclusive of each other and the stereotype that fat people just eat too much candy. Even more cynically though, the filmmakers have assumed that they can put anything on the screen, and if it ends with a contest that the underdogs win, an audience will be satisfied. It is bad enough that HEAVYWEIGHTS has minimal and illogical plotting, and next to no characterization; it's such a joyless film that it often crosses the line into mean-spiritedness.

HEAVYWEIGHTS represents the coming together of seemingly diametrically opposed creative sensibilities. On the one hand, there is cowriter and director Stephen Brill, who created THE MIGHTY DUCKS, perhaps the apotheosis of contemporary, mindless, generic, Disney fare. On the other hand, there are cowriters Judd Apatow and Stiller of TV's great "Ben Stiller Show," which presented sophisticated media parody and satire. The result of the mixture is a truly strange attempt at children's entertainment. (*Violence.*) — P.R.

d, Steven Brill; p, Joe Roth, Roger Birnbaum; exec p, Judd Apatow, Sarah Bowman; assoc p, Jack Giarraputo; co-p, Morgan Michael Fottrell, Charles J.D. Schlissel; w, Judd Apatow, Steven Brill; ph, Victor Hammer; ed, C. Timothy O'Meara; m, J.A.C. Redford; prod d, Stephen Storer; art d, Harry Darrow, Jack D.L. Ballance; set d, Chris Spellman; sound, Mary H. Ellis (mixer); casting, Judy Taylor, Lynda Gordon; cos, Kimberly Tillman; makeup, John Bayless; stunts, Steve Boyum

Comedy/Children's (PR: A MPAA: PG)

HEROIC TRIO 2: EXECUTIONERS
(SEE: EXECUTIONERS)

HEROIC TRIO, THE ★★★½
(Hong Kong) 88m Gordons Film Co. Ltd; China Entertainment Films; Paka Hill Productions ~ Rim Film Distributors c
(DONGFANG SAN XIA)

Anita Mui (*Tung—Wonder Woman*); Maggie Cheung (*Chat—Thief Catcher*); Michelle Yeoh (*San—Invisible Woman*); Damian Lau (*Inspector Lau*); Paul Chin (*Chief of Police*); James Pak (*Inventor*); Ren Shiguan (*Evil Master*); Anthony Wong (*Kau*); Chin Pei; Zhu Mimi; Jiang Haowen; Xu Tao; Ruan Zhaoxiang; Huang Yifei; Chen Zhuoxin; Li Zhaoji; Zheng Ruisheng

Two well-respected actresses (Anita Mui and Maggie Cheung) and a noted actress-stuntwoman (Michelle Yeoh) join with seasoned directors Johnny To (ALL ABOUT AH-LONG) and Ching Siu-Tung (A CHINESE GHOST STORY) to produce a colorful urban fantasy about a trio of costumed superheroines who team up to defeat a supernatural villain dwelling below the city streets.

The abduction of 18 babies in three months leaves the police stumped. Working on the case is Inspector Lau (Damian Lau) who is unaware that his wife Tung (Mui) maintains a separate identity as the lightning-fast, super-powered Wonder Woman; she aids the local police in their efforts to stop the kidnappings.

The culprit, however, has skills to match Tung's. San, the Invisible Woman (Yeoh), is a victim of circumstance. She commits her crimes only to ensure the safety of her scientist boyfriend (James Pak), whose current "robe of invisibility" project is coveted by San's boss, a mysterious being known as the Master (Ren Shiguan). The Master's credo is "China must have a king!" To this end, he has collected the abducted male children in his underground stronghold, hoping to find among them the one who will serve as king; the rest will become ruthless killers, like the Master's sidekick Kau (Anthony Wong).

Into the fray enters Chat (Cheung), the Thief-Catcher. A professional gun-for-hire, Chat assures the chief of police (Paul Chin) that, for a price, she can retrieve his stolen baby boy. After an initial conflict, she unites with Wonder Woman to stop Kau from wreaking havoc in a busy train station.

San finally joins them too, when it becomes apparent that the Master will not spare her boyfriend now that the robe has been perfected. In the ensuing showdown, the seemingly indestructible Master is destroyed by "The Heroic Trio," as Lau dubs them. Tung and Lau resume their happy domesticity, with Lau now aware of his wife's other identity.

With the villain's main goal to have a Chinese king, some reviewers have attempted to see the film's three heroines as metaphorical incarnations of the three Chinas: the mainland, Taiwan, and Hong Kong. This subtext may indeed have been intended by the filmmakers, but the picture's overriding focus on the kipnappings, and the clashes between the superwomen and the bad guys, removes the picture almost entirely from the realm of politics (the film's futuristic sequel EXECUTIONERS has a more direct agenda).

As it stands, THE HEROIC TRIO lingers in one's memory for its more artificial aspects: the eye-catching costumes, the wind-blown urban atmosphere, the TERMINATOR-like skeleton of the Master in the final confrontation, and the kinetic camerawork so familiar from other top-notch Hong Kong action outings. The element that almost single-handedly keeps the proceedings aloft, though, is the playful interaction between the lead performers. Cheung and Wong gleefully make the most of their comic book roles, while Mui and Yeoh reinforce their characters with a dash of melodrama. *(Violence.)* — E.G.

d, To Kei-Fung, Ching Siu-Tung; p, Ching Siu-Tung; exec p, Brian Yip, Cora Cheng, Zheng Jianping; assoc p, Zheng Jianmei; w, Sandy Shaw; ph, Poon Hang-Sang, Tom Lau; ed, Kam Wah Productions; m, William Hu; prod d, Catherine Han, Chan Pui-Wah; art d, Bruce Yu; fx, Bai Le, 3000cc Productions; cos, Bruce Yu; makeup, Wen Xianling, Zheng Fengyan

Fantasy/Martial Arts/Action   (PR: C   MPAA: NR)

HE'S A WOMAN, SHE'S A MAN   ★★
(Hong Kong) 107m United Filmmakers
Organization ~ Peter Chow International c
(GAM TSI YUK YIP)

Leslie Cheung *(Sam Koo)*; Carina Lau *(Rose)*; Anita Yuen *(Ming)*; Eric Tsang *(Yu Lo)*; Lawrence Cheng; Lo Ka-ying

Confusion runs rampant in HE'S A WOMAN, SHE'S A MAN, when a young woman disguises herself as a boy in order to meet her pop-star idol, falls in love with her idol's boyfriend (and he with her), and becomes the latest singing sensation herself.

Ming (Anita Yuen), a fan of the singer Rose (Carina Lau), learns that Rose's producer and boyfriend, Sam Koo (Leslie Cheung), has launched a search for new male talent. Ming's roommate Yu Lo (Eric Tsang) teaches her to walk—and scratch—like a guy, and dresses her in boy's clothing, and she attends the talent contest in the hope of meeting Rose. Ming, now "Wing", completely botches the audition, but Sam signs "him" to get back at Rose, who is angered by his boast that he can make a star of anyone, regardless of talent or looks.

As Sam's protege, Wing moves into the couple's apartment, but finds that they live quite independently. When Sam's tutelage begins to pay off, Rose takes a liking to Wing and even attempts to seduce "him". Wing is entranced but terrified of being found out, and escapes by allowing Rose to think that "he" is gay.

Sam's relationship with Wing also intensifies, and he frets over this chink in his once securely heterosexual identity. He seeks the advice of a flamboyant gay friend, who persuades Sam to explore his feelings. Drunk, Sam tries to kiss Wing, but panics. Wing confesses to Rose that she is in love with Sam and to being female. Rose promises not to betray Ming's secret, but extracts from her a vow to stay away from Sam as long as they officially remain a couple. Ming returns to her small apartment and devoted roommate.

Months later, when Rose announces on television that she is single again, Ming is desperate to return to Sam, but terrified of revealing her true gender. Yu Lo comes to the rescue, again, finding a dress for her to wear and setting the stage for a happy ending.

HE'S A WOMAN, SHE'S A MAN reincarnates a plot familiar from other films in which cross-gendered disguise figures prominently: most obviously VICTOR/VICTORIA. While frustratingly plodding, there is no denying that the film has its charms, which are found mostly in warm if sometimes cartoonish performances. The temperamental diva Rose and anguished artist Sam are predictably drawn, if gamely played. Yuen makes an adorable boy, and pulls off the ruse adequately. She has a comedic grasp on the body language she is taught by her roommate (in fact, she won her second best actress award for this role), but is as childish at the end as when the story began. Ironically, the roommate is the hero of the lot. Tsang in the role is generous and pragmatic, putting his friend's needs first, despite hints of his own unrequited desire for her. His story fails to have a fairy tale ending, but he is the only credible character of them all. *(Sexual situations.)* — C.Ch.

d, Peter Chan; p, Eric Tsang; exec p, Peter Chan; assoc p, Hui Yut-tsan, Hui Yun; w, Chi Lee, James Yuen (from a story by); ph, Chan Tseun-kit; ed, Chan Ki-hop; m, Hui Yun, Tsui Tsang-hei; art d, Hai Tsung-man; cos, Ng Leilou

Romance/Comedy   (PR: C   MPAA: NR)

HIDEAWAY   ★★
(U.S.) 112m S/Q Productions ~ TriStar c

Jeff Goldblum *(Hatch)*; Christine Lahti *(Lindsey)*; Alicia Silverstone *(Regina)*; Jeremy Sisto *(Vassago)*; Alfred Molina *(Dr. Jonas Nyebern)*; Rae Dawn Chong *(Rose Orwetto)*; Kenneth Welsh *(Detective Breech)*; Suzy Joachim *(Dr. Kari Dovell)*; Shirley Broderick *(Miss Dockridge)*; Tom McBeath *(Morton Redlow)*; Joely Collins *(Linda)*; Roger R. Cross *(Harry)*; Michael McDonald *(Young Cop)*; Don S. Davis *(Dr. Martin)*; Rebecca Toolan *(Female Doctor)*; Hiro Kanagawa *(Nurse Nakamura)*;

Jayme Knox *(Mother of Baby)*; Norma Wick *(TV Announcer)*; Michelle Skalnik *(Victim)*; Gaetana Korbin *(Victim)*; Tiffany Foster *(Samantha)*; Mara Duronslet *(Zoe)*

While above-average performers help keep some interest in this adaptation of Dean R. Koontz's bestseller, the film really has little to offer besides a cheesy premise and some flashy visuals.

Satan-worshipping teenager Jeremy, who calls himself Vassago (Jeremy Sisto), murders his mother and sister and then kills himself. Shortly thereafter, antiques dealer Hatch Harrison (Jeff Goldblum) is driving home with his wife Lindsey (Christine Lahti) and daughter Regina (Alicia Silverstone) from a weekend vacation. They get into an accident in which Hatch is apparently killed. Dr. Jonas Nyebern (Alfred Molina) is able to bring Hatch back through a resuscitation technique he's perfected and, after recovering from the experience, Hatch returns to his normal life. But he is soon plagued by frightening visions in which he sees "himself" murdering young women, not knowing at first that he has become psychically linked with Vassago, who has also returned from the dead.

Vassago begins stalking Regina, and Hatch seeks help from psychic Rose Orwetto (Rae Dawn Chong) and Dr. Nyebern. Vassago is also able to see through Hatch's eyes, however, and murders Rose and later Dr. Nyebern. By then, Hatch has found out that the doctor was Vassago's father, who brought his son back to life using the same technique that revived Hatch. Vassago kidnaps Lindsey and Regina and takes them to his lair at an abandoned amusement park; Hatch follows and confronts the killer. With the forces of light on his side, Hatch defeats the demonic villain and saves his wife and daughter.

While HIDEAWAY has its share of intense and striking scenes, it suffers from the fact that the two best ones occur in the first 20 minutes. Vassago's murder/suicide and subsequent trip to hell are powerfully staged, with digital effects representing what awaits Vassago on the other side that are frightening instead of gratuitous. And the car crash that almost claims Hatch's life places in the top ranks of cinematic auto accidents, successfully and scarily evoking the personal terror of the characters involved.

Once the premise has been established, however, the film settles into a more routine story of a man psychically connected with a killer. LAWNMOWER MAN director Brett Leonard is more subtle than some in his handling of the villain's exploits, preferring quick, jolting flashes of the murders to sadistically drawn-out slaughter scenes, and he's got a good cast to work with. Goldblum is just the right actor to portray the increasingly wigged-out Hatch, with Lahti and Silverstone making the most of their underwritten characters. Sisto (who also appeared opposite Silverstone in CLUELESS) is scarily convincing as the reptilian Vassago, a young man who could seduce Regina and slash her throat with equal ease.

Not quite as satisfying is the way the film jettisons the harder-edged horror of Koontz's book for a tamer and more traditional story progression; it's regrettable that co-scripter Andrew Kevin Walker here fails to deliver the complexity and intensity of his script for SEVEN. Though Leonard cranks up the tension in individual scenes, the suspense doesn't accumulate, and the climax is a letdown. Instead of playing out the spiritual conflict between Hatch and Vassago in more emotional, dramatic terms, Leonard overliteralizes it with showy special effects, as computer-generated angels and devils erupt from the characters' heads to do battle. The same conflict between visual spectacle and emotional content—with the latter ultimately suffering—also mars Leonard's second 1995 release, VIRTUOSITY. *(Graphic violence, sexual situations, adult situations, profanity.)* — M.G.

d, Brett Leonard; p, Jerry Baerwitz, Agatha Hanczakowski, Gimel Everett; assoc p, Beau St. Clair; w, Andrew Kevin Walker,

Neal Jimenez (based on the novel by Dean R. Koontz); ph, Gale Tattersall; ed, B.J. Sears; m, Trevor Jones; prod d, Michael Bolton; art d, Sandy Cochrane; set d, Elizabeth Wilcox; sound, Rob Young (mixer); fx, Mike Vezina, Tim McGovern, Jon Townley, Bernice Kenton, Camille Cellucci, Aileen Timmers; casting, Amanda Mackey, Cathy Sandrich; cos, Monique Prudhomme; makeup, Todd McIntosh, Jayne Dancose, Victoria Down; stunts, Jacob Rupp

Horror/Thriller (PR: O   MPAA: R)

HIGH RISK ★★½
(Hong Kong) 104m Wong Jing Workshop ~ Upland Film Corporation c
(SUE DAAM LUNG WAI)

Jet Li *(Lt. Kit Li)*; Jackie Cheung *(Frankie Long)*; Chingmy Yau *(Reporter)*; Wu Ma *(Frankie's Father)*; Charlie Yeung *(Joyce)*; Valerie Chow *(Fai Fai)*; Billy Chau *(Henchman)*; Wong Siu; Lam Kwok-Bun; Charlie Cho; Tuan Wai-Lun; Kwan Sau-Mei; Li Lik-Chee; Vincent Kok; Yuen Tak

After his terrific period-martial arts drama FIST OF LEGEND, Hong Kong star Jet Li takes a step down with this contemporary action film.

Li plays police lieutenant Kit Li, whose wife and son are killed by a bomb set by the Doctor, a criminal mastermind who calls Li by cellular phone during the incident. Two years later, Li has left the force to become the surreptitious stunt double for a popular but basically incompetent martial arts movie star named Frankie Long (Jackie Cheung), and a reporter (Chingmy Yau) is trying to expose him. Long and the reporter are among the attendees at a party in a hi-tech penthouse where a display of priceless diamonds is being unveiled, when the gathering is crashed by the Doctor and his team of armed terrorists. The Doctor plans to steal the diamonds, while one of his henchmen is intent on fighting a match with Long. Li discovers what's happening and infiltrates the party, precipitating a violent cat-and-mouse game with the Doctor and his gang through the building's upper floors. Finally, Li commandeers a police helicopter and crashes it into the penthouse, killing many of the Doctor's men. Long has his showdown with the Doctor's henchman, and with Li's guidance is able to best him; Li himself fights with the Doctor, who manages to escape. Li then finds the reporter strapped to explosives on the building's roof, and the Doctor calls him on a cellular phone to taunt him. Remembering their previous encounter, Li defuses the explosives and informs the Doctor that he tainted him with poison during their fight, correctly surmising that the Doctor would flee too far away to make it to a hospital. The Doctor dies, and Li and Long are celebrated as heroes.

HIGH RISK was directed by one of Hong Kong's busiest filmmakers, Wong Jing, whose work has run the gamut from great drama (GOD OF GAMBLERS, with Chow Yun-Fat) to silly comedy (the Li vehicle LAST HERO IN CHINA) and who here mixes the two in a schizophrenic manner. The story starts as a dead-serious thriller with the deaths of Li's wife and son, then switches to farcical humor in the scenes where Li doubles for Long. But just as the film appears to be developing into a potentially wicked spoof of Asian action filmmaking in general, and Jackie Chan movies in particular, the story switches gears yet again to become a blatant DIE HARD rip-off (right down to the black computer expert who helps crack the lock codes on the diamond display cases).

There are so many supporting characters thrown into the mix that the film is never able to build real tension. Despite an action directing credit for Yuen Kwai, director of the great FONG

SAI-YUK, Li doesn't have enough opportunity to show his stuff; it's 40 minutes before the first major action scene, and Long's character arc requires that he, not Li, has the major climactic martial-arts duel with the number two bad guy. Still, there are a number of funny moments and a few terrific action set pieces, including Li's first attack on the terrorists—in a car he drives into an elevator and rides up to the penthouse—and the climactic chopper assault. Li himself is fine in a comparatively undemanding role, and Cheung is fun as the actor who must prove himself under pressure. This is middling Hong Kong action, suggesting what the genre is capable of without hitting the heights of its best examples. (*Violence, adult situations.*) — M.G.

d, Wong Jing, Yuen Kwai; p, Wong Jing, Pei Hsiang-Chuan; w, Wong Jing

Action/Crime   **(PR: O   MPAA: NR)**

HIGHER LEARNING   ★★★
(U.S.) 127m New Deal Productions; Columbia ~ Columbia c

Omar Epps (*Malik Williams*); Kristy Swanson (*Kristen Connor*); Michael Rapaport (*Remy*); Jennifer Connelly (*Taryn*); Ice Cube (*Fudge*); Jason Wiles (*Wayne*); Tyra Banks (*Deja*); Cole Hauser (*Scott Moss*); Laurence Fishburne (*Professor Maurice Phipps*); Randall Batinkoff (*Chad Shadowhill*); Bradford English (*Officer Bradley*); Regina King (*Monet*); Busta Rhymez (*Dreads*); Jay Ferguson (*Billy*); Andrew Bryniarski (*Knocko*); Trevor St. John (*James*); Talbert Morton (*Erik*); Adam Goldberg (*David Isaacs*); J. Trevor Edmond (*Eddie*); Bridgitte Wilson (*Nicole*); Kari Salin (*Claudia*); John Walton Smith, Jr. (*Coach Davis*); Malcolm Norrington (*Cory*); Antonio Todd (*Adam*); Tim Griffin (*Orientation Advisor*); Patricia Forte (*Counselor*); Sheila Ward (*Counselor*); George LaPorte (*Starting Judge*); Warren Olney (*TV Reporter*); D-Knowledge (*Himself*); Skip O'Brien (*Security Guard*); Joe Bugs (*Security Guard*); Bill Evans (*Security Guard*); Ernie Singleton (*Fudge's Homie*); Dedrick Gobert (*Fudge's Homie*); Bruce Williams (*Fudge's Homie*); Richard D. Alexander (*Big Shorty*); Michael Buchman Silver (*Frat Member*); Graham Galloway (*Frat Member*); Paul Anthony Kropfl (*Frat Member*); James W. Smith (*Race Official*); Walton Greene (*Race Official*); Mary Bakjian (*Race Official*); Mista Grimm (*Drunk Student*); Alicia Stevenson (*Monet's Friend*); Colleen Ann Fitzpatrick (*Festival Singer*); Robby Parker (*Dogman*); Pola Maloles (*Flyer Girl*); Ingrid Walters (*Party Girl*); Kiante Elam (*Black Pepper*); Jamie Jo Medearis (*White Salt*); Rick Avery (*Guard*); Tony Donno (*Gay Victim*); Cole McLarty (*Gay Victim*)

Despite its air of topicality at a time when race and gender are hotly divisive issues on campus, HIGHER LEARNING is a throwback to the earnest college dramas of the '60s and '70s in which idealistic young people learn that higher education isn't exactly what they expected.

The entering freshmen of Columbus College personify the full spectrum of contemporary social ills, divided by race, sex, and class before they ever crack that first book. Sullen Malik (Omar Epps) and his girlfriend, poised and articulate Deja (Tyra Banks), are on athletic scholarships: if they don't run, they've got one-way tickets back to the 'hood. Kristen (Kristy Swanson) is a chronic good girl whose once comfortable upper-middle-class family can barely afford her tuition. Strong-willed pre-med student Monet (Regina King) doesn't trust anyone who claims to have all the answers; lonely Remy (Michael Rappaport) is looking for something to believe in, and finds it with the campus skinheads, whose charismatic leader Scott (Cole Hauser) is the beguiling face of vicious racism. Fudge (Ice Cube) is a sixth-year senior, a glib blowhard who defies authority just to goose the

status quo. Taryn (Jennifer Connelly) is a feminist lesbian; gentle, enlightened Wayne (Jason Wiles) just wants everyone to get along. The imperious Professor Phipps (Laurence Fishburne), who teaches first-year Political Science, holds everyone to the same exacting standards.

Kristen is date-raped and goes to one of Taryn's feminist meetings. She develops a close relationship with Taryn, but is also attracted to Wayne and winds up sleeping with both of them. Fudge, meanwhile, turns Malik onto separatist philosophy; and Remy falls ever deeper into the thrall of the skinheads. Kristen organizes a festival dedicated to peace and racial harmony, hoping it will bring all the students together. But the skinheads disrupt the proceedings and Remy, who has sunk deep into misery and madness, takes to a nearby rooftop with a rifle. He shoots and kills Deja, who's with Malik. Malik chases down Remy, but campus security assumes Malik is the miscreant, and beats him up. Remy shoots himself. Malik and Kristen meet for the first time at Deja's memorial service, where they exchange names and make the first tentative gestures of reconciliation.

HIGHER LEARNING doesn't look promising: the throng of characters is unwieldy, and Singleton's use of dorm room assignments to create initial conflicts screams "plot device." The roomies are mixed and mismatched for maximum friction: backwater white boy Remy in the middle of the Black Power dorm, privileged, unfocused Kristen and scholarship student Monet, smugly self-assured Wayne and Malik, whose racial consciousness is being painfully raised. But what could easily be a Spike Lee diatribe masquerading as discussion blossoms into something messier and more interesting in Singleton's hands.

HIGHER LEARNING tends to preachiness: it opens with a perfectly centered shot of an oversized American flag rippling serenely in the breeze and ends with the same image, skewed and off center. It's flawed, shaggy, and verging on apparent shapelessness, though it's actually carefully structured as a series of opposing pairs whose elements shift in various ways. But its flaws are mostly flaws of ambition, of Singleton's determination to pack into one film everything he's ever thought about the ways young people hurt one another and themselves through ignorance and carelessness and unexamined prejudice. HIGHER LEARNING is a polemical film, and there are times when it's overwhelmed by its didactic agenda. But it's to Singleton's credit that he truly seems to be searching for answers. It's hipper to throw your hands up in despair and say, "This is the way it is—I'm just calling it like I see it," and easier too. Singleton dares to be uncool, and HIGHER LEARNING is a stronger movie for it. (*Sexual situations, adult situations, violence, profanity, substance abuse.*) — M.M.

d, John Singleton; p, John Singleton, Paul Hall; co-p, Dwight Alonzo Williams; w, John Singleton; ph, Peter Lyons Collister; ed, Bruce Cannon; m, Stanley Clarke; prod d, Keith Brian Burns; art d, Richard Holland; set d, Michael C. Claypool; sound, Veda Campbell (mixer); casting, Jaki Brown-Karman, Kimberly Hardin; cos, Carol Oditz; makeup, Alvechia Ewing, Beverly Jo Pryor; stunts, Bob Minor

Drama   **(PR: C   MPAA: R)**

HIGHLANDER: THE FINAL DIMENSION   ★½
(Canada/France/U.K.) 99m Karambole Films Productions; Transfilm; Initial Groupe; Lumiere; Falling Cloud Ltd. ~ Dimension c
(AKA: HIGHLANDER III: THE SORCERER)

Christopher Lambert (*Connor MacLeod/Russell Nash*); Mario Van Peebles (*Kane the Magician*); Deborah Unger (*Alex Johnson/Sarah*); Mako (*Nakano*); Mark Neufeld (*Stenn*); Raoul

Trujillo *(Warrior)*; Jean-Pierre Perusse *(Warrior)*; Frederick Y. Okimura *(Old Japanese Man)*; Daniel Do *(Takamura)*; Gabriel Kakon *(John)*; Louis Bertignac *(Pierre Bouchet)*; Michael Jayston *(Jack Donovan)*; Zhenhu Han *(Innkeeper)*; Akira Inoue *(Innkeeper's Son)*; Darcy Laurie *(Banger)*; George Vitetzakis *(Banger)*; David Francis *(Doctor Malloy)*; Lisa Vitello *(Nurse)*; Matt Holland *(Intern)*; Richard Jutras *(Uniform)*; Liz Macrae *(Interviewer)*; Emidio *(Michetti)*; Andre Oumansky *(Marquis de Condorcet)*; Charles S. Doucet *(Cowboy)*; Garth Gilker *(Cowboy)*; Paul Hopkins *(Tommy)*; Michael McGill *(Medical Examiner)*; Chip Chuipka *(Charlie)*; Patrick Fierry *(Captain)*; Clifford Spencer *(Guillotine Man)*; John Dunn-Hill *(Loony Napoleon)*; Morven Cameron *(Receptionist)*; Vlasta Vrana *(Vorisek)*

HIGHLANDER: THE FINAL DIMENSION promises to be the last in the HIGHLANDER film series, which is just as well, since this entry cannot compete with either the earlier theatrical films or the cult television series.

In the 16th century, Connor MacLeod (Christopher Lambert) receives a spiritual lesson in self-defense from his master, Mako (Nakano), at a mountain retreat. Soon, an evil warrior, Kane the Magician (Mario Van Peebles), confronts and kills Mako in order to obtain his mystical gifts. Three hundred years later, Kane and his three immortal henchmen, reappear in New York City, where they plot to take over the world. When the news reaches a recently widowed MacLeod in Marrakesh, where he is living in 1994 with his son, John (Gabriel Kakon), MacLeod immediately leaves to prepare for battle.

While trying to track down Kane in New York, MacLeod meets Alex Smith (Deborah Unger), a research scientist from the Museum of Ancient History, who is also looking for the destructive warrior. In the midst of their joint search, MacLeod and Alex realize that they were romantically involved during the French Revolution, when her name was Sarah. After finding the old sword that Mako bequeathed him 300 years earlier, MacLeod travels to his ancestral home in Scotland, where he repairs his sword for the ultimate duel with Kane. But he returns to New York once he hears that Kane has kidnapped John. The final confrontation determines the fate of humankind.

This HIGHLANDER might not seem so jaded to the uninitiated, but HIGHLANDER aficionados will immediately recognize how inferior it is next to the earlier movie and current television versions. Although Christopher Lambert repeats his film role as the immortal action hero, he is less dynamic than he was in HIGHLANDER (1986) or even HIGHLANDER 2, THE QUICKENING (1991). He is also far less charismatic and interesting to watch than Adrian Paul of the European television serial. Moreover, in this film, Lambert inexplicably whispers his lines, while the special effects are deafening. Wolf Kroeger's interior production design is slick and colorful, and Scotland is pleasing to look at, but the photography and editing poorly cover the visuals. About the only fun in the picture is watching Mario Van Peebles overplay his villainous role. *(Nudity, sexual situations, mild profanity.)* — E.M.

d, Andrew Morahan; p, Claude Leger; exec p, Guy Collins, Charles L. Smiley; assoc p, Stephen Key; co-p, Jean Cazes, Eric Altmayer, James Daly; w, Paul Ohl (from the story by William N. Panzer and Brad Mirman, based on characters created by Gregory Widen); ph, Steven Chivers; ed, Yves Langlois; m, Peter Robinson; prod d, Wolf Kroeger, Gilles Aird, Ben Morahan; sound, Claude Hazanavicius; fx, Brian Johnson, Stuart Galloway, Louis Craig; casting, Nadja Ross, Vera Miller; cos, Jackie Budin; makeup, Didier Lavergne, Stephan Dupuis, Charle Carter; stunts, Dave McKeown

Fantasy/Adventure   (PR: C MPAA: R)

HOME FOR THE HOLIDAYS   ★★
(U.S.) 103m Egg Pictures; PolyGram ~ Paramount c

Holly Hunter *(Claudia Larson)*; Robert Downey, Jr. *(Tommy Larson)*; Anne Bancroft *(Adele Larson)*; Charles Durning *(Henry Larson)*; Dylan McDermott *(Leo Fish)*; Geraldine Chaplin *(Aunt Glady)*; Steve Guttenberg *(Walter Wedman)*; Cynthia Stevenson *(Joanne Wedman)*; Claire Danes *(Kitt)*; Emily Ann Lloyd *(Brittany Lace)*; Zachary Duhame *(Walter Jr.)*; Austin Pendleton *(Peter Arnold)*; David Strathairn *(Russell Terziak)*; Amy Yasbeck *(Ginny Johnson Drewer)*; James Lecesne *(Ron Drewer)*; Angela Paton *(Woman on Airplane)*; Randy Stone *(Man In Car)*; Sam Slovick *(Jack)*; Susan Lyall *(Woman at Party)*; Shawn Wayne Hatosy *(Counter Boy)*; Nat Benchley *(Airport Cop)*; Molly Austin *(Woman on Airport Phone)*; Vivienne Shub *(Woman No.2 on Airport Phone)*; Julie Ann Mendez *(Woman No.3 on Airport Phone)*; Johnny Tonini *(Young Henry)*; Eva Langsdorf *(Young Adele)*; Wilder Ferguson *(Young Glady)*; Stephanie Francoz *(Young Claudia)*; Blake Hovespian *(Young Tommy)*; Natasha Stanton *(Young Joanne)*

It would be surprising if Jodie Foster understood much about real life in Middle America, but HOME FOR THE HOLIDAYS suggests that she knows nothing except what she's learned from watching "Talk Soup." For her second directorial effort, Foster has chosen a talented ensemble and an ambitious W.D. Richter screenplay that attempts a comic treatment of family dysfunction. The result, however, is confusion and cacophony.

Claudia Larson (Holly Hunter) has returned to Baltimore for Thanksgiving in desperate need of familial comfort. The day before, in Chicago, Claudia lost her job and discovered that her teen-age daughter (Claire Danes) intends to lose her virginity over the holiday. Unfortunately, the Larson family isn't a very comforting lot. Claudia's chain-smoking mother, Adele (Anne Bancroft), is always blowing in her daughter's face and criticizing her life. Her slightly daft father, Henry (Charles Durning), compulsively putters around the house. Claudia's gay and overbearingly obnoxious brother, Tommy (Robert Downey Jr.), and his new "associate," Leo Fish (Dylan McDermott), show up unexpectedly as well.

Rounding out the dinner table are Claudia's prissy sister, Joanne (Cynthia Stevenson), Joanne's boring husband, Walter (Steve Guttenberg), and crazy Aunt Glady (Geraldine Chaplin). Glady kicks things off by revealing her undying love for Henry, unrequited for 43 years. Then Tommy throws the turkey in Joanne's lap and dumps food on her head. With the revelation of Tommy's recent, very public, gay wedding ceremony, Claudia learns that Leo isn't gay: rather, he has come in order to meet her. That evening, Claudia and Leo run errands together—taking leftovers to Joanne and Walter, who earlier fled in terror. They sense an attraction; however, Claudia isn't willing to "take a chance on love" because they live in different time zones. The next day, Leo throws the dice and joins Claudia on her return flight to Chicago.

HOME FOR THE HOLIDAYS is divided into sections, each introduced by a title card identifying the impending fear Claudia will face—e.g., "Flying," "Relatives," and "More Relatives." At precisely the time when a viewer will be wondering if the proceedings have a point, up comes the title: "The Point." This turns out to be that the quality of the memories you receive from family offsets the quantity of indignities they make you suffer. Thus the promise of domestic satire is suddenly reduced to pure Hollywood banality.

Throughout, Foster seems uncertain whether she's engaging in an edgy dissection of '90s family life or simply updating "Capra-corn" for superficially hip contemporary audiences. The result is confusion. We're supposed to identify with Claudia as a sort of eternal child, but she's too bohemian a character. She's an artist who smokes pot and leaves her daughter home alone on a family holiday (Jean Arthur would never have done that.) Foster delights in Robert Downey Jr.'s smugness and scatological ad-libs, but viewers are more likely to sympathize with Joanna, who's cast as the film's heavy. All she wants is a nice Thanksgiving dinner, where everyone behaves, and no one gets food dumped on their head. Is that so wrong? *(Profanity, adult situations.)* — P.R.

d, Jodie Foster; p, Jodie Foster, Peggy Rajski; exec p, Stuart Kleinman; w, W.D. Richter (from the short story by Chris Radant); ph, Lajos Koltai; ed, Lynzee Klingman; m, Mark Isham; prod d, Andrew McAlpine; art d, Jim Tocci; set d, Barbara Drake; sound, Chris Newman (mixer); casting, Avy Kaufman; cos, Susan Lyall; makeup, Kathrine James

Comedy   **(PR: A   MPAA: PG-13)**

HOTEL SORRENTO   ★★½
(Australia) 112m Bayside Pictures; Horizon Films; Australian Film Finance Corporation; Film Victoria ~ Castle Hill c
(AKA: SORRENTO BEACH)

Caroline Goodall *(Meg Moynihan)*; Caroline Gillmer *(Hilary Moynihan)*; Tara Morice *(Pippa Moynihan)*; Joan Plowright *(Marge Morissey)*; John Hargreaves *(Dick Bennett)*; Ray Barrett *(Wal Moynihan)*; Ben Thomas *(Troy Moynihan)*; Nicholas Bell *(Edwin)*

Richard Franklin's HOTEL SORRENTO, a literate, well-acted film, is a Chekhovian drama (appropriately enough, about three sisters) set in a picturesque Victorian beach town near Melbourne. Based on a play by Hannie Rayson, Franklin's ensemble movie does not try to camouflage its theatrical origins, choosing instead to augment them with subtle filmic touches, many of them provided by Geoff Burton's assured cinematography. This is an intelligent, often amusing film which will reward audiences in search of thoughtful, quality fare.

Hilary Moynihan (Caroline Gillmer), a fortyish widow, lives at the beach front house nicknamed "Hotel Sorrento" with her retired father Wal (Ray Barrett) and teenage son Troy (Ben Thomas). Her sister Pippa (Tara Morice) has flown in from New York with a scheme to open an American-style sandwich franchise. In London, third sister Meg (Caroline Goodall), a Booker Prize nominee for her *roman a clef* about a quarrelsome Australian family, decides on an impromptu trip home, accompanied by her English husband Edwin (Nicholas Bell). Rounding out the mix are weekend beach residents Marge (Joan Plowright) and her houseguest Dick (John Hargreaves), the latter a magazine editor hoping for an exclusive story on Meg's homecoming. But a sudden death intervenes, propelling family and friends into a second act full of revelations, accusations and bitter memories.

As scripted by Franklin and Peter Fitzpatrick, HOTEL SORRENTO grapples with a number of issues, including personal loyalty, national insecurity, family rivalry and artistic responsibility. No doubt, some viewers will find it all too talky, but it is witty and perceptive talk delivered with consummate skill by an octet of gifted actors. Gillmer, who played Meg in the original Sydney stage production, is sturdy and reliable as Hilary. Goodall deftly explores Meg's love-hate feelings for her family. Plowright, in the juicy part of a philosophical, seen-it-all type, mines clever-sounding lines ("Australian men don't understand melancholy; they confuse it with depression") for optimum laughs. Thomas is natural and affecting as Troy, who begins to think, at an awkward age, that he may be jinxed by life, and even death.

One of HOTEL SORRENTO's ongoing jokes has the Moynihan telephone always ringing in the middle of the night, such is Australia's apparent remoteness from America and Europe. But there is nothing remote about the ideas and emotions that inform these characters and render them universal. "I'm not a known quantity to my children," confesses Marge, but she and all the others in HOTEL SORRENTO will be known quantities to anyone for whom family has been both a blessing and a burden. — E.K.

d, Richard Franklin; p, Richard Franklin; co-p, Helen Watts; w, Richard Franklin, Peter Fitzpatrick (based on the play by Hannie Rayson); ph, Geoff Burton; ed, David Pulbrook; m, Nerida Tyson-Chew; prod d, Tracy Watt; casting, Greg Apps; cos, Lisa Meagher

Drama   **(PR: A   MPAA: NR)**

HOUSEGUEST   ★
(U.S.) 108m Houseguest Productions; Caravan Pictures ~ Buena Vista c

Sinbad *(Kevin Franklin)*; Phil Hartman *(Gary Young)*; Kim Griest *(Emily Young)*; Chauncey Leopardi *(Jason Young)*; Talia Seider *(Sarah Young)*; Kim Murphy *(Brooke Young)*; Tony Longo *(Joey Gasperini)*; Jeffrey Jones *(Ron Timmerman)*; Stan Shaw *(Larry)*; Ron Glass *(Derek Bond)*; Kevin Jordan *(Steve "ST-3")*; Mason Adams *(Mr. Pike)*; Patricia Fraser *(Nancy Pike)*; Don Brockett *(Happy Marcelli)*; Kevin West *(Vincent Montgomery)*; Wynonna Smith *(Lynn)*; Kirk Baily *(Stuart the Manager)*; Valerie Long *(Sister Mary Winters)*; Jesse Rivera *(Little Kevin)*; Melvin Brentley, II *(Bobby)*; Brandon Alexander *(Kid No. 1)*; B'nard Lewis *(1st Local Guy)*; Janathan Floyd *(2nd Local Guy)*; Vondria Bergen *(Ticket Saleswoman)*; Susan Richards *(Happy's Wife)*; Palma Greenwood *(Myrna)*; Chuck Aber *(Big Spin Host)*; Larry John Meyers *(Mr. Ichabod)*; Jody Savin *(Rosie the Caterer)*; Alex Coleman *(Tom Miller)*; Lee Cass *(Stern Man)*; Marilyn Eastman *(Society Woman)*; John Hall *(Preppy Man)*; Bob Tracey *(Priest)*; Vicki Ross-Norris *(Woman in Red Dress)*; Tina Benko *(Waitress)*; William Cameron *(Jerry Jordan)*; Patti Lesniak *(Jane Jordan)*; Kate Young *(Michelle Castell)*; Randall Miller *(Drunk at Party)*; Donald Joseph Freeman *(Happy's Thug)*; Mindy Reynolds *(Burger Counter Girl)*; Catherine Cuppari *(Kelly)*; Bingo O'Malley *(Ticket Vendor)*; Susan Chapek *(Nurse)*; Ron Newell *(Dr. Kraft)*; Alvin McCray *(Dental Student)*

Comedian Sinbad impersonates Phil Hartman's childhood friend to become his houseguest and hide from some mobsters in this truly awful attempt at family farce.

Good-natured Kevin Franklin (Sinbad) is trying to get rich quick, but things are not going his way. Escaping from loan sharks, he runs into Gary Young (Phil Hartman) at the airport and passes himself off as Derek Bond, an old friend Young has not seen in 25 years. Franklin becomes Young's houseguest, and for the rest of the weekend faces the task of impersonating someone he knows nothing about. He bluffs his way through a Career Day speech, a wine-tasting, a day on the links, and a party in his honor. Everyone but he knows Bond is a famous dentist, well-known wine expert, and golfer. To keep up the ruse, Franklin even agrees to perform dental surgery on Young's mean and racist boss Mr. Pike (Mason Adams).

Along the way, Franklin comes to care for the people he is deceiving, but unfortunately, the Youngs are not a happy family. Young and Emily's (Kim Griest) marriage is strained by their careers: he is a lawyer; she runs a yogurt shop. Franklin convinces Young to stand up to Pike and quit his job in allegiance to Emily. Franklin then injects the Young children with some similar, healthy doses of love and self-esteem. When the real Bond (Ron Glass) shows up, and the loan sharks finally catch up with

Franklin, Young rallies his family to help his new friend. Franklin can escape, but will not because he has learned lessons about honesty and responsibility himself. In the end, he pays off his debt with a winning lottery ticket, but acknowledges that true wealth lies in having friends like the Youngs.

HOUSEGUEST is a movie that defies all expectations. After Sinbad's amazingly unfunny monologue at the opening, the viewer may well expect that things can only get better. They do not. When one scene devolves into a pointless montage of rapid fire nonsensical action, one clings to the belief that the next one cannot as well. It does. Meanwhile, any hopes that each shameless promotional mention of McDonald's just *has* to be the last are repeatedly shattered. Instead, HOUSEGUEST is stuffed with jump cuts, odd camera angles, and frenzied overcranking, in the hope that viewers will be distracted from the fact that nothing funny is going on. They will not. — P.R.

d, Randall Miller; p, Joe Roth, Roger Birnbaum; exec p, Dennis Bishop; co-p, Riley Kathryn Ellis, Jody Savin; w, Lawrence Gay, Michael DeGaetano; ph, Jerzy Zielinski; ed, Eric Sears; m, John Debney; prod d, Paul Peters; art d, Gary Kosko; set d, Amy Wells; sound, David MacMillan; casting, Rick Montgomery, Dan Parada; cos, Jyl Moder; makeup, A. Vechia Trahan; stunts, Jeffrey J. Dashnaw

Comedy   **(PR: A MPAA: PG)**

HOW TO MAKE AN AMERICAN QUILT   ★★½
(U.S.) 109m Amblin Entertainment ~ Universal c

Winona Ryder *(Finn)*; Maya Angelou *(Anna)*; Anne Bancroft *(Glady Joe)*; Ellen Burstyn *(Hy)*; Alfre Woodard *(Marianna)*; Kate Capshaw *(Sally)*; Jean Simmons *(Em)*; Kate Nelligan *(Constance)*; Lois Smith *(Sophia)*; Adam Baldwin *(Finn's Father)*; Dermot Mulroney *(Sam)*; Rip Torn *(Arthur)*; Samantha Mathis *(Young Sophia)*; Clare Danes *(Young Glady Joe)*; Esther Rolle *(Aunt Pauline)*; Derrick O'Connor *(Dean)*; Johnathon Schaech *(Leon)*; Loren Dean *(Preston)*; Mykelti Williamson *(Winston)*; Melinda Dillon *(Mrs. Darling)*; Joanna Going *(Young Em)*; Tim Guinee *(Young Dean)*; Richard Jenkins *(Howell)*; Alicia Goranson *(Young Hy)*; Maria Celedonio *(Young Anna)*; Denis Arndt *(James)*; Matt Zusser *(Pres)*; Ari Meyers *(Duff)*; Kaela Green *(Evie)*; Jared Leto *(Beck)*; Holland Taylor *(Mrs. Rubens)*; Gail Strickland *(The Mrs.)*; Jane Alden *(Em's Mother)*; David Williams *(Em's Father)*; Tamala Jones *(Anna's Great Grandmother)*; Harvey E. Lee, Jr. *(Anna's Great Grandfather)*; Debra Sticklin *(Lady Guest)*; Charles Parks *(Male Guest)*; Will Estes *(Boy at Party)*; Jonah Rooney *(Boy at Party)*; Kaelyn Craddick; Sara Craddick *(Young Finn)*; Rae'ven Larrymore Kelly *(Little Anna)*; Brian McElroy; Michael McElroy *(Baby Pres)*; Paige Kettner; Ryanne Kettner *(Little Evie)*; Annie Mae Hunter *(Little Duff)*; Krysten Lee Wilson; Kellie Lynn Wilson *(Baby Duff)*

HOW TO MAKE AN AMERICAN QUILT offers a sentimental journey through the secret lives, longings and regrets of a multigenerational group of women bound together by the task of creating a quilt. It's a compendium of received wisdom, Hollywood-style—stuffed with morals and meaningful moments, bolstered by a large, well-known cast.

Finn (Winona Ryder) is a young graduate student hiding away for the summer at her grandmother's house, where she has to finish her masters thesis and to decide whether to marry her carpenter boyfriend Sam (Dermot Mulroney). After having changed her thesis topic several times she has settled on the subject of women's craft and ritual and is hoping to gain inspiration from a long-standing quilting bee that her great aunt Gladys (Anne Bancroft) and her grandmother Hy (Ellen Burstyn) have held. As the summer progresses, Finn learns that the theme of the

quilt in progress is "Where Love Resides" and that it is intended to be her wedding quilt. One by one she develops an intimacy with each member of the quilting circle and learns of the loss, regret, and secret liaisons of their pasts, vastly enriching the meaning of each square and leading her to reassess her own hesitant relationship with love. She eventually returns to Sam after having a fling with local stud Leon (Johnathan Schaech).

The intertwining stories of each of the women are told in flashbacks. We learn that the bitter, old Sophia was once a radiant beauty and excellent diver whose dreams of freedom were squashed by years of childbearing and domesticity, while her husband lived the life of adventure they had dreamed of. The group's master quilt maker (Maya Angelou), the daughter of freed slaves and domestic servants, finds love in her mulatto daughter and describes how her ancestors struggled to pass down the quilt that bore the story of their suffering, joy, and love from one generation to the next.

The vignettes exemplify and clarify the notion that pieces make up a whole, and that unity and beauty are achieved through devotion and team effort, a theme at once thoughtful and overbearing. Thematic overkill is evident in the scene in which a storm tears through the house and blows away Finn's thesis, scattering it all over creation. Finn is inclined to quit, but perseveres after the older women find various parts of her paper, iron them, and return them. On the other hand, the opening sequence—in which the camera lingers over what appears to be a rich and varied quilt and then moves away to reveal that we're seeing is a geographical panoramic shot of fields, roads and the patterns and colors of nature—is a subtle and effective rendering of the idea.

The metaphor of the quilt is potentially a good one, representing a narrative history in image and cloth, an art form deeply bound to the tradition and repression of American woman. But the film's script is uninspired and takes few risks, and its flashbacks are for the most part uninteresting and filled with cliches. The film's overarching conservatism and heavy-handed moralizing—despite a scene where Finn shares a joint with grandma Hy and great aunt Gladys—is also disappointing. *(Adult situations.)* — R.C.

d, Jocelyn Moorhouse; p, Sarah Pillsbury, Midge Sanford; exec p, Walter Parkes, Laurie MacDonald, Deborah Jelin Newmyer; co-p, Patricia Whitcher; w, Jane Anderson (based on the novel by Whitney Otto); ph, Janusz Kaminski; ed, Jill Bilcock; m, Thomas Newman; prod d, Leslie Dilley; art d, Ed Verreaux; set d, Marvin March; sound, Russell Williams, II; fx, Martin Becker; casting, Risa Bramon Garcia, Mary Vernieu; cos, Ruth Myers; makeup, Valli O'Reilly; stunts, Dan Bradley

Drama   **(PR: A MPAA: PG-13)**

HOW TO TOP MY WIFE   ★★½
(South Korea) 99m Kang Woo Suk Production Company Ltd. ~ Morning Calm Cinema c
(MANURA CHUGIGI)

Joong-Hoong Park *(Bong-Soo Park)*; Jin-Sil Choi *(So-Young Chang)*; Joung-Hwa Eum *(Heri)*; Chong-Won Choi *(Killer)*; Hyoung-Gi Choi *(Director)*

Though the premise is at times unsettling, this Korean comedy (with English subtitles) takes a light approach to a dark subject matter: murdering a spouse. Reminiscent of the 1960s comedies HOW TO MURDER YOUR WIFE and DIVORCE, ITALIAN STYLE, this feature updates the plot for the 1990s to good effect.

Bong-Soo Park (Joong-Hoon Park) is the president of a film production company. The real boss, however, is his overbearing wife So-Young Chang (Jin-Sil Choi), the head of publicity.

So-Young constantly overrides her husband's decisions on everything from budgets to editing. Bong-Soo's mistress, Heri (Joung-Hwa Eum), pressures him to divorce, but he is afraid of what his vengeful wife would do if she learned he was cheating. He has good reason to fear, since So-Young has already threatened to expose Bong-Soo for embezzling company funds if he ever dares to leave her.

Bong-Soo consults an occultist, who warns that if his wife lives, he will die. After Bong-Soo savagely attacks a voodoo doll representing So-Young, she is rushed to the hospital with chest pains. Bong-Soo is dismayed that the attack was not fatal, but is heartened by the doctor's prognosis—So-Young has a heart condition and should avoid undue excitement and physical exertion, including strenuous sex. This diagnosis leads Bong-Soo to attempt unusual methods of killing his wife—including marathon lovemaking sessions and rollercoaster rides. Exhausted from his efforts—while his wife remains hale and hearty—Bong-Soo finally hires a hit man (Chong-Won Choi). The comedy is only increased when his attempts to murder So-Young repeatedly go awry.

Bong-Soo suddenly has a change of heart when he learns that his wife is expecting his child. He races to the movie set to save her from the hired assassin, but she has already incapacitated the killer and discovered that he was hired by Bong-Soo. So-Young throws Bong-Soo out of her life and their house, but she soon grows lonely without him. Shortly after Bong-Soo moves back in, So-Young discovers that he is having another affair. This time she is the one hiring the hit man, and the film ends with her instructing him to do a better job this time around.

Though he flashes an infectious grin and occasionally redeems himself with moments of warmth, Joong-Hoon Park—saddled with an unsympathetic character—is essentially unlikable. Being outshone at the office by a woman is hardly acceptable grounds for murder in contemporary society—even in Korea. If his wife was portrayed as a shrew, audiences might commiserate with Park's predicament, but Jin-Sil Choi's So-Young is a dynamic, attractive woman whose only shortcoming is her devotion to a chauvinistic husband. The comedy ranges from subtle to slapstick, with the funniest segments those featuring Chong-Won Choi as the hapless hit man.

HOW TO TOP YOUR WIFE enjoyed a slightly wider US release than director Kang's 1994 comedy TWO COPS. As Kang is gaining a reputation as a Korean Billy Wilder, chances are good that more American audiences will get a chance to enjoy his future efforts. *(Violence, sexual situations, adult situations, profanity.)* — B.R.

d, Woo-Suk Kang; p, Woo-Suk Kang; exec p, Mi-Hee Kim; w, Sang-Jim Kim, See-Uk Oh; ph, Kwang-Suk Chong; ed, Hyun Kim; m, Kyung-Shik Choi

Comedy   **(PR: O   MPAA: NR)**

HOWLING: NEW MOON RISING, THE
(U.S.) 90m Allied Vision ~ New Line Home Video c
(AKA: HOWLING G)

Clive Turner *(Ted)*; John Huff *(Father John)*; John Ramsden *(Detective)*; Cheryl Allen *(Cheryl)*; Romy Walthall *(Marie Adams)*; Ernest Kester *(Ernie)*; Elizabeth She *(Mary Lou)*; Jaqueline Armitage *(Jaqueline)*; Jim Lozano *(Jim)*; Robert Morwell *(Bob)*; Jim Brock *(Brock)*; Sally Harkham *(Eveanne)*; Claude "Pappy" Allen *(Pappy)*; Harriet Allen *(Harriet)*; Bonnie Lagassa *(Bonnie)*; Jack Holder *(Jack)*; Leslee Anderson *(Leslee)*; Dolores Silver *(Dolores)*; Jaro Prikopsky *(Jaro)*; Brett Owens *(Brett)*; Gary Ham *(Gary)*; Michelle Stilles *(Michelle)*; Joel

Harkham *(Joel)*; Carl Lagassa *(Carl)*; Larry Gutierrez *(Larry)*; Sybil Ramsden *(Sybil)*

With only one or two exceptions, the long series of films spawned by Joe Dante's 1981 hit has provided little to howl about, but this seventh entry represents a new low for the franchise.

The old-style Western village of Pioneer Town is rocked by the death of one of its residents. At the same time, an Australian named Ted (Clive Turner) arrives in town and strikes up a friendship with some of the locals, including an attractive young woman named Cheryl (Cheryl Allen). Meanwhile, a priest (John Huff), assisting a detective (John Ramsden) investigating another nearby murder, explains to him the history of a werewolf curse that now seems to be plaguing the area. He reveals that Ted was once present at a massacre at a Budapest castle and, as more deaths occur in Pioneer Town, some of the residents come to believe Ted is responsible. Ted is arrested, and it comes out that he is writing an expose of the town, which is said to harbor criminals; the priest and detective claim he is the werewolf and arm his guards with silver bullets. Cheryl helps Ted escape, but then turns on him, revealing that she, in fact, is the werewolf and plans to kill him to cover her identity. But the detective has set her up and loaded her gun with blanks; after she transforms into lupine form, she is killed with silver bullets. Ted goes free, and he and the townspeople forgive each other.

This crashing, unscary bore comes off as less a horror film than a vanity project for star Clive Turner, who also served as writer, producer, supervising editor and postproduction supervisor, in addition to stealing full directing credit from co-director Roger Nall (who, under the circumstances, was probably just as happy to lose it). The genre elements are strictly perfunctory, as much of the movie is devoted to a down-home depiction of the denizens of Pioneer Town, most of whom play themselves. (An amusing end title states that while the movie's events are fictitious, the characters in the town are real.) Long scenes, meandering dialogue, dumb in-jokes (there's an ineffectual running gag about George Jones), and endless country-and-western song interludes are no substitute for scares. Many of the movie's werewolf scenes consist of flashbacks to HOWLINGs IV and V, while the red-tinted point-of-view shots and lackluster effects that make up the new monster footage are mercifully given little screen time. *(Graphic violence, profanity.)* — M.G.

d, Clive Turner; p, Clive Turner; exec p, Edward Simons; assoc p, Kent Adamson, John Ramsden; w, Clive Turner (based on the *Howling* novels by Gary Brandner); ph, Andreas Kossak; ed, Clive Turner; m, Guy Moon; art d, Helen Harwell; sound, Charles Kelly; fx, S.O.T.A. FX; cos, Caroline Mills; makeup, Stephanie Fowler

Horror   **(PR: O   MPAA: R)**

HUNTED, THE   ★★★
(U.S.) 110m Davis Entertainment; The Goldstein Co. ~ Universal c

Christopher Lambert *(Paul Racine)*; John Lone *(Kinjo)*; Joan Chen *(Kirina)*; Yoshio Harada *(Takeda)*; Yoko Shimada *(Mieko)*; Mari Natsuki *(Junko)*; Tak Kubota *(Oshima)*; Masumi Okada *(Lt. Wadakura)*; Tatsuya Irie *(Hiryu)*; Hideyo Amamoto *(Mr. Motogi)*; Michael Warren *(Chase)*; Bart Anderson *(John)*; James Saito *(Nemura)*; Seth Sakai *(Dr. Otozo Yamura)*; Toshishiro Obata *(Ryuma)*; Ken Kensei *(Sujin)*; Hiroyasu Takagi *(Misato)*; Jason Furukawa *(Bartender)*; Naoko Sasaki *(Officer Noako)*; Warren Takeuchi *(Officer at Hospital)*; Dean Choe *(1st Ninja)*; Victor Kimura *(Medical Technician)*; Iris Salmon *(1st Surgeon)*; Jack Mar *(2nd Surgeon)*; Hisami Kaneta *(Nurse)*; Anthony Towe

(Fumio); Kuniharu Tamura *(Noraki)*; Tong Lung *(Detective)*; Reina Reyes *(Small Girl)*; Hiroshi Nakatsuka *(Taxi Driver)*; Jay Ono *(Train Controlman)*; Hiro Kanagawa *(Lieutenant)*; Mercedes Tang *(Mistress)*; Ryoto Sakata *(Officer on Train)*; Ken Shimizu *(Rookie)*; Sumi Mutoh *(Sumi)*; Chieko Sugano *(Dancer)*

Underpraised by mainstream print and media critics hung up on such niceties as plot logic, this pure action film offers contact sports with such lightning-paced eclat that the thrill-seekers for whom the movie is intended will find themselves in a state of blissful battery.

On a business trip to Japan, Paul Racine (Christopher Lambert) uncharacteristically indulges in a one-night stand with Kirina (Joan Chen), the fed-up mistress of an underworld don. Having bonded soulfully with the mysteriously tormented Kirina, Racine is horrified when he witnesses her beheading at the hands of ninja-master Kinjo (John Lone), whose face he sees. The invincible leader of a centuries-old samurai tradition, Kinjo vows to wipe out this witness. Racine initially rejects protection overtures from a modern warrior couple, Takeda (Yoshio Haruda) and Mieko (Yodo Shimada), who are opposed to Kinjo's bloody empire of intimidation, but finally allows himself to be whisked away to their feudal castle training center. Here Takeda seeks the angle that will force Kinjo into personal confrontation. As ruthless as his target, Takeda risks the lives of his disciples to settle a centuries-old feud christened in the blood of his ancestors.

On the island fortress, Racine quickly learns the basics of samurai warfare. Kinjo shows up to slay the gaijin Racine with a secret army of fighters who annihilate Takeda's gentler acolytes. Following the wounding of Mieko, Kinjo employs dirty tricks galore to outdo Takeda but does not count on fast-learner Racine who, after a few rounds, knocks out a temple's supports which crush Kinjo underneath the shrine.

Power-packed from start to finish, THE HUNTED does not succumb to the usual mysticism that retards the progress of so many martial arts machines. The screenplay cleverly exploits the irony that noble Takeda and conscienceless Kinjo are cut from the same unforgiving cloth. Unlike conventional action morality plays armed with black and white characters, THE HUNTED is a film about taking the low road to stay alive in modern times; the moral is that when two opponents are evenly matched, the one willing to cheat may wind up victorious. The combat is so plentiful that the movie seems to drive on a violence-autopilot, but the fight scenes are choreographed and filmed with breathtaking dexterity. In the sweep of its martial artistry, THE HUNTED is so far superior to run-of-the-mill kung fu entries that grateful fans can overlook its weaknesses: the biggest drawback being the Takeda-Kinjo rivalry having to take a back seat to the instant heroism of Racine, although it is clearly the high point of viewer involvement. However, the film packs enough lethal punch to overcome its insistence on putting an American figure in a spotlight better reserved for ninja masters, for whom life is a distant second to prevailing over the enemy. *(Graphic violence.)* — R.P.

d, J.F. Lawton; p, John A. Davis, Gary W. Goldstein; exec p, William Fay; assoc p, Yuriko Matsubara; w, J.F. Lawton; ph, Jack Conroy; ed, Robert A. Ferretti, Eric Strand; m, Motofumi Yamaguchi; prod d, Phil Dagort; art d, Sheila Haley; set d, Lin Macdonald; sound, Larry Sutton (mixer); fx, Bob Comer; casting, Karen Rea, Doreen Lane; cos, Rita Riggs; makeup, Margaret Solomon; stunts, Buddy Joe Hooker, John Wardlow, Tom Muzila

Thriller/Action/Martial Arts   **(PR: C   MPAA: R)**

HYENAS   ★★★½

(Senegal/Switzerland/France) 113m Thelma Film; ADR Productions; George Reinhardt Productions; DRS Television; Channel Four; Filmcompany ~ Kino International c
(HYENES; RAMATOU)

Mansour Diouf *(Dramaan Drameh)*; Ami Diakhate *(Linguere Ramatou)*; Mamadou Mahouredia Gueye *(The Mayor)*; Issa Ramagelissa Samb *(The Professor)*; Faly Drameh; Kaoru Egushi *(Toko)*; Djibril Diop Mambety *(Gaana)*; Hanny Tchelley *(An Amazon)*; Omar Ba *(The Head of Protocol)*; Calgou Fall *(The Priest)*; Abdoulaye Diop *(The Doctor)*; Rama Thiaw

Senegalese director Djibril Diop Mambety adapted this morality tale from Friedrich Durrenmatt's harrowing satirical play, *Der Besuch der alten Dame*. What's interesting here is how well Durrenmatt's themes come through, even when translated into an entirely different culture.

The African village of Colobane becomes severely impoverished when an unknown outsider buys the main factory and closes it down. The townspeople's hopes rise when word comes that the millionairess Linguere Ramatou (Ami Diakhate), a former inhabitant of Colobane, is returning. The Mayor (Mamadou Mahouredia Gueye) prepares a welcoming speech in praise of her and exhorts the inhabitants to be on their best behavior. The visitor turns out to be an ancient, indomitable lady, hobbling on one leg as a result of a plane crash years before.

Ramatou tells the villagers that she will give them $100 million if they fulfill a special request. She demands the life of one Dramaan Drameh (Mansour Diouf), the most popular man in town, destined to be its next mayor. It seems that this humble grocer had been in love with her in the far-off days of their youth. Yet, when she became pregnant, he threw her over in favor of a rich girl. He even went so far as to bribe two friends with wine to say that they, too, had slept with Ramatou. The outcast girl was forced to leave Colobane, in disgrace; she became a prostitute, as did her child.

The whole town, Dramaan included, is at first flabbergasted by this request. However, soon after, Dramaan's sleepy little store becomes a beehive of activity with crowds of villagers coming to buy all sorts of unaffordable luxuries, all on credit. He seeks the help of the local police and clergy, but they wave his fears aside. In desperation, he makes an attempt to leave town by train, but is detained by a threatening group of neighbors. However much they may want to resist Ramatou's influence, the futility of their efforts becomes clear when she reveals that she has indeed bought up the entire town, factory included. The Mayor calls a general meeting, during which he tells Dramaan that he must pay for the wrong he did. He offers Dramaan the option of suicide ("You'd leave the memory of a more or less decent human being") and hands him a gun. Dramaan refuses to give them such an easy out and decides to face the inevitable.

Mambety's translation is quite faithful to the original play and the African setting gives it an added, elemental power. His sure direction recalls the simple force of Zhang Yimou's best work. Matthias Kalin's fine photography keeps pace, with hypnotic imagery: the bleakly beautiful desert; shimmering seascapes; and the milling townspeople in their gaudy, newly-acquired finery. Acting as wordless accompanists to the drama are various native beasts: languorous baboons; quizzical owls; hovering vultures and, of course, the dangerous packs of hyenas which reflect the townspeople's growing rapaciousness. The startling scenes of crass consumerism taking hold of Colobane are every bit as menacingly funny as they were in the original. Waxis Diop's music is a strikingly evocative blend of romantic Spanish guitars and stirring African chants. Diouf's performance as a simple, foolish man who makes some fatally easy choices, grows steadily in tragic stature. Diakhato's stylized acting lends her the grandeur of a Byzantine empress and is effectively impenetrable. Reminiscing about their early love, the two have a banked chemistry that's like a faint, near-dead ember hidden in the ashes. *(Adult situations, violence.)* — D.N.

d, Djibril Diop Mambety; p, Pierre-Alain Meier, Alain Rozanes; assoc p, Maag Daan, George Reinhardt; w, Djibril Diop Mambety (based on the the play "Der Besuch der alten Dame" by Friedrich Durrenmatt, adapted from his novel *Der Besuch*); ph, Matthias Kalin; ed, Loredana Cristelli; m, Wasis Diop; sound, Maguette Salla; cos, Oumou Sy

Drama/Comedy   **(PR: C   MPAA: NR)**

I AM CUBA ★★★★
(Russia/Cuba) 141m Mosfilm; ICAIC ~
Milestone Films c
(YA KUBA)

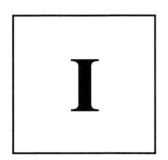

Luz Maria Collazo *(Maria/Betty)*; Jose Gallardo *(Pedro)*; Sergio Corrieri *(Alberto)*; Mario Gonzalez *(Pablo)*; Jean Bouise *(Jim)*; Raul Garcia *(Enrique)*; Celia Rodriguez *(Gloria)*; Salvador Vud; Alberto Morgan; Fausto Mirabel; Roberto Garcia York; Maria de las Mercedes Diez; Barbara Dominguez; Jesus del Monte; Luisa Maria Jimenez; Tony Lopez; Hector Castaneda; Rosando Lamadris; Raquel Revuelta *(Cuba's Voice)*; N. Nikitina *(Russian Text Reader)*; G. Yepifantsev *(Russian Text Reader)*

An epic celebration of the revolution that brought Fidel Castro to power, I AM CUBA is much more than a Cold War-era curiosity. This 1964 Soviet-Cuban co-production, unearthed and released in the US in 1995, is an audaciously stylish movie that dazzles viewers with one spectacularly inventive shot after another.

The film unfolds in four parts, each a didactic tale about the pre-revolutionary era. The first is set in decadent Havana, where by day women parade poolside in bikinis and high-heeled mules for men in dark glasses. By night, everyone has a daiquiri in one hand and a cigar in the other. It is into this world that a poor sweet Havana girl sinks, becoming a prostitute servicing American tourists. In the second story, an old sugar farmer is about to be evicted from his land by the United Fruit Company. He sends his two children to town to spend his last peso, swilling Coca Cola and playing the jukebox, while he sets fire to his house and his cane fields and collapses in despair.

The third section opens with the pronouncement: "Who is responsible for this? Batista." University students demonstrate and plot against the government. Caught red-handed with a copy of *Lenin: The State And Revolution*, they become martyrs to the revolutionary cause. In the final segment, a simple peasant—who only wants to live in peace—is driven from his home by aerial bombings, delivered by Batista's air force. He sees the light about the need to take up arms and heads to a rebel camp in the Sierra Maestra, where Castro's bearded troops welcome him as a comrade. The film's magnificent images are accompanied by a spare poetic narration.

Filming began on Mikhail Kalatozov's I AM CUBA one month after the Cuban Missile Crisis and five years after Fidel Castro had come to power. To the Soviets, Castro's regime then seemed to be a model for the revolutionary transformation of post-colonial states. Influenced by Sergei Eisenstein, Kalatozov created his own POTEMKIN for the people of Cuba. Just as POTEMKIN had celebrated the Russian people's liberation from the Czar, I AM CUBA would glorify that country's liberation from Batista and his greedy, US-backed dictatorship. Kalatozov teamed with his long-time cinematographer Sergei Urusevsky, Cuban novelist Enrique Pineda Barnet, and Soviet poet Yevgeny Yevtushenko to produce 141-minute epic. (Yevtushenko had worked as a correspondent in Cuba for *Pravda* and was at that time a friend of Castro.)

I AM CUBA was not shown outside Cuba and the Soviet Union until the 1992 Telluride Film Festival, where it was screened—without English titles—as part of a special tribute to Mikhail Kalatozov. Kalatozov is best known for THE CRANES ARE FLYING, which won the Golden Palm at the 1958 Cannes Film Festival. Critical reaction to I AM CUBA was strong, and Francis Ford Coppola, Martin Scorsese, and Milestone Film teamed together to subtitle the film in English and release it in the US. The film is immensely entertaining and occasionally inspiring, a delirious combination of Slavic solemnity, Latin exoticism, Communist idealism and breathtakingly beautiful images. It is best enjoyed on the big screen. — J.S.

d, Mikhail Kalatozov; p, Mikhail Kalatozov; w, Yevgeny Yevtushenko, Enrique Pineda Barnet; ph, Sergei Urusevsky; ed, N. Glagoleva; m, Carlos Farinas; sound, V. Sharun

Docudrama/Drama   (PR: A   MPAA: NR)

I CAN'T SLEEP ★★
(France) 110m Arena Films; Orsans Productions; Pyramide Productions; Les Films de Mindif; France 3 Cinema; MG Films; Agora Films; Vega Film ~ New Yorker Films c
(J'AI PAS SOMMEIL)

Katherina Golubeva *(Daiga)*; Richard Courcet *(Camille)*; Vincent Dupont *(Raphael)*; Laurent Grevill *(Le Docteur)*; Ira Mandella-Paul *(Harry)*; Alex Descas *(Theo)*; Irina Grjebina *(Mina)*; Tolsty *(Vassili)*; Patrick Grandperret *(Abel)*; Sophie Simon *(Alice)*; Line Renaud *(Ninon)*; Beatrice Dalle *(Mona)*

Potentially explosive material—the 1987 murders of 20 elderly Parisian women by a gay interracial couple—is tastefully dampened by the arthouse stylings of French director Clair Denis (CHOCOLAT). This docudrama about multicultural Paris is elegant to a fault, slackly paced, and generally tedious. Even the drag show is dull.

I CAN'T SLEEP follows a few loosely connected characters around Paris, where the murders of several elderly women in the 18th District has gripped the city. A young woman immigrant from Vilnius, Daiga (Katerina Golubeva), discovers that one of the murderers is Camille (Richard Courcet), a transvestite from the Antilles who resides at the same hotel where she works as a maid. Camille and his lover, Raphael (Vincent Dupont), continue committing the gruesome crimes—without an apparent motive—but Camille's brother, Theo (Alex Descas), a musician and carpenter, is too distant from Camille to help him. Theo also has his own set of problems to resolve, as he fights with his wife, Mona (Beatrice Dalle), about moving back to Martinique with their child, Harry (Ira Mandella-Paul).

One night, Daiga follows Camille through the city. When she sees that he has been arrested by the police, she returns to his hotel room where she steals his stash of money. Meanwhile, Theo and the rest of Camille's family are summoned to the police station, where they are shocked by Camille's confession to the murders (in his defense, he observes that "the world's gone crazy"). Camille's mother feels anguish and lashes out at her son, while Theo simply walks away from his brother. Daiga flees Paris with the money.

I CAN'T SLEEP curiously fails to make much of its potentially rich thematic material—class, race, gender and sexual identity, etc. Like its handsome anti-hero, it's a stylishly appointed cipher. Denis throws out classical story structure, character development, and the dimestore psychoanalysis of typical serial-killer films. The resultant lack of suspense—indeed, of any narrative interest—is presumably deliberate. Still, the many well-drawn characters provide just enough substance to keep most viewers awake. Denis also scores some points by interpolating shrill television and radio commentary, suggesting society's complicity in the crimes.

On a purely technical level, I CAN'T SLEEP is impressive. The de-saturated color design is pretty, though it won't look like much on video. The absence of traditional scoring accentuates a few canny uses of diegetic music. The performers are generally fine, but Courcet's amateurish performance almost scuttles the whole enterprise. *(Violence, nudity, sexual situations, adult situations, profanity.)*

d, Claire Denis; p, Bruno Pesery; assoc p, Ruth Waldburger, Fabienne Vonier; w, Claire Denis, Jean-Pol Fargeau; ph, Agnes Godard; ed, Nelly Quettier; m, John Pattison; prod d, Thierry Flamand, Arnaud DeMoleron; sound, Vincent Arnardi (mixer), Thierry Lebon (mixer), Jean-Louis Ughetto (engineer), Anne-Marie L'Hote; cos, Claire Fraisse; makeup, Daniele Vaurin

Drama/Crime (PR: O MPAA: NR)

I JUST WASN'T MADE FOR THESE TIMES
(SEE: BRIAN WILSON: I JUST WASN'T MADE FOR THESE TIMES)

I LIKE TO PLAY GAMES ★
(U.S.) 95m Playboy Entertainment; Cameo Films ~ A-Pix Entertainment c

Lisa Boyle *(Suzanne)*; Ken Steadman *(Michael)*; James Dizazzo *(Nick)*; Pamela Dickerson *(Melody)*; Toshiya Agata *(Kobe)*; Tom Druzbick *(Lochran)*; Jennifer Burton *(Tiffany)*; Monique Noel *(Valerie)*; Brittney Kwon *(Asian Girl)*; Cappucino Moore *(Jock)*; Cheryl Rixon *(Sean)*; Kenneth Roussel *(Alexis)*

You won't find any of the characters in this silly sex binge filing sex-harassment lawsuits. It's a softcore flick set in an office in which kinkiness is part of everyone's job description.

Jock ad exec Michael (Ken Steadman) dumps his latest lust-bunny Melody (Pamela Dickerson) because he feels their sex life is dull. Once he eyes the new marketing/media agent Suzanne Bronhill (Lisa Boyle), he's convinced she's the babe who can fly him to moon. Warned by Suzanne's discarded playmate Nick (James Dizazzo) that this ballbuster will feed him through a sexual shredder, Michael nonetheless pursues the teasing tramp. As ambitious as she is controlling, Suzanne drives Michael wild with a series of interrupted pleasures and then finally waxes his surfboard, so to speak, when he should be prepared for a meeting with a Japanese client. Never repeating any sex game twice, Suzanne dazzles Michael by switching from spankable school-girl to dominatrix. Even when dumped Nick drugs himself into a stupor, Michael remains convinced he can handle her. To his chagrin, Suzanne not only outshines his campaign ideas at work, but also sleeps with the important Japanese client. After Suzanne bags Michael when he breaks a cardinal rule by declining a challenge to include Melody in a *menage a trois*, Michael falls apart. He bugs heartless Suzanne until she has him arrested for rape. Striving for ascendancy, Michael hits Suzanne with a fake suicide pact, but she strikes back by persuading her new cop boy toy to arrest him. Only when Michael counters by nearly drowning her does the turbo-slut admit that she loves Michael and is willing to cry uncle!

For all the lip smacks and pelvic thrusts, this ineffectual, childish romp goes where other skinflicks have already gone before. Despite the vexatious vixen's reputation, her methods (bondage, candle wax, public sex) are old hat in the arena of direct-to-video sleaze. Although every cast member, even extras, seems to have spent life at a gym, the actors don't exude any personality—it's as if their only signs of life emanate from erogenous zones. Boyle has a body stacked with sinuous curves, but is stuck with an immature voice and a nagging demeanor; where's Shannon Tweed when you really need her? The preposterous business setting, perhaps a nod to DISCLOSURE, gives fresh meaning to the notion of a leg up the corporate ladder.

(Extreme profanity, extensive nudity, substance abuse, sexual situations.) — R.P.

d, Moctezuma Lobato; p, Nick Zuvic, Vivian Mayhew; w, David Keith Miller; ph, Kim Haun; ed, Josh Kanin; m, Herman Beeftink; prod d, Meike Kopp; art d, Cecil Gentry; sound, Stephen Tibbo (mixer); casting, Lori Cobe

Erotic/Thriller (PR: O MPAA: NR)

I, THE WORST OF ALL ★★★½
(Argentina) 100m Gea Cinematografica ~ First Run Features c
(YO, LA PEOR DE TODAS)

Assumpta Serna *(Sister Juana Ines de la Cruz)*; Dominique Sanda *(Vice-Reine Maria Luisa)*; Hector Alterio *(Viceroy)*; Lautaro Murua *(Archbishop of Mexico)*; Alberto Segado *(Father Miranda)*; Franklin Caicedo *(Santa Cruz—Bishop of Puebla)*; Graciela Araujo *(Sister Ursula)*; Gerardo Romano *(Siguenza)*; Hugo Soto; Margara Alonso; Lidia Catalano; Margarita Padin; Alejandro Colunga; Rosario Blefari; Felisa Rocha; Emma Rivera; Fernando Noy; Jose Martin; Walter Soubrie; Jesus Berenguer; Guillermo Marin; Nicolas Alvarado; Susana Cortinez; Alice Elias; Monica Lacoste; Pedro Cano; Marcos Woinski; Issac Haimovici; Nestor Sacco; Arnaldo Colombaroli; Alejandro Maci; Oscar Milazzo; Nicolas Cardasco; Jean-Piere Reguerraz; Lorena Lopez; Fernanda Ronsisvalli; Andrea Rodriguez; Karina Allegue; Luciana Mastromaura; Victoria Solarz; Scaramuzza; Norma Suzat

Bringing to the screen the tragic true story of 17th-century Mexican writer and poet Sister Juana Ines de la Cruz in I, THE WORST OF ALL, Maria Luisa Bemberg has fashioned an eloquent statement about freedom and repression.

A brilliant freethinker, Sister Juana Ines de la Cruz (Assumpta Serna) entered the convent at the age of 19, as the only alternative to marriage and motherhood for a woman of her class. The convent promised her the freedom to follow her own pursuits, and her lavish room is filled with books, scientific instruments and manuscripts of her poems and plays. Sister Juana enjoys the protection and friendship of the Viceroy (Hector Alterio) and his beautiful, cultured wife, Maria Luisa (Dominique Sanda), and engages in genteel intellectual discussions with dignitaries from the court and the church. But some of her ideas seem dangerously radical; in the shadow of the infamously brutal Inquisition, very little dissent will be tolerated in "New Spain". When a conservative, woman-hating Archbishop (Lautaro Murua) is appointed to Mexico, he makes it his personal mission to punish Sister Juana for her "scientific digressions in the fashion of godless Europe."

Even as the heavy hand of the Inquisition creeps closer to her privileged room where she engages in the "adventure of knowledge", Sister Juana discovers a life beyond that of her mind. She falls in love with Maria Luisa, who becomes her muse as well as her guardian. The two women discuss the arts and sciences—all in an atmosphere charged with unconsummated passion. The Viceroy and Vicereine eventually return to Spain, where the Vicereine publishes Sister Juana's poetry. Sister Juana dies at the age of 44, having survived the Plague, but with her spirit broken.

Sister Juana Ines de la Cruz is considered one of the finest poets in the Spanish language today. Based on the book *The Traps of Faith* by Nobel Prize-winner Octavio Paz, I, THE WORST OF ALL is arguably Maria Luisa Bemberg's most overtly political film and a powerful indictment of religious and political repression. Bemberg, who died in 1995, was one of Argentina's most important filmmakers, and like many of her heroines, battled against conventions. Not only was she a woman who rose to the top of her profession in a national industry rife with machismo, but she did not become involved in theater and film until she was in her late 50s. In 1984, she was nominated for the Best Foreign Film Academy Award for CAMILA. I, THE WORST OF ALL was made in 1990; Bemberg's last film was I DON'T WANT TO TALK ABOUT IT (DE ESO NO SE HABLA) in 1993.

With its cool claustrophobia drawn from the sumptuous austerity of the cloisters, I, THE WORST OF ALL is a fascinating tribute to an extraordinary, unconfined woman. — J.S.

d, Maria Luisa Bemberg; p, Lita Stantic; exec p, Gilbert Marouani; w, Maria Luisa Bemberg, Antonio Larreta (based on the book *The Traps of Faith* by Octavio Paz); ph, Felix Monti; ed, Juan Carlos Macias; m, Luis Maria Serra; prod d, Voytek; art d, Daniel Mora; fx, Enrique Gandaras, Rodolfo Denevi, Hugo Sica; cos, Graciela Galan; makeup, Mirta Blanco

Drama/Biography/Religious   **(PR: A   MPAA: NR)**

IL POSTINO
(SEE: POSTMAN, THE)

IN THE DEEP WOODS   ★
(U.S.) 95m Frederic Golchan Productions;
Leonard Hill Films ~ Atlantic Entertainment c

Rosanna Arquette *(Joanna Warren)*; Anthony Perkins *(Paul Miller)*; Will Patton *(Eric Gaines)*; D.W. Moffatt *(Frank McCarry)*; Chris Rydell *(Tommy Warren)*; Amy Ryan *(Beth)*; Beth Broderick *(Myra Cantrell)*; Harold Sylvester *(George Dunaway)*; Kimberly Beck *(Margot)*; Paul Perri *(Allen Harkins)*; Greg Kean *(Ken Hollister)*; Ned Bellamy *(Jerome Spears)*; Mary Gregory *(Grace Warren)*; David Grant Wright *(Larry Jenner)*; Ava Lazar *(Cynthia Manning)*; Donalee Wood *(Jeanne Donaldson)*; Rochelle Swanson *(Allison Cox)*; D.J. Sullivan *(Sarah Hubbard)*; Mik Scriba *(Mark Cassell)*; Virginia Hawkins *(Helen Resnick)*; Shirley Saunders *(1st Bookstore Manager)*; Ellen Dubin *(2nd Manager)*; Elizabeth Soukop *(Officer Benson)*; Kevin O'Neill *(1st Detective)*; Spike Sorrentino *(2nd Detective)*; Steve Tom *(Master of Ceremonies)*; Janet Haley *(Elderly Woman)*

The video box misleadingly presents IN THE DEEP WOODS as an erotic thriller, when in fact this 1995 video release is actually a tepid 1992 made-for-TV film, with no sex, violence, or substance.

At the start of the film, a number of women have been found dead. Joanna Warren (Rosanna Arquette), a children's author, knows one of the victims, and becomes involved with the police's search for the killer. She is approached by nervous, mysterious private detective Paul Miller (Anthony Perkins), who claims his daughter was one of the victims. Miller suggests to Joanna that her brother Tommy (Chris Rydell) is a suspect in the crime and that he won't stop murdering unless Joanna convinces him to confess. Miller's creepy manner, seeming dishonesty, and penchant for showing up in unexpected places frighten Joanna. She stands by her brother, even though the evidence begins to mount against him. When one of Joanna's friends is killed, Joanna finds evidence that Tommy is guilty. She confronts him, and he confesses. When Joanna and Tommy were children, their father was killed in a boat accident that left Tommy unharmed. From then on, their mother always treated Joanna better than him. The murders were a misguided attempt to get back at Joanna. After confessing, Tommy tries to escape, but is killed.

IN THE DEEP WOODS is a lame psychological thriller. The cinematography is unimaginative and repetitive. The first shot of

Miller, mysteriously watching the action from afar, establishes him as someone not to be trusted. Unfortunately, director Charles Correll feels the necessity to repeat the shot every five minutes, until Miller's hackneyed trench coat and stare become laughable. Similarly, during each killing, the camera cuts to the same static shot of the woods as we hear the victim's screams. Full of plot holes, contrivances, and stupid dialogue, the writing is equally desperate. In one scene, a police officer follows Joanna down a dark street and scares her, only to tell her he was concerned for her safety. The scene's sole purpose, to establish him as a suspect, is never followed up. When Tommy is finally proven to be the actual killer, we discover that his pattern of killing was based upon childhood nursery rhymes, yet it's never explained how that relates to his hatred of women in general and of Joanna in particular. The acting is perfunctory, suggesting that the performers know they're in a turkey and just want to get it over with. Rosanna Arquette is particularly indifferent, though she does show off an amazing collection of sunglasses. *(Violence, adult situations.)* — A.M.

d, Charles Correll; exec p, Frederic Golchan, Leonard Hill, Ron Gilbert, Joel Fields; assoc p, Ardythe Goergens; w, Robert Nathan, Robert Rosenblum (based on the novel by Nicholas Conde); ph, James Glennon; ed, Mark W. Rosenbaum; m, Sylvester Levay; prod d, Johnathan Carlson; set d, Susan Degus; sound, Jay Patterson; casting, Molly Lopata; cos, Robert Eli Bodford, Jr.; makeup, Paula Sutor

Mystery/Thriller   **(PR: A   MPAA: NR)**

IN THE MOUTH OF MADNESS   ★★½
(U.S.) 94m New Line ~ New Line c

Sam Neill *(John Trent)*; Julie Carmen *(Linda Styles)*; Jurgen Prochnow *(Sutter Cane)*; Charlton Heston *(Jackson Harglow)*; David Warner *(Dr. Wrenn)*; John Glover *(Saperstein)*; Bernie Casey *(Robinson)*; Peter Jason *(Paul)*; Frances Bay *(Mrs. Pickman)*; Wilhem von Homburg *(Simon)*; Kevin Rushton *(Guard)*; Gene Mack *(Guard)*; Conrad Bergschneider *(Axe Maniac)*; Marvin Scott *(Reporter)*; Katherine Ashby *(Receptionist)*; Ben Gilbert *(Young Teen)*; Dennis O'Connor *(Cop)*; Paul Brogen *(Scrawny Teen)*; Sharon Dyer *(Homeless Woman)*; Sean Ryan *(Bicycle Boy)*; Lance Paton *(Little Boy)*; Jacelyn Holmes *(Little Girl)*; Hayden Christensen *(Paperboy)*; Garry Robbins *(Truck Driver)*; Sean Roberge *(Desk Clerk)*; Robert Lewis Bush *(Hotel Man)*; Louise Beaven *(Old Lady)*; Cliff Woolner *(Bus Driver)*; Deborah Theaker *(Municipal Woman)*; Chuck Campbell *(Customer)*; Carolyn Tweedle *(Nurse)*; Thom Bell *(Farmer)*; Mark Adriaans *(Window Teen)*; Jack Moore-Wickham *(Simon's Son, Johnny)*; David Austerwell; Richard Kohler; Kieran Sells; Laura Schmidt; Kyle Sheenan; Daniel Verhoeven; Kevin Zegers; Katie Zegers *(Group of Kids)*

John Carpenter tackles more complex material than usual with this film, and the results are entertaining but lack the scary directness of his best work.

From a padded cell, where he has covered the walls and his face and body with crosses, John Trent (Sam Neill) explains to a doctor how he got there. An insurance investigator, Trent is hired by publisher Jackson Harglow (Charlton Heston) to find best-selling horror author Sutter Cane (Jurgen Prochnow), who has vanished before completing his new novel, *In the Mouth of Madness*. Cane's fans have been rioting, and when Trent begins reading Cane's previous books, he suffers from bizarre dreams. From their cover designs, Trent pieces together a map revealing the location of Hobbs End, the novels' fictional setting. Accompanied by Cane's editor, Styles (Julie Carmen), he sets out to drive there.

The trip is unnervingly surreal, and when they arrive at Hobbs End, they discover it is identical to the town in Cane's books. Styles tells the skeptical Trent that they are living out the author's latest novel, and when Cane himself is discovered inside a church, he reveals that his writings have been guided by a race of alien creatures who plot to use them to invade our planet. Styles is overtaken by the evil forces, and Trent manages to escape to the outside world, where he burns Cane's completed manuscript.

He soon finds, however, that the book has already been published and is causing worldwide riots and mutations. Killing a possessed attacker leads Trent to the asylum, and that night he hears horrible sounds beyond his cell. Escaping the next day, he discovers both the asylum and the city beyond deserted and ruined. Venturing into a theater showing IN THE MOUTH OF MADNESS the movie, he watches it and begins to laugh maniacally.

The idea of a horror novelist's writings being based on real evil certainly has potential, but in terms of dramatic construction, IN THE MOUTH OF MADNESS has not been well thought-out. The fatal flaw lies in the characterization of Trent, who spends most of the film voicing his denial of the frightening events he witnesses, believing the whole thing to be a publicity stunt. It is hard to be scared for a character who is not scared himself.

Once the film reaches its third act, as Trent realizes and encounters the widespread effects of Cane's work, it begins to cast the creepy spell it is aiming for, with the kind of chilly open ending that only Carpenter still seems willing to put into horror films these days. It is too bad, though, that for a good deal of the running time, he tries too hard to keep the audience on edge with quick-flash visuals (KNB EFX's apparently extensive creature creations are barely glimpsed) and loud noises; while there is plenty of atmosphere, it is rarely as scary as one hopes from a Carpenter movie. (*Graphic violence, profanity.*) — M.G.

d, John Carpenter; p, Sandy King; exec p, Michael De Luca; assoc p, Artist Robinson; w, Michael De Luca; ph, Gary B. Kibbe; ed, Edward A. Warschilka; m, John Carpenter, Jim Lang ; prod d, Jeff Steven Ginn; art d, Peter Grundy; set d, Elinor Rose Galbraith; sound, John Pospisil (design), Owen A. Langevin (mixer), Ron Bartlett (mixer), Larry Hoki (recordist); fx, Martin Malivoire, Ted Ross, Bruce Nicholson, Industrial Light & Magic; casting, Back Seat Casting; cos, Robert Bush, Robin Michel Bush; makeup, Donald J. Mowat, Robert Kurtzman, Gregory Nicotero, Howard Berger, K.N.B. EFX Group; stunts, Jeff Imada

Horror   **(PR: O   MPAA: R)**

IN THE NAME OF THE EMPEROR   ★★★
(U.S.) 52m Film News Now Foundation ~
Film News Now Foundation c/bw

Robin Brentano; Ted Hannon; Matthew Myers; Lamar Sanders; Sam Schacht (*Narrator*)

This genuinely shocking documentary exposes Japan's WWII war crimes and explores the reasons for the convenient historical amnesia afflicting both Japan and the US.

A Chinese woman, miraculously still alive, her identity lost to history, bends over for the camera, the better to display the mutilation wrought by Japanese soldiers who attempted to behead her. As evidence of man's inhumanity to man (and woman), these few, horrific frames of film are heartstopping. They are also irrefutable proof that history has been host to many holocausts, and not just the ones we are willing to talk about.

In 1937, Japan invaded the Chinese capital of Nanjing and within six weeks, some 300,000 Chinese were killed and 20,000

women raped. As the documentary makes clear, this scourge of history, the "Rape of Nanjing," is barely known today, largely due to the white-washing of WWII era historians, as well as the traditional Japanese educational and political policy of "don't ask, don't tell." The film recounts how the US government helped facilitate this cover-up through insufficient investigation and punishment during the Tokyo war crimes tribunal following WWII.

Christine Choy and Nancy Tong, the directors of this incisive, crucially important documentary, went into the Shinjiku district of today's Tokyo and interviewed young people, all of whom professed total ignorance of these dark events. The filmmakers also interviewed various professors, whose reactions range from complete, shameful denial to the anguished, frustrated attempts of a few brave souls to throw light on the truth.

The Ministry of Education was forbidden to write about the massacre—as a result, textbooks have long been censored. However, invaluable footage of the invasion, which includes the above-mentioned moment, was surreptitiously filmed by the Reverend John Magee, an American missionary. We hear entries from the diary he kept which tell of the harrowing sights witnessed and exhaustive attempts to help the hundreds of refugees who came to his door. Perhaps most chilling of all are the accounts of surviving Japanese soldiers, paragons of the "just following orders" school. They matter-of-factly describe skewering a woman and her two babies like potatoes or hunting people down like rabbits in the street. "It would have been all right if we'd only raped them—I shouldn't say 'all right,'" one recalls. "But we always stabbed and then killed them."

The film is a terse, impassioned flood of terrifying revelations that raise questions of tremendous importance. The Japanese tradition of saving face at all costs—which manifests itself not only in the cover-up of past atrocities but also in recent international skullduggery (e.g., the Daiwa Bank collapse)—reveals itself all too clearly here. This exceptional documentary will enlighten viewers not only about our common past, but also about the world that surrounds us today. (*Violence, adult situations, sexual situations.*) — D.N.

d, Nancy Tong, Christine Choy; p, Nancy Tong; ph, Christine Choy; ed, Nanette Burstein, Dan Tun

Documentary/Historical   **(PR: O   MPAA: NR)**

INCREDIBLY TRUE ADVENTURES   ★★★
OF TWO GIRLS IN LOVE, THE
(U.S.) 95m Smash Pictures ~ Fine Line c

Laurel Holloman (*Randy Dean*); Nicole Parker (*Evie Roy*); Maggie Moore (*Wendy*); Kate Stafford (*Rebecca Dean*); Sabrina Artel (*Vicky*); Toby Poser (*Lena*); Nelson Rodriguez (*Frank*); Dale Dickey (*Regina*); Andrew Wright (*Hayjay*); Stephanie Berry (*Evelyn Roy*); Babs Davy (*Waitress*); John Elson (*Ali*); Katlin Tyler (*Girl No. 1*); Anna Padgett (*Girl No. 2*); Chelsea Cattouse (*Girl No. 3*); Lillian Kiesler (*Old Lady No. 1*); Maryette Charlton (*Old Lady No. 2*); Katlin Tyler

In Maria Maggenti's tender, lighthearted debut feature, two high school seniors fall in love for the first time; the twist is that they are both girls.

A series of comic misadventures is triggered by the unlikely schoolgirl romance between a rebellious, gas-pumping tomboy, Randy Dean (Laurel Hollomon), and one of the smartest, most beautiful girls in the class, Evie Roy (Nicole Parker). One day Evie pulls her Range Rover into the gas station where Randy works part-time. Instantly charmed by each other, the two meet again at school and a romance blossoms. Working class African American Randy lives with her lesbian aunt (Kate Stafford) and her aunt's lover. She's struggling at school and probably won't graduate. Upper class white Evie lives with her mother (Stephanie Berry) in an elegant home. She's a high achiever at school and is headed for college. Randy is a bit of a loner; Evie is one of the most popular girls in the school. Randy knows she's a lesbian, Evie just knows that she has fallen in love with Randy. THE INCREDIBLY TRUE ADVENTURE OF TWO GIRLS IN LOVE follows Randy and Evie as they experience the intense thrill of first love, and encounter the disapproval of family and friends. When Evie's mother goes out of town on business, the two girls decide to consummate their love after an awkward evening of candlelit wining and dining. Discovered *en repose* by Evie's horrified mother, but determined to stick together against all odds, the two girls flee; everything culminates in a showdown at a motel where family and friends converge to keep the young lovers from running away together.

THE INCREDIBLY TRUE ADVENTURE OF TWO GIRLS IN LOVE is a charming romantic comedy about coming-of-age. Essentially a conventional genre picture—carried by the spirit of boundless teen-love optimism—its only real distinguishing feature is that the romance is between two girls. The performances by the young leads, who have previously worked in theater, are captivating in a naturalistic, slightly awkward way. Writer-director Maria Maggenti has achieved excellent production values in this "no-budget" film. While the script reveals an excellent ear for authentic teen dialogue, the climax misfires, playing only as screwball silliness. Though THE INCREDIBLY TRUE ADVENTURE OF TWO GIRLS IN LOVE is likely to be of most interest to lesbians who can identify with its story, it does have broader appeal because of its portrayal of a universal rite of passage. *(Sexual situations.)* — J.S.

d, Maria Maggenti; p, Dolly Hall; assoc p, Zoe Oka Edwards, Mark Huisman, Melissa Painter; co-p, A. John Rath; w, Maria Maggenti; ph, Tami Reiker; ed, Susan Graef; m, Terry Dame; prod d, Ginger Tougas; art d, Betsy Alton; sound, Steven Borne (design); casting, Heidi Griffiths; cos, Cheryl Hurwitz

Drama/Comedy/Romance (PR: C   MPAA: R)

INDIAN IN THE CUPBOARD, THE ★★★½
(U.S.) 96m Kennedy/Marshall Company; Scholastic Productions; Paramount; Columbia ~ Paramount c

Hal Scardino *(Omri)*; Litefoot *(Little Bear)*; Lindsay Crouse *(Jane)*; Richard Jenkins *(Victor)*; Rishi Bhat *(Patrick)*; Steve Coogan *(Tommy)*; David Keith *(Boone)*; Sakina Jaffrey *(Lucy)*; Vincent Kartheiser *(Gillon)*; Nestor Serrano *(Teacher)*; Ryan Olson *(Adiel)*; Leon Tejwani; Lucas Tejwani *(Baby Martin)*; Christopher Conte *(Purple Mohawk)*; Cassandra Brown *(Emily)*; Christopher Moritz *(Sam)*; Beni Malkin *(Ramon)*; Juliet Berman *(Tina)*; Stephen Morales *(Kiron)*; George Randall *(Indian Chief)*; Gia Galeano *(Yard Teacher)*; Kevin Malaro *(School Kid)*; Tom Bewley *("Darth Vader")*; Keii Johnston *("G.I. Joe")*; J.R. Horsting *("Robocop")*; Michael Papjohn *("Cardassian")*; Eric Stabnau *("Firengi")*

THE INDIAN IN THE CUPBOARD is an exemplary work of political correctness that generally avoids being preachy or cloying. Bolstered by strong performances, low-key direction and a playfully nuanced screenplay, the film endeavors to teach life lessons about the validity of unfamiliar cultures and the importance of empathy.

Omri (Hal Scardino) lives with his family in Manhattan's colorful Lower East Side, where he celebrates his ninth birthday. His gifts include an old wooden cupboard salvaged by older brother Gillon (Vincent Kartheiser) and a three-inch plastic fig-

ure of an American Indian brave, a present from best friend Patrick (Rishi Bhat). Omri's mother, Jane (Lindsay Crouse), gives him an old key for the cupboard door. He places the plastic Indian inside, locks the door, and goes to sleep. Awakened by a sound from the cupboard, Omri finds that the Indian has come to life. The English-speaking warrior—a veteran of the French-Indian Wars—is an Iroquois named Little Bear (Litefoot), who initially believes that the giant youngster is an incarnation of the Great Spirit.

Omri initially treats Little Bear like a pet but respects him more as he learns about his culture. He takes him outside to gather materials for a proper house. Briefly unattended, Little Bear is attacked by a bird. Omri borrows a plastic WWI medic from his older brother and brings to life Tommy Atkins (Steve Coogan), a British soldier fresh from the battlefield. Thinking he is dreaming, Tommy attends to the Indian's wounds before being placed back in the cupboard, where is returned to plastic form and transported back to his "real" life.

Omri shares his secret with Patrick, who ignores his warnings and brings a toy horseman to life. The cowboy Boone (David Keith), a teary boozer from the late 19th century, is immediately hostile to Little Bear, but they eventually become buddies. Omri and Patrick clash at school when the latter tries to show the tiny pair to classmates. Back at home, the friends all watch TV. Horrified and disoriented during a Western depicting the slaughter of Indian families, Little Bear shoots the cheering Boone with an arrow. Gillon has taken the cupboard in retaliation for Omri's mistreatment of his pet rat. Omri retrieves the cupboard, but the key is missing, so he is unable to avail himself of its magical powers. Little Bear retrieves the key, narrowly escaping the rat, and Omri brings Tommy back to save Boone.

The boy decides to send Little Bear and Boone back. As Little Bear describes a rite-of-passage through which he had been guiding his nephew before his magical abduction, Omri imagines himself beside his full-sized "uncle" in the forest. Called back to reality, Omri places his little friends in the cupboard and transforms them into toys. He reads aloud the conclusion of his adventure to his classmates at school.

Adapted from the acclaimed 1981 children's book by Lynn Reid Banks, THE INDIAN IN THE CUPBOARD marks the long overdue return of screenwriter Melissa Mathison to movies. Best known for scripting E.T. THE EXTRA-TERRESTRIAL and THE BLACK STALLION, Mathison (aka Mrs. Harrison Ford) excels at conjuring the private world of young boys. Frank Oz, a somewhat prosaic filmmaker, makes do with solid storytelling instead of big action set-pieces, chases, or star power. As rendered by Industrial Light and Magic, the special effects—though first-rate—hark back to the charming low-tech feel of the kiddie fantasies of yesteryear. Only Randy Edelman's over insistent score goes occasionally over-the-top.

The film offers subtle and unexpected pleasures for adult viewers: the tender and understated love expressed by the parents toward Omri; the boy's quiet alliance with his homemaker mother; and the gentle comparisons drawn between the lives of children, women, the elderly, and figures of Otherness. Another plus is the casting. The buck-toothed and beguilingly goofy Scardino (previously seen as a rival chess prodigy in SEARCHING FOR BOBBY FISHER) is a welcome alternative to the standard cute kid star. Keith provides sturdy comic support and Native American rapper Litefoot is properly strong and dignified. — K.G.

d, Frank Oz; p, Kathleen Kennedy, Frank Marshall, Jane Startz; exec p, Robert Harris, Martin Keltz, Bernie Williams; assoc p, Michelle Wright, Arthur F. Repola; w, Melissa Mathison (based on the novel by Lynne Reid Banks); ph, Russell Carpenter; ed,

Ian Crafford; m, Randy Edelman; prod d, Leslie McDonald; art d, Tony Fanning; set d, Chris L. Spellman; sound, Arthur Rochester (mixer); fx, Eric Brevig, David Blitstein, Michael Lanteri, Ginger Theisen, Anne Calanchini, Industrial Light & Magic; casting, Margery Simkin; cos, Deborah L. Scott; makeup, Felicity Bowring; stunts, Dennis R. Scott, Lynn Salvatori

Children's/Fantasy/Adventure   **(PR: AA   MPAA: PG)**

INDICTMENT: THE MCMARTIN TRIAL   ★★★½
(U.S.) 135m HBO Pictures; Ixtlan Productions; Abby Mann Productions; Breakheart Films ~ HBO Home Video c

James Woods *(Danny Davis)*; Mercedes Ruehl *(Lael Rubin)*; Lolita Davidovich *(Kee McFarlane)*; Sada Thompsn *(Virginia McMartin)*; Henry Thomas *(Raymond Buckey)*; Shirley Knight *(Peggy Buckey)*; Mark Blum *(Wayne Satz)*; Alison Elliott *(Peggy Ann Buckey)*; Chelsea Field *(Christine Johnson)*; Joe Urla *(Glenn Stevens)*; Scott Waara *(Dean Gits)*; Valerie Wildman *(Diana Sullivan)*; Richard Bradford *(Ira Reiner)*; Scott Armstrong *(Sean)*; Roberta Bassin *(Judy Johnson)*; Patricia Belcher *(Juror #1)*; Gabrielle Boni *(Tara)*; Kathryn Brock *(Sybil Brand Deputy)*; Betsy Brockhurst *(Angry Parent)*; Dennis Burkley *(George Freeman)*; Katsy Chappell *(Denise)*; Richelle Churchill *(Rubin's Secretary)*; Blake Molino Clausen *(Kid #5)*; Robert Clendenin *(Soundman)*; Sally Crawford *(Betty Raidor)*; James Cromwell *(Judge Pounders)*; Leigh Curran *(Faye)*; Gregg Daniel *(T.V. Reporter)*; Kadina Delejalde *(Sandy)*; Betty Donner *(Mary Ann Jackson)*; Zachary Eginton *(Sam)*; Cassidy Ellis *(Heather)*; Ramsey Ellis *(Jonathan)*; Sean Emslie *(Bailiff)*; Jack English *(Chuck Buckey)*; Nicole Feenstra *(Girl)*; Miriam Flynn *(Judge Bobb)*; Mark Folger *(Bald Guard)*; Cherie Franklin *(Deputy Nell)*; Kate Fuglei *(Parent)*; Avner Garbi *(Fadeel)*; Taylor Gilbert *(Reporter #1)*; Castulo Guerra *(Martinez)*; Michael Haney *(Reporter #14)*; Seth Isler *(Male Parent)*; Denise Johnson *(Jennifer)*; Austin Kottke *(Kid #4)*; Annie La Russa *(Reporter #11)*; Greg Lauren *(Reporter #7)*; Richard B. Lemberger *(Concession Vendor)*; Josefina Lopez *(Female Inmate)*; Colin Patrick Lynch *(Fireman)*; Michael C. Mahon *(Bailiff)*; Kevin Malaro *(Kid #3)*; Mary Mara *(Detective Jane Hoag)*; Sandy Martin *(Deputy Phyllis)*; Courtland Mead *(Malcolm Johnson)*; Adam Meadows *(Kid #8)*; William Mesnik *(Dr. Merrick)*; Rolando Molina *(Court Clerk)*; Michael Monks *(Juror #3)*; Jessica Needham *(Kid #1)*; Tom Nolan *(Courthouse Deputy)*; Joycelyn O'Brien *(Babette Spitler)*; Sarah O'Nan *(Kid #6)*; Vic Polizos *(Jack Andrews)*; Richard Portnow *(Judge George)*; Jack Rader *(Sergeant Noble)*; Heather Ramsay *(Kid #9)*; Kerry Remsen *(Female Parent)*; June Saruwatari *(Reporter #9)*; Danny Schmittler *(Aaron)*; Eileen Seeley *(Pamela Bozanith)*; Arthur Senzy *(Reverend Parker)*; Tony Simotes *(Reporter #13)*; J.W. Smith *(Male Inmate)*; Charlie Stavola *(Juror #2)*; Shane Sweet *(Kid #2)*; Kevin Symons *(Reporter #12)*; A.C. Weary *(Reporter #8)*; David Whalen *(Reporter #5)*; Bernard White *(Reporter #10)*; Kenneth White *(Chief Kuhlmeyer)*; Clayton C. Whitfield *(Knudsen)*; Sanders Witkow *(Kid #7)*

One of the most searing films ever made for television, INDICTMENT recounts the real-life McMartin child abuse case and subtextually parallels the day care scandal with other major witch hunts throughout American history.

As the shocking charges against the McMartin Day Care Center owners and teachers roll in, rational disbelief and benefits-of-the-doubt are mowed down by a media frenzy. Railroaded by careerist prosecutors led by Lael Rubin (Mercedes Ruehl), and convicted by the press before the trial even begins, the falsely charged include grandmother Virginia McMartin (Sada

Thompson), daughter Peggy Buckey (Shirley Knight), grandson Raymond Buckey (Henry Thomas), granddaughter Peggy Ann Buckey (Alison Elliott), and several part-time instructors. Despite his wife's disapproval, naturally combative advocate Danny Davis (James Woods) stops defending drug lords in order to challenge an out-of-control judicial bandwagon. What begins as a grandstanding attempt to get high on controversy ends up resurrecting Davis's soul as he becomes convinced of his unpopular clients' innocence. Bolstered by public opinion, a poorly researched prosecution case proceeds despite misgivings by key players like Glenn Stevens (Joe Urla). Winning, not justice, is all that counts, even though the initial accusation came from Judy Johnson (Roberta Bassin), an alcoholic schizophrenic whose child was actually being molested by her estranged husband. Fueling parental outrage toward the McMartins is the manipulated testimony of the children, whose finger-pointing is orchestrated by an untrained social worker, Kee MacFarlane (Lolita Davidovich), who further compromises her integrity by sleeping with a media hound covering the case. Davis delves deeply enough to realize the alleged events couldn't really have occurred, the children direct wilder and wilder charges against the sheriff's department and townspeople, and the trumped-up prosecution case begins to crumble. Unfortunately, the unraveling of the McMartin miscarriage of justice (which in Raymond Buckey's case lasted 5 years), occurs too late to save the reputations and careers of the accused. Demonstrating that Rubin's case is a tapestry of conjecture and unsubstantiated accusations, and ripping apart inconsistencies in MacFarlane's methodology, Davis succeeds in achieving the Pyrrhic victory of a hung jury for Raymond. Although the legal nightmare ends, the aftershocks of the blanket condemnation of the McMartin day care workers continue to this day.

The indicted McMartin family and their employees were not the only victims of the wave of child abuse hysteria that swept America in the 80s. While there may never be an explanation for what triggered the witch hunts, the lessons are not edifying for zealous prosecutors, sensation-seeking crime addicts, or irresponsible journalists. Compressing a wealth of material that could have been spun out to major miniseries length, INDICTMENT's lynching-by-media scenario (recalling the Lindy Chamberlain case, filmed in 1988 as CRY IN THE DARK) skillfully turns the tables on the tabloid-debased media, incorporating shots of camera equipment and anonymous reporters into the weave of the film. In a controlled cinematic manner unusual in standard TV problem drama, INDICTMENT employs multiple camera angles and mesmerizing extreme closeups in the courtroom sequences, and makes the jaundiced perspective of the TV newsman an integal part of the travesty being depicted. In one dazzling scene, Raymond and Peggy Ann are permitted to view the bizarre, videotaped ramblings of their former charges, the film cutting back abruptly to long-shots so that the snippets of testimony ring hollow in an impersonal courtroom. Rewarded with a richly deserved Emmy as 1995's best made-for-TV movie, this combustible courtroom psychodrama is an unsparingly written horror film about people sacrificed to the hidden agendas and political ambitions of others. INDICTMENT's innovative direction and expertly constructed teleplay are complemented by a superlative ensemble, headed by a patently focused Woods as a hack attorney redeemed by his unflagging stand against hypocrisy and Emmy Best Supporting Actress winner Shirley Knight, who gives a crystalline performance as a woman overwhelmed, unable to even comprehend what's happening to her and her family. *(Violence, profanity, nudity, adult situations, sexual situations.)* — R.P.

d, Mick Johnson; p, Diana Pokorny; exec p, Oliver Stone, Janet Yang, Abby Mann; w, Abby Mann, Myra Mann; ph, Rodrigo Garcia; ed, Richard A. Harris; m, Peter Rodgers Melnick; prod d, Howard Cummings; art d, David Seth Lazan; set d, Susan J. Emshwiller; sound, Mark Deren (mixer); casting, Mali Finn; cos, Shay Cunliffe; makeup, Karen Dahl; stunts, Glory Fioramonti

Docudrama/Drama/Crime　　　　**(PR: C　MPAA: R)**

INNOCENT LIES　　　　　　★★½
(U.K./France) 88m Red Umbrella Films; Septieme Productions; Cinea; PolyGram DA; Le Studio Canal Plus; Sofica Investimage 4 ~ PolyGram Video c

Stephen Dorff *(Jeremy Graves)*; Gabrielle Anwar *(Celia Graves)*; Adrian Dunbar *(Alan Cross)*; Sophie Aubry *(Solange Montfort)*; Joanna Lumley *(Lady Helena Graves)*; Melvil Poupaud *(Louis Bernard)*; Bernard Haller *(Georges Montfort)*; Marianne Denicourt *(Maud Graves)*; Florence Hoath *(Angela Cross)*; Alexis Denisof *(Christopher Wood)*; Donal McCann *(Joe Greene)*; Rosalind Bennett *(Janet Blain)*; Yvon Back *(Inspector Talmi)*; Kate Buffery *(Anna Gross)*; Michel Winogradoff *(Albert/Ferry Captain)*; Gad Bensussan *(Young Policeman)*; Charles Duron *(Beach Boy)*; Alan Cross *(Station Clerk)*; Jacqueline Millot *(Madame Boucau)*; Henri Bedex *(Monsieur Boucau)*; Emmanuelle Boucard *(Daughter Refugee)*; Gaby Juhel *(Mother Refugee)*; Catherine Lachontch *(Montfort's Fiancee)*; Marianne Segol *(Gig)*; Alexandra Monvoisin *(ZaZa)*; Jean Guillaume *(Priest)*; Ryan Gregory *(Blue Pyjama)*; Eliot Gregory *(Red Pyjama)*; Kepia Knightly *(Young Celia)*; Alexandre Desplat *(Pianist)*; Gwenola Daniel *(Singer)*; Tatjana Verdonik *(Maud's Mother)*; Oskar Freitag *(Maud's Father)*; Joel Lebras *(Man Patisserie)*; Josette Guegan *(Bunny Girl)*

There's almost a surfeit of visual style on display here, but murder, mystery, and incest do not quite make effective bedfellows in INNOCENT LIES.

In September, 1938, British Inspector Cross (Adrian Dunbar) travels across the Channel to a palace-like estate in Calais to investigate the murder of his old friend Joe Greene (Donal McCann). The household is headed by the severe, tight-lipped Lady Graves (Joanna Lumley) and includes her son Jeremy (Stephen Dorff), daughter-in-law Maud (Marianne Denicourt), daughter Celia (Gabrielle Anwar), and her fiance Christopher (Alexis Denisof). With the local Prefect Montfort (Bernard Haller) reluctantly cooperating, Cross quickly uncovers previous unexplained deaths in the household, including that of Jeremy's twin brother when he was a child, and Celia's previous fiance. He also observes that there is more than a brother-sister relationship between Jeremy and Celia, with whom Cross is soon helplessly in love.

Lady Graves turns up dead by strangulation, and the evidence implicates Celia, but during hectic lovemaking, Celia confesses to Cross that she and Jeremy killed her together, as they did his twin brother as children. Celia, who is now terrified of Jeremy's deteriorating mental state, is spirited out of jail by Cross, but at the train station where he has deposited her, Jeremy suddenly appears and begins making love to her. When he begins to strangle her, Celia kills him with a pair of scissors. A distraught Cross bursts in to find Celia huddled in a corner, apparently regressing to childhood.

Most films dealing with aberrant sexual psychology are not themselves schizophrenic, but INNOCENT LIES is, since director Patrick DeWolf, who cowrote the screenplay with Kerry Crabbe, completely jettisons his murder-mystery plot in favor of the incest drama. Joe Greene's murder remains unsolved and unexplained. The film has all the elements for a classy tale of

family intrigue, but what is on screen does not impress the viewer, despite stylish direction by DeWolf, who expertly utilizes a slowly revelatory flashback structure for Jeremy and Celia's initial murder, and solid performances by Adrian Dunbar (CRYING GAME, HEAR MY SONG, MY LEFT FOOT) and Gabrielle Anwar (SCENT OF A WOMAN, BODY SNATCHERS, FOR LOVE OR MONEY). 1970s star Joanna Lumley, working on her first film since the 1983 CURSE OF THE PINK PANTHER, is properly, stoically reticent—what a family she has got to contend with, let alone those rumored ties with the Nazis. Up and coming actor Stephen Dorff (BACKBEAT, JUDGMENT NIGHT, S.F.W.) unfortunately remains almost totally uninteresting and unsympathetic; he is not tragically afflicted, just nuts.

While the production's 1938 setting is strongly detailed in the beginning and end, it somewhat oddly disappears in the middle, with Cross's immersion into the beautiful but "haunted" house and its oddball occupants. A British-French coproduction, the movie, superbly shot in wide-screen by Patrick Blossier (DR. PETIOT), was theatrically released in Europe as HALCYON DAYS, before heading to video and pay-cable TV in the US under the literally nonsensical title INNOCENT LIES. *(Violence, nudity, sexual situations, profanity.)* — D.B.

d, Patrick Dewolf; p, Simon Perry, Philippe Guez; exec p, Marvin J. Rosenblum; assoc p, Philippe Carcassonne; w, Kerry Crabbe, Patrick Dewolf; ph, Patrick Blossier; ed, Chris Wimble, Joelle Hache; m, Alexandre Desplat; prod d, Bernd Lepel; art d, Nicolas Prier, Charlie Smith; sound, Ivan Sharrock (mixer), Colin Ritchie, John Hayward, Robin O'Donoghue; casting, Irene Lamb, Suzanne Smith, Natalie Cherron; cos, Tom Rand; makeup, Peter King

Crime/Mystery/Drama　　　　**(PR: O　MPAA: NR)**

INNOCENT, THE　　　　　　★★½
(U.K./Germany) 119m Lakehart; Sievernich Film; Berlin Film Board; Brandenburg Film Board; North Rhine Westfalia Film Board ~ Miramax c

Anthony Hopkins *(Bob Glass)*; Isabella Rossellini *(Maria)*; Campbell Scott *(Leonard Marnham)*; Hart Bochner *(Russell)*; Ronald Nitschke *(Otto)*; James Grant *(MacNamee)*; Jeremy Sinden *(Captain Lofting)*; Richard Durden *(Black)*; Corey Johnson *(Lou)*; Richard Good *(Piper)*; Lena Lessing *(Jenny)*; Dana Golembeck *(Charlotte)*; Susanne Jansen *(Mermaid Singer)*; Christine Gerlach *(Woman With Dog)*; Ludger Pistor *(German Informer)*; Meret Becker *(Ulrike)*; Christiane Flegel *(Frau Eckdorf)*; Klaus-Jurgen Steinmann *(Herr Eckdorf)*; Jessica Cardinahl *(Maria's Child)*; Franziska Brix *(Maria's Child)*; Forest Ashley Knight *(Maria's Child)*; Matthew Burton *(Flight Officer)*; Rupert Chetwynd *(Air Commodore)*; Martin Becker *(Offender at Police Station)*; Natascha Bub *(Offender at Police Station)*; Hans Martin Stier *(Police Inspector)*; Helmut Bernhoffen *(Police Inspector)*; Gerch Hofmann *(Police Inspector)*; Friedrich Solms-Baruth *(Hotel Receptionist)*; Martin Honer *(Left Luggage Officer)*; Vera Ziegler; Jurgen Wink; Helga Petersen; Olaf Meden; Melitta Moritz; Gundula Damerow *(Maria's Neighbors)*; Stefan Taufelder *(East German Checkpoint)*; Hubertus Brand *(East German Border Guard)*; Peter Meseck *(East German Border Guard)*; Mark Valley; Ian Rowles; Robert Lively; Hans Diederich; J.L. Hooper; Harvey Friedman; Nigel Scotting; Steven Moorecraft; Kevin Davenport; Chris Potter *(Tunnel Technicians)*; Jeff Seyfried; John Scott; Tony Estese; Kelly Cole; Arnold Strong *(US Guards)*

Ian McEwan's intense, impressively atmospheric novel might have made a good film, but director John Schlesinger's efforts were undermined by some bizarre miscasting.

1955: Young Englishman Leonard Marnham (Cambell Scott) arrives in West Berlin to work as a communications engineer on a highly classified project, constructing a warehouse tunnel designed to tap telephone lines beneath the Russian sector of the city. His chief partner is Bob Glass (Anthony Hopkins), a hale and hearty American. Glass takes the innocent Leonard under his wing and shows him the ropes, of both their top-secret business and the wicked city.

Leonard, a virgin, embarks on a torrid affair with Maria (Isabella Rossellini), a beautiful office worker. Glass disapproves, seeing their relationship as a security breach. Leonard's burgeoning sexuality takes a turn for the nasty, and he forces Maria to have rough sex with him. Meanwhile, Otto (Ronald Nitschke)—Maria's estranged, alcoholic and abusive husband—looms menacingly over their liaison. An ex-German war hero, his battle record exempts him from the punishment his actions would ordinarily warrant.

Otto surprises the couple in Maria's apartment, drunkenly demanding money and becoming violent. He attacks Maria and Leonard, and as the two men struggle, she caves in Otto's skull with an iron cobbler's last. The lovers cut up Otto's corpse with a saw and pack it into two equipment cases Leonard purloins from work. Over the next two days, he lugs the heavy bags back to the warehouse, pursued relentlessly by sniffing dogs and hateful busybodies who try to guess what's inside. He even has the bad luck to run smack into Glass, whom he tells that the suitcases contain electronic equipment.

Warehouse sentries demand that Leonard open the bags, but he puts them off with some fancy double-talk about security and stows the bags in the tunnel. Finally relieved of his awful burden, Leonard goes into the Russian sector to a cafe frequented by dealers in classified information and sells what he knows about the tunnel. Leonard returns home, and soon receives a call from the frantic Glass: Russians have broken into the tunnel. In the confused days that follow, Leonard is recalled to London and happily plans to leave with his beloved.

Leonard's hopes are dashed at the airport, when Maria tells him she's staying. While Leonard was disposing of the body, Glass got her to reveal the whole story—not just the murder, but also her feelings about Leonard, colored by his sexual abusiveness and unpleasant behavior in the days following Otto's death.

1987: An aged Leonard returns to Germany as the Berlin Wall is crumbling, and meets up with Maria. She is the widow of Bob Glass, and has three grown children. They ruefully reminisce about their past, and are able to smile at the present amidst the hubbub.

Schlesinger deftly recreates the atmosphere of Cold War Berlin, in which people live at a fever pitch amidst government intrigue. Like McEwan's book, the film is as much about the minutiae of spying as Leonard's sexual awaking and the violence that accompanies it. But Schlesinger doesn't stint on the story's Grand Guignol aspects: the murder and subsequent disposal of Otto are scarily gory stuff. The flashback framing device that embeds the main story in Leonard and Maria's present-day reunion is a floridly romantic conceit that might have been better suited to a different film.

THE INNOCENT's great liability is what can only be described as its willfully perverse casting: American Scott as Englishman Leonard, English Hopkins playing American Glass and Italian-Swedish Rossellini as German Maria. Rossellini comes off least badly, while Hopkins wallows in the worst cliches of talking like a Yank, and additionally conceives Glass as some sort of overbaked hipster, snapping his fingers and sashaying through hallways to the strains of "Shake, Rattle and Roll." The result resembles nothing human. Campbell Scott isn't quite up to the demands of his role—the film's most complex—and his English

accent is as uncertain and phony as Hopkins' American one is flamboyant and phony. *(Nudity, violence, profanity, substance abuse, sexual situations, adult situations.)* — D.N.

d, John Schlesinger; p, Norma Heyman, Chris Sievernich, Wieland Schultz-Keil; exec p, Ann Dubinet; w, Ian McEwan (based on his novel); ph, Dietrich Lohmann; ed, Richard Marden; m, Gerald Gouriet; prod d, Luciana Arrighi; art d, Dieter Dohl; set d, Olaf Schiefner; sound, Axel Arft (mixer), Paul Rabjohns (design); fx, Adolf Wojtinek; casting, Noel Davis, Jeremy Zimmerman; cos, Ingrid Zore; makeup, Joan Hills

Spy/Drama/Historical　　　　　　　　　(PR: O　MPAA: NR)

IT TAKES TWO　　　　　　　　　　　　　　★★
(U.S.) 101m Rysher Films; Orr & Cruickshank Productions; Dualstar Productions ~ Warner Bros. c

Kirstie Alley *(Diane Barrow)*; Steve Guttenberg *(Roger Callaway)*; Ashley Olsen *(Alyssa Callaway)*; Mary-Kate Olsen *(Amanda Lemmon)*; Philip Bosco *(Vincenzo)*; Jane Sibbett *(Clarice Kensington)*; Michelle Grisom *(Carmen)*; Desmond Roberts *(Frankie)*; Tiny Mills *(Tiny)*; Shanelle Henry *(Patty)*; Anthony Aiello *(Anthony)*; La Tonya Borsay *(Wanda)*; Michelle Londsdale-Smith *(Michelle)*; Sean Orr *(Jerry)*; Elizabeth Walsh *(Emily)*; Michael Vollans *(Blue Team Kid)*; Paul O'Sullivan *(Bernard Louffier)*; Lawrence Dane *(Mr. Kensington)*; Garrard Parkes *(St. Bart's Priest)*; Gina Clayton *(Muffy Bilderberg)*; Doug O'Keefe *(Craig Bilderberg)*; Mark Huisman *(Waiter at Party)*; Marilyn Boyle *(Miss Van Dyke)*; Ernie Grunwald *(Harry Butkis)*; Ellen Ray Hennessey *(Fanny Butkis)*; Dov Tiefenback *(Harry Butkis, Jr.)*; Annick Obonsawin *(Brenda Butkis)*; Austin Pool *(Billy Butkis)*; Andre Lorant *(Bobby Butkis)*; Philip Williams *(Airport Tractor Driver)*; Vito Rezza *(Butkis' Neighbor)*

IT TAKES TWO showcases the Olsen twins from the television hit "Full House" in a familiar PARENT TRAP-type yarn. As one of the "trapped parents," however, Kirstie Alley at least makes all of her scenes worthwhile.

Once upon a time in New York, there lived two identical strangers—Amanda Lemmon (Mary-Kate Olsen), a poor but tough orphan raised by a school teacher, Diane Barrow (Kirstie Alley), and Alyssa Callaway (Ashley Olsen), the wealthy but sweet-natured daughter of cellular phone company founder Roger Callaway (Steve Guttenberg). After attending her umpteenth interview with some prospective foster parents, Amanda joins her classmates for a week away at a summer camp established by Callaway and located across the lake from his Upstate New York mansion.

During her camp stay, Amanda meets Alyssa while running through the woods. Once they get over their initial shock, the girls decide to trade places for a day. The swap enables the more streetwise Amanda to help Alyssa scare off Callaway's fiance, Clarice Kensington (Jane Sibbett), a gold-digging, child-hating woman. When the girls reunite the next day, they concoct a new plan to fix up Callaway with Barrow while Kensington is out of town. Unfortunately, "Amanda" (actually Alyssa) is adopted suddenly and taken away by her new foster parents. Through the girls' ingenuity and Barrow's helicopter rescue, however, "Amanda" returns in time to help break up Callaway's Manhattan church wedding. Callaway, Barrow and the girls then ride off together, an instant family in the making.

Alternating in the same role, the Olsen twins are never seen together on "Full House," which makes their joint appearances in made-for-TV films and this first theatrical release a special treat for their fans. However, the distaff PRINCE AND THE

PAUPER gimmick fails to work here, chiefly because the tykes are interchangeable from the start, and they seem to forget who's playing what as the narrative ambles along its predictable class-clashing course. It is not the Olsens' fault that screenwriter Deborah Dean Davis has saddled them with so many sappy parent-child scenes to play or that director Andy Tennant has required them to ape Macaulay Culkin's famous gesture of triumph from the HOME ALONE series.

On the brighter side of things, Kirstie Alley shows up intermittently and makes the most of her time. Alley, an underrated screwball heroine (see SIBLING RIVALRY), is particularly funny when a horse she is riding goes berserk, and during a monologue in a field while waiting for her dream date to arrive. One other plus is a sometimes funny musical soundtrack that includes comic variations on everything from Bernard Herrmann's music for PSYCHO to Aaron Copland's "Rodeo." — E.M.

d, Andy Tennant; p, Jim Cruickshank, James Orr; exec p, Keith Samples, Mel Efros; co-p, Laura Friedman, Andy Cohen; w, Deborah Dean Davis; ph, Kenneth D. Zunder; ed, Roger Bondelli; m, Sherman Foote, Ray Foote; prod d, Edward Pisoni; art d, Vlasta Svoboda; set d, Enrico Campana; sound, David Lee; casting, Amy Lippens; cos, Molly McGuiness

Children's/Comedy/Romance   **(PR: A   MPAA: PG)**

JACK-O

(U.S.) 89m American Independent;
Royal Oaks Entertainment ~
Triboro Entertainment Group c

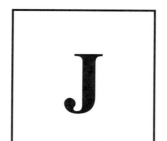

Linnea Quigley *(Carolyn Miller)*; Rebecca Wicks *(Linda Kelly)*; Gary Doles *(David Kelly)*; Ryan Latshaw *(Sean Kelly/Andrew Kelly)*; John Carradine *(Walter Machen)*; Cameron Mitchell *(Dr. Cadaver)*; Brinke Stevens *(Witch)*; Dawn Wildsmith *(Sorceress)*; Catherine Walsh *(Vivian Machen)*; Rachel Carter *(Julie Miller)*; Tom Ferda *(Jim)*; Bill Cross *(Richard Watson)*; Helen Keeling *(Amanda Watson)*; Thor Schwiegerath *(Robbie)*; Christina Connell *(Sarah)*; Kelly Lacy *(Shannon)*; George Castells *(Brent)*; Bernie Fidello *(Simms)*; Michael Walsh *(Paul)*; Mike Conner *(Arthur Kelly)*; Katy Maznicki *(Eunice Kelly)*; Vic Savage *(Cable Installer)*; Ron Bernard *(Rush Gingraw)*; Rick Riggs *(Daniel Kelly)*; Rhonda Riggs *(Jewell Kelly)*; Tom Ferguson *(Tom Mason)*; Dawn Wildsmith *(Sorceress)*; Heidi Kneisl *(Hell Pig)*; Kerrylynn Dekanski *(Hell Pig)*; Joe Solar *(Hell Pig)*; Patrick Moran *(Jack O'Lantern)*

There are plenty of storytelling tricks but no treats in JACK-O, a misbegotten composite rip-off of PUMPKINHEAD and HALLOWEEN.

In 1915, the Kelly family was responsible for putting an end to warlock Walter Machen (John Carradine), but a huge, pumpkin-headed ghoul took revenge for him. Eighty years later, David and Linda Kelly (Gary Doles and Rebecca Wicks) are putting together a "haunted garage" for Halloween while their son, Sean (Ryan Latshaw), is having nightmares about his family's dark past. Vivian (Catherine Walsh), a local woman considered a "witch" by the kids, befriends the Kelly family. This Halloween night, the Kelly's have called Carolyn Miller (Linnea Quigley) to babysit for Sean. Meanwhile, across town, the jack o'lantern demon (Patrick Moran) has returned to life after a young punk removed a wooden cross from his grave, and he begins cutting a bloody swath through the town.

The vengeful monster ultimately tracks down Sean as he is out trick-or-treating with Carolyn, and they flee to the cemetery from whence the monster came. Back at the Kelly house, Vivian reveals that she's a descendant of Walter Machen seeking to destroy the demon, and that she was hoping Sean could lure it out. She and the Kellys race to the cemetery, where Vivian is killed, but David and Sean manage to skewer the creature with the wooden cross, destroying it forever.

JACK-O is the third film (after DARK UNIVERSE and BIO-HAZARD II) directed by Steve Latshaw, a Fred Olen Ray protege whose work up to this point is distinguished by a singular lack of narrative drive. As if aware of the material's meandering nature, Latshaw packs JACK-O with a seemingly endless barrage of flashbacks and dream sequences that serve only to confuse the story. The demon itself (never referred to as "Jack-O" in the movie) and the mayhem he creates remain resolutely not scary, thanks as much to cheesy special effects as to Latshaw's slack direction.

The cast isn't much to speak of—they seem to have been encouraged to do and say everything as slowly as possible—though longtime scream queen Quigley does get in her traditional gratuitous shower scene. Also worth noting is the inclusion of old footage—to no real advantage beyond curiosity value—of deceased thespians John Carradine and Cameron Mitchell. For this and many other reasons, PLAN NINE FROM OUTER SPACE is an appropriate point of reference for JACK-O, though this one isn't even good for many unintentional laughs. *(Graphic violence, extensive nudity, sexual situations, profanity.)* — M.G.

d, Steve Latshaw; p, Patrick Moran, Steve Latshaw; exec p, Fred Olen Ray; w, Patrick Moran (based on a story by Fred Olen Ray and Brad Lineweaver); ph, Maxwell J. Beck; ed, Wayland Strickland; m, Jeffrey Walton; prod d, Guillaume DeLouche; art d, Christopher Clark; sound, Del Casher, Phillip Raves; fx, Todd Palamar, Obscure Artifacts; cos, Patricia McKiou; makeup, Corrina Adkins

Horror **(PR: O MPAA: R)**

JADE ★½

(U.S.) 93m The Robert Evans Company ~ Paramount c

David Caruso *(David Corelli)*; Linda Fiorentino *(Trina Gavin)*; Chazz Palminteri *(Matt Gavin)*; Michael Biehn *(Lt. Bob Hargrove)*; Richard Crenna *(Governor Lew Edwards)*; Donna Murphy *(Karen Heller)*; Ken King *(Petey Vasko)*; Holt McCallany *(Bill Barrett)*; David Hunt *(Pat Callendar)*; Angie Everhart *(Patrice Jacinto)*; Kevin Tighe *(D.A. Arnold Clifford)*; Victor Wong *(Mr. Wong)*; Jay Jacobus *(Justin Henderson)*; Victoria Smith *(Sandy)*; Drew Snyder *(Executive)*; Bud Bostwick *(Justin Henderson's Brother)*; Darryl Chan *(Tommy Loy)*; Graham Cowley *(Deputy Coroner)*; Nellie Cravens *(Governor's Secretary)*; Ron Ulstad *(Kyle Medford)*; Allen Gebhardt *(Forensic Man)*; Garrett Griffin *(Police Officer)*; Julian Hill *(Forensic)*; Budd Joe Hooker; Bobby Bass; Sandra Berumen; Richard Ziker *(Assistant DAs)*; Arthur Johnson; Paul Schlotfeldt; Rene Charles LaPrevotte; John Loftus; Tom Walsh; Howard Weathersby; Kevin Whitfield; John Wyman *(Cops)*; Mini Mehra *(Resident)*; Nicholas Tarvid *(Pilot)*; Harold Morrison *(Co-Pilot)*; William Piletic *(Priest)*; Olimpia Saravia *(Maid)*; Tina J. Spangler *(Secretary)*; Isaac Spivey *(Homeless Man)*; Victor Talmadge *(Lawyer)*; Kenneth Tigar *(Corporate Man)*; Bill Tolliver *(Medical Examiner)*; James Edward Veurink *(Executive)*; Ron Winston Yuan *(Technician)*; The Peter Duchin Orchestra *(Black & White Ball Orchestra)*

JADE, which unites stubbornly sordid screenwriter Joe Eszterhas—of BASIC INSTINCT notoriety—and director William Friedkin, is a fetid tangle of misogynistic fantasies, just what one would expect from Eszterhas. But it's a bit of a shock from Friedkin, once widely considered a filmmaker of considerable skill and intelligence.

JADE opens with a long tracking shot through a riotously luxurious apartment, filled with the sort of pricey knickknacks meant to connote old money and sophisticated tastes. There is an offscreen argument, and then the sounds of someone being brutally murdered: blood stains the expensive rugs and pools on the glossy floor. At a charity ball, we meet three old friends: David Corelli (David Caruso), a crusading young San Francisco DA, Matt Gavin (Chazz Palminteri), a smarmy, philandering lawyer to the rich and infamous and darkly glamorous Trina (Linda Fiorentino), Matt's wife and David's onetime flame, a world-renowned clinical psychologist whose lecture on violence in the workplace is a showstopper. David is called away to the scene of the gory crime, to investigate the circumstances under which a perverted moneybags got himself butchered with a ceremonial ax. The deceased's effects include a collection of pubic hair in precious little boxes, so the search for the killer begins with his sexual contacts. One name haunts the investigation: Jade, a mysterious woman who was the millionaire panderer's partner in a high-level prostitution/blackmail scheme and a particular favorite of San Francisco's rich and powerful back-door men—including the Governor (Richard Crenna), on whose benevolence David's political aspirations rest.

With hard-nosed Detective Bob Hargrove (Michael Biehn), David learns that Trina was in the apartment on the afternoon of the murder, and even handled the murder weapon. Hargrove, whose puritanism colors his approach to the case, considers her the prime suspect. When the dead man's beach house is searched, a videotape of Trina having sex with a stranger is uncovered. She's arrested, but denies that she's the mysterious Jade or has anything to do with the bloody goings-on that dog the investigation. A lesbian prostitute named Patrice Jacinto (Angie Everhardt), who worked with Jade, seems to be a promising lead, but she's run down by a car on her way to meet David. He engages in high-speed chase with the car, but eventually loses it on a deserted pier. A peeping Tom who used to spy on the comings and goings at the beach house is also killed.

David eventually discovers that Trina and Jade are indeed one—her pseudonym seems intended to carry some Orientalist whiff of corrupt sexual allure—and she tells David she got involved with the sordid business as a way of expressing her individuality and sexual power. But she isn't the killer: in a trick ending, David is led to believe that it's the volatile Hargrove, and is forced to rescue Trina from Hargrove's vicious attempt to rape and murder her. But the "surprise" second ending reveals that the real murderer is Matt, who found out about his wife's double life and retaliated by murdering everyone who knew about her sexual transgressions.

JADE is full to bursting with juvenile vulgarity, though Friedkin has given the material a somewhat more successful gloss than Paul Verhoeven—who appears to have embraced the excesses of American popular culture with the enthusiasm of a slumming European—was able to give SHOWGIRLS. It's driven by a potent mixture of disgust with, and attraction to, the very idea of anal sex, and informed throughout by a puerile, voyeuristic loathing of the icky things grown men get up to with the sort of women who let them. JADE's seamy excesses would be conventional in a direct-to-video erotic thriller. In a major studio production, they're just plain embarrassing. *(Violence, nudity, extreme profanity, sexual situations.)* — M.M.

d, William Friedkin; p, Robert Evans, Gary Adelson, Craig Baumgarten; exec p, William J. MacDonald; co-p, George Goodman; w, Joe Eszterhas; ph, Andrzej Bartkowiak; ed, Augie Hess; m, James Horner; prod d, Alex Tavoularis; art d, Charles Breen; set d, Gary Fettis; sound, Kirk Francis (mixer), Gary Rydstrom (design); fx, Lawrence James Cavanaugh, R. Bruce Steinheimer; casting, Ronnie Yeskel; cos, Marilyn Vance; makeup, Robert Ryan, Chris Walas, Inc.; stunts, Buddy Joe Hooker

Erotic/Thriller/Crime   **(PR: O   MPAA: R)**

JAR, THE   ★★★½
(Iran) 85m Institute for the Intellectual Development of Children and Young Adults ~ Artistic License Films c
(KHOMREH)

Behzad Khodaveisi *(Teacher)*; Fatemah Azrah *(Mrs. Khavar)*; Alireza Haji-Ghasemi; Ramazan Molla-Abbasi; Hossein Balai; Abbas Khavanizadeh

A crack in a water jar marks the "inciting incident" in THE JAR, a perceptive, engaging comedy from Iran.

THE JAR is set in a rural desert village in 1967, years before the Islamic Revolution. In the village's one-room schoolhouse, the children share their water from a large terracotta jar, which one day develops a crack along its side. The young school teacher (Behzad Khodaveisi) visits a student's father who may be able to repair the crack, but the man claims he is too busy. The

embarrassed son's refusal to attend class forces the father to agree to fix the jar.

The father instructs all the children to bring ashes and eggs from their homes. A mix of egg whites and ashes will be used to cement the crack. The next day when the teacher finds that the children have brought enough ashes but not enough eggs, he realizes that some of the parents think he is trying to keep the yolks for his own use. Angered by the implied criticism, the teacher solves the problem by feeding the students the yolks while the jar is being repaired.

Waiting for the jar to be fixed, the children drink water from a nearby stream. One of the boys falls into the stream and later becomes ill. His mother, Mrs. Khavar (Fatemeh Azrah), complains to the teacher about the episode, then sets out to raise money from the other parents to buy a new jar for the school. Mrs. Khavar's campaign soon gets mired in malicious gossip, when the other parents insinuate that, with the cooperation of the teacher, Mrs. Khavar has given the collected money to her husband for personal use. The teacher nearly leaves over the imbroglio, but a village elder urges him to stand up to the rumors and stay. The children are delighted when the teacher decides not to move away.

Like THROUGH THE OLIVE TREES and the more popular WHITE BALLOON, THE JAR is a winsome little movie out of Iran that signals a new voice in Middle Eastern cinema (notably, THE JAR takes place before the Islamic Revolution). Also like other recent Iranian imports, THE JAR appears slighter on the surface than it is underneath. The cracked jar provides a basic metaphor that drives the simple narrative, the crack symbolically exposing the social, economic and moral fissures in the society. Expertly developed by writer-director Ebrahim Foruzesh (this is the former producer's second directorial effort), THE JAR says volumes about the far-reaching consequences of challenging a social order.

However, the film compares slightly less favorably to both Abbas Kiarostami's THROUGH THE OLIVE TREES, which was more beautifully shot, and Jafar Panahi's WHITE BALLOON, which better articulated a child's point of view. But what the unadorned production of THE JAR lacks in artistic finesse it makes up for in humanitarian charm, most notably from the ensemble of unknown actors who give refreshingly natural and spontaneous performances. Without sugarcoating its subject, the picture leaves a sweet aftertaste and a fond memory. *(Violence.)* — E.M.

d, Ebrahim Foruzesh; p, Alireza Zarrin; w, Ebrahim Foruzesh; ph, Iraj Safavi; ed, Changiz Sayad; m, Mohammad Reza Aligholi

Comedy/Drama   **(PR: AA   MPAA: NR)**

JEFFERSON IN PARIS   ★★½
(U.S.) 144m Merchant-Ivory Productions;
Touchstone ~ Buena Vista c

Nick Nolte *(Thomas Jefferson)*; Greta Scacchi *(Maria Cosway)*; Jean-Pierre Aumont *(D'Hancarville)*; Simon Callow *(Richard Cosway)*; Seth Gilliam *(James Hemings)*; Thandie Newton *(Sally Hemings)*; James Earl Jones *(Madison Hemings)*; Michael Lonsdale *(Louis XVI)*; Gwyneth Paltrow *(Patsy Jefferson)*; Estelle Eonnet *(Polly Jefferson)*; Todd Boyce *(William Short)*; Nigel Whitmey *(John Trumbull)*; Nicholas Silberg *(Monsieur Petit)*; Catherine Samie *(Cook)*; Lionel Robert *(Cook's Helper)*; Stanislas Carre deMalberg *(Surgeon)*; Jean Rupert *(Surgeon)*; Yvette Petit *(Dressmaker)*; Paolo Mantini *(Hairdresser)*; F. Van Den Driessche *(Mutilated Officer)*; Humbert Balson *(Mutilated Officer)*; Michel Rois *(Mutilated Officer)*; Bob Sessions *(James Byrd)*; Jeffrey Justin Ribier *(Mulatto Boy)*; Marc Tissot *(Con-

struction Foreman); Lambert Wilson *(Marquis de Lafayette)*; Elsa Zylberstein *(Adrienne de Lafayette)*; Christopher Thompson *(Interpreter)*; Jean-Francois Perrier; Eric Genovese; Bruno Putzulu; Philippe Mareuil; Philippe Bouclet *(Liberal Aristocrats)*; Olivier Galfione *(Chevalier de Saint-Colombe)*; Anthony Valentine *(British Ambassador)*; Steve Kalfa *(Dr. Guillotin)*; Andre Julien *(Savant)*; Jacques Herlin *(Savant)*; Elizabeth Kaza *(Card Player)*; Agathe de la Boulaye *(Card Player)*; Abdel Bouthegmes *(Lafayette's Indian)*; Charlotte de Turckheim *(Marie Antoinette)*; Damien Groelle *(The Dauphin)*; Valerie Toledano *(Madame Elizabeth)*; Vernon Dobtchev *(King's Translator)*; Felix Malinbaum *(Captain of the Guard)*; Herve Hiolle *(King's Messenger)*; Philippe Girard *(Post Office Spy)*; Eric Berg *(Post Office Spy)*; Nancy Marchand *(The Abbess)*; Jessica Lloyd *(Julia)*; Daniel Mesguich *(Mesmer)*; Yan Duffas; Thibault de Montalembert; Magali Leiris; Valentine Varella *(Assistants)*; Gabrielle Islwyn *(Singer with Megaphone)*; William Christie *(Conductor)*; Jean-Paul Fouchecourt *(Dardanus)*; Ismail Merchant *(Tipoo Sultan's Ambassador)*; Martine Chevalier *(Mademoiselle Contat)*; Valerie Lang *(Demented Woman)*; Vincent Cassel *(Camille Desmoulins)*; Beatrice Winde *(Mary Hemings)*; Tim Choate *(Reporter)*

This Merchant-Ivory production is an upscale tabloid expose of the skeletons in the famous president's closet that dishes the dirt—the Sally Hemings affair and Jefferson's possible mulatto children—as if it were fact instead of hotly debated supposition. The Great Man's personality remains a mystery in this "Masterpiece Theatre" version of a celebrity roast.

1784. As America settles into hard-won democracy, founding father Thomas Jefferson (Nick Note) accepts the post of ambassador to France. Grieving for his beloved wife, he encourages his clinging daughter Patsy's (Gwyneth Paltrow's) emotional dependency and treats her as a surrogate spouse and hostess. Although he presents himself as a moral arbiter at the court of Louis XVI, Jefferson engages in an adulterous flirtation with the artistic Maria Cosway (Greta Scacchi) and stands by passively as callous Queen Marie Antoinette depletes the treasury with her frivolous spending. As one of the shapers of the Declaration of Independence, Jefferson proclaims the equality of all men. Yet he employs James Hemings (Seth Gilliam), a slave inherited from his wife's family, to run his household in France. The arrival of James's teenage sister Sally (Thandie Newton)—who is also the half-sister of Jefferson's late wife—creates a storm in the Jefferson household.

While possessive Patsy turns a blind eye to her father's affair with Maria, his dalliance with Sally outrages her. She confides in Maria, who bids Jefferson adieu and returns to her effete husband (Simon Callow). The starving French rebel, tumbling the Ancient Regime, and Jefferson's appointment to France winds down. With his daughter and slave-mistress in tow, Jefferson returns to his upcoming glory years as valued statesman and tormented private citizen in America.

JEFFERSON IN PARIS is a rich confection indeed, filled with tidbits about fashion, customs, art, and commerce in 18th-century France and America. But like a meal consisting of nothing but *petits-fours*, this lavish biopic is too much dessert and not enough main course. The Merchant-Ivory team (which includes screenwriter Ruth Prawer Jhabvala) drops incredibly intricate doilies over the architecture of history, and as beautiful as their budget-blowing visualizations are, they don't inspire debate, explain Jefferson's stature abroad or expand the viewer's understanding of the personal contradictions that define his character.

Except for the fact that the figures move, we might as well be exploring a wax museum at Monticello or Versailles. The sets,

costumes and bric-a-brac are spellbindingly photographed, but the glimpses of Jefferson's life hardly add up to a full-fleshed portrait of a complex and deeply paradoxical man. Overrated star Nolte is hampered by a script in which insinuation takes precedence over insight, and while Jefferson's nobility and heroism come naturally to him, he never manages to suggest the presence of a vital man beneath the peruke. As for the remainder of the enormous cast, the idiosyncratic Paltrow is given too few scenes and the vapidly pretty Scacchi too many. Newton resembles an impressionable slave girl less than the young Lena Horne.

More appropriate to examining characters who suppress their external emotions but have rich interior lives, the Merchant-Ivory style is ill-suited to dealing with this man of action. The filmmakers turn a historical dazzler into a wet blanket; a man of infinite variety becomes, in their fussy hands, just another repressed American abroad. *(Violence, profanity, sexual situations, adult situations, nudity.)* — R.P.

d, James Ivory; p, Ismail Merchant; exec p, Donald Rosenfeld, Paul Bradley; assoc p, Donald Rosenfeld; co-p, Humbert Balsan; w, Ruth Prawer Jhabvala; ph, Pierre Lhomme; ed, Andrew Marcus, Isabel Lorente; m, Richard Robbins; prod d, Guy Claude Francois; art d, Thierry Francois; set d, Bernadette Saint Loubert; sound, Mike Shoring (recordist), Laurent Quaglio (designer); casting, Sylvie Brochere, Joanna Merlin, Celestia Fox; cos, Jenny Beavan, John Bright; makeup, Carol Hemming, Tina Earnshaw, Pauline Heys

Romance/Biography/Drama   (PR: A   MPAA: PG-13)

JEFFREY   ★★★
(U.S.) 92m Workin' Man Films; Booking Office ~
Orion Classics c

Steven Weber *(Jeffrey)*; Patrick Stewart *(Sterling)*; Michael T. Weiss *(Steve)*; Bryan Batt *(Darius)*; Sigourney Weaver *(Debra Moorhouse)*; Nathan Lane *(Father Dan)*; Olympia Dukakis *(Mrs. Marcangelo)*; Christine Baranski *(Ann Marwood Bartle)*; Kathy Najimy *(Acolyte)*; Robert Klein *(Skip Winkley)*; Irma St. Paule *(Mother Teresa)*; Victor Garber *(Tim)*; J. Smith Cameron *(Sharon)*; Ethan Phillips *(Dave)*; Michael Duvert *(Sean)*; Peter Maloney *(Dad)*; Debra Monk *(Mom)*; Gregory Jbara *(Angelique)*; Marylouise Burke *(Aunt Phyllis)*; Joe Ponazecki *(Uncle Barney)*; Alice Drummond *(Grandma Rose)*; Henry Stram *(Cousin Gary)*; Lee Mark Nelson *(Crying Guy)*; John Ganun *(Tourist)*; Nicky Paraiso *(Salesman)*; K. Todd Freeman *(Barney's Waiter)*; Patti Ann O'Connell *(Cheryl the Showgirl)*; Patrick Kerr *(Waiter/Actor/Policeman)*; Peter Bartlett *(Casting Director)*; John Seidman *(Boss)*; Barton Heyman *(Elderly Man)*; Darryl Theirse *(Homeboy)*; Camryn Manheim *(Single Woman)*; Nancy Ticotin *(Woman in the Window)*; Marcus Lovett *(Memorial Guest)*; Michele Pawk *(Young Mother)*; Demetri Corbin *(House Manager)*; Alexander Cohen Smith *(Child)*; Peter B. *(Master)*; Albert Macklin *(Slave)*; Alison Sheehy *(Network V.O.)*; Sarah Peterson *(Nurse)*

JEFFREY, Paul Rudnick's hilarious stage farce about, of all things, the AIDS crisis, has made a comfortable transition to the screen. Even taking into account the succinct specificity of its milieu (Manhattan; gay), scene for scene, it delivers more real laughs than most recent movies.

The eponymous Jeffrey (Steven Weber) has decided to foreswear sex in light of his overwhelming fear of AIDS. His resolve is sorely tested by all manner of fleshy temptation rampant in Sin City, particularly a hunky guy, Steve (Michael T. Weiss), he meets at the gym one day. Then there are his friends Sterling (Patrick Stewart), a posh British interior designer, and Sterling's dim but adorable boyfriend Darius (Bryan Batt). They want more than anything for Jeffrey to find a lover and share the connubial bliss they enjoy. Compulsive wisecracking and camping get all three of them through every situation from dealing with the snotty help at Barney's to those endless memorials for stricken friends. Steve showers Jeffrey with attention and would seem to be the perfect mate, but for the fact that he is HIV-positive. Jeffrey manages to stand tough in the face of all who would sway him from his celibate track, but in the process he alienates not only Steve, but Sterling, who loses Darius to AIDS and grows disgusted by his friend's noncommital stance. The film becomes an exhortation to living life to the fullest as Jeffrey eventually comes to terms with his own humanity and fears.

The subject may be definitely unfunny, but Rudnick's comic voice is ever present and cleverly transforms situations when they threaten to become too maudlin. He even provides a wickedly funny send-up of evangelist Marianne Williamson in the person of Debra Moorhouse (Sigourney Weaver), to whom a desperate Jeffrey turns. With her beige-clad acolytes (led by a hysterically obsequious Kathy Najimy) slavering over her every raucously intoned platitude, she's a monster and monstrously funny. His observation of the hothouse arena of urban, urbane gays is demonically accurate. Rudnick only falters in the more emotional moments, where something beyond a ruthlessly clever approach is required.

First-time director Christopher Ashley has done an adequate job in the screen transferral, with occasional inspired moments, like his sudden intercutting of suburban mall jocks reacting with disgust to the first on-screen kiss between two males. (It's the funniest film non sequitur since Truffaut killed off that poor old woman with a heart attack in SHOOT THE PIANO PLAYER.) Ashley also makes full use of such New York gay landmarks as Chelsea Gym, those obnoxious George Segal same-sex couple statues in Sheridan Square, and the annual Stonewall Pride March. Stewart's Sterling is the ultimate bitchy queen, and Batt, recreating his stage role, is engaging and touching.

The main problem with the film lies in its principals, who are devoid of the essential chemistry to lend the proper magic and suspense to their romance. Weber and Weiss do not have either the talent or the personal charisma to be wholly believable in the roles assigned to them. *(Adult situations, sexual situations, profanity, violence.)* — D.N.

d, Christopher Ashley; p, Mark Balsam, Mitchell Maxwell, Victoria Maxwell; exec p, Kevin McCollum; co-p, Paul Rudnick; w, Paul Rudnick (based on his play); ph, Jeffery Tufano; ed, Cara Silverman; m, Stephen Endelman; prod d, Michael Johnston; set d, Andrew Baseman; ch, Jerry Mitchell; sound, Matthew Price (mixer); casting, Marcia Shulman; cos, David C. Woolard; makeup, Debbie Zoller; stunts, George Aguilar

Comedy   **(PR: O   MPAA: R)**

JERKY BOYS: THE MOVIE, THE   ★
(U.S.) 81m Caravan; Touchstone; J.B. Productions ~
Buena Vista c

Johnny Brennan *(Johnny Brennan)*; Kamal Ahmed *(Kamal)*; Alan Arkin *(Lazarro)*; William Hickey *(Uncle Freddy)*; Alan North *(Mickey)*; Brad Sullivan *(Worzic)*; James Lorinz *(Brett Weir)*; Suzanne Shepherd *(Mrs. B.)*; Vincent Pastore *(Tony Scarboni)*; Brian Tarantina *(Geno)*; Peter Appel *(Sonny)*; Ozzy Osbourne *(Band Manager)*; Paul Bartel *(Host)*; Tom Jones *(Himself)*; Daryl Theirse *(Connley)*; David Pittu *(Doorman)*; Frank Senger *(Bouncer)*; Michael Louis Wells *(Roadie)*; Henry Bogdan, Rob Echeverria; Page Nye Hamilton; John Stanier *(Helmet—The Band)*; John Norman Thomas *(The Cabbie)*; Hope Shapiro *(Tolly)*; Danny Dennis *(Comedian)*; Brenda Forbes

(Rich Woman); David Stepkin *(Old Man)*; Robert Weil *(Quigley)*; Joe Lisi *(Foreman)*; Ron Ostrow *(Fast Food Family Man)*; Garfield! *(Guard)*; Susan Blommaert *(Sister Mary)*; Angela Pupello *(Brett's Date)*; Jorjan Fox *(Lozarro's Young Lady)*; Ronald Rand *(Angry Customer)*; David Klein *(Young Johnny Brennan)*; Coach Cox *(Young Kamal)*; Christopher Conte *(Young Brett Weir)*; Charlotte Moore *(Mrs. Weir)*; Dennis Hutchinson *(Newsman)*; Maria A. Corbo *(Newswoman)*; Jerry Dunphy *(Anchorwoman)*; Christopher Harrison *(Sparky the Clown)*; John DiLeo *(Reporter)*; Marc Webster *(Reporter)*; Al Cerullo *(Helicopter Pilot)*

The popular phone pranksters, whose outrageous calls became hits both on underground tapes and on commercial compact discs, come to the screen in this cheap and unfunny comedy.

Johnny and Kamal (Johnny Brennan and Kamal Ahmed) are Queens layabouts who delight in making crank calls. When childhood acquaintance (and victim) Brett Weir (James Lorinz) brags to them about his recently acquired mob employment, the duo put a call in to his higher-ups, setting themselves up as visiting hit men from Chicago. The two are embraced by the Mafiosi, who send them to shake down a bar owner whose refusal to sell out stands in the way of a real estate takeover. Said owner turns out to be Mickey (Alan North), whose place is Johnny and Kamal's favorite hangout, and who beats them up when they reluctantly inform him of their mission. Soon, local boss Lazarro (Alan Arkin) is onto the boys' scheme, but they manage to escape from his underlings by posing as various bizarre characters.

After rescuing Johnny's mother, Mrs. B (Suzanne Shepherd), from the gangsters, the boys call hard-nosed cop Worzic (Brad Sullivan), who's been after them as well, hoping they'll lead him to their fictitious boss. Worzic turns out to be in league with Lazarro, however, and Johnny and Kamal, using the tricks they know best, contrive to tape incriminating statements on the phone. They take their story to the press, which dubs them "The Jerky Boys." When Lazarro and Worzic are busted, the duo are given city office jobs—from which they continue to pull their old pranks.

The idea of a Jerky Boys movie in which the boys spend little time on the phone seems counterproductive, though the filmmakers evidently realized (and rightly so) that watching staged crank calls on screen doesn't have the subversive kick of listening to the real thing being performed on unsuspecting targets. Unfortunately, what they've come up with is a lame movie that pretty much could have starred any pair of second-rate comics. In real life, the Jerkys targeted businesses and posed as outrageous characters, apparently in symbolic retaliation for mistreatment at the hands of job interviewers. But in the film the boys are just a couple of harmless eccentrics who make crank calls because they have nothing better to do.

A similar lack of inspiration pervades the entire film, which takes off from the most obvious premise possible for a Jerky Boys movie and develops it with a distinct lack of comic style and imagination. A good supporting cast (including William Hickey, Paul Bartel, and Tom Jones in a cameo) is wasted, and the Jerkys themselves don't exactly come off as prime comic acting talents. Still, it's hard to ascribe too much blame to the boys themselves; when their private little game became public and Hollywood came calling, who were they to say no? *(Violence, extreme profanity.)* — M.G.

d, James Melkonian; p, Joe Roth, Roger Birnbaum; exec p, Tony Danza, Emilio Estevez; assoc p, Jonathan Glickman; co-p, Randy Ostrow; w, James Melkonian, Rich Wilkes, John G. Brennan, Kamal Ahmed; ph, Ueli Steiger; ed, Dennis M. Hill; m, Ira Newborn; prod d, Dan Leigh; set d, Ronnie von Blomberg;

sound, Michael Barosky (mixer); fx, Steve Kirshoff; casting, Douglas Aibel; cos, John Dunn; makeup, Michal Bigger; stunts, Peter Bucossi

Comedy/Docudrama   **(PR: O   MPAA: R)**

JLG BY JLG   ★★★½
(France/Switzerland) 58m Gaumont; Peripheria ~ Cinema Parallel c

(AKA: JLG/JLG; JLG/JLG—AUTOPORTRAIT DE DECEMBRE)

Jean-Luc Godard; Nathalie Aguillar; Brigitte Bastien; Denis Jadot; Andre Labarthe; Genevieve Pasquier

Jean-Luc Godard takes up the challenge of self-examination in JLG BY JLG. This highly stylized and meditative self-portrait addresses issues ranging from the director's career and life to the nature of cinema and culture.

The film opens in the dark interior of Godard's home in Switzerland. A video camera sits on a tripod, gazing out to the brightness beyond the window. The camera moves in on a portrait of Godard as a boy while the man rasps into a microphone, "I was already in mourning for myself." Godard describes himself as suffering from loss of self, and he represents this state through images of frozen, snow-covered, barren landscapes. The film is subtitled "A Self-portrait in Winter."

Godard is quick to declare that the film is neither a documentary nor an autobiography, but a self-portrait, thus aligning this cinematic gesture with painting and the visual arts instead of literature or commentary (despite frequent references to the written text, e.g., open books and blank pages). Questions about self-examination, identity, and the reflexive nature of cinema arise after Godard asks rhetorically what the words of the title mean. He employs the metaphor of a mirror to describe filmic representation and observes that the title of his film is itself a mirror image.

Godard introduces what he calls his stereo theory of reception, drawing a point of reference—the individual—on a piece of paper, then extending two lines out in opposing directions joined by a common line to form a triangle. At the receiving end he draws another point and another triangle intersecting with the first, creating a figure like the Star of David. Viewer and object, he suggests, are bound by a mutual field of reception and understanding. The object can be a film, an other, or an historical moment or epoch.

Godard conceives of culture as a static, oppressive body. Early in the film he warns that culture is the rule and art the exception, and that the rule desires the death of the exception. On the other hand, Godard proposes that language brings all human beings into a universal community and declares his sole purpose to be the realization of this universality.

As ever, Godard's reflections on the art of cinema are intriguing (where they are not confounding), but what stays with the viewer is the uncompromising frankness of the film's autobiographical elements. The director does not hesitate to reveal hostility, self-absorption, and cynicism about his own endeavors. It is an unforgettable portrait of an aging, lonely, seemingly misanthropic artist who isn't nearly ready to give up the ghost. *(Adult situations.)* — M.F.

d, Jean-Luc Godard; p, Jean-Luc Godard; w, Jean-Luc Godard; ph, Yves Pouliquer, Christian Jaquenod; ed, Christine Cormon; sound, Pierre-Alain Besse

Documentary/Experimental   **(PR: A   MPAA: NR)**

JOHNNY MNEMONIC   ★★½
(Canada/U.S.) 98m Alliance Communications; CineVisions ~ TriStar c

Keanu Reeves *(Johnny Mnemonic)*; Dina Meyer *(Jane)*; Ice-T *(J-Bone)*; Takeshi Kitano *(Takahashi)*; Denis Akiyama *(Shinji)*; Dolph Lundgren *(Street Preacher)*; Henry Rollins *(Spider)*; Barbara Sukowa *(Anna K)*; Udo Kier *(Ralfi)*; Tracy Tweed *(Pretty)*; Falconer Abraham *(Yomamma)*; Don Francks *(Hooky)*; Diego Chambers *(Henson)*; Sherry Miller *(Takahashi's Girlfriend)*; Arthur Eng *(Viet)*; Von Flores *(Viet)*; Victoria Tengelis *(Pharmakom Receptionist)*; Warren Sulatycky *(Yakuza Operator)*; Celina Wu *(Mikiyo)*; Gene Mack *(Laslo)*; Jamie Elman *(Toad)*; Simon Sinn *(Man in Hotel Lobby)*; Caitlin Carmody *(Twin in Hotel Lobby)*; Erin Carmody *(Twin in Hotel Lobby)*; Doug O'Keefe *(Pharmakom Security)*; Marlow Vella *(Lotek Kid)*; Howard Szafer *(Strike)*; Paul Brogren *(Stump)*; Arthi Sambasivan *(Nurse)*; Silvio Oliviero *(Stick)*; Coyote Shivers *(Buddy)*; Lynne Adams *(Rocket Launcher Yakuza)*; Mike Shearer *(Yakuza Partner)*; Susan Tsgkaris *(Opera Singer)*; Christopher Comrie *(Beijing Riot Newscaster)*; Robin Crosby *(Girl in Hotel Room)*

A dystopian future thriller that sets a bare-bones chase plot against elaborate neo-BLADE RUNNER decor, JOHNNY MNEMONIC isn't the total disaster many critics declared, but it's far less than the sum of its rather amazing parts.

In the 21st century, the world is divided sharply between affluent technocrats and the impoverished masses, who live on the filthy streets. A new plague called NAS—nerve attenuation syndrome, which is apparently brought about by information overload—has left much of the world's population with fatal tremors. The information superhighway and the back roads of the human mind are one, and Johnny (Keanu Reeves) is king of the road. His brain filled with high-tech computer chips, Johnny transports information too sensitive to trust to more conventional means. But he's tired of his lonely, alienating job, and increasingly troubled by having given up his memories to make room for circuit boards. Determined to undergo expensive memory reconstruction surgery, Johnny is susceptible to the "one last job" blandishments that always spell trouble in movie narratives.

In a sleek Beijing hotel room, Johnny meets a group of scientists who want to export industrial secrets. Just as the information upload into his brain is completed, a band of Yakuza—sent by ruthless corporate overlord Takahashi ("Beat" Takeshi Kitano) and led by the smoothly vicious Shinji (Denis Akiyama)—bursts in and kills everyone except Johnny. He escapes, but without part of the code that will allow him to download. The program he has uploaded is so massive that he's in imminent danger of total sensory meltdown.

Johnny meets with his sleazy agent, Ralfi (Udo Kier), who plans to kill him and sell the purloined information. Johnny is saved by freelance bodyguard Jane (Dina Meyer), who takes him to the Lo-Teks, anti-technology rebels. They're led by the angry J-Bone (Ice T), and live in a glorified treehouse made of industrial castoffs. In a desperate effort to download the information—which he realizes is the cure for NAS—Johnny goes to Spider (Henry Rollins), a tattooed "flesh mechanic." Before Spider can operate, a $6 million mercenary named Street Preacher (Dolph Lundgren) bursts in and kills him. Jane and Johnny return to the Lo-Teks, and they turn to mysterious codebreaker Jones—a dolphin—for help. Takahashi and his goons attack the Lo-Tek stronghold, but Shinji turns on Takahashi and kills him. Before he dies, Shinji turns over the missing code. The cure for NAS is downloaded, leaving Johnny free to recover his own memories and contemplate his future.

It seems incredible that JOHNNY MNEMONIC should be the first work by novelist William Gibson—who coined the term "cyberspace"—to make it to the screen. His vision of the future, in which a vast electronic frontier is dominated by outlaw hackers and multinational corporations, is dense, compelling, and perfectly in sync with popular preoccupations: virtual reality, emerging diseases, the Internet, the New World Order.

But JOHNNY MNEMONIC doesn't quite live up to its implicit promise. Keanu Reeves was widely blamed: unless carefully directed, he's an actor who fairly radiates blank stupidity, and casting him in a movie in which the plot revolves around what's in his head seems to beg for trouble. But Reeves is actually an asset. With his oddly angular face, lanky frame, and big, awkward feet, Reeves looks startlingly like the generic men in black suits who populate the canvases of painter-turned-director Robert Longo. He brings exactly the right vacuousness to a character whose brain is continually being sucked dry.

The reptilian Kier is self-consciously sleazy as Johnny's agent, and belligerent, tattooed punk poet Henry Rollins is entertaining as renegade surgeon Spider. He-Man Lundgren is a positive revelation as Street Preacher, not just because he caresses a cruciform dagger with such wondrous fervor, but because with shoulder-length, center-parted hair he looks astonishingly like the effete portraits of the suffering Jesus that line the walls of Catholic grammar schools (the Lord's face atop a muscleman's body is a potent fetish image). Barbara Sukowa, best known for her work in Fassbinder films, is relegated to a small role as a dead scientist reborn as a sort of ghost in the machine.

The film's other elements—including its elaborate production design, action set pieces and extensive computer animation—are all fine, but they add up to nothing more than the sum of their parts—perhaps because the BRING ME THE HEAD OF JOHNNY MNEMONIC plot is a bit thin, or perhaps because first-time feature director Longo lacks the skill or the panache to pull it all together.

The film was released in a longer version in Japan. Most of the additional footage included popular Japanese personality Beat Takeshi. *(Violence, substance abuse, profanity.)* — M.M.

d, Robert Longo; p, Don Carmody; exec p, Staffan Ahrenberg, B.J. Rack, Victoria Hamburg, Robert Lantos; w, William Gibson (based on his short story); ph, Francois Protat; ed, Ronald Sanders; m, Brad Fiedel; prod d, Nilo Rodis Jamero; art d, Dennis Davenport; set d, Enrico Campana; sound, Douglas Murray (design), Doug Ganton (mixer); fx, Rory Cutler, John Nelson, Gene Warren, Jr., Fantasy II Film Effects; casting, John Buchan; cos, Olga Dimitrov; makeup, Linda Gill; stunts, Victor Armstrong

Science Fiction/Thriller   (PR: C   MPAA: R)

JON JOST'S FRAMEUP
(SEE: FRAMEUP)

JOURNEY OF AUGUST KING, THE   ★★½
(U.S.) 91m Addis/Wechsler Productions ~ Miramax c

Jason Patric *(August King)*; Thandie Newton *(Annalees Williamsburg)*; Larry Drake *(Olaf Singletary)*; Sam Waterston *(Mooney Wright)*; Sara-Jane Wylde *(Ida Wright)*; Eric Mabius *(Hal Wright)*; Bill Whitlock *(Samuel)*; Muse Watson *(Zimmer)*; John Doman *(Bolton)*; Andrew Stahl *(Harrison)*; Danny Nelson *(Felix)*; Collin Wilcox Paxton *(Mina)*; Dean Rader Duvall *(Gabriel)*; Billy Ray Reynolds *(Ben)*; Marlus C. Harding *(Sims)*; Lisa Roberts *(Meg)*; John Burnett Hall *(Travis)*; Roy Bush Laughter *(Tom)*; Clint Menacof *(Ralph)*; A. Duncan Shirley, III *(Porter)*; Chase Conley *(Harry (Son))*; E. George Betz *(Bridge Attendant)*; Nesbitt Blaisdell *(Mr. Cole)*; Graham Paul *(Wade)*; Joan Cope *(Elsie)*; Terry Nienhuis *(Fisher)*

Like a Disney film from the 1950s, THE JOURNEY OF AUGUST KING whitewashes provocative subject matter; but two lead actors give substance and dignity to this drama about a man who helps a slave girl in the post-Civil War South.

Jason Patric plays August King, a young widower in 1815 in North Carolina, who stops on his way home at a town to buy supplies for his farm. Just after he hears about a male and female slave having escaped from their owner, Olaf Singletary (Larry Drake), August meets Annalees (Thandie Newton), the female runaway. Reluctantly at first, and knowing he is committing a crime, August hides Annalees in his wagon; but, as they travel along the road together, August and Annalees grow closer. When word spreads that the white man helping one of the runaway slaves is also traveling with a milk cow, August kills his cow to cover his tracks. Further along the way, August and Annalees witness Olaf brutally killing the male slave. As they arrive at his home, August points out the trail that will lead Annalees North. The next day, Annalees begins her new journey alone, while August confronts the wealthy landowner, Mooney Wright (Sam Waterston), who joins Olaf in burning his farm as punishment for his crime. August, however, has already discovered that material goods can never replace spiritual wealth.

Based on John Ehle's 1971 novel, THE JOURNEY OF AUGUST KING tells its tale in a manner reminiscent of television shows like DR. QUINN, MEDICINE WOMAN. The politics are "correct" inasmuch as slavery is considered a bad thing, but the issues raised are dealt with so coyly, the film almost insults its audience. The one reference to a sexual relationship between Olaf and Annalees gets so buried, for example, that her speech about her master wanting "his garden hoe" cries out for a Damon Wayans-type satire, which, of course, never comes. Only once, during Olaf's murder of the escaped male slave, does AUGUST KING suggest the more powerful, if less lofty-minded, enterprise that perhaps director John Duigan (FLIRTING, SIRENS) had in mind. But Maya Angelou's voice-over sets the earnest tone early on and Sam Waterston's post-I'LL FLY AWAY cameo clinches it at the end. (Also, the muted earth-tone color scheme throughout gets stifling at times.)

What finally saves THE JOURNEY OF AUGUST KING from complete midcult solemnity is the fine performances by both Patric and Newton (who played Sally Hemmings in JEFFERSON IN PARIS). Patric and Newton are so good together that they make the potentially hackneyed moments believable. The ending is moving thanks primarily to the lead performers' thoughtful and low-key approach to their roles. If nothing else, THE JOURNEY OF AUGUST KING makes one hope that these actors advance to better showcases for their talents in years to come. *(Violence, adult situations.)* — E.M.

d, John Duigan; p, Nick Wechsler, Sam Waterston; exec p, Bob Weinstein, Harvey Weinstein, Richard N. Gladstein; assoc p, Borden Mace; co-p, Kerry Orent; w, John Ehel (based on his novel); ph, Slawomir Idziak; ed, Humphrey Dixon; m, Stephen Endelman; prod d, Patricia Norris; sound, Paul Ledford (mixer); fx, Ray Bivins; casting, Billy Hopkins, Suzanne Smith, Kerry Barden; cos, Patricia Norris; makeup, Lori Hicks, Tony Elwood

Drama/Historical   (PR: C   MPAA: PG-13)

JUDGE DREDD   ★★
(U.S.) 91m Judge Dredd Productions; Edward R. Pressman Film Corportation; Cinergi; Creative Movie Marketing; Hollywood Pictures ~ Buena Vista c

Sylvester Stallone *(Judge Dredd)*; Armand Assante *(Rico)*; Rob Schneider *(Fergie)*; Jurgen Prochnow *(Judge Griffin)*; Max Von Sydow *(Judge Fargo)*; Diane Lane *(Judge Hershey)*; Joanna Miles *(McGruder)*; Joan Chen *(Ilsa)*; Balthazar Getty *(Olmeyer)*; Mitchell Ryan *(Hammond)*; James Remar *(uncredited)*; Maurice Roeves *(Miller)*; Ian Dury *(Geiger)*; Chris Adamson *(Mean Machine)*; Ewen Bremner *(Junior Angel)*; Peter Marinker *(Jude Esposito)*; Angus MacInnes *(Judge Silver)*; Louise Delamere *(Locker Judge)*; Phil Smeeton *(Fink Angel)*; Steve Toussaint *(Hunter Squad Leader)*; Bradley Savelle *(Chief Judge Hunter)*; Mark Morghan *(Judge Killed by Robot)*; Ed Stobart *(Barge Crew Member)*; Huggy Lever *(Brutal Prisoner)*; Alexis Daniel *(Brisco)*; John Blakey *(Border Guard)*; Howard Grace *(Pilot)*; Dig Wayne *(Reggie)*; Martin McDougal *(Twist)*; Ashley Artus *(Squatter No. 1)*; Christopher Glover *(Squatter No. 2)*; Brendan Fleming *(Squatter No. 3)*; Stephen Lord *(Zed Squatter No. 1)*; Phil Kingston *(Zed Squatter No. 2)*; Ewan Bailey *(Aspen Guard)*; Stuart Mullen *(Co-pilot)*; Pat Starr *(Lily Hammond)*; Adam Henderson *(Fuppie)*

An expensive live-action version of a popular British comic book, JUDGE DREDD takes audiences to a vividly rendered dystopian future where uniformed, armed Judges act as police, jury and executioner. A fast pace, clever twists, and dazzling futuristic effects shore up a lightweight story which raises some interesting ethical questions about cloning, but brushes them off in a conventional action climax.

In the crowded, sprawling Mega City One of the far future, Judge Dredd (Sylvester Stallone) is legendary for his fearlessness and strict adherence to the letter of the law. As "block wars" break out with increasing frequency, Judge Griffin (Jurgen Prochnow) of the ruling council urges Chief Justice Fargo (Max Von Sydow) to expand the use of the death penalty. Meanwhile, renegade judge Rico (Armand Assante) escapes from prison and returns to Mega City One, where he hatches a plot with Judge Griffin to bring criminal chaos to the city and enable Griffin to implement totalitarian measures to restore order.

Dredd is framed by Rico—his former best friend—for the murder of a crusading TV reporter (Mitchell Ryan), and is sentenced to life in a penal colony. When the prison shuttle craft is shot down over the "Cursed Earth" desert by pirates, Dredd and fellow prisoner Ferguson (Rob Schneider), a small-time computer hacker, escape and overpower the pirates with the surprise help of Justice Fargo, who has hurried to the site of the crash. Fargo is fatally wounded in the battle, but before he dies he reveals that Dredd is the living result of the Janus Project, a secret experiment designed to create the perfect judge from selected DNA. Rico is Dredd's only blood relation, cloned from the same DNA but inexplicably warped into the perfect criminal.

Back in Mega City One, Dredd escapes police pursuers in a wild air-cycle chase over the city's skyline and meets up with sympathetic Judge Hershey (Diane Lane). Together, Dredd, Hershey and Ferguson raid the secret lab housing the Janus Project. With the help of turncoat biologist Ilsa (Joan Chen), Rico prepares to clone a whole generation of new judges in a matter of hours, replacing the "perfect judge" DNA sample with his own. As the clones begin to hatch prematurely, Dredd, Hershey and Ferguson enter and take on Rico, his robot bodyguard, and Ilsa in a battle to the death. The clones are destroyed, Griffin, Rico and Ilsa are killed, and Dredd emerges from the lab wreckage to learn he's been cleared of all charges.

This hugely expensive film—it's reported to have cost some $75 million—adapted from a cult comic book series delivers the goods to its particular audience. The story moves quickly, the characters are engaging, and the supporting cast is packed with top-level talent. More importantly, the film's vision of a night-marish, densely packed future city boasts some truly imaginative design touches. The pivotal air-cycle chase involves breathtaking aerial maneuvers to dodge the high-rise towers and electronic advertising fields. The overall urban design closely recalls that of BLADE RUNNER, but is much more garish and out-of-control.

The cloning subplot, in which the stoic, bloodless Dredd finds out he was created in a lab, could have been used for greater emotional impact *a la* ROBOCOP, but the filmmakers opted for visual splash and fast-paced action rather than any serious subtext. Stallone effectively meets the physical demands of the title role, but too often comes across as a caricature; he is more cartoonish than the two-dimensional comic book Dredd, whose dark edge is much of his appeal. *(Violence.)* — B.C.

d, Danny Cannon; p, Charles M. Lippincott, Beau E.L. Marks; exec p, Edward R. Pressman, Andrew Vajna; assoc p, Tony Munafo, Susan Nicoletti; w, William Wisher, Steven E. de Souza (from a story by William Wisher and Michael DeLuca, based on characters created by John Wagner and Carlos Ezquerra); ph, Adrian Biddle; ed, Alex Mackie, Harry Keramidas; m, Alan Silvestri; prod d, Nigel Phelps; art d, Les Tompkins; set d, Peter Young; sound, Leslie Shatz (designer), Chris Munro (mixer); fx, Joss Williams, Joel Hynek, Diane Pearlman, Mass. Illusion; casting, Jackie Burch; cos, Emma Porteous; makeup, Nick Dudman; stunts, Marc Boyle

Science Fiction   **(PR: C   MPAA: R)**

JUDICIAL CONSENT   ★★
(U.S.) 101m Prelude Pictures; Rysher Entertainment ~ WarnerVision c

Bonnie Bedelia *(Gwen Warwick)*; Will Patton *(Alan Warwick)*; Dabney Coleman *(Charles Mayron)*; Billy Wirth *(Martin)*; Lisa Blount *(District Attorney)*; Michael Greene; Kevin McCarthy; Jim McMullen; Sheila Hanahan; Henry Brown

William Bindley's debut feature aspires to the John Grisham league of legal thriller but, with a pedestrian plot and a lack of sustained suspense, JUDICIAL CONSENT falls well short. It was released direct to home video after some 1994 festival showings.

Her marriage on the rocks, Judge Gwen Warwick (Bonnie Bedelia) begins an illicit affair with a young library clerk, Martin (Billy Wirth). Her jealous husband Alan (Will Patton) knows Gwen is cheating, but suspects that her lover is attorney Charles Mayron (Dabney Coleman), Gwen's friend and colleague. Charles is found murdered, and one of his many lovers is arrested for the crime. Gwen presides over the case, and discovers that evidence planted at the crime scene links her to the murder. She assumes that her husband has framed her, but then she learns that Martin is the one who set her up. She brings the police to Martin's loft, but he has disappeared. Knowing that her arrest is imminent, Gwen frantically researches her past cases to discover Martin's identity and motive. She learns that she had sentenced Martin's father to life imprisonment. As Gwen tries to find the murder weapon and prove her innocence, Martin returns. Rather than kill Gwen, he wants to see her imprisoned, like his father. But in a scuffle in Gwen's attic, Martin is killed.

Bedelia gives an engaging performance, but her interpretation of the central character may be the film's fatal flaw. It is hard to believe that a woman as intelligent and accomplished as Gwen would fall into Martin's trap. Wirth is effective as the mysterious Martin. Lisa Blount is strong as the ambitious DA briefly suspected of the murder. Coleman, Patton and Kevin McCarthy make the best of underdeveloped characters. *(Violence, nudity, sexual situations, profanity.)* — B.R.

d, William Bindley; p, Douglas Curtis, Mark W. Koch; exec p, Keith Samples, William Hart; w, William Bindley; ph, James Glennon; ed, William Hoy; m, Christopher Young; prod d, Dorian Vernaccio, Deborah Raymond; sound, Jeff Jones; casting, Fern Orenstein; cos, Eleanor Nyquist-Patton; makeup, Elizabeth Colburn

Drama/Thriller (PR: O MPAA: NR)

JUMANJI ★★½
(U.S.) 100m Interscope Communications; Teitler Films; TriStar ~ TriStar c

Robin Williams *(Alan Parrish)*; Jonathan Hyde *(Van Pelt/Sam Parrish)*; Kirsten Dunst *(Judy)*; Bradley Pierce *(Peter)*; Bonnie Hunt *(Sarah)*; Bebe Neuwirth *(Nora)*; David Alan Grier *(Bentley)*; Patricia Clarkson *(Carol Parrish)*; Adam Hann-Byrd *(Young Alan)*; Laura Bell Bundy *(Young Sarah)*; James Handy *(Exterminator)*; Gillian Barber *(Mrs. Thomas)*; Brandon Obray *(Benjamin)*; Cyrus Thiedeke *(Caleb)*; Gary Joseph Thorup *(Billy Jessup)*; Leonard Zola *(Cop)*; Lloyd Berry *(Bum)*; Malcolm Stewart *(Jim Shepherd)*; Annabel Kershaw *(Martha Shepherd)*; Darryl Henriques *(Gun Salesman)*; Robin Driscoll *(Paramedic)*; Peter Bryant *(Paramedic)*; Sarah Gilson *(Girl)*; Florica Vlad *(Girl)*; June Lion *(Baker)*; Brenda Lockmuller *(Pianist)*; Frederick Richardson *(Barber)*

"Jumanji" is the name of a bizarre game of jungle exploration that literally comes to life in the inventive and dazzlingly illustrated children's book by Chris van Allsburg. As a film, unfortunately, JUMANJI has too many snakes and not enough ladders.

It's 1969. Alan (Adam Hann-Byrd) is the son of distant, insensitive Sam Parrish (Jonathan Hyde), a wealthy factory owner in a small New Hampshire town. In a construction site, Alan finds a strange board game (the box emits faint drumming sounds) and convinces his friend Sarah (Laura Bell Bundy) to play it. Alan's turn brings up the message: "In the jungle you must wait, until the die show six or eight." He is immediately sucked into the game board in a howling whirlwind. Sarah drops the dice, inadvertently taking her turn and unleashing a swarm of bats who chase her out into the night.

Twenty-six years later, orphaned siblings Peter and Judy (Bradley Pierce and Kirstin Dunst) move into the now-abandoned house with their aunt Nora (Bebe Neuwirth). They find the game and resume play. Things pick up exactly where they left off: after Peter summons a trio of huge mosquitoes, Judy rolls a six, conjuring up both a gang of vandalizing monkeys and Alan himself, now an adult (Robin Williams), who has survived his jungle exile and knows all the dangers the game has in store. He is both overjoyed to be released and deeply saddened by the sight of his now depressed home town. Judy presses him to continue the game because the rules state that the creatures will only vanish when the game has been won. Just as he relents, he realizes that Sarah must take her turns as well.

They find her, now a New Age adept calling herself "Madame Serene" (Bonnie Hunt). Her turn brings forth the Great White Hunter, Van Pelt (also played by Hyde), whose prey happens to be Alan. This leads the film into a series of chase scenes involving losing and recovering the game several times, and culminating in the ransacking of a strip mall. Pursued by Van Pelt, Aunt Nora, and Carl the cop (David Alan Grier), the quartet manage to complete the last few turns, as monsoons, crocodiles, spiders, and quicksand threaten to do them all in. Alan's final roll wins the game, restoring them in a flash to 1969. Given the chance to start over, Alan and Sarah get married, save the factory and, in a denouement, find Peter and Judy's parents and stop them from taking the ski trip that would have ended their lives.

This piling on of happy endings is indicative of the film's greatest flaw: it over-tells the story, stopping after every action scene to reflect on some important truth and chew over the plot. This jerky pacing undercuts the genuinely outstanding effects (by the same animators who brought JURASSIC PARK to life). The climax, which is so frantic it doesn't give the actors time to talk, is a lot of fun, but becomes a bit too intense for those under the age of eight (Judy gets in the neck). The morbid sense of humor and offhand attitude toward death could have been a strength, were it not for a script full of awkward dialogue, lame jokes about therapy, and other gags pitched toward the adults in the audience.

To his credit, Williams is quite restrained, rarely lapsing into his trademark riffs and mannerisms. The talented Hunt is stuck in a limited role with nothing interesting to do. The four children are terrific — especially Bundy, who actually looks like a young Hunt. Director Joe Johnston (HONEY, I SHRUNK THE KIDS) handles the action scenes with cliffhanger gusto—these, presumably, were what made the film a box-office smash—although dim lighting (to hide the seams from the computer-generated animals) is a drawback. But screenwriters Jonathan Hensleigh (A FAR OFF PLACE), Greg Taylor (PRANCER), and Jim Strain (BINGO) have taken the story far too seriously, infusing it with another ersatz nuclear family metaphor that puts too much pressure on what was originally a goofy fantasy about confronting fear. By compelling JUMANJI to be more than a game, they take all the fun out of it. Just like grown-ups! *(Violence, mild profanity.)* — R.S.

d, Joe Johnston; p, Scott Kroopf, William Teitler; exec p, Ted Field, Robert W. Cort, Larry J. Franco; w, Jonathan Hensleigh, Greg Taylor, Jim Strain (from a story by Greg Taylor, Jim Strain, and Chris Van Allsburg, based on the book by Chris Van Allsburg); ph, Thomas Ackerman; ed, Robert Dalva; m, James Horner; prod d, James Bissell; art d, David Willson, Glen Pearson; set d, Tedd Kuchera, Cynthia T. Lewis; sound, Rob Young (mixer), Randy Thom (design), Gary Rydstrom (design); fx, Stan Parks, Rory Cutler, Stephen L. Price, Ken Ralston, Industrial Light & Magic; casting, Nancy Foy; cos, Martha Wynne Snetsinger; makeup, Sandy Cooper, Tom Woodruff, Jr., Alec Gillis, Charles Porlier; stunts, Betty Thomas

Children's/Fantasy/Adventure (PR: A MPAA: PG)

JUPITER'S WIFE ★★★
(U.S.) 72m Blackridge Productions ~ Artistic License Films c

Maggie Cogan *(Jupiter's Wife)*; Bobbi *(Homeless Friend)*; Dr. James Krumenauer *(Veterinarian)*; Katina Pendleton *(Woman from the Upper East Side)*; Audrey Pendleton *(Katina's Daughter)*; Joan Culpepper *(Psychic Soul Reader)*; Joanne Bergbom *(High School Classmate)*; Charles *(Friend of Maggie)*; Lynn *(Friend of Maggie)*; Edwige Val *(Teacher of Gymnastic Workshop)*; Peter Negroponte *(Filmmaker's Child)*; Ramona Negroponte *(Filmmaker's Child)*

It is not unusual for a documentary to remind one of a mainstream movie, and the thematic soulmate of JUPITER'S WIFE is the 1991 THE FISHER KING. But Michel Negroponte's portrait of a homeless Manhattan mystic is far superior; too bad that its exposure on the festival circuit and Cinemax cable received nowhere near the audiences of the Robin Williams vehicle.

Negroponte, an New York University (NYU) film instructor and documentarian (SPACE COAST), who is apparently never without a video camera, recounts in the first person his meetings with Maggie, a curiously captivating middle-aged woman walking her collection of stray dogs in Central Park. She lives in a crate (she calls it her "Sugar Shack") and speaks in cheerful stream-of-consciousness riddles that blend James Joyce with classical Greek myths.

Maggie matter-of-factly claims to be a daughter of the late Hollywood actor Robert Ryan and a concubine of the god Zeus, for whom she bore quintuplets, now kept hidden from her but in constant contact via ESP. She also makes off-the-wall comments like "Sometimes I forget I have a face."

Negroponte analyzes the strange claims as carefully as police search for clues in a murder case. Inquiries to Robert Ryan's family prove that Maggie, while not a relative, was truly a close friend and frequent companion during the 1960s. Her association with celebrities like Ryan arose from her notable job as the first female horse-and-carriage driver in Central Park. The film's eeriest moments rediscover vintage footage of a young, bespectacled Maggie, guest-starring on the game show "What's My Line?" But her moment in the limelight was followed by a failed marriage (possibly two), after which Maggie lost custody of her children and sank into drugs, schizophrenia, and fantasies in which her ex-husband loomed with Olympian proportions.

Estranged from her own parents, Maggie has been homeless since 1986. A hard winter and bulldozing of the Sugar Shack force Maggie to a safehouse apartment, where social workers, plus a few theater folk who remember the carriage driver of yesteryear, visit to offer their support. But Maggie, almost always upbeat, seems less a pathetic victim and more the holy fool of folklore tradition; Negroponte ends his narrative pondering Maggie's uncanny prediction of the birth of his own child.

Unlike other documentaries, news reports or dramas on the homeless, JUPITER'S WIFE seeks no pity, nor does it express righteous political outrage on behalf of its subject. Rather, it displays a unique and remarkable life altered by mental illness into metaphorical delusions that are nearer the truth than a casual bystander would ever think. As if to drive home the point, Negroponte introduces, without comment, another Central Park regular, Maggie's friend Bobbie. She's a youngish, self-proclaimed Holocaust survivor making very odd statements connecting the Kennedys with the Mafia. What, one asks, lies behind her particular tall tales? *(Profanity, adult situations.)* — C.C.

d, Michel Negroponte; p, Michel Negroponte; co-p, Jane Weiner, Doug Block; w, Michel Negroponte, Gabriel Morgan; ph, Michel Negroponte; ed, Michel Negroponte; m, Brooks Williams; sound, Harmonic Ranch (mixing), Brooks Williams (design), Beo Morales (design)

Documentary (PR: C MPAA: NR)

JURY DUTY ★½
(U.S.) 86m Triumph Films; Weasel Productions; TriStar ~ TriStar c

Pauly Shore *(Tommy)*; Tia Carrere *(Monica)*; Stanley Tucci *(Frank)*; Brian Doyle-Murray *(Harry)*; Abe Vigoda *(Judge Powell)*; Shelley Winters *(Mom)*; Charles Napier *(Jed)*; Richard Edson *(Skeets)*; Richard Riehle *(Principal Beasely)*; Alex Datcher *(Sarah)*; Richard T. Jones *(Nathan)*; Sharon Barr *(Libby Starling)*; Jack McGee *(Murphy)*; Nick Bakay *(Richard Hertz)*; Ernie Lee Banks *(Ray)*; Dick Vitale *(Hal Gibson)*; Billie Bird *(Rose)*; Jorge Luis Abreu *(Jorge)*; Siobhan Fallon *(Heather)*; Gregory Cooke *(Reece Fishburn)*; Mark L. Taylor *(Russell Cadbury)*; Sean Whalen *(Carl Wayne Bishop)*; Laurelyn Scharkey *(Harry's Bombshell)*; Steven Hy Landau *(Tuna Salad Guy)*; Melissa Samuels *(Club Announcer)*; Paul Stork *(Transvestite)*; William Newman *(Judge D'Angelo)*; Susan Lentini *(Judge Swartz)*; Tom Booker *(Press Runner)*; Jay Kogen *(Russell's Assistant)*; Paul

Thorpe *(Goliath)*; Michael Reid Mackay *(Steer Shack Employee)*; David McMillan *(Friendly Falafel Employee)*; Saemi Nakamura *(Wiener Boy Employee)*; Efren Ramirez *(Pirate Pete's Employee)*; J.D. Hall *(Guard)*; Bruce Economou *(Guard)*; Lynn Ziegler *(Mrs. Woodall)*; Yolanda Miro *(Spanish Reporter)*; Y. Hero Abe *(Japanese Reporter)*; Michael Feresten *(Folk Singer)*; Fritz Mashimo *(Japanese Suicide Man)*; George Christy *(Dr. Brookings)*

JURY DUTY, featuring Pauly Shore, is an insipid courtroom comedy slapped together to coincide with the O.J. Simpson murder trial.

Tommy Collins (Shore) is an unemployable slacker who finds himself out on the street when his mother (Shelley Winters) takes their trailer home with her on vacation; a timely jury notice may provide the answer, but only if the trial lasts long enough to require sequestering. Collins manages to land a spot in the trial of Carl Wayne Bishop (Sean Whalen), a.k.a. the drive-through killer, accused of murdering seven former bosses at various fast-food restaurants. Though the court initially puts the jury up in the most dilapidated wing of a nearby hotel, Collins uses some strategically-placed product endorsements to wheedle his way into a plush suite. His comfort level secured, Collins's next challenge is to stretch the apparently open-and-shut case into a nice, lengthy vacation. During the month-long deliberation, he manages—quite by accident—not only to prove the defendant's innocence, but to win the love of a gorgeous cojuror (Tia Carrere).

Though the fact that Hollywood can produce a comedy to capitalize on the macabre media blitz surrounding a murder trial is inherently repugnant, the premise of JURY DUTY—that to someone like Collins serving on the jury of a long trial is more attractive than getting a job—shows some initial promise. But what might have been the film's best chance at comedy falls disappointingly flat. Instead of coming up with creative ways for Collins to stall the jury's rendering of a decision, the twenty-eight-day deliberation is compressed into a soundless, and largely pointless, montage. The bulk of the film relies upon Shore's lowest-common-denominator style of physical humor, which played much better in five-minute MTV segments than it does in a feature film.

JURY DUTY works best when it is skewering America's voyeuristic relationship with the courtroom, evidenced by the series of recently televised sensational trials. In one funny but short scene, sports megamouth Dick Vitale plays a "Justice-TV" commentator, recapping the day's trials in his trademark supersonic patter ("We're talkin' mistrial city, baby!"). It is also no coincidence that, in these few funny scenes, Shore is blissfully offscreen. After his performance in SON-IN-LAW and IN THE ARMY NOW, it is not difficult to understand why his appeal is rapidly waning. Thankfully, JURY DUTY is unlikely to reverse that trend. *(Violence, profanity.)* — B.T.

d, John Fortenberry; p, Yoram Ben-Ami, Peter M. Lenkov; assoc p, Dessie Markovsky, Emile Razpopov; co-p, Stephen L. Bernstein, Richard M. Heller; w, Neil Tolkin, Barbara Williams, Samantha Adams (based on a story by Barbara Williams and Samantha Adams); ph, Avi Karpick; ed, Stephen Semel; m, David Kitay; prod d, Deborah Raymond, Dorian Vernaccio; set d, Nancy S. Fallace; sound, Itzahk Magall (mixer); fx, Frank Ceglia; casting, Ferne Cassell; cos, Terry Dresbach; makeup, Suzanne Sanders; stunts, Dan Bradley

Comedy (PR: C MPAA: PG-13)

JUST CAUSE ★★★
(U.S.) 102m Fountainbridge Films ~ Warner Bros. c

Sean Connery *(Paul Armstrong)*; Laurence Fishburne *(Tanny Brown)*; Kate Capshaw *(Laurie Armstrong)*; Blair Underwood *(Bobby Earl)*; Ed Harris *(Blair Sullivan)*; Christopher Murray *(Wilcox)*; Ruby Dee *(Evangeline)*; Scarlett Johansson *(Kate)*; Daniel J. Travanti *(Warden)*; Ned Beatty *(McNair)*; Kevin McCarthy *(Phil Prestiss)*; Hope Lange *(Libby Prestiss)*; Liz Torres *(Dolores)*; Ida Conklin *(Dolores)*; Lynne Thigpen *(Dolores)*; Taral Nicks *(Lena)*; Victor Slezak *(Sergeant Rogers)*; Chris Sarandon *(Lyle Morgan)*; George Plimpton *(Elder Philips)*; Brooke Alderson *(Dr. Doliveau)*; Colleen Fitzpatrick *(Prosecutor)*; Richard Liberty *(Chaplin)*; Joel S. Ehrenkranz *(Judge)*; Barbara Jean Kane *(Joanie Shriver)*; Maurice Jamasal Brown *(Tanny's Son)*; Patrick Maycock *(Kid Washing Car)*; Jordan F. Vaughn *(Kid Washing Car)*; Francisco Paz *(Concierge)*; Marie Hyman *(Clerk)*; S. Bruce Wilson *(Party Guest)*; Erik Stephan *(Student)*; Melanie Hughes *(Receptionist)*; Megan Meinardus; Melissa Hood-Julien; Jenna Del Buono; Ashley Popelka; Marisa Perry; Augusta Lundsgaard *(Slumber Party Girls)*; Connie Lee Brown *(Prison Guard)*; Clarence Lark, III *(Prison Guard)*; Marie St. James; Gary Landon Mills; Shareef Malnik; Tony Bolano; Angele Maldonade; Fausto Rodriguez *(Prisoners)*; Karen Leeds; Dan Romero; Satcie A. Zinn *(Reporters)*

JUST CAUSE is a powerful excursion into Southern-style paranoia, whose cinematography is so potent that viewers will feel as if they're sweating along with the protagonists. Despite an occasional strangulation of credibility, this melodramatic shocker—benefitting from an uncredited rewrite by Richard Price—provides alert sleuths with a real work-out.

When her grandson Bobby Earl (Blair Underwood) is arrested for killing a child, Evangeline Ferguson (Ruby Dee) treks from the Florida Everglades to Boston where she pleads with capital punishment opponent Paul Armstrong (Sean Connery) to reopen the case. Retired Professor Armstrong refuses until his wife Laurie (Kate Capshaw) persuades him otherwise.

Back in Pachoula, Florida, Armstrong doesn't receive a warm reception from Sheriff Tanny (Laurence Fishburne) and Deputy Wilcox (Christopher Murray) who had beaten a confession out of Bobby Earl and who may have personal reasons for keeping the case closed. As Armstrong investigates, he finds a maelstrom of ambiguities and suppositions regarding Bobby Earl's guilt. Moreover, while visiting the crime scene with Sheriff Tanny, Armstrong feels the brunt of the locals' resentment when Tanny chokes him with a seat belt to demonstrate the killer's method in subduing the child, who was later sexually mutilated.

Fighting for his client even after his car is vandalized, Armstrong reels when his investigation is complicated by some startling developments: (1) Bobby Earl was previously charged with child kidnapping, a case which was (2) prosecuted by Laurie, who used the conviction to enhance her career. Angered by this deception, Armstrong presses on as Bobby Earl lets it slip that another inmate admitted committing the child-murder for which Bobby Earl might be executed. Nicknamed the Angel of Death, Blair Sullivan (Ed Harris), a serial killer, reveals the whereabouts of the murder weapon. With new evidence secured, Bobby Earl goes free, but Sullivan pleads with Armstrong to visit his elderly parents as a quid pro quid for clearing Bobby Earl. When Armstrong discovers the Sullivans' rotting corpses, he fears for his own family's safety. Prodding Sullivan, he discovers that Bobby Earl engineered this false confession in exchange for agreeing to slay Sullivan's parents upon his release. Kidnapping Laurie and their daughter Kate (Scarlet Johansson), Bobby Earl spirits them to his old killing ground. After he murders Deputy Sheriff Wilcox and incapacitates Tanny, Bobby Earl battles Armstrong at a poacher's cabin where Laurie and Kate are being held captive. Because he was castrated during his initial incarceration for kidnapping, Bobby Earl nursed revenge plans against former prosecutor Laurie. However, with the aid of wounded Tanny, Armstrong stabs the madman and an alligator claims his body.

Although JUST CAUSE could be convicted on several counts of audience manipulation, it is not one of those cheesy thrillers that throws in red herrings at the last minute. All the clues arm-chair detectives need are present from the set-up, but the screenplay skillfully draws our attention away from the obvious. Toying with audience perception until the recovery of the murder weapon, JUST CAUSE out-maneuvers the viewer (even if Laurie's withholding of her prior history with Bobby Earl is excessively tricky). Equally shaky is Paul's improbable last-minute rescue of his family in which he and Tanny conveniently zero in on the resourceful Bobby Earl. Reservations aside, JUST CAUSE is an always provocative and often scary journey through small town prejudice and criminal mentality. With an ominous sense of dread exacerbated by sun-baked cinematography, JUST CAUSE is acted powerfully enough to camouflage occasional screenplay indulgences. Moreover, JUST CAUSE challenges our subliminal reaction to factual evidence—we believe Bobby Earl because he's soft-spoken and handsome, whereas the rough-hewn Fishburne seems like a law-and-order race traitor. Without Fishburne, Underwood, and Harris, JUST CAUSE would probably not have been as proficient. However, with these three remarkable actors, the film is elevated to a thinking person's thriller status, enriched by its discussion of capital punishment, intra-race racism, and guilt as the tie that binds only those burdened with a conscience. *(Graphic violence, extreme profanity, sexual situations, adult situations.)* — R.P.

d, Arne Glimcher; p, Lee Rich, Arne Glimcher, Steve Perry; exec p, Sean Connery; assoc p, Rhonda Tollefson, Michael Alden; co-p, Gary Foster, Anna Reinhardt; w, Jeb Stuart, Peter Stone (based on the novel by John Katzenbach); ph, Lajos Koltai; ed, William Anderson; m, James Newton Howard; prod d, Patrizia von Brandenstein; art d, Dennis Bradford; set d, Cloudia Rebar, Maria Nay; sound, James Sabat (mixer); fx, Mike Meinardus; casting, Billy Hopkins, Suzanne Smith, Kerry Barden; cos, Ann Roth, Gary Jones; makeup, Scott Eddo, Shelly Woodhouse, Melanie Hughes; stunts, Chuck Picerni, Picerni

Crime/Drama/Thriller   (PR: O   MPAA: R)

KICKING AND SCREAMING ★★

(U.S.) 96m Castleberg Productions;
Sandollar Productions; Fifth Year Productions;
Trimark Pictures ~ Trimark Pictures c

Josh Hamilton *(Grover)*; Olivia d'Abo *(Jane)*;
Parker Posey *(Miami)*; Chris Eigeman *(Max)*;
Eric Stoltz *(Chet)*; Jason Wiles *(Skippy)*; Cara
Buono *(Kate)*; Carlos Jacott *(Otis)*; Elliot Gould
(Grover's Dad); Sam Gould *(Pete)*; Catherine
Kellner *(Gail)*; Jonathan Baumbach *(Professor)*;
John Lehr *(Louis)*; Peter Czernin *(Lester)*; Eliza
Roberts *(Josselyn)*; Chris Reed *(Friederich)*; Noah Baumbach
(Danny); Jason S. Kassin *(Freddy)*; David Deluise *(Bouncer)*;
Thea Goodman *(Friederich's Date)*; Lauren Katz *(Stephanie)*;
Alexia Landau *(Nose Ring Girl)*; Perrey Reeves *(Amy)*; Anthony
Giglio, Jr. *(Singing Freshman #1)*; Richard Tacchino *(Singing
Freshman #2)*; Nico Baumbach *(Random Freshman)*; Jose Igna-
cio Alvarez *(Stunt Knight #1)*; Solier Fagundez *(Stunt Knight
#2)*; David Kirsch *(Ike)*; Matthew Kaplan *(Omar)*; Dean Cameron
(Zach); Marissa Ribisi *(Charlotte)*; Kaela Dobkin *(Audra)*; Sal
Viscuso *(Bar Teacher)*; Jessica Hecht *(Ticket Woman)*; Nora Perri-
cone *(Door Person)*; Melanie Koch *(Girl at Bark)*

KICKING AND SCREAMING is built around the shallow angst
of a group of young men who seem to have little ambition
beyond whining cynically about their career opportunities and
girlfriends. Though slightly less affected than other recent comedies of this type, this film seems closer to a pretentious episode
of TV's "Friends" than a real slice of life.

KICKING AND SCREAMING begins at a graduation party.
Grover (Josh Hamilton) breaks up with his girlfriend Jane
(Olivia d'Abo) when she tells him she's leaving the United States
to do her post-graduate work in Prague. Jane wants Grover to
come with her, but Grover would rather stay near the college
campus and live with three of his fellow ex-classmates—priggish
Max (Chris Eigeman), neurotic Otis (Carlos Jacott) and immature Skippy (Jason Wiles)—none of whom has quite accepted the
reality of life after graduation.

The friends cling to their student ways in order not to have to
deal with disorienting post-college life. Grover spends his time
reminiscing about his relationship with Jane. Max hesitantly
begins a relationship with Kate (Cara Buono), a local teenage
waitress. Otis forms a two-person book club with Chet (Eric
Stoltz), a perennial student and philosopher of life. And Skippy
tries to hold onto Miami (Parker Posey), the girlfriend who has
outgrown him. With the help of informal encounter sessions and
tough love, the friends all manage to get beyond their personal
and professional plights.

Like Whit Stillman (METROPOLITAN, BARCELONA)
and his imitators, first-time director Noah Baumbach—the
son of *Village Voice* film critic Georgia Brown—takes as his
subject the psychopathology of twentysomething, white yuppie males who have to be dragged, kicking and screaming,
into the world of adult responsibilities. The film's dialogue,
weighted down with allusions to TV, comic books and other
trivialities, is meant to be sharp and cynical, a scintillating
surface that conceals the deeper romantic natures of these
bourgeois college graduates. But most of it simply shows off
Baumbach's talent for glibness. Chris Eigeman—who appeared in both Stillman films as a character very like
Max—tosses off philosophical lines like, "I caught myself
writing 'go to bed' and 'wake up' in my date book as if they
were different events." As Carla, the supposedly unsophisticated waitress points out, all the guys sound like Max, which
is probably to say, all the guys sound like Baumbach. In the
end, KICKING AND SCREAMING is a poor imitation of a
French comedy of manners in the style of Eric
Rohmer. Though the male characters are insuf-
ferable and the more likable women peripheral,
the performances of Hamilton and
d'Abo—whose broken romance (told in flashback) builds to a poignant climax—are impressive. Such better known actors as Stoltz, Posey
and Elliot Gould (who plays Grover's father) do
nice—if uninspired—work in small roles. Only
viewers who have never seen a film of this type
will find KICKING AND SCREAMING fresh
and original. *(Nudity, sexual situations, substance abuse, profanity.)* — E.M.

d, Noah Baumbach; p, Joel Castleberg; exec p, Sandy Gallin,
Carol Baum, Mark Amin; assoc p, Jeremy Kramer, Jason Blum,
Erin Gorman; co-p, Phillip B. Goldfine, Andrew Hersh; w, Noah
Baumbach (from a story by Noah Baumbach and Oliver Berk-
man); ph, Steven Bernstein; ed, J. Kathleen Gibson; m, Phil
Marshall; prod d, Dan Whifler; set d, Gail Bennett; sound, Ed
White; casting, Ellie Kanner; cos, Mary Jane Fort

Comedy/Drama/Romance   **(PR: C   MPAA: R)**

KID IN KING ARTHUR'S COURT, A ★★

(U.S.) 91m Tapestry Films; Trimark Pictures;
Walt Disney ~ Buena Vista c

Thomas Ian Nicholas *(Calvin Fuller)*; Joss Ackland *(King Arthur)*; Art Malik *(Belasco)*; Paloma Baeza *(Katey)*; Kate Winslet
(Princess Sarah); Daniel Craig *(Master Kane)*; David Tysall
(Ratan); Ron Moody *(Merlin)*; Barry Stanton *(Blacksmith)*; Mi-
chael Mehlnan *(Shop Owner)*; Melani Eoettinger *(Peasant
Woman)*; Rebecca Denton *(Washer Woman)*; Michael Kelly *(Ap-
prentice)*; Louise Rosner *(Lady-in-Waiting)*; Paul Rosner *(Peas-
ant Boy)*; Bela Unger *(Head Guard)*; Shane Rimmer *(Coach)*;
Tim Wickham *(Ricky Baker)*; Daniel Bennett *(Howell)*; Deborah
Weston *(Mom)*; Vincent Marzello *(Dad)*; Catherine Blake
(Maya); J.P. Guerin *(Umpire)*

A KID IN KING ARTHUR'S COURT is wholesome wish fulfillment of the blandest kind, in which a young, inept baseball
enthusiast is mistakenly conjured up by Merlin to save Camelot.

Hoping for a miracle to rescue Camelot from the laxity of a
doddering King Arthur (Joss Ackland), Merlin (Ron Moody)
makes magic to catch a 20th century knight. Instead, he accidentally summons young Calvin Fuller (Thomas Ian Nicholas),
whose lack of self-esteem makes him a lousy baseball player. In
the middle of a humiliating game, he finds himself magically
transported into a medieval world of Black Knights and would-
be usurpers like Lord Belasco (Art Malik), who hopes to gain the
throne through marriage to Arthur's daughter, Princess Sarah
(Kate Winslett). Inadvertently rescuing a box belonging to the
King but stolen by the Black Knight, Fuller is regaled at court.
At the Well of Destiny, the out-of-place adolescent learns that his
only escape route to the 20th century lies in participating in
Merlin's Camelot clean-up campaign. Shot by Cupid's arrow,
Fuller enjoys introducing the King's younger daughter Katey
(Paloma Baeza) to modern contraptions like the bicycle much
more than he appreciates his knight-training by a commoner in
love with Sarah. When the elder princess persuades her father to
offer her hand only to a tournament winner, Belasco kidnaps his
reluctant fiancee. After making the King aware of Belasco's
treachery, Fuller and the now regalvanized Arthur rescue Sarah
from her perilous perch in a dungeon.

At the tourney, which the King eventually opens to all free
men, Belasco eliminates all rivals until a dark knight vanquishes
him. The mysterious figure reveals herself to be none other than

Princess Sarah, who claims the combat school instructor for her mate after Arthur banishes Belasco. With Camelot on the mend, thanks in part to his pitching in, a confident Calvin is transported back to the modern-day baseball diamond, where he dazzles his detractors with finesse and proves that heroism is a matter of belief in one's abilities.

While A KID IN KING ARTHUR'S COURT is smartly packaged and executed with Hollywood studio lacquering, it lacks enchantment. The film is aided somewhat by Nicholas, who compensates in comic spunk for what he lacks in spontaneous charm. Unfortunately, he is not bolstered with sterling support by Ackland, who is saddled with interpreting the king as a convalescent home party pooper, or by Malek, whose delivery is far too bombastic. Youngsters will regard as cool Calvin's inventive use of the local blacksmith to impress his girlfriend with newfangled things like rollerblades, but the film does little more than suitably fill up the gaping maw of family entertainment. For most adults, sitting through this whimsy will be like buying back-to-school wardrobes for their kids: more duty than pleasure. *(Mild violence.)* — R.P.

d, Michael Gottlieb; p, Robert L. Levy, Peter Abrams, J.P. Guerin; exec p, Mark Amin; assoc p, Megan Ring; co-p, Andrew Hersh, Jonathon Komack Martin; w, Michael Part, Robert L. Levy; ph, Elemer Ragalyi; ed, Michael Ripps, Anita Brandt-Burgoyne; m, J.A.C. Redford; prod d, Laszlo Gardonyi; set d, Istvan Toth; sound, Otto Olah; fx, Ferenc Ormos, Gabor Balogh; casting, Allison Gordon-Kohler, John Hubbard, Ros Hubbard; cos, Maria Hruby; makeup, Julia Vitrai; stunts, Bela Unger

Children's/Fantasy (PR: A MPAA: PG)

KIDS ★★★

(U.S.) 90m Independent Pictures; The Guys Upstairs ~ Shining Excalibur Pictures c

Leo Fitzpatrick *(Telly)*; Justin Pierce *(Casper)*; Chloe Sevigny *(Jennie)*; Sarah Henderson *(Girl No. 1)*; Rosario Dawson *(Ruby)*; Harold Hunter *(Harold)*; Yakira Peguero *(Darcy)*; Joseph Knofelmacher *(Taxi Driver)*; Joseph Chan *(Ball Owner)*; Jonathan S. Kim *(Korean Guy)*; Adriane Brown *(Little Girl)*; Sajan Bhagat *(Pasul)*

The *cause celebre* of 1995 independent film, KIDS generated heated debate as to the nature of its appeal. Is it a hard-hitting look at the problems of today's youth, or child pornography cloaked in pious cliches?

KIDS looks at 24 hours in the lives of several, mostly middle-class, white New York City teenagers at the beginning of summer. The film opens with Telly (Leo Fitzpatrick), a tough-talking adolescent preoccupied with seducing young virgins, adding another notch to his bedpost. He leaves the girl's apartment and brags about the encounter to his best friend, Casper (Justin Pierce), as they travel to the home of a friend, where a group of young men are engaged in a raunchy discussion about sex.

At the same time, a group of young women—including several of Telly's recent conquests—share their ideas about and experiences of sex. Two of them, Jennie (Chloe Sevigny) and Ruby (Rosario Dawson), agree to go to a clinic to get tested for sexually transmitted diseases. While Ruby discovers she is disease-free, Jennie learns that she is HIV-positive. After absorbing the shocking news, Jennie feels compelled to inform Telly that he, too, must be HIV-positive, since he was her first and only sexual partner.

Jennie tries tracking Telly down by looking for him in his favorite hangouts, including Washington Square Park. But Telly has already moved on to courting another very young woman, whom he escorts to a big apartment party that night. Jennie

arrives at the party, too, after taking drugs that make her drowsy. She finds Telly in the apartment bedroom, but the cocky lothario is already having sex with his latest victim. Jennie walks away from Telly, then falls asleep on a couch next to other tired partygoers. Early that morning, Casper—who spent the night getting drunk at the party—rapes Jennie in her sleep.

Still photographer Larry Clark is known for his grim, murky, sexually-charged pictures of adolescents, most notoriously the portraits that make up his 1983 book, *Teenage Lust*. It's no surprise that his first feature film covers the same provocative territory. In KIDS, Clark effectively captures the apparently self-contained world of aimless, poorly supervised city youths, using a *cinema verite* style that makes even the more contrived moments of the film feel realistic. Clark also elicits honest, un-self-conscious performances from almost all of his young cast.

But KIDS aims to be much more than a cinematic snapshot. Working with a screenplay by 21-year-old skateboard enthusiast Harmony Korine, Clark tells a cautionary tale about sex and drugs in the age of AIDS. Korine's story pays clever—and perhaps unwitting—homage to Arthur Schnitzler's classic "Reigen" which follows the liaisons of a daisy-chain of sex partners. Ironically, the most famous adaptation of "Reigen"—Max Ophuls' LA RONDE (1950)—neglects to mention that this merry-go-round of love is haunted by the specter of syphilis, just as KIDS' world of loveless sex is haunted by AIDS.

Clark's documentary-style rendering of events is generally effective, but eventually wears out its welcome: One yearns for a simple, steady tripod shot and release from the tangential glances at homeless people that suggest a Profound Statement in the making. Korine and Clark's take on contemporary teenage problems (they're generally immoral and have unprotected sex) also lends itself to unbecoming disingenuity—after all, it's not *their* fault if viewers find the sex scenes involving young teenagers arousing. This is, of course, in keeping with traditions that predate the cinema by centuries, but at the very least Clark—who has the better part of three decades on Korine—ought to acknowledge the erotic fillip buried in the stern lesson. In another obvious irony, distributor Miramax—a Disney-owned "independent"—was forced to create a new company, Excalibur Films, in order to release the NC-17-rated film, the better not to upset their family oriented parent company. *(Violence, nudity, sexual situations, adult situations, substance abuse, extreme profanity.)* — E.M.

d, Larry Clark; p, Cary Woods; exec p, Gus Van Sant, Michael Chambers, Patrick Panzarella; co-p, Christine Vachon, Lauren Zalaznick, Cathy Konrad; w, Harmony Korine (from an original story treatment by Larry Clark, Jim Lewis, Leo Fitzpatrick, and Justin Pierce); ph, Eric Alan Edwards; ed, Chris Tellefson; m, Lou Barlow, John Davis; prod d, Kevin Thompson; set d, C. Ford Wheeler; sound, Charles Hunt, Jan McLaughlin; casting, Alysa Wishingrad; cos, Kim Druce

Drama (PR: O MPAA: NC-17)

KILIAN'S CHRONICLE ★★½

(U.S.) 112m Lara Classics ~ Ed Cruea Releasing c

Christopher Johnson *(Kilian)*; Robert McDonough *(Ivar)*; Eva Kim *(Turtle)*; Gino Montesinos *(Contacook)*; Jonah Ming Lee *(Kitchi)*; Robert Mason Ham *(White Eagle)*

A Celtic slave's adventures in a foreign land are charted in KILIAN'S CHRONICLE, a beautifully shot but dramatically uneven independent feature film.

Set 500 years before Columbus journeyed to America, KILIAN'S CHRONICLE tells the story of Kilian (Christopher

Johnson), an indentured slave to a group of Vikings who are sailing across the Atlantic Ocean to conquer new territory. The Irish-born Kilian, who details his adventures in a journal, chafes under the demands of his master, Ivar (Robert McDonough), a particularly cruel warrior. Once the boat reaches the coast, Kilian escapes from his captors and tries to survive on his own in the wilds. Ivar instigates the massacre of a group of Native Americans and his men flee home, fearing reprisals, leaving him behind as punishment. Later, when Kilian is bitten by a snake, the Native Americans rescue him, welcome him into their society and attempt to learn his language. In turn, Kilian learns the tribe's language and helps them with his carpentry know-how, eventually falling in love with Turtle (Eva Kim). Meanwhile, Ivar joins another Viking tribe living on the coast, but never stops thinking about seeking vengeance on Kilian for escaping. When Kilian's tribe plans to trade goods with these nearby Vikings, Ivar ruins the negotiations by killing an Indian, and an all-out war ensues. After the fighting subsides, Kilian decides to return to Ireland, leaving Turtle and her younger brother, Contacook (Gino Montesinos), behind. The night before Kilian is to leave, however, Ivar catches up with him and holds him captive, demanding that he become his slave again. Kilian escapes from Ivar, only to find Ivar holding Contacook hostage on the boat sailing home. Kilian seems ready to return to slavery as long as Ivar frees Contacook, but Kilian tricks Ivar and the two men fight. With Contacook's help, Kilian kills Ivar, and then decides to return to Turtle with her helpful brother.

Less condescending but just as painfully earnest as DANCES WITH WOLVES, the low-budget KILIAN'S CHRONICLE shows Native Americans in a better light than most Hollywood films. It also makes a concerted effort to accurately portray this fascinating and rarely dramatized period. (Writer-director Pamela Berger is a former Boston College professor whose screenplay was informed by up-to-date academic and archeological research.) But though it's rarely didactic, it *is* slow-moving and dramatically uneven. Berger's emphasis on cultural differences (the Indians' orderly, quasi-socialist utopia vs. the Vikings' savage anarchy) comes at the expense of dramatic structure. Ivar, for example, disappears from the narrative for so long after the opening reel that his quest to find Kilian is virtually forgotten; he is almost unrecognizable when he reappears much later in the film. Berger also entirely skips over how Kilian and natives learn each other's languages (Kilian's narration covers what's missing, but it seems like an afterthought). The modern-sounding English dialect that the natives speak so fluently is anachronistic, as is the soft-rock guitar piece played during two separate chase sequences.

Still, if nothing else, KILIAN'S CHRONICLE succeeds visually. Especially considering the film's low budget, the camerawork (by John Hoover) is artful without being arty. Many scenes are visually striking, from the spare opening images of the Vikings' ship against the seascape to the solemn but beautiful Indian burial in the autumnal woods. Berger and production designer John Demeo also effectively transform contemporary settings in Massachusetts and Connecticut into their mid-15th century counterparts. In this way, KILIAN'S CHRONICLE contains more novelty than THE JOURNEY OF AUGUST KING, another 1995 film about a runaway slave.

KILIAN'S CHRONICLE may work better as an educational tool than a stirring drama, but as the former, at least it provides strong visual interest. (*Violence, adult situations.*) — E.M.

d, Pamela Berger; p, Pamela Berger, Mark Donadio; exec p, Barbara Hartwell; assoc p, Krista Thomas; w, Pamela Berger; ph, John Hoover; ed, Jon Neuberger; m, R. Carlos Nakai, Bevan

Manson; prod d, John Demeo; art d, Sophie Carlhian; cos, Dena Popienko; stunts, Coll Anderson

Drama/Historical/Romance   **(PR: AA   MPAA: NR)**

KILLER
(SEE: BULLETPROOF HEART)

KINGDOM, THE   ★★★★
(Denmark) 271m Zentropa Entertainment; Danmarks Radio; Swedish Television; Westdeutscher Rundfunk; ARTE; The Coproduction Office ~ October Films c
(RIGET)

Ernst-Hugo Jaregard *(Stig Helmer)*; Kirsten Rolffes *(Mrs. Drusse)*; Ghita Norby *(Rigmor)*; Soren Pilmark *(Krogen)*; Holger Juul Hansen *(Dr. Moesgaard)*; Annevig Schelde Ebbe *(Mary)*; Jens Okking *(Bulder)*; Otto Brandenburg *(Porter Hansen)*; Baard Owe *(Bondo)*; Solbjorg Hojfeldt *(Camilla)*; Birgitte Raabjerg *(Judith)*; Louise Fribo *(Sanne)*; Peter Mygind *(Mogge)*; Ole Boisen *(Christian)*; Vita Jensen *(Dishwasher 1)*; Morten Rotne Leffers *(Dishwasher 2)*; Michael Simpson *(Man from Haiti)*; Bente Eskesen *(Night Nurse)*; Nis Bank-Mikkelsen *(Priest)*; Dick Kayso *(Security Manager)*; Soren Lenander *(Young Man)*; Finn Nielsen *(Madsen)*; Mette Munk Plum *(Mona's Mother)*; Solveig Sundborg *(Miss Kruger)*; Helle Virkner *(Mrs. Mogensen)*; Else Petersen *(Old Lady)*; Claus Strandberg *(Hypnotized Patient)*; Tova Maes *(Mrs. Zakariasen)*; Kurt Ravn *(Zakariasen's Son)*; Svend Ali Haman *(Haman)*; Morten Elsner *(Mechanic)*; Claus Nissen *(Jensen)*; Gunnvor Nolsoe *(Charlady)*; Henning Jensen *(Hospital Manager)*; Lars Lunoe *(Minister of Health)*; Lea Brogger *(Mary's Mother)*; Laura Christensen *(Mona)*; Udo Kier *(Aage Kruger)*; Soren Elung Jensen *(Man in Top Hat)*; Paul Huttel *(Dr. Stenbaek)*; Holger Perfort *(Professor Ulrich)*; Benny Poulsen *(Senior Registrar)*; Henrik Koefoed *(CT-Scanner Operator)*; Lene Vasegaard *(Gynecologist)*; Klaus Wegener *(Doctor in Casualty)*; Michael Moritzen *(Ear Specialist)*; Julie Wieth *(Pediatric Nurse)*; Annette Ketcher *(Casualty Nurse)*; Birte Tove *(Nurse 1)*; Lise Schroder *(Nurse 2)*; Mette Marckmann *(Young Nurse)*; Thomas Stender *(Student)*; Soren Hauch-Fausboll *(Auxiliary Nurse)*; Soren Steen *(Porter OK)*; Gordon Kennedy *(Assistant, Animal Collection)*; Ole Emil Riisager *(Narrator)*; Ruth Junker *(Voice, Dishwasher 1)*; Peter Gilsfort *(Voice, Dishwasher 2)*; Erik Wedersoe *(Voice, Aage Kruger)*

Made for Danish television, THE KINGDOM is four episodes of an entertainingly cracked medical soap opera-*cum*-ghost story, strung together and released in the US as a theatrical film. The closest thing to it in recent memory is the David Lynch-produced television series "Twin Peaks," but THE KINGDOM works as a theatrical release, despite the segment breaks, episodic story development, and wildly unresolved cliff-hanger ending.

The Kingdom is the name of a huge, crumbling hospital, built on sinister marshland and home to a diverse and eccentric crew of doctors and patients. The action begins with the arrival of Mr. Drusse (Kirsten Rolffes), a sweet, middle-aged woman complaining of vague neurological symptoms. Chief neurosurgeon Stig Helmer (Ernst-Hugo Jaregard)—an arrogant Swede who regularly repairs to the hospital roof to bellow his hatred and contempt for all things Danish—dismisses her as a malingerer. As it happens, he's right: her doltish son (Otto Brandenburg) is a porter at the hospital, and she feigns illness so she can spend time with him. All fairly harmless, if a bit dotty. But Mrs. Drusse, who fancies herself a psychic, soon has another reason to hang around the Kingdom: while riding in one of its elevators she hears the crying of a small child, and the sound seems to come from within the shaft. Mrs. Drusse's quest to contact the child ghost, whose name is Mary (Annevig Schelde Ebbe), and find out why her spirit haunts the hospital forms THE KINGDOM's spine. But all sorts of other dramas take place around it.

Hoping to win additional funding, Head Doctor Moesgaard (Holger Juul Hansen) has cooked up a cheery feel-good program—Operation Morning Air—at the hospital, and has issued an open invitation to a group of government officials to come by for a tour. He's also enamored of the nurse who runs the experimental sleep lab, and concerned about his handsome but rather stupid son Mogge (Peter Mykind), a medical student. Energetic and compassionate Dr. Hook (Soren Pilmark) devotes his energies to fighting waste in the system: he lives in the basement, recycles a wide variety of hospital goods (including eye drops from which he distills cocaine; he sells the drug to staff members then plows the money back into medical supplies) and begins an affair with another doctor, Judith (Birgitte Raabjerg), who's pregnant by the lover who just abandoned her. Hook clashes regularly with Helmer, who is also having an affair with another staff member, Dr. Rigmore (Ghita Norby), and trying to distance himself from the case of Mona (Laura Christensen), a young girl who emerged from one of his operations severely and irreparably brain damaged.

In addition, there's a secret cabal of doctors conducting Masonic rituals in the hospital's basement and performing bizarre transplants on the sly; a phantom ambulance; a pair of Down's syndrome-afflicted dishwashers who empathize with the uneasy spirits that have been set loose; a possessed dog; stuff oozing from the walls; an exorcism; and Judith's pregnancy, which is progressing at an alarming rate.

Mary's story unfolds meanwhile, and by the time she turns up in the flesh—preserved in a huge Ehrlenmeyer flask—we've learned through flashbacks that she was the illegitimate child of Dr. Aage Kruger (Udo Kier), one the first physicians to practice at the Kingdom at the turn of the century. The sickly child was taken to the Kingdom at her father's behest, then hidden in an isolated room and finally murdered. The series ends with Judith going into premature labor—though she's hugely pregnant and looks as though she carries at least full-term twins—and giving birth to Kruger, whose bloody face emerging from between her thighs is the film's closing image.

Prior to THE KINGDOM, director Lars von Trier had distinguished himself primarily for his flamboyant visual style—ZENTROPA is a film of such unremitting gorgeousness that it's positively exhausting—and singular humorlessness. So the great and pleasant surprise of THE KINGDOM is how blackly funny it is. At the same time von Trier manages to work up some real scares: little Mary's first appearance, crouched in a high corner of the elevator shaft and ringing a tiny bell is chilling, as is the scene in which Mrs. Drusse questions a newly dead friend by having her make the buzzing fluorescent lights dim—once for yes, twice for no.

"The Kingdom" is the nickname of the real National State Hospital in Copenhagen, where the series was shot—during working hours and using available light—and the unglamorized cinematography and rough-and-ready looking compositions help eliminate the feeling of preciousness that mars von Trier's earlier work. The 271-minute running time, so daunting when spelled out—four-and-a-half hours!—seems like nothing in the unfolding. (*Violence, nudity, sexual situations, adult situations, profanity.*) — M.M.

d, Lars von Trier; p, Ole Reim; exec p, Svend Abrahamsen, Peter Aalbaek Jensen; assoc p, Ib Tardini, Philippe Bober; w, Lars von Trier, Tomas Gislason (from a story by Lars von Trier and Niels Vorsel); ph, Eric Kress; ed, Jacob Thuesen, Molly Marlene Stensgaard; m, Joachim Holbek; art d, Jette Lehmann; sound, Peter Hansen (recordist), Per Streit (design); fx, Niels Skovgaard, Niels Fly; makeup, Lis Olsson, Birthe Lyngso Sorensen, Kim Olsson

Drama/Horror (PR: C   MPAA: R)

KINGFISH: A STORY OF HUEY P. LONG ★★★
(U.S.) 96m Chris/Rose Productions; Red Bank Films ~ Turner Home Entertainment c

John Goodman (*Huey P. Long, Jr.*); Matt Craven (*Seymour Weiss*); Anne Heche (*Aileen Dumont*); Ann Dowd (*Rose Long*); Jeff Perry (*Earl Long*); Bob Gunton (*Franklin D. Roosevelt*); Bill Cobbs (*Pullman Porter*); Hoyt Axton (*Huey P. Long, Sr.*); Kirk Baltz (*Frank Costello*); Richard Bradford (*Judge Benjamin Pavy*); Jimmie Ray Weeks (*Allen Henderson*); Bill Raymond (*Governor O.K. Allen*); John McConnell ("*Battlin" Bozman*); Ed Bruce (*Governor J.Y. Sanders*); Joe Chrest (*Carl Weiss*); Joe Warfield (*Delesdernier*); Chappy Hardy (*Frank Mendola*); Thomas Keller (*James*); Patrick Cullen (*Antoine Daspit*); Daniel Kamin (*Cecil Christopher*); Bertram Dykes (*Farmer*); Rita Smith (*Farmer's Wife*); Joanne Pankow (*Waitress*); Walter Breaux (*Warren*); Greg Baber (*Tom Frady*); Jack Hazard (*Man at Parade*); James Winder (*Luther*); Stocker Fontelieu (*1st Impeachment Senator*); Graham Timbes (*2nd Impeachment Senator*); Bill Jessup (*3rd Impeachment Senator*); Mary Coulson (*Marguerita Haas*); Katie Planche Friedrichs (*Mary Lou*); Charles McLawhorn (*1st Elderly Senator*); Victoria Edwards (*Chanteuse*); Mary Madeleine Thibeaux (*Nun*); Mike McNally (*Man in Bathroom*)

Made for cable, this biographical film feels like a labor of love on the part of star John Goodman, who proves once again that his considerable talents are not limited merely to situation comedy.

KINGFISH depicts Huey Long as a charismatic speaker whose tireless campaigning and unsinkable loyalty to the working class fueled his climb up the political ladder. Beginning as a railroad commissioner in 1919, it took the wily Long just nine years to oust the governor of Louisiana, then move on to Washington as that state's senator. Along the way, the Kingfish (as Long dubbed himself) assembled a fearsome political machine that threatened even President Franklin Delano Roosevelt—and with good reason, for Long saw himself as the man who could steal the Democratic vote from FDR in the upcoming presidential race. Counterpointing Long's singleminded political ambition is his divided love life, split between his neglected yet loyal wife and his politically savvy mistress, Aileen DuMont (whom, at one point, Long appoints Louisiana's Secretary of State). In the end, the Kingfish's voracious appetite for power destroys him, and he is shot in the halls of the state capital by the son-in-law of a political rival.

As the only A-list actor in an otherwise competent but forgettable cast, the burden of carrying KINGFISH falls squarely on Goodman's shoulders. Luckily, he rises to the occasion, imbuing the politician with the right combination of likability, ferocity, and hubris to justify his vast array of both enemies and supporters. Add to the mixture Goodman's role as producer and it becomes clear that he is the fulcrum upon which the success of the film rests. Fortunately, he is assisted by veteran feature director Thomas Schlamme (MISS FIRECRACKER, SO I MARRIED AN AXE MURDERER), who keeps Goodman's leash just short enough to prevent the star from going overboard. All told, KINGFISH is a satisfying look at the kind of political playmaking whose echoes can still be heard today. (*Violence, sexual situations.*) — B.T.

d, Thomas Schlamme; p, John Goodman, Bob Christiansen, Rick Rosenberg; assoc p, Tina Threadgill; co-p, Daniel Schneider; w, Paul Monash; ph, Alexander Gruszynski; ed, Pall Dixon; m, Patrick Williams; prod d, Thomas A. Walsh; art d, Barbara Ann Jaekel; sound, Walter Holyman (mixer); fx, Bill Purcell, Scott Rushton; casting, Mindy Marin, John Papsidera; cos, Merrily Murray-Walsh; makeup, Bob Harper; stunts, Jeff Jensen

Drama/Biography (PR: C MPAA: NR)

KISS OF DEATH ★★★½
(U.S.) 101m 20th Century Fox ~ 20th Century Fox c

David Caruso *(Jimmy Kilmartin)*; Samuel L. Jackson *(Calvin)*; Nicolas Cage *(Little Junior)*; Helen Hunt *(Bev)*; Kathryn Erbe *(Rosie)*; Stanley Tucci *(Frank Zioli)*; Michael Rapaport *(Ronnie)*; Ving Rhames *(Omar)*; Philip Baker Hall *(Big Junior)*; Anthony Heald *(Jack Gold)*; Angel David *(J.J.)*; John Costelloe *(Cleary)*; Lindsay J. Wrinn *(Corinna)*; Megan L. Wrinn *(Corinna)*; Katie Sagona *(Corinna—4 Years Old)*; Anne Meara *(Bev's Mother)*; Kevin Corrigan *(Kid Selling Infinity)*; Hugh Palmer *(Dancing Naked Man)*; Hope Davis *(Junior's Girlfriend)*; Richard Price *(City Clerk)*; Edward McDonald *(US Attorney)*; Alex Stevens *(Convoy Drunk)*; Mark Hammer *(Judge)*; Joe Lisi *(Agent at Bungalow)*; Frank Dileo *(Big Junior's Friend)*; Jason Andrews *(Johnny A)*; Sean G. Wallace *(Bobby B)*; Ed Trucco *(Calvin's Partner)*; Bernadette Penotti *(Molested Dancer)*; Debra J. Pereira *(Sioux Dancer)*; Shiek Mahmud-Bey *(Federal Agent)*; John C. Vennema *(Angry Federal Agent)*; Tony Cucci; Allen K. Bernstein *(Junior's Crew #2)*; Dame *(J.J.'s Crew #1)*; Jose De Soto *(J.J.'s Crew #2)*; Lloyd Hollar *(Prison Chaplain)*; Nicholas Falcone *(Priest at Funeral)*; James McCauley *(Cop Outside Bar)*; Michael Artura *(Emergency Room Cop)*; Tom Riis Farrell *(EMS Supervisor)*; Juliet Adair Pritner *(Female Agent)*; Henry Yuk *(Chinese Restaurant Owner)*; Chuck Margiotta *(Escort at Cemetery #1)*; Jay Boryea *(Escort at Cemetery #2)*; Joseph Pentangelo *(Riker's Security Officer)*; Alan Jeffrey Gordon *(Riker's Security Officer)*; Dean Rader-Duval *(Sing Sing Guard)*; Willie M. Watford *(Sing Sing Guard)*

Loosely based on the 1947 film of the same name, this sturdy, stylish thriller marks former "NYPD Blue" star David Caruso's debut in a leading role.

Caruso plays Jimmy Kilmartin, a car thief trying to go straight. He lives in Queens with his wife Bev (Helen Hunt)—a recovering alcoholic—and baby daughter Corinna. Jimmy allows himself to be pressured into helping his cousin Ronnie (Michael Rapaport) move stolen cars for neighborhood crime boss Little Junior Brown (Nicolas Cage), a hulking asthmatic with a father fixation. The job gets bungled, the cops show up and while Ronnie escapes, Jimmy is caught. Jimmy earns the undying enmity of Calvin (Samuel L. Jackson), a detective who's wounded during the arrest. As the injured Jimmy lies in the emergency room, he's approached by DA Frank Zioli (Stanley Tucci), who wants to bust Junior. Jimmy refuses to talk and does three years in prison. While he's in, the weasely Ronnie gets Bev drunk and seduces her. She then dies in a car accident, and her baby is taken in by her sister Rose (Kathryn Erbe) and mother. Jimmy makes a deal with Zioli to infiltrate Little Junior's gang in exchange for parole. Jimmy wears a wire to Little Junior's "office," a gaudy strip club called Baby Cakes. Calvin is assigned to the case, and he and Jimmy form a grudging friendship. Jimmy and Rose fall in love. Meanwhile, Junior takes a shine to Jimmy and wants him to help deal with the large, menacing Omar (Ving Rhames), who seems to want to muscle in on Junior's operations.

The unpredictable Junior kills Omar, and Jimmy is picked up by Omar's men. He soon finds he's in even more trouble than he imagined. Omar was an undercover federal agent—which is news to Zioli—and Jimmy is caught in the middle as the representatives of the warring law-enforcement agencies squabble. Zioli promises to protect Jimmy if he betrays Junior, but breaks his promise when the case against Junior falls apart.

Junior's men come after Jimmy and his family, and Jimmy decides he has no choice but to confront Junior at the strip club for a final showdown. In the ensuing free-for-all, Calvin arrests Junior for assaulting a police officer. Zioli plans to let Junior go again, but Jimmy blackmails him into prosecuting.

Strictly speaking, KISS OF DEATH isn't a remake. It keeps the 1947 film's central situation—a petty thief is squeezed by criminals on one side and uncaring law men on the other—but tells an entirely new story. Director Barbet Schroeder emphasizes the ugly, rundown locales and shoots much of the action at night, establishing the film's sleazy, unglamorous tone. Novelist-screenwriter Richard Price—whose credits include SEA OF LOVE, NIGHT AND THE CITY, and CLOCKERS—has a feel for this type of atmosphere, and gives the familiar story a few curves, most memorably the character of Junior. Free of the mumbling and mannerisms for which he's famous, Cage gives one of his best performances, alternately menacing and pitiable. We first see him weight-lifting—using a stripper instead of barbells—and he's filled with New Age-style advice about life and career direction.

There is much familiar territory here—the ambitious, cynical DA, the crook trying to go straight, the detective who has more in common with petty criminals like Jimmy than the sleek guys in suits who really run the world—and the final confrontation, in which Jimmy single-handedly takes on Junior and his men, strains plausibility. Caruso played many supporting film roles prior to attaining TV celebrity in "NYPD Blue," but KISS OF DEATH was his first bid for big screen stardom. Both his performance and the film overall are highly watchable. *(Extreme profanity, graphic violence, adult situations, nudity.)*

d, Barbet Schroeder; p, Barbet Schroeder, Susan Hoffman; exec p, Jack Baran; co-p, Richard Price; w, Richard Price (based on the 1947 screenplay by Ben Hecht and Charles Lederer from a story by Eleazar Lipsky); ph, Luciano Tovoli; ed, Lee Percy; m, Trevor Jones; prod d, Mel Bourne; set d, Roberta J. Holinko; sound, Les Lazarowitz (mixer); fx, Steve Kirshoff; casting, Paula Herold; cos, Theadora Van Runkle; makeup, Allen Weisinger; stunts, Mike Russo

Crime/Drama (PR: C MPAA: R)

KURT VONNEGUT'S HARRISON BERGERON ★★½
(Canada) 99m Atlantis Films Ltd.; Cypress Films; Showtime ~ Republic Pictures Home Video c
(AKA: HARRISON BERGERON)

Sean Astin *(Harrison Bergeron)*; Christopher Plummer *(John Klaxon)*; Miranda de Pencier *(Phillipa)*; Natalie Radford *(Alma)*; Nigel Bennett *(Dr. Eisenstock)*; Buck Henry *(Havlicek)*; Eugene Levy *(President McKloskey)*; Howie Mandel *(Charlie the TV Show Host)*; John Astin; Andrea Martin *(Heather Hoffman)*; Peter Boretski *(Newman)*; David Calderisi *(Commissioner Benson)*; Emmanuelle *(Chriqui)*; Hayden Christensen *(Eric)*; Roger Dunn *(George Bergeron)*; Jayne Eastwood *(Ms. Newbound)*; Matthew Ferguson *(Garth Bergeron)*; Linda Goranson *(Hazel Bergeron)*; Wendy Hopkins *(Jennifer)*; Quyen Hua *(Wang)*; Juliette Jacobs *(Mother)*; Richard Monette *(Eric Shockley)*; Avi Phillips *(Morris Wilkerson)*; Diana Reis *(Miss Hopkins)*

Imagine a society where everyone is average. There is no envy, and therefore no conflict. KURT VONNEGUT'S HARRISON BERGERON is intellectual science fiction with a thoughtful and entertaining premise.

In 2053, after the Second American Revolution, it has been determined that for society to thrive, everyone must be of equal skill and intelligence. All Americans wear headbands that regulate IQ levels, but Harrison Bergeron (Sean Astin) continues to think at a higher grade than classmates and family. Hoping to make him normal, his family takes him in for treatment. The day before brain surgery, a doctor gives Harrison the address of an underground "head house," where he can have conversations with intelligent women. There, he meets Phillipa (Miranda de Pencier), who plays chess with him. The house is raided, and Harrison wakes up at the National Administration Center, which secretly runs the country. Phillipa is a spy, and Harrison has been chosen to join the nation's hidden leaders (his family is told he died on the operating table). He learns that in the late 20th century, after the Cold War, growing technology made most jobs obsolete and unemployment skyrocketed, causing the riots that started the Revolution. The NAC restored order by giving society back to the "common person." Harrison argues they will be better off if freedom and intellectual and artistic stimulation are returned to citizens.

Harrison and Phillipa fall in love. They plan to escape to Mexico, but Phillipa is caught and given the brain operation to become "normal." Harrison is told that he has been chosen to lead the NAC. He balks, locks himself in their TV studio, goes on the air and tells America the truth, then plays them unauthorized music, reads great literature and shows classic films. He controls the airwaves for nearly a day, until guards break into the room; it seems that after his show, 99% of the country put their headbands back on and forgot all he said. Ordered to make a new broadcast telling the remaining 1% that it was all a hoax, Bergeron does so, then kills himself on the air. The audience doesn't understand. Years later, bootlegs of his show circulate among teens, and Harrison Bergeron becomes a hero to a new generation.

While visually plain and lacking author Vonnegut's clever wordplay, KURT VONNEGUT'S HARRISON BERGERON is a superior made-for-cable TV production. The screenplay is biting and often hilarious, making current pop-culture references without tying itself down to any present-day political situation, and unafraid of letting viewers draw their own conclusions. The future envisioned in the film is extreme—but not out of the realm of possibility. Assertions that many people prefer predictability to quality, and power to intelligence ring uncomfortably true. The story offers no easy answers; the Revolution is horrifying, and the oblivious masses are clearly happy being synthetically average. The ending is hopeful but cautious, implying that there will always be a small subculture holding ideals unacceptable to the majority. Astin is a little too incredulous as Harrison, but the other performances are first rate, especially de Pencier's smart, sexy female lead. Several cameos provide clever in-jokes, typical of a film that invites one to think on many different levels. *(Profanity, sexual situations, adult situations, violence.)* — A.M.

d, Bruce Pittman; p, Jonathan Hackett; exec p, Peter Sussman, James Nadler, John Glascoe; w, Arthur Crimm (based on the short story by Kurt Vonnegut); ph, Michael Storey; ed, Ion Webster; m, Lou Natale; prod d, Susan Longmire; art d, Alta Louise Doyle; set d, Carolyn Loucks; sound, David Lee (recordist); fx, Jordan Craig; casting, Darlene Kaplan; cos, Marie-Sylvie Devau; makeup, Linda Preston

Science Fiction/Comedy/Drama   **(PR: C   MPAA: R)**

LAKOTA WOMAN: SIEGE AT WOUNDED KNEE ★★

(U.S.) 113m Fred Berner Films; Fonda Films; Von Zerneck/Sertner Films ~ Turner Home Entertainment c

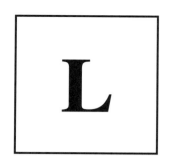

Irene Bedard *(Mary Crow Dog)*; August Schellenberg *(Dick Wilson)*; Joseph Runningfox *(Leonard Crow Dog)*; Floyd Red Crow Westerman *(Grandfather Fool Bull)*; Tantoo Cardinal *(Emily Moore)*; Pato Hoffmann *(Spencer)*; Michael Horse *(Dennis Banks)*; Lawrence Bayne *(Russell Means)*; Nancy Parsons *(Sister Mary Margaret)*; Dean Norris *(Red Arrow)*; Tim Sampson *(Pedro Bissonette)*; Scott Means *(John Standing)*; Gary Bullock *(FBI Agent Rainey)*; John Harnagel *(Father Hochbauer)*; Casey Camp-Horinek *(Aunt Elsie Flood)*; Dawn Levand *(Young Mary)*; Dawn Little Sky *(Grandma Moore)*; Nathan Bison *(Joe Little Horse)*; Virginia Mercado *(Young Barbara)*; Angel McFarland *(Barbara)*; Richard Swallow *(Webster)*; Norman Roach *(Clyde Bellecourt)*; James Abourezk *(District Attorney)*; Richard Whitman *(Carter Camp)*; Michael Spears *(Stat Man)*; Ellen Moves Camp *(Choach Means)*; Archie Little *(Fools Crow)*; Lois Red Elk *(Gladys Bissonette)*; Owen LeBeau *(Buddy Lamont)*; Wi-Waste-Win Conroy *(Little Girl)*; Melanie Two Eagle *(Charlene)*; Amy Moore Davis *(Nadine)*; Jennifer White-Plume *(Receptionist)*; David Bald Eagle *(Old Man at Headquarters)*; Julie Recountre *(Old Woman at Headquarters)*; Mekasi Horinek *(Young Man at Headquarters)*; Vic Camp *(Webster's Friend)*; Mark J. Nelson *(Codelle)*; Van Burnette *(Driver Goon)*

Based on the biography *Lakota Woman*, this made-for-cable film tells the story of Mary Crow Dog and her gradual emergence into political consciousness and activism. The film traces the major events of her life but focuses on her participation in a stand-off between local and federal authorities at Wounded Knee, South Dakota in 1973.

The young Mary (Dawn Lavand) is born on the Rosebud reservation in South Dakota and comes of age in the shadow of the suffering of her ancestors. She is sent to a Christian mission school, where her braids are cut off and the teachers attempt to anglicize her. She becomes a troubled teen who, when unable to find work, turns to drinking and recklessness. Beaten and strung out in a jail cell, an older Mary (Irene Bedard) meets Spencer (Pato Hoffman) who first tells her of AIM, the American Indian Movement, and its intention to reclaim stolen land and fight for the rights of Indians.

With Dick Wilson (August Schellingberg) and his boys running her hometown, Indian lives have become valueless in the face of the law and recourse to justice in the courts is reserved for whites. When the leaders of AIM arrive to address this situation, Wilson and his gang go on the offensive, setting off a battle which climaxes when AIM followers head en masse for Wounded Knee, the site of the 1890 massacre of their ancestors. Federal agents, negotiators, and an army of journalists converge on the scene for a stand-off lasting more than two months. Mary gives birth at Wounded Knee and after a short run as a martyr in a jail cell, is heralded as a brave and heroic woman.

Good intentions aside, the film is corrupted by a terrible script incorporating absurdly stoic voice-over narration by Mary. The acting and character development are so weak that it is impossible to remember or care about people as they change and grow over time. The film fails to present a dynamic historical context, and, instead, resorts to expressing the anguish and anger of American Indians in traditional archetypes of nobility and righteousness, rather than probing more deeply beyond the cliches into the complex subtleties of the subject. *(Violence, adult situations.)* — R.C.

d, Frank Pierson; p, Fred Berner; exec p, Lois Bonfiglio, Frank Von Zerneck, Robert M. Sertner; assoc p, Ari Sloane; co-p, Hanay Geiogamah, Steve Saeta; w, Bill Kerby (based on the book *Lakota Woman* by Mary Crow Dog and Richard Erdoes); ph, Toyomichi Kurita; ed, Katina Zinner; m, Richard Horowitz; prod d, Stephen Marsh; art d, Russ Smith; set d, Robin Peyton; sound, Russell C. Fager (mixer); fx, Rick H. Josephson; casting, Rene Haynes; cos, John Dunn; makeup, Wayne Massarelli; stunts, Gene Hartline

Docudrama (PR: A MPAA: NR)

LAMB ★★★

(U.K.) 110m Limehouse Pictures; Flickers Productions; Channel Four ~ Capitol Entertainment c

Liam Neeson *(Michael Lamb—Brother Sebastian)*; Hugh O'Conor *(Owen Kane)*; Ian Bannen *(Brother Benedict)*; Ronan Wilmot *(Brother Fintan)*; Frances Tomelty *(Mrs. Kane)*; Dudley Sutton *(Haddock)*; Denis Carey *(Mr. Lamb)*; David Gorry *(O'Donnell)*; Stuart O'Conner *(O'Halloran)*; Harry Towb *(Priest)*; Eileen Kennally *(Neighbor Woman)*; Andrew Pickering *(Murphy)*; Ian McElhinney *(Maguire)*; Bernadette McKenna *(Jeweller's Assistant)*; Jessica Saunders *(Bank Teller on Boat)*; Robert Hamilton *(Stranger at Holyhead)*; Roger Booth *(Farmer on Train)*; Marjie Lawrence *(Department Store Assistant)*; Nicola Wright *(Hotel Receptionist)*; Freddie Stuart *(1st Crook)*; Roy Glascock *(2nd Crook)*; Al Ashton *(Aquarium Attendant)*; Doreen Keogh *(Landlady of Cheap Hotel)*; Nick Dunning *(Football Spectator)*; Nigel Humphries *(Policeman)*; Tony Wreddon *(Pharmacist)*; Dudley Sutton *(Haddock)*; Larrington Walker *(Newtan)*; Walter McMonagle *(Carpenter)*; Colum Convey *(Plumber)*; Elmer Gillespie *(Avis Girl)*

Originally produced in 1985 and briefly released in the US ten years later to capitalize on Liam Neeson's stardom, this sensitive and disturbing film proved worth the wait. The screenplay, adapted by Bernard MacLaverty from his novel, concerns a young clergyman who flees his teaching post at a remote Catholic boarding school, taking with him an epileptic boy.

Ten-year-old Owen Kane (Hugh O'Conor) is brought to St. Kiaran's school on the coast of Ireland by his mother (Frances Tomelty), who appears to care little for her son and has physically abused him. Michael Lamb (Liam Neeson), himself troubled by questions of faith, takes Owen under his wing. Lamb protects Owen from injury during an epileptic fit, meets with him to find out how he is adjusting, and impresses him by returning a pack of confiscated cigarettes. He also defends Owen against Brother Benedict (Ian Bannen), the school's superior, when Owen is accused of, and punished for, for an act of graffiti he firmly denies having committed. When Lamb's sick father dies and leaves him a small inheritance, he runs away from the school, taking Owen with him.

They travel to London, stay in a succession of rented rooms, each worse than the last, and eventually become squatters in a flat offered by a lecherous and alcoholic fellow emigrant. In Ireland, Lamb is accused of kidnapping Owen and stealing school funds. When the money runs low, the authorities seem to be closing in, and Lamb cannot refill Owen's prescription for medication against his epileptic attacks, they return to Ireland. There, on an isolated beach, Lamb drowns Owen while he is having an epileptic fit. He then attempts to drown himself but fails. The film concludes with Lamb sitting alone beside Owen's body.

LAMB is a fine but depressing film in which director Colin Gregg investigates the strange relationship between the naive, introspective, and well-intentioned man and the mischievous, maladjusted, lonely boy. Neither seems aware of the depth and complexity of the attachment; yet, each reaches out for emotional support from the other. Filmed in confined interiors, or in haunting isolation against bleak and empty landscapes, the film successfully projects Lamb's timidity and fear and Owen's alienation. *(Adult situations.)* — M.F.

d, Colin Gregg; p, Neil Zeiger; exec p, Al Burgess; assoc p, Martin Procter; w, Bernard MacLaverty (based on his novel); ph, Michael Garfath; ed, Peter Delfgou; m, Van Morrison; prod d, Austen Spriggs; art d, Val Wolstenholme; sound, Bill Burgess (recordist); fx, Gordon Coxon; casting, Simone Reynolds; cos, Monica Howe; makeup, Vivien Placks; stunts, Bill Weston

Drama   **(PR: A   MPAA: NR)**

LAMERICA   ★★★★
(Italy/France) 120m Cecchi Gori Group;
Tiger Cinematografica; Arena Films; Alia Film ~
New Yorker Films c

Enrico Lo Verso *(Gino)*; Michele Placido *(Fiore)*; Carmelo Di Mazzarelli *(Spiro)*; Piro Milkani *(Selimi)*; Elida Janushi *(Selimi's Cousin)*; Sefer Pema *(Prison Warden)*; Nikolin Elezi *(Boy Who Dies)*; Artan Marina *(Ismail)*; Besim Kurti *(Policeman)*; Esmerald Ara *(Little Girl)*

LAMERICA is a boldly chilling portrait of post-Communist Europe in moral eclipse, directed with passion and singular grace by Italian Gianni Amelio (STOLEN CHILDREN).

Just across the Adriatic from Italy, Albania is an isolated, impoverished mountainous region that was once invaded by Mussolini's army. The collapse of a 50-year-old Communist regime now draws a wide range of entrepreneurs, including the Italians Gino (Enrico Lo Verso) and Fiore (Michele Placido). They intend to reap big profits from the Balkan reversion to market capitalism, but the law requires them to act through a local figurehead. Both men are openly contemptuous of the Albanians and are astounded at the waste of resources everywhere evident in the backward land.

In an effort to find a local whom they can control, Gino and Fiore visit a prison, where the inmates are all starving, dirty, scabrous, and half-crazy. One of them, Spiro (Carmelo Di Mazzarelli), is little more than a zombie, even when washed and dressed up in a business suit to become the ostensible chairman of Fiore's paper company. The younger Gino is clearly impatient with minding Spiro, especially when the former political prisoner doffs his suit and flees for Italy.

In the hilly, arid wastes of rural Albania, Gino discovers that Spiro, despite his Albanian papers, is an illiterate Italian army deserter, left stranded years before by an irony of history and his poor addled memories. Gino, his car stripped of its tires, is soon stranded as well. The unlikely pair get a ride on a truck crowded with young migrants eager to get to Italy. Their fellow passengers are a easy-going crowd, although one sickly man dies in Spiro's arms. Spiro is forever kindly, willing to share his food, and optimistic, talking of returning to home and fields. Gino is shaken by the death and warms to Spiro. Then, in a telephone conversation with Fiore, Gino learns that their enterprise has been scuttled. Gino and Spiro are now among the unemployed, like the thousands of Albanians around them.

Gino leaves Spiro and his spare cash to the mercies of an impromptu hostel and returns to his hotel in the capital, only to

be arrested by the police on the charge of corrupting an official. Shaken by his brief stay in an Albanian prison, his stylish Italian clothing now replaced by grimy hand-me-downs, Gino is soon wandering the streets of Tirana. He joins a group of young people who are fervently learning to speak Italian. We see him again aboard an old rusted freighter, the Partizani, loaded with Albanian refugees, among whom he soon spots Spiro. The addled veteran comforts the younger Gino and talks wistfully of their future in America.

Amelio's genuinely moving film deservedly won the European Felix Award and Italy's equivalent of the Oscar (it was also the Italian entry for the 1995 Academy Awards). Its near-hallucinatory portrayal of the chaotic plight of Albania in the grip of a singularly ruthless brand of capitalism is trenchant and unforgettable. LAMERICA's central theme, however, is the timeless hope of the migrant—a dubious dream of spiritual renewal in a real or imagined "Lamerica." Beautifully structured despite an episodic plot, the film is also brilliantly acted, especially by Lo Verso, one of the most gifted actors of his generation. *(Adult situations, profanity.)* — L.R.

d, Gianni Amelio; p, Mario Cecchi Gori, Vittorio Cecchi Gori; exec p, Enzo Porcelli; w, Gianni Amelio, Andrea Porporati, Alessandro Sermoneta; ph, Luca Bigazzi; ed, Simona Paggi; m, Franco Piersanti; prod d, Giuseppe M. Gaudino, Nicola Rubertelli; set d, Giuseppe M. Gaudino; sound, Alessandro Zanon; cos, Liliana Sotira, Claudia Tenaglia

Drama/Political   **(PR: A   MPAA: NR)**

LAST DAYS OF JOHN DILLINGER, THE
(SEE: DILLINGER)

LAST GOOD TIME, THE   ★★★
(U.S.) 90m Apogee Films ~ Samuel Goldwyn Company c

Armin Mueller-Stahl *(Joseph Kopple)*; Maureen Stapleton *(Ida Cutler)*; Lionel Stander *(Howard Singer)*; Olivia d'Abo *(Charlotte Zwicki)*; Adrian Pasdar *(Eddie)*; Zohra Lampert *(Barbara)*; Kevin Corrigan *(Frank)*; Molly Powell *(Dorothy)*; Jody Wilson *(Mrs. Wilder)*; Beatrice Winde *(Nurse Westman)*; Burt Harris *(Supermarket Manager)*; Ken Simmons *(Bartender)*; Gino Lucci *(Bus Driver)*

Actor Bob Balaban's first forays into directing were PARENTS and MY BOYFRIEND'S BACK, bizarre and off-putting pieces of comic-horror juvenilia. A promising change of pace, THE LAST GOOD TIME is a reflective, lyrical tale about rediscovering love near the end of life.

Retired violinist Joseph Kopple (Armin Mueller-Stahl) dwells alone in a fastidiously neat urban flat. Widowed, sixtyish neighbor Ida (Maureen Stapleton) shyly tries to attract his attention, but Kopple sticks to a set routine of reading and conversations with his only friend, who is dying in the hospital (veteran character actor Lionel Stander, in his final performance). During a domestic disturbance, Kopple's upstairs neighbors toss items out the window; Kopple retrieves a lost storage-locker key from the fire escape and hides it. Then Charlotte (Olivia D'Abo), a sexy, streetwise girl seeking refuge from her abusive boyfriend, appears. Kopple takes her in, introduces her to great books and music, recalls his youthful, ill-fated marriage to a dancer, and reveals the $6,000 tax problem that endangers his secure home. Charlotte remains evasive about her underworld associates, who threaten her and finally ransack Kopple's rooms over a mysterious missing object of great importance. At that point, Kopple reluctantly admits to concealing the storage-locker key. Charlotte angrily takes it and storms out, then later reappears and tenderly makes love to the old man. The next day she departs for good, having traded the key for enough cash to pay Kopple's IRS debt. Spirit renewed, Kopple calls on Ida.

Balaban can be commended first for carving a plot out of Richard Bausch's vaporous, elegiac novel, and for keeping a lid on potential crime-thriller elements that might have taken over completely in the hands of a less-disciplined filmmaker. The mystery of the key and the valuable secret it guards remain unspecified and are not really relevant anyway in a story line about intimacy, second chances, and repressed yearning. Mueller-Stahl plays a part similar to that of Anthony Hopkins in THE REMAINS OF THE DAY, a pleasant, civilized man whose perfectly-ordered existence masks an emotional rigidity that has cost him dearly. D'Abo, often cast in routine decorative-blonde roles, shows impressive range as the shady waif, even if a dramatic high point still requires her to bare her voluptuous torso for a May-December sex scene. In outline, THE LAST GOOD TIME does seem more than a little like male wish fulfillment (the aged Kopple gets a young honey before he's forced to settle for the matronly Ida), but heartfelt performances and direction raise the moment above the predictable commonplace.

Though the independent feature won top prize at the 1995 Hampton's Film Festival, its theatrical exposure was even briefer than that of PARENTS and MY BOYFRIEND'S BACK. *(Profanity, sexual situations, adult situations, nudity.)* — C.C.

d, Bob Balaban; p, Bob Balaban, Dean Silvers; exec p, Klaus Volkenborn; assoc p, Ricardo Freixa, Tod Scott Brody; w, Bob Balaban, John McLaughlin (based on the novel by Richard Bausch); ph, Claudia Raschke; ed, Hughes Winborne; m, Jonathan Tunick; prod d, Wing Lee; art d, Michael Shaw; set d, Betsy Alton; sound, Antonio L. Arroyo (mixer); casting, Billy Hopkins, Suzanne Smith, Kerry Barden; cos, Kimberly A. Tillman; makeup, Angela Johnson; stunts, Jim Lovelett

Romance/Drama   **(PR: C   MPAA: NR)**

LAST OF THE DOGMEN   ★★½
(U.S.) 120m Last of the Dog Men Inc.; Carolco;
Savoy Pictures ~ Savoy Pictures c
(AKA: LAST OF THE DOG MEN, THE)

Tom Berenger *(Lewis Gates)*; Barbara Hershey *(Professor Lillian Sloan)*; Kurtwood Smith *(Sheriff Deegan)*; Andrew Miller *(Briggs)*; Steve Reevis *(Yellow Wolf)*; Graham Jarvis *(Pharmacist)*; Helen Calahasen *(Yellow Wolf's Wife)*; Eugene Black Bear *(Spotted Elk)*; Gregory Scott Cummins *(Sears)*; Mark Boone, Jr. *(Tattoo)*; Wilford Brimley *(Narrator)*; Dawn Lavand *(Indian Girl)*; Sidel Standing Elk *(Lean Bear)*; Hunter Bodine *(Kid)*; Parley Baer *(Mr. Hollis)*; Georgie Collins *(Senior Editor)*; Sherwood Price *(Tracker)*; Molly Parker *(Nurse)*; Antony Holland *(Doc Carvey)*; Robert Donley *(Old Timer)*; Brian Stollery *(Grad Student)*; Mitchell LaPlante *(Wild Boy)*

Tom Berenger and Barbara Hershey star in LAST OF THE DOGMEN, a pleasant if overlong adventure picture about a bounty hunter and a historian who discover a secret tribe of Native Americans. It may seem familiar in spots, but it is competently told.

Berenger plays Lewis Gates, a grizzled and widowed bounty hunter who lives and works in Montana. Although Lewis scraps with Sheriff Deegan (Kurtwood Smith)—his ex-father-in-law, who blames Lewis for the death of his daughter—he accepts Deegan's assignment to track down three convicts who have escaped into the mountains.

During his hunt, Lewis witnesses an Indian warrior killing the convicts. Back in town, Lewis tells the skeptical sheriff what he saw, and then consults Dr. Lillian Stone (Barbara Hershey), a

college professor of Native American history. Although she can't believe that Indians still live in the mountains, she tells him the story of a Cheyenne tribe, known as the "Dogmen," who were massacred at nearby Sand Creek many decades earlier.

Lewis sets out to find the Dogmen and Lillian joins him despite their slightly antagonistic relationship. They locate the Indians, who are initially guarded and defensive. Eventually, their leader, Yellow Wolf (Steve Reevis), takes the outsiders to see his son, who was wounded earlier by one of the fugitives. Though afraid of discovery, Yellow Wolf joins Lewis on a journey back to town, where penicillin is available.

Circumstances force Lewis to steal the medicine, which drives the sheriff and his deputies to chase him back into the mountains. After finding the tribe again, Lewis delivers the penicillin and begins absorbing tribal culture. Soon, however, Lewis realizes he must leave his new friends so that the sheriff will not discover the whereabouts of the "lost" clan. While Lillian decides to stay on with the Cheyenne, Lewis deliberately gets himself trapped and arrested. However, he wins his release by saving the sheriff's life and heads back into the mountains.

LAST OF THE DOGMEN recycles elements from the various revisionist Westerns of the 1950s, including DEVIL'S DOORWAY (1950), ACROSS THE WIDE MISSOURI (1951), THE BIG SKY (1952), and THE NAKED SPUR (1953), adding a liberal dose of DANCES WITH WOLVES (1990). The film is laudably conscientious in its re-creation of Native American culture, even if occasionally falls prey to the romanticism that plagues the P.C. Westerns of the 1990s. There are some surprisingly stirring moments, including the first meeting between Lewis and Lillian and the tribe, and some pointedly critical ones, including Lewis's reaction to a mock-Indian candy dispenser he sees in a drug store. The performers lend dignity to these scenes (Berenger is also surprisingly funny with some of his cynical one-liners), and the production, from Richard Halsey's photography to David Arnold's music, further strengthens the drama. *(Violence, profanity.)* — E.M.

d, Tab Murphy; p, Joel B. Michaels; exec p, Mario Kassar; assoc p, Don Heitzer; w, Tab Murphy; ph, Karl Walter Lindenlaub; ed, Richard Halsey; m, David Arnold; prod d, Trevor Williams; art d, Ricardo Spinace; sound, David Ronne (mixer), David M. Kelson (mixer); fx, David Kelsey; casting, Amanda Mackey, Cathy Sandrich; cos, Elsa Zamparelli; makeup, Allan A. Apone; stunts, Chuck Waters

Drama/Romance/Adventure   **(PR: A   MPAA: PG)**

LAST RIDE, THE   ★★
(U.S.) 102m Big Truck Productions; Nu World
Entertainment; HKM Film ~ Evergreen Entertainment c
(AKA: F.T.W.; FUCK THE WORLD)

Mickey Rourke *(Frank T. Wells)*; Lori Singer *(Scarlett Stuart)*; Brion James *(Sheriff Rudy Morgan)*; Peter Berg *(Clem)*; Rodney A. Grant; Aaron Neville; Charlie Sexton

A love story about a hard-luck cowboy and a trigger-happy incest victim, THE LAST RIDE tracks a star-crossed couple's inevitable demise with dreary, predictable results.

Rodeo champ Frank T. Wells (Mickey Rourke) is released from prison and tries to saddle up his career again. Nearby, Scarlett Stewart (Lori Singer), an automechanic, and her violent, possessive brother, Clem (Peter Berg), rob a bank. During the getaway, Clem kills three cops and a bank guard. The cops track down the robbers. Scarlett escapes, but not before she sees a cop kill her brother. When Frank's truck breaks down, he rides a horse to get help and finds Scarlett hiding in a barn. She pulls a gun on him, but eventually ends up fixing his truck. Returning the favor, he offers her a place to stay. The two quickly become intimate. But the climate is hardly romantic; Scarlett is a wanted woman prepared to kill any cop in her way. The pair go on the rodeo circuit. When Frank criticizes Scarlett for robbing a convenience store, she gets violent and reveals her incestuous relationship with her brother. At a three-day rodeo, Scarlett declares it's the "first time I've ever felt alive." Not long after, she provokes a barroom brawl that lands Frank in jail. He gets out in time to ride, but a broken hand makes him a long shot to win. While Frank saddles up for the last ride of the rodeo and winds up winning a $5,000 purse, Scarlett robs a bank. She gets shot after crashing into a cop car, but somehow manages to escape. Frank finds her and decides to take his critically injured lover, on horseback, to Canada. Scarlett dies on the way. Mounted police chase Frank until a helicopter sniper kills him.

There's not much to like about THE LAST RIDE, other than some terrific Big Sky terrain. Mickey Rourke, who once displayed a convincing macho swagger in movies like BAR-FLY, does little more than let a smile flicker across his face. Lori Singer's Scarlett, blessed with automotive skills and physical beauty, is an unsympathetic bundle of contradictions who hates her brother and the cops who killed him alike. But let's not blame the victim. The characters here are supposed to give each other a shot at redemption. Under Micheal Karbelnikoff's direction and Mari Kornhuaser's thin script, they're shooting blanks from the get-go. *(Nudity, violence, extreme profanity, adult situations.)* — S.K.

d, Michael Karbelnikoff; p, Tom Mickel; exec p, Ron Altbach, Avi Lerner, Danny Dimbort; assoc p, Alexis Magagni, Mari Kornhauser; co-p, Joanna Plafsky, Trevor Short; w, Mari Kornhauser, Sir Eddie Cook (from a story by Mari Kornhauser); ph, James L. Carter; ed, Joe D'Augustine; prod d, John Reinhart; casting, Danielle Eskanazi

Drama/Romance (PR: O   MPAA: R)

LAST SAMURAI, THE ★★★
(U.S.) 90m c

John Fujioka *(Yasujiro Endo)*; James Ryan *(Miyagawa)*; Lance Henriksen *(Johnny Congo)*; Arabella Holzbog *(Caro)*; John Saxon *(Haroun Al-Hakim)*; Lisa Eilbacher *(Susan)*

In an apparent homage to masterpieces of the samurai genre, THE LAST SAMURAI opens with an incongruously elegant, black-and-white sequence, in which two unidentified martial artists spar on a seashore. The film settles down more pedestrianly in the office of Yasujiro Endo (John Fujioka), a wealthy Japanese businessman. Endo, a devotee of the martial arts and the disappearing traditions of an earlier era, is haunted by visions of a solitary figure traversing the plains. With his assistant and sparring partner Miyagawa (James Ryan), Endo embarks on a trip to the fictional African nation of Imatzi. Ostensibly traveling to negotiate with silicon miners, Endo also seeks the source of his visions, which he believes to be an ancestor, killed while on a mission to bring Buddhism to Africa. Johnny Congo (Lance Henriksen), a Vietnam vet making his way around the world as a mercenary, also arrives in war-torn Imatzi, accompanied by his girlfriend Caro (Arabella Holzbog). Congo's bravado catches Endo's eye, and he is promptly hired to fly Endo and Miyagawa into guerrilla territory. The party arrives at the luxurious tent dwelling of gunrunner Haroun Al-Hakim (John Saxon) and his wife Susan (Lisa Eilbacher), an American novelist who has converted to her husband's Muslim faith. These unlikely and mutually distrustful comrades pass the time uneasily, jockeying for opportunities to pursue their own agendas—and deriding Congo's violent nature and dishonorable soldier-for-hire status.

Pledging that he is not afraid to die when "the perfect moment" comes, Congo storms from the camp. Hakim is killed by weapons he supplied to the guerrillas, and Johnny finds his perfect moment. In sacrificing himself for the lives of others, he regains his honor in the eyes of his companions.

THE LAST SAMUARI provides adequate action in tandem with director-screenwriter Paul Mayersberg's almost poignant insistence on addressing the themes of honor and cultural displacement, common to his earlier work as a writer on films such as THE MAN WHO FELL TO EARTH and MERRY CHRIST-MAS, MR. LAWRENCE. Still, this film suffers from lack of a clear mission of its own. Endo's desire to avenge his ancestor, originally the driving force of the film, fizzles next to Congo's more complex dual role as action hero and tragic hero. The loose ends of several subplots, raised and quickly dropped, suggest missed opportunities to have some fun—and to give the more wooden characters in the ensemble some depth. Holzbog, underused as a potential foil for Congo, enters the film gamely toughing it up, but soon sheds her boots and jeans for more feminine attire and becomes just a pretty face who needs rescuing. Hers is not the only character suffering from lack of development. This meeting of lost souls from nearly every corner of the globe is marred by its reliance on ethnic stereotypes to propel the narrative, rather than the potentially complex motivations of its troubled characters. *(Violence, nudity, profanity, adult situations.)* — C.Ch.

d, Paul Mayersberg; w, Paul Mayersberg

Action/Adventure/Martial Arts (PR: C   MPAA: NR)

LAST SUMMER IN THE HAMPTONS ★★★
(U.S.) 105m Jagtoria Film Co.; Rainbow Film Co. ~ Rainbow Releasing c

Victoria Foyt *(Oona Hart)*; Viveca Lindfors *(Helena Mora)*; Jon Robin Baitz *(Jake Axelrod)*; Savannah Boucher *(Suzanne)*; Roscoe Lee Browne *(Freddy)*; Andre Gregory *(Ivan Axelrod)*; Nick Gregory *(George)*; Melissa Leo *(Trish Axelrod)*; Roddy McDowall *(Thomas)*; Martha Plimpton *(Chloe Garfield)*; Ron Rifkin *(Eli Garfield)*; Diane Salinger *(Marian Mora Garfield)*; Brooke Smith *(Lois Garfield)*; Kristoffer Tabori *(Nick Mora)*; Holland Taylor *(Davis Mora Axelrod)*; Henry Jaglom *(Max Berger)*; Arnold Leo *(Doctor)*; Joseph Feury *(Producer)*; Barbara Flood *(Wealthy Lady)*; Michael Emil *(House Guest)*; Alexandra Styron *(House Guest)*; Chris Knoblock *(Student Actor)*; Luis de la Garza *(Chauffeur)*; Michele Fleischman *(Waitress at Cafe)*

LAST SUMMER IN THE HAMPTONS celebrates the acting profession in a quirky yet charming way. Henry Jaglom's observant look at a theatrical clan's vacation is one of the director's better films to date.

In the affluent artistic resort community of East Hampton, New York, a large theater family congregates in their sprawling summer home to rehearse Chekhov's "The Seagull". But the knowledge that Helena Mora (Viveca Lindfors), the clan's matriarch, is selling the house, casts a pall over preparations for the play. Everyone realizes that this will be the family's last summer in the Hamptons. Another distraction to the rehearsals comes in the form of Oona Hart (Victoria Foyt), a Hollywood star and unexpected houseguest who causes rifts among some family members. Oona's pursuit of the lead role in the latest play by Helena's grandson (and the family's star playwright) Jake Axelrod (Jon Robin Baitz) forces him to rethink his original concept, while her entreaties to Jake's father, Ivan (Andre Gregory), to become the director of his son's play succeed in revealing the communication chasm between the two men. Meanwhile, Jake must contend with the sexual advances of both his alcoholic sister, Lois (Brooke Smith), and an opportunistic young actor, George (Nick Gregory). Finally, at the family's performance of "The Seagull" for the Hamptons' residents, several of the Chekhovian offstage problems are resolved in dramatic ways.

Henry Jaglom has often been called a West Coast, poor man's Woody Allen, making elaborate home movies starring his actor friends (not helping matters this time is that LAST SUMMER IN THE HAMPTONS recalls Allen's MIDSUMMER NIGHT'S SEX COMEDY, which itself was a tribute to Ingmar Bergman's SMILES OF A SUMMER NIGHT). While both Jaglom and Allen are guilty of self-indulgence, it is Jaglom who has emerged over the years as the more open-ended (and certainly the more naturalistic) of the two. Jaglom is especially preferable to Allen in his development and treatment of women characters (LAST SUMMER was cowritten by Jaglom and its star, Victoria Foyt); it is particularly refreshing that female characters with complex, realistic personalities have dominated Jaglom's last few films (EATING, BABYFEVER) in knowing, funny ways.

Jaglom's characteristic tendency to give loose, improvisational leeway to his actors, female and male, provides an apt approach for a film that feels like a documentary about several well-known theater personalities, but also says much about the masks people don in all types of relationships. The able cast displays a full range of styles and attitudes: Viveca Lindfors revels in the role of a wistful, aging but highly dynamic former Hollywood star, playing off her real-life identity as an aging but highly dynamic former Hollywood star (at one point, Helena, her character, watches herself on television in THE ADVENTURES OF DON JUAN and NIGHT UNTO NIGHT, two Lindfors films of the 1940s); Victoria Foyt cleverly but subtly savages the Michelle Pfeiffer-type of glamor personality who uses method acting exercises to prepare herself for her networking sessions (her animal imitations supply the film's funniest—and oddest—moments); as Jake, playwright Jon Robin Baitz (in his film debut) expertly conveys the occupational hazards of his real-life profession; As Ivan, Andre Gregory lightly sends up his reputation as an enigmatic director-guru; Ron Rifkin's Eli almost steals the show as a vain actor who bickers endlessly with his willful daughter, Chloe (Martha Plimpton); and, finally, Jaglom himself appears in a dead-on cameo as Oona's fast-talking agent, Max Berger.

There are a couple of drawbacks. By using such a large ensemble, Jaglom wastes some of the other performers he has employed, including Roscoe Lee Brown, Roddy McDowall, and Holland Taylor. Also, there are perhaps one too many shocking family revelations (in addition to a few unanswered questions) that arise in the melodramatic climax (which is patterned after Jean Renoir's RULES OF THE GAME).

LAST SUMMER IN THE HAMPTONS is much more than a tribute to the strengths and vulnerabilities of theater people. It is also a shrewd commentary on the roles all people play in both the theater and "everyday" life, and a perceptive interrogation of the boundary between the two. (*Violence, sexual situations, adult situations, profanity.*) — E.M.

d, Henry Jaglom; p, Judith Wolinsky; w, Henry Jaglom, Victoria Foyt; ph, Hanania Baer; ed, Henry Jaglom; m, Rick Baitz; sound, Neil Danziger (mixer); cos, Barbara Flood; makeup, Tracy Warbin

Comedy/Drama   (PR: C   MPAA: R)

LEAVING LAS VEGAS   ★★★
(U.S.) 112m United Artists;
Lumiere Pictures ~
MGM/UA c

Nicolas Cage (*Ben Sanderson*); Elisabeth Shue (*Sera*); Julian Sands (*Yuri*); Richard Lewis (*Peter*); Valeria Golino (*Terri*); Steven Weber (*Marc Nussbaum*); Kim Adams (*Sheila*); Emily Procter (*Debbie*); Graham Beckel (*L.A. Bartender*); R. Lee Ermey (*Conventioneer*); Laurie Metcalf (*Landlady*); David Brisbin (*Landlord*); Xander Berkeley (*Cynical Cabbie*); Lou Rawls (*Concerned Cabbie*); Stuart Regen (*Man at Bar*); Al Henderson (*Man at Strip Bar*); Shashi Bhatia (*Hispanic Prostitute*); Carey Lowell (*Bank Teller*); Anne Lange (*Business Colleague*); Thomas Kopache (*Mr. Simpson*); Vincent Ward (*Business Man #1*); French Stewart (*Business Man #2*); Lucinda Jenney (*Weird Woman*); Mike Figgis (*Mobster #1*); Waldemar Kalinowski (*Mobster #2*); Ed Lauter (*Mobster #3*); David Kriegel (*Hotel Manager*); Bill Thompson (*Midwest Man at Poolside*); Marek Stabrowski (*Pawn Shop Owner*); Mariska Hargitay (*Hooker at Bar*); Danny Huston (*Barman #2*); Shawnee Smith (*Biker Girl*); Paul Quinn (*Biker Guy*); Julian Lennon (*Bartender in Biker Bar*); Tracy Thorne (*Waitress at Mall*); Bob Rafelson (*Man at Mall*); Susan Barnes (*Desk Clerk*); Marc Coppola (*Dealer*); Michael Goorjian (*College Boy #1*); Jeremy Jordan (*College Boy #2*); Davidlee Willson (*College Boy #3*); Sergio Premoli (*Stetson Man at Casino*); Gordon Michaels (*Security Guard*)

One of the most highly praised films of 1995, LEAVING LAS VEGAS is as obsessive, but not so well written, as LAST TANGO IN PARIS or JULES AND JIM, films that are also far more cinematically imaginative. The critical consensus on Mike Figgis's romantic downer hinged on its universal theme—"It's about unconditional love, don't you see?"—suggesting that certain overwhelmed critics really should get out more, and not just to the movies.

When we first meet Ben (Nicolas Cage), he's careening through the aisles of a liquor store, blissfully filling up his cart with bottles. Ben is systematically divesting himself of everything most people care about—his family, his possessions, his job—and intends to blow his severance pay on a final, fatal alcoholic binge in Las Vegas.

While driving drunkenly along the Strip, he meets clean-scrubbed prostitute Sera (Elizabeth Shue), takes her back to his room and promptly passes out. This intrigues her, and after she breaks with her doomed, sadistic Russian pimp (Julian Sands)—he's managed to anger the Russian Mafia, and pays the usual price—she turns to Ben for companionship. Sera makes a solemn promise that she will never ask him to stop drinking, sealing the pact with the gift of a silver hip flask. In exchange, she is accorded a rollicking daily existence defined by dealing with his shakes, incomprehensible slurring, vomiting, and hangovers.

Together they burn their bridges, trashing casinos and motel rooms. She has the added misfortune to be gang-raped by a trio of teenaged goons whom she'd figured as easy marks. Ben and Sera break up, and are finally reunited just before Ben achieves his goal, going into that good night on an orgasmic wave and leaving Sera bereft, with only her patient analyst in whom to confide.

Director-writer Mike Figgis adapted his script from a semi-autobiographical novel by John O'Brien, who committed suicide two weeks after his book was optioned. The writer's father described the book as a suicide note, and the film is an absolute, unredeemed downer from beginning to end, a true masochist's delight. "Don't you think it'll be a little boring, living with a drunk?" Ben asks Sera. LEAVING LAS VEGAS is certainly the answer, as enervating a dead end as other treatments of tortured, sodden jerks—UNDER THE VOLCANO and BARFLY, for example—have been. Figgis's fascination with these lowlifes has brought out the worst in his ear for tripe, witness such gutter profundities as "You're like some kind of antidote that mixes with the liquor and makes everything all right," and "I'm tired of coming home alone to a bottle of mouthwash to get the taste of come out of my mouth." Figgis gives the film his trademark velvet-noir look—a remarkable, if not necessarily laudable achievement, given that it was shot for a pittance on Super 16 film—which belies the grittily nihilistic, verite intentions he professed. The busy jazz score was composed by Renaissance Man Figgis, and features the distinctive and wholly inappropriate vocal stylings of Sting.

Cage, who has proved an effective comedian in RAISING ARIZONA, MOONSTRUCK and VAMPIRE'S KISS, won an Academy Award for his monotonously doomed performance. His weird, San Fernando Valley-boy inflections merely emphasize the thudding banality of Figgis's would-be mordant lines, like "I kept running out of booze, and the store would be closed because I kept forgetting to look at my watch." A scene in which he awakes from a stupor, blinking and simpering at Shue like a huge, obscene baby—"I feel like a prickly pear"—apparently struck many viewers as the height of great acting, rather than profoundly embarrassing self-indulgence. Shue works like the dickens, but she's never convincing as a streetwalker: her Sera is too perfectly groomed, aerobicized and dressed (in a glamorous, skintight collection of corsets and rubber sheaths by Vivienne Westwood). What draws her to Ben is, like his inner torment, a complete mystery. The film features aimless cameo appearances by the likes of Richard Lewis, Steven Weber, Valeria Golino, Julian Lennon, Lou Rawls and Laurie Metcalf. (*Substance abuse, nudity, profanity, adult situations, sexual situations, violence.*) — D.N.

d, Mike Figgis; p, Lila Cazes, Annie Stewart; exec p, Paige Simpson, Stuart Regen; w, Mike Figgis (based on the novel by John O'Brien); ph, Declan Quinn; ed, John Smith; m, Mike Figgis; prod d, Waldemar Kalinowski; art d, Barry M. Kingston; set d, Florence Fellman; sound, Pawel Wdowczak (mixer); fx, William Harrison; casting, Carrie Frazier; cos, Laura Goldsmith, Vivienne Westwood; makeup, Katy Bihr; stunts, Russell Towery

AA Best Actor: Nicolas Cage; *AAN Best Actress:* Elisabeth Shue; *AAN Best Director:* Mike Figgis; *AAN Best Adapted Screenplay:* Mike Figgis

Drama   (PR: O   MPAA: R)

LES MISERABLES   ★★★
(France) 177m Les Films 13; TF1 Films ~
Warner Bros. c

Jean-Paul Belmondo (*Henri Fortin/Jean Valjean/Roger Fortin*); Michel Boujenah (*Andre Ziman*); Alessandra Martines (*Elise Ziman*); Salome Lelouch (*Salome Ziman*); Annie Girardot (*Farmer Woman*); Philippe Leotard (*Farmer*); Clementine Celarie (*Catherine/Fantine*); Philippe Khorsand (*Policeman/Javert*); Ticky Holgado (*The Kind Hoodlum*); Rufus (*Thenardier Father and Son*); Nicole Croisille (*Thenardiere 1830/1900*); William Leymergie (*Toureiffel*); Jean Marais (*Bishop Myriel*); Micheline Presle (*The Mother Superior*); Darry Cowl; Antoine Dulery; Jacques Gamblin; Pierre Vernier; Sylvie Joly; Robert Hossein; Daniel Toscan du Plantier (*Comte de Villenueve*); Cyrielle Claire; Margot Abascal; Paul Belmondo; Jacques Bonnot; Jacques Boudet; Marie Bunel; Mickael Bussinger; Nathalie Cerda; Michael Cohen; Jean-Francois Derec; Max Fournel; Valerio Gamberini; Pierre-Alexis Hollenbeck; Maurice Mons; Anne-Marie Pisani; Wolfgang Pissors; Isabelle Sadoyan; Marie-France Santon; Peter Semler; Guillaume Souchet

In this umpteenth film version of Victor Hugo's LES MISERABLES, director Claude Lelouch sumptuously updates the classic story. Fans of the book and traditional screen epics should be won over, while those expecting something more radical should just stay away.

Hugo's 1862 novel has inspired Lelouch to place some LES MISERABLES characters and themes into a story spanning the first half of the 20th century. Through a clever device, Lelouch also recreates actual scenes from the book and incorporates them into a tale that begins in France, on New Years Eve of 1899. A nobleman, Comte de Villeneuve (Daniel Toscan de Plantier), commits suicide, and his driver, Henri Fortin (Jean-Paul Belmondo), is wrongly imprisoned for murder. Henri is killed trying to escape from jail. His wife, Catherine (Clementine Celarie), becomes a prostitute and eventually kills herself. Their son, Roger, grows up without his parents, and becomes a champion boxer.

Flash forward to 1931. Law student Andre Ziman (Michel Boujenah) marries a ballerina, Elise (Alessandra Martines). Eleven years later, the Zimans and their daughter, Salome (Salome Lelouch), are forced to flee the Nazis with the help of Roger Fortin (Belmondo), now a truck driver. On the trip across France to the Swiss border, the illiterate Roger asks Andre to read portions from his favorite novel, *Les Miserables* (from this point onward, scenes from the novel are interwoven with the narrative).

To protect Salome, the Zimans ask Roger to enter her into a convent school for girls. Soon after, however, Andre and Elise are separated during a Nazi ambush of Jewish refugees at the Swiss border. Over the next months and years, Andre hides on a farm owned by a middle-aged couple (Philippe Leotard and Annie Girardot), Elise is forced to entertain high-ranking Nazi officers, and Roger helps some gangsters-turned-partisans. As D-Day approaches, Roger assists his friends in the Allied attack, while Elise escapes her Nazi captors with the help of a police officer (Philippe Khorsand). Andre, meanwhile, resists the sexual advances of the farmer's wife and eventually leaves the farm.

After the war, Roger honors the Allied victory at his newly-opened cafe, "Chez Jean Valjean," where the Zimans and their daughter reunite. A few years later, Salome marries one of the ex-freedom fighters, and all the surviving characters celebrate liberty, equality, and fraternity.

Compared to his French New Wave brethren, Claude Lelouch, the most unabashed romantic humanist of the bunch, has never received high marks from critics. For this very reason, LES MISERABLES may be his best film to date. Lelouch could find no closer kindred spirit than Victor Hugo, the quintessential Romantic novelist. The updated aspects of this three-hour superproduction in no way compromise Hugo's vision or style.

Lelouch's cinematic tapestry is exceptionally well mounted. Almost every scene—from a large-scale ballroom dance, to a daring prison escape, to the D-Day invasion on the beaches of Normandy—has been appointed with exquisite care by art director Jacques Bufnoir and set decorator Laurent Teysseyre. Lelouch himself (with the help of Philippe Pavans de Ceccatty) handles the mobile camera with a skillful flourish throughout. Belmondo deserves special mention for playing three roles extremely well (in his 60s, he's as sympathetic and charismatic as ever).

Still, to anyone in sympathy with the aspirations of the New Wave—notably its decisive rejection of stuffy, studio-bound efforts by the older French film masters—this LES MISERABLES, good as it is, feels like a backward step. (*Violence, nudity, sexual situations, adult situations, profanity.*) — E.M.

d, Claude Lelouch; p, Claude Lelouch; assoc p, Tania Zazulinski; w, Claude Lelouche (freely adapted from the novel by Victor Hugo); ph, Claude Lelouch; ed, Helene De Luze; m, Francis Lai, Didier Barbelivien, Philippe Servain, Erik Berchot, Michel Legrand; art d, Jacques Bufnoir; set d, Laurent Tesseyre; sound, Gerard Rousseau, Harald Maury; fx, Dominique Colladant, George Demetrau; casting, Arlette Gordon; cos, Dominique Borg; makeup, Charly Koubesserian, Magali Ceyrat; stunts, Daniel Verite

Drama (PR: C MPAA: R)

LESSONS OF DARKNESS ★★★½
(Germany/France/Spain) 50m c
(LEKTIONEN IN FINSTERNIS)

Werner Herzog *(Narrator)*

LESSONS OF DARKNESS takes place predominately in the burning oil fields of the Persian Gulf. By judiciously assembling some remarkable shots, Werner Herzog has created a brilliant, unforgettable documentary-epic.

LESSONS OF DARKNESS is divided into 12 sections, beginning with "A Capital City," a panoramic view of Baghdad prior to the 1990 US bombing of Iraq, and "The War," a fragment of grainy nighttime bombing footage shown on CNN at that time. The remaining 10 sections ("Finds From Torture Chambers," "Satan's National Park," "Dinosaurs on the March," etc.) detail the extraordinary environmental aftereffects of both the bombing and Saddam Hussein's subsequent burning of the Kuwaiti oil fields.

Compared to Rainer Werner Fassbinder and Wim Wenders, Werner Herzog has always been considered the most austere and typically Germanic of the New German Cinema triumvirate. Herzog's story films, including AGUIRRE THE WRATH OF GOD (1973), THE ENIGMA OF KASPER HAUSER (1974) and FITZCARRALDO (1982) have been both damned and praised for their bleak vision and deliberate, symbolic style, while his documentaries, including LA SOUFRIERE (1976), have also divided critics and audiences by using an untraditionally "personal" approach. Yet there is no denying that Herzog's customary method is tremendously effective in his 1992 documentary, LESSONS OF DARKNESS (released in the US in 1995).

Like MEAT (1976), Frederick Wiseman's documentary about the meat-processing industry, LESSONS OF DARKNESS presents simultaneously beautiful and horrific images. Herzog, like Wiseman, thereby opens himself up to criticism that he has created seductive formalism out of tragedy. It is true that cinematographer Paul Berriff's aerial views of the burning landscape are reminiscent of the paintings of Hieronymus Bosch and Max Ernst, and, like a painter with a huge, wide(screen) canvas, Herzog does find a curious magnificence in the roaring fire, billowing smoke, bubbling oil, and steaming earth. The director also emphasizes the grandeur of the spectacle with selections from several musical warhorses, including Wagner's "Parsifal," Grieg's "Peer Gynt," and Verdi's "Requiem."

Herzog meticulously constructs the images in a way that develops a point of view about his subject. It is vital, for example, that the director includes brief interviews early on with two Iraqi women whose families suffered greatly during the massacre. The face of one woman's child, who has lost his entire capacity to speak, haunts the rest of the 50-minute film like a ghostly portent. LESSONS OF DARKNESS never returns to these victims, but it doesn't need to: symbolically, the film goes on to show that no words could ever describe the degree to which the land and people have been destroyed by human folly. (Man's

destruction of nature has been a theme in other Herzog films, including his 1970 FATA MORGANA, which was set in a postapocalyptic African desert.) In a shrewd way, Herzog pays tribute to the power of silent film by refusing to add more than a spare voice-over to the shots, and by using old-fashioned but ironic intertitles to describe each section. Observing the American firefighters at the end, Herzog bitterly remarks (in the voice-over) that man has not learned his lesson from this nightmare: "What are they up to? Are they going to rekindle the blaze? Has life without fire consumed them?. . . Now they are content. Now there is something for them to extinguish again."

Formally rich yet philosophically solid, boldly operatic yet quietly poetic, politically critical yet mystically transcendent, LESSONS OF DARKNESS is pure cinema. *(Adult situations.)* — E.M.

d, Werner Herzog; p, Paul Berriff, Werner Herzog; w, Werner Herzog; ph, Paul Berriff; ed, Rainer Standke

Documentary (PR: A MPAA: NR)

LIE DOWN WITH DOGS ★★
(U.S.) 84m Grainy Pictures; Miramax ~ Miramax c

Wally White *(Tommie)*; James Sexton *(Eddie)*; Darren Dryden *(Ben)*; Vann Jones *(Glen/Herbert)*; Bash Halow *(Guy)*; Randy Becker *(Tom)*; Brian Quirk *(Ru)*; Reno Dakota *(Square Joe)*; Kevin Mayes *(Toby)*; Ken Bonnin *(Chris)*; David Matwljkow *(Charlie)*; Darren Anthony *(Jose)*; Hans Hoppenbrouwers *(Dan)*; Nonny Kulecza *(Bob)*; Ty-Ranne Grimsted *(Carmelota Pessums)*; Jack Hazan *(Simon)*; Wendy Adams *(Sally)*; Michel Richoz *(Michi)*; J.D. Cerna *(Peter/Sal)*; Richard B. Olson *(Jeffrey)*; Carol McDonald *(Margaret)*; Martha J. Cooney *(Doctor)*; Rob Cardazone *("Trip")*; Steve Lent *(Benjamin)*; Charlie Fieran *(Anthony)*; Chester Hinsfield *(Flyerman)*; Al Marz *(Scalper)*; Nevada Belle *(Church Lady)*; Christine Hull *(Tourist Lady)*; Hart F. Faber *(Bob's Voice)*; Julie Wheeler *(Prep Girl)*; Kevin Shenk *(Waitress)*; Scott James Jordan *(Driver/Groper)*; Tim McCarthy *(Dorothy Stratton Killer)*; Jonathan Pauldick *(Political Guy #1)*; Anthony Bennett *(Political Guy #2)*; Devin Quigley *(Political Woman)*; Raymond Capuana *(Dick Guy #1)*; Dennis Davis *(Dick Guy #2)*; Eli Kabillio *(Dick Guy #3)*; Eddie Encarnacion *(Dick Guy #4)*; Matthew Gambino *(Tommie's Body Double)*; Roberto H. Fantauzzi *(Underwear & Sex Boy)*; Clifton Lively, Jr. *(Underwear & Sex Boy)*; Mark Irish *(Underwear & Sex Boy)*; Ricardo Angelico *(Underwear Boy)*; Denis Gawley *(Sex Boy)*; Paul Rex Pierson *(Sex Boy)*; Jesus Cortez *(Stripper)*

A showcase for star-director-writer Wally White, LIE DOWN WITH DOGS follows the summer adventures of a young gay man who exchanges the fetid inferno that is Manhattan for a provincial town's boys and booze. It's moderately charming and wholly forgettable.

Tommie (Wally White) arrives in Provincetown and looks for various transient jobs while making friends with dissolute Eddie and Guy (James Sexton, Bash Halow). They introduce him to denizens of the town, such as the proprietors of various bed-and-breakfasts who are all recovering alcoholics, and a truly obnoxious barfly. He has a fling with sleazy hustler Tom (Randy Becker), and, along with the entire Cape, he has his head turned by Ben (Darren Dryden), a hunky jogger who haunts the dunes. All this carousing ultimately makes Tommie ill, and it is then that he discovers that his new pals are fair weather at best. He staggers back to New York with a pile of experience under his belt, and—who knows?—just might come back again next year.

Slapped together with little or no artistry, LIE DOWN WITH DOGS achieves its admittedly low intentions by delivering mindless fun. The contrast between the quaint, picturesque, sleepy, small town and the flamboyant, dissipated lifestyles of its residents is exploited for maximum laughs. Toothsome White is alternately goofy and appealing as a self-deprecating Everyman. As a director, he has no problem breaking the fourth wall when a laugh is needed. He is constantly addressing the camera, turning a job interview into an imagined porno scene, blocking an intrusive lens during an intimate boudoir moment, and screaming long distance to his unsupportive financial backers. His style is all over the place—hand-helds and wipes, Old Hollywood-style montages, freewheeling naturalism morphing into stylized set pieces—yet the film has a genially tacky kind of appeal. Its insouciance is a celebration of its own basic ethos, as expressed by one character: "The 90s have finally kicked in, so let's have some *fun*." Certainly it is a welcome alternative to the AIDS-afflicted, white-bread dreariness of PHILADELPHIA, LONGTIME COMPANION, AN EARLY FROST, and so on.

Despite the obvious limitations of the script, White does capture the desperation and discomforts of a New York summer and the aching romanticism that infects so many young souls looking for love on the beach. There is some cold truth, too, in the scenes where Tommie is let down by his new friends and realizes that his bond with them is transitory. Meanwhile, Jellybean Benitez's highly serviceable hit-laden score keeps things on the bounce. *(Adult situations, sexual situations, nudity, profanity, substance abuse.)* — D.N.

d, Wally White; p, Anthony Bennett, Wally White; exec p, John Pierson; assoc p, Carijn Lau, Jennifer Ryan Cohen, Eli Kabillo; w, Wally White; ph, George Mitas; ed, Hart F. Faber; m, Jellybean Benitez; art d, Reno Dakota

Comedy/Romance   **(PR: O MPAA: R)**

LIFE AND DEATH OF CHICO MENDES, THE
(SEE: BURNING SEASON, THE)

LITTLE ODESSA   ★★★
(U.S.) 99m Paul Webster/Addis-Wechsler Productions; New Line ~ Fine Line c

Tim Roth *(Joshua Shapira)*; Edward Furlong *(Reuben Shapira)*; Vanessa Redgrave *(Irina Shapira)*; Maximilian Schell *(Arkady Shapira)*; Moira Kelly *(Alla Shustervich)*; Paul Guilfoyle *(Boris Volkoff)*; Natasha Andreichenko *(Natasha)*; David Vadim *(Sasha)*; Mina Bern *(Grandma Tsilya)*; Boris McGiver *(Ivan)*; Mohammed Ghaffari *(Pahlevi)*; Michael Khumrev *(Yuri)*; Dmitry Preyers *(Victor)*; David Ross *(Anatoly)*; Ron Brice *(Man With One Leg)*; Jace Kent *(Mechanic)*; Marianna Lead *(Clara)*; Gene Ruffini *(Janitor)*

Twenty-six-year-old writer-director James Gray made his feature film debut with this bleak gangland tale that demonstrates an admirably disciplined film sense but exudes an off-putting coldness.

Cold pretty much defines everybody here, emotionally or laid out on a slab. Russian-Jewish immigrant Arkady Shapira (Maximilian Schell) lives in the Brooklyn neighborhood nicknamed "Little Odessa." He has disowned his older son Joshua (Tim Roth), who has become a hit man for the Russian mafia. Joshua, who has steered clear of the old neighborhood since he killed the son of local Godfather Volkoff (Paul Guilfoyle), returns reluctantly to Little Odessa to kill an Iranian jeweler. Joshua defies his father by contacting his troubled teenage brother Reuben (Edward Furlong), who tells him that their mother, Irina (Vanessa Redgrave), has terminal brain cancer. The sensitive and intelligent Reuben is struggling to make sense of what has happened to his family: His mother is dying, his brother is a murderer and

his upright father is seeing another woman. Joshua negotiates an uneasy truce with his father, visits his mother—who entrusts Reuben's care to him—and rekindles his romance with a neighborhood girl, Alla (Moira Kelly).

At the 80th birthday party of Reuben and Joshua's grandmother, Volkoff warns Arkady not to hide Joshua. Later, Reuben follows Joshua and his cohorts as they murder the jeweler and incinerate his body. Reuben retrieves the gun they use and hides it. Joshua prepares to leave and visits his father one last time. They fight, and Joshua humiliates him; afterwards, Arkady calls Volkoff and betrays his troublesome son. In the movie's striking climax, Volkoff's men try to ambush Joshua amidst sheet-draped clothes-lines in Alla's dreary backyard. Reuben has gotten wind of the assassination plot, retrieves the gun and rushes to his brother's defense. Reuben and Alla are both killed, and Irina dies. The stunned Joshua burns Reuben's corpse in the junkyard where he regularly dispose of bodies, and envisions a happy reunion with his mother that can never be.

Gray said he patterned his script after Greek tragedy, by way of the ethnic crime culture film embodied in MEAN STREETS and ROCCO AND HIS BROTHERS. LITTLE ODESSA's transplanted Eastern European setting is largely unexplored territory in American cinema, and Gray's Little Odessa is an alienated urban landscape of beachside piers and working-class streets where Joshua can shoot a man in the head in broad daylight before dozens of quiet bystanders, secure in the knowledge that the police will never find one eyewitness. But LITTLE ODESSA is a stark, insular enigma from beginning to end.

The undeniably talented cast members all deliver sullen, onenote performances against mud-colored backdrops of dirty snow and stained wallpaper. Schell's Arkady, a once-proud intellectual who's been defeated on nearly every front and now can barely raise his voice above a choked whisper, is the most rounded character in the film. But while LITTLE ODESSA's minimalist characterizations are simply dreary, its artfully muted style sets it apart from the mob of Quentin Tarantino imitations that rushed theaters in the wake of RESERVOIR DOGS. The kidnapping and murder of the jeweler is made all the more awful by the near-silence and congealed darkness in which it occurs, and the film's traditional Russian score is grimly effective. The final showdown in a maze of billowing white sheets is the film's most striking sequence, and indicates a filmmaker with a clear vision and sure control of the medium. For all its flaws, LITTLE ODESSA can't help being an impressive debut. *(Violence, nudity, sexual situations, adult situations, profanity.)* — C.C.

d, James Gray; p, Paul Webster; exec p, Nick Wechsler, Claudia Lewis, Rolf Mittweg; co-p, Kerry Orent; w, James Gray; ph, Tom Richmond; ed, Dorian Harris; m, Dana Sano; prod d, Kevin Thompson; art d, Judy Rhee; set d, Charles Ford; sound, Tom Paul (mixer), Mark Weingarten (mixer); fx, Drew Jiritano; casting, Douglas Abiel; cos, Michael Clancy; makeup, Karen Nichols; stunts, Roy Farfel

Crime/Drama   **(PR: O MPAA: R)**

LITTLE PRINCESS, A   ★★★
(U.S.) 97m Baltimore Pictures; Mark Johnson Productions ~ Warner Bros. c

Eleanor Bron *(Miss Minchin)*; Liam Cunningham *(Captain Crewe/Prince Rama)*; Liesel Matthews *(Sara Crewe)*; Rusty Schwimmer *(Amelia Minchin)*; Arthur Malet *(Charles Randolph)*; Vanessa Lee Chester *(Becky)*; Errol Sitahal *(Ram Dass)*; Heather DeLoach *(Ermengarde)*; Taylor Fry *(Lavinia)*; Darcie Bradford *(Jesse)*; Rachael Bella *(Betsy)*; Alexandra Rea-Baum *(Gertrude)*; Camilla Belle *(Jane)*; Lauren Blumenfeld *(Rose-

mary); Kelsey Mulrooney *(Lottie)*; Kaitlan Cullum *(Ruth)*; Alison Moir *(Princess Sita)*; Time Winters *(Frances the Milkman)*; Lomax Study *(Monsieur Dufarge)*; Vincent Schiavelli *(Mr. Barrow)*; Pushpa Rawal *(Maya)*; Rahi Azizi *(Laki)*; Ken Palmer *(John Randolph)*; Helen Greenberg *(Flower Lady)*; Norman Merrill *(Doctor in Hospital)*; Peggy Miley *(Mabel the Cook)*; Robert P. Cohen *(Ermengarde's Father)*; William Blomquist *(Rich Boy in Street)*; David Fresco *(Beggar Man in Fantasy)*; Judith D. Drake *(Bakery Woman)*; Chris Ellis *(Policeman)*

This new version of the Frances Hodgson Burnett ("The Secret Garden") novel that inspired one of Shirley Temple's best films tells the tale of a rich girl forced into poverty when her father vanishes during wartime. Despite its fine production values, the new LITTLE PRINCESS doesn't quite capture the magic of the earlier production.

1914, Simla, India: Imaginative 10-year-old Sara Crewe (Liesel Matthews) lives with her wealthy, widowed father (Liam Cunningham), a British Army captain. Sara enjoys her life in exotic India, and reads tales from the Sanskrit epic *Ramayana*, in which the hero, Rama, saves Princess Sita from the monstrous demon Ravana. World War I destroys the tranquillity of Sara's life: her father must rejoin his regiment, and places Sara in Miss Minchin's School for Girls in New York City. Sara immediately wins over most of the other students enrolled in the prestigious school, but stern headmistress Miss Minchin (Eleanor Bron) hates the child's free-spirited ways. She must, however, put up with them because of Sara's father's money.

Captain Crewe is reported killed in battle. Since he will no longer be able to pay Sara's tuition, the vengeful Minchin removes Sara from class, takes away her possessions and forces her to be one of the school's servants. The distraught but still headstrong Sara is no longer allowed to speak to her former classmates, but finds a new friend in her attic roommate, the black servant girl Becky (Vanessa Lee Chester). Meanwhile, in the building next door, Indian manservant Ram Dass (Errol Sitahal)—whom Sara has befriended—takes in a wounded British soldier suffering from amnesia. Sara learns that the soldier is her father and, with Becky and Ram Dass' help, gets him to recover his memory just before Miss Minchin instructs the authorities to take Sara away.

The 1993 success of THE SECRET GARDEN, also based on a Burnett novel, inspired Warner Bros. to remake *Sara Crewe*, which had already been filmed as a vehicle for both Mary Pickford (in 1917) and Shirley Temple (1939). To Warner Bros.' surprise, however, the new LITTLE PRINCESS (later *A LITTLE PRINCESS*) failed to attract substantial audiences, despite its impressive pedigree and critical accolades. In an unusual marketing move, the studio released the film a second time with a new ad campaign, but this still failed to make it a success.

A LITTLE PRINCESS is adapted respectably by screenwriters Richard LaGravenese and Elizabeth Chandler, meticulously produced, opulently designed—particularly in the colorful fantasy sequences—elegantly photographed by cinematographer Emmanuel Lubezki and adequately (in the case of Eleanor Bron, more than adequately) acted. While Shirley Temple is a more appealing youngster than newcomer Liesel Matthews, Matthews is both sassy and unabashedly emotional. And though the new LITTLE PRINCESS is a far darker affair than the 1939 version, Mexican-born director Alfonso Cuaron doesn't make it anywhere near as drab and moody as Agnieszka Holland's more artistically and commercially successful THE SECRET GARDEN. Some viewers may find the political correctness of Sara's relationship with Becky forced and even hypocritical, since the Indian characters are still treated in a stereotypically exoticized way. — E.M.

d, Alfonso Cuaron; p, Mark Johnson; exec p, Alan C. Blomquist, Amy Ephron; co-p, Dalisa Cohen; w, Richard LaGravenese, Elizabeth Chandler (based on the novel *Sara Crewe* by Frances Hodgson Burnett); ph, Emmanuel Lubezki; ed, Steven Weisberg; m, Patrick Doyle; prod d, Bo Welch; art d, Tom Duffield; set d, Cheryl Carasik; sound, Richard Beggs (design), Jose Antonio Garcia (mixer); fx, Alan E. Lorimer; casting, Jill Greenberg Sands; cos, Judianna Makovsky; makeup, Julie Hewitt, Robert N. Norin; stunts, Charles Croughwell

AAN Best Art Direction: Bo Welch (art direction), Cheryl Carasik (set decoration); *AAN Best Cinematography:* Emmanuel Lubezki

Children's/Drama (PR: AA MPAA: G)

LIVING IN OBLIVION ★★★
(U.S.) 91m JDI Productions; Lemon Sky
Productions ~ Sony Pictures Classics c/bw

Steve Buscemi *(Nick Reve)*; James LeGros *(Chad Palomino)*; Catherine Keener *(Nicole Springer)*; Dermot Mulroney *(Wolf)*; Danielle von Zerneck *(Wanda)*; Rica Martens *(Cora)*; Peter Dinklage *(Tito)*; Robert Wightman *(Gaffer)*; Hilary Gilford *(Script)*; Kevin Corrigan *(Assistant Camera)*; Matthew Grace *(Boom)*; Michael Griffiths *(Sound Mixer)*; Tom Jarmusch *(Driver/Intern)*; Ryan Bowker *(Food Service/Clapper)*; Francesca DiMauro *(Food Service Supervisor)*; Norman Field *(Hair/Make-up Artist)*; Lori Tan Chin *(Costume Designer)*; Vincenzo Amelia *(Cook)*; Laurel Thornby *(Nicole's Mother)*

The joys and sorrows of the young auteur are celebrated in this delightful comedy that conveys the realities of filmmaking far better than, say, Francois Truffaut's DAY FOR NIGHT (1973), a lavish love letter to the frustrations of filmmaking.

The guerrilla world of independent filmmaking is thoroughly documented in this sprightly film by Tom DiCillo, which focuses on one mishap-filled day on the set of Nick Reve's (Steve Buscemi) low-budget movie. His crew includes dumb hunk cinematographer Wolf (Dermot Mulroney); bossy assistant director Wanda (Danielle Von Zerneck), who's chosen this most inauspicious moment to break up with Wolf; a viciously ambitious script girl (Hilary Gilford); and a sound squad who bear more than a passing resemblance to the Three Stooges. Nick's cast is equally difficult. He's secretly in love with leading lady Nicole (Catherine Keener) and at his wits' end as to what to do with unbearable leading man Chad Palomino (James LeGros), who's fresh from Hollywood and filled with bright ideas. He's also sleeping with his co-star, and their misbegotten tryst seems to have infected the entire project with malaise. He insists on improvising scenes to the advantage of his character, infuriating Nicole and driving Nick to distraction.

The put-upon director must also suffer the intrusions of his clueless mother, the overweening (and ridiculous) ambitions of his clumsy but ever-watchful crew and the ill-timed tantrums of the temperamental midget who's vital to his Fellini-esque dream sequence. Nick is tormented by nightmares that predict failure for his film, but things are eventually put right with the help of—of all people—Mom. At the end of the day, Nick and Nicole seem ready to embark on a relationship with personal, as well as professional, promise.

The modest LIVING IN OBLIVION evokes with equal accuracy the trials and triumphs of making movies. It depicts the enervating monotony which accompanies the cinematic process without being boring, because it also captures the sensation of watching something fall into shape despite the snafus. If there's anyone who thinks movies just happen magically, LIVING IN OBLIVION will be an educational experience. It should, in fact, be mandatory viewing for all bewildered parents of aspiring filmmakers. DiCillo's script is filled with cliches, but they ring fresh by virtue of the candid desperation of the situation and the director's good humor. For all the cutting satire and obscene outbursts—many of them very funny—LIVING IN OBLIVION is sharply observed (such details as the battered station wagon that serves as production limo and the pathetic buffet table laden with Oreos and doughnuts are right on the money) and filled with heart.

Editor Camila Toniolo must be singled out for her yeoman work in effectively blending the behind-the-scenes and finished-film footage. Frank Prinzi's snazzy photography, which switches from grainy black-and-white to glossy stylized color, is at its most effective in a couple of the best dream sequences ever filmed.

Buscemi—whose look vacillates between Jesus Christ and Don Knotts—makes Nick simultaneously addled and intensely convinced of the importance of what he's doing; few contemporary actors convey exasperation and mounting agitation better than Buscemi. Keener does equally good work as the embattled Nicole, who can go from a quivering bundle of neuroses to tough cookie in the wink of an eye. An early scene in which she experiences an acting breakthrough—one of the most difficult effects to bring off convincingly—has a truly revelatory, deliciously hard-won quality to it.

A startlingly blonde, wildly extemporizing LeGros is the embodiment of every director's worst nightmare: the ultimate Hollywood jerk. Though DeCillo regularly denied it, the resemblance to Brad Pitt, star of DeCillo's JOHNNY SUEDE (1991), was unmistakable. (*Adult situations, sexual situations, profanity.*) — D.N.

d, Tom DiCillo; p, Marcus Viscidi, Michael Griffiths; exec p, Hilary Gilford; assoc p, Danielle von Zerneck, Dermot Mulroney, Jane Gil; co-p, Meredith Zamsky; w, Tom DiCillo; ph, Frank Prinzi; ed, Camilla Toniolo; m, Jim Farmer; prod d, Therese DePrez; art d, Scott Pask, Janine Michelle; sound, Matthew Price (mixer); casting, Marcia Shulman; cos, Ellen Lutter; makeup, Chris Laurence, Laura Tesone

Comedy   **(PR: C MPAA: R)**

LONELY WIFE, THE
(SEE: CHARULATA)

LORD OF ILLUSIONS   ★★½
(U.S.) 109m United Artists ~ MGM/UA c
(AKA: CLIVE BARKER'S LORD OF ILLUSIONS)

Scott Bakula (*Harry D'Amour*); Famke Janssen (*Dorothea Swann*); Trevor Edmond (*Young Butterfield*); Daniel Von Bargen (*Nix*); Kevin J. O'Connor (*Philip Swann*); Joseph Latimore (*Caspar Quaid*); Sheila Tousey (*Jennifer Desiderio*); Susan Traylor (*Maureen Pimm*); Ashley Lyn Cafagna (*Young Dorothea*); Michael Angelo Stuno (*Lead Male Cultist*); Keith Brunsmann (*Snakeman*); Barbara Patrick (*Lead Female Cultist*); Wayne Grace (*Loomis*); Mikey LeBeau (*Exorcised Boy*); Robb Humphreys (*D'Amour's Demon*); James Brandon Shaw (*Motel Bellboy*); Johnny Venokur (*Tapert*); Jordan Marder (*Ray Miller*); Barry Del Sherman (*Butterfield*); McNally Sagal (*Detective Eddison*); Joanna Sanchez (*Clemenzia*); Joel Swetow (*Valentin*); Stephen Weingartner (*Stage Manager*); Daniel Edward Mora, Jr. (*Stage Technician*); Billy McComb (*Walter Wilder*); Vincent Schiavelli (*Vinovich*); Lorin Stewart (*Billy Who*); Barry "Shabaka" Henley (*Dr. Toffler*); Bergen Lynn Williams (*Nurse*); Mike Deak (*Apparition In Repository*); Carrie Ann Inaba; Sarah McAfee; Laurie Kanyok; Jason Yribar; Stephanie LaCause; Lu-

cas Tommassini; Yuri Mageoy (*Dancers*); Joseph Daniel Daley; Stephen Earnhart; Dana Fatigante; Nick Hunter; Tannis Kobrin; Crystal Lujan; Alan McFarland; Ava Stander; D.F. Swatter; Michael L. Swearingen; Colette J. Toomer; Rasool M. Visram; Heidi Wolfe (*Cultists*)

Adapted from his novella *The Last Illusion*, this film from horror author Clive Barker is an effectively chilling marriage of the supernatural and noir genres.

In 1982, Philip Swann (Kevin J. O'Connor), a follower of demonic cult leader Nix (Daniel Von Bargen), leads a group of his fellow devotees in killing and burying the evil guru before he can sacrifice a young girl. In the present day, private eye Harry D'Amour (Scott Bakula) travels from New York to Los Angeles on an insurance fraud case, only to stumble upon one of Nix's former cultists being mutilated by another. Some of the group are intent on raising Nix from the dead, and Dorothea Swann (Famke Janssen), the would-be sacrifice now grown up and married to her savior, hires Harry to look after Philip, now a famous magician. But during one of his performances, Philip is killed by falling swords when an escape trick goes wrong.

The cultists continue to threaten Dorothea, and in the course of protecting her, Harry winds up romantically involved with her. It soon transpires, however, that Philip is still alive, having faked his own death to escape the wrath of Nix's followers. That doesn't stop them from disinterring Nix and reviving him at his old haunt in the desert, where he repays the favor by killing them all. He then turns on Dorothea and Harry, who is powerless against his black magic; it falls to Philip to invoke his own supernatural talents and send Nix to hell forever.

Barker may go too far over the top at times in this, his third directorial outing (after HELLRAISER and NIGHTBREED), but he is to be commended for giving the horror genre some much-needed juice. Instead of falling back on cliched shock effects or cushioning the scares with comic relief, he creates a brooding, gruesome atmosphere. As usual, he has worked up a compelling mythology to undergird his horrors, and the contrast between real magic and stage illusions provides a neat metaphorical device.

The film's production values are top-notch, including Ronn Schmidt's sharp photography and nasty makeup effects by a gallery of artists. Particularly striking is Nix's final incarnation, in which his deformed features sprout demonic growths. Von Bargen's full-blooded performance is complemented by Bakula, who makes a solid hero. There's also good support from Janssen (whose first appearance, swimming across a mansion's pool and emerging in a sexy bathing suit, could have served as an audition for her subsequent appearance in GOLDENEYE), Vincent Schiavelli as an illusionist with an attitude, and Barry Del Sherman and Jordan Marder as two of Nix's twisted followers.

A few of the dramatic developments are unconvincing (particularly when Harry and Dorothea fall into bed together, seemingly only to fulfill genre requirements), and Barker occasionally pushes the horror too hard, resulting in unintentional humor. But for the most part, LORD OF ILLUSIONS is more ambitious, scary, and entertaining than most of the chillers to emerge in the '90s. (*Graphic violence, nudity, sexual situations, profanity.*) — M.G.

d, Clive Barker; p, JoAnne Sellar, Clive Barker; exec p, Steve Golin, Sigurjon Sighvatsson; assoc p, Anna C. Miller; w, Clive Barker (based on his short story "Lord of Illusion"); ph, Ronn Schmidt; ed, Alan Baumgarten; m, Simon Boswell; prod d, Stephen Hardie; art d, Marc Fisichella, Bruce Robert Hill; set d, David A. Koneff; sound, Steven Halbert; fx, Lou Carlucci, Thomas C. Rainone, Fantasy II Film Effects; casting, Sharon Howard-Field; cos, Luke Reichle; makeup, Thomas C. Rainone,

Steve Johnson, Kurtzman Nicotero & Berger EFX Group; stunts, Cliff Cudney

Horror   (PR: O   MPAA: R)

LOSING ISAIAH   ★★½
(U.S.) 108m The Koch Company; Paramount ~
Paramount c

Jessica Lange *(Margaret Lewin)*; Halle Berry *(Khaila Richards)*; David Straithairn *(Charles Lewin)*; Cuba Gooding, Jr. *(Eddie Hughes)*; Daisy Eagan *(Hannah Lewin)*; Marc John Jeffries *(Isaiah)*; Samuel L. Jackson *(Kadar Lewis)*; Joie Lee *(Marie)*; Regina Taylor *(Gussie)*; LaTanya Richardson *(Caroline Jones)*; Jacqueline Brookes *(Judge Silbowitz)*; Donovon Ian H. McKnight *(Amir)*; Rikkia A. Smith *(Josie)*; Paulette McDaniels *(Ethel)*; Velma Austin *(Rehab Leader)*; Glenda Starr Kelley *(Group Leader)*; Joan Kohn *(Toby Fredericks)*; Patrick Clear *(Bill Fredericks)*; Gabriella Santinelli *(Heidi)*; Mike Bacarella *(Liquor Store Clerk)*; Mike Houlihan *(1st Liquor Store Cop)*; John Beasley *(Garbage Man)*; James "Ike" Eichling *(Garbage Man)*; James F. Tillett *(Intern)*; John Judd *(Paramedic)*; Cheryl Hamada *(ER Nurse)*; Valerie Shull *(Mrs. Ianelli)*; Laura Ceron *(NICU Woman)*; Jackie Samuel *(NICU Nurse)*; Deanna Dunagan *(Dr. Goldfein)*; Mike Nussbaum *(Dr. Jamison)*; Margaret Travolta *(Sandra Harris)*; Eddie "Bo" Smith, Jr. *(Alley Junkie)*; Jaqueline Fleming *(File Cabinet Girl)*; Sibyl Offutt *(Tenement Woman)*; Gregory Hollimon *(Tenement Man)*; Rick Worthy *(Alley Man)*; Torrence W. Murphy *(Alley Man)*; Crystal Barnes; Sheila-Marie Robinson; La Taunya Bounds; Tamara Rutledge *(Inmates)*; Valeri Ross *(Day Care Teacher)*; Jacqueline Williams *(Day Care Worker)*; Ora Jones *(Day Care Woman)*; Nicholas Foster *(Boy at Swings)*; Thomica Laquice Simmons *(Neighbor Girl)*; Evan Lionel *(Paramedic)*; Jennifer Crystal *(Park Nanny)*; Matthew Brennan; Denise Aguilar; Christy Lombardi; Hector Matos; Stephanie Mullin; Daniel Nudelman; Elbert Pagan, Jr.; Kate Tash; Christ Tossing *(Singers in School Play)*; Jonathan Rivera *(Cymbals Player)*; Karen Luehne *(Pianist)*; Brian Friedopfer *(Duck)*; Paul Jorjorian *(Duck)*

Two good performance and a few touching moments make LOSING ISAIAH a notch better than most made-for-television movies about child custody battles, but exploitative writing and uneven direction prevent the film from being a superior melodrama.

LOSING ISAIAH is set in two worlds—the ghettos of Chicago and the city's more affluent suburbs, many miles away. The story begins in the inner city, where drug-addicted African-American Khaila Richards (Halle Berry) leaves her baby, Isaiah, inside a garbage can for a few minutes, while she makes a drug deal nearby. When Khaila returns to retrieve Isaiah, she is horrified to discover that he is missing, not knowing that some sanitation workers had found the baby, and taken him away to a Chicago hospital.

The hospital's Caucasian social worker assigned to Isaiah's case, Margaret Lewin (Jessica Lange), takes a special liking to him, and soon convinces her husband, Charles (David Strathairn), and teenaged daughter, Hannah (Daisy Eagan), to adopt Isaiah into their middle-class home, located outside of the city. By the time Isaiah is four (and played by Marc John Jefferies), Margaret secures the adoption. In the meantime, Khaila has recovered from her drug addiction and is struggling to make a new life for herself. By happenstance, she receives news that Isaiah has been found, and, with the help of an activist lawyer, Kadar Lewis (Samuel L. Jackson), she becomes determined to assert her maternal rights and reclaim him.

Margaret and her family are devastated by the news of the lawsuit, but quickly hire their own African-American lawyer to fight back in court. During the proceedings, however, Khaila prevails over the Lewins thanks to her lawyer's shrewd ability to convince the judge that "black babies belong with black mothers." Yet, soon after Khailah takes Isaiah from the Lewins to live with her in her new home, she realizes that the boy misses his "other" mother. Khailah then calls Margaret, who has been distraught ever since losing Isaiah, to help her create a happier life for "their" son.

LOSING ISAIAH appears to be ripped from the headlines regarding recent hotly contested Solomonic child custody suits (Baby M, most notably), but producer-screenwriter Naomi Foner and director Stephen Gyllenhaal (Foner's husband) are savvy enough to use the time-honored techniques of old-style Hollywood melodramas like THE GREAT LIE (1941) and OUR VERY OWN (1950) to tell a tale more successful at stirring emotions than resolving issues. (The added element of race seems to also make ISAIAH topical, but this, too, simply adds another layer to the audience manipulation.) Foner even structures her screenplay toward a classic "when ladies meet" scene between the main protagonists (which takes place in a bathroom during a court break). The moment sparks dramatic interest (and, yes, the fur flies), yet it also exploits and demeans a legitimate debate about the social welfare of children today in non-traditional family units.

Fortunately, Jessica Lange and Halle Berry make the bathroom encounter and the other two-dimensional theatrics throughout much more authentic and honest then they might have been. Berry, in particular, succeeds against the filmmakers' racially stereotypical attitudes in the early scenes, and makes her remarkable transformation later on convincing to watch. Lange has less of a role to work with as Margaret, but she gives a nuanced account of a woman who might just be using her love for the abandoned child as a substitute for her emotionally unstable marriage. The other actors fail to get beyond the thin, stereotyped writing (Samuel L. Jackson is the least persuasive of all) but Cuba Gooding Jr. makes a pleasant impression as Khailah's over-eager, would-be suitor.

The happy ending notwithstanding, LOSING ISAIAH leaves a bitter aftertaste. It also too rarely transcends the heated yet simplistic polemics (Ken Loach's LADYBIRD, LADYBIRD provides a much better example of a recent film dealing meaningfully with related themes). Despite the fine leads and some well-crafted scenes, LOSING ISAIAH is apt to make viewers angry and frustrated no matter where they stand on the issues. *(Violence, nudity, adult situations, substance abuse, profanity.)* — E.M.

d, Stephen Gyllenhaal; p, Howard W. Koch, Jr., Naomi Foner; assoc p, Kimberly Brent, Sharon Owyang; w, Naomi Foner (based on the novel by Seth J. Margolis); ph, Andrzej Bartkowiak; ed, Harvey Rosenstock; m, Mark Isham; prod d, Jeannine Oppewall; art d, Bill Arnold; set d, Jay Hart; sound, Thomas Nelson (mixer); casting, Aleta Chappelle; cos, Marv Malin; stunts, Rick LeFevour

Drama   (PR: C   MPAA: R)

LOVE AND HUMAN REMAINS   ★★★
(Canada) 100m Max Films; Atlantis Films ~
Sony Pictures Classics c

Thomas Gibson *(David)*; Ruth Marshall *(Candy)*; Mia Kirshner *(Benita)*; Cameron Bancroft *(Bernie)*; Rick Roberts *(Robert)*; Joanne Vannicola *(Jerri)*; Matthew Ferguson *(Kane)*; Aidan Devine *(Sal)*; Robert Higden *(Editor)*; Sylvain Morin *(Drag*

Queen); Ben Watt *(Native Boy)*; Karen Young *(Singer)*; Serge Houde *(Cowboy)*; Alex Wylding *(Victim)*; Polly Shannon *(Victim)*; Annie Juneau *(Victim)*; Maurice Podbrey *(Theater Director)*; Genevieve Angers; Josee Boisvert; Aimee Castle; Rod Charlebois; Ellen Cohen; Andy Delisle; Suzanne Desautels; Maximilian Devree; Charles Doucet; Nathalie Goguen; Kim Handysides; Joan Heney; Lisa Hull; Barbara Jones; Luc Leblanc; John Lozano; Gary McKeehan; Michele-Barbara Pelletier; Maxime Roy; Harry Standjofski

LOVE AND HUMAN REMAINS is a dark expose of twenty-something alienation, adapted from Brad Fraser's stage play "Unidentified Human Remains and the True Nature of Love. Denys Arcand's film effectively evokes its characters' feelings of rootlessness and restlessness, but is ultimately unfulfilling as a sociological portrait of modern urban life in crisis.

LOVE AND HUMAN REMAINS revolves around a circle of seven friends, one of whom is discovered to be a vicious serial killer. David (Thomas Gibson) is a handsome gay waiter and childhood TV sitcom star, who lives with his ex-girlfriend, Candy (Ruth Marshall). David is looking for love but terrified of commitment. He and his good-looking, womanizing friend Bernie (Cameron Bancroft) commiserate about their feelings of aimlessness and frustration. After years of unsatisfying sexual encounters at gay bars, David begins a strange liaison with Kane (Matthew Ferguson), a curious and confused 17 year old busboy at the restaurant where David waits tables. Benita (Mia Kirshner), a professional dominatrix with psychic capabilities, provides David with insights about his relationships with Kane and Bernie. Candy, whose feelings for David are not yet fully resolved, is juggling two new relationships—with a clingy lesbian schoolteacher, Jerri (Joanne Vannicola), and a secretive

bartender, Robert (Rick Roberts). Swirling around all these characters is a string of brutal killings of women, the victims' earrings ripped out of their ears and taken as mementos. Clues point to several different killers before the real murderer is revealed.

LOVE AND HUMAN REMAINS is the first English-language film from Canadian director Arcand whose earlier films, DECLINE OF THE AMERICAN EMPIRE and JESUS OF MONTREAL, were both nominated for best foreign-language Oscars. LOVE AND HUMAN REMAINS is tough. It's a grim and disturbing portrayal of a socially estranged generation trying to find meaning in life. Sex has become confused and confusing—a space to play out fears and fantasies about identity, love, power, intimacy, pleasure, pain, and death. The characters wander through their lives in unrelentingly harsh urban landscapes with punishing industrial lighting—bereft of nature and natural light—feeling that they're nothing like anyone else in the world. All of this would be fine, were it not for the shockingly sunny ending which casts a strangely empty shadow over the rest of the film. *(Sexual situations, nudity, violence, adult situations.)* — J.S.

d, Denys Arcand; p, Roger Frappier; exec p, Roger Frappier, Pierre Latour; co-p, Peter Sussman; w, Brad Fraser (based on his play *Unidentified Human Remains and the True Nature of Love*); ph, Paul Sarossy; ed, Alain Baril; m, John McCarthy; prod d, Francois Seguin; set d, Jean Kazemirchuck, Michele Nolet, Ginette Robitaille; sound, Dominique Chartrand, Marcel Pothier; fx, Louis Craig; casting, Deirdre Bowen, Lynn Kressel, Lucie Robitaille, Stuart Aikins; cos, Denis Sperdouklis; makeup, Micheline Trepanier; stunts, Yves Langlois

Crime/Drama/Erotic   **(PR: O   MPAA: R)**

MACHINE DREAMS ★★½

(West Germany) 87m Barfuss Films;
Westdeutscher Rundfunk; Norddeutscher
Rundfunk ~ First Run Features c
(MASCHINENTRAUME)

Rolf Riehm

M

MACHINE DREAMS, a 1988 West German
"intellectual documentary" released to US theaters and home video in 1995, has as its conceit a
sleeping narrator who sees in his "dream" (the
film itself) a historical overview and philosophical dissection of "man's relationship to machine." By turns
brooding and eerie, at first compelling and insightful, the film's
presentation of machines as a manifestation of human longing
and desire (but also of fear and anxiety) eventually grinds into a
reductionist and relentlessly oppressive mire.

An 87-minute experimental film by Peter Krieg, MA-
CHINE DREAMS embarks on a historical and intellectual
tour of ideas about machines, a wide-ranging jaunt that takes
us from a 6th-century monastery (where St. Benedict set the
stage for the idea of man as a machine) to the corridors of MIT
and the frontiers of artificial intelligence and "cyber-evolu-
tion." To present these concepts, Krieg casts a wide net in his
choice of subjects, including interviews with everyone from
German philosophers and space agency administrators to
Japanese robotics designers, from London machine artists to
American military drill sergeants. We also get an eclectic
stream of images, from wooden clock gears to automobile
production lines, from sex acts between constructed performance machines to astronaut space walks, from a half-finished
Marilyn Monroe robot to an R2D2 look-alike security guard.

Krieg, through his omnipresent narrator, presents his idea that
"wish machines" (for example, space travel) and "fear machines" (for example, military arsenal) are the prototypes for all
machines.

MACHINE DREAMS is more successful, and more compelling, in presenting the historical development of the idea
of "man as machine," than it is in presenting its dystopian
view of the ongoing evolution of man-machines and machine-
men. By the time we are halfway through the film, it has more
or less played out its thesis regarding the inevitable evolution
and ensuing dangers of man's symbiotic relationship with the
machine. Completely devoid of a spokesperson for "the human spirit," the film collapses concepts such as artistic inspiration, love, the godhead, and the soul into what Marvin
Minsky, MIT scientist and one of the fathers of artificial
intelligence, calls the "meaningless by-products" of switching from one kind of thinking in the brain to another. This is
exactly the kind of Science-as-Savior, left-brain-only thinking that is taken to task in Diane Keaton's 1995 UNSTRUNG
HEROES—which makes a nice, albeit unwitting, companion
piece to MACHINE DREAMS.

Besides its lack of heart, one of the biggest drawbacks
of the film is the grating techno-industrial soundtrack, with
out-of-focus close-ups slamming into sharpness running a
close second. Nonetheless, despite its questionable production values and ponderous German angst, this could be
just the video you need on a rainy Saturday night to generate a rousing intellectual discussion of man-machine's inhumanity to machine-man. (Adult situations, sexual
situations, violence.) — P.P.

d, Peter Krieg; w, Peter Krieg; ph, Peter Krieg; ed, Peter Krieg;
m, Rolf Riehm; sound, Uthea

Documentary   **(PR: C   MPAA: NR)**

MAD LOVE ★★

(U.S.) 99m MLP Films; Sarbande
Productions; Touchstone ~ Buena Vista c

Chris O'Donnell (Matt); Drew Barrymore
(Casey); Joan Allen (Margaret); Matthew Lil-
lard (Eric); Richard Chaim (Duncan); Robert
Nadir (Coach); Jude Ciccolella (Richard); Amy
Sakasitz (Joanna); T.J. Lowther (Adam); Kevin
Dunn (Clifford); Elaine Miles (Housekeeper);
Sharon Collar (Librarian); Selene H. Vigil;
Valerie M. Agnew; Roisin Dunne; Elizabeth F.
Davis (7 Year Bitch); Todd Sible (Bartender);
Liev Schreiber (Salesman); Angelina Calderon Torres (Land-
lady); Stefan Enriquez (Waiter); Yvonne C. Orona (Mechanic);
Pedro Garcia (Mechanic)

MAD LOVE is a teenage love story which covers familiar
territory—the wild young girl, the ambitious boy dragged down
by love, the attempted suicide, the clueless parents, and the failed
road trip.

When Matt (Chris O'Donnell), a young man with college
aspirations and an interest in astronomy, catches a glimpse in his
telescope of the new girl in town, beautiful and wild Casey
Roberts (Drew Barrymore), his life turns upside down. Matt has
more responsibilities than a teen can handle. Having taken on the
burden of managing the household and caring for his young twin
siblings after his mother's departure, he finds the kind of freedom Casey represents irresistible; when she beckons him away
from his ambitions and duties, he goes willingly.

One day Casey rings the school fire alarm to summon Matt
while he is taking his SAT test. School authorities suspend Casey,
and her parents forbid her to see Matt. When she responds by
attempting suicide, her parents institutionalize her. Matt stages
her escape from the hospital, and together they hit the road.

What follows is a road trip with its full share of adventure,
risk, boredom, and, eventually, the harsh and inescapable realities of life. Casey's mental imbalance gradually becomes undeniable, forcing Matt to seek help from her parents. When Casey
overhears Matt's desperate call from a phone booth outside their
motel, she sets off alone in their stolen car, determined to blow
her brains out. Matt steals another car and follows. After a
melodramatic struggle on the desert sands, Matt manages to
convince Casey to return to her parents and the aid of social
workers.

Director Antonia Bird tries unsuccessfully to capture the rebellious romanticism of Matt and Casey, when compromise and
responsibilities lurk menacingly ahead. The postcard sentimentality which plagues the film reaches its peak in the conclusion.
Casey has returned to Chicago and Matt receives a letter with her
smiling photograph enclosed. In a voice-over, she speaks about
her recovery and growth while flashback images of their romanticized adventure, their beautiful bodies shot during sunset
against gorgeous landscapes, drip from the screen accompanied
by suitably sentimental background music. Highlighting contemporary rock music and fast scenes of risk and adventure, the
film strives to mirror the restless spirit of youth but only approaches the outer shell of this experience, the one which stars
in glossy fashion magazines and the daydreams of preteens.
(Adult situations, sexual situations, profanity.) — R.C.

d, Antonia Bird; p, David Manson; co-p, John Landgraf, Marcus
Viscidi; w, Paula Milne; ph, Fred Tammes; ed, Jeff Freeman; m,
Andy Roberts; prod d, David Brisbin; art d, Mark Worthington;
set d, Gene Serdena; sound, Nelson Stoll (mixer), Fred Runner
(mixer), Scott Kinzey (recordist); casting, Dianne Crittenden;

cos, Eugenie Bafaloukos; makeup, Fern Buchner; stunts, Webster Winery

Romance/Drama   **(PR: C   MPAA: PG-13)**

MAGIC IN THE WATER   ★★
(U.S.) 98m Oxford Film Company; Pacific
Motion Pictures Productions; Triumph Films ~ TriStar c

Mark Harmon *(Jack Black)*; Joshua Jackson *(Joshua Black)*; Harley Jane Kozak *(Dr. Wanda Bell)*; Sarah Wayne *(Ashley Black)*; Willie Nark-Orn *(Hiro)*; Frank Sotonoma Salsedo *(Uncle Kipper)*; Morris Panych *(Mack Miller)*; Ben Cardinal *(Joe Pickled Trout)*; Adrien Dorval *(Wright Hardy)*; Marc Acheson *(Lefty Hardy)*; Anthony Towe *(Taka)*; John Proccacino *(Frank)*; Thomas Cavanaugh *(Simon (1st Patient))*; Garrett Bennett *(Christian (2nd Patient))*; Brian Finney *(Bug-Eyes (3rd Patient))*; David Rasche *(Phillip (4th Patient))*; Tamsin Kelsey *(Sheriff Stevenson)*; Benjamin Ratner *(FX Man)*; Lesley Ewen *(Private Nurse)*; William Sasso *(Shy Young Orderly)*; Teryl Rothery *(Beth)*; Norma Wick *(Reporter)*; Nathan Begg *(Kid in Cowboy Hat)*; Philip Baer *(Boy in Boat)*; Peter Baer *(Boy in Boat)*; Elisa Wayne *(Girl in Tutu)*; Cole Halleran *(Boy on Leash)*

MAGIC IN THE WATER is a Disney confection about a mystical sea monster, Orky, with a sweet tooth for Oreos.

Agreeing in principle to spend quality time with his kids, grade-schooler Ashley (Sarah Wayne) and teenager Joshua (Joshua Jackson), divorced dad Jack Black (Mark Harmon), a caustic radio-show shrink, plans a working vacation in the seaside tourist trap of Glenorky. Ignoring the two products of his broken home, Jack faxes and phones while Joshua pleads for his own wheels and Ashley starts a tentative friendship with Orky, a sea creature whom no one believes in except their Native American neighbor, Uncle Kipper (Frank Sotonama Salsedo). Flirting with the resident psychiatrist, Dr. Wanda Bell (Harley Jane Kozak), hard-bitten Black is unprepared for the life-altering experience awaiting him.

Able to change its form, Orky inhabits Black's body to enable him to rescue Ashley from a fall off a rope ladder. Alternately euphoric and depressed after this possession, Black begins to manifest the symptoms of Orky-projection that Dr. Bell recognizes from patients in her therapy group. Enlisting the aid of Uncle Kipper, her skeptical brother, and Hiro (Willie Nark-Orn), the son of a Japanese researcher, Ashley uncovers the reason Orky has been reaching out to the community. Industrialist Mack Miller (Morris Panych), has been dumping pollutants along Orky's living space; the seriously ill beast is signaling Black and the others for help. Although Miller tries to fool suspicious eyes with a manned mechanical Orky submarine, the contraption sinks with the kids trapped aboard. Rallying his strength (sapped because of sedation following his experience), Black saves the kids inside Orky's cavern after the ailing mammal brings the Orky sub there. The police nail Miller, and Orky eventually recovers and makes a believer out of Dr. Bell.

Fifteen minutes of this sticky-sweet salute to everyone's inner child may make the viewer a confirmed curmudgeon for life. Glowingly photographed, MAGIC IN THE WATER tries to manufacture synthetic magic, but its screenplay is predicated on musty formulas, and its direction is uninspired. Perhaps wisely withholding glimpses of the lovable floating legend until the climax, the movie inevitably disappoints with its presentation of this magical entity; instead of a wondrous creature, the audience gets a slab of grayish dino-rubber that has a saucer-eyed face with way too much similarity to E.T. A fairy tale version of FREE WILLY, this family fare about believing in the impossible only fitfully weaves a spell. Dismayingly simple in its psychol-

ogy and heavy-handed in its typical cartooning of the villain, MAGIC IN THE WATER does not attain the gravity of a true fable which would lead the spellbound into healing introspection. The only question this movie poses for viewers is: how did a great big beastie with no hands open up Oreos, lick off the white-cream fillings, reseal the cookies, and then return them to the dock without breaking them. Now, that is a miracle! *(Violence.)* — R.P.

d, Rick Stevenson; p, Matthew O'Connor, Rick Stevenson; exec p, Karen Murphy, Tony Allard; assoc p, Christian Loubek; w, Rick Stevenson, Icel Dobell Massey (from a story by Ninian Dunnett, Rick Stevenson, and Icel Dobell Massey); ph, Thomas Burstyn; ed, Allan Lee; m, David Schwartz; prod d, Errol Clyde Klotz; art d, Eric Norlin; set d, T. Michael O'Connor; sound, Anke Bakker (design), Michael McGee (mixer); fx, Randy Shymkiw, Rory Cutler, Gene Warren, Jr., Fantasy II Film Effects; casting, Debra Zane, Stuart Aikins; cos, Monique Prudhomme; makeup, Sandy Cooper; stunts, Jim Dunn

Children's/Adventure   **(PR: AA   MPAA: PG)**

MAJOR PAYNE   ★★
(U.S.) 97m Major Payne Productions; Universal; Wife 'n Kids Productions ~ Universal c

Damon Wayans *(Major Benson Winifred Payne)*; Karyn Parsons *(Dr. Emily Walburn)*; Bill Hickey *(Dr. Phillip)*; Michael Ironside *(Lt. Colonel Stone)*; Albert Hall *(General Elias Decker)*; Steve Martini *(Cadet Alex Stone)*; Orlando Brown *(Cadet Tiger Dane)*; Andrew Harrison Leeds *(Cadet Dotson)*; Joda Blare-Hershman *(Cadet Bryan)*; Damien Wayans *(Cadet Williams)*; R. Stephen Wiles *(Cadet Heathcoat)*; Rodney P. Barnes *(Weight Lifter)*; Ross Bickell *(Colonel Braggart)*; Scott "Bam Bam" Bigelow *(Huge Biker)*; Peyton Chesson Fohl *(Cadet Johnson)*; Stephen Coleman *(Cadet Leland)*; Mark Conway *(Police Sergeant)*; David DeHart *(Wellington Cadet Captain)*; Joshua Todd Diveley *(New Cadet)*; Robert Faraoni, Jr. *(Smart-Ass Soldier)*; Michael Gabel *(Lt. Wiseman)*; R.J. Knoll *(Blind Kid)*; Dean Lorey *(Mr. Shipman)*; Mark W. Madison *(Cadet Fox)*; Brad Martin *(M.P.)*; Chris Owen *(Cadet Wuliger)*; Seymour Swan *(Soldier)*; Leonard Thomas *(Bleeding Soldier)*; Hechter Ubarry *(Guerilla Leader)*; Carolyn L.A. Walker *(Woman)*; Tommy Wiles *(Cadet)*; Christopher James Williams *(Marksman)*; Al Cerullo *(Chopper Pilot)*; John Louis Fischer *(Chopper Pilot)*

Damon Wayans carries MAJOR PAYNE, a remake of the 1955 comedy THE PRIVATE WAR OF MAJOR BENSON, but the odd combination of sentiment and rude humor works against the film.

Filling Charlton Heston's army boots, Wayans plays Maj. Benson Payne, a career military man, who is discharged from the army, but finds himself unable to fit into "civilian" life. Payne gets an assignment as commander of a motley group of children, aged six to 16, at the Madison Academy Junior ROTC. But Payne clashes constantly with the boys, who try in several ways to get rid of their harsh, disciplinarian leader.

Finally, Payne makes a deal with the boys that he'll leave as long as they win the upcoming annual Virginia ROTC games. Meanwhile, Payne's nature softens slightly thanks to the efforts of Dr. Emily Walburn (Karyn Parsons), the boys' counselor, and Tiger Dane (Orlando Brown), the youngest cadet. Over time, the boys begin to appreciate Payne's authority, and choose to win the tournament for the sake of team spirit.

Just before the games begin, however, Payne takes a new assignment as a Lieutenant-Colonel in Bosnia. Disheartened but determined, the boys compete in the preliminary rounds, coming in second place to their rivals at the Wellington Academy. Then, in a change of heart, Payne returns to support his troupe in time for the final games, which they win.

Damon Wayans is a gifted comedian (certainly more so than Charlton Heston, the original Maj. Benson). But in MAJOR PAYNE, Wayans (who co-wrote and co-produced this vehicle) sets up two problems for himself that are ultimately insurmountable. First, Wayans has taken his maniacal nerd hall-monitor character from a sketch in his former television series, "In Living Color," and has deposited him in a feature-length story. If MAJOR PAYNE had more of a surrealist or cartoon approach (as it exhibits in Payne's one daydream sequence—a spoof of "The Donna Reed Show"), perhaps the peculiar two-dimensionality of Maj. Payne would work. But the surrounding characters in the story approximate real-world human beings too much, and the contrasts are more odd than funny.

Equally awkward is that Wayan's brand of humor mixes poorly with the sentimental drama at the heart of the picture. Wayans, the comic, may recite—as Payne—a twisted, violent version of "The Little Engine That Could" to taint Tiger, but Wayans, the co-writer, always makes sure that we realize Payne is trying to grow in his patriarchal responsibilities (inside, Payne turns out to be more innocent and childlike than the children he is supervising). Thus, the best satiric moments—e.g. Payne's "robot" dance parody on his date with Dr. Walburn—always precede "heartwarming" follow-up scenes. (This juxtaposition leads to a moment of real hypocrisy, as Payne hits a cadet's father for hitting his son—after a series of scenes where Payne himself has physically tormented the cadets!)

Worst of all, MAJOR PAYNE updates but retains the conservative message of the original film. The story indicates that all the characters' problems are solved when the boys learn to respect Payne's supremacy (Aretha Franklin's rendition of "Respect" accompanies the transformation). Not only are duty, unity and patriotism honored in the film, but the "rap" drill finale led by Tiger co-opts the individualism of the boys, streamlining their abilities into a sort of funky uniform goose-step.

It is hard to believe that the same irreverent comic of "In Living Color" co-created MAJOR PAYNE, but the movie's "rap" drill scene perhaps represents a brilliant metaphor for the way Hollywood is able to co-opt the individuality of talented performers like Daman Wayans. *(Violence, profanity.)* — E.M.

d, Nick Castle; p, Eric L. Gold, Michael Rachmil; exec p, Damon Wayans, Harry Tatelman; co-p, Tracy Carness; w, Dean Lorey, Damon Wayans, Gary Rosen (based on the 1955 screenplay *The Private War of Major Benson* by William Roberts and Richard Alan Simmons from a story by Joe Connelly and Bob Mosher); ph, Richard Bowen; ed, Patrick Kennedy; m, Craig Safan; prod d, Peter Larkin; art d, David Crank; set d, James V. Kent; sound, Rosa Howell-Thornhill (mixer), Charlie Ajar, Jr. (recordist); fx, Joey DiGaetano, III; casting, Aleta Chappelle; cos, Jennifer L. Bryan; makeup, Selena Evans-Miller; stunts, Greg Elam

Comedy   **(PR: A   MPAA: PG-13)**

MALLICIOUS   ★★
(U.S.) 92m International Keystone Entertainment Ltd.; Republic Pictures ~ Republic Pictures Home Video c

Molly Ringwald *(Melissa)*; Patrick McGaw *(Doug Gordon)*; Sarah Lassez *(Laura)*; Ryan Michael *(Mitch)*; Mimi Kuzyk *(Mrs. Gordon)*; John Vernon *(Detective Pronzini)*; Rick Henrickson *(Rich)*; Jennifer Copping *(Judy)*; Joe Maffei *(Professor Lesher)*; Jerry Wasserman *(1st Detective)*; Jay Brazeau *(Orderly)*; Marlene Worrall *(Mrs. Nelson)*; Judith Maxie *(Doctor)*; Stephen E. Miller *(Coach)*; Philip Hayes *(2nd Detective)*; William Sasse *(Heavy Guy)*

After 1980s success as a popular juvenile lead, saucer-eyed Molly Ringwald marches into an unrewarding FATAL ATTRACTION ripoff.

Jock Doug Gordon (Patrick McGaw) has trouble concentrating on sports-medicine studies because fiancee Laura (Sarah Lassez) adheres to a good-girl policy that only gets him to second base. When she goes college shopping out of town, Doug plays relationship hookey and accompanies a pal to a mixer. Vixen Melissa (Ringwald) targets him for her pent-up possessiveness and drives Doug wild with carnal pleasure. The fun carries a price Doug doesn't want to pay when Laura returns. Handling rejection badly, Melissa bugs Doug's nervous mom (Mimi Kuzyk) at his house and makes her presence felt as the teaching assistant in his anatomy class. After Melissa slays his pussycat and deposits it at Laura's place, Doug admits his indiscretion. Worse is to come; Melissa cries rape in front of a baseball scout recruiting Doug, getting him arrested, while engineering his mother's accidental overdose on the sly. Finally Laura's research into Melissa proves to cops that incest abuse unhinged the campus siren enough for her to kill her father (still hung in a home freezer) and institutionalize her mom. Two months later, falsely secure in San Francisco, Laura exercises poor judgment (like everybody in this plot) by choosing supposedly long-gone Melissa as a roommate. She ties Laura up, crushes a patrolman's skull and assaults Doug with a baseball bat. Fortunately Doug's been practicing on the diamond himself, and bats the bitch out the window.

Is the world really filled with so many psychotic vamps with cling-complexes and tumescent chumps who can't keep their peckers zipped? What's most disturbing is MALICIOUS using an incest survivor as looney killer. Refusing to humanize this terminatrix, the script salivates over a history of sex abuse for shock value. If you get your bloodthirsty kicks savoring date-from-hell flicks, MALICIOUS gets sufficient mileage out of its cautionary tale of a college kid learning the cost of cheating on a bride-to-be. But what does it say about hypocritical American sexual values that dalliance is always grounds for a rise in the homicide rate? It would be nice to report that falling star Ringwald transcends her slasher film surroundings, but she doesn't deliver hubba-hubba sex appeal, and her screen presence barely registers a pulse. Without compensatory gifts, Molly fades into the woodwork of a formula aimed at sending oversexed frat brothers back into the arms of their marriage-minded sorority girls. One-night-stand freak-outs like MALICIOUS are just a new form of those explicit Army documentaries warning about social diseases, the same old scare-mongering starring sexual liberty as the boogeyman. *(Graphic violence, extreme profanity, nudity, substance abuse, sexual situations, adult situations.)* — R.P.

d, Ian Corson; p, Robert Vince, William Vince; exec p, Michael Strange; w, George Saunders; ph, Michael Slovis; ed, Richard Martin; m, Graeme Coleman; prod d, Marian Witlak; art d, Lisa Lev; set d, Francesca Dappen; sound, Joe Schliessler (mixer); fx, Andy Chamberlayne; casting, Abra Edelman, Elisa Goodman; stunts, Scott Ateah

Thriller/Erotic   **(PR: O   MPAA: R)**

MALLRATS   ★★
(U.S.) 97m Alphaville Productions; View Askew Productions ~ Gramercy c

Shannen Doherty *(Rene)*; Jeremy London *(T.S. Quint)*; Jason Lee *(Brodie)*; Claire Forlani *(Brandi)*; Ben Affleck *(Shannon)*; Joey Lauren Adams *(Gwen)*; Renee Humphrey *(Tricia)*; Jason Mewes *(Jay)*; Ethan Suplee *(William)*; Stan Lee *(Himself)*; Priscilla Barnes *(Ivannah)*; Michael Rooker *(Svenning)*; Scott

Mosier *(Roddy)*; Kevin Smith *(Silent Bob)*; Carol Banker *(Security Guard)*; Steven Blackwell *(Arresting Cop)*; Terry Hempleman *(Cop)*; Kyle Boe *(Pull Toy Kid)*; David Brinkley *(TV Executive #1)*; Jeff Gadbois *(TV Executive #2)*; Walter Flanagan *(Fan at Comic Store)*; Ethan Flower *(Guy Contestant #1)*; Ed Hapstack *(Guy Contestant #2)*; Chelsea Frye *(Girl with Easter Bunny)*; Art James *(Game Show Host)*; Bryan Johnson *(Employee at Comic Store)*; David Klein *(Fan at Comic Store)*; Tyson Nassauer *(Kid at Poster Kiosk)*; Britt Swenson *(Child at Kiosk #1)*; Mikey Kovar *(Child at Kiosk #2)*; Crystal Muirhead-Manik *(Saleslady at Lingerie Store)*; Brian O'Halloran *(Gill)*; Aaron Preusse *(Passerby in Park Lot)*; Sven Thorsen *(La Fours)*; Mary Woolever *(Teacher)*; Brad Fox; Gino Gori; Zach Perkins; Brad Giddings; Bryce Mack; Christopher O'Larkin *(Team La Fours)*

Writer-director Kevin Smith's 1994 debut, CLERKS, showed that a clever filmmaker with something to say doesn't need a big budget or a particularly talented cast to say it well. Smith's sequel, MALLRATS, has more money and a more talented cast but very little to say—and even that is said poorly.

High school senior T.S. Quint (Jeremy London) fights with his girlfriend Brandi (Claire Forlani) when she blows off a camping trip; that same morning, T.S.'s friend Brodie (Jason Lee) is dumped by girlfriend Rene (Shannon Doherty) because he is more interested in video gaming and his comic book collection than he is in her. Confused and heartbroken, the two young men seek solace in the local mall. There they encounter such colorful personalities as Jay and Silent Bob (the latter played by director Smith), an anarchic pair of philosophers-*cum*-drug dealers; a 15-year-old sexologist; and a topless psychic with a supernumerary nipple. They also discover that their individual love lives are in dire jeopardy: Brandi is about to appear on her father's game-show, "Truth or Date," while Rene is being courted by a smooth mall store manager whose idea of romantic conquest entails anal sex. With help from Jay and Silent Bob, as well some advice from legendary Marvel comic book publisher Stan Lee, T.S. and Brodie succeed in sabotaging the game show and winning back their damsels in distress.

MALLRATS, the second installment in Smith's proposed "New Jersey Trilogy" is a surprising disappointment compared to CLERKS. Beginning with its unpromising double-breakup premise and continuing through its painfully contrived game-show climax, it lacks the bawdy, clever originality of its predecessor. Not that Smith doesn't try to recapture his first film's magic; indeed, the relationship of T.S. and Brodie bears a striking resemblance to that of CLERKS's lovesick Dante and his VCR-junkie buddy Randall. But MALLRATS is missing the hilariously realistic portrayals—annoying customers, underpaid store staff, and completely directionless hangers-on—that made CLERKS such a gem.

Absent, too, are the *faux*-philosophical discourses on bizarre sexual practices and the nature of love; MALLRATS's dialogue is still clever and intelligent, but apart from brief exchanges on Superman's inability to impregnate Lois Lane and the significance of the mall's food court, its cleverness is wasted on propelling the film's ridiculous plot. Another surprise is the mediocre acting in MALLRATS, which only occasionally surpasses that of CLERKS's cast of unknowns. *(Nudity, sexual situations, profanity.)* — B.T.

d, Kevin Smith; p, James Jacks, Sean Daniel, Scott Mosier; w, Kevin Smith; ph, David Klein; ed, Paul Dixon; m, Ira Newborn; prod d, Dina Lipton; art d, Sue Savage; set d, Diana Stoughton; sound, Jose Araujo (mixer), Charlie Ajar, Jr. (recordist), Harry E. Snodgrass (design); fx, Paul Murphy; casting, Don Phillips; cos,

Dana Allyson; makeup, Brigette A. Nyre, Christ Ballas; stunts, Robert Apisa

Comedy (PR: C MPAA: R)

MAN OF THE HOUSE ★★
(U.S.) 98m Forever Girls; All Girl Productions;
Walt Disney ~ Buena Vista c

Chevy Chase *(Jack Sturges)*; Farrah Fawcett *(Sandra Archer)*; Jonathan Taylor Thomas *(Ben Archer)*; George Wendt *(Chet Bronski)*; David Shiner *(Lloyd Small)*; Art LaFleur *(Red Sweeney)*; Richard Portnow *(Joey Renda)*; Richard Foronjy *(Murray)*; Peter Appel *(Tony)*; Chief Leonard George *(Leonard Red Crow)*; George Greif *(Frank Renda)*; Ron Canada *(Bob Younger)*; Chris Miranda *(Hank Sweeney)*; Zachary Browne *(Norman Bronski)*; Spencer Vrooman *(Darryl Small)*; Nicholas Garrett *(Monroe Hill)*; Jimmy Baker *(Young Ben)*; John DiSanti *(Romeo Costanza)*; Walter Marsh *(1st Judge)*; Judith Maxie *(2nd Judge)*; Jim Smith *(Minister)*; Sean Orr *(Bailiff)*; Tony Sampson *(1st Big Kid at School)*; Shane Meier *(2nd Big Kid at School)*

MAN OF THE HOUSE offers passable family entertainment by putting a "minor" obstacle in the way of true love: a 12-year-old boy.

When US Attorney Jack Sturges (Chevy Chase) falls in love with collage artist Sandra Archer (Farrah Fawcett) and plans to marry her, Archer's son, Ben (Jonathan Taylor Thomas), wary of all men in his mother's life since his father's desertion, does everything he can to prevent the match. Ben polices the house at night, making sure everyone stays in separate beds. He scoffs at Jack's attempt to make breakfast ("He's trying to kill us with animal fat!"), and compels his would-be dad to join the very unhip YMCA Indian Guides program with him. Even more potentially dangerous to Jack is a gang of mob members bent on snuffing him out for sending one of theirs to the pen. The Guides, with the help of authentic Chief Leonard Red Crow (Chief Leonard George), join forces to come to the rescue and, in the process, Ben begins to have a grudging respect for Jack.

As corny, predictable and sentimental as the story is, MAN OF THE HOUSE manages to be a respectable entry into the family-entertainment realm. It is good to see characters in this genre driven by something akin to real emotion. The Native American theme lends some substance to the material, although there are a few queasy, commercial lapses which may not delight the more staunchly politically correct (e.g., a rain dance performed to a C&C Music Factory disco hit).

Chase is more appealing than he has been in a while, showing some real heart in a discreetly scripted role. Thomas, who bears an amusingly uncanny likeness to veteran actress and Jerry Lewis sidekick, Kathleen Freeman, does not stint on the obnoxiousness and avoids overt bathos in his character's emotional about-face. Unfortunately, as his gold-haired, crusty-voiced Mom, Fawcett is a timidly peripheral presence. It is no wonder her little brat rules her like a mini-Mussolini, where a smart rap on the skull could put a more adult perspective on things. Chief Leonard George, son of the Oscar-nominated Dan George (LITTLE BIG MAN), brings a bit of welcome authenticity to the show. Probably the best performance of all is given by the city of Vancouver, Canada, which stands in nicely as that current favorite Northwestern paradise of filmmakers, Seattle. — D.N.

d, James Orr; p, Bonnie Bruckheimer, Marty Katz; exec p, Margaret South; assoc p, Casey Grant; w, James Orr, Jim Cruickshank (from a story by David Peckinpah and Richard Jefferies); ph, Jamie Anderson; ed, Harry Keramidas; m, Mark Mancina; prod d, Lawrence G. Paull; art d, David Willson; set d, Rose Marie McSherry; sound, Rob Young (mixer); fx, Mike Vezina,

Michael Lessa; casting, Amy Lippens; cos, Tom Bronson; makeup, Victoria Down; stunts, Betty Thomas

Children's/Comedy (PR: A MPAA: PG)

MANGLER, THE ★★
(U.S.) 106m Distant Horizon; Allied Film
Productions ~ New Line c

Robert Englund (*Bill Gartley*); Ted Levine (*John Hunton*); Daniel Matmor (*Mark Jackson*); Jeremy Crutchley (*Pictureman/Mortician*); Vanessa Pike (*Sherry Ouelette*); Demetre Phillips (*Stanner*); Lisa Morris (*Lin Sue*); Vera Blacker (*Mrs. Frawley*); Ashley Hayden (*Annette Gillian*); Danny Keogh (*Herb Diment*); Ted Leplat (*Doctor Ramos*); Todd Jensen (*Roger Martin*); Sean Taylor (*Derrick Gates*); Gerrit Schoonhoven (*Aaron Rodriguez*); Nan Hamilton (*Mrs. Ellenshaw*); Adrian Waldron (*Mr. Ellenshaw*); Norman Coombes (*Judge Bishop*); Larry Taylor (*Sheriff Hughes*); Irene Franges (*Mrs. Smith*); Megan Wilson (*Ginny Jason*); Odile Rault (*Alberta*); Ron Smerczak (*Officer Steele*)

One more demonstration of the perils of expanding Stephen King's short stories to feature length, this is an atmospheric but dramatically ineffective shocker.

"The Mangler" is the nickname of a giant industrial steam-iron and folding machine that dominates the Blue Ribbon Laundry, overseen by the aged, tyrannical William Gartley (Robert Englund). After Mrs. Frawley (Vera Blacker) is sucked into the machine, local police officer John Hunton (Ted Levine) attempts an investigation but is stymied by Gartley, who seems to have town officials in his pocket and a strange connection to the Mangler. After a young boy suffocates inside an icebox that has had contact with the Mangler, Hunton's brother-in-law Mark Jackson (Daniel Matmor), an expert in the supernatural, theorizes that demonic forces are driving both the machine and Gartley.

It soon transpires that Gartley has a long-standing pact with the Mangler that requires him to make sacrifices to it; the next in line is Gartley's own teenaged niece, Sherry (Vanessa Pike). Hunton and Jackson interrupt the sacrifice and rescue Sherry, while Gartley is chewed up by the machine instead. Jackson attempts to exorcize the evil forces powering the Mangler, but the ritual is unsuccessful, and the mechanical monster slashes Jackson in two. It then takes off after Hunton and Sherry, who are able to defeat it after a long chase.

King's original short story "The Mangler," published in his *Night Shift* collection, stands as a testament to his abilities as a writer; in it, he takes one of the silliest premises imaginable and manages to make it scary. Conveying a sense of horror on screen is trickier business, however, and the film version of King's tale overcomplicates the story with unconvincing twists and characters. In terms of adaptation, the best that can be said of THE MANGLER is that it hews closer to the basics of the author's original than some King films, but it is faithful to a fault. After coming up with its own rationale for the Mangler's murderous activities, the script, by director Tobe Hooper, Stephen Brooks, and Peter Welbeck (a pseudonym for coexecutive producer Harry Alan Towers), for some reason also includes King's silly explanation that the machine receives extra powers from the ingredients in antacid tablets that have been accidentally spilled into it.

The best part of the movie is the fetid, oppressive atmosphere Hooper works up inside the sweatshop that evocatively serves as an industrial hell. The Mangler itself is an imposing creation, and its gory activities (which are more so on an unrated video version) pack an occasional chill, but too much of the movie is

devoted to slack plotting and overstated acting. Though set in the US, THE MANGLER was filmed in South Africa. Towers and producer Anant Singh's next collaboration was the apartheid drama CRY, THE BELOVED COUNTRY. *(Graphic violence, adult situations, extreme profanity.)* — M.G.

d, Tobe Hooper; p, Anant Singh; exec p, Harry Alan Towers; assoc p, Rita Marie Bartlett; w, Tobe Hooper, Stephen Brooks, Peter Welbeck (based on a short story by Stephen King); ph, Amnon Salomon; ed, David Heitner; m, Barrington Pheloung; prod d, David Barkham; sound, Nicky De Beer (design), Richard Sprawson (mixer); fx, Max Poolman, Maximum Effects, Carolyn Soper, Denise Davis, Buena Vista Visual Effects; casting, Christa Schamberger; cos, Moira Anne Meyer; makeup, Tracy Crystal, Scott Wheeler, Scott Coulter; stunts, Gavin Mey

Horror (PR: O MPAA: R)

MARTHA & ETHEL ★★★
(U.S.) 80m Canobie Films ~ Sony Pictures Classics c

Martha Kneifel; Ethel Edwards; Jyll Johnstone; Barbara Ettinger; Ruth Fuglistaller (*Martha's Voice-over*)

A documentary about the nannies who raised filmmakers Jyll Johnstone and Barbara Ettinger, MARTHA & ETHEL is an emotional portrait of two child-rearing experts and the influence they exerted on the lives of their charges. Their methods are as different as their backgrounds and the roles they played in two fundamentally different households.

MARTHA & ETHEL, which cuts back and forth between its two case histories, is a painstaking valentine to the domestic help who helped shape future director Johnstone and co-producer Ettinger. Beginning in the post-WWII era, this exemplary character study examines the nannies' own backgrounds, their working years as adjuncts to the Ettinger and Johnstone families, and finally their retirement years.

Although born Catholic, German Martha finds that her position in a Jewish household makes her *persona non grata* with the Nazis. She emigrates to America, where she settles into the Johnstone family circle. Remembered primarily as a disciplinarian, Martha instills a work ethic and a sense of decorum in the Johnstone children but doesn't provide the affection they crave from her and their absentee socialite mother.

In stark contrast, Ethel leaves her impoverished roots in North Carolina for big city gaiety up North. Welcoming the opportunity to work for the Ettingers, Ethel ends up spending more time with her substitute family than she does with her own relatives. Recalled as a bastion of warmth and understanding—particularly during Mrs. Ettinger's divorce—Ethel freely gives of her heart while maintaining an innate sense of her position as a paid servant. In her twilight years, Ethel reunites briefly with her kinfolk, but chooses to remain with Mrs. Ettinger as paid companion. Retired independently in Queens, Martha reluctantly accepts the Johnstone brood's offer to transplant her to California, since they feel a compulsion to look after her—a reversal of roles that no one had anticipated.

Never once regretting that they didn't raise their own children, Martha and Ethel accept being an integral part of their privileged families without actually being blood relatives. What's most intriguing about this touching documentary is the proof it offers that love is powerful regardless of the package in which it comes.

In addition, the film documents the roles played by women like Mrs. Ettinger and Mrs. Johnstone, of necessity part-time mothers because they were expected to function as social extensions of their prominent husbands. A firm caste system was clearly in place in the Johnstone family: Martha held an important but subservient position. The sad recollections of the

Johnstone children make clear that they were stranded by their busy parents in a netherworld of benign neglect, and they embrace Martha despite her refusal to overstep what she perceived as her bounds. At the other end of the domestic spectrum, Ethel not only brought up the Ettinger children but served as support system for the divorced Mrs. Ettinger, a lady-in-waiting to the discarded princess.

MARTHA & ETHEL also examines the nannies' roles in the context of the changing roles of women in American society. While this documentary never denigrates their effectiveness as surrogate parents, the nannies almost seem like artifacts from another era, when debutantes ruled the earth. What is most reassuring about this complimentary remembrance is that both Johnstone and Ettinger can still embrace two remarkable women who accepted a place in their homes but won a place in their hearts. The film isn't a backhanded compliment to Martha and Ethel. It's an honest attempt to come to terms with pre-feminist child-rearing values upheld by their mothers (one can't help but wonder whether the filmmakers have nannies for their kids, or rely on today's fast-food equivalent: daycare center workers). Without hinting that they love their own mothers less, the filmmakers dedicate this film to their nannies. (Adult situations.) — R.P.

d, Jyll Johnstone; p, Jyll Johnstone; assoc p, Gretchen McGowan, Christina Houlihan; co-p, Barbara Ettinger; w, Jyll Johnstone, Barbara Ettinger, Alysha Cohen, Christina Houlihan, Frank Ortega, Sharon Woods; ph, Joseph Friedman; ed, Toby Shimin; m, Sarah Franklyn, John Casey; sound, John D. McCormick (mixer)

Documentary   **(PR: A   MPAA: G)**

MARTHA AND I   ★★★
(Germany/Italy/France) 107m Idunafilm; TF1 Films
Production; PROGEFI; Zweites Deutsches Fernsehen;
Osterreichischer Rundfunk Fernsehen; Canal Plus; RAI-TV
Channel 2 ~ Cinema Four/Original Cinema c
(MARTHA UND ICH)

Marianne Sagebrecht *(Martha)*; Michel Piccoli *(Dr. Ernst Fuchs)*; Vaclav Chalupa *(Emil—as a Teenager)*; Ondrej Vetchy *(Emil—as an Adult)*; Bozidara Turzonvova *(Rosa Kluge)*; Jana Brezinova *(Ida Fuchs)*; Sona Valentova *(Elsa Fuchs)*; Jana Altmanova *(Kamila Fuchs)*; Zuzana Kocurikova *(Ilona)*; Klaus Grunberg *(Bertl)*; Michael Kausch *(Werner)*; Jiri Menzel *(Dr. Benda)*; Bernhard Wicki *(Narrator)*

This sharply observed small-scale drama is given shape and tragic intensity by the Holocaust. The love story of a Jewish obstetrician and his Sudeten-German wife is narrated by the physician's nephew, a character based on director-writer Jiri Weiss.

Emil (Vaclav Chalupa), a gangling teenager, is sent by his parents in Prague to stay with his uncle Ernst Fuchs (Michel Piccoli) in a small border town. Dr. Fuchs has a dazzling Hungarian wife upon whom he lavishes gifts, but not enough attention (as an obstetrician, he often works odd and long hours). After the good doctor discovers another man in his wife's bed, he gets a divorce. Some time later, he marries his former housekeeper and cook, Martha (Marianne Sagebrecht), who is devoted to him.

The doctor's snobbish sisters cannot abide his choice, and Martha's brothers are little happier. Her older brother, Bertl (Klaus Grunberg), is somewhat flattered by the connection with a respected professional, but younger brother Werner (Michael Kausch), a Nazi, is outraged by his sister's betrayal of her blood and race.

By 1938, Dr. Fuchs is forced to sell his luxurious house and move to Prague. Living with his sisters, Martha proves herself a loyal wife, cunning politician, and dogged helper. Meanwhile, she tries to find relatives in the safe haven of New York.

Worried about Martha's well-being in wartime Prague, Dr. Fuchs arranges with her brothers to protect her; instead, they simply abduct and return her to their Sudeten village. We learn of her sad fate after the war, when an older Emil (Ondrej Vetchy), wearing the uniform of the Czech forces attached to the British Army, drives in to find her.

A memory play haunted by the spectre of history, MARTHA AND I is richly textured and singularly unsentimental, which only makes its calamitous circumstances more deeply affecting. Weiss's approach to anti-Semitism is unusually perceptive, emphasizing the complex interplay of class issues with old-fashioned bigotry. Sagebrecht is marvelous as the canny cook turned sweetheart—with the help of good dental work, a new hairdo, and expensive clothes. (Her performance won awards at film festivals in San Francisco, Seattle, and Venice.)

Weiss has avoided the obvious wartime trappings for this production: not one German uniform is seen, and it is sometimes difficult to discern the passage of time from uneasy peace to outright war. The film received no theatrical release in Germany, reportedly because the producers felt that it would be seen as anti-German. The version of the film released elsewhere in Europe lacked a sequence in which a war-wounded Bertl explains anti-Semitism as a mistake foisted on Hitler by bad advisers. (Sexual situations, adult situations.) — L.R.

d, Jiri Weiss; p, Sabine Tettenborn, Marius Schwarz; exec p, Maurice Kanbar; w, Jiri Weiss; ph, Viktor Ruzicka; ed, Gisela Haller; m, Jiri Stivin; art d, Karel Vacek; cos, Maria Frankova; makeup, Sophie Landry

Drama   **(PR: C   MPAA: NR)**

MAYA LIN: A STRONG CLEAR VISION   ★★½
(U.S.) 96m Sanders & Mock Productions ~
Ocean Releasing c

Maya Lin

MAYA LIN: A STRONG CLEAR VISION is perhaps best known as the film that won the Oscar for Best Documentary in the year (1994) that HOOP DREAMS was not even nominated. This story of a courageous young architect isn't nearly as revealing or memorable as HOOP DREAMS, but it contains rewards of its own.

Maya Lin, a 20-year-old Asian-American Yale student, was thrust into the national spotlight in 1980 when she won a government-commissioned contest to design the Vietnam War Veterans' Memorial in Washington, DC. Lin maintained her dignity while right-wing politicians and some Vietnam War veterans protested against her simple black wall covered with the names of Americans who died in Vietnam. Critics felt the wall symbolized a scar of shame on the nation. Nevertheless, Lin was vindicated by worldwide acceptance of the piece after it was built in 1982.

The remainder of MAYA LIN: A STRONG CLEAR VISION documents the creation of Lin's lesser-known accomplishments since the Vietnam Memorial controversy, including the Morris Dees Civil Rights Memorial in Alabama, the Weber House Museum in Massachusetts, the Charlotte Sports Coliseum in North Carolina, a fountain honoring women graduates back at her alma mater, and a glass landscape sculpture in Ohio. The film ends in 1992, with Lin attending the 10-year anniversary of the dedication of the Vietnam Memorial, still her most famous work.

Those familiar with Lin only through the Vietnam Memorial controversy may be surprised to discover the range and number of other projects she has worked on since then. Director Freida Lee Mock combines archival material with new footage (including many interviews and shots of Lin at work), creating a conscientious, occasionally absorbing portrait.

Unfortunately, the awkward dramatic structure and barely competent technical handling hinder the film from becoming a truly first-rate production. Granted, it is scarcely the director (or Maya Lin's) fault that the most dramatic event in Lin's professional life occurred at the beginning of her career (in rousing footage, Lin elegantly dukes it out with politicians, Vietnam veterans, and even Ross Perot on a segment of "Nightline"). And, yet, this opening material makes the subsequent events covered much less compelling, even anticlimactic.

Director Mock might have given the post-War Memorial scenes greater interest had she looked more closely at some of the ironies in Lin's career: that Lin had fought against erecting a kitschy statue next to the Vietnam Memorial during its creation, yet seems oblivious today to the kitsch her own work has inspired in the veterans who regularly visit the site; that Lin's self-described "special team" that helped her on the Civil Rights memorial in Alabama included no African-Americans.

The main reason that MAYA LIN: A STRONG CLEAR VISION remains worthwhile viewing is that Maya Lin herself transcends many of the film's deficiencies. Her drive, determination, and grace are indeed inspirational. They emphasize that, while this tribute is sometimes bland and conventional, its subject certainly is not. The film had a brief theatrical release in 1995 before going to home video. — E.M.

d, Freida Lee Mock; p, Freida Lee Mock, Terry Sanders; exec p, Eileen Harris Norton; assoc p, Jessica Yu; w, Freida Lee Mock; ph, Don Lenzer, Eddie Marritz; ed, William T. Cartwright, Sr.; m, Charles Bernstein; sound, Steve Flick (design), Rick Ash (mixer), Robyn Hutman, Judy Carp

Documentary/Biography   **(PR: AA   MPAA: NR)**

ME AND THE MOB   ★
(U.S.) 86m RSVP Productions; Writers
Limited Partnership ~ Bullseye Video c
(AKA: WHO DO I GOTTA KILL?)

James Lorinz *(Jimmy Corona)*; Tony Darrow *(Tony Bando)*; John Costelloe *(Billy "Bink-Bink" Borelle)*; Vinny Pastore *(Aldo "Birdman" Bodamo)*; Frank Gio *(Frankie "The Fixer" Giachetti)*; Richard Bright *(Belcher)*; Sandra Bullock *(Lori)*; Stephen Lee *(Bobby Blitzer)*; Gemma Nanni *(Angie Giochetti)*; Ted Sorel *(George Stellaris)*; Louis Giovanetti *(Dick)*; Frank "Butch the Hat" Aqilino *(Joey "Clams" Tantillo)*; Chacha Ciarcia *(Marty "No Neck" Scalia)*; Lee Anne Linfante *(Tina)*; Mario Cantone *(Rico)*; Frankie Cee *(Franco)*; Michael Luciano *(Leary)*; Sandra Colosimo *(Agency Receptionist)*; Lori Rachal *(Jogger)*; Suze Trevitchik *(Girl at George's Bar)*; Johnny Lorinz *(Detective)*; Arthur Nascarella *(Distraught Wiseguy)*; Nicholas Spina *(Carwash Owner)*; Victor Triola *(Exiting Patron)*; Anthony Michael Hall *(Jimmy's Friend)*; Vickie Weinstein *(Publisher's Secretary)*; Roy Frumkes *(Publisher)*; Mary Lynn Hetsko *(Nurse)*; Mario Augusta *(Priest)*; Nellie Zastawna *(Bingo Woman)*; Irma St. Paule *(Woman 2)*; Frances Levy *(Woman Negotiating)*; Steve Buscemi *(Conspiracy Nut—uncredited)*

ME AND THE MOB was released (barely) in 1994 as WHO DO I GOTTA KILL?, and, in an attempt to draw fans of MARRIED TO THE MOB, was renamed for its 1995 video release. No matter what name it goes by, though, this film is a tedious low-budget Mafia comedy that will undoubtedly disappoint those who are lured by the new title.

Jimmy Corona (James Lorinz) is a writer who's down on his luck. He has a lousy agent and no inspiration. His girlfriend leaves him, he is banished from his favorite bar, and he is such a loser that he can't even kill himself.

Desperate, Jimmy takes his agent's advice and decides to write a "real life crime story." He visits his uncle Tony (Tony Darrow), who works for crime boss Frankie "The Fixer"by Giochetti (Frank Gio). Jimmy asks to join "the business," hoping that he'll gather material for his novel. Tony welcomes Jimmy and teams him up with Billy "Bink-Bink" Borelle (John Costelloe). At first, Jimmy is a bumbling fool, but when he visits the bar, his former hangout, he gets tough and beats up the owner.

Soon after, Jimmy is asked to kill a man. He is too afraid to do it, but the man dies of a heart attack as Jimmy and Frankie's men argue. Jimmy is picked up by the police and charged with the "murder." They say they'll let him go if he helps them to nab Frankie. The police hook Jimmy up with a wire, but the wire begins picking up radio broadcasts at the most inopportune time. Jimmy is beaten up and Frankie orders him to be executed.

Tony and Billy take Jimmy away but spare his life. It turns out that Tony had been wired also. This would be great, but the police run out of money and decide to drop the case against Frankie. The three men, in fear of Frankie, hide out while Jimmy writes his book. All three are found and shot by Frankie's men, but they survive. While Jimmy and Tony are in the hospital recuperating, Frankie comes to visit. He too has written a book about the Mafia, and he beat Jimmy to the publisher. As the curtain falls, Tony and Jimmy end up running a fixed bingo game, and are beaten up by several old ladies.

ME AND THE MOB is a silly, hackneyed story, made with little inspiration. Jimmy is not a particularly interesting character, and his predicament never excites the viewer. ME AND THE MOB has occasional clever dialogue, but the emphasis is put on the uninteresting plot and lame sight gags, such as Jimmy trying to slash his wrists with a safety razor. The only funny scene revolves around the mob's discussion of whether Jimmy should be credited with a real kill after his victim's heart attack. If the film had contained more clever conversations of that type, the low budget and cheap sets might not be as noticeable. Unfortunately, the presence of one good scene simply points out how pedestrian the rest of the film is. *(Sexual situations, profanity.)* — A.M.

d, Frank Rainone; p, Frank Rainone; exec p, Nicholas P. Spina; co-p, Vincent Viola; w, Rocco Simonelli, Frank Rainone, James Lorinz; ph, Adam Kimmel; ed, Michelle Gorchow; m, Doug Katsaros; prod d, Susan Bolles; art d, Rachael Weinzimer; set d, Catherine Pierson; sound, Neil Danziger (mixer), Peter Waggoner (mixer); fx, Drew Jiritano; casting, Todd Thaler, Caroline Sinclair; cos, Barbara Kramer, Kim Druce; makeup, Magda Dajani

Comedy   **(PR: O   MPAA: R)**

MEET THE FEEBLES   ★★★
(New Zealand) 94m Wingnut Films ~
Greycat Films c

VOICES OF: Danny Mulheron *(Heidi)*; Donna Akersten; Stuart Devenie; Mark Hadlow; Ross Jolly; Brian Sergent; Peter Vere Jones; Mark Wright

Yes, MEET THE FEEBLES is a one-joke film. But it's a pretty good joke, in a crude kind of way. The Feebles are a troupe of sleazy show business types trying to mount a song-and-dance show they hope will launch them on the road to TV fame and fortune. But they're not human: they're offensive foam puppets who fornicate, abuse drugs and alcohol, and generally behave like the scum of the earth while producing the seedy *Fabulous Feebles Variety Hour*. Naturally, in this simultaneous parody of "The Muppets" television series and the backstage dramas of yore, everything that can go wrong, does.

MEET THE FEEBLES is far less concerned with plot than with stringing together a series of cruel and extremely gross gags. The movie opens as the randy host, Harry the Hare, discovers that he has a loathsome sexually transmitted disease (could it be AIDS?). The stage manager is a worm. Wynyard the frog—who does a knife-throwing act—has Vietnam flashbacks. Sandy the chicken has filed a paternity suit against Sid the juggling elephant, who swears the child isn't his. The show's director, Sebastian the Fox, is a frustrated performer and eventually gets to do his big number, a ditty called "Sodomy" ("*You might think it odd o' me. . .*").The show's really big star, Heidi the hippo, is smarting from her romantic betrayal by disgusting producer Bletch the walrus, who's taken up with a purring Siamese pussy named Samantha.

Bletch is also dealing drugs out of his office, with thuggish Barry the bulldog handling the leg-breaking side of the business. Bletch's assistant, Trevor the rat, makes pornographic movies starring pierced bovines and whip-cracking cockroaches. And to make it all worse, a muckraking fly—the sort of sleazy tabloid journalist who quite literally wallows in excrement—has gotten a whiff of something nasty going on at the Feebles studio and won't leave off investigating until he finds out what it is. Into this den of iniquity stumbles poor, sweet, lisping Robert the hedgehog, fresh out of drama school and ripe to fall in love with imperious dancing poodle Lucille. The various sketches are strung along the spine of Robert's sappy romance, which is as predictable as it ought to be: Lucille falls for Robert, Robert loses Lucille, Lucille and Robert are happily reunited at the end. They're the only ones for whom things end happily, however: The rest of the foam and wire armature cast goes down in a hail of bullets when Heidi decides she's had enough and lets loose with a machine gun.

MEET THE FEEBLES is a film for everyone whose teeth hurt every time they see those terminally sweet, blandly pleasant Muppets. That said, MEET THE FEEBLES wasn't originally intended to be a feature-length film, and it's an idea that would probably have been better served at shorter length. This 1989 film only received theatrical release in the US in 1995, after it became a hot item on the underground video scene. It's the second feature directed by New Zealand bad boy Peter Jackson, whose first and third films—the coarse sci-fi comedy BAD TASTE and over-the-top zombie parody DEAD ALIVE—offered similar mixes of hoary genre cliche and gross-out sight gags. Aggressive tastelessness is a key element in this film's aesthetic, as is grotesque excess; overall, the film's sensibilities are firmly mired in the toilet and the fraternity house, dedicated to grabbing complacently jaded viewers by the scruff and forcing them to gasp, "I can't believe they did that!" Nevertheless, it has moments of undeniable comic genius and is often agonizingly funny. (*Violence, sexual situations, adult situations, substance abuse, profanity.*) — M.M.

d, Peter Jackson; p, Jim Booth, Peter Jackson; w, Frances Walsh, Stephen Sinclair, Danny Mulheron, Peter Jackson; ph, Murray Milne; ed, Jamie Selkirk; m, Peter Dasent; prod d, Mike Kane; sound, Grant Taylor (mixer); fx, Steve Ingram; cos, Glenis Foster

Comedy   **(PR: O   MPAA: NR)**

MESSENGER   ★★
(U.S.) 84m c

Richard Barboza *(Jeff)*; Carolyn Kinebrew *(Tina)*; Scott Ferguson *(John)*; Malika Davis *(Lois)*

MESSENGER has a message to deliver, and it does so with all the drama of mail service. This noble-minded movie is a needless remake of the neo-realist classic THE BICYCLE THIEF, set in New York with an African-American cast.

Jeff Rogers (Richard Barbosa) is trying to go straight after a history of unspecified criminal activity. He already has one child, and his wife Tina (Carolyn Kinebrew) is pregnant with their second. Jeff lands a job as a bicycle messenger, but doesn't have a bike, so Tina pawns her wedding ring for the money to buy one. On Jeff's first day at work, the bike gets stolen. He and Tina figure the thief will show up in Central Park on Saturday, either riding or selling the bike, so they go there intent on catching him. The search seems hopeless, and the couple take their frustrations out on each other. Finally, miraculously, Jeff spots the thief. They track him to his home, but by then the bike is long gone, and Jeff gets beaten up for his trouble. (Director Loftis plays the cop who intercedes on Jeff's behalf.) Desperate, Jeff angrily sends Tina away and attempts to steal a bike. He fails. Tina then goes into labor and, as they ride away in an ambulance, they vow to stay together and persevere.

It's no surprise that MESSENGER suffers in comparison to THE BICYCLE THIEF, but the remake is weaker than it needed to be. Wherever producer, writer, and director Norman Loftis (SMALL TIME) has changed the story, the result is for the worse. In the BICYCLE THIEF, the bike represents the sole means of support for an impoverished family; its loss is genuinely devastating. Here, the bike is little more than a plot device, providing Jeff and Tina an excuse to spend a day in the park (where they roller-skate and eat Belgian waffles). Moreover, the movie's logical and moral parameters are undermined by an early scene in which Jeff gets into an argument in a club, pulls a gun, and has to be restrained from killing the man. Are we then to believe that stealing a bike poses an ethical dilemma for him?

The film awkwardly hammers home its central point: that young black men need to stay alive, stay out of prison, and stay home if they are to become strong husbands and fathers. Benevolent patriarchy, Loftis implies, is a necessary condition for the improvement of the African-American community. If this was the message of 1995's Million Man March on Washington, it is also a cherished belief of those whites who like to believe that black men are responsible for their own predicament. (*Extreme profanity, violence.*) — P.R.

d, Norman Loftis; p, Norman Loftis; w, Norman Loftis; ph, Joe Di Gennaro; ed, John Walters; m, Joe Loduca; sound, David Alvaraz

Drama   **(PR: C   MPAA: NR)**

METAL AND MELANCHOLY   ★★★
(Netherlands/Peru) 80m VPRO Television; Ariel Film c
(AKA: METAL & MELANCOLIA)

Heddy Honigmann's METAL AND MELANCHOLY is a moving look at taxi drivers in Lima, Peru. Winner of the Grand Prix at the prestigious documentary film festival Cinema du Rel, this portrait of life for the city's cab drivers also becomes an insightful statement about Peruvian national identity.

Government corruption and ineptitude have nearly bankrupted Peru. Salaries have not kept up with inflation, and men and women who work as teachers, actors, housewives and government officials moonlight as cab drivers to make ends meet. For the price of a $1.00 "Taxi" sticker, people can put their beat-up old family cars into service as taxis. The director interviews more than a dozen taxi drivers, following them as they drive around the streets of the city, talking about their lives and their work. Most of their cars are very old and in terrible condition. However, the drivers stand proudly beside them, posing for the camera. Some drivers have invented elaborate schemes to secure their cars against the ever-present threat of theft. One can only be started by connecting an intricate system of wires; another has a removable gearstick. In one amusing scene, a police officer who has pulled a taxi over, reveals that he too drives one in his spare time. The drivers talk candidly about their lives—stories of professional disappointments, lost love and sick children. They also talk about their country, revealing the complex mixture of resolve and resignation which seems to characterize the people of Lima.

Director Heddy Honigmann grew up in Lima and emigrated to Holland in her early 20s. METAL AND MELANCHOLY is a loving portrait of her birthplace, an intelligent (if a little sentimental) attempt to understand how Peru came to be in its current state. One of the interview subjects in the film talks of a Spanish poet who once described Peru as being "like metal and melancholy." Pain and poverty have made people as hard as metal, but they are also melancholy because they wish for the good old days. As these taxi drivers cruise around the potholed streets of Lima, revealing the city's decaying architectural grandeur as well as their own poignant stories, METAL AND MELANCHOLY shows with affection and sadness a country which seems to be spiraling downward. — J.S.

d, Heddy Honigmann; p, Susanne van Voorst; w, Heddy Honigmann, Peter Delpeut; ph, Stef Tijdink; ed, Jan Hendricks, Danniel Danniel; sound, Piotr Van Dijl

Documentary   (PR: A   MPAA: NR)

MIAMI RHAPSODY   ★★
(U.S.) 95m Avnet/Kerner Company; Hollywood
Pictures ~ Buena Vista c

Sarah Jessica Parker *(Gwyn)*; Gil Bellows *(Matt)*; Antonio Banderas *(Antonio)*; Mia Farrow *(Nina)*; Paul Mazursky *(Vic)*; Kevin Pollak *(Jordan)*; Barbara Garrick *(Terri)*; Carla Gugino *(Leslie)*; Bo Eason *(Jeff)*; Naomi Campbell *(Kaia)*; Jeremy Piven *(Mitchell)*; Kelly Bishop *(Zelda)*; Mark Blum *(Peter)*; Norman Steinberg *(Charlie)*; Ben Stein *(Rabbi)*; Donal Logue *(Derek)*; Mary Chernoff *(Grandma Lil)*; Elodia Riovega *(Antonio's Mother)*; Chaz Mena *(Ted)*; George Tapia *(Carlos)*; Avery Sommers *(Nurse)*; Ed Arenas *(Photographer)*; Frank Fong *(Chinese Host)*; Lisa Banes *(Gynecologist)*

The specter of Woody Allen hangs heavy over MIAMI RHAPSODY, whose rave coverage in *The New York Times* is doubtless entirely unrelated to the fact that first-time filmmaker David Frankel's father is *Times* editor Max Frankel.

Gwyn Marcus (Sarah Jessica Parker), an advertising copy writer who wants to write sitcoms, doesn't know what to do with herself. Her career ambitions are frustrated, her family is super-dysfunctional and her fiance Matt (Gil Bellows), a handsome zoologist, seems too good to be true.

And things are even worse than she thinks. Mom Nina (Mia Farrow) has just discovered that dad Vic (Paul Mazursky) has been conducting a longtime affair with travel agent Zelda (Kelly Bishop). Sister Leslie (Carla Gugino) recently wed a pro football player (Bo Eason), whose tightfisted ways have sent her flying into the arms of Mitchell (Jeremy Piven). Brother Jordan (Kevin Pollak) is terminally unfaithful to his pregnant wife Terri (Barbara Garrick), most recently with his business partner's wife (Naomi Campbell), a model. And to top it all off, the conventional—if ditsy—Nina has taken up with Antonio (Antonio Ban-

deras), the hunky Latino nurse who's been caring for Gwyn's grandma Lil (Mary Charnoff), recently felled by a stroke.

Everyone suspects everyone else of deceit and betrayal, and before she knows it, Gwyn is tangling the sheets with the irresistible Antonio, upping the ante of all this romantic confusion. But despite the indiscriminate bed-hopping, most of the embattled couples stick it out, helped along by events like Jordan joining his long-suffering wife in the delivery room. Gwyn even gets her career in gear when her script is accepted by a network.

David Frankel's heart is in the right place: he wants to make a sprightly, modern romantic comedy. But he keeps putting his own director's foot in his own hyperactive writer's mouth. He overloads his script with so many one-liners of highly variable quality that the characters—especially heroine Gwyn—resemble chatty automatons more than flesh and blood people. Some of the quips are witty, but trying to sift them out of the verbal diarrhea quickly becomes exhausting. Frankel also fails to create any sort of romantic atmosphere: the trendy Miami of South Beach and Coral Gables may well be one big shopping mall, but that doesn't mean it should look like one. Jack Wallner's cinematography is too muddy to capture what color and Deco design manage to peep through the mass of convenience stores.

Though the cast is filled with talented performers, there are too many of them for the film to contain comfortably. Parker—such a delightful comedienne in L.A. STORY and HONEYMOON IN VEGAS—is hampered by her character's talkativeness: Gwyn might be likable, if only she'd shut up long enough to let the viewer find out. Farrow—her plaintive delivery and mannerisms grafted on to an irritatingly dumb-blonde matron role—is so entirely associated with Woody Allen that her presence in this film is eerie. Most of the rest of the cast weigh in with the expected stuff: Mazursky is blusteringly clueless; Bishop reliable as his inamorata; Banderas all *salsa picante*. Supermodel Campbell makes her screen debut and is amusing as—surprise!—a spoiled mannequin, but is badly served by the inept, dark cinematography. The one performer who manages to come through with any authenticity is Chernoff, who plays feeble Grandma Lil with such simple humanity that she inadvertently shows up the clankingly derivative artificiality of the film. *(Adult situations, sexual situations, profanity.)* — D.N.

d, David Frankel; p, Barry Jossen, David Frankel; exec p, Jon Avnet, Jordan Kerner; assoc p, Joe M. Aguilar; w, David Frankel; ph, Jack Wallner; ed, Steven Weisberg; m, Mark Isham; prod d, J. Mark Harrington; set d, Barbara Peterson; sound, Michael Tromer (mixer); fx, Kevin Harris; casting, Renee Rousselot; cos, Patricia Field; makeup, Isabel Harkins

Comedy/Romance   (PR: C   MPAA: PG-13)

MIDNIGHT TEASE 2   ★
(U.S.) 93m Sunset Films International; Pacific Trust ~
New Horizons Home Video c

Kimberly Kelley *(Jennifer Brennan)*; Jack Turturici *(Paul Douglas)*; Julie K. Smith *(Cherry)*; Ross Hagen *(John Donnelly)*; Tane McClure *(Lacy)*; Brett Baxter Clark *(Joe Martoni)*; Griffen Drew *(Desiree)*; Kim Kopf *(Katlin Clark)*; Tammy Parks *(Misty)*; Hoke Howell *(Harry)*; Lenny Juliano *(Frankie Bono)*; Erin Ashley *(Shane)*; Debra Beatty *(Sandra)*; Antonia Dorian *(Stephanie)*; Kimberley Roberts *(Chris)*; Jim Wynorski *(Drunk at Bar)*

MIDNIGHT TEASE 2 is equally inadequate as thriller and soft-core porn. It's got silly choreographed pole dances that are nude versions of schlocky early '80s music videos; a plot even more flimsy than the costumes; and a script that contains more stripping than talking.

The film is centered around lovely Jen Brennan (Kimberly Kelley), whose go-go dancer sister was murdered by a serial killer in the original MIDNIGHT TEASE. With the aid of John Donnelly (Ross Hagen) a wheelchair-bound detective, Jen goes undercover at the L.A. strip club where her sister was murdered, in the hopes of catching the killer. Jen meets various suspects at the club. Meanwhile, the killer continues to knock off strippers by luring them into private lap dances, only to suffocate them with plastic bags. John ominously warns Jen, "Don't trust anybody."

Joe (Brett Baxter Clark), who has a history of beating up strippers, hires Jen to dance. Bouncer Frankie (Lenny Juliano) promises to protect Jen from patrons who can't keep it in their laps. Jen's peers include top stripper Cherry (Julie K. Smith) and Lacy (Tane McClure), the maternal bartender. Everyone is surprised by how well novice Jen takes to her new profession. She's deemed "a real natural," and given special attention by the club's most popular regular, handsome artist Paul Douglas (Jack Turturici). Thankfully, before we even have time to wonder if Paul is the killer, John clears up that mystery. We are told that another murder took place while Paul was in bed with Jen. John is convinced that Jen can trap the murderer by uncovering his "trigger"—whatever provokes the killer to kill. Finally, Jen rubs up against a clue. It seems that Joe, the owner, has sent the victims, who all happen to have been mothers, out to private parties at the same address. Jen reveals her true identity and her suspicions about Joe to Lacy, only to discover moments later that the address is Lacy's. In homage to BASIC INSTINCT, and a host of other lesbian killer movies, Lacy suddenly appears dressed as a man and wielding a plastic bag. An undercover cop saves Jen from death by suffocation.

The "trigger" is revealed during the synthetic epilogue, in which John conveniently tells us that Lacy was abused by her mother as a child, which is why she only chooses mothers as her victims. This is as ironic as the film gets. MIDNIGHT TEASE 2 teases us with the promise of eroticism and mystery, but all it delivers are mechanical lessons in lap dancing and a plot as artificial as the actresses' breasts. (Graphic violence, extreme profanity, extensive nudity, sexual situations.) — J.D.

d, Richard Styles; p, Richard Gabai, Tony Gutilla; exec p, Jim Wynorski, Alan B. Bursteen; assoc p, Christopher Dempsey; w, Richard Styles; ph, Gary Graver; ed, John Shepphird; prod d, Chris Dempsey; art d, Michael Angelo; set d, Michele Piper; sound, Lee Alexander (mixer); fx, Ray Hairyhoosen; casting, Noble Henri; cos, Maral Kalinian; makeup, Luanne Iannucci, Tim Bellszig; stunts, Smiley Rosenstein, Deborah Rosenstein

Erotic/Thriller/Mystery   (PR: O   MPAA: NR)

MIGHTY APHRODITE   ★★★
(U.S.) 95m Sweetland Films ~ Miramax c

Woody Allen (Lenny); Helena Bonham Carter (Amanda); F. Murray Abraham (Leader); Claire Bloom (Amanda's Mother); Olympia Dukakis (Jocasta); Michael Rapaport (Kevin); Mira Sorvino (Linda Ash); David Ogden Stiers (Laius); Jack Warden (Tiresias); Peter Weller (Jerry Bender); Steven Randazzo (Bud); J. Smith-Cameron (Bud's Wife); Jeffrey Kurland (Oedipus); Donald Symington (Amanda's Father); Jimmy McQuaid (Max); Tucker Robin (Infant Max); Nolan Tuffey (Two-Year Old Max); Yvette Hawkins (School Principal); Karin Haidorfer (Park Avenue Woman); Gary Alper (Park Avenue Man); Rosemary Murphy (Adoption Coordinator); Peter McRobbie (Linda's Ex-Landlord); Kathleen Doyle (Ex-Landlord's Wife); Jennifer Greenhut (Lenny's Secretary); Sondra James (Operator); Paul Giamatti (Extras Guild Researcher); William Addy (Superintendent);

Kenneth Edelson (Ken); Danielle Ferland (Cassandra); Dan Mullane (Messenger); Thomas Durkin (Race Announcer); Dan Moran (Ricky, the Pimp); Paul Herman (Ricky's Friend); Tony Sirico (Boxing Trainer); Tony Darrow (Boxing Trainer); Ray Garvey (Boxing Trainer); Kent Blocher (Voice of Zeus); Joseph P. Coleman (Porno Film Star); Georgette Pasare (Porno Film Star); Bray Poor (Helicopter Pilot)

MIGHTY APHRODITE is a welcome return to contemporary comedy for Woody Allen, in which his usual neurotic Upper East Siders mix with hookers and hustlers while a real Greek chorus looks on.

The film opens with the Greek Chorus—whose members include David Ogden Stiers, F. Murray Abraham and Olympia Dukakis—assembled in an ancient amphitheater. In epic tones, they begin to tell the story of sportswriter Lenny Weinrib (Woody Allen) and his wife Amanda (Helena Bonham Carter), who works in an art gallery. Amanda—who feels she's too busy to have a child the usual way—investigates adoption, despite Lenny's objections. When baby Max becomes available she seizes the opportunity, and Lenny finds himself surprisingly taken with the infant.

Unable to leave well enough alone, Lenny becomes obsessed with finding the child's natural mother, despite the warnings of the Chorus. He surreptitiously tracks down Max's mother and discovers—to his horror—that she's a prostitute and part-time porno actress named Linda Ash (Mira Sorvino). Lenny makes an appointment to see her, and she—quite naturally—assumes he's a customer, albeit a particularly shy one. While Amanda is considering the advances of a sleazy art dealer, Jerry Bender (Peter Weller), Lenny meets several times with Linda, getting her to reveal many details about her past life. Though she finally tells him about the child she gave up, he doesn't tell her about Max.

Lenny begins to feel a sense of paternal responsibility for the good-hearted but dim-witted Linda, and encourages her to give up hooking. He fixes her up with Kevin (Michael Rapaport), a handsome and extremely stupid boxer. Linda and Kevin date, but break up when he learns about her seedy past. Linda is heartbroken, and she and Lenny sleep together. He goes back to Amanda, who realizes she doesn't love Jerry. Linda and Lenny part ways, but in an O. Henry-style epilogue, the now happily-married Linda and her child run into Lenny and Max at FAO Schwartz. Each is blissfully unaware that he/she is the parent of the other's child.

MIGHTY APHRODITE is Woody Allen's funniest film in years, thanks in large part to the character of Linda and the way her good-natured earthiness clashes with Lenny's neurotic repression. Sorvino's performance is an amazing feat of transformation that recalls Judy Holliday's dumb blonde roles, though her helium-tinged voice and raunchy dialogue are even more suggestive of a foul-mouthed Minnie Mouse. Linda's blithe discussions of explicit sexual acts and her sordid past are utterly disarming; she's simultaneously innocent and sexy. The Greek Chorus may be a gimmick, but it's an effective one, and elevates this tale of urban malaise to an examination of love, fate, and man's inability to save himself from his own hubris. The Chorus also illustrates one of Allen's favorite comic devices: mixing the lofty and philosophical with the mundane. Hearing the Chorus pontificate on the subject of Lenny's inconsequentially sordid affair, intoning his name as if he were Zeus, is certainly a funny idea, and one that recalls such early Allen comedies as LOVE AND DEATH and BANANAS.

The story is slight and not without implausibilities—how did Amanda get a baby so quickly, anyway?—but enough of the dialogue is genuinely funny that it doesn't really matter. (Profanity, sexual situations, nudity.)

d, Woody Allen; p, Robert Greenhut; exec p, Jean Doumanian, J.E. Beaucaire; assoc p, Thomas Reilly; co-p, Helen Robin; w, Woody Allen; ph, Carlo DiPalma; ed, Susan E. Morse; m, Dick Hyman; prod d, Santo Loquasto; art d, Tom Warren; set d, Susan Bode; ch, Graciela Daniele; sound, Gary Alper (mixer); casting, Juliet Taylor; cos, Jeffrey Kurland; makeup, Fern Buchner, Rosemarie Zurlo

AA Best Supporting Actress: Mira Sorvino; *AAN Best Original Screenplay:* Woody Allen

Comedy   **(PR: C   MPAA: R)**

MIGHTY MORPHIN POWER RANGERS: ★★★
THE MOVIE
(U.S.) 95m Rita Enterprises; Tengu Productions; 20th Century Fox/Family Films; Saban Entertainment; Toei Company ~ 20th Century Fox c

Karan Ashley *(Aisha/Yellow Ranger)*; Johnny Yong Bosch *(Adam/Black Ranger)*; Steve Cardenas *(Rocky/Red Ranger)*; Jason David Frank *(Tommy/White Ranger)*; Amy Jo Johnson *(Kimberly/Pink Ranger)*; David Yost *(Billy/Blue Ranger)*; Paul Schrier *(Bulk)*; Jason Narvy *(Skull)*; Paul Freeman *(Ivan Ooze)*; Gabrielle Fitzpatrick *(Dulcea)*; Nicholas Bell *(Zordon)*; Peta-Maree Rixon *(Alpha 5)*; Jean Paul Bell *(Mordant)*; Kerry Casey *(Goldar)*; Mark Ginther *(Lord Zedd)*; Julia Cortez *(Rita Repulsa)*; Jamie Croft *(Fred Kelman)*; Paul Pantano *(Kid)*; Mitchell McMahon *(Kid)*; Tim Valka *(Kid)*; Peter Mochrie *(Mr. Kelman)*; Scott McGregor *(Security Guard)*; Paula Morrell *(Reporter)*; Paul Goddard *(Construction Worker)*; Robert Simper *(Construction Worker)*; Robyn Gol *(Zombie Parent Dancer)*

"Mighty Morphin Power Rangers," the cheesy but hugely popular television show about costumed teens who battle alien monsters, has been upgraded for the big screen with a strong plot line, expert special effects, and impressive location filming in Australia. This is more merchandising ploy than movie, but it's surprisingly enjoyable action fluff.

In the city of Angel Grove, construction workers discover an ancient, locked, underground chamber and unwittingly release the evil alien overlord Ivan Ooze (Paul Freeman), who quickly aligns himself with alien villains Lord Zedd (Mark Ginther), Rita Repulsa (Julia Cortez), and Goldar (Kerry Casey). Pitting his oozing purple minions against a local team of six teenaged martial artists (played by a cast of virtually indistinguishable unknowns) who transform themselves into the costumed, superheroic Power Rangers, Ooze attacks and lays waste to the command center of Zordon (Nicholas Bell), the Power Rangers' alien mentor. Now powerless and confronted with the sad sight of a weakened Zordon, the Rangers are sent to the planet Phados, where they must seek out a source of new power.

In Angel Grove, without the Power Rangers to stop him, Ivan Ooze uses his purple ooze to turn the town's parents into zombie slaves, who begin digging up long-buried giant insectoid robots known as Ectomorphs. On Phados, the teens face many obstacles, but they are aided on their journey by a woman warrior, Dulcea (Gabrielle Fitzpatrick), who assigns them new sacred animals. The six succeed in restoring their powers and return to Earth in time to battle Ooze's Ectomorphs and help the children of Angel Grove save their parents. Armed with new Zords—armed flying vehicles—the Power Rangers confront Ooze, who has taken over the body of one of the Ectomorphs, and take him into outer space, where they maneuver him into the path of a speeding comet.

The American series on which this movie is based uses action scenes from a Japanese-produced *sentai* (costumed super team) TV program, intercut with newly-shot scenes of American actors playing the Rangers out of costume. For the movie, the filmmakers put the American actors in new costumes and dispensed with the Japanese footage, creating all-new special effects and fight scenes. The result is a surprisingly engaging action fantasy with a simple yet effective story line, battle scenes inspired by Hong Kong action films, and imaginative special effects depicting a variety of menacing creatures and striking vistas of outer space. In addition, the filmmakers make clever use of Australian outback and rainforest locations to recreate the alien landscape of Phados.

While the TV series aims for broad kiddie appeal, the movie wisely omits the inane high school antics and makes the teen Rangers more serious and dedicated opponents of evil. The American actors lack individual screen presence, but their energy, agility, youthful attractiveness, and strong sense of teamwork prove refreshing and endearing. *(Violence.)* — B.C.

d, Bryan Spicer; p, Haim Saban, Shuki Levy, Suzanne Todd; co-p, David Coatsworth; w, Arne Olsen (from a story by John Kamps and Arne Olsen); ph, Paul Murphy; ed, Wayne Wahrman; m, Graeme Revell; prod d, Craig Stearns; art d, Colin Gibson; set d, Tim Ferrier; sound, Bob Clayton (recordist), Robert Renga (recordist); fx, Tad Pride, Steve Courtley, Erik Henry, Richard Hollander, Steve Dellerson, VIFX; casting, Liz Mullinar, Christine King; cos, Joseph Porro; makeup, Lynn Wheeler; stunts, Rocky McDonald

Children's / Adventure /
Science Fiction   **(PR: A   MPAA: PG)**

MINA TANNENBAUM ★★★
(France) 128m Union Generale du Cinematographique; IMA Films; Christian Bourgois Productions; La Sept Cinema; FCC; Societe Francaise de Production Cinematographique; Les Films de l'Etang; Belbo Film Productions ~ New Yorker Films c

Romane Bohringer *(Mina Tannenbaum)*; Elsa Zylberstein *(Ethel Benegui)*; Florence Thomassin *(Cousin)*; Nils Tavernier *(Francois)*; Stephane Slima *(Didier)*; Chantal Krief *(Daisy)*; Jany Gastaldi *(Gisele)*; Dimitri Furdui *(Henri)*; Eric Defosse *(Serge)*; Jean-Philippe Ecoffey *(Jacques Dana)*; Harry Cleven *(Gerard)*; Alexandre von Sivers *(Devas)*; Artus dePenguern *(Naschich)*; Elise Benroubi *(Mina—Age 10)*; Shirley Kleinman *(Ethel—Age 10)*; Sabrina Germeau *(Mina—Age 5)*; Elodie Grosbris *(Ethel—Age 5)*; Hugues Quester *(Choumachere)*; Tony Cecchinato *(Gypsy)*; Gwenola deLuze *(Muriel)*; Julien Kafaro *(Man in the Street)*; Blanche Aubree; Sylvia Antrop; Massimo Bellini; Mina Buhbinder; Daniel Charlier; Peter Chase; Yves Claessem; Phillippe Chiffre; Bobby Pacha; Lucia Coppola; Bertie Cortez; Marielle Deschamps; Stephanie Degroot; Phillippe Drukman; Pierre Dumaine; Muriel Esser; Daphne Eyles; Jacqueline Ghaye; Madame Gonzales; Serge Gozlan; Richard Guez; Denis Grumbach; Bob Ingaro; Anita Jans; Jean Keutericks; Jacques Korman; Simon Lafon; Jean-Claude Lachkar; Louis Langlet; Gaetan Malrait; Eva Mazauric; Jocya Milshtein; Huguette Ouaknine; Martine Cohen; Francois DePaeuw; Francis Paguet; Isabelle Quadens; Marion Quoilin; Rachel Sabbah; Jean-Louis Sbille; Laurent Scano; Sarah Silvera; Martin Stameschkine; Cathy Tastet; Joseph Tibi Tillie; Jean-Pierre Valere; Isabelle Vander Velde; Christian Vermeullen; Alan Villeval; Rywka Wajsbrot; Emillie Woitchik; Alice Xanadu

MINA TANNENBAUM chronicles a 25-year friendship between two young Jewish women in Paris. Martine Dugowson's directorial debut is charming and enjoyable, although it does have a cinematic awkwardness characteristic of many first films.

Paris, 1968. As students and workers riot, two seven-year-old girls are attending ballet school. Mina is bespectacled and intense; Ethel is chubby and outgoing. Both are outsiders who turn to each other and begin a symbiotic friendship filled with compassion, support, secrets, and love. MINA TANNENBAUM follows them as they move into the comic adventures of their teenage years—rebelling against their parents, trying to find their true identities, and discovering romance. Mina (Romane Bohringer, as a teen and adult) is an aspiring painter, an idealist who believes in sticking to her dreams at all costs. In part, this uncompromising nature gives her integrity and strength, but it also sets the stage for the breakdown of her friendship with Ethel (Elsa Zylberstein, as a teen and adult), who isn't really committed to anything in particular. But Ethel does want to leave her mark on life—as Mina does with her painting—and she becomes a journalist. As they move out of their teens and become adults, their closeness becomes entangled in shifting self-images, jealousies, and resentment. When Ethel marries the man that Mina secretly loves—arrogant art dealer Jacques Dana (Jean-Philippe Ecoffey)—Ethel and Mina angrily part ways. Ethel moves ahead with her life, while Mina loses her confidence in her talents and her will to paint. Having depended on each other for most of their lives, Mina and Ethel are both forced to come to terms with the profound consequences of losing a friend.

MINA TANNENBAUM is an amusing and entertaining drama, an intimate look at the ebb and flow of friendships between women. Both Romane Bohringer and Elsa Zylberstein are widely seen as rising stars on the French movie scene. Bohringer, who won a Cesar (the French Oscar equivalent) for her role in Cyril Collard's SAVAGE NIGHTS (1992, US release 1994), gives a wonderful performance as the intense, raw Mina. Zylberstein, who can also be seen in FARINELLI and JEFFERSON IN PARIS, allows Ethel's character to develop a rich complexity as she juggles her own needs and desires in work, love and friendship. Director and writer Martine Dugowson won the Best Screenplay Award at the 1992 Cannes Film Festival. However, her direction of MINA TANNENBAUM bears the marks of a novice filmmaker, mixing a very traditional episodic style of storytelling with wild, slightly ungainly touches (like the use of movie clips). Unfortunately, MINA TANNENBAUM pales as a portrait of the power and complexity of female friendship in comparison to the work of another female director, Diane Kurys. (*Sexual situations, adult situations.*) — J.S.

d, Martine Dugowson; p, Georges Benayoun; exec p, Paul Rozenberg, Anne-Dominique Toussaint, Pascal Jadecewicz, Georges Benayoun; assoc p, Yves Marmion; w, Martine Dugowson; ph, Dominique Chapuis; ed, Martine Barraque, Dominique Gallieni; m, Peter Chase; art d, Philippe Chiffre; set d, Jean-Claude Bemels; sound, Alain Villeval, Jean-Francois Auger (mixer); casting, Gigi Akoka; cos, Stephane Excoffier; makeup, Nancy Badoux

Drama   **(PR: C   MPAA: NR)**

MONEY TRAIN   ★
(U.S.) 103m Peters Entertainment; Columbia ~
Columbia c

Wesley Snipes (*John*); Woody Harrelson (*Charlie*); Robert Blake (*Patterson*); Jennifer Lopez (*Grace Santiago*); Chris Cooper (*Torch*); Joe Grifasi (*Riley*); Scott Sowers (*Mr. Brown*); Skipp Sudduth (*Kowalski*); Vincent Larensca (*Subway Robber*); Nelson Vasquez (*Subway Robber*); Vincent Patrick (*Bartender Frank*); Aida Turturro (*Woman on Platform*); Alvaleta Guess (*Woman on Platform*); Vincent Pastore (*Gambler*); David Tawil (*Gambler*); Ron Ryan (*Gambler*); Greg McKinney (*Guard*);

Mitch Kolpan (*Guard*); Jeremy Roberts (*Guard*); John Norman Thomas (*Detective*); Oni Faida Lampley (*Dispatcher*); Jack O'Connell (*Dispatcher*); Saul Stein (*Brown's Enforcer*); Manny Siverio (*Brown's Enforcer*); Johnny Centatiempo (*Brown's Enforcer*); Enrico Colantoni (*Dooley*); Christopher Anthony Young (*Guard with Dooley*); Richard Grove (*Motorman*); Steven Randazzo (*Guy at Bar*); William Charlton (*Businessman*); Josefina Diaz (*Young Woman*); Moss Porter (*Mickey*); Keith Leon Williams (*Darryl*); Jose Zuniga (*Victor*); Thomas G. Waites (*Barricade Captain*); Leikili Mark (*Punk Girl*); Kevin Guy Brown (*Punk Guy*); Bill Nunn (*Crash Train Motorman*); Sharon Schaffer (*Token Clerk*); Angel Caban (*Decoy Cop*); Joe Bacino (*Decoy Cop*); Jose Soto (*Hood*); Larry Gilliard, Jr. (*Hood*); Flex (*Hood*); Michael Artura (*Second Captain*); Mark Weil (*Stockbroker*); Joseph Wilson Ayesu (*Little Joe*); Katie Gill (*Crosswalk Child*); Cody Gill (*Crosswalk Child*)

Woody Harrelson and Wesley Snipes, co-stars of the surprise hit WHITE MEN CAN'T JUMP(1992), are reteamed in an empty-headed, and curiously mean-spirited caper-comedy about conflicts between foster brothers that come to a head when one sets out to rob the train that collects the New York City Transit Authority's money. The verbal sparring and good-natured banter between Harrelson and Snipes is undercut by the film's reliance on a series of highly implausible action scenes and a climactic caper that throws any and all credibility out the window.

Foster brothers Charlie (Woody Harrelson) and John (Wesley Snipes) have both grown up to be undercover transit cops. But their relationship becomes strained when both fall in love with their new partner Grace Santiago (Jennifer Lopez). Things get worse when compulsive gambler Charlie runs up a gambling debt of fifteen thousand dollars payable to local mobsters.

A number of high-profile subway crimes lead to run-ins with tyrannical Transit Police boss Donald Patterson (Robert Blake), who is obsessed with the flawless and punctual operation of the "money train," a high-tech subway car assigned to collect revenues from each of the system's stations. John—the responsible brother (at least, comparatively speaking), laughs off Charlie's apparently joking suggestion that that they come up with a plan to rob the money train.

Charlie's personal problems are exacerbated by the realization that Grace loves John rather than him. Charlie is also beaten by mobster Brown (Scott Somers) and his thugs, who threaten to kill John if the debt isn't paid. Angry and desperate, he decides to go ahead with his plan and on New Year's Eve, Charlie hijacks the train. Alerted to the theft by police radio, John races on his motorcycle through the subway tunnels, finds the car and tries to convince Charlie to leave the money and flee. The police are in hot pursuit, the train's brakes are damaged so it can't be stopped and it winds up hot on the tail of a Brooklyn-bound B Express full of late-night passengers.

After a number of maneuvers by both Charlie and transit police boss Patterson, Charlie and John find a way to stop the train, leap to safety and make their escape. Reaching the street, Charlie and John lose themselves in the crowd at Times Square's New Year's celebration. John is astonished to find that Charlie had managed to get away with a half-million dollars stuffed under his coat.

THE MONEY TRAIN is a cynical and lazy attempt to capitalize on the great chemistry Harrelson and Snipes demonstrated in WHITE MEN CAN'T JUMP, with the twist that they're playing a black man and white man who grew up as brothers. Harrelson's Charlie is something of a loser, resentful of always being shown up by the more stable, self-assured John. John's affection and care for Charlie are truly touching—he even goes so far as to back off from love interest Grace in order to give

Charlie a clear field. But what could have been a compelling and witty character study is destroyed by the film's attachment to a sloppily conceived caper plot punctuated by ridiculous stunts: Even Schwarzenegger couldn't make them plausible. It vaguely recalls such early '70s caper comedies as COPS AND ROBBERS, THE HOT ROCK and BANK SHOT, but has little of their wit or intricate plotting.

Following its premiere in New York, MONEY TRAIN was blamed for a series of copycat crimes involving the torching of subway token booths, a crime depicted in detail in the film. *(Violence, profanity, sexual situations.)* — B.C.

d, Joseph Ruben; p, Jon Peters, Neil Canton; exec p, Frederick Pierce, Tracey Barone, Adam Fields; co-p, Doug Claybourne, Michael Steele; w, Doug Richardson, David Loughery (from a story by Doug Richardson); ph, John W. Lindley; ed, George Bowers, Bill Pankow; m, Mark Mancina; prod d, Bill Groom; art d, Dennis Bradford, Sarah Knowles; set d, Beth Rubino; sound, James J. Sabat (mixer); fx, Phil Cory, Tim McGovern; casting, Francine Maisler; cos, Ruth E. Carter; makeup, Laini Thompson, Margot Boccia; stunts, Jack Gill

Action/Comedy/Thriller   **(PR: C   MPAA: R)**

MONTH BY THE LAKE, A   ★★½
(U.S.) 92m Miramax ~ Miramax c

Vanessa Redgrave (*Miss Bentley*); Edward Fox; Uma Thurman (*Miss Beaumont*); Alida Valli (*Mrs. Fascioli*); Alessandro Gassman (*Vittorio*); Carlo Cartier (*Mr. Bonizzoni*); Natalia Bizzi (*Mrs. Bonizzoni*); Paola Lombardi (*Enrico*); Sonia Maertinelli (*Maria*); Frances Nacman (*American Lady*); Veronica Wells (*American Lady*); Riccardo Rossi (*Guido*); Ajanta Barilli (*Italian Girl*); Bianca Tognocchi (*Angel 1*); Carlotta Bresciani (*Angel 2*); Sonia Martinelli; Frances Nacman; Veronica Wells; Riccardo Rossi; Ajanta Barilli; Bianca Tognocchi; Carlotta Bresciani

Vanessa Redgrave and Uma Thurman star in another bland reworking of SUMMERTIME and THE ROMAN SPRING OF MRS. STONE, a dependable formula in which love comes to the middle-aged and lonely in picturesque Italy.

It is 1937, and Miss Bentley (Redgrave) returns to the Lake Como vacation hotel of her youth. There she meets stuffy old Major Wilshaw (Edward Fox), and gamely sets her cap for him, despite his apparent aversion to her. Her case is not helped when she bests him at tennis, is tardy for cocktails, and dares to disagree with him in conversation. She must contend with Miss Beaumont (Thurman), a charming young flirt who decides to have a bit of fun, leading the hopelessly smitten Wilshaw by the nose. Miss Bentley consoles herself by dabbling in amateur photography, a pursuit which leads to a frightening encounter with a group of young Blackshirts.

Meanwhile, poor Wilshaw continues to make a fool of himself, especially when he attempts to perform a magic act during a soiree at the hotel. Eventually, he comes to see Miss Beaumont as a minx and Miss Bentley as a suitable mate.

Nicely dressed characters in a succulent locale work out their minute problems with minimal fuss: it's non-threatening, sexless stuff for middle-aged Anglophiles. Exceptional acting can bring this sort of thing off; here, however, Redgrave is badly miscast in a role better suited to the more acerbic talent of, say, Maggie Smith. She is nevertheless in strapping physical form (shown off to spectacular effect in a bathing suit), and can still bewitch the camera by going from haggard to agelessly radiant in a second. Thurman is suitably stunning in her floaty 1930s summer frocks, dithering and flapping her huge, bony hands like a Fitzgerald belle. It is fun to see these two cinema goddesses face each other across a generation, but the script never delivers the delicious, bitchy confrontation we're breathlessly anticipating. Fox's Major, a pompous old bore, is incomprehensible as a love object for Miss Bentley.

Art-house moguls Harvey and Bob Weinstein bankrolled this upper-middlebrow formula film in a transparent attempt to replicate their success as distributors of 1992's ENCHANTED APRIL. While A MONTH BY THE LAKE delivers the goods (luscious cinematography, tony British accents, costumes to die for) with ruthless efficiency, it's generally tame and uninspired. *(Adult situations, sexual situations.)* — D.N.

d, John Irvin; p, Robert Fox; exec p, Harvey Weinstein, Bob Weinstein; w, Trevor Bentham (based on the novel by H.E. Bates); ph, Pasqualino De Santis; ed, Peter Tanner; m, Nicola Piovani; prod d, Gianni Giovagnoni; set d, Mauro Passi; sound, David Crozier (mixer); casting, Rita Forzano; cos, Lia Morandini; makeup, Nilo Jacoponi; stunts, Franco Salamon

Drama/Comedy   **(PR: A   MPAA: PG)**

MOONLIGHT AND VALENTINO   ★★
(U.S.) 107m Working Title Films; PolyGram ~ Gramercy c

Elizabeth Perkins (*Rebecca Trager Lott*); Whoopi Goldberg (*Sylvie Morrow*); Gwyneth Paltrow (*Lucy Trager*); Kathleen Turner (*Alberta Russell*); Jon Bon Jovi (*The Painter*); Shadia Simmons (*Jenny Morrow*); Erica Luttrell (*Drew Morrow*); Matthew Koller (*Alex Morrow*); Peter Coyote (*Paul—uncredited*); Scott Wickware (*Policeman*); Kelli Fox (*Nurse*); Harrison Liu (*Mr. Wong*); Wayne Lam (*Mr. Wong's Son*); Ken Wong (*Mr. Wong's Father*); Carlton Watson (*Henrik*); Jack Jessop (*Sid*); Josef Sommer (*Thomas Trager*); Trim (*Valentino*); Jeremy Sisto (*Steven*); Alan Clifton (*Street Vendor*); Judah Katz (*Marc*); Julian Richings (*Hairstylist*)

Four middle-class women explore grief and examine personal growth in MOONLIGHT AND VALENTINO. With sparkling actresses in the lead roles, it is easy to overlook the defects and superficialities of this contemporary specimen of what used to be called a "women's movie."

When her husband Ben dies after being struck by a car while jogging, Rebecca (Elizabeth Perkins) seeks solace in her career as professor of English at a local college. Purposely repressing her mourning because she cannot face the permanence of Ben's death, Rebecca leans on the sturdy shoulders of her eccentric younger sister Lucy (Gwyenth Paltrow), her best friend Sylvie (Whoopi Goldberg), and her former stepmother Alberta (Kathleen Turner). Self-absorbed in her "why-me" worldview, Rebecca only steps outside her own misery to referee Lucy's fights with Alberta, who attacks opportunities for mothering in the same way she would tackle a Wall Street campaign.

While Sylvie deals with feelings of inadequacy in her marriage with Paul (Peter Coyote), Lucy falls for one of Rebecca's students. Encouraged by her friends, Rebecca steps out of her shadow-life long enough to bask in an affair with her house painter (pop star John Bon Jovi). The reawakening of romantic longing forces Rebecca to release her pent-up tears and to reveal her unassuaged guilt at denying Ben's desire to have kids. Crippled by their various unresolved issues, the women hold a liberating ceremony by Ben's graveside. In articulating their hidden fears, the quartet feels empowered to face their futures responsibly without any need for rationalizing self-protection.

Screenwriter Ellen Simon (daughter of Neil Simon) has inherited her father's knack for whipping out snappy one-liners. What she has not acquired is a gift for revealing the characters' attitudes through their actions. Baring their souls, Simon's creations chatter themselves and the audience into near-nervous breakdowns. Every line of dialogue seems to be a monologue in the making.

What really hurts MOONLIGHT AND VALENTINO is the self-absorption of its central character, Rebecca. Viewers will be impatient with her veil of self-indulgence. Also, the final grave-yard ritual scene smells of the kind of instant intimacy that puts dabblers in religion and psychology on bestseller lists and trivializes human suffering by denying its mysteries. (Nudity, extreme profanity, adult situations, sexual situations.) — R.P.

d, David Anspaugh; p, Alison Owen, Eric Fellner, Tim Bevan; assoc p, Liza Chasin; co-p, Mary McLaglen; w, Ellen Simon (based on her play); ph, Julio Macat; ed, David Rosenbloom; m, Howard Shore; prod d, Robb Wilson King; art d, David Ferguson; set d, Carol Lavoie; sound, Bruce Carwardine (mixer); fx, Michael Kavanagh; casting, Amanda Mackey, Cathy Sandrich; cos, Denise Cronenberg; makeup, Patricia Green

Romance/Drama (PR: C MPAA: R)

MORTAL KOMBAT ★★½
(U.S.) 101m Threshold Entertainment; New Line ~ New Line c

Christopher Lambert (Lord Rayden); Bridgette Wilson (Sonya Blade); Linden Ashby (Johnny Cage); Talisa Soto (Princess Kitana); Cary-Hiroyuki Tagawa (Shang Tsung); Trevor Goddard (Kano); Robin Shou (Liu Kang); Chris Casamassa (Scorpion); Francois Petit (Sub-Zero); Keith H. Cooke (Reptile); Hakim Alston (Fighting Monk); Kenneth Edwards (Art Lean); John Fujioka (Chief Priest); Daniel Haggard (Assistant Director); Sandy Helberg (Director); Steven Ho (Chan); Peter Jason (Master Boyd); Lloyd Kino (Grandfather); Gregory McKinney (Jaxx); Mikal Moore (Singer at Techno Club); Brice Stephens (Singer at Techno Club); Kevin Richardson (Voice of Goro); Ed Boone (Voice of Scorpion)

Derived from a popular and much-reviled video game, MORTAL KOMBAT all but abandons narrative in favor of non-stop action, the more outlandish, the better.

Mortal Kombat, the biggest martial arts tournament ever, is to be held in the Far East. Three disparate competitors have been summoned by mysterious Lord Rayden (Christopher Lambert). Johnny Cage (Linden Ashby) is a Hollywood action movie star whose bravado conceals performance anxiety. Sonya Blade (Bridgette Wilson) is a blonde, beautiful cop smarting from the death of her partner. Liu Kang (Robin Shou) intends to avenge the death of his little brother Chan (Stephen Ho) at the hands of the wicked Shang Tsung (Cary-Hiroyuki Tagawa). Soul-eating sorcerer Shang comes from an otherworldly wasteland, and will take possession of the Earth if her champions lose this year's competition. Cage, Blade and Liu are the world's last hope.

The three journey to the Temple of Light in China, governed by an unseen Emperor whose gorgeous daughter, Princess Kitana (Talisa Soto), is the 10,000 year-old heir to Outworld. The fighters are pitted against a variety of savage opponents. They include Sonya's nemesis, the one-eyed hunk of Aussie trash (Trevor Goddard) who killed her partner; four-armed colossus Prince Goro, whom Johnny sends hurtling over a cliff; zombie ninjas and a slew of viciously fanged serpents and pterodactyls which morph out of various enemy body parts. Rayden and Kitana act as spiritual advisors throughout; telling their charges they must each overcome their own worst fears: the fear of being a fake (Johnny), fear of trust (Sonya) and fear of one's own destiny (Liu Kang). The climactic showdown is between Liu Kang and Shang Tsung, and it's nearly lost when the spirit of little Chan materializes. But Liu prevails, slaughtering Shang Tsung and recovering his brother's soul. "I gotta tell you something," the enigmatic Rayden says in conclusion. "You guys did great."

MORTAL KOMBAT is not a sophisticated movie. The various plot twists seem to have been imagined by a comic-book besotted fifth-grader ("Let's have the souls of Shang Tsung's victims leave their bodies and enter him through his eyeballs!"); the characters are simply flesh-and-blood incarnations of the little animated figures that scurrying across video game screens. Tagawa dominates the picture (as he did in the misbegotten RISING SUN) with his inexhaustible panoply of arrogant sneers and scornful, evil smiles. Lambert, by contrast, lingers on the sidelines wearing a variety of coolie hats and dispensing nuggets of wisdom in a rasp of a voice that is only slightly less striking that his extraordinary silver wig.

Johnny Cage is the carrier of the obligatory wise-ass humor—"Let's dance," he says to his opponents, "this is where you fall down"—while mushy romantic stuff is avoided at all costs. The all-important action is competently photographed and slickly edited, and Jonathan Carlson's production design is rather appealing, half harem fantasy, half MAD MAX wilderness. The special effects are less special than they ought to be, running the predictable gamut of woozy morphing, deadly foreign objects emerging from human bodies and various lethal beasts that are a bit too literal—all sniping fang and claw—to be truly terrifying. George Clinton's score is a high energy cacophony that would suit the most strenuous aerobics class. (Violence, profanity, adult situations.) — D.N.

d, Paul Anderson; p, Lawrence Kasanoff; exec p, Danny Simon, Bob Engelman; assoc p, Alison Savitch, Lauri Apelian; w, Kevin Droney; ph, John R. Leonetti; ed, Martin Hunter; m, George S. Clinton; prod d, Jonathan Carlson; art d, Jeremy Cassells; set d, Susan L. Degus; sound, Steve Nelson (mixer), Peter Meiselman (mixer), David Farmer (design); fx, Alison Savitch, Stuart Robinson, R/Greenberg Associates West, Inc., Peter Montgomery, Buena Vista Visual Effects, Ron Trost, Class A Special Effects, Frank Welker; casting, Fern Champion, Mark Paladini; cos, Ha Nguyen; makeup, Mony Mansano, Kano/Monk; stunts, Pat E. Johnson

Fantasy/Martial Arts/Action (PR: A MPAA: PG-13)

MOSAIC PROJECT, THE ★★
(U.S.) 89m Artists View Entertainment; Caroli Pictures Productions ~ Monarch Home Video c

Jon Tabler (Ken); Ben Marley (Jeff); Colleen Coffey (Ash); Joe Estevez (Fred); Robert Z'Dar (Harry); Julie Strain (Tess); Neil Delaima (Keller); Lena Osborn (Jill); Sean Donahue (Jerry); Billy Million (Frank); Gino Dentie (Mr. G.); Ashlie Rhey (Stewardess); Chuck Loch (Scientist); Narda Torrealba (Monica); Scott Ziehl (Dead Man); John Sjogren (Dead Man); William Buzick, III (Train Bum); James Zahnd (Train Track Thug); Nickolas Fleming (Train Track Thug); Edwin Larson (Train Track Thug); Dr. Zarif (New Mosaic); Mike Gunther (New Mosaic); Kelly Brown (New Mosaic)

Boys will be be overgrown boys in this Yankee Doodle riff on James Bonding. Since the athletic prowess of the leading men isn't complemented by any similar agility as actors, this globe-trotting adventure seems to be missing a few pieces.

To prevent criminal mastermind Keller (Neil Delaima) from activiating an espionage device pilfered from the US, fed agent Jerry (Sean Donahue) hides The Mosaic Project before taking a rooftop plunge to his death. (Implanting Mosaic computer chips into the brain transforms an average spy into a superhero programmed with multiple languages and a wide range of lethal self-defense capabilities.) By accident, two Fresno ne'er-do-wells, Ken (Jon Tabler) and Jeff (Ben Marley) discover the secret weapon. Whisked away to Washington, DC, Jeff and Ken receive instant brain surgery (instead of a reward) and new careers in the challenging world of espionage. Not cognizant of the fact that their new boss Fred (Joe Estevez) is in league with Keller, the former day laborers embark on a series of dangerous escapades with fellow Mosaic, Ash (Colleen Coffey). After putting a gaggle of martial artists out of commission, Jeff and Ken exit an international crimeworld party with counterfeit forgery plates. Later, a raid on Keller headquarters costs Ash her life, although she does eliminate Keller's first-in-command, Frank (Billy Million), and reveal Fred's treachery to her cospies. Now on the run, the accidental agents realize that Fred plans to subject them to a deadly chip removal operation. Defeating three new-improved Mosaics sent to unemploy them, the James Bond-wannabees allow the feds to think they've been dispatched by one of the human Mosaic bombs. After Keller and Fred re-enact the climax of DUEL IN THE SUN, Ken and Jeff are free to test their implanted dexterities in the upscale job market.

Although this film's premise is flexible enough to supply a TV action show with a season full of plot lines, this direct-to-video just squeezes into the marginally entertaining category. Fortunately, the basic wish fulfillment of two Average Joes becoming Napoleon Solo and Ilya Kuryakin overnight should appeal to college-age action buffs who feel invulnerable after a few beers. Showing its martial artistry during some combative Interpol skirmishes, THE MOSAIC PROJECT kenpos with a lot more vigor than style. What ultimately sinks this escapism is a failure to freshen up stale spy jinks with action ingenuity, and the low wattage of the cast. In addition to the dim contributions of junk veterans like Estevez and Robert Z'Dar, leading men Tabler and Marley demonstrate they need acting chips implanted in their brains before birthing future performances. Despite its sci-fi twist on the How-I-Spent-My-Summer-Vacation fantasy syndrome, THE MOSAIC PROJECT is unable to maximize a series of padded adventures into dynamite bursts of action. As vocational guidance thrillers go, this undistinguished body-blocking pic is light years better than MONEY TO BURN but not nearly as jazzy as IF LOOKS COULD KILL. (*Graphic violence, profanity.*) — R.P.

d, John Sjogren; p, John Sjogren, Scott Ziehl; co-p, Tom Bolger; w, John Sjogren, Scott Ziehl; ph, Steven R. Miles, Kevin McCoy; ed, James Post, Paul Anderson; m, Nigel Holton; prod d, Pat Sjogren; art d, Fred Stuhr, Garrett Pelicastro; fx, FX House; casting, John Sjogren, Scott Ziehl; stunts, Sean Donahue

Action/Martial Arts/Spy   (PR: C   MPAA: R)

MOVING THE MOUNTAIN   ★★★
(U.S./U.K.) 83m Xingu Films ~ October Films c
(AKA: CHINA: MOVING THE MOUNTAIN)

Wang Dan; Wang Chaohua; Wu'er Kaixi; Chai Ling; Li Lu; Zhang Jin-Ming (*Li Lu—Age 10*); Huang Yi-Ming (*Li Lu—Age 4*)

An overview of the history of modern China leading up to the 1989 Tiananmen Square massacre, MOVING THE MOUNTAIN is a strong reminder of a time when China seemed on the brink of a democratic revolution. Dramatic re-creations combine with documentary footage and interviews to produce a dynamic snapshot of the spirit of a generation.

The film focuses on one central character, Li Lu, to take the viewer from the terrors of the Cultural Revolution to the romance of resistance and subsequent reflection. Born one month before Mao launched the Great Proletarian Cultural Revolution in 1966, Li Lu grows up with the contradictions, and sudden reversals, of

Chinese socialism. Following Mao's death (in 1976), and Deng Xiaoping's rise to power, the 1980s are a time of constant struggle and ideological confusion. Li Lu sets about educating himself, reading everything he can find as banned Western and Chinese books become available on the black market. But China's economic growth does not ease the political oppression and, by 1989, the climate is one of bitterness, frustration, and anger.

That year Li Lu boards a train for Beijing, many miles away. Revolution is in the air, and thousands have gathered in Tiananmen Square—the symbolic heart of China—to demand reform. As Li Lu joins the growing movement of resistance, four of the other student leaders are introduced. One of them, Wang Dan, is interviewed in a secret location in Beijing. One of the first and most important student leaders, he served a prison sentence for his involvement in the Tiananmen Square demonstrations and now lives under constant surveillance by the authorities.

Interviewed in New York, united for the first time since they were together in the Square, are Li Lu, Wang Chaohua, Wu'er Kiaxi, and Chai Ling. They reflect on the immediate build-up to June 3, 1989, when martial law was declared and troops converged on Tiananmen Square from all directions.

The final third of the film traces the aftermath: hiding from the authorities, flight, and escape. All the student leaders are still involved in campaigning for Chinese democracy. They note that the movement was not born in 1989, nor was it killed when the tanks rolled into Tiananmen Square. Relating their movement to a Chinese parable, Li Lu predicts that with the continued efforts of his and future generations, one day "the mountain will be moved."

Director Michael Apted is best known for the 7 UP series of documentaries, as well as Hollywood features like COAL MINER'S DAUGHTER, GORILLAS IN THE MIST, and NELL. However, the moving force behind this documentary appears to be its producer, Trudie Styler. Styler and her husband, musician Sting, have long championed humanitarian causes. MOVING THE MOUNTAIN has been accused of oversimplifying some of the issues in this complex and highly-charged history. Some say the film minimizes the ideological differences between the student leaders and glosses over the possible involvement of the Hong King Triads (and even the CIA) in facilitating the escapes from China. Historical debates aside, MOVING THE MOUNTAIN provides a great deal of valuable information and is a fascinating portrait of youth, once fired by the revolutionary spirit, now burdened by exile and struggling to retain hope. (*Adult situations.*) — J.S.

d, Michael Apted; p, Trudie Styler; w, Michael Apted; ph, Maryse Alberti; ed, Susanne Rostock; m, Liu Sola

Documentary/Historical   (PR: A   MPAA: NR)

MURDER IN THE FIRST   ★★½
(U.S.) 122m Le Studio Canal Plus; Wolper Organization ~ Warner Bros. c

Christian Slater (*James Stamphill*); Kevin Bacon (*Henri Young*); Gary Oldman (*Associate Warden Glenn*); Embeth Davidtz (*Mary McCasslin*); Bill Macy (*William McNeil*); Stephen Tobolowsky (*Mr. Henkin*); Brad Dourif (*Byron Stamphill*); R. Lee Ermey (*Judge Clawson*); Mia Kirshner (*Adult Rosetta Young*); Ben Slack (*Jerry Hoolihan*); Stefan Gierasch (*Warden James Humson*); Kyra Sedgwick (*Blanche*); Alexander Bookston (*Alcatraz Doc*); Richie Allan (*Jury Foreman*); Herb Ritts (*Mike Kelly*); Charles Boswell (*Simpson*); David Sterling (*Inmate Rufus "Roy" McCain*); Michael Melvin (*Inmate Arthur "Doc" Barker*); George Maguire (*1st Inmate*); Nick Scoggin (*2nd In-*

mate); Douglas Bennett *(3rd Inmate)*; Joseph Richards *(4th Inmate)*; Julius Varnado *(5th Inmate)*; Tony Barr *(Winthrop)*; Stuart Nisbet *(Harve)*; Gary Ballard *(Alcatraz Guard Swenson)*; Randy Pelish *(Alcatraz Guard Whitney)*; Sonny H. King *(Alcatraz Guard Wimer)*; Eddie Bowz; Brian Leckner; Time Winters; James Keane; Lance Brady; Michael Merrins *(Alcatraz Guards)*; Ray Quartermus; Lee E. Mathis; Wayne Parks; Warren Spottswood *(City Jail Guards)*; Thomas Fenske *(Newsreel Reporter)*; Robert Lee *(Newsreel Reporter)*; Wally Rose *(Shopkeeper)*; Amanda Borden *(Rosetta Young—Age 9)*; Eve Brenner *(Winthrop's Secretary)*; Joseph Cole *(Marshall Gates)*; Richard Kwong *(Chinese Monk)*; Gary Lee Davis *(Giant of a Man)*

A horrors-of-prison-life diatribe that abruptly becomes an earnest courtroom drama, MURDER IN THE FIRST is filled with good intentions. It's based on a true story, but the conflicts are painted in such stark shades of black and white that it seems entirely forced and implausible, despite an excellent performance by Kevin Bacon.

The film opens with a mock newsreel story about the 1938 attempt by four convicts to escape the notorious island prison on Alcatraz. Two died and two were returned to jail, where one ratted to prison authorities. The other, Henri Young (Kevin Bacon), is tortured and thrown into solitary confinement by sadistic Warden Glenn (Gary Oldman). Young spends three years in solitary, lying naked in the dark and filth.

Young is finally released into the general population, where he promptly kills the inmate who betrayed him. He's transferred to a jail in San Francisco to stand trial for first-degree murder, and his case is assigned to an untried eager beaver named James Stamphill (Christian Slater). To everyone but Stamphill, it's clear that the young lawyer has been given the case because it appears open-and-shut: the court-appointed lawyer is expected to do nothing more than grease Young's path to the electric chair. Stamphill's older, savvier brother (Brad Dourif) advises him not to rock the boat. To make matters worse, Young is a most unprepossessing client: withdrawn, silent and crippled (the result of one of Glenn's many savage assaults), he's a pitiful but not necessarily sympathetic figure.

Stamphill takes it all as a personal challenge. First he coaxes Young to talk to him—baseball provides the link that finally brings the two men together—then gets him to tell him how his life took the sorry course it did. After learning that orphaned Young, trying desperately to care for his younger sister, was thrown into prison as a teenager for stealing $5 from a rural post office, Stamphill decides he must help him. His novel tactic: to put the system on trial, shifting the focus off Young and onto a brutal, corrupt penal establishment that gives free reign to sadistic perverts, exemplified by Warden Glenn.

Stamphill succeeds in exposing Glenn's depravity, and wins the case, at least in the sense that Young isn't convicted of first-degree murder. That Young goes back to prison and dies there is downplayed as much as possible, so the audience can leave feeling good that his was the case that "brought down Alcatraz," as the film's promotional materials trumpeted.

Despite its wealth of period detail, MURDER IN THE FIRST feels false. Director Mark Rocco apparently couldn't draw a consistent level of performance from his cast, and star Slater is a large part of the movie's problem. Even in a 1940s haircut and a 1940s suit, his manner is pure, smirking contemporary smart-ass, and it gets in the way of characterization at every turn. Gary Oldman's foaming-at-the-mouth performance—much the same one he delivered in the more straightforwardly outlandish THE PROFESSIONAL—also strains audience credulity: his Warden Glenn is so patently deranged that you have to wonder how he's

stayed out of the psycho ward, let alone managed to hold any sort of job.

Had the film not been released in January, ensuring that it was completely forgotten by the time Academy Award nominations were made, Bacon's performance—even in an undistinguished film—would have been guaranteed an Oscar nomination. He drools, he limps, he grovels, he cries, he stammers—but despite excesses, this is real acting, and it's extremely effective. *(Violence, adult situations, sexual situations.)* — M.M.

d, Marc Rocco; p, Marc Frydman, Mark Wolper; exec p, David L. Wolper, Marc Rocco; co-p, Deborah Lee; w, Dan Gordon; ph, Fred Murphy; ed, Russell Livingstone; m, Christopher Young; prod d, Kirk M. Petruccelli; art d, Michael Rizzo; set d, Greg Grande; sound, Ed White (mixer); casting, Mary Jo Slater; cos, Sylvia Vega-Vasquez; makeup, Lisa Rocco; stunts, Doug Coleman

Drama   **(PR: C   MPAA: R)**

MURIEL'S WEDDING   ★★½
(Australia) 105m House and Moorhouse Films ~
Miramax c

Toni Collette *(Muriel)*; Bill Hunter *(Bill)*; Rachel Griffiths *(Rhonda)*; Jeane Drynan *(Betty)*; Gennie Nevinson *(Deidre)*; Matt Day *(Brice)*; Daniel Lapaine *(David Van Arkle)*; Sophie Lee *(Tania)*; Belina Jarrett *(Janine)*; Rosalind Hammond *(Cheryl)*; Pippa Grandison *(Nicole)*; Chris Haywood *(Ken Blundell)*; Daniel Wyllie *(Perry)*; Gabby Millgate *(Joanie)*; Katie Sauders *(Penelope)*; Dene Kermond *(Malcolm)*; Susan Prior *(Girl at Wedding)*; Nathan Kaye *(Chook)*; Cecily Polson *(Tania's Mother)*; Rob Steele *(Higgins)*; Genevieve Picot *(Store Detective)*; Richard Sutherland *(Constable Saunders)*; Steve Smith *(Constable Gillespie)*; Jeamin Lee *(Chinese Waitress)*; Jon-Claire Lee *(Chinese Maitre D')*; Kuni Hashimoto *(Akira)*; Ken Senga *(Victor Keinosuke)*; Des Rodgers *(Island MC)*; Rohan Jones; Scott Hall-Watson; Craig Olson; Justin Witham *(Restaurant Boys)*; Rodney Arnold *(Ejected Diner)*; Barry Crocker *(Himself)*; Steve Cox *(Criuse Taxi Driver)*; Kevin Copeland *(Sailor)*; James Schramko *(Sailor)*; Richard Morecroft *(Himself)*; Richard Carter *(Federal Policeman)*; John Gaden *(Doctor)*; Heather Mitchell *(Bridal Manageress #1)*; Heidi Lapaine *(Bridal Assistant #1)*; Diane Smith *(Physiotherapist)*; Darrin Klimek *(Rhonda's Taxi Driver)*; Penne Hackforth-Jones *(Bridal Manageress #2)*; Kirsty Hinchcliffe *(Bridal Assistant #2)*; Robert Alexander *(Barrister)*; Troy Hardy *(Young Boy)*; Robyn Pitt Owen *(Singer at Muriel's Wedding)*; Annie Byron *(Rhonda's Mother)*; Jacqueline Linke; Alvaro Marques; Fiona Sullivan; Ineke Rapp; Julian Garner *(Members of the Press)*; Vincent Ball *(Priest)*; John Hoare *(Well Wisher)*; Frankie Davidson *(Sergeant)*; Louise Cullen *(Deidre's Friend)*; Basil Clarke *(Funeral Priest)*; John Walton *(Taxi Driver)*

P.J. Hogan's MURIEL'S WEDDING, one of the surprise hits of early 1995, harks back to the recent US success of other Australian films with its satirical, delightfully campy style. Toni Collette stars as Muriel Heslop, a young ABBA fan who sets out to make a life for herself by leaving her hometown, family and friends.

Muriel is a plump and unhappy woman who dreams of escaping to a new and better life through marriage. She's also a fanatical follower of the Swedish pop band ABBA, whose songs are featured prominently on the soundtrack. She's dumped by friends who look down on her and ridiculed by her father (Bill Hunter) for being useless. When her parents give her a blank check to get her started in business, she seizes the opportunity to reinvent herself, emptying the family bank account and leaving provincial Porpoise Spit. She surprises her vacationing ex-friends by showing up at the same resort they're staying at, but winds up making a new friend in Rhonda (Rachel Griffith). She moves to Sydney, finds a job, changes her name, and embarks on new adventures.

Secretly Muriel feeds her obsession by going to wedding boutiques to fit dresses and by keeping a private photo album of herself in different dresses. Through the personal ads, she meets and marries a wealthy young white South African (David Lapaine) who is trying to secure Australian citizenship so that he can swim in the Olympics. Muriel is thrilled at her wedding, despite the groom's obvious apprehension.

Muriel cannot sustain her dreams. Rhonda is confined to a wheelchair after sudden surgery to remove a cancerous tumor in her back; Muriel's father leaves her mother (Jeanie Drynan) for another woman (Gennie Nevinson) and loses his job; and her mother kills herself with sleeping pills soon after the wedding. Muriel decides she cannot continue to lie. She resumes her true first name, gives up on her marriage, and asks Rhonda, who moves back to Porpoise Spit to live with her mother, to return to Sydney with her.

Like the Australian hits STRICTLY BALLROOM (1993) and THE ADVENTURES OF PRISCILLA, QUEEN OF THE DESERT (1994), MURIEL'S WEDDING projects a cheeky, benevolent satirical spirit, celebrating the dreams of losers and outcasts. The film relies heavily on Toni Collette, who supplies the necessary screen charisma. Her Muriel is emotionally flamboyant, by turns mopish and highly excitable.

Ultimately, the comedy here is grounded in self-hatred, hostility, and despair. Nearly everyone who wanders through this brash and deliberately tasteless film is stupid, ungainly, or grotesquely tragic. But this only heightens the pleasure during moments of delirious merriment, as when Muriel lip-synchs an ABBA song at a karaoke contest, resplendent and unashamed in a tight-fitting white satin jumpsuit. *(Profanity, sexual situations.)* — M.F.

d, P.J. Hogan; p, Lynda House, Jocelyn Moorhouse; assoc p, Michael D. Aglion, Tony Mahood; w, P.J. Hogan; ph, Martin McGrath; ed, Jill Bilcock; m, Peter Best; prod d, Patrick Reardon; art d, High Bateup; set d, Jane Murphy, Glen W. Johnson; ch, John O'Connell; sound, David Lee, Glenn Newnham, Livia Ruzic, Roger Savage; fx, Ray Fowler; casting, Alison Barrett; cos, Terry Ryan; makeup, Noriko Watanabe; stunts, Rocky McDonald

Comedy   (PR: C   MPAA: R)

MUTANT SPECIES   ★
(U.S.) 100m Southern Star Studios ~
LIVE Entertainment c

Leo Rossi *(Hollinger)*; Ted Prior *(Trotter)*; Denise Crosby *(Carol Anne)*; Grant Gelt *(Jordie)*; Powers Boothe *(Frost)*; Wilford Brimley *(Devro)*; Grant James *(Senator Roberts)*; Jackson Bostwick *(Tex)*; Jack Verell *(Jones)*; Mark Krasnoff *(Lozano)*; Jimmy Steger *(Willie)*; Ronald McCall *(McCall)*; Douglas M. Griffin *(Spivak)*; Patrick Gallagher *(Team Leader)*; Jeffrey Graham *(Sizer)*; Gordon Lett *(Maravek)*; John Graham *(Harter)*; Dan Chandler *(Colonel)*; Erik Fallin *(Aide)*; Constance Yelverton *(Officer)*; Samantha Petrey *(Tiffany)*; Melissa McBride *(Tiffany's Mom)*; John McConnell *(Redneck)*; Daryl Arden *(Vogel)*; David G. Bowers *(Pettila)*; Eric Cadora *(NCO)*; Lenny Herb *(Radio Man)*; John Lopez *(MP)*; Adrian Colon; Steve Hale; Buck Kinsaul; Anthony Fleet *(Soldiers)*

This PREDATOR imitation botches an opportunity for arresting sci-fi, veering from a vigorous action audience-pounder into a latent retread of BEAUTY AND THE BEAST. Exceptionally strong production values are nullified by poor acting and by direction that has the professional soullessness of TV car commercials.

When a rocket carrying toxic waste into outer space misfires, a special forces squad is called in to clean up the spill. Unknown to the task force, they have been set up by a crazed bio-design proponent, Frost (Powers Boothe), for a one-way trip to field test a new genetic warfare creation. Obeying orders to absorb the rocket cargo (a mutant DNA strain that transform ordinary men into killing machines) squad leader Hollinger (Leo Rossi) is genetically turned into a fiend who machine guns his own men. As best buddy Trotter (Ted Prior) outwits the mutating soldier and survives the massacre, Hollinger metamorphisizes into the Great White Hunter of Frost's dreams. Discredited by patriotic General Devro (Wilford Brimley), who's vehemently opposed to Frost's devaluing of human life, Frost deviously works to keep his monster-combatant alive while seeking to eliminate witnesses with the Prometheus Plan, in which the crash site environs would be scorched by fire. With the aid of farmer Carol Anne (Denise Crosby) and her quick-witted teenaged brother Jordie (Grant Gelt), Trotter evades the rampaging mutant and Frost's loyal troops. As the monster picks off soldiers with enviable dispatch and regenerates itself after their pitiful strafings, Trotter and Jordie must trick the creature after it kidnaps Carol Anne. In the end, the new super-soldier Hollinger allows himself to be blown up after Trotter manages to reason with what's left of the mutant's human side. As the Prometheus Plan obliterates the monster's killing fields, Trotter, Carol Anne, and Jordie escape and survive to testify against Frost's insane bio-scheme.

While it's conceivable that the Pentagon might develop an unstoppable, artificially molded grunt, it's hard to buy this film's premise that they would do so with such risk of public exposure. That concept is only one of several hard candy balls of exposition apt to get lodged in the throats of even the most cooperative genre devotees. As nonsensical escapism buttressed by specially effective carnage, MUTANT SPECIES initially holds promise. In stumbling over its fantasy terrain, however, it becomes a mutation of a different color, not the antimilitary blast it tries to be but a fatally confused sci-fi revamp of THE MOST DANGEROUS GAME. Marring an already structurally challenged screenplay is what could be called the Star Intrusion Factor. Obviously, Boothe and Brimley were hired only for marquee value, and their scenes carry the irrelevant air of excess dramatic baggage. It's not that they don't help inch the plot along, it's that their scenes are clumsily dropped into the ongoing narrative, serving only as interruptions. Not that MUTANT SPECIES couldn't use some entertaining interruptions. Miscast as the Marine-android, high-strung wise guy Rossi captures neither the cocky demeanor of a born soldier nor the pathos of a frightened man surrendering his humanity to duty. And there is no more ludicrous scene of recent vintage than the pep talk Trotter gives his old-pal-turned-monster about behaving like a true blue Uncle Sammy boy. Looking like a refugee from THE NEVERENDING STORY, the Hollinger-creature blubbers his way into the annals of monster movie camp. *(Graphic violence, extreme profanity.)* — R.P.

d, David A. Prior; p, Robert Willoughby, Michael W. Evans, Jr.; exec p, Patrick Gallagher; w, William Virgil, David A. Prior; ph, Carlos Gonzalez; ed, Tony Malinowski; m, William T. Stromberg; prod d, Andrew Menzies; sound, Palmer "Whit" Norris (mixer); fx, Gary Beall; casting, Billy Da Motta; cos, Quenby Tilloy; makeup, Amanda Wells, Paul Palos, Ben Rock; stunts, Gary Beall

Action/Science Fiction/Horror   (PR: O   MPAA: R)

MUTE WITNESS ★★★

(Germany/U.K./Russia) 90m Comet Films;
Avrora Media; Cobblestone Pictures; Patmos Films ~
Sony Pictures Classics c

Marina Sudina *(Billy Hughes)*; Fay Ripley *(Karen Hughes)*;
Evan Richards *(Andy Clarke)*; Oleg Jankowskij *(Larsen)*; Igor
Volkov *(Arkadi)*; Sergei Karlenkov *(Lyosha)*; Alexander Buriev
(Strohbecker); Alec Guinness *(The Reaper)*; Alexander Piatov
(Wartschuk); Nikoai Pastuhov *(Janitor)*; Stephen Bouser
(Lovett); Valeri Barahtin *(Mitja)*; Nikolai Chindjaikin *(Inspector
Pekar)*; Vasheslav Naumenko *(Officer Mlekov)*; Larisa Husno-
lina *(Victim)*; Olga Tolstetskaya *(Actress)*; Denis Karasiov *(Fake
Policeman)*; Igor Iljin *(Fake Policeman)*; Oleg Abramov *(Dou-
ble)*; Uri Sherstiniov *(Angry Neighbour)*; Ludmilla Makeeva
(Neighbor's Wife); Vladimir Salnikov *(Lab Assistant)*; Sascha
Buchman *(Alex)*; Natalia Poliushkina *(Natasha)*; Konstantin Sit-
nikov *(Angry Props Manager)*; Regina Peter *(Telephone Operator's Voice)*; Norbert Soentgen *(Peeping Tom)*

This offbeat, self-referential genre picture gets off to a great start,
and though it loses steam about two-thirds of the way through,
it's a promising feature debut for writer-director Anthony Waller.

A lone woman is terrorized by a masked intruder, who finally
murders her. Her death throes are protracted and theatrical:
deliberately theatrical, in fact, as we're watching a film-within-
a-film. Mute Billy (Marina Sudina) is a special effects artist. The
cocky director, Andy (Evan Richards), is dating Billy's sister,
Karen (Fay Ripley). They're shooting on cavernous, antiquated
sound stages—the film was actually shot at the Mosfilm studios—with a Russian cast and crew.

That night, Billy goes back to the studio to retrieve something
and gets locked in. Unable to call for help, she goes exploring
and stumbles upon crew members Arkadi (Igor Volkov) and
Lyosha (Sergei Karlenkov), who are shooting a porno movie.
Matters take a sudden, terrifying turn when the porno movie
becomes a snuff film, and a careless move on Billy's part alerts
the murderers to her presence. She leads them on a chase through
winding corridors, elevator shafts, and basement tunnels. Just
when it seems there's nowhere left for her to run, Karen and
Andy arrive and the killers are forced to abandon their pursuit.

The police are called, but Lyosha and Arkadi claim that they
were just testing some special effects. The police are inclined to
believe their countrymen, especially after Billy takes them to the
basement elevator shaft where she saw body parts stuffed in a
garbage bag and they find nothing but ordinary garbage. Only
enigmatic Inspector Larsen (Oleg Jankowskij), formerly of the
KGB, seems to be on the side of the Americans. He warns that if
the Russians were making a snuff movie, they're probably associated with "The Reaper," a shadowy and dangerous organized
crime figure.

Billy returns to her own apartment. While she's bathing, the
pornographers burst in and question her about a mysterious
computer diskette. Larsen rescues Billy and informs her that this
diskette contains damaging information about the Reaper's
criminal enterprises. Larsen's opportune arrival seems suspicious—could he be working for the Russian Mafia?

Billy remembers having seen a diskette at the studio, so
Larsen takes her back there. Andy and Karen also head for the
studio, where the Reaper's minions are gathering in ominous
black cars. Larsen takes the diskette, and Andy and Karen arrive
in time to see Larsen shoot Billy, who collapses in a pool of
blood. The Reaper and his gang drive off, and Billy gets to her
feet: her "death" was a cleverly contrived special effect.

An inventive thriller about innocents abroad, MUTE WIT-
NESS pays homage to the conventions of the genre and eventually trips over its own cleverness. But the first third is a lean,

nail-biting knockout that takes the most cliched of situations—a
girl trapped in a scary place filled with dangerous people—and
gives it a series of fresh, frightening twists. Waller was clearly
inspired by the many Hitchcock films in which fresh-faced
Americans are caught in webs woven by nightmarish foreigners.
Indeed, at its best, his film lives up to the term "Hitchcockian."

The plot contains twists and turns aplenty, and the Russian
locale is a boon (the story was originally set in Chicago, where
it could easily have looked grindingly familiar). Billy is a spunky
and resourceful heroine, even if Waller does strain viewers'
credulity by having her insist on going home alone after her
dreadful ordeal at the studio. And it's a shame to see Billy
reduced to such humiliating inventions as trying to attract the
attention of a neighborhood Peeping Tom by baring her breasts
(the killers are in her apartment and she hopes the voyeur will
call the police). By the time it unveils its final plot reversal,
MUTE WITNESS has stooped to increasingly elaborate impos-
sibilities of the F/X (1986) variety. Still, it's an impressive debut,
and for much of its running time a genuinely fresh and entertaining thriller. *(Violence, adult situations, sexual situations, nudity,
profanity.)* — M.M.

d, Anthony Waller; p, Alexander Buchman, Norbert Soentgen,
Anthony Waller; exec p, Richard Claus; assoc p, Werner Konig,
Pieter Lony; co-p, Grigory Riazhsky, Alexander Atanesjan; w,
Anthony Waller; ph, Egon Werdin; ed, Peter Adam; m, Wilbert
Hirsch; prod d, Matthias Kammermeier; art d, Barbara Becker;
sound, Albert Avramenko (recordist); fx, Victor Orlov, Pavel
Terchov, Christian Burgdorff, Opitical Arts; casting, Nina Sokul-
Matsuk, Elena Denisova; cos, Svetlana Luzanova; makeup, Irina
Morozova; stunts, Sergei Vorobiov

Thriller/Mystery/Drama **(PR: C MPAA: R)**

MY ANTONIA ★★

(U.S.) 92m Gideon Productions; Fast Track Films;
Wilshire Court Productions ~ Paramount Home Video c

Jason Robards *(Grandfather Burden)*; Eva Marie Saint *(Grandmother Burden)*; Neil Patrick Harris *(Jim Burden)*; Elina Lowensohn *(Antonia)*; Jan Triska *(Mr. Shimerda)*; Norbert Weisser
(Otto); Anne Tremko *(Lena)*; Travis Fine *(Harry Paine)*; Mira
Furlan *(Mrs. Shimerda)*; Boris Krutonog *(Pavel)*; Bobby Goldstein *(Ambrosch Shimerda)*; Endre Hules *(Russian Peter)*; Olek
Krupa *(Krajiek)*; T. Max Graham *(Mr. Harling)*; Myra Turley
(Mrs. Harling); John Livingston *(Charley Harling)*; Sarah Bern-
hardt *(Sally Harling)*; Devon Cahill *(Nina Harling)*; Blair Wil-
liamson *(Marek Shimerda)*; Lauren Montgomery *(Yulka
Shimerda)*; Cinnamon Schultz *(Helga)*; Megan Birdsall *(Mar-
garet)*; Lemartt Holman *(Blindman Arnault)*; Abby Sullivan
(Mrs. Carlsen); Betty Laird *(Mrs. Vannis)*; Brendan McCurdy
(Ambrosch Cuzak); Ian Atwood *(Leo Cuzak)*; Kyla Pratt *(Yulka
Cuzak)*; Peggy Friesen *(A Woman)*; Joan Hennecke *(Another
Woman)*; Tom Wees *(Conductor)*

Literary prairie queen Willa Cather hasn't fared too well with
contemporary TV adaptations of her work. The creative personnel behind the stuffy O, PIONEERS and the flat MY ANTONIA
seem transfixed by their reverence for the material, stricken with
Hallmark Hall of Fame-itis and encased in Sunday School ser-
monizing.

Following the smallpox deaths of his parents, Virginian teen
Jimmy Burden (Neil Patrick Harris) finds himself transplanted
to the rolling farmlands of the Midwest during the great immigrant migration of the late 1800s. Though yielding to his strict
grandparents, Mr. and Mrs. Burden (Jason Robards and Eva
Marie Saint), Jimmy finds a soul mate in free-spirited Antonia
Shimerda (Elina Lowensohn) whose Russian immigrant family

is ill-prepared for the prejudices and hardships awaiting them as farmers. Guiding their grandson's future, the Burdens are charitable to the emigree Bohemians but urge Jimmy to confine his relationship with Antonia to tutoring her in English. Defeated by his failure to provide for his large family, Mr. Shimerda (Jan Triska) shoots himself. Come springtime, the Burdens decide to retire to the city so Jimmy can receive a better education. Defying her husband's dictum, Mrs. Burden arranges for Antonia to secure a serving position in the house next door to theirs. Angering her new employers after Jimmy fights with Harry Paine (Travis Fine) over her at a dance, Antonia accepts a declasse hotel job, dismisses Jimmy's romantic interest in her, and encourages him to succeed at Harvard. While Jimmy achieves his ivy-covered goals despite the sexual distraction of Antonia's friend Lena (Anne Tremko), less-fortunate Antonia encounters disgrace and unwed motherhood after her elopement with Paine. Later, attorney Jimmy is overjoyed that his beloved Antonia has found contentment with an upright farmer husband and many children.

Despite all the highlights of Cather's masterful tome—births, deaths, winter storms, decades of unrequited love—this made-for-cable movie has all the impact of a schoolmarm reciting grammatical tables. As restrained and tasteful as a leather-bound copy of Cather, this movie is a rather tidy tribute to the unruly pioneer spirit Cather was celebrating. Because her yarn is so solidly constructed and because Robards and Saint flawlessly embody their rural characters, MY ANTONIA is a pleasant viewing experience if not a memorable one. What's missing (and this can only partially be attributed to Harris's colorless reading of narrative passages from the novel) is the sense of connection between rowdy Antonia and puppy-doggish Jimmy. Through a combination of sincere but foot-dragging direction and a script encumbered with years of piled-up incidents, the innocent friendship-turned-social tragedy never registers in more than flashes. Refusing to condescend to Cather's regional types and elevated by a firm period sense, MY ANTIONIA is an honorable failure. But the rich panorama of the novel deserved more than this Cliff Notes guide to Cather country. (*Violence, profanity, sexual situations.*) — R.P.

d, Joseph Sargent; p, Victoria Riskin; exec p, David Rintels; w, Victoria Riskin (based on the novel by Willa Cather); ph, Robert Primes; ed, Debra Karen; m, David Shire; prod d, James L. Schoppe; set d, Marcia Calosio; sound, Sunny Meyer (mixer), Darin Knight (mixer); fx, Gary King, Ultimate Special Effects; casting, Dan Shaner; cos, Sandra Culotta; makeup, Claudia Thompson

Drama   (PR: A   MPAA: PG)

MY FAMILY: MI FAMILIA   ★★★
(U.S.) 125m Majestic Films; American Playhouse Theatrical Films; American Zoetrope; Newcomm ~ New Line c
(AKA: MY FAMILY)

Jimmy Smits (*Jimmy Sanchez*); Esai Morales (*Chucho*); Eduardo Lopez Rojas (*Jose Sanchez*); Jenny Gago (*Maria Sanchez*); Elpidia Carrillo (*Isabel Magana*); Lupe Ontiveros (*Irene Sanchez*); Jacob Vargas (*Young Jose Sanchez*); Jennifer Lopez (*Young Maria*); Maria Canals (*Young Irene Sanchez*); Leon Singer (*El Californio*); Michael De Lorenzo (*Butch Mejia*); Jonathan Hernandez (*Young Jimmy*); Constance Marie (*Toni Sanchez*); Edward James Olmos (*Paco, the Narrator*); Enrique Castillo (*Memo Sanchez*); Scott Bakula (*David Ronconi*); Mary Steenburgen (*Gloria*); Dedee Pfeiffer (*Karen Gillespie*); Rafael Cortes (*Roberto*); Ivette Reina (*Trini*); Amelia Zapata (*Roberto's

Girlfriend); Emilio Del Haro (*Ox Cart Driver*); Abel Woolrich (*Ox Cart Driver*); Rosalee Mayeux (*Maria's Employer*); Alicia Del Lago (*Maria's Aunt*); Thomas Rosales (*The Boatman*); Anthony Gonzalez (*Baby Paco*); Cassandra Campos (*Baby Irene*); Michael Gonzalez (*Little Paco*); Susanna Campos (*Little Irene*); Benito Martinez (*Young Paco*); Greg Albert (*Young Memo*); Cris Franco; Salvador Hernandez; Samuel Hernandez; Juan Jimenez; Jesus Alberto Guzman; Jose Mario Rodriguez; Arturo Palacios (*Mariachi Band*); Valente Rodriguez (*Chucho's Friend*); Eddie Ayala (*Chucho's Friend*); Romeo Rene Fabian (*Eddie*); Bel Hernandez (*Eddie's Mom*); Jeanette Jurado (*Rosie*); David Salas; Bill Mondragon; Eric Mondragon; Dennis Jimenez; Alex Tanasi (*The Originals*); Seidy Lopez (*Lena*); George Lopez, Jr. (*Ballplayer No. 1*); Moses Saldana (*Ballplayer No. 2*); Brian Lally (*Officer*); Ernie Lively (*Sergeant*); Bart Johnson (*Young Officer*); Peter Mark Vasquez (*Prison Guard*); Ruben Sierra (*Gerardo*); Willie C. Carpenter (*INS Guard*); Delana Michaels (*Judge*); Pete Leal (*Old Man on Balcony*); Valerie Wildman (*Sunny*); Michael Tomlinson (*Dr. McNally*); Saachiko (*Nurse*); Emilio Rivera (*Tamalito*); Paul Robert Langdon (*Carlitos*); Angelina Estrada (*Woman with Groceries*); Bibi Besch (*Mrs. Gillespie*); Bruce Gray (*Mr. Gillespie*)

MY FAMILY: MI FAMILIA warmly tells the story of one Mexican-American family from Los Angeles, and in doing so reveals nearly a century of an American history unknown to most.

The story is narrated by the eldest son, a writer named Paco (Edward James Olmos), and begins in the 1920s with his father, Jose Sanchez (Eduardo Lopez Rojas), travelling on foot for two years from central Mexico to Los Angeles, believing it still to be a part of Mexico. Jose falls in love, marries Maria (Jenny Gago), and has two children (Anthony Gonzalez and Cassandra Campos) when tragedy first strikes. Maria fails to return from the market one day, being one of a group of Mexicans randomly rounded up, regardless of citizenship, and deported to Mexico. Alone, pregnant, and separated from her family by an unsurmountable distance, she vows to return, and two years later, after nearly dying, she does, accompanied by their son Chuchu (Esai Morales).

Chuchu grows up to be the meanest pachuco in town. While the father holds the traditional values of humility and hard work, Chuchu loathes his predicament as a member of an underclass, resents his father's willing servitude, and would rather do the mambo and shine his car than work. Despite being kicked out of the house by his father, he does not lose the devotion of his adoring little brother Jimmy (Jonathan Hernandez), the heart of the family. When Chuchu kills his enemy at a school dance, Jimmy must witness his brother's death at the hands of police.

Jimmy grows up to be a sad and angry man (Jimmy Smits) whose thefts land him in prison. The narrator explains that Jimmy took all the anger upon himself, freeing the other siblings to live less encumbered lives. Jimmy is almost saved by love when his politicized sister, Toni (Constance Marie), arranges for him to marry Isabel (Elpidia Magana), a Salvadorean political refugee, to save her from deportation and certain death, but she dies in childbirth, leaving Jimmy more angry than ever. He is imprisoned again, and his young infant son is left to be raised by his grandparents. Years later, Jimmy tries with difficulty to regain the trust and affection of his young son.

The only sibling to leave the barrio is Memo (Enrique Castillo), a successful lawyer who adopts the anglicized version of his name, Bill. The culture clash resulting when Memo brings home his new Anglo wife and in-laws to meet his family provides an amusing and complex scene dramatizing both the misconceptions Anglos hold regarding Hispanic-Americans and the various ways the members of a group of Hispanics interpret themselves.

Like its title, which hesitates between two languages, the film depicts the fragmented historical and cultural condition of the American Hispanic. The situation of balancing between two worlds is symbolized by the bridge which separates central Los Angeles from the barrio in the east, a bridge which only the Hispanics cross, as they travel to work for low wages every morning in the gardens and homes of the Anglos. The characters' relations to this bridge in many ways determine their fates. Elsewhere, the intersection of old and new worlds is embodied in the mother, who frequently weaves the mystical folklore of her ancestors into their lives to explain the unexplainable.

The film is beautifully photographed by Edward Lachman, capturing the colors and moods of several different decades and styles. Director Gregory Nava, whose acclaimed film EL NORTE (1983) broached some of this territory, portrays the dynamic atmosphere of Hispanic culture, its blend of races and cultures, and particularly the cross-cultural experience of being considered outsiders in their own country. *(Adult situations, violence.)* — R.C.

d, Gregory Nava; p, Anna Thomas; exec p, Guy East, Tom Luddy, Francis Ford Coppola; assoc p, Nancy De Los Santos; w, Gregory Nava, Anna Thomas (from a story by Gregory Nava); ph, Edward Lachman; ed, Nancy Richardson; m, Pepe Avila, Mark McKenzie; prod d, Barry Robison; art d, Troy Myers; set d, Suzette Sheets; sound, Jose Araujo (mixer); casting, Janet Hirschenson, Jane Jenkins, Roger Mussenden; cos, Tracy Tynan; makeup, Ken Diaz, Mark Sanchez; stunts, Dan Bradley

AAN Best Makeup: Ken Diaz, mark Sanchez

Drama   **(PR: C   MPAA: R)**

MY LIFE AND TIMES WITH   ★★½
ANTONIN ARTAUD
(France) 93m Archipel 33; Laura Productions;
La Sept-Arte; France 2 Cinema; Celluloid Dreams ~
Leisure Time Features c/bw
(EN COMPAGNIE D'ANTONIN ARTAUD)

Sami Frey *(Antonin Artaud)*; Marc Barbe *(Jacques Prevel)*; Julie Jezequel; Valerie Jeannet; Charlotte Valandrey; Clotilde De Bayser

MY LIFE AND TIMES WITH ANTONIN ARTAUD is a fictitious account of the final two years of Antonin Artaud's life, based on an autobiographical book by poet Jacques Prevel. Gerard Mordillat's darkly comic docudrama is particularly fascinating for fans of Artaud or for those with an interest in the bohemian life of Paris in the 1940s.

Antonin Artaud (1896-1948) was a French poet, writer, and actor, who is best remembered as the author of *The Theater and Its Double*, a manifesto for his proposed Theater of Cruelty. Prevel's book chronicles the incredible two years he spent with Artaud. MY LIFE AND TIMES WITH ANTONIN ARTAUD begins in 1946, when Artaud (Sami Frey) has just been released from an asylum and returns to his circle of friends. For Jacques Prevel (Marc Barbe), his meeting with Artaud is a revelation. As a young poet, Artaud is his mentor. Prevel follows Artaud around, attending to his every whim (including supplying him with drugs) and listening attentively to his increasingly mad tirades. Prevel shares his life with two women—a pregnant wife and a low-rent mistress—but his main object of worship is Artaud, whose life and thoughts he records until Artaud's death two years later.

Shot in moody black and white, MY LIFE AND TIMES WITH ANTONIN ARTAUD is wonderfully evocative of the edgy elegance of bohemian life in postwar Paris. Nights spent in smoky bars drift into days of intense artistic pursuit, all enhanced by alcohol and drugs. Sami Frey cleverly plays the complexity of Artaud's aging genius—a cocktail of brilliant existential musings and delusional pretentious posturing. Marc Barbe evokes Prevel's character with care. Despite his youthful eagerness and ambition, Prevel will forever live in the shadow of his idol. Artaud's presence and words loom large in this film. While this will be an asset to fans of this artistically significant writer, it makes MY LIFE AND TIMES WITH ANTONIN ARTAUD of less interest to those unfamiliar with his body of work or this period of Paris cultural history. In French, with English subtitles. *(Adult situations, substance abuse.)* — J.S.

d, Gerard Mordillat; p, Denis Freyd, Gerard Guerin, Jerome Prieur; w, Gerard Mordillat, Jerome Prieur (based on the book *En compagnie d'Antonin Artaud* by Jacques Prevel); ph, Francois Catonne; ed, Sophie Rouffio; m, Jean-Claude Petit; prod d, Jean-Pierre Clech; sound, Pierre Lorrain, Dominique Dalmasso; cos, Caroline De Vivaise

Drama/Biography   **(PR: C   MPAA: NR)**

MYSTERY OF RAMPO, THE   ★★★
(Japan) 103m Rampo Production Committee ~
Samuel Goldwyn Company c
(AKA: RAMPO)

Masahiro Motoki *(Kogoro Akechi)*; Naoto Takenaka *(Edogawa Rampo)*; Michiko Hada *(Shizuko/Marquess)*; Teruyuki Kagawa *(Masashi Yokomizo)*; Mikijiro Hira *(Marquis Ogawara)*; Shiro Sano; Ittoku Kishibe; Nekohachi Edoya; Jyunichi Takagi; Charlie Yutani; Kirin Kiki; Yasushi Akimoto; Hiroshi Abe; Genjiro Arato; Riyoko Ideka; Eiji Oshita; Kenji Otsuki; Keiko Oginome; Reiko Okutani; Fumiko Osanai; Hitoshi Ozawa; Narumi Oda; Masay Kato; Maiko Kikuchi; Kazuya Kimura; Toru Kenjyo; Keiko Kono; Ken Sakamura; Ryuzo Saki; Akiko Santo; Rieko Zanma; Julie Dreyfus; Jinichiro Sudo; Tetsuya Tsukushi; Koji Tsutsumi; Rieko Terada; Toshiji Nakayama; Yoko Narahashi; Mariko Hayashi; Yu Hayami; Yoshimi Hara; Yoshio Harada; Kinji Fukasaku; Tsubasa Fukuoka; Tetsuya Bessho; Tomokazu Miura; Akiko Mizuno; Akiko Yagi; Kenichi Yajima; Uyu Yamaguchi; Euchi Yoshikawa; Sergeant Luke Takamura, III; Koji Wakamatsu

"Edogawa Rampo" (the Japanese transliteration of "Edgar Allen Poe") was the *nom de plume* of a prolific Japanese author who flourished before WWII. This film, which is based on some of Rampo's writings, is a bizarre and dazzling excursion into the world of his imagination.

The film quickly demonstrates that Rampo (Naoto Takenaka) is heavily influenced by Western fiction (e.g., Poe, Conan Doyle, Cooper) at a time when the nation is quickly embracing Western culture, including European militarist ideologies. His new story—"The Appearance of Osei" (presented in animation reminiscent of traditional screen paintings), about a woman who murders her sickly husband by allowing him to suffocate in a trunk—is banned by the young Showa government, along with many of his earlier writings. A film based on his character Detective Akechi is about to be released; Rampo's producer encourages him to stick with commercial projects. A depressed Rampo feels himself drawn into a separate reality, described as walking in circles that widen imperceptibly. This impression is deepened by the discovery of a woman named Shizuko (Michiko Hada), who is accused of murdering her husband using the same peculiar method as the supposedly fictional Osei. Rampo's publisher Masachi (Teruyuki Kagawa) encourages him to believe that his fiction is somehow linked to this woman's life, and presses him to write her future.

Rampo concedes and visits Shizuko's shop. She gives him a broken music box which she treasured as a child; he dreams the music box comes to life when Shizuko kills herself. This is the start of their curious, tentative courtship, which is marked by strained conventions and unexpressed longings. Unable to remain in the world of flesh and blood, Rampo quickly escapes into his alternative world, where he is transformed into his alter ego, Akechi (Masahiro Motoki), who is investigating a mad Marquis (Mikijiro Hira) with whom an accused murderess has taken residence. In a virtual parody of Gothic fiction (notably REBECCA, PSYCHO and HOUSE OF USHER), Akechi parachutes into the Marquis' manor, discovering that he is a madman with a bizarre fixation on his deceased mother. The Marquis smokes "Mandrake pollen," tortures guests with readings of Poe accompanied by films of war atrocities, taunts death by racing his stallion toward a cliff only stopping at the last moment, and, dressed as his mother, engages in sadomasochistic sex with the widow while screening homemade bondage films on the body of another woman.

Rampo is pulled away from his interior story by a telegram summoning him to Shizuko's shop; she is hysterical about the reappearance of the trunk in her store, and begs Rampo to stay with her—deeply conflicted, he declines, saying he must complete his writing. When Rampo resumes the story, he discovers that the Marquis indicates his approval for Akechi's feelings toward the young widow, and tumbles over the cliff in his final ride; Akechi inspects the grass at the cliff edge and confronts the widow, who instantly confesses, then asks Akechi to climb into the fateful trunk. Rampo tries to stop Akechi, who rebuffs him. Rampo races to the shop, but Shizuko is gone. His two worlds collide as he races back to the manor to stop the ending of his story, only to find that with Akechi in the trunk, the widow poisons herself before he can pick the lock and burst out. Rampo enters the room just as his imaginary world implodes in a breath-taking array of cinematic pyrotechnics, dissolving into an eternal embrace between the writer and his subject.

RAMPO is an intricate, delicate, and terribly Japanese puzzle, which first-time director Kazuyoshi Okuyama (an established film producer) and cinematographer Yasushi Sasakibara have filmed with skill and energy, investing every shot with cunning photography and technical sophistication. The visual style playfully tweaks the masters of Gothic and mystery films (especially Hitchcock and Corman, but also Huston, Hawks, Lang, and James Whale) in the same way that the story plays with Poe and Chandler. The orchestral score by Akiru Senju (with the Czech Philharmonic) has an old-fashioned lustre that underscores the conflict between traditional and modern imaginations. The ornate production design and recurring leit motifs (mirrors, hope chests, pink roses) build like a symphony to a rapturous crescendo that resolves the conflict without satisfying the conventions of narrative. Ultimately, the film is a celebration of artistic imagination that appreciates the losses and sacrifices which motivate human creativity.

RAMPO was a colossal hit in Japan in 1994, but failed to make a strong impression in the US, despite its liberal borrowings from American film and literature. Perhaps that's the result of the dumbing down of American film; RAMPO requires the active investment of an intelligent, discerning audience, rewarding viewers with a uniquely enchanting experience. (*Nudity, sexual situations, adult situations, violence.*) — R.S.

d, Kazuyoshi Okuyama, Rentaro Mayuzumi; p, Yoshihisa Nakagawa; exec p, Kazuyoshi Okuyama; w, Kazuyoshi Okuyama, Yuhei Enoki (based on an original story by Edogawa Rampo); ph, Yasushi Sasakibara; ed, Akimasa Kawashima; m, Akira Senju; prod d, Kyoko Heya; set d, Masahiro Furuya; anim, Yasuhiro Nakura, Hiroko Misoka; fx, Michihisa Miyashige, Atsuki Sato; cos, Sachico Ito

Drama/Mystery (PR: O MPAA: NR)

NADJA ★★½
(U.S.) 92m Kino Link Productions ~
October Films bw

Elina Lowensohn *(Nadja)*; Suzy Amis *(Cassandra)*; Peter Fonda *(Dr. Van Helsing/Dracula)*; Martin Donovan *(Jim)*; Galaxy Craze *(Lucy)*; Karl Geary *(Renfield)*; Jared Harris *(Edgar)*; David Lynch *(Morgue Receptionist)*; Jack Lotz *(Boxing Coach)*; Nic Ratner *(Bar Victim)*; Rob Gosse *(Garage Mechanic)*; Rome Neal *(Garage Mechanic)*; Jose Zuniga *(Bartender)*; Isabel Gilles *(Waitress)*; Bernadette Jurkowski *(Dracula's Bride)*; Jeff Winner *(Young Dracula)*; Sean *(Bela)*; Giancarlo Roma *(Romanian Kid)*; Anna Roma *(Romanian Mother)*; Thomas Roma *(Romanian Policeman)*; Aleksander Rasic *(Romanian Policeman)*; Miranda Russell *(Lucy's Baby)*

NADJA, written and directed by Michael Almereyda, is an ambitious little art/horror movie about a female Romanian vampire who is transplanted to New York City. This is a doggedly quirky offering, filmed in black-and-white 35mm and Pixelvision—footage shot using the $45 discontinued Fisher-Price toy camera adopted by some of the more precocious indie filmmakers.

As embodied by the charismatic Elina Lowensohn, Nadja lives a melancholy existence amid the darker warrens of downtown Manhattan, feeding off strangers and supplementing her intake with the blood of shark embryos from Mexico. After her father (seen via manipulated footage of Bela Lugosi), also a vampire, is killed by Dr. Van Helsing (Peter Fonda), Nadja grows more world-weary. In a dreary bar, she meets Lucy (Galaxy Craze) and falls in love with her, unaware that Lucy's husband Jim (Martin Donovan) is Van Helsing's nephew. As if that weren't enough coincidence, Nadja also has a twin brother, Edgar (Jared Harris), who is in the care of a woman called Cassandra (Suzy Amis), who is Jim's half-sister.

Lucy, increasingly under Nadja's spell, becomes gravely ill. Nadja flees for Transylvania with Cassandra, closely pursued by the rest of the company. In a final confrontation, Van Helsing kills Nadja and rescues Lucy and Cassandra. Back in the US, Edgar marries Cassandra, who may now be possessed by Nadja's spirit.

"Her emotions are like big storms," says Edgar of his sister, but he could easily be talking about NADJA's narrative. Actually, NADJA is less about narrative than about style and excess. Cinematographer Jim DeNault's moody use of light and shadow suggests an homage to Carl Dreyer's VAMPYR, but NADJA doesn't approach that 1931 horror classic's eerie sense of displacement. Kurt Ossenfort provides some startling production design, particularly in the film's early passages, and Prudence Moriarty's invariably dark costumes are consistently atmospheric. But too often, Almereyda sabotages NADJA's promising look and storyline for a cheap laugh or some campy diversion. Among the actors, Fonda is clearly the worst offender. Amusing at first in his long-haired vampire-killer mode, he soon drifts into a Dennis Hopper impersonation which, however accurate, grows increasingly irritating. Only Lowensohn and Karl Geary, who plays Renfield, seem able to walk a thin line between the film's humor and its serious, if overwrought, convictions.

As for Pixelvision, which is a bit like looking through a glazed shower door, Almereyda employed it in his little-seen 1992 feature ANOTHER GIRL ANOTHER PLANET. In NADJA, where it's meant to provide the vampire's point-of-view, it has the effect of obscuring what ought to be the film's most vivid scenes, hardly a smart idea for a movie which aspires to the horror genre. *(Graphic violence, sexual situations, nudity.)* — E.K.

d, Michael Almereyda; p, Mary Sweeney, Amy Hobby; exec p, David Lynch; assoc p, Andrew Fierberg; w, Michael Almereyda; ph, Jim DeNault; ed, David Leonard; m, Simon Fisher Turner; prod d, Kurt Ossenfort; sound, William Kozy (mixer), Stuart Levy (design); fx, Arthur Jolly; casting, Billy Hopkins, Suzanne Smith, Kerry Barden; cos, Prudence Moriarty; makeup, Dina Doll; stunts, Arthur Jolly

Horror/Drama   (PR: C   MPAA: R)

NAKED KILLER ★★½
(Hong Kong) 88m Wong Jing Workshop Ltd. ~
Rim Film Distributors c
(CHIKLO GOUYEUNG)

Simon Yam *(Tinam)*; Chingmy Yau *(Kitty)*; Carrie Ng *(Princess)*; Kelly Yao *(Baby)*; Svenwara Madoka *(Sister Cindy)*

NAKED KILLER provides gory delight through an action-packed story of a confused detective and his encounter with a Hong Kong-based group of glamorous lesbian-feminist killers out to get the male "rubbish of the world."

In a stylish opening, a cold-blooded female assassin lays a trap for and brutally murders a male victim in a scene complete with a display of martial arts, explosive gun play, and castration—for comic relief. Tinam (Simon Yam) is a detective suffering from flashbacks, and impotence, three months after accidentally killing his brother in the line of duty. He meets Kitty (Chingmy Yau) in a hair salon when she attacks a hairdresser who refuses to take responsibilty for fathering another woman's baby. Despite being overcome with nausea at the prospect of drawing his gun, Tinam manages to keep Kitty from castrating the man. She makes off with Tinam's beeper and calls him for a date to return it, enticing him to escort her on a provocative shopping spree.

Kitty's next mission is to avenge the death of her father, killed by his wife's lover. Leaving half a dozen bodies in her wake, she flees with a hostage who, when Kitty is wounded, helps her blast their way through dozens of thugs in hot pursuit. Kitty's hostage turns out to be Sister Cindy (Suenwara Madoka), a professional killer who offers to train her in the same profession. Kitty is shocked at the proposal and Cindy must entice her with promises of money, power, and a new identity, which, following her recent escapades, she needs desperately. As Cindy's training of Kitty (now known as Shang Hil-Qun) commences, Princess (Carrie Ng), a previous protege of Cindy's, receives orders to kill her old master.

Investigating a series of murders identical to the opening scene's, Tinam meets Shang and recognizes her as Kitty. Their flirtation is renewed and eventually becomes a bond so great that Tinam is unable to conduct his investigation (while he does conquer his impotence). Kitty's love for him is greater than her devotion to her master, but she tries to protect Cindy from Princess, eventually losing her to a kiss of poisoned lipstick from her rival. Kitty and Tinam, unable to escape either Princess or the police, commit suicide locked in a lover's embrace.

NAKED KILLER, even at its most turgidly melodramatic, never takes itself too seriously, remaining a gleeful cartoon of heroic feminist avengers with a penchant for revealing gowns and skintight catsuits. The lesbian angle is played with little offense. After all, if Kitty's loyalty to Cindy had not been strained by her heterosexual liaison with Tinam, these women might have ruled Hong Kong. Tinam's insecurity over his sexual powers is endearing and the castrations that accompany each murder are actually played for laughs! NAKED KILLER may not be the best of the Hong Kong action pictures—John Woo's films provide more bang for your buck—but its good-humored glitz adds diverting twists to a convoluted and ultimately predictable story of obsession and betrayal. *(Violence, nudity, sexual situations.)* — C.Ch.

d, Fok Yiu Leung; p, Wong Jing; assoc p, Dennis Chan; w, Wong Jing; ph, William Yim; ed, Wong Chi-hung; m, Lowell Lo; art d, Ngai Fong Nai; cos, Shirley Chan

Martial Arts/Fantasy/Erotic　　　　**(PR: C　MPAA: NR)**

NATIONAL LAMPOON'S ATTACK OF THE 5'2" ★★★ WOMEN

(U.S.) 82m Imagination Productions ~
Paramount Home Video c
(AKA: ATTACK OF THE 5'2" WOMEN)

TONYA: THE BATTLE OF WOUNDED KNEE: Julie Brown *(Tonya Hardly)*; Stella Stevens *(Lawanda)*; Khrystyne Haje *(Nancy Cardigan)*; John Robert Hoffman *(Jeff Googooly)*; Eric "Sparky" Edwards *(Sean Heckardt)*; Peter Deluise *(Stan Stant)*; Melora Harte *(Tonya's Coach)*; Janice Kent *(Nancy's Coach)*; Susan Watson *(Nancy's Mom)*; Nick Toth *(Nancy's Dad)*; Jennifer Butt *(Oksana Bayou)*; Brianna Weissman *(Little Tonya)*; Sydney Lassick *(Weirdo)*; Margaret Cho *(Connie Tong)*; HE NEVER GAVE ME AN ORGASM: Julie Brown *(Lenora Babbitt)*; Adam Storke *(Juan Wayne Babbitt)*; Sam McMurray *(Dick)*; Bridget Sienna *(Maria)*; Priscilla Barnes *(Crystal)*; Stanley DeSantis *(Dr. Kelloc)*; Lauren Tewes *(Hostess)*; Dick Miller *(Officer Murphy)*; Rick Overton *(Officer Brown)*; Anne DeSalvo *(Cycle Slut)*; Tom Kenny *(Director)*; Liz Torres *(Lenora's Mom)*; Vicki Lawrence *(Herself)*

NATIONAL LAMPOON'S ATTACK OF THE 5'2" WOMEN, made for cable TV and released to home video in 1995, scores a double parody bullseye. Vulgar and hilariously profane, this twin tale of media madness torn from the tabloids is the perfect party video.

In the first story, "Tonya: The Battle of Wounded Knee," Tonya Hardly (Julie Brown) dreams of snaring the Olympic gold medal despite the constant put-downs from her mom (Stella Stevens) and disqualifying threat of weight fluctuations. While prissy Miss Perfect, Nancy Cardigan (Khrystyne Haje), figure-eights ever closer to super-stardom, Tonya feels burdened by her humble trailer park origins. She needs an edge. Rather than hire an image consultant, studly husband Jeff Googooly (John Robert Hoffman) masterminds a scheme to ensure Tonya's victory in the Olympic trials. Hiring inept amateur mercenaries Sean Heckardt (Eric "Sparky" Edwards) and Stan Stant (Peter Deluise), Jeff only succeeds in temporarily sidelining Nancy. Sailing above the scandal resulting from the assault on Cardigan, Tonya does get to compete at Lilliehammer, yet she's plagued by her own second-rate talent and tight-fitting panties. In the perfect anti-climax, Oksana Bayou (Jennifer Butt)—an even bigger princess than Nancy—skates off in tears with the gold medal.

In the second sketch, "He Never Gave Me an Orgasm," Lenora Babbitt (Julie Brown) relates to an interviewer (Sam McMurray) the details of her bloody path to feminist awareness. In flashbacks, we see how the repeated failure of her drunken husband, Juan Wayne Babbitt (Adam Storke), to satisfy her sexually led to the justifiable removal of his penis. When the dismembered organ is located by police but then gobbled up by a pooch, Dr. Kelloc (Stanley DeSantis) performs wonders with a donor penis from a biker. Unfortunately, tempestuous Lenora learns that the biker's widow (Anne DeSalvo) has visitation

rights, so she repeats history live on TV during a re-enactment. While on the daytime talk show "Vick," the now re-emasculated Juan Wayne reveals himself as a transsexual who finally understands the difficulty of being a woman in these tumultuous modern times.

Fans of the versatile Julie Brown (who lampooned Madonna mercilessly in the 1992 cable feature MEDUSA: DARE TO BE TRUTHFUL) know what to expect from her—gut-busting one-liners, comically over-the-top performances, and sight gags so crudely funny they could be called Second City Burlesque. However, those seeking pointed satire about the Tonya Harding/Lorena Bobbitt scandals will be laughing down the wrong drain-pipes. These two sketches are broad bio-parodies in which Julie and her co-creators don't poke fun at deserving targets, but rather rib their subjects to death. If, in real life, Harding wept about broken laces to stall for time, here Tonya Hardly's panties slide up the crack of her butt, prompting a sidesplitting remark from an Olympic judge: "Can you believe the size of her ass?" It's hard to distinguish reality from embellishment once you've enjoyed Julie Brown's wicked put-downs of sacred cows. If the Bobbitt sketch is less hilarious, it's because the filmmakers stray too far from the outline of actual events so outrageous they hardly need comic escalation. Whereas Brown's performance as a horny version of Carmen Miranda is almost solely responsible for powering the Bobbitt send-up, the Tonya Harding segment soars to heights of lunacy in scene after scene.

Much funnier than most Hollywood theatrical comedies, this dual-comedy also features some trademark Julie Brown tunes which are stylish enough for her collaborators Tyng and Coffey to write a full-scale musical. One only wishes that some of the weaker subplots of both sketches had been jettisoned so that Brown might have sunk her talons into a quartet of famous females, perhaps letting Tonya and Lorena keep company with, say, Leona Helmsley and the female cast from "Friends." *(Sexual situations, violence, extreme profanity.)* — R.P.

d, Richard Wenk; p, Peter Manoogian , J. Marina Muhlfriedel; exec p, Julie Brown, David Jablin; assoc p, Charlie Coffey; w, Charlie Coffey, Julie Brown; ph, Rex Nicholson; ed, Debbie Chiate; m, Christopher Tyng; prod d, John Iacovelli; art d, Roland Rosenkranz; sound, Craig Woods (mixer); fx, Gary F. Bentley, Special Effects Systems; casting, Gary Oberst; cos, Mona May; makeup, Cinzia Zanetti

Comedy　　　　　　　　　**(PR: O　MPAA: R)**

NATIONAL LAMPOON'S SENIOR TRIP　　★
(U.S.) 94m Dick Clark Productions; Alliance ~
New Line/New Line c

Matt Frewer *(Principal Moss)*; Valerie Mahaffey *(Miss Tracy Milford)*; Lawrence Dane *(Senator John Lerman)*; Tommy Chong *(Red)*; Jeremy Renner *(Mark "Dags" D'Agostino)*; Rob Moore *(Reggie)*; Sparky Edwards *(Miosky)*; Kevin McDonald *(Travis)*; Fiona Loewi *(Lisa Perkins)*

NATIONAL LAMPOON'S SENIOR TRIP is a dreary combination of 1980s teen sex comedy and 1970s drug comedy. Neither genre was particularly funny in their day, and this 1990s film is mixture of the worst of both.

Fairmount High School in Ohio is every teacher's worst nightmare. The students are disruptive and unruly, and more interested in sex, drinking, and drugs than their studies. Mark D'Agostino (Jeremy Renner) and his pal Reggie (Rob Moore) are the most popular kids in the school, mostly because they are the best at supplying alcohol and drugs. Principal Moss (Matt Frewer) is a high-strung, paranoid man who is incapable of keeping any of the students in line.

When the students break the rules one time too many, their punishment is, as a group, to write an essay about "What's Wrong With Education In America." The essay is sent to the President of the United States, who likes it and decides to use it as an example for the country. He sends Ohio's Senator back home to offer the Fairmount kids a trip to the White House. The Senator is a sneaky Republican with sights on the Presidency, and when he discovers that the Fairmount students are irresponsible hooligans he decides to use the opportunity to unseat the liberal President.

After an eventful bus ride, the students arrive in Washington, DC. There, they party in a posh private hotel suite and humiliate Principal Moss. Class brain Lisa Perkins (Fiona Leowi) discovers the Senator's evil plan. He leaves for the White House with one clueless student, who begins to make a fool of himself and the President. The rest of the students arrive in time to expose the Senator and to prove that they really are role models for our youth. The Fairmount students are heroes, the Senator is disgraced, and the President is more popular than ever.

NATIONAL LAMPOON'S SENIOR TRIP does not have any ideas. While the story of ne'er-do-wells making good is tried and true, it doesn't work with insipid jokes and unlikable protagonists. D'Agostino and Reggie, who are supposed to provide the film with most of its humor, are uninteresting caricatures and completely without charisma. Lisa, the only somewhat likable character, is not well developed and ends up choosing to be friends with the burnouts simply because she wants to lose her virginity before she goes to college. Matt Frewer is horrendously miscast as the bumbling principal. He whines, trips over himself, and takes the material far more seriously than anyone in their right mind would.

The humor consistently reaches for the lowest common denominator. Jokes are about drugs, racial stereotypes, fat kids, and bodily functions. None of the ideas are fresh or even updated (how many times do we have to see an "eat the marijuana before the cop gets to the car" scene before Hollywood figures out it isn't funny?). The film's writers don't even bother to get simple details right. For example, the trip from Columbus to Washington, about six or seven hours in reality, is turned into a 24-hour event in this film. Or maybe it just seems that long. Either way, SENIOR TRIP is a hopeless mess in every way, and a road well deserved of being less travelled. *(Sexual situations, profanity, substance abuse.)* — A.M.

d, Kelly Makin; p, Wendy Grean; exec p, Stephane Reichel, Michel Roy; w, Roger Kumble, I. Marlene King; ph, Francis Protat; ed, Stephen Lawrence; prod d, Gregory Keen; art d, John Dondertman; set d, Jeff Fruitman; cos, Sharon Purdy

Comedy   **(PR: O   MPAA: R)**

NEA   ★★½
(France/West Germany) 103m Films la Boetie;
Multimedia; Telecine ~ Eurotrash Film and Video c
(AKA: YOUNG EMMANUELLE, A)

Sami Frey *(Axel Thorpe)*; Ann Zacharias *(Sybille Ashby)*; Francoise Brion *(Judith)*; Micheline Presle *(Mother)*; Heinz Bennent; Ingrid Caven; Robert Freitag; Chantal Brunner; Martin Provost; Villiers De L'Isle De Cume; Roland Briet; Francine Custer; Nicole Duhamel; Claude Marouski; Francoise Maye; Nelly Kaplan *(Librarian)*; Rose-Marie Nicolas; Lise Ramu; Michel Viala

NEA, released in France in 1976, is a slickly sentimental fantasy about an adolescent girl's sexual awakening. Its 1995 US video release will appeal primarily to cat lovers and fans of sappy escapist romances.

Sybille Ashby (Ann Zacahrias) is a shy, rebellious 16-year-old with a penchant for erotic literature. Axel Thorpe (Sami Frey), a handsome, middle-aged bookstore-owner and publisher, catches her stealing his wares and demands an explanation. She tells him she wants to write and offers him a sample of her work. He is encouraging, but thinks she needs more experience. She becomes his protege.

At her parents' posh suburban villa, Sybille (aided by her cat, Cumes) becomes a methodical voyeur. She spies on her parents making love, then later discovers her mother (Micheline Presle) in bed with her lover, "Aunt" Judith (Francoise Brion). She dutifully transcribes her observations into prose. Her scandalized father also catches Mom and Judith in the act, and Mrs. Ashby decides to leave him as soon as Sybille is old enough. Sybille arranges a rendezvous with Thorpe, who provides her with the experience she needs: she loses her virginity and they become lovers. Inspired, Sybille pens *Nea*, which, with help from Thorpe, becomes an instant success. Thorpe meets the Ashbys but conceals his relationship with Sybille. She catches him in bed with her older sister. Sybille takes revenge by faking a rape and blaming Thorpe, who goes to prison. He escapes and attacks Sybille, threatening to kill her if she doesn't confess to the frame-up. As they struggle, their old passion reappears with predictable results. Reunited, they bury Sybille's manuscripts and leave together, apparently followed by Cumes the cat.

NEA was produced and directed by Nelly Kaplan, who also helped adapt the script from a novel by Emmanuelle Arsan. Technically, the film is almost seamless. The cinematography is lush, the editing is clean and efficient, and the acting is competent. Michel Magne's score is unobtrusive. For the American viewer, NEA's subtitles are almost superfluous; tones of voice, montage, and camerawork tell most of the story on their own. NEA's major flaw is its story, and how Kaplan handles it. It asks the viewer to take impossible situations seriously and accept ridiculous behavior because it is prettily packaged. Any comic elements in NEA are so understated they pass unnoticed. Sybille collects "evidence" of her supposed rape by seducing a schoolboy; this scene could be funny, but instead it's disgustingly clinical. Encounters between the film's various lovers lack emotional depth and erotic tension.

NEA is blatantly commercial; its plot, production values, and tone are reminiscent of daytime soaps, an impression reinforced by its rich, good-looking, and decadent characters, suggesting a view of upper-middle-class life ostensibly tailored to the expectations of French blue-collar audiences. With its understated style wedded to an overblown plot, NEA is polished kitsch. *(Sexual situations, nudity, adult situations.)* — C.M.

d, Nelly Kaplan; p, Andre Genoves, Yvon Guezel; w, Jean Chapot, Nelly Kaplan (based on the novel by Emmanuelle Arsan); ph, Andreas Winding; ed, Helene Plemiannikov; m, Michel Magne; art d, Bernard Evein; sound, William Sivel (recordist); casting, Mamade; cos, Michele Cerf

Romance/Erotic   **(PR: O   MPAA: R)**

NEKROMANTIK   ★
(West Germany) 75m Manfred O. Jelinsky Productions ~
Leisure Time Features c

Daktari Lorenz *(Robert Schmadtke)*; Beatrice M. *(Betty)*; Harald Lundt *(Bruno)*; Susa Kohlstedt *(Vera)*; Heike Surban *(Prostitute)*; Colloseo Schulzendorf *(Joe)*; Henri Boeck; Clemens Schwender; Holger Suhr; Jorg Buttgereit *(Joe's Streetcleaning Agency Team)*; Franz Rodenkirchen *(Pornokiller)*; Volker Hauptvogel; Harald Weis; Patricia Leipold; Elke Fuchs; Margit im Schlaa; Christiane Baumgarten; Heinz Langner; Simone Sporl;

Wilfried Hoog; Michael Bushcke; Manfred Repnow; Daniela Geburtig; Manfred O. Jelinkski; Fritz Fuchs; Lasko; Marion Koob-Liebing; Hagen Koob-Liebing; Heini Walton; Hapunkt Fix; Splat Brose; Mutfak Reisse

Unearthed for midnight bookings in 1995, after creeping around the underground circuit for years, NEKROMANTIK is a pointless and distasteful exercise in a rarely discussed aspect of human behavior.

Robert (Daktari Lorenz) works with a crew which removes bodies from accident sites, but he takes more than a professional interest in his work; he is a necrophile, due at least partially to a traumatic childhood during which he watched his father skin animals. His girlfriend, Betty (Beatrice M.), shares his attraction for the dead, and cavorts with him, bathing in blood and fondling both human and animal organs. He brings a cadaver home from work, and the couple engage in lengthy sex with the corpse.

Then Robert loses his job and Betty leaves him, taking the body with her. Robert starts to slide into despair, and attempts to comfort himself by attending a slasher movie and having sex with the corpse of a prostitute. But nothing works, and he commits suicide by repeatedly stabbing himself in the gut. No sooner has he been buried, however, than a mysterious woman begins digging him up.

NEKROMANTIK's very first shot, of a woman urinating on a roadside, pretty much sums up the movie's approach and its goals. Director-cowriter Jorg Buttgereit clearly intends to rub the audience's face in graphic ugliness, exposing the seamiest possible extremes of human behavior. Some have praised the film for just this reason, applauding its no-holds-barred approach to horror and depravity and appreciating it for "going too far" in the face of increasing banality in mainstream filmmaking.

The fact remains that it is easy to "go too far" in the movies, especially when the budget is low, and NEKROMANTIK is as cheap as they come (at least part of it was filmed in super-8). There are occasional dark chuckles (particularly Betty's note to Robert: "Left for good. Took the corpse."), but by the time NEKROMANTIK reaches its supposed catharsis, with Robert hacking away at his innards and ejaculating blood, it has long since collapsed into a debased freak show. *(Graphic violence, extensive nudity, sexual situations.)* — M.G.

d, Jorg Buttgereit; p, Manfred O. Jelinski; w, Jorg Buttgereit, Franz Rodenkirchen; ph, Uwe Bohrer; ed, Jorg Buttgereit, Manfred O. Jelinski; m, Daktari Lorenz, Hermann Kopp, John Boy Walton; sound, Franz Rodenkirchen, Harald Weiss; fx, Daktari Lorenz, Jorg Buttgereit, Franz Rodenkirchen; casting, Jorg Buttgereit

Horror (PR: O MPAA: NR)

NET, THE ★★½
(U.S.) 118m Columbia ~ Columbia c

Sandra Bullock *(Angela Bennett)*; Jeremy Northam *(Jack Devlin)*; Dennis Miller *(Dr. Alan Champion)*; Diane Baker *(Mrs. Bennett)*; Wendy Gazelle *(Ruth Marks/Imposter)*; Ken Howard *(Bergstrom)*; Ray McKinnon *(Dale)*; Daniel Schorr *(WNN Anchor)*; L. Scott Caldwell *(Public Defender)*; Robert Gossett *(Ben Phillips)*; Kristina Krofft *(1st Nurse)*; Julia Pearlstein *(2nd Nurse)*; Juan Garcia *(Resort Desk Clerk)*; Tony Perez *(Mexican Doctor)*; Margo Winkler *(Mrs. Raines)*; Gene Kirkwood *(Stan Whiteman)*; Christopher Darga *(Cop)*; Charles Winkler *(Cop)*; Rick Snyder *(Russ Melbourne)*; Gerald Berns *(Jeff Gregg)*; Tannis Benedict *(Elevator Woman)*; Vaughn Armstrong *(Trooper)*; Wren T. Brown *(Trooper)*; Lynn Blades *(Remote Reporter)*; Israel Juarbe *(Thief)*; Julia Vera *(Mexican Nun)*; Lewis Dix *(FedEx Man)*; Lili Flanders *(Embassy Worker)*; Adam Winkler

(Computer Nerd); Brian Frankish *(Shuttle Driver)*; Wanda Lee Evans *(Desk Sergeant)*; Kerry Kilbride *(WNN Reporter)*; Roland Gomez *(Limo Driver)*; Melvin Thompson *(Fire Official)*; Rich Bracco *(Fireman)*; Lucy Butler *(Female Officer)*; John Livingston *(Computer Technician)*; David Winkler *(Computer Technician)*; Cam Brainard *(Computer Technician)*; Dennis Richmond *(Newscaster)*; Elaine Corral Kendall *(Newscaster)*; Alfredo Lopez *(Guitar Player)*; Thomas Crawford *(Waiter)*; John Cappon *(ICU Doctor)*; Barbara Abedi *(CCU Nurse)*; Kevin Brown *(The Bunny)*; Hope Parrish *(Security Officer)*; William B. Hill *(Security Officer)*; Danny Breen *(Supervisor)*; Andrew Amador *(Dermot Conley)*; Melissa Bomes *(Reservation Clerk)*

This well conceived thriller pits imperiled individualism against a technology which threatens global takeover. In the 1950s the invader most likely originated from outer space, absorbed souls and multiplied in some gooey biological fashion. In 1995, the monster is the Internet, the global electronic network linking the infrastructure of contemporary society.

Angela Bennett (Sandra Bullock) is a reclusive computer hacker who works out of her home for a software firm. An online friend sends her a diskette containing a video game with hidden software that allows access to some of the most confidential computer systems in the country; he needs her expertise to make sense of what he has uncovered. On his way to meet her, he dies in a plane crash caused by a strange air traffic control computer error. Unaware that he's dead, she leaves for vacation in Mexico, where she meets Jack Devlin (Jeremy Northam), a handsome stranger who takes her out on his boat and seduces her. She discovers that Devlin, who has used deeply personal information gleaned from online conversations to trap her, has been hired to kill her and retrieve the diskette.

Angela narrowly escapes with the diskette, and in order to re-enter the United States must use a visa issued to Ruth Marx, the name that has become mysteriously attached to her social security number. Upon returning home, Angela finds herself enmeshed in a thoroughly modern nightmare. Her identity has been stolen—all important computer systems list her as Ruth Marx, who has a police record for prostitution and possession—her house has been sold, Devlin is after her and everyone to whom she reaches out dies, including her therapist/ex-lover Alan Champion (Dennis Miller), whose computerized medical records are changed with fatal consequences. The only person left to verify her identity is her mother, who suffers from Alzheimer's Disease.

Unable to go to the police because of "Ruth Marx"'s record, Angela realizes that her only escape lies in hunting her hunter. She discovers that news reports of computer tampering on Wall Street and of a new software designed to protect companies and agencies can be traced back to the same source. The software producers have created a market for their product, and installed a back door into their program that will permit them access to sensitive records: The criminal possibilities are endless. Angela sneaks into the software company and goes to work, fixing her identity and saving evidence to diskette. She is chased to a large, crowded expo center where she uses the public computers to send an E-mail to the FBI complete with evidence.

Though attractive (surprisingly so, given her M&M and pizza diet and sedentary lifestyle), Angela is in every other respect the typical computer nerd—the kind of woman who says things like "I don't usually do this on my first date." While THE NET is not a film given to subtlety or understatement, it does revolve around a female protagonist and offers a paranoid but not inaccurate vision of the female condition—defensive, forced to fight for credibility, isolated and marginalized. Like the female lead in SINGLE WHITE FEMALE (1992), Angela has only her own cunning and strength to rely on when men are rendered useless and can no longer save the day. THE NET also accurately explores the problems and nuances of the new online culture, including estrangement from the tangible world, the ease with which identities are hidden under fictitious names like "cyber-bob," and the validity and infallibility readily attributed to computerized information that make it a veritable gold mine for deception. The film also highlights the reality that in contemporary culture, power is bound to information. *(Violence, adult situations.)* — R.C.

d, Irwin Winkler; p, Irwin Winkler, Rob Cowan; w, John Brancato, Michael Ferris; ph, Jack N. Green; ed, Richard Halsey; m, Mark Isham; prod d, Dennis Washington; art d, Tom Targownik; set d, Anne D. McCulley; sound, Richard Lightstone (mixer); fx, Dale L. Martin, Leo Leoncio Solis, Joe Quinlivan, Frank W. Schepler, David Drzewiecki; casting, Mindy Marin; cos, Linda Bass; makeup, Pamela Westmore; stunts, Buddy Van Horn

Thriller/Action   **(PR: C MPAA: PG-13)**

NEVER TALK TO STRANGERS   ★★★

(U.S.) 102m Alliance; Never Talk to Strangers Productions, Inc.; TriStar ~ TriStar c

Rebecca De Mornay *(Dr. Sarah Taylor)*; Antonio Banderas *(Tony Ramirez)*; Dennis Miller *(Cliff Raddison)*; Len Cariou *(Henry Taylor)*; Harry Dean Stanton *(Max Cheski)*; Eugene Lipinski *(Dudakoff)*; Martha Burns *(Maura)*; Beau Starr *(Grogan)*; Phillip Jarrett *(Spatz)*; Tim Kelleher *(Wabash)*; Emma Corosky *(Young Sarah)*; Susan Coyne *(Alison)*; Joseph R. Gannascoli *(Carnival Attendant)*; Reg Dreger *(Flight Attendant)*; Frances Hyland *(Mrs. Slotnick)*; John Bourgeois *(Uniformed Cop)*; Kevin Rushton *(Corridor Guard)*; Kelley *(Grando)*; Bruce Beaton *(Taxi Driver)*; Tony Meyler *(Cop #1)*; Rodger Barton *(Plain Clothes Cop)*; Nolan Jennings *(Waiter)*; Bret Pearson *(Accomplice)*; Teresa Hergert *(Anchorwoman)*

A prim psychiatrist falls for a sexy stranger in NEVER TALK TO STRANGERS, a romantic thriller that offers good, trashy entertainment. What this film lacks in artistry, it makes up in B-movie *divertissement.*

Dr. Sarah Taylor (Rebecca De Mornay), an attractive, single psychiatrist, works at New York's prestigious Veer Institute. Sarah is assigned to evaluate the mental competency of Max Cheski (Harry Dean Stanton), a serial rapist-murderer awaiting trial. One night Sarah meets sexy Tony Ramirez (Antonio Banderas), a security expert who is new to the city. Sarah agrees to go on a date with Tony, but her errant father, Henry Taylor (Len Cariou), shows up unexpectedly at her apartment that same night. Sarah seeks comfort from Tony at his nearby loft after a strained father-daughter encounter. After she reveals her childhood psychic wounds, Tony and Sarah have sex.

As time passes, Tony and Sarah's relationship becomes more complex and sexually involved. However, she begins to suspect Tony of mischief when she receives a mysterious gift of dead flowers at her door. Her fears turn to horror when she later receives another gift: her cat, mutilated, in a box. Tony comes to Sarah's aid and assures her that he is innocent of any wrongdoing. Nevertheless, Sarah hires a private detective to follow him and soon discovers that Tony is actually spying on *her* in order to track down the whereabouts of her previous boyfriend, Benny.

Just as Sarah confronts Tony, Tony shows her videotaped evidence proving that she has a split personality and has, in effect, been stalking herself. She now reveals that she was molested by her father as a child and forced to help him kill her mother. Her father arrives on the scene and Sarah kills both men (just as she had killed Benny). She arranges the crime scene so

as to suggest that the two men killed each other, and gets away with both crimes.

De Mornay and Banderas display real chemistry in this well-crafted vehicle, closely patterned after the 1957 Gerd Oswald classic, SCREAMING MIMI. NEVER TALK TO STRANGERS is at it most engaging when it overplays its hand: in the S&M Lite love scenes set in Tony's "cage" (which recall the Madonna-Willem Dafoe gyrations in BODY OF EVIDENCE), the SILENCE OF THE LAMBS-style head games between Max and Sarah, and that great father-daughter confrontation in the high-pitched climax. All of these melodramatic morsels are set to Pino Donaggio's appropriately edgy score and nicely enhanced by Linda Del Rosario's production design, which emphasizes cool aquas and fiery reds. *(Extreme profanity, graphic violence, nudity, sexual situations, adult situations.)* — E.M.

d, Peter Hall; p, Andras Hamori, Jeffrey R. Neuman, Martin J. Wiley; exec p, Rebecca De Mornay; assoc p, Roberto Silvi, Tom Willey; co-p, Jean Desormeaux, Ralph S. Dietrich; w, Lewis Green, Jordan Rush; ph, Elemer Ragalyi; ed, Roberto Silvi; m, Pino Donaggio; prod d, Linda Del Rosario; set d, Richard Paris; sound, Chaim Gilad; fx, Frank Carere, Jon Campfen; casting, Jon Comerford; cos, Terry Dresbach; makeup, Desne Holland, Greg Nicotero, K.N.B. EFX Group; stunts, Rick Forsythe

Thriller/Erotic/Drama   **(PR: O MPAA: R)**

NEW JERSEY DRIVE   ★★½

(U.S.) 96m 40 Acres And a Mule; Mule Filmworks ~ Gramercy c

Sharron Corley *(Jason Petty)*; Gabriel Casseus *(Midget)*; Saul Stein *(Roscoe)*; Gwen McGee *(Renee Petty)*; Andre Moore *(Ritchie)*; Donald Adeosun Faison *(Tiny Dime)*; Conrad Meertins, Jr. *(P-Nut)*; Devin Eggleston *(Jamal)*; Koran C. Thomas *(Ronnie)*; Michelle Morgan *(Coreen)*; Samantha Brown *(Jackie Petty)*; Christine Baranski *(Prosecutor)*; Robert Jason Jackson *(Lionel Gentry)*; Roscoe Orman *(Judge)*; Dwight Errington Myers *(Bo-Kane)*; Gary DeWitt Marshall *(Jessy)*; Ron Brice *(Tiko)*; Shawn McClean *(Reebo)*; Paulie Schulze *(Booking Sergeant)*; Leslie Nipkow *(Female Officer)*; Arthur Nascarella *(Mr. Chop Shop)*; Michael Tancredi *(Officer Clueless)*; Ian Kelly *(Incarcerated Knucklehead/Young Gun)*; Emilio Mayes *(Young Gun)*; Arabella Field *(Female Jury Member)*; David Butler *(TV Reporter)*; Oran Jones *(Ron Q.'s Dad)*; T.K. Kirkland *(House Rules)*; Leslie Segar *(Angry Resident)*; Kellie Turner *(Agitated Neighbor)*; Maurice Carlton *(Irate Friend)*; Monique Maxwell *(Jackie's Homegirl)*; Monet-Cherise Dunham *(Jackie's Homegirl)*; James McCauley *(Whiteboy in Jeep)*; Teisha Panley *(P.J. Spokesperson)*; Damon Chandler *(Detective)*; Andy Radcliffe *(Buff)*; Ellsworth (Cisco) Davis *(Cisco)*

A bleak film about youthful car thieves at war with the police, NEW JERSEY DRIVE fails to invest its principal characters with the fully fleshed personalities needed to offset their unappealing behavior.

The film opens with Jason Petty (Sharron Corley) in a juvenile home, pondering in voice-over the events that landed him there. Jason, who lives with his working-class family in Newark, fills his spare hours stealing cars and joyriding with his buddies, including Ronnie (Koran C. Thomas), Midget (Gabriel Casseus), Tiny Dime (Donald Adeosun Faison), Ritchie (Andre Moore), and P-Nut (Conrad Meertins Jr.). One night he's cruising with Ronnie, who's under surveillance by the Newark police. The cops open fire on the car, and Ronnie is shot. Jason is arrested and given probation, but warned that any further trouble with the law will land him in the lock-up.

One bad cop, Roscoe (Saul Stein) of the Auto Theft detail, has it in for the car-stealing kids. He and his officers catch Tiny Dime in a stolen vehicle and chase him through the city streets until he smashes up the car, dying in the accident. Roscoe also harasses Jason. In retaliation, Jason, Midget, and Ritchie steal a police car and spend the night screaming through the streets and harassing motorists.

After one fight too many with his concerned mother, Jason moves away from home and in with Midget, who lives in the projects with his grandma. Midget is beaten by the police and graduates to carjacking, at which point the cops set him up: he and P-Nut try to steal yet another car and are ambushed by the police. P-Nut is killed, and Jason goes to jail. Despite her disappointment in his behavior, Jason's mother never loses faith in her son. He and Ronnie testify before a grand jury about Roscoe's wild behavior, and he's suspended from the force.

Jason is released, and Midget offers him the chance to steal a van. Jason declines, and later that evening learns from the news that the police opened fire on the van, killing Midget.

Writer-director Nick Gomez's first film, LAWS OF GRAVITY (1992), a look at poor white crooks eking out a marginal existence in a rundown New York neighborhood, seemed tough, fresh, illuminating and, above all, authentic. So why does his second, about poor black crooks eking out a marginal existence in a rundown New Jersey neighborhood, feel so false? One hesitates to suggest that it's because Gomez isn't black, but perhaps it is; instead of understanding the material intimately, he approaches it through the conventions created and perpetuated by movies, newspaper articles, TV, and popular music, and winds up reconstituting them as his own.

Though apparently sympathetic to its youthful protagonists, NEW JERSEY DRIVE doesn't offer the viewer a single reason to like them, or even to empathize with their narrow and brutally degenerate world view. The 'hood cliches are on view in force: poverty, drugs, drinking 40s on stoops, teenage motherhood, peer pressure, ghetto machismo, racist cops, violence, and alienation. Far from helping the viewer see the world through Jason's eyes, his flat, uninflected voice-over—in which he declares that he and his boys were only out for some fun and games—suggests that he's a juvenile sociopath who deserves worse than he eventually gets. (*Violence, profanity, sexual situations, adult situations.*) — M.M.

d, Nick Gomez; p, Larry Meistrich, Bob Gosse; exec p, Spike Lee; assoc p, David Tuttle; co-p, Rudd Simmons; w, Nick Gomez (based on a story by Nick Gomez and Michel Marriott); ph, Adam Kimmel; ed, Tracy S. Granger; prod d, Lester Cohen; set d, Lynn-Marie Nigro; sound, Jeff Pullman (production mixer); fx, Steve Kirshoff; casting, Tracey Moore, Todd Thaler; makeup, Ellie Winslow; stunts, Phil Neilson

Drama/Crime   (PR: C MPAA: R)

NEW YORK COP   ★
(U.S./Japan) 88m Sun Stripe Productions ~
Columbia TriStar Home Video c
(AKA: N.Y. COP; NEW YORK UNDERCOVER COP)

Chad McQueen (*Hawk*); Mira Sorvino (*Maria*); Toru Nakamura (*Toshi*); Conan Lee (*Konen Li*); Andreas Katsulas (*Ferrara*); Tony Sirico (*Mr. C*); Manny Perez (*Tito*); Jon Seda (*Mario*); Manny Siverio (*Sledge*); Larry Romano (*Emilio*); Laurence Mason (*Danny Boy*); Suzanne Tino (*Marge*); Christine Romeo (*Kate*); Steve Boles (*Capt. Brodsky*); Glenn Miller (*Bad Ass*); Clifford Cudney (*Man in Porno Shop*); Alan Rozelle (*Buster*); Vic Noto (*Biker*); Elisa Anders (*Nancy*); Candace Dian Levertt (*Rosie*); Chuck Zito (*Mafia Hood*); David Lomax (*Mugger*);

Wesley H. Clark (*Mr. Ethan*); George Kee Cheung (*Tong*); Chad Coleman (*Iceman*); Tyrone Jackson (*Sammy T.*); Eric Lutes (*Powell*)

Yet another international coproduction featuring a Japanese leading man, NEW YORK COP doesn't augur well for the future of Yankee-Rising Sun artistic cooperation. Do American sound as comical in Japanese as Nakamura does mangling English? This is not a racist observation; if an actor has to spit out salty urban street talk, he must do so intelligibly. After all, the F-word is the Haiku of American cop movies.

Fresh on the Manhattan beat, rookie cop Toshi (Toru Nakamura) frets about fitting into the force's plans for him to go undercover in order to infiltrate Alphabet City gangs. Ridiculed by a contact for overdressing, Toshi gets swept into the crime maelstrom as a Puerto Rican gang shoos him through several buildings onto the mean streets, where he's rescued by roving sculptress Maria Mendoza (Mira Sorvino). Through this struggling artist, Toshi meets her gangster brother Hawk (Chad McQueen), who leads the gang who tried to kill him. Confounding Hawk's prediction of failure, Toshi uses his karate skills to extract money owed Hawk by a biker and moves himself inside the gang's inner circle, much to the annoyance of Hawk's ambitious second-in-command Tito (Manny Perez). Meanwhile, hit man Iceman (Chad Coleman) is wiping out undercover cops networking with Toshi, including Konen Li (Conan Lee), who manages to wound Hawk's main Mafia connection, Mr. C (Tony Sirico) before being murdered. Toshi secures vital info about Hawk's illegal arms sales, but the bust goes sour, and police precinct snitch Marge (Suzanne Tino) comprises future stings. On the heels of rubouts of Toshi's street liaison and his best buddy Danny Boy (Laurence Mason), Tito backs up his suspicions about Toshi, who has fallen into disfavour with Hawk by sleeping with Maria. When vacillating Hawk backpedals about wanting Toshi dead, Tito eliminates him and takes over the gang. Toshi invades Tito's powermeeting with Mr. C, kills Tito, shoots out Mr. C's tires (which causes a crash-and-burn), and uses Iceman's own high-tech gun on the cop-killing assassin.

Even if this movie is based on fact, this biographical action pic feels derivative and dispiriting, as if a true story had been photocopied endlessly on the Xerox machine of TV cop show schlock. What emerges is a cloudy facsimile of reality—like SERPICO translated into Japanese and then badly retranslated back into English. Where is the magnetic pull of a story line involving a complicated web of snitches, boys in the hood, undercover experts, killer capos, etc.? Has any chance for breakneck excitement been sapped by too many routine car chases, mobster meatball stereotyping, and an insipid cop-meets-good-girl romance? On its own terms, as a souped-up joyride through an urban inferno, NEW YORK COP barely offers enough gratuitous body-bashing to satisfy action junkies. How can you start a genre groupie's heart pumping when none of the bad guys exudes any menace; indeed, the Hell's Angels here are so out of shape they would probably collapse into Richard Simmons's arms at the first mention of a free diet program. Then there's the Nakamura setback from which any movie could not recover; he kickboxes beautifully but puts his talented feet in his mouth every time he speaks. Unmagnetic on camera, Nakamura comes across not as an embattled cop but as a slow-burning tourist knocked silly by a martial arts competition he attended a bit too confidently. He's as uncomfortable with leading-man status as he is with English. (*Graphic violence, extreme profanity, extensive nudity, sexual situations, substance abuse.*) — R.P.

d, Toru Murakawa; p, Simon Tse; exec p, Yoshinori Watanabe, Mitsuru Kurosawa, Joseph Wolf; assoc p, Joe Cirillo, Alex Hapsas; co-p, Randy Jurgensen; w, Hiroshi Kashiwabara (based on the book *New York Undercover Cop* by Jiro Ueno); ph, Peter Fernberger; ed, Barbara Boguski, Larry Marinelli; m, Bob Mithoff; prod d, Susan Boles; set d, Caroline Ghertler; sound, Michael Barosky (mixer); fx, Wilfred Caban, Edward Drohan, III; casting, Lou Di Giamo; cos, David Swaryn; makeup, Jack Engel; stunts, Clifford Cudney, George Kee Cheung

Martial Arts/Action   **(PR: C   MPAA: R)**

NEXT DOOR   ★★½
(U.S.) 95m Nederlander Television and Film Productions; Tudor Entertainment; TriStar Television ~ Columbia TriStar Home Video c

James Woods *(Matt Coler)*; Kate Capshaw *(Karen Coler)*; Randy Quaid *(Lenny Benedetti)*; Lucinda Jenney *(Marci Benedetti)*; Miles Feulner *(Bucky Coler)*; Billy L. Sullivan *(Sparky Benedetti)*; Dan Hildebrand *(Butcher)*; Chantal Coffey *(Student)*; Erik Hyler *(Student)*; Stella Choe *(Student)*; Joe Minjares; Ivory Ocean; Temple Hammett

A video release of a 1994 made-for-cable movie, NEXT DOOR is a disturbing look at class warfare and intellectual snobbery.

Matt Coler (James Woods) and his wife Karen (Kate Capshaw) are college professors who live in the suburbs while awaiting faculty housing. Next door, butcher Lenny Benedetti (Randy Quaid) and his wife Marci (Lucinda Jenney) epitomize the blue-collar lifestyle the Colers look down their noses at. The Benedettis are loud and raucous, make love in the backyard, and have an obsession with lawn watering. When Lenny's incessant watering kills Karen's azaleas, a friendly discussion over the situation escalates into full-scale war. Matt ruins Lenny's patio furniture, Lenny floods Matt's car, and so on. Matt tries to call a truce, but Lenny continues harassing the Colers. After their dog is poisoned, the Colers become frightened and call the police. The cops find no evidence against Lenny and urge the two families to bury the hatchet. The feud spreads to involve the children, and when Matt's son (Miles Feulner) beats up Lenny's son (Billy L. Sullivan), Lenny retaliates by attacking Matt. He later attempts to rape Karen while she is home alone. Matt goes to Lenny's workplace and publicly threatens him, also revealing that Lenny has been laid off. That night Lenny breaks into Matt's home and terrorizes the family, attacking Matt and molesting Karen. To defend his family, Matt desperately fights his bigger, stronger opponent. The bloody battle ends with Lenny being set ablaze by Matt, who tells police that Lenny went too far.

Barney Cohen's script is an amalgam of black comedy, suspense, and social commentary, but NEXT DOOR is never as funny, frightening, or incisive as it is unsettling. As the savagery escalates, the film's tone becomes increasingly uneasy, the filmmakers' message obscured by such disturbing scenes as Lenny swallowing Matt's car keys in one gulp. Rather than challenging social snobbery, NEXT DOOR may actually reinforce it. When the Colers get to know the neighbors they once snubbed, they learn Lenny is not uneducated and unrefined but highly intelligent and psychotically competitive. And while the Colers gain insight about themselves and their social prejudices, the lessons are lost on Lenny, who, despite his high IQ, hates college professors and thinks "words are turds." *(Graphic violence, nudity, sexual situations, adult situations, profanity.)* — B.R.

d, Tony Bill; p, Jay Benson; exec p, Gladys Nederlander, Marty Tudor; assoc p, Dennis Stuart Murphy; w, Barney Cohen; ph, Thomas Del Ruth; ed, Axel Hubert; m, Van Dyke Parks; prod d, Steven Jordan; set d, Donald Light-Harris; sound, Douglas Axtell (mixer); fx, Vincent Montefusco; cast-

ing, Beth Klein; cos, Debra McGuire; makeup, Darcy Knight, Steve Johnson; stunts, Steve Lambert

Drama   **(PR: O   MPAA: R)**

NICK OF TIME   ★★½
(U.S.) 89m Paramount ~ Paramount c

Johnny Depp *(Gene Watson)*; Courtney Chase *(Lynn Watson)*; Charles S. Dutton *(Huey)*; Christopher Walken *(Mr. Smith)*; Roma Maffia *(Ms. Jones)*; Marsha Mason *(Governor Eleanor Grant)*; Peter Strauss *(Brendan Grant)*; Gloria Reuben *(Krista Brooks)*; Bill Smitrovich *(Officer Trust)*; G.D. Spradlin *(Mystery Man)*; Miguel Najera *(Franco—Governor's Bodyguard)*; Jerry Tondo *(Chief Aide)*; Lance Hunter Voorhees *(Weapons Security)*; John Azevedo, Jr. *(Security Associate)*; Lance August *(Personal Security)*; Peter MacKenzie *(JBN Reporter)*; Rick Zieff *(JBN Videographer)*; Tom Bradley *(Himself)*; Michael Chong *(Asian Man)*; Cynthia Noritake *(Asian Woman)*; Holly Kuespert *(Physically Attractive Woman)*; Pamela Dunlap *(Centerpiece Poacher)*; Jan Speck *(Rally Orienter)*; Tom Lawrence *(Personal Waste Facility User)*; Robert Buckingham *(Illegal Security Access Carrier)*; J. Clark Johnson *(Hackney Transportist)*; Antony Sandoval *(Un Homme)*; Isabel Lorca *(Une Femme)*; Nicole Mancera *(Una Nina)*; Yolanda Gonzalez *(Su Madre)*; Antonette Saftler *(Mrs. Wentzel)*; Teddy Beeler *(Union Station Security)*; Alison Stuart *(Verbally Abusive Spouse)*; Yul Vazquez *(Gustino—Guest Services)*; Edith Diaz *(Irene—Domestic Maintenance)*; Armando Ortega *(Hector—Guest Services)*; C.J. Bau *(Mixologist)*; Cynthena Sanders *(Beverage Server)*; Dana Mackey *(Transport Reception Manager)*; Christopher Jacobs *(Comestible Server)*; Charles Carroll *(Sanitation Engineer)*

NICK OF TIME is a gimmicky thriller told in "real time": one minute of fictional time equals, more or less, one minute of real time. Unfortunately, its premise—that a regular guy could be plucked from a crowd and entrusted with the task of assassinating a political figure—never becomes even remotely plausible.

It's noon, and Gene Watson's (Johnny Depp's) train is pulling into the station. Watson is on a business trip, traveling with his small daughter, Lynn (Courtney Chase). A man and a woman—Mr. Smith (Christopher Walken) and Ms. Jones (Roma Maffia)—scan the terminal from a balcony. Smith spots Nick and declares he's the one they're looking for. Pretending to be cops—complete with convincing badges—Smith and Jones accost Watson and his daughter, escorting them outside to a gray van. Once inside, Smith lays out the deal. He wants Watson to murder a woman at the nearby Bonaventure hotel. He gives Watson ID, an itinerary, a picture and a gun. If the woman isn't dead by 1:30, they'll kill little Lynn.

By 12:25, Watson is at the hotel, where he realizes his target is Governor Eleanor Grant (Marsha Mason), who's campaigning for re-election. He tries several times to enlist help, but Smith always appears, warning with increasing intensity that Watson had better get on with the job. Jones parks the van at the curb outside. Watson blows an opportunity to shoot Grant in an elevator, then tries to get help from her security team, only to find they're in on it, too. In desperation, he pulls the gun on Grant's assistant, and persuades her to take him to Grant's husband and campaign manager, Brendan (Peter Strauss). He tells Brendan the story and, to his horror, Brendan and his associate (G.D. Spradlin) call Smith, who kills Grant's assistant and tells Watson to get back to it.

At 1:00, Watson tricks Smith into revealing himself in front of Huey (Charles S. Dutton), a shoeshine man and army veteran. Huey agrees to help. He concocts a plan to convince Smith that Watson is in the toilet, then helps Watson sneak into the Governor's hotel room. At 1:20, he tells her the story and says that if she doesn't believe him, she should try to cancel the next speech on her schedule, the one that will offer Watson his last opportunity to shoot her before the deadline. At 1:23, Watson slips back into the men's room, just in time for Smith to burst in.

Brendan's evasive answers to the governor's questions convince her Watson was telling the truth. She appears for her speech, which Watson disrupts by firing into the ceiling. Smith tries to pull off the assassination himself—there's plenty of evidence against Watson—but misses. Huey tackles Jones and prevents her from murdering Lynn, and Watson kills Smith and rescues his daughter. The media begin reporting on the attempted assassination.

Why would the shadowy forces that want the Governor dead—apparently conservative businessmen who supported her election and feel betrayed by her liberal inclinations—allow Smith to sell them on a plan that involves blackmailing an amateur into doing the deed? Who knows? NICK OF TIME certainly doesn't provide an answer, and the outlandishness of the conceit hangs over the film like a dense fog, damping down whatever suspense might have been wrung from Depp's race against time. While no more preposterously paranoid than, say, THE MANCHURIAN CANDIDATE, NICK OF TIME gets bogged down its gimmick to the detriment of its plot and atmosphere. Despite the claustrophobic location—virtually the entire film takes place inside the hotel—there's plenty of action, but it seems forced and artificial.

In an era of ludicrously overstated action pictures, it would be nice to be able to point at NICK OF TIME as an alternative, but it's simply too deeply flawed. The film's tone is particularly damaged by a gratuitous sequence that begins with Watson shooting Smith and ends with Watson falling from a high balcony to what seems certain death. It turns out to have taken place entirely in Watson's imagination, a cheap ploy to add an spectacular stunt to a movie that otherwise takes pains to keep its scale small and human. *(Violence, profanity.)* — M.M.

d, John Badham; p, John Badham; exec p, D.J. Caruso; assoc p, Cammie Crier; w, Patrick Sheane Duncan; ph, Roy H. Wagner; ed, Frank Morriss, Kevin Stitt; m, Arthur B. Rubinstein; prod d, Philip Harrison; art d, Eric Orbom; set d, Julia Badham; sound, Willie Burton (mixer); fx, Jeff Jarvis; casting, Carol Lewis; cos, Mary E. Vogt; makeup, John Elliott, Jim Scribner, Sheila Evers; stunts, Shane Dixon

Thriller/Crime/Drama (PR: C MPAA: R)

NIGHTMARE ★★
(U.S.) 84m Patchett-Kauffman Entertainment ~
New Horizons Home Video c

Victoria Principal *(Linda Hemmings)*; Paul Sorvino *(Lt. Jake Wilman)*; Jonathan Banks *(Edward Ryter)*; Danielle Harris *(Dana Hemmings)*; Christine Healy *(Susan Fisher)*; Charles Siebert *(District Attorney Gordon)*; Gregg Henry *(Hal Lawrence)*

NIGHTMARE is an unimaginative telling of a generic story—faced with the law's indifference, a mother must seek justice against the man who attacked her daughter.

Teacher and single mother Linda Hemmings (Victoria Principal) faces a parent's worst nightmare when her daughter Dana (Danielle Harris) is kidnapped. Dana escapes and her assailant Edward Ryter (Jonathan Banks) is arrested. But the nightmare has just begun as Hemmings learns that Ryter won't stay imprisoned long, and he threatens to kill Dana if she testifies. Certain that Ryter has killed before but never been caught, Hemmings teams up with police detective Jake Wilman (Paul Sorvino). They discover that Ryter can be linked circumstantially to other cases

of missing girls. Hemmings breaks into Ryter's home to search for evidence against him, and when he unexpectedly returns, she shoots him. She covers her tracks, but Wilman is suspicious. Eventually she confesses her action to Wilman and turns over proof of murders Ryter committed. Satisfied that justice has been done, Wilman rules Ryter's death a suicide.

Produced in 1991 for broadcast in foreign television markets, and now released to video, NIGHTMARE is a movie ideally suited to the Lifetime Cable Network's programming, but even there it would be a subpar offering. The story is wholly unremarkable. The beautiful and willful mother, guided by the determined and paternal cop, takes down the creepy-looking bad guy, while the straightforward plot plods unambiguously to its conclusion. The generic dramatics are made watchable by the cast, and the production values are good, but that's not much of a recommendation, unless you bring low expectations to your rental choices. *(Violence.)* — P.R.

d, John Pasquin; p, Graham Cottle; exec p, Victoria Principal, Kenneth Kaufman, Tom Patchett; w, John Robert Bensink, Rick Husky (based on the novel by Marjorie Dorner); ph, Denis Lewiston; ed, David Campling; m, Dana Kappoff; prod d, Roy Alan Amaral; casting, Beth Hymson

Drama (PR: A MPAA: PG-13)

NINA TAKES A LOVER ★★½
(U.S.) 100m Sharona Productions ~ Triumph Releasing c

Laura San Giacomo *(Nina)*; Paul Rhys *(Photographer)*; Michael O'Keefe *(Journalist)*; Cristi Conaway *(Friend)*; Fisher Stevens *(Paulie)*

NINA TAKES A LOVER is the story of a bored married woman who has an affair while her husband is away on business. Writer-director Alan Jacobs, feeling that 90s films had been dreadfully lacking in romance, set out to fill a void. The film's resulting box-office failure may be more due to the public's distaste for dialogue and subtlety than the fact that his goal was only partially realized.

The film opens with Nina (Laura San Giacomo) telling her tale in flashback to a reporter (Michael O'Keefe) who is writing a story about marital infidelity. Nina feels restless because her marriage lacks romance. When her best friend (Cristi Conaway) begins an affair with Paulie (Fisher Stevens), the owner of a local coffee shop, Nina disapproves but is fascinated. When her husband leaves for a three-week business trip, Nina meets a handsome British photographer (Paul Rhys) in a park. Despite her initial hesitancy, his charm and her attraction to him prevail, and the two begin an affair. Nina insists that her affair is different than her friend's. While Paulie is childish and unreliable, the photographer is mature and attentive. Her friend's affair may be a fling, but Nina's is true love. The affair changes Nina's life. The unpredictability and excitement it brings make her feel important and worthwhile.

One day, while in the photographer's studio, Nina discovers that he has been sleeping with other women. The news reporter doesn't understand her feeling of betrayal, so she admits to him that the photographer is her husband, and the "affair" was simply an attempt to bring some spice into their marriage. Nina reacts to her husband's infidelity by unsuccessfully trying to seduce Paulie. After that failure, she decides to completely reevaluate the marriage. The film ends on a positive note, with Nina and the photographer reunited, determined to bring the romance of their "affair" into their everyday life.

NINA TAKES A LOVER is Jacobs's first feature film, and it shows impressive style. San Francisco's charm is well used; it seems like the most romantic city on earth. The film's use of coffee shops and parks effectively brings the viewer into Nina's world. Nina and the photographer are complex, fully realized characters, and the emotions in the film are believable and powerful. The acting is of high quality, and Stevens is as strong as San Giacomo and Rhys. On the other hand, the flashback technique is a distraction that exists only to expose the film's secret. Nina's voice-overs are often awkward ("I *loved* making love to him"), but the dialogue, which is solid and intelligent, compensates. The film's statement that monogamy is more romantic than infidelity is supported by the chaotic and unfulfilling affair of Laura's friend. However, since much of the film's strength comes from the danger and mystery of Nina's affair, the conclusion seems halfhearted.

Jacobs's biggest fear about the film was that the general public, who usually favor action and sex over dialogue and romance, wouldn't give it a chance. Both leads believed in Jacobs and the script enough to appear in the film for less than their usual fees, and the film is clearly a labor of love. Despite its flaws, NINA TAKES A LOVER shows talent and deserves more attention than it received. *(Sexual situations, nudity, profanity.)* — A.M.

d, Alan Jacobs; p, Jane Hernandez, Alan Jacobs; exec p, Graeme Bretall, Shelby Notkin; assoc p, Clarisse Perrette; w, Alan Jacobs; ph, Phil Parmet; ed, John Nutt; m, Todd Boekelheide; prod d, Don De Fina; set d, Victoria Lewis; sound, Dan Gleich; casting, Billy Pagano, Sharon Bialy, Debi Manwiller; cos, Marianna Astrom-De Fina; makeup, Nancy Marsalis

Romance/Drama　　　　　　　**(PR: C　MPAA: R)**

NINE MONTHS　　　　　　　★★½
(U.S.) 103m 1492 Pictures; 20th Century Fox ~
20th Century Fox c

Hugh Grant *(Samuel Faulkner)*; Julianne Moore *(Rebecca Taylor)*; Tom Arnold *(Marty Dwyer)*; Joan Cusack *(Gail Dwyer)*; Jeff Goldblum *(Sean Fletcher)*; Robin Williams *(Dr. Kosevich)*; Mia Cottet *(Lili)*; Joey Simmrin *(Truman)*; Ashley Johnson *(Shannon Dwyer)*; Alexa Vega *(Molly Dwyer)*; Aislin Roche *(Patsy Dwyer)*; Priscilla Alden *(Older Woman)*; Edward Ivory *(Older Man)*; James M. Brady *(Bicyclist)*; Charles A. Martinet *(Arnie)*; Brendan Columbus *(Little Boy on Beach)*; Eleanor Columbus *(Little Girl in Ballet Class #1)*; Anna Barnathan *(Little Girl in Ballet Class #2)*; Zelda Williams *(Little Girl in Ballet Class #3)*; Peter Bankins *(Tow Truck Driver)*; Betsy Monroe *(Bobbie)*; Ngaio S. Bealum *(Sean's Friend #1)*; Cynthia Urquhart *(Sean's Friend #2)*; Tim Moffet *(Sean's Friend #3)*; Mia Liban *(Sean's Friend #4)*; Kumar Singh *(Sean's Friend #5)*; Amanda Girard *(Praying Mantis)*; Val Diamond *(Dr. Kosevich's Receptionist)*; Jerry Masan *(Clown Outside Toy Store)*; Irene Columbus *(Woman in Toy Store)*; Violet Columbus *(Baby in Toy Store)*; Brittany Radcliffe *(Child #1 at Toy Store)*; Porscha Radcliffe *(Child #2 at Toy Store)*; Cody Lee Dorkin *(Child #3 at Toy Store)*; Emily Gosnell *(Child #4 at Toy Store)*; Bradley Gosnell *(Child #5 at Toy Store)*; Kristin Davis *(Tennis Attendant)*; Angela Hopkins *(Ultrasound Receptionist)*; Emily Yancy *(Dr. Thatcher)*; Hayley Rose Hansen *(Baby in Ultrasound)*; Shawn Cady *(Roller Blade Girl)*; George F. Mauricio *(Moving Man)*; Paul Simon *(Car Salesman)*; Frank P. Verducci *(Car Lot Customer #1)*; Barbara Olson *(Car Lot Customer #2)*; Morgan Miller *(Kid Being Choked in Park)*; Carol De Pasquale *(Maternity Floor Receptionist)*; Bruce Devan *(Doctor in Hallway)*; Cheryl Lee Thorup *(Christine)*; Clarke Devereux *(Emergency Attendant #1)*; Tommy Banks *(Emergency Attendant #2)*; Susan Ilene Johnson *(Delivery Room Head Nurse)*; Maureen McVerry *(Pregnant Woman #1)*; Velina Brown *(Pregnant Woman #2)*; Joy M. Cook

(Pregnant Woman #3); Sue Murphy *(Pregnant Woman #4)*; Lee Ann Manley *(Pregnant Woman #5)*; Diane Amos *(Rebecca's Nurse)*; Betsy Aidem *(Gail's Nurse)*; Terence McGovern *(Anesthesiologist)*; Geoff Bolt *(Male Delivery Room Nurse)*; Gwen Holloway *(Female Delivery Room Nurse)*

A "nuclear family reassurance" comedy from writer-director Chris Columbus of HOME ALONE and MRS. DOUBTFIRE notoriety, NINE MONTHS handles adult subject matter in a profoundly juvenile manner.

English child psychologist Samuel Faulkner (Hugh Grant) and his American girlfriend Rebecca Taylor (Julianne Moore) have a near-perfect relationship, until the day she announces she's pregnant. What's an immature cad to do? He can marry her, and risk ending up like Marty (Tom Arnold), a loud, boorish—but to hear him tell it, blissfully happy—father of three little monsters. Or he can leave her, and risk ending up like his artist friend Sean (Jeff Goldblum)—whose sister Gale (Joan Cusack) is Marty's wife—who has a girlfriend young enough to be his daughter. Lip service is paid to this being a tragic state of affairs, though Sean seems happy as a pig in mud. Samuel truly loves Rebecca, so he puts on a happy face and ignores the problem.

Months pass, and Samuel still hasn't warmed to the idea of fatherhood. Rebecca leaves him and moves in with Gail and Marty. Samuel quickly realizes what he's lost, but Rebecca will have nothing to do with him. Determined to win her back, he dumps his beloved Porsche in favor of a family car, and starts reading baby books. Eventually he proposes, and soon after, the two are married. When the big day comes, Rebecca and Samuel find themselves in the delivery room with Marty and Gale, and a Russian doctor who's only recently switched from animal husbandry to obstetrics (Robin Williams). Samuel argues with Marty (who's trying to videotape both births), screams at the doctor (whose fractured English is incomprehensible), and ends up wrestling on the floor with both of them. In the end, the new daddy couldn't love his new son more.

NINE MONTHS marked the much anticipated major American movie debut of adorably befuddled Hugh Grant, self-deprecating star of the phenomenally successful FOUR WEDDINGS AND A FUNERAL (1994). His charm is considerable, almost sufficient to gloss over the fact that he's playing the sort of man who imagines his newly pregnant girlfriend as a giant, slimy praying mantis about to devour him. Samuel's a heel, and Grant's mission is to make him such an affable gent that viewers will overlook his shortcomings, secure in the knowledge that he'll embrace domesticity eventually.

Shortly before the release of NINE MONTHS, Grant was arrested in Los Angeles for picking up a prostitute. The event generated so much publicity for the picture that it was soon being cynically suggested that the whole sordid business had been a publicity stunt. It also appears to have led to the removal of a sequence in which Grant's character is arrested and booked (for breaking a window to rescue his cat); though footage from the scene was in the trailer, it was not in the finished film. Like Woody Allen's HUSBANDS AND WIVES (1992), NINE MONTHS also lent itself to being read in light of Grant's public indiscretion: the scene in which he tells Rebecca, "I was a disgrace. You had every right to walk out on me," particularly provoked hilarity.

NINE MONTHS is based on the French film NEUF MOIS, and it's a sad comment on the state of American comedy that such a simple-minded premise isn't even an original one. The themes the film addresses are nothing more than the topics one would see on "Donahue" or "Oprah"—"My man won't commit"; "My man fears fatherhood"; "Foreign doctor horror stories"—and it's unfortunate that the idea NINE MONTHS sells so convincingly—a baby will fix a troubled relationship—is also featured on talk shows, in the form of poor, single, teenaged mothers. *(Profanity, violence, sexual situations.)* — P.R.

d, Chris Columbus; p, Anne Francois, Chris Columbus, Mark Radcliffe, Michael Barnathan; exec p, Joan Bradshaw, Christopher Lambert; assoc p, Paula DuPre Pesmen; w, Chris Columbus (based on the film NEUF MOIS written and directed by Patrick Braoude); ph, Donald McAlpine; ed, Raja Gosnell, Stephen Rivkin; m, Hans Zimmer; prod d, Angelo P. Graham; art d, W. Steven Graham; set d, Garrett Lewis; sound, Nelson Stoll (mixer), Scott Kinzey (recordist); fx, John McLeod; casting, Janet Hirshenson, Jane Jenkins; cos, Jay Hurley; makeup, Greg Cannom, Bob Mills; stunts, Glenn R. Wilder

Comedy/Romance   **(PR: A   MPAA: PG-13)**

NIXON   ★★★
(U.S.) 190m Cinergi Productions; Illusion Entertainment Group; Hollywood Pictures ~ Buena Vista c/bw

Anthony Hopkins *(Richard M. Nixon)*; Joan Allen *(Pat Nixon)*; Powers Boothe *(Alexander Haig)*; Ed Harris *(E. Howard Hunt)*; Bob Hoskins *(J. Edgar Hoover)*; E.G. Marshall *(John Mitchell)*; David Paymer *(Ron Ziegler)*; David Hyde Pierce *(John Dean)*; Paul Sorvino *(Henry Kissinger)*; Mary Steenburgen *(Hannah Nixon)*; J.T. Walsh *(John Ehrlichman)*; James Woods *(H.R. Haldeman)*; Brian Bedford *(Clyde Tolson)*; Kevin Dunn *(Charles Colson)*; Fyvush Finkel *(Murray Chotiner)*; Annabeth Gish *(Julie Nixon)*; Tony Goldwyn *(Harold Nixon)*; Larry Hagman *("Jack Jones")*; Ed Herrmann *(Nelson Rockefeller)*; Madeleine Kahn *(Martha Mitchell)*; Saul Rubinek *(Herb Klein)*; Tony Lo Bianco *(Johnny Roselli)*; Corey Carrier *(Richard Nixon at 12)*; Tom Bower *(Frank Nixon)*; David Barry Gray *(Richard Nixon at 19)*; Tony Plana *(Manolo Sanchez)*; Dan Hedaya *(Trini Cardoza)*; John Cunningham *(Bob)*; John C. McGinley *(Earl)*; John Diehl *(Gordon Liddy)*; Robert Beltran *(Frank Sturgis)*; Lenny Vullo *(Bernard Barker)*; Ronald Von Klaussen *(James McCord)*; Kamar De Los Reyes *(Eugenio Martinez)*; Enrique Castillo *(Virgilio Gonzales)*; Victor Rivers *(Cuban Plumber)*; Drew Snyder *(Moderator)*; Sean Stone *(Donald Nixon)*; Joshua Preston *(Arthur Nixon)*; Ian Calip *(Football Player)*; Jack Wallace *(Football Coach)*; Julie Condra Douglas *(Young Pat Nixon)*; Annette Helde *(Happy Rockefeller)*; Howard Platt *(Lawyer at Party)*; Mike Kennedy *(Convention Announcer)*; Harry Murphy *(Fan #1)*; Suzanne Schnulle Murphy *(Fan #2)*; Michael Kaufman *(Fan #3)*; Bridgette Wilson *(Sandy)*; Pamela Dickerson *(Girlfriend)*; O'Neal Compton *(Texas Man)*; John Bedford Lloyd *(Cuban Man)*; Dr. Christian Renna *(Family Doctor)*; Michael Chiklis *(TV Director)*; Wilson Cruz *(Joaquin)*; James Pickens *(Black Orator)*; Mikey Stone *(Edward Nixon)*; Robert Marshall *(Spiro Agnew)*; Marley Shelton *(Tricia Nixon)*; James Karen *(Bill Rogers)*; Richard Fancy *(Mel Laird)*; Peter Carlin *(Student #1)*; Joanna Going *(Young Student)*; Michelle Krusiec *(Student #2)*; Wass Stevens *(Protester)*; Tom Nicoletti *(Secret Service Agent #1)*; Chuck Pfeiffer *(Secret Service Agent #2)*; Alex Butterfield *(White House Staffer)*; Mark Steins *(White House Security)*; Ric Young *(Mao Tse-Tung)*; Bai Ling *(Chinese Interpreter)*; Peter P. Starson, Jr. *(Air Force One Steward)*; Jon Tenney *(Reporter #1)*; Julie Araskog *(Reporter #2)*; Ray Wills *(Reporter #3)*; John Bellucci *(Reporter #4)*; Zoey Zimmerman *(Reporter #5)*; Mary Rudolph *(Rosemary Woods)*; Clayton Townsend *(Floor Manager #1)*; Donna Dixon *(Maureen Dean)*; John Stockwell *(Staffer #1)*; Charlie Haugk *(Staffer #2)*; Boris Sichkin *(Leonid Brezhnev)*; Fima Noveck *(Andre Gromyko)*; Raissa Danilova *(Russian Interpreter)*; Marilyn Rockafellow *(Helen Smith)*; Bill

Bolender *(Bethesda Doctor)*; Melinda Renna *(Bethesda Nurse)*; George Plimpton *(President's Lawyer)*

If the era loosely defined as "the Sixties" truly ended with Watergate, then NIXON should represent director Oliver Stone's last fling with that turbulent period. As much fantasy as history, by turns elegiac, infuriating, and dull, the film is the epitome of Stone's try-everything, "kitchen sink" aesthetic.

The narrative jumps forward and back through time with abandon. In the "present"—August, 1974—President Richard Nixon (Anthony Hopkins) listens to tape recordings that he has been ordered to surrender to the House Judiciary Committee. The tapes prove that in 1972, he illegally ordered the FBI to halt its investigation of the Watergate burglary. His Chief of Staff, Alexander Haig (Powers Boothe) persuades him to resign rather than provoke a Constitutional crisis.

Flashbacks reveal 12-year-old Dick Nixon (Corey Carrier) growing up in an impoverished Quaker home, coping with an unloving father (Tony Goldwyn), a strict, pious mother (Mary Steenburgen), and the deaths of two brothers from tuberculosis. Nixon works his way through college and law school and wins election to Congress, where he becomes prominent by securing the indictment of alleged Communist Alger Hiss. Meanwhile, he has married Pat (Joan Allen), who resents his obsession with politics but resigns herself to playing the loyal wife.

As Eisenhower's Vice President, Nixon is accused of maintaining an illegal slush fund, but saves his career by delivering the "Checkers" speech on national television. His TV savvy deserts him, however, during the 1960 Presidential race, when he is humiliated in debates by a suave JFK. He loses to Kennedy in a remarkably close election—which his aides believe was stolen by the Democrats—and later announces his retirement from politics after losing the 1962 California gubernatorial race.

The social turmoil of the 1960s creates an opening for a conservative candidate. A sinister cabal of businessmen, together with FBI chief J. Edgar Hoover (Bob Hoskins), persuade Nixon to run again, despite his wife's misgivings. He wins the 1968 election, largely because he claims to have a secret plan to end the Vietnam War. After his re-election in 1972, he negotiates the withdrawal of US troops, but National Security Adviser Henry Kissinger (Paul Sorvino) gets the credit. As the Watergate scandal unravels, forcing the resignation of close advisers H.R. Haldeman (James Woods) and John Erlichman (J.T. Walsh), Nixon attempts to salvage his presidency through diplomatic openings to China and Russia. He is nevertheless undone by taped evidence of his crimes and resigns in 1974, bidding a tearful farewell to his staff. President Bill Clinton eulogizes Nixon as the end titles roll.

One's appreciation of the screenplay (by Steve J. Rivele, Christopher Wilkinson, and Stone) will probably depend on one's familiarity with real events. Opening and closing on the ill-starred President's "final days," NIXON loops back and forth through well-trodden historical ground (the Checkers speech, the Nixon-Kennedy debates, the Hiss case, etc.), semi-factual elaborations of little-known events (Nixon's strict Quaker upbringing in Whittier, California, his marital woes), and outright fabrications (a sinister meeting with Hoover at the racetrack, a blackmail attempt by an imaginary Texas power broker played by Larry Hagman, TV's J.R. Ewing). All of it is refracted through Stone's peculiar penchant for seeing diabolical connections everywhere. In this case, a link is made between Nixon's supposed involvement in the Bay of Pigs invasion and his ultimate vulnerability to the "military-industrial complex." Ironically, the film posits a nutty theory of the Kennedy assassination that is completely inconsistent with the equally nutty theory offered in Stone's JFK.

What makes NIXON better than JFK is the centering gravity of Anthony Hopkins's empathetic performance. Though not an obvious choice to play the not-so-great man—his heavy makeup and awkward American accent are often distracting—Hopkins nevertheless manages to wring pathos from a life characterized by self-pity, paranoia, and good intentions gone badly wrong. Unfortunately, when genuine newsreel footage of the historical Richard Nixon appears at the end of the film, the real man instantly dispels all the sympathy Hopkins builds in three hours of screen time.

Of course, it is Oliver Stone and his preoccupations that are the real subjects of NIXON. Nothing but the director's own egoism could have led him to believe that a definitive portrait of Nixon was possible so soon after the man's death. If Stone presents a surprisingly mild portrait, it is perhaps because Stone and Nixon were far closer in temperament than they are politically. Indeed, compared to the political atmosphere at the time of the film's release, Nixon's brand of internationalist Republicanism looked wistfully liberal. In intention, the film might be understood as the CITIZEN KANE Orson Welles would have told if Kane had actually won his governorship. *(Extreme profanity.)* — N.N.

d, Oliver Stone; p, Clayton Townsend, Oliver Stone, Andrew G. Vajna; assoc p, Richard Rutowski; co-p, Eric Hamburg, Dan Halsted; w, Stephen J. Rivele, Christopher Wilkinson, Oliver Stone; ph, Robert Richardson; ed, Brian Berdan, Hank Corwin; m, John Williams; prod d, Victor Kempster; art d, Donald Woodruff, Richard F. Mays, Margery Zweizig; set d, Merideth Boswell; sound, David MacMillan (mixer); fx, F. Lee Stone, Peter Kuran, Christer Hokanson, Chris Loudon; casting, Billy Hopkins, Heidi Levitt, Mary Vernieu; cos, Richard Hornung; makeup, John Blake, Gordon Smith, FX Smith

AAN Best Actor: Anthony Hopkins; *AAN Best Supporting Actress:* Joan Allen; *AAN Best Original Screenplay:* Stephen J. Rivele, Christopher Wilkinson, Oliver Stone; *AAN Best Dramatic Score:* John Williams

Drama/Biography/Political　　　(PR: C　MPAA: R)

NO MERCY　　　★★★½
(Peru/Mexico/France) 117m Inca Films;
Amaranta Foundation of New Latin American
Cinema ~ Inca Films c
(SIN COMPASION)

Diego Bertie *(Ramon Romano)*; Adriana Davila *(Sonia Martinez)*; Jorge Chiarella *(Mayor Portillo)*; Hernan Romero *(Alejandro Velaochaga)*; Marcello Rivera *(Julian Razuri)*; Mariella Trejos *(Senora Aliaga)*; Leandro Martinez *(Ricardo Fernandez)*; Carlos Onetto *(The Priest)*; Augusto Modenesi *(Mr. Aliaga)*

Dostoyevsky's *Crime and Punishment* has been shrewdly transplanted to modern-day Peru for NO MERCY, a grim and gritty drama about a philosophy student who commits a double murder.

In a run-down section of Lima, Ramon Romano (Diego Bertie) scrapes by to pay the rent on his one-room apartment while attending the nearby university. In class, he argues with his professors about Kant and Nietzsche, but otherwise appears to be a likable, soft-spoken young man. Privately, however, Romano rages about his landlady, Mrs. Aliaga (Mariella Trejos), a symbol of nouveau riche excess. On the day Romano visits Mrs. Aliaga to pay his overdue rent, he revolts against her brusque, demanding manner, and kills her in a moment of passion. When the woman's husband happens upon the scene, Romano kills him as well.

Romano tells no one about the crime, not even his most loyal friend, Julian Razuri (Marcello Rivera), but he does go to the police station to report an unrelated accident. While Romano is at the station, a wily police inspector, Mayor Portillo (Jorge Chiarella), begins suspecting that this student is involved in the unsolved murder case. Back home, Romano gives money he had stolen from the Aliagas to his neighbor and girlfriend, Sonia (Adriana Davila), so that she may free herself from a life of prostitution. Portillo, meanwhile, tries to make Romano feel guilty by telling him that the landlady's gardener has confessed to the crime, but Romano still refuses to tell the truth. Finally, Romano confesses after Sonia tells him of her religious devotion. Romano spends eight years in jail, while Sonia waits for him outside.

NO MERCY has much to say about the social, political, religious and economic conditions in Peru today, and yet, Francisco J. Lombardi's production best resembles the late 1960s work of *nouvelle vague* director, Claude Chabrol. Like Chabrol, Lombardi expands upon the style of Alfred Hitchcock's Hollywood thrillers by using unexpected and intrusive shards of self-conscious humor in the midst of morbid and grisly scenes. The first murder itself is graphic and gruesome, and, yet, the difficulty Romano has in completing the bloody task recalls the same darkly humorous approach Hitchcock took in the famous TORN CURTAIN (1966) murder scene, which Chabrol then revised in LA FEMME INFIDELE (1969). NO MERCY makes many other extratextual points throughout, including the Inspector's comment that Romano's apartment looks like the set of "a neorealist film".

NO MERCY also features a great performance by Diego Bertie, who perfectly captures Romano's revolutionary ideals and anti-Christian fervor. It is almost too bad when the film leaves Romano's story to include a subplot about a rich widower (played by Hernan Romero) who also tries to "save" Sonia. Still, most of NO MERCY remains compelling viewing, realistically executed yet reflexively enlightening. *(Graphic violence, nudity, adult situations, profanity.)* — E.M.

d, Francisco Jose Lombardi; p, Francisco Jose Lombardi; exec p, Gustavo Sanchez; w, Augusto Cabada (based on the novel *Crime and Punishment* by Feodor Dostoyevsky); ph, Pili Flores Guerra; ed, Luis Barrios; m, Leopoldo La Rosa; prod d, Cecilia Montiel; sound, Daniel Padilla; casting, Monica Dominguez

Drama/Crime/Political　　　(PR: C　MPAA: NR)

NOBODY LOVES ME　　　★★★
(Germany) 104m Cobra Films ~ CFP Distribution c
(KEINER LIEBT MICH)

Maria Schrader *(Fanny Fink)*; Pierre Sanoussi-Bliss *(Orfeo de Altamar)*; Michael Von Au *(Lothar Sticker)*; Elisabeth Trissenaar *(Madeleine)*; Ingo Naujoks *(Lasse Langsfeld)*; Joachim Krol *(Anton)*; Peggy Parnass *(Mrs. Radebrecht)*; Lorose Keller *(Zsa Zsa)*; Anya Hoffmann *(Charlotte)*; Erwin Grosche *(Mr. Kokkinos)*; Roland Kabelitz *(Mr. Findeis)*; Steffen Grabner *(Benno Kugler)*; Oliver Nagele *(Mr. Froh)*; Ute Maria Lerner *(Sevgi)*; Laura Medinger *(Lisa)*; Stefan Gebelhoff *(Young Man in Cafe)*; Birgit Stein *(Lover I)*; Gruschenka Stevens *(Lover II)*; Claudia Matschulla *(Business Woman)*; Omer Simsek *(Bank Teller)*; Ruth Bruck *(Elderly Woman)*; Karin Johnson *(Waitress)*; Klaus Kohler *(Herbert)*; Peter Bohlke *(Old Man in Church)*

Against the backdrop of Cologne's annual carnival, NOBODY LOVES ME tells the strange and quirky story of Fanny Fink (Maria Schrader), a lonely single woman coping with life in modern-day Germany.

Fink is so glum about her future, that she has enrolled in classes on "conscious dying," and lies supine in a coffin at home at night. Desperate for companionship, she enlists her neighbor, a drag queen and spiritual advisor named Orfeo (Pierre Sanoussi-Bliss), to help her with her man trouble. During a palm reading session, the bizarre but likable Orfeo tells Fanny that she will soon meet Mr. Right, but Fanny mistakes the handsome Lothar (Michael Von Au), her building's new manager, for the man in question, and seeks Orfeo's further assistance to capture Lothar's attention.

After Orfeo casts a love spell that seems to work, Fanny catches Lothar having sex with her best friend, Charlotte (Anya Hoffmann). Meanwhile, Orfeo experiences his own heartbreak when he catches his lover, a television anchor, kissing another man in the middle of the nightclub where Orfeo performs.

On the night of her 30th birthday, Fanny commiserates with Orfeo, whom Lothar has evicted for not paying his rent. Orfeo then tells Fanny that he is about to die and will soon be taken away by UFOs to his home planet of Arcturus. Although skeptical at first, Fanny helps her friend prepare for his heavenly ascent by placing him in her coffin. Orfeo does indeed disappear and Fanny commemorates his life by throwing a party with her other neighbors, one of whom turns out to be the real Mr. Right.

NOBODY LOVES ME marks a comeback for director Doris Dorrie, who seemed to have disappeared from the scene after her 1985 international hit, MEN. Most of Dorrie's more recent features and documentaries have received limited distribution, perhaps due to the failure of her one unspeakably bad foray into Hollywood filmmaking, ME AND HIM (1988), which was about a man and his talking penis. With NOBODY LOVES ME, Dorrie has written and directed a sharp yet wistful meditation on modern-day relationships that is almost as winning as MEN.

NOBODY LOVES ME arrived in U.S. theaters during a cycle of quasi-feminist films about young single women looking for love and happiness (MURIEL'S WEDDING, A CIRCLE OF FRIENDS, PARTY GIRL), but Dorrie's approach has more in common with Percy Adlon's SUGARBABY (1985). In both these German-language films, the women become obsessed with handsome but inappropriate mates and, while NOBODY LOVES ME ends happily for Fanny, both films are tinged with a melancholic and morbid slant on life (SUGARBABY's Marianne is a mortuary attendant.)

In a style falling somewhere between Fassbinder and Fellini, Dorrie and her husband, cinematographer Helge Weindler, create a surreal yet vividly believable portrait of an urban setting undergoing vast changes (the restoration of Fanny's spirit parallels the renovation of her apartment building). Yet, the disquieting subplot about Lothar's eviction of the poorer tenants is a frank reminder that not all changes are necessarily good. (While the film emphasizes the personal over the political, there are a few broadsides against the gentrification of postunification Germany.)

The film provides a number of charming and funny moments. The best of them involve Fanny and Orfeo; whether dancing to Edith Piaf's "*Non, je ne regrette rien,*" or casting a romantic spell on Lothar, they make a delightful team. Maria Schrader and Pierre Sanoussi-Bliss are superb in their roles. The rest of the cast, too, contribute fine work, especially Elisabeth Trissenaar as Fanny's trash novel-writing mother.

NOBODY LOVES ME will hopefully give Doris Dorrie renewed exposure. Her idiosyncratic yet sensitive storytelling makes her a director of note. (*Nudity, sexual situations, extreme profanity.*) — E.M.

d, Doris Dorrie; p, Gerd Huber, Renate Seefeldt; w, Doris Dorrie; ph, Helge Weindler; ed, Inez Regnier; m, Niki Reiser; prod d,

Tom Schlesinger; art d, Claus Kottmann; sound, Wolfgang Wirtz; casting, An Dorthe Braker, Horst D. Scheel; cos, Siegbert Kammerer

Comedy/Drama/Romance   **(PR: O   MPAA: NR)**

NOSTRADAMUS KID, THE   ★★
(Australia) 120m Beyond Films; Simpson; LeMesurier Films ~ LIVE Entertainment c

Noah Taylor (*Ken Elkin*); Miranda Otto (*Jennie O'Brien*); Jack Campbell (*McAllister*); Erick Mitsak (*Wayland*); Alice Garner (*Esther*); Lucy Bell (*Sarai*); Arthur Dignam (*Pastor Anderson*); Jeanette Cronin (*Christy*); Jodie Andrews (*Fat Woman*); Allan Light (*Brother Allison*); Robyn Gurney (*Mrs. Elkin*); Colin Friels (*American Preacher*); Luke Cross (*1st Bikie*); Chris Harding (*2nd Bikie*); Melanie Reeson (*1st Adventist Girl*); Kirilee Trist (*2nd Adventist Girl*); Loene Carmen (*Meryl*); Marie Lloyd (*Shepard's Rod*); Annie Byron (*Mrs. Rod*); Hec McMillan (*Meryl's Mum*); Bartholomew Rose (*Kavanagh*); Greg Simpson (*Mr. O'Brien*); David Ritchie (*Club Waiter*); Marilla Newman (*1st Club Stripper*); Joanne Reid (*2nd Club Stripper*); Judy Schmidt (*3rd Club Stripper*); Norman Galton (*Bus Conductor*); Bob Maza (*Black Man*); Jim McClelland (*Magistrate*); Carmel Mullin (*Customer*); Nan Vernon (*Shopkeeper*); Bob Henderson (*1st Usher*); Philip Brown (*Fuzzy Wuzzy*); Bruno Baldoni (*Italian Grocer*); Kenny Graham (*Elderly Attendant*); Imogen Annesley (*1st Beat Girl*); Pamela Hawken (*Piano Player*)

Basing this screen nostalgia on his own growing pains in the Seventh-Day Adventist Church, Australian writer-director Bob Ellis attempts to find cinematic expression for his boyhood brush with religious fanaticism. Unfortunately, his life story is hardly the stuff of a 120-minute epic comedy.

Although college newspaper editor Ken Elkins (Noah Taylor) ankled his fundamentally righteous religion years ago, he is still haunted by the shades of fire and brimstone. As the film flashes back and forth between his rebellious present and his coming-of-age with more pious friend Wayland (Erick Mitsak), Elkins struggles with the call of the flesh. This religion-sanctioned denial of basic urges drives his childhood sweetheart Esther (Alice Garner) off her mind eventually. Not entirely convinced that the Seventh-Day Adventists are incorrect in predicting Armageddon, Elkins philosophizes with flamboyant poet McAllister (Jack Campbell) and then puts his energy into pursuing rich beauty Jennie O'Brien (Miranda Otto). Stalking O'Brien, he is served with a restraining order, and his friend McAllister dumps him for a cushy position as a rich woman's boy-toy. On the eve of the predicted end of the world, Elkins convinces O'Brien to run away with him where they will be safe from nuclear fallout. During this impractical flight, the sexually compatible couple discover their incompatibility as marriage partners. After Elkins's fears of a war with Cuba peter out along with the famous missile crisis, a pregnant O'Brien marries McAllister, and the confused Elkins invests his zeal in a writing vocation. As the years pass, he becomes a famous playwright and journalist. When he runs into boyhood pal Wayland and his wife Sarai (Lucy Bell), they ask his counsel about breaking with their Church. The specter of the Seventh Day Adventist Church still hangs over their lives.

Is there anything more unappetizing than a specifically regional coming-of-age yarn whose moral lessons its filmmaker fails to make universal? With its nonincisive flashbacks zigzagging from fire-and-brimstone past to guilt-ridden present, and a lifeless narration that makes each comic payoff topple before fruition, THE NOSTRADAMUS KID is about as much fun as waiting for the world to end. The color photography is pretty and the supporting cast faithfully chalks up some acting victories. However, Taylor as Elkins wrecks the film's tiny potential with a charismatic void. Throughout this remembrance of flings past, the viewer gets tired of Elkins's soul-searching combined with hints of his prowess in the sack. When the protagonist's world continues not with a bang but a whimper, we cease caring about him or about the warping effects of organized religions. *(Extreme profanity, nudity, sexual situations.)* — R.P.

d, Bob Ellis; p, Terry Jennings; exec p, Roger LeMesurier, Roger Simpson; w, Bob Ellis; ph, Geoff Burton; ed, Henry Dangar; m, Chris Neal; prod d, Roger Ford; art d, Laurie Faen; sound, David Lee (recordist); casting, Liz Mullinar, Catherine Dodd; cos, Louise Wakefield; makeup, Trish Glover, Paul Pattison; stunts, Bernie Ledger

Comedy/Religious　　　　　　**(PR: C　MPAA: R)**

NOT ANGELS BUT ANGELS　　　　　　★★
(Czechoslovakia/France) 80m Miro Films ~
Water Bearer Films c

Jarda; Peter; Honza; Marek; Radek; Zibor; Robert; Pepa; Mirek; Michael; Lada; Joseph; Marcel; Eda; Roman; Joseph Gregoni

While NOT ANGELS BUT ANGELS opts for reticence as it chronicles the nocturnal odysseys of teen hustlers in Prague, Czechoslovakia, one wishes that a little anger or choked-back sentiment had entered into the equation. A bit exploitative (at times the film seems to have been designed for a Men & Boys travel agency), this documentary is an intriguing but pointlessly arty record of a troubling phenomenon: freelance sex jobs for adolescents after the fall of the Iron Curtain. It bubbles with enough dramatic juice to satisfy those who wish to slum through the lower depths.

In the wake of Russia's emancipation of her Eastern European satellite states, Western-style capitalism invaded the once repressed society of Prague. Now the playground of horny tourists, the Czech city breeds adolescent whores who bare their soul on camera as they justify their lifestyles. For every bisexual like Radek who supports a family by servicing male tricks, there are dozens of young, parentally rejected homosexuals trading their bodies instead of flipping burgers at a Czech MacDonalds. Constitutionally unable to be tolerated by their narrow-minded parents, runaways like Robert, Miko, and Danek play Russian roulette with HIV to earn a living. The youths' monologues about sexual bartering are interrupted by the self-serving spiel of a pimp who haunts the popular train station like a Dolly Levi for older gay men. Once recruited into the life, these doleful male streetwalkers often gamble away their savings at clubs that perpetuate the cycle of love for sale. Whether homosexual or bisexual, the film's subjects seem stunted emotionally by having used themselves as a business franchise in a career that wears out employability rapidly.

Fascinating as these case studies of young men servicing chicken hawks in Eastern Europe are, NOT ANGELS BUT ANGELS is particularly resonant in conveying the combination of economic necessity and low self-esteem that marks the hustler's predisposition for prostitution. The film's strongest suit is how assiduously it highlights the premature adulthood that permeates the interviewees' demeanors. No matter how they boast of high wages or clinically discuss the pitfalls of fleshpeddling, all of the participants seem to share an unfamiliarity with joy. Less edifyingly, the film occasionally seems to revel in its salacious subject matter, with porno still inserts and lingering shots of one youth as he bathes. While hardly a recruitment film for hustling, the film hasn't been fashioned with enough restraint. Its pretentious use of Angel iconography and celestial choirs is a real liability. It takes more than classical music and cherubs to lend heavenly irony to an enterprise that straddles the worlds of concerned social scientist and gawking voyeur. By the end, we're not sure which point of view prevails; only the pain in the young men's eyes lingers in the memory. *(Extreme profanity, extensive nudity, substance abuse, sexual situations.)* — R.P.

d, Wiktor Grodecki; p, Miro Vostar; assoc p, Michael Klein; w, Wiktor Grodecki; ph, Vladimir Holomek; ed, Wiktor Grodecki; sound, Jan Ceneil

Documentary　　　　　　**(PR: O　MPAA: NR)**

NOTHING TO LOSE
(SEE: DEATH IN BRUNSWICK)

NOW AND THEN　　　　　　★★
(U.S.) 96m Moving Pictures Productions ~ New Line c

Demi Moore *(Samantha Albertson)*; Melanie Griffith *(Tina Tercell)*; Rosie O'Donnell *(Roberta Martin)*; Rita Wilson *(Christina Dewitt)*; Christina Ricci *(Young Roberta)*; Thora Birch *(Young Teeny)*; Gaby Hoffmann *(Young Samantha)*; Ashleigh Aston Moore *(Young Chrissy)*; Willa Glen *(Angela Albertson)*; Bonnie Hunt *(Mrs. Dewitt)*; Janeane Garofalo *(Wiladene)*; Lolita Davidovich *(Mrs. Albertson)*; Cloris Leachman *(Grandma Albertson)*; Devon Sawa *(Scott Wormer)*; Travis Robertson *(Roger Wormer)*; Justin Humphrey *(Eric Wormer)*; Bradley Coryell *(Clay Wormer)*; Ric Reitz *(Mr. Albertson)*; Walter Sparrow *(Crazy Pete)*; Kellen Crosby *(Kenny)*; Joey Stinson *(Outfielder)*; James Paul Cleckler *(Catcher)*; Tucker Stone *(Young Morton)*; Jamison B. Dowd *(Jimmy)*; Hank Azaria *(Bud Kent)*; Beverly Shelton *(Eda)*; Geoff McKnight *(Tractor Driver)*; T.S. Morgan *(Limo Driver)*; Carl Espy *(Morton Williams)*; Alice Tew *(Baby)*

A nostalgic reminiscence about the friendship shared by four girls in 1970, NOW AND THEN fairly demands to be viewed as a female STAND BY ME, but pales by the comparison.

Samantha (Demi Moore) and Teeny (Melanie Griffith) have returned to their hometown for a reunion with their childhood friends, Roberta (Rosie O'Donnell) and a very pregnant Chrissy (Rita Wilson). It's an occasion for Sam to recall the friends' last summer of innocence.

In 1970, Shelby, Indiana was still a place where 12-year-old girls could disappear all day and stay out well into the night without alarming their parents. For Sam (Gaby Hoffman), Roberta (Chistina Ricci), Teeny (Thora Birch), and Chrissy (Ashleigh Aston Moore), the summer of that year was a time to enjoy black cows at the malt shop, listen to bubblegum pop on AM radio, play Truth or Dare, ride their bike, and feud with the nasty Wormer brothers. It's also a time for them to start facing some decidedly adult realities.

Sam, whose parents are divorcing, is obsessed with the macabre and regularly drags her friends out to the cemetery to hold midnight seances. Believing they've raised the spirit of a child, known as "Dear Johnny," they begin a quest to discover how he died, but discover it's the town secret. Eventually, they learn Johnny and his mother were brutally murdered. One night, Sam gets trapped in a sewer during a thunderstorm, and is saved by Crazy Pete (Walter Sparrow), a scary hermit who only comes out at night. Sam realizes that Pete is Johnny's father, and he's never recovered from the loss. She won't make the same mistake of loving and losing when she grows up.

With her friends beside her, Chrissy has her baby—a girl. Sam realizes that she's made a mistake pushing people away. All the women vow to remain close from now on, just as they were in 1970.

Childbirth and women's friendships. Sex, death, and Vietnam. NOW AND THEN is a female bonding movie with big ambitions: it wants to provide a metaphor for America's loss of innocence. On that level it fails, mostly because the filmmakers seem to believe that evoking a genuine period feel is simply a matter of slapping the right selection of bubblegum hits on the soundtrack. Nor does it succeed as a humorous, poignant mosaic *a la* THE JOY LUCK CLUB or HOW TO MAKE AN AMERICAN QUILT—it's just too loosely structured. Samantha, who's supposed to be a famous writer, isn't a very good storyteller, and her narration meanders around pointlessly. Hollywood considers movies about girls to be box-office poison. Unfortunately, NOW AND THEN, a very modest success, missed an opportunity to dispel that notion. *(Profanity.)* — P.R.

d, Lesli Linka Glatter; p, Suzanne Todd, Demi Moore; exec p, Jennifer Todd; co-p, Eric McLeod; w, I. Marlene King; ph, Ueli Steiger; ed, Jacqueline Cambas; m, Cliff Eidelman; art d, Gershon Ginsburg; set d, Anne Kuljian; sound, James Thornton (mixer); fx, Morgan Guynes, Andre Ellingson; casting, Valerie McCaffrey; cos, Deena Appel; makeup, Deborah Larsen; stunts, Dean Mumford

Comedy/Drama   (PR: A   MPAA: PG-13)

NUMBER ONE FAN   ★½
(U.S.) 93m MCEG Sterling Entertainment ~
Orion Home Video c

Chad McQueen *(Zane Barry)*; Renee Ammann *(Blair Madsen)*; Catherine Mary Stewart *(Holly Newman)*; Paul Bartel *(Director)*; Eric Da Re *(Randall McSwain)*; Charles Matthau *(Scotty Youngman)*; Hoyt Axton *(Lt. Joe Halsey)*; Dean Norris *(Graham Chandler)*; Mary Woronov *(Wedding Coordinator)*; Mark Duke Dalton *(Billy Larkin)*; Sky Solari *(Gabrielle)*; Shay Duffin *(Bartender)*; J. Allison Foust *(Script Supervisor)*; Barry Nolan *(Lieutenant/Interrogator)*; Kelly Dayton *(Tour Guide)*; Lauren Abels *(Salesgirl)*; Gloria Delaney *(Nurse)*; Dick Miller *(Night Manager)*; Douglas Cavanaugh *(Security Guard)*; Jonathan R. Perkins *(Security Guard)*; Nina Blackwood *(Reporter)*; Kurt Lott *(Thug with a Whip)*

Trashy and opportunistic, NUMBER ONE FAN applies erotic thriller conventions and style to the celebrity-stalker syndrome with sleazy results.

Zane Barry (Chad McQueen) is a hot young action star making his latest film and planning his wedding with his fiancee, movie costumer Holly Newman (Catherine Mary Stewart). At a party, he and gorgeous young Blair Madsen (Renee Ammann)

catch each other's eye, and he allows himself to be seduced by her. She proves to be a childhood friend and longtime fan from his hometown, and the next night she talks Zane into missing the premiere of Holly's first film and sleeping with her again. Assuming this is the last he'll see of Blair, Zane patches things up with Holly, but then Blair accosts him in his dressing room. When Zane's manager Scotty (Charles Matthau) goes to call security, Blair follows and strangles him.

Stepping up her campaign to win Zane, Blair attacks Holly, who refuses to speak to Zane when he visits her in the hospital. Blair then vandalizes his dressing room, kills a security guard there, and torches Zane's car. To make matters worse, Blair's angry husband Billy (Mark Duke Dalton) turns up and attacks Zane. Finally, Blair kidnaps Holly, threatening to kill her if Zane doesn't meet her at the studio. Billy follows Zane there. During the resulting confrontation, a fire erupts, and Zane rescues Holly while Billy runs into the flames to save Blair. But Blair's body is never recovered, and the threat of her presence haunts Zane during his subsequent wedding to Holly.

Despite the presence of a woman director, NUMBER ONE FAN is sexist in any number of ways. This is yet another film in which the male protagonist get to have his cake and eat it too, cheating on his loving girlfriend with a hot two-night stand yet remaining a blameless victim in the film's eyes when the seductress won't let him go. And the male target audience is clearly supposed to lust for Blair as she bares her gorgeous body yet fear her predatory sexuality at the same time.

As a thriller, the film is both predictable and unconvincing, particularly when Blair kills Scotty and the night watchman, and nobody appears to notice their disappearance. Aside from the introduction of Billy, a character whose potential goes largely undeveloped, the story proceeds with barely a hint of surprise. Indeed, considering its tacky exploitation of such stalking cases as the Rebecca Schaefer murder, the biggest mystery in this movie is why Paul Bartel, who directed and costarred with Schaefer in SCENES FROM THE CLASS STRUGGLE IN BEVERLY HILLS, agreed to take part in it as an actor. *(Violence, extensive nudity, sexual situations, profanity.)* — M.G.

d, Jane Simpson; p, Donald P. Borchers; exec p, Kathryn Cass, Daryl Sancton; assoc p, Mark F. Kaplan; w, Anthony Laurence Greene; ph, Sead Mutarevic; ed, Ivan Ladizinsky; m, Robert J. Walsh; prod d, Gary Randall; sound, Oliver L. Moss; fx, Gregg Hendrickson; casting, Linda Francis; cos, Vincent Lapper; makeup, Eryn Krueger

Thriller   (PR: O   MPAA: R)

OH . . . ROSALINDA!! ★★½
(U.K.) 101m Associated British Picture Corporation; Pathe c

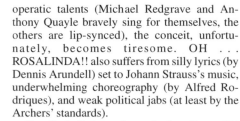

Anthony Quayle *(General Orlovsky)*; Anton Walbrook *(Dr. Falke, the Fledermaus)*; Walter Berry *(Singing Voice of Dr. Falke)*; Richard Marner *(Colonel Lebotov)*; Ludmilla Tcherina *(Rosalinda)*; Sari Barabas *(Singing Voice of Rosalinda)*; Michael Redgrave *(Colonel Eisenstein)*; Mel Ferrer *(Captain Alfred Westerman)*; Alexander Young *(Singing Voice of Alfred Westerman)*; Nicholas Bruce *(Hotel Receptionist)*; Anneliese Rothenberger *(Adele)*; Dennis Price *(Major Frank)*; Dennis Dowling *(Singing Voice of Major Frank)*; Oskar Sima *(Frosh)*

OH. . . ROSALINDA!!, a misfired 1955 British operetta, made its New York debut (in CinemaScope and restored color) in 1995. For all its faults, however, OH . . . ROSALINDA!! offers a welcome respite from today's less accomplished art films.

This modern version of *Die Fledermaus* is set in an unreal, cartoon-colored post-WWII Vienna. The frolic begins when Dr. Falke (Anton Walbrook), a diplomat, lands in political hot water after he is discovered lying on a sacred Russian statue at the Soviet embassy following a night of revelry in the Occupied city. Falke plots revenge for his embarrassment on Eisenstein (Michael Redgrave), the French army colonel who had placed him on the statue.

Falke first visits Eisenstein at the plush Hotel Quadrille, where he informs him of his impending arrest due to his part in the international incident. Falke then pretends that he has arranged a delay in the imprisonment so that Eisenstein may enjoy himself at an embassy ball that night. Eisenstein lies to his wife Rosalinda (Ludmilla Tcherina), saying that he is going directly to jail when, in fact, he is going first to the ball, which is in honor of the Russian general Orlovsky (Anthony Quayle). After her husband leaves, however, Rosalinda entertains Alfred (Mel Ferrer), an American army officer and old flame who is also staying at the hotel.

When the British commandant, Major Frank (Dennis Price), comes to arrest Eisenstein in his hotel room, he mistakes the American lothario for the French colonel. Meanwhile, Falke tips off Rosalinda that her husband has been seen at the embassy. Rosalinda goes to the ball incognito as a redheaded temptress in order to test her husband's fidelity. After she seduces her husband, who does not recognize her, Rosalinda abruptly leaves, and Eisenstein voluntarily goes to prison to serve his time. When he arrives, however, the colonel is alarmed to find Captain Frank in his cell impersonating him (and declaring his love for Rosalinda). Eisenstein leaves the captain in his place in the jail and returns to the hotel to confront his wife. Rosalinda, in turn, accuses Eisenstein of cheating on her. Eventually, however, they forgive each other for their past indiscretions, while the other hotel guests drink the night away.

It is easy to see why OH . . . ROSALINDA!! was never distributed in the United States. The elaborate froufrou is even more frivolous than THE RED SHOES (1948) and TALES OF HOFFMAN (1951), the two earlier musical hits by director Michael Powell and screenwriter Emeric Pressburger (jointly known as The Archers). Whereas THE RED SHOES offered a commonplace backstage melodrama to anchor its fanciful ballets, and TALES OF HOFFMAN presented pure fantasy without any linear narrative at all, OH. . . ROSALINDA!! offers something uncomfortably in between. The film tells its story in the tradition of the most mannered Hollywood musicals—with stars breaking into songs at any given point in the midst of ultrastylized sets. Given that these stars are hardly known for their operatic talents (Michael Redgrave and Anthony Quayle bravely sing for themselves, the others are lip-synced), the conceit, unfortunately, becomes tiresome. OH . . . ROSALINDA!! also suffers from silly lyrics (by Dennis Arundell) set to Johann Strauss's music, underwhelming choreography (by Alfred Rodriques), and weak political jabs (at least by the Archers' standards).

Despite both the major and minor flaws, OH . . .ROSALINDA!! provides at least a few moments of fun—in addition to the crazy, beautiful production design by Hein Heckroth. Anton Walbrook gets to reprise his wry storyteller role, from Max Ophuls's LA RONDE (1950), in a pre-title direct-address sequence. (The Archers also later poke fun at the running "Madame de . . ." joke from Ophuls's 1954 EARRINGS OF MADAME DE . . . .) Dennis Price's drunk scenes are shot in split screen, cleverly mimicking his character's double vision. Mel Ferrer acts surprisingly goofy in a couple of musical moments, although he would be used to better effect in Jean Renoir's similar sexual roundelay, ELENA AND HER MEN (1956). And Ludmilla Tcherina is delightful as Rosalinda, even though her big moment at the ball—when she seduces her husband—is undercut by its brevity.

OH . . . ROSALINDA!! will never attain the status of BLACK NARCISSUS, A MATTER OF LIFE AND DEATH, or THE RED SHOES, but stateside Archer aficionados ought to be grateful to have a "new" work in the canon. *(Sexual situations.)* — E.M.

d, Michael Powell, Emeric Pressburger; p, Michael Powell, Emeric Pressburger; assoc p, Sydney S. Streeter; w, Michael Powell, Emeric Pressburger (based on the operetta *Die Fledermaus* by Johann Strauss); ph, Christopher Challis; ed, Reginald Mills; m, Johann Strauss; prod d, Hein Heckroth; ch, Alfred Rodrigues; sound, Leslie Hammond, Herbert Janeczka; cos, Jean Desses of Paris; makeup, Constance Reeve

Musical/Comedy/Opera (PR: A MPAA: NR)

O.J. SIMPSON STORY, THE ★★½
(U.S.) 90m National Studios ~ FoxVideo c

Bobby Hosea *(O.J. Simpson)*; Jessica Tuck *(Nicole Brown Simpson)*; Bruce Weitz *(Robert Shapiro)*; David Roberson *(A.C. Cowlings)*; Kimberly Russell *(Marguerite)*; James Handy *(Detective Vannatter)*; Paul Witten *(Ronald Goldman)*; Johnathan R. Hoog *(Justin)*; Natassia Yalley *(Sydney)*; Michael C. Gwynne *(Detective Lange)*; Bumper Robinson *(Young O.J.)*; Terrence Howard *(Young A.C.)*; Harvey Jason *(Howard Weitzman)*; Eugene Lee *(Willie Mays)*; Jonathan Steele *(Kato)*; Mariann Aalda *(O.J.'s Mom Eunice)*; Martin Cassidy *(TV Detective)*; Steve Akahoski *(TV Detective No. 2)*; Eliana H. Alexander *(Young Woman)*; Jaques Apollo Bolton *(Teammate)*; John Cann *(Freeway Chris)*; Darwyn Carson *(Woman Prosecutor)*; Gary Cervantes *(Police Spokesman)*; Noel Conlon *(Nicole's Father)*; Pamela Dunlap *(Therapist)*; Richard Fancy *(Ed Ledbetter)*; Leo Greene *(Anchorman No. 2)*; Randy Hamilton; Jonathan R. Hoog; Terrence Howard; Timothy O'Neale Hutchinson; Eugene Lee; Helaine Lembeck; Jarrett Lennon; James Lesure; Gary Lindsey; Barry Livingston; Henry Marshall; Toy Newkirk; Zook Norman; Amy Peck; Timi Prulheire; Bumper Robinson; Brogan Roche; Eamonn Roche; Toni Sawyer; Roger Smith; Jill Stokesbury; Brian Ann Zoccola

THE O.J. SIMPSON STORY is a sincere portrait of the former football star and movie actor, his rise to fame, and his descent into infamy. Bobby Hosea delivers a creditable performance in the title role, and the 1994 Fox Television special released on home video in 1995 suffers less than one might expect for having been rushed to the small screen to capitalize on the surge of publicity following Simpson's arrest for murder.

A frightened dog, its paws covered with blood, runs barking through the quiet streets of Brentwood, California. Nearby, O.J. Simpson (Bobby Hosea) climbs into a waiting limousine. As the limo drives away, a neighborhood couple has followed the dog to the scene of a grisly double murder. Simpson's ex-wife, Nicole (Jessica Tuck), and a visitor, Ron Goldman (Paul Witten), lie dead in Nicole's yard. Simpson is soon under arrest for the slayings. His questioning by police, and by attorney Robert Shapiro (Bruce Weitz), triggers a series of memories, through which we view Simpson's ghetto origins, his rise to fame in professional football, his career as a sportscaster and actor, his two marriages, and a personal life that seemingly deteriorated even as his career soared.

In flashback, we see O.J. meet and marry Nicole. The relationship, at first idyllic, gradually turns into an abusive nightmare. Finally, Nicole ends the marriage, but even then, O.J. continues to terrorize her. The flashback sequences continue through the night of the murder. Meanwhile, the post-arrest story line moves gradually forward, concluding with the well-known "low-speed chase" over the Los Angeles freeways. The film ends with O.J.'s surrender to the police.

Bringing THE O.J. SIMPSON STORY to television required the filmmakers to deal with a number of problems. One of these was that the real-life Simpson drama was still being played out in the courtroom. Since Simpson's guilt or innocence had yet to be established, the filmmakers had the delicate task of developing a character who might be an innocent man or a cold-blooded murderer. Hosea's Simpson is properly enigmatic, with enough flashes of pure goodness, and enough hints of near-psychotic evil, to allow the film to survive the final disposition of the case.

Director Jerrold Freeman is billed pseudonymously as Alan Smithee, suggesting that he wishes to disown the film. But Freeman deserves praise for treating his subject with taste and genuine respect. In all, the film is surprisingly well done, and should satisfy anyone with a continuing taste for O.J. (Adult situations.) — J.W.

d, Jerrold Freeman; p, Bob Lemchen; exec p, Robert Lovenheim; w, Stephen Harrigan; ph, Jeffrey Jur; ed, Kimberly Bennett; m, Harald Kloser; prod d, Linda Pearl; set d, Cece Rodarte; sound, Mark Weingarten (mixer); casting, Alice Cassidy; cos, Bernie White; makeup, DeeDee Altamara; stunts, Bob Minor

Docudrama/Crime/Biography   (PR: C   MPAA: NR)

OLD LADY WHO WALKED   ★★½
IN THE SEA, THE
(France) 95m Blue Dahlia Production; Societe
Financiere de Coproduction; Films A2; Little Bear
Productions; JM Productions ~ Cinepix c
(LA VIELLE QUI MARCHAIT DANS LA MER)

Jeanne Moreau *(Lady M)*; Michel Serrault *(Pompilius)*; Luc Thuillier *(Lambert)*; Geraldine Danon *(Noemie)*; Jean Bouchaud *(Mazurier)*; Marie-Dominique Aumont *(Muriel)*; Hester Wilcox *(Girl)*; Lea Gabrielle *(Alexandra)*; Lara Guirao *(Librarian)*; Mattia Sbragia *(Stern)*

THE OLD LADY WHO WALKED IN THE SEA gives Jeanne Moreau a chance to tear into the tailor-made role of a crusty, aging jewel thief. But the Gallic comedy lacks real style and sophistication.

On the sunny beaches of Guadeloupe, Lady M. (Moreau), a grand but mysterious figure, and her aging partner, Pompilius (Michel Serrault), scour the shore for wealthy blackmail victims.

While looking for juicy targets one day, Lady M. takes a fancy to Lambert (Luc Thullier), a young beach boy and petty thief, whom she wishes to turn into a refined con artist. Lady M. convinces the reluctant Pompilius, who was once her lover, to help with the transformation, but the newly-formed triangle is fraught with jealousy and sexual tension.

The team's first major heist, the theft of a visiting Maharani's crown jewels, seems successful until a clever detective catches up with Lady M., who returns the jewels and claims Pompilius is a kleptomaniac. Distraught by both the accusation and Lady M.'s devotion to Lambert, Pompilius commits suicide. Lady M. becomes mentally and physically unstable over the tragic loss, but she insists on going to Paris for another robbery. The new scheme almost falls apart due to Lady M.'s deteriorating condition; yet, when last seen, Lady M. and Lambert are back on the Guadeloupean sands planning their next heist.

THE OLD LADY WHO WALKED IN THE SEA is likable enough as the story ambles along in the pretty settings, but the film inescapably brings to mind several other, better "heist" films, both comic (TROUBLE IN PARADISE, DESIRE, RAFFLES, BEDTIME STORY, DIRTY ROTTEN SCOUNDRELS) and serious (RIFIFI, TO CATCH A THIEF, PICKPOCKET, THE GRIFTERS). Here, Jeanne Moreau even physically resembles Melina Mercouri, who played the leader of a gang of male thieves in TOPKAPI, Jules Dassin's spoof on his own RIFIFI.

THE OLD LADY WHO WALKED IN THE SEA makes too much of an issue out of Moreau's age (64 when the film was shot in 1992), diluting the caper plot, and making the happy ending (after a hint of tragedy to come) seem forced and unconvincing. On the other hand, the many insults on the subject of age that fly between Lady M. and Pompilius give the film its liveliest moments. (Violence, nudity, sexual situations, adult situations, extreme profanity.) — E.M.

d, Laurent Heynemann; exec p, Gerard Jourd'hui; w, Dominique Roulett (based on the novel *La Vieille Qui Marchait Dans la Mer* by Frederic Dard); ph, Robert Alazraki; ed, Jacques Comets; set d, Valerie Grall; sound, Jean-Pierre Laforce (mixer), Michel Desrois; casting, Shula Siegfried; cos, Catherine Leterrier; makeup, Nurith Barkan, Catherine DeMesmaecker, Anne Bourdiol

Comedy/Drama   (PR: O   MPAA: NR)

ONCE WERE WARRIORS   ★★★
(New Zealand) 99m Communicado; New Zealand
Film Commission; Avalon Studios; New Zealand On Air ~
Fine Line c

Rena Owen *(Beth Heke)*; Temuera Morrison *(Jake Heke)*; Mamaengaroa Kerr-Bell *(Grace Heke)*; Julian Arahanga *(Nig Heke)*; Taungaroa Emile *(Boogie Heke)*; Rachael Morris, Jr. *(Polly Heke)*; Joseph Kairau *(Huata Heke)*; Clifford Curtis *(Bully)*; Pete Smith *(Dooley)*; George Henare *(Bennett)*; Mere Boynton *(Mavis)*; Shannon Williams *(Toot)*; Calvin Tuteao *(Taka)*; Ray Bishop *(King Hitter)*; Ian Mune *(Judge)*; Te Whataniu Skipworth *(Te Tupaea)*; Rangi Motu *(Matawai)*; Robert Pollock *(Policeman)*; Jessica Wilcox *(Policewoman)*; Stephen Hall *(Prosecuting Officer)*; Wiki Oman *(Youth Advocate)*; Israel Williams *(Youth)*; Johnathon Wirem *(Youth)*; Richard Meihana *(Taunter in Court)*; Edna Stirling *(Woman)*; Ngawai Simpson *(Woman)*; Spike Kem *(Old Drunk)*; Arona Rissetto *(Nig's Friend)*; Fran Viveaere *(Nig's Girlfriend)*; Brian Kairau *(Joking Man Outside Club)*; Charlie Tumahai *(Karaoke Singer)*; Tama Renata *(Party Guitarist)*; Guy Moana *(Evicted Partygoer/Pub Customer)*; Maree Moschonas *(Gang Rape Victim)*; Riwia Brown *(Bully's Girlfriend)*; Mac Hona; Percy Robinson;

Jason Kerapa; Robbie Ngauma; James Dean Wilson; Chris Mason (*Core Gang Members*); Brain Kairau; Marshall Kairau; Joseph Te Whiu; Jim Ngaata; David Rare; Donald Allen; Charles Marsh; Winstone Bedgood; Piki Mark; Royal Waa; Jack Grace; Manuel Apiata; George Tiopira; Maru Nihoniho; Jaye Cassidy; Vivienne Wilson; Hiraina Kume; Thomasina Perana (*Jake's Mates*)

A disturbing portrait of domestic violence, ONCE WERE WARRIORS resists the easy conventions of the battered wife film (a genre that flourishes on television) and forces the viewer to contend with characters whose actions and motives are complex and elusive. Though certain details of the story arise from racial issues specific to contemporary New Zealand, its broad outlines are chillingly universal.

Jake and Beth Heke (Temuera Morrison and Rena Owen) and their five children live in a Maori ghetto in Auckland. Though Jake happily plays *pater familias* at the local tavern, he's not much of a father to his own offspring. Eldest son Nig (Julian Arahanga) is already estranged from his family, and has joined a hard-core Maori gang whose members must get elaborate facial tattoos and undergo initiation by torture. Beth's dreams reside in her intelligent and introspective daughter Grace (Mamaengaroa Kerr-Bell), a shy 13-year-old whom Jake accuses of being "too smart for her own good," just like her mother.

Jake loses his job—"so what," he says, contemplating life on the dole—and the ensuing argument with Beth sends him off to the watering hole. That night, he brings the party home. The children huddle together in their bedroom, while the drunken Jake serenades his wife with love songs. Moments later, in a fit of temper, he beats her bloody and drags her off to bed. The next morning, one eye blackened and swollen shut, Beth can't accompany son Boogie (Taungaroa Emile) to juvenile court. As a result, he's remanded into state custody. When he hears the news, Jake responds that Boogie is a mama's boy who needs the "toughening up."

On the day Jake has promised to take Beth to visit Boogie he goes drinking again, stranding his family in the parking lot. That night, during another house party, "Uncle" Bully (Clifford Curtis) sneaks into Grace's bed and rapes her. Grace kills herself. Defying Jake's objections and threats, Beth buries Grace on ancestral Maori lands. Jake refuses to attend the funeral.

Later, Beth reads Grace's diary and learns what drove her daughter to suicide. She takes the evidence to Jake at the tavern, and he in turn beats Bully to death. Beth abandons Jake, leaving him to face the oncoming sirens alone.

The dynamic that holds together the Heke marriage is a complicated one: Jake and Beth still lust for one another after years of marriage, but there's a class wedge between them. To outsiders—white outsiders in particular—they're both members of an economically impoverished and socially marginalized minority, but Beth is pure blooded Maori, while Jake is of mixed heritage—her family considers that she married beneath herself, and Jake has never forgotten it. Beth is intelligent, resourceful and strong, but accepts the notion that the way to a happy marriage is to keep her mouth shut and her legs open. The film ends on a muted note of hope for Beth and her remaining children, but Jake's expulsion from their lives still leaves a gaping hole.

ONCE WERE WARRIORS opens with a shot of happy white people on a sunny beach, from which the camera pulls back to reveal a billboard set against the backdrop of a slum. Jake and Beth are gratifyingly complex characters. Though brutal and bitterly frustrated by the ruin of his life—some of which is his own fault and some of which is not—Jake is no ogre, and Morrison captures his charisma and carnal allure, as well as the

terrifying power of his mercurial rages. Beth is no simpering victim—she's drawn to Jake's fire and understands her own complicity in choosing to live in the furnace.

ONCE WERE WARRIORS takes its title from a remark made by one of Beth's relatives—the Maori people, she says sadly, once were warriors—a phrase that evokes a culture of violence and honor. Jake, the descendant of slaves, believes that honor derives from physical force. Nig, who disdains his father, nonetheless follows in his footsteps, exalting strength of body. Grace's death reminds Beth, the descendant of royalty, that honor resides in the soul and flows from pride in oneself and strength of spirit, lessons that Boogie begins to learn not from his family, but from a teacher at reform school.

ONCE WERE WARRIORS offers American viewers the opportunity to view a pressing concern—family values—through the prism of an alien culture. (*Adult situations, graphic violence, extreme profanity, sexual situations.*) — P.R.

d, Lee Tamahori; p, Robin Scholes; w, Riwia Brown (based on the novel by Alan Duff); ph, Stuart Dryburgh; ed, Michael Horton; m, Murray Grindlay, Murray McNabb; prod d, Michael Kane; art d, Shayne Radford; sound, Graham Morris (recordist), Kit Rollings (design), Michael Hedges (mixer), John Neil; casting, Don Selwyn; cos, Michael Kane; makeup, Debra East, Guy Moana; stunts, Robert Bruce

Drama   (PR: O   MPAA: R)

1-900   ★★★
(Netherlands) 80m Dino Filmprodukties ~
Zeitgeist Films c
(06)

Ariane Schluter (*Sarah*); Ad Van Kempen (*Thomas*)

The sorry state of gender relations isn't much different in the work of Vincent van Gogh and 1-900, a film directed by his distant relative, Theo van Gogh. 1-900 is a depressing but well crafted little movie about two people who communicate exclusively on the telephone.

In this two character drama set in two Amsterdam apartments, Thomas (Ad van Kempen), a 33-year-old architect, chooses Sarah (Ariane Schluter), a thirtyish professor of art, from a selection of voice mail messages supplied by a phone sex service. In their first conversation, the two discover they have a mutual interest in art, but Thomas gets offended by Sarah's laughter during their initial discussion about sex, and hangs up on her. The next morning, Sarah calls Thomas back and they masturbate while talking to one another.

Eventually, Thomas and Sarah make a weekly event out of their phone sex, but Sarah becomes increasingly frustrated with Thomas's arrogant manner during their role-playing. She then threatens to end the relationship when Thomas says he has figured out her last name from a chance meeting with one of her former students. Sarah agrees to continue calling Thomas only if he promises to stop snooping into her private life, but the next time she calls she reaches Wilbert, Thomas's father, who informs her that Thomas has died suddenly. Stunned by the news, Sarah tries to talk about Thomas with his father to ease her pain, but receives an even bigger shock when Thomas reveals himself to be Wilbert, adding that he just wanted to see how much she cared. The relationship ends on this pathetic note.

1-900 originated as an "interactive" play titled "06" (the Dutch equivalent to the US "1-900" number) in which audience members could choose between different phone sex characters to view in different cubicles. For the film version (also originally titled 06), director Theo van Gogh pared down the play to only two characters. Coincidentally, a 1996 American release,

DENISE CALLS UP, which also presented lonely thirtysomething characters who engage in phone sex but never meet, more closely approximated the structure of the play. But whereas DENISE CALLS UP is an empty farce, 1-900 is a provocative drama *about* emotional emptiness.

Surprisingly, 1-900 maintains interest despite its limited (two room) setting and intense focus on two cautiously developed characters. Van Gogh makes the shrewd point that no matter how detached Thomas and Sarah pretend to be from one another, they are actually revealing a great deal and getting very close (phone sex represents only a means to that end). The film is an actor's dream, and Ariane Schluter and Ad van Kempen are always believable, even when their actions are inscrutable (for example, when they suddenly assume the roles of father and daughter during one discussion). Schluter perhaps deserves extra kudos for executing the more emotionally demanding role.

Like his forebear, van Gogh complements his themes with adroit technique. (Amusing references to art history also abound.) The circular camera movements in the opening shots counter the theatricality of the material, while suggesting two scared and lonely characters circling one another. The color schemes of the two apartments suggest the truth about the characters well before the audience gets to know them (Thomas's apartment is a cold, dark blue, while Sarah reclines like "Olympia" on a warm red couch). A chess game late in their relationship mirrors its growing complexity, as well as the different roles they play. Finally, Sarah's fish tank symbolizes both the voyeuristic function of the cinema screen and the glass house appearance of Sarah's life after Thomas finds out more about her than she wants him to know.

Fans of erotica may be disappointed to find that most of the masturbation is off camera and that 1-900 is more rueful than erotic or funny. But for those looking for a different sort of relationship movie, 1-900 is worth picking up. (*Nudity, sexual situations, adult situations, profanity.*) — E.M.

d, Theo Van Gogh; p, Theo Van Gogh; w, Johan Doesberg, Marcel Otten, Ariane Schluter, Ad Van Kempen (based on the play *06* by Johan Doesberg); ph, Tom Erisman; ed, Ot Louw; m, Ruud Bos; art d, Ruud Van Dijk; sound, Ben Zijlstra

Drama/Erotic (PR: O MPAA: NR)

ONLY THE BRAVE ★★½
(Australia) 62m Pickpocket Productions; Film Victoria; Australian Film Commission ~ First Run Features c

Elena Mandalis (*Alex*); Dora Kaskanis (*Vicki*); Maude Davey (*Kate Groves*); Helen Athanasiadis (*Maria*); Tina Zerella (*Sylvie*); Bob Bright (*Reg*); Mary Sitarenos (*Athena*); Petra Brady (*Tammy*); George Harlem (*Mr. Stefanos*); Eugenia Fragos (*Mr. Stefanos*); Paul Valpato (*Evan*); John Brumpton (*Paul*); Karen Hadfield (*Woman Poet*); Don Bridges (*Skeet*); Marcia Ferguson (*Teacher in Classroom*); Melanie Beddil (*Teacher in Office*); Julie Bosevska (*Young Alex*); Nico Lathouris (*Laslo*); Nik Pantazopoulos; Robert Price

Ana Kokkinos's first feature, ONLY THE BRAVE, released in its native Australia in 1994 and in the US in 1995, is a flawed but powerfully realistic look at two Australian teenagers. This coming-of-age film about two high school girls is indifferently scripted and fails to realize the promise of a fresh perspective on a familiar theme.

Alex (Elena Mandalis) and Vicki (Dora Kaskanis) live in suburbs of Melbourne that are as wild and dangerous as the city itself. Outside of their troubled homes, they wander aimlessly, set fires, smoke pot, get drunk, and look for sex.

Despite Alex's lack of academic motivation, one female teacher, Miss Groves (Maude Davey), makes an extra effort with her. Alex develops a crush on Miss Groves, but is uncomfortable about her feelings. Forced to contend with Miss Grove's attachment to her boyfriend, Alex feels betrayed. Meanwhile, Alex's preoccupation with her teacher causes a rift between her and Vicki, who is showing disturbing signs of emotional instability. Alex discovers that Vicki is being sexually molested by her father. When she tries to bring this news to Miss Groves, the teacher is dismissive.

Alex resolves to rescue Vicki and plans to take her friend to Sydney, where Alex's mother lives. She searches for Vicki and finds her atop a cooling tower. She has soaked herself with lighter fluid. Despite Alex's attempts to save her friend, Vicki succeeds in burning herself to death.

A worthy attempt to come to grips with the terrors of adolescence, particularly as they apply to young lesbians, ONLY THE BRAVE is bleak throughout, and offers little in the way of hope or solutions. The acting is creditable, but the dark, static photography tends to further deaden a film that is distressingly grim to begin with. Australia has the highest teen suicide rate in the world, and Kokkinos's film, despite a weak script and certain technical limitations, offers plausible reasons why. (*Substance abuse, profanity.*)

d, Ana Kokkinos; p, Fiona Eagger; assoc p, Rina Reiss; w, Ana Kokkinos, Mira Robertson; ph, James Grant; ed, Mark Atkin; m, Philip Brophy; art d, Georgina Campbell; sound, James Currie (mixer), Jock Healy (recordist), Craig Carter; fx, Peter Stubbs, Jeff Little, Conrad Rothman, Film Trick; casting, Dina Mann, Prototype Casting; cos, Margot McCartney; makeup, Sandy Royce; stunts, Mark Hennessy

Drama (PR: C MPAA: NR)

OPERATION DUMBO DROP ★★
(U.S.) 108m Flying Elephant Productions; Interscope Communications; Walt Disney Pictures; Polygram ~ Buena Vista c

Danny Glover (*Captain Sam Cahill*); Ray Liotta (*Captain T.C. Doyle*); Denis Leary (*David Poole*); Doug E. Doug (*Harvey (H.A.) Ashford*); Corin Nemec (*Lawrence Farley*); Dinh Thien Le (*Linh*); Tcheky Karyo (*Goddard*); Hoang Ly (*Nguyen*); Vo Trung Anh (*Quang*); Marshall Bell (*Pederson*); James Hong (*Y B'ham*); Long Nguyen (*Jhon*); Tim Kelleher (*C-123 Pilot*); Scott N. Stevens (*C-123 Co-Pilot*); Kevin La Rosa (*Huey Pilot #1*); Christopher Ward (*Huey Co-Pilot*); Robert Kevin Miller (*Huey Gunner #1*); Michael Lee (*Village Elder*); Le Minh Tien (*NVA Captain*); Mac Van Nam (*NVA Lieutenant*); Ton Nguyen That (*Feed Salesman*); Somsak Hormsabat (*Bike Driver*); Lionel Douglas (*Lieutenant*); Tien Nguyen Van (*NVA Anti-Aircraft*); Doi Chettawat Kanboon (*Lihn—Six Years Old*); Chern Dao Van (*Lihn's Father*); Steve Countouriotis (*Huey Co-Pilot #2*); Mark S. Bryant (*C-130 Pilot*); Jared Chandler (*C-130 Co-Pilot*); Nick Satriano (*Red*); Hing Hang Quang (*Old Villager*); Thanh Nguyen (*NVA Soldier*); Wichien Nguyen Thi (*Peasant Woman*)

If Stanley Kubrick's FULL METAL JACKET were to be remade by Steven Spielberg, the result might be something like OPERATION DUMBO DROP. This wartime comedy-drama about some Green Berets delivering an elephant to a village in South Vietnam in 1968 is offensive in its attempt to be inoffensive.

Based on the real-life experiences of Jim Morris, OPERATION DUMBO DROP follows tough Captain T.C. Doyle (Ray Liotta) as he tries to ingratiate himself with the residents of a village located near a major Viet Cong supply route. As Doyle replaces his better-liked predecessor, Captain Sam Cahill (Danny Glover), he unwittingly angers an enemy commander, who punishes the Montagnard villagers by killing their beloved elephant.

Doyle and Cahill team up to find another elephant, which they must deliver in time for a ceremonial ritual that is five days away. They convince their commanding officer to bring along two young soldiers, H.A. (Doug E. Doug) and Farley (Corin Nemec). They are also joined by David Poole (Denis Leary), an army supply officer who helps negotiate the sale of the new elephant, and Linh (Dinh Thien Le), a 12-year-old orphan who is the only one able to control and direct the animal.

Linh and the servicemen guide the elephant, Bo-Tat, through 200 miles of dangerous territory, tangling with enemy soldiers along the way. Linh slowly comes to trust the Green Berets, despite the fact that his father had been killed in crossfire. The mission, however, nearly falls apart when the men learn that the village has lost its airplane landing strip and is no longer considered of strategic interest. Against orders, the team decides to fulfill their promise to the village: they put Bo-Tat in a crate attached to a huge parachute and drop her on the village. The plan succeeds and the soldiers rejoice in their ability to do something nice during the war.

OPERATION DUMBO DROP is not only the first comic adventure to be set during the Vietnam War, but it also carries the dubious distinction of being the only Vietnam War film to date to be marketed to families as children's entertainment. Still, even those with only a rudimentary understanding of the conflict will question the approach of a film in which the US military's chief mission is to preserve the lives, happiness, and traditions of Vietnamese villagers. Indeed, this bizarre tale might have made for a memorable black satire (elephants, after all, weren't the only heavy payloads that Uncle Sam was dropping on Vietnamese villages in '68), but it's played strictly for middlebrow yuks and rote male bonding.

Despite the gung-ho cheeriness, not all of the film is as light as the scene where Poole falls into a truck of elephant droppings. Many parts, particularly the Cahill-Linh scenes, are mawkishly sentimental (David Newman's incessant musical score cues the audience for the appropriate responses). But in trying to balance the serious and the carefree—while blithely erasing history—screenwriters Gene Quintano and Jim Kouf, and director Simon Wincer (FREE WILLY), make a mockery of a war that killed some 60,000 Americans and as many as two million Vietnamese.

In recent years Disney has taken over a TV network and tried to buy a Civil War battlefield in Virginia. With OPERATION DUMBO DROP, it refights and wins the Vietnam War, using its patented feel-good style in place of B-52s. (*Violence, adult situations, profanity.*) — E.M.

d, Simon Wincer; p, David Madden, Diane Nabatoff; exec p, Robert W. Cort, Ted Field; co-p, Penelope L. Foster; w, Jim Kouf, Graham Yost, Gene Quintano (from a story by Jim Morris); ph, Russell Boyd; ed, O. Nicholas Brown; m, David Newman; prod d, Paul Peters; art d, Lisette Thomas, Steve Spence; set d, Jim Erickson; sound, Ben Osmo (mixer); fx, Brian Cox, Michael Lessa, Buena Vista Visual Effects; casting, Mike Fenton, Julie Ashton; cos, Rosanna Norton; makeup, Judy Lovell; stunts, Guy Norris

Comedy/Adventure/War (PR: A MPAA: PG)

OPERATION INTERCEPT ★½
(U.S.) 94m Hess/Kallberg Associates ~
Vidmark Entertainment c

Bruce Payne (*Maj. Paul Gordon Pruitt*); Natasha Andreichenko (*Francesca Zaborszin*); John Stockwell (*Maj. Andy Aldrich*); Lance Henriksen (*Bill Stenghel*); Michael Champion (*Johann*); Dennis Christopher (*Victor*); Curt Lowens (*Dr. Alexander Zaborszin*); Corinne Bohrer (*Sharon Pruitt*); Corbin Bernsen; John Prosky; Dean Howell

A technothriller singularly lacking in both thrills and technological wizardry, OPERATION INTERCEPT deals with a villainous Soviet scientist's attempt to destroy America.

Vengeful Francesca Zaborszin (Natasha Andreichenko) believes the U.S. government staged the suicide of her father, a Soviet scientist and defector. The industrious villainess sets up her own base in the deserts of Kazakhstan, wielding powerful electromagnetic pulses channelled though orbiting navigation satellites to attack and bring down civilian aircraft. She also captures the revolutionary high-altitude fighter-bomber Aurora One. Summoned to strike back are two utterly nondescript Top Gunners, Maj. Paul Gordon Pruitt (Bruce Payne) and Maj. Andy Aldrich (John Stockwell), who soar into action in Aurora Two. Forced down by Zaborszin, the pair are caught and tortured by her private army of sinister Slavs, but Pruitt escapes. Eventually, tedious plot twists lead both Zaborszin and Pruitt to take to the skies in separate Auroras. She penetrates D.C. airspace to make a bombing run at the White House, but Pruitt's afterburners turn her into a fireball.

There is a feeble attempt at intrigue over who really killed old Dr. Zaborszin, a matter not resolved until the final scene, by which time it is quite irrelevant who did. Unlike its anti-heroine (played with a certain degree of sympathy by Andreichenko), OPERATION INTERCEPT never once catches fire. There are pursuits and fights aplenty, but it is easy to sense the filmmaker's desperation to stretch the skullduggery to feature length, as hackneyed characters defy all reasonable norms of human behavior and deliver cliched dialogue ("Come on, you can do it!"). The unconvincing airborne sequences rely heavily on computerized flight simulations, and indeed the digital graphics make the Aurora planes amazingly "realistic" in the sense that they sure enough appear solid and three-dimensional, but they look no different from sleek, little toy jets bouncing along on well-concealed wires. Even that has its limits: the camera cuts away to avoid ever showing a landing. In the U.S., OPERATION INTERCEPT taxied directly to home video. (*Profanity, violence.*) — C.C.

d, Paul Levine; p, Kevin M. Kallberg, Oliver G. Hess; exec p, Albert L. Taylor, Kenneth J. Kallberg, Mark Amin; assoc p, Ivan Cat; w, Paul Levine; ph, John Newby; ed, Barry Zetlin; m, Richard Marvin; prod d, Pamela Marcotte; set d, Jeannie Gunn; fx, Steve DeLollis, Bruce Mattox, Wes Mattox; casting, Fern Champion, Dawn Steinberg; cos, Tricia Gray

Action (PR: C MPAA: R)

OTHELLO ★★
(U.K.) 124m Dakota Films; Imminent Films;
Castle Rock ~ Columbia c

Laurence Fishburne (*Othello*); Irene Jacob (*Desdemona*); Kenneth Branagh (*Iago*); Nathaniel Parker (*Cassio*); Michael Maloney (*Roderigo*); Anna Patrick (*Emilia*); Nicholas Farrell (*Montano*); Indra Ove (*Bianca*); Michael Sheen (*Lodovico*); Andre Oumansky (*Gratiano*); Philip Locke (*1st Senator*); John Savident (*2nd Senator*); Gabriele Ferzetti (*The Duke of Venice*); Pierre Vaneck (*Brabantio*)

A good production of Shakespeare's *Othello* should burn like dry wood, but this new film version sinks like a bundle of wet rags. Despite a talented cast and Venice locations, director Oliver Parker's OTHELLO is weak, flat, and conventional.

Although Parker has truncated and rearranged the classic 1602-04 text, the story remains the same. In 16th century Venice, Othello (Laurence Fishburne), a Moorish military leader, provokes the wrath of a Venetian nobleman, Brabantio (Pierre Vaneck), when he elopes with his beautiful daughter, Desdemona (Irene Jacob). Othello quells some of Brabantio's anger after he returns from a successful battle against the Turks in Cyprus. Meanwhile, Brabantio's aide, Iago (Kenneth Branagh), whom Othello passes over for a promotion, begins an elaborate plan to destroy Othello and his happy new marriage.

While Othello and Desdemona honeymoon on a Mediterranean island, Iago enlists the aid of his wife, Emilia (Anna Patrick), who is Desdemona's maid, as well as one of Desdemona's rejected suitors, Roderigo (Michael Maloney), to plant Desdemona's handkerchief in the bedroom of Cassio (Nathaniel Parker), Othello's right-hand man. Iago then proceeds to convince Othello that Desdemona loves Cassio.

Othello rages with jealousy over Iago's insinuations, but he becomes fully convinced of the affair when he sees Cassio brandishing the handkerchief. Brought to the breaking point, Othello confronts and then kills Desdemona, despite her pleas of innocence. Immediately after the murder, Emilia convinces Othello that he has made a mistake, prompting him to take revenge on Iago and kill himself.

Othello has been filmed many times, but never successfully. Orson Welles's 1952 version—still the best—was marred somewhat by the financial difficulties Welles faced during the off-and-on production, and Laurence Olivier's overrated 1965 version suffers more than ever today from its stagy approach and blackface makeup.

First-time director Oliver Parker's OTHELLO errs both in casting and in stylistic choices. With his shaven pate, single earring, and dashing Italian duds, Laurence Fishburne looks as if he's posing for *Gentleman's Quarterly*, while his line readings sound awkwardly amateurish next to the declamatory style of Kenneth Branagh (when not reciting, Fishburne overplays his seizure scenes). Irene Jacob also looks great, but her dark hair and French accent make her seem miscast, while Kenneth Branagh successfully captures the smugness of Iago, but misses his character's evil intensity. Others in the cast are proficient, but only Nathaniel Parker as Cassio gives a really rounded portrait.

A bigger problem with OTHELLO is that it fails to take advantage of the highly topical theme of racism that underlies so much of the tragedy. Fishburne may be the first African-American actor to portray Othello on screen, but Parker never emphasizes the scandalous nature of the interracial union (although he comes close during the couple's first public kiss). Moreover, Parker privileges Branagh's Iago by giving him several direct-address monologues and asides, which undercut Othello's and Desdemona's equally crucial points of view. What this new OTHELLO refuses to acknowledge is that a much more gripping version of a similar story had already played out in 1995: the televised murder trial of O.J. Simpson. *(Violence, nudity, sexual situations, adult situations.)* — E.M.

d, Oliver Parker; p, Luc Roeg, David Barron; exec p, Jonathan Olsberg; w, Oliver Parker (adapted from the play *The Tragedy of Othello: The Moor of Venice* by William Shakespeare); ph, David Johnson; ed, Tony Lawson; m, Charlie Mole; prod d, Tim Harvey; art d, Desmond Crowe, Livia Borgognoni; sound, Peter Glossop (mixer); casting, Debbie McWilliams; cos, Caroline Harris; makeup, Tina Earnshaw

Drama (PR: C   MPAA: R)

OUT OF ANNIE'S PAST ★½
(U.S.) 91m Point of View Productions; Karen Moore Productions; MCA Television Entertainment ~ MCA/Universal Home Video c

Catherine Mary Stewart *(Annie Carver/Natalie Kovacs)*; Scott Valentine *(Michael Carver)*; Dennis Farina *(Charlie Ingall)*; Carsten Norgaard *(Lev Petrovitch)*; Michael Flynn *(Det. Hopkins)*; Ray Oriel *(Pedro Cruz)*; Lilliana Cabal *(Delia)*; Carlos Gomez *(Detective Mendoza)*; Sam Cooper *(Daniel Worth)*; Brett Palmer *(Paul Bradshaw)*; Christy Summerhays *(Morgan Bradshaw)*; Toni Lynn Byrd *(Nancy)*; Bill Osborn *(Dmitri)*; Tony Larimer *(Alexei)*; Declan Pizzino *(Adam)*; Paige Lowry *(Cassie)*; Shawn Nottingham *(1st Man)*; Amanda Bruce *(Banker)*; Richard Jewkes *(Appraiser)*; Jonathan Gochberg *(Doctor)*; Jana McQuay *(Nurse)*; Melinda Clarkson *(Michael's Secretary)*; Curley Green *(Young Cop)*; Michael Scott *(Knight)*; Kevin Rahm *(Young Waiter)*; Dick Mitchell *(Resort Manager)*; Doug Stewart *(Rookie Cop)*; Marge Hilton *(Judge)*; Rosalind Soulam *(Foreman)*; Frank Gerrish *(1st Reporter)*; Carole Mikita *(2nd Reporter)*; Bonnie Baker *(1st Well Wisher)*; Frank Kanig *(Chauffeur)*

This formless thriller serves no other purpose except to offer lingering, tormented close-ups of Catherine Mary Stewart as Annie Carver, a woman whose violent past threatens to change forever her highly respectable and peaceful present.

Carver is a Utah-based art dealer married to a successful architect (Scott Valentine) and leading a blissful life until Charlie Ingall (Dennis Farina) shows up. He is an sleazy investigator who knows Annie is really Natalie, a decade ago the runaway moll of New York gangster Lev Petrovitch (Carsten Norgaard), who is still obsessed with getting her back. Ingall demands $100,000 to keep quiet but fatally hits his head while struggling with Annie.

Unfortunately, Lev has already been alerted and insists on reuniting with a reluctant but resigned Annie. Lev's unsentimental father, the "Russian godfather of Brooklyn," tries to end his son's distraction by sending hit men after Annie. Lev and the assassins conveniently gun each other down, leaving Annie free at last.

OUT OF ANNIE'S PAST feels like a sequence of transitional scenes after the main sections were edited out; everything happens too fast, and the story races to its end. The only time director Stuart Cooper can muster some enthusiasm is in the campy portrayal of a trash-TV show that reenacts Annie's past at hysteria pitch. With so much time spent by Annie on frantically liquidating her assets to pay off Ingall, she does not exactly strike one as a strong and resourceful protagonist. But she does look fetching in lingering, tormented close-ups. *(Violence, sexual situations.)* — C.C.

d, Stuart Cooper; p, Harvey Frand; exec p, Karen Moore; w, Pablo Fenjves; ph, Reed Smoot; ed, Cari Coughlin; m, Charles Bernstein; prod d, Gary Griffin Constable; set d, Donna Stamps; sound, Michael Fowler (mixer); fx, Rolf Larson; casting, Reuben Cannon & Associates; cos, Robert Moore; makeup, Dennis Liddiard; stunts, Bret Davidson

Thriller (PR: C   MPAA: R)

OUT OF SYNC ★★½
(U.S.) 105m United Image Entertainment ~ LIVE Entertainment c

LL Cool J *(Jason "The Saint" St. Julian)*; Victoria Dillard *(Monica Collins)*; Ramy Zada *(Danny Simon)*; Howard Hesseman *(Detective Caldwell)*; Yaphet Kotto; Isaac Hayes; Aries Spears; Debbie Allen; Norm Nixon; Tim Reid

Despite its starring rapper LL Cool J, old-style gangsters and not original gangstas figure prominently in OUT OF SYNC, a traditional noir narrative produced by Black Entertainment Television.

Jason "The Saint" Julian (LL Cool J) was the hottest club DJ in LA before he spent some time in jail and went through alcohol rehab. Bad luck still seems to follow him and he now owes a very angry bookie $30,000. An LAPD detective, Caldwell (Howard Hesseman), coerces Julian to become a police informant and go to work in a dance club owned by drug dealer Danny Simon (Ramy Zada). Julian quickly gets caught up in a dangerous affair with Simon's girlfriend Monica (Victoria Dillard), who enlists his help in her plot to rob Simon. Julian steals $500,000 of Simon's drug money, but Monica double-crosses him and absconds with the loot. Caldwell gives Julian a chance to track Monica down and retrieve the money, but while doing that he must also elude Simon's thugs. When Julian gets the money, Caldwell, who it turns out is on Simon's payroll, tries to steal it. But Julian is no fool, and he has set a trap. In the end, Simon is killed, Caldwell is arrested, and The Saint prepares to begin a new life far away.

OUT OF SYNC is by no means an exceptionally good movie, but it does not lay claims to being one either. Shot in under a month for about $1.5 million by a novice director with a cast of no "major talent," it probably should have been as disappointing as most direct-to-video films are, and no one would have needed to apologize. But the film owes a lot to Robert E. Dorn's script, which manages to incorporate all the plot elements of classic 1940s noir films. Actress-choreographer and TV sitcom director Debbie Allen's first feature competently tells the story, although it lacks the sense of style that is required for the genre. LL Cool J tries for Bogie-like nonchalance in his performance, but comes through as too sedate and often half-asleep.

For the trivia buffs: director Allen appears in one scene as a manicurist, and her husband, former NBA star Norm Nixon, gets hustled by Cool J in a hoops scene; the film's producer, Tim Reid, plays the silent partner of his former "WKRP in Cincinnati" costar Hesseman. Also, the friendship that developed between Allen and Cool J during the making of this film led them to costar in the sitcom "In the House." *(Profanity, violence, nudity, sexual situations.)* — P.R.

d, Debbie Allen; p, Tim Reid; co-p, Butch Lewis, Earl A. Saunders; w, Robert Dorn; ph, Isidore Mankofsky; prod d, Marek Dobrowolski; art d, Nicole Koenningsberg; set d, Penny Barrett; sound, Mike Patillo; casting, Eileen Knight; cos, Winnie Brown

Crime/Drama   **(PR: C   MPAA: R)**

OUTBREAK   ★★½
(U.S.) 128m Arnold Kopelson Productions;
Punch Productions; Warner Bros. ~ Warner Bros. c

Dustin Hoffman *(Colonel Sam Daniels MD)*; Rene Russo *(Dr. Roberta "Robby" Keough)*; Morgan Freeman *(General Billy Ford)*; Cuba Gooding, Jr. *(Major Salt)*; Kevin Spacey *(Major Casey Schuler)*; Patrick Dempsey *(Jimbo Scott)*; Donald Sutherland *(General Donald McClintock)*; Zakes Mokae *(Dr. Benjamin Iwabi)*; Malick Bowens *(Dr. Raswani)*; Susan Lee Hoffman *(Dr. Lisa Aronson)*; Benito Martinez *(Dr. Julio Ruiz)*; Bruce Jarchow *(Dr. Mascelli)*; Leland Hayward, III *(Henry Seward)*; Daniel Chodos *(Rudy Alvarez)*; Dale Dye *(Colonel Briggs)*; Cara Keough *(Sarah Jeffries)*; Gina Menza *(Mrs. Jeffries)*; Per Didrik

Fasmer *(Mr. Jeffries)*; Michelle Joyner *(Sherry Mauldin)*; Donald Forrest *(Mack Mauldin)*; Julie Pierce *(Erica Mauldin)*; Tim Ransom *(Tommy Hull)*; Michelle M. Miller *(Darla Hull)*; Maury Sterling *(Sandman One Pilot)*; Michael Emanuel *(Sandman One Co-Pilot)*; Lucas Dudley *(Viper One Pilot)*; Robet Alan Joseph *(Viper Two Pilot)*; Joseph Latimore *(Viper Two Co-Pilot)*; Michael Sottile *(Gunner Pilot)*; Ed Beechner *(Gunner)*; Matthew Saks *(Sergeant Wolf)*; Diana Bellamy *(Mrs. Pananides)*; Lance Kerwin *(American Mercenary)*; Brett Oliver *(Belgian Mercenary)*; Eric Mungai Nguku *(African Nurse)*; Larry Hine *(Young McClintock)*; Nickolas H. Marshall *(Young Ford)*; Douglas Hebron *(Ju-Ju Man)*; Jae Woo Lee *(Korean Captain)*; Derek Kim *(Seaman Chulso Lee)*; Bill Stevenson *(Biotest Guard)*; Kellie Overbey *(Alice)*; Dana Andersen *(Corinne)*; Patrica Place *(Mrs. Foote)*; Nicholas Pappone *(Little Boy on Plane)*; Traci Odom *(Little Boy's Mother)*; Herbert Jefferson, Jr.; Thomas Crawford; Buzz Barbee *(Boston Doctors)*; Jenna Byrne *(Tracy)*; Brian Reddy *(Tracy's Father)*; Ina Romeo *(Mrs. Logan)*; Teresa Velarde *(Nurse Emma)*; J.J. Chaback *(Nurse Jane)*; Carmela Rappazzo *(Hospital Receptionist)*; Kurt Boesen *(Mayor Gaddis)*; Jack Rader *(Police Chief Fowler)*; Robert Rigamonte *(County Health Official)*; Mimi Doyka *(Frightened Mother)*; C. Jack Robinson *(Biotest Manager)*; Robert Alan Beuth *(George Armistead)*; Gordon Michaels *(Man in Line)*; Peter Looney *(White House Counsel)*; Conrad Bachmann *(California Governor)*; Cary J. Pitts *(Anchorman)*; Cynthia Harrison *(Co-anchor)*; Marcus Hennessy *(Station Manager)*; Albert Owens *(Broadcast Director)*; David Silverbrand *(TV Reporter)*; Julie Araskog *(Janet Adams)*; Frank Rositani *(Senator Rosales)*; George Christy *(Senator)*; Bruce Isacson *(Jaffe)*; Marilyn Brandt *(Ford's Secretary)*; Philip Handy *(Sergeant Meyer)*

A 1995 Ebola virus epidemic in Zaire provided the film OUTBREAK—about a similar virus unleashed in the US—with "ripped from today's headlines" immediacy. But the situation's dramatic potential is lost in a muddle of misplaced action movie cliches.

In a remote village in Zaire, Colonel Sam Daniels (Dustin Hoffman), an Army medical researcher, discovers the most deadly virus he has ever seen. The Motaba virus is extremely contagious, and kills those infected with it within 24 hours. Daniels' superior, General Ford (Morgan Freeman), assures him that because the site of the epidemic was so remote, no one infected could have gotten out alive to pass it on. Still, Daniels has a bad feeling.

A monkey carrying the virus ends up in California, and soon Motaba is spreading through small town Cedar Creek. Daniels and his ex-wife Robby Keough (Rene Russo)—a biohazard specialist with the Center for Disease Control—are both dispatched to the scene. The Army has the town blockaded in a massive quarantine. New victims arrive with frightening speed, and the doctors can't figure out how the virus is spreading so fast. Finally, Daniels discovers the virus has mutated and can now be spread through the air. Their only hope is to find the Motaba virus' original host, since the carrier's body must contain antibodies that can be used to create a cure.

The ugly truth is that Ford doesn't want Motaba cured, because he and General McClintock (Donald Sutherland) plan to use it in germ warfare. To protect this secret, the evil McClintock is willing to blow up Cedar Creek. Keough gets infected, and Daniels becomes a hunted man. He and his assistant, Major Salt (Cuba Gooding, Jr.), take their investigation on the run. With luck and determination, they track the monkey down and capture it. After a helicopter chase, the doctors return to Cedar Creek. They synthesize a vaccine, but the bomb is on the way. They take to the air again and block the bomber's path. Keough is cured, and intimates she and Daniels might reconcile.

Never mind that OUTBREAK bears an uncanny resemblance to George Romero's paranoid, greatly underappreciated THE CRAZIES (1973). It still contains moments of exceptional drama: An apparently innocuous kiss spreads the disease. A coughing moviegoer spews his germs into the air and infects the rest of the audience: See *that* in a dark theater during cold and flu season! A young mother is taken from her home and children to quarantine, and then quickly zipped up in a body bag. When Daniels realizes the virus is airborne, he looks up at an air-conditioning vent, and the camera zooms in and dollies through the duct.

The so-called "disease cowboys" like Keough and Daniels, who eagerly rush into the life threatening situations when others are fleeing, are potentially interesting, and the spread of the Motaba virus is pure INVASION OF THE BODY SNATCHERS. Unfortunately, OUTBREAK is done in by the misconception that the big screen demands big action and flashy pyrotechnics. The military conspiracy and the helicopter antics only take time away from the hunt for the monkey, and in turn make laughable the ease with which one small animal is found in the very big state of California. OUTBREAK boasts the services of a far better than average cast, who still can't overcome the deficiencies of the script. Dustin Hoffman seems out of place as a career Army officer; his iconoclastic image serves him when he's insubordinate, but *Dustin Hoffman: Action Hero*? In true Hollywood fashion, he's old enough to be Rene Russo's father, which adds one more layer of implausibility to a relationship that's already unconvincing.

OUTBREAK was the winner in the race to get an Ebola virus movie to the screen. A rival project, based on the best-selling non-fiction book *The Hot Zone*, fell apart when OUTBREAK began production. Competition to reach the screen first forced OUTBREAK to begin filming before the script was completed, and the effects of this rush are evident in the disjointed final product. (*Violence, profanity, adult situations.*) — P.R.

d, Wolfgang Petersen; p, Arnold Kopelson, Wolfgang Petersen, Gail Katz; exec p, Anne Kopelson, Duncan Henderson; assoc p, Scott Dougherty; co-p, Stephen Brown, Nana Greenwald, Sanford Panitch; w, Lawrence Dworet, Robert Roy Poole; ph, Michael Ballhaus; ed, Stephen Rivkin; m, James Newton Howard; prod d, William Sandell; art d, Nancy Patton, Francis J. Pezza; set d, Rosemary Brandenburg; sound, Richard Lightstone (mixer); fx, John Frazier, Mark Vago, Helen Ostenberg Elswit, Boss Film Studios; casting, Jane Jenkins, Janet Hirshenson; cos, Erica Edell Phillips; makeup, Susan A. Cabral, Ellis Burman, Monty Westmore, Matthew W. Mungle, John E. Jackson; stunts, Buddy Van Horn, Keith Tellez

Drama/Thriller   (PR: C MPAA: R)

OUTSIDE THE LAW   ★★
(U.S.) 95m Nu Image ~ New Line Home Video c

David Bradley (*Brad Kingsbury*); Anna Thompson (*Tanya Borgman*); Ashley Laurence (*Paige/Felicia*); Steven M. Gagnon (*Geoffreys*); Jamie Renee Smith (*Alicia*); Terrance Stone (*Lozano*); William Boyett (*Briskin*); Stephanie Swinney (*Billy*); Robert La Sardo (*Spike*); Paul Boyer (*Dave*); Charlie Holliday (*Garth*); Bill Moseley (*Hank*); Takayo Fisher (*Mrs. Yu*); Sean Moran (*Big John*); Jennifer Anglin (*Nancy*); Patricia Statham (*Stranger*); William Wellman, Jr. (*Palacio*); Annie O'Connell (*Mrs. Kornberg*); Kelly

Galindo (*Greta*); Jim Hudson (*Sheriff*); Maurice Singer (*Preacher*); Anna Davidson (*Tricia*); Nino Tempo (*Priest*)

In some cockeyed sense, OUTSIDE THE LAW is as confused as Tony, its bisexual heroine, who effortlessly moves from lesbianism to preference-altering sex with a studly LAPD detective. Bisexuality is not the only flip-flop here—unrequited love leads to murder, past crimes (cloudily exhumed) resurface to haunt the protagonists, and the volatile hero risks life and pension to bend the law in bed with a suspect. OUTSIDE THE REALM OF REASON might be a better title.

When a councilman's beautiful daughter, Billy Soriana (Stephanie Swinney), is fatally knifed while heading home from a lesbian tryst, dual suspect trails snake from the scene of the crime. While hotheaded detective Brad Kingsbury (David Bradley) points an accusing finger at Spike (Robert LaSardo), Billy's drug-pushing ex-beau, his adoring partner Paige (Ashley Laurence) and rival police force veteran Geoffreys (Steven M. Gagnon) target Billy's dyke dreamboat Tanya Borgman (Anna Thompson). While neglecting his young daughter and ignoring his infatuated partner, hard-drinking Brad finds time for the Hitchcock blonde Tanya even after her green-card husband winds up dead. Burying her grief in Brad's chest, the switch-hitter is haunted by a past incident in which her fiance's death was covered up by arson at his hotel and his former girlfriend Tammy committed suicide. For years, Tammy's nutty sister Felicia (believed to be dead) taunted Tanya with accusations. Meanwhile, when dogged Geoffreys make a play for spurned Paige, he discovers a button at her apartment which matches one found at the second crime scene. Steps ahead of her coworker, unhinged Paige (who's really vengeful Felicia) shoots Geoffreys. At knifepoint, Paige/Felicia rounds up innocent-all-along Tanya for an impromptu birthday party for Brad's daughter. Having figured out Paige's reasons for lying about Felicia's death, Brad races back to town. When Paige/Felicia's gun gets knocked behind a bar during a fracas, Brad's kid hands the pistol to Tanya, who distracts Paige/Felicia with her poor aim. After Paige wounds Tanya, Brad fells his weirded-out partner with a gun blow to the head, thus ending Felicia's long-running campaign of revenge against Tanya.

The skill of the genre piece in continually suturing its gaping plot holes is no match for its resolve to throw Bradley and Thompson on top of each other. Since their clinches are steamy, wolf-whistling action fans will willingly forgive the salivating flick's many lapses in logic and taste. Because Thompson ranks as videodom's most beddable blonde since Virginia Madsen, both male and female girl watchers will receive sufficient arousal stimuli. Of course, one must accept the film's tenet that lesbianism is an vocational pastime for the horny. Apparently, sexist video hucksters really think that all gay- bisexual women need is a romp with a hunk like Bradley to reclaim them for heterosexuality. (*Graphic violence, extreme profanity, extensive nudity, sexual situations, substance abuse.*) — R.P.

d, Boaz Davidson; p, Danny Dimbort, Avi Lerner; exec p, Trevor Short, Lisa Wilson Deitell; w, Dennis Dimster-Denk (from a story by Boaz Davidson and Dennis Dimster-Denk); ph, Avi Karpick; ed, Bruria B. Davidson; m, Blake Leyh; prod d, Ladislaw Wilhelm; art d, Bob Ziliox; sound, Jehuda Maayan (mixer); fx, Gary Bentley; casting, James Tarzia; cos, Caren Berger; makeup, Carrie Garton; stunts, Patrick Statham, Rob King

Erotic/Thriller/Crime   (PR: O MPAA: NR)

PANTHER ★★★½

(U.S.) 125m Working Title;
Tribeca Productions ~ Gramercy c

Kadeem Hardison *(Judge)*; Bokeem Woodbine *(Tyrone)*; Joe Don Baker *(Brimmer)*; Courtney B. Vance *(Bobby Seale)*; Tyrin Turner *(Cy)*; Huey Newton *(Marcus Chong)*; Anthony Griffith *(Eldridge Cleaver)*; Bobby Brown *(Rose)*; Nefertiti *(Alma)*; James Russo *(Rodgers)*; Jenifer Lewis *(Rita)*; Chris Rock *(Drinker #1)*; Roger Guenveur Smith *(Pruitt)*; Michael Wincott *(Tynan)*; Richard Dysart *(Hoover)*; M. Emmet Walsh *(Dorsett)*; Wesley Jonathan *(Little Bobby)*; Kahlil Nelson *(Boy on Bike)*; Thayis Walsh *(Bernadette)*; Anthony Jones *(Sabu)*; Dick Gregory *(Reverend Slocum)*; Kool Moe Dee *(Jamal)*; Lahmard Tate *(Gene McKinney)*; William Fuller *(Sergeant Schreck)*; David Greenlee *(Patrolman)*; Melvin Van Peebles *(Cynical Jail Bird)*; Adam Powers *(White Hippie)*; Sharrif Simmons *(Poet)*; Emory Douglas *(Bret Schaefer)*; Aklam *(Bakar)*; Mark Curry *(Lombard)*; Rob Rule; Eddie Anisko; Robbie Allen; David King *(Berkeley Campus Singers)*; Dario Scardapane *(Student)*; Reginald Ballard *(Brother at Meeting)*; Ralph Ahn *(Mr. Yang)*; James Bigwood *(Grove Street Cop)*; Martin Bright *(Grove Street Cop)*; John "Doo Doo Brown" Gordon *(Recruit)*; Marvin Young *(Recruit)*; D-Knowledge *(Recruit)*; Mark Buntzman *(Pushy Reporter)*; Robert Peters *(Cop at Ramparts)*; Shanice Wilson *(Singer at Punk Panthers)*; Jeffrey Carr *(Denzil Dowell)*; Ann Weldon *(Mrs. Dowell)*; Steven Carl White *(George)*; Brian Turk *(Deputy)*; Charles Cooper *(Sheriff)*; Tony Toni Tone *(Band at Barbecue)*; Dwayne P. Wiggins; Timothy C. Riley; John T. Smith; Elijah Baker; Vincent Lars; Bill Ortiz *(Band at Barbecue)*; Jay Koch *(Governor Reagan)*; Tim Loughrin *(Reporter at Capitol)*; Tony Beard *(Guard at Capitol)*; Jerry Rubin *(Defense Attorney)*; Beau Windham *(Hoover's Aide)*; Jamie Zozzaro *(Girl Buying Drugs)*; Yolanda Whitaker *(Pregnant Junkie)*; Roberto L. Santanta *(Matty)*; Arthur Reed *(Blind Man)*; Gunnar Peterson *(Cop at Gas Station)*; Christopher Michaels *(Reporter at Police Station)*; John Harwood *(Cop at Line Up)*; James LeGros *(Avakian)*; John Knight *(Cop at Panther Office)*; Joseph Culp *(Baby-Faced Cop)*; Erik Kohner *(Nervous Cop)*; Preston L. Holmes *(Prison Guard)*; Robert Culp *(Charles Garry)*; Chris Tucker; John Snyder *(Cop)*; Tracey Costello; Mario Van Peebles *(Stokely Carmichael)*; Jeris Poindexter *(Black Cop)*; Steve Gagnon *(Prosecutor)*; Brent Sincock *(Judge)*; Manny Perry *(Shorty)*; James A. Earley *(Angry Cop)*; William Brennan *(Partner)*

A sprawling, ambitious film about the rise and fall of the Black Panther Party, PANTHER is an alternative history of the 1960s, one in which drugs, popular music, rebellion against authority, and the Vietnam War resonate entirely differently than they do in the work of middle-class white filmmakers.

1966, Oakland, California: a youngster is run down at a street corner that lacks a traffic light. As recalled by Judge (Kadeem Hardison), the incident helps galvanize an African-American community that's regularly shortchanged in services and harassed by the police. Neighborhood firebrands Huey Newton (Marcus Chong) and Bobby Seale (Courtney B. Vance) form the Black Panther Party for Self-Defense, and Judge, a Vietnam veteran uncertain what to do with his life, joins up.

The Panthers organize a variety of community services: free breakfasts for children, sickle-cell anemia testing, and block parties. They finance their activities by selling Mao's Little Red Book to local college students, who see the Panthers as brothers in their fight against the Establishment. The Panthers also arm themselves and stand up to the brutal police. Police Chief Dorsett (M. Emmet Walsh) is pressured to do something about the Panthers, and assigns Brimmer (Joe Don Baker) to spy on them. Newton encourages Judge to manipulate Brimmer so the Panthers will know what the police are up to, but swears him to secrecy; Brimmer in turn thinks he can use Judge to spy on the Panthers. Judge, therefore, is always in danger of being thought a traitor.

When armed Panthers march on the State Capitol, they garner a blizzard of media attention and the enmity of J. Edgar Hoover (Richard Dysart), who plots to destroy them. Eldridge Cleaver (Anthony Griffith) joins the Panthers as minister of information. As the Party becomes increasingly famous, internal chaos and political persecution drives members apart.

Newton is set up for the murder of a cop and thrown in jail. Young Panther Bobby Hutton (Wesley Jonathan) is murdered by police and Cleaver is expelled from the party for advocating violence in the wake of Dr. Martin Luther King's murder. After Newton is acquitted, the FBI makes a deal with the Mafia to flood ghetto neighborhoods with cheap heroin. Disgusted, Brimmer leaks the plan to Judge, but he's unable to do anything to stop it.

Mario van Peebles was born to direct PANTHER, adapted from an unpublished novel by his father—filmmaker and lifelong radical Melvin Van Peebles—whose SWEET SWEETBACK'S BAADASSSS SONG (1971) was a favorite of the Panthers. At the time of its release, PANTHER was caught up in the continuing debate, triggered by such films as Oliver Stone's JFK (1991) and Spike Lee's MALCOLM X (1992), about the responsibility of filmmakers to history—particularly recent history—and the line between perspective and propaganda. Like those films, PANTHER mixes fact and fiction with wild abandon. Van Peebles called his picture "edutainment" aimed at young black Americans "who thought 'Huey Newton' was a cookie." The issue, he argued, isn't so much fidelity to facts as it is one of creating alternative mythologies, popular narratives that may be closer to the truth than supposedly objective "histories" that reflect mainstream ideology. For most of its running time, PANTHER is rousing entertainment, and does offer a sharply different perspective on what may well the most over-mythologized decade in America's past.

The director's determination to invoke a living mythology of the Black Panther Party is manifest throughout. His strategies for bringing the past to life include a painstaking recreation of '60s ambiance, images, and icons—like the famous poster of an armed Newton seated in a fan-backed wicker chair—and effective updatings of '60s pop music, notably the anthemic theme song "Freedom," here sung by an impressive array of '90s rap and hip-hop divas, from Me'Shell Ndege'Ocello to En Vogue to Salt-N-Pepa. The film is peppered with meaningful cameos: the younger Van Peebles appears briefly as Stokely Carmichael, while '60s comedian-turned-political activist Dick Gregory appears as the Reverend Slocum. Former Yippie Jerry Rubin plays a lawyer who defends the Panthers.

Unfortunately—like JFK—PANTHER is derailed by paranoid conspiracy thinking, specifically its contention that the government and the Mafia teamed up to flood black neighborhoods with drugs, which undermined the Black Power movement and produced a generation of complacent junkies. Like all conspiracy thinking, it's tinged with lunacy and undermines everything around it. *(Violence, profanity, adult situations, substance abuse.)* — M.M.

d, Mario Van Peebles; p, Preston Holmes, Mario Van Peebles, Melvin Van Peebles; exec p, Eric Fellner, Tim Bevan; assoc p, Liza Chasin; w, Melvin Van Peebles; ph, Eddie Pei; ed, Earl Watson; m, Larry Robinson; prod d, Richard Hoover; art d,

Bruce Hill; set d, Robert Kensinger; sound, Susumu Tokunow (mixer); fx, Beverly Hardigan; casting, Robi Reed; cos, Paul A. Simmons; makeup, Kim Davis, Diane Hammond; stunts, Bob Minor

Historical/Drama/Political   (PR: C   MPAA: R)

PARTY GIRL ★★★
(U.S.) 98m Party Pictures Inc. ~ First Look c

Parker Posey *(Mary)*; Guillermo Diaz *(Leo)*; Omar Townsend *(Mustafa)*; Sasha von Scherler *(Judy Lindendorf)*; Anthony De Sando *(Derrick)*; Donna Mitchell *(Rene)*; Liev Schreiber *(Nigel)*; Sasha von Scherler *(Mrs. Lindendorf)*; Nicole Bobbitt *(Venus)*; Simon Verhoeven *(Kurt/Karl)*; C. Francis Blackchild *(Wanda)*; L.B. Williams *(Howard)*; Margaret Hall *(Consignment Shop Owner)*; The Lady Bunny *(Itself)*; Natasha Twist *(Herself)*; Tim Duperron; Robert Sorce *(The It Twins)*; Becky Mode *(Ann)*; Richard Topol *(Hannah Arendt Buff)*; Raymond Moy *(Mr. Lu)*; Lum Chang Pang *(Policeman)*; Johnny Ventimiglia *(Tough Guy)*; Irma St. Paule *(Mumbling Library Patron)*; Marion Rosenfeld *(Maid Marion)*; Adam Siegal *(Sheepish Library Patron)*; Beth Koules *(Identical Twin Enthusiast)*; DJ Jazzy Nice *(Papi)*; Anthony Jones *(Stripper)*; Dwight Ewell; Wendell Daugherty; Teresa Lebron *(He-He-Hello Trio)*; Elisa Burchett; Heinrich Zwahlen *(Basscut)*; Ivon Rosas *(Go-Go Boy)*; Eduardo Quinones *(Go-Go Boy)*; Sabah Shayan *(Belly Dancer)*; Elizabeth Beer *(Hi-Tech Falafel Vendor)*

A fluffy comedy about love, responsibility and fabulous clothes, PARTY GIRL barely hides its candy-coated heart beneath a veneer of hip Downtown style.

Twenty-four-year-old Mary (Parker Posey), a feckless, arrogant club kid, is arrested at her Chinatown loft for throwing a rent party. She calls the only responsible person she knows: her stern godmother Judy (Sasha von Scherler), who was a good friend of Mary's late mother. Judy bails her out, but delivers a lecture that plays to Mary's deepest fears: that underneath her fabulous, popular exterior, she is "a woman with no common sense." Desperate for money, Mary takes a job as a clerk at the library where Judy works, but is flummoxed by the complexities of the Dewey decimal system.

Mary's personal life is complicated. She's recently broken up with her English boyfriend Nigel (Liev Schreiber), a bouncer at the popular club Rene's. Her friend Leo (Guillermo Diaz), an aspiring DJ who's between apartments, has moved into her loft. Meanwhile, she's struck up a flirtatious friendship with the handsome Mustafa (Omar Townsend), who was a teacher in his native Lebanon but now sells falafel on the streets of New York. Her friends are a cool collection of gay men, drag queens, and party girls like her. Mary continues living the nightlife while working at the library by day, even helping Leo get a job by introducing him to Rene (Donna Mitchell). But the library exerts a strange pull over her: she's good at her new job, and one evening she breaks in and spends the night learning the Dewey decimal system. She's so enthusiastic that she uses it to rearrange Leo's records. Omar, meanwhile, decides she's too flighty for him, but she persists in her attentions. Their relationship takes off when he comes to the library for information about getting his teaching certificate and finds her at the desk. They make love in the Romance Languages section.

Judy finds out about the amorous escapade and decides that Mary isn't fit to work in the library. Mary, devastated, decides to do what she does best: she throws an exotic, Middle-Eastern themed party, persuading Omar to sell falafel. They have a fight, and she gets so stoned that she passes out on the stairs to her loft, and wakes up with new resolve. She wants to become a profes-

sional librarian, and invites Judy to her apartment to persuade her of her seriousness. Meanwhile, Mary's friends have made Omar's falafel stand a hit. Of course, when Judy arrives there's a raucous 25th birthday bash in progress, complete with a stripper dressed as a policeman. But with Omar's help, Mary convinces Judy that she is a changed woman.

Perky, knowing, and sometimes sweetly funny, PARTY GIRL made online history by being the first feature film to be sneak previewed in its entirety—albeit in short, jerky segments—on the Internet. Written and directed by first-timer Daisy von Scherler Mayer, whose mother plays the imperious Judy, PARTY GIRL is utterly inconsequential, but wears its slightness with such good-natured style that it's hard to dislike. Its low budget is apparent in the underpopulated club scenes, but the cast is uniformly excellent—particularly the relentlessly effervescent Posey—and the modern take on old-fashioned romantic comedy is surprisingly effective.

The script isn't without nuances—Mary's insecurities, particularly her fear that she has no real talents and has just fooled people into thinking she's great, are conveyed without sledgehammer obviousness—but it's mostly played for light laughs. Since first films most often err on the side of pretension, von Sherler Mayer should probably be commended for having the courage to be trivial. *(Profanity, sexual situations, adult situations, substance abuse.)* — M.M.

d, Daisy von Scherler Mayer; p, Harry Brickmayer, Stephanie Koules; w, Daisy von Scherler Mayer, Harry Brickmayer (from a story by Daisy von Scherler Mayer, Harry Brickmayer, and Sheila Gaffney); ph, Michael Slovis; ed, Cara Silverman; m, Anton Sanko; prod d, Kevin Thompson; set d, Jennifer Baime; sound, Antonio Arroyo (mixer); casting, Caroline Sinclair; cos, Michael Clancy; makeup, Angela Johnson

Drama/Comedy   (PR: C   MPAA: R)

PAYBACK ★
(U.S.) 89m Tapestry Films ~ Trimark c

C. Thomas Howell *(Oscar Bonsetter)*; Joan Severance *(Rose Gullerman)*; Marshall Bell *(Tom "Gully" Gullerman)*; Richard Burgi *(Al Keegan)*; John Toles-Bey *(Marcus Jackson)*; R.G. Armstrong *(Old Mac)*; Dave Higgins *(Liquor Store Owner)*; Denise Bessette *(Store Owner's Wife)*; Breckin Meyer *(Store Owner's Son)*; Steve Wilcox *(Tough Punk)*

This dull variation on THE POSTMAN ALWAYS RINGS TWICE runs 90 minutes and feels twice that. It doesn't even deliver enough "erotic content" to justify the attention it might receive from its direct-to-video target audience.

Prison inmate Oscar Bonsetter (C. Thomas Howell) befriends Mac (R.G. Armstrong), an old con with a secret. On his deathbed, Mac reveals that a painting in his cell is really a map to his stolen fortune, the whereabouts of which thuggish guard Gully (Marshall Bell) has been trying to beat out of Mac for years. Oscar vows to avenge Mac and kill Gully. Years later a paroled Oscar tracks Gully down. The former guard is now blind, and operating a seaside diner with sexy wife Rose (Joan Severance). Calling himself "Lee," Oscar gets a job at the diner and begins searching for the painting, which Gully confiscated all those years ago. Rose's come-hither looks and tight outfits prove too much for Oscar to resist. They have sex and fall in love (in that order). Eventually, Oscar finds the painting, the loot, and asks Rose to run off with him, but she won't leave Gully as long as he's blind—or alive. Oscar offers Gully the money to have a sight-restoring operation, but ends up killing him in self-defense. Then Rose slays a surprised Oscar, and takes off with the money.

PAYBACK's biggest problem is miscast leads. First Oscar is a hardened con, willing to kill for vengeance and wealth. Then he becomes Lee, a nebbish with compassion for the brute who tortured him and abuses the woman he loves. With the denouement, Rose is conceptually transformed into a *femme fatale*, but never displays the traits of one. Neither Howell nor Severance can muster the depth to bring off their roles. Instead of a tough guy, he looks like the drummer in a bad, grunge-rock band. She's lovely to look at, but no Jessica Lange, and certainly no Lana Turner. *(Violence, sexual situations, profanity, nudity.)* — P.R.

d, Anthony Hickox; p, Sam Bernard, Natan Zahavi; exec p, Robert L. Levy, Peter Abrams, J.P. Guerin; w, Sam Bernard; ph, David Bridges; ed, Anita Brandt-Burgoyne; m, Anthony Marinelli; prod d, Stuart Blatt; casting, Allison Gordon-Kohler

Thriller (PR: O MPAA: R)

PEBBLE AND THE PENGUIN, THE ★★
(U.S.) 74m Don Bluth Ireland Ltd. ~ MGM/UA c

VOICES OF: Shani Wallis *(Narrator)*; Martin Short *(Hubie)*; James Belushi *(Rocko)*; Tim Curry *(Drake)*; Annie Golden *(Marina)*; Scott Bullock *(Chubby/Gentoo)*; Louise Vallance *(Priscilla/Chinstrap 2)*; Pat Musick *(Pola/Chinstrap 1)*; Angeline Ball *(Gwynne/Chinstrap 3)*; Kenall Cunningham *(Timmy)*; Alisa King *(Petra)*; Michael Nunes *(Beany)*; Neil Ross *(Scrawny)*; Phillip Clarke *(King)*; B.J. Ward *(Magellenic 1)*; Hamilton Camp *(Magellinic 2)*; Will Ryan *(Ryan/Tika)*; Pat Musick *(Chinstrap 1)*; Louise Vallance *(Chinstrap 2)*; Angeline Ball *(Chinstrap 3)*; Stanley Jones *(McCallister)*

Recommended for toddlers who love anything in cartoon form, THE PEBBLE AND THE PENGUIN is a musical about romance and adventure in penguin land, with the underlying message that good little boys have to resort to violence and good little girls must wait around to be valued as prizes.

In Antarctic circles, penguins apparently perform a mating ritual in which the he-bird drops the spiffiest stone he can locate at the webbed feet of his betrothed. Although bashful Hubie (voice of Martin Short) finds a Cartier-equivalent pebble for dream gal Marina (voice of Annie Golden), his courtship does not run smooth. Double-crossed by the most eligible bachelor Drake (voice of Tim Curry), who sandbags Hubie's engagement so he can worm his way into Marina's affections, Hubie is knocked into the ocean. Kidnapped as potential zoo material, and accompanied by growling inmate Rocko (voice of Jim Belushi), unflappable Hubie stages a daring shipboard getaway. Playing on Rocko's desire to be the world's first flying penguin, Hubie persuades his brawny friend to travel with him back to Antarctica. Arriving in the nick of time to claim Marina's flipper in marriage, Hubie must not only battle egotistical Drake, but also navigate past a fearsome seal, who almost dines on him and Rocko after Hubie drops his engagement pebble. Rescuing Marina as Drake's lair crumbles and the wicked penguin perishes with it, brave Hubie completes the prenuptial ceremony. Meanwhile, Rocko finally manages to soar into the penguin book of records.

Adults will probably wonder whether the joys of parenthood outweigh having to endure cartoons like THE PEBBLE AND THE PENGUIN. Several nagging questions present themselves: have anthro-zoologists actually discovered a mating ritual for penguins that involves engagement nuggets? And who are the real-life models for the chatty cast of characters on screen? In no way do they resemble the usual bird immortalized by the likes of Tennessee Tuxedo. With their Karl Malden noses, and Ed Wynn-ish coiffures, the film's leading characters are more like killer clowns. If viewers can overlook that visual downside (the car-

toon's backgrounds are impeccably drawn), there is still the total lack of inventiveness in the script to consider.

While the rich, rainbow-drenched drawing style makes this an acceptable moppet time-waster, the film could have benefited from a topflight song score. Better at ballads than musical comedy, Barry Manilow created a charming score for THUMBELINA. Working in a more treacly vein here, and hampered by the most inane lyrics, Manilow seems to vacillate between ripping off "Les Miserables" or "Sesame Street." — R.P.

d, Don Bluth; p, Russell Boland; exec p, James Butterworth; w, Rachel Koretsky, Steve Whitestone; ed, Thomas V. Moss; m, Barry Manilow; prod d, David Goetz; anim, John Pomeroy, Richard Bazley, Ralf Palmer, Len Simon, Silvia Hoefnagels, John Hill, John Power; fx, David Tidgwell

Children's/Animated/Fantasy (PR: AA MPAA: G)

PENTATHLON ★★
(U.S.) 101m PFG Entertainment; LIVE Entertainment ~ LIVE Entertainment c

Dolph Lundgren *(Eric Brogar)*; Renee Coleman *(Julie)*; Roger E. Mosley *(Creese)*; David Soul *(Mueller)*; Evan James *(Offerman)*; Barry Lynch *(Horst)*; David Drummond *(Hundt)*; Philip Bruns *(Vic)*; Daniel Riordan *(Rhinehardt)*; Bruce Malmuth *(Erhardt)*; Erik Holland *(Rudolph Brogar)*; Gerald Hopkins *(Christian)*; Anthony Pennello *(Cop #1)*; Andreas Renell *(Schubert)*; Alex Rodine *(Ambassador)*; James Paradise *(Rabbi)*; Sandra West *(TV Director)*; Dudley Knight *(Schiller)*; Kevin White *(Freddie)*; Rob Stull *(Bodeen)*; Buddy Joe Hooker *(Otto)*; Jesse Mullen *(Young Eric)*; Michelle Harrell *(Sheila)*; Birgit Nielsen *(Ticket Agent)*; Carl Sundstrom *(Rally Guard)*; John Nabor *(Announcer)*; Angelina Estrada *(Landlady)*; Mel Stewart *(Olympic Athlete)*

Despite the suspense potential of Olympic try outs, East German police ambushes, and Aryan nation conspiracies, PENTATHLON is a standard stuck-in-the-mud action exercise. Flaunting his impressive bulk, Nordic god Dolph Lundgren acts like an industrial strength male model; his ultra-reticent demeanor makes him a liability as an action superstar unless he's cast as an android.

After snagging a 1988 gold medal at Seoul for his fatherland, East German athlete Eric Brogar (Dolph Lundgren) makes a 100-yard-dash for political asylum with the US. Later, Brogar becomes a self-pitying boozehound until his talents are spotted by his diner-owning boss Creese (Roger E. Mosley). Still smarting over his defection, Eric's jingoistic ex-coach Heinrich Mueller (David Soul) beats Brogar's papa to death before flying to the US in search of the pentathlete who got away. While Eric reunites with former main squeeze Julia (Renee Coleman), who hones his endurance skills at her dad's woodland retreat, Mueller joins forces with neo-Nazi sympathizers including Eric's former rival Rinehardt (Daniel Riordan). At a Never-Again peace rally, they plot to assassinate a rabbi and an ambassador while spreading a hate message on cable TV. After viciously beating up Julia's dad and shooting Creese, they kidnap Eric, who thwarts their scheme by wiping out most of the neo-Nazis. Three weeks later, at the pentathlon finals, heroic Eric not only triumphs in his tryout but also wounds the Gestapo-wannabee Mueller with a gun Mueller drops near the finish line due to the timely interference of Julia.

Somehow, PENTATHLON manages to transform Olympian feats of strength and political melodrama into a dreary scenario with the impact of watching out-of-shape men exchange nationalistic insults during an aerobics class. Huffing and puffing through its nationalistic plot twists, the film never gets any adrenalin pumping. Given the constraints of a far-from-generous budget (whose telltale signs include stock footage and a plugged-in electronic score), PENTATHLON still might have roused sports enthusiasts if only its key action sequences had been executed with any oomph. Shapelessly edited, the film's moribund political intrigue is comprised of an unconvincing wolf pack of German superpatriots led by an eye-popping David Soul. Sporting an operetta accent and a flagging intensity, Soul seems badly in need of an injection of Conrad Veidt vitamins. The premise that Berlin cold war hardliners think that live coverage of a political rubout would alter anyone's opinion in this up-to-our-necks-in-terrorists era or that they could seize control of TV transmission long enough to make their point (unless they negotiated with Jenny Jones) is notably ridiculous. Towering over this broken-wheeled CHARIOTS OF FIRE update like an umlaut is impenetrable macho man Lundgren. Carved in muscle, this grunting sphinx only comes to life when he exercises. *(Graphic violence, extreme profanity, substance abuse.)* — R.P.

d, Bruce Malmuth; p, Martin Caan, Dolph Lundgren; exec p, Carol H. Thompson, Ronna B. Wallace, Dolph Lundgren; assoc p, Rob Stull, Mikela Walters, Deborah Gilels; co-p, Jason Clark; w, William Stadiem, Gary MacDonald, Gary Devore (from a story by William Stadiem and Bruce Malmuth); ph, Misha Suslov; ed, Richard Nord; m, David Spear; prod d, James Hynkle; art d, David W. Ford; fx, Frank Ceglia; casting, Rick Montgomery, Dan Parada; cos, Alexandra Welker; makeup, Suzanne Parker Sanders

Action/Martial Arts (PR: C MPAA: R)

PEREZ FAMILY, THE ★★
(U.S.) 91m Samuel Goldwyn Company ~ Samuel Goldwyn Company C

Marisa Tomei *(Dottie Perez)*; Anjelica Huston *(Carmela Perez)*; Alfred Molina *(Juan Raul Perez)*; Chazz Palminteri *(Lieutenant John Pirelli)*; Trini Alvarado *(Teresa Perez)*; Celia Cruz *(Luz Paz)*; Diego Wallraf *(Angel Perez)*; Angela Lanza *(Flavia)*; Jose Philipe Padron; Ranjit Chowdhry; Lazaro Perez

The cast is better than the script in THE PEREZ FAMILY, a seriocomic tale of Cuban immigrants forging a new existence in Miami after the 1980 Mariel boatlift.

Released after 20 years, political prisoner Juan Raul Perez (Alfred Molina) makes his way to Miami in the Mariel boatlift. On the way, he meets Dorita "Dottie" Perez (Marisa Tomei), a prostitute and sugarcane worker with big dreams about America. Entering the US at the same time, they are mistakenly listed by immigration officials as husband and wife. Juan's real wife, Carmela (Anjelica Huston), has waited patiently for two decades to be reunited with her husband, having raised their daughter Teresa (Trini Alvarado) alone. Carmela's brother Angel (Diego Wallraff) fails to recognize Juan at the docks and brings Carmela the devastating news that Juan has not come on the last boatlift.

Dottie learns that single refugees are considered undesirable, while large families are highest on the list to receive sponsors. She convinces Juan they should play husband and wife just until they land a sponsor. In the refugee camp, Dottie corrals two more unrelated Perezes into playing family members. The fabricated Perez family is sponsored by a church and put to work selling flowers on the roadside. Dottie excels at the task due to her vivacious manner. She soon spins dreams of owning a flower shop with her *faux* family.

While mourning her lost husband, Carmela strikes up a flirtation with police officer Pirelli (Chazz Palminteri). Juan finally succeeds in locating Carmela, but after seeing her with Pirelli, he

decides to stay out of her life and settle down with Dottie, with whom he has fallen in love. The foursome are brought together at a festival which erupts into chaos when the long-separated couple is reunited. Though she loves Juan, Dottie steps aside so he can return to his family. Juan and Carmela realize that the changes brought by 20 years have turned them into strangers. They part as friends, Carmela returning to Pirelli, and Juan to an overjoyed Dottie.

Though its core plot is reminiscent of a 1940s screwball comedy, THE PEREZ FAMILY engenders few laughs. The general tone is melancholic, and at times downright tragic, as when Dottie's bogus "son" is murdered. The dichotomy between tone and plot compromises its overall effectiveness. Additionally, the story is hampered by illogical plot twists and inscrutable character motivation, with several questions remaining unanswered at film's end. Brightly colored costumes, picturesque settings, and salsa music give the film a rich cultural flavor, but the flashy surface does not conceal the underlying narrative deficiencies.

The film's strongest asset is its likable cast, headed by Tomei, who gives a gutsy, impassioned performance as free spirit Dottie. The normally waif-like Tomei gained 20 pounds for her role. Mainly clad in halter and bikini tops, her newly voluptuous figure is displayed to good advantage. In embracing her character's ethnicity, Tomei tends to go slightly overboard; her accent occasionally borders on the burlesque. In less showy performances, Huston and Molina acquit themselves well. The only clinker in the cast is Wallraff, who is saddled with a grating, stereotypical character.

The casting of Italian-American Tomei and half-Spanish Huston and Molina as Cubans heated up the controversial debate over ethnic casting. Demonstrators turned out for the film's opening in Manhattan, protesting the casting of non-Cuban actors in the lead roles. Samuel Goldwyn Co. president Meyer Gottlieb defended the casting choices, saying "There's a profession called 'acting.'" Director Mira Nair (who appears in a cameo) claimed to have offered the role of Juan to Andy Garcia and the late Raul Julia, but both declined. For the women's roles, the lack of bankable female Latino stars resulted in the casting of Oscar winners Tomei and Huston, but even their star power failed to boost the film's disappointing box-office return. *(Violence, extensive nudity, sexual situations, profanity.)* — B.R.

d, Mira Nair; p, Michael Nozik, Lydia Dean Pilcher; exec p, Julia Chasman, Robin Swicord; w, Robin Swicord (based on the novel by Christine Bell); ph, Stuart Dryburgh; ed, Bob Estrin; m, Alan Silvestri; prod d, Mark Friedberg; art d, Ken Hardy; set d, Stephanie Carroll; sound, Henry Lopez; casting, Billy Hopkins; cos, Eduardo Castro; makeup, D'Amoure, Jay Canistraci

Comedy/Romance/Drama (PR: C MPAA: R)

PERSUASION ★★★½
(U.K.) 103m BBC Films; WGBH/Mobil Masterpiece Theater; Millesime Productions ~ Sony Pictures Classics c

Amanda Root *(Anne Elliot)*; Ciaran Hinds *(Captain Wentworth)*; Susan Fleetwood *(Lady Russell)*; Corin Redgrave *(Sir Walter Elliot)*; Fiona Shaw *(Mrs. Croft)*; John Woodvine *(Admiral Croft)*; Phoebe Nicholls *(Elizabeth Elliot)*; Samuel West *(Mr. Elliot)*; Sophie Thompson *(Mary Musgrove)*; Judy Cornwell *(Mrs. Musgrove)*; Simon Russell Beale *(Charles Musgrove)*; Felicity Dean *(Mrs. Clay)*; Roger Hammond *(Mr. Musgrove)*; Emma Roberts *(Louisa Musgrove)*; Victoria Hamilton *(Henrietta Musgrove)*; Robert Glenister *(Captain Harville)*; Richard McCabe *(Captain Benwick)*; Helen Schlesinger *(Mrs. Smith)*; Jane Wood *(Nurse Rooke)*; David Collings *(Mr. Shepherd)*; Darlene Johnson *(Lady Dalrymple)*; Cinnamon Faye *(Miss Car-*

teret); Isaac Maxwell-Hunt *(Henry Havter)*; Roger Llewellyn *(Sir Henry Willoughby)*; Sally George *(Mrs. Harville)*; David Acton *(Naval Officer)*; Justin Avoth *(Naval Officer)*; Lonnie James *(Jemima)*; Roger Watkins *(Landlord)*; David Plummer *(Apothecary)*; Bill McGuirk *(Tradesman)*; Niall Refoy *(Tradesman)*; Ken Shorter *(Lady Dalrymple's Butler)*; Dermot Kerrigan *(Footman)*; Tom Rigby *(Little Charles)*; Alex Wilman *(Little Walter)*; Rosa Mannion *(Concert Opera Singer)*

PERSUASION brings Jane Austen's novel to movie screens for the first time. A faithful literary adaptation, PERSUASION is a high-quality period drama featuring strong performances and confident direction.

Set in England in the early 19th century, PERSUASION is the story of Anne Elliot (Amanda Root) and her enduring love for Frederick Wentworth (Ciaran Hinds). At the age of 19 and contrary to her true feelings, Anne rejected Wentworth's marriage proposal, persuaded by the advice of her friend Lady Russell that a penniless naval officer was no match for the daughter of a baronet. The story begins eight years later, when Anne is 27, on the verge of spinsterhood. The Elliot family—including Anne's pompous father, Sir Walter (Corin Redgrave), and her snobbish older sister Elizabeth—has been living beyond its means at lavish Kellynch Hall. They are required to cut costs and go to a smaller residence in fashionable Bath while leasing Kellynch Hall to Admiral Croft (John Woodvine) and his wife (Fiona Shaw), who happens to be Wentworth's sister. When the newly rich Wentworth re-enters Anne's social circle, her feelings for him are rekindled; but Wentworth still feels pain and distrust from their earlier relationship.

Anne's younger sister, Mary (Sophie Thompson), is married to Charles Musgrove (Simon Russell Beale), the heir of a neighboring landed proprietor. Musgrove has two sisters, Louisa (Emma Roberts) and Henrietta (Victoria Hamilton). Wentworth is at first attracted to them both, but soon becomes entangled with Louisa. When Louisa is dangerously injured in a fall at Lyme Regis, Wentworth's partial responsibility for the accident makes him feel an increased obligation to Louisa at the very time his heart is being drawn back to Anne. Fortunately, during her convalescence and Wentworth's absence, Louisa becomes engaged to a friend of Wentworth. In the meantime, Anne is being courted by her cousin William Elliot (Samuel West), the heir presumptive to the Kellynch estate. At the same time that he is paying persistent attention to Anne, William is also having an affair with Mrs. Clay (Felicity Dean), who in turn has matrimonial designs on Sir Walter Elliot. Anne is awakened to Elliot's duplicity by an old friend. Discovering that Anne's love for him remains unshaken, Wentworth takes courage to renew his offer of marriage.

Jane Austen was 40 when she wrote *Persuasion* and 41 when she died. Published posthumously, the novel was popularly supposed to be semi-autobiographical. Although *Persuasion* was made into a television serial in the 1970s, British theater director Roger Miller's production is the first time the story has been made into a feature film. Like its source, PERSUASION has a genteel quality, evoking the quiet, day-to-day life of the upper middle class in 19th-century England. There's none of the lushness of Scorsese's THE AGE OF INNOCENCE; restraint is the order of the day, especially for women who were expected to be demure and passive. The challenging role of Anne Elliot is handled superbly by Amanda Root. Although Anne is the central character, she hardly speaks during the first half of the film; and Root achieves a delicate balance of strength and sadness, without ever making her character pitiful. Other performances are all strong, and the production design is assured. PERSUASION feels much like the novel, a charming portrait of an elegant and refined world, ruled more by manners than the heart. *(Adult situations.)* — J.S.

d, Roger Michell; p, Fiona Finlay; exec p, George Faber, Rebecca Eaton; assoc p, Margot Hayhoe; w, Nick Dear (based on the novel by Jane Austen); ph, John Daly; ed, Kate Evans; m, Jeremy Sams; prod d, William Dudley, Brian Sykes; art d, Linda Ward; ch, Geraldine Stephenson; sound, Terry Elms (recordist); fx, Colin Gorry; casting, Siobhan Bracke; cos, Alexander Byrne; makeup, Jean Speak; stunts, Helen Caldwell

Romance/Drama/Historical   **(PR: A   MPAA: PG)**

PHANTOM LOVER, THE   ★★★½
(Hong Kong) 98m Mandarin Films; Sil-Metropole Company Ltd. ~ Mandarin Films c
(AKA: YE BOON GOH SING)

Leslie Cheung *(Song Danping)*; Wu Chien-Lien *(Du Yunyan)*; Huang Lei *(Wei Qing)*; Lau Lam; Bow Fong; Roy Szeto; Kuo Chui; Roy Szeto

A striking Asian variation on THE PHANTOM OF THE OPERA theme, THE PHANTOM LOVER is Gothic romantic tragedy at its finest.

In 1936 Peking, a theatrical troupe moves into a dilapidated theater where they are to stage their productions. One of the group, Wei Qing (Huang Lei) sees a ghostly figure in the building's shadows, and the place's old caretaker tells him its history. Ten years ago, the structure was an opera house where Song Danping (Leslie Cheung) was the star, an idol to many women in the area. But his heart belonged to Du Yunyan (Wu Chien-Lien), the daughter of a prominent local businessman who disapproved of her consorting with Song. Yunyan was betrothed to the son of politician Mr. Zhao, who had a major deal going with Yunyan's father. A terrible fire burned down the theater, apparently killing Song, and the marriage between Yunyan and Zhao's son went ahead. But when it was discovered she was not a virgin, Yunyan was cast out by her family, who subsequently moved away, and is now a madwoman roaming the city's streets.

Wei soon discovers that the apparition he saw is Song, still alive and hiding in the theater, horribly scarred but still pining for Yunyan, who has come to the building every full moon hoping to see him. Song encourages Wei to mount a production of *Romeo and Juliet*, the opera he was performing before the fire (which he reveals was set by the Dus and the Zhaos). Song assists Wei with the singing from offstage. The Zhaos arrive in town on political business, and when the son discovers Yunyan in the street, he viciously beats her. Wei realizes that Song is attempting to "live again" through him and confronts Song, urging him to step out of the shadows. This he does, and with Wei's help, he exposes the Zhaos' treachery. Song is then reunited with Yunyan and they ride out of town in a carriage together.

While it contains no overt supernatural elements, THE PHANTOM LOVER is very much in the tradition of director Ronny Yu's previous THE BRIDE WITH WHITE HAIR, combining Gothic themes and eerie imagery with a heartfelt story of two lovers torn apart by social and familial forces. While the earlier film concentrated more on special effects, THE PHANTOM LOVER aims directly for the heart.

Hong Kong pop star Cheung is perfectly cast as Song, putting his haunting singing voice to good use. He also collaborated on the songs with composer Chris Babida, whose instrumental score is lush and evocative. Wu is ravishing and heartbreaking as the object of Song's desire, and Huang well captures both Wei's initial naivete and his eventual boldness in forcing Song to reveal himself.

The film's wide-screen visuals are frequently breathtaking, with sumptuous photography by Peter Pau. The 1936 sequences are in sepia tones, while only the lengthy flashback to Song and Yunyan's story is presented in full, rapturous color. The rest of the film is just a notch less compelling, and the climactic events seem a bit rushed, but overall this is an immensely powerful experience. (Violence, sexual situations, adult situations.) — M.G.

d, Ronny Yu; p, Michael Ng, Raymond Wong; exec p, Raymond Wong, Li Ning; co-p, Leslie Cheung; w, Roy Szeto, Raymond Wong, Ronny Yu; ph, Peter Pau; ed, David Wu; m, Chris Babida; prod d, Eddie Ma; cos, William Chang, Yeung Sinling

Drama/Fantasy/Romance   **(PR: C   MPAA: NR)**

PIANO LESSON, THE   ★★
(U.S.) 99m Hallmark Hall of Fame Productions; Craig Anderson Productions ~ Republic Pictures Home Video c

Alfre Woodard (Berniece Charles); Charles Dutton (Boy Willie Charles); Courtney B. Vance (Lymon); Zelda Harris (Maretha); Lou Myers (Winning Boy); Tommy Hollis (Avery); Carl Gordon (Doaker); Rosalyn Coleman (Grace); Tommy LaFitte (Ace); Lynne Innerst (Miss Ophelia); Harold Surratt (Papa Willie Boy); Elva Branson (Mama Berniece); Tim Hartman (Sutter); Ben Tatar (Watermelon Man); Alice Eisner (Watermelon Lady); Bob Tracey (Nolander)

THE PIANO LESSON, a wrenching but flawed cable adaptation of August Wilson's play, is committed to conveying the experience of poor African-Americans caught in a bind between treasuring their heritage and surviving financially.

Traveling up North with a truckload of watermelons he hopes to sell with compatriot Lymon (Courtney B. Vance), irrepressible Boy Willie (Charles Dutton) dreams of purchasing 100 acres of land for $2000. Dropping by unannounced at the home of Uncle Doaker (Carl Gordon) and Boy Willie's sister Berniece (Alfre Woodard), desperate Boy Willie campaigns to sell his mother's hand-carved piano to finance his new start as a property-owner. Whereas Boy Willie only sees the instrument as a cash source, the high-strung Berniece views the disputed object as an heirloom. In the course of this impasse, flashbacks reveal the tortured history of the piano.

Generations ago, slaveowner Sutter (Tim Hartman) traded two of Boy Willie's ancestors for a piano; when his music-loving wife yearned for her two sold slaves, he commissioned a slave artisan to carve their faces into the wood. Because the craftsman ended up whittling in the entire history of this slave clan, Doaker's brother, Boy Willie's father, stole the unique creation and ended up burned to death in a boxcar along with some hobos, in a white man's reprisal against the theft.

Although realist Boy Willie still plans to make off with the piano, the house seems haunted by those who died for this symbolic item and by the spirit of the plantation master Sutter, too. Refusing to capitulate even though she has not touched the keyboard since her mother's death, Berniece remains crippled by the price her parents paid for this symbol of their ancestry. After Preacher Avery (Tommy Hollis) blesses the house, restless ghosts stir themselves. Feeling the power of the past, a chastised Boy Willie reconciles with Berniece, who once again plays the piano and keeps the bittersweet music of the family's history alive.

Bearing a great deal of symbolic weight on those keys, THE PIANO LESSON is another August Wilson folk tale about the legacy of slavery. Sadly, this particular production fails to make any psychological or ectoplasmic ghosts come alive for the audience. It is not because the dramaturgy does not make the playwright's message abundantly clear: both Boy Willie and Berniece are wrong and right. Just as you should not sell off an heirloom that signifies family pride, you also should not shut yourself off emotionally because of what happened in the past. If Boy Willie is trapped by wanting to grab the brass ring, then Berniece is so traumatized by her family's legacy that she only exists as an apparition of repression. The problem with this carefully mapped-out theater piece is its obviousness. Playwright Wilson labors his points, relieves the dreary soul-searching with musical interludes, then returns to dramatic confrontations at an even higher pitch. Shouting as if playing to the balcony, the cast members do little to illuminate this tale of completing the unfinished business of one's forebears. (Violence, adult situations, substance abuse, profanity.) — R.P.

d, Lloyd Richards; p, August Wilson; exec p, Richard Welsh, Craig Anderson; co-p, Brent Shields; w, August Wilson (based on his play); ph, Paul Elliott; ed, Jim Oliver; m, Stephen James Taylor; prod d, Jim Newport; art d, Tim Saternow; set d, Eva Kamienska-Carter; sound, Michael C. Moore; casting, Olivia Harris, Phyllis Huffman; cos, Vicki Sanchez; makeup, Ellie Winslow

Drama   **(PR: C   MPAA: PG)**

PICTURE BRIDE   ★★★½
(U.S.) 90m Thousand Cranes Filmworks ~ Miramax c

Youki Kudoh (Riyo); Akira Takayama (Matsuji); Tamlyn Tomita (Kana); Cary-Hiroyuki Tagawa (Kanzaki); Toshiro Mifune (The Benshi); Yoki Sugi (Aunt Sode)

PICTURE BRIDE is a gentle, lyrical historical drama and a deeply satisfying evocation of one immigrant's experiences in old Hawaii. The film gained accolades at the 1995 Sundance Film Festival but, in the tradition of Sundance winners like CHAMELEON STREET and RUBY IN PARADISE, was ignored by the public.

Riyo (Youki Kudoh), a Japanese teenager circa 1918, tries to escape an unhappy situation with a solution common among girls of the era: being a mail-order bride for a planter in Hawaii. She exchanges photos with Matsuji (Akira Takayama), then nervously voyages to the big island of Oahu only to find her new husband is 20 years older than he was in the portrait he sent her, and dwells in a sharecropper's shack. Though married to him in a civil ceremony, Riyo shuns Matsuji and vows to earn enough as an underpaid field hand to return to Japan.

Thrown into the toil of the sugarcane harvest, Riyo befriends the savvy Kana (Tamlyn Tomita), another relocated Japanese girl, married to an alcoholic worker but persevering as best she can with their child. Kana teaches Riyo survival skills, and Matsuji how to be a better husband, then perishes with her son in a cane field blaze. Finally on guardedly intimate terms with Matsuji, Riyo confesses why she left Japan: her parents died of tuberculosis, making her an outcast in the rigid society. The true turning point comes when Riyo encounters Kana's ghost on the beach. The spirit considers Hawaii, not Japan, her real home and urges Riyo to do the same. A strike looms among plantation employees and, on the first anniversary of her arrival, Riyo donates all her savings to the laborers' communal fund. In a voice-over epilogue, the aged Riyo notes that she and Matsuji had many children during their long life together.

Kayo Hatta's first feature film draws heavily on her own family history. Made with compassion and humanity, the film never descends to mere romantic melodrama or exotic travelogue, but maintains an unabashedly feminist point of view toward events. The narrative is low-key: While the audience is told that Kana's husband beats her, no abuse is shown; the strike stays off-screen. Hints of vice and racism within the plantation's community are also kept at a distance. The scope is restricted to a few main characters, but they attract the sympathy of the viewer.

Actress-model Youki Kudoh—seen in Jim Jarmusch's MYSTERY TRAIN as the Graceland pilgrim who imagined Elvis as Buddha — maintains a fetchingly delicate balance of fragility and determination, while Takayama (in a role based on Hatta's grandfather) is a winningly earnest, if rough-hewn suitor. The lone ostentatious touch is the legendary Toshiro Mifune's cameo as a travelling storyteller, a sort of human cinema who evokes fond memories of faraway Japan for the immigrants. A more nuanced performance comes from the Hawaiian countryside itself. Initially a monotonous wall of sugarcane stalks, it turns into a tropical paradise as Riyoh's attitude warms toward the land and her husband. Though rated PG 13 and released with a deceptively erotic ad campaign, there is nothing in PICTURE BRIDE to render it objectionable for young audiences. — C.C.

d, Kayo Hatta; p, Lisa Onodera, Diane Mei Lin Mark; exec p, Diane Mei Lin Mark; assoc p, Eleanor Nakama; w, Kayo Hatta, Mari Hatta (from a story by Kayo Hatta, Mari Hatta, and Diane Mei Lin Mark); ph, Claudio Rocha; ed, Lynzee Klingman, Mallori Gottlieb; prod d, Paul Guncheon; sound, Susan Chong; casting, Anna Fishburn; cos, Ada Akaji

Drama/Romance/Historical   (PR: A   MPAA: PG-13)

PIGALLE   ★★

(France/Switzerland) 93m Premiere Heure LM; Union Generale Cinematographique; FCC; Delfilm ~ Seventh Art Releasing c

Vera Briole *(Vera)*; Francois Renaund *(Fifi)*; Raymond Gil *(Fernande)*; Philippe Ambrosini *(Le Malfait)*; Blanca Li *(Divine)*; Jean-Claude Grenier *(L'Emereur)*; Bobby Pacha *(La Pahca)*; Younesse Boudache *(Mustaf)*; Patrick Chauvel *(Jesus Le Gitan)*; Jacky Bapps *(Forceps)*; Roger Desprez *(Roger L'Elegant)*; Jean-Michel Fete *(P'tit Fred)*; Olindo Cavadini *(Polo)*; Christian Auger *(Rene)*; Jean-Jacques Jauffret *(Marc-Antoine)*; Philippe Nahon *(Lezzi)*; Christiane Saunier *(Cri-Cri)*; Ursula Deuker *(Marlene)*; Anne Carole *(Pauline)*; Mostefa Zerguine *(Hamad)*; Gerard Lebrun *(L'Africain)*

Karim Dridi's first feature is a portrait of the people who live in Pigalle, the infamous Red Light district of Paris. Unfortunately PIGALLE is plagued by cliched characters, visuals, and dialogue.

Vera (Vera Briole) is a peep-show stripper who lives with one of Pigalle's leading drug dealers, who happens to be called Jesus (Patrick Chauvel). Fifi (Francis Renaud) is a junkie pickpocket who lives with Divine (Blanca Li), a transvestite prostitute. Fifi and Vera are friends who hang out together on the streets. When Fifi starts expressing amorous feelings towards Vera, their easy-going friendship becomes complicated. Divine becomes involved in dealing drugs and is found brutally stabbed, having been tossed half-dead from a black Porsche. Fifi is convinced that the murderer was Jesus. Seeking revenge for Divine's death, Fifi rapes Vera, but both of them are being tricked into becoming pawns in a violent power play between the three big drug barons in the area.

Pigalle, home of the Can-Can and the Moulin Rouge, has attracted the interest of many artists and writers, including Genet and Cendrars. PIGALLE is reportedly the first film ever shot entirely in this neighborhood, and it almost functions as an anthropological docudrama, its handheld camera peeking into the area's strip shows, sex clubs, and back rooms. Many of the people who appear in the film are real residents, lending an air of authenticity. It is the narrative elements of the film which

really fail. The characters are cliched and one-dimensional—the stripper with a heart of gold, the confused hopeless junkie, the tragic drag queen called Divine, and so on. The visual scenery often feels well-worn—e.g., two people having sex in the shadows under the neon lights of Le Plaisir club, or drug deals done in white stretch limos. And the plot is so scant and predictable that what we're really left with are endlessly long dance sequences from peep shows, masturbating voyeurs, scenes of heavy empty sex, and Vera's rape, all set to a throbbing musical track. *(Graphic violence, extensive nudity, sexual situations, substance abuse, extreme profanity.)* — J.S.

d, Karim Dridi; p, Romain Bremond, Patrice Haddad; w, Karim Dridi; ph, John Mathieson; ed, Lise Beaulieu; art d, Gilles Bontemps; sound, Louis Gimel; cos, Jean-Louis Mazabraud; makeup, Huelan Vanduc

Drama   (PR: O   MPAA: NR)

PLAY TIME   ★

(U.S.) 95m Cameo Films ~ Triboro Entertainment Group c

Monique Parent *(Geena)*; Craig Stepp *(Brad)*; Elliot David *(Joe)*; Jennifer Burton *(Lindsey)*; Julie Strain *(Sheraton)*; Tammy Parks *(Michelle)*; Tina Simonsoa *(Receptionist)*; Wendy Hamilton *(Brad's Secretary)*; Robert Lepucki *(Salesman)*; Francis Shanahan *(Young Brad)*; Sani August *(Brad's Dad)*; Ashlie Rhey *(Connie)*

Aside from temporal surface details, this feeble erotica might have been retrieved from a 1970's time capsule marked: "Wife-swapping flick." Lacking the energetic sleaze of that era, this 1990's connubial battery recharger is decked out in sensual pastels and plays like a Kama Sutra video on downers.

Has the spice gone out of the marriage of blonde babe Geena (Monique Parent) and tight-ass hubby Brad (Craig Stepp)? Perhaps a Palm Springs getaway with Brad's business partner Joe (Elliot David) and his orgasmoholic wife Lindsey (Jennifer Burton) will wake up their torpid sex lives. Inducing her inhibited pal Geena to masturbate while they leer at the pool boy, Lindsey indoctrinates her friend into a world where each woman's bed is an orgone box. As a follow-up to lesbian sex at their office, Lindsey sets up a ski weekend in which Joe spies on the fornicating women from a closet. After voyeuristic Joe regales the duo with a similar tale about his cousin Connie (Ashlie Rhey), the adventurous trio threesomes in a hot tub. Plans to melt iceberg Brad falter when he realizes Lindsey's wanton masturbation in a sauna was prearranged. Although Lindsey makes amends for her manipulativeness by providing Brad with oral sex at his office, her plans to save Brad and Joe's troubled business partnership snag when the two couples pair off with each other. Returning to Palm Springs to recapture their nuptial magic, Brad's pals are pleased when he finally spills his guts about his stuck-in-the-mud sexuality, and a flashback reveals how his stepmother Sheraton (Julie Strain) seduced him, only to be discovered by his father. With Brad unburdened of his sexual hang-up, both marriages are saved (and the decks are cleared for further experimentation in the future).

In both its edited and unedited versions, PLAY TIME is about as steamy as blowing one's breath on an icy window in the winter. Never has so much flesh been undraped to so little avail. Although the femme stars undulate like Victoria's Secret models on a vibrating bed, the male leads suggest peckish accountants who've been sex-trained by the Moral Majority. Watching their rather tame fantasies unfold, viewers get the nagging suspicion that these stars are performing in a film financed by former Surgeon General Jocelyn Elders; never has a sexploitation film drooled on so insistently about autoeroticism. Voyeurism comes in a distant second; intercourse seems like an afterthought for these uncoupling couples. Once again, lesbianism is viewed as a heterosexual appetizer for egocentric straight men hungry for instant adultery. The attitude espoused by stud flicks like PLAY TIME reaches its nadir when Geena brags to her rival that, "My breasts are bigger than yours!" Since the gals' measurements do not square off with their IQs, PLAY TIME remains unchallenging turn-on material. It's dull enough to give fidelity a good name. *(Extreme profanity, extensive nudity, sexual situations.)* — R.P.

d, Dale Trevillion; p, Dale Trevillion, Nick Zuvic; w, Mary Ellen Hanover; ph, Sven Kirsten; ed, Anna Maria Szanto; m, Joel Derouin; prod d, Chris Carriveau; casting, Lori Cobe; cos, Jillian Kreiner; makeup, Tarra Day

Erotic   **(PR: O   MPAA: NR)**

POCAHONTAS   ★★★
(U.S.) 87m Walt Disney ~ Buena Vista c

VOICES OF: Irene Bedard *(Pocahontas—Speaking Voice)*; Judy Kuhn *(Pocahontas—Singing Voice)*; Mel Gibson *(Captain John Smith)*; Russell Means *(Chief Powhatan)*; David Ogden Stiers *(John Ratcliffe)*; Linda Hunt *(Grandmother Willow)*; Joe Baker *(Lon)*; Billy Connolly *(Ben)*; Christian Bale *(Thomas)*; John Kassir *(Meeko)*; Danny Mann *(Percy)*; Michelle St. John *(Nakoma)*; Gordon Tootoosis *(Kekata)*; Frank Welker *(Flit)*; James Fall *(Kocoum)*

A technically brilliant piece of animation, Disney's POCAHONTAS recounts the familiar, historically-based tale of selfless love between a young American Indian girl and an English settler. Overall, POCAHONTAS is a triumph as a visual experience, but a disappointment as a film.

To young John Smith (voice of Mel Gibson) and his shipmates, the New World will be a rich, exciting place. At the same time, it will hold many dangers, including bands of unwashed, bloodthirsty redskins. Despite his youth, John Smith is already widely known for his courage and his deadly skill when fighting savages. Governor Ratcliffe (voice of David Ogden Stiers), who is leading the voyage to New England, is glad to have a man like Smith aboard. The pompous, greedy Ratcliffe intends to claim the New World's unmined treasure for himself, and with Smith on the crew, Ratcliffe is sure that no savages will spoil his plans.

As John Smith's ship draws nearer to her homeland, a young native American girl named Pocahontas (voice of Irene Bedard) somehow senses that soon, her world will be forever changed. Her father, Chief Powhatan (voice of Russell Means), has recently arranged a marriage for his daughter. The designated bridegroom is Kocoum, a young warrior who is kind, brave, and decent, but far too serious for the high-spirited Pocahontas.

When the ship lands, and Pocahontas sees John Smith, she is instantly drawn to him. They meet; they somehow learn to communicate; they struggle to overcome their fears and prejudices. Soon, they fall in love. The relationship is quickly discovered. Kocoum and Ratcliffe face off and there is bloodshed; the two sides prepare for a full-scale battle. Just as it seems that John Smith, too, will die, Pocahontas risks her own life to save his, and her courage brings peace to the land.

POCAHONTAS breaks the Disney mold in several small but significant ways. Unlike generations of animated princesses, the capable Pocahontas doesn't waste much time waiting for her prince. She's too busy canoeing over waterfalls, harvesting corn, and chatting with a wise old tree spirit (Linda Hunt). It's also the first Disney film based on the life of a real person, though it's been widely criticized for the many liberties taken with historical fact. And it doesn't have a doggedly happy ending—the chaste

lovers part at the end, returning to their own people rather than running off together to seek improbable bliss. Still, in many respects, POCAHONTAS embodies the Disney style flawlessly. It's technically polished, gently preachy, and a beautifully realized piece of feature-length animation. But it's visually subdued, all cool greens and blues, and the score is unusually bland: there's nothing here to match THE LION KING's toe-tapping "Hakuna Matata" number.

Throughout the film, the realistic animation begs comparison to a live-action motion picture. The perspective, in fact, imitates the roving "eye" of a movie camera: rather than moving within a static box, characters are frequently tracked through the scenery.

Perhaps unfortunately, the pace also seems suited to live action. A spare, minimalist plot is stretched over the movie, leaving lengthy patches with little in the way of action. As in a classic Hollywood romance, such moments are used for long, expressive silences, or wordless but intensely meaningful gestures. However, such pauses were designed to be filled by the expressive faces of human actors. Here, by contrast, it is rather unsettling when the "camera" dollies in on the heroine's stylized, impossibly slanted, fleshless cartoon eyes, and lingers as the painted features soften in a strange imitation of human emotion.

The slowed pace may well affect the video market. As any parent will tell you, most of Disney's major animated features of the 1980s and 1990s can easily stand a hundred viewings on the VCR. POCAHONTAS may not. Children will, for a time, play with the POCAHONTAS action figures; they will wear the POCAHONTAS accessories and carry the POCAHONTAS lunch box; but it seems unlikely that they will be perpetually entranced by the slow, silent, emotion-filled scenes that fill POCAHONTAS. — J.W.

d, Mike Gabriel, Eric Goldberg; p, James Pentecost; assoc p, Baker Bloodworth; w, Carl Binder, Susannah Grant, Philip LaZebnik (from a story by Glen Keane, Joe Grant, Ralph Zondag, Burny Mattinson, Ed Gombert, Kaan Kaylon, Francis Glebas, Robert Gibbs, Bruce Morris, Todd Kurosawa, Duncan Majoribanks, and Chris Buck); ed, H. Lee Peterson; m, Alan Menken, Stephen Schwartz; art d, Michael Giaimo; anim, Glen Keane, John Pomeroy, Duncan Majoribanks, Ruben Aquino, Nik Ranieri, Dave Prulksma, Chris Buck, Ken Duncan; casting, Brian Chavanne, Ruth Lambert, Karen Margiotta

AA Best Musical or Comedy Score: Alan Menken, Stephen Schwartz; *AA Best Original Song:* Alan Menken, Stephen Schwartz "Colors of the Wind"

Animated/Musical/Romance   **(PR: AA   MPAA: G)**

POCAHONTAS: THE LEGEND   ★★
(Canada) 101m ~ GoodTimes Entertainment c

Sandrine Holt *(Pocahontas)*; Miles O'Keefe *(John Smith)*; Tony Goldwyn *(Sir Edwin Wingfield)*; Billy Marasty *(Prince Kocoum)*; Gordon Tootoosis

This Canadian production offers children a naive, romantic vision of the most celebrated Indian princess in history. However, history buffs, realists, and adults, beware.

Powhatan Prince Kocoum (Billy Marasty) sees the arrival of British settlers as the beginning of a prophesied third invasion. His cousin, Princess Pocahontas (Sandrine Holt), views the newcomers through more peaceful eyes. While she is instantly smitten by the sight of handsome John Smith (Miles O'Keefe), Kocoum is enamored by the settlers' "thundersticks."

After their arrival, some settlers fall sick, and Smith visits the Powhatans, hoping to trade rifles for medicine. Ambushed by Kocoum, Smith is badly beaten and later sentenced to death. But

Pocahontas claims him, citing a law permitting her to own a captive. Smith's nemesis, Sir Edwin Wingfeld (Tony Goldwyn), accuses the captured settler of being a traitor. Eventually, Smith sends medicine and a note explaining his situation to the fort. The missive is intercepted by Wingfeld, however, who pockets the note and destroys the medicine.

While Wingfeld slanders Smith, Kocoum urges his chief to declare war. Smith finally returns to the fort and is placed under arrest. His reputation is saved when another settler finds his note hidden in Wingfeld's quarters. Desperate, Wingfeld conspires with Kocoum to kidnap Pocahontas, but their plan backfires when Smith rescues her and wounds Kocoum. Still, Kocoum uses the wound to convince the chief to declare war. Pocahontas asks that she and Kocoum submit to the truth test, which involves holding one's hand over a flame. Kocoum fails and is killed. The Chief offers the settlers peace on one condition—John Smith must return to England with Captain Newport. Pocahontas agrees, and watches her love sail away.

POCAHONTAS, THE LEGEND scores poorly on the historical accuracy meter. History books say Pocahontas was captured by settlers and held hostage in exchange for prisoners. While captive, she converted to Christianity and met John Rolfe, who married her and took her to England. This wide-eyed romance hardly fares much better on the narrative meter, either. This is a classic noble-savage love story, complete with stilted dialogue, easy- reading plot lines, and native American drum thumping. Finally, there are moments, notably a revealing love scene, that seem more mature than this built-for-kids film warrants. *(Adult situations, sexual situations, violence.)* — S.K.

d, Daniele J. Suissa; w, Daniele J. Suissa

Historical/Romance (PR: C MPAA: NR)

POSTCARDS FROM AMERICA ★★½
(U.K.) 89m Normal Films; Channel Four ~ Strand Releasing c

James Lyons *(David Wojnarowicz)*; Michael Tighe *(Teenage David)*; Olmo Tighe *(Young David)*; Michael Imperioli *(The Hustler)*; Michael Ringer *(Father)*; Maggie Low *(Mother)*; John Ventimiglia; David Strickland; Brad Hunt; Jason Emard; Joe Marshall; Jeffrey Steele *(Drivers)*; Paul Germaine-Browne; Dick Callahan; Dennie Carrig; John Corrigan; Steven Mark Friedman *(Johns)*; Les "Linda" Simpson *(Trippy)*; Dean "Sissy Fit" Novotny *(Porn Theater Drag Queen)*; Tom Gilroy *(Adult David's Friend)*; Peter Byrne *(St. Sebastian)*; Bob Romano *(Art Dealer)*; Danny Urbino *(Porn Star)*; Tony Urbino *(Porn Star)*; Patti DiLeo; Maureen Goldfedder; Prudence Wright Holmes; Coco McPherson *(Suburban Moms)*; Oona Brangham-Snell *(Little Girl)*; Colin Blair Fisher *(Young David's Friend)*; Rick Bolton *(Uncle)*; Lane Burgess *(Aunt)*; Zachary Asher Katz *(Little Boy)*; Dimitry Stathas *(Little Boy)*; Matthew Kuran *(Little Boy)*; Joyce George *(Ideal Mom)*; Jay Nickerson *(Ideal Dad)*; Jonathan Turner *(David's Neighbor)*; Lea Gulino *(David's Neighbor)*; Thom Milano *(Policeman)*; Crosby Romberger *(David's Brother)*; Allyson Anne Buckley *(David's Sister)*; Augustus Goertz *(Mugged Man)*; Todd Marsh *(Son with Aids)*; Philip Yenawine; Carol Morgan; Emily Spray; Sam Atkinson *(AIDS Family Member)*

English-born director Steve McClean makes his feature debut with an impressionistic film based on David Wojnarowicz's fictionalized autobiographical writings. POSTCARDS FROM AMERICA is a moody, nostalgic take on coming of age in the age of AIDS.

Wojnarowicz was a little-known multidisciplined East Village artist until his homoerotic work came under fire from conserva-

tive members of the US Congress. When the artist met the attack with a lawsuit and a heart-wrenching essay on the horror of AIDS, he became an international cause celebre overnight.

Wojnarowicz did not live long enough to see the outcome of his suit; he died from AIDS-related complications. His current stature as poet, essayist, video director, painter, and performance artist owes much to the people who came into his life during its last decade and, ultimately, on their success in promoting and marketing his work after his death.

In POSTCARDS FROM AMERICA, a young man, infected and acutely aware of his mortality, replays memories, dreams and fantasies as he drifts along a desert highway having random sexual encounters. Much of the remembered experience is idealized, interwoven with depictions of gratuitous violence and self-destructive acts of sexual and physical abuse. McClean accentuates the darker sides of Wojnarowicz's troubled life: the sadistic, bullying father; the adolescence spent as a vicious street hustler; and the promiscuity of a rootless manhood. Narration using Wojnarowicz's own words punctuates Stephen Endelman's orginal soundtrack.

It is perhaps this dark characterization of Wojnarowicz's growing-up and young adulthood that makes for a very unsympathetic portrait. The ambivalent homoerotic aspects of his relationship with his aggressive, violent father are emphasized, suggesting that the son's later abhorrent behavior stems directly from mistreatment. As a cunning teenage prostitute, he thinks little of threatening and robbing his clients. And as a substance-abusing young adult, he is a desperate man living on the edge.

Ellen Kuras's solid camerawork and the forward and backward juxtaposition of incidents give the film an ethereal poetry that belies its harsh theme and gritty depictions. Serviceable performances from the three actors who play Wojnarowicz at various ages establish and reinforce the strong moods. But the film soon feels repetitive and overlong. More judicious selection and editing would have strengthened the portrait without compromising Wojnarowicz's vision or director-writer McClean's interpretation of it. *(Violence, substance abuse, adult situations, sexual situations.)* — O.L.

d, Steve McLean; p, Christine Vachon, Craig Paull; exec p, Mark Nash; assoc p, Philip Yenawine, Olivier Renaud-Clement, Joel Hinman, Pamela Koffler; co-p, Steve McLean; w, Steve McLean (based on the books *Close to the Knives* and *Memories That Smell Like Gasoline* by David Wojnarowicz); ph, Ellen Kuras; ed, Elizabeth Gazzara; m, Stephen Endelman; prod d, Therese Deprez; art d, Scott Pask; sound, Neil Danziger (mixer), Jan McLaughlin (mixer); casting, Daniel Haughey, Jakki Fink; cos, Sara Slotnick; makeup, Tim Dark, Barri Scinto, Mandy Lyons

Drama (PR: O MPAA: NR)

POSTMAN, THE ★★★½
(Italy/France/Belgium) 113m Cecchi Gori Group; Tiger Cinematographica; Pentafilm; Esterno Mediterraneo Film; Blue Dahlia Productions; Le Studio Canal Plus; K2T ~ Miramax c
(IL POSTINO)

Massimo Troisi *(Mario Ruoppolo)*; Philippe Noiret *(Pablo Neruda)*; Maria Grazia Cucinotta *(Beatrice Russo)*; Linda Moretti *(Donna Rosa)*; Renato Scarpa *(Telegraph Operator)*; Anna Bonaiuto *(Matilde)*; Mariana Rigillo *(Di Cosimo)*; Bruno Alessandro *(Pablo Neruda's Voice)*; Sergio Solli; Carlo di Maio; Nando Neri; Vincenzo di Sauro; Orazio Stracuzzi; Alfredo Cozzolino

In 1952, exiled Chilean dissident and poet Pablo Neruda traveled to Europe, where a nervous, deeply anti-Marxist Italian government tried to kick him out, eventually depositing him on the isle of Capri. That a famous Communist should have found himself living in a rich man's villa, learning about life from the "simplest people in the world," is the arch conceit underlying this finely wrought film.

Massimo Troisi plays Mario Ruoppolo, a listless fellow who lives with his father in a tiny island village where fresh water is scarce and life revolves around subsistence fishing and voting for the local Dons. Mario has never liked fishing, and at his father's urging he finally finds a job as a postman, working for the district's Postmaster (Renato Scarpa), a Marxist. His village has never before needed a postman, but the arrival of Neruda (Philippe Noiret) has changed everything. The Postmaster hails Neruda as a "poet of the people," but Mario reads his verse and, observing the return addresses on his mail, declares him a poet chiefly of women. The shy Mario attempts to ingratiate himself with the writer, and soon begins to learn about the power of "metaphor" and his own ability to create images (he is asked for an adjective to describe fishing nets, and offers "sad"). Mario is impressed by Neruda's wisdom and with his passionate marriage to his beautiful wife. Mario meets his own Beatrice (Maria Grazia Cucinotta) when she challenges him to a game of foosball at her aunt's tavern. He seeks Neruda's advice, then cribs a piece of erotic poetry, which is found by Beatrice's aunt (Linda Moretti), who has to enjoin the local priest to read it for her. When Neruda chastises Mario for the theft, he replies with the novel defense that poetry "belongs not to those who write it but to those who need it." Mario marries Beatrice with Neruda as best man, but at the wedding feast Neruda receives word that his exile has been lifted.

A heartbroken Mario follows his mentor's career through the Postmaster's newspapers, but the only letter the postman receives himself is a request from Neruda's secretary that some possessions be shipped home. Playing with Neruda's Dictaphone, Mario is struck by an idea: creating a literal "tone poem," recording sounds that describe the life of his island community (including waves both large and small, his father's "sad nets" and the "night sky"). There follows a jarring coda in which Neruda returns to the island, only to find that Mario is dead—killed at a Communist demonstration where he was to read a poem entitled "The Song of Pablo Neruda". Listening to the Dictaphone tape (which remarkably preserves Mario's final moments), Neruda reflects ruefully on his own life of idealism and commitment. The film closes with a quote from Neruda identifying the pain from which his poetry originally sprang.

Based on *Burning Patience* by Antonio Skarmeta (set in Chile, not Capri), this film was a labor of love for Troisi, who sought Radford (1984, WHITE MISCHIEF) to direct and who shares a screenplay credit. The film has a gentle political edge, knocking Marxists and Christian Democrats with equal cheerfulness, and shares the peculiar sentimentality of Neapolitan film of the period (beautifully reconstructed by production designer Lorenzo Baraldi). But at the center, there's a serious story—about absent fathers, literal and spiritual—presented with great subtlety by Troisi, whose self-deprecating humor, sly delivery, and melancholic charm are inimitable.

The downbeat coda feels forced and, at least in retrospect, unnecessary. Troisi, who suffered from a congenital heart defect, postponed surgery to complete the film, and died the day after shooting wrapped. Beloved in Italy, Troisi had made 11 other films, directing five, and several TV specials, but this film would mark his American debut. The actor's fate hangs over every minute of THE POSTMAN (which he shot in small bursts, often an hour or less in a day), and necessarily frames the audience's response. When Mario receives the secretary's letter, he shrugs it off, saying he was a fool to expect more. It is impossible to be unmoved by a dying man's despairing assumption that nobody will remember him. *(Adult situations, profanity.)* — R.S.

d, Michael Radford; p, Mario Cecchi Gori, Vittorio Cecchi Gori, Gaetano Daniele; exec p, Alberto Passone; w, Anna Pavignano, Michael Radford, Furio Scarpelli, Giacomo Scarpelli, Massimo Troisi (from a story by Furio Scarpelli and Giacomo Scarpelli based on the novel *Burning Patience* by Antonio Skarmeta); ph, Franco Di Giacomo; ed, Roberto Perpignani; m, Luis Enrique Bacalov; prod d, Lorenzo Baraldi; sound, Massimo Loffredi, Alessandra Perpignani, Angelo Raguseo (mixer); cos, Gianni Gissi; makeup, Alfredo Marazzi, Simone Marazzi, Leone Noel

AAN Best Picture; AAN Best Actor: Massimo Troisi; *AAN Best Director:* Michael Radford; *AAN Best Adapted Screenplay:* Anna Pavignano, Michael Radford, Furio Scarpelli, Giacomo Scarpelli, Massimo Troisi; *AA Best Dramatic Score:* Luis Bacalov

Comedy/Drama (PR: A MPAA: PG)

POWDER ★★★½
(U.S.) 111m Powder Productions; Hollywood Pictures; Caravan Pictures ~ Buena Vista c

Mary Steenburgen *(Jessie Caldwell)*; Sean Patrick Flanery *(Powder)*; Lance Henriksen *(Sheriff Barnum)*; Jeff Goldblum; Brandon Smith *(Duncan)*; Bradford Tatum *(John Box)*; Susan Tyrrell *(Maxine)*; Missy Crider *(Lindsey)*; Ray Wise *(Stipler)*; Esteban Louis Powell *(Mitch)*; Reed Frerichs *(Syke)*; Chad Cox *(Zane)*; Joe Marchman *(Brennan)*; Philip Maurice Hayes *(Greg)*; Dannete McMann *(Emma)*; Tom Tarantini *(Steven Barnum)*; Woody Watson *(Mr. Kelloway)*; Alex Allen Morris *(Dr. Roth)*; Brady Coleman *(Dr. Deggan)*; Barry Berfield *(Paramedic)*; Paula Engel *(Anna)*; Meason Wiley *(Arturo)*; Dee Macaluso *(Nurse #1)*; James Houston *(Doc. Assoc. #1)*; Bill Grant-Minchen *(Doc. Assoc. #2)*; Bonnie Gallup *(Nurse #2)*

This affecting teen-oriented fantasy is unusually sincere: it seems to spring from, rather than pander to, adolescent sensibilities. Sadly, the release of this thoughtful allegory coincided with the revelation of a sex scandal involving its neophyte writer-director.

A pregnant woman is rushed to the hospital after being struck by lightning. She dies, but her baby—an albino with extraordinary brain-wave activity—survives. Nearly two decades later, Sheriff Barnum (Lance Henriksen) summons school administrator Jessie Caldwell (Mary Steenburgen) to a remote Texan farmhouse. The elderly homeowner has died, leaving behind his grandson, called Powder (Sean Patrick Flanery) because of his snow-white skin. Powder has been raised in a cellar away from painful sunlight and prying eyes. He is viewed with suspicion by Barnum's mean-spirited deputy, Duncan (Brandon Smith).

Caldwell has the shy orphan admitted to her school. The other students shun him as a freak, particularly after he demonstrates strange electromagnetic powers. Barnum is interested in Powder's welfare but preoccupied by the failing health of his wife and deteriorating relations with estranged son Steven (Tom Tarantini).

Powder shows further evidence of his powers at a science demonstration led by personable teacher Donald Ripley (Jeff Goldblum). The boy is befriended by Lindsey (Missy Crider), a female classmate. Later, during a deer hunt supervised by Duncan, Powder places his hand on the dying deer and grasps the deputy's arm. Duncan is forced to experience the animal's sensations and later finds himself unable to use a gun. Desiring to go home, Powder wreaks psychic havoc in Caldwell's office but accepts comfort from Ripley, who discovers that the boy's touch is therapeutic. Powder uses his powers to allow Barnum to communicate with his comatose wife, who urges a reconciliation with Steven.

Powder and Lindsey grow closer until the girl's father angrily intervenes. Returning to school, Powder is taunted by a bully. His touch restores the bully's memories of childhood abuse by a father-figure. Enraged, the youth strips Powder and throws him outside into a muddy puddle. During the struggle, Powder's magnetism increases. He attracts an electrical charge which strikes the bully, causing his heart to stop. Powder shocks the boy's heart back into operation and flees.

Barnum, Caldwell, Ripley, and Duncan find Powder back in the empty farmhouse. Seeing storm clouds approaching, Powder runs across an open field with outstretched arms. The others pursue as Powder is joyously consumed by lightning. His light passes through each of them as he is transformed into energy.

In 1987, writer-director Victor Salva plead guilty to having and filming unlawful sex with a minor—Nathan Forrest Winters, the 12-year-old star of his feature debut CLOWNHOUSE (1988). Sentenced to three years, Salva served 15 months and completed parole in 1992. He resumed his film career, writing and directing NATURE OF THE BEAST (1995), before completing his first theatrical feature under the auspices of Caravan Pictures and Disney's Hollywood Pictures. In 1995, the 20-year-old Winters appeared at an industry preview screening of POWDER and urged a boycott of Salva's film.

Knowledge of the filmmaker's past necessarily colors one's perception of POWDER. Even disregarding the explosive issue of intergenerational sex, POWDER unavoidably becomes a parable about the difficulties of being a gay male teen. Powder's upbringing in the cellar becomes a metaphor for "the closet" and the hostility he faces upon his emergence is explicitly linked with homophobia. Powder is taunted by the bully after he is caught staring at a shirtless basketball player splashing his head and torso with cool water at a fountain.

While avoiding the increasingly tired practice of overt pop culture references, POWDER knowingly employs themes and imagery from previous films: an "alien" with unusual powers encounters our world (STARMAN; E.T. THE EXTRA-TER-RESTRIAL); a strange youth raised in a cellar is suddenly propelled outside (Werner Herzog's THE ENIGMA OF KASPAR HAUSER); a mysterious neighborhood eccentric is revealed as benign (TO KILL A MOCKINGBIRD); and a youth's physical difference becomes a lightning rod for intolerance (THE BOY WITH GREEN HAIR). Clearly POWDER reveals a strong organizing intelligence working out personal concerns through the template of pop culture.

POWDER is bolstered by its sober tone, deft scoring (from veteran Jerry Goldsmith), lovely performances, and Salva's undeniable passion and conviction. The film even skirts the usual genre cliches: Powder doesn't win over the kids with his powers; he doesn't get mad and kick butt; he doesn't get the girl. All in all, it's hard to imagine a more humane genre film emerging from contemporary Hollywood. (Profanity, nudity, violence.) — K.G.

d, Victor Salva; p, Roger Birnbaum, Daniel Grodnik; exec p, Riley Kathryn Ellis, Robert Snukal; co-p, Dennis Murphy; w, Victor Salva; ph, Jerzy Zielinski; ed, Dennis M. Hill; m, Jerry Goldsmith; prod d, Waldemar Kalinowski; art d, Barry Kingston; set d, Florence Fellman; sound, Steve C. Aaron (mixer); fx, Ron Trost, Stephanie Powell, Linda Komperda, Out of the Blue Visual Effects; casting, Junie Lowry-Johnson; cos, Betsy Cox; makeup, Kris Evans, Thomas R. Burman, Bari Dreiband-Burman, Steve LaPorte, Barney Burman; stunts, David Sanders

Fantasy/Drama   (PR: C   MPAA: PG-13)

POWER OF ATTORNEY   ★
(U.S.) 97m Osmosis Pictures; Small World Entertainment; CineVu Films ~ Turner Home Entertainment c

Danny Aiello (*Scassi*); Elias Koteas (*Paulie Diehl*); Rae Dawn Chong (*Joan Armstrong*); Roger Wilson (*Frankie*); Nina Siemaszko (*Maria*); Greg Rogers (*Peters*); Hagen Beggs (*Stern*); Andrew Airlie (*Adams*); Babz Chula (*Angela*); Liduin Currell (*Judge Keen*); Harvey Dumansky (*Joey*); Dave "Squatch" Ward (*Buddha*); Alex Green (*Cabbie*); Rick Aiello (*Tito*); Tygh Runyan (*Whoopie*); Howard Himelstein (*Snooks*); Ann Fairlie (*Mama*); Ernie Prentice (*Papa*); Scott Swanson (*Hospital Director*); Giuseppe Bianchi (*Old Man*); Dwight Rosco (*Foreman*); Stuart Davidson (*Donald*); John Tench (*Carlos*)

The tackiest courtroom drama in recent memory, POWER OF ATTORNEY is so carelessly directed, vestigially scripted, and somnabulistically acted that you can only take offense at the lack of care evident in every frame. This rip-off of THE FIRM barely offers the minimum requirements of its genre.

Despite escaping the mean-streets lifestyle that claims his drug-dealing brother Frankie (Roger Wilson), attorney Paulie Diehl (Elias Koteas) considers a career change, shifting from prosecution to defense when he fails to convict a hit man. Falling prey to the blandishments of the Gotti-like mob boss Scassi (Danny Aiello), Paulie ignores the advice of his fiancee Maria (Nina Siemaszko) and convinces himself that shady Scassi is a reformed man filled with remorse for all the deaths he has ordered. On trial for rubbing out a mobster named Vinnie, Scassi gains Paulie's trust until crime witness Frankie proves a fly in the ointment of Paulie's defense strategy. Paulie realizes that Scassi's protestation of innocence is as empty as his promise not to hurt Frankie, but he's forced to keep his commitment to Scassi even after he obtains videotaped proof that the Capo iced Frankie. Playing the game in true Godfather fashion, retainer Paulie bides his time to confront the acquitted Scassi with the video but gets taken for a ride to the gangster's favorite garbage dump/body-disposal site. After Scassi's henchman get nailed by the cops, nonvigilante Paulie saves his guilty former patron for the proper legal channels and resumes his career on the right side of the law.

This incredibly juiceless thriller parades familiar cliches about the Mob and loopholes in the judicial system to little avail. Since the slack screenplay doesn't freshly configure its moral bleakness, none of the Machiavellian intricacies of Scassi's pocketing of the former assistant DA is developed with any suspense. Sans directorial flash or distracting star turns, POWER OF ATTORNEY further weakens its case with bogus ethnicity. At times, its half-baked depiction of earthy, temperamental Italianess ranks with the ersatz Jewish cavorting during the Hebrew wedding ceremony in THOROUGHLY MODERN MILLIE. At least that unkosher film had the excuse of being a musical; this realistic dago-bashing doesn't amount to either a competent evidentiary thriller or an absorbing courtroom drama, and it's hard to root for a dopey hero whose refusal to see the obvious is like a hairshirt of stupidity. (Graphic violence, extreme profanity, adult situations.) — R.P.

d, Howard Himelstein; p, Jeff Barmash, George Erschbamer, Murray Shostak; exec p, Cindy Cowan, Brian Shuster; w, George Erschbamer, Jeff Barmash; ph, Rick Maguire; ed, Frank Faugno; m, Hal Beckett; prod d, Brian Davie; fx, Terry Sanderhoff; casting, Tom McSweeney, Ann Forry; cos, David Lisle; makeup, Joanne Kinchella; stunts, Melissa Stubbs

Crime/Drama   (PR: C   MPAA: R)

PREHYSTERIA! 3 ★½
(U.S.) 85m Moonbeam Entertainment ~
Paramount Home Video c

Whitney Anderson *(Ella MacGregor)*; Fred Willard *(Thomas MacGregor)*; Pamela Matteson *(Michelle MacGregor)*; Bruce Weitz *(Uncle Hal MacGregor)*; Dave Buzzotta *(Heath MacGregor)*; John Fujioka *(Yamamoto)*; Matt Lescher *(Needlemeyer)*; Shannon Dow Smith *(Bush)*; Thomas Emery Dennis *(Dole)*; Owen Bush *(Mr. Cranston)*; Raymond O'Connor; Peter Dennis; Bill Moseley

The helpful quintet of dwarf dinosaurs from the first few PRE-HYSTERIA pics rear their latex heads again. This time their dull presence drags down to the cinematic tar pits a premise that would have played out better without them.

At Kings Road Country Club ex-pro-am golf champion Thomas MacGregor (Fred Willard) dwells in disgrace on an abandoned miniature golf course. Having missed the putt of his life, he now fixes carts for his venal brother "Uncle Hal" MacGregor (Bruce Weitz), proprietor of Kings Road. Thomas's duffer daughter Ella (Whitney Anderson) is determined to become a British Open contender and frequently trespasses on Uncle Hal's greens. After one day of digging divots, she discovers the shrunken saurians, who give Thomas an idea: "Dino-Putt." The MacGregor family revamps their miniature course with a sort of "Flintstones" motif as a diversion for bored rich kids whose parents are busy on Kings Road. The new attraction's success frustrates Uncle Hal, who schemed to acquire the property for an underhanded deal with a visiting Japanese. In a finale awfully familiar to anyone who saw CADDYSHACK, Uncle Hal goes against Ella in a putt-putt showdown over the MacGregor legacy.

Anderson is cute as she effects golf mania right down to a Scottish accent and lovingly-framed portrait of Sean Connery. Grownups trapped into watching might be amused at fairways parodies of THE SWORD IN THE STONE, GODZILLA, and even JFK, though director Julian Breen tends to rerun every gag at least three times. But those diminutive dinosaurs doom PRE-HYSTERIA! 3 to extinction. Anthropomorphized to the extent that crude puppetry techniques allow, the rubbery reptiles tie shoelaces, play charades, and generally behave like no dinosaur ever; they're just surrogates for circus chimps, elves, friendly ghosts/aliens, leprechauns (in fact, the same production outfit did the superior LEAPIN' LEPRECHAUNS!) or any other wonder-working critters in banal children's movies, and hardly merit their painful, lingering closeups. Once the "wee beasties" are revealed, in fact, most other characters simply ignore them.

Just as the original PREHYSTERIA grabbed attention on the direct-to-home-video market for its coincident release while JURASSIC PARK cleaned up in theaters, PREHYSTERIA! 3 uncannily anticipated a boomlet of golf-inspired pics in the mid-1990s, like Adam Sandler's HAPPY GILMORE and Kevin Costner's TIN CUP. *(Violence)* — C.C.

d, Julian Breen; p, Karen L. Spencer; exec p, Charles Band; w, Neil Ruttenberg, Brent V. Friedman, Michael Davis; ph, James Lawrence Spencer; ed, Paul Petschek; m, Michael Wetherwax, Richard Band; prod d, Milo; art d, John Zachary; set d, Nicki Roberts; fx, Mark Rappaport; cos, Dennis McCarthy

Children's/Comedy/Fantasy (PR: AA MPAA: PG)

PRIEST ★★★
(U.K.) 97m BBC Films; Electric Pictures;
Polygram; Distant Horizon ~ Miramax c

Linus Roache *(Father Greg Pilkington)*; Tom Wilkinson *(Father Matthew Thomas)*; Cathy Tyson *(Maria Kerrigan)*; Robert Carlyle *(Graham)*; James Ellis *(Father Ellerton)*; Lesley Sharp *(Mrs. Unsworth)*; Robert Pugh *(Mr. Unsworth)*; Christine Tremarco *(Lisa Unsworth)*; Paul Barber *(Charlie)*; Rio Fanning *(Bishop)*; Jimmy Coleman *(Funeral Director)*; Bill Dean *(Altar Boy)*; Gilly Coman *(Ellie Molloy)*; Fred Pearson *(Patrick)*; Jimmy Gallagher *(Mick Molly)*; Tony Booth *(Tommy)*; Charley Wilde *(Tommy's Child)*; Euan Blair *(Tommy's Child)*; Guiseppe Murphy *(Man in Lift)*; Kim Johnson *(Mrs. Gobshite)*; Keith Cole *(Mr. Gobshite)*; Adrian Luty *(Jehovah's Witness)*; Mandy Walsh *(Guest at Wake)*; Stephanie Roscoe; Ann Haydn-Edwards; Mike Haydn *(Guests at Wake)*; Bobby Martino *(Bobby)*; Rupert Pearson *(Man on Skateboard)*; Victoria Arnold *(Girl in Confessional)*; Gareth Potsig *(Boy Car Thief)*; Ray Williams *(Boy with Stutter)*; Valerie Lilley *(Sister Kevin)*; Kevin Jones *(Boy at Beach)*; Michael Ananins *(Charge Sergeant)*; Mickey Poppins *(Reporter)*; Marsha Thomason *(Nurse)*; Matyelok Gibbs *(Housekeeper)*; John Bennett *(Father Redstone)*

Director Antonia Bird outraged the Catholic Church and embarrassed her film's distributors (Miramax and its parent company, Disney) with this candid portrayal of the moral anguish and development of a young priest (Linus Roache) struggling to come to terms with the sins of his new parish and his own homosexuality.

Father Greg Pilkington arrives in working-class Liverpool and is shocked by the libertine behavior of his fellow clergyman and housemate Matthew Thomas (Tom Wilkinson). When he catches Matthew sleeping with the housekeeper (Cathy Tyson), he erupts with moral indignation. The older priest warns him that he has much to learn.

Father Pilkington's lessons begin when a 14-year-old girl (Christine Tremarco) confesses to him that her father (Robert Pugh) is sexually abusing her. Tortured by the confession, Pilkington must choose between informing the girl's mother and honoring the seal of the confessional. He hesitates too long, and the mother catches her husband in the act. She angrily condemns the young priest for having kept his knowledge silent.

While clinging to the sanctity of church law on this matter, Pilkington has meanwhile been breaking his vows by sleeping with a man (Robert Carlyle) he met at a gay bar. One day, while having sex in a parked car, they are caught by the police and arrested. When the media discover that one of the offenders is a priest, the story becomes front page news. Ostracized from his community and traumatized by disgrace, Pilkington is sent to a retreat in a small village.

Matthew comes to convince him to return and say mass with him before the parish. Many of the flock are outraged by his return, refusing to forgive his transgression and leaving the church in disgust. The two friends continue the service for those who have chosen to forgive, one of whom is the young girl. The film concludes with their embrace, as she comes to take the host.

The three principal sins at issue in this deeply moral film are heterosexual sex within the priesthood, homosexual sex, and incestuous sex. The young priest's certainty regarding the evil of sexual sin is challenged by his discovery that Matthew and the housekeeper share a long-standing, committed loving relationship, as well as by the growing love and friendship between himself and his homosexual lover. He also must contend with the unsettling argument that incest is natural and merely a cultural taboo.

As revealed in the film, the complexity of these issues points up the problematic nature of all ethical claims, the difference between law and justice, and the difficulty of maintaining faith in the midst of cruelty, suffering, and the silence of God.

While the film takes a liberal position, exposing the injustice done to both heterosexual and homosexual love by Catholicism, it is careful to leave difficult questions unanswered, placing more value on the raising of questions and the stimulation of philosophical debate.

Originally made for British television, this well-acted melodrama offers a more candid and bold visual portrayal of homosexual eroticism than American audiences are accustomed to. Refusing to shy away from controversial images, Bird quietly demystifies taboos. Directed with depth and intelligence, PRIEST lucidly delivers its message that sin is a complicated matter, and forgiveness and humility an even greater challenge. *(Nudity, sexual situations, adult situations.)* — R.C.

d, Antonia Bird; p, George Faber, Josephine Ward; exec p, Mark Shivas; assoc p, Joanna Newbery; w, Jimmy McGovern; ph, Fred Tammes; ed, Susan Spivey; m, Andy Roberts; prod d, Raymond Langhorn; art d, Sue Pow; sound, Dennis Cartwright (recordist); casting, Janet Goddard; cos, Jill Taylor; makeup, Ann Humphreys

Drama   (PR: C   MPAA: NR)

PROFESSION: NEO-NAZI   ★★½
(Germany) 87m OST-Film; Hoffman & Loeser
Produktion ~ Drift Distribution c
(BERUF NEONAZI)

Ernst Zundel

This chilling documentary profiles the contemporary neo-Nazi movement of today, specifically two of its leading figures, Ernst Zundel, the self-styled new Fuhrer, and his younger compatriot, Ewald.

The film opens in Toronto at a staid-seeming convention, during which various interested parties converse and proudly display jackets emblazoned with Nazi insignia. We are then admitted into the office of Zundel and given a tour of its swastika-like flags (red with a bold black Z on a white circle), portraits of Hitler, picket signs saying things like "The Holocaust is Pure Hate," and the concentration camp-styled uniform he sports for TV cameras with his phone number displayed on the back. We are then treated to his views about anti-German propaganda ("The Holocaust is a hoax"), the myth of the Jews being a single race ("There are Black Ethiopian Jews, Chinese Jews . . ."), and global domination ("My mouth waters when I plan world rule."). Most important is the audio and video equipment which is used to send his message around the world ("These are my greatest weapons. Khomeini's speeches were distributed to thousands in Iran this way."). We see him opening up letters from supporters, all containing monetary donations of differing amounts ("Every day, we receive thousands of donations, worldwide."). After some generalized but always vehement mutterings about a worldwide struggle being the only means to triumph over "the enemy," the focus shifts.

We are introduced to Ewald, who smirks with false modesty as Zundel describes him as having the world at his feet: "the right age, the right looks, the right stature . . . the noble Teuton, two meters tall, blond, blue eyes." Ewald, who likens himself to Himmler or Heydrich, actually makes Zundel seem a model of self-effacement. He says that, although he'd jump off a bridge for him if asked, "I'm not modest or selfless like him. I don't want to be." The film follows Ewald to Munich, where he says neo-Nazism, which he calls Orthodox National Socialism, is starting up again. "One speaks of a Common Europe," he says. "It's already here. We must understand Hitler in our hearts and minds. What he wanted is still valid." The big set piece is his visit to Auschwitz, which he loudly calls "useless, bullshit." He is con-

fronted by a young American Jewish tourist, outraged by his assertions. He coldly faces him down, calling the Holocaust a fabrication of Jewish media influence. "I won't be guilty for things I didn't do," he tells him.

The direction of this documentary carries objectivity to a fault. No overt judgments of any kind are made by the filmmakers. It could almost be read either way, pro or con, depending on the viewer's convictions. This cold presentation of fact is indeed frightening, but might have worked more successfully had the material been better shaped. There's not enough explanation and identification of people and places. The speakers are thrown into our faces with little or no introduction. It makes the task of absorbing all the fascinating information unduly taxing for the viewer. One's emotional response is put on a slight delay while one tries to figure out what's what. Whatever the creators' opinion, there can be no obfuscation of one's gut reaction to certain scenes, like when a Serbian woman tearfully recounts that 32 members of her family have died. Fixing a hawklike eye on her, Ewald says, "I would say to her, 'Nation and Fatherland.' For the Serbs, it's the equivalent of 'Sieg heil' for the Jews." *(Adult situations)* — D.N.

d, Winfried Bonengel; w, Winfried Bonengel; ph, Johann Feindt; ed, Wolfram Kohler

Documentary/Political   (PR: C   MPAA: NR)

PROMISE, THE   ★★★½
(Germany/Italy/Switzerland) 115m Bioskop-Film;
Odessa Film; Filmola; Westdeutscher Rundfunk;
Les Productions JMH ~ Fine Line c
(AKA: YEAR OF THE WALL; DAS VERSPRECHEN; DIE JAHRE DER MAUER)

Corinna Harfouch *(Sophie Sellman)*; Meret Becker *(Young Sophie)*; August Zirner *(Konrad Richter)*; Anian Zollner *(Young Konrad)*; Jean-Yves Gaultier *(Gerard)*; Eva Mattes *(Barbara)*; Suzanne Uge *(Young Barbara)*; Hans Kremer *(Harald)*; Pierre Besson *(Young Harald)*; Tina Engel *(Sophie's Aunt)*; Otto Sander *(Professor Lorenz)*; Hark Bohm *(Muller)*; Dieter Mann *(Konrad's Father)*; Simone von Zglinicki *(Konrad's Mother)*; Ulrike Krumbiegel; Monika Hansen *(Sophie's Mother)*; Klaus Piontek *(Sophie's Stepfather)*; Christian Herschmann *(Alexander at Age 12)*; Joerg Meister *(Alexander at Age 20)*; Heiko Senst *(Wolfgang)*; Anka Baier *(Monika)*; Sven Lehmann *(Max)*; Udo Kroschwald *(Secret Police Agent)*; Ruth Gloss *(Konrad's Grandmother)*; Elisabeth Trissenaar *(Aunt Marianne)*; Peter Pfefferkorn *(Heinrich)*; Philippe-Morrier Genaud *(Ruhlander)*; Andre Severyn; Franz Vielmann; Hagen Oechel; Christian Schmidt; Wolfgang Winckler; Katrin Heller; Christina Grosse; Karl Kranzkowsi; Horst Heimer; Johanna Neumann

Twentieth-century German history has consistently lent itself to cinematic interpretations. Veteran director Margarethe von Trotta's THE PROMISE is one of the first features out of a reunified Germany to mine the rich source material of dramatic events surrounding the fall of the Berlin Wall.

East German teenage lovers Konrad (Anian Zollner) and Sophie (Meret Becker) are separated during an attempted escape from East Berlin precipitated by the building of the infamous wall in 1961. Sophie manages to flee with some school friends through the divided city's one sewage system, but Konrad, in attempting to cover up their escape route, gets left behind. The plot is discovered by Konrad's father who, out of party loyalty, turns his son over to the Communist authorities. After some routine punishment, Konrad (played as an adult by August Zirner) grows up to be a world-renowned physicist and model East German citizen.

Meanwhile Sophie (played as an adult by Corinna Harfouch) makes her life in West Germany, working as an interpreter and tour guide. The two stay in touch through mutual friends and smuggled messages, finally arranging a brief but passionate reunion in Prague, coincidentally during the tumultuous Soviet invasion of the summer of 1968. The meeting eventually results in the birth of a son. Even though Konrad and Sophie live in the same city, the wall separates them, so the relationship continues to be played out against the escalating and ultimately subsiding tensions between East and West. As travel restrictions for East Germans are relaxed in the 1980s, the couple meets once again. Konrad gets to know his son but discovers that Sophie is now in a long-term relationship with a French journalist.

Von Trotta's thoughtful script, which she cowrote with Peter Schneider, has deftly captured the suffering and stubbornness that characterized relations between the two Germanys during the Cold War. She has pulled credible and moving performances from two sets of actors playing the protagonists, first as teenagers and later as adults. The intense emotional undercurrents that characterize lovers divided both by an ideology and a physical barrier are palpable. The film successfully captures the telling visual details which encapsulate the social and economic differences that marked the separation of the East from the West for nearly 50 years.

A charter member of New German Cinema, the group of filmmakers who emerged in the late 1960s intent upon reviving a moribund German cinema, von Trotta has created an accessible film that would have traveled better internationally had it been made in English, though the subtitled version provides an adequate translation. Sentimental, even Hollywoodish by German standards, THE PROMISE is straightforward storytelling in the best narrative and cinematic tradition. (Adult situations.) — O.L.

d, Margarethe von Trotta; p, Eberhard Junkersdorf, Jean-Marc Henchoz; w, Peter Schneider, Margarethe von Trotta, Felice Laudadio; ph, Franz Rath; ed, Suzanne Baron; m, Jurgen Knieper; prod d, Karel Vacek, Martin Dostal, Katrin Esther Ritterbusch; art d, Benedikt Herforth; set d, Franz Bauer; sound, Christian Moldt; cos, Petra Kay, Yoshio Yabara; makeup, Irmela Holzapfel, Jurgen Holzapfel

Drama/Historical/Romance   (PR: A   MPAA: R)

PROPHECY, THE   ★★★½
(U.S.) 96m Overseas Film; First Look Pictures;
Neo Motion Pictures ~ Dimension c
(AKA: GOD'S ARMY)

Christopher Walken (Angel Gabriel); Elias Koteas (Thomas Dagget); Eric Stoltz (Angel Simon); Virginia Madsen (Katherine); Moriah Shining Dove Snyder (Mary); Adam Goldberg (Jerry); Amanda Plummer (Rachael); Viggo Mortensen (Lucifer); Emma Sheneh (Grandmother); Nik Winterhawk (John); J.C. Quinn (Burrows); Albert Nelson (Grey Horse); Steve Hytner (Joseph); Jeremy Williams-Hurner (Brian); Emily Conforto (Sandra); Nick Gomez (Jason); Christina Holmes (Allison); Sandra Lafferty (Madge); Jeff Cadiente (Usiel); Bobby Lee Hayes (Deputy #1); John Sankovich (Deputy #2); William Buck Hart (Grave Keeper); Randy Adakai-Nez (High School Kid); Sioux-Z Jessup (Nurse)

Filmed in 1993 as GOD'S ARMY, this unusual confrontation between good and evil is a rarity among modern horror films, a chiller that is as much about ideas as the more overt trappings of the supernatural.

Thomas Dagget (Elias Koteas), a priest who lost his faith and became a homicide cop, finds himself caught up in a war on Earth between two bands of angels. On the bad side is Gabriel

(Christopher Walken), who has become envious of the favor God has granted humankind and seeks the soul of a recently deceased general (who had committed atrocities during the Korean War) to aid him in the battle. Simon (Eric Stoltz), representing the good angels, has beaten him to the soul, however, and transferred it into the body of a young Native-American girl, Mary (Moriah Shining Dove Snyder). Gabriel, assisted by Jerry (Adam Goldberg), a suicide he has briefly brought back to life, tracks down Simon and kills him; meanwhile, Dagget arrives in the same Southwestern town and befriends Mary's schoolteacher, Katherine (Virginia Madsen).

After a confrontation with the wrathful Gabriel, during which Jerry is killed once again, Dagget and Katherine take Mary to her tribe's village, where the elders prepare to conduct a ceremony to exorcise the dark soul from the girl's body. Dagget and Katherine receive unexpected counsel from Lucifer (Viggo Mortensen) himself, who is displeased with Gabriel's apparent desire to create a second Hell. Gabriel arrives and attacks Dagget, who calls upon his reaffirmed faith and fends him off; Lucifer destroys Gabriel by pulling out his heart, and the general's soul is successfully purged from Mary's body.

Despite some minor structural and pacing problems, THE PROPHECY is one of the most daring, original and imaginative horror films in quite some time. Gregory Widen, who previously wrote BACKDRAFT and coscripted the original HIGHLANDER, has developed an intriguing theological basis for his directorial debut, based on the observation that angels as presented in the Bible are as potentially destructive as they are spiritual, and elaborates on it in any number of intriguing ways. The film does indeed have the feel of a first feature whose creator had so many good ideas that he cannot assemble them all in an entirely coherent manner; but better too many ideas than not enough, and the movie remains tense and involving throughout, with terrific humorous touches that never get in the way of the seriousness of the basic story.

Helping immeasurably to carry the film is Walken, the only actor one can imagine pulling off the driven yet mordantly humorous character of Gabriel. Whether viciously dispatching his enemies or tossing off the occasional sarcastic quip with equal panache, Walken remains a striking antagonist throughout. Koteas, Madsen,u and Stoltz as the forces of good are equally compelling, and Mortensen provides a wonderfully sardonic turn as Lucifer, who informs Katherine that while entrance to Heaven may be restricted, "we're open every day—even on Christmas." (Graphic violence, adult situations, profanity.) — M.G.

d, Gregory Widen; p, Joel Soisson, W.K. Border, Michael Leary; co-p, Don Phillips; w, Gregory Widen; ph, Bruce D. Johnson, Richard Clabaugh; ed, Sonny Baskin; m, David C. Williams; prod d, Clark Hunter; set d, Michele Spadaro; sound, Al Rizzo (mixer); fx, Jor van Kline; casting, Don Phillips; cos, Dana Allyson; makeup, Martha Cecilia; stunts, Dan Bradley

Horror   (PR: O   MPAA: R)

PROVINCIAL ACTORS   ★★★½
(Poland) 108m X Film Unit; Polish Corporation
for Film Production ~ New Yorker Home Video c
(AKTORZY PROWINCJONALNI)

Tadeusz Huk (Krzystof); Halina Labonarska (Anka); Ewa Dalkowska; Slawa Kwasniewska

PROVINCIAL ACTORS, Agnieszka Holland's first directorial effort, is an outstanding example of Polish cinema's often highly subtle intermingling of the personal and the political. Made in 1979 and released to US home video in 1995, the film uses sharp humor for covert political critique. Ironically, while Poland's recent liberalization may have engendered artistic freedom, subtle films like this one have lost their raison d'etre.

In a provincial town near Lodz, a group of performers prepares to stage *Liberation*, a Polish literary classic distinguished by its enigmatic mixture of symbolic and realist elements. The troupe's prime player, Chris (Tadeusz Huk), is eager to move on to a bigger and better future and sees this play as his big chance for advancement. As a result, he debates the changes made in the script—cuts that minimize the political connotations—and has frequent temper tantrums. Chris's problems are not confined to the theater—his wife, Anka (Halina Labonarska), a puppeteer, is unhappy with their 10-year-old marriage. They bicker constantly and are soon sleeping in separate rooms.

The theater is a snakepit of contending ambitions and weaknesses. One gay actor, a has-been, is appropriately cynical, while another actor hits the bottle. The women gossip about which younger actress is sleeping with the director. Even the prop men are riven by social and personal tensions. When the troupe learns that a critic from Lodz will be at the premiere, the temperature rises significantly.

Anka, a former university student, still reads Heidegger (which Chris ridicules). On a trip to Warsaw, she meets an old school friend who seems to live well, but admits she has achieved success by means of "dagger and poison." After the successful premiere, Chris and the director talk about conforming and getting on with their careers. Anka, however, is fed up with Chris and moves out; Chris then contemplates suicide. He's about to pull the trigger on his shotgun, but instead wrecks a poster announcing the play and heads for Anka's puppet theater, where she comforts him.

The backstage story has the potential for tragedy or farce, but in this Polish variant the pressures of a political dictatorship are never too distant, especially when it comes to success or advancement. Holland and her co-screenwriter, Witold Zatorski, have also suffused the film with a sense of corruption and social decay—ills that can only be tolerated through a reliance on family love. PROVINCIAL ACTORS won the Cannes Film Festival's International Critics Prize. *(Adult situations, profanity.)* — L.R.

d, Agnieszka Holland; w, Agnieszka Holland, Witold Zatorski; ph, Jacek Petrycki; ed, Halina Nawrocka; m, Andrzej Zarycki; prod d, M. Danisz, Renata Czyznikowska, Wladyslaw Bielski; art d, Bogdan Solle; cos, Ludwika Niskiewicz

Drama/Political/Comedy (PR: C MPAA: NR)

PURE FORMALITY, A ★★★
(Italy/France) 108m Cecchi Gori Group; Tiger Cinematografica; Cecchi Gori Film ~ Sony Pictures Classics c
(UNA PURA FORMALITA)

Gerard Depardieu *(Onoff)*; Roman Polanski *(Inspector)*; Sergio Rubini *(Andre—The Young Policeman)*; Nicola DiPinto *(The Captain)*; Paolo Lombardi *(The Warrant Officer)*; Tano Cimarosa *(The Old Attendant)*; Maria Rosa Spagnolo *(Paola)*

Director Guiseppe Tornatore's A PURE FORMALITY is a suspenseful, philosophical drama about the interrogation of a famous writer in a run-down provincial police station following a mysterious event that appears to have happened near the writer's home.

The film opens with the image of a gun turning toward the viewer, and the sound of a shot. Next, a man (Gerard Depardieu) is seen running desperately through the woods during a nighttime storm. Stopped at a police roadblock and taken into custody, the man says he is the famous and reclusive writer Onoff. The inspector who interrogates him (Roman Polanski) is an admirer

of Onoff's work, and tests the man by quoting passages from Onoff's books. The inspector comes to believe his suspect's claim, is impressed and apologetic, but insists he must continue to investigate a murder in the area. Subsequently, Onoff's inconsistent behavior and the film's ambiguous flashbacks both suggest the author may be guilty of a terrible crime.

The station's power fails, plunging everyone into darkness, and candles are lit. Onoff watches what appears to be a heavy body bag being brought in. In desperation he knocks out a young officer and escapes into the woods, but he is recaptured. Next day, the inspector empties a large canvas bag full of photographs belonging to Onoff on the desk between them. The inspector reveals that there never was a murder and that the body bag contained the photographs. c

A PURE FORMALITY is a study in isolation and guilt. Onoff feels guilty about the solitude his writing requires and, at the same time, has doubts about the value of his work. His lover, fearing he will try suicide, arranges for friends and the local police to protect and comfort him. The possibility of a real crime and the guilt associated with it force Onoff to reconsider his situation. He asks himself if one can commit a crime and not remember. The implication is that Onoff has a responsibility toward life and that falsehood, forgetting, and thoughts of suicide are all indicative of his failure to meet that responsibility. He survives his despair and shame and is rejuvenated by the efforts of friends and strangers.

There are many traditional elements to this crime story: the mystery; the isolation; inner conflicts; the storm; and the power failure. But it is the unconventional nature of the progress and resolution of the story, translated into intimate and unusual camera angles, that makes the film a success. As the investigation progresses, the police and Onoff come to know, or presume to know, more and more about one another. But as more is revealed, more questions emerge, with greater uncertainty about what was previously known or assumed. The investigation suggests that all human interaction and understanding involves a complex process of speculation and interpretation. *(Violence, adult situations.)* — M.F.

d, Giuseppe Tornatore; p, Mario Cecchi Gori, Vittorio Cecchi Gori; exec p, Bruno Altissimi, Claudio Saranceni; assoc p, Alexandre Mnouchkine, Jean-Louis Livi; w, Giuseppe Tornatore, Pascal Quignard (based on a story by Giuseppe Tornatore); ph, Blasco Giurato; ed, Giuseppe Tornatore; m, Ennio Morricone; prod d, Andrea Crisanti; sound, Pierre Gamet; cos, Beatrice Bordone

Crime/Drama/Mystery (PR: C MPAA: NR)

PUSHING HANDS ★★½
(Taiwan/U.S.) 100m Central Motion Picture Company; Good Machine Inc.; Ang Lee Productions ~ Cinepix c
(TUI SHOU)

Sihung Lung *(Mr. Chu)*; Lai Wang *(Mrs. Chen)*; Bo Z. Wang *(Alex Chu)*; Deb Snyder *(Martha Chu)*; Lee Haan *(Jeremy Chu)*; Emily Liu *(Yi Cui)*

Fans of director Ang Lee's deservedly acclaimed later films will find much to enjoy in this less polished early effort. While failing to blend domestic tragedy and farce as artfully as he does in his subsequent works, Lee delivers a gentle generational-social gap comedy filled with rueful life lessons and colorful Chinese customs.

Alex Chu (Bo Z. Wang) is torn between caring for his stubborn elderly father, Mr. Chu (Sihung Lung), and loving his high-strung wife Martha (Deb Snyder), who neurotically guards her domestic turf. He is tired of refereeing their arguments after he's had a hard day at the office. Plagued by writer's block, feminist author Martha not only complains about interruptions in her work schedule but actively resents Mr. Chu for interfering in her child-rearing and using her kitchen for traditional cooking. While seeing her son and husband as Americans, she experiences a racist distaste for the old man, whom she treats like an unwanted house guest.

Eventually Mr. Chu decides there is no room for him in his son's life. Bravely, he severs ties and accepts a menial job as a dishwasher but, because of his age, he is abused by his employer. After a confrontation with his cost-cutter boss, Mr. Chu embarks on a much more successful career as a teacher of the Pushing Hands Tai Chi technique. As word of his prowess spreads, he becomes a sought-after teacher, achieves a position of respect in the Manhattan community, and risks a romance with a golden-ager whom he had previously met at a senior recreational center.

Although Ang Lee touches on a variety of troubling issues, this generation-crossroads film is betrayed by its own lack of focus. Lee appears to have so much he wants to get off his chest, that he lets it pour out without lending dramatic shape to his confused feelings. PUSHING HANDS is a film adrift on a wave of anger, much of it directed inward. The family crisis loses credibility because of the biased portrait of Martha, and Snyder's own unappealing screen persona; Martha registers as the daughter-in-law from Hell. Alex's peacemaking dillydallying, meanwhile, leaves the film in dramatic stasis. As a portrait of a courageous old man who refuses to be put out to pasture in a foreign land, PUSHING HANDS fails to succinctly and fairly present the springboard for his journey into empowerment. (Profanity, violence.) — R.P.

d, Ang Lee; p, Ted Hope, James Schamus, Emily Lui, Ang Lee; exec p, Jiang Feng-Chyi; assoc p, Hsu Li-Kong; w, Ang Lee, James Schamus; ph, Jong Lin; ed, Tim Squyres; m, Xiao-Song Qu; prod d, Scott Bradley; art d, Michael Shaw; sound, Paul Thomas Christian; casting, Wendy Ettinger, Jeff Berman; cos, Elizabeth Jenyon

Comedy/Drama (PR: A MPAA: NR)

PYROMANIAC'S LOVE STORY, A ★
(U.S.) 96m Hollywood Pictures ~ Buena Vista c

William Baldwin (Garet); John Leguizamo (Sergio); Sadie Frost (Hattie); Erika Eleniak (Stephanie); Michael Lerner (Perry); Joan Plowright (Mrs. Linzer); Armin Mueller-Stahl (Mr. Linzer); Mike Starr (Sergeant Zikowski); Julio Oscar Mechoso (Jerry); Richard Crenna (Businessman); Floyd Vivino (Man); Babz Chula (Wife); Tony Perri (Man In Car); Randy Butcher (Driver); Lesley Kelly (Jail Police Woman/Desk Officer); Jennifer Roblin (Maid); Elena Kudaba (Mrs. Olden); Michael McCullough (Bartender); Derrick Patterson (1st Man in Bar); Rob Wilson (2nd Man in Bar); Louis Strauss (Old Man); Phillip Williams (Officer in Car); Ann Holloway (Nurse); Gene Mack (Police Officer); Jonathan Allora (Man at Party); Michael Tait (Mr. Potts); Barbara Franklin (Garden Party Woman); Doug Hoyle (Biker)

This is a shrill romantic comedy, set in a bakery, from the creators of TV's "Northern Exposure."

Good-hearted pastry boy Sergio (John Leguizamo) is hopelessly devoted to tough-talking waitress, Hattie (Sadie Frost), even though a spoiled heiress, Stephanie (Erika Eleniak), declares her love for him late one night at the bakery. Fretting over declining business, Sergio's boss, Mr. Linzer (Armin Mueller-Stahl) begs his loyal employee to torch this family shop so that Mrs. Linzer (Joan Plowright) can face a financially secure future.

Although Sergio declines, arson mysteriously destroys the business, and the Linzers and Sergio separately assume the blame.

Sergio's admission follows a meeting with a businessman (Richard Crenna) who offers him $25,000 to take the rap for his pyromaniac son Garet (William Baldwin). Tempted, Sergio does not figure on the wrath of dreamer Garet, who torched the bakery as a love token for haughty Stephanie. Butting into Sergio's romantic affairs after he talks him out of suicide at the train tracks, Garet falls for Hattie. After Stephanie overdramatizes her feelings for Sergio, vacillating swain Garet finally accepts blame for the fire, thus allowing the Linzers to leave jail and enjoy their insurance money. Impressed by Garet's burning ardor, Stephanie vows to wait until he has served his prison stretch; grumpy Hattie finally admits the depth of her affection for true-blue Sergio.

Cannibalism may have been amusing in EATING RAOUL; baby-selling might have been a howl in PINK FLAMINGOS; arson is no laughing matter in A PYROMANIAC'S LOVE STORY. The filmmaker displays questionable taste in creating a starry-eyed romance in which the wanton destruction of property is a display of love. Sinking the already leaden conceit are young actors not likely to gain immortality for their light comic touch. While Leguizamo manages a deadpan sweetness, Eleniak mistakes pouting for charm, Frost seems miscast, and Baldwin cavorts like a high schooler doing a John Barrymore impression. Yeoman work by old pros (Crenna, Plowright, Mueller-Stahl) only hammers home the deficiencies of the young actors. (Violence, profanity.) — R.P.

d, Joshua Brand; p, Mark Gordon; co-p, Allison Lyon Segan, Barbara Kelly; w, Morgan Ward; ph, John Schwartzman; ed, David Rosenbloom; m, Rachel Portman; prod d, Dan Davis; art d, Peter Grundy; set d, Elena Kenney; sound, Bruce Carwardine (mixer); fx, Martin Malivore, Bob Hall, Arthur Langevin; casting, Amanda Mackey, Cathy Sandrich; cos, Bridget Kelly; makeup, Katherine Southern; stunts, Shane Cardwell

Romance/Comedy (PR: A MPAA: PG)

QUICK AND THE DEAD, THE ★★½
(U.S.) 103m IndieProd Company; Japan Satellite Broadcasting ~ TriStar c

Sharon Stone (Ellen); Gene Hackman (Herod); Russell Crowe (Cort); Leonardo DiCaprio (Kid); Tobin Bell (Dog Kelly); Roberts Blossom (Doc Wallace); Kevin Conway (Eugene Dred); Lance Henriksen (Ace Hanlon); Keith David (Sgt. Cantrell); Pat Hingle (Horace the Bartender); Gary Sinise (Marshall); Woody Strode (Charles Moonlight); Mark Boone, Jr. (Scars); Olivia Burnette (Katie); Fay Masterson (Mattie Silk); Raynor Scheine (Ratsy); Jerry Swindall (Blind Boy); Scott Spiegel (Gold Teeth Man); Jonothon Gill (Spotted Horse); Sven-Ole Thorsen (Gutzon); Lennie Loftin (Flat Nose Foy); Matthew Gold (Foy's Boy); Arturo Gastelum (Carlos Montoya); David Cornell (Simp Dixon); Josef Rainer (Virgil Sparks); Stacey Ramsower (Young Ellen); Tony Boggs (Zeb); Scott Ryder (Gunfighter); Timothy Patrick Quill (Man in Bar); Solomon Abrams (Man on Veranda); John Cameron (Bordello Swell); Bruce Campbell (Wedding Shemp); Michael Stone (Counselor); Butch Molina (Saloon Patron); Gregory Goossen (Young Herod's Man); Mick Garris (Young Herod's Man); Oliver Dear (Young Herod's Man)

Part burlesque of Sergio Leone's revisionist westerns, part throwback to the classics of the genre, THE QUICK AND THE DEAD tells the story of a woman who seeks vengeance upon the man who destroyed her family. This jokey feminist twist on the revenge formula starts out tough and funny but becomes strangely insubstantial by the end.

Set in 1878 Arizona, THE QUICK AND THE DEAD follows four days in the life of Ellen (Sharon Stone), a mysterious but rugged stranger who travels to a remote town named Redemption. Ellen signs up to take part in the town's annual shooting tournament, during which the contestants duel each other to death. Ellen hopes to survive her preliminary matches so that she may challenge the town's best fighter, the feared despot John Herod (Gene Hackman). Ellen wants to kill Herod because he is responsible for a family tragedy that occurred in her childhood. However, Ellen, who is not a crack shot, fears that she may not have the guts to carry out the deed when the time comes.

Ellen is not the only person who wishes to kill the tyrannical Herod. The entire town despises their leader, and secretly hires an assassin, Sgt. Cantrell (Keith David), to eliminate him during the contest. After Herod kills Cantrell instead, Herod's son, the Kid (Leonardo DiCaprio), challenges his father. He also loses. Ellen must duel with Herod's ex-partner in crime, the gunfighter-turned-preacher Cort (Russell Crowe), before she may have her showdown with Herod himself. But Cort does not want to participate in the tournament and plots with Ellen to fake her death during their shootout. In the apocalyptic finale, the "dead" Ellen returns by blowing up the town with hidden explosives during Herod's duel against Cort. Finally, she also finds the courage to kill Herod and she leaves Redemption in Cort's capable hands.

For Sharon Stone, THE QUICK AND THE DEAD represents career retrenchment. After BASIC INSTINCT, Stone's "overnight" stardom was tarnished by both salacious press items and bad movie choices (e.g., SLIVER, THE SPECIALIST). By co-producing THE QUICK AND THE DEAD and surrounding herself with top talent, Stone assured that a reasonably respectable film would be made. She also cast herself against type, astutely modifying her "blonde bombshell" image. Stone, like the film, affects a tough exterior that hides a soft center. Ellen's weakness, in particular her inability to kill Herod on several occasions, sets her apart—in an insidiously sexist way—from the Man With No Name of the Sergio Leone films THE QUICK AND THE DEAD so laboriously emulates.

In addition to the Leone references, director Sam Raimi and writer Simon Moore play with a wide range of genre iconography, including Gene Hackman's nasty variation on his UNFORGIVEN role and quotes from JOHNNY GUITAR and THE LEFT-HANDED GUN (Biblical allusions throughout the story are also heavy going). But the homage borders on Mel Brooks-style parody at times (as one gunfighter is shot through the head, his silhouette on the ground reveals sunlight gleaming through the bullet hole before he collapses). The self-conscious cleverness would work better, perhaps, if other scenes weren't played for high seriousness.

While THE QUICK AND THE DEAD ambles along with flashes of effective comedy, horror and melodrama, the scattershot approach never quite jells. Thanks mainly to the strong, poignant performances of Russell Crowe and Leonardo DiCaprio, the tricky but fun camerawork of Dante Spinotti, and the appropriately earthy production design of Patricia von Brandenstein, THE QUICK AND THE DEAD provides more than a few winning moments. *(Violence, profanity, sexual situations.)* — E.M.

d, Sam Raimi; p, Joshua Donen, Allen Shapiro, Patrick Markey; exec p, Toby Jaffe, Robert Tapert; co-p, Chuck Binder, Sharon Stone; w, Simon Moore; ph, Dante Spinotti; ed, Pietro Scalia; m, Alan Silvestri; prod d, Patrizia von Brandenstein; art d, Steve Saklad; set d, Hilton Rosemarin; sound, Dennis L. Maitland (mixer); fx, Al Di Sarro, Peter Donen; casting, Francine Maisler; cos, Judianna Makovsky; makeup, Gary Liddiard, Robert Kurtzman, Greg Nicotero, Howard Berger, Kurtzman, Nicotero & Berger EFX Group ; stunts, Terry Leonard

Western/Drama/Comedy (PR: C   MPAA: R)

RADIO INSIDE ★★★

(U.S.) 95m MGM/UA Communications; Showtime Entertainment; Snowball Productions; Polar Entertainment; Capitol Films ~ MGM/UA Home Video c

William McNamara *(Matthew)*; Elisabeth Shue *(Natalie)*; Dylan Walsh *(Michael)*; Ilse Earl *(Mrs. Piccalo)*; Pee Wee Love *(T.J.)*; Steve Zurk *(Father)*; Ara Madzounian *(Jesus)*; Tony Fabozzi *(Ford)*; Brett Murray *(Young Matthew)*; Justin Taylor *(Young Michael)*; Jonathan Groves *(Leonard)*; Sandra Thigpen *(Gina)*; Glen Trotiner *(Dwight)*; Jennifer Thompson *(Crystal)*; Jessica Elizabeth Forres *(Nadine)*; Estella McNair *(Sara)*; Edgar Allen Poe, IV *(Cabbie)*; Fred Buch *(Uncle Leonard)*; Eleanor Garth *(Aunt Bitsy)*; Paul Sylvan *(Cop at Pool)*; Parris Buckner *(Cop at Pool)*; Leslie Erganian *(Mother)*; Jody Wilson *(Deputy Sheriff)*

RADIO INSIDE is a stylized slice-of-life drama, which blends fantasy, reality, and flashbacks in telling the story of a confused young man involved in a love triangle with his brother and his brother's girlfriend. An expanded version of writer-director Jeffrey Bell's short graduation film, RADIO INSIDE was shown at Cannes in 1994, and debuted on the Showtime cable network later that year.

Matthew Anderson (William McNamara), a recent college graduate from Indiana, moves in with his older brother Michael (Dylan Walsh), a Miami advertising executive. Laid-back Matthew spends most of his time watching fish at the aquarium or soaking in the tub, thinking. Michael thinks Matt should quit daydreaming and join the real world, and offers him work as a copywriter. Instead, Matt takes a job as a lifeguard at a municipal pool, a move Michael thinks unwise, especially since their father drowned a year ago. But Matt would rather supervise the rowdy kids at the pool than join the corporate rat race. Matthew finds a kindred spirit in Michael's girlfriend, Natalie (Elisabeth Shue), a bookstore clerk. As Michael becomes more and more work-obsessed, neglected Natalie pals around with Matthew. After a short while, they fall for each other. Natalie wants to break off her relationship with Michael to be with Matt, but Matt decides that though he loves Natalie he cannot do anything to hurt his big brother.

The three are brought back together when a misunderstanding leads Matt to the conclusion that a boy has drowned at the pool because of his negligence. He takes off in Michael's car, consumed with guilt not only over this incident, but also because he was present when his father drowned and was unable to save him. As Michael and Natalie sit by the phone and worry, Matthew tries to drown himself, but survives. Comforted by his brother's love, Matthew learns to deal with his grief and guilt, and Michael accepts the fact that Matt and Natalie love each other.

The title refers to Michael's observation that Matt's brain is like a bored four-year-old playing with a radio dial, switching stations every few seconds. Matt's flights of fancy include memories of his youth, visions of his deceased father (Steve Zurk), and conversations with a Cuban-speaking Jesus (Ara Madzounian). Matt's internal radio is also fixated on water, and frequent flashes of aquatic imagery add to the film's distinct visual style. The soundtrack features songs by The Cranberries, R.E.M., and Big Head Todd and the Monsters. *(Nudity, sexual situations, profanity.)* — B.R.

d, Jeffrey Bell; p, Mark Tarlov, John Fiedler, Joe Caracciolo; exec p, Sharon Harel, Jane Barclay; assoc p, Glen Trotiner, Dean Garvin; co-p, Margaret Hilliard, Suzanne Smith; w, Jeffrey Bell; ph, Brian Capener; ed, Jim Clark; m, Gil Goldstein; prod d, John

DiMinico; art d, Leslie Erganian; set d, Leslie Ergnaian; sound, Jonathan "Earl" Stein (mixer); casting, Billy Hopkins, Barden Kerry; cos, Jacqui W. Greenhill, Valarie Fusaro; makeup, Lisa Layman

Drama (PR: C MPAA: NR)

RAMPO

(SEE: MYSTERY OF RAMPO, THE)

REASON TO BELIEVE, A ★★

(U.S.) 109m Pioneer Pictures ~ Castle Hill c

Allison Smith *(Charlotte Byrne)*; Jay Underwood *(Jim Current)*; Danny Quinn *(Wesley Grant)*; Georgia Emelin *(Linda Berryman)*; Kim Walker *(Judith)*; Keith Coogan *(Potto)*; Lisa Lawrence *(Alison)*; Christopher Birt *(Gary)*; Obba Babatunde *(Professor Thurman)*; Mark Metcalf *(Dean Kirby)*; Robin Riker *(Constance)*; Holly Marie Combs *(Sharon)*; Afton Smith *(Becky)*; Joe Flanigan *(Eric Sayles)*; David Overlund *(Frehley)*; Jim Keiffer *(Dave Brown)*; Michelle Stratton *(Amy)*; Mary Thomas *(Tracy)*; Rachel Parker *(Donna)*; Sally Kenyon *(Daisy)*; Andy Holcomb *(Harvey)*; Cary Spadafori *(Nancy)*; Terek Puckett *(Lazy Student)*; Matt Johnson *(Hippie Student)*; Heather Weber *(C.J.'s Happy Girl)*; Christopher Trela *(Kinko's Brother)*; Don Handfield *(Nuj)*; Claire Cundiff *(Captain Pepper)*; Christian Meinhardt *(Editor)*; Tulane Chartok *(Dean's Secretary)*; Carol O'Neil *(Feminist)*; Alex Wolfe *(Asshole in Quad)*; Noah Lanich *(Puking Brother)*; Amy Smith *(Bartender)*; Frank Martana *(Scared Brother)*; Jeff Niles *(Treeford Brother)*; Doug Devine *(Tequila Shot Brother)*; Dave Trachtenberg *(Biggest Brother)*; Jon Huffman *(Dean)*; Fathers of the Id *(Bar Band)*; Material Issue *(Band at Viking Party)*

If good intentions were all a film needed, A REASON TO BELIEVE would pass with flying colors—but however well-executed, this campus date-rape drama is entirely too simplistic.

Charlotte (Allison Smith), a coed at a small-town college, is part of a social circle that includes several members of a particularly rowdy fraternity, including her boyfriend, Wesley (Danny Quinn). When he must leave the campus during the weekend that the frat is having a major party, she attends the bash solo, against his wishes. She gets drunk and flirts with Wesley's best friend, Jim (Jay Underwood), who winds up forcing sex on her in an upstairs room. At first traumatized by the incident, Charlotte is slow to say anything about it; meanwhile, Jim boasts that she really "wanted it," which Wesley readily accepts. When Charlotte finally does speak out, she is disbelieved and ostracized by her friends, both male and female.

She finally finds support from Linda (Georgia Emelin), the leader of a campus feminist organization, who nonetheless uses her as a political tool in her quest to get the frat abolished. Ultimately, a hearing before the school's Dean (Mark Metcalf) is called, and although the frat brothers have vowed to stick together and protect Jim, he shows his true colors during the hearing. Jim is expelled, new anti-date rape motions are passed on the campus, and Charlotte is reconciled with Wesley.

A REASON TO BELIEVE clearly has its heart in right place, which is no doubt why first-time writer-director Douglas Tirola, working on a tiny budget, managed to get the technical support to give it crisp, professional production values. He also landed a strong young cast who were likely attracted by its earnest tackling of a genuine social problem—but the film wears its earnestness on its sleeve. If there's such a thing as a generic date-rape drama, this is it; all of the characters behave exactly the way one expects them to, given the situation. The young performers do solid work that makes the film watchable—even moving at a few points—but Tirola's straightforward, realistic approach squeezes out the possibility of any of them behaving in a surprising or complex manner.

In the end, the characters come to represent mouthpieces or emblems for specific ideas instead of flesh-and-blood people. Moreover, the film's conclusion, in which Charlotte all too easily accepts Wesley's apology—and which suggests that all she needs to get over her ordeal is good, healthy sex with someone she really likes—is ridiculous and offensive. It's tempting to call A REASON TO BELIEVE a TV-movie-level treatment of its central issue—except that a TV film (WHEN HE'S NOT A STRANGER, starring Annabeth Gish) already dealt with similar material several years ago with much more dramatic complexity. *(Violence, nudity, sexual situations, adult situations, substance abuse, extreme profanity.)* — M.G.

d, Douglas Tirola; p, Douglas Tirola, Ged Dickersin; co-p, Christopher Trela; w, Douglas Tirola; ph, Sarah Cawley; ed, Sabine Hoffman; prod d, Carol O'Neil; art d, Constance Lemasson; set d, Tracy Keegan; sound, Alex Wolfe (recordist); casting, Laura Adler; cos, Yvens DeThelismond; makeup, Karen Caldwell

Drama   **(PR: O   MPAA: R)**

RECKLESS   ★★½
(U.S.) 90m Playhouse International Pictures; Samuel Goldwyn Company ~ Samuel Goldwyn Company c

Mia Farrow *(Rachel)*; Mary-Louise Parker *(Pooty)*; Scott Glenn *(Lloyd)*; Tony Goldwyn *(Tom)*; Eileen Brennan *(Sister Margaret)*; Giancarlo Esposito *(Game Show Host Tim Timko)*; Stephen Dorff *(Tom, Jr.)*; Juana Barrios *(Female Reporter Re: Fire)*; Mike Heibeck *(Fireman)*; Vee Brown *(Anchor Person Re: Jogger)*; Jack Gilpin *(Weatherman)*; William Duell *(Roy)*; Deborah Rush *(Trish)*; Anthony Pagano *(Small Boy in Therapy)*; Debra Monk *(Therapist)*; Joanne Krispin *(Beautiful Twin)*; Lisa Krispin *(Beautiful Twin)*; Mary Beth Peil *(Bartender)*; Lindsay Mae Sawyer *(Little Rachel)*; William Fichtner *(Rachel's Father)*; William Preston *(Porter)*; John Magill *(Cashier at Liquor Store)*; Zach Grenier *(Anchor Person)*; Lisa Louise Langford *(Anne Lacher-Holden)*; Walter Bryant *(Doctor)*; Doug Barron *(TV Director)*; Maureen Silliman *(Shelter Reporter)*; Ron Bagden *(Young Shelter Volunteer)*; Ladd Patellis *(Man in Mask)*; Pat DiStefano *(TV Technician)*; Elijah Nicole Rosello *(Granddaughter)*; Nancy Marchand *(Grandmother)*; Nesbitt Blaisdell *(Grandfather)*

RECKLESS seeks to provide a darkly comic antidote to the season of good cheer. It is a meandering fable about the strange and whimsical life of a woman abandoned by her husband on Christmas Eve.

Rachel (Mia Farrow) has visions of sugarplums until her husband Tom (Tony Goldwyn) reveals that he has hired a man to kill her and shoves her out the window because he has had a change of heart. Lost in a snowstorm, Rachel is rescued by Lloyd (Scott Glenn), who invites Rachel to move in with him and his wife Pooty (Mary-Louise Parker), a deaf-mute parapalegic. Months pass, and they are all very happy. Eventually, Pooty and Lloyd confess secrets to Rachel; she is not really deaf, he abandoned his first wife and family.

When Christmas comes again, Tom arrives at the cabin. He wants, and their sons need, Rachel back; but before she can decide what to do, Tom and Pooty drink poisoned champagne and die, so Rachel and Lloyd go on the lam. They travel from Springfield to Springfield (every state has one) and finally settle in the desert. When Lloyd, who has been in a drunken stupor and

a Santa suit the whole time, dies too, Rachel ends up in a mission, herself now mute. She is cared for by a nun (Eileen Brennan) and spends years at the mission until she finally speaks again.

Rachel moves to Alaska (where she has always wanted to live because it is always like Christmas) and becomes a psychology professor. Fifteen years after that first, fateful Christmas Eve, a student (Stephen Dorff) approaches her for help with his holiday depression. It is her youngest son, and she offers to help him but does not reveal her true identity.

To work, RECKLESS needs to be like a snowball rolling down a hill, gaining weight and momentum on its way. Instead, it plays like a series of connected sketches, each whimsical in its own way, each revealing a dark side beneath a shining blanket of virgin snow, but no more. It is a parable without a point. RECKLESS, directed by Norman Rene and written by Craig Lucas (adapting his own play), is a film with an interesting premise that lacks a strong narrative follow-through.

The outstanding delight of RECKLESS is Mia Farrow's performance at the head of a very game cast. Set adrift in a sea of quirkiness that brings to mind her plight in Woody Allen's ALICE, Farrow nonetheless shines as if she were born to play the role. With blond curls framing her delicate features and eyeglasses magnifying her wide-eyed innocence, she's picture perfect, as is the work of cinematographer Frederick Elmes and production designer Andrew Jackness. The winter night Farrow is pushed out into is a scene right off a greeting card. Throughout the film, details conspire to present Farrow as an overgrown little girl lost. If only the script had given her somewhere to go. *(Adult situations, profanity.)* — P.R.

d, Norman Rene; p, Amy J. Kaufman; exec p, Lindsay Law; w, Craig Lucas (based on his play); ph, Frederick Elmes; ed, Michael Berenbaum; m, Stephen Endelman; prod d, Andrew Jackness; art d, Philip Messina; set d, Daniel Boxer; sound, Michael Barosky; casting, Billy Hopkins, Suzanne Smith, Kerry Barden; cos, Walker Hicklin

Comedy   **(PR: C   MPAA: PG-13)**

RED FIRECRACKER, GREEN FIRECRACKER   ★★½
(China/Hong Kong) 115m Yung & Associate; Xi'an Film Studio; Beijing Salon Films ~ October Films c
(PAODA SHUANG DENG)

Ning Jing *(Cai Chunzhi—The Master)*; Wu Gang *(Niu Bao—The Painter)*; Zhao Xiaorui *(Man Dihong)*; Gao Yang *(Chief Servant Qiao)*; Xu Zhengyun *(Old Master Xu)*; Zhao Liang *(Hei Liu)*; Ju Xingmao *(Bao Ge)*; Li Yushen *(Manservant)*; Lu Hui *(Old Boss Wang)*; Wang Liyuan *(Wang Ma)*; Zhang Bolin *(Businessman)*

Set in turn-of-the-century China, RED FIRECRACKER, GREEN FIRECRACKER is a classic tale of the struggle between youthful passions and age-old traditions. Winner of three Golden Roosters—China's Oscar equivalent—He Ping's film comes through as an engaging, well-made drama, but lacks the brilliance US audiences have come to expect from Fifth Generation filmmakers.

For many centuries, the Cai family has ruled over the vast territory of Northern China, along the banks of the Yellow River. But in the years leading up to the 1911 revolution, the family is left with one daughter, Chunzhi (Ning Jing), and no male heirs to run its successful fireworks empire. From childhood, an uncomprehending Chunzhi is forced to suppress her femininity and learn the role of an absolute ruler. She is addressed in the masculine form, clothed like a man, and forbidden ever to marry. At 19, she accepts her destiny and ascends to the position of "Master."

Soon after this ascension, Chunzhi hires an itinerant young artist, Niu Bao (Wu Gang), to paint traditional gods for the coming New Year festivities. Finding herself irresistibly attracted to the spirited artist, Chunzhi realizes the price she has paid for her position as Master. When the artist senses his Master's rising passion, he risks his life to win her. Chunzhi's love for Niu Bao tears at the fabric of her society; when their illicit affair becomes known, violence erupts and the Master begins to lose control over her people. To restore order, the family elders reluctantly concede Chunzhi's womanhood, but bind her to a centuries-old tradition of selecting a husband: a death-defying public fire-cracker contest. Chunzhi watches anxiously as Niu Bao, among others, risks his life for her hand in marriage.

Although RED FIRECRACKER, GREEN FIRECRACKER is an enjoyable period drama, it fails at many levels. For example, Chunzhi's transformation from a sadistic, melancholic "man" to a giggly, glamorous woman comes off as campy, not courageous; her life remains ruled by her relationships to men (her father, family elders, Niu Bao). The spectacular cinematography illuminates well the ambivalence Chunzhi feels about her environment—sumptuously elegant and beautiful, yet strangely dark and mausoleum-like—but this is overshadowed by too many heavy-handed metaphors. As soon as Chunzhi loses her virginity, the Yellow River, symbolizing the inexorable flow of history and change, becomes rough. And, of course, there is the metaphor of the fireworks themselves, gray and lifeless on the outside, waiting only to be ignited and explode into an orgasm of color. This film's explosive potential, by contrast, remains unrealized. *(Adult situations, sexual situations.)* — J.S.

d, He Ping; p, Yong Naiming, Chan Chun-Keung; exec p, Yong Naiming; w, Da Ying (based on the novel by Feng Jicai); ph, Yang Lun; ed, Yuan Hong; m, Zhao Jiping; art d, Qian Yunxiu; set d, Zhang Deqin; sound, Gu Changning, Zhang Wen; cos, Chen Changmin; makeup, Ma Shuangyin

Drama/Romance   (PR: C   MPAA: NR)

RED SUN RISING   ★★½
(U.S.) 100m Amritraj Entertainment; RSR Productions ~ Imperial Entertainment c

Don "The Dragon" Wilson *(Thomas Hoshino)*; Terry Farrell *(Karen Ryder)*; Soon-Teck Oh *(Yamata)*; James Lew *(Jaho)*; Mako *(Buntoro Iga)*; Michael Ironside; Edward Albert; Yuji Okumoto; Stoney Jackson

In contrast to most other low-budget American-made martial arts thrillers, RED SUN RISING boasts above-average fight choreography and a strong cast of familiar players in its story of a Japanese cop teaming with a female Los Angeles counterpart to stop a Japanese mobster from fomenting gang war.

Kyoto policeman Thomas Hoshino (Don "The Dragon" Wilson) arrives in Los Angeles seeking to extradite mobster Yamata (Soon-Teck Oh), who escapes police custody before the transfer can be made. Hoshino teams with police detective Karen Ryder (Terry Farrell) to try and track down Yamata before he can succeed in his plan to ignite a gang war between the Chicano Malitos and the black Icemen and profit from selling weapons to both sides. Yamata's henchman Jaho (James Lew), a hypnotic martial artist who employs the lethal "death touch," continually outwits Hoshino and Ryder and leaves a string of bodies in his wake. Hoshino reconnects with Buntoro Iga (Mako), his one-time martial arts instructor, who devotes himself to training Hoshino in the skills necessary to defeat Jaho. Finally, Hoshino learns of a rendezvous between Yamata and the Icemen and attempts to break it up and arrest Yamata, only to be thwarted by a corrupt federal agent (Edward Albert), who has been paid off

by Yamata. The Malitos' timely arrival saves Hoshino from certain death and enables him to engage in one last pitched battle with Jaho. His training pays off when he defeats Jaho by using his own newly learned death touch.

While still a low-budget potboiler with a far-fetched story line, RED SUN RISING is far superior to most similar efforts, including Roger Corman's ongoing series of BLOODFIST films which also star kickboxing champ Don "The Dragon" Wilson. While the fight scenes may be slower and less frenetic than similar scenes in Hong Kong thrillers, they tend to be more carefully filmed and staged (by Wilson himself) than usual for American films and employ actual martial artists. In addition, the film benefits from tight direction and editing and expert performances from such genre favorites as Mako, in his familiar role as a wise Asian elder; Soon-Teck Oh, as a smooth Japanese crime boss; Michael Ironside, in a rare sympathetic turn as a police captain; and Edward Albert as a corrupt BATF agent.

The acting of lead Don "The Dragon" Wilson has gradually improved to the point of adequacy, but he fights skillfully and vigorously and is photographed well, benefiting from dramatic lighting. Terry Farrell, from "Star Trek: Deep Space Nine," is very attractive as the no-nonsense detective with a sense of humor and a warm, feminine side. Rising martial arts star James Lew makes an imposing and formidable villain, with his long hair, black costume, and menacing but graceful moves. *(Violence, profanity.)* — B.C.

d, Francis Megahy; p, Paul Maslak, Neva Friedenn; exec p, Ashok Amritraj; assoc p, Jackie Dadon, James Holt, Kenneth Haker; w, David S. Green (from a story by David S. Green, Neva Friedenn, and Paul Maslak); ph, John Newby; ed, John Weidner; m, John Coda; prod d, Wendy Guidery; art d, Roz Johanna Gross; sound, David Chornow; casting, Ted Warren, Gennette Tondino; cos, Craig Anthony

Action/Martial Arts   (PR: C   MPAA: R)

REDHEADS
(SEE: DESPERATE PREY)

REDWOOD CURTAIN   ★★½
(U.S.) 99m Chris/Rose Productions; Hallmark Hall of Fame Productions, Inc. ~ New Horizons Home Video c

Jeff Daniels *(Lyman Fellers)*; John Lithgow *(Laird Riordan)*; Lea Salonga *(Geri Riordan)*; Debra Monk *(Geneva Simonson)*; Catherine Hicks *(Julia Riordan)*; Vilma Silva *(Zenaida)*; Jonathan Korty *(Dennis McCaw)*; Steve Anthony Jones *(Nate Stone)*; Jarion Monroe *(Leon Shea)*; Shirley Douglas *(Schyler Noyes)*; Joy Carlin *(Mrs. Cole)*; Cab Covay *(Mad John)*; R. Blakeslee *(Colby)*

Based on Lanford Wilson's play of the same name, REDWOOD CURTAIN is the tepid made-for-TV story of a young Amer-Asian woman's search for her identity.

Geri Riordan (Lea Salonga), is an 18-year-old musical prodigy. Born to an American father and a Vietnamese mother during the Vietnam war, Geri was adopted by Laird Riordan (John Lithgow), a Vietnam veteran and his wife Julia (Catherine Hicks), a distant workaholic. The film opens with Geri performing a piano concert, watched by her Dad. Afterwards, he praises her technique but tells her she must "risk everything" to achieve magnificence. After Laird dies from alcoholism, Geri, left alone with her cold foster mother, becomes obsessed with finding out as much as she can about her real parents.

She goes to visit her Aunt Geneva (Debra Monk), in California's Redwood Forest. Before Geri leaves, Julia gives her a box that Laird left, which contains a few clues about Geri's birth parents, including her father's possible name, "Ray Farrow." Geri is intrigued by one of the "men from the forest" who follows her around town. These men, a local tells her, are Vietnam vets who "barely escaped the bamboo curtain, now they just want to get lost behind the Redwood curtain." Geri, convinced that one man can lead her to her real father, invades the forest. She confronts Lyman Fellers (Jeff Daniels), her stalker. He warns her to leave him alone. With help from Geneva, Geri figures out that his name, when pronounced with a Vietnamese accent would sound similar to "Ray Farrow." She deduces that he must be her real father. She is wrong. Lyman reveals that Geri's mother wanted her to have a life in America with her father. Her real father couldn't bring her home with him because he already had a wife in the States. But he wanted to keep Geri. When asked why he didn't, Lyman states: "He did. He just fixed it with the adoption people." Once Geri finds out that Laird was her real father after all she is able to release her grief through her music.

Wilson's play is complex, but the Hallmark Hall of Fame adaption is simplistic. Geneva's running monologues about her late brother's "demons" offer no details let alone insights. What did happen in Vietnam? Not much is revealed in this film. And while Geri is the center of the story, she remains a cipher. Daniels reprises his stage role and gives a noble but limited performance. This movie about a search for one's past stays in the present to the point of stagnation. As Geri realized, after her father drank himself to death while the family looked on: "Maybe we were all too polite." REDWOOD CURTAIN suffers from the same problem. (*Profanity, adult situations.*) — J.D.

d, John Korty; p, Rick Rosenberg, Bob Christiansen; exec p, Richard Welsh; w, Ed Namzug (based on the play by Lanford Wilson); ph, Ronnie Taylor; ed, Scott Vickrey; m, Lawrence Shragge; prod d, Fred Harpman; set d, Robert Benton; sound, Nelson Stoll (mixer); casting, Phyllis Huffman, Olivia Harris; cos, Jennifer Parsons; makeup, Cynthia Bachman

Drama (PR: A MPAA: PG)

REFLECTIONS IN THE DARK ★★½
(U.S.) 84m Saban Entertainment; Concorde-New Horizons; Forrester Films ~ New Horizons Pictures c
(AKA: REFLECTIONS ON A CRIME; REGINA)

Mimi Rogers (*Regina*); Billy Zane (*Colin*); John Terry (*James*); Kurt Fuller (*Howard*); Lee Garlington (*Tina*); Nancy Fish (*Ellen*); Frank Birney (*Doctor*); Adrienne Ragard (*Attorney*); Alain Ohanian (*Daniel*); Ina Parker (*Haircutter*)

Best approached as a showcase for the underappreciated actress Mimi Rogers, the ambitious REFLECTIONS IN THE DARK is a psychological thriller, and the most blistering attack on marriage this side of Ingmar Bergman.

On death row, Regina (Mimi Rogers), convicted of murdering her husband, blithely awaits her execution with wisecracks that mask an inner rage. Aside from unwanted drop-ins by a priest and a physician, her only solace during her final vigil is prison guard Colin (Billy Zane), who pumps Regina for details about her case. Although in no mood to clear up the mystery, she does begin to feed bits and pieces of her life story to Colin, whom she also attempts to seduce. As flashbacks reflect different versions of how she killed her apparently decent husband James (John Terry) on their seventh wedding anniversary, the truth about her motivation assumes greater complexity.

Regina and James were happy enough initially, but the years brought emotional deprivation to them both. Overly-possessive James also wants to wipe out Regina's memories of her first and purest love, Daniel (Alain Ohanian). On their anniversary, James

gives Regina a gag pistol-cigarette lighter with a note allegedly from the long dead Daniel—a thoughtless gesture that encapsulates why Regina might want to kill him. Before she walks that last mile, however, a final flashback reveals that, although she was seething with anger, Regina killed James accidentally. A shard of glass from a broken mirror was lodged in the brush with which she hit James. Liberated from her entrapping marriage, Regina assumes responsibility for the slaying and faces her punishment with no regrets.

Casual viewers may not be able to tune in and out of the equivocal metaphysical mind games played by REFLECTIONS IN THE DARK. As a courtroom-jailhouse mystery, the film is too artful and contrived. But as a bleak musing on the dynamics of marriage, it is an eye-opening chiller, presenting the union as a shared crime of the heart marked by incessant subtle power-plays. By the end of a long dissection of this unholy union, the viewer can see why Regina wanted James dead: just to be rid of him, through an immediate, cleansing erasure of his being.

Having bitten off a concept that might give Antonioni pause, talented writer-director Jon Purdy runs aground in failing to make the jail guard an adequate counterweight to the protagonist. Drably played by Zane, he is merely a one-dimensional sounding board. Although this imbalance places an immense burden on Rogers, she displays a courageous, unrestricted abandon that illuminates her performance. (*Graphic violence, extreme profanity, extensive nudity, adult situations, sexual situations.*) — R.P.

d, Jon Purdy; p, Gwen Field, Barbara Klein, Carol Dunn Trussell, Alida Camp; exec p, Roger Corman, Lance H. Robbins, Mike Elliot; assoc p, Billy Da Mota; w, Jon Purdy; ph, Teresa Medina; ed, Norman Buckley; m, Parmer Fuller; prod d, Arlan Jay Vetter; art d, Roger Belk; sound, Christopher Taylor; casting, Billy Da Mota; cos, Denna Appel; makeup, Suzanne Willet

Drama/Prison (PR: O MPAA: R)

REMOTE CONTROL ★★½
(Iceland) 85m Skifan HF ~
Columbia TriStar Home Video c

Bjorn Jorundur Fridbjornsson (*Axel*); Margret Hugren Gustavsdottir (*Maeja*); Helgi Bjornsson (*Moli*); Soley Eliasdottir (*Unner*); Eggert Thorleifsson

A missing remote control provides the occasion to take a wild ride through Icelandic youth culture.

Axel (Bjorn Jorundur Fridbjornsson) must find his mother's missing remote control before she lets the drain out of the tub and sink where he is storing his aquarium fish. Sister Maja (Margret Hugren Gustavsdottir) thinks she is helping when she sends him off with her girlfriend Unner (Soley Eliasdottir) to find out if Unner's smuggler brother Moli (Helgi Bjornsson) has a spare. Moli does have one last Samsung remote control, but before obtaining it, Axel gets drawn into the political crossfire of rival gangs and, unbeknownst to him, is mistaken for Moli.

Moli would like to store his illegal stereo equipment at Axel's and, while at a headbanger's rock music night club, asks him for his address. Axel shouts it out during the one moment of silence between drum strokes, and his home soon becomes a raging party overrun with gang members and club hoppers, two of whom pack his sleeping mother into a boat and release her into the reservoir.

Meanwhile Unner and Axel are run over by gang leader Aggi (Eggert Thorleifsson) and his thugs just as their love affair begins to blossom. They narrowly escape ending up at the bottom of the river in concrete shoes, since neither Aggi nor his thugs knows the correct way to mix cement. Escaping, Unner and Axel rescue Axel's frazzled mother and retrieve their coveted remote control.

A confusing but somewhat fun film that would have achieved genuine humor with a tighter script. The plot conceit of the missing remote control reveals chaos thriving just beyond the realm of the "control" and convenience of modern technology. Unner is convinced that she can control the volume of the television with her mind—but in reality Maja is always standing behind her with the remote control in hand. Poor Axel just cares about his fish and keeping his mother content. This is a rare peek at some of the fashion and culture of young Iceland. — R.C.

d, Oskar Jonasson; p, Jon Olafsson; w, Oskar Jonasson; ph, Sigurdur Sverrir Palsson; m, Sigurjon Kjartansson; sound, Kjartan Kjartansson

Comedy   (PR: A   MPAA: NR)

RENT-A-KID   ★★
(Canada) 90m Paragon Entertainment; Paul Bernbaum Productions; Viacom ~ Republic Pictures Home Video c

Leslie Nielsen *(Harry)*; Christopher Lloyd *(Lawrence)*; Matt McCoy *(Russ)*; Sherry Miller *(Val)*; Tabitha Lupien *(Molly)*; Amos Crawley *(Brandon)*; Cody Jones *(Kyle)*; Tony Rosato *(Cliff Haber)*

The simple and obvious premise of RENT-A-KID, a 1992 Canadian movie released to US home video in 1995, is pulled off well enough in this children's comedy.

Orphanage owner Cliff Haber (Tony Rosato) goes on vacation, leaving his kids in the hands of his Dad Harry (Leslie Nielsen), whose business is renting everything from single glasses to house pets. While dining out, Harry overhears a young couple debating the pros and cons of having children. He convinces Russ Syracuse (Matt McCoy) and wife Val (Sherry Miller) to try out their parenting skills by renting kids for ten days. The lucky tykes are the Ward family: Brandon (Amos Crawley), aged 13; Kyle (Cody Jones), aged 10, and Molly (Tabitha Lupien), aged five. They are sworn to stay together as a family but have had no luck finding parents who want all three of them. The savvy kids aren't sure whether they're being used to make a buck, or whether this is their last chance to find parents who'll take them. They decide the Syracuses are worth a shot and vow to behave. The rental parents try to give the kids what they want. Val takes Molly to lunch at a fancy restaurant where they both order grilled cheese and milk. Squeamish Russ takes would-be surgeon Kyle to watch live surgery at the local hospital. Bookish Brandon is left in the care of doorman Lawrence Kady (Christopher Lloyd).

All goes well, except for a few major mishaps. The Syracuses forget that they have kids and leave them on their own for a night, only to be saved and chastised by the doorman. Hearing that antique dealer Russ's business is going under, young Molly enters a sweepstakes contest for two million dollars. She unknowingly writes her entry form on the back of one of Russ's treasures: a letter written by Abraham Lincoln. Brandon, a pretty good historian in his own right, swears that the letter is a fake. Disbelieving, Val calls him a liar. In the end the would-be parents wallow in their inferiority complex. They realize the kids are good . . . but who would want them? They're materialistic people. But when Harry comes to retrieve the merchandise, the Syracuses can't let them go. Russ explains, "In the last ten days, we fell in love with these kids, and we became a family." The rental agreement turns into a permanent sale.

The ending is happy and predictable, but RENT-A-KID is still an above-average movie for hip kids who are sick of Macaulay Culkin. Leslie Nielsen's part must have either been ad-libbed or

written as a composite of his AIRPLANE and NAKED GUN characters—and it works. His trademark tics are repeating himself and overstating the obvious. Only his timing could make schtick like this work. RENT-A-KID is no OLIVER TWIST, but it does bring a funny and unsentimental twist to the old orphan story. This is a real comedy for kids. — J.D.

d, Fred Gerber; p, Dan Howard; exec p, Jon Slan; w, Paul Bernbaum; ph, Rene Ohashi; ed, George Ralston; m, Ron Famin; prod d, Jeff Gunn; sound, John J. Thomson

Children's/Comedy   (PR: AA   MPAA: G)

RESTORATION   ★★★
(U.S.) 113m Segue Productions; Avenue Productions ~ Miramax c

Robert Downey, Jr. *(Merivel)*; Sam Neill *(King Charles II)*; David Thewlis *(Pearce)*; Polly Walker *(Celia)*; Meg Ryan *(Katherine)*; Ian McKellen *(Will Gates)*; Hugh Grant *(Finn)*; Ian McDiarmid *(Ambrose)*; Mary Macleod *(Midwife)*; Mark Letheren *(Daniel)*; Sandy McDade *(Hannah)*; Rosalind Bennett *(Eleanor)*; Willie Ross *(Man with Visible Heart)*; David Gant *(Chiffinch)*; Benjamin Whitrow *(Merivel's Father)*; Neville Watchurst *(Latin Doctor)*; Bryan Pringle *(Watchman)*; Roy Evans *(Fleeing Man)*; John Quarmby *(The Chancellor)*; John Dallimore *(The Secretary)*; Roger Ashton-Griffiths *(Mr. Bung)*; Janan Kubba *(Pretty Wench)*; Henrietta Voigts *(Female Patient)*; Simon Taylor *(Second Doctor)*; Selina Giles *(Fair Lady)*; Susanne McKenrick *(Dark Lady)*; Nick Hutchinson *(Pinworth)*; Andrew Havill *(Gallant)*; Tony Gardner *(Gallant)*; David Ryall *(Lord Bathurst)*; Philip Babot; Ena Cohen; Dylan Davies; Jim Ennis; Russell Gomer; Caroline Lamb; Margarlda Morini; Frank Rozelaar-Green; Carol Blade; Jessica Cohen; Alex Edmonds; Stephen Fisher; Timothy Hext; Philip Michell; Belinda Neave *(Whittlesea Dancers)*; Wendy Griffith; Bernadette Iglish; Leonni Pallett; Beryl St. John; Judy Herbert; Philippa Luce; Joanne Redfern; Wendy Woodbridge *(Court Dancers)*

RESTORATION is an old-fashioned, sprawling historical epic with the sudsy emotionality of Dickens and the earthy jocularity of Fielding—the kind of movie they supposedly don't make anymore.

Set in and around London before the Great Fire of 1666—a time of artistic and sensual excess following the oppressive protectorate of Oliver Cromwell—RESTORATION follows the maturation of young Dr. Merivel (Robert Downey, Jr.). A gifted and compassionate healer, Merivel withdraws from his apparent destiny in order to wallow in the fleshly pleasures of being the pampered Court Veterinarian to King Charles II (Sam Neill). Merivel is given the plum assignment of marrying the King's mistress, the stunningly beautiful Celia Clement (Polly Walker). Merivel disobeys his master, however, by falling in love with his haughty, imperious wife. Along with Celia, the King has given Merivel an estate, Bidnold, and he sublimates his hopeless desire for the absent Celia by decorating and throwing parties. Shamed by Celia's unexpected appearance, he puts off revelry and shyly woos her in an awkward, ineffectual manner, until the arrival of a supercilious portraitist (Hugh Grant) sent by the King brings matters to a head. Merivel attempts a clumsy declaration of passion and is directly rebuffed, leading to Celia's departure, and the loss of the King's favor—and with it his beloved Bidnold.

Merivel retreats to Oxfordshire, where his former medical school colleague, Pearce (David Thewlis), and his Quaker friends have a small hospital for the insane. Here he meets the traumatized Katherine (Meg Ryan). They begin an ill-advised affair, and after Pearce dies of tuberculosis, Merivel and Katherine—now pregnant—are asked to leave. Merivel comes to love

Katherine, only to lose her in childbirth. Grief-stricken, he takes his infant daughter back to London, which is gripped by the spread of bubonic plague. Merivel returns to practicing medicine, calling himself "Pearce" as a form of penance. His work comes to the attention of the King, and he is called to court to treat the ailing Celia, who proves to be merely pregnant. He leaves the palace and is trapped in the mass panic of the Great Fire of London, in which he believes he has lost his child. He is found by his former footman Gates (Sir Ian McKellen), and restored not only to his daughter, but to Bidnold and, ultimately, the King's good graces.

RESTORATION owes as much to TOM JONES as to DAVID COPPERFIELD, and its mixture of humorous banter, grubby authenticity and riotous rococo opulence also recalls Richard Lester's brilliant THE THREE MUSKETEERS (1973). Director Michael Hoffman and production designer Eugenio Zanetti create sequences of elaborate splendor teeming with amusing details, but without losing focus on the characters and events they adorn. The film's sumptuous costumes won an Academy Award. Star Downey wisely opted not to burden himself with an English accent, and uses his basset hound eyes to great effect. He manages to carry the film's emotional scenes with the same delicate ease he brings to its comic moments, proving conclusively that he can do more than merely charm his way through a film. Neill's Charles is every inch the King, and Ryan doesn't embarrass herself, despite her cliched Irish brogue.

Rupert Walters' script, based on the novel by Rose Tremain, is genuinely witty, written in a modified modern idiom that never violates the sense of time and place and is punctuated with aphorisms worthy of the best period writers. Oliver Stapleton's luscious cinematography captures London's burnished age in ochres and reds, later shifting to grayish greens in Oxfordshire. The Great Fire is a disappointing puff of smoke—the film ran seriously over budget and shooting was curtailed, compelling Hoffman to reinvent the last reel in editing. Overall, the film benefits from its brevity and tight pace. Though it received only a limited release—distributor Miramax had no faith in its commercial viability—RESTORATION is a disarming delight. Slyly entertaining and intelligent, it deserved far more attention than it received. *(Nudity, profanity, adult situations.)* — R.S.

d, Michael Hoffman; p, Cary Brokaw, Andy Paterson, Sarah Ryan Black; exec p, Kip Hagopian; assoc p, Mark Bentley; co-p, Bob Weinstein, Harvey Weinstein, Donna Gigliotti; w, Rupert Walters (based on the novel by Rose Tremain); ph, Oliver Stapleton; ed, Garth Craven; m, James Newton Howard; prod d, Eugenio Zanetti; art d, Alan Cassie, Lucy Richardson, Jonathan Lee; set d, Eugenio Zanetti; ch, Quincy Sacks, Kate Flatt; sound, Simon Kaye (mixer), Taffy Haines (maintenance); fx, Peter Hutchinson; casting, Mary Selway, Patsy Pollock; cos, James Acheson; makeup, Paul Engelen

AA Best Art Direction: Eugenio Zanetti; *AA Best Costume Design:* James Acheson

Historical/Romance/Comedy (PR: C MPAA: R)

RETURN OF THE GOD OF GAMBLERS ★★★
(Hong Kong) 125m c

Chow Yun-fat *(God of Gamblers)*; Tony Leung *(Little Trumpet)*; Chingmy Yau; Ng Sin-lin

Action takes many forms in RETURN OF THE GOD OF GAMBLERS, a surprisingly comedic sequel to the 1989 Hong Kong hit GOD OF GAMBLERS. A tale of rivalry and revenge directed by Wong Jing, it supplements the expected gunfights and chase scenes with more subtle confrontations over a deck of cards, telekinetic powers, romance, and heartbreak.

Ko Chun, the God of Gamblers (Chow Yun-fat) is enjoying his four-year retirement from gambling as a father-to-be sequestered in a Parisian manison. His seclusion is violently interrupted when an old rival, Chau, attacks the house; Chun fights off a small army only to find his wife Yau dying and his unborn son brutally aborted by Chau's men. On her deathbed, Yau pleads that Chun not gamble or admit to being the God of Gamblers for one year. Desperate to avenge his family's deaths, Chun grows restless as the year since Yau's death nears an end. He travels to Mainland China, where he is befriended by Hoi On, who is, unbeknownst to Chun, an underworld character. Chau attacks Hoi On's yacht, and despite Chun's victory in an fantastically implausible underwater fight, he can rescue only Hoi On's young son Siu Yuen and before the ship explodes promises to take the boy home to Taiwan. Mistaking them for culprits rather than victims of the attack, police arrest Chun and the boy, but they manage to escape and hide out at an inn where they join forces with some new acquaintances, the foremost being Little Trumpet (Tony Leung), who makes an appealignly comic—if crude—sidekick for the suave God of Gamblers.

Upon reaching Taiwan, the boy is kidnapped by Chau's men before his sister, Hoi Tong, can meet him. Hoi Tong, having taken over her father's business, arranges for the rivals to meet in a luxurious casino. Because Chun cannot gamble for three more days without breaking his vow, Little Trumpet must pose as the God of Gamblers, resulting in high slapstick confusion and recurrent attacks by Chau's men. In time for the big showdown, Chun reveals his true identity. While Chau enlists the aide of a telekinetic magician with the power to change cards, the God of Gambler's own psychic powers prevail. Chun not only wins the match but avenges the deaths of his wife and unborn son.

While RETURN OF THE GOD OF GAMBLERS takes an unnecessarily long time to tell its story (125 minutes), a strong and reserved performance by Chow Yun-Fat, and an inversely broad and leering appearance by Tony Leung, make the time pass pleasantly, even in the protracted climactic card game. A subplot involving Little Trumpet's sister's adoration for the God of Gamblers may seem discordantly saccharine, (especially to viewers unfamiliar with the Hong Kong action genre, which frequently incorporates a deeply romantic story line), but Chun's graceful handling of her teenage crush only adds to his appeal as a gentleman as well as a man of action.

Portrayals of the Mainland Chinese are broadly cartoonish. For example, once off the mainland, the police captain taken hostage by our heroes undergoes a fervent conversion, so enamoured of capitalism—and so stupid—that he can't be bothered to remove the price tag from his newly purchased designer sunglasses. A few such misfired attempts at political humor fall vulgarly flat in a film of otherwise high-spirited comedy, action, and heartfelt emotions. *(Graphic violence.)* — C.C.

d, Wong Jing

Martial Arts/Action (PR: C MPAA: NR)

RETURN OF THE NATIVE, THE ★★★
(U.S./U.K.) 99m Signboard Hill Productions; Craig Anderson Productions; Hallmark Hall of Fame Productions ~ Republic Pictures Home Video c

Catherine Zeta-Jones *(Eustacia Vye)*; Ray Stevenson *(Clym Yeobright)*; Joan Plowright *(Mrs. Yeobright)*; Clive Owen *(Damon Wildeve)*; Steven Mackintosh *(Diggory Venn)*; Claire Skinner *(Thomasin)*; Celia Imrie *(Susan Nunsuch)*; Paul Rogers *(Captain Vye)*; Gregg Saunders *(Charley)*; Richard Avery *(Humphrey)*;

Matthew Owen *(Johnny)*; Peter Wight *(Timothy)*; Jeremy Peters *(Sam)*; John Boswall *(Granfer Castle)*; William Waghorn *(Christian Castle)*; Britta Smith *(Olly Dowden)*; John Breslin *(Vicar)*; Daniel Newman *(Mummer)*

A Hallmark Hall of Fame production of Thomas Hardy's classic novel, handsomely staged and faithfully adapted, THE RETURN OF THE NATIVE concerns the tragic fate of a woman whose dreams outreach her destiny.

Eustacia Vye (Catherine Zeta Jones) lives with her grandfather in rustic Egdon Heath. She dreams of escaping the desolate moor and the townspeople who spurn her. Her dalliance with the roguish Damon Wildeve (Clive Owen) leads to scandal when Wildeve leaves his intended bride Thomasin (Claire Skinner) at the altar. Wildeve wants to run off with Eustacia, but returning native Clym Yeobright (Ray Stevenson) captures her fancy. Clym has been living in Paris and working in the diamond business. Eustacia sets out to win Clym's heart and succeeds easily. Clym plans to remain in Egdon Heath and open a school for underprivileged children. Eustacia is convinced Clym will tire of Egdon Heath and take her back with him to Paris. Clym and Eustacia marry, despite the vehement objections of Mrs. Yeobright (Joan Plowright). Eustacia's dreams are dashed when Clym partially loses his sight. Unable to continue his studies, Clym toils in the fields. Living in a small cottage, the wife of a furze cutter, is not the life Eustacia had envisioned for herself. She is once again tempted by Wildeve's attentions. The death of Mrs. Yeobright brings further conflict between Clym and Eustacia. They part, Eustacia returning to live with her grandfather. Months later, Clym writes a letter to Eustacia begging her to come back, but it arrives too late. Eustacia has decided to run off with Wildeve. Waiting for Wildeve in a storm, the distraught Eustacia jumps into the river and drowns. Both Wildeve and Clym try to save her, and Wildeve loses his life in the attempt. After the tragedy, Clym remains in Egdon Heath, teaching and preaching about love, life, beauty, and truth, forever haunted by visions of his wife.

First published in 1878, *The Return of the Native* had never been filmed until this 1994 made-for-TV production. The all-British cast is uniformly fine. Jones is beautiful and beguiling as Hardy's doomed heroine. The story hinges upon the lure of the men she loves, and both Stevenson and Owen measure up to the intensity and magnetism of their literary counterparts. To US audiences, the only familiar cast member is Plowright, who is splendid as Clym's mother. Filmed on location in the windswept countryside of Exmoor, England, the production boasts exquisite photography and production design. — B.R.

d, Jack Gold; p, Nick Gilliot; exec p, Richard Welsh, Craig Andersen; co-p, Brent Shields; w, Robert W. Lenski (based on the novel by Thomas Hardy); ph, Alan Hume; ed, Jim Oliver; m, Carl Davis; prod d, Peter Mullins; art d, David Minty; set d, Peter Howitt; sound, Tony Dawe (mixer); fx, Alan Whibley; casting, Mary Selway; cos, Derek Hyde; makeup, Lois Burwell

Drama   (PR: A   MPAA: PG)

RHYTHM THIEF   ★★★
(U.S.) 88m Film Crash; Film Four International ~ Strand Releasing bw

Jason Andrews *(Simon)*; Eddie Daniels *(Marty)*; Kevin Corrigan *(Fuller)*; Kimberly Flynn *(Cyd)*; Sean Hagerty *(Shayme)*; Mark Alfred *(Mr. Bunch)*; Christopher Cooke *(Jules)*; Bob McGrath *(Rat-Boy)*; Alan Davidson *(Otis)*; Paul Rodriguez *(Eladio)*; Cynthia Sley *(Herself)*; Chip English *(Band Member—1-900-BOXX)*; Stephen Paynes *(Band Member—1-900-BOXX)*; Carla Olla *(Band Member—1-900-BOXX)*; Robin Levine *(Diane)*; Johnny Kretz

(Commuter) ; David Fuhrer *(Druggie)*; Christopher Grimm *(Cigar Guy)*; Katie Bolger *(Razzel)*; Jeff Dypwick *(Party Guy)*

Shot in stark 16mm black-and-white, RHYTHM THIEF sardonically follows the neo-noir fate of Simon (Jason Andrews), an urban loner who surreptitiously tape-records rock concerts and sells the cassettes on the sidewalks of New York's Lower East Side.

Not surprisingly, Simon is beaten up and receives death threats from an all-girl punk band (led by Cynthia Sley, of the Bush Tetras, billed in the credits as herself), who stalk Simon through alleys and into his bleak tenement. Simon has slightly gentler relations with two other women, hostile "Ludlow Street chick" Cyd (Kimberly Flynn), who bursts in for quick, angry bouts of purgative sex, and waiflike Marty (Eddie Daniels), an outpatient from the same mental ward where Simon's mother is institutionalized.

Marty now brings word that his mother, a onetime greeting-card writer, is dead (she still has the old lady's verses transcribed on her bare arms) and tries to love Simon, putting his practiced alienation to the test. Fleeing Sley, the pair wind up in a beach-side idyll at Far Rockaway, but Simon, sensing his number is up, goes back to the Lower East Side to put his affairs, such as they are, in order. Even for fatalist Simon, the city serves up a cruel and sudden end; he is killed not by resentful rockers but a maniac neighbor who falsely blames him for stealing appliances.

RHYTHM THIEF is weakest when it gropes to explain Simon's malaise in vaguely Freudian terms and strongest when it shuts up and shows things, which is fortunately most of the time. Howard Krupa's high-contrast cinematography paints the sun-bleached concrete slabs and Stygian shadows of midsummer Manhattan with a tactile quality, sharply complementing the pitch and pulse of Matthew Harrison's edgy direction. Persistent gallows humor and the sweet nature of Daniels's character offset the downbeat tale's heavy cynicism. Andrews ably discerns between nonacting and not reacting for his poker-faced antihero. Though publicity for RHYTHM THIEF emphasized its $11,000 cost and 11-day shooting schedule, the film seems less a rush job and more a work of seasoned confidence by Harrison, a native New Yorker who began shooting short films in rough parts of town while still a kid and made his feature debut in 1993 with a "bowling noir" called SPARE ME. One critic compared RHYTHM THIEF to Godard's BREATHLESS, though it has more in common with Susan Siedelman's SMITHEREENS, a similarly low-budget look at the downward spiral of a fringe character on the Big Apple punk scene. *(Violence, sex, nudity, adult situations, substance abuse, profanity.)* — C.C.

d, Matthew Harrison; p, Jonathan Starch; exec p, Matthew Harrison; assoc p, Pier Paolo Piccoli, Trula Marcus, Gary Marcus; co-p, Christopher Cooke; w, Christopher Grimm, Matthew Harrison; ph, Howard Krupa; ed, Matthew Harrison; m, Danny Brenner, Hugh O'Donovan, John L. Horn, Kevin Okurland; art d, Daniel Fisher; sound, Charles Hunt (recordist); casting, Meredith Jacobson; cos, Nina Carter; makeup, Angela Johnson, Barri Scinto

Drama   (PR: O   MPAA: NR)

RICHARD III   ★★★½
(U.K./U.S.) 104m Bayly/Pare Productions; United Artists; First Look Pictures ~ MGM/UA c

Ian McKellen *(Richard III)*; Annette Bening *(Queen Elizabeth)*; Maggie Smith *(The Duchess of York)*; Nigel Hawthorne *(Clarence)*; John Wood *(King Edward IV)*; Robert Downey, Jr. *(Earl Rivers)*; Kristin Scott Thomas *(Lady Anne)*; Jim Broadbent *(Buckingham)*; Jim Carter *(Lord Hastings)*; Bill Paterson *(Rich-*

ard Ratcliffe); Adrian Dunbar *(Corporal James Tyrell)*; Edward Jewesbury *(King Henry)*; Christopher Bowen *(Prince Edward)*; Marco Williamson *(Prince of Wales)*; Kate Steavenson-Payne *(Princess Elizabeth)*; Dominic West *(Richmond)*; Tim McInnerny *(Catesby)*; Dennis Lill *(Lord Mayor)*; Edward Hardwicke *(Stanley)*; Ryan Gilmore *(George Stanley)*; Donald Sumpter *(Brackenbury)*; Roger Hammond *(Archbishop)*; Tres Hanley *(Air Hostess)*; Stacey Kent *(Ballroom Singer)*; Andy Rashleigh *(Jailer)*; Bruce Purchase *(City Gentleman)*; James Dreyfus *(1st Subaltern)*; David Antrobus *(2nd Subaltern)*

Ian McKellen's delightfully sinister portrait of a power-hungry sociopath highlights this oddly breezy adaptation of Shakespeare's *Richard III*. This a flawed and far from definitive rendering, but it's dynamic and enjoyably revisionist.

Fragments of Shakespeare's 1592 text are strewn throughout this new version of the classic play, but McKellen and director-co-writer Richard Loncraine have completely re-envisioned the setting of the historical drama. The hunchbacked Duke of Gloucester still malevolently murders his family members one by one, climbing his way to the top to become king, but now his coup takes place among the aristocratic, pro-fascist Cliveden Set of the 1930s.

Richard is first seen leading the troops of the House of York against the reigning King in a re-imagined, modern-day War of the Roses. Richard kills the King and Prince of Wales during the battle, clearing the way for Edward (John Wood), Duke of York, to ascend to the throne. After the celebration in London, however, Edward imprisons a third brother, Clarence (Nigel Hawthorne), on suspicion of treason. Richard immediately consolidates his power by proposing to (and eventually marrying) the widow of the deceased King, Lady Anne (Kristin Scott Thomas).

Richard continues his rise by ordering the murders of several people who are either close to the throne or pose a threat to him. These include not only Clarence, but also Richard's brother-in-law, Rivers (Robert Downey, Jr.), the sons of Edward and Elizabeth (Annette Bening), and an advisor, Hastings (Jim Carter). Eventually, Richard also kills Anne. The only person Richard seems to fear is his mother, the Duchess of York (Maggie Smith), who scolds him for his misdeeds. Finally, Richard manipulates Elizabeth into an arranged marriage that enables him to be crowned King, but Richard's former ally, Buckingham (Jim Broadbent), unleashes his armed forces against Richard's camp, and Richard dies in the ensuing battle.

By reinventing the material in a timely and imaginative way, RICHARD III succeeds where other recent Shakespeare-on-film adaptations fail. This version brazenly moves around chunks of text, shifts the story to a more recent and comprehensible age, and irreverently spoofs the sacrosanct material (the first soliloquy now takes place in a urinal, while the closing sequence uses an old Al Jolson tune, "Sittin' On Top of the World," to recall the climax of WHITE HEAT).

However, the film does not take its revisionist point quite far enough. The look is appropriately elegant, but only a few scenes stand out as truly eye-catching (e.g., a fascist rally shot like TRIUMPH OF THE WILL in 3-strip Technicolor, Richard's fiery death scene). Moreover, the parallels between Richard's ascent and the rise of European fascism make for interesting allegory, but McKellen and Loncraine stop far short of driving the point home with reference to the present day (*a la* Orson Welles's mid-30s stage version of *Julius Caesar*).

The best part of the film is McKellen's lighthanded, carefree way with the text. The actor's asides to the camera have just the witty, sardonic flavor that was missing from Branagh's self-amused addresses to the audience in the 1995 OTHELLO.

McKellen's forceful and frighteningly funny performance is matched by Kristin Scott Thomas's mournful, masochistic Lady Anne. They are both well supported by Nigel Hawthorne, Maggie Smith, and Jim Broadbent in parts that amount to showy cameos. Far less successful are the performances by two American actors clearly added to the film for marquee value, Bening and Downey. *(Violence, nudity, sexual situations, adult situations, substance abuse.)* — E.M.

d, Richard Loncraine; p, Lisa Katselas Pare, Stephen Bayly; exec p, Ellen Dinerman Little, Ian McKellen, Joe Simon, Maria Apodiacos; assoc p, Mary Richards, Michele Tandy; w, Ian McKellen, Richard Loncraine (adapted from the stage production by Richard Eyre, based on the play by William Shakespeare); ph, Peter Biziou; ed, Paul Green; m, Trevor Jones; prod d, Tony Burrough; art d, Choi Ho Man, Richard Bridgland; sound, David Stephenson (recordist); fx, John Evans; casting, Irene Lamb; cos, Shuna Harwood; makeup, Pat Hay, Daniel Parker; stunts, Jim Dowdall

AAN Best Art Direction: Tony Burrough; *AAN Best Costume Design:* Shuna Harwood

Drama/Historical/War   **(PR: C   MPAA: R)**

RIVER OF GRASS   ★★★
(U.S.) 75m Plan B Pictures ~ Strand Releasing c

Lisa Bowman *(Cozy)*; Larry Fessenden *(Lee Ray Harold)*; Dick Russell *(Jimmy Ryder)*; Stan Kaplan *(J.C.)*; Michael Buscemi *(Doug)*; Lisa Robb; Tom Laverack; Bert Yaeger; Mary Glenn; Carol Flakes; Frances Reichardt; George Moore; Mannie Mack; Greg Shroeder; Kyle Hawkins; Heather Florio; Joseph Florio; Duncan Young; Santo Fazio; Monica Davidson; Jerry Utter; Shelley Florio; Sheila Korsi; Lou "Spot" Perdomo; Barbara Bucci; Steven Lezak; Robert Perry; Jerry Reichardt; Kerline Alce; Ricco Jackson; Robert Lawon; Carl Crowder; Barry Shore; T. Colin Dodd; Wayne Ferguson; Roz DeLisi; Mitch Lewis; Patrick Cooke; Harry Epp; Robert Greenbaum; John Ulrich; Will Connelly; Matthew Sigal

Kelly Reichardt's independent RIVER OF GRASS is based on an ambitious idea: a realist version of the American road film, starring two lazy, unintelligent, and disreputable protagonists. Unfortunately, the film suffers the fate of similar portrayals of unremarkable characters: the people never become interesting, nor does the story.

Cozy (Lisa Bowman) is a bored young woman who lives with her husband and children in a working-class neighborhood of the Florida Everglades, and dreams of freedom. Cozy's father, a Miami detective, also miserably uninspired, drinks in his free time. One evening he loses his gun, which finally finds its way to Lee Ray Harold (Larry Fessenden), a jobless young man who lives with his grandparents. Thrown out by his grandmother, Harold ends up in a bar, where he meets Cozy. They drink together, and later sneak into someone's backyard pool. When they accidentally fire the gun at the pool's owner as he steps out into his yard, Harold and Cozy flee, believing they have killed the man. Trying to survive with little money, the two get into various scrapes. Harold later learns that the man they fired at was unharmed, but he does not tell Cozy.

Cozy, convinced she is a murderer on the run, insists they leave Miami. Trying to sneak past a toll booth because they do not have any change, Harold pulls over when cautioned by a guard, obediently turns the car around, and heads back to Miami. He confesses to Cozy that they are not murderers and tells her he will find work and take care of her. Cozy, now carrying the gun, points it at Harold and forces him to jump out of the car before she speeds off.

Reichardt's contribution to the road film genre is a latent satire, or perhaps a negation, of the genre itself: a road movie where the main characters spend most of their time holed up in a motel no more than a few miles from where they started. In place of the exciting and transcendent, she offers the mundane and unfulfilled. Traditionally, road film characters are either villainous outcasts or alienated, restless individuals who go off the deep end. Films like BONNIE AND CLYDE and, more recently, THELMA AND LOUISE, also tend to build up momentum toward a climactic conclusion. Reichardt's film instead portrays the sad and pathetic life of two unattractive losers in a realist, rather than sensational, style. The result is languid, whimsical at best. (Violence, adult situations, profanity.) — M.F.

d, Kelly Reichardt; p, Jesse Hartman, Kelly Reichardt; assoc p, Ralph McKay, Larry Fessenden; w, Kelly Reichardt (from her story); ph, Jim Denault; ed, Larry Fessenden; prod d, David Doernberg; sound, Matthew Sigal (recordist); cos, Sara Slotnick; makeup, Nina Port

Drama/Crime (PR: C   MPAA: NR)

ROB ROY ★★★
(U.S.) 134m Talisman Films; United Artists ~
United Artists c

Liam Neeson (Rob Roy); Jessica Lange (Mary); John Hurt (Montrose); Tim Roth (Cunningham); Eric Stoltz (McDonald); Andrew Keir (Argyll); Brian Cox (Killearn); Brian McCardie (Alasdair); Gilbert Martin (Guthrie); Vicki Masson (Betty); Gilly Gilchrist (Iain); Jason Flemyng (Gregor); Ewan Stewart (Coll); David Hayman (Sibbald); Brian McArthur (Ranald); David Palmer (Duncan); Myra McFadyen (Tinker Woman); Karen Matheson (Ceilidh Singer); Shirley Henderson (Morag); John Murtagh (Referee); Bill Gardiner (Tavern Lad); Valentine Nwanze (Servant Boy); Richard Bonehill (Gutherie's Opponent)

Though less aggressively action-packed than BRAVEHEART, 1995's other epic men-in-kilts movie, ROB ROY offers a hearty and colorful portrayal of a Scottish folk hero.

In 1713 Scotland, Robert Roy MacGregor, better known as Rob Roy (Liam Neeson), heads the renowned MacGregor clan by protecting the livestock of the British Marquis of Montrose (John Hurt). An exceptional cattle drover, Rob kills bandits and rival clan members who try to steal Montrose's property. When not working, Rob lives a quiet life in a small village named Inversnaid, with his wife, Mary of Comar (Jessica Lange), and their two sons (Ewan Stewart, David Palmer).

Rob's life changes dramatically after he arranges to borrow 1000 pounds from Montrose in order to buy cattle to sell at another market for a sizable profit. Rob's second-in-command, McDonald (Eric Stoltz) is ambushed and murdered by Montrose's unscrupulous nephew Archie Cunningham (Tim Roth), who steals the money, and pins the crime on the MacGregors.

Rob is accused of the theft, but Montrose offers him a deal: If Rob will slander the Duke of Argyll (Andrew Keir)—Montrose's rival—as a Jacobite, Montrose will drop the charges. Rob Roy refuses the dishonorable offer, and escapes to become an outlaw. In retaliation, Cunningham rapes Mary, and British soldiers raid and torch Inversnaid.

Montrose's men capture Rob and beat him severely; he returns to Mary—who has come to understand why her husband values honor so highly—and appeals to Argyll for help, revealing Rob's refusal to defame him. The Duke suggests a dual between Rob and Cunningham as a way to end the standoff with Montrose. If Cunningham wins, Rob will be arrested and the Duke will pay

the missing 1000 pounds. If Rob wins, all charges will be dropped. At the climax of the tense, bloody sword fight, Rob kills Cunningham. He leaves to rejoin Mary and their sons at their new home in Balquhidder.

A star vehicle for actor Liam Neeson, ROB ROY also offers above-average drama and adventure. Scottish director Michael Caton-Jones, in his best film since his first, SCANDAL (1989), uses the expansive Highland vistas expressively, yet refrains from overglamorizing the earthy legend. Screenwriter Alan Sharp—whose credits include ULZANA'S RAID (1972) and NIGHT MOVES (1975)—weaves an intricate tale of political intrigue into the story, offering viewers more than the usual mossy romance and flashy swordfights.

The cast performs splendidly and fits well into the early 18th-century landscape. Tim Roth's Cunningham is a chillingly complex villain—he received an Academy Award nomination—and Jessica Lange delivers a fine and understated performance, delineating Mary's ribald pleasure in life with as much clarity as her noble suffering. Liam Neeson, who wears a kilt with astonishing grace and vigor, proves himself as a fine actor in the movie star mold. Despite its violent excesses—the final swordfight is particularly horribly attenuated—ROB ROY is a well-crafted popcorn movie, satisfying on several levels. (Graphic violence, nudity, sexual situations, profanity.) — E.M.

d, Michael Caton-Jones; p, Peter Broughan, Richard Jackson; exec p, Michael Caton-Jones; co-p, Larry DeWaay; w, Alan Sharp; ph, Karl Walter Lindenlaub; ed, Peter Honess; m, Carter Burwell; prod d, Assheton Gorton; art d, John Ralph, Alan Tomkins; set d, Ann Mollo; sound, David John (recordist); fx, Ulrich Nefzer; casting, Susie Figgis; cos, Clare Spragge, Sandy Powell; makeup, Morag Ross; stunts, Vic Armstrong

AAN Best Supporting Actor: Tim Roth

Historical/Adventure/Biography (PR: C   MPAA: R)

ROOMMATES ★★★
(U.S.) 108m Interscope Communications, Inc.;
Unit One Film Partners; Nomura, Babcock & Brown;
PolyGram ~ Buena Vista c

Peter Falk (Rocky); D.B. Sweeney (Michael Holeczak); Julianne Moore (Beth); Ellen Burstyn (Judith); Jan Rubes (Bolek Krupa); Joyce Rheeling (Barbara); Ernie Sabella (Stash); John Cunningham (Burt Shook); Noah Fleiss (Michael—Age 5); Lisa Davis (Betty); Rohn Thomas (Kevin); Karl Mackey (Milan Postevic); Rev. Zygmund Szarnicki (Funeral Priest); Chance Marquez (Bully at Baseball Game); David Cutter (Peanut Vendor); David Tom (Michael—Age 15); Lillian Misko-Coury (Bakery Saleswoman); Kate Young (Nun); Noah Abrams (Stavinski); Ilana Levine (E.R. Nurse); Scott Cohen (Attending Intern); Pattie Carlson (Second E.R. Nurse); Adrienne Wodenka (Third E.R. Nurse); Daniel Corbin Cox (Attending Physician); Joel de la Fuente (Toby); Raymond Wong (Deng); Wanqing Wu (Zhang); Zhe Sun (Liu); Mengze Shi (Fan); Ann Heekin (Cecilia); Scott Kloes (Celilia's Son); Vicki Ross-Norris (Cecilia's Nurse); Frankie Faison (Professor Martin); Peter Klemens (Bartender); Rev. Donald R. Wilson (Reverend at Wedding); Ron Jaye (Good Morning Columbus Host); Courtney Chase (Lisa); Ryan Kelley (Mo); Katie Cardille-Rogal (Papergirl); Willard Scott (Himself); Bernard Canepari (Judith's Lawyer); Dorothy Silver (Housekeeper); Rosa Gamarra-Thomson (Cleaning Lady); Gerry Becker (Dr. Minceberg); Jeffrey Howell (Surgeon); Nelle Stokes (Recovery Room Nurse); Mary Marini (O.R. Nurse); Robert Gardner (Assisting Surgeon); Robert Dyga (Profusionist)

A boxoffice dud that deserved to do better, ROOMMATES is the sentimental story of the exceptional bond between an orphaned boy and his elderly grandfather. The story spans thirty-two years and is disjointed at times, but the larger-than-life performance of Peter Falk as Rocky compensates for the movie's structural shortcomings.

Orphaned at age five, Michael Holeczek (D.B. Sweeney) is taken in by his 75-year-old grandfather, Rocky (Falk). Rocky is a Polish immigrant who works as a baker and has not let his advancing age slow him down. Rocky instills in his grandson his Old World values and work ethic. Twenty years later, the building Rocky has lived in for over 50 years is condemned. Michael, now an intern, invites his grandfather to move in with him. Sharing Michael's cramped basement apartment, the roommates quickly get on each other's nerves. Their biggest source of contention is Beth (Julianne Moore), Michael's blue-blooded girlfriend. After catching the pair trysting on the pullout sofa, Rocky decides that Beth is not a "nice" girl. Michael suspects Rocky is jealous of Beth for coming between them. Still, when Michael gets cold feet about commitment, it is Rocky who engineers his proposal to Beth.

Michael and Beth have two children, while Rocky remains active as a baker until well past his 100th birthday. When Beth suddenly dies in a car accident, it is Rocky who takes over, caring for his grandson and great-grandchildren and keeping the family together in the face of a custody battle with Beth's snooty mother (Ellen Burstyn). Only after Michael's life is back on track does 107-year-old Rocky finally loosen his grip on life.

ROOMMATES is a character-driven piece and Falk as Rocky is in the driver's seat. His powerhouse performance transforms what could have been a marginal film into a solidly entertaining one. Aided by Greg Cannom's convincing makeup design, Falk is surprisingly believable as a 107-year-old codger too busy caring for his family to die. Rocky exasperates those around him while still commanding their respect and winning their love. From the tip of his liver-spotted head to the heels of his well-worn shoes, Falk inhabits Rocky with dignity and authenticity. He doesn't do old geezer shtick—he is the genuine article. Playing in Falk's shadow, Sweeney doesn't get much of a chance to shine, but his is a likeable, albeit bland, character. Moore gives a spirited performance as Beth, whose battle to win Rocky's affections provides some of the film's choicest moments. Burstyn plays the controlling mother-in-law to perfection.

The film loses steam when it changes courses midway. When the focal point shifts from Rocky to Michael, and a series of dramatic events whipsaw emotions, the film begins to ramble and feel overlong. It regains its verve near the end, when cagey Rocky reclaims center stage, taking on Judith and preventing her from splitting up the family.

ROOMMATES is based on Max Apple's autobiographical novel of the same name and was inspired by the author's relationship with his own grandfather. Apple adapted the screenplay with Stephen Metcalfe. At the behest of the producers, Apple changed Rocky's ethnic background (he's a Lithuanian Jew in the book, a Polish Catholic in the film) and other story elements. The homogenized product lacks much of the book's whimsy but still has its heart. (*Violence, sexual situations, profanity.*) — B.R.

d, Peter Yates; p, Ted Field, Scott Kroopf, Robert W. Cort; exec p, Adam Leipzig, Ira Halberstadt; assoc p, Max Apple; w, Max Apple, Stephen Metcalfe (from the novel by Max Apple); ph, Mike Southon; ed, John Tintori; m, Elmer Bernstein; prod d, Dan Bishop; art d, Jefferson Sage; set d, Dianna Freas; sound, Douglas Axtell (mixer); casting, Linda Lowy; cos, Linda Dona-

hue; makeup, Barbie Palmer, Greg Cannom, Bob Laden, Coleen Callaghan; stunts, John C. Meier

AAN Best Makeup: Greg Cannom, Bob Laden, Colleen Callaghan

Drama/Comedy (PR: A MPAA: PG)

ROSWELL: THE U.F.O. COVER-UP ★★★
(U.S.) 91m Citadel Entertainment; Showtime Entertainment; Viacom Pictures ~ Republic Pictures Home Video c
(AKA: ROSWELL)

Kyle MacLachlan *(Major Jesse Marcel)*; Martin Sheen *(Townsend)*; Dwight Yoakam *(Mac Brazel)*; Xander Berkeley *(Sherman Carson)*; Bob Gunton *(Frank Joyce)*; Kim Greist *(Vy Marcel)*; Peter MacNicol *(Lewis Rickett)*; John M. Jackson *(Colonel "Butch" Blanchard)*; Charles Martin *(Smith)*; Nick Searcy *(Mortician)*; J.D. Daniels *(Jessie Marcel, Jr.)*; Eugene Roche *(James Forrestal)*; Lisa Waltz *(Janet Foss)*; Charles Hallahan *(Older Pilot MacIntire)*; Ray McKinnon *(Deputy Joe Pritchard)*; Doug Wert *(Older Jessie Marcel, Jr.)*; David Selburg *(Station Manager)*; Doug McCurry *(Arresting MP)*; Charles M. Kistler *(Interrogator No. 1)*; Daiton Rutowski *(Interrogator No. 2)*; Matthew Faison *(General Ramey)*; John Hostetter *(Colonel Thomas DuBose)*; Michael Bofshever *(Irving Newton)*; Jonathan Mincks *(Younger Stanton)*; F. William Parker *(Older Stanton)*; Peter Radon *(Melvin Brown)*; Gary Bullock *(Eavesdropper)*; Jim Hayne *(Harris)*; Mark Phelan *(Gate Guard)*; Steve Lanza *(Outside Doctor)*; Arthur Kopit *(Inside Doctor)*; Michael Strasser *(Hospital MP)*; Don Fischer *(Outdoor MP)*; Denice Marcel *(Waitress)*; John Mahon *(Red Hat Vet)*; Stanley Grover *(Straw Hat Vet)*; Warren Munson *(Yellow Hat Vet)*; Hansford Rowe *(Chaplain)*; Richard Fancy *(Doctor)*; Paul Davids *(Photographer)*; Philip Baker Hall *(Roswell General)*; Larry Dobkin *(General)*; Edward Penn *(Civilian Advisor)*; Arthur Hiller *(Scientist No. 1)*; Brian Carpenter *(Scientist No. 2)*; George Pentecost *(Civilian Advisor)*; Bruce Gray *(Admiral)*; Frank A. Roys *(General)*; Vernon Blackman *(Aide)*; Brian Cousins *(Medical Officer)*; James G. MacDonald *(Area 51 Officer)*; Robert Harvey *(Admiral)*; Ken Kimmons *(James Harris)*; Cynthia Allison *(TV Commentator at Roswell Inn)*; Hoke Howell *(Bar Vet at Roswell Inn)*; Bruce Ed Morrow *(General at Roswell Inn)*; William Edwards *(Alien Clown at Roswell Inn)*; Layne Beamer *(Soldier)*; Max Trumpower *(Gate Guard)*; Mik Scriba *(Air Mechanic)*; Matt Landers *(Lieutenant Walter Haut)*; George Gray, III *(Deputy)*; Stephen C. Foster *(Gate MP)*; Dave Adams *(Provost Marshal)*; Bill Cook *(Jeep Driver)*; J.W. "Corky" Fornof *(Pilot)*; Charles Beck *(Pilot)*; Randy Gagne *(Pilot)*

With the success of such television programs as "The X-Files" and "Sightings", it's not surprising that films are following suit with "true-life" offerings like FIRE IN THE SKY and ROSWELL, a made-for-cable drama based on the same events that inspired the 1980 cult film HANGAR 18.

Major Jesse Marcel (Kyle MacLachlan) sees a 1977 military reunion in Roswell, New Mexico, as an opportunity to clear his name. Thirty years earlier, Marcel had been the point man in an investigation into the possible crash landing of a flying saucer—a crash that left a crater littered with silvery, foil-like debris that displayed reconstructive properties unlike any earthly alloy. Soon, however, Major Marcel is picked to be the fall guy, covering the incident with an army-issued story about a fallen weather balloon. Three decades later, Marcel—who has been stricken with terminal lung cancer—interrogates former comrades about what, if anything, they saw or heard. He learns of a second, much larger crash site, strewn with several dead aliens—and one still living. In the end, a mysterious man calling himself Townsend (Martin Sheen) reveals what really happened in Roswell, and after.

Drawn from a book documenting "actual" events in 1947, ROSWELL could have easily been a cinematic version of the *Weekly World News*. However, director and co-story-writer Jeremy Paul Kagan (BIG MAN ON CAMPUS, DESCENDING ANGEL) carefully spins the story around Marcel's investigation rather than simply relying upon the spooky details. Only in the end, when Townsend (who may or may not be an Army mouthpiece) relates how the government systematically suppressed information on alien visitors, does the film slip into "Sightings"-like dramatization—and even then, it feels more like an episode of "In Search Of" as directed by Oliver Stone. Kyle MacLachlan, who otherwise looks about eighteen years old, convincingly portrays the maligned and embittered old major looking at his last chance for vindication. *(Profanity.)* — B.T.

d, Jeremy Paul Kagan; p, Ilene Kahn, Jeremy Kagan; exec p, Paul Davids, David R. Ginsberg; co-p, Peter McIntosh; w, Paul Davids, Jeremy Kagan, Arthur Kopit (from a story by Paul Davids, Jeremy Kagan, and Arthur Kopit, based on the book *U.F.O. Crash at Roswell* by Kevin D. Randle and Donald R. Schmidt); ph, Steven Poster; ed, David Holden, Bill Yahraus; m, Elliot Goldenthal; prod d, Michael Z. Hanan, Gene Warren, Jr.; art d, Charles Lagola; set d, David Koneff; sound, Richard G. Schexneyder (mixer); fx, Randy Lee Tarum, Gene Warren, Jr., Fantasy II Film Effects; casting, Amanda Mackey, Cathy Sandrich; cos, May Routh; makeup, Julie Purcell, Manilo Rocchetti; stunts, Seth Arnett, Jim McConnell

Science Fiction/Docudrama   **(PR: C   MPAA: PG-13)**

ROY COHN/JACK SMITH   ★★
(U.S.) 90m Good Machine; Pomodori Foundation; The Laboratory for Icon & Idiom ~ Strand Releasing c

Ron Vawter *(Roy Cohn/Jack Smith)*; Coco McPherson *(Chica)*

Two outrageous one-man shows performed by the late actor Ron Vawter are here transferred to film by director Jill Godmilow. The footage was then edited to provide interwoven portraits of two flamboyant, but very different, mid-20th Century figures—lawyer Roy Cohn and pioneer filmmaker Jack Smith. But there are risks in filming theatrical stagings, and this becomes quickly apparent in ROY COHN/JACK SMITH, an intriguing, but frequently static and ultimately unsatisfying record of live performance.

Vawter captures the fabulous subterfuges of celebrity mouthpiece Roy Cohn and underground film artist Jack Smith, both of whom were apparently consumed by fantasy in their private and public lives. Smith was a relatively benign innovator, but Cohn propelled himself into the public political arena at the infamous McCarthy anti-communist hearings in the early 1950's. Throughout his career, he proved himself capable of doing serious harm.

In director Godmilow's unadorned filming, Vawter attempts to capture the essence of both men. For Cohn, Vawter draws from the lawyer's many speeches, bringing the material together by having him address an imaginary banquet on topics including politics and family values. At one point, Cohn coolly stresses how important it was for the accused spy and mother of two Ethel Rosenberg to be executed because, emotionally, she was stronger than her mild-mannered husband Julius. This is wholly in keeping with Cohn's character. Then, without missing a beat, he bemoans his own single status, lisping on about how the right woman has yet to come into his life, even asking if there might be an interested party in the audience. This type of hypocrisy

pervaded Cohn's life until his death from AIDS in 1993. (The illness also claimed the lives of both Smith and Vawter.)

Intercut with the Cohn material is Vawter's interpretation of Smith's autobiographical performance piece, a monologue which Smith often performed himself. In tacky Egyptian drag and draped across a chaise longue surrounded by mementos from his life and career, Smith chatters incessantly about this and that while his eclectic collection of personal snapshots flash on an upstage scrim behind him.

Smith, who became famous for his early underground film innovations such as FLAMING CREATURES (1962), inspired a generation of rising independents. Such a seminal figure deserves to have his story told in context, which is sorely missing here. Cohn, a ruthless pit bull for whoever could afford his services, was motivated by greed and his own self-aggrandizement; he was more infamous than respected and few mourned his passing.

This filmed stage performance tends to dilute the material's potential and overall impact, though director Godmilow tries to open the proceedings up by using three cameras and shooting audience reaction. Somehow, rather than distracting viewers from an overall claustrophobia that pervades the piece, this contributes to it. Such diverse and driven figures, contemporaries who functioned in separate spheres that may have occasionally intersected, should provide the opportunity for more fascinating portraits. Director Godmilow, who is perhaps best known for the documentary ANTONIA: PORTRAIT OF A WOMAN (1973), seems not only restricted by the material but by the manner in which she chose to approach it.

ROY COHN/JACK SMITH is too often tedious and flat, and a challenge to the casual viewer. Ultimately the filming is valuable as a record of two performances, made even more so by the two controversial personalities it depicts, and the gifted performer who brought unique interpretations to their lives. *(Adult situations.)* — O.L.

d, Jill Godmilow; p, Ted Hope, James Schamus, Marianne Weems; exec p, Jonathan Demme; assoc p, Anthony Bergman, Mary Jane Skalski; w, Ron Vawter (based on the plays *Roy Cohn* by Gary Indiana and *What's Underground About Marshmallows* by Jack Smith); ph, Ellen Kuras; ed, Merril Stern; m, Michael Sahl; prod d, Gregory Mehrten, Clay Shirky, Marianne Weems; sound, Steve Kazmierski (mixer), Chat Gunter (mixer), Lawrence Loewinger (mixer); cos, Ellen McCartney; makeup, Kathryn Nixon

Biography/Documentary/Drama   **(PR: C   MPAA: NR)**

RUN OF THE COUNTRY, THE   ★★½
(U.S./U.K.) 109m Channel Four Films; Castle Rock; One Two Nine Productions ~ Columbia c

Albert Finney *(Father)*; Matt Keeslar *(Danny)*; Victoria Smurfit *(Annagh)*; Anthony Brophy *(Prunty)*; David Kelly *(Father Gaynor)*; Dearbhla Molloy *(Mother)*; Carole Nimmons *(Mrs. Prunty)*; Vinnie McCabe *(Annagh's Uncle)*; Trevor Clark *(Barman)*; Kevin Murphy *(Big Man)*; Michael O'Reilly *(Bouncer Patterson)*; P.J. Brady *(Carolan)*; Miche Doherty *(Dolan)*; Declan Mulholland *(Farmer)*; Dawn Bradfield *(Daphne)*; Paddy McGuiness *(Lookout)*; Christy Mahon *(Man)*; Pat Kinevane *(McQuade)*; Joe Hanley *(Monkey)*; Maureen Dow *(Mrs. McKenna)*; Eileen Ward *(Mrs. Lee)*; Thoams Lappin *(Rennicks)*; Robin Hines *(Soldier)*; Antoine Byrne *(Wench)*; Seamus O'Rourke *(Man at Annagh's)*; Joan Sheehy *(Widdy McGinn)*; Noel Smith *(Goblin Gilmour)*; Hugh B. O'Brien *(Danny's Uncle)*; Aine Ni Mhuiri *(Danny's Aunt)*; Sissy Connolly *(Elderly Lady)*; Mary Reilly *(Woman)*; The Titanic Cinq *(Themselves)*

While THE RUN OF THE COUNTRY succeeds in creating a strong sense of place and culture, this coming-of-age tale of love and loss in rural Ireland suffers from an identity crisis, unable to decide whether it is a lighthearted romance or a full-blown tragedy.

Danny (Matt Keeslar) has just finished high school, and is unsure of whether to go to University, when his mother dies. He is left alone with his father (Albert Finney), a bitter, gruff police sergeant. Danny doesn't take well to being both son and homemaker, and he gravitates toward his older friend Prunty (Anthony Brophy). Danny, whose upbringing was sheltered and simple, enjoys his time with this crude, oversexed, and adventurous friend, and begins to become more worldly and outgoing.

Danny meets Annagh Lee (Victoria Smurfit), who lives just over the border in Northern Ireland, and soon they fall in love. Danny's father wants to send him to America, and discourages the romance. When Annagh becomes pregnant, her family forbids her to see Danny. She disobeys, and the couple try to raise money for an abortion. Annagh has a miscarriage, and her family prepares to send her away. Shortly afterwards, Prunty dies in a tractor accident. Distraught, Danny goes to see Annagh, where he is jumped by members of her family, who tar and feather him for his misdeeds. Danny goes home in shame. He reconciles with his father, who still wants him to go to America, but he chooses to go to Dublin instead, to attend University.

Shane Connaughton wrote the screenplay, based on his novel, and it is obvious that the material was too close to him to be pruned of unnecessary scenes. After a mild beginning, the story rapidly moves into tragedy; however, the romance, which should be the heart of the story, doesn't begin until the film is half over. Moreover, the film's editing is not particularly selective, a political subplot is clumsy and confusing, and a scene where Danny begins to develop his father's worst tendencies is forced and unconvincing.

Finney's performance is strong despite a somewhat one-dimensional role, and Brophy, as Prunty, is even better. His scenes—especially a hilarious one where he convinces Danny to impersonate a priest—are full of life and are the highlight of the film. The film's marketers wishfully tout Keeslar and Smurfit as future stars. She is appropriately winsome and strong, but he is too stiff and uncomfortable to give Danny the hero status Connaughton and director Peter Yates desire (although his Irish accent, especially for an American, is excellent).

Despite the awkward pace, Yates' direction is outstanding. He has a wonderful grasp of how the human face registers emotions, and has an equally good feel for the beauty of the rural Irish landscape. The community that is created in this film is distinct and memorable—it's too bad, though, that the story isn't up to the quality of the visuals. (*Violence, nudity, sexual situations, adult situations, profanity.*) — A.M.

d, Peter Yates; p, Peter Yates, Ruth Boswell; exec p, Nigel Wooll, Morgan O'Sullivan; w, Shane Connaughton (based on his book); ph, Mike Southon; ed, Paul Hodgson; m, Cynthia Millar; art d, Dave Wilson; set d, Mark Geraghty; sound, Ken Weston (mixer); fx, Ian Wingrove; casting, Hubbard Casting; stunts, Eddie Stacey

Drama/Romance   **(PR: C   MPAA: R)**

SABRINA ★★½

(U.S.) 127m Scott Rudin Productions;
Mirage Enterprises; Sandollar Productions;
Constellation Films ~ Paramount c

Harrison Ford *(Linus Larrabee)*; Julia Ormond *(Sabrina Fairchild)*; Greg Kinnear *(David Larrabee)*; Nancy Marchand *(Maude Larrabee)*; John Wood *(Fairchild)*; Richard Crenna *(Patrick Tyson)*; Angie Dickinson *(Ingrid Tyson)*; Lauren Holly *(Elizabeth Tyson)*; Dana Ivey *(Mack)*; Miriam Colon *(Rosa)*; Elizabeth Franz *(Joanna)*; Fanny Ardant *(Irene)*; Valeria Lemercier *(Martine)*; Patrick Bruel *(Louis)*; Becky Ann Baker *(Linda)*; Paul Giamatti *(Scott)*; John C. Vennema *(Ron)*; Gregory Chase *(Ron)*; Margo Martindale *(Nurse)*; J. Smith-Cameron *(Carol)*; Christine Luneau-Lipton *(Ticket Taker)*; Michael Dees *(Singer at Larrabee Party)*; Denis Holmes *(Butler)*; Jo-Jo Lowe *(Red Head)*; Ira Wheeler *(Bartender)*; Philippa Cooper *(Kelly)*; Ayako *(India)*; Francois Genty *(Make-up Assistant)*; Guillaume Gallienne *(Assistant)*; Ines Sastre; Phina; Helena Katia; Andrea Behalikova; Jennifer Herrera; Kristina Kumlin; Eva Linderholm; Stefano Tartini *(Models)*; Carmen Chaplin; Micheline Van de Velde; Joanna Rhodes; Alan Boone; Patrick Forster Delmas; Kentaro Matsuo *(Paris Friends)*; J.B. Benn *(Magician)*; Peter McKernan *(Helicopter Pilot)*; Ed Connelly *(Gulf Stream Pilot)*; Ronald Schwary *(Sheik)*; Kenneth A. MacDonald *(Beggar)*; Alvin Lum *(Tyson Butler)*; Siching Song *(Mother in Hospital)*; Phil Nee *(Father in Hospital)*; Randy Becker *(Trainer)*; Susan Browning *(Secretary)*; Saikat Mondal *(Moroccan Waiter)*; Peter Parks *(Senator)*; La Compagnie Jolie Mome *(Street Singers)*

Billy Wilder buffs muttered "Sacrilege!" when director Sidney Pollack and screenwriter Barbara Benedek tackled SABRINA, his 1954 film of playwright Ernest Lehman's willfully slight Cinderella story. But surprisingly enough, the remake takes the flimsy premise in a new direction, with generally positive results.

This is nominally a SABRINA for the '90s: gone is the family patriarch—now Maude Larrabee (Nancy Marchand) is in charge of the vast family fortune and Long Island Xanadu. But it's still managed by workaholic son Linus (Harrison Ford), little brother David (Greg Kinnear) still chases willowy debutantes, and lovestruck Sabrina (Julia Ormond)—the humble chauffeur's daughter—still watches the cavorting of the very rich from an arboreal perch. David's fiancee, Elizabeth Tyson (Lauren Holly), is a sop to feminism: she's a dedicated physician and only incidentally the daughter of an electronics tycoon with whom Linus seeks a business merger.

The dowdy teenage Sabrina (as convincingly plain as Audrey Hepburn before her) returns from two years working for *Vogue* in Paris, transformed into a ravishing beauty. David doesn't recognize her, but when he learns her identity—and that she's nursed a passionate crush on him since the age of nine—he falls under her spell and prepares to call off the wedding. Linus quickly takes charge: while David convalesces from an embarrassing run-in with a champagne flute, Linus cunningly courts Sabrina himself. His intentions could hardly be more callous: to rescue his deal with Elizabeth's father and, as a bonus, his brother from an impulsive affair.

Linus professes loneliness and dissatisfaction with his success; Sabrina regards him with an amused curiosity, tinged with sympathy. But eventually she begins to succumb to his subtle ploys, and her feelings about both brothers become increasingly ambivalent. When Linus suggests that they go to Paris together, she is genuinely torn.

Forced to choose, she recognizes her infatuation with David as the schoolgirl crush it is. But the calculating Linus has a last minute attack of decency and can't go through with his plan to abandon Sabrina in Paris with a broken heart and $50,000 in the bank. He comes clean and offers the money by way of an apology. Sabrina leaves, shaken but dignified, taking only the ticket to Orly. A reformed David pulls off a clever boardroom coup that not only rescues Linus' merger but resolves their sibling rivalry and convinces Linus of his love for Sabrina. Linus jumps aboard the Concorde to beat Sabrina's plane to Paris so he can meet her for a painful, heartfelt reconciliation.

Wilder's film comes off badly in several key respects: it's cynical and smugly glib, toying casually with suicide and the exploitative manipulation of various characters by others. Benedek makes a number of interesting revisions in Lehman's story, including her rethinking of Sabrina herself: the dizzy, child-like waif of Wilder's film becomes an intelligent, articulate woman who regards Linus with more suspicion than Hepburn's character could muster. Linus' scheming takes on a distinctly unpleasant edge with the sexual coyness of the '50s stripped away, and Benedek's digs at slash-and-burn capitalism hit the mark. How unfortunate, then, that she also softens the earlier film's acute class consciousness by making Sabrina's father as rich (and arguably as amoral) as any Larrabee: he's been trading stocks based on the conversation he overhears while chauffeuring. Overall, the film's humor is gentler, and Angie Dickinson's cameo as Elizabeth's mother—a stewardess turned trophy wife—is a howl.

Benedek and Pollack raise the emotional stakes, and the trade-off they make is that halfway through the film it ceases to be a comedy. Kinnear—erstwhile host of cable TV's "Talk Soup"—makes a stunning debut, utterly out-charming the slick playboy William Holden played in the original. Ford tosses off his patented tough-but-vulnerable routine without difficulty. It's unfair to compare Ormond to Hepburn—Ormond is an actress, Hepburn was a Movie Star—but suffice it to say that Ormond carries the new SABRINA's emotional weight.

No effort or expense was spared in the making of the new SABRINA, which cost more than $50 million and barely broke even at the box office. On many levels it's an improvement over both Lehman's play and Wilder's jaundiced vision, but ultimately it fails to convince. *(Profanity.)* — R.S.

d, Sydney Pollack; p, Scott Rudin, Sydney Pollack; exec p, Ronald Schwary, Lindsay Doran; w, Barbara Benedek, David Rayfiel (based on the 1954 screenplay by Billy Wilder, Samuel Taylor, and Ernest Lehman, from the play *Sabrina Fair* by Samuel Taylor); ph, Giuseppe Rotunno; ed, Frederic Steinkamp; m, John Williams; prod d, Brian Morris; art d, John Kasarda; set d, George DeTitta, Jr., Amy Marshall; sound, Danny Michael (mixer); fx, Industrial Light & Magic; casting, David Rubin; cos, Ann Roth; makeup, Bernadette Mazur

AAN Best Musical or Comedy Score: John Williams; *AAN Best Original Song:* John Williams, Alan and Marilyn Bergman "Moonlight"

Comedy/Romance (PR: A MPAA: PG)

SAFE ★★★★

(U.S.) 123m American Playhouse Theatrical Films; Chemical Films; Good Machine; Kardana; Channel Four Films ~ Sony Pictures Classics c

Julianne Moore *(Carol White)*; Peter Friedman *(Peter)*; Xander Berkeley *(Greg White)*; Susan Norman *(Linda)*; Kate McGregory Stewart *(Claire)*; Mary Carver *(Nell)*; Steven Gilborn *(Dr.*

Hubbard); April Grace *(Susan)*; Peter Crombie *(Dr. Reynolds)*; Ronnie Farer *(Barbara)*; Lorna Scott *(Marilyn)*; James LeGros *(Chris)*; Jessica Harper *(Joyce)*; Rio Hackford *(Lester)*; Brandon Cruz *(Steve)*; Janel Moloney *(Hairdresser)*; Peter Friedman *(Peter Dunning)*; Jodie Markell *(Anita)*; Martha Velez-Johnson *(Fulvia)*; Chauncey Leopardi *(Rory)*; Saachiko *(Dry Cleaners Manager)*; Tim Gardner *(Department Store Dispatcher)*; Wendy Haynes *(Waitress)*; Alan Wasserman *(Client)*; Jean Pflieger *(Client's Wife)*; Brendan Dolan *(Patrolman)*; John Apicella *(Psychiatrist)*; Dana Anderson *(Lynn)*; Wendy Gayle *(Baby Shower Mother)*; Cassy Friel *(Baby Shower Child)*; Frank Dent *(Video Narrator)*; Sarah Davis *(Sarah)*; Beth Grant *(Becky—Auditorium Speaker)*; Jo Wilkinson *(Listener No. 1)*; Gerrielani Miyazaki *(Listener No. 2)*; Edith Meeks *(Patient No. 1)*; Francesca Roberts *(Patient No. 2)*; Elinor O. Caplan *(Patient No. 3)*; Dean Norris *(Mover)*; Julie Burgess *(Aerobics Instructor)*; Joe Comando *(Exterminator)*; Ravi Achar *(Wrenwood Instructor)*; Tricia Dong *(Wrenwood Patient)*; James Lyons *(Cab Driver)*; Eleanor Graham *(Singer)*; Mitch Greenhill *(Accompanist)*

SAFE tells the story of a California housewife's mysterious physical deterioration with an ironic distance that is both humorous and chilling.

SAFE opens in the sterile landscape of San Fernando Valley, where suburban homemaker Carol White (Julianne Moore) slowly discovers that she's allergic to her new sofa. Next, she has a terrifying choking attack caused by exhaust fumes on the freeway. Both Carol's husband Greg (Xander Berkeley) and her physician, Dr. Hubbard (Stephen Gilborn), dismiss the malady as emotional. But Carol continues to experience adverse reactions to everything from her hairspray to the food she eats.

On her own, Carol enters an experimental program for environmental illnesses. She gets medical treatment for the toxic substances in the atmosphere, but her condition continues to worsen. Finally, Carol moves out of her home and into chemical-free community Wrenwood, in Albuquerque, New Mexico. The wellness center offers Carol both medical aid *and* spiritual fulfillment, but her physical decline continues. Neither Wrenwood's inspirational leader, Peter Dunning (Peter Friedman), nor attentive fellow patient Chris (James LeGros) raises her hopes of recovery. Carol ends up living in an isolated igloo, a bleak, uncertain future in store.

SAFE sounds like a disease-of-the-week movie, but it transforms the formulaic material into something original and spellbinding. Much as Douglas Sirk and Rainer Werner Fassbinder reimagined the conventions of melodrama, director Todd Haynes—who was indeed inspired by a TV movie, THE BOY IN THE PLASTIC BUBBLE—takes SAFE from its soap opera potential to unlimited, open-ended possibilities. Haynes—whose SUPERSTAR: THE KAREN CARPENTER STORY (1987) starred Barbie dolls—subverts SAFE's touchy-feely subject matter through viciously satirical writing that's politically incorrect, but essentially above criticism by virtue of its misanthropic evenhandedness. The film's sole African-American woman is glib and theatrical; the person with AIDS—Wrenwood's guru—is venal and unctuous; and just about everyone else is self-absorbed and unappealing. Even Carol is more pathetic than sympathetic, so nondescript that she's defined by her suffering. SAFE's second half provoked more controversy than its first, because it appeared to mock New Age healers and the victims of disease. But SAFE suggests that a larger societal malaise is more at fault than any of its characters.

Haynes carefully keeps viewers at arm's length through the cool detachment of his technique. The film's extended opening shot shows a car ride from Carol's point-of-view before Carol has been introduced, while the subsequent long shots of Carol in

her large but suffocating house make her seem remote and unapproachable. Still later, Carol addresses the camera directly, challenging viewers to confront the social and spiritual malaise of their own lives. Julianne Moore's performance strikes a brilliant balance between physical fragility and bourgeois vacuity. Moore is so good at conveying Carol's failure to understand that there are no safe places, it becomes painful to watch her descent.

SAFE's form and content complement each other throughout. Cinematographer Alex Nepomniaschy's beautiful tableaux-like long takes hint at the silent, unseen poison that infiltrates the atmosphere. Ed Tomney's haunting New Age-style score also suggests the dark elements beneath the bright exteriors, especially when juxtaposed with Haynes's clever selection of sunny pop tunes. *(Sexual situations, adult situations, profanity.)* — E.M.

d, Todd Haynes; p, Christine Vachon, Lauren Zalaznick; exec p, James Schamus, Lindsay Law, Ted Hope; assoc p, Ernest Kerns; w, Todd Haynes; ph, Alex Nepomniaschy; ed, James Lyons; m, Ed Tomney; prod d, David Bomba; art d, Anthony Stabley; set d, Mary E. Gullickson; sound, Neil Danziger (mixer); casting, Jakki Fink; cos, Nancy Steiner; makeup, Deborah Larson, Chris Laurence

Drama (PR: C   MPAA: R)

SAFE PASSAGE ★★
(U.S.) 98m Juno Pix, Inc.; Katja Motion Picture Group; Pacific Western ~ New Line c

Susan Sarandon *(Mag Singer)*; Sam Shepard *(Patrick Singer)*; Robert Sean Leonard *(Alfred Singer)*; Sean Astin *(Izzy Singer)*; Marcia Gay Harden *(Cynthia)*; Nick Stahl *(Simon Singer)*; Jason London *(Gideon Singer)*; Matt Keeslar *(Percival Singer)*; Philip Arthur Ross *(Merle Singer)*; Steven Robert Ross *(Darren Singer)*; Philip Bosco *(Mort)*; Priscilla Reeves *(Mrs. Silverman)*; Joe Lisi *(Dog Owner)*; Marvin Scott; Bill Boggs; Kathryn Kinley; Cindy Hom *(Newspeople)*; Christopher Wynkoop *(Evangelist)*; Jesse Lee *(Percival, Age 9 and 10)*; Jordan Clarke *(Coach)*; Jeffrey DeMunn *(Doctor)*; Rutanya Alda *(Beth)*; Kazuya Takahashi *(TV News Cameraman)*; Lisa Castleman *(TV Reporter)*; Sally Nacker *(TV Reporter)*; Ralph Howard *(Radio Reporter)*; David Leary *(Voice of Marine Spokesman)*; Ralph Byers *(Voice of Sinai Reporter)*

"Safe" is the key word here. In the blandest possible terms, SAFE PASSAGE tells the story of a mother (Susan Sarandon) who has seven devoted sons, an irresponsible husband (Sam Shepard) and scary dreams.

To many, Mag Singer (Sarandon) seems a Super Mom. But she's riddled with doubt, stemming from a sense of frustration and the pressures of caring for a large family. Her husband Patrick (Sam Shepard), an eccentric inventor, is subject to sudden, terrifying fits of blindness. She herself yearns for something more fulfilling than the exclusive motherhood she has known for years, and is apprehensive about the Civil Service test she is about to take.

Her sons are the handful you'd imagine. Alfred (Robert Sean Leonard), the eldest, is worryingly uptight and involved with an older woman (Marcia Gay Harden) with children of her own. Gideon (Jason London), a track star, is a terminal victim of sibling rivalry, who has always railed against Patrick's demanding expectations. Bespectacled, bearded Izzy (Sean Astin) is a teddy-bearish veterinarian. The youngest, Simon (Nick Stahl), feels smothered and has taken to wearing dreadlocks. There's also a set of indistinguishable twins (Philip and Steven Ross). Finally, there's Percival (Matt Keeslar), a serviceman who has been reported missing in action on the Sinai Peninsula. The whole family unites for an excruciating vigil before the television, awaiting the latest news bulletins. During this wary time, conflicts are resolved, Patrick's blindness is miraculously cured, the garage gets cleaned, and all the Singers get the chance to show the strong stuff they're made of.

Director Robert Allan Ackerman comes from the stage; this much is excruciatingly obvious. His shoddily shot film has a 1950s "Philco Playhouse" feel to it, with its few basic sets (the Singer home or car), celebration of WASP family values (that Jewish-sounding surname notwithstanding), and endless, expository dialogues between the characters. Deena Goldstone's trite script is equal parts melodrama, pat resolution, and attempted heart-warming sentimentality. The Singer boys are all basically the same: nice, white-bread and just a tad confused. For variety's sake, couldn't one of them have been gay or a drug abuser or suicidal or *something*?

Under these enervated circumstances, it's a small wonder that Sarandon manages to give any kind of performance and emerge with her dignity intact. The actress's innate good humor is a boon here. She gives full, amusingly loquacious due to the film's single funny moment, a pot-smoking episode with Percival. *(Adult situations, substance abuse, profanity.)* — D.N.

d, Robert Allan Ackerman; p, Gale Anne Hurd; exec p, David Gale, Betsy Beers, Ruth Vitale; w, Deena Goldstone (based on the novel by Ellyn Bache); ph, Ralf Bode; ed, Rick Shaine; m, Mark Isham; prod d, Dan Bishop; art d, Jefferson Sage; set d, Dianna Freas; sound, Tod A. Maitland (mixer), Robin Johnston (recordist); fx, Steve Kirshoff; casting, Pam Dixon Mickelson; cos, Renee Ehrlich Kalfus; makeup, Marilyn Carbone, Michal Bigger; stunts, Glory Fioramonti, Jery Hewit

Drama (PR: C MPAA: PG-13)

SCANNER COP II: VOLKIN'S REVENGE
(SEE: SCANNERS: THE SHOWDOWN)

SCANNERS: THE SHOWDOWN ★★
(U.S.) 95m Image Organization; Showdown Productions, Inc. ~ Republic Pictures Home Video c
(AKA: SCANNER COP II: VOLKIN'S REVENGE)

Daniel Quinn *(Sam Staziak)*; Patrick Kilpatrick *(Karl Volkin)*; Khrystyne Haje *(Carrie Goodart)*; Stephen Mendel *(Jim Mullins)*; Robert Forster *(Capt. Jack Bitters)*; Brenda Swanson *(Glory Avionis)*; Jerry Potter *(Sheriff)*; Jewel Shepherd *(Nurse)*; Tony Fasce *(Pickpocket Jones)*; Terrie Snell *(Washer Woman)*; Jim Blumetti *(Old Cop)*; Eric Chambers *(Young Cop)*; Evan MacKenzie *(J.J.)*; Barbara Tarbuck *(Rachel Staziack)*; Eugene Glazer *(Institute Director)*; Allan Kolman *(Country Doctor)*; Robert Knott *(Deputy)*; Julian Neil *(Kidnapper Leader)*; Frank Uzzolio *(Billy)*; Steve Wilcox *(Craig Volkin)*; Yvette Harding *(Teenage Girl)*; John Walter Davis *(Security Guard)*; Richard Epper *(Janitor)*; Patrick J. Statham *(Forklift Driver)*; Kurt Bryant *(Foreman)*; Richard Assad *(Hotel Clerk)*; Monika Ramirez *(Hotel Maid)*; Kim Delgado *(Sgt. Collins)*; Lisa Comshaw *(Denise)*; Dan Weiss *(Denise's Husband)*; Ellen Dubin *(Cop 1)*; Marlon Archey *(Cop 2)*; Al Goto *(Lobby Cop 1)*; Carl Ciarfalio *(Lobby Cop 2)*; Nicholas Gunn *(Scanned Senior Citizen)*; Aaron Lustig *(Dr. Gordon)*; Elvin Havard *(Orderly)*; Michael Sloane *(Wildman Inmate)*; Brett Jones *(Institute Guard)*; Katie Wagner *(Reporter)*; Lee Mathis *(Attendant)*; Patricia Place *(Old Woman)*; Kane Hodder *(Kidnapper #1)*; Rick Avery *(Kidnapper #2)*; Thomas DeWier *(Kidnapper #3)*

Filmed (and released overseas) as SCANNER COP 2: VOLKIN'S REVENGE, this head splitting film tilts back in the

direction of horror from the more action-oriented previous entry in the series.

Now a detective, scanner Sam Staziak (Daniel Quinn) has become curious about his family and enlists the help of Carrie Goodart (Khrystyne Haje), the director of the Trans Neural Resource Center. While she is looking up information on his past, she is visited by Carl Volkin (Patrick Kilpatrick), a criminal scanner whom Staziak once put away but who is now out, seeking revenge. The encounter leaves Goodart in a coma; visiting her in hospital, Staziak scans her and discovers the identity of her attacker. Volkin begins visiting other scanners around the city, draining their life forces like a psychic vampire, to build up his own in preparation for his confrontation with Staziak.

Goodart recovers and helps Staziak track Volkin, but the villain manages to consistently elude them. At the same time, Staziak and Goodart continue the search for Staziak's mother and track her to a local nursing home. But Volkin finds out and attacks her, threatening to scan her to death. Rather than submit to his psychic assault, she jumps from the roof. The outraged Staziak finally confronts Volkin, and the two engage in a hideous scanning duel. Despite Volkin's incredible powers, Staziak manages to overpower him and finishes him off in the traditional scanner way: by exploding his head.

Some of the dialogue in the film is clumsy and overly expository, which is not helped by the rather flat performance of Quinn, here clothed and coiffed to resemble Mel Gibson in the LETHAL WEAPON movies. The other performers fare better, including the persuasively malevolent Kilpatrick and the appealing Haje (though she appears a bit too young for the character, having just come off the high school sitcom "Head of the Class").

Steve Barnett's direction keeps the story moving, while Mark Sevi's script makes an admirable attempt to develop both the scanner mythology and Staziak's character. Volkin's scanning attacks unfortunately run on too long, overemphasizing John Carl Buechler's ghastly makeup effects to the point where they become gross instead of scary. (There is one bravura set piece, however, involving a female scanner melded with a screen door.) The best scan scene, in fact, is a bloodless one in which Staziak psychically compels the comatose Goodart to draw a picture of her attacker. SCANNERS: THE SHOWDOWN is entertaining exploitation fare, though one has to wonder how much further this idea (which is now five films old) can be stretched. *(Graphic violence, profanity.)* — M.G.

d, Steve Barnett; p, Pierre David; exec p, Rene Malo; assoc p, Meyer Shwarzstein, Lawrence Goebel; co-p, Noel A. Zanitsch; w, Mark Sevi (based upon characters created by David Cronenberg); ph, Thomas Jewett; ed, Patrick Rand; m, Richard Bowers; prod d, Terri Schaetzle; sound, Bruce Nazarian, Scott Wolf, Adam Joseph; fx, John Carl Buechler; casting, Cathy Henderson, Tom McSweeney; cos, Charmian Espinoza; makeup, Deborah McNulty; stunts, Kurt Bryant

Science Fiction/Horror (PR: O MPAA: R)

SCARLET LETTER, THE ★½
(U.S.) 118m Lightmotive; Allied Stars; Cinergi; Moving Pictures ~ Hollywood Pictures c

Demi Moore *(Hester Prynne)*; Gary Oldman *(Arthur Dimmesdale)*; Robert Duvall *(Roger Prynne)*; Lisa Jolliff-Andoh *(Mituba)*; Edward Hardwicke *(John Bellingham)*; Robert Prosky *(Horace Stonehall)*; Roy Dotrice *(Thomas Cheever)*; Joan Plowright *(Harriet Hibbons)*; Malcolm Storry *(Major Dunsmuir)*; Jim Bearden *(Goodman Mortimer)*; Larissa Lapchinski *(Goody Mortimer)*; Amy Wright *(Goody Gotwick)*; George Aguilar *(Johnny Sassamon)*; Tim Woodward *(Brewster*

Stonehall); Joan Gregson *(Elizabeth Cheever)*; Dana Ivey *(Meredith Stonehall)*; Bella Bruce *(Pearl)*; Diane Salinger *(Margaret Bellingham)*; Jocelyn Cunningham *(Mary Rollings)*; Francie Swift *(Sally Short)*; Sheldon Peters Wolfchild *(Moskeegee)*; Eric Schweig *(Metacomet)*; Kristen Fairlie *(Faith Stonehall)*; Sarah Campbell *(Prudence Stonehall)*; Judd Jones *(Mr. Bobbin)*; Anthony Paton *(Town Beadle)*; Marguerite McNeil *(Widow Wormser)*; Kennetch Charlette *(Tarrantine Chief)*; Deborah Tennant *(Quaker Lady)*; Kateri Walker *(Female Sachem)*; Shaun R. Clarke *(Militia Guardsman)*; Jay Carmichael *(Militia Guardsman)*; Jason Parkhill *(First Guardsman)*; Jeremy Keddy *(Drummer Boy)*; Nicholas Rice *(The Clerk)*; Len Doncheff *(Trader)*; Ashley Nolan *(Goody Hunter)*; Stephen Aderneck *(Speaking Native)*; Evelyn Francis *(Algonquin Native)*; Gary Joseph *(Native Rider)*; Stephen Micalchunk *(Passenger No. 1)*; Jeremy Akerman *(Middle Aged Passenger)*; Jodhi May *(Voice of Pearl)*

Director Roland Joffe's Hollywood rendition of THE SCARLET LETTER takes Nathaniel Hawthorne's classic work of American literature and unintentionally turns it into comedy. Actress Demi Moore—who plays the adulterous Hester Prynne—was instrumental in bringing the work to the screen, and it's hard not to see her hand in its rather heavy-handed revisions of the original story. The film bears little resemblance other than caricature to its literary precursor, and trivializes its sophisticated study of the dynamics of morality.

The stubborn and headstrong Hester Prynne (Demi Moore) arrives in the puritan Massachusetts Bay Colony to set up a homestead and await the arrival of her husband. Her independence and strength quickly make the locals uncomfortable. She soon forgets her loveless marriage and falls in love with the Reverend Arthur Dimmesdale (Gary Oldman), and when her husband is reported missing and presumed dead, they consummate their relationship. Hester becomes pregnant, giving the local authorities an excuse to imprison her as an adulteress. She is eventually released into an even greater prison, constant and unrelenting public humiliation in the form of a red letter A, for adultery, she must wear on her chest at all times. Reverend Dimmesdale—depicted here as a romantic, teary-eyed lover—heeds her wish that he keep his role in her troubles secret. He suffers silently as he witnesses her martyred shame.

Hester's husband, Roger Chillingworth (Robert Duvall), is not dead. He was captured by Indians and absorbed into their society, where he learned to enjoy the ritual and abandon of his new culture. When his animality and cruelty surpasses theirs, he is returned to the puritans. He arrives in town to witness Hester's shame and decides to join the community incognito, find out who the father of the child is, and take revenge. He gradually convinces the community that Hester and her friends are witches and should be hanged and burned at the stake. One night he scalps a man, imagining him the Reverend on his way home from a night at Hester's. The murdered man is actually a would-be rapist fleeing her home. When he discovers his mistake he takes his own life.

Hester is about to be hanged when Dimmesdale steps forward, admits the truth, and places the noose around his own neck. The mob demands his death, but a serendipitous Indian attack allows Hester, the Reverend, and their little girl Pearl (Bella Bruce) to ride off into the sunset, dropping the letter A in the dust behind their carriage wheels.

Much of the controversy surrounding this version of *The Scarlet Letter* had to do with this happy ending. In the novel, Dimmesdale dies, torn by moral guilt and by his denial of the will of God. Hester wears the letter A throughout her entire life, its meaning gradually changing to "able." But the pat Hollywood ending is only the last ridiculous guffaw in an adaptation that misses the point at every turn. Hester and her friends are depicted as early feminists, confident, forthright and free-spirited. Neither Hester nor Dimmesdale is very troubled by the central sin of adultery, and their stubborn conviction that they have in fact not committed a sin undermines the complex moral dynamics that the novel sought to elucidate by a depiction of troubled desire, guilt, shame, public and private morality, and the tragic interplay of these forces in an early developing community. *(Adult situations, sexual situations, nudity.)* — R.C.

d, Roland Joffe; p, Roland Joffe, Andrew G. Vajna; exec p, Dodi Fayed, Tova Laiter; assoc p, Jonathan Cornick; co-p, Robert Colesberry; w, Douglas Day Stewart (freely adapted from the novel by Nathaniel Hawthorne); ph, Alex Thomson; ed, Thom Noble; m, John Barry; prod d, Roy Walker; art d, Tony Wollard; set d, Rosalind Shingleton; sound, Doug Ganton (mixer), Tom Hidderly (mixer); fx, Martin Malivoire; casting, Elisabeth Leustig; cos, Gabriella Pescucci; makeup, Fabrizio Sforza; stunts, Brent Woolsey, Jeff Dashaw

Drama/Romance/Historical   (PR: C   MPAA: R)

SEARCH AND DESTROY   ★½
(U.S.) 90m New Image; October Films;
Autumn Pictures ~ October Films c

Griffin Dunne *(Martin Mirkheim)*; Illeana Douglas *(Marie Davenport)*; Dennis Hopper *(Dr. Waxling)*; Christopher Walken *(Kim Ulander)*; John Turturro *(Ron)*; Rosanna Arquette *(Lauren Mirkhein)*; Ethan Hawke *(Roger)*; Martin Scorsese *(The Accountant)*; Jason Ferraro *(Young Daniel Strong)*; Robert Knepper *(Daniel Strong)*; David Thornton *(Rob)*; Linda Wahl *(Party Guest)*; Laurie Godet *(Model)*; Randy Pearlstein; Vincent Angell *(Security Guard)*; Nicole Burdette *(Dorothy)*; Tanya Polkhotte *(Kim's Secretary)*; Karole Armitage *(Red River Valley Dancer)*; Dan Hedaya *(Tailor)*; Ken Simmons *(Nunez)*; Angel David *(Pamfilo)*; Frank Girardeau *(State Trooper)*; Tahnee Welch *(Dead World Girl)*

A comedy of desperation, this film marks the directorial debut of 1980s art world wunderkind, painter David Salle. Trendy to a fault, it tries to poke fun at the drug world, would-be film entrepreneurs, New Age philosophy and what passes today for cafe society. It succeeds only in alienating the viewer.

Martin Mirkheim (Griffin Dunne) is a compulsive dreamer who owes $147,956 in back taxes and is faced with divorce from his fed-up wife (Rosanna Arquette). He is not, however, without a plan. Besotted by the "You can do it" philosophy of Dr. Luthor Waxling (Dennis Hopper), a cable TV self-help guru, Mirkheim determines to acquire the movie rights to Waxling's novel *Daniel Strong*, a primer of self-affirmation. He flies to Dallas to meet Waxling, takes his assistant Marie (Illeana Douglas) out to dinner, and pitches her his idea while she tells him of a preposterously gory movie script she has written. Sparks of romance fly and she sneaks him a backstage pass to see Waxling. The "Great Man" is at first intrigued, but when he discovers Mirkheim has no financing, he throws him out.

The indefatigable Mirkheim talks Marie into accompanying him to New York to seek the necessary funds. While there, they encounter such charming druggie types as Kim (Christopher Walken) and Ron (John Turturro) who lead them on a wild ride through all the city's darkest back alleys. They manage to survive a few near-death situations in the company of these maniacs, including a wild time in the country and a shoot-out involving the police on the highway. They eventually somehow achieve their ends.

With this film, Salle joins the ranks of painters-turned-movie directors, which include names like Salvador Dali, Jean Cocteau,

Picasso and, more recently, David Lynch and Peter Greenaway. Unfortunately, Salle's film is not a patch on even the most indifferent of these men's works. Adapted from a play by Howard Korder, the film—which resolutely remains stagy—works overtime to achieve a satiric, edgy quality, but merely delivers confusion and ennui. Worst of all, Salle, who has painted some provocative representations of suburban life, has made a film bereft of any sensuality or visual style whatsoever. The photography is indifferent, marked by a few glossy fantasy sequences. The production design, which looked so alluring in an *Interview* magazine layout, seems nonexistent. The performances are so underdirected and determinedly tongue-in-cheek that it is impossible to identify with any of the characters. Griffin Dunne has already played to death the part of an anxious yuppie taking an urban walk on the wild side (AFTER HOURS, WHO'S THAT GIRL?). As denizens of the world of contraband, Walken and Turturro seem to be vying with each other in weirdness. The single exception is Illeana Douglas, who, even when saddled with a featherbrained role, comes through with her usual self-deprecating charm and personal style, like a cartoon Audrey Hepburn. Also, in a cameo role as a debonair insurance man, Martin Scorsese invests his one scene with more elegance than is apparent in the entire film. *(Violence, substance abuse, adult situations, sexual situations, profanity.)* — D.N.

d, David Salle; p, Ruth Charny, Dan Lupovitz, Ellie Cohn; exec p, Martin Scorsese, Avi Lerner, Danny Dimbort; assoc p, Trevor Short, Boaz Davidson, Mark Blum; w, Michael Almereyda (based on the play by Howard Korder); ph, Bobby Bukowski, Michael Spiller; ed, Michelle Gorchow; m, Elmer Bernstein; prod d, Robin Standefer; art d, Stephen Alesch; set d, Amy Tapper; sound, Pawel Wdowczak (mixer), Joe Zappala (design); casting, Billy Hopkins, Suzanne Smith, Kerry Barden; cos, Donna Zakowska; makeup, Judy Chin; stunts, Roy Farfel

Comedy/Drama   **(PR: O   MPAA: R)**

SECRET OF ROAN INISH, THE   ★★★½
(U.S.) 102m Skerry Movies Corporation;
Peter Newman Productions ~ First Look Pictures   c

Jeni Courtney *(Fiona Coneelly)*; Mick Lally *(Hugh Coneelly)*; Eileen Colgan *(Tess Coneelly)*; Richard Sheridan *(Eamon)*; John Lynch *(Tadhg)*; Cillian Byrne *(Jamie)*; Susan Lynch *("Selkie" Woman)*; Frankie McCafferty; Fergal McElheron; Brendan Conroy; Dave Duffy; Gerard Rooney *(Liam)*; Susan Lynch *(Selkie)*; Linda Greer; Pat Slowey; Declan Hannigan

A fairy tale for children and adults alike, THE SECRET OF ROAN INISH satisfies completely. This gentle cinematic whimsy, about a young Irish girl who discovers the magical elements of her Celtic family heritage, is writer-director John Sayles's best, most charming film to date.

In late 1940s Ireland, an unemployed widower sends his young daughter, Fiona (Jeni Courtney), to live with her grandparents, Tess (Eileen Colgan) and Hugh Coneelly (Mick Lally), in a northwest coast fishing village. Hugh tells Fiona the story of how, years earlier, her baby brother, Jamie, was swept out to sea in his cradle, and Fiona becomes obsessed with finding the boy.

Fiona's search begins on the nearby island of Roan Inish ("seal island"), where her parents first lost Jamie. Fiona actually spots her baby brother one afternoon while he plays with the seals that have raised him, but she fails to capture the elusive toddler. Back in the fishing village, Fiona learns all about the Celtic legend of the Selkie from Tadhg (John Lynch), a cousin. Tadhg explains to Fiona that many generations ago, an ancestor, Liam Coneelly (Gerard Rooney) married a dark-haired half-human/half-seal creature (Susan Lynch) called a Selkie, whom he

had found swimming in the water. In time, after bearing several children, the Selkie eventually returned to the sea, leaving behind a magic cradle. Some generations later, the cradle became the sea craft that protected Jamie when he was swept away from his parents.

Fiona tells another cousin, Eamon (Richard Sheridan), about seeing Jamie, and asks him to help her rebuild the abandoned family cottage on Roan Inish as a place for the family to live again. Despite the threat of eviction, Tess and Hugh refuse to move to their ancestral home, but once Fiona lets slip that she has seen Jamie on the island, the Coneellys swiftly decide to head to Roan Inish. There they lure Jamie back into the family fold.

During the 1980s, John Sayles earned a reputation as a maker of serious, topical independent films about worthy subjects (e.g., lesbianism in LIANNA, racism in BROTHER FROM ANOTHER PLANET, labor struggle in MATEWAN). Ironically, the director's most satisfying film to date, politically and otherwise, is this seemingly innocuous children's fantasy. Thanks to his earnest, straightforward approach to unlikely material (the source is a 1957 novella, *Secret of the Ron Mor Skerry*, by Rosalie K. Fry), Sayles ends up tempering the excesses of what might have been sentimental blarney. At the same time, he finds a subtler than usual approach to his characteristic political concerns: he scores a key feminist point simply by centering the action on the strong-willed Fiona.

In recent years, Sayles has developed his technical and artistic skills, as evidenced by CITY OF HOPE (1990) and PASSION FISH (1992), but ROAN INISH far exceeds these efforts. It creates a fresh, captivating mise-en-scene, simultaneously realistic and magical (Haskell Wexler's cinematography of the Irish locales is crucial here). A highlight is the Selkie myth, which is depicted with a refreshing minimum of camera tricks and special effects. Another great sequence is the Old Hollywood-style montage illustrating the children's rebuilding of the cottage on Roan Inish. The climactic family reunion with Jamie is genuinely moving and thoroughly exhilarating. — E.M.

d, John Sayles; p, Maggie Renzi, Sarah Green; exec p, John Sloss, Glen Jones, Peter Newman; assoc p, Paul Miller; w, John Sayles (based on the book *The Secret of Ron Mor Skerry* by Rosalie K. Fry); ph, Haskell Wexler; ed, John Sayles; m, Mason Daring; prod d, Adrian Smith; art d, Henry Harris; set d, Tom Conroy; sound, Clive Winter; fx, Trevor Neighbour; casting, John Hubbard, Ros Hubbard; cos, Consolata Boyle; makeup, Morna Ferguson

Fantasy/Romance/Children's   **(PR: AA   MPAA: PG)**

SECRETARY, THE   ★★
(U.S.) 94m Image Organization; Republic Pictures ~ Republic Pictures Home Video   c
(AKA: CRIMINAL INSTINCT)

Mel Harris *(Ellen Bradford)*; Sheila Kelly *(Deidre Bosnell)*; Barry Bostwick *(Eric Bradford)*; James Russo *(Ted Burke)*; Raymond Baker *(Lester Howland)*; Rod McCary *(George Matthias)*; Grainger Hines *(Robert Stiller)*; Mimi Craven *(Marcia Hastings)*; Sondra Currie *(Mary Quinn)*; Ashley Peldon *(Cindy Bradford)*; Richard Herd *(Chuck Bosnell)*; Christopher Kriesa *(James Robinson)*; Robert Lipton *(Richard Josephson)*; Anna Mathias *(June Grayson)*; Madison Wright *(Shari Grayson)*; Aaron Nelms *(Tim Grayson)*; Alan Shearman *(Brad Johnston)*; John Hostetter *(Detective Larry Parkins)*; Jerry DiChiara *(Buchanan)*

A suspense thriller decidedly lacking in thrills, THE SECRETARY stars Sheila Kelley (from TV's "L.A. Law") as an ambitious office worker who'll stop at nothing to get ahead. Produced as a CBS made-for-television movie in 1994, THE SECRETARY was released on video in 1995.

Eight years after witnessing her boss kill himself because she broke off their relationship, former stockbroker Ellen Bradford (Mel Harris) returns to the work force. She meets secretary Deidre (Kelley), who gives her pointers on impressing the boss, Les (Raymond Baker). Les plans to hire the other candidate, Richard Josephson (Robert Lipton), but Deidre wants Ellen to get the job, so she forges a letter from Josephson declining the position. She tells Josephson he has been rejected, and when he demands a meeting with the boss, she kills him; Ellen is hired. Deidre is later passed over for a promotion that would have lifted her out of the secretarial pool after five years, sending her into a fury. Believing Ellen can help her get ahead, Deidre pokes into her background looking for information to use as leverage. Deidre uncovers the suicide of Ellen's former boss and plots an elaborate scheme to recreate the events and blackmail Ellen. She arranges a late-night work meeting between Ellen and a co-worker, Ted (James Russo), then murders Ted and makes it look like a suicide. Deidre warns Ellen that she has evidence which will implicate her in Ted's murder. Ellen realizes that when her past history is revealed, no one will believe she is innocent.

Deidre demands that Ellen help her embezzle six million dollars. To convince her to cooperate, Deidre goes after Ellen's husband Eric (Barry Bostwick), crushing his legs under a jeep. She later abducts their daughter Cindy (Ashley Peldon). Knowing that her daughter's life depends on her compliance, Ellen transfers the funds to Deidre's account, while covertly tape recording Deidre's admission of her crimes. Deidre's father Chuck (Richard Herd), who has been alerted of his daughter's actions by Ellen, arrives in time to talk Deidre out of killing Ellen. Deidre is arrested and Ellen's family is reunited.

There is little that is original in THE SECRETARY. The formulaic plot takes its cues from FATAL ATTRACTION, THE HAND THAT ROCKS THE CRADLE, SINGLE WHITE FEMALE, and other psycho female flicks. As the secretary from Hell, Kelley is appropriately loony, but she lacks the sinister edge which made Glenn Close, Rebecca DeMornay and Jennifer Jason Leigh so frightening in the previously mentioned films. The family she victimizes is sweet and likable, but there isn't enough tension generated to make you feel as though they are in any real danger. There is one spark of originality in a scene in which Ellen outwits Deidre by planting two tape recorders, knowing Deidre will be looking for one and will stop searching when she finds the first device. From there the rest of the action is anticlimactic. *(Violence, sexual situations, profanity.)* — B.R.

d, Andrew Lane; p, Pierre David; assoc p, Lawrence Goebel, Meyer Shwartzstein; co-p, Noel A. Zanitsch, Clark Peterson; w, Graham Flashner; ph, Steven Bernstein; ed, Julian Semilian; m, Louis Febre; prod d, William Ryder; sound, Dan Monihan (mixer); fx, Steve Patino; casting, Cathy Henderson, Tom McSweeney; cos, Charmian Espinoza

Thriller   **(PR: C   MPAA: R)**

SENSE AND SENSIBILITY   ★★★½
(U.S.) 135m Mirage Enterprises ~ Columbia c

Emma Thompson *(Elinor Dashwood)*; Kate Winslet *(Marianne Dashwood)*; Alan Rickman *(Colonel Brandon)*; Hugh Grant *(Edward Ferrars)*; Greg Wise *(John Willoughby)*; Emilie Francois *(Margaret Dashwood)*; Elizabeth Spriggs *(Mrs. Jennings)*; Imogen Stubbs *(Lucy Steele)*; Gemma Jones *(Mrs. Dashwood)*; Harriet Walter *(Fanny Dashwood)*; James Fleet *(John Dashwood)*; Robert Hardy *(Sir John Middleton)*; Imelda Staunton *(Charlotte Palmer)*; Hugh Laurie *(Mr. Palmer)*; Richard

Lumsden *(Robert Ferrars)*; Tom Wilkinson *(Mr. Dashwood)*; Lone Vidahl *(Miss Grey)*; Ian Brimble *(Thomas)*; Isabelle Amyes *(Betsy)*; Oliver Ford Davies *(Doctor Harris)*; Eleanor McCready *(Mrs. Bunting)*; Allan Mitchell *(Pigeon)*; Alexander John *(Curate)*; Josephine Gradwell *(Maid to Mrs. Jennings)*

1995 marked an unusual and unexpected trend in the annals of popular culture—a Jane Austen renaissance. CLUELESS was hailed as a clever update of Austen's EMMA, a TV miniseries adaptation of *Pride and Prejudice* proved popular, and PERSUASION enjoyed a lengthy run on the art-house circuit. Meanwhile, to Hollywood's astonishment, SENSE AND SENSIBILITY was something very close to a blockbuster hit. First-time screenwriter Emma Thompson and director Ang Lee combined their talents for this graceful adaptation of Austen's first full-length novel. If the result is perhaps not quite as sharp as Austen's prose, it is nonetheless as handsome and intelligent an adaptation as one could reasonably expect.

John Dashwood inherits the entirety of his father's estate, Norland, since law does not permit his father to leave property to John's half-sisters. Prodded by his haughty wife Fanny, he minimizes his settlement on his stepmother and her daughters, and the couple moves into Norland. Mrs. Dashwood and her daughters—sensible Elinor (Emma Thompson), passionate Marianne (Kate Winslet), and young tomboy Margaret (Emilie Francois) prepare to vacate their home. Fanny's brother, Edward Ferrars (Hugh Grant), visits for a time, and he and Elinor fall in love. Marianne chides her sister for being too restrained in expressing her feelings, and Fanny sends her brother off to London, informing the Dashwoods that his mother would disinherit him if he married below his station.

Mrs. Dashwood and her daughters move into a cottage on the estate of a boisterous cousin, Sir John (Robert Hardy), who lives with his similarly rowdy mother-in-law Mrs. Jennings (Elizabeth Spriggs). A kindly neighbor who lost a love in his youth, Colonel Brandon (Alan Rickman), is attracted to Marianne, but she finds him too genteel, preferring instead a man closer to her own reckless, poetry-spouting temperament, Mr. Willoughby (Greg Wise). Brandon dashes off abruptly from a picnic and Willoughby completes his conquest, but he too runs off the day before he has promised to propose.

Mrs. Jennings invites Elinor and Marianne to join her at her house in London along with her daughter and son-in-law, and a cousin, Lucy Steele (Imogen Stubbs). Lucy, unaware of Elinor's feelings, confides that she has been secretly engaged to Edward for years. Marianne meet Willoughby at a ball, but he is now engaged to the wealthy Miss Grey (Lone Vidahl). Brandon tells Elinor the reason he ran off: he has helped raise the daughter of his dead love, and found out that she became pregnant by Willoughby. Elinor also discovers that Willoughby lost his inheritance because of his caddish behavior and so needed to court a wealthier woman. Upon hearing the news, a distraught Marianne wanders off in a thunderstorm and develops near-fatal pneumonia. Brandon proves his love during the crisis and Marianne now reciprocates. Lucy, meanwhile, falls for Edward's brother. Edward, now free and set up with a position by Brandon, apologizes to Elinor for romancing her while he was engaged, and the once-reticent couple declare their love.

Beautifully helmed by Lee, SENSE AND SENSIBILITY surprised many who saw the Taiwanese director as an odd choice for this comedy of 19th-century British manners. However, Lee's earlier works—e.g., THE WEDDING BANQUET and EAT DRINK MAN WOMAN—are not as far from Austen's worldview as it might seem. These are delicately wrought studies of social mores; especially where marriage is concerned, a highly structured society forces propriety and money to take precedence over love. Lee's frequently distanced framing works as a cinematic rendering of Austen's coolly ironic prose, and his camera angles and moving shots are splendid. The humor of Margaret's hiding under a table comes from the framing, and a track and tilt fully register Mrs. Dashwood's and Fanny's widely disparate responses to Edward's and Elinor's romance. Lee gets the most out of such hilarious vignettes as one in which all four Dashwood women begin crying.

Lee also elicits uniformly excellent performances from his cast, with Thompson and Winslet particularly fine. Thompson also deserves credit for a faithful, intelligent screenplay which never rushes through Austen's plot. The major differences are ones of tone. It's no surprise that the film's dramatic moments are emphasized more than the novel's. More important, however, Hollywood can never quite take the full measure of Austen's satire. Austen saw marriage as primarily a social and economic institution, but Hollywood is in the business of selling marriage as the ideal of love. Consequently, the film is more romanticized than the novel, and much of the satire is missing. But if the film isn't quite pure Austen, it is more than reasonably mature and entertaining mainstream cinema. *(Adult situations.)* — D.L.

d, Ang Lee; p, Lindsay Doran; exec p, Sydney Pollack; co-p, James Schamus, Laurie Borg; w, Emma Thompson (based on the novel by Jane Austen); ph, Michael Coulter; ed, Tim Squyres; m, Patrick Doyle; prod d, Luciana Arrighi; art d, Philip Elton; set d, Ian Whittaker; sound, Tony Dawe (mixer); fx, Ricky Farns, Randall Balsmeyer; cos, Jenny Beavan, John Bright; makeup, Morag Ross; stunts, Nick Wilkinson

AAN Best Picture; AAN Best Supporting Actress: Kate Winslet; *AAN Best Actress:* Emma Thompson; *AA Best Adapted Screenplay:* Emma Thompson; *AAN Best Cinematography:* Michael Coulter; *AAN Best Costume Design:* Jenny Beavan, John Bright; *AAN Best Dramatic Score:* Patrick Doyle

Drama/Romance (PR: A MPAA: PG)

SEPARATE LIVES ★★
(U.S.) 102m Interscope Communications;
Trimark Pictures ~ Trimark Pictures c

James Belushi *(Tom Beckwith)*; Linda Hamilton *(Lauren Porter/Lena)*; Vera Miles *(Dr. Ruth Goldin)*; Elisabeth Moss *(Ronnie Beckwith)*; Drew Snyder *(Robert Porter)*; Mark Lindsay Chapman *(Keno Sykes)*; Marc Poppel *(Detective Joe Gallo)*; Elizabeth Arlen *(Dee Harris)*; Josh Taylor *(Charles Duffy)*; Ken Kerman *(Detective Boyle)*; Michael Whaley *(Detective Miller)*; Jackie De Batin *(Darlene)*; Joshua Malina *(Randall)*; Lisa Vanderpump *(Heidi Porter)*; Craig Stepp *(David Mills)*; Lisa Chess *(Margaret Porter-Mills)*; Ara Maxwell *(Young Lauren Porter)*; Pat Delany *(Jane Weiss)*; Joseph Gallison *(Paul)*; Tom Morga *(Carl)*; John Rubano *(Gyp)*; Ray Quartermus *(Guard)*; Beverly Costaldo *(Redhead)*; Christine Devine *(News Reporter)*; Joseph Briski *(Arresting Cop)*; Logan Clarke *(Big Ben)*; Athan Maroulis; Rob Morton; Matt Green *(Spawn Ranch)*

This mindless thriller operates on the level of a daytime talk show about multiple personalities. Since any suspense is tangential and there's a distinct lack of chemistry between stars Linda Hamilton and James Belushi, SEPARATE LIVES barely sputters to life.

When Jane Weiss (Pat Delany) tries to reopen a decades-old homicide investigation, she is gunned down on the beach at Malibu. As a young girl, celebrated psychotherapist Lauren Porter (Hamilton) was traumatized when her mother blew away her stepfather with a shotgun and then killed herself. Lauren now teaches criminal behavior at a local college, where she opens up

to one of her students, former cop Tom Beckwith (Belushi). She believes that she may be suffering from multiple personality disorder and persuades Beckwith to keep her under surveillance.

Lauren soon slips into the danger-craving half of her split personality: Lena, a dance-club swinger whose stormy liaison with Keno Sykes (Mark Lindsay Chapman) results in the savage beating of Beckwith. Delving into the past while dealing with a tricky relationship with his own daughter, Ronnie (Elisabeth Moss), Beckwith is shocked when a ballistics report suggests that Lauren killed Jane Weiss. The weapon, however, soon disappears. When Lauren's ex-husband agrees to babysit for her, he winds up the latest murder victim.

Beckwith accosts Lauren as she fades in and out of her aggressive demeanor. Beckwith drives her—against her will—to the family manse where the original crimes took place, and forces the traumatized woman to confront a scarred past. Lauren's father, Robert Porter (Drew Snyder), appears on the scene and admits to having killed Lauren's mother and stepdad. He attempts to kill Lauren/Lena, but Beckwith sends him flying out of the window to his death. Lauren is apparently cured.

In classic film noirs, a femme fatale killed because of some character flaw, but Lauren Porter—like the heroines of many noir updates—just can't help herself: she's damaged goods. In either event, mental illness is exploited to flesh out sketchy characterizations in this underwritten murder mystery. Since Robert's guilt is readily apparent from his first appearance, any attempt to lay the blame at the doorstep of Lauren—in either of her personas—simply prolongs the inevitable. At best, the film is a cynival revamp of superior murder yarns, many with stars more charismatic than beefy bulldozer Belushi and one-expression-fits-every-mood Hamilton. *(Graphic violence, extensive nudity, extreme profanity, sexual situations, adult situations.)* — R.P.

d, David Madden; p, Diane Nabatoff, Guy Riedel; exec p, Mark Amin, Ted Field, Robert W. Cort; co-p, Andrew Hersh; w, Steven Pressfield; ph, Kees Van Ostrum; ed, Janice Hampton; m, William Olvis; prod d, Bernt Capra; art d, Walter Cahall; set d, Karen L. McCaughey; sound, John Sutton, III (mixer), David Farmer (design); fx, Tommy Bellissimo; casting, Mike Fenton, Allison Cowitt; cos, Jacqueline C. Arthur; makeup, Ben Nye, Jr.; stunts, John Moio

Thriller/Crime/Mystery (PR: O MPAA: R)

SERIOUS ABOUT PLEASURE ★★
(France) 100m Dovidis Paris Cannes Production
O.R.T.F. ~ Eurotrash Film and Video c
(SERIEUX COMME LE PLAISIR)

Jane Birkin *(Ariane)*; Richard Leduc *(Bruno)*; Georges Mansart *(Patrice)*; Michel Lonsdale *(Fournier)*; Roland Dubillard *(Berg)*; Pierre Etaix *(Busboy)*; Jean-Claude Carriere *(Chief)*; Serge Gainsbourg *(Unkown One)*; Jean-Luc Bideau *(Suicidal One)*; Andrea Ferreol *(Woman in White)*

Ariane (Jane Birkin) and her two lovers travel across the country in a convertible making a game of life and love in SERIOUS ABOUT PLEASURE. Released in France in 1975, the film was made available in the US home video market in 1995.

Ariane, Patrice (Georges Mansart), and Bruno (Richard Leduc) share the same bed in a Parisian flat and the same sense of friendship and freedom. When they win a cash prize, they set out on a random adventure, stopping only to ask pedestrians which way they should go next. The three lovers enjoy using others as props in their games. In one amusing scene Patrice and Bruno bring home two women, and Ariane pretends to be the English maid. In another, they play on the desires of the hotel guests by creating fictitious roles for each other and arranging amorous rendezvous they will never keep. In one rather surreal scene, they purchase a basket of bad apples and affix them to a leafless tree, playing at a make-believe paradise.

The only moment of seriousness in the film occurs when Ariane becomes pregnant, and a chill of reality passes through the affair. Each sets off alone, only to be reunited with the others on a train. The fun commences all over again. Ten years later they are still together, proud parents of a young boy.

The film is set to sweet light music and coated with the ambiance of 1970s French erotic comedy, light as whipped cream and bubble baths. There is a hollow attempt to portray the characters as living romantic and creative lives—they read poetry in bed, Ariane works in a gallery, and Bruno works for a publisher of illicit literary titles. This is harmless fun, but a frivolous offshoot of Truffaut's infinitely more interesting JULES AND JIM (1962). *(Nudity.)* — R.C.

d, Robert Benayoun; w, Robert Benayoun, Jean-Claude Carriere; ph, Jean Badal; ed, Jean Ravel; m, Michel Berger

Romance/Comedy **(PR: C MPAA: NR)**

SEVEN ★★★½
(U.S.) 107m New Line ~ New Line c

Brad Pitt *(Detective David Mills)*; Morgan Freeman *(Lieutenant William Somerset)*; Gwyneth Paltrow *(Tracy)*; Richard Roundtree *(Talbot)*; John C. McGinley *(California)*; Kevin Spacey *(John Doe)*; John Cassini *(Officer Davis)*; Peter Crombie *(Dr. O'Neill)*; Reg E. Cathey *(Dr. Santiago)*; Richard Portnow *(Dr. Beardsley)*; Daniel Zacapa *(Detective Taylor at 1st Murder)*; Martin Serene *(Wild Bill)*; Endre Hules *(Cab Driver)*; R. Lee Ermey *(Police Captain)*; Richard Schiff *(Mark Swarr)*; Bob Mack *(Gluttony Victim)*; Gene Borkan *(Eli Gould (Sin of Greed))*; Michael Reid MacKay *(Victor (Sin of Sloth))*; Cat Mueller *(Hooker (Sin of Lust))*; Heidi Schanz *(Beautiful Woman (Sin of Pride))*; Andy Walker *(Dead Man at 1st Crime Scene)*; Julie Araskog *(Mrs. Gould)*; George Christy *(Workman at Door of Somerset's Office)*; Hawthorne James *(George the Night Guard at the Library)*; Roscoe Davidson *(First Guard at the Library)*; Bob Collins *(Second Guard at the Library)*; Jimmy Dale Hartsell *(Library Janitor)*; Charline Su *(TV News Reporter)*; Dominique Jennings *(TV News Reporter)*; Allan Kolman *(First Forensic Man in the Law Office)*; Beverly Burke *(TV Anchor Woman)*; Mario Di Donato *(Fingerprint Forensic Man in Law Office)*; Alfonso Freeman *(Fingerprint Technician)*; Harrison White *(Cop on SWAT Team)*; Robert Stephenson *(Cop on SWAT Team)*; Tudor Sherrard *(Coupon Man Outside Pizza Parlor)*; Mark Boone, Junior *(Greasy FBI Man)*; Pamala Tyson *(Thin Vagrant by John Doe's Apartment)*; Lennie Loftin *(Policeman Who Takes Statement From Vagrant)*; Sarah Hale Reinhardt *(Police Sketch Artist)*; Emily Wagner *(Detective Sara at John Doe's Apartment)*; Michael Massee *(Man in Booth at Massage Parlor)*; David Correia *(First Cop at Massage Parlor)*; Ron Blair *(Second Cop at Massage Parlor)*; Leland Orser *(Crazed Man in Massage Parlor)*; Lexie Bigham *(Sweating Cop at Massage Parlor)*; Evan Miranda *(Paramedic at Massage Parlor)*; Paul S. Eckstein *(Paramedic at Massage Parlor)*; Brian Evers *(Duty Sergeant)*; Shannon Wilcox *(Woman Cop Behind Desk)*; Jim Deeth *(Helicopter Pilot)*; John Santini *(Helicopter Pilot)*; Charles Tamburro *(SWAT Helicopter Pilot)*; Richmond Arquette *(Delivery Man)*; Duffy Gaver *(Marksman in Helicopter)*

Bleak and deeply serious, SEVEN forges the formulaic elements of dozens of lousy movies—mismatched cops, a serial killer, noir trappings—into a compelling one. As dark as an anvil and as subtle as a hammer, SEVEN gets the job done—it entertains, if you accept it on its own implacable terms.

The hard rain that pours down daily on the streets of the unnamed metropolis in which SEVEN is set isn't enough to wash the human filth off the streets. Having spent 34 years in the futile task of street cleaning, detective William Somerset (Morgan Freeman) is set to retire. He wants his last week to pass quietly, but he's charged with training his replacement, David Mills (Brad Pitt), an eager hotshot, new to the city. First thing Monday, they're faced with an unusual murder: an obese man has been force-fed spaghetti until he literally burst, and the word "GLUT-TONY" was written in grease on the wall.

The next day, a rich defense lawyer is found dead in his office, missing a pound of flesh. "GREED" is written on the floor in blood. Somerset concludes—hastily but, as it turns out, correctly—that the murders are based on the seven deadly sins, and that killings based on sloth, pride, lust, envy, and wrath will follow.

Wednesday night, Mills's wife Tracy (Gwyneth Paltrow) invites Somerset to dinner, hoping to build a bridge between the antagonistic partners. It works. When the police find "SLOTH" over a man who's been strapped to a bed for a year, Sommerset realizes the killer is toying with them. Clues have been planted to lead the police along, and when the seven are finished, the clever killer will be famous; some will even see him as a prophet. A secret FBI computer that's a conspiracy theorist's worst nightmare (it tracks people who've taken suspicious books out of libraries) leads the detectives to the killer's apartment, but he escapes. Soon after, a prostitute (lust) and a model (pride) are murdered.

On Sunday, Somerset's last day, killer John Doe (Kevin Spacey), turns himself in, and offers to lead the detectives to his last two victims. The three drive out to a sun-drenched field, where Doe reveals he's killed Tracy because he envied her love for Mills. In wrathful retribution, Mills kills Doe.

SEVEN is unnerving from the jarring graphics of the opening credits, set to the electronic pulse of Nine Inch Nails' industrial rock. The stench and filth of the gluttony scene is tangible and nauseating. The sloth episode is horrific, and contains a sickening shock, while the rape-murder of lust is almost unimaginably gruesome. Director David Fincher assaults the audience relentlessly; his "Noir York" is a claustrophobic world, colored from a palette of stark grays and the occasional, dingy yellow. Fincher wants to immerse viewers in the rot of this world, and indict its (and our) malaise for the on-screen sins: John Doe is only a festering symptom.

In his directing debut, ALIEN3, Fincher's visuals were at cross-purposes with both audience expectations and the marketing demands of the production. SEVEN's straightforward story allows Fincher's visuals to achieve maximum effect. SEVEN's cast is up to the demands of competing with a strongly articulated visual schema. Freeman carries the weight of its world, countering Fincher's expressionism with his minimalist performance. Barely speaking above a whisper, Somerset is the moral center of the universe and just about sick to death of it. Still, he ties his tie more purposefully than most actors deliver Hamlet's soliloquy. Creepy Kevin Spacey doesn't disappoint as John Doe.

The film's finale is a bit anti-climactic, though, talking on beyond the point where the outcome is obvious. That we aren't shown Paltrow's mutilated body, or that Pitt doesn't turn his gun on himself and splatter his brains all over Freeman are SEVEN's only concessions to some sort of feel-good ending. Throughout the film, Fincher taunts viewers sadistically, daring them to enjoy themselves, and the fact that a film so awash in nihilism did so well at the box office begs the question of whether it was Pitt's adoring fans, or Quentin Tarantino's, who answered that challenge. *(Graphic violence, adult situations, profanity, nudity.)* — P.R.

d, David Fincher; p, Arnold Kopelson, Phyllis Carlyle; exec p, Gianni Nunnari, Dan Kolsrud, Anne Kopelson; assoc p, Michele Platt; co-p, Stephen Brown, Nana Greenwald, Sanford Panitch; w, Andrew Kevin Walker; ph, Darius Khondji; ed, Richard Francis-Bruce; m, Howard Shore; prod d, Arthur Max; art d, Gary Wissner; set d, Clay A. Griffith; sound, Willie D. Burton (mixer), Ren Klyce, Jack Keller, David Behle; fx, Peter Albiez, Danny Cangemi, Greg Kimble, Tim Thompson; casting, Billy Hopkins, Suzanne Smith, Kerry Borden; cos, Michael Kaplan; makeup, Jean Black, Michael White, Rob Bottin; stunts, Charles Picerni, Picerni

Thriller/Crime/Action (PR: O MPAA: R)

SEX, DRUGS AND DEMOCRACY ★★
(Netherlands/U.S.) 87m Red Hat Productions ~
Red Hat Productions c
(AKA: SEX, DRUGS & DEMOCRACY)

Jonathan Blank *(Interviewer)*; Barclay Powers *(Interviewer)*

This documentary by American filmmakers Jonathan Blank and Barclay Powers gives a portrait of Holland as a modern-day citadel of individual freedom.

Primarily set in Amsterdam, it presents a country where the sale of marijuana and hashish is legally permitted. Prostitution, also permitted, is restricted to red light districts where brothels follow strict health codes and are subject to frequent inspections. The free national health system provides for both abortion and euthanasia. About the only things that *are* forbidden are capital punishment and guns.

This general permissiveness has its roots in the country's earliest charter, a tradition which has long made Amsterdam a haven for the alternatively inclined. A long history of religious and social tolerance has been admirably upheld in this, one of the most densely populated of European countries. Regulation and the law are held up as guidelines which control social problems, and this seems to work. Only three percent of the population under 19 years of age indulge in "soft" drugs. The number of AIDS cases and sexually transmitted diseases is relatively low, and prostitution is far from rampant. Because of its healthy attitude toward sex education, the country can also pride itself on having the lowest rates of abortion and teenage pregnancy in the world, as well as the smallest prison population. Environmental issues, health care, education, and housing are constitutional priorities.

SEX, DRUGS AND DEMOCRACY partly fails as a film because, despite their obvious admiration for the country they are filming, Blank and Powers offer a meandering, laggardly Cook's tour of the city that is alternately impressive and exploitative. The red light district is played up as much as possible. The filmmakers also seem to spend a rather unconscionable amount of time in a sex bar with a nude female writhing in the customers' faces. There are interviews with any number of local characters, from professional pot growers to keepers of the most unlikely sorts of museums. What is amazing here is how complacently boring it all seems after a while. It is as if, without strictures, the populace just drifts off into a universally accepting blandness that is, in its own way, a kind of suffocation. Most of the interviewees have a self-satisfied, smug air about them that engenders a rather unfortunate response in the viewer. Amsterdam seems like a great place for a quick wicked getaway, but there is not much reason to stick around too long. *(Nudity, sexual situations, adult situations, substance abuse.)* — D.N.

d, Jonathan Blank; p, Barclay Powers, Jonathan Blank; ph, Jonathan Blank; ed, Jonathan Blank; m, Philip Foxman, Mark Sterling, Nick Balaban; sound, Jonathan Blank

Documentary (PR: O MPAA: NR)

S.F.W. ★
(U.S.) 92m A & M Films; Propaganda Films;
PolyGram ~ Gramercy Pictures c

Stephen Dorff *(Cliff Spab)*; Reese Witherspoon *(Wendy Pfister)*; Jake Busey *(Morrow Streeter)*; Joey Lauren Adams *(Monica Dice)*; Pamela Gidley *(Janet Streeter)*; David Barry Gray *(Scott Spab)*; Jack Noseworthy *(Joe Dice)*; Richard Portnow *(Gerald Parsley)*; Edward Wiley *(Mr. Spab)*; Lela Ivey *(Mrs. Spab)*; Natasha Gregson Wagner *(Kristen)*; Annie McEnroe *(Dolly)*; Virgil Frye *(Earl)*; Francesca P. Roberts *(Kim Martin)*; Soon Teck Oh *(Milt Morris)*; Blair Tefkin *(Allison Ash)*; Steven Antin *(Dick Zetterland)*; Melissa Lechner *(Sandy Hooten)*; Lenny Wolpe *(Phil Connors)*; Natalie Strauss *(Rita Connors)*; Tobey Maguire *(Al)*; Dana Allan Young *(Johnny)*; John Roarke *(Phil Donahue Clone/Sam Donaldson Clone/Alan Dershowitz Clone/Ted Koppel Clone/Larry King Clone)*; Gary Coleman *(Himself)*; Amber Benson *(Barbara "Babs" Wyler)*; China Kantner *(Female Pantyhose Gunman)*; Kathryn Atwood *(Pebbles Goren)*; Caroline Barclay *(Mindy Lawford)*; Sylvia Short *(Doctor Travis)*; Sandra Phillips *(Female Talent Agent)*; Gary Grossman *(Male Talent Agent)*; Michelle Seipp *(Hotel Receptionist)*; Frank Collison *(Stoner Witness)*; Stephanie Friedman *(Dori Smelling)*; Adam Small *(Burger Boy Manager)*; Ben Slack *(Madison Heights Mayor)*; Carol Hankins *(Nervous Lady on Talkshow)*; Kristen Ernst *(Teenage Girl on Talkshow)*; Mil Nicholson *(Woman at Homecoming)*; Charles Font *(Burger Boy Worker)*; John Chaidez *(Burger Boy Worker)*; Corey Gunnestad *(Burger Boy Worker)*; William Scott Brown; Lisa Dinkins; Amber Edam; Jerome Front; Susan Harney; Philip Moon; Joanne Takahashi; R.W. Wilson *(Reporters)*; Ada Gorn *(Photographer)*; Jon Gudmundsson *(Photographer)*; Bernadette Elise *(Photographer)*

S.F.W. is a miserable entry in the sweepstakes to catch the pulse of Generation X. The title stands for "So Fucking What," and that about sums it up.

Cliff Spab (Stephen Dorff) is the 20-year-old voice of his generation. He's a foulmouthed, disaffected, apathetic slacker, who mindlessly fills his days flipping burgers and getting wasted. Then, for 36 days, Spab is held hostage in a convenience store. His captors videotape everything, and the tapes are broadcast on national TV. The only other survivor is Wendy Pfister (Reese Witherspoon), a pretty, 17-year-old, rich girl whose life Spab saves. We learn about the ordeal in the course of the film through flashbacks and the media.

When he gets back to the real world, Spab discovers he is some sort of hero. Over the 36 days, the talkative Spab has galvanized the nation with his philosophy of saying "so fucking what" in the face of adversity. Everywhere he goes, he is met by a mob of media and cheering crowds, though now he just wants to be left alone. For several days, he wanders around aimlessly interacting with various fans, lowlives, opportunists, and friends, who all want a piece of him. Eventually, he decides to capitalize on his fame, but he misses Wendy, who has become America's heroic cover girl. Finally, he and Wendy reunite. They talk, make love, and share the drink they call loneliness. When they give a public appearance, Spab and Wendy are shot and wounded by a young girl (Amber Benson). Their attacker becomes the media's new flavor of the month, leaving Spab and Wendy free to plan a future together in peace.

The comedy in S.F.W. is supposed to derive from its satire of the celebrity-creating media machine. This is signaled by the casting of one actor (John Roarke) to play all the news figure-heads, from Donahue to Koppel and on. The dramatic import is supposed to derive from how deeply Spab's nihilism and cynicism are felt, signaled by the fact that Spab never cracks a smile. The potentially interesting hostage episode is barely in the picture, and comes off like a pointless "Twilight Zone" episode. Most of the movie consists of long, boring stretches of inaction. It's difficult to convey just how unpleasant it is to spend 90 minutes listening to Cliff Spab's incessant and irritating musings; it's also unimaginable that those well-armed terrorists wouldn't have put him out of his misery fast. (Extreme profanity, sexual situations, nudity, violence.) — P.R.

d, Jefery Levy; p, Dale Pollock; exec p, Sigurjon Sighvatsson; assoc p, Gloria Lopez; co-p, Mike Nelson; w, Danny Rubin, Jefery Levy (based on the novel by Andrew Wellman); ph, Peter Deming; ed, Lauren Zuckerman; m, Graeme Revell; prod d, Eve Cauley; art d, Philip Messina; set d, Sandy Struth; sound, Douglas Murray (design), David B. Chornow (mixer), W. Philip Rogers (recordist); fx, Frank Ceglia; casting, Owens Hill, Rachel Abroms; cos, Debra McGuire; makeup, Cheryl Voss; stunts, Steve M. Davison

Comedy/Drama   **(PR: O MPAA: R)**

SHALLOW GRAVE   ★★½
(U.K.) 94m Figment Film; Film Four; Channel Four Films; Glasgow Film Fund ~ Gramercy c

Kerry Fox *(Juliet Miller)*; Christopher Eccleston *(David Stephens)*; Ewan McGregor *(Alex Law)*; Ken Stott *(Detective McCall)*; Keith Allen *(Hugo)*; John Bett *(Brian McKinley)*; Kenneth Bryans *(Senior Police Officer)*; Elspeth Cameron *(Elderly Woman)*; Jean Marie Coffey *(Goth)*; Tony Curren *(Salesman)*; Bill Denniston *(Master of Cermonies)*; Paul Doonan *(Newspaper Office Boy)*; Victor Eadie *(Freezer Victim)*; Grant Glendinning *(Bath Victim)*; Colin McRedie *(Cameron)*; Jenny McCrindle *(Nurse)*; Victoria Nairn *(Woman Visitor)*; Leonard O'Malley *(Tim)*; Gregor Powrie *(Young Policeman)*; David Alan MacDonald *(Lumsden)*; Billy Riddoch *(Editor)*; Gary Lewis *(Male Visitor)*; Frances Low *(Doctor)*; Peter Mullen *(Andy)*; John Hodge *(Mitchell)*; David Scoular *(Cash Machine Victim)*; John Carmichael & His Band *(Themselves)*

Excessively praised by critics in search of a new master of suspense, SHALLOW GRAVE is undeniably stylish, even though its characters are distinctly cold and unlikable.

Three smarty-pants Edinburgh roommates are looking for a fourth person to share their fabulous apartment. Alex (Ewan McGregor), a journalist, David (Christopher Eccleston), an accountant, and Juliet (Kerry Fox), a doctor, put the applicants through a long and deliberately humiliating interview process that allows them ample opportunity to show off and feel superior. They ultimately accept the somewhat older Hugo (Keith Allen), who moves in and almost immediately dies of a drug overdose. He leaves behind a suitcase crammed with money.

After some debate, the trio decide to cut up Hugo's body, bury it in the woods, and keep the cash. David is the least comfortable with the decision, especially since he draws the short straw and has to do the nastiest part of the job: mutilating the corpse to prevent identification. The murder disrupts the fragile balance of the relationship between the trio: Juliet draws closer to Alex, whom she once dated, and David withdraws, eventually moving into the attic. He takes the money with him and hides it, and begins drilling holes in the floor so he can watch his roommates below. Things begin to get really ugly when two of Hugo's

criminal associates, who want the money, break into the apartment and viciously attack Juliet and Alex. David manages to kill both the interlopers, and they too are dismembered and buried.

The new killings drive a further wedge between the three friends, and David's behavior becomes increasingly erratic. The bodies are discovered, and Alex is assigned to cover the story; the situation unnerves him profoundly. Juliet calculatingly shifts her affections to the awkward and sexually repressed David, and they plan to flee together with the money. Violence erupts: David stabs Alex, and Juliet kills David. She stabs Alex as well, leaving him pinned to the floor through the shoulder, and heads for the airport with the suitcase. Just before leaving the country, she finds that it's full of cut-up copies of Alex's newspaper stories about the uncovered bodies. Lying in the apartment, where he has hidden the money under the floor, Alex smiles as the police arrive.

Even before its UK release, SHALLOW GRAVE was enthusiastically touted by the British press, who hailed director Danny Boyle as a "British Quentin Tarantino." US critics greeted SHALLOW GRAVE with Hitchcock comparisons, ignoring the fact that Hitchcock's protagonists—even the most twisted and murderous—are invariably more sympathetic than SHALLOW GRAVE's self-centered, obnoxious snobs, the British equivalent of yuppie scum. That's not to say that a crime thriller's central characters have be traditionally sympathetic and likable, but SHALLOW GRAVE's protagonists are really hateful, petty and greedy and all too willing to sell one another down the river for money. But their predicament is worked through in a painfully logical manner—once they decide to get rid of the body, the dice are thrown—and their surrender to their own dark impulses (none of the three puts up much of a fight) is both bleakly funny and rigorously nasty. Boyle's always striking compositions characterize him as a director with an eye for evocative imagery, and while the actors could easily have softened their characters, making them more conventionally sympathetic, they instead commit themselves to making them venal, cynical and astonishingly calculating. Unlike PULP FICTION, SHALLOW GRAVE is a film in which the abundant violence and brutality are truly unpleasant rather than hiply thrilling. (Graphic violence, adult situations, profanity.) — M.G.

d, Danny Boyle; p, Andrew Macdonald; exec p, Allan Scott; assoc p, John Downes; w, John Hodge; ph, Brian Tufano; ed, Masahiro Hirakubo; m, Simon Boswell; prod d, Kave Quinn; art d, Zoe MacLeod; sound, Colin Nicholson (mixer); fx, Tony Steers; casting, Sarah Trevis; cos, Kate Carin; makeup, Graham Johnston, Grant Mason; stunts, Clive Curtis

Thriller/Crime   **(PR: C MPAA: R)**

SHANGHAI TRIAD   ★★★½
(China/France) 108m Shanghai Film Studios; Alpha Films; UGC Images; La Sept Cinema ~ Sony Pictures Classics c
(YAO A YAO YAO DAO WAIPO QIAO)

Gong Li *(Bijou—Xiao Jinbao)*; Li Baotian *(Tang, the Triad Boss)*; Wang Xiaoxiao *(Shuisheng, the Boy)*; Li Xuejian *(6th Uncle)*; Sun Chun *(Song, Tang's No. 2)*; Fu Biao *(Tang's No. 3)*; Chen Shu *(Shi Ye)*; Liu Jiang *(Fat Yu)*; Jiang Baoying *(Cuihua, the Widow)*; Yang Qianquan *(Ah Jiao)*; Gao Ying; Gao Weiming; Lian Shuliang; Wang Ya'nan; Zhang Yayun; Guo Hao; Zheng Jiasen; Ni Zengshao; An Xing; Jia Shijun; Jiang Jiankang; Yu Jiangang; Lu Dou

Though Zhang Yimou's SHANGHAI TRIAD lacks the overtly political subtext that distinguished his previous films—including the acclaimed RED SORGHUM (1988), JU DOU (1989), and

RAISE THE RED LANTERN (1991)—it's an absorbing character study of a gangster's moll and her journey of self-discovery.

It's 1930, and Shanghai's underworld is flourishing under Nationalist rule. Mr. Tang (Li Boatian), the godfather of the Green dynasty, controls the city's traffic in opium and prostitution. Mr. Tang's mistress is beautiful Xiao Jinbao (Gong Li), a nightclub singer who goes by the nickname Jewel. Fourteen-year-old Tang Shuisheng (Wang Xiaoxiao), a distant relative of the godfather, is brought from the country by his Uncle Liu (Li Xuejian) to become Xiao Jingboa's servant.

Though paid superficial respect as the boss's concubine, Jewel is despised by Tang's men, and her isolation manifests itself in high-handed affectation and childish tantrums. The watchful Shuisheng soon learns that Jewel is having an affair with Song (Shun Chun), Tang's treacherous right-hand man. Tang, meanwhile, is attempting to negotiate a truce with fellow gangster Fat Yu (Liu Jiang). After a horrific massacre in which Tang is wounded and Shuisheng's uncle killed, Tang moves his inner circle to an isolated island whose only inhabitants are the young peasant widow Cuihua (Jiang Baoying) and her pretty little daughter Ah Jiao (Yang Qianquan).

Though she rails against the island prison, Jewel's conversations with Cuihua and her poignant encounters with Ah Jiao—in whom she recognizes the child she once was—reveal a softer side of her character. The island sojourn also exposes the ruthless brutality beneath Tang's sophisticated veneer: After Jewel flirtatiously reveals that Cuihua has a lover who visits her secretly at night, Tang has the man murdered. Following several days of enforced idleness, Tang announces that Song is coming from the mainland. While crouching in the reeds, Shuisheng hears voices and realizes that Song's men plan to murder Tang. He rushes to warn Tang, only to find that the old man is not surprised. The trip to the island has been a ruse, designed to lure the traitorous Song out into the open. His men are slaughtered, and Song and Jewel are murdered. Before her death, Jewel pleads for Cuihua and Ah Jiao, but Cuihua has already been killed, and Ah Jiao's fate decided.

The film ends with Tang and his entourage preparing to return to the mainland, accompanied by little Ah Jiao, who will be groomed to replace Jewel. Shuisheng is hung upside down from the ship's mast as punishment for having defended Jewel.

Zhang Yimou was criticized for having made a film that lacked the clear political dimension of his earlier pictures, so it's ironic that political controversy surrounded the 1995 New York Film Festival showing of SHANGHAI TRIAD. At the request of the Chinese Government—angered by another festival entry, Tiananmen Square massacre documentary THE GATE OF HEAVENLY PEACE—Zhang had to abandon his plans to attend the Festival. In addition, SHANGHAI TRIAD marked the apparent end of the longtime collaboration of Zhang and star Gong Li, which has often been compared to the intense professional and personal relationship between Josef von Sternberg and Marlene Dietrich. Gong has appeared in all seven of Zhang's features.

By using old Hollywood genre motifs—particularly those of 1930s musicals and gangster pictures—Zhang does indeed soften his usually biting social analysis, but SHANGHAI TRIAD is an effective, intimate drama driven by implicit criticism of repressive patriarchy. It's most interesting and original conceit lies in moving Jewel, who would normally be a supporting character, to the center of the story. The glittery nightclub set of the film's first half contrasts strongly with the natural island location of the second, underlining Jewel's transformation, and Zhang encapsulates her lost innocence in the contrast between the silly nightclub numbers—her signature song is "Pretending"—and the simple but haunting children's tune she teaches Ah Jiao. Gong's moving performance is only one of this well-crafted film's as-

sets. It also features excellent performances from Wang Xiao Xiao as Shuisheng and Li Boatian as the spider-like Mr. Tang. Finally, Lu Yue's cinematography introduces more camera movement than in previous Zhang films, and the director cleverly represents Shuisheng's point of view in many extended shots. (*Violence, sexual situations, adult situations, profanity.*) — E.M.

d, Zhang Yimou; p, Jean-Louis Piel; exec p, Wang Wei, Zhu Yongde; w, Bi Feiyu (freely adapted from the novel *Men Gui (Gang Law)* by Li Xiao); ph, Lu Yue; ed, Du Yuan; m, Zhang Guangtian; prod d, Cao Jiuping; art d, Huang Xinming, Ma Yongming; ch, Wang Qing; sound, Tao Jing (design); cos, Tong Huamiao; makeup, Mi Zide, Yang Yu

AAN Best Cinematography: Lu Yue

Drama/Crime (PR: C MPAA: R)

SHAO LIN POPEYE ★★½
(Taiwan/Hong Kong) Youngtze Film & Video ~ TC Film & Video in Hong Kong Co. c

Ge-Ying Lin (*Spinach*); Shao-Wen Haw (*Chow Sing Chi*); Shiao-Long She (*Li Lan Kit*); Jeng-Yie Chang; Lo-Shen Shu; Chung-Dan Fan; Kuo-Jew Chang; Dee Lew

A lightweight, gag-filled coming-of-age comedy, this farce blatantly lifts the story line of SOME KIND OF WONDERFUL, adding elements from other John Hughes productions (like HOME ALONE) and a silly subplot about a four-year-old kung-fu master. Though it's obvious from the start where the film is headed, its fast pace and softhearted approach toward unrequited adolescent love make for charming, occasionally goofy, entertainment.

Teenage Pi Shi Ting (Ge-Ying Lin), nicknamed Spinach, is romantically hung up on Annie, the well-off granddaughter of his school principal. Spinach's best friend Pearl warns him that he's pursuing a hopeless cause, but the lovesick daydreamer continues to court Annie, despite physical threats from her aggressive boyfriend Eagle, who is the son of a key school official. To settle matters, Eagle challenges Spinach to a one-on-one baseball game. Despite Eagle's victory, he still beats Spinach up over his continuing attention to Annie. In the meantime, Spinach's mother begins to suspect that her husband is cheating on her, so she transforms his casual business trip from Hong Kong to mainland China into a full-blown family vacation. While there, Spinach's baby brother Chow Sing Chi (Shao-Wen Haw) wanders away from the family and encounters Li Lan Kit (Shiao-Long She), a four-year-old monk who agrees to teach Sing kung fu. Spinach accompanies Sing to Kit's temple, hoping that the rigors of the martial arts will improve his self confidence. On his return to Hong Kong, Annie once again rebuffs him, even after he defeats Eagle in a second baseball face-off. Undaunted, he soon supplies her with with a tape on which Eagle's father urges Eagle to marry her in order to facilitate a deal with Japanese businessmen that would sell the school out from under her grandfather's nose. The climactic scene pits Eagle, his crooked dad, and a gang of hoods against Spinach, Sing, and Li Lan Kit. The ensuing confrontation sees the good guys emerge victorious, with Spinach set to make a mature romantic decision: after Annie convinces him they don't belong together, he pledges his love to Pearl, who has been pining for him from the start.

As slight as it is, the film remains watchable, precisely because it is such a shameless crib of Hughes's innately American kiddie fare. The imposition of the "baby fu" subplot renders the proceedings more properly Asian, although its eventual resolution in a slapstick, HOME ALONE vein once again brings up the spectral influence of American pap. That said, the film still has its pleasures, including a cartoonlike opening fantasy sequence, a video-game fight scene, and the silly instances wherein the precocious kids act out various kung fu cliches. (The movie's peculiar title is a complete non sequitur—"Popeye" is the name of Chow's pet dog.) — E.G.

d, Yen-Pin Chiu; p, Shiao-Ping Chang; exec p, Jing-Hwan Lee; w, Ying-Chio Yeh; ph, Rom-Shiw Chen; ed, Bo-Wen Chen; prod d, Pai-Rom

Comedy/Martial Arts/Children's   (PR: A   MPAA: NR)

SHORT FILM ABOUT KILLING, A   ★★★★
(Poland) 84m Polish Corporation for Film Production; Tor Film Unit; Zespoly Filmowe; Telewizja Polska; Sender Freies Berlin ~ Sovcan c
(KROTKI FILM O ZABIJANIU)

Miroslaw Baka (*Jacek Lazar—The Murderer*); Krzysztof Globisz (*Piotr Balicki—The Lawyer*); Peter Jan Tesarz (*Waldemar Rekowski—The Taxi Driver*); Zbigniew Zapasiewicz (*Bar Examiner*); Barbara Dziekan-Vajda (*Girl in Cinema Box Office*); Aleksander Bednarz (*Executioner*); Jerzy Zass (*Court Official*); Zdzislaw Tobiasz (*Judge*); Artur Barcis (*Young Man*); Krystyna Janda; Olgierd Lukaszewicz; L. Andrzejewski; Wendy Bednarz; Z. Borek; W. Byrdy; W. Borsucki; A. Gawronski; H. Guzek; I. Glebicka; E. Helman; B. Hubicki; H. Kowalczykowa; K. Luft; H. Lapinski; B. Niewinowski; B. Marynowski; M. Manteska; M. Maciejewski; A. Mastalerz; J. Mielech; M. Miarczynska; L. Pietrasz; M. Pieczynska; Z. Plato; Z. Rychter; K. Stelmaszyk; K. Stepkowski; M. Szary; C. Switkowski; A. Wolska

A SHORT FILM ABOUT KILLING is an expanded version of episode five of late director Krzysztof Kieslowski's DECALOGUE (1988), a ten-part series made for Polish television interpreting the themes of the biblical Ten Commandments in modern stories. This episode focuses on the fifth commandment "Thou Shalt not Kill" and brilliantly portrays the dynamics between killer, victim, and legal system, implicating all three in a web of violence, hatred, moral anguish, and guilt.

The film opens in the bleak courtyards of a typical Polish housing project. A series of images establish the bond between nature, death, and human cruelty—a piece of fruit covered with insects, children running away giggling after lynching a black cat, a man barely avoiding being hit by an object thrown with ill intent from a window. The camera begins to follow this man, the simple taxi driver Waldemar (Peter Jan Tesarz), as he prepares for his workday. The urban landscape is depicted as a hostile terrain where each isolated person takes pleasure only in the small covert actions they can achieve against others. The taxi driver himself indulges in these little aggressions and, in the course of a day, delights in leaving passengers stranded, frightening poodles, and even feeding poisoned meat to a stray dog.

Two more characters are introduced, Jacek (Miroslaw Baka), a young thug from the countryside, unhappy and restless, who wanders the city aimlessly, and Piotr (Krzysztof Globisz) a young, idealistic law student who takes and passes his bar exams. The film intercuts the lives of these three apparently unrelated figures throughout the course of the day in which their fates will intersect irretrievably. We witness the joy and optimism of the new lawyer, the alienation of the young thug, and the boredom and cruelty of the taxi driver. It is with apparent arbitrariness that Jacek finally hails one cab and not another, instructs the driver to take a desolate alternative route, and then brutally murders him. Jacek will be defended unsuccessfully by the young lawyer Piotr, given the death penalty, and hanged by the state.

The relative speed with which the film moves from the murder to capital punishment serves to highlight their moral equivalence. The long buildup that precedes the murders engenders no sympathy but rather adopts the cold perspective of a stranger. In this sense, Kieslowski relies entirely on the crimes themselves to reveal the meanings of the moral commandment. For instance, the cab driver is unlikeable, yet his particularly grisly murder is emotionally troubling for both the viewer and the murderer. When strangulation fails, Jacek delivers blows to the head, but the man refuses to die. After dragging the corpse to the river, Jacek hears his victim quietly uttering the word "please". In great duress he smashes a boulder repeatedly over the man's skull until he is certain the man is dead.

On the day of his scheduled execution, Jacek requests a visit from his lawyer and unburdens his soul on the tormented Piotr. Piotr's initial joy in his work has gone; his experience with this case has taught him the anguish of his new occupation. Piotr follows Jacek and a group of grim prison officers through dark, barren corridors to the execution chamber, where a noose is placed around his neck and a mechanical hatch opens the floor beneath him. The panic and discomfort of those involved in the execution resembles Jacek's own fumblings with the taxi driver, and the film's final scenes reverberate with the meaning of a life and the moral burden of those who take it.

Released in Poland in 1988, this film preceded the success of Kieslowski's later French films, including THE DOUBLE LIFE OF VERONIQUE (1991) and the much acclaimed trilogy RED (1995), WHITE (1995), and BLUE (1995), which take up similar themes of contingency, fate, and coincidence surrounding and defining human action and responsibility. Distributed in an expanded version in conjunction with A SHORT FILM ABOUT LOVE, both films are superb works. (*Adult situations, profanity, graphic violence.*) — R.C.

d, Krzysztof Kieslowski; p, Ryszard Chutkowski; w, Krzysztof Kieslowski, Krzysztof Piesiewicz; ph, Slawomir Idziak; ed, Ewa Smal; m, Zbigniew Preisner; prod d, Halina Dobrowolska; art d, Grazyna Tkaczyk; set d, Robert Czesak; sound, Malgorzata Jaworska (recordist); cos, Malgorzata Obloza, Hanna Cwiklo; makeup, Dorotta Sewerynska; stunts, Robert Brzezinski, Janusz Chlebowski, Jozef Stefanski

Drama/Political   (PR: O   MPAA: NR)

SHORT FILM ABOUT LOVE, A   ★★★½
(Poland) 87m Tor Film Unit; Telewizja Polska; Polish Corporation for Film Production; Sander Freies Berlin ~ Sovcan c
(KROTKI FILM O MILOSCI)

Olaf Lubaszenko (*Tomek*); Grazyna Szapolowska (*Magda*); Stefania Iwinska (*Gospodyni*); Piotr Machalica (*Roman*); Artur Barcis (*Mlody Mezczyzna*); M. Chojnacka; S. Gawlik; T. Gradowski; R. Imbro; J. Piechocinski; K. Koperski; J. Michalewska; M. Rozniatowska; E. Ziolkowska

A SHORT FILM ABOUT LOVE is an expanded version of episode six of late director Krzysztof Kieslowski's DECALOGUE (1988), a ten-part series made for Polish television that presents the themes of the Ten Commandments in modern stories. Though this episode represents the commandment regarding adultery, Kieslowski focuses more broadly on desire of a distant object, exemplified best in modern life by the figure of the lone voyeur. Unique to this portrayal of voyeurism, desire is redeemed by love.

The young voyeur Tomek (Olaf Lubaszenko) cultivates a private passion for Magda (Grazyna Szapolowska), an older woman living in the apartment opposite his window. He gazes rapturously through his telescope every evening, phones her simply to hear her voice, and sets an alarm to the hour she is expected home. He is particularly moved one evening when he watches her arrive home alone, drop her head to the table, and cry inconsolably. Magda is a single woman with a healthy lovelife, but Tomek is disturbed by her affairs and looks away when she makes love to a man. He even goes as far as to phone the gas company and report a false gas leak in her unit to interrupt her passion. Tomek also takes advantage of his position as a postal clerk to slip phoney notices in her box to lure her to the post office. He also takes an early morning milk delivery job, in hope of coming into contact with her at her doorstep.

One day Tomek courageously reveals the truth to her. She flees in disgust but that evening positions the bed directly in front of the window, undresses, and invites a man into her bed. The next morning Magda meets him at the door when he delivers her milk and tries to assess exactly what he wants from her. His response, "nothing," perplexes her. Out of curiosity, she agrees to meet him at a cafe, where she learns that he has been confiscating her mail, that he has opinions about the various men she has known during the past year, and that he was introduced to her window by his friend before him who also enjoyed her. Further questioning reveals that he no longer masturbates over her or watches her having sex, and that his desire has turned into genuine love.

Cynical about the possibility of love, she decides to seduce him and teach him that love is a myth. He ejaculates in his pants, and she observes that *this* is love, and this is *all* it is. In utter despair he runs home and cuts his wrists. She sees him being taken away by ambulance and begins making inquiries. Now she becomes the voyeur, obsessed with watching his window for his return. When he does return, she rushes over and finds him sleeping. She peers through his telescope and sees herself alone in her apartment, her head on the table, crying inconsolably—she sees herself as the object of his love and care. Rather than teaching the young man her cynicism, he has taught her of the existence of love.

This film is especially interesting because it challenges the traditional interpretation of voyeurism as an assaultive and objectifying gaze. In this film, the gaze becomes increasingly subjective, providing a uniquely intimate viewpoint. It is her lack of self consciousness that allows him to see her as she truly is, and thus allows him to truly love her. The telescope, an instrument of distance and objectivity, dialectically brings him closer to an intimate realm he would otherwise not know. His love overcomes the sin of desire and violation expressed in the religious commandment. Distributed in conjunction with A SHORT FILM ABOUT KILLING, both films predate Kieslowski's recent critically acclaimed films THE DOUBLE LIFE OF VERONIQUE (1991) and the trilogy RED (1995), WHITE, (1995) and BLUE (1995), and both films serve to reveal a remarkable and important filmmaker. *(Adult situations, sexual situations.)* — R.C.

d, Krzysztof Kieslowski; p, Ryszard Chutkowski; w, Krzysztof Kieslowski, Krzysztof Piesiewicz; ph, Witold Adamek; ed, Ewa Smal; m, Zbigniew Preisner; art d, Halina Dobrowolska; set d, Grazyna Tkaczyk, Robert Czesak; sound, Nikodem Wolk-Laniewski (recordist); cos, Malgorzata Obloza, Hanna Cwiklo; stunts, Robert Brzezinski, Andrzej Zaczynski, Janusz Chlebowski, Ryszard Janikowski

Drama (PR: C MPAA: NR)

SHOW, THE ★★
(U.S.) 93m The Show Productions, Inc.; Tollin/Robbins Productions; Rysher Entertainment ~ Savoy Pictures c/bw

Run DMC; Warren G; Naught by Nature; Wu-Tang Clan; Craig Mack; Dr. Dre; Da 5 Footaz; Snoop Doggy Dog; Tha Dog Pound; The Notorious B.I.G.; Afrika Bambaataa; Andre Harrell; Doc Ice; The Furious Five; Kid Capri; Kurtis Blow; Russell Simmons; Sean "Puffy" Combs; Slick Rick; Soulsonic Force; Twinz; Whodini

A documentary so unstructured that it sometimes resembles rushes rather than a finished film, THE SHOW panders to rap and hip-hop fans, never deigning to provide context for or commentary on its subjects—presumably because anyone so uncool as to need it obviously doesn't deserve the time of day. Its attitude is flawless, if obnoxious, but by most conventional documentary standards, THE SHOW is a failure.

Structurally, THE SHOW is a standard-issue, MTV-style music "rockumentary" that mixes concert footage and interviews with artists, record company executives—notably hip-hop pioneer Russell Simmons, one of the film's presenters and its co-executive producer—and various hangers-on. The show of the title is a 1994 concert at the Philadelphia Armory, featuring a stellar lineup of rappers, including most of the artists featured in the interview segments. THE SHOW opens and closes with scenes of Simmons visiting rapper Slick Rick in jail, where he's serving a sentence for second-degree murder. For no apparent reason, the majority of the performance footage—but not all—is in B&W, while the offstage footage is in color.

Perhaps the most interesting thing THE SHOW reveals is the generational and aesthetic differences that divide a world which appears to most outsiders as an uniform realm of throbbing hostility. One particularly telling sequence shows hip-hop elder statesmen like Afrika Bambaataa and Kurtis Blow sitting around a table debating the finer points of rap's history and kvetching about the younger generation, for all the world like a pack of old vaudevillians at the Carnegie Deli, reminiscing and deploring the youth of today. The observations of rap veterans like LL Cool J and members of Run DMC about the increasing hostility of hip-hop are also revealing. The younger artists, almost to a man (there are virtually no women artists on view), appear rancorous, unfocused, and inarticulate in their interviews. To hear one after another mumble, swear, and repeatedly lose his train of thought is to wonder whether director Brian Robinson went out of his way to capture them at their worst. He also records members of Tha Dogg Pound arguing bitterly with him and one another, as well as a minor mutiny among the members of Wu-Tang Clan.

THE SHOW features performance clips of an impressive array of hip-hop's current stars—including Naughty by Nature, Dr. Dre, Notorious B.I.G. and Warren G. But it's extremely repetitive. The concert footage all looks alike, and the interviews are numbingly similar—how many times must we hear that rap is aggressive and expletive-filled because it reflects life in the 'hood? A series of scenes in which Japanese fans mimic rap's cadences and trademark gestures—crude pelvic thrusts and hostile hand gestures—is funny but cheap. *(Extreme profanity.)* — M.M.

d, Brian Robbins; p, Michael Tollin, Robert Johnson; exec p, Russell Simmons, Stan Nathan, Bob Kenneally; assoc p, Marvin Wadlow; co-p, Carmen Ashford; w, Michael Tollin, Brian Robbins; ph, Dasal Banks, Larry Banks, Steven Consentino, Ericson Core, John Demps, Todd A. Dos Reis, Johnny Simmons, Michael Negrin; ed, Michael Schultz; m, Stanley Clarke; prod d, Yoland Busbee; sound, Abdul Malik Abbot, Dwight Brown, Scott Evan, Evan Prettyman, Davis S. McJunkin, Ben Moore

Documentary/Musical (PR: C MPAA: R)

SHOWGIRLS ★½
(U.S.) 131m Chargeurs; Carolco; Vegas Productions;
United Artists ~ MGM/UA c

Elizabeth Berkley *(Nomi Malone)*; Kyle MacLachlan *(Zack Carey)*; Gina Gershon *(Cristal Connors)*; Glenn Plummer *(James Smith)*; Robert Davi *(Al Torres)*; Alan Rachins *(Tony Moss)*; Gina Ravera *(Molly Abrams)*; Lin Tucci *(Henrietta Bazoom)*; Greg Travis *(Phil Newkirk)*; Al Ruscio *(Mr. Karlman)*; Patrick Bristow *(Marty Jacobsen)*; William Shockley *(Andrew Carver)*; Michelle Johnston *(Gay Carpenter)*; Dewey Weber *(Jeff)*; Rena Riffel *(Penny)*; Melinda Songer *(Nicky)*; Melissa Williams *(Julie)*; Lance Davis *(Bell Captain)*; Jack McGee *(Jack the Stagehand)*; Jim Ishida *(Mr. Okida)*; Ungela Brockman *(Annie)*; Bobbie Phillips *(Dee)*; Dante McCarthy *(Carmi)*; Caroline Key Johnson *(Nadia)*; Joan Foley *(Jail Matron)*; Terry Beeman *(Felix)*; Kevin Stea *(Daryl)*; Sebastian La Cause *(Sal)*; Lisa Boyle *(Sonny)*; Alexander Folk *(Booking Sergeant)*; Matt Battaglia *(Andrew Carver's Bodyguard)*; Teo *(Andrew Carver's Bodyguard)*; Elaine Van Betten *(Versace Salesperson)*; Alexander Zale *(Doctor)*; Irene Olga Lopez *(Personnel Woman)*; Julie Pop *(Nurse)*; Jacob Witkin *(Caesar)*; Jana Walker *(Secretary)*; Christina Robinette *(Receptionist)*; Jim Wise *(Cheetah Loudmouth)*; Michael Shure *(Cheetah Drunk)*; Geoff Calla *(Cheetah Drunk)*; Rick Marotta *(Long-Haired Drunk)*; Paul Bates *(Cheetah Bouncer)*; Michael Cooke *(Casino Lecher)*; Jean Barrett *(Change Girl)*; Gary Devaney *(Texan at Spago)*; Gene Ellison-Jone *(Texan at Spago)*; Fernando Celis *(Hector)*; Robert Dunn *(Chimp Trainer)*; Ashley Nation *(Julie's Daughter)*; Cory Melander *(Jule's Son)*; Sean Breen *(Reporter)*; Elizabeth Kennedy *(Photographer)*; Katherine Manning *(Reporter)*; Warren Reno *(Crave Club Bouncer)*; Ken Enomoto *(Cheetah Customer)*; Y. Hero Abe *(Cheetah Customer)*; Odney Ueno *(Cheetah Customer)*; Kathleen McTeague *(Al Torres' Girl)*; Kristen Knittl *(Al Torres' Girl)*; Sage Peart *(Paramedic)*; Gregory R. Goliath *(Cheetah Bouncer)*; Michael Washington *(Crave Club Heckler)*; Judette Warren *(Spelling Dancer)*; Lonetta Pugh *(Baby Fat Dancer)*; Maria Diaz *(Yoga Dancer)*; Madison Clark *(Classes Dancer)*; Bethany Chesser *(Finalist Dancer)*; Kelly St. Romaine *(Melon Dancer)*; Danielle Burgio *(Ear and Nose Dancer)*

The most hyped movie of 1995, SHOWGIRLS was Hollywood's first attempt to mass-market a film with an NC-17 rating. But excoriating reviews scared off everyone but curiosity seekers and the raincoat crowd. Its non-stop display of flesh and sleaze aside, SHOWGIRLS is a cliched and coarsely acted backstage drama whose only possible value lies in its camp posturing.

Nomi (Elizabeth Berkley), a brassy young woman, hitchhikes into Las Vegas determined to become a star showgirl. All her possessions are stolen by the Elvis impersonator from whom she gets a lift. As she sits weeping in a parking lot, she is befriended by Molly (Gina Ravera), a young costumer. Molly invites Nomi to share her trailer, and Nomi quickly begins clawing her way to the top of the Vegas ladder. She gets a job dancing in a sleazy topless club, then begins doing lap dances for bigger pay. After performing for big-time hotel entertainment director Zack Carey (Kyle MacLachlan) and Stardust Hotel revue star Cristal Connors (Gina Gershon), Nomi wins an audition in front of a big-time producer. Molly warns her of the dangers of swimming with sharks. After sleeping with Zack and flirting with Cristal's come-ons, understudy Nomi pushes Cristal down a flight of stairs. She becomes the new star of the Stardust revue.

Now famous and covered with glitter, Nomi is invited to a party with Michael Bolton-like crooner Andrew Carver (William Shockley), Molly's idol. Nomi takes her loyal roommate to Carver's swank affair. Carver flirts with the starstruck Molly, then lures her into a room where he and his brutal bodyguards gang rape her. Zack tries to buy the girls' silence on behalf of "the Vegas family," but Nomi turns from backstabber to vengeance-seeker. With stiletto heels and a switchblade, she beats Carver senseless. Nomi leaves Las Vegas the same way she came in: hitching a ride.

This colossal misfire from the writer-director team of Joe Eszterhas and Paul Verhoeven—who created the erotic thriller BASIC INSTINCT—received the critical censure it so richly merited, but also set back the cause of producing and exhibiting films whose adult subject matter might warrant an NC-17 rating. Verhoeven negotiated an unprecedented studio guarantee that he could make a controversial and graphic movie and not have to cut it for an R rating. Instead of delivering a provocative film for mature audiences, he produced an unpleasant, two-dimensional gawk at the seamy facade and sleazy back rooms of topless Las Vegas.

Verhoeven claimed he intended to show the harsh, corrupted side of this culture of showgirls and the glitzmeisters who exploit them in all its shallowness. The glossy, neon surface of the casinos and strip joints are indeed captured in the film's flashy cinematography, but Eszterhas's story and characters are equally superficial. Rather than offering a critique of the Vegas aesthetic, SHOWGIRLS simply makes us voyeuristic participants in the sleaze. Elizabeth Berkeley's wooden lead performance makes the script's weaknesses all the more obvious. Her Nomi has no range, only extremes: She's either giggling girlishly or shrieking like a brass harpy, suggesting that she suffers from a bipolar disorder. Her character is witlessly unsympathetic—even by comparison with the despicable snakes who surround her—and the fact that she's in virtually every shot makes SHOWGIRLS that much more painful to watch.

When SHOWGIRLS has the opportunity to redeem itself in the final act, it turns from merely bad to reprehensible. The film's only likable character (arguably the film's only real character), the selfless and innocent Molly, is brutally raped in a barely-motivated story twist. Eszterhas claimed this was a "moral tale," because Nomi does the right thing by rejecting Vegas values and avenging the crime. But SHOWGIRLS is no THELMA & LOUISE: It's can't even put its "moral" on screen. While Verhoeven doesn't shy away from the violent display of a gang rape of, not coincidentally, the only story's only African-American woman, he's suddenly coy when the rapist is assaulted. We see only Carver's point of view as Nomi repeatedly kicks him in revenge; the violence is kept off-camera, as if this—of all things—were too horrible to show. If this is redemption, it fails to make Nomi any more sympathetic. *(Extensive nudity, sexual situations, adult situations, profanity, violence, substance abuse.)* — D.S.

d, Paul Verhoeven; p, Alan Marshall, Charles Evans; exec p, Mario Kassar; assoc p, Lynn Ehrensperger; co-p, Ben Myron; w, Joe Eszterhas; ph, Jost Vacano; ed, Mark Goldblatt, Mark Helfrich; m, David A. Stewart; prod d, Allan Cameron; art d, William F. O'Brien; set d, Richard C. Goddard; ch, Marguerite Pomerhn-Derricks; sound, Joseph Geisinger (mixer); fx, Burt Dalton, Special Effects Unlimited, Inc.; casting, Johanna Ray, Elaine Huzzar; cos, Ellen Mirojnick; makeup, David Craig Forrest; stunts, Gary Combs

Erotic/Drama (PR: O MPAA: NC-17)

SILENCE OF THE HAMS ★
(Italy/U.S.) 85m 13 Century Wolf; Concorde-New Horizons; Silvio Berlusconi Communications ~ October Films c
(IL SILENZIO DEI PROSCIUTTI)

Ezio Greggio *(Antonio Motel)*; Dom DeLuise *(Dr. Animal Cannibal Pizza)*; Billy Zane *(Joe Dee Fostar)*; Joanna Pacula *(Lily)*; Charlene Tilton *(Jane)*; Martin Balsam *(Detective Balsam)*; Stuart Pankin *(Pete Putrid)*; John Astin *(Ranger)*; Larry Storch *(Sergeant)*; Bubba Smith *(Olaf)*; Rip Taylor *(Mr. Laurel)*; Phyllis Diller *(Old Secretary)*; Shelley Winters *(Mother)*; Nedra Volz *(Ranger's Wife)*; Rosey Brown *(Motorcycle Cop)*; Henry Silva *(Police Chief)*; Marshall Bell *(Cross Dresser Agent)*; Lee Allan *(First Agent)*; Sal Landi *(Second Agent)*; John Roarke *(George Bush)*; Pat Rick *(Bill Clinton)*; Tony Cox *(Dwarf Guard)*; Joe Dante *(Dying Man)*; John Carpenter *(Trench Coat Man)*; Irwin Keyes *(Guard)*; Jeff Bright *(Mummy)*; Kimber Sissons *(Push-up Lady)*; Eddie Deezen *(Video Cameraman)*; Kenneth Dayitian *(Pavarotti)*; Peter DeLuise *(Checkout Guard)*; Rudy De Luca *(Checkout Maniac)*; Lynn Shirey *(Hillary Clinton)*; John Landis *(FBI Agent)*; David DeLuise *(Policeman 1)*; John Fadule *(Policeman 2)*; Al Ruscio *(Phillip Morris)*; Dom Irrera *(Gas Station Attendant)*; Lance Kinsey *(First Interrogating Officer)*; Jeff Weston *(Agent)*; Shelly Desai *(Trick)*; Seifullah Ziyad, II *(Michael Jackson)*; Lonnie Burr *(Drunk)*; Debra Christofferson *(Misery Woman)*; Linda Lutz *(Housedress Woman)*; Heather Elizabeth Parkhurst *(Beautiful Woman)*; Jim Maniaci *(Rape Culturist 1)*; Manny Molina *(Rape Culturist 2)*; Raymond Serra *(Agent Prostitute 1)*; Robert Muse *(Agent Prostitute 2)*; Daniel McVicar *(Forensic Expert)*; Lana Schwab *(Nurse)*; Wilhelm Von Homburg *(Maitre d')*; Matteo Molinari *(Bell Boy)*; Rino Piccolo *(Ambulance Driver)*

A colossal misfire of the parody genre, this takeoff on thriller movies spoofs a number of classic (PSYCHO, NIGHT OF THE LIVING DEAD) and contemporary (MISERY, BASIC INSTINCT, SILENCE OF THE LAMBS) films. A cast of has-beens and wannabes—headed by an Italian star as yet unknown in the US—fail to breathe life into the stale gags and tired trickery of this direct-to-video release.

For his first big assignment, FBI agent Joe Dee Fostar (Billy Zane) is put on the trail of the Psycho Serial Killer. His quest begins at the Unbelievably Bad Maniacs wing of the Hollywood Nuthouse, where he interviews Dr. Animal Cannibal Pizza (Dom DeLuise) for clues as to the killer's identity. In the meantime, Fostar's girlfriend, Jane (Charlene Tilton), steals $400,000 from her employer, Mr. Laurel (Rip Taylor), and holes up at the Cemetery Motel, where she is stabbed, shot, and drowned by Antonio Motel (Ezio Greggio), the bewigged proprietor. Detective Balsam (Martin Balsam) investigates Jane's disappearance and becomes the next victim. Jane's sister Lily (Joanna Pacula) turns to Joe Dee for help in locating Jane. Joe Dee, more interested in finding the missing money, returns to Dr. Animal for advice. In exchange for his release and his own pizza parlor, Dr. Animal points the FBI man in the direction of Antonio's Motel. Joe Dee and Lily are held in the basement by Antonio's mother (Shelley Winters), who admits to being the psycho killer. After a ranger (John Astin) and his wife (Nedra Volz) come upon the scene, the suspects, victims, and killers take turns pulling off face masks to reveal their true identities. Jane and Inspector Balsam are still alive, Mr. Laurel reclaims the stolen cash, and Antonio's mother wonders who she has really killed.

The parody genre has enjoyed a resurgence in popularity in the past half-decade. Recent entries include HOT SHOTS! (parts one and DEUX), the NAKED GUN series, FATAL INSTINCT, and NATIONAL LAMPOON'S LOADED WEAPON. Despite a few innovative comic bits, THE SILENCE OF THE HAMS cannot keep company with these other films, and essentially falls flat. With his American debut film, writer-director-star Greggio tried to hedge his bets by throwing in everything but the kitchen sink. There are pratfalls, sight gags, word puns, flatulence jokes,

and celebrity impersonators. The TV series "The Addams Family" is even knocked off—its finger-snapping theme song plays whenever Astin (whose character has a pet foot called "Smelly Thing") appears. Greggio, who somehow convinced a number of celebrities and noted filmmakers to appear in cameos, should have kept mum. *(Violence, nudity, sexual situations, profanity.)* — B.R.

d, Ezio Greggio; p, Ezio Greggio, Julie Corman; exec p, Harris Tulchin, Ezio Greggio; w, Ezio Greggio; ph, Jacques Haitkin; ed, Robert Barrere, Andy Horvitch; m, Parmer Fuller; prod d, Jim Newport; art d, Russel Smith; set d, Natalie Kendrick Pope; sound, James R. Einolf (mixer); fx, John Hartigan, Ultimate Effects; casting, Craig Campobasso; cos, Leesa Evans; makeup, Michelle Bloom, David Barton, Modus EFX; stunts, Gary Morgan

Comedy (PR: O MPAA: R)

SISTER MY SISTER ★★★
(U.K.) 89m Film Four International; NFH Productions; Channel Four; British Screen Finance ~ Seventh Art Releasing c

Julie Walters *(Madame Danzard)*; Joely Richardson *(Christine)*; Jodhi May *(Lea)*; Sophie Thursfield *(Isabelle)*; Amelda Brown *(Visitor)*; Lucita Pope *(Visitor)*; Kate Gartside *(Sister Veronica)*; Aimee Schmidt *(Young Lea)*; Gabriella Schmidt *(Young Christine)*

A British dramatization of a famous French crime, SISTER MY SISTER traveled the American arthouse and festival circuit in 1995. Based on the true story of incestuous sisters who murdered their employers in 1932 (previously dramatized in Jean Genet's play, "The Maids"), SISTER MY SISTER is a dark, disturbing film, the kind you cannot forget, no matter how much you'd like to.

Lest anyone unfamiliar with the grisly case believe this tale may end happily, the filmmakers begin the piece with fragmented views of the victims' bodies along a blood-spattered staircase. The story then back-pedals to the day when Lea (Jodhi May) came to work as a maid in the Danzard household, where her elder sister Christine (Joely Richardson) is already employed. Their employers, the exacting Madame (Julie Walters) and her disagreeable daughter Isabelle (Sophie Thursfield), are initially delighted with the sisters, who are submissive, quiet, and efficient. Madame is also thrilled at the terms of their employment and crows, "We'll get two practically for the price of one! They don't even want separate rooms!"

After cutting ties to their emotionally abusive mother, the sisters lead a completely isolated existence. They rarely speak to their employers and have no outside acquaintances. They share a bed in a cramped attic room, to which they retreat whenever they are not needed by Madame Danzard. Their extreme closeness and mutual dependence slowly progresses into a sexual relationship.

Possessively jealous of her sister, Christine becomes enraged when she witnesses Lea and Isabelle exchanging shy smiles. Where Christine was once a perfectionist, her fears over losing Lea cause her to become agitated and distracted from her work. Madame begins to suspect that something is amiss with the sisters.

Tensions escalate to a boiling point when the Danzards are out one afternoon and Lea blows an electrical fuse while ironing. When the Danzards return, they find the house in darkness, and the sisters distressed and disheveled. Madame surmises the nature of the sisters' relationship, and in a heated confrontation on the staircase, she spits at them and threatens to expose their secret. Pushed to the brink of madness, the sisters attack Madame and Isabelle with their bare hands, brutally murdering and dismembering them. When police arrive, they find the sisters in bed together, naked and clutching one another.

A postscript reveals that Lea was imprisoned for twenty years, then worked as a chambermaid until her death in 1982. Christine was sentenced to death by guillotine, but that sentence was commuted and she was committed to an insane asylum, where she died four years later. She never spoke Lea's name again.

Grim subject matter, slow pacing, and a claustrophobic setting combine to make SISTER MY SISTER an overlong, psychologically depleting experience. The dialogue is minimal, and much of the action consists of exchanged looks. Thus, first-time director Meckler wisely focuses on the actors rather than the action, especially since the script holds few surprises once the shock of the initial bloody montage passes. Kesselman (who based the script upon her play, "My Sister in This House") draws interesting parallels between the two relationships, both based on an unhealthy emotional dependence. A particularly effective scene intercuts between the Danzards playing cards in the parlor and the maids upstairs making love.

Richardson and May have meaty roles in the incestuous sisters. Both actresses possess wonderfully expressive faces, useful commodities in a film in which dialogue is sparse. Richardson's commanding presence makes Christine's descent into madness particularly riveting. May blends her character's childlike naivete and desperate neediness to craft the film's most pitiable character. Though Madame Danzard is one of the victims, she is scripted as the villain of the piece, a monstrous woman obsessed with maintaining an immaculate household. Walters teeters on the verge of caricature in her performance.

Backing the all-woman cast is a nearly all-woman production team, topped by producer Norma Heyman. Perhaps one result of this predominantly female collaboration is that neither the sex nor violence is exploitative. The sisters' sexual relationship is discretely and tastefully filmed. Likewise, the murders are conservatively shot, with the more gruesome details of the killings left to the imagination. (*Graphic violence, sexual situations, adult situations.*) — B.R.

d, Nancy Meckler; p, Norma Heyman; assoc p, Joyce Herlihy; w, Wendy Kesselman (based on her play *My Sister In This House*); ph, Ashley Rowe; ed, David Stiven; m, Stephen Warbeck; prod d, Caroline Amies; art d, Frank Walsh; sound, Chris Munro (mixer); Glenn Freemantle; casting, Sara Bird; cos, Lindy Hemming

Drama/Crime (PR: O   MPAA: NR)

SIX DAYS, SIX NIGHTS ★★½
(France/U.K.) 90m New Light Films;
France 3 Cinema ~ Lumiere Pictures c
(AKA: TO THE LIMIT; A LA FOLIE)

Anne Parillaud *(Alice)*; Beatrice Dalle *(Elsa)*; Patrick Aurignac *(Franck)*; Bernard Verley *(Sanders)*; Alain Chabat *(Thomas)*; Jean-Claude DeGoror *(Raymond)*; Marie Guillard *(Betty)*

The old saying about houseguests who stay more than a week is played out with a killer vengeance in this engrossing, well-designed *menage a trois*.

Diane Kurys's film is a Gallic variant of SINGLE WHITE FEMALE. Elsa (Beatrice Dalle) is the visitor from hell who descends upon her artist friend, Alice (Anne Parillaud), and makes herself right at home with her toothbrush, refrigerator, and, of course, her hapless boxer boyfriend, Franck (Patrick Aurignac). As the two women act out their mysterious symbiosis, Frank becomes little more than a pawn. Are the two really

sisters, as one claims? Are they former lovers? What's obvious is the fact that Elsa is more than a little batty, with her constant prevaricating and destructive behavior. The apartment the trio share turns into a veritable inferno of mental and physical game-playing that becomes increasingly dangerous. Before the end of the film Elsa turns Alice into a quivering mass handcuffed to a radiator before a nonplussed Franck. Alice eventually pulls herself together, gives Elsa the heave-ho, and gets her career back on track. She ends up in New York, far from Elsa's demonic dogging of her . . . or is she?

Starting with Vivien Leigh's Blanche Dubois, another houseguest who *should* leave, but never does, films have amply covered this psychosexual terrain. There's nothing particularly enlightening here, nor is anything probed very deeply, but Diane Kurys's direction is surer than it's ever been, and the claustrophobic aura of mystery is quite compelling. (That sub-Hitchcockian ending is risible, however.) Fabio Conversi's camerawork is vital to the conception, with its subtle palette and sinuous moves. Like the film's technicians, the actors also prove themselves well up to the task. With her stars, the director has two of the most compelling presences in French cinema. Waifish Parillaud makes a perfect victim, a Parisian equivalent to Anne Archer, whom she strongly resembles. Dalle, with her intriguing death's head face and a body that is at once emaciated and voluptuous, reprises her BETTY BLUE mania with knifelike precision. Instantly recognizable to the audience as a human minefield, it's a wonder the other characters aren't on to her from the start, but then there would be no movie. Aurignac is also comely, and rather touching as a macho man who is methodically stripped of all his defenses. (*Sexual situations, nudity, profanity, adult situations, substance abuse.*) — D.N.

d, Diane Kurys; p, Alexandre Arcady; exec p, Robert Benmussa; assoc p, Philippe Lievre; w, Diane Kurys, Antoine Lacomblez; ph, Fabio Conversi; ed, Luc Barnier; m, Michael Nyman; prod d, Tony Egry; set d, Marie-Agnes Giafferi; sound, Claude Villand (mixer); fx, Christian Portal, Jean-Francois Cousson, Pierre Bandini, Lionel Callari, Patrick Cauderlier, Jacana; casting, Pierre Amzallag; cos, Mic Cheminal; makeup, Didier Lavergne

Drama (PR: O   MPAA: NR)

SKINNER ★½
(U.S.) 84m Cinequaon Pictures; 5 Kidd Productions; Skinner Films ~ A-Pix Entertainment c

Traci Lords *(Heidi)*; Ted Raimi *(Dennis Skinner)*; Ricki Lake *(Kerry Tate)*; David Warshofsky *(Geoff Tate)*; Richard Schiff *(Eddie)*; Blaire Baron *(Gloria)*; Roberta Eaton *(Sandy)*; Christina Engelharde *(Rachel)*; DeWayne Williams *(Earl)*; Time Winters *(Night Watchman)*; Frederica Keston *(Suzanne)*; Saralee Froton *(Young Woman)*

Unleashed onto home video after two years' confinement on the shelf, SKINNER is an underdeveloped, unpleasant psycho chiller.

In need of extra money, Kerry Tate (Ricki Lake) rents out a spare room to Dennis Skinner (Ted Raimi) while her trucker husband, Geoff (David Warshofsky), is away on a job. Dennis seems like a nice, rather shy young man, but he is actually a cruel psychopath who abducts and skins young women, having witnessed his doctor father performing a post-mortem on his mother when he was a child. He himself is being hunted by Heidi (Traci Lords), a previous victim who escaped, minus some of her skin, before he could kill her. She tracks him down and confronts him as he's prowling for prey, but he overcomes her and butchers yet another innocent girl.

Despite Geoff's suspicions and her own discovery of some tangential evidence, Kerry doesn't suspect Dennis's true nature until it's too late. He takes her to the basement where he skins his victims, but is interrupted by the arrival of Geoff and Heidi. During the ensuing struggle, a security guard appears, mistakenly shoots Heidi dead and wounds Dennis. Although he's incapacitated, Dennis just laughs; he knows he'll be judged insane, and eventually be free to stalk again.

Given that director Ivan Nagy's involvement with Hollywood madam Heidi Fleiss and Lake's talk-show success only came to light after SKINNER's production, its delayed release could be seen as felicitous. But factor in Lords's adult-film past and the backgrounds of the movie's makers are far more interesting than anything that turns up on screen. Almost entirely bereft of plot, SKINNER quickly degenerates into a series of stalk-and-murder scenes involving anonymous female victims, punctuated by such offensive comic relief as Dennis indulging in minstrel-show antics while clad in the skin of a black man. Instead of being scary, the clinical scenes of butchery (excised in the R-rated version) and shots of the half-skinned Lords injecting herself with painkillers are just gross and unsavory; no doubt this isn't the kind of exposed flesh Lords's fans are interested in. She and the other actors do what they can under the circumstances, but are generally undone by characters who are—to stay with the film's prevalent metaphor—only skin-deep. (Graphic violence, extensive nudity, profanity.) — M.G.

d, Ivan Nagy; p, Brad Wyman, Joff Pollon; exec p, Nelson I. Korchak, Mark Beychok, Daniel Sales; assoc p, James H. Rutt; co-p, Tamar E. Glaser; w, Paul Hart-Wilden; ph, Greg Littlewood; ed, Peter Schink, Fred Roth; m, Contagion; prod d, Jonathan Carlson; sound, Dan Monahan; fx, K.N.B. EFX Group; casting, Jakki Fink; cos, John Stavros; makeup, Laurie Schakosky

Horror (PR: O MPAA: NR)

SMOKE ★★★½
(U.S.) 112m Miramax; Nippon Film Development; Smoke Productions; Euro Space Productions; Interal ~ Miramax c

Harvey Keitel (Auggie Wren); William Hurt (Paul Benjamin); Harold Perrineau, Jr. (Thomas "Rashid" Cole); Forest Whitaker (Cyrus Cole); Stockard Channing (Ruby McNutt); Victor Argo (Vinnie); Erica Gimpel (Doreen Cole); Clarice Taylor (Ethel); Ashley Judd (Felicity); Malik Yoba (The Creeper); Mary Ward (April Lee); Jared Harris (Jimmy Rose); Giancarlo Esposito (Tommy); Jose Zuniga (Jerry); Stephen Gevedon (Dennis); Daniel Auster (Book Thief); Dierdre O'Connell (Waitress); Michelle Hurst (Aunt Em); Mel Gorham (Violet); Vincenzo Amelia (Irate Customer); Gilson Heglas (Cyrus Jr.); Howie Rose (Baseball Announcer); Baxter Harris (Lawyer No. 1); Paul Geier (Lawyer No. 2); Walter T. Mead (Roger Goodwin); Murray Moston (Waiter)

Author Paul Auster (THE MUSIC OF CHANCE) teamed up with filmmaker Wane Wang (A GREAT WALL) to create this novel excursion into storytelling.

Auggie Wren (Harvey Keitel) runs a cigar store in the Park Slope neighborhood of Brooklyn, where a colorful assortment of regular customers, including blocked novelist Paul Benjamin (William Hurt), hang out and spin philosophy while puffing on Panatelas. Auggie has a singular hobby: every day for years he's taken a single photo of his store from the exact same spot on the other side of the street. Paul still grieves for his wife, who was killed in a holdup, and dwells obsessively on the contingency of life ("If she hadn't had exact change . . . ").

Paul is saved from a hit-and-run collision by a young man who calls himself Rasheed (Harold Perrineau, Jr.), who has nowhere to live. Paul takes him home for a few days, but finds the

intrusion on his writerly solitude intolerable, and asks him to find his own place. Rasheed leaves, refusing to take money from Paul. Later, a woman searching for the young man explains to Paul that his real name is Tom Cole, and he has been searching for his father, Cyrus, who killed his wife (Tom's mother) in a drunken car wreck 12 years earlier. Tom finds Cyrus (Forrest Whitaker) in Peekskill, where he is trying to reopen a dilapidated gas station. Calling himself Paul Benjamin, Tom charms his way into a job without revealing his identity.

Meanwhile, Auggie's old flame Ruby (Stockard Channing), shows up seeking $3000 to get her daughter—who might be Auggie's—away from her abusive, crack-dealing boyfriend. Auggie reluctantly visits Felicity (Ashley Judd) with Ruby, and finds a foul-mouthed, pregnant crackhead who rejects their offer of assistance. Tom returns to Park Slope and Auggie offers him a job. But Tom accidentally destroys Auggie's secret cache of Cuban cigars, blowing a big deal and costing him $5000. Tom tells Paul that he has a bag of money that was dropped during a robbery. Paul and Tom give the money to Auggie; Auggie gives the money to Ruby to get Felicity into rehab; and everyone retires to Cyrus's garage for some inconvenient truths and a silent, sullen picnic.

Later, Paul asks Auggie to tell him a story to help him over his writer's block. Auggie recounts a bizarre but moving experience (which Auster had previously published as "Auggie Wren's Christmas Story") about trying to find a thief and instead inadvertently impersonating him to humor a blind old woman. The story is told again in silent flashback.

Forget the convolutions of the plot. In SMOKE, narrative is about fiction: invented selves and imagined histories, the lies we tell ourselves to make our lives bearable. Auster's script, which appropriately receives top billing, is unabashedly literary: instead of delivering conventional cross-talk, characters spin yarns or regale each other with elaborate fabrications and opinions. Most of these are refreshing and original enough to carry the film through narrative contrivances and unsubtle performances. Whitaker, Keitel, and particularly Hurt tend to drift into stagy, "actorly" posturing, but they seem to relax about halfway through the film. The immensely gifted Judd steals her scene with ease and leaves an indelible mark of genuine pain.

Wang yields to both the writer and the actors throughout the film, noticeably asserting himself only in the doubled story at the film's conclusion. But his attention to detail is quietly omnipresent and extremely effective: the look, sound, and feel of the locations provide a palpable backdrop against which Auster paints his slightly surreal word pictures.

Wang and Auster enjoyed their collaboration so much that they made a second improvised film on the same set, with many of the same actors, during the few days left after their main shoot wrapped. That film, BLUE IN THE FACE, was released shortly after SMOKE. (Profanity, adult situations.) — R.S.

d, Wayne Wang; p, Greg Johnson, Peter Newman, Hisami Kuriowa, Kenzo Horikoshi; exec p, Bob Weinstein, Harvey Weinstein, Satoru Iseki; w, Paul Auster (based on his story "Auggie Wren's Christmas Story"); ph, Adam Holender; ed, Maisie Hoy; m, Rachel Portman; prod d, Kalina Ivanov; art d, Jeff McDonald; set d, Karin Wiesel; sound, Drew Kunin; casting, Heidi Levitt, Billy Hopkins; cos, Claudia Brown

Comedy/Drama (PR: C MPAA: R)

SOMETHING TO TALK ABOUT ★★★
(U.S.) 106m Spring Creek Productions ~ Warner Bros. c

Julia Roberts (Grace); Dennis Quaid (Eddie); Robert Duvall (Wyly King); Gena Rowlands (Georgia King); Kyra Sedgwick

(Emma Rae); Brett Cullen *(Jamie Johnson)*; Haley Aull *(Caroline)*; Muse Watson *(Hank Corrigan)*; Anne Shropshire *(Aunt Rae)*; Ginnie Randall *(Eula)*; Terence P. Currier *(Dr. Frank Lewis)*; Rebecca Koon *(Babaranelle)*; Rhoda Griffis *(Edna)*; Lisa Roberts *(Kitty)*; Deborah Hobart *(Lorene Tuttle)*; Amy Parrish *(Lucy)*; Helen Baldwin *(Mary Jane)*; Libby Whittemore *(Nadine)*; Punky Leonard *(Norma Leggett)*; Michael Flippo *(Sonny)*; Beau Holden *(Frank)*; Noreen Reardon *(June)*; Bennie L. Jenkins *(Dub)*; Rusty Hendrickson *(Harry)*; J. Don Ferguson *(Announcer)*; Mary Nell Santacroce *(Mrs. Pinkerton)*; Shannon Eubanks *(Jessie Gaines)*; Jamye Price *(Anne)*; Brinley Arden Vickers *(College Friend)*

The second film to come from the pen of THELMA & LOUISE Oscar winner Callie Khouri, SOMETHING TO TALK ABOUT is lively, Southern-style entertainment, with spice and sass, wit and warmth. In her most appealing role since PRETTY WOMAN, Julia Roberts portrays a wealthy Southern woman whose ordered, society-approved life is shattered by her husband's infidelity.

When Grace King Bishon (Roberts) catches her husband Eddie (Dennis Quaid) cheating with a pretty blonde, she takes their daughter Caroline (Haley Aull) and moves back to her family's horse ranch. Her parents, Georgia (Gena Rowlands) and Wyly (Robert Duvall) appear more concerned with public appearances than with their daughter's pain. The compliant Georgia urges Grace to stand by her man despite his digressions, and to keep the matter quiet, rather than giving people "something to talk about." The authoritarian Wyly, who has a history of cheating himself, doesn't understand why Grace is upset. Moreover, he doesn't want Grace's marital problems interfering with a lucrative business deal he's cooking up with Eddie. Only her sister Emma Rae (Kyra Sedgwick) shares Grace's rage (though she also points out that when her sister began dating a guy nicknamed "Hound Dog," she ought to have known what she was getting into), and at the first opportunity gives Eddie a well-placed knee to let him know what she thinks of him.

As the King family prepares for the annual Grand Prix showjumping competition, Grace buries herself in work and flirts with an attractive horse trainer (Brett Cullen). Recognizing that she is partly to blame for their marital problems, she considers taking Eddie back. Their attempt at reconciliation is foiled by the effects of a poisoned meal which Grace prepared for Eddie in a moment of anger. As Grace forges her own identity and pursues the dreams she abandoned when she married, she realizes that there may be room in her life for Eddie after all.

While SOMETHING TO TALK ABOUT has many wonderfully comic moments and some heartrendingly touching ones, the elements don't gel into a completely satisfactory package. Khouri's dialogue is rich and funny, especially the ribald zingers she penned for Emma Rae. Though Khouri has been labeled a feminist writer, SOMETHING TO TALK ABOUT isn't about empowering women or bashing men. What makes the film intriguing is that the apparently black-and-white case of infidelity gradually becomes less clear-cut—Eddie isn't as bad as his nickname implies, and Grace hasn't been the model wife and mother she appears. The central story—of the sacrifices and compromises needed to make a marriage work—is a well-crafted mix of comedy and pathos.

There is also an uninvolving subplot regarding who will ride which horse in the Grand Prix, and whether Wyly and Caroline will win their respective competitions. The equestrian event lacks suspense because there's nothing at stake; the characters involved haven't been fully developed, and the outcome doesn't affect Grace and Eddie's happiness. The action sometimes drags, and there are loose ends all over the place. The run-on conclusion

leaves the impression of a last-minute studio decision to tack on a happy ending. The postscript may have made some viewers happy but it feels unnatural and unnecessary.

In perhaps his most conventional, mainstream film, director Lasse Hallstrom (MY LIFE AS A DOG, WHAT'S EATING GILBERT GRAPE) elicits delicious performances from the ensemble cast. In a stroke of casting genius, Julia Roberts and Kyra Sedgwick play sisters and not only look eerily alike, but also display a familial rapport onscreen. Roberts gives a solid, fan-pleasing performance. As the wisecracking Emma Rae, Sedgwick runs away with nearly every scene she is in. Quaid plays the lovable scoundrel with just the right touch—it's easy to see why Grace wants to forgive Eddie. The company's elder statesmen turn in masterful performances: Duvall is the personification of swaggering superiority, and Rowlands brims with repressed emotion. Shot in South Carolina and Georgia, the film has a genuine Southern flavor and boasts beautiful scenery and luminous cinematography. *(Sexual situations, adult situations, profanity.)* — B.R.

d, Lasse Hallstrom; p, Anthea Sylbert, Paula Weinstein; exec p, Goldie Hawn; co-p, William Beasley; w, Callie Khouri; ph, Sven Nykvist; ed, Mia Goldman; m, Hans Zimmer, Graham Preskett; prod d, Mel Bourne; set d, Roberta Holinko; ch, Toni Basil; sound, Peter F. Kurland (mixer); fx, John D. Milinac; casting, Marion Dougherty; cos, Aggie Guerard Rodgers; makeup, Sarah Mays

Comedy/Drama (PR: C MPAA: R)

SON OF THE SHARK, THE ★★★½
(France/Belgium) 88m Gaumont; Compagnie des Images; France 3 Cinema; Premiere Heure; Saga Films; Invisible Films; Sveriges TV1; TRL ~ Seventh Art Releasing c
(LE FILS DU REQUIN)

Ludovik Vandendaele *(Martin Vanderhoes)*; Erick DaSilva *(Simon Vanderhoes)*; Sandrine Blancke *(Marie)*; Maxime Leroux *(The Father)*

During its brief US tour, this debut feature from Agnes Merlet won was compared to THE 400 BLOWS for its naturalistic depiction of juvenile delinquents. But Francois Truffaut's trouble-prone hero came across as a decent, likeable kid who has had some bad breaks. The protagonists in SON OF A SHARK, by contrast, are two feral children for whom it is nearly impossible to feel any compassion.

Whenever theft or vandalism occurs in the small seaside village of Lignon, odds are that adolescent Martin Vanderhoes (Ludovic Vandendaele) and his younger brother Simon (Erick Da Silva) are the culprits. Their mother walked out on them, and their father, a docile drunkard, barely rates their attention, as the siblings regularly run away from foster homes and reform school to commit more mayhem. They steal a school bus, drive it over a cliff near the beach, and dwell in the wreck until tides flood it. They embark on a vandalism spree (which is all the more disturbing for the childishly innocent fun the pair have). And they stick together with genuine filial love and utmost loyalty, until Martin starts spending time with Marie (Sandrine Blancke), a pretty schoolgirl. Simon is jealous of the interloper and the civilizing influence she tries to exert over the older boy. Eventually Simon, wielding a weapon, forces the terrified Marie to strip naked on the beach in front of Martin, making both an offering and a challenge of her. In a climax that brilliantly blends pathos and cruelty, Martin makes his choice to leave town with his brother.

The title derives from the boys' regular visits to the docks, where they seem to feel sorry for the fishermen's harvest of decapitated fish heads that lie twitching and gasping. In voice-over diary entries, Martin likens himself to a shark, though the context suggests a victim as much as a predator. A disappointingly noncommittal ending shows the duo literally fading away, with the suggestion that they have gone to sea. Reportedly based on actual incidents, SON OF A SHARK has no solutions for its problem children other than basic survival, the key to which is how the brothers stick together. Their bond humanizes these young incorrigibles, however fleetingly. *(Violence, sexual situations, adult situations, nudity, substance abuse, profanity.)* — C.C.

d, Agnes Merlet; p, Francois Fries; assoc p, Hubert Toint, Patrice Haddad; w, Agnes Merlet (from a story by Santiago Amigorena and Agnes Merlet); ph, Gerard Simon; ed, Pierre Choukroun, Guy Lecorne; m, Bruno Coulais; art d, Laurent Allaire; sound, Henri Morelle, Jean-Pierre LaForce

Drama (PR: C MPAA: NR)

SORRENTO BEACH
(SEE: HOTEL SORRENTO)

SPECIES ★★½
(U.S.) 111m MGM ~ MGM/UA c

Ben Kingsley *(Fitch)*; Michael Madsen *(Press)*; Alfred Molina *(Arden)*; Forest Whitaker *(Dan)*; Marg Helgenberger *(Laura)*; Natasha Henstridge *(Sil)*; Michelle Williams *(Young Sil)*; Jordan Lund *(Aide)*; Don Fischer *(Aide)*; Scott McKenna *(Train Hobo)*; Virginia Morris *(Mother)*; Jayne Luke *(Snack Shop Clerk)*; David K. Schroeder *(German Tourist)*; David Jensen *(Conductor)*; Esther Scott *(Female Conductor)*; Shirley Prestia *(Dr. Roth)*; William Utay *(Colleague)*; David Selburg *(Government Man)*; Herta Ware *(Mrs. Morris)*; Melissa Bickerton *(Fitch's Secretary)*; Lucy Rodriguez *(Wedding Dress Saleswoman)*; Scott Sproule *(Team Driver)*; Stogie Kenyatta *(Cop)*; Gary Bullock *(Motel Clerk)*; Susan Hauser *(Lab Worker)*; William Bumiller *(Bouncer)*; Caroline Barclay *(Drunken Girl)*; Matthew Ashford *(Guy in Club)*; Anthony Guidera *(Robbie)*; Sarah S. Leese *(Screaming Woman)*; Whip Hubley *(John Carey)*; Patricia Belcher *(Admittance Clerk)*; Richard Fancy *(Doctor)*; Leslie Ishii *(Nurse)*; Marliese K. Schneider *(Abducted Woman)*; Robert Mendelson *(Homeless Man)*; Pam Cook *(Commercial Model)*; Lisa Liberati *(Bathroom Bimbo)*; Ed Stone *(Waiter)*; Dendrie Taylor *(Marie)*; Kurtis Burow *(Baby Boy)*; Dana Hee *(Creature Performer)*; Frank Welker *(Voice of Alien Sil)*

A cross between ALIEN and BASIC INSTINCT, SPECIES is a perfect illustration of what happens when millions of dollars' worth of technical expertise is brought to bear on a cheap, exploitative script.

In a top-secret Utah laboratory, scientists prepare to murder a young girl named Sil (Michelle Williams) with cyanide gas. But Sil breaks out of her enclosure, flees the lab and hops on a train bound for Los Angeles. Dr. Xavier Fitch (Ben Kingsley), the head of the project, calls in a curious team to catch the fugitive: ex-Marine assassin Press Lennox (Michael Madsen), anthropologist Stephen Arden (Alfred Molina), molecular biologist Laura Baker (Marg Helgenberger) and psychic empath Dan Smithson (Forest Whitaker). He explains what they've been cooking up in the lab: a revolutionary blend of alien and human DNA. The result was Sil, a half-human, half-alien hybrid that is rapidly maturing and must be stopped.

Sil, now a beautiful young woman (Natasha Henstridge) driven to mate and perpetuate her species, arrives in LA. The team tracks her to a nightclub and then to the home of a young man whom Sil intends to seduce. She kills him before achieving her goal and escapes. The team encounters Sil again at the club,

leading to a chase and a fiery crash in which they believe Sil is killed. But she has tricked them and changed her appearance, and lures Arden to a hotel room. There, she mates with and kills him. The rest of the group pursues her into some sewer tunnels.

Metamorphosing into her true, monstrous form, Sil bears a child and kills Fitch before the remaining members of the team are able to kill both her and her baby. They leave without noticing that the creature is still alive within the body of a rat.

Director Roger Donaldson gives SPECIES pace and style, and the production is further shored up by sharp cinematography, a strong musical score, fine special effects and a cast of reliable character actors. But the sleazy material defeats every attempt to dress it up. Dennis Feldman's script sets up all kinds of intriguing possibilities, only to fritter them away with a story that has no more depth and development than the average direct-to-video movie, and less than some. The opening scenes suggest a kind of familial connection between Sil and her "father," Fitch, and the subsequent exposition promises an interesting exploration of how a predatory species from another world might adapt to life on Earth. But most of this material is sublimated to the need for gorgeous alien Henstridge to bare her breasts seductively. The script's wittiest conceit is that such a luscious creature would have any trouble at all finding a stud to father future alien generations, and the obstacles it throws in her path—though hardly plausible—provide the film's most amusing moments.

What it lacks in complexity, SPECIES makes up for in noise and frenetic confusion. Donaldson handles the action with great facility, and the monstrous Sil—courtesy of Steve Johnson's creature creations and Richard Edlund's visual effects—achieves genuinely scary life. One gripping, if gratuitous, sequence involves the scientific SWAT team growing a monster sample out of some unblended DNA and having to fight off the beastly result.

Madsen, Helgenberger, Whitaker, Kingsley and Molina do what they can with their woefully underwritten characters. If model-turned-actress Henstridge has no particular depth as Sil, it hardly matters: she was hired to look great and does. The film's best performance is delivered by Williams, who gives the prepubescent Sil an eerie edge, conveying the curiosity and terror of a stranger in a strange land without a word of dialogue. *(Graphic violence, extensive nudity, sexual situations, adult situations, profanity.)* — M.G.

d, Roger Donaldson; p, Frank Mancuso, Jr., Dennis Feldman; exec p, David Streit, Mark Egerton; w, Dennis Feldman; ph, Andrzej Bartowiak; ed, Conrad Buff; m, Christopher Young; prod d, John Muto; art d, Dan Webster; set d, Jackie Carr; sound, Jay Boekelheide (design); fx, Richard Edlund; casting, Amanda Mackey, Cathy Sandrich; cos, Joe I. Tompkins; makeup, H.R. Giger, Steve Johnson; stunts, Glenn Randall, Randall, Max Kelven

Science Fiction/Action (PR: O MPAA: R)

SPIKE AND MIKE'S FESTIVAL ★★
OF ANIMATION '95
(U.K./Canada/U.S.) 96m ~
Festival Films c

One of several annual animation compilations, this feature includes 13 short animated films from the US, UK, and Canada, purporting to show the best of independent or state-funded animation in a variety of styles and formats. Although the animation in these short films is often quite spectacular, the content is noticeably lacking in wit or substance.

THE BIG STORY, a black and white clay-animated piece spoofing Billy Wilder's THE BIG CARNIVAL (1951), features

Kirk Douglas look-alikes (voiced by Frank Gorshin) playing out a short encounter between a hotshot reporter and his hardened editor.

NOSEHAIR, a line-drawing-on-paper work by Bill Plympton, presents a man's attempt to pull out a nose hair. This results in catastrophe as the hair elongates and transforms into a variety of objects and landscapes, all of which put the hair's owner in peril.

THE VILLAGE is a storybook-style cartoon animation about an isolated fortresslike village, where the residents' intense scrutiny of each other threatens the budding romance of a young couple.

IDDY BITTY BEAT BOY presents a brash, colorful, jazz-inflected short tale of a 1950s beat boy who becomes an overnight sensation only to be tried and convicted of obscenity charges.

TRIANGLE (Erica Russell) shows three dancing figures which become increasingly abstract shapes as they dance to a lively and intricate score of Afro-Caribbean rhythms.

PERSONAL HELL has a young woman listening and responding to phone messages left for her personal ad, as oil paint-on-glass images illustrate her voice-over comments.

SLEEPY GUY is an elaborate computer animation of a man who keeps getting awakened in the middle of a romantic dream.

In LEGACY, computer animation guides viewers through a cave of rock paintings, one of which comes alive temporarily.

BRITANNIA (Joanna Quinn) is a set of pencil drawings on paper satirizing England's imperialist past.

THE JANITOR (Vanessa Schwartz) uses line drawings on paper and a voice-over monologue by actor Geoffrey Lewis to describe how the narrator, sent by God to clean up the earth, botches the job and causes floods.

THE MONK AND THE FISH is a whimsical cel-animated rendition of a monk's vain efforts to catch a feisty fish from the monastery's pond.

BOB'S BIRTHDAY (Alison Snowden and David Fine) is cartoon animation about a dentist who unwittingly ruins his wife's efforts to surprise him with a party.

Nick Park's THE WRONG TROUSERS, a lengthy clay-animated piece, tells the story of an inventor's dog and its rivalry with the inventor's new tenant, a malevolent penguin.

One could argue that a single seven-minute Warner Bros. cartoon from 1946 contains more humor, wit, and excitement than this entire collection of recent animation, which includes two Academy Award winners and four nominees. While some of the selections boast elements of cuteness (PRIVATE HELL), or are simply beautifully designed (TRIANGLE), none offers any sense of purpose. Most simply use the medium to show off animation technique.

The animators' concerns are all rather mundane and might have been better expressed as live-action comedy skits, children's books, short stories, or short, comical cel-animated cartoons. SLEEPY GUY, in particular, and THE WRONG TROUSERS would have been much funnier and more effective had they been done as short cartoons rather than lengthy computer- and clay-animated works. (Adult situations, profanity.) — B.C.

d, Mark Baker, Darren Butts, Michael Dudock de Wit, David Fine, Dana Hanna, Raman Hui, Nick Park, Bill Plympton, Joanna Quinn, Erica Russell, Vanessa Schwartz, Alison Snowden, David Stoten, Tim Watts, Mo Willems

Animated   (PR: C   MPAA: NR)

SPITFIRE   ★
(U.S.) 90m Schmoeller/Karnowski Productions; Filmwerks ~ Trimark Pictures c

Kristie Phillips (Charlie Case); Sarah Douglas (Carla Davis); Tim Thomerson (Rex Beachum); Lance Henriksen (Richard Charles); Simon Poland (Alain); David Wu (Chan); Debra Fondren (Amanda Case); Terri Conn (Vicky); Jackie Brummer (Borakova); Viktor Makhov (Russian Coach); Gary Schmoeller (Coach Crandall)

A female gymnast becomes involved in a not-so-intriguing web of international goings-on in this lackluster video release.

Champion gymnast Charlie Case (Kristie Phillips) is en route to the World Finals in Greece when she acquires the launch codes for some Ukrainian nuclear missiles. In fact, the codes were passed to her by British superspy Richard Charles (Lance Henriksen) before he was taken prisoner by villainess Carla Davis (Sarah Douglas). Unbeknownst to Charlie, Richard is her father. With down-on-his-luck reporter Rex Beachum (Tim Thomerson) in tow, Charlie travels to Hong Kong. Aided by some half-brothers, and her expert karate skills, Charlie is able to elude the evil Carla and her buffoonish thugs. Eventually however, Carla captures Charlie and offers her father's life in exchange for the codes. Can Charlie subdue Carla, save the free world, and still make it to her championship match in Athens that afternoon? You bet. Richard and Rex then thwart a plan by the nasty Romanian gymnasts to drug Charlie. She triumphs and is declared "the greatest gymnast of all time!"

Secret agent romps can be energetic star vehicles, but SPITFIRE has little drama, the tongue-in-cheek humor falls flat, and the action is limp (even though every blow resounds with a "Thwack!"). And who's this Kristie Phillips, anyway? And to what audience is this gymnastics-meets-James-Bond story supposed to appeal? It doesn't contain enough exposed flesh and gratuitous violence to draw such films' traditional (male) viewers, but there's enough "adult content" to make it questionable entertainment for children, to whose juvenile mentality it otherwise seems perfectly suited. (Violence, profanity, adult situations, nudity.) — P.R.

d, Albert Pyun; p, Gary Schmoeller, Tom Karnowski; exec p, Paul Rosenblum; co-p, Ray Zimmerman; w, Albert Pyun, David Yorkin, Christopher Borkgren; ph, George Mooradian; ed, Dennis O'Connor; m, Tony Riparetti; prod d, Rodell Cruz, Rosa Pang; casting, Cathy Henderson, Tom McSweeney; cos, Shelley Busalacchi

Action/Sports/Spy   (PR: C   MPAA: R)

SPY WITHIN, THE   ★
(U.S.) 92m Hillwood Entertainment; Concorde-New Horizons ~ New Horizons Home Video c
(AKA: FLIGHT OF THE DOVE)

Scott Glenn (Will Rickman); Theresa Russell (Alex Canis); Lane Smith (Stephen Hahn); Terence Knox (Jonathan "J.B." Brandeis); Katherine Helmond (Dr. Pamela Schilling); Joe Pantoliano (Attorney Brezner); Alex Rocco (Bartender); Rudy Ramos (Ortiz); Gary Graham (Silver); Angelo DiMascio (Burns); Juan Riojas (Rodas); Bo Eason (Donner); Nicholas Mele (Mailman); Shashawnee Hall (Stocky Workman); Robert Dryer (Tall Workman); Tricia Munford (Co-Counsel); Steve Taub (Truck Driver)

A former secret agent, guilt-ridden over her professional exploits as an S&M-style entrapment specialist, runs from the US government and her own troubled past in THE SPY WITHIN, a tepid suspense film that attempts to blend action spectacle with human insight. Despite considerable sex and violence, the film is unrelentingly tedious; the only elements that might hold some viewers' attention are Theresa Russell's breasts, which are featured prominently.

Alex Canis, alias "The Dove" (Theresa Russell), is trying to extricate herself from her employment within "a covert sector of the NSA," but her former superior, J.B. (Terence Knox), will not allow her to tender a simple resignation. Alex knows too much, and J.B. wants her killed. Alex has done her information-gathering in corsets and spike heels, assuming the role of a high-priced dominatrix; her disciplinary services were recorded on film and later used by NSA agents to ensure their subjects' cooperation. What worries J.B. most is that Alex has recorded her exploits in a manuscript. While her autobiography is not intended for publication (writing it was a therapeutic exercise for Alex), this is irrelevant to J.B.

On the run, with J.B. and his thugs one step behind, Alex suddenly finds herself joined by Will Rickman (Scott Glenn), a demolition expert who, like Alex, is haunted by his past. Rickman is facing a major lawsuit, which is constant reminder that the bodies of a mother and child were found in the rubble of his last demolition job. Alex and Rickman achieve physical intimacy within hours of first meeting. Only gradually, however, do they reveal themselves emotionally. With difficulty, they learn to trust one another, and when J.B. finally catches up with Alex, she and Rickman face him side by side.

THE SPY WITHIN is an apparent attempt to create a sensitive spy movie for the recovery-oriented 1990s. Unfortunately, director Steve Railsback develops his characters by assigning them multiple outbursts of melodramatic self-disclosure, giving the film the emotional tenor of a television talk show.

The actors are limited by Lewis Green's appallingly stilted script; Railsback tries to add interest by throwing in plenty of hot sex, along with car chases, gunplay, a couple of mutilated corpses, and a torture-assisted interrogation. None of this, unfortunately, will be enough to keep most viewers awake throughout the entire picture. *(Violence, extensive nudity, sexual situations, extreme profanity.)* — J.W.

d, Steve Railsback; p, Mike Elliott; exec p, Roger Corman, Chris Peschken, Chris Naumann; w, Lewis Green; ph, Anghel Decca; ed, Roderick Davis; m, David Wurst, Eric Wurst; prod d, Robert de Vico; art d, Kenny Minster; set d, Jordan Steinberg; sound, Christopher Taylor (mixer); casting, Jan Glaser; cos, Tami Mor Wyman, Rina Ramon Fiddler; makeup, Elisabeth Fry; stunts, Patrick Statham

Spy   **(PR: O   MPAA: R)**

SPY WITHIN, THE
(SEE: FLIGHT OF THE DOVE)

STALINGRAD   ★★★½
(Germany) 150m Royal Film; Bavaria Film;
BA Produktion; Perathonom ~ Strand Releasing c

Thomas Kretschmann *(Hans von Witzland)*; Dominique Horwitz *(Fritz Reiser)*; Jochen Nickel *(Rollo Rohleder)*; Karel Hermanek *(Musk)*; Dana Vavrova *(Irina)*; Sebastian Rudolph *(GeGe Muller)*; Martin Benrath *(General Hentz)*; Sylvester Groth *(Otto)*

STALINGRAD recreates Hitler's most bitter military defeat, the nearly four-year siege that dominated the eastern front of WW II. A German production, the film depicts both the tenacity of the German army and its craven submission to the most fearful orders.

Directed by Joseph Vilsmaier, who also worked on the script with Johannes Heide and Jurgen Buscher, the film begins with a squad of German soldiers who are basking in the glow of their recent victories and traveling to the Russian front with their new lieutenant, Hans von Witzland (Thomas Kretschmann). Their

first glimpse of Stalingrad is a sobering experience. Worse than the huddled groups of tired, dirty, and wounded Germans is the brutal handling by the Field Police of Russian prisoners of war. When Witzland reprimands a guard, the lieutenant is manhandled, and his protest to the police captain is greeted with a sneer.

The squad's first clash with the Russians is a Pyrrhic victory: the carnage is dreadful, and Witzland arranges a temporary local truce to retrieve the wounded and the dead. In the melee, a young Russian finds himself among the Germans. Since he is no real threat, they treat him decently, as they listen to Hitler's boastful speech on the radio. Within minutes, a shell crashes into the room and Witzland, the tough Sergeant Rollo Rohleder (Jochen Nickel), the squad cynic Fritz Reiser (Dominique Horwitz), and the latest replacement GeGe Muller (Sebastian Rudolf), fight their way out of a new Russian encirclement.

After another confrontation with the police captain, Witzland is stripped of his officer's epaulets and sent with his friends to a penal battalion that hunts for and defuses land mines in the snow. Offered reinstatement, they participate in a vicious battle, after which they are called upon to execute so-called saboteurs, one of whom is the Russian boy they had once captured. Watched by the police captain, they obediently carry out orders. This event acts as a catalyst; the lieutenant, Geiger and GeGe attempt to find a way out of the Red Army's trap. Having wandered through the snow and the devastation they eventually return to kill the detested police captain, but not before he has disclosed a cache of hoarded food. The men discover shelves full of bread, fuel and supplies, as well as a captured Red Army woman (Dana Vavrova), who had been tied up, tortured and raped. She speaks perfect German and offers to help them escape the city. It is January 1943, the eve of the German Sixth Army's official surrender.

A war film made by Germans about their country's part in WW II, STALINGRAD emphasizes both the horrors of battle and the harsh discipline imposed on the ordinary German soldier. Troops straight from Africa via Italy and a proper Prussian officer are contrasted with the habitual war crimes associated with the war in the east. Obedience was necessary for survival in an atmosphere where military justice meant the execution of about 2,500 soldiers annually, for infractions of military law and political crimes. Like the Wehrmacht, STALINGRAD takes the best tactical position and defends it ably, but only by ignoring the wider causes and nature of the war itself.

Fabulously expensive by European standards, this film began life as a miniseries on German television and was compressed and re-edited for its brief theatrical run in the US. Director Vilsmaier doesn't miss a single cliche of post-Vietnam "anti-war" war movies, but the epic scale compensates for the well-worn material. *(Graphic violence, adult situations, nudity.)* — L.R.

d, Joseph Vilsmaier; p, Joseph Vilsmaier; exec p, Gunter Rohrbach, Bob Arnold, Hanno Huth, Michael Krohne; w, Johannes Heide, Jurgen Buscher, Joseph Vilsmaier; ph, Joseph Vilsmaier, Rolf Greim, Klaus Moderegger, Peter Von Haller; ed, Hannes Nikel; m, Norbert J. Schneider; prod d, Wolfgang Hundhammer, Jindrich Goetz; sound, Milan Bor, Gunther Stadelmann; fx, Karl Baumgartner; cos, Ute Hofinger; stunts, Jaroslav Tomsa, Petr Drozda

War/Historical   **(PR: C   MPAA: NR)**

STARS FELL ON HENRIETTA, THE   ★★½
(U.S.) 110m Malpaso Productions;
Butcher's Run Productions ~ Warner Bros. c

Robert Duvall *(Mr. Cox)*; Aidan Quinn *(Don Day)*; Frances Fisher *(Cora Day)*; Brian Dennehy *(Big Dave)*; Lexi Randall *(Beatrice Day)*; Kaytlyn Knowles *(Pauline Day)*; Francesca Ruth Eastwood *(Mary Day)*

THE STARS FELL ON HENRIETTA tells the Depression-era tale of a wildcat oilman who touches the lives of those around him. As this optimistic oddball character, Robert Duvall saves an otherwise ordinary dust-bowl drama from dullness.

Duvall plays Mr. Cox, a destitute but lovable wheeler-dealer, who travels with just his suitcase and a cat, Matilda, all over Texas during the oil rush of 1935. When Mr. Cox happens upon the rural town of Henrietta, he claims that he can "smell" the oil under the land owned by a poor farm family, Don and Cora Day (Aidan Quinn and Frances Fisher) and their three daughters (Lexi Randall, Kaytlyn Knowles, and Francesca Ruth Eastwood). At first, Don and Cora are skeptical about Mr. Cox's promises of wealth, but over time, Don begins to share his vision and eventually makes a deal to share the profits if oil is ever found. Lacking the funds to buy a rig, Mr. Cox tries to enlist the aid of a wealthy oilman, Big Dave (Brian Dennehy), to invest in the venture. When Big Dave scoffs at the plan, however, Mr. Cox resorts to violence and steals the money from him at a card game in the hotel at which they are both staying. Meanwhile, Don and Cora fight over their bank's threat to foreclose on the farm, and Don's desperate attempt to set a rig up himself, without Mr. Cox's help. In the end, Don and Mr. Cox join forces, using Big Dave's stolen bankroll, and the team strikes oil at the last possible moment.

THE STARS FELL ON HENRIETTA came and went quickly at the box office in 1995, perhaps because audiences were put off by the Depression setting. Yet, despite the milieu and occasional mishaps the characters experience, THE STARS FELL ON HENRIETTA infuses life-affirming sentiments into a story that avoids real disasters (epitomized by the fact that Mr. Cox, apparently killed during the climactic oil gush, proves to have survived for the happy ending).

Clearly, THE STARS FELL ON HENRIETTA fits into a long tradition of inspiring Hollywood melodramas in which tough people battle (and usually win) against Depression-era adversity, from THE GRAPES OF WRATH to PLACES IN THE HEART. Just as in those films, the characters here are stock, but, more detrimentally, the talented cast in STARS has trouble rising above the one-dimensional nature of Philip Railsback's script. While reuniting with Aidan Quinn's Don, Francis Fisher as Cora, for example, must utter the film's worst line: "I want you back where you belong," she says, referring to their marriage bed. Only Robert Duvall transcends the potential flatness of his familiar role—a cross between the con man in THE RAINMAKER and Harry in HARRY AND TONTO (who also traveled with a beloved cat)—by fleshing out his part with welcome nuances. Duvall is especially good at conveying barely expressed hurt followed by cheery resilience after several humiliations are inflicted on Mr. Cox. THE STARS FELL ON HENRIETTA also benefits from a sturdy production that complements the earnest if plodding direction by James Keach (the former actor's first feature film). It is curious and amusing that even in a story set in the 1930s, Warner Bros. inserts '90s product placements, including many references to Coke and a shot of a "Batman" comic book (no small part of Time Warner's franchise). Still, the only really egregious aspect of the film is the trite, superfluous voice-over narration at the opening and closing.

THE STARS FELL ON HENRIETTA hardly makes exciting screen fare, but it does give Robert Duvall a chance to shine in a role that may just inspire capitalist fantasies in all of us. *(Violence, profanity.)* — E.M.

d, James Keach; p, Clint Eastwood, David Valdes; assoc p, Steve Railsback; w, Philip Railsback; ph, Bruce Surtees; ed, Joel Cox; m, David Benoit; prod d, Henry Bumstead; art d, Jack Taylor, Jr.; set d, Alan Hicks; sound, John Pritchett; fx, John Frazier; casting, Phyllis Huffman; cos, Van Broughton Ramsey; makeup, Manlio Rocchetti; stunts, Buddy Van Horn

Drama   **(PR: A   MPAA: PG)**

STEAL BIG, STEAL LITTLE   ★½
(U.S.) 130m Chicago Pacific Entertainment ~ Savoy Pictures c

Andy Garcia *(Ruben Partida Martinez/Robert Martin)*; Alan Arkin *(Lou Perilli)*; Rachel Ticotin *(Laura Martinez)*; Joe Pantoliano *(Eddie Agopian)*; Holland Taylor *(Mona Rowland-Downey)*; Ally Walker *(Bonnie Martin)*; David Ogden Stiers *(Judge Winton Myers)*; Charles Rocket *(Sheriff Otis)*; Richard Bradford *(Nick Zingaro)*; Kevin McCarthy *(Reed Tyler)*; Nathan Davis *(Harry Lordly)*; Dominik Garcia-Lorido *(Maria Martinez)*; Mike Nussbaum *(Sam Barlow)*; Rita Taggart *(Autumn McBride)*; Takaaki Ishibashi *(Yoshi Takamura)*; Tom Wood *(Dan McCann)*; Philip Arthur Ross *(Tinker)*; Steven Robert Ross *(Buzz)*; Natalija Nogulich *(Alice)*; Joe Kosala *(Sheriff Joe)*; Victor Rivers *(Sheriff Vic)*; Sam Vlahos *(Mauricio)*; Andy Romano *(Clifford Downey)*; Ramon Gonzales *(Julian)*; Salvatore Basile *(Luis)*; Fred Asparagus *(Angel)*; William Marquez *(Rafael)*; Nelson Marquez *(Emilio Campos)*; Richard Marquez *(Eduardo)*; Leata Galloway *(Agatha)*; Renee Victor *(Rosa)*; Adam James *(Tyler's Bodyguard)*; Drucilla A. Carlson *(Tonya)*; Nina Beesley *(Brandy)*; Candice Daly *(Melissa)*; Cynthia Mace *(Betty Myers)*; Karen Kondazian *(Mrs. Agopian)*; Miguel Nino *(Guardia Officer)*; Ron Dean *(Nick's Boy)*; Jack Wallace *(Nick's Boy)*; Robert Harris *(Farley)*; Robert Langenbucher *(Bailsman Aames)*; Time Winters *(IRS Agent Cox)*; Tighe Barry *(Glitch)*; Suzanne Goddard *(Shakara)*; Joe Drago *(Inmate)*; Duane Davis *(Jailer)*; Roselynn Pilkington *(Eddie's Secretary)*; Fred Lehto *(Strange Man)*; Cody Glenn *(INS Agent)*; Lee DeBroux *(INS Official)*; Robert Lesser *(Agent Buchanan)*; Pamela Winslow *(Melanie)*; Frank Ray Perilli *(B.J.)*; Mick Pellegrino *(Mission Father)*; Eddie Bo Smith *(Bartender)*; Soren Hansen *(Security Guard)*; Liz Lang *(Court Clerk)*

STEAL BIG, STEAL LITTLE stars Andy Garcia in the dual role of twins battling over an inheritance. This simple comic premise, which recalls the anarchic British farce, THE WRONG BOX, is overblown into a monstrosity of big intentions and little rewards.

Garcia plays Ruben Partida Martinez and his brother Robert Martin. As children, they were found near the La Fortuna ranch in Santa Barbara and raised by the owners. Robert followed in his father's footsteps to become a slimy businessman, with crooked white friends like Reed Tyler (Kevin McCarthy) and Judge Myers (David Ogden Stiers). Ruben emulated his mother, Mona (Holland Taylor), a free-spirited artist. He is a simple, good-hearted, generous man, who lives among the Mexican workers on his ranch. When Mona dies, she leaves everything to Ruben, thwarting Robert's plans to sell off the 40,000 acres to developers. A fight ensues.

Ruben, aided by his estranged wife Laura (Rachel Ticotin), Robert's ex-wife Bonnie (Ally Walker), and friend Lou Perilli (Alan Arkin), proceeds to turn La Fortuna into a self-supporting commune for the people who till its soil. Robert calls in political favors to have Ruben subjected to constant police harassment. After visits from the IRS and INS, Ruben is in trouble. He has trusted his longtime friend, lawyer Eddie Agopian (Joe Pantoliano), with his finances, and soon the ranch is on the block, because Agopian was in Robert's pocket all along. Perilli now convinces Ruben to fight fire with fire. Ruben impersonates Robert to get dirt on Myers and Tyler, and then blackmails the judge. Robert, who's been mistaken for Ruben and jailed, realizes the error of his ways and sets out to save his brother. With La Fortuna safely in Ruben's hands, the brothers agree to work for the little people's benefit.

Essentially a vanity project for director Andrew Davis (he also shares production, story, and screenplay credits), STEAL BIG, STEAL LITTLE is his reward for the success of his last film, 1993's THE FUGITIVE. There, he showed how deftly he could mix drama and humor with action to turn what could have been an overlong and plodding narrative into a fast-paced pleasure. Here, the faults lie not in misguidance, but misconception. The film's core is an overly simplistic parable about class and race antagonisms in California. As it progresses, it mutates into an attempt at epic comedy; every time a character is introduced, a subplot is introduced as well, or the story goes off at a tangent. Flashbacks, romances, suspected infidelities, the entire idea of Perilli's character (though Arkin's performance is a bright spot), and Perilli's connections with the Mob are but a few of the plot's convolutions. Davis mixes it all together, along with a lot of spectacle, and keeps it moving, but following the story becomes a chore. Too much time is wasted showing what a nice guy Ruben is, and Robert never gets established as a force in the film; the gimmick of Garcia's playing two roles is never exploited to any comic effect. (Profanity, violence.) — P.R.

d, Andrew Davis; p, Andrew Davis, Fred Caruso; exec p, Mel Pearl; assoc p, Teresa Tucker-Davies, Maher Ahmad; co-p, Lowell Blank; w, Andrew Davis, Lee Blessing, Jeanne Blake, Terry Kahn (from a story by Andrew Davis, Teresa Tucker-Davies, and Frank Ray Perilli); ph, Frank Tidy; ed, Don Brochu, Tina Hirsch; m, William Olvis; prod d, Michael Haller; art d, Mark E. Zuelzke; set d, Gene Serdena; sound, Scott D. Smith (mixer); fx, Roy Arbogast; casting, Amanda Mackey Johnson, Cathy Sandrich; cos, Jodie Tillen; makeup, Rick Sharp; stunts, Jeff Habberstad

Drama/Action/Comedy   **(PR: A   MPAA: PG-13)**

STRANGE DAYS   ★★½
(U.S.) 145m First Light; Lightstorm Entertainment ~ 20th Century Fox c

Ralph Fiennes (Lenny Nero); Angela Bassett (Lornette "Mace" Mason); Juliette Lewis (Faith Justin); Tom Sizemore (Max Peltier); Michael Wincott (Philo Gant); Vincent D'Onofrio (Burton Steckler); Glenn Plummer (Jeriko One); Brigitte Bako (Iris); Richard Edson (Tick); William Fichtner (Dwayne Engelman); Josef Sommer (Palmer Strickland); Joe Urla (Keith); Nicky Katt (Joey Corto); Michael Jace (Wade Beemer); Louise LeCavalier (Cindy "Vita" Minh); David Carrera (Duncan); Jim Ishida (Mr. Fumitsu); Todd Graff (Tex Arcana); Malcolm Norrington (Replay); Anais Munoz (Diamanda); Ted Haler (Tow Truck Driver); Rio Hackford (Bobby the Bartender); Brook Susan Parker (Cecile); Brandon Hammond (Zander); Donald "Donnie" Young (Young Zander); B.J. Crockett (Young Zander); Dex Elliot Sanders (Curtis); Ronnie Willis (Homeboy); David Packer (Lane); Paulo Tocha (Spaz Diaz); James Muro (Nervous POV); Ron Young (POV Voice); Art Chudabala (Thai Restaurant Owner); Erica Kelly (Restaurant Hostess); Marlana Young (Waitress); Ray Chang (Thai Restaurant Cook); Raul Reformina (Busboy); Chris Douridas (Talk Radio Host); Billy Worley (Dan from Silverlake); Amon Bourne (Dewayne); Lisa Picotte (Lori from Encino); Kylie Ireland (Stoned Looking Girl); Nicole Hilbig (Stoned Girl's Lover); Stefan Arngrim (Skinner); Agustin Rodriguez (Eduardo); Kelly Hu (Anchor Woman); Nynno Anderson (Angry Jeriko Fan); Liat Goodson (Retinal Fetish Bouncer); Honey Labrador (Beach Beauty); Delane Vaughn (Mace's Husband); Mark Arneson (Police Officer); James Acheson (Cop in Bathroom); John Francis (Death); Zoot (Mime); Royce Minor (Angry Black Kid); Milan Reynolds (National Guard Medic #1); Russell W. Smith (National Guard #2); Sarah Abukutsa Marshall; Russell Hines; Michael Jaasi; Maurice Marshall; Carolyn Adunni McPherson; Jennifer Jin-Jin Reeves; Charmain Renata Hubbard; Reginald T. Thornton; Chester A. Whitmore; Lori Simone Wilkerson (African Dancers)

Despite its high-tech trappings, slick surfaces and relentless self-reflexivity, Kathryn Bigelow's STRANGE DAYS is shopworn pulp. Though executed with superior style and showy performances, it fails to realize the potential of its premise.

In the last days of 1999, former vice cop Lenny Nero (Ralph Fiennes) prowls a chaotic Los Angeles dealing illegal "clips." These are contraband recordings of sensory experiences made directly from the brains of individuals equipped with the Superconducting Quantum Interference Device (SQUID), a device easily secreted under a hat or hairpiece. A principled pusher, Lenny refuses to deal in "snuff" clips. He uses the forbidden technology himself to relive his own happier days with Faith Justin (Juliette Lewis) who has since become a rising pop star under the control of menacing promoter Philo Gant (Michael Wincott). Lenny keeps tabs on Faith—whom he still loves—through his friend Max Peltier (Tom Sizemore), a former cop turned bodyguard. In turn, Lenny's friend Lornette "Mace" Mason (Angela Bassett), a formidable limo driver-cum-security specialist, keeps a protective eye on him.

News of the highway shooting of rapper/activist Jeriko One (Glenn Plummer) raises racial tensions. Iris (Brigitte Bako), a sympathetic hooker, warns Lenny that Faith is in danger, but disappears, pursued by police. Lenny later receives a clip that records the rape and murder of Iris. Searching for clues, he recalls that Iris has tossed a clip into his car, which has since been towed. Having broken into a car pound to retrieve the clip, Lenny and Mace narrowly escape murderous rogue cops Steckler (Vincent D'Onofrio) and Engelman (William Fichtner).

Watching the clip, Lenny experiences the murder of Jeriko One from Iris's point-of-view. The culprits are Steckler and Engelman. Fearing the violence that would erupt if word got out, Lenny and Mace go to the New Year's Eve party at the Bonaventure Hotel, where Mace takes the clip to the straight-arrow head of the police force, Palmer Strickland (Josef Sommer). Lenny seeks out Gant but finds him brain-dead from a SQUID OD administered by the treacherous Max, who admits to Iris's murder. They fight and Max falls to his death. Mace flees Steckler and Engelman through streets thronged with revellers. She handcuffs them but is knocked down by National Guardsmen. The crowd riots in her support until Strickland arrives. Having viewed the incriminating clip, he orders the arrest of the crooked cops; Engelman commits suicide and Steckler is shot down while trying to retaliate. Lenny and Mace are reunited as the new century is rung in.

Director Kathryn Bigelow has been conveniently labeled as the female filmmaker who makes stylishly "masculine" genre fare. Here, however, her background as a painter, conceptual artist, and would-be post-structuralist theorist may be more relevant than her gender. She reliably delivers the action goods and F/X fillips—e.g., the innovative use of lightweight and helmet cameras in long, elaborately choreographed, continuous POV shots—but her political understanding and emotional commitment are those of a slumming intellectual.

Bigelow told one interviewer her film "explores the idea of watching and the need to watch, and Lenny is a kind of director-producer of heightened-reality documentaries that put the viewer into the head of the person having a particular experience"—thus establishing her acquaintance with recent academic ideas about spectatorship. Beyond a limited understanding of post-modern theory, however, Bigelow seems ill-equipped to come to grips with the millennial themes and racial politics that her story promises to explore.

A cultural by-product of the videotaped beating of black motorist Rodney King by LA police, the film seems a calculated attempt to restore the audience's faith in (white) police authority. As Bigelow has herself conceded, "the murder [of Jeriko One] is a random, freak situation perpetrated by two individuals—two loose-cannon cops—acting completely outside any authority. Ultimately, justice prevails and the authority figures remain untarnished." This decision to let authority off the hook eliminated any possibility that STRANGE DAYS could make a meaningful statement about the racial, social, and economic meaning of the Rodney King beating and the subsequent LA riots. There's nothing here about how our society actually *works* as the end of the 20th Century approaches. What's left is pure sensation. There's very little at stake; the generic elements function as a template for empty virtuosity.

The impressive ensemble struggles valiantly, but it's a losing game. Bassett is particularly poignant, delivering her portentous lines with sincere intensity. Fiennes isn't precisely miscast, but his role is misconceived. It's hard to imagine that this passive softie was once a vice cop. Though outwardly a cynical sleaze, Lenny is just another fallen idealist trying to regain his lost Faith. By the end of the film, it's hard to care one way or the other. *(Nudity, graphic violence, profanity, adult situations, sexual situations.)* — K.G.

d, Kathryn Bigelow; p, James Cameron, Steven-Charles Jaffe; exec p, Rae Sanchini, Lawrence Kasanoff; co-p, Ira Shuman; w, James Cameron, Jay Cocks (from a story by James Cameron); ph, Matthew F. Leonetti; ed, Howard Smith; m, Graeme Revell; prod d, Lilly Kilvert; art d, John Warnke; set d, Kara Lindstrom; sound, Jeff Wexler (mixer), David Ronne (mixer), Gary Rydstrom (design); fx, Terry Frazee, James Lima, Digital Domain, Michael "Tony" Meagher; casting, Rick Pagano; cos, Ellen Mirojnick; makeup, Mike Germain; stunts, Doug Coleman

Science Fiction/Thriller/Drama (PR: O MPAA: R)

STRANGER, THE ★★★½
(India) 120m National Film Development Corporation of India ~ Filmhaus c
(AGANTUK)

Utpal Dutt *(Manmohan Mitra)*; Deepankar De *(Sudhindra Bose)*; Mamata Shankar *(Anila Bose)*; Bikram Bhattacharya *(Satyaki/Bablu)*; Dhritiman Chatterjee *(Lawyer Sen Gupta)*; Rabi Gosh *(Ranjan Rakshit)*; Subrota Chatterji *(Chhanda Rakshit)*; Promode Ganguly *(Tridib Mukherji)*; Ajit Bannerji *(Mr. Sital)*; Aveek De; Sourav Bannerji; Sambitendu Dutt Majumdar; Sumon Bhaduri; Pitambar Chowdhury; Brahmadev Sharma; Rankanath; Subhas Mondol; Hansi Marondi

Satyajit Ray's last film is a testimony to his growing sense of unease in a world dehumanized by moral degeneration, greed, suspicion, and animosity. The theme was not new for him, but the three films that together form the last phase of his work, all depict with increasing intensity the struggle for individual integrity in a hostile and cynical environment.

Anila (Mamata Shankar), wife of Sudhindra Bose (Deepankar De), suddenly receives a letter from her long lost uncle, Manmohan (Utpal Dutt), who went abroad 35 years ago and did not keep in touch with the family. Now on his way to Australia, having learnt that Anila is his sole surviving relative, he wishes to spend a week in Calcutta as her guest.

Anila and Sudhindra are suspicious of this stranger in their midst. Is he really Manmohan? Why has he surfaced after all these years? What was he doing all this time? The only person who is excited by his arrival is Anila's 11-year-old son, Satyaki (Bikram Bhattacharya). Just when Anila is almost convinced of Manmohan's genuineness, she remembers her grandfather's will. Sudhindra immediately seizes on the idea: of course, Manmohan came to demand a share of the property, and all this show of affection is mere eyewash.

Inquiries reveal that the money is still with Sital Sarkar (Ajit Bannerji), who lives in Bolpur and was the executor of the will. Subsequently Sudhindra calls upon his friend Sen Gupta (Dhritiman Chatterjee) to check out Manmohan. In an embarrassing encounter with Sen Gupta, who is openly superior, suspicious, and cynical, Manmohan admits he is an anthropologist who has spent most of his life among tribal communities of the American continent. Fully aware of the inquisition he faces, Manmohan argues for the savage society he loves and expresses his scorn for civilization as it is understood by the younger man. Sensing his own failure in arguing his case, Sen Gupta in a rage accuses Manmohan of exploiting his friends.

When Manmohan vanishes next morning, Anila and Sudhindra drive down to Bolpur, assuming he has gone to collect his money. They find him in a tribal village, where they make amends and Anila forgets her civilized self long enough to join the tribal women in an exuberant folk dance. Back in Calcutta, before he leaves again, Manmohan hands an envelope to Sudhindra: a small token of gratitude. The gift turns out to be a check, transferring to Anila the entire amount of Manmohan's share in the family property.

The story of THE STRANGER (as the film was entitled for its US release; its original Bengali title is AGANTUK) is a slight but tenacious framework for the core of the film, the confrontation between Manmohan and Sen Gupta. Most of the film builds up to it, and the denouement is therefore predictable and almost insignificant. That is where the film reveals its major flaw: Manmohan argues for the eternally untainted soul of primitive society, ignoring the reality of indigenous communities across the world—brutalized, exploited, and transformed through the centuries by conquerors and kings, traders, and drug peddlers. Given the context, the counterpoint of "progress" may after all have something to say in its favor.

Although the viewer might quarrel with the director's simplistic romanticizing of the noble savage, THE STRANGER harks back to a more vigorous Ray, before his illness confined him to the studio. Made with assistance from his son, filmmaker Sandip Ray, THE STRANGER presents a visual grace and serenity that was missing from his two preceding films, GANASHATRU and SHAKHA PROSHAKHA. It also refines the anger expressed in those films, and manages to convey Ray's disillusionment in more poignant and humane terms.

Ray's protagonist expresses disillusionment with modern civilization, but never despair. His amused tolerance of the family's suspicions never degenerates into cynicism. He can still offer his affection and faith, at first to Satyaki, the innocent child among them, and later even to Anila and Sudhindra, who have so grossly misjudged him.

Of the three last films of Ray, THE STRANGER appears closest to a real comeback. It has the gentle humor present in many of his earlier films, the subtle nuances of character, the unspoken suggestions of veiled histories, and the stark simplicity of the cinematic form that hides nothing behind a startling visual experience. — S.B.

d, Satyajit Ray; p, Satyajit Ray; w, Satyajit Ray; ph, Barun Raha; ed, Dulal Dutt; m, Satyajit Ray; prod d, Ashoke Bose; sound, Sujit Sarkar (design); cos, Lalita Ray; makeup, Ananta Das

Drama   **(PR: AA   MPAA: NR)**

STRAWBERRY AND CHOCOLATE   ★★★
(Cuba) 111m Instituto Cubano del Arte y
Industria Cinematograficos; Instituto Mexicano de
Cinematografia; Tabasco Films; Telemadrid; Sociedad
General de Autores de Espana ~ Miramax c
(FRESA Y CHOCOLATE)

Jorge Perugorria (*Diego*); Vladimir Cruz (*David*); Mirta Ibarra (*Nancy*); Francisco Gattorno (*Miguel*); Joel Angelino (*German*); Marilyn Solaya (*Vivian*); Andres Cortina (*Santeria Priest*); Antonio Carmona (*Boyfriend*); Ricardo Avila (*Taxi Driver*); Maria Elena del Toro (*Passenger*); Zolanda Ovia (*Passenger*); Diana Iris del Puerto (*Neighbor*)

STRAWBERRY AND CHOCOLATE, the story of a friendship between two very different Cuban men, is the most audience-friendly movie to date by Cuba's best-known director, Tomas Guttierrez Alea (MEMORIES OF UNDERDEVELOPMENT). Based on a prize-winning short story by Senel Paz, this surprisingly slight film is a warm and fuzzy plea for tolerance that never becomes fully engaging.

David (Vladimir Cruz) is a political science student on the rebound from a failed romance. He is idealistic, serious, and deeply committed to the revolution. Diego (Jorge Perugorria) is a homosexual artist, hedonistic, flamboyant, naturally rebellious, and grappling with a troubled relationship of his own. The two meet in a Havana ice cream parlor, where Diego tries vainly to pick David up. An unusual friendship commences. They seem complete antagonists at first, but Diego joyously exposes David to the wonders of banned books, local architecture, Maria Callas, John Donne, Johnny Walker Red, and English tea sipped from Sevres cups. David, who had initially planned to spy on Diego and report his subversive behavior to the Party, gradually begins to feel affection for this impenitent rebel, as well as a need to protect him.

Bopping around their periphery is Nancy (Mirta Ibarra), a wild neighbor with suicidal tendencies who blithely rids David of his virginity. Less happily, there is also Miguel (Francisco Gatorno), David's macho, intolerant roommate, who causes grief for Diego after the artist writes an angry letter to the authorities protesting the censorship of an exhibit he is mounting. Ultimately, despite his deep love for his country, Diego realizes he must leave Cuba and bids a wry, fond farewell to his young comrade.

The basic premise here—gay libertine vs. uptight heterosexual Communist—reeks of KISS OF THE SPIDER WOMAN, but without the melodrama. While the central relationship and slim story line are tastefully rendered, perhaps a bit of melodrama would have helped to bring the film to life. Presumably due to censorship, Cuba's long history of homophobic oppression is largely avoided. The film's rather muted political subtext is unfortunately matched by the mildness of the screenplay.

US audiences are likely to find the characters old-fashioned and stereotypical—Diego and David behave in strictly prescribed, predictable ways, the former ever characterized by outrage and dynamic emotions, the latter always reactive and wary. The film seems about to fortuitously shift gears when Diego takes David on a rhapsodic tour of the still-extant glories of Havana, but the sequence is truncated, and we return once more to the site of most of the action, Diego's artifact-filled warren of an apartment. The handsome Perugorria is something of a Cuban

Jean Brodie with his character's endless culture-vulture pronouncements about life, art, and *haute cuisine*. He's amusing and affecting, but the character wants fleshing out. Cruz is okay as the unwilling love object, but the film dwells too much on his narcissistic mooning over his former girlfriend. (*Nudity, adult situations, sexual situations, substance abuse, profanity.*) — D.N.

d, Tomas Gutierrez Alea, Juan Carlos Tabio; exec p, Robert Redford, Miguel Mendoza, Camilo Vives, Frank Cabrera, Georgina Balzaretti; assoc p, Nacho Cobo, Juan Munoz; w, Senel Paz (based on his short story "The Wolf, the Forest and the New Man"); ph, Mario Garcia Joya; ed, Miriam Talavera, Osvaldo Donatien, Rolando Martinez; m, Jose Maria Vitier; prod d, Fernando O'Reylly; set d, Orlando Gonzalez; sound, Germinal Hernandez (design), Silvia Rodriguez (recordist); cos, Miriam Duenas; makeup, Maria Elena del Toro, Graciela Grossas

Drama/Romance/Political   **(PR: O   MPAA: NR)**

STUART SAVES HIS FAMILY   ★★★
(U.S.) 100m Constellation Films; Paramount ~
Paramount c

Al Franken (*Stuart Smalley*); Laura San Giacomo (*Julia*); Vincent D'Onofrio (*Donnie*); Shirley Knight (*Stuart's Mom*); Harris Yulin (*Stuart's Dad*); Lesley Boone (*Jodie*); John Link Graney (*Kyle*); Marjorie Lovett (*Aunt Paula*); Walt Robles (*Smalley Uncle*); Erik Cord (*Smalley Uncle*); Denver Mattson (*Smalley Uncle*); Grant Hoover (*Young Stuart*); Cory Milano (*Young Donnie*); Michelle Horn (*Young Jodie*); Harris Laskawy (*Mr. Dimmit*); Tom Dugan (*Ajax Spokesperson*); Camille Saviola (*Roz Weinstock*); Bess Meyer (*Laurie*); Julia Sweeney (*Mea C.*); Patrick Kerr (*Makeover Artist*); Aaron Lustig (*Fred*); Fred Applegate (*Carl*); Darrell Larson (*Jerry*); Dakin Matthews (*Intervention Counselor*); Jeffrey Joseph (*Lawyer*); Marte Boyle Slout (*Madelyn Doyle*); Joe Flaherty (*Cousin Ray*); Robin Duke (*Cousin Denise*); Lewis Arquette (*Cemetery Official*); Michael G. Hagerty (*Cop*); Peter Torokvei (*Minister*); Allen Garfield (*Maitre d'*); Pamela Brull (*Female Diner*); Walter Olkewicz (*Larry Skoag*); Jeremy Roberts (*Brad Skoag*); Steven Kampmann (*Stan Brunner*); Robert Curtis-Brown (*Andy*); Violet Ramis (*Production Assistant*); Aloma Wright (*Autograph Seeker*); Rachel Miller (*Woman with Subpoena*); Kurt Fuller (*Von Arks*); Walter S. Beaver (*Orville Egeberg*); Michael C. McCarthy (*Merl Egeberg*); David Pasquesi (*Tollefson*); Richard Riehle (*Judge*); R.M. Haley (*Bailiff*); Theodore Raimi (*Hal*); Rogan Wilde (*Ted*)

Stuart Smalley, the "12-stepper's 12-stepper," steps up from television's "Saturday Night Live" to the big screen in this satire of dysfunction and recovery that is on target surprisingly often.

Stuart Smalley (Al Franken) is host of a public access show famous for the ego-reinforcing mantra: "I'm good enough. I'm smart enough. And doggone it, people like me." He is also a member of several 12-step programs, including Overeaters Anonymous, Al-Anon, and Debtors Anonymous. (Though not in debt, he has "money issues.") When his TV show is unceremoniously canceled, Stuart barely has time to make a healing action before he is called home for his aunt's funeral. In Minneapolis, Stuart reunites with his completely dysfunctional family: his father (Harris Yulin), a "big, mean drunk;" his brother Donnie (Vincent D'Onofrio), also an alcoholic, and unemployed; his sister Jodie (Lesley Boone), the partner in several bad marriages; and his mother (Shirley Knight), a master of passive-aggressive guilt inducement.

Aunt Paula's funeral is a fiasco. Dad and Donnie drop the coffin, get into a fight with some relatives, and are arrested.

Stuart, as executor of Paula's estate, becomes embroiled in a legal dispute with the rest of the Smalleys. He returns to Chicago, and with the help and encouragement of his best friend Julia (Laura San Giacomo), devotes his efforts to getting his show, "Daily Affirmation," back on the air. By Christmas, "Daily Affirmation" has become a big hit on cable, and Stuart is celebrating how he has stopped beating himself up over his failure to save his family. After all, he can only heal himself. Then Donnie shows up in Chicago, clean and sober, looking to begin a new life.

Like a very heartfelt Richard Simmons, Stuart Smalley does get rather irksome. At one point, Stuart is involved in a bar fight and he cannot help but suggest his tormentor get in touch with his "powerless and frightened inner child." The weakest parts of the film are those that focus on Stuart and his TV show because the film is unwilling to skewer its star. The best parts are the ones with his family. A particular highlight is a flashback of vacationing Smalleys trying to see all of Hollywood's sights in one day. Finding humor in alcoholism (not drunkenness) is a tricky business, and Al Franken's script cuts close to the bone. Harris Yulin, in the pivotal role, strikes just the right tone. Ironically, this black comedy is more honest about pain than last year's Franken-scripted serious drama, WHEN A MAN LOVES A WOMAN. Harold Ramis (GROUNDHOG DAY) again delivers a strong directorial effort. Also, having talented actors like D'Onofrio and San Giacomo in key roles, instead of "Saturday Night Live" coworkers, is a big plus. (*Profanity, adult situations, substance abuse.*) — P.R.

d, Harold Ramis; p, Lorne Michaels, Trevor Albert; exec p, Dinah Minot, C.O. Erickson; assoc p, Whitney White; w, Al Frankin (based on his book); ph, Lauro Escorel; ed, Pembroke Herring, Craig Herring; m, Marc Shaiman; prod d, Joseph T. Garrity; art d, Thomas P. Wilkins; set d, Dena Roth; sound, Willie Burton (mixer); casting, Nancy Foy; cos, Susie DeSanto; makeup, Bradley Wilder; stunts, Victor Paul, Rick LeFevour

Comedy   **(PR: A   MPAA: PG-13)**

SUBSTITUTE WIFE, THE   ★★½
(U.S.) 92m Frederick S. Pierce Company ~ Vidmark Entertainment c
(AKA: SUBSTITUTE, THE)

Farrah Fawcett (*Pearl Hickson*); Lea Thompson (*Amy Hightower*); Peter Weller (*Martin Hightower*); Karis Bryant (*Jessica Hightower*); Cory Lloyd (*Nathan Hightower*); Colton Conklin (*Jack*); Zeke Mills (*Mr. Honecker*); Annie Suite (*Mrs. Van Der Meer*); Marco Perela (*Mr. Hoffman*); Jill Parker Jones (*Mrs. Hoffman*); Babs George (*Mrs. Parker*); Gena Sleete (*Hattie Donahue*); Gail Cronauer (*Isabel Donahue*); Lou Perryman (*Saloon Keeper*); Jonathan Joss (*Black Deer*); Blue Deckert (*Royal Spencer*); Wally Welch (*Jake*); Guich Koock (*Mr. Van Der Meer*); John S. Davies (*Preacher #1*); Tony Frank (*Major Willows*); John Harrison (*Groom*); Travis Middleton (*Preacher #3*); Katherine Catmull (*Dianne*); Alandra Lancaster (*Older Jessica*); Otis A. Katvedt (*Older Jack*)

Set in 1869 Nebraska, THE SUBSTITUTE WIFE is about a Wild West couple who strike upon an unconventional solution to their misfortune.

When she is stricken with a fatal illness, frontierswoman Amy Hightower (Lea Thompson) fears that her husband Martin (Peter Weller) will not be able to manage the farm and their four young children alone. She sets out to find him a new wife, but single women are so scarce that the only candidate she can find is a tough talking and not so young prostitute named Pearl (Farrah Fawcett). Eager for a change of scenery, Pearl accepts Amy's unusual proposition. She quickly learns that being a wife and

mother entails more work than she had anticipated, but she sticks to the bargain. Amy trains Pearl to cook, clean, care for the children, and perform chores on the farm. She encourages her husband to share Pearl's bed and is glad when he complies.

Just when Pearl is ready to fill Amy's shoes, Amy makes a miraculous recovery. Pearl packs her bags but Amy begs her to stay. She feels indebted to Pearl, whom she has grown to love. The women work out an arrangement whereby they share the farm work as well as Martin's affections. Martin faintly protests that their living situation is ungodly but eventually settles on a weekly bed-swapping schedule. Several months later, Amy suffers a relapse and dies.

In THE SUBSTITUTE WIFE, campy dialogue and offbeat humor are jarringly juxtaposed with emotional outpourings and tender deathbed scenes. It works better when playing for laughs. Of the leads, Fawcett commands the lion's share of attention. She gives a spirited performance and smoothly handles her character's transformation from reluctant understudy to devoted wife and mother. Thompson presents a fine portrait of the dying Amy, at once physically fragile and emotionally powerful, a woman determined that her struggle for her family's wellbeing will not end with her own death. Weller succeeds in winning his laconic homesteader a few moments of regard by letting on that despite his protestations, Martin realizes just how enviable his position is. Filmed on location in Central Texas, the piece features convincing period costumes and production design. (*Sexual situations, profanity*) — B.R.

d, Peter Werner; p, Michael O. Gallant; exec p, Frederick S. Pierce, Keith Pierce, Richard Pierce, Stan Daniels; assoc p, Andrew Golov; w, Stan Daniels; ph, Neil Roach; ed, Martin Nicholson; m, Mark Snow; prod d, Cary White; art d, Michael Sullivan; set d, Barbara Haberecht; sound, Jennifer Murphy (mixer); casting, Barbara Brinkley; cos, Van Broughton Ramsey; makeup, Kate Shorter

Western/Drama/Comedy   **(PR: C   MPAA: PG-13)**

SUBSTITUTE, THE
(SEE: SUBSTITUTE WIFE, THE)

SUDDEN DEATH   ★★½
(U.S.) 110m Signature Films; Baldwin Cohen; Imperial Entertainment ~ Universal c

Jean-Claude Van Damme (*Darren*); Powers Booth (*Joshua Foss*); Raymond J. Barry (*Vice President*); Whittni Wright (*Emily*); Ross Malinger (*Tyler*); Dorian Harewood (*Hallmark*); Kate McNeil (*Kathi*); Michael Gaston (*Hickey*); Audra Lindley (*Mrs. Ferrara*); Brian Delate (*Blair*); Steve Aronson (*Dooley*); Michael Aubele (*Ace*); Karen Baldwin (*TV Director*); Jennifer D. Bowser (*Joan*); Pat Brisson (*Player #2*); Glenda Morgan Brown (*Mrs. Taylor*); Jophery Brown (*Wootton*); William Cameron (*Secret Serviceman*); Bernard Canepari (*Jefferson*); Jay Caufield (*Tolliver*); Alan Clement (*Mr. Wirtz*); Bill Clement (*Pre-Game Announcer*); Bill Dalzell, III (*Spota*); Gil Combs (*Secret Service #1*); Jack Erdie (*Scratch*); Ed Evanko (*Baldwin*); David Flick (*Spectator*); Glenn Alan Gardner (*Sugarman Driver*); John Hall (*Hallmark's Secret Service #2*); Jeff Habbersted (*Lewis*); Mark Hager (*Elevator SS Man*); John Hateley (*Briggs*); Rosine "Ace" Hatem (*Concessionaire*); Jeff Hochendoner (*Duckerman*); Jeffrey Howell (*Usborn*); Brian Hutchison (*Young Agent*); Jeff Jimerson (*Anthem Singer*); Mark Kachowski (*Beaumont*); Callum Keith-King (*Kitchen Assistant*); Rick LeFevour (*Ante Room SS Man*); Tommy LaFitte (*Sugarman Guard*); Raymond Laine (*Foss Man #1*); Mike Lange (*Play by Play Announcer*); Butch Luick (*Fat Man*); Fred Mancuso

(Pratt); Anthony Marino *(Vendor)*; Larry John Meyers *(Box Secret Service #2)*; Ken Milchick *(Coach)*; Faith Minton *(Carla)*; Paul Mochnick *(Andre Ferrara)*; Brad Moniz *(Toowey)*; Jean-Pierre Nutini *(Employee #1)*; Daniel R. Pagath *(Asisstant Coach)*; Manny Perry *(Brody)*; Allan Pinsker *(Older Man)*; Douglas Rees *(Spotter)*; Diane Robin *(Mrs. Baldwin)*; Luc Robitaille *(Himself)*; Thomas Saccio *(Foss Helicopter Pilot)*; Vinnie Sciullo *(Foss Man #2)*; Jack Skelly *(Elderly Guard)*; Brian Smrz *(Thug #2)*; Phil Spano *(Player #1)*; Paul Steigerwald *(Color Commentator)*; John Sterling *(Kitchen Secret Service Agent)*; Harold Surratt *(Hallmark Secret Service Agent #3)*; Rohn Thomas *(Mayor Taylor)*; Milton E. Thompson, Jr. *(Kurtz)*; Dixie Tymitz *(Mrs. Wirtz)*; Fred Waugh *(Bluto)*; Rema D. Webb *(Cindy)*; Dean E. Wells *(Kloner)*

This Jean-Claude Van Damme vehicle, about an ex-firefighter who single-handedly vanquishes villains who have kidnaped his daughter and the Vice President of the United States, is a minor but pleasant effort, with tongue firmly in cheek most of the way.

Darren (Van Damme) is a man getting over both a painful divorce and the loss of his job as a firefighter in present-day Pittsburgh. While working as fire inspector for the city's Civic Arena, Darren makes a special appeal to his ex-wife to let him take their children, Emily (Whittni Wright) and Tyler (Ross Malinger), to the Stanley Cup Finals between the Chicago Black-hawks and the Pittsburgh Penguins at the indoor stadium. When Darren and the children arrive, they observe the Secret Service preparing for a visit from the Vice President (Raymond J. Barry). At the same time, Joshua Foss (Powers Booth), an ex-CIA agent, initiates an elaborate plot to kidnap the Vice President and hold him hostage. Foss plans to detain his captive in the owner's box while, via computer, he funnels frozen government assets from other countries into his own bank account.

Foss's kidnapping scheme works until Emily accidentally becomes a hostage along with the Vice President and his political cronies. Darren immediately joins forces with the Secret Service to find Emily, but is shocked when he discovers that the head of the Secret Service team, Hallmark (Dorian Harewood), is actually working for Foss. Darren kills Hallmark (and some other bad guys), then deactivates several bombs that Foss had planned to detonate around the arena at the conclusion of the game.

After eluding Foss's thugs by pretending to be a hockey player during the rousing match, Darren finally breaks into Foss's stadium suite, where he kills all remaining henchmen and rescues the hostages, including Emily. Foss, meanwhile, tries to flee the stadium in a helicopter, but Darren foils the escape by killing the pilot. The chopper crashes down onto the stadium ice and explodes.

In his second consecutive film with director Peter Hyams (TIME COP), Van Damme has been relegated to almost pure action hero, with very few demands made on him as an actor. Ironically, the Belgian martial arts star gets little opportunity to show off what he does best, and the contrivance of having an ex-firefighter perform perfect roundhouses really stretches the limit.

Happily, most of the jokes in SUDDEN DEATH are more deliberate. Even if Darren displays no comic sense, his fight scenes are hilariously campy; and when he escapes by pretending to be a hockey goalie, the episode is staged to resemble a Danny Kaye routine. With Van Damme as low-key as always, however, Powers Booth becomes the real star, stealing the show as the cynically funny Joshua Foss. *(Violence, profanity.)* — E.M.

d, Peter Hyams; p, Moshe Diamant, Howard Baldwin; exec p, Ash R. Shah, Sundip R. Shah, Anders P. Jensen, Sunil R. Shah; assoc p, Karen Baldwin; co-p, Richard Cohen, Jason Clark, Jack Frost Sanders; w, Gene Quintano (from a story by Karen Baldwin); ph, Peter Hyams; ed, Steven Kemper; m, John Debney; prod d, Philip Harrison; art d, William Barclay; set d, Caryl Heller; sound, Les Lazarowitz (mixer); fx, Garry Elmendorf, Gregory L. McMurry, VIFX; casting, Penny Perry Davis, Deborah Brown; cos, Dan Lester; makeup, Katalin Elek; stunts, Gary M. Hymes

Action/Thriller/Adventure　　　　**(PR: C　MPAA: R)**

SUM OF US, THE　　　　　　★★★
(Australia) 100m Quicksilver Productions;
Southern Star Entertainment; Hal McElroy ~
Samuel Goldwyn Company c

Jack Thompson *(Harry Mitchell)*; Russell Crowe *(Jeff Mitchell)*; John Polson *(Greg)*; Deborah Kennedy *(Joyce Johnson)*; Joss Morony *(Young Jeff)*; Mitch Mathews *(Gran)*; Julie Herbert *(Mary)*; Des James *(Football Coach)*; Mick Campbell *(Footballer)*; Donny Muntz *(Ferry Captain)*; Jan Adele *(Barmaid)*; Rebekah Elmaloglou *(Jenny)*; Lola Nixon *(Desiree)*; Sally Cahill *(Greg's Mother)*; Bob Baines *(Greg's Father)*; Paul Freeman *(George)*; Walter Kennard *(Barman)*; Stuart Campbell *(Leatherman)*; Graham Drake *(Leatherman)*; Elaine Lee *(Woman on Train)*; Ross Anderson *(Gardener)*; Michael Burgess *(Foreman)*; John Rhall *(Dad's Brother)*; Helen Williams *(Brother's Wife)*; Jan Merriman *(Nurse)*

THE SUM OF US, a warm and deeply affecting comedy-drama from down under, centers on the unconventional relationship between widower Harry Mitchell (Jack Thompson), a ferry captain, and his 24-year-old son Jeff (Russell Crowe), a plumber. The twist on this father-and-son tale is that Jeff is openly gay and Harry is boisterously supportive.

When Jeff brings home his date, a handsome gardener named Greg (John Polson), Harry keeps interrupting at inopportune moments. He offers his son's suitor romantic advice, asks how he takes his tea in the morning, and discusses safe sex. Over beers in the backyard, Harry also gets Greg to open up about his feelings and dreams. Greg, who hides his sexual preference from his homophobic parents, cannot adjust to the cozy domesticity at the Mitchells'. Just when Harry finally leaves the lovers alone, Greg leaves. Jeff, who thought he had finally found someone special, is inconsolable and lashes out at his well-intentioned father.

Harry is also looking for love and finds it with Joyce (Deborah Kennedy), an attractive divorcee whom he meets through a dating service. The relationship proceeds swimmingly, and they are soon discussing marriage. Then Joyce learns, to her horror, that Jeff is gay and Harry is not ashamed but proud. She breaks off the relationship, and moments later heartbroken Harry suffers a stroke.

Jeff assumes the responsibility of caring for his father, who, paralyzed and unable to speak, communicates with Jeff using a buzzer rigged to his wheelchair. Harry's spirit and verve have not diminished despite his physical limitations, and he still manages to play matchmaker for his son and Greg. Disowned by his parents after they discover he is gay, Greg becomes more appreciative of Jeff's relationship with his father. As Jeff and Greg resume their romance, no one is happier than dear old Dad.

David Stevens wrote the screenplay based on his award-winning stage play, which enjoyed a successful off-Broadway run in 1990. The film version racked up a slew of awards in Australia, including the best feature award at the 1994 Sydney Film Festival and top honors for the screenplay and star Thompson from the Film Critics Circle of Australia. In adapting the stage play for the screen, Stevens' only blunder was retaining the theatrical device of having the characters speak directly to the audience. A common practice in the theater, this seldom works in film and is a distraction here, especially when a post-stroke Harry delivers speeches about his frustrations at being unable to speak. Kevin Dowling, who directed the stage play, was reenlisted to helm the film version, codirecting with cinematographer Geoff Burton, whose camera is most effective in a series of evanescent black-and-white flashbacks that convey the anguish of Jeff's elderly grandmother and her lesbian lover, who are forced to separate.

Russell Crowe and Jack Thompson are perfectly cast as the devoted father and son. From their "Odd Couple" banter to their wrenching heart-to-hearts, they complement each other in timing, style and temperament. Veteran character actor Thompson (BREAKER MORANT, MAD DOG MORGAN) gives one of his best portrayals here, and Crowe, who appeared in this year's THE QUICK AND THE DEAD, is being touted as the next Mel Gibson.

THE SUM OF US received limited release in the US, its modest box office receipts attributable to its foreign origin and lack of domestic star power. Its subject matter may have also kept mainstream audiences away, and more is the pity. The fact that a father who openly supports his son's homosexuality is still considered aberrant in 1995 is a distressing notion. After all, as Harry says, our children are only the sum of us. *(Sexual situations, adult situations, profanity.)* — B.R.

d, Kevin Dowling, Geoff Burton; p, Hal McElroy; exec p, Errol Sullivan, Hal McElroy; w, David Stevens (based on his play); ph, Geoff Burton; ed, Frans Vandenburg; m, Dave Faulkner; prod d, Graham "Grace" Walker; art d, Ian Gracie; set d, Kerrie Brown; sound, Leo Sullivan (recordist); casting, Faith Martin and Associates; cos, Louise Spargo; makeup, Leslie Rouvray

Comedy/Drama (PR: C MPAA: NR)

SWIMMING WITH SHARKS ★★
(U.S.) 93m Keystone Partners; Cineville; Neofight Film; Mama'z Boy Entertainment ~ Trimark Pictures c
(AKA: BUDDY FACTOR, THE)

Kevin Spacey *(Buddy Ackerman)*; Frank Whaley *(Guy)*; Michelle Forbes *(Dawn Lockard)*; Benicio Del Toro *(Rex)*; T.E. Russell *(Foster Kane)*; Roy Dotrice *(Cyrus Miles)*; Matthew Flynt *(Manny)*; Patrick Fischler *(Moe)*; Jerry Levine *(Jack)*

George Huang's first film, about a perpetually undermined assistant who finally kills his tormenting boss, appears to be primarily an act of revenge against all the egotistical, cruel, manipulative people Huang has worked for, especially notorious Hollywood producer Joel Silver.

Mild-mannered Guy (Frank Whaley) is personal assistant to Buddy Ackerman (Kevin Spacey), a studio big shot who belittles Guy in front of everybody, sends him to do meaningless, degrading chores, and steals his ideas. Guy endures this misery because he worships movies. He also meets and becomes involved with girl-wonder producer Dawn Lockard (Michelle Forbes). Lockard wants to do "serious" films for teenagers; Ackerman is only interested in violent action films. Guy tries to bridge the gap by teaming Lockard's script with Ackerman's hot new director Foster Kane (T.E. Russell), and rewriting the ending. Ackerman sells the film to the head of Keystone Studios without crediting Guy, pausing at his desk to criticize his spelling errors. Tensions grow between Guy and Lockard, who keeps urging him to confront Ackerman or quit. Finally, they split up, and, through a mixed phone line, Guy overhears Lockard and Ackerman arranging a late night tryst. Guy breaks into Ackerman's home, ties him up, and beats and tortures him savagely, recounting every insult and injury he has received. Ackerman not only refuses to apologize, but continues to berate Guy for being spineless. When Lockard arrives and pleads with Guy to stop, Ackerman actually urges Guy to kill him, telling him he has to take action and destroy whatever is making him weak.

The film, structured as a series of flashbacks, opens with Guy standing by a police car as a covered body is hauled off in an ambulance. As the flashbacks move closer to the present, we see Guy more and more from Ackerman's point of view, and throughout the film there are indications that Guy is molding himself in Ackerman's image. The resolution, featuring a bogus "surprise" ending, is less a twist than a twitch.

Spacey, who coproduced the film, clearly saw Ackerman as a perfect role for himself, and almost succeeds in making the character a real human being. But neither Whaley nor the script offer a compelling protagonist. Lockard's relationship with Guy lacks credibility; we cannot understand what she sees in this human beanbag. The conflict is artificial, so the denouement lacks force.

Huang has a derivative directorial style that matches his derivative, if moderately entertaining, script. There are some genuinely funny lines amid the clutter of Hollywood inside jokes, but that's about as far as it goes. *(Extreme profanity, graphic violence, sexual situations.)* — R.S.

d, George Huang; p, Steve Alexander, Joanne Moore; exec p, Jay Cohen, Stephen Israel; assoc p, Kevin Reidy; co-p, Kevin Spacey, Buzz Hays; w, George Huang; ph, Steven Finestone; ed, Ed Marx; m, Tom Heil; prod d, Veronika Merlin, Cecil Gentry; art d, Karen Haase; sound, Giovanni DiSimone (mixer); fx, Dennis Dion, Martin Mercer; casting, Andrea Stone Guttfreund, Laurel Smith; cos, Kirsten Everberg; makeup, Sarah Gaye Deal; stunts, Mike Kirton

Comedy (PR: O MPAA: R)

TALES FROM THE CRYPT: DEMON KNIGHT ★★★
(U.S.) 92m Universal ~ Universal c
(AKA: DEMON KNIGHT)

John Kassir *(Voice of the Crypt Keeper)*; Billy Zane *(The Collector)*; William Sadler *(Brayker)*; Jada Pinkett *(Jeryline)*; Brenda Bakke *(Cordelia)*; CCH Pounder *(Irene)*; Dick Miller *(Uncle Willy)*; Thomas Haden Church *(Roach)*; John Schuck *(Sheriff Tupper)*; Gary Farmer *(Deputy Bob Martel)*; Charles Fleisher *(Wally Enfield)*; Tim deZarn *(Homer)*; Sherrie Rose *(Wanda)*; Ryan Sean O'Donohue; Tony Salome *(Sirach)*; Ken Baldwin *(Dickerson)*; Tiffany Anne; Reda Beebe; Te-See Bender; Traci Bingham; Ponti Butler; Veronica Culver; Tina Hollimon; Elaine Marks; Mim Parker *(Party Babes)*; Graham Galloway *(Fred)*; Dale Swann *(Bus Driver)*; Mark D. Kennerly *(Other Collector)*; Peggy Trentini *(Amanda)*; Kathy Barbour *(Crypt Keeper Starlet)*; Tina New *(Crypt Keeper Starlet)*; Stephanie Sain *(Radio Voice/Mavis)*

The first of three planned theatrical features based on HBO's popular EC Comics-inspired series, DEMON KNIGHT is an energetic retelling of a standard horror story.

In a framing device, the Crypt Keeper (voiced by John Kassir) introduces his tale of terror. Fleeing from evil pursuers, a man named Brayker (William Sadler) arrives at the Mission Hotel, where the residents include the proprietor Irene (CCH Pounder), a prostitute Cordelia (Brenda Bakke), her no-good boyfriend Roach (Thomas Haden Church), old drunk Willy (Dick Miller), postal clerk Enfield (Charles Fleisher), and a young woman named Jeryline (Jada Pinkett), who is on a work-release program from jail. A mysterious man called the Collector (Billy Zane) arrives with the local sheriff, seeking a large, mystical key in Brayker's possession. A fight breaks out, during which the Collector kills the sheriff and leaves, returning with an army of demons that attack the hotel.

After helping the others fend the monsters off and "sealing" all the entrances with blood from the key, Brayker reveals that it is the blood of Jesus Christ, and that the key has been passed down for centuries in an effort to keep it from the Collector, who can use it to unleash Hell on Earth. Seduced by the Collector's spirit, Cordelia becomes a demon, kills Enfield, and disfigures Irene before being dispatched herself. The Collector then tempts Jeryline, who resists him; Willy does not, however, and must be decapitated. Roach steals the key and hands it over to the Collector to save his own skin, but he dies at the demons' claws. The creatures' new invasion leaves only Jeryline and the mortally wounded Brayker alive; refilling the key with his own blood, Brayker passes it on to Jeryline before expiring. She uses the key to kill the Collector, then sets the hotel ablaze and departs, but with a new Collector seemingly on her trail.

HBO's "Tales From the Crypt" won a sizable following for its mixture of full-bore gruesomeness and tongue-in-cheek humor, a combination effectively preserved in this feature-length expansion. Instead of taking its story inspiration from the EC comics, however, this one adapts the tried-and-true formula of a group of innocents trapped in an enclosed space besieged by monsters, and spices it up with an interesting religious background, well-sketched characters, and plenty of well-executed special effects and makeup. Director Ernest Dickerson (marking a vast improvement on his previous SURVIVING THE GAME) punches the script across with style and a sharp sense of humor.

As the demons' creepy-charming human leader, Zane makes a great villain, while Sadler is equally solid as his longtime quarry and Pinkett proves to be one of the horror genre's more memorable feisty heroines. An extra bonus for B-movie devotees is the appearance of longtime character actor Miller, here receiving one of his biggest roles in a while; the scene in which the Collector gives Willy a taste of his ultimate fantasy, placing him in a bar surrounded by topless babes, is worth the price of admission for fans. In a horror-film market overcrowded with filmmakers attempting to "elevate" the genre or deny it, DEMON KNIGHT's straightforward, unabashed, and energetic approach is as welcome as it is entertaining. *(Graphic violence, nudity, sexual situations, profanity.)* — M.G.

d, Ernest Dickerson; p, Gilbert Adler; exec p, Richard Donner, David Giler, Walter Hill, Joel Silver, Robert Zemeckis; assoc p, Alexander B. Collett, Dan Cracchiolo; co-p, Scott Nimerfro, Wendy Wanderman, Alan Katz; w, Ethan Riff, Cyrus Voris, Mark Bishop; ph, Rick Bota; ed, Stephen Lovejoy; m, Ed Shearmur, Danny Elfman; prod d, Christiaan Wagener; art d, Colin Irwin; set d, George Toomer; anim, January Nordman, Laurel Klick, Alan Wolfson, W.L. Arance; sound, Tim Cooney (mixer); fx, Scott Coulter, Scott Patton, Thomas "Brooklyn" Bellisimo, Charles "Gris Gris" Belardinelli, John T. Van Vliet; casting, Jaki Brown-Karman; cos, Warden Neil; makeup, Justin Henderson, Donna-Lou Henderson, Scott Wheeler, Todd Masters; stunts, Shane Dixon

Horror **(PR: O MPAA: R)**

TALES FROM THE HOOD ★★½
(U.S.) 97m 40 Acres and a Mule Filmworks ~
Savoy Pictures c

Clarence Williams, III *(Mr. Simms)*; Joe Torry *(Stack)*; Wings Hauser *(Strom)*; Tom Wright *(Martin Moorehouse)*; David Alan Grier *(Carl)*; Brandon Hammond *(Walter)*; Corbin Bernsen *(Duke Metger)*; Roger Smith *(Rhodie)*; Rosalind Cash *(Dr. Cushing)*; Lamont Bentley *(Crazy K)*; De'Aundre Bonds *(Ball)*; Samuel Monroe, Jr. *(Bulldog)*; Anthony Griffith *(Clarence)*; Michael Massee *(Newton)*; Duane Whitaker *(Billy)*; Rusty Cundieff *(Richard)*; Paula Jai Parker *(Sissy)*; Art Evans *(Eli)*

An affectionate homage to anthology horror movies with a twist—that all the stories concern African-Americans—TALES FROM THE HOOD is glossy, clever, and occasionally fun.

A trio of trash-talking homeboys (Joe Torry, De'Aundre Bonds, Samuel Monroe Jr.) muscles into the spooky funeral home of Mr. Simms (Clarence Williams III) looking for drugs they think have been hidden there. The eccentric Simms refuses to be intimidated, instead telling them four tales of poetic justice, each of which ends with someone in one of his coffins.

In "Rogue Cop Revelation," Clarence (Anthony Griffith), a Black rookie, is torn between loyalty to the police force and loyalty to his race when he finds himself privy to the doings of three corrupt white cops, led by brutal Officer Strom (Wings Hauser). Strom and his lackeys murder Black community leader Martin Moorehouse (Tom Wright), then make his death look like a car accident brought about by drug abuse. Clarence watches, horrified, but fails to breach the blue wall of silence. Moorehouse returns from the grave as a zombie, taking revenge on his murderers and on Clarence, whose silence damns him.

The second segment, "Boys Do Get Bruised," tackles child abuse. Young Walter (Brandon Hammond) often comes to school with injuries that he blames on a monster. Concerned teacher Richard (Rusty Cundieff) pays a visit to Walter's home and speaks with his mother, Sissy (Paula Jai Parker), who assures him that everything is fine. But the arrival of stepfather Carl

(David Alan Grier) leads Richard to believe—correctly—that the man beats his wife and child. Walter's pictures of the "monster" eventually save him: he crumples one up, and Carl is crumpled into a broken mass of flesh and bone.

In "KKK Comeuppance," loathsome David Duke-like politician Duke Metger (Corbin Bernsen) takes up residence in the home of a long dead voodoo woman. One wall is decorated with an eerie mural of the woman surrounded by dolls; legend has it that her dolls contained the souls of murdered slaves. Metger scoffs at the stories, even after political consultant Rhodie (Roger Smith), a Black man willing to ignore Metger's heinous politics to advance his own career, dies in a suspicious accident in the house. Metger finally gets what he deserves at the hands of the scampering hoard of voodoo dolls.

The fourth and final segment, "Hard Core Convert," concerns dope-dealing gangster Crazy K (Lamont Bentley). A tough street hood who doesn't care about anyone or anything, Crazy K is nearly killed by rival gangsters and winds up in jail, still unrepentant. Hoping to work the system to his advantage, he volunteers for an experimental treatment program and finds himself in Dr. Cushing's (Rosalind Cash's) House of High Fashion Horrors. Cushing's CLOCKWORK ORANGE-style efforts at behavior modification are still not enough to make Crazy K see the error of his ways, so he's visited by the vengeful ghosts of everyone who's died at his hands or because of his criminal misbehavior.

After the last tale, the gangbangers grow impatient with Mr. Simms and his moral lessons. They threaten him until he promises to take them to where the drugs are hidden. Imagine their surprise when he suddenly transforms himself into a winged, horned being—the very Devil himself—and tells them that they're all in Hell.

TALES FROM THE HOOD makes clear the exact nature of actor-writer-director Rusty Cundieff's misspent youth: he spent it watching pictures like TALES FROM THE CRYPT (1972) and dreaming that someday he'd make his own multi-part horror picture. TALES FROM THE HOOD is a great genre idea: Cundieff probably couldn't believe his luck when he realized that, despite BLACULA (1972), BLACKENSTEIN (1973), and DR. BLACK AND MR. WHITE (1976), no one had ever made a Black anthology horror movie. But it's not a great film. It suffers from the perpetual plague of the omnibus form—some segments are far stronger than others—and the whole project feels more than a little self-conscious. But it's pretty solidly entertaining, even when its ambitions exceed its reach.

It's an affectionate reworking of genre conventions, of course, but each tale is also meant to pack a powerful and racially specific moral punch. Drugs, gangster culture, black-on-black violence, and racism are all worked into Cundieff's TALES, and if the lessons are obvious, at least two of them—"KKK Comeuppance" and "Hard Core Convert"—are delivered with considerable flair. And who can resist a film in which "The Mod Squad"'s Clarence Williams III is the Devil? (Violence, profanity, adult situations, substance abuse.) — M.M.

d, Rusty Cundieff; p, Darin Scott; exec p, Spike Lee; w, Rusty Cundieff, Darin Scott; ph, Anthony B. Richmond; ed, Charles Bornstein; m, Christopher Young; prod d, Stuart Blatt; sound, Oliver Moss; fx, Kenneth Hall; casting, Robi Reed-Humes; makeup, Kenneth Hall, Screaming Mad George, KNB EFX Group

Horror (PR: C MPAA: R)

TALL TALE: THE UNBELIEVABLE ADVENTURES OF PECOS BILL ★★★
(U.S.) 98m Caravan Pictures; Walt Disney Company; Tall Tales Productions ~ Buena Vista c
(AKA: TALL TALE: THE INCREDIBLE ADVENTURE)

Patrick Swayze (Pecos Bill); Oliver Platt (Paul Bunyan); Roger Aaron Brown (John Henry); Nick Stahl (Daniel Hackett); Scott Glenn (J.P. Stiles); Stephen Lang (Jonas Hackett); Jared Harris (Head Thug Pug); Catherine O'Hara (Calamity Jane); Moira Harris (Sarah Hackett); Joseph Grifasi (Man in Top Hat); John P. Ryan (Grub); Scott Wilson (Zeb); Bert Kramer (Bronson); Eric Lawson (Sheriff); Bill Rodgers (Captain of Industry); Susan Barnes (Hag in Alley); John Nance (Doctor); Mike Moroff (Bar Room Bully); Richard Zobel (Barkeep); Michael J. Kosta (Farmer #1); Timothy Glenn Riley (Farmer #2); Darwyn Swalve (Lumberjack #1); Jay S. York (Lumberjack #2); Kevin Brown (Bettor #1); E.B. Meyers (Bettor #2); James Oscar Lee (Spectator); Sal Jenco (Big Jim)

Grandly produced and providing a photocopy of the panoramic sweep of classic westerns, TALL TALE performs a neat balancing act between tongue-in-cheek revisionism and standard folkloric hero-worship, agreeably mixing family values, high adventure, and bustling low comedy. If the young protagonist's father strikes one as a cloying frontier savior and if the villain huffs and puffs like a personality-less desperado, the film achieves unfettered distinction in scaling the heroic dimensions of its three American legends, Pecos Bill, Paul Bunyan, and John Henry, to a modern measure.

Dreaming of adventure, young Daniel Hackett (Nick Stahl) feels trapped on his family homestead and estranged from his pragmatic father Jonas (Stephen Lang). When Jonas is wounded defending the Hackett property, Daniel flees with a land deed coveted by snake-in-the-grass J.P Stiles (Scott Glenn). Determined to gobble up land for his railroad bosses, Stiles and his honchos pursue the lad as he drifts downriver and lands in a desert where two galoots nearly gun him down for fun. Rescued by Pecos Bill (Patrick Swayze), who rides in on a cyclone, Daniel rejects the tall tales he learned from his father. A born cynic, Daniel grates on the nerves of Pecos Bill's companion, Paul Bunyan (Oliver Platt), whom Pecos has shamed out of retirement. When the semi-mythical men encounter another frontier legend, John Henry (Roger Aaron Brown), the weak-willed Daniel disappoints the trio during John Henry's stake-driving competition. Although Pecos Bill eludes the wrath of Clamity Jane (Catherine O'Hara) and her claims of breach of promise, he has his hands full with Stiles's mercenaries, who badger Daniel so relentlessly he thinks of giving up. Despite Paul Bunyan's misgivings, Daniel comes through and becomes a role model for his entire fearful community as he confronts Stiles, who comes barreling through on a locomotive. Forcing Stiles backward into a tunnel where he meets a crushing demise, Daniel and his three prairie heroes prove that courage can be a group effort. Having stood the test of bravery against overwhelming odds, Daniel is relieved to find that his dad has recovered from his wounds. Finally comprehending the true worth of his family's land, the now mature Daniel can bid farewell to his larger-than-life friends who taught him the necessity of taking a stand.

Slammed by some critics for inappropriately imbuing legendary characters with politically correct attitudes, TALL TALE rather seems a case of legitimate revamping of folklore for contemporary tastes. A feast for sore eyes, this rambunctious western fantasia is the most diverting Disney live-action in some time. Swayze's blustering combination of Foghorn Leghorn and Frank Butler is engaging; more surprisingly, Oliver Platt succeeds in making Paul Bunyan less a giant do-gooder than a curmudgeonly dropout from Weight Watchers, capable of great feats during fits of pique. In this re-telling, the stature of these folk favorites lies in their fortitude and courage rather in than their amazing physical feats, like effortlessly chopping down redwoods. Instead of outdistancing Daniel, the three caballeros seem earthbound enough for the sassy boy to force them to put up or shut up. With its 1940s serial-style cliff-hangers and galloping chase sequences, TALL TALE is one family entertainment that grown-ups needn't roll their eyes at. In particular, fathers and sons in search of quality video time need look no further than this film's camaraderie, broad heroics, and scenic splendor. It's a bucking bronco of a children's film, full of tough varmints, slapstick mythologizing, and the feel-good triumph of a David over corporate Goliaths. The Disney conglomerate is often chastised for grinding out formula films like so many theme parks. TALL TALE demonstrates that the formula sometimes still works. *(Violence, profanity.)* — R.P.

d, Jeremiah Chechik; p, Joe Roth, Roger Birnbaum; exec p, Bill Badalato; assoc p, Kirsten W. Welles; w, Steven L. Bloom, Robert Rodat; ph, Janusz Kaminski; ed, Richard Chew; m, Randy Edelman; prod d, Eugenio Zanetti; art d, Rick Heinrichs, Jim R. Dultz; set d, Jerie Kelter; sound, Tim Chau (design), Robert Janiger (mixer); fx, Terry Frazee, Erik Henry, Steve Dellerson; casting, Jackie Burch; cos, Wayne Finkelman; makeup, Ken Chase, Dennis Glass, Sheri P. Short; stunts, Ernie Orsatti

Action/Adventure/Children's   **(PR: A   MPAA: PG)**

TANK GIRL   ★★½
(U.S.) 103m Trilogy Entertainment Group;
United Artists ~ United Artists c

Lori Petty *(Rebecca Buck—Tank Girl)*; Ice-T *(T-Saint—The Rippers)*; Naomi Watts *(Jet Girl)*; Don Harvey *(Sergeant Small)*; Jeff Kober *(Booga—The Rippers)*; Reg E. Cathey *(Deetee—The Rippers)*; Scott Coffey *(Donner—The Rippers)*; Malcolm McDowell *(Kesslee)*; Ann Magnuson *(Madam)*; Iggy Pop *(Rat Face)*; Staci Linn Ramsower *(Sam)*; Ann Cusack *(Sub Girl)*; Brian Wimmer *(Richard)*; Dawn Robinson *(Model)*; Billy L. Sullivan *(Max)*; James Hong *(Che'tsai)*; Charles Lucia *(Captain Derouche)*; Harlan Clark; Doug Jones; Ata Scanlan; Alvarez Wortham *(Additional Rippers)*; Roz Witt *(Dr. Nikita)*; Brixton Karnes *(Pilot)*; Will Nahkohe Strickland *(Razor Ray)*; Charles Robert Harden *(Zack)*; Tom Noga *(Foreman)*; Bo Jesse Christopher *(Town)*; John David Bland *(Trooper Wayne)*; Jo Farkas *(Sand Hermit)*; Stanton Davis *(Father)*; Jillian Balch *(Mother)*; Richard Schiff *(Trooper in Trench)*; Kane Picoy *(Trooper No. 1)*; Troy Startoni *(Jet Pilot)*; Beth DePatie *(Prostitute)*; Clayton Landey *(Guard)*; Roger Bohman *(Technician)*; Frank Walton *(Trooper In Basement)*; Richard Scott Sarafian *(Flyer Trooper)*; Aaron Kuhr *(Trooper at Pump Hangar)*; Kelly Cousineau *(Young Rebecca)*; Chief Gordon *(Trooper)*; Kelly Kerby *(Trooper)*; Jim Sullivan *(Semi Driver)*; William A. Doyle *(Dig Site Worker)*; Robert "Rock" Galotti *(Long Hair)*; Peer Ebbighausen *(Flyer Pilot)*; Bruce Spaulding Fuller; Shane Mahan; Mark Maitre; J. Alan Scott; Aurorah Allain; Kristie Canavan; Anne Fletcher; Carla Garrido; Heather Hendricks; Carolyn Kusian; Letha Lamb; Larissa Lanoue; Holly Manville; Cory William May; Mary Oedy; Kristianne Reed; Lynette Ruiz; Ryoko Sawaishi; Joie Shettler; Wes Veldnink; Dee Dee Weathers; Anacia Weiskittel; Nikki Whitfield; Kimberly Wolfe *("Liquid Silver" Dancers)*

A frenetic pastiche of everything from THE ROAD WARRIOR to SNOW WHITE, TANK GIRL is a woman-oriented action film

placed in a post-apocalyptic future, whose strange terrors are happily diluted by the comic book presentation of the story.

Earth, 2033. Water is scarce, and worth fighting and dying for. The evil utility company, Water and Power, run by megalomaniac Kesslee (Malcolm McDowell), controls almost all of the precious liquid. Only the Rippers, nonhuman creatures who stage guerrilla attacks on WP facilities, stand between Kesslee and absolute power. Rebecca Buck (Lori Petty) is among the handful of footloose renegades who scavenge the desert for survival. When she is captured by WP troops, Kesslee, who likes her spirit, offers her the opportunity to work for him fighting the Rippers. She refuses, and Kesslee tortures her and puts her to work in the mines. There Buck befriends timid fellow prisoner Jet (Naomi Watts). Eventually, they escape, taking a tank and a jet with them. Free in the desert, they transform themselves into Tank Girl and Jet Girl.

Tank Girl learns that Sam (Staci Linn Ramsower), a 10-year-old girl she is close to, is being held by an evil madam (Ann Magnuson) at the lavish Liquid Silver brothel. The girls go to rescue Sam, but Kesslee's men show up too, and take Sam away. To save Sam, the girls seek out the Rippers, who turn out to be a group of poetry-loving, half-kangaroo, half-human soldiers, genetically designed by the military during the last war. Their ranks include the angry, militant T-Saint (Ice-T) and the gentle, stupid Booga (Jeff Kober). After hijacking a WP arms shipment, the girls and the Rippers launch an assault on the WP headquarters. While Jet pays back an old tormentor, Tank kills Kesslee, and rescues Sam from certain death.

Many action movies are cartoonish, but one that halts its action to stage a Busby Berkeley style production number to Cole Porter's "Let's Do It" is knowingly silly. If TANK GIRL ever took itself at all seriously, it would be a disaster, but it never does. The result is a fun film all about attitude and aesthetic, but never about story or character. Relishing TANK GIRL's comic book origins, talented director Rachel Talalay packs the film with terrific, colorful visuals and scatters a flurry of animation sequences throughout. The hyperactive editing would be dizzying if NATURAL BORN KILLERS had not kicked that door in already. Unfortunately, the movie just seems to be in a big hurry to go nowhere.

The relentless pace of TANK GIRL is propelled by Lori Petty's sheer force in the title role. Embodying the sassy nihilism of the neo-punk attitude so prevalent in contemporary music, and on the soundtrack, Petty is a blast. Ever kinetic, she is playful and sexy, tough and funny, churlish and heroic. Straddling the tank's huge gun shaft in fashion shoot poses, platinum-blond Petty bears a striking resemblance to Madonna, sans Madonna's eroticism. It is too bad this female empowerment fantasy did not have more teeth, and go beyond its "be assertive, take control," message to, at least, mildly satirize the male-oriented action film cliches it is so full of. *(Profanity, violence.)* — P.R.

d, Rachel Talalay; p, Pen Densham, John Watson, Richard B. Lewis; exec p, Tom Astor, Aron Warner; co-p, Christian L. Rehr; w, Tedi Sarafian (based on the comic book by Jamie Hewlett and Alan Martin); ph, Gale Tattersall; ed, James R. Symons; m, Graeme Revell; prod d, Catherine Hardwicke; art d, Phillip Toolin, Charles D. Lee, Richard Yanez-Toyon, Jim Dultz; set d, Cindy Carr; sound, Ed Novick (recordist); fx, Peter Crosman, Rochelle Gross, Ken Pepiot; casting, Pam Dixon Mickelson; cos, Arianne Phillips; makeup, Deborah Larsen, Cheri Montesanto Medcaf; stunts, Walter Scott

Science Fiction/Action/Comedy   **(PR: C   MPAA: R)**

TENDERFOOT, THE
(SEE: BUSHWHACKED)

TERESA'S TATTOO ★

(U.S.) 95m CineTel Films; Yankee Entertainment Group ~ Vidmark Entertainment c

Adrienne Shelly (*Teresa/Gloria*); C. Thomas Howell (*Carl*); Nancy McKeon (*Sara*); Lou Diamond Phillips (*Wheeler*); Casey Siemaszko (*Michael*); Jonathan Silverman (*Rick*); Joe Pantoliano (*Bruno*); Sean Astin; Deidrich Bader; Majel Barrett; Anthony Clark; Brian Davila; Melissa Etheridge; Nanette Fabray; Tippi Hedren; k d lang; Mary Kay Place; Mare Winningham; Kiefer Sutherland

TERESA'S TATTOO is a bizarre and comic tale of underworld rivalry, spiced with abductions and escapes, fraudulent FBI agents, and national secrets hidden in a pair of earrings. An unpalatable concoction, the film went straight to video after a few poorly received festival showings.

Teresa (Adrienne Shelly), a mousy math whiz, is kidnapped, along with her fun-loving pal Sara (Nancy McKeon), by thugs headed by frozen-food magnate Carl (C. Thomas Howell). Carl needs a quick replacement for his recently deceased hostage Gloria (also played by Shelly) in order to pull off an extortion scheme. The girls are drugged and when Teresa wakes up, she has been made up to resemble Gloria, with bimbo attire, red hair, and a dragon tattooed on her chest.

At a back-alley meeting with rival thug Wheeler (Lou Diamond Phillips) and Gloria's brother (Casey Siemaszko), Carl offers Teresa in exchange for stolen holographs, unaware that the holographs are hidden in the earrings they left on Gloria's corpse. Teresa escapes only to find that the FBI agent she turns to for help is running Carl's operation. Her budding flame Rick (Jonathan Silverman) comes to her aid but is abducted by Wheeler, just as Teresa is reapprehended by Carl.

Teresa and Sara discover Gloria's body in Carl's factory, take the holographic earrings, and escape once again. Back in Teresa's home, her roommate Bruno (Joe Pantoliano) sets to work decoding the holographs, which contain top secret details of the space program. The various goons and crooked federal agents converge on Teresa's home, but she announces that the space-program data has been transmitted to the university and the media, and the bad guys retreat.

Saddled with witless dialogue and flat characterizations, TERESA'S TATTOO is an unredeemable mess, far more interesting for its behind-the-scenes goings-on than its onscreen inanity. In her feature film directorial debut, music video director Julie Cypher cast both her longtime companion Melissa Etheridge, and her ex-husband Lou Diamond Phillips (they divorced in 1991 after Cypher fell in love with Etheridge). Etheridge, who appears in a cameo role as a hooker, also contributed five original songs to the score, arguably the film's strongest selling point. Coproducer Philip McKeon, a former child actor, recruited his sister Nancy for a key role. McKeon, who appears to be having a great time as wild girl Sara, almost makes TERESA'S TATTOO enjoyable in spots. The rest of the acting ranges from bad to worse. Almost all the characters appear to be intellectually challenged and are excruciatingly overacted—in Phillips's case, bizarrely accented as well. (*Violence*) — B.R.

d, Julie Cypher; p, Lisa Hansen, Phil McKeon; exec p, Marc Rocco, Paul Hertzberg; assoc p, Georgie Huntington; co-p, Catalaine Knell, Don McKeon; w, Georgie Huntington; ph, Sven Kirsten; ed, Christopher Rouse; m, Andrew Keresztes; prod d, Rando Schmook; art d, Lisa Deutch; sound, Geoffrey Patterson, John S. Coffey; casting, Mary Jo Slater

Comedy (PR: C MPAA: R)

THINGS TO DO IN DENVER WHEN YOU'RE DEAD ★★

(U.S.) 114m Woods Entertainment; Miramax ~ Miramax c

Andy Garcia (*Jimmy "The Saint" Tosnia*); Christopher Lloyd (*Pieces*); William Forsythe (*Franchise*); Bill Nunn (*Easy Wind*); Treat Williams (*Critical Bill*); Jack Warden (*Joe Heff*); Steve Buscemi (*Mister Shhh*); Fairuza Balk (*Lucinda*); Gabrielle Anwar (*Dagney*); Christopher Walken (*The Man with the Plan*); Michael Nicolosi (*Bernard*); Bill Cobbs (*Malt*); Marshall Bell (*Lt. Atwater*); Glenn Plummer (*Baby Sinister*); Don Stark (*Gus*); Harris Laskawy (*Ellie*); William Garson (*Cuffy*); David Stratton (*Alex*); Deborah Strang (*Dodie*); Sarah Trigger (*Meg*); Jenny McCarthy (*Blonde Nurse*); Buddy Guy; Ray Allison; Scott Holt; Greg Rzab (*House Band*); Wiley Harker (*Boris Carlotti*); Joe Drago (*Maitre d'*); Chuck Bacino (*Accordion Player*); Don Cheadle (*Rooster*); Tiny Lister, Jr. (*House*); Bill Long (*The "Dead Beat" Man*); Cheree Jaeb (*Little Girl*); Sarah Levy Arbess (*Girl #1*); Larissa Michieli (*Girl #2*); Larry Raben (*Young Man*); Lynn Appelbaum (*Young Woman*); Taylor Hale (*Stevie*); Archie Smith (*Mr. Jergen*); Harriet Medin (*Old Woman*); Bill Bolender (*Stevie's Dad*); Susan Merson (*Woman with Cancer*); Bill Erwin (*70 Year Old Man*); Nate Ingram (*Alley Hood*); Jacob Bergener (*Alley Hood*); Larry Curry, Jr. (*Black Youth*); Ruthay (*Receptionist*); Selina Mathews (*Cynthia*); Phil Boardman (*Gym Teacher*); William Denis (*Businessman*); Danny Romo (*Montirez Brother*)

THINGS TO DO IN DENVER WHEN YOU'RE DEAD, a black-comic thriller by first-time feature director Gary Fleder, is yet another Quentin Tarantino knockoff, but one that is lacquered with a certain dizzy romanticism.

Ex-gangster Jimmy The Saint (Andy Garcia) is summoned out of retirement by his onetime boss (Christopher Walken), known only as The Man With The Plan. The Man offers Jimmy money to put a scare into a kid who is romancing his son's former girlfriend. It's a simple "action," The Man explains, but Jimmy, a generous fellow and an ex-seminarian to boot, rounds up several of his down-on-their-luck pals to share the wealth and make the "action" a reunion of sorts. As luck would have it, Jimmy has just fallen instantly in love with Dagney (Gabrielle Anwar), a nice, beautiful woman intrigued by his bon-vivant, if somewhat fatuous, charm. Naturally, the "action" goes awry when one of Jimmy's unstable cronies opens fire on a cop. Angered by the screw-up, The Man pronounces a death sentence on Jimmy and his crew, and Jimmy's budding romance starts looking like a non-starter.

Scott Rosenberg's screenplay has a self-conscious originality, which it often camouflages with cliches. Director Fleder has a knack for assembling colorful images on the screen, but the movie, which runs nearly two hours, is too languorous for the lean, pared-down genre it inhabits. Garcia's performance doesn't help: too good an actor to walk through a part, he glides, trusting in Rosenberg's faux hard-boiled script to carry the day—which it doesn't. Walken offers his now patented wacko-criminal turn, but it remains for Treat Williams and Fairuza Balk (the younger sister in GAS FOOD LODGING) to jack up the movie's energy, the former as an edgy mortician who gives new meaning to the term "loose cannon," and the latter almost unrecognizable as a streetwalker with an attitude.

THINGS TO DO IN DENVER WHEN YOU'RE DEAD is stylish and entertaining up to a point. But there's a smug irony inherent in its deferring to classic film noir while positioning itself as a contemporary black comedy. It may have satisfied the cravings of casual Tarantino buffs, but hard-core Quentin addicts probably weren't fooled. (*Violence, sexual situations, adult situations, profanity.*) — E.K.

d, Gary Fleder; p, Cary Woods; exec p, Marie Cantin, Bob Weinstein, Harvey Weinstein; assoc p, Scott Rosenberg; co-p, Cathy Konrad; w, Scott Rosenberg; ph, Elliot Davis; ed, Richard Marks; m, Michael Convertino; prod d, Nelson Coates; art d, Burton Rencher; set d, Anne D. McCulley; sound, Jim Steube (mixer); fx, Tim Drnec; casting, Ronnie Yeskel; cos, Abigail Murray; makeup, Rick Sharp, Steve Artmont, Todd Masters; stunts, John Branagan

Crime/Drama   **(PR: O   MPAA: R)**

3 NINJAS KNUCKLE UP   ★
(U.S.) 94m Sheen Productions; TriStar ~
Columbia TriStar Home Video c

Victor Wong *(Grandpa)*; Charles Napier *(Jack Harding)*; Michael Treanor *(Rocky)*; Max Elliott Slade *(Colt)*; Chad Power *(Tum Tum)*; Crystle Lightning *(Jo)*; Patrick Kilpatrick *(J.J.)*; Donald L. Shanks *(Charlie)*; Sheldon Peters Wolfchild *(Lee)*; Nickolas G. Ramus *(Chief Roundcreek)*; Donal Logue *(Jimmy)*; Scott MacDonald *(Eddy)*; Vincent Schiavelli *(Mayor)*; Selina Jayne *(Jo's Mother)*; Kait Lyn Mathews *(Theresa)*; Don Stark *(Sheriff)*; Dennis Holman *(EPA Man)*; Michael Hungerford *(Truck Driver)*; Cathy Perry *(Reporter)*; Wayne Collins, Jr.; Jamie Melissa Gunderson; Danuel Pipoly; Amanda Nicole Power *(Kids)*; Erin Treanor *(Pizza Parlor Girl)*; Gary Epper *(Biker)*; Eric Mansker *(Biker)*; Ted Pitsis *(Town Man)*; Stuart "Proud Eagle" Grant *(Indian)*; Jeff Cadiente *(Indian)*

This martial arts slapstick can only appeal to children who crave pint-sized role models who can throttle adults. Grown-ups will come away feeling violated by the film's clumsy comedy, ancient plot, and unimaginative action sequences.

During summer vacation with Grandpa (Victor Wong), the Ninja trio, Rocky (Michael Treanor), Colt (Max Elliott Slade), and Tum Tum (Chad Power), rescue Jo (Crystle Lightning), a young Native American damsel in distress, whose tribe is battling pollution. What the boys do not initially realize is that Jo's persecutors, led by J.J. (Patrick Kilpatrick), provide muscle for Jack Harding (Charles Napier), whose company dumps toxic waste in the countryside. Kidnapped by Harding's minions, Jo's dad Charlie (Donald L. Shanks) confiscates a computer disc that can draw unfavorable media attention to Harding's misdeeds. In a town of scared adults, Rocky, Colt, and Tum Tum learn to perform their good deeds unselfishly without clamoring for approbation.

Surely even children packed off to weekend karate classes expect more than this indifferently choreographed Lilliputian action film. Laced with Eastern versions of tea-bag homilies, the civic lesson on Native American affairs is a combination of low blows and high moral posturing. There is also a ludicrous tribal dance number inspired by Disney on Parade that can only be described as "Ninjarobics." Atrociously acted, word-processed rather than screenwritten, and directed as if the crew were out of breath from too many kick-boxing demos, 3 NINJAS KNUCKLE UP will have viewers knuckling under. — R.P.

d, Sang Okk Sheen ; p, Martha Chang; exec p, Simon B. Sheen, James Kang; w, Alex Sangok Kim; ph, Eugene Shlugleit; ed, Pam Choules; m, Gary Stevan Scott; prod d, Don Day; art d, Phil Brandes; casting, Gary Oberst; cos, Scillia A. Hernandez; makeup, Nancy Cassett; stunts, Al Jones

Children's/Martial Arts/Action   (PR: A   MPAA: PG-13)

THREE WISHES   ★★½
(U.S.) 105m Rysher Entertainment ~ Savoy Pictures c

Patrick Swayze *(Jack)*; Mary Elizabeth Mastrantonio *(Jeanne)*; Joseph Mazzello *(Tom)*; Seth Mumy *(Gunny)*; David Marshall Grant *(Phil)*; Jay O. Sanders *(Coach Schramka)*; Michael O'Keefe *(Adult Tom)*; John Diehl *(Leland's Dad)*; Diane Venora *(Joyce)*; David Zahorsky *(Little Leland)*; Brian Flannery *(Brian)*; Brock Pierce *(Scott)*; Davin Jacob Carey *(Sackin)*; David Hart *(Brian's Father)*; Scott Patterson *(Scott's Father)*; Michael Laskin *(Sackin's Father)*; Robert Starr *(Hank)*; Simone Study *(Brian's Mother)*; Lauren Sinclair *(Scott's Mother)*; Annabelle Gurwitch *(Leland's Mother)*; Moira Harris *(Katherine Holman)*; Neil McDonough *(Policeman)*; Brad Parker *(Passerby)*; Philip Levien *(Tool and Die Coach)*; Lawrence R. Baca *(Colony Drive-In Coach)*; Bill Mumy *(Neighbor)*; Colleen Camp *(Neighbor's Wife)*; Brandon LaCroix *(Little Magician)*; Jamie Cronin *(Cindy)*; Alexander Roos *(Hide and Seek Boy)*; Garette Ratliff Hensen *(Neighborhood Teenager)*; Jay Gerber *(Dr. Pavlick)*; William G. Schilling *(Doctor)*; Tiffany Lubran *(Holman Daughter)*; Kathryn Lubran *(Holman Daughter)*; Marc Shelton *(X-ray Technician)*; Vivien Strauss *(Bystander)*; Loanne Bishop *(Bystander)*; John DeVoe *(Teenager on Roof)*; Ethan Jensen *(Teenager on Roof)*; Robb Turner *(Man with Rake)*; Rosa *(Betty Jane)*; Nathanial Dunlap; Todd DeLevie; Jonathan Higashi; Spencer Gordon; Michael Nesbit; Peter Tuber; John-Michael Baca; Matthew Castle; Scott Drake; Justine Gentile; David Teroaka; Gregg Wallis *(Northridge 1994 USA Little League Champs)*

Though mostly set in a thoughtfully reconstructed middle-class suburb of the 1950s, THREE WISHES reflects a more telling nostalgia for recent film history—namely the late 1970s and early '80s family-oriented fantasies of Steven Spielberg.

On Memorial Day in present-day Edendale, California, Tom Holman (Michael O'Keefe) and his family face the prospect of bankruptcy. While out driving with the brood, Tom nearly runs over a little dog, which then follows a street person into a nearby cemetery. As Tom pursues him, he flashes back to 1955.

Eleven-year-old Tom (Joseph Mazzello) lives in Edendale with his war-widow mother, Jeanne (Mary Elizabeth Mastrantonio), and five-year-old brother Gunny (Seth Mumy). This group also has a near-miss on a holiday drive, sideswiping hobo Jack McCloud (Patrick Swayze) while swerving to avoid a dog. The police chase off the wounded transient, but Jeanne feels obligated to take him in until his broken leg heals. Her friends and family are scandalized.

Jack and the dog, whose name is Betty Jane, grow close to the family. Coaching Tom's baseball team, Jack teaches them how to win by meditating and not trying so hard. Stricken with cancer, Gunny has a vision of Betty Jane transforming into a magical genie in an explosion of lights and color. Jack tells him that a genie once granted him three wishes. When Jack was unable to decide, the genie wished that Jack would always be at his side. Gunny wishes to fly and gets his chance during a fireworks show. Jeanne wishes for Gunny to recover; he does. Angered that Jack intends to leave, Tom refuses to make a wish, so the transient makes a secret wish for him. After Jack has left, the father of the Holman clan returns from Korea, where he had been held prisoner.

Back in the present, the adult Tom discovers that the man he has has been following is Jack, who appears unchanged. Jack tells him the secret wish he made in 1955: that Tom would always be happy with his life. Renewed, Tom rejoins his family and goes to face up to his troubles. The camera reveals a gravestone with Jack's name and life dates, suggesting that he actually died in WWII.

With its single suburban Mom struggling to raise her kids on her own, absent father supplanted by a magical playmate, and curious child facing the first intimations of mortality, THREE WISHES aims to be a second E.T. THE EXTRA-TERRESTRIAL, but falls far short of the mark. Though the films trots out the obligatory depiction of a young boy's sense of exclusion and yearning for a father, the execution lacks Spielberg's poetry, resonance, and conviction.

Striving for a new take on familiar material, helmer Martha Coolidge succeeds in keeping the sentiment down to an acceptable level. Moreover, she and Mastrantonio beef up the role of the mother, a figure usually neglected in these tales of sons and their virtual fathers. While the actress glows with warmth, intelligence, and strength, she can't transcend the mediocrity of the script. Intended to be ambiguous, the fantastic elements feel generic and gratuitous in the context of the larger film. On the kiddie front, Joseph Mazzello suffers convincingly and dares to be unsympathetic; young Seth Mumy, son of Bill (formerly Billy) Mumy of "Lost in Space" fame, is adorable and touching as the sickly younger brother.

Although the setting is Edendale, the film does not view 1950s suburbia as paradise lost. THREE WISHES presents happy dreams of sunny vistas and innocent pop culture, but never elides the era's oppressive conformity and unquestioned patriarchy. Ultimately, THREE WISHES is a bit predictable and heavy-handed for adults and too glum and long-winded for young children. While the endeavor is not without merit, most will leave the film comparing it unfavorably to Spielberg at his peak. *(Adult situations, nudity.)* — K.G.

d, Martha Coolidge; p, Gary Lucchesi, Clifford Green, Ellen Green; exec p, Keith Samples, Larry Y. Albucher; w, Elizabeth Anderson (from a story by Clifford Green and Ellen Green); ph, Johnny E. Jensen; ed, Steven Cohen; m, Cynthia Millar; prod d, John Vallone; art d, Gae Buckley; set d, Robert Gould; sound, Lee Orloff (mixer), Leslie Schatz (design); fx, Phil Tippett, David P. Kelsey, Lauren Alexandra Ritchie, Jon Farhat, R/Greenberg Associates West, Inc.; casting, Aleta Chappelle; cos, Shelley Komarov; makeup, John Elliot; stunts, Lisa Cain

Fantasy/Drama (PR: A MPAA: PG)

THROUGH THE OLIVE TREES ★★★
(Iran/France) 108m CiBy 2000 ~ Miramax c
(ZIRE DARAKHTAN ZEYTON)

Hossein Rezai *(Hossein)*; Tahereh Ladania *(Tahereh)*; Mohamad Ali Keshavarz *(Film Director)*; Zarifeh Shiva *(Mrs. Shiva)*; Farhad Kheradmand *(Farhad)*; Mahbanou Darabi; Ahmad Ahmadpour; Babk Ahmadpour

THROUGH THE OLIVE TREES is a slight, pleasant variation on Francois Truffaut's DAY FOR NIGHT. Iranian director Abbas Kiarostami fails to take full advantage of his film-within-a-film construct, but he tells his simple story well.

Just outside Tehran, a production crew prepares for a film shoot. The director, Mohamad (Mohamad Ali Keshavarz), begins his first day by selecting Tahereh (Tahereh Ladania) out of a group of women for the part of the ingenue. Later, during the filming of the first shot, Mohamad discovers that the leading man in the scene has a stuttering problem, so he dispatches his executive assistant, Mrs. Shiva (Zarifeh Shiva), to find another male lead quickly.

Mrs. Shiva picks out Hossein (Hossein Rezai), a poor but earnest young worker, little knowing that Hossein is already in love with Tahereh. She also fails to realize that Tahereh refuses to speak to Hossein because her grandmother disapproves of his class standing, and because he had once proposed marriage on

the eve of an earthquake that killed her parents. The gap in communication between the two actors causes new problems on the set, which Mohamad seeks to remedy by ending the workday early and by threatening to replace his young leads. The plan works, and both actors show up the next day for filming. Before the camera rolls, however, Mohamad listens to Hossein's poignant wish to marry the more cultured Tahereh, and decides to play matchmaker. Cunningly, Mohamad arranges for Hossein to walk Tahereh home after the shoot is finished. During the walk, Hossein pleads with Tahereh to answer his proposal of marriage, but she ignores him for most of the way, until, finally, she gives him his answer.

THROUGH THE OLIVE TREES is a small-scale film with modest ambitions, but it very well may mark a turning point in the Western acceptance of Iranian cinema. The film is an agreeable, humanistic comedy that makes no serious political statement, but provides just the sort of nonthreatening product to be praised (perhaps a bit overpraised) in the US and some parts of Europe, where Iran is still considered an outlaw country.

To be fair, OLIVE TREES is not entirely without political implications. It makes a few passing observations about Old versus New World values, the state of contemporary class conflicts, and the growing feminist awareness among young Iranian women. Notably, the argument between Mrs. Shiva and Tahereh about whether to wear a peasant dress for her big scene suggests a generational clash among Iranian women. Also, the expectation that Hossein should serve the film crew tea between takes, even though he stars in their production, points up the inequities in the persistent caste system. And Tahereh's refusal to call Hossein "Mister" in their scene together represents the disintegration of at least one old patriarchal custom.

Messages aside, THROUGH THE OLIVE TREES is a well-crafted film. Several sweeping shots by cinematographers Hossein Djafarian and Farhad Saba capture the beauty of the landscape, and many simpler shots are artfully composed and angled. The performances are natural and engaging. If director Kiarostami (who also wrote, produced and edited) misses some prime opportunities for physical comedy in the film-within-a-film segments, he at least knows how to build up to a good verbal joke. THROUGH THE OLIVE TREES may be a minor effort, but it is satisfying on its own limited terms. — E.M.

d, Abbas Kiarostami; p, Abbas Kiarostami; w, Abbas Kiarostami; ph, Hossein Djafarian, Farhad Saba; ed, Abbas Kiarostami; sound, Tchangiz Sayyad (mixing), Mahmoud Samakbashi, Yadollah Najafi

Drama/Comedy (PR: AA MPAA: G)

TIE-DIED: ROCK 'N' ROLL'S ★★★
MOST DEADICATED FANS
(U.S.) 88m Padded Cell Pictures; Arrowood Productions ~ ISA Releasing c

Jahree Sullivan; Dianna Evans Sullivan; John Coit; Jertzy Hanley; Jeremy Grosbard; Ryan Massey; Lee Jones; Al Dickens; Toni Brown; Chris Fitzgerald; Cathleen Porter; Brock Dewitt; Natelie Carrigton; Michael Koetters; Michaelle Peters; Laura Lambrecht; Cartoon Danny; Jasper; JD; Turtle; Leef; Mother Earth; Ridley Walker; Ed Masson; Dan Adkins; Chris Bowers; Trash Captain; John Scott; Bagitta Hodgson; Tom Bus Mechanic; Zane Kesey; Cassie; Fast Eddie; Thin Man; Carver Dan; Patrick Wayman; P.J. Kovach; Michael Magimo; Stephanie Gates; Xylie Edelman; Morning Davis; Chris Smiley; Nikki Badua; Lush; Golden Eagle; Winter Wells; Jennie Kim; Jerilyn Lee Brandelius; N. Lawsen; Gail Harte; Paul Doherty; Patrick Biehler; Pat Corbin; Kat O'Sullivan; Teresa Avila; David Bilgre;

Jeff Bounds; Thomas J. Espe; Summer Hirschfel; Sarah Meadows; Chris Hennessey; Hugh Hamill; Harold Berlowe; Uncle Sam; Daniel Gamel; Monica Pratt; Peter Gorman; Mark Mirkos; Angelina Gargano; David Hussey; Sandra Jacobson

Andrew Behar's feature-length investigation of the Deadheads charts the progress of an extraordinary cultural phenomenon: the survivors of the Dead, an estimated two million fans who had followed the rock band Grateful Dead worldwide, from one concert to another, for three decades. The "Long, Strange Trip" of the band ended on August 9, 1995, when middle-aged frontman Jerry Garcia died of heart failure at a rehab clinic.

Behar's lens focuses on the impromptu carnival in parking lots and meadows adjacent to any Dead show. During the 1994 summer tour, the Deadheads put on their own performances, with guitars, bagpipes, drums, even didgeridoos. Vans and buses testify to years on the road, while tie-dyed Deadheads and their children greet each other with easy familiarity. Many have indeed met before, at concerts thousands of miles apart. Some are working professionals; others map their existence around the Grateful Dead. The Deadheads come across at first as a friendly extended family of free spirits whose sunny attitudes evoke the good feelings of the 1960s flower children.

Later on in the film there emerges a darker portrait. Veteran Deadheads admit there has been a change for the worse in the late 1980s, when the band's lone chart-topper, "Touch of Gray," attracted a younger crowd interested less in flower power and more in hard drugs and violence. The band's reputation as a magnet for narcotics and liquor is hardly unearned, but Behar counterpoints dope-addled zombies and nitrous oxide inhalers with groups like the Wharf Rats, a subsection of the Deadheads pledged to sobriety.

Draconian federal antidrug operations have targeted Dead concerts (Behar had to convince some of his subjects that his camera crew were not undercover DEA agents), but a rural policeman and a shopkeeper testify that they personally have had no problems with the swarming fans. TIE-DIED concludes with various Deadheads naming their favorite Dead song, including a tot's amusing vote for "I Want My MTV."

While TIE-DIED was in post-production, lawyers for the Grateful Dead sought an injunction against the film, in what Behar later said was a simple misunderstanding over music rights, but which the press blew up into a conspiracy to suppress any hint of drugs and decadence. In fact, while not ignoring the negatives, TIE-DIED ultimately favors the Deadheads and their mellow fellowship, typified by the recurring appearance of "Jahree from Boston," a young New Englander in dreadlocks. When first seen, he is endearingly eccentric. His next appearance, searching for his dog lost somewhere along the tour route, seems forlorn and pathetic. In a final, post-credit visit, Jahree repeats the dog's description and optimistically gives his actual phone number out to the (presumably Deadhead) viewers. His simple trust suggests the Deadheads are indeed onto something, a sense of belonging that transcends mere recording-industry demographics.

The Grateful Dead's 1995 concerts were marred by untypical riots in Indiana, and several patrons were fatally struck by lightning in Washington. Garcia's demise confirmed the end of an era in rock culture to which the film bears testimony. (*Substance abuse, profanity, adult situations.*) — C.C.

d, Andrew Behar; p, Marsha Oglesby, James Deutch; exec p, Joseph A. Kim, Sara Sackner, Jennifer Fish; assoc p, Peter Shapiro; ph, Hamid Shams; ed, Andrew Behar, Sara Sackner; m, Peter Fish

Documentary/Musical   (PR: C   MPAA: R)

TIE THAT BINDS, THE   ★★★
(U.S.) 98m Interscope Communications; Hollywood Pictures ~ Buena Vista c

Daryl Hannah *(Leann Netherwood)*; Keith Carradine *(John Netherwood)*; Moira Kelly *(Dana Clifton)*; Vincent Spano *(Russell Clifton)*; Julia Devin *(Janie)*; Ray Reinhardt *(Sam Bennett)*; Barbara Tarbuck *(Jean Bennett)*; Cynda Williams *(Lisa-Marie Chandler)*; Bruce A. Young *(Gil Chandler)*; Ned Vaughn *(Officer Carey)*; Jenny Gago *(Maggie)*; Carmen Argenziano *(Phil Hawkes)*; Laurie Lathem *(Alex)*; Willie Garson *(Ray Tanton)*; Kerrie Cullen *(Female Police Officer)*; Bob Minor *(Male Police Officer)*; George Marshall Ruge *(Detective No. 1)*; Tommy Rosales, Jr. *(Detective No. 2)*; Laura Lee Kelly *(Aide)*; Marquis Nunley *(Boy Russell)*; Benjamin Mouton *(Father in Restaurant)*; Jack Johnson *(Boy in Restaurant)*; Melanie MacQueen *(Waitress)*; Greg Collins *(Bartender)*; Dana Gladstone *(Dr. Bradford)*; Jesse Hays *(Boy in School)*; Andrea Sandahl *(Tina)*; Chris Ellis *(Security Guard No. 1)*; Coleen Maloney *(Security Guard No. 2)*; Shawne Rowe *(Ogre's Wife)*; Melissa Hays *(Princess)*; Steve Rosenbaum *(The Ogre)*; Suzanne Krull *(The Fox)*; Kevin Bourland *(Man in Range Rover)*; Taylor Allbright *(Girl in Schoolyard)*; Gene Lythgow *(Detective Lorenz)*; Lynn Wanlass *(Nurse)*; Kenny Alexander *(Officer Wright)*

Directed by screenwriter Wesley Strick (TRUE BELIEVER, FINAL ANALYSIS), THE TIE THAT BINDS is an efficient, well-acted thriller predicated on one of the most powerful of bourgeois fears about adoption: that an adopted child might have "bad blood."

Malevolent modern day hippies Leann (Daryl Hannah) and John Netherwood (Keith Carradine) roam America with their little girl Janie (Julia Devin) in tow, terrorizing the middle class through robbery, vandalism and murder. But they're caught while burgling the home of an old couple, and while wounded John and scary soul-mate Leann manage to get away, the police take Janie into custody.

Aided by adoption agency case worker Maggie (Jennie Gago), struggling architect Russell Clifton (Vincent Spano) and his photographer wife Dana (Moira Kelly) welcome the traumatized six-year-old into their home. Though intelligent and charming, Janie's behavior is disturbing: She hides in closets, cuts herself, steals food and draws monstrous pictures of the "Tooth Fairy," of whom she's terrified. Russell and Dana believe that with love she'll forget her past, though they secretly worry about what that past might involve. Meanwhile, the Netherwoods begin planning to reclaim their child. Leann picks up the hapless policeman who rescued Janie, and John tortures the name of the adoption agency where Janie was placed out of the man before slitting his throat. They then force Maggie to tell them about the Cliftons, and murder her as well.

Meanwhile, Russell and Dana have done some amateur sleuthing, and have begun to get an idea what Janie's real parents are like. Leann tries to snatch Janie from school, and the Cliftons go into hiding. The Netherwoods track down the Clifton's friends, the Chandlers, and threatens to hurt their newborn: Desperate new mother Lisa Marie (Cynda Williams) reveals the location of the Cliftons' hiding place, a half-built model home Russell designed. Russell and Dana fight the murderous couple to the death, and return home with Janie.

Much meaner than the polished lullaby thriller, THE HAND THAT ROCKS THE CRADLE, this good family-bad family chiller (which plays on middle-class fears of the underclass with more ferocity than insight) packs a really nasty punch, primarily because of the feral performances of Carradine and Hannah. Carradine gives white trash patriarch John Netherwood a demonic presence that's as compelling as it is terrifying, and vacant doll Hannah—in her suede vest and faintly fetishistic jewelry—looks eerily like a high-fashion Manson girl. The moment when she tenderly positions her thumb over the soft spot on a newborn's head, smiling tenderly as she makes it clear that if she doesn't get the information she wants she's going to *push*—is diabolically conceived and flawlessly played.

Lushly photographed and art directed, THE TIE THAT BINDS has aspirations to being a real-life fairy tale—the Netherwoods are the flesh-and-blood embodiments of the monsters under the bed that terrify small children—and comes surprisingly close to pulling it off. Though it's classic direct-to-video material, the film's relatively high profile cast earned it a token theatrical release. It performed badly, probably because it was too nasty for mainstream audiences and a bit polished for down-and-dirty crazed killer buffs. (*Graphic violence; extreme profanity, adult situations.*)

d, Wesley Strick; p, David Madden, Patrick Markey, Susan Zachary, John Morrissey; exec p, Ted Field, Jon Brown, Robert W. Cort; w, Michael Auerbach; ph, Bobby Bukowski; ed, Michael Knue; m, Graeme Revell; prod d, Marcia Hinds-Johnson; art d, Bo Johnson; set d, Don Diers; sound, Robert Eber (mixer); casting, Marci Liroff; cos, Betsy Heimann; makeup, Jean A. Black; stunts, John Moio

Horror/Thriller (PR: C MPAA: R)

TO CROSS THE RUBICON ★★½
(U.S.) 107m Lensman Company ~ MTI Home Video bw

Patricia Royce (*Kendall Byrne*); Lorraine Devon (*Claire Runyan*); J.D. Souther (*David Berry*); John Halpern (*Wade Madsen*); Billy Burke (*James Bird*); Bruce P. Young (*Lee Wilke*)

TO CROSS THE RUBICON was filmed in 1991, shown at film festivals in 1992, given theatrical release in select cities in 1994, and released on home video in 1995. It's a heartfelt but flawed story about single women in their 30s, looking for romance.

Claire (Lorraine Devon) and Kendall (Patricia Royce) have successful careers but are unsatisfied because they are single. While both women are intelligent, Claire is book-smart and Kendall is street-smart. Though they have little problem finding men to date, none of the men are stable, ready for commitment, or willing to be with a successful career woman. The two women have a strong bond, which is tested when Claire begins to date Kendall's ex-lover David (J.D. Souther). Kendall reacts by dating a 20-year-old musician who is exciting but irresponsible. Both women eventually end the relationships, deciding that it's all right to hold out for what they really want. They remain close friends with each other and are happy with their careers and their independence.

TO CROSS THE RUBICON is talky but not dull. The screenplay, written by Devon and Royce, is literate though occasionally silly. Character development is strong, and Claire's and Kendall's strengths and flaws are well-developed and authentic. The female point of view is a treat for viewers who are used to seeing films written by and for men, but it also contributes to the film's major flaw. For example, in one scene, the musician begins weeping uncontrollably when he realizes that when his romance with Kendall fails, the two can no longer be friends. The scene is a female fantasy, much as teenage sex comedies are filled with male fantasies, and satisfying as it may be, it is not as realistic as the actions of the female characters. The open ending compensates somewhat. It affirms the strength in both women but does not take the easy way out by having either of them find Mr. Right.

For a low-budget independent production, TO CROSS THE RUBICON has very strong performances. The black-and-white cinematography is also high quality, though the setting, Seattle, which is usually gorgeous on film, is not used to advantage. While the film is not completely satisfying, it is interesting and original. It was a labor of love for Devon, Royce, and director Barry Caillier, and shows promise for their future projects. (*Sexual situations, profanity.*) — A.M.

d, Barry Caillier; exec p, Jim Clapp; assoc p, Patricia Royce, Barry Caillier, Tom Hechim; w, Patricia Royce, Lorriane Devon; ph, Christopher Tufty; ed, Patrick Barber; m, Paul Speer, David Lanz; prod d, Michael Anderson; cos, Ron Leamon

Drama/Romance (PR: C MPAA: NR)

TO DIE FOR ★★★
(U.S.) 100m LH Productions; Laura Ziskin Productions; Columbia ~ Columbia c

Nicole Kidman (*Suzanne Stone*); Matt Dillon (*Larry Maretto*); Joaquin Phoenix (*Jimmy Emmett*); Casey Affleck (*Russell Hines*); Illeana Douglas (*Jancie Maretto*); Alison Folland (*Lydia Mertz*); Dan Hedaya (*Joe Maretto*); Wayne Knight (*Ed Grant*); Kurtwood Smith (*Earl Stone*); Holland Taylor (*Carol Stone*); Susan Traylor (*Faye Stone*); Maria Tucci (*Angela Maretto*); Tim Hopper (*Mike Warden*); Michael Rispoli (*Ben DeLuca*); Buck Henry (*Mr. Finlaysson*); Gerry Quigley (*George*); Tom Forrester (*Fisherman*); Alan Edward Lewis (*Fisherman*); Nadine MacKinnon (*Sexy Woman*); Conrad Coates (*Weaselly Guy*); Ron Gabriel (*Sal*); Ian Heath (*Student*); Graeme Millington (*Student*); Sean Ryan (*Student*); Nicholas Pasco (*Detective*); Joyce Maynard (*Lawyer*); David Collins (*Reporter*); Eve Crawford (*Reporter*); Janet Lo (*Reporter*); David Cronenberg (*Man at Lake*); Tom Quinn (*Skating Promoter*); Peter Glenn (*Priest*); Amber-Lee Campbell (*Suzanne at Five*); Colleen Williams (*Valerie Mertz*); Simon Richards (*Chester*); Philip Williams (*Babe Hines*); Susan Backs (*June Hines*); Kyra Harper (*Mary Emmett*); Adam Roth (*Band Member*); Andrew Scott (*Band Member*); Tamara Gorski (*Girl at Bar*); Katie Griffin (*Girl at Bar*); Carla Renee (*Girl at Bar*)

Not *just* another facile attempt to blame societal ills on TV, TO DIE FOR leavens its heavy-handed satire of mainstream American values with genuine empathy for its marginal characters. Adapted from Joyce Maynard's fact-based novel about a New Hampshire teacher who bullied her teenaged lover into murdering her husband, TO DIE FOR was a comeback of sorts for both director Gus Van Sant—whose EVEN COWGIRLS GET THE BLUES (1994) was a genuine debacle—and screenwriter Buck Henry, who hadn't written a critical or commercial hit since 1978's HEAVEN CAN WAIT.

Little Hope, New Hampshire, is the center of a media whirlwind involving lovely local weathergirl Suzanne Stone (Nicole Kidman) and murder most foul. All the relevant relatives, in-laws, and townspeople are interviewed on TV, while Suzanne tells her story to an unseen listener.

Ambitious, shallow, and obsessed with television, Suzanne marries Larry Maretto, a likable, salt-of-the-earth guy whose family owns the local Italian restaurant. Larry's sister Janice (Illeana Douglas), a budding pro ice skater, distrusts Suzanne from the start.

Suzanne gets a job at a local cable station and overwhelms station manager Ed Grant (Wayne Knight) with her desire to present the weather. Having tasted on-air glory, she's bursting with ideas for new programming, including a documentary on local high school students. The project is approved, and Suzanne focuses on three underachieving outcasts: Jimmy (Joaquin Phoenix), Russell (Casey Affleck), and Lydia (Alison Folland). Both Jimmy and Lydia develop crushes on their glamorous interviewer.

Larry upsets Suzanne's game plan by pressuring her to start a family. She retaliates by seducing Jimmy, telling him heartbreaking tales of domestic abuse and suggesting that everything would be fine if he would just kill Larry. Eventually caving in under the relentless pressure, Jimmy and Russell borrow Lydia's father's gun and do the deed.

Suzanne's footage leads the police to her teenage accomplices, who quickly confess. Suzanne claims innocence and is released on bail. She goes to the media with a wild story of a drug deal gone wrong, casting Larry as a junkie and Jimmy and Russell as his suppliers. Finishing her story before a camcorder, Suzanne takes the videotape and drives off to meet a man she believes to be a Hollywood producer (David Cronenberg). He's actually a mob hit man who, after dispatching Suzanne, telephones Larry's father (Dan Hedaya) to report that his daughter-in-law is secreted under the ice of a frozen lake.

Now a local celebrity, Lydia appears on TV talking about teenage dieting while Janice practices skating on the lake.

While a filmmaker can critique the patriarchy through a female antagonist, TO DIE FOR opts to finger the usual suspects: TV, unseemly ambition, and some generalized flaw in the American character. Moreover, by ending with Donovan warbling "The Season of the Witch," the film reveals itself as just another horror story about an ambitious woman. Kidman's Suzanne Stone is simply a monster, the chicly dressed go-getter from Hell. Her wildly overrated performance shows some comic flair, but the part is woefully underwritten. Stone suggests Faith Ford's ever perky Corky from TV's "Murphy Brown" more than any genuine human being. Dillon fares better in a role that could easily have descended into caricature: his death scene has a tragic humanity that the film rarely achieves with the other "straight" characters. Douglas is another standout as Larry's no-nonsense sister.

Van Sant and Henry's contempt for Middle America rivals Robert Altman's at its worst; they can't even be bothered to get the details right. For example, the sequence in which the Stones and Marettos appear together on a daytime talk show fails to capture any of the crazy confessional energy of that peculiarly American forum. In fact, none of the film's TV recreations have the ring of truth, a substantial liability in this media-mad context.

Van Sant's specialty is films about edgy outsiders from the demimonde like MALA NOCHE (1985), DRUGSTORE COWBOY (1989), and MY OWN PRIVATE IDAHO (1991), and TO DIE FOR picks up whenever the "troubled" teens come on screen. The film renders their anomie with sympathy and understanding, and both Phoenix and Folland deliver hauntingly memorable performances. If Henry's screenplay were worthy of the film's generally strong performances and sensitive direction, TO DIE FOR would linger much longer in the memory. *(Violence, profanity, adult situations, sexual situations.)* — K.G.

d, Gus Van Sant; p, Laura Ziskin; exec p, Jonathan Taplin, Joseph M. Caracciolo; co-p, Sandy Isaac, Leslie Morgan; w, Buck Henry (based on the novel by Joyce Maynard); ph, Eric Alan Edwards; ed, Curtiss Clayton; m, Danny Elfman; prod d, Missy Stewart; art d, Vlasta Svoboda; set d, Carol A. Lavoie; sound, Robert Fernandez, Bill Jackson, Owen Langevin; fx, Laird McMurray Film Services; casting, Howard Feuer; cos, Beatrix Aruna Pasztor; makeup, Patricia Green

Crime/Comedy/Drama **(PR: C MPAA: R)**

TO THE LIMIT
(SEE: SIX DAYS, SIX NIGHTS)

TO WONG FOO, THANKS FOR EVERYTHING! JULIE NEWMAR ★★
(U.S.) 108m Amblin Entertainment ~ Universal c

Wesley Snipes *(Noxeema Jackson)*; Patrick Swayze *(Vida Boheme)*; John Leguizamo *(Chi Chi Rodriguez)*; Stockard Channing *(Carol Ann)*; Blythe Danner *(Beatrice)*; Arliss Howard *(Virgil)*; Jason London *(Bobby Ray)*; Chris Penn *(Sheriff Dollard)*; Melinda Dillon *(Merna)*; Beth Grant *(Loretta)*; Alice Drummond *(Clara)*; Marceline Hugot *(Katina)*; Jennifer Milmore *(Bobby Lee)*; Jamie Harrold *(Billy Budd)*; Mike Hodge *(Jimmy Joe)*; Michael Vartan *(Tommy)*; RuPaul *(Rachel Tensions)*; Julie Newmar *(Herself)*; Joel Story *(Little Earnest)*; Abie Hope Hyatt *(Donna Lee)*; Jamie Leigh Wolbert *(Sandra Lee)*; Shea Degan *(State Trooper)*; Dean Houser *(State Trooper)*; Joe Grojean *(State Trooper)*; Keith Reddin *(Motel Manager)*; Naomi Campbell *(Girl)*; William P. Hopkins *(Small Guy)*; Dayton Callie *(Crazy Elijah)*; Ron Carley *(Old Man)*; Shea R. Bredenkamp; Michael A. Tushaus; Patrick Tuttle; Timothy A. Zimmerman; Tim Keller *(Rude Boys)*; Alexander Heimberg *(Miss Understood)*; Joey Arias *(Justine)*; Allen Hidalgo *(Chita Riviera)*; Mishell Chandler *(Miss Missy)*; Catiria Reyes *(Herself)*; David Drumgold *(Cappuccino Commotion)*; Clinton Leupp *(Miss Coco Peru)*; Lionel Tiburcio *(Laritza Dumont)*; Bernard A. Mosca *(Olympia)*; Daniel T. "Sweetie" Boothe *(Announcer)*; David Barton *(Boy in Chains)*; Susanne Bartsch; Quentin Crisp; Kevin "Flotilla DeBarge" Joseph; Matthew Kasten; Widow Norton *(NY Pageant Judges)*; Charles Ching *(Coco LaChine)*; Mike Fulk *(Victoria Weston)*; Niasse N. Mamadou *(Lola)*; Brendan McDanniel *(Candis Cayne)*; Shelton McDonald *(Princess Diandra)*; Richard Ogden *(Kabuki)*; James Palacio *(Fiona James)*; Steven Polito *(Hedda Lettuce)*; Philip Stoehr *(Philomena)*; Martha Flynn *(Vida's Mother)*; Billie J. Diekman *(Florist)*; Shari Shell-True *(Dance Teacher)*

The first contemporary Hollywood film to tackle the flamboyant world of drag queens, TO WONG FOO . . . was saddled with high expectations. But its bizarre mix of comedy and drama is neither convincing nor consistently funny and, worst of all, entirely lacks the outrageousness that is the hallmark of a true drag diva.

At a transvestite beauty pageant in New York, Noxeema Jackson (Wesley Snipes) and Vida Boheme (Patrick Swayze) tie for first place, winning a trip to Los Angeles to compete in a national drag championship. Poor little Chi Chi Rodriguez (John Leguizamo) is left crying on the stairs, and the munificent winners agree to take her along with them. For luck, they steal the signed photo that gives the film its title, and prop it on the dashboard like a plastic saint.

On a deserted back road somewhere in the heartland, they're stopped by redneck Officer Dollard (Chris Penn), who figures that a car full of career girls is an opportunity to get fresh. Vida decks him, and they flee. Later, their car breaks down in the middle-of-nowhere town of Snydersville. While waiting for it to be fixed, they give the town some much-needed lessons in fabulousness. Vida befriends the mechanic's wife, Carol Ann (Stockard Channing), and discovers she's being abused. Noxeema gets a mute woman to speak by swapping film trivia with her. Chi Chi begins a flirtation with the callow Bobby Ray (Jason London), though she delivers him sagely into the hands of sweet little real girl Bobby Lee (Jennifer Millmore) before anything untoward takes place.

Realizing—to his utter horror—that he's looking for three men in drag, Dollard furiously searches the sort of places he imagines homosexuals would congregate: beauty salons, florist's shops, ballet schools, and the like. By the time he tracks down Vida, Noxeema and Chi-Chi, all Snydersville has succumbed to their charms, and the townspeople drive him away. The trio then drive off to LA, where Chi-Chi is crowned winner of the National Drag Queen Championship.

WONG FOO's plot hinges on two incredible premises. First, that drag queens are in drag all the time, even while driving on back roads at night in less enlightened areas of the country. And second, that almost no one in Snydersville realizes or cares that these strapping women are exactly what they look like: men in frocks. The action seems to unfold in some weird alternate universe in which Angels in Drag can solve all problems: heal the mute, turn gangs of would-be rapists into polite young men, liberate battered women, transform wallflowers into the belles of the ball, and bring joy and laughter to the downtrodden.

The film wants to have it both ways: it wants to be a sort of fairy tale—pardon the expression—in which drag queens wave their wands over a dusty backwater and magically transform it, and at the same time it wants to be a real-life drama dealing with such problems as domestic violence and homophobia. But it handles these issues in an infuriatingly simplistic way: one well-aimed punch from Vida is all it takes to make the wife abuser slink out of town, and some wise words from Chi Chi convince Bobby Ray—who's been seduced by Chi Chi's exotic allure—that he'd much rather have shy local tomboy Bobby Lee.

To its credit, WONG FOO doesn't hide the fact that its characters are gay, but only Chi Chi is allowed libido and, perhaps not coincidentally, Leguizamo all but steals the movie. There are clever lines and funny situations in TO WONG FOO . . ., but not nearly enough of the caustic wit in which real drag queens specialize. *(Profanity, sexual situations, violence, adult situations.)*

d, Beeban Kidron; p, G. Mac Brown; exec p, Bruce Cohen; assoc p, Mitchell Kohn; w, Douglas Carter Beane; ph, Steve Mason; ed, Andrew Mondshein; m, Rachel Portman; prod d, Wynn Thomas; art d, Robert Guerra; set d, Ted Glass; sound, Michael Barosky (mixer), Harry Higgins (recordist), Ted Clark (recordist); casting, Billy Hopkins, Suzanne Smith, Kerry Barden; cos, Marlene Stewart; makeup, J. Roy Helland

Comedy **(PR: C MPAA: PG-13)**

TOM AND HUCK ★★
(U.S.) 93m Walt Disney Pictures ~ Buena Vista c

Jonathan Taylor Thomas *(Tom Sawyer)*; Brad Renfro *(Huck Finn)*; Eric Schweig *(Injun Joe)*; Charles Rocket *(Judge Thatcher)*; Amy Wright *(Aunt Polly)*; Michael McShane *(Muff Potter)*; Marian Seldes *(Widow Douglas)*; Rachael Leigh Cook *(Becky Thatcher)*; Lanny Flaherty *(Emmett)*; Courtland Mead *(Sid)*; Peter MacKenzie *(Mr. Sneed)*; Heath Lamberts *(Schoolmaster Dobbins)*; William Newman *(Doc Robinson)*; Joey Stinson *(Joe Harper)*; Blake Heron *(Ben Rodgers)*; Jim Aycock *(Defense Lawyer)*; Andy Stahl *(Sheriff)*; Adrian Roberts *(Welshman)*; Tiffany Lynn Clark *(Suzy Harper)*; Kellen Hathaway *(Billy Newton)*; Mark Cabus *(Farmer)*; Bronwen Murray *(Mary)*; Paul Anthony Kropfl *(Impatient Trial Spectator)*; Newell Alexander; Tommy Lamey; David Cowgill; Stuart K. Robinson *(Search Party)*; Mitch Carter; Ike Eisenmann; Matthew Valencia; Blake Ewing *(Taverners)*; Rosemary Alexander; Sherry Hursey; Philece Sampler; Wendy Cutler; Tamra Mellow; Edie Mirman; Toby Ganger; Austin Kottke; Courtney Pelton; Katherine Zarimba *(Townsfolk)*

No great film has ever been made from *The Adventures of Tom Sawyer*, but TOM AND HUCK must rate as one of the weakest screen versions of the Mark Twain classic.

In Pre-Civil War Hannibal, Missouri, circa 1840, Tom Sawyer (Jonathan Taylor Thomas) causes no end of grief for his guard-

ian, Aunt Polly (Amy Wright). When Tom sneaks out of bed one night, Polly punishes him by having him paint a fence; but Tom cleverly cons his neighborhood friends into doing his chore for him. Meanwhile, he flirts with his schoolmate, Becky Thatcher (Rachael Leigh Cook), and visits his closest friend, Huckleberry Finn (Brad Renfro), another trouble-making youth, who hides out in the woods, away from the town where he feels he is not wanted.

Together in a graveyard one night, Tom and Huck witness Injun Joe (Eric Schweig), another local outcast, murder the town doctor over an argument about some buried loot. The boys flee the scene after seeing Joe take the treasure. Back at Huck's hideaway, the friends promise each other never to tell anyone what they have seen.

Yet, later, when Muff Potter (Michael McShane), the town drunk, is accused of the crime and sent to trial, Tom breaks his vow and takes the witness stand to reveal the identity of the real murderer. While Tom is cheered by the court attendees for saving Muff, Injun Joe flees the town.

Huck resents Tom for going back on his word, but, during a picnic celebration, he rescues his friend when Injun Joe chases Tom and Becky through a cave, where Joe has buried the treasure. Huck fights off Joe, who dies from a fall in the cave, and recovers the valuable coins. Subsequently, Huck's heroism wins the heart of Widow Douglas (Marian Seldes), who adopts the youth and brings him back to the town.

Screenwriters Stephen Sommers and David Loughery have retained most but not all of the basic elements of the original story in this adaptation. Thomas, who became famous at a tender age in the hit sitcom "Home Improvement," seems just right for the role, until his child-star line readings start sounding artificial next to the brooding naturalism of THE CLIENT's Renfro, who plays a strikingly older Huck. Thomas also finds the dramatic scenes in the latter half of the film far beyond his capability.

Other cast members look unconvincing, particularly Cook as the pallid Becky, who will make viewers yearn for Jodie Foster's spunky, prefeminist Becky from the second of two 1973 film versions. Also, the depiction of Injun Joe may revive the debate about Twain and racism, while the conspicuous absence of slave characters attempts to sweep that issue under the rug. One other disturbing element: the film's schizophrenic attitude toward child abuse, which is played for both laughs and sympathy. Despite the Disney gloss, sloppy direction, editing, and camerawork contribute to the dispiriting feeling. *(Violence, profanity.)* — E.M.

d, Peter Hewitt; p, Laurence Mark, John Baldecchi; exec p, Barry Bernardi, Stephen Sommers; assoc p, Howard Ellis; w, Stephen Sommmers, David Loughery (based on the novel *The Adventures of Tom Sawyer* by Mark Twain); ph, Bobby Bukowski; ed, David Freeman; m, Stephen Endelman; prod d, Gemma Jackson; art d, Michael Rizzo; set d, Ellen J. Brill; sound, Walter P. Anderson (mixer); fx, Michael Nathan Arbogast, Smoke & Mirrors Ltd.; casting, Gail Levin, Tricia Tomey; cos, Marie France; makeup, Harriette Landau

Adventure/Children's/Comedy **(PR: A MPAA: PG)**

TOMMY BOY ★★½
(U.S.) 96m Broadway Video; Paramount ~ Paramount c

Chris Farley *(Tommy Callahan)*; David Spade *(Richard Hayden)*; Brian Dennehy *(Big Tom Callahan)*; Bo Derek *(Beverly)*; Dan Aykroyd *(Zalinsky)*; Julie Warner *(Michelle)*; Sean McCann *(Rittenhauer)*; Zach Grenier *(Reilly)*; James Blendick *(Gilmore)*; Clinton Turnbull *(Young Tommy)*; Ryder Britton *(Young Richard)*; Paul Greenberg *(Skittish Student)*; Graeme Millington;

Michael Cram; Dean Marshall; Philip McMullen *(Frat Boys)*; Philip Williams *(Danny)*; David "Skippy" Malloy *(Sammy)*; Roy Lewis *(Louis)*; Austin Pool *(Obnoxious Bus Kid)*; Willian Dunlop *(R.T.)*; Jack Jessop *(Priest)*; Michael Dunston *(Singer at Wedding)*; David Hemblen *(Archer)*; George Kinamis *(Kid at Lake)*; Dov Tiefenbach *(Kid at Lake)*; Mark Zador *(Kid at Lake)*; Helen Hughes *(Boardroom Lady)*; J.R. Zimmerman *(Boardroom Man)*; Robert K. Weiss *("No" Manager)*; Reg Dreger *("No" Manager)*; Lloyd White *("No" Manager)*; David Huband *(Gas Attendant)*; Hayley Gibbins *(Little Girl at Carnival)*; Julianne Gilles *(Brady's Receptionist)*; Addison Bell *(Mr. Brady)*; Cory Sevier *(Boy in Commercial)*; Maria Vacratsis *(Helen)*; Colin Fox *(Nelson)*; Lorri Bagley *(Woman at Pool)*; Lynn Cunningham *(Pretty Hitchiker)*

Of the glut of "Saturday Night Live"-derived feature films (CONEHEADS, IT'S PAT, STUART SAVES HIS FAMILY, BILLY MADISON) to flood the market in the wake of the commercial success of WAYNE'S WORLD, TOMMY BOY is the freshest and funniest. Though not directly based on "SNL" characters or sketches, TOMMY BOY features two of its current stars, Chris Farley and David Spade, as well as original troupe member Dan Aykroyd, and was produced by "SNL" creator-producer Lorne Michaels, and scripted by Bonnie and Terry Turner (WAYNE'S WORLD, WAYNE'S WORLD 2, CONEHEADS) with "SNL" staff writer Fred Wolf.

After seven years of college, Tom Callahan Jr. (Farley) finally graduates, with a D+ average. No one is more proud than his father, Tom Sr. (Brian Dennehy), president of a large auto parts empire, who puts Tommy Boy on the payroll and gives him his own office. More surprises are in store for Tommy—his father is getting remarried to a "10" named Beverly (Bo Derek) whose son Paul (Rob Lowe) will be the brother Tommy always wanted. The foursome never quite becomes a family, as Big Tom dies of a heart attack on his wedding day. Without its president and chief salesman, Callahan Auto Parts is in danger of going under. The bank turns down a loan that would keep the company solvent during the transition to new leadership. Tommy puts up his share of the company and his father's house as collateral for the loan and announces he will take his father's place on an upcoming sales trip. Richard Hayden (David Spade), Big Tom's former assistant, is drafted to accompany overwhelmingly underqualified Tommy. Snide and supercilious, Richard is an unlikely partner for the good-natured oaf Tommy. Their sales trip starts out disastrously, as one client after another rejects their sales pitch and one mishap after another wreaks havoc on Richard's prized car.

Tommy's natural charm eventually wins out, and the pair start racking up sales. Their efforts are sabotaged by Paul, who changes the shipping orders in the company computer. Beverly and Paul, in reality a husband-and-wife con team, conspire to sell the company to rival auto-parts king Zalinsky (Dan Aykroyd). Having lost his company stock to the bank, Tommy makes one last-ditch effort to save the company. Posing as flight attendants, Tommy and Richard finagle a trip to Chicago, arriving at Zalinsky's office just as Beverly is about to sign over the company. Using quick thinking and phony explosives, Tommy hijacks the meeting, bringing national media attention to his plight. He exposes Beverly and Paul, regains control of the company, and extracts a huge order from Zalinsky for Callahan brake pads.

Though the comedy is decidedly lowbrow, this laugh-a-minute rouser features hilarious sight gags and slapstick comedy, particularly in the road sequences. The demolition of Richard's car by—among other things—a deer, and Tommy's overzealous sales pitch, replete with burning props, earn two of the biggest belly laughs. Director Peter Segal (NAKED GUN 33 1/3) keeps

the action rolling and the laughs coming. The script has a good share of fat jokes at the expense of star Farley, but on the whole it is inoffensive fun. The paper-thin plot doesn't hold up to dissection (in a company that large, Tom Sr. was the only salesman?), but TOMMY BOY was not intended as a literary breakthrough. In fact, it is only when it takes itself seriously that the screenplay blunders, such as in Richard's syrupy declaration of friendship for Tommy at film's end.

TOMMY BOY marks the first star turn for both Farley (CONEHEADS, AIRHEADS) and Spade (CONEHEADS, PCU, REALITY BITES). Spade is a master at snappy wisecracks, and Farley is a fine physical comedian. Together, they are a winning comedy team whether brawling over their differences or bawling over a Carpenters song. The fine supporting cast is topped by Lowe, who takes nearly as many pratfalls as Farley. Dennehy is terrific as the bighearted Dad, Derek is radiant as the conniving stepmom, and Julie Warner is beautiful but bland as Farley's unbelievable love interest. *(Violence, sexual situations, profanity.)* — B.R.

d, Peter Segal; p, Lorne Michaels; exec p, Robert K. Weiss; assoc p, Michael Ewing; co-p, Barnaby Thompson; w, Bonnie Turner, Terry Turner, Fred Wolf; ph, Victor J. Kemper; ed, William Kerr; m, David Newman; prod d, Stephen Lineweaver; art d, Alicia Keywan; set d, Gordon Sim; sound, Hank Garfield (sound mixer); fx, Michael Kavanagh; casting, Pamela Basker; cos, Patti Unger; makeup, Irene Kent; stunts, Branko Racki

Comedy   **(PR: A   MPAA: PG-13)**

TOO OUTRAGEOUS ANIMATION   ★★
(U.S./Italy/Japan/Poland/U.K./France) 88m c

TOO OUTRAGEOUS ANIMATION is an 88-minute compilation of 33 short animated films linked by their reliance on sexual, scatological, and violent themes. While the films are generally well executed, the majority of them are designed strictly for the titillation of college boy audiences, replacing genuine wit with shock tactics, tastelessness, and bathroom humor.

Ranging from a few seconds to several minutes each, these 33 segments from the US, England, Italy, France, Poland, and Japan feature a wide variety of animation styles. Highlights include:

"The Expiration Date," in which a dog's "cartoon license" expires, enabling the cat, its perennial victim, to inflict on the dog escalating levels of permanent damage.

"Liver Lust or Louie," done in brightly colored 1950s animation style, focuses on a sexually-frustrated woman who achieves satisfaction with Louie, a slick-haired young man she meets on the street. When they both suffer multiple amputations and wind up in the hospital together, their lovemaking continues unabated.

"They Gave Us a . . . but We Lost the Instruction Booklet," illustrates anal imagery as manifested in modern industry, which frequently replicates the function of the anus and deposits waste products onto the earth.

"The Four Wishes" adapts the classic tale of a poor farmer and his wife being granted four wishes, only to use them up in an angry dispute resulting in the growth of multiple genitalia over each other's bodies.

DNA Productions' "Captain Weird Beard" consists of linking segments spread throughout the film, and follows the gradual dismemberment and mutilation of a tavern kitchen boy by a group of pirates after the boy has expressed a wish to be a pirate.

Other representative titles in the group include "Guano: Who Calcutta the Cheese?," about flatulent cartoon characters; "Yes, Timmy, There is a Santa Claus," a shaggy dog tale culminating in a cruel joke played by Santa on a legless boy; "Little Red Riding Hood and the Wolf," exploring the sexual possibilities suggested by the title coupling; and "Let's Chop Soo-e," a cartoon game show in which a piglet desperately tries to avoid the butcher's cleaver.

Opening with the legend, "Reality is for people who can't handle animation," TOO OUTRAGEOUS ANIMATION is a far cry from the once-outrageous works of the 1970s, such as the celebrated one-joke "Bambi Meets Godzilla" and even Ralph Bakshi's X-rated FRITZ THE CAT. These new shorts, dating from 1989-1994, reveal no restraints in displays of blood, dismemberment, sexual activity, release of excrement, flatulence, and cruel jokes at the expense of the disabled. While such subjects can certainly be funny at times, most of the filmmakers here show little interest in creating anything beyond a single, naughty, attention-getting gag.

What's remarkable about this compilation, however, is the truly breathtaking level of skill and mastery of the medium. In addition to some expertly-executed 3-D model animation and at least one example of computer animation, the majority of the pieces are done in traditional cartoon cel animation in a wide variety of styles. Some of the shorts are quite clever and use their imagery to make a point—most notably "They Gave Us a. . . but We Lost the Instruction Booklet" by veteran Italian animator Guido Manuli, as well as Michel Ocelot's "Four Wishes," both cited above. "The Expiration Date" is quite amusing for the way it takes a traditional cartoon premise to its violent but logical conclusion.

Ultimately, however, the effect of putting so many of these shorts together in a compilation is numbing, undermining the chances of the less outrageous shorts in the group to stand out more memorably. *(Graphic violence, nudity, sexual situations, profanity.)* — B.C.

d, DNA Productions , Michel Ocelot, Cassandra Einstein, Mike Grimshaw, Vincent Lavacherry, Vincenzo Gionala, Webster Colcord, Aaron Tardo, Federico Vitali, Eric Pigors; p, Benjamin Levy; exec p, Terry Thoren

Animated (PR: O MPAA: R)

TOO YOUNG TO DIE? ★★½
(U.S.) 92m Von Zerneck/Sertner Films ~
Repbublic Pictures Home Video c

Juliette Lewis *(Amanda Sue Bradley)*; Michael Tucker *(Buddy Thorton)*; Brad Pitt *(Billy Canton)*; Michael O'Keefe *(Mike Medwicki)*; Yvette Heyden *(Annie Meechan)*; J. Stephen Brady *(Brian Davidson)*; Laurie O'Brien *(Wanda Sledge)*; Dean Abston *(Harvey Sledge)*; Emily Longstreth *(Jean)*; Alan Fudge *(Mark Calhoun)*; Mark Davenport *(Mickey)*; Lew Hopson *(Star)*; Annabelle Weenick *(Birdie Jewel)*; Charles C. Stevenson, Jr. *(Pastor)*; Charles David Richards *(Billings)*; Hank Woessner *(Boss)*; Tim DeZarn *(Patron)*; Jeremy Bailey *(Police Officer)*; C.W. Hemingway *(Gas Station Attendant)*; Taylor Fry *(Sally)*; Bradley Pierce *(Web)*; Don Pugsley *(Booking Officer)*; James Schendel *(Foreman)*; Redmond Gleeson *(Janitor)*; Tom Everett

Before either became a box office superstar, Brad Pitt and Juliette Lewis teamed up for this controversial made-for-television drama about a teenager facing the death penalty. TOO YOUNG TO DIE? aired on NBC in 1990, one year prior to Pitt's breakout role in THELMA AND LOUISE and Lewis's Oscar-nominated performance in CAPE FEAR. Released to home video in 1995 to capitalize on Pitt's escalating appeal, TOO YOUNG TO DIE? is an interesting, fact-inspired drama, highlighted by a riveting performance by then 16-year-old Lewis.

Amanda Sue Bradley (Lewis) is arrested at a trailer park. Charged with murder and kidnapping, she will face the death penalty if tried as an adult. The events leading up to her arrest are revealed in a series of extended flashbacks, punctuated by interviews with her well-meaning but inexperienced public defender, Buddy Thornton (Michael Tucker).

Raised by an uncaring mother and a drunken, abusive stepfather, Amanda leaves home at fourteen to marry her boyfriend. Amanda's young husband abandons her soon after their marriage to enlist in the Army. Returning to her mother's trailer, Amanda learns that mom and stepdad have moved and left no forwarding address. With no money and nowhere to live, Amanda wanders from one place to another looking for a job. She becomes the easy prey of low-life drifter Billy (Pitt). Billy puts her to work dancing in a strip joint and feeds her drugs to help her overcome her inhibitions. Soon he has lured her into a life of prostitution. Still too young to get a real job, Amanda clings to Billy out of desperation. She meets Mike Medwicki (Michael O'Keefe), a kind, divorced Army sergeant, who offers her room and board with no strings attached. Amanda falls in love with Mike and thrives in her new domestic environment. When his relationship with Amanda is discovered, Mike faces court-martial. Though he loves her, he sends Amanda away. She returns, heartbroken and defeated, to her life with Billy. Billy persuades Amanda to exact revenge on Mike and his new girlfriend. They break into Mike's home and kidnap the couple, taking them out to an oil field. In a drug-induced jealous rage, Amanda stabs Mike to death. Despite her attorney's heartfelt pleas, Amanda is tried as an adult. She is found guilty and sentenced to death.

Though his character was really a supporting player, Michael Tucker received top billing because he was a TV star ("L.A. Law") when TOO YOUNG TO DIE? aired, while his two costars were virtually unknown. Tucker is effective as a sympathetic lawyer who defends and befriends Amanda, but his contributions are overshadowed by Pitt's unbridled intensity and Lewis's needy vulnerability. TOO YOUNG TO DIE? effectively builds suspense—and audience sympathy—by leaving the identity of the murder victim and the question of Amanda's guilt or innocence unknown until well into the story. After this revelation, the film turns into a courtroom drama for its final, and weakest, act, which promotes the filmmakers' message that troubled minors are victims of society and should not be held accountable for capital offenses. *(Violence, sexual situations, adult situations, substance abuse, profanity.)* — B.R.

d, Robert Markowitz; p, Susan Weber-Gold, Julie Anne Weitz; exec p, Frank Von Zerneck, Robert M. Sertner; assoc p, Paul Alan Mones, Timothy McFlynn; w, David Hill, George Rubino (from a story by David Hill); ph, Eric Van Haren Noman; ed, Harvey Rosenstock, Eric Sears; m, Charles Bernstein; prod d, Donald Light-Harris; set d, William Vail; sound, Jacob Goldstein (mixer); casting, Susan Glicksman, Fern Orenstein; cos, Shari Feldman; makeup, Davida Simon

Drama (PR: O MPAA: R)

TOP DOG ★★
(U.S.) 87m Top Dog Productions; Tanglewood Entertainment Group; LIVE Entertainment ~
LIVE Entertainment c

Chuck Norris *(Jake Wilder)*; Peter Savard Moore *(Karl Koller)*; Clyde Kusatsu *(Captain Callahan)*; Michele Lamar Richards *(Savannah Boyette)*; Erik von Detten *(Matthew Swanson)*; Carmine Caridi *(Lou Swanson)*; Herta Ware *(Jake's Mother)*; Kai Wulff *(Otto Dietrich)*; Francesco Quinn *(Mark Curtains)*; Timothy Bottoms *(Nelson Houseman)*

Dealing with bomb-and-building demolitions by homegrown hate groups, this Chuck Norris would-be comedy is a victim of bad timing (it was released shortly after the Oklahoma City bombing) as well as its own inherent bad taste.

After neo-Nazis kill his owner, heroic police dog Reno (played by Hollywood stunt dog Reno) gets reassigned to non-conformist, loose-cannon officer Jake Wilder (Chuck Norris). Multi-talented, the bomb-sniffing Briard (a French herding dog) lends his paws to solving his owner's murder and to cracking down on the white supremacists fanning out over San Diego. As Jake and Reno narrow in on conspiracy plans, thugs disguised as killer clowns assault Jake and canine-specialist Detective Boyette (Michele Lamar Richards) near Jake's home.

Inspired by fearmonger Kurt Koller (Peter Savard Moore) and drilled by mercenary Nelson Houseman (Timothy Bottoms), white supremacists plan to target several synagogues and the Coalition for Racial Unity on Hitler's birthday. At Koller's headquarters, Reno grabs an incriminating notebook which he hides before untying his captured partner Jake. Tipped off by the notebook, Jake stymies the racial disharmony offensive while Boyette chases down Koller. Thanks to the teamwork of the shaggy cop and Reno, the police round up the entire network of racially-divisive anarchists.

If you thought pooches removing infants from burning buildings went out with silent movie shorts, prepare yourself for the TOP DOG experience. The latest in an unwelcome series of Man's Best Friend police flicks (TURNER & HOOCH, K-9), this movie's dramaturgy dates back to the 1920's—only the slick car chases and cutting-edge technology identify it as contemporary. To say that this movie doesn't quite jell would be understatement. In a family film, viewers may be jarred by the ripped-from-today's-headlines villains who are not played for cartoonish laughs. What is one to make of that heavy artillery attack by a death squad of killer clowns? Since TOP DOG doesn't appear to be confronting children's subliminal fears of clowns, genocide, or death of a beloved relative, it's obvious this movie is just a confused grab at the commercial brass ring. On the plus side, charismatic pooch Reno easily out-stunts and out-acts his co-star Norris.

In the end, this mutt of a movie suffers from several kinds of artistic mongrelism. After this confused entertainment, one wonders if BEETHOVEN IN BOSNIA will be the next doggy caper suitable for politically-involved families everywhere. (Violence, profanity, adult situations.) — R.P.

d, Aaron Norris; p, Andy Howard; exec p, Tom Steinmetz, Seth Willenson; w, Ron Swanson (based on a story by Aaron Norris and Tim Grayem); ph, Joao Fernandes; ed, Peter Schink; prod d, Norm Baron; set d, Bill Volland; sound, Jim Thornton; casting, Penny Perry; cos, Verkina Flower-Crow

Children's/Action/Martial Arts   (PR: A   MPAA: PG-13)

TOTAL ECLIPSE   ★★½
(U.K./France) 110m F.I.T. Productions;
Portman Productions ~ Fine Line c

Leonardo DiCaprio (Arthur Rimbaud); David Thewlis (Paul Verlaine); Romane Bohringer (Mathilde Verlaine); Dominique Blanc (Isabelle Rimbaud); Felicie Pasotti Cabarbaye (Isabelle as a Child); Nita Klein (Rimbaud's Mother); James Thieree (Frederic); Emmanuelle Oppo (Vitalie); Denise Chalem (Mrs. Maute de Fleurville); Andrzej Seweryn (Mr. Maute de Fleurville); Christopher Thompson (Carjat); Bruce van Barthold (Aicard); Christopher Chaplin (Charles Cros); Christopher Hampton (The Judge); Mathias Jung (Andre); Kettly Noel (Somalian Woman); Cheb Han (Djami)

The lives of two 19th-century French poets, Arthur Rimbaud and Paul Verlaine, are portrayed in TOTAL ECLIPSE, a refreshingly

rude antidote to the stiff biographical screen dramas of Great Artists. Still, with its emphasis on sex and bad manners, Christopher Hampton's screenplay does an injustice to two important literary figures.

In 1871 Paris, during the reign of Napoleon III, teenaged poet Arthur Rimbaud (Leonardo DiCaprio) arrives from his mother's modest country home to become the protege of established bard Paul Verlaine (David Thewlis). Despite his marriage to pregnant Mathilde (Romane Bohringer), Paul is so taken with the impetuous, handsome youth that he sets him up in a garret in the city, where they begin a passionate love affair.

Paul's personal and professional fascination with Arthur diminishes after Mathilde gives birth. Paul takes his wife to Brussels to rekindle their relationship. But Arthur follows them and seduces Paul into joining him in London. Finally, Mathilde leaves Paul, suing him for divorce. Paul again leaves Arthur after a misunderstanding, but Arthur later tracks him down in Brussels, where Paul shoots and injures Arthur during a fight. The incident attracts the police and Paul is later imprisoned for two years on a charge of sodomy.

Upon Paul's release from jail, the men meet in the Black Forest of Germany. Paul has found religion, but Arthur is more cynical than ever and they break up for good. Living on his own in the African desert, Arthur develops a tumor on his knee, which kills him. After Arthur's death, a relative appeals to Paul to destroy Arthur's "profane" manuscripts, but Paul refuses.

TOTAL ECLIPSE has the lavish look of a Merchant-Ivory period production. The colorful and picturesque view of late 19th-century Europe is augmented by Yorgos Arvanitis's camerawork, Dan Weil's production design, Francoise Benoit-Fresco's set decoration and Pierre-Yves Gayraud's costumes. However, the depiction of the two main characters runs against the grain of this marvelously recreated epoch. Director Agnieszka Holland and screenwriter Christopher Hampton upset the usual conventions of the biopic by presenting the "heroes" in a most unflattering light, while still appealing for a certain amount of audience empathy and understanding.

It represents quite an achievement that the filmmakers were able to shock so much (TOTAL ECLIPSE received harshly critical reviews when released) by showing so little (there is some nudity in the film, but very little graphic sex). Holland, who created a different sort of uproar with 1991's EUROPA, EUROPA (about a real-life Jew who masqueraded as an Aryan during World War II), pushes the envelope this time by showing the sadomasochistic gay love affair in an uncompromising way.

TOTAL ECLIPSE stumbles dramatically in its failure to construct a well-rounded portrait of its subjects. Hampton's focus on the romantic relationships comes at the expense of illuminating the work of Rimbaud and Verlaine. Of course, representing the work of writers presents serious difficulties for filmmakers, but Hampton might have thought to include more than one (interrupted) reading of a poem. (Violence, nudity, sexual situations, substance abuse, extreme profanity.) — E.M.

d, Agnieszka Holland; p, Jean-Pierre Ramsay Levi; exec p, Jean-Yves Asselin, Staffan Ahrenberg, Pascale Faubert; w, Christopher Hampton; ph, Yorgos Arvanitis; ed, Isabel Lorente; m, Jan A.P. Kaczmarek; prod d, Dan Weil; sound, Francois Groult (mixer); cos, Pierre-Yves Gayraud; makeup, Odile Fourquin

Biography/Drama   (PR: O   MPAA: R)

TOUR OF DUTY
(SEE: BREACH OF CONDUCT)

TOY STORY ★★★½
(U.S.) 80m Walt Disney Pictures; PIXAR Productions ~
Buena Vista c

VOICES OF: Tom Hanks *(Woody)*; Tim Allen *(Buzz Lightyear)*;
Don Rickles *(Mr. Potato Head)*; Jim Varney *(Slinky Dog)*; Wallace Shawn *(Rex)*; John Ratzenberger *(Hamm)*; Annie Potts *(Bo Peep)*; John Morris *(Andy)*; Erik Von Detten *(Sid)*; Laurie Metcalf *(Mrs. Davis)*; R. Lee Ermey *(Sergeant)*; Sarah Freeman *(Hannah)*; Penn Jillette *(TV Announcer)*

An astonishing technical accomplishment, TOY STORY combines sophisticated computer animation with lively characters and a charming story. The result is a slick, amusing film that will redefine the prevailing standards for animated features.

Six-year-old Andy's toybox doesn't reveal too many surprises: a Mr. Potato Head, a Slinky dog, a plastic dinosaur, and a bucketful of tiny molded soldiers, etc. Once Andy is out of the room, though, the toys have a life of their own. The head hombre is Woody (voiced by Tom Hanks), a floppy cowboy with a pull-string voice who enjoys "favorite toy" status. Woody's hold on the top spot loosens when Andy receives a new toy for his birthday, the cartoon action figure "Buzz Lightyear: Space Ranger" (Tim Allen). This high-tech plaything comes complete with laser beam (a wrist-mounted flashing diode) and spring-loaded wings. Buzz quickly climbs to the top of the toy totem, threatening to oust Woody as Andy's favorite toy; what's more, Buzz begins to win favor among the other toys with his spaceman gadgets and his "just doing my job, ma'am" chivalry. Stripped of both status and authority, Woody sulks and plots his rival's elimination.

En route to a restaurant, Woody gets his chance. During a stop at a gas station, Buzz wanders out of the family car and gets lost. Woody wrestles with his conscience and decides to fetch Buzz, but both toys are left behind when the family car drives off. The rivals make a virtue of necessity and join forces to find Andy. Just when salvation seems within reach, Buzz falls into the clutches of Andy's next-door neighbor, the evil, toy-torturing Sid. Woody marches alone into Sid's attic bedroom, a dark funhouse of crazy angles, naked wood, and Heavy Metal posters. Hidden under his bed are the results of his sadistic experiments: mutant toys pieced together out of dolls, cars, and household items.

With the help of the mutant toys, Buzz and Woody make their escape—but not before teaching Sid a lesson that should end his toy-torturing days forever. Once again within reach of their goal, they discover that Andy and his family have loaded their belongings into a van and are even now traveling to a new home. With the help of a battery-powered car and a bottle rocket, Buzz and Woody, now reconciled, fly to the safety of Andy's toybox.

TOY STORY, billed as the first feature film constructed entirely of computer animation, TOY STORY is a visual masterpiece that must truly be seen to be believed. The brainchild of director John Lasseter and his team of computer animators at Pixar, TOY STORY genuinely makes viewers forget they're watching an animated film. For its considerable achievements—which took four years and an army of computer animators to complete—TOY STORY was given a special Academy Award. Its bravura set pieces—notably the astonishing toy's-eye-view flying sequence—mark new milestones in animation.

Adding to TOY STORY's appeal is a witty screenplay, written by Joel Cohen and Alex Sokolow and revised by Joss Whedon. At its heart, the film is a classic buddy movie, with two clashing personalities forced to resolve their differences. The toys' personalities are persuasively fleshed out, and the resulting chemistry makes TOY STORY not only a successful children's movie, but also one of the most enjoyable comedies of its year.

TOY STORY is primarily intended for kids, but it is craftily pitched toward adult audiences as well. Many of the jokes are aimed way over the heads of young moviegoers (e.g., Mr. Potato Head's rearranging his features and proclaiming himself a Picasso). Additionally, some of the images are potentially too intense for the youngest viewers. Sid's mutant toys in particular are truly grotesque and often scary (at times, this sequence resembles the disturbing experimental films of the Brothers Quay). Overall, though, TOY STORY is one of the most entertaining films of 1995, hinting at wonderful possibilities for the future of animated cinema. — B.T.

d, John Lasseter; p, Ralph Guggenheim, Bonnie Arnold; exec p, Edwin Catmull, Steven Jobs; w, Joss Whedon, Andrew Stanton, Joel Cohen, Alec Sokolow (from an original story by John Lasseter, Pete Docter, Andrew Stanton, and Joe Ranft); ed, Robert Gordon, Lee Unkrich; m, Randy Newman; art d, Ralph Eggleston; anim, Pete Docter, Rich Quade, Ash Brannon, Pixar Animation Studios; sound, Gary Rydstrom (design); casting, Ruth Lambert

AAN Best Original Screenplay: Joss Whedon, Andrew Stanton, Joel Cohen, Alec Sokolow; story by John Lasseter, Peter Docter, Andrew Stanton, Joe Ranft; *AAN Best Musical or Comedy Score:* Randy Newman; *AAN Best Original Song:* Randy Newman "You've Got a Friend"

Animated/Fantasy/Children's (PR: AA MPAA: G)

TRAPS ★★★
(Australia) 98m Ayer Productions Pty. Ltd.;
Australian Film Commission ~ Filmopolis Pictures c

Saskia Reeves *(Louise Duffield)*; Robert Reynolds *(Michael Duffield)*; Sami Frey *(Daniel Renouard)*; Jacqueline McKenzie *(Viola Renouard)*; Kiet Lam *(Tuan)*; Hoa To *(Tatie Chi)*; Nguyen Minh Tri *(Thief)*; Thierry Marquet *(Captain Brochard)*; Tran Duy An *(Bao)*; Ho Thu Nga *(Kim)*; Vu T Le Thi *(Bao's Mother)*; Nguyen Ngoc Dang *(Bao's Grandfather)*; Jean Louis Beaulieu *(French Officer)*; Claude Holweger *(French Soldier)*; Tat Binh *(Vietminh Captain)*; Trieu Xuan Sam *(Vietminh in Hut)*; Ly Thai Dung *(Vietminh Executioner)*

TRAPS takes place in the politically charged atmosphere of Vietnam in the 1950s, focusing on the personal lives of several western "visitors" to the region. While the film features intriguing characters in a provocative story and setting, it is marred by weak dialogue and an overly melodramatic plot.

Louise Duffield (Saskia Reeves), an Australian photographer, accompanies Michael (Robert Reynolds), her husband, on his assignment to write economic reports about rubber plantation operations in 1950 Indochina. The underlying problems in Louise and Michael's marriage become more apparent in their new environment, a country house occupied by their hosts, Daniel Renouard (Sami Frey), a French plantation owner, and Viola Renouard (Jacqueline McKenzie), Daniel's willful daughter.

While tensions mount among the four sexually frustrated characters, the Vietnamese Communists living outside the residence begin retaliating against the westerners for the mistreatment of a house servant. After Louise and Viola barely escape being killed by soldiers in the jungle, they rejoin Michael and Daniel at the house, where they are forced to kill a soldier who threatens to warn his comrades of their whereabouts. Louise also realizes her marriage is over when she discovers that Michael has been influenced by Daniel's French imperialist views (and that he has shared Daniel's bed). Daniel forces a bloody confrontation with Louise, Michael, and Viola as the three try to escape the area, but, ultimately, he loses in the showdown.

In her first feature film, director Pauline Chan effectively evokes the Vietnam of her youth through authentic clothes and hairstyles, and location cinematography. Although TRAPS is based on Kate Grenville's book, *Dreamhouse*, which was set in Tuscany, Chan cleverly changes the setting, adding a new dramatic dimension to the story, and offering wise observations about culture clashes, uneasy alliances, and the effects of the political on the personal.

But Chan is less successful in building upon her innovative premise, in part because she sometimes writes cliched dialogue, which diminishes the impact of some big scenes. In the film's last quarter, Chan also pushes the action to a hyperbolic extreme: the group-killing of the soldier, the two lead male characters having sex, Louise's epiphany about her marriage, and the last brutal acts all occur within a very short time frame.

For the bulk of the film, Chan proves herself both a thoughtful and sensual stylist, with a good eye for details and a sure feeling for various types of characters. Her obvious talent, though it assures a solid future for the director, makes the ending of TRAPS all the more disappointing. *(Violence, extensive nudity, sexual situations, adult situations, profanity.)* — E.M.

d, Pauline Chan; p, Jim McElroy; w, Pauline Chan, Robert Carter (based on the novel *Dreamhouse* by Kate Grenville); ph, Kevin Hayward; ed, Nick Beauman; m, Stephen Rae; prod d, Michael Philips; art d, Philip Drake; sound, John Schiefelbein (recordist); casting, Mike Fenton; cos, David Rowe; makeup, Margaret Stevenson

Drama/Historical/Political   **(PR: O   MPAA: R)**

TWELVE MONKEYS   ★★★½
(U.S./U.K./Germany/Japan/France) 130m Atlas Entertainment; BBC; Polygram; Classico; Shochiku; Telemunchen; UGC; Universal ~ Universal c
(AKA: 12 MONKEYS)

Bruce Willis *(James Cole)*; Madeleine Stowe *(Kathryn Railly)*; Brad Pitt *(Jeffrey Goines)*; Christopher Plummer *(Dr. Goines)*; Jon Seda *(Jose)*; David Morse *(Dr. Peters)*; Frank Gorshin *(Dr. Fletcher)*; Irma St. Paule *(Poet)*; Joey Perillo *(Detective Franki)*; Harry O'Toole *(Louie/Raspy Voice)*; Joseph Melito *(Young Cole)*; Michael Chance *(Scarface)*; Vernon Campbell *(Tiny)*; Paul Meshejian *(Detective Dalva)*; Christopher Meloni *(Lt. Halperin)*; Rozwill Young *(Billings)*; Robert O'Neill *(Wayne)*; Fred Strother *(L.J. Washington)*; Joseph McKenna *(Wallace)*; Rick Warner *(Dr. Casey)*; Anthony "Chip" Brienza *(Dr. Goodin)*; Kevin Thigpen *(Kweskin)*; Michael Ryan Segal *(Weller)*; Charles Techman *(Professor)*; Jann Ellis *(Marilou)*; H. Michael Walls *(Botanist)*; Bob Adrian *(Geologist)*; Simon Jones *(Zoolologist)*; Carol Florence *(Astrophysicist)*; Bill Raymond *(Microbiologist)*; Ernest Abuba *(Engineer)*; Bruce Kirkpatrick *(Policeman No. 1)*; Wilfred Williams *(Policeman No. 2)*; Nell Johnson *(Ward Nurse)*; Joilet Harris *(Harassed Mother)*; Drucie McDaniel *(Waltzing Woman Patient)*; John Blaisse *(Old Man Patient)*; Louis Lippa *(Patient at Gate)*; Stan Kang *(X-Ray Doctor)*; Pat Dias *(WWI Captain)*; Aaron Michael Lacey *(WWI Sergeant)*; Johnnie Hobbs, Jr. *(Officer No. 1)*; Janet L. Zappala *(Anchorwoman)*; Thomas Roy *(Evangelist)*

It was an act of sheer hubris to remake Chris Marker's experimental short LA JETEE (1962)—a futuristic meditation on *temps perdu* told almost entirely in still images—as a big-budget, mainstream picture starring Bruce Willis. That Terry Gilliam, working from a script by David Webb Peoples and Janet Peoples, managed to make TWELVE MONKEYS into a clever, complex, and poignant success is as astonishing as it is satisfying.

2035: A plague has devastated the Earth, and the remnants of humanity live in dirty underground cities beneath what was once Philadelphia. James Cole (Willis), an brutal sociopath confined to a hellish prison, is "volunteered" to don a contamination suit and comb the frozen surface for bugs and small animals—anything that might help scientists discover a plague cure. Cole completes his mission, only to find that authorities have further plans for him. Cole has vivid dreams (or are they memories?) of the past: a small boy in an airport, a blond woman screaming, a running man felled by a bullet. By virtue of his intense imagination, he has been selected for a time-travel experiment that will send him back to the year 1996. Once there, he is to track down the mysterious Army of the Twelve Monkeys, a group of animal rights fanatics suspected of having unleashed the virus that appeared suddenly in cities all over the world.

Cole's first trip back is a disaster: he's six years early, and his apocalyptic raving lands him in an insane asylum. His fellow inmates include Jeffrey Goines (Brad Pitt), the gibbering son of a rich and powerful medical researcher (Christopher Plummer). Cole also meets psychiatrist Dr. Kathryn Railly (Madeleine Stowe), an intense brunette who treats him sympathetically but still diagnoses him as having a "Cassandra Complex." The future scientists snatch Cole back and try again.

Cole is sent back to 1996, and again meets up with Dr. Railly, who's written a book on millennial madness and the history of apocalyptic delusions. Cole kidnaps her, hoping to convince her that the world as she knows it really is about to end. He finds the Army of the Twelve Monkeys quartered in an abandoned storefront and realizes to his horror that Jeffrey Goines is its leader—could Cole's rants have encouraged the unbalanced Goines to destroy the world with a virus stolen from his father? Menahwile, Cole is haunted by the past and the future: he sees sinister emissaries in sunglasses, is bedevilled by an apparent madman who warns him that he's being tracked through implants in his teeth, and is thrown back to WWI trenches, where he's shot in the leg. Cole gradually persuades Railly that he's not mad (the WWI-era bullet in his flesh is a key piece of evidence). He knows they can't stop the plague, so he and Railly decide to flee to the Florida Keys and enjoy their last days.

The Army of the Twelve Monkeys carries out its plan—nothing more than a stunt that involves freeing the animals in the Philadelphia Zoo—as Railly and Cole head for the airport. There they realize that Dr. Goines's assistant, a religious zealot who's stolen a virulent virus from the lab, is the real agent of the plague. In a last, futile attempt to change the future, they try to stop him boarding his plane: Cole is shot to death as Railly—in the blond wig she's bought as a disguise—screams and a small boy watches.

Despite Brad Pitt's Academy Award nomination, his performance—a riot of the tics and twitches so often mistaken for real acting—is TWELVE MONKEYS's weakest element. Its greatest strength is the almost palpable sense of destiny that drives Cole and Railly and the world to an inevitable appointment with doom. Intensely romantic and bitterly fatalistic, TWELVE MONKEYS is filled with eerily beautiful images—like the escaped zoo animals on the highway—and frighteningly apt ones. The moment when Railly looks a WWI photo she's used in her book, only to suddenly notice Cole in the background, is truly chilling. *(Violence, adult situations, sexual situations, profanity, nudity.)* — M.M.

d, Terry Gilliam; p, Charles Roven; exec p, Robert Cavallo, Gary Levinsohn, Robert Kosberg; assoc p, Kelley Smith-Wait, Mark Egerton; co-p, Lloyd Phillips; w, David Peoples, Janet Peoples (inspired by the film LA JETTE written by Chris Marker); ph, Roger Pratt; ed, Mick Audsley; m, Paul Buckmaster; prod d,

Jeffrey Beecroft; art d, William Ladd Skinner; set d, Crispian Sallis; sound, Jay Meagher (mixer); fx, Anthony Simonaitas, Vincent Montefusco, Kent Houston, Susi Roper, Peerless Camera Co.; casting, Margery Simkin; cos, Julie Weiss; makeup, Christina Beveridge, Alan Weisinger; stunts, Phil Neilson

AAN Best Supporting Actor: Brad Pitt; *AAN Best Costume Design:* Julie Weiss

Science Fiction/Fantasy/Drama   **(PR: C   MPAA: R)**

TWENTY SOMETHING   ★★½
(Hong Kong) 96m c
(AKA: FROM NINE TO FIVE; MAN 9 JIU 5)

Valerie Chow; Moses Chan; Farini Cheung; Jordan Chan; Yau Chau-Yuet; Bak Ka-Sin; Yip Hon-Leung; Cheung Hung-On

TWENTY SOMETHING chronicles the exploits of a group of well-heeled but restless young Hong Kong professionals who frequent a bar called Berlin. The film starts as a melodramatic, if accurately detailed, portrait of restless young adults approaching various crossroads in their lives. Before it ends, it becomes a harsh morality tale.

Jennifer, Alice, Tom, Mick, Pat, Sue, and Bo are friends who meet new lovers, drink until they're sick, and occasionally find the wherewithal to nurse one another through crises. Pat, the group's overweight matchmaker and gossipmonger who cannot get a date herself, organizes endless drinking games, karaoke parties, and friendly group breakfasts to fortify these young people before they go to work. Alice falls for Mick, whose girlfriend has left him to immigrate to Canada. Although Mick vows to avoid commitment, soon the two are settled into a domesticity that descends into tedium.

Alice's best friend, Sue, whose capacity for self-destruction is the most extreme of any in the group, catches Mick's wandering eye, bringing things to a boiling point when Alice agrees to let Sue and Mick sleep together. In this painful turn of events, Alice waits outside while Sue climbs into Mick's bed. They make passionate love but, before they reach orgasm, Alice comes back into the room and takes Sue's place. Sue returns to Berlin, distraught, and Bo offers a shoulder for her to cry on. She goes with him to a rooftop. Drunk, he propositions her, and ignoring her protests, rapes her. As they struggle, he loses his grip on her and she falls off the roof's ledge.

Sue's death is the end of an era. Bo blames himself, but the group as a whole is forgiving, taking the tragedy as an expected wake-up call to get on with their lives. Alice and Mick get married, and the occasion becomes a bittersweet reunion.

Generations clash in the film's whirlwind opening scenes. Inside a Jeep parked on a hilltop against a sweeping Hong Kong vista, Jennifer is performing oral sex on Tom, as a group of elderly men and women practicing Tai Chi veers dangerously close, and Tom, an ambitious insurance agent who is eventually transferred to Singapore, fends off his mother, who calls him on his car phone. Taking all interruptions in their stride, the pair finish and scurry off to work. This pattern of all-night parties and rude reawakenings in the workaday world jobs serves as TWENTY SOMETHING's motif.

At first TWENTY SOMETHING may seem meandering, even plotless, and only minimally concerned with character development. But soon it forges ahead, depicting with irony and almost anthropological curiosity the group's behavior. Then the climactic tragedy occurs, and the film hurries to a too-neat conclusion that belies the chaos of its characters' lives. *(Sexual situations, adult situations, nudity, substance abuse.)* — C.Ch.

d, Teddy Chan; p, Peter Chan; w, James Yuen

Drama   **(PR: O   MPAA: NR)**

TWO BITS   ★★
(U.S.) 93m Arthur Cohn Productions; Connexion Films; Capella International ~ Miramax c
(AKA: DAY TO REMEMBER, A)

Al Pacino *(Grandpa)*; Mary Elizabeth Mastrantonio *(Luisa)*; Jerry Barone *(Gennaro)*; Alec Baldwin *(Narrator)*; Patrick Borriello *(Tullio)*; Andy Romano *(Dr. Bruna)*; Donna Mitchell *(Mrs. Bruna)*; Mary Lou Rosato *(Aunt Carmela)*; Joe Grifasi *(Uncle Joe)*; Rosemary DeAngelis *(Mrs. Conte)*; Ronald McLarty *(Irish)*; Charles Scalies *(Ballyhoo Driver)*; Joanna Merlin *(Guendolina)*; Geoff Pierson *(Dr. Wilson)*; Karen Shallo *(Woman in Red)*; Nick Discenza *(Father of Deceased)*; Rik Colliti *(Vottima)*; Rose Arrick *(Mother of Deceased)*; Joy Pinizotto *(Bride)*; Louis Lippa *(Father of the Bride)*; Johnny C. *(Head Pallbearer)*; Gene D'Allesandro *(Brother of Deceased)*; Anthony DeSando *(Victor)*; Sheila Murphy *(Mary Linguini)*; Jayne Haynes *(Mrs. Rizzo)*; Mikey Viso *(Petey)*; Joe Fersedi *(Player #1)*; Rick Faugno *(Player #2)*; Jon Napolitano *(Player #3)*; Nicole Molina *(Little Girl)*; Mario D'Elia *(Petey's Dad)*; Mary Testa *(Housewife)*; Ted Brunetti *(Guendolina's Youngest Son)*; Tony Rosa *(Guendolina's Eldest Son)*; Lynn Battaglia *(Guendolina's Son's Wife)*; Joey Perillo *(Ballyhoo Replacement Driver)*; Dominic Leporarti *(Freddie)*; Skip Rose *(Ball Player)*

Lovingly photographed and sensitively composed, TWO BITS is a visually enterprising 1930's coming-of-age yarn about a young boy grappling with financial desperation and the terminal heart disease of his tale-spinning grandpa. Unfortunately, the narrative texture of this sentimental confection is a bit too rich for consumption.

In the midst of the Depression, hard-headed twelve-year-old Gennaro (Jerry Barone) kids around with his Grandpa (Al Pacino) who has promised to leave him a quarter when he dies. While Gennaro's mother, Luisa (Mary Elizabeth Mastrantonio), strives to cope with a variety of hardships, Gennaro becomes obsessed with attending the opening of South Philly's grand movie palace, La Paloma. The price of admission is two bits. He picks up some pennies singing on the street, but his aunt (Mary Lou Rosato) confiscates his earnings. A job offer—cleaning up for his grandfather's physician, Doctor Bruna (Andy Romano)—is jeopardized when Bruna's disturbed wife (Donna Mitchell) makes an awkward pass at the astonished lad and later hangs herself. As Grandpa comforts his frustrated grandson, he begs Gennaro to visit Gwendolina (Joanna Merlin), a woman he seduced and abandoned many years ago. Obtaining the embittered woman's forgiveness in his proxy role, Gennaro earns the final dime he needs, arrives at the theater too late for the early bird price, and trudges back home where his grandpa is failing rapidly. Gennaro confesses that that all-important quarter no longer seems earth-shattering, but wise gramps counsels him to hang on to his desires. That evening, when grandpa finally expires and Gennaro picks up his inheritance, he pools it with his earnings to attend the late show at La Paloma, honoring the old man's belief that one should never defer one's dreams.

A blaring truck hawking the wonders of the La Paloma Theater snakes through this gentle film's plot, along with dozens of other symbols of shabby hope and sad surrender. A labor of love for all concerned, TWO BITS never jells. The film strives fussily for the impact of an Americanized CINEMA PARADISO, but TWO BITS fails to convey the spiritual connection to cinema that informed its model. Instead, colorful, quirky incidents pile up as if the audience were visiting a theme park called Saroyan-

Land. In this dreamy vision of a Technicolor Depression, the few bizarre excursions into despair are so jarring that they feel oddly mean-spirited.

Pacino's stab at extending his range is sincerely meant, but it comes off like an acting-class experiment. Barone is pleasant, but like the movie he fails to keep aloft, he never penetrates too deeply into adolescent angst or personal loss. From the screenwriter of PSCYHO and the director of AT CLOSE RANGE, this film represents a holiday from violence, both emotional and physical. For the audience, it's a feel-good wallow that leaves little more than a nagging respect for what a quarter used to buy. *(Profanity, sexual situations, adult situations.)* — R.P.

d, James Foley; p, Arthur Cohn; exec p, Joseph Stefano, Willi Baer, David Korda; assoc p, Rolf Deyhle; w, Joseph Stefano; ph, Juan Ruiz-Anchia; ed, Howard Smith; m, Carter Burwell; prod d, Jane Musky; art d, Tom Warren; set d, Robert J. Franco; sound, Drew Kunin (mixer); fx, Norman B. Dodge, Jr., Bob Vazquez; casting, Glenn Daniels; cos, Claudia Brown; makeup, Luigi Rocchetti

Drama   **(PR: A   MPAA: PG-13)**

TWOGETHER   ★★
(U.S.) 122m Dream Catcher Entertainment Group; Twogether Limited Partnership ~ Columbia TriStar Home Video c

Nick Cassavetes *(John Madler)*; Brenda Bakke *(Allison McKenzie)*; Jeremy Piven *(Arnie)*; Jim Beaver *(Oscar)*; Tom Dugan *(Paul)*; Damian London *(Mark Saffron)*; William Bumiller *(Donald Walters)*; Jennifer Bassey *(Mrs. McKenzie)*; Jerry Bossard *(Bartender)*; Deborah Driggs *(Melissa)*; Christian Bocher *(David)*

TWOGETHER is about a couple thrown together by coincidence and kept together by circumstance. It is a quality production, but the care that went into the filming of this romantic drama does not compensate for the mediocre script. The premise and style are interesting, but the characters are unpleasant, and the film, which is over two hours long, rambles.

John Madler (Nick Cassavetes) is a talented but irresponsible painter. He has trouble paying the rent in his oceanside apartment, and the quality and quantity of his work is uneven. At an exhibition of his paintings, he meets Allison McKenzie (Brenda Bakke), who volunteers at the gallery. Their sexual attraction overcomes them, and they leave the show. The next morning, they wake up in Las Vegas, hung over and married. They decide the marriage is a mistake and celebrate the divorce papers with a sexual tryst that results in pregnancy. Allison moves in with John, planning to stay until the baby is born. Though they sleep together, they plan no romantic future together and are free to see other people.

Allison is wealthy but unconfident. Her idealism clashes with John's pessimism, and, though they grow close, their differences remain problematic. After the baby is born, Allison moves back in with her parents. John's building is sold to developers, and he decides to leave California for an isolated, "problem-free" island. As he goes to the airport, Allison tries to talk him into staying. Wary of commitment, he leaves. Four years later, he is back. The couple decide to get married for a second, and permanent, time.

TWOGETHER's story is interesting but inconsistent. After two hours of extensive character development and growth, it ends abruptly, never explaining why John chose to return. The ambitious attempt to tie together several threads at once is not handled well. Many of the film's subplots are vehicles for allowing us to understand John and Allison, but they take up too much screen time and take focus away from the heart of the film. Some of the film's best scenes, such as John's disc jockey friend deciding to broadcast only "good news" for a day, are enjoyable but rushed and inconsequential.

Though the writing is pretentious and the story is often silly, the film's style is creative and original. Scenes rarely flow together in a traditional way. Some begin in the middle of the action, without explanation, while others don't appear to fit the narrative at all. Nightmare sequences don't reveal themselves as such until the characters wake up, and we see plot progress through conversation rather than action. With time, the audience learns about the characters and has little problem following the story. The technique saves the film from tedium. The acting is strong, but the dialogue is often terrible, particularly during the sex scenes. Many of the characters' "deep" conversations will baffle viewers. The unusual nature of the romance spices up the film, but the bland and self-absorbed couple don't arouse much audience sympathy. The video box stresses the erotic nature of the film, and while there are plenty of sex scenes, the fluffy advertising undermines the serious nature of the film. *(Extensive nudity, sexual situations, extreme profanity.)* — A.M.

d, Andrew Chiaramonte; p, Emmett Alston, Andrew Chiaramonte; assoc p, Fred Pierson, Linda Scannardi, Louis J. Zivet; co-p, Todd Fisher; w, Andrew Chiaramonte; ph, Eugene Shlugleit; ed, Todd Fisher, Andrew Chiaramonte; m, Nigel Holton; prod d, Philip Michael Brandes; art d, Phil Zarling; sound, Kip Gynn; casting, Lori Cobe; cos, Jacqueline Johnson; makeup, Karen Dahl

Drama/Romance   **(PR: O   MPAA: R)**

UNDER SIEGE 2: DARK TERRITORY

★★½

(U.S.) 100m The Goldstein Company; Regency Enterprises; Nasso Production ~ Warner Bros. c

Steven Seagal *(Casey Ryback)*; Eric Bogosian *(Travis Dane)*; Katherine Heigl *(Sarah Ryback)*; Morris Chestnut *(Bobby Zachs)*; Everett McGill *(Penn)*; Kurtwood Smith *(General Stanley Cooper)*; Nick Mancuso *(Tom Breaker)*; Andy Romano *(Admiral Bates)*; Brenda Bakke *(Gilder)*; Sandra Taylor *(Sandi Korn)*; Jonathan Banks *(Scotty)*; David Gianopoulos *(David Trilling)*; Dale Dye *(Col. Darza)*; Royce D. Applegate *(Ryback's Cook)*; Todd O. Russell *(Ryback's Driver)*; Nick Mancuso *(Breaker)*; Peter Greene *(Merc No. 1)*; Patrick Kilpatrick *(Merc No. 2)*; Scott Sowers *(Merc No. 3)*; Afifi *(Female Merc)*; Denis L. Stewart *(Holy-Merc)*; Christopher Darga *(Cook No. 1)*; Don Blakely *(Cook No. 2)*; Jim Clark *(Train Consultant)*; Stan Garner *(Train Consultant)*; Silan Smith *(Friendly Faced Engineer No. 1)*; Rick Wiles *(Conductor)*; Jim Dirker *(Helicopter Pilot)*; Warren Tabata *(Bartender)*; Ginger Lewis *(Lady Hostage)*; Phyllis Davis *(Hostage No. 2)*; Julius Nasso *(Hostage No. 3)*; James V. Caciola *(Hostage No. 4)*; Greg Collins *(Huey Pilot)*; Ken Vieira *(Helicopter Pilot)*; Wren T. Brown *(Captain No. 1)*; D.C. Douglas *(Technician No. 1)*; Thom Adcox Hernandez *(Technician No. 2)*; Catherine NacNeal *(Assistant)*; Frank Roman *(Aide)*; Al Sapienza *(Captain No. 2)*; Jennifer Starr *(ATAC Assistant No. 2)*; Ping Wu *(SYSOS Officer)*

Almost matching its 1992 predecessor where thrills, pace, and action are concerned, UNDER SIEGE 2: DARK TERRITORY tells a tale of high-tech terrorists hijacking a train while a lone hero whittles down their numbers. Rapid-fire cross-cutting and constant movement keep the suspense going through all sorts of contrivances and plot holes.

En route from Denver to Los Angeles, the Grand Continental, a high speed passenger train, is stopped and boarded by a band of renegade soldiers. They're led by crazed weapons designer/computer genius Travis Dane (Eric Bogosian), who intends to use a portable transmitter to get control of Grazer-One, a secret military satellite armed with a particle-beam weapon of Dane's creation. With all the passengers held hostage in the rear cars, Dane sets up his equipment, gains control of the satellite, and demonstrates its power by targeting and blowing up a secret weapons factory in China. US military and intelligence brass can only watch in horror from the ATAC Command Center. Dane is prepared to blow up the Pentagon and all of Washington, DC in exchange for a payment of one billion dollars from his foreign clients.

On board the train, an undetected passenger—former Navy SEAL-turned-master chef Casey Ryback (Steven Seagal)—enlists the aid of a porter, Bobby (Morris Chestnut), in a campaign to eliminate the terrorists one by one and stop Dane's mad plan.

After programming Grazer-One to target the Pentagon, Dane arranges for an escape by helicopter and sets the train on a collision course with the oncoming Nevada Petrol Express. Casey and Bobby overpower the hostage guards and uncouple the train cars carrying the hostages, freeing them from danger. They then confront the remaining terrorists, including ex-soldier Penn (Everett McGill), who has made a hostage of Casey's niece, Sarah (Katherine Heigl). After Bobby commandeers Dane's helicopter, Casey kills Penn in a furious knife and hand-to-hand duel and sends Sarah up the ladder to the 'copter. Casey then stops Dane and shoots a hole through his computer, effectively ending Dane's control over the satellite only seconds before the destructive beam is to hit Washington. The train collides with the

Petrol Express and Casey races back to the last car and leaps through the open door, catching the ladder of the waiting helicopter.

The decision to set this sequel on a passenger train speeding through the Rockies allows for all sorts of breathtaking stunts, fast motion, and impressive scenery that were not possible with the static battleship setting of the original. At times, the film plays like a condensed version of an old Republic cliffhanger. In addition, the high-pitched cross-cutting between three different sets of characters gives the viewer little time to pause for breath or question the logic of the proceedings.

The villains here steal the show, with Eric Bogosian channeling his stage-perfected ranting to create a wonderfully crazed mad scientist. McGill, as Dane's sadistic lieutenant, sports a tall, lean frame, steely expression and close-cropped white hair, giving him a strong resemblance to '30s pulp hero Doc Savage.

On the heroic side, Seagal merely zips through his role, breaking necks, throwing thugs off the train, and spraying automatic weapons fire in close quarters (ignoring, as UNDER SIEGE did, the inevitability of ricochet), wasting little time on dialogue or characterization. Morris Chestnut (BOYZ N THE HOOD) offers forced comic relief as the cocky sidekick. Coming off best is Heigl, who stands up to the heavies with a show of spunk and courage that gives the film a small slice of emotional heft. *(Violence, profanity.)* — B.C.

d, Geoff Murphy; p, Steven Seagal, Arnon Milchan, Steve Perry; exec p, Gary W. Goldstein, Jeffrey Neuman, Martin Wiley; assoc p, Edward McDonnell, Dan Romero, Doug Metzger; co-p, Julius R. Nasso; w, Richard Hatem, Matt Reeves (based on characters created by J.F. Lawton); ph, Robbie Greenberg; ed, Michael Tronick; m, Basil Poledouris; prod d, Albert Brenner; art d, Carol Wood; set d, Kathe Klopp; sound, Edward Tise (mixer), Christopher Boyes (designer); fx, Dale L. Martin, Richard Yuricich; casting, Louis DiGiaimo; cos, Richard Bruno; makeup, Jef Simons; stunts, Dick Ziker

Action/Drama (PR: C MPAA: R)

UNDERCOVER

★

(U.S.) 93m Axis Films International; Axis-Davis Joint Venture ~ A-Pix Entertainment c

Athena Massey *(Cindy)*; Jeffrey Dean Morgan *(Ramone)*; Meg Foster *(Mrs. V.)*; Tom Tayback *(Sgt. Gold)*; Rena Riffel *(Rain)*; Anthony Guidera *(Hunt)*; Mark Kiely *(Jefferson)*; Mari Morrow *(Victoria)*; Elena Olanson *(Tracy)*; John Higginson *(Bernard)*; Joe Petruzzi *(Mr. Rosten)*; Tate Stringer *(Ty)*; Norman Saleet *(Dr. Freeman)*; Kevin McLaughlin *(Man)*

Clint Eastwood's TIGHTROPE, it appears, is a seminal film for the direct-to-video marketplace. In this retwisting of that film noir, a promising female detective muddies the waters of morality by enjoying her walk on the wild side as a hooker just a little too much.

Miffed at being regarded a just one of the boys in blue, tomboyish Cindy (Athena Massey) leaps at the opportunity to tackle a big homicide case by donning high-priced call girl regalia. Over the objections of her skeptical detective partner, Cindy chooses to use the vice connections of her superior officer, Sgt. Gold (Tom Tayback), to get hired in a brothel run by the sarge's former flame, Mrs. V. (Meg Foster). Apparently, one of this establishment's bright lights, Tracy (Elena Olanson), ran a blackmail sideline, a franchise shut down permanently by the wealthy john she victimized. Impressing her madam, Cindy investigates suspects with so much relish she occasionally gets saddled with paying customers instead of plants sent by Sgt. Gold. Willing to give her all, the hooker-cop selectively grills Tracy's coworkers like Rain (Rena Riffel) who's afraid she'll end up the next casualty, but lets the resident bouncer Ramone (Jeffrey Dean Morgan) shoulder some of the crimebusting heat after she learns he was the late Tracy's brother. With Ramone's cooperation, Cindy plans to draw out the perp with false news about the location of Tracy's missing blackmail negative. The plan works all too well, and in short order, the mysterious killer strong-arms Rain into locating the missing photos and snuffs out Ramone in a hit-and-run attack outside Cindy's pad. While covering for another prostitute, Cindy discovers Rain tied up in a bathtub and realizes that mild-mannered customer Jefferson (Mark Kiely) is the murderer. Fortuitously, Mrs. V. arrives and shortens her client list by shooting Jefferson in the back. At last, Cindy not only proves she has the right stuff for solving homicides but finally attracts the romantic eye of her partner. Working as a whore has been a real learning experience for the rookie cop.

Soft-core film purveyors will do anything to work in their steamy skinflick sequences. At the very least, UNDERCOVER deserves credit for finding an excuse in its scenario for lots of heterosexual wish fulfillment. However, the movie's approach to the heroine's search for career-and-libido legitimacy is almost Pollyannaish. When confronted with a real customer, this sexually inexperienced cookie just closes her eyes and thinks of the Department. And isn't it lucky that intercourse is never the first priority of her first regulars, who seem to be timid castoffs from BELLE DU JOUR. UNDERCOVER is recommended only for those stag-movie diehards for whom a little nudity goes a long way. (*Extensive nudity, profanity, violence, sexual situations.*) — R.P.

d, Gregory Hippolyte; p, Andrew Garroni; w, Oola Bloome, Lalo Wolf; ph, Philip Hurn; ed, Kent Smith; m, Ashley Irwin; prod d, Jeffrey Texas Shell; set d, Robin McMullan; sound, Bill Reinhardt (mixer); casting, Sue Swan; cos, Bonnie Stauch; makeup, Lori Gattuso

Action/Crime/Erotic (PR: O MPAA: NR)

UNDERNEATH, THE ★★★½
(U.S.) 99m Populist Pictures ~ Gramercy c

Peter Gallagher (*Michael Chambers*); Alison Elliot (*Rachel*); William Fichtner (*Tommy Dundee*); Adam Trese (*David Chambers*); Joe Don Baker (*Clay Hinkle*); Paul Dooley (*Ed Dutton*); Elisabeth Shue (*Susan*); Anjanette Comer (*Mrs. Chambers*); Dennis Hill (*Guard (Tom)*); Harry Goaz (*Guard (Casey)*); Mark Feltch (*Guard (George)*); Jules Sharp (*Hinkle's Assistant*); Kenneth D. Harris (*Mantrap Guard*); Vincent Gaskins (*Michael's Partner*); Cliff Haby (*Turret Operator*); Tonie Perensky (*Ember Waitress*); Randall Brady (*Ember Bartender*); Richard Linklater (*Ember Doorman*); Helen Cates (*Susan's Friend*); Kevin Crutchfield (*VIP Room Flunky*); Brad Leland (*Man Delivering Money*); John Martin (*Justice of the Peace*); Rick Perkins (*TV Delivery Man #1*); Paul Wright (*TV Delivery Man #2*); David Jensen (*Satellite Dish Installer*); Jordy Hultberg (*TV Sports Reporter*); Steve Shearer (*Detective*); Fred Ellis (*Detective's Partner*); Joe Chrest (*Mr. Rodman*); Cowboy Mouth (*Band #1*); Wheel (*Band #2*); Gal's Panic (*Band #3*); Herman the German (*Band #4*)

Steven Soderbergh's THE UNDERNEATH fuses steamy ironic elements of his debut feature, SEX, LIES, AND VIDEOTAPE, with a wide-screen film noir tale of betrayal and greed based on the 1949 Robert Siodmak picture CRISS CROSS. Soderbergh, under the pseudonym Sam Lowry (the name of the Jonathan Pryce character in Terry Gilliam's BRAZIL), shares screenwriting credit with CRISS CROSS scenarist Daniel Fuchs for this moody tale, moved from Los Angeles to Austin, Texas.

Onetime chronic gambler Michael Chambers (Peter Gallagher) is back in town, with an eye toward reuniting with ex-wife Rachel (Alison Elliott), now linked to Tommy Dundee (William Fichtner), a ruthless nightclub owner. Chambers's mother (Anjanette Comer) is about to marry Ed (Paul Dooley), who happens to work for an armored-car company, an affiliation Chambers finds hard to resist once Ed offers him a job there. Meanwhile, Rachel tempts fate by hooking up with Chambers again. When Dundee finds out, Chambers, to save his skin, suggests a robbery, an inside job which he can engineer as driver of the armored vehicle. Tommy agrees, but the heist does not go smoothly, clearing the decks for some fast and shifty maneuvering by all three principals.

THE UNDERNEATH is hardly a movie to be watched casually. Its complex narrative, replete with recurring flashbacks, continually challenges viewer concentration. Perhaps to provide a counterpoint, but also with a bow to Siodmak, Soderbergh includes a remarkable centerpiece in which a hospitalized Chambers, coming down off painkillers, struggles to separate reality from distorted imagery and to distinguish between those who would help and those who would harm him. Cinematographer Elliot Davis's shifting of colors here is as subtle as it is disquieting. Moviegoers expecting the relentless pace of big-budget action pictures may be turned off by this sequence, and, indeed, by THE UNDERNEATH's character-driven plot, which veers repeatedly into psychological explorations and stylistic flourishes.

Gallagher brings intelligence and charisma to the part of Chambers, expertly distilling that character's devious charm. Relative newcomer Elliott is a major discovery, alluring and enigmatic as Rachel, whose next move is anybody's guess. Fichtner creates a magnetic villain in Tommy, one whose coldblooded fury is never far from the surface. Adam Trese, as Chambers's brother, David, captures the simmering anger and frustration of a sibling who plays by the rules only to be overshadowed in his mother's affections by his less deserving brother. Veterans Dooley and Joe Don Baker add class to the proceedings, as does Comer, fondly remembered for her youthful appearances in THE LOVED ONE and THE APPALOOSA.

THE UNDERNEATH is more cerebral but no less eccentric than the melodramas it arguably resembles. Soderbergh takes considerable chances here and succeeds with a smart, unnerving thriller that handsomely rewards the viewer attentive to its twisting chronicle of avarice, deception and envy. (*Violence, profanity, adult situations.*) — E.K.

d, Steven Soderbergh; p, John Hardy; exec p, Joshua Donen, William Reid, Lionel Wigram; w, Sam Lowry, Daniel Fuchs (based on the screenplay "Criss Cross" by Daniel Fuchs, from the novel by Don Tracy); ph, Elliot Davis; ed, Stan Salfas; m, Cliff Martinez; prod d, Howard Cummings; art d, John Frick; set d, Jeanette Scott; sound, Paul Ledford; casting, Ronnie Yeskel; cos, Karyn Wagner, Kristen Anacker; makeup, Lizbeth Williamson; stunts, Bobby Sargent

Crime/Drama/Thriller (PR: C MPAA: R)

UNSTRUNG HEROES ★★½
(U.S.) 93m Hollywood Pictures; Roth/Arnold Productions ~ Buena Vista c

Andie MacDowell (*Selma Lidz*); John Turturro (*Sid Lidz*); Michael Richards (*Danny Lidz*); Maury Chaykin (*Arthur Lidz*); Nathan Watt (*Steven/Franz Lidz*); Kendra Krull (*Sandy Lidz*); Joey Andrews (*Ash*); Celia Weston (*Amelia*); Jack McGee (*Lindquist*); Candice Azzara (*Joanie*); Anne DeSalvo (*May*); Lillian Adams (*Aunt Estelle*); Lou Cutell (*Uncle Melvin*); Sumer

Stamper *(Nancy Oppenheim)*; Sean P. Donahue *(Ralph Crispi)*; Rabbi Harold M. Schulweis *(Rabbi Blaustein)*; Zoaunne LeRoy *(Mrs. Kantruitz)*; Vince Melocchi *(Inspector Marshall)*; Charles Patrick *(In-Crowd Boy)*; Alison Chalmers *(In-Crowd Girl)*; Chris Warfield *(Mr. Clements)*; Wayne Duvall *(Mr. Crispi)*; Andrew Craig *(Man in Line)*; Becky Ann Baker *(Mrs. Harris)*; Mary Mercier *(Waitress)*; Len Costanza *(Second Doctor)*; Peter Kaitlyn *(Dr. Feldman)*; Julie Pinson *(Nurse Franklin)*

Even clever, amusing puns are quickly forgotten, and UNSTRUNG HEROES is a pun of a movie. Sentimental and entertaining in a lighthearted way, it fades from the memory even as the credits roll. It's unfortunate that the efforts of Keaton and her cast weren't put into something more durable.

Los Angeles, the early 1960s. Twelve-year-old Steven Lidz (Nathan Watt) adores his mother Selma (Andie MacDowell) while harboring more ambivalent feelings about his father, eccentric inventor Sidney (John Turturro). When Selma develops cancer and the foundation of Steven's world is shaken, Sidney—always more interested in his gadgets than his children—is too preoccupied to help. So Steven gravitates towards his father's supportive, but even more eccentric brothers. Paranoid Uncle Danny (Michael Richards) sees anti-Semitic conspiracies everywhere—he's convinced "Idaho" is an Indian word for "Jew-hater"—while while Uncle Arthur (Maury Chaykin) is an overgrown, innocent simpleton and the sweetest of souls.

Steven moves in with his uncles, whose apartment is bursting with stacks of old newspapers, photographs, and Arthur's meticulously catalogued "treasures"—what ordinary people would call junk. Arthur's prize is a collection of balls he's fished from the sewers, in which he says he can hear the joy of children. Much to his parents' dismay, Steven becomes "one of *them*," wearing disguises and calling himself "Franz." He helps Danny and Arthur elude their landlord and outsmart a city inspector.

The already tenuous familial bonds are strained when Danny convinces Franz to begin instruction for his bar mitzvah. Sidney, who has abandoned his faith (and his people, Danny charges) in favor of science and reason, is outraged. As Selma's condition worsens, Sidney struggles with the irrationality of the inevitable loss. Franz "becomes a man," and begins to emerge from his shell at school. Danny has a nervous breakdown and commits himself. After Selma's death, it's Franz who shows his father that their memories can provide the strength they need to go on.

There's no resonance to the coming-of-age story UNSTRUNG HEROES tells, because even though it's presented as a reminiscence by the adult Steven/Franz, he never tells us what it all meant to him. Tellingly, author Franz Lidz has distanced himself from this fictionalized account of his 1991 memoir. Remember the old admonition: "Just because the story's true doesn't mean it'll make a good movie." Had UNSTRUNG HEROES delved more deeply into the history and relationships of the brothers, it would be a more interesting picture. As it stands, this trifling character study still hinges on the portrayals of Danny and Sidney. Turturro gives Sidney the right obsessive edge, but Richards—famous for playing hipster doofus Kramer on TV's "Seinfeld"—plays Danny as an irritable doofus. In his hands, Danny's mental problems are little more than an excuse for slapstick pratfalls.

UNSTRUNG HEROES is Diane Keaton's first feature film as director—her previous credits include the documentary HEAVEN and episodes of "China Beach" and "Twin Peaks" for television—and in collaboration with cinematographer Phedon Papamichael, she crafted a movie filled with lovely and lyrical images and scenes. With a stronger story at her disposal, she could be a directing force with which to reckon. *(Adult situations.)* — P.R.

d, Diane Keaton; p, Donna Roth, Susan Arnold, William Badalato; assoc p, Joe Kelly, Jackie Rubin; w, Richard LaGravenese (based on the book by Franz Lidz); ph, Phedon Papamichael; ed, Lisa Churgin; m, Thomas Newman; prod d, Garreth Stover; art d, Chris Cornwell; set d, Larry Dias; sound, Robert J. Anderson, Jr. (mixer); casting, Gail Levin; cos, Jill Ohanneson; makeup, Patricia A. Gerhardt; stunts, Ernie Orsatti, Fred Lerner

AAN Best Musical or Comedy Score: Thomas Newman

Comedy/Drama   **(PR: A   MPAA: PG)**

UNZIPPED   ★★★½
(U.S.) 80m Hachette Filipacchi Productions; Elle Magazine ~ Miramax c

Isaac Mizrahi; Nina Santisi; Eartha Kitt; Sandra Bernhard; Naomi Campbell; Mark Morris; Madonna; Roseanne

UNZIPPED is a stylish, highly entertaining documentary portrait of New York fashion designer Isaac Mizrahi.

UNZIPPED opens with a dark and dejected Mizrahi, having just read the overwhelmingly negative reviews of his 1994 spring collection. This engaging documentary traces the development of his next collection. It reveals Mizrahi's design process and how he often draws inspiration from movies and television. For this collection, he is inspired by NANOOK OF THE NORTH and CALL OF THE WILD, wanting to create a "50s cheesecake meets Eskimo" look, or "Giselle meets Fred Flintstone." UNZIPPED provides a behind-the-scenes look at the technical process of fashion design—sketching, making patterns, choosing fabrics and accessories, tailoring—as well as the business of fashion: the models, the high-profile clients, the shows, the media. UNZIPPED shows Mizrahi shooting a magazine cover with Cindy Crawford and arguing with Naomi Campbell about removing her navel ring. He meets with Eartha Kitt about making gowns for her, and hangs out with his friends, performer Sandra Bernhard and choreographer Mark Morris. He courts Candy Pratts from *Vogue* and Polly Mellen from *Allure*. The colorful Mizrahi confides his faith in the ouija board for design direction, his love of Mary Tyler Moore's spirit and style ("along with Jackie Kennedy she shaped American taste"), and his admiration for the cool gentility of Anton Walbrook's character in THE RED SHOES. The chubby Jewish boy from Brooklyn jokes around with his proud mother, Sarah Mizrahi, who has been an inspiration to his career. The creative genius tussles with his vice president and creative director, Nina Santisi, about his wild ideas for staging the show. Then just days before Mizrahi is about to unveil his collection, the trade magazine *WWD* features a front-page story announcing that the theme of the latest collection by French designer Jean-Paul Gaultier is "Eskimo Chic." Mizrahi plummets into the dumps again. How could another designer have exactly the same idea at the same time? The movie builds to a fitting climax, with a witty and colorful runway show. UNZIPPED ends with Mizrahi reading the reviews the following morning; the show and the collection are a triumph.

Winner of the Audience Award at the Sundance Film Festival, UNZIPPED is the first film from fashion photographer Douglas Keeve. His affectionately ambivalent approach to the fashion industry is refreshing after Robert Altman's seriously dull satire READY TO WEAR and the sheer self-promotion of fashion television shows. UNZIPPED also works as a playful, intimate profile of Isaac Mizrahi and a good suspense thriller as the countdown to Mizrahi's fall collection takes place. Beautifully filmed by Ellen Kuras, UNZIPPED mixes grainy black-and-white, video, and brilliant Technicolor to amazing effect. UN-ZIPPED is funny and flamboyant, camp and creative, warm and whimsical, hip and happening, just like its subject. (Profanity.) — J.S.

d, Douglas Keeve; p, Michael Alden; exec p, David J. Pecker, Nina Santisi; co-p, Paul DeBenedictis, Keith Estabrook; ph, Ellen Kuras; ed, Paula Heredia

Documentary (PR: C MPAA: R)

UP TO A CERTAIN POINT ★★★
(Cuba) 70m Instituto Cubana Del Arte y Industria Cinematograficos; Habana ~ New Yorker Video c
(HASTA CIERTO PUNTO)

Oscar Alvarez (Oscar); Mirta Ibarra (Lina); Coralia Veloz (Marian); Omar Valdes (Arturo); Ana Vina (Flora); Rogelio Blain (Diego); Claudio A. Tamayo (Claudio); Luis Celeiro (Quinones); Lazaro Nunez (Funcionario); Elsa Medina (Vecina); Marisela Justiz (Obrera)

This subtly acted docudrama is by veteran filmmaker Tomas Gutierrez Alea, whose dazzling STRAWBERRY AND CHOCO-LATE won Cuba's first Best Foreign Film nomination in Hollywood's 1995 Oscar derby. Though far from Oscar caliber, this thought-provoker snakes around the hard truths a film director-protagonist avoids, both in his private life and in the documentary he toys with finishing.

In the midst of a successful career, multitalented writer Oscar (Oscar Alvarez) scratches his seven-year itch while researching a documentary about machismo in the labor class. In attempting to get under the skin of the common man and investigate how his views were affected by the Revolution, Oscar becomes infatuated with vibrant Lina (Mirta Ibarra), who works side by side with the dockworkers. He even bases a role for his actress wife Marian (Coralia Veloz) on Lina. Both a dedicated single mother and a dedicated activist, Lina fills Oscar in on the workers movement and her own progress defying female stereotypes. Selfishly resisting any reflection upon the damage to his marriage or the way he's compromising his film project, Oscar is furious when his partner Arturo (Omar Valdes) decides to complete the complex film essay himself. Like some of the interviewed workers who favor complacency over action, Oscar will only commit himself up to a certain point. Despite his education, he falls prey to the same unreasoning macho jealousy as the common folk. By limiting himself to a worldview that only emphasizes his needs, Oscar's up-to-a-certain point mentality leaves all his relationships in limbo.

Large chunks of footage are devoted to interviews with real-life blue collar males, who offer invaluable insights into Castro's Cuba and the day-to-day existence of the working poor under his regime. Equally revealing is this movie's glimpse into the attitudes of the intelligentsia slumming among the less privileged for artistic validation. Made on the 25th anniversary of the Revolution and released to US home video in 1995, this ambitious drama charts the course of changing mind-sets through the decades; it makes the perfect bookend for Alea's earlier art-house classic, MEMORIES OF UNDERDEVELOPMENT (1968). Although UP TO A CERTAIN POINT does not jell, its mass of contradictions are worth consideration. The film is a brave attempt to equate the resistance to male-female equality in the lower middle classes with the larger issue of the set-in-its-ways government's control of its citizenry. Professing to love Lina, Oscar wishes to imprison her as a traditional mistress; his self-serving neediness reflects poorly on his enlightenment. Although the movie ends ambiguously with Lina symbolically boarding a plane, the protagonist Oscar has more in common with the

traditionalist workmen than he might want to admit. One interviewee boasts: "I've changed up to a certain point. I'm probably at 80 percent, but they'll never get me to 100 percent. No way." Obviously, sexist political attitudes changed quite slowly during this 25-year period. For better or worse, this unresolved diary of a filmmaker is 80 percent adept soul-searching and 20 percent artistic indecisiveness by an acclaimed moviemaker. (Profanity, violence, sexual situations.) — R.P.

d, Tomas Gutierrez Alea; p, Humberto Hernandez; w, Juan Carlos Tabio, Serafin Quinones, Tomas Gutierrez Alea; ph, Mario Garcia Joya; ed, Miriam Talavera; m, Leo Brouwer; prod d, Pedro Lopez; sound, Germinal Hernandez; cos, Jose Manuel Villa; makeup, Grisell Cordero, Lisette Revilla

Drama/Political/Docudrama (PR: C MPAA: NR)

USUAL SUSPECTS, THE ★★★
(U.S.) 96m Rosco Film GMBH; Blue Parrott Productions; Bad Hat Harry Productions; PolyGram; Spellings Films International ~ Gramercy c

Stephen Baldwin (McManus); Gabriel Byrne (Dean Keaton); Benicio Del Toro (Fenster); Kevin Pollak (Hockney); Kevin Spacey (Roger "Verbal" Kint); Chazz Palminteri (Kujan); Pete Postlethwaite (Kobayashi); Suzy Amis (Edie); Giancarlo Esposito (Jack Baer); Dan Hedaya (Sgt. Rabin); Paul Bartel (Smuggler); Carl Bressler (Saul Berg); Phillip Simon (Fortier); Jack Shearer (Renault); Christine Estabrook (Dr. Plummer); Clark Gregg (Dr. Walters); Morgan Hunter (Arkosh Kovash); Ken Daly (Translator); Michelle Clunie (Sketch Artist); Louis Lombardi (Strausz); Frank Medrano (Rizzi); Ron Gilbert (Daniel Metz-Heiser); Smadar Hanson (Keyser Soze's Wife); Vito D'Ambrosio (Customer); Gene Lythgow (Cop on Pier); Bob Elmore (Bodyguard #1); David Powledge (Bodyguard #2); Bob Pennetta (Bodyguard #3); Bill Bates (Bodyguard #4); Castulo Guerra (Arturro Marquez); Peter Rocca (Arturro's Bodyguard); Bert Williams (Old Cop)

This twisty and twisted yarn is one of the more successful entries in the post-Tarantino cycle of hip, violent crime flicks. Since Bryan Singer's only previous directing credit is 1993's PUBLIC ACCESS, which played festivals but never found a distributor, THE USUAL SUSPECTS marks a promising major-league debut.

Special investigator Kujan (Chazz Palminteri) grills "Verbal" Kint (Kevin Spacey), a crippled con-man who is the lone survivor of an LA boat explosion that claimed more than 20 victims. Kujan wants to confirm that his nemesis, the rogue cop Keaton (Gabriel Byrne), is actually dead.

Kint relates the majority of the film in flashback, beginning with the fateful day when five shifty guys meet in a police-station lineup in New York City. Along with dour Keaton, Kint encounters cheerfully sociopathic McManus (Stephen Baldwin), mordantly sarcastic Hockney (Kevin Pollak), and Fenster (Benicio Del Toro), whose speech is virtually incomprehensible. Together they plot to steal a small fortune in gems from "New York's Finest Taxi Service"—crooked cops who provide escort service for visiting drug kingpins.

They head for LA, where McManus connects with his fence, Redfoot (Peter Greene), who double-crosses them into killing a lawyer. The murder draws the attention of a nebulous underground figure named Keyser Soze. Kobayashi (Pete Postlethwaite), Soze's agent, informs the gang that their meeting was no accident: they were brought together because each one has stolen something from Soze. They are ordered to repay their debt by stealing $90 million in cocaine from a boatload of Hungarians. Fenster balks, and is found dead soon after. Keaton, an apparently reluctant participant, urges the rest to go forward with the job. They pull off the robbery with great flair, but they're soon being picked off one by one, presumably by Soze.

Meanwhile, FBI agent Baer (Giancarlo Esposito) is searching for Soze. A Hungarian survivor fished out of the bay claims to have seen Soze. Kint describes Soze as unimaginably evil, but Kujan is only interested in Keaton and dismisses Soze as a criminal bogey man.

Kujan browbeats Kint into admitting that his sympathetic portrait of Keaton is false, and even suggests that Keaton himself is Soze and has faked his own death. After Kint is released, Kujan notices that many of the names in Kint's story can be found on the office bulletin board. Baer rushes in with a new explanation of the boat caper: it was an elaborate scheme to murder a Federal informant who knew Soze. A faxed sketch of Soze comes in: it's Kint. Kujan races to the street, but he's too late.

THE USUAL SUSPECTS is an intricately plotted, densely layered story, and although the resolution of Soze's identity is dramatically fulfilling—and not all that surprising—it has the effect of undermining the entire narrative. It's possible that none of the characters besides Kint and Keaton are "real"—and even if they are, we know the Keaton we've been watching isn't the "real" Keaton. But fans of taut, self-consciously clever puzzles will find this film a delightful excursion through a narrative maze, full of talented actors having great fun with their quirky, nasty characters. Pollak shines early, though his good lines diminish as the film progresses, and Baldwin is surprisingly chilling. Byrne holds the center with his patented brooding intensity, and Del Toro is simply hysterical as a jumble of visual and verbal tics. But it's Spacey who carries the weight of the film, and he rises admirably to the challenge of epitomizing pure evil with a blandly human face.

If the audience tumbles to the McGuffin before the cops do, that's par for the genre. The script (by Singer's longtime friend and partner Christopher McQuarrie) is spiced with juicy moments, even if it is occasionally lapses into dull, exposition-laden speeches. While it's inevitable that every new crime film will be compared to Tarantino, Singer's true influences appear to be much more traditional filmmakers, like George Roy Hill, Don Siegel and, of course, Hitchcock (with a few obvious nods to the Coen brothers and John Woo). From them he culls a variety of techniques that keep the film moving visually even when the story seems to be wandering or confused. It's a remarkably assured film for a 28-year-old whiz kid (enhanced by John Ottman's superb editing job), and it bodes well for his career. (*Violence, profanity, adult situations.*) — R.S.

d, Bryan Singer; p, Bryan Singer, Michael McDonnell; exec p, Robert Jones, Hans Brockmann, Francois Duplat, Art Horan; co-p, Kenneth Kokin; w, Christopher McQuarrie; ph, Newton Thomas Sigel; ed, John Ottman; m, John Ottman; prod d, Howard Cummings; art d, David Lazan; set d, Sara Andrews; sound, Geoffrey Patterson (mixer), Jack Keller (recordist), David Behle (recordist); fx, Roy Downey; casting, Francine Maisler; cos, Louise Mingenbach; makeup, Michelle Buhler, David Barton; stunts, Gary Jensen

AA Best Supporting Actor: Kevin Spacey; *AA Best Original Screenplay:* Christopher McQuarrie

Crime/Thriller (PR: O MPAA: R)

VALLEY OF ABRAHAM, THE ★★½
(Portugal/France/Switzerland) 187m Madragoa Films; Gemini Films; Light Night ~ Artificial Eye c
(VALE ABRAAO)

Maria Barroso *(Narrator)*; Leonor Silveira *(Ema Cardeano)*; Cecile Sanz de Alba *(Young Ema)*; Luis Miguel Cintra *(Carlos de Paiva)*; Rui de Carvalho *(Paulino Cardeano)*; Luis Lima Barreto *(Pedro Lumiares)*; Micheline Larpin *(Simona)*; Diogo Doria *(Fernando Osorio)*; Jose Pinto *(Caires)*; Filipe Cochofel *(Fortunato)*; Joao Perry *(Padre Dossem)*; Gloria de Matos *(Maria Do Loreto)*; Antonio Reis *(Semblano)*; Isabel Ruth *(Ritinha)*; Laura Soveral *(Tia Augusta)*; Monique Dodd *(Chelinha)*; Juliana Samarine *(Nelson's Wife)*; Miguel Guilherme *(Motorcyclist)*; Nuno Vieira de Almeida *(Nelson)*; Isabel de Castro *(Melo Sister)*; J'lia Bulsel *(Melo Sister)*; Dina Treno *(Branca)*; Dalila Carmo e Sousa *(Marina)*; Paula Seabra *(Alice)*; Vanda Fernandes *(Lolota as a Young Child)*; Sofia Alves *(Lolota as a Little Girl)*; Leonor Viseu *(Luisona as a Young Child)*; Beatriz Batarda *(Luisona as a Little Girl)*; Antonio Wagner *(Baltazar)*; Argentina Rocha *(Carlos' First Wife)*; Josefina Hungaro *(Nelson's Mother)*; Fernando Bento *(Dr. Carmesim)*; Manuel Enes *(Homero)*; Ana Queirus *(Paiva Sister)*; Mercedes Brawand *(Paiva Sister)*; David Cardoso *(Gardener)*; Vaz Mendes *(Teenage Boy)*; Rui Oliveira *(Teenage Boy)*; Joaquim Nogueira *(Narciso)*; Lurdes Rocha *(Dressmaker)*; Marques de Aredo *(Padre)*; Padre Pires *(Padre)*

Veteran Portuguese director Manoel de Oliveira transplants the 19th century into the present in THE VALLEY OF ABRAHAM, a loose rendition of Flaubert's classic novel *Madame Bovary*. This is Oliveira's 13th film, but the first to be distributed to a US audience. Born in 1908, Oliveira is one of the few living directors whose career reaches back to the silent era—his first film, HARD LABOR ON THE RIVER DOURO (1931), was a silent documentary.

The narrative recounts the life of Ema, from young girlhood through adulthood to death. The defining experience of the young Ema (Cecil Sanz de Alba) is the intoxication experienced while standing on the veranda in her white dress and causing car crashes with her astounding beauty. On her way to meet two veteran society women, she catches her reflection in a mirror and is mesmerized. The women size her up and determine that she will be dangerous. At age 14, she meets the respectable doctor Carlos de Paiva (Luis Miguel Cintra) while dining with her father, and is not impressed. Several years later, she marries him and enters a life of bourgeois drawing rooms, convention, and the boredom of leisure.

It is in this social environment that the mature Ema (Leonor Silveira) begins to feed insatiably on the power her beauty exerts over men. She drifts from affair to affair and becomes increasingly estranged from her husband and two daughters. Her lovers range considerably in age and social status, the only prerequisite being that they desire her. None of these relationships proves to be either fulfilling or even remotely interesting. Her independence and alienation trouble family members, who are ultimately helpless in the face of her desire. Through the years, she periodically returns to the estate of her first lover despite his absence. It is here that her heavily foreshadowed death occurs when she falls through two weak boards on the pier.

Director Oliveira has said that this film is about how a woman's poetic outlook leads systematically to her ruin, but Ema's outlook is never firmly established as poetic, and bears closer resemblances to severe narcissism. Like her counterparts in the 19th century, she lives through men—their status, their gaze, and their desires; her only resistance is domestic sexual transgression, sighs, aloofness, and silence. As a portrayal of a woman, the character is oddly displaced in the 20th century and even inappropriate, and the film never clearly establishes a reason for this gesture.

In the tradition of the 19th-century novel, the film is narrated by an unnamed male, and like *Madame Bovary*, it offers a distinctly male and modernist interpretation of women. If there is a poetic vision represented in the film, it is to be found here, in the romanticism which extols the fascination, mystery, and unbearable beauty of a woman—a description that never quite seems to fit the Ema presented. When one of the men in the film compares Ema to Flaubert's character, she disagrees, but unfortunately this is not pursued.

At over three hours in length, the film lingers with painstaking detail on a social class characterized by boredom and pretension. A great deal of screen time is devoted to the false intellectualism and forced mannerisms of dinner party conversations, as Ema listens intently with studied grace, self-consciousness, and feminine poise. The one moment of relief is offered when husband Carlos loses his composure and yanks a purring cat from the lap of his sensual wife and throws it violently at the camera, momentarily exposing the stifled anger and patronizing misogyny lurking behind the pedestal. (Sexual situations.) — R.C.

d, Manoel de Oliveira; p, Paulo Branco; w, Manoel de Oliveira (based on the novel Vale Abraao by Augustina Bessa-Luis); ph, Mario Barroso; ed, Manoel de Oliveira, Valerie Loiseleux; prod d, Maria Jose Branco; sound, Christophe Winding (mixer), Henri Maikoff; casting, Agnes Fierobe; cos, Isabel Branco; makeup, Michelle Bernet

Drama   **(PR: C   MPAA: NR)**

VAMPIRE IN BROOKLYN   ★★
(U.S.) 103m Eddie Murphy Productions;
Paramount ~ Paramount c

Eddie Murphy (Maximillian/Preacher Pauley/Guido); Angela Bassett (Rita); Allen Payne (Justice); Kadeem Hardison (Julius); John Witherspoon (Silas); Zakes Mokae (Dr. Zeko); Joanna Cassidy (Dewey); Simbi Khali (Nikki); Messiri Freeman (Eva); Kelly Cinnante (Officer); Nick Corri (Anthony); W. Earl Brown (Thrasher); Ayo Adeyemi (Bartender); Troy Curvey, Jr. (Choir Leader); Vickilyn Reynolds (Mrs. Brown); William Blount (Deacon Brown); Joe Costanza (Bear); John La Motta (Lizzy); Marcelo Tubert (Waiter); Nick DeMauro (Caprisi); Jerry Hall (Woman in Park); Mark Haining (Man in Park); Wendy Robie (Zealot in Police Station); Alyse Mandel (Cop); Larry Paul Marshall (Greeter at Church); Vince Micelli (Checker Player); Oren Waters; Carlton Davis; Clive Ross; Michael Hyde; Maxine Waters Willard; Josef Powell; Roy Galloway; Carmen Carter; Julie Waters Tillman; Carmen Twillie (Singers); Ray Combs (Game Show Host)

An attempt by comic star Eddie Murphy to expand his range, VAMPIRE IN BROOKLYN never quite commits to either scares or laughs. The result is a film that tries to appeal to two audiences and doesn't satisfy either.

Maximillian (Murphy), the last of a race of Caribbean vampires, comes to Brooklyn in search of a half-human, half-vampire woman he intends to make his bride. Rita (Angela Bassett) is a no-nonsense cop who's unaware of her blood-sucking heritage, and is involved in a burgeoning romantic relationship with her partner, Justice (Allan Payne). Maximilian transforms street punk Julius (Kadeem Hardison) into his reluctant, slowly decomposing right-hand ghoul, and sets out to seduce Rita. He first wins over her sluttish roommate Nikki (Simbi Khali), whom he kills.

Justice, suspicious of Maximilian, consults with supernatural expert Dr. Zeko (Zakes Mokae) as Rita falls ever deeper under Maximilian's spell. Though she resists at first, Rita eventually succumbs to his bite and becomes a full-fledged vampire. Justice arrives at Maximilian's lair and, fending off Julius's attacks, convinces Rita to turn away from the dark side. Maximilian ends

up with a stake in his heart. Freed from his spell, Rita leaves with Justice, while Julius looks forward to enjoying his status as the foremost ghoul in town.

After a series of comedies that performed below expectations, VAMPIRE IN BROOKLYN was intended to mark Murphy's shift into a more serious leading role, with fright veteran Wes Craven at the helm to assure that the horror elements wouldn't be subjugated to guffaws. But it's clear that someone, whether Murphy or Paramount Pictures, wasn't entirely comfortable with the star entirely leaving his humorous persona behind. In keeping with the tradition of his previous foreigner-in-New-York comedy, COMING TO AMERICA, Murphy also appears in a pair of heavily made-up comic supporting roles. As jittery street hood Guido and Preacher Pauley, who exhorts that "evil is good," Murphy reaffirms his talent for his hilarious mimicry. But the comic cameos distract from his straightforward leading performance, which isn't bad at all.

VAMPIRE IN BROOKLYN is also hurt by the fact that, beyond the gimmick of casting Murphy as a vampire, the movie doesn't have any new thoughts about vampires. That said, Bassett brings considerable strength and intelligence to her familiar role, and Hardison—a kind of homeboy Renfield—has some very funny bits. Craven drenches the film in eerie mood, though shooting it in LA precluded capturing the New York atmosphere that might have helped distinguish it. The picture also lacks the social concerns that gave depth to Craven's underrated THE PEOPLE UNDER THE STAIRS (1991). Though VAMPIRE IN BROOKLYN makes it evident that Murphy and Craven aren't such strange bedfellows as they may at first seem, the movie would have been more successful had one of them given himself over more entirely to the artistic approach of the other.

During the film's production, 32-year-old stuntwoman Sonja Davis died while doubling for Bassett in a 45-foot fall from a rooftop, prompting an investigation by the California Occupational Safety and Health Administration and a suit filed by Davis's family against Eddie Murphy, Paramount Pictures, Wes Craven and others involved with the production. (Graphic violence, nudity, sexual situations, extreme profanity.) — M.G.

d, Wes Craven; p, Eddie Murphy, Mark Lipsky; exec p, Marianne Maddalena, Stuart M. Besser; assoc p, Jeffrey Fenner; co-p, Ray Murphy, Jr., Dixie J. Capp; w, Charles Murphy, Christopher Parker, Michael Lucker (from a story by Charles Murphy, Eddie Murphy, and Vernon Lynch, Jr.); ph, Mark Irwin; ed, Patrick Lussier; m, J. Peter Robinson; art d, Gary Diamond, Cynthia Charette; set d, Robert Kensinger; ch, Eartha Robinson; sound, Jim Stuebe (mixer), Paul Clay (design); fx, Jessica L. Huebner, Gene Warren, Fantasy II, Peter M. Chesney, Image Engineering; casting, Eileen Mack Knight; cos, Ha Nguyen; makeup, Bernadine M. Anderson, Marie Carter, Erin Haggerty, Karrie Aubuchon, Kurtzman, Nicotero & Berger EFX Group; stunts, Alan Oliney

Horror/Comedy   **(PR: C   MPAA: R)**

VAMPIRES AND OTHER STEREOTYPES   ★★
(U.S.) 87m Brimstone Productions ~
Brimstone Productions c/bw

William White (Ivan); Wendy Bednarz (Kirsten); Ed Hubbard (Harry); Rick Poli (Albert); Anna DiPace (Linda); Suzanne Scott (Jennifer); Mick McCleery (Erik); Laura McLauchlin (Rosa); Monica Baxavanis (Adriana); Bean Miller (Lizard King); Mike Memphis (The King); Fia Perera (She Demon); Sally Narkis (Waitress from Hell); Rutger Powell (Bug Monster); Kevin J. Lindenmuth (Swamp Monster); Lawrence McCleery (No-Face); Brett Heniss (The Hand); Scott Sliger (Snot-Head); Tim Kehlenbach (*Headless Corpse*); J.B. Macabre (*Dead-Head Voice*); Tim Schoeber (*Boyfriend #1*); Pat Ryan (*Boyfriend #2*); Ken Nocito (*Boyfriend #3*); John Innocenzo (*Boyfriend #4*); Gary Putz (*Boyfriend #5*); John Collins (*Boyfriend #6*)

Only partially true to its title, this direct-to-video horror film deals just briefly with vampires but contains an unfortunate number of genre stereotypes.

In a Manhattan warehouse, demon hunters Ivan (William White) and Harry (Ed Hubbard) rescue the irascible Albert (Rick Poli) from a supernatural executioner. They are soon joined by college gals Kirsten (Wendy Bednarz), Linda (Anna DiPace), and Jennifer (Suzanne Scott), who have been led there by Kirsten's new boyfriend, Erik (Mick McCleery), in search of a party. However, the warehouse is actually a gateway to hell, and when Jennifer cuts her hand and bleeds on the floor, the place is thrust into a netherworld between the two regions. Erik appears to escape through a glowing passage, but Albert (who is Kirsten's father) dies trying to follow.

As supernatural creatures assault the group, it transpires that Albert promised Kirsten to the underworld before her birth, and Erik is in fact the demon supposed to deliver her. Kirsten, however, is rescued by Ivan, who has fallen for her. Both he and Harry turn out to be vampires who protect humans from hell's spawn on Earth. Not quite up to the task, though, Harry succumbs to "the hunger" and kills Linda, and Ivan in turn kills him. The sun rises, and Ivan and Kirsten escape the warehouse—but the injured Jennifer is left behind, and the demons claim her.

An opening scene shot in black-and-white and the climactic discussions of the vampires' place on Earth suggest slight aspirations to art, but for the most part VAMPIRES AND OTHER STEREOTYPES is typical low-budget horror, clearly inspired in both story and sensibility by Sam Raimi's EVIL DEAD II. Although well-produced for a movie of this kind—with slick-looking video photography transferred to film—this production lacks the pace and originality to make up for its lackadaisical plotting. More often than not, the humor is simply goofy, and—as in so many films of this type—the approach to the makeup effects favors quantity over quality.

The acting is a mixed bag, with the leads registering stronger than the supporting cast, though they all have their share of awkward line readings. Moreover, the twist on genre standards indicated by the title might have carried more resonance had Ivan and Harry's true identities been established earlier instead of being withheld for a last-act surprise. (*Graphic violence, profanity.*) — M.G.

d, Kevin J. Lindenmuth; p, Kevin J. Lindenmuth; w, Kevin J. Lindenmuth; ph, Tullio Tedeschi; ed, Kevin J. Lindenmuth; m, The Krypt; prod d, One By One Film and Video; fx, Scott Sliger, Scott Hart, Imageffects Studios

Horror **(PR: O MPAA: NR)**

VILLAGE OF THE DAMNED ★★
(U.S.) 99m Alphaville Productions ~ Universal c

Christopher Reeve (*Alan Chaffee*); Kirstie Alley (*Dr. Susan Verner*); Linda Kozlowski (*Jill McGowan*); Michael Pare (*Frank McGowan*); Meredith Salenger (*Melanie Roberts*); Mark Hamill (*Reverend George*); Pippa Pearthree (*Mrs. Sarah Miller*); Peter Jason (*Ben Blum*); Constance Forslund (*Callie Blum*); Karen Kahn (*Barbara Chaffee*); Thomas Dekker (*David*); Lindsey Haun (*Mara*); Cody Dorkin (*Robert*); Trishalee Hardy (*Julie*); Jessye Quarry (*Dorothy*); Adam Robbins (*Isaac*); Chelsea DeRidder Simms (*Matt*); Renee Rene Simms (*Casey*); Danielle Wiener (*Lily*); Hillary Harvey (*Mara—Age 1*); Bradley Wilhelm (*David—Age 9 Months*); Jennifer Wilheim (*Mara/David—Age 4*

Months); Buck Flower (*Carlton*); Squire Fridell (*The Sheriff*); Darryl Jones (*CHP*); Ed Corbett (*Older Deputy*); Ross Martineau (*Younger Deputy*); Skip Richardson (*Deputy*); Tony Haney (*Dr. Bush*); Montgomery Hom (*Technician*); Steve Chambers (*Trooper No. 1*); Ron Kaell (*Trooper No. 2*); Lane Nishikawa (*Scientist*); Michael Halton (*Station Attendant Harold*); Julie Eccles (*Eileen Moore*); Lois Saunders (*Doctor at Clinic*); Sidney Baldwin (*Labor Room Physician*); Wendolyn Lee (*Nurse No. 5*); Kathleen Turco-Lyon (*Nurse No. 3*); Abigail Van Alyn (*Nurse No. 1*); Roy Conrad (*Oliver*); Dan Belzer (*Young Husband*); Dena Martinez (*Young Wife*); Alice Barden (*Woman at Town Hall*); John Brebner (*Man at Town Hall*); Ralph Miller (*Villager*); Rip Haight (*Man at Gas Station Phone*)

In John Carpenter's VILLAGE OF THE DAMNED a quaint old village becomes host to an alien species in the form of white haired children sharing the same soul and possessing destructive powers.

Problems begin in the peaceful coastal village of Midwich when one day all the villagers collapse simultaneously. Officials arrive but no one can enter the village without losing consciousness. When the blackout is lifted, all the women, including a virgin, are pregnant. The government wants to study the children and agrees to pay each woman to take her baby to term. All the children survive but one, who is whisked away for a private autopsy by Dr. Susan Verner (Kirstie Alley), an ambitious research scientist, who keeps secret the knowledge that the corpse reverts to alien form.

The children resemble humans physically, except for their white hair and flaming eyes, but lack feelings, exhibit superior intelligence, share a group consciousness, and tend to walk in line in male and female pairs. One of the children, David (Thomas Dekker), does not have a partner as a result of the stillbirth and begins to stray away from the others and develop human feelings. The children display certain mental powers: they can read minds and redirect the will so that their victims bring on their own destruction. Suicides begin occurring throughout the village, and it seems no one can stop the children, until the town doctor (Christopher Reeve) discovers that he can block his mind and slip some dynamite into their den. The dynamite destroys the children, but David is rescued by his mother (Linda Kozlowski), opening up the possibility for a sequel.

Based on the novel *The Midwich Cuckoos* by John Wyndham and the 1960 English film of the same title, the story follows a traditional theme best rendered in INVASION OF THE BODY SNATCHERS (1956), which some critics interpreted as being representative of cold war fears, especially the threat Communism poses to individualism.

In a broader sense, VILLAGE OF THE DAMNED projects the most basic of human terrors: the fear of group power overtaking individual will is expressed in the children as well as in the government and medical establishment which intervene in the realm of the body by manipulating reproductive decisions. In the homogeneous setting of the village, any difference is a radical threat, and the children exemplify that difference in its most extreme form. The scene where all the women give birth simultaneously makes even the natural processes of life itself terrifying. And the destruction wrought by the children is merely predicated by their biological need to survive at any cost and to eliminate anything which impedes that goal. (*Adult situations, sexual situations, violence, profanity.*) — R.C.

d, John Carpenter; p, Michael Preger, Sandy King; exec p, Shep Gordon, Andre Blay, Ted Vernon; co-p, David Chakler; w, David Himmelstein (based on the novel *The Midwich Cuckoos* by John Wyndham and the 1960 screenplay by Stirling Silliphant, Wolf

Rilla, and George Barclay); ph, Gary B. Kibbe; ed, Edward A. Warschilka; m, Dave Davies, John Carpenter; prod d, Rodger Maus; art d, Christa Munro; set d, Don De Fina, Rick Brown; sound, Thomas Causey (mixer); fx, Bruce Nicholson, Industrial Light & Magic; casting, Reuben Cannon; makeup, Ken Chase, Erin Haggerty, K.N.B. EFX Group; stunts, Jeff Imada

Science Fiction/Horror (PR: C MPAA: R)

VIRTUOSITY ★★½
(U.S.) 105m Paramount ~ Paramount c

Denzel Washington *(Parker Barnes)*; Kelly Lynch *(Madison Carter)*; Russell Crowe *(Sid 6.7)*; Stephen Spinella *(Lindenmeyer)*; William Forsythe *(William Cochran)*; Louise Fletcher *(Elizabeth Deane)*; William Fichtner *(Wallace)*; Costas Mandylor *(John Donovan)*; Kevin J. O'Connor *(Clyde Reilly)*; Kaley Cuoco *(Karin)*; Christopher Murray *(Matthew Grimes)*; Heidi Schanz *(Sheila 3.2)*; Traci Lords *(Media Zone Singer)*; J. Gordon Noice *(Big Red)*; Mari Morrow *(Linda Barnes)*; Miracle Unique Vincent *(Christine Barnes)*; Mara Duronslet *(Beautiful Woman at Olympic Stadium)*; Michael Buffer *(Emcee)*; Karen Annarino *(ISTV Reporter)*; Miguel Najera *(Rafael Debaca)*; Danny Goldring *(John Symes)*; Randall Fontana *(Ed)*; Allen Scotti *(Surgeon)*; Dwayne Chattman *(Stripped Man in Media Zone)*; Ed Marques *(Blonde Punk in Media Zone)*; Cheryl Lawson *(Pretty Woman in Media Zone)*; Kevin Loreque *(Animatronic Bartender)*; Eiko Nijo *(Geisha Hostess)*; Gauravani Buchwald *(Burly Man in Video Store)*; Rolando Molina *(Video Store Salesman)*; Gary Anthony Sturgis *(Officer at Video Store)*; Monica Allison *(Woman on Train)*; Susan Mohun *(Bystander)*; David Asman *(Metrolink Cop)*; Anthony C. Hall *(Locator Technician)*; Amy Smallman *(Aide in Cochran's Office)*; Ahmed Ahmed *(Cameraman)*; Marva Hicks *(Onscreen Talent)*; Juan A. Riojas *(Metromedia Cop)*; Steven R. Barnett *(Metromedia Cop)*; John Walcutt *(SWAT Captain)*; Michael Buchman Silver *(Undercover Cop)*; Jordan Marder *(Prison Transport Guard)*; Brogan Young *(Monitor Prison Guard)*; Laura Leigh Hughes *(Suburban Reporter)*; Dustin Nguyen *(Suburban Reporter)*; Tony Winters *(Male Newcaster)*; Virginia Watson *(Anchorwoman)*; Beverly Cohen *(Female Tabloid TV Host)*; Margot Hope *(Paula)*; Una Damon *(Woman with Video Camera)*

VIRTUOSITY begins, confusingly, in cyberspace, where it even more confusingly returns from time to time, telling an involved tale of cops and computer generated robbers played out in virtual reality.

Ex-policeman Parker Barnes (Denzel Washington) has been released from maximum security prison into interactive virtual reality to hunt down Sid 6.7 (Russell Crowe), a computer-generated sadistic criminal. Barnes's imprisonment had stemmed from his attempt to rescue his wife and child, who were kidnapped and killed by Mathew Grimes (Christopher Murray), a maniacal political assassin. Barnes had managed to track Grimes down and kill him, but, in the process, lost an arm and accidentally shot a couple of TV news reporters. His "second chance" is vouchsafed him by Elizabeth Deane (Louise Fletcher), the beleaguered head of the Law Enforcement Technical Advancement Center.

Her job is not made easier by the vicious scheming of her assistant Lindenmayer (Stephen Spinella), who releases Sid 6.7 into the real world and tries to control him, even though he is a composite of the personalitites of such unsavory characters as Charles Manson, John Wayne Gacy, Jeffrey Dahmer, and Ted Bundy. The fact that Grimes's persona has also been prgrammed into Sid only makes Barnes's mission that much more personal. Adding to the difficulty is Sid's indestructibility, namely his ability to regenerate any injured body parts with shattered glass.

Barnes is led on a high-speed chase, accompanied by Dr. Madison Carter (Kelly Lynch), a criminal psychologist doing research. Sid somehow eludes them at every turn, leaving a bloody trail of senselessly slaughtered victims. Eventually he kidnaps Carter's little girl and takes control of a cable TV station. There, he introduces a little program called "Death TV," an interactive platform for his brutal agenda. Carter confronts and kills Lindenmayer, Barnes rescues her daughter and finally manages to destroy Sid.

Years from now, people will probably look back on 1995's spate of cyberspace thrillers such as this one, JOHNNY MNEMOMIC, and STRANGE DAYS, and find them as quaint as any 1950s sci-fi epic. With their mystifyingly involved plots, cartoonish characters and endless techno-babble, they may perhaps find a cult among the more committedly nostalgic net nerds of the future. One can only marvel at the facility with which the actors can spout lines like "The sensitivity calibrations must have slipped just a tad!" or Sid's introductory "I'm a 50 terra-byte, self-evolving neuro network backflip off the high platform." As these things go, VIRTUOSITY is not bad, provided no one takes the technoid peregrinations too seriously.

The film is surprisingly well-acted, and the cinematography and editing are often ruthlessly clever. Washington brings a lot more conviction and deep inner turmoil to his cliched role than it probably deserves and is very game in the hair-raising action scenes. Lynch, who appears in a variety of impeccable Armani working woman ensembles, evinces a dry intelligence in the most nonsensical of parts. Spinella is a creepy caricature, another in a long and dishonorable line of effetely gay villains. The always watchable Kevin O'Connor makes an amusing lot of his tiny bit as an absolute sleaze of a hacker. But it is Crowe who is the real wild card here. Impeccably buffed and groomed, the image of Aryan pitilessness, his demented high spirits and physical grace call up James Cagney in his malevolently leering pre-Code heyday. *(Violence, sexual situations, adult situations, profanity.)* — D.N.

d, Brett Leonard; p, Gary Lucchesi; exec p, Howard W. Koch, Jr.; assoc p, Robert McMinn; co-p, Gimel Everett; w, Eric Bernt; ph, Gale Tattersall; ed, B.J. Sears, Rob Kobrin; m, Christopher Young; prod d, Nilo Rodis; art d, Richard Yanez-Toyon; set d, Jay Hart; sound, Thomas D. Causey (mixer), Frank Serafine (design); fx, Kenneth D. Pepiot, Jon Townley, L2 Communications; casting, Deborah Aquila, Jane Shannon; cos, Francine Jamison-Tanchuck; makeup, Edna M. Sheen, Chris Walas, Inc.; stunts, Mic Rodgers, John C. Meier, Lance Gilbert

Science Fiction/Thriller/Action (PR: O MPAA: R)

VOYAGE EN DOUCE ★★½
(France) 95m Prospectacle; Gaumont; Elefilm ~ New Yorker Video c
(AKA: TRAVELS ON THE SLY)

Dominique Sanda *(Helene)*; Geraldine Chaplin *(Lucie)*

In the 1979 French production VOYAGE EN DOUCE, released to US home video in 1995, two long-time friends travel together to the south of France to look for a summer house; during their trip, the two women remember events from their past, reveal long-held secrets, catch up with each other, and enjoy the present.

Helen (Dominique Sanda), a writer, invites her friend Lucie (Geraldine Chaplin) to accompany her on a search for a summer house after she returns home one evening and finds Lucie sulking outside her apartment door. The two women spend the evening talking about why Lucie is unhappy with her lover Francois and why she wants to leave him. Helen and Lucie then travel through countryside and small villages and visit a few houses before Helen finds a place that inspires her. The women stay in a small hotel and make three separate visits to the house at different times on consecutive days.

Helen and Lucie explore the empty house, stroll the grounds and neighboring countryside, and make trips to a town market and outdoor restaurant. They flirt with each other in bed at night, as well as with a young male waiter who delivers breakfast, and with a stranger at a restaurant. One night, after she remembers her first kiss and only sexual encounter with a woman, Lucie tries to initiate a kiss with Helen, but Helen laughs and turns away. The next day, however, Helen photographs Lucie in stages of undress on the house grounds and unbuttons Lucie's blouse.

The women return to Helen's home and family after a few days, and Lucie spends another evening before she returns to her apartment with Francois. The film concludes with Helen preparing to sneak off. She removes her panties from under her dress, stuffs extra clothes into a bag, puts on an overcoat, and leaves her apartment, but then stops and sits outside the door. It isn't clear whether she intends to go to Lucie or out into the world.

In VOYAGE EN DOUCE, the women's conversations and encounters revolve around the nature of desire and the life of the mind, the erotic and intellectual life they know and create. But the women are also quite different from each other, and this difference enriches the discussions and makes the film interesting and unpredictable. Helen is intelligent, reflective, condescending, and malicious. Lucie, on the other hand, is a more stereotypical feminine character, portrayed as whimsical, flirtatious, and more honest, though weaker. Lucie is also more daring and speaks of real events—though often with great embarrassment—while Helen is given more to fantasizing and fictionalizing her personal narratives.

While the mise-en-scene in general is reminiscent of the films of Truffaut, the film does contain several unique scenes. Most notable, screenwriter and director Michel Deville represents two events through partial flashbacks: Helen's encounter with a stranger is represented both by a sequence of still shots, like a collage of filmic images, and by her narration (which is often at odds with the images presented). On the other hand, a rape that Lucie survived is represented by the sounds of the rape juxtaposed to the images of the countryside surrounding the summer home. In the first case, the images dominate, in the second the sounds.

Another example of Deville's talent is shown in an amusing, charming, and symbolic scene which occurs at the hotel. In bed one morning Lucie imagines a new lover, and when a young man arrives with breakfast, she maneuvers him first into holding her and then kissing her. Helen directs the kiss as she imagines and perhaps desires it. Helen, ultimately unwilling or unable to betray her husband, symbolically kisses Lucie through this nameless, young male. It is to the director's credit that Helen's ambiguity is further complicated by the film's ending, where she is poised to embark on a new beginning which is uncertain to the audience, and perhaps to Helen herself. (*Nudity, sexual situations.*) — M.F.

d, Michel Deville; p, Maurice Bernart; w, Michel Deville, Francois-Regis Bastide, Camille Bourniquel, Muriel Cerf, Jean Chalon, Pierrette Fleutiaux, Patrick Gainville, Yves Navarre, Jacques Perry, Maurice Pons, Beatrice Privat, Suzanne Prou, Frederic Rey, Dominique Rolin, Isaure DeSaint-Pierre; ph, Claude Lecomte; ed, Raymonde Guyot; m, Quentin Demanne; art d, Catherine Ardouin; sound, Henry Moline, Joel Beldent

Drama   (PR: O   MPAA: NR)

WAITING TO EXHALE ★★½
(U.S.) 121m Schindler-Swerdlow
Productions ~ 20th Century Fox c

Whitney Houston *(Savannah)*; Angela Bassett *(Bernadine)*; Loretta Devine *(Gloria)*; Lela Rochon *(Robin)*; Gregory Hines *(Marvin)*; Dennis Haysbert *(Kenneth)*; Mykelti Williamson *(Troy)*; Michael Beach *(John, Sr.)*; Leon *(Russell)*; Wendell Pierce *(Michael)*; Donald Adeosun Faison *(Tarik)*; Jeffrey D. Sams *(Lionel)*; Jazz Raycole *(Onika)*; Brandon Hammond *(John, Jr.)*; Kenya Moore *(Denise)*; Lamont Johnson *(Joseph)*; Wren T. Brown *(Minister)*; Theo *(On Air D.J.)*; Ken Love *(D.J. at the Hermosa)*; Graham Galloway *(Fireman)*; Starletta DuPois *(Savannah's Mother)*; Shari L. Carpenter *(Savannah's Assistant)*; Thomas R. Leander *(Interviewer)*; Cordell Conway; Lee Wells, Jr.; Hope Brown *(People at Hermosa Table)*; Delaina Mitchell *(Tarik's Girl Friend)*; Luis Sharpe *(Herbert)*; Joseph S. Myers *(Security Guard at John's Office)*; Ezra Swerdlow *(Wild Bill)*; Ellin La Var *(Hairdresser)*; Patricia Anne Fox *(Customer at Hair Salon)*; Wally Bujack *(Judge)*

A surprise hit that inspired reams of puzzled cultural analysis, WAITING TO EXHALE follows a year in the lives of four African-American women living in Arizona. Though irresistibly watchable, this adaptation of Terry McMillan's best-selling book is ultimately unsatisfying—it's the movie equivalent of junk food.

Each of the four women suffers the pain of romantic heartbreak, but they're nourished and sustained by their friendships with one another. The most dramatic trouble is Bernadine's (Angela Bassett): her wealthy husband (Michael Beach) leaves her for his Caucasian bookkeeper. Once she gets over her initial fury—by setting fire to his expensive car, with all his chic clothes inside—Bernadine fights her husband in divorce court, while cautiously starting a new relationship with handsome stranger (Wesley Snipes).

Bernadine's friend Savannah (Whitney Houston), a stunningly beautiful local TV news producer, dates a married man (Dennis Haysbert) with her mother's wholehearted approval, but doesn't feel good about herself. Vivacious Robin (Lela Rochon) goes out with a dismal series of losers—including another married man—and her life is further complicated by an unplanned pregnancy. Plump Gloria (Loretta Devine), the oldest of the group, pins her romantic hopes on a handsome new neighbor (Gregory Hines), whom she would also like to be a father figure to her 17-year-old son.

In due time, the women sort out their problems. Bernadine's attorney helps her win a large settlement from her soon-to-be ex-husband. Savannah dismisses her philandering boyfriend and tells her mother to stop interfering in her life. Robin also says good-bye to her married boyfriend, but decides to keep her baby. And Gloria wins her man, while adjusting to her son's need to start living his own life. In the end, the four women join together to celebrate their new lives.

In all ways but one, WAITING TO EXHALE is a conventional—make that cliched—women's picture, a glossy melodrama about the ups and downs of female lives with strong emphasis on romance. The one difference is that the women are upper-middle-class African-Americans, but that appears to have been enough to convince 20th Century Fox that it had limited commercial potential, despite the enormous success of Terry McMillan's novel and the casting of pop diva Whitney Houston—whose 1992 THE BODYGUARD was a blockbuster—as Savannah.

But surprise, surprise: it became both a *cause celebre*—feminist writers debated its images of women at extraordinary length—and a sort of '90s "happening" for African-American women. Reports had groups of friends returning again and again, talking back to the screen and engaging in intense discussions of Savannah, Bernadine, Robin and Gloria's adventures in the land of no-good men. It was hyperbolically dubbed a Million Man March for women, but a more apt comparison might be with THE ROCKY HORROR PICTURE SHOW.

If there were more movies in which charismatic African-American actresses like Angela Bassett and Lela Rochon took center stage, instead of being relegated to the sidelines playing crack whores, welfare mothers and gang girls, WAITING TO EXHALE would not have caused such a fuss. Its own merits are modest; the film most closely resembles a string of Black Entertainment Television music videos strung together. It's not that the characters or the performers playing them are inherently uninteresting. But actor-turned-director Forest Whitaker and screenwriters McMillan and Ronald Bass (co-writer of THE JOY LUCK CLUB) have taken serious contemporary issues of gender and race and turned them into a cynically romantic soap opera that hooks (and panders to) the viewer with hot-button phrases, musical cues and happy endings for everybody. Life isn't like that, and neither is good melodrama. *(Violence, nudity, sexual situations, substance abuse, extreme profanity.)* — E.M.

d, Forest Whitaker; p, Ezra Swerdlow, Deborah Schindler; exec p, Terry McMillan, Ronald Bass; assoc p, Caron K; w, Terry McMillan, Ronald Bass (based upon the novel by Terry McMillan); ph, Toyomichi Kurita; ed, Richard Chew; m, Kenneth "Babyface" Edmonds; prod d, David Gropman; art d, Marc Fisichella; set d, Michael W. Foxworthy; sound, Tim Chau, Russell Williams, II (mixer); fx, Thomas C. Ford; casting, Jaki Brown-Karman; cos, Judy L. Ruskin; makeup, Ellie Winslow; stunts, Rawn Hutchinson, Brandon Sebek

Drama (PR: C MPAA: R)

WALK IN THE CLOUDS, A ★★★
(U.S.) 103m Zucker Brothers Production ~
20th Century Fox c

Keanu Reeves *(Paul Sutton)*; Aitana Sanchez-Gijon *(Victoria Aragon)*; Anthony Quinn *(Don Pedro Aragon)*; Giancarlo Giannini *(Alberto Aragon)*; Angelica Aragon *(Marie Jose Aragon)*; Evangelina Elizondo *(Guadelupe Aragon)*; Freddy Rodriguez *(Pedro Aragon, Jr.)*; Debra Messing *(Betty Sutton)*; Febronio Covarrubias *(Jose Manuel)*; Roberto Huerta *(Jose Luis)*; Juan Jimenez *(Jose Marie)*; Ismael Gallegos *(Jose's Musical Son)*; Alejandra Flores *(Consuelo)*; Gema Sandoval *(Maria)*; Don Amendolia *(Father Coturri)*; Gregory Martin *(Armistead Knox)*; Mary Pat Gleason *(Bus Driver)*; John Dennis Johnston *(Lout #1)*; Joseph Lindsey *(Lout #2)*; Mark Matheisen *(Soldier #1)*; Brad Rea *(Soldier #2)*; Macon McCalman *(Conductor)*; Ivory Ocean *(Truck Driver)*; Fred Burri *(Swiss Yodler)*; Stephanie Maislen *(USO Woman)*; Joe Troconis *(Man at Gate)*; Loren Sitomer *(Ten-Year-Old Boy)*

Mexican director Alfonso Arau's American debut—made possible by the unexpected success of LIKE WATER FOR CHOCOLATE (1992), the highest-grossing foreign film in US history—is a lushly photographed, resolutely old-fashioned romance capped off with a lavish Maurice Jarre score that italicizes every overwrought emotion.

After WWII, Paul Sutton (Keanu Reeves)—an orphan longing for love and stability—leaves the service eager to rekindle his wartime marriage to Betty (Debra Messing) and get on with his life. The pragmatic Betty, who's been enjoying the favors of other men while Paul was at war, has persuaded his old boss to give him back his job as a traveling chocolate salesman.

While on a sales trip, Paul's life intersects with that of California vineyard heiress Victoria Aragon (Aitana Sanchez-Gijon). She has been seduced and abandoned while away at college, and fears the wrath of her rigid father Alberto (Giancarlo Gianni) when she returns home. Paul proposes a masquerade: he'll pose as Victoria's husband, spend a few days with her family, then run away under cover of night. Though she'll be an object of pity, she won't be scorned.

There is, however, an unexpected pitfall. Paul grows to love her bustling family, particularly earthy grandpa Don Pedro (Anthony Quinn), and finds himself falling in love with her. Even though Paul helps save the family's grapes from frost and participates in the harvest, Victoria's strict father refuses to embrace his new son-in-law. Feeling guilty that he has abandoned Betty, Paul tries to go home. But he runs into the whole Aragon clan at a local fete and, to everyone's surprise, Alberto announces his intention of marrying off his daughter properly in church.

Victoria must reveal the truth, and Paul goes home, to find Betty in bed with another man. He realizes his obligations to her are minimal and goes back to the Aragon homestead. But Alberto refuses to forgive Paul, and in his rage knocks over a lantern that burns down the vineyards. Paul restores his honor by rescuing Victoria's brother Pedro (Freddy Rodriguez) from the flames, and by pointing out that the original, retired Aragon grape root isn't too damaged to give life to future harvests. Victoria has a devoted husband, Paul has found true love and a caring family, and the Aragon vineyards will flourish again.

A remake of Alessandro Blasetti's bittersweet QUATTRO PASSI FRA LE NUVOLE (1942), A WALK IN THE CLOUDS is a virtual compendium of romance movie cliches. But Arau approaches the material with the fervor of a true believer, and he's backed up by all the technical geegaws a big studio budget can buy. The result is awesomely beautiful, if not entirely satisfying. Though Latin himself, the director seems to subscribe to a remarkable number of hot-blooded cliches—Giannini's mustache-twirling histrionics verge on the ludicrous—and leads Reeves and Sanchez-Gijon lack the studio-groomed incandescence that stars like Hedy Lamarr and Robert Walker once radiated. But their amorous ardor is still convincing, and the scrupulously choreographed sequence in which Paul and Victoria don silk butterfly wings, with which they fan life-giving heat onto the grapes is breathtaking. Even more erotic—because it feels as though it was improvised—is the lovemaking that follows Paul and Victoria's frolic in the wine vats: it's a messy and effective evocation of sexual abandon. (Violence, sexual situations, adult situations.) — R.P.

d, Alfonso Arau; p, Gil Netter, David Zucker, Jerry Zucker; exec p, James D. Brubaker; assoc p, Stephen Lytle; co-p, Bill Johnson; w, Robert Mark Kamen, Mark Miller, Harvey Weitzman (based on the 1942 screenplay *Quattro Passi Fra le Nuvole* by Piero Tellini, Cesare Zavattini, and Vittorio de Benedetti); ph, Emmanuel Lubezki; ed, Don Zimmerman; m, Maurice Jarre; prod d, David Gropman; art d, Daniel Maltese; set d, Denise Pizzini; sound, Jose Antonio Garcia (mixer); fx, John McLeod, Bruno Van Zeebroeck, Syd Dutton, Bill Taylor, Illusion Arts; casting, John Lyons, Christine Sheaks; cos, Judy L. Ruskin; makeup, Julie Hewett; stunts, Jake Crawford

Drama/Romance   **(PR: C   MPAA: PG-13)**

WALKING DEAD, THE   ★★
(U.S.) 89m Walking Dead Productions; Jackson-McHenry Company; Price Entertainment ~ Savoy Pictures c

Allen Payne *(PFC Cole Evans)*; Eddie Griffin *(Pvt. Hoover Blanche)*; Joe Morton *(Sgt. Barkley)*; Vonte Sweet *(PFC Joe Brooks)*; Roger Floyd *(Cpl. Pippins)*; Ion Overman *(Shirley Evans)*; Kyley Jackman *(Sandra Evans)*; Bernie Mac *(Ray)*; Jean Lamarre *(Pvt. Earl Anderson)*; Lena Sang *(Barbara Jean)*; Wendy Raquel Robinson *(Celeste)*; Dana Point *(Edna)*; Doil Williams *(Harold)*; Damon Jones *(Second Lt. Duffy)*; Kevin Jackson *(Deuce)*; Vivienne Sendaydiego *(Vietnamese Woman)*; Hank Stone *(First Sgt. Hall)*; Velma Thompson *(Brenda)*; Wilmer Calderon *(Angelo)*; Carlos Joshua Agrait *(Carlos)*; Frank Price *(Mr. Dutkiewicz)*; Susan Ursitti *(Ms. Glusac)*; Sharon Parra *(Zarla)*; Frank Eugene Matthews, Jr. *(Mr. Lake)*; Joshua Armstrong *(Marine Recruiter)*; Terrence King *(Brenda's Lover)*; Nicole Avant *(Rhonda)*; Lisa Walker *(Pippins' Girlfriend)*

This drama about the black experience in Vietnam is an exercise in excess. Directed with a total lack of discipline, it lets every scene overstay its welcome and allows the actors to run amok.

During a not-so-routine mission in the Nam jungles, several soldiers talk about their battles against Caucasian oppression and their skirmishes against emotional short-circuiting. As soul-searching and enemy fire both rage in the background, rigid Sgt. Barkley (Joe Morton) and pragmatic Pvt. Hoover Blanche (Eddie Griffin) quibble about blind duty versus survival. While the debate continues, PFC Cole Evans (Allen Payne) recalls prejudicial housing practices that led to his family's low status. Disgraced after being fired for stealing some hamburger meat from his white boss, the foul-mouthed loner Hoover wound up in the Service. Many more such stories later, the former Reverend Barkley admits giving up his religious calling after wiping out his adulterous wife and her lover. Soon after, the enemy open fire again. Uncharacteristically, Blanche returns from safety to rescue Barkley. Evans, Barkley, and Blanche dodge death and dash away to their headquarters in a rescue helicopter.

Since few films have concentrated almost exclusively on how societal pressures forced poor African Americans to consider Vietnam a stepping stone out of crime and poverty, it is regrettable that these insights into the African American predicament wind up in a film so artlessly written and crassly directed. Instead of drawing the audience inexorably into the internal hell of each new revelation, the haphazardly inserted flashbacks disrupt the flow of the narration and take away from the poignancy of the wartime experience. Worse than the ragged editing, static camera setups, and collapsible screenplay is that 1990s action movie staple: obscenely macho insult exchanges distilled into vulgar poetry, the poorly directed cast members making them sound even more spurious. Aside from the reliably restrained Joe Morton, who seems like an actual tortured human being, the cast behaves like street preachers who declaim rather than create characters. (Graphic violence, adult situations, extreme profanity, sexual situations, substance abuse.) — R.P.

d, Preston A. Whitmore, II; p, Frank Price, George Jackson, Douglas McHenry; co-p, Bill Carraro; w, Preston A. Whitmore, II; ph, John Demps; ed, William C. Carruth, Don Brochu; m, Gary Chang; prod d, George Costello; art d, Joseph M. Altadonna; set d, Bill Cimino; sound, Adam Joseph (mixer); fx, David H. Watkins; casting, Jaki Brown-Karman, Kimberly Kardin; cos, Ileane Meltzer; makeup, Stacye P. Branche, Greg Nicotero, Gino Crognale, Mark Tavarres, KNB EFX Group; stunts, Randy Fife

Drama/War   **(PR: O   MPAA: R)**

WATER ENGINE, THE ★★★½
(U.S.) 88m Brandman Productions; Amblin Television ~
Turner Home Entertainment c

Charles Durning *(Guide)*; Patti LuPone *(Rita Lang)*; William H.
Macy *(Charles Lang)*; John Mahoney *(Mason Gross)*; Joe Mantegna *(Lawrence Oberman)*; Joanna Miles *(Mrs. Varec)*; Mike
Nussbaum *(Mr. Wallace)*; Treat Williams *(Dave Murray)*; J.J.
Johnston *(White Haired Man)*; David Mamet *(Brown Haired
Man)*; Andrea Marcovicci *(Singer in Dance Hall)*; John Capodice *(Kegan)*; Peter Michael Goetz *(Soapbox Speaker One)*;
Natalija Nogulich *(Soapbox Speaker Two)*; Ricky Jay *(Ratty
Inventor)*; Lucinda Jenney *(Gross's Secretary)*; Rebecca Pidgeon
(Connie); Tim Farrell *(Bernie)*; Horton Foote, Jr. *(Grey)*; Felicity
Huffman *(Dance Hall Girl)*; Hawthorne James *(Factory
Worker)*; Martin Sheen *(Chain Letter Voice)*; Lionel Mark Smith
(Mailman); Mike Vitar *(Copyboy)*; Bill Feeney *(Security
Guard)*; Alexander Bookston *(Elevator Operator)*; Marge Kotlisky *(Woman One)*; Barbara Tarbuck *(Woman Two)*; Maggie
Soboil *(Heckler)*; Jordan Lage *(Chauffeur)*; John Putch *(Moderator)*; Larry Marko *(Clothes Pedlar)*; Sandy Martin *(Custodial
Woman)*; Alexander Scott; Judith Piquet; Augusta Copullari
(Opera Singers); John Boyle *(Lecturer)*; Vicent Guastaferro *(Policeman)*; Alan Shearman *(Homeless
Man)*; Sharon Watroba *(Customer)*; Michael Carter *(Paperboy)*;
Greg Finley

An impressive cast of veteran stage performers inhabits this
stylized production of David Mamet's stage play. Set in Depression-era Chicago, Mamet's fable imparts a chilling message
about corporate greed and the defenselessness of the individual
who opposes Big Business. Produced for the cable network TNT
as the inaugural episode of its "Screenworks" series, THE
WATER ENGINE first aired in 1992, and was released to the
home video market in 1995.

Drill press operator Charles Lang (William H. Macy) has
invented an engine that derives its energy from water. He plans
to patent his invention and use the proceeds to lift himself and his
blind sister Rita (Patti LuPone) out of the slums of Chicago. He
demonstrates the engine for patent attorney Mason Gross (John
Mahoney), who brings Lawrence Oberman (Joe Mantegna), an
attorney claiming to represent "outside interests," into the negotiations. Distrustful of both men, Charles hides his engine and the
blueprints. Using threats and intimidation, Oberman tries to get
Charles to turn over the engine and the plans. Charles refuses to
give in to Oberman's threats and finds himself pursued by Oberman's henchmen as well as the police. He contacts newspaper
reporter Dave Murray (Treat Williams) and arranges an appointment to discuss his invention and Oberman's efforts to suppress
it. Oberman kidnaps Rita and prevents Charles from keeping his
appointment with Murray. Charles manages to deposit the blueprints in a mailbox before he is trapped by Oberman. Charles
refuses to answer Oberman's questions unless Rita is released.
The next day, the bodies of a mutilated man and woman are
found in the river. Charles' young friend Bernie (Tim Farrell)
receives a set of blueprints in the mail for a water-powered
engine which he may one day build.

The integrity of THE WATER ENGINE has not been compromised in its transition from stage to screen. It remains Broadway-calibre entertainment with outstanding performances and
first-rate production values. Director Steven Schacter retained
the style and artiness of a stage production. While distancing
some viewers, this approach imparts a sense of resonating importance to the proceedings. Mamet, who adapted the script from his
1976 play, peppers the piece with cryptic dialogue, including a
bizarre conversation overheard on a bus, and an ominous chain
letter which snakes through town (read as a voice-over by Martin

Sheen). Its Kafka-esque elements aside, THE WATER ENGINE
is an intense, gripping drama.

Macy's doomed protagonist is a well-crafted, intense portrayal. Mantegna is suitably sinister. LuPone is refreshingly
upbeat, a lone ray of sunshine in a somber piece. A wealth of
accomplished performers are on hand in supporting and
cameo roles. Betty Madden's costumes and Barry Robison's
set pieces convincingly reflect the period. *(Adult situations,
violence.)* — B.R.

d, Steven Schachter; p, Donald P. Borchers; exec p, Michael
Brandman; assoc p, Sarah Bowman; co-p, Leanne Moore; w,
David Mamet (based on his play); ph, Bryan England; ed, Martin
Hunter; m, Alaric Jans; prod d, Barry Robison; art d, Douglas
Hall; set d, Sara Andrews; sound, Richard Schexnayder (mixer);
fx, John Hartigan; casting, Risa Bramon, Billy Hopkins, Juel
Bestrop, Mary Vernieu; cos, Betty Madden; makeup, Belinda
Bryant; stunts, Kurt Bryant

Drama   (PR: C   MPAA: NR)

WATERWORLD ★★½
(U.S.) 134m King Kona Productions;
The Gordon Company; TIG Productions; Davis Entertainment;
Licht/Mueller Film Corp.; Universal ~ Universal c

Kevin Costner *(Mariner)*; Dennis Hopper *(Deacon)*; Jeanne
Tripplehorn *(Helen)*; Tina Majorino *(Enola)*; Michael Jeter *(Gregor)*; Gerard Murphy *(Nord)*; R.D. Call *(Enforcer)*; Chaim
Jeraffi *(Drifter #1)*; Kim Coates *(Drifter #2)*; John Fleck *(Doctor)*; Robert Joy *(Ledger Guy)*; Jack Black *(Pilot)*; John Toles-Bey *(Plane Gunner)*; Zitto Kazann *(Elder #3/Survivior #1)*;
Zakes Mokae *(Priam)*; Sab Shimono *(Elder #1)*; Leonardo
Cimino *(Elder #2)*; Zitto Kazann *(Elder #3/Survivor #1)*; Ric
Aviles *(Gatesman)*; Henry Kapono Ka'aihue *(Gatesman)*; Tracy
Anderson *(Gatesman)*; Luke Ka'illi, Jr. *(Boy)*; Anthony DeMasters *(Boy)*; Willy Petrovic *(Boy)*; Jack Kehler *(Banker)*; Lanny
Flaherty *(Trader)*; Robert Silverman *(Hydroholic)*; Rita Zohar
(Atoller); Chris Douridas *(Atoller)*; August Neves *(Old Atoller)*;
Neil Giuntoli *(Hellfire Gunner)*; David Finnegan *(Toby)*; Gregory B. Goossen *(Sawzall Smoker)*; Guy William Preston *(Depth
Gauge)*; Ari Barak *(Atoll Man)*; Alexa Jago *(Atoll Woman)*; Sean
Whalen *(Bone)*; Robert LeSardo *(Smitty)*; Lee Arenberg *(Djeng)*;
Doug Spinuzza *(Truan)*

Thematically modest but logistically ambitious, this seagoing
science-fiction adventure was originally envisioned as a Roger
Corman-produced quickie. The thrifty mogul eventually demurred, concerned that the production would exceed his maximum budget by several million dollars. WATERWORLD's
eventual price tag: $175 million.

In the future, the polar ice caps have melted and flooded the
Earth. The Mariner (Kevin Costner) has adapted well to this
watery new world, sailing in a specially designed trimaran and
salvaging treasures from the sea. After fending off some scavengers, the Mariner visits the Atoll, a floating, armored settlement,
where he trades soil for a plant and some water. Detained after
refusing to impregnate a local girl, he is revealed as a mutant with
working gills and webbed feet. He is about to be "recycled" by
the Atoll-dwellers when their floating shanty town is attacked by
the marauding Smokers, who terrorize the seas in their oil-powered vessels. Trader Helen (Jeanne Tripplehorn) rescues him.

In return, she wants safe transport for her adoptive daughter
Enola (Tina Majorino) and herself. Head Smoker Deacon (Dennis Hopper) wants Enola for the tattoo on her back—a map that's
said to lead to Dryland.

The Mariner doesn't enjoy having traveling companions and
goes so far as to throw Enola—who can't swim—overboard. He

refuses Helen's offer of sex for the girl's passage, but eventually agrees to let them both stay. The Mariner and Enola gradually become friends as he teaches her the ways of the sea. After eluding a trap set by the Smokers, the Mariner places Helen in an improvised diving bell and shows her the vast ruin of a metropolitan city under the waves. They resurface to find that Deacon and his Smokers have boarded his trimaran. The Mariner and Helen escape, but the Smokers burn the ship and kidnap Enola. Amidst the wreckage, the Mariner finds a drawing by Enola that matches a landscape in one of his ancient issues of *National Geographic.*

The Mariner and Helen are rescued by Gregor (Michael Jeter), an eccentric balloonist from the Atoll. After reuniting Helen with other Atoll survivors, the Mariner rescues Enola from Deacon's stronghold aboard the rusting oil tanker Exxon Valdez. They figure out the map and use the balloon to float to Dryland, where Enola was born. Uncomfortable on terra firma, the Mariner heads back out to sea alone.

As news of a monumentally troubled shoot whose production costs were skyrocketing drifted in from far-off Hawaii, the movie industry buzzed that WATERWORLD would be a disaster of legendary proportions and would bring successful actor-producer Kevin Costner down a peg in the Hollywood pecking order. Wags whispered "Fish-tar" and "Kevin's Gate" as director Kevin Reynolds quit during post-production. Despite the negative hype, the film is far from horrendous and managed to turn a modest profit, despite its enormous cost. But its sheer mediocrity will relegate it to the ranks of forgotten extravaganzas.

Can we see all that money on the screen? Yes, sort of: WATERWORLD is simultaneously overproduced and insufficiently imagined. Shooting on water is expensive under the best of circumstances, and WATERWORLD's circumstances were difficult: storms slowed production, and the entire Atoll set sank and had to be rebuilt. The battle scenes are frenetic and stunt-filled, but the most satisfying special effect is the relatively low-tech trimaran, a marvel of Rube Goldberg-inspired pulleys and levers. There are several splendid moments and sequences—an undersea swimming lesson; an unusual fishing maneuver; the tour of the underwater city—but they're fleeting. The film's cleverest gag occurs before the opening credits: the spinning Earth of the Universal Pictures logo segues seamlessly into the opening shot, the camera approaching the globe as its land masses sink beneath the sea.

Any major motion picture that opens with its superstar protagonist drinking his own urine—distilled, granted, but pee none the less—has something going for it. WATERWORLD aspires to laud ecological values—the villains burn oil, smoke cigarettes and eat a processed meat product called "Smeat," while the hero lives at peace with the sea—but its sheer profligacy undermines the message. Everything could be forgiven were WATERWORLD more thrilling and original, but it's a lavish, soggy retread of the futuristic Australian action classic THE ROAD WARRIOR. Ironically, if Corman *had* made WATERWORLD, genre fans would probably be toasting its modest pleasures. As a major motion picture, however, it's a bit of a washout. *(Nudity, graphic violence, profanity, adult situations, sexual situations.)* — K.G.

d, Kevin Reynolds; p, Charles Gordon, John A. Davis, Kevin Costner; exec p, Andy Licht, Jeff Mueller, Ilona Herzberg; assoc p, David Fulton; w, David Twohy, Peter Rader, Joss Whedon (uncredited); ph, Dean Semler; ed, Peter Boyle; m, James Newton Howard; prod d, Dennis Gassner; art d, David Klassen; set d, Nancy Haigh; sound, Keith A. Webster (mixer); fx, Martin R. Bresin, Michael J. McAlister, Sean Phillips, Boss Film Studios, Brad C. Kuehn, Jamie Price, Cinesite; casting, David Rubin,

Jakki Fink; cos, John Bloomfield; makeup, Frank Perez, Jim McCoy, The Burman Studio; stunts, R.A. Rondell

AAN Best Sound: Steve Maslow, Gregg Landaker, Keith A. Wester

Adventure / Action / Science Fiction   **(PR: A   MPAA: PG-13)**

WHEN BILLY BROKE HIS   ★★★½
HEAD ... AND OTHER TALES OF WONDER
(U.S.) 58m Independent Television Company ~ Tara Releasing c

Billy Golfus; Wade Blank; Kay Gaddis; Larry Kegan; Barb Knowlen; Paul Longmore; Joy Mincy-Powell; Ed Roberts; Robert Stephens; Lee Swenson

One part personal essay and one part road picture, WHEN BILLY BROKE HIS HEAD sheds much-needed light on an often ignored segment of the population, those with physical and developmental disabilities.

Unlike other Hollywood and independent films about this topic, WHEN BILLY BROKE HIS HEAD is unique in that it has been made by someone with a disability himself. Billy Golfus is a former Minneapolis radio show host who, in 1984, suffered paralysis and brain injury in a motor scooter accident. In this documentary, Golfus takes viewers on a road trip around the country to meet (among others) a blind woman unable to fill out government forms to maintain her benefits, a disability activist who fights for public transportation accessibility in Denver, a musician who has founded a program for "attitude reassessment about disability and sexuality," and a professor of history at San Francisco State College who notes similarities between the treatment of persons with disabilities and other "minorities." Golfus's journey ultimately becomes a challenge to viewers to confront their own prejudices.

As its irreverent title suggests, WHEN BILLY BROKE HIS HEAD looks and sounds like Michael Moore's 1989 documentary hit, ROGER AND ME. The film's stock quality (blown up from 16mm) is harsh and grainy, yet the low-budget "feel" complements the likeable, raffish spirit of the production. Also echoing the Moore film, Billy Golfus has written and narrated his piece with wit and candor, and his Kerouac-like road trip has been expertly (but not slickly) photographed by Slawomir Grunberg and edited by David E. Simpson.

What sets BILLY apart from ROGER AND ME is that it evokes a poignancy that was missing in Michael Moore's film. Highlights of the hour-long film include: Billy's two difficult visits with his father, a crusty man who refuses to acknowledge his own physical limitations, yet clearly harbors a prejudice against others with disabilities ("You're not that disabled," he tells his son. "It's a matter of determination."); Billy's visit with the state bureaucrat who methodically yet confusingly explains why Billy should get less than five hundred dollars a month from the government; and the superb montage of scenes from films and television shows (including FREAKS, PASSION FISH, "Star Trek," and Jerry Lewis's "Muscular Dystrophy Telethon") that represent people with disabilities in stereotypical ways.

Billy Golfus succeeds with his small film where RAIN MAN failed as a big film (as Billy might say, RAIN MAN represented just another "inspirational cripple story"). WHEN BILLY BROKE HIS HEAD may not be always easy to watch, but it is the kind of film that should be watched, and widely. *(Adult situations.)* — E.M.

d, David E. Simson, Billy Golfus; p, David E. Simson, Billy Golfus; w, Billy Golfus; ph, Slawomir Grunberg; ed, David E. Simpson; sound, Tom Blakemore (mixer)

Documentary (PR: A MPAA: NR)

WHEN NIGHT IS FALLING ★★½

(Canada) 94m Crucial Pictures, Inc.; Telefilm Canada; The Ontario Film Development Corporation; Alliance Communications Corportation ~ October Films c

Pascale Bussieres *(Camille)*; Rachael Crawford *(Petra)*; Henry Czerny *(Martin)*; David Fox *(Reverend DeBoer)*; Don McKellar *(Timothy)*; Tracy Wright *(Tory)*; Clare Coulter *(Tillie)*; Karyne Steben *(Trapeze Artist)*; Sarah Steben *(Trapeze Artist)*; Jonathan Potts *(Hang Glider)*; Tom Melissis *(Hang Glider)*; Stuart Clow *(Hang Glider)*; Richard Farrell *(Board President)*; Fides Krucker *(Roaring Woman)*; Thom Sokoloski *(Man with Goatee)*; Jennifer Roblin *(Waitress)*; Jacqueline Casey *(Iron Swinger)*; Sigrid Johnson *(Iron Swinger)*

The title of Patricia Rozema's second film (her first was the 1987 crowd-pleaser I'VE HEARD THE MERMAIDS SINGING) is taken from the closing lines of Bergman's FANNY AND ALEXANDER, a paean to living life to the fullest before time grows short. This lighthearted fantasy of lesbian attraction, which cleverly twits its own pretensions but can't resist a little bit of preaching, doesn't quite live up to Bergman's resonant phrase.

Camille (Pascale Bussieres) and boyfriend Martin (Henry Czerny) are teachers at a small Christian college in Canada—she teaches mythology (read "heart"), he theology (read "head"). The chaplain (David Fox) informs them that he'd like to recommend them both jointly for his soon-to-be-vacated position, but cautions that they would have to be married for the school to allow them to cohabit. After her dog dies suddenly, a distraught Camille is comforted in a Laundromat by Petra (Rachael Crawford), an attractive young stranger, who encourages her to embrace life. Camille discovers that their loads of laundry were switched, but decides to wear one of Camille's sexy tops to an interview with the Chaplain. Later, she calls Petra after finding her business card—for a post-modern performance troupe called "Sirkus of Sorts"—in the laundry bag.

In her trailer, Petra confesses to switching the laundry, and flirts aggressively with an intrigued but ultimately affronted Camille. Petra pursues Camille apologetically, and they have a passionate kiss in a doorway that Camille cuts short. Martin proposes marriage, explaining that the job offer is a blessing in disguise, before leaving for a convention in Chicago. Left to herself, Camille fantasizes about Petra, returning to the circus and asking Petra if they can be "friends." Petra responds by taking Camille hang-gliding. Confused by her feelings, Camille seeks guidance from the Chaplain, who overcomes his own admitted qualms about homosexuality as best he can and suggests that they pray together. Instead, Camille flees to the circus and has sex with Petra. Their passion faces an immediate test when the manager (Don McKellar) informs Petra that they will be going to San Francisco for an international competition.

Martin returns early from Chicago, finds Petra's number and goes looking for Camille, spying them in a clinch. Back in Camille's kitchen, they have a confrontation, during which he urges her not to say anything but to consider consequences first. Camille decides to bury the dog in the woods where she and Petra flew, drinks half a bottle of cherry brandy, and passes out. Found at the last minute by Petra's friends, she is saved from hypothermia by Petra's body heat, and leaves town that night with the circus.

From the opening dream images through the closing montage, writer/director Rozema makes a strong impression as a visual stylist. Much of her technique is derivative (there is more than a hint of Atom Egoyan—credited as a "friend of the film"—and outright quotes from MY BEAUTIFUL LAUNDRETTE and WINGS OF DESIRE), but she adds a jaunty, cheerful personality that animates the film. Her transitions and segues are brilliant and often amusing, and her use of multi-layered light to create emotional backdrops is mature and effective. The film is studded with funny offhand dialogue and throw-away jokes that, unfortunately, tend to underscore the poverty of writing in the rather heavy-handed "message moments."

The actresses are both charming, but their characters are poorly developed—Petra in particular is given to such air-headed aphorisms as "Without music life would be a mistake" or "Fear is the price you pay for adventure." Their attraction is never explored beyond the physical level, leaving the resolution somewhat forced and almost trivial.

Though the central love story disappoints, there are enough original and marvelous moments in the film to not only make it passably entertaining but also to suggest that Rozema is a filmmaker to watch. *(Nudity, sexual situations, profanity.)* — R.S.

d, Patricia Rozema; p, Barbara Tranter; assoc p, Sandra Cunningham; w, Patricia Rozema; ph, Douglas Koch; ed, Susan Shipton; m, Lesley Barber; prod d, John Dondertman; set d, Megan Less, Rob Hepburn; sound, Alan Geldart (recordist); fx, Performance Solutions; casting, Lucie Robitaille, Billy Hopkins, Kenny Barden, John Buchan; cos, Linda Muir; makeup, Stephen Lynch

Drama (PR: O MPAA: NR)

WHILE YOU WERE SLEEPING ★★★

(U.S.) 100m SST Productions; Caravan Pictures; Hollywood Pictures ~ Buena Vista c

Sandra Bullock *(Lucy Moderatz)*; Bill Pullman *(Jack)*; Peter Gallagher *(Peter)*; Peter Boyle *(Ox)*; Jack Warden *(Saul)*; Glynis Johns *(Elsie)*; Michael Rispoli *(Joe Jr.)*; Jason Bernard *(Jerry)*; Micole Mercurio *(Midge)*; Ally Walker *(Ashley Bacon)*; Monica Keena *(Mary)*; Ruth Rudnick *(Wanda)*; Marcia Wright *(Celeste)*; Dick Cusack *(Dr. Rubin)*; Thomas Q. Morris *(Man in Peter's Room)*; Bernie Landis *(Doorman)*; James Krag *(Dalton Clarke)*; Dick Worthy *(Orderly)*; Marc Grapey *(Intern)*; Joel Hatch *(Priest)*; Mike Bacarella *(Mr. Fusco)*; Peter Siragusa *(Hot Dog Vendor)*; Gene Janson *(Man in Chuch)*; Krista Lally *(Phyllis)*; Kevin Gudahl *(Cop at ICU)*; Ann Whitney *(Blood Donor Nurse)*; Margaret Travolta *(Admitting Nurse)*; Shea Farrell *(Ashely's Husband)*; Kate Reindres *(Beth)*; Susan Messing *(Celeste's Friend)*; Richard Pickren *(Lucy's Father)*; Megan Schaiper *(Young Lucy)*

This warm, sentimental romantic comedy manages to remain winning despite the occasional misstep. The engaging Sandra Bullock and Bill Pullman carry the proceedings over those bumps with no apparent effort.

Lucy (Bullock), a lonely Chicago subway token clerk still mourning the recent death of her father, has a crush on regular customer Peter Callahan (Peter Gallagher), a dashingly handsome lawyer. He barely notices her. On Christmas Eve, he's mugged by two thugs and thrown onto the tracks. Lucy witnesses the crime from her booth and springs into action, moving his unconscious body out of the way of an oncoming train.

The comatose Peter is taken to the hospital, where an overzealous nurse mistakes Lucy for his fiancee, kicking off a series of misunderstandings. Lucy suddenly finds herself embraced by Peter's loving, if slightly eccentric, working-class family, who quickly accustom themselves to the notion that the aloof Peter never saw fit to mention his engagement.

The Callahans ask Lucy to spend Christmas with them, and she accepts rather than return to her own miserable apartment. Things become more awkward with the arrival of Peter's brother, Jack (Pullman), who doesn't quite buy her story. His suspicions deepen after a visit to her apartment, where the landlord's irritating son, Joe Jr. (Michael Rispoli), pretends that *he's* Lucy's boyfriend.

Lucy finds an ally in Peter's godfather Saul (Jack Warden), who tells her he knows her secret, but that since the family loves her so much he'll keep it to himself. Jack later comes to Lucy's apartment to deliver a gift from his parents, and they wind up spending the evening together: it's clear that they're meant for each other. Meanwhile, the complications pile up. Lucy's friends think Jack is her fiance. Peter's real fiancee, Ashley Bacon (Ally Walker), is leaving messages on his answering machine. And Peter wakes up and, of course, doesn't recognize Lucy. His family assumes he has amnesia.

Chastened by his brush with death, Peter proposes to Lucy and the Callahans arrange for a wedding in the hospital. Unable to keep on lying, Lucy confesses and runs off in tears, but Jack tracks her down and proposes as his beaming family looks on.

Working from a script by Daniel G. Sullivan and Fredric Lebow, director Jon Turteltaub keeps WHILE YOU WERE SLEEPING moving along at an even clip, using comic relief to mitigate scenes that could easily collapse into mawkishness or over-the-top sentimentality. Phedon Papamichael's straightforward camera work and Bruce Green's judicious editing also contribute to propelling the proceedings along. The story runs out of steam about three-quarters of the way through, and there aren't enough clever twists or jokes to sustain it. But despite the wintry Chicago backdrop, it's all as cuddly as a basket of puppies. Bullock is consistently engaging, while Pullman's slightly fuzzy good looks and wry smile make it easy to believe she'd fall for him. The rest of the cast, which includes Glynis Johns and Peter Boyle as the doting parents, Walker as a surgically enhanced harpy, and the scene-stealing Rispoli as Lucy's inept and unwanted suitor—who's at one point caught hiding out in Lucy's closet, trying on her high heels—give the adorable leads strong support. *(Profanity)* — O.L.

d, Jon Turteltaub; p, Joe Roth, Roger Birnbaum; exec p, Steve Barron, Arthur Sarkissian; assoc p, Jonathan Glickman, Elaine Johnson; co-p, Charles J.D. Schlissel, Susan Stremple; w, Daniel G. Sullivan, Fredric Lebow; ph, Phedon Papamichael; ed, Bruce Green; m, Randy Edelman; prod d, Garreth Stover; art d, Chris Cornwell; set d, Larry Dias; sound, Curt Frisk (mixer); fx, Guy Clayton, Jr.; casting, Amanda Mackey, Cathy Sandrich; cos, Betsy Cox; makeup, Pamela Westmore

Comedy/Romance   **(PR: A   MPAA: PG)**

WHITE MAN'S BURDEN   ★★
(U.S.) 89m UGC; A Band Apart Productions;
Lawrence Bender Productions; Rysher Entertainment ~
Savoy Pictures c

John Travolta *(Pinnock)*; Harry Belafonte *(Thaddeus)*; Kelly Lynch *(Marsha)*; Margaret Avery *(Megan)*; Tom Bower *(Stanley)*; Andrew Lawrence *(Donnie)*; Bumper Robinson *(Martin)*; Tom Wright *(Lionel)*; Sheryl Lee Ralph *(Roberta)*; Judith Drake *(Dorothy)*; Robert Gossett *(John)*; Wesley Thompson *(Williams)*; Tom Nolan *(Johansson)*; Willie Carpenter *(Marcus)*; Michael Beach *(Policeman #1 Outside Bar)*; Lee Duncan *(Policeman #2 Outside Bar)*; Wanda Lee Evans *(Renee)*; Lawrence A. Mandley *(Sheriff #1 at Eviction)*; William Hendry *(Sheriff #2 at Eviction)*;

Thom Barry *(Landlord)*; Carrie Snodgress *(Josine)*; Brian Brophy *(Bank Teller)*; Chelsea Lagos *(Cheryl)*; Duane R. Shepard, Sr. *(Maitre d' at Fashion Show)*; Bert Remsen *(Hot Dog Vendor)*; Steve Wilcox *(First Youth at Hot Dog Stand)*; Jason Kristopher *(Youth at Hot Dog Stand)*; Seth Green *(Youth at Hot Dog Stand)*; Alexis Arquette *(Panhandler)*; Larry Nash *(Policeman at Gas Station)*; Mae Elvis *(Eleven-year-old Girl)*; Dean Hallo *(Charles)*; Kerry Remsen *(Pregnant Woman at Bus Stop)*; Googy Gress *(Bystander at Bus Stop)*; Lisa Dinkins *(Shooting Policewoman)*; Lawrence T. Wrentz *(Shooting Policeman)*; Steve Larson *(Bottle Thrower)*; Lawrence Bender *(Bar Patron #1)*; Matt O'Toole *(Bar Patron #2)*; Iain Jones *(Bar Patron #3)*; Janet Hubert *(Dinner Guest)*; Attallah Shabazz *(Dinner Guest)*; Willette Klausner *(Dinner Guest)*; David C. Harvey *(Factory Worker)*; Amy Powell *(Newscaster)*; Keith Collier *(Dancer on TV)*; Annamarie Simmons *(Dancer on TV)*; Rosie Tenison *(Detective on TV)*; Manny Jacobson *(Himself)*; Dondre Whitfield *(Terrence)*; Ingrid Rogers *(Taylor)*

Racial power is inverted in WHITE MAN'S BURDEN, the directorial debut of Desmond Nakano, best known as the screenwriter of LAST EXIT TO BROOKLYN (1990) and BOULEVARD NIGHTS (1979). The result is predictable and unmoving.

Louis Pinnock (John Travolta), a white factory worker and devoted family man, sees his life gradually destroyed after he makes a delivery to the posh suburban home of sophisticated black factory owner Thaddeus Thomas (Harry Belafonte). An outspoken bigot, Thaddeus catches Louis glancing through an open window at his half-dressed wife (Margaret Avery). Thaddeus complains to Louis's boss, and the wheels of disaster are set in motion. First Louis loses his job. Then he's brutally beaten by the police. Finally, unable to find work, he and his family are evicted from their home. Louis' wife (Kelly Lynch) and two children move in with his mother-in-law, and he takes up shelter in an abandoned building.

In a fit of desperation and anger, Louis goes to Thaddeus's home, where Louis demands at gunpoint the money he believes Thaddeus owes him. Since Thaddeus doesn't have the cash, they drive to the bank, which is closed for the weekend. Louis insists they spend the weekend together, and Thaddeus sees the squalor of life in the white ghetto as Louis visits his son, drives past his former home, and crashes in his miserable tenement squat. Thaddeus suffers a heart attack trying to escape, and Louis reveals his underlying good nature by trying to get him to the hospital.

Louis's truck breaks down, and he puts his own life in danger by firing shots into store windows to get the attention of police. The police arrive, but when they see an armed white man standing over a fallen black man, they open fire and kill Louis. Thaddeus recovers and returns to his life of privilege with a broader perspective on race and social class. He visits Louis's widow and offers her money, but she refuses to take it, disgusted by the assumption that money could compensate for the loss of her husband.

WHITE MAN'S BURDEN is clearly well intentioned, but so unsophisticated that it's hard to imagine precisely what its intentions are. Its strategy is simplicity itself: the pervasive cliches of white and black culture are left intact but inverted, as though this alone will cause people to see the world in a whole new light. It doesn't work, though it does make it tediously easy to see where each scene is leading.

WHITE MAN'S BURDEN deals only with the symptoms of cultural conflict and never even attempts to deal with the complex history of African-Americans. Its assumption that crime and violence are triggered merely by a chain of individual misfortunes is misleading, and the apparent hope that white viewers—shown a familiar story in which all the bad guys are white and the decent, hard-working people black—will abandon their deep-rooted prejudices and sympathize with the historically underprivileged is without foundation.

Some small effort has been made to guess how a black-dominated society might differ from a white one, but "small" is the operative word. Women's fashions, for example, bear a passing resemblance to some traditional African attire. But on the whole it's the WASP world order in blackface. This simplified approach can work if played for comic effect—witness TRADING PLACES (1983)—but WHITE MAN'S BURDEN aspires to serious drama and fails. *(Profanity, violence, adult situations.)* — M.F.

d, Desmond Nakano; p, Lawrence Bender; exec p, Yves Marmon; assoc p, Joann Fregalette Jansen; co-p, Paul Hellerman; w, Desmond Nakano; ph, Willy Kurant; ed, Nancy Richardson; m, Howard Shore; prod d, Naomi Shohan; art d, John Ivo Gilles; set d, Evette F. Siegel; sound, Ken King (mixer); casting, Barbara Cohen, Mary Gail Artz; cos, Isis Mussenden; makeup, Judy Murdock; stunts, Ken Lesco

Drama/Fantasy   **(PR: C   MPAA: R)**

WHO DO I GOTTA KILL?
(SEE: ME AND THE MOB)

WICKED CITY   ★★★
(Japan) 90m Japan Home Video ~
Streamline Pictures c

VOICES OF: Greg Snegoff; Mike Reynolds; Gaye Kruger; Edie Mirman

A futuristic tale of a precarious peace treaty between the earth and an alternate "black world" dimension, WICKED CITY is Japanese animation at its most stylized, crafting an eerie, darkly beautiful cityscape bursting with sex, violence, grotesque monsters, romance, and some occasional humor.

In late 20th century Tokyo, Taki is a human "Black Guard" who is assigned a female partner, Makie, from the parallel "Black World" dimension, whose denizens have monstrous forms and special powers, but can adopt human appearances. Their job is to guard the thousand-year-old mediator, Guiseppe Mayart, as he prepares to preside over peace treaty negotiations between the human dimension and the Black World.

The diminutive Mayart's predilection for sex and fun leaves him open to attack by Black World "radicals" who seek to derail the peace process. Makie has to fend off assaults by two former lovers from the Black World and is abducted and raped by one group of radicals. Taki leaves Mayart in order to rescue Makie and is ordered off the job by his supervisor.

Driving away on their own, Taki and Makie are attacked by monsters again, only this time they are saved by Mayart who reveals his super powers. The two are enveloped in a cloud of white energy and wind up in a dreamlike state in a church where they make love. Mayart arrives and explains that it was his job all along to protect the two because they have been chosen, by virtue of their genetic makeup, to create a cross-dimensional baby to increase the chances for interdimensional co-operation. After one last battle with Black World monsters on the roof of the church, the two lovers leave to create a new world of love and harmony between the two races.

Directed by Yoshiaki Kawajiri (DEMON CITY SHINJUKU, NINJA SCROLL)—one of a handful of innovative Japanese animators striving to give *anime* a new look—WICKED CITY is especially noteworthy for its nightmarish cityscape and surreal backgrounds. The sci-fi noir tone is underscored by Taki's voice-

over narration and frequent drives through nighttime city streets and deserted highways. The Black World characters dress like typical underworld denizens—gangsters and hookers—dropping their human facades in an instant to reveal gaping jaws, gigantic slashing claws, and rapacious tentacles. With their deadpan expressions and sleek character design, Taki and Makie seem fairly normal against such a background.

The frequent doses of sex and violence will attract some viewers because of their exquisite rendering and baroque character, while repelling others because of their misogyny. Although Makie is a strong, assertive character, she's subjected to repeated, brutal rapes—including one by a monstrous tentacled parasite—leaving a foul taste which even the romantic ending can't erase.

A live action remake of WICKED CITY was produced in 1993 by Hong Kong filmmaker Tsui Hark. Toning down the sex and violence while pumping up the romanticism, it offered stylish production values and extraordinary makeup effects to match the other-worldly tone of the animated original. *(Graphic violence, nudity, sexual situations, profanity.)* — B.C.

d, Yoshiaki Kawajiri, Carl Macek; p, Carl Macek; w, Kiseo Choo (from his story)

Animated/Science Fiction   **(PR: O   MPAA: NR)**

WIGSTOCK: THE MOVIE   ★★★
(U.S.) 80m Goldstreet Pictures ~
Samuel Goldwyn Company c

RuPaul; Alexis Arquette; Jackie Beat; Deee-lite; The Lady Bunny; Lypsinka; Mistress Formika; Crystal Waters; Joey Arias; Perfidia; John Kelly; Donna Giles; Leigh Bowery; Coco Peru; The Duelling Bankheads; Tabboo!; Flotilla de Barge; Girlina; Wendy Wild; Floyd; Candis Cayne; Daisy

WIGSTOCK: THE MOVIE celebrates New York's annual drag festival with absolutely FAB-ulous performances intercut with a fascinating peek behind-the-scenes. Like many performance-based films, WIGSTOCK: THE MOVIE doesn't have the excitement of the live event, but it does capture well the spirit of Wigstock—a call for individuality, tolerance, fun, and style. Wigstock is Woodstock without the bad hair.

On Labor Day each year, drag queens defy the unflattering light of day to strut their stuff on stage before an audience of thousands. Wigstock started out in Tompkins Square Park in the East Village, but became so big that in 1994 it was moved to the Christopher Street Piers. Director Barry Shils has sifted through two years of great performances, capturing some of the most entertaining and hair-raising moments. One of the creators of Wigstock, The Lady Bunny, performs as well as plays the role of sassy Mistress of Ceremonies for a cast of other spectacular characters including: RuPaul ("Supermodel of the World"); Lypsinka (aka John Epperson), who has been acclaimed for his one-(wo)man shows and as a model for designers Thierry Mugler and Valentino; Joey Arias, who "channels" the spirit of Billie Holliday; and Mistress Formika, whose brilliant rendition of "The Age of Aquarius" opens the movie. Other highlights include the late Leigh Bowery's outrageous "birthing" sequence, Grammy-nominated dance recording artist Crystal Waters performing in male drag, and the musical group Deee-Lite. Live performances are intercut with a backstage look at the performers, rehearsals, and the critical process of choosing a wig. Actor Alexis Arquette (PULP FICTION, LAST EXIT TO BROOKLYN), drag performer Eva Destruction, and Jo Beat (GRIEF) provide dramatic links between sequences.

WIGSTOCK: THE MOVIE is high on entertainment and provides a rare opportunity to watch some incredibly talented and unique performers. In an age when drag is skirting the Hollywood mainstream (e.g., MRS. DOUBTFIRE; PRISCILLA: QUEEN OF THE DESERT; and TO WONG FOO, THANKS FOR EVERYTHING! JULIE NEWMAR), WIGSTOCK: THE MOVIE remains a unique and moving reminder of a time when drag was not just sensational frocks and Size 14 pumps—a time when drag was about disrupting gender and defying discrimination, about celebrating diversity and the spirit of adventure. *(Profanity.)* — J.S.

d, Barry Shils; p, Dean Silver, Marlen Hecht; exec p, Klaus Volkenborn, Susan Ripps, Barry Shils; assoc p, Gary Kauffman, George Larkin, Claudia Lorka, Cheryl Miller Houser; co-p, David Sweeney, Tom Parziale; ph, Wolfgang Held; ed, Marlen Hecht, Todd Scott Brody, Barry Shils; m, Peter Fish, Robert Reale; art d, Linda del Rosario, Richard Paris

Documentary (PR: C   MPAA: NR)

WILD BILL ★★★
(U.S.) 98m The Zanuck Company; United Artists ~ MGM/UA c

Jeff Bridges *(James Butler "Wild Bill" Hickok)*; Ellen Barkin *(Calamity Jane)*; John Hurt *(Charley Prince)*; Diane Lane *(Susannah Moore)*; David Arquette *(Jack McCall)*; Keith Carradine *(Buffalo Bill Cody)*; Christina Applegate *(Lurline)*; Bruce Dern *(Will Plummer)*; James Gammon *(California Joe)*; James Remar *(Donnie Lonigan)*; Marjoe Gortner *(Preacher)*; Robert Knott *(Dave Tutt)*; Karen Huie *(Song Lew)*; Steve Reevis *(Sioux Chief Whistler)*; Pato Hoffmann *(Cheyenne Leader)*; Patrick Gorman *(Doctor)*; Lee DeBroux *(Carl Mann)*; Stoney Jackson *(Jubal Pickett)*

Widely regarded as the conclusion of a trilogy of Western biographies—following THE LONG RIDERS (1980) and GERONIMO: AN AMERICAN LEGEND (1993)—by veteran director Walter Hill, WILD BILL is an old man's Western, contemplative and tinged with regret.

The film opens at the funeral of William Hickock (Jeff Bridges), better known as "Wild Bill." As longtime friend Charley Prince (John Hurt) mournfully assesses Hickock's short, fabled career, various aspects of his life and legend are explored in flashback.

A montage of shoot-outs and brawls spanning the years 1867-76 establishes the legend of Wild Bill; these scenes include a near-fatal fight with some soldiers, a barroom stunt in which Bill shoots a shot glass off a dog's head while standing with his back turned, and an ignominious street fight in which Sheriff Hickock accidentally kills his own deputy. Hickock also appears on-stage with Buffalo Bill's Wild West Show and makes a poor go of it. No matter how carefully Buffalo Bill (Keith Carradine) prompts him, Wild Bill on-stage is as wooden and awkward as he is captivating and forceful in real life.

Most of the film's present-time action takes place in the last few days of Bill's life. He and Charley go to Deadwood, South Dakota—a muddy, violent, gold rush town that Charley compares to Sodom—to see Bill's old flame, Calamity Jane (Ellen Barkin) and consider what the future holds for a drink-sodden gunfighter who's slowing down and going blind. Bill well knows that the curse of the gunfighter is the succession of young hot shots looking to outdraw him, but he has a personal nemesis: Jack McCall (David Arquette), whose mother, Susannah Moore (Diane Lane), Bill once seduced and abandoned. Encouraged by the vindictive prostitute Lurline (Christina Applegate), McCall is determined to avenge his mother's disgrace at gunpoint, but isn't up to killing Bill by himself. He hires a gang of killers—led by the brutal Donnie Lonnigan (James Remar)—to help him.

Bill retreats to the opium den on the outskirts of town, and his drug-induced haze prompts more flashbacks. These include his relationship with the fragile Susannah—the great love of his life—and his bizarre shoot-out with the vicious, wheelchair-bound Bill Plummer (Bruce Dern). In order to level the playing field, Bill has himself tied to a chair and still wins. "Things are coming back to haunt me," Bill mumbles miserably to the Chinese woman who runs the opium den.

In the film's third act, Bill and Jane meet up in a bar and recapture some of their old spark. They begin to make love on a bar table, but are rudely interrupted by McCall and Lonnigan's gang. As the night wears on, McCall and Wild Bill spar verbally. Finally, Bill tells the boy to go ahead and kill him. He does.

Poorly received by audiences and critics, WILD BILL recalls the mordantly elegiac UNFORGIVEN (1992) in its tone and thematic underpinnings. But where UNFORGIVEN's screenplay was seamless, WILD BILL's—assembled from a novel (Pete Dexter's *Deadwood*), a play (Thomas Babe's *Fathers and Sons*), and Hill's own original research—is an awkward pastiche. And while UNFORGIVEN had at its center the near-mythic Clint Eastwood—who comes with with a gold mine of Western associations—WILD BILL revolves around Jeff Bridges, a fine actor but a considerably less resonant presence. Nevertheless, his Bill is a complex, contradictory character, not particularly likable, but always strangely compelling.

The supporting cast is unusually strong, from Dern and Marjoe Gortner (playing Deadwood's fire-and-brimstone preacher) in small parts, to Barkin, who manages to banish all thoughts of Doris Day rootin' and tootin' her way through CALAMITY JANE (1953). Keith Carradine's one-scene cameo as huckster Buffalo Bill is particularly striking.

Hill's most successful technical conceit is his use of high-contrast black-and-white video transferred to film for Hickock's most intense memories, including a haunting encounter with an Indian brave in a blinding blizzard, and the sequences involving Savannah, the great love he destroyed. *(Violence, profanity, nudity, sexual situations, adult situations.)* — M.M.

d, Walter Hill; p, Richard D. Zanuck, Lili Fini Zanuck; co-p, Gary Daigler; w, Walter Hill (based on the novel *Deadwood* by Pete Dexter and the play *Fathers and Sons* by Thomas Babe); ph, Lloyd Ahern; ed, Freeman Davies; m, Van Dyke Parks; prod d, Joseph Nemec, III; art d, Daniel Olexiewicz; set d, Gary Fettis; sound, Lee Orloff (recordist); fx, Lawrence J. Cavanaugh, Casey Cavanaugh, Joseph P. Mercurio; casting, Shari Rhodes, Joseph Middleton; cos, Dan Moore; makeup, Gary Liddiard; stunts, Allan Graf

Western / Historical / Biography (PR: C   MPAA: R)

WILD REEDS ★★★★
(France) 110m IMA Films; Les Films Alain Sarde; Le Canal Plus; La Sept/Arte; IMA Productions; SFP Productions ~ Gala Films c

Frederic Gorny *(Henri)*; Gael Morel *(Francois)*; Elodie Bouchez *(Maite)*; Stephane Rideau *(Serge)*; Michele Moretti *(Madame Alvarez)*; Nathalie Vigne *(Young Bride)*; Laurent Groulout *(The Photographer)*; Jacques Nolot *(Monsieur Morelli)*; Eric Kreikenmayer *(Young Bridegroom)*; Michel Ruhl *(Monsieur Cassagne)*; Fatia Maite *(Aicha)*; Claudine Taulere *(Nurse)*; Elodie Soulinhac *(Girl at Party)*; Dominique Bovard *(Guard)*; Paul Simonet *(Bridegroom's Father)*; Bordes Fernand Raouly *(Bridegroom's Mother)*; Charles Picot *(Headmaster)*; Christophe Maitre *(Gym Instructor)*; Michel Voisin *(Priest)*; Denis Bergonhe *(Plump Attendant)*

Andre Techine's lovely coming-of-age film—set in 1962, near the end of the Algerian war for independence—evokes the vulnerability and desperation of adolescence through the stories of a group of teenagers whose lives intersect at a boarding school in southwestern France. The title derives from La Fontaine's fable "The Oak and the Reeds" and serves to place the characters within the broader context of nature: Techine often frames them within a landscape of rolling hills and pans gently across the frame, giving the film the wistful flow of reeds in the wind.

There are four youngsters: Maite (Elodie Bouchez), the feminist, Communist daughter of the school's literature instructor; timid, intelligent Francois (Gael Morel), who's discovering his homosexuality; Serge (Stephane Rideau), the passionate and physical son of emigre Italian farmers; and Henri (Frederic Gorny), older than the rest and an Algerian refugee who supports the reactionary OAS.

The film opens with the wedding of Serge's older brother Pierre, a soldier fighting in Algeria and a former student of Maite's mother, Mme. Alvarez (Michele Moretti). Pierre marries to obtain a leave-of-absence, hoping to defect with Mme. Alvarez's help, but she refuses. He later dies in combat, and his death affects the lives of all the characters.

Serge is expected to assume additional family responsibilities, and becomes intensely suspicious of Henri. Overwhelmed by guilt, Mme Alvarez has a breakdown, leaving Maite overwhelmed and alone. She moves into the local Communist Party headquarters during her mother's absence. Francois and Serge have a brief, ambivalent sexual encounter that leads Francois to confront his sexuality: "I'm a faggot," he tells his reflection, and goes on to share his inner tumult with Maite and the town shoe salesman, who is also gay. Meanwhile, Henri's obsession with the war affects his studies, and he eventually decides to leave school and rejoin his mother in Algeria. He wanders through town burning Communist Party signs, but stops at party headquarters when he sees Maite inside. They talk and nearly overcome their political differences.

The following day, Francois, Maite, and Serge decide to go swimming to pass the time while they wait for their exam results. They bump into Henri and invite him along. Francois and Serge swim and joke around in their underwear, and Serge tells Francois that what happened between them won't happen again, and that he shouldn't think about it. Henri and Maite make love, but she then encourages him to leave town. Their lives and friendships reflect a terrifying mixture of innocence, desire, and idleness, as well as a growing urgency and seriousness.

WILD REEDS was produced as part of a series called "*Tous les garcons et les filles de leur age*" (all the boys and girls of their time), for which nine directors were invited to make films about teenagers, set in the periods of their own youth. It won four 1994 Cesar awards (the French equivalent of the Oscar), including Best Picture, Director and Screenplay, and was France's official entry that year for the Academy Award for Best Foreign Language Film. It also received the 1994 *Prix Dullac*, awarded by a highly respected panel of French film critics, and played the film festival circuit to international acclaim.

WILD REEDS is particularly effective in its depiction of the vulnerability of young people to conflict and the suffering of family and friends. Though their friendship is a refuge from the world around them, it also brings into sharp relief the things that isolate them from one another: Francois can't share his desire; Maite, her despair at her mother's breakdown; Serge, his frustration at his adult responsibilities to his family; and Henri, the rage he feels during his native country's struggle for independence.

American audiences will be particularly struck by the independence and thoughtfulness of Techine's teenagers. They are, of course, the products of a particularly volatile time and place,

shaped by personal and family crises, national events, the unique atmosphere of boarding school, and the fact that they are all in some way excluded from mainstream society. Techine focuses on the teenagers' friendships, as well as the abyss that often divides adults and youths. (*Sexual situations, adult situations.*) — M.F.

d, Andre Techine; p, Alain Sarde, Georges Benayoun; exec p, Jean-Jacques Albert; assoc p, Paul Rozenberg, Chantal Poupaud; w, Andre Techine, Gilles Taurand, Olivier Massart; ph, Jeanne Lapoirie; ed, Martine Giordano; set d, Pierre Soula; sound, Pierre Lorrain, Jean-Paul Mugel; casting, Michel Nasri; cos, Elisabeth Tavernier

Drama   (PR: C   MPAA: NR)

WINDOW TO PARIS   ★★★
(Russia/France) 87m Fontaine; Films du Bouloi; Sodaperaga ~ Sony Pictures Classics c

Agnes Soral (*Nicole*); Sergei Dontsov (*Nikolai Tchijov*); Victor Mikhailov (*Gorokhov*); Nina Oussatova (*Vera*); Kira Kreylis-Petrova (*Gorokhov's Mother-in-Law*); Natalia Ipatova (*Gorokhov's Daughter*); Viktor Gogolev (*Kouzmitch*); Tamara Timofeeva (*Maria Olegovna*); Andrei Ourgante (*Gouliaiev*); Jean Rupert (*Mousieur Prevost*); Malka Rybowaka (*Lady in Black*); Bernard Cassus-Soulanis (*Alarm Installer*); Vladimir Kaliche (*Ivanov*); Alexei Zalivalov (*Petrov*); Alexei Kozodaev (*Sidorov*); Elena Drapeko (*Vice-Principal*); Valentine Boukine (*Headmaster*); Varvara Chebalina (*Prostitute*); Anatoli Slivnikov (*Police Chief*); Serguei Labyrine (*Police Lieutenant*); Anatoli Chvedersky (*Orchestra Conductor*); Tatiana Golodovitch (*Headmistress*); Maxime Demtchenko (*Professor*)

A grim subtext—the bleakness of life in post-Soviet Russia—lies beneath this charming fantasy about a magical window in St. Petersburg that opens onto the rooftops of Paris.

A communal apartment in what was once called Leningrad is dominated by Gorokhov (Viktor Michailov), whose family is loud, voracious, and cunning in the tradition of Gogol's wily peasantry. Their boarder, an older woman, has mysteriously disappeared, so they rent the room to Tchijov (Sergei Dontsov). A sweet-tempered music teacher, Tchijov works in a school where the formulaic obeisance to Communism has been neatly swapped for an equally slavish worship of capitalism: the walls are adorned with huge, iconic photographs of foreign currency and slogans. On the night Tchijov moves in, there's a drunken party, with Gorokhov and his friends proclaiming themselves fellow musicians (the film opens with a grotesque parade, led by Gorokhov's troupe, marching to a tinny rendition of "The Internationale").

They're awakened from a drunken stupor by the sudden appearance of the mysterious former tenant, who has a strange story to tell. Her clothing cabinet, it seems, hides a window that leads directly to Paris.

Although it takes a while before the soused Petersburgers realize their momentous discovery, the Gorokhov family is soon taking lusty advantage of the magical window to collect all sorts of Western luxuries, including a Citroen 2-CV. Gorokhov even rigs a hand-cranked organ to play Tchaikovsky, picking up spare change on the streets of Paris. Their stereotypically Parisian rooftop neighbor, a bohemian taxidermist named Nicole (Agnes Soral), quickly learns to dislike the boorish Russian intruders. But when she removes a strategic fire-escape ladder, the practical Gorokhovs simply use her apartment to get to and from the City of Light. Enraged, Nicole follows them into their rooms and soon finds herself trapped in St. Petersburg, totally bewildered and unprepared for the casual cruelties of contemporary Russian life.

Tchijov, who's been fired from his school job, lands a gig in Paris, but quits when he learns that he's to play in a chamber orchestra that performs in a strip club. He returns to Russia just in time to save Nicole from the clutches of the local police. To celebrate, Nicole and Tchijov treat his class to a field trip in Paris, though he needs to exert all his charms to get them to return. The final scene shows Tchijov and the Gorokhovs all hammering at a wall in an effort to discover another fantastic window.

With his co-scriptwriter, Arkadi Tigai, director Yuri Mamin has created a surprisingly incisive magic realist comedy about the appeal of a wealthy, cosmopolitan, and perhaps foolishly spoiled society to perpetually strapped urban Russians. St. Petersburg appears, to Nicole and to us, as a grim, shabby, dangerous slum, while Paris is shown as a veritable candy shop to famished children. It's not the real Paris, of course—the French capital has pronounced social problems of its own—but Paris as it exists in the fevered imaginations of former Soviets. Thus Mamin's film can also be read as a sly critique of contemporary Russia's misguided idealization of the West. Ultimately, Tchijov's decision to return home may be as realistic as it is sentimental. *(Adult situations, profanity.)* — L.R.

d, Yuri Mamin; p, Guy Seligmann; w, Yuri Mamin, Arkadi Tigai; ph, Sergei Nekrassov, Anatoly Lapchov; ed, Olga Andrianova, Joele Van Effenterre; m, Yuri Mamin, Aleksei Zalivalov; prod d, Vera Zelinskaia; sound, Leonide Gavritchenko; fx, Igor Plaksine, Victor Okovity, Vladimir Smirnov, Zalman Zelkine, Jean-Pierre Toffolon, Olivier Nigay, Jean-Marc Segura; casting, Maria Vereschak, Katerina Petrenko, Bernard Szabo; cos, Natalya Zamakhina; makeup, Alexandra Kouzmina

Comedy/Fantasy/Romance   (PR: C   MPAA: PG-13)

WINGS OF COURAGE   ★★

(U.S.) 40m TriStar; IMAX Corporation ~ Sony Pictures Classics c

Craig Sheffer *(Henri Guillaumet)*; Elizabeth McGovern *(Noelle Guillaumet)*; Tom Hulce *(Antoine de Saint-Exupery)*; Val Kilmer *(Jean Mermoz)*; Ken Pogue *(Pierre Deley)*; Ron Sauve *(Jean-Rene Lefebvre)*

The first fiction feature made in IMAX-3D, WINGS OF COURAGE is a technological landmark, but not much of a movie.

The year: 1930. Antoine de St. Exupery (Tom Hulce) and celebrity flyer Jean Mermoz (Val Kilmer) have formed the first company to fly mail between France and South America, over dangerous, mountainous terrain. New pilot Henri Guillaumet (Craig Sheffer) joins the company, despite the worries of his wife Noelle (Elizabeth McGovern) back in France.

On a run between Santiago and Buenos Aires, the worst happens: Henri runs into a storm, his plane crashes, and he's stranded in the barren, snow-covered Andes. He tries to call for help, and at first stays with the plane and waits. But after he sees St. Exupery's plane fly over, apparently without noticing the tiny wreck in the snow, Guillaumet he begins walking. Hungry, frost-bitten, and exhausted, he eventually collapses in the snow. But at the 11th hour he's rescued, and returns home to his wife.

Directed by French filmmaker Jean-Jacques Annaud—whose earlier credits include THE NAME OF THE ROSE (1986) and THE BEAR (1989)—WINGS OF COURAGE is the first narrative movie shot in the IMAX-3D process, which produces images vastly superior to anything possible using older 3-D systems. The film can only be enjoyed in theaters specially equipped with expensive IMAX technology, and the viewer must wear a helmet that is somewhat distracting by virtue of its sheer bulk. Nevertheless, it's an improvement over traditional 3-D glasses, allowing viewers—even those who wear corrective

glasses—to see a pretty fair approximation of a three-dimensional image.

This 40-minute featurette is hardly a great film, but it showcases the technical process with great competence. It delivers a more convincing approximation of a "real movie" that 1995's other 3-D fiction feature, ACROSS THE SEA OF TIME, which shills for Sony's technology (and New York City) far more crudely. Some of the film's insipidity is no doubt due to the G rating—necessary in order to maximize the potential audience—but not all.

Not surprisingly, WINGS OF COURAGE is filled with shots designed to wow the viewer with natural spectacle rendered in startling 3-D, and Annaud carefully composed many shots with objects of interest in all three focal planes, heightening the impact of the film's three-dimensionality. Interestingly, the film's least effective sequence is an interior set in a club, in which a couple seen dancing in the foreground has a distinctly ghostly look.

The drama, however, based loosely on the adventures of real-life flyers, is painfully simplistic—Guillaumet gets lost and is found—and the characters (unlike the scenery) are entirely without depth or shading. Mermoz is smug. Guillaumet is determined. Noelle is worried. So wooden are their characters that Kilmer, Sheffer, and McGovern are all easily upstaged by an adorable little dog. Viewed flat, one suspects, WINGS OF COURAGE would be very flat indeed. The film played at several Sony-owned theaters throughout 1995, earning per-screen grosses that regularly surpassed every major studio release. — M.M.

d, Jean-Jacques Annaud; p, Jean-Jacques Annaud; exec p, Antoine Compin, Charis Horton; co-p, Richard Briggs; w, Alain Godard, Jean-Jacques Annaud; ph, Robert Fraisse; ed, Louise Rubacky; prod d, Ian Thomas; art d, Douglasann Menchions; set d, Lesley Beale; sound, George Tarrant (mixer); fx, Neil Trifunovich; casting, Mary Jo Slater; cos, Aggie Rodgers; makeup, Stephan Dupuis

Adventure/Drama   (PR: AA   MPAA: G)

WINGS OF HONNEAMISE: ★★½
ROYAL SPACE FORCE

(Japan) 121m Gainax Production Company; Bandai Company; Manga Entertainment; Heolo Ltd.; Animaze ~ Tara Releasing/Manga Entertainment c (HONNEAMISE NO TSUBASA)

VOICES OF: Robert Matthews *(Shirotsugh Lhadatt)*; Melody Lee *(Riquinni Nonderaiko)*; Stevie Beeline *(General Khaidenn)*; Lee Stone *(Matti)*; Arnie Hinks *(Karrock)*; Alfred Thev *(Dr. Gnnom)*; Steve Blum; Warren Daniels; Rudy Luzion; Sunley Gurd, Jr.; Simon Isaacson; Anthony Mordy; Christophe de Groot; Jonathan Charles; Jeff Frayer; Joe Montine; Mimi Woods; Werdee Day; Jack Emmet; Dorothy Melendres; Tom Charles; Helen Storm; Richard George; Doug Stone; Thomas White; Don Martin; Jayne Allen; Bambi Durron; Joe Romersa; Lena Gale; Anthony Sintacrose; Jill Lyons; Dougary Grant; Anthony Mordy

A groundbreaking Japanese feature by a group of young animators, THE WINGS OF HONNEAMISE was released to US home video in 1995 in an English language version. This tale of a young man who volunteers to be his planet's first man in space offers breathtaking animation, spectacular design, and a carefully constructed imaginary culture—although its deliberately paced, meandering storyline demands extraordinary patience.

The film posits an alternate world incorporating Japanese, American, European, and Third World cultural elements and a level of technological achievement on a par with that of the

1950s. Shiro Lhadatt, an aspiring pilot, enters into the Royal Space Force of Honneamano, a ragtag band of rejects from the other armed services thrust into a fledgling space program marked by low morale and underfunding.

When Shiro meets Leiqunni, a poor, plain-looking girl who distributes religious pamphlets, he is inspired by her enthusiasm for the space program and volunteers to pilot the first rocket to orbit the planet. Put through extensive and expensive training, he becomes a public hero thanks to a campaign carefully orchestrated by the royal family and the media.

When Shiro discovers that the rocket launch is being used to provoke a war with the neighboring Republic, he becomes disillusioned and goes AWOL. After Leiqunni fends off his fumbling attempt to rape her, Shiro returns to the city where an attack on him by an agent of the Republic convinces him to return to the base and continue his preparation for the flight.

The launch is officially called off after enemy troops cross the border, but General Khaidenn, Shiro's commander, defies orders and begins the countdown. The rocket is successfully launched and the warfare stops temporarily. Looking out over the earth, Shiro proclaims the absence of borders and makes a plea for world peace.

THE WINGS OF HONNEAMISE is an ambitious animated feature that succeeds best at creating an elaborate alternate world in which a society stands poised between traditional culture and high technology. The detailed production design and intricate imagery of cityscapes, rural countryside, and the primitive rocket base are imaginatively executed with numerous clever touches.

The character of Shiro, however, is never fleshed out enough to make the viewer really care about his frequent bouts with self-doubt and disillusion. His response to Leiqunni's enthusiasm is rather sudden and not convincingly motivated. In fact, Leiqunni remains the most interesting character in the film. Her religious devotion is rather touching in such an uncaring society and it ultimately has a profound effect on Shiro. Also, the fact that she's drawn realistically and not in the *kawaii* (i.e., cute) fashion so favored by Japanese animators makes her stand out as a recognizable character. However, the scripters' decision to block any potential romance between the two main characters reduces the film's emotional impact.

One final production note: The fact that the film was made by a small group of young animators who formed their own company and got a major toy company, Bandai, to bankroll its $50 million budget parallels the story's focus on a small group of young people who embark on a hugely expensive, risky project financed in the film by the royal family. *(Sexual situations, profanity.)* — B.C.

d, Hiroyuki Yamaga; p, Makoto Yamashina, Taro Yoshida, Keiji Kusano, Ken Iyadomi, Makoto Yamashina, Yutaka Maseba, Hirohiko Sueyoshi, Hiroaki Inoue; exec p, Toshio Okada, Shigeru Watanabe; w, Horoyuki Yamaga, Quint Lancaster, Mary Mason; ph, Hiroshi Isagawa; ed, Harutoshi Ogata; m, Ryuichi Sakamoto; art d, Hiromasa Ogura; anim, Yoshiyuki Sadamoto, Fumo Ild000a, Hideaki Anno, Yuji Moriyama; sound, Shohei Hayashi (recordist); casting, Doug Stone Enterprises

Animated/Drama/Science Fiction   **(PR: C   MPAA: NR)**

WITHOUT ANESTHESIA   ★★½
(Poland) 131m Film Unit X ~ New Yorker Video c
(BEZ ZNIECZULENIA)

Zbigniew Zapasiewicz *(Jerzy Michalowski)*; Ewa Datkowska *(Eva Michalowski)*; Andrzej Seweryn *(Jacek)*; Krystyna Janda *(Agato)*; Roman Wilhelmi; Emilia Krakowska; Kazimierz Kaczor; Magda Teresa Wojcik; Jerzy Stuhr

Director Andrzej Wajda—who first gained international attention for his bleak and powerful portrayal of the futility of escape from German-occupied Poland in KANAL (1956)—turns his gaze to contemporary Polish consciousness in the 1979 WITHOUT ANESTHESIA, released to US home video in 1995. This is a story about a successful foreign correspondent who returns from abroad to discover that his wife has left him for another man—what he has assumed was the perfect life gradually reveals itself to have been merely a refuge.

The film begins with a televised interview of journalist Jerzy Michalowski (Zbigniew Zapasiewicz), a household name in Poland. Confident and proud, he glibly pontificates about the revolutions he has witnessed abroad and the times he has risked his life for the story. When questioned about why he covers events in the Third World and not those in Poland, he prefers to skip to the next question.

Jerzy's wife (Ewa Datkowska) picks him up at the airport and informs him that she and their young daughter have moved out. He is taken completely by surprise. As the weeks pass, he finds himself increasingly estranged and ostracized from his community. The courses he has planned to teach at the University have been cancelled and he is not given any new assignments. He is stranded without anesthesia, so to speak. When the divorce goes to court he listens silently as a series of witnesses commit perjury to bolster his wife's case. Jerzy, the confident professional who is never without a rhetorical speech, is speechless, and leaves the courthouse alone. Later, ambulances arrive at his home and remove his corpse.

The film takes a critical look at Poles who have turned their attention to the exterior world in an effort to distance themselves from the humiliation and suffering of their homeland. In the film's opening interview, Jerzy frequently uses the concerns of private life to illustrate political events, and yet he has failed to make this vital connection in his own life. In a drunken conversation with students at his apartment, he discusses his broken marriage but when challenged, fails to see how the political petition resembles the marital contract. When he faces the deceit and corruption of the Polish judicial system, he finds he is defenseless and that he has overestimated his own strength.

In a realist manner, the camera follows Jerzy through the long days of his despair as he occupies a seemingly unending array of dark, dingy, poorly-planned interiors. The result is a painfully slow film which lacks sufficient visual interest. Thus, in the end, the engaging premise of the film is buried somewhere beneath volumes of unnecessary and dreary footage. — R.C.

d, Andrzej Wajda; p, Barbara Pec-Slesicka; w, Agnieszka Holland, Andrzej Wajda; ph, Edward Klosinski; ed, Halina Prugar; m, Jerzy Derfel, Wojciech Mlynarski; prod d, Allan Starski; sound, Piotr Zawadski

Drama   **(PR: A   MPAA: NR)**

WIZARD OF DARKNESS   ★★
(Japan) 82m Gaga Communications;
Tsuburaya Eizo Company c
(EKO EKO ARAZAKU)

Kimika Yoshino *(Misa)*; Miho Kanno *(Mizuno)*; June Takagi *(Miss Shirai)*; Knori Kanomatsu *(Wami)*

Hell breaks loose at a Japanese high school when the students become intrigued with a ghastly string of Satanic murders. While director Shimako Sato's second feature—which was based on a Japanese comic book—is primarily a slasher film, she has also laced WIZARD OF DARKNESS with a few unexpected twists as well as a glancing examination of the horrors of teenage sexual and cultural anxieties.

Any illusion that order prevails at the school is soon broken for the viewer. For starters, the teacher Mr. Numata not only greets but gropes the girls each morning as they arrive, and Ms. Shirai (June Takagi), the homeroom advisor, is involved in a lesbian affair with her student Kazumi. Class troublemaker, Mizuno (Miho Kanno), foments interest in the occult among his classmates, and proposes to put a curse on Mr. Numata. The new girl, Misa (Kimika Yoshino), helps deploy the spell. When Numata falls ill, rumors fly that Misa's supernatural powers are all too real. Only Shindo, the class hunk who has a crush on Misa, and Mizuki, her first friend at the school, stand by her.

Ms. Shirai asks her students to stay after school to take a test, and leaves them alone in the classroom. When she fails to return, they drift off, only to discover that all doors and windows are sealed. Misa, Shindo, and Mizuki set out to find a viable exit; the others follow troublemaker Mizuno, whose escape efforts lead to a fatal fire, a decapitation, and his own madness. He turns on his fellow students, slits Shindo's throat, and is killed himself.

When only Misa and Mizuki are left, the ruse is revealed: Mizuki's supernatural powers rival Misa's. The two girls square off in a battle of unearthly forces that threatens to destroy the entire city. Finally Misa defeats Mizuki, and locates Shirai, a Satanist who has been behind the murders all along. While she is unable to save Kazumi, who is only a pawn and one of Shirai's intended sacrifices, Misa triumphantly prevents evil from getting the upper hand.

Even at only 81 minutes, WIZARD OF DARKNESS still stalls now and then. But the film accumulates enough atmospheric detail to rouse a good fright: clean-cut victims clad in school uniforms, claustrophobic classrooms, ominously-darkened hallways, and violence replete with fountains of spurting blood.

While some elements of the film suggest that the real evil is Mr. Numata's abuse of the girls, or corrupting Western influences, pinning the bizarre and violent events on Ms. Shirai's predatory and power-mongering lesbianism seems trite. Every sexual option presented to these ill-fated adolescents—Numata's lasciviousness, Shirai's homosexuality, even Shindo's adolescent attraction to Misa—leads to death, destruction, and chaos. Given this, one might guess that the real evil is a cultural fear of sexuality. But whatever the cause of cataclysmic disruption, Order (predictably) must be restored; that a teenage girl gets to do the job is about the only welcome change of pace in this otherwise politically status quo production. (Nudity, sexual situations, graphic violence.) — C.Ch.

d, Shimako Sato; p, Yoshi Chiba, Shun Kobayashi, Tomoyuki Imai; exec p, Hiroshi Yamaji, Akira Tsuburaya; w, Shimako Sato, Junki Takegami (based on the comic book series *Wizard of Darkness*); ph, Shoei Sudo; ed, Shimako Sato; m, Ali Project

Horror   (PR: O   MPAA: NR)

WOMAN AT WAR, A   ★★★
(France/U.K.) 115m Palace Pictures; Canal Plus Productions; BBC ~ Republic Pictures Home Video c

Martha Plimpton *(Helene Mozkiewicz)*; Eric Stoltz *(Franz Boehler)*; Olgierd Lukaszewicz *(Schwenke)*

The war is WWII. The woman is Helene Moszkiewicz (Martha Plimpton), a 19-year-old Jewish girl in Nazi-occupied Brussels, who infiltrates the Gestapo. Based on Moszkiewicz's book, *Inside the Gestapo*, A WOMAN AT WAR is an absorbing, true account of heroism and sacrifice in the tradition of SCHINDLER'S LIST.

The daughter of a Jewish shopkeeper, young Moszkiewicz swiftly comes to a sobering maturity when her homeland surrenders to Nazi rule in 1940. Moszkiewicz draws attention to herself by standing up to a Gestapo officer, for which she nearly gets arrested. Franz Boehler (Eric Stoltz), a Nazi collaborator and profiteer who is also a leader in the Resistance, is impressed by her boldness and her fluency in the German language and recruits her to work with his group. After her parents and sister are arrested by the Gestapo, Moszkiewicz assumes the identity of Olga Richter (with false identity papers procured by Boehler) and works in the Gestapo headquarters. One of her duties is reviewing the files of suspected Jews and deciding who should be arrested now, and who later.

Moszkiewicz gains a reputation as a trusted and efficient worker while secretly sabotaging files and warning Jews who are on the arrest lists. Her actions are discovered by Jacques, a "Jew hunter," who is killed by Boehler before he can expose her. Boehler is the next to come under suspicion, and to save him, Moszkiewicz kills his accuser, Schwenke (Olgierd Lukaszewicz). Once lovers, Moszkiewicz and Boehler part when she learns that he is helping Nazi officers to flee the crumbling Third Reich in exchange for a handsome payment. When Belgium is liberated, Moszkiewicz is arrested as a Nazi collaborator. She clears her name and then is used by the Allies to lead Boehler into a trap that results in his death.

A WOMAN AT WAR was produced as a BBC miniseries in 1991. Its home video release in 1995, perhaps prompted by the success of SCHINDLER'S LIST, unearthed this British treasure for U.S. audiences to enjoy. Filmed on location in Poland and lensed in subdued tones, it offers an impressive recreation of wartime Belgium. This powerful adaptation of Moszkiewicz's story by Reg Gadney and Edward Bennett (who also directed) contains some exquisitely painful and poignant moments: when the Allies storm the Gestapo building, everybody has escaped except Moszkiewicz, who has remained to safeguard the files and instruct the soldiers on the importance of the records. She explains that each file is a person and, if destroyed, will be forgotten, as there will be no evidence. As Moszkiewicz is dragged away by the soldiers, she sees the files being tossed out of the windows and set ablaze.

Plimpton is superb in a challenging role which requires dual accents and a wide range of emotions. Less convincing is Stoltz, who comes across as distinctly American and too happy-go-lucky for a man treading dangerous waters. (*Violence, adult situations.*) — B.R.

d, Edward Bennett; p, Patrick Cassavetti, Martyn Auty; exec p, Nik Powell, Anat Birnbaum; w, Edward Bennett, Reg Gadney (based the book *Inside the Gestapo* by Helene Moszkiewicz); ed, Robin Sales; m, Stanislas Syrrvicz

Drama / War / Historical   (PR: C   MPAA: PG-13)

WOODEN MAN'S BRIDE, THE   ★★★
(China/Taiwan) 105m Long Shong Film Production Company ~ Arrow Releasing c

Chang Shih *(Kui)*; Wang Lan *(Young Mistress)*; Wang Yumei *(Madame Liu)*; Kao Mingjun *(Chief Tang)*

Set in a remote village in Northwestern China during the 1920s—and directed by Huang Jianxin, one of China's "Fifth Generation" of contemporary filmmakers—THE WOODEN MAN'S BRIDE is a strikingly beautiful tale of passionate love, repressive traditions, and the spirit of resistance.

The film opens with the wealthy Liu family preparing a traditional arranged wedding for their son. The important job of carrying the bride (Wang Lan) from her village to the Liu mansion is given to a local peasant named Kui (Chang Shih). Dressed in red with her face covered by a scarf, the bride is carried into the groom's village on a chair strapped to Kui's back. On route, the caravan is attacked by a gang of bandits. Although Kui tries to carry the bride to safety, she surrenders to the gang in order to save Kui's life. Kui hastens to the Liu mansion with news of the kidnapping. The young groom rushes for his rifle, and accidentally sets off an explosion which kills him. Deciding he must save the young mistress, Kui goes to the bandits' hideout. Impressed by his innocence and bravery, the bandits release the young women unharmed and Kui fulfills his duty of carrying her to the Liu home.

Upon their return, Madame Liu (Wang Yumei) hires Kui as a long term worker at her tofu mill as a reward for saving the young mistress. The bride, however, is subjected to a crude test of her virginity by Madame Liu, and forced to marry a wooden replica of the dead bridegroom. She is expected to remain faithful to the wooden image, and to be committed to the Liu family for the rest of her life. The bond between Kui and the now-miserable young mistress grows stronger and their relationship develops into a passionate affair. When this is discovered, Kui is driven from the village and the young mistress's ankles are broken, both as punishment and to prevent her from committing adultery again. Kui, beaten and desperate, returns to the bandits' hideout for refuge. One year later, a band of outlaws appears from the desert and marches to the Liu mansion. The group is led by Kui, who orders Madame Liu to be executed, and the young mistress is freed. Kui then changes into his ragged carrier's clothes, and with the young bride dressed in red on a chair strapped to his back, walks away from the village towards an uncertain future.

Both the story and style of THE WOODEN MAN'S BRIDE will feel familiar—and perhaps less successful—to anyone who has seen Chen Kiage's YELLOW EARTH, or Zhang Yimou's RED SORGHUM, JU DOU, or RAISE THE RED LANTERN. In all these films, age-old Chinese traditions oppress passionate young lovers, who survive even the most inhumane circumstances. The rugged Chinese landscape—bleached of color, bathed in golden light—throws into relief the elaborate, brightly colored trappings of "civilized" life. However, somewhat hidden in THE WOODEN MAN'S BRIDE is also a sense of deadpan absurdity, most evident as the young bride lives, eats, and sleeps with a wooden statue. This sensibility is reminiscent of Huang Jianxin's first film, THE BLACK CANNON INCIDENT, a satirical treatment of the bureaucratic system in China and one of the only films from the Fifth Generation to deal overtly with contemporary issues. *(Violence, sexual situations, adult situations.)* — J.S.

d, Huang Jianxin; p, Wang Ying Hsiang; w, Yang Zhengguang (based on the novel by Jia Pingua); ph, Zhang Xiaoguang; ed, Lei Qin; m, Zhang Dalong; cos, Du Longxi

Romance/Drama (PR: C MPAA: NR)

WORLD AND TIME ENOUGH ★★½
(U.S.) 90m One In Ten Films ~ Strand Releasing c

Matt Guidry *(Matt)*; Gregory G. Giles *(Joey)*; Kraig Swartz *(David)*; Peter Macon *(Mike)*; Bernadette Sullivan *(Marie)*; John Patrick Martin *(Mr. Quincy)*; Adam Mikelson *(Young Mark)*; Kathleen Fuller *(Mrs. Quincy)*

This homegrown Minneapolis gay drama, the feature debut of 29-year-old Eric Mueller, opens with a fresh attitude but succumbs to tedium in the home stretch.

Mark Quincy (Matt Guidry) and Joey Brown (Gregory G. Giles) are young gay lovers in the American midwest. Mark, a moody "conceptual sculptor," litters the community with unauthorized guerrilla artwork designed to draw attention to the HIV virus he carries. Key to his worldview is the childhood loss of his mother to a toppling cathedral crucifix: afterwards, his father withdrew into a private world, building model churches. Joey, meanwhile, is an HIV-free garbage collector who fills their shared apartment with colorful found objects. Angrily disowned by his homophobic adoptive parents, Joey wants to find his real family but meets with little success. When Mark learns that his father is dead, he embarks on a mad project to construct a mighty cathedral all by himself in the middle of a field, an obsession that strains his relationship with Joey. When his makeshift scaffolding collapses, Mark is laid up in the hospital. Joey, deciding a cathedral need not be of eternal stone and mortar, lovingly constructs a whimsical outdoor shrine, and wheels a recovering Mark out to see it.

Putting a congenial spin on all the histrionics—well, some of the histrionics—is Kraig Swartz, as a skeptical pal who interrupts the story at irregular intervals with asides that, for example, snidely dismiss manic Mark as a "drama queen." This unofficial narrator even gets snippy with the filmmakers themselves. When, in the film's second half, Swartz largely disappears, he is truly missed. WORLD ENOUGH AND TIME ENOUGH goes from an agreeable mixture of camp and sincerity to a fairly straightforward picture that reruns such familiar bits as the traumatic coming-out scene and the predictable punchout of a gay-basher. This technique—the sly segue from outrageous comedy that opens one's guard to harder-hitting material—is a familiar gambit in queer cinema (or, for that matter, any film that deals with oft-stereotyped minorities). Sometimes the trick works, sometimes it doesn't, and this plucky contender can't quite pull off the changes. Though Swartz plays his part with swishy sarcasm, the principle actors avoid the fey mannerisms of queer stereotypes, which is refreshing. What is not are the recurring slurs against non-gays. With the exception of Joey's nurturing stepsister (Bernadette Sullivan), straights everywhere are depicted as morons and bimbos. The substitution of heterophobia for homophobia hardly spells progress. *(Adult situations, violence, profanity.)* — C.C.

d, Eric Mueller; p, Julie Hartley, Andrew Peterson; assoc p, Emily Stevens; co-p, David Haugland; w, Eric Mueller; ph, Kyle Bergersen; ed, Laura Stokes; m, Eugene Huddleston; prod d, Heather McElhatton; sound, Johnny Hagen (design); casting, Lynn Blumenthal

Drama (PR: C MPAA: NR)

YEAR OF THE WALL
(SEE: PROMISE, THE)

YOUNG EMMANUELLE, A
(SEE: NEA)

YOUNGER & YOUNGER ★★
(Germany/France/Canada) 99m Younger
Enterprises; Pelemele Film; Kushner-Locke
Company ~ Paramount Home Video c

YZ

Donald Sutherland *(Jonathan Younger)*; Lolita
Davidovich *(Penelope Younger)*; Brendan Fraser *(Winston
Younger)*; Sally Kellerman *(Zig Zag Lilian)*; Julie Delpy
(Melodie); Linda Hunt *(Frances)*; Nicholas Gunn; Matt Damon;
Kim Little; Pit Kruger

Percy Adlon's film YOUNGER & YOUNGER strives to satirize
both contemporary American culture and German acculturiza-
tion in the strange and magical environment of Hollywood and
its obsession with fame, glamour, and beauty.

German immigrant Jonathan Younger (Donald Sutherland)
owns a rental storage facility with his American wife Penelope
(Lolita Davidovich) in a suburb of Hollywood. Jonathan social-
izes, flirts with women, plays an organ located above the office,
and flees on a motorcycle whenever business or personal conflicts raise their head. When famous European actress ZigZag
Lilian (Sally Kellerman) arrives with her daughter Melodie
(Julie Delpy) to rent space, Younger manages to introduce himself to the girl.

His wife, meanwhile, haggard and miserable, runs the office
and pops pills for a bad heart. Following an argument, Younger
takes an old acquaintance of hers to his room above the office,
probably to punish his wife, but when she overhears them she
dies.

Their son Winston (Brendan Fraser) returns from business
training abroad. He is fond of his father but quickly loses all
illusions about him when he learns his father knows nothing of
management, his mother has always run the business, and his
father's infidelity precipitated her death. He is comforted by his
growing friendship with Melodie.

Younger begins to imagine he sees his wife, each time looking
younger and prettier. He becomes increasingly nostalgic and
guilty and eventually drives his motorcycle off a road with an
image of his young wife in his mind. Winston and Melodie take
over the business, marry, and have a child.

Director Adlon enjoys indulging in the eccentricity of
seemingly ordinary people. He satirizes the sentimentality
invested in the images people have of themselves and others
and the relationships they form with things. Jonathan copes
with his wife's death by imagining her youth and their early
love. And he does not actually play the organ—it plays ballads automatically—though he permits others, including his
son, to believe he does.

Much of the film is shot in soft light and colors, warm pastels
well-suited to the languid mood of the film. However, while
Adlon's drama is often visually pleasing, the story and humor are
regrettably dull. — M.F.

d, Percy Adlon; p, Eleonore Adlon; exec p, Howard Hurst, Aziz
Oggeh; assoc p, Christopher Webster; w, Percy Adlon, Felix O.
Adlon; ph, Bernd Heinl; ed, Suzanne Fenn; m, Hans Zimmer;
prod d, Steven Legler; art d, Nancy B. Roberts; set d, Barbara
Cassel; sound, Jose Araujo; casting, Jerold Franks; cos, Sharen
Davis

Comedy (PR: A   MPAA: R)

ZOOMAN ★★½
(U.S.) 95m Manheim Company;
Logo Productions ~ Republic Pictures
Home Video c

Louis Gossett, Jr. *(Rueben Tate)*; Charles S. Dut-
ton *(Emmett)*; Cynthia Martells *(Rachel)*; Khalil
Kain *(Zooman)*; Hill Harper *(Victor)*; CCH Poun-
der *(Ash)*; Vondie Curtis Hall *(Davis)*; Tommy Hol-
lis *(Mr. Washington)*; Julio Mechoso *(Cruz)*; Kasi
Lemmons *(Grace)*; Joe Lala *(Cortez)*; Sully Diaz
(Monita); Vicellous Shannon *(Russell)*; Alberto
Vazquez *(Alex)*; Alyssa Ashley Nichols (Jackie);
Sam Bottoms *(Policeman)*; John Pittman *(Mr. Miller)*; Angelina
Estrada *(Mrs. Gonzales)*; Lisa Rhoden *(TV Reporter)*; Destinee De-
Walt *(Girl #15)*; Marcus Salgado *(Bartender)*; Jorge Pupo *(NYPD
Policeman)*

ZOOMAN is director Leon Ichaso's adaptation of Pulitzer Prize
winner Charles Fuller's play about the impact of inner city
violence.

Zooman (Khalil Kain) roams the streets of New York delivering a freewheeling monologue on his wild life. Meanwhile,
Rachel Tate (Cynthia Martells) orders her daughter Jackie
(Alyssa Ashely Nichols) out of the house. She goes out on the
stoop. When Zooman spots an opponent in the crowded street,
he pulls out a gun and starts shooting, accidentally killing Jackie.
Rueben Tate (Lou Gossett Jr.), Rachel's estranged husband,
comes home to grieve, and police canvass the neighborhood for
witnesses. No one admits to seeing a thing, although Jackie's
older brother Victor (Hill Harper) hears the murderer is named
Zooman. For his part, Zooman is unrepentant, blaming the death
on the girl being in the wrong place at the wrong time.

Frustrated by the lack of witnesses, Victor decides to put up a
sign on his house to shame his neighbors into talking. It reads:
"The killers of our Jackie are free because our neighbors will not
identity them."

The sign backfires, enraging most neighbors and attracting
TV crews. Meanwhile, Victor gets a gun to kill Zooman. Soon
after the tearful memorial service, Zooman returns to the 'hood.
He checks out the sign but retreats when a neighbor confronts
him. Later that night he returns and fires a shot at the sign. Victor
comes out of the house, and Zooman aims his gun at him. Just as
he's about to pull the trigger, someone else in the neighborhood
shoots him dead.

ZOOMAN's best moments rise from its title character's enraged, homeboy-Brechtian rants. Khalil Kain's disturbing portrait has a crazy charisma that benefits from Charles Fuller's
caustic pen. On the home front, however, the Tates fall prey to
that well-documented affliction of stage-to-movie adaptations—stiffness. With much of the action confined to the house,
and much of the dialogue confined to grief and justice, Ichaso's
film cannot shed the shackles of the theater. His one other major
problem is the conveniently ignored plotting glitch—if Victor
knows Zooman killed his sister, why does he not tell his own
family? Still, thanks to the compelling conflict at its center,
ZOOMAN almost triumphs despite its little inconsistencies.
(Profanity, adult situations.) — S.K.

d, Leon Ichaso; p, James B. Freydberg, Michael Manheim; assoc
p, Ron Parker; w, Charles Fuller (based on his play *Zooman and
the Sign*); ph, Jeffrey Jur; ed, Gary Karr; m, Daniel Licht; prod d,
Richard Hoover; art d, Keith Cox; set d, Sandy Struth; sound, Rolf
Pardula (mixer); fx, W. Bruce Mattox; casting, Beth Klein; cos,
Sharen Davis; makeup, June Josef-Sparks; stunts, Julius LeFlore

Drama (PR: C   MPAA: R)

Academy Awards

ACADEMY AWARDS

68th AWARDS OF THE ACADEMY OF MOTION PICTURE ARTS AND SCIENCES

(Listings in italics indicate winners)

Best Picture

Mel Gibson, Alan Ladd, Jr., Bruce Davey, BRAVEHEART
Brian Grazer, APOLLO 13
George Miller, Doug Mitchell, Bill Miller, BABE
Mario Cecchi Gori, Vittorio Cecchi Gori, Gaetano
   Daniele, THE POSTMAN (IL POSTINO)
Lindsay Doran, SENSE AND SENSIBILITY

Best Performance by an Actor in a Leading Role

Nicolas Cage, LEAVING LAS VEGAS
Sean Penn, DEAD MAN WALKING
Richard Dreyfuss, MR. HOLLAND'S OPUS
Anthony Hopkins, NIXON
Massimo Troisi, THE POSTMAN (IL POSTINO)

Best Performance by an Actress in a Leading Role

Susan Sarandon, DEAD MAN WALKING
Meryl Streep, THE BRIDGES OF MADISON COUNTY
Sharon Stone, CASINO
Elisabeth Shue, LEAVING LAS VEGAS
Emma Thompson, SENSE AND SENSIBILITY

Best Performance by an Actor in a Supporting Role

Kevin Spacey, THE USUAL SUSPECTS
Ed Harris, APOLLO 13
James Cromwell, BABE
Tim Roth, ROB ROY
Brad Pitt, TWELVE MONKEYS

Best Performance by an Actress in a Supporting Role

Mira Sorvino, MIGHTY APHRODITE
Kathleen Quinlan, APOLLO 13
Mare Winningham, GEORGIA
Joan Allen, NIXON
Kate Winslet, SENSE AND SENSIBILITY

Best Achievement in Directing

Mel Gibson, BRAVEHEART
Chris Noonan, BABE
Tim Robbins, DEAD MAN WALKING
Mike Figgis, LEAVING LAS VEGAS
Michael Radford, THE POSTMAN (IL POSTINO)

Best Achievement in Writing (Screenplay Written Directly for the Screen)

Christopher McQuarrie, THE USUAL SUSPECTS
Randall Wallace, BRAVEHEART
Woody Allen, MIGHTY APHRODITE
Stephen J. Rivele, Christopher Wilkinson, Oliver Stone,
   NIXON
Joss Whedon, Andrew Stanton, Joel Cohen, Alec
   Sokolow, TOY STORY

Best Achievement in Writing (Screenplay Based on Material Previously Produced or Published)

Emma Thompson, SENSE AND SENSIBILITY

William Broyles, Jr., Al Reinert, APOLLO 13
George Miller, Chris Noonan, BABE
Mike Figgis, LEAVING LAS VEGAS
Anna Pavignano, Michael Radford, Furio Scarpelli,
   Giacomo Scarpelli, Massimo Troisi, THE POSTMAN
   (IL POSTINO)

Best Foreign Language Film

ANTONIA'S LINE (The Netherlands)
ALL THINGS FAIR (Sweden)
DUST OF LIFE (Algeria)
O QUATRILHO (Brazil)
THE STAR MAKER (Italy)

Best Achievement in Art Direction

Eugenio Zanetti, RESTORATION
Michael Corenblith, Merideth Boswell, APOLLO 13
Roger Ford, Kerrie Brown, BABE
Bo Welch, Cheryl Carasik, A LITTLE PRINCESS
Tony Burrough, RICHARD III

Best Achievement in Cinematography

John Toll, BRAVEHEART
Stephen Goldblatt, BATMAN FOREVER
Emmanuel Lubezki, A LITTLE PRINCESS
Michael Coulter, SENSE AND SENSIBILITY
Lu Yue, SHANGHAI TRIAD

Best Achievement in Costume Design

James Acheson, RESTORATION
Charles Knode, BRAVEHEART
Shuna Harwood, RICHARD III
Jenny Beavan, John Bright, SENSE AND SENSIBILITY
Julie Weiss, TWELVE MONKEYS

Best Achievement in Documentary Features

Jon Blair, ANNE FRANK REMEMBERED
Thomas Lennon, Michael Epstein, THE BATTLE OVER
   CITIZEN KANE
Allan Miller, Walter Scheuer, FIDDLEFEST — ROBERTA
   TZAVARAS AND HER EAST HARLEM VIOLIN
   PROGRAM
Mike Tollin, Fredric Golding, HANK AARON: CHASING
   THE DREAM
Jeanne Jordan, Steven Ascher, TROUBLESOME CREEK:
   A MIDWESTERN

Best Achievement in Documentary Short Subjects

Kary Antholis, ONE SURVIVOR REMEMBERS
Nancy Dine, Richard Stilwell, JIM DINE: A
   SELF-PORTRAIT ON THE WALLS
Greg MacGillivray, Alec Lorimore, THE LIVING SEA
Terry Sanders, Freida Lee Mock, NEVER GIVE UP: THE
   20th CENTURY ODYSSEY OF HERBERT ZIPPER
Charles Guggenheim, THE SHADOW OF HATE

Best Achievement in Film Editing
Mike Hill, Dan Hanley, APOLLO 13
Marcus D'Arcy, Jay Friedkin, BABE
Steven Rosenblum, BRAVEHEART
Chris Lebenzon, CRIMSON TIDE
Richard Francis-Bruce, SEVEN

Best Achievement in Makeup
Peter Frampton, Paul Pattison, Lois Burwell,
 BRAVEHEART
Ken Diaz, Mark Sanchez, MY FAMILY: MI FAMILIA
Greg Cannom, Bob Laden, Colleen Callaghan,
 ROOMMATES

Best Achievement in Music (Original Dramatic Score)
Luis Bacalov, THE POSTMAN (IL POSTINO)
James Horner, APOLLO 13
James Horner, BRAVEHEART
John Williams, NIXON
Patrick Doyle, SENSE AND SENSIBILITY

Best Achievement in Music (Original Musical or Comedy Score)
Alan Menken, Stephen Schwartz, POCAHONTAS
Marc Shaiman, THE AMERICAN PRESIDENT
John Williams, SABRINA
Randy Newman, TOY STORY
Thomas Newman, UNSTRUNG HEROES

Best Achievement in Music (Original Song)
Alan Menken, Stephen Schwartz, "Colors of the Wind"
 (POCAHONTAS)
Bruce Springsteen, "Dead Man Walkin'" (DEAD MAN
 WALKING)
Michael Kamen, Bryan Adams, Robert John Lange,
 "Have You Ever Really Loved a Woman" (DON JUAN
 DEMARCO)
John Williams, Alan Bergman, Marilyn Bergman,
 "Moonlight" (SABRINA)
Randy Newman, "You've Got a Friend" (TOY STORY)

Best Achievement in Animated Short Films
Nick Park, A CLOSE SHAVE
John R. Dilworth, THE CHICKEN FROM OUTERSPACE
Chris Landreth, Robin Bargar, THE END
Alexij Kharitidi, GAGARIN
Chris Bailey, RUNAWAY BRAIN

Best Achievement in Live Action Short Films
Christine Lahti, Jana Sue Memel, LIEBERMAN IN LOVE
Luke Cresswell, Steve McNicholas, BROOMS
Griffin Dunne, Thom Colwell, DUKE OF GROOVE
Jeff Goldblum, Tikki Goldberg, LITTLE SURPRISES
Dianne Houston, Joy Ryan, TUESDAY MORNING RIDE

Best Achievement in Sound
Rick Dior, Steve Pederson, Scott Millan, David
 MacMillan, APOLLO 13
Donald O. Mitchell, Frank A. Montano, Michael
 Herbick, Petur Hliddal, BATMAN FOREVER
Andy Nelson, Scott Millan, Anna Behlmer, Brian
 Simmons, BRAVEHEART
Kevin O'Connell, Rick Kline, Gregory H. Watkins,
 William B. Kaplan, CRIMSON TIDE
Steve Maslow, Gregg Landaker, Keith A. Wester,
 WATERWORLD

Best Achievement in Sound Effects Editing
Lon Bender, Per Hallberg, BRAVEHEART
John Leveque, Bruce Stambler, BATMAN FOREVER
George Watters, II, CRIMSON TIDE

Best Achievement in Visual Effects
Scott E. Anderson, Charles Gibson, Neal Scanlan, John
 Cox, BABE
Robert Legato, Michael Kanfer, Leslie Ekker, Matt
 Sweeney, APOLLO 13

Honorary Awards
Kirk Douglas
Chuck Jones

Obituaries

OBITUARIES

(January 1 to December 31, 1995)

by Frank Lovece

Abbott, George

born: June 25, 1887, Forestville, NY
died: Jan. 31, 1995, Miami Beach, FL, age 107
educ: University of Rochester; Harvard

The Colossus at Broadway, whose contributions as writer, actor, director, producer and impresario in the theater and secondarily film will long remain unsurpassed.

George Francis Abbott, the force behind such enduring American works as *Chicago, Twentieth Century, Room Service, Pal Joey, Sweet Charity, On the Town, A Tree Grows in Brooklyn, Pajama Game, Once Upon a Mattress, Fiorello!, A Funny Thing Happened on the Way to the Forum* and *Damn Yankees* was a quintessential damn Yankee himself. Tall and imposing, yet big-hearted and modest, Abbott melded the universal and the topical to win over audiences and critics through succeeding generations. He was active even toward the end, co-directing his off-Off-Broadway play *Frankie* at 102; contributing revisions to what became a hit revival of *Damn Yankees* at 106, and, less than two weeks before his death, dictating revisions for a projected revival of *Pajama Game.*

Abbott, the eldest of three children of George Burwell and May MacLaury Abbott, moved with his family to Cheyenne, WY when he was 11. He worked as a Western Union messenger and as a ranch cowboy before being sent to Kearney Military Academy in Nebraska. In his teens, in Hamburg, NY, he grew to love theater, and nurtured his interest at the University of Rochester, where he played football and joined the Dramatic Club. He studied playwriting at Harvard's renowned George Pierce Baker workshop, and in 1912 won a $100 prize for his play *The Man in the Manhole.* The following year he tried tackling Broadway, which tackled him back; he landed a role as a drunken collegian in *The Misleading Lady,* then languished for two years before being hired as a Boy Friday and de facto casting associate/assistant producer. He returned to acting in 1923, winning acclaim as a cowboy in *Zander the Great,* and as acting work increased, gradually turned his attention to scripts and production. He co-wrote his first Broadway plays, *The Fall Guy* and *A Holy Terror,* in 1925, and scored his first hit as co-director and co-writer of *Broadway* (1926), which was adapted to film in both 1929 (in a production utilizing a landmark new type of camera crane allowing for unprecedented moving shots) and 1942.

Abbott came to Hollywood with the talkies, directing and writing or co-writing the script adaptations for WHY BRING THAT UP? and HALF-WAY TO HEAVEN (1929), MANSLAUGHTER (also producer) and THE SEA GOD (1930), STOLEN HEAVEN, SECRETS OF A SECRETARY and MY SIN (1931); directing THE CHEAT (1931), and earning an Oscar screenwriting nomination for Best Picture-winner ALL QUIET ON THE WESTERN FRONT (1930). Abbott devoted his full attention to theater during the following decade, but eventually added to his film portfolio as director and producer of TOO MANY GIRLS (1940)—where he introduced Lucille Ball to Desi Arnaz—and as co-director and co-producer (with Stanley Donen) of his stage-musical adaptations THE PAJAMA GAME (1957) and DAMN YANKEES (1958), writing or co-writing the scripts. He produced films including BOY MEETS GIRL and ROOM SERVICE (1938) and PRIMROSE PATH (1940).

The films to date adapted from plays and musicals he co-wrote are THE SATURDAY NIGHT KID, NIGHT PARADE, COQUETTE (for which Mary Pickford earned a Best Actress Oscar), and BROADWAY (1929), THE FALL GUY (1930), THOSE WE LOVE (1932), LILLY TURNER (1933), STRAIGHT IS THE WAY (1934), HEAT LIGHTING (1934; remade as 1941's HIGHWAY WEST), THREE MEN ON A HORSE (1936), ON YOUR TOES (1939), THE BOYS FROM SYRACUSE (1940), the remake of BROADWAY (1942), BEAT THE BAND (1947) and WHERE'S CHARLEY? (1952).

Among the stars he helped establish with early big breaks were Eddie Albert, Shirley Booth, Tom Bosley, Carol Burnett, Jose Ferrer, Jack Gilford, Van Johnson, Garson Kanin, Gene Kelly, Shirley MacLaine, Butterfly McQueen, Paul Muni and Jean Stapleton; among the behind-the-scenes unknowns were Leonard Bernstein, Betty Comden & Adolph Green, Bob Fosse, Harold Prince and Jerome Robbins. Among his honors and awards were a shared Pulitzer Prize, the Drama Critics Circle Award and two Tony Awards for *Fiorello!* (1959); Tonys for *The Pajama Game* (1955), *Damn Yankees* (1956) and *A Funny Thing Happened on the Way to the Forum* (1963), plus a special lifetime-career Tony and the Kennedy Center Lifetime Achievement Award. He is the namesake, and was the initial recipient, of the Society of Stage Directors & Choreographers top award.

Abbott was once widowed and once divorced, and married third wife Joy Valderrama in 1983. Abbott died of a stroke.

Adams, Elizabeth

aka: Madam Alex
born: c. 1935, The Philippines
died: July 8, 1995, Los Angeles, CA, age 60

Beverly Hills' Madam Alex, whose brothel's clientele included movie-industry men for two decades.

Elizabeth Adams, who gave an early career break to the flamboyant Heidi Fleiss, traded information on murder suspects, drug dealers and others in exchange for a 1991 plea bargain; she received 18 months probation, then returned to business in a house close by the West Hollywood sheriff's office. Adams had life-support measures terminated following heart surgery.

Adamson, Al

born: 1929, Los Angeles, CA
died: c. June 1995, Indio, CA, age 66; body found Aug. 2, 1995

Cult-favorite horror/exploitation director.

The son of Hollywood parents—father Victor Adamson aka Denver Dixon aka Art Mix was a one-time cowboy star, and mother Delores Booth an actress—Albert Victor Adamson, Jr. specialized in drive-in features and the bottom halves of double-bills with such micro-budget classics-of-their-kind as SATAN'S SADISTS (made for $50,000) and NURSE SHERRI. He'd dabbled in acting, appearing at age 12 in his father's feature MORMAN CONQUEST (1941), and in his own first two films as producer-director. But he found his niche as a canny exploitation hand who churned out horror, black-action, naughty-nurse and psycho-biker movies—often reediting, retitling and redistributing them, with or without new scenes, in a plethora of versions. Many featured his wife, the late Regina Carrol (aka Regina Carrol Gelfen). Most were self-distributed through his Independent International company, formed in 1968 with partners Sam Sherman and Dan Kennis. By the late 1980s, Adamson had turned to family pictures—one of which, LOST, boasted his biggest budget ever, $475,000—and owned a Hollywood restaurant, the Houston Pit Barbecue. Adamson, who gave early (albeit Anglicized) breaks to Vilmos Zsigmund ("William Zsigmond") and Laszlo ("Leslie") Kovacs, was a Sam Arkoff for the seventies.

As in one of his own films, Adamson's life ended horrifically: his body was discovered entombed beneath a whirlpool tub, under cement and tiles, after he'd been missing for five weeks. Fred Fulford, a contractor living at Adamson's home while remodeling it, was charged with homicide.

Aldridge, Kay

born: c. 1917
died: Jan. 12, 1995, Rockport, ME, age 77

Model-actress among the most photographed women of the 1930s, who decorated several B-pictures.

Kay Aldridge, who graced the covers of *Life, Ladies' Home Journal, Redbook* and *Look* magazines, appeared in 18 films from 1937-45—mostly bottom-bill programmers, but occasional A-pictures such as LOUISIANA PURCHASE (1941) and DU BARRY WAS A LADY (1943). She appeared in musicals, dramas and thrillers, with her most notable screen roles in ROY ROGERS' GOLDEN HOOFS (1941), THE

PHANTOM OF 42nd STREET and THE MAN WHO WALKED ALONE (1945). Her other films include ROSALIE (1937), HOTEL FOR WOMEN and HERE I AM A STRANGER (1939), YESTERDAY'S HEROES, SHOOTING HIGH, SAILOR'S LADY, GIRL IN 313, GIRL FROM AVENUE A, DOWN ARGENTINE WAY, and FREE, BLONDE AND 21 (1940), and YOU'RE IN THE ARMY NOW, and NAVY BLUES (1941).

Aldridge, known off-camera as Kay Aldridge Tucker upon her marriage to the second of her three husbands, died of a heart attack.

Alexander, Ronald

born: Ronald George Alexander Ungerer, c. 1917, West New York, N.J.
died: April 24, 1995, New York, NY, age 78
Well-regarded Broadway playwright who wrote two Hollywood screenplays.

Ronald George Alexander Ungerer toiled as a factory worker, boxer, singer and Broadway organizer for the United Service Organizations before becoming a bit player on the stage and in a film, THE LADY IN QUESTION aka IT HAPPENED IN PARIS (1940). Turning to writing, he scored particular successes with the comedies *Time Out for Ginger* (1952), starring Melvyn Douglas as the father of three daughters—as was Alexander himself—and *Nobody Loves an Albatross,* a satire of the TV industry that starred Robert Preston. Alexander adapted the former into the film BILLIE (1965). His other screenplays include RETURN TO PEYTON PLACE (1961), REQUIEM FOR A GUNFIGHTER and THE BOUNTY KILLER (1965). The film HOLIDAY FOR LOVERS (1959) was adapted from his same-name play. At his death, Alexander was collaborating with composer Diane Leslie on two musicals and an animated-film screenplay.

Alexander died of cancer.

Allan, Ted

born: Jan. 25, 1916, Montreal, Canada,
died: June 29, 1995, Toronto, Canada, age 79
Novelist and screenwriter best known for his Academy Award-nominated screenplay LIES MY FATHER TOLD ME (1975), in which he also played a supporting role.

Ted Allan had previously scripted a 1960 UK version of director Jan Kadar's 1920s Jewish-Canadian boyhood, this one incongruously set among Christian Dubliners; he remade the remake as a stage version, in 1986. Allan had likewise turned to real life for inspiration with his mid-1950s book *The Scalpel, The Sword: The Story of Dr. Norman Bethune,* which he adapted into both the 1990 Canada-France-China co-production BETHUNE aka DR. BETHUNE: THE MAKING OF A HERO, and a 1977 Canadian telefilm, BETHUNE, both starring Donald Sutherland. Allan's experiences alongside the controversial Bethune in the Canadian Mackenzie-Papineau Battalion medical unit of the International Brigades during the Spanish Civil War formed the basis of a novel, *This Time a Better Earth.*

Allan also wrote short stories for *The New Yorker, Harper's* and other magazines, a popular children's book, *Willie, the Squowse,* and plays including *The Money Makers, The Ghost Writers, Oh! What a Lovely War* (adapted into a 1969 UK film with John Lennon), *I've Seen You Cut Lemons, Secret of the World, Legend of Pepito, Double Image* and *Gog and Magog,* as well as the book for the musical *Chu Chem.* He co-adapted his play *Love Streams* with director John Cassavetes for Cassavetes' 1984 film. Allan also wrote the screenplay for THE WEBSTER BOY aka MIDDLE OF NOWHERE (U.K. 1962), and co-wrote FALLING IN LOVE AGAIN (1980).

Allan died of respiratory failure.

Andrews, Maxene

born: Jan. 3, 1916, Minneapolis, MN
died: Oct. 21, 1995, Hyannis, MA, age 79
Singer with the iconic WWII harmonizing trio The Andrews Sisters, who played themselves in 17 films.

Maxene (sometimes listed as Maxine in movie credits) Andrews organized the singing sisters in 1932, recruiting 21-year-old LaVerne and 14-year-old Patty. Maxene, "the one on the left," hit the high notes, with LaVerne on the low-end and Patty in midrange. The quintessential girls-next-door went from local talent shows to a vaudeville troupe, the Larry Rich Unit Show, and became stars in 1937 with a part-English version of

the Yiddish song "Bei Mir Bist du Schoen." Despite their not reading music, the trio enjoyed a succession of smashes including "Boogie-Woogie Bugle Boy" (a hit cover for Bette Midler in the 1970s), "The Jumping Jive," "Ti-Pi-Tin," "Hold Tight," "The Beer Barrel Polka" (followed by "The Pennsylvania Polka" and "Strip Polka"), the ballad "Apple Blossom Time," boogie-woogie tunes like "Rhumboogie" and "Beat Me, Daddy, Eight to the Bar" (inspiration for the tile of their radio show, Eight-to-a-Bar Ranch) and the WWII smashes "Don't Sit Under the Apple Tree" and "Rum and Coca-Cola." Through the 1940s, they sold more than 50 million records and earned at least 17 gold records.

After a brief break-up in the early 1950s, the occasionally estranged sisters regrouped and performed until LaVerne's death in 1967. Maxene and Patty, who endured a rocky relationship, last performed together with a fill-in "sister" in the 1974 Broadway musical Over Here, which ran for more than a year. Maxene—who was named dean of women at Tahoe Paradise College in Lake Tahoe, CA in 1970—then fostered a solo club career, released a 1990 album, *Maxene: An Andrews Sister,* and appeared as herself for four weeks in 1995 during the ongoing run of the off-Broadway musical *Swing Time Canteen.* Shortly before her death, she joined President Clinton and Bob Hope in singing "America the Beautiful" at an anniversary celebration to mark the end of WWII.

The sisters' films were ARGENTINE NIGHTS (1940), BUCK PRIVATES, HOLD THAT GHOST aka OH, CHARLIE, and IN THE NAVY (1941), WHAT'S COOKIN'?, PRIVATE BUCKAROO, and GIVE OUT, SISTERS (1942), ALWAYS A BRIDESMAID, HOW'S ABOUT IT? and SWINGTIME JOHNNY (1943), FOLLOW THE BOYS, HOLLYWOOD CANTEEN, and MOONLIGHT AND CACTUS (1944), HER LUCKY NIGHT (1945), MAKE MINE MUSIC (voices in animated film; 1946), ROAD TO RIO (1947), and MELODY TIME (voices in animated film; 1948)

Maxene, known as Mackie to family and friends, died of a heart attack.

Arnold, Danny

born: Arnold Rothman, Jan. 23 1925, New York City
died: Aug. 19, 1995, Los Angeles, CA, age 70
Co-creator and visionary force behind the classic TV series "Barney Miller," and a recipient of the Writers Guild of America lifetime achievement honor.

Best known for his television writing, the one-time Danny Arnold began as a summer-stock and vaudeville actor and comedian. After serving in the Marines during WWII, he became a sound-effects editor at Columbia and then a Hollywood utility player, involved in editing, writing and production. He acted in films including BREAKTHROUGH (1950), and the Dean Martin-Jerry Lewis film SAILOR BEWARE (1951), then wrote the story and co-wrote the screenplay for the comic duo's THE CADDY (1953). Arnold also wrote or co-wrote the screenplays for DESERT SANDS and FORT YUMA (1955), REBEL IN TOWN and OUTSIDE THE LAW (1956) and THE LADY TAKES A FLYER (1958), and wrote and produced the James Thurber-inspired THE WAR BETWEEN MEN AND WOMEN (1972), in which Arnold had a cameo as a police officer.

After breaking into television writing for Tennessee Ernie Ford and Rosemary Clooney in the 1950s, Arnold went on to write, direct and produce sitcoms, beginning with the final season of "The Real McCoys" in 1963. He worked on "Bewitched" and "That Girl," created the acclaimed Thurberesque seriocomedy "My World and Welcome to It" (NBC 1969-70), for which he won an Emmy Award, and co-created "Barney Miller" (ABC 1975-82), winning an Emmy for the 1981-82 season. Though he shared creator credit with Theodore J. Flicker for that show, the two were not collaborators and Flicker remained uninvolved; the self-described workaholic Arnold orchestrated every aspect of that literate, topical, often bleakly witty sitcom starring Hal Linden as a beleaguered but patriarchal New York city precinct captain. Arnold's subsequent series, "Joe Bash" and "Stat," were both short-lived. The Writers Guild honored him with its lifetime Paddy Chayefsky Award in 1985.

Arnold, who'd had a heart attack and bypass operation in 1979, died of heart failure.

Aviles, Rick

born: c. 1954, New York City
died: March 17, 1995, Los Angeles, age 41

Stand-up comic who made occasional forays into both comic and dramatic films.

After starting in stand-up in and around Greenwich Village, Rick Aviles appeared in cable-comedy programs such as HBO's "One Night Stand," and was a recurring regular on the 1987-88 season of the syndicated TV variety series "It's Showtime at the Apollo." Aviles appeared in the miniseries THE STAND (1994), and in films including CANNONBALL RUN (1984), MONDO NEW YORK (1987), SPIKE OF BENSON-HURST (1988), MYSTERY TRAIN and IDENTITY CRISIS (1989), GHOST, THE GODFATHER: PART III, and GREEN CARD (1990), and CARLITO'S WAY (1993)

After filming one of his most visible roles, as a floating town's council leader in WATERWORLD (1995), Aviles died of heart failure before the movie's release. He had also worked on another film prior to his death, JOE'S APARTMENT.

No cause of death was given.

Barrett, Kay Brown

born: c. 1901, Hastings-on-Hudson, NY
died: Jan. 18, 1995, Highstown, NJ, age 93
educ: Wellesley College

Talent scout and agent who secured the movie rights to *Gone With the Wind*, and helped change David O. Selznick's opinion that, "A Civil War story won't go."

Kay Brown Barrett, working at such agencies as ICM, Leland Hayward, and MCA, represented such performers and authors as Montgomery Clift, Isak Dinesen, Alec Guinness, John Gielgud, Lillian Hellman, Ralph Richardson, Rex Harrison, Fredric March, Arthur Miller (for 40 years), and Patricia Neal. She helped bring such novels as Edna Ferber's *Cimarron* and Daphne du Maurier's *Rebecca* to the screen, and was instrumental in luring European stars Ingrid Bergman and Laurence Olivier to Hollywood, and—though her claim was disputed by Hitchcock collaborator Charles Bennett, who credited himself—in persuading director Alfred Hitchcock to sign with Selznick.

Upon her 1924 graduation from Wellesley, where she majored in English, she began work with the Mary Arden Theater School in Peterborough, NH. When Joseph P. Kennedy and the school's other owners bought a movie company, the Film Booking Office, Barrett began reading stories and scouting for film rights. The company evolved into RKO, for which Barrett secured the rights to *Cimarron*, which won the 1932 Academy Awards for picture and screenplay

Barrett died following a stroke.

Beck, Thomas

born: c. 1909
died: Sept. 23, 1995, Miami Shores, FL, age 86

Contract player in 1930s films, who worked to promote the nascent Screen Actors Guild and left movies in 1939 after a studio rollback of his wages.

After beginning as a New York stage actor, Thomas Beck appeared in a variety of parts in Fox's "Charlie Chan" and "Mr. Moto" film series. Among his notable other roles were the village priest in Shirley Temple's HEIDI (1937), and a soldier who dies in Ronald Colman's arms in UNDER TWO FLAGS (1936).

No cause of death was reported.

Begelman, David

born: Aug. 26, 1921, New York, NY
died: Aug. 7, 1995, Los Angeles, CA, age 73

One-time president of Columbia Pictures, who oversaw the making of such hits as THE WAY WE WERE and CLOSE ENCOUNTERS OF THE THIRD KIND, yet became iconic for precipitating one of Hollywood's most infamous financial scandals.

The troubled David Begelman—who in his self-created history claimed to have graduated from Yale and gone on to Yale Law School, though he'd done neither—was president of Columbia Pictures when he forged actor Cliff Robertson's signature on a Sept. 2, 1976 check for $10,000. In what became known as the "Indecent Exposure" scandal, after the best-selling book by Wall Street Journal reporter David McClin-

tick, authorities found Begelman had also cashed two other checks, totaling $30,000, made out to director Martin Ritt and to Ma Maison maitre d' Pierre Groleau. In addition, Begelman padded his expense account by at least $23,000.

Begelman pleaded no contest in 1978 to felony grand theft; he was fined $5,000, placed on three years probation, and, as a condition of sentence, produced the documentary short "Angel Death," about the dangers of the drug PCP ("angel dust"). That film prompted Burbank Municipal Judge Thomas C. Murphy, in 1979, to reduce the charge to a misdemeanor, enter a not-guilty plea to the new charge, dismiss the case, and revoke the last two years of probation. The case's repercussions were felt beyond Begelman, however, as Los Angeles District Attorney John Van de Kamp established a task force that ferreted out more embezzlement in the movie industry.

Begelman, raised in the Bronx as a Manhattan tailor's son, spent WWII in the Air Force, including a brief stint in a technical training program on the campus of Yale University. Begelman briefly attended New York University after the war, then dropped out and drifted into insurance. In 1948, he joined MCA as an agent, becoming vice president of special projects after 11 years. In 1960, he and fellow MCA staffer Freddie Fields left to form what would eventually be Creative Management Associates, where Begelman's clients included Judy Garland and Barbra Streisand. Begelman became president of Columbia Pictures in 1973, where he greenlighted, in addition to the aforementioned, such films as TOMMY, FUNNY LADY, SHAMPOO and MURDER BY DEATH.

Begelman was forced to resign during the scandal, but went on to be named president of MGM in December 1979. His tenure there included the flops PENNIES FROM HEAVEN and WHOSE LIFE IS IT ANYWAY? and the hit POLTERGEIST. Ousted July 1982 from what was now MGM/UA, he formed Sherwood Productions with Los Angeles Kings owner Bruce McNall and Texas billionaires the Hunt brothers; films here included the hit MR. MOM, cult-fave THE ADVENTURES OF BUCKAROO BANZAI: ACROSS THE EIGHTH DIMENSION, and the dismal BLAME IT ON RIO. Begelman formed Gladden Entertainment in May 1984; despite hits including WEEKEND AT BERNIE'S and MANNEQUIN, the company went bankrupt after a decade, owing some $4.1 million to directors, writers and actors including Michelle Pfeiffer and Jeff Bridges.

At about 8:30 on the evening of Monday, Aug. 7, Begelman telephoned a friend, Danny Welks, to speak about putting affairs in order. Afterward, distraught over business reverses, and with a history of leaving friends fearful of his suicide, Begeleman died of a self-inflicted gunshot wound at his Century City home.

Bemberg, Maria Luisa

born: April 14, 1922 (some sources give 1940), Buenos Aires, Argentina
died: May 7, 1995, Buenos Aires, Argentina, age 73

Argentine director of the Oscar-nominated CAMILLA (1984).

In her 40s—after a wealthy childhood, marriage to an architect, raising four children, then becoming divorced—Marisa Luisa Bemberg co-founded the theater company Teatro del Globo, directed two short films, and, at age 48, wrote her first screenplay, "Cronica de Una Senora"; she followed this five years later with "Triangular de Cuatro." After brief studies with Lee Strasberg in New York, she co-founded a production company with Lita Stantic, and self-financed her first two features: MOMENTOS (Argentina 1981) and SENORA DE NADIE (Argentina 1982), the latter reportedly the first Argentine feature to include a specifically gay character.

Her other films as director and, generally, co-writer, included CAMILA (Argentina/Spain 1984), the semiautobiographical MISS MARY (Argentina 1986), YO, LA PEOR DE TODOS/I, THE WORST OF ALL (Argentina 1990), and I DON'T WANT TO TALK ABOUT IT (Argentina/Italy 1992). Before her death, she had completed the screenplay "A Strange Summer," based on a short story by Silvino Campo.

No cause of death was reported.

Bennett, Charles

born: Aug. 2, 1899, Shoreham-by-Sea, England
died: June 15, 1995, Los Angeles, age 95

Oscar-nominated screenwriter who collaborated with Alfred Hitchcock and Irwin Allen.

Entering theater intending to be an actor, and winding up a playwright, Charles Bennett co-adapted his play *Blackmail* with Alfred Hitchcock for the director's first sound picture, in 1929. Bennett, alone or with others, then fruitfully collaborated on a succession of popular Hitchcock thrillers, many now considered classics: THE MAN WHO KNEW TOO MUCH (UK 1934), THE 39 STEPS (UK 1935), SECRET AGENT (UK 1936), SABOTAGE aka THE WOMAN ALONE, and YOUNG AND INNOCENT aka THE GIRL WAS YOUNG (UK 1937). After establishing himself with both Hitchcock and others, Bennett joined what became known as Hollywood's "British Colony," where he collaborated with Hitchcock on FOREIGN CORRESPONDENT (1940) and SABOTEUR (1942), taking no credit for the latter. It was his and Hitchcock's last collaboration, though they reportedly remained friends and Bennett ascribed the situation to mutually busy schedules.

Bennett's prodigious output of more than 45 films also included, for producer/director Irwin Allen, THE BIG CIRCUS (1959), THE LOST WORLD (1960), VOYAGE TO THE BOTTOM OF THE SEA (1961) and FIVE WEEKS IN A BALLOON (1962). Bennett wrote episodes of Allen's spinoff TV series, "Voyage to the Bottom of the Sea" and for Allen's "Land of the Giants," as well as for "The Wild Wild West" and the dramatic anthologies "Cavalcade of America" and "The Dick Powell Show." His last theatrical film was CITY UNDER THE SEA aka WAR GODS OF THE DEEP (US/UK 1965), though 20th Century Fox hired him in the early 1990s to write an eventually unproduced remake of BLACKMAIL. Bennett directed two self-written features, MADNESS OF THE HEART (1949) and ESCAPE (1953). In March, 1995, he was honored with the Writers Guild of America West's Screen Laurel lifetime-achievement award.

Bennett, whose first wife was actress-aviatrix Faith Bennett, died of natural causes.

Blackburn, Clarice

born: c. 1921, San Francisco, CA
died: Aug. 5, 1995, New York City, age 74
educ: Texas State College for Women
Stage actress and television writer who appeared in a handful of films

Clarice Blackburn made her professional debut in a 1947 Martha's Vineyard production, *The Circle of Chalk*. After understudying in Broadway's *The Happy Time*, she played lead roles in *The Grass Harp* and *American Gothic* at Circle in the Square in 1953, and was Shirley Booth's wiseacre co-worker in the Broadway hit *Desk Set* (1955). She won acclaim for her role as Zeena in a 1960 television production of "Ethan Frome." Blackburn, a TV soap opera regular, appeared in both the serialized horror drama "Dark Shadows" and in the second of two spinoff movies. She shared 1985 and 1988 Daytime Emmy Awards as part of the writing team for the soap opera "All My Children." Her films include: THE VIOLATORS (1957), PRETTY POISON (1968), NIGHT OF DARK SHADOWS aka CURSE OF DARK SHADOWS (1971), and MAN ON A SWING (1974).

Blackburn died of cancer.

Blackwell, Charles

aka: Charles Allen Blackwell
born: c. 1929, Philadelphia, PA
died: June 2, 1995, New York City, age 66
educ: Oberlin College
Broadway dancer, choreographer and stage manager, who also performed in, and composed for, film.

After touring overseas with the Pearl Primus School of African Dance, Charles Blackwell had a brief career in business before returning to the theater as a solo dancer in *Fanny*, beginning an 18-year association with producer David Merrick. Blackwell was the stage manager for shows including *Sugar*, *The Wiz*, *Sunday in the Park With George*, *Jerome Robbins's Broadway*, *Annie Get Your Gun* and *Promises, Promises*. He earned a Tony nomination for the book of the musical *The Tap Dance Kid*. He was also an advisor to, and one of the founders of, the Alvin Ailey Dance Company.

In film, Blackwell wrote the screenplay for the Bill Cosby-Sidney Poitier caper comedy A PIECE OF THE ACTION (1977), and appeared in the movies TIMES SQUARE (1980) and THE FAN (1981), as well as in TV shows such as "Law & Order." He served as composer or musical director for films including CANDIDATE FOR MURDER (1962), A

PLACE TO GO (1964), THE SINISTER MAN and WHAT'S NEW PUSSYCAT? (1965).

Blackwell died of cancer.

Blaine, Vivian

born: Vivienne Stapleton, Nov. 21, 1921, Newark, NJ
died: Dec. 9, 1995, New York City, age 74
Singer-showstopper who left her mark as Miss Adelaide in the Broadway, London and movie productions of *Guys and Dolls*.

Playing the quintessential *New Yawkese* chanteuse in the acclaimed Frank Loesser-Abe Burrows musical adaptation of Damon Runyon's stories, Vivian Blaine capped a singing career that stretched as long as Miss Adelaide's engagement to Nathan Detroit. A vaudeville child-singer at age 3, she was performing professionally at nightclubs while still in elementary school. At 14, she joined the Halsey Miller Orchestra, and upon graduating from Southside High School, hit the road as a band singer. In 1941, after a talent scout saw a picture of her performing at Manhattan's Governor Clinton Hotel, she won a screen test and a contract at 20th Century-Fox. After a couple of middling years, Blaine threatened to quit, prompting the studio to relaunch her career as "the cherry blonde." The leads or co-leads in the musicals that followed—including GREENWICH VILLAGE (1944), DOLL FACE (1945, based on the Louise Hovick aka Gypsy Rose Lee play *The Naked Genius*), THREE LITTLE GIRLS IN BLUE (1946) and IF I'M LUCKY (1946)—proved forgettable. She shone, however, as singer Emily in Rodgers and Hammerstein's STATE FAIR (1945).

Blaine, after having been turned down for *Guys and Dolls*' Miss Sarah Brown, the Mission Doll, ran into producers Cy Feuer and Ernest Martin some months later on Broadway. She auditioned again, and won what was then the small role of Miss Adelaide. Little by little during rehearsals, she suggested bits and routines that wound up wowing. Blaine's songs "A Bushel and a Peck," "Take Back Your Mink" and the bring-the-house-down "Adelaide's Lament" helped make the show the sensation of 1950. Blaine continued as Miss Adelaide for five years (with an interlude for the 1952 film SKIRTS AHOY!) and reprised the role for the 1955 film version.

Blaine, in addition to further Broadway work, also appeared on TV in such dramatic anthologies as "Philco Television Playhouse," "Center Stage" and, appropriately, "Damon Runyon Theater" (in its 1958 adaptation of "Pick the Winner"). She starred with Pinky Lee in the twice-weekly, 15-minute primetime sitcom "Those Two" (NBC 1951-53), about a nightclub singer and her unrequited accompanist (turning over the role to another actress in May 1952). Blaine's few episodic credits include "Route 66," "Fantasy Island", "The Love Boat," and "Murder, She Wrote," and the soap operas "One Life to Live" and "Mary Hartman, Mary Hartman." Her other films include THRU DIFFERENT EYES and GIRL TROUBLE (1942), JITTERBUGS and HE HIRED THE BOSS (1943), SOMETHING FOR THE BOYS (1944), NOB HILL (1945), MAIN STREET TO BROADWAY (cameo, 1955), PUBLIC PIGEON NO. 1 (1957), RICHARD (cameo, 1972), THE DARK (1979), and PARASITE (1982).

Blaine died of pneumonia and congestive heart failure.

Blane, Ralph

born: Ralph Blane Hunsecker, c. 1914, Broken Arrow, OK
died: Nov. 13, 1995, Broken Arrow, OK, age 81
Composer and lyricist best known for the Hollywood musical MEET ME IN ST. LOUIS.

Ralph Blane began as a tenor on NBC radio shows of the 1930s, before becoming one of Broadway's *New Faces of 1936*. He met future collaborator Hugh Martin as a fellow backup vocalist in *Louisiana Purchase*, and the two went on to land a hit the first time out with the musical *Best Foot Forward* (1941, filmed 1943, and revived as a vehicle for a young Liza Minnelli in 1963). MGM's MEET ME IN ST. LOUIS (1944), starring Minnelli's mother, Judy Garland, introduced the songs "Have Yourself a Merry Little Christmas," "The Boy Next Door" and the Oscar-nominated "The Trolley Song." The duo was also nominated for "Pass That Peace Pipe," from GOOD NEWS (1947).

Blane and Martin together contributed songs to films including BEST FOOT FORWARD and THOUSANDS CHEER (1943), BROADWAY RHYTHM (1944), the vaudeville-like ZIEGFELD FOLLIES (1945; also as two of the 36 credited co-writers), ATHENA (1954), THE GIRL RUSH (1955) and THE GIRL MOST LIKELY

(1957). The partnership dissolved, but the two reunited to write 10 new songs for a 1989 stage adaptation of MEET ME IN ST. LOUIS. Blane's other films as a collaborative songwriter or score composer include THRILL OF A ROMANCE (1945), EASY TO WED and NO LEAVE, NO LOVE (1946), ONE SUNDAY AFTERNOON and SUMMER HOLIDAY (1948), MY BLUE HEAVEN (1950), SKIRTS AHOY! (1952) and DOWN AMONG THE SHELTERING PALMS (1953).

Blane died after a long battle with Parkinson's disease.

Blaustein, Julian
born: c. 1913, New York, NY
died: June 20, 1995, Beverly Hills, CA, age 82
educ: Boston Latin School; Harvard University
Producer and film-industry booster.

Julian C. Blaustein—who helped shepherd the science-fiction classic THE DAY THE EARTH STOOD STILL (1951), resisting pressures to blacklist supporting star Sam Jaffee—flourished for 40 years as both an old-line studio producer and as an independent. A reader and later story-department head at Universal, he worked in similar capacity for MCA and Paramount in the late 1930s. After his WWII service—in which he worked in various capacities on more than 250 training and informational films for the Army Signal Corps photo center—he joined David O. Selznick Productions as editorial supervisor, and from 1949-52 served as a producer and an executive producer for 20th Century-Fox. Leaving in 1952, he produced films independently for studios including MGM, Columbia, United Artists and Universal.

His films include: BROKEN ARROW and MISTER 880 (1950), THE GUY WHO CAME BACK, HALF ANGEL and TAKE CARE OF MY LITTLE GIRL (1951), DON'T BOTHER TO KNOCK and THE OUTCASTS OF POKER FLAT (1952), DESIREE (1954), THE RACERS aka in Britain SUCH MEN ARE DANGEROUS (1955), STORM CENTER (1956), COWBOY and BELL, BOOK AND CANDLE (1958), THE WRECK OF THE MARY DEARE (1959), TWO LOVES (1961), KHARTOUM (1966), THREE INTO TWO WON'T GO (UK 1969). He co-wrote the stories for FOR LOVE OR MONEY aka TOMORROW AT MIDNIGHT (1939) and Abbott & Costello's THE NOOSE HANGS HIGH (1948). In 1995, in one of his last public efforts, he brought imporant historical reminiscences to the special-edition laserdisc of THE DAY THE EARTH STOOD STILL.

A member of the Academy of Motion Picture Arts and Sciences since 1946, he helped establish the Academy's Don and Gee Nicholl Fellowships for screenwriting. From 1987 to his death, he served as a trustee of the Motion Picture & Television Fund.

Blaustein died of cancer.

Blum, Edwin
born: c. 1906, Atlantic City, NJ; raised San Francisco, CA
died: May 2, 1995, Santa Monica, CA, age 89
Screen and TV scripter, and a founding member of the Writers Guild of America.

Edwin Blum began in film in 1933 as a ghost writer for Ernest Pascal, third president of the Writers Guild, and co-author of the Blum stage plays *The Kick Back* (1936) and *I Am My Youth* (1938). His 15 screenplays included that of STALAG 17 (1953), co-adapted with producer-director Billy Wilder from the Broadway play by Donald Bevan and Edmund Trzcinski. Writing mostly adaptations in collaboration, Blum also wrote the screenplays for THE NEW ADVENTURES OF TARZAN (1935), TARZAN AND THE GREEN GODDESS (1938), KIDNAPPED (1938), THE ADVENTURES OF SHERLOCK HOLMES (1939), YOUNG PEOPLE (1940), THE GREAT AMERICAN BROADCAST (1941), THE BOOGIE MAN WILL GET YOU (1942), HENRY ALDRICH GETS GLAMOUR (1942), THE CANTERVILLE GHOST (1944), MAN ALIVE (1945), DOWN TO EARTH (1947), STALAG 17 and SOUTH SEA WOMAN (1953), THE BAMBOO PRISON (1955) and THE MIDNIGHT STORY (1957). For television, he wrote scripts for "The Man from U.N.C.L.E.," "77 Sunset Strip," "The Roaring 20's" and "Hawaii Five-O." In 1960, his play *The Saving Grace* won a Ford Foundation Prize; it was produced off-Broadway in 1963.

Blum, a Democratic Party activist, managed several Congressional campaigns, and wrote jokes and speeches for Adlai Stevenson and Hubert H. Humphrey.

No cause of death was reported.

Bolt, Robert
born: Aug. 15, 1924, Sale (near Manchester), England
died: Feb. 20, 1995, near Petersfield, Hampshire, UK, age 70
educ: Exeter; Manchester University
Oscar-winning writer of epics for the screen and stage.

Robert Oxton Bolt began writing radio and later stage plays while an English teacher at the tony Millfield School, in Somerset. Bolt enjoyed London successes with the comedy *Flowering Cherry* (later brought to Broadway) and *The Tiger and the Horse*, but it was his historical drama *A Man For All Seasons* (1961) that established his reputation. Bolt's study of the star-crossed confrontation between King Henry VIII and his Lord Chancellor, Sir Thomas More, traveled to Broadway in 1962 to win five Tony Awards, including for play and for author (dramatic). In cinematic parallel, the 1966 U.K. film version—adapted by Bolt and Constance Willis and again starring Tony-winner Paul Scofield as More—took six Academy Awards, including for picture and for adapted screenplay.

By that time, Bolt had already broken into films, and earned an Academy Award nomination, with David Lean's seven-Oscar epic LAWRENCE OF ARABIA (UK 1962), based on T.E. Lawrence's book *The Seven Pillars of Wisdom*. Bolt had initially been called in for seven weeks' dialogue work, after the departure of the blacklisted "Hollywood Ten" expatriate Michael Wilson, who'd written three drafts; Bolt stayed on more than a year, and received solo screenwriting credit despite Wilson's argument that the movie adhered to his original structure. Bolt followed LAWRENCE with another Lean epic, DOCTOR ZHIVAGO (1965), based on the Boris Pasternak novel. Screenwriter Bolt won his first Academy Award; the film took five. He and Lean again collaborated on RYAN'S DAUGHTER (UK 1970), Bolt's first original screenplay; it starred then-wife Sarah Miles, whom Bolt had married in 1967 after his 18-year marriage to painter Celia Ann Roberts had ended. (He and Miles separated in 1975; after a subsequent marriage to actress Anne Zane ended, Bolt remarried Miles; she was with him at his death.) Bolt had another stage success with *Vivat! Vivat Regina!* (1970), starring Miles as Mary, Queen of Scots; she attained an Oscar nomination reprising the role in his film adaptatation LADY CAROLINE LAMB (UK 1972), which Bolt also directed. Bolt and Lean afterward began work on a cinematic diptych of the infamous *HMS Bounty* mutiny, with the scripts "The Law Breakers" and "The Long Arm." Yet before the latter could be finished, Bolt suffered a heart attack on April 12, 1979, followed by a stroke two days later. The first script was rescued for the 1984 film THE BOUNTY.

Bolt's final screen credit was for THE MISSION (UK 1986). Before his death, he was adapting for BBC television the novel *Wild Swans* by Jung Chang, and adapting his own children's play *The Thwarting of Baron Bollingrew* (1966) into a children's novel. He had just completed work on an HBO telefilm about a young Richard Nixon.

Bolt—who declined to be labeled one of Britain's "Angry Young Men," saying he was "anxious rather than angry"—was nonetheless imprisoned for at least two weeks on civil disobedience charges in September 1961, for attending a nuclear disarmament protest in London.

Bolt died after continuing to be plagued by heart trouble.

Borboni, Paola
born: Jan. 1, 1900, Parma, Italy
died: April 9, 1995, Bodio Lomnago, Varese, Italy, age 95
Italian theater actress known as one of the country's foremost performers of Pirandello.

Paola Borboni, who began onstage in Milan at 16, played minor film roles in silent cinema before developing as a comic lead with Armando Falconi's theater troupe. Her triumphs with the work of playwright Luigi Pirandello led her in 1942 to form the first Pirandello theater company. She gained television fame in the 1960s with her popular show "Donna Paola Fermo Posta." Among her handful of films are Fellimni's I VITELLONI (1953), and ROMAN HOLIDAY (1953), as the grumpy cleaning lady who discovers Audrey Hepburn in Gregory Peck's bathtub.

Borboni died after a stroke.

Borsos, Philip
born: 1953, Tasmania
died: Feb. 2, 1995, Vancouver, B.C., Canada, age 41
Canadian writer-director.

Philip Borsos, who earned an Academy Award nomination for the 1979 documetnary short "Nails," won critical acclaim and swept the Canadian

Genie Awards with his first feature, the turn-of-century Western THE GREY FOX (Canada 1982). He went on to direct the American thriller THE MEAN SEASON and the well-received holiday story ONE MAGIC CHRISTMAS (1985), BETHUNE aka DR. BETHUNE aka BETHUNE: THE MAKING OF A HERO (Canada-France-China 1990), and FAR FROM HOME: THE ADVENTURES OF YELLOW DOG (Canada 1996). He had just completed production on the latter, in March 1994, when he learned he had leukemia.

Borsos died following complications from a bone-marrow transplant on Oct. 28, 1994.

Brett, Jeremy

born: Jeremy Huggins, Nov. 3, 1935, Berkswell, England
died: Sept. 12, 1995, age 59
educ: Eton College

British light leading man best known for his acclaimed TV portrayals of Sherlock Holmes, and as Audrey Hepburn's suitor in MY FAIR LADY (1964).

Jeremy Brett, the son of a colonel, appeared in British theater with such productions as *Richard II, Troilus and Cressida, Meet Me by Moonlight, Variations on a Theme, Mr. Fox of Venice, St. Joan, Hamlet, A Measure of Cruelty, Hedda Gabler, A Voyage Round My Father* and *The Way of the World*, and on Broadway in *Aren't We All?*. His film career was slight, reaching its zenith with the Academy Award-winning Best Picture MY FAIR LADY, in which he came to prominence as the callow but sweetly sincere Freddy Eynsford-Hill; dubbed by Bill Shirley, he introduced the song "On the Street Where You Live." Most prominently, he played for a decade what has been termed the definitive Sherlock Holmes, in a series of Granada Television productions beginning in 1984 and running on the PBS "Mystery!" series beginning a year later. Set in 19th-century London, and considered true to the spirit of Sir Arthur Conan Doyle's stories, they co-starred David Burke as Dr. Watson. His additional British TV work includes D'Artagnan in the 10-episode series "The Three Musketeers" (BBC, 1966-67)

In addition to numerous US and UK telefilms, Brett's movies include WAR AND PEACE (US-Italy 1956), THE WILD AND THE WILLING aka YOUNG AND WILLING (UK 1961, released in U.S. 1962), MAC-BETH (US-UK 1963), THE VERY EDGE (UK 1963), GIRL IN THE HEADLINES aka THE MODEL MURDER CASE (UK 1964) and THE MEDUSA TOUCH (UK-France 1978). He married actress Anna Massey in 1958, divorcing after four years.

Brett died in his sleep, of heart failure.

Brinegar, Paul

born: c. 1918
died: March 27, 1995, age 77

Movie and TV supporting player best known for his role as Wishbone on the Clint Eastwood Western series "Rawhide" (CBS 1959-66).

Paul Brinegar was also a cast-member on three other series, playing Jim "Dog" Kelly from 1956-58 on "The Life and Legend of Wyatt Earp" (ABC 1955-61), grouchy ranchhand Jelly Hoskins on the second season of "Lancer" (CBS 1968-71), and querulous cowboy Lamar Pettybone on the first season of the modern-day "Matt Houston" (ABC 1982-85). Largely retired afterward, he returned to play the Stage Driver as one of several old TV-Western cowpokes to cameo in MAVERICK (1994).

Brinegar's films include LARCENY (1948), THE GAL WHO TOOK THE WEST, SWORD IN THE DESERT and TAKE ONE FALSE STEP (1949), STORM WARNING (1950), JOURNEY INTO LIGHT (1951), THE CAPTIVE CITY, PAT AND MIKE and HERE COME THE NEL-SONS aka MEET THE NELSONS (1952), FAST COMPANY and SO BIG (1953), DAWN AT SOCORRO, HUMAN DESIRE and ROGUE COP (1954), I DIED A THOUSAND TIMES (1955), FLIGHT TO HONG KONG and WORLD WITHOUT END (1956), COPPER SKY, HELL ON DEVIL'S ISLAND, THE SPIRIT OF ST. LOUIS and THE VAMPIRE aka MARK OF THE VAMPIRE (1957), CATTLE EMPIRE and HOW TO MAKE A MONSTER (1958), COUNTRY BOY aka HERE COMES THAT NASHVILLE SOUND (1966), CHARRO! (1969), HIGH PLAINS DRIFTER (1973) and CHATTANOOGA CHOO CHOO (1984).

Brinegar died of emphysema.

Brody, Estelle

born: c. 1905, New York, NY or Montreal, Ont., Canada
died: June 3, 1995, Malta, age 90

British silent-movie star who did character roles in sound films.

Estelle Brody played romantic female leads in British silent films, receiving high critical acclaim for her title role in MADEMOISELLE FROM ARMENTIERES (UK 1926). Much later, she appeared in character roles in LILLI MARLENE and THEY WERE NOT DIVIDED (UK 1951), LUXURY GIRLS (Italy 1953), THE STORY OF ESTHER COSTELLO aka GOLDEN VIRGIN (UK 1957) and NEVER TAKE CANDY FROM A STRANGER aka THE MOLESTER (UK 1961), among other films.

No cause of death was reported.

Bronson, Lillian

born: Oct. 21, 1902, Lockport, NY
died: Aug. 1, 1995, San Clemente, CA, age 92

Prolific 1940s movie supporting actress who successfully segued to a TV character-acting career for at least three decades more.

Lillian Bronson—whose roles encompassed everything from Clark Gable's secretary in THE HUCKSTERS (1947) to a motorcyle (grand)mama on an episode of TV's "Happy Days"—found unexpected fame late in life when she served as the model for a building-sized mural by artist Kent Twitchell on the side of the Prince Hotel, near the Hollywood Freeway. A county arts project financed by the National Endowment for the Arts, the mural was painted over with a billboard in 1986, leading to Twitchell's winning an out-of-court settlement for the mural's restoration.

Bronson played Grandma in the primetime soap "Kings Row" (ABC 1955-56), seen approximately every third week as a rotating segment of "Warner Brothers Presents", and neighbor Mrs. Drake in the Betty White young-marrieds sitcom "Date with the Angels" (ABC 1957-58). She thereafter guested in series including "Perry Mason."

Her films include the classics GASLIGHT (1944), A TREE GROWS IN BROOKLYN (1945) and FATHER OF THE BRIDE (1950), as well as HAPPY LAND (1943), ENTER ARSENE LUPIN, HERE COME THE WAVES, MADEMOISELLE FIFI, THE PEARL OF DEATH, WHAT A MAN! and IN THE MEANTIME, DARLING (1944), CHRISTMAS IN CONNECTICUT, THE GIRL OF THE LIMBER-LOST, HOLLYWOOD AND VINE, JUNIOR MISS, MOLLY AND ME, OVER 21 and ROAD TO ALCATRAZ (1945), DRESSED TO KILL, MURDER IN THE MUSIC HALL, NOCTURNE and SENTIMENTAL JOURNEY (1946), DEAD RECKONING, THE SHOCKING MISS PILGRIM, THEY WON'T BELIEVE ME and WELCOME STRANGER (1947), FAMILY HONEYMOON and SLEEP, MY LOVE (1948), IN THE GOOD OLD SUMMERTIME and RUSTY'S BIRTH-DAY (1949), DAKOTA LIL, JOE PALOOKA MEETS HUMPHREY and THE NEXT VOICE YOU HEAR (1950), EXCUSE MY DUST, PASSAGE WEST, and THE SWORD OF MONTE CRISTO (1951), HERE COME THE NELSONS, NO ROOM FOR THE GROOM, ROSE OF CIMARRON and ROOM FOR ONE MORE (1952), AFFAIR WITH A STRANGER and SO THIS IS LOVE (1953), FOXFIRE (1955), BATTLE AT BLOODY BEACH (1961), WALK ON THE WILD SIDE (1962) and SPENCER'S MOUNTAIN (1963, as Henry Fonda's mother).

No cause of death was reported.

Brooks, Phyllis

born: c. 1915, Boise, ID
died: Aug. 1, 1995, Cape Neddick, ME, age 80

Popular one-time model, actress and socialite, who was engaged to Cary Grant before marrying a future Congressman.

Phyllis Brooks went from artist's model for the likes of illustrator James Montgomery Flagg to modeling as the "Ipana toothpaste girl." Segueing to Hollywood, she adorned several minor movies and also appeared in two of the popular Charlie Chan series and in a pair of Shirley Temple films, REBECCA OF SUNNYBROOK FARM and LITTLE MISS BROADWAY (1938). In summer 1939 — by which time magazines had been calling her "the next Mrs. Grant" for three years—she and the celebrated star announced their engagement. It sputtered for months, amid breakups and reconciliations, until Grant hooked up with Barbara Hutton, whom he married in 1942. After their final breakup, an infuriated

Brooks reportedly smashed a framed picture of herself over Grant's head during a party at his house.

Brooks' films include ANOTHER FACE, I'VE BEEN AROUND, LADY TUBBS, THE MAN WHO RECLAIMED HIS HEAD, McFADDEN'S FLATS, STRANGE WIVES and TO BEAT THE BAND (1935), DANGEROUSLY YOURS and YOU CAN'T HAVE EVERYTHING (1937), CHARLIE CHAN IN HONOLULU, CITY GIRL, IN OLD CHICAGO, UP THE RIVER, WALKING DOWN BROADWAY and STRAIGHT, PLACE AND SHOW (1938), CHARLIE CHAN IN RENO and LUCKY TO ME (1939), THE FLYING SQUAD and SLIGHTLY HONORABLE (1940), THE SHANGHAI GESTURE and HI'YA, SAILOR (1941), NO PLACE FOR A LADY and SILVER SPURS (1943), DANGEROUS PASSAGE and LADY IN THE DARK (1944), HIGH POWERED and THE UNSEEN (1945). She did well on Broadway, finding success in the George S. Kaufman-Edna Ferber play Stage Door (1936) and the Ethel Merman musical hit *Panama Hattie* (1940).

Brooks retired in 1945 to marry WWII hero and wealthy former college football star Torbert H. Macdonald, a college roommate of John F. Kennedy at Harvard; the president was their eldest son's godfather. Macdonald served 11 straight terms as a Massachusetts Representative, from 1954 to his death in 1976. Brooks, who remained home in Malden, MA rather than relocate to Washington, became a popular political hostess.

No cause of death was reported.

Carew, Peter

born: c. 1922
died: Aug. 9, 1995, Paramus, NJ, age 73
Film, TV and theater actor-singer.

Peter Carew, who worked as a teacher and an athletics coach as well as a performer, guested on series including "Barney Miller," "Cannon," "Car 54, Where Are You?" "Kojak," "Naked City" and "The Rockford Files." His films include NOTHING BUT A MAN (1964), HARVEY MIDDLEMAN, FIREMAN (1965), BLUE VELVET and PLAYING FOR KEEPS (1986), SOMEONE TO WATCH OVER ME (1987), MASQUERADE (1988), and SCENT OF A WOMAN (1992).

Carew died of a heart attack at home.

Carotenuto, Mario

born: 1916, Rome, Italy
died: April 14, 1995, Rome, Italy, age 79
Italian character actor in more than one hundred films.

Mario Carotenuto was born into an acting family, with father Nello performing in numerous Italian silent films, and late brother Memmo often appearing as a working stiff. Carotenuto's theater work included Giogio Stehler-staged productions of *The Threepenny Opera* (1956) and Puigi Pirandello's *The Mountain Giants* (1966), as well as roles in Neil Simon's *Promises, Promises* and *The Sunshine Boys*, Moliere's *The Miser*, Harold Pinter's *The Homecoming*, and, as Eliza Doolittle's scalawag dad, *My Fair Lady*.

Carotenuto's film career, which began in the early 1950s, includes the movies THE BEACH (1954), SCANDAL IN SORRENTO (Italy-France 1955, released US 1957), with Sophia Loren and Vittorio De Sica, POOR BUT BEAUTIFUL (1956), IT HAPPENED IN ROME (Italy 1959), IL MATTATORE: L'HOMME AUX CENT VISAGES/LOVE AND LARCENY (Italy-France 1963), JEUX D'ADULTES/THE HEAD OF THE FAMILY (Italy-France 1967), with Nino Manfredi and Leslie Caron, IF IT'S TUESDAY, THIS MUST BE BELGIUM (1969), ASSASSINS OF ROME (1971) and LO SCOPANE SCIENTIFICO/THE SCIENTIFIC CARDPLAYER (Italy 1972) with Silvana Mangano, Joseph Cotten and Bette Davis.

Carotenuto died of cancer.

Cash, Rosalind

born: Dec. 31, 1938, Atlantic City, NJ
died: Oct. 31, 1995, Los Angeles, CA, age 56
educ: City College of New York
Esteemed theater actress and an original member of the Negro Ensemble Company, who fought against stereotypical film roles.

Rosalind Cash had made her stage debut in *The Wayward Stork* (1996) and was already an established young New York stage performer when she joined the Negro Ensemble Company in 1968; indeed, already cast

in *The Great White Hope* at the Arena Stage in Washington, she left and paid the Arena the equivalent of two weeks' salary in order to join the new theater company instead. Her NEC work included roles in *The Song of the Lusitanian Bogey, Kongi's Harvest, Sweet Daddy Goodness,* Samm-Art Williams' *The 16th Round*, and her signature role, the strong-willed barber's daughter and primary family wage-earner in Lonne Elder III's *Ceremonies in Dark Old Men;* she reprised the role in a 1975 ABC TV production. Cash had made her Broadway debut in *The Wayward Stork* (1966), and appeared opposite Glenda Jackson in both the London play and the 1978 US/UK film, THE CLASS OF MISS MACMICHAEL.

Cash played the matriarchal Mary Mae Ward during a stint on the soap opera "General Hospital." Other prominent TV work included "Sophisticated Gents" (PBS 1981), Maya Angelou's "Sister, Sister," the miniseries "The Guyana Tragedy: The Story of Jim Jones," the PBS "American Playhoues" production "Keeping On" 1981; later released theatrically), and the PBS "Wonderworks" offering, "The Mighty Pawns." Cash guested on series including "Barney Miller," "Cagney and Lacey," "China Beach," "Hill Street Blues," "Kojak," "The Mary Tyler Moore Show" and "thirtysomething."

Vocally, if not always successfully, she fought the often-stereotyped Hollywood depiction of African-American women; in the Richard Brooks satire WRONG IS RIGHT (1982), Cash played the first black female vice president of the United States. Her other films include KLUTE and THE OMEGA MAN (1971), HICKEY AND BOGGS, MELINDA and THE NEW CENTURIONS (1972), THE ALL-AMERICAN BOY (1973), AMAZING GRACE and UPTOWN SATURDAY NIGHT (1974), CORNBREAD, EARL AND ME (1975), DEATH DRUG (made 1978, released direct-to-video 1983), THE MONKEY HUSTLE and DR. BLACK, MR. HYDE (1976), THE ADVENTURES OF BUCKAROO BANZAI: ACROSS THE EIGHTH DIMENSION (1984), GO TELL IT ON THE MOUNTAIN (1984; theatrical release of an "American Playhouse" production running on PBS Jan. 14, 1985), DEATH SPA (1987), and the horror anthologies THE OFFSPRING aka FROM A WHISPER TO A SCREAM (1987) and TALES FROM THE HOOD (1995).

Cash's honors included the Black American Cinema Society's Phoenix Award (1987), and induction into the Black Filmmakers Hall of Fame (1992).

Cash died of cancer.

Chaplin, Lita Grey

aka: Lillita Louise McMurray
born: 1908, Hollywood, CA
died: Dec. 29, 1995, Woodland Hills, CA, age 88
Second wife of Charlie Chaplin, and his last surviving former spouse.

Under her birth name of Lillita Louise McMurray, she had appeared with Chaplin at age 12 in the comedy short "The Idle Class" (1921) and again that year in the classic feature THE KID (as, amazingly, the dream-sequence vixen who tempts The Little Tramp). She adopted the professional name Lita Grey for THE GOLD RUSH (1925), in which the 15-year-old (reported as 19 by the studio) was cast as the leading lady, in a role initially set for Edna Purviance; though scenes with her were filmed, the part was eventually played by Georgia Hale after Grey became pregnant, compelling Chaplin to marry her (in Empalme, Mexico, Nov. 26, 1924). Their predictably troubled marriage ended with a highly publicized, January 1927 divorce filing (a salacious 52-page document that became an underground paperback best-seller titled *The Complaint of Lita*) and a settlement of $600,000 plus a $100,000 trust fund for each of their two children: Charles Chaplin Jr. (1925-1968) and former actor Sydney Chaplin (b. 1926). It was the largest such settlement in American legal history to that time. Mrs. Chaplin was portrayed by Deborah Maria Moore in the 1992 US/UK film biography, CHAPLIN.

Mrs. Chaplin went on to a singing career in the U.S. and U.K., performing for eight years in the Radio Keith Orpheum vaudeville circuit. She starred in the film THE DEVIL'S SLEEP (1951) before retiring to found the Lita Grey Chaplin Talent Agency. With co-author Morton Cooper, she wrote the biography *My Life With Chaplin* (1966); reportedly unhappy with the book, she later began writing another set of memoirs, which she completed before her death. Mrs. Chaplin died after a lengthy illness.

Chia, Lee

See under "L"

Cicognini, Alessandro

born: c. 1905
died: nov. 9, 1995, Rome, Italy, age 90

Italian film music composer of THE BICYCLE THIEF and other neorealist classics.

Cicognini, who walked away from film composition in the 1960s, was most closely identified with master director Vittorio De Sica, scoring such classics as SCIUSCIA/SHOESHINE (Italy 1946), LADRI DI BICICLETTE/THE BICYCLE THIEF (Italy 1948), MIRACOLO A MILANO/MIRACLE IN MILAN (Italy 1951), UMBERTO D. (1952) and IL TETTO/THE ROOF (Italy 1955), as well for some of De Sica's lesser films, STAZIONE TERMINI/TERMINAL STATION, INDISCRETION aka INDISCRETION OF AN AMERICAN WIFE (US-Italy 1954), L'ORO DI NAPOLI/THE GOLD OF NAPLES (Italy 1954; a six-episode anthology with two episodes deleted for US version), IL GIUDIZIO UNIVERSALE/THE UNIVERSAL JUDGEMENT (Italy 1961).

His other films includes ETTORE FIERAMOSCA (Italy 1938), I GRANDI MAGAZZINI (Italy 1939), QUATTRO PASSI TRA LE NUVOLE (1942), NESSUNO TORNA INDIETRO (1945), STORMBOUND (Italy 1951), DUE SOLDI DI SPERANZA/TWO PENNIES WORTH OF HOPE (Italy 1952), THE THIEF OF VENICE (1952), ALTRI TEMPI/TIMES GONE BY, RING AROUND THE CLOCK and PANE, AMORE E FANTASIA/BREAD, LOVE AND DREAMS (Italy 1953) and THE LITTLE WORLD OF DON CAMILLO (France-Italy 1953), TOO BAD SHE'S BAD and BUON GIORNO, ELEFANTE!/HELLO, ELEPHANT aka PARDON MY TRUNK (Italy 1954), FRISKY, LA FORTUNA DI ESSERE DONNA/LUCKY TO BE A WOMAN and ULISSE/ULYSSES (Italy 1955), SUMMERTIME (1955), LOSER TAKES ALL (UK 1956), ANNA OF BROOKLYN (1958; with De Sica as co-composer), THE BLACK ORCHID (1959), IT STARTED IN NAPLES and A BREATH OF SCANDAL (1960), FAST AND SEXY (France-Italy 1960) and THE PIGEON THAT TOOK ROME (1962).

No cause of death was reported.

Clayton, Jack

born: March 1, 1921, Brighton, England
died: Feb. 25, 1995, Slough, England, age 73

Director whose work initiated Britain's social-realist "Kitchen Sink" era of filmmaking.

With A ROOM AT THE TOP (UK 1959), starring Laurence Harvey and Simone Signoret in a sexually and socially frank adaptation John Braine's novel of class-consciousness and rampant capitalism's human costs, Jack Clayton brought a freshly naturalistic, if downbeat, perspective to contemporary British subject matter. The film was nominated for a Best Picture Academy Award, and Clayton for director (with actress Signoret and screenwriter Neil Paterson each winning a statuette) and spawned two non-Clayton sequels, LIFE AT THE TOP (UK 1965) and MAN AT THE TOP (UK 1975), the latter a spinoff of the same-name Brit TV series featuring the character Harvey had played. As the kineticism of Jean-Luc Godard's BREATHLESS would spark the French New Wave, the sobering naturalism of ROOM AT THE TOP impacted heavily on such contemporary British directors as Lindsay Anderson, Tony Richardson and Karel Reisz.

Clayton began in movies in 1936, as a messenger boy for London Films. During WWII, he worked on documentaries with the Royal Air Force film unit. Afterward, he rose through the British films ranks as production manager (as on Alexander Korda's 1948 film AN IDEAL HUSBAND), associate producer, and producer. He debuted as a director with the medium length THE BESPOKE OVERCOAT (1955; also producer), which won a prize at the Venice Film Festival. Clayton's third wife and widow, Israeli actress Haya Harareet, appeared as Esther in BEN HUR (1959)—ironically, the film that won out over ROOM for Best Picture.

Clayton died after suffering from heart and liver problems.

Colon, Alex

born: c. 1941, Puerto Rico
died: Jan. 6, 1995, Los Angeles, CA, age 53

Theater actor-director with a nearly quarter-century body of film work.

Colon made his film and his New York stage debut the same year, 1970, with the movie THE CROSS AND THE SWITCHBLADE and the Neil Simon play *The Gingerbread Lady*. His extensive theater work included directing an L.A. Actors Theater workshop of Miguel Pinero's acclaimed prison drama *Short Eyes*, as well as serving as director for the Nosotros Theater and New York City's Puerto Rican Traveling Theater. He appeared in a slew of TV-movies and miniseries, including "The Marcus-Nelson Murders" (1973), "The Law" (1974), "Hustling" and "Sky Heist" (1975), "Raid on Entebbe" and "Tarantulas: The Deadly Cargo" (1977), "Siege" and "Battered" (1978) and "Women of San Quentin" (1983), as well as the 26 1/2-hour limited series "Centennial" (NBC 1978-79). He guested on TV shows including "Murder, She Wrote."

Colon's films include THE HOSPITAL (1971), THE TAKING OF PELHAM ONE TWO THREE and THE SUPER COPS (1974), THE ULTIMATE WARRIOR (1975), SPECIAL DELIVERY (1976), WHEN YOU COMIN' BACK, RED RYDER? (1979), BACK ROADS (1981), DEAL OF THE CENTURY (1983), DEATH OF AN ANGEL and INVASION U.S.A. (1985), THE MIGHTY QUINN and RED SCORPION (1989), DEEP COVER (1992) and THE GETAWAY (1994)

Colon died after what was reported as an extended illness.

Cook, Elisha Jr.

born: Dec. 26, 1906 (some accounts give 1902), San Francisco, CA; raised Chicago, IL
died: May 18, 1995, Big Pine, CA, age reportedly 91

Weasely yet beloved character actor and film heavy best known as the gunsel Wilmer in THE MALTESE FALCON (1941).

Elisha Cook Jr.—whose other signature parts included those of the doomed patsy Jonesy in THE BIG SLEEP (1946), a murdered homesteader in SHANE (1953), the satanic apartment manager in ROSEMARY'S BABY (1968), and the henpecked little racetrack teller in Stanley Kubrick's THE KILLING (1956)—was the son of an actress. He began performing at age 14, in stock and vaudeville, before being picked by Eugene O'Neill for the juvenile lead in Broadway's "Ah Wilderness!" He went on to a more than 60-year career in more than a hundred theatrical features and an euqal number of TV roles—the latter starting with a guest apperance on ABC's "Dick Tracy" in 1950, and stretching to TV-movies and to memorable epidodic appearances on "The Adventures of Superman," "The Odd Couple," "ALF," "Alfred Hitchcock Presents" and "Star Trek," among many other shows. Cook also appeared in a 1966 ABC pilot, "McNab's Lab." He capped his career with the recurring role of shady Francis "Ice Pick" Hofstetler from 1983-88 on "Magnum, PI" (CBS 1980-88). Cook—who would modestly explain he landed the role of Wilmer by having the same agent as MALTESE FALCON star Humphrey Bogart and writer-director John Huston—suffered a stroke five years before his death.

Cook had been in failing health for several months.

Cook, Peter

born: Nov. 17, 1937, Torquay, England
died: Jan. 9, 1995, London, England, age 57
educ: Cambridge

Comedian and comic writer whose irreverent revues helped export the absurdist-intellectual British humor epitomized by such later troupes as Monty Python's Flying Circus.

Peter Cook, with fellow writer-performers Alan Bennett, Jonathan Miller and Dudley Moore, scored early critical and commerical acclaim with their hit London revue *Beyond the Fringe*, which in 1962 successfully translated to Broadway and earned its members a 1963 Special Tony Award, plus a special citation from the New York Drama Critics Circle; the cast album was a 1962 Grammy nominee for Comedy Performance. Cook and longtime occasional partner Moore repeated their success with Broadway's long-running *Good Evening* (1973), winning 1974 Special Tony Awards, as well as the 1974 Grammy for Spoken Word Recording. The duo appeared in further revues, made comedy albums—many featuring their boorish characters Derek and Clive — appeared together in the British sitcom "Not Only—But Also. . . " (BBC, 1965-66 and 1970, plus two 1971 specials), and did a 1993 Derek-and-Clive comedy video. For American TV, Cook starred as a pompously efficient butler on the sitcom "The Two of Us" (CBS 1981-82), and won a 1984 Emmy Award as producer of the Outstanding Limited Series, "Concealed Enemies" (made for PBS' "American Playhouse"). Cook's other TV work includes the Mad Hatter role in the 1966 BBC special "Alice in Wonderland."

In film, Cook and Moore teamed up on THE WRONG BOX (UK 1966), THE BED SITTING ROOM (UK 1969), THOSE DARING

YOUNG MEN IN THEIR JAUNTY JALOPIES aka QUEI TEMERARI SULLE LORO PAZZE, SCATENATE, SCALCINATE CARRIOLE aka MONTE CARLO OR BUST (Italy-France-UK 1969), the Sherlock Holmes spoof, THE HOUND OF THE BASKERVILLES (UK 1980), co-written by Cook and Moore with director Paul Morrissey, and their best-known film, the comic fantasy BEDAZZLED (UK 1967), a Cook and Moore-written tour de force with the two each playing multiple characters.

Cook—who also published the satiric magazine *Private Eye,* and founded the satirical London nightclub the Establishment and its spinoff New York club and off-Broadway revue—additionally starred in the title role of THE RISE AND RISE OF MICHAEL RIMMER (UK 1970), a political satire he co-wrote with Monty Python's John Cleese and Graham Chapman, and Kevin Billington. His other films include A DANDY IN ASPIC (1968), THE SECRET POLICEMAN'S OTHER BALL (UK 1982), YELLOWBEARD (1983, also co-writer with Chapman), SUPER-GIRL (UK 1984), THE PRINCESS BRIDE (1987), WHOOPS APOCA-LYPSE (UK 1987), WITHOUT A CLUE (UK 1988), GETTING IT RIGHT and GREAT BALLS OF FIRE (1989) and BLACK BEAUTY (1994). One of his final projects was the video "Peter Cook Talks Golf Balls."

Cook died of a gastrointestinal hemorrhage.

Corseaut, Aneta

born: Nov. 3, 1933, Hutchinson, KS
died: Nov. 6, 1995, age 62

Actress best known as Sheriff Andy Taylor's girlfriend and eventual wife, teacher Helen Crump, on "The Andy Griffith Show" Aneta Corseaut had regular roles on three TV series—"The Gertrude Berg Show" aka "Mrs. G. Goes to College" (CBS 1961-62), "The Andy Griffith Show" (CBS 1960-68), from 1964-68, and "House Calls" (CBS 1979-82). In films, Corseaut is immortalized as Steve McQueen's girlfriend, Judy, in THE BLOB (1958); she also appeared in THE TOOLBOX MURDERS (1978).

Corseaut died of cancer.

Cottrell, William H.D. Jr.

born: c. 1906
died: Dec. 22, 1995, Burbank, CA, age 89

Disney animator and writer turned company executive.

Cottrell began with Disney as a cameraperson before going on to become one of six animation directors on the landmark animated feature SNOW WHITE AND THE SEVEN DWARFS (1937). He was also on the writing teams of animated features including PINOCCHIO (1940), THE RELUCTANT DRAGON (1941), THE THREE CABALLEROS (1944), MELODY TIME (1948) and ALICE IN WONDERLAND (1951). Cottrell later led the division that spearheaded the design and construction of Disneyland, and went on to spend 18 years running the Disney business division Retlaw before retiring in 1982. His father, William (aka Bill) Cottrell, was a movie supporting player in films including THE NAKED CITY (1948), LES MISERABLES (1952) and JULIUS CAESAR (1953)

No cause of death was reported.

Craven, John

born: June 22, 1916, New York, NY
died: Nov. 22, 1995, Salt Point, NY, age 79

Film and Broadway actor who originated the role of George Gibbs in Thornton Wilder's Pulitzer Prize-winning *Our Town* (1938).

The 21-year-old Craven's critical success (alongside his playwright-actor father Frank Craven, as the Stage Manager), led to a solid career in such Broadway fare as *The Happiest Days,* playing the lead opposite Uta Hagen, *Delicate Story, Two on an Island,* the revival of Sidney Howard's *They Knew What They Wanted, Babes in Arms, Glory for All, The Happiest Days, Candide* and, again with his father, *Village Green* (1941).

Craven staged USO shows while stationed in Naples during WWII. From 1951-52, he co-starred with Pat Kirkland as Bob and Betty Mac-Donald in CBS' live, 15-minute, weekday noontime serial "The Egg and I," TV's first comedic soap opera (based on Betty MacDonald's book and on the 1947 film). Craven also appeared in TV guest roles on series including "Alfred Hitchcock Presents," "Ford Theater," "Gunsmoke," "Playhouse 90," "The Twilight Zone" (1960s) and "Wyatt Earp." In 1968,

Craven moved to Barcelona for seven years to teach drama and direct theater.

In his prominent film roles, Craven played a college student-cum-surrogate grandson to feisty widow Mabel Paige in SOMEONE TO RE-MEMBER (1943), and in director Don Siegel's COUNT THE HOURS aka in Britain EVERY MINUTE COUNTS (1953), played a migrant farm worker unjustly accused of murder. His other films include HER FIRST MATE (1933), OVER THE GOAL (1937), DR. GILLESPIE'S CRIMI-NAL CASE and THE HUMAN COMEDY (1943), MEET THE PEOPLE and THE PURPLE HEART (1944), FLIGHT TO NOWHERE and SWELL GUY (1946), SECURITY RISK (1954), BATTLE STATIONS, FRIENDLY PERSUASION, HOLD BACK THE NIGHT and NAVY WIFE (1956), LET'S MAKE LOVE and OCEAN'S ELEVEN (1960), and THE WILD SCENE (1970).

No cause of death was reported.

Crosby, Gary

born: June 25, 1933, Los Angeles, California
died: Aug. 24, 1995, Burbank, CA, age 62
educ: Stanford University

Actor son of screen legend Bing Crosby, who wrote a scathing childhood memoir in 1983.

As a child, Crosby—the eldest of the four sons of crooner Bing and first wife Dixie Lee Crosby — appeared with his siblings Lindsay and twins Philip and Dennis as themselves in Bing's STAR SPANGLED RHYTHM (1942) and the star-cameo-studded DUFFY'S TAVERN (1945), and in the Eddie Bracken-Veronica Lake musical OUT OF THIS WORLD (1945), as children in the audience. After college, Crosby returned to movies as a supporting actor, often in war films, and formed an unsuccessful 1950s pop group. He'd previously dueted with his father on the music industry's first double-sided gold record, "Sam's Song" b/w "Play a Simple Melody" (1950). A one-time Hollywood hellion and self-acknowledged alcoholic, Crosby recalled in his autobiography, *Going My Own Way,* that he was regularly beaten by his abusive father for such transgressions as being chubby; Gary played Bing in the 1983 TV-movie based on the book. Crosby's brothers Lindsay and Dennis committed suicide in 1989 and 1991, respectively.

Crosby made his TV debut on "The Jack Benny Show" in 1955, then played a successions of Eds: Eddie the bellhop on the first-season cast of "The Bill Dana Show" (NBC 1963-65); Officer Ed Wells on "Adam 12" (NBC 1968-75; semi-regular); and Officer Ed Rice on "Chase" (NBC 1973-74; semi-regular). He guested on series including "The Flying Nun," "Hunter," "Matlock," "Murder, She Wrote," "Perry Mason" and "The Twilight Zone," in the memorable 1964 episode, "Come Wander With Me." His films include MARDI GRAS (1958), HOLIDAY FOR LOVERS and A PRIVATE'S AFFAIR (1959), BATTLE AT BLOODY BEACH and THE RIGHT APPROACH (1961), TWO TICKETS TO PARIS (1962), OPERATION BIKINI aka THE SEAFIGHTERS (1963), GIRL HAPPY and MORITURI aka THE SABOTEUR: CODE NAME MORITURI (1965), WHICH WAY TO THE FRONT? (1970) and THE NIGHT STALKER (1987; no relation to the Darren McGavin TV-movie or series).

Crosby died of lung cancer.

Darden, Severn

born: Nov. 9, 1929
died: May 26, 1995, Santa Fe, NM, age 65

Film actor and Second City co-founder, whose masterful comic improvisations and barbed intellectualist humor stamped a vein of American satire reaching its apotheosis with the early "Saturday Night Live."

Severn Darden, who influenced countless Second City comics and had the respect of more commercially successful peers as Mike Nichols and Alan Arkin, was a flamboyant collegian given to sporting a cape and cane. In the mid-1950s, after leaving the University of Chicago, he joined the city's new satiric improv-comedy troupe The Compass Players, the forerunner to Second City. Here he created such popular characters as his signature German expert-on-everything, Professor Valter von de Vogelweide. In 1959, Darden, with Howard Alk, Roger Bowen, Andrew Duncan, Barbara Harris, Mina Kolb and Eugene Troobnick, formed the premiere Second City cast, and, like an intellectual John Belushi, formed the group's mad-genius hub.

Darden continued his association with and satiric and improv humor in the 1961 Broadway revue *From the Second City,* for which he was

Tony-nominated as Supporting or Featured Actor (Musical), and Sills & Co., New York City's de facto Second City branch, which went to Broadway in 1969 with the Tony-nominated *Story Theatre*; the cast was spun off into a same-name sketch-comedy series (syndicated 1971). Darden also spent three seasons at the American Shakespeare Festival, and his theater work included *A Murderer Among Us*, *A P.S. 193*, *A Leda Had a Little Swan* and *A The Front Page*.

His films include two independent Chicago efforts by a fledgling Philip Kaufman, GOLDSTEIN (1964) and FEARLESS FRANK aka FRANK'S GREATEST ADVENTURE (1967), as well as DOUBLE-BARRELLED DETECTIVE STORY (1965), DEAD HEAT ON A MERRY-GO-ROUND (1966), LUV and THE PRESIDENT'S ANALYST (1967, playing the Russian spy), THEY SHOOT HORSES, DON'T THEY? (1969), CISCO PIKE, THE HIRED HAND, THE LAST MOVIE, VANISHING POINT and WEREWOLVES ON WHEELS (1971), CONQUEST OF THE PLANET OF THE APES, DIRTY LITTLE BILLY, EVERY LITTLE CROOK AND NANNY, PLAY IT AS IT LAYS, and THE WAR BETWEEN MEN AND WOMEN (1972) BATTLE FOR THE PLANET OF THE APES and THE DAY OF THE DOLPHIN (1973). JACKSON COUNTY JAIL and MOTHER, JUGS & SPEED (1976), HOPSCOTCH (1980), SATURDAY THE 14TH (1981), YOUNG GIANTS (1983), REAL GENIUS (1985), BACK TO SCHOOL (1986) and THE TELEPHONE (1988). He co-wrote and co-produced THE VIRGIN PRESIDENT (1968), featuring Second City members and Peter Boyle's film debut.

Darden died of heart failure.

De Mille, Katherine

born: Katherine Lester, June 29, 1911, Vancouver, BC
died: April 27, 1995, Tucson, AZ, age 83

Supporting actress of the 1930s and '40s, and adopted daughter of Cecil B. De Mille.

As Katherine Lester, Katherine De Mille was adopted from a Hollywood orphanage by the famed producer-director when she was nine. She made her film debut in her father's MADAME SATAN (1930), and appeared twice more in his pictures, in THE CRUSADES (1935) and UNCONQUERED (1947). Married from 1938-53 to Anthony Quinn, she starred opposite him as his wife in BLACK GOLD (1947) and appeared in a cameo in his MAN FROM DEL RIO (1956), after she'd left acting. De Mille often played tormented women, such as Dorothy Lamour's jealous native-girl rival in ALOMA OF THE SOUTH SEAS (1941), but she also appeared in musicals and comedies.

De Mille died of Alzheimer's disease.

Dean, Mary

aka: Mary Dean Lauria
born: c. 1923
died: Dec. 19, 1995, Toluca Lake, CA, age 72
educ: University of Wisconsin

Multifaceted actress, singer, lyricist and impresario.

Mary Dean's career stretched to 1937, with a role as one of Madrigal Singers in the Fred Astaire-Burns & Allen musical A DAMSEL IN DISTRESS. Between then and the 1970-1980s — when, as Mary Dean Lauria, she provided voiceovers on Ralph Bakshi's animated FRITZ THE CAT (1972), HEAVY TRAFFIC (1973) and HEY, GOOD LOOKIN' (1982)—she wrote the lyrics for the #1 Cher hit "Half-Breed" (1973), acted in such 1950s TV series as "The Cisco Kid," "The Life of Riley," "Dragnet" and "Space Patrol," contributed to NBC's 1950s weekday magazine series "Home" and appeared in one other musical, CINDERELLA JONES (made 1944, released 1946). Dean reportedly helped discover the popular '60s rock group The Cowsills, and also reportedly hosted the shows "What's the Name of That Song," "Time It" and "Jean and Dean," which appear to have been either pilots or obscure local-TV shows.

Dean died of emphysema.

Denner, Charles

born: May 29, 1926, Tarnow, Poland
died: Sept. 10, 1995, Dreux, France, age 69

Leading man and supporting star whose more than two dozen French films included the title role of Francois Truffaut's L'HOMME QUI AIMAIT LES FEMMES/THE MAN WHO LOVED WOMEN (1977).

Charles Denner studied in Paris with Charles Dullin 1945, and four years later joined the National Popular Theater. His films for such directors as Truffaut, Claude Chabrol, Costa-Gavras, Claude Lelouch and Louis Malle include leading roles in LANDRU aka BLUEBEARD (France-Italy 1963), LA VIE A L'ENVERS/LIFE UPSIDE DOWN aka INSIDE OUT (1965), and LE CORPS DE DIANE/DIANE'S BODY (France-Czechoslovakia 1969). He also appeared in films including MATA HARI (France 1965), COMPARTIMENT TUEURS/THE SLEEPING CAR MURDER (France 1966), LE VIEIL HOMME ET L'ENFANT/THE TWO OF US aka THE OLD MAN AND THE BOY (France 1967), LE VOLEUR/THE THIEF OF PARIS and LA MARIEE ETAIT EN NOIR/THE BRIDE WORE BLACK (France-Italy 1967), Z (France 1969), LE VOYOU/THE CROOK (France 1971), UNE BELLE FILLE COMME MOI/SUCH A GORGEOUS KID LIKE ME aka in Britain A GORGEOUS BIRD LIKE ME (France 1973), AND NOW MY MY LOVE (France 1975), THE FIRST TIME (France 1978) and GOLDEN EIGHTIES (France-Belgium-Switzerland 1986).

Denner died of cancer.

Dermit, Edouard

born: 1925
died: May 1995, age 70

The last lover and heir of the artist-writer-poet-filmmaker Jean Cocteau, who appeared in major roles in three of Cocteau's legendary films: the Cocteau written-directed OPRHEE/ORPHEUS (France 1949; US release 1950), LES ENFANTS TERRIBLES/THE STRANGE ONES (France 1950), co-adapted by Cocteau from his 1929 novel, and the Cocteau written-directed LE TESTAMENT D'ORPHEE/THE TESTAMENT OF ORPHEUS (France 1959, US release 1960). No cause of death was reported.

Dickson, Dorothy

born: 1902 or July 25, 1893 (sources differ), U.S.
died: Sept. 1995, London, England

American actress-dancer who worked primarily in England.

Dorothy Dickson, a London theater star, introduced the song "Look for the Silver Lining" in London in the Jerome Kern musical *Sally* (1921). Other London stage works included *Red Letter Day* and *As Long As They're Happy*. Dickson also performed in New York City and in the Ziegfeld Follies. She last performed onstage at a 1980 gala to commemorate 75 years of *Peter Pan*.

Dickson's films include the silent MONEY MAD (UK 1917), and LA ROUTE EST BELLE aka THE ROAD IS FINE (France; US release 1930), CHANNEL CROSSING (UK 1932, US release 1933), DANNY BOY (UK 1934; star) and SWORD OF HONOUR (UK 1938).

No cause of death was reported.

Easdale, Brian

born: Aug. 1909
died: Oct. 1995, age 86

British composer, who worked mostly on Michael Powell-Emeric Pressburger films.

Brian Easdale, whose score for the Powell-Pressburger classic THE RED SHOES (UK 1948) won him an Academy Award, began scoring films with Britain GPO Film Unit shorts from 1934-38. He scored the Powell-Pressburger films BLACK NARCISSUS (UK 1946; also musical conductor), THE SMALL BACK ROOM aka HOUR OF GLORY (UK 1949), THE ELUSIVE PIMPERNEL aka THE FIGHTING PIMPERNEL (UK 1950), GONE TO EARTH aka THE WILD HEART aka GYPSY BLOOD (UK 1950, US release 1952) and THE BATTLE OF THE RIVER PLATE aka PURSUIT OF THE GRAF SPEE (UK 1956, US release 1957).

Easdale's other features include FERRY PILOT (UK 1942), Carol Reed's OUTCAST OF THE ISLANDS (UK 1951; US release 1952), THE GREEN SCARF (UK 1954), the Pressburger written-produced MIRACLE IN SOHO (UK 1956, US release 1957), the Powell directed-produced PEEPING TOM aka FACE OF FEAR (UK 1960; also music director), THE QUEEN'S GUARDS (UK 1961, US release 1963), and RETURN TO THE EDGE OF THE WORLD (UK 1978).

No cause of death was reported.

Egan, Eddie

born: Jan. 3, 1930, Queens, NY
died: Nov. 5, 1995, Fort Lauderdale, FL, age 65

New York City police detective turned bit-player and technical advisor, and the inspiration for Gene Hackman's Popeye Doyle in THE FRENCH CONNECTION (1971)

Raised by his grandmother after being orphaned at age 12, Eddie Egan joined the Marines and played center field on the New York Yankees Triple-A minor-league club before joining the Port Authority Police, transferring to the N.Y.P.D. in 1955, and being appointed a narcotics detective a year later. His colorful exploits earned him the nickname Popeye, and his work with partner Sonny Grosso on the 1962 "French Connection" heroin case inspired a novel by Robin Moore and the subsequent Academy Award-winning Best Picture by director William Friedkin and screenwriter Ernest Tidyman, themselves Oscar-winners. Egan played a bit role in the film. Egan also played a bit part and served as technical advisor on BADGE 373 (1973), in which Robert Duvall played an Egan-like cop.

Egan was dismissed from the Police Department after the real-life French Connection case for allegedly withholding drugs, then failing to appear in court to testify. The dismissal was later reversed in court, and Egan formally retired to work as an actor (in films including 1972's PRIME CUT and 1987's COLD STEEL), producer, and technical advisor, often on telefilms and TV series.

Egan died of colon cancer.

Ende, Michael

born: 1929, Garmisch-Partenkirchen, Bavaria
died: Aug. 28, 1995, Stuttgart, Germany, age 65

Acclaimed children's fantasy author whose book *The Neverending Story* was adapted into a worldwide hit movie that has spawned two sequels to date.

Michael Ende, the son of surrealist artist Edgar Ende, is equally well-known in literary circles for *Momo*, about a little girl who retrieves hours stolen by "time thieves," and which itself was a late-1970s/early-1980s opera and play before being adapted as a 1985 movie (thus far unreleased in the US). DIE UNENDLICHE GESCHICHTE/THE NEVERENDING STORY (West Germany 1984) was directed and co-adapted by Wolfgang Petersen in his English-language debut. It was followed by films based on Ende's characters, THE NEVERENDING STORY II: THE NEXT CHAPTER/AUF DER SUCHE NACH PHANTASIEN (US-West Germany 1990, released in US 1991), directed by George Miller, and DIE UNENDISCHE GESCHICHTE III/THE NEVERENDING STORY III (Germany 1994, direct-to-video US 1995), directed by Peter Macdonald."

Ende, who was displeased with the initial film adaptation and removed his name from the credits, died after treatment for stomach cancer.

Endfield, Cy

aka: C. Raker; C. Raker Endfield, Hugh Baker
born: Cyril Raker Endfield, November 1914, Scranton, PA
died: April 16, 1995, Shipston-on-Stour, Warwickshire, England, age 80
educ: Yale; New Theater School, New York City

Writer-director of crime thrillers and adventure yarns, who thrived in England after being blacklisted in the United States.

Cy Endfield was a child-prodigy magician who—after teaching drama and producing for the stage in New York and Montreal, the moving to Los Angeles—met Orson Welles in a Hollywood Boulevard magic shop; the meeting led to Welles (then working on THE MAGNIFICENT AMBERSONS) giving Endfield an assistant's job at his Mercury company. During WWII, Endfield served with the Army Signal Corps; his first film, the 15-minute short "Inflation," was commissioned by the Office of War Information but rejected as anti-capitalistic. In 1945, Endfield began directing "Passing Parade" shorts for MGM, and began writing features. Some reference sources and his *Variety* obit erroneously list him as having made his directorial debut with GENTLEMAN JOE PALOOKA aka JOE PALOOKA, CHAMP (1946), which was in fact helmed by studio director Reginald LeBorg (1902-89, who directed several of the comic-strip-based "Joe Palooka" films and worked from 1943-73; Enfield did, however, co-write the script, with Albert DePina. His actual feature debut was STORK BITES MAN (1947), which he also scripted.

For the next few years, Endfield worked in radio and television as well as in film, but it was the supposed leftist slant of his movies that in 1951 put him on the Hollywood blacklist prompted by the House Un-American Activities Committee. One, THE ARGYLE SECRETS (1948), which he directed and adapted from his own "Suspense" radio play "The Argyle Album," suggested (accurately) the U.S. secretly brought Nazi scientists here to work for the military. Endfield emigrated to England, working under pseudonym or else uncredited entirely on a half-dozen films before placing his name on HELL DRIVERS (UK 1958). With that film's star, Stanley Baker, Endfield formed a production company under which Endfield co-produced, directed and wrote or co-wrote the films ZULU (UK 1964), which helped lead Michael Caine to stardom, and SANDS OF THE KALAHARI (UK 1965). In an interesting sidelight, Endfield in 1978 invented an electronic pocket-typewriter.

Endfield's other films as writer-director include: MR. HEX (1946; writer only), HARD BOILED MAHONEY (1947; writer only), SLEEP, MY LOVE (1948; writer only), THE ARGYLE SECRETS (1948), JOE PALOOKA IN THE COUNTERPUNCH (1949; writer only), JOE PALOOKA IN THE BIG FIGHT (1949), THE UNDERWORLD STORY aka THE WHIPPED (1950), THE SOUND OF FURY aka TRY AND GET ME (1951; director only), TARZAN'S SAVAGE FURY (1952), THE LIMPING MAN, (UK 1953; uncredited co-director with Charles De Lautour), COLONEL MARCH INVESTIGATES (UK 1953; director only; theatrical release of three episodes of Boris Karloff British TV series "Colonel March of Scotland Yard"), THE MASTER PLAN (UK 1954, as "Hugh Baker"), IMPULSE (UK 1955; uncredited co-director with Charles De Lautour), THE SECRET (UK 1955), CHILD IN THE HOUSE (UK 1956; as "C. Raker Endfield"), SEA FURY and JET STORM aka KILLING URGE (UK 1959), MYSTERIOUS ISLAND (UK 1961), HIDE AND SEEK (UK 1964), DAS AUSSCHWEIFENDE LEBEN DES MARQUIS DE SADE/DE SADE (West Germany-US 1969; reportedly co-directed with uncredited Roger Corman and Gordon Hessler), UNIVERSAL SOLDIER (UK 1971) and ZULU DAWN (UK 1980, co-writer only).

Endfield died of cerebral vascular disease.

Ergas, Moris

born: c. 1922, Thessaloniki, Greece
died: Feb. 8, 1995, Rome, Italy, age 72

Producer of primarily Italian-language films in the 1950s and '60s.

During WWII, Moris Ergas, who'd left his hometown to study film in Belgrade, was imprisoned in the Ferramonti Tarsia concentration camp for Jews in Italy. During his active film-production period, he was a frequent target of paparazzi for his tempestuous, 11-year relationship with actress Sandra Milo, with whom he had actress daughter Debora Ergas. He left the film industry in the 1970s for entrepreneurial ventures in construction and solar energy, and returned in the 1990s as a producer and distributor of Czech cinema.

His films as producer include writer-director Roberto Rossellini's IL GENERALE DELLA ROVERE/GENERAL DELLA ROVERE (Italy-France 1959), LA STEPPA/STEPPE, THE (Italy-France 1963), KAPO (Italy-France-Yugoslavia 1960, US release 1964), an Academy Award nominee for Foreign Language Film, ADUA E LE COMPAGNE/LOVE A LA CARTE (Italy 1965), with Simone Signoret, Marcello Mastroianni and Milo, LA VISITA (Italy-France 1966), starring Milo, and ZBEHOVIA A PUTNICI/THE DESERTER AND THE NOMADS (Czechoslovakia-Italy, 1969).

Everett, Kenny

born: Maurice James Christopher Cole, c. 1945
died: April 4, 1995, age 50

British comedian and DJ whose "The Kenny Everett Video Show" was an inspiration for MTV. Everett—whose BBC show began in 1978 and was aired in the US as well—began in radio in the 1960s, and claimed to have coined the BBC nickname "The Beeb." He appeared in the music-world crime drama DATELINE DIAMONDS (UK; US released 1966) and starred in the horror parody BLOODBATH AT THE HOUSE OF DEATH (UK; US release 1983), with Vincent Price and Pamela Stephenson.

Everett died of complications from AIDS.

Fabrizi, Franco

born: c. 1916, Cortemaggiore (near Piacenza), Italy
died: Oct. 18, 1995, Cortemaggiore, Italy, age 79

Rakish supporting star and occasional lead in a reported 150 or so film comedies and dramas

Fabrizi, best-known as a provincial Casanova in Federico Fellini's I VITELLONI (Italy 1953), began in plays and revues in 1947. He made his film debut with Francesco De Robertis' CARICA EROICA (Italy 1952). Fabrizi, a staple of gossip columns who often squired actresses and society girls, went on to appear in Fellini's IL BIDONE/THE SWINDLE (Italy-France 1955), as the henchman Roberto, and GINGER AND FRED (Italy-France-West Germany 1986), as the TV-show host. He also appeared in Michelangelo Antonioni's LE AMICHE/THE GIRL-FRIENDS (Italy 1955, released US 1962), Luchino Visconti's MORTE A VENEZIA/DEATH IN VENICE (Italy-France 1971), and Roberto Benigni's THE LITTLE DEVIL (Italy 1988).

Fabrizi died of cancer.

Farrar, David

born: 1908, Forest Gate, England
died: Aug. 31, 1995, South Africa, age 87

Romantic lead of BLACK NARCISSUS (UK 1946) and other British films, whose attempts at crossover stardom led to playing American-film heavies.

The tall, virile and vaguely sinister-looking Farrar came to the stage at age 12 in *A Midsummer Night's Dream*, and then quit school at 14 to work briefly for British newspapers before devoting himself to acting. By BLACK NARCISSUS, Farrar was already somewhat known in the U.S. as the star of British melodramas and two entries in the UK's "Sexton Blake" sleuthing series (1944's MEET SEXTON BLAKE and 1945's THE ECHO MURDERS, after having played a bit part in 1938's SEXTON BLAKE AND THE HOODED TERROR). But after his Michael Powell-Emeric Pressburger masterpiece and the director-producer duo's THE SMALL BACK ROOM aka HOUR OF GLORY (UK 1948, US release 1949), Farrar often found himself third-billed in American films behind domestic leads—among them, Tony Curtis and Janet Leigh in THE BLACK SHIELD OF FALWORTH (1954), and John Wayne and Lana Turner in THE SEA CHASE (1955). Farrar, soon relegated to supporting and cameo roles, made his last film in 1962. His autobiography: *No Royal Road* (1948).

No cause of death was reported

Finney, Jack

born: Walter Braden Finney, 1911, Milwaukee, WI
died: Nov. 14, 1995, Greenbrae, CA, age 84
educ: Knox College, Galesburg, IL

Cult-favorite novelist whose books were adapted into popular films.

Finney—whose critically acclaimed hit *Time After Time* (1970) was in development by Robert Redford for a movie adaptation during 1995—wrote the science-fiction novel *The Body Snatchers* (1955); it was filmed twice as INVASION OF THE BODY SNATCHERS (the 1956 classic and a 1978 remake) and once as BODY SNATCHERS (1993), and the novel itself was reissued under the original film's title. Critics found the film an incisive allegory for Cold War-hysteria, but Finney—who'd sold all film rights for $7,500—insisted the novel was only meant as popular entertainment.

Finney's first book, the caper-thriller *Five Against the House*, was filmed in 1955, with Guy Madison and Kim Novak. His *House of Numbers* was made into a 1957 film with Jack Palance playing the story's twins. Finney's 1963 novel *Good Neighbor Sam*, based on his own experiences in the advertising business, was adapted into the 1964 Jack Lemmon movie, and *Assault on a Queen*, another caper, into the 1966 Frank Sinatra movie, with a script by Rod Serling. Yet though Finney would write about the real world with verisimilitude, he otherwise specialized in time-travel themes, often with an adman as protagonist. His short-story collection *The Third Level* included two time-travel tales, and he returned to that theme in *The Woodrow Wilson Dime* (1968) and *Time After Time*, a detailed and richly researched story of an advertising artist transported to 1880s New York. Finney published a sequel, *From Time to Time*, in 1995. Among his other fantasy-dramas is the novel *Marion's Wall* (1973), about a silent-movie actress who tries to revive her career by swapping bodies with a young woman. It was adapted into the 1985 Glenn Close movie *MAXIE*.

Finney, who lived in Mill Valley, CA, died of pneumonia.

Flanders, Ed

born: Dec. 29, 1934, Minneapolis, MN
died: Feb. 22, 1995, Denny, CA, age 60

Tony- and three-time Emmy-Award-winning actor best known as the avuncular Dr. Donald Westphall on "St. Elsewhere" (NBC 1982-88).

Flanders began as a hometown stage actor in the 1950s and soon reached Broadway, where he won a 1974 supporting-actor Tony Award as the crusty Irish father in the revival of Eugene O'Neill's *A Moon for the Misbegotten*; he won an Emmy reprising the role for a 1976 "ABC Theatre" presentation. Flanders' other Broadway appearances included *The Trial of the Catonsville Nine*, later made into a 1972 film in which he reprised his role as activist priest Father Daniel J. Berrigan. A member of San Diego's Globe Theater company, he segued to TV beginning with an episode of "Cimarron Strip" in 1967, and appearing several times on "Hawaii Five-O." Yet he specialized in telefilms, miniseries and dramatic specials, particularly White House dramas such as "Eleanor and Franklin" (1976), PBS' "Harry S Truman: Plain Speaking" (1977), winning an Emmy for the title role), "Backstairs at the White House" (1979), for which he was Emmy-nominated, "Blind Ambition" (1979), and "The Final Days" (1989).

In the fall of 1987, Flanders left "St. Elsewhere" ensemble, in which he played the chief of staff at an inner-city Boston hospital. He returned for the May 1988 series finale, delivering a long, unscripted soliloquy on death that took his fellow actors and the show's displeased producers by surprise; the speech was nonetheless kept in. He won his final Emmy (Actor—Drama Series) in 1983, and was nominated again in 1985, 1986 and 1987.

Flanders' others films: THE GRASSHOPPER (1970), MacARTHUR (1977), THE NINTH CONFIGURATION aka TWINKLE, TWINKLE, KILLER KANE (1980), THE PURSUIT OF D.B. COOPER and TRUE CONFESSIONS (1981) and a starring role with George C. Scott in THE EXORCIST III (1990).

Flanders died of a self-inflicted gunshot wound to the head.

Fleet, Preston

born: c. 1935, Buffalo, NY
died: Jan. 31, 1995, Santa Barbara, CA, age 60

Inventor of the audience-surrounding Omnimax projection system.

Fleet, the son of a wealthy aircraft manufacturer, founded the drive-through photo-development kiosk-chain Fotomat in 1968. In 1973, he helped establish the Reuben H. Fleet Space Theater and Space Museum, in San Diego, for which he devised a projection system to surround audiences with sight and sound using large, tilted-dome screens. The projectors, now manufactured by the Toronto-based manufacturer, Imax, are currently installed in more than 100 theaters worldwide. Fleet also helped produce the Imax film "Chronos" (1985), a time-lapse short by director/cinematographer Ron Fricke that won a 1987 award at the first international festival for large-format films.

Fleet, who lived in Santa Maria, CA, died of cancer.

Fleetwood, Susan

born: Sept. 21, 1944, St. Andrews, Scotland
died: Sept. 29, 1995, Salisbury, England, age 51
educ: Royal Academy of Dramatic Art, London, England

Royal Shakespeare Company actress who played supporting roles in prominent British and American films.

Fleetwood, the sister of Mick Fleetwood of the pop-rock group Fleetwood Mac, won the RADA's highest prize, the Bancroft Gold Medal, before helping found the 1960s theater group the Liverpool Everyman. She performed with the RSC beginning in 1967-68, and joined the National Theatre Company in 1975, drawing acclaim throughout her career for work in such plays as John Osborne's *Look Back in Anger* and *Watch It Come Down*, *Playboy of the Western World* (opposite Stephen Rea at the Old Vic), *Hamlet* (as Ophelia opposite Albert Finney in a Peter Hall production), and others including *Tamburlaine the Great*, *The Plough and the Stars*, *Lavender Blue*, *Cinderella*, *The Women*, *The Cherry Orchard* and *The Seagull*. For British TV, she co-starred in the "Cagney and Lacey"-like series "Chandler and Co.," and appeared in dramatic productions including "The Watercress Girl," "Between the Wars," "Strangers and Brothers," "Summer's Lease" and "The Good Soldier." Her films include CLASH OF THE TITANS (UK 1981), HEAT AND DUST (UK 1983), YOUNG SHERLOCK HOLMES (1985), Andrei

Tarkovsky's OFFRET-SA CRIFICATIO/THE SACRIFICE (France-Sweden 1986), WHITE MISCHIEF (UK 1988), THE KRAYS (UK 1990) and PERSUASION (UK 1995).

Fleetwood died of cancer, which she'd been battling for 10 years.

Flemyng, Gordon

born: 1934, Glasgow, Scotland
died: 1995

British director, who came into films from TV.

Gordon Flemyng was among the directors whose episodes of the cult-hit British adventure series "The Avengers" (1961-69) aired in the US (ABC 1966-69); he also directed episodes of the British-made series "The Saint" (syndicated 1963-66, NBC 1967-69). Flemying's other UK TV work includes the "Women Beware Women" segment of the two-play special "Blood and Thunder" (Granada TV 1965), starring future "Avenger" Diana Rigg; the "Six Shades of Black" production of "A Loving Disposition" (Granada TV 1965); and the "Screenplay" production of "The Sound of the Guns" (Granada TV 1979). He also directed the telefilms "Philby, Burgess and Maclean" (Granada TV 1977) and "Cloud Waltzing" (Yorkshire Television 1987). He directed two big-screen features spun-off from the BBC series "Doctor Who": DR. WHO AND THE DALEKS (UK 1965) and DALEKS—INVASION EARTH 2150 A.D. aka INVASION EARTH 2150 A.D. (UK 1966).

Flemyng's films include SOLO FOR SPARROW (UK 1962, US release 1966), JUST FOR FUN and FIVE TO ONE (UK 1963), THE SPLIT (1968), GREAT CATHERINE (UK 1968) and THE LAST GRENADE aka GRIGSBY (UK 1970).

No cause of death was reported.

Flemyng, Robert

born: Jan. 1912
died: May 1995, age 83

British actor.

Robert Flemyng often played leading or top-billed support roles as professional or military men. He made his stage debut in 1931, and was the co-lead of his first film, the musical HEAD OVER HEELS aka HEAD OVER HEELS IN LOVE (UK 1936, US release 1937). Flemyng is best known among horror fans as the title character of director Riccardo Freda's L'ORRIBILE SEGRETO DEL DR. HICHCOCK/THE HORRIBLE DR. HICHCOCK aka in Britain THE TERROR OF DR. HICHCOCK (Italy 1962, US release 1964). Flemyng appeared on TV as early as 1949, with the BBC production of the comic play "By Candlelight," and performed to the end, playing the role of John Godwin in the 1995 BBC-WGBH/Boston miniseries "The Choir." Other British TV work include the miniseries "Vanity Fair" (1971), "Rebecca" (1978) and "Memento Mori" (1992).

Flemyng's films include BOND STREET (UK 1948), THE BLUE LAMP, CONSPIRATOR and THE GUINEA PIG aka THE OUTSIDER (UK 1949), BLACKMAILED (UK 1950), THE MAGIC BOX (UK 1951, US release 1952), THE HOLLY AND THE IVY (UK 1952, US release 1954), CAST A DARK SHADOW (UK 1954, US release 1955), THE MAN WHO NEVER WAS (UK 1956), FUNNY FACE (1957), LET'S BE HAPPY (UK 1957), WINDOM'S WAY (UK 1957, US release 1958), BLIND DATE aka CHANCE MEETING (UK 1959), A TOUCH OF LARCENY (UK 1959, US release 1960), MYSTERY SUBMARINE aka DECOY (UK 1962, US release 1963), THE DEADLY AFFAIR and THE SPY WITH A COLD NOSE (UK 1966), THE QUILLER MEMORANDUM (US-UK 1966), THE BLOOD BEAST TERROR aka THE VAMPIRE BEAST CRAVES BLOOD (UK 1967), BATTLE OF BRITAIN (UK 1969), THE BODY STEALERS (US-UK 1969), THE FIRE-CHASERS (UK 1970), THE DARWIN ADVENTURE (UK 1971), YOUNG WINSTON (UK 1972), TRAVELS WITH MY AUNT (1972), GOLDEN RENDEZVOUS aka NUCLEAR TERROR (1977), THE THIRTY-NINE STEPS (UK 1978), THE MEDUSA TOUCH (UK-France 1978), KAFKA (US-France 1991) and SHADOWLANDS (1993).

No cause of death was reported.

Ford, Derek

born: c. 1933
died: May 19, 1995, Bromly, Kent, England, age 62

British exploitation writer-director.

In the 1960s, after working with brother Donald on radio and TV scripts beginning 1948, Ford collaborated with his sibling on mildly naughty girls'-school and horror pictures, eventually specializing in popular softcore sex comedies. His films, usually co-written with Donald in the '60s, include: as writer—THE BLACK TORMENT, THE YELLOW TEDDYBEARS aka GUTTER GIRLS aka THRILL SEEKERS, and SATURDAY NIGHT OUT (UK 1964), A STUDY IN TERROR aka FOG (UK 1965), CORRUPTION (UK 1967), HELL BOATS (UK 1970), SCREAM AND DIE aka THE HOUSE THAT VANISHED (UK 1974), and DON'T OPEN TILL CHRISTMAS (UK 1984). As writer-director—A PROMISE OF BED aka THIS, THAT AND THE OTHER, THE WIFE SWAPPERS aka THE SWAPPERS, and GROUPIE GIRL aka I AM A GROUPIE (UK 1970), SUBURBAN WIVES (UK 1973), and THE GIRL FROM STARSHIP VENUS (UK 1975).

Foss-Lawrence, Fanya

aka: Fanya Foss, Fanya Roberts, Fanya Lawrence
born: c. 1906, Odessa, Russia; raised New York, NY
died: Dec. 12, 1995, Palm Springs, CA, age 89
educ: Juilliard School of Music

Screenwriter, poet and novelist.

In the late 1930s, Foss-Lawrence, while a librarian at Columbia University, met and secretly married writer Edward Dahlberg. She subsequently wrote the semiautobiographical novel *Ask No Return*, which RKO Pictures optioned for director Garson Kanin; Foss, offered a contract to write the screenplay, moved to Hollywood in 1940 and turned out bright, amusing minor pictures, such as the Victor Jory comedy THE STORK PAYS OFF (1941). In 1942, Foss wed Marc Lawrence, a prolific character actor in movies from 1932 through the '90s. In 1951, she moved with him and their two children to Italy, where Lawrence acted in films and Foss eventually wrote scripts for the NBC series "Captain Gallant of the Foreign Legion," which filmed there for a season. In 1957, they returned to Hollywood, where Foss-Lawrence wrote scripts for TV shows including "Have Gun Will Travel" and "The Rifleman"; she additionally wrote for the British series "Ivanhoe," syndicated here. Known for her short stories and poetry, Foss-Lawrence also wrote the novel *Passport to Life* and the play *Adam Ate the Apple*.

Foss-Lawrence's films include: GIRLS UNDER TWENTY-ONE (1940), THE RICHEST MAN IN TOWN and AFFECTIONATELY YOURS (1941), HI' YA, SAILOR (1941, as Fanya Roberts, co-writer with Stanley Roberts), WHY GIRLS LEAVE HOME (1945, as Fanya Lawrence), NIGHTMARE IN THE SUN (1964, with husband Marc Lawrence as director, co-producer, co-writer) and PIGS aka DADDY'S DEADLY DARLINGS (1973, with Lawrence; apparently unreleased).

Foss-Lawrence died of natural causes.

Frank, Richard Edward

aka: Richard Frank
born: c. 1953, Boston, MA
died: died Aug. 27, 1995, Los Angeles, CA, age 42
educ: University of Michigan (graduated 1974), Juilliard School of Drama (graduated 1978)

Stage and TV supporting actor who played Salieri's priest and confidant, Father Vogler, in AMADEUS (1984).

Frank was best known for his role as Jules Bennett, the dryly put-upon assistant to magazine editor Catherine Hughes (Ann Magnuson) in the popular sitcom "Anything But Love" (ABC 1989-92), starring Jamie Lee Curtis and Richard Lewis. (His character's last name was Kramer in the show's initial spring 1989 tryout run.) Frank also wrote *The 'R' Coloring Book* and three volumes of *The Struggling Actor's Coloring Book*.

Frank died of complications from AIDS.

Freleng, Friz

born: Isadore Freleng, Aug. 21, 1906, Kansas City, MO
died: May 26, 1995, Los Angeles, CA, age 88

Legendary Warner Bros. animation director.

Freleng, with such "Termite Terrace" compatriots as Chuck Jones, Tex Avery, Bob Clampett, and Robert McKimson, helped change the face of animation with slick, irreverent, witty and technically masterful cartoon shorts starring such iconic characters as Bugs Bunny, Daffy Duck, Porky Pig, the Coyote and Road Runner, Pepe LePew, and the volatile, pint-sized Yosemite Sam — whom writer Michael Maltese actually patterned after the sometimes hot-tempered Freleng (who was also, like Sam, on the short side, and who sported a small red mustache).

The self-taught Freleng began as an animator with a fledgling Walt Disney, joining his fellow hometown boy's Kansas City coterie in Los Angeles. There he helped draw Oswald the Lucky Rabbit cartoons with fellow animators Hugh Harman and Rudolf Ising. In 1930, the three and production executive Leon Schlesinger inaugurated the Warner Bros. animation department, launching the "Looney Tunes" series; "Merrie Melodies," initially differentiated from Looney Tunes by being in color, soon followed. Freleng's first effort as director, the Looney Tune "Bosko in Dutch," was released March 1933. When the Harman-Ising team split with Schlesinger over money that same year, Freleng stayed and (after a brief dalliance at MGM in the late 1930s) became part of arguably the greatest conglomerate of animation talent at one company before or since.

Freleng himself directed the first Porky Pig short, "I Haven't Got a Hat" (1935), in which stuttering young school-pig Porky is paired with a cat named Beans. Freleng, with a half-dozen other directors variously, directed Bugs and Daffy cartoons through the 1940s and '50s, and helped the characters evolve. It was Freleng who paired an occasionally used canary character with a recent feline creation to launch the Tweety and Sylvester series, starting with the Academy Award-winning "Tweetie Pie" (May 1947); Freleng went on to direct virtually every Tweety Bird short. Freleng also redesigned an unnamed Latino mouse from a 1953 cartoon to create Speedy Gonzales, who debuted in a titular 1955 short which likewise won an Oscar.

Statuettes also went to Freleng for the shorts for "Birds Anonymous" (1957) and "Knighty Knight Bugs" (1958). And remarkably, an 11-minute Public Health Service short that Freleng wrote with director Jones, "So Much for So Little" (1949), became the only cartoon to win an Academy Award for documentary.

Some of Freleng's other notable shorts during his Warners period include "You Ought to be in Pictures" (1940), in which a live-action Schlesinger interacts with a cartoon Daffy and Porky; the Oscar-nominated "Rhapsody in Rivets" (1941), a brilliantly executed, no-dialogue opus of a construction site set to Liszt's "Hungarian Rhapsody," with the foreman inadvertently "conducting" the workers (and physical gags) in time to the score; "Little Red Riding Rabbit" (1943); "Hare Trigger" (1944), which introduced Yosemite Sam; "Racketeer Rabbit" (1946); "Buccaneer Bunny" (1948); "Hare Brush" (1955); the unique, jazz-scored "The Three Little Bops," with narration by Stan Freberg (1957); "Show Biz Bugs" (1957); and, as producer, the Oscar-nominated Speedy short "The Pied Piper of Guadalupe" (1961).

When the Warner Bros. animation studio closed down in 1963, Freleng joined with Warners executive David H. DePatie to form DePatie-Freleng Enterprises. A year later, Warner Bros. ironically contracted them to revive Looney Tunes and Merrie Melodies, at half the budget; the once-great legacy carried on tarnished until Warners abandoned cartoons once more in 1969. Throughout this time, DePatie-Freleng gained acclaim for their animated title sequence to the Blake Edwards film THE PINK PANTHER (1964), and the spinoff theatrical-cartoon series featuring that urbane feline. The Freleng-directed short "The Pink Phink" (1964) won Freleng the fifth and final Oscar with which he was associated; DePatie-Freleng received another nomination in 1966, for "The Pink Blueprint." DePatie and Freleng also garnered two Emmy Awards and six additional nominations from 1975 to 1982 for their Pink Panther and Dr. Seuss cartoons, and an ABC afterschool special. Through the early 1980s, Freleng helped produce Warner Bros. cartoon compilation movies, some with new framing sequences, and TV specials.

Freleng's feature-film work also includes TWO GUYS FROM TEXAS (1948; directed dream sequence in which Bugs Bunny gives advice to a cartoon Jack Carson) and MY DREAM IS YOURS (1949; directed dream sequence in which Bugs Bunny sings and dances with live-action Jack Carson and Doris Day).

No cause of death was reported.

Gabor, Eva

born: Feb. 11, 1921, Budapest, Hungary
died: July 4, 1995, Los Angeles, CA, age 74

Light comic actress beloved by baby-boomers as Lisa Douglas on TV's "Green Acres."

Eva Gabor, less flamboyant and more accomplished than her actress sister Zsa Zsa (nee Sari), was the eldest of the three celebrated Gabor siblings whose glamor brought them a quirky fame in the 1930s and '40s.

Eva, the first to arrive, had been a cafe singer and ice skater in her native Hungary, and upon emigrating in Hollywood in 1939 signed on with Paramount as a contract player. Her combination of porcelain beauty and unintimidating comic grace made her the glamor-girl-next-door. It was a role she played to perfection on "Green Acres" (CBS 1968-71), as a Park Avenue socialite who folows her attorney husband (Eddie Albert) to his dream life as a farmer — albeit on an exaggeratedly rundown farm with increasingly surreal, comically Kafkaesque touches as the series went on. She reprised her role in the TV-movie "Return to Green Acres" (1990).

Gabor played the romantic female lead in her second film, FORCED LANDING (1941), and again in LOVE ISLAND (1952) and CAPTAIN KIDD AND THE SLAVE GIRL (1954). But mostly, she served as a decorative supporting player in such films as THE WIFE OF MONTE CRISTO (1946), ARTISTS AND MODELS (1955), the remake of MY MAN GODFREY (1957), and GIGI (1958). In the 1970s, she was in demand as vocal talent in animated features. Her major career break came with the 1950 Broadway show *The Happy Time*, in which she earned raves playing an unemployed acrobat. Her success there led to "The Eva Gabor Show," an interview program which, per various references, was either on local New York TV or on ABC daytime from 1950-51, and to a Las Vegas nightclub act with Zsa Zsa and socialite-sister Magda.

Eva had already made her live-TV dramatic debut, in a 1949 installment of the NBC anthology "Your Show Time"; her multitude of TV credits include "Studio One," "U.S. Steel Hour," "Masterpiece Playhouse" (in "Uncle Vanya"), "The Defenders," "Here's Lucy," "Fantasy Island" and "Hart to Hart," as Lisa Douglas in crossover episodes of "Petticoat Junction," "The Beverly Hillbillies," and TV pilots including "Mickey and the Contessa" (CBS 1963), "Almost Heaven" (ABC 1978) and "The Gregory Harrison Show" (CBS 1989). She also co-starred in the 1986 CBS sitcom, "Bridges to Cross." In 1983, she made her last Broadway appearance, succeeding Colleen Dewhurst in *You Can't Take It With You*. Afterward, while continuing to act occasionally, she spent her time running a multimillion-dollar wig company she'd founded, and, after several marriages, accompanying entertainment mogul Merv Griffin. Her autobiography: *Orchids and Salamis* (1951).

Her other films include: MIDNIGHT ANGEL aka PACIFIC BLACK-OUT (1941), A ROYAL SCANDAL a.k.a. in Britain CZARINA (1945), SONG OF SURRENDER (1949), LOVE ISLAND (1952), PARIS MODEL (1953), THE LAST TIME I SAW PARIS and THE MAD MAGICIAN (1954), DON'T GO NEAR THE WATER (1957), THE TRUTH ABOUT WOMEN (UK 1958), IT STARTED WITH A KISS (1959), A NEW KIND OF LOVE a.k.a SAMANTHA (1963), YOUNGBLOOD HAWKE (1964) and THE PRINCESS ACADEMY (US-Yugoslavia-France 1987), and the animated features THE ARISTOCATS (1970), THE RESCUERS (1977), NUTCRACKER FANTASY (1979) and THE RESCUERS DOWN UNDER (1990).

Gabor, who is survived by her sisters and their mother, died of respiratory distress and other infections, after having broken a hip in a fall in Mexico on June 21.

Garfield, David

born: c. 1944
died: Nov. 24, 1995, age 51

Film editor son of blacklisted actor John Garfield (1913-52) and Roberta Garfield, and stepson of New York City labor attorney Sidney Cohn. His films include HERO AT LARGE (1980), THE CHOSEN (1982), ALL THE RIGHT MOVES and THE STING II (1983), FLASHPOINT (1984), SYLVESTER (1985), DESERT BLOOM and THE KARATE KID PART II (1986), VICE VERSA (1988) and SCORCHERS (1992).

Garrison, Ellen

born: c. 1899, Boston, MA
died: June 2, 1995, age 96
educ: The Brearley School

One-shot actress who, at age 83, delighted audiences with her role as the older self of Dr. Eudora Fletcher (Mia Farrow) in the Woody Allen film ZELIG (1983). As the psychiatrist for Allen's character, the older Fletcher delivers a series of monologues throughout the film. Garrison—a direct descendant of John Jay, and the widow of prominent attorney and civil-rights advocate Lloyd K. Garrison—was recommended for the part by a mutual friend of the casting director.

No cause of death was reported.

Gazzo, Michael V.

born: c. 1923
died: Feb. 14, 1995, Los Angeles, CA, age 71
Character actor and playwright.

Michael V. Gazzo came to prominence in 1955 with his play *A Hatful of Rain*, a groundbreakingly frank and sympathetic portrait of a drug addict struggling to kick his habit. Starring Ben Gazzarra, Shelley Winters and Tony (then billed as Anthony) Franciosa, the critically lauded play ran 390 performances and was adapted into both an acclaimed 1957 film starring Eva Marie Saint, Don Murray and Oscar-nominee Franciosa, with a script co-written by Gazzo, and a 1967 ABC dramatic special. Gazzo also wrote the Broadway play *Night Circus* (1958) and co-wrote the script for the Elvis Presley movie KING CREOLE (1958). Gazzo, who often played Mafiosi, received a supporting actor Academy Award nomination for THE GODFATHER, PART II (1974).

His other films as actor include A MAN CALLED ADAM (1966), THE GANG THAT COULDN'T SHOOT STRAIGHT (1971), BLACK SUNDAY (1977), FINGERS and KING OF THE GYPSIES (1978), THE FISH THAT SAVED PITTSBURGH (1979), LOVE AND BULLETS (UK 1979), ALLIGATOR and CUBA CROSSING aka KILL CASTRO (1980), BACK ROADS and BODY AND SOUL (1981), CANNONBALL RUN II and FEAR CITY (1984), COOKIE (1989), LAST ACTION HERO (1993), and RING OF THE MUSKETEERS (direct-to-video 1994).

Gazzo died of complications following a stroke.

Giannetti, Alfredo

born: c. 1924
died: July 30, 1995, Rome, Italy, age 71
Italian screenwriter and sometime director, who shared a screenwriting Oscar for the international hit DIVORZIO ALL'ITALIANA/DIVORCE, ITALIAN STYLE (Italy 1961, US release 62). Alfredo Giannetti made his screenwriting debut with director Giuseppe De Santis' UN MARITO PER ANNA ZACCHERO/A HUSBAND FOR ANNA (Italy 1953), and shortly afterward began a fertile collaboration with director Pietro Germi, beginning with IL FERROVIERE/THE RAILROAD MAN aka MAN OF IRON (Italy 1956) and continuing with L'UOMO DEL PAGLIA/THE STRAW MAN (Italy 1957), UN MALEDETTO IMBROGLIO/THE FACTS OF MURDER aka A SORDID AFFAIR (Italy 1957, US release 1965), DIVORCE, ITALIAN STYLE (1962), L'IMMORALE/THE CLIMAX aka TOO MUCH FOR ONE MAN (Italy-France 1967), and SERAFINO (Italy-France 1968, US release 1970). Giannetti began directing with GIORNO PER GIORNO DISPERATAMENTE (Italy 1961). He later made Italian telefilms, in particular a series about women in historial time periods that often coaxed star actresses such as Anna Magnani out of semi-retirement; these include "1870," "The Chanteuse," "1943: An Encounter" and "The Automobile."

Giannetti died following a stroke.

Godunov, Alexander

born: Boris Alexander Godunov, Nov. 28, 1949, Sakhalin Island, USSR
died: found dead May 18, 1995, West Hollywood, CA, age 45
World-renowned ballet star and bad-boy jet-setter who also acted in films.

Alexander Godunov's brooding looks and flowing locks became best known outside the dance world for his supporting roles as Kelly McGillis' stoic Amish suitor in WITNESS (1985) and a terrorizing henchman in DIE HARD (1988). At age 9, his mother enrolled him at the Riga State Ballet School, where one classmate was Mikhail Baryshnikov. Upon graduation, Godunov joined Igor Moiseyev's Young Ballet, and in the 1970s became a star with the Bolshoi. Godunov defected to the US on Aug. 21, 1979, prompting a split from his ballet-dancer wife Ludmila (sometimes transliterated Lyudmila) Vlasova that led to their formal divorce in 1982; he later took up with actress Jacqueline Bisset.

After his defection, Godunov danced with the American Ballet Theater in New York for three years, but his sometimes stubborn and prickly personality and a feud with ABT artistic director Baryshnikov led to his departure from the company. Godunov went on to perform with the Asami Maki Ballet of Japan, the Israel Ballet, Maurice Bejart's Ballet of the Twentieth Century, and briefly with an ensemble called Godunov & Stars before retiring from dance. He then studied with Stella Adler and at the Juilliard School of Music before making his well-received film debut in

WITNESS. Godunov became a US citizen in 1987, and was the subject of a 1980s documentary, "Godunov: The World to Dance In."

His other films were THE MONEY PIT (1986), WAXWORK II: LOST IN TIME (direct-to-video 1992), the critically well-received THE RUNESTONE (direct-to-video 1992 after one Los Angeles playdate and film festivals), and NORTH (1994), a comic-fantasy in which he and Kelly McGillis essentially reprised their roles from WITNESS. Weeks before his death, Godunov was filming a movie in Budapest, Hungary.

Godunov, around the time of his death, had been regularly attended by a home nurse, who discovered his body on May 18; his physician listed death as by natural causes.

Gordon, Gale

born: Charles Aldrich Jr. (some sources give Gaylord Aldrich), Feb. 2, 1906, New York, NY
died: June 30, 1995, Escondido, CA, age 89
Character actor of radio, TV and film, whose dignified fussiness, slow burns, and withering gazes were put to superb use opposite the inspired comedienne Lucille Ball.

Gale Gordon, who appeared in films beginning 1942 and was a major performer in 1950s radio, found a lasting niche in American television history playing Lucy's foil in three series: as Theodore J. Mooney on "The Lucy Show" (CBS 1963-68), Harrison Otis Carter on "Here's Lucy" (CBS 1968-74) and Curtis McGibbon on "Life with Lucy" (ABC 1986). He had been Ball's first choice to play neighbor Fred Mertz, but he was already committed to "Our Miss Brooks" (CBS 1952-56), in which he reprised the role of Principal Osgood Conklin that he'd originated on radio.

The son of show-business parents—father Charles T. Aldrich was a noted vaudevillian, mother Gloria Gordon played boardinghouse owner Mrs. O'Reilly on "My Friend Irma" (CBS 1952-54) — Gordon attended schools in New York and England before taking up the family business. He appeared in one film, HERE WE GO AGAIN (1942), then turned his talents elsewhere. By the 1950s, he was performing regular roles in several weekly radio shows, including "Our Miss Brooks," "The Great Gildersleeve" (as Rumson Bullard), "The Alice Faye-Phil Harris Show," "The Dennis Day Show," Lucille Ball's "My Favorite Husband" (as Rudolph Atterbury) and "Fibber McGee and Molly," in which, as Mayor LaTrivia, he could always be counted on to sputter exasperatedly, "McGeeeeeee!" (Years later, Gordon become the real-life honorary mayor of the resort area Borrego Springs, CA.) He made his TV debut in two 1952 episodes of "I Love Lucy," playing Ricky Ricardo's stuffy boss at the Tropicana Club. Gordon was also a cast-member of the series "The Brothers" (CBS 1956-57), "Sally" (NBC 1958), "Peter and Gladys" (CBS 1960-62), and "Dennis the Menace" (CBS 1959-63), in which he replaced the late Joseph Kearns' neighbor, George Wilson, as his brother, John Wilson, beginning May 1962. Among his episodic-TV credits is a 1962 CBS pilot, "For the Love of Mike." He retired in 1986, except for local stage roles; among his final parts was a 1991 cameo appearnce as Mr. Mooney in the sitcom "Hi Honey, I'm Home!".

Gordon's films include A WOMAN OF DISTINCTION (1950), HERE COME THE NELSONS aka MEET THE NELSONS (1952), FRANCIS COVERS THE BIG TOWN (1953), OUR MISS BROOKS (1956), RALLY 'ROUND THE FLAG, BOYS! (1958), DON'T GIVE UP THE SHIP and THE 30 FOOT BRIDE OF CANDY ROCK (1959), VISIT TO A SMALL PLANET (1960), ALL HANDS ON DECK, ALL IN A NIGHT'S WORK and DONDI (1961), SERGEANT DEADHEAD (1965), SPEEDWAY (1968) and THE 'BURBS (1989).

Gordon died of cancer, only weeks after the death of his actress wife, Virgina Curley, to whom he'd been married 55 years.

Granger, Dorothy

born: c. 1911, Ohio
died: Jan. 4, 1995, Los Angeles, age 83
Founding SAG member and minor actress in well over 75 films.

Dorothy Granger, born into a vaudeville family, won a Texas beauty pageant at age 13, and performed in touring companies before making her film debut in the short "The Sophomore" (1929). A voluptuous redhead in her youth, she often played dance-hall girls, hat-check girls, chorus girls and other tootsies before segueing into comic roles with billings such as "Fat Girl" (in the Paulette Goddard-Luise Rainer DRAMATIC SCHOOL, 1938) and "Fat Bridesmaid" (NEW MOON, 1940). She then settled into neighbors, wives and, in the lavish Elizabeth Taylor-

Montgomery Clift RAINTREE COUNTY (1957), her last film appearance, as stately Mademoiselle Gaubert. Granger also guested on 1950s TV shows, including "The Abbott and Costllo Show," "I Married Joan," "Father Knows Best," "Lassie," "The Jack Benny Show" and "Death Valley Days," and for more than 40 years ran a Los Angeles firm that served as upholsterers-to-the-stars. In 1993, with the 60th anniversary of the Screen Actors Guild, she was honored with other charter members who'd been issued the first SAG cards. After appearing in installments of the Hal Roach comedy-short series "The Boy Friends," three Laurel & Hardy two-reelers (including 1930's "The Laurel and Hardy Murder Case") and other comic shorts including W.C. Fields' "The Dentist" (1932), she had roles in numerous feature films from the 1930s through the 1950s.

Granger died of cancer.

Grau, Doris

born: 1924, Brooklyn, NY
died: Dec. 30, 1995, Los Angeles, CA, age 71
Film and TV script supervisor turned senior actress.

She began her career at Columbia Pictures and in later years worked on TV series including "Cheers" and the "The Tracey Ullman Show." Turning to acting later in life, she appeared in the Eddie Murphy comedy THE DISTINGUISHED GENTLEMAN (1992), and did voiceover work on the TV series "The Simpsons" and "The Critic," and the movie BABE (Australia 1995).

Grau died of respiratory failure.

Greene, John L.

born: Buffalo, NY; raised Fremont, OH
died: Oct. 4, 1995, Los Angeles, CA, age 82
educ: University of Iowa (M.A. journalism)
Creator of the TV series "My Favorite Martian" (CBS 1963-66), who dabbled in movies.

A short story writer who moved on to children's radio shows, John L. Greene went to Hollywood in 1938 to write for "Texaco Star Theater" and other radio programs. He later segued to television, writing for series including "Ozzie and Harriet," "Blondie," "The Real McCoys," "The Flying Nun," "I Dream of Jeannie," "The Andy Griffith Show" and "Green Acres." The fondly remembered "My Favorite Martian" starred Ray Walston as an avuncular spaceman who lived with reporter Bill Bixby while trying to repair his downed spacecraft, while both tried keep to "Uncle Martin's" real nature hidden from other earthlings. Greene, not to be confused with actor John T. Greene, co-wrote the movies PLUNDERS OF PAINTED FLATS (1959) and the Bob Hope-Phyllis Diller outing THE PRIVATE WAR OF SGT. O'FARRELL (1968).

No cause of death was reported.

Griffin, Eleanore

born: c. 1904
died: July 26, 1995, Woodland Hills, CA, age 91
Academy Award-winning co-writer of BOYS TOWN (1938).

Eleanore Griffin had been in Hollywood very shortly before writing (with Dore Schary and John Meehan) that sentimental orphanage-drama favorite of Newt Gingrich's. She went on to a remarkably lengthy career, highlighted by Judy Garland's first starring role, in THOROUGHBREDS DON'T CRY (1937); Garland's musical classic THE HARVEY GIRLS (1946); Lana Turner's IMITATION OF LIFE (1959), and (uncredited, as was fellow scripter William Rankin) the Howard Hawks classic ONLY ANGELS HAVE WINGS (1939), starring Cary Grant and Jean Arthur.

Griffin's other films include: LOVE IN A BUNGALOW, TIME OUT FOR ROMANCE and WHEN LOVE IS YOUNG (1937), ST. LOUIS BLUES and STREET OF MISSING MEN (1939), BLONDIE IN SOCIETY and I WANTED WINGS (1941), John Wayne's IN OLD OKLAHOMA aka WAR OF THE WILDCATS (1943), HI, BEAUTIFUL! (1944), NOB HILL (1945), TENTH AVENUE ANGEL (1948), A MAN CALLED PETER and GOOD MORNING, MISS DOVE (1955), THIRD MAN ON THE MOUNTAIN aka BANNER IN THE SKY (1959), the second remake of BACK STREET (1961), starring Susan Hayward, and ONE MAN'S WAY (1964).

Griffin died after what was reported as a long illness.

Guardino, Harry

born: Dec. 22 or 23 (accounts differ), 1925, New York, NY
died: July 17, 1995, Palm Springs, CA age 69
Handsomely weathered actor often cast as smoothly tough, urbane bad guys and investigators.

Born on the Lower East Side and later raised in Brooklyn, Harry Guardino began acting at age 12 in Police Athletic League productions. He left high school to help support his parents and five siblings, working unloading flatcars for the New York central Railroad and, variously through the years, as a truck driver, house painter, carpenter, usher, dishwasher and gas station attendant. Guardino served in the Navy during WWII, seeing action in Iwo Jima and Okinawa as a gunner's mate. Afterward, he joined the Merchant Marine, and eventually entered a New York drama workshop alongside fellow students Tony Curtis and Ben Gazzara; Guardino would later understudy Gazzara in the acclaimed 1955 play *A Hatful of Rain,* and perform the role in the road tour.

Guardino had already worked in films by that time, with PURPLE HEART DIARY and Humphrey Bogart's SIROCCO (both 1951), and classmate Curtis' FLESH AND FURY (1952). Guardino made his Broadway debut with *End as a Man,* and appeared in such plays as *The Seven Descents of Myrtyle, The Rose Tattoo, Natural Affection, Anyone Can Whistle, Woman of the Year* (1981), *One More River,* in which he earned a 1960 Tony nomination, and the comedy *The Pigeon That Took Rome,* for which he garnered a Golden Globe nomination; Guardino co-starred with Charlton Heston in the 1962 film version. Among his final projects was the comedy *Breaking Legs,* performed on tour with Danny Aiello.

Guardino was especially prolific in television, where he'd debuted on the "Kaiser Aluminum Hour" installment "The Deadly Silence" (NBC 1957). He starred as "The Reporter" (CBS 1964) and in the title role of "Monty Nash" (syndicated 1971-72), and co-starred in "The New Adventures of Perry Mason" (CBS 1973-74), as Mason's courtroom nemesis, Hamilton Burger. The unaired drama "Stranded" was released theatrically with 40 additional minutes as VALLEY OF MYSTERY (1967).

Guardino's other films include THE BIG TIP OFF and HOLD BACK TOMORROW (1955), HOUSEBOAT (1958), THE FIVE PENNIES and PORK CHOP HILL (1959), FIVE BRANDED WOMEN (1960), KING OF KINGS (1961), HELL IS FOR HEROES (1962), RHINO! (1964), in which he starred, OPERAZIONE SAN GENNARO/TREASURE OF SAN GENNARO (Italy-France-West Germany 1966, US release 1968), THE ADVENTURES OF BULLWHIP GRIFFIN (1967), THE HELL WITH HEROES, JIGSAW, and MADIGAN (1968), LOVERS AND OTHER STRANGERS (1970), RED SKY AT MORNING (1971), THEY ONLY KILL THEIR MASTERS (1972), CAPONE and WHIFFS (1975), ST. IVES (1976), ROLLERCOASTER (1977), MATILDA (1978), GOLDENGIRL (1979), ANY WHICH WAY YOU CAN (1980), FIST OF HONOR (direct-to-video 1993), and two Clint Eastwood movies as San Francisco police detective Lt. Bressler, DIRTY HARRY (1971) and THE ENFORCER (1976).

Guardino died of lung cancer.

Hackett, Albert

born: Feb. 16, 1900, New York, NY
died: March 16, 1995, New York, NY, age 95
Pulitzer Prize-winning playwright and screenwriter who, with first wife Florence Goodrich, wrote such enduring classics as *The Diary of Anne Frank,* THE THIN MAN (1934), IT'S A WONDERFUL LIFE (1946), EASTER PARADE (1948), FATHER OF THE BRIDE (1950) and SEVEN BRIDES FOR SEVEN BROTHERS (1954). Goodrich predeceased him in 1984; Hackett remarried the following year.

The son of theater and film actress Florence Hackett (1882-1954) and the brother of actor Raymond Hackett (1902-1958), Albert Hackett made his stage debut at age six, playing a girl in *Lottie, the Poor Saleslady.* He later toured in vaudeville and with Maude Adams in *Peter Pan,* and grew into mostly comic adult roles in silent films and on stage. He and the twice-married Goodrich were both actors when they met in 1924; they began writing together, and found success with their critically well-received Broadway comedy *Up Pops the Devil,* in which Hackett also acted. The play was adapted by other writers into the 1931 Carole Lombard film of the same name, and the 1938 Bob Hope picture THANKS FOR THE MEMORY. Hackett and Goodrich were married in 1931 and soon relocated to Hollywood. They made their screenwriting debut with THE SECRET OF MADAME BLANCHE (1933). Always writing together, occasionally with a collaborator (such as Ogden Nash on 1937's THE

FIREFLY), they wrote both original scripts and adaptations of comedies, musicals and dramas.

Hackett and Goodrich—who'd written plays including *Bridal Wise* (1932), a moderate success, and *The Great Big Doorstep* (1942), a flop—triumphed with Broadway's *The Diary of Anne Frank*, which opened at the Cort Theater on Oct. 5, 1955, ran 717 performances and won a Pulitzer Prize, a Tony Award for best play, and the New York Drama Critics Circle Award. Based on the book *Anne Frank: The Diary of a Young Girl*, the play took several years and eight drafts to complete. Goodrich and Hackett adapted it themselves for the 1959 movie, which won three Oscars and was nominated for Best Picture.

Hackett and Goodrich ironically were not Oscar-nominated themselves for ANNE FRANK, but for THE THIN MAN and AFTER THE THIN MAN (1936), FATHER OF THE BRIDE and SEVEN BRIDES FOR SEVEN BROTHERS; all but AFTER THE THIN MAN were also Best Picture nominees.

Hackett's other films as writer, all with Goodrich, include: PENT-HOUSE aka in Britain CROOKS IN CLOVER (1933), FUGITIVE LOVERS and HIDE-OUT (1934), NAUGHTY MARIETTA and AH, WILDERNESS! (1935), ROSE MARIE aka INDIAN LOVE CALL and SMALL TOWN GIRL aka ONE HORSE TOWN (1936), ANOTHER THIN MAN and SOCIETY LAWYER (1939), THE HITLER GANG and LADY IN THE DARK (1944), THE VIRGINIAN (1946), THE PIRATE and SUMMER HOLIDAY (1948), IN THE GOOD OLD SUMMER-TIME (1949), FATHER'S LITTLE DIVIDEND and TOO YOUNG TO KISS (1951), GIVE A GIRL A BREAK (1953), THE LONG, LONG TRAILER (1954), A CERTAIN SMILE (1958), and FIVE FINGER EXERCISE (1962). The two 1990s FATHER OF THE BRIDE movies were based on the Goodrich-Hackett originals. Additionally, Hackett, who acted in silent films, also appeared as an actor in the both the Broadway musical and the 1930 movie adaptation, WHOOPEE.

Hackett died of pneumonia.

Halas, John

born: April 16, 1912, Hungary
died: Jan. 1995, age 82
Animator.

John Halas and his wife, Joy Batchelor, worked in Britain as an animation writer-director-producer duo. They worked together on several cartoon shorts, as well as on features—one of which, the George Orwell adaptation ANIMAL FARM (UK 1955; Halas and Batchelor co-writers, co-directors, co-producers), stands as Britain's first feature-length animated film. They also produced director Alberto Cavalcanti's live-action-and-animated THE MONSTER OF HIGHGATE PONDS (UK; US release 1961). Among Halas' other works is the feature AUTOMANIA 2000 (UK 1963).

No cause of death was reported.

Harman, Estelle Karchmer

born: c. 1923
died: April 30, 1995, Hollywood, CA, age 72
Acting teacher and one-time head of Universal Studios talent department, who trained Carol Burnett, Tony Curtis, Rock Hudson and others.

Estelle Harman had helped found the theater-arts department at UCLA before going to work for Universal. While at the unviersity, she directed plays including *Alice in Wonderland*, *All My Sons* and *Henry IV*, and was one of the founding directors of the Circle Theater. At Universal, her students in addition to the aforementioned included Sharon Gless, Michael Landon, Lee Majors, Hugh O'Brian, Victoria Principal, Mamie Van Doren, and Dennis Weaver.

No cause of death was reported.

Harris, Phil

born: June 24, 1904, coal-mining camp outside Linton, IN
died: Aug. 11, 1995, Rancho Mirage, CA, age 91
Bandleader and fresh-mouthed Jack Benny sidekick, immortalized as the voice of Baloo the Bear in Disney's animated THE JUNGLE BOOK (1967).

Phil Harris grew up in a musical environment when his father, a circus bandmaster and vaudeville musician, moved the family to Nashville, TN when Harris was five or six. Harris took up drums, and eventually formed a touring band called the Dixie Syncopaters, followed in 1932 an orchstra

that proved popular enough on the big-band circuit to find work in radio. Harris spun off into movie parts, occasionally playing himself, and joined the radio troupe of renowned comedian Jack Benny from 1936-52; Harris and actress wife Alice Faye (b. 1912) also had their own radio program from 1946-54. He also appeared in the Jack Benny films MAN ABOUT TOWN (1939) and BUCK BENNY RIDES AGAIN (1940). Harris' biggest musical hit was the almost tap-like song "The Thing," and he also popularized such loony tunes as "That's What I Like About the South," "Is It True What They Say About Dixie?" "Woodman, Spare that Tree," "The Preacher and the Bear," and "Smoke, Smoke That Cigarette." Nonetheless, he was retired and mostly forgotten when Disney brought him in for Baloo; reportedly, it was at Harris' improvisational suggestion that the script was rewritten to incorporate the slang and particular personalities of the vocal performers. The song "The Bare Necessities," which Harris performed in the film, was nominated for an Oscar.

No cause of death was reported.

Harris, Robert

born: 1900
died: May 18, 1995, London, England, age 95
educ: Royal Academy of Dramatic Art
British classical actor with a five-decade career.

Robert Harris—not to be confused with the 1930s producer Robert Harris, the costumer Robert Harris, or American character actor Robert H. Harris—made his stage debut in J.M. Barrie's *The Will* (1923), and his Broadway debut two years, in Noel Coward's *Easy Virtue*. He joined the Old Vic company in 1931, playing Mark Antony in *Julius Caesar*, and *Hamlet*. Among his Broadway plays are George Bernard Shaw's *Candide* (1937), as Marchbanks, opposite Katharine Cornell, and *Edwina Black* (1950). From 1963-64, he toured the US as Sir Thomas More in Robert Bolt's acclaimed play *A Man for All Seasons*. His last stage appearance came in *Make No Mistake* (1971), in the London suburb of Guildford.

Harris's films include (with accompanying years those of US release): THE "W" PLAN (UK 1931), UNDERCOVER aka UNDERGROUND GUERRILLAS aka CHETNIK(UK 1944), THE LIFE AND DEATH OF COLONEL BLIMP (UK 1945), MR. DREW aka FOR THEM THAT TRESPASS (UK 1949), LAUGHING ANNE (UK-US 1954), BUNDLE OF JOY (1956), THE BIG CAPER (UK 1957), OSCAR WILDE (UK 1960), GIRL IN THE HEADLINES aka THE MODEL MURDER CASE (UK 1964), THE SECRET OF MY SUCCESS (UK 1965), DECLINE AND FALL aka DECLINE AND FALL. . . OF A BIRD WATCHER (UK 1968), YOUNG WINSTON (UK 1972), LADY CAROLINE LAMB (UK-UK-Italy 1972), MASSACRE IN ROME (Italy 1973), and RANSOM aka THE TERRORISTS (UK 1975).

No cause of death was reported.

Harrison, Kathleen

born: 1898, Lancashire, England
died: Dec. 1995, age c. 97
British character actress.

Kathleen Harrison made her stage debut in 1926, and through her films—starting with HOBSON'S CHOICE (UK 1931)—developed a slightly batty yet ultimately warm and motherly persona that made her a national figure. Harrison co-starred as Ethel Huggett in the three-picture Huggett family series, with a young Petula Clark playing one of her daughters: HERE COME THE HUGGETTS (UK 1948), VOTE FOR HUGGETT (UK 1948) and THE HUGGETTS ABROAD (UK 1949). She was as adept in such serious leading role as an an abandoned wife in WATERFRONT aka WATERFRONT WOMEN (UK 1950, US release 1952) as she was in such comedies as THE HAPPY FAMILY aka MR. LORD SAYS NO (UK 1952) or MRS. GIBBONS' BOYS (UK 1962). Among her at least 74 films is one American movie, NIGHT MUST FALL (1937). On British television, Harrison starred as a Cockney charwoman who came into a fortune in the 25-episode, 55-minute seriocomedy "Mrs. Thursday" (ATV 1966-67); she also appeared in the 1977 miniseries "Our Mutual Friend."

No cause of death was reported.

Hawkins, Yvette

born: c. 1941
died: April 10, 1995, New York, NY, age 54
Theater, film and TV actress and writer.

Yvette Hawkins appeared in the Broadway plays *The Amen Corner*, *Ain't Supposed to Die a Natural Death* and *Checkmates*, and Off-Broadway in *The Strong Breed*, *The Trials of Brother Jero*, *The Resurrection of Lady Lester*, *The Last Street Play* and *Before It Hits Home*, as well as in regional theater. Her TV work includes the daytime serials "As the World Turns" and "The Guiding Light," and the series "Cagney and Lacey" and "Law & Order." She did writing for the Children's Television Workshop, and was a co-writer of the book *A Guide to the Black Apple*.

Her films include NIGHTHAWKS (1981), ZEBRAHEAD (1992) and MISSISSIPPI MASALA (US-UK 1992).

Hawkins died of lung cancer.

Heifitz, Josef

aka: Iosif Kheifits; Iosif Kheyfits
born: Dec. 17, 1905, Minsk, Russia
died: April 24, 1995, St. Peterburg, Russia, age 90
educ: Leningrad School of Film Arts aka Leningrad Technicum of Screen Arts

Director from the early Soviet cinema "golden age."

Heifitz, whose name transliterates variously from the Russian Cyrillic alphabet, joined the Sovkino studio in the former Leningrad in 1928, where he and two-decade collaborator Alexander Zarkhi collaborated on several scripts, ending with TRANSPORT OGNYA (USSR 1930); they also co-directed two shorts around this time. Moving to LenFilm, Heiftiz and Zarkhi began a co-directing collaboration that would last nearly two decades. Most notably, they co-wrote and co-directed the major historical work DEPUTAT BALTIKI/BALTIC DEPUTY aka DEPUTY OF THE BALTIC (USSR 1937), a forerunner of Soviet cinema's "historic realism" school. Their partnership ended in 1950, with prominent Jewish figure Heiftiz largely unable to work until after dictator Joseph Stalin's death in 1954.

No cause of death was reported.

Helmore, Tom

born: Jan. 4, 1904, England
died: Sept. 12, 1995, Longboat Key, FL, age 91

Dapper Broadway actor who brought his debonair British style to several Hollywood films.

Tom Helmore began as a movie extra in his native England while apprenticing in his father's accountancy firm. He went on to the London stage, and, beginning 1930, credited film roles. He made his Broadway debut in 1939 in S.N. Behrman's *No Time for Comedy*, opposite Katharine Cornell, and married Cornell's understudy, Mary Drayton, six years later. Helmore was Rex Harrison's standby in the original production of *My Fair Lady*, in which he later toured. In 1965, Helmore appeared in the stage thriller *The Playroom*, by his actress-turned-playwright wife, who died in 1994. Helmore's TV work included the live dramas "Playhouse 90" and "Studio One," and a dramatic special adaptation of *Of Human Bondage*. He also wrote a novel, *Affair at Quala* (1964), published by Simon & Schuster.

Helmore's films include (with US-release dates for the UK films): WHITE CARGO (UK 1930), THE HOUSE OF UNREST (UK 1931), THE BARTON MYSTERY and MY WIFE'S FAMILY aka THE WIFE'S FAMILY (UK 1932), THE KING'S CUP and UP FOR THE DERBY (UK 1933), THE FEATHERED SERPENT, THE SCOOP, SONG AT EVENTIDE and VIRGINIA'S HUSBAND (UK 1934), THE RIGHT AGE TO MARRY and THE RIVERSIDE MURDER (UK 1935), LUCK OF THE TURF and Alfred Hitchcock's SECRET AGENT (UK 1936), MERRY COMES TO STAY aka MERRY COMES TO TOWN (UK 1937), EASY RICHES and PAID IN ERROR (UK 1938), SHADOWED EYES and NOT WANTED ON VOYAGE aka TREACHERY ON THE HIGH SEAS (UK 1939), THE BIRDS AND THE BEES aka THREE DARING DAUGHTERS (UK 1948), SCENE OF THE CRIME (1949), SHADOW ON THE WALL (1950), LET'S DO IT AGAIN (UK 1953), TROUBLE ALONG THE WAY (1953), THE TENDER TRAP and LUCY GALLANT aka OIL TOWN (1955), DESIGNING WOMAN and THIS COULD BE THE NIGHT (1957), Hitchcock's VERTIGO (1958), as the school chum who hires James Stewart to keep an eye on Kim Novak, COUNT YOUR BLESSINGS and THE MAN IN THE NET (1959), THE TIME MACHINE (US-UK 1960), ADVISE AND CONSENT (1962) and FLIPPER'S NEW ADVENTURE aka FLIPPER AND THE PIRATES (1964).

No cause of death was reported.

Highsmith, Patricia

born: Jan. 12, 1921, Fort Worth, TX; raised New York, NY
died: Feb. 5, 1995, Locarno, Switzerland, age 74

Popular author whose novels of mannered pathological obsessions became the basis several films including Alfred Hitchcock's STRANGERS ON A TRAIN (1951).

Patricia Highsmith published seven short-story collections and 20 novels, five of which featured the intelligent, cultured, yet amoral Tom Ripley, who murders when he feels it necessary. Under the pseudonym Claire Morgan, she also wrote the lesbian novel *The Price of Salt* (1951). Highsmith's first novel, *Strangers on a Train* (1950), was filmed twice: first as the Hitchcock classic (which in turn inspired the 1987 black comedy THROW MOMMA FROM THE TRAIN), and then as ONCE YOU KISS A STRANGER (1969). *The Talented Mr. Ripley* was filmed by Rene Clement as PLEIN SOLEIL/PURPLE NOON aka LUST FOR EVIL (France-Italy 1959, US release 1961, US re-release 1996), starring Alain Delon. *Ripley's Game* was adapted by writer-director Wim Wenders as THE AMERICAN FRIEND (West Germany 1977), starring Dennis Hopper as Ripley. *The Blunderer* became LE MEURTRIER/ENOUGH ROPE aka THE MURDERER (France-Italy-West Germany, US release 1966), and *The Cry of the Owl* became the same-name French-Italian film (LE CRI DU HIBOU) by writer-director Claude Chabrol, released here 1992.

No cause of death was reported for Highsmith, who'd lived in Locarno since 1982.

Hively, Jack

aka: Jack B. Hively
born: c. 1910
died: Dec. 19, 1995, Hollywood, CA, age 85

Editor and director.

Jack Hively, a contract hand at RKO, was best known for directing three features starring George Sanders as Leslie Charteris' suave detective "The Saint": THE SAINT TAKES OVER and THE SAINT'S DOUBLE TROUBLE (1940) and THE SAINT IN PALM SPRINGS (1941). Hively moved to Paramount in 1942, after the highly publicized failure of the Gloria Swanson comeback vehicle FATHER TAKES A WIFE (1941); after one film there, he served in the U.S. Army Signal corps during WWII, attaining the rank of major. After a final feature, for Universal, in 1948, Hively turned to television; there he directed numerous episodes of series including "Death Valley Days," "Timmy and Lassie," "Lassie," "Eight is Enough" and "Greatest Heroes of the Bible." Hively also directed two "Classics Illustrated" telefilms that aired the same month, "The Adventures of Huckleberry Finn (NBC 1981), which was shot at least two years prior, and "California Gold Rush" (NBC 1981).

Hively died following a short illness.

Hogan, Dick

born: c. 1918
died: Aug. 18, 1995, age 77

Minor supporting actor who played freshmen, bellhops, cadets, and the unfortunate young David Kentley, murdered in the opening of Alfred Hitchcock's classic ROPE (1948). Dick Hogan retired from film soon afterward.

Hogan died of a heart attack.

Hordern, Michael

born: Oct. 3, 1911, Berkhampsted, Hertfordshire, England
died: May 2, 1995, Oxford, England, age 83
educ: Brighton College

British classical actor who played character roles in more than 90 films—often as a world-weary authority figure, and once as the afterworld-weary Jacob Marley.

After stints in his early 20s as a schoolmaster, salesperson, and amateur actor, Michael Hordern — who was knighted Jan. 1, 1983—made his London debut as Lodovico in *Othello* (1937). He made his first film in 1939, then after WWII service in the Royal Navy returned to a highly prolific stage and movie career spanning more than 50 years. A well-recognized supporting actor in film, his stage roles nonetheless included the likes of King Lear, Prospero and Macbeth, and the title character of Chekhov's *Ivanov* (1950); he also originated the role of the flustered philosopher in the London premiere of Tom Stoppard *Jumpers*. Other prominent plays among his 80 include Stoppard's *Enter a Free Man*, *A Doll's House*, *Toad of Toad Hall*, and *The Rivals*; he made his Broadway debut in Marcel Ayme's *Moonbirds* (1959). Hodern's British TV work stretches back to a 1946 BBC production of the play "Morning Departure" and a 1947 "Rebecca," as well as productions of "Don Juan in Hell," "Memento Mori," "Middlemarch," "Tartuffe," "The Zany Adventures of Robin Hood," Evelyn Waugh's "Scoop" (1987), "The Green Man" (BBC/A&E 1990), and many Shakespeare plays, as well as voiceovers in animated series and specials including "The Wind in the Willows" (Thames TV 1983). He co-starred in the series "Paradise Postponed" (Thames TV 1986).

Hordern's film roles include Marley, opposite Alastair Sim, in SCROOGE aka A CHRISTMAS CAROL (UK 1951); Errol Flynn's father, King Edward III, in THE DARK AVENGER aka THE WARRIORS (UK 1955); Banquo in MACBETH (US-UK; NBC "Hallmark Hall of Fame" production 1960, theatrical release 1963), opposite Maurice Evans and Judith Anderson; and Baptista, Elizabeth Taylor's father, in THE TAMING OF THE SHREW/LA BISBETICA DOMATA (US-Italy 1967). Other films include PASSPORT TO PIMLICO (UK 1948, US release 1949), TOM BROWN'S SCHOOLDAYS (1951), THE HEART OF THE MATTER (UK 1953, US release 1954), THE BEACHCOMBER (UK 1954, US release 1955), ALEXANDER THE GREAT, THE MAN WHO NEVER WAS, and PACIFIC DESTINY (UK 1956), SINK THE BISMARCK! (UK 1960), MAN IN THE MOON, (UK 1961), EL CID (US-Italy 1961), CLEOPATRA (1963), THE YELLOW ROLLS-ROYCE, and THE SPY WHO CAME IN FROM THE COLD (UK 1965), CAST A GIANT SHADOW, KHARTOUM (UK 1966), A FUNNY THING HAPPENED ON THE WAY TO THE FORUM (1966), HOW I WON THE WAR (UK 1967), WHERE EAGLES DARE, ANNE OF THE THOUSAND DAYS, THE BED SITTING ROOM (UK 1969), ALICE'S ADVENTURES IN WONDERLAND and THE PIED PIPER (UK 1972), THE POSSESSION OF JOEL DELANEY (1972), ENGLAND MADE ME (UK 1972, US release 1973), THE MACKINTOSH MAN and THEATRE OF BLOOD (UK 1973), MR. QUILP aka THE OLD CURIOSITY SHOP (UK 1974, US release 1975), BARRY LYNDON (UK 1975; narration), ROYAL FLASH (UK 1975), LUCKY LADY (1975), THE SLIPPER AND THE ROSE aka THE STORY OF CINDERELLA (UK 1976, US release 1977), THE WILDCATS OF ST. TRINIAN'S (UK 1980), GANDHI (UK-India 1982), THE MISSIONARY (UK 1982), YELLOWBEARD (UK 1983), YOUNG SHERLOCK HOLMES (1985), LADY JANE (UK 1986), and LABYRINTH (1986).

Hordern died of kidney disease; his actress wife, Grace Eveline Mortimer, died in 1986.

Hornung, Richard

born: 1950, Bethlehem, Pa.
died: Dec. 30, 1995, Los Angeles, CA, age 45
educ: University of Illinois

Oscar-nominated costume designer.

Richard Hornung began his career in New York City, designing for Broadway and Off-Broadway plays, including a revival of Shaw's *Candide* (1981) and the Jeff Conaway musical *The News* (1985). He made his film debut in Joel and Ethan Coen's RAISING ARIZONA (1986), and worked with the Coen brothers again on MILLER'S CROSSING (1990), BARTON FINK (1991) and THE HUDSUCKER PROXY (1994), the latter of which earned him an Academy Award nomination.

Hornung's other films include CHINA GIRL and LESS THAN ZERO (1987), PATTY HEARST and YOUNG GUNS (1988), DOC HOLLYWOOD and SLEEPING WITH THE ENEMY (1991), HERO and LIGHT SLEEPER (1992), DAVE and THIS BOY'S LIFE (1993) and Oliver Stone's NATURAL BORN KILLERS (1994) and NIXON (1995).

Hornung died of complications from AIDS.

Howard, John

born: John R. Cox Jr., April 14, 1913, Cleveland, OH
died: Feb. 19, 1995, Santa Rosa, CA, age 82
educ: Western Reserve University, Ohio (Phi Beta Kappa)

Productive film supporting player best known as investigator Bulldog Drummond, and for not getting the girl in the classics LOST HORIZON and THE PHILADELPHIA STORY.

John Howard appeared onstage in his native Cleveland before becoming a Paramount contract player and making his screen debut in AN-

NAPOLIS FAREWELL aka in Britain GENTLEMEN OF THE NAVY (1935). A stalwart leading-man type, he found himself starring in mostly B-pictures and such programmers as the "Bulldog Drummond" series, succeeding Ronald Colman, Ralph Richardson and Ray Milland as the adventurous ex-British Army officer Capt. Hugh "Bulldog" Drummond. Howard, the most prolific Drummond, starred in seven of these roughly hour-long films until the series' demise in 1939. (There were unsuccessful attempts at reviving the character in the 1940s and '60s.) Howard was memorable as Colman's doomed brother in Frank Capra's LOST HORIZON (1937), and as Katharine Hepburn snobbish fiance in George Cukor's THE PHILADELPHIA STORY (1940)—in both cases being specifically requested by the director, and, ironically, disliking the character he played. He was also notable in John Wayne's THE FIGHTING KENTUCKIAN (1949), as the friendly nemesis competing with Wayne for Vera Ralston, and BORDER FLIGHT (1936), in which he co-starred with Frances Farmer.

In the 1950s, Howard starred on several TV series: On "Crawford Mystery Theatre" aka "Public Prosecutor" (DuMont 1951, New York City local program 1951-52), a half-hour quiz show with guests deducing solutions to detective filmlets. He starred as Dr. Wayne Hudson in "Dr. Hudson's Secret Journal" (syndicated; produced 1955-57), and as modern-day Caribbean-skipper John Hawk in "The Adventures of the Sea Hawk" (syndicated; produced 1958-59). He also played the recurring role of Dave Welch from 1965-67 on "My Three Sons" (ABC/CBS 1960-72). Howard retired from acting in the early 1970s, and became a teacher at a Northridge, CA school before moving to Santa Rosa in the early 1990s.

Howard died of heart failure.

Hurd, Hugh

aka: Harry Tampa
born: c. 1925
died: July 15, 1995, New York (Greenwich Village), NY, age 70
educ: High School of Music and Art; New York University

Actor and prominent civil-rights activist.

Hugh Hurd was already a known stage actor in the 1950s when he, actor Godfrey Cambridge and writer Maya Angelou organized one of the first New York City benefits for the Rev. Dr. Martin Luther King Jr., raising $9,000 for his civil-rights movement; Angelou later wrote of the Village Gate benefit in her book *The Heart of a Woman*. In 1962, Hurd and Cambridge went on to found the Committee for the Employment of Negro Performers, leading Congressman Adam Clayton Powell Jr. to hold hearings on racial discrimination in the entertainment industry.

Hurd (who may or may not be the same Hugh Hurd who served as set designer on the 1950 film CRISIS), made an auspicious film debut in John Cassavetes' first feature as director, the improvisational SHADOWS (1960). Based largely on improvs by members of the Variety Arts Studio, the strikingly frank film about a jazz trumpeter (Hurd) forced to play seedy strip clubs and other dives while serving as father-figure to his pass-for-white younger sister and brother was disdained by Hollywood until winning the Critics Award at Cannes. Hurd worked again with Cassavetes on A WOMAN UNDER THE INFLUENCE (1974). Bookending Hurd's career was his last film appearance, 20 years later, in a French documentary on Cassavetes.

Hurd, whose many theater roles include that of Mack the Knife in a 1968 production of *The Threepenny Opera* at Washington, D.C.'s Arena Stage, also appeared in TV dramas, soap operas, and commercials. His other films include FOR LOVE OF IVY (1968), BLADE (1973) and LIEBESTRAUM (UK 1991). A "Hugh L. Hurd" appears in WHO'S THE MAN? (1993).

Hurd died of complications from hypertension and kidney failure.

Hurwitz, Harry

born: c. 1938, New York, NY
died: Sept. 21, 1995, Los Angeles, CA, age 57
educ: High School of Music and Art; New York University

Idiosyncratic independent writer-director, and painter.

Harry Hurwitz was initially a film and art teacher at New York City's Cooper Union, Parsons School of Design, and New York University. A lifelong fan of silent film, he began his own filmmaking career with the TV documentary "The Eternal Tramp" aka "Chaplinesque, My Life and Hard Times." His first feature, the heartfelt comedy THE PROJECTIONIST (1971), became a minor classic by anticipating the likes of ZELIG, THE PURPLE ROSE OF CAIRO and several famous 1990s cola commercials by inserting a projectionist (Chuck McCann) into old-movie scenes and having him interact with the likes of Humphrey Bogart in CASABLANCA and Ruby Keeler and Dick Powell in DAMES. The $160,000 movie, part of the permanent collection of the Museum of Modern Art, also marked the first film appearance of comedian Rodney Dangerfield. Hurwitz, who wrote, directed, produced and edited, also had a bit part as the Friendly Usher. In other films, he served in various capacities as producer/director/writer, including being one of five credited co-writers on UNDER THE RAINBOW (1981). Under the pseudonym Harry Tampa, he wrote and directed what he called "disco vampire movies" including FAIRYTALES and AUDITIONS (1978), and NOCTURNA aka NOCTURNA, GRANDDAUGHTER OF DRACULA (1979).

His other films include THE COMEBACK TRAIL (made 1971, released 1982; producer, co-writer, director, editor), RICHARD (1972; co-writer, co-director), SAFARI 3000 (1982; director), THE BIG SCORE (1983; executive producer), THE ROSEBUD BEACH HOTEL (1984; producer-director), THAT'S ADEQUATE (1990; writer-director) and FLESHTONE (1994 direct-to-video; writer-director). At the time of his death he was preparing the film REMAKE, with commitments from actors Johnny Depp, Peter Riegert, Carrie Fisher, Richard Lewis and Susan Dey and executive producer Arnold Kopelson. Of Hurwitz's three sons, Samuel is a director-producer and Michael an actor.

Hurwitz died of heart failure while awaiting a heart transplant.

Ives, Burl

born: Burl Icles Ivanhoe Ives, June 14, 1909, Hunt City, Hunt Township, or Jasper County (accounts differ), IL
died: April 14, 1995, Anacortes, WA, age 85
educ: Newton High School; Eastern Illinois State Teachers College; New York University

Beloved balladeer and Academy Award-winning actor.

Burl Ives—the mountainous, avuncular tenor who popularized American folk songs and became known to generations of children through his voice in a perennial animated Christmas special—was singing professionally, for quarters, by age four. Ives dropped out of college after three years to hitchhike around the country, supporting himself with odd jobs and, billed as the Vagabond Lover, with his banjo and singing. In the early 1930s, he came to New York City to study with vocal coach Ekka Toedt, and briefly attended NYU (1937-38). In 1938 Ives began working professionally with a theater group in Carmel, NY. That year he made his Broadway debut in a small, non-singing role in the Rodgers and Hart musical *The Boys From Syracuse*; he went on to the road company of the duo's *I Married an Angel*. Ives earned plaudits during a four-month engagement at the Village Vanguard, and by 1940, had his own radio show, *The Wayfarin' Stranger*. He made his film debut as a singing cowboy in SMOKEY (1946). His most famous movie role—that of Big Daddy in the 1955 stage and 1958 screen version of CAT ON A HOT TIN ROOF—came indirectly, from scuffling with a heckler at the Village Vanguard; according to Ives' widow, director Elia Kazan witnessed the contretemps, and decided to cast Ives in the fatherly but potentially explosive role. Ives won a supporting-actor Oscar playing a feudal-lord rancher in the 1958 Western THE BIG COUNTRY, starring Gregory Peck and Jean Simmons.

Ives—who popularized such songs as "Blue Tail Fly," "Big Rock Candy Mountain," "Holly Jolly Christmas" and "A Little Bitty Tear" on dozens of albums including *Christmas Eve With Burl Ives*, *Songs of the West*, *Songs I Sang in Sunday School*, and his last, 1993's *The Magic Balladeer*—debuted on television with the "U.S. Steel Hour" drama, "To Die Alone" (CBS 1/6/57). Ives may be best remembered as the voice of the model-animated Sam the Snowman in the holiday evergreen "Rudolph the Red-Nosed Reindeer" (first telecast NBC 1964). Among his 13 Broadway productions are *This Is the Army* (1942), *Sing Out, Sweet Land* (1944), *She Stoops to Conquer* (1949), *Show Boat* (1954 revival), and *Dr. Cook's Garden* (1967). Ives, who wrote nine books, described his road experienced alongside Woody Guthrie and others in his autobiography, *Wayfarin' Stranger* (1948).

Ives's other films include GREEN GRASS OF WYOMING and STATION WEST (1948), SO DEAR TO MY HEART (1949), SIERRA (1950), EAST OF EDEN (1955), THE POWER AND THE PRIZE (1956), DESIRE UNDER THE ELMS and WIND ACROSS THE EVERGLADES (1958), DAY OF THE OUTLAW (1959), LET NO MAN WRITE MY EPITAPH (1960), OUR MAN IN HAVANA (UK 1960), THE SPIRAL ROAD (1962), SUMMER MAGIC (1963), THE BRASS

BOTTLE and ENSIGN PULVER (1964), JUST YOU AND ME, KID (1979), EARTHBOUND (1981), WHITE DOG (1982), UPHILL ALL THE WAY (1986) and TWO-MOON JUNCTION (1988).

Ives, who had been in a coma since April 12, died of complications of mouth cancer.

James, Edward

born: c. 1909
died: March 6, 1995, Escondido, CA, age 86
Screenwriter, primarily for television.

Ed James wrote mostly 60- to 70-minute programmers for Universal, Fox, Republic and RKO in the late 1930s to early 1940s before shifting to radio and later TV. He wrote the pilot episode of "Father Knows Best" for NBC radio in 1949, creating the characters on which the TV series was based. With Seaman Jacobs, he co-wrote the TV pilots of "The Addams Family" and "F-Troop," as well as episodes of such TV sitcoms as "The Bill Dana Show," "The Danny Thomas Show," "Family Affair," "Leave it to Beaver," "The Many Loves of Dobie Gillis," "Mr. Roberts," "My Favorite Martian," "My Three Sons," "No Time for Sergeants," "Petticoat Junction," "The Real McCoys," "Run, Buddy, Run" and "Tycoon." James retired in 1972.

His films include YOUNG FUGITIVES (1938), which was based on his short story "Afraid to Talk"), and OVER MY DEAD BODY and PRIVATE BUCKAROO (1942), ADVENTURES OF A ROOKIE, HOOSIER HOLIDAY and ROOKIES IN BURMA (1943) and SO THIS IS WASHINGTON (1943, co-story only).

James died of heart failure.

Jeakins, Dorothy

born: Jan. 11, 1914, San Diego, CA; raised Los Angeles
died: Nov. 21, 1995, Santa Barbara, CA, age 81
Three-time Oscar-winning costume designer.

Dorothy Jeakins—whose career was, remarkably for the time, as a freelancer rather than studio designer—won a scholarship to the Otis Art Institute and later worked as an animation cel painter for Disney. Her job drawing fashion designs for the I. Magnin department store brought her to the attention of movie art director Richard Dey, and in turn, director Victor Fleming. Hired to serve as sketch artist for the designer Barbara Karinska on Fleming's JOAN OF ARC (1948), Jeakins was quickly promoted and replaced her; the two did, however, share the film's Academy Award for Costume Design. She went on to win Academy Awards for producer-director Cecil B. DeMille's SAMSON AND DELILAH (1949), sharing it with four others including the renowned Edith Head, and, for director/co-writer, John Huston THE NIGHT OF THE IGUANA (1964), winning solo.

Jeakins also earned four shared and five solo Oscar nominations for MY COUSIN RACHEL (1952), starring Olivia de Havilland and Richard Burton; DeMille's THE GREATEST SHOW ON EARTH (1952) and THE TEN COMMANDMENTS (1956); William Wyler's THE CHILDREN'S HOUR aka in Britain THE LOUDEST WHISPER (1961); THE SOUND OF MUSIC (1965); HAWAII (1966); THE WAY WE WERE (1973), and THE DEAD (1987).

Jeakins, equally esteemed in other media, designed New York stage productions of *South Pacific*, *Affairs of State*, *King Lear*, *Too Late the Phalarope*, *Major Barbara*, *Winesburg, Ohio* and *The World of Suzie Wong*; from 1953 to 1963, she designed for the Los Angeles Civic Light Opera Company, with a year off in Japan to study traditional costumes of Noh drama on a Guggenheim fellowship, in 1961. For television, she costumed Mary Martin in *Annie Get Your Gun* and Audrey Hepburn and Mel Ferrer in *Mayerling*. Jeakins served as curator of textiles at the Los Angeles County Museum of Art from 1967 to 1970 and, after her retirement, advised the costume department at Santa Barbara City College. In 1987, she won the Women in Film Crystal Award for professional achievement. A 1940 marriage to Raymond Eugene Dane, a 20th Century Fox publicity director, ended in divorce in 1946.

Jeakins, who lived in Montecito, CA before moving to a care home, died of complications related to Alzheimer's and Parkinson's diseases.

Julian, Arthur

born: c. 1923
died: Jan. 30, 1995, age 71
Screenwriter.

Arthur Julian wrote for such widely varied TV series as "Amen," "F-Troop," "Maude," "December Bride," "Gimme a Break," "Hogan's Heroes" and "The Carol Burnett Show" (the team of which shared a 1970/71 Emmy nomination for Writing—Variety or Music). He also wrote or co-wrote the features THE HAPPY ROAD (1957), directed by Gene Kelly, THE BEATNIKS (1960), and THE BOATNIKS (1970). Playing Dr. Melamed, he appeared in the cult-classic beach movie HOW TO STUFF A WILD BIKINI (1965).

Julian died of heart failure.

Kaidanovsky, Aleksandr

aka: Alexander Kaidanovsky
born: June 23, 1946, southern USSR
died: Dec. 3, 1995, Moscow, Russia, age 59
educ: Rostov Theater School; Shchukhin Institute, Moscow
Actor.

Aleksandr Kaidanovsky was best known in the West as the title character in director-production designer Andrei Tarkovsky's STALKER (USSR 1979; US release 1982). After his graduation in 1971 from the Shchukhin Institute, Kaidanovsky became successful as a Moscow stage actor with the companies of the Vakhtangov Theater and the Moscow Arts Theater. After becoming a Soviet film and TV star, he gave up acting in 1980 to take directing courses under Tarkovsky at Moscow's Institute of Cinema. After directing several highly-regarded shorts and films, including the masterpiece ZHENA KEROZINSHCHIKA/THE KEROSENE SELLER'S WIFE (USSR 1988; also writer), he returned to work as an actor throughout Europe. Kaidanovsky was a jury member of the 1994 Cannes Festival.

Kaidanovsky died of a heart attack.

Kelly, Nancy

born: March 25, 1921, Lowell, MA
died: Jan. 2, 1995, Bel Air, CA, age 73
educ: The Bentley School for Girls
Acting-family scion best known as the mother in THE BAD SEED.

Nancy Kelly, the daughter of actress and artist's model Nan Kelly Yorke (1895-1978) and the brother of actor Jack Kelly (b. 1927), moved to New York with her family shortly after birth, and began a successful career as a child model and actress, appearing onstage in Broadway's *Give Me Yesterday* and other plays, and in films of the mid- to late-1920s. After segueing to radio work, she returned to movies as a romantic female lead, often in war pictures but also in such domestic comedies as HE MAR-RIED HIS WIFE (1940), opposite Joel McCrea. She appeared in major roles in numerous Broadway plays. Her most acclaimed role was Mrs. Christine Penmark, mother of eight-year-old homicidal psychotic Rhoda (Patty McCormack) in both the 1954 play and 1956 film of Maxwell Anderson's Broadway play *The Bad Seed*. Kelly, who won a Tony Award for her stage performance, earned a Best Actress Academy Award nomination for the movie—her last, age 35. She made her TV debut in 1950, on the CBS "Silver Theater" live drama "Minor Incident," and earned a 1956 Emmy nomination for playing a nun in the "Studio One" drama "The Pilot; after a spate of anthology dramas including "Philco Television Playhouse" and "The Alfred Hitchcock Hour," Kelly left TV from 1963-74, when she returned to do an episode each of "Medical Center" and "Bronk" and a pair of TV-movies before retiring from the screen in 1977.

Kelly's films include the silent films UNTAMED LADY, MISMATES and THE GREAT GATSBY (1926) and the sound features THE GIRL ON THE BARGE (1929), CONVENTION GIRL (1935), SUBMARINE PATROL (1938), JESSE JAMES, TAIL SPIN, FRONTIER MARSHAL and STANLEY AND LIVINGSTONE (1939), SAILOR'S LADY, ONE NIGHT IN THE TROPICS and PRIVATE AFFAIRS (1940), SCOT-LAND YARD, PARACHUTE BATTALION and A VERY YOUNG LADY (1941), TO THE SHORES OF TRIPOLI, FRIENDLY ENEMIES and FLY BY NIGHT aka in Britain SECRETS OF G32 (1942), TAR-ZAN'S DESERT MYSTERY, TORNADO and WOMEN IN BONDAGE aka HITLER'S WOMEN (1943), SHOW BUSINESS, DOUBLE EXPO-SURE and GAMBLER'S CHOICE (1944).

Kelly died of diabetes-related illness.

Kheyfits, Iosif

aka: Iosif Kheifits
See Heifitz, Iosif

Kingsley, Sidney

born: Sidney Kirshner, Oct. 18, 1906, New York, NY
died: March 20, 1995, Oakland, NJ, age 88
educ: Townsend Harris High School; Cornell University
Playwright whose works inspired long-running characters and helped establish enduring genre structures.

Sidney Kingsley won the 1933 Pulitzer Prize for his first Broadway play, *Men in White*, which, together with *Detective Story* (1949), serves as the archetype for most medical and detective films and TV shows. As well, Kingsley's 1935 Broadway drama of slum life, *Dead End*, introduced young street toughs played by Gabriel Dell, Leo Gorcey, Huntz Hall, Billy Halop and others who, known alternately as the Dead End Kids, the East Side Kids and the Bowery Boys, would become pop-culture icons and some of filmdom's most enduring characters. All three plays were made into films.

Kingsley's began writing one-act plays while attending Cornell on a scholarship. After graduating with a B.A. in 1928, he spent four months acting with a stock company in the Bronx. Later, while spending three years crafting *Men in White*, he worked as a play reader in New York and as a scenario reader for Columbia Pictures in Hollywood. Famously slow and meticulous in his craft, Kingsley followed *Men in White* (produced by the legendary Group Theater and staged by Lee Strasberg) with only eight more produced plays, among them the box-office flops *10 Million Ghosts* (1936), about arms merchants, and *The World We Make* (1939), about a woman's voyage through madness and sanity; the American Revolution-set allegory *The Patriots* (1943), which won a New York Drama Critics Circle Award; *Darkness at Noon* (1951), which earned a second Drama Critics prize; *Lunatics and Lovers* (1954); and *Night Life* (1962). Kingsley directed nearly all, and produced several.

Kingsley, who in 1977 became founding chairman of New Jersey's Motion Picture and Television Development Commission, was a president of the Dramatists Guild, a board member of both La Mama Experimental Theater and the Martha Graham dance company, and a WWII Army lieutenant. He was married in 1939 to popular actress Madge Evans, who retired from the screen in 1938 and from the stage in 1943. He was inducted into the Theater Hall of Fame in 1983, and received the William Inge Award for lifetime achievement in the American theater in 1988. New York Senator Robert F. Wagner Sr. credited *Dead End* with adding major impetus to slum clearance.

The films adapted from Kingsley's works are MEN IN WHITE (1934), starring Clark Gable and Myrna Loy; DEAD END aka CRADLE OF CRIME (1937), adapted by Lillian Hellman; HOMECOMING (1948), starring Gable and Lana Turner, and based on the Kingsley story "The Homecoming of Ulysses"; and DETECTIVE STORY (1951), starring Kirk Douglas in one of his finest performances.

Kingsley died of a stroke.

Kirby, George

born: June 8, 1924, Chicago, IL
died: Sept. 30, 1995, Las Vegas, NV, age 71
Comedian, singer and impressionist.

The portly, African-American George Kirby developed a reported more than one hundred impressions, including those of actors Humphrey Bogart and James Cagney, and singers including Billy Eckstine, Sarah Vaughan, and the perennially requested Pearl Bailey. By 1952, he was appearing with the Count Basie show in Las Vegas and later performed solo there, and made his TV debut on "The Ed Sullivan Show" in 1957. He hosted his own series, "Half the George Kirby Comedy Hour" (syndicated 1972), where a young Steve Martin had some of his earliest TV exposure, and co-starred in the impressionist all-star ensemble The Kopykats on "The ABC Comedy Hour" (ABC 1972), with their segments later syndicated as the half-hour sketch series, "The Kopykats." After a 3-1/2-year stint in a California Federal prison, following a conviction for selling cocaine and heroin to a Government undercover agent in Las Vegas, Kirby resumed his career in 1982. He later hosted a documentary, "Amos 'n' Andy, Anatomy of a Controversy."

Kirby, not to be confused with the minor 1930s-40s actor, claimed to be "the first black stand-up comedian—before me, they were buck and wing"; whether or not that assertion is accurate, he was unquestionably a pioneer in his field and one of the first African-American stand-up comedians to win national attention. His films include OH DAD, POOR DAD, MAMA'S HUNG YOU IN THE CLOSET AND I'M FEELIN' SO

SAD (1967), THE SHAGGY D.A. (1976), TROUBLE IN MIND (1985) and LEONARD PART 6 (1987).

Kirby died of Parkinson's disease.

Knowles, Patric

born: Reginald Lawrence Knowles, Nov. 11, 1911, Horsforth or Leeds (sources vary), England
died: Dec. 23, 1995, Woodland Hills, CA, age 84

Patrician, highly prolific second lead.

Patric Knowles, who'd dropped out of school to work for his father's publishing company, eventually joined the repertory group of the Playhouse Theater in Oxford, England. During his London stage debut, *By Appointment*, he was spotted by a Warner Bros. executive and signed as a contract player at the Warner studio in nearby Teddington. The studio exported Knowles to Hollywood for THE CHARGE OF THE LIGHT BRIGADE (1936), in which he played the military captain who won Olivia de Havilland from Errol Flynn, and he went on to appear with Flynn in the 1938 films THE SISTERS, FOUR'S A CROWD and THE ADVENTURES OF ROBIN HOOD, in which he played the dashing Will Scarlett. Knowles played romantic leads in films including LADY IN A JAM (1942), opposite Irene Dunne, and the POW-camp drama THREE CAME HOME (1950), opposite Claudette Colbert, and appeared as well in musicals, comedies—including Abbott and Costello's WHO DONE IT? (1942) and HIT THE ICE aka OH, DOCTOR (1943)—and in the lead role as a detective in films including FAIR EXCHANGE (UK; US release 1936), THE PATIENT IN ROOM 18 (1938) and THE STRANGE CASE OF DR. RX (1942). Knowles was also a Universal contract player, appearing in such horror classics as THE WOLF MAN (1941), and as the scientist who revives Frankenstein's monster in FRANKENSTEIN MEETS THE WOLF MAN (1943). During WWII, Knowles enlisted in the Royal Canadian Air Force, as a flying instructor, and later joined the U.S. Army Air Force as a civilian instructor.

Knowles died of a cerebral hemorrhage.

Knox, Alexander

born: Jan. 16, 1907, Strathroy, Ontario, Canada
died: April 25, 1995, Northumberland, England, age 88
educ: University of Western Ontario (degree, English literature)

Alexander Knox, who garnered an Academy Award nomination in the lead role of President Woodrow Wilson in the historical drama WILSON (1944), made his stage debut in 1929 in Boston. Relocating to England, he made his film debut in THE GAUNT STRANGER aka THE PHANTOM STRIKES (UK 1938, US release 1939). The outbreak of WWII prompted a return to the U.S., where he appeared in several Broadway plays including Laurence Olivier's production of *Romeo and Juliet* (1940), as Friar Laurence, Katharine Cornell's production of *The Three Sisters* (1942), *Jupiter Laughs* (1940), *Jason* (1942) and *The Closing Door* (1949), which he wrote. He also penned the plays *Old Master* and *Trafalgar Square*, several novels, including *Bride of Quietness* (1933) and *Night of the White Bear* (1971), and two films, as co-scripter: SISTER KENNY (1946), in which he was co-star opposite Rosalind Russell, and THE JUDGE STEPS OUT aka INDIAN SUMMER (1949), in both of which he also appeared. Knox made his American TV debut in 1954, in ABC's British-produced dramatic anthology series "The Vise." He also appeared in several telefilms, the "Masterpiece Theater" miniseries "The Last Place on Earth" (PBC 1985), and in a 1965 episode of the British-produced series "The Saint," aired in US in syndication. His widow is former actress Doris Nolan, who, except for one 1975 film, retired from the screen upon marrying Knox in the mid-1940s.

Knox's films include THE FOUR FEATHERS (UK 1939), THE SEA WOLF (1941), TOKYO JOE (1949), THE VIKINGS (1958), THE WRECK OF THE MARY DEARE and PASSIONATE SUMMER (1959) CRACK IN THE MIRROR (1960), OPERATION AMSTERDAM and OSCAR WILDE (UK 1960), THE LONGEST DAY (1962), KHARTOUM (1966), MODESTY BLAISE (UK 1966), ACCIDENT, HOW I WON THE WAR and the James Bond film YOU ONLY LIVE TWICE, playing the American president (UK 1967), NICHOLAS AND ALEXANDRA and PUPPET ON A CHAIN (UK 1971), GORKY PARK (1983) and JOSHUA THEN AND NOW (Canada 1985).

Knox, who had homes in London and Berwick-Upon-Tweed, died of bone cancer.

Koch, Howard

born: Dec. 12, 1902, New York, NY
died: Aug. 17, 1995, Kingston, NY, age 92
educ: St. Stephens (now Bard) College; Columbia University Law School

Renowned yet blacklisted screenwriter who co-scripted CASABLANCA (1942) and the infamous radio broadcast *The War of the Worlds* (1938).

Howard Koch, who with Julius J. Epstein and Philip G. Epstein adapted an unproduced play into what is generally considered the best-loved American film, began in writing plays while a practicing lawyer in Hartsdale, NY. Neither of his initial two Broadway efforts, *Great Scott!* (1929) and *Give Us This Day* (1933) were successful, and while Koch continued writing plays, including *Straitjacket* and the much later *Dead Letters*, he also turned to radio scripts and books. For Orson Welles' and John Houseman's Mercury Theater of the Air he adapted and updated the H.G. Wells novel *The War of the Worlds*, setting a Martian invasion in New Jersey with a prankish Welles playing it mostly as a real news report; the Halloween broadcast caused widespread panic, which Koch later wrote about in a book *Portrait of an Event*. Moving on to Warner Bros., Koch wrote or co-wrote screenplays for several films including SERGEANT YORK (1941), for which he shared an Original Screenplay Oscar nomination, and collaborated with John Huston on the acclaimed Broadway historical drama, *In Time to Come* (1941).

Koch's film MISSION TO MOSCOW (1943)—made at the time of the U.S.-Soviet World War II alliance, and at Jack and Harry Warners' dictate that Russians be depicted sympathetically — was turned against the writer eight years later by Jack Warner himself at Senator Joseph McCarthy's witch-hunting House Un-American Activities Committee; he cited it as evidence of Koch's supposed Communist leanings, and Koch was subsequently blacklisted by the American Legion. Koch and his wife moved to France in 1952, hoping to collaborate with director Max Ophuls in adapting Thomas Mann's novel *The Magic Mountain*. There and in Italy, Germany and England—where Koch was set to script Arthur Rank productions until witch-hunters fingered him to American investors, who then terminated their backing—Koch wrote mostly unproduced screenplays pseudonymously. As "Howard Rodney" and "Peter Howard," he scripted THE INTIMATE STRANGER aka the 10-minute-shorter US version FINGER OF GUILT (UK 1956), directed by fellow pseudonymous blacklistee Joseph Losey. Koch returned that year to the US, where prominent attorney Edward Bennett Williams threatened to sue the American Legion for $1 million unless Koch were removed from their blacklist; the Legion complied, but Koch by this time could not recapture his golden career. Moving to Woodstock, NY, he remained productive writing and producing locally staged plays, and penning his late-1970s memoirs, *As Time Goes By*. In December, 1994, the nonagenarian Koch had his CASABLANCA Oscar auctioned for $184,000 at Christie's in New York, saying the proceeds would help pay for a granddaughter's graduate-school education. Among his final projects was an uncompleted novel, *Invasion from Mars*.

Koch died of pneumonia.

Kramerov, Savelly

aka: Savely Kramarov
born: c. 1935, Moscow, USSR
died: June 6, 1995, San Francisco, age 60

Beloved Russian movie comedian, who traded stardom for religious freedom when he emigrated to small character roles in U.S. films.

In the course of his 42 Soviet films, Savelly Kramerov (whose name transliterates variously from the Russian Cyrillic alphabet) endeared himself to millions with his bumbling, cross-eyed visage—a genuine medical condition he had corrected upon his arrival in the US. He generally portrayed a stock Russian archetype known colloquially as "Crazy Ivan," the beleaguered everyman who finds the only way to survive nonsensical bureaucracies and officials is to be a little crazy himself.

Kramerov, whose parents were Jewish, was listed as Russian by his mother on his internal passport after his attorney father was arrested in a Stalinist purge and died in internal exile. In 1979, he reclaimed his Orthodox Jewish roots, and sought to emigrate to Israel. The authorities denied him a visa and removed his films from theaters and television, prompting Kramerov to launch a successful publicity campaign for his cause. Kramerov emigrated to Los Angeles rather than Israel, but maintained Jewish Orthodox rituals. After arriving here c. 1982, Kramerov made his American film debut in 1984, playing the KGB operative trying to keep Robin Williams from defecting in MOSCOW ON THE HUDSON, and played a Russian cosmonaut in 2010. His movies have again become popular in the former USSR.

Kramerov's USSR films include IVAN VASILYEVICH CHANGES HIS PROFESSION, TWELVE CHAIRS, MY FRIEND KOLKA, GENTLEMEN OF FORTUNE, LONG RECESS and AFONYA. An "S. Kramarov" appears in the credits of the dramas PROSHCHAYTE/FAREWELL, DOVES and NA SEMI VETRAKH/THE HOUSE ON THE FRONT LINE, released in the US in 1962 and 1963, respectively. Kramerov's other American films include ARMED AND DANGEROUS (1986), RED HEAT (1988), TANGO AND CASH (1989) and LOVE AFFAIR (1994). He also appeared in television roles.

Kramerov, who lived in Forest Knolls, Marin County, died of cancer, endocarditis, and complications from cancer surgery.

Lane, Priscilla

born: Priscilla Mullican, June 12, 1917, Indianola, Iowa
died: April 4, 1995, Andover, MA, age 76
educ: Simpson College, Des Moines, Iowa

Engaging, wholesomely pretty actress who played the romantic lead in Alfred Hitchcock's SABOTEUR (1942), and who with actress siblings Rosemary and Lola Lane co-starred in a popular series of films about four sisters

Priscilla Lane, the youngest and generally considered prettiest of the actress sisters, was one of five daughters of a Midwestern dentist. After attending a music conservatory in Des Moines, vocalists Priscilla and Rosemary toured with the popular big band Fred Waring's Pennsylvanians; they broke into film with the group in VARSITY SHOW (1937). The two were signed as Warner Bros. contract players, joining established sister Lola. Keenly independent, Priscilla was suspended at least twice for refusing what she felt were unsuitable roles. Her 1939 comedy YES, MY DARLING DAUGHTER, adapted from the proto-feminist play, caused a publicity-building outburst when the Board of Censors demanded cuts in the story, which involves a young woman determined to spend a weekend with her boyfriend, who's departing for a job in Europe. Lane also played Cary Grant's fiancee in ARSENIC AND OLD LACE (1944) and a girlfriend in the cadet comedies BROTHER RAT (1938) and BROTHER RAT AND A BABY (1940). Most prominently, she co-starred with her three sisters and Gale Page in the Academy Award Best Picture nominee FOUR DAUGHTERS (1938), playing small-town sis Thea Lemp; based on the Fannie Hurst novel *Sister Act*. This film spun off two sequel melodramas—FOUR WIVES (1939) and FOUR MOTHERS (1941)—as well as the copycat DAUGHTERS COURAGEOUS (1939), with the same main cast, original director and original screenwriter, and the sisters renamed Masters. Lane retired after marrying Air Force Colonel Joseph A. Howard, and left Hollywood in 1950, surfacing again briefly in show business to host the local Boston TV program, "The Priscilla Lane Show" (1958). Sisters Rosemary and Lola, who between them made dozens of films, died in 1974 and 1976, respectively.

Lane died after what her family described as a brief illness.

Lathrop, Philip

aka: Philip H. Lathrop
born: 1916
died: April 12, 1995, Los Angeles, age 83

Oscar-nominated cinematographer who shot more than 60 features.

Philip Lathrop worked in Hollywood from 1934, beginning as an assistant cameraperson at Universal Studios, and progressing to camera loader until cinematographer Joseph A. Valentine (THE WOLF MAN; SABOTEUR) made Lathrop his assistant. Lathrop later assisted the celebrated Russell Metty for ten years, last working together on Orson Welles' TOUCH OF EVIL (1958). Lathrop became a full-fledged cinematographer starting with the live-action sequences of the weekly daytime cartoon series "The Woody Woodpecker Show" (ABC 1957-58), in which animator and host Walter Lantz discussed his craft. Lathop went on to shoot the Blake Edwards series "Peter Gunn" (NBC/ABC 1958-61), leading to collaborations with the writer-director on his films THE PERFECT FURLOUGH aka in Britain STRICTLY FOR PLEASURE (1958), EXPERIMENT IN TERROR (1962), the acclaimed DAYS OF WINE AND ROSES (1962), THE PINK PANTHER (1964) and WHAT DID YOU DO IN THE WAR, DADDY? (1966). Lathrop photographed several Steve McQueen films, including SOLDIER IN THE RAIN (1963)

and THE CINCINNATI KID (1965), as well as the three AIRPORT sequels. Lathrop garnered Academy Award nominations for THE AMERICANIZATION OF EMILY (1964) and EARTHQUAKE (1974), and four Emmy nominations for his telefilms, winning in 1984-85 for "Malice in Wonderland" and in 1986-87 for "Christmas Snow." He served as co-chairman of the American Society of Cinematographers' Achievement Awards committee, and received the ASC's Lifetime Achievement honor in 1991.

Lathrop died of cancer.

Lawrence, Bruno

born: c. 1941
died: June 9, 1995, North Island, NZ, age 54

New Zealand musician turned acclaimed actor.

Bruno Lawrence was a jazz drummer in the 1950s; he moved to Sydney, Australia in the mid-1960s and became a member of the rock band Max Meritt & the Meteors before turning to acting in the following decade. In addition to playing critically lauded leads in such films as Roger Donaldson's SMASH PALACE (New Zealand 1981; US release 1982) and Geoff Murphy's THE QUIET EARTH (New Zealand 1985; co-scripted by Lawrence), he also appeared in Australian sitcoms.

Lawrence's movies include two others by leading New Zealand director Murphy—GOODBYE PORK PIE (New Zealand 1981) and UTU (New Zealand 1983, US release 1984)—as well as BEYOND REASONABLE DOUBT (New Zealand 1980), RACE TO THE YANKEE ZEPHYR aka TREASURE OF THE YANKEE ZEPHYR (Australia-New Zealand 1981, US release 1984), BATTLETRUCK aka WARLORDS OF THE 21ST CENTURY (1982), WILD HORSES and HEART OF THE STAG (New Zealand 1984), PALLET ON THE FLOOR (New Zealand 1984; music composer only), AN INDECENT OBSESSION (Australia; US release 1985), RIKKY AND PETE (Australia 1988), THE EFFICIENCY EXPERT aka in Britain SPOTSWOOD (Australia 1992), and JACK BE NIMBLE (New Zealand 1994).

Lawrence was at work on the feature COSI when he was diagnosed with his ultimately fatal lung cancer.

Lee Chia

born: c. 1924, Fujian province, China
died: mid-January, 1995, Taipei, Taiwan, age 71

Influential Taiwanese filmmaker of the 1950s and '60s. Chia began his career as a journalist in China before moving to Taiwan in 1947. There, beginning 1951, he wrote scripts for agricultural documentaries. Three years later, he became a script-editor for the state-run Central Motion Picture Corp. Eventually rising to director, he helmed some two dozen Mandarin-dialect movies, including OYSTER GIRL (1964; co-director), ORCHIDS AND MY LOVE (1965), FIRE BULLS (1966; co-director) and TIAO CHAN/THE BAIT OF BEAUTY (1967; co-director). He made his final film in 1981.

No cause of death was reported.

Leustig, Elizabeth

born: c. 1945, France
died: Dec. 19, 1995, Moscow, Russia, age 50

Casting director.

Elizabeth Leustig began her career at the Los Angeles Actors Theater and then Zoetrope Studios, where she did extras casting; she went on to the Casting Company before freelancing. A member of the Casting Society of America, Leustig won the CSA's Artios Award for dramatic feature casting, for Kevin Costner's DANCES WITH WOLVES (1990). She worked on multiple projects for Costner's TIG Productions, including THE BODYGUARD (1992), RAPA NUI (1993) and the multipart CBS documentary "500 Nations," directed and co-produced by her husband, Jack Leustig. Leustig was CSA-nominated both for "500 Nations" and A RIVER RUNS THROUGH IT (1992). Her other films include Roland Joffee's THE SCARLET LETTER (1995), Robert Altman's KANSAS CITY, as well as David and Jerry Zucker's HIGH SCHOOL HIGH; the latter two were still upcoming at the time of her death.

Leustig was killed by a hit-and-run driver in Moscow, where she was casting the Phillip Noyce feature THE SAINT.

Lin Tsui, Jeanette

born: Tseng Ch'i-chen, c. 1934, Shanghai, China
died: Feb. 22, 1995, Taipei, Taiwan, age 60
Singer-actress star of 1950s and '60s Hong Kong film.

Jeanette Lin Tsui was a major leading lady who reportedly made some 50 films. She moved with her family to Hong Kong after WWII, developing an interest in acting while in high school there. Lin signed with Liberty Studio in 1954, and became famous overnight with her first movie, A DAUGHTER'S HEART; she married its director Chun Kim, in 1959. Lin retired in the late 1960s. In 1967, she divorced Chun, who later committed suicide; she then married Taiwanese action star Jimmy Wang Yu, whom she divorced in 1975.

Lin, who had suffered from asthma since childhood, died of heart failure following an asthma attack.

Lindfors, Viveca

born: Elsa Viveca Torstensdotter Lindfors, Dec. 29, 1920, Uppsala, Sweden
died: Oct. 25, 1995, Uppsala, Sweden, age 74
educ: Royal Dramatic Theater, Stockholm
Beautiful, eminent film and stage actress, who turned to character roles after Hollywood failed to mold her to leading-lady stardom.

Viveca Lindfors, the daughter of art-book publisher Torsten and painter Karen, studied acting in Stockholm for three years before going on to eight Swedish films and many theater productions. She embarked for the US in 1946, signing with Warner Bros. two years later. Yet after starring in mostly undistinguished Hollywood fare and playing the Queen in the Errol Flynn swashbuckler ADVENTURES OF DON JUAN (1948), Lindfors pursued a career of character roles in American movies, leading roles in theater and international productions, and stately guest appearances on television. She wrote, directed and starred in the 65-minute, American Film Institute drama UNFINISHED BUSINESS (1987).

Lindfors won the Special Award at the Venice Film Festival as the romantic lead in Morris Engel's acclaimed independent feature, WEDDINGS AND BABIES (1960), and acting awards at the Berlin Film Festival as star of the war drama DIE VIER IM JEEP/FOUR IN A JEEP (Switzerland 1951) and as the lesbian seducer in the Jean-Paul Sarte adaptation HUIS CLOS/NO EXIT aka SINNERS GO TO HELL (US-Argentina 1962). The latter was adapted by Hungarian-born New York playwright-director George Tabori, Lindfors' fourth husband, whom she married in 1954. She was wed to Swedish cinematographer Henry Hasso and Swedish attorney Folke Rogard, having a child by each, and, in 1949, American director Don Siegel. She and Siegel, who directed her films NIGHT UNTO NIGHT (1949) and NO TIME FOR FLOWERS (1952), divorced in 1953. Their son, Kristoffer Tabori (b. Aug. 4, 1952), is an actor-director who appeared with Lindfors in her final film, LAST SUMMER IN THE HAMPTONS (1996).

Lindfors made an electrifying Broadway debut in the title role of *Anastasia* (1955), winning a Drama League award. She drew raves performing plays by Shakespeare, Brecht, Tennessee Williams and others, including *Miss Julie* (1955), *Brecht on Brecht* (1961), and her solo show *I Am a Woman* (1973). In 1966, she was a founder and artistic director of the Berkshire Theater Festival in Stockbridge, MA. Lindfors made her American TV debut in the "Lux Video Theater" drama "Autumn Nocturne" (CBS 1953), and in several other dramatic anthology series such as "Playhouse 90" ("The Last Tycoon," 1957), "U.S. Steel Hour" ("The Vanishing Point," 1953; "They Never Forget," 1957; "Dangerous Episode," 1959) and "You Are There" ("The Court-Martial of Mata Hari," 1954). After appearing in a 1959 episode of "Rawhide," she went on to guest in some two dozen series including "Naked City," "The Untouchables," "The Defenders," "The Nurses," "Bonanza," "Ben Casey," "Dynasty," "Hotel," and "Life Goes On," for which she won the 1989-90 Emmy Award as Outstanding Guest Actress in a Drama Series. Lindfors was also Emmy-nominated for a supporting role in the 1978 telefilm "A Question of Guilt," one of her several TV movies. She remained a prominent actress to the end, with a spirited role in the hit STARGATE (1994), and a poignant summing-up as an acclaimed actress-matriarch in LAST SUMMER IN THE HAMPTONS, in which the still-beautiful star played a semiautobiographical role that showed her character starring as the Queen in Lindfors' ADVENTURES OF DON JUAN. Lindfors was slashed in the face in 1990 by a razor-wielding attacker while she strolled in Greenwich Village; her wounds required 28 stitches. The actress, who lived in Manhattan, had been in Sweden since July 1995 to perform her one-woman stage production, *In Search of Strindberg*.

She died of pneumonic complications from rheumatoid arthritis.

Linn, Michael

died: March 23, 1995, Los Angeles, CA
educ: New England Conservatory of Music
Composer for TV and film.

Michael Linn majored in jazz trumpet while in school, and went on to play trumpet and piano and compose tunes for such big bands as Jaki Byard's Apollo Stompers, Rocking Chair, Ultimate Spinach, and Mason-Dixon & the Line. He moved to Hollywood in the 1980s, and reportedly assisted composers on films including EATING RAOUL (1982), THAT'S LIFE (1986), and A TIME OF DESTINY (1988). He reportedly scored his first feature, the apparently unreleased TRIAL BY TERROR, in 1985. He's credited as composer, sometimes in collaboration, on the films AMERICAN NINJA and RAPPIN' (1985), ALLAN QUATERMAIN AND THE LOST CITY OF GOLD (1987) and INFINITY (1991). Linn was vice president of Cannon's music division during the late 1980s, and went solo in 1990, providing music to film and TV. In 1994, Linn and producer partner Michael Alden formed A Novel Production Co. Inc., which at the time of Linn's death was involved with the planned film VEECK AS IN WRECK, a film biography of White Sox owner Bill Veeck to star Bill Murray.

Linn died after a long battle with cancer.

Locke, Katherine

born: c. 1910, Russia
died: Sept. 12, 1995, Thousand Oaks, CA, age 85
Film and celebrated stage actress, and wife of the writer-producer Norman Corwin.

Katherine Locke's parents, wanting her to become a concert pianist, enrolled her in the Damrosch Academy conservatory in New York City. Locke instead fled to Los Angeles to join the actors group The Potboilers and to work as a movie extra. She had made her stage debut in *The Joy of Serpents* (1928) at the Provincetown Playhouse in Greenwich Village, and later performed small roles in *Firebird*, with Judith Anderson, *Halfway to Hell* and *If a Body*. Her great success starring opposite John Garfield in Arthur Kober's Broadway comedy, *Having Wonderful Time* (1937) led to major roles in Maurice Evans' *Hamlet*, playing Ophelia to critical acclaim, *Fifth Column*, and *Clash by Night*. Other plays include *Balloon*, *The Late Christopher Bean* and *Crime and Punishment*. She worked with Corwin on at least one of his radio plays, "El Capitan and the Corporal" (July 25, 1944).

Locke's films include STRAIGHT FROM THE SHOULDER (1936), WILSON and THE SEVENTH CROSS aka THE SEVEN CROSSES (1944), THE SNAKE PIT (1948), THE SOUND OF FURY, aka TRY AND GET ME (1950), PEOPLE WILL TALK (1951), FLESH AND FURY (1952) and A CERTAIN SMILE (1958).

Loew, Arthur Jr.

aka: Arthur M. Loew Jr.
born: c. 1926, New York, NY
died: Nov. 10, 1995, Amado, AZ, age 69
Producer and scion of a film-industry dynasty.

Arthur Loew Jr. was the son of one-time MGM president Arthur Loew Sr. (1897-1976), as well as the nephew of independent producer and film executive David Loew (1897-1973), the paternal grandson of Marcus Loew (1870-1927)—the theater-chain head who bought Metro Pictures in 1924 and merged with the Goldwyn company and Louis B. Meyer Pictures to form MGM—and the maternal grandson of Paramount Pictures founder Adolph Zukor (1873-1976). His family relocated to Tucson when he was a child. After a year at the University of Arizona, Loew became a newspaper drama critic and sports reporter, then moved to California in 1947. There he performed as a comedian, and for the family-run MGM played the small role of the Studio Production Man in the TO PLEASE A LADY aka RED HOT WHEELS (1950), and other bit parts in SUMMER STOCK aka in Britain IF YOU FEEL LIKE SINGING (1950), and A LIFE OF HER OWN (1951). Loew debuted as a producer with director Fred Zinnemann's MGM film THERESA (1951), and went on to produce a handful of films through 1966. Loew was married from 1959-63 to Deborah Jean Power, the widow of actor

Tyrone Power, adopting the infant son born after Powers' death. With Deborah Jean and second wife Regina, a former model-actress, Loew had three more sons and two daughters. When not involved in film, Loew raised and trained show horses. In 1984, he was appointed chairman of the Advisory Board of the National Association of Film Commissioners; he also served as chairman of Arizona Governor Bruce Babbit's Motion Picture and Television Advisory Board.

Loew's films as producer include THE AFFAIRS OF DOBIE GILLIS (1953), ARENA (1953; also story; originally released in 3D), THE MARAUDERS (1955), THE RACK (1956)—an early Paul Newman film adapted by Stewart Stern from Rod Serling's acclaimed teleplay—and PENELOPE (1966).

Loew, who died in his sleep, had recently begun treatment for lung cancer.

Lorimer, Louise

born: c. 1898
died: Aug. 12, 1995, Newton, MA, age 97
educ: Leland Powers School of Drama, Boston, MA
Bit-part actress who continued performing into her 80s.

Louise Lorimer made her professional acting debut in a 1926 Greenwich Village revival of the 19th-century drama *East Lynne*, and later went on to Broadway with a leading role in the comedy *Feathers in a Gale* (1943) and parts in *I Remember Mama* (1944) and *My Fair Lady*. She was also active in the USO, journeying to the Pacific theater during WWII, and helping in the post-war Berlin air-lift. She made her movie debut in 1939, and though often playing secretaries and nurses, appeared as Miss Porter in the Kirk Douglas-Jane Wyman THE GLASS MENAGERIE (1950) and was featured as the seen-it-all dowager, rewrite-woman Bernice Valentine in director-producer Jack Webb's newspaper drama —30— aka in Britain DEADLINE MIDNIGHT (1959). Lorimer also regularly guested on TV series including "Alfred Hitchcock Presents," "Dennis the Menace," "Profiles in Courage," "Dragnet" (as an informal stock player), "Battlestar Galactica" (in the 1978 premiere of which the 82-year-old Lorimer played her final screen part), and in the recurring role of Stagecoach Sal in 1951-52 made-for-TV episodes of the afternoon children's series "Hopalong Cassidy" (NBC/syndicated 1949-54, mostly featuring edited versions of the movie features). She also taught at the Leland Powers School on Martha's Vineyard. Lorimer's films include Alfred Hitchcock's MARNIE (1964) and FAMILY PLOT (1976), and Richard Fleischer's COMPULSION (1959).

Lorimer died after an extended illness.

Loy, Nanni

born: Giovanni Loy, Oct. 23, 1925, Cagliari, Sardinia
died: Aug. 21, 1995, Fregene, near Rome, Italy, age 69
Leading Italian director and outspoken film-industry advocate, equally adept at comedies and war dramas.

Nanni Loy graduated with a law degree before taking a course in documentary production at Rome's *Centro Sperimentale di Cinematografia* film school, where he much later returned to teach directing. He became an assistant to such directors as Augusto Genina and Luigi Zampa, then made two documentaries before his feature debut in the mid-1950s. Among his most notable films are the Italian-Resistance drama LE QUATTRO GIORNATE DI NAPOLI aka IL BATTAGLIA DI NAPOLI/THE FOUR DAYS OF NAPLES (Italy 1962, US release by MGM 1963), for which director and co-writer Loy garnered Academy Award nominations for Original Screenplay and Foreign Language Film; and the comedies IL CAFFE E UN PIACERE. . . SE NON E BUONO CHE PIACERE E?/CAFE EXPRESS (Italy 1978, US release 1980), starring Nino Manfredi, and PICONE SENT ME aka WHERE'S PICONE? (Italy 1983, US release 1984; also co-writer), starring Giancarlo Giannini. The two latter films exemplify Loy's popular use of a stock Italian character, the beleaguered but adaptable Neapolitan who always lands on his feet. Loy left film for a short while in 1963 to work in television, creating the "Candid Camera"-like series "*Specchio Segreto*" and the later "*Viaggio in Seconda Classe*."

Loy was on vacation at a beach resort when he suffered a fatal heart attack.

Lubin, Arthur

born: July 25, 1899 or 1901, Los Angeles, CA
died: May 11, 1995, Glendale, CA, age 94 or 96
educ: Carnegie Tech (now Carnegie-Mellon University), Pittsburgh, PA
Wide-ranging director-producer best known for his "Francis the Talking Mule" films and for the classic, talking-horse TV series, "Mister Ed."

Arthur Lubin, said companion Critt Davis after Lubin's death, had consistently shaved two years off his age, accounting for the 1901 birthdate in reference books. Lubin graduated from Carnegie Tech in 1922, and appeared as an actor in the mid-1920s onstage at the Pasadena Playhouse and elsewhere, and in silent and early sound films. In 1925, he and fellow actors were arrested by the Los Angeles Police for performing an "obscene" play, Eugene O'Neill's *Desire Under the Elms*. Lubin found his calling in directing, first for the stage and then at various studios before finding a longtime home at Universal. He directed a fledgling John Wayne in four non-Westerns—CALIFORNIA STRAIGHT AHEAD, I COVER THE WAR, the hockey story IDOL OF THE CROWDS, and ADVENTURE'S END (all 1937)—and Claude Rains in the generally well-regarded first sound version of PHANTOM OF THE OPERA (1943). Lubin also helped popular vaudeville and radio comedians Abbott and Costello become film stars, directing a string of their seminal movies: BUCK PRIVATES aka in Britain ROOKIES—their second feature and first successful one—ABBOTT AND COSTELLO IN THE NAVY aka IN THE NAVY, HOLD THAT GHOST aka OH, CHARLIE and KEEP 'EM FLYING (all 1941) and RIDE 'EM COWBOY (1942). Years later, Lubin directed the children's live-action/animation cult-classic, THE INCREDIBLE MR. LIMPET (1964).

It was Lubin's films about a talking Army mule, however, that ensured him his spot in film history: His deal for "Francis," a legendarily hard sell to Universal executives, inadvertently helped establish an industry practice: Lubin made the film only after he'd agreed to accept a percentage of profits in lieu of part of his normal fee. Then, ironically, the low-budget hit series helped keep the financially troubled Universal afloat during a difficult time. The first six of the seven-film series were directed by Lubin and starred Donald O'Connor as WWII second lieutenant Peter Stirling, with Chill Wills providing Francis's voice. (An unsuccessful seventh entry, 1956's FRANCIS IN THE HAUNTED HOUSE, had a different director, star, and voice.) They were based on the 1946 novel *Francis* by the real-life Stirling, writing pseudonymously as David Stern.

Despite Lubin's talking-animal track record, "Mister Ed" was an equally tough pitch. CBS secretary Sonia Chernus had read some of the 28 "Mister Ed" stories by Walter Brooks in *The Saturday Evening Post* and *Liberty* magazines, and in 1957 brought them to Lubin's attention; she went on to receive "Format Developed by" screen credit and a small royalty. Lubin convinced comedian-producer George Burns to have his McCadden Productions put up $75,000 for the 1958 pilot, filmed but unaired, which was scripted by four writers, directed by Lubin, and produced by Lubin and Burns. The eventual series, which starred Allan Young as Wilbur Post and an uncredited Rocky Lane providing Ed's voice, began in first-run syndication beginning January 1961; it proved so popular that it made the virtually unprecedented leap to network in October that year, running on CBS through Sept. 4, 1966. Lubin directed all but the first two episodes. He went on to direct films through 1971, and TV series including "77 Sunset Strip,""Bonanza," "Bronco," "Cheyenne," "Maverick," and the sitcom pilots "You're Only Young Twice" (CBS 1960) and "Little Lulu" (ABC 1978), the latter a live-action sitcom based on the comic-strip character.

Lubin suffered a stroke in December 1994, and had since lived at a Glendale, CA nursing home, where his condition deteriorated the night of May 11.

Lukas, Karl

born: c. 1919
died: Jan. 16, 1995, Agoura Hills, CA, age 75
Stage, film and TV actor for 40 years.

Karl Lukas's acting career began at the Barter Theater in Abingdon, VA, where his many credits included *Much Ado About Nothing*. His most memorable role was as Lindstrom opposite Henry Fonda in Joshua Logan's acclaimed Broadway production of *Mister Roberts* (1948). Lukas appeared opposite Jackie Cooper in Broadway's *Remains to Be Seen* (1951). In episodic television, Lukas played recurring roles on the TV series "St. Elsewhere," "Family Affair" and "Shane," and guested on series including "Playhouse 90," "Climax," "Alfred Hitchcock Presents,"

"The Untouchables," "Ben Casey," "Bonanza," "Gunsmoke," "Then Came Bronson," "Little House on the Prairie," and "Cannon."

Lukas's films include THE LONG, LONG TRAILER (1954), UNDER FIRE (1957), ONIONHEAD and THE TRUE STORY OF LYNN STUART (1958), TALL STORY (1960), THERE WAS A CROOKED MAN and WATERMELON MAN aka THE NIGHT THE SUN CAME OUT (1970), TORA! TORA! TORA! (US-Japan 1970), OKLAHOMA CRUDE and EMPEROR OF THE NORTH POLE aka EMPEROR OF THE NORTH (1973), 99 AND 44/100% DEAD aka in Britain CALL HARRY CROWN (1974), HUSTLE (1975), LAS VEGAS LADY (1976), TWO-MINUTE WARNING (1976), THE SHAGGY D.A. (1976; voice only), and BIG TROUBLE (1986). No cause of death was reported.

Lupino, Ida

born: Feb. 4, 1918, London, England
died: Aug. 3, 1995, Burbank, CA, age 77
educ: Royal Academy of Dramatic Art
Powerful actress and pioneering woman director.

A major film presence from the 1930s through the 1950s, Lupino went from ingenue to great actress to respected director. She was born into a multigeneration acting family that had emigrated from Italy in the 17th century. Her father was British comedian Stanley Lupino (1893-1942); also in show business were her mother, Connie Emerald, her uncles Harry, Mark and Barry, and her cousin Lupino Lane. After enrolling at RADA at 13, she made her film debut as the Lolita-like star of HER FIRST AFFAIRE (UK 1933); per differing accounts, she either got the role when director Allan Dwan saw her perform onstage, or when Dwan auditioned the girlish-looking Emerald, and cast instead the daughter who'd accompanied her. Lupino, who'd already appeared as a movie extra, quickly churned out five more British features before Paramount brought her to US to play the title role of in ALICE IN WONDERLAND (1933). Though the studio changed its mind and gave the role to Charlotte Henry instead, Paramount kept Lupino on contract. Yet by the end of the decade, after she'd appeared in several films of little note, contracted polio, and wed actor Louis Hayward (in 1938, divorcing him in 1945), Lupino switched to Warner Bros.

Ironically, she received her first major critical acclaim in a Paramount picture, as the spiteful Cockney prostitute in the THE LIGHT THAT FAILED (1939). Lupino reaped plaudits again the next year as a crazed wife in Warner's film THEY DRIVE BY NIGHT aka in Britain ROAD TO FRISCO, co-starring Humphrey Bogart, George Raft and Ann Sheridan. She went on to excel in a string of films including the Bogart classic HIGH SIERRA (1941); THE HARD WAY (1942), for which she took the New York Film Critics Best Actress Award in a role Bette Davis had declined, and WOMAN IN HIDING (1949), in which she co-starred for the first time with future husband Howard Duff (1917-90). They were married from 1951-83, though separated after 1972. Their other films together were: 1953's JENNIFER; 1955's WOMEN'S PRISON, 1956's WHILE THE CITY SLEEPS, and 1954's PRIVATE HELL 36, co-written by Lupino and her ex-husband Collier Young, a producer to whom she'd been married from 1948-50 and with whom she founded, in 1949, the production company Emerald Pictures, later renamed Filmmakers. Though Lupino's broad acting range encompassed even comedy and musicals—she sang the theme song, "Blame It on the Danube," in 1937's FIGHT FOR YOUR LADY—the actress found her greatest popularity playing tough, earthy or emotionally scarred women.

Lupino made her uncredited directing debut with the Emerald production NOT WANTED aka STREETS OF SIN (1949), starring Sally Forrest and Keefe Brasselle, with Lupino in a supporting role; credited director Elmer Clifton suffered a heart attack three days into production, prompting co-producer and co-scripter Lupino to take the reins. Her first credited film as director is OUTRAGE (1950), a rape drama co-written by Lupino, Collier and Malvin Wald, and produced by Collier. Lupino went on to direct the polio drama NEVER FEAR aka THE YOUNG LOVERS (1950), which she co-wrote with Collier, and produced; HARD, FAST, AND BEAUTIFUL (1951), which Collier produced; THE HITCH-HIKER (1953), a rare example of a film noir directed by a woman, produced by Collier and co-scripted by Lupino, Collier and Robert L. Holmes; THE BIGAMIST (1953), also produced by Collier and co-written by him and Lupino, who additionally starred alongside Edmond O'Brien and Joan Fontaine; and THE TROUBLE WITH ANGELS aka MOTHER SUPERIOR (1966), her sole studio production. The musically accomplished Lupino—whose concert piece "Aladdin's Lamp" was per-

formed by the Los Angeles Philharmonic in 1937—composed the piano tune "Didn't You Know" for OUTRAGE. Lupino also directed more than 100 television episodes, for series as diverse as "The Untouchables," "Gilligan's Island" and "Have Gun, Will Travel," along with anthology series such as "Alfred Hitchcock Presents" and "Screen Directors Playhouse."

Lupino guested in several dozen TV series, up through the 1977 "Charlie's Angels" episode "I Will Be Remembered," in which she played an old movie actress. She made her TV debut in December 1953, as one of four rotating headliners (with David Niven, Dick Powell and Charles Boyer) in the weekly anthology series "Four Star Playhouse" (CBS 1952-56). Lupino also appeared on such dramatic anthologies as "Climax," "Zane Grey Theater," "Lux Playhouse," and "The Twilight Zone" as well such episodic series as "Bonanza," "The Wild Wild West," "The Mod Squad," "Family Affair," "Columbo," "Medical Center," "Switch," "Police Woman" and "Batman," as the villainess Dr. Cassandra. Lupino hosted the anthology series "The Ida Lupino Theater" (syndicated 1956), and produced "Mr. Adams and Eve" (CBS 1957-1958), a semiautobiographical, shortlived sitcom in which she and husband Howard Duff played married movie stars. Lupino became a naturalized US citizen in 1948.

Lupino, who in the mid-1990s had spent six months in the Motion Picture Home undergoing physical therapy, was diagnosed with cancer in June 1995. She suffered a stroke July 23 before eventually succumbing to cancer.

Lynn, Jeffrey

born: Ragnar Godfrey Lind, Feb. 16, 1906 or 1909 (sources differ), Auburn, MA
died: Nov. 24, 1995, age 86 or 89
educ: Bates College
Boyishly handsome leading man of the 1930s and '40s.

Jeffrey Lynn appeared in silent films, acted in stock, and taught high school before a role in a touring production of *Brother Rat* led to a screen test and a Warner Bros. contract, in 1937. He appeared in several leading roles, including one in the controversial, proto-feminist comedy YES, MY DARLING DAUGHTER (1939), about a young woman (Priscilla Lane) determined to spend a weekend with her boyfriend; it garnered much publicity when the Board of Censors demanded cuts. Lynn had earlier starred opposite Lane as the innocent heartbreaker Felix Deitz, in the Best Picture Oscar-nominee FOUR DAUGHTERS (1938); he reprised the role of Lane's fiance and husband, in the sequels FOUR WIVES (1939) and FOUR MOTHERS (1941), and the near-sequel DAUGHTERS COURAGEOUS (1939), in which the same cast played a different family. Lynn and Lane also appeared together in COWBOY FROM BROOKLYN aka in Britain ROMANCE AND RHYTHM (1938) and THE ROARING TWENTIES (1939). Yet after a prominent role in the Best Picture Oscar-nominee A LETTER TO THREE WIVES (1949), made for Fox after his MGM contract expired, Lynn saw his film popularity wane, and he segued to stage and television. His Broadway shows included *Lo and Behold!* (1951), *A Call on Kuprin* (1961), and *Dinner at Eight* (1966 revival).

Lynn died of complications from a stroke.

Maley, Alan

born: c. 1932, England
died: May 13, 1995. Belvedere, CA age 63
Oscar-winning special-effects technician.

Alan Maley began in British films as an assistant sign painter, and was the set designer of A VERY IMPORTANT PERSON aka A COMING-OUT PARTY (UK 1961). By the time of DR. STRANGELOVE OR: HOW I LEARNED TO STOP WORRYING AND LOVE THE BOMB (UK 1964), he was a matte artist responsible for helping achieve such effects as Slim Pickens's ride atop a nuclear missile. Maley was named a supervising matte artist at Disney in 1964, where he did special effects for films including THE LOVE BUG (1968) and HERBIE RIDES AGAIN (1974), and shared a Visual Effects Academy Award with two colleagues for the live-action/animated BEDKNOBS AND BROOMSTICKS (1971). He later helped establish the matte painting department for Lucasfilm's in-house special-effects division, Industrial Light & Magic. Maley's other films include THE SPY WHO LOVED ME (1977).

Maley died of a heart attack.

Malle, Louis

born: Oct. 30, 1932, Thumieres Nord, France
died: Nov. 23, 1995, Beverly Hills, CA, age 63

Internationally renowned writer-director of such thoughtful, often provocative modern classics as MURMUR OF THE HEART, ATLANTIC CITY, MY DINNER WITH ANDRE and AU REVOIR, LES ENFANTS. The husband of American actress Candice Bergen, Malle was also an acclaimed documentarist and a figure of the influential French New Wave who nonetheless shunned that movement's emphasis on flashy directorial style in favor of quietly passionate, substantial stories. From historical everyman dramas to wistful contemporary fables to reflective yet erotic studies of sexual need, Malle—as director and writer or co-writer—developed a body of work that was remarkably often both commercially and artistically victorious.

A child of privilege, Louis Malle was one of seven children of a sugar heiress and a father who directed sugar refineries. In 1944, anticipating close combat between Allied forces seeking to liberate German-occupied Paris, his parents sent Malle to a Jesuit boarding school in Fontainbleau; there a kitchen worker betrayed the monks' sheltering of Jewish students, leading to the deaths of the children and the headmaster. These events became the basis of AU REVOIR, LES ENFANTS/GOODBYE, CHILDREN (France 1987; also co-producer), a heartfelt indictment of French collaborators that earned Malle Academy Award nominations for Best Original Screenplay and Best Foreign Language Film; it won seven French Cesar awards, and the Golden Lion at the Venice Film Festival.

After high school, Malle studied political science at the Sorbonne, but soon transferred to the Institut des Hautes Etudes Cinematographiques film school (1951-53). Afterward, he became an assistant to oceanographer Jacques-Yves Cousteau, and filmed undersea expeditions in 1954 and 1955 that lead to the Academy Award-winning documentary feature LE MONDE DU SILENCE/THE SILENT WORLD (France 1956; co-director and co-photographer with Cousteau). The fledgling Malle also directed two shorts (1953's "Fontaine de Vaucluse" and 1955's "Station 307"), assisted Robert Bresson on UN CONDAMNE A MORT S'EST ECHAPPE/A MAN ESCAPED (France 1956), was a cameraperson for the Jacques Tati comedy MON ONCLE/MY UNCLE (France 1958), and then helmed his first solo feature ASCENSEUR POUR L'ECHAFAUD/FRANTIC aka ELEVATOR TO THE GALLOWS (France 1958; also executive producer). The successful thriller earned Malle the *Prix Delluc* award, and helped establish the great actress Jeanne Moreau, who became a star with Malle's next film, LES AMANTS/THE LOVERS (France 1959; also executive producer), a sexually charged study of a wife and mother who trade her ennui-filled, middle-class life for a hopeful yet uncertain future after a night of erotic abandon. The lyrical yet highly daring film resulted in a notorious censorship case against a suburban Cleveland theater manager, with the charge eventually thrown out by the Supreme Court.

From 1962 to 1964, Malle took a hiatus from film to become an on-air foreign correspondent for French television, reporting from Algeria, Vietnam, and Thailand. After returning to movies with a trio of films, Malle accepted an offer from the BBC to shoot a documentary; after divorcing first wife Anne-Marie Deschodt, he spent six months in India with a 16mm cameraperson and a sound engineer. Malle returned home to produce, write and narrate an acclaimed and controversially hard-hitting seven-part series, "L'Indie fantome"/"Phantom India," shown on British TV c. 1969-70, as well as a feature documentary, CALCUTTA (UK 1969) and a six-hour theatrical version of the series, billed both under the original French and English titles and as L'INDIE 68 and LOUIS MALLE'S INDIA (UK 1972).

Malle swept back into fictional cinema with the seriocomic tale of painful adolescent sexuality and mother-son incest, LE SOUFFLE AU COEUR/MURMUR OF THE HEART (France-Italy-West Germany 1971; co-produced by Malle's producer-brother Vincent Malle); it earned Malle his fourth Oscar nomination, this one for Adapted Screenplay. Years later he again broached taboo sexuality, this time between a father and his son's fiancee, in DAMAGE (France-UK 1992; producer-director only; Vincent Malle co-producer); threatened with an NC-17 rating in the US, the uncut film is available on videodisc. LACOMBE, LUCIEN (France 1974; also producer) was Malle's first look at what was, for France, a taboo theme—that of French collaborators with the Nazis, a blow to the myth of a purely resistant nation. Yet while Malle's portrait of a teenaged collaborator was nominated for Foreign Language Film, it enraged his homeland; the controversy, along with the huge failure of Malle's experimental fantasy BLACK MOON (France 1976; also producer), prompted his move to the US Here he made a series of successful films, and met future wife Bergen, whom he married in 1980 and with whom he had a daughter, Chloe. (Malle also had relationships with German actress Gila von Weiterhausen and Canadian actress Alexandra Stewart, having a child by each.) Malle's many English-language films include the controversial PRETTY BABY (1978; producer-director-co-story only), a languid tale of life in a 1917 New Orleans brothel, featuring Susan Sarandon and Brooke Shields (in her second film) as a prostitute and her soon-to-be-deflowered 12-year-old. Malle scored acclaim for the audacious, essentially two-person/one-set drama MY DINNER WITH ANDRE (1981; director only), in which his camera and a fascinating script by stars Wallace Shawn and Andre Gregory kept a 110-minute dinner conversation lively; and modern classic ATLANTIC CITY aka ATLANTIC CITY, U.S.A. (US-Canada 1981; director), starring Burt Lancaster and Sarandon as two hard-nosed dreamers in that faded yet changing resort town. The latter earned Oscar nominations for Picture, Actor, Actress, Director and Screenplay (by John Guare). Malle's next film, the comedy CRACKERS (1984; director only), was one of his few outright flops. Malle appeared very occasionally as a cameo actor, as in Nelly Kaplan's LA FIANCEE DU PIRATE/A VERY CURIOUS GIRL aka DIRTY MARY (France 1969), Aki Kaurismaki's LA VIE DE BOHEME (Finland-France-Sweden 1993), and a 1994 episode of Bergen's sitcom, "Murphy Brown."

Malle's other films include ZAZIE DANS LE METRO/ZAZIE aka ZAZIE IN THE UNDERGROUND (France 1960, US release 1961; also producer), LA VIE PRIVEE/A VERY PRIVATE AFFAIR (France-Italy 1962), LE FEU FOLLET/THE FIRE WITHIN (France-Italy 1963, US release 1964), VIVA MARIA (France-Italy 1965; also producer), LE VOLEUR/THE THIEF OF PARIS (France-Italy 1967; also producer), HISTOIRES EXTRAORDINAIRES/SPIRITS OF THE DEAD (France-Italy 1968, US release 1969; "William Wilson" episode in Poe anthology), ALAMO BAY (1985; director and, with Vincent Malle, co-producer only), MILOU EN MAI/MAY FOOLS (France 1990; executive producer Vincent Malle) and VANYA ON 42ND STREET (1994; director only). He also made the feature documentaries HUMAIN, TROP HUMAIN (France 1972), PLACE DE LA REPUBLIQUE (France 1973) and AND THE PURSUIT OF HAPPINESS aka GOD'S COUNTRY (1985).

Malle—who lived seven months a year in France, returning to his and Bergen's Los Angeles home monthly—was diagnosed with cancer of the lymph nodes in August 1995. He died of resultant complications.

Marchant, William

born: c. 1923, Allentown, PA
died: Nov. 5, 1995, Paramus, NJ, age 72
educ: Temple University; Yale University School of Drama

Playwright and screenwriter.

William Marchant was best known for the Broadway comedy *The Desk Set* (1955), the basis for the popular 1957 Spencer Tracy-Katharine Hepburn movie. After college and his WWII Army service, Marchant had his play *Within a Glass Bell* (1950) produced at the Westport Country Playhouse in 1950. His Broadway play *To Be Continued* (1952) had among its stars Dorothy Stickney, with whom he would later live before his tragic, impoverished final years. Aside from his plays and at least two produced screenplays—for TRIPLE CROSS (France-UK 1966, US release 1967), starring Christopher Plummer, Romy Schneider and Trevor Howard, and MY LOVER, MY SON (US-UK 1970), with Schneider and Dennis Waterman—Marchant wrote magazine articles, novels (including *Firebird*), TV scripts for the soap opera "One Life to Live," and a book about his friendship with Noel Coward, *The Pleasure of His Company*.

Marchant lived in Stanton, NJ for a decade with Stickney, and later at the Actors Fund of America Nursing and Retirement Home in Englewood, NJ before moving to the Bergen Pines County Hospital in 1994. His body lay unclaimed for six weeks, with the hospital prepared to bury him in a pauper's grave until a social worker sifted through documents and found someone who made arrangements for his cremation and a memorial service. No cause of death was reported.

Martin, Dean

born: Dino Paul Crocetti, June 7, 1917, Steubenville, OH
died: Dec. 25, 1995, Beverly Hills, CA, age 78

Singer, dramatic actor, comic straight-man, and icon of swinging bachelorhood.

With his effortless charm and devil-may-care manner, Dean Martin epitomized the urbane American-male image in the 1950s and '60s—all the while winking at that romanticized fantasy. Martin found his first success as handsome straight-man to the manic slapstick of Jerry Lewis, with whom he appeared in 17 films, 14 of them as leads; after their split, he continued as an established recording star in the crooner mode, as well as recreating himself as a dramatic actor and, later, as a long-running TV variety-show host. He was part of Frank Sinatra's "Rat Pack," a clique that also included Sammy Davis Jr., Joey Bishop, Shirley MacLaine and Peter Lawford, whose ties to President John F. Kennedy reputedly helped forge the now-established bridge between the worlds of politics and Hollywood.

The son of an Italian immigrant barber, Martin began his singing career by imitating Bing Crosby for friends. Leaving high school, he worked briefly in a steel mill, as a gas station attendant, and as a nightclub croupier, and boxed as a teenaged amateur welterweight. He began singing ballads and pop standards at dance halls and clubs, adopting the pseudonym Dino Martini when he sang with the Ernie McKay dance band in Columbus, Ohio in 1939; he had it Americanized to Dean Martin when he joined Cleveland's Sammy Watkins and His Orchestra in 1940. Martin made a successful New York City club debut in 1943, and two years later met young comic Lewis. Their teaming was serendipitous—each was coincidentally booked on the same bill at the 500 Club in Atlantic City, NJ in 1946; they found huge success with an ad-libbed routine of Lewis playing a bumbling, dish-dropping busboy comically interrupting Martin's singing act. The comic chemistry netted them a six-week smash run at the New York club the Copacabana, which lead producer Hal Wallis to sign them to a Paramount contract. Additionally, Martin—who'd released records on the Diamond, Apollo and Embassy labels from 1946-47—was signed to big-name Capitol Records in 1948; he landed approximately 40 singles on the "Billboard" pop chart between 1950 and 1969.

Martin and Lewis made their film debut in supporting roles in MY FRIEND IRMA (1949), stealing the film; they appeared in expanded roles in MY FRIEND IRMA GOES WEST (1950). The duo headlined their next film, AT WAR WITH THE ARMY (1951), and went on to a half-decade run of 15 more commercial hits: THAT'S MY BOY (1951), SAILOR BEWARE and JUMPING JACKS (1952), THE STOOGE, SCARED STIFF and THE CADDY (1953), MONEY FROM HOME, LIVING IT UP and THREE RING CIRCUS aka JERRICO, THE WONDER CLOWN (1954), YOU'RE NEVER TOO YOUNG and ARTISTS AND MODELS (1955), PARDNERS and HOLLYWOOD OR BUST (1956); they also made a cameo appearance in the Bob Hope-Bing Crosby ROAD TO BALI (1953). Martin's songs in THE CADDY included a duet with Lewis, "That's Amore," which earned an Oscar nomination for writers Harry Warren and Jack Brooks, and became a two-million-selling Martin signature. It was revived in 1987 as the theme to MOONSTRUCK. Martin and Lewis were also among the rotating hosts of the TV variety show "The Colgate Comedy Hour" (NBC 1950-55). Yet by the time the duo was shooting HOLLYWOOD OR BUST, the animosity that had grown over the years between them reached a flashpoint with Martin's objections to a script eventually filmed as THE DELICATE DELINQUENT (1957); Darren McGavin played the Martin role in that Jerry Lewis film.

Martin, already ensconced in a hit recording career, continued to flourish in movies after the breakup, turning in a lauded performance as co-star, with Marlon Brando and Montgomery Clift, in the WWII drama THE YOUNG LIONS (1958). He went on to give equally deft, appealing performances in such films as the Westerns RIO BRAVO (1959) and THE SONS OF KATIE ELDER (1965), the character study SOME CAME RUNNING (1959), and the granddaddy of disaster movies, AIRPORT (1970). He was charming as a James Bondian superspy in the tongue-in-cheek Matt Helm pictures THE SILENCERS (1966), MURDERER'S ROW (1966), THE AMBUSHERS (1967) and THE WRECKING CREW (1968); likewise in the kitschy-cool if self-indulgent Rat Pack films OCEAN'S ELEVEN (1960), SERGEANTS 3 aka SOLDIERS 3 (1962), 4 FOR TEXAS (1963) and ROBIN AND THE SEVEN HOODS (1964). Yet in other films, Martin could just as easily sleepwalk through a role, seemingly anxious to leave and enjoy a martini and a round of golf. (He was not, however, at least after his early years, the convivial boozehound of his screen persona.)

Martin hosted the long-running variety series "The Dean Martin Show" (NBC 1965-74), which was retitled and slightly reformatted as "The Dean Martin Comedy Hour" in 1973. Martin also lent his name, if not his presence, to several summer-replacement series, such as "Dean Martin Presents The Golddiggers" and "The Dean Martin Summer Show."

Martin released at least 62 solo, movie-soundtrack, and compilation albums, from the 78 rpm *Manhattan at Midnight* (Diamond 1956) to the CD *Swingin' Down Yonder* (Capitol 1991). Among his hit songs are the number-one singles "Memories Are Made of This" (1955) and "Everybody Loves Somebody" (1964, later to become his variety-show theme), as well as "Return to Me," "Volare (Nel Blu Dipinto Di Blu)," "You're Nobody Till Somebody Loves You" and "I Will." While never considered a major song interpreter, his languid crooning was nonetheless a strong influence on Elvis Presley and others. He made his only music video, for "Since I Met You Baby," in 1983, with son Ricci Martin directing. Martin's last major public appearance was a musical one: March 20, 1988, and the second concert of the Martin-Sinatra-Davis Together Again Tour. He quit that tour immediately after the show; though the official cause was kidney-related health reasons, Martin, according to Nick Tosches' lauded 1992 biography *Dino: Living High in the Dirty Business of Dreams*, simply and inexplicably felt like quitting. Notably, it was the one-year anniversary of a son's death.

Martin had four children by first wife Elizabeth Anne McDonald, whom he married in 1940 and divorced in 1949. His 1949-73 second marriage, to model and 1947 Orange Bowl Queen Jeanne (nee Jean) Biegger, produced three children, among them Dean Paul (Dino) Martin (1951-87), who like his father would have careers in music and as an actor (Dean Martin's last wife was beauty-salon receptionist Kathy Hawn (nee Catherine Mae Conaster), to whom he was married from 1973 to 1977.

Martin died of acute respiratory failure.

Mathews, Carmen

born: c. 1911
died: Aug. 31, 1995, West Redding, CT, age 84
educ: Royal Academy of Dramatic Art, London
Actress and humanitarian.

The classically trained Carmen Mathews appeared in many British stage productions, including *Hamlet* with Maurice Evans and *Richard III*, and on Broadway in works including *Beaux Stratagem*, *A Holiday for Lovers*, *Zenda*, *A Delicate Balance*, *Dear World* and *David Copperfield*. Her prolific television career began with a production of "Dark Fleece" on the CBS live-drama anthology "Schlitz Playhouse of Stars," and included a huge number of such dramas for such series as "US Steel Hour," "Studio One," "Playhouse 90," "You Are There," "Danger," "Suspense," and "Hallmark Hall of Fame," as well as at least a half-dozen episodes of "Alfred Hitchcock Presents." In 1985, Mathews founded an education center on her 100-acre property in West Redding, New Pond Farm, and ran a residential summer camp for underprivileged there since 1975; before her death, she gave a perpetual conservation easement over the property to the Redding Land trust, to ensure the land remains uncommercialized. In 1987, the United Nations named her one of Connecticut's Outstanding Women.

Mathews' films include BUTTERFIELD 8 (1960), A RAGE TO LIVE (1965), RABBIT, RUN (1970), Academy Award Best Picture-nominee SOUNDER (1972)—as the humanitarian white woman who gives Kevin Hooks's character a chance at a good education—and DANIEL (1983).

Mathews died of natural causes.

McClure, Doug

born: May 11, 1935, Glendale, CA
died: Feb. 5, 1995, Sherman Oaks, CA, age 59
educ: UCLA
TV actor and one-time movie heartthrob.

Perennially boyish Doug McClure began riding horses at age eight, and as a teen spent summers on a Nevada cattle ranch and as a bronco-buster in occasional rodeos—experiences that would serve him well in numerous Western movies and as a star of the TV series "The Virginian." He made his small-screen debut in a 1957 episode of the syndicated anthology "Men of Annapolis," and appeared later that same year in the hit Western "Maverick"—the big-screen version of which, in 1994, would ironically be McClure's final film. McClure's first movie, THE ENEMY BELOW, also came in 1957. He gained his first attention playing William Bendix's sidekick in "The Overland Trail" (NBC 1960) and began a long career in television. McClure starred or co-starred in five more series: the private-eye drama "Checkmate" (CBS 1960-62); as James Drury's young sidekick Trampas in "The Virginian" (NBC 1962-71; retitled "The Men from Shiloh" its final season), the secret-agent series "Search" (NBC 1972-73), co-starring with Hugh O'Brian and Tony Franciosa, the San Francisco period adventure "The Barbary Coast" (ABC 1975-76), and the sitcom "Out of This World" (first-run syndication 1987-91), co-starring as an egocentric former TV star turned small-town mayor. McClure's many telefilms and miniseries include "The Judge and Jake Wyler" (NBC 1972), the pilot for a series starring Bette Davis as a retired judge-turned-detective and McClure as her parolee legman. Married at least three times, including once to actress Barbara Luna, McClure was also a boyfriend of Nancy Sinatra. In a weird form of flattery, McClure's last name went to Troy McClure, a washed-up star in the satirical animated series "The Simpsons." In December, 1994, McClure received a star on the Hollywood Walk of Fame.

McClure's films include THE LAND THAT TIME FORGOT (UK 1975), AT THE EARTH'S CORE (UK 1976) and THE PEOPLE THAT TIME FORGOT (UK 1977), as well as a co-starring role with James Stewart in SHENANDOAH (1965). He also appeared in SOUTH PACIFIC (1958), GIDGET (1959), THE HOUSE WHERE EVIL DWELLS (1982), CANNONBALL RUN II (1984), 52 PICK-UP (1986), OMEGA SYNDROME (1987), and TAPEHEADS (1988).

McClure, who was thought to have recovered from lung cancer, collapsed on the Hawaii set of the feature ONE WEST WAIKIKI on Jan. 8; doctors found the cancer had spread to his liver and bones.

McCowan, George

born: c. 1927, Winnipeg, Manitoba, Canada
died: Nov. 1, 1995, age 68

Director of TV episodic dramas and telefilms, and occasional theatrical releases. George McCowan directed the TV-movies "Cannon," and "Return to Fantasy Island," which each led to series. He also directed episodes of "The Mod Squad," "The Invaders," "The Starlost," "Barnaby Jones," "The Streets of San Francisco," "Starsky and Hutch," "Charlie's Angels," "S.W.A.T.," "The Love Boat" and other shows, as well as TV movies, including "The Monk" (ABC 1969; his debut), "The Return of Mod Squad" (ABC 1979) and the Canadian telefilm "Sanity Clause" (CBC 1990; co-director with David Barlow).

McCowan's theatrical films include the sequel Western THE MAGNIFICENT SEVEN RIDE! and FROGS (1972), THE INNBREAKER (Canada 1974), SHADOW OF THE HAWK (Canada 1976) and the remake THE SHAPE OF THINGS TO COME (Canada 1979).

McGowan died of heart failure and emphysema.

Mclean, David

born: May 19, 1922, Akron, OH
died: Oct. 12, 1995, Los Angeles, CA, age 73

Actor and Marlboro Man.

David McLean began acting on stage in Ohio and later Los Angeles, where he settled after his WWII service and worked also as a cartoonist and sketch artist. He gained much notice as star of the TV Western "Tate" (NBC 1960), a summer replacement series, even appearing on a June 1960 cover of TV Guide. The show quickly faded, but McLean found himself guesting on Westerns shows, including "Bonanza," "The Westerner," "High Chaparral," "The Virginian" and "Gunsmoke," as well as such dramas as "The Fugitive," "Ironside" and "The Streets of San Francisco," and sitcoms including "That Girl." He was one of several featured cowboy types ridin' and ropin' on Marlboro cigarettes commercials, before developing lung cancer and turning into a prominent anti-cigarette crusader. In recent years, he retired from acting and worked in architectural design.

McLean's films include X-15, THE RIGHT APPROACH, THE SILENT CALL and VOYAGE TO THE BOTTOM OF THE SEA (1961), THE STRANGLER (1964), NEVADA SMITH (1966), KINGDOM OF THE SPIDERS (1977) and DEATHSPORT (1978).

McLean died of lung cancer.

McQueen, Butterfly

born: Thelma McQueen, Jan. 8, 1911, Tampa, FL
died: Dec. 22, 1995, outside Augusta, GA, age 84
educ: City College of New York

Actress best known as Prissy in GONE WITH THE WIND.

Butterfly McQueen, who adopted her nickname after dancing in the Butterfly Ballet in a production of A Midsummer Night's Dream, was the daughter of a stevedore and a domestic worker. When her parents separated, she moved first to Augusta, GA and then to Babylon, L.I. and New York City with her mother. As a teen, she joined a Harlem theater group. Later, after a brief stint in nursing school, McQueen made her Broadway debut in George Abbott's Brown Sugar (1937), becoming a member of the Abbot Acting Company. Abbott tailored a role for her in Broadway's What a Life; during an intermission at a Philadelphia performance, she received the contract for the role that would embed her in cinematic Americana, that of Scarlett O'Hara's tearful slave "who didn't know nuthin' 'bout birthin' babies" in GONE WITH THE WIND (1939). She found herself so identified with the sobbing-maid stereotype that in her next film, AFFECTIONATELY YOURS (1941), her character's name was Butterfly. Tiring of the image, she left films after DUEL IN THE SUN (1946), laboring in various menial jobs between sporadic theater, radio and TV work. She worked as a companion for a Long Island woman, sold toys at Macy's, waitressed, and worked as a receptionist and dance teacher at New York's Mount Morris Park Recreation Center. McQueen received her bachelor's degree in political science from CCNY in 1975, at age 64.

McQueen made her small-screen debut with a 1950 production of the CBS live-drama series "Studio One," titled "Give Us Our Dreams," and co-starred on the first two seasons of the landmark sitcom "Beulah" (ABC 1950-53), the first fictional TV-series starring African-Americans; she played Oriole, the friend of ever-resourceful housemaid Beulah (initially played by Ethel Waters). She also appeared in a 1959 "Hallmark Hall of Fame" production, "The Green Pastures," and won a 1979/80 Daytime Emmy Award for her performance in "ABC Afterschool Special: The Seven Wishes of a Rich Kid." Her final TV appearance was in the 1986 PBS limited series, "The Adventures of Huckleberry Finn."

McQueen's films include CABIN IN THE SKY and I DOOD IT aka in Britain BY HOOK OR BY CROOK (1943), FLAME OF THE BARBARY COAST and MILDRED PIERCE (1945), THE PHYNX (1970; one of 34 celebrity cameos), AMAZING GRACE (1974), and THE MOSQUITO COAST (1986), as Ma Kennywick. McQueen died of second- and third-degree burns over more than 70 percent of her body, after being caught in a fire ignited by a kerosene heater at her small Georgia home six miles south of Augusta.

Meadow, Herb

born: c. 1912
died: March 1, 1995, Los Angeles, CA, age 83

Film and TV writer, and series creator.

Herb Meadow started out as a radio announcer at WMIL/Brooklyn. He reportedly moved to Hollywood on the advice of producer-director Mervyn LeRoy, who was said to have given Meadow the assignment of writing a screenplay based on Lloyd C. Douglas' novel The Robe, a project that apparently never materialized. (The Frank Ross-produced 1953 Best Picture THE ROBE was written by Philip Dunne.) Meadow made his screenwriting debut with THE STRANGE WOMAN (1946), and showed much flexibility in subject matter and studio, turning out the Errol Flynn adventure THE MASTER OF BALLANTRAE for Warner Bros. in 1953, and the potboiler HIGHWAY DRAGNET for Roger Corman in 1954. Meadow had his biggest success in television, for which he co-created the Richard Boone Western "Have Gun Will Travel" (CBS 1957-63). He afterward helped develop "Arrest and Trial" (ABC 1953-64), a 90-minute weekly series that was a precursor to the 1990s series "Law & Order," and developed and produced the Western insurance-investigator series "The Man From Blackhawk" (ABC 1959-60). He also wrote the pilot script for the trucker adventure series "Movin' On" (NBC 1974-76). Meadow was producer-director of the unsold pilot "Collectors Item" (CBS 1958), starring Vincent Price as a detective-art-gallery owner, and Peter Lorre as his underworld-connected assistant.

Meadow's films include SALLY AND SAINT ANNE (1952), THE REDHEAD FROM WYOMING (1953), COUNT THREE AND PRAY, THE LONE RANGER (a big-screen adaptation of the TV series) and STRANGER ON HORSEBACK (1955), EVERYTHING BUT THE TRUTH and THE UNGUARDED MOMENT (1956), and MAN AFRAID (1957). At the time of Meadows' death, his screenplay ANNE OF THE SPANISH MAIN was in pre-production at Miramax.

Meadow died of a heart attack.

Meddings, Derek

born: Jan. 1931
died: Sept. 1995
British special-effects technician.

Derek Meddings first gained prominence designing the special effects for several of Gerry and Sylvia Anderson's much-loved sci-fi puppet series, including "Supercar" (ATV 1961-62), "Fireball XL5" (ATV 1962-63) and "Thunderbirds" (ATV 1965-66; special effects supervisor). Meddings first two features were the spin-offs THUNDERBIRD 6 and THUNDERBIRDS ARE GO (UK; US releases 1968). He later worked on the teams that provided special effects for SUPERMAN (1978) and several James Bond movies.

Meddings's films include DOPPELGANGER aka JOURNEY TO THE FAR SIDE OF THE SUN (UK 1969), Z.P.G. aka ZERO POPULATION GROWTH (1972), LIVE AND LET DIE (UK 1973), THE MAN WITH THE GOLDEN GUN (UK 1974), THE LAND THAT TIME FORGOT (UK 1975), SHOUT AT THE DEVIL (UK 1976), ACES HIGH and THE SPY WHO LOVED ME (UK 1977), MOONRAKER (UK 1979), FOR YOUR EYES ONLY (UK 1981), BANZAI (France; US release 1983), KRULL (UK 1983), SPIES LIKE US (1985; also actor), HIGH SPIRITS (US-UK 1988), BATMAN (1989), THE NEVERENDING STORY II: THE NEXT CHAPTER/AUF DER SUCHE NACH PHANTASIEN (US-West Germany 1990, released in US 1991) and DIE UNENDISCHE GESCHICHTE III/THE NEVERENDING STORY III (Germany 1994, direct-to-video US 1995).

No cause of death was reported.

Megna, John

born: c. 1953, New York City
died: Sept. 4, 1995, Los Angeles, CA, age 42
educ: Cornell University, Ithaca, NY (BA, performing arts)
Child actor who continued into adult roles.

As a boy, John Megna appeared in Broadway plays including *All the Way Home*, in several TV shows, and in the classic film TO KILL A MOCKINGBIRD (1962), playing neighbor boy Dill Harris, a friend of Scout and Jem Finch's (Mary Badham, Phillip Alford). He'd made his screen debut on the NBC dramatic anthology "DuPont Show of the Month" in January 1962. He went on to juvenile appearances on such series as "The Alfred Hitchcock Hour,""Dr. Kildare," "Ben Casey," "Star Trek" and "I Spy," moving onto at least four grown-up appearances on "Police Woman" from 1975-77. He shot an unsold pilot, "Hollywood High," for NBC in 1977. One of Megna's sisters is the actress Connie Stevens (nee Concetta Ann Ingolia).

Megna's films include HUSH. . . HUSH, SWEET CHARLOTTE (1964), BLINDFOLD (1966), GO TELL THE SPARTANS (1978), SMOKEY AND THE BANDIT II aka in Britain SMOKEY AND THE BANDIT RIDE AGAIN (1980) and THE CANNONBALL RUN (1981).

Megna died of complications from AIDS.

Meisner, Gunter

born: c. 1929
died: Dec. 5, 1995, Berlin, Germany, age 66
educ: State Conservatory, Dusseldorf
German character actor who played lots of Nazis.

Gunter Meisner was a sculptor and painter before studying acting under Gustaf Grundgens, who inspired the protagonist of the film MEPHISTO (1981). In his stage work, he specialized in theater-of-the-absurd—establishing in 1962 the Diogenes Studio Theater, devoted to that form—and classical theater; he toured the US in 1964 in Franz Kafka's *Report to the Academy*, and appeared Off-Broadway in *Fairwell* that same year. His TV work included the ABC miniseries "The Winds of War," the telefilm "Love and Honor," and appearances in the soap operas "One Life to Live" and "The Edge of Night." Among the other arts organizations he founded are Berlin's Gallery Diogenes (1959) and the International Association for Arts & Sciences (1961).

Meisner's films include BABETTE S'EN VA-T-EN GUERRE/BABETTE GOES TO WAR (France 1959), FRAGE 7/QUESTION 7 (US-West Germany 1961), THE COUNTERFEIT TRAITOR (1962), THE QUILLER MEMORANDUM (US-UK 1966), PARIS BRULE-T-IL?/IS PARIS BURNING? (US-France 1966), FUNERAL IN BERLIN (UK 1966), THE BRIDGE AT REMAGEN (1969), WILLY WONKA AND THE CHOCOLATE FACTORY (1971), as the villain, Mr. Slugworth,

THE ODESSA FILE (UK-West Germany 1974), INSIDE OUT aka HITLER'S GOLD (UK 1975), VOYAGE OF THE DAMNED (UK 1976), DAS SCHLANGENEI/THE SERPENT'S EGG (US-West Germany 1977), THE BOYS FROM BRAZIL (US-UK 1978), JUST A GIGOLO (West Germany 1979), AVALANCHE EXPRESS (1979), THE AMERICAN SUCCESS COMPANY aka SUCCESS (1980), L'AS DES AS/ ACE OF ACES (France-West Germany; US release 1982), NIGHT CROSSING (1982), UNDER THE VOLCANO (1984), DREI GEGEN DREI (West Germany; US release 1985), IN A GLASS CAGE (Spain; US release 1989), and MAGDALENE (1990). He also directed the 1970 films DON'T LOOK FOR ME WHERE I CAN'T BE FOUND and BEGA DWA BEGA/ONE FOR ALL, the latter in Swahili for Tanzanian Film Unit.

Meisner died of heart failure.

Meltzer, Lewis

born: c. 1911, New York, NY
died: Feb. 23, 1995, Albuquerque, NM, age 84
educ: New York University (BA, English)
Prolific screenwriter.

Lewis Meltzer was born into a show business family: father Isidor Meltzer was a comedian in Yiddish theater, and brother Sid Melton is a character actor best known as Alf Monroe on "Green Acres" and "Uncle Charley" Halper on "The Danny Thomas Show." He reportedly moved to Hollywood in 1938 at the request of the director Rouben Mamoulian, and wrote in a variety of genres for several studios through 1959. He wrote a 1958 play, *Come and Kiss Me*, whose original title he gave to Alan Jay Lerner at the lyricist's request, for his musical adaptation of Shaw's *Pygmalion: My Fair Lady*. Meltzer's most famous screenplay credits are for GOLDEN BOY (1939) and THE MAN WITH THE GOLDEN ARM (1955). As Lou Meltzer, he wrote for such early TV series as "Dagmar's Canteen" and "The Morey Amsterdam Show."

Meltzer lost his eyesight in the mid-1980s. Meltzer's films include THOSE HIGH GREY WALLS (1939), THE LADY IN QUESTION aka IT HAPPENED IN PARIS (1940), NEW YORK TOWN and TEXAS (1941), THE TUTTLES OF TAHITI (1942), DESTROYER and FIRST COMES COURAGE (1943), ONCE UPON A TIME (1944), LADIES' MAN (1947), MAN-EATER OF KUMAON and TEXAS, BROOKLYN AND HEAVEN aka in Britain THE GIRL FROM TEXAS (1948), THE LADY GAMBLES (1949; co-story only), COMANCHE TERRITORY (1950), ALONG THE GREAT DIVIDE (1951), DESERT LEGION, THE JAZZ SINGER and SHARK RIVER (1953), NEW ORLEANS UNCENSORED aka in Britain RIOT ON PIER 6 (1955), AUTUMN LEAVES (1956), THE BROTHERS RICO (1957), HIGH SCHOOL CONFIDENTIAL! aka THE YOUNG HELLIONS (1958) and THE BEAT GENERATION aka THIS REBEL AGE (1959).

Meltzer died of pneumonia.

Michael, Ralph

born: Ralph Champion Shotter, 1907
died: 1995, age c. 88
Longtime British character actor, often in stiff-upper-lip roles.

Ralph Michael played the romantic lead in THE GIRL WHO FORGOT (UK; US release 1939) and starred in the war drama FOR THOSE IN PERIL (UK 1944). His other films include FALSE EVIDENCE (UK; US release 1937), JOHN HALIFAX—GENTLEMAN (UK 1938), FRONT LINE KIDS, GERT AND DAISY CLEAN UP and WOMEN AREN'T ANGELS (UK; US release 1942), SAN DEMETRIO, LONDON (UK 1943; US release 1947), THEY CAME TO A CITY (UK 1944), DEAD OF NIGHT (UK 1945), JOHNNY FRENCHMAN (UK 1945; US release 1946), EUREKA STOACKADE (UK 1948), A SONG FOR TOMORROW (UK; US release 1948), THE ASTONISHED HEART and THE HASTY HEART (UK 1949), THE SOUND BARRIER aka BREAKING THE SOUND BARRIER (UK 1952), BLONDE BAIT aka WOMEN WITHOUT MEN (US-UK 1956), SEVEN WAVES AWAY aka ABANDON SHIP! (UK 1957), A NIGHT TO REMEMBER (UK 1958), DATE AT MIDNIGHT and A TASTE OF MONEY (UK; US release 1960), THE COURT MARTIAL OF MAJOR KELLER (UK; US release 1961), L'AFFONDAMENTO DELLA VALIANT/THE VALIANT (UK-Italy; US release 1962), PRIVATE POTTER (UK; US release 1963), CHILDREN OF THE DAMNED and A JOLLY BAD FELLOW aka THEY ALL DIED LAUGHING (UK 1964), MURDER MOST FOUL (UK; US release 1964), THE HEROES OF TELEMARK aka THE

UNKNOWN BATTLE (UK; US release 1965), HE WHO RIDES A TIGER (UK; US release 1966), GRAND PRIX and KHARTOUM (1966), THE ASSASSINATION BUREAU (UK 1968 or 1969), HOUSE OF CARDS (UK 68; US release 1969), THE COUNT OF MONTE CRISTO (UK 1975; released as telefilm in US), EMPIRE OF THE SUN (1987) and LIONHEART (very brief release 1987, direct-to-video 1990).

No cause of death was reported.

Miller, Patsy Ruth

born: Paricia Ruth Miller, June 22, 1905, St. Louis, MO
died: July 16, 1995, Palm Desert, CA, age 91

Actress best known as the Gypsy dancing girl in the silent classic THE HUNCHBACK OF NOTRE DAME (1923).

Convent-educated Patsy Ruth Miller was 16 and vacationing with her family in Hollywood when she met film star Alla Nazimova at a party; Nazimova helped the youngster win a part in Rudolph Valentino's CAMILLE (1921). In her most famous role, she played Esmeralda to Lon Chaney's tragic Quasimodo. Miller went on to fame in a string of mostly silent films, and in real life as the "most engaged girl in Hollywood." She was married three times: to writer-director Tay Garnett (1945's THE POSTMAN ALWAYS RINGS TWICE, 1947's A CONNECTICUT YANKEE IN KING ARTHUR'S COURT) and screenwriter John Lee Mahin (1932's SCARFACE, 1937's CAPTAINS COURAGEOUS), both of whom she divorced, and businessman E.S. Deans, who died in 1986. She did a string of five comedies in which she co-starred with or played support to Edward Everett Horton—THE HOTTENTOT, THE SAP and THE AVIATOR (1929), WIDE OPEN (1930) and LONELY WIVES (1931)—but retired from acting soon after the advent of sound. She turned to writing radio scripts, a novel (*The Flanagan Girl*) and the book for a Broadway musical about Tchaikovsky, *Music in My Heart;* she won three O. Henry awards for her short stories. Miller later appeared briefly on Broadway, and made a cameo apperance in the film QUEBEC (1951), which, she wrote in her autobiography, she did as a lark.

Miller died of heart failure.

Moctezuma, Juan Lopez

died: Aug. 2, 1995, age 63

Mexican actor, radio personality, painter, and horror director.

A lifelong lover of horror and fantasy in all their forms, Juan Lopez Moctezuma had directed for television and for surrealist theater before making his feature-film directorial debut with DR. TARR'S TORTURE DUNGEON (Mexico; US release 1972), a surreal horror movie based on Edgar Allan Poe's "The System of Doctor Tarr and Prof. Fether." His other films include the bisexual vampire flick MARY, MARY, BLOODY MARY (US-Mexico 1975), starring Cristina Ferrare in the title role and John Carradine as her father, and TO KILL A STRANGER (1985 direct-to-video), featuring Dean Stockwell, Donald Pleasence, and famed cartoonist Sergio Aragones. He also directed SISTERS OF SATAN (Mexico c. 1973; US release 1975), with Tina Romero and Claudio Brook. At the time of his death, Moctezuma was struggling to complete THE CURE FOR FEAR, based on the true story of a woman who, in the 1950s, made tamales with the flesh of children. The production had been plagued with financial troubles.

Montgomery, Elizabeth

born: April 15, 1933, Los Angeles, CA
died: May 18, 1995, Los Angeles, CA, age 62
educ: The Westlake School for Girls, Beverly Hills, CA; the Spence School, New York, NY; American Academy of Dramatic Arts, New York, NY

Star of TV's "Bewitched," who went on to a career in challenging, often socially conscious telefilms.

Elizabeth Montgomery, who masked her glamorous looks beneath wifely attire, post-apocalyptic grime, or whatever else a role demanded, was the daughter of actor-director-producer Robert Montgomery (1904-1981) and stage actress Elizabeth Allan. Despite her father's attempts to dissuade her from pursuing acting, he eventually let her apprentice on his anthology series "Robert Montgomery Presents" (NBC 1950-57); she made her debut, playing Robert's daughter, in the 1951 production "Top Secret," then went on to become one of several repertory players during two of its seasons. Montgomery, whose acting career spanned more than 40 years, made countless appearances on such series as "Studio One,"

"Armstrong Circle Theater," "Climax," "DuPont Show of the Month" (1958's "Harvey," opposite Art Carney), "Alfred Hitchcock Presents," "Cimarron City" (her episodic-series debut), "The Untouchables" (the 1960 episode "The Rusty Heller Story," for which she earned the first of nine Emmy Award nominations), "Burke's Law," "Rawhide," "77 Sunset Strip," "The Flintstones" (voice only, in the episode "Samantha") and "The Twilight Zone," in which she and a young Charles Bronson memorably performed in a two-character *tour de force*, "Two." Montgomery also appeared in the TV pilot "The Boston Terrier" (ABC 1963).

She was best-known, however, as Samantha Stephens, the beautiful blond witch who only wanted to be a suburban housewife, in the hit series "Bewitched" (ABC 1964-72). The series was produced and directed by William Asher, Montgomery's husband at the time. She garnered Emmy nominations for comedy-series actress five years running, beginning in the 1965-66 season. Afterward, she became a high priestess of TV-movies, beginning with "The Victim" (ABC 1972) and the TV-movie pilot "Mrs. Sundance" (ABC 1974), and continuing through Emmy-nominated turns in "A Case of Rape" (NBC 1974), "The Legend of Lizzie Borden" (ABC 1975) and the miniseries "The Awakening Land" (ABC 1978).

Before marrying and divorcing Asher, Montgomery was married briefly to socially prominent New Yorker Frederick Gallatin Gammann, and then from 1957-63 to actor Gig Young, with whom she starred in the "Theater '62" TV production "The Spiral Staircase" (1961). At the time of her death she was married to actor Robert Foxworth, whom she met on "Mrs. Sundance" and with whom she appeared in the telefilm "Face to Face" (1990) and in New York and Los Angeles stage productions of *Love Letters. The New York Times* obituary erroneously gave Montgomery's birth year as 1938 and her age as 57.

Montgomery's films were THE COURT-MARTIAL OF BILLY (1955), WHO'S BEEN SLEEPING IN MY BED?, in which she co-starred opposite Dean Martin, JOHNNY COOL (1963), produced and directed by husband-to-be Asher, and the Academy Award-winning Documentary Feature THE PANAMA DECEPTION (1992), which she narrated.

Montgomery had undergone surgery for colon cancer, and in April 1995 had surgery for the removal of what was described as a small malignant tumor. Montgomery died of cancer.

Moses, Gilbert

born: Aug. 20, 1942, Cleveland, OH
died: April 14, 1995, New York, NY, age 52

Esteemed stage and TV director-producer.

Gilbert Moses began acting in Cleveland community theater at age 9. He spent a year at the Sorbonne in Paris while studying at Oberlin College, then left college to join the Civil Rights movement. Committed to socially relevant theater, he co-founded the Free Southern Theater with John O'Neal, and toured the South in the 1960's with plays ranging from *In White America* to *Waiting for Godot.* Death threats by white Southerners and the arrests of company members pushed him to leave the company. He went on to direct such theater works as *Every Night When the Sun Goes Down, Louis,* a musical about Louis Armstrong, *Rigoletto,* for the San Francisco Opera Company, and Toni Morrison's *Dreaming Emmett.* He won an Obie Award for his Off-Broadway production of LeRoi Jones' *Slave Ship* (1969) at the Chelsea Theater center, and directed Ed Bullins' *Taking of Miss Janie,* winner of the 1975 New York Drama Critics Circle Award for Best new American play. For Broadway, he directed Melvin Van Peebles' *Ain't Supposed to Die a Natural Death* (1971), and, with George Faison, directed, staged, and choreographed the Leonard Bernstein-Alan Jay Lerner musical *1600 Pennsylvania Avenue* (1976). In 1977, Moses directed two episodes of the miniseries "Roots," and has helmed episodes of "Benson" and "Law & Order," and the telefilms "The Greatest Thing That Almost Happened"(1977), "A Fight for Jenny" (1986) and "Runaway" (1989); he also produced network afterschool specials, and taught both theater and film. Two of his three wives were the actress Denise Nicholas and the actress-singer Dee Dee Bridgewater.

Moses' movies are WILLIE DYNAMITE (1973) and THE FISH THAT SAVED PITTSBURGH (1979).

Moses died of multiple myeloma.

Muir, Esther

born: 1895, New York, NY
died: Aug. 1, 1995, Mount Kisco, NY, age c. 100

Actress and one-time wife of Busby Berkeley.

Petite blond Esther Muir began modeling while still a high school student, and broke into theater with such plays and musicals as *Greenwich Village Follies*, *Earl Carroll's Vanities*, *Queen High*, *Honeymoon Lane* and *Baby Blue*, and found stage stardom as the leading lady of Broadway's *My Girl Friday* (1929) (not to be confused with the film HIS GIRL FRIDAY, adapted from the play *The Front Page*). Shortly thereafter, columnist Walter Winchell introduced Muir to then-choreographer Busby Berkeley, whom she divorced in 1931. She was later married to composer-producer Sam Coslow (1945's OUT OF THIS WORLD, 1947's COPACABANA), whom she divorced in 1948; their daughter, Jacqueline Coslow, is an actress. Muir appeared in dozens of films, often playing bit or supporting roles like "The Tart" (in 1933's THE BOWERY), "Blonde Woman" (in 1938's THE TOY WIFE), "Prostitute" (in 1941's HONKY TONK) and "Prima Donna" (twice, in 1936's THE GREAT ZIEGFELD and 1938's ROMANCE IN THE DARK). Muir was memorable in the Marx Brothers classic, A DAY AT THE RACES (1937), as "Flo."

No cause of death was given for Muir, who lived in Somers, NY.

Mullard, Arthur

born: 1920 or Nov. 10, 1913
died: Dec. 1995

Cockney character comedian.

Big and bluff Arthur Mullard generally played either a cop or a robber in numerous films since the 1940s, and was a British television star in the '70s. His TV work in the UK included the sitcom "The Arthur Askey Show" (ATV 1961), "Whizzkid's Guide" (1981) and "Romany Jones" (1973).

Mullard's movies include OPERATION DIAMOND (UK; US release 1948), SKIMPY IN THE NAVY (UK; US release 1949), the Ealing Studio classic THE LAVENDER HILL MOB (UK 1951), OH ... ROSALINDA!! (UK 1955), THE BANK RAIDERS (UK 1958), THE MAN WHO LIKED FUNERALS (UK 1959), TWO WAY STRETCH (UK 1960), BAND OF THIEVES (UK; US release 1962), CROOKS ANONYMOUS, THE LONELINESS OF THE LONG DISTANCE RUNNER, POSTMAN'S KNOCK and Richard Lester's IT'S TRAD, DAD! aka RING-A-DING RHYTHM (UK 1962), LADIES WHO DO, SPARROWS CAN'T SING and THE WRONG ARM OF THE LAW (UK 1963), FATHER CAME TOO aka WE WANT TO LIVE ALONE (UK; US release 1964), ALLEZ FRANCE!/THE COUNTERFEIT CONSTABLE (France 1964) CUCKOO PATROL (UK; US release 1965), THE GREAT ST. TRINIAN'S TRAIN ROBBERY and MORGAN: A SUITABLE CASE FOR TREATMENT aka MORGAN! (UK 1966), SMASHING TIME (UK 1967), CHITTY CHITTY BANG BANG (UK 1968), LOCK UP YOUR DAUGHTERS (UK 1969), CROOKS AND CORONETS/SOPHIE'S PLACE (US-UK 1969; US release 1970), THE VAULT OF HORROR aka TALES FROM THE CRYPT II (UK 1973) and ADVENTURES OF A PLUMBER'S MATE (UK 1978).

The cause of Mullard's death was not available.

Murphy, Joan

aka: Joan Murphy Adler
born: c. 1931
died: March 8, 1995, age 55

Miami-based actress.

Joan Murphy was the waitress who served Dustin Hoffman and Jon Voight in MIDNIGHT COWBOY (1969). She guested in supporting roles on such TV series as "Miami Vice," and appeared in the films DON'T DRINK THE WATER (1969), LIMBO aka CHAINED TO YESTERDAY (1972), THE MEAN SEASON (1985), BAND OF THE HAND (1986) and HIDDEN FEARS (Canada 1994).

Murphy died of cancer.

Nukanen, Ernest

born: July 18, 1919, near Cardiff, Wales
died: Feb. 26, 1995, Belfast, ME, age 75
educ: Black Mountain College, NC

Documentary filmmaker.

Ernest Nukanen was the son of a Welsh mother, who died young, and a Finnish father. He was raised for a time in New York City by his English stepmother, but went to sea on a British oil tanker at the start of WWII. When poor eyesight disqualified him for Royal Air Force service, he served on a US merchant vessel as an electrician and radio operator. Years later, as a combat cameraperson, he covered the US Marine landings in the Dominican Republic in 1965, as well the war in Vietnam and Cambodia for ABC News.

Nukanen began his career as an assistant cameraperson on "Dreams That Money Can Buy," a short surrealist film directed by Hans Richter and featuring sequences by Fernand Leger, Alexander Calder, Max Ernst and Marcel Duchamp. Nukanen journeyed to the North Pole in 1957 to film a return expedition by Lowell Thomas, Peter Freuchen, Admiral Donald MacMillan and Sir Hubert Wilkins, then later trekked to Suriname to shoot and co-produce JOURNEY TO CHILANE, a documentary on the Oyanan forest tribe. He also made biographical documentaries about bandleader Duke Ellington and statesman Hubert H. Humphrey. From 1979 until his retirement in 1991, Nukanen taught at the University of Southern California, and helped create the school's documentary film program.

Nukanen had been in failing health for some time.

O'Shea, Tessie

born: March 13, 1913, 1917 or 1918 (sources vary) Cardiff, Wales
died: April 21, 1995, Lessburg, FL, age 77, 78, or 82

Mirthful, girthful music-hall performer, whose signature song was "Two-Ton Tessie from Tennessee."

Tessie O'Shea began singing and dancing as a child, and reportedly made her first tour of music halls and variety theaters—the British equivalent to vaudeville—at age seven. She later appeared in a starring role at the Bristol Hippodrome. She first performed "Two-Ton Tessie from Tennessee" while singing in a Blackpool, England revue. O'Shea went on to become a headliner of such British revues as *On With the Show* and *High Time*, the latter of which played the London Palladium in the 1940's. O'Shea sang a command performance for Princess Elizabeth and Princess Margaret in 1944, entertained British and American troops during WWII, and produced the revues *Tessie's Big Show* and *Tess and Bill*, which was adapted into a BBC radio series. She made her US stage debut as a Cockney fish-and-chips peddler in the musical *The Girl Who Came to Supper*; her mere 12 minutes onstage, singing a medley of four Noel Coward songs, won her a 1964 Tony Award as musical supporting/featured actress, and led to appearances on "The Ed Sullivan Show" and Johnny Carson "Tonight" show. Her subsequent Broadway shows were *A Time for Singing* (1966), *Something's Afoot* (1976) and *Broadway Follies* (1981). During 1964, O'Shea was a regular on the variety series "The Entertainers" (CBS 1964-65), and garnered a 1967/68 Emmy Award nomination for dramatic supporting actress her role as music-hall entertainer "Tessie O'Toole" in the 2 1/2-hour dramatic special "The Strange Case of Dr. Jekyll and Mr. Hyde" (ABC 1968).

After playing herself in her film debut, Carol Reed's THE IMMORTAL BATTALION aka THE WAY AHEAD (UK 1944), and a character called "Tessie" in LONDON TOWN aka MY HEART GOES CRAZY (UK 1946, US release 1953), O'Shea went on to films including HOLIDAYS WITH PAY (UK 1948), SOMEWHERE IN POLITICS (UK 1949), THE SHIRALEE (UK 1957), Academy Award Best-Picture nominee THE RUSSIANS ARE COMING, THE RUSSIANS ARE COMING (1966), as the prim Boston telephone operator, THE BEST HOUSE IN LONDON (UK 1969), and BEDKNOBS AND BROOMSTICKS (1971). O'Shea also appeared as herself in her one American telefilm, "The Word" (CBS 1978).

O'Shea, who lived in East Lake Weir, FL, died of congestive heart failure.

Okada, Eiji

born: June 13, 1920, Japan
died: Sept. 14, 1995, age 75

Leading man of Japanese stage and screen, best known in the West for HIROSHIMA, MON AMOUR.

Eiji Okada served in the Japanese Army during WWII, then worked as a traveling salesperson and as a miner before making his film debut in UNTIL THE DAY WE MEET AGAIN (Japan 1950). He gained international prominence as the co-star, with Emmanuele Riva, of director Alain Resnais' politicized erotic drama HIROSHIMA, MON AMOUR (France-Japan 1959). Okada went on to co-star with Marlon Brando as the sympathetic Communist-rebel leader in THE UGLY AMERICAN (1963), and as the entrapped but ultimately ennobled entomologist of SUNA NO ONNA/WOMAN IN THE DUNES aka WOMAN OF THE DUNES (Japan 1964), an Academy Award Best Foreign-Language Picture nominee. In later years, Okada devoted less time to film than to the stage, founding a theater company with his wife, Aiko Wasa.

No cause of death was given.

Olaf, Pierre

born: July 14, 1928
died: Sept. 1995, age 67

Actor, cabaret artist and clown. Pierre Olaf's films include writer-director Jean Renoir's FRENCH CANCAN aka ONLY THE FRENCH CAN (France; US release 1955), WILD AND WONDERFUL aka MONSIEUR COGNAC (1964), ALLEZ FRANCE!/THE COUNTERFEIT CONSTABLE (France 1964), THE ART OF LOVE (1965), CAMELOT (1967), THE GAMBLERS and DON'T DRINK THE WATER (1969), LE PETIT THEATRE DE JEAN RENOIR/THE LITTLE THEATER OF JEAN RENOIR (1969 French telefilm; US theatrical release 1974), UN NUAGE ENTRE LES DENTS (France 1974), RETENEZ-MOI. . . OU JE FAIS UN MALHEUR! (France 1983), AMERICAN DREAMER and CHEECH AND CHONG'S THE CORSICAN BROTHERS (1984). Olaf also appeared in the telefilms "Lace" (1984) and "Around the World in 80 Days" (1989). No cause of death was available.

Oliver, Gordon

born: c. 1910, Los Angeles, CA
died: Jan. 26, 1995, Los Angeles, age 84

Film actor and TV producer.

Gordon Oliver began his film-acting career in 1935. He played a leading man in such B-pictures as YOUTH ON PAROLE and WHITE BONDAGE (both 1937) and starred as a misanthropic Marine in THE MARINES ARE HERE (1938) before settling into supporting status. Oliver appeared mostly in Warner Bros. films during the mid-1930s—including SAN QUENTIN (1937), with Humphrey Bogart and Pat O'Brien—and in Columbia pictures later in the decade. He left acting in the early 1950s to produce such TV series as "Douglas Fairbanks, Jr. Presents" (syndicated; produced 1952-57, premiered January 1953) and the limited docudrama series "Profiles in Courage" (NBC 1964-65), and to serve as executive producer on such series as "Peter Gunn" (NBC/ABC 1958-61), "Mr. Lucky" (CBS 1959-60) and "It Takes a Thief" (ABC 1968-70), as well as for the pilots of "The Seven Little Foys" (NBC 1964), the spy-adventure "Code Name: Heraclitus" (NBC 1967), the legal drama "Guilty or Not Guilty" (NBC 1966), and the Don Knotts sitcom "The Reason Nobody Hardly Ever Sees a Fat Outlaw in the Old West is as Follows" (NBC 1967). These pilots for prospective series ran on the summer anthology program "The Bob Hope Chrysler Theatre." Gordon also produced, and had a small part in, the Bob Hope feature CANCEL MY RESERVATION (1972).

Oliver died of emphysema.

Parrish, Robert

born: Jan. 4, 1916, Columbus, GA
died: Dec. 4, 1995, Southampton, Long Island, NY, age 79

Oscar-winning film editor turned well-regarded director.

At age eight, Robert Parrish moved with his family to Hollywood, where he and his three siblings consistently found after-school work as extras, set-dismantlers and the like. In his memoirs, "Growing Up in Hollywood" (1976) and "Hollywood Doesn't Live Here Anymore" (1988), he described appearing as a juvenile actor in films including Charlie Chaplin's CITY LIGHTS (1931), in which he played a newsboy. Director John Ford, with whom Parrish worked as a bit player on several films, apprenticed him as an assistant editor on MARY OF SCOTLAND (1936) and as sound editor on YOUNG MR. LINCOLN and DRUMS ALONG THE MOHAWK (1939), THE GRAPES OF WRATH and THE LONG VOYAGE HOME (1940) and TOBACCO ROAD (1941). Parrish did WWII service alongside Ford in the Navy's Field Photography Branch, and worked on the director's Oscar-winning documentary shorts "The Battle of Midway" (1942; co-editor with Ford) and "December 7th" (editor). Parrish himself co-directed, with Garson Kanin, the documentary GERMAN MANPOWER (1943). He returned to share an Academy Award, with Francis Lyon, on his first feature as editor, Robert Rossen's classic BODY AND SOUL (1947); he later co-edited Rossen's Oscar-winning Best Picture, ALL THE KING'S MEN (1949). Parrish made a promising start as director with such films as CRY DANGER (1951), THE PURPLE PLAIN (UK 1954), starring Gregory Peck, and the

Western THE WONDERFUL COUNTRY (1959), starring Robert Mitchum, but his work in the 1960s was highly inferior. Parrish mostly worked in England in his later years, and was one of five credited directors on the misconceived James Bond parody CASINO ROYALE (UK 1967). Parrish's mother was minor actress Laura Parrish (nee Laura Virginia Reese), and his sister the popular child actress and later B-movie lead Helen Parrish (1922-1959).

No cause of death was given for Parrish, who lived in Sag Harbor, Long Island.

Patrick, John

aka: Jack Patrick
born: John Goggin, or O'Goggan (accounts differ), May 17, 1905, Louisville, KY
died: Nov. 7, 1995, Delray Beach, FL, age 90
educ: Our Lady of Holy Cross College, New Orleans, LA; Columbia University, New York, NY

Pulitzer Prize-winning playwright and screenwriter.

John Patrick—not to be confused with playwright-screenwriter John Patrick Shanley—wrote radio scripts for NBC in San Francisco from 1933-36. He broke into films with EDUCATING FATHER (1936), scripting mostly for Fox (generally with writing partner Lou Breslow) through the early 1950s. Patrick went on to a distinguished and commercially successful career in both movies and the stage. His first two produced plays—*Hell Freezes Over* (1935), directed by Josh Logan, and *The Willow and I* (1942)—were Broadway flops. Yet his comedy *Teahouse of the August Moon* (1953), adapted from a novel by Vern J. Sneider, was a major hit that brought him not only the Pulitzer, but a Tony and a New York Drama Critics Circle Award. Patrick then adapted it himself for the 1956 movie starring Marlon Brando and Glenn Ford. His other plays include the often-produced *The Hasty Heart* (1945) and *Curious Savage* (1950), as well as *Love Is a Time of Day* (1969), *Good as Gold, Everybody's Girl, Scandal Point, A Barrelful of Pennies, Opal is a Diamond, Macbeth Did it, A Bad Year for Tomatoes, Noah's Animals* and, as director also, *Enigma*. *The Hasty Heart*, based on Patrick's experiences in a WWII ambulance unit, was adapted into a 1949 British movie starring Ronald Reagan and Patricia Neal. As a screenwriter, his prominent films include the musicals LES GIRLS (1957), which won him a Screen Writers Guild award, and HIGH SOCIETY (1956), and the romantic dramas THREE COINS IN THE FOUNTAIN (1954) and LOVE IS A MANY-SPLENDORED THING (1955).

Patrick, who lived in Suffern, NY until moving to an adult care center in Delray Beach, FL in 1993, was found dead with a plastic bag over his head; his death was ruled a suicide.

Pennell, Nicholas

born: c. 1938, Brixham, Devon, England
died: Feb. 22, 1995, Stratford, Ontario, Canada, age 56
educ: Royal Academy of Dramatic Art

Venerable Shakespearean actor.

Nicholas Pennell, for 23 years a versatile mainstay of Canada's esteemed Stratford Festival, appeared in more than 75 plays for the company, including the title roles in *Macbeth, Richard II*, and *Hamlet*. He also played Orlando in *As You Like It* and Berowne in *Love's Labour's Lost*, and in non-Shakespearean roles appeared in such works as *The Cherry Orchard, The Importance of Being Earnest* and *World of Wonders*. In 1980, he played Leonard Woolf opposite Maggie Smith as Virginia Woolf in the world premiere of Edna O'Brien's *Virginia*. He toured with a one-man show, *A Variable Passion*, and appeared on television, most notably as Michael Mont on "The Forsyte Saga" (BBC 1967; aired in US on PBS-precursor NET, 1969-70). He was slated to appear during the 1995 Stratford season in *Macbeth, The Country Wife* and *Amadeus*, but illness prevented him from attending the start of rehearsals, two days before his death.

Pennell's films include RASPUTIN—THE MAD MONK (UK 1966), ONLY WHEN I LARF and ISADORA aka THE LOVES OF ISADORA (UK 1968), BATTLE OF BRITAIN (UK 1969), DAVID COPPERFIELD (UK 1970) and CRY OF THE PENGUINS aka MR. FORBUSH AND THE PENGUINS (UK; US release 1971).

Pennell died of cancer.

Perry, Frank

born: Aug. 21, 1930, New York, NY
died: Aug. 29, 1995, New York, NY, age 65
educ: University of Miami, Miami, FL

Esteemed director of intimate, humanist independent films, and splashy Hollywood productions.

Frank Perry remains best known for two remarkably different films: the sensitive, low-budget drama of two mentally disturbed teens, DAVID AND LISA (1962; also co-executive producer), and the rollicking Joan Crawford biopic MOMMIE DEAREST (1981; also co-writer). Perry began in the theater, parking cars at Connecticut's Westport Country Playhouse, progressing to stage manager, associate producer for the Theater Guild, and eventually producer, with Off-Broadway's *The Pretenders*. After military service during the Korean War, he broke into film as a production assistant; a Frank Perry is credited as art designer on ISLAND WOMEN aka ISLAND WOMAN (1958). That year, Perry met and married Eleanor Baylor, with whom he raised $200,000 to make DAVID AND LISA, a sleeper hit was one of the first successful non-exploitation films to be independently produced and distributed. Directed by Perry and adapted by Eleanor Perry from the book by Dr. Theodore Isaac Rubin, the film won the Best New Director award at the Venice Film Festival and earned Academy Award nominations for director and for adapted screenplay; stars Keir Dullea and Janet Margolin were named best actress and actor at the San Francisco Film Festival.

The Perrys were less successful with such follow-up films as their harrowing $320,000 indie LADYBUG, LADYBUG (1963; also producer), or their artful, brutal, originally X-rated LAST SUMMER (1969), both scripted by Eleanor. But they scored another critical and commercial hit with DIARY OF A MAD HOUSEWIFE (1970), also produced and directed by Frank from an adapted script by Eleanor. The couple ended their personal and professional relationship that same year. Eleanor continued as a playwright and screenwriter until her death, and Frank as a director; he later married and divorced novelist Barbara Goldsmith, and was married to third wife Virginia at the time of his death.

After the split, Perry made his first studio film, Universal's PLAY IT AS IT LAYS (1972; also co-producer). Five years before his death, Perry was diagnosed with terminal cancer and given a year to live; beating the odds, he spent the next few years making the documentary/personal journal ON THE BRIDGE (1993), a critically acclaimed film-festival success. Perry- not to be confused with actor Frank Perry (1942's RIO RITA, 1969's MY SIDE OF THE MOUNTAIN)—made his Broadway directing debut with Paul Zindel's *Ladies of the Alamo* (1977), and reportedly hosted and co-produced an early public-TV documentary series, "Playwrights at Work." He was also producer-director, again working from Eleanor Perry scripts, on the "A Christmas Memory" (ABC 1966) and the sequel "Thanksgiving Visitor" (ABC 1968), one-hour specials adapted from Truman Capote stories; the former, which was Emmy-nominated for best dramatic program, was later included in the Perry's theatrical release TRUMAN CAPOTE'S TRILOGY (1969).

Perry's other films include THE SWIMMER (1968; also co-producer; one scene directed by Sydney Pollack; script adaptation by Eleanor Perry), DOC (1971; also producer), MAN ON A SWING (1974), RANCHO DELUXE (1975), MONSIGNOR (1982), COMPROMISING POSITIONS (1985; also producer) and HELLO AGAIN (1987; also co-producer). Perry also directed the well-regarded telefilm "Dummy" (1979) and telefilm/series-opener "Skag" (1980), for which he was Emmy-nominated for director, drama series.

Perry, who lived in Aspen, CO, died of prostate cancer.

Phillips, John

born: c. 1915
died: 1995, age 80

British actor particularly noted among horror-movie aficionados for his supporting roles in such films as VILLAGE OF THE DAMNED (UK 1960), THE MUMMY'S SHROUD (UK 1967)—as rich industrialist Stanley Preston—and TORTURE GARDEN (UK 1968). He also appeared in more prestigious works such as BECKET (UK 1964), THE ROMAN SPRING OF MRS. STONE (US-UK 1961) and ROMANOFF AND JULIET (1961). John Phillips is not to be confused with minor American actor John Phillips (1948's KEY LARGO), the musician-composer John Phillips (1990's AIR AMERICA), or the British producer John I. Phillips (1964's THE SICILIANS).

Phillips' films include DIAL RED O and THE DARK AVENGER aka THE WARRIORS (UK 1955), RICHARD III (UK 1955, US release 1956), THE SHIRALEE and FORTUNE IS A WOMAN aka SHE PLAYED WITH FIRE (UK 1957), FLOODS OF FEAR and I ACCUSE! (UK 1958), JOHN PAUL JONES (UK 1959), FOLLOW THAT HORSE! (UK 1960), MAN IN THE MOON (UK 1960, US release 1961), OFF-BEAT aka THE DEVIL INSIDE (UK 1961), A PRIZE OF ARMS (UK 1961, US release 1962), WE JOINED THE NAVY (UK 1962), THE MOUSE ON THE MOON (UK 1963), JOEY BOY (UK 1965), and ASCENDANCY (UK 1982).

No cause of death was reported.

Pleasence, Donald

born: Oct. 5, 1919, Worksop, Nottinghamshire, England; raised Sheffield, England
died: Feb. 2, 1995, St. Paul de Vence, France, age 75

Acclaimed, highly flexible actor, equally well-known for his command of Pinter onstage and for playing Dr. Sam Loomis in the HALLOWEEN movies.

Donald Pleasence came from a railway family, and left school in his late teens to work briefly as a railroad clerk himself. He had already appeared on stage as Caesar in a student production of Shaw's *Caesar and Cleopatra*, and was soon hired as an assistant stage manager at the Playhouse, on the Channel island of Jersey. Pleasence made his professional debut there in 1939, as Hareton in *Wuthering Heights*. Three years later, he made his London debut as Valentine in *Twelfth Night*. After WWII service with the Royal Air Force—he was shot down over France in 1944 and spent a year in a German POW camp—he appeared in a Peter Brook production of *The Brothers Karamazov*, and afterward made his Broadway debut in Laurence Olivier and Vivien Leigh's double-bill of *Caesar and Cleopatra* and *Antony and Cleopatra*. Yet he won his greatest acclaim in 1960 as the manipulative, individualistic tramp, Davies, in Harold Pinter's London production of *The Caretaker*. He reprised his role on Broadway the following year, as well in the 1963 British movie (retitled THE GUEST in America) and in the 1991 London revival. His Broadway Davies earned Pleasence a Tony Award nomination, and he went on to further nominations in 1965, 1969 and 1972 for his roles in Jean Anouilh's *Poor Bitos*, Robert Shaw's *The Man in the Glass Booth*, and Simon Gray's *Wise Child*, respectively. The latter, in which he played a transvestite, marked his last Broadway appearance. His other plays include *Hobson's Choice* and his own adaptation of Robert Louis Stevenson's *Ebb Tide*, as well as several Shakespeare productions at Stratford-on-Avon.

Pleasence broke into film with BEACHCOMBER (UK 1954), and soon established himself as a versatile character actor who could play both heroic scientists and world-beating villains. Among his many memorable roles were forger Dr. Absalon in THE GREAT ESCAPE (1963, followed by the 1988 miniseries sequel "The Great Escape II: The Untold Story"); Ernst Stavro Blofeld in the Sean Connery James Bond film YOU ONLY LIVE TWICE (UK 1967); a miniaturized scientist killed in FANTASTIC VOYAGE (1966); one of the futuristic drones in George Lucas' seminal THX 1138 (1971); the 1940s father of a raped, impregnated daughter in WEDDING IN WHITE (Canada 1972), and as psychiatrist Dr. Loomis in HALLOWEEN (1978), HALLOWEEN II (1981), HALLOWEEN IV: THE RETURN OF MICHAEL MYERS (1988), HALLOWEEN 5: THE REVENGE OF MICHAEL MYERS (1989) and HALLOWEEN: THE CURSE OF MICHAEL MYERS (1995). A self-admitted compulsive, Pleasence, even at the height of his career, was willing to work in low-budget horror films as the only name star. Many of these were still unreleased in the US at the time of his death.

On television, Pleasence co-starred as the protagonistic Prince John in the British-shot series "The Adventures of Robin Hood" (CBS 1955-58). His many miniseries roles included Salomon Van der Merwe in the nine-hour "Master of the Game" (CBS 1984), and heroic Reverend Septimus Harding in the "Masterpiece Theatre" seven-parter "The Barchester Chronicles" (PBS 1984). Among Pleasence's several telefilms and dramatic specials are "The Diary of Anne Frank" (ABC 1967); "The Defection of Simas Kudirka" (1978 CBS), for which he earned an Emmy nomination; "Hallmark Hall of Fame: All Quiet on the Western Front" (NBC 1979), later released theatrically; the Dennis Potter-scripted "Blade on a Feather" aka "Deep Cover" (London Weekend Television 1988), released as a direct-to-video movie here in 1989; and "Guinevere" (1994), in which he played Merlin in one of his final screen appearances.

Pleasence was married four times; his actress daughter Angela played one of his daughters in "The Barchester Chronicles."

Pleasence had recently completed work on the British Channel 4 telefilm "Safe Haven" with his youngest daughter, Miranda, and was scheduled to tour in "King Lear" with daughters Angela, Miranda and Holly.

Pleasence died unexpectedly and in relatively good health, possibly due to complications following a heart-valve replacement operation.

Porter, Eric

born: April 8, 1928, London, England
died: May 15, 1995, London, England, age 67
educ: Wimbledon College

British actor and occasional character lead, best-known as a star of TV's "The Forsyte Saga."

Porter, a member of the Royal Shakespeare Company, made his professional debut in 1945, in the time-honored role of spear-carrier. He went on to appear in many 1950s plays directed by John Gielgud, and in the title roles in *King Lear* and *Uncle Vanya*. Porter appeared on Broadway in *The Visit* (1958), and in such Shakespeare plays as *Twelfth Night*, *Richard III* and *Macbeth*. He won accolades playing Big Daddy in *Cat on a Hot Tin Roof* at London's National Theater in 1988, and as Sere-bryakov in a 1992 production of *Uncle Vanya* there. Though he appeared in several films, he was more widely known for his television work. Porter played the leading role of lawyer Soames Forsyte in the 26-part literary adaptation "The Forsyte Saga" (BBC 1967; aired in US on PBS-precursor NET, 1969-70), as well as Polonius in "Hamlet" (BBC 1980), a Russian adviser in "The Jewel in the Crown" (PBS 1984 in US), and Fagin in "Oliver Twist" (PBS 1986 in US).

Porter—not to be confused with Australian animator Eric Porter nor fellow English stage and film actor Eric Portman—played leads in the films THE LOST CONTINENT (UK 1968), HANDS OF THE RIPPER (UK 1971) and THE BELSTONE FOX aka FREE SPIRIT (UK 1973). His other films include THE FALL OF THE ROMAN EMPIRE (1964), THE PUMPKIN EATER (UK 1964), THE HEROES OF TELEMARK aka THE UNKNOWN BATTLE (UK 1965), KALEIDOSCOPE (UK 1966), NICHOLAS AND ALEXANDRA (UK 1971), ANTONY AND CLEOPATRA (UK 1972), THE DAY OF THE JACKAL (UK-France 1973), HITLER: THE LAST TEN DAYS (UK-Italy 1973), MARCO POLO JUNIOR (UK 1973), CALLAN (UK 1974; a big-screen version of the TV series), HENNESSY (UK 1975) and THE THIRTY-NINE STEPS (UK 1978).

Porter died of colon cancer.

Powell, Dilys

born: c. 1901
died: June 3, 1995, age 93

Dilys Powell, the influential film critic for Britain's Sunday "Times," began reviewing movies in 1939, and throughout the 1940s and '50s was one of the most prominent and powerful voices in her field. She stopped reviewing new releases in 1976, when she was 75, and began reviewing films on television; she continued doing so until her death. Her final review, of a TV showing of BARRY LYNDON, appeared the day afterward. Her newspaper career spanned 71 years.

Precht, Andrew

born: c. 1950, Scarsdale, NY
died: Feb. 21, 1995, Grenada, age 45
educ: USC; Southern Californian Institute of Architecture (master's degree)

Art director.

Andrew Precht, the grandson of legendary TV producer-host Ed Sullivan and the son of TV producer Robert Precht, was co-set designer of THE ABYSS (1989) and art director or co-art director on HOOK (1991), BRAM STOKER'S DRACULA (1992), BEING HUMAN and LEGENDS OF THE FALL (1994), after having apprenticed on earlier films. At the time of his death, Precht was in Grenada working on Ridley Scott's WHITE SQUALL (1996). No cause of death was disclosed.

Price, Steven Lee

born: c. 1931
died: May 22, 1995, age 34

Visual Effects Supervisor at Lucasfilm's Industrial Light & Magic division.

Stephen Lee Price had worked at ILM since HOOK (1991), after having worked at post-production houses in Chicago, Miami and Los Angeles on projects including the film GHOST (1990) and the TV series "Star Trek: The Next Generation." He supervised the special effects in films including DEATH BECOMES HER (1992), SCHINDLER'S LIST (1993) and JUMANJI (1995), and served as a key animator in JURASSIC PARK (1993). His widow is ILM executive in charge of production Patricia Blau. Price died of pancreatic cancer.

Quinn, Katherine De Mille

See under "D"

Rene, Allio

born: 1924, Marseille, France
died: March 27, 1995, age 71

Director and screenwriter whose feisty and independent rural characters sought to transcend the peasant life he'd himself known in childhood.

Rene Allio segued into feature filmmaking in his 40s, following a celebrated career as a painter, theatrical director, and set designer. After directing a 1962 animated short, "Le Meule/The Haystack," he adapted a Bertolt Brecht story for his first and best-known feature, LA VIEILLE DAME INDIGNE/THE SHAMELESS OLD LADY (1964); it starred the single-name French actress Sylvie as a rural widow determined to enjoy life's pleasures unabashedly before she dies. Allio's painterly films include L'UNE ET L'AUTRE/THE OTHER ONE (1967)—which, like his previous film, featured his actress wife Malka Ribovska—PIERRE ET PAUL (1969), LES CAMISARDS (1971), RUDE JOURNEE SUR LA REINE (1973) and MOI PIERRE RIVIERE/I, PIERRE RIVIERE, HAVING SLIT THE THROATS OF MY MOTHER, MY SISTER AND MY FATHER (1976).

Allio, who worked in theater with the Comedie Francaise, the Paris Opera, the La Scala Opera and the Royal Shakespeare Theater, and helped design the interior of the recent new zoology gallery at the Natural History Museum in Paris, died after a long illness.

Robin, Dany

born: April 14, 1927, Clamart, France
died: May 25, 1995, Paris, France, age 68

French actress.

The petite, blond Dany Robin was a Gallic heartthrob in the 1940s and '50s, often playing an adorably lovestruck young woman. She began her career as a dancer with the Paris Opera company, and went on to act in light dramas and comedies, including title roles in LA FETE A HEN-RIETTE/HOLIDAY FOR HENRIETTA aka HENRIETTE'S HOLIDAY (France 1952, US release 1955), JULIETTA (France 1953, US release 1957) and FROU-FROU (France-Italy 1955). Robin was married to French star Georges Marchal, and to British producer Michael Sullivan.

Robin's films include LUNEGARDE (France 1946), Marcel Carne's LES PORTES DE LA NUIT/GATES OF THE NIGHT (France 1946; US release 1950), L'EVENTAIL/NAUGHTY MARTINE and Rene Clair's LE SILENCE EST D'OR/MAN ABOUT TOWN (France 1947), LES AMOUREUX SONT SEULS AU MONDE/MONELLE (France 1948), LA PASSAGERE (France 1949), LA SOIF DES HOMMES/THE THIRST OF MEN (France 1950), JUPITER (France; US release 1952) LES AMANTS DES MINUIT, TEMPI NOSTRI/THE ANATOMY OF LOVE (France 1953), ACT OF LOVE (US-France 1953), opposite Kirk Douglas, CADET-ROUSSELLE (France; US release 1954), ESCALE A ORLY and NAPOLEON (France 1955), as Desiree Clary, PARIS CO-QUIN/MAID IN PARIS (France 1956), MIMI PINSON (France 1958), LES DRAGUEURS/THE CHASERS (France 1959), LA FRANCAISE ET L'AMOUR/LOVE AND THE FRENCHWOMAN (France 1960, US release 1961), LES AMOURS CELEBRES (France 1961), WALTZ OF THE TOREADORS aka THE AMOROUS GENERAL (UK 1962), LES PARSIENNES/TALES OF PARIS aka OF BEDS AND BROADS (France-Italy 1962), FOLLOW THE BOYS (1963), DON'T LOSE YOUR HEAD (UK; US release 1967), THE BEST HOUSE IN LONDON (UK 1969) and Alfred Hitchcock's TOPAZ (1969).

Robin died of injuries suffered in a fire at her home, which also critically injured Sullivan.

Robinson, Darren

aka: Buffy Robinson; The Human Beat Box
born: c. 1967
died: Dec. 10, 1995, Rosedale, Queens, NY, age 28
Rap star who appeared in films.

Darren "Buffy" Robinson was a 450-pound rapper who recorded hit records in the 1980s as part of the aptly named trio The Fat Boys. With Mark "Prince Markie Dee" Morales and Damon "Kool Rock" Wimbley, Robinson performed on rap hits including "Crushin'" and "Wipeout." The group played supporting roles in the 1985 films KNIGHTS OF THE CITY and KRUSH GROOVE, and starred with Ralph Bellamy in the Three Stooges-like slapstick comedy DISORDERLIES (1987).

Robinson died of apparent cardiac arrest after falling from a couch at his home.

Rocca, Daniela

born: c. 1938, Catania, Sicily
died: May 28, 1995, Milo, Sicily, age 57
Italian actress best known as the unfortunate wife in the comedy DIVORCE, ITALIAN STYLE.

Daniela Rocca escaped her poverty-ridden working-class background by winning Italian beauty contests. She made her film debut in writer-director Maurice Cloche's MARCHANDS DE FILLES/SELLERS OF GIRLS aka GIRL MERCHANTS (France 1957, US release 1967). Four years later, her work in Mario Bonnard's I MASNADIERI (Italy 1961) prompted writer-director Pietro Germi to have Rocca hide her sultriness behind dowdy frocks to play Marcello Mastroianni's whiny, sex-crazed Sicilian wife in DIVORZIO ALL'ITALIANA/DIVORCE, ITALIAN STYLE (Italy 1962), an international hit that won an Academy Award for original screenplay. Yet by the mid-1960s, Rocca found few new offers; at age 35, she became chronically depressed and branded insane in the press. Rocca recovered sometime later to play a small role in the Marco Bellocchio Italian telefilm "La Macchina del Cinema," and to perform in theater. Rocca published three novels, a volume of poetry, and a non-fiction book, *Psychoanalysis, Dreams and Fantasies Hidden in the Mind*, for which Bellocchio wrote a preface.

Rocca died of heart failure.

Rogers, Ginger

born: Virginia Katherine McMath, June 16, 1911, Independence, MO; raised Kansas City, MO, Fort Worth, TX
died: April 25, 1995, Rancho Mirage, CA
Academy Award-winning dramatic actress, and half of film's most famous dance team.

Ginger Rogers, who triumphed in dramas, comedies, and even thrillers but became iconic for her 10 movie-musicals with Fred Astaire, was groomed for stardom from childhood. Her mother, Lela Owens McMath (d. 1977) was divorced from William McMath shortly after Ginger's birth. Rogers, who was called "Ginger" from childhood, took her last name from John Rogers, who was briefly her stepfather. She took dancing and singing lessons at age five, and a year later went first to Hollywood and then New York City with her mother, who became a screenwriter at Fox. Lela later became a pioneering reporter and drama critic in Fort Worth, where Rogers made her professional debut at 14, filling-in for a week as a dancer with Eddie Foy's vaudeville troupe. The following year, she won a local Charleston contest, for which top prize was a one-month booking on the Texas-Oklahoma vaudeville circuit; Rogers, with her mother chaperoning, toured in an act called "Ginger and Her Redheads" which was extended to 21 weeks. In 1928, she again toured briefly in vaudeville with her first husband, dancer Jack Pepper aka Jack Culpepper or Edward Culpepper, whom she divorced in 1931. She again appeared in a solo act, with the Eddie Lowry band in Chicago and the Paul Ash orchestra in New York. During this time she made her movie debut, filming at least four shorts, including the Rudy Vallee three-reeler "Campus Sweethearts."

A major career break came in 1929, when Rogers became the second female lead in the Broadway musical *Top Speed*. During this and her next Broadway musical, George Gershwin's *Girl Crazy* (1930-31), Rogers began appearing in New York-shot features for Paramount, starting with the Claudette Colbert melodrama YOUNG MAN OF MANHATTAN

(1930). She played wisecracking flapper Puff Randolph, whose line, "Cigarette me, big boy," became one of the most popular catch-phrases of the decade. Rogers made her screen singing debut in her second effort, QUEEN HIGH (1930), then after a succession of minor roles, won release from her contract in 1931. With THE TIP-OFF aka in Britain LOOKING FOR TROUBLE (1931), she made the first of several features for RKO, where she would establish herself as a musical star. Two years later, playing a supporting role in the Dolores Del Rio musical FLYING DOWN TO RIO, Rogers would team up with well-known dancer Fred Astaire, who was making his second film. (They had met in 1930, when he gave her dance instruction for *Girl Crazy*.) Their bouyant, graceful, effortlessly elegant dancing stole the film, and the duo—despite a sometimes contentious working relationship—went on to nine more movie-musicals together, including such classics as THE GAY DIVORCEE (1934) and Academy Award Best Picture-nominee TOP HAT (1935). The other Astaire-Rogers films are ROBERTA (1935), FOLLOW THE FLEET and SWING TIME (1936), SHALL WE DANCE (1937), CAREFREE (1938), THE STORY OF VERNON AND IRENE CASTLE (1939) and, in a reunion after original star Judy Garland left due to a breakdown, THE BARKLEYS OF BROADWAY (1949).

With their popularity beginning to wane after nine films in seven years, Rogers and Astaire went their own ways in 1939. Rogers, choosing a dramatic change-of-pace, won a Best Actress Oscar the following year in the title role of the sentimental classic KITTY FOYLE (1940). Indeed, though her musicals with Astaire overshadowed most of her career, Rogers often won accolades in dramas such as Best Picture nominee STAGE DOOR (1937) and PRIMROSE PATH (1940), and comedies, including BACHELOR MOTHER (1939), TOM, DICK AND HARRY (1941) and THE MAJOR AND THE MINOR (1942); in 1945, she was reportedly Hollywood's highest-paid star. Segueing primarily to stage and television roles in the 1950s, she won kudos in the otherwise panned Broadway comedy *Love and Let Love* (1951), which she financed herself. (Another dud, *The Pink Jungle*, never made it to New York.) Rogers made her TV dramatic debut with the "Producer's Showcase" production of Noel Coward's "Tonight at 8:30" (NBC 1954). Rogers won acclaim succeeding Carol Channing in the title role of Broadway's *Hello, Dolly!* in 1965, playing the role for more than two years; in 1969, she introduced *Mame* to London. Rogers also starred regularly in summer-stock productions, and even directed a 1980s Tarrytown, NY production of *Babes in Arms*.

On television, Rogers played herself in the 1956 "Climax" production "The Louella Parsons Story," and guested on "The Jack Benny Program," "The June Allyson Show," "Zane Grey Theater," "Here's Lucy," "The Love Boat," "Glitter" and "Hotel" (in 1987); she also starred in the unsold pilot "The Ginger Rogers Show" aka "A Love Affair for Just Three" (CBS 1963), and in a handful of specials. In the 1970s, she developed a successful nightclub act, and was a fashion consultant to the J.C. Penney department-store chain. Her 1991 autobiography was called *Ginger, My Story*. Rogers was a 1992 recipient of the Kennedy Center Honors for lifetime achievement. Her other four marriages, all ending in divorce, were to actor Lew Ayres (1934-40), aviator Jack Briggs (1943-1949), French actor Jacques Bergerac (1953-57), with whom she appeared in BEAUTIFUL STRANGER aka TWIST OF FATE (UK 1954), and producer-director William Marshall (1961-67), who co-produced her QUICK, LET'S GET MARRIED aka THE CONFESSION aka SEVEN DIFFERENT WAYS (1965).

Rogers died of natural causes.

Rose, Jack

born: Warsaw, Poland, Nov. 4, 1907 or 1911
died: Oct. 20, 1995, Los Angeles, CA, age 87 or 84
educ: Ohio University
Comedy writer-producer.

Jack Rose was the youngest of 13 children who, at age five, emigrated with his family from Poland to Brooklyn. After college, he worked as a press agent in New York, planting *bon mots* under his clients' names in newspaper columns. He later wrote for comedian Milton Berle, and relocated to Hollywood in the 1940s, where he penned gags for Bob Hope's weekly radio show. Rose's first movie script (co-written with Edmund Beloin) was the Hope-Crosby ROAD TO RIO (1947); he went on to do screenplays for Hope's MY FAVORITE BRUNETTE (1947), THE PALEFACE (1948), THE GREAT LOVER and SORROWFUL JONES (1949), THE SEVEN LITTLE FOYS (1955; also producer), and

BEAU JAMES (1957; also producer). Beginning with the Cary Grant comedy, ROOM FOR ONE MORE aka THE EASY WAY (1952), Rose began an 18-year writing collaboration with fellow Hope gagster Melville Shavelson, who later began directing the films that Rose produced. The two garnered an Academy Award nomination for Original Screenplay for THE SEVEN LITTLE FOYS; they would be nominated again for the Cary Grant-Sophia Loren HOUSEBOAT (1958; also producer). Rose earned a third nomination, with co-writer Mel Frank, for A TOUCH OF CLASS (1973), and a Writers Guild Award nomination for I'LL SEE YOU IN MY DREAMS (1951). Rose's other writing projects include, with Shavelson and Ernest Lehman, the scripts for several Academy Award shows. Rose is not to be confused with the minor, Chicago-born actor also named Jack Rose.

Rose died of cancer.

Rosenblum, Ralph

born: Oct. 13, 1925, New York, NY
died: Sept. 4, 1995, New York, NY

Esteemed film editor, best-known for his six Woody Allen pictures.

Ralph Rosenblum, who also directed TV-movies, taught, and wrote a book on editing, broke into feature-film editing with the 1960 exploitation movies MURDER, INC. and PRETTY BOY FLOYD, and worked his way to such A-pictures as FAIL SAFE (1964), THE PAWNBROKER and A THOUSAND CLOWNS (1965). Rosenblum and Juan Jose Marino are variously credited as editor on the post-Civil War psychological drama THE FOOL KILLER aka VIOLENT JOURNEY (1965), which was re-edited and re-released by Jack Dreyfus, Jr. in 1969. Rosenblum was one of four editors on his first film for Allen, TAKE THE MONEY AND RUN (1969). He went on to cut SLEEPER (1973), LOVE AND DEATH (1975), Academy Award Best Picture winner ANNIE HALL (1977) and INTERIORS (1978), his last four films as an editor, and was associate producer—though not editor—on Allen's BANANAS (1971). Rosenblum then directed the PBS "American Short Story" productions "The Greatest Man in the World" (1979) and "Any Friend of Nicholas Nickleby is a Friend of Mine" (1982), as well as Henry Fonda's last project, the ABC telefilm "Summer Solstice" (1981), and a 1986 telefilm, "Stiffs." He also consulted on the films THE GREY FOX (Canada 1982) and MARVIN AND TIGE (1983), and the TV-movies PLAYING FOR TIME (1980) and JACOBO TIMERMAN: PRISONER WITHOUT A NAME, CELL WITHOUT A NUMBER (1983). With Robert Karen, he was co-author of the book *When the Shooting Stops . . . the Cutting Begins* (1979). For the past several years, Rosenblum also taught at Columbia University's graduate film school, and at summer film workshops in Rockport, ME.

Rosenblum died of heart failure.

Rowland, Roy

born: Dec. 31, 1910, New York, NY
died: June 1995, age 84
educ: USC

Director.

Roy Rowland started in film in the early 1930s as a script clerk, and soon became an assistant director. By the late '30s, he was directing shorts, including Peter Benchley's famed "How To" series, "Pete Smith Specialities" and "Crime Doesn't Pay." The competent Rowland's films include the highly regarded Edward G. Robinson picture OUR VINES HAVE TENDER GRAPES (1945) and the cult classic THE 5,000 FINGERS OF DR. T. (1953). Rowland's wife, Laura Cummings, is the sister of producer Jack Cummings and the niece of Louis B. Mayer. Their son, Steve Rowland, is an actor whose films include Rowland's LOS PISTOLEROS DE CASA GRANDE/GUNFIGHTERS OF CASA GRANDE (US-Spain 1964, US release 1965).

Rowland's films include HOLLYWOOD PARTY (1934; uncredited co-director), A STRANGER IN TOWN (1943), LOST ANGEL (1944), BOYS' RANCH (1946), THE ROMANCE OF ROSY RIDGE and KILLER MCCOY (1947), TENTH AVENUE ANGEL (1948), SCENE OF THE CRIME (1949), THE OUTRIDERS and TWO WEEKS WITH LOVE (1950), EXCUSE MY DUST (1951), BUGLES IN THE AFTERNOON (1952), AFFAIR WITH A STRANGER and THE MOONLIGHTER (1953), ROGUE COP and WITNESS TO MURDER (1954), MANY RIVERS TO CROSS and HIT THE DECK (1955), SLANDER, THESE WILDER YEARS and MEET ME IN LAS VEGAS aka in Britain VIVA LAS VEGAS (1956), GUN GLORY (1957), THE SEVEN HILLS

OF ROME (US-Italy 1958), THE GIRL HUNTERS aka THE CHASERS (UK 1963; also co-writer), SIE NANNTEN IHN GRINGO (Germany-Italy 1966 or Germany-Spain 1965; sources differ), SURCOUF, LE TIGRE DES SEPT MERS/THE SEA PIRATE (France-Spain-Italy 1967; also producer; credited as co-director with Sergio Bergonzelli), and LAND RAIDERS aka DAY OF THE LANDGRABBERS (1970; associate producer only).

No cause of death was available.

Rozsa, Miklos

born: April 18, 1907, Budapest, Hungary
died: July 27, 1995, Los Angeles, CA, age 88
educ: Leipzig Conservatory

Legendary film composer.

Miklos Rozsa scored 89 films, including a parade of classics, earning three Academy Awards and an additional 13 nominations. He worked first for producer Alexander Korda in 1930s England, then under contract for MGM through the 1950s. His Oscar-recognized films alone include some of Hollywood's greatest spectacles, intimate dramas, and psychological thrillers. He won Academy Awards for SPELLBOUND (1945), A DOUBLE LIFE (1947) and Best Picture BEN-HUR (1959), and received nominations for the classic fantasy THE THIEF OF BAGHDAD (UK 1940), SUNDOWN (1941), LYDIA (1941), the live-action THE JUNGLE BOOK aka RUDYARD KIPLING'S JUNGLE BOOK (1942), DOUBLE INDEMNITY (1944), A SONG TO REMEMBER (1945, with music director Morris Stoloff), Best Picture THE LOST WEEKEND (1945), THE KILLERS (1946), QUO VADIS (1951), IVANHOE (UK 1952), JULIUS CAESAR (1953), and EL CID (US-Italy 1961), for both score and song ("The Falcon and the Dove," lyrics by Paul Francis Webster).

Child prodigy Miklos Rozsa began composing music and playing the violin at age five. His father insisted Rozsa study chemistry at the University of Budapest; Rozsa did so, but concurrently studied at the Music Conservatory. Later, he studied composition and violin in Leipzing, Germany. He continued his education in Paris and London; there he was introduced to fellow Hungarian Korda, who commissioned him to write the score for KNIGHT WITHOUT ARMOR (UK 1937). Reportedly, another fellow Hungarian, scriptwriter Akos Tolnay, asked Rozsa to score the film titled THUNDER IN THE CITY, but that movie appears in no standard reference source, even under alternate titles. Rozsa's first Hollywood film was THAT HAMILTON WOMAN aka in Britain LADY HAMILTON (1941; also music director). He also composed several concert works, including tone poems, rhapsodies, variations and concertos; his "Concerto for Violin" (1956) was given its premiere by Jascha Heifetz, and he composed his "Sinfonia Concertante" (1966) for Gregor Piatigorsky. His autobiography is called *A Double Life* (1982).

Rozsa, who suffered from a nerve disorder, died of pneumonia. Three weeks prior he'd had a stroke, and had been on life support thereafter.

Santa Cruz, Abel

born: c. 1915, Buenos Aires, Argentina
died: Feb. 4, 1995, Buenos Aires, Argentina, age 79
educ: Faculty of Philosophy & Letters, Buenos Aires, Argentina

Highly prolific Argentine screenwriter and playwright.

Abel Santa Cruz wrote a reported 84 movies, 60 plays and hundreds of radio and TV scripts in a career that began in 1939. He'd begun writing professionally two years earlier in the humor magazine "Patoruzu" under the pseudonym Dr. Lepido Frias; here he created the schoolroom tales of "Jacinta Pichimahuida," which years later became a popular *telenovela*. In 1939 he began writing for radio, where he created the 20-year-running hit sitcom "Que pareja!"/"What a Couple!" He began writing for film the following year, and for theater in 1942, beginning with *Esta Noche, Filmacion/Tonight, Filming*. He was so popular and prolific that eight films in 1956 alone were released with Santa Cruz as writer or co-writer; similarly, he had four TV series airing simultaneously in 1973. Santa Cruz's many films include MALEVO, EL RAFA, NAZARENO REYES, EL ORIENTAL and JUAN WITHOUT NAME. Among the popular stars of his films were Luis Sandrini, who starred as a recurring professor character in three, and singer Lolita Torres, who appeared in Santa Cruz comedies. Santa Cruz's fifth wife was actress Eve Ziegler. He died of complications from leukemia.

Santi, Lionello

aka: Nello Santi
born: c. 1918, Tuscany region, Italy
died: Dec. 10, 1995, Rome, Italy, age 77

Leading Italian film producer.

Lionello Santi, either himself or through production companies including Galatea Cinematografica, produced a reported 60 features, many of them distributed internationally. He was involved in a production capacity on films ranging from sword-and-sandal epics to serious dramas. His most illustrious achievement may be the unprecedented Italy-USSR partnership he brokered for the Giuseppe De Santis-directed ITALIANI BRAVA GENTE aka ITALIANO BRAVA GENTE/ATTACK AND RE-TREAT (Italy-USSR 1965), which he produced with an international cast including Americans Arthur Kennedy and Peter Falk. This, and his support of Russian director Gleb Panfilov, helped earn Santi special honors at the Moscow Film Festival in 1995. Santi was also president of Cinecitta Studios from 1972-77. He died after what was reported as a long illness.

Scott, Allan

born: Arlington, NJ
died: April 13, 1995, Santa Monica, CA, age 88
educ: Amherst College; Oxford University

Screenwriter whose career stretched from Astaire-Rogers musicals to such 1990s films as THE WITCHES.

Allan Scott, who worked well into his 80s, started out on Broadway as co-writer of the comedy *Goodbye Again* (1933), which featured a fledgling James Stewart; the play was revived in 1943 and 1956, and adapted into both the 1933 film of the same name and a remake, HON-EYMOON FOR THREE (1941). Scott made his screenwriting debut in 1934, co-adapting the Vincent Lawrence play *Sour Grapes* into the film LET'S TRY AGAIN aka in Britain MARRIAGE SYMPHONY (1934). Shortly thereafter, he found a niche as co-scripter of six consecutive Fred Astaire-Ginger Rogers musicals: ROBERTA, Academy Award Best Picture nominee TOP HAT (both 1935), FOLLOW THE FLEET and SWING TIME (both 1936), SHALL WE DANCE (1937), and CARE-FREE (1938). He went on to write scripts for Rogers, including FIFTH AVENUE GIRL (1939), LUCKY PARTNERS and PRIMROSE PATH (both 1940). Altogether, he was credited on at least 45 films, and as a well-known script doctor made uncredited but acknowledged contributions to dozens of others, including HOLIDAY INN (1942), SINCE YOU WENT AWAY (1944), THE PARADINE CASE and PORTRAIT OF JENNIE (1948), THE CAINE MUTINY (1954), THE DEFIANT ONES (1958) and the Astaire-Rogers vehicle THE GAY DIVORCEE (1934). Scott's war drama SO PROUDLY WE HAIL (1943) received an Oscar nomination for Best Original Screenplay. He co-wrote, with Theodor Geisel—better known as Dr. Seuss—the children's film THE 5,000 FINGERS OF DR. T. (1953), which, though Geisel denounced the final product, remains a cult favorite. Other prominent movies include IMITA-TION OF LIFE (1959; co-adapted with Eleanore Griffin), DON'T LOOK NOW (UK-Italy 1973), and THE WITCHES (US-UK 1990).

No cause of death was reported.

Scott, Timothy

born: c. 1938; raised New Mexico
died: June 14, 1995, Los Angeles, age 57

Character actor and 1994 inductee into the Cowboy Hall of Fame.

Timothy Scott moved to Los Angeles to study acting in 1959, and found roles on television and, beginning 1967, in film. Cast as everything from a Nazi general to a Cajun chef, he most often played cowboys, ranch hands and, in modern-day roles, rural locals. He co-founded, with James Gammon, the MET Theatre in Los Angeles, and was a supporting cast-member of the sitcom "Down Home" (NBC 1990-91) and two Western series: "Wildside" (ABC 1985) and, billed as Tim Scott, "Ned Blessing—The Story of My Life & Times" (CBS 1993). Scott is not to be confused with a younger actor also named Timothy Scott, who appeared in A CHORUS LINE (1985) and elsewhere.

Scott's films include IN THE HEAT OF THE NIGHT and THE WAY WEST (1967), THE BALLAD OF JOSIE aka MEANWHILE BACK AT THE RANCH and THE PARTY (1968), BUTCH CASSIDY AND THE SUNDANCE KID (1969), ONE MORE TRAIN TO ROB and VANISH-ING POINT (1971), WELCOME HOME, SOLDIER BOYS aka FIVE DAYS HOME (1972), LOLLY-MADONNA XXX aka THE LOLLY-MADONNA WAR (1973), MACON COUNTY LINE (1974), THE FARMER and KID VENGEANCE (1977), DAYS OF HEAVEN (1978), THE ELECTRIC HORSEMAN (1979), THE BALLAD OF GRE-GORIO CORTEZ, EUREKA and NIGHTMARES (1983).

Scott died of lung cancer.

Shulman, Irving

born: May 21, 1913, Brooklyn, NY
died: March 23, 1995, Sherman Oaks, CA, age 81
educ: Ohio University; Columbia University; UCLA (Ph.D., English)

Novelist and screenwriter who wrote the story treatment for REBEL WITHOUT A CAUSE.

Irving Shulman made an early name for himself with his first and most successful novel, *The Amboy Dukes* (1947), which he co-adapted into the 1949 film CITY ACROSS THE RIVER. Establishing himself as a street-bred chronicler of gritty urban life, Shulman went on to write 14 more novels, including *The Big Brokers* (1951), *Good Deeds Must Be Punished* (1956) and *The Velvet Knife* (1959), the latter about Hollywood, where he was briefly a contract writer at Warner Bros. Shulman also wrote three biographies; his and Arthur Landau's best-seller *Harlow: An Intimate Biography* (1964) became the basis for the 1965 biopic starring Carroll Baker. Shulman was also a pioneer of novelizations, adapting the WEST SIDE STORY screenplay into a book. As a screenwriter, Shulman's credits include adapting the story "The Blind Run," by Dr. Robert M. Lindner, into the treatment from which Stewart Stern wrote the script to REBEL WITHOUT A CAUSE (1955); oddly, the movie's Academy Award nomination for Best Motion Picture Story went to director Nicho-las Ray. Shulman returned to college late in life to earn a Ph.D. in English, at age 59.

Shulman's films include JOURNEY INTO LIGHT (1951), THE RING, (1952; adapted from his novel *The Square Trap*), CHAMP FOR A DAY (1953), TERROR AT MIDNIGHT (1956; story only), BABY FACE NELSON (1957; story only), CRY TOUGH (1959; original novel basis only), and the Mamie Van Doren cult classic COLLEGE CONFI-DENTIAL (1960).

Shulman died of Alzheimer's disease.

Sinclair, Madge

aka: Madge Dorita Sinclair-Compton
born: April 28, 1938, Kingston, Jamaica, West Indies
died: Dec. 20, 1995, Los Angeles, CA, age 57
educ: Shortwood Teacher Training College, Jamaica

Regal, award-winning actress who provided the voice of queen-mother Sarabi in THE LION KING.

Madge Sinclair spent six years as a teacher in her native Jamaica before moving to New York City at age 30. She performed with the New York Shakespearean Festival and Off-Broadway for several years before making her movie debut in CONRACK (1974). She's appeared often opposite James Earl Jones, playing queen to his king in both the animated hit THE LION KING (1994) and in the Eddie Murphy comedy COMING TO AMERICA (1988); Sinclair also won a supporting-actress Emmy Award playing diner-owner "Empress" Josephine Austin, who married the lead character, played by Jones, on "Gabriel's Fire" and its successor series, "Pros and Cons" (ABC 1990-92). Sinclair appeared in the miniseries "Roots" (ABC 1977), garnering an Emmy nomination, and the series "Grandpa Goes to Washington" (NBC 1978-79), "Trapper John, M.D." (CBS 1979-1986), in which she earned a 1982/83 Emmy nomination playing Nurse Ernestine Shoop, and "Me and the Boys" (ABC 1994); she was also a semi-regular during 1987 on "Ohara" (ABC 1987-88). Other TV works includes the telefilms "The Autobiography of Miss Jane Pittman" (CBS 1974) and Maya Angelou's "I Know Why the Caged Bird Sings" (CBS 1979), and the special "Backwards—The Riddle of Dys-lexia." Among Sinclair's theater performances is *Division Street* at Los Angeles' Mark Taper Forum.

In addition to her Emmy, Sinclair was received two NAACP Image Awards, the Los Angeles Drama Critics' Award and, from the prime minister of Jamaica, The Order of Distinction, Rank of Commander.

Sinclair's films include CORNBREAD, EARL AND ME (1975), I WILL. . . I WILL. . . FOR NOW and LEADBELLY (1976), CONVOY and UNCLE JOE SHANNON (1978), STAR TREK IV: THE VOYAGE

HOME (1986), as Captain of the *Saratoga*, and THE END OF INNO-CENCE (1991).

Sinclair died of leukemia.

Smith, John

born: Robert Earl Van Orden, March 6, 1931, Los Angeles, CA
died: Jan. 25 1995, Los Angeles, CA, age 63

Blond, boyish supporting actor and TV-Western co-star, who legally changed his name at the behest of the agent who helped christen Rock Hudson and Tab Hunter.

He began his career as Robert Van Orden, one of the Bob Mitchell Boys' Choir who sang in the Bing Crosby films GOING MY WAY (1944) and THE BELLS OF ST. MARY'S (1946); he also used his original name to play James Stewart's kid brother in the crime drama/inventor's-biography CARBINE WILLIAMS (1952). He left acting afterward, but, according to legend, was lured back by talent agent Henry Wilson, who suggested the novel name-change. (A young actor named John Smith had already, however, played an unnamed "Boy" in both the film 1950 film A WOMAN OF DISTINCTION and 1951's THE GUY WHO CAME BACK.) Smith gained attention as one of the passengers in the airplane epic THE HIGH AND THE MIGHTY (1954), and subsequently had a recurring role in the 1954-55 season of the sitcom "That's My Boy" (CBS 1954-59). Smith went on to numerous movie supporting parts through the 1950s before landing a co-starring role as Deputy Sheriff Lane Temple in the Western "Cimarron City" (NBC 1958-60), quickly followed by the co-lead role of rancher Slim Sherman in "Laramie" (NBC 1959-63). His more prominent movie roles include the handsome young medical officer who gets the girl in the classic WE'RE NO ANGELS (1955), and the lead in the boxing drama THE CROOKED CIRCLE (1958).

Smith, who was married from 1960 until 1964 to actress Luana Patten, died of cirrhosis of the liver, possibly in conjunction with heart problems.

Sonbert, Warren

born: c. 1948, New York, NY
died: May 31, 1995, San Francisco, CA, age 46 or 47 (sources differ)
educ: New York University

Acclaimed experimental filmmaker.

Warren Sonbert began making films in 1966 while a student at NYU. Most of his 18 shorts, which were generally shown at film festivals, were silent or accompanied by music tracks, and often utilized everyday imagery edited to surreal effect. His 16mm films reflected his interests in travel, classical music and other performing and visual arts, at their best achieving what one critic called "a complex sense of the exotic and the ordinary in life." In 1973, Sonbert's "Carriage Trade" (1968-72) was shown at the Whitney Museum of American Art, and "The Cup and the Lip" was included in the Museum of Modern Art's 1986 Cineprobe series of avant-garde films. His "Honor and Obey" was one of five filmlets screened under the umbrella title "Avant-Garde Voice" at the 1988 New York Film Festival; "Friendly Witness" (32 minutes) played there the following year, and "Short Fuse" (1991; 37 minutes), a montage of rage in the era of AIDS, played in 1992. Sonbert's work is in the permanent collection at MoMA, as well as at the British Film Institute in London and the Vienna Film Museum. He was the subject of retrospectives at the Berlin Film Festival, the Norsk Film Institute in Oslo, Norway, and Anthology Film Archives in New York City. He won a Special Jury Award for Experimental Film at the 1987 San Francisco Film Festival, and a Rockefeller Foundation Fellowship in 1991.

Sonbert moved to San Francisco in the early 1970s; there he taught filmmaking at the San Francisco Art Institute, and wrote reviews of operas and films for publications including the *Bay Area Reporter* and the *San Francisco Sentinel*. His other shorts include "Noblesse Oblige" (1981; 25 minutes).

Sonbert died of complications from AIDS.

Southern, Terry

born: May 1, 1924, Alvarado, TX
died: Oct. 29, 1995, New York, NY, age 71
educ: Southern Methodist University; University of Chicago; Northwestern University (B.A., 1948); The Sorbonne, Paris (1948-50)

Eclectic screenwriter and novelist who co-wrote the screenplays of DR. STRANGELOVE and EASY RIDER, and is one the past and present

cultural icons on the cover of the Beatles album *Sgt. Pepper's Lonely Hearts Club Band*.

Terry Southern, whose gently absurd satirical sense influenced a generation of comic writers, began penning short stories at age 11. He attended high school in Dallas, briefly tried college, then served in the Army from 1943-45 and returned to college on the GI Bill. He went on to study at the Sorbonne, remaining in Paris until 1955. By the end of the 1950s, he'd published three novels: *Flash and Filigree*; *Candy*, an erotic satire co-written (under the pseudonym Maxwell Kenton) with Mason Hoffenberg; and *The Magic Christian*. *Candy* became a U.S. bestseller a few years after its original publication in France, though ironically the authors received no royalties for its sales here since the book hadn't been registered for American copyright. It was eventually adapted by Buck Henry and director Christian Marquand into the all-star fiasco CANDY (Italy-France 1968). Southern himself co-wrote the script to THE MAGIC CHRISTIAN (UK 1969; US release 1970) with collaborators Graham Chapman and John Cleese of "Monty Python's Flying Circus," Peter Sellers, and director Joseph McGrath; it met with mixed response.

By that time, however, Southern was already established as a youth-culture legend both for his books and for two landmark films. The nuclear-age satire DR. STRANGELOVE OR: HOW I LEARNED TO STOP WORRYING AND LOVE THE BOMB (UK 1963), directed by Stanley Kubrick and adapted by Kubrick, Southern and Peter George from George's novel *Red Alert*, is perhaps cinema's finest black comedy. Its skewed-intellectual sensibility did much to bring underground film-making themes and techniques into the commercial mainstream, and STRANGELOVE garnered four Academy Award nominations, among them for Best Picture and Best Adapted Screenplay; it also won the Writers Guild Award for screenplay. Southern was also part of the writing triumvirate on EASY RIDER (1969), for which he shared an original-screenplay Oscar nomination with producer-co-writer Peter Fonda and director-co-writer Dennis Hopper. A critical and commercial phenomenon, EASY RIDER's sex, drugs and rock 'n' roll concerns—in front of and behind the camera—was in many ways the flashpoint between the fading studio factory system and the rise of independent A-movie production.

Though Southern's sensibility went out of fashion in the 1980s, he continued to write for a variety of media. His books include the anthology *Red-Dirt Marijuana and Other Tastes* (1967), and the novels *Blue Movie* (1970) and *Texas Summer* (1992). He was a staff writer, from 1981-82, on the late-night sketch-comedy series "Saturday Night Live," and taught screenwriting through the 1980s and '90s first at New York University and then Columbia University. Southern additionally wrote the text for *Virgin*, a pictorial history of Virgin Records.

Southern's films, often written in collaboration, include THE LOVED ONE and THE CINCINNATI KID (1965), CASINO ROYALE (UK 1967), BARBARELLA (France-Italy 1968), END OF THE ROAD (US; also co-producer) and THE TELEPHONE (1988 direct-to-video). He also worked on a reported 40 or so unproduced screenplays.

Southern, who lived in East Canaan, CT, fell ill on Oct. 25 while on his way to teach at Columbia, and died at a Manhattan hospital four days later of respiratory failure.

Spence, Irv

born: Irven Spence, April 24, 1909
died: Sept. 21, 1995, Dallas, TX, age 86

Animator.

Irv Spence was a high-school newspaper artist alongside fellow student William Hanna, later to become half of animation giant Hanna-Barbera. Spence joined the Charles Mence Studios as an animator, and by the early 1930s was recruited by fabled animation director Ub Iwerks to work on MGM's "Flip the Frog" theatrical-cartoon series. After the undistinguished Flip's demise, Spence moved within the company to work on the complete run of Bill Hanna and Joe Barbera's seven-time Academy Award-winning "Tom & Jerry" shorts. After MGM shuttered its animation department in 1957, Spence spent the next 30 years with Hanna-Barbera Productions, working on such TV cartoon series as "The Flintstones," "The Jetsons," "Yogi Bear" and "Scooby-Doo." Spence also served as an animator on the feature films GAY PURR-EE (1962), THE PHANTOM TOLLBOOTH (1970), and Ralph Bakshi's WIZARDS (1977) and HEY, GOOD LOOKIN' (1982).

Spence died of natural causes.

Squire, Katherine

born: c. 1903, Defiance, OH
died: March 29, 1995, Lake Hill, NY, age 92
educ: Ohio Wesleyan

Longtime actress best known for her prolific theater work.

Katherine Squire made her professional acting debut at the Cleveland Play House, then after attending the American Laboratory Theater made her Broadway debut in the comedy *Goodbye Again* in 1932. Other Broadway credits include *The Traveling Lady* by Horton Foote, and *The Sin of Pat Muldoon.* She co-starred in Tyrone Guthrie's landmark Phoenix Theater production of *Six Characters in Search of an Author* (1955). Among her countless other roles in New York and in regional theater, where she often played leads, Squire appeared in the 1958 Actors Studio production of Sean O'Casey's *Shadow of a Gunman,* and as the mother in the 1961 New York premiere of Arnold Wesker's *Roots.* On television, Squire appeared in several dramas by playwright Foote, as well as in the telefilm "Eric" (NBC 1975) and the soap operas "The Doctors" and "One Life to Live."

In films she often played mothers, including Rita Hayworth's in THE STORY ON PAGE ONE (1959) and Dirk Bogarde's in SONG WITHOUT END (1960). Squire was married to actor George Mitchell, who died in 1972 shortly after playing a memorable role as The Old Man in THE ANDROMEDA STRAIN. The couple appeared together in RIDE IN THE WHIRLWIND (1966) and TWO-LANE BLACKTOP (1971). Squire's other films include STUDS LONIGAN (1960), DAYS OF WINE AND ROSES (1962), THIS SAVAGE LAND aka THE ROAD WEST (1969), LOLLY-MADONNA XXX aka THE LOLLY-MA-DONNA WAR (1973) and WHEN HARRY MET SALLY. . . (1989), as a member of the "Documentary Couples." No cause of death was reported.

Stark, Wilbur

born: Aug. 10, 1922, Brooklyn, NY
died: Aug. 11, 1995, New York, NY, age 83
educ: Manual Training High School; Columbia University

Radio, TV and film producer, and the father of photographer and former soft-porn actress Koo Stark.

Wilbur Stark, who reportedly produced more than 1,500 TV shows, began his career in 1935 at radio station WMCA. In 1946, after having become a leading salesperson there, he left to form a radio production company. In that medium he produced several series, including "Teen Canteen," "Escape With Me" and "Anybody Home?" For early television, he produced such series as "Newsstand Theater" (ABC 1952) and "True Story" (NBC 1957-58), the police/detective series "Crime Without Father" (ABC 1951-52) and "The Brothers Brannagan" (syndicated 1960), the soap opera "Modern Romances" (ABC 1954-58), the daytime variety series "Ladies' Choice" (NBC 1953), and the sitcom "Adventures of Colonel Flack" aka "Colonel Humphrey Flack" aka "Fabulous Fraud" aka "The Impostor" (DuMont 1953-54, syndicated 1958). The bulk of his output was in producing/developing/packaging game shows, including the early, extremely short-lived (three-episode) "Cut" (DuMont 1949; also director), the Dick Clark-hosted "The Object Is" (ABC 1963-64), and the hour-long, primetime "Spin the Picture" (DuMont 1949-50).

Stark's films as producer include the Romy Schneider drama MY LOVER, MY SON (US-UK 1970, partly based on Stark's story "Second Level"), the stylish Hammer horror film VAMPIRE CIRCUS (UK 1972), and, as executive producer, THE THING (1982).

Stark died of cancer.

Stephens, Sir Robert

born: July 14, 1931, Bristol, England
died: Nov. 12, 1995, London, England, age 64

Acclaimed yet self-destructive Shakespearean actor.

Sir Robert Stephens, who was knighted during the last year of his life, was considered the one-time heir to Sir Laurence Olivier, then director of the National Theater, until quarrels led Stephens to leave his associate director post in 1970. His marriage to distinguished actress Maggie Smith, his third wife, likewise disintegrated, due to the alcoholism, adultery, and suicidal tendencies he detailed in his 1995 autobiography, *Knight Errant.* Yet Sir Robert accomplished a triumphant late-life comeback when the Royal Shakespeare Company invited the half-forgotten

actor to play Falstaff in its 1991-92 productions of both parts of *Henry IV,* and, two years later, the title role in *King Lear.*

After a poor and violence-scarred childhood, Stephens, a laborer's son, became involved in amateur theatricals and eventually won a scholarship to a drama school in Yorkshire. In 1956, after doing provincial repertory work, he joined the fledgling English Stage Company, the troupe which helped revitalize and shock British theater with its production of John Osborne's *Look Back in Anger.* Though Stephens did not appear in that play, he won a role in Osborne's The Entertainer, and understudied mentor-to-be Olivier in the title role. Stephens' first major success came with *Epitaph for George Dillon* (1958) by Osborne and Anthony Creighton; though the subsequent Broadway version flopped, Stephens received warm reviews. In 1963, Olivier invited him to join the new National Theater Company, where Stephens established himself as one of his generation's leading actors. On film, Stephens starred with Maggie Smith starred in THE PRIME OF MISS JEAN BRODIE (UK 1969) and TRAVELS WITH MY AUNT (1972). They were married in 1967, broke up in 1973, and formally divorced two or three years later.

Stephens' movie career was less eminent than his stage work, if equally long-lived. He debuted in a small role in WAR AND PEACE (US-Italy 1956), and later co-starred with Vanessa Redgrave and David Warner as one-third of the romantic triangle in MORGAN: A SUITABLE CASE FOR TREATMENT aka MORGAN! (UK 1966). Playing the title role in Billy Wilder's revisionist comedy-mystery THE PRIVATE LIFE OF SHERLOCK HOLMES (US-UK 1970), a box-office disaster, did not transfer his ascendant star from theater to film, and its failure drove the troubled Stephens to attempt suicide. His many problems led him on a downward spiral of bit parts until his professional and personal recovery in the '90s. He won a 1992 Olivier Award, the British equivalent of the Tony, and married fourth wife Patricia Quinn, an actress best known as Magenta in THE ROCKY HORROR PICTURE SHOW (1975). Stephens had four children; his two sons by Smith, Toby and Christopher, are actors.

Stephens died after having undergone a liver and kidney transplant, and suffering organ-rejection problems.

Stewart, Douglas

born: Samuel Douglas Stewart, c. 1919
died: March 3, 1995, Los Angeles, CA, age 75

Oscar-winning film editor.

Douglas Stewart broke into feature-film editing with THE HITCH-HIKER (1953), and subsequently cut 15 more features over the next 30 years. He shared an Oscar with four other editors on his last film, Philip Kaufman's THE RIGHT STUFF (1983); he'd previously edited INVASION OF THE BODY SNATCHERS (1978) for Kaufman. Among Stewart's best work is John Wayne's last film, THE SHOOTIST (1976), an elegiac summing-up of a gunfighter's, and an actor's, career.

Stewart's films include EIGHTEEN AND ANXIOUS aka NO GREATER SIN (1957), GIRL IN THE WOODS (1958), NIGHTMARE IN THE SUN (1964; co-editor), GAMES (1967), Elvis Presley's CHANGE OF HABIT (1969), THE GREAT NORTHFIELD, MINNESOTA RAID (1972), THE WHITE DAWN (1974), TELEFON (1977), WALK PROUD aka GANG (1979), ROUGH CUT (UK 1980), FAST-WALKING and JINXED! (1982).

Stewart died of Parkinson's disease.

Stone, Christopher

born: Oct. 4, 1940, Manchester, NH
died: Oct. 29, 1995, Los Angeles, CA, age 55

Highly prolific TV actor who appeared in a number of films.

Christopher Stone began as a contract player at Screen Gems, which eventually merged into Columbia Television. His TV debut was a 1968 episode of "The Outcasts." Stone then made three appearances on "Here Come the Brides" and one on "The Mod Squad" before co-starring in the ensemble drama "The Interns" (CBS 1970-71). Stone also starred in the series "Spencer's Pilots" (CBS 1976) and, with actress wife Dee Wallace Stone in the "The New Lassie" (syndicated; 48 episodes produced 1989-91), on which he was also a director. Stone also appeared in the pilot "Wheeler and Murdoch" (ABC 1973). He appeared with Dee Wallace in three films: THE HOWLING (1981), CUJO (1983), and LEGEND OF THE WHITE HORSE (made 1985, released 1991).

Stone, not to be confused with movie composer Christopher L. Stone, also appeared in several other films, including THE GRASSHOPPER and THE NOTORIOUS CLEOPATRA (1970), LOVE ME DEADLY (1972), THE JUNKMAN (1982) and THE ANNIHILATORS (1985).

Stone died of a heart attack.

Stoneburner, Sam

born: c. 1929, Virginia
died: Nov. 29, 1995, New York, NY, age 66
educ: Georgetown University; American Academy of Dramatic Arts

Actor.

The gentlemanly Sam Stoneburner made his Broadway debut in *Different Times*, and returned to Broadway in *Bent*; the 1981 Lincoln Center production of *Macbeth*; the musical *The First* (1981), and in both the 1990 Broadway and 1993 film versions of John Guare's *Six Degrees of Separation* (1990). He additionally appeared in the national and Broadway companies of *Annie*. TV roles include the part of Soames on the ABC soap opera "Loving." In film, Stoneburner had small roles in TOOTSIE (1982), MOSCOW ON THE HUDSON (1984), STEPHEN KING'S SILVER BULLET (1985), 84 CHARING CROSS ROAD and WEEDS (1987), and JFK (1991) and LOVE HURTS (1992).

Stoneburner died of esophageal cancer.

Sutton, Grady

born: Grady Harwell Sutton, April 5, 1908 or 1906, Chattanooga, TN
died: Sept. 17, 1995, Woodland Hills, CA, age 87 or 89

Character comedian and a favorite W.C. Fields foil, who appeared in at least 123 features and countless comedy shorts, TV shows and commercials.

Grady Sutton's chubby jowls, drawling manner, flabby frame and desire—usually vain—to keep dignity intact made him a classic comic patsy. After he came to California on vacation in 1924, director-friend William Seiter offered him film work, and soon Sutton was appearing in shorts by producers Mack Sennett and Hal Roach; among his typical roles was the haplessly clueless Alabam' in director George Stevens' early-1930s comedy-short series "The Boy Friends." Sutton made his feature debut with a bit part in THE MAD WHIRL (1925).

Sutton met Fields when they appeared together in the Sennett short "The Pharmacist" (1933); afterward, Fields insisted Sutton appear in all his films. Sutton played Fields' smarmy stepson in THE MAN ON THE FLYING TRAPEZE aka in Britain THE MEMORY EXPERT (1935), circus hand Chester Dalrymple in YOU CAN'T CHEAT AN HONEST MAN (1939) and, most memorably, as queasy future son-in-law Og Oggilby in THE BANK DICK aka in Britain THE BANK DETECTIVE (1940). Playing male secretaries, expectant fathers, comic tipplers and tradesman, Sutton gave comic support to—or stole scenes from—the likes of Harold Lloyd, Laurel and Hardy, Katharine Hepburn, Carole Lombard and Elvis Presley. One of his earliest roles was a bit part in Lloyd's THE FRESHMAN (1925); he later appeared in Lloyd's MOVIE CRAZY (1932), in the role of Man Afraid of Mice. Sutton appeared with Laurel and Hardy in PACK UP YOUR TROUBLES (1932), reluctantly stepped on Hepburn's foot for a dance scene in ALICE ADAMS (1935)—prompting the star to send him the note, "Dearest Grady, you can dance with me anytime"—and played the befuddled rich collegian, Charlie Van Rumple, whom Carole Lombard teases in MY MAN GODFREY (1936). He also played Cedric Weehunt in three of the six films based on the popular "Lum 'n' Abner" radio series: THE BASHFUL BACHELOR (1942), GOIN' TO TOWN (1944), and PARTNERS IN TIME (1946), and played roles in the Elvis movies TICKLE ME (1965) and PARADISE, HAWAIIAN STYLE (1966). All told, by one count, Sutton appeared in more than 180 features and shorts. On television, he played Sturgis the butler in the sitcom "The Pruitts of Southampton" (ABC 1966-67), and guested on "The Odd Couple" and many other series. Sutton retired from films in 1971, but came back to play the School Board President in the cult hit ROCK 'N' ROLL HIGH SCHOOL (1979). A generation who may not otherwise have seen him was exposed to Sutton, playing a comic-relief ranch-hand, in TV's "Mystery Science Theater 3000" screening of LAST OF THE WILD HORSES (1948).

Sutton died of natural causes.

Sylvester, William

born: Jan. 31, 1922, Oakland, CA
died: Jan. 25, 1995

American actor mostly seen in British films.

William Sylvester, best known as the diplomat-scientist Dr. Heywood Floyd in 2001: A SPACE ODYSSEY (US-UK 1968), also co-starred as spy-agency boss Leonard Driscoll in the present-day science-fiction series "Gemini Man" (NBC 1976). He made his film debut in GIVE US THIS DAY aka SALT TO THE DEVIL (UK 1950), and often played the lead role in British programmers, such as THE STRANGER CAME HOME aka THE UNHOLY FOUR (UK 1954) and OFFBEAT aka THE DEVIL INSIDE (UK 1960, US release 1961).

Tedrow, Irene

born: Aug. 3, 1907, Denver, CO
died: March 10, 1995, age 87

Actress active in radio, film and TV.

Irene Tedrow played a host of minor Mrs. roles in the course of 24 films across four decades. A noted radio performer, she gained fame in that medium as mom Janet Archer on the popular "Meet Corliss Archer" (CBS radio, 1943 through the early 1950s). Tedrow came to TV as early as 1949, when for a couple of months she was the first of two actresses to co-star as housewife Margaret on the sitcom "The Ruggles" (ABC 1949-52). In 1952, Tedrow was the second of three actresses to play Janet Archer on "Meet Corliss Archer" (CBS 1951-52, syndicated 1954-55). She also played the recurring roles of Mrs. Elkins on "Dennis the Menace" (CBS 1959-63) and teacher Mrs. Ring in some 1965 episodes of "Mr. Novak" (NBC 1963-65). She garnered a 1977/78 Emmy Award nomination as Outstanding Lead Actress for a Single Appearance in a Drama or Comedy Series, for her guest role on "James at 15."

Tedrow's films include THE MOON AND SIXPENCE (1942), SONG OF THE OPEN ROAD (1944), UNCLE HARRY aka THE STRANGE AFFAIR OF UNCLE HARRY (1945), JUST BEFORE DAWN (1946), THEY WON'T BELIEVE ME (1947), AIR HOSTESS and THIEVES' HIGHWAY (1949), THE COMPANY SHE KEEPS (1950), A LION IS IN THE STREETS aka A LION IN THE STREETS (1953), SANTA FE PASSAGE (1955), THE TEN COMMANDMENTS (1956), LOVING YOU (1957), HOT SPELL and SADDLE THE WIND (1958), PLEASE DON'T EAT THE DAISIES (1960), A THUNDER OF DRUMS (1961), DEADLY DUO (1962), THE CINCINNATI KID (1965), FOR PETE'S SAKE! (1966), GETTING STRAIGHT (1970), MANDINGO (1975), EMPIRE OF THE ANTS (1977), FOUL PLAY (1978) and MIDNIGHT MADNESS (1980).

Tedrow died of complications from a stroke.

Thomas, Rachel

born: Feb. 9, 1905, Wales
died: Feb. 9, 1995, Cardiff, Wales, age 90

Welsh character actress.

Rachel Thomas, who specialized in playing fiery Welsh matrons, made her film debut in THE PROUD VALLEY (UK 1940, US release 1941), starring Paul Robeson. Her final film released here, the U.S. independent HAPPY AS THE GRASS WAS GREEN (1973), was re-released in 1978 as HAZEL'S PEOPLE. Thomas' films include UNDERCOVER aka UNDERGROUND GUERRILLAS aka CHETNIK (UK 1943, US release 1944), THE HALF-WAY HOUSE (UK 1943 or 1944, US release 1945), THE CAPTIVE HEART (UK 1946), BLUE SCAR (UK; US release 1949), VALLEY OF SONG aka MEN ARE CHILDREN TWICE (UK; US release 1953), TIGER BAY (1959), CATACOMBS aka THE WOMAN WHO WOULDN'T DIE (UK 1965), SKY WEST AND CROOKED aka GYPSY GIRL (UK 1966) and UNDER MILK WOOD (UK 1973).

Thomas, who had been ill for an extended time following a fall, died on her 90th birthday.

Thomas, Ross

born: c. 1926, Oklahoma City, OK
died: Dec. 18, 1995, Santa Monica, CA, age 69
educ: University of Oklahoma, Norman, OK (B.A. English, 1949)

Novelist and screenwriter.

Ross Thomas, who also wrote under the pseudonym Oliver Bleeck, turned his career as foreign correspondent and government spokesperson into the basis for stylish political thrillers. His many novels include *The Cold War Swap* (1965), a CIA story that won the Mystery Writers of America's Edgar Award for best first novel, as well as *Cast a Yellow Shadow* (1967), *The Porkchoppers* (1972), and *Briarpatch* (1985), which won that year's Edgar for best mystery novel. As Bleeck, Thomas wrote novels featuring professional go-between Philip St. Ives; one of them, *The Procane Chronicle*, was the basis for the Charles Bronson film ST. IVES (1976). As a screenwriter, Thomas and Dennis O'Flaherty co-wrote the adapted screenplay to Wim Wenders's HAMMETT (1982). Thomas also wrote the story treatment for BOUND BY HONOR aka BLOOD IN, BLOOD OUT (1993) and the screenplay to BAD COMPANY (1995).

Thomas, who lived in Malibu, died of cancer.

Tobin, Genevieve

aka: Genevieve Tobin Keighley
born: Nov. 29, 1901, New York, NY
died: July 31, 1995, Los Angeles, CA, age 93

Perky, attractive blond actress of the 1930s, who in both comedies and melodramas often played either a divorcing wife or the reason for another wife's divorce.

Tobin, who was in real life married to director William Keighley from 1938 until his death in 1972, began her career on stage as a child actress. After her education in New York and Paris, she opened in the Broadway musical *Oh, Look!* (1918); in 1920, she appeared in *Little Old New York*, in which she then played on the road for more than two years. Tobin also appeared in Cole Porter's *Fifty Million Frenchmen*, and made her film debut in the silent NO MOTHER TO GUIDE HER (1923).

Tobin remained primarily a stage actress before signing on as a contract player with Universal and making her sound-film debut in A LADY SURRENDERS aka in Britain BLIND WIVES (1930). In a prolific decade of playing married women, tootsies, and married tootsies, she cheated onscreen with Maurice Chevalier in ONE HOUR WITH YOU (1932), wouldn't give Edward G. Robinson a divorce in I LOVED A WOMAN (1933), left Robinson for his gambling in DARK HAZARD (1934), was the bimbo creation of beauty-clinic doctor Cary Grant in KISS AND MAKE UP (1934), and was the rich wife among Humphrey Bogart's hostages in THE PETRIFIED FOREST (1936). Keighley directed her in three comedies: EASY TO LOVE (1934), in which she starred opposite Adolphe Menjou; the controversial proto-sex-romp YES, MY DARLING DAUGHTER (1939), in which Tobin played support; and her final film, NO TIME FOR COMEDY aka GUY WITH A GRIN (1940), in which she co-starred as the other woman who tries to come between Jimmy Stewart and Roz Russell. Tobin and Keighley later moved to Paris, where they lived for many years.

Tobin died of natural causes.

Toeplitz, Jerzy

born: c. 1910, Kharkov, Ukraine
died: July 24, 1995, Warsaw, Poland, age 85
educ: University of Warsaw

Film historian and film-school founder

Jerzy Toeplitz co-founded and was the first director (1949-1952, returning 1957-68) of the highly regarded Lodz Film School; among its students during that time were future directors Roman Polanski, Andrzej Wajda and Jerzy Skolimowski. Toeplitz had previously worked at the newly founded Film Polski during the mid-1940s. He was forced leave his Lodz position in 1968, reportedly because of anti-Semitism, and subsequently became the first director of the Australian Film, Television and Radio School, in Sydney, serving from 1973 until his retirement in 1979. Toeplitz also wrote several books, including *Hollywood and After*, the six-volume *History of Cinematographic Art*, and, as co-author, *The History of Polish Film*.

No cause of death was reported.

Tony, Azito

born: New York City
died: May 26, 1995, New York, NY, age 46

Stage and occasional movie actor, who reprised onscreen his Tony Award-nominated role as the Sergeant in the New York Shakespeare Festival's 1981 operetta revival The Pirates of Penzance. Aside from that 1983 film adaptation, his movies include UNION CITY, PRIVATE RESORT, MOONSTRUCK, BLOODHOUNDS OF BROADWAY and THE ADDAMS FAMILY. His TV guest work included "Miami Vice."

Azito died of complications from AIDS.

Totten, Robert

born: Feb. 5, 1937, Los Angeles, CA
died: Jan. 27, 1995, Sherman Oaks, CA, age 57

Film and television writer-director and sometime actor, who specialized in Westerns.

Robert Totten first gained attention with the low-budget WWII drama THE QUICK AND THE DEAD (1963), on which he was director, co-writer, and possibly art designer: the credit for the latter reads "Totten, O.R.C." His solidly shot, $100,000 independent feature netted him a six-month contract at Warner Bros., where he directed episodes of the TV series "Hawaiian Eye" and "77 Sunset Strip," and was second-unit director on SPENCER'S MOUNTAIN (1963) and YOUNGBLOOD HAWKE (1964). Totten, who'd debuted in films as an actor in the psychological-horror film TRAUMA (1962), went on to direct many TV series.

Totten's films include, as director, RIDE A NORTHBOUND HORSE (1969), THE WILD COUNTRY aka THE NEWCOMERS (1971) and PONY EXPRESS RIDER (1976), and, as actor, THE APPLE DUMPLING GANG RIDES AGAIN (1979). Totten also directed half of DEATH OF A GUNFIGHTER (1969), before being let go at the behest of star Richard Widmark and replaced by Don Siegel.

Totten died of a heart attack.

Tsui, Jeannette Lin

See under "L"

Turner, Lana

born: Julia Jean Mildred Frances Turner, Feb. 8, 1920, Wallace, ID
died: June 29, 1995, Los Angeles, CA, age 75

Screen legend.

Lana Turner—an MGM glamor queen whose sultry, smoldering image obviated her thespian shortcomings—enjoyed and endured a life of glitter and grief surpassing those of her movie-melodrama characters. Her life included eight marriages to seven men; the murder of her reputed-mobster boyfriend by her teenaged daughter; a suicide attempt; two abortions and three stillbirths; alcoholism, and a 1980 religious awakening. She also starred opposite the cream of Hollywood leading men, was one of MGM's biggest stars, appeared in some legendary films, and was nominated for an Academy Award for her role in PEYTON PLACE (1957).

Myth has it that Turner was discovered in 1936 by a talent scout who noticed her at Schwab's Drug Store, later a world-famous LA mecca for would-be starlets. She was in fact spotted by *Hollywood Reporter* publisher W.R. "Billy" Wilkerson at either Currie's ice cream parlor or at the Top Hat Cafe (per Turner's memoirs)—in either case, across from Hollywood High School—while cutting a secretarial class. Wilkerson's recommendation led to her being signed by a talent agency run by the famed Zeppo Marx, and introduced to producer-director Mervyn LeRoy. Her studio sobriquet was "The Sweater Girl,"and the well-shaped Turner wore a memorable one as the sultry, soda-sipping high schooler in her first credited film, LeRoy's THEY WON'T FORGET (1937). She had previously appeared, unbilled, as a featured extra in 1934's A STAR IS BORN, as one of two women at the Santa Anita racetrack. It was LeRoy who suggested she change her name, though Turner herself chose "Lana."

Turner was the daughter an initerant father, John Turner, who was found dead of a fractured skull while in San Francisco, and Mildred Cowan Turner. After appearing in LeRoy's THE GREAT GARRICK (1937), Turner joined Leroy when he jumped from Warner Bros. to MGM—her home studio for the next 17 years. There she was given bigger and bigger roles as she was groomed for stardom. Though her one scene in THE CHASER (1938) was left on the cutting-room floor (except for a brief shot of her sitting with legs provocatively crossed in a lawyer's waiting room), she had a major supporting role in the LeRoy-produced DRAMATIC SCHOOL (1938), a co-leading role (with Lew Ayres) in the seriocomedy THESE GLAMOUR GIRLS (1939), and her first starring role in the musical comedy DANCING CO-ED aka in Britain EVERY OTHER INCH A LADY (1939). Also appearing in DANCING CO-ED was bandleader Artie Shaw; he and Turner were married in 1940, separating after about seven months and divorcing in 1942.

Turner went on to star in such prominent films as ZIEGFELD GIRL (1941), making a well-received dramatic breakthrough playing a forlorn, consumptive showgirl; HONKY TONK (1941), the first of four films she did with Clark Gable (after having flunked a screen test with him in 1938);

SOMEWHERE I'LL FIND YOU (1942), also with Gable; director LeRoy's JOHNNY EAGER (1942), IMITATION OF LIFE (1959) and, in arguably her two greatest performances as an actress rather than a star, THE POSTMAN ALWAYS RINGS TWICE (1946), with John Garfield, and director Vincente Minnelli's THE BAD AND THE BEAUTIFUL (1952), starring Turner, Kirk Douglas and Dick Powell. Turner's remake of MADAME X (1966) was a production of her short-lived independent company, Eltee.

In the public eye from the time she was dubbed "Queen of the Nightclubs" in the late 1930s, Turner had a highly publicized affair with lawyer Greg Bautzer while married to Shaw, and a romantic relationship with billionaire Howard Hughes. Her other marriages were to actor-turned-restaurateur Stephen Crane in 1943 (with an annulment soon after and a short remarriage weeks later); playboy millionaire and sportsman Henry J. "Bob" Topping (948-1952); movie Tarzan Lex Barker (1953-1957); hotelier and rancher Fred May (1960-1962); producer and businessperson Robert P. Eaton (1965-1969), and nightclub hypnotist Ronald Dante (1969-1972). Among the many men with whom she was romantically linked were actor Fernando Lamas, singer Tony Martin, and Johnny Stompanto, whom Turner met under his alias John Steele. On April 4, 1958, during a violent argument at Turner's home in which he reportedly threatened to disfigure the star, Stompanto was knifed to death by Turner's daughter Cheryl Crane (b. July 1943); a jury exonerated Crane with a finding of justifiable homicide. Crane wrote of the events in her own memoir, *Detour*, in which she also accused Barker of molesting her. Turner's rocky relationship with her daughter, now a real-estate agent, eventually found reconciliation.

Turner continued to make films through the 1970s, then wrote her memoir, *Lana: The Lady, the Legend, the Truth* (1982). She starred as Tracy Carlyle Hastings in the TV series "Harold Robbins' The Survivors" (ABC 1969-70), a flop prime-time soap, and the recurring role of Jacqueline Perrault, mother of good-guy Chase Gioberti (Robert Foxworth), in several 1982-83 episodes of "Falcon Crest" (CBS 1981-90). She'd made her TV debut playing herself in the 1956 "Climax" production "The Louella Parsons Story," later appearing in the occasional Bob Hope or Circus of the Stars special, as well as on "The Smothers Brothers Comedy Hour" in 1967, and in the 1985 "The Love Boat" episode "Call Me Grandma." She also toured in stage works, including *Forty Carats* (1971), *Legendary Ladies,* and *The Pleasure of His Company*.

Turner died of throat cancer, after years of treatment for the disease.

Urquhart, Robert

born: 1922
died: March, 1995
Scottish character actor.

Robert Urquhart debuted in films with YOU'RE ONLY YOUNG TWICE (UK 1951, US 1952) after having begun his career onstage. His handful of lead roles include a homicidal writer in YOU CAN'T ESCAPE (UK 1955), and one of two brothers leading settlers through Africa in GOLDEN IVORY aka WHITE HUNTRESS (UK 1957). He was also prominent as a headmaster in both P'TANG, YANG, KIPPERBANG aka KIPPERBANG (1982 UK telefilm; US theatrical release 1984) and PLAYING AWAY (UK; US release 1986). Urquhart was a cast-member of the British TV series "The Pathfinders" (1972) and "The Amazing Mr. Goodall" (1974).

No cause of death was available.

Vasquez, Joseph B.

born: c. 1962, New York, NY
died: Dec. 16, 1995, Chula Vista, CA, age 33
educ: City University of New York
Promising young independent filmmaker whose HANGIN' WITH THE HOMEBOYS won the screenwriting award at the 1991 Sundance Film Festival.

Joseph B. Vasquez earned a film degree at CUNY and went on to make three low-budget films that focus on violence-scarred Bronx minority youths. STREET STORY, which he produced, directed, wrote, shot and edited, was seen primarily at festivals in 1988. He next wrote, directed and starred in THE BRONX WAR, made in 1989 and released direct-to-video in 1992, after the success of his critically lauded HANGIN' WITH THE HOMEBOYS (1991; writer-director), a $2 million sleeper reportedly written in just three days and shot in 30. At the time of his death,

Vasquez had recently completed work on the film MANHATTAN MERENGUE.

Vasquez, who lived in Hollywood, died of complications from AIDS.

Venuta, Benay

born: Benvenuta Rose Crooke, 1911, San Francisco, CA
died: Sept. 1, 1995, New York, NY, age 84
Actress-singer.

Benay Venuta, who had a New York theater career stretching across more than 50 years, dropped out of a Geneva finishing school and returned to the US to discover her family impoverished by the Depression. Her father dead, she performed in nightclubs, on radio, and as a dancer to help support her family. Venuta's break came in 1935, when, as a virtual unknown, she succeeded Ethel Merman in Cole Porter's Broadway musical *Anything Goes*. She went on to leading roles in Broadway shows including *By Jupiter, Nellie Bly, Hazel Flagg, Kiss the Boys Goodbye,* and *Copper and Brass*. Benuta also played much stock and regional theater, and appeared in Lincoln Center revivals of *Carousel* and *Annie Get Your Gun*; she also appeared, as Dolly Tate, in the 1950 film version of the latter. Venuta painted and made Plexiglas sculptures; during the 1970s, her sculptures were sold at Bonwit Teller in Manhattan.

Venuta's films include REPEAT PERFORMANCE (1947), EASTER PARADE and I, JANE DOE aka in Britain DIARY OF A BRIDE (1948), CALL ME MISTER (1951), STARS AND STRIPES FOREVER aka in Britain MARCHING ALONG (1952), RICOCHET ROMANCE (1954), and THE FUZZY PINK NIGHTGOWN (1957). Venuta died of lung cancer.

Visconti, Empirando

born: c. 1933
died: May 26, 1995, Pavia, Italy, age 62
Director-screenwriter nephew of filmmaker Luchino Visconti. Empirando Visconti came into the film industry as assistant director on his uncle's segment of the anthology film SIAMO DONNE/WE THE WOMEN (Italy 1952; in US, added to another film, 1953's QUESTA E LA VITA/OF LIFE AND LOVE). The younger Visconti also assisted directors Luciano Emmer and Renato Castellani before debuting as a screenwriter on Franceso Maselli's GLI SBANDATI (Italy 1955). His first feature as director was UNA STORIA MILANESE (Italy 1962). Generally regarded as an adequate filmmaker unable to break free from his uncle's shadow, Empirando Visconti wrote and-or directed nine features, including UNA STORIA LOMBARDA aka LA MONICA DI MONZA/THE LADY OF MONZA aka THE NUN OF MONZA (Italy 1969; US release 1970), starring American actress Anne Heywood, and the well-regarded MALAMORE (Italy 1982), his last film.

Visconti died of pulmonary emphysema.

Wallach, Ira

born: c. 1912-13, New York, NY; raised New Rochelle, NY
died: Dec. 2, 1995, New York, NY, age 82 or 83
Versatile comic writer-screenwriter.

Ira Wallach briefly attended Cornell University, then later worked in the potash industry in what was then Palestine, and rose to the rank of US Army sergeant during his WWII service in the Pacific. Though his first book, *The Horn and the Rose* (1947) was a serious novel, he became a satirist and a clever comic observer of popular trends. His best-known novel, *Muscle Beach* (1959), was a humorous tale about the Southern California body-building cult; he co-adapted it into the film DON'T MAKE WAVES (1967; not to be confused with the unrelated 1964 film MUSCLE BEACH PARTY). Wallach's other books include the sendups *How to Be Deliriously Happy* (1950), *Hopalong-Freud* (1951), *Hopalong-Freud Rides Again* (1952) and *Gutenberg's Folly* (1954) and the comic novel *Absence of a Cello* (1960), which was adapted into a 1964 Off-Broadway play. Wallach also contributed sketches to Broadway revues; co-wrote the Broadway comedy *Drink to Me Only* (1958), wrote the book for the Off-Broadway musical *Smiling, the Boy Fell Dead* (1961) and both book and lyrics for *Kaboom!* (1974).

Wallach's films include BOYS' NIGHT OUT (1962; co-writer), THE WHEELER DEALERS aka in Britain SEPARATE BEDS (1963; co-writer), and HOT MILLIONS (UK 1968), for which Wallach and Peter Ustinov shared an Academy Award nomination for Original Screenplay, and won the Writers' Guild of Great Britain's award for comedy screenplay.

Wallach died of pneumonia.

Warner, Jack M.

born: c. 1915
died: April 1, 1995, Los Angeles, CA, age 79
educ: University of Southern California

Producer and studio-executive son of Warner Bros. co-founder Jack L. Warner (1892-1978).

Jack M. Warner joined the Warner short-subject department after college, and moved to the studio's distribution company after WWII. He personally produced a small number of films including the United Artists film THE ADMIRAL WAS A LADY and Fox's THE MAN WHO CHEATED HIMSELF (both 1950). In 1958, after a falling-out with his father over the latter's divorce and remarriage, Jack M. Warner coldly learned from the trade papers that his father had fired him. These and other events informed his novel *Bijou Dream*.

Jack M. Warner, not to be confused with the British actor Jack Warner, died of cancer of the lymph nodes.

Waterman, Willard

born: c. 1914, Madison, WI
died: Feb. 2, 1995, Burlingame, CA, age 80

Actor and radio star.

Willard Waterman studied electrical engineering at the University of Wisconsin, where he appeared in college theater and radio productions before dropping out to pursue acting. He quickly became busy in 1930s-'40s radio productions, and performed on such popular series as "Amos 'n' Andy," "The Guiding Light," "Little Orphan Annie," "Lux Radio Theater," and "The Real McCoys." He succeeded Hal Peary as the pompous and humorously blustery politician Throckmorton P. Gildersleeve on radio's "The Great Gildersleeve" (1941 through the 1950s). Waterman continued on in the role in the TV sitcom version (syndicated 1955-56). He also played the recurring role of Mr. Quigley on "Dennis the Menace" (CBS 1959-63). He played Mr. Upton in the movie comedy AUNTIE MAME (1958) and played small but pungent supporting roles in a host of films including FATHER OF THE BRIDE (1950), THREE COINS IN THE FOUNTAIN (1954), Martin and Lewis' HOLLYWOOD OR BUST (1956) and THE APARTMENT (1960).

Waterman died of bone marrow disease.

Wayne, David

born: Wayne James McMeekan, Jan. 30, 1914, Traverse City, MI
died: Feb. 9, 1995, Santa Monica, CA, age 81

Elfin, highly respected character actor, and winner of one of the first Tony Awards for acting.

David Wayne, the son of an insurance executive, lost his mother when he was four years old. Raised by close family friends, he eventually spent two years at Western Michigan University in nearby Kalamazoo, before moving to Cleveland and working briefly as a statistician. He joined Cleveland's famed Shakespearean repertory company in 1936, making his professional debut in *As You Like It*. He moved to New York City in 1938, landed a small role in *The American Way* (1939), and married actress Jane Gordon two years later. Rejected for WWII Army service, he volunteered to serve as an ambulance driver in North Africa with the American Field Service.

Two years after his discharge, he debuted on Broadway as the leprechaun, Og, in *Finian's Rainbow* (1947). The role won him the inaugural Tony Award for supporting actor in a musical. In 1948, he played Ensign Pulver in another critical and commercial hit, *Mister Roberts*, starring Henry Fonda. Wayne won critical praise for major roles in such productions as *The Ponder Heart* and *The Loud Red Patrick* (both 1956), and starring roles in *Teahouse of the August Moon*, for which he earned a 1956 Tony Award as lead actor in a drama, playing the wily Sakini, *Say Darling* (1958), *Send Me No Flowers* (1960), *Too Good To Be True* (1963) and *The Happy Time*, for which he earned a 1967 Tony nomination as lead actor in a musical. For the Lincoln Center Repertory Company, he appeared in *After the Fall*, *Marco's Millions*, *But for Whom Charlie* and *Incident at Vichy*.

Wayne made his movie debut in 1948 with PORTRAIT OF JENNIE aka TIDAL WAVE a.k.a in Britain JENNIE, and his television bow the

same year, with the "Theater Guild Television Playhouse" production of "Great Catherine" (NBC 5/2/48) and the "Actors' Studio" production of "The Thousand Dollar Bill" (CBS 10/17/48). He starred or co-starred in several TV series and was nominated for a guest-actor Emmy Award for a 1957 episode of NBC's "Suspicion."

Alternating for the most part between third-billed support and character leads, Wayne twice played Marilyn Monroe's screen love—her husband in WE'RE NOT MARRIED (1952), her suitor in HOW TO MARRY A MILLIONAIRE (1953)—and was Joanne Woodward's insensitive husband opposite her Academy Award-winning performance in THE THREE FACES OF EVE (1957). He was a solid, highly effective lead in both dramas and comedies alike, including Joseph Losey's well-regarded remake of M (1951), the sentimental drama WAIT TILL THE SUN SHINES, NELLIE (1952), and (with Tom Ewell) the military buddy-comedy hit UP FRONT (1951).

Wayne, whose wife died in 1993, died of lung cancer.

Welsh, Patricia

born: c. 1915
died: Jan. 26, 1995, Tucson, AZ, age 79

One-time San Francisco radio soap-opera star who was the primary provider of the title character's voice in E.T. THE EXTRA-TERRESTRIAL (1982).

The gravel-voiced Welsh, who uttered the famous phrases "E.T. phone home" and "Be good," went uncredited in the film at the behest of director Steven Spielberg. She was additionally sworn to secrecy during the movie's theatrical run, and ordered not to casually mention the famous words, which she was paid to dub in English, Spanish, French and German. Two other people, as well as a sea otter and a dog, provided various aspects of E.T.'s voice. Welsh, who lived in Green Valley, AZ, died of pneumonia at a Tucson hospital.

White, Slappy

born: Melvin White, c. 1921, Baltimore, MD
died: Nov. 7 or Nov. 8, 1995, Brigantine, NJ, age 74

Comedian.

Slappy White was a pioneering African-American comedian, who in the 1950s, with such colleagues as Nipsey Russell and Redd Foxx, helped bridge the gap between the "chitlin' circuit" of predominantly black nightclubs and what was then the predominantly white mainstream. In doing so, he significantly helped to integrate both the clubs and the culture; indeed, his signature bit used a white glove and a black glove to promote racial harmony.

White began his career by dancing on the street for coins; he was often partnered with Foxx, with whom he later had a two-man comedy act in the '50s. Working the chitlin' circuit, he opened for such stars as singer Dinah Washington; later, as African-American humor moved into the mainstream, White became a regular in Las Vegas, performing frequently in the 1960s with the likes of Dean Martin. He later appeared often in TV specials and celebrity roasts. White played the recurring role of Melvin during 1972 on Foxx's "Sanford and Son" (NBC 1972-76) and was a semi-regular on the comedy-variety series "Redd Foxx" (ABC 1977-78); he co-starred with Foxx on the sitcom pilot "My Buddy" (NBC 1979), and played talent agent Benjamin White in the regular cast of the Martin Short-William Allen Young pilot about an interracial comedy team, "White and Reno" (NBC 1981). He was an Honor Board Member of the National Comedy Hall of Fame.

White's films include THE MAN FROM O.R.G.Y., aka THE REAL GONE GIRLS (1970), AMAZING GRACE (1974), and MR. SATURDAY NIGHT (1992).

White died of a heart attack at his home.

Whitney, John Sr.

aka: John Whitney
born: April 8, 1917, Altadena, CA
died: Sept. 22, 1995, age 78
educ: Pomona College, Claremont, CA

Legendary experimental filmmaker, widely regarded as "the father of computer graphics."

John Whitney Sr. melded art, music and technology into a new and integrated discipline. His pioneering explorations and abstract films established many of the principles of motion-control computer techniques now used routinely in movie production, and he influenced a generation of filmmakers; Whitney's "slit-scan" technique helped make possible Douglas Trumbull's "stargate" sequence in 2001: A SPACE ODYSSEY. Whitney's own commercial applications included collaborating with Saul Bass on the titles to Hitchcock's VERTIGO (1958).

Whitney's multifaceted childhood interests led to his making rudimentary 8mm abstract films after college. In the early 1940s, while a factory worker at Lockheed Aircraft, Whitney began collaborating with his brother James (b. Dec. 1921), a painter, in a series of 8mm animated shorts. Their mid-1940s "Film Exercises" series were widely shown in the U.S. and Europe, bringing them prominence in the world of art and experimental film, and winning an award at the first Experimental Film Festival, held in Belgium in 1949. In 1945, the brothers began separate filmmaking careers. Whitney, in the early 1950s, took various films assignments such as production engineering films on missile projects for Douglas Aircraft, while also performing stage shows of music set to real-time, abstract "oil-wipe" imagery. He produced three "Gerald McBoing-Boing" TV shorts for the UPA animation studio in 1955 (the remake "Lion Hunt" and, with Ernie Pintoff, "Blues Pattern" and "Performing Painter"). In 1957, Whitney helped designer Charles Eames create a seven-screen film presentation for the Buckminster Fuller Dome in Moscow. He then spent two years designing and building his first computerized graphics system, and founded his Motion Graphics, Inc. in 1960, to produce computer-assisted title sequences and commercials. Whitney taught at the California Institute of Technology in 1971, and taught computer graphics at UCLA from 1975-85. A grand old man of computer art, he was honored at conferences and festivals, and was the subject of the 1984 videodisc "The World of John Whitney: Pioneer of Visual Music." Whitney—not to be confused with the 1940s actor John Whitney—was the recipient of countless grants and honors, including the rarely bestowed Medal of Commendation from the Academy of Motion Picture Arts and Sciences, an IBM artist-in-residence research grant (1966-69), two Guggenheim grants, and several from the National Endowment for the Arts. Whitney wrote the book *Digital Harmony: On the Complementarity of Music and Visual Art* (1980). His sons John, Jr. (b. 1946), Michael (b. 1947) and Mark (b. 1950) have themselves been involved in award-winning filmmaking and animation.

No cause of death was available.

Wickes, Mary

born: Mary Isabelle Wickenhauser (some sources give Wickenhausen), June 13, 1910, 1912 or 1916, St. Louis, MO
died: Oct. 22, 1995, Los Angeles, CA, age 85, 83 or 79
educ: Washington University, St. Louis, MO; UCLA (master's degree, theater)

Comic actress with a 52-year career in movies.

Mary Wickes gamefully used her equine looks to play a procession of man-hungry spinsters, no-nonsense nuns and wisecracking housekeepers. Best known as Nurse Preen in THE MAN WHO CAME TO DINNER (1942)—taking Monty Woolley's wicked barbs and giving back as good as she got—Wickes was the woman on call whenever producers needed some comically acerbic dame as girlfriend to a Lou Costello, Shemp Howard, or Larry Linville. She was a regular in the plays of George S. Kaufman, who called her his favorite comedienne. She began her career in the mid-1930s at the Berkshire Playhouse in Stockbridge, MA, later moving to New York and landing a small role in Broadway's *The Farmer Takes a Wife*. She went on to do some two dozen Broadway plays and musicals, including Philip Barry's *Spring Dance*, Kaufman and Edna Ferber's *Stage Door* (1936), *Father Malady's Miracle (1937),* Kaufman and Moss Hart's *The Man Who Came to Dinner* (1939)—repeating her role in both the movie and a 1972 telefilm with Orson Welles—*Jackpot* (1944), *Town House* (1948) and *Show Boat* (1952), and *Oklahoma!* (1979 revival). She reportedly performed than 200 regional and stock productions, in everything from *You Can't Take It With You* at the American Conservatory Theater in San Francisco, to *Henry IV, Part I* at the American Shakespeare Theater in Stratford, Conn.

Wickes made her TV debut in 1949, becoming the first actress to play the title role in "Mary Poppins," in a production for "Studio One." She was a cast regular in several series: the variety show "Inside USA with Chevrolet" (CBS 1949-50); "The Peter and Mary Show" aka "The Peter Lind Hayes Show" (NBC 1950-51), during the 1950 portion; "Bonino" (NBC 1953); "The Halls of Ivy" (CBS 1954-55); "Mrs. G. Goes to College" aka "The Gertrude Berg Show" (CBS 1961-62), for which

Wickes was Emmy nominated for her supporting role as boardinghouse owner Maxfield; "Julia" (NBC 1968-71); "Doc" (CBS 1975-76), and "Father Dowling Mysteries." Wickes also played the recurring role of Miss Esther Cathcart from 1959-61 on "Dennis the Menace" (CBS 1959-63). Among her memorable TV guest appearances are as ballet teacher Madame Lamonde on "I Love Lucy," and as a senior officer with an eye for Major Frank Burns on "M*A*S*H."

On the movie side, Wickes was so memorable that by many accounts she was the Disney animators' model for the voice and mannerisms of Cruella De Vil in ONE HUNDRED AND ONE DALMATIANS (1961), for which Wickes provided the voice of another character. She played Sister Mary Lazarus in SISTER ACT (1992) and SISTER ACT 2: BACK IN THE HABIT (1993), garnering, for the former, an American Comedy Award nomination for funniest supporting female in a motion picture. Among other notable roles, White played Emma in WHITE CHRISTMAS (1954), Sister Clarissa in THE TROUBLE WITH ANGELS aka MOTHER SUPERIOR (1966) and WHERE ANGELS GO. . . TROUBLE FOLLOWS (1968), Meryl Streep's Grandma in POSTCARDS FROM THE EDGE (1990) and Aunt March in LITTLE WOMEN (1994). She taught acting seminars at her alma mater.

Wickes died of complications following surgery.

Willingham, Calder

born: Calder Baynard Willingham, Jr., Dec. 23, 1922, Atlanta, GA; raised Rome, GA
died: Feb. 19, 1995, Laconia, NH, age 72
educ: University of Virginia

Novelist and screenwriter who THE GRADUATE and other films.

Calder Willingham was behind the typewriter of some of America's most powerful and enduring films. One of the generation of young, post-war, naturalistic novelists that included Norman Mailer and James Jones, Willingham exploded onto the scene with his first novel, *End as a Man* (1947), an account of sadism at a military academy; Willingham had himself gone to The Citadel for a year before attending the University of Virginia. He adapted his hit novel—over which obscenity charges were famously filed by the New York Society for the Suppression of Vice—into both a 1953 Off-Broadway play and the film THE STRANGE ONE aka in Britain END AS A MAN (1957). Willingham wrote nine more novels including *To Eat a Peach* (1955), *Rambling Rose* (1972), *The Big Nickel* (1975; his final novel) and two best-sellers, *Providence Island* and 1963's *Eternal Fire*.

The same year as THE STRANGE ONE, Willingham and collaborators Jim Thompson and Stanley Kubrick wrote the adapted screenplay for Kubrick's classic PATHS OF GLORY (1957). He co-wrote the adapted screenplays for THE VIKINGS (1958), the Marlon Brando-directed ONE-EYED JACKS (1961), the coming-of-age classic THE GRADUATE (1967), for which he received an Academy Award nomination, and the critically acclaimed LITTLE BIG MAN (1970). Willingham also co-wrote with Joan Tewkesbury and Robert Altman the script to Altman's THIEVES LIKE US (1974), and adapted his own semiautobiographical novel into the script for RAMBLING ROSE (1991), both highly lauded films. He collaborated with director David Lean on the script for BRIDGE ON THE RIVER KWAI (1957), but Willingham's credit was removed after an argument with producer Sam Speigel. At the time of his death, Willingham had recently completed an original screenplay for Amblin Entertainment.

Calder, who lived in New Hampton, NH, died of lung cancer.

Wolfman Jack

born: Robert Smith, Jan. 21, 1938, Brooklyn, NY
died: July 1, 1995, Belvidere, NC, ag age 57

Renowned disk jockey, who appeared in several films and TV shows.

Wolfman Jack, who had his name legally changed, was one of the nation's best-known radio personalities. Early in his career, in 1960 and '61, he was Daddy Jules on WTID/Norfolk, VA, and in 1962, he was Big Smith With the Records at country station KCIJ/Shreveport, LA. He created the Wolfman Jack persona while one of several legendary DJs of "border radio"—stations just over the border in Mexico, which broadcast at a country-sweeping 250,000 watts, at the time five times the legal limit for American stations. Wolfman Jack—broadcasting from 1963-66 on XERF-AM/Via Cuna Cohuilla and afterward from XERB/Rosarito—became an airwave hero to countless youths. Among them was George Lucas, who had Wolfman Jack play himself, poignantly and magnetically, in AMERICAN GRAFFITI (1973). He had previously played himself in the little-seen THE SEVEN MINUTES (1971). In the early 1970s, Wolfman Jack moved to New York City to work for about a year at WNBC, then shifted to Los Angeles to host his own syndicated radio show, and to serve as announcer on the latenight music series "The Midnight Special" (NBC 1973-81). He was mentioned in songs, such as the Guess Who hit "Clap for the Wolfman," and in recent times made about 150 appearances a year, serving as host at a variety of events. He did TV informercials for music collections, and just before his death he had returned home from a 20-day tour to promote his autobiography, *Have Mercy: Confessions of the Original Rock-and-Roll Animal.* He had also recently done a guest spot on the sitcom "Married. . . With Children."

Wolfman Jack's movies include SGT. PEPPER'S LONELY HEARTS CLUB BAND (1978), MORE AMERICAN GRAFFITI (1979), and, in character roles, MOTEL HELL (1980) and MORTUARY ACADEMY (1992).

Wolfman Jack died of a heart attack.

Youngerman, Joseph

born: c. 1906, South Chicago, IL
died: Nov. 22, 1995, Los Angeles, CA, age 89
Assistant director and beloved Hollywood fix-it man.

Joseph Youngerman, who helped build the Directors Guild of America into a film-industry force, moved to Los Angeles in 1923 as an electrician's assistant. He backed into the movies three years later, with a job in the Paramount prop department. His affable personality and quick mastery of studio nuts-and-bolts, from managing budgets to knowing which switches to flip, made him a favorite of stars and directors. Director Norman Taurog, for whom Youngerman worked as prop man on SKIPPY (1930), promoted him to first assistant director with Bing Crosby's RHYTHM ON THE RANGE (1936). Youngerman went on to work as first assistant director for such directors as Cecil B. De Mille, Ernst Lubitsch, Rouben Mamoulian, Josef von Sternberg, and William Wellman—for whom he did five films, and was so highly regarded that Wellman entrusted him with directing the elaborate battle scenes between the British Army and the Fuzzy Wuzzies in THE LIGHT THAT FAILED (1939). Youngerman also directed a series of films for the Army Signal Corps during WWII, including the short "Safeguarding Military Information," starring Walter Huston, and one on cryptographic security.

After working on almost 100 movies, Youngerman became Paramount's head of backlot operations, working as assistant to studio head

Henry Ginsberg. In 1950, after five years in that position, he switched careers to become executive secretary of what was then the Screen Directors Guild—at the time, a relatively small group of 900 directors and assistant directors. During his tenure, Youngerman achieved such milestones as a late-1950s merger with the Radio and Television Directors Guild to form the DGA; it currently numbers more than 10,000 members. He also devised and current Guild pension plan—mapping out the complicated formula one sleepless night in 1960 — and spearheaded the construction of the DGA's 1955-88 headquarters. Youngerman served until 1977, after which he became a consultant and national executive secretary emeritus. He was also executive secretary-treasurer of the Directors Guild Educational and Benevolent Foundation. He was the subject of a DGA book of interviews, *My Seventy Years at Paramount Studios and the Directors Guild of America* (1995).

Youngerman's many films as first assistant director include BEAU GESTE (1936), MEN WITH WINGS (1938), BUCK BENNY RIDES AGAIN (1940), SULLIVAN'S TRAVELS (1941), SO PROUDLY WE HAIL (1943), and FOR WHOM THE BELL TOLLS (1943).

Youngerman died after suffering a stroke.

Zhang Nuanxin

born: c. 1941, Huhhot, Mongolia
died: May 28, 1995, Peking, China, age 54
educ: Peking Film Academy
Chinese director best known for her art-house hit SACRIFICE OF YOUTH (China 1985).

Zhang Nuanxin was born into a family from Liaoning province, and after study at Peking Film Academy, stayed on to teach. She later learned French when sent to the countryside during the Cultural Revolution. She debuted in features with the female-athlete drama THE DRIVE TO WIN (China 1981), following it with the melodrama SACRIFICE OF YOUTH, about the Dai minority in southern China; it played film festivals and was distributed in the West. Zhang then studied film in Paris before returning to China to teach and direct. Her husband was the writer-critic Li Tuo, with whom she wrote a controversial 1979 article on the modernization of film language.

Zhang' other films include PALANQUIN OF TEARS, THE STORY OF YUNNAN, and GOOD MORNING, BEIJING.

No cause of death was reported.

Indices

MASTER INDEX FOR MPG ANNUALS

Listed below are the titles of all films reviewed since 1984, with their year of release in thr US. This date will enable you to locate the *Motion Picture Guide* volume in which the film appears. All films released in 1984 can be found in volume IX of the original *Motion Picture Guide*. Films released during or after 1985 can be found in the *Motion Picture Guide Annual* for the year *following* the film's year of release (i.e. films of 1986 are reviewed in the 1987 *Annual*, films of 1987 in the 1988 *Annual*, etc.).

If a film has been reviewed, but is absent from the list below, the title in question was released prior to 1984 and may be found in the original, ten-volume set, which is arranged alphabetically by title.

A

A COR DO SEU DESTINO (SEE: COLOR OF DESTINY, THE)(1988)
A CORPS PERDU (SEE: STRAIGHT TO THE HEART)(1988)
A HORA DA ESTRELA (SEE: HOUR OF THE STAR)(1986)
A LA MODE (1994)
A NAGY GENERACIO (SEE: GREAT GENERATION, THE)(1986)
ABOUT LAST NIGHT (1986)
ABOVE THE LAW (1988)
ABOVE THE RIM (1994)
ABRAXAS: GUARDIAN OF THE UNIVERSE (1993)
ABSOLUTE BEGINNERS (1986)
ABYSS, THE (1989)
ACCA (SEE: ASSA)(1988)
ACCIDENTAL TOURIST, THE (1988)
ACCOMPANIST, THE (1993)
ACCUMULATOR 1 (1995)
ACCUSED, THE (1988)
ACE VENTURA: PET DETECTIVE (1994)
ACE VENTURA: WHEN NATURE CALLS (1995)
ACES: IRON EAGLE III (1992)
ACHALGAZRDA KOMPOZITORIS MOGZAUROBA (SEE: YOUNG COMPOSER'S ODYSSEY)(1986)
ACQUA E SAPONE (1985)
ACROSS THE MOON (1995)
ACROSS THE SEA OF TIME: NEW YORK 3D (1995)
ACROSS THE TRACKS (1991)
ACTION JACKSON (1988)
ADAM'S RIB (1992)
ADDAMS FAMILY VALUES (1993)
ADDAMS FAMILY, THE (1991)
ADDICTION, THE (1995)
ADJUSTER, THE (1992)
ADUEFUE (1988)
ADULT EDUCATION (SEE: HIDING OUT)(1987)
ADVENTURES IN BABYSITTING (1987)
ADVENTURES IN DINOSAUR CITY (1992)
ADVENTURES IN SPYING (1992)
ADVENTURES OF A GNOME NAMED GNORM, THE (1994)
ADVENTURES OF BARON MUNCHAUSEN, THE (1989)
ADVENTURES OF FORD FAIRLANE, THE (1990)
ADVENTURES OF HERCULES (SEE: HERCULES II)(1985)
ADVENTURES OF HUCK FINN, THE (1993)
ADVENTURES OF MARK TWAIN, THE (1985)
ADVENTURES OF MATT THE GOOSEBOY, THE (1995)
ADVENTURES OF MILO AND OTIS, THE (1989)
ADVENTURES OF PRISCILLA, QUEEN OF THE DESERT, THE (1994)

ADVENTURES OF THE AMERICAN RABBIT, THE (1986)
ADVOCATE, THE (1994)
AEROBICIDE (SEE: KILLER WORKOUT)(1987)
AFFENGEIL (1992)
AFRAID OF THE DARK (1992)
AFTER DARK, MY SWEET (1990)
AFTER HOURS (1985)
AFTER MIDNIGHT (1989)
AFTER SCHOOL (1989)
AFTERSHOCK (1990)
AGATHA CHRISTIE'S TEN LITTLE INDIANS (SEE: TEN LITTLE INDIANS)(1990)
AGE ISN'T EVERYTHING (1991)
AGE OF INNOCENCE, THE (1993)
AGENT ON ICE (1986)
AGNES OF GOD (1985)
AI CITY (1995)
AILEEN WUORNOS: THE SELLING OF A SERIAL KILLER (1994)
AILSA (1995)
AIR AMERICA (1990)
AIR UP THERE, THE (1994)
AIRBORNE (1993)
AIRHEADS (1994)
AKE AND HIS WORLD (1985)
AKIRA (1991)
AKIRA KUROSAWA'S DREAMS (SEE: DREAMS)(1990)
ALADDIN (1987)
ALADDIN (1992)
ALAMO BAY (1985)
ALAN & NAOMI (1992)
ALBERTO EXPRESS (1992)
ALEXA (1989)
ALICE (1988)
ALICE (1990)
ALIENS (1986)
ALIEN3 (1992)
ALIEN FROM L.A. (1988)
ALIEN INTRUDER (1993)
ALIEN NATION (1988)
ALIEN PREDATOR (1987)
ALIEN SPACE AVENGER (SEE: SPACE AVENGER)(1991)
ALIENATOR (1990)
ALIVE (1993)
ALL-AMERICAN MURDER (1992)
ALL DOGS GO TO HEAVEN (1989)
ALL I WANT FOR CHRISTMAS (1991)
ALL THE VERMEERS IN NEW YORK (1992)
ALL TIED UP (1994)
ALLAN QUATERMAIN AND THE LOST CITY OF GOLD (1987)
ALLIGATOR EYES (1990)
ALLIGATOR II: THE MUTATION (1991)
ALLNIGHTER, THE (1987)
ALLONSANFAN (1985)
ALMOST (1991)
ALMOST AN ANGEL (1990)

ALMOST BLUE (1993)
ALMOST DEAD (1995)
ALMOST HOLLYWOOD (1994)
ALMOST PREGNANT (1992)
ALOHA SUMMER (1988)
ALWAYS (1985)
ALWAYS (1989)
AMANT, L (SEE: LOVER, THE)(1992)
AMATEUR (1995)
AMAZING GRACE AND CHUCK (1987)
AMAZING PANDA ADVENTURE, THE (1995)
AMAZON (1991)
AMAZON WOMEN ON THE MOON (1987)
AMAZONIA—THE CATHERINE MILES STORY (SEE: WHITE SLAVE)(1986)
AMAZONIA: VOICES FROM THE RAINFOREST (1993)
AMAZONS (1987)
AMBITION (1991)
AMBULANCE, THE (1993)
AMERICA 3000 (1986)
AMERICA'S DEADLIEST HOME VIDEO (1995)
AMERICAN ANTHEM (1986)
AMERICAN AUTOBAHN (1989)
AMERICAN BLUE NOTE (1991)
AMERICAN BOYFRIENDS (1990)
AMERICAN COMMANDOS (1986)
AMERICAN COP (1995)
AMERICAN CYBORG: STEEL WARRIOR (1994)
AMERICAN DREAM (1992)
AMERICAN EAGLE (1990)
AMERICAN FABULOUS (1992)
AMERICAN FLYERS (1985)
AMERICAN FRIENDS (1993)
AMERICAN GOTHIC (1988)
AMERICAN HEART (1993)
AMERICAN JUSTICE (1986)
AMERICAN KICKBOXER 1 (1991)
AMERICAN ME (1992)
AMERICAN NIGHTMARES (SEE: COMBAT SHOCK)(1986)
AMERICAN NINJA (1985)
AMERICAN NINJA 2: THE CONFRONTATION (1987)
AMERICAN NINJA 3: BLOOD HUNT (1989)
AMERICAN NINJA 4: THE ANNIHILATION (1991)
AMERICAN PRESIDENT, THE (1995)
AMERICAN RICKSHAW (1991)
AMERICAN SHAOLIN: KING OF THE KICKBOXERS II (1993)
AMERICAN SUMMER, AN (1991)
AMERICAN TAIL: FIEVEL GOES WEST, AN (1991)
AMERICAN TAIL, AN (1986)
AMERICAN WAY, THE (SEE: RIDERS OF THE STORM)(1988)
AMIGOS (1986)
AMITYVILLE 1992: IT'S ABOUT TIME (1992)
AMONG THE CINDERS (1985)

BEASTMASTER 2: THROUGH THE PORTAL OF TIME (1992)
BEAT, THE (1988)
BEATING HEART, A (1992)
BEATRICE (1988)
BEAUTIFUL DREAMERS (1992)
BEAUTY AND THE BEAST (1991)
BEBE'S KIDS (1992)
BECOMING COLETTE (1992)
BED & BREAKFAST (1992)
BED YOU SLEEP IN, THE (1995)
BEDROOM EYES II (1990)
BEDROOM WINDOW, THE (1987)
BEER (1986)
BEETHOVEN (1992)
BEETHOVEN LIVES UPSTAIRS (1992)
BEETHOVEN'S 2ND (1993)
BEETLEJUICE (1988)
BEFORE AND AFTER (1985)
BEFORE SUNRISE (1995)
BEFORE THE RAIN (1995)
BEGINNER'S LUCK (1986)
BEING AT HOME WITH CLAUDE (1993)
BEING HUMAN (1994)
BELIEVERS, THE (1987)
BELIZAIRE THE CAJUN (1986)
BELL DIAMOND (1987)
BELLE EPOQUE (1993)
BELLY OF AN ARCHITECT, THE (1987)
BENEFIT OF THE DOUBT (1993)
BENJI THE HUNTED (1987)
BENNY & JOON (1993)
BERLIN AFFAIR, THE (1985)
BERNARD AND THE GENIE (1992)
BERRY GORDY'S THE LAST DRAGON (SEE: LAST DRAGON, THE)(1985)
BERSERKER (1988)
BERT RIGBY, YOU'RE A FOOL (1989)
BEST INTENTIONS, THE (1992)
BEST OF THE BEST (1989)
BEST OF THE BEST II (1993)
BEST OF TIMES, THE (1986)
BEST SELLER (1987)
BETRAYAL (1995)
BETRAYAL OF THE DOVE (1993)
BETRAYED (1988)
BETSY'S WEDDING (1990)
BETTER OFF DEAD (1985)
BETTER OFF DEAD (1995)
BETTER TOMORROW, A (1994)
BETTY (1993)
BETTY BLUE (1986)
BETWEEN HEAVEN AND EARTH (1993)
BETWEEN THE TEETH (1994)
BEVERLY HILLBILLIES, THE (1993)
BEVERLY HILLS BRATS (1989)
BEVERLY HILLS COP II (1987)
BEVERLY HILLS COP III (1994)
BEYOND DARKNESS (1992)
BEYOND JUSTICE (1992)
BEYOND RANGOON (1995)
BEYOND SUSPICION (1994)
BEYOND THE DOOR III (1991)
BEYOND THE LAW (1994)
BEYOND THE RISING MOON (SEE: STAR QUEST: BEYOND THE RISING MOON)(1990)
BEYOND THE WALLS (1985)
BEYOND THERAPY (1987)
BHAJI ON THE BEACH (1994)
BIAN ZHOU BIAN CHANG (SEE: LIFE ON A STRING)(1992)
BIG (1988)
BIG BAD JOHN (1990)
BIG BAD MAMA II (1987)

BIG BANG, THE (1991)
BIG BLUE, THE (1988)
BIG BLUE, THE (1989)
BIG BUSINESS (1988)
BIG DIS, THE (1990)
BIG EASY, THE (1987)
BIG GIRLS DON'T CRY ... THEY GET EVEN (1992)
BIG GREEN, THE (1995)
BIG MAN ON CAMPUS (1991)
BIG MAN, THE (SEE: CROSSING THE LINE)(1991)
BIG PARADE, THE (1987)
BIG PICTURE, THE (1989)
BIG SHOTS (1987)
BIG SLICE, THE (1991)
BIG SWEAT, THE (1991)
BIG TOP PEE-WEE (1988)
BIG TOWN, THE (1987)
BIG TROUBLE (1986)
BIG TROUBLE IN LITTLE CHINA (1986)
BIGFOOT: THE UNFORGETTABLE ENCOUNTER (1995)
BIKINI BISTRO (1995)
BIKINI CARWASH COMPANY II, THE (1993)
BIKINI CARWASH COMPANY, THE (1992)
BIKINI GENIE (SEE: WILDEST DREAMS)(1990)
BIKINI ISLAND (1991)
BIKINI SHOP, THE (SEE: MALIBU BIKINI SHOP)(1987)
BIKINI SUMMER (1991)
BIKINI SUMMER 2 (1992)
BILL & TED'S BOGUS JOURNEY (1991)
BILL & TED'S EXCELLENT ADVENTURE (1989)
BILLY BATHGATE (1991)
BILLY MADISON (1995)
BILOXI BLUES (1988)
BINGO (1991)
BIRD (1988)
BIRD ON A WIRE (1990)
BIRDS II: LAND'S END, THE (1994)
BIRDS OF PREY (1987)
BIRDS OF PREY (1988)
BIRUMA NO TATEGOTO (SEE: BURMESE HARP, THE)(1985)
BITTER HARVEST (1993)
BITTER MOON (1994)
BITTER VENGEANCE (1995)
BLACK AND WHITE (1986)
BLACK BEAUTY (1994)
BLACK CAULDRON, THE (1985)
BLACK FOX (1995)
BLACK ICE (1992)
BLACK IS ... BLACK AIN'T (1995)
BLACK MAGIC WOMAN (1991)
BLACK MOON RISING (1986)
BLACK RAIN (1989)
BLACK RAIN (1990)
BLACK ROBE (1991)
BLACK ROSES (1989)
BLACK SNOW (1994)
BLACK WATER (1994)
BLACK WIDOW (1987)
BLACKBELT (1992)
BLACKOUT (1988)
BLADE IN THE DARK, A (1986)
BLADES (1990)
BLAKE EDWARDS' SON OF THE PINK PANTHER (1993)
BLAME IT ON THE BELLBOY (1992)
BLANK CHECK (1994)
BLANKMAN (1994)
BLASTFIGHTER (1985)

BLAZE (1989)
BLESSING (1995)
BLIND CHANCE (1987)
BLIND DATE (1987)
BLIND DIRECTOR, THE (1986)
BLIND FURY (1990)
BLIND JUSTICE (1994)
BLIND TRUST (SEE: INTIMATE POWER)(1986)
BLIND VISION (1992)
BLINDFOLD: ACTS OF OBSESSION (1994)
BLINK (1994)
BLINK OF AN EYE (1992)
BLISS (1985)
BLOB, THE (1988)
BLOCK NOTES-DIE UN REGISTA-APPUNTI (SEE: INTERVISTA)(1987)
BLOOD AND CONCRETE - A LOVE STORY (1991)
BLOOD DINER (1987)
BLOOD GAMES (1991)
BLOOD IN THE FACE (1991)
BLOOD IN, BLOOD OUT (SEE: BOUND BY HONOR)(1993)
BLOOD OATH (SEE: PRISONERS OF THE SUN)(1991)
BLOOD OF HEROES (1990)
BLOOD ON THE BADGE (1992)
BLOOD ON THE MOON (SEE: COP)(1988)
BLOOD RED (1990)
BLOOD RELATIONS (1990)
BLOOD SALVAGE (1990)
BLOOD SCREAMS (1991)
BLOOD SISTERS (1987)
BLOODFIST (1989)
BLOODFIST IV: DIE TRYING (1992)
BLOODFIST III: FORCED TO FIGHT (1992)
BLOODFIST II (1991)
BLOODHOUNDS OF BROADWAY (1989)
BLOODMATCH (1991)
BLOODMOON (1991)
BLOODSPORT (1988)
BLOODSTONE: SUBSPECIES II (1993)
BLOODSUCKERS FROM OUTER SPACE (1987)
BLOODSUCKING PHAROAHS IN PITTSBURGH (1991)
BLOODY BIRTHDAY (1986)
BLOODY POM POMS (1988)
BLOODY WEDNESDAY (1987)
BLOWBACK (1991)
BLOWN AWAY (1994)
BLU ELETTRICO (SEE: ELECTRIC BLUE)(1988)
BLUE (1993)
BLUE (1994)
BLUE CHIPS (1994)
BLUE CITY (1986)
BLUE DESERT (1991)
BLUE HEAT (SEE: LAST OF THE FINEST)(1990)
BLUE HEAVEN (1985)
BLUE IGUANA, THE (1988)
BLUE IN THE FACE (1995)
BLUE JEAN COP (SEE: SHAKEDOWN)(1988)
BLUE KITE, THE (1994)
BLUE MONKEY (1988)
BLUE SKY (1994)
BLUE STEEL (1990)
BLUE TIGER (1995)
BLUE TORNADO (1991)
BLUE VELVET (1986)
BLUE VILLA, THE (1995)
BLUES LA-CHOFESH HAGODOL (SEE: LATE SUMMER BLUES)(1988)
BOB MARLEY: TIME WILL TELL (1992)
BOB ROBERTS (1992)

C

CASTLE FREAK (1995)
CASUAL SEX? (1988)
CASUALTIES OF WAR (1989)
CAT CHASER (1991)
CATCH THE HEAT (1987)
CATHOLIC BOYS (SEE: HEAVEN HELP US)(1985)
CAT'S EYE (1985)
CAUGHT (1987)
CAVEGIRL (1985)
CB4 (1993)
CEASE FIRE (1985)
CELLAR DWELLER (1988)
CEMENT GARDEN, THE (1994)
CEMENTERIO DEL TERROR (1985)
CEMETERY CLUB, THE (1993)
CENTER OF THE WEB (1992)
CENTURY (1995)
CERTAIN FURY (1985)
C'EST LA VIE (1990)
CHAIN, THE (1985)
CHAIN GANG (1985)
CHAIN LETTERS (1985)
CHAIN OF DESIRE (1993)
CHAINED HEAT II (1993)
CHAINS OF GOLD (1992)
CHAINSAW HOOKERS (SEE: HOLLYWOOD CHAINSAW HOOKERS)(1988)
CHAIR, THE (1991)
CHALLENGERS, THE (1994)
CHAMELEON STREET (1991)
CHANCES ARE (1989)
CHAPLIN (1992)
CHARULATA (1995)
CHASE, THE (1994)
CHASERS (1994)
CHASING DREAMS (1989)
CHATTAHOOCHEE (1990)
CHEAP SHOTS (1991)
CHEATIN' HEARTS (1993)
CHECK IS IN THE MAIL, THE (1986)
CHECKING OUT (1989)
CHEERLEADER CAMP (SEE: BLOODY POM POMS)(1988)
CHEETAH (1989)
CHERRY 2000 (1985)
CHEYENNE WARRIOR (1994)
CHICAGO JOE AND THE SHOWGIRL (1990)
CHICKEN HAWK: MEN WHO LOVE BOYS (1994)
CHIDAMBARAM (1986)
CHILDREN OF A LESSER GOD (1986)
CHILDREN OF NATURE (1994)
CHILDREN OF THE CORN II: THE FINAL SACRIFICE (1993)
CHILDREN OF THE CORN III: URBAN HARVEST (1995)
CHILDREN OF THE DUST (SEE: GOOD DAY TO DIE, A)(1995)
CHILDREN OF THE NIGHT (1992)
CHILDREN, THE (1992)
CHILD'S PLAY (1988)
CHILD'S PLAY 2 (1990)
CHILD'S PLAY 3 (1991)
CHINA GIRL (1987)
CHINA MOON (1994)
CHINA O'BRIEN II (1992)
CHINA O'BRIEN (1991)
CHINA WHITE (1991)
CHINA: MOVING THE MOUNTAIN (SEE: MOVING THE MOUNTAIN)(1995)
CHING SE (SEE: GREEN SNAKE)(1994)
CHIPMUNK ADVENTURE, THE (1987)
CHOCOLATE WAR, THE (1988)
CHOKE CANYON (1986)

CHOPPER CHICKS IN ZOMBIETOWN (1991)
CHOPPING MALL (1986)
CHORUS LINE, A (1985)
CHORUS OF DISAPPROVAL, A (1989)
CHRISTMAS REUNION, A (1994)
CHRISTOPHER COLUMBUS: THE DISCOVERY (1992)
CHRONICLE OF A DEATH FORETOLD (1987)
CHRONICLE OF THE WARSAW GHETTO UPRISING ACCORDING TO MAREK EDELMAN (1995)
C.H.U.D. II: BUD THE C.H.U.D. (1989)
CHUNG ON TSOU (SEE: CRIME STORY)(1994)
CHURCH, THE (1991)
CIA—CODE NAME ALEXA (1993)
C.I.A. II TARGET: ALEXA (1994)
CIAO, PROFESSORE! (1994)
CINEMA PARADISO (1990)
CIRCLE OF FRIENDS (1995)
CIRCUITRY MAN (1990)
CIRCUITRY MAN II (1994)
CIRCUMSTANCES UNKNOWN (1995)
CITIZEN X (1995)
CITY AND THE DOGS, THE (1985)
CITY LIMITS (1985)
CITY OF BLOOD (1988)
CITY OF HOPE (1991)
CITY OF JOY (1992)
CITY OF LOST CHILDREN, THE (1995)
CITY SLICKERS (1991)
CITY SLICKERS II: THE LEGEND OF CURLY'S GOLD (1994)
CITY UNPLUGGED (1995)
CITY ZERO (1991)
CLAIRE OF THE MOON (1993)
CLAN OF THE CAVE BEAR, THE (1986)
CLANDESTINOS (SEE: LIVING DANGEROUSLY)(1988)
CLARA'S HEART (1988)
CLASS ACT (1992)
CLASS ACTION (1991)
CLASS OF '61 (1995)
CLASS OF 1999 II: THE SUBSTITUTE (1994)
CLASS OF 1999 (1990)
CLASS OF NUKE 'EM HIGH (1986)
CLASS OF NUKE 'EM HIGH PART 2: SUBHUMANOID MELTDOWN (1991)
CLASS RELATIONS (1986)
CLEAN AND SOBER (1988)
CLEAN SLATE (1994)
CLEAN, SHAVEN (1995)
CLEAR AND PRESENT DANGER (1994)
CLEARCUT (1992)
CLERKS (1994)
CLIENT, THE (1994)
CLIFFHANGER (1993)
CLIFFORD (1994)
CLIMATE FOR KILLING, A (1991)
CLIVE BARKER'S LORD OF ILLUSIONS (SEE: LORD OF ILLUSIONS)(1995)
CLOCKERS (1995)
CLOCKWISE (1986)
CLOSE MY EYES (1991)
CLOSE TO EDEN (1992)
CLOSER, THE (1991)
CLOSET LAND (1991)
CLUB EARTH (SEE: GALACTIC GIGOLO)(1988)
CLUB EXTINCTION (1991)
CLUB FED (1991)
CLUB LIFE (1987)
CLUB PARADISE (1986)
CLUB, THE (1994)
CLUE (1985)
CLUELESS (1995)

COASTWATCHER (SEE: LAST WARRIOR, THE)(1989)
COBB (1994)
COBRA (1986)
COCA-COLA KID, THE (1985)
COCAINE WARS (1986)
COCKTAIL (1988)
COCOON (1985)
COCOON: THE RETURN (1988)
CODE NAME: CHAOS (1992)
CODE NAME: EMERALD (1985)
CODE NAME VENGEANCE (1989)
CODE NAME ZEBRA (1987)
CODE OF SILENCE (1985)
CODICE PRIVATO (SEE: PRIVAE ACCESS)(1988)
COEUR QUI BAT, UN (SEE: BEATING HEART, A)(1992)
COHEN AND TATE (1989)
COLD FEET (1990)
COLD HEAVEN (1992)
COLD JUSTICE (1992)
COLD STEEL (1987)
COLDBLOODED (1995)
COLLISION COURSE (1992)
COLONEL CHABERT (1994)
COLONEL REDL (1985)
COLOR ADJUSTMENT (1992)
COLOR OF DESTINY, THE (1988)
COLOR OF MONEY, THE (1986)
COLOR OF NIGHT (1994)
COLOR PURPLE, THE (1985)
COLORADO COWBOY: THE BRUCE FORD STORY (1995)
COLORS (1988)
COMBAT SHOCK (1986)
COMBINATION PLATTER (1993)
COME AND SEE (1986)
COME SEE THE PARADISE (1990)
COMEDIE! (SEE: COMEDY!)(1987)
COMEDY! (1987)
COMET BUTTERFLY AND SWORD (1994)
COMFORT OF STRANGERS, THE (1991)
COMIC MAGAZINE (1986)
COMING OUT UNDER FIRE (1994)
COMING TO AMERICA (1988)
COMING UP ROSES (1986)
COMMANDO (1985)
COMMANDO SQUAD (1987)
COMMENT FAIRE L'AMOUR AVEC UN NEGRE SANS SE FATIGUER (SEE: HOW TO MAKE LOVE TO A NEGRO WITHOUT GETTING TIRED)(1990)
COMMITMENTS, THE (1991)
COMMON BONDS (1992)
COMMUNION (1989)
COMO AGUA PARA CHOCOLATE (SEE: LIKE WATER FOR CHOCOLATE)(1993)
COMPANION, THE (1995)
COMPANY BUSINESS (1991)
COMPANY OF STRANGERS, THE (SEE: STRANGERS IN GOOD COMPANY)(1991)
COMPANY OF WOLVES, THE (1985)
COMPLEX WORLD (1992)
COMPROMISING POSITIONS (1985)
COMRADES (1987)
COMRADES IN ARMS (1992)
CONCIERGE, THE (SEE: FOR LOVE OR MONEY)(1993)
CONCRETE ANGELS (1987)
CONEHEADS (1993)
CONFESSIONS OF A HIT MAN (1994)
CONFESSIONS OF A SERIAL KILLER (1992)
CONGO (1995)
CONGRESS OF PENGUINS, THE (1995)
CONJUGAL BED, THE (1994)

CONSEIL DE FAMILLE (SEE: FAMILY BUSINESS)(1987)
CONSENTING ADULTS (1992)
CONSUMING PASSIONS (1988)
CONTACTO CHICANO (1986)
CONTAR HASTA TEN (1986)
CONVENT, THE (1995)
CONVICT COWBOY (1995)
CONVICTION, THE (1994)
CONVICTS (1991)
COOK, THE THIEF, HIS WIFE & HER LOVER, THE (1989)
COOKIE (1989)
COOL AS ICE (1991)
COOL RUNNINGS (1993)
COOL WORLD (1992)
COP (1988)
COP AND A HALF (1993)
COP AND THE GIRL, THE (1985)
COPS AND ROBBERSONS (1994)
COPYCAT (1995)
CORPORATE AFFAIRS (1991)
CORRINA, CORRINA (1994)
COSMIC EYE, THE (1986)
COSMIC SLOP (1995)
COUCH TRIP, THE (1988)
COUNTDOWN (1985)
COUNTRY LIFE (1995)
COUPE DE VILLE (1990)
COURAGE MOUNTAIN (1990)
COURT OF THE PHARAOH, THE (1985)
COUSIN BOBBY (1992)
COUSINS (1989)
COVER ME (1995)
COVER STORY (1995)
COVER-UP (1991)
COVERT ASSASSIN (1994)
COW, THE (1995)
COWBOY WAY, THE (1994)
COWS (1994)
CRACK HOUSE (1989)
CRACKERJACK (1995)
CRASH AND BURN (1991)
CRASH LANDING: THE RESCUE OF FLIGHT 232 (SEE: THOUSAND HEROES, A)(1994)
CRAWLERS, THE (1994)
CRAWLSPACE (1986)
CRAZY BOYS (1987)
CRAZY FAMILY, THE (1986)
CRAZY JOE (SEE: DEAD CENTER)(1994)
CRAZY LOVE (SEE: LOVE IS A DOG FROM HELL)(1987)
CRAZY PEOPLE (1990)
CRAZYSITTER, THE (1995)
CREATION OF ADAM (1995)
CREATOR (1985)
CREATURE (1985)
CREEP (1995)
CREEPERS (1985)
CREEPOZOIDS (1987)
CREEPSHOW 2 (1987)
CREW, THE (1995)
CRI DU HIBOU, LE (SEE: CRY OF THE OWL, THE)(1992)
CRIME BROKER (1994)
CRIME LORDS (1991)
CRIME OF HONOR (1987)
CRIME STORY (1994)
CRIME ZONE (1989)
CRIMES AND MISDEMEANORS (1989)
CRIMES OF THE HEART (1986)
CRIMEWAVE (1985)
CRIMINAL LAW (1989)
CRIMINAL PASSION (1994)
CRIMSON TIDE (1995)

CRIMSON WOLF (1995)
CRISSCROSS (1992)
CRITICAL CONDITION (1987)
CRITTERS (1986)
CRITTERS 2: THE MAIN COURSE (1988)
CRITTERS 4 (1992)
CRITTERS 3 (1991)
"CROCODILE" DUNDEE (1986)
"CROCODILE" DUNDEE II (1988)
CRONACA DI UNA MORTE ANNUNCIIATA (SEE: CHRONICLE OF A DEATH FORETOLD)(1987)
CRONOS (1994)
CROOKED HEARTS (1991)
CROOKLYN (1994)
CROSS MY HEART (1987)
CROSS MY HEART (1991)
CROSSING DELANCEY (1988)
CROSSING GUARD, THE (1995)
CROSSING THE BRIDGE (1992)
CROSSING THE LINE (1991)
CROSSING, THE (1992)
CROSSOVER DREAMS (1985)
CROSSROADS (1986)
CROW, THE (1994)
CRUDE OASIS, THE (1995)
CRUMB (1995)
CRUSH (1993)
CRUSH, THE (1993)
CRUSOE (1989)
CRY-BABY (1990)
CRY FREEDOM (1987)
CRY IN THE DARK, A (1988)
CRY IN THE NIGHT, A (1993)
CRY IN THE WILD, A (1991)
CRY OF THE OWL, THE (1992)
CRY, THE BELOVED COUNTRY (1995)
CRY WILDERNESS (1987)
CRYING GAME, THE (1992)
CRYSTAL HEART (1987)
CTHULHU MANSION (1992)
CUP FINAL (1992)
CURE, THE (1995)
CURFEW (1989)
CURFEW (1994)
CURLY SUE (1991)
CURSE, THE (1987)
CURSE IV: THE ULTIMATE SACRIFICE (1993)
CURSE OF THE CRYSTAL EYE (1993)
CURSE OF THE STARVING CLASS (1995)
CURSE III: BLOOD SACRIFICE (1991)
CUSTODIAN, THE (1994)
CUT AND RUN (1986)
CUTTHROAT ISLAND (1995)
CUTTING CLASS (1989)
CUTTING EDGE, THE (1992)
CYBER BANDITS (1995)
CYBER NINJA (1994)
CYBER TRACKER (1994)
CYBORG (1989)
CYBORG 2 (1993)
CYCLONE (1987)
CYRANO DE BERGERAC (1990)
LORD OF ILLUSIONS (1995)

D

D.O.A. (1988)
DA (1988)
DA YUE BING (SEE: BIG PARADE, THE)(1987)
DAD (1989)
DADDY AND THE MUSCLE ACADEMY (1992)
DADDY NOSTALGIA (1991)
DADDY'S BOYS (1988)

DADDY'S DYIN' . . . WHO'S GOT THE WILL? (1990)
DAHONG DENGLONG GAOGAO GUA (SEE: RAISE THE RED LANTERN)(1992)
DALLAS DOLL (1995)
DAMAGE (1992)
DAMNATION (1988)
DAMNED IN THE USA (1992)
DAMNED RIVER (1990)
DANCE MACABRE (1992)
DANCE ME OUTSIDE (1995)
DANCE OF THE DAMNED (1989)
DANCE WITH A STRANGER (1985)
DANCE WITH DEATH (1992)
DANCER, THE (1995)
DANCERS (1987)
DANCES WITH WOLVES (1990)
DANCING IN THE DARK (1986)
DANCING WITH DANGER (1994)
DANGER OF LOVE (1995)
DANGER ZONE, THE (1987)
DANGER ZONE II: REAPER'S REVENGE (1989)
DANGER ZONE III: STEEL HORSE WAR (1991)
DANGEROUS GAME (1993)
DANGEROUS HEART (1994)
DANGEROUS LIAISONS (1988)
DANGEROUS MINDS (1995)
DANGEROUS TOUCH (1994)
DANGEROUS WOMAN, A (1993)
DANGEROUS, THE (1995)
DANGEROUSLY CLOSE (1986)
DANIELLE STEELE'S "KALEIDOSCOPE" (SEE: KALEIDOSCOPE)(1994)
DANZON (1992)
DAO MA DAN (SEE: PEKING OPERA BLUES)(1986)
DARK ANGEL (SEE: I COME IN PEACE)(1990)
DARK ANGEL: THE ASCENT (1994)
DARK BACKWARD, THE (1991)
DARK DEALER (1995)
DARK EYES (1987)
DARK HALF, THE (1993)
DARK HORSE (1992)
DARK OBSESSION (1991)
DARK RIDER (1991)
DARK SIDE OF GENIUS, THE (1995)
DARK SIDE OF THE MOON (1990)
DARK TOWER (1989)
DARK WIND, THE (1993)
DARK, THE (1994)
DARKMAN (1990)
DARKMAN 2: THE RETURN OF DURANT (1995)
DARKNESS (1994)
DARKNESS IN TALLINN (SEE: CITY UNPLUGGED)(1995)
D.A.R.Y.L. (1985)
DAS HAUS AM FLUSS (1986)
DAS SCHWEIGEN DES DICHTERS (SEE: POET'S SILENCE, THE)(1987)
DATE WITH AN ANGEL (1987)
DAUGHTER OF DARKNESS (1994)
DAUGHTER OF THE NILE (1988)
DAUGHTERS OF THE DUST (1992)
DAVE (1993)
DAWANDEH (SEE: RUNNER, THE)(1991)
DAWNING, THE (1993)
DAY IN OCTOBER, A (1992)
DAY MY PARENTS RAN AWAY, THE (1994)
DAY OF ATONEMENT (1993)
DAY OF THE COBRA, THE (1985)
DAY OF THE DEAD (1985)
DAY THE SUN TURNED COLD, THE (1995)

DAY TO REMEMBER, A (SEE: TWO BITS)(1995)
DAY YOU LOVE ME, THE (1988)
DAYS OF THUNDER (1990)
DAZED AND CONFUSED (1993)
DE BRUIT ET DE FUREUR (SEE: SOUND AND FURY)(1988)
DE MISLUKKING (SEE: FAILURE, THE)(1986)
DE SABLE ET DE SANG (SEE: SAND AND BLOOD)(1989)
DE VLASCHAARD (SEE: FLAXFIELD, THE)(1985)
DEAD, THE (1987)
DEAD AGAIN (1991)
DEAD AIM (1990)
DEAD ALIVE (1993)
DEAD-BANG (1989)
DEAD CALM (1989)
DEAD CENTER (1994)
DEAD CERTAIN (1992)
DEAD CONNECTION (1994)
DEAD-END DRIVE-IN (1986)
DEAD END KIDS (1986)
DEAD FUNNY (1995)
DEAD HEAT (1988)
DEAD MAN WALKING (1988)
DEAD MAN WALKING (1995)
DEAD MAN'S REVENGE (1994)
DEAD MATE (1989)
DEAD MEN DON'T DIE (1991)
DEAD OF WINTER (1987)
DEAD ON (1994)
DEAD ON SIGHT (1994)
DEAD PIT (1990)
DEAD POETS SOCIETY (1989)
DEAD POOL, THE (1988)
DEAD PRESIDENTS (1995)
DEAD RINGERS (1988)
DEAD TIRED (SEE: GROSSE FATIGUE)(1995)
DEAD WOMEN IN LINGERIE (1991)
DEADBOLT (1992)
DEADFALL (1993)
DEADLINE (1987)
DEADLY BET (1992)
DEADLY CURRENTS (1992)
DEADLY CURRENTS (1994)
DEADLY DAPHNE'S REVENGE (1994)
DEADLY DREAMS (1988)
DEADLY EXPOSURE (1993)
DEADLY EXPOSURE (1994)
DEADLY FRIEND (1986)
DEADLY ILLUSION (1987)
DEADLY MARIA (1995)
DEADLY OBSESSION (1989)
DEADLY PASSION (1985)
DEADLY POSSESSION (1989)
DEADLY PREY (1987)
DEADLY PURSUIT (SEE: SHOOT TO KILL)(1988)
DEADLY RIVALS (1993)
DEADLY SECRET, THE (1994)
DEADLY STRANGERS (SEE: BORDER HEAT)(1988)
DEADLY TARGET (1994)
DEADLY TWINS (1988)
DEADSPACE (1991)
DEADTIME STORIES (1987)
DEALERS (1989)
DEATH AND THE MAIDEN (1994)
DEATH BECOMES HER (1992)
DEATH BEFORE DISHONOR (1987)
DEATH HOUSE (1992)
DEATH IN BRUNSWICK (1995)
DEATH MACHINE (1995)
DEATH MAGIC (1993)

DEATH MATCH (1994)
DEATH OF A SOLDIER (1986)
DEATH OF AN ANGEL (1985)
DEATH OF EMPEDOCLES, THE (1986)
DEATH OF MARIO RICCI, THE (1985)
DEATH PENALTY (SEE: SATAN KILLER, THE)(1993)
DEATH RING (1993)
DEATH SENTENCE (1986)
DEATH WARRANT (1990)
DEATH WISH 3 (1985)
DEATH WISH 4: THE CRACKDOWN (1987)
DEATH WISH V: THE FACE OF DEATH (1994)
DEATHROW GAMESHOW (1987)
DEATHSTALKER AND THE WARRIORS FROM HELL (1989)
DEATHSTALKER IV: MATCH OF TITANS (1992)
DEBT, THE (SEE: VERONICO CRUZ)(1990)
DECEIT (1993)
DECEIVED (1991)
DECEIVERS, THE (1988)
DECEMBER (1991)
DECEMBER BRIDE (1994)
DECEPTION (1993)
DECLINE OF THE AMERICAN EMPIRE, THE (1986)
DECONSTRUCTING SARAH (1995)
DECOY (1995)
DEEP BLUES (1992)
DEEP COVER (1992)
DEEPSTAR SIX (1989)
DEF BY TEMPTATION (1990)
DEF-CON 4 (1985)
DEFENCE OF THE REALM (1985)
DEFENDING YOUR LIFE (1991)
DEFENSELESS (1991)
DEJA VU (1985)
DELICATESSEN (1992)
DELIRIOUS (1991)
DELOS ADVENTURE, THE (1987)
DELTA FORCE, THE (1986)
DELTA FORCE 2 (1990)
DELTA FORCE COMMANDO 2 (1991)
DELTA FORCE 3: YOUNG COMMANDOS (1991)
DELTA HEAT (1992)
DELUSION (1991)
DEMOLITION MAN (1993)
DEMON IN MY VIEW, A (1992)
DEMON KEEPER (1994)
DEMON KNIGHT (SEE: TALES FROM THE CRYPT: DEMON KNIGHT)(1995)
DEMON WIND (1990)
DEMONI 2—L'INCUBO RITORNA (SEE: DEMONS 2—THE NIGHTMARE RETURNS)(1986)
DEMONIC TOYS (1992)
DEMONS (1986)
DEMONS (1987)
DEMONS 2: THE NIGHTMARE RETURNS (1986)
DEMONSTONE (1990)
DENIAL (1991)
DENNIS THE MENACE (1993)
DER BULLE UND DAS MAEDCHEN (SEE: COP AND THE GIRL, THE)(1985)
DER FLIEGER (SEE: FLYER, THE)(1987)
DER HIMMEL UBER BERLIN (SEE: WINGS OF DESIRE)(1987)
DER JOKER (SEE: LETHAL OBSESSION)(1988)
DER OLYMPISCHE SOMMER (SEE: OLYMPIC SUMMER, THE)(1994)
DER ROSENKONIG (1986)
DER TOD DES EMPEDOKLES (SEE: DEATH OF EMPEDOCLES, THE)(1988)

DESERT BLOOM (1986)
DESERT HEARTS (1985)
DESERT KICKBOXER (1992)
DESERT STEEL (1994)
DESERT WARRIOR (1985)
DESIRE AND HELL AT SUNSET MOTEL (1992)
DESPERADO (1995)
DESPERATE HOURS (1990)
DESPERATE MOTIVE (1993)
DESPERATE MOVES (1986)
DESPERATE PREY (1995)
DESPERATE REMEDIES (1994)
DESPERATE TRAIL, THE (1994)
DESPERATELY SEEKING SUSAN (1985)
DESTINY (SEE: TIME OF DESTINY, A)(1988)
DESTINY TURNS ON THE RADIO (1995)
DETECTIVE (1985)
DETECTIVE KID, THE (SEE: GUMSHOE KID, THE)(1990)
DETECTIVE SCHOOL DROPOUTS (1986)
DEVIL IN A BLUE DRESS (1995)
DEVIL IN THE FLESH (1986)
DEVIL'S DAUGHTER, THE (1992)
DEVIL'S ODDS (SEE: WILD PAIR, THE)(1987)
DIALOGUES WITH MADWOMEN (1994)
DIAMOND SKULLS (SEE: DARK OBSESSION)(1991)
DIARY OF A HITMAN (1992)
DICE RULES (1991)
DICK TRACY (1990)
DIE BLEIERNE ZEIT (SEE: MARIANNE AND JULIANE)(1994)
DIE HARD (1988)
DIE HARD 2: DIE HARDER (1990)
DIE HARD WITH A VENGEANCE (1995)
DIE KAMELIENDAME (SEE: LADY OF THE CAMELIAS)(1987)
DIE MACHT DER BILER: LENI RIEFENSTAHL (SEE: WONDERFUL, HORRIBLE LIFE OF LENI RIEFENSTAHL, THE)(1994)
DIE MITLAUFER (SEE: FOLLOWING THE FUHRER)(1986)
DIE REISE (SEE: JOURNEY, THE)(1986)
DIE WANNSEEKONFERENZ (SEE: WANNSEE CONFERENCE, THE)(1987)
DIE WATCHING (1993)
DIE XUE SHUANG XIONG (SEE: KILLER, THE)(1991)
DIGGER (1995)
DIGGSTOWN (1992)
DILLINGER (1995)
DILLINGER AND CAPONE (1995)
DIM SUM: A LITTLE BIT OF HEART (1985)
DINGO (1991)
DINOSAUR ISLAND (1994)
DIPLOMATIC IMMUNITY (1991)
DIRECT HIT (1994)
DIRT BIKE KID, THE (1986)
DIRTY DANCING (1987)
DIRTY LAUNDRY (1987)
DIRTY MONEY (1995)
DIRTY ROTTEN SCOUNDRELS (1988)
DISAPPEARANCE OF CHRISTINA, THE (1994)
DISCLOSURE (1994)
DISCRETION ASSURED (1994)
DISORDERLIES (1987)
DISORGANIZED CRIME (1989)
DISTANT COUSINS (SEE: DESPERATE MOTIVE)(1993)
DISTANT THUNDER (1988)
DISTANT VOICES, STILL LIVES (1989)
DISTINGUISHED GENTLEMAN, THE (1992)
DISTURBANCE, THE (1990)
DISTURBED (1991)

DIVERTIMENTO (SEE: LA BELLE NOISEUSE)(1993)
DIVING IN (1991)
DIXIELAND DAIMYO (1986)
DO OR DIE (1992)
DO THE RIGHT THING (1989)
DOC HOLLYWOOD (1991)
DOCTEUR JEKYLL ET LES FEMMES (SEE: DR. JEKYLL)(1985)
DOCTEUR M. (SEE: CLUB EXTINCTION)(1991)
DR. ALIEN (1989)
DOCTOR AND THE DEVILS, THE (1985)
DR. BETHUNE (1993)
DR. CALIGARI (1990)
DR. GIGGLES (1992)
DR. HACKENSTEIN (1989)
DR. JEKYLL (1985)
DR. JEKYLL & MS. HYDE (1995)
DOCTOR MORDRID (1992)
DR. OTTO AND THE RIDDLE OF THE GLOOM BEAM (1986)
DR. PETIOT (1994)
DOCTOR, THE (1991)
DOES THIS MEAN WE'RE MARRIED? (1992)
DOG TAGS (1990)
DOGFIGHT (1991)
DOIN' TIME (1985)
DOIN' TIME ON PLANET EARTH (1989)
DOLLMAN (1991)
DOLLMAN VS. DEMONIC TOYS (1993)
DOLLS (1987)
DOLLY DEAREST (1992)
DOLORES CLAIBORNE (1995)
DOMINICK AND EUGENE (1988)
DOMINION TANK POLICE: PART 2 (1993)
DON JUAN DEMARCO (1995)
DON JUAN, MY LOVE (1991)
DON JUAN, MI QUERIDO FANTASMA (SEE: DON JUAN, MY LOVE)(1991)
DON'T HANG UP (1994)
DONA HERLINDA AND HER SON (1986)
DON'T TELL HER IT'S ME (1990)
DON'T TELL MOM THE BABYSITTER'S DEAD (1991)
DOOM GENERATION, THE (1995)
DOOMED TO DIE (1985)
DOOMSDAY GUN (1995)
DOORS: THE SOFT PARADE - A RETROSPECTIVE, THE (1991)
DOORS, THE (1991)
DOPPELGANGER (1993)
DORMIRE (1985)
DOT AND THE KOALA (1985)
DOUBLE BLAST (1994)
DOUBLE CROSS (1994)
DOUBLE, DOUBLE, TOIL AND TROUBLE (1995)
DOUBLE DRAGON (1994)
DOUBLE EDGE (1992)
DOUBLE EXPOSURE (1994)
DOUBLE HAPPINESS (1995)
DOUBLE IDENTITY (1991)
DOUBLE IMPACT (1991)
DOUBLE LIFE OF VERONIQUE, THE (1991)
DOUBLE O KID, THE (1993)
DOUBLE OBSESSION (1994)
DOUBLE THREAT (1993)
DOUBLE TROUBLE (1992)
DOUBLE VISION (1992)
DOWN AND OUT IN BEVERLY HILLS (1986)
DOWN BY LAW (1986)
DOWN THE DRAIN (1990)
DOWN TWISTED (1989)
DOWNTOWN (1990)

DRACHENFUTTER (SEE: DRAGON'S FOOD)(1988)
DRACULA: DEAD AND LOVING IT (1995)
DRACULA RISING (1993)
DRACULA'S WIDOW (1988)
DRAGNET (1987)
DRAGON FIRE (1993)
DRAGON: THE BRUCE LEE STORY (1993)
DRAGONFIGHT (1993)
DRAGON'S FOOD (1988)
DRAGONWORLD (1994)
DREAM A LITTLE DREAM (1989)
DREAM A LITTLE DREAM 2 (1995)
DREAM GIRLS (1994)
DREAM LOVER (1986)
DREAM LOVER (1994)
DREAM MACHINE, THE (1991)
DREAM TEAM, THE (1989)
DREAMANIAC (1987)
DREAMCHILD (1985)
DREAMING OF RITA (1995)
DREAMS (1990)
DREI GEGEN DREI (1985)
DRIFTER, THE (1988)
DRIVE (1992)
DRIVING ME CRAZY (1991)
DRIVING MISS DAISY (1989)
DROP DEAD FRED (1991)
DROP SQUAD (1994)
DROP ZONE (1994)
DROWNING BY NUMBERS (1991)
DRUGSTORE COWBOY (1989)
DRY WHITE SEASON, A (1989)
D2: THE MIGHTY DUCKS (1994)
DU MICH AUCH (SEE: SAME TO YOU)(1987)
DUCKTALES: THE MOVIE—TREASURE OF THE LOST LAMP (1990)
DUDES (1988)
DUE OCCHI DIBOLICI (SEE: TWO EVIL EYES)(1990)
DUET FOR ONE (1986)
DUMB & DUMBER (1994)
DUMB DICKS (SEE: DETECTIVE SCHOOL DROPOUTS)(1986)
DUNE WARRIORS (1991)
DUNGEONMASTER (1985)
DUST (1985)
DUST DEVIL (1993)
DUTCH (1991)
DUTCH TREAT (1987)
DYING YOUNG (1991)
DYNAMO (1994)
TWO BITS (1995)

E

EAR, THE (1992)
EARTH GIRLS ARE EASY (1989)
EAST OF THE WALL (1986)
EASY WHEELS (1989)
EAT A BOWL OF TEA (1990)
EAT AND RUN (1986)
EAT DRINK MAN WOMAN (1994)
EAT THE PEACH (1987)
EATING (1991)
EBBTIDE (1994)
ECHO PARK (1986)
ECHOES OF PARADISE (1989)
ECLIPSE (1995)
ED WOOD (1994)
EDDIE AND THE CRUISERS II: EDDIE LIVES! (1989)
EDGAR ALLAN POE'S MASQUE OF THE RED DEATH (SEE: MASQUE OF THE RED DEATH)(1990)

EDGE OF HELL, THE (SEE: ROCK 'N' ROLL NIGHTMARE)(1987)
EDGE OF HONOR (1991)
EDGE OF SANITY (1989)
EDWARD SCISSORHANDS (1990)
EDWARD II (1992)
EFFICIENCY EXPERT, THE (1992)
800 LEAGUES DOWN THE AMAZON (1993)
EIGHT MEN OUT (1988)
8 MILLION WAYS TO DIE (1986)
8 SECONDS (1994)
8 SECONDS TO GLORY (SEE: 8 SECONDS)(1994)
18 AGAIN! (1988)
84 CHARING CROSS ROAD (1987)
84 CHARLIE MOPIC (1989)
EIN BLICK—UND DIE LIEBE BRICHT AUS (1986)
EIN MANN WIE EVA (SEE: MAN LIKE EVA, A)(1985)
EIN VIRUS KENNT KEINE MORAL (SEE: VIRUS KNOWS NO MORALS, A)(1986)
EL AMOR BRUJO (1986)
EL AMOR ES UNA MUJER GORDA (SEE: LOVE IS A FAT WOMAN)(1988)
EL ANO DE LAS LUCES (SEE: YEAR OF AWAKENING, THE)(1987)
EL IMPERIO DE LA FORTUNA (SEE: REALM OF FORTUNE, THE)(1987)
EL MARIACHI (1993)
EL PATRULLERO (SEE: HIGHWAY PATROLMAN)(1993)
EL TESORO DEL AMAZONES (SEE: TREASURE OF THE AMAZON, THE)(1985)
ELECTRIC BLUE (1988)
ELENI (1985)
ELIMINATORS (1986)
ELLA (SEE: MONKEY SHINES: AN EXPERIMENT IN FEAR)(1988)
ELLIOT FAUMAN, PH.D. (1990)
ELSA (SEE: AILSA)(1995)
ELVIRA: MISTRESS OF THE DARK (1988)
EMANON (1987)
EMBRACE OF THE VAMPIRE (1995)
EMBRYOS (1985)
EMERALD FOREST, THE (1985)
EMINENT DOMAIN (1991)
EMMANUELLE 5 (1987)
EMMANUELLE 6 (1992)
EMPIRE OF THE SUN (1987)
EMPIRE RECORDS (1995)
ENCHANTED APRIL (1992)
ENCINO MAN (1992)
END OF INNOCENCE, THE (1991)
END OF THE LINE (1988)
ENDANGERED (1994)
ENDLESS DESCENT (1991)
ENDLESS SUMMER II: THE JOURNEY CONTINUES, THE (1994)
ENEMIES, A LOVE STORY (1989)
ENEMY GOLD (1994)
ENEMY MINE (1985)
ENEMY TERRITORY (1987)
ENEMY UNSEEN (1991)
ENEMY WITHIN, THE (1995)
ENID IS SLEEPING (SEE: OVER HER DEAD BODY)(1992)
ENORMOUS CHANGES AT THE LAST MINUTE (1985)
ENRICO IV (SEE: HENRY IV)(1985)
ENTANGLED (1993)
EQUALIZER 2000 (1987)
EQUINOX (1993)
ERIK THE VIKING (1989)
ERMO (1995)
ERNEST GOES TO CAMP (1987)
ERNEST GOES TO JAIL (1990)

ERNEST GOES TO SCHOOL (1994)
ERNEST RIDES AGAIN (1993)
ERNEST SAVES CHRISTMAS (1988)
ERNEST SCARED STUPID (1991)
EROTIQUE (1995)
ESCAPE FROM ... SURVIVAL ZONE (1992)
ESCAPE FROM THE BRONX (1985)
ESCAPES (1987)
ESCORT GIRL (SEE: HALF MOON STREET)(1986)
ESPECIALLY ON SUNDAY (1993)
ESPERAME EN EL CIELO (SEE: WAIT FOR ME IN HEAVEN)(1988)
ETERNITY (1995)
ETHAN FROME (1993)
EUROPA (SEE: ZENTROPA)(1992)
EUROPA, EUROPA (1991)
EVE OF DESTRUCTION (1991)
EVEN COWGIRLS GET THE BLUES (1994)
EVERY BREATH (1994)
EVERY OTHER WEEKEND (1991)
EVERY TIME WE SAY GOODBYE (1986)
EVERYBODY WINS (1990)
EVERYBODY'S ALL-AMERICAN (1988)
EVERYBODY'S FINE (1991)
EVIL CLUTCH (1992)
EVIL DEAD 2: DEAD BY DAWN (1987)
EVIL SPIRITS (1991)
EVIL WITHIN, THE (1994)
EVILS OF THE NIGHT (1985)
EVOLVER (1995)
EXCESSIVE FORCE (1993)
EXECUTION PROTOCOL, THE (1993)
EXECUTIONERS (1995)
EXILED IN AMERICA (1992)
EXIT TO EDEN (1994)
EXORCIST III, THE (1990)
EXOTICA (1995)
EXPERT, THE (1995)
EXPERTS, THE (1989)
EXPLORERS (1985)
EXPOSURE (1991)
EXTERMINATORS OF THE YEAR 3000, THE (1985)
EXTRAMUROS (1991)
EXTREME PREJUDICE (1987)
EXTREME VENGEANCE (1994)
EXTREMITIES (1986)
EYE OF THE EAGLE 3 (1992)
EYE OF THE STORM (1992)
EYE OF THE STRANGER (1993)
EYE OF THE TIGER (1986)
EYES OF A WITNESS (1994)
EYES OF AN ANGEL (1994)
EYES OF THE BEHOLDER (1993)
EYES OF THE SERPENT (1994)
EYEWITNESS TO MURDER (1993)

F

FABULOUS BAKER BOYS, THE (1989)
FACE OF THE ENEMY (1990)
FACES OF WOMEN (1995)
FAILURE, THE (1986)
FAIR GAME (1985)
FAIR GAME (1986)
FAIR GAME (1991)
FAIR GAME (1995)
FAITH (1993)
FALCON AND THE SNOWMAN, THE (1985)
FALLING, THE (SEE: ALIEN PREDATOR)(1987)
FALLING DOWN (1993)
FALLING FROM GRACE (1992)
FALSE IDENTITY (1990)

FAMILY, THE (1987)
FAMILY BUSINESS (1987)
FAMILY BUSINESS (1989)
FAMILY PRAYERS (1993)
FAMINE WITHIN, THE (1991)
FANDANGO (1985)
FAR AND AWAY (1992)
FAR FROM HOME (1989)
FAR FROM HOME: THE ADVENTURES OF YELLOW DOG (1995)
FAR NORTH (1988)
FAR OFF PLACE, A (1993)
FAR OUT MAN (1990)
FARAWAY, SO CLOSE (1993)
FAREWELL TO THE KING (1989)
FAREWELL, MY CONCUBINE (1993)
FARINELLI (1995)
FARM, THE (SEE: CURSE, THE)(1987)
FARM OF THE YEAR (SEE: MILES FROM HOME)(1988)
FAST FOOD (1989)
FAST FORWARD (1985)
FAST GETAWAY (1991)
FAST GETAWAY 2 (1994)
FAT GUY GOES NUTZOID!! (1986)
FAT MAN AND LITTLE BOY (1989)
FATAL ATTRACTION (1987)
FATAL BEAUTY (1987)
FATAL BOND (1993)
FATAL INSTINCT (1992)
FATAL INSTINCT (1993)
FATAL JUSTICE (1993)
FATAL PAST (1994)
FATE (1992)
FATHER (1992)
FATHER AND SCOUT (1995)
FATHER HOOD (1993)
FATHER OF THE BRIDE (1991)
FATHER OF THE BRIDE PART II (1995)
FATHERLAND (1995)
FATHERS AND SONS (1992)
FATHER'S ON A BUSINESS TRIP (SEE: WHEN FATHER WAS AWAY ON BUSINES)(1985)
FAUST (1994)
FAUSTO (SEE: A LA MODE)(1994)
FAVOR, THE (1994)
FAVORITES OF THE MOON (1985)
FAVOUR, THE WATCH, AND THE VERY BIG FISH, THE (1992)
FEAR (1989)
FEAR, ANXIETY AND DEPRESSION (1989)
FEAR OF A BLACK HAT (1994)
FEAR, THE (1995)
FEARLESS (1993)
FEAST OF JULY (1995)
FEDERAL HILL (1994)
FEDERICO FELLINI'S INTERVISTA (SEE: INTERVISTA)(1987)
FEDS (1988)
FEED (1992)
FEEL THE HEAT (SEE: CATCH THE HEAT)(1987)
FELDMANN CASE, THE (1987)
FEMALE MISBEHAVIOR (1993)
FEMME FATALE (1991)
FEMMES DE PERSONNE (1986)
FERNGULLY: THE LAST RAINFOREST (1992)
FEROCIOUS FEMALE FREEDOM FIGHTERS (1989)
FERRIS BUELLER'S DAY OFF (1986)
FEUD, THE (1990)
FEVER PITCH (1985)
FEW DAYS WITH ME, A (1989)
FEW GOOD MEN, A (1992)
FIELD, THE (1990)

FIELD OF DREAMS (1989)
FIELD OF FIRE (1992)
FIFTH MONKEY, THE (1991)
50-50 (1993)
52 PICK-UP (1986)
FILOFAX (SEE: TAKING CARE OF BUSINESS)(1990)
FINAL ANALYSIS (1992)
FINAL APPROACH (1991)
FINAL EMBRACE (1994)
FINAL EXECUTIONER, THE (1986)
FINAL IMPACT (1992)
FINAL JUSTICE (1985)
FINAL MISSION (1994)
FINAL ROUND (1994)
FINAL SACRIFICE, THE (SEE: QUEST FOR THE LOST CITY)(1994)
FINAL TAKE: THE GOLDEN AGE OF MOVIES (1986)
FINE MESS, A (1986)
FINE ROMANCE, A (1992)
FINEST HOUR, THE (1992)
FINISHING TOUCH, THE (1992)
FIORILE (1994)
FIRE AND ICE (1987)
FIRE BIRDS (1990)
FIRE FESTIVAL (SEE: HIMATSURI)(1985)
FIRE IN EDEN (SEE: TUSKS)(1990)
FIRE IN THE NIGHT (1986)
FIRE IN THE SKY (1993)
FIRE THIS TIME, THE (1994)
FIRE WITH FIRE (1986)
FIREHAWK (1993)
FIREHEAD (1991)
FIREHOUSE (1987)
FIRES WITHIN (1991)
FIREWALKER (1986)
FIRING LINE, THE (1991)
FIRM, THE (1993)
FIRST DEGREE (1995)
FIRST KNIGHT (1995)
FIRST POWER, THE (1990)
FISH CALLED WANDA, A (1988)
FISHER KING, THE (1991)
FIST FIGHTER (1989)
FIST OF HONOR (1993)
FIST OF STEEL (1993)
FIST OF THE NORTH STAR (1991)
FIT TO KILL (1993)
FIVE CORNERS (1988)
FIVE HEARTBEATS, THE (1991)
FIX, THE (1985)
FLAME IN MY HEART, A (1990)
FLANAGAN (1985)
FLASHBACK (1990)
FLATLINERS (1990)
FLAXFIELD, THE (1985)
FLESH AND BLOOD (1985)
FLESH AND BONE (1993)
FLESH GORDON 2 (SEE: FLESH GORDON MEETS THE COSMIC CHEERLEADERS)(1993)
FLESH GORDON MEETS THE COSMIC CHEERLEADERS (1993)
FLESHTONE (1994)
FLETCH LIVES (1989)
FLICKS (1987)
FLIGHT OF THE INNOCENT (1993)
FLIGHT OF THE INTRUDER (1991)
FLIGHT OF THE NAVIGATOR (1986)
FLINCH (1994)
FLINTSTONES, THE (1994)
FLIRTING (1992)
FLOUNDERING (1994)
FLOWERS IN THE ATTIC (1987)

GOD AFTON, HERR WALLENBERG (SEE: GOOD EVENING, MR. WALLENBERG)(1993)
GOD IS MY WITNESS (1994)
GOD'S ARMY (SEE: PROPHECY, THE)(1995)
GODFATHER, PART III, THE (1990)
GODS MUST BE CRAZY II, THE (1990)
GODZILLA 1985 (1985)
GODZILLA VS. BIOLLANTE (1992)
GOING AND COMING BACK (1985)
GOING HOME (1988)
GOING UNDER (1991)
GOING UNDERCOVER (1989)
GOKIBURI (SEE: TWILIGHT OF THE COCKROACHES)(1990)
GOLD DIGGERS: THE SECRET OF BEAR MOUNTAIN (1995)
GOLDEN BRAID, THE (1991)
GOLDEN CHILD, THE (1986)
GOLDEN DART HERO (1994)
GOLDEN EIGHTIES (1986)
GOLDEN GATE (1994)
GOLDENEYE (1995)
GOOD DAY TO DIE, A (1995)
GOOD EVENING, MR. WALLENBERG (1993)
GOOD FATHER, THE (1987)
GOOD GIRLS DON'T (1995)
GOOD MAN IN AFRICA, A (1994)
GOOD MORNING, BABYLON (1987)
GOOD MORNING, VIETNAM (1987)
GOOD MOTHER, THE (1988)
GOOD OLD BOY (SEE: RIVER PIRATES, THE)(1994)
GOOD SON, THE (1993)
GOOD WIFE, THE (1986)
GOOD WOMAN OF BANGKOK, THE (1991)
GOODBYE, CHILDREN (SEE: AU REVOIR LES ENFANTS)(1988)
GOODBYE, NEW YORK (1985)
GOODFELLAS (1990)
GOOFBALLS (1987)
GOOFY MOVIE, A (1995)
GOONIES, THE (1985)
GOR (1989)
GORDY (1995)
GORILLA BATHES AT NOON (1995)
GORILLAS IN THE MIST (1988)
GOSPEL ACCORDING TO VIC, THE (1986)
GOTCHA! (1985)
GOTHIC (1987)
GRAFFITI BRIDGE (1990)
GRAND CANYON (1991)
GRAND HIGHWAY, THE (1988)
GRANDMOTHER'S HOUSE (1989)
GRANNY, THE (1995)
GRAVEYARD SHIFT (1987)
GRAVEYARD SHIFT (1990)
GREAT AMERICAN SEX SCANDAL, THE (1994)
GREAT BALLS OF FIRE (1989)
GREAT BIKINI OFF-ROAD ADVENTURE, THE (1994)
GREAT DAY IN HARLEM, A (1995)
GREAT ELEPHANT ESCAPE, THE (1995)
GREAT GENERATION, THE (1986)
GREAT MOUSE DETECTIVE, THE (1986)
GREAT OUTDOORS, THE (1988)
GREAT WALL, A (1986)
GREEDY (1994)
GREEN CARD (1990)
GREEN MONKEY (SEE: BLUE MONKEY)(1988)
GREEN SNAKE (1994)
GREMLINS 2: THE NEW BATCH (1990)
GRIEF (1994)

GRIFTERS, THE (1990)
GRIM PRAIRIE TALES (1990)
GROSS ANATOMY (1989)
GROSS MISCONDUCT (1995)
GROSSE FATIGUE (1995)
GROUND ZERO (1989)
GROUNDHOG DAY (1993)
GRUMPIER OLD MEN (1995)
GRUMPY OLD MEN (1993)
GRUNT! THE WRESTLING MOVIE (1985)
GUARDIAN, THE (1990)
GUARDIAN ANGEL (1994)
GUARDIAN OF HELL (1985)
GUARDING TESS (1994)
GUELWAAR (1993)
GUILIA E GUILIA (SEE: JULIA AND JULIA)(1988)
GUILTY AS CHARGED (1992)
GUILTY AS SIN (1993)
GUILTY BY SUSPICION (1991)
GUMBY: THE MOVIE (1995)
GUMSHOE KID, THE (1990)
GUN IN BETTY LOU'S HANDBAG, THE (1992)
GUNG HO (1986)
GUNMEN (1994)
GUNPOWDER (1987)
GUNRUNNER, THE (1989)
GUNS (1991)
GUNS OF HONOR (1994)
GUYVER II: DARK HERO, THE (1994)
GUYVER, THE (1992)
GYMKATA (1985)

H

H.P. LOVECRAFT'S LURKING FEAR (SEE: LURKING FEAR)(1994)
H.P. LOVECRAFT'S THE UNNAMABLE II: THE STATEMENT OF RANDOLPH CARTER (SEE: UNNAMABLE II, THE)(1993)
HAAKON HAAKONSEN (SEE: SHIPWRECKED)(1991)
HACKERS (1995)
HAIL CAESAR (1994)
HAIL, MARY (1985)
HAIRDRESSER'S HUSBAND, THE (1992)
HAIRSPRAY (1988)
HALF JAPANESE: THE BAND THAT WOULD BE KING (1993)
HALF MOON STREET (1986)
HALLOWEEN IV: THE RETURN OF MICHAEL MYERS (1988)
HALLOWEEN 5: THE REVENGE OF MICHAEL MYERS (1989)
HALLOWEEN: THE CURSE OF MICHAEL MYERS (1995)
HALLOWEEN TREE, THE (1994)
HAMBURGER HILL (1987)
HAMBURGER...THE MOTION PICTURE (1986)
HAMLET (1990)
HAMOUN (1991)
HAND THAT ROCKS THE CRADLE, THE (1992)
HANDFUL OF DUST, A (1988)
HANDMAID'S TALE, THE (1990)
HANDS OF STEEL (1986)
HANGFIRE (1991)
HANGIN' WITH THE HOMEBOYS (1991)
HANNAH AND HER SISTERS (1986)
HANNA'S WAR (1988)
HANOI HILTON, THE (1987)
HANS CHRISTIAN ANDERSEN'S THUMBELINA (1994)
HANUSSEN (1989)
HANY AZ ORA, VEKKER UR? (SEE: WHAT'S THE TIME, MR. CLOCK?)(1985)

HAPPILY EVER AFTER (1993)
HAPPY HELL NIGHT (1992)
HAPPY HOUR (1987)
HAPPY NEW YEAR (1987)
HAPPY TOGETHER (1990)
HARD DRIVE (1994)
HARD HUNTED (1993)
HARD LABOUR (1994)
HARD PROMISES (1992)
HARD TARGET (1993)
HARD TICKET TO HAWAII (1987)
HARD TIMES (1988)
HARD TO DIE (1993)
HARD TO KILL (1990)
HARD TRAVELING (1985)
HARD TRUTH, THE (1994)
HARD VICE (1994)
HARD WAY, THE (1991)
HARD-BOILED (1992)
HARDBODIES 2 (1986)
HARDCASE AND FIST (1989)
HARDWARE (1990)
HAREM (1985)
HARLEM DIARY: NINE VOICES OF RESILIENCE (1995)
HARLEM NIGHTS (1989)
HARLEY DAVIDSON AND THE MARLBORO MAN (1991)
HARMONY CATS (1994)
HARRISON BERGERON (SEE: KURT VONNEGUT'S HARRISON BERGERON)(1995)
HARRY AND THE HENDERSONS (1987)
HARVEST, THE (1993)
HATTA ISHAAR AKHAR (SEE: CURFEW)(1994)
HAUNTED HONEYMOON (1986)
HAUNTING FEAR (1991)
HAUNTING OF HAMILTON HIGH, THE (SEE: HELLO MARY LOU: PROM NIGHT II)(1987)
HAUNTING OF MORELLA, THE (1990)
HAVANA (1990)
HAWK, THE (1993)
HE SAID, SHE SAID (1991)
HEAD OFFICE (1986)
HEADS (1994)
HEAR MY SONG (1991)
HEAR NO EVIL (1993)
HEARING VOICES (1991)
HEART AND SOULS (1993)
HEART CONDITION (1990)
HEART IN WINTER, A (SEE: UN COEUR EN HIVER)(1993)
HEART OF DIXIE (1989)
HEART OF MIDNIGHT (1989)
HEARTBREAK HOTEL (1988)
HEARTBREAK RIDGE (1986)
HEARTBURN (1986)
HEARTS OF FIRE (1987)
HEARTSTONE (SEE: DEMONSTONE)(1990)
HEAT (1987)
HEAT (1995)
HEAT AND SUNLIGHT (1988)
HEATHCLIFF: THE MOVIE (1986)
HEATHERS (1989)
HEAVEN AND EARTH (1990)
HEAVEN AND EARTH (1993)
HEAVEN HELP US (1985)
HEAVEN IS A PLAYGROUND (1992)
HEAVENLY BODIES (1985)
HEAVENLY CREATURES (1994)
HEAVENLY KID, THE (1985)
HEAVENLY PURSUITS (SEE: GOSPEL ACCORDING TO VIC, THE)(1986)

HEAVEN'S A DRAG (1995)
HEAVYWEIGHTS (1995)
HEIMAT (1985)
HELAS POUR MOI (1994)
HELL COMES TO FROGTOWN (1988)
HELL HIGH (1989)
HELL MASTER (1992)
HELL SQUAD (1986)
HELLBOUND: HELLRAISER II (1988)
HELLHOLE (1985)
HELLO AGAIN (1987)
HELLO MARY LOU: PROM NIGHT II (1987)
HELLRAISER (1987)
HELLRAISER III: HELL ON EARTH (1992)
HELLROLLER (1992)
HENRY & JUNE (1990)
HENRY: PORTRAIT OF A SERIAL KILLER
    (1989)
HENRY V (1989)
HER ALIBI (1989)
HERCULES II (1985)
HERDSMEN OF THE SUN (1991)
HERE COME THE LITTLES (1985)
HERO (1992)
HERO AND THE TERROR (1988)
HEROIC TRIO 2: EXECUTIONERS (SEE:
    EXECUTIONERS)(1995)
HEROIC TRIO, THE (1995)
HE'S A WOMAN, SHE'S A MAN (1995)
HE'S MY GIRL (1987)
HEXED (1993)
HEY BABU RIBA (1987)
HIDDEN, THE (1987)
HIDDEN II, THE (1994)
HIDDEN AGENDA (1990)
HIDDEN FEARS (1994)
HIDDEN OBSESSION (1993)
HIDDEN VISION (SEE: NIGHT EYES)(1990)
HIDEAWAY (1995)
HIDER IN THE HOUSE (1991)
HIDING OUT (1987)
HIGH DESERT KILL (1990)
HIGH HEELS (1991)
HIGH HOPES (1988)
HIGH LONESOME: THE STORY OF
    BLUEGRASS MUSIC (1994)
HIGH RISK (1995)
HIGH SCHOOL II (1994)
HIGH SEASON (1988)
HIGH SPEED (1986)
HIGH SPIRITS (1988)
HIGH STAKES (1989)
HIGH STRUNG (1994)
HIGH TIDE (1987)
HIGHER LEARNING (1995)
HIGHLANDER (1986)
HIGHLANDER: THE FINAL DIMENSION
    (1995)
HIGHLANDER 2: THE QUICKENING (1991)
HIGHWAY PATROLMAN (1993)
HIGHWAY 61 (1992)
HIGHWAY TO HELL (1992)
HILLS HAVE EYES II, THE (1985)
HIMATSURI (1985)
HIMMO, KING OF JERUSALEM (1988)
HIRED TO KILL (1992)
HISTORY (1988)
HIT, THE (1985)
HIT LIST (1990)
HIT THE DUTCHMAN (1993)
HITCHER, THE (1986)
HITMAN (SEE: AMERICAN
    COMMANDOES)(1986)
HITMAN, THE (1991)

HIUCH HA'GDI (SEE: SMILE OF THE LAMB,
    THE)(1986)
HOCUS POCUS (1993)
HOFFA (1992)
HOL VOLT, HOL NEM VOLT (SEE:
    HUNGARIAN FAIRY TALE, A)(1989)
HOLCROFT COVENANT, THE (1985)
HOLD ME THRILL ME KISS ME (1993)
HOLLYWEIRD (SEE: FLICKS)(1987)
HOLLYWOOD BOULEVARD II (1991)
HOLLYWOOD CHAINSAW HOOKERS (1988)
HOLLYWOOD HARRY (1985)
HOLLYWOOD HOT TUBS II: EDUCATING
    CRYSTAL (1990)
HOLLYWOOD SHUFFLE (1987)
HOLLYWOOD VICE SQUAD (1986)
HOLLYWOOD ZAP! (1986)
HOLY MATRIMONY (1994)
HOMBRE MIRANDO AL SUDESTE (SEE:
    MAN FACING SOUTHEAST)(1986)
HOME ALONE (1990)
HOME ALONE 2: LOST IN NEW YORK (1992)
HOME FOR THE HOLIDAYS (1995)
HOME FRONT (SEE: MORGAN STEWART'S
    COMING HOME)(1987)
HOME IS WHERE THE HART IS (1987)
HOME IS WHERE THE HEART IS (SEE:
    SQUARE DANCE)(1987)
HOME OF ANGELS (1994)
HOME OF OUR OWN, A (1993)
HOME SWEET HOME (1994)
HOMEBOY (1989)
HOMEBOYS (1992)
HOMER & EDDIE (1990)
HOMEWARD BOUND: THE INCREDIBLE
    JOURNEY (1993)
HOMICIDAL IMPULSE (1992)
HOMICIDE (1991)
HONEY, I BLEW UP THE KID (1992)
HONEY, I SHRUNK THE KIDS (1989)
HONEYMOON ACADEMY (1990)
HONEYMOON IN VEGAS (1992)
HONG GAOLIANG (SEE: RED
    SORGHUM)(1988)
HONG KONG '97 (1994)
HONOR AND GLORY (1993)
HOOK (1991)
HOOP DREAMS (1994)
HOOSIERS (1986)
HOPE AND GLORY (1987)
HORROR SHOW, THE (1989)
HORSEPLAYER (1991)
HOSTAGE (1993)
HOSTAGE (1987)
HOSTAGE: DALLAS (SEE: GETTING
    EVEN)(1986)
HOSTAGE FOR A DAY (1994)
HOSTILE HOSTAGES (SEE: REF, THE)(1994)
HOSTILE TAKEOVER (1990)
HOT AND COLD (SEE: WEEKEND AT
    BERNIE'S)(1989)
HOT CHILD IN THE CITY (1987)
HOT CHILI (1986)
HOT CHOCOLATE (1992)
HOT PURSUIT (1987)
HOT RESORT (1985)
HOT SEAT (SEE: CHAIR, THE)(1989)
HOT SHOT (1987)
HOT SHOTS! (1991)
HOT SHOTS! PART DEUX (1993)
HOT SPOT, THE (1990)
HOT TARGET (1985)
HOT TO TROT (1988)
HOTEL COLONIAL (1987)
HOTEL NEW YORK (1985)
HOTEL SORRENTO (1995)

HOUR OF THE ASSASSIN (1987)
HOUR OF THE PIG, THE (SEE: ADVOCATE,
    THE)(1994)
HOUR OF THE STAR, THE (1986)
HOURS AND TIMES, THE (1992)
HOUSE (1986)
HOUSE IV (1992)
HOUSE IN THE HILLS, A (1993)
HOUSE OF ANGELS (1993)
HOUSE OF CARDS (1993)
HOUSE OF GAMES (1987)
HOUSE OF THE DARK STAIRWAY (SEE:
    BLADE IN THE DARK, A)(1986)
HOUSE OF THE SPIRITS, THE (1994)
HOUSE OF USHER, THE (1992)
HOUSE ON CARROLL STREET, THE (1988)
HOUSE ON THE EDGE OF THE PARK (1985)
HOUSE ON TOMBSTONE HILL, THE (1992)
HOUSE PARTY (1990)
HOUSE PARTY 3 (1994)
HOUSE PARTY 2 (1991)
HOUSE II: THE SECOND STORY (1987)
HOUSEGUEST (1995)
HOUSEHOLD SAINTS (1993)
HOUSEKEEPER, THE (1987)
HOUSEKEEPING (1987)
HOUSESITTER (1992)
HOUSEWIFE FROM HELL (1994)
HOW I GOT INTO COLLEGE (1989)
HOW TO GET AHEAD IN ADVERTISING
    (1989)
HOW TO MAKE AN AMERICAN QUILT (1995)
HOW TO MAKE LOVE TO A NEGRO
    WITHOUT GETTING TIRED (1990)
HOW TO TOP MY WIFE (1995)
HOW U LIKE ME NOW (1993)
HOWARD THE DUCK (1986)
HOWARDS END (1992)
HOWLING TWO: YOUR SISTER IS A
    WEREWOLF (1985)
HOWLING III, THE (1987)
HOWLING IV . . . THE ORIGINAL
    NIGHTMARE (1988)
HOWLING 5: THE REBIRTH, THE (1989)
HOWLING VI - THE FREAKS (1991)
HOWLING: NEW MOON RISING, THE (1995)
HUCK AND THE KING OF HEARTS (1994)
HUDSON HAWK (1991)
HUDSUCKER PROXY, THE (1994)
HUGH HEFNER: ONCE UPON A TIME (1992)
HUMAN SHIELD, THE (1992)
HUNGARIAN FAIRY TALE, A (1989)
HUNK (1987)
HUNT FOR RED OCTOBER, THE (1990)
HUNTED, THE (1995)
HUNTER'S BLOOD (1987)
HUNTING (1992)
HUOZHE (SEE: TO LIVE)(1994)
HURRICANE SMITH (1992)
HUSBANDS AND LOVERS (1992)
HUSBANDS AND WIVES (1992)
HUSTRUER, 2—TI AR ETTER (SEE:
    WIVES—TEN YEARS AFTER)(1985)
HYENAS (1995)
HYPERSPACE (1990)
WINGS OF HONNEAMISE: ROYAL SPACE
    FORCE (1995)

I

BRIAN WILSON: I JUST WASN'T MADE FOR
    THESE TIMES (1995)
I AM CUBA (1995)
I AM MY OWN WOMAN (1994)
I CAN'T SLEEP (1995)
I COME IN PEACE (1990)

I DON'T BUY KISSES ANYMORE (1992)
I DON'T WANT TO TALK ABOUT IT (1994)
I JUST WASN'T MADE FOR THESE TIMES
    (SEE: BRIAN WILSON: I JUST WASN'T
    MADE FOR THESE TIMES)(1995)
I LIKE IT LIKE THAT (1994)
I LIKE TO PLAY GAMES (1995)
I LOVE A MAN IN A UNIFORM (SEE: A MAN
    IN UNIFORM)(1994)
I LOVE N.Y. (1987)
I LOVE TROUBLE (1994)
I LOVE YOU TO DEATH (1990)
I, MADMAN (1989)
I ONLY WANT YOU TO LOVE ME (1994)
I PHOTOGRAPHIA (SEE: PHOTOGRAPH,
    THE)(1987)
I, THE WORST OF ALL (1995)
I WAS A TEENAGE T.V. TERRORIST (1987)
I WAS A TEENAGE ZOMBIE (1987)
ICE (1994)
ICE PALACE, THE (1987)
ICE RUNNER, THE (1993)
ICH BIN MEINE EIGENE FRAU (SEE: I AM
    MY OWN WOMAN)(1994)
ICH UND ER (SEE: ME AND HIM)(1990)
ICH WILL DOCH NUR, DAS IHR MICH LIEBT
    (SEE: I ONLY WANT YOU TO LOVE
    ME)(1994)
ICICLE THIEF, THE (1990)
IDENTITY CRISIS (1991)
IDI I SMOTRI (SEE: COME AND SEE)(1986)
IF LOOKS COULD KILL (1991)
IL CASO MORO (SEE: MORO AFFAIR,
    THE)(1987)
IL DIAVOLO IN CORPO (SEE: DEVIL IN THE
    FLESH)(1986)
IL LADRO DI BAMBINI (SEE: STOLEN
    CHILDREN, THE)(1993)
IL POSTINO (SEE: POSTMAN, THE)(1995)
I'LL DO ANYTHING (1994)
ILLEGALLY YOURS (1988)
ILLUSIONIST, THE (1985)
ILLUSIONS (1992)
ILLUSTRIOUS ENERGY (1988)
I'M GONNA GIT YOU SUCKA (1988)
IMAGEMAKER, THE (1986)
IMAGEN LATENTE (SEE: LATENT
    IMAGE)(1988)
IMAGINARY CRIMES (1994)
IMMEDIATE FAMILY (1989)
IMMORTAL BELOVED (1994)
IMMORTAL COMBAT (1994)
IMPORTANCE OF BEING EARNEST, THE
    (1992)
IMPORTED BRIDEGROOM, THE (1990)
IMPROMPTU (1990)
IMPROPER CONDUCT (1994)
IMPULSE (1990)
IN A GLASS CAGE (1989)
IN A MOMENT OF PASSION (1993)
IN BED WITH MADONNA (SEE: TRUTH OR
    DARE)(1991)
IN COUNTRY (1989)
IN CUSTODY (1994)
IN DE SCHADUW VAN DE OVERWINNING
    (SEE: SHADOW OF VICTORY)(1986)
IN GOLD WE TRUST (1992)
IN THE ARMY NOW (1994)
IN THE COLD OF THE NIGHT (1991)
IN THE DEEP WOODS (1995)
IN THE EYE OF THE SNAKE (1994)
IN THE HANDS OF THE ENEMY (1994)
IN THE HEAT OF PASSION (1992)
IN THE HEAT OF PASSION 2: UNFAITHFUL
    (1994)
IN THE LAND OF THE DEAF (1994)
IN THE LINE OF FIRE (1993)

IN THE MOOD (1987)
IN THE MOUTH OF MADNESS (1995)
IN THE MOUTH OF THE WOLF (1988)
IN THE NAME OF THE EMPEROR (1995)
IN THE NAME OF THE FATHER (1993)
IN THE SHADOW OF KILIMANJARO (1986)
IN THE SHADOW OF THE STARS (1991)
IN THE SOUP (1992)
IN THE SPIRIT (1990)
IN THE WILD MOUNTAINS (1986)
IN TOO DEEP (1991)
IN WEITER FERNE SO NAH (SEE: FARAWAY,
    SO CLOSE)(1993)
INCIDENT AT OGLALA (1992)
INCREDIBLY TRUE ADVENTURES OF TWO
    GIRLS IN LOVE, THE (1995)
INDECENT BEHAVIOR (1993)
INDECENT BEHAVIOR 2 (1994)
INDECENT OBSESSION, AN (1985)
INDECENT PROPOSAL (1993)
INDIAN IN THE CUPBOARD, THE (1995)
INDIAN RUNNER, THE (1991)
INDIAN SUMMER (1993)
INDIANA JONES AND THE LAST CRUSADE
    (1989)
INDICTMENT: THE MCMARTIN TRIAL (1995)
INDIO 2 - THE REVOLT (1992)
INDOCHINE (1992)
INFERNO IN DIRETTA (SEE: CUT AND
    RUN)(1986)
INFESTED (SEE: TICKS)(1994)
INFINITY (1991)
INHERITOR (1990)
INKWELL, THE (1994)
INNER CIRCLE, THE (1991)
INNER SANCTUM (1991)
INNER SANCTUM 2 (1994)
INNERSPACE (1987)
INNOCENT, THE (1988)
INNOCENT BLOOD (1992)
INNOCENT LIES (1995)
INNOCENT MAN, AN (1989)
INNOCENT MOVES (SEE: SEARCHING FOR
    BOBBY FISCHER)(1993)
INNOCENT VICTIM (1990)
INNOCENT, THE (1995)
INSIDE EDGE (1992)
INSIDE MONKEY ZETTERLAND (1993)
INSIDE OUT (1986)
INSIGNIFICANCE (1985)
INSOMNIACS (1986)
INSPECTOR LAVARDIN (1992)
INSTANT JUSTICE (1986)
INSTANT KARMA (1991)
INTENT TO KILL (1993)
INTERNAL AFFAIRS (1990)
INTERROGATION, THE (1990)
INTERSECTION (1994)
INTERVIEW WITH THE VAMPIRE (1994)
INTERVISTA (1987)
INTIMATE POWER (1986)
INTO THE NIGHT (1985)
INTO THE SUN (1992)
INTO THE WEST (1993)
INVADERS (1993)
INVADERS FROM MARS (1986)
INVASION OF THE SPACE PREACHERS (1992)
INVASION U.S.A. (1985)
INVISIBLE KID, THE (1988)
INVISIBLE: THE CHRONICLES OF
    BENJAMIN KNIGHT (1994)
IO SPERIAMO CHE ME LO CAVO (SEE: CIAO,
    PROFESSORE!)(1994)
I.Q. (1994)
IRON & SILK (1991)

IRON EAGLE (1986)
IRON EAGLE II (1988)
IRON MAZE (1991)
IRON MONKEY (1994)
IRON TRIANGLE, THE (1989)
IRON WILL (1994)
IRONWEED (1987)
IS-SLOTTET (SEE: ICE PALACE, THE)(1988)
ISHTAR (1987)
ISLAND FURY (1994)
ISTANBUL, KEEP YOUR EYES OPEN (1990)
ISTORIYA AS: KLYACHIMOL (SEE: ASYA'S
    HAPPINESS)(1988)
IT COULD HAPPEN TO YOU (1994)
IT COULDN'T HAPPEN HERE (1988)
IT DON'T PAY TO BE AN HONEST CITIZEN
    (1985)
IT RUNS IN THE FAMILY (1994)
IT TAKES TWO (1995)
IT'S ALL TRUE: BASED ON AN UNFINISHED
    FILM BY ORSON WELLES (1993)
IT'S ALIVE III: ISLAND OF THE ALIVE (1988)
IT'S PAT (1994)
IVAN AND ABRAHAM (1994)

J

JACK BE NIMBLE (1994)
JACK KEROUAC'S AMERICA (SEE:
    KEROUAC)(1985)
JACK THE BEAR (1993)
JACKALS (SEE: AMERICAN JUSTICE)(1986)
JACKNIFE (1989)
JACK-O (1995)
JACK'S BACK (1988)
JACOB'S LADDER (1990)
JACQUES AND NOVEMBER (1985)
JACQUOT (1993)
JACQUOT DE NANTES (SEE: JACQUOT)(1993)
JADE (1995)
JAGGED EDGE (1985)
JAILBIRD ROCK (1988)
JAKE SPEED (1986)
JAMES JOYCE'S WOMEN (1985)
JAMON JAMON (1993)
JANUARY MAN, THE (1989)
JAR, THE (1995)
JASON GOES TO HELL: THE FINAL FRIDAY
    (1993)
JASON LIVES: FRIDAY THE 13TH PART VI
    (SEE: FRIDAY THE 13TH PART VII—THE
    NEW BLOOD)(1988)
JASON'S LYRIC (1994)
JATSZANI KELL (SEE: LILY IN LOVE)(1985)
JAWS: THE REVENGE (1987)
JE VOUS SALUE, MAFIA (SEE: HAIL
    MAFIA)(1985)
JEAN DE FLORETTE (1986)
JEAN DE FLORETTE 2 (SEE: MANON OF THE
    SPRING)(1986)
JEANNE, PUTAIN DU ROI (SEE: KING'S
    WHORE, THE)(1993)
JEFFERSON IN PARIS (1995)
JEFFREY (1995)
JENATSCH (1987)
JENNIFER EIGHT (1992)
JENNY KISSED ME (1985)
JERICHO FEVER (1994)
JERKY BOYS: THE MOVIE, THE (1995)
JERSEY GIRL (1994)
JESTER, THE (1987)
JESUS OF MONTREAL (1990)
JETSONS: THE MOVIE (1990)
JEWEL OF THE NILE, THE (1985)
JEZEBEL'S KISS (1990)
JFK (1991)

JIMMY HOLLYWOOD (1994)
JIMMY REARDON (SEE: NIGHT IN THE LIFE OF JIMMY REARDON, A)(1988)
JIT (1993)
JLG BY JLG (1995)
JO JO DANCER, YOUR LIFE IS CALLING (1986)
JOCKS (1987)
JOE VERSUS THE VOLCANO (1990)
JOEY BREAKER (1993)
JOHNNY BE GOOD (1988)
JOHNNY HANDSOME (1989)
JOHNNY MNEMONIC (1995)
JOHNNY STECCHINO (1992)
JOHNNY SUEDE (1992)
JON JOST'S FRAMEUP (SEE: FRAMEUP)(1995)
JOSH AND S.A.M. (1993)
JOSHUA THEN AND NOW (1985)
JOURNEY, THE (1986)
JOURNEY OF AUGUST KING, THE (1995)
JOURNEY OF HONOR (1992)
JOURNEY OF HOPE (1991)
JOURNEY OF NATTY GANN, THE (1985)
JOURNEY TO SPIRIT ISLAND (1988)
JOY LUCK CLUB, THE (1993)
JU DOU (1991)
JUDGE DREDD (1995)
JUDGEMENT IN STONE, A (SEE: HOUSEKEEPER, THE)(1987)
JUDGMENT IN BERLIN (1988)
JUDGMENT NIGHT (1993)
JUDICIAL CONSENT (1995)
JUICE (1992)
JULIA AND JULIA (1988)
JULIA HAS TWO LOVERS (1991)
JUMANJI (1995)
JUMPIN' AT THE BONEYARD (1992)
JUMPIN' JACK FLASH (1986)
JUNGLE BOOK, THE (1994)
JUNGLE FEVER (1991)
JUNGLE RAIDERS (1986)
JUNIOR (1994)
JUPITER'S WIFE (1995)
JURASSIC PARK (1993)
JURY DUTY (1995)
JURY DUTY: THE COMEDY (SEE: GREAT AMERICAN SEX SCANDAL, THE)(1994)
JUST ANOTHER GIRL ON THE I.R.T. (1993)
JUST BETWEEN FRIENDS (1986)
JUST CAUSE (1995)
JUST LIKE A WOMAN (1994)
JUST LIKE IN THE MOVIES (1992)
JUST ONE OF THE GUYS (1985)

K

K-9 (1989)
K2 (1992)
KADISBELLAN (SEE: SLINGSHOT, THE)(1994)
KAFKA (1991)
KALEIDOSCOPE (1994)
KALIFORNIA (1993)
KAMATA KOSHINKYOKU (SEE: FALL GUY)(1985)
KANDYLAND (1988)
KANGAROO (1986)
KANSAS (1988)
KAOS (1985)
KARATE KID PART II, THE (1986)
KARATE KID PART III, THE (1989)
KARATE TIGER 5 (SEE: AMERICAN SHAOLIN: KING OF THE KICKBOXERS II)(1993)
KARHOZAT (SEE: DAMNATION)(1988)

KARMA (1986)
KEROUAC (1985)
KEY EXCHANGE (1985)
KICK OR DIE (1992)
KICKBOXER (1989)
KICKBOXER 4: THE AGGRESSOR (1994)
KICKBOXER 3: THE ART OF WAR (1992)
KICKBOXER 2 (1991)
KICKING AND SCREAMING (1995)
KID (1991)
KID IN KING ARTHUR'S COURT, A (1995)
KIDS (1995)
KIKA (1994)
KILIAN'S CHRONICLE (1995)
KILL CRUISE (1992)
KILL LINE (1992)
KILL ME AGAIN (1990)
KILL-OFF, THE (1990)
KILL ZONE (1985)
KILL ZONE (1993)
KILLBOTS (SEE: CHOPPING MALL)(1986)
KILLER (SEE: BULLETPROOF HEART)(1995)
KILLER IMAGE (1992)
KILLER INSTINCT (SEE: MAD DOG COLL)(1993)
KILLER KLOWNS FROM OUTER SPACE (1988)
KILLER LOOKS (1994)
KILLER NERD (1991)
KILLER PARTY (1986)
KILLER TOMATOES EAT FRANCE! (1992)
KILLER TOMATOES STRIKE BACK (1991)
KILLER WORKOUT (1987)
KILLER, THE (1991)
KILLERS EDGE, THE (1991)
KILLING AFFAIR, A (1985)
KILLING BEACH, THE (1993)
KILLING EDGE, THE (SEE: INVADERS)(1993)
KILLING OBSESSION (1994)
KILLING STREETS, THE (1991)
KILLING ZOE (1994)
KILLING ZONE, THE (1991)
KINDER KADER KOMMANDEURE (SEE: STRICTLY PROPAGANDA)(1993)
KINDERGARTEN COP (1990)
KINDRED, THE (1987)
KINEMA NO TENCHI (SEE: FINAL TAKE: THE GOLDEN AGE OF MOVIES)(1986)
KING AND HIS MOVIE, A (1986)
KING DAVID (1985)
KING KONG LIVES (1986)
KING LEAR (1988)
KING OF NEW YORK (1990)
KING OF THE HILL (1993)
KING OF THE KICKBOXERS, THE (1991)
KING OF THE STREETS (1986)
KING RALPH (1991)
KING SOLOMON'S MINES (1985)
KING'S WHORE, THE (1993)
KINGDOM, THE (1995)
KINGFISH: A STORY OF HUEY P. LONG (1995)
KINJITE: FORBIDDEN SUBJECTS (1989)
KISS, THE (1988)
KISS BEFORE DYING, A (1991)
KISS GOODNIGHT, A (1994)
KISS ME A KILLER (1992)
KISS OF DEATH (1995)
KISS OF DEATH, THE (1994)
KISS OF THE SPIDER WOMAN (1985)
KLASSENVERHALTNISSE (SEE: CLASS RELATIONS)(1986)
KNIGHT MOVES (1993)
KNIGHTS OF THE CITY (1985)

KOKS I KULISSEN (SEE: LADIES ON THE ROCKS)(1985)
KOMIKKU ZASSHI NANKA IRANI (SEE: COMIC MAGAZINE)(1986)
KONBU FINZE (SEE: TERRORIZERS, THE)(1987)
KONEKO MONGATARI (SEE: ADVENTURES OF MILO AND OTIS, THE)(1990)
KOOTENAI BROWN (SEE: SHOWDOWN AT WILLIAMS CREEK)(1991)
KORCZAK (1991)
KRAYS, THE (1990)
KRUSH GROOVE (1985)
KUFFS (1992)
KUNG FU MASTER (1989)
KUROI AME (SEE: BLACK RAIN)(1990)
KURT VONNEGUT'S HARRISON BERGERON (1995)
KVITEBJORN KONG VALEMAN (SEE: POLAR BEAR KING, THE)(1994)

L

L'ELEGANT CRIMINEL (1992)
L.627 (1994)
L.A. STREETFIGHTERS (SEE: NINJA TURF)(1986)
LA BAMBA (1987)
LA BELLE NOISEUSE (1991)
LA BOCA DEL LOBO (SEE: IN THE MOUTH OF THE WOLF)(1988)
L.A. BOUNTY (1989)
LA CAGE AUX FOLLES 3: THE WEDDING (1985)
LA CARTE DU TENDRE (SEE: MAP OF THE HUMAN HEART)(1993)
LA CASA CON LA SCALA NEL BUIO (SEE: BLADE IN THE DARK, A)(1986)
LA CASA NEL PARCO (SEE: HOUSE ON THE EDGE OF THE PARK)(1985)
LA CHASSE AUX PAPILLONS (1993)
LA CHEVRE (1985)
LA CHIESA (SEE: CHURCH, THE)(1991)
LA CIUDAD Y LOS PERROS (SEE: CITY AND THE DOGS, THE)(1987)
LA CONDANNA (SEE: CONVICTION, THE)(1994)
LA CORSA DELL'INNOCENTE (SEE: FLIGHT OF THE INNOCENT)(1993)
LA CORTE DE FARAON (SEE: COURT OF THE PHARAOH, THE)(1985)
LA DISCRETE (1992)
LA DOUBLE VIE DE VERONIQUE (SEE: DOUBLE LIFE OF VERONIQUE, THE)(1991)
LA DUEDA INTERNA (SEE: VERONICO CRUZ)(1990)
LA FAMIGLIA (SEE: FAMILY, THE)(1987)
LA FEMME NIKITA (1991)
LA FRACTURE DU MYOCARDE (SEE: CROSS MY HEART)(1991)
LA GLOIRE DE MON PERE (SEE: MY FATHER'S GLORY)(1991)
L.A. GODDESS (1993)
LA GRIETA (SEE: ENDLESS DESCENT)(1991)
L.A. HEAT (1989)
LA HISTORIA OFICIAL (SEE: OFFICIAL STORY, THE)(1985)
LA LECTRICE (1989)
LA LEGENDA DEL RUDIO MALESE (SEE: JUNGLE RAIDERS)(1986)
LA LEI DEL DESEO (SEE: LAW OF DESIRE, THE)(1987)
LA MESSA E FINITA (SEE: MASS IS ENDED, THE)(1988)
LA MORT DE MARIO RICCI (SEE: DEATH OF MARIO RICCI, THE)(1985)
LA PASSION BEATRICE (SEE: BEATRICE)(1988)
LA PELICULA DEL REY (SEE: KING AND HIS MOVIE, A)(1986)

LA PESTE (SEE: PLAGUE, THE)(1993)
LA REINE MARGOT (SEE: QUEEN MARGOT)(1994)
LA SCARLATINE (1985)
LA SCORTA (1994)
LA SEGUA (1985)
L.A. STORY (1991)
LA VIE DE BOHEME (1993)
LA VIE EST RIEN D'AUTRE (SEE: LIFE AND NOTHING BUT)(1990)
L.A. WARS (1994)
LABYRINTH (1986)
LABYRINTH OF PASSION (1990)
L'ACCOMPAGNATRICE (SEE: ACCOMPANIST, THE)(1993)
L'ADDITION (1985)
LADIES CLUB, THE (1986)
LADIES OF THE LOTUS (1987)
LADIES ON THE ROCKS (1985)
LADRI DI SAPONETTE (SEE: ICICLE THIEF, THE)(1990)
LADY DRAGON (1992)
LADY DRAGON 2 (1993)
LADY IN WAITING (1994)
LADY IN WHITE (1988)
LADY JANE (1986)
LADY OF THE CAMELIAS (1987)
LADYBIRD, LADYBIRD (1994)
LADYBUGS (1992)
LADYHAWKE (1985)
LAIR OF THE WHITE WORM, THE (1988)
LAKOTA WOMAN: SIEGE AT WOUNDED KNEE (1995)
LAMB (1995)
LAMBADA (1990)
LAMERICA (1995)
L'AMI DE MON AMIE (SEE: BOYFRIENDS AND GIRLFRIENDS)(1988)
LAMP, THE (SEE: OUTING, THE)(1987)
LAN FENGZHENG (SEE: BLUE KITE, THE)(1994)
LAND BEFORE TIME, THE (1988)
LAND BEFORE TIME II: THE GREAT VALLEY ADVENTURE, THE (1994)
LAND OF DOOM (1986)
LANDSCAPE IN THE MIST (1990)
LANDSCAPE SUICIDE (1986)
LANDSLIDE (1992)
L'ANNEE DES MEDUSES (1987)
LAS VEGAS WEEKEND (1985)
LASER MAN, THE (1988)
LASER MOON (1992)
LASSIE (1994)
LAST ACTION HERO (1993)
LAST BOY SCOUT, THE (1991)
LAST BUTTERFLY, THE (1993)
LAST CALL (1991)
LAST DAYS OF CHEZ NOUS, THE (1993)
LAST DAYS OF JOHN DILLINGER, THE (SEE: DILLINGER)(1995)
LAST DRAGON, THE (1985)
LAST EMPEROR, THE (1987)
LAST EXIT TO BROOKLYN (1989)
LAST FLIGHT TO HELL (1991)
LAST GOOD TIME, THE (1995)
LAST HOUR, THE (1991)
LAST KLEZMER, THE (1994)
LAST KLEZMER: LEOPOLD KOZLOWSKI, HIS LIFE AND HIS MUSIC, THE (SEE: LAST KLEZMER, THE)(1994)
LAST OF ENGLAND, THE (1987)
LAST OF THE DOGMEN (1995)
LAST OF THE FINEST, THE (1990)
LAST OF THE MOHICANS, THE (1992)
LAST PARTY, THE (1993)
LAST RESORT (1986)

LAST RIDE, THE (1991)
LAST RIDE, THE (1995)
LAST RITES (1988)
LAST SAMURAI, THE (1995)
LAST SEDUCTION, THE (1994)
LAST STRAW, THE (1987)
LAST SUMMER IN THE HAMPTONS (1995)
LAST TEMPTATION OF CHRIST, THE (1988)
LAST TIME OUT (1994)
LAST WARRIOR, THE (1989)
LATCHO DROM (1994)
LATE FOR DINNER (1991)
LATE SUMMER BLUES (1988)
LATENT IMAGE (1988)
LATINO (1985)
LAW OF DESIRE (1987)
LAWNMOWER MAN, THE (1992)
LAWS OF GRAVITY (1992)
LE CHATEAU DE MA MERE (SEE: MY MOTHER'S CASTLE)(1991)
LE CHENE (SEE: OAK, THE)(1993)
LE COMPLOT (SEE: TO KILL A PRIEST)(1989)
LE CRI DU PAPILLON (SEE: LAST BUTTERFLY, THE)(1993)
LE DECLIN DE L'EMPIRE AMERICAIN (SEE: DECLINE OF THE AMERICAN EMPIRE, THE)(1986)
LE DOCTEUR PETIOT (SEE: DR. PETIOT)(1994)
LE DUE VITE DI MATTIA PASCAL (SEE: TWO LIVES OF MATTIA PASCAL, THE)(1985)
LE GRAND BLEU (SEE: BIG BLUE, THE)(1988)
LE GRAND CHEMIN (SEE: GRAND HIGHWAY, THE)(1988)
LE GRAND PARDON II (SEE: DAY OF ATONEMENT)(1993)
LE JEUNE MARIE (1985)
LE JUPON ROUGE (SEE: MANUELA'S LOVES)(1987)
LE LIEU DU CRIME (SEE: SCENE OF THE CRIME)(1986)
LE PAYS DES SOURDS (SEE: IN THE LAND OF THE DEAF)(1994)
LE PETIT AMOUR (SEE: KUNG FU MASTER)(1989)
LE POUVOIR DU MAL (SEE: POWER OF EVIL, THE)(1985)
LE THE AU HAREM D'ARCHIMEDE (SEE: TEA IN THE HAREM OF ARCHIMEDE)(1985)
LEAGUE OF THEIR OWN, A (1992)
LEAN ON ME (1989)
LEAP OF FAITH (1992)
LEATHER JACKETS (1992)
LEATHERFACE: THE TEXAS CHAINSAW MASSACRE III (1990)
LEAVING LAS VEGAS (1995)
LEAVING NORMAL (1992)
LEGAL EAGLES (1986)
LEGAL TENDER (1991)
LEGEND (1985)
LEGEND OF BILLIE JEAN, THE (1985)
LEGEND OF FONG SAI-YUK, THE (SEE: FONG SAI-YUK)(1993)
LEGEND OF SURAM FORTRESS (1985)
LEGEND OF THE OVERFIEND (1993)
LEGEND OF THE WHITE HORSE (1991)
LEGEND OF WOLF MOUNTAIN, THE (1993)
LEGENDS OF THE FALL (1994)
LEKCE FAUST (SEE: FAUST)(1994)
LEMON SISTERS, THE (1990)
LENA'S HOLIDAY (1991)
L'ENFER (1994)
LEOLO (1993)
LEON (SEE: PROFESSIONAL, THE)(1994)
LEON THE PIG FARMER (1993)

LEONARD PART 6 (1987)
LEPRECHAUN (1993)
LEPRECHAUN 2 (1994)
LES FAVORIS DE LA LUNE (SEE: FAVORITES OF THE MOON)(1985)
LES GUERISSEURS (SEE: ADUEFUE)(1988)
LES INNOCENTS (SEE: INNOCENT, THE)(1988)
LES MISERABLES (1995)
LES NOCES DE PAPIER (SEE: PAPER WEDDING)(1991)
LES NUITS FAUVES (SEE: SAVAGE NIGHTS)(1994)
LES PLOUFFE (1985)
LES PORTES TOURNANTES (SEE: REVOLVING DOORS, THE)(1988)
LES VEUFS (SEE: ENTANGLED)(1993)
LES YEUX D'UN ANGE (SEE: EYES OF AN ANGEL)(1994)
LESS THAN ZERO (1987)
LESSONS OF DARKNESS (1995)
LET HIM HAVE IT (1991)
LET IT RIDE (1989)
L'ETAT SAUVAGE (1990)
LETHAL OBSESSION (1988)
LETHAL WEAPON (1987)
LETHAL WEAPON 3 (1992)
LETHAL WEAPON 2 (1989)
LET'S GET HARRY (1987)
LETTER TO BREZHNEV (1986)
LEVIATHAN (1989)
L'HOMME BLESSE (1985)
LIARS' CLUB, THE (1994)
LICENCE TO KILL (1989)
LICENSE TO DRIVE (1988)
LIE DOWN WITH DOGS (1995)
LIEBESTRAUM (1991)
LIFE AND DEATH OF CHICO MENDES, THE (SEE: BURNING SEASON,THE)(1995)
LIFE AND NOTHING BUT (1990)
LIFE AND TIMES OF ALLEN GINSBERG, THE (1994)
LIFE IS A LONG QUIET RIVER (1990)
LIFE IS CHEAP...BUT TOILET PAPER IS EXPENSIVE (1990)
LIFE IS SWEET (1991)
LIFE OF SIN, A (1993)
LIFE ON A STRING (1992)
LIFE ON THE EDGE (1992)
LIFE STINKS (1991)
LIFE WITH MIKEY (1993)
LIFEFORCE (1985)
LIGHT IN THE JUNGLE, THE (1992)
LIGHT OF DAY (1987)
LIGHT SLEEPER (1992)
LIGHT YEARS (1988)
LIGHTHORSEMEN, THE (1988)
LIGHTNING JACK (1994)
LIGHTNING—THE WHITE STALLION (1986)
LIGHTSHIP, THE (1986)
LIKE FATHER, LIKE SON (1987)
LIKE WATER FOR CHOCOLATE (1993)
LILY IN LOVE (1985)
LILY WAS HERE (1992)
LIMIT UP (1989)
LINGUINI INCIDENT, THE (1992)
LINK (1986)
LION KING, THE (1994)
LIONHEART (1990)
LIONHEART (1991)
LIPSTICK CAMERA, THE (1994)
LISA (1990)
LISTEN TO ME (1989)
LITTLE BIG LEAGUE (1994)
LITTLE BUDDHA (1994)

LITTLE DORRIT (1988)
LITTLE FLAMES (1985)
LITTLE GIANTS (1994)
LITTLE HEROES (1991)
LITTLE MAN TATE (1991)
LITTLE MERMAID, THE (1989)
LITTLE MISS MILLIONS (1994)
LITTLE NEMO: ADVENTURES IN
  SLUMBERLAND (1992)
LITTLE NIKITA (1988)
LITTLE NOISES (1992)
LITTLE ODESSA (1995)
LITTLE PRINCESS, A (1995)
LITTLE RASCALS, THE (1994)
LITTLE SHOP OF HORRORS (1986)
LITTLE SISTER, THE (1985)
LITTLE SISTER (1992)
LITTLE STIFF, A (1994)
LITTLE THIEF, THE (1989)
LITTLE TREASURE (1985)
LITTLE VEGAS (1992)
LITTLE VERA (1988)
LITTLE WOMEN (1994)
LIVE BY THE FIST (1993)
LIVIN' LARGE (1991)
LIVING DANGEROUSLY (1988)
LIVING DAYLIGHTS, THE (1987)
LIVING END, THE (1992)
LIVING IN OBLIVION (1995)
LIVING ON TOKYO TIME (1987)
LIVING PROOF: HIV AND THE PURSUIT OF
  HAPPINESS (1994)
LIVING TO DIE (1991)
LO ZIO INDEGNO (SEE: SLEAZY UNCLE,
  THE)(1991)
LOCK 'N' LOAD (1991)
LOCK UP (1989)
LOCKED-UP TIME (1992)
L'ODEUR DE LA PAPAYE VERTE (SEE:
  SCENT OF GREEN PAPAYA, THE)(1994)
LONDON (1994)
LONDON KILLS ME (1992)
LONE JUSTICE (1994)
LONELY HEARTS (1992)
LONELY IN AMERICA (1993)
LONELY PASSION OF JUDITH HEARNE, THE
  (1988)
LONELY WIFE, THE (SEE:
  CHARULATA)(1995)
LONELY WOMAN SEEKS LIFE COMPANION
  (1990)
LONG DAY CLOSES, THE (1993)
LONG WALK HOME, THE (1991)
LONGSHOT, THE (1986)
LONGTIME COMPANION (1990)
LOOK WHO'S TALKING (1989)
LOOK WHO'S TALKING NOW (1993)
LOOK WHO'S TALKING TOO (1990)
LOOKING FOR EILEEN (1987)
LOOSE CANNONS (1990)
LOOSE JOINTS (SEE: FLICKS)(1987)
LOOSE SCREWS (1985)
LORD OF THE FLIES (1990)
LORDS OF MAGICK, THE (1990)
LORDS OF THE STREET, THE (SEE:
  ADUEFUE)(1988)
LORENZO'S OIL (1992)
LOS INSOMNES (SEE: INSOMNIACS)(1986)
LOS MONJES SANGRIENTOS (SEE: BLOOD
  SCREAMS)(1991)
LOSER TAKE ALL (SEE: STRIKE IT
  RICH)(1990)
LOSER, THE HERO, THE (1985)
LOSING ISAIAH (1995)
LOST ANGELS (1989)
LOST BOYS, THE (1987)

LOST EMPIRE, THE (1985)
LOST IN AMERICA (1985)
LOST IN YONKERS (SEE: NEIL SIMON'S
  LOST IN YONKERS)(1993)
LOST WORDS, THE (1994)
LOVE AFFAIR (1994)
LOVE AFTER LOVE (1994)
LOVE AND A .45 (1994)
LOVE AND HUMAN REMAINS (1995)
LOVE & MURDER (1991)
LOVE AT LARGE (1990)
LOVE, CHEAT & STEAL (1994)
LOVE CRIMES (1992)
LOVE FIELD (1992)
LOVE HURTS (1992)
LOVE IS A DOG FROM HELL (1987)
LOVE IS A FAT WOMAN (1988)
LOVE IS A GUN (1994)
LOVE POTION NO. 9 (1992)
LOVE SONGS (1986)
LOVE TILL FIRST BLOOD (1986)
LOVE WITHOUT PITY (1991)
LOVE YOUR MAMA (1993)
LOVER, THE (1992)
LOVERBOY (1989)
LOVERS (1992)
LOVERS' LOVERS (1994)
LOW BLOW (1986)
LOW DOWN DIRTY SHAME (1994)
LOWER LEVEL (1992)
LOYALTIES (1986)
LUCAS (1986)
LUCKIEST MAN IN THE WORLD, THE (1989)
LUCKY LUKE: DAISY TOWN (1994)
LUNA PARK (1994)
LUNATIC, THE (1992)
LUNATICS, THE (1986)
LUNATICS: A LOVE STORY (1992)
LURKING FEAR (1994)
LUST IN THE DUST (1985)
LYRICAL NITRATE (1991)

M

ENGLISHMAN WHO WENT UP A HILL BUT
  CAME DOWN A MOUNTAIN, THE (1995)
M. BUTTERFLY (1993)
MAC (1993)
MAC AND ME (1988)
MACARONI (1985)
MACARTHUR'S CHILDREN (1985)
MACCHERONI (SEE: MACARONI)(1985)
MACHINE DREAMS (1995)
MACK THE KNIFE (1990)
MAD AT THE MOON (1993)
MAD DOG AND GLORY (1993)
MAD DOG COLL (1993)
MAD LOVE (1995)
MAD MAX BEYOND THUNDERDOME (1985)
MADAME BOVARY (1991)
MADAME SOUSATZKA (1988)
MADE IN AMERICA (1993)
MADE IN HEAVEN (1987)
MADE IN USA (1989)
MADHOUSE (1990)
MADNESS OF KING GEORGE, THE (1994)
MAGDALENE (1990)
MAGIC IN THE WATER (1995)
MAGIC KID, THE (1994)
MAGIC KID 2 (1994)
MAGICAL WORLD OF CHUCK JONES, THE
  (1992)
MAHABHARATA, THE (1990)
MAID TO ORDER (1987)
MAID, THE (1991)

MAJOR LEAGUE (1989)
MAJOR LEAGUE II (1994)
MAJOR PAYNE (1995)
MAKING MR. RIGHT (1987)
MAKING OF "...AND GOD SPOKE," THE
  (SEE: ...AND GOD SPOKE)(1994)
MAKIOKA SISTERS, THE (1985)
MALA NOCHE (1985)
MALANDRO (1986)
MALAYUNTA (SEE: BAD COMPANY)(1986)
MALCOLM (1986)
MALCOLM X (1992)
MALENKAYA VERA (SEE: LITTLE
  VERA)(1989)
MALIBU BIKINI SHOP, THE (1987)
MALICE (1993)
MALICIOUS (1995)
MALLRATS (1995)
MALONE (1987)
MAMA, THERE'S A MAN IN YOUR BED
  (1990)
MAMBO KINGS, THE (1992)
MAN AND A WOMAN: 20 YEARS LATER, A
  (1986)
MAN BITES DOG (1993)
MAN FACING SOUTHEAST (1986)
MAN FROM LEFT FIELD, THE (1994)
MAN IN LOVE, A (1987)
MAN IN THE MOON, THE (1991)
MAN IN UNIFORM, A (1994)
MAN INSIDE, THE (1990)
MAN LIKE EVA, A (1985)
MAN OF NO IMPORTANCE, A (1994)
MAN OF THE HOUSE (1995)
MAN ON FIRE (1987)
MAN OUTSIDE (1988)
MAN TROUBLE (1992)
MAN UNDER SUSPICION (1985)
MAN WHO ENVIED WOMEN, THE (1985)
MAN WITH ONE RED SHOE, THE (1985)
MAN WITHOUT A FACE, THE (1993)
MANCHURIAN AVENGER (1985)
MANDROID (1993)
MANGIATI VIVI (SEE: DOOMED TO
  DIE)(1985)
MANGLER, THE (1995)
MANHATTAN BABY (1986)
MANHATTAN BY NUMBERS (1994)
MANHATTAN MURDER MYSTERY (1993)
MANHATTAN PROJECT, THE (1986)
MANHUNT, THE (1986)
MANHUNTER (1986)
MANIAC COP (1988)
MANIAC COP 3: BADGE OF SILENCE (1993)
MANIAC COP 2 (1991)
MANIAC WARRIORS (1992)
MANKILLERS (1987)
MANNEQUIN (1987)
MANNEQUIN TWO: ON THE MOVE (1991)
MANNER (SEE: MEN)(1985)
MANON (1987)
MANON OF THE SPRING (1987)
MAN'S BEST FRIEND (1993)
MANUELA'S LOVES (1987)
MANUFACTURING CONSENT: NOAM
  CHOMSKY AND THE MEDIA (1993)
MAP OF THE HUMAN HEART (1993)
MAPANTSULA (1989)
MARDI GRAS FOR THE DEVIL (1993)
MARI DE LA COIFFEUSE, LA (SEE:
  HAIRDRESSER'S HUSBAND, THE)(1992)
MARIANNE AND JULIANE (1994)
MARIA'S LOVERS (1985)
MARIA'S STORY (1991)
MARIE (1985)

MARK TWAIN (SEE: ADVENTURES OF
  MARK TWAIN, THE)(1985)
MARKED FOR DEATH (1990)
MARQUIS (1993)
MARRIED PEOPLE, SINGLE SEX PART 2:
  FOR BETTER OR WORSE (1994)
MARRIED TO IT (1993)
MARRIED TO THE MOB (1988)
MARRYING MAN, THE (1991)
MARSUPIALS: THE HOWLING III (SEE:
  HOWLING III, THE)(1987)
MARTHA & ETHEL (1995)
MARTHA AND I (1995)
MARTHA JELLNECK (1988)
MARTIAL LAW (1991)
MARTIAL LAW 2: UNDERCOVER (1992)
MARTIANS GO HOME! (1990)
MARTIN LAWRENCE YOU SO CRAZY (SEE:
  YOU SO CRAZY)(1994)
MARTIN'S DAY (1985)
MARUSA NO ONNA (SEE: TAXING WOMAN,
  A)(1987)
MARUSA NO ONNA II (SEE: TAXING
  WOMAN'S RETURN, A)(1988)
MARY SHELLEY'S FRANKENSTEIN (1994)
MASALA (1993)
MASCARA (1987)
MASK (1985)
MASK, THE (1994)
MASQUE OF THE RED DEATH (1990)
MASQUE OF THE RED DEATH, THE (1991)
MASQUERADE (1988)
MASS IS ENDED, THE (1988)
MASTERBLASTER (1987)
MASTERS OF MENACE (1991)
MASTERS OF THE UNIVERSE (1987)
MATA HARI (1985)
MATCH FACTORY GIRL, THE (1992)
MATEWAN (1987)
MATINEE (1993)
MATT RIKER (SEE: MUTANT HUNT)(1987)
MATTER OF DEGREES, A (1991)
MAURICE (1987)
MAUVAIS SANG (SEE: BAD BLOOD)(1987)
MAVERICK (1994)
MAXIE (1985)
MAXIM XUL (1991)
MAXIMUM BREAKOUT (1992)
MAXIMUM FORCE (1992)
MAXIMUM OVERDRIVE (1986)
MAY FOOLS (1990)
MAY WINE (1991)
MAYA LIN: A STRONG CLEAR VISION (1995)
MAYBE BABY (SEE: FOR KEEPS)(1988)
MAZEPPA (1993)
MCBAIN (1991)
MCGUFFIN, THE (1985)
ME AND HIM (1990)
ME AND THE KID (1994)
ME AND THE MOB (1995)
ME & VERONICA (1993)
MEACHOREI HASORAGIM (SEE: BEOND
  THE WALLS)(1985)
MEAN SEASON, THE (1985)
MEATBALLS III (1987)
MEATBALLS 4 (1992)
MEDICINE MAN (1992)
MEDICINE RIVER (1994)
MEDITERRANEO (1992)
MEET THE APPLEGATES (1991)
MEET THE FEEBLES (1995)
MEET THE HOLLOWHEADS (1989)
MEETING VENUS (1991)
MEGAVILLE (1992)
MEIER (1987)

MELO (1988)
MEMED MY HAWK (1987)
MEMOIRS OF AN INVISIBLE MAN (1992)
MEMORIES OF ME (1988)
MEMPHIS BELLE (1990)
MEN (1986)
MEN AT WORK (1990)
MEN DON'T LEAVE (1990)
MEN IN LOVE (1990)
MEN OF RESPECT (1991)
MENACE II SOCIETY (1993)
MEN'S CLUB, THE (1986)
MERCENARY FIGHTERS (1988)
MERLIN (1994)
MERMAIDS (1990)
MERY PER SEMPRE (SEE: FOREVER
  MARY)(1991)
MESSENGER (1995)
MESSENGER OF DEATH (1988)
METAL AND MELANCHOLY (1995)
METAMORPHOSIS: THE ALIEN FACTOR
  (1993)
METEOR MAN, THE (1993)
METISSE (SEE: CAFE AU LAIT)(1994)
METROPOLITAN (1990)
MI VIDA LOCA—MY CRAZY LIFE (1994)
MIAMI BLUES (1990)
MIAMI RHAPSODY (1995)
MIDNIGHT CABARET (1991)
MIDNIGHT CLEAR, A (1992)
MIDNIGHT COP (1989)
MIDNIGHT CROSSING (1988)
MIDNIGHT EDITION (1994)
MIDNIGHT FEAR (1992)
MIDNIGHT KISS (1993)
MIDNIGHT RUN (1988)
MIDNIGHT STING (SEE: DIGGSTOWN)(1992)
MIDNIGHT TEASE (1994)
MIDNIGHT TEASE 2 (1995)
MIDNIGHT 2: SEX, DEATH AND VIDEOTAPE
  (1993)
MIGHTY APHRODITE (1995)
MIGHTY DUCKS, THE (1992)
MIGHTY MORPHIN POWER RANGERS: THE
  MOVIE (1995)
MIGHTY QUINN, THE (1989)
MIKAN NO TAIKYOKU (SEE: GO MASTERS,
  THE)(1985)
MIKEY (1992)
MILAGRO BEANFIELD WAR, THE (1988)
MILES FROM HOME (1988)
MILK MONEY (1994)
MILLENNIUM (1989)
MILLER'S CROSSING (1990)
MILLION DOLLAR MYSTERY (1987)
MILOU EN MAI (SEE: MAY FOOLS)(1990)
MILWR BYCHAN (SEE: BOY SOLDIER)(1987)
MINA TANNENBAUM (1995)
MINBO NO ONNA (SEE: MINBO - OR THE
  GENTLE ART OF JAPANESE
  EXTORTION)(1994)
MINBO - OR THE GENTLE ART OF
  JAPANESE EXTORTION (1994)
MIND, BODY & SOUL (1992)
MINDWALK (1991)
MINDWARP (1992)
MINISTRY OF VENGEANCE (1989)
MIRACLE BEACH (1992)
MIRACLE MILE (1989)
MIRACLE ON 34TH STREET (1994)
MIRACLE, THE (1991)
MIRACLES (1987)
MIRROR IMAGES (1992)
MIRROR, MIRROR (1991)
MIRROR, MIRROR 2: RAVEN DANCE (1994)

MISADVENTURES OF MR. WILT, THE (1990)
MISCHIEF (1985)
MISERY (1990)
MISFIT BRIGADE, THE (1988)
MISHIMA (1985)
MISS FIRECRACKER (1989)
MISS MARY (1986)
MISS MONA (1987)
MISSING IN ACTION 2—THE BEGINNING
  (1985)
MISSING PARENTS (SEE: DAY MY PARENTS
  RAN AWAY, THE)(1994)
MISSION, THE (1986)
MISSION KILL (1987)
MISSION OF JUSTICE (1992)
MISSISSIPPI BURNING (1988)
MISSISSIPPI MASALA (1992)
MR. AND MRS. BRIDGE (1990)
MR. BASEBALL (1992)
MR. DESTINY (1990)
MR. FROST (1990)
MISTER JOHNSON (1991)
MR. JONES (1993)
MR. LOVE (1986)
MR. NANNY (1993)
MR. NORTH (1988)
MR. SATURDAY NIGHT (1992)
MR. WONDERFUL (1993)
MR. WRITE (1994)
MISTRESS (1992)
MITT LIV SOM HUND (SEE: MY LIFE AS A
  DOG)(1987)
MITTEN INS HERZ (SEE: STRAIGHT
  THROUGH THE HEART)(1985)
MIXED NUTS (1994)
MO' BETTER BLUES (1990)
MO' MONEY (1992)
MOB WAR (1989)
MOBSTERS (1991)
MODEL BY DAY (1994)
MODERN GIRLS (1986)
MODERN LOVE (1990)
MODERNS, THE (1988)
MOM (1991)
MOM AND DAD SAVE THE WORLD (1992)
MONA LISA (1986)
MONEY FOR NOTHING (1993)
MONEY MAN (1993)
MONEY PIT, THE (1986)
MONEY TO BURN (1994)
MONEY TRAIN (1995)
MONEY TREE, THE (1993)
MONKEY BOY (1992)
MONKEY SHINES: AN EXPERIMENT IN
  FEAR (1988)
MONKEY TROUBLE (1994)
MONSIEUR HIRE (1989)
MONSTER DOG (1986)
MONSTER HIGH (1990)
MONSTER IN A BOX (1992)
MONSTER IN THE CLOSET (1987)
MONSTER SHARK (1986)
MONSTER SQUAD, THE (1987)
MONTANA RUN, THE (1992)
MONTH BY THE LAKE, A (1995)
MOON 44 (1991)
MOON IN SCORPIO (1987)
MOON OVER PARADOR (1988)
MOONLIGHT AND VALENTINO (1995)
MOONSTRUCK (1987)
MORGAN STEWART'S COMING HOME (1987)
MORGEN GRAUEN (SEE: TIME
  TROOPERS)(1990)
MORNING AFTER, THE (1986)
MORNING GLORY (1993)

MORNING TERROR (SEE: TIME TROOPERS)(1990)
MORO AFFAIR, THE (1986)
MORONS FROM OUTER SPACE (1985)
MORTAL KOMBAT (1995)
MORTAL THOUGHTS (1991)
MORTUARY ACADEMY (1992)
MOSAIC PROJECT, THE (1995)
MOSQUITO COAST, THE (1986)
MOTEL VACANCY (SEE: TALKING WALLS)(1987)
MOTHER'S BOYS (1994)
MOTORAMA (1993)
MOUNTAINS OF THE MOON (1990)
MOUNTAINTOP MOTEL MASSACRE (1986)
MOVERS AND SHAKERS (1985)
MOVIE HOUSE MASSACRE (1986)
MOVING (1988)
MOVING TARGETS (1987)
MOVING THE MOUNTAIN (1995)
MOVING VIOLATIONS (1985)
MRS. DOUBTFIRE (1993)
MRS. PARKER AND THE VICIOUS CIRCLE (1994)
MUCH ADO ABOUT NOTHING (1993)
MUI DU DU XANH (SEE: SCENT OF GREEN PAPAYA, THE)(1994)
MUNCHIE (1992)
MUNCHIE STRIKES BACK (1994)
MUNCHIES (1987)
MUPPET CHRISTMAS CAROL, THE (1992)
MURDER BY NUMBERS (1990)
MURDER-IN-LAW (1993)
MURDER IN THE FIRST (1995)
MURDER ONE (1988)
MURIEL'S WEDDING (1995)
MURPHY'S LAW (1986)
MURPHY'S ROMANCE (1985)
MUSIC BOX (1989)
MUSIC OF CHANCE, THE (1993)
MUTANT HUNT (1987)
MUTANT ON THE BOUNTY (1989)
MUTANT SPECIES (1995)
MUTATOR (1991)
MUTE WITNESS (1995)
MUTILATOR, THE (1985)
MY AMERICAN COUSIN (1985)
MY ANTONIA (1995)
MY BEAUTIFUL LAUNDRETTE (1986)
MY BLUE HEAVEN (1990)
MY BOYFRIEND'S BACK (1993)
MY BROTHER'S WIFE (1994)
MY CHAUFFEUR (1986)
MY COUSIN VINNY (1992)
MY DARK LADY (1987)
MY DEMON LOVER (1987)
MY FAMILY: MI FAMILIA (1995)
MY FATHER IS COMING (1992)
MY FATHER, THE HERO (1994)
MY FATHER'S GLORY (1991)
MY FIRST WIFE (1985)
MY GIRL (1991)
MY GIRL 2 (1994)
MY GRANDPA IS A VAMPIRE (1992)
MY HEROES HAVE ALWAYS BEEN COWBOYS (1991)
MY LEFT FOOT (1989)
MY LIFE (1993)
MY LIFE AND TIMES WITH ANTONIN ARTAUD (1995)
MY LIFE AS A DOG (1985)
MY LIFE'S IN TURNAROUND (1994)
MY LITTLE PONY (1986)
MY MAN ADAM (1986)
MY MOTHER'S CASTLE (1991)

MY NEIGHBOR TOTORO (1993)
MY NEW GUN (1992)
MY OWN PRIVATE IDAHO (1991)
MY SAMURAI (1993)
MY SCIENCE PROJECT (1985)
MY STEPMOTHER IS AN ALIEN (1988)
MY SWEET LITTLE VILLAGE (1985)
MY 20TH CENTURY (1989)
MY UNCLE'S LEGACY (1990)
MYSTERY DATE (1991)
MYSTERY OF ALEXINA, THE (1985)
MYSTERY OF RAMPO, THE (1995)
MYSTERY TRAIN (1989)
MYSTIC PIZZA (1988)
NIGHT OF LOVE, A (1988)

N

NADINE (1987)
NADJA (1995)
NAIL GUN MASSACRE (1988)
NAKED (1993)
NAKED CAGE, THE (1986)
NAKED GUN: FROM THE FILES OF POLICE SQUAD!, THE (1988)
NAKED GUN 33 1/3: THE FINAL INSULT (1994)
NAKED GUN 2 1/2: THE SMELL OF FEAR, THE (1991)
NAKED IN NEW YORK (1994)
NAKED KILLER (1995)
NAKED LUNCH (1991)
NAKED OBSESSION (1992)
NAKED VENGEANCE (1986)
NAME OF THE ROSE, THE (1986)
NARROW MARGIN (1990)
NASTY GIRL, THE (1990)
NATIONAL LAMPOON'S LOADED WEAPON 1 (1993)
NATIONAL LAMPOON'S ATTACK OF THE 5'2" WOMEN (1995)
NATIONAL LAMPOON'S CHRISTMAS VACATION (1989)
NATIONAL LAMPOON'S EUROPEAN VACATION (1985)
NATIONAL LAMPOON'S LAST RESORT (1994)
NATIONAL LAMPOON'S SENIOR TRIP (1995)
NATIVE SON (1986)
NATURAL BORN KILLERS (1994)
NAVIGATOR, THE (1989)
NAVY SEALS (1990)
NEA (1995)
NEAR DARK (1987)
NEAR MISSES (1992)
NECESSARY ROUGHNESS (1991)
NECO Z ALENKY (SEE: ALICE)(1988)
NECROMANCER (1989)
NECROPOLIS (1987)
NEEDFUL THINGS (1993)
NEIGHBOR, THE (1993)
NEIL SIMON'S LOST IN YONKERS (1993)
NEIL SIMON'S THE SLUGGER'S WIFE (SEE: SLUGGER'S WIFE, THE)(1985)
NEKROMANTIK (1995)
NELL (1994)
NEMESIS (1993)
NEON CITY (1992)
NEON MANIACS (1986)
NERVOUS TICKS (1993)
NET, THE (1995)
NETHERWORLD (1992)
NEUROTIC CABARET (1991)
NEVER CRY DEVIL (SEE: NIGHT VISITOR)(1990)
NEVER LEAVE NEVADA (1991)

NEVER TALK TO STRANGERS (1995)
NEVER TOO YOUNG TO DIE (1986)
NEVERENDING STORY II: THE NEXT CHAPTER, THE (1991)
NEW ADVENTURES OF PIPPI LONGSTOCKING, THE (1988)
NEW AGE, THE (1994)
NEW CRIME CITY: LOS ANGELES 2020 (1994)
NEW EDEN (1994)
NEW JACK CITY (1991)
NEW JERSEY DRIVE (1995)
NEW KIDS, THE (1985)
NEW LIFE, A (1988)
NEW YEAR'S DAY (1989)
NEW YORK COP (1995)
NEW YORK STORIES (1989)
NEW YORK'S FINEST (1988)
NEWSIES (1992)
NEXT DOOR (1995)
NEXT KARATE KID, THE (1994)
NEXT OF KIN (1989)
NGATI (1987)
NI-LO-HO NU-ERH (SEE: DAUGHTER OF THE NILE)(1988)
NICE GIRLS DON'T EXPLODE (1987)
NICK OF TIME (1995)
NICKEL & DIME (1992)
NICKEL MOUNTAIN (1985)
NIGHT AND DAY (1992)
NIGHT AND THE CITY (1992)
NIGHT ANGEL (1990)
NIGHT ANGELS (1987)
NIGHT EYES (1990)
NIGHT EYES III (1993)
NIGHT EYES 2 (1992)
NIGHT FIRE (1994)
NIGHT GAME (1989)
NIGHT IN THE LIFE OF JIMMY REARDON, A (1988)
NIGHT IS YOUNG, THE (SEE: BAD BLOOD)(1987)
NIGHT LIFE (1991)
'NIGHT, MOTHER (1986)
NIGHT OF THE CREEPS (1986)
NIGHT OF THE DEMONS (1989)
NIGHT OF THE DEMONS 2 (1994)
NIGHT OF THE LIVING DEAD (1990)
NIGHT OF THE RUNNING MAN (1994)
NIGHT OF THE SHARKS (1990)
NIGHT OF THE WARRIOR (1991)
NIGHT ON EARTH (1992)
NIGHT RHYTHMS (1992)
NIGHT STALKER, THE (1987)
NIGHT VISITOR (1990)
NIGHT WE NEVER MET, THE (1993)
NIGHT ZOO (1988)
NIGHTBREED (1990)
NIGHTFALL (1988)
NIGHTFLYERS (1987)
NIGHTFORCE (1987)
NIGHTMARE (1995)
NIGHTMARE ON ELM STREET 7 (SEE: WES CRAVEN'S NEW NIGHTMARE)(1994)
NIGHTMARE ON ELM STREET PART 2: FREDDY'S REVENGE, A (1985)
NIGHTMARE ON ELM STREET 3: DREAM WARRIORS, A (1987)
NIGHTMARE ON ELM STREET 4: THE DREAM MASTER, A (1988)
NIGHTMARE ON ELM STREET 5: THE DREAM CHILD, A (1989)
NIGHTMARE WEEKEND (1986)
NIGHTMARE'S PASSENGERS (1986)
NIGHTWARS (1988)
NIKITA (SEE: LA FEMME NIKITA)(1991)
NINA TAKES A LOVER (1995)

9 1/2 NINJAS (1991)
NINE 1/2 WEEKS (1986)
9 DEATHS OF THE NINJA (1985)
NINE MONTHS (1995)
976-EVIL (1989)
976-EVIL II (1992)
1918 (1985)
1991: THE YEAR PUNK BROKE (1992)
1969 (1988)
90 DAYS (1986)
NINJA TURF (1986)
NIXON (1995)
NO DEAD HEROES (1987)
NO DESSERT DAD, 'TIL YOU MOW THE LAWN (1994)
NO ESCAPE (1994)
NO ESCAPE NO RETURN (1994)
NO HOLDS BARRED (1989)
NO MAN'S LAND (1987)
NO MERCY (1986)
NO MERCY (1995)
NO PLACE TO HIDE (1993)
NO RETREAT, NO SURRENDER (1986)
NO RETREAT, NO SURRENDER 3 - BLOOD BROTHERS (1991)
NO RETREAT, NO SURRENDER II (1989)
NO SAFE HAVEN (1989)
NO SECRETS (1991)
NO SKIN OFF MY ASS (1991)
NO SURRENDER (1986)
NO WAY OUT (1987)
NOBODY LOVES ME (1995)
NOBODY'S FOOL (1986)
NOBODY'S FOOL (1994)
NOBODY'S PERFECT (1990)
NOCE IN GALILEE (SEE: WEDDING IN GALILEE)(1988)
NOI TRE (SEE: WE THREE)(1985)
NOIR ET BLANC (SEE: BLACK AND WHITE)(1986)
NOIR ET BLANC (1991)
NOISES OFF (1992)
NOMADS (1985)
NORTH (1994)
NORTH SHORE (1987)
NOSTRADAMUS (1994)
NOSTRADAMUS KID, THE (1995)
NOT ANGELS BUT ANGELS (1995)
NOT OF THIS EARTH (1988)
NOT QUITE JERUSALEM (1985)
NOT SINCE CASANOVA (1988)
NOT WITHOUT MY DAUGHTER (1991)
NOTEBOOK ON CITIES AND CLOTHES (1991)
NOTHING BUT TROUBLE (1991)
NOTHING IN COMMON (1986)
NOTHING TO LOSE (SEE: DEATH IN BRUNSWICK)(1995)
NOVEMBER MEN (1994)
NOW AND THEN (1995)
NOWHERE TO HIDE (1987)
NOWHERE TO RUN (1989)
NOWHERE TO RUN (1993)
NUIT ET JOUR (SEE: NIGHT AND DAY)(1992)
NUMBER ONE FAN (1995)
NUMBER ONE WITH A BULLET (1987)
NUNS ON THE RUN (1990)
NUOVO CINEMA PARADISO (SEE: CINEMA PARADISO)(1990)
NUTCRACKER PRINCE, THE (1990)
NUTCRACKER: THE MOTION PICTURE (1986)
NUTS (1987)

O

O BOBO (SEE: JESTER, THE)(1987)
O.C. AND STIGGS (1987)
OAK, THE (1993)
OBERST REDL (SEE: COLONEL REDL)(1985)
OBJECT OF BEAUTY, THE (1991)
OBLIVION (1994)
OBSESSED (1989)
OCEAN DRIVE WEEKEND (1986)
OCI CIORNIE (SEE: DARK EYES)(1987)
OCTOBER 32ND (SEE: MERLIN)(1994)
ODD JOBS (1986)
ODDBALL HALL (1992)
OF MICE AND MEN (1992)
OFF BEAT (1986)
OFF LIMITS (1988)
OFFERINGS (1989)
OFFICE PARTY (SEE: HOSTILE TAKEOVER)(1990)
OFFICIAL DENIAL (1994)
OFFICIAL STORY, THE (1985)
OFFRET-SA CRIFICATIO (SEE: SACRIFICE)(1986)
OFFSPRING, THE (1987)
OH ... ROSALINDA!! (1995)
OH, WHAT A NIGHT (1992)
O.J. SIMPSON STORY, THE (1995)
OKOGE (1993)
OLD EXPLORERS (1991)
OLD GRINGO (1989)
OLD LADY WHO WALKED IN THE SEA, THE (1995)
OLEANNA (1994)
OLIVER & COMPANY (1988)
OLIVIER, OLIVIER (1993)
OLYMPIC SUMMER, THE (1994)
OMEGA SYNDROME (1987)
ON DEADLY GROUND (1994)
ON THE BLOCK (1991)
ON THE EDGE (1985)
ON VALENTINE'S DAY (1986)
ONCE AROUND (1991)
ONCE BITTEN (1985)
ONCE UPON A CRIME (1992)
ONCE UPON A FOREST (1993)
ONCE UPON A TIME IN CHINA (1992)
ONCE UPON A TIME IN CHINA II (1994)
ONCE UPON A TIME IN CHINA III (1994)
ONCE WERE WARRIORS (1995)
ONE CRAZY NIGHT (1993)
ONE CRAZY SUMMER (1986)
ONE FALSE MOVE (1992)
ONE FOR SORROW, TWO FOR JOY (SEE: SIGNS OF LIFE)(1989)
ONE GOOD COP (1991)
ONE LAST RUN (1992)
ONE LOOK AND LOVE BEGINS (SEE: EIN BLICK—UND DIE LIEBE BRICHT AUS)(1987)
ONE MAGIC CHRISTMAS (1985)
ONE MINUTE TO MIDNIGHT (1988)
ONE MORE SATURDAY NIGHT (1986)
ONE NIGHT ONLY (1986)
1-900 (1995)
ONE-WAY TICKET, A (1988)
ONLY THE BRAVE (1994)
ONLY THE BRAVE (1995)
ONLY THE LONELY (1991)
ONLY YOU (1992)
ONLY YOU (1994)
OPEN DOORS (1991)
OPEN HOUSE (1987)
OPERA DO MALANDRO (SEE: MALANDRO)(1986)
OPERATION DUMBO DROP (1995)

OPERATION GOLDEN PHOENIX (1994)
OPERATION INTERCEPT (1995)
OPPONENT, THE (1990)
OPPORTUNITY KNOCKS (1990)
OPPOSING FORCE (1987)
OPPOSITE SEX AND HOW TO LIVE WITH THEM, THE (1993)
OPTIONS (1989)
ORIANE (1985)
ORIGINAL INTENT (1992)
ORLANDO (1993)
ORMENS VAG PA HALLEBERGET (SEE: SERPENT'S WAY)(1987)
ORPHANS (1987)
OSA (1985)
OSCAR (1991)
OTAC NA SLUZBENOH PUTU (SEE: WHEN FATHER WAS AWAY ON BUSINES)(1985)
OTELLO (1986)
OTHELLO (1995)
OTHER PEOPLE'S MONEY (1991)
OTHER WOMAN, THE (1992)
OTOKOWA TSURAIYOO TORAIJIRO KOKORO NO TABIJI (SEE: TORA-SAN GOES TO VIENNA)(1986)
OTRA HISTORIA DE AMOR (SEE: ANOTHER LOVE STORY)(1986)
OTRA VUELTA DE TUERCA (SEE: TURN OF THE SCREW)(1985)
OUR FATHER (1985)
OUT COLD (1989)
OUT FOR BLOOD (1992)
OUT FOR JUSTICE (1991)
OUT OF AFRICA (1985)
OUT OF ANNIE'S PAST (1995)
OUT OF BOUNDS (1986)
OUT OF CONTROL (1985)
OUT OF MY WAY (SEE: STORY OF FAUSTA)(1988)
OUT OF ORDER (1985)
OUT OF ROSENHEIM (SEE: BAGDAD CAFE)(1987)
OUT OF SYNC (1995)
OUT OF THE RAIN (1991)
OUT ON A LIMB (1992)
OUTBREAK (1995)
OUTER HEAT (SEE: ALIEN NATION)(1988)
OUTFIT, THE (1993)
OUTING, THE (1987)
OUTRAGEOUS FORTUNE (1987)
OUTREMER (SEE: OVERSEAS)(1991)
OUTSIDE THE LAW (1995)
OUTSIDERS, THE (1987)
OVER EXPOSED (1990)
OVER GRENSEN (SEE: FELDMANN CASE, THE)(1987)
OVER HER DEAD BODY (1992)
OVER THE HILL (1993)
OVER THE SUMMER (1986)
OVER THE TOP (1987)
OVERBOARD (1987)
OVERKILL (1987)
OVERSEAS (1991)
OVIRI (SEE: WOLF AT THE DOOR, THE)(1986)
OX, THE (1992)

P

P.K. AND THE KID (1987)
P.O.W. THE ESCAPE (1986)
PACIFIC HEIGHTS (1990)
PACKAGE, THE (1989)
PAGEMASTER, THE (1994)
PAINT IT BLACK (1990)
PAINTING THE TOWN (1992)
PALE BLOOD (1992)

PALE RIDER (1985)
PALERMO CONNECTION, THE (1991)
PAMELA PRINCIPLE, THE (1992)
PANAMA DECEPTION, THE (1992)
PANTHER (1995)
PANTHER SQUAD (1986)
PAPER MASK (1991)
PAPER WEDDING (1991)
PAPER, THE (1994)
PAPERBOY, THE (1994)
PAPERHOUSE (1989)
PARADISE (1991)
PARADISE MOTEL (1985)
PARENTHOOD (1989)
PARENTS (1989)
PARIS, FRANCE (1994)
PARIS IS BURNING (1991)
PARKING (1985)
PARTING GLANCES (1986)
PARTIR REVENIR (SEE: GOING AND
  COMING BACK)(1985)
PARTY CAMP (1987)
PARTY GIRL (1995)
PARTY PLANE (1991)
PASAJEROS DE UNA PESADILLA (SEE:
  MIGHTMARE'S PASSENGERS)(1986)
PASCALI'S ISLAND (1988)
PASS THE AMMO (1988)
PASSED AWAY (1992)
PASSENGER 57 (1992)
PASSION FISH (1992)
PASSION TO KILL, A (1994)
PAST TENSE (1994)
PASTIME (1991)
PATAKIN (1985)
PATHFINDER (1990)
PATRIOT, THE (1986)
PATRIOT GAMES (1992)
PATTI ROCKS (1988)
PATTY HEARST (1988)
PATUL CONJUGAL (SEE: CONJUGAL BED,
  THE)(1994)
PAUL BOWLES: THE COMPLETE OUTSIDER
  (1994)
PAVLOVA—A WOMAN FOR ALL TIME (1985)
PAYBACK (1991)
PAYBACK (1995)
PCU (1994)
PEACEMAKER (1990)
PEBBLE AND THE PENGUIN, THE (1995)
PEE-WEE'S BIG ADVENTURE (1985)
PEEPHOLE (1994)
PEGGY SUE GOT MARRIED (1986)
PEKING OPERA BLUES (1986)
PELICAN BRIEF, THE (1993)
PELLE THE CONQUEROR (1987)
PENITENT, THE (1988)
PENITENTIARY III (1987)
PENN & TELLER GET KILLED (1989)
PENTATHLON (1995)
PEOPLE UNDER THE STAIRS, THE (1991)
PEPI, LUCI, BOM AND OTHER GIRLS ON
  THE HEAP (1992)
PEPI, LUCI, BOM Y OTRAS CHICAS DEL
  MONTON (SEE: PEPI, LUCI, BOM AND
  OTHER GIRLS ON THE HEAP)(1992)
PEREZ FAMILY, THE (1995)
PERFECT (1985)
PERFECT MATCH, THE (1987)
PERFECT MODEL, THE (1989)
PERFECT MURDER, THE (1990)
PERFECT WEAPON, THE (1991)
PERFECT WORLD, A (1993)
PERFECTLY NORMAL (1991)
PERIL (1985)

PERILS OF P.K., THE (1986)
PERMANENT RECORD (1988)
PERSONAL FOUL (1987)
PERSONAL SERVICES (1987)
PERSUASION (1995)
PET SEMATARY (1989)
PET SEMATARY II (1992)
PETER'S FRIENDS (1992)
PETIT CON (1985)
PHANTASM II (1988)
PHANTASM III: LORD OF THE DEAD (1994)
PHANTOM LOVER, THE (1995)
PHANTOM OF THE MALL: ERIC'S REVENGE
  (1989)
PHANTOM OF THE OPERA (1989)
PHANTOM OF THE RITZ (1992)
PHENOMENA (SEE: CREEPERS)(1985)
PHILADELPHIA (1993)
PHILADELPHIA ATTRACTION, THE (1985)
PHILADELPHIA EXPERIMENT 2, THE (1993)
PHOBIA (1988)
PHONE CALL, THE (1991)
PHOTOGRAPH, THE (1987)
PHYSICAL EVIDENCE (1989)
PIANO LESSON, THE (1995)
PIANO, THE (1993)
PICCOLI FUOCHI (SEE: LITTLE
  FLAMES)(1985)
PICK-UP ARTIST, THE (1987)
PICKLE, THE (1993)
PICTURE BRIDE (1995)
PICTURES FROM A REVOLUTION (1992)
PIGALLE (1995)
PIGS (1993)
PIN (1989)
PINK CADILLAC (1989)
PINK NIGHTS (1985)
PINOCCHIO AND THE EMPEROR OF THE
  NIGHT (1987)
PIRATES (1986)
PIT AND THE PENDULUM, THE (1991)
PIZZA MAN (1991)
PLACE FOR ANNIE, A (1994)
PLACE IN THE WORLD, A (1994)
PLACE OF WEEPING (1986)
PLAGUE, THE (1993)
PLANES, TRAINS, AND AUTOMOBILES (1987)
PLATOON (1986)
PLATOON LEADER (1988)
PLAY DEAD (1986)
PLAY MURDER FOR ME (1992)
PLAY NICE (1992)
PLAY TIME (1995)
PLAYBOYS, THE (1992)
PLAYER, THE (1992)
PLAYING AWAY (1986)
PLAYING FOR KEEPS (1986)
PLAYMAKER (1994)
PLEDGE NIGHT (1991)
PLENTY (1985)
PLOT AGAINST HARRY, THE (1990)
PLUGHEAD REWIRED: CIRCUITRY MAN II
  (SEE: CIRCUITRY MAN II)(1994)
POCAHONTAS (1995)
POCAHONTAS: THE LEGEND (1995)
POETIC JUSTICE (1993)
POET'S SILENCE, THE (1987)
POINT BREAK (1991)
POINT OF NO RETURN (1993)
POISON (1991)
POISON IVY (1992)
POKAYANIYE (SEE: REPENTANCE)(1987)
POLAR BEAR KING, THE (1994)
POLICE (1986)

POLICE ACADEMY 2: THEIR FIRST
  ASSIGNMENT (1985)
POLICE ACADEMY 3: BACK IN TRAINING
  (1986)
POLICE ACADEMY 4: CITIZENS ON PATROL
  (1987)
POLICE ACADEMY 5: ASSIGNMENT MIAMI
  BEACH (1988)
POLICE ACADEMY 6: CITY UNDER SIEGE
  (1989)
POLTERGEIST II (1986)
POLTERGEIST III (1988)
PONTIAC MOON (1994)
POPCORN (1991)
POPE MUST DIE!, THE (SEE: POPE MUST
  DIET!, THE)(1992)
POPE MUST DIET!, THE (1992)
PORKY'S REVENGE (1985)
PORTE APERTE (SEE: OPEN DOORS)(1991)
POSITIVE I.D. (1986)
POSSE (1993)
POSSESSED BY THE NIGHT (1994)
POSTCARDS FROM AMERICA (1995)
POSTCARDS FROM THE EDGE (1990)
POSTMAN, THE (1995)
POTOMOK BELONGO BARSSA (SEE:
  DESCENDANT OF THE SNOW LEOPARD,
  THE)(1986)
POUND PUPPIES AND THE LEGEND OF BIG
  PAW (1988)
POUR SACHA (1992)
POUVOIR INTIME (SEE: INTIMATE
  POWER)(1986)
POWDER (1995)
POWER (1986)
POWER OF ATTORNEY (1995)
POWER OF EVIL, THE (1985)
POWER OF ONE, THE (1992)
PRANCER (1989)
PRAY FOR DEATH (1986)
PRAYER FOR THE DYING, A (1987)
PRAYER OF THE ROLLERBOYS (1991)
PREDATOR (1987)
PREDATOR 2 (1990)
PREHYSTERIA (1993)
PREHYSTERIA! 2 (1994)
PREHYSTERIA! 3 (1995)
PRELUDE TO A KISS (1992)
PRESENCE, THE (1994)
PRESIDIO, THE (1988)
PRESUMED INNOCENT (1990)
PRETTY IN PINK (1986)
PRETTY SMART (1987)
PRETTY WOMAN (1990)
PRETTYKILL (1987)
PREY FOR THE HUNTER (1993)
PRICK UP YOUR EARS (1987)
PRIEST (1995)
PRIMAL RAGE (1990)
PRIMAL SCREAM (1988)
PRIMARY MOTIVE (1992)
PRIMARY TARGET (1990)
PRIME RISK (1985)
PRIME TARGET (1991)
PRIMO BABY (1992)
PRINCE JACK (1985)
PRINCE OF DARKNESS (1987)
PRINCE OF TIDES, THE (1991)
PRINCES IN EXILE (1991)
PRINCESS ACADEMY, THE (1987)
PRINCESS AND THE GOBLIN, THE (1994)
PRINCESS BRIDE, THE (1987)
PRINCESS CARABOO (1994)
PRINCIPAL, THE (1987)
PRISON (1988)
PRISON PLANET (1993)

PRISON SHIP (SEE: STAR SLAMMER: THE ESCAPE)(1988)
PRISONERS OF THE SUN (1991)
PRIVATE ACCESS (1988)
PRIVATE FUNCTION, A (1985)
PRIVATE LESSONS—ANOTHER STORY (1994)
PRIVATE RESORT (1985)
PRIVATE SHOW (1985)
PRIVATE WARS (1993)
PRIVILEGE (1991)
PRIZZI'S HONOR (1985)
PROBLEM CHILD (1990)
PROBLEM CHILD 2 (1991)
PROFESSION: NEO-NAZI (1995)
PROFESSIONAL, THE (1992)
PROFESSIONAL, THE (1994)
PROGRAM, THE (1993)
PROGRAMMED TO KILL (1987)
PROJECT: ALIEN (1991)
PROJECT: GENESIS (1994)
PROJECT: SHADOWCHASER (1992)
PROJECT X (1987)
PROM NIGHT IV - DELIVER US FROM EVIL (1992)
PROMISE, THE (1995)
PROMISED LAND (1988)
PROOF (1992)
PROPHECY, THE (1995)
PROSPERO'S BOOKS (1991)
PROTECTOR, THE (1985)
PROVINCIAL ACTORS (1995)
PRZESLUCHANIE (SEE: INTERROGATION, THE)(1990)
PRZYPADEK (SEE: BLIND CHANCE)(1987)
PSY (SEE: PIGS)(1993)
PSYCHIC (1992)
PSYCHO III (1986)
PSYCHO COP 2 (1994)
PSYCHOS IN LOVE (1987)
PUBLIC EYE, THE (1992)
PUERTO RICAN MAMBO (NOT A MUSICAL), THE (1992)
PULP FICTION (1994)
PULSE (1988)
PULSEBEAT (1986)
PUMP UP THE VOLUME (1990)
PUMPKINHEAD (1988)
PUMPKINHEAD 2: BLOOD WINGS (1994)
PUNCHLINE (1988)
PUNISHER, THE (1991)
PUPPET MASTER 4 (1993)
PUPPET MASTER 5: THE FINAL CHAPTER (1994)
PUPPET MASTER III: TOULON'S REVENGE (1991)
PUPPET MASTER II (1991)
PUPPET MASTERS, THE (SEE: ROBERT A. HEINLEIN'S THE PUPPET MASTERS)(1994)
PURE COUNTRY (1992)
PURE FORMALITY, A (1995)
PURE LUCK (1991)
PURPLE ROSE OF CAIRO, THE (1985)
PUSHED TO THE LIMIT (1992)
PUSHING HANDS (1995)
PYRATES (1991)
PYROMANIAC'S LOVE STORY, A (1995)

Q

Q&A (1990)
QIU JU (SEE: STORY OF QIU JU, THE)(1993)
QUALCOSA DI BIONDO (1985)
QUARREL, THE (1992)
QUARTIERE (1987)
QUEEN MARGOT (1994)

QUEEN OF HEARTS (1989)
QUEENS LOGIC (1991)
QUEST FOR THE LOST CITY (1994)
QUESTION OF COLOR, A (1993)
QUICK (1994)
QUICK AND THE DEAD, THE (1995)
QUICK CHANGE (1990)
QUICKSILVER (1986)
QUIET COOL (1986)
QUIET EARTH, THE (1985)
QUIGLEY DOWN UNDER (1990)
QUIZ SHOW (1994)

R

R.O.T.O.R. (1988)
RABID GRANNIES (1989)
RACE FOR GLORY (1989)
RACHEL PAPERS, THE (1989)
RACHEL RIVER (1989)
RAD (1986)
RADIO DAYS (1987)
RADIO FLYER (1992)
RADIO INSIDE (1995)
RADIOACTIVE DREAMS (1986)
RADIOLAND MURDERS (1994)
RAGE AND HONOR (1993)
RAGE AND HONOR II: HOSTILE TAKEOVER (1993)
RAGE IN HARLEM, A (1991)
RAGE OF HONOR (1987)
RAGGEDY RAWNEY, THE (1990)
RAIN KILLER, THE (1991)
RAIN MAN (1988)
RAIN WITHOUT THUNDER (1993)
RAINBOW, THE (1989)
RAINBOW BRITE AND THE STAR STEALER (1985)
RAINING STONES (1994)
RAISE THE RED LANTERN (1992)
RAISING ARIZONA (1987)
RAISING CAIN (1992)
RAMBLING ROSE (1991)
RAMBO: FIRST BLOOD, PART II (1985)
RAMBO III (1988)
RAMPAGE (1992)
RAMPO (SEE: MYSTERY OF RAMPO, THE)(1995)
RAN (1985)
RAPA NUI (1994)
RAPID FIRE (1992)
RAPPIN' (1985)
RAPTURE, THE (1991)
RASPAD (1992)
RASPUTIN (1985)
RATBOY (1986)
RAW DEAL (1986)
RAW JUSTICE (1994)
RAW NERVE (1991)
RAWHEAD REX (1987)
RE-ANIMATOR (1985)
READY TO WEAR (PRET-A-PORTER) (1994)
REAL BULLETS (1990)
REAL GENIUS (1985)
REAL MCCOY, THE (1993)
REALITY BITES (1994)
REALM OF FORTUNE, THE (1986)
REASON TO BELIEVE, A (1995)
REBEL (1985)
REBEL LOVE (1986)
REBRO ADAMA (SEE: ADAM'S RIB)(1992)
RECKLESS (1995)
RECKLESS KELLY (1994)
RECRUITS (1986)
RED (1994)

RED FIRECRACKER, GREEN FIRECRACKER (1995)
RED HEADED STRANGER (1987)
RED HEAT (1988)
RED HEAT (1988)
RED KISS (1986)
RED OCEAN (SEE: MONSTER SHARK)(1986)
RED ROCK WEST (1994)
RED SCORPION (1989)
RED SHOE DIARIES 4: AUTO EROTICA (1994)
RED SONJA (1985)
RED SORGHUM (1988)
RED SUN RISING (1995)
RED SURF (1990)
RED X (SEE: STEPPING RAZOR - RED X)(1993)
REDHEADS (SEE: DESPERATE PREY)(1995)
REDL EZREDES (SEE: COLONEL REDL)(1985)
REDWOOD CURTAIN (1995)
REF, THE (1994)
REFLECTING SKIN, THE (1991)
REFLECTIONS IN THE DARK (1995)
REFORM SCHOOL GIRLS (1986)
REFRIGERATOR, THE (1992)
REGARDING HENRY (1991)
REGENERATED MAN, THE (1994)
REINCARNATION OF GOLDEN LOTUS, THE (1990)
RELENTLESS (1989)
RELENTLESS III (1993)
RELENTLESS 4: ASHES TO ASHES (1994)
REMAINS OF THE DAY, THE (1993)
REMANDO AL VIENTO (SEE: ROWING WITH THE WIND)(1988)
REMBETIKO (1985)
REMBRANDT LAUGHING (1989)
REMO WILLIAMS: THE ADVENTURE BEGINS ... (1985)
REMOTE (1993)
REMOTE CONTROL (1988)
REMOTE CONTROL (1995)
RENAISSANCE MAN (1994)
RENDEZVOUS (1985)
RENEGADES (1989)
RENT-A-COP (1988)
RENT-A-KID (1995)
RENTED LIPS (1988)
REPENTANCE (1988)
REPLIKATOR (1994)
REPOSSESSED (1990)
REQUIEM FOR DOMINIC (1991)
REQUIEM FUR DOMINIC (SEE: REQUIEM FOR DOMINIC)(1991)
RESCUE, THE (1988)
RESCUERS DOWN UNDER, THE (1990)
RESERVOIR DOGS (1992)
RESIDENT ALIEN (1991)
RESISTANCE (1994)
RESTLESS CONSCIENCE, THE (1991)
RESTORATION (1995)
RESURRECTED, THE (1992)
RETALIATOR (SEE: PROGRAMMED TO KILL)(1987)
RETRIBUTION (1988)
RETURN (1986)
RETURN OF JAFAR, THE (1994)
RETURN OF JOSEY WALES, THE (1987)
RETURN OF SUPERFLY, THE (1990)
RETURN OF SWAMP THING, THE (1989)
RETURN OF THE GOD OF GAMBLERS (1995)
RETURN OF THE KILLER TOMATOES (1988)
RETURN OF THE LIVING DEAD (1985)
RETURN OF THE LIVING DEAD III (1993)
RETURN OF THE LIVING DEAD PART II (1988)

RETURN OF THE NATIVE, THE (1995)
RETURN TO FROGTOWN (SEE: FROGTOWN II)(1993)
RETURN TO HORROR HIGH (1987)
RETURN TO OZ (1985)
RETURN TO SALEM'S LOT, A (1988)
RETURN TO SNOWY RIVER (1988)
RETURN TO THE BLUE LAGOON (1991)
RETURN TO THE LOST WORLD (1994)
RETURN TO TWO MOON JUNCTION (1994)
RETURN TO WATERLOO (1985)
RETURNING, THE (1991)
REUNION (1991)
REVENGE (1990)
REVENGE (1986)
REVENGE OF THE INNOCENTS (SEE: SOUTH BRONX HEROES)(1985)
REVENGE OF THE NERDS II: NERDS IN PARADISE (1987)
REVENGE OF THE TEENAGE VIXENS FROM OUTER SPACE, THE (1986)
REVERSAL OF FORTUNE (1990)
REVOLUTION (1985)
REVOLUTION! (1991)
REVOLVING DOORS, THE (1988)
RHAPSODY IN AUGUST (1991)
RHOSYN A RHITH (SEE: COMING UP ROSES)(1986)
RHYTHM THIEF (1995)
RICH GIRL (1991)
RICH IN LOVE (1993)
RICHARD III (1995)
RICHIE RICH (1994)
RICKY 1 (1988)
RICOCHET (1991)
RIDERS OF THE STORM (1988)
RIFF-RAFF (1993)
RIKKY AND PETE (1988)
RIKYU (1991)
RING OF FIRE (1991)
RING OF FIRE II: BLOOD AND STEEL (1993)
RING OF STEEL (1994)
RING OF THE MUSKETEERS (1994)
RISING SUN (1993)
RISK (1994)
RITA, SUE AND BOB TOO! (1987)
RIVER OF DEATH (1990)
RIVER OF GRASS (1995)
RIVER PIRATES, THE (1994)
RIVER RUNS THROUGH IT, A (1992)
RIVER WILD, THE (1994)
RIVERBEND (1990)
RIVER'S EDGE (1987)
ROAD HOUSE (1989)
ROAD KILL USA (1994)
ROAD TO RUIN (1992)
ROAD TO WELLVILLE, THE (1994)
ROAD TRIP (SEE: JOCKS)(1987)
ROADSIDE PROPHETS (1992)
ROB ROY (1995)
ROBERT A. HEINLEIN'S THE PUPPET MASTERS (1994)
ROBIN HOOD: MEN IN TIGHTS (1993)
ROBIN HOOD: PRINCE OF THIEVES (1991)
ROBINSON'S GARDEN (1988)
ROBOCOP (1987)
ROBOCOP 2 (1990)
ROBOCOP 3 (1993)
ROBOT HOLOCAUST (1987)
ROBOT JOX (1990)
ROBOT WARS (1993)
ROCK-A-DOODLE (1992)
ROCK & ROLL COWBOYS (1992)
ROCK HUDSON'S HOME MOVIES (1993)

ROCK 'N' ROLL HIGH SCHOOL FOREVER (1991)
ROCK 'N' ROLL NIGHTMARE (1987)
ROCK SOUP (1992)
ROCKET GIBRALTAR (1988)
ROCKETEER, THE (1991)
ROCKIN' ROAD TRIP (1986)
ROCKY IV (1985)
ROCKY V (1990)
RODNIK DLIA ZHAZHDUSHCHIKH (SEE: SPRING FOR THE THIRSTY, A)(1988)
RODRIGO D. - NO FUTURE (1991)
RODRIGO D. - NO FUTURO (SEE: RODRIGO D. - NO FUTURE)(1991)
ROGER CORMAN'S FRANKENSTEIN UNBOUND (SEE: FRANKENSTEIN UNBOUND)(1990)
ROLLER BLADE (1986)
ROMANCE DA EMPREGADA (SEE: STORY OF FAUSTA)(1988)
ROMEO IS BLEEDING (1994)
ROMERO (1989)
ROMPER STOMPER (1993)
ROOFTOPS (1989)
ROOKIE, THE (1990)
ROOKIE OF THE YEAR (1993)
ROOM WITH A VIEW, A (1986)
ROOMMATES (1995)
ROOTS OF EVIL (1992)
ROSALIE GOES SHOPPING (1989)
ROSARY MURDERS, THE (1987)
ROSE GARDEN, THE (1989)
ROSENCRANTZ AND GUILDENSTERN ARE DEAD (1991)
ROSWELL: THE U.F.O. COVER-UP (1995)
ROUGE (1990)
ROUGE BAISER (SEE: RED KISS)(1985)
ROUGE OF THE NORTH (1988)
ROUND MIDNIGHT (1986)
ROUND TRIP TO HEAVEN (1992)
ROVER DANGERFIELD (1992)
ROWING WITH THE WIND (1989)
ROXANNE (1987)
ROY COHN/JACK SMITH (1995)
ROYCE (1994)
RUBIN & ED (1992)
RUBY (1992)
RUBY IN PARADISE (1993)
RUDE AWAKENING (1989)
RUDY (1993)
RUDYARD KIPLING'S THE JUNGLE BOOK (SEE: JUNGLE BOOK, THE)(1994)
RULE #3 (1994)
RUMPELSTILTSKIN (1987)
RUN (1991)
RUN OF THE COUNTRY, THE (1995)
RUNAWAY TRAIN (1985)
RUNAWAYS, THE (SEE: SOUTH BRONX HEROES)(1985)
RUNESTONE, THE (1992)
RUNNER, THE (1991)
RUNNING COOL (1993)
RUNNING FREE (1994)
RUNNING MAN, THE (1987)
RUNNING ON EMPTY (1988)
RUNNING OUT OF LUCK (1986)
RUNNING SCARED (1986)
RUSH (1991)
RUSH WEEK (1991)
RUSSIA HOUSE, THE (1990)
RUSSKIES (1987)
RUSTLERS' RHAPSODY (1985)
RUTANGA TAPES, THE (1991)
RUTHLESS PEOPLE (1986)
RYDER, P.I. (1986)

S

SABRINA (1995)
SACRED HEARTS (1985)
SACRIFICE, THE (1986)
SADY SKORPIONA (SEE: GARDEN OF SCORPIONS)(1993)
SAFE (1995)
SAFE PASSAGE (1995)
SAIGON (SEE: OFF LIMITS)(1988)
ST. ELMO'S FIRE (1985)
SAINT OF FORT WASHINGTON, THE (1993)
SALAAM BOMBAY! (1988)
SALMONBERRIES (1994)
SALOME (1986)
SALOME'S LAST DANCE (1988)
SALSA (1988)
SALUTE OF THE JUGGER, THE (SEE: BLOOD OF HEROES)(1990)
SALVADOR (1986)
SALVATION! (1987)
SAM AND SARAH (1991)
SAMANTHA (1993)
SAME TO YOU (1987)
SAMMY AND ROSIE GET LAID (1987)
SAND AND BLOOD (1989)
SANDLOT, THE (1993)
SANKOFA (1994)
SANS ESPOIR DE RETOUR (SEE: STREET OF NO RETURN)(1991)
SANS TOIT NI LOI (SEE: VAGABOND)(1985)
SANTA CLAUS: THE MOVIE (1985)
SANTA CLAUSE, THE (1994)
SANTA SANGRE (1990)
SARAFINA! (1992)
SARRAOUNIA (1994)
SATAN KILLER, THE (1993)
SATAN'S PRINCESS (1991)
SATIN VENGEANCE (SEE: NAKED VENGEANCE)(1986)
SATISFACTION (1988)
SATURDAY NIGHT AT THE PALACE (1987)
SATURDAY NIGHT SPECIAL (1994)
SATURDAY THE 14TH STRIKES BACK (1989)
SAVAGE BEACH (1990)
SAVAGE INSTINCT (1992)
SAVAGE ISLAND (1985)
SAVAGE LUST (1993)
SAVAGE NIGHTS (1994)
SAVE ME (1994)
SAVING GRACE (1986)
SAXO (1988)
SAY ANYTHING (1989)
SAY YES (1986)
SCANDAL (1989)
SCANNER COP (1994)
SCANNER COP II: VOLKIN'S REVENGE (SEE: SCANNERS: THE SHOWDOWN)(1995)
SCANNERS: THE SHOWDOWN (1995)
SCANNERS III: THE TAKEOVER (1992)
SCANNERS II: THE NEW ORDER (1991)
SCARECROWS (1988)
SCARLET LETTER, THE (1995)
SCAVENGERS (1988)
SCENE OF THE CRIME (1986)
SCENES FROM A MALL (1991)
SCENES FROM THE CLASS STRUGGLE IN BEVERLY HILLS (1989)
SCENES FROM THE GOLDMINE (1988)
SCENT OF A WOMAN (1992)
SCENT OF GREEN PAPAYA, THE (1994)
SCHACHZUGE (SEE: KNIGHT MOVES)(1993)
SCHINDLER'S LIST (1993)
SCHOOL DAZE (1988)
SCHOOL SPIRIT (1985)

SCHOOL TIES (1992)
SCISSORS (1991)
SCORCHERS (1992)
SCORNED (1994)
SCOUT, THE (1994)
SCREAMPLAY (1986)
SCREAMTIME (1986)
SCREEN TEST (1986)
SCREWBALL HOTEL (1989)
SCREWFACE (SEE: MARKED FOR
    DEATH)(1990)
SCROOGED (1988)
SEA OF LOVE (1989)
SEARCH AND DESTROY (1995)
SEARCH FOR SIGNS OF INTELLIGENT LIFE
    IN THE UNIVERSE, THE (1991)
SEARCHING FOR BOBBY FISCHER (1993)
SEASON OF DREAMS (SEE: STACKING)(1987)
SEASON OF FEAR (1989)
SEBASTIAN STAR BEAR: FIRST MISSION
    (1993)
SECOND BEST (1994)
SECRET ADMIRER (1985)
SECRET ADVENTURES OF TOM THUMB,
    THE (1994)
SECRET FRIENDS (1992)
SECRET GAMES (1992)
SECRET GAMES 2: THE ESCORT (1993)
SECRET GARDEN, THE (1993)
SECRET OF MY SUCCESS, THE (1987)
SECRET OF NIKOLA TESLA, THE (1985)
SECRET OF ROAN INISH, THE (1995)
SECRET OF THE SWORD, THE (1985)
SECRET PLACES (1985)
SECRET RAPTURE, THE (1994)
SECRETARY, THE (1995)
SECRETS IN THE ATTIC (1994)
SECRETS SECRETS (1985)
SECUESTRO: A STORY OF A KIDNAPPING
    (1994)
SEDUCE ME (1994)
SEDUCTION: THE CRUEL WOMAN (1989)
SEE NO EVIL, HEAR NO EVIL (1989)
SEE YOU IN THE MORNING (1989)
SEEDPEOPLE (1992)
SEGRETI SEGRETI (SEE: SECRETS
    SECRETS)(1985)
SENSE AND SENSIBILITY (1995)
SENSE OF FREEDOM, A (1985)
SENTIMIENTOS: MIRTA DE LINIERS A
    ESTAMBUL (1987)
SEPARATE LIVES (1995)
SEPARATE VACATIONS (1986)
SEPARATION (SEE: DON'T HANG UP)(1994)
SEPTEMBER (1987)
SERE CUALQUIER COSA PERO TE QUIERO
    (1986)
SERIAL MOM (1994)
SERIOUS ABOUT PLEASURE (1995)
SERPENT AND THE RAINBOW, THE (1988)
SERPENT OF DEATH, THE (1991)
SERPENT'S WAY, THE (1987)
SESAME STREET PRESENTS: FOLLOW THAT
    BIRD (1985)
SETTA, LA (SEE: DEVIL'S DAUGHTER,
    THE)(1992)
SEVEN (1995)
SEVEN HOURS TO JUDGEMENT (1988)
SEVEN MINUTES IN HEAVEN (1986)
SEVENTH COIN, THE (1993)
SEVENTH SIGN, THE (1988)
SEVERED TIES (1992)
SEX AND ZEN (1993)
SEX APPEAL (1986)
SEX CRIMES (1992)
SEX, DRUGS AND DEMOCRACY (1995)

SEX, DRUGS, ROCK & ROLL (1991)
SEX, LIES, AND VIDEOTAPE (1989)
SEX O'CLOCK NEWS, THE (1986)
SEX OF THE STARS, THE (1994)
SEXUAL INTENT (1994)
SEXUAL OUTLAWS (1994)
SEXUAL RESPONSE (1992)
S.F.W. (1995)
SHADEY (1987)
SHADOW OF THE RAVEN, THE (1990)
SHADOW OF THE WOLF (1993)
SHADOW OF VICTORY (1986)
SHADOW PLAY (1986)
SHADOW, THE (1994)
SHADOWFORCE (1993)
SHADOWHUNTER (1993)
SHADOWLANDS (1993)
SHADOWS AND FOG (1992)
SHADOWS IN THE CITY (1991)
SHADOWS OF THE PEACOCK (SEE: ECHOES
    OF PARADISE)(1989)
SHADOWS RUN BLACK (1986)
SHADOWZONE (1990)
SHAG (1989)
SHAKEDOWN (1988)
SHAKES THE CLOWN (1992)
SHAKING THE TREE (1992)
SHALLOW GRAVE (1995)
SHAME (1988)
SHAME (1994)
SHAMELESS (1993)
SHANGHAI SURPRISE (1986)
SHANGHAI TRIAD (1995)
SHAO LIN POPEYE (1995)
SHATTER DEAD (1994)
SHATTERED (1991)
SHAWSHANK REDEMPTION, THE (1994)
SHE (1985)
SHE-DEVIL (1989)
SHELTERING SKY, THE (1990)
SHERLOCK BONES, UNDERCOVER DOG
    (1994)
SHERLOCK: UNDERCOVER DOG (SEE:
    SHERLOCK BONES, UNDERCOVER
    DOG)(1994)
SHE'S BACK (1991)
SHE'S GOTTA HAVE IT (1986)
SHE'S HAVING A BABY (1988)
SHE'S OUT OF CONTROL (1989)
SHINING THROUGH (1992)
SHIPWRECKED (1991)
SHIRLEY VALENTINE (1989)
SHOCK 'EM DEAD (1991)
SHOCK TO THE SYSTEM, A (1990)
SHOCKER (1989)
SHOOT FOR THE SUN (1986)
SHOOT TO KILL (1988)
SHOOTFIGHTER: FIGHT TO THE DEATH
    (1993)
SHOOTING ELIZABETH (1992)
SHOOTING PARTY, THE (1985)
SHORT CIRCUIT (1986)
SHORT CIRCUIT 2 (1988)
SHORT CUTS (1993)
SHORT FILM ABOUT KILLING, A (1995)
SHORT FILM ABOUT LOVE, A (1995)
SHORT TIME (1990)
SHOUT (1991)
SHOW OF FORCE, A (1990)
SHOW, THE (1995)
SHOWDOWN (1993)
SHOWDOWN AT WILLIAMS CREEK (1991)
SHOWDOWN IN LITTLE TOKYO (1991)
SHOWGIRLS (1995)
SHRIMP ON THE BARBIE, THE (1990)

SHRUNKEN HEADS (1994)
SHY PEOPLE (1988)
SIBLING RIVALRY (1990)
SICILIAN, THE (1987)
SID AND NANCY (1986)
SIDE OUT (1990)
SIDEKICKS (1993)
SIDEWALK STORIES (1989)
SIESTA (1987)
SIGNE CHARLOTTE (SEE: SINCERELY
    CHARLOTTE)(1986)
SIGNS OF LIFE (1989)
SILENCE OF THE HAMS (1995)
SILENCE OF THE LAMBS, THE (1991)
SILENCER, THE (1993)
SILENT ASSASSINS (1988)
SILENT FALL (1994)
SILENT NIGHT, DEADLY NIGHT PART II
    (1987)
SILENT NIGHT, DEADLY NIGHT 5: THE TOY
    MAKER (1991)
SILENT NIGHT, DEADLY NIGHT 3: BETTER
    WATCH OUT! (1989)
SILENT TONGUE (1994)
SILENT TOUCH, THE (1993)
SILIP (1985)
SILK (1986)
SILK DEGREES (1994)
SILK 'N' SABOTAGE (1994)
SILK ROAD, THE (1992)
SILVER BRUMBY, THE (SEE: SILVER
    STALLION, THE)(1994)
SILVER CITY (1985)
SILVER STALLION, THE (1994)
SILVERADO (1985)
SILVERLAKE LIFE: THE VIEW FROM HERE
    (1994)
SIMPLE MEN (1992)
SIMPLE TWIST OF FATE, A (1994)
SIN VERGUENZA (SEE: SHAMELESS)(1993)
SINCERELY CHARLOTTE (1986)
SING (1989)
SINGLE WHITE FEMALE (1992)
SINGLES (1992)
SINS OF DESIRE (1993)
SINS OF THE NIGHT (1993)
SIOUX CITY (1994)
SIRENS (1994)
SISTER ACT (1992)
SISTER ACT 2: BACK IN THE HABIT (1993)
SISTER MY SISTER (1995)
SISTER OF LOVE (SEE: BAR 51—SISTER OF
    LOVE)(1986)
SISTER, SISTER (1988)
SISTERS (SEE: SOME GIRLS)(1989)
SIUNIN WONG FEI-HUNG TSI TITMALAU
    (SEE: IRON MONKEY)(1994)
SIX DAYS, SIX NIGHTS (1995)
SIX DEGREES OF SEPARATION (1993)
'68 (1988)
SIZZLE BEACH, U.S.A. (1986)
SJECAS LI SE DOLLY BELL? (SEE: DO YOU
    REMEMBER DOLLY BELL?)(1986)
SKATEBOARD KID, THE (1993)
SKEETER (1994)
SKELETON COAST (1989)
SKI PATROL (1990)
SKI SCHOOL (1991)
SKIN ART (1994)
SKIN DEEP (1989)
SKINHEADS—THE SECOND COMING OF
    HATE (1990)
SKINNER (1995)
SKY BANDITS (1986)
SLACKER (1991)
SLAMDANCE (1987)

SLASH DANCE (1989)
SLAUGHTER HIGH (1987)
SLAUGHTER OF THE INNOCENTS (1994)
SLAUGHTERHOUSE (1988)
SLAUGHTERHOUSE ROCK (1988)
SLAVES OF NEW YORK (1989)
SLEAZY UNCLE, THE (1991)
SLEEP WITH ME (1994)
SLEEPAWAY CAMP 2: UNHAPPY CAMPERS (1988)
SLEEPAWAY CAMP 3: TEENAGE WASTELAND (1989)
SLEEPING CAR, THE (1990)
SLEEPING WITH STRANGERS (1994)
SLEEPING WITH THE ENEMY (1991)
SLEEPLESS IN SEATTLE (1993)
SLINGSHOT, THE (1994)
SLIPPING INTO DARKNESS (1989)
SLIPSTREAM (1990)
SLIVER (1993)
SLUGGER'S WIFE, THE (1985)
SLUMBER PARTY MASSACRE 3 (1992)
SLUMBER PARTY MASSACRE II (1987)
SMALL KILL (1993)
SMALL TIME (1991)
SMILE OF THE LAMB, THE (1986)
SMOKE (1995)
SMOOTH TALK (1985)
SMOOTH TALKER (1992)
SNAKEEATER III ... HIS LAW (1992)
SNAKEEATER II: THE DRUG BUSTER (1991)
SNAPPER, THE (1993)
SNEAKERS (1992)
SNIPER (1993)
SNO-LINE (1986)
SO I MARRIED AN AXE MURDERER (1993)
SOAPDISH (1991)
SOCIETY (1992)
SODBUSTERS (1994)
SOFIA (1987)
SOFIE (1993)
SOFT KILL, THE (1994)
SOLAR CRISIS (1993)
SOLARBABIES (1986)
SOLDIER'S TALE, A (1992)
SOLDIER'S FORTUNE (1992)
SOLDIER'S REVENGE (1986)
SOME GIRLS (1989)
SOME KIND OF WONDERFUL (1987)
SOMEONE TO LOVE (1988)
SOMEONE TO WATCH OVER ME (1987)
SOMETHING SPECIAL (1987)
SOMETHING TO DO WITH THE WALL (1991)
SOMETHING TO TALK ABOUT (1995)
SOMETHING WILD (1986)
SOMMERSBY (1993)
SON-IN-LAW (1993)
SON OF THE PINK PANTHER (SEE: BLAKE EDWARDS' SON OF THE PINK PANTHER)(1993)
SON OF THE SHARK, THE (1995)
SONDAGSBARN (SEE: SUNDAY'S CHILDREN)(1994)
SONNY BOY (1990)
SORORITY GIRLS AND THE CREATURES FROM HELL (1991)
SORORITY HOUSE MASSACRE (1986)
SORORITY HOUSE MASSACRE 2 (1992)
SORRENTO BEACH (SEE: HOTEL SORRENTO)(1995)
SOUL MAN (1986)
SOULTAKER (1991)
SOUND AND FURY (1988)
SOURSWEET (1988)

SOUS LE SOLEIL DE SATAN (SEE: UNDER SATAN'S SUN)(1988)
SOUTH (1988)
SOUTH BEACH (1993)
SOUTH BRONX HEROES (1985)
SOUTH CENTRAL (1992)
SPACE 2074 (SEE: STAR QUEST: BEYOND THE RISING MOON)(1990)
SPACE AVENGER (1991)
SPACE RAGE (1987)
SPACEBALLS (1987)
SPACECAMP (1986)
SPACED INVADERS (1990)
SPANKING THE MONKEY (1994)
SPEAKING PARTS (1989)
SPECIALIST, THE (1994)
SPECIALMENTE LA DOMENICA (SEE: ESPECIALLY ON SUNDAY)(1993)
SPECIES (1995)
SPEECHLESS (1994)
SPEED (1994)
SPEED ZONE (1989)
SPELLBINDER (1988)
SPIDER AND THE FLY, THE (1994)
SPIES LIKE US (1985)
SPIKE AND MIKE'S FESTIVAL OF ANIMATION '95 (1995)
SPIKE OF BENSONHURST (1988)
SPIKER (1986)
SPIRIT OF THE EAGLE (1991)
SPIRITS (1992)
SPIRIT OF '76, THE (1991)
SPITFIRE (1995)
SPLIT DECISIONS (1988)
SPLIT SECOND (1992)
SPLITTING HEIRS (1993)
SPONTANEOUS COMBUSTION (1990)
SPOORLOOS (SEE: VANISHING, THE)(1991)
SPOTSWOOD (SEE: EFFICIENCY EXPERT, THE)(1992)
SPRING FOR THE THIRSTY, A (1988)
SPY WITHIN, THE (1995)
SPY WITHIN, THE (SEE: FLIGHT OF THE DOVE)(1995)
SQUAMISH FIVE, THE (1988)
SQUANTO: A WARRIOR'S TALE (1994)
SQUARE DANCE (1987)
SQUEEZE, THE (1987)
STACKING (1987)
STAKEOUT (1987)
STALINGRAD (1995)
STAMMHEIM (1986)
STAND ALONE (1985)
STAND AND DELIVER (1988)
STAND BY ME (1986)
STAND-IN, THE (1985)
STANLEY AND IRIS (1990)
STANNO TUTTI BENE (SEE: EVERYBODY'S FINE)(1991)
STAR CRYSTAL (1986)
STAR QUEST: BEYOND THE RISING MOON (1990)
STAR SLAMMER: THE ESCAPE (1988)
STAR TREK IV: THE VOYAGE HOME (1986)
STAR TREK V: THE FINAL FRONTIER (1989)
STAR TREK VI: THE UNDISCOVERED COUNTRY (1991)
STAR TREK: GENERATIONS (1994)
STARCHASER: THE LEGEND OF ORIN (1985)
STARGATE (1994)
STARLIGHT HOTEL (1987)
STARS AND BARS (1988)
STARS FELL ON HENRIETTA, THE (1995)
STATE OF GRACE (1990)
STATIC (1985)

STATION, THE (1992)
STAY TUNED (1992)
STAYING TOGETHER (1989)
STAZIONE, LA (SEE: STATION, THE)(1992)
STEAL AMERICA (1992)
STEAL BIG, STEAL LITTLE (1995)
STEALING HEAVEN (1989)
STEALING HOME (1988)
STEAMING (1985)
STEEL AND LACE (1991)
STEEL DAWN (1987)
STEEL MAGNOLIAS (1989)
STEELE JUSTICE (1987)
STEELE'S LAW (1992)
STEFANO QUANTESTORIE (1994)
STELLA (1990)
STEPFATHER, THE (1987)
STEPFATHER 2: MAKE ROOM FOR DADDY (1989)
STEPHEN KING'S GRAVEYARD SHIFT (SEE: GRAVEYARD SHIFT)(1990)
STEPHEN KING'S SILVER BULLET (1985)
STEPHEN KING'S SLEEPWALKERS (1992)
STEPMONSTER (1993)
STEPPING OUT (1991)
STEPPING RAZOR - RED X (1993)
STEWARDESS SCHOOL (1986)
STICK (1985)
STICKY FINGERS (1988)
STILL LIFE: THE FINE ART OF MURDER (1993)
STITCHES (1985)
STOLEN CHILDREN, THE (1993)
STONE COLD (1991)
STONED AGE, THE (1994)
STOOGEMANIA (1986)
STOP! OR MY MOM WILL SHOOT (1992)
STORIA DI RAGAZZI E DI RAGAZZE (SEE: STORY OF BOYS AND GIRLS)(1991)
STORM (1989)
STORMS OF AUGUST, THE (1988)
STORMY MONDAY (1988)
STORMYYD AWST (SEE: STORMS OF AUGUST, THE)(1988)
STORY OF BOYS AND GIRLS (1991)
STORY OF FAUSTA, THE (1988)
STORY OF QIU JU, THE (1993)
STORY OF WOMEN (1989)
STORYVILLE (1992)
STRAIGHT OUT OF BROOKLYN (1991)
STRAIGHT TALK (1992)
STRAIGHT THROUGH THE HEART (1985)
STRAIGHT TO HELL (1987)
STRAIGHT TO THE HEART (1988)
STRANDED (1987)
STRANGE DAYS (1995)
STRANGER, THE (1987)
STRANGER AMONG US, A (1992)
STRANGER BY NIGHT (1994)
STRANGER, THE (1995)
STRANGERS IN GOOD COMPANY (1991)
STRANGLEHOLD (1994)
STRAPLESS (1989)
STRAWBERRY AND CHOCOLATE (1995)
STREET ASYLUM (1990)
STREET CRIMES (1992)
STREET FIGHTER (1994)
STREET HUNTER (1991)
STREET JUSTICE (1989)
STREET KNIGHT (1993)
STREET LEGAL (SEE: LAST OF THE FINEST)(1990)
STREET OF NO RETURN (1991)
STREET SMART (1987)
STREET SOLDIERS (1991)

STREET STORY (1988)
STREET TRASH (1987)
STREET WARS (1994)
STREETS (1990)
STREETS OF GOLD (1986)
STREETWALKIN' (1985)
STRICTLY BALLROOM (1993)
STRICTLY BUSINESS (1991)
STRICTLY PROPAGANDA (1993)
STRIKE IT RICH (1990)
STRIKING DISTANCE (1993)
STRIPPED TO KILL (1987)
STRIPPED TO KILL II: LIVE GIRLS (1989)
STRIPPER (1986)
STROKE OF MIDNIGHT (1991)
STUART SAVES HIS FAMILY (1995)
STUFF STEPHANIE IN THE INCINERATOR (1990)
STUFF, THE (1985)
SUBSPECIES (1991)
SUBSTITUTE WIFE, THE (1995)
SUBSTITUTE, THE (SEE: SUBSTITUTE WIFE, THE)(1995)
SUBURBAN COMMANDO (1991)
SUBWAY (1985)
SUCCESSFUL MAN, A (1987)
SUDDEN DEATH (1985)
SUDDEN DEATH (1995)
SUGAR HILL (1994)
SUGARBABY (1985)
SUICIDE CLUB, THE (1988)
SUM OF US, THE (1995)
SUMMER (1986)
SUMMER (1988)
SUMMER CAMP NIGHTMARE (1987)
SUMMER HEAT (1987)
SUMMER HOUSE, THE (1993)
SUMMER RENTAL (1985)
SUMMER SCHOOL (1987)
SUMMER STORY, A (1988)
SUMMER VACATION: 1999 (1990)
SUNDAY'S CHILDREN (1994)
SUNDOWN: THE VAMPIRE IN RETREAT (1991)
SUNSET (1988)
SUNSET GRILL (1993)
SUNSET STRIP (1985)
SUNSET STRIP (1992)
SUPER MARIO BROS. (1993)
SUPER, THE (1991)
SUPERCOP: POLICE STORY III (1992)
SUPERFANTAGENIO (SEE: ALADDIN)(1987)
SUPERMAN IV: THE QUEST FOR PEACE (1987)
SUPERNATURALS, THE (1987)
SUPERSTAR: THE LIFE AND TIMES OF ANDY WARHOL (1991)
SUPERSTITION (1985)
SUR (SEE: SOUTH)(1988)
SUR LA TERRE COMME AU CIEL (SEE: BETWEEN HEAVEN AND EARTH)(1993)
SURE FIRE (1994)
SURE THING, THE (1985)
SURF NAZIS MUST DIE (1987)
SURF NINJAS (1993)
SURPRISE PARTY (1985)
SURRENDER (1987)
SURVIVAL QUEST (1990)
SURVIVING THE GAME (1994)
SUSPECT (1987)
SUTURE (1994)
SWAN LAKE - THE ZONE (1991)
SWAN PRINCESS, THE (1994)
SWEET COUNTRY (1987)
SWEET DREAMS (1985)

SWEET HEARTS DANCE (1988)
SWEET JUSTICE (1993)
SWEET KILLING (1993)
SWEET LIBERTY (1986)
SWEET LIES (1989)
SWEET LORRAINE (1987)
SWEET MURDER (1993)
SWEET REVENGE (1987)
SWEET TALKER (1991)
SWEETIE (1989)
SWIMMER, THE (1988)
SWIMMING TO CAMBODIA (1987)
SWIMMING WITH SHARKS (1995)
SWING KIDS (1993)
SWITCH (1991)
SWITCHING CHANNELS (1988)
SWOON (1992)
SWORD OF HEAVEN (1985)
SWORD OF HONOR (1994)
SWORDSMAN, THE (1993)
SYLVESTER (1985)
SYLVIA (1985)
SZAMARKOHOGES (SEE: WHOOPING COUGH)(1987)
SZERELEM ELSO VERIG (SEE: LOVE TILL FIRST BLOOD)(1985)

T

ABDUCTED 2: THE REUNION (1995)
T2 (SEE: TERMINATOR 2: JUDGEMENT DAY)(1991)
TACONES LEJANOS (SEE: HIGH HEELS)(1991)
TAFFIN (1988)
TAI-PAN (1986)
TAKING CARE OF BUSINESS (1990)
TAKING OF BEVERLY HILLS, THE (1991)
TAKING THE HEAT (1994)
TALE OF RUBY ROSE, THE (1987)
TALE OF SPRINGTIME, A (1992)
TALE OF WINTER, A (1994)
TALENT FOR THE GAME (1991)
TALES FROM THE CRYPT: DEMON KNIGHT (1995)
TALES FROM THE DARKSIDE: THE MOVIE (1990)
TALES FROM THE HOOD (1995)
TALES OF THE THIRD DIMENSION (1985)
TALK RADIO (1988)
TALKIN' DIRTY AFTER DARK (1991)
TALKING TO STRANGERS (1988)
TALKING WALLS (1987)
TALL GUY, THE (1989)
TALL TALE: THE UNBELIEVABLE ADVENTURES OF PECOS BILL (1995)
TALONS OF THE EAGLE (1992)
TALVISOTA (1989)
TAMMY AND THE T-REX (1994)
TAMPOPO (1986)
TANGO AND CASH (1989)
TANGO BAR (1989)
TANK GIRL (1995)
TAP (1989)
TAPEHEADS (1988)
TARGET (1985)
TAROT (1986)
TATIE DANIELLE (1991)
TATTOO CONNECTION, THE (1994)
TAX SEASON (1990)
TAXI BLUES (1991)
TAXI DANCERS (1993)
TAXING WOMAN, A (1988)
TAXING WOMAN'S RETURN, A (1988)
TC 2000 (1993)
TEA IN THE HAREM OF ARCHIMEDE (1985)

TEARS IN THE RAIN (1994)
TED & VENUS (1991)
TEEN WITCH (1989)
TEEN WOLF (1985)
TEEN WOLF TOO (1987)
TEENAGE EXORCIST (1994)
TEENAGE MUTANT NINJA TURTLES (1990)
TEENAGE MUTANT NINJA TURTLES III (1993)
TELEPHONE, THE (1988)
TEMP, THE (1993)
TEMPO DI UCCIDERE (SEE: TIME TO KILL)(1991)
TEMPOS DIFICEIS (SEE: HARD TIMES)(1988)
TEMPTATION (1994)
TEMPTATION OF A MONK, THE (1994)
TEN LITTLE INDIANS (1990)
TENANTS, THE (1991)
TENDERFOOT, THE (SEE: BUSHWHACKED)(1995)
TEQUILA SUNRISE (1988)
TERESA'S TATTOO (1995)
TERMINAL BLISS (1992)
TERMINAL CHOICE (1985)
TERMINAL VELOCITY (1994)
TERMINATOR 2: JUDGMENT DAY (1991)
TERMINI STATION (1991)
TERROR AT THE OPERA (1991)
TERROR IN BEVERLY HILLS (1991)
TERROR WITHIN, THE (1989)
TERROR WITHIN II, THE (1991)
TERRORGRAM (1991)
TERRORVISION (1986)
TEST OF LOVE (SEE: ANNIE'S COMING OUT)(1985)
TESTAMENT (1988)
TETSUO: THE IRON MAN (1992)
TEXAS CHAINSAW MASSACRE PART 2, THE (1986)
TEXAS TENOR: THE ILLINOIS JACQUET STORY (1992)
TEXASVILLE (1990)
THANK YOU AND GOOD NIGHT! (1992)
THAT NIGHT (1993)
THAT WAS THEN...THIS IS NOW (1985)
THAT'S ENTERTAINMENT! PART III (1994)
THAT'S LIFE! (1986)
THELMA & LOUISE (1991)
THERE GOES THE NEIGHBORHOOD (1993)
THERE'S NOTHING OUT THERE (1992)
THERESE (1986)
THESE FOOLISH THINGS (SEE: DADDY NOSTALGIA)(1991)
THEY LIVE (1988)
THEY STILL CALL ME BRUCE (1987)
THEY WATCH (1994)
THING CALLED LOVE, THE (1993)
THINGS CHANGE (1988)
THINGS TO DO IN DENVER WHEN YOU'RE DEAD (1995)
35 UP (1992)
36 FILLETTE (1988)
THIRTY-TWO SHORT FILMS ABOUT GLENN GOULD (1994)
THIS BOY'S LIFE (1993)
THIS IS MY LIFE (1992)
THOUSAND HEROES, A (1994)
THOUSAND PIECES OF GOLD (1991)
THRASHIN' (1986)
THREE AMIGOS (1986)
THREE COLORS: BLUE (SEE: BLUE)(1993)
THREE COLORS: RED (SEE: RED)(1994)
THREE COLORS: WHITE (SEE: WHITE)(1994)
3:15, THE MOMENT OF TRUTH (1986)
THREE FOR THE ROAD (1987)

THREE FUGITIVES (1989)
3 MEN AND A BABY (1987)
THREE MEN AND A CRADLE (1985)
3 MEN AND A LITTLE LADY (1990)
THREE MUSKETEERS, THE (1993)
3 NINJAS (1992)
3 NINJAS KICK BACK (1994)
3 NINJAS KNUCKLE UP (1995)
THREE O'CLOCK HIGH (1987)
THREE OF HEARTS (1993)
THREE WISHES (1995)
THREEPENNY OPERA, THE (SEE: MACK THE KNIFE)(1990)
THREESOME (1994)
THROUGH THE OLIVE TREES (1995)
THROW MOMMA FROM THE TRAIN (1987)
THUMBELINA (SEE: HANS CHRISTIAN ANDERSEN'S THUMBELINA)(1994)
THUNDER IN PARADISE 2 (1994)
THUNDER RUN (1986)
THUNDER WARRIOR (1986)
THUNDERHEART (1992)
TICKET (1987)
TICKS (1994)
TIDES OF WAR (1994)
TIE-DIED: ROCK 'N' ROLL'S MOST DEADICATED FANS (1995)
TIE ME UP! TIE ME DOWN! (1990)
TIE THAT BINDS, THE (1995)
TIGER CLAWS (1992)
TIGER WARSAW (1988)
TIGER'S TALE, A (1988)
TIGRERO: A FILM THAT WAS NEVER MADE (1994)
TIGRESS (1993)
TILL MURDER DO US PART (1994)
TILL THERE WAS YOU (1992)
TIM BURTON'S THE NIGHTMARE BEFORE CHRISTMAS (1993)
TIME AFTER TIME (1985)
TIME BOMB (1991)
TIME GUARDIAN, THE (1990)
TIME INDEFINITE (1993)
TIME OF DESTINY, A (1988)
TIME OF THE GYPSIES (1990)
TIME RUNNER (1993)
TIME TO DIE, A (1985)
TIME TO DIE, A (1991)
TIME TO KILL (1991)
TIME TRACKERS (1989)
TIME TROOPERS (1990)
TIMECOP (1994)
TIN MEN (1987)
TINA: WHAT'S LOVE GOT TO DO WITH IT (SEE: WHAT'S LOVE GOT TO DO WITH IT)(1993)
TITAN FIND (SEE: CREATURE)(1985)
TITO AND ME (1993)
TITO I YA (SEE: TITO AND ME)(1993)
TO BE THE BEST (1993)
TO CROSS THE RUBICON (1995)
TO DENDRO POU PLIGONAME (SEE: TREE WE HURT, THE)(1987)
TO DIE FOR (1989)
TO DIE FOR (1995)
TO DIE FOR 2: SON OF DARKNESS (1991)
TO KILL A PRIEST (1989)
TO KILL A STRANGER (1985)
TO LIVE (1994)
TO LIVE AND DIE IN L.A. (1985)
TO PROTECT AND SERVE (1992)
TO RENDER A LIFE (1992)
TO SLEEP WITH A VAMPIRE (1993)
TO SLEEP WITH ANGER (1990)
TO THE DEATH (1993)

TO THE LIMIT (SEE: SIX DAYS, SIX NIGHTS)(1995)
TO WONG FOO, THANKS FOR EVERYTHING! JULIE NEWMAR (1995)
TOBY MCTEAGUE (1986)
TOGETHER ALONE (1992)
TOKYO DECADENCE (1993)
TOKYO POP (1988)
TOM AND HUCK (1995)
TOM AND JERRY - THE MOVIE (1993)
TOM & VIV (1994)
TOMB, THE (1986)
TOMBOY (1985)
TOMBSTONE (1993)
TOMCAT: DANGEROUS DESIRES (1993)
TOMMY BOY (1995)
TONARI NO TOTORO (SEE: MY NEIGHBOR TOTORO)(1993)
TONG TANA - A JOURNEY TO THE HEART OF BORNEO (1991)
TOO BEAUTIFUL FOR YOU (1989)
TOO MUCH SUN (1991)
TOO OUTRAGEOUS ANIMATION (1995)
TOO SCARED TO SCREAM (1985)
TOO YOUNG TO DIE? (1995)
TOP DOG (1995)
TOP GUN (1986)
TORA-SAN GOES TO VIENNA (1989)
TORCH SONG TRILOGY (1988)
TORMENT (1986)
TORN APART (1990)
TORRENTS OF SPRING (1990)
TOTAL ECLIPSE (1995)
TOTAL EXPOSURE (1991)
TOTAL RECALL (1990)
TOTO LE HEROS (1992)
TOUCH AND DIE (1992)
TOUCH AND GO (1986)
TOUCH OF A STRANGER (1990)
TOUGH GUYS (1986)
TOUGH GUYS DON'T DANCE (1987)
TOUGHER THAN LEATHER (1988)
TOUR OF DUTY (SEE: BREACH OF CONDUCT)(1995)
TOUS LES MATINS DU MONDE (1992)
TOXIC AVENGER, THE (1985)
TOXIC AVENGER, PART II, THE (1989)
TOXIC AVENGER PART III: THE LAST TEMPTATION OF TOXIE, THE (1989)
TOY SOLDIERS (1991)
TOY STORY (1995)
TOYS (1992)
TRACES OF RED (1992)
TRACK 29 (1988)
TRADING HEARTS (1988)
TRADING MOM (1994)
TRAIN OF DREAMS (1987)
TRAINED TO FIGHT (1992)
TRAINED TO KILL (1994)
TRANCERS (1985)
TRANCERS 5: SUDDEN DETH (1994)
TRANCERS III: DETH LIVES (1992)
TRANCERS II: THE RETURN OF JACK DETH (1991)
TRANSFORMERS: THE MOVIE, THE (1986)
TRANSYLVANIA 6-5000 (1985)
TRAPPED IN PARADISE (1994)
TRAPPED IN SPACE (1994)
TRAPS (1995)
TRAUMA (1994)
TRAVELLING AVANT (1988)
TRAVELLING NORTH (1988)
TRAXX (1988)
TREACHEROUS (1994)
TREASURE OF THE AMAZON, THE (1985)

TREE OF HANDS, THE (SEE: INNOCENT VICTIM)(1990)
TREE WE HURT, THE (1986)
TREMORS (1990)
TRESPASS (1992)
TRIAL BY JURY (1994)
TRIAL, THE (1993)
TRIBULATION 99: ALIEN ANOMALIES UNDER AMERICA (1991)
TRICK OR TREAT (1986)
TRIGGER FAST (1994)
TRIP TO BOUNTIFUL, THE (1985)
TRIPLE IMPACT (1993)
TRIUMPH OF THE SPIRIT (1989)
TROIS COULEURS: BLANC (SEE: WHITE)(1994)
TROIS COULEURS: BLEU (SEE: BLUE)(1993)
TROIS COULEURS: ROUGE (SEE: RED)(1994)
TROLL (1986)
TROLL 3 (SEE: CRAWLERS, THE)(1994)
TROLL IN CENTRAL PARK, A (1994)
TROLL 2 (1992)
TROOP BEVERLY HILLS (1989)
TROP BELLE POUR TOI (SEE: TOO BEAUTIFUL FOR YOU)(1990)
TROPICAL HEAT (1993)
TROUBLE BOUND (1993)
TROUBLE IN MIND (1985)
TROUBLE WITH DICK, THE (1987)
TRUE BELIEVER (1989)
TRUE BLOOD (1989)
TRUE COLORS (1991)
TRUE IDENTITY (1991)
TRUE LIES (1994)
TRUE LOVE (1989)
TRUE ROMANCE (1993)
TRUE STORIES (1986)
TRULY, MADLY, DEEPLY (1991)
TRUST (1991)
TRUST ME (1989)
TRUSTING BEATRICE (1993)
TRUTH OR DARE (1991)
TRYST (1994)
TUCKER: THE MAN AND HIS DREAM (1988)
TUFF TURF (1985)
TULITIKKUTEHTAAN TYTTO (SEE: MATCH FACTORY GIRL, THE)(1992)
TUNE IN TOMORROW (1990)
TUNE, THE (1992)
TURK 182! (1985)
TURN OF THE SCREW (1985)
TURNER & HOOCH (1989)
TURTLE DIARY (1985)
TUSKS (1990)
TWEENERS (SEE: TRADING HEARTS)(1988)
TWELVE MONKEYS (1995)
TWENTY BUCKS (1993)
TWENTY DOLLAR STAR (1991)
24 HOURS TO MIDNIGHT (1992)
24TH INTERNATIONAL TOURNEE OF ANIMATION, THE (1994)
29TH STREET (1991)
TWENTY-ONE (1991)
TWENTY SOMETHING (1995)
TWICE DEAD (1989)
TWICE IN A LIFETIME (1985)
TWILIGHT OF THE COCKROACHES (1990)
TWIN PEAKS: FIRE WALK WITH ME (1992)
TWIN SISTERS (1992)
TWINS (1988)
TWIST (1993)
TWISTED (1991)
TWISTED JUSTICE (1990)
TWISTED OBSESSION (1990)
TWISTER (1989)

TWO EVIL EYES (1990)
TWO JAKES, THE (1990)
TWO LIVES OF MATTIA PASCAL, THE (1985)
TWO SMALL BODIES (1994)
2020 TEXAS GLADIATORS (1985)
2002: THE RAPE OF EDEN (1994)
TWO TO TANGO (1989)
TWO-MOON JUNCTION (1988)
TWOGETHER (1995)

U

UCHO (SEE: EAR, THE)(1992)
UFORIA (1985)
UHF (1989)
ULTERIOR MOTIVES (1993)
ULTIMATE DESIRES (1992)
ULTRAVIOLET (1992)
UMBRELLA WOMAN, THE (SEE: GOOD WIFE, THE)(1986)
UN COEUR EN HIVER (1993)
UN ETE INOUBLIABLE (SEE: UNFORGETTABLE SUMMER, AN)(1994)
UN HOMBRE DE EXITO (SEE: SUCCESSFUL MAN, A)(1987)
UN HOMBRE VIOLENTE (1986)
UN HOMME AMOUREUX (SEE: MAN IN LOVE, A)(1987)
UN HOMME ET UNE FEMME: VINGT ANS DEJA (SEE: MAN AND A WOMAN: 20 YEARS LATER, A)(1986)
UN LUGAR EN EL MUNDO (SEE: PLACE IN THE WORLD, A)(1994)
UN MONDE SANS PITIE (SEE: LOVE WITHOUT PITY)(1991)
UN PASAJE DE IDA (SEE: ONE-WAY TICKET, A)(1988)
UN WEEK-END SUR DEUX (SEE: EVERY OTHER WEEKEND)(1991)
UN ZOO LA NUIT (SEE: NIGHT ZOO)(1987)
UNBEARABLE LIGHTNESS OF BEING, THE (1988)
UNBELIEVABLE TRUTH, THE (1990)
UNBORN II, THE (1994)
UNBORN, THE (1991)
UNCLE BUCK (1989)
UNCONSCIOUS (SEE: FEAR)(1986)
UNDER COVER (1987)
UNDER SATAN'S SUN (1988)
UNDER SIEGE (1992)
UNDER SIEGE 2: DARK TERRITORY (1995)
UNDER SUSPICION (1992)
UNDER THE BOARDWALK (1990)
UNDER THE CHERRY MOON (1986)
UNDER THE GUN (1989)
UNDERCOVER (1995)
UNDERCOVER BLUES (1993)
UNDERCOVER COP (1994)
UNDERNEATH, THE (1995)
UNDYING LOVE (1991)
UNE FLAME DANS MON COEUR (SEE: FLAME IN MY HEART, A)(1990)
UNEARTHING, THE (1994)
UNFAITHFUL (SEE: IN THE HEAT OF PASSION 2: UNFAITHFUL)(1994)
UNFINISHED BUSINESS (1985)
UNFINISHED BUSINESS... (1987)
UNFORGETTABLE SUMMER, AN (1994)
UNFORGIVEN (1992)
UNHOLY, THE (1988)
UNINVITED, THE (1988)
UNINVITED (1993)
UNIVERSAL SOLDIER (1992)
UNLAWFUL ENTRY (1992)
UNNAMABLE II, THE (1993)
UNREMARKABLE LIFE, AN (1989)
UNSTRUNG HEROES (1995)

UNTAMED HEART (1993)
UNTERGANGENS ARKITEKTUR (SEE: ARCHITECTURE OF DOOM)(1991)
UNTIL THE END OF THE WORLD (1991)
UNTOUCHABLES, THE (1987)
UNVEILED (1994)
UNZIPPED (1995)
UP TO A CERTAIN POINT (1995)
UPHILL ALL THE WAY (1986)
URAMISTEN (SEE: PHILADELPHIA ATTRACTION, THE)(1985)
URANUS (1991)
URBAN CROSSFIRE (1994)
URGA (SEE: CLOSE TO EDEN)(1992)
UROTSUKIDOJI (SEE: LEGEND OF THE OVERFIEND)(1993)
USED PEOPLE (1992)
USUAL SUSPECTS, THE (1995)
UTZ (1993)

V

VACAS (SEE: COWS)(1994)
VAGABOND (1985)
VAGRANT, THE (1992)
VALENTINO RETURNS (1989)
VALET GIRLS (1987)
VALHALLA (1986)
VALLEY OF ABRAHAM, THE (1995)
VALMONT (1989)
VALS, THE (1985)
VAMP (1986)
VAMPIRE HUNTER D (1992)
VAMPIRE IN BROOKLYN (1995)
VAMPIRES AND OTHER STEREOTYPES (1995)
VAMPIRES IN HAVANA (1985)
VAMPIRE'S KISS (1989)
VAN GOGH (1992)
VANISHING, THE (1991)
VANISHING, THE (1993)
VANYA ON 42ND STREET (1994)
VASECTOMY: A DELICATE MATTER (1986)
VEGAS IN SPACE (1993)
VENDETTA (1986)
VENICE/VENICE (1992)
VERA (1987)
VERNE MILLER (1988)
VERONICO CRUZ (1990)
VERRIEGELTE ZEIT (SEE: LOCKED-UP TIME)(1992)
VERY CLOSE QUARTERS (1986)
VESNICKO MA STREDISKOVA (SEE: MY SWEET LITTLE VILLAGE)(1985)
V.I. WARSHAWSKI (1991)
VIA APPIA (1991)
VICE ACADEMY (1989)
VICE ACADEMY III (1991)
VICE VERSA (1988)
VICOLI E DELITTI (SEE: CAMORRA)(1986)
VICTOR ONE (SEE: UNDERCOVER COP)(1994)
VIDEO DEAD (1987)
VIEW TO A KILL, A (1985)
VILLA DEL VENERDI, LA (SEE: HUSBANDS AND LOVERS)(1992)
VILLAGE OF THE DAMNED (1995)
VILLE ETRANGERE (SEE: FOREIGN CITY, A)(1988)
VINCENT AND THEO (1990)
VINDICATOR (SEE: DESERT WARRIOR)(1985)
VIOLATED (1986)
VIOLENT BREED, THE (1986)
VIOLETS ARE BLUE (1986)
VIRGIN HIGH (1991)

VIRGIN QUEEN OF ST. FRANCIS HIGH, THE (1987)
VIRTUOSITY (1995)
VIRUS KNOWS NO MORALS, A (1986)
VISA U.S.A. (1987)
VISION QUEST (1985)
VISIONS OF LIGHT: THE ART OF CINEMATOGRAPHY (1993)
VISSZASZAMLALAS (SEE: COUNTDOWN)(1985)
VITAL SIGNS (1990)
VLCI BOUDA (SEE: WOLF'S HOLE)(1987)
VOICES FROM THE FRONT (1992)
VOLERE VOLARE (1993)
VOLUNTEERS (1985)
VOODOO DAWN (1991)
VOYAGE EN DOUCE (1995)
VOYAGER (1992)
VOYEUR, THE (1994)
VROEGER IS DOOD (SEE: BYGONES)(1988)

W

WAGONS EAST! (1994)
WAIT FOR ME IN HEAVEN (1988)
WAIT UNTIL SPRING, BANDINI (1991)
WAITING FOR THE MOON (1987)
WAITING TO EXHALE (1995)
WALK IN THE CLOUDS, A (1995)
WALK LIKE A MAN (1987)
WALK ON THE MOON, A (1987)
WALKER (1987)
WALKING DEAD, THE (1995)
WALKING ON WATER (SEE: STAND AND DELIVER)(1988)
WALKING THE EDGE (1985)
WALL STREET (1987)
WALTZING REGITZE (1991)
WANNSEE CONFERENCE, THE (1987)
WANTED: DEAD OR ALIVE (1987)
WAR AND LOVE (1985)
WAR BIRDS (1989)
WAR OF THE ROSES, THE (1989)
WAR PARTY (1989)
WAR REQUIEM (1989)
WAR ROOM, THE (1993)
WAR ZONE (SEE: DEADLINE)(1987)
WAR, THE (1994)
WARDOGS (1987)
WARLOCK (1991)
WARLOCK: THE ARMAGEDDON (1993)
WARM NIGHTS ON A SLOW MOVING TRAIN (1987)
WARNING SIGN (1985)
WARRIOR QUEEN (1987)
WATCH IT (1993)
WATCHERS (1988)
WATCHERS III (1994)
WATER (1985)
WATER AND SOAP (SEE: ACQUA E SAPONE)(1985)
WATER ENGINE, THE (1995)
WATERDANCE, THE (1992)
WATERLAND (1992)
WATERWORLD (1995)
WAXWORK (1988)
WAXWORK II: LOST IN TIME (1992)
WAYNE'S WORLD (1992)
WAYNE'S WORLD 2 (1993)
WE THE LIVING (1989)
WE THINK THE WORLD OF YOU (1989)
WE THREE (1985)
WEDDING BAND (1990)
WEDDING BANQUET, THE (1993)
WEDDING GIFT, THE (1994)
WEDDING IN GALILEE (1988)

WEEDS (1987)
WEEKEND AT BERNIE'S (1989)
WEEKEND AT BERNIE'S II (1993)
WEEKEND WARRIORS (1986)
WEININGER'S LAST NIGHT (1991)
WEININGERS NACHT (SEE: WEININGER'S LAST NIGHT)(1991)
WEIRD SCIENCE (1985)
WELCOME HOME (1989)
WELCOME HOME, ROXY CARMICHAEL (1990)
WELCOME IN VIENNA (1988)
WELCOME TO 18 (1986)
WELCOME TO GERMANY (1988)
WELCOME TO OBLIVION (1992)
WENDY CRACKED A WALNUT (SEE: ALMOST)(1991)
WE'RE BACK! A DINOSAUR'S STORY (1993)
WE'RE NO ANGELS (1989)
WE'RE TALKIN' SERIOUS MONEY (1992)
WES CRAVEN'S NEW NIGHTMARE (1994)
WESTLER (SEE: EAST OF THE WALL)(1986)
WET AND WILD SUMMER (1993)
WETHERBY (1985)
WHALES OF AUGUST, THE (1987)
WHAT ABOUT BOB? (1991)
WHAT COMES AROUND (1986)
WHAT HAPPENED WAS ... (1994)
WHAT WAITS BELOW (1986)
WHAT'S LOVE GOT TO DO WITH IT (1993)
WHATEVER IT TAKES (1986)
WHAT'S EATING GILBERT GRAPE? (1993)
WHAT'S THE TIME, MR. CLOCK? (1985)
WHEELS OF FIRE (SEE: DESERT WARRIOR)(1985)
WHEELS OF TERROR (SEE: MISFIT BRIGADE, THE)(1988)
WHEN A MAN LOVES A WOMAN (1994)
WHEN BILLY BROKE HIS HEAD ... AND OTHER TALES OF WONDER (1995)
WHEN FATHER WAS AWAY ON BUSINESS (1985)
WHEN HARRY MET SALLY... (1989)
WHEN NATURE CALLS (1985)
WHEN NIGHT IS FALLING (1995)
WHEN THE PARTY'S OVER (1993)
WHEN THE RAVEN FLIES (1985)
WHEN THE WHALES CAME (1989)
WHEN THE WIND BLOWS (1988)
WHERE ANGELS FEAR TO TREAD (1992)
WHERE ARE THE CHILDREN? (1986)
WHERE SLEEPING DOGS LIE (1993)
WHERE THE DAY TAKES YOU (1992)
WHERE THE HEART IS (1990)
WHERE THE RED FERN GROWS, PART 2 (1994)
WHERE THE RIVER RUNS BLACK (1986)
WHERE THE RIVERS FLOW NORTH (1994)
WHEREVER YOU ARE (1988)
WHILE YOU WERE SLEEPING (1995)
WHISPERS (1991)
WHISPERS IN THE DARK (1992)
WHISTLE BLOWER, THE (1987)
WHITE (1994)
WHITE FANG (1991)
WHITE FANG 2: MYTH OF THE WHITE WOLF (1994)
WHITE GHOST (1988)
WHITE GIRL, THE (1990)
WHITE HUNTER, BLACK HEART (1990)
WHITE LIGHT (1991)
WHITE MAN'S BURDEN (1995)
WHITE MEN CAN'T JUMP (1992)
WHITE MILE (1994)
WHITE MISCHIEF (1988)

WHITE NIGHTS (1985)
WHITE OF THE EYE (1988)
WHITE PALACE (1990)
WHITE SANDS (1992)
WHITE SLAVE (1986)
WHITE TRASH (1992)
WHITE WATER SUMMER (1987)
WHITE WOLVES: A CRY IN THE WILD II (1993)
WHO DO I GOTTA KILL? (SEE: ME AND THE MOB)(1995)
WHO FRAMED ROGER RABBIT (1988)
WHO SHOT PATAKANGO? (1992)
WHOOPEE BOYS, THE (1986)
WHOOPING COUGH (1987)
WHORE (1991)
WHORE 2 (1994)
WHO'S HARRY CRUMB? (1989)
WHO'S THAT GIRL (1987)
WHO'S THE MAN? (1993)
WHY HAS BODHI-DHARMA LEFT FOR THE EAST? (1993)
WHY ME? (1990)
WICKED CITY (1995)
WICKED GAMES (1994)
WICKED STEPMOTHER (1989)
WICKED, THE (1991)
WIDE EYED AND LEGLESS (SEE: WEDDING GIFT, THE)(1994)
WIDE SARGASSO SEA (1993)
WIDOWS' PEAK (1994)
WIGSTOCK: THE MOVIE (1995)
WILD AT HEART (1990)
WILD BILL (1995)
WILD CACTUS (1993)
WILD GEESE II (1985)
WILD HEARTS CAN'T BE BROKEN (1991)
WILD ORCHID (1990)
WILD ORCHID 2: TWO SHADES OF BLUE (1992)
WILD PAIR, THE (1987)
WILD REEDS (1995)
WILD THING (1987)
WILD WHEELS (1992)
WILDCATS (1986)
WILDER NAPALM (1993)
WILDEST DREAMS (1990)
WILDFIRE (1992)
WILDROSE (1985)
WILLIES, THE (1991)
WILLOW (1988)
WILLS AND BURKE (1985)
WILLY MILLY (SEE: SOMETHING SPECIAL!)(1987)
WILT (SEE: MISADVENTURES OF MR. WILT, THE)(1990)
WIND (1992)
WIND, THE (1987)
WINDOW TO PARIS (1995)
WINGS OF COURAGE (1995)
WINGS OF DESIRE (1987)
WINGS OF THE APACHE (SEE: FIRE BIRDS)(1990)
WINNERS TAKE ALL (1987)
WINTER IN LISBON, THE (1992)
WINTER PEOPLE (1989)
WINTER WAR, THE (SEE: TALVISOTA)(1989)
WIRED (1989)
WIRED TO KILL (1986)
WISDOM (1986)
WISE GUYS (1986)
WISECRACKS (1992)
WISH YOU WERE HERE (1987)
WISHFUL THINKING (1993)
WITCH, THE (SEE: SUPERSTITION)(1985)

WITCHBOARD (1987)
WITCHBOARD 2: THE DEVIL'S DOORWAY (1993)
WITCHCRAFT III: THE KISS OF DEATH (1991)
WITCHCRAFT IV: VIRGIN HEART (1992)
WITCHCRAFT V: DANCE WITH THE DEVIL (1993)
WITCHCRAFT 6: THE DEVIL'S MISTRESS (1994)
WITCHES, THE (1990)
WITCHES OF EASTWICK, THE (1987)
WITCHFIRE (1986)
WITH HONORS (1994)
WITHNAIL & I (1987)
WITHOUT A CLUE (1988)
WITHOUT ANESTHESIA (1995)
WITHOUT YOU, I'M NOTHING (1990)
WITNESS (1985)
WIT'S END (SEE: G.I. EXECUTIONER, THE)(1985)
WITTGENSTEIN (1993)
WIVES—TEN YEARS AFTER (1985)
WIZARD, THE (1989)
WIZARD OF DARKNESS (1995)
WIZARD OF LONELINESS, THE (1988)
WIZARDS OF THE DEMON SWORD (1991)
WIZARDS OF THE LOST KINGDOM (1985)
WOLF (1994)
WOLF AT THE DOOR, THE (1987)
WOLF'S HOLE (1986)
WOMAN AT WAR, A (1995)
WOMAN, HER MEN AND HER FUTON, A (1992)
WOMAN OBSESSED, A (1989)
WOMAN SCORNED: THE BETTY BRODERICK STORY, A (SEE: TILL MURDER DO US PART)(1994)
WOMAN WITH A PAST (1994)
WOMAN'S TALE, A (1991)
WOMEN FROM THE LAKE OF SCENTED SOULS (1994)
WOMEN ON THE VERGE OF A NERVOUS BREAKDOWN (1988)
WOMEN'S PRISON MASSACRE (1986)
WONDERFUL, HORRIBLE LIFE OF LENI RIEFENSTAHL, THE (1994)
WONDERLAND (1988)
WONG FEI-HUNG (SEE: ONCE UPON A TIME IN CHINA)(1992)
WONG FEI-HUNG II (SEE: ONCE UPON A TIME IN CHINA II)(1994)
WONG FEI-HUNG III (SEE: ONCE UPON A TIME IN CHINA III)(1994)
WOODEN MAN'S BRIDE, THE (1995)
WOODSTOCK: THE DIRECTOR'S CUT (1994)
WOODSTOCK: THREE DAYS OF PEACE AND MUSIC (SEE: WOODSTOCK: THE DIRECTOR'S CUT)(1994)
WORKING GIRL (1988)
WORKING GIRLS (1986)
WORLD AND TIME ENOUGH (1995)
WORLD APART, A (1988)
WORLD GONE WILD (1988)
WORTH WINNING (1989)
WRAITH, THE (1986)
WRESTLING ERNEST HEMINGWAY (1993)
WRITE TO KILL (1991)
WRONG GUYS, THE (1988)
WYATT EARP (1994)
WYROK SMIERCI (SEE: DEATH SENTENCE)(1986)

X

XIANG HUN NU (SEE: WOMEN FROM THE LAKE OF SCENTED SOULS)(1994)
XIYAN (SEE: WEDDING BANQUET, THE)(1993)

XTRO 2: THE SECOND ENCOUNTER (1991)
XYZ MURDERS, THE (SEE: CRIMEWAVE)(1985)

Y

YAABA (1989)
YANZHI KOU (SEE: ROUGE)(1990)
YASEMIN (1988)
YASHA (1985)
YE SHAN (SEE: IN THE WILD MOUNTAINS)(1986)
YEAR MY VOICE BROKE, THE (1988)
YEAR OF AWAKENING, THE (1986)
YEAR OF THE COMET (1992)
YEAR OF THE DRAGON (1985)
YEAR OF THE GUN (1991)
YEAR OF THE WALL (SEE: PROMISE, THE)(1995)
YEARLING, THE (1994)
YEELEN (SEE: BRIGHTNESS)(1988)
YELLOW EARTH (1986)

YINGXIONG BENSE (SEE: BETTER TOMORROW, A)(1987)
YOU CAN'T HURRY LOVE (1988)
YOU ONLY DIE ONCE (SEE: DEAD MAN'S REVENGE)(1994)
YOU SO CRAZY (1994)
YOUNG AMERICANS, THE (1994)
YOUNG COMPOSER'S ODYSSEY, A (1986)
YOUNG EINSTEIN (1989)
YOUNG EMMANUELLE, A (SEE: NEA)(1995)
YOUNG GUNS (1988)
YOUNG GUNS II (1990)
YOUNG NURSES IN LOVE (1989)
YOUNG SHERLOCK HOLMES (1985)
YOUNG SOUL REBELS (1991)
YOUNGBLOOD (1986)
YOUNGER & YOUNGER (1995)

Z

ZABUDNITE NA MOZARTA (SEE: FORGET MOZART!)(1985)

ZAMRI OUMI VOSKRESNI (SEE: FREEZE—DIE—COME TO LIFE)(1990)
ZANDALEE (1991)
ZEBRAHEAD (1992)
ZED & TWO NOUGHTS, A (1985)
ZELLY AND ME (1988)
ZENTROPA (1992)
ZERO BOYS, THE (1987)
ZERO PATIENCE (1994)
ZINA (1985)
ZIPPERFACE (1993)
ZIVOT SA STRICEM (SEE: MY UNCLE'S LEGACY)(1990)
ZOEKEN NAAR EILEEN (SEE: LOOKING FOR EILEEN)(1987)
ZONE TROOPERS (1986)
ZONING (1986)
ZOO GANG, THE (1985)
ZOO RADIO (1991)
ZOOMAN (1995)
ZUCKERBABY (SEE: SUGARBABY)(1985)

FILMS BY COUNTRY OF ORIGIN

A bullet before the title indicates a film co-produced by more than one country

Argentina
I, THE WORST OF ALL

Australia
BABE
COUNTRY LIFE
DALLAS DOLL
• DARK SIDE OF GENIUS, THE
DEATH IN BRUNSWICK
DESPERATE PREY
ETERNITY
• GROSS MISCONDUCT
HOTEL SORRENTO
MURIEL'S WEDDING
NOSTRADAMUS KID, THE
ONLY THE BRAVE
SUM OF US, THE
TRAPS

Austria
FOR GOD AND COUNTRY

Belgium
• BLUE VILLA, THE
• FARINELLI
• POSTMAN, THE
• SON OF THE SHARK, THE

Brazil
• BOCA
• CARMEN MIRANDA: BANANAS IS MY
BUSINESS

Canada
• BOULEVARD
CIRCUMSTANCES UNKNOWN
CRACKERJACK
• DANCE ME OUTSIDE
• DARKMAN 2: THE RETURN OF DURANT
• DIGGER
DOUBLE HAPPINESS
• ECLIPSE
EXOTICA
• FIRST DEGREE
• FUN
• HIGHLANDER: THE FINAL DIMENSION
• JOHNNY MNEMONIC
KURT VONNEGUT'S HARRISON
BERGERON
LOVE AND HUMAN REMAINS
POCAHONTAS: THE LEGEND
RENT-A-KID
• SPIKE AND MIKE'S FESTIVAL OF
ANIMATION '95
WHEN NIGHT IS FALLING
• YOUNGER & YOUNGER

China
• ERMO
• RED FIRECRACKER, GREEN
FIRECRACKER
• SHANGHAI TRIAD
• WOODEN MAN'S BRIDE, THE

Cuba
• I AM CUBA
STRAWBERRY AND CHOCOLATE
UP TO A CERTAIN POINT

Czechoslovakia
ACCUMULATOR 1
COW, THE
• NOT ANGELS BUT ANGELS

Denmark
• BETRAYAL
KINGDOM, THE

Finland
• CITY UNPLUGGED

France
• AILSA
• AMATEUR
AUGUSTIN
• BEFORE THE RAIN
• BLUE VILLA, THE
• BURNT BY THE SUN
• BUSINESS AFFAIR, A
• CARRINGTON
• CITY OF LOST CHILDREN, THE
• CONVENT, THE
• FARINELLI
• FRANKIE STARLIGHT
• FRIENDS
• GEORGIA
• GLASS SHIELD, THE
GROSSE FATIGUE
• HIGHLANDER: THE FINAL DIMENSION
• HYENAS
I CAN'T SLEEP
• INNOCENT LIES
• JLG BY JLG
• LAMERICA
LES MISERABLES
• LESSONS OF DARKNESS
• MARTHA AND I
MINA TANNENBAUM
MY LIFE AND TIMES WITH ANTONIN
ARTAUD
• NEA
• NO MERCY
• NOT ANGELS BUT ANGELS
OLD LADY WHO WALKED IN THE SEA,
THE
• PIGALLE
• POSTMAN, THE
• PURE FORMALITY, A
SERIOUS ABOUT PLEASURE
• SHANGHAI TRIAD
• SIX DAYS, SIX NIGHTS
• SON OF THE SHARK, THE
• THROUGH THE OLIVE TREES
• TOO OUTRAGEOUS ANIMATION
• TOTAL ECLIPSE
• TWELVE MONKEYS
• VALLEY OF ABRAHAM, THE
VOYAGE EN DOUCE
WILD REEDS
• WINDOW TO PARIS
• WOMAN AT WAR, A
• YOUNGER & YOUNGER

Germany
• AILSA
• BUSINESS AFFAIR, A

• CITY OF LOST CHILDREN, THE
DEADLY MARIA
• ECLIPSE
• EROTIQUE
• GORILLA BATHES AT NOON
• INNOCENT, THE
• LESSONS OF DARKNESS
• MARTHA AND I
• MUTE WITNESS
NOBODY LOVES ME
PROFESSION: NEO-NAZI
• PROMISE, THE
STALINGRAD
• TWELVE MONKEYS
• YOUNGER & YOUNGER

Hong Kong
ASHES OF TIME
DAY THE SUN TURNED COLD, THE
• ERMO
EXECUTIONERS
HEROIC TRIO, THE
HE'S A WOMAN, SHE'S A MAN
HIGH RISK
NAKED KILLER
PHANTOM LOVER, THE
• RED FIRECRACKER, GREEN
FIRECRACKER
RETURN OF THE GOD OF GAMBLERS
• SHAO LIN POPEYE
TWENTY SOMETHING

Hungary
ADVENTURES OF MATT THE
GOOSEBOY, THE
• CITIZEN X

Iceland
REMOTE CONTROL

India
• BANDIT QUEEN
CHARULATA
STRANGER, THE

Iran
JAR, THE
• THROUGH THE OLIVE TREES

Ireland
• AILSA
• AWFULLY BIG ADVENTURE, AN
• CIRCLE OF FRIENDS
• FRANKIE STARLIGHT

Italy
• FARINELLI
• LAMERICA
• MARTHA AND I
• POSTMAN, THE
• PROMISE, THE
• PURE FORMALITY, A
• SILENCE OF THE HAMS
• TOO OUTRAGEOUS ANIMATION

Ivory Coast
FACES OF WOMEN

Japan
AI CITY

BAREFOOT GEN
CRIMSON WOLF
MYSTERY OF RAMPO, THE
• NEW YORK COP
TALE OF GENJI, THE
• TOO OUTRAGEOUS ANIMATION
• TWELVE MONKEYS
WICKED CITY
WINGS OF HONNEAMISE: ROYAL SPACE FORCE
WIZARD OF DARKNESS

Macedonia
• BEFORE THE RAIN

Mexico
• NO MERCY

Netherlands
• METAL AND MELANCHOLY
1-900
• SEX, DRUGS AND DEMOCRACY

New Zealand
MEET THE FEEBLES
ONCE WERE WARRIORS

Peru
• METAL AND MELANCHOLY
• NO MERCY

Poland
CHRONICLE OF THE WARSAW GHETTO UPRISING ACCORDING TO MAREK EDELMAN
PROVINCIAL ACTORS
SHORT FILM ABOUT KILLING, A
SHORT FILM ABOUT LOVE, A
• TOO OUTRAGEOUS ANIMATION
WITHOUT ANESTHESIA

Portugal
• CONVENT, THE
• VALLEY OF ABRAHAM, THE

Russia
• BURNT BY THE SUN
CREATION OF ADAM
• I AM CUBA
• MUTE WITNESS
• WINDOW TO PARIS

Senegal
• HYENAS

South Africa
• FRIENDS

South Korea
HOW TO TOP MY WIFE

Spain
• BUSINESS AFFAIR, A
• CITY OF LOST CHILDREN, THE
• LESSONS OF DARKNESS

Sweden
• BETRAYAL
• CITY UNPLUGGED
DANCER, THE
DREAMING OF RITA

Switzerland
• BLUE VILLA, THE
CONGRESS OF PENGUINS, THE
• HYENAS
• JLG BY JLG
• PIGALLE
• PROMISE, THE
• VALLEY OF ABRAHAM, THE

Taiwan
• PUSHING HANDS
• SHAO LIN POPEYE
• WOODEN MAN'S BRIDE, THE

U.K.
• AMATEUR
ARABIAN KNIGHT
• AWFULLY BIG ADVENTURE, AN
• BANDIT QUEEN
• BEFORE THE RAIN
• BETRAYAL
• BUSINESS AFFAIR, A
• CARRINGTON
CENTURY
• DEAD FUNNY
DEATH MACHINE
ENGLISHMAN WHO WENT UP A HILL BUT CAME DOWN A MOUNTAIN, THE
• FRANKIE STARLIGHT
• FRIENDS
FUNNY BONES
GLORY BOYS, THE
HEAVEN'S A DRAG
• HIGHLANDER: THE FINAL DIMENSION
• INNOCENT LIES
• INNOCENT, THE
LAMB
• MOVING THE MOUNTAIN
• MUTE WITNESS
OH ... ROSALINDA!!
• OTHELLO
PERSUASION
POSTCARDS FROM AMERICA
PRIEST
• RETURN OF THE NATIVE, THE
• RICHARD III
• RUN OF THE COUNTRY, THE
SHALLOW GRAVE
SISTER MY SISTER
• SIX DAYS, SIX NIGHTS
• SPIKE AND MIKE'S FESTIVAL OF ANIMATION '95
• TOO OUTRAGEOUS ANIMATION
• TOTAL ECLIPSE
• TWELVE MONKEYS
• WOMAN AT WAR, A

U.S.
ABDUCTED 2: THE REUNION
ACE VENTURA: WHEN NATURE CALLS
ACROSS THE MOON
ACROSS THE SEA OF TIME: NEW YORK 3D
ADDICTION, THE
ALMOST DEAD
• AMATEUR
AMAZING PANDA ADVENTURE, THE
AMERICA'S DEADLIEST HOME VIDEO
AMERICAN COP
AMERICAN PRESIDENT, THE
ANDROID AFFAIR, THE
ANGUS
APOLLO 13
ARIZONA DREAM
ARMAGEDDON: THE FINAL CHALLENGE
ART FOR TEACHERS OF CHILDREN
ASCENT, THE
ASSASSINS
ATTACK OF THE 60-FOOT CENTERFOLD
AVENGING ANGEL
BABY-SITTERS CLUB, THE
BABYSITTER, THE
BAD BLOOD
BAD BOYS

BAD COMPANY
BALLET
BALLISTIC
BALLOT MEASURE 9
BALTO
BAR GIRLS
BASKETBALL DIARIES, THE
BATMAN FOREVER
BED YOU SLEEP IN, THE
BEFORE SUNRISE
BETTER OFF DEAD
BEYOND RANGOON
BIG GREEN, THE
BIGFOOT: THE UNFORGETTABLE ENCOUNTER
BIKINI BISTRO
BILLY MADISON
BITTER VENGEANCE
BLACK FOX
BLACK IS ... BLACK AIN'T
BLESSING
BLUE IN THE FACE
BLUE TIGER
• BOCA
BODILY HARM
BODY CHEMISTRY 4: FULL EXPOSURE
BODY SHOT
BODY STROKES
BORN TO BE WILD
• BOULEVARD
BOYS ON THE SIDE
BRADY BUNCH MOVIE, THE
BRAVEHEART
BREACH OF CONDUCT
BREAK, THE
BRIAN WILSON: I JUST WASN'T MADE FOR THESE TIMES
BRIDGES OF MADISON COUNTY, THE
BROKEN TRUST
BROTHERS MCMULLEN, THE
BUFFALO GIRLS
BULLETPROOF HEART
BURNING SEASON, THE
BUSHWHACKED
BYE BYE, LOVE
CAGED HEARTS
CAGED HEAT 3000
CANADIAN BACON
CANDYMAN: FAREWELL TO THE FLESH
• CARMEN MIRANDA: BANANAS IS MY BUSINESS
CASINO
CASPER
CASTLE FREAK
CHILDREN OF THE CORN III: URBAN HARVEST
• CIRCLE OF FRIENDS
• CITIZEN X
• CITY UNPLUGGED
CLASS OF '61
CLEAN, SHAVEN
CLOCKERS
CLUELESS
COLDBLOODED
COLORADO COWBOY: THE BRUCE FORD STORY
COMPANION, THE
CONGO
CONVICT COWBOY
COPYCAT
COSMIC SLOP
COVER ME
COVER STORY
CRAZYSITTER, THE
CREEP

CREW, THE
CRIMSON TIDE
CROSSING GUARD, THE
CRUDE OASIS, THE
CRUMB
CRY, THE BELOVED COUNTRY
CURE, THE
CURSE OF THE STARVING CLASS
CUTTHROAT ISLAND
CYBER BANDITS
• DANCE ME OUTSIDE
DANGER OF LOVE
DANGEROUS MINDS
DANGEROUS, THE
DARK DEALER
• DARK SIDE OF GENIUS, THE
• DARKMAN 2: THE RETURN OF DURANT
• DEAD FUNNY
DEAD MAN WALKING
DEAD PRESIDENTS
DECONSTRUCTING SARAH
DECOY
DESPERADO
DESTINY TURNS ON THE RADIO
DEVIL IN A BLUE DRESS
DIE HARD WITH A VENGEANCE
• DIGGER
DILLINGER
DILLINGER AND CAPONE
DIRTY MONEY
DR. JEKYLL & MS. HYDE
DOLORES CLAIBORNE
DON JUAN DEMARCO
DOOM GENERATION, THE
DOOMSDAY GUN
DOUBLE, DOUBLE, TOIL AND TROUBLE
DRACULA: DEAD AND LOVING IT
DREAM A LITTLE DREAM 2
EMBRACE OF THE VAMPIRE
EMPIRE RECORDS
ENEMY WITHIN, THE
• EROTIQUE
EVOLVER
EXPERT, THE
FAIR GAME
FAR FROM HOME: THE ADVENTURES OF
    YELLOW DOG
FATHER AND SCOUT
FATHER OF THE BRIDE PART II
FATHERLAND
FEAR, THE
FEAST OF JULY
• FIRST DEGREE
FIRST KNIGHT
FLUKE
FOOL AND HIS MONEY, A
FORGET PARIS
FOUR ROOMS
FRAMEUP
FRANK & JESSE
FRANK AND OLLIE
FREE WILLY 2: THE ADVENTURE HOME
FRENCH KISS
FRIDAY
• FUN
GALAXIS
• GEORGIA
GET SHORTY
GETTING OUT
GHOST BRIGADE
GIRL IN THE CADILLAC
• GLASS SHIELD, THE
GOLD DIGGERS: THE SECRET OF BEAR
    MOUNTAIN

GOLDENEYE
GOOD DAY TO DIE, A
GOOD GIRLS DON'T
GOOFY MOVIE, A
GORDY
GRANNY, THE
GREAT DAY IN HARLEM, A
GREAT ELEPHANT ESCAPE, THE
• GROSS MISCONDUCT
GRUMPIER OLD MEN
GUMBY: THE MOVIE
HACKERS
HALLOWEEN: THE CURSE OF MICHAEL
    MYERS
HARLEM DIARY: NINE VOICES OF
    RESILIENCE
HEAT
HEAVYWEIGHTS
HIDEAWAY
HIGHER LEARNING
HOME FOR THE HOLIDAYS
HOUSEGUEST
HOW TO MAKE AN AMERICAN QUILT
HOWLING: NEW MOON RISING, THE
HUNTED, THE
I LIKE TO PLAY GAMES
IN THE DEEP WOODS
IN THE MOUTH OF MADNESS
IN THE NAME OF THE EMPEROR
INCREDIBLY TRUE ADVENTURES OF
    TWO GIRLS IN LOVE, THE
INDIAN IN THE CUPBOARD, THE
INDICTMENT: THE MCMARTIN TRIAL
IT TAKES TWO
JACK-O
JADE
JEFFERSON IN PARIS
JEFFREY
JERKY BOYS: THE MOVIE, THE
• JOHNNY MNEMONIC
JOURNEY OF AUGUST KING, THE
JUDGE DREDD
JUDICIAL CONSENT
JUMANJI
JUPITER'S WIFE
JURY DUTY
JUST CAUSE
KICKING AND SCREAMING
KID IN KING ARTHUR'S COURT, A
KIDS
KILIAN'S CHRONICLE
KINGFISH: A STORY OF HUEY P. LONG
KISS OF DEATH
LAKOTA WOMAN: SIEGE AT WOUNDED
    KNEE
LAST GOOD TIME, THE
LAST OF THE DOGMEN
LAST RIDE, THE
LAST SAMURAI, THE
LAST SUMMER IN THE HAMPTONS
LEAVING LAS VEGAS
LIE DOWN WITH DOGS
LITTLE ODESSA
LITTLE PRINCESS, A
LIVING IN OBLIVION
LORD OF ILLUSIONS
LOSING ISAIAH
MAD LOVE
MAGIC IN THE WATER
MAJOR PAYNE
MALICIOUS
MALLRATS
MAN OF THE HOUSE
MANGLER, THE

MARTHA & ETHEL
MAYA LIN: A STRONG CLEAR VISION
ME AND THE MOB
MESSENGER
MIAMI RHAPSODY
MIDNIGHT TEASE 2
MIGHTY APHRODITE
MIGHTY MORPHIN POWER RANGERS:
    THE MOVIE
MONEY TRAIN
MONTH BY THE LAKE, A
MOONLIGHT AND VALENTINO
MORTAL KOMBAT
MOSAIC PROJECT, THE
• MOVING THE MOUNTAIN
MURDER IN THE FIRST
MUTANT SPECIES
MY ANTONIA
MY FAMILY: MI FAMILIA
NADJA
NATIONAL LAMPOON'S ATTACK OF THE
    5'2" WOMEN
NATIONAL LAMPOON'S SENIOR TRIP
NET, THE
NEVER TALK TO STRANGERS
NEW JERSEY DRIVE
• NEW YORK COP
NEXT DOOR
NICK OF TIME
NIGHTMARE
NINA TAKES A LOVER
NINE MONTHS
NIXON
NOW AND THEN
NUMBER ONE FAN
O.J. SIMPSON STORY, THE
OPERATION DUMBO DROP
OPERATION INTERCEPT
• OTHELLO
OUT OF ANNIE'S PAST
OUT OF SYNC
OUTBREAK
OUTSIDE THE LAW
PANTHER
PARTY GIRL
PAYBACK
PEBBLE AND THE PENGUIN, THE
PENTATHLON
PEREZ FAMILY, THE
PIANO LESSON, THE
PICTURE BRIDE
PLAY TIME
POCAHONTAS
POWDER
POWER OF ATTORNEY
PREHYSTERIA! 3
PROPHECY, THE
• PUSHING HANDS
PYROMANIAC'S LOVE STORY, A
QUICK AND THE DEAD, THE
RADIO INSIDE
REASON TO BELIEVE, A
RECKLESS
RED SUN RISING
REDWOOD CURTAIN
REFLECTIONS IN THE DARK
RESTORATION
• RETURN OF THE NATIVE, THE
RHYTHM THIEF
• RICHARD III
RIVER OF GRASS
ROB ROY
ROOMMATES
ROSWELL: THE U.F.O. COVER-UP

ROY COHN/JACK SMITH
● RUN OF THE COUNTRY, THE
SABRINA
SAFE
SAFE PASSAGE
SCANNERS: THE SHOWDOWN
SCARLET LETTER, THE
SEARCH AND DESTROY
SECRET OF ROAN INISH, THE
SECRETARY, THE
SENSE AND SENSIBILITY
SEPARATE LIVES
SEVEN
● SEX, DRUGS AND DEMOCRACY
S.F.W.
SHOW, THE
SHOWGIRLS
● SILENCE OF THE HAMS
SKINNER
SMOKE
SOMETHING TO TALK ABOUT
SPECIES
● SPIKE AND MIKE'S FESTIVAL OF
ANIMATION '95
SPITFIRE
SPY WITHIN, THE
STARS FELL ON HENRIETTA, THE
STEAL BIG, STEAL LITTLE
STRANGE DAYS
STUART SAVES HIS FAMILY

SUBSTITUTE WIFE, THE
SUDDEN DEATH
SWIMMING WITH SHARKS
TALES FROM THE CRYPT: DEMON
KNIGHT
TALES FROM THE HOOD
TALL TALE: THE UNBELIEVABLE
ADVENTURES OF PECOS BILL
TANK GIRL
TERESA'S TATTOO
THINGS TO DO IN DENVER WHEN
YOU'RE DEAD
3 NINJAS KNUCKLE UP
THREE WISHES
TIE-DIED: ROCK 'N' ROLL'S MOST
DEADICATED FANS
TIE THAT BINDS, THE
TO CROSS THE RUBICON
TO DIE FOR
TO WONG FOO, THANKS FOR
EVERYTHING! JULIE NEWMAR
TOM AND HUCK
TOMMY BOY
● TOO OUTRAGEOUS ANIMATION
TOO YOUNG TO DIE?
TOP DOG
TOY STORY
● TWELVE MONKEYS
TWO BITS
TWOGETHER
UNDER SIEGE 2: DARK TERRITORY

UNDERCOVER
UNDERNEATH, THE
UNSTRUNG HEROES
UNZIPPED
USUAL SUSPECTS, THE
VAMPIRE IN BROOKLYN
VAMPIRES AND OTHER STEREOTYPES
VILLAGE OF THE DAMNED
VIRTUOSITY
WAITING TO EXHALE
WALK IN THE CLOUDS, A
WALKING DEAD, THE
WATER ENGINE, THE
WATERWORLD
WHEN BILLY BROKE HIS HEAD ... AND
OTHER TALES OF WONDER
WHILE YOU WERE SLEEPING
WHITE MAN'S BURDEN
WIGSTOCK: THE MOVIE
WILD BILL
WINGS OF COURAGE
WORLD AND TIME ENOUGH
ZOOMAN

West Germany
MACHINE DREAMS
● NEA
NEKROMANTIK

Yugoslavia
● GORILLA BATHES AT NOON

FILMS BY DISTRIBUTOR

A-PIX ENTERTAINMENT
AMERICAN COP
BODY STROKES
DANCE ME OUTSIDE
DESPERATE PREY
FEAR, THE
I LIKE TO PLAY GAMES
SKINNER
UNDERCOVER

ARIES
DARK DEALER

ARROW HOME VIDEO
COVER STORY

ARROW RELEASING
BANDIT QUEEN
ERMO
GUMBY: THE MOVIE
WOODEN MAN'S BRIDE, THE

ARTIFICIAL EYE
VALLEY OF ABRAHAM, THE

ARTISTIC LICENSE FILMS
DALLAS DOLL
JAR, THE
JUPITER'S WIFE

ATLANTIC ENTERTAINMENT
IN THE DEEP WOODS

AUGUST ENTERTAINMENT
FUN

BFS VIDEO
GLORY BOYS, THE

BRIMSTONE PRODUCTIONS
VAMPIRES AND OTHER STEREOTYPES

BUENA VISTA

Walt Disney Productions
Hollywood Pictures
Touchstone Pictures

BAD COMPANY
BIG GREEN, THE
CRIMSON TIDE
DANGEROUS MINDS
DEAD PRESIDENTS
FATHER OF THE BRIDE PART II
FEAST OF JULY
FRANK AND OLLIE
FUNNY BONES
GOOFY MOVIE, A
HEAVYWEIGHTS
HOUSEGUEST
JEFFERSON IN PARIS
JERKY BOYS: THE MOVIE, THE
JUDGE DREDD
KID IN KING ARTHUR'S COURT, A
MAD LOVE
MAN OF THE HOUSE
MIAMI RHAPSODY
NIXON

OPERATION DUMBO DROP
POCAHONTAS
POWDER
PYROMANIAC'S LOVE STORY, A
ROOMMATES
SCARLET LETTER, THE
TALL TALE: THE UNBELIEVABLE
   ADVENTURES OF PECOS BILL
TIE THAT BINDS, THE
TOM AND HUCK
TOY STORY
UNSTRUNG HEROES
WHILE YOU WERE SLEEPING

BULLSEYE VIDEO
ABDUCTED 2: THE REUNION
BIKINI BISTRO
ME AND THE MOB

CABIN FEVER ENTERTAINMENT
ASCENT, THE
BLACK FOX
BUFFALO GIRLS
GREAT ELEPHANT ESCAPE, THE

CAPITOL ENTERTAINMENT
LAMB

CASTLE HILL
BUSINESS AFFAIR, A
GREAT DAY IN HARLEM, A
HOTEL SORRENTO
REASON TO BELIEVE, A

CFP DISTRIBUTION
NOBODY LOVES ME

CHRISTA SAREDI WORLD SALES
CONGRESS OF PENGUINS, THE

CINE ELECTRA
AILSA

CINEMA FOUR/ORIGINAL CINEMA
MARTHA AND I

CINEMA PARALLEL
COW, THE
JLG BY JLG

CINEPIX
DEAD FUNNY
OLD LADY WHO WALKED IN THE SEA,
   THE
PUSHING HANDS

COLUMBIA
AMERICAN PRESIDENT, THE
BABY-SITTERS CLUB, THE
BAD BOYS
BEFORE SUNRISE
BEYOND RANGOON
DESPERADO
DOLORES CLAIBORNE
DRACULA: DEAD AND LOVING IT
FIRST KNIGHT
FORGET PARIS

HIGHER LEARNING
MONEY TRAIN
NET, THE
OTHELLO
RUN OF THE COUNTRY, THE
SENSE AND SENSIBILITY
TO DIE FOR

COLUMBIA TRISTAR HOME VIDEO
BLUE TIGER
CYBER BANDITS
DEATH IN BRUNSWICK
DREAM A LITTLE DREAM 2
NEW YORK COP
NEXT DOOR
REMOTE CONTROL
3 NINJAS KNUCKLE UP
TWOGETHER

DIMENSION
CHILDREN OF THE CORN III: URBAN
   HARVEST
HALLOWEEN: THE CURSE OF MICHAEL
   MYERS
HIGHLANDER: THE FINAL DIMENSION
PROPHECY, THE

DISCOVERY COMMUNICATIONS
HARLEM DIARY: NINE VOICES OF
   RESILIENCE

DOR FILM
FOR GOD AND COUNTRY

DRIFT DISTRIBUTION
PROFESSION: NEO-NAZI

ED CRUEA RELEASING
KILIAN'S CHRONICLE

EUROTRASH FILM AND VIDEO
NEA
SERIOUS ABOUT PLEASURE

EVERGREEN ENTERTAINMENT
LAST RIDE, THE

FESTIVAL FILMS
SPIKE AND MIKE'S FESTIVAL OF
   ANIMATION '95

FILM BRIDGE INTERNATIONAL
ACCUMULATOR 1

FILM NEWS NOW FOUNDATION
IN THE NAME OF THE EMPEROR

FILMHAUS
BED YOU SLEEP IN, THE
CITY UNPLUGGED
STRANGER, THE

FILMOPOLIS PICTURES
TRAPS

FILMS TRANSIT INTERNATIONAL
BLUE VILLA, THE

FINE LINE

AWFULLY BIG ADVENTURE, AN
DOUBLE HAPPINESS
FRANKIE STARLIGHT
INCREDIBLY TRUE ADVENTURES OF
  TWO GIRLS IN LOVE, THE
LITTLE ODESSA
ONCE WERE WARRIORS
PROMISE, THE
TOTAL ECLIPSE

FIRST LOOK PICTURES

PARTY GIRL
SECRET OF ROAN INISH, THE

FIRST RUN FEATURES

DREAMING OF RITA
FRIENDS
HEAVEN'S A DRAG
I, THE WORST OF ALL
MACHINE DREAMS
ONLY THE BRAVE

FOX SEARCHLIGHT PICTURES

BROTHERS MCMULLEN, THE

FOXVIDEO

O.J. SIMPSON STORY, THE

FULL MOON HOME ENTERTAINMENT

CASTLE FREAK

GALA FILMS

WILD REEDS

GOODTIMES ENTERTAINMENT

POCAHONTAS: THE LEGEND

GRAMERCY PICTURES

BEFORE THE RAIN
CANADIAN BACON
CANDYMAN: FAREWELL TO THE FLESH
CARRINGTON
DEAD MAN WALKING
MALLRATS
MOONLIGHT AND VALENTINO
NEW JERSEY DRIVE
PANTHER
S.F.W.
SHALLOW GRAVE
UNDERNEATH, THE
USUAL SUSPECTS, THE

GREYCAT FILMS

MEET THE FEEBLES

GROUP ONE DISTRIBUTION

EROTIQUE

HALLMARK HOME ENTERTAINMENT

GETTING OUT

HBO HOME VIDEO

CITIZEN X
COSMIC SLOP
DOOMSDAY GUN
ENEMY WITHIN, THE
INDICTMENT: THE MCMARTIN TRIAL

HEMDALE HOME VIDEO

ACROSS THE MOON

IMPERIAL ENTERTAINMENT

BALLISTIC
RED SUN RISING

INCA FILMS

NO MERCY

INTERNATIONAL CINEMA

CARMEN MIRANDA: BANANAS IS MY
  BUSINESS

IRS MEDIA

COLDBLOODED

ISA RELEASING

TIE-DIED: ROCK 'N' ROLL'S MOST
  DEADICATED FANS

JANE BALFOUR FILMS

DEADLY MARIA
GORILLA BATHES AT NOON

JUST FOR KIDS HOME VIDEO

ADVENTURES OF MATT THE
  GOOSEBOY, THE

KEYSTONE PICTURES

BULLETPROOF HEART

KINO INTERNATIONAL

AUGUSTIN
DAY THE SUN TURNED COLD, THE
HYENAS

KIT PARKER FILMS

ARIZONA DREAM

LEISURE TIME FEATURES

MY LIFE AND TIMES WITH ANTONIN
  ARTAUD
NEKROMANTIK

LIVE ENTERTAINMENT

BAD BLOOD
CREW, THE
MUTANT SPECIES
NOSTRADAMUS KID, THE
OUT OF SYNC
PENTATHLON
TOP DOG

LIVE HOME VIDEO

BOULEVARD

LUMIERE PICTURES

SIX DAYS, SIX NIGHTS

MANDARIN FILMS

PHANTOM LOVER, THE

MCA/UNIVERSAL HOME VIDEO

ANDROID AFFAIR, THE
BREACH OF CONDUCT
CLASS OF '61
COMPANION, THE
DARKMAN 2: THE RETURN OF DURANT
DECONSTRUCTING SARAH
OUT OF ANNIE'S PAST

MGM/UA

CUTTHROAT ISLAND
FLUKE
GET SHORTY
GOLDENEYE
HACKERS
LEAVING LAS VEGAS
LORD OF ILLUSIONS
PEBBLE AND THE PENGUIN, THE
RICHARD III
SHOWGIRLS
SPECIES
WILD BILL

MGM/UA HOME VIDEO

CONVICT COWBOY
RADIO INSIDE

MILESTONE FILMS

I AM CUBA

MIRAMAX

ARABIAN KNIGHT
BLUE IN THE FACE
COUNTRY LIFE
CROSSING GUARD, THE
CRUDE OASIS, THE
CRY, THE BELOVED COUNTRY
ENGLISHMAN WHO WENT UP A HILL
  BUT CAME DOWN A MOUNTAIN, THE
EXOTICA
FOUR ROOMS
GEORGIA
GLASS SHIELD, THE
GORDY
GROSSE FATIGUE
INNOCENT, THE
JOURNEY OF AUGUST KING, THE
LIE DOWN WITH DOGS
MIGHTY APHRODITE
MONTH BY THE LAKE, A
MURIEL'S WEDDING
PICTURE BRIDE
POSTMAN, THE
PRIEST
RESTORATION
SMOKE
STRAWBERRY AND CHOCOLATE
THINGS TO DO IN DENVER WHEN
  YOU'RE DEAD
THROUGH THE OLIVE TREES
TWO BITS
UNZIPPED

MONARCH

ALMOST DEAD

MONARCH HOME VIDEO

MOSAIC PROJECT, THE

MORNING CALM CINEMA

HOW TO TOP MY WIFE

MTI HOME VIDEO

TO CROSS THE RUBICON

NEW HORIZONS HOME VIDEO

ATTACK OF THE 60-FOOT CENTERFOLD
BODY CHEMISTRY 4: FULL EXPOSURE
CAGED HEAT 3000
CRAZYSITTER, THE
DILLINGER AND CAPONE
MIDNIGHT TEASE 2
NIGHTMARE

REDWOOD CURTAIN
SPY WITHIN, THE

NEW HORIZONS PICTURES
REFLECTIONS IN THE DARK

NEW LINE
ANGUS
BASKETBALL DIARIES, THE
DON JUAN DEMARCO
FRIDAY
IN THE MOUTH OF MADNESS
MANGLER, THE
MORTAL KOMBAT
MY FAMILY: MI FAMILIA
NATIONAL LAMPOON'S SENIOR TRIP
NATIONAL LAMPOON'S SENIOR TRIP
NOW AND THEN
SAFE PASSAGE
SEVEN

NEW LINE HOME VIDEO
EMBRACE OF THE VAMPIRE
HOWLING: NEW MOON RISING, THE
OUTSIDE THE LAW

NEW YORKER FILMS
I CAN'T SLEEP
LAMERICA
MINA TANNENBAUM

NEW YORKER VIDEO
FACES OF WOMEN
PROVINCIAL ACTORS
UP TO A CERTAIN POINT
VOYAGE EN DOUCE
WITHOUT ANESTHESIA

NORTHERN ARTS ENTERTAINMENT
DIRTY MONEY

OCEAN RELEASING
MAYA LIN: A STRONG CLEAR VISION

OCTOBER FILMS
ADDICTION, THE
KINGDOM, THE
MOVING THE MOUNTAIN
NADJA
RED FIRECRACKER, GREEN
    FIRECRACKER
SEARCH AND DESTROY
SILENCE OF THE HAMS
WHEN NIGHT IS FALLING

ORION CLASSICS
BAR GIRLS
JEFFREY

ORION HOME VIDEO
DANGEROUS, THE
EXPERT, THE
NUMBER ONE FAN

PALOMAR PICTURES
BRIAN WILSON: I JUST WASN'T MADE
    FOR THESE TIMES

PARAMOUNT
BRADY BUNCH MOVIE, THE
BRAVEHEART
CLUELESS
CONGO
HOME FOR THE HOLIDAYS

INDIAN IN THE CUPBOARD, THE
JADE
LOSING ISAIAH
NICK OF TIME
SABRINA
STUART SAVES HIS FAMILY
TOMMY BOY
VAMPIRE IN BROOKLYN
VIRTUOSITY

PARAMOUNT HOME VIDEO
BITTER VENGEANCE
CIRCUMSTANCES UNKNOWN
COVER ME
DARK SIDE OF GENIUS, THE
DIGGER
MY ANTONIA
NATIONAL LAMPOON'S ATTACK OF THE
    5'2" WOMEN
PREHYSTERIA! 3
YOUNGER & YOUNGER

PETER CHOW INTERNATIONAL
HE'S A WOMAN, SHE'S A MAN

POLYGRAM VIDEO
CENTURY
FIRST DEGREE
INNOCENT LIES

PRO/REP
GROSS MISCONDUCT

RAINBOW RELEASING
LAST SUMMER IN THE HAMPTONS

RANDUM FILMS AND
ENTERTAINMENT
AMERICA'S DEADLIEST HOME VIDEO

RED HAT PRODUCTIONS
SEX, DRUGS AND DEMOCRACY

REPUBLIC PICTURES HOME VIDEO
BIGFOOT: THE UNFORGETTABLE
    ENCOUNTER
BOCA
CRACKERJACK
KURT VONNEGUT'S HARRISON
    BERGERON
MALICIOUS
PIANO LESSON, THE
RENT-A-KID
RETURN OF THE NATIVE, THE
ROSWELL: THE U.F.O. COVER-UP
SCANNERS: THE SHOWDOWN
SECRETARY, THE
TOO YOUNG TO DIE?
WOMAN AT WAR, A
ZOOMAN

RIGHT STUF INTERNATIONAL
AI CITY

RIM FILM DISTRIBUTORS
HEROIC TRIO, THE
NAKED KILLER

SAMUEL GOLDWYN COMPANY
DOOM GENERATION, THE
LAST GOOD TIME, THE
MYSTERY OF RAMPO, THE
PEREZ FAMILY, THE
RECKLESS

SUM OF US, THE
WIGSTOCK: THE MOVIE

SAVOY PICTURES
CIRCLE OF FRIENDS
DESTINY TURNS ON THE RADIO
DR. JEKYLL & MS. HYDE
LAST OF THE DOGMEN
SHOW, THE
STEAL BIG, STEAL LITTLE
TALES FROM THE HOOD
THREE WISHES
WALKING DEAD, THE
WHITE MAN'S BURDEN

SEVENTH ART RELEASING
PIGALLE
SISTER MY SISTER
SON OF THE SHARK, THE

SHINING EXCALIBUR PICTURES
KIDS

SONY PICTURES CLASSICS
ACROSS THE SEA OF TIME: NEW YORK
    3D
AMATEUR
BURNT BY THE SUN
CHARULATA
CITY OF LOST CHILDREN, THE
CRUMB
FARINELLI
LIVING IN OBLIVION
LOVE AND HUMAN REMAINS
MARTHA & ETHEL
MUTE WITNESS
PERSUASION
PURE FORMALITY, A
SAFE
SHANGHAI TRIAD
WINDOW TO PARIS
WINGS OF COURAGE

SOVCAN
SHORT FILM ABOUT KILLING, A
SHORT FILM ABOUT LOVE, A

SPELLING FILMS INTERNATIONAL
BABYSITTER, THE

STARR VALLEY FILMS
BLESSING

STRAND RELEASING
CLEAN, SHAVEN
CONVENT, THE
ECLIPSE
POSTCARDS FROM AMERICA
RHYTHM THIEF
RIVER OF GRASS
ROY COHN/JACK SMITH
STALINGRAD
WORLD AND TIME ENOUGH

STREAMLINE PICTURES
BAREFOOT GEN
CRIMSON WOLF
WICKED CITY

SVENSKA FILMINSTITUTET
DANCER, THE

SVT INTERNATIONAL
BETRAYAL

TARA RELEASING
BLACK IS ... BLACK AIN'T
WHEN BILLY BROKE HIS HEAD ... AND
    OTHER TALES OF WONDER

TARA RELEASING/MANGA ENTERTAINMENT
WINGS OF HONNEAMISE: ROYAL SPACE
    FORCE

TC FILM & VIDEO IN HONG KONG CO.
SHAO LIN POPEYE

TRIBORO ENTERTAINMENT GROUP
BODY SHOT
JACK-O
PLAY TIME

TRIMARK PICTURES
KICKING AND SCREAMING
PAYBACK
SEPARATE LIVES
SPITFIRE
SWIMMING WITH SHARKS

TRISTAR
DEVIL IN A BLUE DRESS
HIDEAWAY
JOHNNY MNEMONIC
JUMANJI
JURY DUTY
MAGIC IN THE WATER
NEVER TALK TO STRANGERS
QUICK AND THE DEAD, THE

TRIUMPH RELEASING
NINA TAKES A LOVER

TURNER HOME ENTERTAINMENT
AVENGING ANGEL
BETTER OFF DEAD
BROKEN TRUST
DECOY
FATHER AND SCOUT
GALAXIS
GHOST BRIGADE
GIRL IN THE CADILLAC
KINGFISH: A STORY OF HUEY P. LONG
LAKOTA WOMAN: SIEGE AT WOUNDED
    KNEE
POWER OF ATTORNEY
WATER ENGINE, THE

20TH CENTURY FOX
BUSHWHACKED
BYE BYE, LOVE
DIE HARD WITH A VENGEANCE
FAR FROM HOME: THE ADVENTURES OF
    YELLOW DOG
FRENCH KISS
KISS OF DEATH
MIGHTY MORPHIN POWER RANGERS:
    THE MOVIE
NINE MONTHS
STRANGE DAYS
WAITING TO EXHALE
WALK IN THE CLOUDS, A

TWISTED ILLUSIONS, INC.
CREEP

UNITED ARTISTS
ROB ROY
TANK GIRL

UNIVERSAL
APOLLO 13
BABE
BALTO
BILLY MADISON
CASINO
CASPER
CLOCKERS
CURE, THE
GOLD DIGGERS: THE SECRET OF BEAR
    MOUNTAIN
HOW TO MAKE AN AMERICAN QUILT
HUNTED, THE
MAJOR PAYNE
SUDDEN DEATH
TALES FROM THE CRYPT: DEMON
    KNIGHT
TO WONG FOO, THANKS FOR
    EVERYTHING! JULIE NEWMAR
TWELVE MONKEYS
VILLAGE OF THE DAMNED
WATERWORLD

UPLAND FILM CORPORATION
HIGH RISK

VIDMARK ENTERTAINMENT
BREAK, THE
CURSE OF THE STARVING CLASS
DANGER OF LOVE
DEATH MACHINE
EVOLVER
FOOL AND HIS MONEY, A
FRANK & JESSE
GOOD DAY TO DIE, A

OPERATION INTERCEPT
SUBSTITUTE WIFE, THE
TERESA'S TATTOO

WARNER BROS.
ACE VENTURA: WHEN NATURE CALLS
AMAZING PANDA ADVENTURE, THE
ASSASSINS
BATMAN FOREVER
BORN TO BE WILD
BOYS ON THE SIDE
BRIDGES OF MADISON COUNTY, THE
COPYCAT
EMPIRE RECORDS
FAIR GAME
FREE WILLY 2: THE ADVENTURE HOME
GRUMPIER OLD MEN
HEAT
IT TAKES TWO
JUST CAUSE
LES MISERABLES
LITTLE PRINCESS, A
MURDER IN THE FIRST
OUTBREAK
SOMETHING TO TALK ABOUT
STARS FELL ON HENRIETTA, THE
UNDER SIEGE 2: DARK TERRITORY

WARNER HOME VIDEO
BURNING SEASON, THE
DILLINGER
DOUBLE, DOUBLE, TOIL AND TROUBLE
FATHERLAND

WARNERVISION
BODILY HARM
GRANNY, THE
JUDICIAL CONSENT

WATER BEARER FILMS
CREATION OF ADAM
NOT ANGELS BUT ANGELS

WORLD ARTISTS HOME VIDEO
FRAMEUP

YORK HOME VIDEO
ARMAGEDDON: THE FINAL CHALLENGE

ZEITGEIST FILMS
ART FOR TEACHERS OF CHILDREN
BALLOT MEASURE 9
1-900

ZIPPORAH FILMS
BALLET

FILMS BY STAR RATING

All films in this volume are listed below by their star ratings. The ratings are:

★★★★★ = Masterpiece;   ★★★★ = Excellent;   ★★★ = Good;   ★★ = Fair;   ★ = Poor;   No Star Rating = Without Merit

★★★★★

CHARULATA

★★★★

BEFORE THE RAIN
BLACK IS ... BLACK AIN'T
CLUELESS
CRUMB
DEVIL IN A BLUE DRESS
FUNNY BONES
HEAT
I AM CUBA
KINGDOM, THE
LAMERICA
SAFE
SHORT FILM ABOUT KILLING, A
WILD REEDS

★★★½

ADDICTION, THE
APOLLO 13
ARABIAN KNIGHT
ARIZONA DREAM
ASHES OF TIME
BABE
BANDIT QUEEN
BED YOU SLEEP IN, THE
BEFORE SUNRISE
CARMEN MIRANDA: BANANAS IS MY
    BUSINESS
CHRONICLE OF THE WARSAW GHETTO
    UPRISING ACCORDING TO MAREK
    EDELMAN
CITIZEN X
CITY OF LOST CHILDREN, THE
CONGRESS OF PENGUINS, THE
CRIMSON TIDE
DAY THE SUN TURNED COLD, THE
ERMO
FRAMEUP
GEORGIA
GLASS SHIELD, THE
HEROIC TRIO, THE
HYENAS
I, THE WORST OF ALL
INDIAN IN THE CUPBOARD, THE
INDICTMENT: THE MCMARTIN TRIAL
JAR, THE
JLG BY JLG
KISS OF DEATH
LESSONS OF DARKNESS
NO MERCY
PANTHER
PERSUASION
PICTURE BRIDE
POSTMAN, THE
POWDER
PROMISE, THE
PROPHECY, THE
PROVINCIAL ACTORS
RICHARD III

SECRET OF ROAN INISH, THE
SENSE AND SENSIBILITY
SEVEN
SHANGHAI TRIAD
SHORT FILM ABOUT LOVE, A
SMOKE
SON OF THE SHARK, THE
STALINGRAD
STRANGER, THE
TOY STORY
TWELVE MONKEYS
UNDERNEATH, THE
UNZIPPED
WATER ENGINE, THE
WHEN BILLY BROKE HIS HEAD ... AND
    OTHER TALES OF WONDER

★★★

ACCUMULATOR 1
ACE VENTURA: WHEN NATURE CALLS
AILSA
AMATEUR
ART FOR TEACHERS OF CHILDREN
AUGUSTIN
BALLET
BEYOND RANGOON
BLUE VILLA, THE
BOYS ON THE SIDE
BRADY BUNCH MOVIE, THE
BRAVEHEART
BRIAN WILSON: I JUST WASN'T MADE FOR
    THESE TIMES
BRIDGES OF MADISON COUNTY, THE
BROTHERS MCMULLEN, THE
BUFFALO GIRLS
BULLETPROOF HEART
BURNING SEASON, THE
BURNT BY THE SUN
CARRINGTON
CASINO
CASPER
CITY UNPLUGGED
CLEAN, SHAVEN
COLORADO COWBOY: THE BRUCE FORD
    STORY
COPYCAT
COUNTRY LIFE
COW, THE
CREATION OF ADAM
CROSSING GUARD, THE
CURE, THE
DALLAS DOLL
DEAD MAN WALKING
DEATH MACHINE
DESPERADO
DOLORES CLAIBORNE
DOUBLE HAPPINESS
ETERNITY
EXECUTIONERS
EXPERT, THE
FACES OF WOMEN
FAR FROM HOME: THE ADVENTURES OF
    YELLOW DOG

FOR GOD AND COUNTRY
FRANK AND OLLIE
FRENCH KISS
FRIDAY
GET SHORTY
GOLDENEYE
GORILLA BATHES AT NOON
GREAT DAY IN HARLEM, A
GROSSE FATIGUE
HIGHER LEARNING
HUNTED, THE
IN THE NAME OF THE EMPEROR
INCREDIBLY TRUE ADVENTURES OF TWO
    GIRLS IN LOVE, THE
JEFFREY
JUPITER'S WIFE
JUST CAUSE
KIDS
KINGFISH: A STORY OF HUEY P. LONG
LAMB
LAST GOOD TIME, THE
LAST SAMURAI, THE
LAST SUMMER IN THE HAMPTONS
LEAVING LAS VEGAS
LES MISERABLES
LITTLE ODESSA
LITTLE PRINCESS, A
LIVING IN OBLIVION
LOVE AND HUMAN REMAINS
MARTHA & ETHEL
MARTHA AND I
MEET THE FEEBLES
METAL AND MELANCHOLY
MIGHTY APHRODITE
MIGHTY MORPHIN POWER RANGERS: THE
    MOVIE
MINA TANNENBAUM
MOVING THE MOUNTAIN
MUTE WITNESS
MY FAMILY: MI FAMILIA
MYSTERY OF RAMPO, THE
NATIONAL LAMPOON'S ATTACK OF THE
    5'2" WOMEN
NEVER TALK TO STRANGERS
NINJA SCROLL
NIXON
NOBODY LOVES ME
ONCE WERE WARRIORS
1-900
PARTY GIRL
PHANTOM LOVER, THE
POCAHONTAS
PRIEST
PURE FORMALITY, A
RADIO INSIDE
RESTORATION
RETURN OF THE GOD OF GAMBLERS
RETURN OF THE NATIVE, THE
RHYTHM THIEF
RIVER OF GRASS
ROB ROY
ROOMMATES
ROSWELL: THE U.F.O. COVER-UP

SISTER MY SISTER
SOMETHING TO TALK ABOUT
STRAWBERRY AND CHOCOLATE
STUART SAVES HIS FAMILY
SUM OF US, THE
TALES FROM THE CRYPT: DEMON KNIGHT
TALL TALE: THE UNBELIEVABLE
 ADVENTURES OF PECOS BILL
THROUGH THE OLIVE TREES
TIE-DIED: ROCK 'N' ROLL'S MOST
 DEADICATED FANS
TIE THAT BINDS, THE
TO DIE FOR
TRAPS
UP TO A CERTAIN POINT
USUAL SUSPECTS, THE
WALK IN THE CLOUDS, A
WHILE YOU WERE SLEEPING
WICKED CITY
WIGSTOCK: THE MOVIE
WILD BILL
WINDOW TO PARIS
WOMAN AT WAR, A
WOODEN MAN'S BRIDE, THE

★★½

AI CITY
ALMOST DEAD
AMERICAN PRESIDENT, THE
ANGUS
ASCENT, THE
AWFULLY BIG ADVENTURE, AN
BABY-SITTERS CLUB, THE
BABYSITTER, THE
BAD BLOOD
BAD BOYS
BAD COMPANY
BAREFOOT GEN
BASKETBALL DIARIES, THE
BATMAN FOREVER
BETRAYAL
BETTER OFF DEAD
BLESSING
BLUE IN THE FACE
BLUE TIGER
BODY SHOT
BREACH OF CONDUCT
BROKEN TRUST
BUSINESS AFFAIR, A
BYE BYE, LOVE
CENTURY
CIRCLE OF FRIENDS
CIRCUMSTANCES UNKNOWN
CLASS OF '61
CLOCKERS
COLDBLOODED
COMPANION, THE
CONVENT, THE
CONVICT COWBOY
CRIMSON WOLF
CRUDE OASIS, THE
CRY, THE BELOVED COUNTRY
CURSE OF THE STARVING CLASS
CUTTHROAT ISLAND
DANGEROUS, THE
DARK SIDE OF GENIUS, THE
DEAD PRESIDENTS
DEADLY MARIA
DECOY
DIE HARD WITH A VENGEANCE
DIGGER
DON JUAN DEMARCO
DOOM GENERATION, THE

DREAMING OF RITA
ECLIPSE
ENEMY WITHIN, THE
ENGLISHMAN WHO WENT UP A HILL BUT
 CAME DOWN A MOUNTAIN, THE
EROTIQUE
EXOTICA
FARINELLI
FATHERLAND
FEAR, THE
FEAST OF JULY
FIRST KNIGHT
FLUKE
FORGET PARIS
FRANK & JESSE
FRANKIE STARLIGHT
FREE WILLY 2: THE ADVENTURE HOME
FRIENDS
FUN
GETTING OUT
GOLD DIGGERS: THE SECRET OF BEAR
 MOUNTAIN
GOOD DAY TO DIE, A
GOOFY MOVIE, A
GREAT ELEPHANT ESCAPE, THE
GROSS MISCONDUCT
GRUMPIER OLD MEN
GUMBY: THE MOVIE
HACKERS
HARLEM DIARY: NINE VOICES OF
 RESILIENCE
HIGH RISK
HOTEL SORRENTO
HOW TO MAKE AN AMERICAN QUILT
HOW TO TOP MY WIFE
IN THE MOUTH OF MADNESS
INNOCENT LIES
INNOCENT, THE
JEFFERSON IN PARIS
JOHNNY MNEMONIC
JOURNEY OF AUGUST KING, THE
JUMANJI
KILIAN'S CHRONICLE
KURT VONNEGUT'S HARRISON BERGERON
LAST OF THE DOGMEN
LORD OF ILLUSIONS
LOSING ISAIAH
MACHINE DREAMS
MAYA LIN: A STRONG CLEAR VISION
MONTH BY THE LAKE, A
MORTAL KOMBAT
MURDER IN THE FIRST
MURIEL'S WEDDING
MY LIFE AND TIMES WITH ANTONIN
 ARTAUD
NADJA
NAKED KILLER
NEA
NET, THE
NEW JERSEY DRIVE
NEXT DOOR
NICK OF TIME
NINA TAKES A LOVER
NINE MONTHS
OH ... ROSALINDA!!
O.J. SIMPSON STORY, THE
OLD LADY WHO WALKED IN THE SEA, THE
ONLY THE BRAVE
OUT OF SYNC
OUTBREAK
POSTCARDS FROM AMERICA
PROFESSION: NEO-NAZI
PUSHING HANDS
QUICK AND THE DEAD, THE

RECKLESS
RED FIRECRACKER, GREEN FIRECRACKER
RED SUN RISING
REDWOOD CURTAIN
REFLECTIONS IN THE DARK
REMOTE CONTROL
RUN OF THE COUNTRY, THE
SABRINA
SHALLOW GRAVE
SHAO LIN POPEYE
SIX DAYS, SIX NIGHTS
SPECIES
STARS FELL ON HENRIETTA, THE
STRANGE DAYS
SUBSTITUTE WIFE, THE
SUDDEN DEATH
TALES FROM THE HOOD
THREE WISHES
TO CROSS THE RUBICON
TOMMY BOY
TOO YOUNG TO DIE?
TOTAL ECLIPSE
TOWARD THE TERRA
TWENTY SOMETHING
UNDER SIEGE 2: DARK TERRITORY
UNSTRUNG HEROES
VALLEY OF ABRAHAM, THE
VIRTUOSITY
VOYAGE EN DOUCE
WAITING TO EXHALE
WATERWORLD
WHEN NIGHT IS FALLING
WINGS OF HONNEAMISE: ROYAL SPACE
 FORCE
WITHOUT ANESTHESIA
WORLD AND TIME ENOUGH
ZOOMAN

★★

ACROSS THE MOON
ACROSS THE SEA OF TIME: NEW YORK 3D
AMAZING PANDA ADVENTURE, THE
AMERICA'S DEADLIEST HOME VIDEO
AMERICAN COP
ANDROID AFFAIR, THE
ASSASSINS
AVENGING ANGEL
BALLISTIC
BALLOT MEASURE 9
BALTO
BAR GIRLS
BIG GREEN, THE
BIGFOOT: THE UNFORGETTABLE
 ENCOUNTER
BITTER VENGEANCE
BLACK FOX
BODILY HARM
BODY CHEMISTRY 4: FULL EXPOSURE
BORN TO BE WILD
BREAK, THE
CANADIAN BACON
CASTLE FREAK
CHILDREN OF THE CORN III: URBAN
 HARVEST
CONGO
CRACKERJACK
DANCE ME OUTSIDE
DANCER, THE
DANGEROUS MINDS
DARKMAN 2: THE RETURN OF DURANT
DEATH IN BRUNSWICK
DESTINY TURNS ON THE RADIO
DILLINGER

DILLINGER AND CAPONE
DOOMSDAY GUN
DOUBLE, DOUBLE, TOIL AND TROUBLE
DREAM A LITTLE DREAM 2
EMBRACE OF THE VAMPIRE
EMPIRE RECORDS
EVOLVER
FAIR GAME
FATHER AND SCOUT
FATHER OF THE BRIDE PART II
FIRST DEGREE
GIRL IN THE CADILLAC
GLORY BOYS, THE
GRANNY, THE
HEAVEN'S A DRAG
HE'S A WOMAN, SHE'S A MAN
HIDEAWAY
HOME FOR THE HOLIDAYS
I CAN'T SLEEP
IT TAKES TWO
JUDGE DREDD
JUDICIAL CONSENT
KICKING AND SCREAMING
KID IN KING ARTHUR'S COURT, A
LAKOTA WOMAN: SIEGE AT WOUNDED
   KNEE
LAST RIDE, THE
LIE DOWN WITH DOGS
MAD LOVE
MAGIC IN THE WATER
MAJOR PAYNE
MALICIOUS
MALLRATS
MAN OF THE HOUSE
MANGLER, THE
MESSENGER
MIAMI RHAPSODY
MOONLIGHT AND VALENTINO
MOSAIC PROJECT, THE
MY ANTONIA
NIGHTMARE
NOSTRADAMUS KID, THE
NOT ANGELS BUT ANGELS
NOW AND THEN
OPERATION DUMBO DROP
OTHELLO
OUTSIDE THE LAW
PEBBLE AND THE PENGUIN, THE
PENTATHLON
PEREZ FAMILY, THE
PIANO LESSON, THE
PIGALLE
POCAHONTAS: THE LEGEND
REASON TO BELIEVE, A
RENT-A-KID

ROY COHN/JACK SMITH
SAFE PASSAGE
SCANNERS: THE SHOWDOWN
SECRETARY, THE
SEPARATE LIVES
SERIOUS ABOUT PLEASURE
SEX, DRUGS AND DEMOCRACY
SHOW, THE
SPIKE AND MIKE'S FESTIVAL OF
   ANIMATION '95
SWIMMING WITH SHARKS
TANK GIRL
THINGS TO DO IN DENVER WHEN YOU'RE
   DEAD
TO WONG FOO, THANKS FOR
   EVERYTHING! JULIE NEWMAR
TOM AND HUCK
TOO OUTRAGEOUS ANIMATION
TOP DOG
TWO BITS
TWOGETHER
VAMPIRE IN BROOKLYN
VAMPIRES AND OTHER STEREOTYPES
VILLAGE OF THE DAMNED
WALKING DEAD, THE
WHITE MAN'S BURDEN
WINGS OF COURAGE
WIZARD OF DARKNESS
YOUNGER & YOUNGER

★½

ATTACK OF THE 60-FOOT CENTERFOLD
CANDYMAN: FAREWELL TO THE FLESH
COSMIC SLOP
COVER ME
CRAZYSITTER, THE
CYBER BANDITS
DECONSTRUCTING SARAH
DR. JEKYLL & MS. HYDE
FOUR ROOMS
GHOST BRIGADE
GORDY
HIGHLANDER: THE FINAL DIMENSION
JADE
JURY DUTY
NUMBER ONE FAN
OPERATION INTERCEPT
OUT OF ANNIE'S PAST
PREHYSTERIA! 3
SCARLET LETTER, THE
SEARCH AND DESTROY
SHOWGIRLS
SKINNER
STEAL BIG, STEAL LITTLE

##

ADVENTURES OF MATT THE GOOSEBOY,
   THE
BILLY MADISON
BOCA
BODY STROKES
BOULEVARD
BUSHWHACKED
CREEP
DANGER OF LOVE
DARK DEALER
DEAD FUNNY
DESPERATE PREY
DIRTY MONEY
DRACULA: DEAD AND LOVING IT
FOOL AND HIS MONEY, A
GALAXIS
HALLOWEEN: THE CURSE OF MICHAEL
   MYERS
HEAVYWEIGHTS
HOUSEGUEST
I LIKE TO PLAY GAMES
IN THE DEEP WOODS
JERKY BOYS: THE MOVIE, THE
ME AND THE MOB
MIDNIGHT TEASE 2
MONEY TRAIN
MUTANT SPECIES
NATIONAL LAMPOON'S SENIOR TRIP
NEKROMANTIK
NEW YORK COP
PAYBACK
PLAY TIME
POWER OF ATTORNEY
PYROMANIAC'S LOVE STORY, A
S.F.W.
SILENCE OF THE HAMS
SPITFIRE
SPY WITHIN, THE
TERESA'S TATTOO
3 NINJAS KNUCKLE UP
UNDERCOVER

NO STAR RATING

ABDUCTED 2: THE REUNION
ARMAGEDDON: THE FINAL CHALLENGE
BIKINI BISTRO
CAGED HEARTS
CAGED HEAT 3000
COVER STORY
CREW, THE
GOOD GIRLS DON'T
HOWLING: NEW MOON RISING, THE
JACK-O

FILMS BY GENRE

Films belonging to more than one genre are listed under each appropriate category

Action

ABDUCTED 2: THE REUNION
AMERICAN COP
ASSASSINS
BAD BLOOD
BAD BOYS
BALLISTIC
BATMAN FOREVER
BLUE TIGER
CONVICT COWBOY
CRACKERJACK
CRIMSON TIDE
CRIMSON WOLF
CUTTHROAT ISLAND
DANGEROUS, THE
DARKMAN 2: THE RETURN OF DURANT
DECOY
DESPERADO
DIE HARD WITH A VENGEANCE
EXPERT, THE
FAIR GAME
GALAXIS
GOLDENEYE
GOOD GIRLS DON'T
HEROIC TRIO, THE
HIGH RISK
HUNTED, THE
LAST SAMURAI, THE
MONEY TRAIN
MORTAL KOMBAT
MOSAIC PROJECT, THE
MUTANT SPECIES
NET, THE
NEW YORK COP
OPERATION INTERCEPT
PENTATHLON
RED SUN RISING
RETURN OF THE GOD OF GAMBLERS
SEVEN
SPECIES
SPITFIRE
STEAL BIG, STEAL LITTLE
SUDDEN DEATH
TALL TALE: THE UNBELIEVABLE
    ADVENTURES OF PECOS BILL
TANK GIRL
3 NINJAS KNUCKLE UP
TOP DOG
UNDER SIEGE 2: DARK TERRITORY
UNDERCOVER
VIRTUOSITY
WATERWORLD

Adventure

ACE VENTURA: WHEN NATURE CALLS
ACROSS THE SEA OF TIME: NEW YORK 3D
ADVENTURES OF MATT THE GOOSEBOY,
    THE
AMAZING PANDA ADVENTURE, THE
ASCENT, THE
BALTO
BATMAN FOREVER
BEYOND RANGOON

BIGFOOT: THE UNFORGETTABLE
    ENCOUNTER
BORN TO BE WILD
BRAVEHEART
CONGO
CUTTHROAT ISLAND
CYBER BANDITS
DANCE ME OUTSIDE
DECOY
DIE HARD WITH A VENGEANCE
DIRTY MONEY
DREAMING OF RITA
FAR FROM HOME: THE ADVENTURES OF
    YELLOW DOG
FIRST KNIGHT
FREE WILLY 2: THE ADVENTURE HOME
GOLD DIGGERS: THE SECRET OF BEAR
    MOUNTAIN
GREAT ELEPHANT ESCAPE, THE
HIGHLANDER: THE FINAL DIMENSION
INDIAN IN THE CUPBOARD, THE
JUMANJI
LAST OF THE DOGMEN
LAST SAMURAI, THE
MAGIC IN THE WATER
MIGHTY MORPHIN POWER RANGERS: THE
    MOVIE
OPERATION DUMBO DROP
ROB ROY
SUDDEN DEATH
TALL TALE: THE UNBELIEVABLE
    ADVENTURES OF PECOS BILL
TOM AND HUCK
WATERWORLD
WINGS OF COURAGE

Animated

ADVENTURES OF MATT THE GOOSEBOY,
    THE
AI CITY
ARABIAN KNIGHT
BALTO
BAREFOOT GEN
CRIMSON WOLF
GOOFY MOVIE, A
GUMBY: THE MOVIE
PEBBLE AND THE PENGUIN, THE
POCAHONTAS
SPIKE AND MIKE'S FESTIVAL OF
    ANIMATION '95
TALE OF GENJI, THE
TOO OUTRAGEOUS ANIMATION
TOY STORY
WICKED CITY
WINGS OF HONNEAMISE: ROYAL SPACE
    FORCE

Biography

BANDIT QUEEN
BURNING SEASON, THE
CARMEN MIRANDA: BANANAS IS MY
    BUSINESS
CARRINGTON
COLORADO COWBOY: THE BRUCE FORD
    STORY
CRUMB

DILLINGER
ETERNITY
FARINELLI
I, THE WORST OF ALL
JEFFERSON IN PARIS
KINGFISH: A STORY OF HUEY P. LONG
MAYA LIN: A STRONG CLEAR VISION
MY LIFE AND TIMES WITH ANTONIN
    ARTAUD
NIXON
O.J. SIMPSON STORY, THE
ROB ROY
ROY COHN/JACK SMITH
TOTAL ECLIPSE
WILD BILL

Children's

ACROSS THE SEA OF TIME: NEW YORK 3D
ADVENTURES OF MATT THE GOOSEBOY,
    THE
AMAZING PANDA ADVENTURE, THE
ANGUS
ARABIAN KNIGHT
BABE
BABY-SITTERS CLUB, THE
BALTO
BIG GREEN, THE
BIGFOOT: THE UNFORGETTABLE
    ENCOUNTER
BORN TO BE WILD
CASPER
CRAZYSITTER, THE
DIGGER
DOUBLE, DOUBLE, TOIL AND TROUBLE
FAR FROM HOME: THE ADVENTURES OF
    YELLOW DOG
FATHER AND SCOUT
FREE WILLY 2: THE ADVENTURE HOME
GOLD DIGGERS: THE SECRET OF BEAR
    MOUNTAIN
GOOFY MOVIE, A
GORDY
GREAT ELEPHANT ESCAPE, THE
GUMBY: THE MOVIE
HEAVYWEIGHTS
INDIAN IN THE CUPBOARD, THE
IT TAKES TWO
JUMANJI
KID IN KING ARTHUR'S COURT, A
LITTLE PRINCESS, A
MAGIC IN THE WATER
MAN OF THE HOUSE
MIGHTY MORPHIN POWER RANGERS: THE
    MOVIE
PEBBLE AND THE PENGUIN, THE
PREHYSTERIA! 3
RENT-A-KID
SECRET OF ROAN INISH, THE
SHAO LIN POPEYE
TALL TALE: THE UNBELIEVABLE
    ADVENTURES OF PECOS BILL
3 NINJAS KNUCKLE UP
TOM AND HUCK
TOP DOG
TOY STORY

Comedy

ACCUMULATOR 1
ACE VENTURA: WHEN NATURE CALLS
ACROSS THE MOON
AMERICAN PRESIDENT, THE
ANGUS
ARIZONA DREAM
ATTACK OF THE 60-FOOT CENTERFOLD
AUGUSTIN
BABE
BABY-SITTERS CLUB, THE
BAD BOYS
BEFORE SUNRISE
BIG GREEN, THE
BIKINI BISTRO
BILLY MADISON
BLUE IN THE FACE
BORN TO BE WILD
BOYS ON THE SIDE
BRADY BUNCH MOVIE, THE
BROTHERS MCMULLEN, THE
BUSHWHACKED
BUSINESS AFFAIR, A
BYE BYE, LOVE
CANADIAN BACON
CASPER
CLUELESS
COSMIC SLOP
COUNTRY LIFE
CRAZYSITTER, THE
DALLAS DOLL
DEAD FUNNY
DEATH IN BRUNSWICK
DESTINY TURNS ON THE RADIO
DR. JEKYLL & MS. HYDE
DON JUAN DEMARCO
DOOM GENERATION, THE
DOUBLE, DOUBLE, TOIL AND TROUBLE
DOUBLE HAPPINESS
DRACULA: DEAD AND LOVING IT
DREAM A LITTLE DREAM 2
EMPIRE RECORDS
ENGLISHMAN WHO WENT UP A HILL BUT
    CAME DOWN A MOUNTAIN, THE
ERMO
EROTIQUE
FATHER AND SCOUT
FATHER OF THE BRIDE PART II
FOOL AND HIS MONEY, A
FORGET PARIS
FOUR ROOMS
FRANKIE STARLIGHT
FRENCH KISS
FRIDAY
FUNNY BONES
GET SHORTY
GOOD GIRLS DON'T
GORDY
GORILLA BATHES AT NOON
GROSSE FATIGUE
GRUMPIER OLD MEN
HEAVEN'S A DRAG
HEAVYWEIGHTS
HE'S A WOMAN, SHE'S A MAN
HOME FOR THE HOLIDAYS
HOUSEGUEST
HOW TO TOP MY WIFE
HYENAS
INCREDIBLY TRUE ADVENTURES OF TWO
    GIRLS IN LOVE, THE
IT TAKES TWO
JAR, THE
JEFFREY

JERKY BOYS: THE MOVIE, THE
JURY DUTY
KICKING AND SCREAMING
KURT VONNEGUT'S HARRISON BERGERON
LAST SUMMER IN THE HAMPTONS
LIE DOWN WITH DOGS
LIVING IN OBLIVION
MAJOR PAYNE
MALLRATS
MAN OF THE HOUSE
ME AND THE MOB
MEET THE FEEBLES
MIAMI RHAPSODY
MIGHTY APHRODITE
MONEY TRAIN
MONTH BY THE LAKE, A
MURIEL'S WEDDING
NATIONAL LAMPOON'S ATTACK OF THE
    5'2" WOMEN
NATIONAL LAMPOON'S SENIOR TRIP
NINE MONTHS
NOBODY LOVES ME
NOSTRADAMUS KID, THE
NOW AND THEN
OH ... ROSALINDA!!
OLD LADY WHO WALKED IN THE SEA, THE
OPERATION DUMBO DROP
PARTY GIRL
PEREZ FAMILY, THE
POSTMAN, THE
PREHYSTERIA! 3
PROVINCIAL ACTORS
PUSHING HANDS
PYROMANIAC'S LOVE STORY, A
QUICK AND THE DEAD, THE
RECKLESS
REMOTE CONTROL
RENT-A-KID
RESTORATION
ROOMMATES
SABRINA
SEARCH AND DESTROY
SERIOUS ABOUT PLEASURE
S.F.W.
SHAO LIN POPEYE
SILENCE OF THE HAMS
SMOKE
SOMETHING TO TALK ABOUT
STEAL BIG, STEAL LITTLE
STUART SAVES HIS FAMILY
SUBSTITUTE WIFE, THE
SUM OF US, THE
SWIMMING WITH SHARKS
TANK GIRL
TERESA'S TATTOO
THROUGH THE OLIVE TREES
TO DIE FOR
TO WONG FOO, THANKS FOR
    EVERYTHING! JULIE NEWMAR
TOM AND HUCK
TOMMY BOY
UNSTRUNG HEROES
VAMPIRE IN BROOKLYN
WHILE YOU WERE SLEEPING
WINDOW TO PARIS
YOUNGER & YOUNGER

Crime

ACE VENTURA: WHEN NATURE CALLS
AMATEUR
AMERICA'S DEADLIEST HOME VIDEO
BAD BLOOD
BAD BOYS

BLUE TIGER
BODILY HARM
BODY SHOT
BROKEN TRUST
BULLETPROOF HEART
CASINO
CIRCUMSTANCES UNKNOWN
CITIZEN X
CITY UNPLUGGED
CLEAN, SHAVEN
CLOCKERS
COLDBLOODED
COPYCAT
COVER STORY
DANGEROUS, THE
DEAD PRESIDENTS
DESPERADO
DESTINY TURNS ON THE RADIO
DEVIL IN A BLUE DRESS
DIE HARD WITH A VENGEANCE
DILLINGER
DILLINGER AND CAPONE
DIRTY MONEY
DOOM GENERATION, THE
DREAM A LITTLE DREAM 2
FIRST DEGREE
FUN
GET SHORTY
GIRL IN THE CADILLAC
GLASS SHIELD, THE
HEAT
HIGH RISK
I CAN'T SLEEP
INDICTMENT: THE MCMARTIN TRIAL
INNOCENT LIES
JADE
JUST CAUSE
KISS OF DEATH
LITTLE ODESSA
LOVE AND HUMAN REMAINS
NEW JERSEY DRIVE
NICK OF TIME
NO MERCY
O.J. SIMPSON STORY, THE
OUT OF SYNC
OUTSIDE THE LAW
POWER OF ATTORNEY
PURE FORMALITY, A
RIVER OF GRASS
SEPARATE LIVES
SEVEN
SHALLOW GRAVE
SHANGHAI TRIAD
SISTER MY SISTER
THINGS TO DO IN DENVER WHEN YOU'RE
    DEAD
TO DIE FOR
UNDERCOVER
UNDERNEATH, THE
USUAL SUSPECTS, THE

Docudrama

ACROSS THE SEA OF TIME: NEW YORK 3D
ART FOR TEACHERS OF CHILDREN
BALLET
BLACK IS ... BLACK AIN'T
CHRONICLE OF THE WARSAW GHETTO
    UPRISING ACCORDING TO MAREK
    EDELMAN
CITIZEN X
CONGRESS OF PENGUINS, THE
DANGER OF LOVE
DOOMSDAY GUN

ETERNITY
GORILLA BATHES AT NOON
I AM CUBA
INDICTMENT: THE MCMARTIN TRIAL
JERKY BOYS: THE MOVIE, THE
LAKOTA WOMAN: SIEGE AT WOUNDED
    KNEE
O.J. SIMPSON STORY, THE
ROSWELL: THE U.F.O. COVER-UP
UP TO A CERTAIN POINT

Documentary

BALLOT MEASURE 9
BETRAYAL
BLACK IS ... BLACK AIN'T
BRIAN WILSON: I JUST WASN'T MADE FOR
    THESE TIMES
CARMEN MIRANDA: BANANAS IS MY
    BUSINESS
COLORADO COWBOY: THE BRUCE FORD
    STORY
CRUMB
DANCER, THE
FRANK AND OLLIE
GREAT DAY IN HARLEM, A
HARLEM DIARY: NINE VOICES OF
    RESILIENCE
IN THE NAME OF THE EMPEROR
JLG BY JLG
JUPITER'S WIFE
LESSONS OF DARKNESS
MACHINE DREAMS
MARTHA & ETHEL
MAYA LIN: A STRONG CLEAR VISION
METAL AND MELANCHOLY
MOVING THE MOUNTAIN
NOT ANGELS BUT ANGELS
PROFESSION: NEO-NAZI
ROY COHN/JACK SMITH
SEX, DRUGS AND DEMOCRACY
SHOW, THE
TIE-DIED: ROCK 'N' ROLL'S MOST
    DEADICATED FANS
UNZIPPED
WHEN BILLY BROKE HIS HEAD ... AND
    OTHER TALES OF WONDER
WIGSTOCK: THE MOVIE

Drama

ACROSS THE MOON
ADDICTION, THE
AILSA
AMATEUR
AMERICAN PRESIDENT, THE
APOLLO 13
ARIZONA DREAM
ART FOR TEACHERS OF CHILDREN
ASHES OF TIME
AWFULLY BIG ADVENTURE, AN
BABY-SITTERS CLUB, THE
BABYSITTER, THE
BAD COMPANY
BANDIT QUEEN
BAR GIRLS
BAREFOOT GEN
BASKETBALL DIARIES, THE
BED YOU SLEEP IN, THE
BEFORE SUNRISE
BEFORE THE RAIN
BETTER OFF DEAD
BEYOND RANGOON
BLESSING
BLUE IN THE FACE
BLUE VILLA, THE

BOCA
BOULEVARD
BOYS ON THE SIDE
BRAVEHEART
BREAK, THE
BRIDGES OF MADISON COUNTY, THE
BROKEN TRUST
BROTHERS MCMULLEN, THE
BULLETPROOF HEART
BURNING SEASON, THE
BURNT BY THE SUN
BUSINESS AFFAIR, A
CASINO
CENTURY
CHARULATA
CIRCLE OF FRIENDS
CITY UNPLUGGED
CLASS OF '61
CLEAN, SHAVEN
CLOCKERS
CONVENT, THE
CONVICT COWBOY
COUNTRY LIFE
COW, THE
CREATION OF ADAM
CREW, THE
CROSSING GUARD, THE
CRUDE OASIS, THE
CRY, THE BELOVED COUNTRY
CURE, THE
CURSE OF THE STARVING CLASS
DANCE ME OUTSIDE
DANGEROUS MINDS
DAY THE SUN TURNED COLD, THE
DEAD MAN WALKING
DEAD PRESIDENTS
DEADLY MARIA
DEATH IN BRUNSWICK
DESPERADO
DESPERATE PREY
DEVIL IN A BLUE DRESS
DIGGER
DIRTY MONEY
DOLORES CLAIBORNE
DON JUAN DEMARCO
DOOM GENERATION, THE
DREAMING OF RITA
ECLIPSE
EMPIRE RECORDS
ERMO
EROTIQUE
EXOTICA
FACES OF WOMEN
FAR FROM HOME: THE ADVENTURES OF
    YELLOW DOG
FARINELLI
FATHER OF THE BRIDE PART II
FEAST OF JULY
FIRST DEGREE
FIRST KNIGHT
FLUKE
FOR GOD AND COUNTRY
FOUR ROOMS
FRAMEUP
FRANKIE STARLIGHT
FRIENDS
FUN
FUNNY BONES
GEORGIA
GETTING OUT
GLASS SHIELD, THE
GROSS MISCONDUCT
HEAT

HEAVEN'S A DRAG
HIGHER LEARNING
HOTEL SORRENTO
HOW TO MAKE AN AMERICAN QUILT
HYENAS
I AM CUBA
I CAN'T SLEEP
I, THE WORST OF ALL
INCREDIBLY TRUE ADVENTURES OF TWO
    GIRLS IN LOVE, THE
INDICTMENT: THE MCMARTIN TRIAL
INNOCENT LIES
INNOCENT, THE
JAR, THE
JEFFERSON IN PARIS
JOURNEY OF AUGUST KING, THE
JUDICIAL CONSENT
JUST CAUSE
KICKING AND SCREAMING
KIDS
KILIAN'S CHRONICLE
KINGDOM, THE
KINGFISH: A STORY OF HUEY P. LONG
KISS OF DEATH
KURT VONNEGUT'S HARRISON BERGERON
LAMB
LAMERICA
LAST GOOD TIME, THE
LAST OF THE DOGMEN
LAST RIDE, THE
LAST SUMMER IN THE HAMPTONS
LEAVING LAS VEGAS
LES MISERABLES
LITTLE ODESSA
LITTLE PRINCESS, A
LOSING ISAIAH
LOVE AND HUMAN REMAINS
MAD LOVE
MARTHA AND I
MESSENGER
MINA TANNENBAUM
MONTH BY THE LAKE, A
MOONLIGHT AND VALENTINO
MURDER IN THE FIRST
MUTE WITNESS
MY ANTONIA
MY FAMILY: MI FAMILIA
MY LIFE AND TIMES WITH ANTONIN
    ARTAUD
MYSTERY OF RAMPO, THE
NADJA
NEVER TALK TO STRANGERS
NEW JERSEY DRIVE
NEXT DOOR
NICK OF TIME
NIGHTMARE
NINA TAKES A LOVER
NIXON
NO MERCY
NOBODY LOVES ME
NOW AND THEN
OLD LADY WHO WALKED IN THE SEA, THE
ONCE WERE WARRIORS
1-900
ONLY THE BRAVE
OTHELLO
OUT OF SYNC
OUTBREAK
PANTHER
PARTY GIRL
PEREZ FAMILY, THE
PERSUASION
PHANTOM LOVER, THE
PIANO LESSON, THE

PICTURE BRIDE
PIGALLE
POSTCARDS FROM AMERICA
POSTMAN, THE
POWDER
POWER OF ATTORNEY
PRIEST
PROMISE, THE
PROVINCIAL ACTORS
PURE FORMALITY, A
PUSHING HANDS
QUICK AND THE DEAD, THE
RADIO INSIDE
REASON TO BELIEVE, A
RED FIRECRACKER, GREEN FIRECRACKER
REDWOOD CURTAIN
REFLECTIONS IN THE DARK
RETURN OF THE NATIVE, THE
RHYTHM THIEF
RICHARD III
RIVER OF GRASS
ROOMMATES
ROY COHN/JACK SMITH
RUN OF THE COUNTRY, THE
SAFE
SAFE PASSAGE
SCARLET LETTER, THE
SEARCH AND DESTROY
SENSE AND SENSIBILITY
S.F.W.
SHANGHAI TRIAD
SHORT FILM ABOUT KILLING, A
SHORT FILM ABOUT LOVE, A
SHOWGIRLS
SISTER MY SISTER
SIX DAYS, SIX NIGHTS
SMOKE
SOMETHING TO TALK ABOUT
SON OF THE SHARK, THE
STARS FELL ON HENRIETTA, THE
STEAL BIG, STEAL LITTLE
STRANGE DAYS
STRANGER, THE
STRAWBERRY AND CHOCOLATE
SUBSTITUTE WIFE, THE
SUM OF US, THE
THINGS TO DO IN DENVER WHEN YOU'RE DEAD
THREE WISHES
THROUGH THE OLIVE TREES
TO CROSS THE RUBICON
TO DIE FOR
TOO YOUNG TO DIE?
TOTAL ECLIPSE
TRAPS
TWELVE MONKEYS
TWENTY SOMETHING
TWO BITS
TWOGETHER
UNDER SIEGE 2: DARK TERRITORY
UNDERNEATH, THE
UNSTRUNG HEROES
UP TO A CERTAIN POINT
VALLEY OF ABRAHAM, THE
VOYAGE EN DOUCE
WAITING TO EXHALE
WALK IN THE CLOUDS, A
WALKING DEAD, THE
WATER ENGINE, THE
WHEN NIGHT IS FALLING
WHITE MAN'S BURDEN
WILD REEDS
WINGS OF COURAGE

WINGS OF HONNEAMISE: ROYAL SPACE FORCE
WITHOUT ANESTHESIA
WOMAN AT WAR, A
WOODEN MAN'S BRIDE, THE
WORLD AND TIME ENOUGH
ZOOMAN

Erotic

ATTACK OF THE 60-FOOT CENTERFOLD
BABYSITTER, THE
BIKINI BISTRO
BOCA
BODY CHEMISTRY 4: FULL EXPOSURE
BODY SHOT
BODY STROKES
CAGED HEARTS
CAGED HEAT 3000
COVER ME
DECONSTRUCTING SARAH
ECLIPSE
EMBRACE OF THE VAMPIRE
EROTIQUE
I LIKE TO PLAY GAMES
JADE
LOVE AND HUMAN REMAINS
MALICIOUS
MIDNIGHT TEASE 2
NAKED KILLER
NEA
NEVER TALK TO STRANGERS
1-900
OUTSIDE THE LAW
PLAY TIME
SHOWGIRLS
UNDERCOVER

Experimental

JLG BY JLG

Fantasy

ACCUMULATOR 1
ARABIAN KNIGHT
BABE
BODY STROKES
CASPER
CITY OF LOST CHILDREN, THE
CONGRESS OF PENGUINS, THE
CRIMSON WOLF
DESTINY TURNS ON THE RADIO
DIGGER
DOUBLE, DOUBLE, TOIL AND TROUBLE
EXECUTIONERS
FLUKE
FOR GOD AND COUNTRY
GORDY
GUMBY: THE MOVIE
HEROIC TRIO, THE
HIGHLANDER: THE FINAL DIMENSION
INDIAN IN THE CUPBOARD, THE
JUMANJI
KID IN KING ARTHUR'S COURT, A
MORTAL KOMBAT
NAKED KILLER
PEBBLE AND THE PENGUIN, THE
PHANTOM LOVER, THE
POWDER
PREHYSTERIA! 3
SECRET OF ROAN INISH, THE
THREE WISHES
TOY STORY
TWELVE MONKEYS

WHITE MAN'S BURDEN
WINDOW TO PARIS

Historical

APOLLO 13
AVENGING ANGEL
BRAVEHEART
BURNT BY THE SUN
CARRINGTON
CENTURY
CHRONICLE OF THE WARSAW GHETTO UPRISING ACCORDING TO MAREK EDELMAN
CLASS OF '61
CONGRESS OF PENGUINS, THE
DILLINGER
DILLINGER AND CAPONE
FRANK & JESSE
IN THE NAME OF THE EMPEROR
INNOCENT, THE
JOURNEY OF AUGUST KING, THE
KILIAN'S CHRONICLE
MOVING THE MOUNTAIN
NINJA SCROLL
PANTHER
PERSUASION
PICTURE BRIDE
POCAHONTAS: THE LEGEND
PROMISE, THE
RESTORATION
RICHARD III
ROB ROY
SCARLET LETTER, THE
STALINGRAD
TALE OF GENJI, THE
TRAPS
WILD BILL
WOMAN AT WAR, A

Horror

ADDICTION, THE
CANDYMAN: FAREWELL TO THE FLESH
CASTLE FREAK
CHILDREN OF THE CORN III: URBAN HARVEST
CREEP
DARK DEALER
DARKMAN 2: THE RETURN OF DURANT
DEATH MACHINE
DR. JEKYLL & MS. HYDE
DRACULA: DEAD AND LOVING IT
EMBRACE OF THE VAMPIRE
EVOLVER
FEAR, THE
GHOST BRIGADE
GRANNY, THE
HALLOWEEN: THE CURSE OF MICHAEL MYERS
HIDEAWAY
HOWLING: NEW MOON RISING, THE
IN THE MOUTH OF MADNESS
JACK-O
KINGDOM, THE
LORD OF ILLUSIONS
MANGLER, THE
MUTANT SPECIES
NADJA
NEKROMANTIK
PROPHECY, THE
SCANNERS: THE SHOWDOWN
SKINNER
TALES FROM THE CRYPT: DEMON KNIGHT
TALES FROM THE HOOD

TIE THAT BINDS, THE
VAMPIRE IN BROOKLYN
VAMPIRES AND OTHER STEREOTYPES
VILLAGE OF THE DAMNED
WIZARD OF DARKNESS

Martial Arts

ASHES OF TIME
BAD BLOOD
BALLISTIC
DANGEROUS, THE
DECOY
EXECUTIONERS
EXPERT, THE
HEROIC TRIO, THE
HUNTED, THE
LAST SAMURAI, THE
MORTAL KOMBAT
MOSAIC PROJECT, THE
NAKED KILLER
NEW YORK COP
PENTATHLON
RED SUN RISING
RETURN OF THE GOD OF GAMBLERS
SHAO LIN POPEYE
3 NINJAS KNUCKLE UP
TOP DOG

Musical

BRIAN WILSON: I JUST WASN'T MADE FOR
    THESE TIMES
FARINELLI
GEORGIA
GREAT DAY IN HARLEM, A
OH ... ROSALINDA!!
POCAHONTAS
SHOW, THE
TIE-DIED: ROCK 'N' ROLL'S MOST
    DEADICATED FANS

Mystery

CONVENT, THE
DEAD FUNNY
DEVIL IN A BLUE DRESS
DOLORES CLAIBORNE
EXOTICA
FIRST DEGREE
IN THE DEEP WOODS
INNOCENT LIES
MIDNIGHT TEASE 2
MUTE WITNESS
MYSTERY OF RAMPO, THE
PURE FORMALITY, A
SEPARATE LIVES

Opera

OH ... ROSALINDA!!

Political

BANDIT QUEEN
BEFORE THE RAIN
BEYOND RANGOON
BOCA
BURNING SEASON, THE
BURNT BY THE SUN
CANADIAN BACON
ENEMY WITHIN, THE
FATHERLAND
GLORY BOYS, THE
GORILLA BATHES AT NOON
LAMERICA

NIXON
NO MERCY
PANTHER
PROFESSION: NEO-NAZI
PROVINCIAL ACTORS
SHORT FILM ABOUT KILLING, A
STRAWBERRY AND CHOCOLATE
TRAPS
UP TO A CERTAIN POINT

Prison

ACROSS THE MOON
ASCENT, THE
BETTER OFF DEAD
CAGED HEARTS
CAGED HEAT 3000
EXPERT, THE
GETTING OUT
REFLECTIONS IN THE DARK

Religious

CONVENT, THE
I, THE WORST OF ALL
NOSTRADAMUS KID, THE

Romance

AMERICAN COP
AMERICAN PRESIDENT, THE
BAR GIRLS
BEFORE SUNRISE
BRIDGES OF MADISON COUNTY, THE
BROTHERS MCMULLEN, THE
BUSINESS AFFAIR, A
BYE BYE, LOVE
CARRINGTON
CIRCLE OF FRIENDS
CLUELESS
COMPANION, THE
COUNTRY LIFE
CUTTHROAT ISLAND
DON JUAN DEMARCO
DREAMING OF RITA
ENGLISHMAN WHO WENT UP A HILL BUT
    CAME DOWN A MOUNTAIN, THE
FAIR GAME
FEAST OF JULY
FIRST KNIGHT
FORGET PARIS
FRANKIE STARLIGHT
FRENCH KISS
GIRL IN THE CADILLAC
GRUMPIER OLD MEN
HEAVEN'S A DRAG
HE'S A WOMAN, SHE'S A MAN
INCREDIBLY TRUE ADVENTURES OF TWO
    GIRLS IN LOVE, THE
IT TAKES TWO
JEFFERSON IN PARIS
KICKING AND SCREAMING
KILIAN'S CHRONICLE
LAST GOOD TIME, THE
LAST OF THE DOGMEN
LAST RIDE, THE
LIE DOWN WITH DOGS
MAD LOVE
MIAMI RHAPSODY
MOONLIGHT AND VALENTINO
NEA
NINA TAKES A LOVER
NINE MONTHS
NOBODY LOVES ME
PEREZ FAMILY, THE

PERSUASION
PHANTOM LOVER, THE
PICTURE BRIDE
POCAHONTAS
POCAHONTAS: THE LEGEND
PROMISE, THE
PYROMANIAC'S LOVE STORY, A
RED FIRECRACKER, GREEN FIRECRACKER
RESTORATION
RUN OF THE COUNTRY, THE
SABRINA
SCARLET LETTER, THE
SECRET OF ROAN INISH, THE
SENSE AND SENSIBILITY
SERIOUS ABOUT PLEASURE
STRAWBERRY AND CHOCOLATE
TALE OF GENJI, THE
TO CROSS THE RUBICON
TWOGETHER
WALK IN THE CLOUDS, A
WHILE YOU WERE SLEEPING
WINDOW TO PARIS
WOODEN MAN'S BRIDE, THE

Science Fiction

ACCUMULATOR 1
AI CITY
ANDROID AFFAIR, THE
ARMAGEDDON: THE FINAL CHALLENGE
ATTACK OF THE 60-FOOT CENTERFOLD
BIGFOOT: THE UNFORGETTABLE
    ENCOUNTER
CAGED HEAT 3000
COMPANION, THE
CYBER BANDITS
DEATH MACHINE
EVOLVER
GALAXIS
HACKERS
JOHNNY MNEMONIC
JUDGE DREDD
KURT VONNEGUT'S HARRISON BERGERON
MIGHTY MORPHIN POWER RANGERS: THE
    MOVIE
MUTANT SPECIES
ROSWELL: THE U.F.O. COVER-UP
SCANNERS: THE SHOWDOWN
SPECIES
STRANGE DAYS
TANK GIRL
TWELVE MONKEYS
VILLAGE OF THE DAMNED
VIRTUOSITY
WATERWORLD
WICKED CITY
WINGS OF HONNEAMISE: ROYAL SPACE
    FORCE

Sports

BIG GREEN, THE
BREAK, THE
SPITFIRE

Spy

AMERICAN COP
BAD COMPANY
DOOMSDAY GUN
GLORY BOYS, THE
GOLDENEYE
INNOCENT, THE
MOSAIC PROJECT, THE

SPITFIRE
SPY WITHIN, THE

Thriller

ALMOST DEAD
AMATEUR
AMERICA'S DEADLIEST HOME VIDEO
ASSASSINS
BABYSITTER, THE
BAD COMPANY
BALLISTIC
BITTER VENGEANCE
BLUE TIGER
BODILY HARM
BODY CHEMISTRY 4: FULL EXPOSURE
BODY SHOT
BREACH OF CONDUCT
BULLETPROOF HEART
CIRCUMSTANCES UNKNOWN
CITIZEN X
CITY UNPLUGGED
COMPANION, THE
COPYCAT
COVER ME
COVER STORY
CRACKERJACK
CREW, THE
CRIMSON TIDE
DANGER OF LOVE
DARK SIDE OF GENIUS, THE
DECONSTRUCTING SARAH
DESPERATE PREY

DOOMSDAY GUN
DREAM A LITTLE DREAM 2
ENEMY WITHIN, THE
FAIR GAME
FATHERLAND
GLORY BOYS, THE
GOLDENEYE
HACKERS
HIDEAWAY
HUNTED, THE
I LIKE TO PLAY GAMES
IN THE DEEP WOODS
JADE
JOHNNY MNEMONIC
JUDICIAL CONSENT
JUST CAUSE
MALICIOUS
MIDNIGHT TEASE 2
MONEY TRAIN
MUTE WITNESS
NET, THE
NEVER TALK TO STRANGERS
NICK OF TIME
NUMBER ONE FAN
OUT OF ANNIE'S PAST
OUTBREAK
OUTSIDE THE LAW
PAYBACK
SECRETARY, THE
SEPARATE LIVES
SEVEN
SHALLOW GRAVE
STRANGE DAYS

SUDDEN DEATH
TIE THAT BINDS, THE
UNDERNEATH, THE
USUAL SUSPECTS, THE
VIRTUOSITY

War

ASCENT, THE
BEFORE THE RAIN
CHRONICLE OF THE WARSAW GHETTO
    UPRISING ACCORDING TO MAREK
    EDELMAN
CLASS OF '61
CRIMSON TIDE
DEAD PRESIDENTS
FOR GOD AND COUNTRY
OPERATION DUMBO DROP
RICHARD III
STALINGRAD
WALKING DEAD, THE
WOMAN AT WAR, A

Western

AVENGING ANGEL
BLACK FOX
BUFFALO GIRLS
FRANK & JESSE
GHOST BRIGADE
GOOD DAY TO DIE, A
QUICK AND THE DEAD, THE
SUBSTITUTE WIFE, THE
WILD BILL

FILMS BY MPAA RATING

The Motion Picture Association of America (MPAA) currently grades films according to the following codes:

G GENERAL AUDIENCES (All ages admitted)
PG PARENTAL GUIDANCE SUGGESTED (Some material may not be suitable for children)
PG-13 PARENTS STRONGLY CAUTIONED (Some material may be inappropriate for children under 13)
R RESTRICTED (Under 17 requires accompanying parent or adult guardian)
NC-17 NO CHILDREN UNDER 17 ADMITTED
NR NOT RATED

G

ACROSS THE SEA OF TIME: NEW YORK 3D
ARABIAN KNIGHT
BABE
BALTO
GOOFY MOVIE, A
GORDY
GUMBY: THE MOVIE
LITTLE PRINCESS, A
MARTHA & ETHEL
PEBBLE AND THE PENGUIN, THE
POCAHONTAS
RENT-A-KID
THROUGH THE OLIVE TREES
TOY STORY
WINGS OF COURAGE

PG

AMAZING PANDA ADVENTURE, THE
APOLLO 13
ASCENT, THE
BABY-SITTERS CLUB, THE
BIG GREEN, THE
BIGFOOT: THE UNFORGETTABLE
  ENCOUNTER
BORN TO BE WILD
CANADIAN BACON
CASPER
CRY, THE BELOVED COUNTRY
DARK DEALER
DIGGER
DR. JEKYLL & MS. HYDE
ENGLISHMAN WHO WENT UP A HILL BUT
  CAME DOWN A MOUNTAIN, THE
FAR FROM HOME: THE ADVENTURES OF
  YELLOW DOG
FATHER AND SCOUT
FATHER OF THE BRIDE PART II
FLUKE
FRANK AND OLLIE
FREE WILLY 2: THE ADVENTURE HOME
GOLD DIGGERS: THE SECRET OF BEAR
  MOUNTAIN
HEAVYWEIGHTS
HOUSEGUEST
INDIAN IN THE CUPBOARD, THE
IT TAKES TWO
JUMANJI
KID IN KING ARTHUR'S COURT, A
LAST OF THE DOGMEN
MAGIC IN THE WATER
MAN OF THE HOUSE
MIGHTY MORPHIN POWER RANGERS: THE
  MOVIE
MONTH BY THE LAKE, A
MY ANTONIA

OPERATION DUMBO DROP
PERSUASION
PIANO LESSON, THE
POSTMAN, THE
PREHYSTERIA! 3
PYROMANIAC'S LOVE STORY, A
REDWOOD CURTAIN
RETURN OF THE NATIVE, THE
ROOMMATES
SABRINA
SECRET OF ROAN INISH, THE
SENSE AND SENSIBILITY
STARS FELL ON HENRIETTA, THE
TALL TALE: THE UNBELIEVABLE
  ADVENTURES OF PECOS BILL
THREE WISHES
TOM AND HUCK
UNSTRUNG HEROES
WHILE YOU WERE SLEEPING

PG-13

ACE VENTURA: WHEN NATURE CALLS
AMERICAN COP
AMERICAN PRESIDENT, THE
ANDROID AFFAIR, THE
ANGUS
BATMAN FOREVER
BILLY MADISON
BRADY BUNCH MOVIE, THE
BREACH OF CONDUCT
BREAK, THE
BRIDGES OF MADISON COUNTY, THE
BUSHWHACKED
BYE BYE, LOVE
CIRCLE OF FRIENDS
CLUELESS
CONGO
COUNTRY LIFE
CRAZYSITTER, THE
CURE, THE
CUTTHROAT ISLAND
DON JUAN DEMARCO
DOUBLE HAPPINESS
DRACULA: DEAD AND LOVING IT
DREAM A LITTLE DREAM 2
EMPIRE RECORDS
FIRST KNIGHT
FORGET PARIS
FRENCH KISS
GLASS SHIELD, THE
GOLDENEYE
GRUMPIER OLD MEN
HACKERS
HOME FOR THE HOLIDAYS
HOW TO MAKE AN AMERICAN QUILT

JEFFERSON IN PARIS
JOURNEY OF AUGUST KING, THE
JURY DUTY
MAD LOVE
MAJOR PAYNE
MIAMI RHAPSODY
MORTAL KOMBAT
NET, THE
NIGHTMARE
NINE MONTHS
NOW AND THEN
PICTURE BRIDE
POWDER
RECKLESS
ROSWELL: THE U.F.O. COVER-UP
SAFE PASSAGE
STEAL BIG, STEAL LITTLE
STUART SAVES HIS FAMILY
SUBSTITUTE WIFE, THE
3 NINJAS KNUCKLE UP
TO WONG FOO, THANKS FOR
  EVERYTHING! JULIE NEWMAR
TOMMY BOY
TOP DOG
TWO BITS
WALK IN THE CLOUDS, A
WATERWORLD
WINDOW TO PARIS
WOMAN AT WAR, A

R

ABDUCTED 2: THE REUNION
ACROSS THE MOON
AMATEUR
ASSASSINS
ATTACK OF THE 60-FOOT CENTERFOLD
AWFULLY BIG ADVENTURE, AN
BABYSITTER, THE
BAD BLOOD
BAD BOYS
BAD COMPANY
BALLISTIC
BAR GIRLS
BASKETBALL DIARIES, THE
BEFORE SUNRISE
BEYOND RANGOON
BITTER VENGEANCE
BLUE IN THE FACE
BLUE TIGER
BOCA
BODILY HARM
BODY CHEMISTRY 4: FULL EXPOSURE
BODY SHOT
BOULEVARD
BOYS ON THE SIDE

BRAVEHEART
BROTHERS MCMULLEN, THE
BURNT BY THE SUN
CAGED HEAT 3000
CANDYMAN: FAREWELL TO THE FLESH
CARRINGTON
CASINO
CASTLE FREAK
CENTURY
CHILDREN OF THE CORN III: URBAN
   HARVEST
CIRCUMSTANCES UNKNOWN
CITY OF LOST CHILDREN, THE
CLEAN, SHAVEN
CLOCKERS
COLDBLOODED
CONVICT COWBOY
COPYCAT
COSMIC SLOP
COVER ME
CRACKERJACK
CREW, THE
CRIMSON TIDE
CROSSING GUARD, THE
CRUDE OASIS, THE
CRUMB
CYBER BANDITS
DANGER OF LOVE
DANGEROUS MINDS
DARK SIDE OF GENIUS, THE
DARKMAN 2: THE RETURN OF DURANT
DEAD FUNNY
DEAD MAN WALKING
DEAD PRESIDENTS
DEATH IN BRUNSWICK
DEATH MACHINE
DECONSTRUCTING SARAH
DECOY
DESPERADO
DESPERATE PREY
DESTINY TURNS ON THE RADIO
DEVIL IN A BLUE DRESS
DIE HARD WITH A VENGEANCE
DILLINGER AND CAPONE
DOLORES CLAIBORNE
EVOLVER
EXOTICA
EXPERT, THE
FAIR GAME
FARINELLI
FEAR, THE
FEAST OF JULY
FIRST DEGREE
FOOL AND HIS MONEY, A
FOUR ROOMS
FRANK & JESSE
FRANKIE STARLIGHT
FRIDAY
FUNNY BONES
GALAXIS
GEORGIA
GET SHORTY
GHOST BRIGADE
GIRL IN THE CADILLAC
GOOD DAY TO DIE, A
GRANNY, THE
GROSS MISCONDUCT
GROSSE FATIGUE
HALLOWEEN: THE CURSE OF MICHAEL
   MYERS
HEAT
HIDEAWAY
HIGHER LEARNING
HIGHLANDER: THE FINAL DIMENSION

HOWLING: NEW MOON RISING, THE
HUNTED, THE
IN THE MOUTH OF MADNESS
INCREDIBLY TRUE ADVENTURES OF TWO
   GIRLS IN LOVE, THE
INDICTMENT: THE MCMARTIN TRIAL
JACK-O
JADE
JEFFREY
JERKY BOYS: THE MOVIE, THE
JOHNNY MNEMONIC
JUDGE DREDD
JUST CAUSE
KICKING AND SCREAMING
KINGDOM, THE
KISS OF DEATH
KURT VONNEGUT'S HARRISON BERGERON
LAST RIDE, THE
LAST SUMMER IN THE HAMPTONS
LEAVING LAS VEGAS
LES MISERABLES
LIE DOWN WITH DOGS
LITTLE ODESSA
LIVING IN OBLIVION
LORD OF ILLUSIONS
LOSING ISAIAH
LOVE AND HUMAN REMAINS
MALICIOUS
MALLRATS
MANGLER, THE
ME AND THE MOB
MIGHTY APHRODITE
MONEY TRAIN
MOONLIGHT AND VALENTINO
MOSAIC PROJECT, THE
MURDER IN THE FIRST
MURIEL'S WEDDING
MUTANT SPECIES
MUTE WITNESS
MY FAMILY: MI FAMILIA
NADJA
NATIONAL LAMPOON'S ATTACK OF THE
   5'2" WOMEN
NATIONAL LAMPOON'S SENIOR TRIP
NEA
NEVER TALK TO STRANGERS
NEW JERSEY DRIVE
NEW YORK COP
NEXT DOOR
NICK OF TIME
NINA TAKES A LOVER
NIXON
NOSTRADAMUS KID, THE
NUMBER ONE FAN
ONCE WERE WARRIORS
OPERATION INTERCEPT
OTHELLO
OUT OF ANNIE'S PAST
OUT OF SYNC
OUTBREAK
PANTHER
PARTY GIRL
PAYBACK
PENTATHLON
PEREZ FAMILY, THE
POWER OF ATTORNEY
PROMISE, THE
PROPHECY, THE
QUICK AND THE DEAD, THE
REASON TO BELIEVE, A
RED SUN RISING
REFLECTIONS IN THE DARK
RESTORATION
RICHARD III

ROB ROY
RUN OF THE COUNTRY, THE
SAFE
SCANNERS: THE SHOWDOWN
SCARLET LETTER, THE
SEARCH AND DESTROY
SECRETARY, THE
SEPARATE LIVES
SEVEN
S.F.W.
SHALLOW GRAVE
SHANGHAI TRIAD
SHOW, THE
SILENCE OF THE HAMS
SMOKE
SOMETHING TO TALK ABOUT
SPECIES
SPITFIRE
SPY WITHIN, THE
STRANGE DAYS
SUDDEN DEATH
SWIMMING WITH SHARKS
TALES FROM THE CRYPT: DEMON KNIGHT
TALES FROM THE HOOD
TANK GIRL
TERESA'S TATTOO
THINGS TO DO IN DENVER WHEN YOU'RE
   DEAD
TIE-DIED: ROCK 'N' ROLL'S MOST
   DEADICATED FANS
TIE THAT BINDS, THE
TO DIE FOR
TOO OUTRAGEOUS ANIMATION
TOO YOUNG TO DIE?
TOTAL ECLIPSE
TRAPS
TWELVE MONKEYS
TWOGETHER
UNDER SIEGE 2: DARK TERRITORY
UNDERNEATH, THE
UNZIPPED
USUAL SUSPECTS, THE
VAMPIRE IN BROOKLYN
VILLAGE OF THE DAMNED
VIRTUOSITY
WAITING TO EXHALE
WALKING DEAD, THE
WHITE MAN'S BURDEN
WILD BILL
YOUNGER & YOUNGER
ZOOMAN

NC-17

SHOWGIRLS

NR

ACCUMULATOR 1
ADDICTION, THE
ADVENTURES OF MATT THE GOOSEBOY,
   THE
AI CITY
AILSA
ALMOST DEAD
AMERICA'S DEADLIEST HOME VIDEO
ARIZONA DREAM
ARMAGEDDON: THE FINAL CHALLENGE
ART FOR TEACHERS OF CHILDREN
ASHES OF TIME
AUGUSTIN
AVENGING ANGEL
BALLET
BALLOT MEASURE 9
BANDIT QUEEN

BAREFOOT GEN
BED YOU SLEEP IN, THE
BEFORE THE RAIN
BETRAYAL
BETTER OFF DEAD
BIKINI BISTRO
BLACK FOX
BLACK IS ... BLACK AIN'T
BLESSING
BLUE VILLA, THE
BODY STROKES
BRIAN WILSON: I JUST WASN'T MADE FOR
    THESE TIMES
BROKEN TRUST
BUFFALO GIRLS
BULLETPROOF HEART
BURNING SEASON, THE
BUSINESS AFFAIR, A
CAGED HEARTS
CARMEN MIRANDA: BANANAS IS MY
    BUSINESS
CHARULATA
CHRONICLE OF THE WARSAW GHETTO
    UPRISING ACCORDING TO MAREK
    EDELMAN
CITIZEN X
CITY UNPLUGGED
CLASS OF '61
COLORADO COWBOY: THE BRUCE FORD
    STORY
COMPANION, THE
CONGRESS OF PENGUINS, THE
CONVENT, THE
COVER STORY
COW, THE
CREATION OF ADAM
CREEP
CRIMSON WOLF
CURSE OF THE STARVING CLASS
DALLAS DOLL
DANCE ME OUTSIDE
DANCER, THE
DANGEROUS, THE
DAY THE SUN TURNED COLD, THE
DEADLY MARIA
DILLINGER
DIRTY MONEY
DOOM GENERATION, THE
DOOMSDAY GUN
DOUBLE, DOUBLE, TOIL AND TROUBLE
DREAMING OF RITA
ECLIPSE
EMBRACE OF THE VAMPIRE
ENEMY WITHIN, THE
ERMO
EROTIQUE
ETERNITY
EXECUTIONERS
FACES OF WOMEN

FATHERLAND
FOR GOD AND COUNTRY
FRAMEUP
FRIENDS
FUN
GETTING OUT
GLORY BOYS, THE
GOOD GIRLS DON'T
GORILLA BATHES AT NOON
GREAT DAY IN HARLEM, A
GREAT ELEPHANT ESCAPE, THE
HARLEM DIARY: NINE VOICES OF
    RESILIENCE
HEAVEN'S A DRAG
HEROIC TRIO, THE
HE'S A WOMAN, SHE'S A MAN
HIGH RISK
HOTEL SORRENTO
HOW TO TOP MY WIFE
HYENAS
I AM CUBA
I CAN'T SLEEP
I LIKE TO PLAY GAMES
I, THE WORST OF ALL
IN THE DEEP WOODS
IN THE NAME OF THE EMPEROR
INNOCENT LIES
INNOCENT, THE
JAR, THE
JLG BY JLG
JUDICIAL CONSENT
JUPITER'S WIFE
KIDS
KILIAN'S CHRONICLE
KINGFISH: A STORY OF HUEY P. LONG
LAKOTA WOMAN: SIEGE AT WOUNDED
    KNEE
LAMB
LAMERICA
LAST GOOD TIME, THE
LAST SAMURAI, THE
LESSONS OF DARKNESS
MACHINE DREAMS
MARTHA AND I
MAYA LIN: A STRONG CLEAR VISION
MEET THE FEEBLES
MESSENGER
METAL AND MELANCHOLY
MIDNIGHT TEASE 2
MINA TANNENBAUM
MOVING THE MOUNTAIN
MY LIFE AND TIMES WITH ANTONIN
    ARTAUD
MYSTERY OF RAMPO, THE
NAKED KILLER
NEKROMANTIK
NO MERCY
NOBODY LOVES ME
NOT ANGELS BUT ANGELS

OH ... ROSALINDA!!
O.J. SIMPSON STORY, THE
OLD LADY WHO WALKED IN THE SEA, THE
1-900
ONLY THE BRAVE
OUTSIDE THE LAW
PHANTOM LOVER, THE
PIGALLE
PLAY TIME
POCAHONTAS: THE LEGEND
POSTCARDS FROM AMERICA
PRIEST
PROFESSION: NEO-NAZI
PROVINCIAL ACTORS
PURE FORMALITY, A
PUSHING HANDS
RADIO INSIDE
RED FIRECRACKER, GREEN FIRECRACKER
REMOTE CONTROL
RETURN OF THE GOD OF GAMBLERS
RHYTHM THIEF
RIVER OF GRASS
ROY COHN/JACK SMITH
SERIOUS ABOUT PLEASURE
SEX, DRUGS AND DEMOCRACY
SHAO LIN POPEYE
SHORT FILM ABOUT KILLING, A
SHORT FILM ABOUT LOVE, A
SISTER MY SISTER
SIX DAYS, SIX NIGHTS
SKINNER
SON OF THE SHARK, THE
SPIKE AND MIKE'S FESTIVAL OF
    ANIMATION '95
STALINGRAD
STRANGER, THE
STRAWBERRY AND CHOCOLATE
SUM OF US, THE
TO CROSS THE RUBICON
TWENTY SOMETHING
UNDERCOVER
UP TO A CERTAIN POINT
VALLEY OF ABRAHAM, THE
VAMPIRES AND OTHER STEREOTYPES
VOYAGE EN DOUCE
WATER ENGINE, THE
WHEN BILLY BROKE HIS HEAD ... AND
    OTHER TALES OF WONDER
WHEN NIGHT IS FALLING
WICKED CITY
WIGSTOCK: THE MOVIE
WILD REEDS
WINGS OF HONNEAMISE: ROYAL SPACE
    FORCE
WITHOUT ANESTHESIA
WIZARD OF DARKNESS
WOODEN MAN'S BRIDE, THE
WORLD AND TIME ENOUGH

FILMS BY PARENTAL RECOMMENDATION (PR)

AA – good for children; A – acceptable for children;
C – cautionary, some scenes may be objectionable for children; O – objectionable for children

AA

ADVENTURES OF MATT THE GOOSEBOY, THE
AMERICAN PRESIDENT, THE
ANGUS
APOLLO 13
ARIZONA DREAM
ASCENT, THE
BABE
BABY-SITTERS CLUB, THE
BALLET
BALLOT MEASURE 9
BETRAYAL
BIG GREEN, THE
BLUE IN THE FACE
BORN TO BE WILD
BRADY BUNCH MOVIE, THE
BRIAN WILSON: I JUST WASN'T MADE FOR THESE TIMES
BUSHWHACKED
BYE BYE, LOVE
CANADIAN BACON
CARMEN MIRANDA: BANANAS IS MY BUSINESS
CASPER
CHARULATA
CONGO
CRAZYSITTER, THE
CRY, THE BELOVED COUNTRY
CUTTHROAT ISLAND
DANCER, THE
DAY THE SUN TURNED COLD, THE
ENGLISHMAN WHO WENT UP A HILL BUT CAME DOWN A MOUNTAIN, THE
ERMO
ETERNITY
FAR FROM HOME: THE ADVENTURES OF YELLOW DOG
FATHER OF THE BRIDE PART II
FIRST KNIGHT
FLUKE
FOOL AND HIS MONEY, A
FORGET PARIS
FRANKIE STARLIGHT
FRENCH KISS
GOLD DIGGERS: THE SECRET OF BEAR MOUNTAIN
GRUMPIER OLD MEN
HARLEM DIARY: NINE VOICES OF RESILIENCE
HEAVYWEIGHTS
HOME FOR THE HOLIDAYS
HOTEL SORRENTO
HOUSEGUEST
HOW TO MAKE AN AMERICAN QUILT
I AM CUBA
I, THE WORST OF ALL
IN THE DEEP WOODS
IT TAKES TWO
JEFFERSON IN PARIS
JLG BY JLG
JUMANJI

KID IN KING ARTHUR'S COURT, A
LAKOTA WOMAN: SIEGE AT WOUNDED KNEE
LAMB
LAMERICA
LAST OF THE DOGMEN
LESSONS OF DARKNESS
MAJOR PAYNE
MAN OF THE HOUSE
MARTHA & ETHEL
METAL AND MELANCHOLY
MIGHTY MORPHIN POWER RANGERS: THE MOVIE
MONTH BY THE LAKE, A
MORTAL KOMBAT
MOVING THE MOUNTAIN
MY ANTONIA
NIGHTMARE
NINE MONTHS
NOW AND THEN
OH ... ROSALINDA!!
OPERATION DUMBO DROP
PERSUASION
PICTURE BRIDE
POSTMAN, THE
PROMISE, THE
PUSHING HANDS
PYROMANIAC'S LOVE STORY, A
REDWOOD CURTAIN
REMOTE CONTROL
RETURN OF THE NATIVE, THE
ROOMMATES
SABRINA
SENSE AND SENSIBILITY
SHAO LIN POPEYE
STARS FELL ON HENRIETTA, THE
STEAL BIG, STEAL LITTLE
STUART SAVES HIS FAMILY
TALL TALE: THE UNBELIEVABLE ADVENTURES OF PECOS BILL
3 NINJAS KNUCKLE UP
THREE WISHES
TOM AND HUCK
TOMMY BOY
TOP DOG
TWO BITS
UNSTRUNG HEROES
WATERWORLD
WHEN BILLY BROKE HIS HEAD ... AND OTHER TALES OF WONDER
WHILE YOU WERE SLEEPING
WITHOUT ANESTHESIA
YOUNGER & YOUNGER

A

ACROSS THE SEA OF TIME: NEW YORK 3D
AMAZING PANDA ADVENTURE, THE
ARABIAN KNIGHT
BALTO
BIGFOOT: THE UNFORGETTABLE ENCOUNTER

COLORADO COWBOY: THE BRUCE FORD STORY
DIGGER
DOUBLE, DOUBLE, TOIL AND TROUBLE
DREAMING OF RITA
FATHER AND SCOUT
FRANK AND OLLIE
FREE WILLY 2: THE ADVENTURE HOME
GOOFY MOVIE, A
GORDY
GREAT DAY IN HARLEM, A
GREAT ELEPHANT ESCAPE, THE
GUMBY: THE MOVIE
INDIAN IN THE CUPBOARD, THE
JAR, THE
KILIAN'S CHRONICLE
LITTLE PRINCESS, A
MAGIC IN THE WATER
MAYA LIN: A STRONG CLEAR VISION
PEBBLE AND THE PENGUIN, THE
POCAHONTAS
PREHYSTERIA! 3
RENT-A-KID
SECRET OF ROAN INISH, THE
STRANGER, THE
THROUGH THE OLIVE TREES
TOY STORY
WINGS OF COURAGE

C

ACE VENTURA: WHEN NATURE CALLS
AI CITY
ALMOST DEAD
AMATEUR
AMERICAN COP
ANDROID AFFAIR, THE
ASHES OF TIME
ASSASSINS
AUGUSTIN
AVENGING ANGEL
AWFULLY BIG ADVENTURE, AN
BAR GIRLS
BAREFOOT GEN
BASKETBALL DIARIES, THE
BATMAN FOREVER
BED YOU SLEEP IN, THE
BEFORE SUNRISE
BEFORE THE RAIN
BEYOND RANGOON
BILLY MADISON
BITTER VENGEANCE
BLACK FOX
BLACK IS ... BLACK AIN'T
BLESSING
BLUE VILLA, THE
BOYS ON THE SIDE
BREACH OF CONDUCT
BREAK, THE
BRIDGES OF MADISON COUNTY, THE
BROKEN TRUST
BROTHERS MCMULLEN, THE

BUFFALO GIRLS
BULLETPROOF HEART
BURNING SEASON, THE
BURNT BY THE SUN
BUSINESS AFFAIR, A
CENTURY
CHRONICLE OF THE WARSAW GHETTO
    UPRISING ACCORDING TO MAREK
    EDELMAN
CIRCLE OF FRIENDS
CIRCUMSTANCES UNKNOWN
CITIZEN X
CITY OF LOST CHILDREN, THE
CITY UNPLUGGED
CLASS OF '61
CLUELESS
COMPANION, THE
CONGRESS OF PENGUINS, THE
CONVENT, THE
CONVICT COWBOY
COUNTRY LIFE
COW, THE
CREATION OF ADAM
CREW, THE
CRIMSON TIDE
CRUDE OASIS, THE
CRUMB
CURE, THE
CURSE OF THE STARVING CLASS
DANCE ME OUTSIDE
DANGER OF LOVE
DANGEROUS MINDS
DARKMAN 2: THE RETURN OF DURANT
DEAD MAN WALKING
DEATH IN BRUNSWICK
DECOY
DESPERADO
DESTINY TURNS ON THE RADIO
DEVIL IN A BLUE DRESS
DIE HARD WITH A VENGEANCE
DILLINGER AND CAPONE
DR. JEKYLL & MS. HYDE
DOLORES CLAIBORNE
DON JUAN DEMARCO
DOOMSDAY GUN
DOUBLE HAPPINESS
DRACULA: DEAD AND LOVING IT
DREAM A LITTLE DREAM 2
EMPIRE RECORDS
ENEMY WITHIN, THE
EXECUTIONERS
FACES OF WOMEN
FAIR GAME
FATHERLAND
FEAST OF JULY
FOR GOD AND COUNTRY
FRAMEUP
FRANK & JESSE
FRIDAY
FRIENDS
FUN
FUNNY BONES
GALAXIS
GEORGIA
GET SHORTY
GETTING OUT
GHOST BRIGADE
GIRL IN THE CADILLAC
GLASS SHIELD, THE
GLORY BOYS, THE
GOLDENEYE
GOOD DAY TO DIE, A
GORILLA BATHES AT NOON
GROSSE FATIGUE

HACKERS
HEAVEN'S A DRAG
HEROIC TRIO, THE
HE'S A WOMAN, SHE'S A MAN
HIGHER LEARNING
HIGHLANDER: THE FINAL DIMENSION
HUNTED, THE
HYENAS
INCREDIBLY TRUE ADVENTURES OF TWO
    GIRLS IN LOVE, THE
INDICTMENT: THE MCMARTIN TRIAL
JOHNNY MNEMONIC
JOURNEY OF AUGUST KING, THE
JUDGE DREDD
JUPITER'S WIFE
JURY DUTY
KICKING AND SCREAMING
KINGDOM, THE
KINGFISH: A STORY OF HUEY P. LONG
KISS OF DEATH
KURT VONNEGUT'S HARRISON BERGERON
LAST GOOD TIME, THE
LAST SAMURAI, THE
LAST SUMMER IN THE HAMPTONS
LES MISERABLES
LIVING IN OBLIVION
LOSING ISAIAH
MACHINE DREAMS
MAD LOVE
MALLRATS
MARTHA AND I
MESSENGER
MIAMI RHAPSODY
MIGHTY APHRODITE
MINA TANNENBAUM
MONEY TRAIN
MOONLIGHT AND VALENTINO
MOSAIC PROJECT, THE
MURDER IN THE FIRST
MURIEL'S WEDDING
MUTE WITNESS
MY FAMILY: MI FAMILIA
MY LIFE AND TIMES WITH ANTONIN
    ARTAUD
NADJA
NAKED KILLER
NET, THE
NEW JERSEY DRIVE
NEW YORK COP
NICK OF TIME
NINA TAKES A LOVER
NIXON
NO MERCY
NOSTRADAMUS KID, THE
O.J. SIMPSON STORY, THE
ONLY THE BRAVE
OPERATION INTERCEPT
OTHELLO
OUT OF ANNIE'S PAST
OUT OF SYNC
OUTBREAK
PANTHER
PARTY GIRL
PENTATHLON
PEREZ FAMILY, THE
PHANTOM LOVER, THE
PIANO LESSON, THE
POCAHONTAS: THE LEGEND
POWDER
POWER OF ATTORNEY
PRIEST
PROFESSION: NEO-NAZI
PROVINCIAL ACTORS
PURE FORMALITY, A

QUICK AND THE DEAD, THE
RADIO INSIDE
RECKLESS
RED FIRECRACKER, GREEN FIRECRACKER
RED SUN RISING
RESTORATION
RETURN OF THE GOD OF GAMBLERS
RICHARD III
RIVER OF GRASS
ROB ROY
ROSWELL: THE U.F.O. COVER-UP
ROY COHN/JACK SMITH
RUN OF THE COUNTRY, THE
SAFE
SAFE PASSAGE
SCARLET LETTER, THE
SECRETARY, THE
SERIOUS ABOUT PLEASURE
SHALLOW GRAVE
SHANGHAI TRIAD
SHORT FILM ABOUT LOVE, A
SHOW, THE
SMOKE
SOMETHING TO TALK ABOUT
SON OF THE SHARK, THE
SPIKE AND MIKE'S FESTIVAL OF
    ANIMATION '95
SPITFIRE
STALINGRAD
SUBSTITUTE WIFE, THE
SUDDEN DEATH
SUM OF US, THE
TALE OF GENJI, THE
TALES FROM THE HOOD
TANK GIRL
TERESA'S TATTOO
TIE-DIED: ROCK 'N' ROLL'S MOST
    DEADICATED FANS
TIE THAT BINDS, THE
TO CROSS THE RUBICON
TO DIE FOR
TO WONG FOO, THANKS FOR
    EVERYTHING! JULIE NEWMAR
TWELVE MONKEYS
UNDER SIEGE 2: DARK TERRITORY
UNDERNEATH, THE
UNZIPPED
UP TO A CERTAIN POINT
VALLEY OF ABRAHAM, THE
VAMPIRE IN BROOKLYN
VILLAGE OF THE DAMNED
WAITING TO EXHALE
WALK IN THE CLOUDS, A
WATER ENGINE, THE
WHITE MAN'S BURDEN
WIGSTOCK: THE MOVIE
WILD BILL
WILD REEDS
WINDOW TO PARIS
WINGS OF HONNEAMISE: ROYAL SPACE
    FORCE
WOMAN AT WAR, A
WOODEN MAN'S BRIDE, THE
WORLD AND TIME ENOUGH
ZOOMAN

O

ABDUCTED 2: THE REUNION
ACCUMULATOR 1
ACROSS THE MOON
ADDICTION, THE
AILSA
AMERICA'S DEADLIEST HOME VIDEO
ARMAGEDDON: THE FINAL CHALLENGE

ART FOR TEACHERS OF CHILDREN
ATTACK OF THE 60-FOOT CENTERFOLD
BABYSITTER, THE
BAD BLOOD
BAD BOYS
BAD COMPANY
BALLISTIC
BANDIT QUEEN
BETTER OFF DEAD
BIKINI BISTRO
BLUE TIGER
BOCA
BODILY HARM
BODY CHEMISTRY 4: FULL EXPOSURE
BODY SHOT
BODY STROKES
BOULEVARD
BRAVEHEART
CAGED HEARTS
CAGED HEAT 3000
CANDYMAN: FAREWELL TO THE FLESH
CARRINGTON
CASINO
CASTLE FREAK
CHILDREN OF THE CORN III: URBAN
  HARVEST
CLEAN, SHAVEN
CLOCKERS
COLDBLOODED
COPYCAT
COSMIC SLOP
COVER ME
COVER STORY
CRACKERJACK
CREEP
CRIMSON WOLF
CROSSING GUARD, THE
CYBER BANDITS
DALLAS DOLL
DANGEROUS, THE
DARK DEALER
DARK SIDE OF GENIUS, THE
DEAD FUNNY
DEAD PRESIDENTS
DEADLY MARIA
DEATH MACHINE
DECONSTRUCTING SARAH
DESPERATE PREY
DILLINGER
DIRTY MONEY
DOOM GENERATION, THE

ECLIPSE
EMBRACE OF THE VAMPIRE
EROTIQUE
EVOLVER
EXOTICA
EXPERT, THE
FARINELLI
FEAR, THE
FIRST DEGREE
FOUR ROOMS
GOOD GIRLS DON'T
GRANNY, THE
GROSS MISCONDUCT
HALLOWEEN: THE CURSE OF MICHAEL
  MYERS
HEAT
HIDEAWAY
HIGH RISK
HOW TO TOP MY WIFE
HOWLING: NEW MOON RISING, THE
I CAN'T SLEEP
I LIKE TO PLAY GAMES
IN THE MOUTH OF MADNESS
IN THE NAME OF THE EMPEROR
INNOCENT LIES
INNOCENT, THE
JACK-O
JADE
JEFFREY
JERKY BOYS: THE MOVIE, THE
JUDICIAL CONSENT
JUST CAUSE
KIDS
LAST RIDE, THE
LEAVING LAS VEGAS
LIE DOWN WITH DOGS
LITTLE ODESSA
LORD OF ILLUSIONS
LOVE AND HUMAN REMAINS
MALICIOUS
MANGLER, THE
ME AND THE MOB
MEET THE FEEBLES
MIDNIGHT TEASE 2
MUTANT SPECIES
MYSTERY OF RAMPO, THE
NATIONAL LAMPOON'S ATTACK OF THE
  5'2" WOMEN
NATIONAL LAMPOON'S SENIOR TRIP
NEA
NEKROMANTIK
NEVER TALK TO STRANGERS

NEXT DOOR
sNOBODY LOVES ME
NOT ANGELS BUT ANGELS
NUMBER ONE FAN
OLD LADY WHO WALKED IN THE SEA, THE
ONCE WERE WARRIORS
1-900
OUTSIDE THE LAW
PAYBACK
PIGALLE
PLAY TIME
POSTCARDS FROM AMERICA
PROPHECY, THE
REASON TO BELIEVE, A
REFLECTIONS IN THE DARK
RHYTHM THIEF
SCANNERS: THE SHOWDOWN
SEARCH AND DESTROY
SEPARATE LIVES
SEVEN
SEX, DRUGS AND DEMOCRACY
S.F.W.
SHORT FILM ABOUT KILLING, A
SHOWGIRLS
SILENCE OF THE HAMS
SISTER MY SISTER
SIX DAYS, SIX NIGHTS
SKINNER
SPECIES
SPY WITHIN, THE
STRANGE DAYS
STRAWBERRY AND CHOCOLATE
SWIMMING WITH SHARKS
TALES FROM THE CRYPT: DEMON KNIGHT
THINGS TO DO IN DENVER WHEN YOU'RE
  DEAD
TOO OUTRAGEOUS ANIMATION
TOO YOUNG TO DIE?
TOTAL ECLIPSE
TRAPS
TWENTY SOMETHING
TWOGETHER
UNDERCOVER
USUAL SUSPECTS, THE
VAMPIRES AND OTHER STEREOTYPES
VIRTUOSITY
VOYAGE EN DOUCE
WALKING DEAD, THE
WHEN NIGHT IS FALLING
WICKED CITY
WIZARD OF DARKNESS

NAME INDEX

Individuals included in the cast or credit sections of the film reviews in this volume are listed below. Names are arranged alphabetically by function as follows:

Actors
Animators
Art Directors
Associate Producers
Casting
Choreographers
Cinematographers

Co-producers
Costumes
Directors
Editors
Executive Producers
Makeup/ FX makeup
Music Composers
Producers

Production Designers
Screenwriters
Set Decorators
Sound
Source Authors
Special Effects
Stunts

ACTORS

"Sniff"
FUNNY BONES
Aalda, Mariann
O.J. SIMPSON STORY, THE
Abascal, Margot
LES MISERABLES
Abatemarco, Tony
DECONSTRUCTING SARAH
Abbott, Bruce
DILLINGER
Abbott, Jennifer M.
CASINO
Abdul-Jabbar, Kareem
FORGET PARIS
Abdullah, Siti
BEYOND RANGOON
Abe, Hiroshi
MYSTERY OF RAMPO, THE
Abe, Y. Hero
JURY DUTY
SHOWGIRLS
Abedi, Barbara
NET, THE
Abelar, Michael
CROSSING GUARD, THE
Abell, Tim
ATTACK OF THE 60-FOOT CENTERFOLD
Abels, Lauren
CURSE OF THE STARVING CLASS
NUMBER ONE FAN
Aber, Chuck
HOUSEGUEST
Abourezk, James
LAKOTA WOMAN: SIEGE AT WOUNDED KNEE
Abraham, F. Murray
DILLINGER AND CAPONE
MIGHTY APHRODITE
Abraham, Falconer
FIRST DEGREE
JOHNNY MNEMONIC
Abrahams, Jon
DEAD MAN WALKING
Abramov, Oleg
MUTE WITNESS
Abrams, Noah
ROOMMATES
Abrams, Solomon
QUICK AND THE DEAD, THE
Abreu, Jorge Luis
JURY DUTY
Abston, Dean
TOO YOUNG TO DIE?
Abuba, Ernest
TWELVE MONKEYS
Achar, Ravi
SAFE

Acheson, James
STRANGE DAYS
Acheson, Marc
MAGIC IN THE WATER
Acheson, Mark
BULLETPROOF HEART
Ackerman, Forrest J.
ATTACK OF THE 60-FOOT CENTERFOLD
Ackland, Joss
CITIZEN X
KID IN KING ARTHUR'S COURT, A
Ackroyd, Gayle
FIRST DEGREE
Ackroyd, Jack
GOOD DAY TO DIE, A
Acres, Mary
BABE
Acton, David
PERSUASION
Adakai-Nez, Randy
PROPHECY, THE
Adam, Marie Christine
FRENCH KISS
Adams, Blake
BODY STROKES
Adams, Brooke
BABY-SITTERS CLUB, THE
Adams, Dave
ROSWELL: THE U.F.O. COVER-UP
Adams, Frederick B.
FUN
Adams, Jane
FATHER OF THE BRIDE PART II
Adams, Joey Lauren
MALLRATS
S.F.W.
Adams, Jojo
BIGFOOT: THE UNFORGETTABLE ENCOUNTER
Adams, Kim
LEAVING LAS VEGAS
Adams, Lillian
UNSTRUNG HEROES
Adams, Lynne
JOHNNY MNEMONIC
Adams, Mason
HOUSEGUEST
Adams, Michael
DESPERATE PREY
Adams, Phillip
DALLAS DOLL
Adams, Timothy
DIE HARD WITH A VENGEANCE
Adams, Wendy
FOOL AND HIS MONEY, A
LIE DOWN WITH DOGS
Adamson, Chris
CUTTHROAT ISLAND
JUDGE DREDD

Adamson, Frank
DOLORES CLAIBORNE
Adamson, Shayne
BREACH OF CONDUCT
Addy, William
MIGHTY APHRODITE
Adele, Jan
SUM OF US, THE
Adelson, Steve
FUN
Aderneck, Stephen
SCARLET LETTER, THE
Adewale
ACE VENTURA: WHEN NATURE CALLS
CONGO
Adeyemi, Ayo
VAMPIRE IN BROOKLYN
Adioukrou People of Lopou Village
FACES OF WOMEN
Adisa, Lawrence B.
CLOCKERS
Adkins, Dan
TIE-DIED: ROCK 'N' ROLL'S MOST DEADICATED FANS
Adler, Cynthia
CARMEN MIRANDA: BANANAS IS MY BUSINESS
Adonis, Frank
CASINO
Adriaans, Mark
IN THE MOUTH OF MADNESS
Adrian, Bob
TWELVE MONKEYS
Adric, Daniel
CITY OF LOST CHILDREN, THE
Affleck, Ben
MALLRATS
Affleck, Casey
TO DIE FOR
Afifi
UNDER SIEGE 2: DARK TERRITORY
Agarwal, Anirudh
BANDIT QUEEN
Agata, Toshiya
I LIKE TO PLAY GAMES
Agnew, Valerie M.
MAD LOVE
Agrait, Carlos Joshua
WALKING DEAD, THE
Aguilar, Denise
LOSING ISAIAH
Aguilar, George
SCARLET LETTER, THE
Aguillar, Nathalie
JLG BY JLG
Ahern, Tim
FORGET PARIS
Ahlers, Ozzie
GUMBY: THE MOVIE

Ahmadpour, Ahmad
  THROUGH THE OLIVE TREES
Ahmadpour, Babk
  THROUGH THE OLIVE TREES
Ahmed, Ahmed
  VIRTUOSITY
Ahmed, Kamal
  JERKY BOYS: THE MOVIE, THE
Ahn, Ralph
  PANTHER
Ahwesh, Peggy
  ART FOR TEACHERS OF CHILDREN
Aidem, Betsy
  NINE MONTHS
Aiello, Anthony
  IT TAKES TWO
Aiello, Danny
  POWER OF ATTORNEY
Aiello, Rick
  CLOCKERS
  POWER OF ATTORNEY
Airlie, Andrew
  POWER OF ATTORNEY
Akahoski, Steve
  O.J. SIMPSON STORY, THE
Akar, Haydar
  DEATH IN BRUNSWICK
Akerman, Jeremy
  SCARLET LETTER, THE
Akersten, Donna
  MEET THE FEEBLES
Akey, William
  FATHER OF THE BRIDE PART II
Akimoto, Yasushi
  MYSTERY OF RAMPO, THE
Akiyama, Denis
  JOHNNY MNEMONIC
Akkus, Orhan
  DEATH IN BRUNSWICK
Aklam
  PANTHER
Alan, Lori
  BOYS ON THE SIDE
  FATHER OF THE BRIDE PART II
Alanis, Samantha
  BABY-SITTERS CLUB, THE
Alaskey, Joe
  CASPER
Albanese, Frank
  DEAD PRESIDENTS
Albarran, Gerardo
  BURNING SEASON, THE
Albert, Edward
  RED SUN RISING
Albert, Greg
  MY FAMILY: MI FAMILIA
Albert, Larry
  BORN TO BE WILD
Albert, Marv
  FORGET PARIS
Albert, Robert
  CLEAN, SHAVEN
Albert, Shari
  BROTHERS MCMULLEN, THE
Alberto, Jorge
  DIRTY MONEY
Alce, Kerline
  RIVER OF GRASS
Alda, Alan
  CANADIAN BACON
Alda, Rutanya
  SAFE PASSAGE
Alden, Jane
  BABE
  BABYSITTER, THE
  HOW TO MAKE AN AMERICAN QUILT

Alden, Priscilla
  NINE MONTHS
Alderson, Brooke
  JUST CAUSE
Alessandro, Bruno
  POSTMAN, THE
Alessi, J.T.
  HEAVYWEIGHTS
Alexander, Brandon
  HOUSEGUEST
Alexander, Bruce
  CENTURY
Alexander, Diane
  FORGET PARIS
Alexander, Eliana H.
  O.J. SIMPSON STORY, THE
Alexander, Jace
  CLUELESS
Alexander, Karen
  BAD BOYS
Alexander, Kenny
  TIE THAT BINDS, THE
Alexander, Michael G.
  AMERICAN PRESIDENT, THE
Alexander, Newell
  TOM AND HUCK
Alexander, Richard D.
  HIGHER LEARNING
Alexander, Robert
  MURIEL'S WEDDING
Alexander, Rosemary
  TOM AND HUCK
Alexander, Terry
  AMATEUR
Alfaro, Manny
  BASKETBALL DIARIES, THE
Alfred, Mark
  RHYTHM THIEF
Alhanko, Anneli
  DANCER, THE
Alia
  ERMO
Alianak, Hrant
  BILLY MADISON
Allain, Aurorah
  TANK GIRL
Allain, Jean
  FRENCH KISS
Allan, Lee
  SILENCE OF THE HAMS
Allan, Richie
  MURDER IN THE FIRST
Allbright, Taylor
  TIE THAT BINDS, THE
Allegue, Karina
  I, THE WORST OF ALL
Allen, Cheryl
  HOWLING: NEW MOON RISING, THE
Allen, Claude "Pappy"
  HOWLING: NEW MOON RISING, THE
Allen, Debbie
  OUT OF SYNC
Allen, Donald
  ONCE WERE WARRIORS
Allen, Eugene
  COSMIC SLOP
Allen, Georgia
  FLUKE
Allen, Harriet
  HOWLING: NEW MOON RISING, THE
Allen, Ivan
  APOLLO 13
Allen, Janet
  HEAVEN'S A DRAG
Allen, Jayne
  WINGS OF HONNEAMISE: ROYAL SPACE
    FORCE

Allen, Joan
  MAD LOVE
  NIXON
Allen, Kayla
  ACE VENTURA: WHEN NATURE CALLS
  EROTIQUE
Allen, Keith
  SHALLOW GRAVE
Allen, Penny
  CROSSING GUARD, THE
Allen, Richard V.
  DIE HARD WITH A VENGEANCE
Allen, Robbie
  PANTHER
Allen, Ronnie
  EXPERT, THE
Allen, Sabrina
  EMBRACE OF THE VAMPIRE
Allen, Sage
  FRANKIE STARLIGHT
Allen, Steve
  CASINO
Allen, Tim
  TOY STORY
Allen, Weldon
  DOLORES CLAIBORNE
Allen, Woody
  MIGHTY APHRODITE
Alley, Kirstie
  IT TAKES TWO
  VILLAGE OF THE DAMNED
Allison, Bill
  CASINO
Allison, Cynthia
  ROSWELL: THE U.F.O. COVER-UP
Allison, Frankie
  CASINO
Allison, Monica
  VIRTUOSITY
Allison, Ray
  THINGS TO DO IN DENVER WHEN
    YOU'RE DEAD
Allora, Jonathan
  PYROMANIAC'S LOVE STORY, A
Allwine, Wayne
  GOOFY MOVIE, A
Almodovar, Robert
  CONGO
Alonso, Margara
  I, THE WORST OF ALL
Alper, Gary
  MIGHTY APHRODITE
Alston, Hakim
  MORTAL KOMBAT
Altamura, John
  BIKINI BISTRO
Altenburg, Leopold
  FOR GOD AND COUNTRY
Alterio, Hector
  I, THE WORST OF ALL
Altman, John
  HEAVEN'S A DRAG
Altmanova, Jana
  MARTHA AND I
Altschuler, Robert
  GREAT DAY IN HARLEM, A
Alvarado, David
  DESPERADO
Alvarado, Nicolas
  I, THE WORST OF ALL
Alvarado, Trini
  PEREZ FAMILY, THE
Alvarez, Elizabeth
  BITTER VENGEANCE
Alvarez, Jose Ignacio
  KICKING AND SCREAMING
Alvarez, Oscar
  UP TO A CERTAIN POINT

Alvarez, Roberto
  DANGEROUS MINDS
Alvarez, Roma
  COSMIC SLOP
Alves, Sofia
  VALLEY OF ABRAHAM, THE
Amador, Andrew
  NET, THE
Amakye, Willie
  CONGO
Amalfitano, Richard
  CASINO
Amamoto, Hideyo
  HUNTED, THE
Amato, Angela
  DIE HARD WITH A VENGEANCE
Amatrudo, Ed
  BAD BOYS
Ambrosini, Philippe
  PIGALLE
Amelia, Vincenzo
  LIVING IN OBLIVION
  SMOKE
Amendolia, Don
  DECONSTRUCTING SARAH
  WALK IN THE CLOUDS, A
Ames, Kenner
  CANADIAN BACON
Amiel, Wayne
  HEAVEN'S A DRAG
Amis, Suzy
  NADJA
  USUAL SUSPECTS, THE
Ammann, Renee
  NUMBER ONE FAN
Ammouchi, Ali
  DEATH IN BRUNSWICK
Amos, Beth
  CANADIAN BACON
Amos, Diane
  COPYCAT
  NINE MONTHS
Amos, Keith
  BREACH OF CONDUCT
Amron, Marcia
  FOOL AND HIS MONEY, A
Amurri, Eva
  DEAD MAN WALKING
Amyes, Isabelle
  SENSE AND SENSIBILITY
Amyot, Marc
  CITY OF LOST CHILDREN, THE
Amzuliscu, Radu
  CITIZEN X
An Xing
  SHANGHAI TRIAD
Ananins, Michael
  PRIEST
Anbeh, Susan
  FRENCH KISS
Andel, Pavel
  FATHERLAND
Andelin, James
  GRUMPIER OLD MEN
Anderle, David
  BRIAN WILSON: I JUST WASN'T MADE
    FOR THESE TIMES
Anders, Elisa
  NEW YORK COP
Andersen, Dana
  OUTBREAK
Anderson, Axel
  ASSASSINS
Anderson, Bart
  HUNTED, THE
Anderson, Buddy
  CROSSING GUARD, THE

Anderson, Christopher
  DOUBLE, DOUBLE, TOIL AND TROUBLE
Anderson, Colin
  ETERNITY
Anderson, Dana
  SAFE
Anderson, Daniel
  BODY STROKES
Anderson, Daryl
  BREAK, THE
Anderson, Deke
  BALLISTIC
Anderson, Erich
  GLASS SHIELD, THE
Anderson, Greg
  CASINO
Anderson, J.J.
  CASPER
Anderson, Jaime
  FUN
Anderson, Jeff Scott
  CASINO
Anderson, Jeffrey
  AMERICAN PRESIDENT, THE
Anderson, Joel
  CURSE OF THE STARVING CLASS
Anderson, Kenneth
  FEAST OF JULY
Anderson, Larry
  COSMIC SLOP
Anderson, Leslee
  HOWLING: NEW MOON RISING, THE
Anderson, Lisa Arrindell
  CLOCKERS
Anderson, Nynno
  STRANGE DAYS
Anderson, Richard
  GLASS SHIELD, THE
Anderson, Ross
  SUM OF US, THE
Anderson, Sascha
  BETRAYAL
Anderson, Stanley
  CANADIAN BACON
Anderson, Tracy
  WATERWORLD
Anderson, Whitney
  PREHYSTERIA! 3
Andre, Charles
  GOOD DAY TO DIE, A
Andreichenko, Natasha
  LITTLE ODESSA
  OPERATION INTERCEPT
Andreozzi, Jack
  DECONSTRUCTING SARAH
Andrews, David
  APOLLO 13
  DECONSTRUCTING SARAH
Andrews, Jason
  KISS OF DEATH
  RHYTHM THIEF
Andrews, Jodie
  NOSTRADAMUS KID, THE
Andrews, Jody
  ABDUCTED 2: THE REUNION
Andrews, Joey
  UNSTRUNG HEROES
Andric, Branko
  BEFORE SUNRISE
Andrzejewski, L.
  SHORT FILM ABOUT KILLING, A
Angel, Jack
  BALTO
Angelico, Ricardo
  LIE DOWN WITH DOGS
Angelina, Diana
  COVER STORY

Angelino, Joel
  STRAWBERRY AND CHOCOLATE
Angell, Vincent
  SEARCH AND DESTROY
Angelo, Dom
  CASINO
Angelou, Maya
  HOW TO MAKE AN AMERICAN QUILT
Angers, Genevieve
  LOVE AND HUMAN REMAINS
Angiolini, Steven
  HACKERS
Anglin, Jennifer
  OUTSIDE THE LAW
Anholt, Christien
  CLASS OF '61
Anisko, Eddie
  PANTHER
Ankowitsch, Christian
  BEFORE SUNRISE
Ann-Margret
  GRUMPIER OLD MEN
Annarino, Karen
  VIRTUOSITY
Anne, Tiffany
  TALES FROM THE CRYPT: DEMON
    KNIGHT
Annesley, Imogen
  NOSTRADAMUS KID, THE
Annis, Francesca
  DOOMSDAY GUN
Anomaiprasert, Lisa
  ART FOR TEACHERS OF CHILDREN
Anska, Marianne
  FRENCH KISS
Ant, Adam
  CYBER BANDITS
Anthony, Brian
  DANGEROUS MINDS
Anthony, Darren
  LIE DOWN WITH DOGS
Anthony, David
  CONGO
Anthony, Kathy
  FATHER OF THE BRIDE PART II
Anthony, Lysette
  DR. JEKYLL & MS. HYDE
  DRACULA: DEAD AND LOVING IT
Anthony, Marc
  HACKERS
Anthony, Paul
  COSMIC SLOP
Antin, Steven
  S.F.W.
Antonenko, Dina
  AMERICAN COP
Antonucci, Christopher "Critter"
  CONGO
Antounutti, Omero
  FARINELLI
Antrobus, David
  RICHARD III
Antrop, Sylvia
  MINA TANNENBAUM
Anwar, Gabrielle
  INNOCENT LIES
  THINGS TO DO IN DENVER WHEN
    YOU'RE DEAD
Anyie, Lutang
  BEYOND RANGOON
Anzalone, Nancy Ellen
  ADDICTION, THE
Anzilotti, Perry
  ANGUS
Apatow, Judd
  HEAVYWEIGHTS
Apiata, Manuel
  ONCE WERE WARRIORS

Apicella, John
ACROSS THE MOON
SAFE

Appel, Peter
JERKY BOYS: THE MOVIE, THE
MAN OF THE HOUSE

Appelbaum, Lynn
THINGS TO DO IN DENVER WHEN
YOU'RE DEAD

Appelgate, Royce D.
UNDER SIEGE 2: DARK TERRITORY

Appleby, Matt
DOLORES CLAIBORNE

Applegate, Christina
ACROSS THE MOON
WILD BILL

Applegate, Fred
STUART SAVES HIS FAMILY

Aquilino, Frank "Butch the Hat"
ADDICTION, THE
ME AND THE MOB

Aquino, Amy
BOYS ON THE SIDE

Ara, Esmerald
LAMERICA

Aragon, Angelica
WALK IN THE CLOUDS, A

Arahanga, Julian
ONCE WERE WARRIORS

Arahna, Ray
DIE HARD WITH A VENGEANCE

Aranguiz, Manuel
ECLIPSE

Aranha, Ray
DEAD MAN WALKING

Araskog, Julie
NIXON
OUTBREAK
SEVEN

Arato, Genjiro
MYSTERY OF RAMPO, THE

Araujo, Graciela
I, THE WORST OF ALL

Arbess, Sarah Levy
THINGS TO DO IN DENVER WHEN
YOU'RE DEAD

Archer, Beverly
BRADY BUNCH MOVIE, THE

Archerd, Selma
BRADY BUNCH MOVIE, THE

Archey, Marlon
SCANNERS: THE SHOWDOWN

Archie, John
CREW, THE

Archuleta, Ismael
DANGEROUS MINDS

Archuleta, Michael
DANGEROUS MINDS

Ardant, Fanny
SABRINA

Ardell, Mark
HEAVEN'S A DRAG

Arden, Daryl
MUTANT SPECIES

Arden, Noby
BATMAN FOREVER

Arenas, Ed
MIAMI RHAPSODY

Arenberg, Lee
WATERWORLD

Arevado, Mario
BURNING SEASON, THE

Arevalo, Robert
DESPERADO

Argenziano, Carmen
BURNING SEASON, THE
DON JUAN DEMARCO
TIE THAT BINDS, THE

Argiro, Vinny
DEVIL IN A BLUE DRESS

Argo, Victor
BLUE IN THE FACE
SMOKE

Arias, Joey
TO WONG FOO, THANKS FOR
EVERYTHING! JULIE NEWMAR
WIGSTOCK: THE MOVIE

Arizmendi, Yareli
BIG GREEN, THE

Arkhipova, Nina
BURNT BY THE SUN

Arkin, Alan
DOOMSDAY GUN
JERKY BOYS: THE MOVIE, THE
STEAL BIG, STEAL LITTLE

Arklie, Thomas
HEAVEN'S A DRAG

Arlen, Elizabeth
SEPARATE LIVES

Armitage, Jaqueline
HOWLING: NEW MOON RISING, THE

Armitage, Karole
SEARCH AND DESTROY

Armstrong, Alun
AWFULLY BIG ADVENTURE, AN
BRAVEHEART

Armstrong, Bryan
CANADIAN BACON

Armstrong, Joshua
WALKING DEAD, THE

Armstrong, Lyle
FRANK & JESSE

Armstrong, Pat
CIRCUMSTANCES UNKNOWN

Armstrong, R.G.
PAYBACK

Armstrong, Scott
INDICTMENT: THE MCMARTIN TRIAL

Armstrong, Vaughn
NET, THE

Arndt, Denis
HOW TO MAKE AN AMERICAN QUILT

Arneson, Mark
STRANGE DAYS

Arnett, Jr., Isaac T.
FREE WILLY 2: THE ADVENTURE HOME

Arngrim, Stefan
STRANGE DAYS

Arnold, Rodney
MURIEL'S WEDDING

Arnold, Tom
NINE MONTHS

Arnold, Victoria
PRIEST

Aronberg, Chuck
GHOST BRIGADE

Arone, James
BYE BYE, LOVE
DECONSTRUCTING SARAH

Aronson, Steve
SUDDEN DEATH

Arquette, Alexis
FRANK & JESSE
GHOST BRIGADE
WHITE MAN'S BURDEN
WIGSTOCK: THE MOVIE

Arquette, David
GHOST BRIGADE
WILD BILL

Arquette, Lewis
STUART SAVES HIS FAMILY

Arquette, Patricia
BEYOND RANGOON
DILLINGER

Arquette, Richmond
SEVEN

Arquette, Rosanna
IN THE DEEP WOODS
SEARCH AND DESTROY

Arrick, Rose
TWO BITS

Arroyave, Karina
DANGEROUS MINDS

Artel, Sabrina
INCREDIBLY TRUE ADVENTURES OF
TWO GIRLS IN LOVE, THE

Arthur, Carol
DRACULA: DEAD AND LOVING IT

Arthur, Michelle
GOLDENEYE

Arthur, Rebeca
GET SHORTY

Artura, Michael
KISS OF DEATH
MONEY TRAIN

Artus, Ashley
JUDGE DREDD

Arzoumanian, Suren
FORGET PARIS

Asenjo, Alfonso
FARINELLI

Asharri, Kalique
CYBER BANDITS

Ashby, Katherine
IN THE MOUTH OF MADNESS

Ashby, Linden
MORTAL KOMBAT

Ashe, Paddy
AILSA

Asher, Tony
BRIAN WILSON: I JUST WASN'T MADE
FOR THESE TIMES

Ashford, Matthew
SPECIES

Ashley, Akiko
BASKETBALL DIARIES, THE

Ashley, Erin
MIDNIGHT TEASE 2

Ashley, Karan
MIGHTY MORPHIN POWER RANGERS:
THE MOVIE

Ashton, Al
LAMB

Ashton, Michelle
CREEP

Ashton-Griffiths, Roger
RESTORATION

Ashwood, Jermaine
HARLEM DIARY: NINE VOICES OF
RESILIENCE

Askew, Luke
FRANK & JESSE

Askew, Mari
FRANK & JESSE

Askwith, Johnny
DANCE ME OUTSIDE

Asman, David
VIRTUOSITY

Asner, Kate
DR. JEKYLL & MS. HYDE

Asparagus, Fred
GALAXIS
STEAL BIG, STEAL LITTLE

Assad, Richard
FORGET PARIS
SCANNERS: THE SHOWDOWN

Assan, Azmi
BEYOND RANGOON

Assante, Armand
JUDGE DREDD

Astin, John
KURT VONNEGUT'S HARRISON
BERGERON
SILENCE OF THE HAMS

Astin, Sean
KURT VONNEGUT'S HARRISON
BERGERON
SAFE PASSAGE
TERESA'S TATTOO
Athanasiadis, Helen
ONLY THE BRAVE
Atherton, Simon
CUTTHROAT ISLAND
Atherton, William
BROKEN TRUST
FRANK & JESSE
Atkinson, III, Fort
BABYSITTER, THE
Atkinson, Jayne
FREE WILLY 2: THE ADVENTURE HOME
Atkinson, Phil
FUNNY BONES
Atkinson, Sam
POSTCARDS FROM AMERICA
Atwood, Ian
MY ANTONIA
Atwood, Kathryn
S.F.W.
Aubele, Michael
SUDDEN DEATH
Auberjonois, Rene
BATMAN FOREVER
Aubin, Colette
DIGGER
Aubin, Cyril
CITY OF LOST CHILDREN, THE
Aubree, Blanche
MINA TANNENBAUM
Aubry, Sophie
INNOCENT LIES
Auger, Christian
PIGALLE
August, Lance
NICK OF TIME
August, Sani
PLAY TIME
Augusta, Mario
ME AND THE MOB
Augustine, Scott
GOLD DIGGERS: THE SECRET OF BEAR
MOUNTAIN
Aull, Haley
SOMETHING TO TALK ABOUT
Aumont, Jean-Pierre
JEFFERSON IN PARIS
Aumont, Marie-Dominique
OLD LADY WHO WALKED IN THE SEA,
THE
Aung
BEYOND RANGOON
Aurel, Lucinda
CUTTHROAT ISLAND
Aurignac, Patrick
SIX DAYS, SIX NIGHTS
Auster, Daniel
SMOKE
Austerwell, David
IN THE MOUTH OF MADNESS
Austin, Julie
BRAVEHEART
Austin, Molly
HOME FOR THE HOLIDAYS
Austin, Velma
LOSING ISAIAH
Avalon, Frankie
CASINO
Avant, Nicole
WALKING DEAD, THE
Averill, Heidi
FATHER OF THE BRIDE PART II

Avery, Brian
BIGFOOT: THE UNFORGETTABLE
ENCOUNTER
Avery, James
BRADY BUNCH MOVIE, THE
Avery, Joni
EXPERT, THE
Avery, Margaret
WHITE MAN'S BURDEN
Avery, Richard
RETURN OF THE NATIVE, THE
Avery, Rick
HEAT
HIGHER LEARNING
SCANNERS: THE SHOWDOWN
Avila, Cynthia
DANGEROUS MINDS
Avila, Jose Luis
ARIZONA DREAM
Avila, Ricardo
STRAWBERRY AND CHOCOLATE
Avila, Teresa
TIE-DIED: ROCK 'N' ROLL'S MOST
DEADICATED FANS
Aviles, Angel
DESPERADO
Aviles, Ric
WATERWORLD
Avoth, Justin
PERSUASION
Axton, Hoyt
KINGFISH: A STORY OF HUEY P. LONG
NUMBER ONE FAN
Ayako
SABRINA
Ayala, Eddie
MY FAMILY: MI FAMILIA
Aycock, Jim
TOM AND HUCK
Ayers, Sam
BAD BOYS
Ayesu, Joseph Wilson
MONEY TRAIN
Aykroyd, Dan
CASPER
TOMMY BOY
Aylward, Rory
ENEMY WITHIN, THE
Aylward, Tom
COVER STORY
Ayoub, Michael
BILLY MADISON
Azaria, Hank
HEAT
NOW AND THEN
Azevedo, Jr., John
NICK OF TIME
Azikiwe, Jason
FATHER AND SCOUT
Azizi, Rahi
LITTLE PRINCESS, A
Azrah, Fatemah
JAR, THE
Azzara, Candice
UNSTRUNG HEROES
Azzinaro, Christian A.
CASINO
B-Fine
COSMIC SLOP
B., Heather
DEAD PRESIDENTS
B., Tairrie
EROTIQUE
Ba, Omar
HYENAS
Babatunde, Obba
BORN TO BE WILD
REASON TO BELIEVE, A

Baber, Greg
KINGFISH: A STORY OF HUEY P. LONG
Babic-Zoric, Natasa
GORILLA BATHES AT NOON
Babnoitis, Con
DEATH IN BRUNSWICK
Babot, Philip
RESTORATION
Babson, Thomas W.
GLASS SHIELD, THE
Baca, John-Michael
THREE WISHES
Baca, Lawrence R.
THREE WISHES
Bacarella, Mike
LOSING ISAIAH
WHILE YOU WERE SLEEPING
Bachmann, Conrad
OUTBREAK
Bacino, Chuck
THINGS TO DO IN DENVER WHEN
YOU'RE DEAD
Bacino, Joe
MONEY TRAIN
Back, Yvon
INNOCENT LIES
Backs, Susan
TO DIE FOR
Bacon, Kevin
APOLLO 13
BALTO
MURDER IN THE FIRST
Badalucco, Michael
CLOCKERS
Bader, Deidrich
TERESA'S TATTOO
Badie, Mina
GEORGIA
Badua, Nikki
TIE-DIED: ROCK 'N' ROLL'S MOST
DEADICATED FANS
Baer, G. Gordon
ATTACK OF THE 60-FOOT CENTERFOLD
Baer, Parley
LAST OF THE DOGMEN
Baer, Peter
MAGIC IN THE WATER
Baer, Philip
MAGIC IN THE WATER
Baerwald, David
CROSSING GUARD, THE
Baeza, Paloma
KID IN KING ARTHUR'S COURT, A
Bagby, Laura
COVER STORY
Bagden, Ron
RECKLESS
Bagley, Lorri
TOMMY BOY
Bagley, Ross
BABE
Bagley, Tim
CRAZYSITTER, THE
Bahns, Maxine
BROTHERS MCMULLEN, THE
Bai Li
ASHES OF TIME
Baier, Anka
PROMISE, THE
Bailey, Akida
HARLEM DIARY: NINE VOICES OF
RESILIENCE
Bailey, Bill
BALTO
Bailey, Ewan
JUDGE DREDD
Bailey, Frederick
BODY SHOT

Bailey, Janet
BLACK FOX
Bailey, Jeremy
TOO YOUNG TO DIE?
Bailey, Kimberly
BABE
Bailey, Kyle
BILLY MADISON
Bailey, Tiffany
BAR GIRLS
Bailie, David
CUTTHROAT ISLAND
Baily, Kirk
HOUSEGUEST
Bain, Monte
DANGEROUS, THE
Bainbridge, Sunshine
EROTIQUE
Baines, Bob
SUM OF US, THE
Baird, Samuel
DEAD FUNNY
Baitz, Jon Robin
LAST SUMMER IN THE HAMPTONS
Bajaj, Aseem
BANDIT QUEEN
Bajpai, Manjoj
BANDIT QUEEN
Bak Ka-Sin
TWENTY SOMETHING
Baka, Miroslaw
SHORT FILM ABOUT KILLING, A
Bakaba, Sidiki
FACES OF WOMEN
Bakar, Dion Abu
BEYOND RANGOON
Bakay, Nick
JURY DUTY
Baker, Alan
ATTACK OF THE 60-FOOT CENTERFOLD
Baker, Becky Ann
SABRINA
UNSTRUNG HEROES
Baker, Blanche
DEAD FUNNY
Baker, Bonnie
OUT OF ANNIE'S PAST
Baker, Bubba
FAIR GAME
Baker, Diane
NET, THE
Baker, Elijah
PANTHER
Baker, Jim
CONVICT COWBOY
Baker, Jimmy
MAN OF THE HOUSE
Baker, Joan
DALLAS DOLL
Baker, Joe
POCAHONTAS
Baker, Joe Don
CONGO
GOLDENEYE
PANTHER
UNDERNEATH, THE
Baker, Mickey
FUNNY BONES
Baker, Raymond
SECRETARY, THE
Baker, Roger
CARMEN MIRANDA: BANANAS IS MY
BUSINESS
Bakjian, Mary
HIGHER LEARNING
Bakke, Brenda
TALES FROM THE CRYPT: DEMON
KNIGHT

TWOGETHER
UNDER SIEGE 2: DARK TERRITORY
Baklan, Nickolai
AMERICAN COP
Baklan, Stas
AMERICAN COP
Bako, Brigitte
STRANGE DAYS
Bakula, Scott
LORD OF ILLUSIONS
MY FAMILY: MI FAMILIA
Balai, Hossein
JAR, THE
Balasko, Josiane
GROSSE FATIGUE
Balch, Jillian
TANK GIRL
Bald Eagle, David
LAKOTA WOMAN: SIEGE AT WOUNDED
KNEE
Baldoni, Bruno
NOSTRADAMUS KID, THE
Baldridge, Brad
HEAT
Baldwin, Adam
HOW TO MAKE AN AMERICAN QUILT
Baldwin, Alec
TWO BITS
Baldwin, Daniel
BODILY HARM
Baldwin, Helen
SOMETHING TO TALK ABOUT
Baldwin, Karen
SUDDEN DEATH
Baldwin, Ken
TALES FROM THE CRYPT: DEMON
KNIGHT
Baldwin, Rebecca
FEAR, THE
Baldwin, Sidney
VILLAGE OF THE DAMNED
Baldwin, Stephen
USUAL SUSPECTS, THE
Baldwin, William
FAIR GAME
PYROMANIAC'S LOVE STORY, A
Bale, Christian
POCAHONTAS
Balfour, Noelle
COSMIC SLOP
Balint, Andras
CITIZEN X
Balk, Fairuza
DANGER OF LOVE
THINGS TO DO IN DENVER WHEN
YOU'RE DEAD
Balkay, Geza
CITIZEN X
Balkaya, Huriye
DEATH IN BRUNSWICK
Ball, Angeline
PEBBLE AND THE PENGUIN, THE
Ball, Vincent
MURIEL'S WEDDING
Ballace, Elaine
DRACULA: DEAD AND LOVING IT
Ballantine, Leah Kourtne
FUN
Ballard, Doug
FREE WILLY 2: THE ADVENTURE HOME
Ballard, Gary
MURDER IN THE FIRST
Ballard, Reginald
PANTHER
Ballet Folklorica Azteca
BOYS ON THE SIDE
Balogh, Laszlo Varadi
CITIZEN X

Balsam, Martin
SILENCE OF THE HAMS
Balsam, Talia
COLDBLOODED
COMPANION, THE
Balson, Humbert
JEFFERSON IN PARIS
Baltz, Kirk
KINGFISH: A STORY OF HUEY P. LONG
Bama, Desire
FACES OF WOMEN
Bambaataa, Afrika
SHOW, THE
Bancroft, Anne
DRACULA: DEAD AND LOVING IT
HOME FOR THE HOLIDAYS
HOW TO MAKE AN AMERICAN QUILT
Bancroft, Cameron
LOVE AND HUMAN REMAINS
Banderas, Antonio
ASSASSINS
DESPERADO
FOUR ROOMS
MIAMI RHAPSODY
NEVER TALK TO STRANGERS
Bane, Monty
GLASS SHIELD, THE
Banes, Lisa
MIAMI RHAPSODY
Bank-Mikkelsen, Nis
KINGDOM, THE
Banker, Carol
MALLRATS
Bankins, Peter
NINE MONTHS
Banks, Bonnie
BETTER OFF DEAD
DANGER OF LOVE
Banks, Ernie Lee
GLASS SHIELD, THE
JURY DUTY
Banks, Jonathan
BODY SHOT
NIGHTMARE
UNDER SIEGE 2: DARK TERRITORY
Banks, Lenore
DEAD MAN WALKING
Banks, Tommy
NINE MONTHS
Banks, Tyra
HIGHER LEARNING
Banlaki, Andras
FUNNY BONES
Bannen, Ian
BRAVEHEART
LAMB
Bannerji, Ajit
STRANGER, THE
Bannerji, Sourav
STRANGER, THE
Banning, Jack
BITTER VENGEANCE
Bapps, Jacky
PIGALLE
Baptiste, Victor
DECOY
Barabas, Sari
OH ... ROSALINDA!!
Barahtin, Valeri
MUTE WITNESS
Barak, Ari
WATERWORLD
Baranski, Christine
JEFFREY
NEW JERSEY DRIVE
Barbaro, Nicholas
EXPERT, THE

Barbe, Marc
MY LIFE AND TIMES WITH ANTONIN
ARTAUD
Barbee, Buzz
OUTBREAK
Barber, Gillian
GOLD DIGGERS: THE SECRET OF BEAR
MOUNTAIN
JUMANJI
Barber, Paul
PRIEST
Barbieri, Paula
DANGEROUS, THE
Barbour, Kathy
TALES FROM THE CRYPT: DEMON
KNIGHT
Barboza, Richard
MESSENGER
Barcis, Artur
SHORT FILM ABOUT KILLING, A
SHORT FILM ABOUT LOVE, A
Barclay, Caroline
CANDYMAN: FAREWELL TO THE FLESH
S.F.W.
SPECIES
Barden, Alice
VILLAGE OF THE DAMNED
Baresch, Pia
FOR GOD AND COUNTRY
Barilli, Ajanta
MONTH BY THE LAKE, A
Barkely, Charles
FORGET PARIS
Barker, Patronella Q.
FATHERLAND
Barkett, Steve
ATTACK OF THE 60-FOOT CENTERFOLD
Barkin, Ellen
BAD COMPANY
WILD BILL
Barlow, Allan
BETTER OFF DEAD
Barnard, John
DARK SIDE OF GENIUS, THE
Barnathan, Anna
NINE MONTHS
Barnes, Christopher Daniel
BRADY BUNCH MOVIE, THE
Barnes, Crystal
LOSING ISAIAH
Barnes, Donna
DR. JEKYLL & MS. HYDE
Barnes, Herbie
DANCE ME OUTSIDE
Barnes, Priscilla
CROSSING GUARD, THE
EROTIQUE
MALLRATS
Barnes, Rodney P.
MAJOR PAYNE
Barnes, Susan
LEAVING LAS VEGAS
TALL TALE: THE UNBELIEVABLE
ADVENTURES OF PECOS BILL
Barnett, Gemini
BABE
Barnett, Steven R.
VIRTUOSITY
Barnwell, Jean Marie
BORN TO BE WILD
Baron, Blaire
SKINNER
Baron, Ramonale
EXPERT, THE
Barone, Jerry
TWO BITS
Barr, Sharon
JURY DUTY

Barr, Tony
MURDER IN THE FIRST
Barras, David
CENTURY
Barreto, Erick
CARMEN MIRANDA: BANANAS IS MY
BUSINESS
Barreto, Luis Lima
VALLEY OF ABRAHAM, THE
Barrett, Benjamin
BILLY MADISON
Barrett, Jean
SHOWGIRLS
Barrett, Majel
TERESA'S TATTOO
Barrett, Ray
HOTEL SORRENTO
Barrios, Juana
RECKLESS
Barron, Doug
RECKLESS
Barroso, Maria
VALLEY OF ABRAHAM, THE
Barry, Charlie
DESPERATE PREY
Barry, Jason
CIRCLE OF FRIENDS
Barry, Matt
CRIMSON TIDE
DEVIL IN A BLUE DRESS
Barry, Raymond J.
DEAD MAN WALKING
SUDDEN DEATH
Barry, Scooter
FORGET PARIS
Barry, Thom
AMERICAN PRESIDENT, THE
APOLLO 13
CONGO
WHITE MAN'S BURDEN
Barry, Tighe
STEAL BIG, STEAL LITTLE
Barry, Tony
COUNTRY LIFE
Barrymore, Drew
BATMAN FOREVER
BOYS ON THE SIDE
MAD LOVE
Bartel, Paul
JERKY BOYS: THE MOVIE, THE
NUMBER ONE FAN
USUAL SUSPECTS, THE
Barth, Lawrence
BASKETBALL DIARIES, THE
Barthelemy, Briac
CITY OF LOST CHILDREN, THE
Bartlett, Charles
BABE
Bartlett, Nick
CUTTHROAT ISLAND
Bartlett, Peter
JEFFREY
Bartlett, Robin
DANGEROUS MINDS
Barton, David
TO WONG FOO, THANKS FOR
EVERYTHING! JULIE NEWMAR
Barton, Rodger
NEVER TALK TO STRANGERS
Barton, Tony
FUNNY BONES
Bartsch, Susanne
TO WONG FOO, THANKS FOR
EVERYTHING! JULIE NEWMAR
Basco, Dante
GOOFY MOVIE, A
Basco, Darion
BRADY BUNCH MOVIE, THE

Bashoff, Blake
BUSHWHACKED
Basile, Joe
BYE BYE, LOVE
Basile, Salvatore
STEAL BIG, STEAL LITTLE
Basler, Marianne
FARINELLI
Bass, Bobby
JADE
Bass, Suzi
GETTING OUT
Basset, Skye
DANGEROUS MINDS
Bassett, Angela
STRANGE DAYS
VAMPIRE IN BROOKLYN
WAITING TO EXHALE
Bassey, Jennifer
TWOGETHER
Bassin, Roberta
INDICTMENT: THE MCMARTIN TRIAL
Bastien, Brigitte
JLG BY JLG
Batarda, Beatriz
VALLEY OF ABRAHAM, THE
Bateke, Fidel
CONGO
Bateman, Amy
FUN
Bateman, Geoffrey
BUFFALO GIRLS
Bates, Bill
USUAL SUSPECTS, THE
Bates, Kathy
ANGUS
CURSE OF THE STARVING CLASS
DOLORES CLAIBORNE
Bates, Mychael
FATHER OF THE BRIDE PART II
Bates, Paul
SHOWGIRLS
Bates, Rupert
FEAST OF JULY
Bates-Campbell, Lola
BALTO
Batinkoff, Randall
HIGHER LEARNING
Batiste, David
CLOCKERS
Batt, Bryan
JEFFREY
Battaglia, Lynn
TWO BITS
Battaglia, Matt
SHOWGIRLS
Battistone, Catherine
BAREFOOT GEN
Battle, David Wade
GHOST BRIGADE
Battle, Patrice F.
FUN
Bau, C.J.
NICK OF TIME
Bauchau, Patrick
DARK SIDE OF GENIUS, THE
Bauer, Kristin
GALAXIS
Bauer, Michelle
ATTACK OF THE 60-FOOT CENTERFOLD
Baumbach, Jonathan
KICKING AND SCREAMING
Baumbach, Nico
KICKING AND SCREAMING
Baumbach, Noah
KICKING AND SCREAMING

Baumgardner, Genelle Lee
FORGET PARIS
Baumgarten, Christiane
NEKROMANTIK
Baxavanis, Monica
VAMPIRES AND OTHER STEREOTYPES
Baxley, Jr., Craig
AVENGING ANGEL
Baxley, Kristin
DECONSTRUCTING SARAH
Baxter, Amy Lynn
BIKINI BISTRO
Bay, Frances
IN THE MOUTH OF MADNESS
Bayle, Jack
AWFULLY BIG ADVENTURE, AN
Bayne, Lawrence
LAKOTA WOMAN: SIEGE AT WOUNDED
KNEE
Bazeley, Mark
FEAST OF JULY
Beach, Adam
DANCE ME OUTSIDE
Beach, Michael
BAD COMPANY
WAITING TO EXHALE
WHITE MAN'S BURDEN
Beal, Gary
DANGEROUS, THE
Beale, Chris
COPYCAT
Beale, Simon Russell
PERSUASION
Beals, Jennifer
ARABIAN KNIGHT
DEVIL IN A BLUE DRESS
FOUR ROOMS
Bealum, Ngaio S.
NINE MONTHS
Beamer, Layne
ROSWELL: THE U.F.O. COVER-UP
Bean, Sean
GOLDENEYE
Beard, Tony
PANTHER
Bearden, Jim
SCARLET LETTER, THE
Bearse, Amanda
DOOM GENERATION, THE
Beasley, John
CURE, THE
LOSING ISAIAH
Beat, Jackie
WIGSTOCK: THE MOVIE
Beaton, Bruce
NEVER TALK TO STRANGERS
Beatty, Debra
CAGED HEAT 3000
MIDNIGHT TEASE 2
Beatty, Jon
GHOST BRIGADE
Beatty, Ned
JUST CAUSE
Beaubian, Susan
FATHER OF THE BRIDE PART II
Beaudin, Rene
CLEAN, SHAVEN
Beaudoin, Michelle
BAD COMPANY
Beaulieu, Jean Louis
TRAPS
Beautier, Philippe
CITY OF LOST CHILDREN, THE
Beaven, Louise
IN THE MOUTH OF MADNESS
Beaver, Jim
TWOGETHER

Beaver, Walter S.
STUART SAVES HIS FAMILY
Bechtel, Jesse
EMPIRE RECORDS
Beck, Charles
ROSWELL: THE U.F.O. COVER-UP
Beck, Dixie
BODY STROKES
Beck, Kimberly
IN THE DEEP WOODS
Beck, Maria
DEATH IN BRUNSWICK
Beckel, Graham
LEAVING LAS VEGAS
Becker, Gerry
DIE HARD WITH A VENGEANCE
ROOMMATES
Becker, Martin
INNOCENT, THE
Becker, Meret
INNOCENT, THE
PROMISE, THE
Becker, Randy
LIE DOWN WITH DOGS
SABRINA
Beckford, Roxanne
FATHER OF THE BRIDE PART II
Bedard, Irene
LAKOTA WOMAN: SIEGE AT WOUNDED
KNEE
POCAHONTAS
Beddil, Melanie
ONLY THE BRAVE
Bedelia, Bonnie
JUDICIAL CONSENT
Bedex, Henri
INNOCENT LIES
Bedford, Brian
NIXON
Bedgood, Winstone
ONCE WERE WARRIORS
Bednarz, Aleksander
SHORT FILM ABOUT KILLING, A
Bednarz, Wendy
SHORT FILM ABOUT KILLING, A
VAMPIRES AND OTHER STEREOTYPES
Bedrosian, Hunter
FEAR, THE
Beebe, Reda
TALES FROM THE CRYPT: DEMON
KNIGHT
Beechner, Ed
OUTBREAK
Beeler, Teddy
NICK OF TIME
Beeline, Stevie
WINGS OF HONNEAMISE: ROYAL SPACE
FORCE
Beeman, Terry
SHOWGIRLS
Beer, Dickey
CUTTHROAT ISLAND
Beer, Elizabeth
PARTY GIRL
Beesley, Nina
STEAL BIG, STEAL LITTLE
Beeson, Joel
BALLISTIC
Beevers, Geoffrey
CENTURY
Bega, Leslie Rae
AMERICAN PRESIDENT, THE
Begeja, Victoria
FRANKIE STARLIGHT
Begg, Nathan
MAGIC IN THE WATER
Beggs, Hagen
POWER OF ATTORNEY

Begley, Jr., Ed
BATMAN FOREVER
CRAZYSITTER, THE
Behalikova, Andrea
SABRINA
Belafonte, Harry
WHITE MAN'S BURDEN
Belcher, David
FEAST OF JULY
Belcher, Patricia
INDICTMENT: THE MCMARTIN TRIAL
SPECIES
Bell, Addison
TOMMY BOY
Bell, E.E.
FORGET PARIS
Bell, Eileen
FUNNY BONES
Bell, Jean Paul
MIGHTY MORPHIN POWER RANGERS:
THE MOVIE
Bell, Lucy
NOSTRADAMUS KID, THE
Bell, Marshall
OPERATION DUMBO DROP
PAYBACK
SILENCE OF THE HAMS
THINGS TO DO IN DENVER WHEN
YOU'RE DEAD
Bell, Nicholas
GROSS MISCONDUCT
HOTEL SORRENTO
MIGHTY MORPHIN POWER RANGERS:
THE MOVIE
Bell, Thom
IN THE MOUTH OF MADNESS
Bell, Tobin
QUICK AND THE DEAD, THE
Bell, Tom
FEAST OF JULY
Bella, Rachael
LITTLE PRINCESS, A
Bellaflores, Eddie
ASSASSINS
Bellamy, Diana
OUTBREAK
Bellamy, Ned
IN THE DEEP WOODS
Bellantoni, Nantino
CIRCUMSTANCES UNKNOWN
Bellany, Jr., Nathaniel
FORGET PARIS
Belle, Camilla
DECONSTRUCTING SARAH
LITTLE PRINCESS, A
Belle, Nevada
LIE DOWN WITH DOGS
Belleville, Donna
GOOD DAY TO DIE, A
Bellini, Massimo
MINA TANNENBAUM
Bellows, Gil
MIAMI RHAPSODY
Bellucci, John
NIXON
Belmondo, Jean-Paul
LES MISERABLES
Belmondo, Paul
LES MISERABLES
Belousov, Vladimir
BURNT BY THE SUN
Belton, Cathy
CIRCLE OF FRIENDS
Beltran, Robert
NIXON
Beltzman, Mark
BILLY MADISON

Belushi, James
CANADIAN BACON
DESTINY TURNS ON THE RADIO
PEBBLE AND THE PENGUIN, THE
SEPARATE LIVES
Belzer, Dan
VILLAGE OF THE DAMNED
Ben-Tal, Sharon
FUN
Benchley, Nat
HOME FOR THE HOLIDAYS
Bender, Lawrence
FOUR ROOMS
WHITE MAN'S BURDEN
Bender, Te-See
TALES FROM THE CRYPT: DEMON
KNIGHT
Benedict, Tannis
NET, THE
Benes, Michelle
BRIDGES OF MADISON COUNTY, THE
Benevides, Rob
CLEAN, SHAVEN
Beninati, Anthony
CLUELESS
Bening, Annette
AMERICAN PRESIDENT, THE
RICHARD III
Benko, Tina
HOUSEGUEST
Benlloch, Marisa
BUSINESS AFFAIR, A
Benn, J.B.
SABRINA
Bennent, Heinz
NEA
Bennett, Anthony
LIE DOWN WITH DOGS
Bennett, Daniel
KID IN KING ARTHUR'S COURT, A
Bennett, Douglas
BIGFOOT: THE UNFORGETTABLE
ENCOUNTER
MURDER IN THE FIRST
Bennett, Garrett
MAGIC IN THE WATER
Bennett, John
PRIEST
Bennett, Joseph
CENTURY
Bennett, Marcia
BILLY MADISON
BOULEVARD
Bennett, Matt
FAR FROM HOME: THE ADVENTURES OF
YELLOW DOG
Bennett, Nigel
KURT VONNEGUT'S HARRISON
BERGERON
Bennett, Rosalind
INNOCENT LIES
RESTORATION
Benrath, Martin
STALINGRAD
Benroubi, Elise
MINA TANNENBAUM
Benscoter, Robert
COPYCAT
Benskin, Tyrone
CONVICT COWBOY
Benson, Amber
BYE BYE, LOVE
S.F.W.
Benson, Chris
BLACK FOX
Benson, Deborah
DANGER OF LOVE

Benson, Michael
CLEAN, SHAVEN
Bensussan, Gad
INNOCENT LIES
Bentall, Paul
BUSINESS AFFAIR, A
FIRST KNIGHT
Bentley, Lamont
TALES FROM THE HOOD
Bentley, Laura
DALLAS DOLL
Bento, Fernando
VALLEY OF ABRAHAM, THE
Benton, Robert
GREAT DAY IN HARLEM, A
Bercovici, Luca
GRANNY, THE
Berdot, Trisha
CAGED HEARTS
Berenger, Chelsea
AVENGING ANGEL
Berenger, Chloe
AVENGING ANGEL
Berenger, Tom
AVENGING ANGEL
LAST OF THE DOGMEN
Berenguer, Jesus
I, THE WORST OF ALL
Berezin, Tanya
DEAD FUNNY
Berfield, Barry
POWDER
Berg, Eric
JEFFERSON IN PARIS
Berg, Peter
ACROSS THE MOON
LAST RIDE, THE
Bergbom, Joanne
JUPITER'S WIFE
Bergen, Bob
CRIMSON WOLF
Bergen, Polly
DR. JEKYLL & MS. HYDE
Bergen, Vondria
HOUSEGUEST
Bergener, Jacob
THINGS TO DO IN DENVER WHEN
YOU'RE DEAD
Berger, Sarah
FATHERLAND
Bergeron, Michael
CANDYMAN: FAREWELL TO THE FLESH
Bergonhe, Denis
WILD REEDS
Bergschneider, Conrad
IN THE MOUTH OF MADNESS
Berkeley, Xander
APOLLO 13
DILLINGER
HEAT
LEAVING LAS VEGAS
ROSWELL: THE U.F.O. COVER-UP
SAFE
Berkic, Boris
DEATH IN BRUNSWICK
Berkley, Elizabeth
SHOWGIRLS
Berkoff, Steven
FAIR GAME
Berlowe, Harold
TIE-DIED: ROCK 'N' ROLL'S MOST
DEADICATED FANS
Berman, Josh
BABY-SITTERS CLUB, THE
Berman, Juliet
INDIAN IN THE CUPBOARD, THE
Bern, Mina
LITTLE ODESSA

Bernard, Ed
GIRL IN THE CADILLAC
Bernard, Jason
COSMIC SLOP
WHILE YOU WERE SLEEPING
Bernard, Joseph
GRANNY, THE
Bernard, Ron
JACK-O
Bernhard, Sandra
DALLAS DOLL
UNZIPPED
Bernhardt, Sarah
MY ANTONIA
Bernhoffen, Helmut
INNOCENT, THE
Bernie, Steve
APOLLO 13
Berns, Gerald
NET, THE
Bernsen, Corbin
COVER ME
GHOST BRIGADE
OPERATION INTERCEPT
TALES FROM THE HOOD
Bernstein, Allen K.
KISS OF DEATH
Bernstein, Sheryl
GOOFY MOVIE, A
Berrard, Pamela
FAIR GAME
Berry, Bertice
COSMIC SLOP
Berry, Halle
LOSING ISAIAH
Berry, Lloyd
JUMANJI
Berry, Stephanie
INCREDIBLY TRUE ADVENTURES OF
TWO GIRLS IN LOVE, THE
Berry, Walter
OH ... ROSALINDA!!
Bersen, Collin
COVER ME
Bertie, Diego
NO MERCY
Bertignac, Louis
HIGHLANDER: THE FINAL DIMENSION
Bertrand, Rachel
DR. JEKYLL & MS. HYDE
Berumen, Sandra
JADE
Besch, Bibi
MY FAMILY: MI FAMILIA
Besnehard, Dominique
GROSSE FATIGUE
Bessette, Denise
PAYBACK
Bessho, Tetsuya
MYSTERY OF RAMPO, THE
Besson, Pierre
PROMISE, THE
Best, Katherine
CENTURY
Bett, Joanne
BRAVEHEART
Bett, John
SHALLOW GRAVE
Bettenfeld, Dominique
CITY OF LOST CHILDREN, THE
Betts, Christopher
DESPERATE PREY
Betts, Daniel
CARRINGTON
Betts, Eric
BASKETBALL DIARIES, THE
Betts, Jack
BATMAN FOREVER

Betts, Robert M.
FORGET PARIS
Betz, E. George
JOURNEY OF AUGUST KING, THE
Betzing, Josef
FARINELLI
Beuth, Robert Alan
OUTBREAK
Bevan, Julie
BUFFALO GIRLS
Bewley, Tom
INDIAN IN THE CUPBOARD, THE
Bezak
CITY OF LOST CHILDREN, THE
Bezuidenhout, Frik
FRIENDS
Bhaduri, Sumon
STRANGER, THE
Bhagat, Sajan
KIDS
Bhandari, Satish Chand
BEYOND RANGOON
Bharti, Pallavi
BANDIT QUEEN
Bhasker
BUSINESS AFFAIR, A
Bhat, Rishi
INDIAN IN THE CUPBOARD, THE
Bhatia, Shashi
LEAVING LAS VEGAS
Bhatt, Kamla
BANDIT QUEEN
Bhatt, Puran
BANDIT QUEEN
Bhatt, Sunita
BANDIT QUEEN
Bhattacharya, Bikram
STRANGER, THE
Bianca, Raquel
ABDUCTED 2: THE REUNION
Bianchi, Giuseppe
POWER OF ATTORNEY
Bickell, Ross
MAJOR PAYNE
Bickerton, Melissa
SPECIES
Bicknell, Andrew
BUFFALO GIRLS
Bideau, Jean-Luc
SERIOUS ABOUT PLEASURE
Bidlas, Jan
FATHERLAND
Bie, Sherry
BAD COMPANY
Biehler, Patrick
TIE-DIED: ROCK 'N' ROLL'S MOST
DEADICATED FANS
Biehn, Michael
JADE
Bieler, Lynn
CRUDE OASIS, THE
Bienfait, Charlotte
CITY OF LOST CHILDREN, THE
Bierbichler, Josef
DEADLY MARIA
Big Al
BALTO
Bigelow, Scott "Bam Bam"
MAJOR PAYNE
Biggs, Casey
BODILY HARM
Biggs, Jerry
CURSE OF THE STARVING CLASS
Bigham, Lexie
SEVEN
Bigwood, James
PANTHER

Bilderback, Nicole
CLUELESS
Bilgre, David
TIE-DIED: ROCK 'N' ROLL'S MOST
DEADICATED FANS
Billeter, Ken
BRIDGES OF MADISON COUNTY, THE
Billing, Roy
DALLAS DOLL
Billings, Earl
CRIMSON TIDE
Billingslea, Beau
AMERICAN PRESIDENT, THE
Billingsly, John
BORN TO BE WILD
Billington, Stephen
BRAVEHEART
Billod-Morel, Guillaume
CITY OF LOST CHILDREN, THE
Bingham, Gena
COPYCAT
Bingham, Traci
TALES FROM THE CRYPT: DEMON
KNIGHT
Binkley, Gregg
DRACULA: DEAD AND LOVING IT
Binyon, Dory
DIE HARD WITH A VENGEANCE
Birch, Chirstopher
CARRINGTON
Birch, Peter
BUFFALO GIRLS
Birch, Thora
NOW AND THEN
Bird, Billie
JURY DUTY
Bird, Sandy
CANDYMAN: FAREWELL TO THE FLESH
Birdsall, Megan
MY ANTONIA
Birkett, Jeremiah Wayne
CROSSING GUARD, THE
Birkin, Jane
SERIOUS ABOUT PLEASURE
Birney, Frank
REFLECTIONS IN THE DARK
Biro, Cathleen
CLEAN, SHAVEN
Biro, Zsolt
CITIZEN X
Birt, Christopher
CRIMSON TIDE
REASON TO BELIEVE, A
Bishop, Donald
BYE BYE, LOVE
Bishop, Kelly
MIAMI RHAPSODY
Bishop, Loanne
THREE WISHES
Bishop, Ray
ONCE WERE WARRIORS
Bishop, Tyler
BIG GREEN, THE
Bison, Nathan
LAKOTA WOMAN: SIEGE AT WOUNDED
KNEE
Bissonnette, Joel
BOULEVARD
Biswas, Seema
BANDIT QUEEN
Bizzi, Natalia
MONTH BY THE LAKE, A
Bjorner, Katja
DANCER, THE
Bjornsson, Helgi
REMOTE CONTROL
Black Bear, Eugene
LAST OF THE DOGMEN

Black, Jack
BYE BYE, LOVE
DEAD MAN WALKING
WATERWORLD
Black, Ryan Rajendra
DANCE ME OUTSIDE
Blackchild, C. Francis
PARTY GIRL
Blacker, Vera
MANGLER, THE
Blackholly, Amanda
FUN
Blackman, Vernon
ROSWELL: THE U.F.O. COVER-UP
Blackwell, Rus
CLASS OF '61
Blackwell, Steven
MALLRATS
Blackwood, John
BLACK FOX
Blackwood, Nina
NUMBER ONE FAN
Blade, Carol
RESTORATION
Blades, Lynn
NET, THE
Blades, Richard Scott
AMERICA'S DEADLIEST HOME VIDEO
Blain, Rogelio
UP TO A CERTAIN POINT
Blaine, Hal
BRIAN WILSON: I JUST WASN'T MADE
FOR THESE TIMES
Blair, Bre
BABY-SITTERS CLUB, THE
Blair, Euan
PRIEST
Blair, Nicky
CROSSING GUARD, THE
Blair, Ron
SEVEN
Blair, Tom
BED YOU SLEEP IN, THE
Blaisdell, Brad
BODY CHEMISTRY 4: FULL EXPOSURE
EVOLVER
Blaisdell, Nesbitt
DEAD MAN WALKING
JOURNEY OF AUGUST KING, THE
RECKLESS
Blaisse, John
TWELVE MONKEYS
Blake, Catherine
KID IN KING ARTHUR'S COURT, A
Blake, Geoffrey
APOLLO 13
Blake, Maudie
FUNNY BONES
Blake, Nicholas
BABE
Blake, Robert
MONEY TRAIN
Blakely, Don
UNDER SIEGE 2: DARK TERRITORY
Blakemore, Michael
COUNTRY LIFE
Blakey, Art
GREAT DAY IN HARLEM, A
Blakey, John
FIRST KNIGHT
JUDGE DREDD
Blanc, Dominique
TOTAL ECLIPSE
Blanc, Jennifer
BRADY BUNCH MOVIE, THE
Blanc, Michel
GROSSE FATIGUE

Blanchard, Brianna
CANDYMAN: FAREWELL TO THE FLESH
Blanchard, Ron
COUNTRY LIFE
Blanckaert, Eglantine
CITY OF LOST CHILDREN, THE
Blancke, Sandrine
SON OF THE SHARK, THE
Bland, John David
TANK GIRL
Blank, Jonathan
SEX, DRUGS AND DEMOCRACY
Blank, Wade
WHEN BILLY BROKE HIS HEAD ... AND
OTHER TALES OF WONDER
Blankfield, Mark
DRACULA: DEAD AND LOVING IT
Blanning, Adam
DREAMING OF RITA
Blare-Hershman, Joda
MAJOR PAYNE
Blatch, Helen
CARRINGTON
Blefari, Rosario
I, THE WORST OF ALL
Blendick, James
TOMMY BOY
Bliss, Ian
COUNTRY LIFE
Bliss, Jonah
BABY-SITTERS CLUB, THE
Blocher, Kent
MIGHTY APHRODITE
Blommaert, Susan
JERKY BOYS: THE MOVIE, THE
Blomquist, William
LITTLE PRINCESS, A
Bloom, Claire
MIGHTY APHRODITE
Bloom, John
CASINO
Bloom, Tom
BAD BLOOD
Blossom, Roberts
QUICK AND THE DEAD, THE
Blount, Lisa
JUDICIAL CONSENT
Blount, William
VAMPIRE IN BROOKLYN
Blow, Kurtis
SHOW, THE
Blowers, Sean
FIRST KNIGHT
Blue, Corinne
FRANKIE STARLIGHT
Bluhm, Brady
CRAZYSITTER, THE
Blum, Jack
EXOTICA
Blum, Mark
INDICTMENT: THE MCMARTIN TRIAL
MIAMI RHAPSODY
Blum, Richard
ASSASSINS
Blum, Steve
WINGS OF HONNEAMISE: ROYAL SPACE
FORCE
Blumenfeld, Lauren
LITTLE PRINCESS, A
Blumetti, Jim
DARK DEALER
SCANNERS: THE SHOWDOWN
Blundell, Jack
DALLAS DOLL
Blunt, Augie
AMERICAN PRESIDENT, THE

Blythe, Jr., Lenny
CREEP
Blythe, Peter
CARRINGTON
Blythe, Robert
ENGLISHMAN WHO WENT UP A HILL
BUT CAME DOWN A MOUNTAIN, THE
Boardman, Phil
THINGS TO DO IN DENVER WHEN
YOU'RE DEAD
Boatman, Michael
GLASS SHIELD, THE
Bobbi
JUPITER'S WIFE
Bobbie Roberts & Elephants
FUNNY BONES
Bobbitt, Nicole
PARTY GIRL
Bobst, Brandon
BRIDGES OF MADISON COUNTY, THE
Bocca, Julio
BALLET
Bocher, Christian
TWOGETHER
Bochner, Hart
GOOD DAY TO DIE, A
INNOCENT, THE
Bode, Ben
APOLLO 13
EMPIRE RECORDS
Bodegaard, Christian
FAIR GAME
Bodine, Hunter
LAST OF THE DOGMEN
Bodison, Wolfgang
EXPERT, THE
Boe, Gary "Buddy"
DEAD MAN WALKING
Boe, Kyle
MALLRATS
Boeck, Henri
NEKROMANTIK
Boen, Earl
COMPANION, THE
Boersma, Casey
FATHER OF THE BRIDE PART II
Boersma, Dylan
FATHER OF THE BRIDE PART II
Boesen, Kurt
OUTBREAK
Boesen, Kurt A.
AMERICAN PRESIDENT, THE
Bofshever, Michael
BYE BYE, LOVE
ROSWELL: THE U.F.O. COVER-UP
Bogart, Keith
HALLOWEEN: THE CURSE OF MICHAEL
MYERS
Bogdan, Henry
JERKY BOYS: THE MOVIE, THE
Boggs, Bill
SAFE PASSAGE
Boggs, Tony
QUICK AND THE DEAD, THE
Bogosian, Eric
ARABIAN KNIGHT
DOLORES CLAIBORNE
UNDER SIEGE 2: DARK TERRITORY
Boguski, Thomas "Doc"
BLUE TIGER
Bohlke, Peter
NOBODY LOVES ME
Bohm, Hark
PROMISE, THE
Bohman, Roger
TANK GIRL
Bohrer, Corinne
OPERATION INTERCEPT

Bohringer, Romane
MINA TANNENBAUM
TOTAL ECLIPSE
Boht, Jean
HEAVEN'S A DRAG
Boisen, Ole
KINGDOM, THE
Boisvert, Josee
LOVE AND HUMAN REMAINS
Bolano, Tony
BAD BOYS
JUST CAUSE
Bolen, Gary
EMPIRE RECORDS
Bolender, Bill
NIXON
THINGS TO DO IN DENVER WHEN
YOU'RE DEAD
Boles, Steve
DEAD MAN WALKING
NEW YORK COP
Bolger, Katie
RHYTHM THIEF
Bolland, Wally
CANADIAN BACON
Bollman, Ryan
GRANNY, THE
Bologna, Joseph
DANGER OF LOVE
Bologna, Marlene
BATMAN FOREVER
Bolt, Geoff
NINE MONTHS
Bolton, Buddy
BAD BOYS
Bolton, Jaques Apollo
O.J. SIMPSON STORY, THE
Bolton, Rick
POSTCARDS FROM AMERICA
Bolz, Catharine
BROTHERS MCMULLEN, THE
Bomes, Melissa
NET, THE
Bon Jovi, Jon
MOONLIGHT AND VALENTINO
Bonacki, Lou
BODILY HARM
Bonaduce, Danny
AMERICA'S DEADLIEST HOME VIDEO
Bonaduce, Gretchen
AMERICA'S DEADLIEST HOME VIDEO
Bonaiuto, Anna
POSTMAN, THE
Bonanni, Roberto
FORGET PARIS
Bond, Samantha
GOLDENEYE
Bonds, De'Aundre
TALES FROM THE HOOD
Bonehill, Richard
ROB ROY
Bones, Ken
CUTTHROAT ISLAND
Bonham, Bill
COPYCAT
Bonham Carter, Helena
MIGHTY APHRODITE
Boni, Gabrielle
INDICTMENT: THE MCMARTIN TRIAL
Bonner, Robert
COVER STORY
Bonnin, Ken
LIE DOWN WITH DOGS
Bonnot, Jacques
LES MISERABLES
Bono, Chastity
BAR GIRLS

Bono, Joseph
 CASINO
Bonsall, Brian
 FATHER AND SCOUT
Booker, Tom
 JURY DUTY
Bookston, Alexander
 MURDER IN THE FIRST
 WATER ENGINE, THE
Boone, Alan
 SABRINA
Boone, Ed
 MORTAL KOMBAT
Boone, Jr., Mark
 LAST OF THE DOGMEN
 QUICK AND THE DEAD, THE
 SEVEN
Boone, Lesley
 STUART SAVES HIS FAMILY
Boorman, Charley
 BEYOND RANGOON
Booth, Powers
 SUDDEN DEATH
Booth, Roger
 CUTTHROAT ISLAND
 LAMB
Booth, Tony
 PRIEST
Boothe, Daniel T. "Sweetie"
 TO WONG FOO, THANKS FOR
  EVERYTHING! JULIE NEWMAR
Boothe, Powers
 MUTANT SPECIES
 NIXON
Bordeltier, Clotiel
 CANDYMAN: FAREWELL TO THE FLESH
Borden, Amanda
 MURDER IN THE FIRST
Borek, Z.
 SHORT FILM ABOUT KILLING, A
Boret, Peter
 FIRST DEGREE
Boretski, Peter
 KURT VONNEGUT'S HARRISON
  BERGERON
Borghese, Paul
 BIKINI BISTRO
Borkan, Gene
 SEVEN
Borriello, Patrick
 DIE HARD WITH A VENGEANCE
 TWO BITS
Borsay, La Tonya
 IT TAKES TWO
Borsucki, W.
 SHORT FILM ABOUT KILLING, A
Borter, Rebecca
 DILLINGER
Boryea, Jay
 KISS OF DEATH
Bosch, Johnny Yong
 MIGHTY MORPHIN POWER RANGERS:
  THE MOVIE
Bosco, Philip
 IT TAKES TWO
 SAFE PASSAGE
Bose, Dilip
 CHARULATA
Bosevska, Julie
 ONLY THE BRAVE
Bossard, Jerry
 TWOGETHER
Bostwick, Barry
 SECRETARY, THE
Bostwick, Bud
 JADE
Bostwick, Jackson
 MUTANT SPECIES

Boswall, John
 RETURN OF THE NATIVE, THE
Boswell, Charles
 MURDER IN THE FIRST
Botero, Rodriego
 FATHER OF THE BRIDE PART II
Bottoms, Sam
 ZOOMAN
Bottoms, Timothy
 DIGGER
 TOP DOG
Boucard, Emmanuelle
 INNOCENT LIES
Bouchard, Raphaele
 CITY OF LOST CHILDREN, THE
Bouchaud, Jean
 OLD LADY WHO WALKED IN THE SEA,
  THE
Boucher, Savannah
 LAST SUMMER IN THE HAMPTONS
Bouchez, Elodie
 WILD REEDS
Bouclet, Philippe
 JEFFERSON IN PARIS
Bouda, Djamila
 CITY OF LOST CHILDREN, THE
Boudache, Younesse
 PIGALLE
Boudet, Jacques
 FARINELLI
 LES MISERABLES
Bouise, Jean
 I AM CUBA
Boujenah, Michel
 LES MISERABLES
Boukine, Valentine
 WINDOW TO PARIS
Boulenger, Rachel
 CITY OF LOST CHILDREN, THE
Boulet, Rene
 AUGUSTIN
Bounds, Jeff
 TIE-DIED: ROCK 'N' ROLL'S MOST
  DEADICATED FANS
Bounds, La Taunya
 LOSING ISAIAH
Bouquet, Carole
 BUSINESS AFFAIR, A
 GROSSE FATIGUE
Bourg, John
 BIG GREEN, THE
Bourgeois, John
 NEVER TALK TO STRANGERS
Bourland, Kevin
 TIE THAT BINDS, THE
Bourne, Amon
 STRANGE DAYS
Bouser, Stephen
 MUTE WITNESS
Bouthegmes, Abdel
 JEFFERSON IN PARIS
Boutsikaris, Dennis
 BOYS ON THE SIDE
Bouyala, Gaetan
 CITY OF LOST CHILDREN, THE
Bovard, Dominique
 WILD REEDS
Bovino, Rachel
 ALMOST DEAD
Bow Fong
 PHANTOM LOVER, THE
Bowden, Karen
 EXPERT, THE
Bowe, David
 HEAVYWEIGHTS
Bowen, Christopher
 RICHARD III

Bowen, Dennis
 BYE BYE, LOVE
Bowens, Malick
 OUTBREAK
Bower, Tom
 AVENGING ANGEL
 DILLINGER
 FAR FROM HOME: THE ADVENTURES OF
  YELLOW DOG
 GEORGIA
 NIXON
 WHITE MAN'S BURDEN
Bowers, Chris
 TIE-DIED: ROCK 'N' ROLL'S MOST
  DEADICATED FANS
Bowers, David G.
 MUTANT SPECIES
Bowery, Leigh
 WIGSTOCK: THE MOVIE
Bowker, Ryan
 LIVING IN OBLIVION
Bowman, Lisa
 RIVER OF GRASS
Bowser, Jennifer D.
 SUDDEN DEATH
Bowz, Eddie
 FEAR, THE
 MURDER IN THE FIRST
Boxcar Willie
 GORDY
Boxer, Stephen
 CARRINGTON
Boyce, Jim
 CRIMSON TIDE
 GLASS SHIELD, THE
Boyce, Todd
 JEFFERSON IN PARIS
Boyd, Cameron
 BYE BYE, LOVE
Boyd, Lynda
 DOUBLE, DOUBLE, TOIL AND TROUBLE
Boyden, Peter
 ACROSS THE SEA OF TIME: NEW YORK
  3D
Boyer, Paul
 OUTSIDE THE LAW
Boyett, William
 OUTSIDE THE LAW
Boylan, John
 FIRST DEGREE
Boyle, John
 WATER ENGINE, THE
Boyle, Lisa
 BAD BOYS
 I LIKE TO PLAY GAMES
 SHOWGIRLS
Boyle, Marilyn
 IT TAKES TWO
Boyle, Peter
 BORN TO BE WILD
 BULLETPROOF HEART
 WHILE YOU WERE SLEEPING
Boynton, Mere
 ONCE WERE WARRIORS
Boyraz, Suleyman
 GORILLA BATHES AT NOON
Bozovic, Petar
 GORILLA BATHES AT NOON
Bracco, Lorraine
 BASKETBALL DIARIES, THE
 HACKERS
Bracco, Rich
 NET, THE
Bracken, Heather
 ADDICTION, THE
Bradfield, Dawn
 RUN OF THE COUNTRY, THE

Bradford, Darcie
LITTLE PRINCESS, A
Bradford, Jesse
FAR FROM HOME: THE ADVENTURES OF
YELLOW DOG
HACKERS
Bradford, Richard
CROSSING GUARD, THE
INDICTMENT: THE MCMARTIN TRIAL
KINGFISH: A STORY OF HUEY P. LONG
STEAL BIG, STEAL LITTLE
Bradley, Dan
BLUE TIGER
Bradley, David
OUTSIDE THE LAW
Bradley, Kathleen
FRIDAY
Bradley, Tom
NICK OF TIME
Bradnum, Dick
HEAVEN'S A DRAG
Brady, J. Stephen
TOO YOUNG TO DIE?
Brady, James M.
NINE MONTHS
Brady, Lance
MURDER IN THE FIRST
Brady, P.J.
RUN OF THE COUNTRY, THE
Brady, Petra
ONLY THE BRAVE
Brady, Randall
UNDERNEATH, THE
Brady, Terry
COUNTRY LIFE
Braga, Sonia
BURNING SEASON, THE
Bragger, Klee
GOOFY MOVIE, A
Brags, Ian
DOUBLE, DOUBLE, TOIL AND TROUBLE
Brainard, Cam
NET, THE
Brake, Richard
DEATH MACHINE
Bramble, Adam
DARKMAN 2: THE RETURN OF DURANT
Brams, Julian
COMPANION, THE
Branagh, Kenneth
OTHELLO
Brancato, Jr., Lillo
CRIMSON TIDE
Brand, Hubertus
INNOCENT, THE
Brande, Peter
FUNNY BONES
Brandelius, Jerilyn Lee
TIE-DIED: ROCK 'N' ROLL'S MOST
DEADICATED FANS
Brandenberg, Larry
DILLINGER
Brandenburg, Otto
KINGDOM, THE
Brando, Marlon
DON JUAN DEMARCO
Brandt, Marilyn
OUTBREAK
Brandy, Moe
GORDY
Brangham-Snell, Oona
POSTCARDS FROM AMERICA
Branklyn, Charles
COPYCAT
Brannen, Ralph
DESTINY TURNS ON THE RADIO
Branner, Djola Bernard
BLACK IS ... BLACK AIN'T

Branning, Penelope
ALMOST DEAD
Branson, Elva
PIANO LESSON, THE
Braquet, Jean-Claude
FRENCH KISS
Brasselle, Melissa
BODY CHEMISTRY 4: FULL EXPOSURE
Braugher, Andre
CLASS OF '61
Brawand, Mercedes
VALLEY OF ABRAHAM, THE
Brazeau, Jay
GOLD DIGGERS: THE SECRET OF BEAR
MOUNTAIN
MALICIOUS
Breaux, Jr., Walter
DANGEROUS, THE
DEAD MAN WALKING
Breaux, Walter
KINGFISH: A STORY OF HUEY P. LONG
Brebner, John
VILLAGE OF THE DAMNED
Breck, Peter
DECOY
Bredenkamp, Shea R.
TO WONG FOO, THANKS FOR
EVERYTHING! JULIE NEWMAR
Breen, Danny
NET, THE
Breen, Patrick
GET SHORTY
Breen, Sean
SHOWGIRLS
Breese, Art
BRIDGES OF MADISON COUNTY, THE
Bremner, Ewen
JUDGE DREDD
Brendon, Nicholas
CHILDREN OF THE CORN III: URBAN
HARVEST
Brennan, Eileen
RECKLESS
Brennan, John H.
GALAXIS
Brennan, Johnny
JERKY BOYS: THE MOVIE, THE
Brennan, Matthew
LOSING ISAIAH
Brennan, Wayne
AVENGING ANGEL
Brennan, William
PANTHER
Brenneman, Amy
BYE BYE, LOVE
CASPER
HEAT
Brenner, Eve
MURDER IN THE FIRST
Brentano, Robin
IN THE NAME OF THE EMPEROR
Brentley, II, Melvin
HOUSEGUEST
Bresciani, Carlotta
MONTH BY THE LAKE, A
Breslau, Susan
FIRST KNIGHT
Breslin, John
RETURN OF THE NATIVE, THE
Bresliski, Ljupco
BEFORE THE RAIN
Bresnan, Bill
BIKINI BISTRO
Bresse, Shanna
BILLY MADISON
Bressler, Carl
USUAL SUSPECTS, THE

Bretherick, Andrea
FUNNY BONES
Brewer, Carl
DIE HARD WITH A VENGEANCE
Brewer, Jason C.
BRIDGES OF MADISON COUNTY, THE
Brewer, Juliette
BALTO
Brewerton, Kevin
HACKERS
Brezinova, Jana
MARTHA AND I
Briar, Jamian
GEORGIA
Brice, Ron
CLOCKERS
LITTLE ODESSA
NEW JERSEY DRIVE
Brickman, Greg
ENEMY WITHIN, THE
Bridgers, Arthur
DEAD MAN WALKING
Bridges, Don
ONLY THE BRAVE
Bridges, Jeff
WILD BILL
Brienza, Anthony "Chip"
TWELVE MONKEYS
Brierly, Roger
BUSINESS AFFAIR, A
Briet, Roland
NEA
Bright, Bob
ONLY THE BRAVE
Bright, Jeff
SILENCE OF THE HAMS
Bright, Martin
PANTHER
Bright, Richard
ME AND THE MOB
Brigitte, Anny
FACES OF WOMEN
Brigman, Karen
EMPIRE RECORDS
Brimble, Ian
SENSE AND SENSIBILITY
Brimley, Wilford
LAST OF THE DOGMEN
MUTANT SPECIES
Brinkley, David
MALLRATS
Brinton, Marty
FORGET PARIS
Briole, Vera
PIGALLE
Brion, Francoise
NEA
Brisbin, David
LEAVING LAS VEGAS
Briski, Joseph
SEPARATE LIVES
Brisson, Pat
SUDDEN DEATH
Bristow, Patrick
SHOWGIRLS
Britton, Connie
BROTHERS MCMULLEN, THE
Britton, Ryder
TOMMY BOY
Brix, Franziska
INNOCENT, THE
Broadbent, Jim
RICHARD III
Brock, Jim
HOWLING: NEW MOON RISING, THE
Brock, Kathryn
INDICTMENT: THE MCMARTIN TRIAL

Brock-Abraham, Cleo
BABY-SITTERS CLUB, THE
Brockett, Don
HOUSEGUEST
Brockhurst, Betsy
INDICTMENT: THE MCMARTIN TRIAL
Brockman, Ungela
SHOWGIRLS
Brocksmith, Roy
ALMOST DEAD
Broder, Andrew
CURE, THE
Broderich, Colleen
BAR GIRLS
Broderick, Beth
IN THE DEEP WOODS
Broderick, Matthew
ARABIAN KNIGHT
Broderick, Shirley
HIDEAWAY
Brogen, Paul
IN THE MOUTH OF MADNESS
Brogger, Lea
KINGDOM, THE
Brogren, Paul
JOHNNY MNEMONIC
Brolin, James
EXPERT, THE
Bron, Eleanor
LITTLE PRINCESS, A
Bronze, The
HEAVEN'S A DRAG
Brooke, Jayne
BYE BYE, LOVE
Brooke, Sarah
BORN TO BE WILD
Brookes, Jacqueline
LOSING ISAIAH
Brooks, Adam
FRENCH KISS
Brooks, Alex
DEATH MACHINE
Brooks, Carlos
AMERICAN COP
Brooks, Dana
CANADIAN BACON
Brooks, Dustin
GOLD DIGGERS: THE SECRET OF BEAR
MOUNTAIN
Brooks, Hadda
CROSSING GUARD, THE
Brooks, Jeff
FREE WILLY 2: THE ADVENTURE HOME
Brooks, Lori
AMERICA'S DEADLIEST HOME VIDEO
Brooks, Mark A.
BRIDGES OF MADISON COUNTY, THE
Brooks, Mel
DRACULA: DEAD AND LOVING IT
Brooks, Susan
FREE WILLY 2: THE ADVENTURE HOME
Brophy, Anthony
RUN OF THE COUNTRY, THE
Brophy, Brian
WHITE MAN'S BURDEN
Brose, Splat
NEKROMANTIK
Brosnan, Pierce
GOLDENEYE
Brou, Kouadio
FACES OF WOMEN
Brower, Jordan
BIG GREEN, THE
Brown, Adriane
KIDS
Brown, Amelda
SISTER MY SISTER

Brown, Andre Rosey
FORGET PARIS
Brown, Bernard
FORGET PARIS
Brown, Bobby
PANTHER
Brown, Cassandra
INDIAN IN THE CUPBOARD, THE
Brown, Claire
BETTER OFF DEAD
DANGER OF LOVE
Brown, Clancy
DEAD MAN WALKING
Brown, Connie Lee
JUST CAUSE
Brown, Dwier
DECONSTRUCTING SARAH
Brown, Gary
GLORY BOYS, THE
Brown, Glenda Morgan
SUDDEN DEATH
Brown, Graham
CLOCKERS
Brown, Henry
JUDICIAL CONSENT
Brown, Hope
WAITING TO EXHALE
Brown, Japhery
EXPERT, THE
Brown, Jophery
SUDDEN DEATH
Brown, Julie
CLUELESS
GOOFY MOVIE, A
NATIONAL LAMPOON'S ATTACK OF THE
5'2" WOMEN
Brown, Karlie M. Gavino
BYE BYE, LOVE
Brown, Kelly
MOSAIC PROJECT, THE
Brown, Kevin
NET, THE
TALL TALE: THE UNBELIEVABLE
ADVENTURES OF PECOS BILL
Brown, Kevin Guy
MONEY TRAIN
Brown, Kirstie R. Gavino
BYE BYE, LOVE
Brown, Maurice Jamasal
JUST CAUSE
Brown, Miquel
FRENCH KISS
Brown, Orlando
MAJOR PAYNE
Brown, Philip
NOSTRADAMUS KID, THE
Brown, Riwia
ONCE WERE WARRIORS
Brown, Roger Aaron
GALAXIS
TALL TALE: THE UNBELIEVABLE
ADVENTURES OF PECOS BILL
Brown, Roscoe Lee
BABE
Brown, Rosey
SILENCE OF THE HAMS
Brown, Samantha
NEW JERSEY DRIVE
Brown, Terry
COPYCAT
Brown, Toni
TIE-DIED: ROCK 'N' ROLL'S.MOST
DEADICATED FANS
Brown, Vee
RECKLESS
Brown, Velina
NINE MONTHS

Brown, W. Earl
VAMPIRE IN BROOKLYN
Brown, William Scott
S.F.W.
Brown, Wren
ALMOST DEAD
Brown, Wren T.
NET, THE
UNDER SIEGE 2: DARK TERRITORY
WAITING TO EXHALE
Browne, Ethan
HACKERS
Browne, Roscoe Lee
LAST SUMMER IN THE HAMPTONS
Browne, Scoville
GREAT DAY IN HARLEM, A
Browne, Zachary
MAN OF THE HOUSE
Browning, Susan
SABRINA
Bruce, Amanda
OUT OF ANNIE'S PAST
Bruce, Bella
SCARLET LETTER, THE
Bruce, Ed
KINGFISH: A STORY OF HUEY P. LONG
Bruce, James
DIRTY MONEY
Bruce, Nicholas
OH ... ROSALINDA!!
Bruck, Ruth
NOBODY LOVES ME
Bruckner, Douglas J.O.
CASPER
Bruckschwaiger, Karl
BEFORE SUNRISE
Bruel, Patrick
SABRINA
Bruhanski, Alex
CONVICT COWBOY
Brull, Pamela
STUART SAVES HIS FAMILY
Brummer, Jackie
SPITFIRE
Brumpton, John
ONLY THE BRAVE
Brunet, Genevieve
CITY OF LOST CHILDREN, THE
Brunetti, Ted
TWO BITS
Brunner, Chantal
NEA
Bruno, Jon
APOLLO 13
Bruns, Philip
PENTATHLON
Brunsmann, Keith
LORD OF ILLUSIONS
Bruskotter, Eric
CRIMSON TIDE
Brustyn, Ellen
GETTING OUT
Bryan, Zachery Ty
BIGFOOT: THE UNFORGETTABLE
ENCOUNTER
Bryans, Kenneth
SHALLOW GRAVE
Bryant, Karis
SUBSTITUTE WIFE, THE
Bryant, Kurt
BAD BLOOD
SCANNERS: THE SHOWDOWN
Bryant, Mark S.
OPERATION DUMBO DROP
Bryant, Molly
DEAD MAN WALKING
Bryant, Peter
JUMANJI

Bryant, Walter
RECKLESS
Brychta, Edita
ACCUMULATOR 1
Bryggman, Larry
DIE HARD WITH A VENGEANCE
Bryniarski, Andrew
HIGHER LEARNING
Bryniarski, Bruno
DANCE ME OUTSIDE
Bryson, Edith
COPYCAT
Bub, Natascha
INNOCENT, THE
Bucci, Barbara
RIVER OF GRASS
Buch, Fred
RADIO INSIDE
Buchanan, Russell
CANDYMAN: FAREWELL TO THE FLESH
Buchart, Nicholas
ABDUCTED 2: THE REUNION
Buchman, Sascha
MUTE WITNESS
Buchwald, Gauravani
DANGEROUS MINDS
BRADY BUNCH MOVIE, THE
VIRTUOSITY
Bucio, Julian
BURNING SEASON, THE
Buck, Cory
BUSHWHACKED
Buck, Justin Page
BREAK, THE
Buckingham, Lindsey
BRIAN WILSON: I JUST WASN'T MADE
FOR THESE TIMES
Buckingham, Robert
NICK OF TIME
Buckley, Allyson Anne
POSTCARDS FROM AMERICA
Buckley, Ralph
DIE HARD WITH A VENGEANCE
Buckley, Robert
ACROSS THE SEA OF TIME: NEW YORK
3D
Buckner, Parris
RADIO INSIDE
Buday, Zoltan
DECOY
Budig, Rebecca
BATMAN FOREVER
Buffalo Child
BLACK FOX
Buffer, Michael
VIRTUOSITY
Buffery, Kate
INNOCENT LIES
Buffett, Jimmy
CONGO
Bugden, Sue
GETTING OUT
Bugs, Joe
HIGHER LEARNING
Buhbinder, Mina
MINA TANNENBAUM
Buice, Michael
BIGFOOT: THE UNFORGETTABLE
ENCOUNTER
Buik, Owen
COUNTRY LIFE
Bujack, Wally
WAITING TO EXHALE
Bujang, Kuswadinath
BEYOND RANGOON
Buktenica, Ray
HEAT

Bulani, Ashok
BANDIT QUEEN
Bullock, Gary
LAKOTA WOMAN: SIEGE AT WOUNDED
KNEE
ROSWELL: THE U.F.O. COVER-UP
SPECIES
Bullock, Sandra
FOOL AND HIS MONEY, A
ME AND THE MOB
NET, THE
WHILE YOU WERE SLEEPING
Bullock, Scott
PEBBLE AND THE PENGUIN, THE
Bulsel, J'lia
VALLEY OF ABRAHAM, THE
Bumiller, William
SPECIES
TWOGETHER
Bunce, Stuart
FATHERLAND
FIRST KNIGHT
Bundy, Laura Bell
JUMANJI
Bunel, Marie
LES MISERABLES
Bunting, Lisa
CRACKERJACK
Buntzman, Mark
PANTHER
Buono, Cara
KICKING AND SCREAMING
Burchett, Elisa
PARTY GIRL
Burczek, Hubert
FARINELLI
Burdette, Nicole
SEARCH AND DESTROY
Burger, Cody
HEAVYWEIGHTS
Burgers, Michele
FRIENDS
Burgess, Julie
SAFE
Burgess, Lane
POSTCARDS FROM AMERICA
Burgess, Michael
SUM OF US, THE
Burghardt, Arthur
COSMIC SLOP
Burgi, Richard
PAYBACK
Burgio, Danielle
SHOWGIRLS
Buriev, Alexander
MUTE WITNESS
Burke, Betsy
BAR GIRLS
Burke, Beverly
SEVEN
Burke, Billy
TO CROSS THE RUBICON
Burke, Carlease
GET SHORTY
Burke, Marylouise
JEFFREY
Burkholder, Scott
ACROSS THE MOON
CLASS OF '61
CRIMSON TIDE
Burkley, Dennis
INDICTMENT: THE MCMARTIN TRIAL
Burks, Jernard
DEVIL IN A BLUE DRESS
Burmester, Leo
GREAT ELEPHANT ESCAPE, THE
Burnett, Kelly
DOLORES CLAIBORNE

Burnette, Olivia
QUICK AND THE DEAD, THE
Burnette, Van
LAKOTA WOMAN: SIEGE AT WOUNDED
KNEE
Burns, Edward
BROTHERS MCMULLEN, THE
Burns, James
CYBER BANDITS
Burns, Martha
NEVER TALK TO STRANGERS
Burow, Kurtis
SPECIES
Burr, Lonnie
SILENCE OF THE HAMS
Burrell, Michael
CENTURY
Burri, Fred
WALK IN THE CLOUDS, A
Burris, Pete
DEAD MAN WALKING
Burroughs, Coles
ART FOR TEACHERS OF CHILDREN
Burrows, Saffron
CIRCLE OF FRIENDS
Burstyn, Ellen
BABY-SITTERS CLUB, THE
HOW TO MAKE AN AMERICAN QUILT
ROOMMATES
Burton, Corey
GOOFY MOVIE, A
Burton, Jennifer
I LIKE TO PLAY GAMES
PLAY TIME
Burton, Matthew
INNOCENT, THE
Burton, Zoe
BABE
Buscemi, Michael
RIVER OF GRASS
Buscemi, Steve
DESPERADO
LIVING IN OBLIVION
ME AND THE MOB
THINGS TO DO IN DENVER WHEN
YOU'RE DEAD
Busey, Jake
S.F.W.
Bush, Owen
PREHYSTERIA! 3
Bush, Robert Lewis
IN THE MOUTH OF MADNESS
Bush, Tommy
CRIMSON TIDE
Bushcke, Michael
NEKROMANTIK
Bussieres, Pascale
WHEN NIGHT IS FALLING
Bussinger, Mickael
CITY OF LOST CHILDREN, THE
LES MISERABLES
Busta Rhymez
HIGHER LEARNING
Butcher, Randy
PYROMANIAC'S LOVE STORY, A
Butler, David
NEW JERSEY DRIVE
Butler, Lucy
FATHER AND SCOUT
NET, THE
Butler, Ponti
TALES FROM THE CRYPT: DEMON
KNIGHT
Butrum, Pat
GOOFY MOVIE, A
Butterfield, Alex
NIXON

Buttgereit, Jorg
NEKROMANTIK
Buttinger, Haymon Maria
BEFORE SUNRISE
Buzhardt, Toni Nichelle
DANGEROUS MINDS
Buzick, III, William
MOSAIC PROJECT, THE
Buzzotta, Dave
PREHYSTERIA! 3
Bye, Simon
CARRINGTON
Byers, Ralph
SAFE PASSAGE
Byfield, Trevor
GOLDENEYE
Bynum, Nate
CANDYMAN: FAREWELL TO THE FLESH
Byrd, Tom
CLOCKERS
Byrd, Toni Lynn
OUT OF ANNIE'S PAST
Byrdy, W.
SHORT FILM ABOUT KILLING, A
Byrne, Allie
CENTURY
Byrne, Antoine
RUN OF THE COUNTRY, THE
Byrne, Cillian
SECRET OF ROAN INISH, THE
Byrne, Gabriel
BUFFALO GIRLS
FRANKIE STARLIGHT
USUAL SUSPECTS, THE
Byrne, J. Dixon
CLEAN, SHAVEN
Byrne, Jenna
OUTBREAK
Byrne, Michael
BRAVEHEART
Byrne, Michael P.
BUSHWHACKED
Byrne, Peter
POSTCARDS FROM AMERICA
Byrne, Rose
DALLAS DOLL
Byrnes, Britany
BABE
Byrns, Ryan
CONVICT COWBOY
Byron, Annie
MURIEL'S WEDDING
NOSTRADAMUS KID, THE
Cabal, Lilliana
OUT OF ANNIE'S PAST
Caban, Angel
AMATEUR
MONEY TRAIN
Cabarbaye, Felicie Pasotti
TOTAL ECLIPSE
Cabus, Mark
EXPERT, THE
TOM AND HUCK
Caciola, James V.
UNDER SIEGE 2: DARK TERRITORY
Cada, James
GRUMPIER OLD MEN
Cade, John
BIGFOOT: THE UNFORGETTABLE
ENCOUNTER
Cadell, Pauline
FRANKIE STARLIGHT
Cadiente, Jeff
PROPHECY, THE
3 NINJAS KNUCKLE UP
Cadora, Eric
CANDYMAN: FAREWELL TO THE FLESH
MUTANT SPECIES

Cady, Shawn
NINE MONTHS
Cafagna, Ashley Lyn
LORD OF ILLUSIONS
Cage, Nicolas
KISS OF DEATH
LEAVING LAS VEGAS
Cahill, Devon
MY ANTONIA
Cahill, Sally
DALLAS DOLL
SUM OF US, THE
Cai Jiguang
BLUE VILLA, THE
Caicedo, Franklin
I, THE WORST OF ALL
Cains, Fraser
ENGLISHMAN WHO WENT UP A HILL
BUT CAME DOWN A MOUNTAIN, THE
Cajano, Pasquale
CASINO
Cake, Jonathan
FIRST KNIGHT
Calahasen, Helen
LAST OF THE DOGMEN
Calderisi, David
KURT VONNEGUT'S HARRISON
BERGERON
Calderon, Paul
ADDICTION, THE
CLOCKERS
FOUR ROOMS
Calderon, Wilmer
WALKING DEAD, THE
Caldwell, Diane
BETTER OFF DEAD
Caldwell, Janette
FORGET PARIS
Caldwell, L. Scott
DEVIL IN A BLUE DRESS
NET, THE
Cale, John
BRIAN WILSON: I JUST WASN'T MADE
FOR THESE TIMES
Calevas, Eleni
FORGET PARIS
Calhoun, Jr., William L.
FRIDAY
Calip, Ian
NIXON
Call, R.D.
WATERWORLD
Calla, Geoff
SHOWGIRLS
Callahan, Dick
POSTCARDS FROM AMERICA
Callas, Charlie
DRACULA: DEAD AND LOVING IT
Callie, Dayton
TO WONG FOO, THANKS FOR
EVERYTHING! JULIE NEWMAR
Callow, Simon
ACE VENTURA: WHEN NATURE CALLS
JEFFERSON IN PARIS
Calloway, Vanessa Bell
CRIMSON TIDE
Calvey, Mhairi
BRAVEHEART
Camacho, Mark
DR. JEKYLL & MS. HYDE
Camareno, Joe
BREACH OF CONDUCT
Camenish, Oren
BALLOT MEASURE 9
Cameron, Dean
GHOST BRIGADE
KICKING AND SCREAMING

Cameron, Elspeth
SHALLOW GRAVE
Cameron, J. Smith
JEFFREY
Cameron, John
CONGO
QUICK AND THE DEAD, THE
Cameron, Morven
HIGHLANDER: THE FINAL DIMENSION
Cameron, William
HOUSEGUEST
SUDDEN DEATH
Camp, Colleen
BABY-SITTERS CLUB, THE
DIE HARD WITH A VENGEANCE
THREE WISHES
Camp, Hamilton
PEBBLE AND THE PENGUIN, THE
Camp, Vic
LAKOTA WOMAN: SIEGE AT WOUNDED
KNEE
Camp-Horinek, Casey
LAKOTA WOMAN: SIEGE AT WOUNDED
KNEE
Campbell, Alan
DALLAS DOLL
Campbell, Amber-Lee
TO DIE FOR
Campbell, Bruce
CONGO
QUICK AND THE DEAD, THE
Campbell, Chuck
IN THE MOUTH OF MADNESS
Campbell, Colin
AMERICA'S DEADLIEST HOME VIDEO
Campbell, David
ANDROID AFFAIR, THE
Campbell, Desmond
ANDROID AFFAIR, THE
Campbell, G. Smokey
DEVIL IN A BLUE DRESS
Campbell, Greg
BOULEVARD
Campbell, J. Kenneth
COSMIC SLOP
Campbell, Jack
NOSTRADAMUS KID, THE
Campbell, Lindsey
GOOD DAY TO DIE, A
Campbell, Mick
SUM OF US, THE
Campbell, Naomi
MIAMI RHAPSODY
TO WONG FOO, THANKS FOR
EVERYTHING! JULIE NEWMAR
UNZIPPED
Campbell, Sarah
SCARLET LETTER, THE
Campbell, Scott Michael
FAIR GAME
Campbell, Stuart
SUM OF US, THE
Campbell, Vernon
TWELVE MONKEYS
Campedelli, Lauren
AMERICA'S DEADLIEST HOME VIDEO
Campenella, Christina
ADDICTION, THE
Campos, Cassandra
MY FAMILY: MI FAMILIA
Campos, Gustavo
BURNING SEASON, THE
Campos, Susanna
MY FAMILY: MI FAMILIA
Camuccio, Andrew
HEAT
Camuccio, Brian
HEAT

Canada, Ron
AMERICAN PRESIDENT, THE
MAN OF THE HOUSE
Canals, Maria
MY FAMILY: MI FAMILIA
Canavan, Kristie
TANK GIRL
Candy, John
CANADIAN BACON
Canemaker, John
FRANK AND OLLIE
Canepari, Bernard
ROOMMATES
SUDDEN DEATH
Cann, John
O.J. SIMPSON STORY, THE
Cannon, John
HEAVEN'S A DRAG
Cano, Pedro
I, THE WORST OF ALL
Canton, Joanna
EMPIRE RECORDS
Cantone, Mario
ME AND THE MOB
Canzoneri, Adrian
FATHER OF THE BRIDE PART II
Capizzi, Bill
DON JUAN DEMARCO
Caplan, Claire
DOUBLE, DOUBLE, TOIL AND TROUBLE
Caplan, Elinor O.
SAFE
Caplan, Twink
CLUELESS
Capodice, John
WATER ENGINE, THE
Capone, Nadia
FIRST DEGREE
Cappon, John
NET, THE
Capponi, Pier Paolo
FARINELLI
Capra, Chanel
FREE WILLY 2: THE ADVENTURE HOME
Capra, Francis
FREE WILLY 2: THE ADVENTURE HOME
Caprari, Toni
ARMAGEDDON: THE FINAL CHALLENGE
Capshaw, Kate
HOW TO MAKE AN AMERICAN QUILT
JUST CAUSE
NEXT DOOR
Capuana, Raymond
LIE DOWN WITH DOGS
Caputo, Jay
CONGO
Caramitru, Ion
CITIZEN X
Cardasco, Nicolas
I, THE WORST OF ALL
Cardazone, Rob
LIE DOWN WITH DOGS
Cardenas, Steve
MIGHTY MORPHIN POWER RANGERS:
THE MOVIE
Cardille-Rogal, Katie
ROOMMATES
Cardillo, Pamela
CIRCLE OF FRIENDS
Cardinahl, Jessica
INNOCENT, THE
Cardinal, Ben
MAGIC IN THE WATER
Cardinal, Tantoo
LAKOTA WOMAN: SIEGE AT WOUNDED
KNEE
Cardoso, David
VALLEY OF ABRAHAM, THE

Carey, Davin Jacob
THREE WISHES
Carey, Denis
LAMB
Carey, Tom
ART FOR TEACHERS OF CHILDREN
BLESSING
Carhart, Timothy
CANDYMAN: FAREWELL TO THE FLESH
Carides, Gia
BAD COMPANY
Carides, Zoe
DEATH IN BRUNSWICK
Caridi, Carmine
TOP DOG
Cariou, Len
CLASS OF '61
NEVER TALK TO STRANGERS
Carl, George
FUNNY BONES
Carley, Ron
TO WONG FOO, THANKS FOR
EVERYTHING! JULIE NEWMAR
Carlin, Joy
REDWOOD CURTAIN
Carlin, Nancy
FRAMEUP
Carlin, Peter
NIXON
Carlisle, Steve
DEAD MAN WALKING
Carlo, Johann
FAIR GAME
Carlson, Chris
GEORGIA
Carlson, Drucilla A.
STEAL BIG, STEAL LITTLE
Carlson, Pattie
ROOMMATES
Carlton, Maurice
NEW JERSEY DRIVE
Carlyle, Robert
PRIEST
Carmen, Julie
CYBER BANDITS
IN THE MOUTH OF MADNESS
Carmen, Loene
NOSTRADAMUS KID, THE
Carmichael, Jay
SCARLET LETTER, THE
Carmody, Caitlin
JOHNNY MNEMONIC
Carmody, Erin
JOHNNY MNEMONIC
Carmona, Antonio
STRAWBERRY AND CHOCOLATE
Carney, Laura
CLASS OF '61
Carney, Liam
BRAVEHEART
Carney, Marcus J.
FOR GOD AND COUNTRY
Caro, Marc
CITY OF LOST CHILDREN, THE
Carol, Ann
COLDBLOODED
Carol, Terri
FUNNY BONES
Carole, Anne
PIGALLE
Caron, Leslie
FUNNY BONES
Carothers, Ronald
BLACK FOX
Carpenter, Brian
ROSWELL: THE U.F.O. COVER-UP
Carpenter, John
SILENCE OF THE HAMS

Carpenter, Shari L.
WAITING TO EXHALE
Carpenter, Willie
MY FAMILY: MI FAMILIA
WHITE MAN'S BURDEN
Carr, Jeffrey
PANTHER
Carr, Michael
EROTIQUE
Carracedo, Claudette
DOUBLE HAPPINESS
Carradine, John
JACK-O
Carradine, Keith
TIE THAT BINDS, THE
WILD BILL
Carrasco, Carlos
BURNING SEASON, THE
Carrasco, Jonathan
BURNING SEASON, THE
Carrera, David
STRANGE DAYS
Carrere, Tia
JURY DUTY
Carrey, Jim
ACE VENTURA: WHEN NATURE CALLS
BATMAN FOREVER
Carrier, Corey
BUSHWHACKED
NIXON
Carriere, Jean-Claude
SERIOUS ABOUT PLEASURE
Carrig, Dennie
POSTCARDS FROM AMERICA
Carrigton, Natelie
TIE-DIED: ROCK 'N' ROLL'S MOST
DEADICATED FANS
Carrillo, Elpidia
MY FAMILY: MI FAMILIA
Carroll, Aarron
DARK DEALER
Carroll, Charles
DARK DEALER
NICK OF TIME
Carroll, Janet
BORN TO BE WILD
DESTINY TURNS ON THE RADIO
Carroll, Jim
BASKETBALL DIARIES, THE
Carroll, Luke
DALLAS DOLL
Carroll, Pat
GOOFY MOVIE, A
Carroll, Rocky
CRIMSON TIDE
Carruth, Kelley
EMPIRE RECORDS
Carson, Darwyn
O.J. SIMPSON STORY, THE
Carson, Lisa Nicole
DEVIL IN A BLUE DRESS
Carter, Brian
HEAVEN'S A DRAG
Carter, Carmen
VAMPIRE IN BROOKLYN
Carter, Deshanda
DANGEROUS MINDS
Carter, Gary
CURSE OF THE STARVING CLASS
Carter, Jason
GEORGIA
Carter, Jim
RICHARD III
Carter, Michael
WATER ENGINE, THE
Carter, Mitch
TOM AND HUCK

Carter, Nell
CRAZYSITTER, THE
Carter, Rachel
JACK-O
Carter, Richard
MURIEL'S WEDDING
Cartier, Carlo
MONTH BY THE LAKE, A
Cartlidge, Katrin
BEFORE THE RAIN
Cartoon Danny
TIE-DIED: ROCK 'N' ROLL'S MOST
DEADICATED FANS
Cartwright, Veronica
CANDYMAN: FAREWELL TO THE FLESH
Caruso, David
JADE
KISS OF DEATH
Carver Dan
TIE-DIED: ROCK 'N' ROLL'S MOST
DEADICATED FANS
Carver, Mary
SAFE
Casabonne, Guy
AUGUSTIN
Casamassa, Chris
MORTAL KOMBAT
Casarin, Angel
BURNING SEASON, THE
Casey, Bernie
GLASS SHIELD, THE
IN THE MOUTH OF MADNESS
Casey, Betty
AWFULLY BIG ADVENTURE, AN
Casey, Jacqueline
WHEN NIGHT IS FALLING
Casey, Kerry
MIGHTY MORPHIN POWER RANGERS:
THE MOVIE
Casey, Paddy
AWFULLY BIG ADVENTURE, AN
Cash, Rosalind
TALES FROM THE HOOD
Casillas, Rosendo
DON JUAN DEMARCO
Casillo, Lisa
ADDICTION, THE
Cass, Lee
HOUSEGUEST
Cassamier, Idella
DEAD MAN WALKING
Cassavetes, Nick
TWOGETHER
Cassel, Seymour
DARK SIDE OF GENIUS, THE
Cassel, Vincent
JEFFERSON IN PARIS
Casseus, Gabriel
NEW JERSEY DRIVE
Cassidy, Jaye
ONCE WERE WARRIORS
Cassidy, Joanna
VAMPIRE IN BROOKLYN
Cassidy, Martin
O.J. SIMPSON STORY, THE
Cassie
TIE-DIED: ROCK 'N' ROLL'S MOST
DEADICATED FANS
Cassini, Frank
CRACKERJACK
Cassini, John
SEVEN
Casson, Christopher
FRANKIE STARLIGHT
Cassus-Soulanis, Bernard
WINDOW TO PARIS
Castaneda, Hector
I AM CUBA

Castanon, Gabriel Eduardo
BURNING SEASON, THE
Castell, Dominik
BEFORE SUNRISE
Castelloe, Molly
CLEAN, SHAVEN
Castells, George
JACK-O
Castillo, Enrique
MY FAMILY: MI FAMILIA
NIXON
Castle, Aimee
LOVE AND HUMAN REMAINS
Castle, Danny
BATMAN FOREVER
Castle, Father Robert
ADDICTION, THE
Castle, Matthew
THREE WISHES
Castleman, Lisa
SAFE PASSAGE
Catalano, Lidia
I, THE WORST OF ALL
Cates, Georgina
AWFULLY BIG ADVENTURE, AN
FRANKIE STARLIGHT
Cates, Helen
UNDERNEATH, THE
Cathey, Reg E.
SEVEN
TANK GIRL
Catmull, Katherine
SUBSTITUTE WIFE, THE
Cattouse, Chelsea
INCREDIBLY TRUE ADVENTURES OF
TWO GIRLS IN LOVE, THE
Caufield, Jay
SUDDEN DEATH
Cauldwell, Brendan
AILSA
Caulfield, Maxwell
EMPIRE RECORDS
Caulfield, Melissa
EMPIRE RECORDS
Cavadini, Olindo
PIGALLE
Cavanagh, Megan
DRACULA: DEAD AND LOVING IT
Cavanaugh, Christine
BABE
Cavanaugh, Douglas
NUMBER ONE FAN
Cavanaugh, Thomas
MAGIC IN THE WATER
Cavanaugh, Timothy Patrick
DIRTY MONEY
Caven, Ingrid
NEA
Cavestani, Frank
AMERICAN PRESIDENT, THE
Caviezel, James
GOOD DAY TO DIE, A
Cawley, Tanya
CIRCLE OF FRIENDS
Cayne, Candis
WIGSTOCK: THE MOVIE
Cea, Rob
BORN TO BE WILD
Cecchinato, Tony
MINA TANNENBAUM
Cecere, Fulvio
ASSASSINS
Cedar, Jon
BODY SHOT
Cederberg, Bjorn
BETRAYAL
Cee, Frankie
ME AND THE MOB

Cejas, Juan
BAD BOYS
Celarie, Clementine
LES MISERABLES
Celedonio, Maria
HOW TO MAKE AN AMERICAN QUILT
Celeiro, Luis
UP TO A CERTAIN POINT
Celis, Fernando
SHOWGIRLS
Cellier, Caroline
FARINELLI
Cellucci, Claire
BILLY MADISON
Centatiempo, Johnny
MONEY TRAIN
Centenara, Eliza
DOUBLE, DOUBLE, TOIL AND TROUBLE
Cephers, Troy A.
CRIMSON TIDE
Cerda, Nathalie
LES MISERABLES
Cerna, J.D.
LIE DOWN WITH DOGS
Cerny, Daniel
CHILDREN OF THE CORN III: URBAN
HARVEST
Ceron, Laura
LOSING ISAIAH
Cerullo, Al
JERKY BOYS: THE MOVIE, THE
MAJOR PAYNE
Cervantes, Gary
O.J. SIMPSON STORY, THE
Chaback, J.J.
APOLLO 13
OUTBREAK
Chabat, Alain
SIX DAYS, SIX NIGHTS
Chadwick, Sarah
GROSS MISCONDUCT
Chai Ling
MOVING THE MOUNTAIN
Chaidez, John
S.F.W.
Chaim, Richard
MAD LOVE
Chalem, Denise
TOTAL ECLIPSE
Chalk, Garry
CIRCUMSTANCES UNKNOWN
Challis, Tom
FEAR, THE
Chalmers, Alison
UNSTRUNG HEROES
Chalupa, Vaclav
MARTHA AND I
Chama, Sydney
CRY, THE BELOVED COUNTRY
Chamberlain, Ardwight
BAREFOOT GEN
Chamberlain, Jill
CLEAN, SHAVEN
Chamberlin, Kevin
DIE HARD WITH A VENGEANCE
Chambers, David Kirk
AVENGING ANGEL
Chambers, Diego
JOHNNY MNEMONIC
Chambers, Eric
SCANNERS: THE SHOWDOWN
Chambers, Marilyn
BIKINI BISTRO
Chambers, Rebecca
FATHER OF THE BRIDE PART II
Chambers, Steve
VILLAGE OF THE DAMNED

Champa, Jo
DON JUAN DEMARCO
Champion, Michael
EVOLVER
OPERATION INTERCEPT
Chan, Darryl
JADE
Chan, Jordan
TWENTY SOMETHING
Chan, Joseph
KIDS
Chan, Michael Paul
BATMAN FOREVER
BODY CHEMISTRY 4: FULL EXPOSURE
GALAXIS
Chan, Moses
TWENTY SOMETHING
Chance, Carlton
CENTURY
Chance, Michael
TWELVE MONKEYS
Chancellor, Anna
CENTURY
Chandler, Damon
NEW JERSEY DRIVE
Chandler, Dan
EXPERT, THE
MUTANT SPECIES
Chandler, Erin
BITTER VENGEANCE
Chandler, Jared
OPERATION DUMBO DROP
Chandler, Kyle
CONVICT COWBOY
Chandler, Mishell
TO WONG FOO, THANKS FOR
EVERYTHING! JULIE NEWMAR
Chandra, Mahesh
BANDIT QUEEN
Chang, Jeng-Yie
SHAO LIN POPEYE
Chang, Kuo-Jew
SHAO LIN POPEYE
Chang, Ray
STRANGE DAYS
Chang Shih
WOODEN MAN'S BRIDE, THE
Chang, Stephen
DOUBLE HAPPINESS
Channing, Stockard
SMOKE
TO WONG FOO, THANKS FOR
EVERYTHING! JULIE NEWMAR
Chapek, Susan
HOUSEGUEST
Chaplin, Ben
FEAST OF JULY
Chaplin, Carmen
SABRINA
Chaplin, Christopher
TOTAL ECLIPSE
Chaplin, Geraldine
HOME FOR THE HOLIDAYS
VOYAGE EN DOUCE
Chapman, Duggie
FUNNY BONES
Chapman, Mark Lindsay
SEPARATE LIVES
Chapman, Vernon
BILLY MADISON
Chapman, Wes
BALLET
Chappell, Crystal
BIGFOOT: THE UNFORGETTABLE
ENCOUNTER
Chappell, Katsy
INDICTMENT: THE MCMARTIN TRIAL

Charlebois, Rod
LOVE AND HUMAN REMAINS
Charles
JUPITER'S WIFE
Charles, Jonathan
WINGS OF HONNEAMISE: ROYAL SPACE
FORCE
Charles, Josh
COLDBLOODED
Charles, Tom
DECOY
WINGS OF HONNEAMISE: ROYAL SPACE
FORCE
Charlette, Kennetch
SCARLET LETTER, THE
Charlier, Daniel
MINA TANNENBAUM
Charlton, Maryette
INCREDIBLY TRUE ADVENTURES OF
TWO GIRLS IN LOVE, THE
Charlton, William
MONEY TRAIN
Chartok, Tulane
REASON TO BELIEVE, A
Chase, Carl
CUTTHROAT ISLAND
Chase, Chevy
MAN OF THE HOUSE
Chase, Courtney
NICK OF TIME
ROOMMATES
Chase, Gregory
SABRINA
Chase, Peter
MINA TANNENBAUM
Chasse, Eric
CONVICT COWBOY
Chatterjee, Dhritiman
STRANGER, THE
Chatterjee, Soumitra
CHARULATA
Chatterji, Subrota
STRANGER, THE
Chattman, Dwayne
VIRTUOSITY
Chau, Billy
HIGH RISK
Chau, Francois
BLUE TIGER
Chaudhry, Ranjit
BANDIT QUEEN
Chauvel, Patrick
PIGALLE
Chaykin, Maury
CUTTHROAT ISLAND
DEVIL IN A BLUE DRESS
UNSTRUNG HEROES
Chazel, Marie Ann
GROSSE FATIGUE
Cheadle, Don
DEVIL IN A BLUE DRESS
THINGS TO DO IN DENVER WHEN
YOU'RE DEAD
Cheah, Johnny
BEYOND RANGOON
Chebalina, Varvara
WINDOW TO PARIS
Chen Baochang
ERMO
Chen, Greg
DOUBLE HAPPINESS
Chen, Joan
HUNTED, THE
JUDGE DREDD
Chen, Larissa
DESPERATE PREY
Chen Shu
SHANGHAI TRIAD

Chen Zhuoxin
HEROIC TRIO, THE
Cheng, Lawrence
HE'S A WOMAN, SHE'S A MAN
Chern Dao Van
OPERATION DUMBO DROP
Chernoff, Mary
MIAMI RHAPSODY
Chess, Lisa
SEPARATE LIVES
Chesser, Bethany
SHOWGIRLS
Chester, Vanessa Lee
LITTLE PRINCESS, A
Chestnut, Morris
UNDER SIEGE 2: DARK TERRITORY
Chestnutt, James
DANGER OF LOVE
Chetwynd, Rupert
INNOCENT, THE
Cheung, Farini
TWENTY SOMETHING
Cheung, George Kee
GALAXIS
NEW YORK COP
Cheung Hung-On
TWENTY SOMETHING
Cheung, Jacky
ASHES OF TIME
HIGH RISK
Cheung, Leslie
ASHES OF TIME
HE'S A WOMAN, SHE'S A MAN
PHANTOM LOVER, THE
Cheung, Maggie
ASHES OF TIME
EXECUTIONERS
HEROIC TRIO, THE
Chevalier, Martine
JEFFERSON IN PARIS
Chevallier, Dominique
CITY OF LOST CHILDREN, THE
Cheyne, Hank
BAD BLOOD
DECONSTRUCTING SARAH
Chiarella, Jorge
NO MERCY
Chibber, Deepak
BANDIT QUEEN
Chick, Tom
FRANK & JESSE
Chief-Moon, Byron
GOOD DAY TO DIE, A
Chiefcalf, Calvert
DECOY
Chieffo, Michael
BABYSITTER, THE
CRIMSON TIDE
Chiefmoon, Byron
BLACK FOX
Chiffre, Phillippe
MINA TANNENBAUM
Chiklis, Michael
NIXON
Childress, Helen
AMERICAN COP
Childs, Lucy
DILLINGER
Chiles, Linden
GLASS SHIELD, THE
Chiles, Lois
BABYSITTER, THE
Chin, Lori Tan
LIVING IN OBLIVION
Chin, Paul
HEROIC TRIO, THE
Chin Pei
HEROIC TRIO, THE

Chindjaikin, Nikolai
MUTE WITNESS
Ching, Charles
TO WONG FOO, THANKS FOR
EVERYTHING! JULIE NEWMAR
Chingmy Yau
HIGH RISK
RETURN OF THE GOD OF GAMBLERS
Chinyamurindi, Michael
CONGO
Chisholm, Jimmy
BRAVEHEART
Chiverton, Fred
BRAVEHEART
Chlumsky, Anna
GOLD DIGGERS: THE SECRET OF BEAR
MOUNTAIN
Cho, Charlie
HIGH RISK
Cho, Margaret
DOOM GENERATION, THE
Cho, Peter
BRIDGES OF MADISON COUNTY, THE
Choate, Tim
JEFFERSON IN PARIS
Chodos, Daniel
OUTBREAK
Choe, Dean
HUNTED, THE
Choe, Stella
NEXT DOOR
Choi Hark-kin
EROTIQUE
**Choir of the Guardian Angel National
School**
AILSA
Chojnacka, M.
SHORT FILM ABOUT LOVE, A
Chong, Michael
NICK OF TIME
Chong, Rae Dawn
BOCA
BOULEVARD
BREAK, THE
HIDEAWAY
POWER OF ATTORNEY
Chong, Tommy
NATIONAL LAMPOON'S SENIOR TRIP
Chong-Won Choi
HOW TO TOP MY WIFE
Choua Moua
CURSE OF THE STARVING CLASS
Chow, Valerie
HIGH RISK
TWENTY SOMETHING
Chow Yun-fat
RETURN OF THE GOD OF GAMBLERS
Chowdhry, Ranjit
PEREZ FAMILY, THE
Chowdhury, Pitambar
STRANGER, THE
Chrest, Joe
KINGFISH: A STORY OF HUEY P. LONG
UNDERNEATH, THE
Chriqui, Emmanuelle
KURT VONNEGUT'S HARRISON
BERGERON
Christ, Bill
DIE HARD WITH A VENGEANCE
Christensen, Hayden
IN THE MOUTH OF MADNESS
KURT VONNEGUT'S HARRISON
BERGERON
Christensen, Laura
KINGDOM, THE
Christian, Wolf
FIRST KNIGHT

Christie, Sabrinah
ACE VENTURA: WHEN NATURE CALLS
Christie, William
JEFFERSON IN PARIS
Christmas, Eric
ALMOST DEAD
Christoff, Russ
COPYCAT
Christofferson, Debra
SILENCE OF THE HAMS
Christopher, Bo Jesse
TANK GIRL
Christopher, Dennis
OPERATION INTERCEPT
Christopher, Julian
BROKEN TRUST
Christopher, June
FREE WILLY 2: THE ADVENTURE HOME
Christopherson, Kyle
GRUMPIER OLD MEN
Christy, George
JURY DUTY
OUTBREAK
SEVEN
Chua, Jeni
COPYCAT
Chudabala, Art
STRANGE DAYS
Chuipka, Chip
HIGHLANDER: THE FINAL DIMENSION
Chula, Babz
DOUBLE, DOUBLE, TOIL AND TROUBLE
POWER OF ATTORNEY
PYROMANIAC'S LOVE STORY, A
Church, Thomas Haden
TALES FROM THE CRYPT: DEMON
KNIGHT
Churchill, Richelle
INDICTMENT: THE MCMARTIN TRIAL
Chvedersky, Anatoli
WINDOW TO PARIS
Chye, Yeoh Keat
BEYOND RANGOON
Ciafalio, Carl N.
CANDYMAN: FAREWELL TO THE FLESH
Ciarcia, Chacha
ME AND THE MOB
Ciarfalio, Carl
SCANNERS: THE SHOWDOWN
Ciccelella, Jude
BOYS ON THE SIDE
Cicchetti, Mike
HACKERS
Ciccolella, Jude
MAD LOVE
Cimarosa, Tano
PURE FORMALITY, A
Cimino, Leonardo
WATERWORLD
Cinnante, Kelly
VAMPIRE IN BROOKLYN
Cintra, Luis Miguel
CONVENT, THE
VALLEY OF ABRAHAM, THE
Circo Maromero
DIRTY MONEY
Cisneros, Roman J.
DANGEROUS MINDS
Citti, Franco
MAMMA ROMA
Claessem, Yves
MINA TANNENBAUM
Clair, Jon
CHILDREN OF THE CORN III: URBAN
HARVEST
Claire, Cyrielle
LES MISERABLES

Claire, Janet
GLASS SHIELD, THE
Clancy, Brian
DANCE ME OUTSIDE
Clark, Anthony
TERESA'S TATTOO
Clark, Brett Baxter
MIDNIGHT TEASE 2
Clark, Harlan
TANK GIRL
Clark, Jane
GALAXIS
Clark, Jim
UNDER SIEGE 2: DARK TERRITORY
Clark, Jonathan
HEAVYWEIGHTS
Clark, Madison
SHOWGIRLS
Clark, Matt
CANDYMAN: FAREWELL TO THE FLESH
Clark, Roy
GORDY
Clark, Tiffany Lynn
TOM AND HUCK
Clark, Trevor
RUN OF THE COUNTRY, THE
Clark, Wesley H.
NEW YORK COP
Clarke, Basil
MURIEL'S WEDDING
Clarke, Graham
ARMAGEDDON: THE FINAL CHALLENGE
Clarke, John
DEATH IN BRUNSWICK
Clarke, Jordan
SAFE PASSAGE
Clarke, Kal
EROTIQUE
Clarke, Lars
HEAVYWEIGHTS
Clarke, Logan
SEPARATE LIVES
Clarke, Phillip
PEBBLE AND THE PENGUIN, THE
Clarke, Shaun R.
SCARLET LETTER, THE
Clarkson, Melinda
OUT OF ANNIE'S PAST
Clarkson, Patricia
JUMANJI
Clausen, Blake Molino
INDICTMENT: THE MCMARTIN TRIAL
Clavier, Christian
GROSSE FATIGUE
Claxton, Richard
FIRST KNIGHT
Clay, Tony
ATTACK OF THE 60-FOOT CENTERFOLD
Clayton, Buck
GREAT DAY IN HARLEM, A
Clayton, Gina
IT TAKES TWO
Clear, Patrick
LOSING ISAIAH
Cleckler, James Paul
NOW AND THEN
Clemenson, Christian
APOLLO 13
Clement, Alan
SUDDEN DEATH
Clement, Bill
SUDDEN DEATH
Clemente, Aixa
BABY-SITTERS CLUB, THE
Clendenin, Robert
INDICTMENT: THE MCMARTIN TRIAL

Cleveland, Dan "Rattlehead"
CREEP
Cleven, Harry
MINA TANNENBAUM
Clifford, Richard
CARRINGTON
Clifton, Alan
MOONLIGHT AND VALENTINO
Clinis, Marty
CLEAN, SHAVEN
Clink, Carl
GHOST BRIGADE
Clinton, George
COSMIC SLOP
Clokey, Art
GUMBY: THE MOVIE
Clokey, Gloria
GUMBY: THE MOVIE
Clow, Stuart
WHEN NIGHT IS FALLING
Clunie, Michelle
EROTIQUE
USUAL SUSPECTS, THE
Cluzet, Francois
FRENCH KISS
Coates, Conrad
TO DIE FOR
Coates, Kim
BLACK FOX
WATERWORLD
Cobb, Julie
DR. JEKYLL & MS. HYDE
Cobbs, Bill
FLUKE
KINGFISH: A STORY OF HUEY P. LONG
THINGS TO DO IN DENVER WHEN
YOU'RE DEAD
Coburn, James
AVENGING ANGEL
Cochofel, Filipe
VALLEY OF ABRAHAM, THE
Cochran, Michele
CURSE OF THE STARVING CLASS
Cochrane, Rory
EMPIRE RECORDS
Cockburn, Ian
COUNTRY LIFE
Cocktails, Johnny
DRACULA: DEAD AND LOVING IT
Cody, Marissa
COVER STORY
Coffey, Chantal
NEXT DOOR
Coffey, Colleen
MOSAIC PROJECT, THE
Coffey, Jean Marie
FIRST KNIGHT
SHALLOW GRAVE
Coffey, Scott
TANK GIRL
Cogan, Maggie
JUPITER'S WIFE
Cognard, Lili
CITY OF LOST CHILDREN, THE
Cohan, Robert
DANCER, THE
Cohen, Beverly
VIRTUOSITY
Cohen, Ellen
LOVE AND HUMAN REMAINS
Cohen, Ena
RESTORATION
Cohen, Jessica
RESTORATION
Cohen, Martine
MINA TANNENBAUM
Cohen, Michael
LES MISERABLES

Cohen, Robert P.
LITTLE PRINCESS, A
Cohen, Scott
ROOMMATES
Coit, John
TIE-DIED: ROCK 'N' ROLL'S MOST
DEADICATED FANS
Colantoni, Enrico
MONEY TRAIN
Colby, R. Blakeslee
REDWOOD CURTAIN
Cole, Gary
BRADY BUNCH MOVIE, THE
Cole, Joseph
MURDER IN THE FIRST
Cole, Keith
BILLY MADISON
PRIEST
Cole, Kelly
INNOCENT, THE
Coleman, Alex
HOUSEGUEST
Coleman, Avron
ADDICTION, THE
Coleman, Brady
POWDER
Coleman, Chad
NEW YORK COP
Coleman, Dabney
JUDICIAL CONSENT
Coleman, Gary
S.F.W.
Coleman, Jimmy
PRIEST
Coleman, Joseph P.
MIGHTY APHRODITE
Coleman, Marilyn
BETTER OFF DEAD
Coleman, Renee
PENTATHLON
Coleman, Rosalyn
PIANO LESSON, THE
Coleman, Stephen
MAJOR PAYNE
Coles, Stan
CANADIAN BACON
Colgan, Eileen
SECRET OF ROAN INISH, THE
Coli, Daniel
BRAVEHEART
Colin, Gregoire
BEFORE THE RAIN
Colitti, Rik
DEAD PRESIDENTS
Collar, Sharon
MAD LOVE
Collazo, Luz Maria
I AM CUBA
Collette, Toni
ARABIAN KNIGHT
MURIEL'S WEDDING
Collier, Drake
BETTER OFF DEAD
BORN TO BE WILD
Collier, Keith
WHITE MAN'S BURDEN
Collier, Marian
ASSASSINS
Collings, David
PERSUASION
Collins, Bob
SEVEN
Collins, David
TO DIE FOR
Collins, Georgie
LAST OF THE DOGMEN
Collins, Grace
COVER STORY

Collins, Greg
TIE THAT BINDS, THE
UNDER SIEGE 2: DARK TERRITORY
Collins, Jesse
DARKMAN 2: THE RETURN OF DURANT
Collins, Joely
HIDEAWAY
Collins, John
VAMPIRES AND OTHER STEREOTYPES
Collins, Jr., Wayne
3 NINJAS KNUCKLE UP
Collins, Phil
BALTO
Collison, Frank
S.F.W.
Colliti, Rik
TWO BITS
Colombarolli, Arnaldo
I, THE WORST OF ALL
Colon, Adrian
DEAD MAN WALKING
MUTANT SPECIES
Colon, Miriam
SABRINA
Colosimo, Sandra
ME AND THE MOB
Coltrane, Robbie
GOLDENEYE
Columbus, Brendan
NINE MONTHS
Columbus, Eleanor
NINE MONTHS
Columbus, Irene
NINE MONTHS
Columbus, Violet
NINE MONTHS
Colunga, Alejandro
I, THE WORST OF ALL
Colwell, Chase
FATHER OF THE BRIDE PART II
Colwell, John
DARK DEALER
Colwell, K.C.
FATHER OF THE BRIDE PART II
Colwell, Sue
FATHER OF THE BRIDE PART II
Coman, Gilly
PRIEST
Comando, Joe
SAFE
Combs, David
ENEMY WITHIN, THE
Combs, Gil
SUDDEN DEATH
Combs, Holly Marie
REASON TO BELIEVE, A
Combs, Jeffrey
CASTLE FREAK
DILLINGER AND CAPONE
Combs, Ray
VAMPIRE IN BROOKLYN
Combs, Sean "Puffy"
SHOW, THE
Comer, Anjanette
UNDERNEATH, THE
Commelin, Elizabeth
FRENCH KISS
Compton, David
EXPERT, THE
Compton, O'Neal
NIXON
Comrie, Christopher
JOHNNY MNEMONIC
Comshaw, Lisa
SCANNERS: THE SHOWDOWN
Conaway, Cristi
NINA TAKES A LOVER

Conforto, Emily
   PROPHECY, THE
Conklin, Colton
   SUBSTITUTE WIFE, THE
Conklin, Ida
   JUST CAUSE
Conley, Chase
   JOURNEY OF AUGUST KING, THE
Conley, Jack
   APOLLO 13
   GET SHORTY
Conlon, Noel
   O.J. SIMPSON STORY, THE
Conmee, Marie
   CIRCLE OF FRIENDS
Conn, Terri
   SPITFIRE
Conna, Ed
   ADDICTION, THE
Connell, Christina
   JACK-O
Connell, Jane
   DR. JEKYLL & MS. HYDE
Connelly, Ed
   SABRINA
Connelly, Jennifer
   HIGHER LEARNING
Connelly, Will
   RIVER OF GRASS
Conner, Mike
   JACK-O
Connery, Phillip
   DRACULA: DEAD AND LOVING IT
Connery, Sean
   FIRST KNIGHT
   JUST CAUSE
Connick, Jr., Harry
   COPYCAT
Connolly, Billy
   POCAHONTAS
Connolly, Kevin
   ANGUS
Connolly, Sissy
   RUN OF THE COUNTRY, THE
Connors, Kathleen
   CONGO
Connors, Michael
   DRACULA: DEAD AND LOVING IT
Conrad, Roy
   VILLAGE OF THE DAMNED
Conrad, Shane
   BRADY BUNCH MOVIE, THE
Conroy, Brendan
   AILSA
   AWFULLY BIG ADVENTURE, AN
   CIRCLE OF FRIENDS
   SECRET OF ROAN INISH, THE
Conroy, Wi-Waste-Win
   LAKOTA WOMAN: SIEGE AT WOUNDED
      KNEE
Considine, John
   FREE WILLY 2: THE ADVENTURE HOME
Constantino, Landry M.
   HEAVYWEIGHTS
Conte, Christopher
   INDIAN IN THE CUPBOARD, THE
   JERKY BOYS: THE MOVIE, THE
Conte, Daniel P.
   CASINO
Conti, Peter
   CASINO
   COVER ME
Conti, Richard
   COPYCAT
Contino, Merri
   BODILY HARM
Conto, Marcia
   BOCA

Contreras, Adria
   BOYS ON THE SIDE
Contreras, Victor
   GLASS SHIELD, THE
Convey, Colum
   LAMB
Conway, Cordell
   WAITING TO EXHALE
Conway, Kevin
   QUICK AND THE DEAD, THE
Conway, Mark
   MAJOR PAYNE
Coogan, Keith
   REASON TO BELIEVE, A
Coogan, Steve
   INDIAN IN THE CUPBOARD, THE
Cook, Bill
   ROSWELL: THE U.F.O. COVER-UP
Cook, Jared
   BILLY MADISON
Cook, Joy M.
   NINE MONTHS
Cook, Kelly
   BODY STROKES
Cook, Pam
   SPECIES
Cook, Rachael Leigh
   BABY-SITTERS CLUB, THE
   TOM AND HUCK
Cook, Vincent
   EROTIQUE
Cooke, Christopher
   RHYTHM THIEF
Cooke, Gregory
   JURY DUTY
Cooke, Keith H.
   MORTAL KOMBAT
Cooke, Matt
   CANADIAN BACON
Cooke, Michael
   SHOWGIRLS
Cooke, Patrick
   RIVER OF GRASS
Cooke, Vanessa
   FRIENDS
Coombes, Norman
   MANGLER, THE
Cooney, Kevin
   DEAD MAN WALKING
Cooney, Martha J.
   LIE DOWN WITH DOGS
Cooper, Bobby
   CROSSING GUARD, THE
Cooper, Brian
   DIRTY MONEY
Cooper, Charles
   PANTHER
Cooper, Chris
   MONEY TRAIN
Cooper, Philippa
   SABRINA
Cooper, Roy
   BASKETBALL DIARIES, THE
   DOLORES CLAIBORNE
Cooper, Sam
   OUT OF ANNIE'S PAST
Cooper, Trevor
   CENTURY
Cope, Joan
   JOURNEY OF AUGUST KING, THE
Cope, Richard
   HEAVEN'S A DRAG
Copeland, Kevin
   MURIEL'S WEDDING
Copeland, Marissa
   AMATEUR

Copello, Bert
   FORGET PARIS
Copeman, Michael
   CANADIAN BACON
Coppin, Nick
   FUNNY BONES
Copping, Jennifer
   MALICIOUS
Coppola, Lucia
   MINA TANNENBAUM
Coppola, Marc
   LEAVING LAS VEGAS
Copullari, Augusta
   WATER ENGINE, THE
Corbeil, Luc
   BLACK FOX
Corbett, Ed
   VILLAGE OF THE DAMNED
Corbett, Susannah
   FIRST KNIGHT
Corbin, Demetri
   JEFFREY
Corbin, Pat
   TIE-DIED: ROCK 'N' ROLL'S MOST
      DEADICATED FANS
Corbitt, Wayne T.
   BLACK IS ... BLACK AIN'T
Corbo, Maria A.
   JERKY BOYS: THE MOVIE, THE
Cord, Erik
   STUART SAVES HIS FAMILY
Cordray, Lisa
   DRACULA: DEAD AND LOVING IT
Corduner, Allan
   BUSINESS AFFAIR, A
Corello, Nicky
   DEVIL IN A BLUE DRESS
Cork, Malcolm
   DESPERATE PREY
Corke, Fiona
   GROSS MISCONDUCT
Corkrean, Jana
   BRIDGES OF MADISON COUNTY, THE
Corley, Al
   DON JUAN DEMARCO
Corley, Annie
   BRIDGES OF MADISON COUNTY, THE
Corley, Sharron
   NEW JERSEY DRIVE
Corman, Roger
   APOLLO 13
Corman, Rosemary
   CURE, THE
Cornell, David
   QUICK AND THE DEAD, THE
Cornwell, Judy
   PERSUASION
Corone, Antoni
   FAIR GAME
Corosky, Emma
   NEVER TALK TO STRANGERS
Corre, Sadie
   FUNNY BONES
Correia, David
   SEVEN
Corri, Nick
   VAMPIRE IN BROOKLYN
Corrieri, Sergio
   I AM CUBA
Corrigan, John
   POSTCARDS FROM AMERICA
Corrigan, Kevin
   BAD BOYS
   KISS OF DEATH
   LAST GOOD TIME, THE
   LIVING IN OBLIVION
   RHYTHM THIEF

Corrigan, Patrica
COVER STORY
Corsini, Silvana
MAMMA ROMA
Corso, Jean
FRENCH KISS
Cort, Bud
GIRL IN THE CADILLAC
Cortegiani, Rolando
CASTLE FREAK
Cortes, Rafael
MY FAMILY: MI FAMILIA
Cortez, Bertie
MINA TANNENBAUM
Cortez, Jesus
LIE DOWN WITH DOGS
Cortez, Julia
MIGHTY MORPHIN POWER RANGERS:
THE MOVIE
Cortina, Andres
STRAWBERRY AND CHOCOLATE
Cortinez, Susana
I, THE WORST OF ALL
Coryell, Bradley
NOW AND THEN
Cosmo, James
BRAVEHEART
Costaldo, Beverly
SEPARATE LIVES
Costantino, Fausto
FRENCH KISS
Costanza, Donna Marie
BAR GIRLS
Costanza, Joe
VAMPIRE IN BROOKLYN
Costanza, Len
UNSTRUNG HEROES
Costanzo, Robert
FORGET PARIS
Costello, Tracey
PANTHER
Costelloe, John
KISS OF DEATH
ME AND THE MOB
Costner, Anne
BABY-SITTERS CLUB, THE
Costner, Kevin
WATERWORLD
Costner, Lily
BABY-SITTERS CLUB, THE
Cote, Tina
DARK SIDE OF GENIUS, THE
Cothran, Jr., John
GET SHORTY
Cotone, Mark
DEVIL IN A BLUE DRESS
Cottet, Mia
NINE MONTHS
Cottingham, Paul
HEAVEN'S A DRAG
Coulson, Mary
KINGFISH: A STORY OF HUEY P. LONG
Coulter, Clare
WHEN NIGHT IS FALLING
Council, Richard
CANADIAN BACON
DIE HARD WITH A VENGEANCE
Countouriotis, Steve
OPERATION DUMBO DROP
Courcet, Richard
I CAN'T SLEEP
Courtney, Jeni
SECRET OF ROAN INISH, THE
Cousineau, Kelly
TANK GIRL
Cousins, Brian
ROSWELL: THE U.F.O. COVER-UP

Cousins, Michael
HARLEM DIARY: NINE VOICES OF
RESILIENCE
Covarrubias, Febronio
WALK IN THE CLOUDS, A
Covay, Cab
REDWOOD CURTAIN
Cover, Franklin
COSMIC SLOP
Covert, Allen
HEAVYWEIGHTS
Cowboy Mouth
UNDERNEATH, THE
Cowgill, David
TOM AND HUCK
Cowl, Darry
LES MISERABLES
Cowley, Graham
JADE
Cox, Alan
AWFULLY BIG ADVENTURE, AN
Cox, Brian
BRAVEHEART
ROB ROY
Cox, Chad
POWDER
Cox, Coach
JERKY BOYS: THE MOVIE, THE
Cox, Daniel Corbin
ROOMMATES
Cox, Doug
GIRL IN THE CADILLAC
Cox, Frank
FUNNY BONES
Cox, Freddie
FUNNY BONES
Cox, Jennifer Elise
BRADY BUNCH MOVIE, THE
Cox, Shawn
GEORGIA
Cox, Steve
MURIEL'S WEDDING
Cox, Tony
FRIDAY
SILENCE OF THE HAMS
Cox, Veanne
DIRTY MONEY
Coy, Ric
DRACULA: DEAD AND LOVING IT
Coyle, Brendan
AILSA
Coyne, Ria
BATMAN FOREVER
Coyne, Susan
NEVER TALK TO STRANGERS
Coyote, Peter
BREACH OF CONDUCT
BUFFALO GIRLS
MOONLIGHT AND VALENTINO
Cozzolino, Alfredo
POSTMAN, THE
Crachy, Rick
CASINO
Craddick, Kaelyn
HOW TO MAKE AN AMERICAN QUILT
Craddick, Sara
HOW TO MAKE AN AMERICAN QUILT
Craig, Andrew
UNSTRUNG HEROES
Craig, Daniel
KID IN KING ARTHUR'S COURT, A
Craigie, Ingrid
CIRCLE OF FRIENDS
Cram, Michael
TOMMY BOY
Crampton, Barbara
CASTLE FREAK

Cranston, Bryan
COMPANION, THE
EROTIQUE
Craven, Matt
BULLETPROOF HEART
CRIMSON TIDE
KINGFISH: A STORY OF HUEY P. LONG
Craven, Mimi
SECRETARY, THE
Craven, Wes
FEAR, THE
Cravens, Nellie
JADE
Cravotta, Lorella
CITY OF LOST CHILDREN, THE
Crawford, Brandon
EMPIRE RECORDS
Crawford, Cindy
FAIR GAME
Crawford, Eve
TO DIE FOR
Crawford, Kathi
AMERICA'S DEADLIEST HOME VIDEO
Crawford, Lisa
CROSSING GUARD, THE
Crawford, Rachael
WHEN NIGHT IS FALLING
Crawford, Sally
INDICTMENT: THE MCMARTIN TRIAL
Crawford, Sam
FORGET PARIS
Crawford, Thomas
NET, THE
OUTBREAK
Crawford, Wayne
AMERICAN COP
Crawley, Amos
BILLY MADISON
RENT-A-KID
Craze, Galaxy
NADJA
Creery, Don
BETTER OFF DEAD
Crenna, Richard
JADE
PYROMANIAC'S LOVE STORY, A
SABRINA
Cressen, Marnie
BOYS ON THE SIDE
Cribb, Reg
COUNTRY LIFE
Crider, Missy
POWDER
Crisp, Quentin
TO WONG FOO, THANKS FOR
EVERYTHING! JULIE NEWMAR
Cristofer, Michael
DIE HARD WITH A VENGEANCE
Cristos
DESPERADO
Crivello, Anthony
DILLINGER AND CAPONE
Crocker, Barry
MURIEL'S WEDDING
Crockett, B.J.
STRANGE DAYS
Croft, Bill
CONVICT COWBOY
Croft, Jamie
MIGHTY MORPHIN POWER RANGERS:
THE MOVIE
Croisille, Nicole
LES MISERABLES
Crombie, Peter
SAFE
SEVEN

Cromwell, James
BABE
INDICTMENT: THE MCMARTIN TRIAL
Cronauer, Gail
SUBSTITUTE WIFE, THE
Cronenberg, David
TO DIE FOR
Cronin, Craig
DESPERATE PREY
Cronin, Jamie
THREE WISHES
Cronin, Jeanette
NOSTRADAMUS KID, THE
Cronin, Laurel
DILLINGER
Cronyn, Tandy
GETTING OUT
Crosby, David
BRIAN WILSON: I JUST WASN'T MADE
FOR THESE TIMES
Crosby, Denise
MUTANT SPECIES
Crosby, Kellen
NOW AND THEN
Crosby, Robin
JOHNNY MNEMONIC
Cross, Alan
INNOCENT LIES
Cross, Ben
ASCENT, THE
FIRST KNIGHT
Cross, Bill
JACK-O
Cross, Chloe
CAGED HEARTS
Cross, David
DESTINY TURNS ON THE RADIO
Cross, Luke
NOSTRADAMUS KID, THE
Cross, Pierre Kenneth
FIRST DEGREE
Cross, Roger R.
GOLD DIGGERS: THE SECRET OF BEAR
MOUNTAIN
HIDEAWAY
Crouse, Lindsay
BYE BYE, LOVE
INDIAN IN THE CUPBOARD, THE
Crowder, Carl
RIVER OF GRASS
Crowe, Russell
QUICK AND THE DEAD, THE
SUM OF US, THE
VIRTUOSITY
Crumb, Beatrice
CRUMB
Crumb, Charles
CRUMB
Crumb, Dana
CRUMB
Crumb, Jesse
CRUMB
Crumb, Max
CRUMB
Crumb, Robert
CRUMB
Crumb, Sophie
CRUMB
Crutchfield, Kevin
UNDERNEATH, THE
Crutchley, Jeremy
MANGLER, THE
Cruz, Brandon
SAFE
Cruz, Celia
PEREZ FAMILY, THE
Cruz, Vladimir
STRAWBERRY AND CHOCOLATE

Cruz, Wilson
NIXON
Cruze, Robyn
COUNTRY LIFE
Crystal, Billy
FORGET PARIS
Crystal, Jennifer
AMERICAN PRESIDENT, THE
DRACULA: DEAD AND LOVING IT
LOSING ISAIAH
Csapo, Balazs
CITIZEN X
Csuja, Imre
CITIZEN X
Cuartero-Giordano, Dana
FORGET PARIS
Cuc Dinh
DEAD PRESIDENTS
Cucci, Tony
KISS OF DEATH
Cucinotta, Maria Grazia
POSTMAN, THE
Cudney, Clifford
NEW YORK COP
Cudney, Roger
BURNING SEASON, THE
Culhane, John
FRANK AND OLLIE
Culkin, Kieran
FATHER OF THE BRIDE PART II
Culkin, Michael
CANDYMAN: FAREWELL TO THE FLESH
Cullen, Brett
APOLLO 13
SOMETHING TO TALK ABOUT
Cullen, Kerrie
TIE THAT BINDS, THE
Cullen, Louise
MURIEL'S WEDDING
Cullen, Michael
CLOCKERS
DEAD MAN WALKING
Cullen, Patrick
KINGFISH: A STORY OF HUEY P. LONG
Cullison, Barry
CLASS OF '61
Cullum, Kaitlan
LITTLE PRINCESS, A
Culp, Joseph
APOLLO 13
PANTHER
Culp, Robert
PANTHER
Culpepper, Joan
JUPITER'S WIFE
Culver, Veronica
TALES FROM THE CRYPT: DEMON
KNIGHT
Cumberbatch, Scott
BAD BOYS
Cumming, Alan
CIRCLE OF FRIENDS
GOLDENEYE
Cummings, Diarra
HARLEM DIARY: NINE VOICES OF
RESILIENCE
Cummings, Jim
BALTO
GOOFY MOVIE, A
Cummins, Gregory Scott
LAST OF THE DOGMEN
Cundieff, Rusty
TALES FROM THE HOOD
Cundiff, Claire
REASON TO BELIEVE, A
Cunningham, James
COPYCAT

Cunningham, Jocelyn
SCARLET LETTER, THE
Cunningham, John
NIXON
ROOMMATES
Cunningham, Kenall
PEBBLE AND THE PENGUIN, THE
Cunningham, Liam
FIRST KNIGHT
LITTLE PRINCESS, A
Cunningham, Lynn
TOMMY BOY
Cuoco, Kaley
VIRTUOSITY
Cuppari, Catherine
HOUSEGUEST
Curdy, Olivier
FRENCH KISS
Curr, Philip
HEAVEN'S A DRAG
Curran, Leigh
INDICTMENT: THE MCMARTIN TRIAL
Currell, Liduin
POWER OF ATTORNEY
Curren, Tony
SHALLOW GRAVE
Currie, Brian
GHOST BRIGADE
Currie, Sondra
SECRETARY, THE
Currier, Terence P.
SOMETHING TO TALK ABOUT
Curry, Christopher
BUSHWHACKED
BYE BYE, LOVE
Curry, Jr., Larry
THINGS TO DO IN DENVER WHEN
YOU'RE DEAD
Curry, Mark
PANTHER
Curry, Tim
CONGO
PEBBLE AND THE PENGUIN, THE
Curteis, Anne
CRY, THE BELOVED COUNTRY
FRIENDS
Curtis, Clifford
ONCE WERE WARRIORS
Curtis, Jed
BATMAN FOREVER
Curtis, Liane
EROTIQUE
Curtis, Vicky
AWFULLY BIG ADVENTURE, AN
Curtis-Brown, Robert
ANGUS
STUART SAVES HIS FAMILY
Curto, Vinnie J.
BAD BLOOD
Curvey, Jr., Troy
VAMPIRE IN BROOKLYN
Cusack, Ann
TANK GIRL
Cusack, Dick
WHILE YOU WERE SLEEPING
Cusack, Joan
NINE MONTHS
Custer, Francine
NEA
Cutell, Lou
UNSTRUNG HEROES
Cuthbert, Jon
BROKEN TRUST
Cutler, Wendy
TOM AND HUCK
Cutter, David
ROOMMATES

Cvetkovic, Svetozar
GORILLA BATHES AT NOON
Cypriano, Tania
CARMEN MIRANDA: BANANAS IS MY
BUSINESS
Czarnecki, Jim
CANADIAN BACON
Czernin, Peter
KICKING AND SCREAMING
Czerny, Henry
WHEN NIGHT IS FALLING
d'Abo, Olivia
BIG GREEN, THE
KICKING AND SCREAMING
LAST GOOD TIME, THE
D'Agostino, Liza
BAR GIRLS
D'Allesandro, Gene
TWO BITS
D'Almeida, Duarte
CONVENT, THE
D'Ambrose, Stephen
CURE, THE
D'Ambrosio, Vito
USUAL SUSPECTS, THE
D'Angelo, Beverly
CRAZYSITTER, THE
D'Angelo, Sonny
CASINO
D'Arcy, Jan
BETTER OFF DEAD
DANGER OF LOVE
D'Elia, Mario
TWO BITS
D'Oliveira, Damon
EXOTICA
d'Oliviera, Gael
BEYOND RANGOON
d'Oliviera, Gilles
BEYOND RANGOON
d'Oliviera, Pascale
BEYOND RANGOON
D'Onofrio, Vincent
STRANGE DAYS
STUART SAVES HIS FAMILY
D-Knowledge
HIGHER LEARNING
PANTHER
D.J. Pooh
FRIDAY
Da 5 Footaz
SHOW, THE
Da Re, Eric
NUMBER ONE FAN
Dacombe, Georgiana
CARRINGTON
Dahlgren, Tom
AMERICAN PRESIDENT, THE
Daily, E.G.
GOOFY MOVIE, A
Daisy
WIGSTOCK: THE MOVIE
Dakota, Reno
LIE DOWN WITH DOGS
Dale, Teddy
BABY-SITTERS CLUB, THE
Daley, Joseph Daniel
LORD OF ILLUSIONS
Dalkowska, Ewa
PROVINCIAL ACTORS
Dalle, Beatrice
I CAN'T SLEEP
SIX DAYS, SIX NIGHTS
Dallimore, John
RESTORATION
Dalton, Mark
DESPERADO

Dalton, Mark Duke
NUMBER ONE FAN
Dalton, Stephen
COVER STORY
Dalton, Wally
ASSASSINS
FREE WILLY 2: THE ADVENTURE HOME
Daly, Candice
STEAL BIG, STEAL LITTLE
Daly, Ken
USUAL SUSPECTS, THE
Daly, Rad
CRIMSON TIDE
Daly, Tim
DR. JEKYLL & MS. HYDE
Dalzell, III, Bill
SUDDEN DEATH
Dame
KISS OF DEATH
Damerow, Gundula
INNOCENT, THE
Damevski, Moni
BEFORE THE RAIN
Damon, Matt
YOUNGER & YOUNGER
Damon, Una
VIRTUOSITY
Danaher, Thomas Kevin
BOYS ON THE SIDE
Dance, Charles
CENTURY
Dane, Lawrence
BLACK FOX
DARKMAN 2: THE RETURN OF DURANT
IT TAKES TWO
NATIONAL LAMPOON'S SENIOR TRIP
Danes, Claire
HOME FOR THE HOLIDAYS
HOW TO MAKE AN AMERICAN QUILT
Dangerfield, Rodney
CASPER
Daniel, Alexis
CENTURY
JUDGE DREDD
Daniel, Cynthia
BASKETBALL DIARIES, THE
Daniel, Gregg
BREACH OF CONDUCT
INDICTMENT: THE MCMARTIN TRIAL
Daniel, Gwenola
INNOCENT LIES
Daniels, Danny D.
ACE VENTURA: WHEN NATURE CALLS
Daniels, Eddie
RHYTHM THIEF
Daniels, J.D.
ROSWELL: THE U.F.O. COVER-UP
Daniels, Jeff
REDWOOD CURTAIN
Daniels, Max
HEAT
Daniels, Nada
DEADLY MARIA
Daniels, Warren
WINGS OF HONNEAMISE: ROYAL SPACE
FORCE
Danilova, Raissa
NIXON
Danner, Blythe
TO WONG FOO, THANKS FOR
EVERYTHING! JULIE NEWMAR
Danny Boy
HEAVEN'S A DRAG
Danon, Geraldine
OLD LADY WHO WALKED IN THE SEA,
THE
Dante, Joe
SILENCE OF THE HAMS

Danza, Roberta
DON JUAN DEMARCO
Dao, Catherine
CYBER BANDITS
Dapkunaite, Ingeborga
BURNT BY THE SUN
Darabi, Mahbanou
THROUGH THE OLIVE TREES
Darbo, Patrika
BABE
Darby, Kim
HALLOWEEN: THE CURSE OF MICHAEL
MYERS
Dare, Debra
ATTACK OF THE 60-FOOT CENTERFOLD
Darga, Christopher
CRAZYSITTER, THE
NET, THE
UNDER SIEGE 2: DARK TERRITORY
Dark Angel
HEAVEN'S A DRAG
Darrow, Tony
ME AND THE MOB
MIGHTY APHRODITE
Dash, Stacey
CLUELESS
DaSilva, Erick
SON OF THE SHARK, THE
DaSilva, Henrique
HEAVEN'S A DRAG
Datcher, Alex
EXPERT, THE
JURY DUTY
Datkowska, Ewa
WITHOUT ANESTHESIA
Daugherty, Wendell
PARTY GIRL
Dave Flame & the Barbarians
FUNNY BONES
Davenport, Kevin
INNOCENT, THE
Davenport, Mark
TOO YOUNG TO DIE?
Davey, Maude
ONLY THE BRAVE
Davey, Moyra
ART FOR TEACHERS OF CHILDREN
Davey, Nicholas
BYE BYE, LOVE
Davey, Rachel
BABE
Davi, Robert
DANGEROUS, THE
SHOWGIRLS
Davic, Aleksander
GORILLA BATHES AT NOON
David, Angel
KISS OF DEATH
SEARCH AND DESTROY
David, Elliot
PLAY TIME
David, Keith
BLUE IN THE FACE
CLOCKERS
DEAD PRESIDENTS
QUICK AND THE DEAD, THE
Davidovich, Lolita
INDICTMENT: THE MCMARTIN TRIAL
NOW AND THEN
YOUNGER & YOUNGER
Davids, Paul
ROSWELL: THE U.F.O. COVER-UP
Davidson, Alan
RHYTHM THIEF
Davidson, Anna
OUTSIDE THE LAW
Davidson, Frankie
MURIEL'S WEDDING

Davidson, Monica
RIVER OF GRASS
Davidson, Roscoe
SEVEN
Davidson, Stuart
CIRCUMSTANCES UNKNOWN
POWER OF ATTORNEY
Davidson, Tommy
ACE VENTURA: WHEN NATURE CALLS
Davidtz, Embeth
FEAST OF JULY
MURDER IN THE FIRST
Davies, Dylan
RESTORATION
Davies, John
FRANKIE STARLIGHT
Davies, John S.
SUBSTITUTE WIFE, THE
Davies, Oliver Ford
SENSE AND SENSIBILITY
Davies, Rudi
FRANKIE STARLIGHT
Davies, Stephen
DILLINGER AND CAPONE
Davila, Adriana
NO MERCY
Davila, Brian
TERESA'S TATTOO
Davin, Robert Gwyn
FIRST KNIGHT
Davis, Amy Moore
LAKOTA WOMAN: SIEGE AT WOUNDED
KNEE
Davis, Angela
BLACK IS ... BLACK AIN'T
Davis, Ann B.
BRADY BUNCH MOVIE, THE
Davis, Carlton
VAMPIRE IN BROOKLYN
Davis, Dennis
LIE DOWN WITH DOGS
Davis, Don S.
BLACK FOX
HIDEAWAY
Davis, Duane
STEAL BIG, STEAL LITTLE
Davis, Elizabeth F.
MAD LOVE
Davis, Ellsworth (Cisco)
NEW JERSEY DRIVE
Davis, Frank
DEVIL IN A BLUE DRESS
Davis, Freddie
FUNNY BONES
Davis, Gary Lee
MURDER IN THE FIRST
Davis, Geena
CUTTHROAT ISLAND
Davis, Heather
BAD BOYS
Davis, Hope
KISS OF DEATH
Davis, John Walter
SCANNERS: THE SHOWDOWN
Davis, Kristin
NINE MONTHS
Davis, Lance
SHOWGIRLS
Davis, Lisa
ROOMMATES
Davis, Malika
MESSENGER
Davis, Morning
TIE-DIED: ROCK 'N' ROLL'S MOST
DEADICATED FANS
Davis, Nathan
STEAL BIG, STEAL LITTLE

Davis, Ossie
ANDROID AFFAIR, THE
Davis, Phyllis
UNDER SIEGE 2: DARK TERRITORY
Davis, Sammi
FOUR ROOMS
Davis, Sarah
SAFE
Davis, Sonny Carl
FAIR GAME
Davis, Stanton
TANK GIRL
Davis, Ted
CRAZYSITTER, THE
Davis, Viveka
BODY SHOT
Davis, William B.
CIRCUMSTANCES UNKNOWN
Davis, Worthy
BOYS ON THE SIDE
Davison, Bruce
BABY-SITTERS CLUB, THE
CURE, THE
FAR FROM HOME: THE ADVENTURES OF
YELLOW DOG
Davison, Michelle
BABE
Davy, Babs
INCREDIBLY TRUE ADVENTURES OF
TWO GIRLS IN LOVE, THE
Davydov, Anatoly
ASSASSINS
Dawson, Kamala
BURNING SEASON, THE
Dawson, Kim
BAD BLOOD
Dawson, Mark
GHOST BRIGADE
Dawson, Rosario
KIDS
Day, Matt
MURIEL'S WEDDING
Day, Werdee
WINGS OF HONNEAMISE: ROYAL SPACE
FORCE
Dayitian, Kenneth
SILENCE OF THE HAMS
Dayton, Kelly
NUMBER ONE FAN
de Alba, Cecile Sanz
VALLEY OF ABRAHAM, THE
de Almeida, Joaquim
DESPERADO
de Almeida, Nuno Vieira
VALLEY OF ABRAHAM, THE
de Aredo, Marques
VALLEY OF ABRAHAM, THE
De, Aveek
STRANGER, THE
de Barge, Flotilla
WIGSTOCK: THE MOVIE
De Batin, Jackie
SEPARATE LIVES
De Bayser, Clotilde
MY LIFE AND TIMES WITH ANTONIN
ARTAUD
de Cadenet, Amanda
FOUR ROOMS
de Carvalho, Rui
VALLEY OF ABRAHAM, THE
de Castro, Isabel
VALLEY OF ABRAHAM, THE
De, Deepankar
STRANGER, THE
de Groot, Christophe
WINGS OF HONNEAMISE: ROYAL SPACE
FORCE

De Hoyos, Jaime
DESPERADO
De Jesus, Wanda
GLASS SHIELD, THE
De L'Isle De Cume, Villiers
NEA
de la Boulaye, Agathe
JEFFERSON IN PARIS
de la Fuente, Joel
ROOMMATES
de la Garza, Luis
LAST SUMMER IN THE HAMPTONS
De Lancie, John
EVOLVER
de las Mercedes Diez, Maria
I AM CUBA
De Lorenzo, Michael
MY FAMILY: MI FAMILIA
De Los Reyes, Kamar
NIXON
De Luca, Rudy
DRACULA: DEAD AND LOVING IT
SILENCE OF THE HAMS
De Martino, Kelly
COPYCAT
de Matos, Gloria
VALLEY OF ABRAHAM, THE
de Montalembert, Thibault
JEFFERSON IN PARIS
De Mornay, Rebecca
NEVER TALK TO STRANGERS
de Mouroux, Hedwige
FORGET PARIS
De Niro, Robert
CASINO
HEAT
De Oliveira, Luma
BOCA
De Oliveira, Patrick
BOCA
De Pasquale, Carol
NINE MONTHS
de Pencier, Miranda
KURT VONNEGUT'S HARRISON
BERGERON
De Pinto, Joey
CASINO
De Sando, Anthony
PARTY GIRL
De Soto, Jose
KISS OF DEATH
De Souza, Noel
ACE VENTURA: WHEN NATURE CALLS
De Souza, Ruth
BOCA
de Turckheim, Charlotte
JEFFERSON IN PARIS
de Victor, Claudio
BULLETPROOF HEART
De'Ath, Charles
FATHERLAND
FEAST OF JULY
Deadrick, Jr., Vince
HEAT
Deak, Mike
LORD OF ILLUSIONS
Dean, Bill
PRIEST
Dean, Felicity
PERSUASION
Dean, Loren
APOLLO 13
HOW TO MAKE AN AMERICAN QUILT
Dean, Ron
STEAL BIG, STEAL LITTLE
Deane, Frederick
DIRTY MONEY

DeAngel, Miguel
BUSINESS AFFAIR, A
DeAngelis, Rosemary
TWO BITS
Dear, Eliza
CIRCLE OF FRIENDS
Dear, Oliver
QUICK AND THE DEAD, THE
Dearth, Bill
GLASS SHIELD, THE
DeBroux, Lee
STEAL BIG, STEAL LITTLE
WILD BILL
Decegli, Nicholas
ADDICTION, THE
Deckert, Blue
SUBSTITUTE WIFE, THE
DeCourcey, Michael
ASSASSINS
Dee Lew
SHAO LIN POPEYE
Dee, Ruby
JUST CAUSE
Deee-lite
WIGSTOCK: THE MOVIE
Deering, Barbara
GEORGIA
Dees, Michael
SABRINA
Deeth, Jim
SEVEN
Deezen, Eddie
SILENCE OF THE HAMS
DeFazio, Anthony
DEATH IN BRUNSWICK
Defosse, Eric
MINA TANNENBAUM
Degan, Shea
TO WONG FOO, THANKS FOR
EVERYTHING! JULIE NEWMAR
DeGoror, Jean-Claude
SIX DAYS, SIX NIGHTS
Degroot, Stephanie
MINA TANNENBAUM
DeHart, David
MAJOR PAYNE
DeJanerand, Philippe
GROSSE FATIGUE
Dejean, Sr., Eddie
BRIDGES OF MADISON COUNTY, THE
Dejong, Sandra Lee
BORN TO BE WILD
Dekanski, Kerrylynn
JACK-O
Dekker, Thomas
VILLAGE OF THE DAMNED
Del Buono, Jenna
JUST CAUSE
Del Haro, Emilio
MY FAMILY: MI FAMILIA
Del Lago, Alicia
MY FAMILY: MI FAMILIA
Del Mar, Marcia
GLASS SHIELD, THE
Del Mar, Maria
ECLIPSE
del Monte, Jesus
I AM CUBA
del Puerto, Diana Iris
STRAWBERRY AND CHOCOLATE
Del Sherman, Barry
LORD OF ILLUSIONS
del Sol, Laura
CREW, THE
Del Toro, Benicio
SWIMMING WITH SHARKS
USUAL SUSPECTS, THE

del Toro, Maria Elena
STRAWBERRY AND CHOCOLATE
Delaima, Neil
MOSAIC PROJECT, THE
Delamere, Louise
JUDGE DREDD
Delaney, Chris
BAR GIRLS
Delaney, Gloria
NUMBER ONE FAN
Delaney, Kim
DARKMAN 2: THE RETURN OF DURANT
Delany, Dana
ENEMY WITHIN, THE
Delany, Pat
SEPARATE LIVES
Delany, Pauline
CIRCLE OF FRIENDS
Delate, Brian
SUDDEN DEATH
Delcevski, Boris
BEFORE THE RAIN
Delejalde, Kadina
INDICTMENT: THE MCMARTIN TRIAL
DeLevie, Todd
THREE WISHES
Delgado, Kim
SCANNERS: THE SHOWDOWN
DeLisi, Roz
RIVER OF GRASS
Delisle, Andy
LOVE AND HUMAN REMAINS
Dellapiccola, Armin
EROTIQUE
Delmas, Patrick Forster
SABRINA
DeLoach, Heather
LITTLE PRINCESS, A
Delova, Lence
BEFORE THE RAIN
Delpy, Julie
BEFORE SUNRISE
YOUNGER & YOUNGER
DeLuise, David
DRACULA: DEAD AND LOVING IT
KICKING AND SCREAMING
SILENCE OF THE HAMS
DeLuise, Dom
SILENCE OF THE HAMS
DeLuise, Peter
SILENCE OF THE HAMS
deLuze, Gwenola
MINA TANNENBAUM
deMalberg, Stanislas Carre
JEFFERSON IN PARIS
DeMasters, Anthony
WATERWORLD
DeMauro, Nick
VAMPIRE IN BROOKLYN
DeMeo, William
HACKERS
DeMille, Agnes
BALLET
DeMornay, Rebecca
GETTING OUT
Dempsey, Martin
BRAVEHEART
Dempsey, Patrick
OUTBREAK
Demtchenko, Maxime
WINDOW TO PARIS
DeMunn, Jeffrey
CITIZEN X
SAFE PASSAGE
Dench, Jeffery
FIRST KNIGHT

Dench, Judi
GOLDENEYE
Deneuve, Catherine
CONVENT, THE
Denicourt, Marianne
DOOMSDAY GUN
INNOCENT LIES
Denis, William
THINGS TO DO IN DENVER WHEN
YOU'RE DEAD
Denisof, Alexis
FIRST KNIGHT
INNOCENT LIES
Denison, Liz
DANGER OF LOVE
Denman, Tony
ANGUS
Dennehy, Brian
STARS FELL ON HENRIETTA, THE
TOMMY BOY
Dennis, Alfred
GET SHORTY
Dennis, Danny
JERKY BOYS: THE MOVIE, THE
Dennis, Peter
PREHYSTERIA! 3
Dennis, Thomas Emery
PREHYSTERIA! 3
Denniston, Bill
SHALLOW GRAVE
Dent, Frank
SAFE
Dentie, Gino
MOSAIC PROJECT, THE
Denton, Rebecca
KID IN KING ARTHUR'S COURT, A
DePaeuw, Francois
MINA TANNENBAUM
Depardieu, Gerard
PURE FORMALITY, A
DePatie, Beth
TANK GIRL
dePenguern, Artus
MINA TANNENBAUM
Depp, Johnny
ARIZONA DREAM
DON JUAN DEMARCO
NICK OF TIME
Derec, Jean-Francois
LES MISERABLES
Derek, Bo
TOMMY BOY
Dern, Bruce
WILD BILL
DeRose, Chris
BLUE TIGER
Derryberry, Debi
BABE
Desai, Shelly
SILENCE OF THE HAMS
DeSalvo, Anne
UNSTRUNG HEROES
DeSando, Anthony
TWO BITS
DeSantis, Stanley
BROKEN TRUST
Desautels, Suzanne
LOVE AND HUMAN REMAINS
Descas, Alex
I CAN'T SLEEP
DeScenna, Linda
FATHER OF THE BRIDE PART II
Deschamps, Louise
FRENCH KISS
Deschamps, Marielle
MINA TANNENBAUM
Deschenes, Manon
DR. JEKYLL & MS. HYDE

Desplat, Alexandre
INNOCENT LIES
Despotovich, Nada
DON JUAN DEMARCO
Desprez, Roger
PIGALLE
Deuker, Ursula
PIGALLE
Devan, Bruce
NINE MONTHS
Devaney, Gary
SHOWGIRLS
Deveaux, Nathaniel
CONVICT COWBOY
DeVeillers, John
ASCENT, THE
Deveney, John X.
DANGER OF LOVE
Devenie, Stuart
MEET THE FEEBLES
DeVenney, Scott
COPYCAT
Devereux, Clarke
NINE MONTHS
Devin, Julia
TIE THAT BINDS, THE
Devine, Aidan
LOVE AND HUMAN REMAINS
Devine, Alan
FRANKIE STARLIGHT
Devine, Christine
SEPARATE LIVES
Devine, Doug
REASON TO BELIEVE, A
Devine, Loretta
WAITING TO EXHALE
DeVito, Danny
GET SHORTY
DeVito, Tommy
CASINO
Devitt, Conor
BILLY MADISON
Devlin, Billy
CRIMSON TIDE
DeVoe, John
THREE WISHES
Devon, Lorraine
TO CROSS THE RUBICON
Devon, Ron
CYBER BANDITS
Devree, Maximilian
LOVE AND HUMAN REMAINS
DeWalt, Destinee
ZOOMAN
Dewey, Kevin
GETTING OUT
DeWier, Thomas
SCANNERS: THE SHOWDOWN
Dewitt, Brock
TIE-DIED: ROCK 'N' ROLL'S MOST
DEADICATED FANS
DeYoung, William
DANGER OF LOVE
deZarn, Tim
TALES FROM THE CRYPT: DEMON
KNIGHT
DeZarn, Tim
TOO YOUNG TO DIE?
Di Cesare, Eva
DALLAS DOLL
Di Donato, Mario
SEVEN
di Maio, Carlo
POSTMAN, THE
Di Mazzarelli, Carmelo
LAMERICA
Di Santi, John
ALMOST DEAD

di Sauro, Vincenzo
POSTMAN, THE
Diab, John
BODY SHOT
Diakhate, Ami
HYENAS
Diamant, Sigal
BAD BLOOD
Diamond, Reed
ASSASSINS
Diamond, Val
NINE MONTHS
Dias, Antoinette
CITY OF LOST CHILDREN, THE
Dias, Pat
TWELVE MONKEYS
Diaz, Edith
NICK OF TIME
Diaz, Guillermo
PARTY GIRL
Diaz, Josefina
MONEY TRAIN
Diaz, Maria
SHOWGIRLS
Diaz, Sully
ZOOMAN
DiCaprio, Leonardo
BASKETBALL DIARIES, THE
QUICK AND THE DEAD, THE
TOTAL ECLIPSE
DiChiara, Jerry
SECRETARY, THE
Dickens, Al
TIE-DIED: ROCK 'N' ROLL'S MOST
DEADICATED FANS
Dickerson, Pamela
I LIKE TO PLAY GAMES
NIXON
Dickey, Dale
INCREDIBLY TRUE ADVENTURES OF
TWO GIRLS IN LOVE, THE
Dickinson, Angie
SABRINA
Dickinson, Misty
APOLLO 13
Dickinson, Sandra Searles
BALTO
Dickman, Karl-Heinz
FARINELLI
Diederich, Hans
INNOCENT, THE
Diehl, John
ALMOST DEAD
BUFFALO GIRLS
NIXON
THREE WISHES
Diekman, Billie J.
TO WONG FOO, THANKS FOR
EVERYTHING! JULIE NEWMAR
Dignam, Arthur
NOSTRADAMUS KID, THE
Dignam, Dr. William
CROSSING GUARD, THE
Dignam, Erin
CROSSING GUARD, THE
DiGregorio, Ben
DANGER OF LOVE
Dileo, Frank
KISS OF DEATH
DiLeo, John
JERKY BOYS: THE MOVIE, THE
DiLeo, Patti
POSTCARDS FROM AMERICA
Dill, Deena
HEAVYWEIGHTS
Dillard, Victoria
GLASS SHIELD, THE
OUT OF SYNC

Diller, Phyllis
SILENCE OF THE HAMS
Diller, Steven
AMERICA'S DEADLIEST HOME VIDEO
Dillingham, Jazzmine
BABE
Dillman, Pamela
BYE BYE, LOVE
Dillon, Hugh
DANCE ME OUTSIDE
Dillon, Matt
FRANKIE STARLIGHT
TO DIE FOR
Dillon, Melinda
HOW TO MAKE AN AMERICAN QUILT
TO WONG FOO, THANKS FOR
EVERYTHING! JULIE NEWMAR
Dillon, Paul
CUTTHROAT ISLAND
FAIR GAME
DiMascio, Angelo
SPY WITHIN, THE
DiMauro, Francesca
LIVING IN OBLIVION
Din, Ismail
BEYOND RANGOON
Dinh Thien Le
OPERATION DUMBO DROP
Dinkins, Lisa
S.F.W.
WHITE MAN'S BURDEN
Dinklage, Peter
LIVING IN OBLIVION
DiNunzio, Aurelio
CIRCUMSTANCES UNKNOWN
Diols, Williams
FRENCH KISS
Dion, Nicole
BAR GIRLS
Dionisi, Stefano
FARINELLI
Diop, Abdoulaye
HYENAS
Diouf, Mansour
HYENAS
DiPace, Anna
VAMPIRES AND OTHER STEREOTYPES
DiPinto, Nicola
PURE FORMALITY, A
Dirker, Jim
UNDER SIEGE 2: DARK TERRITORY
DiSanti, John
MAN OF THE HOUSE
Discenza, Nick
TWO BITS
Dishy, Bob
DON JUAN DEMARCO
DiStefano, Pat
RECKLESS
Diveley, Joshua Todd
MAJOR PAYNE
Dix, Lewis
NET, THE
Dixit, G.B.
BANDIT QUEEN
Dixon, Donna
NIXON
Dizazzo, James
I LIKE TO PLAY GAMES
DJ Jazzy Nice
PARTY GIRL
Do, Daniel
HIGHLANDER: THE FINAL DIMENSION
Dobkin, Kaela
KICKING AND SCREAMING
Dobkin, Larry
ROSWELL: THE U.F.O. COVER-UP

Dobtchev, Vernon
JEFFERSON IN PARIS
Doc Ice
SHOW, THE
Dodd, Monique
VALLEY OF ABRAHAM, THE
Dodd, T. Colin
RIVER OF GRASS
Dodds, John
BLACK FOX
Doe, John
GEORGIA
Dog Pound, Tha
SHOW, THE
Doherty, Miche
RUN OF THE COUNTRY, THE
Doherty, Paul
TIE-DIED: ROCK 'N' ROLL'S MOST
DEADICATED FANS
Doherty, Shannen
ALMOST DEAD
MALLRATS
Doi Chettawat Kanboon
OPERATION DUMBO DROP
Dolabella, Carlos
BOCA
Dolan, Brendan
SAFE
Dolenz, Micky
BRADY BUNCH MOVIE, THE
Doles, Gary
JACK-O
Dollar, Aubrey
HEAVYWEIGHTS
Dollarhide, Jessica
CASTLE FREAK
Dollase, David
ASSASSINS
Dolson, Edna
BRIDGES OF MADISON COUNTY, THE
Doman, John
DIE HARD WITH A VENGEANCE
JOURNEY OF AUGUST KING, THE
Domange, Francois
FUNNY BONES
Dombasle, Arielle
BLUE VILLA, THE
Dominguez, Barbara
I AM CUBA
Dominguez, Narcisco
ARIZONA DREAM
Dominguez, Wade
DANGEROUS MINDS
EROTIQUE
Donadio, James
GORDY
Donahoo, Nicole
GEORGIA
Donahue, Don
CRUMB
Donahue, Sean
MOSAIC PROJECT, THE
Donahue, Sean P.
UNSTRUNG HEROES
Donald R. Smith and the Golden Voices Gospel Choir of St. Francis De Sales Catholic Church
DEAD MAN WALKING
Donaldson, Patricia
ENEMY WITHIN, THE
Donato, Marc
BILLY MADISON
Doncheff, Len
SCARLET LETTER, THE
Dondertman, John
DANCE ME OUTSIDE
Dong, Tricia
SAFE

Donley, Robert
BUSHWHACKED
LAST OF THE DOGMEN
DonLucas, Esperanza
DON JUAN DEMARCO
Donner, Betty
INDICTMENT: THE MCMARTIN TRIAL
Donno, Tony
HIGHER LEARNING
Donovan, Elisa
CLUELESS
Donovan, Helena
BAR GIRLS
Donovan, Martin
AMATEUR
NADJA
Dontsov, Sergei
WINDOW TO PARIS
Dooley, Paul
EVOLVER
UNDERNEATH, THE
Doolin, Robbie
AWFULLY BIG ADVENTURE, AN
Doonan, Paul
SHALLOW GRAVE
Dorff, Stephen
INNOCENT LIES
RECKLESS
S.F.W.
Doria, Diogo
VALLEY OF ABRAHAM, THE
Dorian, Antonia
MIDNIGHT TEASE 2
Dorkin, Cody Lee
NINE MONTHS
VILLAGE OF THE DAMNED
Dorn, Franchelle Stewart
DIE HARD WITH A VENGEANCE
Dorsey, Kevin
ARABIAN KNIGHT
Dorval, Adrien
MAGIC IN THE WATER
Dostal, Christoph
FOR GOD AND COUNTRY
Dotrice, Roy
SCARLET LETTER, THE
SWIMMING WITH SHARKS
Dott, Amy
GETTING OUT
Dottore, Paul
CASINO
Doucet, Charles
HIGHLANDER: THE FINAL DIMENSION
LOVE AND HUMAN REMAINS
Doucette, Jeff
ACROSS THE MOON
Doug, Doug E.
OPERATION DUMBO DROP
Dougherty, Doc
BASKETBALL DIARIES, THE
Douglas, D.C.
UNDER SIEGE 2: DARK TERRITORY
Douglas, Diane
BILLY MADISON
Douglas, Emory
PANTHER
Douglas, Illeana
SEARCH AND DESTROY
TO DIE FOR
Douglas, Julie Condra
NIXON
Douglas, Lionel
OPERATION DUMBO DROP
Douglas, Michael
AMERICAN PRESIDENT, THE
Douglas, Pavel
GOLDENEYE

Douglas, Sam
HACKERS
Douglas, Sarah
SPITFIRE
Douglas, Shirley
REDWOOD CURTAIN
Douridas, Chris
STRANGE DAYS
WATERWORLD
Dourif, Brad
DEATH MACHINE
MURDER IN THE FIRST
Dow, Maureen
RUN OF THE COUNTRY, THE
Dowd, Ann
BUSHWHACKED
KINGFISH: A STORY OF HUEY P. LONG
Dowd, Jamison B.
NOW AND THEN
Dowling, Dennis
OH ... ROSALINDA!!
Downey, James
BILLY MADISON
Downey, Jr., Robert
HOME FOR THE HOLIDAYS
RESTORATION
RICHARD III
Dowse, Denise
ENEMY WITHIN, THE
Doyka, Mimi
OUTBREAK
Doyle, Chris
GALAXIS
Doyle, John
BABE
Doyle, Kathleen
MIGHTY APHRODITE
Doyle, Tony
CIRCLE OF FRIENDS
Doyle, William A.
TANK GIRL
Doyle-Murray, Brian
JURY DUTY
Dozsa, Zoltan
CITIZEN X
Dr. Dre
SHOW, THE
Dr. Zarif
MOSAIC PROJECT, THE
Drago, Joe
STEAL BIG, STEAL LITTLE
THINGS TO DO IN DENVER WHEN
YOU'RE DEAD
Dragonas, Sakis
DEATH IN BRUNSWICK
Drake, Graham
SUM OF US, THE
Drake, Judith
WHITE MAN'S BURDEN
Drake, Judith D.
LITTLE PRINCESS, A
Drake, Larry
DARKMAN 2: THE RETURN OF DURANT
JOURNEY OF AUGUST KING, THE
Drake, Patricia
DECOY
Drake, Scott
THREE WISHES
Drameh, Faly
HYENAS
Drapeko, Elena
WINDOW TO PARIS
Draper, Polly
GOLD DIGGERS: THE SECRET OF BEAR
MOUNTAIN
Draper, Ralph
FRIENDS

Drea, Marguerite
CIRCLE OF FRIENDS
Dreger, Reg
NEVER TALK TO STRANGERS
TOMMY BOY
Dreisbach, Jeffrey
DIE HARD WITH A VENGEANCE
Drew, Griffen
MIDNIGHT TEASE 2
Dreyfus, James
RICHARD III
Dreyfus, Jean-Claude
CITY OF LOST CHILDREN, THE
Dreyfus, Julie
MYSTERY OF RAMPO, THE
Dreyfuss, Richard
AMERICAN PRESIDENT, THE
Driessche, F. Van Den
JEFFERSON IN PARIS
Driggs, Deborah
TWOGETHER
Drinkwater, Carol
AWFULLY BIG ADVENTURE, AN
Driscoll, Christopher
BUSINESS AFFAIR, A
Driscoll, Robin
JUMANJI
Driver, Minnie
CIRCLE OF FRIENDS
GOLDENEYE
Drukman, Phillippe
MINA TANNENBAUM
Drumgold, David
TO WONG FOO, THANKS FOR
EVERYTHING! JULIE NEWMAR
Drummond, Alice
JEFFREY
TO WONG FOO, THANKS FOR
EVERYTHING! JULIE NEWMAR
Drummond, Brian
BAD COMPANY
Drummond, David
PENTATHLON
Drummond, John
AWFULLY BIG ADVENTURE, AN
Druzbick, Tom
I LIKE TO PLAY GAMES
Dryden, Darren
LIE DOWN WITH DOGS
Dryer, Robert
SPY WITHIN, THE
Drynan, Jeane
MURIEL'S WEDDING
Drysdale, Cliff
BREAK, THE
Du Hui
ERMO
du Peloux de Saint Romain, Renaud
FARINELLI
Dube, Lillian
CRY, THE BELOVED COUNTRY
Dube, Wilfred
DECOY
Dubillard, Roland
SERIOUS ABOUT PLEASURE
Dubin, Ellen
IN THE DEEP WOODS
SCANNERS: THE SHOWDOWN
Dubrow, Michael
CASPER
Duckette, Larry
BLACK IS ... BLACK AIN'T
Dudduth, Skipp
CLOCKERS
Dudgeon, Neil
FATHERLAND
Dudley, Lucas
OUTBREAK

Duell, William
RECKLESS
Duelling Bankheads, The
WIGSTOCK: THE MOVIE
Dufeu, Camille
CITY OF LOST CHILDREN, THE
Duffas, Yan
JEFFERSON IN PARIS
Duffin, Shay
NUMBER ONE FAN
Duffy, Dave
SECRET OF ROAN INISH, THE
Dugan, Tom
STUART SAVES HIS FAMILY
TWOGETHER
Dughi, Mikal
BROKEN TRUST
CIRCUMSTANCES UNKNOWN
Duhame, Zachary
HOME FOR THE HOLIDAYS
Duhamel, Nicole
NEA
Dukakis, Olympia
DIGGER
JEFFREY
MIGHTY APHRODITE
Duke, Charles
HEAT
Duke, Robin
STUART SAVES HIS FAMILY
Dulce, Maria
BOCA
Dulery, Antoine
LES MISERABLES
Dumaine, Pierre
MINA TANNENBAUM
Dumansky, Harvey
POWER OF ATTORNEY
Dumas, Charles
DIE HARD WITH A VENGEANCE
Dunagan, Deanna
LOSING ISAIAH
Dunaway, Faye
ARIZONA DREAM
DON JUAN DEMARCO
Dunbar, Adrian
INNOCENT LIES
RICHARD III
Duncan, Lee
WHITE MAN'S BURDEN
Duncan, Rachel
CRAZYSITTER, THE
Dunham, Christine
BALLET
Dunham, Monet-Cherise
NEW JERSEY DRIVE
Dunlap, Nathanial
THREE WISHES
Dunlap, Pamela
NICK OF TIME
O.J. SIMPSON STORY, THE
Dunlop, Willian
TOMMY BOY
Dunn, Beverly
GROSS MISCONDUCT
Dunn, Kevin
MAD LOVE
NIXON
Dunn, Mkeba W.
GLASS SHIELD, THE
Dunn, Robert
SHOWGIRLS
Dunn, Roger
CANADIAN BACON
KURT VONNEGUT'S HARRISON
BERGERON
Dunn, Stephen
CANDYMAN: FAREWELL TO THE FLESH

Dunn-Hill, John
HIGHLANDER: THE FINAL DIMENSION
Dunne, Griffin
ANDROID AFFAIR, THE
SEARCH AND DESTROY
Dunne, Martin
BRAVEHEART
FRANKIE STARLIGHT
Dunne, Roisin
MAD LOVE
Dunning, Nick
LAMB
Dunphy, Elaine
CIRCLE OF FRIENDS
Dunphy, Jerry
JERKY BOYS: THE MOVIE, THE
Dunst, Kirsten
JUMANJI
Dunston, Michael
TOMMY BOY
Duong Bl
FLUKE
Duperron, Tim
PARTY GIRL
DuPois, Starletta
WAITING TO EXHALE
Dupont, Daniel
CANDYMAN: FAREWELL TO THE FLESH
Dupont, Vincent
I CAN'T SLEEP
Duppin, Andy
BOYS ON THE SIDE
Dupree, Leigh
GLASS SHIELD, THE
Duran, Elvis
DIE HARD WITH A VENGEANCE
Duran, Micki
CLUELESS
Durand, Guillaume
GROSSE FATIGUE
Durand, Jared
BILLY MADISON
Durden, Richard
INNOCENT, THE
Durkin, Thomas
MIGHTY APHRODITE
Durning, Charles
HOME FOR THE HOLIDAYS
WATER ENGINE, THE
Duron, Charles
INNOCENT LIES
Duronslet, Mara
HIDEAWAY
VIRTUOSITY
Durron, Bambi
WINGS OF HONNEAMISE: ROYAL SPACE
FORCE
Dury, Ian
JUDGE DREDD
Dusek, Zenek
COW, THE
Dushku, Eliza
BYE BYE, LOVE
Dutt, Utpal
STRANGER, THE
Dutton, Charles
PIANO LESSON, THE
Dutton, Charles S.
CRY, THE BELOVED COUNTRY
NICK OF TIME
ZOOMAN
Dutton, Danny
DIE HARD WITH A VENGEANCE
Duval, James
DOOM GENERATION, THE
Duvall, Dean Rader
JOURNEY OF AUGUST KING, THE

Duvall, Robert
SCARLET LETTER, THE
SOMETHING TO TALK ABOUT
STARS FELL ON HENRIETTA, THE
Duvall, Wayne
APOLLO 13
UNSTRUNG HEROES
Duvert, Michael
JEFFREY
Dwyer, David
FLUKE
GETTING OUT
Dye, Dale
COVER STORY
OUTBREAK
UNDER SIEGE 2: DARK TERRITORY
Dyer, Micah
FRANK & JESSE
Dyer, Sharon
IN THE MOUTH OF MADNESS
Dyga, Robert
ROOMMATES
Dykes, Bertram
KINGFISH: A STORY OF HUEY P. LONG
Dypwick, Jeff
RHYTHM THIEF
Dysart, Richard
PANTHER
Dziekan-Vajda, Barbara
SHORT FILM ABOUT KILLING, A
Dzundza, George
CRIMSON TIDE
DANGEROUS MINDS
ENEMY WITHIN, THE
Eadie, Victor
SHALLOW GRAVE
Eagan, Daisy
LOSING ISAIAH
Earl, Barbaree
DRACULA: DEAD AND LOVING IT
Earl, Ilse
RADIO INSIDE
Earle, Katie
BABY-SITTERS CLUB, THE
Earley, James A.
PANTHER
Earnhart, Stephen
LORD OF ILLUSIONS
Eason, Bo
MIAMI RHAPSODY
SPY WITHIN, THE
Eastman, Marilyn
HOUSEGUEST
Eastwood, Clint
BRIDGES OF MADISON COUNTY, THE
CASPER
Eastwood, Francesca Ruth
STARS FELL ON HENRIETTA, THE
Eastwood, Jayne
KURT VONNEGUT'S HARRISON
BERGERON
Eastwood, Kyle
BRIDGES OF MADISON COUNTY, THE
Eaton, Roberta
CRUDE OASIS, THE
SKINNER
Ebbe, Annevig Schelde
KINGDOM, THE
Ebbighausen, Peer
TANK GIRL
Eccles, Julie
VILLAGE OF THE DAMNED
Eccleston, Christopher
SHALLOW GRAVE
Echanove, Josefina
BURNING SEASON, THE
Echeverria, Rob
JERKY BOYS: THE MOVIE, THE

Eckert, Andrea
BEFORE SUNRISE
Eckert, Charmagne
DIRTY MONEY
Eckert, Daniella
CLUELESS
Eckstein, Paul S.
SEVEN
Ecoffey, Jean-Philippe
MINA TANNENBAUM
Economou, Bruce
JURY DUTY
Eda
NOT ANGELS BUT ANGELS
Edam, Amber
S.F.W.
Edelman, Xylie
TIE-DIED: ROCK 'N' ROLL'S MOST
DEADICATED FANS
Edelson, Kenneth
MIGHTY APHRODITE
Eder, Horst
FOR GOD AND COUNTRY
Edmond, J. Trevor
HIGHER LEARNING
Edmond, Trevor
LORD OF ILLUSIONS
Edmonds, Alex
RESTORATION
Edoya, Nekohachi
MYSTERY OF RAMPO, THE
Edson, Richard
DESTINY TURNS ON THE RADIO
JURY DUTY
STRANGE DAYS
Edward-Stevens, Michael
BABE
Edwards, Craig
EMPIRE RECORDS
Edwards, Daryl
DIE HARD WITH A VENGEANCE
Edwards, Edward
COSMIC SLOP
Edwards, Ethel
MARTHA & ETHEL
Edwards, Kenneth
MORTAL KOMBAT
Edwards, Malika
BOYS ON THE SIDE
Edwards, Mark Prince
DANGEROUS MINDS
Edwards, Sparky
NATIONAL LAMPOON'S SENIOR TRIP
Edwards, Stacy
FEAR, THE
Edwards, Victoria
KINGFISH: A STORY OF HUEY P. LONG
Edwards, Vince
DILLINGER
FEAR, THE
Edwards, William
ROSWELL: THE U.F.O. COVER-UP
Egan, Aeryk
CURE, THE
Egan, Robert
FATHER AND SCOUT
Eggleston, Devin
NEW JERSEY DRIVE
Egi, Stan
BOYS ON THE SIDE
Eginton, Zachary
FORGET PARIS
INDICTMENT: THE MCMARTIN TRIAL
Egushi, Kaoru
HYENAS
Ehde, Christel
CROSSING GUARD, THE

Ehrenkranz, Joel S.
JUST CAUSE
Eichhorn, Christoph
EROTIQUE
Eichler, Gerd
FOR GOD AND COUNTRY
Eichling, James "Ike"
LOSING ISAIAH
Eigeman, Chris
KICKING AND SCREAMING
Eiland, Michael
BUFFALO GIRLS
Eilbacher, Lisa
LAST SAMURAI, THE
Eilers, Letitia
FRIENDS
Eilertson, Dean
DOLORES CLAIBORNE
Eirik, Sten
DARKMAN 2: THE RETURN OF DURANT
Eisenmann, Ike
TOM AND HUCK
Eisner, Alice
PIANO LESSON, THE
Elam, Kiante
HIGHER LEARNING
Elder, Judyann
FORGET PARIS
Elek, Jozsa
CITIZEN X
Elek, Marton
CITIZEN X
Eleniak, Erika
GIRL IN THE CADILLAC
PYROMANIAC'S LOVE STORY, A
Elezi, Nikolin
LAMERICA
Elfmont, Thomas
HEAT
Elias, Alice
I, THE WORST OF ALL
Elias, Maria
BAR GIRLS
Elias, Michael
GOOD DAY TO DIE, A
Eliasdottir, Soley
REMOTE CONTROL
Elise, Bernadette
S.F.W.
Elizondo, Evangelina
WALK IN THE CLOUDS, A
Elliot, Alison
UNDERNEATH, THE
Elliot, Barr "Star Dragon"
HARLEM DIARY: NINE VOICES OF
RESILIENCE
Elliot, Beverly
BLACK FOX
Elliott, Alison
INDICTMENT: THE MCMARTIN TRIAL
Elliott, Peter
CONGO
Elliott, Sam
BUFFALO GIRLS
Elliott, Sean
FORGET PARIS
Ellis, Cassidy
INDICTMENT: THE MCMARTIN TRIAL
Ellis, Chris
APOLLO 13
CRIMSON TIDE
LITTLE PRINCESS, A
TIE THAT BINDS, THE
Ellis, Fred
UNDERNEATH, THE
Ellis, James
PRIEST

Ellis, Jann
TWELVE MONKEYS
Ellis, Ramsey
BATMAN FOREVER
INDICTMENT: THE MCMARTIN TRIAL
Ellis, Terry
BATMAN FOREVER
Ellison-Jone, Gene
SHOWGIRLS
Ellwand, Greg
ECLIPSE
Elmaloglou, Rebekah
SUM OF US, THE
Elman, Jamie
JOHNNY MNEMONIC
Elmore, Bob
USUAL SUSPECTS, THE
Elsner, Morten
KINGDOM, THE
Elson, John
INCREDIBLY TRUE ADVENTURES OF
TWO GIRLS IN LOVE, THE
Elvis, Mae
WHITE MAN'S BURDEN
Emanuel, Michael
OUTBREAK
Emard, Jason
POSTCARDS FROM AMERICA
Emelin, Georgia
REASON TO BELIEVE, A
Emerson, Jonathan
FATHER AND SCOUT
FATHER OF THE BRIDE PART II
Emery, Angela
BAR GIRLS
Emil, Michael
LAST SUMMER IN THE HAMPTONS
Emile, Taungaroa
ONCE WERE WARRIORS
Emilfork, Daniel
CITY OF LOST CHILDREN, THE
Emmet, Jack
WINGS OF HONNEAMISE: ROYAL SPACE
FORCE
Emslie, Sean
INDICTMENT: THE MCMARTIN TRIAL
Enbom, John
GHOST BRIGADE
Encarnacion, Eddie
LIE DOWN WITH DOGS
Endoso, Kenny
DEVIL IN A BLUE DRESS
HEAT
Endresz, Jr., Laci
FUNNY BONES
Endrovski, Vladimir
BEFORE THE RAIN
Enes, Manuel
VALLEY OF ABRAHAM, THE
Eney, Woody
DANGER OF LOVE
Eng, Arthur
JOHNNY MNEMONIC
Engel, Paula
POWDER
Engel, Tina
PROMISE, THE
Engelharde, Christina
SKINNER
England, Rodney W.
CURE, THE
English, Bradford
HALLOWEEN: THE CURSE OF MICHAEL
MYERS
HIGHER LEARNING
English, Chip
RHYTHM THIEF

English, Deirdre
CRUMB
English, Jack
INDICTMENT: THE MCMARTIN TRIAL
English, Jeff
DARK DEALER
Englund, Robert
MANGLER, THE
Ennis, Jim
RESTORATION
Enomoto, Ken
SHOWGIRLS
Enriquez, Stefan
ASSASSINS
MAD LOVE
Ensign, Michael
CHILDREN OF THE CORN III: URBAN
HARVEST
Eoettinger, Melani
KID IN KING ARTHUR'S COURT, A
Eonnet, Estelle
JEFFERSON IN PARIS
Epp, Harry
RIVER OF GRASS
Epper, Gary
3 NINJAS KNUCKLE UP
Epper, Richard
EXPERT, THE
SCANNERS: THE SHOWDOWN
Epps, Omar
HIGHER LEARNING
Erbe, Kathryn
KISS OF DEATH
Erbe, Kathryne
ADDICTION, THE
Erdie, Jack
SUDDEN DEATH
Erganian, Leslie
RADIO INSIDE
Erickson, Orion
DEATH IN BRUNSWICK
Ermey, R. Lee
DEAD MAN WALKING
LEAVING LAS VEGAS
MURDER IN THE FIRST
SEVEN
TOY STORY
Ernst, Kristen
S.F.W.
Ersgard, Patrik
DREAMING OF RITA
Erwin, Bill
THINGS TO DO IN DENVER WHEN
YOU'RE DEAD
Eshkibok, Gloria May
DANCE ME OUTSIDE
Eskesen, Bente
KINGDOM, THE
Espe, Thomas J.
TIE-DIED: ROCK 'N' ROLL'S MOST
DEADICATED FANS
Espinosa, Pablo
BOYS ON THE SIDE
Esposito, Giancarlo
BLUE IN THE FACE
RECKLESS
SMOKE
USUAL SUSPECTS, THE
Espy, Carl
NOW AND THEN
Esquival, Anthony
BIG GREEN, THE
Esser, Muriel
MINA TANNENBAUM
Estabrook, Christine
USUAL SUSPECTS, THE
Estes, Will
HOW TO MAKE AN AMERICAN QUILT

Estese, Tony
INNOCENT, THE
Estevez, Joe
DILLINGER AND CAPONE
MOSAIC PROJECT, THE
Estevez, Ramon
EXPERT, THE
Estevez, Renee
GOOD GIRLS DON'T
Estrada, Angelina
MY FAMILY: MI FAMILIA
PENTATHLON
ZOOMAN
Estrada, Jose Antonio
BURNING SEASON, THE
Etaix, Pierre
SERIOUS ABOUT PLEASURE
Etheridge, Melissa
TERESA'S TATTOO
Etienne, Babeth
CITY OF LOST CHILDREN, THE
Etienne, Charlotte
FORGET PARIS
Ettinger, Martha
MARTHA & ETHEL
Eubanks, Shannon
SOMETHING TO TALK ABOUT
Evangelisti, Noel
BABYSITTER, THE
Evanko, Ed
SUDDEN DEATH
Evans, Art
TALES FROM THE HOOD
Evans, Bill
HIGHER LEARNING
Evans, Fred
FUNNY BONES
Evans, Howell
ENGLISHMAN WHO WENT UP A HILL
BUT CAME DOWN A MOUNTAIN, THE
Evans, Josh
GHOST BRIGADE
Evans, Lee
FUNNY BONES
Evans, Roy
RESTORATION
Evans, T.J.
ACROSS THE MOON
Evans, Troy
BODILY HARM
BORN TO BE WILD
FATHER AND SCOUT
Evans, Wanda Lee
DECONSTRUCTING SARAH
NET, THE
WHITE MAN'S BURDEN
Evans, William Michael
FRANK & JESSE
Evanson, David
CLOCKERS
Evenson, Wayne A.
GRUMPIER OLD MEN
Everett, Dale Andre Lee
CRIMSON TIDE
Everett, Lee
BAR GIRLS
Everett, Tom
TOO YOUNG TO DIE?
Everhart, Angie
JADE
Evers, Brian
SEVEN
Evers, Bruce
GETTING OUT
Everson, Cory
BALLISTIC
Ewan, Murray
CITIZEN X

Ewell, Dwight
AMATEUR
PARTY GIRL
Ewen, Lesley
DOUBLE HAPPINESS
MAGIC IN THE WATER
Ewing, Blake
TOM AND HUCK
Ewing, Patrick
FORGET PARIS
Eyles, Daphne
MINA TANNENBAUM
Eziashi, Maynard
ACE VENTURA: WHEN NATURE CALLS
Faber, Christian
DIRTY MONEY
Faber, Hart F.
LIE DOWN WITH DOGS
Faberman, Shane
BILLY MADISON
Fabian, Romeo Rene
MY FAMILY: MI FAMILIA
Fabozzi, Tony
RADIO INSIDE
Fabray, Nanette
TERESA'S TATTOO
Fadule, John
SILENCE OF THE HAMS
Faesch, Pierre-Quentin
CITY OF LOST CHILDREN, THE
Faessler, Pearl
BRIDGES OF MADISON COUNTY, THE
Faessler, R.E. "Stick"
BRIDGES OF MADISON COUNTY, THE
Fagundez, Solier
KICKING AND SCREAMING
Fain, Bobby
HEAVYWEIGHTS
Fairbrass, Craig
GALAXIS
Fairchild, Krisha
BETTER OFF DEAD
DANGER OF LOVE
Fairlie, Ann
POWER OF ATTORNEY
Fairlie, Kristen
SCARLET LETTER, THE
Fairs, Nigel
HEAVEN'S A DRAG
Faison, Donald Adeosun
CLUELESS
NEW JERSEY DRIVE
WAITING TO EXHALE
Faison, Frankie
ROOMMATES
Faison, Matthew
ROSWELL: THE U.F.O. COVER-UP
Falco, Edie
ADDICTION, THE
Falcone, Nicholas
KISS OF DEATH
Falk, Peter
ROOMMATES
Fall, Calgou
HYENAS
Fall, James
POCAHONTAS
Fallin, Erik
MUTANT SPECIES
Fallo, Kasey Olsen
DARK DEALER
Fallon, Siobhan
JURY DUTY
Falvay, Klara
CITIZEN X
Fan, Chung-Dan
SHAO LIN POPEYE

Fancy, Richard
NIXON
O.J. SIMPSON STORY, THE
ROSWELL: THE U.F.O. COVER-UP
SPECIES
Fanning, Dennis
CROSSING GUARD, THE
Fanning, Rio
PRIEST
Fantauzzi, Roberto H.
LIE DOWN WITH DOGS
Faraday, Robin
CRIMSON TIDE
Faraoni, Jr., Robert
MAJOR PAYNE
Farer, Ronnie
SAFE
Farfan, Alex
EROTIQUE
Farha, Clint
DANCER, THE
Farid, Zaid
BODY SHOT
Farina, Dennis
GET SHORTY
OUT OF ANNIE'S PAST
Farkas, Jo
FORGET PARIS
TANK GIRL
Farley, Chris
TOMMY BOY
Farmer, Art
GREAT DAY IN HARLEM, A
Farmer, Bill
GOOFY MOVIE, A
Farmer, Gary
TALES FROM THE CRYPT: DEMON
KNIGHT
Farre, Antonio
DIRTY MONEY
Farrell, Nicholas
OTHELLO
Farrell, Perry
DOOM GENERATION, THE
Farrell, Richard
WHEN NIGHT IS FALLING
Farrell, Shea
WHILE YOU WERE SLEEPING
Farrell, Terry
RED SUN RISING
Farrell, Tim
WATER ENGINE, THE
Farrell, Tom Riis
KISS OF DEATH
Farrington, Charles
GUMBY: THE MOVIE
Farris, Cynthia
FUN
Farrow, Mia
MIAMI RHAPSODY
RECKLESS
Fasce, Tony
SCANNERS: THE SHOWDOWN
Fasmer, Per Didrik
OUTBREAK
Fast Eddie
TIE-DIED: ROCK 'N' ROLL'S MOST
DEADICATED FANS
Fathers of the Id
REASON TO BELIEVE, A
Fatigante, Dana
LORD OF ILLUSIONS
Faugno, Rick
TWO BITS
Faulcon, Kent
DIE HARD WITH A VENGEANCE
Favreau, Jon
BATMAN FOREVER

Fawcett, Farrah
GOOD DAY TO DIE, A
MAN OF THE HOUSE
SUBSTITUTE WIFE, THE
Fawzi, Amir
FUNNY BONES
Faye, Cinnamon
PERSUASION
Fazio, Santo
RIVER OF GRASS
Fedoro, Olegario
HACKERS
Feeney, Bill
WATER ENGINE, THE
Feenstra, Nicole
INDICTMENT: THE MCMARTIN TRIAL
Fega, Russ
GALAXIS
Fehr, Dorothy
CIRCUMSTANCES UNKNOWN
Feig, Paul
HEAVYWEIGHTS
Feldman, Corey
DREAM A LITTLE DREAM 2
Fella, Michael
ADDICTION, THE
Felt, Asbestos
CREEP
Feltch, Mark
UNDERNEATH, THE
Fenn, Sherilyn
DILLINGER
Fenske, Thomas
MURDER IN THE FIRST
Fenyes, Erika
CITIZEN X
Ferda, Tom
JACK-O
Feresten, Michael
JURY DUTY
Ferguson, David
COPYCAT
Ferguson, J. Don
SOMETHING TO TALK ABOUT
Ferguson, Jay
HIGHER LEARNING
Ferguson, John Pyper
FRANK & JESSE
GOOD DAY TO DIE, A
Ferguson, Marcia
ONLY THE BRAVE
Ferguson, Matthew
BILLY MADISON
ECLIPSE
KURT VONNEGUT'S HARRISON
BERGERON
LOVE AND HUMAN REMAINS
Ferguson, Scott
MESSENGER
Ferguson, Tom
JACK-O
Ferguson, Wayne
RIVER OF GRASS
Ferguson, Wilder
HOME FOR THE HOLIDAYS
Ferland, Danielle
MIGHTY APHRODITE
Fernandes, Vanda
VALLEY OF ABRAHAM, THE
Fernandez, Juan
DANGEROUS, THE
Ferraez, Marcos A.
COLDBLOODED
Ferraro, Jason
SEARCH AND DESTROY
Ferratti, Rebecca
EMBRACE OF THE VAMPIRE

Ferrell, Tyra
BETTER OFF DEAD
Ferreol, Andrea
SERIOUS ABOUT PLEASURE
Ferrer, Mel
OH ... ROSALINDA!!
Ferrero, Martin
GET SHORTY
HEAT
Ferret, Gregory Steven
FUN
Ferri, Alessandra
BALLET
Ferry, David
DARKMAN 2: THE RETURN OF DURANT
Fersedi, Joe
TWO BITS
Ferstenberg, Bernard
ACROSS THE SEA OF TIME: NEW YORK
3D
Ferzetti, Gabriele
OTHELLO
Fessenden, Larry
RIVER OF GRASS
Fete, Jean-Michel
PIGALLE
Fetters, Cliff
FREE WILLY 2: THE ADVENTURE HOME
Feulner, Miles
NEXT DOOR
Feury, Joseph
LAST SUMMER IN THE HAMPTONS
Fiara, Christi
BODILY HARM
Fichtner, William
HEAT
RECKLESS
STRANGE DAYS
UNDERNEATH, THE
VIRTUOSITY
Fickert, Mark
DARK DEALER
Fickes, Mary Holt
HEAVYWEIGHTS
Fidello, Bernie
JACK-O
Field, Arabella
NEW JERSEY DRIVE
Field, Chelsea
INDICTMENT: THE MCMARTIN TRIAL
Field, Norman
LIVING IN OBLIVION
Field, Todd
FRANK & JESSE
Fields, Christopher John
APOLLO 13
Fields, Maurie
COUNTRY LIFE
Fields, Tony
ACROSS THE MOON
Fieldsted, Robert
ACROSS THE MOON
Fiennes, Ralph
STRANGE DAYS
Fieran, Charlie
LIE DOWN WITH DOGS
Fierry, Patrick
HIGHLANDER: THE FINAL DIMENSION
Fierstein, Harvey
DR. JEKYLL & MS. HYDE
Fieweger, Thomas J.
COPYCAT
Figgis, Mike
LEAVING LAS VEGAS
Figueroa, Efrain
COSMIC SLOP
Fiji, Ali
BEYOND RANGOON

Filberto, Ramirez
DON JUAN DEMARCO
Filippo, Fab
CANADIAN BACON
Fine, Travis
MY ANTONIA
Fink, John
BATMAN FOREVER
Finkel, Fyvush
NIXON
Finley, Greg
WATER ENGINE, THE
Finley, Margot
FAR FROM HOME: THE ADVENTURES OF
YELLOW DOG
Finnegan, David
WATERWORLD
Finnegan, Tom
COSMIC SLOP
Finney, Albert
RUN OF THE COUNTRY, THE
Finney, Brian
MAGIC IN THE WATER
Finnigan, A.
EXPERT, THE
Fioramonti, Glory
BATMAN FOREVER
Fiorella, Kristen
CURSE OF THE STARVING CLASS
Fiorentino, Linda
BODILY HARM
JADE
Firth, Colin
CIRCLE OF FRIENDS
Firth, Peter
AWFULLY BIG ADVENTURE, AN
Fischer, Denise
FUN
Fischer, Don
ROSWELL: THE U.F.O. COVER-UP
SPECIES
Fischer, John Louis
MAJOR PAYNE
Fischler, Patrick
SWIMMING WITH SHARKS
Fish, Nancy
REFLECTIONS IN THE DARK
Fishburne, Laurence
BAD COMPANY
HIGHER LEARNING
JUST CAUSE
OTHELLO
Fisher, Colin Blair
POSTCARDS FROM AMERICA
Fisher, Frances
STARS FELL ON HENRIETTA, THE
Fisher, Jennifer
BAR GIRLS
Fisher, Joely
COMPANION, THE
Fisher, Stephen
RESTORATION
Fisher, Takayo
DANGEROUS, THE
OUTSIDE THE LAW
Fisk, Madison
BABY-SITTERS CLUB, THE
Fisk, Schuyler
BABY-SITTERS CLUB, THE
Fithi, Ahmad
BEYOND RANGOON
Fitzgerald, Chris
TIE-DIED: ROCK 'N' ROLL'S MOST
DEADICATED FANS
Fitzgerald, Tara
ENGLISHMAN WHO WENT UP A HILL
BUT CAME DOWN A MOUNTAIN, THE

Fitzhugh, Katherine
COPYCAT
Fitzpatrick, Colleen
HIGHER LEARNING
JUST CAUSE
Fitzpatrick, Gabrielle
MIGHTY MORPHIN POWER RANGERS:
THE MOVIE
Fitzpatrick, James
CURSE OF THE STARVING CLASS
GLASS SHIELD, THE
Fitzpatrick, Leo
KIDS
Fix, Hapunkt
NEKROMANTIK
Flaherty, Joe
STUART SAVES HIS FAMILY
Flaherty, Lanny
TOM AND HUCK
WATERWORLD
Flakes, Carol
RIVER OF GRASS
Flanagan, Tommy
BRAVEHEART
Flanagan, Walter
MALLRATS
Flanders, Ed
BYE BYE, LOVE
Flanders, Lili
NET, THE
Flanery, Sean Patrick
FRANK & JESSE
POWDER
Flanigan, Joe
REASON TO BELIEVE, A
Flannery, Brian
THREE WISHES
Flaster, Andy
FORGET PARIS
Fleck, John
WATERWORLD
Fleeks, Eric
EVOLVER
GLASS SHIELD, THE
Fleet, Anthony
MUTANT SPECIES
Fleet, James
SENSE AND SENSIBILITY
Fleetwood, Susan
PERSUASION
Flegel, Christiane
INNOCENT, THE
Fleischer, Charles
TALES FROM THE CRYPT: DEMON
KNIGHT
Fleischer, Rudolph
FATHERLAND
Fleischman, Michele
LAST SUMMER IN THE HAMPTONS
Fleiss, Heidi
DOOM GENERATION, THE
Fleiss, Noah
ROOMMATES
Fleming, Brendan
JUDGE DREDD
Fleming, Jaqueline
LOSING ISAIAH
Fleming, Nickolas
MOSAIC PROJECT, THE
Fleming, Rico
EMPIRE RECORDS
Flemyng, Jason
ROB ROY
Fletcher, Alan
GROSS MISCONDUCT
Fletcher, Andrea
BATMAN FOREVER

Fletcher, Anne
TANK GIRL
Fletcher, John
CLOCKERS
Fletcher, Louise
VIRTUOSITY
Flex
MONEY TRAIN
Flick, David
SUDDEN DEATH
Flip
DIE HARD WITH A VENGEANCE
Flippo, Michael
SOMETHING TO TALK ABOUT
Flood, Barbara
LAST SUMMER IN THE HAMPTONS
Florence, Carol
TWELVE MONKEYS
Flores, Alejandra
WALK IN THE CLOUDS, A
Flores, Serafino
ARIZONA DREAM
Flores, Von
ECLIPSE
JOHNNY MNEMONIC
Florio, Heather
RIVER OF GRASS
Florio, Joseph
RIVER OF GRASS
Florio, Shelley
RIVER OF GRASS
Flower, Buck
VILLAGE OF THE DAMNED
Flower, Ethan
MALLRATS
Flowers, Jennifer
DESPERATE PREY
Flowers, Jim
FRANK & JESSE
Floyd
WIGSTOCK: THE MOVIE
Floyd, Janathan
HOUSEGUEST
Floyd, Roger
WALKING DEAD, THE
Fluga, Alexandra
BAR GIRLS
Flunder, Yvette
BLACK IS ... BLACK AIN'T
Flynn, Kimberly
HEAT
RHYTHM THIEF
Flynn, Martha
TO WONG FOO, THANKS FOR
EVERYTHING! JULIE NEWMAR
Flynn, Michael
OUT OF ANNIE'S PAST
Flynn, Miriam
BABE
INDICTMENT: THE MCMARTIN TRIAL
Flynn, Patrick
ACROSS THE SEA OF TIME: NEW YORK
3D
Flynt, Matthew
SWIMMING WITH SHARKS
Fohl, Peyton Chesson
MAJOR PAYNE
Foley, Joan
SHOWGIRLS
Folger, Mark
INDICTMENT: THE MCMARTIN TRIAL
Folk, Alexander
SHOWGIRLS
Folk, Wayne
DECOY
Folland, Alison
TO DIE FOR

Fonda, Bridget
BALTO
Fonda, Peter
NADJA
Fondren, Debra
SPITFIRE
Fong, Donald
DOUBLE HAPPINESS
Fong, Frank
MIAMI RHAPSODY
Fong, Nathan
DOUBLE HAPPINESS
Font, Charles
S.F.W.
Fontana, Randall
VIRTUOSITY
Fontana, Tess
DECONSTRUCTING SARAH
Fontelieu, Stocker
KINGFISH: A STORY OF HUEY P. LONG
Foody, Ralph
DILLINGER
Foote, Jr., Horton
WATER ENGINE, THE
Forbes, Brenda
JERKY BOYS: THE MOVIE, THE
Forbes, Greg
FORGET PARIS
Forbes, Michelle
SWIMMING WITH SHARKS
Forbes, Shang
BYE BYE, LOVE
Ford, Bruce
COLORADO COWBOY: THE BRUCE FORD
STORY
Ford, Dalvin
DEAD MAN WALKING
Ford, Harrison
SABRINA
Ford, Maria
DILLINGER AND CAPONE
Ford, Ron
FEAR, THE
Ford, Steven
HEAT
Forde, Seamus
CIRCLE OF FRIENDS
Forke, Farrah
HEAT
Forlani, Claire
MALLRATS
Forman, Petr
ACCUMULATOR 1
Forney, Jay Speed
CONGO
Fornof, J.W. "Corky"
ROSWELL: THE U.F.O. COVER-UP
Foronjy, Richard
MAN OF THE HOUSE
Forres, Jessica Elizabeth
RADIO INSIDE
Forrest, Donald
OUTBREAK
Forrest, Kathy
BAR GIRLS
Forrester, Tom
TO DIE FOR
Fors, John R.
BRADY BUNCH MOVIE, THE
Forslund, Constance
VILLAGE OF THE DAMNED
Forster, Robert
COVER STORY
SCANNERS: THE SHOWDOWN
Forsythe, Julie
BABE

Forsythe, William
THINGS TO DO IN DENVER WHEN
YOU'RE DEAD
VIRTUOSITY
Fortag, Sonje
DRACULA: DEAD AND LOVING IT
Forte, Patricia
GLASS SHIELD, THE
HIGHER LEARNING
Fortea, Isabella
BIKINI BISTRO
Foster, Frances
CLOCKERS
Foster, Meg
UNDERCOVER
Foster, Nicholas
LOSING ISAIAH
Foster, Stan
BREACH OF CONDUCT
Foster, Stephen C.
ROSWELL: THE U.F.O. COVER-UP
Foster, Tiffany
HIDEAWAY
Fouchecourt, Jean-Paul
JEFFERSON IN PARIS
Fouille, Robinson
CITY OF LOST CHILDREN, THE
Fournel, Max
LES MISERABLES
Foust, J. Allison
NUMBER ONE FAN
Fow, Paul
DOOM GENERATION, THE
Fowler, Isaac
CLOCKERS
Fowler, Jennifer
DIRTY MONEY
Fowler, Larned
DIRTY MONEY
Fowler, Lizzie
DIRTY MONEY
Fox, Brad
MALLRATS
Fox, Colin
TOMMY BOY
Fox, David
BLACK FOX
WHEN NIGHT IS FALLING
Fox, Edward
MONTH BY THE LAKE, A
Fox, Gordon
DARK DEALER
Fox, James
DOOMSDAY GUN
Fox, Jonathan
FARINELLI
Fox, Jorjan
DEAD FUNNY
JERKY BOYS: THE MOVIE, THE
Fox, Kelli
DOUBLE, DOUBLE, TOIL AND TROUBLE
MOONLIGHT AND VALENTINO
Fox, Kerry
COUNTRY LIFE
FRIENDS
SHALLOW GRAVE
Fox, Michael J.
AMERICAN PRESIDENT, THE
BLUE IN THE FACE
COLDBLOODED
Fox, Patricia Anne
WAITING TO EXHALE
Fox, Shayna
CONGO
Foxcroft, Les
ETERNITY
Foye, Janet
BABE

Foyt, Victoria
LAST SUMMER IN THE HAMPTONS
Fragos, Eugenia
ONLY THE BRAVE
Frain, James
AWFULLY BIG ADVENTURE, AN
Francis, David
HIGHLANDER: THE FINAL DIMENSION
Francis, Evelyn
SCARLET LETTER, THE
Francis, John
STRANGE DAYS
Francisco, Vernon
BOYS ON THE SIDE
Francks, Don
JOHNNY MNEMONIC
Francks, Dov
FIRST DEGREE
Francks, Rainbow
BLACK FOX
Franco, Cris
MY FAMILY: MI FAMILIA
Franco, Tony
ATTACK OF THE 60-FOOT CENTERFOLD
Francois, Emilie
SENSE AND SENSIBILITY
Francoz, Stephanie
HOME FOR THE HOLIDAYS
Franges, Irene
MANGLER, THE
Frank, Brian
BYE BYE, LOVE
Frank, Jason David
MIGHTY MORPHIN POWER RANGERS:
THE MOVIE
Frank, Tony
SUBSTITUTE WIFE, THE
Franke, Peter
DEADLY MARIA
Franken, Al
STUART SAVES HIS FAMILY
Frankfurt, Steve
GREAT DAY IN HARLEM, A
Frankish, Brian
NET, THE
Franklin, Barbara
PYROMANIAC'S LOVE STORY, A
Franklin, Cherie
DRACULA: DEAD AND LOVING IT
INDICTMENT: THE MCMARTIN TRIAL
Franklin, Daniel
FEAR, THE
Franklin, Hardy R.
EROTIQUE
Franklyn-Robbins, John
DR. JEKYLL & MS. HYDE
Franz, Elizabeth
SABRINA
Franzo, Jimmy
BAD BOYS
Fraser, Brendan
YOUNGER & YOUNGER
Fraser, Brent
DARK SIDE OF GENIUS, THE
Fraser, Danielle
DIGGER
Fraser, Duncan
CIRCUMSTANCES UNKNOWN
CRACKERJACK
Fraser, Patricia
HOUSEGUEST
Frawly, John
DALLAS DOLL
Frayer, Jeff
WINGS OF HONNEAMISE: ROYAL SPACE
FORCE
Frazier, Kim
DARK DEALER

Fredro
CLOCKERS
Freeman, Alfonso
SEVEN
Freeman, Bud
GREAT DAY IN HARLEM, A
Freeman, Cheryl
DEAD PRESIDENTS
Freeman, Don
GRANNY, THE
Freeman, Donald Joseph
HOUSEGUEST
Freeman, J.E.
COPYCAT
Freeman, K. Todd
JEFFREY
Freeman, Messiri
VAMPIRE IN BROOKLYN
Freeman, Morgan
OUTBREAK
SEVEN
Freeman, Paul
MIGHTY MORPHIN POWER RANGERS:
THE MOVIE
SUM OF US, THE
Freeman, Sarah
TOY STORY
Freeman, Yvette
ANGUS
CHILDREN OF THE CORN III: URBAN
HARVEST
Freitag, Oskar
INNOCENT LIES
Freitag, Robert
NEA
French, Delphine
CURE, THE
Frerichs, Reed
POWDER
Frerot, Alain
FRENCH KISS
Fresco, David
LITTLE PRINCESS, A
Freund, Jeremie
CITY OF LOST CHILDREN, THE
Frewer, Matt
NATIONAL LAMPOON'S SENIOR TRIP
Frey, Chery
BLUE TIGER
Frey, Sami
MY LIFE AND TIMES WITH ANTONIN
ARTAUD
NEA
TRAPS
Fribo, Louise
KINGDOM, THE
Fridbjornsson, Bjorn Jorundur
REMOTE CONTROL
Fridell, Squire
VILLAGE OF THE DAMNED
Friedman, Harvey
INNOCENT, THE
Friedman, Peter
SAFE
Friedman, Stephanie
S.F.W.
Friedman, Steven Mark
POSTCARDS FROM AMERICA
Friedopfer, Brian
LOSING ISAIAH
Friedrichs, Katie Planche
KINGFISH: A STORY OF HUEY P. LONG
Friel, Cassy
SAFE
Friels, Colin
NOSTRADAMUS KID, THE
Friesen, Peggy
MY ANTONIA

Frissung, Jean Claude
FRANKIE STARLIGHT
Fritsch, Hannes
HEAT
Fritz, Nikki
ATTACK OF THE 60-FOOT CENTERFOLD
Frizzelle, Zed
GET SHORTY
Front, Jerome
S.F.W.
Frosslova, Marketa
ACCUMULATOR 1
Frost, Sadie
PYROMANIAC'S LOVE STORY, A
Frost, Stephen
FEAST OF JULY
Froton, Saralee
SKINNER
Frumkes, Roy
ME AND THE MOB
Fry, Taylor
LITTLE PRINCESS, A
TOO YOUNG TO DIE?
Frye, Chelsea
MALLRATS
Frye, Virgil
S.F.W.
Fu Biao
SHANGHAI TRIAD
Fuchs, Elke
NEKROMANTIK
Fuchs, Fritz
NEKROMANTIK
Fudge, Alan
GALAXIS
TOO YOUNG TO DIE?
Fuega, Russ
GALAXIS
Fuelner, Miles
AVENGING ANGEL
Fuglei, Kate
INDICTMENT: THE MCMARTIN TRIAL
Fuglistaller, Ruth
MARTHA & ETHEL
Fuhrer, David
RHYTHM THIEF
Fujioka, John
LAST SAMURAI, THE
MORTAL KOMBAT
PREHYSTERIA! 3
Fukasaku, Kinji
MYSTERY OF RAMPO, THE
Fukuoka, Tsubasa
MYSTERY OF RAMPO, THE
Fulk, Mike
TO WONG FOO, THANKS FOR
EVERYTHING! JULIE NEWMAR
Fuller, Bruce Spaulding
TANK GIRL
Fuller, Cameron Corwin
BABYSITTER, THE
Fuller, Jonathan
CASTLE FREAK
Fuller, Kathleen
WORLD AND TIME ENOUGH
Fuller, Kurt
REFLECTIONS IN THE DARK
STUART SAVES HIS FAMILY
Fuller, William
PANTHER
Funches, Garvin
CHILDREN OF THE CORN III: URBAN
HARVEST
Fundacaro, Phil
DOUBLE, DOUBLE, TOIL AND TROUBLE
Funke, Ulrich
FRANKIE STARLIGHT

Fuqua, Ardie
DIE HARD WITH A VENGEANCE
Furdui, Dimitri
MINA TANNENBAUM
Furious Five, The
SHOW, THE
Furlan, Mira
MY ANTONIA
Furlong, Edward
LITTLE ODESSA
Furukawa, Jason
HUNTED, THE
Fustakian, Bryan
CONVICT COWBOY
Futterman, Dan
CLASS OF '61
Fylking, Gertt
DREAMING OF RITA
Gabel, Michael
MAJOR PAYNE
Gaberman, Alexander
BASKETBALL DIARIES, THE
Gabriel, Ron
TO DIE FOR
Gabrielle, Lea
OLD LADY WHO WALKED IN THE SEA,
THE
Gabrielli, Elisa Pensler
BRADY BUNCH MOVIE, THE
Gadbois, Jeff
MALLRATS
Gaddis, Kay
WHEN BILLY BROKE HIS HEAD ... AND
OTHER TALES OF WONDER
Gaddis, Marshall
BED YOU SLEEP IN, THE
Gaden, John
MURIEL'S WEDDING
Gaekwad, Sunil
BANDIT QUEEN
Gaetani, Nick
BASKETBALL DIARIES, THE
Gage, Kevin
HEAT
Gage, Patricia
FIRST DEGREE
Gagne, Randy
ROSWELL: THE U.F.O. COVER-UP
Gagnon, Steve
PANTHER
Gagnon, Steven M.
OUTSIDE THE LAW
Gago, Jenny
MY FAMILY: MI FAMILIA
TIE THAT BINDS, THE
Gainsbourg, Charlotte
GROSSE FATIGUE
Gainsbourg, Serge
SERIOUS ABOUT PLEASURE
Gal's Panic
UNDERNEATH, THE
Galan, Alfonso
BUSINESS AFFAIR, A
Galan, Mapi
CITY OF LOST CHILDREN, THE
Galasso, Chandra
ANDROID AFFAIR, THE
Galbacs, Zoltan
CITIZEN X
Gale, Lena
WINGS OF HONNEAMISE: ROYAL SPACE
FORCE
Gale, Lorena
BROKEN TRUST
CIRCUMSTANCES UNKNOWN
Galeano, Gia
INDIAN IN THE CUPBOARD, THE

Galeota, Michael
BUSHWHACKED
Galfione, Olivier
JEFFERSON IN PARIS
Galindo, Kelly
OUTSIDE THE LAW
Galko, Balazs
CITIZEN X
Gallacher, Frank
DALLAS DOLL
Gallagher, David Drew
AMERICAN PRESIDENT, THE
Gallagher, Jimmy
PRIEST
Gallagher, Maureen
BAD BOYS
Gallagher, Patrick
MUTANT SPECIES
Gallagher, Peter
UNDERNEATH, THE
WHILE YOU WERE SLEEPING
Gallant, Tom
DOLORES CLAIBORNE
Gallardo, Carlos
DESPERADO
Gallardo, Jose
I AM CUBA
Gallegos, Ismael
WALK IN THE CLOUDS, A
Gallienne, Guillaume
SABRINA
Gallison, Joseph
SEPARATE LIVES
Gallo, Vincent
ARIZONA DREAM
Galloway, Don
DOOM GENERATION, THE
Galloway, Graham
HIGHER LEARNING
TALES FROM THE CRYPT: DEMON
KNIGHT
WAITING TO EXHALE
Galloway, Leata
STEAL BIG, STEAL LITTLE
Galloway, Roy
VAMPIRE IN BROOKLYN
Gallup, Bonnie
POWDER
Galotti, Robert "Rock"
TANK GIRL
Galton, Norman
NOSTRADAMUS KID, THE
Galvez, Desire
DANGEROUS MINDS
Gamarra-Thomson, Rosa
ROOMMATES
Gamberini, Valerio
LES MISERABLES
Gambill, Art
GHOST BRIGADE
Gambino, Matthew
LIE DOWN WITH DOGS
Gamblin, Jacques
LES MISERABLES
Gamel, Daniel
TIE-DIED: ROCK 'N' ROLL'S MOST
DEADICATED FANS
Gammon, James
WILD BILL
Gandolfini, James
CRIMSON TIDE
GET SHORTY
Ganger, Toby
TOM AND HUCK
Ganguly, Promode
STRANGER, THE
Gannascoli, Joseph R.
NEVER TALK TO STRANGERS

Gannon, Lisa
FORGET PARIS
Gant, David
BRAVEHEART
RESTORATION
Gant, Robert
BITTER VENGEANCE
Ganun, John
JEFFREY
Ganzel, Teresa
GRANNY, THE
Gao Songhai
ERMO
Gao Weiming
SHANGHAI TRIAD
Gao Yang
RED FIRECRACKER, GREEN
FIRECRACKER
Gao Ying
SHANGHAI TRIAD
Gaona, Richie
DESPERADO
Garber, Dennis
CRIMSON TIDE
Garber, Victor
EXOTICA
JEFFREY
Garbi, Avner
INDICTMENT: THE MCMARTIN TRIAL
Garces, Paula
DANGEROUS MINDS
Garcia, Albert
BAD BLOOD
Garcia, Andy
STEAL BIG, STEAL LITTLE
THINGS TO DO IN DENVER WHEN
YOU'RE DEAD
Garcia, Cesar
DIRTY MONEY
Garcia, Juan
NET, THE
Garcia, Malquele
FUN
Garcia, Pedro
MAD LOVE
Garcia, Raul
I AM CUBA
Garcia, Rick
AMERICAN PRESIDENT, THE
Garcia, Santiago
DON JUAN DEMARCO
Garcia-Lorido, Dominik
STEAL BIG, STEAL LITTLE
Gardener, Kimberly
CURSE OF THE STARVING CLASS
Gardiner, Bill
ROB ROY
Gardiner, Iain
DESPERATE PREY
Gardner, Devin
HALLOWEEN: THE CURSE OF MICHAEL
MYERS
Gardner, Glenn Alan
SUDDEN DEATH
Gardner, Robert
ROOMMATES
Gardner, Tim
SAFE
Gardner, Tony
RESTORATION
Garfield, Allen
DESTINY TURNS ON THE RADIO
STUART SAVES HIS FAMILY
Garfield!
JERKY BOYS: THE MOVIE, THE
Gargano, Angelina
TIE-DIED: ROCK 'N' ROLL'S MOST
DEADICATED FANS

Garito, Ken
CLOCKERS
Garlington, Lee
BABYSITTER, THE
REFLECTIONS IN THE DARK
Garmon, Pamela
DEAD MAN WALKING
Garms, Justin
BYE BYE, LOVE
GORDY
Garner, Alice
NOSTRADAMUS KID, THE
Garner, Julian
MURIEL'S WEDDING
Garner, Stan
UNDER SIEGE 2: DARK TERRITORY
Garnett, Richard
DOOMSDAY GUN
Garnier, Phillippe
FRENCH KISS
Garofalo, Ettore
MAMMA ROMA
Garofalo, Janeane
BYE BYE, LOVE
COLDBLOODED
NOW AND THEN
Garrett, Brad
CASPER
Garrett, Nicholas
MAN OF THE HOUSE
Garrett, Steve
GALAXIS
Garrick, Barbara
MIAMI RHAPSODY
Garrido, Carla
TANK GIRL
Garrido, Joaquin
BURNING SEASON, THE
Garris, Mick
QUICK AND THE DEAD, THE
Garrivier, Victor
FRENCH KISS
Garson, William
THINGS TO DO IN DENVER WHEN
YOU'RE DEAD
Garson, Willie
TIE THAT BINDS, THE
Garth, Eleanor
RADIO INSIDE
Gartside, Kate
SISTER MY SISTER
Garver, David
BUFFALO GIRLS
Garvey, Ray
MIGHTY APHRODITE
Gary, Laura
FREE WILLY 2: THE ADVENTURE HOME
Gaskill, Andy
FRANK AND OLLIE
Gaskins, Vincent
DARK DEALER
UNDERNEATH, THE
Gaskins, Yolanda
ENEMY WITHIN, THE
Gassman, Alessandro
MONTH BY THE LAKE, A
Gasso, Jim
FORGET PARIS
Gastaldi, Jany
MINA TANNENBAUM
Gastelum, Arturo
QUICK AND THE DEAD, THE
Gaston, Michael
AMATEUR
HACKERS
SUDDEN DEATH

Gates, Stephanie
TIE-DIED: ROCK 'N' ROLL'S MOST
DEADICATED FANS
Gatinois, Jonathan
CITY OF LOST CHILDREN, THE
Gattorno, Francisco
STRAWBERRY AND CHOCOLATE
Gaudet, Desiree
DANGEROUS, THE
Gaultier, Jean-Yves
PROMISE, THE
Gaver, Duffy
SEVEN
Gavin, James W.
ASSASSINS
Gawley, Denis
LIE DOWN WITH DOGS
Gawlik, S.
SHORT FILM ABOUT LOVE, A
Gawronski, A.
SHORT FILM ABOUT KILLING, A
Gayle, Wendy
SAFE
Gaynor, Joey
GALAXIS
Gazelle, Wendy
NET, THE
Gazzara, Ben
CONVICT COWBOY
Ge Zhijun
ERMO
Geary, Karl
NADJA
Gebelhoff, Stefan
NOBODY LOVES ME
Gebhardt, Allen
JADE
Geburtig, Daniela
NEKROMANTIK
Gee, Sandra
ACROSS THE MOON
Geeves, Peter
CUTTHROAT ISLAND
Geier, Paul
SMOKE
Geldenhuys, Gustav
FRIENDS
Gelt, Grant
MUTANT SPECIES
Genaud, Philippe-Morrier
PROMISE, THE
Geneste, Joris
CITY OF LOST CHILDREN, THE
Genevie, Michael
CLASS OF '61
Genovese, Eric
JEFFERSON IN PARIS
Genovesi, Linda
CANADIAN BACON
Gentile, Justine
THREE WISHES
Genty, Francois
SABRINA
Genzel, Carrie
CAGED HEARTS
Geoffrey, Lauren
CITY OF LOST CHILDREN, THE
George, Babs
SUBSTITUTE WIFE, THE
George, Chief Leonard
MAN OF THE HOUSE
George, Denise
HACKERS
George, Joyce
POSTCARDS FROM AMERICA
George, Richard
WINGS OF HONNEAMISE: ROYAL SPACE
FORCE

George, Sally
PERSUASION
Georgiadis, George
BOYS ON THE SIDE
Gera, Zoltan
CITIZEN X
Geraghty, Bridget Kate
BABY-SITTERS CLUB, THE
Geraghty, Marita
DON JUAN DEMARCO
Gerardi, Joan
BIKINI BISTRO
Gerber, Jay
THREE WISHES
Gere, Richard
FIRST KNIGHT
Gerlach, Christine
INNOCENT, THE
Germaine, Maeve
BABE
Germaine-Browne, Paul
POSTCARDS FROM AMERICA
Germeau, Sabrina
MINA TANNENBAUM
Germon, Nane
CITY OF LOST CHILDREN, THE
Gero, Jono
CITIZEN X
Gerolmo, Chris
CITIZEN X
Gerrish, Frank
OUT OF ANNIE'S PAST
Gershon, Gina
SHOWGIRLS
Gerulaitas, Vitas
BREAK, THE
Geter, Leo
HALLOWEEN: THE CURSE OF MICHAEL
MYERS
Getty, Balthazar
JUDGE DREDD
Gevai, Simon
CITIZEN X
Gevedon, Stephen
BLUE IN THE FACE
BOYS ON THE SIDE
SMOKE
Ghaffari, Mohammed
LITTLE ODESSA
Ghaye, Jacqueline
MINA TANNENBAUM
Ghosal, Syamal
CHARULATA
Ghosh, Bankim
CHARULATA
Giaimo, Anthony
FAIR GAME
Giamatti, Paul
MIGHTY APHRODITE
SABRINA
Giangrando, Anthony
ADDICTION, THE
Giannini, Giancarlo
WALK IN THE CLOUDS, A
Gianopoulos, David
CANDYMAN: FAREWELL TO THE FLESH
UNDER SIEGE 2: DARK TERRITORY
Gibault, Thierry
CITY OF LOST CHILDREN, THE
Gibbins, Hayley
TOMMY BOY
Gibbs, Keith
FORGET PARIS
Gibbs, Matyelok
PRIEST
Gibbs, Nigel
DEVIL IN A BLUE DRESS

Gibson, Donal
BRAVEHEART
Gibson, Gayle
BAR GIRLS
Gibson, Henry
CYBER BANDITS
Gibson, Mel
BRAVEHEART
CASPER
POCAHONTAS
Gibson, Thomas
LOVE AND HUMAN REMAINS
Giddings, Brad
MALLRATS
Gidley, Pamela
CREW, THE
S.F.W.
Gielgud, John
FIRST KNIGHT
Gierasch, Stefan
MURDER IN THE FIRST
Gierl, Craig
CURE, THE
Gifaldi, Sam
FLUKE
Gifford, Alec
DEAD MAN WALKING
Gifford, Gloria
ACROSS THE MOON
Giftos, Elaine
BODY CHEMISTRY 4: FULL EXPOSURE
Giglio, Jr., Anthony
KICKING AND SCREAMING
Gil, Raymond
PIGALLE
Gilbert, Ben
IN THE MOUTH OF MADNESS
Gilbert, John
ECLIPSE
Gilbert, Ron
USUAL SUSPECTS, THE
Gilbert, Taylor
INDICTMENT: THE MCMARTIN TRIAL
Gilborn, Steven
BRADY BUNCH MOVIE, THE
SAFE
Gilchrist, Gilly
ROB ROY
Giles, Donna
WIGSTOCK: THE MOVIE
Giles, Gregory G.
WORLD AND TIME ENOUGH
Giles, Selina
RESTORATION
Gilford, Hilary
LIVING IN OBLIVION
Gilker, Garth
HIGHLANDER: THE FINAL DIMENSION
Gill, Cody
MONEY TRAIN
Gill, Earl
AWFULLY BIG ADVENTURE, AN
Gill, Jonothon
QUICK AND THE DEAD, THE
Gill, Katie
MONEY TRAIN
Gillen, Aidan
CIRCLE OF FRIENDS
Gilles, Isabel
NADJA
Gilles, Julianne
TOMMY BOY
Gilles, Marcel Jean
BILLY MADISON
Gillespie, Dizzy
GREAT DAY IN HARLEM, A

Gillespie, Elmer
LAMB
Gillett, Chris
FUN
Gillette, Anita
BOYS ON THE SIDE
Gilley, Mickey
GORDY
Gilliam, Burton
BORN TO BE WILD
Gilliam, Elizabeth
CROSSING GUARD, THE
Gilliam, Seth
JEFFERSON IN PARIS
Gilliard, Jr., Larry
MONEY TRAIN
Gillmer, Caroline
HOTEL SORRENTO
Gilmore, Ryan
RICHARD III
Gilpin, Jack
RECKLESS
Gilroy, Jack
AMERICAN PRESIDENT, THE
Gilroy, Tom
POSTCARDS FROM AMERICA
Gilsfort, Peter
KINGDOM, THE
Gilson, Sarah
JUMANJI
Gimpel, Erica
AMATEUR
SMOKE
Ginga, Kazuhiro
AI CITY
Ginther, Mark
MIGHTY MORPHIN POWER RANGERS:
THE MOVIE
Gio, Frank
ME AND THE MOB
Giovanetti, Louis
ME AND THE MOB
Girard, Amanda
NINE MONTHS
Girard, Philippe
JEFFERSON IN PARIS
Girardeau, Frank
SEARCH AND DESTROY
Girardot, Annie
LES MISERABLES
Girlina
WIGSTOCK: THE MOVIE
Gish, Annabeth
NIXON
Gitlin, Michael
ART FOR TEACHERS OF CHILDREN
Gitonga, Jackson
CONGO
Gittelson, Larry
DILLINGER
Gittoes, George
ETERNITY
Giuntoli, Neil
WATERWORLD
Givens, Steven
FUN
Gladstone, Dana
TIE THAT BINDS, THE
Glascock, Roy
LAMB
Glasgow, Gil
BIG GREEN, THE
Glass, Ron
HOUSEGUEST
Glasser, Isabel
CIRCUMSTANCES UNKNOWN
ENEMY WITHIN, THE

Glazer, Eugene
SCANNERS: THE SHOWDOWN
Gleason, Mary Pat
WALK IN THE CLOUDS, A
Gleaves, Nicholas
CENTURY
Glebicka, I.
SHORT FILM ABOUT KILLING, A
Gleeson, Brendan
BRAVEHEART
Gleeson, Redmond
TOO YOUNG TO DIE?
Glen, Willa
NOW AND THEN
Glendinning, Grant
SHALLOW GRAVE
Glenister, Robert
PERSUASION
Glenn, Cody
STEAL BIG, STEAL LITTLE
Glenn, Mary
RIVER OF GRASS
Glenn, Peter
TO DIE FOR
Glenn, Scott
RECKLESS
SPY WITHIN, THE
TALL TALE: THE UNBELIEVABLE
ADVENTURES OF PECOS BILL
Globisz, Krzysztof
SHORT FILM ABOUT KILLING, A
Gloss, Ruth
PROMISE, THE
Glover, Christopher
JUDGE DREDD
Glover, Danny
OPERATION DUMBO DROP
Glover, Joan
DEAD MAN WALKING
Glover, John
IN THE MOUTH OF MADNESS
Glover, Susan
DR. JEKYLL & MS. HYDE
Gluxam, Wolfgang
BEFORE SUNRISE
Glynn, Carlin
BLESSING
Goaz, Harry
UNDERNEATH, THE
Gobert, Dedrick
HIGHER LEARNING
Gochberg, Jonathan
OUT OF ANNIE'S PAST
Godard, Jean-Luc
JLG BY JLG
Goddard, Beth
BUSINESS AFFAIR, A
Goddard, Paul
BABE
MIGHTY MORPHIN POWER RANGERS:
THE MOVIE
Goddard, Suzanne
STEAL BIG, STEAL LITTLE
Goddard, Trevor
BREAK, THE
MORTAL KOMBAT
Godet, Laurie
SEARCH AND DESTROY
Godwin, Stephen
DANGER OF LOVE
Goepen, Willie
CONVICT COWBOY
Goertz, Augustus
POSTCARDS FROM AMERICA
Goetz, Peter Michael
FATHER OF THE BRIDE PART II
WATER ENGINE, THE

Goff, D.C. "Dash"
FRANK & JESSE
Goffe, Rusty
FUNNY BONES
Gofman, Betty
BOCA
Gogolev, Viktor
WINDOW TO PARIS
Goguen, Nathalie
LOVE AND HUMAN REMAINS
Going, Joanna
GOOD DAY TO DIE, A
HOW TO MAKE AN AMERICAN QUILT
NIXON
Gol, Robyn
MIGHTY MORPHIN POWER RANGERS:
THE MOVIE
Gold, Glori
EMBRACE OF THE VAMPIRE
Gold, L. Harvey
BAD COMPANY
BROKEN TRUST
Gold, Matthew
QUICK AND THE DEAD, THE
Goldberg, Adam
HIGHER LEARNING
PROPHECY, THE
Goldberg, Brent Michael
CRIMSON TIDE
Goldberg, Whoopi
BOYS ON THE SIDE
MOONLIGHT AND VALENTINO
Goldblatt, Max
BUSHWHACKED
HEAVYWEIGHTS
Goldblum, Jeff
HIDEAWAY
NINE MONTHS
POWDER
Golden, Annie
PEBBLE AND THE PENGUIN, THE
Golden Eagle
TIE-DIED: ROCK 'N' ROLL'S MOST
DEADICATED FANS
Goldfedder, Maureen
POSTCARDS FROM AMERICA
Goldman, David
HEAVYWEIGHTS
Goldring, Danny
VIRTUOSITY
Goldstein, Bobby
MY ANTONIA
Goldstein, Herb
DR. JEKYLL & MS. HYDE
Goldstein, Jenette
FAIR GAME
Goldthwait, Bobcat
DESTINY TURNS ON THE RADIO
Goldwyn, Tony
DOOMSDAY GUN
NIXON
POCAHONTAS: THE LEGEND
RECKLESS
Golembeck, Dana
INNOCENT, THE
Golfus, Billy
WHEN BILLY BROKE HIS HEAD ... AND
OTHER TALES OF WONDER
Goliath, Gregory R.
SHOWGIRLS
Golino, Valeria
FOUR ROOMS
LEAVING LAS VEGAS
Golodovitch, Tatiana
WINDOW TO PARIS
Golson, Benny
GREAT DAY IN HARLEM, A

Golubeva, Katherina
I CAN'T SLEEP
Gomer, Russell
RESTORATION
Gomez, Carlos
BITTER VENGEANCE
DESPERADO
OUT OF ANNIE'S PAST
Gomez, Consuelo
DESPERADO
Gomez, Eduardo
BILLY MADISON
Gomez, Glen
CANDYMAN: FAREWELL TO THE FLESH
Gomez, Jaime
CRIMSON TIDE
Gomez, Marga
BATMAN FOREVER
Gomez, Nick
PROPHECY, THE
Gomez, Roland
NET, THE
Gomez, Sergio
DANGEROUS, THE
Goncalves, Gilberto
CONVENT, THE
Gong Li
SHANGHAI TRIAD
Gonini, Luciano
MAMMA ROMA
Gontijo, Athos
CARMEN MIRANDA: BANANAS IS MY
BUSINESS
Gonzales, Arturo
DIRTY MONEY
Gonzales, Benjamin S.
ARIZONA DREAM
Gonzales, Ramon
STEAL BIG, STEAL LITTLE
Gonzalez, Anthony
MY FAMILY: MI FAMILIA
Gonzalez, Clifton Gonzalez
DEAD PRESIDENTS
Gonzalez, Mario
I AM CUBA
Gonzalez, Marisela
DANGEROUS MINDS
Gonzalez, Michael
MY FAMILY: MI FAMILIA
Gonzalez, Ralph
BAD BOYS
Gonzalez, Steven
AMERICAN PRESIDENT, THE
Gonzalez, Yolanda
NICK OF TIME
Good, Meagan
FRIDAY
Good, Richard
INNOCENT, THE
Goodall, Caroline
HOTEL SORRENTO
Goodall, Matthew
APOLLO 13
Goodall, Taylor
APOLLO 13
Goodell, Kathy
CRUMB
Gooding, Jr., Cuba
LOSING ISAIAH
OUTBREAK
Goodloe, J. Mills
ASSASSINS
Goodman, Hazelle
HEAT
Goodman, John
KINGFISH: A STORY OF HUEY P. LONG
Goodman, Oscar
CASINO

Goodman, Thea
KICKING AND SCREAMING
Goodson, Barbara
BAREFOOT GEN
CRIMSON WOLF
Goodson, Liat
STRANGE DAYS
Goodstriker, Leon
BLACK FOX
Goold, Jane
BUFFALO GIRLS
Goorjian, Michael
LEAVING LAS VEGAS
Goossen, Gergory
QUICK AND THE DEAD, THE
Goossen, Gregory B.
GET SHORTY
WATERWORLD
Goran
BEFORE THE RAIN
Goranson, Alicia
HOW TO MAKE AN AMERICAN QUILT
Goranson, Linda
KURT VONNEGUT'S HARRISON
BERGERON
Gordon, Alan Jeffrey
KISS OF DEATH
Gordon, Carl
PIANO LESSON, THE
Gordon, Carolyn
CASTLE FREAK
Gordon, Chief
TANK GIRL
Gordon, Jillian
CASTLE FREAK
Gordon, John "Doo Doo Brown"
PANTHER
Gordon, Joyce
BILLY MADISON
Gordon, Margaret
CASTLE FREAK
Gordon, Serena
GOLDENEYE
Gordon, Spencer
THREE WISHES
Gordon, Suzanna
CASTLE FREAK
Gordon-Levitt, Joseph
GREAT ELEPHANT ESCAPE, THE
Gorham, Mel
BLUE IN THE FACE
SMOKE
Gori, Gino
MALLRATS
Gorman, Patrick
AVENGING ANGEL
WILD BILL
Gorman, Peter
TIE-DIED: ROCK 'N' ROLL'S MOST
DEADICATED FANS
Gormley, Peggy
BLUE IN THE FACE
Gorn, Ada
S.F.W.
Gorny, Frederic
WILD REEDS
Gorry, David
LAMB
Gorshin, Frank
TWELVE MONKEYS
Gorski, Tamara
TO DIE FOR
Gortner, Marjoe
WILD BILL
Gosh, Rabi
STRANGER, THE
Gosnell, Bradley
NINE MONTHS

Gosnell, Emily
NINE MONTHS
Gosse, Rob
NADJA
Gossett, Jr., Louis
CURSE OF THE STARVING CLASS
ZOOMAN
Gossett, Robert
NET, THE
WHITE MAN'S BURDEN
Goswami, Mandakini
BANDIT QUEEN
Goto, Al
SCANNERS: THE SHOWDOWN
Gottheimer, Ruth
CLEAN, SHAVEN
Gotti, Roberta
HACKERS
Gottlieb, Carl
CLUELESS
Gotz, Harald
FARINELLI
Goudy, Ed
CHILDREN OF THE CORN III: URBAN
HARVEST
Gough, Karen
BABE
Gough, Michael
BATMAN FOREVER
Gould, Elliot
DANGEROUS, THE
GLASS SHIELD, THE
KICKING AND SCREAMING
Gould, Elliott
COVER ME
Gould, Joe
BEFORE THE RAIN
Gould, Sam
KICKING AND SCREAMING
Gover, Dominic
FEAST OF JULY
Gow, Claire
DALLAS DOLL
Gozlan, Serge
MINA TANNENBAUM
Grabner, Steffen
NOBODY LOVES ME
Grabosky, Victor
AMERICAN COP
Grace, April
SAFE
Grace, Howard
JUDGE DREDD
Grace, Jack
ONCE WERE WARRIORS
Grace, Matthew
LIVING IN OBLIVION
Grace, Wayne
LORD OF ILLUSIONS
Gracen, Elizabeth
EXPERT, THE
Gradowski, T.
SHORT FILM ABOUT LOVE, A
Gradwell, Josephine
SENSE AND SENSIBILITY
Graf, David
BRADY BUNCH MOVIE, THE
FATHER AND SCOUT
Graff, Todd
STRANGE DAYS
Graham, Currie
AMATEUR
Graham, Eleanor
SAFE
Graham, Gary
SPY WITHIN, THE
Graham, Gerrit
BREAK, THE

Graham, Jeffrey
MUTANT SPECIES
Graham, Jim
ASSASSINS
Graham, John
MUTANT SPECIES
Graham, Kenny
NOSTRADAMUS KID, THE
Graham, T. Max
MY ANTONIA
Grahn, Nancy Lee
CHILDREN OF THE CORN III: URBAN
HARVEST
Grandison, Pippa
MURIEL'S WEDDING
Grando, Kelley
NEVER TALK TO STRANGERS
Grandperret, Patrick
I CAN'T SLEEP
Graney, John Link
STUART SAVES HIS FAMILY
Granger, Bernard
EMPIRE RECORDS
Granger, Philip
BROKEN TRUST
Grant, Beth
SAFE
TO WONG FOO, THANKS FOR
EVERYTHING! JULIE NEWMAR
Grant, David Marshall
THREE WISHES
Grant, Dougary
WINGS OF HONNEAMISE: ROYAL SPACE
FORCE
Grant, Hugh
AWFULLY BIG ADVENTURE, AN
ENGLISHMAN WHO WENT UP A HILL
BUT CAME DOWN A MOUNTAIN, THE
NINE MONTHS
RESTORATION
SENSE AND SENSIBILITY
Grant, James
INNOCENT, THE
Grant, Raymond
DANGEROUS MINDS
Grant, Richard
DANGEROUS MINDS
Grant, Rodney A.
LAST RIDE, THE
Grant, Salim
ANGUS
Grant, Stuart "Proud Eagle"
3 NINJAS KNUCKLE UP
Grant, Vince
DRACULA: DEAD AND LOVING IT
Grant-Minchen, Bill
POWDER
Grapentien, Elizabeth
EMPIRE RECORDS
Grapey, Marc
WHILE YOU WERE SLEEPING
Grau, Doris
COLDBLOODED
Graves, Amanda
HEAT
Graves, Emily
HEAT
Graves, Rupert
DOOMSDAY GUN
Gray, Bruce
MY FAMILY: MI FAMILIA
ROSWELL: THE U.F.O. COVER-UP
Gray, Caroline
AILSA
Gray, David Barry
DEAD PRESIDENTS
NIXON
S.F.W.

Gray, David Myers
EMPIRE RECORDS
Gray, F. Gary
FRIDAY
Gray, III, George
ROSWELL: THE U.F.O. COVER-UP
Gray, Sheila
CANADIAN BACON
Gray, Spalding
BAD COMPANY
BEYOND RANGOON
Greaves, James
HEAVEN'S A DRAG
Greco, Joe
DILLINGER
Green, Alex
DOUBLE, DOUBLE, TOIL AND TROUBLE
POWER OF ATTORNEY
Green, Calvin
EXOTICA
Green, Curley
OUT OF ANNIE'S PAST
Green, Kaela
HOW TO MAKE AN AMERICAN QUILT
Green, Matt
SEPARATE LIVES
Green, Seth
WHITE MAN'S BURDEN
Greenbaum, Robert
RIVER OF GRASS
Greenberg, Ari
BUSHWHACKED
Greenberg, Helen
LITTLE PRINCESS, A
Greenberg, Paul
TOMMY BOY
Greene, Arlon G.
COPYCAT
Greene, Bob
COPYCAT
Greene, Graham
DIE HARD WITH A VENGEANCE
Greene, Jim
FAIR GAME
Greene, Kim Morgan
DR. JEKYLL & MS. HYDE
Greene, Leo
O.J. SIMPSON STORY, THE
Greene, Michael
JUDICIAL CONSENT
Greene, Peter
CLEAN, SHAVEN
UNDER SIEGE 2: DARK TERRITORY
Greene, Walton
HIGHER LEARNING
Greenhill, Mitch
SAFE
Greenhut, Jennifer
MIGHTY APHRODITE
Greenlee, David
PANTHER
Greenspan, David
AMATEUR
Greenwood, Bruce
BITTER VENGEANCE
COMPANION, THE
EXOTICA
Greenwood, Palma
HOUSEGUEST
Greer, Dustin
HEAVYWEIGHTS
Greer, Linda
SECRET OF ROAN INISH, THE
Greer, Stuart
EXPERT, THE
Greet, Christopher
FUNNY BONES

Gregg, Clark
USUAL SUSPECTS, THE
Greggio, Ezio
DRACULA: DEAD AND LOVING IT
SILENCE OF THE HAMS
Gregoni, Joseph
NOT ANGELS BUT ANGELS
Gregory, Andre
LAST SUMMER IN THE HAMPTONS
Gregory, Constantine
GOLDENEYE
Gregory, Dick
PANTHER
Gregory, Eliot
INNOCENT LIES
Gregory, Ian
EVOLVER
Gregory, Ken
BABE
Gregory, Mary
IN THE DEEP WOODS
Gregory, Michael
GLASS SHIELD, THE
Gregory, Nick
LAST SUMMER IN THE HAMPTONS
Gregory, Peter
BABY-SITTERS CLUB, THE
Gregory, Ryan
INNOCENT LIES
Gregson, Joan
SCARLET LETTER, THE
Greif, George
MAN OF THE HOUSE
Greist, Kim
ROSWELL: THE U.F.O. COVER-UP
Grenier, Jean-Claude
PIGALLE
Grenier, Zach
RECKLESS
TOMMY BOY
Grennel, Nick
AWFULLY BIG ADVENTURE, AN
Grennell, Aidan
FRANKIE STARLIGHT
Gress, Googy
AMERICAN PRESIDENT, THE
APOLLO 13
WHITE MAN'S BURDEN
Grevill, Laurent
I CAN'T SLEEP
Grevioux, Kevin
CONGO
Grey, Joel
DANGEROUS, THE
Greyeyes, Michael
DANCE ME OUTSIDE
Gribbin, Tristin
FRANKIE STARLIGHT
Grieco, Dominick
CASINO
Grier, David Alan
JUMANJI
TALES FROM THE HOOD
Gries, Jon
GET SHORTY
Griest, Kim
HOUSEGUEST
Grifasi, Joe
BATMAN FOREVER
MONEY TRAIN
TWO BITS
Grifasi, Joseph
TALL TALE: THE UNBELIEVABLE
ADVENTURES OF PECOS BILL
Griffin, Douglas M.
MUTANT SPECIES
Griffin, Eddie
WALKING DEAD, THE

Griffin, Garrett
JADE
Griffin, Johnny
GREAT DAY IN HARLEM, A
Griffin, Joseph
FIRST DEGREE
Griffin, Kathy
FOUR ROOMS
Griffin, Katie
BOULEVARD
TO DIE FOR
Griffin, Tim
EVOLVER
HIGHER LEARNING
Griffin, Tony
DRACULA: DEAD AND LOVING IT
Griffis, Guy
BLESSING
Griffis, Melora
BLESSING
Griffis, Rhoda
SOMETHING TO TALK ABOUT
Griffith, Anthony
PANTHER
TALES FROM THE HOOD
Griffith, Bill
CRUMB
Griffith, Kenneth
ENGLISHMAN WHO WENT UP A HILL
BUT CAME DOWN A MOUNTAIN, THE
Griffith, Melanie
BUFFALO GIRLS
NOW AND THEN
Griffith, Thomas Ian
CRACKERJACK
Griffith, Wendy
RESTORATION
Griffiths, Michael
LIVING IN OBLIVION
Griffiths, Rachel
MURIEL'S WEDDING
Griffiths, Reg
FUNNY BONES
Griffiths, Richard
FUNNY BONES
Griggs, Camila
BAR GIRLS
Grimes, Scott
CRIMSON TIDE
Grimm, Christopher
RHYTHM THIEF
Grimm, Mista
HIGHER LEARNING
Grimm, Tim
DILLINGER
Grimsted, Ty-Ranne
LIE DOWN WITH DOGS
Grindemann, Wolfgang
FARINELLI
Grisom, Michelle
IT TAKES TWO
Grivna, Lawrence
GRUMPIER OLD MEN
Grjebina, Irina
I CAN'T SLEEP
Grocholski, Czeslaw
CITIZEN X
Grodenchik, Max
APOLLO 13
Grodin, Jed
GHOST BRIGADE
Groelle, Damien
JEFFERSON IN PARIS
Grojean, Joe
TO WONG FOO, THANKS FOR
EVERYTHING! JULIE NEWMAR

Grosbard, Jeremy
TIE-DIED: ROCK 'N' ROLL'S MOST
DEADICATED FANS
Grosbris, Elodie
MINA TANNENBAUM
Grosche, Erwin
NOBODY LOVES ME
Grose, Peter
DESPERATE PREY
Grosse, Christina
PROMISE, THE
Grossman, Gary
S.F.W.
Groth, Sylvester
STALINGRAD
Grouezas, Giorgos
BLUE VILLA, THE
Groulout, Laurent
WILD REEDS
Grout, Tanya
BILLY MADISON
Grove, Richard
MONEY TRAIN
Grover, Stanley
ROSWELL: THE U.F.O. COVER-UP
Groves, Jonathan
RADIO INSIDE
Gruber, Juliette
AILSA
Grumbach, Denis
MINA TANNENBAUM
Grunberg, Klaus
MARTHA AND I
Grunke, Thomas
ACE VENTURA: WHEN NATURE CALLS
Grunwald, Ernie
IT TAKES TWO
Guastaferro, Vicent
WATER ENGINE, THE
Gudahl, Kevin
WHILE YOU WERE SLEEPING
Guddi
BANDIT QUEEN
Gudgell, Wally
ASSASSINS
Gudmundsson, Jon
S.F.W.
Guegan, Josette
INNOCENT LIES
Guerin, J.P.
KID IN KING ARTHUR'S COURT, A
Guerra, Castulo
BODILY HARM
INDICTMENT: THE MCMARTIN TRIAL
USUAL SUSPECTS, THE
Guerra, Saverio
BAD BOYS
Guervo, Fernando Guillen
BUSINESS AFFAIR, A
Guess, Alvaleta
MONEY TRAIN
Guess, Alvaletah
DEAD PRESIDENTS
Gueye, Mamadou Mahouredia
HYENAS
Guez, Richard
MINA TANNENBAUM
Gugino, Carla
MIAMI RHAPSODY
Guidera, Anthony
SPECIES
UNDERCOVER
Guidry, Matt
WORLD AND TIME ENOUGH
Guilbert, Ann
GRUMPIER OLD MEN

Guilfoyle, Paul
CLASS OF '61
LITTLE ODESSA
Guilherme, Miguel
VALLEY OF ABRAHAM, THE
Guillard, Marie
SIX DAYS, SIX NIGHTS
Guillaume, Jean
INNOCENT LIES
Guillaume, Robert
COSMIC SLOP
GOOD DAY TO DIE, A
Guinee, Tim
HOW TO MAKE AN AMERICAN QUILT
Guinness, Alec
MUTE WITNESS
Guirao, Lara
OLD LADY WHO WALKED IN THE SEA,
THE
Guiton, Richard
BABY-SITTERS CLUB, THE
Gulbe, Milena
CITY UNPLUGGED
Gulino, Lea
POSTCARDS FROM AMERICA
Gunderson, Jamie Melissa
3 NINJAS KNUCKLE UP
Gunderson, Rick
FORGET PARIS
Gunn, Nicholas
SCANNERS: THE SHOWDOWN
YOUNGER & YOUNGER
Gunn, Peter
FUNNY BONES
Gunn, Vincenetta
COPYCAT
Gunnestad, Corey
S.F.W.
Gunther, Mike
MOSAIC PROJECT, THE
Gunton, Bob
ACE VENTURA: WHEN NATURE CALLS
DOLORES CLAIBORNE
KINGFISH: A STORY OF HUEY P. LONG
ROSWELL: THE U.F.O. COVER-UP
Gunton, Robert
COSMIC SLOP
Guo Hao
SHANGHAI TRIAD
Guo Shuguang
ERMO
Gupta, Pawan
BANDIT QUEEN
Gupta, Pradeep
BANDIT QUEEN
Gupta, Yogesh
BANDIT QUEEN
Gupton, Eric
BLACK IS ... BLACK AIN'T
Gurd, Jr., Sunley
WINGS OF HONNEAMISE: ROYAL SPACE
FORCE
Gurney, Robyn
NOSTRADAMUS KID, THE
Gurwitch, Annabelle
THREE WISHES
Gusman, Daniel
BAD BLOOD
Gustavsdottir, Margret Hugren
REMOTE CONTROL
Gutierrez, Alfredo
BURNING SEASON, THE
Gutierrez, Larry
HOWLING: NEW MOON RISING, THE
Gutman, Jason
DANGEROUS MINDS
Gutstein, Ken
DON JUAN DEMARCO

Guttenberg, Steve
BIG GREEN, THE
HOME FOR THE HOLIDAYS
IT TAKES TWO
Guy, Buddy
THINGS TO DO IN DENVER WHEN
YOU'RE DEAD
Guzaldo, Joe
DILLINGER
Guzek, H.
SHORT FILM ABOUT KILLING, A
Guzman, Jesus Alberto
MY FAMILY: MI FAMILIA
Guzman, Luis
BURNING SEASON, THE
Gwaliori, Ddhawal
BANDIT QUEEN
Gwar
EMPIRE RECORDS
Gwynne, Michael C.
DILLINGER AND CAPONE
O.J. SIMPSON STORY, THE
Haan, Lee
PUSHING HANDS
Habbersted, Jeff
SUDDEN DEATH
Habib, Nora
AUGUSTIN
Haby, Cliff
UNDERNEATH, THE
Hack, Olivia
BRADY BUNCH MOVIE, THE
Hackford, Rio
SAFE
STRANGE DAYS
Hackforth-Jones, Penne
MURIEL'S WEDDING
Hackman, Gene
CRIMSON TIDE
GET SHORTY
QUICK AND THE DEAD, THE
Hada, Michiko
MYSTERY OF RAMPO, THE
Hadfield, Karen
ONLY THE BRAVE
Hadfield, Mark
CENTURY
Hadji-Lazaro, Francois
CITY OF LOST CHILDREN, THE
Hadlow, Mark
MEET THE FEEBLES
Hagan, Jr., Earl
FOOL AND HIS MONEY, A
Hagan, Marianne
HALLOWEEN: THE CURSE OF MICHAEL
MYERS
Hagan, Mary Anne
FLUKE
Hagen, Ross
ATTACK OF THE 60-FOOT CENTERFOLD
MIDNIGHT TEASE 2
Hager, Mark
SUDDEN DEATH
Hagerty, Michael G.
STUART SAVES HIS FAMILY
Hagerty, Sean
RHYTHM THIEF
Haggard, Daniel
MORTAL KOMBAT
Haggerty, Dan
ABDUCTED 2: THE REUNION
Hagler, Nik
BIG GREEN, THE
Hagman, Larry
NIXON
Hagon, Garrick
BALTO
FATHERLAND

Hahn, Archie
BRADY BUNCH MOVIE, THE
Haid, Charles
BROKEN TRUST
Haidorfer, Karin
MIGHTY APHRODITE
Haight, Rip
VILLAGE OF THE DAMNED
Haim, Corey
DREAM A LITTLE DREAM 2
Haimovici, Issac
I, THE WORST OF ALL
Haining, Mark
VAMPIRE IN BROOKLYN
Haje, Khrystyne
SCANNERS: THE SHOWDOWN
Haje, Richard
FORGET PARIS
Haji-Ghasemi, Alireza
JAR, THE
Hale, Birdie M.
DIE HARD WITH A VENGEANCE
Hale, Steve
MUTANT SPECIES
Hale, Taylor
THINGS TO DO IN DENVER WHEN
YOU'RE DEAD
Haler, Ted
STRANGE DAYS
Haley, Janet
EROTIQUE
IN THE DEEP WOODS
Haley, R.M.
STUART SAVES HIS FAMILY
Hall, Albert
DEVIL IN A BLUE DRESS
MAJOR PAYNE
Hall, Anthony C.
FORGET PARIS
VIRTUOSITY
Hall, Anthony Michael
ME AND THE MOB
Hall, Brad
BYE BYE, LOVE
Hall, Bug
BIG GREEN, THE
Hall, Ernie
ASSASSINS
Hall, Herb
CLUELESS
Hall, J.D.
JURY DUTY
Hall, Jerry
VAMPIRE IN BROOKLYN
Hall, John
HOUSEGUEST
SUDDEN DEATH
Hall, John Burnett
JOURNEY OF AUGUST KING, THE
Hall, Margaret
PARTY GIRL
Hall, Michael Keys
ALMOST DEAD
Hall, Philip Baker
KISS OF DEATH
ROSWELL: THE U.F.O. COVER-UP
Hall, Shashawnee
SPY WITHIN, THE
Hall, Stephen
ONCE WERE WARRIORS
Hall, Vondie Curtis
ZOOMAN
Hall-Watson, Scott
MURIEL'S WEDDING
Hallahan, Charles
ROSWELL: THE U.F.O. COVER-UP
Haller, Bernard
INNOCENT LIES

Halleran, Cole
MAGIC IN THE WATER
Halliday, Christopher
CUTTHROAT ISLAND
Halliday, David
GROSSE FATIGUE
Halliday, Estelle
GROSSE FATIGUE
Halligan, Tim
FORGET PARIS
Hallo, Dean
BLUE TIGER
WHITE MAN'S BURDEN
Hallowell, Todd
APOLLO 13
Halme, Tony
DIE HARD WITH A VENGEANCE
Halow, Bash
LIE DOWN WITH DOGS
Halpern, John
TO CROSS THE RUBICON
Halsey, Brett
FIRST DEGREE
Halton, Michael
VILLAGE OF THE DAMNED
Ham, Gary
HOWLING: NEW MOON RISING, THE
Ham, Robert Mason
KILIAN'S CHRONICLE
Hamada, Cheryl
LOSING ISAIAH
Haman, Svend Ali
KINGDOM, THE
Hamblyn, Kate
FEAST OF JULY
Hamid, Yusof Abdul
BEYOND RANGOON
Hamill, Hugh
TIE-DIED: ROCK 'N' ROLL'S MOST
DEADICATED FANS
Hamill, Mark
VILLAGE OF THE DAMNED
Hamilton, Gabrielle
BEFORE THE RAIN
Hamilton, Harlan
CLEAN, SHAVEN
Hamilton, Josh
KICKING AND SCREAMING
Hamilton, Linda
SEPARATE LIVES
Hamilton, Nan
MANGLER, THE
Hamilton, Page Nye
JERKY BOYS: THE MOVIE, THE
Hamilton, Randy
O.J. SIMPSON STORY, THE
Hamilton, Robert
LAMB
Hamilton, Victoria
PERSUASION
Hamilton, Wendy
PLAY TIME
Hammer, Mark
KISS OF DEATH
Hammett, Temple
NEXT DOOR
Hammil, John
BLUE TIGER
Hammond, Brandon
STRANGE DAYS
TALES FROM THE HOOD
WAITING TO EXHALE
Hammond, Roger
DOOMSDAY GUN
PERSUASION
RICHARD III
Hammond, Rosalind
MURIEL'S WEDDING

Hamper, Ben
CANADIAN BACON
Hampton, Christopher
TOTAL ECLIPSE
Hampton, Richard
BUSINESS AFFAIR, A
Han, Cheb
TOTAL ECLIPSE
Hanafi, Hani Mohsin
BEYOND RANGOON
Hanahan, Sheila
JUDICIAL CONSENT
Hance, James
CLEAN, SHAVEN
Hancock, Robin
DANGEROUS, THE
Hancock, Sheila
BUSINESS AFFAIR, A
Handevidt, Dale
CURE, THE
Handfield, Don
REASON TO BELIEVE, A
Handwerger, Jeb
HACKERS
Handy, James
JUMANJI
O.J. SIMPSON STORY, THE
Handy, Philip
OUTBREAK
Handysides, Kim
LOVE AND HUMAN REMAINS
Haney, Anne
AMERICAN PRESIDENT, THE
Haney, Michael
INDICTMENT: THE MCMARTIN TRIAL
Haney, Tony
COPYCAT
VILLAGE OF THE DAMNED
Hankin, Larry
BILLY MADISON
Hankins, Carol
S.F.W.
Hanks, Jeremy
AVENGING ANGEL
Hanks, Tom
APOLLO 13
TOY STORY
Hanley, Jertzy
TIE-DIED: ROCK 'N' ROLL'S MOST
DEADICATED FANS
Hanley, Joe
RUN OF THE COUNTRY, THE
Hanley, Maureen
APOLLO 13
Hanley, Tres
RICHARD III
Hanlon, Peter
CIRCUMSTANCES UNKNOWN
Hanly, Peter
BRAVEHEART
Hann-Byrd, Adam
DIGGER
JUMANJI
Hannah, Daryl
GRUMPIER OLD MEN
TIE THAT BINDS, THE
Hannah, Duncan
ART FOR TEACHERS OF CHILDREN
Hannigan, Declan
SECRET OF ROAN INISH, THE
Hannon, Mary Ann
ADDICTION, THE
Hannon, Ted
IN THE NAME OF THE EMPEROR
Hansard, Bart
FLUKE
Hansen, Hayley Rose
NINE MONTHS

Hansen, Holger Juul
KINGDOM, THE
Hansen, Lauren
BAR GIRLS
Hansen, Monika
PROMISE, THE
Hansen, Soren
STEAL BIG, STEAL LITTLE
Hanson, Dian
CRUMB
Hanson, Smadar
USUAL SUSPECTS, THE
Hapstack, Ed
MALLRATS
Hara, Yoshimi
MYSTERY OF RAMPO, THE
Harada, Yoshio
HUNTED, THE
MYSTERY OF RAMPO, THE
Harcombe, Sebastian
CARRINGTON
Hardaway, Tim
FORGET PARIS
Harden, Charles Robert
TANK GIRL
Harden, Marcia Gay
CONVICT COWBOY
SAFE PASSAGE
Harder, D.J.
DARK SIDE OF GENIUS, THE
Hardie, Jim
GLASS SHIELD, THE
Harding, Chris
NOSTRADAMUS KID, THE
Harding, Jan Leslie
AMATEUR
Harding, Jeff
HACKERS
Harding, Marlus C.
JOURNEY OF AUGUST KING, THE
Harding, Mike
EMPIRE RECORDS
Harding, Yvette
SCANNERS: THE SHOWDOWN
Hardison, Kadeem
PANTHER
VAMPIRE IN BROOKLYN
Hardwicke, Edward
RICHARD III
SCARLET LETTER, THE
Hardy, Chappy
KINGFISH: A STORY OF HUEY P. LONG
Hardy, Robert
SENSE AND SENSIBILITY
Hardy, Trishalee
VILLAGE OF THE DAMNED
Hardy, Troy
MURIEL'S WEDDING
Harewood, Dorian
SUDDEN DEATH
Harfouch, Corinna
PROMISE, THE
Hargitay, Mariska
LEAVING LAS VEGAS
Hargreaves, John
COUNTRY LIFE
HOTEL SORRENTO
Harish
BANDIT QUEEN
Harker, Wiley
THINGS TO DO IN DENVER WHEN
YOU'RE DEAD
Harkham, Joel
HOWLING: NEW MOON RISING, THE
Harkham, Sally
HOWLING: NEW MOON RISING, THE
Harlem, George
ONLY THE BRAVE

Harley, Graham
FIRST DEGREE
Harmon, Mark
DILLINGER
MAGIC IN THE WATER
Harms, John
ASSASSINS
FREE WILLY 2: THE ADVENTURE HOME
Harnagel, John
LAKOTA WOMAN: SIEGE AT WOUNDED
KNEE
Harnell, Jess
CASPER
Harnesberger, Robert
BUFFALO GIRLS
Harney, Susan
S.F.W.
Harper, Bill
BREACH OF CONDUCT
Harper, Hill
ZOOMAN
Harper, Jessica
SAFE
Harper, Kyra
TO DIE FOR
Harrell, Andre
SHOW, THE
Harrell, Michelle
PENTATHLON
Harrelson, Woody
MONEY TRAIN
Harris, Aaron
GLORY BOYS, THE
Harris, Baxter
SMOKE
Harris, Bruklin
DANGEROUS MINDS
Harris, Burt
LAST GOOD TIME, THE
Harris, Danielle
NIGHTMARE
Harris, Ed
APOLLO 13
JUST CAUSE
NIXON
Harris, Epatha
ANGUS
Harris, Henry
ACROSS THE MOON
Harris, Jared
BLUE IN THE FACE
NADJA
SMOKE
TALL TALE: THE UNBELIEVABLE
ADVENTURES OF PECOS BILL
Harris, Joilet
TWELVE MONKEYS
Harris, Kenneth D.
UNDERNEATH, THE
Harris, Mel
SECRETARY, THE
Harris, Michael
BAR GIRLS
Harris, Mike
BABE
Harris, Moira
TALL TALE: THE UNBELIEVABLE
ADVENTURES OF PECOS BILL
THREE WISHES
Harris, Neil Patrick
MY ANTONIA
Harris, Niki
HEAT
Harris, Richard
CRY, THE BELOVED COUNTRY
Harris, Ricky
HEAT

Harris, Robert
STEAL BIG, STEAL LITTLE
Harris, Zelda
BABY-SITTERS CLUB, THE
PIANO LESSON, THE
Harrison, Christopher
JERKY BOYS: THE MOVIE, THE
Harrison, Cynthia
OUTBREAK
Harrison, Daniel
BRIAN WILSON: I JUST WASN'T MADE
FOR THESE TIMES
Harrison, John
SUBSTITUTE WIFE, THE
Harrison, Nicholas
HEAVEN'S A DRAG
Harrold, Jamie
AMATEUR
TO WONG FOO, THANKS FOR
EVERYTHING! JULIE NEWMAR
Harrold, Kathryn
COMPANION, THE
Hart, Blaine
DECOY
Hart, Calvin
CLOCKERS
Hart, David
THREE WISHES
Hart, Ian
ENGLISHMAN WHO WENT UP A HILL
BUT CAME DOWN A MOUNTAIN, THE
Hart, Linda
GET SHORTY
Hart, Monica
BORN TO BE WILD
Hart, William Buck
PROPHECY, THE
Harte, Gail
TIE-DIED: ROCK 'N' ROLL'S MOST
DEADICATED FANS
Harte, Jerry
FRENCH KISS
Hartman, Phil
CRAZYSITTER, THE
HOUSEGUEST
Hartman, Ron
ANDROID AFFAIR, THE
Hartman, Steven
ANGUS
CANDYMAN: FAREWELL TO THE FLESH
Hartman, Tim
PIANO LESSON, THE
Hartsell, Jimmy Dale
SEVEN
Harvey, Cynthia
BALLET
Harvey, David C.
WHITE MAN'S BURDEN
Harvey, Don
BETTER OFF DEAD
GLASS SHIELD, THE
TANK GIRL
Harvey, Frank
FUNNY BONES
Harvey, Hillary
VILLAGE OF THE DAMNED
Harvey, Robert
ROSWELL: THE U.F.O. COVER-UP
Harvey, Ted
HEAT
Harwood, John
PANTHER
Hashim, Rudzuan
BEYOND RANGOON
Hashimoto, Kuni
DALLAS DOLL
MURIEL'S WEDDING

Haskins, James Douglas
ASSASSINS
Hassan, Faisal
DIE HARD WITH A VENGEANCE
Hasse, Kim
BRADY BUNCH MOVIE, THE
Hastings, Nigel
DOOMSDAY GUN
Hatashita, Heidi
ANDROID AFFAIR, THE
Hatch, Joel
WHILE YOU WERE SLEEPING
Hatcher, Martha
DARK DEALER
Hatcher, Shirley J.
DIE HARD WITH A VENGEANCE
Hatcher-Travis, Elizabeth
FRANK & JESSE
Hateley, John
SUDDEN DEATH
Hatem, Rosine "Ace"
SUDDEN DEATH
Hathaway, Kellen
TOM AND HUCK
Hathorn, Florrie
DEAD MAN WALKING
Hatosy, Shawn Wayne
HOME FOR THE HOLIDAYS
Hatton, David
FATHERLAND
Hauch-Fausboll, Soren
KINGDOM, THE
Hauer, Rutger
FATHERLAND
Haugk, Charlie
NIXON
Haun, Darla
DRACULA: DEAD AND LOVING IT
Haun, Lindsey
VILLAGE OF THE DAMNED
Hauptvogel, Volker
NEKROMANTIK
Hauser, Cole
HIGHER LEARNING
Hauser, Fay
CANDYMAN: FAREWELL TO THE FLESH
Hauser, Susan
SPECIES
Hauser, Wings
TALES FROM THE HOOD
Hausserman, Mischa
DIE HARD WITH A VENGEANCE
Havard, Elvin
SCANNERS: THE SHOWDOWN
Havers, Nigel
BURNING SEASON, THE
Havill, Andrew
RESTORATION
Haw, Shao-Wen
SHAO LIN POPEYE
Hawke, Ethan
BEFORE SUNRISE
SEARCH AND DESTROY
Hawken, Pamela
BABE
NOSTRADAMUS KID, THE
Hawker, Cheryl
GRUMPIER OLD MEN
Hawkes, John
CONGO
Hawkins, Kyle
RIVER OF GRASS
Hawkins, Virginia
BITTER VENGEANCE
IN THE DEEP WOODS
Hawkins, Yvette
MIGHTY APHRODITE

Hawksley, Dominic
DEATH MACHINE
Hawley, Norman
FRANK & JESSE
Hawthorne, Nigel
RICHARD III
Hawtrey, Nicholas
FRENCH KISS
Hayami, Yu
MYSTERY OF RAMPO, THE
Hayashi, Mariko
MYSTERY OF RAMPO, THE
Haydar, Sahin Ali
FOR GOD AND COUNTRY
Hayden, Ashley
MANGLER, THE
Haydn, Mike
PRIEST
Haydn-Edwards, Ann
PRIEST
Hayek, Salma
DESPERADO
FAIR GAME
FOUR ROOMS
Hayes, Bobby Lee
PROPHECY, THE
Hayes, Isaac
OUT OF SYNC
Hayes, Philip
BULLETPROOF HEART
DECOY
MALICIOUS
Hayes, Philip Maurice
POWDER
Hayman, David
ROB ROY
Hayne, Jim
ROSWELL: THE U.F.O. COVER-UP
Haynes, Jayne
TWO BITS
Haynes, Wendy
SAFE
Haynie, Jim
BRIDGES OF MADISON COUNTY, THE
Hays, Jesse
TIE THAT BINDS, THE
Hays, Melissa
TIE THAT BINDS, THE
Hays, Robert
CYBER BANDITS
Haysbert, Dennis
HEAT
WAITING TO EXHALE
Hayward, III, Leland
OUTBREAK
Hayward, Leland
FEAR, THE
Hayward, Wade
BABE
Haywood, Chris
MURIEL'S WEDDING
Hazan, Jack
LIE DOWN WITH DOGS
Hazard, Jack
KINGFISH: A STORY OF HUEY P. LONG
Head, Christina
HARLEM DIARY: NINE VOICES OF
RESILIENCE
Heady, Lena
CENTURY
Heal, Mark
FEAST OF JULY
Heald, Anthony
BUSHWHACKED
KISS OF DEATH
Healy, Christine
NIGHTMARE

Healy, David
DOOMSDAY GUN
Healy, Patricia
HEAT
Heames, Darin
FEAR, THE
Heath, Ian
TO DIE FOR
Heath, Robin Lynn
ANGUS
Heather, Chris
AMERICA'S DEADLIEST HOME VIDEO
Heather, Dan
AMERICA'S DEADLIEST HOME VIDEO
Heather, Larry
AMERICA'S DEADLIEST HOME VIDEO
Heaton, Rebecca
AVENGING ANGEL
Heaton, Tom
CONVICT COWBOY
Heaton, Will
AVENGING ANGEL
Hebron, Douglas
OUTBREAK
Heche, Anne
KINGFISH: A STORY OF HUEY P. LONG
Hecht, Alexander
FUN
Hecht, Elizabeth
FUN
Hecht, Jessica
KICKING AND SCREAMING
Heck, Brad
DECOY
Hedaya, Dan
CLUELESS
NIXON
SEARCH AND DESTROY
TO DIE FOR
USUAL SUSPECTS, THE
Hedge, Douglas
DALLAS DOLL
Hedren, Tippi
TERESA'S TATTOO
Hee, Dana
SPECIES
Heekin, Ann
ROOMMATES
Heffeman, Anthony
DESPERATE PREY
Heglas, Gilson
SMOKE
Heibeck, Mike
RECKLESS
Heigl, Katherine
UNDER SIEGE 2: DARK TERRITORY
Heilbron, Jerry
GHOST BRIGADE
Heilo
HEAVEN'S A DRAG
Heimberg, Alexander
TO WONG FOO, THANKS FOR
EVERYTHING! JULIE NEWMAR
Heimer, Horst
PROMISE, THE
Heinemann, Juliane
DEADLY MARIA
Heiner, Thomasine
FRENCH KISS
Helberg, Sandy
GRANNY, THE
MORTAL KOMBAT
Helde, Annette
NIXON
Helgeland, Thomas
ASSASSINS

Helgenberger, Marg
BAD BOYS
SPECIES
Heller, Eve
ART FOR TEACHERS OF CHILDREN
Heller, Katrin
PROMISE, THE
Hellerman, Quinn Thomas
FOUR ROOMS
Helman, E.
SHORT FILM ABOUT KILLING, A
Helmond, Katherine
SPY WITHIN, THE
Hemblen, David
EXOTICA
TOMMY BOY
Hembrow, Mark
DESPERATE PREY
Hemingway, Anthony
EMPIRE RECORDS
Hemingway, C.W.
TOO YOUNG TO DIE?
Hemmerich, Valerie
FATHER OF THE BRIDE PART II
Hemphill, Essex
BLACK IS ... BLACK AIN'T
Hempleman, Terry
MALLRATS
Henare, George
ONCE WERE WARRIORS
Henderson, Adam
JUDGE DREDD
Henderson, Al
LEAVING LAS VEGAS
Henderson, Bob
NOSTRADAMUS KID, THE
Henderson, Fred
BAD COMPANY
Henderson, Sarah
KIDS
Henderson, Shirley
ROB ROY
Hendricks, Heather
TANK GIRL
Hendricks, Samantha
GRANNY, THE
Hendrickson, Rusty
SOMETHING TO TALK ABOUT
Hendry, William
WHITE MAN'S BURDEN
Heney, Joan
LOVE AND HUMAN REMAINS
Heniss, Brett
VAMPIRES AND OTHER STEREOTYPES
Henley, Barry "Shabaka"
DESTINY TURNS ON THE RADIO
LORD OF ILLUSIONS
Henley, Barry Shabanka
DEVIL IN A BLUE DRESS
Hennecke, Joan
MY ANTONIA
Hennessey, Chris
TIE-DIED: ROCK 'N' ROLL'S MOST
DEADICATED FANS
Hennessey, Ellen Ray
IT TAKES TWO
Hennessy, Marcus
OUTBREAK
Henninger, Corie
COPYCAT
Henrickson, Rick
MALICIOUS
Henriksen, Lance
BOULEVARD
LAST SAMURAI, THE
OPERATION INTERCEPT
POWDER

QUICK AND THE DEAD, THE
SPITFIRE
Henriques, Darryl
JUMANJI
Henry, Buck
KURT VONNEGUT'S HARRISON
BERGERON
TO DIE FOR
Henry, Gregg
BODILY HARM
NIGHTMARE
Henry, Shanelle
IT TAKES TWO
Hensen, Garette Ratliff
THREE WISHES
Hensley, Sonya
BITTER VENGEANCE
Henson, Garette Ratliff
CASPER
Henson, Lisa
FUNNY BONES
Henson, Sudie
FRANK & JESSE
Henstridge, Natasha
SPECIES
Hentoff, Nat
GREAT DAY IN HARLEM, A
Herb, Lenny
MUTANT SPECIES
Herbert, Judy
RESTORATION
Herbert, Julie
SUM OF US, THE
Herd, Richard
COSMIC SLOP
SECRETARY, THE
Hergert, Teresa
NEVER TALK TO STRANGERS
Herlihy, Tim
BILLY MADISON
Herlin, Jacques
JEFFERSON IN PARIS
Herman, Glenn
DIE HARD WITH A VENGEANCE
Herman, Paul
CASINO
HEAT
MIGHTY APHRODITE
Herman the German
UNDERNEATH, THE
Hermanek, Karel
STALINGRAD
Hernandez, Bel
MY FAMILY: MI FAMILIA
Hernandez, Joelle
DEAD PRESIDENTS
Hernandez, Jonathan
MY FAMILY: MI FAMILIA
Hernandez, Jordan
DEAD PRESIDENTS
Hernandez, Jose
DON JUAN DEMARCO
Hernandez, Salvador
MY FAMILY: MI FAMILIA
Hernandez, Samuel
MY FAMILY: MI FAMILIA
Hernandez, Thom Adcox
UNDER SIEGE 2: DARK TERRITORY
Heron, Blake
TOM AND HUCK
Herrera, Christina
ASSASSINS
Herrera, Jennifer
SABRINA
Herrmann, Ed
NIXON
Herron, Cindy
BATMAN FOREVER

Herschmann, Christian
PROMISE, THE
Hershey, Barbara
LAST OF THE DOGMEN
Herzog, Werner
LESSONS OF DARKNESS
Heslov, Grant
CONGO
Hess, Erica
BABY-SITTERS CLUB, THE
Hess, Jayne
ENEMY WITHIN, THE
Hesseman, Howard
OUT OF SYNC
Hessey, Horace
AWFULLY BIG ADVENTURE, AN
Hester, Helen
DEAD MAN WALKING
Heston, Charlton
AVENGING ANGEL
IN THE MOUTH OF MADNESS
Hetsko, Mary Lynn
ME AND THE MOB
Hewett, Dorothy
ETERNITY
Hewitt, Don
BOYS ON THE SIDE
Hewlett, Roger
BREACH OF CONDUCT
Hext, Timothy
RESTORATION
Heyden, Yvette
TOO YOUNG TO DIE?
Heyman, Barton
BASKETBALL DIARIES, THE
DEAD MAN WALKING
JEFFREY
Hibler, Amber
FRANKIE STARLIGHT
Hickenlooper, George
GHOST BRIGADE
Hickey, Bill
MAJOR PAYNE
Hickey, Tom
AWFULLY BIG ADVENTURE, AN
CIRCLE OF FRIENDS
Hickey, William
FORGET PARIS
JERKY BOYS: THE MOVIE, THE
Hickox, Anthony
GRANNY, THE
Hicks, Catherine
DILLINGER AND CAPONE
REDWOOD CURTAIN
Hicks, Chuck
ENEMY WITHIN, THE
Hicks, Kahlil
HARLEM DIARY: NINE VOICES OF
RESILIENCE
Hicks, Kevin
DANCE ME OUTSIDE
Hicks, Marva
VIRTUOSITY
Hicks, Richard
FEAST OF JULY
Hicks, Shari
ATTACK OF THE 60-FOOT CENTERFOLD
Hicks, Tommy
GLASS SHIELD, THE
Hickson, Joan
CENTURY
Hidalgo, Allen
TO WONG FOO, THANKS FOR
EVERYTHING! JULIE NEWMAR
Higa, Jimmy
BIG GREEN, THE
Higashi, Jonathan
THREE WISHES

Higden, Robert
LOVE AND HUMAN REMAINS
Higgins, Clare
FATHERLAND
Higgins, Dave
PAYBACK
Higgins, David Anthony
COLDBLOODED
Higginson, John
UNDERCOVER
Highmore, Edward
DOOMSDAY GUN
Hilbig, Nicole
STRANGE DAYS
Hildebrand, Dan
NEXT DOOR
Hildreth, Kevin L.
FORGET PARIS
Hill, Alfie
COVER STORY
Hill, Barbara K.
BODY CHEMISTRY 4: FULL EXPOSURE
Hill, Dennis
UNDERNEATH, THE
Hill, Julian
JADE
Hill, Lauren
HEAVYWEIGHTS
Hill, Tom
HACKERS
Hill, William B.
NET, THE
Hiller, Arthur
ROSWELL: THE U.F.O. COVER-UP
Hilton, Marge
OUT OF ANNIE'S PAST
Himelstein, Howard
POWER OF ATTORNEY
Hinchcliffe, Kirsty
MURIEL'S WEDDING
Hinde, John
DALLAS DOLL
Hinds, Ciaran
CIRCLE OF FRIENDS
PERSUASION
Hine, Larry
OUTBREAK
Hines, Grainger
SECRETARY, THE
Hines, Gregory
WAITING TO EXHALE
Hines, Robin
RUN OF THE COUNTRY, THE
Hines, Russell
STRANGE DAYS
Hing Hang Quang
OPERATION DUMBO DROP
Hingle, Pat
BATMAN FOREVER
QUICK AND THE DEAD, THE
Hinkle, Tanya Blood
BAR GIRLS
Hinks, Arnie
WINGS OF HONNEAMISE: ROYAL SPACE
FORCE
Hinsfield, Chester
LIE DOWN WITH DOGS
Hinton, Milt
GREAT DAY IN HARLEM, A
Hinton, Mona
GREAT DAY IN HARLEM, A
Hiolle, Herve
JEFFERSON IN PARIS
Hipkiss, Barbara
DIE HARD WITH A VENGEANCE
Hira, Mikijiro
MYSTERY OF RAMPO, THE

Hiroyuki-Tagawa, Cary
DANGEROUS, THE
Hirschfel, Summer
TIE-DIED: ROCK 'N' ROLL'S MOST
DEADICATED FANS
Hlarmendaris, Sergio
ARIZONA DREAM
Ho, Steven
MORTAL KOMBAT
Ho Thu Nga
TRAPS
Hoa To
TRAPS
Hoang Ly
OPERATION DUMBO DROP
Hoare, John
MURIEL'S WEDDING
Hoath, Florence
INNOCENT LIES
Hobart, Deborah
FLUKE
GORDY
SOMETHING TO TALK ABOUT
Hobbs, Jr., Johnnie
TWELVE MONKEYS
Hochendoner, Jeff
SUDDEN DEATH
Hocke, Bernard
GET SHORTY
Hocking, Kristen
BITTER VENGEANCE
Hodder, Kane
SCANNERS: THE SHOWDOWN
Hodge, Aldis
DIE HARD WITH A VENGEANCE
Hodge, Edwin
DIE HARD WITH A VENGEANCE
Hodge, John
SHALLOW GRAVE
Hodge, Mike
DR. JEKYLL & MS. HYDE
TO WONG FOO, THANKS FOR
EVERYTHING! JULIE NEWMAR
Hodges, Cory
BAD BOYS
Hodges, David U.
BATMAN FOREVER
Hodges, Tom
HEAVYWEIGHTS
Hodgson, Bagitta
TIE-DIED: ROCK 'N' ROLL'S MOST
DEADICATED FANS
Hodgson, Michael
FIRST KNIGHT
Hoffeurt, Alysia
CITY OF LOST CHILDREN, THE
Hoffman, Avi
ACROSS THE SEA OF TIME: NEW YORK
3D
Hoffman, Dustin
OUTBREAK
Hoffman, Mark
AMERICA'S DEADLIEST HOME VIDEO
Hoffman, Susan Lee
OUTBREAK
Hoffman, Wendy
BAR GIRLS
Hoffmann, Anya
NOBODY LOVES ME
Hoffmann, Gaby
NOW AND THEN
Hoffmann, Pato
LAKOTA WOMAN: SIEGE AT WOUNDED
KNEE
WILD BILL
Hoflin, David
DEATH IN BRUNSWICK

Hofmann, Gerch
INNOCENT, THE
Hohenstein, Don
BETTER OFF DEAD
Hojfeldt, Solbjorg
KINGDOM, THE
Holcomb, Andy
REASON TO BELIEVE, A
Holden, Beau
SOMETHING TO TALK ABOUT
Holden, Marjean
BALLISTIC
Holder, Jack
HOWLING: NEW MOON RISING, THE
Holgado, Ticky
CITY OF LOST CHILDREN, THE
FUNNY BONES
LES MISERABLES
Holiday, Fred
BODY CHEMISTRY 4: FULL EXPOSURE
Holihan, Ryan
APOLLO 13
FATHER AND SCOUT
Holland, Antony
LAST OF THE DOGMEN
Holland, Erik
PENTATHLON
Holland, Floyd Gale
COPYCAT
Holland, Matt
HIGHLANDER: THE FINAL DIMENSION
Holland, Sean
CLUELESS
Hollar, Lloyd
KISS OF DEATH
Hollenbeck, Pierre-Alexis
LES MISERABLES
Holliday, Carol
GOOFY MOVIE, A
Holliday, Charlie
OUTSIDE THE LAW
Hollimon, Gregory
LOSING ISAIAH
Hollimon, Tina
TALES FROM THE CRYPT: DEMON
KNIGHT
Hollinger, Robert
ANDROID AFFAIR, THE
Hollis, Tommy
PIANO LESSON, THE
ZOOMAN
Holloman, Laurel
INCREDIBLY TRUE ADVENTURES OF
TWO GIRLS IN LOVE, THE
Holloway, Ann
PYROMANIAC'S LOVE STORY, A
Holloway, Gwen
NINE MONTHS
Holloway, Mary
FLUKE
Holly, Lauren
SABRINA
Holman, Dennis
3 NINJAS KNUCKLE UP
Holman, Lemartt
MY ANTONIA
Holmes, Christina
PROPHECY, THE
Holmes, Denis
SABRINA
Holmes, Jacelyn
BILLY MADISON
IN THE MOUTH OF MADNESS
Holmes, Preston L.
PANTHER
Holmes, Prudence Wright
POSTCARDS FROM AMERICA

Holness, Deborah
CAGED HEARTS
Holst, Yaba
DREAMING OF RITA
Holt, Sandrine
DANCE ME OUTSIDE
POCAHONTAS: THE LEGEND
Holt, Scott
THINGS TO DO IN DENVER WHEN
YOU'RE DEAD
Holub, Radek
COW, THE
Holweger, Claude
TRAPS
Holzbog, Arabella
LAST SAMURAI, THE
Holzman, Edward
BODY STROKES
Hom, Cindy
SAFE PASSAGE
Hom, Montgomery
VILLAGE OF THE DAMNED
Hommen, Peter
DEADLY MARIA
Hona, Mac
ONCE WERE WARRIORS
Honer, Martin
INNOCENT, THE
Honeywell, Helen
BROKEN TRUST
Hong, James
BAD COMPANY
OPERATION DUMBO DROP
TANK GIRL
Honza
NOT ANGELS BUT ANGELS
Hood-Julien, Melissa
JUST CAUSE
Hoog, Johnathan R.
O.J. SIMPSON STORY, THE
Hoog, Jonathan R.
O.J. SIMPSON STORY, THE
Hoog, Wilfried
NEKROMANTIK
Hooker, Buddy Joe
JADE
PENTATHLON
hooks, bell
BLACK IS ... BLACK AIN'T
Hooper, J.L.
INNOCENT, THE
Hooper, Joy
GHOST BRIGADE
Hootkins, William
DEATH MACHINE
FUNNY BONES
Hoover, Grant
ANGUS
STUART SAVES HIS FAMILY
Hope, Gary Francis
FAIR GAME
Hope, Leslie
AVENGING ANGEL
FIRST DEGREE
FUN
Hope, Margot
VIRTUOSITY
Hope, Richard
FEAST OF JULY
Hopkins, Angela
NINE MONTHS
Hopkins, Anthony
INNOCENT, THE
NIXON
Hopkins, Gerald
PENTATHLON
Hopkins, Paul
HIGHLANDER: THE FINAL DIMENSION

Hopkins, Wendy
KURT VONNEGUT'S HARRISON
BERGERON
Hopkins, William P.
TO WONG FOO, THANKS FOR
EVERYTHING! JULIE NEWMAR
Hoppenbrouwers, Hans
LIE DOWN WITH DOGS
Hopper, Dennis
SEARCH AND DESTROY
WATERWORLD
Hopper, Tim
TO DIE FOR
Hopson, Lew
TOO YOUNG TO DIE?
Horinek, Mekasi
LAKOTA WOMAN: SIEGE AT WOUNDED
KNEE
Horiuchi, Yoshitake
AI CITY
Hormel, Smokey
GEORGIA
Hormsabat, Somsak
OPERATION DUMBO DROP
Horn, Michelle
STUART SAVES HIS FAMILY
Horne, J.R.
DIE HARD WITH A VENGEANCE
Horneff, Wil
BORN TO BE WILD
Horse, Michael
LAKOTA WOMAN: SIEGE AT WOUNDED
KNEE
Horsfall, Bernard
BRAVEHEART
Horsford, Anna Maria
FRIDAY
Horst, Arthur L.
GLASS SHIELD, THE
Horsting, J.R.
INDIAN IN THE CUPBOARD, THE
Horton, Marlon
DEAD MAN WALKING
Horton, Peter
BABY-SITTERS CLUB, THE
Horwitz, Dominique
STALINGRAD
Hosea, Bobby
O.J. SIMPSON STORY, THE
Hoskins, Bob
BALTO
NIXON
Hossein, Robert
LES MISERABLES
Hostetter, John
ROSWELL: THE U.F.O. COVER-UP
SECRETARY, THE
Hoszouski, Truman
CONVICT COWBOY
Houde, Serge
LOVE AND HUMAN REMAINS
Hough, Adrian
CANADIAN BACON
Houlihan, Mike
LOSING ISAIAH
Houser, Dean
TO WONG FOO, THANKS FOR
EVERYTHING! JULIE NEWMAR
Houston, James
POWDER
Houston, Whitney
WAITING TO EXHALE
Houzelot, Eric
CITY OF LOST CHILDREN, THE
Hovespian, Blake
HOME FOR THE HOLIDAYS
Howard, Anna
BEYOND RANGOON

Howard, Arliss
TO WONG FOO, THANKS FOR
EVERYTHING! JULIE NEWMAR
Howard, Clint
APOLLO 13
BIGFOOT: THE UNFORGETTABLE
ENCOUNTER
DILLINGER AND CAPONE
FORGET PARIS
Howard, Jean Speagle
APOLLO 13
Howard, Jeremy
CURE, THE
Howard, Jr., James J.
FUN
Howard, Julia
EMPIRE RECORDS
Howard, Ken
NET, THE
Howard, Mary C.
BAR GIRLS
Howard, Ralph
SAFE PASSAGE
Howard, Rance
APOLLO 13
BIGFOOT: THE UNFORGETTABLE
ENCOUNTER
CHILDREN OF THE CORN III: URBAN
HARVEST
Howard, Terrence
DEAD PRESIDENTS
O.J. SIMPSON STORY, THE
Howell, C. Thomas
PAYBACK
TERESA'S TATTOO
Howell, Dean
OPERATION INTERCEPT
Howell, Hoke
MIDNIGHT TEASE 2
ROSWELL: THE U.F.O. COVER-UP
Howell, Jeffrey
ROOMMATES
SUDDEN DEATH
Howell, Margaret
CANDYMAN: FAREWELL TO THE FLESH
Hoyle, Doug
PYROMANIAC'S LOVE STORY, A
Hoyt, John
BASKETBALL DIARIES, THE
DIE HARD WITH A VENGEANCE
Hu, Kelly
STRANGE DAYS
Huang Lei
PHANTOM LOVER, THE
Huang Yi-Ming
MOVING THE MOUNTAIN
Huang Yifei
HEROIC TRIO, THE
Huband, David
TOMMY BOY
Hubbard, Charmain Renata
STRANGE DAYS
Hubbard, Ed
VAMPIRES AND OTHER STEREOTYPES
Hubbard-Boone, Jean
GLASS SHIELD, THE
Huber, Rhys
CIRCUMSTANCES UNKNOWN
Hubert, Janet
WHITE MAN'S BURDEN
Hubicki, B.
SHORT FILM ABOUT KILLING, A
Hubley, Whip
SPECIES
Hudson, Ernie
BASKETBALL DIARIES, THE
CONGO
Hudson, Jim
OUTSIDE THE LAW

Huemer, Peter Ily
BEFORE SUNRISE
Huerta, Chris
CITY OF LOST CHILDREN, THE
Huerta, Roberto
WALK IN THE CLOUDS, A
Huff, John
HOWLING: NEW MOON RISING, THE
Huffman, Felicity
HACKERS
WATER ENGINE, THE
Huffman, Jon
REASON TO BELIEVE, A
Huffman, Rosanna
BABE
Hughes, Finola
DARK SIDE OF GENIUS, THE
Hughes, Frank John
BAD BOYS
Hughes, Helen
BILLY MADISON
TOMMY BOY
Hughes, Laura Leigh
VIRTUOSITY
Hughes, Melanie
JUST CAUSE
Hughes, Miko
APOLLO 13
Hughes, Robert
CRUMB
Hughes, Tresa
DON JUAN DEMARCO
Hugot, Marceline
TO WONG FOO, THANKS FOR
EVERYTHING! JULIE NEWMAR
Huie, Karen
WILD BILL
Huisman, Mark
IT TAKES TWO
Huk, Tadeusz
PROVINCIAL ACTORS
Hulce, Tom
WINGS OF COURAGE
Hules, Endre
APOLLO 13
MY ANTONIA
SEVEN
Hull, Christine
LIE DOWN WITH DOGS
Hull, Jr., Richard
DARK DEALER
Hull, Lisa
LOVE AND HUMAN REMAINS
Hultberg, Jordy
UNDERNEATH, THE
Humphrey, Justin
NOW AND THEN
Humphrey, Renee
CURE, THE
DEVIL IN A BLUE DRESS
FRENCH KISS
FUN
MALLRATS
Humphreys, Alf
BROKEN TRUST
Humphreys, Robb
LORD OF ILLUSIONS
Humphries, Nigel
LAMB
Hungaro, Josefina
VALLEY OF ABRAHAM, THE
Hungerford, Michael
3 NINJAS KNUCKLE UP
Hunt, Bonnie
JUMANJI
NOW AND THEN
Hunt, Brad
POSTCARDS FROM AMERICA

Hunt, David
JADE
Hunt, Helen
KISS OF DEATH
Hunt, Linda
POCAHONTAS
YOUNGER & YOUNGER
Hunt, Thomas
AMERICA'S DEADLIEST HOME VIDEO
Hunter, Annie Mae
HOW TO MAKE AN AMERICAN QUILT
Hunter, Bill
MURIEL'S WEDDING
Hunter, Bruce
CANADIAN BACON
Hunter, Harold
KIDS
Hunter, Holly
COPYCAT
HOME FOR THE HOLIDAYS
Hunter, Jr., Robert
FORGET PARIS
Hunter, Morgan
USUAL SUSPECTS, THE
Hunter, Nick
LORD OF ILLUSIONS
Hunyadkurthy, Istvan
CITIZEN X
Huppert, Isabelle
AMATEUR
Hurlbutt, John
DEAD MAN WALKING
Hursey, Sherry
TOM AND HUCK
Hurst, Michelle
SMOKE
Hurt, John
BETRAYAL
ROB ROY
WILD BILL
Hurt, William
SMOKE
Huse, Tom
BITTER VENGEANCE
Husnolina, Larisa
MUTE WITNESS
Huss, Toby
BASKETBALL DIARIES, THE
Hussain, Nazim
BANDIT QUEEN
Hussey, David
TIE-DIED: ROCK 'N' ROLL'S MOST
DEADICATED FANS
Huston, Anjelica
BUFFALO GIRLS
CROSSING GUARD, THE
PEREZ FAMILY, THE
Huston, C.W.
GEORGIA
Huston, Danny
LEAVING LAS VEGAS
Hutchinson, Dennis
JERKY BOYS: THE MOVIE, THE
Hutchinson, Mark
HEAVEN'S A DRAG
Hutchinson, Nick
RESTORATION
Hutchinson, Timothy O'Neale
O.J. SIMPSON STORY, THE
Hutchison, Brian
SUDDEN DEATH
Hutchison, Stephen
DEATH IN BRUNSWICK
Huttel, Paul
KINGDOM, THE
Hutton, Danny
BRIAN WILSON: I JUST WASN'T MADE
FOR THESE TIMES

Hutton, Peter
ART FOR TEACHERS OF CHILDREN
Hutton, Rif
BIGFOOT: THE UNFORGETTABLE
ENCOUNTER
CHILDREN OF THE CORN III: URBAN
HARVEST
Hutton, Timothy
FRENCH KISS
Hyatt, Abie Hope
TO WONG FOO, THANKS FOR
EVERYTHING! JULIE NEWMAR
Hyatt, Ron
DANGEROUS, THE
Hyde, Jonathan
JUMANJI
Hyde, Michael
VAMPIRE IN BROOKLYN
Hyland, Frances
NEVER TALK TO STRANGERS
Hylands, Scott
DECOY
Hyler, Erik
NEXT DOOR
Hyman, Marie
JUST CAUSE
Hyoung-Gi Choi
HOW TO TOP MY WIFE
Hytner, Steve
PROPHECY, THE
Iannini, Lisa
FEAR, THE
Ibarra, Mirta
STRAWBERRY AND CHOCOLATE
UP TO A CERTAIN POINT
Ibraheem, Rahman
DANGEROUS MINDS
Ice Cube
FRIDAY
GLASS SHIELD, THE
HIGHER LEARNING
Ice-T
JOHNNY MNEMONIC
TANK GIRL
Ideka, Riyoko
MYSTERY OF RAMPO, THE
Idle, Eric
CASPER
Idoni, Marzio
CARRINGTON
Igawa, Togo
BUSINESS AFFAIR, A
Iglish, Bernadette
RESTORATION
Iles, Douglas W.
HACKERS
Iljin, Igor
MUTE WITNESS
Ilyin, Vladimir
BURNT BY THE SUN
Imbro, R.
SHORT FILM ABOUT LOVE, A
Imperioli, Michael
ADDICTION, THE
AMATEUR
BAD BOYS
BASKETBALL DIARIES, THE
CLOCKERS
DEAD PRESIDENTS
POSTCARDS FROM AMERICA
Imrie, Celia
RETURN OF THE NATIVE, THE
Inaba, Carrie Ann
LORD OF ILLUSIONS
Indrikson, Villem
CITY UNPLUGGED
Ineson, Ralph
FIRST KNIGHT

Ingall, Mark
ASCENT, THE
Ingaro, Bob
MINA TANNENBAUM
Ingersoll, James
GLASS SHIELD, THE
Ingersoll, Mary
BITTER VENGEANCE
Ingram, David
HEAVEN'S A DRAG
Ingram, Nate
THINGS TO DO IN DENVER WHEN
YOU'RE DEAD
Innerst, Lynne
PIANO LESSON, THE
Innocenzo, John
VAMPIRES AND OTHER STEREOTYPES
Inoue, Akira
HIGHLANDER: THE FINAL DIMENSION
Inouye, Julie
FREE WILLY 2: THE ADVENTURE HOME
Inwood, Steve
ALMOST DEAD
Iorio, Gary
BASKETBALL DIARIES, THE
Ipale, Aharon
DOOMSDAY GUN
Ipatova, Natalia
WINDOW TO PARIS
Ireland, Celia
DALLAS DOLL
Ireland, Kylie
STRANGE DAYS
Irie, Tatsuya
HUNTED, THE
Irish, Mark
LIE DOWN WITH DOGS
Irons, Jeremy
DIE HARD WITH A VENGEANCE
Ironside, Michael
GLASS SHIELD, THE
MAJOR PAYNE
RED SUN RISING
Irrera, Dom
SILENCE OF THE HAMS
Irvine, Andrea
AILSA
Irvine, Anthony
FUNNY BONES
Irvine, Blanaid
AILSA
Isaac, Alberto
BURNING SEASON, THE
Isaacson, Simon
WINGS OF HONNEAMISE: ROYAL SPACE
FORCE
Isacson, Bruce
OUTBREAK
Ish, Kathryn
AMERICAN PRESIDENT, THE
Ishibashi, Ryo
BLUE TIGER
CROSSING GUARD, THE
Ishibashi, Takaaki
STEAL BIG, STEAL LITTLE
Ishida, Jim
SHOWGIRLS
STRANGE DAYS
Ishii, Leslie
SPECIES
Isler, Seth
INDICTMENT: THE MCMARTIN TRIAL
Islwyn, Gabrielle
JEFFERSON IN PARIS
Ismail, Johari
BEYOND RANGOON
Ismail, Norlela
BEYOND RANGOON

Isobel, Katherine
GOOD DAY TO DIE, A
Israel, Al
DANGEROUS MINDS
Isyanov, Ravil
GOLDENEYE
HACKERS
Itzin, Gregory
BORN TO BE WILD
Ivey, Dana
CLASS OF '61
SABRINA
SCARLET LETTER, THE
Ivey, Lela
S.F.W.
Ivory, Edward
NINE MONTHS
Iwanaga, Yumiko
DALLAS DOLL
Iwinska, Stefania
SHORT FILM ABOUT LOVE, A
Jaasi, Michael
STRANGE DAYS
Jabraud, Anne-Marie
GROSSE FATIGUE
Jace, Michael
STRANGE DAYS
Jacev, Vladimir
BEFORE THE RAIN
Jackman, Kyley
WALKING DEAD, THE
Jackson, Aisleagh
GEORGIA
Jackson, Chubby
GREAT DAY IN HARLEM, A
Jackson, Eldon
CONGO
Jackson, Ernie
CONVICT COWBOY
Jackson, Gregory Paul
FORGET PARIS
Jackson, John M.
ROSWELL: THE U.F.O. COVER-UP
Jackson, Joshua
DIGGER
MAGIC IN THE WATER
Jackson, Kevin
WALKING DEAD, THE
Jackson, Kyle-Scott
GLASS SHIELD, THE
Jackson, Michael A.
DANGER OF LOVE
DIE HARD WITH A VENGEANCE
Jackson, Palmer
DEAD MAN WALKING
Jackson, Ricco
RIVER OF GRASS
Jackson, Robert Jason
NEW JERSEY DRIVE
Jackson, Rose
DEAD PRESIDENTS
Jackson, Samuel L.
DIE HARD WITH A VENGEANCE
FLUKE
KISS OF DEATH
LOSING ISAIAH
Jackson, Stoney
RED SUN RISING
WILD BILL
Jackson, Tim
BATMAN FOREVER
Jackson, Tyrone
NEW YORK COP
Jacob, Gilles
GROSSE FATIGUE
Jacob, Irene
OTHELLO

Jacobs, Christopher
NICK OF TIME
Jacobs, Juliette
KURT VONNEGUT'S HARRISON
BERGERON
Jacobs, Muriel
BLUE VILLA, THE
Jacobson, Manny
WHITE MAN'S BURDEN
Jacobson, Sandra
TIE-DIED: ROCK 'N' ROLL'S MOST
DEADICATED FANS
Jacobus, Jay
COPYCAT
JADE
Jacott, Carlos
KICKING AND SCREAMING
Jacquelina, Tiara
BEYOND RANGOON
Jadot, Denis
JLG BY JLG
Jaeb, Cheree
THINGS TO DO IN DENVER WHEN
YOU'RE DEAD
Jaffe, Susan
BALLET
Jaffrey, Sakina
INDIAN IN THE CUPBOARD, THE
Jaglom, Henry
LAST SUMMER IN THE HAMPTONS
Jago, Alexa
WATERWORLD
James, Adam
STEAL BIG, STEAL LITTLE
James, Art
MALLRATS
James, Brion
COMPANION, THE
LAST RIDE, THE
James, Debbie
BIGFOOT: THE UNFORGETTABLE
ENCOUNTER
James, Des
SUM OF US, THE
James, Errol Kenya
HARLEM DIARY: NINE VOICES OF
RESILIENCE
James, Evan
PENTATHLON
James, Grant
MUTANT SPECIES
James, Hawthorne
SEVEN
WATER ENGINE, THE
James, Lonnie
PERSUASION
James, Marcus
ABDUCTED 2: THE REUNION
James, Sondra
MIGHTY APHRODITE
Janda, Krystyna
SHORT FILM ABOUT KILLING, A
WITHOUT ANESTHESIA
Jankowskij, Oleg
MUTE WITNESS
Janney, Allison
DEAD FUNNY
Janowitz, Tama
FOOL AND HIS MONEY, A
Jans, Anita
MINA TANNENBAUM
Jansen, Susanne
INNOCENT, THE
Janson, Gene
WHILE YOU WERE SLEEPING
Janssen, Famke
GOLDENEYE
LORD OF ILLUSIONS

Januschke, Peter Max
FOR GOD AND COUNTRY
Janushi, Elida
LAMERICA
Jarchow, Bruce
OUTBREAK
Jarda
NOT ANGELS BUT ANGELS
Jardini, Adriana
DON JUAN DEMARCO
Jaregard, Ernst-Hugo
KINGDOM, THE
Jarmusch, Jim
BLUE IN THE FACE
Jarmusch, Tom
LIVING IN OBLIVION
Jarret, Gabriel
AMERICAN PRESIDENT, THE
APOLLO 13
Jarrett, Belina
MURIEL'S WEDDING
Jarrett, Phillip
CONVICT COWBOY
DARKMAN 2: THE RETURN OF DURANT
NEVER TALK TO STRANGERS
Jarrett, Ron Ben
ASSASSINS
Jarvet, Juri
CITY UNPLUGGED
Jarvis, Graham
LAST OF THE DOGMEN
Jason, Donna
ABDUCTED 2: THE REUNION
Jason, Harvey
O.J. SIMPSON STORY, THE
Jason, Peter
CONGO
DECONSTRUCTING SARAH
IN THE MOUTH OF MADNESS
MORTAL KOMBAT
VILLAGE OF THE DAMNED
Jasper
TIE-DIED: ROCK 'N' ROLL'S MOST
DEADICATED FANS
Jauffret, Jean-Jacques
PIGALLE
Jaupart, Jean-Paul
FRENCH KISS
Jay, Michael
BODY STROKES
Jay, Ricky
WATER ENGINE, THE
Jaye, Ron
ROOMMATES
Jayne, Selina
3 NINJAS KNUCKLE UP
Jaynes, Jonathan
FIRST KNIGHT
Jayston, Michael
HIGHLANDER: THE FINAL DIMENSION
Jbara, Gregory
JEFFREY
JD
TIE-DIED: ROCK 'N' ROLL'S MOST
DEADICATED FANS
Jeannet, Valerie
MY LIFE AND TIMES WITH ANTONIN
ARTAUD
Jefferson, Jr., Herbert
OUTBREAK
Jefferson, Mike
DIE HARD WITH A VENGEANCE
Jeffrey, Lachlan
DEATH IN BRUNSWICK
Jeffries, Chuck
ADDICTION, THE
Jeffries, Marc John
LOSING ISAIAH

Jelinkski, Manfred O.
NEKROMANTIK
Jemison, Kimble
GLASS SHIELD, THE
Jenco, Sal
ARIZONA DREAM
TALL TALE: THE UNBELIEVABLE
ADVENTURES OF PECOS BILL
Jenkins, Bennie L.
SOMETHING TO TALK ABOUT
Jenkins, Richard
GETTING OUT
HOW TO MAKE AN AMERICAN QUILT
INDIAN IN THE CUPBOARD, THE
Jenkins, Sam
CREW, THE
Jenney, Lucinda
LEAVING LAS VEGAS
NEXT DOOR
WATER ENGINE, THE
Jennings, Dominique
SEVEN
Jennings, Nolan
NEVER TALK TO STRANGERS
Jennings, Rory
FATHERLAND
Jensen, Brian
CONVICT COWBOY
GOOD DAY TO DIE, A
Jensen, Dave
AVENGING ANGEL
Jensen, David
SPECIES
UNDERNEATH, THE
Jensen, Ethan
THREE WISHES
Jensen, Henning
KINGDOM, THE
Jensen, Julie
BAR GIRLS
Jensen, Soren Elung
KINGDOM, THE
Jensen, Todd
ARMAGEDDON: THE FINAL CHALLENGE
MANGLER, THE
Jensen, Tully
BRADY BUNCH MOVIE, THE
Jensen, Vita
KINGDOM, THE
Jenson, Sasha
DILLINGER AND CAPONE
Jeraffi, Chaim
WATERWORLD
Jerido, Ebony
DANGEROUS MINDS
Jeschim, Bilge
BEFORE SUNRISE
Jessica, Taffara
DOLORES CLAIBORNE
Jessop, Jack
MOONLIGHT AND VALENTINO
TOMMY BOY
Jessup, Bill
KINGFISH: A STORY OF HUEY P. LONG
Jessup, Sioux-Z
PROPHECY, THE
Jet Li
HIGH RISK
Jeter, Michael
WATERWORLD
Jewesbury, Edward
RICHARD III
Jewkes, Richard
AVENGING ANGEL
OUT OF ANNIE'S PAST
Jezek, Robert
DEATH MACHINE

Jezequel, Julie
MY LIFE AND TIMES WITH ANTONIN
ARTAUD
Jia Shijun
SHANGHAI TRIAD
Jiang Baoying
SHANGHAI TRIAD
Jiang Haowen
HEROIC TRIO, THE
Jiang Jiankang
SHANGHAI TRIAD
Jillette, Penn
HACKERS
TOY STORY
Jimenez, Dennis
MY FAMILY: MI FAMILIA
Jimenez, Gladys
BAD BLOOD
Jimenez, Jr., Frankie R.
ASSASSINS
Jimenez, Juan
MY FAMILY: MI FAMILIA
WALK IN THE CLOUDS, A
Jimenez, Luisa Maria
I AM CUBA
Jimerson, Jeff
SUDDEN DEATH
Jimmy Z.
GEORGIA
Jin-Sil Choi
HOW TO TOP MY WIFE
Joachim, Suzy
CIRCUMSTANCES UNKNOWN
HIDEAWAY
Joe, Tricia
BABY-SITTERS CLUB, THE
Johansen, Peter
BROTHERS MCMULLEN, THE
Johansson, Scarlett
JUST CAUSE
John, Alexander
SENSE AND SENSIBILITY
John Carmichael & His Band
SHALLOW GRAVE
John, Gottfried
GOLDENEYE
John Lurie National Orchestra, The
BLUE IN THE FACE
Johnny C.
TWO BITS
Johns, Bill
GEORGIA
Johns, Glynis
WHILE YOU WERE SLEEPING
Johns, Mike
FRENCH KISS
Johnson, Amy Jo
MIGHTY MORPHIN POWER RANGERS:
THE MOVIE
Johnson, Anthony
FRIDAY
Johnson, Arthur
JADE
Johnson, Ashley
NINE MONTHS
Johnson, Bart
MY FAMILY: MI FAMILIA
Johnson, Bryan
MALLRATS
Johnson, Carl
GRUMPIER OLD MEN
Johnson, Caroline Key
SHOWGIRLS
Johnson, Christopher
KILIAN'S CHRONICLE
Johnson, Corey
INNOCENT, THE

Johnson, Darlene
PERSUASION
Johnson, Denise
INDICTMENT: THE MCMARTIN TRIAL
Johnson, Hassan
CLOCKERS
Johnson, J. Clark
NICK OF TIME
Johnson, Jack
TIE THAT BINDS, THE
Johnson, Jeffrey Paul
FRANK & JESSE
Johnson, Karin
NOBODY LOVES ME
Johnson, Ken
FORGET PARIS
Johnson, Kevin
FORGET PARIS
Johnson, Kim
PRIEST
Johnson, Kirsten
ECLIPSE
Johnson, Lamont
COSMIC SLOP
WAITING TO EXHALE
Johnson, Leroy
ADDICTION, THE
Johnson, Marcus
FORGET PARIS
Johnson, Mark
COVER STORY
Johnson, Matt
REASON TO BELIEVE, A
Johnson, Michelle
BODY SHOT
Johnson, Nell
TWELVE MONKEYS
Johnson, P. Lynn
BROKEN TRUST
DIGGER
Johnson, Penny
CLASS OF '61
Johnson, Sigrid
WHEN NIGHT IS FALLING
Johnson, Susan Ilene
NINE MONTHS
Johnston, Bobby
BODY STROKES
Johnston, Chris
CUTTHROAT ISLAND
Johnston, J.J.
BODY SHOT
WATER ENGINE, THE
Johnston, John Dennis
WALK IN THE CLOUDS, A
Johnston, Keii
INDIAN IN THE CUPBOARD, THE
Johnston, Marie E.
FRANK AND OLLIE
Johnston, Michelle
GRUMPIER OLD MEN
SHOWGIRLS
Johnston, Ollie
FRANK AND OLLIE
Johnston, Shaun
CONVICT COWBOY
Johnston, Shirley
CRY, THE BELOVED COUNTRY
Johnstone, Jyll
MARTHA & ETHEL
Jolie, Angelina
HACKERS
Jolliff-Andoh, Lisa
SCARLET LETTER, THE
Jolly, Ross
MEET THE FEEBLES

Joly, Roget
CLEAN, SHAVEN
Joly, Sylvie
LES MISERABLES
Jonathan, Wesley
PANTHER
Jones, Anthony
PANTHER
PARTY GIRL
Jones, Barbara
LOVE AND HUMAN REMAINS
Jones, Bill T.
BLACK IS ... BLACK AIN'T
Jones, Brett
SCANNERS: THE SHOWDOWN
Jones, Cody
RENT-A-KID
Jones, Damon
WALKING DEAD, THE
Jones, Darryl
VILLAGE OF THE DAMNED
Jones, Davy
BRADY BUNCH MOVIE, THE
Jones, Doug
TANK GIRL
Jones, Dug
BAD BOYS
Jones, Gary
DOUBLE, DOUBLE, TOIL AND TROUBLE
Jones, Gemma
FEAST OF JULY
SENSE AND SENSIBILITY
Jones, Grace
CYBER BANDITS
Jones, Hank
GREAT DAY IN HARLEM, A
Jones, Iain
WHITE MAN'S BURDEN
Jones, James Earl
CRY, THE BELOVED COUNTRY
JEFFERSON IN PARIS
Jones, Jeffrey
AVENGING ANGEL
HOUSEGUEST
Jones, Jill Parker
SUBSTITUTE WIFE, THE
Jones, Jona
FUNNY BONES
Jones, Judd
SCARLET LETTER, THE
Jones, Kevin
PRIEST
Jones, L.Q.
CASINO
Jones, Laurie
BAR GIRLS
Jones, Lee
TIE-DIED: ROCK 'N' ROLL'S MOST
DEADICATED FANS
Jones, Maxine
BATMAN FOREVER
Jones, Ora
LOSING ISAIAH
Jones, Oran
NEW JERSEY DRIVE
Jones, Patrice
BOYS ON THE SIDE
Jones, Peter Vere
MEET THE FEEBLES
Jones, Richard T.
JURY DUTY
Jones, Rohan
MURIEL'S WEDDING
Jones, Rupert Penry
FATHERLAND
Jones, Sam
BALLISTIC

Jones, Sannye
FORGET PARIS
Jones, Simon
TWELVE MONKEYS
Jones, Stanley
PEBBLE AND THE PENGUIN, THE
Jones, Steve Anthony
REDWOOD CURTAIN
Jones, Tamala
HOW TO MAKE AN AMERICAN QUILT
Jones, Tom
JERKY BOYS: THE MOVIE, THE
Jones, Tommy Lee
BATMAN FOREVER
Jones, Vann
LIE DOWN WITH DOGS
Jones, Wayson R.
BLACK IS ... BLACK AIN'T
Jonhson, Ken
BUSHWHACKED
Joong-Hoong Park
HOW TO TOP MY WIFE
Jordan, Don
DR. JEKYLL & MS. HYDE
Jordan, Jeremy
LEAVING LAS VEGAS
Jordan, Jr., Taft
GREAT DAY IN HARLEM, A
Jordan, Kevin
HOUSEGUEST
Jordan, Scott James
LIE DOWN WITH DOGS
Jorgensen, Ben
BASKETBALL DIARIES, THE
BREAK, THE
Jorjorian, Paul
LOSING ISAIAH
Josef, Philip
GOLD DIGGERS: THE SECRET OF BEAR
MOUNTAIN
Joseph
NOT ANGELS BUT ANGELS
Joseph, Al
FORGET PARIS
Joseph, Gary
SCARLET LETTER, THE
Joseph, Jeffrey
STUART SAVES HIS FAMILY
Joseph, Kevin "Flotilla DeBarge"
TO WONG FOO, THANKS FOR
EVERYTHING! JULIE NEWMAR
Joseph, Ralph
CANDYMAN: FAREWELL TO THE FLESH
Joseph, Robet Alan
OUTBREAK
Josephson, Erland
DANCER, THE
Josifovski, Josif
BEFORE THE RAIN
Joss, Jonathan
SUBSTITUTE WIFE, THE
Jostyn, Jennifer
BROTHERS MCMULLEN, THE
Joung-Hwa Eum
HOW TO TOP MY WIFE
Jourden, Brynna
BETTER OFF DEAD
Journee, Bruno
CITY OF LOST CHILDREN, THE
Jovanovski, Meto
BEFORE THE RAIN
Jovanovski, Mile
BEFORE THE RAIN
Joy, Robert
WATERWORLD
Joyce, Gloria
BAR GIRLS

Joydeb
CHARULATA
Joyner, Michelle
OUTBREAK
Jozefson, Jack
ALMOST DEAD
Ju Xingmao
RED FIRECRACKER, GREEN
FIRECRACKER
Juarbe, Israel
NET, THE
Judd, Ashley
HEAT
SMOKE
Judd, John
LOSING ISAIAH
Jugbe, Ayo Ade
CONGO
Jugnot, Gerard
GROSSE FATIGUE
Juhel, Gaby
INNOCENT LIES
Juiff, Patrice
FRENCH KISS
Juillot, Ghislaine
FRENCH KISS
Julia, Raul
BURNING SEASON, THE
Juliano, Lenny
MIDNIGHT TEASE 2
Julien, Andre
JEFFERSON IN PARIS
Julien, Jay
ADDICTION, THE
Julien, Robbin
EMBRACE OF THE VAMPIRE
Juma, Lenny
GREAT ELEPHANT ESCAPE, THE
Jump, Gordon
BITTER VENGEANCE
Juneau, Annie
LOVE AND HUMAN REMAINS
Jung, Mathias
TOTAL ECLIPSE
Jung, Nathan
GALAXIS
Junior, Enzo
HACKERS
Junker, Ruth
KINGDOM, THE
Jurado, Jeanette
MY FAMILY: MI FAMILIA
Jurek, Delia
CURE, THE
Jurkowski, Bernadette
NADJA
Justiz, Marisela
UP TO A CERTAIN POINT
Jutras, Richard
HIGHLANDER: THE FINAL DIMENSION
Ka'aihue, Henry Kapono
WATERWORLD
Ka'illi, Jr., Luke
WATERWORLD
Kabelitz, Roland
NOBODY LOVES ME
Kabillio, Eli
LIE DOWN WITH DOGS
Kabler, Roger
CLUELESS
Kachowski, Mark
SUDDEN DEATH
Kaczor, Kazimierz
WITHOUT ANESTHESIA
Kadamani, Daniel
DEATH IN BRUNSWICK

Kadi, Nicholas
CONGO
Kaell, Ron
COPYCAT
VILLAGE OF THE DAMNED
Kafaro, Julien
MINA TANNENBAUM
Kagawa, Teruyuki
MYSTERY OF RAMPO, THE
Kahan, Stephen
ASSASSINS
Kahan, Steve
FREE WILLY 2: THE ADVENTURE HOME
Kahl, Rolf Peter
DEADLY MARIA
Kahn, Karen
VILLAGE OF THE DAMNED
Kahn, Madeleine
NIXON
Kain, Khalil
ZOOMAN
Kairau, Brian
ONCE WERE WARRIORS
Kairau, Joseph
ONCE WERE WARRIORS
Kairau, Marshall
ONCE WERE WARRIORS
Kaiser, Henry
DRACULA: DEAD AND LOVING IT
Kaiser, Suki
CIRCUMSTANCES UNKNOWN
Kaitlyn, Peter
UNSTRUNG HEROES
Kakon, Gabriel
HIGHLANDER: THE FINAL DIMENSION
Kalanzo, Kass
HARLEM DIARY: NINE VOICES OF
    RESILIENCE
Kalfa, Steve
JEFFERSON IN PARIS
Kaliche, Vladimir
WINDOW TO PARIS
Kalinowski, Waldemar
LEAVING LAS VEGAS
Kamin, Daniel
KINGFISH: A STORY OF HUEY P. LONG
Kaminsky, Max
GREAT DAY IN HARLEM, A
Kamle, Raj Kumar
BANDIT QUEEN
Kampmann, Steven
STUART SAVES HIS FAMILY
Kamuyu, Andrew
CONGO
Kanagawa, Hiro
HIDEAWAY
HUNTED, THE
Kandal, Nancy
AMERICAN PRESIDENT, THE
Kane, Barbara Jean
JUST CAUSE
Kane, Carol
CRAZYSITTER, THE
Kane, Kathleen
DRACULA: DEAD AND LOVING IT
Kaneshiro, Takeshi
EXECUTIONERS
Kaneta, Hisami
HUNTED, THE
Kang, Stan
TWELVE MONKEYS
Kanig, Frank
OUT OF ANNIE'S PAST
Kanno, Miho
WIZARD OF DARKNESS
Kanomatsu, Knori
WIZARD OF DARKNESS

Kantner, China
S.F.W.
Kantymir, Kenneth
ABDUCTED 2: THE REUNION
Kanyok, Laurie
LORD OF ILLUSIONS
Kao Mingjun
WOODEN MAN'S BRIDE, THE
Kaplan, Matthew
KICKING AND SCREAMING
Kaplan, Nelly
NEA
Kaplan, Seth
FATHER OF THE BRIDE PART II
Kaplan, Stan
RIVER OF GRASS
Karabatsos, Ron
GET SHORTY
Karahisarus, Kris
DEATH IN BRUNSWICK
Karasiov, Denis
MUTE WITNESS
Karels, Eugene
GRUMPIER OLD MEN
Karen, James
COMPANION, THE
CONGO
NIXON
Karenga, Maulana
BLACK IS ... BLACK AIN'T
Karin, Anna
FEAR, THE
Kark, Tonu
CITY UNPLUGGED
Karlenkov, Sergei
MUTE WITNESS
Karnes, Brixton
TANK GIRL
Karr, Tom
CREEP
Kartheiser, Vincent
INDIAN IN THE CUPBOARD, THE
Karvan, Claudia
DESPERATE PREY
Karyo, Tcheky
BAD BOYS
GOLDENEYE
OPERATION DUMBO DROP
Kasem, Casey
COSMIC SLOP
Kaskanis, Dora
ONLY THE BRAVE
Kasper, Gary
BATMAN FOREVER
Kassin, Jason S.
KICKING AND SCREAMING
Kassir, John
CASPER
POCAHONTAS
TALES FROM THE CRYPT: DEMON
    KNIGHT
Kasten, Matthew
TO WONG FOO, THANKS FOR
    EVERYTHING! JULIE NEWMAR
Kastrati, Arben
BEFORE THE RAIN
Kates, Kimberley
BAD BLOOD
Katia, Helena
SABRINA
Kato, Masay
MYSTERY OF RAMPO, THE
Katsulas, Andreas
NEW YORK COP
Katt, Nicky
BABYSITTER, THE
CURE, THE

DOOM GENERATION, THE
STRANGE DAYS
Katt, William
AMERICAN COP
Katvedt, Otis A.
SUBSTITUTE WIFE, THE
Katz, Brian
FLUKE
Katz, Cindy
HEAT
Katz, Dr. Edward L.
CROSSING GUARD, THE
Katz, Dr. Louis A.
ADDICTION, THE
Katz, Judah
MOONLIGHT AND VALENTINO
Katz, Lauren
KICKING AND SCREAMING
Katz, Zachary Asher
POSTCARDS FROM AMERICA
Kaufman, Evan
ANGUS
Kaufman, Michael
NIXON
Kaufmann, Joshka
CITY OF LOST CHILDREN, THE
Kausch, Michael
MARTHA AND I
Kavanagh, John
BRAVEHEART
CIRCLE OF FRIENDS
Kavner, Julie
FORGET PARIS
Kavner, Steven
FATHER AND SCOUT
Kaye, Nathan
MURIEL'S WEDDING
Kayman, Lee
CLEAN, SHAVEN
Kayso, Dick
KINGDOM, THE
Kaza, Elizabeth
CASTLE FREAK
JEFFERSON IN PARIS
Kazann, Zitto
WATERWORLD
WATERWORLD
Kazanskaia, Alla
BURNT BY THE SUN
Kean, Greg
IN THE DEEP WOODS
Keane, Bryan
ART FOR TEACHERS OF CHILDREN
Keane, Christine
FRANKIE STARLIGHT
Keane, Dillie
HEAVEN'S A DRAG
Keane, Glen
FRANK AND OLLIE
Keane, James
ANGUS
MURDER IN THE FIRST
Keane, Sean
AILSA
Keast, Brent
CAGED HEARTS
Keaton, Diane
FATHER OF THE BRIDE PART II
Keddy, Jeremy
SCARLET LETTER, THE
Keegan, Rose
FIRST KNIGHT
Keeling, Helen
JACK-O
Keena, Monica
WHILE YOU WERE SLEEPING
Keener, Catherine
LIVING IN OBLIVION

Keenlyside, Eric
GOOD DAY TO DIE, A
Keeslar, Matt
RUN OF THE COUNTRY, THE
SAFE PASSAGE
Kegan, Larry
WHEN BILLY BROKE HIS HEAD ... AND
OTHER TALES OF WONDER
Kehlenbach, Tim
VAMPIRES AND OTHER STEREOTYPES
Kehler, Jack
ACROSS THE MOON
WATERWORLD
Keiffer, Jim
REASON TO BELIEVE, A
Keir, Andrew
ROB ROY
Keitel, Harvey
BLUE IN THE FACE
CLOCKERS
GET SHORTY
SMOKE
Keith, David
GOLD DIGGERS: THE SECRET OF BEAR
MOUNTAIN
INDIAN IN THE CUPBOARD, THE
Keith-King, Callum
SUDDEN DEATH
Keketse, Lizzy
FRIENDS
Kelk, Christopher
BILLY MADISON
Kelleher, Tim
CLOCKERS
NEVER TALK TO STRANGERS
OPERATION DUMBO DROP
Keller, Elizabeth
CIRCLE OF FRIENDS
FRANKIE STARLIGHT
Keller, Heidi
CASINO
Keller, Lorose
NOBODY LOVES ME
Keller, Thomas
KINGFISH: A STORY OF HUEY P. LONG
Keller, Tim
TO WONG FOO, THANKS FOR
EVERYTHING! JULIE NEWMAR
Kellerman, Sally
YOUNGER & YOUNGER
Kelley, Glenda Starr
LOSING ISAIAH
Kelley, Kimberly
MIDNIGHT TEASE 2
Kelley, Ryan
ROOMMATES
Kelley, Sheila
DECONSTRUCTING SARAH
Kelley, Tom
HEAVYWEIGHTS
Kellner, Catherine
KICKING AND SCREAMING
Kelly, Arthur
FEAST OF JULY
Kelly, Brendan
CLOCKERS
DEVIL IN A BLUE DRESS
Kelly, Cheryl A.
BOYS ON THE SIDE
Kelly, Daniel Hugh
BAD COMPANY
Kelly, Darragh
AILSA
Kelly, David
RUN OF THE COUNTRY, THE
Kelly, Erica
STRANGE DAYS

Kelly, Ian
NEW JERSEY DRIVE
Kelly, Joan
ALMOST DEAD
Kelly, John
WIGSTOCK: THE MOVIE
Kelly, June
CLEAN, SHAVEN
Kelly, Laura Lee
TIE THAT BINDS, THE
Kelly, Lesley
PYROMANIAC'S LOVE STORY, A
Kelly, Michael
KID IN KING ARTHUR'S COURT, A
Kelly, Moira
LITTLE ODESSA
TIE THAT BINDS, THE
Kelly, Phil
BRAVEHEART
CIRCLE OF FRIENDS
FUNNY BONES
Kelly, Rae'ven
CLASS OF '61
Kelly, Rae'ven Larrymore
HOW TO MAKE AN AMERICAN QUILT
Kelly, Sheila
SECRETARY, THE
Kelly-Young, Leonard
ENEMY WITHIN, THE
Kelsey, Harley
BUSHWHACKED
Kelsey, Tamsin
MAGIC IN THE WATER
Kem, Spike
ONCE WERE WARRIORS
Kemp, Martin
BOCA
CYBER BANDITS
EMBRACE OF THE VAMPIRE
Kemp, Stephanie
GET SHORTY
Kendall, Elaine Corral
NET, THE
Kendall, Kendrick
COVER STORY
Kenevey, Chris
AWFULLY BIG ADVENTURE, AN
Kenjyo, Toru
MYSTERY OF RAMPO, THE
Kennally, Eileen
LAMB
Kennard, Walter
SUM OF US, THE
Kennedy, Andrew
HEAVEN'S A DRAG
Kennedy, Deborah
DEATH IN BRUNSWICK
SUM OF US, THE
Kennedy, Dev
ACE VENTURA: WHEN NATURE CALLS
Kennedy, Elizabeth
SHOWGIRLS
Kennedy, Gordon
KINGDOM, THE
Kennedy, Ken
HEAVEN'S A DRAG
Kennedy, Merle
ACROSS THE MOON
Kennedy, Mike
NIXON
Kennedy, Patricia
COUNTRY LIFE
Kennedy, Shannon
FATHER OF THE BRIDE PART II
Kennedy, William Jimmy
COVER STORY

Kennerly, Mark D.
TALES FROM THE CRYPT: DEMON
KNIGHT
Kenny, Jack
EVOLVER
Kenny, Shannon
BODILY HARM
Kensei, Ken
DEAD FUNNY
HUNTED, THE
Kent, Anne
AILSA
Kent, Jace
LITTLE ODESSA
Kent, Stacey
RICHARD III
Kente, Dambisa
CRY, THE BELOVED COUNTRY
FRIENDS
Kenyatta, Stogie
SPECIES
Kenyon, Randall Lee
BETTER OFF DEAD
Kenyon, Sally
REASON TO BELIEVE, A
Keo, Kim
ARIZONA DREAM
Keogh, Danny
MANGLER, THE
Keogh, Doreen
LAMB
Keogh, Jimmy
BRAVEHEART
Keough, Cara
OUTBREAK
Kerapa, Jason
ONCE WERE WARRIORS
Kerby, Kelly
TANK GIRL
Kerman, Ken
SEPARATE LIVES
Kermond, Dene
MURIEL'S WEDDING
Kern, Peter
EROTIQUE
Kerr, Addison Grant
AMERICA'S DEADLIEST HOME VIDEO
Kerr, Patrick
JEFFREY
STUART SAVES HIS FAMILY
Kerr-Bell, Mamaengaroa
ONCE WERE WARRIORS
Kerrigan, Dermot
PERSUASION
Kershaw, Annabel
JUMANJI
Kershner, Irvin
ANGUS
Kerwin, Brian
GOLD DIGGERS: THE SECRET OF BEAR
MOUNTAIN
Kerwin, Lance
OUTBREAK
Kesey, Zane
TIE-DIED: ROCK 'N' ROLL'S MOST
DEADICATED FANS
Keshavarz, Mohamad Ali
THROUGH THE OLIVE TREES
Kessler, Zale
DRACULA: DEAD AND LOVING IT
Kester, Ernest
HOWLING: NEW MOON RISING, THE
Keston, Frederica
SKINNER
Ketcher, Annette
KINGDOM, THE
Kettlewell, Ruth
FUNNY BONES

Kettner, Paige
HOW TO MAKE AN AMERICAN QUILT
Kettner, Ryanne
HOW TO MAKE AN AMERICAN QUILT
Keutericks, Jean
MINA TANNENBAUM
Kevin, Paul
HEAVEN'S A DRAG
Key, Tom
GORDY
Keye, Jay
GEORGIA
Keyes, Irwin
SILENCE OF THE HAMS
Khali, Simbi
VAMPIRE IN BROOKLYN
Khan, George
FUNNY BONES
Khan, Namir
DANCE ME OUTSIDE
Khanjian, Arsinee
EXOTICA
Kharisma
DIE HARD WITH A VENGEANCE
Khavanizadeh, Abbas
JAR, THE
Kheradmand, Farhad
THROUGH THE OLIVE TREES
Khilling, Rhed
FRANK & JESSE
Khmelnitski, Aleksander
DANCER, THE
Khodaveisi, Behzad
JAR, THE
Kholman, Rolf
AWFULLY BIG ADVENTURE, AN
Kholmann, Udo
FOR GOD AND COUNTRY
Khorsand, Philippe
LES MISERABLES
Khumalo, Leleti
CRY, THE BELOVED COUNTRY
Khumalo, Macbeth
FRIENDS
Khumrev, Michael
LITTLE ODESSA
Kid Capri
SHOW, THE
Kidman, Nicole
BATMAN FOREVER
TO DIE FOR
Kiely, Mark
UNDERCOVER
Kier, Udo
JOHNNY MNEMONIC
KINGDOM, THE
Kiesler, Lillian
INCREDIBLY TRUE ADVENTURES OF
TWO GIRLS IN LOVE, THE
Kiet Lam
TRAPS
Kiki, Kirin
MYSTERY OF RAMPO, THE
Kikuchi, Maiko
MYSTERY OF RAMPO, THE
Kilbride, Kerry
NET, THE
Kilian, Brian
FORGET PARIS
Kilmer, Val
BATMAN FOREVER
HEAT
WINGS OF COURAGE
Kilpatrick, Patrick
GRANNY, THE
SCANNERS: THE SHOWDOWN
3 NINJAS KNUCKLE UP
UNDER SIEGE 2: DARK TERRITORY

Kim, Derek
OUTBREAK
Kim, Eva
KILIAN'S CHRONICLE
Kim, Jennie
TIE-DIED: ROCK 'N' ROLL'S MOST
DEADICATED FANS
Kim, Jonathan S.
KIDS
Kim, Karen
COVER ME
Kim, Peter Y.
HACKERS
Kimbrough, Matthew
BABYSITTER, THE
Kimmons, Ken
ROSWELL: THE U.F.O. COVER-UP
Kimura, Kazuya
MYSTERY OF RAMPO, THE
Kimura, Victor
HUNTED, THE
Kinamis, George
TOMMY BOY
Kincannon, Kit
FRANKIE STARLIGHT
Kinebrew, Carolyn
MESSENGER
Kinevane, Pat
RUN OF THE COUNTRY, THE
King, Alan
CASINO
King, Alisa
PEBBLE AND THE PENGUIN, THE
King, Carlyle
BABE
King, Casey
DRACULA: DEAD AND LOVING IT
King, David
PANTHER
King, Jeff
ASSASSINS
King, Jerry
BUFFALO GIRLS
King, Joel
DANCE ME OUTSIDE
King, Ken
JADE
King, Lawrence
ABDUCTED 2: THE REUNION
King, Matthew Bradley
HEAVYWEIGHTS
King, Regina
FRIDAY
HIGHER LEARNING
King, Sonny H.
MURDER IN THE FIRST
King, Terrence
WALKING DEAD, THE
King, Wendy
DANCE ME OUTSIDE
King, Yolanda
FLUKE
Kingsley, Ben
SPECIES
Kingston, Alex
CARRINGTON
Kingston, Phil
JUDGE DREDD
Kinison, Malika
DANGEROUS, THE
Kinley, Kathryn
SAFE PASSAGE
Kinnear, Greg
DILLINGER
SABRINA
Kinney, Terry
DEVIL IN A BLUE DRESS

Kino, Lloyd
MORTAL KOMBAT
Kinsaul, Buck
MUTANT SPECIES
Kinsey, Lance
SILENCE OF THE HAMS
Kinski, Nastassja
CRACKERJACK
Kinyon, Bert
COPYCAT
Kiraly, Attila
CITIZEN X
Kirandziska, Suzana
BEFORE THE RAIN
Kirby, Bruno
BASKETBALL DIARIES, THE
Kirk, Amy
GOLD DIGGERS: THE SECRET OF BEAR
MOUNTAIN
Kirk, Tommy
ATTACK OF THE 60-FOOT CENTERFOLD
Kirkland, T.K.
NEW JERSEY DRIVE
Kirkpatrick, Bruce
TWELVE MONKEYS
Kirkwood, Craig
COSMIC SLOP
Kirkwood, Gene
CROSSING GUARD, THE
NET, THE
Kirsch, David
KICKING AND SCREAMING
Kirshner, Mia
EXOTICA
LOVE AND HUMAN REMAINS
MURDER IN THE FIRST
Kirton, Mike
BAD BOYS
Kirzinger, Ken
ACE VENTURA: WHEN NATURE CALLS
Kishibe, Ittoku
MYSTERY OF RAMPO, THE
Kistler, Charles M.
ROSWELL: THE U.F.O. COVER-UP
Kitano, Takeshi
JOHNNY MNEMONIC
Kitchen, Michael
DOOMSDAY GUN
FATHERLAND
GOLDENEYE
Kitt, Eartha
UNZIPPED
Klanfer, Francois
FIRST DEGREE
Klar, Gary
HACKERS
Klausner, Willette
WHITE MAN'S BURDEN
Klebel, Barbara
BEFORE SUNRISE
Klein, Barbara Anne
ASSASSINS
Klein, David
JERKY BOYS: THE MOVIE, THE
MALLRATS
Klein, Jill
BOYS ON THE SIDE
Klein, Joanne
DANGER OF LOVE
Klein, Kristin
BAR GIRLS
Klein, Nita
TOTAL ECLIPSE
Klein, Robert
JEFFREY
Kleinman, Shirley
MINA TANNENBAUM

Klemens, Peter
ROOMMATES
Klementowicz, Paul
HACKERS
Klemp, Marcus
GRUMPIER OLD MEN
Klimek, Darrin
MURIEL'S WEDDING
Kline, Kevin
FRENCH KISS
Klingler, Rebecca Jane
COPYCAT
Kloes, Scott
ROOMMATES
Klooren, Enn
CITY UNPLUGGED
Klotz, Heidi
DEADLY MARIA
Kluger, Jeffrey S.
APOLLO 13
Klyn, Vincent
BALLISTIC
Knapp, Alex
DECONSTRUCTING SARAH
Knaster, Jeremy
DEAD MAN WALKING
Kneifel, Martha
MARTHA & ETHEL
Kneisl, Heidi
JACK-O
Knepper, Robert
GETTING OUT
SEARCH AND DESTROY
Knickerbocker, Will
BAD BOYS
Knight
DEATH IN BRUNSWICK
Knight, Christopher
BRADY BUNCH MOVIE, THE
DOOM GENERATION, THE
GOOD GIRLS DON'T
Knight, Dudley
PENTATHLON
Knight, Forest Ashley
INNOCENT, THE
Knight, John
PANTHER
Knight, Shirley
GOOD DAY TO DIE, A
INDICTMENT: THE MCMARTIN TRIAL
STUART SAVES HIS FAMILY
Knight, Tuesday
BABYSITTER, THE
COVER STORY
Knight, Victor
DR. JEKYLL & MS. HYDE
Knight, Wayne
TO DIE FOR
Knightly, Kepia
INNOCENT LIES
Knittl, Kristen
SHOWGIRLS
Knittle, Kristen
BODY STROKES
Knoblock, Chris
LAST SUMMER IN THE HAMPTONS
Knofelmacher, Joseph
KIDS
Knoll, R.J.
CRIMSON TIDE
DEVIL IN A BLUE DRESS
MAJOR PAYNE
Knotkova, Viktorie
COW, THE
Knott, Robert
SCANNERS: THE SHOWDOWN
WILD BILL

Knowlen, Barb
WHEN BILLY BROKE HIS HEAD ... AND
OTHER TALES OF WONDER
Knowles, Kaytlyn
STARS FELL ON HENRIETTA, THE
Knox, Jayme
HIDEAWAY
Knox, Terence
SPY WITHIN, THE
Ko, U Aung
BEYOND RANGOON
Kobayashi, Kiyoshi
AI CITY
Kober, Jeff
TANK GIRL
Kobrin, Tannis
LORD OF ILLUSIONS
Kocevska, Katerina
BEFORE THE RAIN
Koch, Jay
COSMIC SLOP
PANTHER
Koch, Melanie
KICKING AND SCREAMING
Koch, Peter
BODY SHOT
Kochin, Sveta
AMERICAN COP
Kocurikova, Zuzana
MARTHA AND I
Kodet, Jiri
ACCUMULATOR 1
Kodoulis, Panaiotis
BLUE VILLA, THE
Koefoed, Henrik
KINGDOM, THE
Koenig, Tommy
DRACULA: DEAD AND LOVING IT
Koetters, Michael
TIE-DIED: ROCK 'N' ROLL'S MOST
DEADICATED FANS
Kogen, Jay
COLDBLOODED
JURY DUTY
Kohler, Klaus
NOBODY LOVES ME
Kohler, Richard
IN THE MOUTH OF MADNESS
Kohlstedt, Susa
NEKROMANTIK
Kohn, Joan
LOSING ISAIAH
Kohner, Erik
PANTHER
Kohout, Jan
FATHERLAND
Koiwai, Jay
CROSSING GUARD, THE
Kok, Vincent
HIGH RISK
Kolarova, Daniela
ACCUMULATOR 1
Kolb, Hayley
BIG GREEN, THE
Kolb, Mina
BYE BYE, LOVE
Koller, Matthew
MOONLIGHT AND VALENTINO
Kollmann, Johannes
FOR GOD AND COUNTRY
Kolman, Allan
FORGET PARIS
SCANNERS: THE SHOWDOWN
SEVEN
Kolpakova, Irina
BALLET
Kolpan, Mitch
MONEY TRAIN

Koman, Jacek
DESPERATE PREY
Kominsky, Alice
CRUMB
Kondazian, Karen
STEAL BIG, STEAL LITTLE
Konig, Tex
BILLY MADISON
Kono, Keiko
MYSTERY OF RAMPO, THE
Konoval, Karin
DOUBLE, DOUBLE, TOIL AND TROUBLE
Konowal, Brian
CLOCKERS
Kontargyris, Sandy
CITY OF LOST CHILDREN, THE
Konupek, Ingrid
DECONSTRUCTING SARAH
Koob-Liebing, Hagen
NEKROMANTIK
Koob-Liebing, Marion
NEKROMANTIK
Koock, Guich
SUBSTITUTE WIFE, THE
Kool Moe Dee
PANTHER
Koon, Rebecca
SOMETHING TO TALK ABOUT
Kopache, Thomas
LEAVING LAS VEGAS
Koperski, K.
SHORT FILM ABOUT LOVE, A
Kopf, Kim
MIDNIGHT TEASE 2
Kopit, Arthur
ROSWELL: THE U.F.O. COVER-UP
Kopit, Lauren
BYE BYE, LOVE
Kopp, Lee
COPYCAT
Kora, Surendra
BANDIT QUEEN
Korba, Fran
CURE, THE
Korbin, Gaetana
HIDEAWAY
Korbin, Joyce R.
BASKETBALL DIARIES, THE
Korman, Harvey
DRACULA: DEAD AND LOVING IT
Korman, Jacques
MINA TANNENBAUM
Korognai, Karoly
CITIZEN X
Korsi, Sheila
RIVER OF GRASS
Korty, Jonathan
REDWOOD CURTAIN
Korzenko, Melissa
BILLY MADISON
Kosala, Joe
STEAL BIG, STEAL LITTLE
Kosinski, Jerzy
FOOL AND HIS MONEY, A
Kosta, Michael J.
TALL TALE: THE UNBELIEVABLE
ADVENTURES OF PECOS BILL
Kosterman, Mitch
DOUBLE, DOUBLE, TOIL AND TROUBLE
Koteas, Elias
EXOTICA
POWER OF ATTORNEY
PROPHECY, THE
Kotecki, Robert
EROTIQUE
Kotere, Brazylia
DEVIL IN A BLUE DRESS

Koti, Kati
CITIZEN X
Kotlisky, Marge
WATER ENGINE, THE
Kotowich, Brennan Leo
CIRCUMSTANCES UNKNOWN
Kottke, Austin
INDICTMENT: THE MCMARTIN TRIAL
TOM AND HUCK
Kotto, Yaphet
OUT OF SYNC
Koules, Beth
PARTY GIRL
Kovach, P.J.
TIE-DIED: ROCK 'N' ROLL'S MOST
DEADICATED FANS
Kovacs, Danny
COPYCAT
Kovar, Mikey
MALLRATS
Kowalczykowa, H.
SHORT FILM ABOUT KILLING, A
Koyal, Bholanath
CHARULATA
Koyama, Fumi
AI CITY
Kozak, Harley Jane
ANDROID AFFAIR, THE
MAGIC IN THE WATER
Kozlowski, Linda
VILLAGE OF THE DAMNED
Kozodaev, Alexei
WINDOW TO PARIS
Krabbe, Jeroen
FARINELLI
Kraft, Jonathan
CASINO
Krag, James
WHILE YOU WERE SLEEPING
Krakowska, Emilia
WITHOUT ANESTHESIA
Kramer, Bert
TALL TALE: THE UNBELIEVABLE
ADVENTURES OF PECOS BILL
Kramer, Eric Allen
CRAZYSITTER, THE
Kramer, Joni
DON JUAN DEMARCO
Kramer, Michael
BOULEVARD
Krantz, Peter
EXOTICA
Kranzkowsi, Karl
PROMISE, THE
Krape, Evelyn
BABE
Krasnoff, Mark
MUTANT SPECIES
Krawic, Michael
DILLINGER
Kreikenmayer, Eric
WILD REEDS
Kremer, Hans
PROMISE, THE
Kretchmer, Harry
ENGLISHMAN WHO WENT UP A HILL
BUT CAME DOWN A MOUNTAIN, THE
Kretschmann, Thomas
STALINGRAD
Kretz, Johnny
RHYTHM THIEF
Krevoy, Cecile
COLDBLOODED
Kreylis-Petrova, Kira
WINDOW TO PARIS
Krief, Chantal
MINA TANNENBAUM

Kriegel, David
LEAVING LAS VEGAS
Kriesa, Christopher
DILLINGER AND CAPONE
SECRETARY, THE
Kriski, Mark
BIGFOOT: THE UNFORGETTABLE
ENCOUNTER
Krispin, Joanne
RECKLESS
Krispin, Lisa
RECKLESS
Kristofer, Jason
CROSSING GUARD, THE
WHITE MAN'S BURDEN
Kriuchkova, Svetlana
BURNT BY THE SUN
Krochmal, Jenny
DEAD MAN WALKING
Krofft, Kristina
NET, THE
Krol, Joachim
DEADLY MARIA
NOBODY LOVES ME
Kroon, Christopher
BRIDGES OF MADISON COUNTY, THE
Kropfl, Paul Anthony
HIGHER LEARNING
TOM AND HUCK
Kroschwald, Udo
PROMISE, THE
Krstevski, Mladen
BEFORE THE RAIN
Krucker, Fides
WHEN NIGHT IS FALLING
Kruger, Gaye
WICKED CITY
Kruger, Pit
YOUNGER & YOUNGER
Krull, Kendra
UNSTRUNG HEROES
Krull, Suzanne
TIE THAT BINDS, THE
Krumbiegel, Ulrike
PROMISE, THE
Krumenauer, Dr. James
JUPITER'S WIFE
Krupa, Olek
FAIR GAME
MY ANTONIA
Krupas, John
AMERICA'S DEADLIEST HOME VIDEO
Kruper, Karen
FAR FROM HOME: THE ADVENTURES OF
YELLOW DOG
Kruse, Daniel
DEAD PRESIDENTS
Krusiec, Michelle
NIXON
Krutonog, Boris
MY ANTONIA
Kubatsi, Joe
FRIENDS
Kubba, Janan
RESTORATION
Kubeka, Abigail
CRY, THE BELOVED COUNTRY
Kubeke, Peter
FRIENDS
Kubota, Tak
HUNTED, THE
Kudaba, Elena
PYROMANIAC'S LOVE STORY, A
Kuderna, Josef
FOR GOD AND COUNTRY
Kudoh, Youki
PICTURE BRIDE

Kudrow, Lisa
CRAZYSITTER, THE
Kuespert, Holly
NICK OF TIME
Kuhn, Judy
POCAHONTAS
Kuhn, Thomas
GEORGIA
Kuhr, Aaron
TANK GIRL
Kulecza, Nonny
LIE DOWN WITH DOGS
Kulich, Vladimir
DECOY
Kuloglu, Ekrem
DEATH IN BRUNSWICK
Kulterer, Hubert Fabian
BEFORE SUNRISE
Kume, Hiraina
ONCE WERE WARRIORS
Kumlin, Kristina
SABRINA
Kunene, Vusi
CRY, THE BELOVED COUNTRY
FRIENDS
Kunz, Simon
GOLDENEYE
Kuo Chui
PHANTOM LOVER, THE
Kuran, Matthew
POSTCARDS FROM AMERICA
Kurland, Jeffrey
MIGHTY APHRODITE
Kurti
BEFORE SUNRISE
Kurti, Besim
LAMERICA
Kurtz, Joyce
BAREFOOT GEN
Kusatsu, Clyde
DECONSTRUCTING SARAH
TOP DOG
Kushch, Alexander
AMERICAN COP
Kushida, Alice
AMERICAN PRESIDENT, THE
Kusian, Carolyn
TANK GIRL
Kuss, Richard
GLASS SHIELD, THE
Kuwaar, Sanjeev
BANDIT QUEEN
Kux, Bill
DIE HARD WITH A VENGEANCE
Kuzyk, Mimi
MALICIOUS
Kwan Sau-Mei
HIGH RISK
Kwasniewska, Slawa
PROVINCIAL ACTORS
Kwei-Armah, Kwame
CUTTHROAT ISLAND
Kwon, Brittney
I LIKE TO PLAY GAMES
Kwon, Sue
BUSHWHACKED
Kwong, Kenny
COPYCAT
Kwong, Richard
MURDER IN THE FIRST
Kyd, Susan
BUSINESS AFFAIR, A
Kynman, Paul
FIRST KNIGHT
La Cause, Sebastian
SHOWGIRLS

La Compagnie Jolie Mome
SABRINA
La Due, Joe
CASINO
La Marre, Jean Claude
DEAD PRESIDENTS
La Motta, John
VAMPIRE IN BROOKLYN
La Paglia, Vittorio
MAMMA ROMA
La Rosa, Brian
CONGO
La Rosa, Diego
FLUKE
La Rosa, Kevin
OPERATION DUMBO DROP
La Russa, Annie
INDICTMENT: THE MCMARTIN TRIAL
La Sardo, Robert
OUTSIDE THE LAW
La Var, Ellin
WAITING TO EXHALE
La Von, Breta
BOYS ON THE SIDE
Labadie, Jean-Philippe
CITY OF LOST CHILDREN, THE
Labarthe, Andre
JLG BY JLG
Labatut, Marta
ASSASSINS
LaBelle, Rob
BROKEN TRUST
Labonarska, Halina
PROVINCIAL ACTORS
Labrador, Honey
STRANGE DAYS
Labranche, Erin
CANDYMAN: FAREWELL TO THE FLESH
LaBrecque, Patrick
HEAVYWEIGHTS
Labuda, Marian
ACCUMULATOR 1
Labyrine, Serguei
WINDOW TO PARIS
LaCarruba, Manny
GUMBY: THE MOVIE
LaCause, Stephanie
LORD OF ILLUSIONS
Lacey, Aaron Michael
TWELVE MONKEYS
Lacey, Deborah
DEVIL IN A BLUE DRESS
Lachkar, Jean-Claude
MINA TANNENBAUM
Lachontch, Catherine
INNOCENT LIES
Lackaff, Peter Sebastian
ASSASSINS
Lacoco, Joe
CASINO
Lacoste, Monica
I, THE WORST OF ALL
LaCroix, Brandon
THREE WISHES
LaCroix, Denis
BLACK FOX
LaCroix, Lisa
DANCE ME OUTSIDE
Lacusta, Deb
FORGET PARIS
Lacy, Kelly
JACK-O
Lada
NOT ANGELS BUT ANGELS
Ladania, Tahereh
THROUGH THE OLIVE TREES

Ladd, Jordan
EMBRACE OF THE VAMPIRE
Lady Bunny, The
PARTY GIRL
WIGSTOCK: THE MOVIE
Laes, Vaino
CITY UNPLUGGED
Laffan, Pat
AWFULLY BIG ADVENTURE, AN
Lafferty, Sandra
PROPHECY, THE
LaFitte, Tommy
PIANO LESSON, THE
SUDDEN DEATH
LaFleur, Art
MAN OF THE HOUSE
Lafon, Simon
MINA TANNENBAUM
Lagassa, Bonnie
HOWLING: NEW MOON RISING, THE
Lagassa, Carl
HOWLING: NEW MOON RISING, THE
Lage, Jordan
WATER ENGINE, THE
Lagercrantz, Marika
DREAMING OF RITA
Lagerfelt, Caroline
BYE BYE, LOVE
FATHER OF THE BRIDE PART II
Lagos, Chelsea
WHITE MAN'S BURDEN
Lahti, Christine
HIDEAWAY
Lai Wang
PUSHING HANDS
Lail, Leah
HEAVYWEIGHTS
Laimbeer, Bill
FORGET PARIS
Laine, Raymond
SUDDEN DEATH
Laird, Betty
MY ANTONIA
Lajous, Cmdt. Olivier
GOLDENEYE
Lake, Ricki
SKINNER
Lala, Joe
ZOOMAN
Lally, Brian
MY FAMILY: MI FAMILIA
Lally, Krista
WHILE YOU WERE SLEEPING
Lally, Mick
CIRCLE OF FRIENDS
SECRET OF ROAN INISH, THE
Lam Kwok-Bun
HIGH RISK
Lam, Wayne
MOONLIGHT AND VALENTINO
Lamadris, Rosando
I AM CUBA
Lamar, John
ASSASSINS
Lamarre, Jean
WALKING DEAD, THE
Lamas, Lorenzo
BAD BLOOD
Lamb, Caroline
RESTORATION
Lamb, Letha
TANK GIRL
Lambert, Christopher
HIGHLANDER: THE FINAL DIMENSION
HUNTED, THE
MORTAL KOMBAT
Lambert, Javier
BURNING SEASON, THE

Lambert, Major
CIRCLE OF FRIENDS
Lamberts, Heath
TOM AND HUCK
Lambrecht, Laura
TIE-DIED: ROCK 'N' ROLL'S MOST
DEADICATED FANS
Lamey, Tommy
TOM AND HUCK
Lampert, Zohra
LAST GOOD TIME, THE
Lampley, Oni Faida
MONEY TRAIN
Lancaster, Alandra
SUBSTITUTE WIFE, THE
Land, Kena
CAGED HEAT 3000
Landau, Alexia
KICKING AND SCREAMING
Landau, Steven Hy
JURY DUTY
Landers, Matt
ROSWELL: THE U.F.O. COVER-UP
Landesberg, Steve
CRAZYSITTER, THE
Landey, Clayton
TANK GIRL
Landi, Sal
SILENCE OF THE HAMS
Landis, Bernie
WHILE YOU WERE SLEEPING
Landis, John
SILENCE OF THE HAMS
Lane, Cristy
GORDY
Lane, Diane
JUDGE DREDD
WILD BILL
Lane, Margaret
DEAD MAN WALKING
Lane, Nathan
JEFFREY
Lane, Susan
DOLORES CLAIBORNE
Lang, Archie
ENEMY WITHIN, THE
Lang, Gerard
DECOY
lang, k. d.
TERESA'S TATTOO
Lang, Liz
STEAL BIG, STEAL LITTLE
Lang, Stephen
AMAZING PANDA ADVENTURE, THE
TALL TALE: THE UNBELIEVABLE
ADVENTURES OF PECOS BILL
Lang, Valerie
JEFFERSON IN PARIS
Langdon, Paul Robert
MY FAMILY: MI FAMILIA
Lange, Anne
LEAVING LAS VEGAS
Lange, Hope
JUST CAUSE
Lange, Jack
DECONSTRUCTING SARAH
Lange, Jessica
LOSING ISAIAH
ROB ROY
Lange, Mike
SUDDEN DEATH
Langedijk, Jack
DARKMAN 2: THE RETURN OF DURANT
Langella, Frank
BAD COMPANY
CUTTHROAT ISLAND
DOOMSDAY GUN

Langenbucher, Robert
STEAL BIG, STEAL LITTLE
Langenfeld, Todd A.
DIE HARD WITH A VENGEANCE
Langer, Allison A.J.
GHOST BRIGADE
Langford, Lisa Louise
RECKLESS
Langlet, Louis
MINA TANNENBAUM
Langley, Teresa
BODY STROKES
Langner, Heinz
NEKROMANTIK
Langsdorf, Eva
HOME FOR THE HOLIDAYS
Lanich, Noah
REASON TO BELIEVE, A
Lannon, Emma
CIRCLE OF FRIENDS
Lanoue, Larissa
TANK GIRL
Lanz, Elisabeth
FOR GOD AND COUNTRY
Lanz, Gary
GEORGIA
Lanza, Angela
DESPERADO
PEREZ FAMILY, THE
Lanza, Steve
ROSWELL: THE U.F.O. COVER-UP
LaPaglia, Anthony
BULLETPROOF HEART
EMPIRE RECORDS
Lapaine, Daniel
MURIEL'S WEDDING
Lapaine, Heidi
MURIEL'S WEDDING
Lapchinski, Larissa
SCARLET LETTER, THE
Lapinski, H.
SHORT FILM ABOUT KILLING, A
LaPlante, Mitchell
GOOD DAY TO DIE, A
LAST OF THE DOGMEN
LaPorte, George
HIGHER LEARNING
Lappin, Thoams
RUN OF THE COUNTRY, THE
LaPresle, Kevin
BOYS ON THE SIDE
LaPrevotte, Rene Charles
JADE
Larensca, Vincent
MONEY TRAIN
Larimer, Tony
OUT OF ANNIE'S PAST
Lark, III, Clarence
JUST CAUSE
Larkin, Sheena
DR. JEKYLL & MS. HYDE
Larou, Liz
COSMIC SLOP
Larpin, Micheline
VALLEY OF ABRAHAM, THE
Larriva, Tito
BOYS ON THE SIDE
DESPERADO
Lars, Vincent
PANTHER
Larson, Darrell
STUART SAVES HIS FAMILY
Larson, Edwin
MOSAIC PROJECT, THE
Larson, Liz
DR. JEKYLL & MS. HYDE

Larson, Michael R.
GLASS SHIELD, THE
Larson, Steve
WHITE MAN'S BURDEN
LaScala, David
BIKINI BISTRO
Laskawy, Harris
FATHER OF THE BRIDE PART II
STUART SAVES HIS FAMILY
THINGS TO DO IN DENVER WHEN
YOU'RE DEAD
Laskin, Michael
THREE WISHES
Lasko
NEKROMANTIK
Lassez, Sarah
MALICIOUS
Lathem, Laurie
TIE THAT BINDS, THE
Lathouris, Nico
DEATH IN BRUNSWICK
ONLY THE BRAVE
Latimer, Randy Sue
BLESSING
Latimore, Joseph
AMERICAN PRESIDENT, THE
DEVIL IN A BLUE DRESS
LORD OF ILLUSIONS
OUTBREAK
Latko, Romney
DIRTY MONEY
LaTour, Nick
DON JUAN DEMARCO
Latshaw, Ryan
JACK-O
Lau, Carina
HE'S A WOMAN, SHE'S A MAN
Lau Ching-Wan
EXECUTIONERS
Lau, Damian
EXECUTIONERS
HEROIC TRIO, THE
Lau Lam
PHANTOM LOVER, THE
Laughter, Roy Bush
JOURNEY OF AUGUST KING, THE
Laumeister, Shannah
BRADY BUNCH MOVIE, THE
Laupen, Andrew
CITY OF LOST CHILDREN, THE
Lauren, Ashley Michael
FUN
Lauren, Greg
BATMAN FOREVER
INDICTMENT: THE MCMARTIN TRIAL
Laurence, Ashley
AMERICAN COP
OUTSIDE THE LAW
Laurie, Darcy
HIGHLANDER: THE FINAL DIMENSION
Laurie, Hugh
SENSE AND SENSIBILITY
Laurie, Piper
CROSSING GUARD, THE
Lauter, Ed
GIRL IN THE CADILLAC
LEAVING LAS VEGAS
Lavanant, Dominique
GROSSE FATIGUE
Lavand, Dawn
LAST OF THE DOGMEN
Laverack, Tom
RIVER OF GRASS
LaVetta, Robert
BAD BLOOD
Lavie, Efrat
AMERICAN PRESIDENT, THE

Law, Phyllida
BEFORE THE RAIN
Law, Salleyanne
GLORY BOYS, THE
Lawhorn, John
FLUKE
Lawley, Yvonne
DEATH IN BRUNSWICK
Lawlor, Sean
BRAVEHEART
Lawner, Damon
COPYCAT
Lawon, Robert
RIVER OF GRASS
Lawrence, Andrew
WHITE MAN'S BURDEN
Lawrence, Joey
GOOFY MOVIE, A
Lawrence, Lisa
REASON TO BELIEVE, A
Lawrence, Marjie
LAMB
Lawrence, Mark Christopher
CRIMSON TIDE
Lawrence, Martin
BAD BOYS
Lawrence, Tom
NICK OF TIME
Lawsen, N.
TIE-DIED: ROCK 'N' ROLL'S MOST
DEADICATED FANS
Lawson, Cheryl
VIRTUOSITY
Lawson, Eric
TALL TALE: THE UNBELIEVABLE
ADVENTURES OF PECOS BILL
Lazar, Ava
IN THE DEEP WOODS
LaZar, John
ATTACK OF THE 60-FOOT CENTERFOLD
Lazar, Paul
BUFFALO GIRLS
Le Berre, Sandrine
BLUE VILLA, THE
Le Brun, Robert
BODY SHOT
Le Minh Tien
OPERATION DUMBO DROP
Lea, Nicholas
BAD COMPANY
Leachman, Cloris
DOUBLE, DOUBLE, TOIL AND TROUBLE
NOW AND THEN
Lead, Marianna
LITTLE ODESSA
Leader, Dave
CONVICT COWBOY
Leaf, David
BRIAN WILSON: I JUST WASN'T MADE
FOR THESE TIMES
Leaf, Richard
BRAVEHEART
CUTTHROAT ISLAND
Leahy, Jonathon
DALLAS DOLL
Leal, Pete
MY FAMILY: MI FAMILIA
Leander, Thomas R.
WAITING TO EXHALE
Leard, Jim
ABDUCTED 2: THE REUNION
Learning, Carren
GOLD DIGGERS: THE SECRET OF BEAR
MOUNTAIN
Leary, David
SAFE PASSAGE
Leary, Denis
OPERATION DUMBO DROP

Leatche, Alexis
  FACES OF WOMEN
Leavitt, David
  CASINO
LeBeau, Mikey
  LORD OF ILLUSIONS
LeBeau, Owen
  LAKOTA WOMAN: SIEGE AT WOUNDED
    KNEE
Leblanc, Carl
  CANDYMAN: FAREWELL TO THE FLESH
Leblanc, Luc
  LOVE AND HUMAN REMAINS
LeBlanc, Matt
  GHOST BRIGADE
Lebras, Joel
  INNOCENT LIES
Lebron, Juan Manuel
  ASSASSINS
Lebron, Teresa
  PARTY GIRL
Lebrun, Gerard
  PIGALLE
LeCavalier, Louise
  STRANGE DAYS
Lecesne, James
  HOME FOR THE HOLIDAYS
Lechner, Melissa
  S.F.W.
Leckner, Brian
  MURDER IN THE FIRST
LeClair, John
  FAR FROM HOME: THE ADVENTURES OF
    YELLOW DOG
Leclerc, Agathe
  CLEAN, SHAVEN
Ledbetter, Melinda
  BRIAN WILSON: I JUST WASN'T MADE
    FOR THESE TIMES
Leduc, Richard
  SERIOUS ABOUT PLEASURE
Lee, Casey
  BIG GREEN, THE
Lee Chong-Lin
  BLUE VILLA, THE
Lee, Conan
  NEW YORK COP
Lee, Darren
  HACKERS
Lee, Diane
  DON JUAN DEMARCO
Lee, Elaine
  DALLAS DOLL
  SUM OF US, THE
Lee, Eugene
  O.J. SIMPSON STORY, THE
Lee, Jae Woo
  OUTBREAK
Lee, James Oscar
  TALL TALE: THE UNBELIEVABLE
    ADVENTURES OF PECOS BILL
Lee, Jason
  MALLRATS
Lee, Jeamin
  MURIEL'S WEDDING
Lee Jellyhead & the Ballet Hooligans
  FUNNY BONES
Lee, Jesse
  BRADY BUNCH MOVIE, THE
  SAFE PASSAGE
Lee, Joie
  LOSING ISAIAH
Lee, Jon-Claire
  MURIEL'S WEDDING
Lee, Jonah Ming
  KILIAN'S CHRONICLE
Lee, Jr., Harvey E.
  HOW TO MAKE AN AMERICAN QUILT

Lee, Larry A.
  BATMAN FOREVER
Lee, Melody
  WINGS OF HONNEAMISE: ROYAL SPACE
    FORCE
Lee, Michael
  OPERATION DUMBO DROP
Lee, Robert
  DALLAS DOLL
  MURDER IN THE FIRST
Lee, Ruta
  FUNNY BONES
Lee, Sophie
  MURIEL'S WEDDING
Lee, Spike
  CLOCKERS
Lee, Stan
  MALLRATS
Lee, Stephen
  ME AND THE MOB
Lee, Taryn
  DANGER OF LOVE
Lee, Wendee
  BAREFOOT GEN
Lee, Wendolyn
  VILLAGE OF THE DAMNED
Leeds, Andrew Harrison
  MAJOR PAYNE
Leeds, Karen
  JUST CAUSE
Leeds, Sue-Ann
  CLASS OF '61
Leef
  TIE-DIED: ROCK 'N' ROLL'S MOST
    DEADICATED FANS
Leese, Sarah S.
  SPECIES
Lefebvre, Stephane
  DR. JEKYLL & MS. HYDE
LeFevour, Rick
  SUDDEN DEATH
Leffers, Morten Rotne
  KINGDOM, THE
Legend, Johnny
  CHILDREN OF THE CORN III: URBAN
    HARVEST
LeGros, James
  DESTINY TURNS ON THE RADIO
  LIVING IN OBLIVION
  PANTHER
  SAFE
Leguizamo, John
  PYROMANIAC'S LOVE STORY, A
  TO WONG FOO, THANKS FOR
    EVERYTHING! JULIE NEWMAR
Lehmann, Sven
  PROMISE, THE
Lehr, John
  KICKING AND SCREAMING
Lehto, Fred
  STEAL BIG, STEAL LITTLE
Leibowitch, Julie
  FRENCH KISS
Leigh, Brenda
  COMPANION, THE
Leigh, Cassandra
  CAGED HEAT 3000
Leigh, Jennifer Jason
  DOLORES CLAIBORNE
  GEORGIA
Leigh, Taylor
  CAGED HEARTS
Leipold, Patricia
  NEKROMANTIK
Leiris, Magali
  JEFFERSON IN PARIS
Leisure, David
  BRADY BUNCH MOVIE, THE

Leland, Brad
  UNDERNEATH, THE
Lelouch, Salome
  LES MISERABLES
Lembeck, Helaine
  O.J. SIMPSON STORY, THE
Lemberger, Richard B.
  INDICTMENT: THE MCMARTIN TRIAL
Lemercier, Valeria
  SABRINA
Lemmon, Jack
  GRUMPIER OLD MEN
Lemmons, Kasi
  ZOOMAN
Lemole, Samantha
  CURE, THE
Lemore, George
  CANDYMAN: FAREWELL TO THE FLESH
Lenander, Soren
  KINGDOM, THE
Lengyel, Ferenc
  CITIZEN X
Lennix, Harry
  CLOCKERS
Lennon, Jarrett
  O.J. SIMPSON STORY, THE
Lennon, Julian
  LEAVING LAS VEGAS
Lennox, Kai
  CRIMSON TIDE
  DEVIL IN A BLUE DRESS
Lent, Steve
  LIE DOWN WITH DOGS
Lenthall, David
  EMPIRE RECORDS
Lentini, Susan
  JURY DUTY
Leo, Arnold
  LAST SUMMER IN THE HAMPTONS
Leo, Melissa
  LAST SUMMER IN THE HAMPTONS
Leon
  WAITING TO EXHALE
Leonard, Punky
  SOMETHING TO TALK ABOUT
Leonard, Robert Sean
  SAFE PASSAGE
Leonard, Sherlyn
  DANGEROUS, THE
Leoni, Tea
  BAD BOYS
Leontiev, Avangard
  BURNT BY THE SUN
Leopardi, Chauncey
  BIG GREEN, THE
  CASPER
  HOUSEGUEST
  SAFE
Leotard, Philippe
  LES MISERABLES
LePere, Trevie Jean
  FRIENDS
Leplat, Ted
  MANGLER, THE
Leporarti, Dominic
  TWO BITS
Lepucki, Robert
  PLAY TIME
Leras, Anibal O.
  ASSASSINS
Lerner, Ken
  BODILY HARM
Lerner, Michael
  GIRL IN THE CADILLAC
  PYROMANIAC'S LOVE STORY, A
Lerner, Ute Maria
  NOBODY LOVES ME

Lerner-Ellis, Daniel
BILLY MADISON
Lerner-Ellis, Jordan
BILLY MADISON
Leroux, Maxime
SON OF THE SHARK, THE
LeRoy, Gloria
BAD BLOOD
LeRoy, Zoaunne
UNSTRUNG HEROES
LeSardo, Robert
WATERWORLD
Lescher, Matt
PREHYSTERIA! 3
Lesene, Charles E.
DEAD PRESIDENTS
Lesniak, Patti
HOUSEGUEST
Lesser, Robert
ACROSS THE MOON
STEAL BIG, STEAL LITTLE
Lessing, Lena
INNOCENT, THE
Lester, Tom
GORDY
Lestyan, Katalin
CITIZEN X
Lesure, James
CRIMSON TIDE
O.J. SIMPSON STORY, THE
Letheren, Mark
RESTORATION
Leto, Jared
HOW TO MAKE AN AMERICAN QUILT
Lett, Gordon
MUTANT SPECIES
Lett, Sean
BILLY MADISON
Letts, Dennis
FRANK & JESSE
Leung Chiu-Wai, Tony
ASHES OF TIME
Leung, Tony
ASHES OF TIME
RETURN OF THE GOD OF GAMBLERS
Leupp, Clinton
TO WONG FOO, THANKS FOR
EVERYTHING! JULIE NEWMAR
Leutgeb, Gerhard
FOR GOD AND COUNTRY
Levand, Dawn
LAKOTA WOMAN: SIEGE AT WOUNDED
KNEE
Leventon, Annabel
BUSINESS AFFAIR, A
Lever, Huggy
JUDGE DREDD
Levertt, Candace Dian
NEW YORK COP
Levi, Nino
BEFORE THE RAIN
Levien, Philip
THREE WISHES
Levine, Allison
GRUMPIER OLD MEN
Levine, Ilana
ROOMMATES
Levine, Jerry
SWIMMING WITH SHARKS
Levine, Robin
RHYTHM THIEF
Levine, Ted
GEORGIA
HEAT
MANGLER, THE
Levinson, Brian
FATHER AND SCOUT

Levitt, Alice
CLEAN, SHAVEN
Levry, Carmen
FACES OF WOMEN
Levy, Eugene
FATHER OF THE BRIDE PART II
KURT VONNEGUT'S HARRISON
BERGERON
Levy, Frances
ME AND THE MOB
Levy, Philip
ACROSS THE SEA OF TIME: NEW YORK
3D
Lew, James
BALLISTIC
RED SUN RISING
Lewgoy, Jose
BOCA
Lewis, Abby
ACROSS THE SEA OF TIME: NEW YORK
3D
Lewis, Alan Edward
TO DIE FOR
Lewis, B'nard
HOUSEGUEST
Lewis, Charlotte
DECOY
EMBRACE OF THE VAMPIRE
Lewis, Fred
DANGEROUS, THE
Lewis, Gary
SHALLOW GRAVE
Lewis, Gilbert
DON JUAN DEMARCO
Lewis, Ginger
UNDER SIEGE 2: DARK TERRITORY
Lewis, Jenifer
DEAD PRESIDENTS
DECONSTRUCTING SARAH
PANTHER
Lewis, Jerry
ARIZONA DREAM
FUNNY BONES
Lewis, Juliette
BASKETBALL DIARIES, THE
STRANGE DAYS
TOO YOUNG TO DIE?
Lewis, Mitch
RIVER OF GRASS
Lewis, Oliver
FIRST KNIGHT
Lewis, Richard
DANGER OF LOVE
LEAVING LAS VEGAS
Lewis, Roy
TOMMY BOY
Leymergie, William
LES MISERABLES
Leyne, Aisling
FRANKIE STARLIGHT
Leyshon, Glynis
DOUBLE, DOUBLE, TOIL AND TROUBLE
Lezak, Steven
RIVER OF GRASS
Lhermitte, Thierry
AUGUSTIN
GROSSE FATIGUE
Li Baotian
SHANGHAI TRIAD
Li, Blanca
PIGALLE
Li Guiming
ERMO
Li Hu
DAY THE SUN TURNED COLD, THE
Li Lai
BLUE VILLA, THE

Li Lik-Chee
HIGH RISK
Li Lu
MOVING THE MOUNTAIN
Li Xuejian
SHANGHAI TRIAD
Li Yong'gui
ERMO
Li Yushen
RED FIRECRACKER, GREEN
FIRECRACKER
Li Zhaoji
HEROIC TRIO, THE
Lian Shuliang
SHANGHAI TRIAD
Liban, Mia
NINE MONTHS
Libby, Brian
HEAT
Liberati, Lisa
SPECIES
Liberato, Mark
DARK DEALER
Liberty, Richard
JUST CAUSE
Lichtefeld, Peter
DEADLY MARIA
Licon, Jeffrey
BURNING SEASON, THE
Lidstone, Nicholas
BABE
Liebeler, Joanne K.
GLASS SHIELD, THE
Lieber, Paul
ACROSS THE MOON
Lifford, Tina
BABE
Light, Allan
NOSTRADAMUS KID, THE
Lightning, Crystle
3 NINJAS KNUCKLE UP
Lightstone, Gillian
FUN
Lightstone, Jonathan
FUN
Ligosh, Max
HACKERS
Lill, Dennis
RICHARD III
Lillard, Matthew
HACKERS
MAD LOVE
Lilley, Clay
BIGFOOT: THE UNFORGETTABLE
ENCOUNTER
Lilley, Valerie
PRIEST
Lima, Kevin
GOOFY MOVIE, A
Limbaugh, Rush
FORGET PARIS
Limpo, Wilson
DANGEROUS MINDS
Lin, Brigitte
ASHES OF TIME
Lin, Ge-Ying
SHAO LIN POPEYE
Lin, Maya
MAYA LIN: A STRONG CLEAR VISION
Linares, Aida
CLUELESS
Linaweaver, Brad
ATTACK OF THE 60-FOOT CENTERFOLD
Lincoln, Scott
DEVIL IN A BLUE DRESS
Lindberg, Chad
BORN TO BE WILD

Lindeman, Penelope
BAR GIRLS
Lindenmuth, Kevin J.
VAMPIRES AND OTHER STEREOTYPES
Linderholm, Eva
SABRINA
Lindfors, Viveca
LAST SUMMER IN THE HAMPTONS
Lindley, Audra
SUDDEN DEATH
Lindo, Delroy
CLOCKERS
GET SHORTY
Lindsay, Mary
DALLAS DOLL
Lindsey, Gary
O.J. SIMPSON STORY, THE
Lindsey, Joseph
WALK IN THE CLOUDS, A
Linfante, Lee Anne
ME AND THE MOB
Ling, Bai
NIXON
Ling, Bal
DEAD FUNNY
Linke, Jacqueline
MURIEL'S WEDDING
Linklater, Richard
UNDERNEATH, THE
Linley, Chad
FRANK & JESSE
Linn, Rex
CUTTHROAT ISLAND
Linney, Laura
CLASS OF '61
CONGO
Lino, Sergio
DIRTY MONEY
Linou, Christos
DEATH IN BRUNSWICK
Lion, June
JUMANJI
Lionel, Evan
LOSING ISAIAH
Liotta, Ray
OPERATION DUMBO DROP
Lipe, Dan
BRADY BUNCH MOVIE, THE
Lipinski, Eugene
NEVER TALK TO STRANGERS
Lippa, Louis
TWELVE MONKEYS
TWO BITS
Lipscombe, Jesse
GOOD DAY TO DIE, A
Lipshultz, Andrew
APOLLO 13
Lipskin, Mike
GREAT DAY IN HARLEM, A
Lipton, Robert
SECRETARY, THE
Lisi, Joe
JERKY BOYS: THE MOVIE, THE
KISS OF DEATH
SAFE PASSAGE
Liska, Stephen
ASSASSINS
Listenbee, Ann
BAR GIRLS
Lister, Jr., Tiny
DON JUAN DEMARCO
FRIDAY
THINGS TO DO IN DENVER WHEN
YOU'RE DEAD
Litefoot
INDIAN IN THE CUPBOARD, THE
Lithgow, John
REDWOOD CURTAIN

Little, Archie
LAKOTA WOMAN: SIEGE AT WOUNDED
KNEE
Little, Kim
YOUNGER & YOUNGER
Little, Michelle
APOLLO 13
Little Sky, Dawn
LAKOTA WOMAN: SIEGE AT WOUNDED
KNEE
Littman, Greg
FEAR, THE
Liu, Carina
ASHES OF TIME
Liu, Emily
PUSHING HANDS
Liu, Harrison
MOONLIGHT AND VALENTINO
Liu Jiang
SHANGHAI TRIAD
Liu Peiqi
ERMO
Lively, Ernie
MY FAMILY: MI FAMILIA
Lively, Jr., Clifton
LIE DOWN WITH DOGS
Lively, Robert
INNOCENT, THE
Lively, Robyn
DREAM A LITTLE DREAM 2
Lively, Scott
BALLOT MEASURE 9
Livingston, Barry
O.J. SIMPSON STORY, THE
Livingston, Benjamin
DRACULA: DEAD AND LOVING IT
Livingston, John
MY ANTONIA
NET, THE
Livingston, Paul
BABE
Livingston, Stanley
ATTACK OF THE 60-FOOT CENTERFOLD
LL Cool J
OUT OF SYNC
Llewellyn, Roger
PERSUASION
Llewelyn, Desmond
GOLDENEYE
Lloyd, Christopher
RENT-A-KID
THINGS TO DO IN DENVER WHEN
YOU'RE DEAD
Lloyd, Cory
SUBSTITUTE WIFE, THE
Lloyd, Emily Ann
APOLLO 13
HOME FOR THE HOLIDAYS
Lloyd, Jessica
JEFFERSON IN PARIS
Lloyd, John Bedford
FAIR GAME
NIXON
Lloyd, Marie
NOSTRADAMUS KID, THE
Lo Bianco, Tony
ASCENT, THE
NIXON
Lo, Janet
TO DIE FOR
Lo Ka-ying
HE'S A WOMAN, SHE'S A MAN
Lo Verso, Enrico
FARINELLI
LAMERICA
Loch, Chuck
MOSAIC PROJECT, THE

Lochran, Derek Mark
DRACULA: DEAD AND LOVING IT
Locke, Eddie
GREAT DAY IN HARLEM, A
Locke, Philip
OTHELLO
Lockmuller, Brenda
JUMANJI
Lockwood, Dean
FAR FROM HOME: THE ADVENTURES OF
YELLOW DOG
Lockyer, Thomas
CUTTHROAT ISLAND
Lodge, David
GLASS SHIELD, THE
Loewi, Fiona
NATIONAL LAMPOON'S SENIOR TRIP
Loftin, Lennie
AMATEUR
QUICK AND THE DEAD, THE
SEVEN
Loftus, John
JADE
Logan, George
COSMIC SLOP
Loggia, Robert
COLDBLOODED
Logue, Donal
CREW, THE
MIAMI RHAPSODY
3 NINJAS KNUCKLE UP
Lohmeyer, Peter
EROTIQUE
Lohnes, Peter
BETTER OFF DEAD
Loiano, Luisa
MAMMA ROMA
Lomax, David
NEW YORK COP
Lombard, Andre
FRIENDS
Lombardi, Christy
LOSING ISAIAH
Lombardi, Louis
USUAL SUSPECTS, THE
Lombardi, Paola
MONTH BY THE LAKE, A
Lombardi, Paolo
PURE FORMALITY, A
London, Damian
TWOGETHER
London, Jason
SAFE PASSAGE
TO WONG FOO, THANKS FOR
EVERYTHING! JULIE NEWMAR
London, Jeremy
BABYSITTER, THE
MALLRATS
London, Tony
HEAVEN'S A DRAG
Londsdale-Smith, Michelle
IT TAKES TWO
Lone, John
HUNTED, THE
Long, Amy
DEAD MAN WALKING
Long, Bill
THINGS TO DO IN DENVER WHEN
YOU'RE DEAD
Long, Matthew
BABE
Long Nguyen
OPERATION DUMBO DROP
Long, Nia
FRIDAY
Long, Shelley
BRADY BUNCH MOVIE, THE

Long, Tom
COUNTRY LIFE
Long, Trevor
DON JUAN DEMARCO
Long, Valerie
HOUSEGUEST
Longley, Victoria
DALLAS DOLL
Longman, Mike
DEAD MAN WALKING
Longmore, Paul
WHEN BILLY BROKE HIS HEAD ... AND
OTHER TALES OF WONDER
Longo, Tony
HOUSEGUEST
Longstreth, Emily
TOO YOUNG TO DIE?
Lonsdale, Michael
JEFFERSON IN PARIS
Lonsdale, Michel
SERIOUS ABOUT PLEASURE
Looney, Peter
OUTBREAK
Lopata, Dean
BRAVEHEART
Lopez, Alfredo
NET, THE
Lopez, Carmen
FAIR GAME
Lopez, Irene Olga
SHOWGIRLS
Lopez, Jennifer
MONEY TRAIN
MY FAMILY: MI FAMILIA
Lopez, John
MUTANT SPECIES
Lopez, Josefina
INDICTMENT: THE MCMARTIN TRIAL
Lopez, Jr., George
MY FAMILY: MI FAMILIA
Lopez, Lorena
I, THE WORST OF ALL
Lopez, Sal
BLUE TIGER
Lopez, Seidy
MY FAMILY: MI FAMILIA
Lopez, Tony
I AM CUBA
Lopez-Dawson, Kamala
EROTIQUE
Lorant, Andre
IT TAKES TWO
Lorca, Isabel
NICK OF TIME
Lord, James
AUGUSTIN
Lord, Stephen
JUDGE DREDD
Lords, Traci
SKINNER
VIRTUOSITY
Lorea, Tony
ATTACK OF THE 60-FOOT CENTERFOLD
Loren, Eric
HACKERS
Loren, Sophia
GRUMPIER OLD MEN
Lorenz, Daktari
NEKROMANTIK
Loreque, Kevin
VIRTUOSITY
Lorey, Dean
MAJOR PAYNE
Lorillard, Elaine
GREAT DAY IN HARLEM, A
Lorinz, James
JERKY BOYS: THE MOVIE, THE
ME AND THE MOB

Lorinz, Johnny
ME AND THE MOB
Lott, Kurt
NUMBER ONE FAN
Lotz, Jack
NADJA
Lou Bowlegged
COSMIC SLOP
Loughridge, Graham
CENTURY
Loughridge, Gregg
DANGER OF LOVE
Loughrin, Tim
PANTHER
Louiso, Todd
APOLLO 13
Lounibos, Tim
EROTIQUE
Loury, Larry
BRIDGES OF MADISON COUNTY, THE
Love, Faizon
FRIDAY
Love, Ken
WAITING TO EXHALE
Love, Patti
AWFULLY BIG ADVENTURE, AN
BUSINESS AFFAIR, A
Love, Pee Wee
CLOCKERS
RADIO INSIDE
Lovett, Bob
DALLAS DOLL
Lovett, Marcus
JEFFREY
Lovett, Marjorie
STUART SAVES HIS FAMILY
Low, Frances
SHALLOW GRAVE
Low, Maggie
POSTCARDS FROM AMERICA
Lowe, Alan
HEAVEN'S A DRAG
Lowe, Jo-Jo
SABRINA
Lowe, John Alexander
CONGO
Lowe, Rob
FIRST DEGREE
FRANK & JESSE
Lowell, Carey
LEAVING LAS VEGAS
Lowens, Curt
OPERATION INTERCEPT
Lowensohn, Elina
AMATEUR
MY ANTONIA
NADJA
Lowry, Paige
OUT OF ANNIE'S PAST
Lowther, T.J.
AVENGING ANGEL
MAD LOVE
Lozano, Jim
HOWLING: NEW MOON RISING, THE
Lozano, John
LOVE AND HUMAN REMAINS
Lozano, Vince
FATHER OF THE BRIDE PART II
Lozoff, Josh
CLUELESS
Lu Dou
SHANGHAI TRIAD
Lu Hui
RED FIRECRACKER, GREEN
FIRECRACKER
Lubas, Randy
COVER STORY

Lubaszenko, Olaf
SHORT FILM ABOUT LOVE, A
Lubran, Kathryn
THREE WISHES
Lubran, Tiffany
THREE WISHES
Lucas, Joshua
CLASS OF '61
Lucas, Peter
CLEAN, SHAVEN
Lucci, Gino
LAST GOOD TIME, THE
Luce, Philippa
RESTORATION
Lucia, Charles
TANK GIRL
Luciano, Michael
ME AND THE MOB
Lucien, Joseph
CITY OF LOST CHILDREN, THE
Lucius, Andreas
GORILLA BATHES AT NOON
Lucy, Tom
FIRST KNIGHT
Ludwig, Brian
DECOY
Luehne, Karen
LOSING ISAIAH
Luessenhop, John
DIRTY MONEY
Luft, K.
SHORT FILM ABOUT KILLING, A
Luick, Butch
SUDDEN DEATH
Lujan, Che
DESTINY TURNS ON THE RADIO
Lujan, Crystal
LORD OF ILLUSIONS
Lukaszewicz, Olgierd
SHORT FILM ABOUT KILLING, A
WOMAN AT WAR, A
Luke, Jayne
SPECIES
Lukyanenko, Anatoli
AMERICAN COP
Lum, Alvin
SABRINA
Lumadue, Roy
ART FOR TEACHERS OF CHILDREN
Lumley, Joanna
INNOCENT LIES
Lumsden, Richard
SENSE AND SENSIBILITY
Lund, Jordan
AMERICAN PRESIDENT, THE
SPECIES
Lunden, Joan
FREE WILLY 2: THE ADVENTURE HOME
Lundgren, Dolph
JOHNNY MNEMONIC
PENTATHLON
Lundsgaard, Augusta
JUST CAUSE
Lundt, Harald
NEKROMANTIK
Luneau-Lipton, Christine
SABRINA
Lung, Tong
HUNTED, THE
Lunoe, Lars
KINGDOM, THE
Luong, Ham-Chau
CITY OF LOST CHILDREN, THE
Lupien, Tabitha
RENT-A-KID
Lupiere, Marz
DEATH IN BRUNSWICK

LuPone, Patti
WATER ENGINE, THE
Lupone, Robert
DEAD PRESIDENTS
Lupton, John
BODY SHOT
Lush
TIE-DIED: ROCK 'N' ROLL'S MOST
DEADICATED FANS
Lust, Andreas
FOR GOD AND COUNTRY
Lustig, Aaron
BOYS ON THE SIDE
SCANNERS: THE SHOWDOWN
STUART SAVES HIS FAMILY
Lutes, Eric
NEW YORK COP
Lutsepp, Ain
CITY UNPLUGGED
Luttrell, Erica
MOONLIGHT AND VALENTINO
Luty, Adrian
PRIEST
Lutz, Adelle
BEYOND RANGOON
DEAD FUNNY
Lutz, Linda
SILENCE OF THE HAMS
Luv, Ram
COVER STORY
Luz, Franc
DON JUAN DEMARCO
Luzion, Rudy
WINGS OF HONNEAMISE: ROYAL SPACE
FORCE
Ly Thai Dung
TRAPS
Lyall, Susan
HOME FOR THE HOLIDAYS
Lydon, Gary
AILSA
Lynch, Barry
ENEMY WITHIN, THE
PENTATHLON
Lynch, Colin Patrick
INDICTMENT: THE MCMARTIN TRIAL
Lynch, David
NADJA
Lynch, John
CURE, THE
SECRET OF ROAN INISH, THE
Lynch, Kelly
VIRTUOSITY
WHITE MAN'S BURDEN
Lynch, Susan
SECRET OF ROAN INISH, THE
Lynde, Janice
BIGFOOT: THE UNFORGETTABLE
ENCOUNTER
Lynn
JUPITER'S WIFE
Lynn, Chelsea
FATHER OF THE BRIDE PART II
Lyon, Liese
BEFORE SUNRISE
Lyons, James
POSTCARDS FROM AMERICA
SAFE
Lyons, Jill
WINGS OF HONNEAMISE: ROYAL SPACE
FORCE
Lyons, Phyllis
BRIDGES OF MADISON COUNTY, THE
Lypsinka
WIGSTOCK: THE MOVIE
Lyster, Maureen
CIRCLE OF FRIENDS

Lythgow, Gene
TIE THAT BINDS, THE
USUAL SUSPECTS, THE
M'Cormac, Frederick
GREAT ELEPHANT ESCAPE, THE
M'Saidie, Fackry
CITY OF LOST CHILDREN, THE
M., Beatrice
NEKROMANTIK
Ma Jingwu
DAY THE SUN TURNED COLD, THE
Mabius, Eric
JOURNEY OF AUGUST KING, THE
Mabohi, Maphiki
FRIENDS
Mabon, Bonnie
BALLOT MEASURE 9
Mabon, Lon
BALLOT MEASURE 9
Mabuya, Noaxie
FRIENDS
Mac, Bernie
FRIDAY
WALKING DEAD, THE
Mac Van Nam
OPERATION DUMBO DROP
Macabre, J.B.
VAMPIRES AND OTHER STEREOTYPES
Macaluso, Dee
POWDER
Macaulay, Marc
BAD BOYS
FAIR GAME
Maccone, Ronald
CASINO
MacDonald, David Alan
SHALLOW GRAVE
MacDonald, James G.
ROSWELL: THE U.F.O. COVER-UP
MacDonald, Jennifer
BAD BLOOD
CLEAN, SHAVEN
MacDonald, Karen
CLEAN, SHAVEN
MacDonald, Kenneth A.
SABRINA
MacDonald, Norm
BILLY MADISON
MacDonald, Ryan
ENEMY WITHIN, THE
MacDonald, Sandy
DOLORES CLAIBORNE
MacDonald, Scott
3 NINJAS KNUCKLE UP
MacDonald, Tony
HEAVEN'S A DRAG
MacDougall, Martin
DEATH MACHINE
MacDowell, Andie
UNSTRUNG HEROES
MacDuff, Janet
GUMBY: THE MOVIE
Mace, Cynthia
STEAL BIG, STEAL LITTLE
Machalica, Piotr
SHORT FILM ABOUT LOVE, A
Maci, Alejandro
I, THE WORST OF ALL
Maciejewski, M.
SHORT FILM ABOUT KILLING, A
MacInnes, Angus
JUDGE DREDD
MacIntyre, David
BETTER OFF DEAD
BORN TO BE WILD
MacIvor, Daniel
ECLIPSE

Mack, Bob
SEVEN
Mack, Bryce
MALLRATS
Mack, Craig
SHOW, THE
Mack, Gene
IN THE MOUTH OF MADNESS
JOHNNY MNEMONIC
PYROMANIAC'S LOVE STORY, A
Mack, Mannie
RIVER OF GRASS
Mack, Shelton
CONGO
Mackay, Denis
DALLAS DOLL
MacKay, Michael Reid
ACE VENTURA: WHEN NATURE CALLS
Mackay, Michael Reid
JURY DUTY
MacKay, Michael Reid
SEVEN
MacKenzie, Evan
SCANNERS: THE SHOWDOWN
MacKenzie, J.C.
CLOCKERS
MacKenzie, Peter
NICK OF TIME
TOM AND HUCK
Mackenzie, Phillip
CIRCUMSTANCES UNKNOWN
Mackey, Dana
NICK OF TIME
Mackey, Karl
ROOMMATES
MacKinnon, Nadine
TO DIE FOR
Mackintosh, Steven
RETURN OF THE NATIVE, THE
Macklin, Albert
JEFFREY
MacLachlan, Kyle
ROSWELL: THE U.F.O. COVER-UP
SHOWGIRLS
Macleod, Mary
RESTORATION
MacMillian, Hec
BABE
MacNicol, Peter
DRACULA: DEAD AND LOVING IT
ROSWELL: THE U.F.O. COVER-UP
Macon, Peter
WORLD AND TIME ENOUGH
MacQueen, Melanie
TIE THAT BINDS, THE
Macrae, Liz
HIGHLANDER: THE FINAL DIMENSION
MacRae, Michael
BETTER OFF DEAD
BORN TO BE WILD
DANGER OF LOVE
Macy, Bill
MURDER IN THE FIRST
Macy, William H.
EVOLVER
WATER ENGINE, THE
Madame Gonzales
MINA TANNENBAUM
Madio, James
BASKETBALL DIARIES, THE
Madison, Mark W.
MAJOR PAYNE
Madoka, Svenwara
NAKED KILLER
Madonna
BLUE IN THE FACE
UNZIPPED

Madsen, Michael
FREE WILLY 2: THE ADVENTURE HOME
SPECIES
Madsen, Virginia
BITTER VENGEANCE
BLUE TIGER
PROPHECY, THE
Madueno, Theo
CITY OF LOST CHILDREN, THE
Madzirov, Igor
BEFORE THE RAIN
Madzounian, Ara
RADIO INSIDE
Maertinelli, Sonia
MONTH BY THE LAKE, A
Maes, Tova
KINGDOM, THE
Maeser, Jean
DEADLY MARIA
Maffei, Joe
MALICIOUS
Maffia, Roma
NICK OF TIME
Mageoy, Yuri
LORD OF ILLUSIONS
Mager, Monika
CITY UNPLUGGED
Magill, John
RECKLESS
Magimo, Michael
TIE-DIED: ROCK 'N' ROLL'S MOST
DEADICATED FANS
Magnani, Anna
MAMMA ROMA
Magnuson, Ann
TANK GIRL
Maguire, George
MURDER IN THE FIRST
Maguire, Tobey
EMPIRE RECORDS
S.F.W.
Mah, Johnny
DOUBLE HAPPINESS
Mahaffey, Valerie
NATIONAL LAMPOON'S SENIOR TRIP
Mahan, Shane
TANK GIRL
Mahar, Dan
DANGER OF LOVE
Maher, Joseph
BULLETPROOF HEART
Maher, Louise
CIRCLE OF FRIENDS
Mahile, Veronique
FACES OF WOMEN
Mahmud-Bey, Shiek
KISS OF DEATH
Mahon, Christy
RUN OF THE COUNTRY, THE
Mahon, John
AMERICAN PRESIDENT, THE
ROSWELL: THE U.F.O. COVER-UP
Mahon, Michael C.
INDICTMENT: THE MCMARTIN TRIAL
Mahoney, John
AMERICAN PRESIDENT, THE
WATER ENGINE, THE
Maillet, Christian
BLUE VILLA, THE
Maina, Khunni Lal
BANDIT QUEEN
Maini, Al
BILLY MADISON
Maislen, Stephanie
WALK IN THE CLOUDS, A
Maite, Fatia
WILD REEDS

Maitre, Christophe
WILD REEDS
Maitre, Mark
TANK GIRL
Majer, Peter
GOLDENEYE
Majerle, Dan
FORGET PARIS
Majorino, Tina
WATERWORLD
Majumdar, Sambitendu Dutt
STRANGER, THE
Makaj, Steve
GOLD DIGGERS: THE SECRET OF BEAR
MOUNTAIN
Makeeva, Ludmilla
MUTE WITNESS
Makhene, Ramolao
CRY, THE BELOVED COUNTRY
Makhov, Viktor
SPITFIRE
Mako
HIGHLANDER: THE FINAL DIMENSION
RED SUN RISING
Maksut, Dzemail
BEFORE THE RAIN
Malahide, Patrick
CUTTHROAT ISLAND
Malang
CONGO
Malaro, Kevin
INDIAN IN THE CUPBOARD, THE
INDICTMENT: THE MCMARTIN TRIAL
Maldonade, Angele
JUST CAUSE
Malet, Arthur
LITTLE PRINCESS, A
Malick, Wendie
AMERICAN PRESIDENT, THE
Malicki-Sanchez, Kerman
BOULEVARD
Malik, Art
KID IN KING ARTHUR'S COURT, A
Malina, Joshua
AMERICAN PRESIDENT, THE
SEPARATE LIVES
Malinbaum, Felix
JEFFERSON IN PARIS
Malinger, Ross
BYE BYE, LOVE
SUDDEN DEATH
Malkin, Beni
INDIAN IN THE CUPBOARD, THE
Malkovich, John
CONVENT, THE
Mallet, Odile
CITY OF LOST CHILDREN, THE
Malloy, David "Skippy"
TOMMY BOY
Malloy, Matt
ACROSS THE SEA OF TIME: NEW YORK
3D
Malmuth, Bruce
PENTATHLON
Malnik, Shareef
JUST CAUSE
Maloles, Pola
HIGHER LEARNING
Maloncon, Gary
BIGFOOT: THE UNFORGETTABLE
ENCOUNTER
FORGET PARIS
Maloney, Coleen
TIE THAT BINDS, THE
Maloney, Michael
OTHELLO
Maloney, Peter
JEFFREY

Malota, Michael
DON JUAN DEMARCO
Malrait, Gaetan
MINA TANNENBAUM
Mamadou, Niasse N.
TO WONG FOO, THANKS FOR
EVERYTHING! JULIE NEWMAR
Mambety, Djibril Diop
HYENAS
Mamet, David
WATER ENGINE, THE
Mamet, Tony
BODY SHOT
Man, Hayley
EROTIQUE
Manahan, Anna
BUSINESS AFFAIR, A
Manca, John
CASINO
Mancera, Nicole
NICK OF TIME
Mancic, Anita
GORILLA BATHES AT NOON
Mancuso, Fred
SUDDEN DEATH
Mancuso, Nick
UNDER SIEGE 2: DARK TERRITORY
Mandalis, Elena
ONLY THE BRAVE
Mandel, Alyse
VAMPIRE IN BROOKLYN
Mandel, Howie
KURT VONNEGUT'S HARRISON
BERGERON
Mandell, Michael
FOOL AND HIS MONEY, A
Mandella-Paul, Ira
I CAN'T SLEEP
Mandin, Manisah
BEYOND RANGOON
Mandley, Lawrence A.
WHITE MAN'S BURDEN
Mandvi, Aasif
DIE HARD WITH A VENGEANCE
Mandylor, Costas
ALMOST DEAD
VIRTUOSITY
Manetti, Larry
BODY CHEMISTRY 4: FULL EXPOSURE
Manfredonia, John F.
BOYS ON THE SIDE
Mangold, Erni
BEFORE SUNRISE
Manheim, Camryn
JEFFREY
Maniaci, Jim
SILENCE OF THE HAMS
Maniatis, Michalis
BLUE VILLA, THE
Manitowabi, Vince
DANCE ME OUTSIDE
Mankiewicz, Christopher
BODY SHOT
Mankuma, Blu
CONVICT COWBOY
Manley, Lee Ann
NINE MONTHS
Mann, Danny
BABE
BALTO
POCAHONTAS
Mann, Dieter
PROMISE, THE
Mann, Gene
DARK DEALER
Mann, Wesley
ANGUS

Mannen, Monique
FEAR, THE
Manni, Vic
BAD BOYS
Manning, Edward
CIRCLE OF FRIENDS
Manning, Katherine
SHOWGIRLS
Mannion, Rosa
PERSUASION
Mansart, Georges
SERIOUS ABOUT PLEASURE
Mansker, Eric
3 NINJAS KNUCKLE UP
Manson, Ted
GORDY
Mansor, Roslee
BEYOND RANGOON
Mantegna, Joe
FORGET PARIS
WATER ENGINE, THE
Mantel, Henriette
BRADY BUNCH MOVIE, THE
Mantell, Michael
DEAD FUNNY
Manteska, M.
SHORT FILM ABOUT KILLING, A
Mantini, Paolo
JEFFERSON IN PARIS
Manuel, Fidelis
BOYS ON THE SIDE
Manville, Holly
TANK GIRL
Manza, Ralph
GET SHORTY
Mapson, Darrell
BIGFOOT: THE UNFORGETTABLE
ENCOUNTER
Mar, Jack
HUNTED, THE
Mara, Mary
INDICTMENT: THE MCMARTIN TRIAL
Marais, Jean
LES MISERABLES
Marasty, Billy
POCAHONTAS: THE LEGEND
Marceau, Sophie
BRAVEHEART
Marcel
NOT ANGELS BUT ANGELS
Marcel, Denice
ROSWELL: THE U.F.O. COVER-UP
Marchand, Nancy
JEFFERSON IN PARIS
RECKLESS
SABRINA
Marchman, Joe
POWDER
Marckmann, Mette
KINGDOM, THE
Marcovicci, Andrea
WATER ENGINE, THE
Marder, Jordan
LORD OF ILLUSIONS
VIRTUOSITY
Mardirosian, Tom
DON JUAN DEMARCO
Marek
NOT ANGELS BUT ANGELS
Mareski, Cvetko
BEFORE THE RAIN
Mareuil, Philippe
JEFFERSON IN PARIS
Margiotta, Chuck
KISS OF DEATH
Margolyes, Miriam
BABE
BALTO

Mari, Gina
DARK SIDE OF GENIUS, THE
Mariac, Morgan
CITY OF LOST CHILDREN, THE
Mariano, Bridget
DON JUAN DEMARCO
Marie, Constance
MY FAMILY: MI FAMILIA
Marie, Louisa
APOLLO 13
Marin, Cheech
DESPERADO
Marin, Guillermo
I, THE WORST OF ALL
Marina, Artan
LAMERICA
Marine, Jeanne
BRAVEHEART
Marini, Mary
ROOMMATES
Marinker, Peter
JUDGE DREDD
Marino, Anthony
SUDDEN DEATH
Marino, Vincent
BILLY MADISON
Marisco, Tony
GEORGIA
Maritz, Albert
FRIENDS
Mark, Dana
BAD BOYS
Mark, Leikili
MONEY TRAIN
Mark, Piki
ONCE WERE WARRIORS
Markam, Agesh
BANDIT QUEEN
Markell, Jodie
SAFE
Markinson, Brian
APOLLO 13
Marko, Larry
WATER ENGINE, THE
Marks, Elaine
TALES FROM THE CRYPT: DEMON
KNIGHT
Marks, Roger
COSMIC SLOP
Marks, Shae
COVER ME
Marley, Ben
APOLLO 13
MOSAIC PROJECT, THE
Marner, Richard
OH ... ROSALINDA!!
Marondi, Hansi
STRANGER, THE
Marotta, Rick
SHOWGIRLS
Maroulis, Athan
SEPARATE LIVES
Marouski, Claude
NEA
Marquant, Rene
CITY OF LOST CHILDREN, THE
Marquardt, Peter
DESPERADO
Marques, Alvaro
MURIEL'S WEDDING
Marques, Ed
VIRTUOSITY
Marquet, Thierry
TRAPS
Marquez, Chance
ROOMMATES

Marquez, Nelson
STEAL BIG, STEAL LITTLE
Marquez, Richard
STEAL BIG, STEAL LITTLE
Marquez, William
STEAL BIG, STEAL LITTLE
Marra, Kindra
BAR GIRLS
Marsden, Jason
GOOFY MOVIE, A
Marsh, Charles
ONCE WERE WARRIORS
Marsh, Jamie
EVOLVER
Marsh, Jean
FATHERLAND
Marsh, Todd
POSTCARDS FROM AMERICA
Marsh, Walter
MAN OF THE HOUSE
Marsh, William
DEATH MACHINE
Marshall, Bryan
COUNTRY LIFE
Marshall, Dean
TOMMY BOY
Marshall, E.G.
NIXON
Marshall, Gary DeWitt
NEW JERSEY DRIVE
Marshall, Henry
O.J. SIMPSON STORY, THE
Marshall, James P.
ARIZONA DREAM
Marshall, Joe
POSTCARDS FROM AMERICA
Marshall, Larry Paul
VAMPIRE IN BROOKLYN
Marshall, Maurice
STRANGE DAYS
Marshall, Mona
ARABIAN KNIGHT
Marshall, Nickolas H.
OUTBREAK
Marshall, Penny
GET SHORTY
Marshall, Robert
NIXON
Marshall, Ruth
DOLORES CLAIBORNE
LOVE AND HUMAN REMAINS
Marshall, Sarah Abukutsa
STRANGE DAYS
Marshall, Tom
FEAST OF JULY
Marshall-Day, Cindy
DRACULA: DEAD AND LOVING IT
Marsily, Caroline
CITY OF LOST CHILDREN, THE
Martana, Frank
REASON TO BELIEVE, A
Martells, Cynthia
BROKEN TRUST
ZOOMAN
Martens, Layton
DANGEROUS, THE
Martens, Rica
LIVING IN OBLIVION
Martin, Andrea
KURT VONNEGUT'S HARRISON
BERGERON
Martin, Brad
MAJOR PAYNE
Martin, Dan
HEAT
Martin, David P.
DIE HARD WITH A VENGEANCE

Martin, Don
WINGS OF HONNEAMISE: ROYAL SPACE
FORCE
Martin, Gilbert
ROB ROY
Martin, Gregory
WALK IN THE CLOUDS, A
Martin, John
UNDERNEATH, THE
Martin, John Patrick
GRUMPIER OLD MEN
WORLD AND TIME ENOUGH
Martin, Jose
I, THE WORST OF ALL
Martin, Kamilah
AMERICAN PRESIDENT, THE
Martin, Karen
APOLLO 13
Martin, Kellie
GOOFY MOVIE, A
Martin, Marta
BODY CHEMISTRY 4: FULL EXPOSURE
Martin, Peter
FUNNY BONES
Martin, Sandy
INDICTMENT: THE MCMARTIN TRIAL
WATER ENGINE, THE
Martin, Steve
FATHER OF THE BRIDE PART II
Martindale, Margo
DEAD MAN WALKING
SABRINA
Martineau, Ross
VILLAGE OF THE DAMNED
Martines, Alessandra
LES MISERABLES
Martinet, Charles A.
NINE MONTHS
Martinez, A.
DECONSTRUCTING SARAH
Martinez, Benedict
BOYS ON THE SIDE
Martinez, Benito
MY FAMILY: MI FAMILIA
OUTBREAK
Martinez, Dena
VILLAGE OF THE DAMNED
Martinez, Leandro
NO MERCY
Martini, Steve
MAJOR PAYNE
Martino, Bobby
PRIEST
Maruyama, Karen
AMERICAN PRESIDENT, THE
Marynowski, B.
SHORT FILM ABOUT KILLING, A
Marz, Al
LIE DOWN WITH DOGS
Marzan, Rick
HEAT
Marzello, Vincent
KID IN KING ARTHUR'S COURT, A
Masamune, Tohuru
BIGFOOT: THE UNFORGETTABLE
ENCOUNTER
Masan, Jerry
NINE MONTHS
Mashimo, Fritz
JURY DUTY
Mason, Bob
FATHERLAND
Mason, Candyce
ARIZONA DREAM
Mason, Chris
ONCE WERE WARRIORS

Mason, Laurence
HACKERS
NEW YORK COP
Mason, Maria
CANDYMAN: FAREWELL TO THE FLESH
Mason, Marsha
BROKEN TRUST
NICK OF TIME
Mason, Tom
BREACH OF CONDUCT
Massari, Christina
BYE BYE, LOVE
Massee, Michael
SEVEN
TALES FROM THE HOOD
Massey, Athena
UNDERCOVER
Massey, Ryan
TIE-DIED: ROCK 'N' ROLL'S MOST
DEADICATED FANS
Masson, Ed
TIE-DIED: ROCK 'N' ROLL'S MOST
DEADICATED FANS
Masson, Vicki
ROB ROY
Masson, William
BRAVEHEART
Mastalerz, A.
SHORT FILM ABOUT KILLING, A
Masterson, Chris
CUTTHROAT ISLAND
Masterson, Danny
BYE BYE, LOVE
Masterson, Fay
AVENGING ANGEL
QUICK AND THE DEAD, THE
Mastrantonio, Mary Elizabeth
THREE WISHES
TWO BITS
Mastromaura, Luciana
I, THE WORST OF ALL
Mastrototaro, Michel
DEAD FUNNY
Masur, Richard
FORGET PARIS
Mat, Senol
DEATH IN BRUNSWICK
Matarazzo, Neal
FREE WILLY 2: THE ADVENTURE HOME
Material Issue
REASON TO BELIEVE, A
Matheisen, Mark
WALK IN THE CLOUDS, A
Mather, Jack
BILLY MADISON
CANADIAN BACON
Matheson, Christian
BILLY MADISON
Matheson, Karen
ROB ROY
Mathews, Kait Lyn
3 NINJAS KNUCKLE UP
Mathews, Mitch
SUM OF US, THE
Mathews, Selina
THINGS TO DO IN DENVER WHEN
YOU'RE DEAD
Mathias, Anna
SECRETARY, THE
Mathis, Lee
SCANNERS: THE SHOWDOWN
Mathis, Lee E.
MURDER IN THE FIRST
Mathis, Samantha
AMERICAN PRESIDENT, THE
HOW TO MAKE AN AMERICAN QUILT
Matlock, Norman
CLOCKERS

Matmor, Daniel
MANGLER, THE
Matos, Hector
LOSING ISAIAH
Matos, Nikki
HARLEM DIARY: NINE VOICES OF
RESILIENCE
Matschulla, Claudia
NOBODY LOVES ME
Matsuhisa, Nobu
CASINO
Matsui, Blythe
FORGET PARIS
Matsuo, Kentaro
SABRINA
Mattes, Eva
PROMISE, THE
Matteson, Pamela
PREHYSTERIA! 3
Matthau, Charles
NUMBER ONE FAN
Matthau, Walter
GRUMPIER OLD MEN
Matthews, Dakin
ENEMY WITHIN, THE
STUART SAVES HIS FAMILY
Matthews, Hillary
COVER ME
Matthews, Jr., Frank Eugene
WALKING DEAD, THE
Matthews, Liesel
LITTLE PRINCESS, A
Matthews, Robert
WINGS OF HONNEAMISE: ROYAL SPACE
FORCE
Matthews, Terrence
CHILDREN OF THE CORN III: URBAN
HARVEST
Matthews, Zook
CONVICT COWBOY
Mattson, Denver
STUART SAVES HIS FAMILY
Maturazzo, Neal
BIGFOOT: THE UNFORGETTABLE
ENCOUNTER
Matusek, Lee Anne
APOLLO 13
Matwljkow, David
LIE DOWN WITH DOGS
Mauceri, Patricia
DIE HARD WITH A VENGEANCE
DON JUAN DEMARCO
Maul, Bill
HACKERS
Mauricio, George F.
NINE MONTHS
Maxie, Judith
MALICIOUS
MAN OF THE HOUSE
Maxwell, Ara
SEPARATE LIVES
Maxwell, Felix
GREAT DAY IN HARLEM, A
Maxwell, Monique
NEW JERSEY DRIVE
Maxwell, Norman Max
BAD BOYS
Maxwell, Roberta
DEAD MAN WALKING
Maxwell-Hunt, Isaac
PERSUASION
May, Cory William
TANK GIRL
May, Jodhi
SCARLET LETTER, THE
SISTER MY SISTER
May, Mathilda
GROSSE FATIGUE

Mayberry, Mariann
DILLINGER
Maycock, Patrick
JUST CAUSE
Maye, Francoise
NEA
Mayes, Colin
FEAST OF JULY
Mayes, Emilio
NEW JERSEY DRIVE
Mayes, Kevin
LIE DOWN WITH DOGS
Mayeux, Rosalee
MY FAMILY: MI FAMILIA
Maynard, Joyce
TO DIE FOR
Maynard, Richard
FRANK & JESSE
Mays, Jefferson
GHOST BRIGADE
Mayweather, Joshua Gibran
CANDYMAN: FAREWELL TO THE FLESH
Maza, Bob
NOSTRADAMUS KID, THE
Mazar, Debi
BATMAN FOREVER
EMPIRE RECORDS
Mazauric, Eva
MINA TANNENBAUM
Mazel, Stefan
FARINELLI
Mazet, Arthur
CITY OF LOST CHILDREN, THE
Mazioud, Rahim
AUGUSTIN
Maznicki, Katy
JACK-O
Mazursky, Paul
MIAMI RHAPSODY
Mazzello, Joseph
CURE, THE
THREE WISHES
McAfee, Sarah
LORD OF ILLUSIONS
McAllister, David
FATHERLAND
McArthur, Brian
ROB ROY
McAteer, Gerry
DOUBLE, DOUBLE, TOIL AND TROUBLE
McBeath, Tom
HIDEAWAY
McBride, Chi
COSMIC SLOP
McBride, Melissa
MUTANT SPECIES
McBurney, Simon
BUSINESS AFFAIR, A
McCabe, Richard
PERSUASION
McCabe, Ruth
AWFULLY BIG ADVENTURE, AN
CIRCLE OF FRIENDS
McCabe, Vinnie
RUN OF THE COUNTRY, THE
McCafferty, Frankie
AILSA
SECRET OF ROAN INISH, THE
McCall, Ronald
MUTANT SPECIES
McCall, T.J.
BAR GIRLS
McCallany, Holt
AMATEUR
JADE
McCalman, Macon
WALK IN THE CLOUDS, A

McCamus, Tom
FIRST DEGREE
McCann, Chuck
DRACULA: DEAD AND LOVING IT
McCann, Donal
INNOCENT LIES
McCann, Sean
TOMMY BOY
McCant, Reed
BETTER OFF DEAD
McCardie, Brian
ROB ROY
McCarthy, Andrew
DEAD FUNNY
McCarthy, Dante
SHOWGIRLS
McCarthy, Jenny
THINGS TO DO IN DENVER WHEN
YOU'RE DEAD
McCarthy, Kevin
JUDICIAL CONSENT
JUST CAUSE
STEAL BIG, STEAL LITTLE
McCarthy, Michael C.
STUART SAVES HIS FAMILY
McCarthy, Neil
FRIENDS
McCarthy, Tim
LIE DOWN WITH DOGS
McCarty, Michael
CASPER
McCary, Rod
SECRETARY, THE
McCauley, James
AMATEUR
KISS OF DEATH
NEW JERSEY DRIVE
McCay, Cole
BAD BLOOD
McClean, Shawn
NEW JERSEY DRIVE
McClean, Unruly Julie
FOUR ROOMS
McCleery, Lawrence
VAMPIRES AND OTHER STEREOTYPES
McCleery, Mick
VAMPIRES AND OTHER STEREOTYPES
McClelland, Jim
NOSTRADAMUS KID, THE
McClements, Catherine
DESPERATE PREY
McClure, Marc
APOLLO 13
McClure, Tane
CAGED HEARTS
MIDNIGHT TEASE 2
McColl, St. Clair
FAR FROM HOME: THE ADVENTURES OF
YELLOW DOG
McComb, Billy
LORD OF ILLUSIONS
McConaughey, Matthew
BOYS ON THE SIDE
McConnell, John
KINGFISH: A STORY OF HUEY P. LONG
MUTANT SPECIES
McConnohie, Amike
BAREFOOT GEN
McCool, Dennis
BRIDGES OF MADISON COUNTY, THE
McCormack, Catherine
BRAVEHEART
McCormack, Colin
FIRST KNIGHT
McCormack, Eric
DOUBLE, DOUBLE, TOIL AND TROUBLE
McCoy, Larry
DEAD PRESIDENTS

McCoy, Matt
BIGFOOT: THE UNFORGETTABLE
ENCOUNTER
RENT-A-KID
McCracken, Paul
FORGET PARIS
McCrae, Margie
DALLAS DOLL
McCray, Alvin
HOUSEGUEST
McCready, Eleanor
SENSE AND SENSIBILITY
McCrindle, Jenny
SHALLOW GRAVE
McCullough, Michael
PYROMANIAC'S LOVE STORY, A
McCurdy, Brendan
MY ANTONIA
McCurry, Doug
ROSWELL: THE U.F.O. COVER-UP
McCusker, Mary
CURE, THE
McDade, Sandy
RESTORATION
McDancer, Buck
COLDBLOODED
McDanger, Buck
EXPERT, THE
McDaniel, Drucie
TWELVE MONKEYS
McDaniels, Paulette
LOSING ISAIAH
McDanniel, Brendan
TO WONG FOO, THANKS FOR
EVERYTHING! JULIE NEWMAR
McDavid, David
CURSE OF THE STARVING CLASS
McDavid, Stacie
CURSE OF THE STARVING CLASS
McDermott, Dylan
DESTINY TURNS ON THE RADIO
HOME FOR THE HOLIDAYS
McDiarmid, Ian
RESTORATION
McDole, Richard Loewll
BOYS ON THE SIDE
McDonald, Carol
LIE DOWN WITH DOGS
McDonald, Christopher
COVER STORY
FAIR GAME
McDonald, Edward
KISS OF DEATH
McDonald, Jodie
FORGET PARIS
McDonald, Kevin
NATIONAL LAMPOON'S SENIOR TRIP
McDonald, Michael
HIDEAWAY
McDonald, Roseann
DALLAS DOLL
McDonald, Shelton
TO WONG FOO, THANKS FOR
EVERYTHING! JULIE NEWMAR
McDonnell, Caitlin Grace
ART FOR TEACHERS OF CHILDREN
McDonnell, Leverne
GROSS MISCONDUCT
McDonough, John
ACROSS THE SEA OF TIME: NEW YORK
3D
McDonough, Neil
THREE WISHES
McDonough, Robert
KILIAN'S CHRONICLE
McDormand, Frances
BEYOND RANGOON

McDougal, Martin
JUDGE DREDD

McDougall, Ken
EXOTICA

McDowall, Roddy
LAST SUMMER IN THE HAMPTONS

McDowell, Malcolm
TANK GIRL

McElheron, Fergal
SECRET OF ROAN INISH, THE

McElhinney, Ian
LAMB

McElroy, Brian
HOW TO MAKE AN AMERICAN QUILT

McElroy, Michael
HOW TO MAKE AN AMERICAN QUILT

McElveen, Gwynne
CIRCLE OF FRIENDS

McEnroe, Annie
S.F.W.

McEntire, Reba
BUFFALO GIRLS

McEvily, John Vincent
ADDICTION, THE

McFadden, Thom
BREACH OF CONDUCT

McFadyen, Angus
BRAVEHEART

McFadyen, Myra
ROB ROY

McFall, Rod
GLASS SHIELD, THE

McFarland, Alan
LORD OF ILLUSIONS

McFarland, Angel
LAKOTA WOMAN: SIEGE AT WOUNDED
  KNEE

McFee, Dwight
GOLD DIGGERS: THE SECRET OF BEAR
  MOUNTAIN

McGarry, Mary Ann
BOYS ON THE SIDE

McGavin, Darren
BILLY MADISON

McGaw, Patrick
BASKETBALL DIARIES, THE
MALICIOUS

McGee, Gwen
NEW JERSEY DRIVE

McGee, Jack
JURY DUTY
SHOWGIRLS
UNSTRUNG HEROES

McGee, Mike
FORGET PARIS

McGeown, Anne
AILSA

McGill, Everett
UNDER SIEGE 2: DARK TERRITORY

McGill, Michael
HIGHLANDER: THE FINAL DIMENSION

McGinley, John C.
BORN TO BE WILD
NIXON
SEVEN

McGinley, Sean
BRAVEHEART
CIRCLE OF FRIENDS

McGiver, Boris
LITTLE ODESSA

McGlone, Mike
BROTHERS MCMULLEN, THE

McGonagle, Richard F.
AMERICAN PRESIDENT, THE

McGoohan, Patrick
BRAVEHEART

McGovern, Barry
BRAVEHEART

McGovern, Elizabeth
BROKEN TRUST
WINGS OF COURAGE

McGovern, Terence
NINE MONTHS

McGowan, Rose
DOOM GENERATION, THE

McGowan, Tom
HEAVYWEIGHTS

McGrath, Alethea
DALLAS DOLL

McGrath, Bob
RHYTHM THIEF

McGrath, Brian
AWFULLY BIG ADVENTURE, AN

McGrath, J.B.
BODY SHOT

McGraw, Christine
GLASS SHIELD, THE

McGregor, Ewan
SHALLOW GRAVE

McGregor, Scott
MIGHTY MORPHIN POWER RANGERS:
  THE MOVIE

McGregor-Stewart, Kate
FATHER OF THE BRIDE PART II

McGruther, Michael
CLOCKERS

McGuiness, Paddy
RUN OF THE COUNTRY, THE

McGuinness, Dave
ART FOR TEACHERS OF CHILDREN

McGuirk, Bill
PERSUASION

McHattie, Stephen
CONVICT COWBOY

McInerney, Bernie
AMERICAN PRESIDENT, THE

McInnerny, Tim
RICHARD III

McIntosh, Bill
HEAT

McIntyre, Marvin J.
BORN TO BE WILD

McKay, Cole
FRANK & JESSE

McKay, David
BRAVEHEART

McKay, Elizabeth P.
BROTHERS MCMULLEN, THE

McKean, Michael
ACROSS THE MOON
BRADY BUNCH MOVIE, THE

McKee, Todd
BREACH OF CONDUCT

McKeehan, Gary
LOVE AND HUMAN REMAINS

McKeel, Mark
APOLLO 13

McKellar, Don
EXOTICA
WHEN NIGHT IS FALLING

McKellen, Ian
HEAVEN'S A DRAG
RESTORATION
RICHARD III

McKenna, Bernadette
LAMB

McKenna, Debra
BAR GIRLS

McKenna, Joseph
TWELVE MONKEYS

McKenna, Scott
SPECIES

McKenrick, Susanne
RESTORATION

McKenzie, Jacqueline
TRAPS

McKenzie, Sally
DESPERATE PREY

McKenzie, Suzie
DESPERATE PREY

McKeon, Nancy
TERESA'S TATTOO

McKernan, Peter
SABRINA

McKinney, Greg
MONEY TRAIN

McKinney, Gregory
MORTAL KOMBAT

McKinnon, Ray
APOLLO 13
NET, THE
ROSWELL: THE U.F.O. COVER-UP

McKissack, Lana
FOUR ROOMS

McKnight, David
GLASS SHIELD, THE

McKnight, Donovon Ian H.
LOSING ISAIAH

McKnight, Geoff
NOW AND THEN

McKoy, Ruby
CROSSING GUARD, THE

McKune, Mike
DILLINGER

McLarty, Cole
HIGHER LEARNING

McLarty, Ronald
TWO BITS

McLauchlin, Laura
VAMPIRES AND OTHER STEREOTYPES

McLaughlin, Ellen
BED YOU SLEEP IN, THE

McLaughlin, Heath
EVOLVER

McLaughlin, Kevin
UNDERCOVER

McLawhorn, Charles
KINGFISH: A STORY OF HUEY P. LONG

McLean, Shawn
CLOCKERS

McLellan, Nora
DOUBLE, DOUBLE, TOIL AND TROUBLE

McLeod, Michael
ANGUS

McLoughlin, Marian
BUSINESS AFFAIR, A

McLoughlin, Ned
AILSA

McMahon, Mitchell
MIGHTY MORPHIN POWER RANGERS:
  THE MOVIE

McMann, Dannete
POWDER

McMillan, David
JURY DUTY

McMillan, Hec
NOSTRADAMUS KID, THE

McMillan, Tanya
DALLAS DOLL

McMonagle, Walter
LAMB

McMullen, Jim
JUDICIAL CONSENT

McMullen, Philip
TOMMY BOY

McNabb, Billie
BRIDGES OF MADISON COUNTY, THE

McNair, Estella
RADIO INSIDE

McNally, Mike
KINGFISH: A STORY OF HUEY P. LONG

McNamara, Peter
FUNNY BONES

McNamara, William
COPYCAT
GIRL IN THE CADILLAC
RADIO INSIDE
McNeice, Ian
ACE VENTURA: WHEN NATURE CALLS
ENGLISHMAN WHO WENT UP A HILL
BUT CAME DOWN A MOUNTAIN, THE
FUNNY BONES
McNeice, Maisie
ENGLISHMAN WHO WENT UP A HILL
BUT CAME DOWN A MOUNTAIN, THE
McNeil, Kate
SUDDEN DEATH
McNeil, Marguerite
SCARLET LETTER, THE
McNulty, Craig
CLOCKERS
McNulty, Kevin
BROKEN TRUST
GOOD DAY TO DIE, A
McPartland, Marian
GREAT DAY IN HARLEM, A
McPherson, Carolyn Adunni
STRANGE DAYS
McPherson, Coco
POSTCARDS FROM AMERICA
ROY COHN/JACK SMITH
McPherson, Graham
BLACK FOX
McQuaid, Jimmy
MIGHTY APHRODITE
McQuay, Jana
OUT OF ANNIE'S PAST
McQueen, Chad
NEW YORK COP
NUMBER ONE FAN
McRedie, Colin
SHALLOW GRAVE
McRobbie, Peter
MIGHTY APHRODITE
McShane, Michael
TOM AND HUCK
McSorely, Gerard
AWFULLY BIG ADVENTURE, AN
McSorley, Gerard
BRAVEHEART
McSorley, Marty
BAD BOYS
FORGET PARIS
McTeague, Kathleen
SHOWGIRLS
McTeer, Janet
CARRINGTON
McTiernan, Sr., John
DIE HARD WITH A VENGEANCE
McVerry, Maureen
NINE MONTHS
McVicar, Daniel
SILENCE OF THE HAMS
Mead, Courtland
BABE
INDICTMENT: THE MCMARTIN TRIAL
TOM AND HUCK
Mead, Walter T.
SMOKE
Meadoff, Randy
CROSSING GUARD, THE
Meadows, Adam
INDICTMENT: THE MCMARTIN TRIAL
Meadows, Jayne
CASINO
Meadows, Sarah
TIE-DIED: ROCK 'N' ROLL'S MOST
DEADICATED FANS
Meaney, Colm
ENGLISHMAN WHO WENT UP A HILL
BUT CAME DOWN A MOUNTAIN, THE

Means, Angela
FRIDAY
Means, Reed Clark
BUSHWHACKED
Means, Russell
BUFFALO GIRLS
POCAHONTAS
Means, Scott
LAKOTA WOMAN: SIEGE AT WOUNDED
KNEE
Meara, Anne
HEAVYWEIGHTS
KISS OF DEATH
Mechoso, Julio
ZOOMAN
Mechoso, Julio Oscar
BAD BOYS
GLASS SHIELD, THE
PYROMANIAC'S LOVE STORY, A
Mecredi, Morningstar
BLACK FOX
Medalis, Joseph G.
COSMIC SLOP
Medearis, Jamie Jo
HIGHER LEARNING
Meden, Olaf
INNOCENT, THE
Medin, Harriet
THINGS TO DO IN DENVER WHEN
YOU'RE DEAD
Medina, Elsa
UP TO A CERTAIN POINT
Medinger, Laura
NOBODY LOVES ME
Medrano, Frank
COVER ME
FAIR GAME
USUAL SUSPECTS, THE
Medved, Calli
ASSASSINS
Medway, Heather
FEAR, THE
Meehan, T.K.
BYE BYE, LOVE
Meeks, Edith
SAFE
Meertins, Jr., Conrad
NEW JERSEY DRIVE
Mehlnan, Michael
KID IN KING ARTHUR'S COURT, A
Mehra, Mini
JADE
Mei, Chris
BILLY MADISON
Meier, Shane
MAN OF THE HOUSE
Meihana, Richard
ONCE WERE WARRIORS
Meiler, Bill
DOUBLE, DOUBLE, TOIL AND TROUBLE
Meinardus, Megan
JUST CAUSE
Meinhardt, Christian
REASON TO BELIEVE, A
Meintjes, Tertius
FRIENDS
Meira, Tarcisio
BOCA
Meissel, Petr
FATHERLAND
Meister, Joerg
PROMISE, THE
Mejia, Enio
DIRTY MONEY
Mekas, Adolfas
ART FOR TEACHERS OF CHILDREN
Melander, Cory
SHOWGIRLS

Mele, Nicholas
SPY WITHIN, THE
Melendez, Ron
CHILDREN OF THE CORN III: URBAN
HARVEST
Melendres, Dorothy
WINGS OF HONNEAMISE: ROYAL SPACE
FORCE
Melissis, Tom
WHEN NIGHT IS FALLING
Melito, Joseph
TWELVE MONKEYS
Mellet, Laurent
FRANKIE STARLIGHT
Mello, Tamara
BRADY BUNCH MOVIE, THE
Mellow, Tamra
TOM AND HUCK
Melocchi, Vince
BITTER VENGEANCE
UNSTRUNG HEROES
Meloni, Christopher
TWELVE MONKEYS
Melvin, Michael
MURDER IN THE FIRST
Melvin, Murray
DOOMSDAY GUN
Memphis, Mike
VAMPIRES AND OTHER STEREOTYPES
Mena, Chaz
MIAMI RHAPSODY
Menacof, Clint
JOURNEY OF AUGUST KING, THE
Menchhofer, Mark
EMPIRE RECORDS
Menchikov, Oleg
BURNT BY THE SUN
Mendel, Sharon
BREACH OF CONDUCT
Mendel, Stephen
SCANNERS: THE SHOWDOWN
Mendelson, Robert
SPECIES
Mendes, Vaz
VALLEY OF ABRAHAM, THE
Mendez, Julie Ann
HOME FOR THE HOLIDAYS
Mengze Shi
ROOMMATES
Menyuk, Erick
BABYSITTER, THE
Menza, Gina
OUTBREAK
Menzel, Jiri
MARTHA AND I
Menzies, Benjamin
DEATH IN BRUNSWICK
Merasty, Billy
EXOTICA
Mercado, Virginia
LAKOTA WOMAN: SIEGE AT WOUNDED
KNEE
Mercedes, Ana
COSMIC SLOP
Mercer, Ernestine
CASPER
Merchant, Ismail
JEFFERSON IN PARIS
Mercier, Mary
UNSTRUNG HEROES
Mercurio, Micole
WHILE YOU WERE SLEEPING
Meredith, Burgess
ACROSS THE MOON
GRUMPIER OLD MEN
Meredith, David Lloyd
ENGLISHMAN WHO WENT UP A HILL
BUT CAME DOWN A MOUNTAIN, THE

Mergenthaler, Carl
  BURNING SEASON, THE
Merlin, Joanna
  TWO BITS
Merlin, Serge
  CITY OF LOST CHILDREN, THE
Merrill, Norman
  LITTLE PRINCESS, A
Merriman, Jan
  SUM OF US, THE
Merrins, Michael
  MURDER IN THE FIRST
Merrins, Michael Lee
  DIE HARD WITH A VENGEANCE
Merrison, Clive
  AWFULLY BIG ADVENTURE, AN
Merrit, Carl
  DARK DEALER
Merritt, Theresa
  BILLY MADISON
Merson, Susan
  THINGS TO DO IN DENVER WHEN
    YOU'RE DEAD
Mesa, Arthur
  GALAXIS
Meseck, Peter
  INNOCENT, THE
Mesguich, Daniel
  JEFFERSON IN PARIS
Meshejian, Paul
  TWELVE MONKEYS
Meskimen, Jim
  APOLLO 13
Mesnick, William
  FATHER AND SCOUT
Mesnik, William
  BATMAN FOREVER
  INDICTMENT: THE MCMARTIN TRIAL
Messerer, Michael
  DANCER, THE
Messing, Debra
  WALK IN THE CLOUDS, A
Messing, Susan
  WHILE YOU WERE SLEEPING
Metcalf, Laurie
  LEAVING LAS VEGAS
  TOY STORY
Metcalf, Mark
  REASON TO BELIEVE, A
Metcalfe, Rebecca
  FUNNY BONES
Metchik, Aaron
  BABY-SITTERS CLUB, THE
Metchik, Asher
  BABY-SITTERS CLUB, THE
Metlitskaya, Irina
  CREATION OF ADAM
Mette, Nancy
  BABY-SITTERS CLUB, THE
Metzler, Jim
  CHILDREN OF THE CORN III: URBAN
    HARVEST
Mewes, Jason
  MALLRATS
Meyer, Bess
  STUART SAVES HIS FAMILY
Meyer, Breckin
  CLUELESS
  PAYBACK
Meyer, Dina
  JOHNNY MNEMONIC
Meyer, Tara
  CANADIAN BACON
Meyering, Jr., Ralph
  AMERICAN PRESIDENT, THE
Meyers, Ari
  HOW TO MAKE AN AMERICAN QUILT

Meyers, E.B.
  TALL TALE: THE UNBELIEVABLE
    ADVENTURES OF PECOS BILL
Meyers, Larry John
  HOUSEGUEST
  SUDDEN DEATH
Meyers-Shyer, Annie
  FATHER OF THE BRIDE PART II
Meyers-Shyer, Hallie
  FATHER OF THE BRIDE PART II
Meyler, Tony
  NEVER TALK TO STRANGERS
Mgwenya, Archie
  FRIENDS
Miarczynska, M.
  SHORT FILM ABOUT KILLING, A
Micalchunk, Stephen
  SCARLET LETTER, THE
Micelli, Vince
  VAMPIRE IN BROOKLYN
Michael
  NOT ANGELS BUT ANGELS
Michael, Garon
  CONGO
Michael, Ryan
  MALICIOUS
Michaels, Christopher
  PANTHER
Michaels, Delana
  MY FAMILY: MI FAMILIA
Michaels, Gordon
  DESTINY TURNS ON THE RADIO
  LEAVING LAS VEGAS
  OUTBREAK
Michaels, Janna
  BUSHWHACKED
Michaels, Suzanne
  AMERICAN PRESIDENT, THE
Michalewska, J.
  SHORT FILM ABOUT LOVE, A
Michel, Jr., Albert
  DESPERADO
Michele, Delaune
  DIRTY MONEY
Michell, Philip
  RESTORATION
Michelman, Jordan
  BORN TO BE WILD
Michetti, Emidio
  HIGHLANDER: THE FINAL DIMENSION
Michieli, Larissa
  THINGS TO DO IN DENVER WHEN
    YOU'RE DEAD
Mickelson, Jennifer
  FORGET PARIS
Mickler, Patrick
  APOLLO 13
Middleton, Travis
  SUBSTITUTE WIFE, THE
Midwood, Ramsay
  DILLINGER
Mielech, J.
  SHORT FILM ABOUT KILLING, A
Mifune, Toshiro
  PICTURE BRIDE
Miguel, Nigel
  FORGET PARIS
Mihulova, Alena
  COW, THE
Mikelson, Adam
  WORLD AND TIME ENOUGH
Mikhailov, Victor
  WINDOW TO PARIS
Mikhalkov, Nadia
  BURNT BY THE SUN
Mikhalkov, Nikita
  BURNT BY THE SUN

Mikic, Aleksander
  BEFORE THE RAIN
Mikita, Carole
  OUT OF ANNIE'S PAST
Miklosy, Gyorgy
  CITIZEN X
Milano, Alyssa
  EMBRACE OF THE VAMPIRE
Milano, Cory
  STUART SAVES HIS FAMILY
Milano, Thom
  POSTCARDS FROM AMERICA
Milanovich, Vladimir
  GOLDENEYE
Milazzo, Oscar
  I, THE WORST OF ALL
Milchick, Ken
  SUDDEN DEATH
Milder, Andy
  APOLLO 13
Miles, Chuck
  AMERICA'S DEADLIEST HOME VIDEO
Miles, Dido
  FIRST KNIGHT
Miles, Elaine
  MAD LOVE
Miles, Joanna
  JUDGE DREDD
  WATER ENGINE, THE
Miles, Vera
  SEPARATE LIVES
Miley, Peggy
  LITTLE PRINCESS, A
Milfont, Denise
  BOCA
Milford, John
  BROKEN TRUST
Milhoan, Michael
  CRIMSON TIDE
  CRIMSON TIDE
Milian, Tomas
  BURNING SEASON, THE
Milkani, Piro
  LAMERICA
Millar, Gavin
  FUNNY BONES
Miller, Andrew
  LAST OF THE DOGMEN
Miller, Bean
  VAMPIRES AND OTHER STEREOTYPES
Miller, Calvin
  FLUKE
Miller, Dennis
  NET, THE
  NEVER TALK TO STRANGERS
Miller, Dick
  NUMBER ONE FAN
  TALES FROM THE CRYPT: DEMON
    KNIGHT
Miller, Gabrielle
  DIGGER
Miller, Glenn
  NEW YORK COP
Miller, Haley
  BIG GREEN, THE
Miller, Ira
  DRACULA: DEAD AND LOVING IT
Miller, Jo
  GEORGIA
Miller, Jonny Lee
  HACKERS
Miller, Jonty
  FIRST KNIGHT
Miller, Joseph Wayne
  HEAVYWEIGHTS
Miller, Maxine
  BROKEN TRUST

Miller, Michelle M.
OUTBREAK
Miller, Morgan
NINE MONTHS
Miller, Rachel
STUART SAVES HIS FAMILY
Miller, Ralph
VILLAGE OF THE DAMNED
Miller, Randall
HOUSEGUEST
Miller, Reggie
FORGET PARIS
Miller, Robert Kevin
OPERATION DUMBO DROP
Miller, Sherry
JOHNNY MNEMONIC
RENT-A-KID
Miller, Stan
BAD BOYS
Miller, Stephanie
FATHER OF THE BRIDE PART II
Miller, Stephen E.
MALICIOUS
Miller, Terry
HEAT
Millgate, Gabby
MURIEL'S WEDDING
Millington, Graeme
TO DIE FOR
TOMMY BOY
Millington, James
DARKMAN 2: THE RETURN OF DURANT
Million, Billy
MOSAIC PROJECT, THE
Millot, Jacqueline
INNOCENT LIES
Mills, Gary Landon
JUST CAUSE
Mills, Jordan
DEATH IN BRUNSWICK
Mills, Tiny
IT TAKES TWO
Mills, Zeke
SUBSTITUTE WIFE, THE
Milmore, Jennifer
TO WONG FOO, THANKS FOR
EVERYTHING! JULIE NEWMAR
Milne, Gordon
HEAVEN'S A DRAG
Milshtein, Jocya
MINA TANNENBAUM
Milton, Dominique
FLUKE
Minckler, Sydney D.
BATMAN FOREVER
Mincks, Jonathan
ROSWELL: THE U.F.O. COVER-UP
Mincy-Powell, Joy
WHEN BILLY BROKE HIS HEAD ... AND
OTHER TALES OF WONDER
Mindy, John
BEYOND RANGOON
Ming, Benji
FUNNY BONES
Minjares, Joe
NEXT DOOR
Minor, Asia
DANGEROUS MINDS
Minor, Bob
ASSASSINS
TIE THAT BINDS, THE
Minor, Royce
STRANGE DAYS
Minovich, Tory
BAR GIRLS
Minter, Kelly Jo
COSMIC SLOP

Minton, Faith
SUDDEN DEATH
Mirabel, Fausto
I AM CUBA
Miranda, Chris
MAN OF THE HOUSE
Miranda, Dianna
EMPIRE RECORDS
EROTIQUE
Miranda, Evan
SEVEN
Miranda, Heloisa
CONVENT, THE
Mircevski, Petar
BEFORE THE RAIN
Mirek
NOT ANGELS BUT ANGELS
Mirikitami, Alan
BOYS ON THE SIDE
Mirkos, Mark
TIE-DIED: ROCK 'N' ROLL'S MOST
DEADICATED FANS
Mirman, Edie
TOM AND HUCK
WICKED CITY
Miro, Yolanda
JURY DUTY
Mironov, Evgenii
BURNT BY THE SUN
Mishler, Tania
BRIDGES OF MADISON COUNTY, THE
Mishra, Hemnat
BANDIT QUEEN
Miskimmin, Peter
DANCE ME OUTSIDE
Misko-Coury, Lillian
ROOMMATES
Mistress Formika
WIGSTOCK: THE MOVIE
Mitchell, Allan
SENSE AND SENSIBILITY
Mitchell, Billy J.
GOLDENEYE
Mitchell, Cameron
JACK-O
Mitchell, Daryl
COSMIC SLOP
Mitchell, Delaina
WAITING TO EXHALE
Mitchell, Dick
OUT OF ANNIE'S PAST
Mitchell, Donna
PARTY GIRL
TWO BITS
Mitchell, Heather
MURIEL'S WEDDING
Mitchell, Susan
ADDICTION, THE
Mitchell-Leon, Carol
GETTING OUT
Mitevska, Labina
BEFORE THE RAIN
Mitri, Paul
DANGER OF LOVE
Mitsak, Erick
NOSTRADAMUS KID, THE
Mitsch, Jack
GRUMPIER OLD MEN
Miura, Tomokazu
MYSTERY OF RAMPO, THE
Miyazaki, Gerrielani
SAFE
Miyeni, Eric
CRY, THE BELOVED COUNTRY
Miyori, Kim
BODY SHOT
Mizrahi, Isaac
UNZIPPED

Mizuno, Akiko
MYSTERY OF RAMPO, THE
Moana, Guy
ONCE WERE WARRIORS
Mochnick, Paul
SUDDEN DEATH
Mochrie, Peter
MIGHTY MORPHIN POWER RANGERS:
THE MOVIE
Mode, Becky
PARTY GIRL
Modenesi, Augusto
NO MERCY
Modine, Matthew
BYE BYE, LOVE
CUTTHROAT ISLAND
FLUKE
Moegi, Gideon
FRIENDS
Moffatt, D.W.
IN THE DEEP WOODS
Moffet, Tim
NINE MONTHS
Moffett, Michelle
ANDROID AFFAIR, THE
Mofokeng, Jerry
CRY, THE BELOVED COUNTRY
FRIENDS
Mohd, Rashidi
BEYOND RANGOON
Mohlamme, Emmanuel
FRIENDS
Mohun, Susan
CLUELESS
VIRTUOSITY
Mohyeddin, Zia
DOOMSDAY GUN
Moir, Alison
LITTLE PRINCESS, A
Mokae, Zakes
OUTBREAK
VAMPIRE IN BROOKLYN
WATERWORLD
Molcik, Antonin
COW, THE
Molee, Casper
CASINO
Molina, Alfred
HIDEAWAY
PEREZ FAMILY, THE
SPECIES
Molina, Butch
QUICK AND THE DEAD, THE
Molina, Ernesto V.
DON JUAN DEMARCO
Molina, Manny
SILENCE OF THE HAMS
Molina, Nicole
TWO BITS
Molina, Rolando
INDICTMENT: THE MCMARTIN TRIAL
VIRTUOSITY
Molinari, Matteo
SILENCE OF THE HAMS
Molinaro, Joe
CASINO
Moll, Richard
GALAXIS
Molla-Abbasi, Ramazan
JAR, THE
Moller, Frank
EROTIQUE
Molloy, Dearbhla
FRANKIE STARLIGHT
RUN OF THE COUNTRY, THE
Moloney, Janel
SAFE

Monahan, Debi A.
DILLINGER AND CAPONE
Mondal, Saikat
SABRINA
Mondol, Subhas
STRANGER, THE
Mondragon, Bill
MY FAMILY: MI FAMILIA
Mondragon, Eric
MY FAMILY: MI FAMILIA
Monette, Richard
KURT VONNEGUT'S HARRISON
BERGERON
Monev, Sando
BEFORE THE RAIN
Monica, Monica L.
CANDYMAN: FAREWELL TO THE FLESH
Moniot, Robert
FRANK & JESSE
Monitor, James
DANGER OF LOVE
Moniz, Brad
SUDDEN DEATH
Monk, Debra
JEFFREY
RECKLESS
REDWOOD CURTAIN
Monks, Darren
FRANKIE STARLIGHT
Monks, Michael
INDICTMENT: THE MCMARTIN TRIAL
Monroe, Betsy
COVER ME
NINE MONTHS
Monroe, Jarion
REDWOOD CURTAIN
Monroe, Jr., Samuel
TALES FROM THE HOOD
Monroe, Kimber
EMPIRE RECORDS
Mons, Maurice
LES MISERABLES
Montalvo, Xavier
GET SHORTY
Montana, Chris
AMERICA'S DEADLIEST HOME VIDEO
Monte, Leticia
CARMEN MIRANDA: BANANAS IS MY
BUSINESS
Monte, Ted
ATTACK OF THE 60-FOOT CENTERFOLD
Montell, Jermaine
CLUELESS
Montemer, Gary
BOYS ON THE SIDE
Montesinos, Gino
KILIAN'S CHRONICLE
Montgomery, Chuck
AMATEUR
Montgomery, Jennifer
ART FOR TEACHERS OF CHILDREN
Montgomery, Lauren
MY ANTONIA
Montgomery, Poppy
DEVIL IN A BLUE DRESS
Montgomery, Ritchie
BODY SHOT
Montgomery, Ruth S.
ART FOR TEACHERS OF CHILDREN
Montine, Joe
WINGS OF HONNEAMISE: ROYAL SPACE
FORCE
Montpetit, Pascale
ECLIPSE
Monvoisin, Alexandra
INNOCENT LIES
Moody, Ron
KID IN KING ARTHUR'S COURT, A

Moon, Philip
BATMAN FOREVER
S.F.W.
Moore, Andre
NEW JERSEY DRIVE
Moore, Anthony
COPYCAT
Moore, Ashleigh Aston
GOLD DIGGERS: THE SECRET OF BEAR
MOUNTAIN
NOW AND THEN
Moore, Barbara
CYBER BANDITS
Moore, Brian Joseph
CANDYMAN: FAREWELL TO THE FLESH
Moore, Cappucino
I LIKE TO PLAY GAMES
Moore, Charles
CAGED HEAT 3000
Moore, Charlotte
JERKY BOYS: THE MOVIE, THE
Moore, Demi
NOW AND THEN
SCARLET LETTER, THE
Moore, Denis
DEATH IN BRUNSWICK
Moore, George
RIVER OF GRASS
Moore, Julianne
ASSASSINS
NINE MONTHS
ROOMMATES
SAFE
Moore, Kelsey Binder
CANADIAN BACON
Moore, Kenya
WAITING TO EXHALE
Moore, Leah Binder
CANADIAN BACON
Moore, Maggie
INCREDIBLY TRUE ADVENTURES OF
TWO GIRLS IN LOVE, THE
Moore, Michael
CANADIAN BACON
Moore, Mikal
MORTAL KOMBAT
Moore, Peter
BITTER VENGEANCE
CURE, THE
Moore, Peter Savard
TOP DOG
Moore, Rob
NATIONAL LAMPOON'S SENIOR TRIP
Moore, Sheila
CIRCUMSTANCES UNKNOWN
Moore, Steve
GOOFY MOVIE, A
Moore, Thurston
BRIAN WILSON: I JUST WASN'T MADE
FOR THESE TIMES
Moore-Wickham, Jack
IN THE MOUTH OF MADNESS
Moorecraft, Steven
INNOCENT, THE
Mora, Jr., Daniel Edward
LORD OF ILLUSIONS
Morales, Esai
BURNING SEASON, THE
MY FAMILY: MI FAMILIA
Morales, Stephen
INDIAN IN THE CUPBOARD, THE
Moran, Dan
MIGHTY APHRODITE
Moran, Israel
DIRTY MONEY
Moran, Patrick
JACK-O

Moran, Sean
OUTSIDE THE LAW
Morange, Geoffroy
CITY OF LOST CHILDREN, THE
Mordy, Anthony
WINGS OF HONNEAMISE: ROYAL SPACE
FORCE
Moreau, Jeanne
OLD LADY WHO WALKED IN THE SEA,
THE
Moreau, Marguerite
FREE WILLY 2: THE ADVENTURE HOME
Morecroft, Richard
MURIEL'S WEDDING
Morel, Gael
WILD REEDS
Moreno, Daysi
CROSSING GUARD, THE
Moreno, Fernando C.
DON JUAN DEMARCO
Moreno, Miguel
ARIZONA DREAM
Moreno, Rita
ANGUS
Moretti, Linda
POSTMAN, THE
Moretti, Michele
WILD REEDS
Moreu, Kristin
HACKERS
Morga, Tom
SEPARATE LIVES
Morgan, Alberto
I AM CUBA
Morgan, Carol
POSTCARDS FROM AMERICA
Morgan, Cindy
GALAXIS
Morgan, Garfield
ENGLISHMAN WHO WENT UP A HILL
BUT CAME DOWN A MOUNTAIN, THE
Morgan, Jeffrey Dean
UNDERCOVER
Morgan, Michelle
NEW JERSEY DRIVE
Morgan, Peter
FUNNY BONES
Morgan, T.S.
NOW AND THEN
Morghan, Mark
JUDGE DREDD
Morgia, Piero
MAMMA ROMA
Mori, Naoko
HACKERS
Moriarty, Cathy
CASPER
FORGET PARIS
Moriarty, Michael
GOOD DAY TO DIE, A
Morice, Tara
HOTEL SORRENTO
Morin, Sylvain
LOVE AND HUMAN REMAINS
Morini, Margarlda
RESTORATION
Moritz, Christopher
INDIAN IN THE CUPBOARD, THE
Moritz, Louisa
GALAXIS
Moritz, Melitta
INNOCENT, THE
Moritz, Reinhold
FOR GOD AND COUNTRY
Moritzen, Michael
KINGDOM, THE
Morocco, Beans
AMERICAN PRESIDENT, THE

Moroff, Mike
DESPERADO
TALL TALE: THE UNBELIEVABLE
ADVENTURES OF PECOS BILL
Morony, Joss
SUM OF US, THE
Morrell, Paula
MIGHTY MORPHIN POWER RANGERS:
THE MOVIE
Morris, Alex Allen
POWDER
Morris, Grinnell
DRACULA: DEAD AND LOVING IT
Morris, Iona
BAREFOOT GEN
Morris, Jane
BUSHWHACKED
Morris, Jason
BAR GIRLS
Morris, Jeff
CROSSING GUARD, THE
Morris, John
TOY STORY
Morris, John Charles
COPYCAT
Morris, Jr., Rachael
ONCE WERE WARRIORS
Morris, Kevin
FORGET PARIS
Morris, Lisa
MANGLER, THE
Morris, Mark
UNZIPPED
Morris, Paula
GREAT DAY IN HARLEM, A
Morris, Thomas
BED YOU SLEEP IN, THE
Morris, Thomas Q.
WHILE YOU WERE SLEEPING
Morris, Victor
BETTER OFF DEAD
Morris, Virginia
SPECIES
Morrison, Harold
JADE
Morrison, Shauna
FORGET PARIS
Morrison, Temuera
ONCE WERE WARRIORS
Morrisson, Doug
COPYCAT
Morrow, Bruce Ed
ROSWELL: THE U.F.O. COVER-UP
Morrow, Mari
BODILY HARM
CHILDREN OF THE CORN III: URBAN
HARVEST
UNDERCOVER
VIRTUOSITY
Morse, David
CROSSING GUARD, THE
TWELVE MONKEYS
Morse, Patti
GUMBY: THE MOVIE
Mortensen, Henry
BLUE TIGER
CRIMSON TIDE
Mortensen, Viggo
CREW, THE
CRIMSON TIDE
PROPHECY, THE
Morton, Billy
BLACK FOX
Morton, Joe
WALKING DEAD, THE
Morton, Rob
SEPARATE LIVES

Morton, Talbert
HIGHER LEARNING
Morwell, Robert
HOWLING: NEW MOON RISING, THE
Mosca, Bernard A.
TO WONG FOO, THANKS FOR
EVERYTHING! JULIE NEWMAR
Moschonas, Maree
ONCE WERE WARRIORS
Moscoso, Gerardo
DESPERADO
Moseley, Bill
OUTSIDE THE LAW
PREHYSTERIA! 3
Moser, Jeff
BILLY MADISON
Moses, Billy
ALMOST DEAD
Moses, William R.
CIRCUMSTANCES UNKNOWN
FUN
Mosier, Scott
MALLRATS
Mosley, Roger E.
PENTATHLON
Moss, Elisabeth
SEPARATE LIVES
Moss, Jesse
GOLD DIGGERS: THE SECRET OF BEAR
MOUNTAIN
Moss, Michael H.
FLUKE
Mosse, Mireille
CITY OF LOST CHILDREN, THE
Mossley, Robin
BROKEN TRUST
Mostel, Josh
BASKETBALL DIARIES, THE
BILLY MADISON
Moston, Murray
SMOKE
Mother Earth
TIE-DIED: ROCK 'N' ROLL'S MOST
DEADICATED FANS
Motoki, Masahiro
MYSTERY OF RAMPO, THE
Motu, Michel
CITY OF LOST CHILDREN, THE
Motu, Rangi
ONCE WERE WARRIORS
Mouss
FUNNY BONES
Mouton, Benjamin
TIE THAT BINDS, THE
Moves Camp, Ellen
LAKOTA WOMAN: SIEGE AT WOUNDED
KNEE
Moy, Raymond
PARTY GIRL
Moyer, Paul
HEAT
Moyle, James
CLASS OF '61
Mpute, Mia
FRIENDS
Mr. Rogers
CASPER
Mueller, Cat
SEVEN
Mueller-Stahl, Armin
LAST GOOD TIME, THE
PYROMANIAC'S LOVE STORY, A
Muglia, Nick
ACROSS THE SEA OF TIME: NEW YORK
3D
Muhoro, Kahara
CONGO

Mui, Anita
EXECUTIONERS
HEROIC TRIO, THE
Muirhead, Oliver
GHOST BRIGADE
Muirhead-Manik, Crystal
MALLRATS
Mukherjee, Madhabi
CHARULATA
Mukherjee, Sailen
CHARULATA
Mukherjee, Suku
CHARULATA
Mulcahy, Jack
BROTHERS MCMULLEN, THE
Mulheron, Danny
MEET THE FEEBLES
Mulholland, Declan
RUN OF THE COUNTRY, THE
Mullan, Peter
BRAVEHEART
Mullane, Dan
MIGHTY APHRODITE
Mullane, Larry
CLOCKERS
Mullen, Georgia
AILSA
Mullen, Jesse
PENTATHLON
Mullen, Marie
CIRCLE OF FRIENDS
Mullen, Peter
SHALLOW GRAVE
Mullen, Stuart
JUDGE DREDD
Muller, Martin
CRUMB
Mulligan, Gerry
GREAT DAY IN HARLEM, A
Mullin, Carmel
NOSTRADAMUS KID, THE
Mullin, Stephanie
LOSING ISAIAH
Mullion, Annabel
CARRINGTON
Mulroney, Dermot
COPYCAT
HOW TO MAKE AN AMERICAN QUILT
LIVING IN OBLIVION
Mulrooney, Kelsey
LITTLE PRINCESS, A
Mulwa, David
GREAT ELEPHANT ESCAPE, THE
Mumy, Bill
THREE WISHES
Mumy, Seth
THREE WISHES
Mune, Ian
ONCE WERE WARRIORS
Munford, Tricia
SPY WITHIN, THE
Mungai, David
CONGO
Munoz, Anais
STRANGE DAYS
Munro, Caroline
HEAVEN'S A DRAG
Munro, Lochlyn
DIGGER
Munson, Warren
ROSWELL: THE U.F.O. COVER-UP
Muntz, Donny
SUM OF US, THE
Murad, Jit
BEYOND RANGOON
Murcell, George
CUTTHROAT ISLAND

Murdoch, Bill
BRAVEHEART
Murdock, George
AMERICAN PRESIDENT, THE
Murnik, Peter
CLASS OF '61
Muro, James
STRANGE DAYS
Murphy, Brittany
CLUELESS
Murphy, Donna
JADE
Murphy, Eddie
VAMPIRE IN BROOKLYN
Murphy, Gerard
WATERWORLD
Murphy, Guiseppe
PRIEST
Murphy, Harry
NIXON
Murphy, Kevin
RUN OF THE COUNTRY, THE
Murphy, Kim
HOUSEGUEST
Murphy, Larry
AWFULLY BIG ADVENTURE, AN
Murphy, Martin
BRAVEHEART
FRANKIE STARLIGHT
Murphy, Rosemary
MIGHTY APHRODITE
Murphy, Sheila
TWO BITS
Murphy, Sue
NINE MONTHS
Murphy, Suzanne Schnulle
NIXON
Murphy, Terry
CASPER
Murphy, Torrence W.
LOSING ISAIAH
Murphy, Wendy
ANDROID AFFAIR, THE
Murphy, William John
CONGO
Murray, Brett
RADIO INSIDE
Murray, Bronwen
TOM AND HUCK
Murray, Christopher
JUST CAUSE
VIRTUOSITY
Murray, Jeff
ATTACK OF THE 60-FOOT CENTERFOLD
Murray, Mary Gordon
EVOLVER
Murray, Stella
DOLORES CLAIBORNE
Murtagh, John
BRAVEHEART
ROB ROY
Murua, Lautaro
I, THE WORST OF ALL
Muse, Robert
SILENCE OF THE HAMS
Musick, Pat
PEBBLE AND THE PENGUIN, THE
PEBBLE AND THE PENGUIN, THE
Musser, Larry
BAD COMPANY
Muth, Ellen
DOLORES CLAIBORNE
Mutoh, Sumi
HUNTED, THE
Mutune, Anthony
CONGO

Mwangi, Sylvester
CONGO
Myers, Dwight Errington
NEW JERSEY DRIVE
Myers, Johnny
HACKERS
Myers, Joseph S.
WAITING TO EXHALE
Myers, Joshua
GOOD DAY TO DIE, A
Myers, Lou
PIANO LESSON, THE
Myers, Matthew
IN THE NAME OF THE EMPEROR
Mygind, Peter
KINGDOM, THE
Myint, Cho Cho
BEYOND RANGOON
Myint, Ye
BEYOND RANGOON
Myles, Eileen
ART FOR TEACHERS OF CHILDREN
Myslivyi, Valentin
AMERICAN COP
N'Guessan, Albertine
FACES OF WOMEN
Nabor, John
PENTATHLON
Nacerino, Anthony
CLOCKERS
Nacker, Sally
SAFE PASSAGE
Nacman, Frances
MONTH BY THE LAKE, A
NacNeal, Catherine
UNDER SIEGE 2: DARK TERRITORY
Nadir, Robert
BETTER OFF DEAD
DANGER OF LOVE
MAD LOVE
Nadler, Larry E.
CASINO
Naeberg, Kurt
DILLINGER
Naessens, Edward
FRANKIE STARLIGHT
Nagai, Ichirou
AI CITY
Nagai, Toru
CASINO
Nagele, Oliver
NOBODY LOVES ME
Nagle, Margaret
FORGET PARIS
Nagy, Michelle
EXPERT, THE
Nahon, Philippe
PIGALLE
Nahra, Nancy
FAIR GAME
Nairn, Victoria
SHALLOW GRAVE
Najera, Miguel
NICK OF TIME
VIRTUOSITY
Najimy, Kathy
JEFFREY
Nakama, Yuriko
BLUE VILLA, THE
Nakamura, Jessica
BILLY MADISON
Nakamura, Saemi
DANGEROUS, THE
JURY DUTY
Nakamura, Toru
BLUE TIGER
NEW YORK COP

Nakashima, Frank
BILLY MADISON
Nakatsuka, Hiroshi
HUNTED, THE
Nakayama, Toshiji
MYSTERY OF RAMPO, THE
Nakumara, Lawrence
BILLY MADISON
Namdeo, Govind
BANDIT QUEEN
Nance, Jack
ACROSS THE MOON
Nance, John
TALL TALE: THE UNBELIEVABLE
ADVENTURES OF PECOS BILL
Nance, Jr., Cortez
DEAD MAN WALKING
Nannarone, Chris
CONVICT COWBOY
Nanni, Gemma
ME AND THE MOB
Napier, Charles
BALLISTIC
BODY SHOT
JURY DUTY
3 NINJAS KNUCKLE UP
Napier, Marshall
BABE
Napolitano, Jon
TWO BITS
Naprous, Daniel
FIRST KNIGHT
Narahashi, Yoko
MYSTERY OF RAMPO, THE
Narayan, Lakshmi
BANDIT QUEEN
Narita, Richard
GALAXIS
Nark-Orn, Willie
MAGIC IN THE WATER
Narkis, Sally
VAMPIRES AND OTHER STEREOTYPES
Narvy, Jason
MIGHTY MORPHIN POWER RANGERS:
THE MOVIE
Nascarella, Arthur
CLOCKERS
ME AND THE MOB
NEW JERSEY DRIVE
Nash, Graham
BRIAN WILSON: I JUST WASN'T MADE
FOR THESE TIMES
Nash, Larry
BREACH OF CONDUCT
WHITE MAN'S BURDEN
Nash, Niecy
BOYS ON THE SIDE
Nassauer, Tyson
MALLRATS
Nassira, Nicola
EVOLVER
Nasso, Julius
UNDER SIEGE 2: DARK TERRITORY
Nation, Ashley
SHOWGIRLS
Natsuki, Mari
HUNTED, THE
Naught by Nature
SHOW, THE
Naujoks, Ingo
NOBODY LOVES ME
Naumenko, Vasheslav
MUTE WITNESS
Navarro, Demetrius
FRIDAY
Navarro, Erika
FAIR GAME

Navarro, Lolo
  BURNING SEASON, THE
Navin, Jr., John P.
  CLASS OF '61
Nazri, Mohd Wan
  BEYOND RANGOON
Ndaba, Themba
  CRY, THE BELOVED COUNTRY
Neal, David
  FEAST OF JULY
Neal, Dennis F.
  DEAD MAN WALKING
Neal, Rome
  NADJA
Neave, Belinda
  RESTORATION
Neave, Gordon
  FAR FROM HOME: THE ADVENTURES OF
    YELLOW DOG
Nedovodin, Nickolai
  AMERICAN COP
Nee, Phil
  SABRINA
Needham, Jessica
  BABY-SITTERS CLUB, THE
  INDICTMENT: THE MCMARTIN TRIAL
Needham, Peter
  BEFORE THE RAIN
Neeson, Liam
  LAMB
  ROB ROY
Nefertiti
  PANTHER
Neff, Mary
  FRANK & JESSE
Negroponte, Peter
  JUPITER'S WIFE
Negroponte, Ramona
  JUPITER'S WIFE
Negulesco, Julian
  FRANKIE STARLIGHT
Neidorf, David
  DILLINGER
Neil, Julian
  BOYS ON THE SIDE
  SCANNERS: THE SHOWDOWN
Neill, Sam
  COUNTRY LIFE
  DEATH IN BRUNSWICK
  IN THE MOUTH OF MADNESS
  RESTORATION
Neilsen, Brigitte
  GALAXIS
Nelligan, Kate
  HOW TO MAKE AN AMERICAN QUILT
Nelms, Aaron
  SECRETARY, THE
Nelson, Adam
  DEAD MAN WALKING
Nelson, Albert
  PROPHECY, THE
Nelson, Danny
  JOURNEY OF AUGUST KING, THE
Nelson, Judd
  CIRCUMSTANCES UNKNOWN
Nelson, Kahlil
  PANTHER
Nelson, Kelly
  CHILDREN OF THE CORN III: URBAN
    HARVEST
Nelson, Lee Mark
  JEFFREY
Nelson, Mark J.
  LAKOTA WOMAN: SIEGE AT WOUNDED
    KNEE
Nelson, Novela
  DEAD FUNNY

Nelson, Raymond
  CURE, THE
Nelson, Sandy
  BRAVEHEART
Nelson, Tim Blake
  AMATEUR
  HEAVYWEIGHTS
Nemade, Avinash
  BANDIT QUEEN
Nemec, Corin
  OPERATION DUMBO DROP
Neri, Nando
  POSTMAN, THE
Nesbit, Michael
  THREE WISHES
Neufeld, Mark
  HIGHLANDER: THE FINAL DIMENSION
Neuhaus, Ingo
  BIGFOOT: THE UNFORGETTABLE
    ENCOUNTER
Neumann, Johanna
  PROMISE, THE
Neumayr, Rudolf
  FOR GOD AND COUNTRY
Neuwirth, Bebe
  JUMANJI
Neves, August
  WATERWORLD
Neville, Aaron
  LAST RIDE, THE
Neville, Daphne
  BUFFALO GIRLS
  FEAST OF JULY
Neville, John
  DANGEROUS MINDS
Nevinson, Genni
  BABE
Nevinson, Gennie
  MURIEL'S WEDDING
Nevolina, Anzhelika
  CREATION OF ADAM
New, Jennifer
  ATTACK OF THE 60-FOOT CENTERFOLD
New Kiva Motions Puppet Theater
  BOYS ON THE SIDE
New, Tina
  TALES FROM THE CRYPT: DEMON
    KNIGHT
Newbern, George
  FATHER OF THE BRIDE PART II
Newberry, Kymberly S.
  AMERICAN PRESIDENT, THE
Newcott, Rosemary
  GETTING OUT
Newell, Ron
  HOUSEGUEST
Newkirk, Toy
  O.J. SIMPSON STORY, THE
Newlin, Dika
  CREEP
Newman, Daniel
  RETURN OF THE NATIVE, THE
Newman, Danny
  BEFORE THE RAIN
Newman, Marilla
  NOSTRADAMUS KID, THE
Newman, Mark D.
  APOLLO 13
Newman, Mike
  FUNNY BONES
Newman, Randy
  BRIAN WILSON: I JUST WASN'T MADE
    FOR THESE TIMES
Newman, Robert
  CLASS OF '61
Newman, Robert L.
  BODY STROKES

Newman, William
  JURY DUTY
  TOM AND HUCK
Newmar, Julie
  TO WONG FOO, THANKS FOR
    EVERYTHING! JULIE NEWMAR
Newmaster, Hanna
  CROSSING GUARD, THE
Newsom, Ted
  ATTACK OF THE 60-FOOT CENTERFOLD
Newton, Huey
  PANTHER
Newton, Thandie
  JEFFERSON IN PARIS
  JOURNEY OF AUGUST KING, THE
Ng, Carrie
  NAKED KILLER
Ng Sin-lin
  RETURN OF THE GOD OF GAMBLERS
Ngaata, Jim
  ONCE WERE WARRIORS
Ngakane, Sam
  CRY, THE BELOVED COUNTRY
Ngauma, Robbie
  ONCE WERE WARRIORS
Ngoombujarra, David
  DALLAS DOLL
Nguku, Eric Mungai
  OUTBREAK
Nguyen, Dustin
  DOOM GENERATION, THE
  VIRTUOSITY
Nguyen Minh Tri
  TRAPS
Nguyen Ngoc Dang
  TRAPS
Nguyen-McCormick, Mitchell
  HACKERS
Ni King
  ASHES OF TIME
Ni Mhuiri, Aine
  RUN OF THE COUNTRY, THE
Ni Zengshao
  SHANGHAI TRIAD
Nicholas, Harold
  FUNNY BONES
Nicholas, Hassan
  FATHER AND SCOUT
Nicholas, Robin
  BUFFALO GIRLS
Nicholas, Thomas Ian
  KID IN KING ARTHUR'S COURT, A
Nicholls, Phoebe
  PERSUASION
Nichols, Alyssa Ashley
  ZOOMAN
Nichols, John Cannon
  CURSE OF THE STARVING CLASS
Nichols, Steven
  COVER ME
Nichols, Taylor
  AMERICAN PRESIDENT, THE
  CONGO
  DIRTY MONEY
Nicholson, Jack
  CROSSING GUARD, THE
Nicholson, Mil
  S.F.W.
Nicholson, Scott
  DIE HARD WITH A VENGEANCE
Nickel, Jochen
  STALINGRAD
Nickerson, Jay
  POSTCARDS FROM AMERICA
Nicks, Taral
  JUST CAUSE
Nicolas, Rose-Marie
  NEA

Nicoletti, Tom
NIXON
Nicolosi, Dino
DEATH IN BRUNSWICK
Nicolosi, Michael
DREAM A LITTLE DREAM 2
THINGS TO DO IN DENVER WHEN
YOU'RE DEAD
Nicols, David B.
FIRST DEGREE
Nielsen, Birgit
PENTATHLON
Nielsen, Finn
KINGDOM, THE
Nielsen, Leslie
DIGGER
DRACULA: DEAD AND LOVING IT
RENT-A-KID
Nielsen, Maura
DRACULA: DEAD AND LOVING IT
Nielsen, Thea
DRACULA: DEAD AND LOVING IT
Nienhuis, Terry
JOURNEY OF AUGUST KING, THE
Nies, Eric
BRADY BUNCH MOVIE, THE
Nieves, Benny
AMATEUR
Niewinowski, B.
SHORT FILM ABOUT KILLING, A
Nihoniho, Maru
ONCE WERE WARRIORS
Nijo, Eiko
VIRTUOSITY
Nikitina, N.
I AM CUBA
Niles, Jeff
REASON TO BELIEVE, A
Nilsson, Rob
COPYCAT
Nimmons, Carole
RUN OF THE COUNTRY, THE
Ning Jing
RED FIRECRACKER, GREEN
FIRECRACKER
Nino, Miguel
STEAL BIG, STEAL LITTLE
Nipkow, Leslie
NEW JERSEY DRIVE
Nipote, Joe
CASPER
Nirmalker, Ram Charan
BANDIT QUEEN
Nisbet, Stuart
CASINO
MURDER IN THE FIRST
Nishi, Toshiyuki
DECONSTRUCTING SARAH
Nishikawa, Lane
VILLAGE OF THE DAMNED
Nissen, Claus
KINGDOM, THE
Nitschke, Ronald
INNOCENT, THE
Nix, Tommy
DESPERADO
Nixon, Lola
SUM OF US, THE
Nixon, Norm
OUT OF SYNC
Noa, Jorge
AMERICAN PRESIDENT, THE
Noah, James
COSMIC SLOP
Nocito, Ken
VAMPIRES AND OTHER STEREOTYPES
Noday, Patt
EMPIRE RECORDS

Noel, Kettly
TOTAL ECLIPSE
Noel, Monique
I LIKE TO PLAY GAMES
Noga, Tom
TANK GIRL
Nogueira, Joaquim
VALLEY OF ABRAHAM, THE
Nogulich, Natalija
GLASS SHIELD, THE
STEAL BIG, STEAL LITTLE
WATER ENGINE, THE
Noh, Lorene
CONGO
Noice, J. Gordon
VIRTUOSITY
Noiret, Philippe
GROSSE FATIGUE
POSTMAN, THE
Nolan, Ashley
SCARLET LETTER, THE
Nolan, Barry
NUMBER ONE FAN
Nolan, Tom
INDICTMENT: THE MCMARTIN TRIAL
WHITE MAN'S BURDEN
Nolasco, E.O.
CLOCKERS
Nolot, Jacques
WILD REEDS
Nolsoe, Gunnvor
KINGDOM, THE
Nolte, Nick
JEFFERSON IN PARIS
Noonan, Polly
ARIZONA DREAM
Noonan, Tom
HEAT
Norby, Ghita
KINGDOM, THE
Norgaard, Carsten
OUT OF ANNIE'S PAST
Noritake, Cynthia
NICK OF TIME
Norman, Susan
SAFE
Norman, Zook
O.J. SIMPSON STORY, THE
Norment, Mary Ann
FUN
Norrington, Malcolm
HIGHER LEARNING
STRANGE DAYS
Norris, Buckley
EROTIQUE
Norris, Chuck
TOP DOG
Norris, Dean
LAKOTA WOMAN: SIEGE AT WOUNDED
KNEE
NUMBER ONE FAN
SAFE
Norstrom, Tomas
DREAMING OF RITA
North, Alan
JERKY BOYS: THE MOVIE, THE
North, J.J.
ATTACK OF THE 60-FOOT CENTERFOLD
Northam, Jeremy
CARRINGTON
NET, THE
**Northfield Mount Hermon Gymnastics
Team**
ART FOR TEACHERS OF CHILDREN
Northrup, Cindie
FUN
Norton, Alex
BRAVEHEART

Norton, Kristen
ACE VENTURA: WHEN NATURE CALLS
Norton, Widow
TO WONG FOO, THANKS FOR
EVERYTHING! JULIE NEWMAR
Norwood, Jr., Willie
ENEMY WITHIN, THE
Noseworthy, Jack
BRADY BUNCH MOVIE, THE
S.F.W.
Nossek, Ralph
CITIZEN X
Noto, Vic
NEW YORK COP
Notorious B.I.G., The
SHOW, THE
Nottingham, Shawn
OUT OF ANNIE'S PAST
Nousianen, Pandora J.
EMPIRE RECORDS
Noveck, Fima
NIXON
Novello, Don
CASPER
Novi, Enrique
BURNING SEASON, THE
Novotny, Dean "Sissy Fit"
POSTCARDS FROM AMERICA
Nowicki, Tom
CLASS OF '61
Noy, Fernando
I, THE WORST OF ALL
Nozawa, Nachi
AI CITY
Nucci, Danny
CRIMSON TIDE
Nudelman, Daniel
LOSING ISAIAH
Nundra, Michael Aniel
ACROSS THE MOON
Nunes, Michael
PEBBLE AND THE PENGUIN, THE
Nunez, Deborah
DARK DEALER
Nunez, Lazaro
UP TO A CERTAIN POINT
Nunley, Marquis
TIE THAT BINDS, THE
Nunn, Bill
CANADIAN BACON
CANDYMAN: FAREWELL TO THE FLESH
MONEY TRAIN
THINGS TO DO IN DENVER WHEN
YOU'RE DEAD
Nussbaum, Mike
LOSING ISAIAH
STEAL BIG, STEAL LITTLE
WATER ENGINE, THE
Nutini, Jean-Pierre
SUDDEN DEATH
Nwanze, Valentine
ROB ROY
Nyutho, Edwin
GREAT ELEPHANT ESCAPE, THE
O'Brien, Austin
APOLLO 13
BABY-SITTERS CLUB, THE
O'Brien, Hannah
DALLAS DOLL
O'Brien, Hugh B.
RUN OF THE COUNTRY, THE
O'Brien, Joycelyn
INDICTMENT: THE MCMARTIN TRIAL
O'Brien, Laurie
TOO YOUNG TO DIE?
O'Brien, Mariah
HALLOWEEN: THE CURSE OF MICHAEL
MYERS

O'Brien, Neill
AILSA

O'Brien, Niall
BRAVEHEART
CLASS OF '61

O'Brien, Patrick Thomas
BRADY BUNCH MOVIE, THE
FORGET PARIS

O'Brien, Skip
HIGHER LEARNING

O'Bryan, Sean
CRIMSON TIDE

O'Byrne, Niamh
CIRCLE OF FRIENDS

O'Connell, Annie
OUTSIDE THE LAW

O'Connell, Dierdre
SMOKE

O'Connell, Jack
MONEY TRAIN

O'Connell, Kay
COLDBLOODED

O'Connell, Patti Ann
JEFFREY

O'Conner, Stuart
LAMB

O'Connor, Dennis
IN THE MOUTH OF MADNESS

O'Connor, Derrick
HOW TO MAKE AN AMERICAN QUILT

O'Connor, Gladys
BILLY MADISON

O'Connor, Jeanette
GIRL IN THE CADILLAC

O'Connor, Kevin J.
CANADIAN BACON
LORD OF ILLUSIONS
VIRTUOSITY

O'Connor, Raymond
PREHYSTERIA! 3

O'Connor, Renee
DARKMAN 2: THE RETURN OF DURANT

O'Conor, Hugh
LAMB

O'Donnell, Bob
DILLINGER

O'Donnell, Chris
BATMAN FOREVER
CIRCLE OF FRIENDS
MAD LOVE

O'Donnell, Fergus
BUSINESS AFFAIR, A

O'Donnell, Katy
AWFULLY BIG ADVENTURE, AN

O'Donnell, Rosie
NOW AND THEN

O'Donohue, Ryan Sean
TALES FROM THE CRYPT: DEMON
KNIGHT

O'Farrell, Dervla
CIRCLE OF FRIENDS

O'Grady, Monty
ANGUS

O'Grady, Patricia
ARIZONA DREAM

O'Haco, Daniel
HEAT

O'Halloran, Brian
MALLRATS

O'Hara, Catherine
TALL TALE: THE UNBELIEVABLE
ADVENTURES OF PECOS BILL

O'Hara, Coleen
GEORGIA

O'Hara, David
BRAVEHEART

O'Hurley, Shannon
COPYCAT

O'Keefe, Doug
IT TAKES TWO
JOHNNY MNEMONIC

O'Keefe, Michael
NINA TAKES A LOVER
THREE WISHES
TOO YOUNG TO DIE?

O'Keefe, Miles
POCAHONTAS: THE LEGEND

O'Kelly, Diane
AILSA

O'Larkin, Christopher
MALLRATS

O'Leary, William
CANDYMAN: FAREWELL TO THE FLESH
ENEMY WITHIN, THE

O'Malley, Bingo
HOUSEGUEST

O'Malley, Leonard
SHALLOW GRAVE

O'Mara, George
BIGFOOT: THE UNFORGETTABLE
ENCOUNTER

O'Nan, Sarah
INDICTMENT: THE MCMARTIN TRIAL

O'Neal, Brian E.
DEVIL IN A BLUE DRESS

O'Neal, Dink
CAGED HEARTS
GIRL IN THE CADILLAC

O'Neil, Carol
REASON TO BELIEVE, A

O'Neill, David Michael
BODY SHOT

O'Neill, Errol
DESPERATE PREY

O'Neill, Karen
CIRCLE OF FRIENDS

O'Neill, Kevin
IN THE DEEP WOODS

O'Neill, Margaret
CIRCLE OF FRIENDS

O'Neill, Michael
BUSHWHACKED

O'Neill, Padraig
AILSA

O'Neill, Robert
TWELVE MONKEYS

O'Raghallaigh, Padraig
AWFULLY BIG ADVENTURE, AN

O'Rawe, Geraldine
CIRCLE OF FRIENDS

O'Reilly, Lance
BABY-SITTERS CLUB, THE

O'Reilly, Michael
RUN OF THE COUNTRY, THE

O'Rourke, Mick
HACKERS

O'Rourke, Seamus
RUN OF THE COUNTRY, THE

O'Sullivan, James
CHILDREN OF THE CORN III: URBAN
HARVEST

O'Sullivan, Kat
TIE-DIED: ROCK 'N' ROLL'S MOST
DEADICATED FANS

O'Sullivan, Paul
IT TAKES TWO

O'Toole, Darren
AILSA

O'Toole, Harry
TWELVE MONKEYS

O'Toole, Matt
WHITE MAN'S BURDEN

O. Sanders, Jay
BIG GREEN, THE

Oakley, Charles
FORGET PARIS

Oates, William
COPYCAT

Obata, Toshiro
BLUE TIGER

Obata, Toshishiro
HUNTED, THE

Oberman, Milt
BIG GREEN, THE

Obermann, Nikola
FRENCH KISS

Obonsawin, Annick
IT TAKES TWO

Obray, Brandon
JUMANJI

Ocean, Ivory
NEXT DOOR
WALK IN THE CLOUDS, A

Oda, Narumi
MYSTERY OF RAMPO, THE

Odom, Todd
AMERICAN PRESIDENT, THE

Odom, Traci
OUTBREAK

Oechel, Hagen
PROMISE, THE

Oedy, Mary
FORGET PARIS
TANK GIRL

Offerman, Inge
FRENCH KISS

Offidani, Raffaella
CASTLE FREAK

Offutt, Sibyl
LOSING ISAIAH

Ogden, Richard
TO WONG FOO, THANKS FOR
EVERYTHING! JULIE NEWMAR

Oginome, Keiko
MYSTERY OF RAMPO, THE

Oglesby, Randy
CANDYMAN: FAREWELL TO THE FLESH

Oh, Sandra
DOUBLE HAPPINESS

Oh, Soon-Teck
RED SUN RISING
S.F.W.

Ohanian, Alain
REFLECTIONS IN THE DARK

Ohmer, Tom
FORGET PARIS

Oja, Peeter
CITY UNPLUGGED

Okada, Masumi
HUNTED, THE

Okimura, Frederick Y.
HIGHLANDER: THE FINAL DIMENSION

Okita, Clyde
AMERICA'S DEADLIEST HOME VIDEO

Okita, Patsy
AMERICA'S DEADLIEST HOME VIDEO

Okking, Jens
KINGDOM, THE

Okonedo, Sophie
ACE VENTURA: WHEN NATURE CALLS

Okumoto, Yuji
BLUE TIGER
RED SUN RISING

Okutani, Reiko
MYSTERY OF RAMPO, THE

Olanson, Elena
UNDERCOVER

Oldman, Gary
MURDER IN THE FIRST
SCARLET LETTER, THE

Oleynik, Larisa
BABY-SITTERS CLUB, THE

Oliveira, Rui
VALLEY OF ABRAHAM, THE

Oliver, Brett
OUTBREAK
Oliver, Christian
BABY-SITTERS CLUB, THE
Oliver, James Louis
ASSASSINS
Oliver, Michael
DILLINGER AND CAPONE
Oliver, Shirley
ASSASSINS
Oliver, Sylvester
BOYS ON THE SIDE
Olivero, Silvio
FIRST DEGREE
Olivia, J. Michael
BUFFALO GIRLS
Oliviero, Silvio
JOHNNY MNEMONIC
Olkewicz, Walter
STUART SAVES HIS FAMILY
Olla, Carla
RHYTHM THIEF
Olmos, Edward James
BURNING SEASON, THE
MY FAMILY: MI FAMILIA
Olney, Warren
CRIMSON TIDE
HIGHER LEARNING
Olsen, Amy
EXPERT, THE
Olsen, Ashley
DOUBLE, DOUBLE, TOIL AND TROUBLE
IT TAKES TWO
Olsen, Mary-Kate
DOUBLE, DOUBLE, TOIL AND TROUBLE
IT TAKES TWO
Olson, Barbara
NINE MONTHS
Olson, Craig
MURIEL'S WEDDING
Olson, Jamie
HEAVYWEIGHTS
Olson, Richard B.
LIE DOWN WITH DOGS
Olson, Ryan
INDIAN IN THE CUPBOARD, THE
Olson, Wallace
GRUMPIER OLD MEN
Oman, Wiki
ONCE WERE WARRIORS
Omar, Zaidi
BEYOND RANGOON
Onetto, Carlos
NO MERCY
Ong, Alannah
DOUBLE HAPPINESS
Ono, Jay
HUNTED, THE
Ontiveros, Lupe
MY FAMILY: MI FAMILIA
Opaterny, Patrick
FATHERLAND
Opinato, Mario
DANGEROUS, THE
Oppo, Emmanuelle
TOTAL ECLIPSE
Orange, Gerald
FOOL AND HIS MONEY, A
Orbach, Ron
CLUELESS
EROTIQUE
Orchid, Bruce R.
ASSASSINS
Orchid, Christina
ASSASSINS
FREE WILLY 2: THE ADVENTURE HOME
Orenstein, Peggy
CRUMB

Oriel, Ray
EROTIQUE
OUT OF ANNIE'S PAST
Orlandersmith, Dael
AMATEUR
Orman, Roscoe
NEW JERSEY DRIVE
Ormond, Julia
FIRST KNIGHT
SABRINA
Ornstein, Max Ryan
BYE BYE, LOVE
Orona, Yvonne C.
MAD LOVE
Orosz, Anna
CITIZEN X
Orr, Sean
IT TAKES TWO
MAN OF THE HOUSE
Orrison, George
BRIDGES OF MADISON COUNTY, THE
Orrison, Robert
BIGFOOT: THE UNFORGETTABLE
ENCOUNTER
Orser, Leland
COVER STORY
GIRL IN THE CADILLAC
SEVEN
Orta, Choco
ASSASSINS
Ortega, Armando
NICK OF TIME
Ortega, Sabrina
FUN
Ortiz, April
FATHER OF THE BRIDE PART II
Ortiz, Bill
PANTHER
Osanai, Fumiko
MYSTERY OF RAMPO, THE
Osborn, Bill
AVENGING ANGEL
OUT OF ANNIE'S PAST
Osborn, Lena
MOSAIC PROJECT, THE
Osborne, Rhonda J.
ASSASSINS
Osbourne, Ozzy
JERKY BOYS: THE MOVIE, THE
Oscarsson, Per
DREAMING OF RITA
Oshita, Eiji
MYSTERY OF RAMPO, THE
Osman, Nyak
BEYOND RANGOON
Ostrow, Ron
JERKY BOYS: THE MOVIE, THE
Otsuki, Kenji
MYSTERY OF RAMPO, THE
Otto, Miranda
NOSTRADAMUS KID, THE
Otto, Victoria
DANGER OF LOVE
Ouaknine, Huguette
MINA TANNENBAUM
Oumansky, Andre
HIGHLANDER: THE FINAL DIMENSION
OTHELLO
Ourgante, Andrei
WINDOW TO PARIS
Oussatova, Nina
WINDOW TO PARIS
Outerbridge, Paul
ANDROID AFFAIR, THE
Ove, Indra
OTHELLO
Overbey, Kellie
OUTBREAK

Overlund, David
REASON TO BELIEVE, A
Overman, Ion
WALKING DEAD, THE
Ovia, Zolanda
STRAWBERRY AND CHOCOLATE
Ovsyanko, Yury
CREATION OF ADAM
Owe, Baard
KINGDOM, THE
Owen, Chris
ANGUS
MAJOR PAYNE
Owen, Clive
CENTURY
CLASS OF '61
DOOMSDAY GUN
RETURN OF THE NATIVE, THE
Owen, Matthew
RETURN OF THE NATIVE, THE
Owen, Megan
CLEAN, SHAVEN
Owen, Rena
ONCE WERE WARRIORS
Owen, Robyn Pitt
MURIEL'S WEDDING
Owens, Albert
OUTBREAK
Owens, Brett
HOWLING: NEW MOON RISING, THE
Owens, Theodor Scott
BUSHWHACKED
Ozawa, Hitoshi
MYSTERY OF RAMPO, THE
Pacha, Bobby
MINA TANNENBAUM
PIGALLE
Pacifici, Federico
FLUKE
Pacino, Al
HEAT
TWO BITS
Pacitti, Dena J.
FUN
Packer, David
STRANGE DAYS
Pacula, Joanna
SILENCE OF THE HAMS
Padgett, Anna
INCREDIBLY TRUE ADVENTURES OF
TWO GIRLS IN LOVE, THE
Padilha, Maria
BOCA
Padin, Margarita
I, THE WORST OF ALL
Padron, Jose Philipe
PEREZ FAMILY, THE
Paez, Jorge "Maromero"
DIRTY MONEY
Pagan, Jr., Elbert
LOSING ISAIAH
Pagano, Anthony
RECKLESS
Pagath, Daniel R.
SUDDEN DEATH
Page, Bobbi
ARABIAN KNIGHT
Page, Jean-Claude
DR. JEKYLL & MS. HYDE
Page, Lawanda
FRIDAY
Pagett, Nicola
AWFULLY BIG ADVENTURE, AN
Paguet, Francis
MINA TANNENBAUM
Pai, Lianna
DEAD FUNNY

Pailhas, Geraldine
  DON JUAN DEMARCO
Pain, Frankie
  CITY OF LOST CHILDREN, THE
Paitina, Ivan
  AMERICAN COP
Pak, James
  HEROIC TRIO, THE
Palacio, James
  TO WONG FOO, THANKS FOR
    EVERYTHING! JULIE NEWMAR
Palacios, Arturo
  MY FAMILY: MI FAMILIA
Paladino, Dennis
  BATMAN FOREVER
Palance, Jack
  BUFFALO GIRLS
Palchek, Alexei
  CREATION OF ADAM
Paley, Andy
  BRIAN WILSON: I JUST WASN'T MADE
    FOR THESE TIMES
Palfenier, Shane
  CIRCUMSTANCES UNKNOWN
Palfrey, Lisa
  ENGLISHMAN WHO WENT UP A HILL
    BUT CAME DOWN A MOUNTAIN, THE
Pallett, Leonni
  RESTORATION
Pallister, Joseph
  BIKINI BISTRO
Palmer, Brett
  OUT OF ANNIE'S PAST
Palmer, David
  ROB ROY
Palmer, Ernest "Chili"
  GET SHORTY
Palmer, Hugh
  AMATEUR
  KISS OF DEATH
Palmer, Joel
  FAR FROM HOME: THE ADVENTURES OF
    YELLOW DOG
Palmer, Ken
  LITTLE PRINCESS, A
Palminteri, Chazz
  JADE
  PEREZ FAMILY, THE
  USUAL SUSPECTS, THE
Paltrow, Gwyneth
  JEFFERSON IN PARIS
  MOONLIGHT AND VALENTINO
  SEVEN
Pam-Grant, Susan
  FRIENDS
Panchal, Sitaram
  BANDIT QUEEN
Pandey, Hemnat
  BANDIT QUEEN
Pandey, Nirmal
  BANDIT QUEEN
Pang, Lum Chang
  PARTY GIRL
Pankin, Stuart
  CONGO
  FATHER AND SCOUT
  SILENCE OF THE HAMS
Pankow, Joanne
  KINGFISH: A STORY OF HUEY P. LONG
Pankratiev, Sergey
  AMERICAN COP
Panley, Teisha
  NEW JERSEY DRIVE
Pantano, Paul
  MIGHTY MORPHIN POWER RANGERS:
    THE MOVIE
Pantazopoulos, Nik
  ONLY THE BRAVE

Pantoliano, Joe
  BAD BOYS
  SPY WITHIN, THE
  STEAL BIG, STEAL LITTLE
  TERESA'S TATTOO
Panych, Morris
  MAGIC IN THE WATER
Papademetriou, Nicholas
  DEATH IN BRUNSWICK
Papiris, Jimmy
  BASKETBALL DIARIES, THE
Papjohn, Michael
  INDIAN IN THE CUPBOARD, THE
Pappone, Nicholas
  OUTBREAK
Paradise, James
  PENTATHLON
Paradise, James R.
  CONGO
Paraiso, Nicky
  JEFFREY
Pardee, Janelle
  GRANNY, THE
Pare, Michael
  DANGEROUS, THE
  VILLAGE OF THE DAMNED
Parent, Monique
  PLAY TIME
Parfitt, Judy
  DOLORES CLAIBORNE
Parillaud, Anne
  FRANKIE STARLIGHT
  SIX DAYS, SIX NIGHTS
Parilo, Marcos
  CANADIAN BACON
Park, Peyton
  CURSE OF THE STARVING CLASS
Parker, Andrew B.
  DIGGER
Parker, Brad
  THREE WISHES
Parker, Brook Susan
  STRANGE DAYS
Parker, F. William
  ROSWELL: THE U.F.O. COVER-UP
Parker, Ina
  REFLECTIONS IN THE DARK
Parker, Lisa
  BAR GIRLS
Parker, Mary-Louise
  BOYS ON THE SIDE
  RECKLESS
Parker, Mim
  TALES FROM THE CRYPT: DEMON
    KNIGHT
Parker, Molly
  LAST OF THE DOGMEN
Parker, Nathaniel
  OTHELLO
Parker, Nicole
  INCREDIBLY TRUE ADVENTURES OF
    TWO GIRLS IN LOVE, THE
Parker, Paula Jai
  COSMIC SLOP
  FRIDAY
  TALES FROM THE HOOD
Parker, Rachel
  REASON TO BELIEVE, A
Parker, Robby
  HIGHER LEARNING
Parker, Sarah Jessica
  MIAMI RHAPSODY
Parkes, Garrard
  IT TAKES TWO
Parkhill, Jason
  SCARLET LETTER, THE
Parkhouse, Bruck
  CONVICT COWBOY

Parkhurst, Heather Elizabeth
  GRANNY, THE
  SILENCE OF THE HAMS
Parks, Charles
  HOW TO MAKE AN AMERICAN QUILT
Parks, Dino
  GLASS SHIELD, THE
Parks, Peter
  SABRINA
Parks, Tammy
  ATTACK OF THE 60-FOOT CENTERFOLD
  MIDNIGHT TEASE 2
  PLAY TIME
Parks, Van Dyke
  BRIAN WILSON: I JUST WASN'T MADE
    FOR THESE TIMES
Parks, Wayne
  MURDER IN THE FIRST
Parnass, Peggy
  NOBODY LOVES ME
Parnell, David
  FRANKIE STARLIGHT
Parr, Stephen
  BIG GREEN, THE
Parra, Sharon
  WALKING DEAD, THE
Parrish, Amy
  SOMETHING TO TALK ABOUT
Parrish, Hope
  NET, THE
Parrish, Steve
  COVER STORY
Parsons, Estelle
  BOYS ON THE SIDE
Parsons, Karyn
  MAJOR PAYNE
Parsons, Nancy
  LAKOTA WOMAN: SIEGE AT WOUNDED
    KNEE
Parton, Julia
  GOOD GIRLS DON'T
Pasare, Georgette
  MIGHTY APHRODITE
Pasco, Nicholas
  TO DIE FOR
Pasdar, Adrian
  GHOST BRIGADE
  LAST GOOD TIME, THE
Pasquesi, David
  STUART SAVES HIS FAMILY
Pasquier, Genevieve
  JLG BY JLG
Passard, Colleen
  DEATH MACHINE
Passero, Lisa
  EVOLVER
Pastko, Earl
  ECLIPSE
Pastore, Vincent
  JERKY BOYS: THE MOVIE, THE
  MONEY TRAIN
Pastore, Vinny
  ME AND THE MOB
Pastuhov, Nikoai
  MUTE WITNESS
Patel, Nazim
  BANDIT QUEEN
Patel, Usha
  BUSINESS AFFAIR, A
Patellis, Ladd
  RECKLESS
Paterson, Bill
  RICHARD III
Paterson, Robert
  BRAVEHEART
Paton, Angela
  HOME FOR THE HOLIDAYS

Paton, Anthony
SCARLET LETTER, THE
Paton, Lance
IN THE MOUTH OF MADNESS
Patore, Vinnie
BASKETBALL DIARIES, THE
Patric, Jason
JOURNEY OF AUGUST KING, THE
Patrick, Anna
OTHELLO
Patrick, Barbara
BODY SHOT
LORD OF ILLUSIONS
Patrick, Charles
UNSTRUNG HEROES
Patrick, Robert
BODY SHOT
DECOY
Patrick, Vincent
MONEY TRAIN
Patten, Jamie
ART FOR TEACHERS OF CHILDREN
Patten, Moultrie
BETTER OFF DEAD
Patterson, Cindy
BALLOT MEASURE 9
Patterson, Derrick
PYROMANIAC'S LOVE STORY, A
Patterson, Rocky
DARK DEALER
Patterson, Scott
THREE WISHES
Patton, Will
COPYCAT
DILLINGER
IN THE DEEP WOODS
JUDICIAL CONSENT
Paul, Alexandra
CYBER BANDITS
Paul, Graham
JOURNEY OF AUGUST KING, THE
Paul, Patricia
CREEP
Pauldick, Jonathan
LIE DOWN WITH DOGS
Paulsen, Rob
GOOFY MOVIE, A
Pavlis, Joanna
FRENCH KISS
Pawk, Michele
JEFFREY
Pawn Boy
CREEP
Paxton, Bill
APOLLO 13
FRANK & JESSE
Paxton, Collin Wilcox
FLUKE
JOURNEY OF AUGUST KING, THE
Paxton, John
FRANK & JESSE
Paymer, David
AMERICAN PRESIDENT, THE
GET SHORTY
NIXON
Payne, Allen
VAMPIRE IN BROOKLYN
WALKING DEAD, THE
Payne, Arthur
AMERICAN COP
Payne, Bruce
OPERATION INTERCEPT
Payne, Janet
FORGET PARIS
Payne, Julie
BRADY BUNCH MOVIE, THE
Paynes, Stephen
RHYTHM THIEF

Paz, Francisco
JUST CAUSE
Peach, Mary
CUTTHROAT ISLAND
Pearlman, Stephen
DIE HARD WITH A VENGEANCE
Pearlstein, Julia
NET, THE
Pearlstein, Randy
SEARCH AND DESTROY
Pearson, Bret
NEVER TALK TO STRANGERS
Pearson, Fred
PRIEST
Pearson, Malachi
CASPER
Pearson, Rupert
PRIEST
Peart, Sage
SHOWGIRLS
Pearthree, Pippa
VILLAGE OF THE DAMNED
Pecher, Claude
AUGUSTIN
Peck, Amy
O.J. SIMPSON STORY, THE
Peck, Anthony
DIE HARD WITH A VENGEANCE
ENEMY WITHIN, THE
Peck, Brian
CHILDREN OF THE CORN III: URBAN
HARVEST
Peck, Jim
CLASS OF '61
Peck, Tony
BAD BLOOD
Peers, Tony
FUNNY BONES
Pegahmagabow, Robert Frank
DANCE ME OUTSIDE
Pegler, Mary
CUTTHROAT ISLAND
Peguero, Yakira
KIDS
Peil, Mary Beth
RECKLESS
Peimontese, Marie
CITY OF LOST CHILDREN, THE
Peldon, Ashley
SECRETARY, THE
Pelish, Randy
MURDER IN THE FIRST
Pelka, Valentine
FIRST KNIGHT
Pellay, Pat
FRIENDS
Pellegrino, Mark
CLASS OF '61
Pellegrino, Mick
STEAL BIG, STEAL LITTLE
Pelletier, Michele-Barbara
LOVE AND HUMAN REMAINS
Pelly, Wilma
GOOD DAY TO DIE, A
Pelton, Courtney
TOM AND HUCK
Pema, Sefer
LAMERICA
Pena, E.J. de la
BABY-SITTERS CLUB, THE
Pena, Elizabeth
ACROSS THE MOON
DEAD FUNNY
FREE WILLY 2: THE ADVENTURE HOME
Pendleton, Audrey
JUPITER'S WIFE
Pendleton, Austin
HOME FOR THE HOLIDAYS

Pendleton, Katina
JUPITER'S WIFE
Penn, Chris
TO WONG FOO, THANKS FOR
EVERYTHING! JULIE NEWMAR
Penn, Edward
ROSWELL: THE U.F.O. COVER-UP
Penn, Leo
CROSSING GUARD, THE
Penn, Sean
DEAD MAN WALKING
Pennello, Anthony
PENTATHLON
Penner, Jonathan
FOOL AND HIS MONEY, A
Pennetta, Bob
USUAL SUSPECTS, THE
Penny, Joe
DANGER OF LOVE
Penotti, Bernadette
KISS OF DEATH
Pentangelo, Joseph
KISS OF DEATH
Pentecost, George
ROSWELL: THE U.F.O. COVER-UP
Pentony, Alan
FRANKIE STARLIGHT
Pepa
NOT ANGELS BUT ANGELS
Pepper, Bob
ANGUS
Perana, Thomasina
ONCE WERE WARRIORS
Perdomo, Lou "Spot"
RIVER OF GRASS
Perdue, Evelyn
DANGER OF LOVE
Pereira, Debra J.
KISS OF DEATH
Perela, Marco
SUBSTITUTE WIFE, THE
Perensky, Tonie
UNDERNEATH, THE
Perera, Fia
VAMPIRES AND OTHER STEREOTYPES
Perevra, Rene
BURNING SEASON, THE
Perez, Jose
BURNING SEASON, THE
Perez, Lazaro
PEREZ FAMILY, THE
Perez, Manny
NEW YORK COP
Perez, Selena
DON JUAN DEMARCO
Perez, Tony
BURNING SEASON, THE
NET, THE
Perfidia
WIGSTOCK: THE MOVIE
Perfort, Holger
KINGDOM, THE
Pergnerova, Tereza
ACCUMULATOR 1
Perilli, Frank Ray
STEAL BIG, STEAL LITTLE
Perillo, Joey
TWELVE MONKEYS
TWO BITS
Perkins, Anthony
GLORY BOYS, THE
IN THE DEEP WOODS
Perkins, Elizabeth
MOONLIGHT AND VALENTINO
Perkins, Jonathan R.
NUMBER ONE FAN
Perkins, Millie
BODILY HARM

Perkins, Rick
UNDERNEATH, THE
Perkins, Zach
MALLRATS
Perlich, Max
GEORGIA
Perlman, Rhea
CANADIAN BACON
Perlman, Ron
CITY OF LOST CHILDREN, THE
FLUKE
Perri, Paul
IN THE DEEP WOODS
Perri, Tony
FIRST DEGREE
PYROMANIAC'S LOVE STORY, A
Perricone, Nora
KICKING AND SCREAMING
Perrier, Jean-Francois
JEFFERSON IN PARIS
Perrin, Alan
FEAST OF JULY
Perrin, Tim
FEAST OF JULY
Perrine, Valerie
BREAK, THE
GIRL IN THE CADILLAC
Perrineau, Jr., Harold
SMOKE
Perron, Fred
CONVICT COWBOY
Perry, Cathy
3 NINJAS KNUCKLE UP
Perry, Freda
DOUBLE, DOUBLE, TOIL AND TROUBLE
Perry, Jeff
KINGFISH: A STORY OF HUEY P. LONG
Perry, Joao
VALLEY OF ABRAHAM, THE
Perry, Manny
PANTHER
SUDDEN DEATH
Perry, Marisa
JUST CAUSE
Perry, Robert
RIVER OF GRASS
Perryman, Lou
SUBSTITUTE WIFE, THE
Persky, Lisa Jane
DEAD FUNNY
DESTINY TURNS ON THE RADIO
Peru, Coco
WIGSTOCK: THE MOVIE
Perugorria, Jorge
STRAWBERRY AND CHOCOLATE
Perusse, Jean-Pierre
HIGHLANDER: THE FINAL DIMENSION
Pesci, Joe
CASINO
Peter
NOT ANGELS BUT ANGELS
Peter B.
JEFFREY
Peter Duchin Orchestra, The
JADE
Peter, Regina
MUTE WITNESS
Peters, Brock
COSMIC SLOP
Peters, Jeremy
RETURN OF THE NATIVE, THE
Peters, Michaelle
TIE-DIED: ROCK 'N' ROLL'S MOST
DEADICATED FANS
Peters, Robert
PANTHER
Petersen, Else
KINGDOM, THE

Petersen, Helga
INNOCENT, THE
Peterson, Alan C.
BAD COMPANY
BROKEN TRUST
Peterson, Craig
ART FOR TEACHERS OF CHILDREN
Peterson, Dennis
BAR GIRLS
Peterson, Gunnar
PANTHER
Peterson, Robert
CRUDE OASIS, THE
Peterson, Sarah
JEFFREY
Petersons, Alexander
DESPERATE PREY
Petherbridge, Edward
AWFULLY BIG ADVENTURE, AN
Petit, Francois
MORTAL KOMBAT
Petit, Yvette
JEFFERSON IN PARIS
Petlock, John
FATHER AND SCOUT
Petrey, Samantha
MUTANT SPECIES
Petri, Andreas
DEADLY MARIA
Petri, Nina
DEADLY MARIA
Petrillo, Salvatore
CASINO
Petrovic, Willy
WATERWORLD
Petrozza, Luigi
ACROSS THE SEA OF TIME: NEW YORK
3D
Petruzzi, Joe
UNDERCOVER
Petty, Kamala
CROSSING GUARD, THE
Petty, Lori
GLASS SHIELD, THE
TANK GIRL
Petty, Tom
BRIAN WILSON: I JUST WASN'T MADE
FOR THESE TIMES
Pfefferkorn, Peter
PROMISE, THE
Pfeiffer, Chuck
NIXON
Pfeiffer, Dedee
MY FAMILY: MI FAMILIA
Pfeiffer, Michelle
DANGEROUS MINDS
Pfeiffer, Peter
COVER STORY
Pfieffer, Chuck
FOOL AND HIS MONEY, A
Pflieger, Jean
SAFE
Pfoff, Brent
GALAXIS
Phage-Wright, Joel
BLACK FOX
Phann, Quynh
DEAD PRESIDENTS
Phelan, Anthony
DESPERATE PREY
Phelan, Mark
ROSWELL: THE U.F.O. COVER-UP
Phetoe, David
FRIENDS
Phifer, Mekhi
CLOCKERS
Phifer, Zack
GET SHORTY

Philbin, John
CREW, THE
DILLINGER
Philibert, Angelique
CITY OF LOST CHILDREN, THE
Phillippe, Ryan
CRIMSON TIDE
Phillips, Avi
KURT VONNEGUT'S HARRISON
BERGERON
Phillips, Betty
GOLD DIGGERS: THE SECRET OF BEAR
MOUNTAIN
Phillips, Bobbie
SHOWGIRLS
Phillips, Demetre
MANGLER, THE
Phillips, Dorothea
CENTURY
Phillips, Ethan
JEFFREY
Phillips, Keith
COPYCAT
Phillips, Kristie
SPITFIRE
Phillips, Linda
BABE
Phillips, Lou Diamond
BOULEVARD
TERESA'S TATTOO
Phillips, Neville
CARRINGTON
FIRST KNIGHT
Phillips, Renee
AMERICAN PRESIDENT, THE
Phillips, Sam
DIE HARD WITH A VENGEANCE
Phillips, Sam Motoana
ACE VENTURA: WHEN NATURE CALLS
Phillips, Sandra
S.F.W.
Phina
SABRINA
Phoenix, Joaquin
TO DIE FOR
Piatov, Alexander
MUTE WITNESS
Piazza, Ivonne
ASSASSINS
Picard, Dorothee
FRENCH KISS
Piccoli, Michel
MARTHA AND I
Piccolo, Rino
GET SHORTY
SILENCE OF THE HAMS
Picerni, Steve
CANDYMAN: FAREWELL TO THE FLESH
Pickells, Michael
BEYOND RANGOON
Pickens, James
NIXON
Pickens, Jr., James
DEAD PRESIDENTS
Pickering, Andrew
LAMB
Pickett, Cindy
EVOLVER
Pickett, Tom
CIRCUMSTANCES UNKNOWN
Pickren, Richard
WHILE YOU WERE SLEEPING
Picot, Charles
WILD REEDS
Picot, Genevieve
MURIEL'S WEDDING
Picotte, Lisa
STRANGE DAYS

Picoy, Kane
TANK GIRL
Pidgeon, Rebecca
WATER ENGINE, THE
Piechocinski, J.
SHORT FILM ABOUT LOVE, A
Pieczynska, M.
SHORT FILM ABOUT KILLING, A
Piekarski, Wojciech
CITIZEN X
Pierce, Bradley
JUMANJI
TOO YOUNG TO DIE?
Pierce, Brock
THREE WISHES
Pierce, David Hyde
NIXON
Pierce, Julie
OUTBREAK
Pierce, Justin
KIDS
Pierce, Katie
FATHER OF THE BRIDE PART II
Pierce, Linda
GETTING OUT
Pierce, Wendell
BYE BYE, LOVE
HACKERS
WAITING TO EXHALE
Pierre, Gabriel
CITY OF LOST CHILDREN, THE
Pierre, Marie-Helene
DR. JEKYLL & MS. HYDE
Pierson, Eric
CANDYMAN: FAREWELL TO THE FLESH
Pierson, Geoff
TWO BITS
Pierson, Paul Rex
LIE DOWN WITH DOGS
Pietragallo, Gene
BODY SHOT
Pietrasz, L.
SHORT FILM ABOUT KILLING, A
Pietro, Brian
AMERICAN PRESIDENT, THE
Pike, Vanessa
MANGLER, THE
Pilato, Bradley
DEATH IN BRUNSWICK
Piletic, William
JADE
Pilkington, Roselynn
STEAL BIG, STEAL LITTLE
Pilmark, Soren
KINGDOM, THE
Pimental, Brian
GOOFY MOVIE, A
Pine, Larry
DEAD MAN WALKING
Ping Wu
UNDER SIEGE 2: DARK TERRITORY
Pinhey, Christopher Mark
BULLETPROOF HEART
Pinizotto, Joy
TWO BITS
Pinkett, Jada
TALES FROM THE CRYPT: DEMON
KNIGHT
Pinon, Dominique
CITY OF LOST CHILDREN, THE
Pinsker, Allan
SUDDEN DEATH
Pinson, Julie
UNSTRUNG HEROES
Pinto, Jose
VALLEY OF ABRAHAM, THE
Piontek, Klaus
PROMISE, THE

Piper, Beverly
FORGET PARIS
Pipoly, Danuel
3 NINJAS KNUCKLE UP
Piquet, Judith
WATER ENGINE, THE
Piras, Tunny
CASTLE FREAK
Pires, Padre
VALLEY OF ABRAHAM, THE
Pirkle, Joan
BODY SHOT
Pirouzkar, Ali
CASINO
Pisani, Anne-Marie
LES MISERABLES
Pissors, Wolfgang
FRENCH KISS
LES MISERABLES
Pistor, Ludger
INNOCENT, THE
Pitillo, Maria
BYE BYE, LOVE
FRANK & JESSE
Pitsis, Ted
3 NINJAS KNUCKLE UP
Pitt, Brad
SEVEN
TOO YOUNG TO DIE?
TWELVE MONKEYS
Pittman, ChaChi
FATHER AND SCOUT
Pittman, John
ZOOMAN
Pitts, Cary J.
OUTBREAK
Pittu, David
JERKY BOYS: THE MOVIE, THE
Piven, Jeremy
DR. JEKYLL & MS. HYDE
HEAT
MIAMI RHAPSODY
TWOGETHER
Pivot, Alexis
CITY OF LOST CHILDREN, THE
Pivot, Berangere
CITY OF LOST CHILDREN, THE
Pivot, Rene
CITY OF LOST CHILDREN, THE
Pizzino, Declan
OUT OF ANNIE'S PAST
Place, Mary Kay
TERESA'S TATTOO
Place, Patrica
OUTBREAK
Place, Patricia
SCANNERS: THE SHOWDOWN
Placido, Michele
LAMERICA
Plana, Tony
BURNING SEASON, THE
NIXON
Platias, Dina
BILLY MADISON
Plato, Z.
SHORT FILM ABOUT KILLING, A
Platt, Howard
NIXON
Platt, Oliver
FUNNY BONES
TALL TALE: THE UNBELIEVABLE
ADVENTURES OF PECOS BILL
Platt, Richard
FUNNY BONES
Plaza, Begonya
HEAT

Pleasence, Donald
ARABIAN KNIGHT
HALLOWEEN: THE CURSE OF MICHAEL
MYERS
Pleshette, John
BORN TO BE WILD
Plimpton, George
FOOL AND HIS MONEY, A
JUST CAUSE
NIXON
Plimpton, Martha
LAST SUMMER IN THE HAMPTONS
WOMAN AT WAR, A
Plowright, Joan
HOTEL SORRENTO
PYROMANIAC'S LOVE STORY, A
RETURN OF THE NATIVE, THE
SCARLET LETTER, THE
Plum, Mette Munk
KINGDOM, THE
Plummer, Amanda
PROPHECY, THE
Plummer, Christopher
CRACKERJACK
DOLORES CLAIBORNE
KURT VONNEGUT'S HARRISON
BERGERON
TWELVE MONKEYS
Plummer, David
PERSUASION
Plummer, Glenn
CONVICT COWBOY
SHOWGIRLS
STRANGE DAYS
THINGS TO DO IN DENVER WHEN
YOU'RE DEAD
Podbrey, Maurice
LOVE AND HUMAN REMAINS
Podemski, Jennifer
DANCE ME OUTSIDE
Podemski, Tamara
DANCE ME OUTSIDE
Podosin, Lisa
BAR GIRLS
Poe, IV, Edgar Allen
RADIO INSIDE
Pogue, Ken
WINGS OF COURAGE
Poindexter, Jeris
PANTHER
Poindexter, Jeris Lee
DEVIL IN A BLUE DRESS
Poindexter, Larry
BODY CHEMISTRY 4: FULL EXPOSURE
Point, Dana
WALKING DEAD, THE
Poitier, Sidney
GOOD DAY TO DIE, A
Pokatilov, Aleksei
BURNT BY THE SUN
Polan, Claire
ATTACK OF THE 60-FOOT CENTERFOLD
Poland, Greg
AMERICAN PRESIDENT, THE
Poland, Simon
SPITFIRE
Polanski, Roman
GROSSE FATIGUE
PURE FORMALITY, A
Polczwartek, Eric
ARIZONA DREAM
Poli, Rick
VAMPIRES AND OTHER STEREOTYPES
Polito, Jon
BUSHWHACKED
FLUKE
Polito, Steven
TO WONG FOO, THANKS FOR
EVERYTHING! JULIE NEWMAR

Poliushkina, Natalia
MUTE WITNESS
Polizos, Vic
INDICTMENT: THE MCMARTIN TRIAL
Polkhotte, Tanya
SEARCH AND DESTROY
Pollack, Paige
BABE
Pollak, Kevin
CANADIAN BACON
CASINO
GRUMPIER OLD MEN
MIAMI RHAPSODY
USUAL SUSPECTS, THE
Pollard, Michael J.
ARIZONA DREAM
Pollet, Will
HEAVEN'S A DRAG
Polley, Sarah
EXOTICA
Pollock, Daniel
DEATH IN BRUNSWICK
Pollock, Robert
ONCE WERE WARRIORS
Polson, Cecily
MURIEL'S WEDDING
Polson, John
SUM OF US, THE
Polusen, David
CONVICT COWBOY
Pomeranc, Max
FLUKE
Pomers, Scarlett
BABY-SITTERS CLUB, THE
Pommier, Michael C.
BRIDGES OF MADISON COUNTY, THE
Ponazecki, Joe
JEFFREY
Ponzio, Carla
BAR GIRLS
Pool, Austin
BILLY MADISON
IT TAKES TWO
TOMMY BOY
Poor, Bray
CLOCKERS
DIE HARD WITH A VENGEANCE
MIGHTY APHRODITE
Pop, Iggy
TANK GIRL
Pop, Julie
SHOWGIRLS
Pope, Lucita
SISTER MY SISTER
Popelka, Ashley
JUST CAUSE
Popeye
DIRTY MONEY
Poppel, Marc
SEPARATE LIVES
Poppins, Mickey
PRIEST
Porizkova, Paulina
ARIZONA DREAM
Porretta, Matthew
DRACULA: DEAD AND LOVING IT
Porter, Cathleen
TIE-DIED: ROCK 'N' ROLL'S MOST
DEADICATED FANS
Porter, Moss
MONEY TRAIN
Porter, Rich
FORGET PARIS
Porter, Terry
HACKERS
Portlock, David
EMBRACE OF THE VAMPIRE

Portman, Natalie
HEAT
Portnow, Richard
ACROSS THE MOON
INDICTMENT: THE MCMARTIN TRIAL
MAN OF THE HOUSE
SEVEN
S.F.W.
Poschl, Hanno
BEFORE SUNRISE
Poser, Toby
INCREDIBLY TRUE ADVENTURES OF
TWO GIRLS IN LOVE, THE
Posey, Parker
AMATEUR
DOOM GENERATION, THE
KICKING AND SCREAMING
PARTY GIRL
Postlethwaite, Pete
USUAL SUSPECTS, THE
Potsig, Gareth
PRIEST
Potter, Chris
INNOCENT, THE
Potter, Jerry
SCANNERS: THE SHOWDOWN
Potter, Tom
BALLOT MEASURE 9
Potts, Annie
TOY STORY
Potts, Jonathan
WHEN NIGHT IS FALLING
Potts, Michael
HACKERS
Pouget, Ely
DEATH MACHINE
Poulikakos, Dimitri
BLUE VILLA, THE
Poulsen, Benny
KINGDOM, THE
Pounder, CCH
TALES FROM THE CRYPT: DEMON
KNIGHT
ZOOMAN
Poupaud, Melvil
INNOCENT LIES
Pourtash, Alexander
BRADY BUNCH MOVIE, THE
Povik, Boleslav
ACCUMULATOR 1
Powell, Amy
WHITE MAN'S BURDEN
Powell, Andrea
EMPIRE RECORDS
Powell, Clifton
DEAD PRESIDENTS
Powell, Esteban Louis
POWDER
Powell, Everard
GREAT DAY IN HARLEM, A
Powell, Josef
VAMPIRE IN BROOKLYN
Powell, Molly
LAST GOOD TIME, THE
Powell, Rutger
VAMPIRES AND OTHER STEREOTYPES
Powell, Tim
CLASS OF '61
Power, Amanda Nicole
3 NINJAS KNUCKLE UP
Power, Chad
3 NINJAS KNUCKLE UP
Power, Derry
FRANKIE STARLIGHT
Powers, Adam
PANTHER
Powers, Barclay
SEX, DRUGS AND DEMOCRACY

Powledge, David
USUAL SUSPECTS, THE
Pownall, Peter
ANDROID AFFAIR, THE
Powrie, Gregor
SHALLOW GRAVE
Prairie, Tanner Lee
ANGUS
Prataris, George
DEATH IN BRUNSWICK
Pratt, Bianca
ADDICTION, THE
Pratt, Kyla
BABY-SITTERS CLUB, THE
MY ANTONIA
Pratt, Monica
TIE-DIED: ROCK 'N' ROLL'S MOST
DEADICATED FANS
Praxmarer, Monika
FOR GOD AND COUNTRY
Preece, Tim
FEAST OF JULY
Premoli, Sergio
LEAVING LAS VEGAS
Prentice, Ernie
POWER OF ATTORNEY
Presle, Micheline
LES MISERABLES
NEA
Pressley, Paizhe
EMPIRE RECORDS
Pressman, Lawrence
ANGUS
ENEMY WITHIN, THE
Prestia, Shirley
SPECIES
Preston, Cyndy
BLACK FOX
Preston, Guy William
WATERWORLD
Preston, Joshua
FATHER OF THE BRIDE PART II
NIXON
Preston, William
RECKLESS
Preusse, Aaron
MALLRATS
Preyers, Dmitry
LITTLE ODESSA
Price, Dennis
OH ... ROSALINDA!!
Price, Frank
WALKING DEAD, THE
Price, Jamye
SOMETHING TO TALK ABOUT
Price, Lindsay
ANGUS
Price, Richard
KISS OF DEATH
Price, Robert
ONLY THE BRAVE
Price, Sherwood
LAST OF THE DOGMEN
Price, Steve
GHOST BRIGADE
Price, Vincent
ARABIAN KNIGHT
Priestly, Jason
COLDBLOODED
Priestly, Justine
BULLETPROOF HEART
Prikopsky, Jaro
HOWLING: NEW MOON RISING, THE
Prince, Akili
DIE HARD WITH A VENGEANCE
Prince, Hansford
COPYCAT

Principal, Victoria
NIGHTMARE
Prine, Andrew
AVENGING ANGEL
Pringle, Bryan
RESTORATION
Prior, Susan
MURIEL'S WEDDING
Prior, Ted
MUTANT SPECIES
Pritchett, Harry
FLUKE
Pritner, Juliet Adair
KISS OF DEATH
Procaccino, John
ASSASSINS
BORN TO BE WILD
Proccacino, John
MAGIC IN THE WATER
Prochnow, Jurgen
IN THE MOUTH OF MADNESS
JUDGE DREDD
Prockter, Colin
FEAST OF JULY
Procter, Emily
LEAVING LAS VEGAS
Proffer, Tony
CANADIAN BACON
Prophet, Melissa
CASINO
Props, Renee
GET SHORTY
Prosky, John
OPERATION INTERCEPT
Prosky, Robert
DEAD MAN WALKING
SCARLET LETTER, THE
Protheroe, Julian
FEAST OF JULY
Proval, David
BRADY BUNCH MOVIE, THE
FOUR ROOMS
Provost, Martin
NEA
Pruett, Harrison
EMBRACE OF THE VAMPIRE
Prulheire, Timi
O.J. SIMPSON STORY, THE
Pryce, Jonathan
BUSINESS AFFAIR, A
CARRINGTON
Pryor, Mowava
ACROSS THE MOON
Pryor, Nicholas
BROKEN TRUST
Psaltirov, Metodi
BEFORE THE RAIN
Puckett, Terek
REASON TO BELIEVE, A
Pugh, Lonetta
SHOWGIRLS
Pugh, Robert
ENGLISHMAN WHO WENT UP A HILL
BUT CAME DOWN A MOUNTAIN, THE
PRIEST
Pugin, Bill
CONGO
Pugsley, Don
TOO YOUNG TO DIE?
Pullman, Bill
CASPER
WHILE YOU WERE SLEEPING
Pupello, Angela
JERKY BOYS: THE MOVIE, THE
Pupo, Jorge
ZOOMAN
Purchase, Bruce
RICHARD III

Purefoy, James
FEAST OF JULY
Purro, Richard
HACKERS
Puskas, Tamas
CITIZEN X
Putch, John
WATER ENGINE, THE
Putz, Gary
VAMPIRES AND OTHER STEREOTYPES
Putzulu, Bruno
JEFFERSON IN PARIS
Py, Olivier
FUNNY BONES
Pyle, Denver
FATHER AND SCOUT
Pyles, Joe
BOYS ON THE SIDE
Qiu Lin
BLUE VILLA, THE
Quadens, Isabelle
MINA TANNENBAUM
Quaid, Dennis
SOMETHING TO TALK ABOUT
Quaid, Randy
BYE BYE, LOVE
CURSE OF THE STARVING CLASS
NEXT DOOR
Quarmby, John
RESTORATION
Quarry, Jessye
VILLAGE OF THE DAMNED
Quartermus, Ray
MURDER IN THE FIRST
SEPARATE LIVES
Quayle, Anthony
OH ... ROSALINDA!!
Queirus, Ana
VALLEY OF ABRAHAM, THE
Quester, Hugues
MINA TANNENBAUM
Quigley, Devin
LIE DOWN WITH DOGS
Quigley, Gerry
TO DIE FOR
Quigley, Linnea
JACK-O
Quill, Timothy Patrick
QUICK AND THE DEAD, THE
Quinlan, Kathleen
APOLLO 13
Quinn, Aidan
STARS FELL ON HENRIETTA, THE
Quinn, Anthony
WALK IN THE CLOUDS, A
Quinn, Chance
EVOLVER
Quinn, Daniel
AMERICAN COP
AVENGING ANGEL
SCANNERS: THE SHOWDOWN
Quinn, Danny
REASON TO BELIEVE, A
Quinn, Francesco
TOP DOG
Quinn, J.C.
PROPHECY, THE
Quinn, Paul
LEAVING LAS VEGAS
Quinn, Tom
TO DIE FOR
Quinones, Eduardo
PARTY GIRL
Quintanilla, Rudy
BITTER VENGEANCE
Quirk, Brian
LIE DOWN WITH DOGS

Quittman, David
BABY-SITTERS CLUB, THE
Quittman, Jeffrey
BABY-SITTERS CLUB, THE
Quoilin, Marion
MINA TANNENBAUM
Quyen Hua
KURT VONNEGUT'S HARRISON
BERGERON
Raabjerg, Birgitte
KINGDOM, THE
Raag, Andres
CITY UNPLUGGED
Rabasa, Ruben
FAIR GAME
Raben, Larry
THINGS TO DO IN DENVER WHEN
YOU'RE DEAD
Rachal, Lori
ME AND THE MOB
Rachins, Alan
SHOWGIRLS
Radcliffe, Andy
NEW JERSEY DRIVE
Radcliffe, Brittany
NINE MONTHS
Radcliffe, Porscha
NINE MONTHS
Radek
NOT ANGELS BUT ANGELS
Rader, Jack
INDICTMENT: THE MCMARTIN TRIAL
OUTBREAK
Rader-Duval, Dean
KISS OF DEATH
Radford, Natalie
ANDROID AFFAIR, THE
KURT VONNEGUT'S HARRISON
BERGERON
Radon, Peter
ROSWELL: THE U.F.O. COVER-UP
Radu, Victoria
FUN
Rae, Cassidy
EVOLVER
Rae, Debra
BODILY HARM
Raekwar, Rakesh
BANDIT QUEEN
Raekwar, Savitri
BANDIT QUEEN
Rafelson, Bob
LEAVING LAS VEGAS
Raffles, Mr. Mark
FUNNY BONES
Raffles, Mrs. Mark
FUNNY BONES
Ragard, Adrienne
REFLECTIONS IN THE DARK
Raghuvanshi, Dilip
BANDIT QUEEN
Ragsdale, Christopher
ANGUS
Rahm, Kevin
OUT OF ANNIE'S PAST
Raimi, Sam
GALAXIS
Raimi, Ted
SKINNER
Raimi, Theodore
STUART SAVES HIS FAMILY
Rainer, Josef
QUICK AND THE DEAD, THE
Raines, Pam
BAR GIRLS
Raistrick, George
FUNNY BONES

Rajna, Mari
CITIZEN X
Rajoli, Haji Mahod
BEYOND RANGOON
Rakharebe, Moses
CRY, THE BELOVED COUNTRY
Ralph, Sheryl Lee
WHITE MAN'S BURDEN
Rambis, Kurt
FORGET PARIS
Rambo, T. Mychael
CURE, THE
Ramessar, Ronald
CRIMSON TIDE
Ramirez, Efren
JURY DUTY
Ramirez, Ismael
CLEAN, SHAVEN
Ramirez, Monika
SCANNERS: THE SHOWDOWN
Ramis, Violet
STUART SAVES HIS FAMILY
Ramono, Calos
BURNING SEASON, THE
Ramos, Richard Russell
DIE HARD WITH A VENGEANCE
Ramos, Rudy
SPY WITHIN, THE
Ramsay, Heather
INDICTMENT: THE MCMARTIN TRIAL
Ramsden, John
HOWLING: NEW MOON RISING, THE
Ramsden, Sybil
HOWLING: NEW MOON RISING, THE
Ramsower, Stacey
BABY-SITTERS CLUB, THE
QUICK AND THE DEAD, THE
TANK GIRL
Ramu, Lise
NEA
Ramus, Nickolas G.
3 NINJAS KNUCKLE UP
Rand, Ronald
JERKY BOYS: THE MOVIE, THE
Randall, Ethan
EMPIRE RECORDS
EVOLVER
Randall, George
INDIAN IN THE CUPBOARD, THE
Randall, Ginnie
SOMETHING TO TALK ABOUT
Randall, Kessia
EMPIRE RECORDS
Randall, Lexi
STARS FELL ON HENRIETTA, THE
Randall, Paul
DEATH MACHINE
Randall, Stacie
COMPANION, THE
DREAM A LITTLE DREAM 2
Randall, Theresa
BAD BOYS
Randazzo, Steven
DEVIL IN A BLUE DRESS
MIGHTY APHRODITE
MONEY TRAIN
Randolph, Bonnie
GUMBY: THE MOVIE
Rands, Jonathan
CRY, THE BELOVED COUNTRY
Rankanath
STRANGER, THE
Rankin, Steve
APOLLO 13
Ransom, Tim
OUTBREAK
Rao, Gajraj
BANDIT QUEEN

Raouly, Bordes Fernand
WILD REEDS
Rapaport, Michael
BASKETBALL DIARIES, THE
HIGHER LEARNING
KISS OF DEATH
MIGHTY APHRODITE
Rapp, Ineke
MURIEL'S WEDDING
Rappazzo, Carmela
OUTBREAK
Rare, David
ONCE WERE WARRIORS
Ras, Eva
GORILLA BATHES AT NOON
Rasche, David
BIGFOOT: THE UNFORGETTABLE
ENCOUNTER
MAGIC IN THE WATER
Rasco, Rachel
GEORGIA
Rashed, Sharif
BLUE IN THE FACE
Rashidi, Sabastian
CLUELESS
Rashleigh, Andy
FUNNY BONES
RICHARD III
Rasic, Aleksander
NADJA
Ratchford, Jerry
CONVICT COWBOY
Rathebe, Dolly
CRY, THE BELOVED COUNTRY
FRIENDS
Ratner, Benjamin
MAGIC IN THE WATER
Ratner, Nic
NADJA
Ratzenberger, John
TOY STORY
Rault, Odile
MANGLER, THE
Rauscher, Mark
AMERICA'S DEADLIEST HOME VIDEO
Ravera, Gina
SHOWGIRLS
Ravn, Kurt
KINGDOM, THE
Rawal, Pushpa
LITTLE PRINCESS, A
Rawat, Basant
BANDIT QUEEN
Rawls, Lou
LEAVING LAS VEGAS
Ray, Amy
BOYS ON THE SIDE
Ray, I, William Earl
BETTER OFF DEAD
Ray, Ron
EROTIQUE
Raya, Patty
APOLLO 13
Raycole, Jazz
WAITING TO EXHALE
Raymond, Bill
KINGFISH: A STORY OF HUEY P. LONG
TWELVE MONKEYS
Raysses, Michael
BREACH OF CONDUCT
Rea, Brad
WALK IN THE CLOUDS, A
Rea, Peggy
DEVIL IN A BLUE DRESS
Rea, Stephen
CITIZEN X
Rea-Baum, Alexandra
LITTLE PRINCESS, A

Read, Trevor
BABE
Reardon, Noreen
SOMETHING TO TALK ABOUT
Recountre, Julie
LAKOTA WOMAN: SIEGE AT WOUNDED
KNEE
Rector, Jeff
BALLISTIC
GALAXIS
Rector, Jerry
DIRTY MONEY
Red Elk, Lois
LAKOTA WOMAN: SIEGE AT WOUNDED
KNEE
Red Wing, Donna
BALLOT MEASURE 9
Reddin, Keith
TO WONG FOO, THANKS FOR
EVERYTHING! JULIE NEWMAR
Reddy, Brian
COSMIC SLOP
OUTBREAK
Redfern, Joanne
RESTORATION
Redgrave, Corin
PERSUASION
Redgrave, Michael
OH ... ROSALINDA!!
Redgrave, Vanessa
LITTLE ODESSA
MONTH BY THE LAKE, A
Reece, Georgia
DOOMSDAY GUN
Reed, Arthur
PANTHER
Reed, Ben
BALLISTIC
Reed, Chris
KICKING AND SCREAMING
Reed, Cliff
FORGET PARIS
Reed, Darryl Alan
AMERICAN PRESIDENT, THE
Reed, Fawn
BAD BOYS
Reed, Kristianne
TANK GIRL
Reed, Lou
BLUE IN THE FACE
Reed, Merrifield
BODY CHEMISTRY 4: FULL EXPOSURE
Reed, Nancy
DIRTY MONEY
Reed, Oliver
FUNNY BONES
Reed, Shirlee
DON JUAN DEMARCO
Rees, Douglas
SUDDEN DEATH
Reeson, Melanie
NOSTRADAMUS KID, THE
Reeve, Christopher
BLACK FOX
VILLAGE OF THE DAMNED
Reeves, Jennifer Jin-Jin
STRANGE DAYS
Reeves, Keanu
JOHNNY MNEMONIC
WALK IN THE CLOUDS, A
Reeves, Perrey
KICKING AND SCREAMING
Reeves, Priscilla
SAFE PASSAGE
Reeves, Richard
FARINELLI
Reeves, Saskia
TRAPS

Reevis, Steve
LAST OF THE DOGMEN
WILD BILL
Reformina, Raul
STRANGE DAYS
Refoy, Niall
PERSUASION
Regalbuto, Joe
BODILY HARM
Regen, Stuart
LEAVING LAS VEGAS
Regine
GROSSE FATIGUE
Regnier, Dominique
FRENCH KISS
Reguerraz, Jean-Piere
I, THE WORST OF ALL
Reichardt, Frances
RIVER OF GRASS
Reichardt, Jerry
RIVER OF GRASS
Reichert, Daniel
BATMAN FOREVER
Reid, Joanne
NOSTRADAMUS KID, THE
Reid, Michael Earl
BALLISTIC
Reid, R.D.
FIRST DEGREE
Reid, Tim
OUT OF SYNC
Reidy, Joseph
CASINO
Reilly, John C.
DOLORES CLAIBORNE
GEORGIA
Reilly, Mary
RUN OF THE COUNTRY, THE
Reina, Ivette
MY FAMILY: MI FAMILIA
Reindres, Kate
WHILE YOU WERE SLEEPING
Reiner, Rob
BYE BYE, LOVE
Reiner, Tracy
APOLLO 13
Reinhardt, Ray
TIE THAT BINDS, THE
Reinhardt, Sarah Hale
SEVEN
Reis, Antonio
VALLEY OF ABRAHAM, THE
Reis, Diana
KURT VONNEGUT'S HARRISON
BERGERON
Reiser, Paul
BYE BYE, LOVE
Reisse, Mutfak
NEKROMANTIK
Reiter, Otto
BEFORE SUNRISE
Reiter, Wilbirg
BEFORE SUNRISE
Reitman, Joseph D.
CLUELESS
Reitz, Ric
NOW AND THEN
Rejah, Jamaludin
BEYOND RANGOON
Remar, James
ACROSS THE MOON
BOYS ON THE SIDE
JUDGE DREDD
WILD BILL
Rempel, Nick
DRACULA: DEAD AND LOVING IT
Remsberg, Calvin
WATER ENGINE, THE

Remsen, Bert
DILLINGER AND CAPONE
WHITE MAN'S BURDEN
Remsen, Kerry
INDICTMENT: THE MCMARTIN TRIAL
WHITE MAN'S BURDEN
Ren Fengwu
ERMO
Ren Shiguan
HEROIC TRIO, THE
Rena, Alexia
ARIZONA DREAM
Renata, Tama
ONCE WERE WARRIORS
Renaud, Line
I CAN'T SLEEP
Renaund, Francois
PIGALLE
Rene, Angie
FLUKE
Renee, Carla
TO DIE FOR
Renell, Andreas
PENTATHLON
Renfro, Brad
CURE, THE
TOM AND HUCK
Renfro, Brian
FIRST DEGREE
Renfro, Bryan
ANDROID AFFAIR, THE
Renna, Dr. Christian
NIXON
Renna, Melinda
NIXON
Renna, Patrick
BIG GREEN, THE
Renner, Jeremy
NATIONAL LAMPOON'S SENIOR TRIP
Rennie, Callum
DOUBLE HAPPINESS
Reno, Jean
FRENCH KISS
Reno, Warren
SHOWGIRLS
Renteria, Carrie
AMERICA'S DEADLIEST HOME VIDEO
Renteria, Danny
AMERICA'S DEADLIEST HOME VIDEO
Renteria, Justin
AMERICA'S DEADLIEST HOME VIDEO
Repnow, Manfred
NEKROMANTIK
Reuben, Gloria
NICK OF TIME
Revill, Clive
ARABIAN KNIGHT
DRACULA: DEAD AND LOVING IT
Revoner, Justin
FRIDAY
Revuelta, Raquel
I AM CUBA
Rey, Renaldo
FRIDAY
Reyes, Catiria
TO WONG FOO, THANKS FOR
EVERYTHING! JULIE NEWMAR
Reyes, Reina
HUNTED, THE
Reynolds, Billy Ray
JOURNEY OF AUGUST KING, THE
Reynolds, Hilary
AWFULLY BIG ADVENTURE, AN
Reynolds, Mike
BAREFOOT GEN
CRIMSON WOLF
WICKED CITY

Reynolds, Milan
STRANGE DAYS
Reynolds, Mindy
HOUSEGUEST
Reynolds, Robert
TRAPS
Reynolds, Vickilyn
FRIDAY
VAMPIRE IN BROOKLYN
Rezai, Hossein
THROUGH THE OLIVE TREES
Reznick, Rhonda
BITTER VENGEANCE
Reznik, Peter
ACROSS THE SEA OF TIME: NEW YORK
3D
Rezza, Vito
IT TAKES TWO
Rhall, John
SUM OF US, THE
Rhames, Ving
KISS OF DEATH
Rhee, Simon
BAD BLOOD
Rheeling, Joyce
ROOMMATES
Rhey, Ashlie
MOSAIC PROJECT, THE
PLAY TIME
Rhoades, Michael
BLACK FOX
Rhoden, Lisa
ZOOMAN
Rhodes, Joanna
SABRINA
Rhys, Iuean
ENGLISHMAN WHO WENT UP A HILL
BUT CAME DOWN A MOUNTAIN, THE
Rhys, Paul
NINA TAKES A LOVER
Riabov, Vladimir
BURNT BY THE SUN
Riach, Ralph
BRAVEHEART
Ribaud-Chevrey, Charlotte
CITY OF LOST CHILDREN, THE
Ribier, Jeffrey Justin
JEFFERSON IN PARIS
Ribisi, Marissa
BRADY BUNCH MOVIE, THE
KICKING AND SCREAMING
Ricci, Christina
CASPER
GOLD DIGGERS: THE SECRET OF BEAR
MOUNTAIN
NOW AND THEN
Rice, Jennifer
HACKERS
Rice, Nicholas
SCARLET LETTER, THE
Richard, Jean-Louis
GROSSE FATIGUE
Richards, Ariana
ANGUS
Richards, Bethany
ANGUS
Richards, Charles David
TOO YOUNG TO DIE?
Richards, Evan
MUTE WITNESS
Richards, Joseph
MURDER IN THE FIRST
Richards, Michael
UNSTRUNG HEROES
Richards, Michele Lamar
COSMIC SLOP
TOP DOG

Richards, Robyn
GOOFY MOVIE, A
Richards, Simon
TO DIE FOR
Richards, Susan
HOUSEGUEST
Richardson, David
BALLET
Richardson, Frederick
JUMANJI
Richardson, III, Edward C.K.
GOOD DAY TO DIE, A
Richardson, Jay
ATTACK OF THE 60-FOOT CENTERFOLD
Richardson, Joely
SISTER MY SISTER
Richardson, Kevin
MORTAL KOMBAT
Richardson, LaTanya
LOSING ISAIAH
Richardson, Miranda
CENTURY
FATHERLAND
Richardson, Skip
VILLAGE OF THE DAMNED
Richardson, Sy
GLASS SHIELD, THE
Richings, Julian
MOONLIGHT AND VALENTINO
Richman, Ester
GRANNY, THE
Richmond, Dennis
COPYCAT
NET, THE
Richoz, Michel
LIE DOWN WITH DOGS
Richter, Jason James
FREE WILLY 2: THE ADVENTURE HOME
Rick, Pat
SILENCE OF THE HAMS
Rickles, Don
CASINO
TOY STORY
Rickman, Alan
AWFULLY BIG ADVENTURE, AN
SENSE AND SENSIBILITY
Riddoch, Billy
SHALLOW GRAVE
Rideau, Stephane
WILD REEDS
Ridley, Ruth
ETERNITY
Riedlinger, John
EMBRACE OF THE VAMPIRE
Rieffel, Lisa
FORGET PARIS
Riegert, Peter
COLDBLOODED
Riehle, Richard
JURY DUTY
STUART SAVES HIS FAMILY
Riehm, Rolf
MACHINE DREAMS
Riffel, Rena
SHOWGIRLS
UNDERCOVER
Rifkin, Ron
LAST SUMMER IN THE HAMPTONS
Rigamonte, Robert
OUTBREAK
Rigano, Joseph
CASINO
Rigby, Terence
FUNNY BONES
Rigby, Tom
PERSUASION
Riggs, Marlon
BLACK IS ... BLACK AIN'T

Riggs, Rhonda
JACK-O
Riggs, Rick
JACK-O
Rigillo, Mariana
POSTMAN, THE
Riisager, Ole Emil
KINGDOM, THE
Riker, Robin
REASON TO BELIEVE, A
Riley, Bus
AVENGING ANGEL
Riley, Michael
FRENCH KISS
Riley, Timothy C.
PANTHER
Riley, Timothy Glenn
TALL TALE: THE UNBELIEVABLE
ADVENTURES OF PECOS BILL
Rimmer, Shane
KID IN KING ARTHUR'S COURT, A
Ringer, Michael
POSTCARDS FROM AMERICA
Ringham, Nancy
HEAVYWEIGHTS
Ringheim, Lise
DREAMING OF RITA
Ringwald, Molly
MALICIOUS
Riojas, Juan
SPY WITHIN, THE
Riojas, Juan A.
VIRTUOSITY
Riordan, Daniel
PENTATHLON
Riovega, Elodia
MIAMI RHAPSODY
Ripley, Fay
MUTE WITNESS
Rise, Josiah
CONVICT COWBOY
Riser, Ronn
FRIDAY
Rispoli, Michael
TO DIE FOR
WHILE YOU WERE SLEEPING
Rissetto, Arona
ONCE WERE WARRIORS
Rist, Robbie
BALTO
Ristoski, Kiril
BEFORE THE RAIN
Ritchie, Anne
ANDROID AFFAIR, THE
Ritchie, David
NOSTRADAMUS KID, THE
Ritts, Herb
MURDER IN THE FIRST
Ritz, Jim
APOLLO 13
Rivera, Emilio
MY FAMILY: MI FAMILIA
Rivera, Emma
I, THE WORST OF ALL
Rivera, Geraldo
GRUMPIER OLD MEN
Rivera, Jesse
HOUSEGUEST
Rivera, Jonathan
LOSING ISAIAH
Rivera, Marcello
NO MERCY
Rivers, James
BRIDGES OF MADISON COUNTY, THE
Rivers, Victor
NIXON
STEAL BIG, STEAL LITTLE

Rivers-Bland, Mansell
BEYOND RANGOON
Rixon, Cheryl
I LIKE TO PLAY GAMES
Rixon, Peta-Maree
MIGHTY MORPHIN POWER RANGERS:
THE MOVIE
Roach, Norman
LAKOTA WOMAN: SIEGE AT WOUNDED
KNEE
Roache, Linus
PRIEST
Roarke, John
S.F.W.
SILENCE OF THE HAMS
Robards, Jason
ENEMY WITHIN, THE
MY ANTONIA
Robb, Lisa
RIVER OF GRASS
Robb, R.D.
BRADY BUNCH MOVIE, THE
Robbins, Adam
VILLAGE OF THE DAMNED
Robbins, Adele
DEAD MAN WALKING
Robbins, Garry
IN THE MOUTH OF MADNESS
Robbins, Gil
DEAD MAN WALKING
Robbins, Jack Henry
DEAD MAN WALKING
Robbins, Jane
FIRST KNIGHT
Robbins, Mary
DEAD MAN WALKING
Robbins, Miles Guthrie
DEAD MAN WALKING
Robbins, Trina
CRUMB
Roberge, Sean
IN THE MOUTH OF MADNESS
Roberson, David
O.J. SIMPSON STORY, THE
Robert
NOT ANGELS BUT ANGELS
Robert, Laura
CITY OF LOST CHILDREN, THE
Robert, Lionel
JEFFERSON IN PARIS
Roberts, Adrian
FLUKE
TOM AND HUCK
Roberts, Bruce
BATMAN FOREVER
Roberts, Dafydd Wyn
ENGLISHMAN WHO WENT UP A HILL
BUT CAME DOWN A MOUNTAIN, THE
Roberts, Desmond
IT TAKES TWO
Roberts, Ed
WHEN BILLY BROKE HIS HEAD ... AND
OTHER TALES OF WONDER
Roberts, Eliza
KICKING AND SCREAMING
Roberts, Emma
PERSUASION
Roberts, Francesca
SAFE
Roberts, Francesca P.
S.F.W.
Roberts, Ian
CRY, THE BELOVED COUNTRY
Roberts, Jeremy
MONEY TRAIN
STUART SAVES HIS FAMILY
Roberts, Julia
SOMETHING TO TALK ABOUT

Roberts, Kimberley
MIDNIGHT TEASE 2
Roberts, Kimberly
BODY CHEMISTRY 4: FULL EXPOSURE
Roberts, Lisa
JOURNEY OF AUGUST KING, THE
SOMETHING TO TALK ABOUT
Roberts, Mario
HEAT
Roberts, Rick
LOVE AND HUMAN REMAINS
Roberts, Sally Ann
DEAD MAN WALKING
Roberts, William
BALTO
Roberts, Wren
BROKEN TRUST
Robertson, Alan
BAD COMPANY
Robertson, Jenny
DANGER OF LOVE
Robertson, Jessie
BIG GREEN, THE
Robertson, Robbie
CROSSING GUARD, THE
Robertson, Travis
NOW AND THEN
Robie, Wendy
VAMPIRE IN BROOKLYN
Robin, Diane
SUDDEN DEATH
Robin, Tucker
MIGHTY APHRODITE
Robinette, Christina
SHOWGIRLS
Robinson, Allison
BILLY MADISON
Robinson, Bumper
O.J. SIMPSON STORY, THE
WHITE MAN'S BURDEN
Robinson, C. Jack
BODY SHOT
OUTBREAK
Robinson, Carl
HEAVEN'S A DRAG
Robinson, David
FORGET PARIS
Robinson, Dawn
BATMAN FOREVER
TANK GIRL
Robinson, Jack
CRY, THE BELOVED COUNTRY
Robinson, James
BRAVEHEART
Robinson, Les
CONGO
Robinson, Percy
ONCE WERE WARRIORS
Robinson, Phillip
HEAT
Robinson, Robby
EXPERT, THE
Robinson, Scot Anthony
CLOCKERS
Robinson, Shane
FUNNY BONES
Robinson, Sheila-Marie
LOSING ISAIAH
Robinson, Stuart K.
TOM AND HUCK
Robinson, Wendy Raquel
WALKING DEAD, THE
Robitaille, Luc
SUDDEN DEATH
Robles, Veronica
DANGEROUS MINDS

Robles, Walt
STUART SAVES HIS FAMILY
Roblin, Jennifer
PYROMANIAC'S LOVE STORY, A
WHEN NIGHT IS FALLING
Robson, Sterling
GRUMPIER OLD MEN
Robson, Wayne
DOLORES CLAIBORNE
DOUBLE, DOUBLE, TOIL AND TROUBLE
Rocca, Peter
USUAL SUSPECTS, THE
Rocco, Alex
SPY WITHIN, THE
Rocha, Argentina
VALLEY OF ABRAHAM, THE
Rocha, Felisa
I, THE WORST OF ALL
Rocha, Lurdes
VALLEY OF ABRAHAM, THE
Rochand, Caroline
CITY OF LOST CHILDREN, THE
Roche, Aislin
NINE MONTHS
Roche, Brogan
O.J. SIMPSON STORY, THE
Roche, Eamonn
O.J. SIMPSON STORY, THE
Roche, Eugene
ROSWELL: THE U.F.O. COVER-UP
Roche, Tudi
BREACH OF CONDUCT
Rochelin, Charles
FORGET PARIS
Rochon, Debbie
ABDUCTED 2: THE REUNION
Rochon, Lela
WAITING TO EXHALE
Rock, Chris
PANTHER
Rock, Rick
ART FOR TEACHERS OF CHILDREN
Rockafellow, Marilyn
NIXON
Rocket, Charles
STEAL BIG, STEAL LITTLE
TOM AND HUCK
Rockett, Eliot
CLEAN, SHAVEN
Rodenkirchen, Franz
NEKROMANTIK
Roderick, David
CENTURY
Roderick, Rochelle
FUN
Rodgers, Bill
TALL TALE: THE UNBELIEVABLE
ADVENTURES OF PECOS BILL
Rodgers, Bob
BILLY MADISON
Rodgers, Des
MURIEL'S WEDDING
Rodine, Alex
PENTATHLON
Rodrigo, Al
GLASS SHIELD, THE
Rodriguez, Agustin
STRANGE DAYS
Rodriguez, Andrea
I, THE WORST OF ALL
Rodriguez, Celia
I AM CUBA
Rodriguez, Chanaia
ARIZONA DREAM
Rodriguez, David
ARIZONA DREAM

Rodriguez, Elizabeth
DEAD PRESIDENTS
DESPERADO
Rodriguez, Fausto
JUST CAUSE
Rodriguez, Freddy
DEAD PRESIDENTS
WALK IN THE CLOUDS, A
Rodriguez, Jose Mario
MY FAMILY: MI FAMILIA
Rodriguez, Lucy
SPECIES
Rodriguez, Marco
BURNING SEASON, THE
Rodriguez, Nelson
INCREDIBLY TRUE ADVENTURES OF
TWO GIRLS IN LOVE, THE
Rodriguez, Patricia Vonne
FOUR ROOMS
Rodriguez, Paul
RHYTHM THIEF
Rodriguez, Robert Polanco
DON JUAN DEMARCO
Rodriguez, Spain
CRUMB
Rodriguez, Valente
MY FAMILY: MI FAMILIA
Rodriquez, Gloria
FORGET PARIS
Roe, Karen
DRACULA: DEAD AND LOVING IT
Roe, Owen
FRANKIE STARLIGHT
Roeder, Peggy
DILLINGER
Roemer, Sylvia
FRANK AND OLLIE
Roescher, Michael
GORDY
Roeves, Maurice
JUDGE DREDD
Rogers, Dulcy
FATHER OF THE BRIDE PART II
Rogers, Greg
POWER OF ATTORNEY
Rogers, Ingrid
WHITE MAN'S BURDEN
Rogers, Mimi
BULLETPROOF HEART
FAR FROM HOME: THE ADVENTURES OF
YELLOW DOG
REFLECTIONS IN THE DARK
Rogers, Paul
RETURN OF THE NATIVE, THE
Rohilla, Ajai
BANDIT QUEEN
Rohmig, Alexandra
GORILLA BATHES AT NOON
Rois, Michel
JEFFERSON IN PARIS
Rojanatavorn, Kawan
EMPIRE RECORDS
Rojas, Eduardo Lopez
MY FAMILY: MI FAMILIA
Rojas, Victor
DIE HARD WITH A VENGEANCE
Roker, Roxie
COSMIC SLOP
Roland, Eugenie Cisse
FACES OF WOMEN
Rolf, Frederick
CLASS OF '61
Rolffes, Kirsten
KINGDOM, THE
Rolle, Esther
HOW TO MAKE AN AMERICAN QUILT

Rollins, Henry
HEAT
JOHNNY MNEMONIC
Rollins, Sonny
GREAT DAY IN HARLEM, A
Roma, Anna
NADJA
Roma, Giancarlo
NADJA
Roma, Thomas
NADJA
Romaldi, John
GALAXIS
Roman
NOT ANGELS BUT ANGELS
Roman, Frank
UNDER SIEGE 2: DARK TERRITORY
Romano, Andy
STEAL BIG, STEAL LITTLE
TWO BITS
UNDER SIEGE 2: DARK TERRITORY
Romano, Bob
POSTCARDS FROM AMERICA
Romano, Gerardo
I, THE WORST OF ALL
Romano, Joey
BAD BOYS
Romano, Larry
NEW YORK COP
Romberger, Crosby
POSTCARDS FROM AMERICA
Romeo, Christine
NEW YORK COP
Romeo, Ina
OUTBREAK
Romero, Briana
BURNING SEASON, THE
Romero, Dan
JUST CAUSE
Romero, Hernan
NO MERCY
Romero, Santos
ARIZONA DREAM
Romersa, Joe
WINGS OF HONNEAMISE: ROYAL SPACE
FORCE
Romo, Danny
THINGS TO DO IN DENVER WHEN
YOU'RE DEAD
Ronsisvalli, Fernanda
I, THE WORST OF ALL
Ronstadt, Linda
BRIAN WILSON: I JUST WASN'T MADE
FOR THESE TIMES
Rooker, Michael
MALLRATS
Rooney, Gerard
SECRET OF ROAN INISH, THE
Rooney, Jonah
HOW TO MAKE AN AMERICAN QUILT
Rooney, Stephen
CIRCLE OF FRIENDS
Roos, Alexander
THREE WISHES
Root, Amanda
PERSUASION
Rosa
THREE WISHES
Rosa, Tony
TWO BITS
Rosales, Gilbert
COLDBLOODED
Rosales, Jr., Thomas
HEAT
MY FAMILY: MI FAMILIA
TIE THAT BINDS, THE
Rosario, Jose
GLASS SHIELD, THE

Rosas, Ivon
PARTY GIRL
Rosas, Misty
CONGO
Rosato, Mary Lou
TWO BITS
Rosato, Tony
RENT-A-KID
Rosco, Dwight
POWER OF ATTORNEY
Roscoe, Stephanie
PRIEST
Rose, Bartholomew
NOSTRADAMUS KID, THE
Rose, David
CASINO
Rose, Howie
SMOKE
Rose, Lenny
CAGED HEARTS
Rose, Natalie
CANADIAN BACON
Rose, Peter Pamela
FUNNY BONES
Rose, Sherrie
TALES FROM THE CRYPT: DEMON
KNIGHT
Rose, Skip
TWO BITS
Rose, Wally
MURDER IN THE FIRST
Roseanne
BLUE IN THE FACE
UNZIPPED
Roselius, John
DEVIL IN A BLUE DRESS
Rosello, Elijah Nicole
RECKLESS
Roseman, Romy
CONGO
Rosemore, Terrence
CANDYMAN: FAREWELL TO THE FLESH
Rosen, Edward J.
ASSASSINS
FREE WILLY 2: THE ADVENTURE HOME
Rosenbaum, Steve
TIE THAT BINDS, THE
Rosenfeld, Marion
PARTY GIRL
Rosenthal, Robin
COVER STORY
Rositani, Frank
OUTBREAK
Rosner, Louise
KID IN KING ARTHUR'S COURT, A
Rosner, Paul
KID IN KING ARTHUR'S COURT, A
Ross, Brian
HEAVEN'S A DRAG
Ross, Clarinda
FLUKE
Ross, Clive
VAMPIRE IN BROOKLYN
Ross, David
LITTLE ODESSA
Ross, J. Michael
BITTER VENGEANCE
Ross, Jaclyn
GRUMPIER OLD MEN
Ross, Kimberly Ann
FUN
Ross, Muriel
DECOY
Ross, Natanya
BABY-SITTERS CLUB, THE
Ross, Neil
PEBBLE AND THE PENGUIN, THE

Ross, Philip Arthur
SAFE PASSAGE
STEAL BIG, STEAL LITTLE
Ross, Ricco
HACKERS
Ross, Ron
FORGET PARIS
Ross, Steven Robert
SAFE PASSAGE
STEAL BIG, STEAL LITTLE
Ross, Valeri
LOSING ISAIAH
Ross, Willie
RESTORATION
Ross-Norris, Vicki
HOUSEGUEST
ROOMMATES
Rossellini, Isabella
INNOCENT, THE
Rossi, Enzo
BEYOND RANGOON
Rossi, Leo
MUTANT SPECIES
Rossi, Riccardo
MONTH BY THE LAKE, A
Rossianov, Christofor
DOOM GENERATION, THE
Rossovich, Rick
COVER ME
Roszyk, Greg "B.D."
FEAR, THE
Rota, Carlo
FIRST DEGREE
Roth, Adam
TO DIE FOR
Roth, Tim
FOUR ROOMS
LITTLE ODESSA
ROB ROY
Rothenberger, Anneliese
OH ... ROSALINDA!!
Rothery, Teryl
MAGIC IN THE WATER
Rothman, John
COPYCAT
Rothman, Malcolm
DILLINGER
Rothwell, Robert
BRADY BUNCH MOVIE, THE
Rounds, Tahmus
COPYCAT
Roundtree, Richard
BALLISTIC
SEVEN
Rourke, Mickey
LAST RIDE, THE
Roussel, Kenneth
I LIKE TO PLAY GAMES
Roussouw, Wilmien
FRIENDS
Rowan, Kelly
ASSASSINS
BLACK FOX
CANDYMAN: FAREWELL TO THE FLESH
Rowatt, Graham
DARKMAN 2: THE RETURN OF DURANT
Rowden, David
BIGFOOT: THE UNFORGETTABLE
ENCOUNTER
Rowe, Hansford
ROSWELL: THE U.F.O. COVER-UP
Rowe, Ian
FUNNY BONES
Rowe, Shawne
TIE THAT BINDS, THE
Rowlands, Gena
SOMETHING TO TALK ABOUT

Rowlands, Joanna
ARMAGEDDON: THE FINAL CHALLENGE
Rowles, Ian
INNOCENT, THE
Roy, Del
CURSE OF THE STARVING CLASS
Roy, Gitali
CHARULATA
Roy, Maxime
LOVE AND HUMAN REMAINS
Roy, Thomas
TWELVE MONKEYS
Royce, Patricia
TO CROSS THE RUBICON
Royds, Cameron
ANGUS
Roys, Frank A.
ROSWELL: THE U.F.O. COVER-UP
Rozelaar-Green, Frank
RESTORATION
Rozelle, Alan
NEW YORK COP
Rozniatowska, M.
SHORT FILM ABOUT LOVE, A
Ruan Zhaoxiang
HEROIC TRIO, THE
Rubalcava, Carmina
FUN
Rubano, John
SEPARATE LIVES
Rubes, Jan
ROOMMATES
Rubin, Ed
DOLORES CLAIBORNE
Rubin, Jerry
PANTHER
Rubinek, Saul
ANDROID AFFAIR, THE
NIXON
Rubini, Sergio
PURE FORMALITY, A
Rubinowitz, Tex
BEFORE SUNRISE
Rubion, Leo
CITY OF LOST CHILDREN, THE
Ruck, Alan
BORN TO BE WILD
Rudd, Paul
CLUELESS
HALLOWEEN: THE CURSE OF MICHAEL
MYERS
Rudder, Michael
DR. JEKYLL & MS. HYDE
Rudneva, Liubov
BURNT BY THE SUN
Rudnick, Ruth
WHILE YOU WERE SLEEPING
Rudolph, Mary
NIXON
Rudolph, Sebastian
STALINGRAD
Rudy, Reed
APOLLO 13
Ruehl, Mercedes
INDICTMENT: THE MCMARTIN TRIAL
Ruffalo, Ed
GLASS SHIELD, THE
Ruffini, Gene
CASINO
LITTLE ODESSA
Rufus
CITY OF LOST CHILDREN, THE
LES MISERABLES
Ruge, George Marshall
ENEMY WITHIN, THE
TIE THAT BINDS, THE

Ruge, Steven
APOLLO 13
ENEMY WITHIN, THE
Ruhl, Michel
WILD REEDS
Ruiz, Jorge
DIRTY MONEY
Ruiz, Lynette
TANK GIRL
Ruiz, Manuel
ARIZONA DREAM
Rule, Rob
PANTHER
Run DMC
SHOW, THE
Runningfox, Joseph
LAKOTA WOMAN: SIEGE AT WOUNDED
KNEE
Runyan, Tygh
POWER OF ATTORNEY
RuPaul
BLUE IN THE FACE
BRADY BUNCH MOVIE, THE
TO WONG FOO, THANKS FOR
EVERYTHING! JULIE NEWMAR
WIGSTOCK: THE MOVIE
Rupert, Jean
JEFFERSON IN PARIS
WINDOW TO PARIS
Ruscio, Al
SHOWGIRLS
SILENCE OF THE HAMS
Rush, Deborah
RECKLESS
Rush, Laura
FOUR ROOMS
Rushton, Kevin
IN THE MOUTH OF MADNESS
NEVER TALK TO STRANGERS
Russ, Tim
BITTER VENGEANCE
Russ, Tom
BIKINI BISTRO
Russell, Anthony
CASINO
Russell, Betsy
BREAK, THE
Russell, Brian
COPYCAT
Russell, Clive
FATHERLAND
Russell, Dick
RIVER OF GRASS
Russell, Greg
CLUELESS
Russell, Kimberly
O.J. SIMPSON STORY, THE
Russell, Miranda
NADJA
Russell, Robert
AMERICA'S DEADLIEST HOME VIDEO
Russell, T.E.
SWIMMING WITH SHARKS
Russell, Theresa
SPY WITHIN, THE
Russell, Todd O.
UNDER SIEGE 2: DARK TERRITORY
Russo, James
PANTHER
SECRETARY, THE
Russo, Rene
GET SHORTY
OUTBREAK
Russomanno, Zak
CITY OF LOST CHILDREN, THE
Rusumny, Jay
FORGET PARIS

Ruth, Isabel
VALLEY OF ABRAHAM, THE
Ruthay
THINGS TO DO IN DENVER WHEN
YOU'RE DEAD
Rutledge, Tamara
LOSING ISAIAH
Rutowski, Daiton
ROSWELL: THE U.F.O. COVER-UP
Ryall, David
CARRINGTON
FATHERLAND
RESTORATION
Ryan, Amy
IN THE DEEP WOODS
Ryan, Eileen
CROSSING GUARD, THE
Ryan, James
LAST SAMURAI, THE
Ryan, John P.
TALL TALE: THE UNBELIEVABLE
ADVENTURES OF PECOS BILL
Ryan, John T.
BAD BLOOD
Ryan, Lee
GLASS SHIELD, THE
Ryan, Leslie
BODY CHEMISTRY 4: FULL EXPOSURE
Ryan, Mark
FIRST KNIGHT
Ryan, Matthew
CROSSING GUARD, THE
Ryan, Meg
FRENCH KISS
RESTORATION
Ryan, Michael
CROSSING GUARD, THE
Ryan, Mitchell
HALLOWEEN: THE CURSE OF MICHAEL
MYERS
JUDGE DREDD
Ryan, Pat
VAMPIRES AND OTHER STEREOTYPES
Ryan, Ron
MONEY TRAIN
Ryan, Sean
IN THE MOUTH OF MADNESS
TO DIE FOR
Ryan, Shawna
EMBRACE OF THE VAMPIRE
Ryan, Will
PEBBLE AND THE PENGUIN, THE
Rybowaka, Malka
WINDOW TO PARIS
Rychter, Z.
SHORT FILM ABOUT KILLING, A
Rydell, Chris
IN THE DEEP WOODS
Ryder, Amy
CANDYMAN: FAREWELL TO THE FLESH
Ryder, Scott
QUICK AND THE DEAD, THE
Ryder, Winona
HOW TO MAKE AN AMERICAN QUILT
Rzab, Greg
THINGS TO DO IN DENVER WHEN
YOU'RE DEAD
Saachiko
MY FAMILY: MI FAMILIA
SAFE
Saadat, Kathleen
BALLOT MEASURE 9
Saalman, Raelyn
ATTACK OF THE 60-FOOT CENTERFOLD
Sabbah, Rachel
MINA TANNENBAUM
Sabella, Ernie
ROOMMATES

Saccio, Thomas
SUDDEN DEATH
Sacco, Nestor
I, THE WORST OF ALL
Sachs, Leslie
DRACULA: DEAD AND LOVING IT
Sadler, Nick
FRANK & JESSE
Sadler, William
TALES FROM THE CRYPT: DEMON
KNIGHT
Sadoyan, Isabelle
LES MISERABLES
Safaraba, Pamela
BIKINI BISTRO
Safe-T-Man
FORGET PARIS
Saffran, Jason
GLASS SHIELD, THE
Safir, Shari-Lyn
DIE HARD WITH A VENGEANCE
Saftler, Antonette
NICK OF TIME
Sagal, McNally
LORD OF ILLUSIONS
Sagebrecht, Marianne
EROTIQUE
MARTHA AND I
Saget, Bob
FATHER AND SCOUT
Sagona, Katie
GRUMPIER OLD MEN
KISS OF DEATH
Sahu, Anil
BANDIT QUEEN
Sain, Oliver
COVER STORY
Sain, Stephanie
TALES FROM THE CRYPT: DEMON
KNIGHT
Saint, Eva Marie
MY ANTONIA
Saito, James
DIE HARD WITH A VENGEANCE
HUNTED, THE
Sakai, Seth
HUNTED, THE
Sakamura, Ken
MYSTERY OF RAMPO, THE
Sakasitz, Amy
MAD LOVE
Sakata, Ryoto
HUNTED, THE
Saki, Ryuzo
MYSTERY OF RAMPO, THE
Saks, Matthew
AMERICAN PRESIDENT, THE
OUTBREAK
Salas, David
MY FAMILY: MI FAMILIA
Salcido, Raphael
ARIZONA DREAM
Saldana, Moses
MY FAMILY: MI FAMILIA
Saleet, Norman
UNDERCOVER
Salenger, Meredith
GIRL IN THE CADILLAC
VILLAGE OF THE DAMNED
Salengro, Christophe
CITY OF LOST CHILDREN, THE
Salgado, Marcus
COSMIC SLOP
ZOOMAN
Sali, Richard
CRACKERJACK
Saliers, Emily
BOYS ON THE SIDE

Salin, Kari
HIGHER LEARNING
Salinger, Diane
LAST SUMMER IN THE HAMPTONS
SCARLET LETTER, THE
Salja, Abdurahman
BEFORE THE RAIN
Sall, Fatou
FACES OF WOMEN
Salley, John Spider
BAD BOYS
Salmon, Iris
HUNTED, THE
Salnikov, Vladimir
MUTE WITNESS
Salome, Tony
TALES FROM THE CRYPT: DEMON
KNIGHT
Salonga, Lea
REDWOOD CURTAIN
Salsedo, Frank Sotonoma
MAGIC IN THE WATER
Samarine, Juliana
VALLEY OF ABRAHAM, THE
Samb, Issa Ramagelissa
HYENAS
Sambasivan, Arthi
JOHNNY MNEMONIC
Sambrano, Libia
BAR GIRLS
Samie, Catherine
JEFFERSON IN PARIS
Samko
BEYOND RANGOON
Sample, Mar'qus
CLOCKERS
Sample, Mar'rece
CLOCKERS
Sampler, Philece
TOM AND HUCK
Sampson, Tim
LAKOTA WOMAN: SIEGE AT WOUNDED
KNEE
Sampson, Tony
MAN OF THE HOUSE
Sams, Jeffrey D.
WAITING TO EXHALE
Samuel, Jackie
LOSING ISAIAH
Samuels, Melissa
JURY DUTY
Samuels, Tiffany
BAD BOYS
San Giacomo, Laura
NINA TAKES A LOVER
STUART SAVES HIS FAMILY
Sanchez, Cary
ASSASSINS
Sanchez, Joanna
LORD OF ILLUSIONS
Sanchez, Mario Ernesto
BAD BOYS
Sanchez-Gijon, Aitana
WALK IN THE CLOUDS, A
Sanchez-Waggoner, Ramona
BEYOND RANGOON
Sand, Paritosh
BANDIT QUEEN
Sanda, Dominique
I, THE WORST OF ALL
VOYAGE EN DOUCE
Sandahl, Andrea
TIE THAT BINDS, THE
Sander, Otto
PROMISE, THE
Sanders, Cynthena
NICK OF TIME

Sanders, Dex Elliot
STRANGE DAYS
Sanders, Elizabeth
BATMAN FOREVER
Sanders, Jay O.
THREE WISHES
Sanders, Lamar
IN THE NAME OF THE EMPEROR
Sanders, Robert
ASSASSINS
Sandler, Adam
BILLY MADISON
Sandorn, David
FORGET PARIS
Sandoval, Antony
NICK OF TIME
Sandoval, Gema
WALK IN THE CLOUDS, A
Sandoval, Miguel
FAIR GAME
GET SHORTY
Sandoval, Selim Running Bear
DANCE ME OUTSIDE
Sands, Julian
GREAT ELEPHANT ESCAPE, THE
LEAVING LAS VEGAS
Sang, Lena
WALKING DEAD, THE
Sangde, Ravi
BANDIT QUEEN
Sanjay
DON JUAN DEMARCO
Sankovich, John
PROPHECY, THE
Sannella, Kathryn
BED YOU SLEEP IN, THE
FRAMEUP
Sano, Shiro
MYSTERY OF RAMPO, THE
Sanoussi-Bliss, Pierre
NOBODY LOVES ME
Sansone, Patricia
CANDYMAN: FAREWELL TO THE FLESH
Santacroce, Mary Nell
CLASS OF '61
SOMETHING TO TALK ABOUT
Santana, Valentin
BURNING SEASON, THE
Santanta, Roberto L.
PANTHER
Santiago, Renoly
DANGEROUS MINDS
HACKERS
Santinelli, Gabriella
LOSING ISAIAH
Santini, John
SEVEN
Santisi, Nina
UNZIPPED
Santo, Akiko
MYSTERY OF RAMPO, THE
Santon, Marie-France
LES MISERABLES
Sapienza, Al
FREE WILLY 2: THE ADVENTURE HOME
UNDER SIEGE 2: DARK TERRITORY
Sarafian, Richard
CROSSING GUARD, THE
DON JUAN DEMARCO
Sarafian, Richard Scott
TANK GIRL
Sarandon, Chris
JUST CAUSE
Sarandon, Susan
DEAD MAN WALKING
SAFE PASSAGE
Saravia, Olimpia
JADE

Sarchielli, Massimo
CASTLE FREAK
Sarrasin, Donna
DR. JEKYLL & MS. HYDE
Sarsgaard, Peter
DEAD MAN WALKING
Saruwatari, June
DANGEROUS, THE
INDICTMENT: THE MCMARTIN TRIAL
Sasaki, Naoko
HUNTED, THE
Sasso, William
MAGIC IN THE WATER
Sassor, William
MALICIOUS
Sastre, Ines
SABRINA
Sather, Eric
ASSASSINS
Satriano, Nick
OPERATION DUMBO DROP
Satta, Alessandro Sebastian
CASTLE FREAK
Sauders, Katie
MURIEL'S WEDDING
Saunders, Gregg
RETURN OF THE NATIVE, THE
Saunders, Jerry
FRANK & JESSE
Saunders, Jessica
LAMB
Saunders, Lois
VILLAGE OF THE DAMNED
Saunders, Rainell
HEAT
Saunders, Shirley
IN THE DEEP WOODS
Saunier, Christiane
PIGALLE
Sauve, Ron
WINGS OF COURAGE
Savage, John
CROSSING GUARD, THE
DANGEROUS, THE
Savage, Vic
JACK-O
Savard, Zachary
GOOD DAY TO DIE, A
Savelle, Bradley
JUDGE DREDD
Savident, John
OTHELLO
Savin, Jody
HOUSEGUEST
Savina, Valentina
DANCER, THE
Savino, Joe
BRAVEHEART
Saviola, Camille
STUART SAVES HIS FAMILY
Savoy, David
DRACULA: DEAD AND LOVING IT
Savoy, Sharon
DRACULA: DEAD AND LOVING IT
Saw, William
BEYOND RANGOON
Sawa, Devon
CASPER
NOW AND THEN
Sawaishi, Ryoko
TANK GIRL
Sawiris, Jackie
DEATH MACHINE
Sawyer, Lindsay Mae
RECKLESS
Sawyer, Toni
O.J. SIMPSON STORY, THE

Saxon, John
LAST SAMURAI, THE
Sayer, Bob
EMPIRE RECORDS
Sbille, Jean-Louis
MINA TANNENBAUM
Sbragia, Mattia
OLD LADY WHO WALKED IN THE SEA,
THE
Scacchi, Greta
COUNTRY LIFE
JEFFERSON IN PARIS
Scales, Prunella
AWFULLY BIG ADVENTURE, AN
Scalies, Charles
TWO BITS
Scanlan, Ata
TANK GIRL
Scanlon, Patricia
AMATEUR
Scanlon, Patty
DEAD FUNNY
Scano, Laurent
MINA TANNENBAUM
Scaramanga, Pandeas
BLUE VILLA, THE
Scaramuzza
I, THE WORST OF ALL
Scardapane, Dario
PANTHER
Scardino, Hal
INDIAN IN THE CUPBOARD, THE
Scarpa, Renato
POSTMAN, THE
Scarr, Derani
COUNTRY LIFE
Scarritt, Hunt
CANDYMAN: FAREWELL TO THE FLESH
Scarwid, Diana
CURE, THE
GOLD DIGGERS: THE SECRET OF BEAR
MOUNTAIN
Schacht, Sam
IN THE NAME OF THE EMPEROR
Schaech, Johnathon
DOOM GENERATION, THE
HOW TO MAKE AN AMERICAN QUILT
Schaff, Brenda
AMERICA'S DEADLIEST HOME VIDEO
Schaff, Lora
AMERICA'S DEADLIEST HOME VIDEO
Schaffer, Sharon
MONEY TRAIN
Schaiper, Megan
WHILE YOU WERE SLEEPING
Schanley, Tom
GOOD DAY TO DIE, A
Schanz, Heidi
SEVEN
VIRTUOSITY
Scharkey, Laurelyn
JURY DUTY
Schaub, Mary Christine
AVENGING ANGEL
Schaub, Sarah
AVENGING ANGEL
Scheine, Raynor
QUICK AND THE DEAD, THE
Schell, Herta
FOR GOD AND COUNTRY
Schell, Maximilian
LITTLE ODESSA
Schellenberg, August
FREE WILLY 2: THE ADVENTURE HOME
LAKOTA WOMAN: SIEGE AT WOUNDED
KNEE

Schellhardt, Mary Kate
APOLLO 13
FREE WILLY 2: THE ADVENTURE HOME
Schendel, James
TOO YOUNG TO DIE?
Schiavelli, Vincent
LITTLE PRINCESS, A
LORD OF ILLUSIONS
3 NINJAS KNUCKLE UP
Schiff, Richard
SEVEN
SKINNER
TANK GIRL
Schilling, William
CRAZYSITTER, THE
Schilling, William G.
THREE WISHES
Schlaa, Margit im
NEKROMANTIK
Schleinzer, Markus
FOR GOD AND COUNTRY
Schlesinger, Helen
PERSUASION
Schlingensief, Christoph
EROTIQUE
Schlotfeldt, Paul
JADE
Schluter, Ariane
1-900
Schmidt, Aimee
SISTER MY SISTER
Schmidt, Chris
COVER STORY
Schmidt, Christian
PROMISE, THE
Schmidt, Gabriella
SISTER MY SISTER
Schmidt, Judy
NOSTRADAMUS KID, THE
Schmidt, Laura
IN THE MOUTH OF MADNESS
Schmit, Rolf
GREAT ELEPHANT ESCAPE, THE
Schmitt, Sarah Kathryn
BRIDGES OF MADISON COUNTY, THE
Schmitt, Walfriede
DEADLY MARIA
Schmittler, Danny
INDICTMENT: THE MCMARTIN TRIAL
Schmoeller, Gary
SPITFIRE
Schnarre, Monika
BULLETPROOF HEART
Schneck, Stephen
ACROSS THE MOON
Schneider, Carol
DEAD FUNNY
Schneider, John E.
BREAK, THE
Schneider, Marliese K.
SPECIES
Schneider, Rob
JUDGE DREDD
Schoeber, Tim
VAMPIRES AND OTHER STEREOTYPES
Schofield, Drew
DOOMSDAY GUN
Schollhammer, Georg
BEFORE SUNRISE
Schoonhoven, Gerrit
MANGLER, THE
Schoppert, Bill
CURE, THE
Schorr, Daniel
NET, THE
Schrader, Maria
NOBODY LOVES ME

Schramko, James
MURIEL'S WEDDING
Schreiber, Avery
DRACULA: DEAD AND LOVING IT
Schreiber, Liev
BUFFALO GIRLS
MAD LOVE
PARTY GIRL
Schrier, Paul
MIGHTY MORPHIN POWER RANGERS:
THE MOVIE
Schroder, Lise
KINGDOM, THE
Schroeder, Barbara
CANADIAN BACON
Schroeder, David K.
SPECIES
Schroeder, T.W.
ANDROID AFFAIR, THE
Schuck, John
TALES FROM THE CRYPT: DEMON
KNIGHT
Schuelke, David
ALMOST DEAD
Schuelke, Jimmy
ALMOST DEAD
Schueneman, Warren
GRUMPIER OLD MEN
Schulman, Ann
ARIZONA DREAM
Schulman, Rick
EXPERT, THE
Schultz, Cinnamon
MY ANTONIA
Schulweis, Rabbi Harold M.
UNSTRUNG HEROES
Schulz, Barbara
FRENCH KISS
Schulze, Paul
AMATEUR
CLOCKERS
NEW JERSEY DRIVE
Schulzendorf, Colloseo
NEKROMANTIK
Schuneman, Gregory
GRUMPIER OLD MEN
Schusted, Denny
GRUMPIER OLD MEN
Schwab, Lana
BRIDGES OF MADISON COUNTY, THE
SILENCE OF THE HAMS
Schwartz, Aaron
HEAVYWEIGHTS
Schwartz, Alan Craig
DEVIL IN A BLUE DRESS
Schwary, Ronald
SABRINA
Schweig, Eric
SCARLET LETTER, THE
TOM AND HUCK
Schweiger, Constanze
BEFORE SUNRISE
Schweiger, Peter
CONGRESS OF PENGUINS, THE
Schwender, Clemens
NEKROMANTIK
Schwiegerath, Thor
JACK-O
Schwimmer, Rusty
LITTLE PRINCESS, A
Sciorra, Annabella
ADDICTION, THE
CURE, THE
Sciullo, Vinnie
SUDDEN DEATH
Scoggin, Nick
COPYCAT
MURDER IN THE FIRST

Scorsese, Catherine
CASINO
Scorsese, Catherine T.
CASINO
Scorsese, Martin
SEARCH AND DESTROY
Scorsiani, Joseph
ANDROID AFFAIR, THE
Scorupco, Izabella
GOLDENEYE
Scott, Alexander
WATER ENGINE, THE
Scott, Amy
BORN TO BE WILD
Scott, Andrew
TO DIE FOR
Scott, Campbell
INNOCENT, THE
Scott, Dawan
FORGET PARIS
Scott, Donna W.
GET SHORTY
Scott, Esther
DON JUAN DEMARCO
SPECIES
Scott, George C.
ANGUS
Scott, J. Alan
TANK GIRL
Scott, John
INNOCENT, THE
TIE-DIED: ROCK 'N' ROLL'S MOST
DEADICATED FANS
Scott, Judith
BOULEVARD
Scott, Kimberly
BATMAN FOREVER
FATHER AND SCOUT
Scott, Lorna
SAFE
Scott, Marvin
IN THE MOUTH OF MADNESS
SAFE PASSAGE
Scott, Michael
OUT OF ANNIE'S PAST
Scott, Suzanne
VAMPIRES AND OTHER STEREOTYPES
Scott Thomas, Kristin
RICHARD III
Scott, Tim
CLASS OF '61
Scott, Willard
ROOMMATES
Scott, William Barry
EXPERT, THE
Scott-Perry, Eva
AMERICA'S DEADLIEST HOME VIDEO
Scotti, Allen
VIRTUOSITY
Scotti, Vito
GET SHORTY
Scotting, Nigel
INNOCENT, THE
Scoular, David
SHALLOW GRAVE
Scranton, Michael
BATMAN FOREVER
Scriba, Mik
IN THE DEEP WOODS
ROSWELL: THE U.F.O. COVER-UP
Scullin, Kevin
ADDICTION, THE
Seabra, Paula
VALLEY OF ABRAHAM, THE
Seagal, Steven
UNDER SIEGE 2: DARK TERRITORY
Seamon, Edward
DEAD FUNNY

Sean
NADJA
Searcy, Nick
ROSWELL: THE U.F.O. COVER-UP
Seboko, Louis
CRY, THE BELOVED COUNTRY
FRIENDS
Seda, Jon
BOYS ON THE SIDE
NEW YORK COP
TWELVE MONKEYS
Sedgwick, Kyra
MURDER IN THE FIRST
SOMETHING TO TALK ABOUT
Sedgwick, Rob
DIE HARD WITH A VENGEANCE
Seeley, Eileen
BATMAN FOREVER
INDICTMENT: THE MCMARTIN TRIAL
Segado, Alberto
I, THE WORST OF ALL
Segal, George
BABYSITTER, THE
Segal, Josh
BOYS ON THE SIDE
Segal, Michael Ryan
TWELVE MONKEYS
Segan, K.D.
BANDIT QUEEN
Segar, Leslie
NEW JERSEY DRIVE
Segerstrom, Mikael
DREAMING OF RITA
Segol, Marianne
INNOCENT LIES
Seibel, Alexandra
BEFORE SUNRISE
Seibert, Scott
BALLOT MEASURE 9
Seider, Talia
HOUSEGUEST
Seidman, John
JEFFREY
Seidman, Michele
EMPIRE RECORDS
Seifertova, Zdena
FATHERLAND
Seipp, Michelle
S.F.W.
Sekely, Steve
DEVIL IN A BLUE DRESS
Selburg, David
ROSWELL: THE U.F.O. COVER-UP
SPECIES
Seldes, Marian
TOM AND HUCK
Self, Elise
BALLOT MEASURE 9
Self, Jim
BALLOT MEASURE 9
Sell, Rod
DILLINGER
Selleck, Tom
BROKEN TRUST
Sells, Kieran
IN THE MOUTH OF MADNESS
Selma
BOCA
Selstad, Jonathan
FATHER OF THE BRIDE PART II
Selstad, Thomas
FATHER OF THE BRIDE PART II
Selzer, Josef
FOR GOD AND COUNTRY
Semler, Peter
LES MISERABLES
Sendaydiego, Vivienne
WALKING DEAD, THE

Senga, Ken
DALLAS DOLL
MURIEL'S WEDDING
Senger, Frank
JERKY BOYS: THE MOVIE, THE
Senst, Heiko
PROMISE, THE
Senzy, Arthur
AMERICAN PRESIDENT, THE
APOLLO 13
INDICTMENT: THE MCMARTIN TRIAL
Serbedzija, Rade
BEFORE THE RAIN
Serene, Martin
SEVEN
Sergei, Ivan
DANGEROUS MINDS
Sergent, Brian
MEET THE FEEBLES
Serna, Assumpta
I, THE WORST OF ALL
Serra, Raymond
SILENCE OF THE HAMS
Serrano, Nestor
BAD BOYS
INDIAN IN THE CUPBOARD, THE
Serrault, Michel
OLD LADY WHO WALKED IN THE SEA,
THE
Sesheta, Greta
GLASS SHIELD, THE
Sessions, Bob
HACKERS
JEFFERSON IN PARIS
Severance, Joan
PAYBACK
Severenson, Karen
AMERICA'S DEADLIEST HOME VIDEO
Severyn, Andre
PROMISE, THE
Sevier, Cory
TOMMY BOY
Sevigny, Chloe
KIDS
Sewell, Rufus
CARRINGTON
Seweryn, Andrzej
TOTAL ECLIPSE
WITHOUT ANESTHESIA
Sexton, Brendan
EMPIRE RECORDS
Sexton, Charlie
LAST RIDE, THE
Sexton, James
LIE DOWN WITH DOGS
Seyfried, Jeff
INNOCENT, THE
Seymour, Carolyn
CONGO
Seymour, M. Jane
BRIDGES OF MADISON COUNTY, THE
Shabazz, Attallah
WHITE MAN'S BURDEN
Shabazz, Salaim
HARLEM DIARY: NINE VOICES OF
RESILIENCE
Shadix, Glenn
DARK SIDE OF GENIUS, THE
Shai, Patrick
CRY, THE BELOVED COUNTRY
Shakh, Eugene
AMERICAN COP
Shakunov, Ilya
CREATION OF ADAM
Shalita, Nelson
CONGO
Shallo, Karen
TWO BITS

Shanahan, Francis
PLAY TIME
Shaner, Michael
EXPERT, THE
Shankar, Mamata
STRANGER, THE
Shanks, Donald L.
3 NINJAS KNUCKLE UP
Shannon, Michael J.
FATHERLAND
Shannon, Polly
LOVE AND HUMAN REMAINS
Shannon, Vicellous
ZOOMAN
Shannon-Burnett, Gaye
GLASS SHIELD, THE
Shapiro, Alan
FUN
Shapiro, Hope
JERKY BOYS: THE MOVIE, THE
Shapiro, Michael
GEORGIA
Shapiro, Whitey
ASSASSINS
Sharian, John
DEATH MACHINE
Shark, David
ASSASSINS
Sharma, Ashok
BANDIT QUEEN
Sharma, Brahmadev
STRANGER, THE
Sharma, Subrata Sen
CHARULATA
Sharp, Jules
UNDERNEATH, THE
Sharp, Lesley
PRIEST
Sharp, Martin
ETERNITY
Sharp, Monti
DEAD PRESIDENTS
Sharpe, Dick
DIRTY MONEY
Sharpe, Luis
WAITING TO EXHALE
Shastri, Jeetendra
BANDIT QUEEN
Shaver, Chris
FORGET PARIS
Shaver, Helen
BORN TO BE WILD
Shaw, Fiona
PERSUASION
Shaw, Ian
CENTURY
Shaw, James Brandon
LORD OF ILLUSIONS
Shaw, Stan
CUTTHROAT ISLAND
HOUSEGUEST
Shawn, Wallace
CLUELESS
GOOFY MOVIE, A
TOY STORY
Shayan, Sabah
PARTY GIRL
Shayna the Monkey
CUTTHROAT ISLAND
She, Elizabeth
HOWLING: NEW MOON RISING, THE
She, Shiao-Long
SHAO LIN POPEYE
Shear, Mike
HEAVEN'S A DRAG
Shearer, Jack
USUAL SUSPECTS, THE

Shearer, Johnetta
COPYCAT
Shearer, Mike
JOHNNY MNEMONIC
Shearer, Steve
UNDERNEATH, THE
Shearman, Alan
BLACK FOX
SECRETARY, THE
WATER ENGINE, THE
Shebib, Suzanna
BILLY MADISON
Sheehan, Patti
BAR GIRLS
Sheehy, Alison
JEFFREY
Sheehy, Joan
RUN OF THE COUNTRY, THE
Sheen, Martin
AMERICAN PRESIDENT, THE
BOCA
BREAK, THE
DILLINGER AND CAPONE
GHOST BRIGADE
ROSWELL: THE U.F.O. COVER-UP
WATER ENGINE, THE
Sheen, Michael
OTHELLO
Sheenan, Kyle
IN THE MOUTH OF MADNESS
Sheffer, Craig
WINGS OF COURAGE
Sheffield, Jamie
COVER STORY
Shell-True, Shari
TO WONG FOO, THANKS FOR
EVERYTHING! JULIE NEWMAR
Shellen, Stephen
DR. JEKYLL & MS. HYDE
Shelley, Sue
CURSE OF THE STARVING CLASS
Shelly, Adrienne
TERESA'S TATTOO
Shelton, Beverly
NOW AND THEN
Shelton, Brad
BED YOU SLEEP IN, THE
Shelton, Marc
THREE WISHES
Shelton, Marley
NIXON
Shen Enshen
ERMO
Sheneh, Emma
PROPHECY, THE
Shenk, Kevin
LIE DOWN WITH DOGS
Shepard, Robin
DRACULA: DEAD AND LOVING IT
Shepard, Sam
SAFE PASSAGE
Shepard, Sr., Duane R.
WHITE MAN'S BURDEN
Shepherd, Jewel
SCANNERS: THE SHOWDOWN
Shepherd, Suzanne
JERKY BOYS: THE MOVIE, THE
Sherayo, Peter
GHOST BRIGADE
Sheridan, Liz
FORGET PARIS
Sheridan, Millicent
CASINO
CROSSING GUARD, THE
Sheridan, Richard
SECRET OF ROAN INISH, THE
Sherman, Natalie
BUSINESS AFFAIR, A

Sherrard, Tudor
SEVEN
Sherstiniov, Uri
MUTE WITNESS
Shettler, Joie
FORGET PARIS
TANK GIRL
Shi Kuifan
BLUE VILLA, THE
Shields, Aaron
CRUDE OASIS, THE
Shields, Loraine
DRACULA: DEAD AND LOVING IT
Shimada, Yoko
HUNTED, THE
Shimizu, Ken
HUNTED, THE
Shimono, Sab
WATERWORLD
Shine, Stephanie
GEORGIA
Shiner, David
MAN OF THE HOUSE
Shirey, Lynn
SILENCE OF THE HAMS
Shirley, III, A. Duncan
JOURNEY OF AUGUST KING, THE
Shiva, Zarifeh
THROUGH THE OLIVE TREES
Shivers, Coyote
EMPIRE RECORDS
JOHNNY MNEMONIC
Shivpuri, Gyan
BANDIT QUEEN
Shockley, William
GIRL IN THE CADILLAC
SHOWGIRLS
Shore, Barry
RIVER OF GRASS
Shore, Pauly
JURY DUTY
Short, John
APOLLO 13
Short, Martin
FATHER OF THE BRIDE PART II
PEBBLE AND THE PENGUIN, THE
Short, Sylvia
S.F.W.
Shorter, Ken
PERSUASION
Shou, Robin
MORTAL KOMBAT
Shpoudeiko, Vlad
AMERICAN COP
Shrapnel, John
FATHERLAND
Shroder, Rick
CRIMSON TIDE
Shroeder, Greg
RIVER OF GRASS
Shropshire, Anne
SOMETHING TO TALK ABOUT
Shroyer, Stephanie
BYE BYE, LOVE
Shu, Lo-Shen
SHAO LIN POPEYE
Shu Zhong
DAY THE SUN TURNED COLD, THE
Shub, Vivienne
HOME FOR THE HOLIDAYS
Shue, Elisabeth
LEAVING LAS VEGAS
RADIO INSIDE
UNDERNEATH, THE
Shuffield, James
BOYS ON THE SIDE
Shukla, Saurabh
BANDIT QUEEN

Shukla, Vijay
BANDIT QUEEN
Shull, Valerie
LOSING ISAIAH
Shum, Jean
FORGET PARIS
Shuman, Danielle
BOYS ON THE SIDE
Shure, Michael
SHOWGIRLS
Shyam, Anupam
BANDIT QUEEN
Sibay, Mussef
CRUDE OASIS, THE
Sibbald, Tony
HACKERS
Sibbett, Jane
IT TAKES TWO
Sibertin-Blanc, Jean-Chretien
AUGUSTIN
Sible, Todd
MAD LOVE
Sibony, Clement
FRENCH KISS
Sichkin, Boris
NIXON
Sicignano, Renee
DON JUAN DEMARCO
Siddal, Brianne
BAREFOOT GEN
Siebel, Lynn Philip
EMBRACE OF THE VAMPIRE
Siebert, Charles
NIGHTMARE
Siefers, Aaron
ANGUS
Siegal, Adam
PARTY GIRL
Siemaszko, Casey
TERESA'S TATTOO
Siemaszko, Nina
AMERICAN PRESIDENT, THE
POWER OF ATTORNEY
Siemon, Clovis
BLESSING
Sierra, Ruben
MY FAMILY: MI FAMILIA
Sigal, Matthew
RIVER OF GRASS
Sigl, Hans
FOR GOD AND COUNTRY
Sigrun, Ragna
ASSASSINS
Sihung Lung
PUSHING HANDS
Sikwayo, Tobias
CRY, THE BELOVED COUNTRY
Silberg, Nicholas
JEFFERSON IN PARIS
Silberg, Tusse
CITIZEN X
Silliman, Maureen
RECKLESS
Sillman, Amy
ART FOR TEACHERS OF CHILDREN
Silva, Henry
SILENCE OF THE HAMS
Silva, Vilma
REDWOOD CURTAIN
Silveira, Leonor
CONVENT, THE
VALLEY OF ABRAHAM, THE
Silver, Dolores
HOWLING: NEW MOON RISING, THE
Silver, Dorothy
ROOMMATES

Silver, Horace
GREAT DAY IN HARLEM, A
Silver, Michael Buchman
ENEMY WITHIN, THE
HIGHER LEARNING
VIRTUOSITY
Silvera, Sarah
MINA TANNENBAUM
Silverbrand, David
OUTBREAK
Silverman, David Michael
COPYCAT
Silverman, Jonathan
TERESA'S TATTOO
Silverman, Robert
WATERWORLD
Silverstone, Alicia
BABYSITTER, THE
CLUELESS
HIDEAWAY
Silverstone, Monty
BABYSITTER, THE
Silvestri, Sandra
FATHER OF THE BRIDE PART II
Sima, Oskar
OH ... ROSALINDA!!
Simacek, Milan
FATHERLAND
Siman, Eva Toth
CITIZEN X
Simma, Andreas
FOR GOD AND COUNTRY
Simmons, Annamarie
WHITE MAN'S BURDEN
Simmons, Jamel "Redrum"
ADDICTION, THE
Simmons, Jean
HOW TO MAKE AN AMERICAN QUILT
Simmons, Ken
LAST GOOD TIME, THE
SEARCH AND DESTROY
Simmons, Michael
BODY STROKES
Simmons, Russell
SHOW, THE
Simmons, Shadia
MOONLIGHT AND VALENTINO
Simmons, Sharrif
PANTHER
Simmons, Thomica Laquice
LOSING ISAIAH
Simmrin, Joey
NINE MONTHS
Simmrin, Mike
CASPER
Simms, Chelsea DeRidder
VILLAGE OF THE DAMNED
Simms, Renee Rene
VILLAGE OF THE DAMNED
Simon, Paul
DIE HARD WITH A VENGEANCE
NINE MONTHS
Simon, Phillip
USUAL SUSPECTS, THE
Simon, Sophie
I CAN'T SLEEP
Simon, Zipporah
FUNNY BONES
Simonds, David
AMATEUR
Simonet, Paul
WILD REEDS
Simons, Keaton
BYE BYE, LOVE
Simons, Tom
AMERICA'S DEADLIEST HOME VIDEO
Simonsoa, Tina
PLAY TIME

Simotes, Tony
  FATHER OF THE BRIDE PART II
  INDICTMENT: THE MCMARTIN TRIAL
Simper, Robert
  MIGHTY MORPHIN POWER RANGERS:
    THE MOVIE
Simpson, Greg
  NOSTRADAMUS KID, THE
Simpson, Les "Linda"
  POSTCARDS FROM AMERICA
Simpson, Michael
  KINGDOM, THE
Simpson, Ngawai
  ONCE WERE WARRIORS
Simpson, Richard
  BUFFALO GIRLS
Simsek, Omer
  NOBODY LOVES ME
Simson, Camilla
  FUNNY BONES
Sinbad
  HOUSEGUEST
Sinclair, Lauren
  THREE WISHES
Sinclair, Laurie A.
  CURE, THE
Sincock, Brent
  PANTHER
Sinden, Donald
  BALTO
Sinden, Jeremy
  INNOCENT, THE
Singer, Leon
  MY FAMILY: MI FAMILIA
Singer, Lori
  LAST RIDE, THE
Singer, Maurice
  OUTSIDE THE LAW
Singer, Stephen
  DON JUAN DEMARCO
Singh, Kumar
  NINE MONTHS
Singletary, Dennis
  BIGFOOT: THE UNFORGETTABLE
    ENCOUNTER
Singleton, Eleva
  COPYCAT
Singleton, Ernie
  HIGHER LEARNING
Singleton, Kenitra
  DEAD MAN WALKING
Sinise, Gary
  APOLLO 13
  QUICK AND THE DEAD, THE
Sinitta
  HEAVEN'S A DRAG
Sinn, Simon
  JOHNNY MNEMONIC
Sintacrose, Anthony
  WINGS OF HONNEAMISE: ROYAL SPACE
    FORCE
Siqin Gaowa
  DAY THE SUN TURNED COLD, THE
Siragusa, Peter
  WHILE YOU WERE SLEEPING
Siraswal, Chotelal
  BANDIT QUEEN
Sirico, Tony
  DEAD PRESIDENTS
  MIGHTY APHRODITE
  NEW YORK COP
Sissons, Kimber
  SILENCE OF THE HAMS
Sisto, Jeremy
  CLUELESS
  CREW, THE
  HIDEAWAY
  MOONLIGHT AND VALENTINO

Sitahal, Errol
  LITTLE PRINCESS, A
Sitarenos, Mary
  ONLY THE BRAVE
Sithole, Chippa
  FRIENDS
Sitnikov, Konstantin
  MUTE WITNESS
Sitomer, Loren
  WALK IN THE CLOUDS, A
Siverio, Manny
  MONEY TRAIN
  NEW YORK COP
Sizemore, Tom
  DEVIL IN A BLUE DRESS
  HEAT
  STRANGE DAYS
Sjogren, John
  MOSAIC PROJECT, THE
Skaggs, Jimmie F.
  CUTTHROAT ISLAND
Skaggs, Norm
  GETTING OUT
Skalnik, Michelle
  HIDEAWAY
Skalsky, Kerry
  ASSASSINS
Skelly, Jack
  SUDDEN DEATH
Skemp, Paul
  FOUR ROOMS
Skinner, Claire
  RETURN OF THE NATIVE, THE
Skinner, Thomas
  DOLORES CLAIBORNE
Skinny Puppy
  DOOM GENERATION, THE
Skipworth, Te Whataniu
  ONCE WERE WARRIORS
Skoric, Greg A.
  DIE HARD WITH A VENGEANCE
Skoric, Ivan
  DIE HARD WITH A VENGEANCE
Sky, Seigel
  BODY STROKES
Skye, Ione
  FOUR ROOMS
Slack, Ben
  MURDER IN THE FIRST
  S.F.W.
Slade, Max Elliott
  APOLLO 13
  3 NINJAS KNUCKLE UP
Slater, Christian
  MURDER IN THE FIRST
Slater, Justine
  BAR GIRLS
Slater, Ryan
  AMAZING PANDA ADVENTURE, THE
  BABYSITTER, THE
Slattery, Tony
  HEAVEN'S A DRAG
Slayton, Bobby
  GET SHORTY
Sleete, Gena
  SUBSTITUTE WIFE, THE
Sley, Cynthia
  RHYTHM THIEF
Slezak, Victor
  BEYOND RANGOON
  BRIDGES OF MADISON COUNTY, THE
  JUST CAUSE
Slick Rick
  SHOW, THE
Sliger, Scott
  VAMPIRES AND OTHER STEREOTYPES
Slima, Stephane
  MINA TANNENBAUM

Slivnikov, Anatoli
  WINDOW TO PARIS
Sloane, Michael
  SCANNERS: THE SHOWDOWN
Sloss, John
  BEFORE SUNRISE
Slout, Marte Boyle
  COSMIC SLOP
  STUART SAVES HIS FAMILY
Slovick, Sam
  HOME FOR THE HOLIDAYS
Slovo, Robyn
  FRIENDS
Slowey, Pat
  SECRET OF ROAN INISH, THE
Slowick, Bill
  ART FOR TEACHERS OF CHILDREN
Slusser, Martin
  DIRTY MONEY
Slusser, Wendelin
  DIRTY MONEY
Small, Adam
  S.F.W.
Smallman, Amy
  VIRTUOSITY
Smart, Jean
  BRADY BUNCH MOVIE, THE
Smeeton, Phil
  JUDGE DREDD
Smerczak, Ron
  CRY, THE BELOVED COUNTRY
  MANGLER, THE
Smigel, Robert
  BILLY MADISON
Smiley, Chris
  TIE-DIED: ROCK 'N' ROLL'S MOST
    DEADICATED FANS
Smith, Afton
  REASON TO BELIEVE, A
Smith, Alexander Cohen
  JEFFREY
Smith, Allison
  REASON TO BELIEVE, A
Smith, Amy
  REASON TO BELIEVE, A
Smith, Anna Deavere
  AMERICAN PRESIDENT, THE
Smith, Archie
  THINGS TO DO IN DENVER WHEN
    YOU'RE DEAD
Smith, Barbara
  BLACK IS ... BLACK AIN'T
Smith, Brandon
  POWDER
Smith, Britta
  CIRCLE OF FRIENDS
  RETURN OF THE NATIVE, THE
Smith, Brittany Alyse
  GOOFY MOVIE, A
Smith, Brooke
  LAST SUMMER IN THE HAMPTONS
Smith, Bubba
  SILENCE OF THE HAMS
Smith, Charles Martin
  ROSWELL: THE U.F.O. COVER-UP
Smith, Colin
  BILLY MADISON
Smith, David Alan
  CURE, THE
Smith, Diane
  MURIEL'S WEDDING
Smith, Ebonie
  COSMIC SLOP
Smith, Eddie Bo
  STEAL BIG, STEAL LITTLE
Smith, Emmy
  FORGET PARIS

Smith, Fred
CASINO
Smith, Hanley
BUFFALO GIRLS
Smith, J.D.
BITTER VENGEANCE
DEVIL IN A BLUE DRESS
Smith, J.W.
HIGHER LEARNING
INDICTMENT: THE MCMARTIN TRIAL
Smith, Jamie Renee
OUTSIDE THE LAW
Smith, Jason Bose
FRIDAY
Smith, Jeffrey L.
GRUMPIER OLD MEN
Smith, Jim
MAN OF THE HOUSE
Smith, John T.
PANTHER
Smith, Jr., Eddie "Bo"
LOSING ISAIAH
Smith, Jr., John Walton
HIGHER LEARNING
Smith, Julie K.
MIDNIGHT TEASE 2
Smith, Juney
BYE BYE, LOVE
Smith, Kellita
CROSSING GUARD, THE
Smith, Kevin
MALLRATS
Smith, Kurtwood
LAST OF THE DOGMEN
TO DIE FOR
UNDER SIEGE 2: DARK TERRITORY
Smith, Lane
SPY WITHIN, THE
Smith, Lionel Mark
WATER ENGINE, THE
Smith, Lois
DEAD MAN WALKING
HOW TO MAKE AN AMERICAN QUILT
Smith, Maggie
RICHARD III
Smith, Melissa
DIRTY MONEY
Smith, Nikki
COVER STORY
Smith, Noel
RUN OF THE COUNTRY, THE
Smith, Pete
ONCE WERE WARRIORS
Smith, Richard T.
CASINO
Smith, Rikkia A.
LOSING ISAIAH
Smith, Rita
KINGFISH: A STORY OF HUEY P. LONG
Smith, Robert
DEAD PRESIDENTS
Smith, Roger
O.J. SIMPSON STORY, THE
TALES FROM THE HOOD
Smith, Roger Guenveur
COSMIC SLOP
PANTHER
Smith, Russell W.
STRANGE DAYS
Smith, Shannon Dow
PREHYSTERIA! 3
Smith, Shawnee
LEAVING LAS VEGAS
Smith, Silan
UNDER SIEGE 2: DARK TERRITORY
Smith, Stephanie
COPYCAT

Smith, Stephen Wolfe
DRACULA: DEAD AND LOVING IT
Smith, Steve
MURIEL'S WEDDING
Smith, Victoria
JADE
Smith, Will
BAD BOYS
Smith, Willie
AWFULLY BIG ADVENTURE, AN
Smith, Wynonna
HOUSEGUEST
Smith-Cameron, J.
MIGHTY APHRODITE
SABRINA
Smitrovich, Bill
BODILY HARM
NICK OF TIME
Smits, Jimmy
GROSS MISCONDUCT
MY FAMILY: MI FAMILIA
Smock, Ashley
CRIMSON TIDE
Smolianoff, Michel
CITY OF LOST CHILDREN, THE
Smothers, Dick
CASINO
Smrz, Brian
SUDDEN DEATH
Smurfit, Victoria
RUN OF THE COUNTRY, THE
Sneed, Maurice
CLOCKERS
Snegoff, Greg
WICKED CITY
Snell, Terrie
SCANNERS: THE SHOWDOWN
Snipes, Wesley
MONEY TRAIN
TO WONG FOO, THANKS FOR
EVERYTHING! JULIE NEWMAR
Snodgress, Carrie
WHITE MAN'S BURDEN
Snoop Doggy Dog
SHOW, THE
Snyder, Chris
HEAVYWEIGHTS
Snyder, Deb
PUSHING HANDS
Snyder, Drew
BREACH OF CONDUCT
GLASS SHIELD, THE
JADE
NIXON
SEPARATE LIVES
Snyder, John
PANTHER
Snyder, Moriah
BRADY BUNCH MOVIE, THE
Snyder, Moriah Shining Dove
PROPHECY, THE
Snyder, Rick
NET, THE
So Yee Shum
DOUBLE HAPPINESS
Soboil, Maggie
WATER ENGINE, THE
Soeberg, Camilla
EROTIQUE
Soentgen, Norbert
MUTE WITNESS
Sokol, Marilyn
BASKETBALL DIARIES, THE
Sokoloff, Marla
BABY-SITTERS CLUB, THE
Sokoloski, Thom
WHEN NIGHT IS FALLING

Solanki, Girish
BANDIT QUEEN
Solar, Joe
JACK-O
Solari, Sky
NUMBER ONE FAN
Solarz, Victoria
I, THE WORST OF ALL
Solaya, Marilyn
STRAWBERRY AND CHOCOLATE
Solberg, Helena
CARMEN MIRANDA: BANANAS IS MY
BUSINESS
Solberg, Russell
BIGFOOT: THE UNFORGETTABLE
ENCOUNTER
Solli, Sergio
POSTMAN, THE
Solms-Baruth, Friedrich
INNOCENT, THE
Somerville, Geraldine
BUSINESS AFFAIR, A
Somes, Michael
BALLET
Sommer, Josef
ENEMY WITHIN, THE
MOONLIGHT AND VALENTINO
STRANGE DAYS
Sommers, Avery
MIAMI RHAPSODY
Somrack, F. Daniel
BODY SHOT
Son, Joe
BAD BLOOD
Song, Siching
SABRINA
Songer, Melinda
SHOWGIRLS
Soni, Deepak
BANDIT QUEEN
Sonkkila, Paul
GROSS MISCONDUCT
Sonnenfeld, Barry
GET SHORTY
Sonwani, Malabai
BANDIT QUEEN
Sook Yin Lee
BAD COMPANY
Soper, Karla Jo
BRIDGES OF MADISON COUNTY, THE
Soral, Agnes
WINDOW TO PARIS
Sorce, Robert
PARTY GIRL
Sorel, Nancy
BLACK FOX
Sorel, Ted
ME AND THE MOB
Soremekun, Kai
HEAT
Sorensen, Tony
CAGED HEARTS
Sorge, Paula
BAR GIRLS
Sorkin, Aaron
AMERICAN PRESIDENT, THE
Sorrentino, Spike
IN THE DEEP WOODS
Sorvino, Mira
BLUE IN THE FACE
MIGHTY APHRODITE
NEW YORK COP
Sorvino, Paul
COVER ME
NIGHTMARE
NIXON
Soto, Garrett E.
DANGEROUS, THE

Soto, Hugo
I, THE WORST OF ALL
Soto, Jose
MONEY TRAIN
Soto, Talisa
DON JUAN DEMARCO
MORTAL KOMBAT
Sottile, Michael
OUTBREAK
Soubrie, Walter
I, THE WORST OF ALL
Souchet, Guillaume
LES MISERABLES
Soukop, Elizabeth
IN THE DEEP WOODS
Soul, David
PENTATHLON
Soulam, Rosalind
OUT OF ANNIE'S PAST
Soulinhac, Elodie
WILD REEDS
Soulsonic Force
SHOW, THE
Sousa, Barry
FORGET PARIS
Sousa, Dalila Carmo e
VALLEY OF ABRAHAM, THE
Souther, J.D.
TO CROSS THE RUBICON
Southerland, Boots
BUFFALO GIRLS
Soveral, Laura
VALLEY OF ABRAHAM, THE
Sowers, Scott
DEAD MAN WALKING
MONEY TRAIN
UNDER SIEGE 2: DARK TERRITORY
Soyez, Florence
FRENCH KISS
Spacey, Kevin
DOOMSDAY GUN
OUTBREAK
SEVEN
SWIMMING WITH SHARKS
USUAL SUSPECTS, THE
Spadafori, Cary
REASON TO BELIEVE, A
Spade, David
TOMMY BOY
Spagnolo, Maria Rosa
PURE FORMALITY, A
Spangler, Tina J.
JADE
Spanjers, Barbara
CASINO
Spano, Joe
APOLLO 13
Spano, Phil
SUDDEN DEATH
Spano, Vincent
ASCENT, THE
TIE THAT BINDS, THE
Sparber, Herschel
GOOFY MOVIE, A
Sparks, Robert
DESTINY TURNS ON THE RADIO
Sparks, Willis
DIE HARD WITH A VENGEANCE
Sparrow, Walter
NOW AND THEN
Speakman, Jeff
EXPERT, THE
Spears, Aries
OUT OF SYNC
Spears, Michael
LAKOTA WOMAN: SIEGE AT WOUNDED
KNEE

Spears, Peter
FATHER OF THE BRIDE PART II
Speck, Jan
NICK OF TIME
Spellos, Peter
BODY SHOT
Spence, Bruce
ACE VENTURA: WHEN NATURE CALLS
Spencer, Clifford
HIGHLANDER: THE FINAL DIMENSION
Spencer, Dorian
FATHER OF THE BRIDE PART II
Spencer, III, Robert E.
HEAVYWEIGHTS
Spencer, John
FORGET PARIS
Spicer, Jerry
BAD BLOOD
BIGFOOT: THE UNFORGETTABLE
ENCOUNTER
Spiegel, Scott
QUICK AND THE DEAD, THE
Spieler, Ortwin
DEADLY MARIA
Spiess, Tom
DEADLY MARIA
Spillane, Des
AILSA
Spiller, Tom
BETTER OFF DEAD
Spina, Nicholas
ME AND THE MOB
Spinali, S.J.
COPYCAT
Spinella, Stephen
VIRTUOSITY
Spinuzza, Doug
WATERWORLD
Spirkovski-Dzumerko, Blagoja
BEFORE THE RAIN
Spivey, Isaac
JADE
Sporl, Simone
NEKROMANTIK
Spotts, Lara
DANGEROUS MINDS
Spottswood, Warren
MURDER IN THE FIRST
Spound, Michael
BYE BYE, LOVE
Spradlin, G.D.
CANADIAN BACON
NICK OF TIME
Spray, Emily
POSTCARDS FROM AMERICA
Spriggs, Elizabeth
SENSE AND SENSIBILITY
Spriggs, Larry
FORGET PARIS
Sproule, Scott
SPECIES
Spur, Andy
HEAVEN'S A DRAG
Srivastava, Aditya
BANDIT QUEEN
Sroka, Warren
ACE VENTURA: WHEN NATURE CALLS
St. Clair, Julie
BALLISTIC
St. James, David
FORGET PARIS
St. James, Marie
JUST CAUSE
St. John, Beryl
RESTORATION
St. John, Gina
BREACH OF CONDUCT

CHILDREN OF THE CORN III: URBAN
HARVEST
St. John, Marco
DANGEROUS, THE
St. John, Michelle
POCAHONTAS
St. John, Trevor
CRIMSON TIDE
HIGHER LEARNING
St. Laurent, Seth
HEAVYWEIGHTS
St. Paul, Stuart
DEATH MACHINE
St. Paule, Irma
JEFFREY
ME AND THE MOB
PARTY GIRL
TWELVE MONKEYS
St. Pierre, David
CONGO
St. Romaine, Kelly
SHOWGIRLS
Stabnau, Eric
INDIAN IN THE CUPBOARD, THE
Stabrowski, Marek
LEAVING LAS VEGAS
Stadiem, William
BUSINESS AFFAIR, A
Stafford, Jim
GORDY
Stafford, Kate
INCREDIBLY TRUE ADVENTURES OF
TWO GIRLS IN LOVE, THE
Stahl, Andrew
CLASS OF '61
JOURNEY OF AUGUST KING, THE
Stahl, Andy
TOM AND HUCK
Stahl, Nick
SAFE PASSAGE
TALL TALE: THE UNBELIEVABLE
ADVENTURES OF PECOS BILL
Stahl, Richard
AMERICAN PRESIDENT, THE
Stait, Brent
BROKEN TRUST
FAR FROM HOME: THE ADVENTURES OF
YELLOW DOG
GOOD DAY TO DIE, A
Staite, Jewel
GOLD DIGGERS: THE SECRET OF BEAR
MOUNTAIN
Stallone, Sylvester
ASSASSINS
JUDGE DREDD
Stameschkine, Martin
MINA TANNENBAUM
Stamper, Sumer
UNSTRUNG HEROES
Stander, Ava
LORD OF ILLUSIONS
Stander, Lionel
LAST GOOD TIME, THE
Standifer, Damon
ACE VENTURA: WHEN NATURE CALLS
Standing Elk, Sidel
LAST OF THE DOGMEN
Standish, Kimbra
HACKERS
Standjofski, Harry
LOVE AND HUMAN REMAINS
Stanier, John
JERKY BOYS: THE MOVIE, THE
Stansbury, Caitlan
BAR GIRLS
Stansova, Dagmar
DIRTY MONEY
Stanton, Barry
KID IN KING ARTHUR'S COURT, A

Stanton, Harry Dean
BLUE TIGER
NEVER TALK TO STRANGERS
Stanton, Maria
DR. JEKYLL & MS. HYDE
Stanton, Natasha
HOME FOR THE HOLIDAYS
Stapleton, Maureen
LAST GOOD TIME, THE
Staribacher, Wolfgang
BEFORE SUNRISE
Stark, Don
THINGS TO DO IN DENVER WHEN
YOU'RE DEAD
3 NINJAS KNUCKLE UP
Stark, Lauren
BODILY HARM
Starks, John
FORGET PARIS
Starr, Beau
BAD BLOOD
DEVIL IN A BLUE DRESS
NEVER TALK TO STRANGERS
Starr, Fredro
ADDICTION, THE
Starr, Jennifer
UNDER SIEGE 2: DARK TERRITORY
Starr, Mike
CLOCKERS
PYROMANIAC'S LOVE STORY, A
Starr, Pat
JUDGE DREDD
Starr, Robert
THREE WISHES
Starson, Jr., Peter P.
NIXON
Startoni, Troy
TANK GIRL
Statham, Patricia
OUTSIDE THE LAW
Statham, Patrick J.
SCANNERS: THE SHOWDOWN
Stathas, Dimitry
POSTCARDS FROM AMERICA
Staunton, Imelda
CITIZEN X
SENSE AND SENSIBILITY
Staunton, Kim
HEAT
Stavola, Charlie
INDICTMENT: THE MCMARTIN TRIAL
Stea, Kevin
SHOWGIRLS
Steadman, Ken
I LIKE TO PLAY GAMES
Steavenson-Payne, Kate
RICHARD III
Steben, Karyne
WHEN NIGHT IS FALLING
Steben, Sarah
WHEN NIGHT IS FALLING
Steel, Andrew
ACE VENTURA: WHEN NATURE CALLS
AMERICAN PRESIDENT, THE
Steele, Jeffrey
POSTCARDS FROM AMERICA
Steele, Jonathan
O.J. SIMPSON STORY, THE
Steele, Rob
COUNTRY LIFE
MURIEL'S WEDDING
Steele, Vernon
DOLORES CLAIBORNE
Steeley, Derek
DEAD MAN WALKING
Steen, Soren
KINGDOM, THE

Steenburgen, Mary
MY FAMILY: MI FAMILIA
NIXON
POWDER
Stefano, Kathleen
COPYCAT
Stefanovski, Ilko
BEFORE THE RAIN
Steffanelli, Marco
CASTLE FREAK
Steger, Jimmy
MUTANT SPECIES
Steiger, Rod
GLORY BOYS, THE
Steigerwald, Paul
SUDDEN DEATH
Stein, Ben
CASPER
MIAMI RHAPSODY
Stein, Birgit
NOBODY LOVES ME
Stein, Saul
MONEY TRAIN
NEW JERSEY DRIVE
Steinbach, Victor
ACROSS THE SEA OF TIME: NEW YORK
3D
Steinberg, Norman
MIAMI RHAPSODY
Steinberg, Rob
COVER ME
Steinemann, Duke
FLUKE
Steinmann, Klaus-Jurgen
INNOCENT, THE
Steins, Mark
NIXON
Steis, William
BODY SHOT
Steitzer, Jeff
GEORGIA
Stelmaszyk, K.
SHORT FILM ABOUT KILLING, A
Stender, Thomas
KINGDOM, THE
Stephan, Erik
JUST CAUSE
Stephan, Jeffrey J.
GET SHORTY
Stephens, Brice
MORTAL KOMBAT
Stephens, Brittany English
BABYSITTER, THE
Stephens, Buck
CASINO
Stephens, Louanne
BIG GREEN, THE
Stephens, Robert
CENTURY
WHEN BILLY BROKE HIS HEAD ... AND
OTHER TALES OF WONDER
Stephenson, Lt. Donald
CLOCKERS
Stephenson, Robert
SEVEN
Stepkin, David
JERKY BOYS: THE MOVIE, THE
Stepkowski, K.
SHORT FILM ABOUT KILLING, A
Stepp, Craig
PLAY TIME
SEPARATE LIVES
Sterling, David
MURDER IN THE FIRST
Sterling, John
SUDDEN DEATH
Sterling, Maury
OUTBREAK

Stern, Daniel
BUSHWHACKED
Sterrenberg, Jay
BROKEN TRUST
Sterz, Benjamin
HEAVEN'S A DRAG
Steven, Jennifer
ATTACK OF THE 60-FOOT CENTERFOLD
Stevens, Alex
KISS OF DEATH
Stevens, Andrew
BODY CHEMISTRY 4: FULL EXPOSURE
Stevens, Brinke
JACK-O
Stevens, Fisher
HACKERS
NINA TAKES A LOVER
Stevens, Gruschenka
NOBODY LOVES ME
Stevens, Scott N.
OPERATION DUMBO DROP
Stevens, Stella
BODY CHEMISTRY 4: FULL EXPOSURE
GRANNY, THE
Stevens, Warren
BAD BLOOD
Stevens, Wass
NIXON
Stevenson, Alicia
HIGHER LEARNING
Stevenson, Bill
OUTBREAK
Stevenson, Cynthia
FORGET PARIS
HOME FOR THE HOLIDAYS
Stevenson, Jr., Charles C.
TOO YOUNG TO DIE?
Stevenson, Ray
RETURN OF THE NATIVE, THE
Stewardson, Dean
FRIENDS
Stewart, Catherine Mary
NUMBER ONE FAN
OUT OF ANNIE'S PAST
Stewart, Dave
HACKERS
Stewart, Denis L.
UNDER SIEGE 2: DARK TERRITORY
Stewart, Doug
OUT OF ANNIE'S PAST
Stewart, Ewan
ROB ROY
Stewart, French
LEAVING LAS VEGAS
Stewart, Jackie
FRANK & JESSE
Stewart, Kate McGregory
SAFE
Stewart, Lorin
LORD OF ILLUSIONS
Stewart, Lynne
CRAZYSITTER, THE
Stewart, Malcolm
JUMANJI
Stewart, Mel
PENTATHLON
Stewart, Nils Allen
CYBER BANDITS
Stewart, Pamela
AMATEUR
Stewart, Patrick
JEFFREY
Stewart, Richard Alan
DRACULA: DEAD AND LOVING IT
Steyn, Jennifer
CRY, THE BELOVED COUNTRY

Sticklin, Debra
HOW TO MAKE AN AMERICAN QUILT
Stickney, Phyllis Yvonne
DIE HARD WITH A VENGEANCE
Sticky Fingaz
CLOCKERS
DEAD PRESIDENTS
Stier, Hans Martin
INNOCENT, THE
Stier, Laszlo
CITIZEN X
Stiers, David Ogden
BAD COMPANY
MIGHTY APHRODITE
POCAHONTAS
STEAL BIG, STEAL LITTLE
Stiller, Ben
HEAVYWEIGHTS
Stiller, Jerry
HEAVYWEIGHTS
Stilles, Michelle
HOWLING: NEW MOON RISING, THE
Stimely, Brett
DECONSTRUCTING SARAH
Stinson, Joey
NOW AND THEN
TOM AND HUCK
Stiritz, John
FRANK & JESSE
Stirling, Edna
ONCE WERE WARRIORS
Stirling, Helen
CASTLE FREAK
Stobart, Ed
JUDGE DREDD
Stockenstroom, Wilma
FRIENDS
Stockton, Scott
CURE, THE
Stockwell, John
NIXON
OPERATION INTERCEPT
Stoehr, Philip
TO WONG FOO, THANKS FOR
EVERYTHING! JULIE NEWMAR
Stojanova, Milica
BEFORE THE RAIN
Stojanovska, Silvija
BEFORE THE RAIN
Stokes, Nelle
ROOMMATES
Stokesbury, Jill
O.J. SIMPSON STORY, THE
Stole, Mink
CRAZYSITTER, THE
Stolle, Fred
BREAK, THE
Stollery, Brian
LAST OF THE DOGMEN
Stoltz, Andre
FRIENDS
Stoltz, Eric
FLUKE
KICKING AND SCREAMING
PROPHECY, THE
ROB ROY
WOMAN AT WAR, A
Stone, Bob
CRIMSON TIDE
Stone, Doug
GORDY
WINGS OF HONNEAMISE: ROYAL SPACE
FORCE
Stone, Ed
SPECIES
Stone, Eric
FIRST KNIGHT

Stone, Hank
FAIR GAME
WALKING DEAD, THE
Stone, Lee
WINGS OF HONNEAMISE: ROYAL SPACE
FORCE
Stone, Michael
QUICK AND THE DEAD, THE
Stone, Mikey
NIXON
Stone, Randy
HOME FOR THE HOLIDAYS
Stone, Sean
NIXON
Stone, Sharon
CASINO
QUICK AND THE DEAD, THE
Stone, Terrance
OUTSIDE THE LAW
Stone, Tucker
NOW AND THEN
Storch, Larry
SILENCE OF THE HAMS
Storey, Howard
BROKEN TRUST
Stork, Paul
JURY DUTY
Storm, Helen
WINGS OF HONNEAMISE: ROYAL SPACE
FORCE
Storm, Michael
BOYS ON THE SIDE
Storry, Malcolm
SCARLET LETTER, THE
Storsberg, Kris
FORGET PARIS
Story, Joel
TO WONG FOO, THANKS FOR
EVERYTHING! JULIE NEWMAR
Stott, Ken
SHALLOW GRAVE
Stover, George
ATTACK OF THE 60-FOOT CENTERFOLD
Stowe, Madeleine
TWELVE MONKEYS
Stracuzzi, Orazio
POSTMAN, THE
Strafella, Richard F.
CASINO
Strain, Julie
MOSAIC PROJECT, THE
PLAY TIME
Straithairn, David
LOSING ISAIAH
Stram, Henry
JEFFREY
Strandberg, Claus
KINGDOM, THE
Strang, Deborah
THINGS TO DO IN DENVER WHEN
YOU'RE DEAD
Strasser, Michael
ROSWELL: THE U.F.O. COVER-UP
Strathairn, David
DOLORES CLAIBORNE
HOME FOR THE HOLIDAYS
Stratton, David
THINGS TO DO IN DENVER WHEN
YOU'RE DEAD
Stratton, Michelle
REASON TO BELIEVE, A
Strauss, Louis
PYROMANIAC'S LOVE STORY, A
Strauss, Natalie
S.F.W.
Strauss, Peter
NICK OF TIME

Strauss, Vivien
THREE WISHES
Streczyn, Anna
BAR GIRLS
Streep, Meryl
BRIDGES OF MADISON COUNTY, THE
Strickland, David
POSTCARDS FROM AMERICA
Strickland, Gail
AMERICAN PRESIDENT, THE
HOW TO MAKE AN AMERICAN QUILT
Strickland, Will Nahkohe
TANK GIRL
Stringer, Tate
UNDERCOVER
Strizhenov, Alexander
CREATION OF ADAM
Strode, Woody
QUICK AND THE DEAD, THE
Stroh, Lindsey
FRIENDS
Strong, Arnold
INNOCENT, THE
Strong, Mark
CENTURY
Strother, Fred
TWELVE MONKEYS
Stroud, Don
DILLINGER AND CAPONE
Stroud, Duke
CHILDREN OF THE CORN III: URBAN
HARVEST
Stuart, Alison
NICK OF TIME
Stuart, Freddie
LAMB
Stuart, Jason
CYBER BANDITS
Stubbs, Imogen
SENSE AND SENSIBILITY
Stuber, Scott
ASSASSINS
FREE WILLY 2: THE ADVENTURE HOME
Studi, Wes
HEAT
Studt, Katya
DEADLY MARIA
Study, Lomax
LITTLE PRINCESS, A
Study, Simone
THREE WISHES
Stuhr, Jerzy
WITHOUT ANESTHESIA
Stuke, Neil
CENTURY
Stull, Rob
PENTATHLON
Stuno, Michael Angelo
LORD OF ILLUSIONS
Sturges, Pat
GRANNY, THE
Sturgis, Gary Anthony
VIRTUOSITY
Sturtz, Robert
HEAVEN'S A DRAG
Styron, Alexandra
LAST SUMMER IN THE HAMPTONS
Su, Charline
SEVEN
Su Tak-Fu
ASHES OF TIME
Sudduth, Skipp
MONEY TRAIN
Sudina, Marina
MUTE WITNESS
Sudo, Jinichiro
MYSTERY OF RAMPO, THE

Sugano, Chieko
HUNTED, THE
Sugi, Yoki
PICTURE BRIDE
Suhor, Yvonne
DILLINGER
Suhr, Brendon
GROSS MISCONDUCT
Suhr, Holger
NEKROMANTIK
Suite, Annie
SUBSTITUTE WIFE, THE
Sukowa, Barbara
JOHNNY MNEMONIC
Sulatycky, Warren
JOHNNY MNEMONIC
Suli, Ania
FUN
Sullivan, Abby
MY ANTONIA
Sullivan, Bernadette
WORLD AND TIME ENOUGH
Sullivan, Billy L.
BIG GREEN, THE
NEXT DOOR
TANK GIRL
Sullivan, Brad
BUSHWHACKED
CANADIAN BACON
JERKY BOYS: THE MOVIE, THE
Sullivan, D.J.
IN THE DEEP WOODS
Sullivan, Dail
CENTURY
Sullivan, Dianna Evans
TIE-DIED: ROCK 'N' ROLL'S MOST
DEADICATED FANS
Sullivan, Fiona
MURIEL'S WEDDING
Sullivan, Jahree
TIE-DIED: ROCK 'N' ROLL'S MOST
DEADICATED FANS
Sullivan, Jim
TANK GIRL
Sullivan, Walter
DALLAS DOLL
Summerhays, Christy
OUT OF ANNIE'S PAST
Summerour, Lisa
ENEMY WITHIN, THE
Summers, Neil
BIGFOOT: THE UNFORGETTABLE
ENCOUNTER
Sumpter, Donald
RICHARD III
Sun Chun
SHANGHAI TRIAD
Sundborg, Solveig
KINGDOM, THE
Sundstrom, Carl
PENTATHLON
Suplee, Ethan
MALLRATS
Surban, Heike
NEKROMANTIK
Suriano, Phillip
CASINO
Surly, Norma
BOCA
Surratt, Harold
PIANO LESSON, THE
SUDDEN DEATH
Susman, Todd
BODILY HARM
Sutera, Paul
BRADY BUNCH MOVIE, THE
Sutherland, Donald
CITIZEN X

OUTBREAK
YOUNGER & YOUNGER
Sutherland, Kiefer
TERESA'S TATTOO
Sutherland, Richard
MURIEL'S WEDDING
Suttles, M. Darnell
CONGO
Sutton, Carol
CANDYMAN: FAREWELL TO THE FLESH
Sutton, Dudley
LAMB
LAMB
Sutton, Lee Etta
EMPIRE RECORDS
Sutton, Lisa
BRADY BUNCH MOVIE, THE
Suzat, Norma
I, THE WORST OF ALL
Suzuoki, Hirotaka
AI CITY
Sverak, Zdenek
ACCUMULATOR 1
Swain, Howard
FRAMEUP
Swallow, Richard
LAKOTA WOMAN: SIEGE AT WOUNDED
KNEE
Swalve, Darwyn
TALL TALE: THE UNBELIEVABLE
ADVENTURES OF PECOS BILL
Swan, Seymour
MAJOR PAYNE
Swann, Dale
TALES FROM THE CRYPT: DEMON
KNIGHT
Swann, Robert
BUSINESS AFFAIR, A
Swanson, Brenda
SCANNERS: THE SHOWDOWN
Swanson, Jack
GETTING OUT
Swanson, Kristy
HIGHER LEARNING
Swanson, Rochelle
IN THE DEEP WOODS
Swanson, Scott
BROKEN TRUST
POWER OF ATTORNEY
Swartz, Kraig
WORLD AND TIME ENOUGH
Swatter, D.F.
LORD OF ILLUSIONS
Swayze, Patrick
TALL TALE: THE UNBELIEVABLE
ADVENTURES OF PECOS BILL
THREE WISHES
TO WONG FOO, THANKS FOR
EVERYTHING! JULIE NEWMAR
Swearingen, Michael L.
LORD OF ILLUSIONS
Swedberg, Heidi
FATHER AND SCOUT
Sweeney, D.B.
ROOMMATES
Sweeney, Julia
STUART SAVES HIS FAMILY
Sweeney, Sean
GETTING OUT
Sweet, Ann
BALLOT MEASURE 9
Sweet, Shane
INDICTMENT: THE MCMARTIN TRIAL
Sweet, Vonte
WALKING DEAD, THE
Sweetman, Alex
DESPERATE PREY

Swenson, Britt
MALLRATS
Swenson, Lee
WHEN BILLY BROKE HIS HEAD ... AND
OTHER TALES OF WONDER
Swerdlow, Ezra
WAITING TO EXHALE
Swetow, Joel
LORD OF ILLUSIONS
Swid, Robin
BABY-SITTERS CLUB, THE
Swift, Francie
SCARLET LETTER, THE
Swift, Keith
BORN TO BE WILD
Swift, Susan
HALLOWEEN: THE CURSE OF MICHAEL
MYERS
Swindall, Jerry
QUICK AND THE DEAD, THE
Swindell, Rasheem
HARLEM DIARY: NINE VOICES OF
RESILIENCE
Swinney, Stephanie
OUTSIDE THE LAW
Switkowski, C.
SHORT FILM ABOUT KILLING, A
Sylvan, Paul
RADIO INSIDE
Sylvester, Harold
IN THE DEEP WOODS
Symington, Donald
MIGHTY APHRODITE
Symons, Kevin
INDICTMENT: THE MCMARTIN TRIAL
Syner, David
DIRTY MONEY
Szabados, Mihaly
CITIZEN X
Szabo, Petra
CITIZEN X
Szafer, Howard
JOHNNY MNEMONIC
Szapolowska, Grazyna
SHORT FILM ABOUT LOVE, A
Szarnicki, Rev. Zygmund
ROOMMATES
Szary, M.
SHORT FILM ABOUT KILLING, A
Szekely, B. Miklos
CITIZEN X
Szervet, Tibor
CITIZEN X
Szeto, Roy
PHANTOM LOVER, THE
Szubanski, Magda
BABE
Tabata, Warren
UNDER SIEGE 2: DARK TERRITORY
Tabboo!
WIGSTOCK: THE MOVIE
Tabler, Jon
MOSAIC PROJECT, THE
Tabobondung, Leslie
DANCE ME OUTSIDE
Tabori, Kristoffer
LAST SUMMER IN THE HAMPTONS
Tacchino, Richard
KICKING AND SCREAMING
Tadross, Michael
DIE HARD WITH A VENGEANCE
Tagawa, Cary-Hiroyuki
MORTAL KOMBAT
PICTURE BRIDE
Tager, Aron
DR. JEKYLL & MS. HYDE
Taggart, Rita
STEAL BIG, STEAL LITTLE

Tahitia
EVOLVER

Tait, Michael
PYROMANIAC'S LOVE STORY, A

Takagi, Hiroyasu
HUNTED, THE

Takagi, June
WIZARD OF DARKNESS

Takagi, Jyunichi
MYSTERY OF RAMPO, THE

Takahashi, Joanne
S.F.W.

Takahashi, Kazuya
SAFE PASSAGE

Takamura, III, Sergeant Luke
MYSTERY OF RAMPO, THE

Takayama, Akira
PICTURE BRIDE

Takenaka, Naoto
MYSTERY OF RAMPO, THE

Takeuchi, Warren
HUNTED, THE

Talbert, Charles
ANGUS

Talifero, Michael
BAD BOYS

Talmadge, Victor
COPYCAT
JADE

Tamayo, Claudio A.
UP TO A CERTAIN POINT

Tamblyn, Russ
ATTACK OF THE 60-FOOT CENTERFOLD

Tambor, Jeffrey
HEAVYWEIGHTS

Tamburro, Charles
SEVEN

Tamura, Kuniharu
HUNTED, THE

Tan, Philip
CONGO

Tanasi, Alex
MY FAMILY: MI FAMILIA

Tancredi, Michael
NEW JERSEY DRIVE

Tang, Mercedes
HUNTED, THE

Tanimura, Yukari
DALLAS DOLL

Tao Chung-Hua
DAY THE SUN TURNED COLD, THE

Tapia, George
MIAMI RHAPSODY

Tarantina, Brian
JERKY BOYS: THE MOVIE, THE

Tarantini, Tom
POWDER

Tarantino, Quentin
DESPERADO
DESTINY TURNS ON THE RADIO
FOUR ROOMS

Tarbuck, Barbara
SCANNERS: THE SHOWDOWN
TIE THAT BINDS, THE
WATER ENGINE, THE

Tardi, Balazs
CITIZEN X

Tare, Nello
EMPIRE RECORDS

Tartini, Stefano
SABRINA

Tarvid, Nicholas
JADE

Tash, Kate
LOSING ISAIAH

Tastet, Cathy
MINA TANNENBAUM

Tat Binh
TRAPS

Tatar, Ben
PIANO LESSON, THE

Tate, Lahmard
PANTHER

Tate, Larenz
DEAD PRESIDENTS

Tatum, Bradford
POWDER

Taub, Steve
SPY WITHIN, THE

Taufelder, Stefan
INNOCENT, THE

Taulere, Claudine
WILD REEDS

Taurer, Robert
FOR GOD AND COUNTRY

Tavernier, Nils
MINA TANNENBAUM

Tawil, David
MONEY TRAIN

Tayback, Tom
UNDERCOVER

Taylor, Christine
BRADY BUNCH MOVIE, THE

Taylor, Clarice
SMOKE

Taylor, Colin
COUNTRY LIFE

Taylor, Corey Joshua
EMPIRE RECORDS

Taylor, Courtney
COMPANION, THE
COVER ME

Taylor, Dendrie
SPECIES

Taylor, Diana
EMPIRE RECORDS

Taylor, Frank
BLESSING

Taylor, Holland
HOW TO MAKE AN AMERICAN QUILT
LAST SUMMER IN THE HAMPTONS
STEAL BIG, STEAL LITTLE
TO DIE FOR

Taylor, Jennifer
CRUDE OASIS, THE

Taylor, Josh
SEPARATE LIVES

Taylor, Justin
RADIO INSIDE

Taylor, Larry
MANGLER, THE

Taylor, Lili
ADDICTION, THE
ARIZONA DREAM
FOUR ROOMS

Taylor, Mark L.
JURY DUTY

Taylor, Meshach
DOUBLE, DOUBLE, TOIL AND TROUBLE

Taylor, Noah
NOSTRADAMUS KID, THE

Taylor, Regina
CLOCKERS
GOOD DAY TO DIE, A
LOSING ISAIAH

Taylor, Rip
SILENCE OF THE HAMS

Taylor, Russie
BABE

Taylor, Sandra
UNDER SIEGE 2: DARK TERRITORY

Taylor, Sean
MANGLER, THE

Taylor, Simon
RESTORATION

Taylor, William
CRACKERJACK

Taylor-Gordon, Hannah
BUFFALO GIRLS

Tchelley, Hanny
HYENAS

Tcherina, Ludmilla
OH ... ROSALINDA!!

Techman, Charles
TWELVE MONKEYS

Teed, Jill
BAD COMPANY

Tefkin, Blair
S.F.W.

Tejwani, Leon
INDIAN IN THE CUPBOARD, THE

Tejwani, Lucas
INDIAN IN THE CUPBOARD, THE

Telsey, Bernard
DEAD PRESIDENTS

Templeton, Claudia
BLUE TIGER

Tempo, Nino
OUTSIDE THE LAW

Tench, John
POWER OF ATTORNEY

Tengelis, Victoria
JOHNNY MNEMONIC

Tenison, Rosie
WHITE MAN'S BURDEN

Tennant, Deborah
SCARLET LETTER, THE

Tenney, Jon
FREE WILLY 2: THE ADVENTURE HOME
NIXON

Tennor, Adria
AMATEUR

Teo
SHOWGIRLS

Ter Kuile, Bill
DANGER OF LOVE

Terada, Rieko
MYSTERY OF RAMPO, THE

Teri, Sandor
CITIZEN X

Teroaka, David
THREE WISHES

Terry, John
BIG GREEN, THE
REFLECTIONS IN THE DARK

Tesarz, Peter Jan
SHORT FILM ABOUT KILLING, A

Tessi, Andreas
FORGET PARIS

Testa, Mary
TWO BITS

Tetzlaff, Robert C.
CASINO

Tew, Alice
NOW AND THEN

Tewes, Lauren
DOOM GENERATION, THE

Thaissart, Sebastien
CITY OF LOST CHILDREN, THE

Thanh Nguyen
OPERATION DUMBO DROP

Thaw, Albert
BEYOND RANGOON

Theaker, Deborah
IN THE MOUTH OF MADNESS

Thedford, Marcello
CRIMSON TIDE
DANGEROUS MINDS

Theirse, Darryl
JEFFREY
JERKY BOYS: THE MOVIE, THE

Theis, Phil
DIE HARD WITH A VENGEANCE
Theo
WAITING TO EXHALE
Therisod, Frederick
FRENCH KISS
Theus, Reggie
FORGET PARIS
Thev, Alfred
WINGS OF HONNEAMISE: ROYAL SPACE
FORCE
Thewlis, David
RESTORATION
TOTAL ECLIPSE
Thiaw, Rama
HYENAS
Thibeaux, Mary Madeleine
KINGFISH: A STORY OF HUEY P. LONG
Thiedeke, Cyrus
JUMANJI
Thieree, James
TOTAL ECLIPSE
Thigpen, Kevin
TWELVE MONKEYS
Thigpen, Lynne
JUST CAUSE
Thigpen, Sandra
RADIO INSIDE
Thin Man
TIE-DIED: ROCK 'N' ROLL'S MOST
DEADICATED FANS
Thirloway, Greg
BROKEN TRUST
Thomas, Anthony
DIE HARD WITH A VENGEANCE
Thomas, Ben
HOTEL SORRENTO
Thomas, Dana Maria
FUN
Thomas, David Jean
DIRTY MONEY
Thomas, Frank
FRANK AND OLLIE
Thomas, Henry
CURSE OF THE STARVING CLASS
INDICTMENT: THE MCMARTIN TRIAL
Thomas, Hong-Mai
CITY OF LOST CHILDREN, THE
Thomas, II, Eric E.
ANGUS
Thomas, Isiah
FORGET PARIS
Thomas, Jeanette A.
FRANK AND OLLIE
Thomas, John Norman
JERKY BOYS: THE MOVIE, THE
MONEY TRAIN
Thomas, Johnathan
DEAD MAN WALKING
Thomas, Jonathan Taylor
MAN OF THE HOUSE
TOM AND HUCK
Thomas, Koran C.
NEW JERSEY DRIVE
Thomas, Leonard
CLOCKERS
MAJOR PAYNE
Thomas, Mary
REASON TO BELIEVE, A
Thomas, Melissa
DALLAS DOLL
Thomas, Rohn
ROOMMATES
SUDDEN DEATH
Thomas, Salvatore
BIKINI BISTRO
Thomason, Bryce Anthony
FRANK & JESSE

Thomason, Marsha
PRIEST
Thomassin, Florence
MINA TANNENBAUM
Thomerson, Tim
SPITFIRE
Thompsn, Sada
INDICTMENT: THE MCMARTIN TRIAL
Thompson, Andy
FUNNY BONES
Thompson, Anna
ANGUS
OUTSIDE THE LAW
Thompson, Bill
LEAVING LAS VEGAS
Thompson, Christopher
JEFFERSON IN PARIS
TOTAL ECLIPSE
Thompson, Emma
CARRINGTON
SENSE AND SENSIBILITY
Thompson, Jack
SUM OF US, THE
Thompson, Jennifer
RADIO INSIDE
Thompson, Jr., Milton E.
SUDDEN DEATH
Thompson, Kenan
HEAVYWEIGHTS
Thompson, Lea
SUBSTITUTE WIFE, THE
Thompson, Mark
AMERICAN PRESIDENT, THE
Thompson, Melvin
NET, THE
Thompson, Michael S.
AMERICA'S DEADLIEST HOME VIDEO
Thompson, Sophie
PERSUASION
Thompson, Velma
WALKING DEAD, THE
Thompson, Wesley
CASPER
WHITE MAN'S BURDEN
Thomson, Anna
BAD BOYS
Thorleifsson, Eggert
REMOTE CONTROL
Thorn, Frankie
BAD BLOOD
Thornby, Laurel
LIVING IN OBLIVION
Thorne, Tracy
LEAVING LAS VEGAS
Thorne-Smith, Courtney
BREACH OF CONDUCT
Thornton, Billy Bob
GHOST BRIGADE
Thornton, David
SEARCH AND DESTROY
Thornton, Kirk
BAREFOOT GEN
CRIMSON WOLF
Thornton, Reginald T.
STRANGE DAYS
Thorpe, Paul
JURY DUTY
Thorsen, Sven
MALLRATS
Thorsen, Sven-Ole
DANGEROUS, THE
QUICK AND THE DEAD, THE
Thorup, Cheryl Lee
NINE MONTHS
Thorup, Gary Joseph
JUMANJI
Throsby, Margaret
DALLAS DOLL

Thrush, Michelle
GOOD DAY TO DIE, A
Thuillier, Luc
OLD LADY WHO WALKED IN THE SEA,
THE
Thurman, Uma
MONTH BY THE LAKE, A
Thursfield, Sophie
SISTER MY SISTER
Thurston, Robert
BROKEN TRUST
Tiburcio, Lionel
TO WONG FOO, THANKS FOR
EVERYTHING! JULIE NEWMAR
Ticotin, Nancy
HACKERS
JEFFREY
Ticotin, Rachel
DECONSTRUCTING SARAH
DON JUAN DEMARCO
STEAL BIG, STEAL LITTLE
Tidwell, Harvey E.
FORGET PARIS
Tiefenbach, Dov
TOMMY BOY
Tiefenback, Dov
IT TAKES TWO
Tielsch, Thomas
EROTIQUE
Tien Nguyen Van
OPERATION DUMBO DROP
Tiernan, Michael
CONVICT COWBOY
Tierney, Lawrence
DILLINGER
Tierney, Malcolm
BRAVEHEART
Tigar, Kenneth
JADE
Tighe, Kevin
AVENGING ANGEL
BETTER OFF DEAD
JADE
Tighe, Michael
POSTCARDS FROM AMERICA
Tighe, Olmo
POSTCARDS FROM AMERICA
Tikaram, Ramon
CUTTHROAT ISLAND
Tikaram, Tanita
EROTIQUE
Tikhonov, Viacheslav
BURNT BY THE SUN
Tilden, Leif
ACE VENTURA: WHEN NATURE CALLS
Tillery, Linda
BLACK IS ... BLACK AIN'T
Tillett, James F.
LOSING ISAIAH
Tillie, Joseph Tibi
MINA TANNENBAUM
Tillman, Julie Waters
VAMPIRE IN BROOKLYN
Tillotson, John Robert
DIE HARD WITH A VENGEANCE
Tilly, Jennifer
EMBRACE OF THE VAMPIRE
Tilmant, Francois Xavier
FRENCH KISS
Tilton, Charlene
SILENCE OF THE HAMS
Timbes, Graham
KINGFISH: A STORY OF HUEY P. LONG
Timbrook, Corbin
GLASS SHIELD, THE
Times, Temise
CRY, THE BELOVED COUNTRY

Timofeeva, Tamara
WINDOW TO PARIS
Tino, Suzanne
NEW YORK COP
Tiopira, George
ONCE WERE WARRIORS
Tippo, Patti
ACE VENTURA: WHEN NATURE CALLS
Tissot, Marc
JEFFERSON IN PARIS
Titanic Cinq, The
RUN OF THE COUNTRY, THE
Tiwari, Vinod
BANDIT QUEEN
Tobey, Kenneth
BODY SHOT
Tobiasz, Zdzislaw
SHORT FILM ABOUT KILLING, A
Tobolowsky, Stephen
DR. JEKYLL & MS. HYDE
MURDER IN THE FIRST
Tocha, Paulo
STRANGE DAYS
Tocktuo, Vincent
ARIZONA DREAM
Todd, Antonio
FEAR, THE
HIGHER LEARNING
Todd, Ryan
FIRST KNIGHT
Todd, Tony
BLACK FOX
CANDYMAN: FAREWELL TO THE FLESH
Todeschini, Claudio
FRENCH KISS
Todorovski, Ljupco
BEFORE THE RAIN
Tognocchi, Bianca
MONTH BY THE LAKE, A
Togunde, Victor
CRIMSON TIDE
Toibin, Niall
FRANKIE STARLIGHT
Toledano, Valerie
JEFFERSON IN PARIS
Toles-Bey, John
PAYBACK
WATERWORLD
Tolliver, Bill
JADE
Tolstetskaya, Olga
MUTE WITNESS
Tolsty
I CAN'T SLEEP
Tom Bus Mechanic
TIE-DIED: ROCK 'N' ROLL'S MOST
DEADICATED FANS
Tom, David
ROOMMATES
Tom, Steve
IN THE DEEP WOODS
Tomei, Marisa
FOUR ROOMS
PEREZ FAMILY, THE
Tomelty, Frances
LAMB
Tomita, Tamlyn
FOUR ROOMS
PICTURE BRIDE
Tomlin, Lily
BLUE IN THE FACE
Tomlinson, Michael
MY FAMILY: MI FAMILIA
Tommassini, Lucas
LORD OF ILLUSIONS
Ton Nguyen That
OPERATION DUMBO DROP

Tondo, Jerry
NICK OF TIME
Tone Loc
HEAT
Tonini, Johnny
HOME FOR THE HOLIDAYS
Tony Toni Tone
PANTHER
Toolan, Rebecca
HIDEAWAY
Toomer, Colette J.
LORD OF ILLUSIONS
Toorvald, Sven
DIE HARD WITH A VENGEANCE
Tootoosis, Gordon
POCAHONTAS
POCAHONTAS: THE LEGEND
Topol, Richard
PARTY GIRL
Tordjman, Charles
BLUE VILLA, THE
Tork, Peter
BRADY BUNCH MOVIE, THE
Torn, Rip
CANADIAN BACON
HOW TO MAKE AN AMERICAN QUILT
Toro, Mimi
BOYS ON THE SIDE
Torokvei, Peter
STUART SAVES HIS FAMILY
Torrealba, Narda
MOSAIC PROJECT, THE
Torrens, Glen
DEATH IN BRUNSWICK
Torres, Angelina Calderon
MAD LOVE
Torres, Jose
FOOL AND HIS MONEY, A
Torres, Liz
BODY SHOT
JUST CAUSE
Torry, Joe
TALES FROM THE HOOD
Tortu, Angela
CRIMSON TIDE
Toscan du Plantier, Daniel
LES MISERABLES
Tossing, Christ
LOSING ISAIAH
Toste, Andrea
FORGET PARIS
Toth, Nick
AMERICAN PRESIDENT, THE
Toub, Shaun
BAD BOYS
Touliatos, George
CRACKERJACK
Tousey, Sheila
LORD OF ILLUSIONS
Toussaint, Lorraine
CLASS OF '61
DANGEROUS MINDS
Toussaint, Steve
JUDGE DREDD
Toussant, Beth
BREACH OF CONDUCT
Tove, Birte
KINGDOM, THE
Towb, Harry
LAMB
Towe, Anthony
HUNTED, THE
MAGIC IN THE WATER
Townsend, Clayton
NIXON
Townsend, Omar
PARTY GIRL

Townsend, Tammy
BRADY BUNCH MOVIE, THE
Trabucco, Candy
BABY-SITTERS CLUB, THE
Tracey, Bob
HOUSEGUEST
PIANO LESSON, THE
Trachtenberg, Dave
REASON TO BELIEVE, A
Traer, Doug
CAGED HEARTS
Trainor, Mary Ellen
CONGO
Tran Duy An
TRAPS
Trash Captain
TIE-DIED: ROCK 'N' ROLL'S MOST
DEADICATED FANS
Trask, David
BRIDGES OF MADISON COUNTY, THE
Trask, Judy
BRIDGES OF MADISON COUNTY, THE
Travanti, Daniel J.
JUST CAUSE
Travers, Joi
CROSSING GUARD, THE
Travis, Abbie
BAR GIRLS
Travis, Greg
SHOWGIRLS
Travis, Lara
EMPIRE RECORDS
Travis, Nancy
DESTINY TURNS ON THE RADIO
FLUKE
Travis, Randy
FRANK & JESSE
Travis, Tony
DIE HARD WITH A VENGEANCE
Traviss, Sheila
CRAZYSITTER, THE
Travolta, John
GET SHORTY
WHITE MAN'S BURDEN
Travolta, Margaret
LOSING ISAIAH
WHILE YOU WERE SLEEPING
Traylor, Susan
HEAT
LORD OF ILLUSIONS
TO DIE FOR
Treanor, Erin
3 NINJAS KNUCKLE UP
Treanor, Michael
3 NINJAS KNUCKLE UP
Treend, Chloe
FUNNY BONES
Trees, Amanda
BATMAN FOREVER
Trejo, Danny
DESPERADO
HEAT
Trejos, Mariella
NO MERCY
Trela, Christopher
REASON TO BELIEVE, A
Tremarco, Christine
PRIEST
Tremelay, Kay
FIRST DEGREE
Tremko, Anne
MY ANTONIA
Treno, Dina
VALLEY OF ABRAHAM, THE
Trent, Buck
GORDY

Trentini, Peggy
  TALES FROM THE CRYPT: DEMON
    KNIGHT
Trenton, "Poorman" Jim
  BODY SHOT
Trese, Adam
  UNDERNEATH, THE
Trevitchik, Suze
  ME AND THE MOB
Trichardt, Carel
  FRIENDS
Trieu Xuan Sam
  TRAPS
Trigger, Sarah
  DESTINY TURNS ON THE RADIO
  THINGS TO DO IN DENVER WHEN
    YOU'RE DEAD
Trim
  MOONLIGHT AND VALENTINO
Trimble, Jerry
  HEAT
Trinidad, Arsenio "Sonny"
  ACE VENTURA: WHEN NATURE CALLS
Trintignant, Jean-Louis
  CITY OF LOST CHILDREN, THE
Triola, Victor
  ME AND THE MOB
Tripp, Chet
  BODY STROKES
Tripplehorn, Jeanne
  WATERWORLD
Triska, Jan
  MY ANTONIA
Trissenaar, Elisabeth
  NOBODY LOVES ME
  PROMISE, THE
Trist, Kirilee
  NOSTRADAMUS KID, THE
Tritremmel, Maria
  FOR GOD AND COUNTRY
Troconis, Joe
  WALK IN THE CLOUDS, A
Troisi, Massimo
  POSTMAN, THE
Trotiner, Glen
  RADIO INSIDE
Troup, David
  AMATEUR
Trucco, Ed
  KISS OF DEATH
Trudeau, Rose Marie
  DANCE ME OUTSIDE
True, Rachel
  EMBRACE OF THE VAMPIRE
Truesdale, Teresa
  BITTER VENGEANCE
Trujillo, Raoul
  BLACK FOX
  HIGHLANDER: THE FINAL DIMENSION
Trump, Donald
  ACROSS THE SEA OF TIME: NEW YORK
    3D
Trumpower, Max
  ROSWELL: THE U.F.O. COVER-UP
Trustman, Susan
  DR. JEKYLL & MS. HYDE
Tsagkaris, Susan
  JOHNNY MNEMONIC
Tsang, Eric
  HE'S A WOMAN, SHE'S A MAN
Tse, Barbara
  DOUBLE HAPPINESS
Tshoaedo, Innocentia
  FRIENDS
Tsou, Cece
  BAR GIRLS
Tsukushi, Tetsuya
  MYSTERY OF RAMPO, THE

Tsutsumi, Koji
  MYSTERY OF RAMPO, THE
Tuan Wai-Lun
  HIGH RISK
Tuber, Peter
  THREE WISHES
Tubert, Marcelo
  VAMPIRE IN BROOKLYN
Tucci, Lin
  SHOWGIRLS
Tucci, Maria
  TO DIE FOR
Tucci, Stanley
  JURY DUTY
  KISS OF DEATH
Tuck, Jessica
  BATMAN FOREVER
  O.J. SIMPSON STORY, THE
Tucker, Chris
  DEAD PRESIDENTS
  FRIDAY
  PANTHER
Tucker, Michael
  TOO YOUNG TO DIE?
Tucker, Paul
  BRAVEHEART
Tuerpe, Paul
  ASSASSINS
  FREE WILLY 2: THE ADVENTURE HOME
Tuffey, Nolan
  MIGHTY APHRODITE
Tufield, Lynn
  GRANNY, THE
Tumahai, Charlie
  ONCE WERE WARRIORS
Tunney, Robin
  EMPIRE RECORDS
Turco, Paige
  DEAD FUNNY
Turco-Lyon, Kathleen
  VILLAGE OF THE DAMNED
Turk, Brian
  PANTHER
Turkel, Ann
  FEAR, THE
Turley, Frank
  ARIZONA DREAM
Turley, Myra
  MY ANTONIA
Turnbull, Clinton
  TOMMY BOY
Turner, Arnold
  BRADY BUNCH MOVIE, THE
Turner, Ashlee
  BABY-SITTERS CLUB, THE
Turner, Clive
  HOWLING: NEW MOON RISING, THE
Turner, Frank
  CRACKERJACK
Turner, Gary
  CARRINGTON
Turner, Jim
  COLDBLOODED
Turner, Jonathan
  POSTCARDS FROM AMERICA
Turner, Kathleen
  MOONLIGHT AND VALENTINO
Turner, Kellie
  NEW JERSEY DRIVE
Turner, Robb
  THREE WISHES
Turner, Rodney
  BROKEN TRUST
Turner, Tyrin
  PANTHER
Turtle
  TIE-DIED: ROCK 'N' ROLL'S MOST
    DEADICATED FANS

Turturici, Jack
  MIDNIGHT TEASE 2
Turturro, Aida
  MONEY TRAIN
Turturro, John
  CLOCKERS
  SEARCH AND DESTROY
  UNSTRUNG HEROES
Turturro, Nicholas
  COSMIC SLOP
Turzonvova, Bozidara
  MARTHA AND I
Tushaus, Michael A.
  TO WONG FOO, THANKS FOR
    EVERYTHING! JULIE NEWMAR
Tushingham, Rita
  AWFULLY BIG ADVENTURE, AN
Tuteao, Calvin
  ONCE WERE WARRIORS
Tuttle, Patrick
  TO WONG FOO, THANKS FOR
    EVERYTHING! JULIE NEWMAR
Twala, Louisa
  FRIENDS
Twala, Mary
  FRIENDS
Tweed, Shannon
  BODY CHEMISTRY 4: FULL EXPOSURE
Tweed, Tracy
  JOHNNY MNEMONIC
Tweedle, Carolyn
  IN THE MOUTH OF MADNESS
Twillie, Carmen
  VAMPIRE IN BROOKLYN
Twinz
  SHOW, THE
Twist, Natasha
  PARTY GIRL
Two Eagle, Melanie
  LAKOTA WOMAN: SIEGE AT WOUNDED
    KNEE
Tyelele, Motshabi
  FRIENDS
Tyler, Katlin
  INCREDIBLY TRUE ADVENTURES OF
    TWO GIRLS IN LOVE, THE
Tyler, Liv
  EMPIRE RECORDS
Tymitz, Dixie
  SUDDEN DEATH
Tyrrell, Susan
  POWDER
Tyrus
  GRANNY, THE
Tysall, David
  KID IN KING ARTHUR'S COURT, A
Tyson, Cathy
  PRIEST
Tyson, Matthew
  EXPERT, THE
Tyson, Pamala
  SEVEN
U Kyaw Win
  BEYOND RANGOON
Ubach, Alanna
  BRADY BUNCH MOVIE, THE
Ubarry, Hechter
  MAJOR PAYNE
Ueda, Yuki
  AI CITY
Ueno, Odney
  SHOWGIRLS
Uge, Suzanne
  PROMISE, THE
Ujlaky, Denes
  CITIZEN X
Ulianova, Inna
  BURNT BY THE SUN

Ulich, Andreas
FARINELLI
Ulrich, John
RIVER OF GRASS
Ulstad, Ron
JADE
Umansky, Andre
BURNT BY THE SUN
Uncle Sam
TIE-DIED: ROCK 'N' ROLL'S MOST
DEADICATED FANS
Underwood, Blair
JUST CAUSE
Underwood, Jay
REASON TO BELIEVE, A
Unger, Bela
KID IN KING ARTHUR'S COURT, A
Unger, Deborah
HIGHLANDER: THE FINAL DIMENSION
Urbino, Danny
POSTCARDS FROM AMERICA
Urbino, Tony
POSTCARDS FROM AMERICA
Urla, Joe
INDICTMENT: THE MCMARTIN TRIAL
STRANGE DAYS
Urquhart, Cynthia
NINE MONTHS
Urrea, Juan
ARIZONA DREAM
Ursitti, Susan
WALKING DEAD, THE
Urungus, Oderus
EMPIRE RECORDS
Usher, Tonia
BROKEN TRUST
Usic, William
DALLAS DOLL
Usko, Renate
DEADLY MARIA
Utay, William
BODILY HARM
SPECIES
Utesch, Christopher
EMBRACE OF THE VAMPIRE
Utter, Jerry
RIVER OF GRASS
Uukkivi, Ivo
CITY UNPLUGGED
Uzzolio, Frank
SCANNERS: THE SHOWDOWN
Vacratsis, Maria
TOMMY BOY
Vadim, David
LITTLE ODESSA
Vaibhav, Vibanshu
BANDIT QUEEN
Vaish, Uma
BANDIT QUEEN
Val, Edwige
JUPITER'S WIFE
Valandrey, Charlotte
MY LIFE AND TIMES WITH ANTONIN
ARTAUD
Valdes, Omar
UP TO A CERTAIN POINT
Vale, Jerry
CASINO
Valencia, Matthew
TOM AND HUCK
Valentin, Cesar
CARMEN MIRANDA: BANANAS IS MY
BUSINESS
Valentine, Anthony
JEFFERSON IN PARIS
Valentine, Graham
FARINELLI

Valentine, Scott
OUT OF ANNIE'S PAST
Valentova, Sona
MARTHA AND I
Valere, Jean-Pierre
MINA TANNENBAUM
Valeriani, Richard
CRIMSON TIDE
Valka, Tim
MIGHTY MORPHIN POWER RANGERS:
THE MOVIE
Vallance, Louise
PEBBLE AND THE PENGUIN, THE
Valley, Mark
INNOCENT, THE
Valli, Alida
MONTH BY THE LAKE, A
Valpato, Paul
ONLY THE BRAVE
Van, Alex
CLASS OF '61
Van Alyn, Abigail
VILLAGE OF THE DAMNED
van Barthold, Bruce
TOTAL ECLIPSE
Van Betten, Elaine
SHOWGIRLS
Van Damme, Jean-Claude
SUDDEN DEATH
Van Damme, Nicola
DEATH MACHINE
van Dantzig, Rudi
DANCER, THE
Van de Velde, Micheline
SABRINA
Van Denzen, Steve
DANCE ME OUTSIDE
Van Der Beek, James
ANGUS
Van Dissel, Peter
BUSINESS AFFAIR, A
Van Dyke, Sandee
DECONSTRUCTING SARAH
Van Hoffman, Brent
GRANNY, THE
Van Kempen, Ad
1-900
Van Oy, Jenna
GOOFY MOVIE, A
Van Patten, Dick
BREAK, THE
Van Patten, Nels
BREAK, THE
Van Patten, Pat
BREAK, THE
Van Patten, Vincent
BREAK, THE
Van Peebles, Mario
HIGHLANDER: THE FINAL DIMENSION
PANTHER
Van Peebles, Melvin
PANTHER
Van Wervike, Thirry
FOR GOD AND COUNTRY
Van Zyl, Dee Dee
DANGER OF LOVE
Vance, Courtney B.
DANGEROUS MINDS
PANTHER
PIANO LESSON, THE
Vance, Gregg
EMBRACE OF THE VAMPIRE
Vance, Ladd
EMBRACE OF THE VAMPIRE
Vance, Scott
GIRL IN THE CADILLAC

Vandendaele, Ludovik
SON OF THE SHARK, THE
Vandernoot, Alexandra
DOOMSDAY GUN
Vanderpump, Lisa
SEPARATE LIVES
Vaneck, Pierre
OTHELLO
Vannicola, Joanne
LOVE AND HUMAN REMAINS
Vansittart, Rupert
BRAVEHEART
CUTTHROAT ISLAND
Vansprang, Alan
BLACK FOX
Varda, Brenda
BLUE TIGER
Varella, Valentine
JEFFERSON IN PARIS
Vargas, Jacob
CRIMSON TIDE
GET SHORTY
MY FAMILY: MI FAMILIA
Varnado, Julius
MURDER IN THE FIRST
Varnagy, Katalin
CITIZEN X
Varney, Jim
EXPERT, THE
TOY STORY
Vartan, Michael
TO WONG FOO, THANKS FOR
EVERYTHING! JULIE NEWMAR
Vascansellos, Anselmo
BOCA
Vasegaard, Lene
KINGDOM, THE
Vasquez, Nelson
MONEY TRAIN
Vasquez, Peter Mark
MY FAMILY: MI FAMILIA
Vasut, Marek
FATHERLAND
Vaughan, Hugh
ENGLISHMAN WHO WENT UP A HILL
BUT CAME DOWN A MOUNTAIN, THE
Vaughan, Tudor
ENGLISHMAN WHO WENT UP A HILL
BUT CAME DOWN A MOUNTAIN, THE
Vaughn, Cesarina
BUSHWHACKED
Vaughn, Delane
STRANGE DAYS
Vaughn, Jordan F.
JUST CAUSE
Vaughn, Kelly
BATMAN FOREVER
Vaughn, Ned
APOLLO 13
TIE THAT BINDS, THE
Vaughn, Peter
FATHERLAND
Vaughn, Terry J.
FRIDAY
Vaughn, Victoria
BAR GIRLS
Vavrova, Dana
STALINGRAD
Vawter, Ron
ROY COHN/JACK SMITH
Vazeos, Antonios
BLUE VILLA, THE
Vazquez, Alberto
ZOOMAN
Vazquez, Angel
ASSASSINS
Vazquez, Yul
NICK OF TIME

Vega, Alexa
  NINE MONTHS
Vekony, Zoltan
  CITIZEN X
Velarde, Teresa
  OUTBREAK
Velasquez, Maribel
  BAR GIRLS
Velde, Isabelle Vander
  MINA TANNENBAUM
Veldnink, Wes
  TANK GIRL
Velez, Eddie
  BITTER VENGEANCE
Velez-Johnson, Martha
  SAFE
Velkov, Dejan
  BEFORE THE RAIN
Vella, Marlow
  JOHNNY MNEMONIC
Vella, Vinny
  CASINO
Veloz, Coralia
  UP TO A CERTAIN POINT
Veltri, Gino
  BILLY MADISON
Venard, Shriley
  CURE, THE
Vendramini, Bella
  DESPERATE PREY
Vendramini, Josie
  DESPERATE PREY
Vennema, John
  BASKETBALL DIARIES, THE
Vennema, John C.
  DIE HARD WITH A VENGEANCE
  KISS OF DEATH
  SABRINA
Vennera, Chick
  BODY CHEMISTRY 4: FULL EXPOSURE
Venokur, Johnny
  LORD OF ILLUSIONS
Venora, Diane
  HEAT
  THREE WISHES
Ventimiglia, John
  PARTY GIRL
  POSTCARDS FROM AMERICA
Vera, Julia
  NET, THE
Verama, Guy
  FRANKIE STARLIGHT
Verbraeken, Buster
  CITY OF LOST CHILDREN, THE
Verdecchia, Guillermo
  CIRCUMSTANCES UNKNOWN
Verdonik, Tatjana
  INNOCENT LIES
Verducci, Frank P.
  NINE MONTHS
Verdugo, Rey
  HEAT
Verduzco, Abraham
  DESPERADO
Verduzco, Danny
  FOUR ROOMS
Verell, Jack
  BITTER VENGEANCE
  MUTANT SPECIES
Verge, Crystal
  GOOD DAY TO DIE, A
Verhoeven, Daniel
  IN THE MOUTH OF MADNESS
Verhoeven, Simon
  PARTY GIRL
Verica, Tom
  BREACH OF CONDUCT

Verley, Bernard
  SIX DAYS, SIX NIGHTS
Vermeulen, Charles
  FRIENDS
Vermeullen, Christian
  MINA TANNENBAUM
Vernier, Pierre
  LES MISERABLES
Vernon, John
  MALICIOUS
Vernon, Nan
  NOSTRADAMUS KID, THE
Vernon, Thom
  BREACH OF CONDUCT
Vetchy, Ondrej
  MARTHA AND I
Veurink, James Edward
  JADE
Viacheslavvornin
  AMERICAN COP
Viala, Michel
  NEA
Vibert, Angela
  CLEAN, SHAVEN
Vibert, Grace
  CLEAN, SHAVEN
Vickers, Brinley Arden
  SOMETHING TO TALK ABOUT
Vickery, John
  DECONSTRUCTING SARAH
Victor, Harry
  GET SHORTY
Victor, Renee
  STEAL BIG, STEAL LITTLE
Vidahl, Lone
  SENSE AND SENSIBILITY
Vidale, Thea
  DR. JEKYLL & MS. HYDE
Vieira, Ken
  UNDER SIEGE 2: DARK TERRITORY
Vielmann, Franz
  PROMISE, THE
Vigil, Selene H.
  MAD LOVE
Vignari, Steve
  CASINO
Vigne, Nathalie
  WILD REEDS
Vigoda, Abe
  JURY DUTY
Villanueva, Enrique
  CITY OF LOST CHILDREN, THE
Villari, Libby
  BIG GREEN, THE
Villeval, Alan
  MINA TANNENBAUM
Villiers, Chris
  FIRST KNIGHT
Villiers, Jay
  BEFORE THE RAIN
Vimpierre, Jacqueline
  AUGUSTIN
Vina, Ana
  UP TO A CERTAIN POINT
Vincent, Craig
  CASINO
Vincent, Frank
  CASINO
Vincent, Jan-Michael
  ABDUCTED 2: THE REUNION
Vincent, Miracle Unique
  VIRTUOSITY
Vinogradov, Serghei
  CREATION OF ADAM
Vintas, Gustav
  FAIR GAME

Virchis, William Alejandro
  BITTER VENGEANCE
Virkner, Helle
  KINGDOM, THE
Viscuso, Sal
  KICKING AND SCREAMING
Viseu, Leonor
  VALLEY OF ABRAHAM, THE
Viso, Mikey
  TWO BITS
Visram, Rasool M.
  LORD OF ILLUSIONS
Vitale, Dick
  JURY DUTY
Vitanov, Jordan
  BEFORE THE RAIN
Vitar, Mike
  WATER ENGINE, THE
Vitello, Lisa
  HIGHLANDER: THE FINAL DIMENSION
Viterelli, Joe
  CROSSING GUARD, THE
Viteri, Jorge
  BURNING SEASON, THE
Vitetzakis, George
  HIGHLANDER: THE FINAL DIMENSION
Vitt, David
  DIE HARD WITH A VENGEANCE
Vittet, Judith
  CITY OF LOST CHILDREN, THE
Viveaere, Fran
  ONCE WERE WARRIORS
Vivek, Rajesh
  BANDIT QUEEN
Vivino, Floyd
  PYROMANIAC'S LOVE STORY, A
Vlad, Florica
  JUMANJI
Vlahos, Sam
  STEAL BIG, STEAL LITTLE
Vlasak, Jan
  FATHERLAND
Vo Trung Anh
  OPERATION DUMBO DROP
Vodin, Olga
  AMERICAN COP
Vogel, Carlo
  CLOCKERS
Vogel, Darlene
  DECOY
Vogel, Laurent Spiel
  FRENCH KISS
Vogt, Peter
  COSMIC SLOP
Voight, Jon
  CONVICT COWBOY
  HEAT
Voigts, Henrietta
  RESTORATION
Voisin, Michel
  WILD REEDS
Voland, Mark
  GIRL IN THE CADILLAC
Volkov, Igor
  MUTE WITNESS
Vollans, Michael
  IT TAKES TWO
Volponi, Paolo
  MAMMA ROMA
Volz, Nedra
  SILENCE OF THE HAMS
Von Au, Michael
  NOBODY LOVES ME
Von Bargen, Daniel
  CRIMSON TIDE
  LORD OF ILLUSIONS

Von Champorcin, Andre
DEADLY MARIA
Von Detten, Erik
TOP DOG
TOY STORY
Von Franckenstein, Clement
AMERICAN PRESIDENT, THE
Von Homburg, Wilhelm
SILENCE OF THE HAMS
von Homburg, Wilhelm
IN THE MOUTH OF MADNESS
Von Huene, Walter
APOLLO 13
Von Klaussen, Ronald
NIXON
von Scherler, Sasha
PARTY GIRL
PARTY GIRL
von Sivers, Alexandre
MINA TANNENBAUM
von Sydow, Max
CITIZEN X
Von Sydow, Max
JUDGE DREDD
Von Tagen, Erika
CASINO
von Zerneck, Danielle
LIVING IN OBLIVION
von Zglinicki, Simone
PROMISE, THE
Vonhoff, Astrid
DEADLY MARIA
Vonne, Patricia
DESPERADO
Vooren, Gerrit
DIE HARD WITH A VENGEANCE
Voorhees, Lance Hunter
NICK OF TIME
Vortex
DEATH IN BRUNSWICK
Vosloo, Arnold
DARKMAN 2: THE RETURN OF DURANT
Vrana, Vlasta
HIGHLANDER: THE FINAL DIMENSION
Vrooman, Spencer
CASPER
MAN OF THE HOUSE
Vu T Le Thi
TRAPS
Vud, Salvador
I AM CUBA
Vullo, Lenny
NIXON
Waa, Royal
ONCE WERE WARRIORS
Waara, Scott
INDICTMENT: THE MCMARTIN TRIAL
Wacks, Michael
ART FOR TEACHERS OF CHILDREN
Waddell, Alison
GET SHORTY
Waddell, Amber
GET SHORTY
Waddington, Steven
CARRINGTON
Wafford, Shannon
DIRTY MONEY
Waghorn, William
RETURN OF THE NATIVE, THE
Wagner, Antonio
VALLEY OF ABRAHAM, THE
Wagner, Emily
SEVEN
Wagner, Katie
SCANNERS: THE SHOWDOWN
Wagner, Maggie
FOOL AND HIS MONEY, A

Wagner, Natasha Gregson
S.F.W.
Wahah, Asmi
BEYOND RANGOON
Wahl, Linda
SEARCH AND DESTROY
Wahlberg, Mark
BASKETBALL DIARIES, THE
Wahlheim, Charles
FORGET PARIS
Waiglein, Harold
BEFORE SUNRISE
Wailbel, Sabine
FOR GOD AND COUNTRY
Waites, Thomas G.
MONEY TRAIN
Wajsbrot, Rywka
MINA TANNENBAUM
Wakamatsu, Koji
MYSTERY OF RAMPO, THE
Walbrook, Anton
OH ... ROSALINDA!!
Walcutt, John
BREACH OF CONDUCT
VIRTUOSITY
Waldoch, Ryan
GRUMPIER OLD MEN
Waldron, Adrian
MANGLER, THE
Waldron, Shawna
AMERICAN PRESIDENT, THE
Walken, Christopher
ADDICTION, THE
BUSINESS AFFAIR, A
NICK OF TIME
PROPHECY, THE
SEARCH AND DESTROY
THINGS TO DO IN DENVER WHEN
  YOU'RE DEAD
Walker, Ally
STEAL BIG, STEAL LITTLE
WHILE YOU WERE SLEEPING
Walker, Andy
SEVEN
Walker, Ann
FATHER OF THE BRIDE PART II
Walker, Carolyn L.A.
MAJOR PAYNE
Walker, Corban
FRANKIE STARLIGHT
Walker, Jana
SHOWGIRLS
Walker, Justin
CLUELESS
Walker, Kateri
SCARLET LETTER, THE
Walker, Kerry
BABE
Walker, Kevin
DARK DEALER
Walker, Kim
REASON TO BELIEVE, A
Walker, Larrington
LAMB
Walker, Lisa
WALKING DEAD, THE
Walker, Liza
CENTURY
HACKERS
Walker, Matthew
DOUBLE, DOUBLE, TOIL AND TROUBLE
Walker, Polly
RESTORATION
Walker, Ridley
TIE-DIED: ROCK 'N' ROLL'S MOST
  DEADICATED FANS
Walker, Trent
EXPERT, THE

Wallace, Basil
FREE WILLY 2: THE ADVENTURE HOME
GOOD DAY TO DIE, A
Wallace, Bill
FEAR, THE
Wallace, George
ALMOST DEAD
BATMAN FOREVER
COSMIC SLOP
Wallace, Jack
NIXON
STEAL BIG, STEAL LITTLE
Wallace, John
COVER STORY
Wallace, Josephine
DIRTY MONEY
Wallace, Michele
BLACK IS ... BLACK AIN'T
Wallace, Sean G.
KISS OF DEATH
Wallace, William
COVER STORY
Wallis, Gregg
THREE WISHES
Wallis, Shani
PEBBLE AND THE PENGUIN, THE
Wallraf, Diego
PEREZ FAMILY, THE
Walls, H. Michael
TWELVE MONKEYS
Walsh, Catherine
JACK-O
Walsh, Dylan
CONGO
RADIO INSIDE
Walsh, Elizabeth
IT TAKES TWO
Walsh, Gerry
CIRCLE OF FRIENDS
Walsh, J.T.
BABYSITTER, THE
NIXON
Walsh, Joseph
GLASS SHIELD, THE
Walsh, M. Emmet
FREE WILLY 2: THE ADVENTURE HOME
GLASS SHIELD, THE
PANTHER
Walsh, Mandy
PRIEST
Walsh, Michael
JACK-O
Walsh, Ruth
BETTER OFF DEAD
Walsh, Sydney
DANGER OF LOVE
Walsh, Thayis
PANTHER
Walsh, Tom
JADE
Walsh, Wendy L.
HEAT
Walter, Harriet
SENSE AND SENSIBILITY
Walter, Tracey
BUFFALO GIRLS
COMPANION, THE
DESTINY TURNS ON THE RADIO
Walters, Ingrid
HIGHER LEARNING
Walters, Jack
ENGLISHMAN WHO WENT UP A HILL
  BUT CAME DOWN A MOUNTAIN, THE
Walters, Julie
SISTER MY SISTER
Walters, Melora
AMERICA'S DEADLIEST HOME VIDEO

Walters, Perla
BODY CHEMISTRY 4: FULL EXPOSURE
Walthall, Romy
HOWLING: NEW MOON RISING, THE
Walton, Bill
FORGET PARIS
Walton, Frank
TANK GIRL
Walton, Heini
NEKROMANTIK
Walton, John
MURIEL'S WEDDING
Waltz, Lisa
ROSWELL: THE U.F.O. COVER-UP
Wang, Bo Z.
PUSHING HANDS
Wang Chaohua
MOVING THE MOUNTAIN
Wang Dan
MOVING THE MOUNTAIN
Wang Fei
AMAZING PANDA ADVENTURE, THE
Wang Jinbao
ERMO
Wang Lan
WOODEN MAN'S BRIDE, THE
Wang Liyuan
RED FIRECRACKER, GREEN
FIRECRACKER
Wang Shiling
ERMO
Wang Wenzhi
ERMO
Wang Xiaoxiao
SHANGHAI TRIAD
Wang Ya'nan
SHANGHAI TRIAD
Wang Yumei
WOODEN MAN'S BRIDE, THE
Wanlass, Lynn
TIE THAT BINDS, THE
Wannamaker, Josh
FAR FROM HOME: THE ADVENTURES OF
YELLOW DOG
Wanqing Wu
ROOMMATES
Ward, Adam
GRUMPIER OLD MEN
Ward, B.J.
PEBBLE AND THE PENGUIN, THE
Ward, Christopher
OPERATION DUMBO DROP
Ward, Dave "Squatch"
POWER OF ATTORNEY
Ward, Eileen
RUN OF THE COUNTRY, THE
Ward, Fred
BLUE VILLA, THE
Ward, Mary
SMOKE
Ward, Megan
BRADY BUNCH MOVIE, THE
Ward, Paddy
FEAST OF JULY
Ward, Rachel
ASCENT, THE
Ward, Sheila
HIGHER LEARNING
Ward, Sophie
CLASS OF '61
Ward, Vincent
LEAVING LAS VEGAS
Warden, Jack
MIGHTY APHRODITE
THINGS TO DO IN DENVER WHEN
YOU'RE DEAD
WHILE YOU WERE SLEEPING

Warder, Frederick
FEAST OF JULY
Ware, Frank Andre
DIE HARD WITH A VENGEANCE
Ware, Herta
SPECIES
TOP DOG
Warfield, Chris
UNSTRUNG HEROES
Warfield, Joe
KINGFISH: A STORY OF HUEY P. LONG
Warloe, Bryan
ANGUS
Warnat, Kimberley
GOLD DIGGERS: THE SECRET OF BEAR
MOUNTAIN
Warner, David
IN THE MOUTH OF MADNESS
Warner, Julie
TOMMY BOY
Warner, Rick
TWELVE MONKEYS
Waronker, Lenny
BRIAN WILSON: I JUST WASN'T MADE
FOR THESE TIMES
Warren G
SHOW, THE
Warren, Jennifer Leigh
CROSSING GUARD, THE
Warren, Judette
SHOWGIRLS
Warren, Michael
HUNTED, THE
Warshofsky, David
SKINNER
Washington, Denzel
CRIMSON TIDE
DEVIL IN A BLUE DRESS
VIRTUOSITY
Washington, Isaiah
CLOCKERS
Washington, Michael
SHOWGIRLS
Washington, Sharon
DIE HARD WITH A VENGEANCE
Washington, William
BAD BLOOD
Washko, Jr., Frank
CASINO
Wasman, David
DANGER OF LOVE
Wasserman, Alan
SAFE
Wasserman, Irving
FORGET PARIS
Wasserman, Jerry
MALICIOUS
Watanabe, Gede
BOYS ON THE SIDE
Watanabe, Takeshi
AI CITY
Watchurst, Neville
RESTORATION
Waters, Crystal
WIGSTOCK: THE MOVIE
Waters, Oren
VAMPIRE IN BROOKLYN
Waterston, Sam
ENEMY WITHIN, THE
JOURNEY OF AUGUST KING, THE
Waterstone, Ilene
FATHER OF THE BRIDE PART II
Watford, Monica
BAR GIRLS
Watford, Willie M.
KISS OF DEATH
Watkins, Roger
PERSUASION

Watroba, Sharon
WATER ENGINE, THE
Watson, Alberta
HACKERS
Watson, Armand
CRIMSON TIDE
Watson, Carlton
CANADIAN BACON
MOONLIGHT AND VALENTINO
Watson, Muse
ASSASSINS
JOURNEY OF AUGUST KING, THE
SOMETHING TO TALK ABOUT
Watson, Virginia
VIRTUOSITY
Watson, Woody
POWDER
Watt, Ben
LOVE AND HUMAN REMAINS
Watt, Nathan
UNSTRUNG HEROES
Watts, Mandy
BILLY MADISON
Watts, Naomi
GROSS MISCONDUCT
TANK GIRL
Waugh, Fred
SUDDEN DEATH
Wayans, Damien
MAJOR PAYNE
Wayans, Damon
MAJOR PAYNE
Wayman, Patrick
TIE-DIED: ROCK 'N' ROLL'S MOST
DEADICATED FANS
Wayne, Big Daddy
GET SHORTY
Wayne, Dig
JUDGE DREDD
Wayne, Elisa
MAGIC IN THE WATER
Wayne, Sarah
MAGIC IN THE WATER
Weakley, Ann
FRANKIE STARLIGHT
Weary, A.C.
INDICTMENT: THE MCMARTIN TRIAL
Weatherred, Michael
CRIMSON TIDE
Weathers, Dee Dee
TANK GIRL
Weathersby, Howard
JADE
Weaver, Fritz
BROKEN TRUST
Weaver, Sigourney
COPYCAT
JEFFREY
Weaving, Hugo
BABE
Webb, Brian
FUNNY BONES
Webb, David
BABE
DANCE ME OUTSIDE
Webb, Rema D.
SUDDEN DEATH
Webb, Spud
FORGET PARIS
Webb, William
BASKETBALL DIARIES, THE
Weber, Catherine
BODY STROKES
Weber, Dewey
DOOM GENERATION, THE
SHOWGIRLS
Weber, Heather
REASON TO BELIEVE, A

Weber, Kal
HACKERS
Weber, Steven
DRACULA: DEAD AND LOVING IT
JEFFREY
LEAVING LAS VEGAS
Webster, Marc
JERKY BOYS: THE MOVIE, THE
Wedersoe, Erik
KINGDOM, THE
Weeks, Christopher
CYBER BANDITS
Weeks, Jimmie Ray
KINGFISH: A STORY OF HUEY P. LONG
Weenick, Annabelle
TOO YOUNG TO DIE?
Wees, Tom
MY ANTONIA
Wegener, Janine
FOR GOD AND COUNTRY
Wegener, Klaus
KINGDOM, THE
Wei Zhi
DAY THE SUN TURNED COLD, THE
Weil, Mark
MONEY TRAIN
Weil, Robert
JERKY BOYS: THE MOVIE, THE
Weilguny, Albert
FOR GOD AND COUNTRY
Weiner, Sabrina
BAD BLOOD
Weingartner, Hans
BEFORE SUNRISE
Weingartner, Stephen
LORD OF ILLUSIONS
Weinstein, Vickie
ME AND THE MOB
Weir, David
CARMEN MIRANDA: BANANAS IS MY
BUSINESS
Weis, Harald
NEKROMANTIK
Weiskittel, Anacia
TANK GIRL
Weisman, Daniel
BYE BYE, LOVE
Weisman, Marguerite
BYE BYE, LOVE
Weiss, Dan
SCANNERS: THE SHOWDOWN
Weiss, Erick
FEAR, THE
Weiss, Joel
CONGO
Weiss, Michael T.
JEFFREY
Weiss, Robert K.
TOMMY BOY
Weiss, Shaun
HEAVYWEIGHTS
Weissenborn, Jennifer
FAR FROM HOME: THE ADVENTURES OF
YELLOW DOG
Weisser, Norbert
MY ANTONIA
Weissman, Cliff
DON JUAN DEMARCO
Weisz, Rachel
DEATH MACHINE
Weitz, Bruce
O.J. SIMPSON STORY, THE
PREHYSTERIA! 3
Welch, Ariel
BIG GREEN, THE
Welch, Ashley
BIG GREEN, THE

Welch, Tahnee
SEARCH AND DESTROY
Welch, Wally
SUBSTITUTE WIFE, THE
Weldon, Ann
PANTHER
Welker, Frank
GOOFY MOVIE, A
POCAHONTAS
SPECIES
Weller, Peter
DECOY
MIGHTY APHRODITE
SUBSTITUTE WIFE, THE
Welliver, Titus
BORN TO BE WILD
Wellman, Jr., William
OUTSIDE THE LAW
Wells, Dean E.
SUDDEN DEATH
Wells, Jr., Lee
WAITING TO EXHALE
Wells, Michael Louis
JERKY BOYS: THE MOVIE, THE
Wells, Veronica
MONTH BY THE LAKE, A
Wells, Winter
TIE-DIED: ROCK 'N' ROLL'S MOST
DEADICATED FANS
Welsh, Kenneth
HIDEAWAY
Wendt, George
MAN OF THE HOUSE
Went, Johanna
DOOM GENERATION, THE
Wert, Doug
ROSWELL: THE U.F.O. COVER-UP
Wesley, Michael
ANGUS
Wesson, Jessica
CASPER
West, Cornel
BLACK IS ... BLACK AIN'T
West, Dominic
RICHARD III
West, Don
COPYCAT
West, Kevin
HOUSEGUEST
West, Natalie
BUSHWHACKED
West, Red
EXPERT, THE
West, Samuel
CARRINGTON
PERSUASION
West, Sandra
PENTATHLON
West, Stephen
BETTER OFF DEAD
West, Tegan
BAD COMPANY
Westerman, Floyd Red Crow
BUFFALO GIRLS
LAKOTA WOMAN: SIEGE AT WOUNDED
KNEE
Weston, Amber Lea
BOULEVARD
Weston, Celia
DEAD MAN WALKING
UNSTRUNG HEROES
Weston, Deborah
KID IN KING ARTHUR'S COURT, A
Weston, Jeff
SILENCE OF THE HAMS
Westphal, Paul
FORGET PARIS

Weyers, Marius
FRIENDS
Whalen, David
INDICTMENT: THE MCMARTIN TRIAL
Whalen, Sean
CRAZYSITTER, THE
JURY DUTY
WATERWORLD
Whalen, Sr., James Patrick
DIE HARD WITH A VENGEANCE
Whaley, Frank
SWIMMING WITH SHARKS
Whaley, Michael
SEPARATE LIVES
Wheal, Stacey
BILLY MADISON
Wheatle, Mark
FAIR GAME
Wheel
UNDERNEATH, THE
Wheeler, Andrew
GOLD DIGGERS: THE SECRET OF BEAR
MOUNTAIN
Wheeler, Ira
SABRINA
Wheeler, Julie
LIE DOWN WITH DOGS
Wheeler, Mark
APOLLO 13
Wheeler-Nicholson, Dana
BYE BYE, LOVE
FRANK & JESSE
Whelehan, Mark
FEAST OF JULY
Whirry, Shannon
GRANNY, THE
Whitaker, Duane
TALES FROM THE HOOD
Whitaker, Forest
ENEMY WITHIN, THE
SMOKE
SPECIES
Whitaker, Yolanda
PANTHER
White, Bernard
INDICTMENT: THE MCMARTIN TRIAL
White, Harrison
SEVEN
White, James Randall
BRADY BUNCH MOVIE, THE
White, Jerri Rose
FATHER OF THE BRIDE PART II
White, Ken
ACROSS THE MOON
White, Kenneth
APOLLO 13
INDICTMENT: THE MCMARTIN TRIAL
White, Kevin
PENTATHLON
White, Lloyd
TOMMY BOY
White, Michael
BALLISTIC
BITTER VENGEANCE
White, Robert James
BETTER OFF DEAD
White, Steve
CLOCKERS
White, Steven Carl
PANTHER
White, Tam
BRAVEHEART
CUTTHROAT ISLAND
White, Terri
BOYS ON THE SIDE
White, Thomas
WINGS OF HONNEAMISE: ROYAL SPACE
FORCE

White, Tom
DILLINGER
White, Wally
LIE DOWN WITH DOGS
White, William
VAMPIRES AND OTHER STEREOTYPES
White-Plume, Jennifer
LAKOTA WOMAN: SIEGE AT WOUNDED
KNEE
Whitehead, O.Z.
AILSA
Whiteley, John
CRY, THE BELOVED COUNTRY
Whitfield, Clayton C.
INDICTMENT: THE MCMARTIN TRIAL
Whitfield, Dondre
WHITE MAN'S BURDEN
Whitfield, Kevin
JADE
Whitfield, Nikki
TANK GIRL
Whitford, Bradley
BILLY MADISON
Whithead, Robert
CRY, THE BELOVED COUNTRY
Whitlock, Bill
JOURNEY OF AUGUST KING, THE
Whitman, Mae
BYE BYE, LOVE
Whitman, Richard
LAKOTA WOMAN: SIEGE AT WOUNDED
KNEE
Whitmey, Nigel
JEFFERSON IN PARIS
Whitmore, Chester A.
STRANGE DAYS
Whitney, Ann
WHILE YOU WERE SLEEPING
Whitrow, Benjamin
RESTORATION
Whitson, Robert
HEAVEN'S A DRAG
Whittemore, Libby
FLUKE
SOMETHING TO TALK ABOUT
Whitworth, Johnny
BYE BYE, LOVE
EMPIRE RECORDS
Whiu, Joseph Te
ONCE WERE WARRIORS
Whodini
SHOW, THE
Whyte, Mal
BRAVEHEART
Wichien Nguyen Thi
OPERATION DUMBO DROP
Wick, Norma
CIRCUMSTANCES UNKNOWN
HIDEAWAY
MAGIC IN THE WATER
Wickham, Tim
KID IN KING ARTHUR'S COURT, A
Wicki, Bernhard
MARTHA AND I
Wicks, Rebecca
JACK-O
Wickware, Scott
MOONLIGHT AND VALENTINO
Wiegert, Alison
BRIDGES OF MADISON COUNTY, THE
Wiener, Danielle
VILLAGE OF THE DAMNED
Wieth, Julie
KINGDOM, THE
Wiggins, Chris
BLACK FOX
Wiggins, Dwayne P.
PANTHER

Wight, Peter
RETURN OF THE NATIVE, THE
Wightman, Robert
LIVING IN OBLIVION
Wilborn, Carlton
DEAD PRESIDENTS
Wilbur, George P.
HALLOWEEN: THE CURSE OF MICHAEL
MYERS
Wilcox, Hester
OLD LADY WHO WALKED IN THE SEA,
THE
Wilcox, Jessica
ONCE WERE WARRIORS
Wilcox, Shannon
SEVEN
Wilcox, Steve
PAYBACK
SCANNERS: THE SHOWDOWN
WHITE MAN'S BURDEN
Wild, Wendy
WIGSTOCK: THE MOVIE
Wilde, Charley
PRIEST
Wilde, Rogan
STUART SAVES HIS FAMILY
Wilder, Alan
BIGFOOT: THE UNFORGETTABLE
ENCOUNTER
Wilder, Nick
CAGED HEARTS
Wildman, Dan
GOOD GIRLS DON'T
Wildman, David
DESPERATE PREY
Wildman, Valerie
INDICTMENT: THE MCMARTIN TRIAL
MY FAMILY: MI FAMILIA
Wildsmith, Dawn
JACK-O
Wiles, Jason
HIGHER LEARNING
KICKING AND SCREAMING
Wiles, R. Stephen
MAJOR PAYNE
Wiles, Rick
UNDER SIEGE 2: DARK TERRITORY
Wiles, Tommy
MAJOR PAYNE
Wiley, Ed
CLASS OF '61
Wiley, Edward
S.F.W.
Wiley, Meason
POWDER
Wilheim, Bradley
VILLAGE OF THE DAMNED
Wilheim, Jennifer
VILLAGE OF THE DAMNED
Wilhelmi, Roman
WITHOUT ANESTHESIA
Wilkerson, Lori Simone
STRANGE DAYS
Wilkerson, Marti
CLEAN, SHAVEN
Wilkes, Melissa
BEFORE THE RAIN
Wilkins, Ernie
GREAT DAY IN HARLEM, A
Wilkinson, Jo
SAFE
Wilkinson, Tom
BUSINESS AFFAIR, A
PRIEST
SENSE AND SENSIBILITY
Willard, Fred
PREHYSTERIA! 3

Willard, J. Greg
FORGET PARIS
Willard, Maxine Waters
VAMPIRE IN BROOKLYN
Willets, Kathy
CREEP
Willett, Blake
HACKERS
Williams, Anwen
ENGLISHMAN WHO WENT UP A HILL
BUT CAME DOWN A MOUNTAIN, THE
Williams, Barbara
DIGGER
Williams, Barry
BRADY BUNCH MOVIE, THE
Williams, Bergen Lynn
LORD OF ILLUSIONS
Williams, Bert
USUAL SUSPECTS, THE
Williams, Bruce
HIGHER LEARNING
Williams, Caroline
DECONSTRUCTING SARAH
Williams, Chino Eats
COSMIC SLOP
Williams, Christopher James
MAJOR PAYNE
Williams, Colleen
TO DIE FOR
Williams, Cress
DOOM GENERATION, THE
Williams, Cynda
GHOST BRIGADE
TIE THAT BINDS, THE
Williams, Damon
HARLEM DIARY: NINE VOICES OF
RESILIENCE
Williams, David
HOW TO MAKE AN AMERICAN QUILT
Williams, Dean
BYE BYE, LOVE
Williams, Denalda
DOUBLE, DOUBLE, TOIL AND TROUBLE
Williams, DeWayne
SKINNER
Williams, Doil
WALKING DEAD, THE
Williams, Eugene
EVOLVER
Williams, Fred
ADDICTION, THE
Williams, Gareth
BLESSING
Williams, Gene
ACE VENTURA: WHEN NATURE CALLS
Williams, Harvey
CLOCKERS
Williams, Helen
SUM OF US, THE
Williams, Ian
HEAVEN'S A DRAG
Williams, III, Clarence
TALES FROM THE HOOD
Williams, Irma
COSMIC SLOP
Williams, Israel
ONCE WERE WARRIORS
Williams, Jacqueline
LOSING ISAIAH
Williams, James
ATTACK OF THE 60-FOOT CENTERFOLD
Williams, Jennifer
ART FOR TEACHERS OF CHILDREN
Williams, Johnny
FORGET PARIS
Williams, Jordan
CLASS OF '61

Williams, Keith Leon
MONEY TRAIN
Williams, Kimberly
COLDBLOODED
FATHER OF THE BRIDE PART II
Williams, L.B.
PARTY GIRL
Williams, Larry
APOLLO 13
Williams, Lloyd
HEAVEN'S A DRAG
Williams, Meadow
APOLLO 13
Williams, Melissa
SHOWGIRLS
Williams, Michelle
SPECIES
Williams, Mollena
AMERICA'S DEADLIEST HOME VIDEO
Williams, Nerissa E.
ASSASSINS
Williams, Philip
IT TAKES TWO
PYROMANIAC'S LOVE STORY, A
TO DIE FOR
TOMMY BOY
Williams, Ray
PRIEST
Williams, Robin
JUMANJI
NINE MONTHS
Williams, Ross
GROSS MISCONDUCT
Williams, Ryan
DEAD PRESIDENTS
Williams, Shannon
ONCE WERE WARRIORS
Williams, Tom
COSMIC SLOP
Williams, Treat
THINGS TO DO IN DENVER WHEN
YOU'RE DEAD
WATER ENGINE, THE
Williams, Wilfred
TWELVE MONKEYS
Williams, Zelda
NINE MONTHS
Williams-Foster, Amir
HARLEM DIARY: NINE VOICES OF
RESILIENCE
Williams-Hurner, Jeremy
PROPHECY, THE
Williamson, Blair
MY ANTONIA
Williamson, Kate
BYE BYE, LOVE
Williamson, Kevin
DIRTY MONEY
Williamson, Marco
RICHARD III
Williamson, Mykelti
FREE WILLY 2: THE ADVENTURE HOME
HEAT
HOW TO MAKE AN AMERICAN QUILT
WAITING TO EXHALE
Willinger, Jason
GOOFY MOVIE, A
Willis, Bruce
DIE HARD WITH A VENGEANCE
FOUR ROOMS
TWELVE MONKEYS
Willis, Jerome
BUSINESS AFFAIR, A
Willis, Ronnie
STRANGE DAYS
Wills, James "Kimo"
EMPIRE RECORDS

Wills, Ray
NIXON
Willson, Davidlee
LEAVING LAS VEGAS
Wilman, Alex
PERSUASION
Wilmot, John D.
DEAD MAN WALKING
Wilmot, Ronan
LAMB
Wilson, Audree
BRIAN WILSON: I JUST WASN'T MADE
FOR THESE TIMES
Wilson, Brian
BRIAN WILSON: I JUST WASN'T MADE
FOR THESE TIMES
Wilson, Bridgette
BILLY MADISON
MORTAL KOMBAT
NIXON
Wilson, Bridgitte
HIGHER LEARNING
Wilson, Carl
BRIAN WILSON: I JUST WASN'T MADE
FOR THESE TIMES
Wilson, Carnie
BRIAN WILSON: I JUST WASN'T MADE
FOR THESE TIMES
Wilson, Carol
CASINO
Wilson, Corey
FEAR, THE
Wilson, Dale
BLACK FOX
GOOD DAY TO DIE, A
Wilson, Don "The Dragon"
BATMAN FOREVER
RED SUN RISING
Wilson, Donnice
GLASS SHIELD, THE
Wilson, James Dean
ONCE WERE WARRIORS
Wilson, James R.
ARIZONA DREAM
Wilson, Jody
LAST GOOD TIME, THE
RADIO INSIDE
Wilson, Kellie Lynn
HOW TO MAKE AN AMERICAN QUILT
Wilson, Kristen
DEAD FUNNY
Wilson, Krysten Lee
HOW TO MAKE AN AMERICAN QUILT
Wilson, Lambert
JEFFERSON IN PARIS
Wilson, Marc
FORGET PARIS
Wilson, Marilyn
BRIAN WILSON: I JUST WASN'T MADE
FOR THESE TIMES
Wilson, Megan
MANGLER, THE
Wilson, R.W.
S.F.W.
Wilson, Reno
COSMIC SLOP
Wilson, Rev. Donald R.
ROOMMATES
Wilson, Rita
NOW AND THEN
Wilson, Rob
PYROMANIAC'S LOVE STORY, A
Wilson, Rod
DARKMAN 2: THE RETURN OF DURANT
Wilson, Roger
GHOST BRIGADE
POWER OF ATTORNEY

Wilson, S. Bruce
JUST CAUSE
Wilson, Scott
DEAD MAN WALKING
TALL TALE: THE UNBELIEVABLE
ADVENTURES OF PECOS BILL
Wilson, Shanice
PANTHER
Wilson, Tom
BORN TO BE WILD
Wilson, Vivienne
ONCE WERE WARRIORS
Wilson, Wendy
BRIAN WILSON: I JUST WASN'T MADE
FOR THESE TIMES
Wilson, Yvette
FRIDAY
Wilton, Penelope
CARRINGTON
Wimmer, Brian
TANK GIRL
Win, Peter
BEYOND RANGOON
Winbush, Camille
DANGEROUS MINDS
Winchester, Maud
AMERICAN PRESIDENT, THE
Winchester, Maude
DRACULA: DEAD AND LOVING IT
Winckler, Wolfgang
PROMISE, THE
Wincott, Michael
PANTHER
STRANGE DAYS
Winde, Beatrice
DANGEROUS MINDS
JEFFERSON IN PARIS
LAST GOOD TIME, THE
Winder, James
KINGFISH: A STORY OF HUEY P. LONG
Windham, Beau
PANTHER
Wine, Landon
BETTER OFF DEAD
Winfield, Rodney
DEAD PRESIDENTS
Winger, Debra
FORGET PARIS
Wingert, David
BORN TO BE WILD
Wink, Jurgen
INNOCENT, THE
Winkelspecht, Micah
CASPER
Winkler, Adam
NET, THE
Winkler, Bill
FEAR, THE
Winkler, Charles
NET, THE
Winkler, David
NET, THE
Winkler, Margo
NET, THE
Winkler, Mel
DEVIL IN A BLUE DRESS
Winkler, William
COVER STORY
Winkless, Jeff
CRIMSON WOLF
Winner, Jeff
NADJA
Winningham, Mare
BETTER OFF DEAD
GEORGIA
TERESA'S TATTOO
Winogradoff, Michel
INNOCENT LIES

Winslet, Kate
KID IN KING ARTHUR'S COURT, A
SENSE AND SENSIBILITY
Winslow, Pamela
STEAL BIG, STEAL LITTLE
Winter, Ralph
HACKERS
Winterfeld, Georg
DEADLY MARIA
Winterhawk, Nik
PROPHECY, THE
Winters, Jonathan
ARABIAN KNIGHT
Winters, Shelley
JURY DUTY
SILENCE OF THE HAMS
Winters, Time
DILLINGER AND CAPONE
LITTLE PRINCESS, A
MURDER IN THE FIRST
SKINNER
STEAL BIG, STEAL LITTLE
Winters, Tony
VIRTUOSITY
Wirem, Johnathon
ONCE WERE WARRIORS
Wirth, Billy
BOYS ON THE SIDE
GOOD DAY TO DIE, A
JUDICIAL CONSENT
Wirth, Bruce
GEORGIA
Wisdom, Bob
COSMIC SLOP
Wise, Greg
FEAST OF JULY
SENSE AND SENSIBILITY
Wise, Jim
SHOWGIRLS
Wise, Ray
BODY SHOT
CREW, THE
GHOST BRIGADE
POWDER
Wise, Sue Carolyn
ASSASSINS
Wisniewski, Andreas
DEATH MACHINE
Witham, Justin
MURIEL'S WEDDING
Withers, Googie
COUNTRY LIFE
Witherspoon, Jimmy
GEORGIA
Witherspoon, John
COSMIC SLOP
FRIDAY
VAMPIRE IN BROOKLYN
Witherspoon, Reese
S.F.W.
Witkin, Jacob
SHOWGIRLS
Witkow, Sanders
INDICTMENT: THE MCMARTIN TRIAL
Witt, Alicia
FOUR ROOMS
FUN
Witt, Roz
TANK GIRL
Witten, Paul
O.J. SIMPSON STORY, THE
Wladyka, Margo
BILLY MADISON
Wodenka, Adrienne
ROOMMATES
Woessner, Hank
TOO YOUNG TO DIE?

Woinski, Marcos
I, THE WORST OF ALL
Woitchik, Emillie
MINA TANNENBAUM
Wojcik, Magda Teresa
WITHOUT ANESTHESIA
Wolbert, Jamie Leigh
TO WONG FOO, THANKS FOR
EVERYTHING! JULIE NEWMAR
Wolf, Kedrick
GRANNY, THE
Wolf, Troy S.
BATMAN FOREVER
Wolfchild, Sheldon Peters
SCARLET LETTER, THE
3 NINJAS KNUCKLE UP
Wolfe, Alex
REASON TO BELIEVE, A
Wolfe, Christine
DON JUAN DEMARCO
Wolfe, Heidi
LORD OF ILLUSIONS
Wolfe, Kimberly
TANK GIRL
Wolfe, Nancy Allison
BAR GIRLS
Wolodarsky, Marc
COLDBLOODED
Wolos-Fonteno, David
DEVIL IN A BLUE DRESS
Wolpe, Lenny
S.F.W.
Wolpert, Jay
FATHER OF THE BRIDE PART II
Wolska, A.
SHORT FILM ABOUT KILLING, A
Wong, Anthony
EXECUTIONERS
HEROIC TRIO, THE
Wong, B.D.
FATHER OF THE BRIDE PART II
Wong, James
CYBER BANDITS
Wong, Ken
MOONLIGHT AND VALENTINO
Wong, Raymond
ROOMMATES
Wong Siu
HIGH RISK
Wong, Victor
JADE
3 NINJAS KNUCKLE UP
Wood, Donalee
IN THE DEEP WOODS
Wood, Gary
GLASS SHIELD, THE
Wood, Jane
PERSUASION
Wood, John
CITIZEN X
RICHARD III
SABRINA
Wood, Tom
APOLLO 13
BUSHWHACKED
STEAL BIG, STEAL LITTLE
Woodard, Alfre
HOW TO MAKE AN AMERICAN QUILT
PIANO LESSON, THE
Woodard, Charlayne
BUFFALO GIRLS
Woodbine, Bokeem
DEAD PRESIDENTS
PANTHER
Woodbridge, Wendy
RESTORATION
Woodel, Norm
EXPERT, THE

Woodford, Mark
ASSASSINS
Woodhall, Geoffrey
BYE BYE, LOVE
Woodington, Albie
FIRST KNIGHT
Woodruff, Rod
BEFORE THE RAIN
Woods, Andrea
BLACK IS ... BLACK AIN'T
Woods, Barbara Alyn
FRANKIE STARLIGHT
Woods, James
CASINO
CURSE OF THE STARVING CLASS
INDICTMENT: THE MCMARTIN TRIAL
NEXT DOOR
NIXON
Woods, Kevin
BABE
Woods, Michael
CANADIAN BACON
Woods, Mimi
WINGS OF HONNEAMISE: ROYAL SPACE
FORCE
Woodvine, John
FATHERLAND
PERSUASION
Woodward, Meredith
BROKEN TRUST
Woodward, Tim
SCARLET LETTER, THE
Woolever, Mary
MALLRATS
Woolner, Cliff
IN THE MOUTH OF MADNESS
Woolrich, Abel
MY FAMILY: MI FAMILIA
Woolsey, Brent
CONVICT COWBOY
Woolvett, Jaimz
DEAD PRESIDENTS
Woren, Dan
GRANNY, THE
Workman, Jason
GHOST BRIGADE
Worley, Billy
STRANGE DAYS
Worley, Jo Anne
GOOFY MOVIE, A
Woronov, Mary
GOOD GIRLS DON'T
NUMBER ONE FAN
Worrall, Marlene
MALICIOUS
Wortham, Alvarez
TANK GIRL
Worthington, Wendy
FATHER OF THE BRIDE PART II
Worthy, Dick
WHILE YOU WERE SLEEPING
Worthy, Rick
LOSING ISAIAH
Woven, Dan
BAREFOOT GEN
Woven, Daniel
CRIMSON WOLF
Wray, Dean
CONVICT COWBOY
Wreddon, Tony
LAMB
Wrentz, Lawrence T.
CONGO
WHITE MAN'S BURDEN
Wright, Adrian
GROSS MISCONDUCT
Wright, Aloma
STUART SAVES HIS FAMILY

Wright, Amy
SCARLET LETTER, THE
TOM AND HUCK
Wright, Andrew
INCREDIBLY TRUE ADVENTURES OF
TWO GIRLS IN LOVE, THE
Wright, Angus
CUTTHROAT ISLAND
FIRST KNIGHT
Wright, Bruce
APOLLO 13
BODY SHOT
BORN TO BE WILD
Wright, David Grant
IN THE DEEP WOODS
Wright, Madison
SECRETARY, THE
Wright, Marcia
WHILE YOU WERE SLEEPING
Wright, Mark
MEET THE FEEBLES
Wright, Max
GRUMPIER OLD MEN
Wright, N'Bushe
DEAD PRESIDENTS
Wright, Nicola
LAMB
Wright, Paul
UNDERNEATH, THE
Wright, Robin
CROSSING GUARD, THE
Wright, Steven
CANADIAN BACON
Wright, Tom
FORGET PARIS
TALES FROM THE HOOD
WHITE MAN'S BURDEN
Wright, Tracy
WHEN NIGHT IS FALLING
Wright, Whittni
SUDDEN DEATH
Wrinn, Lindsay J.
KISS OF DEATH
Wrinn, Megan L.
KISS OF DEATH
Wu, Celina
JOHNNY MNEMONIC
Wu Chien-Lien
PHANTOM LOVER, THE
Wu, David
SPITFIRE
Wu Gang
RED FIRECRACKER, GREEN
FIRECRACKER
Wu, Janet
FREE WILLY 2: THE ADVENTURE HOME
Wu, Joe
DECOY
Wu Jun
ERMO
Wu Ma
HIGH RISK
Wu'er Kaixi
MOVING THE MOUNTAIN
Wu-Tang Clan
SHOW, THE
Wuhl, Robert
DR. JEKYLL & MS. HYDE
Wuhrer, Kari
BOULEVARD
CROSSING GUARD, THE
Wulff, Kai
ASSASSINS
TOP DOG
Wyatt, Dennis
FORGET PARIS
Wylde, Sara-Jane
JOURNEY OF AUGUST KING, THE

Wylding, Alex
LOVE AND HUMAN REMAINS
Wyllie, Daniel
MURIEL'S WEDDING
Wyman, John
JADE
Wyman, Nick
DIE HARD WITH A VENGEANCE
Wynhoff, Lou
AMERICA'S DEADLIEST HOME VIDEO
Wynhoff, Mick
AMERICA'S DEADLIEST HOME VIDEO
Wynkoop, Christopher
CLOCKERS
SAFE PASSAGE
Wynkoop, Joel D.
CREEP
Wynorski, Jim
ATTACK OF THE 60-FOOT CENTERFOLD
BODY CHEMISTRY 4: FULL EXPOSURE
MIDNIGHT TEASE 2
Xanadu, Alice
MINA TANNENBAUM
Xavier, Nelson
BOCA
Xisolo, Washington
FRIENDS
Xu Tao
HEROIC TRIO, THE
Xu Zhengyun
RED FIRECRACKER, GREEN
FIRECRACKER
Xuereb, Emmanuel
AMATEUR
BAD BOYS
Xuereb, Salvator
DOOM GENERATION, THE
Yadav, Raghuvir
BANDIT QUEEN
Yaeger, Bert
RIVER OF GRASS
Yager, Missy
DEAD MAN WALKING
Yagi, Akiko
MYSTERY OF RAMPO, THE
Yahyajedidi, Lotfi
CITY OF LOST CHILDREN, THE
Yajima, Kenichi
MYSTERY OF RAMPO, THE
Yale, Stanley
BAD BLOOD
Yalley, Natassia
O.J. SIMPSON STORY, THE
Yam, Simon
NAKED KILLER
Yamaguchi, Uyu
MYSTERY OF RAMPO, THE
Yamamoto, Yoshinori
HACKERS
Yan Zhenguo
ERMO
Yanami, Shigeru
AI CITY
Yancy, Emily
NINE MONTHS
Yang, Ginny
CLOCKERS
Yang Qianquan
SHANGHAI TRIAD
Yang Shenxia
ERMO
Yang Wenming
ERMO
Yang Xiao
ERMO
Yang Xiaoxia
ERMO

Yao, Kelly
NAKED KILLER
Yaroshefsky, Lois
HEAVYWEIGHTS
Yasbeck, Amy
DILLINGER
DRACULA: DEAD AND LOVING IT
HOME FOR THE HOLIDAYS
Yau Chau-Yuet
TWENTY SOMETHING
Yau, Chingmy
NAKED KILLER
Yeager, Biff
DIRTY MONEY
GLASS SHIELD, THE
Yee, Kelvin Han
COPYCAT
Yee, Stuart W.
COPYCAT
Yelverton, Constance
MUTANT SPECIES
Yen Chin Grow
DEAD PRESIDENTS
Yenawine, Philip
POSTCARDS FROM AMERICA
Yeoh, Michelle
EXECUTIONERS
HEROIC TRIO, THE
Yepifantsev, G.
I AM CUBA
Yesso, Don
FAIR GAME
Yeung, Charlie
HIGH RISK
Yi Ding
AMAZING PANDA ADVENTURE, THE
Yip Hon-Leung
TWENTY SOMETHING
Yoakam, Dwight
ROSWELL: THE U.F.O. COVER-UP
Yoba, Malik
BLUE IN THE FACE
SMOKE
York, Jay S.
TALL TALE: THE UNBELIEVABLE
ADVENTURES OF PECOS BILL
York, Roberto Garcia
I AM CUBA
Yorke, Carl Gabriel
APOLLO 13
Yoshida, Richard
DECOY
Yoshikawa, Euchi
MYSTERY OF RAMPO, THE
Yoshino, Kimika
WIZARD OF DARKNESS
Yost, David
MIGHTY MORPHIN POWER RANGERS:
THE MOVIE
You, Frances
DOUBLE HAPPINESS
Younane, Doris
DEATH IN BRUNSWICK
Young, Alexander
OH ... ROSALINDA!!
Young, Alice
GUMBY: THE MOVIE
Young, Brogan
VIRTUOSITY
Young, Bruce A.
TIE THAT BINDS, THE
Young, Bruce P.
TO CROSS THE RUBICON
Young, Charlie
ASHES OF TIME
Young, Christopher Anthony
MONEY TRAIN

Young, Damian
AMATEUR
Young, Dana Allan
S.F.W.
Young, Dave
ASSASSINS
Young, Donald "Donnie"
STRANGE DAYS
Young, Duncan
RIVER OF GRASS
Young, Karen
LOVE AND HUMAN REMAINS
Young, Kate
HOUSEGUEST
ROOMMATES
Young, Keone
BRADY BUNCH MOVIE, THE
Young, Kristy
GORDY
Young, Marlana
STRANGE DAYS
Young, Marvin
PANTHER
Young, Norris
DANGEROUS MINDS
Young, Ric
NIXON
Young, Ron
STRANGE DAYS
Young, Rozwill
TWELVE MONKEYS
Young, Sean
DR. JEKYLL & MS. HYDE
Young, William Allen
ALMOST DEAD
Younger, Brandi
DANGEROUS MINDS
Youngman, James
FUN
Youssef, Marcus
BAD COMPANY
Yoxall, Tina
FUNNY BONES
Yribar, Jason
LORD OF ILLUSIONS
Yu, Emmy
BABY-SITTERS CLUB, THE
Yu Jiangang
SHANGHAI TRIAD
Yuan, Ron Winston
JADE
Yue Guizhi
ERMO
Yuen, Anita
HE'S A WOMAN, SHE'S A MAN
Yuen Tak
HIGH RISK
Yuk, Henry
KISS OF DEATH
Yulin, Harris
BABY-SITTERS CLUB, THE
CUTTHROAT ISLAND
STUART SAVES HIS FAMILY
Yutani, Charlie
MYSTERY OF RAMPO, THE
Yvan, Carolane
CITY OF LOST CHILDREN, THE
Z'Dar, Robert
MOSAIC PROJECT, THE
Zaar, Tony
EMPIRE RECORDS
Zabriskie, Grace
CREW, THE
GOOD DAY TO DIE, A
Zacapa, Daniel
SEVEN

Zacharias, Ann
NEA
Zada, Ramy
OUT OF SYNC
Zador, Mark
TOMMY BOY
Zahn, Steve
CRIMSON TIDE
Zahnd, James
MOSAIC PROJECT, THE
Zahorsky, David
THREE WISHES
Zahrn, Will
DILLINGER
Zale, Alexander
SHOWGIRLS
Zalivalov, Alexei
WINDOW TO PARIS
Zalkind, Robert
HEAVYWEIGHTS
Zaloom, Joe
DIE HARD WITH A VENGEANCE
Zanden, Philip
DREAMING OF RITA
Zane, Billy
REFLECTIONS IN THE DARK
SILENCE OF THE HAMS
TALES FROM THE CRYPT: DEMON
KNIGHT
Zanma, Rieko
MYSTERY OF RAMPO, THE
Zapasiewicz, Zbigniew
SHORT FILM ABOUT KILLING, A
WITHOUT ANESTHESIA
Zapata, Amelia
MY FAMILY: MI FAMILIA
Zappa, Moon
DARK SIDE OF GENIUS, THE
Zappala, Janet L.
TWELVE MONKEYS
Zarimba, Katherine
TOM AND HUCK
Zass, Jerzy
SHORT FILM ABOUT KILLING, A
Zastawna, Nellie
ME AND THE MOB
Zawadska, Valerie
COW, THE
Zawaski, Ski
FAIR GAME
Zay, Tim
DEAD PRESIDENTS
Zboyovski, Matthew R.
HEAVYWEIGHTS
Zegers, Katie
IN THE MOUTH OF MADNESS
Zegers, Kevin
IN THE MOUTH OF MADNESS
Zellweger, Renee
EMPIRE RECORDS
Zentout, Delphine
FARINELLI
Zepeda, Jorge
BURNING SEASON, THE
Zerella, Tina
ONLY THE BRAVE
Zerguine, Mostefa
PIGALLE
Zerkowski, Ted
BOYS ON THE SIDE
Zeta-Jones, Catherine
RETURN OF THE NATIVE, THE
Zeus
HEAVEN'S A DRAG
Zhang Bolin
RED FIRECRACKER, GREEN
FIRECRACKER

Zhang Guizhi
ERMO
Zhang Haiyan
ERMO
Zhang Jin-Ming
MOVING THE MOUNTAIN
Zhang, Stephanie
AUGUSTIN
Zhang Xiaoyan
ERMO
Zhang Yayun
SHANGHAI TRIAD
Zhang Yiying
ERMO
Zhao Liang
RED FIRECRACKER, GREEN
FIRECRACKER
Zhao Xiaorui
RED FIRECRACKER, GREEN
FIRECRACKER
Zhe Sun
ROOMMATES
Zheng Jiasen
SHANGHAI TRIAD
Zheng Ruisheng
HEROIC TRIO, THE
Zhenhu Han
HIGHLANDER: THE FINAL DIMENSION
Zhi Yanyan
ERMO
Zhu Mimi
HEROIC TRIO, THE
Zibor
NOT ANGELS BUT ANGELS
Zieff, Rick
NICK OF TIME
Ziegler, Lynn
JURY DUTY
Ziegler, Vera
INNOCENT, THE
Ziehl, Scott
MOSAIC PROJECT, THE
Ziker, Richard
JADE
Zima, Vanessa
BABY-SITTERS CLUB, THE
Zima, Yvonne
HEAT
Ziman, Richard
CLOCKERS
HACKERS
Zimbalist, Stephanie
GREAT ELEPHANT ESCAPE, THE
Zimmer, Diana
ANDROID AFFAIR, THE
Zimmerman, J.R.
TOMMY BOY
Zimmerman, Timothy A.
TO WONG FOO, THANKS FOR
EVERYTHING! JULIE NEWMAR
Zimmerman, Zoey
NIXON
Zingaretti, Luca
CASTLE FREAK
Zinn, Satcie A.
JUST CAUSE
Ziolkowska, E.
SHORT FILM ABOUT LOVE, A
Zirner, August
PROMISE, THE
Zito, Chuck
BAD BLOOD
NEW YORK COP
Ziyad, II, Seifullah
SILENCE OF THE HAMS
Zmuda, Bob
BATMAN FOREVER

Zobel, Richard
TALL TALE: THE UNBELIEVABLE
ADVENTURES OF PECOS BILL
Zoccola, Brian Ann
O.J. SIMPSON STORY, THE
Zohar, Rita
WATERWORLD
Zola, Anne Marie
DEATH MACHINE
Zola, Annemarie
HACKERS
Zola, Leonard
JUMANJI
Zollner, Anian
PROMISE, THE
Zoot
STRANGE DAYS
Zorner, Rick
BITTER VENGEANCE
Zozzaro, Jamie
PANTHER
Zucker, Bob
FIRST KNIGHT
Zucker, Burt
FIRST KNIGHT
Zucker, Charlotte
FIRST KNIGHT
Zucker, Kate
FIRST KNIGHT
Zundel, Ernst
PROFESSION: NEO-NAZI
Zuniga, Jose
BLUE IN THE FACE
MONEY TRAIN
NADJA
SMOKE
Zurk, Steve
RADIO INSIDE
Zusser, Matt
HOW TO MAKE AN AMERICAN QUILT
Zwahlen, Heinrich
PARTY GIRL
Zylberstein, Elsa
FARINELLI
JEFFERSON IN PARIS
MINA TANNENBAUM

ANIMATORS

Anno, Hideaki
WINGS OF HONNEAMISE: ROYAL SPACE
FORCE
Aquino, Ruben
POCAHONTAS
Arance, W.L.
TALES FROM THE CRYPT: DEMON
KNIGHT
Armstrong, Eric
CASPER
Babbitt, Art
ARABIAN KNIGHT
Bazley, Richard
PEBBLE AND THE PENGUIN, THE
Belzer, Mike
GUMBY: THE MOVIE
Bolger, Paul
ARABIAN KNIGHT
Bowers, David
BALTO
Boyle, Neil
ARABIAN KNIGHT
Brannon, Ash
TOY STORY
Buck, Chris
POCAHONTAS
Buckley, Stephen
GUMBY: THE MOVIE

Byers-Brown, David
ARABIAN KNIGHT
Calvert, Fred
ARABIAN KNIGHT
Clokey, Art
GUMBY: THE MOVIE
Docter, Pete
TOY STORY
Duncan, Ken
POCAHONTAS
Ersoz, Sahin
BALTO
Finn, William
GOOFY MOVIE, A
Glocka, Angie
GUMBY: THE MOVIE
Grieve, Margaret
ARABIAN KNIGHT
Guenoden, Rodolphe
BALTO
Guillaumet, Ramon
ARABIAN KNIGHT
Hamilton, Alyson
ARABIAN KNIGHT
Hanson, Kurt
GUMBY: THE MOVIE
Harris, Ken
ARABIAN KNIGHT
Hawkins, Emery
ARABIAN KNIGHT
Hill, John
PEBBLE AND THE PENGUIN, THE
Hoefnagels, Silvia
PEBBLE AND THE PENGUIN, THE
Holliday, Carole
GOOFY MOVIE, A
Iguchi, Chuichi
AI CITY
Ilda, Fumo
WINGS OF HONNEAMISE: ROYAL SPACE
FORCE
Jankovics, Marcell
ADVENTURES OF MATT THE
GOOSEBOY, THE
Jeannette, Daniel
BALTO
Keane, Glen
POCAHONTAS
Kleinow, Peter
GUMBY: THE MOVIE
Klick, Laurel
TALES FROM THE CRYPT: DEMON
KNIGHT
Koboyashi, Mitsutoshi
CRIMSON WOLF
Kurtz, Bob
FOUR ROOMS
Laudati, Tony
GUMBY: THE MOVIE
Majoribanks, Duncan
POCAHONTAS
Mann, Alex
GOOFY MOVIE, A
Marlet, Nicolas
BALTO
Mason, Dan
GUMBY: THE MOVIE
Mate, Patrick
BALTO
Misoka, Hiroko
MYSTERY OF RAMPO, THE
Moriyama, Yuji
WINGS OF HONNEAMISE: ROYAL SPACE
FORCE
Nakura, Yasuhiro
MYSTERY OF RAMPO, THE

Nepp, Joszef
ADVENTURES OF MATT THE
GOOSEBOY, THE
Nibbelink, Phil
CASPER
Nordman, January
TALES FROM THE CRYPT: DEMON
KNIGHT
Odell, Brent
ARABIAN KNIGHT
Pablos, Sergio
GOOFY MOVIE, A
Palmer, Ralf
PEBBLE AND THE PENGUIN, THE
Pixar Animation Studios
TOY STORY
Pomeroy, John
PEBBLE AND THE PENGUIN, THE
POCAHONTAS
Power, John
PEBBLE AND THE PENGUIN, THE
Prulksma, Dave
POCAHONTAS
Quade, Rich
TOY STORY
Ranieri, Nik
POCAHONTAS
Rhythm & Hues
BABE
Sadamoto, Yoshiyuki
WINGS OF HONNEAMISE: ROYAL SPACE
FORCE
Salazar, William
BALTO
Schmidt, Erik
BALTO
Scott, Bob
GOOFY MOVIE, A
Serrand, Kristof
BALTO
Simon, Len
PEBBLE AND THE PENGUIN, THE
Smith, Bruce
GOOFY MOVIE, A
Stevenhagen, Rob
BALTO
Tomisawa, Kazuo
BAREFOOT GEN
Varab, Jeffrey J.
BALTO
Walton, Harry
GUMBY: THE MOVIE
Willard, Ken
GUMBY: THE MOVIE
Williams, Richard
ARABIAN KNIGHT
Wolfson, Alan
TALES FROM THE CRYPT: DEMON
KNIGHT
Zondag, Dick
BALTO

ART DIRECTORS

Alesch, Stephen
SEARCH AND DESTROY
Allaire, Laurent
SON OF THE SHARK, THE
Altadonna, Joseph M.
WALKING DEAD, THE
Alton, Betsy
INCREDIBLY TRUE ADVENTURES OF
TWO GIRLS IN LOVE, THE
Angelo, Michael
MIDNIGHT TEASE 2
Arai, Torao
AI CITY

Ardouin, Catherine
VOYAGE EN DOUCE
Arnold, Bill
LOSING ISAIAH
Arnold, Steve
GET SHORTY
Arnold, William
BRIDGES OF MADISON COUNTY, THE
Aronin, Vladimir
BURNT BY THE SUN
Bailey, Justin
BRIAN WILSON: I JUST WASN'T MADE
FOR THESE TIMES
Baker, Maria
FRIDAY
Ballance, Jack D.L.
HEAVYWEIGHTS
Band, Richard
CASTLE FREAK
Barclay, William
SUDDEN DEATH
Barnes, Gordon
BILLY MADISON
Barrows, James R.
FATHER AND SCOUT
Bateup, High
MURIEL'S WEDDING
Becker, Barbara
MUTE WITNESS
Begovich, Patrice
EROTIQUE
Belk, Roger
REFLECTIONS IN THE DARK
Berke, Mayne Schuyler
FOUR ROOMS
Bhagat, Ashok
BANDIT QUEEN
Bolton, Gregory
FREE WILLY 2: THE ADVENTURE HOME
Bomba, David
APOLLO 13
Bontemps, Gilles
PIGALLE
Borgognoni, Livia
OTHELLO
Bradford, Dennis
JUST CAUSE
MONEY TRAIN
Branco, Ze
CONVENT, THE
Brandes, Phil
ALMOST DEAD
BODY SHOT
3 NINJAS KNUCKLE UP
Breen, Charles
JADE
Bridgland, Richard
RICHARD III
Brock, Ian
DARKMAN 2: THE RETURN OF DURANT
Brunsmann, Keith
BAR GIRLS
Buckley, Gae
THREE WISHES
Buckwald, Scott
GOOD GIRLS DON'T
Bufnoir, Jacques
LES MISERABLES
Burian-Mohr, Chris
BATMAN FOREVER
Cahall, Walter
SEPARATE LIVES
Cain, Roger
CUTTHROAT ISLAND
Campbell, Georgina
ONLY THE BRAVE
Campbell, Tony
ETERNITY

Carlhian, Sophie
KILIAN'S CHRONICLE
Caro, Marc
CITY OF LOST CHILDREN, THE
Carter, Joel
GLASS SHIELD, THE
Cassells, Jeremy
MORTAL KOMBAT
Cassie, Alan
DOOMSDAY GUN
RESTORATION
Chandragupta, Bansi
CHARULATA
Charette, Cynthia
VAMPIRE IN BROOKLYN
Chennaux, Alain
BLUE VILLA, THE
Chiffre, Philippe
MINA TANNENBAUM
Chodak, Randy
BROKEN TRUST
Clark, Christopher
JACK-O
Cochrane, Sandy
HIDEAWAY
Coelho, Gioconda
BOCA
Collum, Charles
BABY-SITTERS CLUB, THE
Cornwell, Chris
DECONSTRUCTING SARAH
UNSTRUNG HEROES
WHILE YOU WERE SLEEPING
Cortese, Tom
BAD BLOOD
Cox, Keith
ZOOMAN
Crank, David
MAJOR PAYNE
Crawley, Allen
ANDROID AFFAIR, THE
Crone, Bruce
BUSHWHACKED
Crowe, Desmond
OTHELLO
Cruse, William
FORGET PARIS
Curtis, Beth
ADDICTION, THE
da Silva, Ana Vaz
CONVENT, THE
Dakota, Reno
LIE DOWN WITH DOGS
Darrow, Harry
BIG GREEN, THE
HEAVYWEIGHTS
Davenport, Dennis
JOHNNY MNEMONIC
del Paso, Felipe Fernandez
DESPERADO
del Rosario, Linda
WIGSTOCK: THE MOVIE
Deutch, Lisa
TERESA'S TATTOO
Deverell, Tamara
CANADIAN BACON
ECLIPSE
Diamond, Gary
VAMPIRE IN BROOKLYN
Dickens, Candice
DOUBLE HAPPINESS
Dobrowolska, Halina
SHORT FILM ABOUT LOVE, A
Dohl, Dieter
INNOCENT, THE
Dondertman, John
NATIONAL LAMPOON'S SENIOR TRIP

Donhauser, Andreas
FOR GOD AND COUNTRY
Dorrance, Dan
BRAVEHEART
Dorrance, Daniel T.
ASSASSINS
Doyle, Alta Louise
KURT VONNEGUT'S HARRISON
BERGERON
Drake, Philip
TRAPS
Duffield, Tom
LITTLE PRINCESS, A
Dultz, Jim
TANK GIRL
Dultz, Jim R.
TALL TALE: THE UNBELIEVABLE
ADVENTURES OF PECOS BILL
Durrell, Jr., William J.
BRADY BUNCH MOVIE, THE
Eggleston, Ralph
TOY STORY
Elias, Patricia
BALLISTIC
Elton, Philip
SENSE AND SENSIBILITY
Erganian, Leslie
RADIO INSIDE
Evein, Bernard
NEA
Faen, Laurie
NOSTRADAMUS KID, THE
Fanning, Tony
INDIAN IN THE CUPBOARD, THE
Ferguson, David
MOONLIGHT AND VALENTINO
Fisher, Daniel
RHYTHM THIEF
Fisichella, Marc
LORD OF ILLUSIONS
WAITING TO EXHALE
Fleming, Garth
CRACKERJACK
Fojo, Richard
FLUKE
Fong, Darryl
BAR GIRLS
Ford, David W.
PENTATHLON
Francois, Thierry
JEFFERSON IN PARIS
Frankish, John
HACKERS
Fraser, Eric A.
GOLD DIGGERS: THE SECRET OF BEAR
MOUNTAIN
Frick, John
UNDERNEATH, THE
Garcia, Wilma
BOCA
Gentry, Cecil
I LIKE TO PLAY GAMES
Giaimo, Michael
POCAHONTAS
Gibbens, Dennis
BODILY HARM
Gibson, Colin
BABE
MIGHTY MORPHIN POWER RANGERS:
THE MOVIE
Gilles, John Ivo
WHITE MAN'S BURDEN
Ginsburg, Gershon
NOW AND THEN
Goetz, Gretchen
DARK DEALER
Goldfield, Daniel
DEAD FUNNY

Gracie, Ian
SUM OF US, THE
Graham, W. Steven
NINE MONTHS
Griffiths, Pauline
DOOMSDAY GUN
Grobler, Daniel
AMERICAN COP
Gross, Roz Johanna
RED SUN RISING
Grundy, Peter
IN THE MOUTH OF MADNESS
PYROMANIAC'S LOVE STORY, A
Guerra, Robert
TO WONG FOO, THANKS FOR
EVERYTHING! JULIE NEWMAR
Gunvordahl, Terry
CONVICT COWBOY
Guterres, Candi
EVOLVER
Haase, Karen
SWIMMING WITH SHARKS
Hai Tsung-man
HE'S A WOMAN, SHE'S A MAN
Haley, Sheila
HUNTED, THE
Hall, Douglas
WATER ENGINE, THE
Haras, Jill
DOUBLE HAPPINESS
Hardy, Ken
PEREZ FAMILY, THE
Hardy, Kenneth A.
DEAD PRESIDENTS
Harris, Henry
CENTURY
SECRET OF ROAN INISH, THE
Harwell, Helen
HOWLING: NEW MOON RISING, THE
Hazelwood, Ken
GROSS MISCONDUCT
Hebb, Fontaine Beauchamp
EMBRACE OF THE VAMPIRE
Heinrichs, Rick
TALL TALE: THE UNBELIEVABLE
ADVENTURES OF PECOS BILL
Herforth, Benedikt
PROMISE, THE
Heslup, Willie
AMAZING PANDA ADVENTURE, THE
BAD COMPANY
Hill, Bruce
DRACULA: DEAD AND LOVING IT
LORD OF ILLUSIONS
PANTHER
Hiney, William
CLUELESS
Hole, Fred
DOOMSDAY GUN
Holland, Richard
CONGO
HIGHER LEARNING
Huang, David K.
COVER ME
Huang Xinming
SHANGHAI TRIAD
Huke, John
EMPIRE RECORDS
Hunter, Roland
CRY, THE BELOVED COUNTRY
Hurst, Yvonne J.
DIGGER
FAR FROM HOME: THE ADVENTURES OF
YELLOW DOG
Irwin, Colin
TALES FROM THE CRYPT: DEMON
KNIGHT

Ishiura, Maya
CIRCUMSTANCES UNKNOWN
Jaekel, Barbara Ann
KINGFISH: A STORY OF HUEY P. LONG
Javor, Lorand
CITIZEN X
Jennings, Jack
ALMOST DEAD
Jensen, John R.
DIE HARD WITH A VENGEANCE
Johnson, Bo
TIE THAT BINDS, THE
Johnson, Brad
GHOST BRIGADE
Karman, Steve
COSMIC SLOP
Kasarda, John
SABRINA
Kaufman, Claire
GALAXIS
Kelly, Errol
BEYOND RANGOON
Kendall, Peter
GREAT ELEPHANT ESCAPE, THE
Keywan, Alicia
TOMMY BOY
Kingston, Barry
POWDER
Kingston, Barry M.
LEAVING LAS VEGAS
Kirkpatrick, T.K.
HALLOWEEN: THE CURSE OF MICHAEL
MYERS
Klassen, David
WATERWORLD
Klaus, Sonja
FEAST OF JULY
Knipp, Jeff
ANGUS
DON JUAN DEMARCO
Knowles, Sarah
MONEY TRAIN
Koenningsberg, Nicole
OUT OF SYNC
Kohout, Milos
ACCUMULATOR 1
Kosko, Gary
HOUSEGUEST
Kottmann, Claus
NOBODY LOVES ME
Krantz, Michael
DOOM GENERATION, THE
Lagola, Charles
BURNING SEASON, THE
ROSWELL: THE U.F.O. COVER-UP
Laing, Bob
FIRST KNIGHT
Lalande, Guy
DR. JEKYLL & MS. HYDE
Lamont, Neil
GOLDENEYE
Larson, Ken
ACROSS THE MOON
Lazan, David
USUAL SUSPECTS, THE
Lazan, David Seth
INDICTMENT: THE MCMARTIN TRIAL
Lee, Charles D.
TANK GIRL
Lee, Jonathan
RESTORATION
Lehmann, Jette
KINGDOM, THE
Leker, Lawrence
GOOFY MOVIE, A
Lemasson, Constance
REASON TO BELIEVE, A

Lev, Lisa
MALICIOUS
Lin, Jessinta
DAY THE SUN TURNED COLD, THE
Lowe, Chris
ENGLISHMAN WHO WENT UP A HILL
BUT CAME DOWN A MOUNTAIN, THE
Lucas, Ken
BIGFOOT: THE UNFORGETTABLE
ENCOUNTER
Lucky, Joseph P.
BATMAN FOREVER
Luebbe, Wendell
GOOFY MOVIE, A
Ma Yongming
SHANGHAI TRIAD
Mackintosh, Woods
DIE HARD WITH A VENGEANCE
MacLeod, Zoe
SHALLOW GRAVE
Maltese, Daniel
CASPER
WALK IN THE CLOUDS, A
Maly, Martin
FATHERLAND
Man, Choi Ho
RICHARD III
Martin, Renate
FOR GOD AND COUNTRY
Marty, Jack
DARK DEALER
Matthews, William F.
FAIR GAME
Mayhew, Ina
CLOCKERS
Mays, Richard F.
NIXON
McDonald, Jeff
BLUE IN THE FACE
SMOKE
McNab, Eric
BULLETPROOF HEART
McShirley, Margie Stone
HEAT
Medesto, Claudia
BOCA
Menchions, Douglasann
WINGS OF COURAGE
Messina, Philip
RECKLESS
S.F.W.
Michelle, Janine
LIVING IN OBLIVION
Miller, Bruce Allan
APOLLO 13
Minster, Kenny
SPY WITHIN, THE
Minty, David
RETURN OF THE NATIVE, THE
Mora, Daniel
I, THE WORST OF ALL
Mosselli, Michael
CRAZYSITTER, THE
Munro, Andrew
FUNNY BONES
Munro, Christa
VILLAGE OF THE DAMNED
Murakami, James J.
CRIMSON TIDE
Myers, Troy
MY FAMILY: MI FAMILIA
Naisbitt, Roy
ARABIAN KNIGHT
Naylor, Kave
BUSINESS AFFAIR, A
Ngai Fong Nai
NAKED KILLER

Norlin, Eric
MAGIC IN THE WATER
Nowak, Christopher
ACE VENTURA: WHEN NATURE CALLS
O'Brien, William F.
BOYS ON THE SIDE
SHOWGIRLS
O'Neill, Padraig
AILSA
Oga, Kazuo
BAREFOOT GEN
Ogura, Hiromasa
WINGS OF HONNEAMISE: ROYAL SPACE
FORCE
Olexiewicz, Daniel
WILD BILL
Orbom, Eric
NICK OF TIME
Pain, Keith
CUTTHROAT ISLAND
Papalia, Greg
BYE BYE, LOVE
FATHER OF THE BRIDE PART II
Paris, Richard
WIGSTOCK: THE MOVIE
Parker, III, Charles L.
COMPANION, THE
Pascale, Jan
ARIZONA DREAM
Pask, Scott
LIVING IN OBLIVION
POSTCARDS FROM AMERICA
Patton, Nancy
DANGEROUS MINDS
OUTBREAK
Pearson, Glen
JUMANJI
Pelicastro, Garrett
MOSAIC PROJECT, THE
Pezza, Francis J.
OUTBREAK
Phelps, D. Gary
BIKINI BISTRO
Phillips, Jim
DECOY
Plauche, Scott
FRANK & JESSE
Politanoff, Peter
BAD BOYS
Pow, Sue
PRIEST
Prier, Nicolas
INNOCENT LIES
Qian Yunxiu
RED FIRECRACKER, GREEN
FIRECRACKER
Radford, Shayne
ONCE WERE WARRIORS
Ralph, John
ROB ROY
Rea, Bill
GRUMPIER OLD MEN
Reay, Kerrie
DALLAS DOLL
Rencher, Burton
THINGS TO DO IN DENVER WHEN
YOU'RE DEAD
Rhee, Judy
LITTLE ODESSA
Richardson, Lucy
RESTORATION
Rizzo, Michael
MURDER IN THE FIRST
TOM AND HUCK
Roberts, Nanci B.
BRADY BUNCH MOVIE, THE
Roberts, Nancy B.
YOUNGER & YOUNGER

Rosenkranz, Roland
NATIONAL LAMPOON'S ATTACK OF THE
5'2" WOMEN
Sage, Jefferson
ROOMMATES
SAFE PASSAGE
Saklad, Steve
QUICK AND THE DEAD, THE
Samulekine, Alexandre
BURNT BY THE SUN
Sasaki, Hiroshi
CRIMSON WOLF
Saternow, Tim
PIANO LESSON, THE
Savage, Sue
MALLRATS
Scott, Jan
GETTING OUT
Seagers, Chris
CIRCLE OF FRIENDS
COPYCAT
Sharp, Geoff
HEAVEN'S A DRAG
Shaw, Michael
LAST GOOD TIME, THE
PUSHING HANDS
Shepps, Rob
COVER ME
Sinski, Bruce J.
GOOD DAY TO DIE, A
Sizemore, Troy
CURE, THE
Skinner, William Ladd
TWELVE MONKEYS
Smith, Caroline
FEAST OF JULY
Smith, Charlie
INNOCENT LIES
Smith, Easton Michael
DESTINY TURNS ON THE RADIO
Smith, Russ
LAKOTA WOMAN: SIEGE AT WOUNDED
KNEE
SILENCE OF THE HAMS
Solle, Bogdan
PROVINCIAL ACTORS
Sowards, Andrew
BODY CHEMISTRY 4: FULL EXPOSURE
FEAR, THE
Spence, Steve
OPERATION DUMBO DROP
Spinace, Ricardo
LAST OF THE DOGMEN
Stabley, Anthony
BLUE TIGER
SAFE
Stannard, Roy
FEAST OF JULY
Stebler, Dawn Snyder
CANDYMAN: FAREWELL TO THE FLESH
Stefanovic, Jasna
FIRST DEGREE
Stuhr, Fred
MOSAIC PROJECT, THE
Sullivan, Michael
BUFFALO GIRLS
SUBSTITUTE WIFE, THE
Svoboda, Vlasta
IT TAKES TWO
TO DIE FOR
Tabor, William
BREAK, THE
Targownik, Tom
NET, THE
Taylor, Jr., Jack G.
CASINO
STARS FELL ON HENRIETTA, THE

Thomas, Lisette
OPERATION DUMBO DROP
Tilley, Quenby
DANGEROUS, THE
Tkaczyk, Grazyna
SHORT FILM ABOUT KILLING, A
Tocci, Jim
HOME FOR THE HOLIDAYS
Tomkins, Alan
ROB ROY
Tompkins, Les
JUDGE DREDD
Toolin, Phillip
TANK GIRL
Tougas, Ginger
AMATEUR
Tuttle, Guy
CLASS OF '61
Vacek, Karel
MARTHA AND I
Van Dijk, Ruud
1-900
Verreaux, Ed
CASPER
HOW TO MAKE AN AMERICAN QUILT
Viard, Gerard
FRENCH KISS
Wachter, Theresa
BURNING SEASON, THE
Wagner, Dianne
CRIMSON TIDE
Walsh, Frank
CARRINGTON
SISTER MY SISTER
Ward, Linda
PERSUASION
Warnke, John
AMERICAN PRESIDENT, THE
STRANGE DAYS
Warren, Tom
DEAD MAN WALKING
MIGHTY APHRODITE
TWO BITS
Webster, Dan
DEVIL IN A BLUE DRESS
SPECIES
Weinzimer, Rachael
ME AND THE MOB
Whitaker, Susan
DEATH MACHINE
White, Julianne
DESPERATE PREY
White, Michael
FIRST KNIGHT
Wilby, Mark
FRIENDS
Wilkins, Thomas P.
STUART SAVES HIS FAMILY
Willson, David
JUMANJI
MAN OF THE HOUSE
Wilson, Dave
AWFULLY BIG ADVENTURE, AN
RUN OF THE COUNTRY, THE
Wissner, Gary
SEVEN
Wollard, Tony
SCARLET LETTER, THE
Wolstenholme, Val
LAMB
Wong, Gilbert
BORN TO BE WILD
Wood, Carol
UNDER SIEGE 2: DARK TERRITORY
Woodruff, Donald
NIXON
Worthington, Mark
MAD LOVE

Wymark, Dominic
DESTINY TURNS ON THE RADIO
GRANNY, THE
Yanez-Toyon, Richard
TANK GIRL
VIRTUOSITY
Yarhi, Dan
DOLORES CLAIBORNE
Yu, Bruce
EXECUTIONERS
HEROIC TRIO, THE
Zachary, John
PREHYSTERIA! 3
Zarling, Phil
TWOGETHER
Zhang Daqian
ERMO
Zhanjia, Yang
ASHES OF TIME
Ziliox, Bob
OUTSIDE THE LAW
Zuelzke, Mark E.
STEAL BIG, STEAL LITTLE
Zweizig, Margery
NIXON

ASSOCIATE PRODUCERS

Adamson, Kent
HOWLING: NEW MOON RISING, THE
Aglion, Michael D.
GLASS SHIELD, THE
MURIEL'S WEDDING
Aguilar, Joe M.
MIAMI RHAPSODY
Ahmad, Maher
STEAL BIG, STEAL LITTLE
Akkad, Malek
HALLOWEEN: THE CURSE OF MICHAEL
MYERS
Alden, Michael
JUST CAUSE
Apelian, Lauri
MORTAL KOMBAT
Apple, Max
ROOMMATES
Arons, Rich
BALTO
Backes, Michael
CONGO
Bailey, Frederick
BODY SHOT
Baker, Michael
DOOMSDAY GUN
Baldwin, Bill
BROTHERS MCMULLEN, THE
Baldwin, Karen
SUDDEN DEATH
Barteleme, Jane
CUTTHROAT ISLAND
Bartlett, Rita Marie
MANGLER, THE
Beckner, Stephen
BLUE VILLA, THE
Bedi, Varsha
BANDIT QUEEN
Bell, Fran
DANGER OF LOVE
Bentley, Mark
RESTORATION
Bergman, Anthony
ROY COHN/JACK SMITH
Bester, Rocky
GROSS MISCONDUCT
Billings, Jennifer Graham
BORN TO BE WILD
Blinken, Antony
ADDICTION, THE

Bloodworth, Baker
POCAHONTAS
Blum, Jason
KICKING AND SCREAMING
Blum, Mark
SEARCH AND DESTROY
Blumenfeld, Gina
DOLORES CLAIBORNE
Bober, Philippe
KINGDOM, THE
Borghese, Paul
BIKINI BISTRO
Bostick, Michael
APOLLO 13
Bowman, Sarah
WATER ENGINE, THE
Bregman, Anthony
BROTHERS MCMULLEN, THE
Brent, Kimberly
LOSING ISAIAH
Brody, Tod Scott
LAST GOOD TIME, THE
Brook, Diana Costes
BUSINESS AFFAIR, A
Brook, Simon
FOOL AND HIS MONEY, A
Brown, Ray
DALLAS DOLL
Brown, Robert Latham
DRACULA: DEAD AND LOVING IT
Caillier, Barry
TO CROSS THE RUBICON
Caplan, Twink
CLUELESS
Carcassonne, Philippe
INNOCENT LIES
Caron K
WAITING TO EXHALE
Carr, Warren
BAD COMPANY
Cassidy, Esther
BALLOT MEASURE 9
Cat, Ivan
OPERATION INTERCEPT
Cesaretti, Gusmano
HEAT
Chan, Dennis
NAKED KILLER
Chasin, Liza
FRENCH KISS
MOONLIGHT AND VALENTINO
PANTHER
Cirillo, Joe
NEW YORK COP
Clark, Linda
BOCA
Cobo, Nacho
STRAWBERRY AND CHOCOLATE
Coffey, Charlie
NATIONAL LAMPOON'S ATTACK OF THE
5'2" WOMEN
Cohen, Jennifer Ryan
LIE DOWN WITH DOGS
Collett, Alexander B.
TALES FROM THE CRYPT: DEMON
KNIGHT
Cornick, Jonathan
SCARLET LETTER, THE
Cowel, Eileen
BABY-SITTERS CLUB, THE
Cracchiolo, Dan
TALES FROM THE CRYPT: DEMON
KNIGHT
Crane, Julie B.
FATHER OF THE BRIDE PART II
Crier, Cammie
NICK OF TIME

Cuddy, Carol
ACROSS THE SEA OF TIME: NEW YORK
3D
Cunningham, Sandra
WHEN NIGHT IS FALLING
Cussons, Jane
FEAST OF JULY
Da Mota, Billy
REFLECTIONS IN THE DARK
Daan, Maag
HYENAS
Dadon, Jackie
RED SUN RISING
Dauterive, Mitchell
BATMAN FOREVER
Davidson, Boaz
SEARCH AND DESTROY
Davis, Nick
GALAXIS
De Los Santos, Nancy
MY FAMILY: MI FAMILIA
Deason, Paul
CASPER
CONGO
Deatherage, Joleen
BALLISTIC
Dellal, Jasmine
BLACK IS ... BLACK AIN'T
Dempsey, Christopher
MIDNIGHT TEASE 2
Deyhle, Rolf
TWO BITS
Di Paolo, Vincent
DECOY
DiFranco, Paul
CRAZYSITTER, THE
DJ Pooh
FRIDAY
Donohue, Walter
BEYOND RANGOON
dos Santos, Paulo Jose Cardoso
CARMEN MIRANDA: BANANAS IS MY
BUSINESS
Dougherty, Scott
OUTBREAK
Downes, John
SHALLOW GRAVE
Draper, Jeanette
COVER ME
Durk, Julie
ASSASSINS
Edelman, Abra
BULLETPROOF HEART
Edwards, Zoe Oka
INCREDIBLY TRUE ADVENTURES OF
TWO GIRLS IN LOVE, THE
Egerton, Mark
BEYOND RANGOON
TWELVE MONKEYS
Ehrensperger, Lynn
SHOWGIRLS
Ellis, Howard
TOM AND HUCK
Ewing, Michael
TOMMY BOY
Fadely, Sherry
FREE WILLY 2: THE ADVENTURE HOME
Fenner, Jeffrey
VAMPIRE IN BROOKLYN
Ferraro, Terri
FLUKE
Ferreira, Caique Martin
BOCA
Fessenden, Larry
RIVER OF GRASS
Fields, Karyn
ASSASSINS

Fierberg, Andrew
NADJA
Filon, Rick
EMBRACE OF THE VAMPIRE
Freixa, Ricardo
LAST GOOD TIME, THE
Friedman, Roberta
COVER STORY
Fulton, David
WATERWORLD
Furches, Breaker
AMERICAN COP
Garvin, Dean
RADIO INSIDE
Giarraputo, Jack
BILLY MADISON
HEAVYWEIGHTS
Gigliotti, Donna
DEVIL IN A BLUE DRESS
Gil, Jane
LIVING IN OBLIVION
Gilels, Deborah
PENTATHLON
Gillen, Maria
BABY-SITTERS CLUB, THE
Glickman, Jonathan
JERKY BOYS: THE MOVIE, THE
WHILE YOU WERE SLEEPING
Goebel, Lawrence
SCANNERS: THE SHOWDOWN
SECRETARY, THE
Goergens, Ardythe
IN THE DEEP WOODS
Golov, Andrew
SUBSTITUTE WIFE, THE
Goodloe, J. Mills
ASSASSINS
Gorman, Erin
KICKING AND SCREAMING
Gould, Jean Russo
DEAD FUNNY
Grant, Casey
MAN OF THE HOUSE
Gruberg, Benjamin
COVER STORY
Haddad, Patrice
SON OF THE SHARK, THE
Haker, Kenneth
RED SUN RISING
Hanson, Marla
ADDICTION, THE
Hapsas, Alex
NEW YORK COP
Harbert, Tim
ASCENT, THE
CLASS OF '61
Hayhoe, Margot
PERSUASION
Hechim, Tom
TO CROSS THE RUBICON
Heitzer, Don
LAST OF THE DOGMEN
Herlihy, Joyce
SISTER MY SISTER
Hicks, Kahlil
HARLEM DIARY: NINE VOICES OF
RESILIENCE
Hinkley, Matt
BABYSITTER, THE
Hinman, Joel
POSTCARDS FROM AMERICA
Holt, James
RED SUN RISING
Houlihan, Christina
MARTHA & ETHEL
House, Lynda
DEATH IN BRUNSWICK

Houser, Cheryl Miller
WIGSTOCK: THE MOVIE
Howard, Kelsey T.
BULLETPROOF HEART
Hsu Li-Kong
PUSHING HANDS
Hui Yun
HE'S A WOMAN, SHE'S A MAN
Hui Yut-tsan
HE'S A WOMAN, SHE'S A MAN
Huisman, Mark
INCREDIBLY TRUE ADVENTURES OF
TWO GIRLS IN LOVE, THE
Huntington, Georgie
TERESA'S TATTOO
Imperato, Thomas A.
DEVIL IN A BLUE DRESS
Irving, Brian
BAD BLOOD
Jacobs, Gregory
BEFORE SUNRISE
Jansen, Joann Fregalette
WHITE MAN'S BURDEN
Johnson, Elaine
WHILE YOU WERE SLEEPING
Jorissen, B.B.
BALLOT MEASURE 9
Joyce, Bernadette
DARKMAN 2: THE RETURN OF DURANT
Kabillo, Eli
LIE DOWN WITH DOGS
Kantymir, Kenneth
ABDUCTED 2: THE REUNION
Kaplan, Mark F.
NUMBER ONE FAN
Karr, Tom
CREEP
Kauffman, Gary
WIGSTOCK: THE MOVIE
Kavanaugh, Russ
BOYS ON THE SIDE
Kelly, Joe
UNSTRUNG HEROES
Kerns, Ernest
SAFE
Key, Stephen
HIGHLANDER: THE FINAL DIMENSION
Klein, Michael
NOT ANGELS BUT ANGELS
Koffler, Pamela
POSTCARDS FROM AMERICA
Kohn, Mitchell
TO WONG FOO, THANKS FOR
EVERYTHING! JULIE NEWMAR
Konig, Werner
MUTE WITNESS
Kornhauser, Mari
LAST RIDE, THE
Kramer, Jeremy
COVER ME
KICKING AND SCREAMING
Larkin, George
WIGSTOCK: THE MOVIE
Lau, Carijn
LIE DOWN WITH DOGS
Lawless, Louie Edward
ABDUCTED 2: THE REUNION
Lemer, Robert H.
DIE HARD WITH A VENGEANCE
Lester, Heidi
DEATH MACHINE
Levinson, Art
DILLINGER
Levy, Adam
FEAR, THE
Lievre, Philippe
SIX DAYS, SIX NIGHTS

Lightstone, Monika
FUN
Livi, Jean-Louis
PURE FORMALITY, A
Lony, Pieter
MUTE WITNESS
Lopata, Dean
BRAVEHEART
Lopez, Gloria
S.F.W.
Lorka, Claudia
WIGSTOCK: THE MOVIE
Loubek, Chirstian
MAGIC IN THE WATER
Lytle, Stephen
WALK IN THE CLOUDS, A
Mace, Borden
JOURNEY OF AUGUST KING, THE
Magagni, Alexis
LAST RIDE, THE
Mahood, Tony
MURIEL'S WEDDING
Maltby, Barbara
AMERICAN PRESIDENT, THE
Marcus, Gary
RHYTHM THIEF
Marcus, Trula
RHYTHM THIEF
Markovsky, Dessie
JURY DUTY
Marmion, Yves
MINA TANNENBAUM
Marshall, Mark
FREE WILLY 2: THE ADVENTURE HOME
Martell, Lloyd
DECOY
Martin, Leann
AVENGING ANGEL
Masters, Sue
DALLAS DOLL
Matsubara, Yuriko
HUNTED, THE
Maurer, Michael
BRIDGES OF MADISON COUNTY, THE
McDermott, Kathryn J.
FIRST KNIGHT
McDonnell, Edward
UNDER SIEGE 2: DARK TERRITORY
McFlynn, Timothy
TOO YOUNG TO DIE?
McGowan, Gretchen
MARTHA & ETHEL
McKay, Ralph
RIVER OF GRASS
McMillan, Peter
FUNNY BONES
McMinn, Robert
VIRTUOSITY
Merrifield, Douglas C.
FREE WILLY 2: THE ADVENTURE HOME
Merrill, Robert A.
GLASS SHIELD, THE
Metzger, Doug
UNDER SIEGE 2: DARK TERRITORY
Mikhalkov, Nikita
BURNT BY THE SUN
Miller, Anna C.
CANDYMAN: FAREWELL TO THE FLESH
LORD OF ILLUSIONS
Miller, Paul
SECRET OF ROAN INISH, THE
Miller, Terry
CANADIAN BACON
Milne, Sheila Fraser
BEFORE THE RAIN
Mnouchkine, Alexandre
PURE FORMALITY, A

Mones, Paul Alan
TOO YOUNG TO DIE?
Moore, Michael D.
CREEP
Mosley, Walter
DEVIL IN A BLUE DRESS
Mulroney, Dermot
LIVING IN OBLIVION
Munafo, Tony
ASSASSINS
JUDGE DREDD
Munoz, Juan
STRAWBERRY AND CHOCOLATE
Murphy, Dennis Stuart
NEXT DOOR
Nakama, Eleanor
PICTURE BRIDE
Nancoff, David
DANCE ME OUTSIDE
Neber, Cynthia L.
ASSASSINS
Newbery, Joanna
PRIEST
Nicholls, Allan
DEAD MAN WALKING
Nicoletti, Susan
JUDGE DREDD
Norrington, Stephen
DEATH MACHINE
Novick, Susan E.
BORN TO BE WILD
Oleszczuk, Alicia E.
BLUE TIGER
Owyang, Sharon
LOSING ISAIAH
Painter, Melissa
CLEAN, SHAVEN
INCREDIBLY TRUE ADVENTURES OF
TWO GIRLS IN LOVE, THE
Parker, Ron
ZOOMAN
Pemrick, Donald Paul
CHILDREN OF THE CORN III: URBAN
HARVEST
Perakis, Christine
AMERICAN COP
Perrette, Clarisse
NINA TAKES A LOVER
Pesmen, Paula DuPre
NINE MONTHS
Piccoli, Pier Paolo
RHYTHM THIEF
Pierson, Fred
TWOGETHER
Platt, Michele
SEVEN
Porter, Aldric
APOLLO 13
Poupaud, Chantal
WILD REEDS
Procter, Martin
LAMB
Quaid, Evi
CURSE OF THE STARVING CLASS
Railsback, Steve
STARS FELL ON HENRIETTA, THE
Rainone, Thomas C.
CHILDREN OF THE CORN III: URBAN
HARVEST
Ramsden, John
HOWLING: NEW MOON RISING, THE
Razpopov, Emile
JURY DUTY
Reagan, Patrick
GOOFY MOVIE, A
Redbird, Duke
DANCE ME OUTSIDE

Redman, David
BEFORE THE RAIN
Reher, Kevin
GUMBY: THE MOVIE
Reidy, Joseph
CASINO
Reidy, Kevin
SWIMMING WITH SHARKS
Reilly, Thomas
MIGHTY APHRODITE
Reinhardt, George
HYENAS
Reiss, Rina
ONLY THE BRAVE
Renaud-Clement, Olivier
POSTCARDS FROM AMERICA
Repola, Arthur F.
INDIAN IN THE CUPBOARD, THE
Reutlinger, Ilyse A.
ASSASSINS
Richards, Mary
RICHARD III
Richter, Judy
BROTHERS MCMULLEN, THE
Ring, Megan
KID IN KING ARTHUR'S COURT, A
Ringo, Susan
GET SHORTY
Roberts, Selwyn
HACKERS
Robinson, Artist
IN THE MOUTH OF MADNESS
Robinson, Elizabeth
BRAVEHEART
Robinson, Jr., Andre
FRIDAY
Romero, Dan
UNDER SIEGE 2: DARK TERRITORY
Rooker, Tom
BRIDGES OF MADISON COUNTY, THE
Rosen, Josie
AMAZING PANDA ADVENTURE, THE
Rosenberg, Scott
THINGS TO DO IN DENVER WHEN
YOU'RE DEAD
Rosenfeld, Donald
FEAST OF JULY
JEFFERSON IN PARIS
Roy, Fran
CURSE OF THE STARVING CLASS
Royce, Patricia
TO CROSS THE RUBICON
Rozenberg, Paul
WILD REEDS
Rubin, Jackie
UNSTRUNG HEROES
Rutowski, Richard
NIXON
Rutt, James H.
SKINNER
Sackman, Jeff
FUN
Saint Clair, Barrie
AMERICAN COP
Salgado, Carlos
CARMEN MIRANDA: BANANAS IS MY
BUSINESS
Samuels, Stuart
GREAT DAY IN HARLEM, A
Sarony, Paul
ENGLISHMAN WHO WENT UP A HILL
BUT CAME DOWN A MOUNTAIN, THE
Savitch, Alison
MORTAL KOMBAT
Scannardi, Linda
TWOGETHER
Schecter, Alan
FAIR GAME

Schmid, Regine
ECLIPSE
Schoenberg, Arthur
ARMAGEDDON: THE FINAL CHALLENGE
Seydoux, Michel
BURNT BY THE SUN
Shapiro, Peter
TIE-DIED: ROCK 'N' ROLL'S MOST
DEADICATED FANS
Shea, Kathleen M.
HEAT
Short, Trevor
SEARCH AND DESTROY
Shwarzstein, Meyer
SECRETARY, THE
SCANNERS: THE SHOWDOWN
Silvi, Roberto
NEVER TALK TO STRANGERS
Simons, Jimmy
BYE BYE, LOVE
Skalski, Mary Jane
ROY COHN/JACK SMITH
Sklaski, Mary Jane
BROTHERS MCMULLEN, THE
Skotchdopole, James W.
CRIMSON TIDE
Sloane, Ari
BROKEN TRUST
LAKOTA WOMAN: SIEGE AT WOUNDED
KNEE
Smith-Wait, Kelley
TWELVE MONKEYS
Snowden, Bill
FOOL AND HIS MONEY, A
Spiotta, Elena
GRUMPIER OLD MEN
Spring, Helena
CRY, THE BELOVED COUNTRY
St. Clair, Beau
HIDEAWAY
Stark, Jim
DOOM GENERATION, THE
Stevens, Emily
WORLD AND TIME ENOUGH
Streeter, Sydney S.
OH ... ROSALINDA!!
Stull, Rob
PENTATHLON
Surpin, Shelley
DOOM GENERATION, THE
Suttle, Craig Thurman
EXPERT, THE
Tandy, Michele
RICHARD III
Tardini, Ib
KINGDOM, THE
Thomas, Krista
KILIAN'S CHRONICLE
Thompson, Chris
CARRINGTON
Threadgill, Tina
KINGFISH: A STORY OF HUEY P. LONG
Toint, Hubert
SON OF THE SHARK, THE
Tollefson, Rhonda
JUST CAUSE
Tripp-Haith, James
FRIDAY
Trotiner, Glen
RADIO INSIDE
Tucker-Davies, Teresa
STEAL BIG, STEAL LITTLE
Tuttle, David
NEW JERSEY DRIVE
Van Patten, Nels
BREAK, THE
von Zerneck, Danielle
LIVING IN OBLIVION

Vonier, Fabienne
  I CAN'T SLEEP
Wadlow, Marvin
  SHOW, THE
Waldburger, Ruth
  I CAN'T SLEEP
Walters, Mikela
  PENTATHLON
Warren, Andrew
  AWFULLY BIG ADVENTURE, AN
Waye, Anthony
  GOLDENEYE
Webb, David
  EXOTICA
Webster, Christopher
  YOUNGER & YOUNGER
Weiss, Bruce
  CURSE OF THE STARVING CLASS
Welles, Kirsten W.
  TALL TALE: THE UNBELIEVABLE
    ADVENTURES OF PECOS BILL
Wertheim, Allan
  GOLD DIGGERS: THE SECRET OF BEAR
    MOUNTAIN
White, Whitney
  STUART SAVES HIS FAMILY
Willey, Tom
  NEVER TALK TO STRANGERS
Wilton, Ralph
  CENTURY
Wright, Michelle
  INDIAN IN THE CUPBOARD, THE
Yenawine, Philip
  POSTCARDS FROM AMERICA
Yu, Jessica
  MAYA LIN: A STRONG CLEAR VISION
Zadiko, Brian
  BIKINI BISTRO
Zappy, Leah
  DRACULA: DEAD AND LOVING IT
Zazulinski, Tania
  LES MISERABLES
Zheng Jianmei
  HEROIC TRIO, THE
Zisman, Leonid
  FATHERLAND
Zivet, Louis J.
  TWOGETHER

CHOREOGRAPHERS

Basil, Toni
  SOMETHING TO TALK ABOUT
Daniele, Graciela
  MIGHTY APHRODITE
Flatt, Kate
  RESTORATION
Johnson, Alan
  DRACULA: DEAD AND LOVING IT
Mitchell, Jerry
  JEFFREY
Moore, Claudia
  EXOTICA
O'Connell, John
  MURIEL'S WEDDING
Pomerhn-Derricks, Marguerite
  SHOWGIRLS
Robinson, Eartha
  VAMPIRE IN BROOKLYN
Rodrigues, Alfred
  OH ... ROSALINDA!!
Romano, Patrick
  CLUELESS
Sacks, Quincy
  RESTORATION
Stephenson, Geraldine
  PERSUASION

Wang Qing
  SHANGHAI TRIAD

CINEMATOGRAPHERS

Ackerman, Thomas
  JUMANJI
Adamek, Witold
  SHORT FILM ABOUT LOVE, A
Ahern, Lloyd
  WILD BILL
Ahlberg, Mac
  BRADY BUNCH MOVIE, THE
Alazraki, Robert
  OLD LADY WHO WALKED IN THE SEA,
    THE
Alberti, Maryse
  CRUMB
  HARLEM DIARY: NINE VOICES OF
    RESILIENCE
  MOVING THE MOUNTAIN
Anderson, Jamie
  MAN OF THE HOUSE
Aronson, John
  DILLINGER AND CAPONE
Arvanitis, Yorgos
  TOTAL ECLIPSE
Atherton, Howard
  BAD BOYS
Badal, Jean
  SERIOUS ABOUT PLEASURE
Baer, Hanania
  LAST SUMMER IN THE HAMPTONS
Baffa, Christopher
  CRAZYSITTER, THE
Ballhaus, Michael
  OUTBREAK
Banks, Dasal
  SHOW, THE
Banks, Larry
  EROTIQUE
  SHOW, THE
Barroso, Mario
  CONVENT, THE
  VALLEY OF ABRAHAM, THE
Bartkowiak, Andrzej
  JADE
  LOSING ISAIAH
Bartowiak, Andrzej
  SPECIES
Baszak, Miroslaw
  DANCE ME OUTSIDE
  ECLIPSE
Beck, Maxwell J.
  JACK-O
Beebe, Dion
  ETERNITY
Bergersen, Kyle
  WORLD AND TIME ENOUGH
Beristain, Gabriel
  DOLORES CLAIBORNE
Bernstein, Steven
  KICKING AND SCREAMING
  SECRETARY, THE
Berriff, Paul
  LESSONS OF DARKNESS
Berryman, Ross
  GOLD DIGGERS: THE SECRET OF BEAR
    MOUNTAIN
Biddle, Adrian
  JUDGE DREDD
Bigazzi, Luca
  LAMERICA
Biziou, Peter
  RICHARD III
Blakey, Ken
  BIGFOOT: THE UNFORGETTABLE
    ENCOUNTER

Blank, Jonathan
  SEX, DRUGS AND DEMOCRACY
Blossier, Patrick
  INNOCENT LIES
Bode, Ralf D.
  BIG GREEN, THE
  DON JUAN DEMARCO
  SAFE PASSAGE
Bohrer, Uwe
  NEKROMANTIK
Bota, Rick
  BABYSITTER, THE
  COMPANION, THE
  TALES FROM THE CRYPT: DEMON
    KNIGHT
Bowen, Richard
  FAIR GAME
  MAJOR PAYNE
Boyd, Russell
  OPERATION DUMBO DROP
Brabec, F.A.
  ACCUMULATOR 1
Bridges, David
  PAYBACK
Buckley, Michael
  DIGGER
Bukowski, Bobby
  SEARCH AND DESTROY
  TIE THAT BINDS, THE
  TOM AND HUCK
Burgess, Don
  FORGET PARIS
Burstyn, Thomas
  MAGIC IN THE WATER
Burton, Geoff
  HOTEL SORRENTO
  NOSTRADAMUS KID, THE
  SUM OF US, THE
Byers, Frank
  BITTER VENGEANCE
Byrne, Bobby
  DANGER OF LOVE
Capener, Brian
  RADIO INSIDE
Carpenter, Russell
  INDIAN IN THE CUPBOARD, THE
Carter, James
  DESTINY TURNS ON THE RADIO
Carter, James L.
  CONVICT COWBOY
  LAST RIDE, THE
Catonne, Francois
  MY LIFE AND TIMES WITH ANTONIN
    ARTAUD
Cawley, Sarah
  REASON TO BELIEVE, A
Challis, Christopher
  OH ... ROSALINDA!!
Chan Tseun-kit
  HE'S A WOMAN, SHE'S A MAN
Chapuis, Dominique
  FRIENDS
  MINA TANNENBAUM
Chen, Rom-Shiw
  SHAO LIN POPEYE
Chivers, Steven
  HIGHLANDER: THE FINAL DIMENSION
Choy, Christine
  IN THE NAME OF THE EMPEROR
Clabaugh, Richard
  PROPHECY, THE
Clokey, Art
  GUMBY: THE MOVIE
Collister, Peter Lyons
  HIGHER LEARNING
Connell, David
  ASCENT, THE
  BUFFALO GIRLS

GROSS MISCONDUCT
Conroy, Jack
HUNTED, THE
Consentino, Steven
SHOW, THE
Conversi, Fabio
SIX DAYS, SIX NIGHTS
Core, Ericson
SHOW, THE
Corradi, Pio
CONGRESS OF PENGUINS, THE
Coulter, Michael
SENSE AND SENSIBILITY
Crockett, Todd
DEAD FUNNY
Cundey, Dean
APOLLO 13
CASPER
Daarstad, Erik
FRANK AND OLLIE
Daly, John
PERSUASION
Daniel, Lee
BEFORE SUNRISE
Daviau, Allen
CONGO
Davis, Elliot
GLASS SHIELD, THE
THINGS TO DO IN DENVER WHEN
YOU'RE DEAD
UNDERNEATH, THE
de Borman, John
DEATH MACHINE
de Buitlear, Cian
AILSA
De Santis, Pasqualino
MONTH BY THE LAKE, A
Deakins, Roger A.
DEAD MAN WALKING
Decca, Anghel
SPY WITHIN, THE
Del Ruth, Thomas
NEXT DOOR
delli Colli, Tonino
MAMMA ROMA
Deming, Peter
COSMIC SLOP
S.F.W.
Demps, John
SHOW, THE
WALKING DEAD, THE
Denault, Jim
NADJA
RIVER OF GRASS
Di Gennaro, Joe
MESSENGER
Di Giacomo, Franco
POSTMAN, THE
Dickson, Billy
HALLOWEEN: THE CURSE OF MICHAEL
MYERS
DiGregorio, Rick
DIRTY MONEY
Dintenfass, Andrew
CURE, THE
DiPalma, Carlo
MIGHTY APHRODITE
Djafarian, Hossein
THROUGH THE OLIVE TREES
Dos Reis, Todd A.
SHOW, THE
Doyle, Christopher
ASHES OF TIME
Drake, John
FOOL AND HIS MONEY, A
Dreujou, Marie
AUGUSTIN

Dryburgh, Stuart
ONCE WERE WARRIORS
PEREZ FAMILY, THE
Dunning, Steve
DARK DEALER
Dylewska, Jolanta
CHRONICLE OF THE WARSAW GHETTO
UPRISING ACCORDING TO MAREK
EDELMAN
Eder, Fabian
FOR GOD AND COUNTRY
Edwards, Eric Alan
KIDS
TO DIE FOR
Elliott, Paul
PIANO LESSON, THE
Elmes, Frederick
RECKLESS
England, Bryan
WATER ENGINE, THE
Erisman, Tom
1-900
Escorel, Lauro
STUART SAVES HIS FAMILY
Faber, Christian
DIRTY MONEY
Farkas, Pedro
BOCA
Fealy, Jim
DOOM GENERATION, THE
Feindt, Johann
PROFESSION: NEO-NAZI
Fernandes, Joao
DECONSTRUCTING SARAH
TOP DOG
Fernberger, Peter
NEW YORK COP
Ferris, Michael
BAR GIRLS
Filac, Vilko
ARIZONA DREAM
Finestone, Steven
SWIMMING WITH SHARKS
Fisher, Dick
BROTHERS MCMULLEN, THE
Flynn, Frank P.
BREAK, THE
Fraisse, Robert
CITIZEN X
WINGS OF COURAGE
Fraker, William A.
FATHER OF THE BRIDE PART II
Francesco, Bill
AMERICA'S DEADLIEST HOME VIDEO
Frazee, David
BOULEVARD
Friedman, Joseph
MARTHA & ETHEL
Fujimoto, Tak
DEVIL IN A BLUE DRESS
GRUMPIER OLD MEN
Garcia, Rodrigo
FOUR ROOMS
INDICTMENT: THE MCMARTIN TRIAL
Gardner, James
FAR FROM HOME: THE ADVENTURES OF
YELLOW DOG
Garfath, Michael
LAMB
Gentil, Dominique
FACES OF WOMEN
Gerull, Helga
CAGED HEARTS
Gilpin, Paul
CRY, THE BELOVED COUNTRY
Giurato, Blasco
PURE FORMALITY, A

Glennon, James
IN THE DEEP WOODS
JUDICIAL CONSENT
Godard, Agnes
I CAN'T SLEEP
Goldblatt, Stephen
BATMAN FOREVER
Gonzalez, Carlos
MUTANT SPECIES
Goodnoff, Irv
DANGEROUS, THE
Grant, James
ONLY THE BRAVE
Graver, Gary
ATTACK OF THE 60-FOOT CENTERFOLD
MIDNIGHT TEASE 2
Green, Jack N.
AMAZING PANDA ADVENTURE, THE
BAD COMPANY
BRIDGES OF MADISON COUNTY, THE
NET, THE
Greenberg, Adam
FIRST KNIGHT
Greenberg, Robbie
UNDER SIEGE 2: DARK TERRITORY
Greim, Rolf
STALINGRAD
Griebe, Frank
DEADLY MARIA
Grunberg, Slawomir
WHEN BILLY BROKE HIS HEAD ... AND
OTHER TALES OF WONDER
Gruszynski, Alexander
ANGUS
KINGFISH: A STORY OF HUEY P. LONG
Guerra, Pili Flores
NO MERCY
Hagstrand, Lisa
DANCER, THE
Haitkin, Jacques
EVOLVER
SILENCE OF THE HAMS
Hammer, Victor
BILLY MADISON
HEAVYWEIGHTS
Hansen, Ellen
BALLOT MEASURE 9
Haun, Kim
BODY STROKES
I LIKE TO PLAY GAMES
Hayes, Bob
GOOD GIRLS DON'T
Hayward, Kevin
TRAPS
Heinl, Bernd
FEAR, THE
YOUNGER & YOUNGER
Held, Wolfgang
WIGSTOCK: THE MOVIE
Henrik, Iren
ADVENTURES OF MATT THE
GOOSEBOY, THE
Henriques, Samuel
HARLEM DIARY: NINE VOICES OF
RESILIENCE
Hertz, Richard
CREEP
Hochstatter, Zoran
ALMOST DEAD
BODY CHEMISTRY 4: FULL EXPOSURE
Hojda, Petr
COW, THE
Holender, Adam
BLUE IN THE FACE
SMOKE
Holomek, Vladimir
NOT ANGELS BUT ANGELS

Hoover, John
KILIAN'S CHRONICLE
Hou Young
DAY THE SUN TURNED COLD, THE
Hume, Alan
RETURN OF THE NATIVE, THE
Hurn, Philip
UNDERCOVER
Hyams, Peter
SUDDEN DEATH
Idziak, Slawomir
JOURNEY OF AUGUST KING, THE
SHORT FILM ABOUT KILLING, A
Irwin, Mark
AVENGING ANGEL
VAMPIRE IN BROOKLYN
Isaacks, Levie
EXPERT, THE
Isagawa, Hiroshi
WINGS OF HONNEAMISE: ROYAL SPACE
FORCE
Ishikawa, Kinichi
BAREFOOT GEN
Jacquet, Luc
CONGRESS OF PENGUINS, THE
Jaquenod, Christian
JLG BY JLG
Jensen, Johnny E.
THREE WISHES
Jewett, Thomas
SCANNERS: THE SHOWDOWN
Johnson, Bruce D.
PROPHECY, THE
Johnson, David
OTHELLO
Jong Lin
PUSHING HANDS
Jost, Jon
BED YOU SLEEP IN, THE
FRAMEUP
Joya, Mario Garcia
STRAWBERRY AND CHOCOLATE
UP TO A CERTAIN POINT
Jur, Jeffrey
O.J. SIMPSON STORY, THE
ZOOMAN
Kalin, Matthias
HYENAS
Kaliuta, Vilen
BURNT BY THE SUN
Kallberg, Per
DANCER, THE
Kallstrom, Gunnar
DANCER, THE
Kaminski, Janusz
CLASS OF '61
HOW TO MAKE AN AMERICAN QUILT
TALL TALE: THE UNBELIEVABLE
ADVENTURES OF PECOS BILL
Karpick, Avi
JURY DUTY
OUTSIDE THE LAW
Kazmierski, Stephen
BLESSING
Kelsch, Ken
ADDICTION, THE
Kemper, Victor J.
TOMMY BOY
Khondji, Darius
CITY OF LOST CHILDREN, THE
SEVEN
Kibbe, Gary B.
IN THE MOUTH OF MADNESS
VILLAGE OF THE DAMNED
Kiesser, Jan
GEORGIA

Kimmel, Adam
ME AND THE MOB
NEW JERSEY DRIVE
Kirsten, Sven
PLAY TIME
TERESA'S TATTOO
Kitzanuk, Andrew
ACROSS THE SEA OF TIME: NEW YORK
3D
Klein, David
MALLRATS
Kliewer, Linda
BALLOT MEASURE 9
Klosinski, Edward
WITHOUT ANESTHESIA
Koch, Douglas
WHEN NIGHT IS FALLING
Koltai, Lajos
HOME FOR THE HOLIDAYS
JUST CAUSE
Kossak, Andreas
HOWLING: NEW MOON RISING, THE
Kotov, Rein
CITY UNPLUGGED
Kovacs, Laszlo
COPYCAT
FREE WILLY 2: THE ADVENTURE HOME
Kranhouse, John
DECOY
Kress, Eric
KINGDOM, THE
Krieg, Peter
MACHINE DREAMS
Krupa, Howard
RHYTHM THIEF
Kurant, Willy
BABY-SITTERS CLUB, THE
BUSINESS AFFAIR, A
WHITE MAN'S BURDEN
Kuras, Ellen
POSTCARDS FROM AMERICA
ROY COHN/JACK SMITH
UNZIPPED
Kurita, Toyomichi
LAKOTA WOMAN: SIEGE AT WOUNDED
KNEE
WAITING TO EXHALE
Kwang-Suk Chong
HOW TO TOP MY WIFE
Lachman, Edward
MY FAMILY: MI FAMILIA
Lagerroos, Khell
DREAMING OF RITA
Lapchov, Anatoly
WINDOW TO PARIS
Lapoirie, Jeanne
WILD REEDS
Laskus, Jacek
COVER ME
Lau, Tom
HEROIC TRIO, THE
Laufer, Paul
FRANKIE STARLIGHT
Lautore, Ronald
GREAT ELEPHANT ESCAPE, THE
Layton, Vernon
ENGLISHMAN WHO WENT UP A HILL
BUT CAME DOWN A MOUNTAIN, THE
Leatherbarrow, John
ARABIAN KNIGHT
Lecomte, Claude
VOYAGE EN DOUCE
Leiterman, Richard
DOUBLE, DOUBLE, TOIL AND TROUBLE
Lelouch, Claude
LES MISERABLES
Lenoir, Denis
CARRINGTON

Lenzer, Don
MAYA LIN: A STRONG CLEAR VISION
Leonetti, John R.
BURNING SEASON, THE
MORTAL KOMBAT
Leonetti, Matthew F.
STRANGE DAYS
Lesnie, Andrew
BABE
Letarte, Pierre
DANGEROUS MINDS
Levy, Peter
CUTTHROAT ISLAND
Lewiston, Denis
NIGHTMARE
Lhomme, Pierre
JEFFERSON IN PARIS
Lindenlaub, Karl Walter
LAST OF THE DOGMEN
ROB ROY
Lindenmaier, Patrick
CONGRESS OF PENGUINS, THE
Lindley, John W.
MONEY TRAIN
Littlewood, Greg
SKINNER
Lively, Gerry
CHILDREN OF THE CORN III: URBAN
HARVEST
FRIDAY
Lloyd, Walt
EMPIRE RECORDS
FRANK & JESSE
Lohmann, Dietrich
INNOCENT, THE
Lu Gengxin
ERMO
Lu Yue
SHANGHAI TRIAD
Lubezki, Emmanuel
LITTLE PRINCESS, A
WALK IN THE CLOUDS, A
Macat, Julio
MOONLIGHT AND VALENTINO
MacDonald, Heather
BALLOT MEASURE 9
Machilsky, Serghei
CREATION OF ADAM
MacMillan, Ken
CIRCLE OF FRIENDS
MacPherson, Glenn
FIRST DEGREE
Magierski, Tomasz
CARMEN MIRANDA: BANANAS IS MY
BUSINESS
Maguire, Rick
POWER OF ATTORNEY
Mahoney, Denis
CYBER BANDITS
Maniaci, Teodoro
CLEAN, SHAVEN
Mankofsky, Isidore
FATHER AND SCOUT
OUT OF SYNC
Marker, Spike
BIKINI BISTRO
Marritz, Eddie
MAYA LIN: A STRONG CLEAR VISION
Mason, Steve
DESPERATE PREY
TO WONG FOO, THANKS FOR
EVERYTHING! JULIE NEWMAR
Mathieson, John
PIGALLE
May, Bradford
DARKMAN 2: THE RETURN OF DURANT
Mayers, Michael
DIRTY MONEY

McAlpine, Donald
NINE MONTHS
McCoy, Kevin
MOSAIC PROJECT, THE
McGrath, Martin
MURIEL'S WEDDING
Medencevic, Suki
EMBRACE OF THE VAMPIRE
Medina, Teresa
REFLECTIONS IN THE DARK
Meheux, Phil
GOLDENEYE
Mehta, Ashok
BANDIT QUEEN
Meier, Hans
BLUE VILLA, THE
Menzies, Peter
DIE HARD WITH A VENGEANCE
Mertes, Raffaele
FLUKE
Michalak, Richard
GORDY
Mickens, Michael
CRAZYSITTER, THE
Migeat, Francois
FACES OF WOMEN
Mikesch, Elfi
EROTIQUE
Miles, Steven R.
MOSAIC PROJECT, THE
Milne, Murray
MEET THE FEEBLES
Milosevic, Miodrag
GORILLA BATHES AT NOON
Mitas, George
LIE DOWN WITH DOGS
Mitra, Subrata
CHARULATA
Moderegger, Klaus
STALINGRAD
Montgomery, Jennifer
ART FOR TEACHERS OF CHILDREN
Monti, Felix
I, THE WORST OF ALL
Mooradian, George
SPITFIRE
Morgan, Donald M.
BORN TO BE WILD
DILLINGER
Murphy, Fred
MURDER IN THE FIRST
Murphy, Paul
DALLAS DOLL
MIGHTY MORPHIN POWER RANGERS:
THE MOVIE
Mutarevic, Sead
NUMBER ONE FAN
Navarro, Guillermo
DESPERADO
FOUR ROOMS
Negrin, Michael
SHOW, THE
Negroponte, Michel
JUPITER'S WIFE
Nekrassov, Sergei
WINDOW TO PARIS
Nepomniaschy, Alex
SAFE
New, Robert C.
GALAXIS
Newby, John
OPERATION INTERCEPT
RED SUN RISING
Nicholson, Rex
NATIONAL LAMPOON'S ATTACK OF THE
5'2" WOMEN

Nowak, Danny
ABDUCTED 2: THE REUNION
CRACKERJACK
Nykvist, Sven
SOMETHING TO TALK ABOUT
O'Shea, Michael D.
DRACULA: DEAD AND LOVING IT
Ohashi, Rene
RENT-A-KID
Okazaki, Hideo
CRIMSON WOLF
Orieux, Ron
BROKEN TRUST
GOOD DAY TO DIE, A
Ornelas, Michael
CREEP
Palermo, Spence
BALLOT MEASURE 9
Palsson, Sigurdur Sverrir
REMOTE CONTROL
Papamichael, Phedon
UNSTRUNG HEROES
WHILE YOU WERE SLEEPING
Papamicheal, Phedon
DARK SIDE OF GENIUS, THE
Parmet, Phil
FOUR ROOMS
NINA TAKES A LOVER
Pau, Peter
PHANTOM LOVER, THE
Pei, Eddie
PANTHER
Peterman, Don
GET SHORTY
Petkovic, Aleksander
GORILLA BATHES AT NOON
Petropoulos, Steve
GREAT DAY IN HARLEM, A
Petrycki, Jacek
PROVINCIAL ACTORS
Pfister, Wally
GRANNY, THE
Phillips, David
BASKETBALL DIARIES, THE
Poon Hang Sang
EXECUTIONERS
HEROIC TRIO, THE
Pope, Bill
CLUELESS
Pope, Dick
AWFULLY BIG ADVENTURE, AN
Porath, Gideon
BREACH OF CONDUCT
Poster, Steven
ROSWELL: THE U.F.O. COVER-UP
Pouliquer, Yves
JLG BY JLG
Pratt, Roger
TWELVE MONKEYS
Priestley, Tom
DR. JEKYLL & MS. HYDE
Primes, Robert
MY ANTONIA
Prinzi, Frank
LIVING IN OBLIVION
Protat, Francois
JOHNNY MNEMONIC
NATIONAL LAMPOON'S SENIOR TRIP
Pyrah, Allan
GLORY BOYS, THE
Quale, Steven
CRUDE OASIS, THE
Quinlan, Dick
CURSE OF THE STARVING CLASS
Quinn, Declan
LEAVING LAS VEGAS

Ragalyi, Elemer
KID IN KING ARTHUR'S COURT, A
NEVER TALK TO STRANGERS
Raha, Barun
STRANGER, THE
Raschke, Claudia
LAST GOOD TIME, THE
Rath, Franz
PROMISE, THE
Reiker, Tami
INCREDIBLY TRUE ADVENTURES OF
TWO GIRLS IN LOVE, THE
Reynolds, Buster
ARMAGEDDON: THE FINAL CHALLENGE
Richardson, Robert
CASINO
NIXON
Richmond, Anthony B.
TALES FROM THE HOOD
Richmond, Tom
LITTLE ODESSA
Rinzler, Lisa
DEAD PRESIDENTS
Roach, Neil
SUBSTITUTE WIFE, THE
Rocha, Claudio
PICTURE BRIDE
Roed, Jan
BETRAYAL
Roizman, Owen
FRENCH KISS
Rotunno, Giuseppe
SABRINA
Rowe, Ashley
SISTER MY SISTER
Ruiz-Anchia, Juan
TWO BITS
Ruzicka, Viktor
MARTHA AND I
Ryan, Ellery
DEATH IN BRUNSWICK
Saba, Farhad
THROUGH THE OLIVE TREES
Safavi, Iraj
JAR, THE
Salomon, Amnon
MANGLER, THE
Salzmann, Bernard
ANDROID AFFAIR, THE
BAD BLOOD
Sandtroen, Morton
COLORADO COWBOY: THE BRUCE FORD
STORY
Sarossy, Paul
EXOTICA
LOVE AND HUMAN REMAINS
Sasakibara, Yasushi
MYSTERY OF RAMPO, THE
Sayeed, Malik Hassan
CLOCKERS
Schliesser, Tobias
CANDYMAN: FAREWELL TO THE FLESH
Schliessler, Tobias
BULLETPROOF HEART
Schmidt, Ronn
LORD OF ILLUSIONS
Schreiber, Nancy
GIRL IN THE CADILLAC
Schwartzman, John
PYROMANIAC'S LOVE STORY, A
Seale, John
AMERICAN PRESIDENT, THE
BEYOND RANGOON
Sekula, Andrzej
ACROSS THE MOON
FOUR ROOMS
HACKERS

Semler, Dean
WATERWORLD
Serra, Eduardo
FUNNY BONES
GROSSE FATIGUE
Shams, Hamid
TIE-DIED: ROCK 'N' ROLL'S MOST
DEADICATED FANS
Shepard, Robert
BLACK IS ... BLACK AIN'T
Shlugleit, Eugene
3 NINJAS KNUCKLE UP
TWOGETHER
Sigel, Newton Thomas
USUAL SUSPECTS, THE
Simmons, Johnny
SHOW, THE
Simon, Gerard
SON OF THE SHARK, THE
Sinkovics, Geza
CREW, THE
Slovis, Michael
MALICIOUS
PARTY GIRL
Smith, Doyle
BODILY HARM
Smith, Gregg
COVER STORY
Smoot, Reed
OUT OF ANNIE'S PAST
Southon, Mike
ROOMMATES
RUN OF THE COUNTRY, THE
Sova, Peter
FATHERLAND
FEAST OF JULY
Spencer, James Lawrence
PREHYSTERIA! 3
Spiller, Michael
AMATEUR
SEARCH AND DESTROY
Spinotti, Dante
HEAT
QUICK AND THE DEAD, THE
Stapleton, Oliver
RESTORATION
Steiger, Ueli
BETTER OFF DEAD
JERKY BOYS: THE MOVIE, THE
NOW AND THEN
Stok, Witold
CENTURY
Storey, Michael
KURT VONNEGUT'S HARRISON
BERGERON
Sturup, Jens
FUN
Sudo, Shoei
WIZARD OF DARKNESS
Surtees, Bruce
STARS FELL ON HENRIETTA, THE
Suslov, Misha
PENTATHLON
Tammes, Fred
MAD LOVE
PRIEST
Tattersall, Gale
HIDEAWAY
TANK GIRL
VIRTUOSITY
Taylor, Ronnie
REDWOOD CURTAIN
Tedeschi, Tullio
VAMPIRES AND OTHER STEREOTYPES
Teran, Manuel
BEFORE THE RAIN
Thomson, Alex
SCARLET LETTER, THE

Thorin, Donald E.
ACE VENTURA: WHEN NATURE CALLS
BOYS ON THE SIDE
Tidy, Frank
BLACK FOX
STEAL BIG, STEAL LITTLE
Tijdink, Stef
METAL AND MELANCHOLY
Toll, John
BRAVEHEART
Tovoli, Luciano
KISS OF DEATH
Troll, Wyatt
BRIAN WILSON: I JUST WASN'T MADE
FOR THESE TIMES
Tufano, Brian
SHALLOW GRAVE
Tufano, Jeffery
JEFFREY
Tufty, Christopher
TO CROSS THE RUBICON
Urusevsky, Sergei
I AM CUBA
Vacano, Jost
SHOWGIRLS
Van de Sande, Theo
BUSHWHACKED
Van Haren Noman, Eric
TOO YOUNG TO DIE?
Van Oostrum, Kees
ENEMY WITHIN, THE
Van Ostrum, Kees
SEPARATE LIVES
Vanden Ende, Walther
FARINELLI
Velazquez, Elaine
BALLOT MEASURE 9
Vilsmaier, Joseph
STALINGRAD
Von Haller, Peter
STALINGRAD
Von Sternberg, Nicholas
AMERICAN COP
BODY SHOT
Vulpiani, Mario
CASTLE FREAK
Wages, William
GETTING OUT
Wagner, Ian C.
DARK DEALER
Wagner, Roy H.
NICK OF TIME
Wakeford, Kent
GHOST BRIGADE
Walling, Christopher
BLUE TIGER
DANGEROUS, THE
Wallner, Jack
MIAMI RHAPSODY
Ward, John
HEAVEN'S A DRAG
Weber, Alicia
BALLOT MEASURE 9
Weindler, Helge
NOBODY LOVES ME
Werdin, Egon
MUTE WITNESS
Wexler, Haskell
CANADIAN BACON
SECRET OF ROAN INISH, THE
Wilson, Ian
DOOMSDAY GUN
Winding, Andreas
NEA
Windon, Stephen
COUNTRY LIFE
Wiseman, Frederick
BALLET

Wolfe, Gerald
BALLISTIC
Wolski, Dariusz
CRIMSON TIDE
Wong, Arthur
EROTIQUE
Worrall, Bruce
CIRCUMSTANCES UNKNOWN
Wunstorf, Peter
DOUBLE HAPPINESS
Yang Lun
RED FIRECRACKER, GREEN
FIRECRACKER
Yeoman, Robert
COLDBLOODED
Yim, William
NAKED KILLER
Zhang Xiaoguang
WOODEN MAN'S BRIDE, THE
Zielinski, Jerzy
HOUSEGUEST
POWDER
Zsigmond, Vilmos
ASSASSINS
CROSSING GUARD, THE
Zunder, Kenneth
BYE BYE, LOVE
IT TAKES TWO

C0-PRODUCERS

Altmayer, Eric
HIGHLANDER: THE FINAL DIMENSION
Ashford, Carmen
SHOW, THE
Atanesjan, Alexander
MUTE WITNESS
Atkinson, Nicole
BLACK IS ... BLACK AIN'T
Avellan, Elizabeth
DESPERADO
Baer, Randy C.
BETTER OFF DEAD
Baker, W.E.
FRIDAY
Baldecchi, John
CUTTHROAT ISLAND
Balsan, Humbert
JEFFERSON IN PARIS
Baschet, Marc
BEFORE THE RAIN
Base, Ron
FIRST DEGREE
Beasley, William
SOMETHING TO TALK ABOUT
Bennett, Michael
DEAD PRESIDENTS
Bennett, Valerie
COMPANION, THE
Berenger, Tom
AVENGING ANGEL
Berg, Barry
BRADY BUNCH MOVIE, THE
CLUELESS
Bernstein, Stephen L.
JURY DUTY
Binder, Chuck
QUICK AND THE DEAD, THE
Blank, Lowell
STEAL BIG, STEAL LITTLE
Block, Bruce A.
FATHER OF THE BRIDE PART II
Block, Doug
JUPITER'S WIFE
Bolger, Tom
MOSAIC PROJECT, THE

Borg, Laurie
FUNNY BONES
SENSE AND SENSIBILITY
Bradley, Stephen
AILSA
Brick, Richard
ARIZONA DREAM
Briggs, Richard
WINGS OF COURAGE
Brightman, Adam
DEAD FUNNY
Brown, Stephen
OUTBREAK
SEVEN
Burdis, Ray
DEATH MACHINE
Calverts, Fred
ARABIAN KNIGHT
Cann, Nicole
BURNT BY THE SUN
Capp, Dixie J.
VAMPIRE IN BROOKLYN
Caracciolo, Jr., Joseph M.
COPYCAT
Carcassonne, Philippe
AUGUSTIN
Carness, Tracy
MAJOR PAYNE
Caroselli, Grazia
BETTER OFF DEAD
Carraro, Bill
WALKING DEAD, THE
Carreras, Raquel
DESTINY TURNS ON THE RADIO
Cazes, Jean
HIGHLANDER: THE FINAL DIMENSION
Chakler, David
VILLAGE OF THE DAMNED
Cheung, Leslie
PHANTOM LOVER, THE
Chisolm, David
BREACH OF CONDUCT
Clark, Jason
PENTATHLON
SUDDEN DEATH
Claybourne, Doug
MONEY TRAIN
Coatsworth, David
MIGHTY MORPHIN POWER RANGERS:
THE MOVIE
Cohen, Andy
IT TAKES TWO
Cohen, Dalisa
LITTLE PRINCESS, A
Cohen, Richard
SUDDEN DEATH
Colesberry, Robert
SCARLET LETTER, THE
Collett, Alexander
ASSASSINS
Cooke, Christopher
RHYTHM THIEF
Cooper, Stuart
BITTER VENGEANCE
Cracchiolo, Dan
ASSASSINS
Daigler, Gary
WILD BILL
Daly, James
HIGHLANDER: THE FINAL DIMENSION
Deane, Frederick
DIRTY MONEY
DeBenedictis, Paul
UNZIPPED
Desormeaux, Jean
NEVER TALK TO STRANGERS
DeWaay, Larry
ROB ROY

DeWitt, Elmo
ARMAGEDDON: THE FINAL CHALLENGE
Dickerson, III, Albert
CYBER BANDITS
Dietrich, Ralph S.
NEVER TALK TO STRANGERS
Diller, Steven
AMERICA'S DEADLIEST HOME VIDEO
Dumas-Zajdela, Frederique
BEFORE THE RAIN
Edwards, Rona
COMPANION, THE
Ellis, Riley Kathryn
HOUSEGUEST
Estabrook, Keith
UNZIPPED
Ettinger, Barbara
MARTHA & ETHEL
Everett, Gimel
VIRTUOSITY
Fisher, Todd
TWOGETHER
Folsey, George
GRUMPIER OLD MEN
Foster, Gary
JUST CAUSE
Foster, Penelope L.
OPERATION DUMBO DROP
Fottrell, Morgan Michael
HEAVYWEIGHTS
Franklin, Jeffrey
CASPER
Franklin, Spencer
BABYSITTER, THE
Friedman, Laura
IT TAKES TWO
Gallardo, Carlos
DESPERADO
Geiogamah, Hanay
LAKOTA WOMAN: SIEGE AT WOUNDED
KNEE
Gigliotti, Donna
RESTORATION
Glaser, Tamar E.
SKINNER
Glynn, Kathleen
CANADIAN BACON
Glynn, Victor
AWFULLY BIG ADVENTURE, AN
Goldfine, Phillip B.
KICKING AND SCREAMING
Goodman, George
JADE
Graham, Janet
HACKERS
Greenwald, Nana
OUTBREAK
SEVEN
Hadida, Victor
EXPERT, THE
Halfon, Neal
CRUMB
Halsted, Dan
NIXON
Hamburg, Eric
NIXON
Hansson, Borje
CITY UNPLUGGED
Harrington, Conor
AWFULLY BIG ADVENTURE, AN
Haugland, David
WORLD AND TIME ENOUGH
Hays, Buzz
SWIMMING WITH SHARKS
Heller, Richard M.
JURY DUTY

Hellerman, Paul
FOUR ROOMS
WHITE MAN'S BURDEN
Hersh, Andrew
EVOLVER
FRANK & JESSE
KICKING AND SCREAMING
KID IN KING ARTHUR'S COURT, A
SEPARATE LIVES
Hilliard, Margaret
RADIO INSIDE
Holzman, Edward
BODY STROKES
Isaac, Frank K.
DR. JEKYLL & MS. HYDE
Isaac, Sandy
TO DIE FOR
Jenkel, Brad
GHOST BRIGADE
Johnson, Bill
WALK IN THE CLOUDS, A
Jurgensen, Randy
NEW YORK COP
Katz, Alan
TALES FROM THE CRYPT: DEMON
KNIGHT
Kelly, Barbara
PYROMANIAC'S LOVE STORY, A
Kennedy, Tatiana
DALLAS DOLL
King, Rob
DECOY
Knell, Catalaine
TERESA'S TATTOO
Kokin, Kenneth
USUAL SUSPECTS, THE
Konrad, Cathy
KIDS
THINGS TO DO IN DENVER WHEN
YOU'RE DEAD
Korchok, David
FIRST DEGREE
Kuroiwa, Hisami
BLUE IN THE FACE
Kurta, Paul
EMPIRE RECORDS
La Marca, Andrew G.
ACE VENTURA: WHEN NATURE CALLS
Lambert, Scott
FOUR ROOMS
Landgraf, John
MAD LOVE
Lasker, Alex
BEYOND RANGOON
Lee, Damian
FUN
Lee, Deborah
MURDER IN THE FIRST
Lennon, Kathryn
AILSA
Lewis, Butch
OUT OF SYNC
Lexton, Alexandra
DIGGER
Lindeman, Doug
BAR GIRLS
Lowe, Rob
FRANK & JESSE
MacDonald, Michael
BYE BYE, LOVE
Maguire, Gerard
GROSS MISCONDUCT
Mann, Mary Beth
HARLEM DIARY: NINE VOICES OF
RESILIENCE
Marcus, Robert
DEAD FUNNY

Marmion, Yves
DOOM GENERATION, THE
Martin, Jonathon Komack
KID IN KING ARTHUR'S COURT, A
McCormick, Patrick
BOYS ON THE SIDE
McIntosh, Peter
ROSWELL: THE U.F.O. COVER-UP
McKeon, Don
TERESA'S TATTOO
McLaglen, Mary
MOONLIGHT AND VALENTINO
McLean, Steve
POSTCARDS FROM AMERICA
McLeod, Eric
NOW AND THEN
Mesa, William
GALAXIS
Moore, Leanne
WATER ENGINE, THE
Morgan, Leslie
TO DIE FOR
Murphy, Dennis
POWDER
Murphy, Jr., Ray
VAMPIRE IN BROOKLYN
Myron, Ben
SHOWGIRLS
Nasso, Julius R.
UNDER SIEGE 2: DARK TERRITORY
Nelson, Mike
S.F.W.
Nimerfro, Scott
TALES FROM THE CRYPT: DEMON
KNIGHT
Orent, Kerry
JOURNEY OF AUGUST KING, THE
LITTLE ODESSA
Ostrow, Randy
JERKY BOYS: THE MOVIE, THE
Paillard, Jerome
BLUE VILLA, THE
Panitch, Sanford
OUTBREAK
SEVEN
Parziale, Tom
WIGSTOCK: THE MOVIE
Peters, Lance
GROSS MISCONDUCT
Peterson, Clark
SECRETARY, THE
Phillips, Don
BLUE TIGER
PROPHECY, THE
Phillips, Lloyd
TWELVE MONKEYS
Piel, Jean-Louis
BURNT BY THE SUN
Pierreux, Jacqueline
BLUE VILLA, THE
Place, Graham
GET SHORTY
Plafsky, Joanna
LAST RIDE, THE
Podeswa, Jeremy
ECLIPSE
Price, Richard
CLOCKERS
KISS OF DEATH
Ramml, Wolfgang
BEFORE SUNRISE
Ramsey, Robert
DESTINY TURNS ON THE RADIO
Rath, A. John
INCREDIBLY TRUE ADVENTURES OF
TWO GIRLS IN LOVE, THE
Rehr, Christian L.
TANK GIRL

Reinhardt, Anna
JUST CAUSE
Reynolds, Raimond
BODY CHEMISTRY 4: FULL EXPOSURE
Riazhsky, Grigory
MUTE WITNESS
Robin, Helen
MIGHTY APHRODITE
Rubenstein, Bill
BEYOND RANGOON
Rudnick, Paul
JEFFREY
Ruey, Gerard
BLUE VILLA, THE
Saeta, Steve
LAKOTA WOMAN: SIEGE AT WOUNDED
KNEE
Sager, Ray
FIRST DEGREE
Sanders, Jack Frost
SUDDEN DEATH
Saunders, Earl A.
OUT OF SYNC
Savin, Jody
HOUSEGUEST
Schaffler, Gernot
BEFORE SUNRISE
Schamus, James
SENSE AND SENSIBILITY
Schlissel, Charles J.D.
HEAVYWEIGHTS
WHILE YOU WERE SLEEPING
Schneider, Daniel
KINGFISH: A STORY OF HUEY P. LONG
Schneier, Diane
CONVICT COWBOY
Schroeder, Adam
CLUELESS
Sedov, Vladimir
BURNT BY THE SUN
Segan, Allison Lyon
PYROMANIAC'S LOVE STORY, A
Seig, Matthew
GREAT DAY IN HARLEM, A
Shields, Brent
GETTING OUT
PIANO LESSON, THE
RETURN OF THE NATIVE, THE
Short, Trevor
LAST RIDE, THE
Shuman, Ira
STRANGE DAYS
Simmons, Rudd
NEW JERSEY DRIVE
Smith, Bette L.
ARABIAN KNIGHT
Smith, Diane
BURNING SEASON, THE
Smith, John J.
GRUMPIER OLD MEN
Smith, Suzanne
RADIO INSIDE
Solomon, Richard
ASSASSINS
FREE WILLY 2: THE ADVENTURE HOME
Spacey, Kevin
SWIMMING WITH SHARKS
Sperber, Elaine
DOOMSDAY GUN
Spinks, Lynwood
CUTTHROAT ISLAND
Steele, Michael
MONEY TRAIN
Stern, Tina
BABY-SITTERS CLUB, THE
Stone, Matthew
DESTINY TURNS ON THE RADIO

Stone, Robert
CITIZEN X
Stone, Sharon
QUICK AND THE DEAD, THE
Stone, Webster
CITIZEN X
Stremple, Susan
WHILE YOU WERE SLEEPING
Sussman, Peter
LOVE AND HUMAN REMAINS
Sweeney, David
WIGSTOCK: THE MOVIE
Thompson, Barnaby
TOMMY BOY
Topping, Jenno
BRADY BUNCH MOVIE, THE
Tozija, Gorjan
BEFORE THE RAIN
Trela, Christopher
REASON TO BELIEVE, A
Trodd, Kenith
CIRCLE OF FRIENDS
Turner, Ann
DALLAS DOLL
Upton, Mike
CRAZYSITTER, THE
Vachon, Christine
KIDS
Van Horn, Kelly
FORGET PARIS
Van Patten, James
BREAK, THE
Viola, Vincent
ME AND THE MOB
Viscidi, Marcus
MAD LOVE
Vogel, Heidi
FOUR ROOMS
Wanderman, Wendy
TALES FROM THE CRYPT: DEMON
KNIGHT
Waterman, Steve
CASPER
Watts, Helen
HOTEL SORRENTO
Weiner, Jane
JUPITER'S WIFE
Weinstein, Bob
RESTORATION
Weinstein, Harvey
RESTORATION
Wellington, Jacob
FEAR, THE
Wendl, Ellen Winn
BEFORE SUNRISE
Whitcher, Patricia
HOW TO MAKE AN AMERICAN QUILT
Williams, Cindy
FATHER OF THE BRIDE PART II
Williams, Dwight Alonzo
HIGHER LEARNING
Williams, Terry
HARLEM DIARY: NINE VOICES OF
RESILIENCE
Willis, David
DIE HARD WITH A VENGEANCE
Wisnievitz, David
BUSHWHACKED
Zalaznick, Lauren
KIDS
Zamsky, Meredith
LIVING IN OBLIVION
Zanitsch, Noel A.
SCANNERS: THE SHOWDOWN
SECRETARY, THE
Zimmerman, Ray
SPITFIRE

Zozzora, Carmine
DIE HARD WITH A VENGEANCE

COSTUMES

Acheson, James
RESTORATION
Ahluwalia, Dolly
BANDIT QUEEN
Akaji, Ada
PICTURE BRIDE
Allyson, Dana
MALLRATS
PROPHECY, THE
Anacker, Kristen
COVER ME
UNDERNEATH, THE
Anthony, Craig
RED SUN RISING
Appel, Deena
NOW AND THEN
REFLECTIONS IN THE DARK
Arthur, Jacqueline C.
SEPARATE LIVES
Astrom-De Fina, Marianna
NINA TAKES A LOVER
Aulisi, Joseph G.
DIE HARD WITH A VENGEANCE
Auth, Victoria
BREACH OF CONDUCT
Bafaloukos, Eugenie
MAD LOVE
Baker, Maxine
BULLETPROOF HEART
Bardon, Antonia
FAR FROM HOME: THE ADVENTURES OF
YELLOW DOG
Barton, Shawn
FRIDAY
Baskerville, Derek
DECOY
Bass, Linda
NET, THE
Beavan, Jenny
JEFFERSON IN PARIS
SENSE AND SENSIBILITY
Beraldo, Elisabetta
FLUKE
Berg, Eric
BIGFOOT: THE UNFORGETTABLE
ENCOUNTER
Berger, Caren
OUTSIDE THE LAW
Bergin, Joan
AWFULLY BIG ADVENTURE, AN
FRANKIE STARLIGHT
Berlutti, Olga
FARINELLI
Bernay, Lynn
DECONSTRUCTING SARAH
Bertram, Susan
BODY SHOT
FOUR ROOMS
Bloomfield, John
WATERWORLD
Bodford, Jr., Robert Eli
IN THE DEEP WOODS
Bordone, Beatrice
PURE FORMALITY, A
Borg, Dominique
LES MISERABLES
Boulton, Tracey
CRACKERJACK
Bowers, Marjorie
GETTING OUT
Boyd, Mike
CLASS OF '61

Boyle, Consolata
SECRET OF ROAN INISH, THE
Branco, Isabel
CONVENT, THE
VALLEY OF ABRAHAM, THE
Bridges, Mark
CHILDREN OF THE CORN III: URBAN
HARVEST
Bright, John
JEFFERSON IN PARIS
SENSE AND SENSIBILITY
Bronson, Tom
MAN OF THE HOUSE
Brown, Claudia
BLUE IN THE FACE
COPYCAT
SMOKE
TWO BITS
Brown, Winnie
OUT OF SYNC
Bruno, Richard
UNDER SIEGE 2: DARK TERRITORY
Bryan, Jennifer L.
MAJOR PAYNE
Bryant, Janie
BLESSING
Budin, Jackie
HIGHLANDER: THE FINAL DIMENSION
Burton, Roger
HACKERS
Busalacchi, Shelley
SPITFIRE
Bush, Robert
IN THE MOUTH OF MADNESS
Bush, Robin Michel
IN THE MOUTH OF MADNESS
Butler, Helen
DILLINGER
Byrne, Alexander
PERSUASION
Cacavas, Lisa
BAD BLOOD
Carin, Kate
SHALLOW GRAVE
Carter, Nina
RHYTHM THIEF
Carter, Ruth
CLOCKERS
MONEY TRAIN
Castro, Eduardo
PEREZ FAMILY, THE
Cecchi, Nana
FIRST KNIGHT
Centuri, John
COVER STORY
Cerf, Michele
NEA
Chan, Marjorie
AMAZING PANDA ADVENTURE, THE
Chan, Shirley
NAKED KILLER
Chang, William
PHANTOM LOVER, THE
Cheminal, Mic
SIX DAYS, SIX NIGHTS
Chen Changmin
RED FIRECRACKER, GREEN
FIRECRACKER
Chuck, Wendy
COUNTRY LIFE
Clancy, Michael
LITTLE ODESSA
PARTY GIRL
Clevenger, Morgan
DANGEROUS, THE
Collie, Stephanie
DEATH MACHINE

Cooper-Thoman, Catherine
DOOM GENERATION, THE
Corstens, Bernadette
BLUE VILLA, THE
Cox, Betsy
COMPANION, THE
POWDER
WHILE YOU WERE SLEEPING
Cranstoun, Caroline
CRACKERJACK
Cronenberg, Denise
MOONLIGHT AND VALENTINO
Culotta, Sandra
MY ANTONIA
Cunliffe, Shay
DOLORES CLAIBORNE
INDICTMENT: THE MCMARTIN TRIAL
Cwiklo, Hanna
SHORT FILM ABOUT KILLING, A
SHORT FILM ABOUT LOVE, A
Dare, Daphne
CENTURY
Davis, Rondi Hillstrom
BIG GREEN, THE
Davis, Sharen
DEVIL IN A BLUE DRESS
YOUNGER & YOUNGER
ZOOMAN
de Gaye, Phoebe
FEAST OF JULY
de la Fontaine, Jacqueline
CREW, THE
de Laugardiere, Anne
FARINELLI
De Vivaise, Caroline
MY LIFE AND TIMES WITH ANTONIN
ARTAUD
DeCaro, Charles
BAD COMPANY
DeLaval, Susan
DIGGER
DeSanto, Susie
BABY-SITTERS CLUB, THE
STUART SAVES HIS FAMILY
DeThelismond, Yvens
REASON TO BELIEVE, A
Devau, Marie-Sylvie
KURT VONNEGUT'S HARRISON
BERGERON
Deveau, Marie-Bylvie
BILLY MADISON
Dimitrov, Olga
JOHNNY MNEMONIC
Donahue, Linda
ROOMMATES
Dresbach, Terry
JURY DUTY
NEVER TALK TO STRANGERS
Druce, Kim
KIDS
ME AND THE MOB
Du Longxi
WOODEN MAN'S BRIDE, THE
Duenas, Miriam
STRAWBERRY AND CHOCOLATE
Dunn, John
CASINO
JERKY BOYS: THE MOVIE, THE
LAKOTA WOMAN: SIEGE AT WOUNDED
KNEE
Elias, Reynaldo
BOCA
Engelsman, Julie Rae
DARK SIDE OF GENIUS, THE
Eshelman, Melinda
ADDICTION, THE

Espinoza, Charmian
SCANNERS: THE SHOWDOWN
SECRETARY, THE
Evans, Leesa
SILENCE OF THE HAMS
Everberg, Kirsten
DON JUAN DEMARCO
SWIMMING WITH SHARKS
Excoffier, Stephane
MINA TANNENBAUM
Fakhry-Smith, Camila
GRANNY, THE
Feldman, Shari
TOO YOUNG TO DIE?
Ferrin, Ingrid
BABYSITTER, THE
BATMAN FOREVER
BORN TO BE WILD
Fiddler, Rina Ramon
SPY WITHIN, THE
Field, Patricia
MIAMI RHAPSODY
Filipe, Ruy
CRY, THE BELOVED COUNTRY
Finkelman, Wayne
TALL TALE: THE UNBELIEVABLE
ADVENTURES OF PECOS BILL
Finlayson, Bruce
CANDYMAN: FAREWELL TO THE FLESH
Flood, Barbara
LAST SUMMER IN THE HAMPTONS
Flower-Crow, Verkina
TOP DOG
Flynt, Cynthia
ACROSS THE SEA OF TIME: NEW YORK
3D
Ford, Roger
BABE
Fort, Mary Jane
KICKING AND SCREAMING
Foster, Glenis
MEET THE FEEBLES
Fraisse, Claire
I CAN'T SLEEP
France, Marie
TOM AND HUCK
Francis, Joan
CAGED HEARTS
Frankova, Maria
MARTHA AND I
Friedman, Vicki
DEATH IN BRUNSWICK
Frogley, Louise
CURE, THE
DANGER OF LOVE
FAIR GAME
Fusaro, Valarie
RADIO INSIDE
Galan, Graciela
I, THE WORST OF ALL
Gaultier, Jean-Paul
CITY OF LOST CHILDREN, THE
Gayraud, Pierre-Yves
TOTAL ECLIPSE
Gilmore, Aline
ECLIPSE
Gissi, Gianni
POSTMAN, THE
Glynn, Kathleen
CANADIAN BACON
Goldsmith, Laura
LEAVING LAS VEGAS
Gray, Tricia
OPERATION INTERCEPT
Greenhill, Jacqui W.
RADIO INSIDE

Gresham, Gloria
AMERICAN PRESIDENT, THE
BOYS ON THE SIDE
Haders, Nadine
BODY CHEMISTRY 4: FULL EXPOSURE
Hannan, Mary Claire
FOUR ROOMS
Harris, Caroline
BEFORE THE RAIN
OTHELLO
Harris, Enid
FATHER OF THE BRIDE PART II
Harwood, Shuna
RICHARD III
Heimann, Betsy
GET SHORTY
TIE THAT BINDS, THE
Hemming, Lindy
FUNNY BONES
GOLDENEYE
SISTER MY SISTER
Hernandez, Scillia A.
3 NINJAS KNUCKLE UP
Hicklin, Walker
RECKLESS
Hofinger, Ute
STALINGRAD
Hood, Rosalea
DALLAS DOLL
Hornung, Richard
NIXON
Howe, Monica
LAMB
Hruby, Maria
CITIZEN X
KID IN KING ARTHUR'S COURT, A
Hui, Ann
DAY THE SUN TURNED COLD, THE
Hurley, Jay
NINE MONTHS
Hurwitz, Cheryl
INCREDIBLY TRUE ADVENTURES OF
TWO GIRLS IN LOVE, THE
Hyde, Derek
RETURN OF THE NATIVE, THE
Ito, Sachico
MYSTERY OF RAMPO, THE
Ivanova, Natalia
BURNT BY THE SUN
Jacobs, Monica
DEADLY MARIA
Jacobsen, Matthew
COLDBLOODED
GHOST BRIGADE
Jamison-Tanchuck, Francine
VIRTUOSITY
Jean Desses of Paris
OH ... ROSALINDA!!
Jensen, Judi
BALLISTIC
Jensen, Lisa
GRUMPIER OLD MEN
Jenyon, Elizabeth
PUSHING HANDS
Jimenez, Jolie
EROTIQUE
Johnson, Jacqueline
TWOGETHER
Johnston, Joanna
FRENCH KISS
Johnston, Renee
FUN
Jones, Gary
JUST CAUSE
Jones-Faison, Violette
COSMIC SLOP

Kalfus, Renee Ehrlich
DEAD MAN WALKING
SAFE PASSAGE
Kalinian, Maral
MIDNIGHT TEASE 2
Kammerer, Siegbert
NOBODY LOVES ME
Kane, Michael
ONCE WERE WARRIORS
Kaplan, Michael
SEVEN
Kay, Petra
PROMISE, THE
Keating, Trish
BROKEN TRUST
Kelly, Bridget
PYROMANIAC'S LOVE STORY, A
Kelsall, Colleen
BRIDGES OF MADISON COUNTY, THE
Kitos, Emily Jane
EXPERT, THE
Klein, Beverly
DESTINY TURNS ON THE RADIO
Klindtwordt, Susann
EROTIQUE
Knode, Charles
BRAVEHEART
Komarov, Shelley
THREE WISHES
Kondos, Aphrodite
GROSS MISCONDUCT
Kramer
BEYOND RANGOON
Kramer, Barbara
ME AND THE MOB
Kreiner, Jillian
PLAY TIME
Kurland, Jeffrey
MIGHTY APHRODITE
La Gorce, Deborah
BEYOND RANGOON
Lambert, Anne
HALLOWEEN: THE CURSE OF MICHAEL
MYERS
Landry, Noreen
DARKMAN 2: THE RETURN OF DURANT
Lane, Barbara
FATHERLAND
Lapper, Vincent
NUMBER ONE FAN
Lavery, Gwen
ATTACK OF THE 60-FOOT CENTERFOLD
Lawson, Merrie
BODY STROKES
Leamon, Ron
TO CROSS THE RUBICON
Lednicky, Tanela
DARK DEALER
Lester, Dan
SUDDEN DEATH
Leterrier, Catherine
OLD LADY WHO WALKED IN THE SEA,
THE
Libby, P. Zjene
CYBER BANDITS
Lisle, David
POWER OF ATTORNEY
Little, George
CRIMSON TIDE
Liu Qingli
ERMO
Lloyd, Fred
DON JUAN DEMARCO
Long, Fred
GREAT ELEPHANT ESCAPE, THE
Luk Ha-Fong
ASHES OF TIME

Lutter, Ellen
LIVING IN OBLIVION
Luzanova, Svetlana
MUTE WITNESS
Lyall, Susan
EMPIRE RECORDS
HOME FOR THE HOLIDAYS
Madden, Betty
WATER ENGINE, THE
Madden, Betty Pecha
FRANK & JESSE
Maginnis, Molly
DR. JEKYLL & MS. HYDE
Makovsky, Judianna
LITTLE PRINCESS, A
QUICK AND THE DEAD, THE
Malin, Marv
LOSING ISAIAH
Mancini, Tiziana
CASTLE FREAK
Matthews, Marilyn
CONGO
May, Mona
CLUELESS
NATIONAL LAMPOON'S ATTACK OF THE
5'2" WOMEN
Mazabraud, Jean-Louis
PIGALLE
Mazon, Graciela
DESPERADO
McBride, Elizabeth
ASSASSINS
McCarthy, Dennis
PREHYSTERIA! 3
McCartney, Ellen
ROY COHN/JACK SMITH
McCartney, Margot
ONLY THE BRAVE
McConaghy, Resa
FIRST DEGREE
McGuiness, Molly
IT TAKES TWO
McGuire, Debra
NEXT DOOR
S.F.W.
McKiou, Patricia
JACK-O
McLeod, Mary
GOLD DIGGERS: THE SECRET OF BEAR
MOUNTAIN
Meagher, Lisa
HOTEL SORRENTO
Melton, Giovanna Ottobre
ACROSS THE MOON
Meltzer, Ileane
WALKING DEAD, THE
Meyer, Moira
FRIENDS
Meyer, Moira Anne
MANGLER, THE
Miller, Robert
GALAXIS
Miller, Vicki
CREEP
Mills, Caroline
HOWLING: NEW MOON RISING, THE
Mingenbach, Louise
USUAL SUSPECTS, THE
Mirojnick, Ellen
SHOWGIRLS
STRANGE DAYS
Moder, Jyl
HOUSEGUEST
Moore, Dan
WILD BILL
Moore, Robert
BITTER VENGEANCE
OUT OF ANNIE'S PAST

Morandini, Lia
MONTH BY THE LAKE, A
Moriarty, Prudence
NADJA
Morrison, Kathryn
CURSE OF THE STARVING CLASS
Muir, Linda
EXOTICA
WHEN NIGHT IS FALLING
Murray, Abigail
THINGS TO DO IN DENVER WHEN
YOU'RE DEAD
Murray-Walsh, Merrily
KINGFISH: A STORY OF HUEY P. LONG
Mussenden, Isis
WHITE MAN'S BURDEN
Myers, Ruth
HOW TO MAKE AN AMERICAN QUILT
Neil, Warden
TALES FROM THE CRYPT: DEMON
KNIGHT
Ng Leilou
HE'S A WOMAN, SHE'S A MAN
Nguyen, Ha
MORTAL KOMBAT
VAMPIRE IN BROOKLYN
Nicholls, Tiny
DOOMSDAY GUN
Nieradzik, Anushia
CENTURY
CIRCLE OF FRIENDS
Niskiewicz, Ludwika
PROVINCIAL ACTORS
Norris, Patricia
JOURNEY OF AUGUST KING, THE
Norton, Rosanna
BRADY BUNCH MOVIE, THE
CASPER
OPERATION DUMBO DROP
Nyquist-Patton, Eleanor
JUDICIAL CONSENT
Obloza, Malgorzata
SHORT FILM ABOUT KILLING, A
SHORT FILM ABOUT LOVE, A
Oditz, Carol
BETTER OFF DEAD
GEORGIA
HIGHER LEARNING
Ohanneson, Jill
ANGUS
CROSSING GUARD, THE
UNSTRUNG HEROES
Ohanneson, Jill M.
ARIZONA DREAM
Olah, Thomas
FOR GOD AND COUNTRY
Palmer, Barbara
BODILY HARM
Parsons, Jennifer
REDWOOD CURTAIN
Partridge, Wendy
BLACK FOX
CONVICT COWBOY
GOOD DAY TO DIE, A
Pasternak, Beth
DANCE ME OUTSIDE
Pasztor, Beatrix Aruna
TO DIE FOR
Pecharova, Jaroslava
ACCUMULATOR 1
Pescucci, Gabriella
SCARLET LETTER, THE
Phillips, Arianne
TANK GIRL
Phillips, Erica Edell
FREE WILLY 2: THE ADVENTURE HOME
OUTBREAK

Pollack, Leonard
CREW, THE
Popienko, Dena
KILIAN'S CHRONICLE
Porro, Joseph
MIGHTY MORPHIN POWER RANGERS:
THE MOVIE
Porteous, Emma
JUDGE DREDD
Powell, Sandy
ROB ROY
Prudhomme, Monique
HIDEAWAY
MAGIC IN THE WATER
Purdy, Sharon
NATIONAL LAMPOON'S SENIOR TRIP
Ramsey, Van Broughton
BUFFALO GIRLS
STARS FELL ON HENRIETTA, THE
SUBSTITUTE WIFE, THE
Rand, Tom
BUSINESS AFFAIR, A
INNOCENT LIES
Ray, Lalita
STRANGER, THE
Read, Bobbie
BAD BOYS
DANGEROUS MINDS
Reicher, Robyn
ALMOST DEAD
Reichle, Luke
LORD OF ILLUSIONS
Richards, Reve
FEAR, THE
Riggs, Rita
HUNTED, THE
Ringwood, Bob
BATMAN FOREVER
Robinson, David C.
BASKETBALL DIARIES, THE
Rodgers, Aggie
WINGS OF COURAGE
Rodgers, Aggie Guerard
SOMETHING TO TALK ABOUT
Rose, Penny
CARRINGTON
Rosenberg, Sharon
GALAXIS
Roth, Ann
JUST CAUSE
SABRINA
Routh, May
ROSWELL: THE U.F.O. COVER-UP
Rowe, David
TRAPS
Ruskin, Judy
FORGET PARIS
WAITING TO EXHALE
WALK IN THE CLOUDS, A
Ryack, Rita
APOLLO 13
CASINO
Ryan, Terry
MURIEL'S WEDDING
Ryrie, Elizabeth
ASCENT, THE
Sabbatini, Enrico
CUTTHROAT ISLAND
Sams, Houston
BAR GIRLS
Sanchez, Vicki
PIANO LESSON, THE
Sapunova, Andzhela
CREATION OF ADAM
Schuve, Joyce
BOULEVARD

Scott, Deborah L.
  HEAT
  INDIAN IN THE CUPBOARD, THE
Sequeira, Luis
  ANDROID AFFAIR, THE
Shannon-Burnett, Gaye
  GLASS SHIELD, THE
Shemanek, Kathryn
  BLUE TIGER
Shepard, Dodie
  DRACULA: DEAD AND LOVING IT
Shissler, Richard
  BAD COMPANY
Simmons, Paul A.
  DEAD PRESIDENTS
  PANTHER
Sinling, Yeung
  PHANTOM LOVER, THE
Slotnick, Sara
  DEAD FUNNY
  POSTCARDS FROM AMERICA
  RIVER OF GRASS
Smetanova, Jana
  COW, THE
Snetsinger, Martha Wynne
  JUMANJI
Sotira, Liliana
  LAMERICA
Spargo, Louise
  SUM OF US, THE
Sperdouklis, Denis
  LOVE AND HUMAN REMAINS
Spragge, Clare
  ROB ROY
Stauch, Bonnie
  UNDERCOVER
Stavros, John
  SKINNER
Steiner, Nancy
  SAFE
Stewart, Marlene
  TO WONG FOO, THANKS FOR
    EVERYTHING! JULIE NEWMAR
Still, Jane
  DOUBLE, DOUBLE, TOIL AND TROUBLE
Summers, Cynthia
  CIRCUMSTANCES UNKNOWN
  DOUBLE HAPPINESS
Summers, Ray
  BURNING SEASON, THE
Sundeen, Maria
  CRAZYSITTER, THE
Swaryn, David
  NEW YORK COP
Sy, Oumou
  HYENAS
Tavernier, Elisabeth
  GROSSE FATIGUE
  WILD REEDS
Taylor, Jill
  PRIEST
Tenaglia, Claudia
  LAMERICA
Tierney, Marie
  AILSA
Tillen, Jodie
  STEAL BIG, STEAL LITTLE
Tillman, Kimberly
  HEAVYWEIGHTS
  LAST GOOD TIME, THE
Tilloy, Quenby
  MUTANT SPECIES
Tompkins, Joe I.
  SPECIES
Tong Huamiao
  SHANGHAI TRIAD
Tynan, Tracy
  MY FAMILY: MI FAMILIA

Unger, Patti
  TOMMY BOY
Van Runkle, Theadora
  KISS OF DEATH
Vance, Marilyn
  JADE
Vega-Vasquez, Sylvia
  MURDER IN THE FIRST
Viennings, Pierre
  ARMAGEDDON: THE FINAL CHALLENGE
Villa, Jose Manuel
  UP TO A CERTAIN POINT
Vogt, Mary E.
  NICK OF TIME
Vukasovic-Madenica, Marina
  GORILLA BATHES AT NOON
Wagner, Cathryn
  GIRL IN THE CADILLAC
Wagner, Karyn
  UNDERNEATH, THE
Waite, Barcie
  GORDY
Wakefield, Louise
  NOSTRADAMUS KID, THE
Wallace, Ross
  DESPERATE PREY
Wallstrom, Lenamari
  DREAMING OF RITA
Walsh, Denise
  BREAK, THE
Weiss, Julie
  TWELVE MONKEYS
Welker, Alexander
  AMATEUR
Welker, Alexandra
  DIRTY MONEY
  PENTATHLON
Welley, Florentina
  BEFORE SUNRISE
Westwood, Vivienne
  LEAVING LAS VEGAS
Wetherbee, Amy
  BIGFOOT: THE UNFORGETTABLE
    ENCOUNTER
White, Bernie
  O.J. SIMPSON STORY, THE
Williams, Shirlene
  COSMIC SLOP
Woods, Dana R.
  EMBRACE OF THE VAMPIRE
Woolard, David C.
  JEFFREY
Wyman, Tami Mor
  SPY WITHIN, THE
Yabara, Yoshio
  PROMISE, THE
Yates, Janty
  ENGLISHMAN WHO WENT UP A HILL
    BUT CAME DOWN A MOUNTAIN, THE
Yelland, Sue
  BEFORE THE RAIN
Yoon, Seok Halley
  FATHER AND SCOUT
Yu, Bruce
  HEROIC TRIO, THE
Zakowska, Donna
  SEARCH AND DESTROY
Zamakhina, Natalya
  WINDOW TO PARIS
Zamparelli, Elsa
  ACE VENTURA: WHEN NATURE CALLS
  AVENGING ANGEL
  LAST OF THE DOGMEN
Zophres, Mary
  BUSHWHACKED
Zore, Ingrid
  INNOCENT, THE

DIRECTORS

Ackerman, Robert Allan
  SAFE PASSAGE
Adams, Daniel
  FOOL AND HIS MONEY, A
Adlon, Percy
  YOUNGER & YOUNGER
Alexander, Tom
  DARK DEALER
Allen, Debbie
  OUT OF SYNC
Allen, Woody
  MIGHTY APHRODITE
Almereyda, Michael
  NADJA
Amelio, Gianni
  LAMERICA
Amiel, John
  COPYCAT
Anders, Allison
  FOUR ROOMS
Anderson, Paul
  MORTAL KOMBAT
Annaud, Jean-Jacques
  WINGS OF COURAGE
Anspaugh, David
  MOONLIGHT AND VALENTINO
Apted, Michael
  MOVING THE MOUNTAIN
Araki, Gregg
  DOOM GENERATION, THE
Arau, Alfonso
  WALK IN THE CLOUDS, A
Arcand, Denys
  LOVE AND HUMAN REMAINS
Ashley, Christopher
  JEFFREY
Auster, Paul
  BLUE IN THE FACE
Avancini, Walter
  BOCA
Avery, Rick
  EXPERT, THE
Bach, Jean
  GREAT DAY IN HARLEM, A
Badgely, Christiane
  BLACK IS ... BLACK AIN'T
Badham, John
  NICK OF TIME
Baker, Mark
  SPIKE AND MIKE'S FESTIVAL OF
    ANIMATION '95
Balaban, Bob
  LAST GOOD TIME, THE
Baran, Jack
  DESTINY TURNS ON THE RADIO
Barba, Norberto
  BLUE TIGER
Barker, Clive
  LORD OF ILLUSIONS
Barnett, Steve
  SCANNERS: THE SHOWDOWN
Barnette, M. Neema
  BETTER OFF DEAD
Bass, Kim
  BALLISTIC
Baumbach, Noah
  KICKING AND SCREAMING
Baxley, Craig R.
  AVENGING ANGEL
  DECONSTRUCTING SARAH
Bay, Michael
  BAD BOYS
Beeman, Greg
  BUSHWHACKED

Behar, Andrew
TIE-DIED: ROCK 'N' ROLL'S MOST
DEADICATED FANS
Bell, Jeffrey
RADIO INSIDE
Bemberg, Maria Luisa
I, THE WORST OF ALL
Benayoun, Robert
SERIOUS ABOUT PLEASURE
Bennett, Edward
WOMAN AT WAR, A
Bercovici, Luca
GRANNY, THE
Berger, Pamela
KILIAN'S CHRONICLE
Bigelow, Kathryn
STRANGE DAYS
Bill, Tony
NEXT DOOR
Bindley, William
JUDICIAL CONSENT
Bird, Antonia
MAD LOVE
PRIEST
Blakemore, Michael
COUNTRY LIFE
Blanc, Michel
GROSSE FATIGUE
Blank, Jonathan
SEX, DRUGS AND DEMOCRACY
Bluth, Don
PEBBLE AND THE PENGUIN, THE
Bonengel, Winfried
PROFESSION: NEO-NAZI
Boorman, John
BEYOND RANGOON
Borden, Lizzie
EROTIQUE
Boris, Robert
FRANK & JESSE
Borsos, Phillip
FAR FROM HOME: THE ADVENTURES OF
YELLOW DOG
Boyle, Danny
SHALLOW GRAVE
Brand, Joshua
PYROMANIAC'S LOVE STORY, A
Brandstrom, Charlotte
BUSINESS AFFAIR, A
Breathnach, Paddy
AILSA
Breen, Julian
PREHYSTERIA! 3
Brill, Steven
HEAVYWEIGHTS
Brooks, Mel
DRACULA: DEAD AND LOVING IT
Bruce, James
DIRTY MONEY
Buitenhuis, Penelope
BOULEVARD
Burnett, Charles
GLASS SHIELD, THE
Burns, Edward
BROTHERS MCMULLEN, THE
Burton, Geoff
SUM OF US, THE
Buttgereit, Jorg
NEKROMANTIK
Butts, Darren
SPIKE AND MIKE'S FESTIVAL OF
ANIMATION '95
Caillier, Barry
TO CROSS THE RUBICON
Cain, Chris
AMAZING PANDA ADVENTURE, THE
Campbell, Martin
GOLDENEYE

Cannon, Danny
JUDGE DREDD
Carlei, Carlo
FLUKE
Caro, Marc
CITY OF LOST CHILDREN, THE
Carpenter, John
IN THE MOUTH OF MADNESS
VILLAGE OF THE DAMNED
Castle, Nick
MAJOR PAYNE
Caton-Jones, Michael
ROB ROY
Cederberg, Bjorn
BETRAYAL
Chan, Pauline
TRAPS
Chan, Peter
HE'S A WOMAN, SHE'S A MAN
Chan, Teddy
TWENTY SOMETHING
Chappelle, Joe
HALLOWEEN: THE CURSE OF MICHAEL
MYERS
Charr, Henri
CAGED HEARTS
Chechik, Jeremiah
TALL TALE: THE UNBELIEVABLE
ADVENTURES OF PECOS BILL
Chelsom, Peter
FUNNY BONES
Chiaramonte, Andrew
TWOGETHER
Ching Siu-Tung
EXECUTIONERS
HEROIC TRIO, THE
Chiu, Yen-Pin
SHAO LIN POPEYE
Chopra, Joyce
DANGER OF LOVE
Choy, Christine
IN THE NAME OF THE EMPEROR
Clark, Larry
KIDS
Clokey, Art
GUMBY: THE MOVIE
Colcord, Webster
TOO OUTRAGEOUS ANIMATION
Collins, Boon
ABDUCTED 2: THE REUNION
Colpaert, Carl-Jan
CREW, THE
Columbus, Chris
NINE MONTHS
Condon, Bill
CANDYMAN: FAREWELL TO THE FLESH
Coolidge, Martha
THREE WISHES
Cooper, Stuart
BITTER VENGEANCE
OUT OF ANNIE'S PAST
Corbiau, Gerard
FARINELLI
Correll, Charles
IN THE DEEP WOODS
Corson, Ian
MALICIOUS
Craven, Wes
VAMPIRE IN BROOKLYN
Crawford, Wayne
AMERICAN COP
Crystal, Billy
FORGET PARIS
Cuaron, Alfonso
LITTLE PRINCESS, A
Cundieff, Rusty
TALES FROM THE HOOD

Cypher, Julie
TERESA'S TATTOO
Dante, Maria
DANGEROUS, THE
Darby, Jonathan
ENEMY WITHIN, THE
Dargay, Attila
ADVENTURES OF MATT THE
GOOSEBOY, THE
Davidson, Boaz
OUTSIDE THE LAW
Davis, Andrew
STEAL BIG, STEAL LITTLE
Davis, Tamra
BILLY MADISON
de Clercq, Dimitri
BLUE VILLA, THE
de Oliveira, Manoel
CONVENT, THE
VALLEY OF ABRAHAM, THE
de Wit, Michael Dudock
SPIKE AND MIKE'S FESTIVAL OF
ANIMATION '95
Denis, Claire
I CAN'T SLEEP
Deutch, Howard
GRUMPIER OLD MEN
Deville, Michel
VOYAGE EN DOUCE
Dewolf, Patrick
INNOCENT LIES
DiCillo, Tom
LIVING IN OBLIVION
Dickerson, Ernest
TALES FROM THE CRYPT: DEMON
KNIGHT
DNA Productions
TOO OUTRAGEOUS ANIMATION
Dobson, Kevin James
GOLD DIGGERS: THE SECRET OF BEAR
MOUNTAIN
Donaldson, Roger
SPECIES
Donner, Richard
ASSASSINS
Dorrie, Doris
NOBODY LOVES ME
Dowling, Kevin
SUM OF US, THE
Dridi, Karim
PIGALLE
Dugowson, Martine
MINA TANNENBAUM
Duigan, John
JOURNEY OF AUGUST KING, THE
Dylewska, Jolanta
CHRONICLE OF THE WARSAW GHETTO
UPRISING ACCORDING TO MAREK
EDELMAN
Eastwood, Clint
BRIDGES OF MADISON COUNTY, THE
Ecare, Desire
FACES OF WOMEN
Egoyan, Atom
EXOTICA
Einstein, Cassandra
TOO OUTRAGEOUS ANIMATION
Elgort, Arthur
COLORADO COWBOY: THE BRUCE FORD
STORY
Ellis, Bob
NOSTRADAMUS KID, THE
Elmar, Luis
ADVENTURES OF MATT THE
GOOSEBOY, THE
Eubanks, Corey Michael
BIGFOOT: THE UNFORGETTABLE
ENCOUNTER

Feldman, John
DEAD FUNNY
Ferguson, Michael
GLORY BOYS, THE
Ferland, Guy
BABYSITTER, THE
Ferrara, Abel
ADDICTION, THE
Feuer, Donya
DANCER, THE
Figgis, Mike
LEAVING LAS VEGAS
Fincher, David
SEVEN
Fine, David
SPIKE AND MIKE'S FESTIVAL OF
ANIMATION '95
Fleder, Gary
COMPANION, THE
THINGS TO DO IN DENVER WHEN
YOU'RE DEAD
Fleming, Erik
CYBER BANDITS
Fok Yiu Leung
NAKED KILLER
Foley, James
TWO BITS
Fontaine, Anne
AUGUSTIN
Fortenberry, John
JURY DUTY
Foruzesh, Ebrahim
JAR, THE
Foster, Jodie
HOME FOR THE HOLIDAYS
Frankel, David
MIAMI RHAPSODY
Frankenheimer, John
BURNING SEASON, THE
Franklin, Carl
DEVIL IN A BLUE DRESS
Franklin, Richard
HOTEL SORRENTO
Freeman, Jerrold
O.J. SIMPSON STORY, THE
Friedkin, William
JADE
Gabriel, Mike
POCAHONTAS
Garcia, Michael
ARMAGEDDON: THE FINAL CHALLENGE
Geralmo, Chris
CITIZEN X
Gerber, Fred
RENT-A-KID
Gibson, Mel
BRAVEHEART
Gilliam, Terry
TWELVE MONKEYS
Gionala, Vincenzo
TOO OUTRAGEOUS ANIMATION
Giovanni, Marita
BAR GIRLS
Glatter, Lesli Linka
NOW AND THEN
Glimcher, Arne
JUST CAUSE
Godard, Jean-Luc
JLG BY JLG
Godmilow, Jill
ROY COHN/JACK SMITH
Gold, Jack
RETURN OF THE NATIVE, THE
Goldberg, Eric
POCAHONTAS
Golfus, Billy
WHEN BILLY BROKE HIS HEAD ... AND
OTHER TALES OF WONDER

Gomez, Nick
NEW JERSEY DRIVE
Gordon, Stuart
CASTLE FREAK
Gottlieb, Lisa
ACROSS THE MOON
Gottlieb, Michael
KID IN KING ARTHUR'S COURT, A
Goursaud, Anne
EMBRACE OF THE VAMPIRE
Graves, Alex
CRUDE OASIS, THE
Gray, F. Gary
FRIDAY
Gray, James
LITTLE ODESSA
Gray, John
BORN TO BE WILD
Greeen, David
GOOD DAY TO DIE, A
Gregg, Colin
LAMB
Greggio, Ezio
SILENCE OF THE HAMS
Grimshaw, Mike
TOO OUTRAGEOUS ANIMATION
Grodecki, Wiktor
NOT ANGELS BUT ANGELS
Grosbard, Ulu
GEORGIA
Gutierrez Alea, Tomas
STRAWBERRY AND CHOCOLATE
UP TO A CERTAIN POINT
Gyllenhaal, Stephen
LOSING ISAIAH
Hackford, Taylor
DOLORES CLAIBORNE
Hall, Peter
NEVER TALK TO STRANGERS
Hallstrom, Lasse
SOMETHING TO TALK ABOUT
Hampton, Christopher
CARRINGTON
Hanna, Dana
SPIKE AND MIKE'S FESTIVAL OF
ANIMATION '95
Hardy, Rod
BUFFALO GIRLS
Harlin, Renny
CUTTHROAT ISLAND
Harris, Damian
BAD COMPANY
Harrison, Matthew
RHYTHM THIEF
Hartley, Hal
AMATEUR
Hatta, Kayo
PICTURE BRIDE
Haynes, Todd
SAFE
He Ping
RED FIRECRACKER, GREEN
FIRECRACKER
Heckerling, Amy
CLUELESS
Herzog, Werner
LESSONS OF DARKNESS
Hewitt, Peter
TOM AND HUCK
Hewitt, Rod
DANGEROUS, THE
Heynemann, Laurent
OLD LADY WHO WALKED IN THE SEA,
THE
Hickenlooper, George
GHOST BRIGADE
Hickox, Anthony
PAYBACK

Hickox, James D.R.
CHILDREN OF THE CORN III: URBAN
HARVEST
Hill, Walter
WILD BILL
Himelstein, Howard
POWER OF ATTORNEY
Hippolyte, Gregory
UNDERCOVER
Hoblit, Gregory
CLASS OF '61
Hoffman, Michael
RESTORATION
Hogan, P.J.
MURIEL'S WEDDING
Holcomb, Rod
CONVICT COWBOY
Holland, Agnieszka
PROVINCIAL ACTORS
TOTAL ECLIPSE
Holzman, Edward
BODY STROKES
Honigmann, Heddy
METAL AND MELANCHOLY
Hooper, Tobe
MANGLER, THE
Horton, Peter
CURE, THE
Howard, Ron
APOLLO 13
Huang, George
SWIMMING WITH SHARKS
Huang Jianxin
WOODEN MAN'S BRIDE, THE
Hudlin, Reginald
COSMIC SLOP
Hudlin, Warrington
COSMIC SLOP
Hughes, Albert
DEAD PRESIDENTS
Hughes, Allen
DEAD PRESIDENTS
Hui, Raman
SPIKE AND MIKE'S FESTIVAL OF
ANIMATION '95
Hyams, Peter
SUDDEN DEATH
Ichaso, Leon
ZOOMAN
Irvin, John
MONTH BY THE LAKE, A
Ivory, James
JEFFERSON IN PARIS
Jackson, Peter
MEET THE FEEBLES
Jacobs, Alan
NINA TAKES A LOVER
Jaglom, Henry
LAST SUMMER IN THE HAMPTONS
Jarvilaturi, Ilkka
CITY UNPLUGGED
Jeunet, Jean-Pierre
CITY OF LOST CHILDREN, THE
Joffe, Roland
SCARLET LETTER, THE
Johnson, Mick
INDICTMENT: THE MCMARTIN TRIAL
Johnson, Patrick Read
ANGUS
Johnston, Joe
JUMANJI
Johnston, Lawrence
ETERNITY
Johnstone, Jyll
MARTHA & ETHEL
Jonasson, Oskar
REMOTE CONTROL

Jost, Jon
BED YOU SLEEP IN, THE
FRAMEUP
Kachyna, Karel
COW, THE
Kagan, Jeremy Paul
ROSWELL: THE U.F.O. COVER-UP
Kalatozov, Mikhail
I AM CUBA
Kalvert, Scott
BASKETBALL DIARIES, THE
Kaplan, Nelly
NEA
Kapur, Shekhar
BANDIT QUEEN
Karbelnikoff, Michael
LAST RIDE, THE
Kasdan, Lawrence
FRENCH KISS
Katzin, Lee H.
BREAK, THE
Kawajiri, Yoshiaki
WICKED CITY
Keach, James
STARS FELL ON HENRIETTA, THE
Keaton, Diane
UNSTRUNG HEROES
Keeve, Douglas
UNZIPPED
Kerrigan, Lodge H.
CLEAN, SHAVEN
Kiarostami, Abbas
THROUGH THE OLIVE TREES
Kidron, Beeban
TO WONG FOO, THANKS FOR
    EVERYTHING! JULIE NEWMAR
Kieslowski, Krzysztof
SHORT FILM ABOUT KILLING, A
SHORT FILM ABOUT LOVE, A
Kletter, Richard
ANDROID AFFAIR, THE
Kokkinos, Ana
ONLY THE BRAVE
Korty, John
GETTING OUT
REDWOOD CURTAIN
Krieg, Peter
MACHINE DREAMS
Kurys, Diane
SIX DAYS, SIX NIGHTS
Kusturica, Emir
ARIZONA DREAM
Lane, Andrew
SECRETARY, THE
Lasseter, John
TOY STORY
Latshaw, Steve
JACK-O
Lavacherry, Vincent
TOO OUTRAGEOUS ANIMATION
Law, Clara
EROTIQUE
Lawton, J.F.
HUNTED, THE
Lee, Ang
PUSHING HANDS
SENSE AND SENSIBILITY
Lee, Spike
CLOCKERS
Lelouch, Claude
LES MISERABLES
Lemmo, James
BODILY HARM
DREAM A LITTLE DREAM 2
Leonard, Brett
HIDEAWAY
VIRTUOSITY

Leven, Jeremy
DON JUAN DEMARCO
Levine, Paul
OPERATION INTERCEPT
Levy, Jefery
S.F.W.
Lewis, Mark
GORDY
Lewis, Robert
CIRCUMSTANCES UNKNOWN
Lima, Kevin
GOOFY MOVIE, A
Lindenmuth, Kevin J.
VAMPIRES AND OTHER STEREOTYPES
Lindsay-Hogg, Michael
FRANKIE STARLIGHT
Lindstrom, Jon
DREAMING OF RITA
Linklater, Richard
BEFORE SUNRISE
Litten, Peter Mackenzie
HEAVEN'S A DRAG
Little, Dwight
FREE WILLY 2: THE ADVENTURE HOME
Lobato, Moctezuma
I LIKE TO PLAY GAMES
Loftis, Norman
MESSENGER
Logothetis, Dimitri
BODY SHOT
Lombardi, Francisco Jose
NO MERCY
Loncraine, Richard
RICHARD III
Longo, Robert
JOHNNY MNEMONIC
Low, Stephen
ACROSS THE SEA OF TIME: NEW YORK
    3D
Macek, Carl
CRIMSON WOLF
WICKED CITY
Madden, David
SEPARATE LIVES
Maggenti, Maria
INCREDIBLY TRUE ADVENTURES OF
    TWO GIRLS IN LOVE, THE
Makavejev, Dusan
GORILLA BATHES AT NOON
Makin, Kelly
NATIONAL LAMPOON'S SENIOR TRIP
Malmuth, Bruce
PENTATHLON
Malone, Mark
BULLETPROOF HEART
Mambety, Djibril Diop
HYENAS
Mamin, Yuri
WINDOW TO PARIS
Manchevski, Milcho
BEFORE THE RAIN
Mann, Michael
HEAT
Margolin, Stuart
DOUBLE, DOUBLE, TOIL AND TROUBLE
Markowitz, Robert
TOO YOUNG TO DIE?
Marshall, Frank
CONGO
Mashimo, Koichi
AI CITY
Masuo, Shoichi
CRIMSON WOLF
Matheson, Tim
BREACH OF CONDUCT
May, Bradford
DARKMAN 2: THE RETURN OF DURANT

Mayer, Daisy von Scherler
PARTY GIRL
Mayersberg, Paul
LAST SAMURAI, THE
Mayron, Melanie
BABY-SITTERS CLUB, THE
Mayuzumi, Rentaro
MYSTERY OF RAMPO, THE
Mazo, Michael
CRACKERJACK
McClary, J. Michael
CURSE OF THE STARVING CLASS
McDonald, Bruce
DANCE ME OUTSIDE
McDonald, Heather
BALLOT MEASURE 9
McDonald, Michael James
CRAZYSITTER, THE
McLean, Steve
POSTCARDS FROM AMERICA
McTiernan, John
DIE HARD WITH A VENGEANCE
Meckler, Nancy
SISTER MY SISTER
Megahy, Francis
RED SUN RISING
Melkonian, James
JERKY BOYS: THE MOVIE, THE
Menaul, Chris
FEAST OF JULY
Menaul, Christopher
FATHERLAND
Merlet, Agnes
SON OF THE SHARK, THE
Mesa, William
GALAXIS
Michaels, Richard
FATHER AND SCOUT
Michell, Roger
PERSUASION
Mikhalkov, Nikita
BURNT BY THE SUN
Miller, George
GREAT ELEPHANT ESCAPE, THE
GROSS MISCONDUCT
Miller, Randall
HOUSEGUEST
Mock, Freida Lee
MAYA LIN: A STRONG CLEAR VISION
Monger, Chris
ENGLISHMAN WHO WENT UP A HILL
    BUT CAME DOWN A MOUNTAIN, THE
Montgomery, Jennifer
ART FOR TEACHERS OF CHILDREN
Moore, Michael
CANADIAN BACON
Moorhouse, Jocelyn
HOW TO MAKE AN AMERICAN QUILT
Morahan, Andrew
HIGHLANDER: THE FINAL DIMENSION
Mordillat, Gerard
MY LIFE AND TIMES WITH ANTONIN
    ARTAUD
Moyle, Allan
EMPIRE RECORDS
Mueller, Eric
WORLD AND TIME ENOUGH
Murakawa, Toru
NEW YORK COP
Murnberger, Wolfgang
FOR GOD AND COUNTRY
Murphy, Geoff
UNDER SIEGE 2: DARK TERRITORY
Murphy, Tab
LAST OF THE DOGMEN
Nagy, Ivan
SKINNER

Nair, Mira
PEREZ FAMILY, THE
Nakano, Desmond
WHITE MAN'S BURDEN
Nava, Gregory
MY FAMILY: MI FAMILIA
Negroponte, Michel
JUPITER'S WIFE
Newell, Mike
AWFULLY BIG ADVENTURE, AN
Noonan, Chris
BABE
Norrington, Stephen
DEATH MACHINE
Norris, Aaron
TOP DOG
O'Connor, Pat
CIRCLE OF FRIENDS
Ocelot, Michel
TOO OUTRAGEOUS ANIMATION
Oedekerk, Steve
ACE VENTURA: WHEN NATURE CALLS
Okuyama, Kazuyoshi
MYSTERY OF RAMPO, THE
Orr, James
MAN OF THE HOUSE
Oz, Frank
INDIAN IN THE CUPBOARD, THE
Papamichael, Phedon
DARK SIDE OF GENIUS, THE
Park, Nick
SPIKE AND MIKE'S FESTIVAL OF
ANIMATION '95
Parker, Oliver
OTHELLO
Pasolini, Pier Paolo
MAMMA ROMA
Pasquin, John
NIGHTMARE
Pavlov, Yuri
CREATION OF ADAM
Penn, Sean
CROSSING GUARD, THE
Perez, Jack
AMERICA'S DEADLIEST HOME VIDEO
Petersen, Wolfgang
OUTBREAK
Pierson, Frank
LAKOTA WOMAN: SIEGE AT WOUNDED
KNEE
Pigors, Eric
TOO OUTRAGEOUS ANIMATION
Pittman, Bruce
KURT VONNEGUT'S HARRISON
BERGERON
Platt, Lucas
GIRL IN THE CADILLAC
Plympton, Bill
SPIKE AND MIKE'S FESTIVAL OF
ANIMATION '95
Podeswa, Jeremy
ECLIPSE
Poliakoff, Stephen
CENTURY
Pollack, Sydney
SABRINA
Powell, Michael
OH ... ROSALINDA!!
Pressburger, Emeric
OH ... ROSALINDA!!
Preuss, Ruben
ALMOST DEAD
Price, David
DR. JEKYLL & MS. HYDE
Prior, David A.
MUTANT SPECIES
Proctor, Elaine
FRIENDS

Purdy, Jon
DILLINGER AND CAPONE
REFLECTIONS IN THE DARK
Pyun, Albert
SPITFIRE
Quinn, Joanna
SPIKE AND MIKE'S FESTIVAL OF
ANIMATION '95
Radford, Michael
POSTMAN, THE
Railsback, Steve
SPY WITHIN, THE
Raimi, Sam
QUICK AND THE DEAD, THE
Rainone, Frank
ME AND THE MOB
Rambaldi, Victor
DECOY
Ramis, Harold
STUART SAVES HIS FAMILY
Ray, Fred Olen
ATTACK OF THE 60-FOOT CENTERFOLD
Ray, Satyajit
CHARULATA
STRANGER, THE
Reichardt, Kelly
RIVER OF GRASS
Reiner, Rob
AMERICAN PRESIDENT, THE
Rene, Norman
RECKLESS
Reynolds, Kevin
WATERWORLD
Richards, Lloyd
PIANO LESSON, THE
Riggs, Marlon
BLACK IS ... BLACK AIN'T
Ritter, Tim
CREEP
Robbe-Grillet, Alain
BLUE VILLA, THE
Robbins, Brian
SHOW, THE
Robbins, Tim
DEAD MAN WALKING
Robert, Vincent
FEAR, THE
Rocco, Marc
MURDER IN THE FIRST
Rockwell, Alexandre
FOUR ROOMS
Rodriguez, Robert
DESPERADO
FOUR ROOMS
Roodt, Darrell James
CRY, THE BELOVED COUNTRY
Rosman, Mark
EVOLVER
Ross, Herbert
BOYS ON THE SIDE
Rozema, Patricia
WHEN NIGHT IS FALLING
Ruane, John
DEATH IN BRUNSWICK
Ruben, Joseph
MONEY TRAIN
Russell, Erica
SPIKE AND MIKE'S FESTIVAL OF
ANIMATION '95
Salle, David
SEARCH AND DESTROY
Salva, Victor
POWDER
Sang Okk Sheen
3 NINJAS KNUCKLE UP
Santiago, Cirio
CAGED HEAT 3000

Sargent, Joseph
MY ANTONIA
Sato, Shimako
WIZARD OF DARKNESS
Sauer, Ernest G.
BIKINI BISTRO
Sax, Geoffrey
BROKEN TRUST
Sayles, John
SECRET OF ROAN INISH, THE
Schachter, Steven
WATER ENGINE, THE
Schlamme, Thomas
KINGFISH: A STORY OF HUEY P. LONG
Schlesinger, John
INNOCENT, THE
Schroeder, Barbet
KISS OF DEATH
Schroeder, Michael
COVER ME
Schumacher, Joel
BATMAN FOREVER
Schwartz, Vanessa
SPIKE AND MIKE'S FESTIVAL OF
ANIMATION '95
Scorsese, Martin
CASINO
Scott, Tony
CRIMSON TIDE
Segal, Peter
TOMMY BOY
Shebib, Donald
ASCENT, THE
Shils, Barry
WIGSTOCK: THE MOVIE
Shinzaki, Mamoru
BAREFOOT GEN
Shlumpf, Hans-Ulrich
CONGRESS OF PENGUINS, THE
Shum, Mina
DOUBLE HAPPINESS
Shyer, Charles
FATHER OF THE BRIDE PART II
Silberling, Brad
CASPER
Simpson, Jane
NUMBER ONE FAN
Simson, David E.
WHEN BILLY BROKE HIS HEAD ... AND
OTHER TALES OF WONDER
Singer, Bryan
USUAL SUSPECTS, THE
Singleton, John
HIGHER LEARNING
Sipes, Andrew
FAIR GAME
Sjogren, John
MOSAIC PROJECT, THE
Sloan, Holly Goldberg
BIG GREEN, THE
Sloane, Rick
GOOD GIRLS DON'T
Smith, Gregg
COVER STORY
Smith, John N.
DANGEROUS MINDS
Smith, Kevin
MALLRATS
Snowden, Alison
SPIKE AND MIKE'S FESTIVAL OF
ANIMATION '95
Soderbergh, Steven
UNDERNEATH, THE
Softley, Iain
HACKERS
Solberg, Helena
CARMEN MIRANDA: BANANAS IS MY
BUSINESS

Sonnenfeld, Barry
GET SHORTY
Spicer, Bryan
MIGHTY MORPHIN POWER RANGERS:
THE MOVIE
Stack, Jonathan
HARLEM DIARY: NINE VOICES OF
RESILIENCE
Stern, Steven H.
BLACK FOX
Stevenson, Rick
MAGIC IN THE WATER
Stone, Oliver
NIXON
Stoten, David
SPIKE AND MIKE'S FESTIVAL OF
ANIMATION '95
Strick, Wesley
TIE THAT BINDS, THE
Styles, Richard
MIDNIGHT TEASE 2
Suissa, Daniele J.
POCAHONTAS: THE LEGEND
Sullivan, Kevin Rodney
COSMIC SLOP
Sverak, Jan
ACCUMULATOR 1
Tabio, Juan Carlos
STRAWBERRY AND CHOCOLATE
Takacs, Tibor
BAD BLOOD
Talalay, Rachel
TANK GIRL
Tamahori, Lee
ONCE WERE WARRIORS
Tarantino, Quentin
FOUR ROOMS
Tardo, Aaron
TOO OUTRAGEOUS ANIMATION
Techine, Andre
WILD REEDS
Tennant, Andy
IT TAKES TWO
Thomas, Betty
BRADY BUNCH MOVIE, THE
Thomas, Theodore
FRANK AND OLLIE
Tirola, Douglas
REASON TO BELIEVE, A
To Kei-Fung
EXECUTIONERS
HEROIC TRIO, THE
Tong, Nancy
IN THE NAME OF THE EMPEROR
Tornatore, Giuseppe
PURE FORMALITY, A
Treut, Monika
EROTIQUE
Trevillion, Dale
PLAY TIME
Turner, Ann
DALLAS DOLL
Turner, Clive
HOWLING: NEW MOON RISING, THE
Turner, Robert
DIGGER
Turteltaub, Jon
WHILE YOU WERE SLEEPING
Tykwer, Tom
DEADLY MARIA
Van Gogh, Theo
1-900
Van Peebles, Mario
PANTHER
Van Sant, Gus
TO DIE FOR
Vendramini, Danny
DESPERATE PREY

Verhoeven, Paul
SHOWGIRLS
Vilsmaier, Joseph
STALINGRAD
Vitali, Federico
TOO OUTRAGEOUS ANIMATION
von Krusenstjerna, Fredrik
BETRAYAL
von Trier, Lars
KINGDOM, THE
von Trotta, Margarethe
PROMISE, THE
Wainwright, Rupert
DILLINGER
Wajda, Andrzej
WITHOUT ANESTHESIA
Waller, Anthony
MUTE WITNESS
Wang, Wayne
BLUE IN THE FACE
SMOKE
Was, Don
BRIAN WILSON: I JUST WASN'T MADE
FOR THESE TIMES
Watts, Tim
SPIKE AND MIKE'S FESTIVAL OF
ANIMATION '95
Weisman, Sam
BYE BYE, LOVE
Weiss, Jiri
MARTHA AND I
Wells, Simon
BALTO
Wenk, Richard
NATIONAL LAMPOON'S ATTACK OF THE
5'2" WOMEN
Werneck, Sandra
BOCA
Werner, Peter
SUBSTITUTE WIFE, THE
Whitaker, Forest
WAITING TO EXHALE
White, Wally
LIE DOWN WITH DOGS
Whitmore, II, Preston A.
WALKING DEAD, THE
Widen, Gregory
PROPHECY, THE
Willems, Mo
SPIKE AND MIKE'S FESTIVAL OF
ANIMATION '95
Williams, Richard
ARABIAN KNIGHT
Winberg, Wynn
DARK DEALER
Wincer, Simon
OPERATION DUMBO DROP
Winkler, Irwin
NET, THE
Wiseman, Frederick
BALLET
Wolodarsky, M. Wallace
COLDBLOODED
Wong Jing
HIGH RISK
RETURN OF THE GOD OF GAMBLERS
Wong Kar-Wai
ASHES OF TIME
Woo-Suk Kang
HOW TO TOP MY WIFE
Woolnough, Jeff
FIRST DEGREE
Wynorski, Jim
BODY CHEMISTRY 4: FULL EXPOSURE
Yamaga, Hiroyuki
WINGS OF HONNEAMISE: ROYAL SPACE
FORCE

Yates, Peter
ROOMMATES
RUN OF THE COUNTRY, THE
Yim Ho
DAY THE SUN TURNED COLD, THE
Young, Robert
DOOMSDAY GUN
Yu, Ronny
PHANTOM LOVER, THE
Yuen Kwai
HIGH RISK
Zehrer, Paul
BLESSING
Zhang Yimou
SHANGHAI TRIAD
Zhou Xiaowen
ERMO
Zielinsky, Rafal
FUN
Zucker, Jerry
FIRST KNIGHT
Zwigoff, Terry
CRUMB

EDITORS

Adair, Sandra
BEFORE SUNRISE
Adam, Peter
MUTE WITNESS
Akers, George
CARRINGTON
Albert, Ross
BUSHWHACKED
Allen, Stanford C.
DILLINGER
Alvor, Jonathan
DANGEROUS, THE
Andersen, Niels Pagh
BETRAYAL
Anderson, Paul
MOSAIC PROJECT, THE
Anderson, William
JUST CAUSE
Andrianova, Olga
WINDOW TO PARIS
Anwar, Tariq
DOOMSDAY GUN
FATHERLAND
Appleby, George
DOUBLE, DOUBLE, TOIL AND TROUBLE
Araki, Gregg
DOOM GENERATION, THE
Arsenault, Jeffrey
HEAVEN'S A DRAG
Atkin, Mark
ONLY THE BRAVE
Audsley, Mick
TWELVE MONKEYS
Badgely, Christiane
BLACK IS ... BLACK AIN'T
Baragli, Nino
MAMMA ROMA
Barber, Patrick
TO CROSS THE RUBICON
Baril, Alain
LOVE AND HUMAN REMAINS
Barnier, Luc
SIX DAYS, SIX NIGHTS
Baron, Suzanne
PROMISE, THE
Barrachin, Nicholas
FACES OF WOMEN
Barraque, Martine
MINA TANNENBAUM
Barrere, Robert
CRAZYSITTER, THE

DIRTY MONEY
SILENCE OF THE HAMS
Barrios, Luis
NO MERCY
Baskin, Sonny
PROPHECY, THE
Bassett, Craig
COLDBLOODED
Baumgarten, Alan
LORD OF ILLUSIONS
Beatty, David
BETTER OFF DEAD
Beaulieu, Lise
PIGALLE
Beauman, Nicholas
COUNTRY LIFE
Beauman, Nick
TRAPS
Behar, Andrew
TIE-DIED: ROCK 'N' ROLL'S MOST
DEADICATED FANS
Bell, Geraint
BIGFOOT: THE UNFORGETTABLE
ENCOUNTER
Bennett, Kimberly
O.J. SIMPSON STORY, THE
Benwick, Richard
CRACKERJACK
Berdan, Brian
NIXON
Berenbaum, Michael
RECKLESS
Beyda, Kent
FORGET PARIS
Bilcock, Jill
EROTIQUE
HOW TO MAKE AN AMERICAN QUILT
MURIEL'S WEDDING
Blank, Jonathan
SEX, DRUGS AND DEMOCRACY
Blunden, Christopher
HACKERS
Boguski, Barbara
NEW YORK COP
Bond, Peter
ARABIAN KNIGHT
Bondelli, Roger
BYE BYE, LOVE
IT TAKES TWO
Bonnot, Francoise
BURNING SEASON, THE
Bornstein, Charles
TALES FROM THE HOOD
Bowers, George
MONEY TRAIN
Boyle, Peter
WATERWORLD
Bracken, Richard
BUFFALO GIRLS
Brandon, Maryann
BORN TO BE WILD
GRUMPIER OLD MEN
Brandt-Burgoyne, Anita
KID IN KING ARTHUR'S COURT, A
PAYBACK
Bricker, Randy
HALLOWEEN: THE CURSE OF MICHAEL
MYERS
Brochu, Don
STEAL BIG, STEAL LITTLE
WALKING DEAD, THE
Brody, Todd Scott
WIGSTOCK: THE MOVIE
Bromwell, Lisa
ANDROID AFFAIR, THE
Brown, Casey
FATHER AND SCOUT

Brown, Michael
FATHER AND SCOUT
Brown, O. Nicholas
OPERATION DUMBO DROP
Brown, Robert
FREE WILLY 2: THE ADVENTURE HOME
Brown, Steve
EROTIQUE
Bruce, James
DIRTY MONEY
Buba, Pasquale
HEAT
Buckley, Norma
DILLINGER AND CAPONE
Buckley, Norman
REFLECTIONS IN THE DARK
Buff, Conrad
SPECIES
Burstein, Nanette
IN THE NAME OF THE EMPEROR
Butler, Stephen W.
GOLD DIGGERS: THE SECRET OF BEAR
MOUNTAIN
Buttgereit, Jorg
NEKROMANTIK
Cahn, Daniel
DARKMAN 2: THE RETURN OF DURANT
Cambas, Jacqueline
NOW AND THEN
Camp, Kathryn
FRANK AND OLLIE
Campbell, Malcolm
ACE VENTURA: WHEN NATURE CALLS
Campling, David
NIGHTMARE
Candib, Richard
COSMIC SLOP
Cannon, Bruce
HIGHER LEARNING
Carnochan, John
COMPANION, THE
Carr, Adrian
DANGEROUS, THE
Carruth, William C.
WALKING DEAD, THE
Carter, John
FRIDAY
Cartwright, Sr., William T.
MAYA LIN: A STRONG CLEAR VISION
Cassidy, Jay
CROSSING GUARD, THE
Chan Ki-hop
HE'S A WOMAN, SHE'S A MAN
Chandler, Michael
DIGGER
EMPIRE RECORDS
Chang, William
ASHES OF TIME
Chao Ying-Wu
DAY THE SUN TURNED COLD, THE
Charr, Henri
CAGED HEARTS
Chen, Bo-Wen
SHAO LIN POPEYE
Chew, Richard
TALL TALE: THE UNBELIEVABLE
ADVENTURES OF PECOS BILL
WAITING TO EXHALE
Chiaramonte, Andrew
TWOGETHER
Chiate, Debra
CLUELESS
NATIONAL LAMPOON'S ATTACK OF THE
5'2" WOMEN
Choukroun, Pierre
SON OF THE SHARK, THE
Choules, Pam
3 NINJAS KNUCKLE UP

Churgin, Lisa
UNSTRUNG HEROES
Churgin, Lisa Zeno
DEAD MAN WALKING
Clark, Jim
COPYCAT
RADIO INSIDE
Clayton, Curtiss
GLASS SHIELD, THE
TO DIE FOR
Coates, Anne V.
CONGO
Cohen, Steven
THREE WISHES
Comets, Jacques
OLD LADY WHO WALKED IN THE SEA,
THE
Congdon, Dana
BASKETBALL DIARIES, THE
Conte, Mark
FLUKE
Cormon, Christine
JLG BY JLG
Corwin, Hank
NIXON
Coughlin, Cari
BITTER VENGEANCE
OUT OF ANNIE'S PAST
Cox, Joel
BRIDGES OF MADISON COUNTY, THE
STARS FELL ON HENRIETTA, THE
Crafford, Ian
INDIAN IN THE CUPBOARD, THE
Craven, Garth
RESTORATION
Cristelli, Loredana
HYENAS
Currin, John
ALMOST DEAD
Curtis, Jim
DARK DEALER
D'Arcy, Marcus
BABE
D'Augustine, Joe
LAST RIDE, THE
Dalva, Robert
JUMANJI
Dangar, Henry
GROSS MISCONDUCT
NOSTRADAMUS KID, THE
Danniel, Daniel
METAL AND MELANCHOLY
Davalos, Raul
DESTINY TURNS ON THE RADIO
Davey, Annette
ETERNITY
Davidson, Bruria B.
OUTSIDE THE LAW
Davies, Freeman
WILD BILL
Davis, Roderick
SPY WITHIN, THE
Davis, Ron
BEYOND RANGOON
De Luze, Helene
LES MISERABLES
de Oliveira, Manoel
CONVENT, THE
VALLEY OF ABRAHAM, THE
DeHaven, Cater
BAR GIRLS
Delfgou, Peter
LAMB
Dixon, Humphrey
JOURNEY OF AUGUST KING, THE
Dixon, Pall
KINGFISH: A STORY OF HUEY P. LONG

Dixon, Paul
MALLRATS
Dje-Dje, Madame
FACES OF WOMEN
Donatien, Osvaldo
STRAWBERRY AND CHOCOLATE
Dringenberg, Katja
DEADLY MARIA
Du Yuan
SHANGHAI TRIAD
DuBois, Victor
COSMIC SLOP
Duez, Hans
BLUE VILLA, THE
Dutta, Dulal
CHARULATA
STRANGER, THE
Endacott, Paul
DEATH MACHINE
Eriksdotter, Kerstin
DANCER, THE
Estrin, Bob
PEREZ FAMILY, THE
Evan-Jones, Sim
BALTO
Evans, Kate
PERSUASION
Faber, Hart F.
LIE DOWN WITH DOGS
Fallick, Mort
BODY SHOT
Farr, Glenn
BROKEN TRUST
Faugno, Frank
POWER OF ATTORNEY
Fenn, Suzanne
YOUNGER & YOUNGER
Ferretti, Robert A.
HUNTED, THE
Fessenden, Larry
RIVER OF GRASS
Feuerman, Tod
GOOD DAY TO DIE, A
Fields, Richard
EROTIQUE
Finfer, David
FAIR GAME
Finkle, Claudia
CIRCUMSTANCES UNKNOWN
Fisarek, Alois
ACCUMULATOR 1
Fisher, Dick
BROTHERS MCMULLEN, THE
Fisher, Todd
TWOGETHER
Flaer, Howard
BIGFOOT: THE UNFORGETTABLE
ENCOUNTER
Flaum, Seth
GRUMPIER OLD MEN
Fletcher, Nick
BALTO
Forner, Nancy
FEAR, THE
Foster, Ruth
FRANKIE STARLIGHT
Francis-Bruce, Richard
SEVEN
Frazer, Lindsay
GORDY
Freeman, David
TOM AND HUCK
Freeman, Jeff
DECONSTRUCTING SARAH
MAD LOVE
Friedkin, Jay
BABE

Gadmer, Sylvie
AUGUSTIN
Gallieni, Dominique
MINA TANNENBAUM
Gannon, Steve
GLORY BOYS, THE
Gaster, Nicolas
BEFORE THE RAIN
Gazzara, Elizabeth
POSTCARDS FROM AMERICA
Gibbs, Tony
DON JUAN DEMARCO
Gibson, J. Kathleen
KICKING AND SCREAMING
Giordano, Martine
WILD REEDS
Glagoleva, N.
I AM CUBA
Glatstein, Bert
CASTLE FREAK
Goldblatt, Mark
SHOWGIRLS
Goldenberg, William
CITIZEN X
HEAT
Goldman, Mia
SOMETHING TO TALK ABOUT
Goldstein, Roushell
FIRST DEGREE
Goodhill, Dean
CURSE OF THE STARVING CLASS
Goodspeed, Margie
FOUR ROOMS
Gorchow, Michelle
ME AND THE MOB
SEARCH AND DESTROY
Gordon, Robert
TOY STORY
Gosnell, Raja
NINE MONTHS
Gottlieb, Mallori
PICTURE BRIDE
Grace, Alison
DOUBLE HAPPINESS
Graef, Susan
INCREDIBLY TRUE ADVENTURES OF
TWO GIRLS IN LOVE, THE
Granger, Tracy S.
NEW JERSEY DRIVE
Graves, Alex
CRUDE OASIS, THE
Green, Bruce
WHILE YOU WERE SLEEPING
Green, Paul
RICHARD III
Greenbury, Christopher
BABY-SITTERS CLUB, THE
FRANK & JESSE
Gregory, Jon
AWFULLY BIG ADVENTURE, AN
Grodecki, Wiktor
NOT ANGELS BUT ANGELS
Guyot, Raymonde
VOYAGE EN DOUCE
Hache, Joelle
FARINELLI
INNOCENT LIES
Hai Kit-Wai
ASHES OF TIME
Haller, Gisela
MARTHA AND I
Halsey, Richard
LAST OF THE DOGMEN
NET, THE
Hamilton, Steve
AMATEUR
Hampton, Janice
ANGUS

SEPARATE LIVES
Hanley, Daniel
APOLLO 13
Happ, Magda
ADVENTURES OF MATT THE
GOOSEBOY, THE
Harris, Dorian
LITTLE ODESSA
Harris, Richard A.
INDICTMENT: THE MCMARTIN TRIAL
Harrison, Matthew
RHYTHM THIEF
Hecht, Marlen
WIGSTOCK: THE MOVIE
Heim, Alan
COPYCAT
Heitner, David
CRY, THE BELOVED COUNTRY
MANGLER, THE
Helfrich, Mark
AVENGING ANGEL
SHOWGIRLS
Hellman, Monte
GHOST BRIGADE
Hendricks, Jan
METAL AND MELANCHOLY
Heredia, Paula
COLORADO COWBOY: THE BRUCE FORD
STORY
UNZIPPED
Herring, Craig
STUART SAVES HIS FAMILY
Herring, Pembroke
STUART SAVES HIS FAMILY
Hess, Augie
JADE
Hickox, Emma E.
CREW, THE
Hill, Dennis M.
JERKY BOYS: THE MOVIE, THE
POWDER
Hill, Michael
APOLLO 13
Hiltzik, Richard
COSMIC SLOP
Hirakubo, Masahiro
SHALLOW GRAVE
Hirsch, Tina
STEAL BIG, STEAL LITTLE
Hobson, Gregory
GALAXIS
Hodgson, Paul
RUN OF THE COUNTRY, THE
Hoenig, Dov
HEAT
Hoffman, Sabine
REASON TO BELIEVE, A
Hofstra, Jack
AMAZING PANDA ADVENTURE, THE
Holden, David
ROSWELL: THE U.F.O. COVER-UP
Hollyn, Norman D.
GIRL IN THE CADILLAC
Homolkova, Maria
FOR GOD AND COUNTRY
Honess, Peter
ROB ROY
Honey, Mike
DALLAS DOLL
Horton, Michael
ONCE WERE WARRIORS
Horvitch, Andy
BOCA
SILENCE OF THE HAMS
Hoy, Maisie
SMOKE
Hoy, William
JUDICIAL CONSENT

Hubert, Axel
NEXT DOOR
Hunter, Martin
MORTAL KOMBAT
WATER ENGINE, THE
Hutshing, Joe
FRENCH KISS
Hyun Kim
HOW TO TOP MY WIFE
Ibold, Doug
BREAK, THE
Irvine, Frank
DECOY
Jaglom, Henry
LAST SUMMER IN THE HAMPTONS
Jelinski, Manfred O.
NEKROMANTIK
Jewhurst, Allen
GLORY BOYS, THE
Jones, Sherwood
GRANNY, THE
Jorissen, B.B.
BALLOT MEASURE 9
Jost, Jon
BED YOU SLEEP IN, THE
FRAMEUP
Jympson, John
CIRCLE OF FRIENDS
Kahn, Michael
CASPER
Kam Wah Productions
HEROIC TRIO, THE
Kanin, Josh
I LIKE TO PLAY GAMES
Karen, Debra
MY ANTONIA
Karr, Gary
ZOOMAN
Katz, Virginia
CANDYMAN: FAREWELL TO THE FLESH
Kawashima, Akimasa
MYSTERY OF RAMPO, THE
Kemper, Steven
FAIR GAME
SUDDEN DEATH
Kennedy, Patrick
MAJOR PAYNE
Keramidas, Harry
JUDGE DREDD
MAN OF THE HOUSE
Kerr, William
TOMMY BOY
Kiarostami, Abbas
THROUGH THE OLIVE TREES
Kling, Elizabeth
GEORGIA
Klingman, Lynzee
HOME FOR THE HOLIDAYS
PICTURE BRIDE
Knue, Michael
TIE THAT BINDS, THE
Kobrin, Rob
VIRTUOSITY
Kohler, Wolfram
PROFESSION: NEO-NAZI
Kravetz, Carole
DEVIL IN A BLUE DRESS
Kress, Carl
BODILY HARM
Krieg, Peter
MACHINE DREAMS
Kwong Chi-Leung
ASHES OF TIME
Ladizinsky, Ivan
NUMBER ONE FAN
Lafferty, John
COVER ME

Lahti, James
ACROSS THE SEA OF TIME: NEW YORK
3D
Langlois, Yves
HIGHLANDER: THE FINAL DIMENSION
Larsen, Albert
BODY STROKES
Lawrence, Stephen
NATIONAL LAMPOON'S SENIOR TRIP
Lawson, Tony
FRIENDS
OTHELLO
Lebental, Dan
DEAD PRESIDENTS
Lebenzon, Chris
CRIMSON TIDE
Lecorne, Guy
SON OF THE SHARK, THE
Lee, Allan
MAGIC IN THE WATER
Lei Qin
WOODEN MAN'S BRIDE, THE
Leighton, Robert
AMERICAN PRESIDENT, THE
Leonard, David
NADJA
Liechti, Fee
CONGRESS OF PENGUINS, THE
Lightstone, Monika
FUN
Lindenmuth, Kevin J.
VAMPIRES AND OTHER STEREOTYPES
Lines, Wayne
AMERICAN COP
Link, John
BIG GREEN, THE
Lissova, Raisa
CREATION OF ADAM
Livingston, Victor
CRUMB
Livingstone, Russell
MURDER IN THE FIRST
Lo, Mayin
ADDICTION, THE
Loiseleux, Valerie
CONVENT, THE
VALLEY OF ABRAHAM, THE
Lombardo, Tony
DR. JEKYLL & MS. HYDE
Lorente, Isabel
JEFFERSON IN PARIS
TOTAL ECLIPSE
Louw, Ot
1-900
Lovejoy, Stephen
TALES FROM THE CRYPT: DEMON
KNIGHT
Lowe, Helen
BRIAN WILSON: I JUST WASN'T MADE
FOR THESE TIMES
Lowenthal, Daniel
ACROSS THE MOON
Lukovac, Vuksan
GORILLA BATHES AT NOON
Lussier, Patrick
GALAXIS
VAMPIRE IN BROOKLYN
Lyons, James
SAFE
MacDonald, Heather
BALLOT MEASURE 9
Macias, Juan Carlos
I, THE WORST OF ALL
Mackie, Alex
JUDGE DREDD
Maganini, Elena
FOUR ROOMS

Maggi, Susan
ECLIPSE
Malinowski, Tony
MUTANT SPECIES
Mancilla, Jess
CAGED HEARTS
Marcus, Andrew
JEFFERSON IN PARIS
Marden, Richard
INNOCENT, THE
Marinelli, Larry
NEW YORK COP
Marks, Richard
ASSASSINS
THINGS TO DO IN DENVER WHEN
YOU'RE DEAD
Marsh, Donovan
ARMAGEDDON: THE FINAL CHALLENGE
Martin, David
ENGLISHMAN WHO WENT UP A HILL
BUT CAME DOWN A MOUNTAIN, THE
Martin, Richard
MALICIOUS
Martin, Rick
ABDUCTED 2: THE REUNION
Martinez, Rolando
STRAWBERRY AND CHOCOLATE
Marx, Ed
SWIMMING WITH SHARKS
McNaughton, Steve
CREEP
Melnick, Mark
BALLISTIC
Meniconi, Enzo
BURNT BY THE SUN
Menke, Sally
FOUR ROOMS
Mery-Clark, Laurence
BUSINESS AFFAIR, A
Meyer, David
CARMEN MIRANDA: BANANAS IS MY
BUSINESS
Miller, Jim
GET SHORTY
Miller, Michael R.
BOYS ON THE SIDE
Miller, Peter
ATTACK OF THE 60-FOOT CENTERFOLD
Mills, Reginald
OH ... ROSALINDA!!
Miracle, Jay
DECOY
Miski, Giselle
FACES OF WOMEN
Mondshein, Andrew
TO WONG FOO, THANKS FOR
EVERYTHING! JULIE NEWMAR
Montgomery, Jennifer
ART FOR TEACHERS OF CHILDREN
Monthieux, Maryline
GROSSE FATIGUE
Moradian, Vanice
BODY CHEMISTRY 4: FULL EXPOSURE
Morreale, Andrew
BLESSING
Morriss, Frank
NICK OF TIME
Morse, Susan E.
MIGHTY APHRODITE
Moss, Thomas V.
PEBBLE AND THE PENGUIN, THE
Murawski, Bob
EXPERT, THE
Murch, Walter
FIRST KNIGHT
Nawrocka, Halina
PROVINCIAL ACTORS

Negroponte, Michel
JUPITER'S WIFE
Nelson, Christopher
CONVICT COWBOY
Neuberger, Jon
KILIAN'S CHRONICLE
Nicholson, Martin
DANGER OF LOVE
SUBSTITUTE WIFE, THE
Nikel, Hannes
STALINGRAD
Noble, Thom
SCARLET LETTER, THE
Nord, Richard
PENTATHLON
Noveck, Fima
BAD BLOOD
Nutt, John
NINA TAKES A LOVER
O'Connor, Dennis
SPITFIRE
O'Meara, C. Timothy
HEAVYWEIGHTS
Ogata, Harutoshi
WINGS OF HONNEAMISE: ROYAL SPACE
FORCE
Oliver, Jim
GETTING OUT
PIANO LESSON, THE
RETURN OF THE NATIVE, THE
Ornelas, Michael
CREEP
Ottman, John
USUAL SUSPECTS, THE
Pacek, Michael
DANCE ME OUTSIDE
Paggi, Simona
LAMERICA
Pankow, Bill
MONEY TRAIN
Pappe, Stuart
BAD COMPANY
Paris, Bob
BLACK IS ... BLACK AIN'T
Parkinson, Michael
CENTURY
Peehl, Susan
GREAT DAY IN HARLEM, A
Peppe, Chris
CHILDREN OF THE CORN III: URBAN
HARVEST
Percy, Lee
KISS OF DEATH
Perez, Jack
AMERICA'S DEADLIEST HOME VIDEO
Perler, Gregory
GOOFY MOVIE, A
Perpignani, Roberto
POSTMAN, THE
Peterson, H. Lee
POCAHONTAS
Petrucelli, Britton J.
DARK SIDE OF GENIUS, THE
Petschek, Paul
PREHYSTERIA! 3
Plemiannikov, Helene
NEA
Pollard, Sam
CLOCKERS
Post, James
MOSAIC PROJECT, THE
Prior, Jim
BABYSITTER, THE
Prugar, Halina
WITHOUT ANESTHESIA
Puett, Dallas
FREE WILLY 2: THE ADVENTURE HOME

Pulbrook, David
HOTEL SORRENTO
Quettier, Nelly
I CAN'T SLEEP
Rabinowitz, Jay
CLEAN, SHAVEN
Ralston, George
RENT-A-KID
Rand, Patrick
SCANNERS: THE SHOWDOWN
Ravel, Jean
SERIOUS ABOUT PLEASURE
Rawlings, Terry
GOLDENEYE
Regnier, Inez
NOBODY LOVES ME
Reynolds, Enar
AILSA
Richardson, Nancy
MY FAMILY: MI FAMILIA
WHITE MAN'S BURDEN
Ripps, Michael
KID IN KING ARTHUR'S COURT, A
Ritson, Tim
GLORY BOYS, THE
Ritter, Tim
CREEP
Rivkin, Stephen
NINE MONTHS
OUTBREAK
Rodriguez, Robert
DESPERADO
FOUR ROOMS
Rogers, John
BIKINI BISTRO
Rolf, Tom
DANGEROUS MINDS
HEAT
Rondinella, Thomas R.
FOOL AND HIS MONEY, A
Rosenbaum, Mark W.
IN THE DEEP WOODS
Rosenbloom, David
CLASS OF '61
MOONLIGHT AND VALENTINO
PYROMANIAC'S LOVE STORY, A
Rosenblum, Steven
BRAVEHEART
Rosenstock, Harvey
LOSING ISAIAH
TOO YOUNG TO DIE?
Ross, Caroline
BLUE TIGER
Ross, Rebecca
CYBER BANDITS
Rostock, Susanne
MOVING THE MOUNTAIN
Rostock, Susanne Szabo
HARLEM DIARY: NINE VOICES OF
RESILIENCE
Roth, Fred
SKINNER
Rotter, Stephen A.
FATHER OF THE BRIDE PART II
Rotundo, Nick
BOULEVARD
Rouffio, Sophie
MY LIFE AND TIMES WITH ANTONIN
ARTAUD
Rouse, Christopher
BREACH OF CONDUCT
TERESA'S TATTOO
Rubacky, Louise
WINGS OF COURAGE
Rubell, Paul
BURNING SEASON, THE
Russell, Esther P.
GHOST BRIGADE

Russell, Robin
BULLETPROOF HEART
Sackner, Sara
TIE-DIED: ROCK 'N' ROLL'S MOST
DEADICATED FANS
Sales, Robin
WOMAN AT WAR, A
Salfas, Stan
UNDERNEATH, THE
Saluja, Renu
BANDIT QUEEN
Sanders, Ronald
JOHNNY MNEMONIC
Sato, Shimako
WIZARD OF DARKNESS
Sayad, Changiz
JAR, THE
Sayles, John
SECRET OF ROAN INISH, THE
Scalia, Pietro
QUICK AND THE DEAD, THE
Schink, Peter
SKINNER
TOP DOG
Schneid, Herve
CITY OF LOST CHILDREN, THE
Schoenfeld, Brent
EVOLVER
Schoonmaker, Thelma
CASINO
Schultz, Michael
SHOW, THE
Sears, B.J.
HIDEAWAY
VIRTUOSITY
Sears, Eric
HOUSEGUEST
TOO YOUNG TO DIE?
Selkirk, Jamie
MEET THE FEEBLES
Semel, Stephen
COSMIC SLOP
JURY DUTY
Semilian, Julian
SECRETARY, THE
Shaine, Rick
SAFE PASSAGE
Shepphird, John
MIDNIGHT TEASE 2
Sherin, Anthony
CURE, THE
Shils, Barry
WIGSTOCK: THE MOVIE
Shimin, Toby
MARTHA & ETHEL
Shipton, Susan
EXOTICA
WHEN NIGHT IS FALLING
Shropshire, Terilyn A.
EMBRACE OF THE VAMPIRE
Silverman, Cara
JEFFREY
PARTY GIRL
Silvi, Roberto
NEVER TALK TO STRANGERS
Simpson, David E.
WHEN BILLY BROKE HIS HEAD ... AND
OTHER TALES OF WONDER
Smal, Ewa
SHORT FILM ABOUT KILLING, A
SHORT FILM ABOUT LOVE, A
Smith, Gregg
COVER STORY
Smith, Howard
STRANGE DAYS
TWO BITS
Smith, John
LEAVING LAS VEGAS

Smith, Kent
UNDERCOVER
Spivey, Susan
PRIEST
Squyres, Tim
PUSHING HANDS
SENSE AND SENSIBILITY
Standke, Rainer
LESSONS OF DARKNESS
Stanzler, Wendy
CANADIAN BACON
Stein, Howard Scott
COSMIC SLOP
Steinkamp, Frederic
SABRINA
Stensgaard, Molly Marlene
KINGDOM, THE
Stern, Merril
ROY COHN/JACK SMITH
Stevenson, Lynn
GUMBY: THE MOVIE
Stitt, Kevin
NICK OF TIME
Stiven, David
SISTER MY SISTER
Stokes, Laura
WORLD AND TIME ENOUGH
Strand, Eric
HUNTED, THE
Strickland, Wayland
JACK-O
Svoboda, Jan
COW, THE
Symons, James R.
TANK GIRL
Szanto, Anna Maria
PLAY TIME
Talavera, Miriam
STRAWBERRY AND CHOCOLATE
UP TO A CERTAIN POINT
Tam, Patrick
ASHES OF TIME
Tanner, Peter
MONTH BY THE LAKE, A
Tellefsen, Chris
BLUE IN THE FACE
CITY UNPLUGGED
KIDS
Teschner, Peter
BRADY BUNCH MOVIE, THE
Thuesen, Jacob
KINGDOM, THE
Thumpston, Neil
DEATH IN BRUNSWICK
Tintori, John
ROOMMATES
Toniolo, Camilla
LIVING IN OBLIVION
Tornatore, Giuseppe
PURE FORMALITY, A
Tronick, Michael
UNDER SIEGE 2: DARK TERRITORY
Tun, Dan
IN THE NAME OF THE EMPEROR
Turner, Clive
HOWLING: NEW MOON RISING, THE
Unkrich, Lee
TOY STORY
Urioste, Frank J.
CUTTHROAT ISLAND
Van Buren, Marc
DESPERATE PREY
Van Effenterre, Joele
WINDOW TO PARIS
Van Wyk, Gerrie
ARMAGEDDON: THE FINAL CHALLENGE

Vandenburg, Frans
SUM OF US, THE
Vickrey, Scott
REDWOOD CURTAIN
Virkler, Dennis
BATMAN FOREVER
Wagner, Christian
BAD BOYS
FAIR GAME
Wahrman, Wayne
MIGHTY MORPHIN POWER RANGERS:
THE MOVIE
Walsh, Martin
FUNNY BONES
HACKERS
Walters, John
MESSENGER
Warner, Mark
DOLORES CLAIBORNE
Warschilka, Edward A.
IN THE MOUTH OF MADNESS
VILLAGE OF THE DAMNED
Watson, Earl
PANTHER
Weber, Billy
GRUMPIER OLD MEN
Webster, Ion
KURT VONNEGUT'S HARRISON
BERGERON
Weidner, John
RED SUN RISING
Weisberg, Steven
LITTLE PRINCESS, A
MIAMI RHAPSODY
Weiss, Adam
DRACULA: DEAD AND LOVING IT
Westerlund, Einar
DEAD FUNNY
Wimble, Chris
FEAST OF JULY
INNOCENT LIES
Winborne, Hughes
LAST GOOD TIME, THE
Winters, Ralph E.
CUTTHROAT ISLAND
Wiseman, Frederick
BALLET
Wisman, Ron
ASCENT, THE
BLACK FOX
GREAT ELEPHANT ESCAPE, THE
Wolf, Jeffrey
BILLY MADISON
Wolinsky, Sidney
DANGER OF LOVE
FAR FROM HOME: THE ADVENTURES OF
YELLOW DOG
Wong Chi-hung
NAKED KILLER
Wong Yi-Sun
DAY THE SUN TURNED COLD, THE
Wright, John
DIE HARD WITH A VENGEANCE
Wu, David
PHANTOM LOVER, THE
Yahraus, Bill
ROSWELL: THE U.F.O. COVER-UP
Yuan Hong
RED FIRECRACKER, GREEN
FIRECRACKER
Zasranovic, Andrlja
ARIZONA DREAM
Zeman, Wanda
CHRONICLE OF THE WARSAW GHETTO
UPRISING ACCORDING TO MAREK
EDELMAN
Zetlin, Barry
OPERATION INTERCEPT

Zherer, Paul
BLESSING
Zhong Furong
ERMO
Zimmer, Peter
ENEMY WITHIN, THE
Zimmerman, Don
WALK IN THE CLOUDS, A
Zinner, Katina
LAKOTA WOMAN: SIEGE AT WOUNDED
KNEE
Zinoman, Amanda
CARMEN MIRANDA: BANANAS IS MY
BUSINESS
Zuckerman, Lauren
S.F.W.

EXECUTIVE PRODUCERS

Abraham, Marc
BABY-SITTERS CLUB, THE
Abrahamsen, Svend
KINGDOM, THE
Abrams, Peter
PAYBACK
Adams, Daniel
FOOL AND HIS MONEY, A
Ahrenberg, Staffan
JOHNNY MNEMONIC
TOTAL ECLIPSE
Akkad, Moustapha
HALLOWEEN: THE CURSE OF MICHAEL
MYERS
Albert, Jean-Jacques
WILD REEDS
Albucher, Larry Y.
THREE WISHES
Allard, Tony
BLACK FOX
MAGIC IN THE WATER
Altbach, Ron
LAST RIDE, THE
Altissimi, Bruno
PURE FORMALITY, A
Amin, Mark
CURSE OF THE STARVING CLASS
EVOLVER
FRANK & JESSE
KICKING AND SCREAMING
KID IN KING ARTHUR'S COURT, A
OPERATION INTERCEPT
SEPARATE LIVES
Amritraj, Ashok
RED SUN RISING
Andersen, Craig
RETURN OF THE NATIVE, THE
Anderson, Craig
PIANO LESSON, THE
Andrews, Dale A.
DIGGER
Apatow, Judd
HEAVYWEIGHTS
Apodiacos, Maria
RICHARD III
Arbib, Nicole
DOOM GENERATION, THE
Arnold, Bob
STALINGRAD
Asselin, Jean-Yves
TOTAL ECLIPSE
Astor, Tom
TANK GIRL
Avnet, Jon
MIAMI RHAPSODY
Badalato, Bill
TALL TALE: THE UNBELIEVABLE
ADVENTURES OF PECOS BILL

Baer, Willi
BUSINESS AFFAIR, A
TWO BITS
Baker, Todd
CURE, THE
Balzaretti, Georgina
STRAWBERRY AND CHOCOLATE
Band, Albert
CASTLE FREAK
Band, Charles
CASTLE FREAK
PREHYSTERIA! 3
Bantle, Robert
ASCENT, THE
Baran, Jack
KISS OF DEATH
Barber, Gary
ACE VENTURA: WHEN NATURE CALLS
Barclay, Jane
RADIO INSIDE
Barenholtz, Ben
GEORGIA
Barker, Clive
CANDYMAN: FAREWELL TO THE FLESH
Barone, Tracey
MONEY TRAIN
Barron, Steve
WHILE YOU WERE SLEEPING
Baruc, Robert
FEAR, THE
Bass, Ronald
WAITING TO EXHALE
Baum, Carol
FATHER OF THE BRIDE PART II
KICKING AND SCREAMING
Beach, Jim
DEATH MACHINE
Beaucaire, J.E.
MIGHTY APHRODITE
Becker, Richard
GROSS MISCONDUCT
Beers, Betsy
SAFE PASSAGE
Benayoun, Georges
MINA TANNENBAUM
Benmussa, Robert
SIX DAYS, SIX NIGHTS
Beresford, Bruce
CURSE OF THE STARVING CLASS
Berger, Albert
CRUMB
Bernardi, Barry
TOM AND HUCK
Bernstein, Armyan
BABY-SITTERS CLUB, THE
Besser, Stuart M.
VAMPIRE IN BROOKLYN
Bevan, Tim
DEAD MAN WALKING
PANTHER
Beychok, Mark
SKINNER
Bickford, Laura
CITIZEN X
Birnbaum, Anat
WOMAN AT WAR, A
Bishop, Dennis
BIG GREEN, THE
HOUSEGUEST
Black, Christopher J.
DREAM A LITTLE DREAM 2
Blackwell, Chris
BASKETBALL DIARIES, THE
Blay, Andre
VILLAGE OF THE DAMNED
Bliss, Thomas A.
BABY-SITTERS CLUB, THE

Blomquist, Alan C.
LITTLE PRINCESS, A
Boespflug, Francis
CARRINGTON
Bonfiglio, Lois
BROKEN TRUST
LAKOTA WOMAN: SIEGE AT WOUNDED
KNEE
Borden, Bill
CURE, THE
Border, W.K.
BLUE TIGER
Boswell, Chris
DIGGER
Bovino, Jerald
ALMOST DEAD
Bowman, Sarah
HEAVYWEIGHTS
Bradley, Paul
FEAST OF JULY
JEFFERSON IN PARIS
Bradshaw, Joan
NINE MONTHS
Brandman, Michael
WATER ENGINE, THE
Bretall, Graeme
NINA TAKES A LOVER
Brockmann, Hans
USUAL SUSPECTS, THE
Brown, Jon
TIE THAT BINDS, THE
Brown, Julie
NATIONAL LAMPOON'S ATTACK OF THE
5'2" WOMEN
Brownstein, Jerome
AMATEUR
Brubaker, James D.
WALK IN THE CLOUDS, A
Brugge, Pieter Jan
HEAT
Bruno, Mark
ARMAGEDDON: THE FINAL CHALLENGE
Burgess, Al
LAMB
Burns, Edward J.
BROTHERS MCMULLEN, THE
Burns, Steve
HARLEM DIARY: NINE VOICES OF
RESILIENCE
Bursteen, Alan B.
MIDNIGHT TEASE 2
Butterworth, James
PEBBLE AND THE PENGUIN, THE
Byrne, J. Dixon
CLEAN, SHAVEN
Cabrera, Frank
STRAWBERRY AND CHOCOLATE
Cady, Fitch
BILLY MADISON
Caleb, Ruth
CENTURY
Callender, Colin
DOOMSDAY GUN
Cantin, Marie
THINGS TO DO IN DENVER WHEN
YOU'RE DEAD
Caracciolo, Joseph M.
TO DIE FOR
Carcassonne, Philippe
CARRINGTON
Caruso, D.J.
NICK OF TIME
Cass, Kathryn
NUMBER ONE FAN
Catmull, Edwin
TOY STORY
Caton-Jones, Michael
ROB ROY

Caucheteux, Pascal
DOOM GENERATION, THE
Cavallo, Robert
ANGUS
TWELVE MONKEYS
Cazes, Lila
CYBER BANDITS
Chambers, Michael
KIDS
Chan, Peter
HE'S A WOMAN, SHE'S A MAN
Chapman, Matthew
CITIZEN X
Chapman, Peggy
DALLAS DOLL
Charr, Henri
CAGED HEARTS
Chase, Marianne
EROTIQUE
Chasman, Julia
PEREZ FAMILY, THE
Cheng, Cora
HEROIC TRIO, THE
Choi, Eung Pyo
GALAXIS
Clapp, Jim
TO CROSS THE RUBICON
Claus, Richard
MUTE WITNESS
Clegg, Terence
CIRCLE OF FRIENDS
Cohen, Bruce
TO WONG FOO, THANKS FOR
EVERYTHING! JULIE NEWMAR
Cohen, Jay
SWIMMING WITH SHARKS
Coleman, Tom
FLUKE
Collier, Barry
DECOY
GALAXIS
Collins, Guy
HIGHLANDER: THE FINAL DIMENSION
Colwell, Thom
ANDROID AFFAIR, THE
Compin, Antoine
WINGS OF COURAGE
Connery, Sean
JUST CAUSE
Copeland, III, Miles
CYBER BANDITS
Coppola, Francis Ford
MY FAMILY: MI FAMILIA
Corman, Roger
BODY CHEMISTRY 4: FULL EXPOSURE
CRAZYSITTER, THE
DILLINGER AND CAPONE
REFLECTIONS IN THE DARK
SPY WITHIN, THE
Cort, Robert W.
JUMANJI
OPERATION DUMBO DROP
SEPARATE LIVES
TIE THAT BINDS, THE
Cowan, Cindy
POWER OF ATTORNEY
Craig, Sid
BREAK, THE
Cuddihy, Christopher A.
BLESSING
Cunliffe, David
GLORY BOYS, THE
d'Oliveira, Carlos
CARMEN MIRANDA: BANANAS IS MY
BUSINESS
Daniels, Stan
SUBSTITUTE WIFE, THE

Danza, Tony
JERKY BOYS: THE MOVIE, THE
Davids, Paul
ROSWELL: THE U.F.O. COVER-UP
De Laurentiis, Dino
ASSASSINS
De Luca, Michael
DON JUAN DEMARCO
IN THE MOUTH OF MADNESS
De Mann, Freddy
CANADIAN BACON
De Mornay, Rebecca
NEVER TALK TO STRANGERS
Deakin, Michael
DOOMSDAY GUN
Deitell, Lisa Wilson
OUTSIDE THE LAW
Delfiner, Gary
BULLETPROOF HEART
CRACKERJACK
Demme, Jonathan
DEVIL IN A BLUE DRESS
ROY COHN/JACK SMITH
DePasse, Suzanne
BUFFALO GIRLS
Devenn, Lucus E.
DARK SIDE OF GENIUS, THE
DeWalt, Kevin
DECOY
Dimbort, Danny
LAST RIDE, THE
SEARCH AND DESTROY
Donen, Joshua
UNDERNEATH, THE
Donner, Richard
FREE WILLY 2: THE ADVENTURE HOME
TALES FROM THE CRYPT: DEMON
KNIGHT
Doran, Lindsay
SABRINA
Douglas, Peter
ENEMY WITHIN, THE
Doumanian, Jean
MIGHTY APHRODITE
Dubinet, Ann
INNOCENT, THE
Duplat, Francois
USUAL SUSPECTS, THE
East, Guy
MY FAMILY: MI FAMILIA
Eaton, Rebecca
PERSUASION
Eberts, Jake
ARABIAN KNIGHT
Efros, Mel
IT TAKES TWO
Egerton, Mark
SPECIES
Elgort, Arthur
COLORADO COWBOY: THE BRUCE FORD
STORY
Eliason, Joyce
GOOD DAY TO DIE, A
Elliott, Mike
ATTACK OF THE 60-FOOT CENTERFOLD
CAGED HEAT 3000
REFLECTIONS IN THE DARK
Ellis, Riley Kathryn
POWDER
Emerson, Sasha
FATHER AND SCOUT
Engelman, Bob
MORTAL KOMBAT
Ephron, Amy
LITTLE PRINCESS, A
Epstein, Allen
DOUBLE, DOUBLE, TOIL AND TROUBLE

Erickson, C.O.
STUART SAVES HIS FAMILY
Esparza, Moctesuma
AVENGING ANGEL
Estes, Larry
COLDBLOODED
Estevez, Emilio
JERKY BOYS: THE MOVIE, THE
Faber, George
DALLAS DOLL
PERSUASION
Faubert, Pascale
TOTAL ECLIPSE
Fay, William
HUNTED, THE
Fayed, Dodi
SCARLET LETTER, THE
Feitshans, Buzz
DIE HARD WITH A VENGEANCE
Fellner, Eric
DEAD MAN WALKING
PANTHER
Ferro, Matt
EMBRACE OF THE VAMPIRE
Fiedler, John
COPYCAT
Field, Ted
JUMANJI
OPERATION DUMBO DROP
SEPARATE LIVES
TIE THAT BINDS, THE
Fields, Adam
MONEY TRAIN
Fields, Joel
IN THE DEEP WOODS
Fish, Jennifer
TIE-DIED: ROCK 'N' ROLL'S MOST
DEADICATED FANS
Forte, Deborah
BABY-SITTERS CLUB, THE
Foster, Lucas
BAD BOYS
CRIMSON TIDE
DANGEROUS MINDS
Franco, Larry J.
JUMANJI
Frank, Ilana
BOULEVARD
Frappier, Roger
LOVE AND HUMAN REMAINS
Freyermuth, Ortwin
BODY SHOT
Friedland, Dennis
COVER STORY
Frye, Nicholas
FUNNY BONES
Furie, Jonathan
AMERICA'S DEADLIEST HOME VIDEO
Gale, David
SAFE PASSAGE
Gallagher, Patrick
MUTANT SPECIES
Gallin, Sandy
FATHER OF THE BRIDE PART II
KICKING AND SCREAMING
Garbutta, Stephen
HEAVEN'S A DRAG
Gellis, Andrew
ACROSS THE SEA OF TIME: NEW YORK
3D
Genetti, Dan
BASKETBALL DIARIES, THE
Gernert, Walter
BODY STROKES
EXPERT, THE
Gerson, Laura
FATHER AND SCOUT

Gil, David
ABDUCTED 2: THE REUNION
Gilbert, Ron
IN THE DEEP WOODS
Giler, David
TALES FROM THE CRYPT: DEMON
KNIGHT
Gilford, Hilary
LIVING IN OBLIVION
Ginsberg, David R.
ROSWELL: THE U.F.O. COVER-UP
Ginsburg, David R.
CITIZEN X
DANGER OF LOVE
Gladstein, Richard
CROSSING GUARD, THE
JOURNEY OF AUGUST KING, THE
Glascoe, John
KURT VONNEGUT'S HARRISON
BERGERON
Glickman, Rana Joy
FUN
Goddard, Melissa
FATHER AND SCOUT
Golchan, Frederic
IN THE DEEP WOODS
Gold, James M.
DEAD FUNNY
Goldberg, Emanuel
FOOL AND HIS MONEY, A
Goldstein, David
CURSE OF THE STARVING CLASS
Goldstein, Gary W.
UNDER SIEGE 2: DARK TERRITORY
Golin, Steve
LORD OF ILLUSIONS
Gordon, Shep
VILLAGE OF THE DAMNED
Granims, Tony
CREEP
Green, Jim
DOUBLE, DOUBLE, TOIL AND TROUBLE
Greggio, Ezio
SILENCE OF THE HAMS
Gruberg, Benjamin
ABDUCTED 2: THE REUNION
Guerin, J.P.
PAYBACK
Gurian, Paul R.
ARIZONA DREAM
Guttenberg, Linda
FARINELLI
Hadida, Samuel
EXPERT, THE
Hagopian, Kip
RESTORATION
Halberstadt, Ira
ROOMMATES
Halfon, Lianne
CRUMB
Hallowell, Todd
APOLLO 13
Halmi, Jr., Robert
ASCENT, THE
BLACK FOX
Halmi, Sr., Robert
GETTING OUT
Hamburg, Victoria
JOHNNY MNEMONIC
Hammel, Thomas M.
FAIR GAME
Harel, Sharon
RADIO INSIDE
Harris, Robert
INDIAN IN THE CUPBOARD, THE
Harrison, Matthew
RHYTHM THIEF

Hart, William
JUDICIAL CONSENT
Hartwell, Barbara
KILIAN'S CHRONICLE
Hawn, Goldie
SOMETHING TO TALK ABOUT
Hayward, Sarah
DANCE ME OUTSIDE
Heller, Rosilyn
BETTER OFF DEAD
Henderson, Duncan
OUTBREAK
Henkel, Christoph
CREW, THE
Hertzberg, Paul
TERESA'S TATTOO
Herzberg, Ilona
WATERWORLD
Hibbin, Sally
ENGLISHMAN WHO WENT UP A HILL
BUT CAME DOWN A MOUNTAIN, THE
Hickox, Anthony L.V.
CHILDREN OF THE CORN III: URBAN
HARVEST
Hill, Leonard
IN THE DEEP WOODS
Hill, Walter
TALES FROM THE CRYPT: DEMON
KNIGHT
Holmes, Preston
ADDICTION, THE
Hope, Ted
BROTHERS MCMULLEN, THE
SAFE
Horan, Art
USUAL SUSPECTS, THE
Horton, Charis
WINGS OF COURAGE
Hudlin, Reginald
COSMIC SLOP
Hudlin, Warrington
COSMIC SLOP
Hurst, Howard
YOUNGER & YOUNGER
Huth, Hanno
STALINGRAD
Ice Cube
FRIDAY
Ichise, Taka
BLUE TIGER
Iseki, Satoru
SMOKE
Israel, Stephen
SWIMMING WITH SHARKS
Jablin, David
NATIONAL LAMPOON'S ATTACK OF THE
5'2" WOMEN
Jadecewicz, Pascal
MINA TANNENBAUM
Jaffe, Toby
QUICK AND THE DEAD, THE
Janne, Dominique
FARINELLI
Jarvilaturi, Ilkka
CITY UNPLUGGED
Jensen, Anders P.
SUDDEN DEATH
Jensen, Peter Aalbaek
KINGDOM, THE
Jewison, Norman
DANCE ME OUTSIDE
Jiang Feng-Chyi
PUSHING HANDS
Jobs, Steven
TOY STORY
Jones, Glen
SECRET OF ROAN INISH, THE

Jones, Robert
ENGLISHMAN WHO WENT UP A HILL
BUT CAME DOWN A MOUNTAIN, THE
USUAL SUSPECTS, THE
Jourd'hui, Gerard
OLD LADY WHO WALKED IN THE SEA,
THE
Kallberg, Kenneth J.
OPERATION INTERCEPT
Kanbar, Maurice
MARTHA AND I
Kang, James
3 NINJAS KNUCKLE UP
Karlan, Patricia
BOYS ON THE SIDE
Kasanoff, Lawrence
STRANGE DAYS
Kassar, Mario
CUTTHROAT ISLAND
LAST OF THE DOGMEN
SHOWGIRLS
Katz, Robert
AVENGING ANGEL
Kaufman, Kenneth
NIGHTMARE
Keitel, Harvey
BLUE IN THE FACE
Kelleher, John
AWFULLY BIG ADVENTURE, AN
Keltz, Martin
BABY-SITTERS CLUB, THE
INDIAN IN THE CUPBOARD, THE
Kenneally, Bob
SHOW, THE
Kennedy, Kathleen
BALTO
Ker, Jonathon
BRIAN WILSON: I JUST WASN'T MADE
FOR THESE TIMES
Kerner, Jordan
MIAMI RHAPSODY
Kim, Joseph A.
TIE-DIED: ROCK 'N' ROLL'S MOST
DEADICATED FANS
King, Zalman
BOCA
Kirshbaum, Jeff
FUN
Kleinman, Stuart
HOME FOR THE HOLIDAYS
Koch, Jr., Howard W.
VIRTUOSITY
Kolsrud, Dan
SEVEN
Konigsberg, Frank
GOOD DAY TO DIE, A
Kopelson, Anne
OUTBREAK
SEVEN
Korchak, Nelson I.
SKINNER
Korda, David
BODY SHOT
TWO BITS
Kosberg, Robert
TWELVE MONKEYS
Krohne, Michael
STALINGRAD
Kuehnert, Fred
GHOST BRIGADE
Kurosawa, Mitsuru
NEW YORK COP
Ladd, Jr., Alan
BRADY BUNCH MOVIE, THE
Lado, Aldo
FARINELLI
Laiter, Tova
SCARLET LETTER, THE

Lambert, Christopher
NINE MONTHS
Landau, Susan
ANGUS
Landsburg, Alan
GLORY BOYS, THE
Lantos, Robert
JOHNNY MNEMONIC
Latour, Pierre
LOVE AND HUMAN REMAINS
Lau, Jeff
ASHES OF TIME
Law, Lindsay
AMATEUR
RECKLESS
SAFE
Lawenda, Jeff
ASCENT, THE
Lawrence, Robert
DIE HARD WITH A VENGEANCE
Lee, Jing-Hwan
SHAO LIN POPEYE
Lee, Spike
NEW JERSEY DRIVE
TALES FROM THE HOOD
Leipzig, Adam
ROOMMATES
LeMesurier, Roger
NOSTRADAMUS KID, THE
Lerner, Avi
LAST RIDE, THE
SEARCH AND DESTROY
Levine, Joel
AMERICAN COP
Levinsohn, Gary
ANGUS
TWELVE MONKEYS
Levy, Robert L.
PAYBACK
Lewis, Claudia
LITTLE ODESSA
Li Ran
ERMO
Licht, Andy
WATERWORLD
Little, Ellen Dinerman
RICHARD III
Lovenheim, Robert
O.J. SIMPSON STORY, THE
Luddy, Tom
MY FAMILY: MI FAMILIA
Luger, Lois
DANGER OF LOVE
Lundgren, Dolph
PENTATHLON
Lynch, David
NADJA
MacDonald, Laurie
HOW TO MAKE AN AMERICAN QUILT
MacDonald, William J.
JADE
Mackay, Anne-Marie
BRIAN WILSON: I JUST WASN'T MADE
FOR THESE TIMES
Maddalena, Marianne
VAMPIRE IN BROOKLYN
Malo, Rene
SCANNERS: THE SHOWDOWN
Mann, Abby
INDICTMENT: THE MCMARTIN TRIAL
Mark, Diane Mei Lin
PICTURE BRIDE
Marlow, David
DEAD FUNNY
Marmion, Yves
AMATEUR
Marmon, Yves
WHITE MAN'S BURDEN

Marouani, Gilbert
I, THE WORST OF ALL
Martinelli, Gabriella
AMAZING PANDA ADVENTURE, THE
Maruc, Robert
DEAD FUNNY
Matheson, Tim
BREACH OF CONDUCT
McCollum, Kevin
JEFFREY
McCord, Jonas
CLASS OF '61
McElroy, Hal
SUM OF US, THE
McEveety, Stephen
BRAVEHEART
McKellen, Ian
RICHARD III
McMillan, Terry
WAITING TO EXHALE
Meek, Scott
AMATEUR
Meieran, David
BALLOT MEASURE 9
Melniker, Benjamin
BATMAN FOREVER
Memel, Jana Sue
ANDROID AFFAIR, THE
Mendoza, Miguel
STRAWBERRY AND CHOCOLATE
Menzies, Bryce
DEATH IN BRUNSWICK
Merchant, Ismail
FEAST OF JULY
Mi-Hee Kim
HOW TO TOP MY WIFE
Milchan, Arnon
FREE WILLY 2: THE ADVENTURE HOME
HEAT
Minot, Dinah
STUART SAVES HIS FAMILY
Mittweg, Rolf
LITTLE ODESSA
Moder, Mike
CRIMSON TIDE
Molen, Gerald R.
CASPER
Molito, Thomas
ASCENT, THE
Montgomery, Jeffrey A.
CASPER
Moore, Karen
OUT OF ANNIE'S PAST
Morgan, Peter
FATHER AND SCOUT
Morrissey, John
DR. JEKYLL & MS. HYDE
Mueller, Jeff
WATERWORLD
Murphy, Karen
MAGIC IN THE WATER
Nadler, James
KURT VONNEGUT'S HARRISON
BERGERON
Naidenova, Oliga
CREATION OF ADAM
Nash, Mark
POSTCARDS FROM AMERICA
Nathan, Stan
SHOW, THE
Nathanson, Michael
COPYCAT
Naumann, Chris
DILLINGER AND CAPONE
SPY WITHIN, THE
Nederlander, Gladys
NEXT DOOR

Nelson, Peter Martin
DESTINY TURNS ON THE RADIO
Netter, Gil
FIRST KNIGHT
Neuman, Jeffrey
UNDER SIEGE 2: DARK TERRITORY
Newirth, Charles
AMERICAN PRESIDENT, THE
Newman, Paul L.
DEAD FUNNY
GALAXIS
Newman, Peter
SECRET OF ROAN INISH, THE
Newmyer, Deborah Jelin
HOW TO MAKE AN AMERICAN QUILT
Ning, Li
PHANTOM LOVER, THE
Norton, Eileen Harris
MAYA LIN: A STRONG CLEAR VISION
Notkin, Shelby
NINA TAKES A LOVER
Nunnari, Gianni
SEVEN
O'Boyle, William B.
CURSE OF THE STARVING CLASS
O'Sullivan, Morgan
RUN OF THE COUNTRY, THE
Oggeh, Aziz
YOUNGER & YOUNGER
Okada, Toshio
WINGS OF HONNEAMISE: ROYAL SPACE
FORCE
Okun, Charles
FRENCH KISS
Okuyama, Kazuyoshi
MYSTERY OF RAMPO, THE
Olsberg, Jonathan
OTHELLO
Oppenheimer, Peer
BOULEVARD
Panzarella, Patrick
KIDS
Parkes, Walter
HOW TO MAKE AN AMERICAN QUILT
Passone, Alberto
POSTMAN, THE
Patchett, Tom
NIGHTMARE
Pearl, Mel
STEAL BIG, STEAL LITTLE
Pecker, David J.
UNZIPPED
Pensa, Laura
FOOL AND HIS MONEY, A
Peschken, Chris
DILLINGER AND CAPONE
SPY WITHIN, THE
Pevsner, Tom
GOLDENEYE
Phillips, Michael
COMPANION, THE
Piel, Jean-Louis
BURNT BY THE SUN
Pierce, Frederick S.
MONEY TRAIN
SUBSTITUTE WIFE, THE
Pierce, Keith
SUBSTITUTE WIFE, THE
Pierce, Richard
SUBSTITUTE WIFE, THE
Pierson, John
LIE DOWN WITH DOGS
Pinchuk, Sheldon
BREACH OF CONDUCT
Pollack, Sydney
SENSE AND SENSIBILITY
Porcelli, Enzo
LAMERICA

Porter, Darryl
DEAD PRESIDENTS
Powell, Nik
WOMAN AT WAR, A
Powell, Norman S.
BLACK FOX
Pragjee, Sudhir
CRY, THE BELOVED COUNTRY
Prazasky, Premysl
ACCUMULATOR 1
Pressman, Edward R.
JUDGE DREDD
Preuss, Werner
ALMOST DEAD
Principal, Victoria
NIGHTMARE
Pustin, Bruce S.
BAD BOYS
Putnam, David
BURNING SEASON, THE
Rabins, Sandra
DANGEROUS MINDS
Rack, B.J.
JOHNNY MNEMONIC
Radford, Bonne
BALTO
Raimi, Sam
DARKMAN 2: THE RETURN OF DURANT
Rambaldi, Carlo
DECOY
Rattray, Eric
FIRST KNIGHT
Ray, Fred Olen
JACK-O
Redford, Robert
STRAWBERRY AND CHOCOLATE
Regen, Stuart
LEAVING LAS VEGAS
Reichel, Stephane
NATIONAL LAMPOON'S SENIOR TRIP
Reid, William
UNDERNEATH, THE
Reilly, Brian
BORN TO BE WILD
Ridge, Maripat
AMERICA'S DEADLIEST HOME VIDEO
Rintels, David
MY ANTONIA
Ripps, Susan
WIGSTOCK: THE MOVIE
Robbins, Lance H.
CRAZYSITTER, THE
REFLECTIONS IN THE DARK
Rocco, Marc
MURDER IN THE FIRST
TERESA'S TATTOO
Rockwell, Alexandre
FOUR ROOMS
Rohrbach, Gunter
STALINGRAD
Roos, Don
BOYS ON THE SIDE
Rose, Lee
DECONSTRUCTING SARAH
Rosenblum, Marvin J.
INNOCENT LIES
Rosenblum, Paul
SPITFIRE
Rosenfeld, Donald
JEFFERSON IN PARIS
Ross, Monty
CLOCKERS
Roy, Michel
NATIONAL LAMPOON'S SENIOR TRIP
Rozenberg, Paul
MINA TANNENBAUM

Ryerson, Sean
BEYOND RANGOON
Sackner, Sara
TIE-DIED: ROCK 'N' ROLL'S MOST
DEADICATED FANS
Saget, Bob
FATHER AND SCOUT
Sales, Daniel
SKINNER
Samples, Keith
BODILY HARM
DESTINY TURNS ON THE RADIO
IT TAKES TWO
JUDICIAL CONSENT
THREE WISHES
Sanchez, Gustavo
NO MERCY
Sanchini, Rae
STRANGE DAYS
Sancton, Daryl
NUMBER ONE FAN
Santisi, Nina
UNZIPPED
Saranceni, Claudio
PURE FORMALITY, A
Sarkissian, Arthur
WHILE YOU WERE SLEEPING
Sauer, Ernest G.
BIKINI BISTRO
Saxon, Edward
DEVIL IN A BLUE DRESS
Schamus, James
BROTHERS MCMULLEN, THE
SAFE
Schindler, Peter
DRACULA: DEAD AND LOVING IT
FORGET PARIS
Schneier, Paul Frederick
CONVICT COWBOY
Schumacher, Joel
BABYSITTER, THE
Schwary, Ronald
SABRINA
Scorsese, Martin
SEARCH AND DESTROY
Scott, Allan
SHALLOW GRAVE
Sedov, Vladimir
BURNT BY THE SUN
Sertner, Robert M.
LAKOTA WOMAN: SIEGE AT WOUNDED
KNEE
TOO YOUNG TO DIE?
Shah, Ash R.
SUDDEN DEATH
Shah, Sundip R.
SUDDEN DEATH
Shah, Sunil R.
SUDDEN DEATH
Sheen, Simon B.
3 NINJAS KNUCKLE UP
Sheng, Richard
DARK SIDE OF GENIUS, THE
Shils, Barry
WIGSTOCK: THE MOVIE
Shivas, Mark
AWFULLY BIG ADVENTURE, AN
CENTURY
PRIEST
Short, Trevor
OUTSIDE THE LAW
Shuler-Donner, Lauren
ASSASSINS
Shuster, Brian
BALLISTIC
POWER OF ATTORNEY
Sighvatsson, Sigurjon
CANADIAN BACON

LORD OF ILLUSIONS
S.F.W.
Sigman, Robert
BULLETPROOF HEART
CRACKERJACK
Silver, Joel
TALES FROM THE CRYPT: DEMON
KNIGHT
Simandl, Lloyd A.
CRACKERJACK
Simmons, Russell
ADDICTION, THE
SHOW, THE
Simon, Danny
MORTAL KOMBAT
Simon, Joe
RICHARD III
Simons, Edward
HOWLING: NEW MOON RISING, THE
Simpson, Paige
LEAVING LAS VEGAS
Simpson, Roger
NOSTRADAMUS KID, THE
Singh, Sanjeev
CRY, THE BELOVED COUNTRY
Sivers, John
AWFULLY BIG ADVENTURE, AN
Slan, Jon
RENT-A-KID
Sloss, John
BEFORE SUNRISE
SECRET OF ROAN INISH, THE
Smiley, Charles L.
HIGHLANDER: THE FINAL DIMENSION
Smyth, A. William
CRACKERJACK
Snukal, Robert
POWDER
Sofronski, Bernard
DILLINGER
Softley, Iain
HACKERS
Soisson, Joel
BLUE TIGER
Sommers, Stephen
TOM AND HUCK
Sonnenfeld, Barry
GET SHORTY
Sorlat, Gregoire
DOOM GENERATION, THE
South, Margaret
MAN OF THE HOUSE
Spielberg, Steven
BALTO
CASPER
CLASS OF '61
Spina, Nicholas P.
ME AND THE MOB
Steele, Jim
CREW, THE
Stefano, Joseph
TWO BITS
Steinem, Gloria
BETTER OFF DEAD
Steinhardt, Michael
GIRL IN THE CADILLAC
Steinmetz, Tom
TOP DOG
Stern, Daniel
BUSHWHACKED
Stevens, Leslie
GORDY
Stone, Oliver
INDICTMENT: THE MCMARTIN TRIAL
Stoneman, Rod
AILSA
CIRCLE OF FRIENDS

Stott, Jeffrey
AMERICAN PRESIDENT, THE
Strange, Michael
BULLETPROOF HEART
MALICIOUS
Strawn, Mick
GHOST BRIGADE
Streit, David
SPECIES
Stroller, Louis A.
GOLD DIGGERS: THE SECRET OF BEAR
MOUNTAIN
Sullivan, Errol
SUM OF US, THE
Sussman, Peter
KURT VONNEGUT'S HARRISON
BERGERON
Swedin, Rosalie
CLOCKERS
Swicord, Robin
PEREZ FAMILY, THE
Takacs, Tibor
BAD BLOOD
Takao, Hiroshi
CRIMSON WOLF
Tapert, Robert
DARKMAN 2: THE RETURN OF DURANT
QUICK AND THE DEAD, THE
Taplin, Jonathan
TO DIE FOR
Tarantino, Quentin
FOUR ROOMS
Tatelman, Harry
MAJOR PAYNE
Tavares, Paulo
CARMEN MIRANDA: BANANAS IS MY
BUSINESS
Taylor, Albert L.
OPERATION INTERCEPT
Tejada-Flores, Miguel
ALMOST DEAD
Thenoz, Stephane
FARINELLI
Thompson, Carol H.
PENTATHLON
Thoren, Terry
TOO OUTRAGEOUS ANIMATION
Tichy, Wolfram
ECLIPSE
Todd, Jennifer
NOW AND THEN
Toussaint, Anne-Dominique
MINA TANNENBAUM
Towers, Harry Alan
CRY, THE BELOVED COUNTRY
MANGLER, THE
Tsuburaya, Akira
WIZARD OF DARKNESS
Tudor, Marty
NEXT DOOR
Tulchin, Harris
SILENCE OF THE HAMS
Turner, Bryan
FRIDAY
Turner, Terrence
FIRST DEGREE
Turtle, Jon
FLUKE
Unger, Bill
CRIMSON TIDE
Uslan, Michael E.
BATMAN FOREVER
Vajna, Andrew
JUDGE DREDD
Vajna, Andrew G.
DIE HARD WITH A VENGEANCE
Van Sant, Gus
KIDS

Van Wyck, Jim
    FREE WILLY 2: THE ADVENTURE HOME
Vance, Ladd
    EMBRACE OF THE VAMPIRE
Vendramini, Danny
    DESPERATE PREY
Vereshchagin, Leonid
    BURNT BY THE SUN
Vernon, Ted
    VILLAGE OF THE DAMNED
Vincent, Tony
    DANGEROUS, THE
Vitale, Ruth
    DON JUAN DEMARCO
    SAFE PASSAGE
Vives, Camilo
    STRAWBERRY AND CHOCOLATE
Volkenborn, Klaus
    LAST GOOD TIME, THE
    WIGSTOCK: THE MOVIE
Von Zerneck, Frank
    LAKOTA WOMAN: SIEGE AT WOUNDED
        KNEE
    TOO YOUNG TO DIE?
Vonier, Fabienne
    CARRINGTON
Walker, Chet
    GLASS SHIELD, THE
Wallace, Ronna
    CREW, THE
Wallace, Ronna B.
    PENTATHLON
Wang Wei
    SHANGHAI TRIAD
Wansbrough, Martha
    BUSINESS AFFAIR, A
Warner, Aron
    TANK GIRL
Warren, John
    GIRL IN THE CADILLAC
Watanabe, Shigeru
    WINGS OF HONNEAMISE: ROYAL SPACE
        FORCE
Watanabe, Yoshinori
    NEW YORK COP
Wayans, Damon
    MAJOR PAYNE
Wechsler, Nick
    LITTLE ODESSA
Weinstein, Bob
    BLUE IN THE FACE
    CROSSING GUARD, THE
    ENGLISHMAN WHO WENT UP A HILL
        BUT CAME DOWN A MOUNTAIN, THE
    JOURNEY OF AUGUST KING, THE
    MONTH BY THE LAKE, A
    SMOKE
    THINGS TO DO IN DENVER WHEN
        YOU'RE DEAD
Weinstein, Harvey
    BLUE IN THE FACE
    CROSSING GUARD, THE
    ENGLISHMAN WHO WENT UP A HILL
        BUT CAME DOWN A MOUNTAIN, THE
    JOURNEY OF AUGUST KING, THE
    MONTH BY THE LAKE, A
    SMOKE
    THINGS TO DO IN DENVER WHEN
        YOU'RE DEAD
Weiss, Robert K.
    TOMMY BOY
Welsh, Richard
    GETTING OUT
    GREAT ELEPHANT ESCAPE, THE
    PIANO LESSON, THE
    REDWOOD CURTAIN
    RETURN OF THE NATIVE, THE
Westwell, James R.
    CRACKERJACK

Wigram, Lionel
    UNDERNEATH, THE
Wiley, Martin
    UNDER SIEGE 2: DARK TERRITORY
Wilkinson, Lawrence
    CRUMB
Willenson, Seth
    TOP DOG
Williams, Bernie
    INDIAN IN THE CUPBOARD, THE
Winberg, Ted N.
    DARK DEALER
Wolf, Joseph
    NEW YORK COP
Wolper, David L.
    DILLINGER
    MURDER IN THE FIRST
Wong, Raymond
    PHANTOM LOVER, THE
Wooll, Nigel
    RUN OF THE COUNTRY, THE
Wynorski, Jim
    MIDNIGHT TEASE 2
Yablans, Frank
    CONGO
Yamaji, Hiroshi
    WIZARD OF DARKNESS
Yang, Janet
    INDICTMENT: THE MCMARTIN TRIAL
Yip, Brian
    HEROIC TRIO, THE
Yong Naiming
    RED FIRECRACKER, GREEN
        FIRECRACKER
Zemeckis, Robert
    TALES FROM THE CRYPT: DEMON
        KNIGHT
Zheng Jianping
    HEROIC TRIO, THE
Zhu Yongde
    SHANGHAI TRIAD
Zucker, Janet
    FIRST KNIGHT

MAKEUP/FX MAKEUP

Abrums, Stephen
    BYE BYE, LOVE
    CROSSING GUARD, THE
Adams, Cynthia F.
    BODY SHOT
Adams, Susie
    FEAST OF JULY
Adkins, Corrina
    JACK-O
Altamara, DeeDee
    O.J. SIMPSON STORY, THE
Anderson, Bernadine M.
    VAMPIRE IN BROOKLYN
Anderson, Beverly
    BAR GIRLS
Anderson, Lance
    DEAD PRESIDENTS
Andrews, Joceline
    ENGLISHMAN WHO WENT UP A HILL
        BUT CAME DOWN A MOUNTAIN, THE
Androff, Patty
    DECONSTRUCTING SARAH
Apone, Allan A.
    LAST OF THE DOGMEN
Artmont, Steve
    THINGS TO DO IN DENVER WHEN
        YOU'RE DEAD
Athayde, Pamela M.
    BULLETPROOF HEART
    GOOD DAY TO DIE, A
Aubuchon, Karrie
    VAMPIRE IN BROOKLYN

Avdiushko, Larissa
    BURNT BY THE SUN
Bachman, Cynthia
    REDWOOD CURTAIN
Badoux, Nancy
    MINA TANNENBAUM
Baker, Rick
    BATMAN FOREVER
Balazs, Charles
    ARIZONA DREAM
    CITIZEN X
Ballas, Christ
    MALLRATS
Barber, Lynn
    FLUKE
    GETTING OUT
Barczewska, Elizabeth
    CYBER BANDITS
Barkan, Nurith
    OLD LADY WHO WALKED IN THE SEA,
        THE
Bartels, Annie
    FRIENDS
Bartolucci, Cristina
    FOUR ROOMS
Barton, David
    SILENCE OF THE HAMS
    USUAL SUSPECTS, THE
Bayless, John
    HEAVYWEIGHTS
Beigel, Patty
    GRANNY, THE
Belcher, Suzanne
    ASCENT, THE
Bellszig, Tim
    MIDNIGHT TEASE 2
Benevides, Rob
    CLEAN, SHAVEN
Bennett, Jill
    DECONSTRUCTING SARAH
Berger, Howard
    BAD COMPANY
    DARKMAN 2: THE RETURN OF DURANT
    IN THE MOUTH OF MADNESS
    QUICK AND THE DEAD, THE
Berkeley, Ron
    DON JUAN DEMARCO
Bernet, Michelle
    VALLEY OF ABRAHAM, THE
Beveridge, Christina
    CARRINGTON
    TWELVE MONKEYS
Bigger, Michal
    DEAD MAN WALKING
    JERKY BOYS: THE MOVIE, THE
    SAFE PASSAGE
Bihr, Katy
    LEAVING LAS VEGAS
Black, Jean
    SEVEN
    TIE THAT BINDS, THE
Blaise, Andre
    CURSE OF THE STARVING CLASS
Blake, John
    NIXON
Blanco, Mirta
    I, THE WORST OF ALL
Bloom, Michelle
    SILENCE OF THE HAMS
Blundell, Christine
    HACKERS
Blynder, Karen
    FATHER OF THE BRIDE PART II
Boccia, Margot
    MONEY TRAIN
Boni, Lisa
    DEATH MACHINE

Bottin, Rob
SEVEN
Bourdiol, Anne
OLD LADY WHO WALKED IN THE SEA,
THE
Bowring, Felicity
ACROSS THE MOON
BEYOND RANGOON
INDIAN IN THE CUPBOARD, THE
Branche, Stacye P.
WALKING DEAD, THE
Browski, Anais
CIRCUMSTANCES UNKNOWN
Brumberger, Tom
DIGGER
Bryant, Belinda
WATER ENGINE, THE
Bryant, Janie
BLESSING
Buchanan, Ann
AWFULLY BIG ADVENTURE, AN
Buchner, Fern
BOYS ON THE SIDE
MAD LOVE
MIGHTY APHRODITE
Buechler, John
HALLOWEEN: THE CURSE OF MICHAEL
MYERS
Buhler, Michelle
USUAL SUSPECTS, THE
Buono, Lisa
BLUE TIGER
CHILDREN OF THE CORN III: URBAN
HARVEST
Burman, Barney
POWDER
Burman, Ellis
OUTBREAK
Burman Studio, The
WATERWORLD
Burman, Thomas R.
POWDER
Burwell, Lois
DOOMSDAY GUN
RETURN OF THE NATIVE, THE
Cabral, Susan A.
OUTBREAK
Caglione, Jr., John
HEAT
Caldwell, Karen
REASON TO BELIEVE, A
Canistraci, Jay
PEREZ FAMILY, THE
Cannom, Greg
NINE MONTHS
ROOMMATES
Carbone, Marilyn
SAFE PASSAGE
Carter, Charle
HIGHLANDER: THE FINAL DIMENSION
Carter, Marie
VAMPIRE IN BROOKLYN
Cassett, Nancy
3 NINJAS KNUCKLE UP
Cecilia, Martha
PROPHECY, THE
Ceyrat, Magali
LES MISERABLES
Chase, Ken
TALL TALE: THE UNBELIEVABLE
ADVENTURES OF PECOS BILL
VILLAGE OF THE DAMNED
Chin, Judy
AMATEUR
SEARCH AND DESTROY
Chris Walas, Inc.
JADE
VIRTUOSITY

Cicatelli-Lewis, Donna
EMBRACE OF THE VAMPIRE
Colburn, Elizabeth
JUDICIAL CONSENT
Colton, Tyler
BOCA
Cooper, Sandy
JUMANJI
MAGIC IN THE WATER
Cordero, Grisell
UP TO A CERTAIN POINT
Costello, Cindy
FRANK AND OLLIE
Coulter, Scott
MANGLER, THE
Cournoyer, Sylvain
ECLIPSE
Crognale, Gino
WALKING DEAD, THE
Crognale, Gino B.
CITIZEN X
Crown, Lisa
FIRST DEGREE
Crystal, Tracy
MANGLER, THE
D'Amoure
PEREZ FAMILY, THE
Dahan, Raqueli
EROTIQUE
Dahl, Karen
INDICTMENT: THE MCMARTIN TRIAL
TWOGETHER
Dajani, Magda
ME AND THE MOB
Dancose, Jayne
DOUBLE, DOUBLE, TOIL AND TROUBLE
HIDEAWAY
Dark, Tim
POSTCARDS FROM AMERICA
Das, Ananta
STRANGER, THE
Dashiell, Rene
GHOST BRIGADE
DaSilva, Rosalina
BROKEN TRUST
Davis, Kim
GLASS SHIELD, THE
PANTHER
Daxauer, Liz
HACKERS
Day, Tarra
PLAY TIME
De Winne, Kezia
ENGLISHMAN WHO WENT UP A HILL
BUT CAME DOWN A MOUNTAIN, THE
Deak, Patty
COVER STORY
Deal, Sarah Gaye
SWIMMING WITH SHARKS
Defazio, Dina
BRADY BUNCH MOVIE, THE
del Toro, Maria Elena
STRAWBERRY AND CHOCOLATE
Demers, Nicole
EXOTICA
DeMesmaecker, Catherine
OLD LADY WHO WALKED IN THE SEA,
THE
Devetta, Linda
GOLDENEYE
Diaz, Ken
MY FAMILY: MI FAMILIA
Doll, Dina
NADJA
Down, Victoria
BAD COMPANY
HIDEAWAY
MAN OF THE HOUSE

Dreiband-Burman, Bari
POWDER
Dudman, Nick
JUDGE DREDD
Dunst, Karen
BEFORE SUNRISE
Dupuis, Stephan
COPYCAT
HIGHLANDER: THE FINAL DIMENSION
WINGS OF COURAGE
Earnshaw, Tina
FEAST OF JULY
JEFFERSON IN PARIS
OTHELLO
East, Debra
ONCE WERE WARRIORS
Eddo, Scott
JUST CAUSE
Edmonds, Stan
FAR FROM HOME: THE ADVENTURES OF
YELLOW DOG
Elek, Katalin
SUDDEN DEATH
Elliott, John
NICK OF TIME
THREE WISHES
Ellis, Anya
DOUBLE HAPPINESS
Elsey, David
DEATH MACHINE
Elwood, Tony
JOURNEY OF AUGUST KING, THE
Engel, Jack
NEW YORK COP
Engelen, Paul
CUTTHROAT ISLAND
RESTORATION
Evans, Kris
POWDER
Evans-Miller, Selena
MAJOR PAYNE
Evers, Sheila
NICK OF TIME
Ewing, Alvechia
HIGHER LEARNING
Ferber, Fe
EROTIQUE
Ferguson, Morna
SECRET OF ROAN INISH, THE
Ferriera, Luiz
CARMEN MIRANDA: BANANAS IS MY
BUSINESS
Fiomi, Sabrina
CARMEN MIRANDA: BANANAS IS MY
BUSINESS
Fischer, Denise
FUN
Forrest, David Craig
SHOWGIRLS
Fourquin, Odile
TOTAL ECLIPSE
Fowler, Stephanie
HOWLING: NEW MOON RISING, THE
Fox, Pam
GLORY BOYS, THE
Frampton, Peter
BRAVEHEART
Friedman, Alan "Doc"
BRADY BUNCH MOVIE, THE
CLUELESS
DRACULA: DEAD AND LOVING IT
Fry, Elisabeth
SPY WITHIN, THE
Garton, Carrie
OUTSIDE THE LAW
Gattuso, Lori
UNDERCOVER

George, Screaming Mad
TALES FROM THE HOOD
George, Tracy Lynn
DECOY
Gerhardt, Patricia A.
UNSTRUNG HEROES
Germain, Michael
BOYS ON THE SIDE
STRANGE DAYS
Giger, H.R.
SPECIES
Gill, Linda
JOHNNY MNEMONIC
Gillis, Alec
JUMANJI
Glass, Dennis
TALL TALE: THE UNBELIEVABLE
ADVENTURES OF PECOS BILL
Glover, Trish
NOSTRADAMUS KID, THE
Goodwin, Jeff
EMPIRE RECORDS
Green, Dovi
DARK DEALER
Green, Patricia
MOONLIGHT AND VALENTINO
TO DIE FOR
Griesbrect, Shauna
BODY CHEMISTRY 4: FULL EXPOSURE
Grobe, Evelyn
EROTIQUE
Grossas, Graciela
STRAWBERRY AND CHOCOLATE
Grotsky, Heidi
ATTACK OF THE 60-FOOT CENTERFOLD
Guiliano, Tyla
BODY STROKES
Hagen, Kathleen
FATHER AND SCOUT
Haggerty, Erin
VAMPIRE IN BROOKLYN
VILLAGE OF THE DAMNED
Hall, Kenneth
TALES FROM THE HOOD
Hammond, Diane
CLOCKERS
PANTHER
BASKETBALL DIARIES, THE
Hancock, Michael
BRIDGES OF MADISON COUNTY, THE
Hardy, Linda
GIRL IN THE CADILLAC
Harkins, Isabel
MIAMI RHAPSODY
Harman, Lee
ASSASSINS
Harper, Bob
KINGFISH: A STORY OF HUEY P. LONG
Harvey, April
DESPERATE PREY
Hay, Pat
FUNNY BONES
RICHARD III
Hedgcock, Alan
DEATH MACHINE
Helland, J. Roy
BRIDGES OF MADISON COUNTY, THE
TO WONG FOO, THANKS FOR
EVERYTHING! JULIE NEWMAR
Hemming, Carol
JEFFERSON IN PARIS
Henderson, Donna-Lou
TALES FROM THE CRYPT: DEMON
KNIGHT
Henderson, Justin
TALES FROM THE CRYPT: DEMON
KNIGHT

Hewett, Julie
LITTLE PRINCESS, A
WALK IN THE CLOUDS, A
Heys, Pauline
JEFFERSON IN PARIS
Hicks, Lori
JOURNEY OF AUGUST KING, THE
Hills, Joan
BEFORE THE RAIN
INNOCENT, THE
Hirsch-Smith, Katharina
BORN TO BE WILD
Holland, Desne
NEVER TALK TO STRANGERS
Holzapfel, Irmela
PROMISE, THE
Holzapfel, Jurgen
PROMISE, THE
Hughes, Melanie
BABYSITTER, THE
JUST CAUSE
Humphreys, Ann
PRIEST
Iannucci, Luanne
MIDNIGHT TEASE 2
Iverson, Karen
ALMOST DEAD
Jackson, John E.
CONGO
OUTBREAK
Jacoponi, Nilo
MONTH BY THE LAKE, A
Jakots, Katalin
CITIZEN X
James, Kathrine
HOME FOR THE HOLIDAYS
James, Whitney
FREE WILLY 2: THE ADVENTURE HOME
Jenae, Jori
BIGFOOT: THE UNFORGETTABLE
ENCOUNTER
Joette
CARMEN MIRANDA: BANANAS IS MY
BUSINESS
Johnson, Angela
LAST GOOD TIME, THE
PARTY GIRL
RHYTHM THIEF
Johnson, Steve
LORD OF ILLUSIONS
NEXT DOOR
SPECIES
Johnston, Graham
SHALLOW GRAVE
Josef-Sparks, June
ZOOMAN
K.N.B. EFX Group
BAD COMPANY
CASINO
CITIZEN X
DARKMAN 2: THE RETURN OF DURANT
FOUR ROOMS
IN THE MOUTH OF MADNESS
LORD OF ILLUSIONS
NEVER TALK TO STRANGERS
TALES FROM THE HOOD
VAMPIRE IN BROOKLYN
VILLAGE OF THE DAMNED
WALKING DEAD, THE
Kano/Monk
MORTAL KOMBAT
Kastner-Delago, Eileen
FATHERLAND
Kelly, Kathryn
BABY-SITTERS CLUB, THE
Kennedy, Gail
CONVICT COWBOY
Kent, Irene
TOMMY BOY

Kinchella, Joanne
POWER OF ATTORNEY
King, Peter
INNOCENT LIES
Knight, Darcy
CURE, THE
NEXT DOOR
Koubesserian, Charly
LES MISERABLES
Kouzmina, Alexandra
WINDOW TO PARIS
Krueger, Eryn
NUMBER ONE FAN
Kurtzman, Robert
DARKMAN 2: THE RETURN OF DURANT
IN THE MOUTH OF MADNESS
QUICK AND THE DEAD, THE
Lacagnina, Francesca
DANGER OF LOVE
Laden, Bob
ROOMMATES
Landau, Harriette
CLASS OF '61
TOM AND HUCK
Landry, Sophie
MARTHA AND I
LaPorte, Steve
POWDER
Larsen, Deborah
NOW AND THEN
SAFE
TANK GIRL
Laurence, Chris
LIVING IN OBLIVION
SAFE
Lavergne, Didier
HIGHLANDER: THE FINAL DIMENSION
SIX DAYS, SIX NIGHTS
Lavett, Brent
ASCENT, THE
Layman, Lisa
RADIO INSIDE
le Marinel, Paul
FARINELLI
Lennox, Helen
HEAVEN'S A DRAG
Lestang, Benoit
CITY OF LOST CHILDREN, THE
Liddiard, Dennis
OUT OF ANNIE'S PAST
Liddiard, Gary
QUICK AND THE DEAD, THE
WILD BILL
Lind, Oona
FRANK AND OLLIE
Lonergan, Brendan
DEATH MACHINE
Love, Lisa
CRACKERJACK
Lovell, Judy
OPERATION DUMBO DROP
Lu Yingchun
ERMO
Lygratte, William
EROTIQUE
Lynch, Stephen
WHEN NIGHT IS FALLING
Lyons, Mandy
POSTCARDS FROM AMERICA
Ma Shuangyin
RED FIRECRACKER, GREEN
FIRECRACKER
Makeup Effects Lab
CANDYMAN: FAREWELL TO THE FLESH
Malouf, Kerry
BRIAN WILSON: I JUST WASN'T MADE
FOR THESE TIMES

Mansano, Dee
BAD BLOOD
Mansano, Mony
MORTAL KOMBAT
Marazzi, Alfredo
POSTMAN, THE
Marazzi, Simone
POSTMAN, THE
Mari, Cassi
FRIDAY
Marsalis, Nancy
NINA TAKES A LOVER
Mason, Grant
SHALLOW GRAVE
Massarelli, Wayne
LAKOTA WOMAN: SIEGE AT WOUNDED
KNEE
Masters, Todd
TALES FROM THE CRYPT: DEMON
KNIGHT
THINGS TO DO IN DENVER WHEN
YOU'RE DEAD
Mays, Sarah
SOMETHING TO TALK ABOUT
Mazur, Bernadette
SABRINA
McCarron, Bob
DALLAS DOLL
McCormack, Lynda
DANCE ME OUTSIDE
McCoy, Jim
WATERWORLD
McInally, Randy
ANDROID AFFAIR, THE
McIntosh, Todd
BRADY BUNCH MOVIE, THE
HIDEAWAY
McNulty, Deborah
SCANNERS: THE SHOWDOWN
Medcaf, Cheri Montesanto
TANK GIRL
Mi Zide
SHANGHAI TRIAD
Michaels, Myke
GREAT ELEPHANT ESCAPE, THE
Miller-Jones, Bill
EXPERT, THE
Mills, Bob
NINE MONTHS
Moana, Guy
ONCE WERE WARRIORS
Modus EFX
SILENCE OF THE HAMS
Molnar, Gabriella
CRY, THE BELOVED COUNTRY
Montagna, Peter
FORGET PARIS
Moos, Angela
BUSHWHACKED
Morozova, Irina
MUTE WITNESS
Mowat, Donald J.
IN THE MOUTH OF MADNESS
Mungle, Matthew W.
CONGO
OUTBREAK
Murdock, Judy
COSMIC SLOP
WHITE MAN'S BURDEN
Narcisse, Marietta Carter
DANGEROUS MINDS
Neill, Ve
BATMAN FOREVER
Nelson, Christopher
GRANNY, THE
Ni Mhaonaigh, Linda
AILSA

Nichols, Karen
LITTLE ODESSA
Nicotero, Gregory
CITIZEN X
DARKMAN 2: THE RETURN OF DURANT
IN THE MOUTH OF MADNESS
NEVER TALK TO STRANGERS
QUICK AND THE DEAD, THE
WALKING DEAD, THE
Nieradzik, Dorka
CENTURY
CIRCLE OF FRIENDS
Nixon, Kathryn
ROY COHN/JACK SMITH
Noel, Leone
POSTMAN, THE
Norin, Robert N.
LITTLE PRINCESS, A
Nye, Jr., Ben
SEPARATE LIVES
Nyre, Brigette A.
MALLRATS
O'Quinn, Marilyn
ANDROID AFFAIR, THE
O'Reilly, Valli
HOW TO MAKE AN AMERICAN QUILT
O'Sullivan, Marie
FRANKIE STARLIGHT
Olsson, Kim
KINGDOM, THE
Olsson, Lis
KINGDOM, THE
Optic Nerve
CASTLE FREAK
Ospina, Ermahn
DESPERADO
FOUR ROOMS
Palmer, Barbie
ROOMMATES
Palmer, Carla
BIG GREEN, THE
Palos, Paul
MUTANT SPECIES
Panchuk, Vladimir
AMERICAN COP
Parker, Connie
BLACK FOX
GOLD DIGGERS: THE SECRET OF BEAR
MOUNTAIN
Parker, Daniel
RICHARD III
Pattison, Paul
NOSTRADAMUS KID, THE
Peoples, Marylin
DIE HARD WITH A VENGEANCE
Perez, Frank
WATERWORLD
Pfluegl, Edelgarde K.
BILLY MADISON
Phillips, Darren
HEAVEN'S A DRAG
Phillips, Debra
CARMEN MIRANDA: BANANAS IS MY
BUSINESS
Placks, Vivien
LAMB
Polson, Colin
CRY, THE BELOVED COUNTRY
Porlier, Charles
JUMANJI
Port, Nina
RIVER OF GRASS
Poulsen-Wells, Amanda
DANGEROUS, THE
Preston, Linda
KURT VONNEGUT'S HARRISON
BERGERON

Pryor, Beverly Jo
HIGHER LEARNING
Ptak, Sheryl Leigh
ACE VENTURA: WHEN NATURE CALLS
Purcell, Julie
DESTINY TURNS ON THE RADIO
ROSWELL: THE U.F.O. COVER-UP
Quist, Gerald
BUFFALO GIRLS
Rail, Jason
DOOM GENERATION, THE
Rainone, Thomas C.
LORD OF ILLUSIONS
Reeve, Constance
OH ... ROSALINDA!!
Revilla, Lisette
UP TO A CERTAIN POINT
Ritter, Kathleen
CREEP
Robb-King, Peter
FIRST KNIGHT
Rocchetti, Luigi
DOLORES CLAIBORNE
TWO BITS
Rocchetti, Manlio
ROSWELL: THE U.F.O. COVER-UP
STARS FELL ON HENRIETTA, THE
Rocco, Lisa
MURDER IN THE FIRST
Rock, Ben
MUTANT SPECIES
Rodier, Suzanne
GALAXIS
Roesler, Tina K.
CURSE OF THE STARVING CLASS
Rorvik, Tone
ABDUCTED 2: THE REUNION
Ross, Morag
BEFORE THE RAIN
BUSINESS AFFAIR, A
ROB ROY
SENSE AND SENSIBILITY
Rouvray, Lesley
COUNTRY LIFE
SUM OF US, THE
Rowbottom, Amanda
GROSS MISCONDUCT
Royce, Sandy
ONLY THE BRAVE
Ryan, Robert
JADE
Sanchez, Mark
MY FAMILY: MI FAMILIA
Sanders, Stacy
BAD BLOOD
Sanders, Suzanne
EVOLVER
JURY DUTY
PENTATHLON
Schakosky, Laurie
SKINNER
Schlegelmilch, Kuno
FARINELLI
Schon, Karin
FOR GOD AND COUNTRY
Scinto, Barri
DEAD FUNNY
POSTCARDS FROM AMERICA
RHYTHM THIEF
Scott, David
FIRST DEGREE
Scribner, Jim
NICK OF TIME
Sewerynska, Dorotta
SHORT FILM ABOUT KILLING, A
Sforza, Fabrizio
SCARLET LETTER, THE

Sharp, Rick
GRUMPIER OLD MEN
STEAL BIG, STEAL LITTLE
THINGS TO DO IN DENVER WHEN
YOU'RE DEAD
Sheen, Edna M.
DEVIL IN A BLUE DRESS
VIRTUOSITY
Sheikh, Mohd Iqbal
BANDIT QUEEN
Short, Sheri P.
CANDYMAN: FAREWELL TO THE FLESH
TALL TALE: THE UNBELIEVABLE
ADVENTURES OF PECOS BILL
Shorter, Kate
SUBSTITUTE WIFE, THE
Silva, Rea Ann
FRIDAY
Simard, Diane
DR. JEKYLL & MS. HYDE
Simon, Davida
TOO YOUNG TO DIE?
Simons, Jef
UNDER SIEGE 2: DARK TERRITORY
Smith, Christina
CASPER
CONGO
Smith, FX
NIXON
Smith, Gordon
NIXON
Smith-Ojeil, Jo-Anne
CASINO
Solomon, Margaret
HUNTED, THE
Sorensen, Birthe Lyngso
KINGDOM, THE
Southern, Katherine
CANADIAN BACON
PYROMANIAC'S LOVE STORY, A
Spann, Marvella
DARK DEALER
Speak, Jean
PERSUASION
Stevenson, Margaret
TRAPS
Striepeke, Daniel
AMERICAN PRESIDENT, THE
APOLLO 13
Sutor, Paula
IN THE DEEP WOODS
Syner, David
DIRTY MONEY
Tavarres, Mark
WALKING DEAD, THE
Tenoglio, Pietro
CASTLE FREAK
Tenuta, Carme
BITTER VENGEANCE
Tesone, Laura
LIVING IN OBLIVION
Thompson, Claudia
MY ANTONIA
Thompson, Laini
BAD BOYS
MONEY TRAIN
Thurston, Wanda
DARK DEALER
Tissier, Nathalie
CITY OF LOST CHILDREN, THE
Tomasino, Michael
ANGUS
Tooker, Lori
BLESSING
Toth, Wayne
BAD COMPANY
Trahan, A. Vechia
HOUSEGUEST

Trepanier, Micheline
GEORGIA
LOVE AND HUMAN REMAINS
Tripodi, Chiara
DALLAS DOLL
Tyrer, Carolyn
BABE
Vanduc, Huelan
PIGALLE
Vaurin, Daniele
I CAN'T SLEEP
Vitrai, Julia
KID IN KING ARTHUR'S COURT, A
Voss, Cheryl
ARIZONA DREAM
AVENGING ANGEL
S.F.W.
W.M. Creations, Inc.
ACE VENTURA: WHEN NATURE CALLS
Walas, Mark
COPYCAT
Wallace, Cliff
DEATH MACHINE
Warbin, Tracy
LAST SUMMER IN THE HAMPTONS
Watanabe, Noriko
DEATH IN BRUNSWICK
MURIEL'S WEDDING
Weisinger, Allen
KISS OF DEATH
TWELVE MONKEYS
Wells, Amanda
MUTANT SPECIES
Wen Xianling
HEROIC TRIO, THE
Westgate, Randy
CHILDREN OF THE CORN III: URBAN
HARVEST
Westmore, Monty
OUTBREAK
Westmore, Pamela
FREE WILLY 2: THE ADVENTURE HOME
NET, THE
WHILE YOU WERE SLEEPING
Wheeler, Lynn
MIGHTY MORPHIN POWER RANGERS:
THE MOVIE
Wheeler, Scott
MANGLER, THE
TALES FROM THE CRYPT: DEMON
KNIGHT
White, Douglas
DESPERADO
White, Jimi
DILLINGER
White, Michael
SEVEN
Wilder, Bradley
STUART SAVES HIS FAMILY
Willet, Suzanne
BULLETPROOF HEART
REFLECTIONS IN THE DARK
Williams, Edwin
BANDIT QUEEN
Williams, Gigi
BETTER OFF DEAD
Williamson, Lizbeth
FOUR ROOMS
UNDERNEATH, THE
Winslow, Ellie
DEAD PRESIDENTS
NEW JERSEY DRIVE
PIANO LESSON, THE
WAITING TO EXHALE
Winston, Stan
CONGO
Wong, Ellen
CRIMSON TIDE
GET SHORTY

Woodhouse, Shelly
JUST CAUSE
Woodruff, Jr., Tom
JUMANJI
Wright, Victoria
HEAVEN'S A DRAG
Yagher, Kevin
DR. JEKYLL & MS. HYDE
Yang Yu
SHANGHAI TRIAD
York, Patti
ARIZONA DREAM
Zanetti, Cinzia
NATIONAL LAMPOON'S ATTACK OF THE
5'2" WOMEN
Zheng Fengyan
HEROIC TRIO, THE
Zoe
BREACH OF CONDUCT
Zoller, Debbie
JEFFREY
Zurlo, Rosemarie
MIGHTY APHRODITE

MUSIC COMPOSERS

, Jim Lang
IN THE MOUTH OF MADNESS
Adler, Mark
DECOY
Alcorn, Keith
DARK DEALER
Ali Khan, Nusrat Fateh
BANDIT QUEEN
Aligholi, Mohammad Reza
JAR, THE
Allen, Peter
CRACKERJACK
Altman, John
FUNNY BONES
Alucarda
CREEP
Ambrosio, Marco
GUMBY: THE MOVIE
Anastasia
BEFORE THE RAIN
Arnold, David
LAST OF THE DOGMEN
Artemiev, Eduard
BURNT BY THE SUN
Avila, Pepe
MY FAMILY: MI FAMILIA
Babida, Chris
PHANTOM LOVER, THE
Bacalov, Luis Enrique
POSTMAN, THE
Badalamenti, Angelo
CITY OF LOST CHILDREN, THE
Baitz, Rick
LAST SUMMER IN THE HAMPTONS
Balaban, Nick
SEX, DRUGS AND DEMOCRACY
Band, Richard
CASTLE FREAK
PREHYSTERIA! 3
Barbelivien, Didier
LES MISERABLES
Barber, Lesley
WHEN NIGHT IS FALLING
Barlow, Lou
KIDS
Barnes, John
BETTER OFF DEAD
COSMIC SLOP
Barone, Markus
COVER ME

Barrere, Paul
DIRTY MONEY
Barry, John
ACROSS THE SEA OF TIME: NEW YORK
3D
CRY, THE BELOVED COUNTRY
SCARLET LETTER, THE
Bartek, Steve
COLDBLOODED
Bates, Tyler
BALLISTIC
Beckett, Hal
POWER OF ATTORNEY
Beeftink, Herman
I LIKE TO PLAY GAMES
Bell, David
CONVICT COWBOY
Belling, Andrew
EROTIQUE
Bellis, Richard
DOUBLE, DOUBLE, TOIL AND TROUBLE
Benitez, Jellybean
LIE DOWN WITH DOGS
Benoit, David
STARS FELL ON HENRIETTA, THE
Berchot, Erik
LES MISERABLES
Berger, Michel
SERIOUS ABOUT PLEASURE
Bernstein, Charles
MAYA LIN: A STRONG CLEAR VISION
OUT OF ANNIE'S PAST
TOO YOUNG TO DIE?
Bernstein, Elmer
CANADIAN BACON
DEVIL IN A BLUE DRESS
FRANKIE STARLIGHT
ROOMMATES
SEARCH AND DESTROY
Bernstein, Peter
CANADIAN BACON
Best, Peter
COUNTRY LIFE
MURIEL'S WEDDING
Bini, Rene Mark
GROSSE FATIGUE
Blanchard, Terence
CLOCKERS
Boeddinghaus, David
CRUMB
Boekelheide, Todd
DIGGER
NINA TAKES A LOVER
Bolton, Roger
HEAVEN'S A DRAG
Bos, Ruud
1-900
Boswell, Simon
ANDROID AFFAIR, THE
HACKERS
LORD OF ILLUSIONS
SHALLOW GRAVE
Bowers, Richard
SCANNERS: THE SHOWDOWN
Bramson, Steven
CRUDE OASIS, THE
Brauner, Arthur
CHRONICLE OF THE WARSAW GHETTO
UPRISING ACCORDING TO MAREK
EDELMAN
Bregovic, Goran
ARIZONA DREAM
Brenner, Danny
RHYTHM THIEF
Bronskill, Richard
BODY STROKES
Brophy, Philip
ONLY THE BRAVE

Brouwer, Leo
UP TO A CERTAIN POINT
Bryant, John
CURSE OF THE STARVING CLASS
Buckmaster, Paul
TWELVE MONKEYS
Bullard, Kim
BREAK, THE
Burwell, Carter
BAD COMPANY
GOOFY MOVIE, A
ROB ROY
TWO BITS
Cannella, Anthony
COVER STORY
Carpenter, John
HALLOWEEN: THE CURSE OF MICHAEL
MYERS
IN THE MOUTH OF MADNESS
VILLAGE OF THE DAMNED
Casey, John
MARTHA & ETHEL
Cervenka, Exene
ACROSS THE MOON
Chan, Frankie
ASHES OF TIME
Chang, Gary
AVENGING ANGEL
BURNING SEASON, THE
FATHERLAND
WALKING DEAD, THE
Chase, Peter
MINA TANNENBAUM
Cis, Franz
ADVENTURES OF MATT THE
GOOSEBOY, THE
Clarke, Stanley
HIGHER LEARNING
SHOW, THE
Clinton, George S.
COSMIC SLOP
MORTAL KOMBAT
Coda, John
RED SUN RISING
Coleman, Graeme
BULLETPROOF HEART
MALICIOUS
Combustible Edison
FOUR ROOMS
Contagion
SKINNER
Conti, Bill
BUSHWHACKED
Convertino, Michael
THINGS TO DO IN DENVER WHEN
YOU'RE DEAD
Coulais, Bruno
SON OF THE SHARK, THE
D'Andrea, John
GHOST BRIGADE
D'Avi, Ted
DARK DEALER
Dame, Terry
INCREDIBLY TRUE ADVENTURES OF
TWO GIRLS IN LOVE, THE
Danna, Mychael
DANCE ME OUTSIDE
EXOTICA
Daring, Mason
GETTING OUT
SECRET OF ROAN INISH, THE
Dasent, Peter
MEET THE FEEBLES
Davies, Dave
VILLAGE OF THE DAMNED
Davis, Carl
RETURN OF THE NATIVE, THE
Davis, John
DARK DEALER

KIDS
DeBeasi, Joseph S.
BLESSING
Debney, John
CLASS OF '61
CUTTHROAT ISLAND
HOUSEGUEST
SUDDEN DEATH
Delia, Joe
ADDICTION, THE
ENEMY WITHIN, THE
Demanne, Quentin
VOYAGE EN DOUCE
Derfel, Jerzy
WITHOUT ANESTHESIA
Dermarderosian, Alan
GOOD GIRLS DON'T
Derouin, Joel
PLAY TIME
Desplat, Alexandre
INNOCENT LIES
Di Franco, Paul
BODY CHEMISTRY 4: FULL EXPOSURE
DiIulio, Ron
DARK DEALER
Dikker, Loek
BABYSITTER, THE
Diop, Wasis
HYENAS
Donaggio, Pino
NEVER TALK TO STRANGERS
Donnellan, James
ALMOST DEAD
Doyle, Patrick
LITTLE PRINCESS, A
SENSE AND SENSIBILITY
Edelman, Randy
BIG GREEN, THE
BILLY MADISON
CITIZEN X
INDIAN IN THE CUPBOARD, THE
TALL TALE: THE UNBELIEVABLE
ADVENTURES OF PECOS BILL
WHILE YOU WERE SLEEPING
Edmonds, Kenneth "Babyface"
WAITING TO EXHALE
Edwards, Ross
ETERNITY
Egan, Seamus
BROTHERS MCMULLEN, THE
Eidelman, Cliff
NOW AND THEN
Elfman, Danny
DARKMAN 2: THE RETURN OF DURANT
DEAD PRESIDENTS
TALES FROM THE CRYPT: DEMON
KNIGHT
TO DIE FOR
Endelman, Stephen
ENGLISHMAN WHO WENT UP A HILL
BUT CAME DOWN A MOUNTAIN, THE
JEFFREY
JOURNEY OF AUGUST KING, THE
POSTCARDS FROM AMERICA
RECKLESS
TOM AND HUCK
English, Jon A.
FRAMEUP
Ersoff, Isaac
AMERICA'S DEADLIEST HOME VIDEO
Famin, Ron
RENT-A-KID
Farinas, Carlos
I AM CUBA
Farmer, Jim
LIVING IN OBLIVION
Faulkner, Dave
SUM OF US, THE

Febre, Louis
BIGFOOT: THE UNFORGETTABLE
ENCOUNTER
SECRETARY, THE
Feldman, Richard
BOCA
Fiedel, Brad
JOHNNY MNEMONIC
Figgis, Mike
LEAVING LAS VEGAS
Fisch, Irwin
ASCENT, THE
Fish, Peter
TIE-DIED: ROCK 'N' ROLL'S MOST
DEADICATED FANS
WIGSTOCK: THE MOVIE
Folk, Robert
ACE VENTURA: WHEN NATURE CALLS
ARABIAN KNIGHT
Foote, Ray
IT TAKES TWO
Foote, Sherman
IT TAKES TWO
Fowler, Bruce
FIRST DEGREE
Fox, Charles
GORDY
Foxman, Philip
SEX, DRUGS AND DEMOCRACY
Foxx, Felicity
DESPERATE PREY
Frank, David Michael
BABY-SITTERS CLUB, THE
BITTER VENGEANCE
Franklyn, Sarah
MARTHA & ETHEL
Fuller, Parmer
REFLECTIONS IN THE DARK
SILENCE OF THE HAMS
Gallo, Don
DOOM GENERATION, THE
Garcia, James Edward
AMERICA'S DEADLIEST HOME VIDEO
Garcia, Roel A.
ASHES OF TIME
Gargoni, Adam
BOCA
Garternicht, Klaus
DEADLY MARIA
Gerber, Jerry
GUMBY: THE MOVIE
Gibbs, Michael
CENTURY
Gimbel, Norman
ARABIAN KNIGHT
Glass, Philip
CANDYMAN: FAREWELL TO THE FLESH
Goldenthal, Elliot
BATMAN FOREVER
HEAT
ROSWELL: THE U.F.O. COVER-UP
Goldsmith, Jerry
CONGO
FIRST KNIGHT
POWDER
Goldsmith, Joel
BAD BLOOD
Goldstein, Gil
RADIO INSIDE
Gouriet, Gerald
INNOCENT, THE
Green Day
ANGUS
Grindlay, Murray
ONCE WERE WARRIORS
Grusin, Dave
CURE, THE

Hada, Kentaro
BAREFOOT GEN
Hapka, Petr
COW, THE
Hartley, Richard
AWFULLY BIG ADVENTURE, AN
Harvey, Richard
DOOMSDAY GUN
Heil, Tom
SWIMMING WITH SHARKS
Hicks, John
HARLEM DIARY: NINE VOICES OF
RESILIENCE
Hidden Faces
FRIDAY
Hiel, Tom
DARK SIDE OF GENIUS, THE
Hirsch, Wilbert
MUTE WITNESS
Hirschfelder, David
DALLAS DOLL
Holbek, Joachim
KINGDOM, THE
Holdridge, Lee
BUFFALO GIRLS
Holton, Nigel
MOSAIC PROJECT, THE
TWOGETHER
Homes, Frank
CURSE OF THE STARVING CLASS
Horn, John L.
RHYTHM THIEF
Horner, James
APOLLO 13
BALTO
BRAVEHEART
CASPER
JADE
JUMANJI
Horowitz, Richard
BROKEN TRUST
LAKOTA WOMAN: SIEGE AT WOUNDED
KNEE
Howard, James Newton
FRENCH KISS
JUST CAUSE
OUTBREAK
RESTORATION
WATERWORLD
Howarth, Alan
HALLOWEEN: THE CURSE OF MICHAEL
MYERS
Hu, William
HEROIC TRIO, THE
Huddleston, Eugene
WORLD AND TIME ENOUGH
Hui Yun
HE'S A WOMAN, SHE'S A MAN
Hunter, Steve
CYBER BANDITS
Hyman, Dick
MIGHTY APHRODITE
Irwin, Ashley
EXPERT, THE
UNDERCOVER
Isham, Mark
HOME FOR THE HOLIDAYS
LOSING ISAIAH
MIAMI RHAPSODY
NET, THE
SAFE PASSAGE
Jans, Alaric
WATER ENGINE, THE
Jarre, Maurice
WALK IN THE CLOUDS, A
Jones, Trevor
HIDEAWAY
KISS OF DEATH
RICHARD III

Judd, Philip
DEATH IN BRUNSWICK
Kaczmarek, Jan A.P.
TOTAL ECLIPSE
Kamen, Michael
CIRCLE OF FRIENDS
DIE HARD WITH A VENGEANCE
DON JUAN DEMARCO
Kappoff, Dana
NIGHTMARE
Katsaros, Doug
ME AND THE MOB
Keresztes, Andrew
TERESA'S TATTOO
Kitay, David
CLUELESS
FATHER AND SCOUT
JURY DUTY
Kjartansson, Sigurjon
REMOTE CONTROL
Kloser, Harald
O.J. SIMPSON STORY, THE
Knieper, Jurgen
PROMISE, THE
Kopp, Hermann
NEKROMANTIK
Krausz, Mischa
FOR GOD AND COUNTRY
Krypt, The
VAMPIRES AND OTHER STEREOTYPES
Kypourgos, Nikos
BLUE VILLA, THE
Kyung-Shik Choi
HOW TO TOP MY WIFE
La Rosa, Leopoldo
NO MERCY
Laas, Johan
ARMAGEDDON: THE FINAL CHALLENGE
Lai, Francis
LES MISERABLES
Lanz, David
TO CROSS THE RUBICON
Laxton, Julian
AMERICAN COP
Legrand, Michel
LES MISERABLES
Lerios, Cory
GHOST BRIGADE
Levay, Sylvester
IN THE DEEP WOODS
Leyh, Blake
OUTSIDE THE LAW
Licht, Daniel
CHILDREN OF THE CORN III: URBAN
HARVEST
ZOOMAN
Linda and the Family Values
BALLOT MEASURE 9
Liu Sola
MOVING THE MOUNTAIN
Llewellyn-Jones, Brynmor
GORILLA BATHES AT NOON
Lo, Lowell
NAKED KILLER
Loduca, Joe
MESSENGER
Lorenz, Daktari
NEKROMANTIK
Los Lobos
DESPERADO
Lurie, John
BLUE IN THE FACE
GET SHORTY
Mader
CITY UNPLUGGED
Magne, Michel
NEA

Magness, Clif
BODY SHOT
Mamin, Yuri
WINDOW TO PARIS
Mancina, Marc
FAIR GAME
Mancina, Mark
ASSASSINS
BAD BOYS
MAN OF THE HOUSE
MONEY TRAIN
Manilow, Barry
PEBBLE AND THE PENGUIN, THE
Mann, Hummie
DRACULA: DEAD AND LOVING IT
Manson, Bevan
KILIAN'S CHRONICLE
Marinelli, Anthony
PAYBACK
Marinelli, Dario
AILSA
Marshall, Phil
KICKING AND SCREAMING
Martin, Billy
BLUE IN THE FACE
Martin, Kip
FOOL AND HIS MONEY, A
Martinez, Cliff
UNDERNEATH, THE
Marvin, Richard
OPERATION INTERCEPT
McCarthy, John
LOVE AND HUMAN REMAINS
McHugh, David
DILLINGER
McKenzie, Mark
DR. JEKYLL & MS. HYDE
FRANK & JESSE
MY FAMILY: MI FAMILIA
McNabb, Murray
ONCE WERE WARRIORS
McNeely, Joel
GOLD DIGGERS: THE SECRET OF BEAR
MOUNTAIN
Melnick, Peter Rodgers
INDICTMENT: THE MCMARTIN TRIAL
Menken, Alan
POCAHONTAS
Mennonna, Joey
BIKINI BISTRO
Merrell, Crispin
DEATH MACHINE
Millar, Cynthia
RUN OF THE COUNTRY, THE
THREE WISHES
Miller, Randy
DARKMAN 2: THE RETURN OF DURANT
Mithoff, Bob
NEW YORK COP
Mlynarski, Wojciech
WITHOUT ANESTHESIA
Mole, Charlie
OTHELLO
Moon, Guy
BRADY BUNCH MOVIE, THE
HOWLING: NEW MOON RISING, THE
Morricone, Ennio
PURE FORMALITY, A
Morrison, Van
LAMB
Nakai, R. Carlos
KILIAN'S CHRONICLE
Natale, Lou
KURT VONNEGUT'S HARRISON
BERGERON
Neal, Chris
NOSTRADAMUS KID, THE

Newborn, Ira
JERKY BOYS: THE MOVIE, THE
MALLRATS
Newman, David
BOYS ON THE SIDE
OPERATION DUMBO DROP
TOMMY BOY
Newman, Randy
TOY STORY
Newman, Thomas
HOW TO MAKE AN AMERICAN QUILT
UNSTRUNG HEROES
Niehaus, Lennie
BRIDGES OF MADISON COUNTY, THE
Nitzsche, Jack
CROSSING GUARD, THE
Nyman, Michael
CARRINGTON
SIX DAYS, SIX NIGHTS
O'Donovan, Hugh
RHYTHM THIEF
Ogasawara, Kan
CRIMSON WOLF
Okurland, Kevin
RHYTHM THIEF
Olvis, William
SEPARATE LIVES
STEAL BIG, STEAL LITTLE
Ototmo, Yoshihide
DAY THE SUN TURNED COLD, THE
Ottman, John
USUAL SUSPECTS, THE
Parker, Alan
GLORY BOYS, THE
Parks, Van Dyke
NEXT DOOR
WILD BILL
Pattison, John
I CAN'T SLEEP
Peake, Don
DANGEROUS, THE
Petit, Jean-Claude
MY LIFE AND TIMES WITH ANTONIN
ARTAUD
Pheloung, Barrington
MANGLER, THE
Piersanti, Franco
LAMERICA
Piovani, Nicola
MONTH BY THE LAKE, A
Plumeri, Terry
BREACH OF CONDUCT
Poledouris, Basil
UNDER SIEGE 2: DARK TERRITORY
Portman, Rachel
FRIENDS
PYROMANIAC'S LOVE STORY, A
SMOKE
TO WONG FOO, THANKS FOR
EVERYTHING! JULIE NEWMAR
Pouldouris, Basil
FREE WILLY 2: THE ADVENTURE HOME
Preisner, Zbigniew
FEAST OF JULY
SHORT FILM ABOUT KILLING, A
SHORT FILM ABOUT LOVE, A
Preskett, Graham
SOMETHING TO TALK ABOUT
Project, Ali
WIZARD OF DARKNESS
Rae, Stephen
TRAPS
Ragland, Robert O.
FEAR, THE
Ray, Satyajit
CHARULATA
STRANGER, THE

Reale, Robert
WIGSTOCK: THE MOVIE
Redford, J.A.C.
BYE BYE, LOVE
HEAVYWEIGHTS
KID IN KING ARTHUR'S COURT, A
Reiser, Niki
NOBODY LOVES ME
Revell, Graeme
BASKETBALL DIARIES, THE
MIGHTY MORPHIN POWER RANGERS:
THE MOVIE
S.F.W.
STRANGE DAYS
TANK GIRL
TIE THAT BINDS, THE
Reynolds, John
FRANK AND OLLIE
Riehm, Rolf
MACHINE DREAMS
Riparetti, Tony
SPITFIRE
Robbins, David
DEAD MAN WALKING
Robbins, Richard
JEFFERSON IN PARIS
Roberts, Andy
MAD LOVE
PRIEST
Robertson, Eric N.
BLACK FOX
Robinson, J. Peter
HIGHLANDER: THE FINAL DIMENSION
VAMPIRE IN BROOKLYN
Robinson, Larry
PANTHER
Ross, William
AMAZING PANDA ADVENTURE, THE
Rowe, Hahn
CLEAN, SHAVEN
Rowland, Bruce
GREAT ELEPHANT ESCAPE, THE
GROSS MISCONDUCT
Rubinstein, Arthur B.
NICK OF TIME
Russell, Julian Dylan
BALLOT MEASURE 9
Rustichelli, Carlo
MAMMA ROMA
Safan, Craig
MAJOR PAYNE
Sagisu, Shiro
AI CITY
Sahl, Michael
ROY COHN/JACK SMITH
Sakamoto, Ryuichi
WINGS OF HONNEAMISE: ROYAL SPACE
FORCE
Sams, Jeremy
PERSUASION
Sanko, Anton
GIRL IN THE CADILLAC
PARTY GIRL
Sano, Dana
LITTLE ODESSA
Schmidt, Kendall
GRANNY, THE
Schneider, Norbert J.
STALINGRAD
Schwartz, David
MAGIC IN THE WATER
Schwartz, Stephen
POCAHONTAS
Scott, Gary Stevan
3 NINJAS KNUCKLE UP
Scott, John
FAR FROM HOME: THE ADVENTURES OF
YELLOW DOG

Scott, Tom
DECONSTRUCTING SARAH
Senju, Akira
MYSTERY OF RAMPO, THE
Serra, Eric
GOLDENEYE
Serra, Luis Maria
I, THE WORST OF ALL
Servain, Philippe
LES MISERABLES
Shadowy Men on a Shadowy Planet
DOUBLE HAPPINESS
Shaiman, Marc
AMERICAN PRESIDENT, THE
FORGET PARIS
STUART SAVES HIS FAMILY
Shearmur, Ed
TALES FROM THE CRYPT: DEMON
KNIGHT
Shire, David
COMPANION, THE
MY ANTONIA
Shore, Howard
MOONLIGHT AND VALENTINO
SEVEN
WHITE MAN'S BURDEN
Shragge, Lawrence
REDWOOD CURTAIN
Sighle, Andrei
CREATION OF ADAM
Siliotto, Carlo
FLUKE
Silver, Sheila
DEAD FUNNY
Silvestri, Alan
FATHER OF THE BRIDE PART II
GRUMPIER OLD MEN
JUDGE DREDD
PEREZ FAMILY, THE
QUICK AND THE DEAD, THE
Skyedancer, Sunny McHale
BALLOT MEASURE 9
Snow, Mark
BORN TO BE WILD
DANGER OF LOVE
GOOD DAY TO DIE, A
SUBSTITUTE WIFE, THE
Soles, Steve
DESTINY TURNS ON THE RADIO
Soukup, Ondrej
ACCUMULATOR 1
Spear, David
PENTATHLON
Speer, Paul
TO CROSS THE RUBICON
Spoerri, Bruno
CONGRESS OF PENGUINS, THE
Sprayberry, Robert
BODILY HARM
Sterling, Mark
SEX, DRUGS AND DEMOCRACY
Stewart, David A.
SHOWGIRLS
Stiegler, Robert
FOR GOD AND COUNTRY
Stivin, Jiri
MARTHA AND I
Stone, Christopher
GALAXIS
Strauss, Johann
OH ... ROSALINDA!!
Stromberg, William T.
MUTANT SPECIES
Svoboda, Jiri
ACCUMULATOR 1
Syrrvicz, Stanislas
WOMAN AT WAR, A

Tats Lau
EROTIQUE
Taylor, Jeff
AMATEUR
Taylor, Stephen James
GLASS SHIELD, THE
PIANO LESSON, THE
Thomas, Ian
BOULEVARD
Tollar, Ernie
ECLIPSE
Tomney, Ed
SAFE
Tschanz, Marc
FUN
Tsui Tsang-hei
HE'S A WOMAN, SHE'S A MAN
Tunick, Jonathan
LAST GOOD TIME, THE
Turner, Simon Fisher
NADJA
Tykwer, Tom
DEADLY MARIA
Tyng, Christopher
ACROSS THE MOON
EVOLVER
NATIONAL LAMPOON'S ATTACK OF THE
5'2" WOMEN
Tyson-Chew, Nerida
HOTEL SORRENTO
Ure, Midge
BOCA
Vasseur, Didier
BUSINESS AFFAIR, A
Vitier, Jose Maria
STRAWBERRY AND CHOCOLATE
Walsh, Robert J.
NUMBER ONE FAN
Walton, Jeffrey
ATTACK OF THE 60-FOOT CENTERFOLD
JACK-O
Walton, John Boy
NEKROMANTIK
Warbeck, Stephen
SISTER MY SISTER
Warner, Mark
DOLORES CLAIBORNE
Watkins, Mary
BLACK IS ... BLACK AIN'T
Weiss, Ronald J.
ABDUCTED 2: THE REUNION
Wendy & Lisa
DANGEROUS MINDS
Westlake, Nigel
BABE
Weston, Calvin
BLUE IN THE FACE
Wetherwax, Michael
PREHYSTERIA! 3
Wilkinson, Alex
BAD BLOOD
Williams, Brooks
JUPITER'S WIFE
Williams, David C.
PROPHECY, THE
Williams, John
NIXON
SABRINA
Williams, Joseph
EMBRACE OF THE VAMPIRE
Williams, Patrick
KINGFISH: A STORY OF HUEY P. LONG
Wilson, Brian
BRIAN WILSON: I JUST WASN'T MADE
FOR THESE TIMES
Wold, Erling
BED YOU SLEEP IN, THE

Wolf, Larry
CAGED HEARTS
Wong, Cacine
EXECUTIONERS
Worrell, Bernard
COSMIC SLOP
Wurman, Alex
CREW, THE
Wurst, David
CRAZYSITTER, THE
DILLINGER AND CAPONE
SPY WITHIN, THE
Wurst, Eric
CRAZYSITTER, THE
DILLINGER AND CAPONE
SPY WITHIN, THE
Xiao-Song Qu
PUSHING HANDS
Yamaguchi, Motofumi
HUNTED, THE
Young, Christopher
COPYCAT
JUDICIAL CONSENT
MURDER IN THE FIRST
SPECIES
TALES FROM THE HOOD
VIRTUOSITY
Zalivalov, Aleksei
WINDOW TO PARIS
Zarycki, Andrzej
PROVINCIAL ACTORS
Zehren, John
AMERICA'S DEADLIEST HOME VIDEO
Zhang Dalong
WOODEN MAN'S BRIDE, THE
Zhang Guangtian
SHANGHAI TRIAD
Zhao Jiping
RED FIRECRACKER, GREEN
FIRECRACKER
Zhou Xiaowen
ERMO
Zimmer, Hans
BEYOND RANGOON
CRIMSON TIDE
NINE MONTHS
SOMETHING TO TALK ABOUT
YOUNGER & YOUNGER

PRODUCERS

Abramowitz, Richard
DEAD FUNNY
Abrams, Peter
KID IN KING ARTHUR'S COURT, A
Adelson, Gary
JADE
Adler, Gilbert
TALES FROM THE CRYPT: DEMON
KNIGHT
Adlon, Eleonore
YOUNGER & YOUNGER
Albert, Trevor
STUART SAVES HIS FAMILY
Alden, Michael
UNZIPPED
Alexander, Steve
SWIMMING WITH SHARKS
Almond, Peter O.
BABY-SITTERS CLUB, THE
Alston, Emmett
TWOGETHER
Amiel, Alan
BAD BLOOD
Anciano, Dominic
DEATH MACHINE
Annaud, Jean-Jacques
WINGS OF COURAGE

Araki, Gregg
DOOM GENERATION, THE
Arcady, Alexandre
SIX DAYS, SIX NIGHTS
Arndt, Stefan
DEADLY MARIA
Arnold, Bonnie
TOY STORY
Arnold, Susan
UNSTRUNG HEROES
Auty, Martyn
WOMAN AT WAR, A
Avneri, Ronit
COLORADO COWBOY: THE BRUCE FORD
STORY
Bach, Jean
GREAT DAY IN HARLEM, A
Bacino, Mark
DOUBLE, DOUBLE, TOIL AND TROUBLE
Badalato, William
UNSTRUNG HEROES
Badham, John
NICK OF TIME
Baer, Thomas
GIRL IN THE CADILLAC
Baerwitz, Jerry
HIDEAWAY
Balaban, Bob
LAST GOOD TIME, THE
Baldecchi, John
TOM AND HUCK
Baldwin, Howard
SUDDEN DEATH
Balsam, Mark
JEFFREY
Bansal, R.D.
CHARULATA
Barbaro, Nicholas
EXPERT, THE
Barker, Clive
LORD OF ILLUSIONS
Barmash, Jeff
POWER OF ATTORNEY
Barnathan, Michael
NINE MONTHS
Barron, David
OTHELLO
Baumgarten, Craig
JADE
Bayly, Stephen
RICHARD III
Beaton, Jesse
DEVIL IN A BLUE DRESS
Bedi, Sundeep Singh
BANDIT QUEEN
Belling, Davina
BUSINESS AFFAIR, A
Belmont, Vera
FARINELLI
Ben-Ami, Yoram
JURY DUTY
Benayoun, Georges
MINA TANNENBAUM
WILD REEDS
Bender, Lawrence
FOUR ROOMS
WHITE MAN'S BURDEN
Bennett, Anthony
LIE DOWN WITH DOGS
Benson, Jay
AVENGING ANGEL
NEXT DOOR
Berger, Pamela
KILIAN'S CHRONICLE
Berman, Richard C.
GRUMPIER OLD MEN

Bernard, Sam
GRANNY, THE
PAYBACK
Bernart, Maurice
VOYAGE EN DOUCE
Berner, Fred
LAKOTA WOMAN: SIEGE AT WOUNDED
KNEE
Berriff, Paul
LESSONS OF DARKNESS
Bevan, Tim
FRENCH KISS
MOONLIGHT AND VALENTINO
Bini, Alfredo
MAMMA ROMA
Birnbaum, Roger
BIG GREEN, THE
HEAVYWEIGHTS
HOUSEGUEST
JERKY BOYS: THE MOVIE, THE
POWDER
TALL TALE: THE UNBELIEVABLE
ADVENTURES OF PECOS BILL
WHILE YOU WERE SLEEPING
Black, Sarah Ryan
RESTORATION
Blank, Jonathan
SEX, DRUGS AND DEMOCRACY
Boland, Russell
PEBBLE AND THE PENGUIN, THE
Boorman, John
BEYOND RANGOON
Booth, Jim
MEET THE FEEBLES
Borchers, Donald P.
NUMBER ONE FAN
WATER ENGINE, THE
Borden, Bill
DESPERADO
Border, W.K.
PROPHECY, THE
Boswell, Ruth
RUN OF THE COUNTRY, THE
Brams, Richard
COMPANION, THE
Branco, Paulo
CONVENT, THE
VALLEY OF ABRAHAM, THE
Brandes, Richard
FEAR, THE
Bregman, Martin
GOLD DIGGERS: THE SECRET OF BEAR
MOUNTAIN
Bregman, Michael S.
GOLD DIGGERS: THE SECRET OF BEAR
MOUNTAIN
Bremond, Romain
PIGALLE
Brice, Sandra Saxon
BUFFALO GIRLS
Brickmayer, Harry
PARTY GIRL
Broccoli, Barbara
GOLDENEYE
Brokaw, Cary
RESTORATION
Brooks, Mel
DRACULA: DEAD AND LOVING IT
Brost, Fred
GORDY
Broughan, Peter
ROB ROY
Brown, David
CANADIAN BACON
Brown, G. Mac
TO WONG FOO, THANKS FOR
EVERYTHING! JULIE NEWMAR
Bruce, James
DIRTY MONEY

Bruckheimer, Bonnie
MAN OF THE HOUSE
Bruckheimer, Jerry
BAD BOYS
CRIMSON TIDE
DANGEROUS MINDS
Buchman, Alexander
MUTE WITNESS
Burg, Mark
CURE, THE
Burns, Edward
BROTHERS MCMULLEN, THE
Burton, Tim
BATMAN FOREVER
Byrnes, Thomas
GLASS SHIELD, THE
Caan, Martin
PENTATHLON
Cameron, James
STRANGE DAYS
Camp, Alida
REFLECTIONS IN THE DARK
Canton, Neil
MONEY TRAIN
Caracciolo, Joe
RADIO INSIDE
Carlyle, Phyllis
SEVEN
Carmody, Don
JOHNNY MNEMONIC
Carson, Joan
ANDROID AFFAIR, THE
Caruso, Fred
STEAL BIG, STEAL LITTLE
Cassavetti, Patrick
WOMAN AT WAR, A
Castleberg, Joel
KICKING AND SCREAMING
Cazes, Lila
LEAVING LAS VEGAS
Cecchi Gori, Mario
LAMERICA
POSTMAN, THE
PURE FORMALITY, A
Cecchi Gori, Vittorio
LAMERICA
POSTMAN, THE
PURE FORMALITY, A
Chalon, Jerome
GROSSE FATIGUE
Chan Chun-Keung
RED FIRECRACKER, GREEN
FIRECRACKER
Chan, Peter
TWENTY SOMETHING
Chang, Martha
3 NINJAS KNUCKLE UP
Chang, Shiao-Ping
SHAO LIN POPEYE
Charbonnet, Patricia
FRIDAY
Charny, Ruth
SEARCH AND DESTROY
Chelsom, Peter
FUNNY BONES
Chen Kunming
ERMO
Chernov, Jeffrey
BAD COMPANY
Chiaramonte, Andrew
TWOGETHER
Chiba, Yoshi
WIZARD OF DARKNESS
Ching Siu-Tung
EXECUTIONERS
HEROIC TRIO, THE
Choi, Patrick
GALAXIS

Christiansen, Bob
KINGFISH: A STORY OF HUEY P. LONG
REDWOOD CURTAIN
Chutkowski, Ryszard
SHORT FILM ABOUT KILLING, A
SHORT FILM ABOUT LOVE, A
Clapham, Adam
DOOMSDAY GUN
Clokey, Art
GUMBY: THE MOVIE
Clokey, Gloria
GUMBY: THE MOVIE
Cohn, Arthur
TWO BITS
Cohn, Ellie
SEARCH AND DESTROY
Colichman, Paul
CYBER BANDITS
Collins, Boon
ABDUCTED 2: THE REUNION
Columbus, Chris
NINE MONTHS
Conner, Gary P.
BIKINI BISTRO
Coppola, Francis Ford
DON JUAN DEMARCO
Corman, Julie
SILENCE OF THE HAMS
Cort, Robert W.
ROOMMATES
Cortese, Antonio
DECOY
Costner, Kevin
WATERWORLD
Coston, Suzanne
BUFFALO GIRLS
Cottle, Graham
NIGHTMARE
Counihan, Judy
BEFORE THE RAIN
Cowan, Rob
NET, THE
Cruickshank, Jim
IT TAKES TWO
Crystal, Billy
FORGET PARIS
Curtis, Bruce Cohn
BODILY HARM
Curtis, Douglas
JUDICIAL CONSENT
Curtis, Patrick
AVENGING ANGEL
Curtis, Sara
ENGLISHMAN WHO WENT UP A HILL
BUT CAME DOWN A MOUNTAIN, THE
Dalton, Robin
COUNTRY LIFE
Daniel, Sean
MALLRATS
Daniele, Gaetano
POSTMAN, THE
Daou, Diane
DANGEROUS, THE
Davey, Bruce
BRAVEHEART
David, Pierre
SCANNERS: THE SHOWDOWN
SECRETARY, THE
Davis, Andrew
STEAL BIG, STEAL LITTLE
Davis, John A.
GRUMPIER OLD MEN
HUNTED, THE
WATERWORLD
de Clercq, Jacques
BLUE VILLA, THE
De Fina, Barbara
CASINO

Dennis, Brian
DANCE ME OUTSIDE
Densham, Pen
TANK GIRL
DePew, Gary
CHILDREN OF THE CORN III: URBAN
HARVEST
Deutch, James
TIE-DIED: ROCK 'N' ROLL'S MOST
DEADICATED FANS
DeVito, Danny
GET SHORTY
Deyhle, Rolf
GOLD DIGGERS: THE SECRET OF BEAR
MOUNTAIN
Diamant, Moshe
SUDDEN DEATH
Dickersin, Ged
REASON TO BELIEVE, A
Dimbort, Danny
OUTSIDE THE LAW
Donadio, Mark
KILIAN'S CHRONICLE
Donen, Joshua
QUICK AND THE DEAD, THE
Donner, Richard
ASSASSINS
Dor, Milan
FOR GOD AND COUNTRY
Doran, Lindsay
SENSE AND SENSIBILITY
Eagger, Fiona
ONLY THE BRAVE
Eastwood, Clint
BRIDGES OF MADISON COUNTY, THE
STARS FELL ON HENRIETTA, THE
Ecare, Desire
FACES OF WOMEN
Egoyan, Atom
EXOTICA
Eilts, Mary
CIRCUMSTANCES UNKNOWN
Eisner, Eric
CURE, THE
Elliott, Mike
CRAZYSITTER, THE
DILLINGER AND CAPONE
SPY WITHIN, THE
Elwes, Cassian
FRANK & JESSE
Erschbamer, George
POWER OF ATTORNEY
Evans, Bruce A.
ASSASSINS
Evans, Charles
SHOWGIRLS
Evans, Jr., Michael W.
MUTANT SPECIES
Evans, Robert
JADE
Everett, Gimel
HIDEAWAY
Faber, George
PRIEST
Faure, Brigitte
AUGUSTIN
Feinberg, Gregg D.
CANDYMAN: FAREWELL TO THE FLESH
Feldman, Dennis
SPECIES
Fellner, Eric
FRENCH KISS
MOONLIGHT AND VALENTINO
Fiedler, John
RADIO INSIDE
Field, Gwen
REFLECTIONS IN THE DARK

Field, Ted
ROOMMATES
Fields, Simon
FUNNY BONES
Fienberg, Gregg
CLASS OF '61
Finlay, Fiona
PERSUASION
Fisher, Dick
BROTHERS MCMULLEN, THE
Fitzpatrick, Gary
HEAVEN'S A DRAG
Foner, Naomi
LOSING ISAIAH
Fong, Eddie
EROTIQUE
Foster, Gary
AMAZING PANDA ADVENTURE, THE
Foster, Jodie
HOME FOR THE HOLIDAYS
Fox, Michael J.
COLDBLOODED
Fox, Robert
MONTH BY THE LAKE, A
Francois, Anne
NINE MONTHS
Frand, Harvey
OUT OF ANNIE'S PAST
Frankel, David
MIAMI RHAPSODY
Frankenheimer, John
BURNING SEASON, THE
Franklin, Richard
HOTEL SORRENTO
Frappier, Roger
LOVE AND HUMAN REMAINS
Freeman, Paul
HALLOWEEN: THE CURSE OF MICHAEL
MYERS
Freyd, Denis
MY LIFE AND TIMES WITH ANTONIN
ARTAUD
Freydberg, James B.
ZOOMAN
Frieberg, Camelia
ECLIPSE
EXOTICA
Friedenn, Neva
RED SUN RISING
Fries, Francois
SON OF THE SHARK, THE
Frydman, Marc
MURDER IN THE FIRST
Fuchs, Fred
DON JUAN DEMARCO
Gabai, Richard
MIDNIGHT TEASE 2
Gabrielsson, Lisabeth
DANCER, THE
Galan, Kathryn F.
FRENCH KISS
Gallant, Michael O.
DANGER OF LOVE
SUBSTITUTE WIFE, THE
Garroni, Andre
EXPERT, THE
Garroni, Andrew
BODY STROKES
UNDERCOVER
Genoves, Andre
NEA
Geoffray, Jeff
EVOLVER
Gibson, Mel
BRAVEHEART
Gideon, Raynold
ASSASSINS

Gilliot, Nick
RETURN OF THE NATIVE, THE
Gilmore, William S.
CURSE OF THE STARVING CLASS
Giovanni, Marita
BAR GIRLS
Glimcher, Arne
JUST CAUSE
Glynn, Michael
GLORY BOYS, THE
Godard, Jean-Luc
JLG BY JLG
Goetzman, Gary
DEVIL IN A BLUE DRESS
Gold, Eric L.
MAJOR PAYNE
Goldberg, Gary David
BYE BYE, LOVE
Goldstein, Gary W.
HUNTED, THE
Goldstein, Harel
CURSE OF THE STARVING CLASS
Golfus, Billy
WHEN BILLY BROKE HIS HEAD ... AND
OTHER TALES OF WONDER
Golin, Steve
CANADIAN BACON
CANDYMAN: FAREWELL TO THE FLESH
Goodman, John
KINGFISH: A STORY OF HUEY P. LONG
Gordon, Charles
WATERWORLD
Gordon, Mark
PYROMANIAC'S LOVE STORY, A
Gorman, James
CUTTHROAT ISLAND
Gosse, Bob
NEW JERSEY DRIVE
Goudreau, Richard
ABDUCTED 2: THE REUNION
Graves, Alex
CRUDE OASIS, THE
Grazer, Brian
APOLLO 13
Grean, Wendy
NATIONAL LAMPOON'S SENIOR TRIP
Green, Clifford
THREE WISHES
Green, Ellen
THREE WISHES
Green, Sarah
SECRET OF ROAN INISH, THE
Greenhut, Robert
MIGHTY APHRODITE
Greggio, Ezio
SILENCE OF THE HAMS
Griffin, Christopher
BITTER VENGEANCE
Griffiths, Michael
LIVING IN OBLIVION
Grodnik, Daniel
POWDER
Grosbard, Ulu
GEORGIA
Guerin, Gerard
MY LIFE AND TIMES WITH ANTONIN
ARTAUD
Guerin, J.P.
KID IN KING ARTHUR'S COURT, A
Guez, Philippe
INNOCENT LIES
Guezel, Yvon
NEA
Guggenheim, Ralph
TOY STORY
Guiney, Ed
AILSA

Gutilla, Tony
MIDNIGHT TEASE 2
Haboush, Ray
DARK SIDE OF GENIUS, THE
Hackett, Jonathan
KURT VONNEGUT'S HARRISON
BERGERON
Hackford, Taylor
DOLORES CLAIBORNE
Haddad, Patrice
PIGALLE
Hall, Brad
BYE BYE, LOVE
Hall, Dolly
INCREDIBLY TRUE ADVENTURES OF
TWO GIRLS IN LOVE, THE
Hall, Paul
HIGHER LEARNING
Hamburger, David S.
CROSSING GUARD, THE
Hammel, Thomas M.
BURNING SEASON, THE
Hamori, Andras
NEVER TALK TO STRANGERS
Hanczakowski, Agatha
HIDEAWAY
Hann, Denis
ADDICTION, THE
Hannay, David
DEAD FUNNY
GROSS MISCONDUCT
Hansen, Lisa
TERESA'S TATTOO
Hansson, Borje
DREAMING OF RITA
Hardy, John
UNDERNEATH, THE
Harlin, Renny
CUTTHROAT ISLAND
Hartley, Hal
AMATEUR
Hartley, Julie
WORLD AND TIME ENOUGH
Hartman, Jesse
RIVER OF GRASS
Hassid, Daniel
CREW, THE
Heath, Hilary
AWFULLY BIG ADVENTURE, AN
Hecht, Marlen
WIGSTOCK: THE MOVIE
Hegyes, Stephen
DOUBLE HAPPINESS
Heller, Liz
BASKETBALL DIARIES, THE
Heller, Rosilyn
BETTER OFF DEAD
Henchoz, Jean-Marc
PROMISE, THE
Herbert, Henry
FEAST OF JULY
Herman, Vicky
EROTIQUE
Hernandez, Humberto
UP TO A CERTAIN POINT
Hernandez, Jane
NINA TAKES A LOVER
Hertzberg, Paul
DREAM A LITTLE DREAM 2
Herzog, Werner
LESSONS OF DARKNESS
Hess, Oliver G.
OPERATION INTERCEPT
Heyman, Norma
INNOCENT, THE
SISTER MY SISTER
Hickner, Steve
BALTO

Hill, Michael Jay
COSMIC SLOP
Hinchcliffe, Philip
AWFULLY BIG ADVENTURE, AN
Hobby, Amy
NADJA
Hoffman, Lauran
BAR GIRLS
Hoffman, Susan
KISS OF DEATH
Holmes, Preston
PANTHER
Hope, Ted
AMATEUR
PUSHING HANDS
ROY COHN/JACK SMITH
Horikoshi, Kenzo
SMOKE
Hornickel, Cindy
FATHER AND SCOUT
House, Lynda
MURIEL'S WEDDING
Howard, Andy
TOP DOG
Howard, Dan
RENT-A-KID
Huber, Gerd
NOBODY LOVES ME
Hughes, Albert
DEAD PRESIDENTS
Hughes, Allen
DEAD PRESIDENTS
Hui, Ann
DAY THE SUN TURNED COLD, THE
Hunt, Judith
FRIENDS
Hurd, Gale Anne
SAFE PASSAGE
Hurmer, Alfred
GORILLA BATHES AT NOON
Ice Cube
FRIDAY
Imai, Tomoyuki
WIZARD OF DARKNESS
Inoue, Hiroaki
WINGS OF HONNEAMISE: ROYAL SPACE
FORCE
Ireland, Dan
CREW, THE
Iwase, Yasuteru
BAREFOOT GEN
Iyadomi, Ken
WINGS OF HONNEAMISE: ROYAL SPACE
FORCE
Jacks, James
MALLRATS
Jackson, George
WALKING DEAD, THE
Jackson, Peter
MEET THE FEEBLES
Jackson, Richard
ROB ROY
Jacobs, Alan
NINA TAKES A LOVER
Jacquier, Philippe
AUGUSTIN
Jaffe, Steven-Charles
STRANGE DAYS
Jelinski, Manfred O.
NEKROMANTIK
Jenkel, Brad
COLDBLOODED
Jennings, Terry
NOSTRADAMUS KID, THE
Joffe, Roland
SCARLET LETTER, THE
Johnson, Ernest
COSMIC SLOP

Johnson, Greg
BLUE IN THE FACE
SMOKE
Johnson, Mark
LITTLE PRINCESS, A
Johnson, Robert
SHOW, THE
Johnstone, Jyll
MARTHA & ETHEL
Jossen, Barry
MIAMI RHAPSODY
Josten, Walter
EVOLVER
Junkersdorf, Eberhard
PROMISE, THE
Kagan, Jeremy
ROSWELL: THE U.F.O. COVER-UP
Kahn, Ilene
ROSWELL: THE U.F.O. COVER-UP
Kalatozov, Mikhail
I AM CUBA
Kallberg, Kevin M.
OPERATION INTERCEPT
Kamandar, Dzhavabshir
CREATION OF ADAM
Karago, Njeri
ASCENT, THE
GREAT ELEPHANT ESCAPE, THE
Karnowski, Tom
SPITFIRE
Kasanoff, Lawrence
MORTAL KOMBAT
Kasimov, Anatoli
CREATION OF ADAM
Kastner, Elliot
FRANK & JESSE
Kato, Hiroshi
AI CITY
Katz, Gail
OUTBREAK
Katz, Marty
MAN OF THE HOUSE
Kaufman, Amy J.
RECKLESS
Kaufman, Gary
DECOY
Kennedy, Kathleen
BRIDGES OF MADISON COUNTY, THE
CONGO
INDIAN IN THE CUPBOARD, THE
Kerrigan, Lodge H.
CLEAN, SHAVEN
Khan, Ilene
FATHERLAND
Kiarostami, Abbas
THROUGH THE OLIVE TREES
Kilik, Jon
CLOCKERS
DEAD MAN WALKING
Kimber, Les
BLACK FOX
King, Sandy
IN THE MOUTH OF MADNESS
VILLAGE OF THE DAMNED
Kirkpatrick, David
BRADY BUNCH MOVIE, THE
Klein, Barbara
REFLECTIONS IN THE DARK
Kobayashi, Shun
WIZARD OF DARKNESS
Koch, Jr., Howard W.
LOSING ISAIAH
Koch, Mark W.
JUDICIAL CONSENT
Kolar, Cedomir
ARIZONA DREAM
BEFORE THE RAIN

Komine, Aki
BLUE TIGER
Kopelson, Arnold
OUTBREAK
SEVEN
Koules, Stephanie
PARTY GIRL
Krausz, Danny
FOR GOD AND COUNTRY
Krevoy, Brad
COLDBLOODED
COVER ME
GHOST BRIGADE
Kroopf, Scott
JUMANJI
ROOMMATES
Kuriowa, Hisami
SMOKE
Kusano, Keiji
WINGS OF HONNEAMISE: ROYAL SPACE
FORCE
Kushnick, Ken
BRIAN WILSON: I JUST WASN'T MADE
FOR THESE TIMES
Kwan, Teddie Robin
EROTIQUE
Ladd, Jr., Alan
BRAVEHEART
Larere, Xavier
BUSINESS AFFAIR, A
Later, Adria
DOUBLE, DOUBLE, TOIL AND TROUBLE
Latshaw, Steve
JACK-O
Lawrence, Robert
CLUELESS
Lazar, Andrew
ASSASSINS
Leahy, Michael
BLUE TIGER
Leary, Michael
PROPHECY, THE
Ledoux, Patrice
GROSSE FATIGUE
Lee, Ang
PUSHING HANDS
Lee, Spike
CLOCKERS
Leger, Claude
HIGHLANDER: THE FINAL DIMENSION
Leider, Jerry
DR. JEKYLL & MS. HYDE
Leigh, Jennifer Jason
GEORGIA
Lelouch, Claude
LES MISERABLES
Lemchen, Bob
O.J. SIMPSON STORY, THE
Lenkov, Peter M.
JURY DUTY
Lerner, Avi
OUTSIDE THE LAW
Levi, Jean-Pierre Ramsay
TOTAL ECLIPSE
Levy, Benjamin
TOO OUTRAGEOUS ANIMATION
Levy, Robert L.
KID IN KING ARTHUR'S COURT, A
Levy, Shuki
MIGHTY MORPHIN POWER RANGERS:
THE MOVIE
Lewis, Richard B.
TANK GIRL
Lindenmuth, Kevin J.
VAMPIRES AND OTHER STEREOTYPES
Linson, Art
HEAT

Lippincott, Charles M.
JUDGE DREDD
Lipsky, Mark
VAMPIRE IN BROOKLYN
Loftis, Norman
MESSENGER
Logothetis, Dimitri
BODY SHOT
Lombardi, Francisco Jose
NO MERCY
Low, Stephen
ACROSS THE SEA OF TIME: NEW YORK
3D
Lowe, Heather
AVENGING ANGEL
Lowry, Hunt
FIRST KNIGHT
Lowry, Richard O.
FIRST DEGREE
Lucchesi, Gary
THREE WISHES
VIRTUOSITY
Ludwig, Tony
EMPIRE RECORDS
Lui, Emily
PUSHING HANDS
Lundgren, Dolph
PENTATHLON
Lupovitz, Dan
SEARCH AND DESTROY
Macdonald, Andrew
SHALLOW GRAVE
Macek, Carl
BAREFOOT GEN
CRIMSON WOLF
WICKED CITY
MacGregor-Scott, Peter
BATMAN FOREVER
MacKinnon, Susan
ETERNITY
MacLean, Robert K.
DIGGER
Madden, David
OPERATION DUMBO DROP
TIE THAT BINDS, THE
Maggi, Maurizio
CASTLE FREAK
Mailer, Michael
FOOL AND HIS MONEY, A
Mancilla, Jess
CAGED HEARTS
Mancuso, Jr., Frank
SPECIES
Manheim, Michael
ZOOMAN
Mann, Michael
HEAT
Manoogian, Peter
NATIONAL LAMPOON'S ATTACK OF THE
5'2" WOMEN
Manson, David
MAD LOVE
Manulis, John Bard
BASKETBALL DIARIES, THE
Margoulis, Gene
BODY SHOT
Marijan, Bojana
GORILLA BATHES AT NOON
Maris, Peter
BALLISTIC
Mark, Diane Mei Lin
PICTURE BRIDE
Mark, Laurence
CUTTHROAT ISLAND
TOM AND HUCK
Markey, Patrick
QUICK AND THE DEAD, THE
TIE THAT BINDS, THE

Marks, Beau E.L.
JUDGE DREDD
Marmion, Yves
ARIZONA DREAM
Marshall, Alan
SHOWGIRLS
Marshall, Frank
INDIAN IN THE CUPBOARD, THE
Marx, Timothy
CITIZEN X
Maseba, Yutaka
WINGS OF HONNEAMISE: ROYAL SPACE
FORCE
Maslak, Paul
RED SUN RISING
Maslansky, Paul
FLUKE
Mason, Richard
DESPERATE PREY
Matthews, Ross
DALLAS DOLL
Maxwell, Mitchell
JEFFREY
Maxwell, Victoria
JEFFREY
Mayhew, Vivian
I LIKE TO PLAY GAMES
McDonald, Bruce
DANCE ME OUTSIDE
McDonald, Heather
BALLOT MEASURE 9
McDonnell, Michael
USUAL SUSPECTS, THE
McElroy, Hal
SUM OF US, THE
McElroy, Jim
TRAPS
McGlothen, Steve
BROKEN TRUST
McGrath, John
CARRINGTON
McHenry, Douglas
WALKING DEAD, THE
McKeon, Phil
TERESA'S TATTOO
McTiernan, John
DIE HARD WITH A VENGEANCE
Meier, Pierre-Alain
HYENAS
Meistrich, Larry
NEW JERSEY DRIVE
Mercer, Sam
CONGO
Merchant, Ismail
JEFFERSON IN PARIS
Merhi, Joseph
BIGFOOT: THE UNFORGETTABLE
ENCOUNTER
Messick, Kevin J.
BABYSITTER, THE
Meyer, David
CARMEN MIRANDA: BANANAS IS MY
BUSINESS
Meyers, Nancy
FATHER OF THE BRIDE PART II
Michaels, Joel B.
CUTTHROAT ISLAND
LAST OF THE DOGMEN
Michaels, Lorne
STUART SAVES HIS FAMILY
TOMMY BOY
Mickel, Tom
LAST RIDE, THE
Mickelson, Robert
ACROSS THE MOON
Mikhalkov, Nikita
BURNT BY THE SUN

Milchan, Arnon
BOYS ON THE SIDE
COPYCAT
EMPIRE RECORDS
UNDER SIEGE 2: DARK TERRITORY
Miller, Bill
BABE
Miller, George
BABE
Mitchell, Doug
BABE
Mock, Freida Lee
MAYA LIN: A STRONG CLEAR VISION
Montgomery, Jennifer
ART FOR TEACHERS OF CHILDREN
Moore, Demi
NOW AND THEN
Moore, Joanne
SWIMMING WITH SHARKS
Moore, Michael
CANADIAN BACON
Moorhouse, Jocelyn
MURIEL'S WEDDING
Moran, Patrick
JACK-O
Morrissey, John
TIE THAT BINDS, THE
Mosier, Scott
MALLRATS
Mruvka, Alan
EMBRACE OF THE VAMPIRE
Muhlfriedel, J. Marina
NATIONAL LAMPOON'S ATTACK OF THE
5'2" WOMEN
Muller, Frederick
FATHERLAND
Mulvehill, Charles
DOLORES CLAIBORNE
Murphy, Eddie
VAMPIRE IN BROOKLYN
Nabatoff, Diane
OPERATION DUMBO DROP
SEPARATE LIVES
Nakagawa, Yoshihisa
MYSTERY OF RAMPO, THE
Nakazawa, Keiji
BAREFOOT GEN
Nathanson, Michael
EMPIRE RECORDS
Neame, Christopher
FEAST OF JULY
Negroponte, Michel
JUPITER'S WIFE
Netter, Gil
WALK IN THE CLOUDS, A
Neuman, Jeffrey R.
NEVER TALK TO STRANGERS
Newman, Peter
BLUE IN THE FACE
SMOKE
Newmyer, Robert
BORN TO BE WILD
Ng, Michael
PHANTOM LOVER, THE
Niami, Nile
GALAXIS
Nomuva, Kazufumi
CRIMSON WOLF
Nozik, Michael
PEREZ FAMILY, THE
O'Brian, Peter
FAR FROM HOME: THE ADVENTURES OF
YELLOW DOG
O'Connor, Matthew
MAGIC IN THE WATER
O'Donnell, Lynn
CRUMB

Oglesby, Marsha
TIE-DIED: ROCK 'N' ROLL'S MOST
DEADICATED FANS
Okubo, Kuniko
FRANK AND OLLIE
Olafsson, Jon
REMOTE CONTROL
Onodera, Lisa
PICTURE BRIDE
Ornelas, Michael
CREEP
Orr, James
IT TAKES TWO
Ossard, Claudie
ARIZONA DREAM
CITY OF LOST CHILDREN, THE
Owen, Alison
MOONLIGHT AND VALENTINO
Palmer, Patrick
DON JUAN DEMARCO
Papazian, Robert A.
ENEMY WITHIN, THE
Pare, Lisa Katselas
RICHARD III
Parsons, Clive
BUSINESS AFFAIR, A
Passick, David
BRIAN WILSON: I JUST WASN'T MADE
FOR THESE TIMES
Paterson, Andy
RESTORATION
Paull, Craig
POSTCARDS FROM AMERICA
Pearson, Noel
FRANKIE STARLIGHT
Pec-Slesicka, Barbara
WITHOUT ANESTHESIA
Pei Hsiang-Chuan
HIGH RISK
Penn, Sean
CROSSING GUARD, THE
Pentecost, James
POCAHONTAS
Pepin, Richard
BIGFOOT: THE UNFORGETTABLE
ENCOUNTER
Perry, Simon
INNOCENT LIES
Perry, Steve
BABYSITTER, THE
JUST CAUSE
UNDER SIEGE 2: DARK TERRITORY
Pesery, Bruno
I CAN'T SLEEP
Peters, Jon
MONEY TRAIN
Petersen, Wolfgang
OUTBREAK
Peterson, Andrew
WORLD AND TIME ENOUGH
Petrie, Dorothea G.
GETTING OUT
Peyser, Michael
HACKERS
Phillips, Diana
BLUE IN THE FACE
Pickard, Therese
CENTURY
Piel, Jean-Louis
SHANGHAI TRIAD
Pilcher, Lydia Dean
PEREZ FAMILY, THE
Pillsbury, Sarah
HOW TO MAKE AN AMERICAN QUILT
Pleskow, Eric
BEYOND RANGOON
Podeswa, Jeremy
ECLIPSE

Pokorny, Diana
INDICTMENT: THE MCMARTIN TRIAL
Pollack, Sydney
SABRINA
Pollock, Dale
S.F.W.
Pollon, Joff
SKINNER
Powell, Melissa
BLESSING
Powell, Michael
OH ... ROSALINDA!!
Powell, Norman S.
CONVICT COWBOY
Powers, Barclay
SEX, DRUGS AND DEMOCRACY
Preger, Michael
VILLAGE OF THE DAMNED
Pressburger, Emeric
OH ... ROSALINDA!!
Preuss, Ruben
ALMOST DEAD
Price, Frank
CIRCLE OF FRIENDS
WALKING DEAD, THE
Prieur, Jerome
MY LIFE AND TIMES WITH ANTONIN
ARTAUD
Rachmil, Michael
MAJOR PAYNE
Radcliffe, Mark
NINE MONTHS
Rainone, Frank
ME AND THE MOB
Rajski, Peggy
HOME FOR THE HOLIDAYS
Ray, Fred Olen
ATTACK OF THE 60-FOOT CENTERFOLD
Ray, Satyajit
STRANGER, THE
Reichardt, Kelly
RIVER OF GRASS
Reid, Tim
OUT OF SYNC
Reim, Ole
KINGDOM, THE
Reiner, Rob
AMERICAN PRESIDENT, THE
Renzi, Maggie
SECRET OF ROAN INISH, THE
Reuther, Steven
BOYS ON THE SIDE
Rich, Lee
AMAZING PANDA ADVENTURE, THE
JUST CAUSE
Riche, Alan
EMPIRE RECORDS
Riedel, Guy
SEPARATE LIVES
Riggs, Marlon
BLACK IS ... BLACK AIN'T
Riskin, Victoria
MY ANTONIA
Robbins, Tim
DEAD MAN WALKING
Robinson, James G.
ACE VENTURA: WHEN NATURE CALLS
Robson, Sybil
GORDY
Rodrigues, Jofre
BOCA
Rodriguez, Robert
DESPERADO
Roeg, Luc
OTHELLO
Roessell, David
DARKMAN 2: THE RETURN OF DURANT

Rosenberg, Rick
KINGFISH: A STORY OF HUEY P. LONG
REDWOOD CURTAIN
Rosenthal, Henry S.
BED YOU SLEEP IN, THE
FRAMEUP
Ross, Herbert
BOYS ON THE SIDE
Roth, Donna
UNSTRUNG HEROES
Roth, Joe
HEAVYWEIGHTS
HOUSEGUEST
JERKY BOYS: THE MOVIE, THE
TALL TALE: THE UNBELIEVABLE
ADVENTURES OF PECOS BILL
WHILE YOU WERE SLEEPING
Rotholz, Ron
CANADIAN BACON
Rothstein, Ron
ALMOST DEAD
Rouleau, Lilli
CYBER BANDITS
Rounds, Dan
GOOFY MOVIE, A
Roven, Charles
TWELVE MONKEYS
Rozanes, Alain
HYENAS
Rudin, Scott
CLUELESS
SABRINA
Ryan, Lata
FLUKE
Ryan, Meg
FRENCH KISS
Saarinen, Lasse
CITY UNPLUGGED
Saban, Haim
MIGHTY MORPHIN POWER RANGERS:
THE MOVIE
Sager, Ray
BOULEVARD
Sanders, Terry
MAYA LIN: A STRONG CLEAR VISION
Sanford, Midge
HOW TO MAKE AN AMERICAN QUILT
Sarde, Alain
WILD REEDS
Schamus, James
PUSHING HANDS
ROY COHN/JACK SMITH
Schiff, Paul
BUSHWHACKED
Schindler, Deborah
WAITING TO EXHALE
Schmoeller, Gary
SPITFIRE
Scholes, Robin
ONCE WERE WARRIORS
Schroeder, Barbet
KISS OF DEATH
Schroeder, Carolyn
GLASS SHIELD, THE
Schultz-Keil, Wieland
INNOCENT, THE
Schwartz, Lloyd J.
BRADY BUNCH MOVIE, THE
Schwartz, Sherwood
BRADY BUNCH MOVIE, THE
Schwarz, Marius
MARTHA AND I
Scorsese, Martin
CLOCKERS
Scott, Darin
TALES FROM THE HOOD
Seagal, Steven
UNDER SIEGE 2: DARK TERRITORY

Seefeldt, Renate
NOBODY LOVES ME
Seggerman, Henry
EVOLVER
Seligmann, Guy
WINDOW TO PARIS
Sellar, JoAnne
LORD OF ILLUSIONS
Sellers, Arlene
CIRCLE OF FRIENDS
Sellers, Dylan
AMAZING PANDA ADVENTURE, THE
Seydoux, Michel
BURNT BY THE SUN
Shamberg, Michael
GET SHORTY
Shapiro, Allen
QUICK AND THE DEAD, THE
Shapiro, Larry
BRIAN WILSON: I JUST WASN'T MADE
FOR THESE TIMES
Shapiro, Robert
DR. JEKYLL & MS. HYDE
Shedlo, Ronald
CARRINGTON
Sheffield-MacClure, Richard
GROSS MISCONDUCT
Sher, Stacey
GET SHORTY
Shostak, Murray
POWER OF ATTORNEY
Shuler-Donner, Lauren
FREE WILLY 2: THE ADVENTURE HOME
Sievernich, Chris
INNOCENT, THE
Sighvatsson, Joni
CANDYMAN: FAREWELL TO THE FLESH
Silver, Dean
WIGSTOCK: THE MOVIE
Silver, Jeffery
BORN TO BE WILD
Silver, Joel
ASSASSINS
FAIR GAME
Silvers, Dean
LAST GOOD TIME, THE
Simandl, Lloyd A.
CRACKERJACK
Simmons, Rudd
DEAD MAN WALKING
Simonds, Robert
BILLY MADISON
Simpson, Don
BAD BOYS
CRIMSON TIDE
DANGEROUS MINDS
Simpson, Peter
BOULEVARD
Simson, David E.
WHEN BILLY BROKE HIS HEAD ... AND
OTHER TALES OF WONDER
Singer, Bryan
USUAL SUSPECTS, THE
Singh, Anant
CRY, THE BELOVED COUNTRY
MANGLER, THE
Singleton, John
HIGHER LEARNING
Sjogren, John
MOSAIC PROJECT, THE
Skorpik, Karel
COW, THE
Sloane, Rick
GOOD GIRLS DON'T
Small, Gregory
AMERICAN COP
Smith, Gregg
COVER STORY

Soentgen, Norbert
MUTE WITNESS

Soisson, Joel
PROPHECY, THE

Solberg, Helena
CARMEN MIRANDA: BANANAS IS MY
BUSINESS

Sombetzki, Michael
EROTIQUE

Soukup, Petr
ACCUMULATOR 1

Southwick, Brad
CHILDREN OF THE CORN III: URBAN
HARVEST

Spencer, Karen L.
PREHYSTERIA! 3

Sperling, Andrea
DOOM GENERATION, THE

Spikings, Barry
BEYOND RANGOON

Stabler, Steve
COLDBLOODED
GHOST BRIGADE

Stabler, Steven
COVER ME

Stack, Jonathan
HARLEM DIARY: NINE VOICES OF
RESILIENCE

Stantic, Lita
I, THE WORST OF ALL

Starch, Jonathan
RHYTHM THIEF

Startz, Jane
BABY-SITTERS CLUB, THE
INDIAN IN THE CUPBOARD, THE

Steel, Dawn
ANGUS

Stern, Adam
CREW, THE

Stevens, Andrew
BODY CHEMISTRY 4: FULL EXPOSURE

Stevenson, Rick
MAGIC IN THE WATER

Stewart, Annie
LEAVING LAS VEGAS

Stone, Oliver
NIXON

Styler, Trudie
MOVING THE MOUNTAIN

Sueyoshi, Hirohiko
WINGS OF HONNEAMISE: ROYAL SPACE
FORCE

Sugiyama, Kiyoshi
CRIMSON WOLF

Sulichin, Fernando
ADDICTION, THE

Sutton, Imogen
ARABIAN KNIGHT

Sweeney, Mary
NADJA

Swerdlow, Ezra
WAITING TO EXHALE

Sykorova, Helena
COW, THE

Sylbert, Anthea
SOMETHING TO TALK ABOUT

Tadross, Michael
DIE HARD WITH A VENGEANCE

Tan, Jimmy
ERMO

Tarlov, Mark
COPYCAT
RADIO INSIDE

Taub, Lori-Etta
BREACH OF CONDUCT

Taylor, Sam
BEFORE THE RAIN

Teitler, William
JUMANJI

Tettenborn, Sabine
MARTHA AND I

Thomas, Anna
MY FAMILY: MI FAMILIA

Thomas, Theodore
FRANK AND OLLIE

Tichenor, Harold
GOOD DAY TO DIE, A

Tirola, Douglas
REASON TO BELIEVE, A

To, Johnny
EXECUTIONERS

Todd, Suzanne
MIGHTY MORPHIN POWER RANGERS:
THE MOVIE
NOW AND THEN

Tollin, Michael
SHOW, THE

Tolmach, Matt
COLDBLOODED

Tong, Nancy
IN THE NAME OF THE EMPEROR

Townsend, Clayton
NIXON

Tranter, Barbara
WHEN NIGHT IS FALLING

Treut, Monika
EROTIQUE

Trevillion, Dale
PLAY TIME

Trussell, Carol Dunn
REFLECTIONS IN THE DARK

Tsai Sung-Lin
ASHES OF TIME

Tsang, Eric
HE'S A WOMAN, SHE'S A MAN

Tse, Simon
NEW YORK COP

Tugend, Jennie Lew
FREE WILLY 2: THE ADVENTURE HOME

Turner, Barbara
GEORGIA

Turner, Clive
HOWLING: NEW MOON RISING, THE

Tykwer, Tom
DEADLY MARIA

Ursini, Amedeo
BAD COMPANY

Vachon, Christine
POSTCARDS FROM AMERICA
SAFE

Vajna, Andrew G.
NIXON
SCARLET LETTER, THE

Valdes, David
STARS FELL ON HENRIETTA, THE

Van Gogh, Theo
1-900

Van Patten, Vincent
BREAK, THE

Van Peebles, Mario
PANTHER

Van Peebles, Melvin
PANTHER

van Voorst, Susanne
METAL AND MELANCHOLY

Van Wyck, James
ASSASSINS

Vance, Marylin
EMBRACE OF THE VAMPIRE

Villiers, Cat
BEFORE THE RAIN

Vilsmaier, Joseph
STALINGRAD

Vince, Robert
BULLETPROOF HEART

MALICIOUS

Vince, William
BULLETPROOF HEART
MALICIOUS

Viscidi, Marcus
LIVING IN OBLIVION

von Krusenstjerna, Fredrick
BETRAYAL

Von Vietinghoff, Joachim
GORILLA BATHES AT NOON

Vostar, Miro
NOT ANGELS BUT ANGELS

Waddell, Rose Lam
DOUBLE HAPPINESS

Walker-McBay, Anne
BEFORE SUNRISE

Wallace, William
COVER STORY

Waller, Anthony
MUTE WITNESS

Wang Ying Hsiang
WOODEN MAN'S BRIDE, THE

Ward, Josephine
PRIEST

Was, Don
BRIAN WILSON: I JUST WASN'T MADE
FOR THESE TIMES

Waterston, Sam
JOURNEY OF AUGUST KING, THE

Watson, John
TANK GIRL

Weber-Gold, Susan
TOO YOUNG TO DIE?

Webster, Paul
LITTLE ODESSA

Wechsler, Nick
JOURNEY OF AUGUST KING, THE

Weems, Marianne
ROY COHN/JACK SMITH

Weinstein, Paula
SOMETHING TO TALK ABOUT

Weisman, Sam
BYE BYE, LOVE

Weitz, Julie Anne
TOO YOUNG TO DIE?

Wessler, Charles B.
BUSHWHACKED

White, Timothy
DEATH IN BRUNSWICK

White, Wally
LIE DOWN WITH DOGS

Wilcox, John
AMAZING PANDA ADVENTURE, THE

Wiley, Martin J.
NEVER TALK TO STRANGERS

Williams, Richard
ARABIAN KNIGHT

Willoughby, Robert
MUTANT SPECIES

Wilson, August
PIANO LESSON, THE

Wilson, Colin
CASPER

Wilson, Michael G.
GOLDENEYE

Winberg, Wynn
DARK DEALER

Winitsky, Alex
CIRCLE OF FRIENDS

Winkler, Irwin
NET, THE

Winter, Ralph
HACKERS

Winters, David
DANGEROUS, THE

Wiseman, Frederick
BALLET

Wolinsky, Judith
  LAST SUMMER IN THE HAMPTONS
Wolper, Mark
  DILLINGER
  MURDER IN THE FIRST
Wong Jing
  HIGH RISK
  NAKED KILLER
Wong, Raymond
  PHANTOM LOVER, THE
Woo-Suk Kang
  HOW TO TOP MY WIFE
Wood, Christopher
  EROTIQUE
Woods, Cary
  KIDS
  THINGS TO DO IN DENVER WHEN
    YOU'RE DEAD
Wyman, Brad
  SKINNER
Wynhoff, Michael L.
  AMERICA'S DEADLIEST HOME VIDEO
Yamashina, Makoto
  WINGS OF HONNEAMISE: ROYAL SPACE
    FORCE
Yates, Peter
  RUN OF THE COUNTRY, THE
Yim Ho
  DAY THE SUN TURNED COLD, THE
Yong Naiming
  RED FIRECRACKER, GREEN
    FIRECRACKER
Yoshida, Taro
  WINGS OF HONNEAMISE: ROYAL SPACE
    FORCE
Yoshimoto, Takanori
  BAREFOOT GEN
Young, Jeff
  BOCA
Young, Sally
  DECONSTRUCTING SARAH
Zachary, Susan
  TIE THAT BINDS, THE
Zahavi, Natan
  GRANNY, THE
  PAYBACK
Zalaznick, Lauren
  SAFE
Zanuck, Lili Fini
  WILD BILL
Zanuck, Richard D.
  WILD BILL
Zarrin, Alireza
  JAR, THE
Zehrer, Paul
  BLESSING
Zeiger, Neil
  LAMB
Zhigu, Cheng
  ASHES OF TIME
Ziehl, Scott
  MOSAIC PROJECT, THE
Zielinsky, Rafal
  FUN
Zimmerman, Gloria
  DESTINY TURNS ON THE RADIO
Ziskin, Laura
  TO DIE FOR
Zucker, David
  WALK IN THE CLOUDS, A
Zucker, Jerry
  WALK IN THE CLOUDS, A
Zuvic, Nick
  I LIKE TO PLAY GAMES
  PLAY TIME
Zwigoff, Terry
  CRUMB

PRODUCTION DESIGNERS

Ackland-Snow, Terry
  DOOMSDAY GUN
Adam, Ken
  BOYS ON THE SIDE
Aichele, Ken
  EVOLVER
Aird, Gilles
  HIGHLANDER: THE FINAL DIMENSION
Allen, James
  DILLINGER
Allen, Linda
  DANGER OF LOVE
Amaral, Roy Alan
  NIGHTMARE
Amies, Caroline
  CARRINGTON
  SISTER MY SISTER
Anderson, Michael
  TO CROSS THE RUBICON
Arrighi, Luciana
  INNOCENT, THE
  SENSE AND SENSIBILITY
Bacher, Hans
  BALTO
Baraldi, Lorenzo
  POSTMAN, THE
Barkham, David
  CRY, THE BELOVED COUNTRY
  MANGLER, THE
Baron, Norm
  TOP DOG
Barrett, Penny
  GLASS SHIELD, THE
Baugh, Michael
  ASCENT, THE
Beal, Charley
  ACROSS THE SEA OF TIME: NEW YORK
    3D
Beard, John
  HACKERS
Becher, Sophie
  BUSINESS AFFAIR, A
Beecroft, Jeffrey
  TWELVE MONKEYS
Bellamy, Bruce
  FRIDAY
Bennett, Ellen
  ABDUCTED 2: THE REUNION
Bennett, Laurence
  COMPANION, THE
Bielski, Wladyslaw
  PROVINCIAL ACTORS
Binns, Leslie
  GREAT ELEPHANT ESCAPE, THE
Bishop, Dan
  ROOMMATES
  SAFE PASSAGE
Bissell, James
  JUMANJI
Bjornson, Michael
  DOUBLE HAPPINESS
Blackie, John
  BLACK FOX
Blake, Perry
  BILLY MADISON
Blass, Dave
  BODY CHEMISTRY 4: FULL EXPOSURE
Blatt, Stuart
  PAYBACK
  TALES FROM THE HOOD
Bolles, Susan
  ME AND THE MOB
  NEW YORK COP
Bolton, Michael
  GOLD DIGGERS: THE SECRET OF BEAR
    MOUNTAIN

  HIDEAWAY
Bomba, David
  SAFE
Bose, Ashoke
  STRANGER, THE
Bourne, Mel
  KISS OF DEATH
  SOMETHING TO TALK ABOUT
Box, John
  FIRST KNIGHT
Bradley, Scott
  PUSHING HANDS
Branco, Maria Jose
  VALLEY OF ABRAHAM, THE
Brandes, Philip Michael
  TWOGETHER
Brenner, Albert
  UNDER SIEGE 2: DARK TERRITORY
Brisbin, David
  DEAD PRESIDENTS
  MAD LOVE
Bumstead, Henry
  STARS FELL ON HENRIETTA, THE
Burns, Keith
  BETTER OFF DEAD
Burns, Keith Brian
  HIGHER LEARNING
Burrough, Tony
  RICHARD III
Burt, Donald Graham
  DANGEROUS MINDS
Busbee, Yoland
  SHOW, THE
Callaway, Clay
  EXPERT, THE
Cameron, Allan
  SHOWGIRLS
Canter, Markus
  BLUE TIGER
Cao Jiuping
  SHANGHAI TRIAD
Capra, Bernt
  SEPARATE LIVES
Carlson, Johnathan
  IN THE DEEP WOODS
Carlson, Jonathan
  MORTAL KOMBAT
  SKINNER
Carriveau, Chris
  PLAY TIME
Cauley, Eve
  S.F.W.
Chan Pui Wah
  EXECUTIONERS
Chang, William
  ASHES OF TIME
Clay, Jim
  CIRCLE OF FRIENDS
  COPYCAT
Clech, Jean-Pierre
  MY LIFE AND TIMES WITH ANTONIN
    ARTAUD
Clokey, Gloria
  GUMBY: THE MOVIE
Coates, Nelson
  THINGS TO DO IN DENVER WHEN
    YOU'RE DEAD
Cohen, Lester
  GEORGIA
  NEW JERSEY DRIVE
Collins, Carmel
  FRIENDS
Constable, Gary Griffin
  BITTER VENGEANCE
  OUT OF ANNIE'S PAST
Conti, Carlos
  GROSSE FATIGUE

Conway, Frank
FRANKIE STARLIGHT
Corenblith, Michael
APOLLO 13
Costello, George
WALKING DEAD, THE
Crisanti, Andrea
PURE FORMALITY, A
Cristante, Ivo
ACROSS THE MOON
Crozier, David
GLORY BOYS, THE
Cruz, Rodell
SPITFIRE
Cummings, Howard
INDICTMENT: THE MCMARTIN TRIAL
UNDERNEATH, THE
USUAL SUSPECTS, THE
Czyznikowska, Renata
PROVINCIAL ACTORS
Dagort, Phil
HUNTED, THE
Danisz, M.
PROVINCIAL ACTORS
Davie, Brian
POWER OF ATTORNEY
Davis, Dan
PYROMANIAC'S LOVE STORY, A
Day, Don
BODY SHOT
3 NINJAS KNUCKLE UP
De Fina, Don
NINA TAKES A LOVER
de Vico, Robert
DILLINGER AND CAPONE
SPY WITHIN, THE
Dedaux, Dawn
DANGEROUS, THE
DeGovia, Jackson
DIE HARD WITH A VENGEANCE
Del Rosario, Linda
EXOTICA
NEVER TALK TO STRANGERS
DeLouche, Guillaume
JACK-O
Demeo, John
KILIAN'S CHRONICLE
DeMoleron, Arnaud
I CAN'T SLEEP
Dempsey, Chris
MIDNIGHT TEASE 2
Deprez, Therese
DOOM GENERATION, THE
LIVING IN OBLIVION
POSTCARDS FROM AMERICA
DeScenna, Linda
BYE BYE, LOVE
FATHER OF THE BRIDE PART II
Deskin, Andrew
DECOY
Despotovic, Veljko
GORILLA BATHES AT NOON
Dilley, Leslie
CASPER
HOW TO MAKE AN AMERICAN QUILT
DiMinico, John
RADIO INSIDE
Dobrowolska, Halina
SHORT FILM ABOUT KILLING, A
Dobrowolski, Marek
OUT OF SYNC
Doernberg, David
RIVER OF GRASS
Dondertman, John
DANCE ME OUTSIDE
WHEN NIGHT IS FALLING
Dostal, Martin
PROMISE, THE

Dowding, Jon
GROSS MISCONDUCT
Dudley, William
PERSUASION
Duffy, Tim
BREAK, THE
Eastwood, Laurence
COUNTRY LIFE
Edwards, Chris
DEATH MACHINE
Egry, Tony
SIX DAYS, SIX NIGHTS
Ensley, David
BREACH OF CONDUCT
Erstam, Staffan
DREAMING OF RITA
Ferretti, Dante
CASINO
Ferrier, Tania
CLEAN, SHAVEN
Fischer, David
DOUBLE, DOUBLE, TOIL AND TROUBLE
Flamand, Thierry
I CAN'T SLEEP
Ford, Roger
BABE
NOSTRADAMUS KID, THE
Fox, Rae
COLDBLOODED
Francois, Guy Claude
JEFFERSON IN PARIS
Freeborn, Mark S.
DIGGER
FAR FROM HOME: THE ADVENTURES OF
YELLOW DOG
Friedberg, Mark
PEREZ FAMILY, THE
Frutkoff, Gary
DEVIL IN A BLUE DRESS
FOUR ROOMS
GRUMPIER OLD MEN
Fulton, Larry
BABY-SITTERS CLUB, THE
Gallo, Carmi
ANDROID AFFAIR, THE
Ganz, Armin
CURE, THE
Gardonyi, Laszlo
KID IN KING ARTHUR'S COURT, A
Garrad, Charles
ENGLISHMAN WHO WENT UP A HILL
BUT CAME DOWN A MOUNTAIN, THE
Garrity, Joseph T.
STUART SAVES HIS FAMILY
Garwood, Norman
CUTTHROAT ISLAND
Gassner, Dennis
WATERWORLD
Gaudino, Giuseppe M.
LAMERICA
Gentry, Cecil
SWIMMING WITH SHARKS
Geraghty, Mark
AWFULLY BIG ADVENTURE, AN
Ginn, Jeff Steven
IN THE MOUTH OF MADNESS
Giovagnoni, Gianni
MONTH BY THE LAKE, A
Goetz, David
PEBBLE AND THE PENGUIN, THE
Goetz, Jindrich
STALINGRAD
Gorton, Assheton
ROB ROY
Graham, Angelo P.
NINE MONTHS
Groom, Bill
MONEY TRAIN

Gropman, David
WAITING TO EXHALE
WALK IN THE CLOUDS, A
Guidery, Wendy
RED SUN RISING
Guncheon, Paul
PICTURE BRIDE
Gunn, Jeff
RENT-A-KID
Guterres, Candi
ATTACK OF THE 60-FOOT CENTERFOLD
Hadfield, Veronica
FATHERLAND
Haller, Michael
CROSSING GUARD, THE
STEAL BIG, STEAL LITTLE
Han, Catherine
HEROIC TRIO, THE
Hanan, Michael Z.
BURNING SEASON, THE
ROSWELL: THE U.F.O. COVER-UP
Hanania, Caroline
FUNNY BONES
Hardie, Stephen
LORD OF ILLUSIONS
Hardwicke, Catherine
TANK GIRL
Harman, Holly
GUMBY: THE MOVIE
Harpman, Fred
REDWOOD CURTAIN
Harrington, J. Mark
MIAMI RHAPSODY
Harrison, Philip
NICK OF TIME
SUDDEN DEATH
Harvey, Tim
OTHELLO
Heckroth, Hein
OH ... ROSALINDA!!
Heya, Kyoko
MYSTERY OF RAMPO, THE
Hinds-Johnson, Marcia
TIE THAT BINDS, THE
Hoover, Richard
DEAD MAN WALKING
PANTHER
ZOOMAN
Hun, Catherine
EXECUTIONERS
Hundhammer, Wolfgang
STALINGRAD
Hunter, Clark
PROPHECY, THE
Hutman, Jon
FRENCH KISS
Hynkle, James
PENTATHLON
Iacovelli, John
NATIONAL LAMPOON'S ATTACK OF THE
5'2" WOMEN
Imakaki, Isamu
CRIMSON WOLF
Ivanov, Kalina
BLUE IN THE FACE
SMOKE
Jackness, Andrew
RECKLESS
Jackson, Gemma
TOM AND HUCK
Jamero, Nilo Rodis
JOHNNY MNEMONIC
Jamison, Peter
EMPIRE RECORDS
Johnston, Michael
JEFFREY
Jones, Bryan
COSMIC SLOP

Jordan, Steven
  BRADY BUNCH MOVIE, THE
  CLUELESS
  NEXT DOOR
Jost, Jon
  BED YOU SLEEP IN, THE
Kalinowski, Waldemar
  LEAVING LAS VEGAS
  POWDER
Kammermeier, Matthias
  MUTE WITNESS
Kane, Michael
  ONCE WERE WARRIORS
Kane, Mike
  MEET THE FEEBLES
Kasch, Brian
  CYBER BANDITS
Kaufman, Claire
  GRANNY, THE
Keen, Gregory
  NATIONAL LAMPOON'S SENIOR TRIP
Kelber, Sybille
  DEADLY MARIA
Kempster, Victor
  NIXON
Kennedy, Chris
  DEATH IN BRUNSWICK
Kia, Frank
  CAGED HEARTS
Kilvert, Lilly
  AMERICAN PRESIDENT, THE
  STRANGE DAYS
King, Robb Wilson
  MOONLIGHT AND VALENTINO
Kljakovic, Miljen
  ARIZONA DREAM
Klotz, Errol Clyde
  MAGIC IN THE WATER
Kobayashi, Reiko
  CRAZYSITTER, THE
Kopp, Meike
  I LIKE TO PLAY GAMES
Korink, Petra
  EROTIQUE
Kroeger, Wolf
  HIGHLANDER: THE FINAL DIMENSION
Lagola, Charles
  ADDICTION, THE
Lalande, Guy
  CIRCUMSTANCES UNKNOWN
Lamofsky, Sharon
  BEFORE THE RAIN
Lamont, Peter
  GOLDENEYE
Langhorn, Raymond
  PRIEST
Larkin, Peter
  GET SHORTY
  MAJOR PAYNE
Lee, Wing
  LAST GOOD TIME, THE
Legler, Steven
  YOUNGER & YOUNGER
Leigh, Dan
  JERKY BOYS: THE MOVIE, THE
Leonard, Phil
  AVENGING ANGEL
  BABYSITTER, THE
Lepel, Bernd
  INNOCENT LIES
Lewis, Richard B.
  CLASS OF '61
Light-Harris, Donald
  ENEMY WITHIN, THE
  TOO YOUNG TO DIE?
Lineweaver, Stephen J.
  ACE VENTURA: WHEN NATURE CALLS
  TOMMY BOY

Ling, Barbara
  BATMAN FOREVER
Lipton, Dina
  MALLRATS
Longmire, Susan
  KURT VONNEGUT'S HARRISON
    BERGERON
Lopez, Pedro
  UP TO A CERTAIN POINT
Loquasto, Santo
  MIGHTY APHRODITE
Lucas, Ken
  BIGFOOT: THE UNFORGETTABLE
    ENCOUNTER
Ma, Eddie
  PHANTOM LOVER, THE
Mansbridge, Mark W.
  BUSHWHACKED
Marcotte, Pamela
  GIRL IN THE CADILLAC
  OPERATION INTERCEPT
Marsh, Stephen
  LAKOTA WOMAN: SIEGE AT WOUNDED
    KNEE
Marsh, Terence
  FORGET PARIS
Martin, Blair A.
  CHILDREN OF THE CORN III: URBAN
    HARVEST
Maus, Rodger
  VILLAGE OF THE DAMNED
Mavrakis, Eve
  BANDIT QUEEN
Max, Arthur
  SEVEN
McAlpine, Andrew
  BAD COMPANY
  CLOCKERS
  HOME FOR THE HOLIDAYS
McCabe, Brian
  FEAR, THE
McDonald, Leslie
  INDIAN IN THE CUPBOARD, THE
McElhatton, Heather
  WORLD AND TIME ENOUGH
McLoughlin, Ed
  AILSA
Meadows, Devin
  BAD BLOOD
Mehrten, Gregory
  ROY COHN/JACK SMITH
Melton, Gregory
  DR. JEKYLL & MS. HYDE
Menzies, Andrew
  MUTANT SPECIES
Merlin, Veronika
  SWIMMING WITH SHARKS
Messina, Philip
  GORDY
Mestroni, Vally
  FUN
Miller, Lawrence
  ANGUS
Milo
  PREHYSTERIA! 3
Mittlestadt, Tom
  CRUDE OASIS, THE
Mok, Eddie
  EROTIQUE
Montiel, Cecilia
  DESPERADO
  NO MERCY
Morahan, Ben
  HIGHLANDER: THE FINAL DIMENSION
Morris, Brian
  SABRINA
Mullins, Peter
  RETURN OF THE NATIVE, THE

Munns, David
  BEFORE THE RAIN
Musky, Jane
  TWO BITS
Muto, John
  SPECIES
Nemec, III, Joseph
  WILD BILL
Newport, Jim
  PIANO LESSON, THE
  SILENCE OF THE HAMS
Norris, Patricia
  JOURNEY OF AUGUST KING, THE
North, Marcus
  DALLAS DOLL
Nowak, Christopher
  BASKETBALL DIARIES, THE
O'Neil, Carol
  REASON TO BELIEVE, A
O'Reylly, Fernando
  STRAWBERRY AND CHOCOLATE
One By One Film and Video
  VAMPIRES AND OTHER STEREOTYPES
Oppewall, Jeannine
  BRIDGES OF MADISON COUNTY, THE
  LOSING ISAIAH
Ossenfort, Kurt
  NADJA
Pai-Rom
  SHAO LIN POPEYE
Pang, Rosa
  SPITFIRE
Paris, Richard
  EXOTICA
Paull, Lawrence G.
  MAN OF THE HOUSE
Pearce, Michael
  BODY STROKES
Pearl, Linda
  O.J. SIMPSON STORY, THE
Perry, Michael T.
  FRANK & JESSE

Peters, Paul
HOUSEGUEST
OPERATION DUMBO DROP
Petruccelli, Kirk M.
MURDER IN THE FIRST
Phelps, Nigel
JUDGE DREDD
Philips, Michael
TRAPS
Pickwoad, Michael
CENTURY
Pisoni, Edward
IT TAKES TWO
Pratt, Anthony
BEYOND RANGOON
Prazsky, Premysl
ACCUMULATOR 1
Pui-Wah, Chan
HEROIC TRIO, THE
Quaranta, Gianni
FARINELLI
Quinn, Kave
SHALLOW GRAVE
Randall, Gary
NUMBER ONE FAN
Raymond, Deborah
JUDICIAL CONSENT
JURY DUTY
Reardon, Patrick
MURIEL'S WEDDING
Reichmann, Florian
BEFORE SUNRISE
Reinhart, John
LAST RIDE, THE
Ridolfi, Paola
FOOL AND HIS MONEY, A
Ritterbusch, Katrin Esther
PROMISE, THE
Riva, J. Michael
CONGO
Robilliard, Christopher
FEAST OF JULY
Robison, Barry
CANDYMAN: FAREWELL TO THE FLESH
MY FAMILY: MI FAMILIA
WATER ENGINE, THE
Rodis, Nilo
VIRTUOSITY
Romvari, Jozsef
CITIZEN X
Rosenzweig, Steve
AMATEUR
BLESSING
Rubeo, Bruno
DOLORES CLAIBORNE
Rubertelli, Nicola
LAMERICA
Ryder, William
SECRETARY, THE
Ryman, Bryan
HALLOWEEN: THE CURSE OF MICHAEL
MYERS
Sakash, Evelyn
BIG GREEN, THE
Sanchez, Vigil
CREW, THE
Sandell, William
OUTBREAK
Sanders, Tom
ASSASSINS
BRAVEHEART
Saygel, Attila
DEADLY MARIA
Schaetzle, Terri
SCANNERS: THE SHOWDOWN
Schlesinger, Tom
NOBODY LOVES ME

Schmook, Rando
TERESA'S TATTOO
Schoppe, James L.
MY ANTONIA
Seguin, Francois
LOVE AND HUMAN REMAINS
Seymour, Sharon
DON JUAN DEMARCO
Shaw, Michael
DEAD FUNNY
Shell, Jeffrey Texas
UNDERCOVER
Shirky, Clay
ROY COHN/JACK SMITH
Shohan, Naomi
WHITE MAN'S BURDEN
Sjogren, Pat
MOSAIC PROJECT, THE
Smith, Adrian
SECRET OF ROAN INISH, THE
Smith, Elaine
FIRST DEGREE
Smith, Roy Forge
BORN TO BE WILD
DRACULA: DEAD AND LOVING IT
Sole, Alfred
BODILY HARM
Spencer, James
FAIR GAME
Spier, Carol
CANADIAN BACON
Spisak, Neil
HEAT
Spriggs, Austen
LAMB
Standefer, Robin
SEARCH AND DESTROY
Stark, Hilda
FLUKE
Starski, Allan
WITHOUT ANESTHESIA
Stearns, Craig
MIGHTY MORPHIN POWER RANGERS:
THE MOVIE
Steele, Jon Gary
DARK SIDE OF GENIUS, THE
Stefanovic, Jasna
BOULEVARD
Stewart, Jane Ann
EROTIQUE
Stewart, Missy
TO DIE FOR
Stolz, Peter
EMBRACE OF THE VAMPIRE
Stopkewich, Lynne
BULLETPROOF HEART
Storer, Stephen
HEAVYWEIGHTS
Stover, Garreth
DECONSTRUCTING SARAH
UNSTRUNG HEROES
WHILE YOU WERE SLEEPING
Strawn, C.J.
FATHER AND SCOUT
GHOST BRIGADE
Suetake, Yasumitsu
CRIMSON WOLF
Suzdalov, Mikhail
CREATION OF ADAM
Sykes, Brian
PERSUASION
Sylbert, Paul
FREE WILLY 2: THE ADVENTURE HOME
Tabayoyong, II, Wesley
AMERICAN COP
Tavoularis, Alex
JADE

Thomas, Brent
BROKEN TRUST
Thomas, Ian
WINGS OF COURAGE
Thomas, Wynn
TO WONG FOO, THANKS FOR
EVERYTHING! JULIE NEWMAR
Thompson, Kevin
KIDS
LITTLE ODESSA
PARTY GIRL
Tougas, Ginger
INCREDIBLY TRUE ADVENTURES OF
TWO GIRLS IN LOVE, THE
Vacek, Karel
PROMISE, THE
Vallone, John
BAD BOYS
THREE WISHES
Veneziano, Sandy
BUSHWHACKED
Vernaccio, Dorian
JUDICIAL CONSENT
JURY DUTY
Vetter, Arlan Jay
REFLECTIONS IN THE DARK
von Brandenstein, Patrizia
JUST CAUSE
QUICK AND THE DEAD, THE
Voytek
I, THE WORST OF ALL
Wagener, Christiaan
TALES FROM THE CRYPT: DEMON
KNIGHT
Walker, Graham "Grace"
SUM OF US, THE
Walker, Roy
SCARLET LETTER, THE
Wallace, Ross
DESPERATE PREY
Walsh, Thomas A.
KINGFISH: A STORY OF HUEY P. LONG
Warren, Jr., Gene
ROSWELL: THE U.F.O. COVER-UP
Warter, Fred
GOOFY MOVIE, A
Washington, Dennis
NET, THE
Watt, Tracy
HOTEL SORRENTO
Weems, Marianne
ROY COHN/JACK SMITH
Weil, Dan
TOTAL ECLIPSE
Welch, Bo
LITTLE PRINCESS, A
Whifler, Dan
KICKING AND SCREAMING
White, Cary
BUFFALO GIRLS
SUBSTITUTE WIFE, THE
White, Michael
CRIMSON TIDE
Wilheim, Ladislav
CURSE OF THE STARVING CLASS
Wilhelm, Ladislaw
OUTSIDE THE LAW
Willett, John
AMAZING PANDA ADVENTURE, THE
Williams, Trevor
GOOD DAY TO DIE, A
LAST OF THE DOGMEN
Wilson, Andrew
CRACKERJACK
Wilson, Gary
ARMAGEDDON: THE FINAL CHALLENGE
Witlak, Marian
MALICIOUS

Wood, Charles
GALAXIS
Young, Annie
BOCA
Zanetti, Eugenio
RESTORATION
TALL TALE: THE UNBELIEVABLE
ADVENTURES OF PECOS BILL
Zavrel, Jiri
COW, THE
Zelinskaia, Vera
WINDOW TO PARIS

SCREENWRITERS

Abbott, Scott
BREACH OF CONDUCT
Adams, Daniel
FOOL AND HIS MONEY, A
Adams, Samantha
JURY DUTY
Adlon, Felix O.
YOUNGER & YOUNGER
Adlon, Percy
YOUNGER & YOUNGER
Adrien, Gilles
CITY OF LOST CHILDREN, THE
Ahmed, Kamal
JERKY BOYS: THE MOVIE, THE
Alexander, Tom
DARK DEALER
Allen, Woody
MIGHTY APHRODITE
Almereyda, Michael
NADJA
SEARCH AND DESTROY
Amelio, Gianni
LAMERICA
Anders, Allison
FOUR ROOMS
Anderson, Elizabeth
THREE WISHES
Anderson, Jane
HOW TO MAKE AN AMERICAN QUILT
Annaud, Jean-Jacques
WINGS OF COURAGE
Apatow, Judd
HEAVYWEIGHTS
Apple, Max
ROOMMATES
Apted, Michael
MOVING THE MOUNTAIN
Araki, Gregg
DOOM GENERATION, THE
Armogida, Steve
ATTACK OF THE 60-FOOT CENTERFOLD
Atkins, David
ARIZONA DREAM
Auerbach, Michael
TIE THAT BINDS, THE
Auster, Paul
BLUE IN THE FACE
SMOKE
Bach, Jean
GREAT DAY IN HARLEM, A
Bafaro, Michael
CRACKERJACK
Baker, Kyle
COSMIC SLOP
Balaban, Bob
LAST GOOD TIME, THE
Barendse, Ronda
BODILY HARM
Barker, Clive
LORD OF ILLUSIONS
Barmash, Jeff
POWER OF ATTORNEY

Barnet, Enrique Pineda
I AM CUBA
Barrie, Michael
BAD BOYS
Base, Ron
FIRST DEGREE
Bass, Ronald
DANGEROUS MINDS
ENEMY WITHIN, THE
WAITING TO EXHALE
Bastide, Francois-Regis
VOYAGE EN DOUCE
Batchler, Janet Scott
BATMAN FOREVER
Batchler, Lee
BATMAN FOREVER
Baumbach, Noah
KICKING AND SCREAMING
Beane, Douglas Carter
TO WONG FOO, THANKS FOR
EVERYTHING! JULIE NEWMAR
Beard, Winston
CYBER BANDITS
Bell, Jeffrey
RADIO INSIDE
Bemberg, Maria Luisa
I, THE WORST OF ALL
Benayoun, Robert
SERIOUS ABOUT PLEASURE
Benedek, Barbara
SABRINA
Bennett, Edward
WOMAN AT WAR, A
Bensink, John Robert
NIGHTMARE
Bentham, Trevor
MONTH BY THE LAKE, A
Bercovici, Luca
GRANNY, THE
Beresford, Bruce
CURSE OF THE STARVING CLASS
Berger, Pamela
KILIAN'S CHRONICLE
Bernard, Sam
PAYBACK
Bernbaum, Paul
RENT-A-KID
Bernstein, Walter
DOOMSDAY GUN
Bernt, Eric
VIRTUOSITY
Bi Feiyu
SHANGHAI TRIAD
Biderman, Ann
COPYCAT
Binder, Carl
POCAHONTAS
Binder, John
BLACK FOX
Bindley, William
JUDICIAL CONSENT
Bishop, Mark
TALES FROM THE CRYPT: DEMON
KNIGHT
Bitzelberger, Rick
EMBRACE OF THE VAMPIRE
Blackwell, Sam
DANGER OF LOVE
Blake, Jeanne
STEAL BIG, STEAL LITTLE
Blakemore, Michael
COUNTRY LIFE
Blanc, Michel
GROSSE FATIGUE
Blechman, Corey
FREE WILLY 2: THE ADVENTURE HOME
Blessing, Lee
STEAL BIG, STEAL LITTLE

Bloom, Steven L.
TALL TALE: THE UNBELIEVABLE
ADVENTURES OF PECOS BILL
Bloome, Oola
UNDERCOVER
Bonengel, Winfried
PROFESSION: NEO-NAZI
Borden, Lizzie
EROTIQUE
Boris, Robert
FRANK & JESSE
Borkgren, Christopher
SPITFIRE
Borsos, Phillip
FAR FROM HOME: THE ADVENTURES OF
YELLOW DOG
Bosley, James
FUN
Bourne, Lindsay
ABDUCTED 2: THE REUNION
Bourniquel, Camille
VOYAGE EN DOUCE
Brancato, John
NET, THE
Brennan, John G.
JERKY BOYS: THE MOVIE, THE
Brickmayer, Harry
PARTY GIRL
Bright, Susie
EROTIQUE
Brill, Steven
HEAVYWEIGHTS
Brooks, Adam
FRENCH KISS
Brooks, Carlos
AMERICAN COP
Brooks, Mel
DRACULA: DEAD AND LOVING IT
Brooks, Stephen
MANGLER, THE
Brown, Julie
NATIONAL LAMPOON'S ATTACK OF THE
5'2" WOMEN
Brown, Michael Henry
DEAD PRESIDENTS
Brown, Riwia
ONCE WERE WARRIORS
Broyles, Jr., William
APOLLO 13
Bull, Sheldon
FATHER AND SCOUT
Bunzel, John
BORN TO BE WILD
Burnett, Charles
GLASS SHIELD, THE
Burns, Edward
BROTHERS MCMULLEN, THE
Buscher, Jurgen
STALINGRAD
Butcher, Oliver
DR. JEKYLL & MS. HYDE
Buttgereit, Jorg
NEKROMANTIK
Byers, Danny
BUSHWHACKED
Byrne, Joe
BLACK FOX
Byrne, Johnny
HEAVEN'S A DRAG
Cabada, Augusto
NO MERCY
Cabradek, Karel
COW, THE
Caine, Jeffrey
GOLDENEYE
Cameron, James
STRANGE DAYS

Canaan, Christopher
GREAT ELEPHANT ESCAPE, THE
Carlei, Carlo
FLUKE
Caro, Marc
CITY OF LOST CHILDREN, THE
Carriere, Jean-Claude
SERIOUS ABOUT PLEASURE
Carrington, James
FLUKE
Carter, Robert
TRAPS
Cerf, Muriel
VOYAGE EN DOUCE
Chalon, Jean
VOYAGE EN DOUCE
Chamberlain, Ardwight
BAREFOOT GEN
CRIMSON WOLF
Chan, Pauline
TRAPS
Chan, Susanne
EXECUTIONERS
Chandler, Elizabeth
LITTLE PRINCESS, A
Chandler, Michael
DIGGER
Chapot, Jean
NEA
Chelsom, Peter
FUNNY BONES
Chetwynd, Lionel
DOOMSDAY GUN
Chi Lee
HE'S A WOMAN, SHE'S A MAN
Chiaramonte, Andrew
TWOGETHER
Chong, Rae Dawn
BOULEVARD
Choo, Kiseo
WICKED CITY
Clokey, Art
GUMBY: THE MOVIE
Clokey, Gloria
GUMBY: THE MOVIE
Coady, Nicole
EMBRACE OF THE VAMPIRE
Cocks, Jay
STRANGE DAYS
Coffey, Charlie
NATIONAL LAMPOON'S ATTACK OF THE
5'2" WOMEN
Cohen, Alysha
MARTHA & ETHEL
Cohen, Barney
NEXT DOOR
Cohen, David Steven
BALTO
Cohen, Joel
TOY STORY
Collins, Boon
ABDUCTED 2: THE REUNION
Collins, Max Allan
EXPERT, THE
Colpaert, Carl-Jan
CREW, THE
Columbus, Chris
NINE MONTHS
Connaughton, Shane
RUN OF THE COUNTRY, THE
Cook, Sir Eddie
LAST RIDE, THE
Copp, Rick
BRADY BUNCH MOVIE, THE
Corbiau, Andree
FARINELLI

Corbiau, Gerard
FARINELLI
Corr, Eugene
GETTING OUT
Coto, Manny
EVOLVER
Crabbe, Kerry
INNOCENT LIES
Crimm, Arthur
KURT VONNEGUT'S HARRISON
BERGERON
Cruickshank, Jim
MAN OF THE HOUSE
Crystal, Billy
FORGET PARIS
Cundieff, Rusty
TALES FROM THE HOOD
D.J. Pooh
FRIDAY
Da Ying
RED FIRECRACKER, GREEN
FIRECRACKER
Daniels, Stan
SUBSTITUTE WIFE, THE
Dargay, Attila
ADVENTURES OF MATT THE
GOOSEBOY, THE
Davids, Paul
ROSWELL: THE U.F.O. COVER-UP
Davies, Andrew
CIRCLE OF FRIENDS
Davies, William
DR. JEKYLL & MS. HYDE
Davis, Andrew
STEAL BIG, STEAL LITTLE
Davis, Deborah Dean
IT TAKES TWO
Davis, Michael
PREHYSTERIA! 3
Davis, Nick
GALAXIS
de Clercq, Dimitri
BLUE VILLA, THE
De Luca, Michael
IN THE MOUTH OF MADNESS
De Luca, Rudy
DRACULA: DEAD AND LOVING IT
de Oliveira, Manoel
CONVENT, THE
VALLEY OF ABRAHAM, THE
de Souza, Steven E.
JUDGE DREDD
Deane, Frederick
DIRTY MONEY
Dear, Nick
PERSUASION
DeGaetano, Michael
HOUSEGUEST
Delpeut, Peter
METAL AND MELANCHOLY
Denis, Claire
I CAN'T SLEEP
DeSaint-Pierre, Isaure
VOYAGE EN DOUCE
Deville, Michel
VOYAGE EN DOUCE
Devon, Lorriane
TO CROSS THE RUBICON
Devore, Gary
PENTATHLON
Dewolf, Patrick
INNOCENT LIES
DiCillo, Tom
LIVING IN OBLIVION
Didion, Joan
BROKEN TRUST
Dimster-Denk, Dennis
OUTSIDE THE LAW

Dobell Massey, Icel
MAGIC IN THE WATER
Doesberg, Johan
1-900
Dorn, Robert
OUT OF SYNC
Dorrie, Doris
NOBODY LOVES ME
Dridi, Karim
PIGALLE
Droney, Kevin
MORTAL KOMBAT
Druxman, Michael B.
DILLINGER AND CAPONE
Dugowson, Martine
MINA TANNENBAUM
Duncan, Patrick Sheane
NICK OF TIME
Dunne, John Gregory
BROKEN TRUST
Dworet, Lawrence
OUTBREAK
Dylewska, Jolanta
CHRONICLE OF THE WARSAW GHETTO
UPRISING ACCORDING TO MAREK
EDELMAN
Eaton, Halle
EMBRACE OF THE VAMPIRE
Ecare, Desire
FACES OF WOMEN
Edwards, Paul F.
DILLINGER
Egoyan, Atom
EXOTICA
Ehel, John
JOURNEY OF AUGUST KING, THE
Elehwany, Laurice
AMAZING PANDA ADVENTURE, THE
BRADY BUNCH MOVIE, THE
Elgort, Arthur
COLORADO COWBOY: THE BRUCE FORD
STORY
Eliason, Joyce
GOOD DAY TO DIE, A
Ellis, Bob
NOSTRADAMUS KID, THE
Ellis, Trey
COSMIC SLOP
Enoki, Yuhei
MYSTERY OF RAMPO, THE
Erschbamer, George
POWER OF ATTORNEY
Eszterhas, Joe
JADE
SHOWGIRLS
Ettinger, Barbara
MARTHA & ETHEL
Eubanks, Corey Michael
BIGFOOT: THE UNFORGETTABLE
ENCOUNTER
Fargeau, Jean-Pol
I CAN'T SLEEP
Farrands, Daniel
HALLOWEEN: THE CURSE OF MICHAEL
MYERS
Feirstein, Bruce
GOLDENEYE
Feldman, Dennis
SPECIES
Feldman, John
DEAD FUNNY
Fenjves, Pablo
BITTER VENGEANCE
OUT OF ANNIE'S PAST
Ferland, Guy
BABYSITTER, THE
Ferris, Michael
NET, THE

Feuer, Donya
DANCER, THE
Figgis, Mike
LEAVING LAS VEGAS
Fitzpatrick, Peter
HOTEL SORRENTO
Flannery, Peter
FUNNY BONES
Flashner, Graham
SECRETARY, THE
Fletcher, Charlie
FAIR GAME
Fleutiaux, Pierrette
VOYAGE EN DOUCE
Foner, Naomi
LOSING ISAIAH
Fong, Eddie
EROTIQUE
Fontaine, Anne
AUGUSTIN
Ford, Ron
FEAR, THE
Forman, Susan
DREAM A LITTLE DREAM 2
Foruzesh, Ebrahim
JAR, THE
Foyt, Victoria
LAST SUMMER IN THE HAMPTONS
Frank, Scott
GET SHORTY
Frankel, David
MIAMI RHAPSODY
Frankin, Al
STUART SAVES HIS FAMILY
Franklin, Carl
DEVIL IN A BLUE DRESS
Franklin, Richard
HOTEL SORRENTO
Fraser, Brad
LOVE AND HUMAN REMAINS
French, Margaret
ARABIAN KNIGHT
Friedman, Brent V.
PREHYSTERIA! 3
Frizell, John
DANCE ME OUTSIDE
Fuchs, Daniel
UNDERNEATH, THE
Fuller, Charles
ZOOMAN
Gadney, Reg
WOMAN AT WAR, A
Gainville, Patrick
VOYAGE EN DOUCE
Ganz, Lowell
FORGET PARIS
Garcia, George
ARMAGEDDON: THE FINAL CHALLENGE
Garcia, Michael
ARMAGEDDON: THE FINAL CHALLENGE
Gay, Lawrence
HOUSEGUEST
Gellis, Andrew
ACROSS THE SEA OF TIME: NEW YORK
3D
Geralmo, Chris
CITIZEN X
Gibbons, Rodney
DIGGER
Gibson, William
JOHNNY MNEMONIC
Gilroy, Tony
DOLORES CLAIBORNE
Gislason, Tomas
KINGDOM, THE
Glasser, Barry
GOLD DIGGERS: THE SECRET OF BEAR
MOUNTAIN

Godard, Alain
WINGS OF COURAGE
Godard, Jean-Luc
JLG BY JLG
Goldberg, Gary David
BYE BYE, LOVE
Goldberg, Michael
BUSHWHACKED
Goldsman, Akiva
BATMAN FOREVER
Goldstone, Deena
SAFE PASSAGE
Golfus, Billy
WHEN BILLY BROKE HIS HEAD ... AND
OTHER TALES OF WONDER
Goluboff, Bryan
BASKETBALL DIARIES, THE
Gomez, Nick
NEW JERSEY DRIVE
Gordon, Dan
MURDER IN THE FIRST
Gordon, Jill
ANGUS
Grant, Susannah
POCAHONTAS
Graves, Alex
CRUDE OASIS, THE
Gray, James
LITTLE ODESSA
Green, David S.
RED SUN RISING
Green, Lewis
NEVER TALK TO STRANGERS
SPY WITHIN, THE
Greenberg, Matt
GHOST BRIGADE
Greene, Anthony Laurence
NUMBER ONE FAN
Greggio, Ezio
SILENCE OF THE HAMS
Grimm, Christopher
RHYTHM THIEF
Grodecki, Wiktor
NOT ANGELS BUT ANGELS
Gutierrez Alea, Tomas
UP TO A CERTAIN POINT
Haberman, Steve
DRACULA: DEAD AND LOVING IT
Hall, Brad
BYE BYE, LOVE
Hampton, Christopher
CARRINGTON
TOTAL ECLIPSE
Hanover, Mary Ellen
PLAY TIME
Harrigan, Stephen
O.J. SIMPSON STORY, THE
Harrison, Matthew
RHYTHM THIEF
Hart-Wilden, Paul
SKINNER
Hartley, Hal
AMATEUR
Harwood, Ronald
CRY, THE BELOVED COUNTRY
Hatem, Richard
UNDER SIEGE 2: DARK TERRITORY
Hatta, Kayo
PICTURE BRIDE
Hatta, Mari
PICTURE BRIDE
Haynes, Todd
SAFE
Heckerling, Amy
CLUELESS
Heide, Johannes
STALINGRAD

Heikkinen, Carol
EMPIRE RECORDS
Helgeland, Brian
ASSASSINS
Henry, Buck
TO DIE FOR
Hensleigh, Jonathan
DIE HARD WITH A VENGEANCE
JUMANJI
Herlihy, Tim
BILLY MADISON
Herzog, Werner
LESSONS OF DARKNESS
Hewitt, Rod
DANGEROUS, THE
Hill, David
TOO YOUNG TO DIE?
Hill, Walter
WILD BILL
Hilsman, Hoyt
FATHER AND SCOUT
Himmelstein, David
VILLAGE OF THE DAMNED
Hodge, John
SHALLOW GRAVE
Hoffman, Lauran
BAR GIRLS
Hogan, P.J.
MURIEL'S WEDDING
Hohler, Franz
CONGRESS OF PENGUINS, THE
Holland, Agnieszka
PROVINCIAL ACTORS
WITHOUT ANESTHESIA
Holst, Rita
DREAMING OF RITA
Honigmann, Heddy
METAL AND MELANCHOLY
Hood, Thomas
CIRCUMSTANCES UNKNOWN
Hooper, Tobe
MANGLER, THE
Houlihan, Christina
MARTHA & ETHEL
Huang, George
SWIMMING WITH SHARKS
Hudlin, Warrington
COSMIC SLOP
Huntington, Georgie
TERESA'S TATTOO
Husky, Rick
NIGHTMARE
Hutchinson, Ron
BURNING SEASON, THE
FATHERLAND
Ibragimbekov, Rustam
BURNT BY THE SUN
Ice Cube
FRIDAY
Jackson, Peter
MEET THE FEEBLES
Jacobs, Alan
NINA TAKES A LOVER
Jaglom, Henry
LAST SUMMER IN THE HAMPTONS
Janszen, Karen
FREE WILLY 2: THE ADVENTURE HOME
Jenkins, Dan
BREAK, THE
Jeunet, Jean-Pierre
CITY OF LOST CHILDREN, THE
Jhabvala, Ruth Prawer
JEFFERSON IN PARIS
Jimenez, Neal
HIDEAWAY
John, Tim
DR. JEKYLL & MS. HYDE

Johnson, Mark Steven
GRUMPIER OLD MEN
Johnson, Steve
COVER ME
Johnston, Lawrence
ETERNITY
Johnstone, Jyll
MARTHA & ETHEL
Jonasson, Oskar
REMOTE CONTROL
Jordan, John
BUSHWHACKED
Jost, Jon
BED YOU SLEEP IN, THE
FRAMEUP
Kachyna, Karel
COW, THE
Kagan, Jeremy
ROSWELL: THE U.F.O. COVER-UP
Kahn, Terry
STEAL BIG, STEAL LITTLE
Kamen, Robert Mark
WALK IN THE CLOUDS, A
Kaplan, Nelly
NEA
Kashiwabara, Hiroshi
NEW YORK COP
Kelly, Karen
BODY CHEMISTRY 4: FULL EXPOSURE
Kerby, Bill
LAKOTA WOMAN: SIEGE AT WOUNDED
KNEE
Kerrigan, Lodge H.
CLEAN, SHAVEN
Kesselman, Wendy
SISTER MY SISTER
Khouri, Callie
SOMETHING TO TALK ABOUT
Kiarostami, Abbas
THROUGH THE OLIVE TREES
Kieslowski, Krzysztof
SHORT FILM ABOUT KILLING, A
SHORT FILM ABOUT LOVE, A
Kim, Alex Sangok
3 NINJAS KNUCKLE UP
King, I. Marlene
NATIONAL LAMPOON'S SENIOR TRIP
NOW AND THEN
King, Robert
CUTTHROAT ISLAND
Kletter, Richard
ANDROID AFFAIR, THE
Kokkinos, Ana
ONLY THE BRAVE
Kolsby, Paul
CITY UNPLUGGED
Kopit, Arthur
ROSWELL: THE U.F.O. COVER-UP
Koretsky, Rachel
PEBBLE AND THE PENGUIN, THE
Korine, Harmony
KIDS
Kornhauser, Mari
LAST RIDE, THE
Kouf, Jim
OPERATION DUMBO DROP
Krieg, Peter
MACHINE DREAMS
Krizan, Kim
BEFORE SUNRISE
Kruger, Mark
CANDYMAN: FAREWELL TO THE FLESH
Kuhn, Robert
CURE, THE
Kumble, Roger
NATIONAL LAMPOON'S SENIOR TRIP
Kurys, Diane
SIX DAYS, SIX NIGHTS

Kusturica, Emir
ARIZONA DREAM
Lacomblez, Antoine
SIX DAYS, SIX NIGHTS
LaGravenese, Richard
BRIDGES OF MADISON COUNTY, THE
LITTLE PRINCESS, A
UNSTRUNG HEROES
Lamoureaux, Donald
BALLISTIC
Lancaster, Quint
WINGS OF HONNEAMISE: ROYAL SPACE
FORCE
Lang Yun
ERMO
Larreta, Antonio
I, THE WORST OF ALL
Lasker, Alex
BEYOND RANGOON
Laudadio, Felice
PROMISE, THE
Lawton, J.F.
HUNTED, THE
LaZebnik, Philip
POCAHONTAS
Lebow, Fredric
WHILE YOU WERE SLEEPING
Lee, Ang
PUSHING HANDS
Lee, Spike
CLOCKERS
Lelouche, Claude
LES MISERABLES
Lemmo, James
BODILY HARM
Lenski, Robert W.
RETURN OF THE NATIVE, THE
Lesser, Elana
BALTO
Leven, Jeremy
DON JUAN DEMARCO
Levenson, Dode B.
CHILDREN OF THE CORN III: URBAN
HARVEST
Levine, Paul
OPERATION INTERCEPT
Levy, Jefery
S.F.W.
Levy, Robert L.
KID IN KING ARTHUR'S COURT, A
Lindenmuth, Kevin J.
VAMPIRES AND OTHER STEREOTYPES
Lindsay, Jim
CONVICT COWBOY
Lindstrom, Jon
DREAMING OF RITA
Linklater, Richard
BEFORE SUNRISE
Loftis, Norman
MESSENGER
Loncraine, Richard
RICHARD III
Lorey, Dean
MAJOR PAYNE
Lorinz, James
ME AND THE MOB
Loughery, David
MONEY TRAIN
TOM AND HUCK
Lowry, Sam
UNDERNEATH, THE
Lucas, Craig
RECKLESS
Lucker, Michael
VAMPIRE IN BROOKLYN
MacDonald, Gary
PENTATHLON

Macek, Carl
CRIMSON WOLF
MacLaverty, Bernard
LAMB
Madsen, David
COPYCAT
Maggenti, Maria
INCREDIBLY TRUE ADVENTURES OF
TWO GIRLS IN LOVE, THE
Magon, Jymn
GOOFY MOVIE, A
Maguire, Gerard
GROSS MISCONDUCT
Mailer, Michael
FOOL AND HIS MONEY, A
Makavejev, Dusan
GORILLA BATHES AT NOON
Mambety, Djibril Diop
HYENAS
Mamet, David
WATER ENGINE, THE
Mamin, Yuri
WINDOW TO PARIS
Manchevski, Milcho
BEFORE THE RAIN
Mandel, Babaloo
FORGET PARIS
Mann, Abby
INDICTMENT: THE MCMARTIN TRIAL
Mann, Michael
HEAT
Mann, Myra
INDICTMENT: THE MCMARTIN TRIAL
Maslov, Vladimir
CREATION OF ADAM
Mason, Mary
WINGS OF HONNEAMISE: ROYAL SPACE
FORCE
Massart, Olivier
WILD REEDS
Mastrosimone, William
BURNING SEASON, THE
Masuo, Shoichi
CRIMSON WOLF
Matheson, Chris
GOOFY MOVIE, A
Mathison, Melissa
INDIAN IN THE CUPBOARD, THE
Mattson, John
FREE WILLY 2: THE ADVENTURE HOME
May, Elaine
DANGEROUS MINDS
Mayer, Daisy von Scherler
PARTY GIRL
Mayersberg, Paul
LAST SAMURAI, THE
McCord, Jonas
CLASS OF '61
McDonald, Bruce
DANCE ME OUTSIDE
McDonald, Michael James
CRAZYSITTER, THE
McEwan, Ian
INNOCENT, THE
McGovern, Jimmy
PRIEST
McKay, Steve
DARKMAN 2: THE RETURN OF DURANT
McKellar, Don
DANCE ME OUTSIDE
McKellen, Ian
RICHARD III
McLaughlin, John
LAST GOOD TIME, THE
McLean, Steve
POSTCARDS FROM AMERICA
McMillan, Terry
WAITING TO EXHALE

McQuarrie, Christopher
USUAL SUSPECTS, THE
Melbourne, Gordon
BULLETPROOF HEART
Melkonian, James
JERKY BOYS: THE MOVIE, THE
Merlet, Agnes
SON OF THE SHARK, THE
Metcalfe, Stephen
ROOMMATES
Meyer, Marlane X.
BETTER OFF DEAD
Meyers, Nancy
FATHER OF THE BRIDE PART II
Michaelian, Michael
BLACK FOX
Mikhalkov, Nikita
BURNT BY THE SUN
Miller, David Keith
I LIKE TO PLAY GAMES
Miller, George
BABE
Miller, Mark
WALK IN THE CLOUDS, A
Milne, Paula
MAD LOVE
Mock, Freida Lee
MAYA LIN: A STRONG CLEAR VISION
Monash, Paul
KINGFISH: A STORY OF HUEY P. LONG
Monger, Chris
ENGLISHMAN WHO WENT UP A HILL
BUT CAME DOWN A MOUNTAIN, THE
Montgomery, Jennifer
ART FOR TEACHERS OF CHILDREN
Moore, Michael
CANADIAN BACON
Moore, Simon
QUICK AND THE DEAD, THE
Moran, Patrick
JACK-O
Mordillat, Gerard
MY LIFE AND TIMES WITH ANTONIN
ARTAUD
Moreu, Rafael
HACKERS
Morgan, Gabriel
JUPITER'S WIFE
Moscowitz, April
BODY STROKES
Moskalenko, Vitaly
CREATION OF ADAM
Mueller, Eric
WORLD AND TIME ENOUGH
Mulheron, Danny
MEET THE FEEBLES
Mulholland, Jim
BAD BOYS
Murnberger, Wolfgang
FOR GOD AND COUNTRY
Murphy, Charles
VAMPIRE IN BROOKLYN
Murphy, Tab
LAST OF THE DOGMEN
Nakano, Desmond
WHITE MAN'S BURDEN
Nakazawa, Keiji
BAREFOOT GEN
Namzug, Ed
REDWOOD CURTAIN
Nathan, Robert
IN THE DEEP WOODS
Nava, Gregory
MY FAMILY: MI FAMILIA
Navarre, Yves
VOYAGE EN DOUCE
Neame, Christopher
FEAST OF JULY

Negroponte, Michel
JUPITER'S WIFE
Nemec, Dennis
AVENGING ANGEL
Nepp, Jozsef
ADVENTURES OF MATT THE
GOOSEBOY, THE
Nicholson, William
FIRST KNIGHT
Noonan, Chris
BABE
Norman, Marc
CUTTHROAT ISLAND
Norrington, Stephen
DEATH MACHINE
O'Connor, Joseph
AILSA
O'Leary, Ronan
FRANKIE STARLIGHT
Oederkerk, Steve
ACE VENTURA: WHEN NATURE CALLS
Ohl, Paul
HIGHLANDER: THE FINAL DIMENSION
Okuyama, Kazuyoshi
MYSTERY OF RAMPO, THE
Oliver, Deanna
CASPER
Olsen, Arne
MIGHTY MORPHIN POWER RANGERS:
THE MOVIE
Orr, James
MAN OF THE HOUSE
Ortega, Frank
MARTHA & ETHEL
Osborne, William
DR. JEKYLL & MS. HYDE
Oswin, Cindy
DEAD FUNNY
Otten, Marcel
1-900
Oxlade, Boyd
DEATH IN BRUNSWICK
Paoli, Dennis
CASTLE FREAK
Parker, Christopher
VAMPIRE IN BROOKLYN
Parker, Oliver
OTHELLO
Part, Michael
KID IN KING ARTHUR'S COURT, A
Pasolini, Pier Paolo
MAMMA ROMA
Pavignano, Anna
POSTMAN, THE
Paz, Senel
STRAWBERRY AND CHOCOLATE
Peehl, Susan
GREAT DAY IN HARLEM, A
Penn, Sean
CROSSING GUARD, THE
Peoples, David
TWELVE MONKEYS
Peoples, Janet
TWELVE MONKEYS
Perez, Jack
AMERICA'S DEADLIEST HOME VIDEO
Perry, Jacques
VOYAGE EN DOUCE
Peters, Lance
GROSS MISCONDUCT
Pfarrer, Chuck
DARKMAN 2: THE RETURN OF DURANT
Piesiewicz, Krzysztof
SHORT FILM ABOUT KILLING, A
SHORT FILM ABOUT LOVE, A
Pileggi, Nicholas
CASINO

Pimental, Brian
GOOFY MOVIE, A
Podeswa, Jeremy
ECLIPSE
Poliakoff, Stephen
CENTURY
Ponicsan, Darryl
ENEMY WITHIN, THE
Pons, Maurice
VOYAGE EN DOUCE
Poole, Robert Roy
OUTBREAK
Porporati, Andrea
LAMERICA
Powell, Michael
OH ... ROSALINDA!!
Pressburger, Emeric
OH ... ROSALINDA!!
Pressfield, Steven
SEPARATE LIVES
Price, Richard
CLOCKERS
KISS OF DEATH
Prieur, Jerome
MY LIFE AND TIMES WITH ANTONIN
ARTAUD
Prior, David A.
MUTANT SPECIES
Privat, Beatrice
VOYAGE EN DOUCE
Proctor, Elaine
FRIENDS
Prou, Suzanne
VOYAGE EN DOUCE
Purdy, Jon
REFLECTIONS IN THE DARK
Pyun, Albert
SPITFIRE
Quastrel, Jonas
CRACKERJACK
Quignard, Pascal
PURE FORMALITY, A
Quinones, Serafin
UP TO A CERTAIN POINT
Quintano, Gene
OPERATION DUMBO DROP
SUDDEN DEATH
Rader, Peter
WATERWORLD
Radford, Michael
POSTMAN, THE
Railsback, Philip
STARS FELL ON HENRIETTA, THE
Rainone, Frank
ME AND THE MOB
Ramsey, Robert
DESTINY TURNS ON THE RADIO
Ravich, Rand
CANDYMAN: FAREWELL TO THE FLESH
Ray, Satyajit
CHARULATA
STRANGER, THE
Rayfiel, David
SABRINA
Raymo, Chet
FRANKIE STARLIGHT
Reeves, Matt
UNDER SIEGE 2: DARK TERRITORY
Reichardt, Kelly
RIVER OF GRASS
Reinert, Al
APOLLO 13
Rey, Frederic
VOYAGE EN DOUCE
Richardson, Doug
BAD BOYS
MONEY TRAIN

Richter, W.D.
HOME FOR THE HOLIDAYS
Riff, Ethan
TALES FROM THE CRYPT: DEMON
KNIGHT
Riskin, Victoria
MY ANTONIA
Ritter, Tim
CREEP
Rivele, Stephen J.
NIXON
Robbe-Grillet, Alain
BLUE VILLA, THE
Robbins, Brian
SHOW, THE
Robbins, Tim
DEAD MAN WALKING
Robertson, Mira
ONLY THE BRAVE
Robinson, James
CYBER BANDITS
Rockwell, Alexandre
FOUR ROOMS
Rodat, Robert
TALL TALE: THE UNBELIEVABLE
ADVENTURES OF PECOS BILL
Rodenkirchen, Franz
NEKROMANTIK
Rodriguez, Robert
DESPERADO
FOUR ROOMS
Rolin, Dominique
VOYAGE EN DOUCE
Romhan, Jozsef
ADVENTURES OF MATT THE
GOOSEBOY, THE
Roos, Don
BOYS ON THE SIDE
Rose, Lee
DECONSTRUCTING SARAH
Rosebrook, Jeb
BLACK FOX
Rosen, Gary
MAJOR PAYNE
Rosenberg, Scott
THINGS TO DO IN DENVER WHEN
YOU'RE DEAD
Rosenblum, Robert
IN THE DEEP WOODS
Rosman, Mark
EVOLVER
Rothberg, Jeff
AMAZING PANDA ADVENTURE, THE
Roulett, Dominique
OLD LADY WHO WALKED IN THE SEA,
THE
Royce, Patricia
TO CROSS THE RUBICON
Rozema, Patricia
WHEN NIGHT IS FALLING
Ruane, John
DEATH IN BRUNSWICK
Rubenstein, Bill
BEYOND RANGOON
Rubin, Danny
S.F.W.
Rubino, George
TOO YOUNG TO DIE?
Ruby, Cliff
BALTO
Rudnick, Paul
JEFFREY
Rush, Jordan
NEVER TALK TO STRANGERS
Ruttenberg, Neil
BAD BLOOD
PREHYSTERIA! 3

Salva, Victor
POWDER
Sandler, Adam
BILLY MADISON
Sang-Jim Kim
HOW TO TOP MY WIFE
Sarafian, Tedi
TANK GIRL
Sarno, Robert
DECOY
Sato, Shimako
WIZARD OF DARKNESS
Saunders, George
MALICIOUS
Sayles, John
APOLLO 13
SECRET OF ROAN INISH, THE
Scarpelli, Furio
POSTMAN, THE
Scarpelli, Giacomo
POSTMAN, THE
Schamus, James
PUSHING HANDS
Schiffer, Michael
CRIMSON TIDE
Schluter, Ariane
1-900
Schneck, Stephen
ACROSS THE MOON
Schneider, Peter
PROMISE, THE
Schulman, Roger S.H.
BALTO
Scorsese, Martin
CASINO
Scott, Darin
TALES FROM THE HOOD
See-Uk Oh
HOW TO TOP MY WIFE
Seeberg, Ian
COMPANION, THE
Seig, Matthew
GREAT DAY IN HARLEM, A
Sen, Mala
BANDIT QUEEN
Sermoneta, Alessandro
LAMERICA
Sevi, Mark
SCANNERS: THE SHOWDOWN
Shanley, John Patrick
CONGO
Shapiro, Ruth
GETTING OUT
Sharp, Alan
ROB ROY
Shaw, Sandy
HEROIC TRIO, THE
Shlumpf, Hans-Ulrich
CONGRESS OF PENGUINS, THE
Shoemaker, Emily
CIRCUMSTANCES UNKNOWN
Shum, Mina
DOUBLE HAPPINESS
Shyer, Charles
FATHER OF THE BRIDE PART II
Sibertin-Blanc, Jean-Chretien
AUGUSTIN
Silverstein, Ed
BOCA
Simon, Ellen
MOONLIGHT AND VALENTINO
Simonelli, Rocco
ME AND THE MOB
Sinclair, Stephen
MEET THE FEEBLES
Singleton, John
HIGHER LEARNING

Sjogren, John
MOSAIC PROJECT, THE
Sloan, Holly Goldberg
BIG GREEN, THE
Sloane, Rick
GOOD GIRLS DON'T
Slovak, Jan
ACCUMULATOR 1
Smith, Gregg
COVER STORY
Smith, Kevin
MALLRATS
Smith, Lance
CREW, THE
Soisson, Joel
BLUE TIGER
Sokolow, Alec
TOY STORY
Sommmers, Stephen
TOM AND HUCK
Sonoda, Hideki
AI CITY
Sorkin, Aaron
AMERICAN PRESIDENT, THE
St. John, Nicholas
ADDICTION, THE
Stadiem, William
BUSINESS AFFAIR, A
PENTATHLON
Stanton, Andrew
TOY STORY
Stefano, Joseph
TWO BITS
Stevens, David
SUM OF US, THE
Stevens, Leslie
GORDY
Stevenson, Rick
MAGIC IN THE WATER
Stewart, Douglas Day
SCARLET LETTER, THE
Stone, Matthew
DESTINY TURNS ON THE RADIO
Stone, Oliver
NIXON
Stone, Peter
JUST CAUSE
Stoner, Sherri
CASPER
Strain, Jim
JUMANJI
Strauss, Robert Ian
BODY SHOT
Stroppel, Fredrick J.
DARK SIDE OF GENIUS, THE
Stuart, Jeb
JUST CAUSE
Styles, Richard
MIDNIGHT TEASE 2
Suissa, Daniele J.
POCAHONTAS: THE LEGEND
Sullivan, Daniel G.
WHILE YOU WERE SLEEPING
Sverak, Jan
ACCUMULATOR 1
Sverak, Zdenek
ACCUMULATOR 1
Swanson, Ron
TOP DOG
Sweet, John
GREAT ELEPHANT ESCAPE, THE
Swerdlow, Tommy
BUSHWHACKED
Swicord, Robin
PEREZ FAMILY, THE
Szeto, Roy
PHANTOM LOVER, THE

Tabio, Juan Carlos
UP TO A CERTAIN POINT
Takegami, Junki
WIZARD OF DARKNESS
Tarantino, Quentin
FOUR ROOMS
Taurand, Gilles
WILD REEDS
Taylor, Greg
JUMANJI
Techine, Andre
WILD REEDS
Tejada-Flores, Miguel
ALMOST DEAD
Thomas, Anna
MY FAMILY: MI FAMILIA
Thomas, Ross
BAD COMPANY
Thomas, Theodore
FRANK AND OLLIE
Thompson, Emma
SENSE AND SENSIBILITY
Tigai, Arkadi
WINDOW TO PARIS
Tirola, Douglas
REASON TO BELIEVE, A
Tolkin, Michael
BURNING SEASON, THE
Tolkin, Neil
JURY DUTY
Tollin, Michael
SHOW, THE
Tornatore, Giuseppe
PURE FORMALITY, A
Treut, Monika
EROTIQUE
Troisi, Massimo
POSTMAN, THE
Turner, Ann
DALLAS DOLL
Turner, Barbara
GEORGIA
Turner, Bonnie
BRADY BUNCH MOVIE, THE
TOMMY BOY
Turner, Clive
HOWLING: NEW MOON RISING, THE
Turner, Terry
BRADY BUNCH MOVIE, THE
TOMMY BOY
Twohy, David
WATERWORLD
Tykwer, Tom
DEADLY MARIA
Unger, Matt
BIKINI BISTRO
Van Kempen, Ad
1-900
Van Patten, Vincent
BREAK, THE
Van Peebles, Melvin
PANTHER
Vawter, Ron
ROY COHN/JACK SMITH
Vendramini, Danny
DESPERATE PREY
Vilsmaier, Joseph
STALINGRAD
Virgil, William
MUTANT SPECIES
von Trier, Lars
KINGDOM, THE
von Trotta, Margarethe
PROMISE, THE
Voris, Cyrus
TALES FROM THE CRYPT: DEMON
KNIGHT

Wachowski, Andy
ASSASSINS
Wachowski, Larry
ASSASSINS
Wajda, Andrzej
WITHOUT ANESTHESIA
Walker, Andrew Kevin
HIDEAWAY
SEVEN
Wallace, Randall
BRAVEHEART
Waller, Anthony
MUTE WITNESS
Walsh, Frances
MEET THE FEEBLES
Walters, Rupert
RESTORATION
Wang, Wayne
BLUE IN THE FACE
Ward, Morgan
PYROMANIAC'S LOVE STORY, A
Warren, John
GIRL IN THE CADILLAC
Warren, Stephanie
BREAK, THE
Watson, Ara
DANGER OF LOVE
Way, Rick
CONVICT COWBOY
Wayans, Damon
MAJOR PAYNE
Weiser, Stanley
FATHERLAND
Weiss, Jiri
MARTHA AND I
Weissman, David
DREAM A LITTLE DREAM 2
Weitzman, Harvey
WALK IN THE CLOUDS, A
Welbeck, Peter
MANGLER, THE
Whaley, Joseph
BODILY HARM
Whedon, Joss
TOY STORY
WATERWORLD
Whitcomb, Cynthia
BUFFALO GIRLS
White, Wally
LIE DOWN WITH DOGS
Whitestone, Steve
PEBBLE AND THE PENGUIN, THE
Whitmore, II, Preston A.
WALKING DEAD, THE
Widen, Gregory
PROPHECY, THE
Wilkes, Rich
JERKY BOYS: THE MOVIE, THE
Wilkinson, Christopher
NIXON
Williams, Barbara
JURY DUTY
Williams, Richard
ARABIAN KNIGHT
Williams, Terry
HARLEM DIARY: NINE VOICES OF
RESILIENCE
Wilson, August
PIANO LESSON, THE
Wiltse, David
ASCENT, THE
Winberg, Wynn
DARK DEALER
Wisher, William
JUDGE DREDD
Wolf, Fred
TOMMY BOY

Wolf, Lalo
UNDERCOVER
Wolff, Jurgen
DOUBLE, DOUBLE, TOIL AND TROUBLE
Wolodarsky, M. Wallace
COLDBLOODED
Wong Hing-Dong
DAY THE SUN TURNED COLD, THE
Wong Jing
HIGH RISK
NAKED KILLER
Wong Kar-Wai
ASHES OF TIME
Wong, Raymond
PHANTOM LOVER, THE
Wood, Charles
AWFULLY BIG ADVENTURE, AN
Woods, Sharon
MARTHA & ETHEL
Yamaga, Horoyuki
WINGS OF HONNEAMISE: ROYAL SPACE
FORCE
Yang Zhengguang
WOODEN MAN'S BRIDE, THE
Yeh, Ying-Chio
SHAO LIN POPEYE
Yevtushenko, Yevgeny
I AM CUBA
Yim Ho
DAY THE SUN TURNED COLD, THE
Yim, Taesung
CAGED HEARTS
Yorkin, David
SPITFIRE
Yost, Graham
OPERATION DUMBO DROP
Young, Dalene
BABY-SITTERS CLUB, THE
Young, Paul
BORN TO BE WILD
Yu, Ronny
PHANTOM LOVER, THE
Yuen, James
HE'S A WOMAN, SHE'S A MAN
TWENTY SOMETHING
Zatorski, Witold
PROVINCIAL ACTORS
Zherer, Paul
BLESSING
Ziehl, Scott
MOSAIC PROJECT, THE
Ziller, Paul
CAGED HEAT 3000

SET DECORATORS

Adams, James
GIRL IN THE CADILLAC
Ahrens, Anne H.
HEAT
Alton, Betsy
LAST GOOD TIME, THE
Andrews, Sara
FOUR ROOMS
USUAL SUSPECTS, THE
WATER ENGINE, THE
Arnold, Nancy
DARK SIDE OF GENIUS, THE
Athanasius, Colin
ASCENT, THE
GREAT ELEPHANT ESCAPE, THE
Badham, Julia
NICK OF TIME
Baime, Jennifer
AMATEUR
PARTY GIRL
Barrett, Penny
OUT OF SYNC

Barris, Jon
BODY STROKES
Baseman, Andrew
JEFFREY
Bauer, Franz
PROMISE, THE
Beale, Lesley
WINGS OF COURAGE
Bell, Jeff
CYBER BANDITS
Bemels, Jean-Claude
MINA TANNENBAUM
Bennett, Gail
KICKING AND SCREAMING
Benton, Robert
REDWOOD CURTAIN
Bishop, Tana
DARK DEALER
Blackie-Goodine, Janice
BLACK FOX
CONVICT COWBOY
Bloom, Leslie
DIE HARD WITH A VENGEANCE
Bode, Susan
MIGHTY APHRODITE
Bonetto, Aline
CITY OF LOST CHILDREN, THE
Boswell, Meredith
APOLLO 13
Boswell, Merideth
NIXON
Boutillier, Lisa
GLASS SHIELD, THE
Bowin, Claire
CURE, THE
Boxer, Daniel
RECKLESS
Brandenburg, Rosemary
CASPER
OUTBREAK
Brill, Ellen J.
TOM AND HUCK
Britten, Helen
BIG GREEN, THE
Brown, Donna
COUNTRY LIFE
Brown, Kerrie
BABE
SUM OF US, THE
Brown, Kevin
CRACKERJACK
Brown, Rick
VILLAGE OF THE DAMNED
Buono, Susanna
CHILDREN OF THE CORN III: URBAN
HARVEST
Calosio, Marcia
MY ANTONIA
Campana, Enrico
BILLY MADISON
IT TAKES TWO
JOHNNY MNEMONIC
Campbell, Georgina
GROSS MISCONDUCT
Carasik, Cheryl
LITTLE PRINCESS, A
Carnegie, Doug
AMAZING PANDA ADVENTURE, THE
Carr, Cindy
TANK GIRL
Carr, Jackie
SPECIES
Carroll, Stephanie
PEREZ FAMILY, THE
Cassel, Barbara
YOUNGER & YOUNGER
Chan, Raymond
EXECUTIONERS

Cimino, Bill
WALKING DEAD, THE
Claypool, Michael C.
HIGHER LEARNING
Colahan, Tim
ACROSS THE MOON
Colohan, Tim
COLDBLOODED
Conroy, Tom
SECRET OF ROAN INISH, THE
Corbett, Ann Marie
DIGGER
Cressman, Kara
DEAD FUNNY
Cummings, Peg
GRUMPIER OLD MEN
Czesak, Robert
SHORT FILM ABOUT KILLING, A
SHORT FILM ABOUT LOVE, A
Danis, Francine
DR. JEKYLL & MS. HYDE
Dappen, Francesca
MALICIOUS
Davis, Catherine
COPYCAT
De Fina, Don
VILLAGE OF THE DAMNED
Dean, Lisa
ASSASSINS
Degus, Susan
IN THE DEEP WOODS
Degus, Susan L.
MORTAL KOMBAT
DeTitta, Jr., George
SABRINA
Deutsch, Lisa R.
DESTINY TURNS ON THE RADIO
Dias, Larry
DECONSTRUCTING SARAH
UNSTRUNG HEROES
WHILE YOU WERE SLEEPING
Diers, Don
EMBRACE OF THE VAMPIRE
TIE THAT BINDS, THE
Downes, Cindy E.
BREACH OF CONDUCT
Drake, Barbara
HOME FOR THE HOLIDAYS
Duane, Clare Papetti
BREAK, THE
Emshwiller, Susan J.
INDICTMENT: THE MCMARTIN TRIAL
Ergnaian, Leslie
RADIO INSIDE
Erickson, Jim
OPERATION DUMBO DROP
Fallace, Nancy S.
JURY DUTY
Farr, Judy
CIRCLE OF FRIENDS
Fellman, Florence
LEAVING LAS VEGAS
POWDER
Ferrier, Tim
MIGHTY MORPHIN POWER RANGERS:
THE MOVIE
Fettis, Gary
JADE
WILD BILL
Fischer, Lisa
CONGO
Ford, Charles
LITTLE ODESSA
Ford, Michael
GOLDENEYE
Fowlie, Eddie
BEYOND RANGOON

Foxworthy, Michael W.
WAITING TO EXHALE
Franco, Robert J.
TWO BITS
Frazier, Erica
BODILY HARM
Freas, Dianna
ROOMMATES
SAFE PASSAGE
Fruitman, Jeff
NATIONAL LAMPOON'S SENIOR TRIP
Furuya, Masahiro
MYSTERY OF RAMPO, THE
Galbraith, Elinor Rose
IN THE MOUTH OF MADNESS
Gallacher, Tracey
FUNNY BONES
Gaudino, Giuseppe M.
LAMERICA
Gentile, Jennifer
DOOM GENERATION, THE
Geraghty, Mark
RUN OF THE COUNTRY, THE
Ghertler, Caroline
NEW YORK COP
Giafferi, Marie-Agnes
SIX DAYS, SIX NIGHTS
Glass, Ted
TO WONG FOO, THANKS FOR
EVERYTHING! JULIE NEWMAR
Goddard, Richard C.
SHOWGIRLS
Gonzalez, Orlando
STRAWBERRY AND CHOCOLATE
Gould, Robert
THREE WISHES
Grall, Valerie
OLD LADY WHO WALKED IN THE SEA,
THE
Grande, Greg
MURDER IN THE FIRST
Gray, Maggie
CUTTHROAT ISLAND
Griffith, Clay A.
SEVEN
Gullickson, Mary E.
SAFE
Gunn, Jeannie
OPERATION INTERCEPT
Haberecht, Barbara
BUFFALO GIRLS
SUBSTITUTE WIFE, THE
Haigh, Nancy
WATERWORLD
Hallenbeck, Casey
FREE WILLY 2: THE ADVENTURE HOME
Hart, Jay R.
BRIDGES OF MADISON COUNTY, THE
LOSING ISAIAH
VIRTUOSITY
Heller, Caryl
SUDDEN DEATH
Hepburn, Rob
WHEN NIGHT IS FALLING
Hicks, Alan
STARS FELL ON HENRIETTA, THE
Hill, Derek R.
ACE VENTURA: WHEN NATURE CALLS
CROSSING GUARD, THE
Holinko, Roberta
SOMETHING TO TALK ABOUT
Holinko, Roberta J.
KISS OF DEATH
Hollie, Michele Harding
FRIDAY
Hotte, Paul
DR. JEKYLL & MS. HYDE

Howitt, Peter
  BRAVEHEART
  RETURN OF THE NATIVE, THE
Inget, Shirley
  DOUBLE, DOUBLE, TOIL AND TROUBLE
Ivey, Don K.
  FAIR GAME
Johnson, Glen W.
  MURIEL'S WEDDING
Jones, Tina
  ENGLISHMAN WHO WENT UP A HILL
    BUT CAME DOWN A MOUNTAIN, THE
Kamienska-Carter, Eva
  PIANO LESSON, THE
Kaplan, Marianne
  FAR FROM HOME: THE ADVENTURES OF
    YELLOW DOG
Kazemirchuck, Jean
  LOVE AND HUMAN REMAINS
Keegan, Tracy
  REASON TO BELIEVE, A
Keith, Katterina
  COVER ME
Kelter, Jerie
  TALL TALE: THE UNBELIEVABLE
    ADVENTURES OF PECOS BILL
Kenney, Elena
  PYROMANIAC'S LOVE STORY, A
Kensinger, Robert
  PANTHER
  VAMPIRE IN BROOKLYN
Kent, James V.
  MAJOR PAYNE
Kirkpatrick, Tim
  DANGER OF LOVE
Klopp, Kathe
  UNDER SIEGE 2: DARK TERRITORY
Koneff, David
  LORD OF ILLUSIONS
  ROSWELL: THE U.F.O. COVER-UP
Kuchera, Tedd
  JUMANJI
Kuljian, Anne
  NOW AND THEN
Lamore, Jim
  FIRST DEGREE
Lando, Peter
  BROKEN TRUST
  FAR FROM HOME: THE ADVENTURES OF
    YELLOW DOG
Lavoie, Carol
  CANADIAN BACON
  MOONLIGHT AND VALENTINO
  TO DIE FOR
Lee, Dayna
  FLUKE
Leonard, Larry
  AVENGING ANGEL
  BABYSITTER, THE
Less, Megan
  WHEN NIGHT IS FALLING
Lewis, Cynthia T.
  JUMANJI
Lewis, Garrett
  NINE MONTHS
Lewis, Ty
  EXPERT, THE
Lewis, Victoria
  NINA TAKES A LOVER
Light-Harris, Donald
  NEXT DOOR
Lindstrom, Kara
  FRENCH KISS
  STRANGE DAYS
Litsch, Joseph
  GETTING OUT
Loucks, Carolyn
  KURT VONNEGUT'S HARRISON
    BERGERON

Macdonald, Lin
  HUNTED, THE
Mann, Catherine
  DANGEROUS MINDS
March, Marvin
  HOW TO MAKE AN AMERICAN QUILT
Marshall, Amy
  SABRINA
Martin, Maggie
  DON JUAN DEMARCO
McCaughey, Karen L.
  SEPARATE LIVES
McCulley, Anne D.
  NET, THE
  THINGS TO DO IN DENVER WHEN
    YOU'RE DEAD
McElvin, Ric
  BYE BYE, LOVE
  FATHER OF THE BRIDE PART II
McMullan, Robin
  UNDERCOVER
McShane, Michael
  ECLIPSE
McSherry, Rose Marie
  DIGGER
  MAN OF THE HOUSE
Mey, Gavin
  CRY, THE BELOVED COUNTRY
Michaels, Mickey S.
  CRIMSON TIDE
Milly, Francois
  DOUBLE HAPPINESS
Mitchell, Joe
  BUSHWHACKED
Mollo, Ann
  ROB ROY
Mowat, Douglas
  BABY-SITTERS CLUB, THE
Murphy, Jane
  MURIEL'S WEDDING
Nay, Maria
  JUST CAUSE
Nigro, Lynn-Marie
  NEW JERSEY DRIVE
Niskanen, Lia
  BAR GIRLS
Nolet, Michele
  DR. JEKYLL & MS. HYDE
  LOVE AND HUMAN REMAINS
O'Connor, T. Michael
  MAGIC IN THE WATER
O'Hara, Karen
  AMERICAN PRESIDENT, THE
Paris, Richard
  NEVER TALK TO STRANGERS
Pascale, Jan
  ARIZONA DREAM
  BORN TO BE WILD
  DRACULA: DEAD AND LOVING IT
Passi, Mauro
  MONTH BY THE LAKE, A
Patrick, Elizabeth
  BULLETPROOF HEART
Peters, Kathryn
  DEVIL IN A BLUE DRESS
Peters, Olivia
  DILLINGER
Peterson, Barbara
  MIAMI RHAPSODY
Peyton, Robin
  LAKOTA WOMAN: SIEGE AT WOUNDED
    KNEE
Pierson, Catherine
  ME AND THE MOB
Piper, Michele
  MIDNIGHT TEASE 2
Pizzini, Denise
  WALK IN THE CLOUDS, A

Pope, Natalie Kendrick
  SILENCE OF THE HAMS
Quertier, Jill
  FEAST OF JULY
Rebar, Cloudia
  ANGUS
  JUST CAUSE
Richardson, Nick
  CIRCUMSTANCES UNKNOWN
Rivera, Irina
  FATHER AND SCOUT
Roberts, Nicki
  PREHYSTERIA! 3
Robitaille, Ginette
  DR. JEKYLL & MS. HYDE
  LOVE AND HUMAN REMAINS
Rodarte, Cece
  O.J. SIMPSON STORY, THE
Rollins, Leslie E.
  GET SHORTY
Rosemarin, Hilton
  QUICK AND THE DEAD, THE
Rosen, Andrew
  BAR GIRLS
Roth, Dena
  STUART SAVES HIS FAMILY
Rowland, Elise "Cricket"
  BATMAN FOREVER
Rubino, Beth
  MONEY TRAIN
Saint Loubert, Bernadette
  JEFFERSON IN PARIS
Sallis, Crispian
  TWELVE MONKEYS
Schiefner, Olaf
  INNOCENT, THE
Schutt, Debra
  CLOCKERS
Scott, Jeanette
  UNDERNEATH, THE
Scott, Laurie
  CLASS OF '61
Seirton, William
  FORGET PARIS
Serdena, Gene
  MAD LOVE
  STEAL BIG, STEAL LITTLE
Sharma, Sujata
  BANDIT QUEEN
Sheets, Suzette
  CANDYMAN: FAREWELL TO THE FLESH
  MY FAMILY: MI FAMILIA
Shewchuk, Steve
  DOLORES CLAIBORNE
Shingleton, Rosalind
  SCARLET LETTER, THE
Siegel, Evette F.
  WHITE MAN'S BURDEN
Sim, Gordon
  TOMMY BOY
Simpson, Rick
  BOYS ON THE SIDE
  CASINO
Sless, Maureen
  DANCE ME OUTSIDE
Smith, J. Grey
  CURSE OF THE STARVING CLASS
Soula, Pierre
  WILD REEDS
Spadaro, Michele
  PROPHECY, THE
Spellman, Chris
  HEAVYWEIGHTS
  INDIAN IN THE CUPBOARD, THE
Spheeris, Linda
  EMPIRE RECORDS

Stamps, Donna
  BITTER VENGEANCE
  OUT OF ANNIE'S PAST
Starks, Shirley
  BODY SHOT
Steinberg, Jordan
  SPY WITHIN, THE
Stone, Malcolm
  FIRST KNIGHT
Stoughton, Diana
  MALLRATS
Struth, Sandy
  S.F.W.
  ZOOMAN
Sullivan, Kate
  BAD BOYS
Swiderski, Robin
  GOOD DAY TO DIE, A
Tapia, Rafael
  BODILY HARM
Tapper, Amy
  AMATEUR
  SEARCH AND DESTROY
Tesseyre, Laurent
  LES MISERABLES
Tkaczyk, Grazyna
  SHORT FILM ABOUT LOVE, A
Toomer, George
  TALES FROM THE CRYPT: DEMON
    KNIGHT
Toth, Istvan
  CITIZEN X
  KID IN KING ARTHUR'S COURT, A
Tucker, Rondi
  BETTER OFF DEAD
Vail, William
  TOO YOUNG TO DIE?
Vivanco, Daniel J.
  EVOLVER
Volland, Bill
  TOP DOG
von Blomberg, Ronnie
  JERKY BOYS: THE MOVIE, THE
Webb, Mark
  DECOY
Weber, Carla
  EROTIQUE
Wells, Amy
  CLUELESS
  HOUSEGUEST
Wheeler, C. Ford
  KIDS
Whittaker, Ian
  SENSE AND SENSIBILITY
Wiesel, Karin
  BLUE IN THE FACE
  DEAD PRESIDENTS
  SMOKE
Wilcox, Elizabeth
  BAD COMPANY
  GOLD DIGGERS: THE SECRET OF BEAR
    MOUNTAIN
  HIDEAWAY
Wolverton-Parker, Lynn
  BRADY BUNCH MOVIE, THE
Woollard, Joanne
  HACKERS
Young, Peter
  DOOMSDAY GUN
  JUDGE DREDD
Zanetti, Eugenio
  RESTORATION
Zhang Deqin
  RED FIRECRACKER, GREEN
    FIRECRACKER
Zucker, Harriet
  BASKETBALL DIARIES, THE

SOUND

Aaron, Steve C.
  POWDER
Abbot, Abdul Malik
  SHOW, THE
Abbot, Robert
  BLACK FOX
Adams, Nick
  FRANKIE STARLIGHT
Ajar, Jr., Charlie
  MAJOR PAYNE
  MALLRATS
Alencar, Heron
  CARMEN MIRANDA: BANANAS IS MY
    BUSINESS
Alexander, Lee
  MIDNIGHT TEASE 2
Allen, James
  GUMBY: THE MOVIE
Alper, Gary
  MIGHTY APHRODITE
Alvaraz, David
  MESSENGER
Alvarez, Luis
  DIRTY MONEY
Anderson, Jr., Robert
  ANGUS
  BETTER OFF DEAD
  UNSTRUNG HEROES
Anderson, Walter P.
  ASCENT, THE
  GREAT ELEPHANT ESCAPE, THE
  TOM AND HUCK
Antunes, Firmino
  CARMEN MIRANDA: BANANAS IS MY
    BUSINESS
Araujo, Jose
  MALLRATS
  MY FAMILY: MI FAMILIA
  YOUNGER & YOUNGER
Arft, Axel
  INNOCENT, THE
Arnardi, Vincent
  ARIZONA DREAM
  BURNT BY THE SUN
  CITY OF LOST CHILDREN, THE
  I CAN'T SLEEP
Arroyo, Antonio
  LAST GOOD TIME, THE
  PARTY GIRL
Ash, Rick
  MAYA LIN: A STRONG CLEAR VISION
Atkinson, Dan
  GLORY BOYS, THE
Auger, Jean-Francois
  MINA TANNENBAUM
Avramenko, Albert
  MUTE WITNESS
Axtell, Douglas
  EMPIRE RECORDS
  NEXT DOOR
  ROOMMATES
Bakker, Anke
  MAGIC IN THE WATER
Barker, Alan
  CARMEN MIRANDA: BANANAS IS MY
    BUSINESS
Barnett, Darren
  EROTIQUE
Barosky, Michael
  JERKY BOYS: THE MOVIE, THE
  NEW YORK COP
  RECKLESS
  TO WONG FOO, THANKS FOR
    EVERYTHING! JULIE NEWMAR
Barsony, Peter
  ADVENTURES OF MATT THE
    GOOSEBOY, THE

Bartlett, Ron
  IN THE MOUTH OF MADNESS
Bass, Andy
  DOLORES CLAIBORNE
Befve, Pierre
  GROSSE FATIGUE
Beggs, Richard
  LITTLE PRINCESS, A
Behle, David
  SEVEN
  USUAL SUSPECTS, THE
Beldent, Joel
  VOYAGE EN DOUCE
Bell, Denise
  DOLORES CLAIBORNE
Bender, Jesse
  BAR GIRLS
Benjamin, Judy
  GREAT DAY IN HARLEM, A
Bentley, Peter
  CLASS OF '61
Besse, Pierre-Alain
  JLG BY JLG
Betz, Tom
  EROTIQUE
Birshadsky, Alexander
  CREATION OF ADAM
Blakemore, Tom
  WHEN BILLY BROKE HIS HEAD ... AND
    OTHER TALES OF WONDER
Blank, Jonathan
  SEX, DRUGS AND DEMOCRACY
Boekelheide, Jay
  DIGGER
  SPECIES
Bor, Milan
  STALINGRAD
Borne, Steven
  INCREDIBLY TRUE ADVENTURES OF
    TWO GIRLS IN LOVE, THE
Boudaud, Laurent
  FARINELLI
Boudry, Mike
  GOOFY MOVIE, A
Bowring, Max
  DESPERATE PREY
Boyes, Christopher
  UNDER SIEGE 2: DARK TERRITORY
Bradford, Bonnie
  DARK DEALER
Breindel, Scott
  CRUMB
Brodin, Gail
  DREAMING OF RITA
Brodin, Jan
  DREAMING OF RITA
Brown, Arnold
  FUN
Brown, Dwight
  SHOW, THE
Brown, Lance
  BATMAN FOREVER
Brownlow, David
  BUFFALO GIRLS
Brownrigg, Stacy
  ACE VENTURA: WHEN NATURE CALLS
Buckle, Rudi
  DEATH MACHINE
Burgess, Bill
  LAMB
Burton, Willie
  BRIDGES OF MADISON COUNTY, THE
  NICK OF TIME
  SEVEN
  STUART SAVES HIS FAMILY
Bush, Chuck
  DANGEROUS, THE

Butler, William
DECOY
Byer, Allan
BILLY MADISON
CITIZEN X
Campbell, Colin
AMERICA'S DEADLIEST HOME VIDEO
Campbell, Veda
GLASS SHIELD, THE
HIGHER LEARNING
Carp, Judy
MAYA LIN: A STRONG CLEAR VISION
Carrick, Lloyd
DEATH IN BRUNSWICK
Carter, Craig
ONLY THE BRAVE
Cartwright, Dennis
PRIEST
Carwardine, Bruce
MOONLIGHT AND VALENTINO
PYROMANIAC'S LOVE STORY, A
Casher, Del
JACK-O
Causey, Thomas
CROSSING GUARD, THE
VILLAGE OF THE DAMNED
VIRTUOSITY
Ceneil, Jan
NOT ANGELS BUT ANGELS
Charles, Colin
DOOMSDAY GUN
FIRST KNIGHT
Chartrand, Dominique
LOVE AND HUMAN REMAINS
Chatterjee, Atul
CHARULATA
Chau, Tim
TALL TALE: THE UNBELIEVABLE
ADVENTURES OF PECOS BILL
WAITING TO EXHALE
Chong, Susan
PICTURE BRIDE
Chornow, David
COSMIC SLOP
FRANK & JESSE
RED SUN RISING
S.F.W.
Christian, Paul Thomas
PUSHING HANDS
Church, Dick
FAIR GAME
Clark, Ted
CANADIAN BACON
TO WONG FOO, THANKS FOR
EVERYTHING! JULIE NEWMAR
Clay, Paul
VAMPIRE IN BROOKLYN
Clayton, Bob
MIGHTY MORPHIN POWER RANGERS:
THE MOVIE
Coffey, John S.
TERESA'S TATTOO
Colwell, John
ALMOST DEAD
Coogan, Paul
FEAR, THE
Cooney, Tim
BUSHWHACKED
TALES FROM THE CRYPT: DEMON
KNIGHT
Coufal, Don
DRACULA: DEAD AND LOVING IT
FORGET PARIS
GET SHORTY
Creagh, Gethin
DALLAS DOLL
Crozier, David
MONTH BY THE LAKE, A

Cultherbert, Keith
CANADIAN BACON
Currie, James
ONLY THE BRAVE
Cyr, David
CRACKERJACK
Dagaberto, Juarez
BOCA
Dalmasso, Dominique
MY LIFE AND TIMES WITH ANTONIN
ARTAUD
Daniels, Dan
FIRST DEGREE
Danziger, Neil
LAST SUMMER IN THE HAMPTONS
ME AND THE MOB
POSTCARDS FROM AMERICA
SAFE
Davenport, Robert
FRIDAY
Dawe, Tony
RETURN OF THE NATIVE, THE
SENSE AND SENSIBILITY
De Beer, Nicky
MANGLER, THE
DeMorant, Francois
AUGUSTIN
Deren, Mark
DOOM GENERATION, THE
INDICTMENT: THE MCMARTIN TRIAL
Desrois, Michel
OLD LADY WHO WALKED IN THE SEA,
THE
Deutsch, Stuart
HARLEM DIARY: NINE VOICES OF
RESILIENCE
Devenney, Mary Jo
EVOLVER
FEAR, THE
Devlin, Peter
BAD BOYS
FAIR GAME
DiIulio, Ron
DARK DEALER
DiSimone, Giovanni
COLDBLOODED
CONVICT COWBOY
SWIMMING WITH SHARKS
Dreebin, Bob
BRIAN WILSON: I JUST WASN'T MADE
FOR THESE TIMES
Eber, Robert
AMERICAN PRESIDENT, THE
TIE THAT BINDS, THE
Edwards, Peter
CENTURY
Egan, Liam
ETERNITY
Eidenbenz, Florian
CONGRESS OF PENGUINS, THE
Einolf, James
BODY CHEMISTRY 4: FULL EXPOSURE
Einolf, James R.
SILENCE OF THE HAMS
Elliot, Keith
DANCE ME OUTSIDE
Ellis, Mary
GORDY
Ellis, Mary H.
HEAVYWEIGHTS
Elms, Terry
PERSUASION
Evan, Scott
SHOW, THE
Excoffier, Pierre
CITY OF LOST CHILDREN, THE

Fager, Russell
CARMEN MIRANDA: BANANAS IS MY
BUSINESS
LAKOTA WOMAN: SIEGE AT WOUNDED
KNEE
Farmer, David
MORTAL KOMBAT
SEPARATE LIVES
Felska, Derek
BLESSING
Fernandez, Robert
TO DIE FOR
Fiege, William
ACROSS THE MOON
Flick, Steve
MAYA LIN: A STRONG CLEAR VISION
Foglia, Joe
BREAK, THE
Fowler, Michael
OUT OF ANNIE'S PAST
Francis, Kirk
JADE
Fredriksz, Mike
BRIAN WILSON: I JUST WASN'T MADE
FOR THESE TIMES
Freemantle, Glenn
SISTER MY SISTER
French, Stuart
ANDROID AFFAIR, THE
Frisk, Curt
WHILE YOU WERE SLEEPING
Gamet, Pierre
PURE FORMALITY, A
Ganton, Douglas
CANADIAN BACON
JOHNNY MNEMONIC
SCARLET LETTER, THE
Garcia, Jose Antonio
LITTLE PRINCESS, A
WALK IN THE CLOUDS, A
Garcia, Mario
CARMEN MIRANDA: BANANAS IS MY
BUSINESS
Garfield, Hank
TOMMY BOY
Gauthier, Glen
DOLORES CLAIBORNE
Gavritchenko, Leonide
WINDOW TO PARIS
Geisinger, Joseph
SHOWGIRLS
Geldart, Alan
WHEN NIGHT IS FALLING
Gettinger, Neil
GREAT DAY IN HARLEM, A
Gilad, Chaim
NEVER TALK TO STRANGERS
Gimel, Louis
PIGALLE
Gleich, Dan
NINA TAKES A LOVER
Glossop, Peter
OTHELLO
Goldstein, Jacob
FATHERLAND
TOO YOUNG TO DIE?
Goodman, Richard B.
FATHER OF THE BRIDE PART II
Gordon, Albee
CARMEN MIRANDA: BANANAS IS MY
BUSINESS
Gossett, Gary
BRIAN WILSON: I JUST WASN'T MADE
FOR THESE TIMES
Griffith, Patrick M.
CASTLE FREAK
Griffiths, Frank
DIGGER

Groult, Francois
TOTAL ECLIPSE
Grubbs, Stephen
GETTING OUT
Gu Changning
RED FIRECRACKER, GREEN
FIRECRACKER
Gunter, Chat
ROY COHN/JACK SMITH
Gynn, Kip
TWOGETHER
Hagen, Johnny
WORLD AND TIME ENOUGH
Haines, Taffy
RESTORATION
Halaby, John
GIRL IN THE CADILLAC
Halbert, Steven
LORD OF ILLUSIONS
Hall, Mike
BIGFOOT: THE UNFORGETTABLE
ENCOUNTER
Hallberg, Per
CROSSING GUARD, THE
Hammond, Leslie
OH ... ROSALINDA!!
Hansen, Peter
KINGDOM, THE
Hardy, Gerard
CITY OF LOST CHILDREN, THE
Harmonic Ranch
JUPITER'S WIFE
Harris, Robin
FRIENDS
Hayashi, Shohei
WINGS OF HONNEAMISE: ROYAL SPACE
FORCE
Hayward, John
INNOCENT LIES
Hazanavicius, Claude
HIGHLANDER: THE FINAL DIMENSION
Healy, Jock
ONLY THE BRAVE
Hedges, Michael
ONCE WERE WARRIORS
Hennequin, Dominique
FARINELLI
GROSSE FATIGUE
Hernandez, Germinal
STRAWBERRY AND CHOCOLATE
UP TO A CERTAIN POINT
Hertzog, Steven
GREAT DAY IN HARLEM, A
Hidderly, Tom
SCARLET LETTER, THE
Higgins, Harry
CANADIAN BACON
TO WONG FOO, THANKS FOR
EVERYTHING! JULIE NEWMAR
Hliddal, Petur
ASSASSINS
BATMAN FOREVER
Hobbs, Aidan
BEFORE THE RAIN
Hoki, Larry
BASKETBALL DIARIES, THE
IN THE MOUTH OF MADNESS
Holden, Mark
BROKEN TRUST
Holland, Gary
DRACULA: DEAD AND LOVING IT
FORGET PARIS
GET SHORTY
Holland, Joel
DEAD MAN WALKING
Holyman, Walter
KINGFISH: A STORY OF HUEY P. LONG

Hong Yi
ERMO
Horgan, Kieran
FRANKIE STARLIGHT
Horton, David
ECLIPSE
Howell-Thornhill, Rosa
MAJOR PAYNE
Hoylman, Walter
CANDYMAN: FAREWELL TO THE FLESH
Hunt, Charles
KIDS
RHYTHM THIEF
Hurst, John
BLUE IN THE FACE
Husby, David
BULLETPROOF HEART
GOOD DAY TO DIE, A
Hutman, Robyn
MAYA LIN: A STRONG CLEAR VISION
Iorillo, Victor
BASKETBALL DIARIES, THE
Jackson, Bill
TO DIE FOR
Janeczka, Herbert
OH ... ROSALINDA!!
Janiger, Robert
FREE WILLY 2: THE ADVENTURE HOME
TALL TALE: THE UNBELIEVABLE
ADVENTURES OF PECOS BILL
Jaworska, Malgorzata
SHORT FILM ABOUT KILLING, A
John, David
GOLDENEYE
ROB ROY
Johnson, Melanie
DEAD FUNNY
Johnston, Jason
BODY STROKES
Johnston, Robin
SAFE PASSAGE
Jones, Jeff
JUDICIAL CONSENT
Jordan, John
CARMEN MIRANDA: BANANAS IS MY
BUSINESS
Joseph, Adam
BODILY HARM
SCANNERS: THE SHOWDOWN
WALKING DEAD, THE
Judd, Phil
COUNTRY LIFE
Judkins, Ronald
CONGO
Kaba, Jean-Pierre
FACES OF WOMEN
Kaiser, Reinhold
FOR GOD AND COUNTRY
Kaplan, William B.
CRIMSON TIDE
Kaye, Simon
RESTORATION
Kazmierski, Steve
ROY COHN/JACK SMITH
Keller, Jack
SEVEN
USUAL SUSPECTS, THE
Kelly, Charles
HOWLING: NEW MOON RISING, THE
Kelly, Peter
DANCE ME OUTSIDE
Kelsey, John
CLEAN, SHAVEN
Kelson, David
BYE BYE, LOVE
LAST OF THE DOGMEN
King, II, Robert L.
DANGER OF LOVE

King, Ken
FRANK AND OLLIE
WHITE MAN'S BURDEN
Kinzey, Scott
MAD LOVE
NINE MONTHS
Kjartansson, Kjartan
REMOTE CONTROL
Klyce, Ren
SEVEN
Kniest, Frank
BATMAN FOREVER
Knight, Darin
MY ANTONIA
Korra, Mark
EROTIQUE
Kovacevic, Uros
GORILLA BATHES AT NOON
Koyama, Andy
FUN
Kozy, William
NADJA
Kuenzi, Hans
CONGRESS OF PENGUINS, THE
Kunin, Drew
BLUE IN THE FACE
SMOKE
TWO BITS
Kurland, Peter F.
SOMETHING TO TALK ABOUT
L'Hote, Anne-Marie
I CAN'T SLEEP
Laforce, Jean-Pierre
AUGUSTIN
OLD LADY WHO WALKED IN THE SEA,
THE
SON OF THE SHARK, THE
Langevin, Owen
TO DIE FOR
Langevin, Owen A.
IN THE MOUTH OF MADNESS
Lazarowitz, Les
KISS OF DEATH
SUDDEN DEATH
Lebon, Thierry
BURNT BY THE SUN
CITY OF LOST CHILDREN, THE
I CAN'T SLEEP
Ledford, Paul
JOURNEY OF AUGUST KING, THE
UNDERNEATH, THE
Lee, David
IT TAKES TWO
KURT VONNEGUT'S HARRISON
BERGERON
MURIEL'S WEDDING
NOSTRADAMUS KID, THE
Lengacher, Dieter
CONGRESS OF PENGUINS, THE
Levy, Stuart
NADJA
Lievsay, Skip
CLOCKERS
Lightstone, Richard
DON JUAN DEMARCO
NET, THE
OUTBREAK
Lindauer, Jack
FEAR, THE
GRANNY, THE
Lindsay, Peter
CARRINGTON
FUNNY BONES
HACKERS
Loewinger, Lawrence
ROY COHN/JACK SMITH
Loffredi, Massimo
POSTMAN, THE

Lopez, Henry
PEREZ FAMILY, THE
Lorrain, Pierre
MY LIFE AND TIMES WITH ANTONIN
ARTAUD
WILD REEDS
Maayan, Jehuda
OUTSIDE THE LAW
Maciel, Cristiano
CARMEN MIRANDA: BANANAS IS MY
BUSINESS
MacMillan, David
APOLLO 13
HOUSEGUEST
NIXON
Magal, Itzhak
ENEMY WITHIN, THE
JURY DUTY
Maikoff, Henri
VALLEY OF ABRAHAM, THE
Maitland, Dennis L.
QUICK AND THE DEAD, THE
Maitland, Kim
DIE HARD WITH A VENGEANCE
Maitland, Sr., Dennis
DIE HARD WITH A VENGEANCE
Maitland, Tod A.
CLOCKERS
DEAD MAN WALKING
SAFE PASSAGE
Mangini, Mark
FLUKE
Marcel, Leonard
CREW, THE
DARK SIDE OF GENIUS, THE
FRIDAY
Marquette, David
DOLORES CLAIBORNE
Marson, Mike
BROTHERS MCMULLEN, THE
Martin, Walt
BREACH OF CONDUCT
Martinez, Tony
CLEAN, SHAVEN
Maury, Harald
LES MISERABLES
McCloy, Crosby
ART FOR TEACHERS OF CHILDREN
McCormick, John D.
MARTHA & ETHEL
McGee, Michael
FAR FROM HOME: THE ADVENTURES OF
YELLOW DOG
MAGIC IN THE WATER
McGrath, Steve
COVER STORY
McJunkin, Davis S.
SHOW, THE
McLaughlin, Jan
KIDS
POSTCARDS FROM AMERICA
McLean, Susan
DOLORES CLAIBORNE
McNabb, Mark Hopkins
DECONSTRUCTING SARAH
HALLOWEEN: THE CURSE OF MICHAEL
MYERS
Meagher, Jay
TWELVE MONKEYS
Meiselmann, Peter
GHOST BRIGADE
MORTAL KOMBAT
Meyer, Dieter
CONGRESS OF PENGUINS, THE
Meyer, Sunny
MY ANTONIA
Michael, Danny
SABRINA

Michaels, Senator Mike
BODY SHOT
Miguel, Ann-Marie
FRAMEUP
Mikulik, Zbynek
ACCUMULATOR 1
Miller, Jonathan
CHILDREN OF THE CORN III: URBAN
HARVEST
Moldt, Christian
PROMISE, THE
Moline, Henry
VOYAGE EN DOUCE
Monahan, Dan
SKINNER
Monihan, Dan
BODY CHEMISTRY 4: FULL EXPOSURE
SECRETARY, THE
Moore, Ben
SHOW, THE
Moore, Mervyn
FUNNY BONES
HACKERS
Moore, Michael C.
PIANO LESSON, THE
Moores, James
CREEP
Morales, Beo
JUPITER'S WIFE
Morelle, Henri
SON OF THE SHARK, THE
Morris, Graham
ONCE WERE WARRIORS
Moser, Stuart
FEAST OF JULY
Moss, Oliver
NUMBER ONE FAN
TALES FROM THE HOOD
Mugel, Jean-Paul
CONVENT, THE
FARINELLI
WILD REEDS
Munro, Chris
BUSINESS AFFAIR, A
JUDGE DREDD
SISTER MY SISTER
Munro, Steve
EXOTICA
Murdoch, Shaun
AMERICAN COP
Murphey, John
BED YOU SLEEP IN, THE
Murphy, Jennifer
SUBSTITUTE WIFE, THE
Murray, Douglas
JOHNNY MNEMONIC
S.F.W.
Musy, Francois
BLUE VILLA, THE
Najafi, Yadollah
THROUGH THE OLIVE TREES
Nazarian, Bruce
SCANNERS: THE SHOWDOWN
Negrete, Mark
DARK DEALER
Neil, John
ONCE WERE WARRIORS
Nelson, Dave
FUN
Nelson, Steve
FATHER AND SCOUT
MORTAL KOMBAT
Nelson, Thomas
LOSING ISAIAH
Newman, Chris
COPYCAT
HOME FOR THE HOLIDAYS

Newnham, Glenn
MURIEL'S WEDDING
Nicholson, Colin
SHALLOW GRAVE
Norris, Palmer "Whit"
MUTANT SPECIES
Novak, Jaroslav
COW, THE
Novick, Ed
TANK GIRL
Nyznik, Bruce
FAR FROM HOME: THE ADVENTURES OF
YELLOW DOG
O'Donoghue, Robin
INNOCENT LIES
Olah, Otto
KID IN KING ARTHUR'S COURT, A
Orloff, Lee
HEAT
THREE WISHES
WILD BILL
Osmo, Ben
BABE
COUNTRY LIFE
OPERATION DUMBO DROP
Padilla, Daniel
NO MERCY
Pardula, Rolf
ZOOMAN
Parker, Ralph
GOLD DIGGERS: THE SECRET OF BEAR
MOUNTAIN
Parsons, Michael
CLEAN, SHAVEN
Patillo, Mike
OUT OF SYNC
Patterson, Geoffrey
BABYSITTER, THE
TERESA'S TATTOO
USUAL SUSPECTS, THE
Patterson, Jay
IN THE DEEP WOODS
Patterson, Kevin
APOLLO 13
Patton, Rick
DOUBLE, DOUBLE, TOIL AND TROUBLE
Paul, Nripen
CHARULATA
Paul, Tom
LITTLE ODESSA
Pecker, Al
EROTIQUE
Pellern, Daniel
DANCE ME OUTSIDE
Perpignani, Alessandra
POSTMAN, THE
Perry, Matthew
CLEAN, SHAVEN
Pierce, Steuart P.
DESTINY TURNS ON THE RADIO
Pilcher, Jim
DILLINGER
Pitt, John
BRAVEHEART
Popovic, Serge
EMBRACE OF THE VAMPIRE
Porporino, Mario
BROTHERS MCMULLEN, THE
Pospisil, John
IN THE MOUTH OF MADNESS
Pothier, Marcel
LOVE AND HUMAN REMAINS
Prettyman, Evan
SHOW, THE
Price, Matthew
JEFFREY
LIVING IN OBLIVION

Pritchett, John
BORN TO BE WILD
FRENCH KISS
STARS FELL ON HENRIETTA, THE
Pullman, Jeff
AMATEUR
NEW JERSEY DRIVE
Purcell, Peter
DALLAS DOLL
Quaglio, Laurent
JEFFERSON IN PARIS
Quast, Matthew
CURE, THE
Rabjohns, Paul
INNOCENT, THE
Raguseo, Angelo
POSTMAN, THE
Ramage, Andrew
GROSS MISCONDUCT
Raves, Phillip
JACK-O
Rea, Peter
CRUDE OASIS, THE
Redfern, Ross
EXOTICA
Reinhardt, Bill
BODY STROKES
UNDERCOVER
Renga, Robert
MIGHTY MORPHIN POWER RANGERS:
THE MOVIE
Richards, George
ENGLISHMAN WHO WENT UP A HILL
BUT CAME DOWN A MOUNTAIN, THE
Richardson, Tim
DOUBLE HAPPINESS
Rigaut, Andre
BURNT BY THE SUN
Ritchie, Colin
INNOCENT LIES
Rizzo, Al
PROPHECY, THE
Robbins, Bill
CYBER BANDITS
Rochester, Arthur
INDIAN IN THE CUPBOARD, THE
Rodenkirchen, Franz
NEKROMANTIK
Rodriguez, Silvia
STRAWBERRY AND CHOCOLATE
Rogers, W. Philip
S.F.W.
Rollings, Kit
ONCE WERE WARRIORS
Ronne, David
BABY-SITTERS CLUB, THE
CLUELESS
DANGEROUS MINDS
LAST OF THE DOGMEN
STRANGE DAYS
Ross, Kenneth B.
GETTING OUT
Rousseau, Gerard
LES MISERABLES
Runner, Fred
MAD LOVE
Ruzic, Livia
MURIEL'S WEDDING
Rydstrom, Gary
CASPER
JADE
JUMANJI
STRANGE DAYS
TOY STORY
Sabat, James J.
JUST CAUSE
MONEY TRAIN

Salla, Maguette
HYENAS
Samakbashi, Mahmoud
THROUGH THE OLIVE TREES
Samuels, Alan
ATTACK OF THE 60-FOOT CENTERFOLD
Sapire, Juana
CARMEN MIRANDA: BANANAS IS MY
BUSINESS
Sarkar, Sujit
CHARULATA
STRANGER, THE
Sarokin, William
BASKETBALL DIARIES, THE
Savage, Roger
DEATH IN BRUNSWICK
MURIEL'S WEDDING
Sayyad, Tchangiz
THROUGH THE OLIVE TREES
Scharf, Larry
BLUE TIGER
Schatz, Leslie
THREE WISHES
Schexnayder, Richard
DIRTY MONEY
WATER ENGINE, THE
Schexneyder, Richard
ROSWELL: THE U.F.O. COVER-UP
Schiefelbein, John
TRAPS
Schliessler, Joe
MALICIOUS
Schorr, Richard
FARINELLI
Schremp, Mike
EROTIQUE
Schukrafft, Wolfgang
EROTIQUE
Segal, Ken
DEVIL IN A BLUE DRESS
Sephton, Robert L.
BYE BYE, LOVE
Serafine, Frank
VIRTUOSITY
Seretti, Phillip
GALAXIS
Sharrock, Ivan
CUTTHROAT ISLAND
INNOCENT LIES
Sharun, V.
I AM CUBA
Shatz, Leslie
BORN TO BE WILD
JUDGE DREDD
Shepard, Sekou
BLACK IS ... BLACK AIN'T
Shoring, Mike
FEAST OF JULY
JEFFERSON IN PARIS
Sigal, Matthew
RIVER OF GRASS
Simmons, Brian
BRAVEHEART
CIRCLE OF FRIENDS
Sivel, William
NEA
Smith, Scott D.
STEAL BIG, STEAL LITTLE
Snodgrass, Harry E.
GOLD DIGGERS: THE SECRET OF BEAR
MOUNTAIN
MALLRATS
Sprawson, Richard
CRY, THE BELOVED COUNTRY
MANGLER, THE
Springman, Stefan
BROTHERS MCMULLEN, THE

Stadelmann, Gunther
STALINGRAD
Stafeckis, Roger
CIRCUMSTANCES UNKNOWN
Stein, Jonathan "Earl"
AVENGING ANGEL
RADIO INSIDE
Stephenson, David
RICHARD III
Stettner, Frank
DEAD PRESIDENTS
Steube, Jim
THINGS TO DO IN DENVER WHEN
YOU'RE DEAD
Stoll, Nelson
MAD LOVE
NINE MONTHS
REDWOOD CURTAIN
Streit, Per
KINGDOM, THE
Strzelecki, Piotr
CHRONICLE OF THE WARSAW GHETTO
UPRISING ACCORDING TO MAREK
EDELMAN
Stuebe, Jim
VAMPIRE IN BROOKLYN
Sullivan, Leo
SUM OF US, THE
Summanen, Lasse
DANCER, THE
Sutton, III, John
SEPARATE LIVES
Sutton, Larry
BAD COMPANY
HUNTED, THE
Sutton, Peter
AWFULLY BIG ADVENTURE, AN
Szabolcs, Thomas
BEFORE SUNRISE
Tao Jing
SHANGHAI TRIAD
Tarrant, George
WINGS OF COURAGE
Taylor, Christopher
REFLECTIONS IN THE DARK
SPY WITHIN, THE
Taylor, Grant
MEET THE FEEBLES
Taylor, Robert
BANDIT QUEEN
Taz, Robert
ADDICTION, THE
Thai, Roland
BATMAN FOREVER
Thillaye, Peter
ACROSS THE SEA OF TIME: NEW YORK
3D
Thom, Randy
JUMANJI
Thomson, John J.
RENT-A-KID
Thornton, James
EROTIQUE
NOW AND THEN
Thornton, Jim
TOP DOG
Tibblin, Zsa-Zsa
DANCER, THE
Tibbo, Stephen
I LIKE TO PLAY GAMES
Tise, Edward
GRUMPIER OLD MEN
UNDER SIEGE 2: DARK TERRITORY
Tokunow, Susumu
PANTHER
Tracy, Nancy
FUN

Trew, Glen
BURNING SEASON, THE
Tromer, Michael
MIAMI RHAPSODY
Troutman, Jim
DOUBLE, DOUBLE, TOIL AND TROUBLE
Tukan, Vladimir
DIRTY MONEY
Uchida, Kerry
BULLETPROOF HEART
Ughetto, Jean-Louis
I CAN'T SLEEP
Ulano, Mark
BITTER VENGEANCE
DESPERADO
Umansky, Jean
BURNT BY THE SUN
Uthea
MACHINE DREAMS
Van Dijl, Piotr
METAL AND MELANCHOLY
Vantanen, J. Sergio
CITY UNPLUGGED
Varga, Thomas
BODILY HARM
Villand, Claude
SIX DAYS, SIX NIGHTS
Villeval, Alain
MINA TANNENBAUM
Waggoner, Peter
ME AND THE MOB
Wald, Robert Alan
BIG GREEN, THE
CURSE OF THE STARVING CLASS
Wassmer, Laurent
FUN
Wdowczak, Pawel
CARMEN MIRANDA: BANANAS IS MY
  BUSINESS
FOUR ROOMS
LEAVING LAS VEGAS
SEARCH AND DESTROY
Webb, Jim
BOYS ON THE SIDE
Webster, Keith A.
WATERWORLD
Weingarten, Mark
GEORGIA
LITTLE ODESSA
O.J. SIMPSON STORY, THE
Weiss, Harald
NEKROMANTIK
Wells, Simon J.
AILSA
Weston, Ken
RUN OF THE COUNTRY, THE
Wexler, Jeff
DRACULA: DEAD AND LOVING IT
FORGET PARIS
GET SHORTY
STRANGE DAYS
White, Ed
KICKING AND SCREAMING
MURDER IN THE FIRST
Wilborn, Charles
CASINO
CASPER
Wilkins, Ben
CANDYMAN: FAREWELL TO THE FLESH
Wilkins, Gary
BEYOND RANGOON
EROTIQUE
Williams, Brooks
JUPITER'S WIFE
Williams, II, Russell
BRADY BUNCH MOVIE, THE
HOW TO MAKE AN AMERICAN QUILT
WAITING TO EXHALE

Winding, Christophe
VALLEY OF ABRAHAM, THE
Wintcher, Jeffrey
DANGEROUS, THE
Winter, Clive
SECRET OF ROAN INISH, THE
Wirtz, Wolfgang
NOBODY LOVES ME
Wiskes, Andy
AMAZING PANDA ADVENTURE, THE
Wolf, Scott
SCANNERS: THE SHOWDOWN
Wolfe, Alex
REASON TO BELIEVE, A
Wolk-Laniewski, Nikodem
SHORT FILM ABOUT LOVE, A
Wood, Nicholas
DALLAS DOLL
Woods, Craig
NATIONAL LAMPOON'S ATTACK OF THE
  5'2" WOMEN
Yarme, Andrew
BROTHERS MCMULLEN, THE
Yewdall, David Lewis
DR. JEKYLL & MS. HYDE
EVOLVER
Young, Rob
HIDEAWAY
JUMANJI
MAN OF THE HOUSE
Zanon, Alessandro
LAMERICA
Zappala, Joe
BROKEN TRUST
SEARCH AND DESTROY
Zawadski, Piotr
WITHOUT ANESTHESIA
Zhang Wen
RED FIRECRACKER, GREEN
  FIRECRACKER
Zijlstra, Ben
1-900

SOURCE AUTHORS

Adams, Daniel
FOOL AND HIS MONEY, A
Adams, Samantha
JURY DUTY
Alldredge, Steven
AMAZING PANDA ADVENTURE, THE
Amigorena, Santiago
SON OF THE SHARK, THE
Apple, Max
ROOMMATES
Arsan, Emmanuelle
NEA
Asimov, Isaac
ANDROID AFFAIR, THE
Austen, Jane
PERSUASION
SENSE AND SENSIBILITY
Auster, Paul
SMOKE
Babe, Thomas
WILD BILL
Bache, Ellyn
SAFE PASSAGE
Baer, Randy C.
BETTER OFF DEAD
Bailey, II, Charles Waldo
ENEMY WITHIN, THE
Bainbridge, Beryl
AWFULLY BIG ADVENTURE, AN
Baldwin, Karen
SUDDEN DEATH
Band, Charles
CASTLE FREAK

Banks, Lynne Reid
INDIAN IN THE CUPBOARD, THE
Barclay, George
VILLAGE OF THE DAMNED
Barker, Clive
CANDYMAN: FAREWELL TO THE FLESH
LORD OF ILLUSIONS
Batchler, Janet Scott
BATMAN FOREVER
Batchler, Lee
BATMAN FOREVER
Bates, H.E.
FEAST OF JULY
MONTH BY THE LAKE, A
Baumbach, Noah
KICKING AND SCREAMING
Bausch, Richard
LAST GOOD TIME, THE
Beaulieu, Marcel
FARINELLI
Beckner, Michael Frost
CUTTHROAT ISLAND
Bell, Christine
PEREZ FAMILY, THE
Bell, Derrick
COSMIC SLOP
Bercovici, Luca
GRANNY, THE
Berkman, Oliver
KICKING AND SCREAMING
Bernard, Sam
GRANNY, THE
Bessa-Luis, Agustina
CONVENT, THE
VALLEY OF ABRAHAM, THE
Binchy, Maeve
CIRCLE OF FRIENDS
Blier, Bertrand
GROSSE FATIGUE
Bosley, James
FUN
Brandner, Gary
HOWLING: NEW MOON RISING, THE
Brandstrom, Charlotte
BUSINESS AFFAIR, A
Braoude, Patrick
NINE MONTHS
Braun, Matt
BLACK FOX
Brickman, Harry
PARTY GIRL
Brown, Michael Henry
DEAD PRESIDENTS
Buck, Chris
POCAHONTAS
Burnett, Frances Hodgson
LITTLE PRINCESS, A
Byers, Danny
BUSHWHACKED
Cain, James M.
GIRL IN THE CADILLAC
Cameron, James
STRANGE DAYS
Cameron, Lorne
FIRST KNIGHT
Carlile, Clancy
GOOD DAY TO DIE, A
Carroll, Jim
BASKETBALL DIARIES, THE
Cather, Willa
MY ANTONIA
Cha, Louis
ASHES OF TIME
Chan, Peter
HE'S A WOMAN, SHE'S A MAN
Charr, Henri
CAGED HEARTS

Chekhov, Anton
COUNTRY LIFE
Chevillat, Dick
GORDY
Choo, Kiseo
WICKED CITY
Clark, Larry
KIDS
Clokey, Art
GUMBY: THE MOVIE
Conde, Nicholas
IN THE DEEP WOODS
Connaughton, Shane
RUN OF THE COUNTRY, THE
Connelly, Joe
MAJOR PAYNE
Conner, Gary P.
BIKINI BISTRO
Coover, Robert
BABYSITTER, THE
Corbiau, Andree
FARINELLI
Corbiau, Gerard
FARINELLI
Cowell, Adrian
BURNING SEASON, THE
Crichton, Michael
CONGO
Cronenberg, David
SCANNERS: THE SHOWDOWN
Crow Dog, Mary
LAKOTA WOMAN: SIEGE AT WOUNDED
KNEE
Crutcher, Chris
ANGUS
Cullen, Robert
CITIZEN X
Dard, Frederic
OLD LADY WHO WALKED IN THE SEA,
THE
Davids, Paul
ROSWELL: THE U.F.O. COVER-UP
Davidson, Boaz
OUTSIDE THE LAW
Davis, Andrew
STEAL BIG, STEAL LITTLE
de Benedetti, Vittorio
WALK IN THE CLOUDS, A
De Luca, Rudy
DRACULA: DEAD AND LOVING IT
DeLuca, Michael
JUDGE DREDD
Dexter, Pete
WILD BILL
Dimster-Denk, Dennis
OUTSIDE THE LAW
Docter, Pete
TOY STORY
Doesberg, Johan
1-900
Dorner, Marjorie
NIGHTMARE
Dostoyevsky, Feodor
NO MERCY
Duff, Alan
ONCE WERE WARRIORS
Dunnett, Ninian
MAGIC IN THE WATER
Durrenmatt, Friedrich
HYENAS
Ehel, John
JOURNEY OF AUGUST KING, THE
Eisele, Robert
DARKMAN 2: THE RETURN OF DURANT
Erdoes, Richard
LAKOTA WOMAN: SIEGE AT WOUNDED
KNEE

Erhat, Teff
FARINELLI
Evans, Bruce A.
CUTTHROAT ISLAND
Eyre, Richard
RICHARD III
Ezquerra, Carlos
JUDGE DREDD
Fazekas, Mihaly
ADVENTURES OF MATT THE
GOOSEBOY, THE
Feng Jicai
RED FIRECRACKER, GREEN
FIRECRACKER
Fessler, Michel
FARINELLI
Fitzpatrick, Leo
KIDS
Fleming, Ian
GOLDENEYE
Ford, Ron
FEAR, THE
France, Michael
GOLDENEYE
Frankin, Al
STUART SAVES HIS FAMILY
Fraser, Brad
LOVE AND HUMAN REMAINS
Friedenn, Neva
RED SUN RISING
Fry, Rosalie K.
SECRET OF ROAN INISH, THE
Fuchs, Daniel
UNDERNEATH, THE
Fuller, Charles
ZOOMAN
Gaffney, Sheila
PARTY GIRL
Gallo, George
BAD BOYS
Gatsy, Jill
EXPERT, THE
Gibbs, Robert
POCAHONTAS
Gibson, William
JOHNNY MNEMONIC
Gideon, Raynold
CUTTHROAT ISLAND
Glebas, Francis
POCAHONTAS
Gombert, Ed
POCAHONTAS
Gomez, Nick
NEW JERSEY DRIVE
Goodrich, Francis
FATHER OF THE BRIDE PART II
Gordon, Stuart
CASTLE FREAK
Gorman, James
CUTTHROAT ISLAND
Gosling, Paula
FAIR GAME
Grant, Joe
POCAHONTAS
Grayem, Tim
TOP DOG
Green, Clifford
THREE WISHES
Green, David S.
RED SUN RISING
Green, Ellen
THREE WISHES
Grenville, Kate
TRAPS
Haberman, Steve
DRACULA: DEAD AND LOVING IT
Hackett, Albert
FATHER OF THE BRIDE PART II

Hardy, Thomas
RETURN OF THE NATIVE, THE
Harris, Robert
FATHERLAND
Hatta, Kayo
PICTURE BRIDE
Hatta, Mari
PICTURE BRIDE
Hawthorne, Nathaniel
SCARLET LETTER, THE
Hecht, Ben
KISS OF DEATH
Heckler, Jonellen
CIRCUMSTANCES UNKNOWN
Henrick, Richard P.
CRIMSON TIDE
Herbert, James
FLUKE
Hertzog, Lawrence
DARKMAN 2: THE RETURN OF DURANT
Hewlett, Jamie
TANK GIRL
Hill, David
TOO YOUNG TO DIE?
Himes, Chester
COSMIC SLOP
Hoffman, Lauran
BAR GIRLS
Holroyd, Michael
CARRINGTON
Hostelton, David
FIRST KNIGHT
Hughes, Albert
DEAD PRESIDENTS
Hughes, Allen
DEAD PRESIDENTS
Hugo, Victor
LES MISERABLES
Hui Yun
HE'S A WOMAN, SHE'S A MAN
Ichise, Taka
BLUE TIGER
Indiana, Gary
ROY COHN/JACK SMITH
Itahashi, Shuho
AI CITY
Jefferies, Richard
MAN OF THE HOUSE
Jia Pingua
WOODEN MAN'S BRIDE, THE
Johnson, LouAnne
DANGEROUS MINDS
Johnson, Mark Steven
GRUMPIER OLD MEN
Jordan, John
BUSHWHACKED
Kagan, Jeremy
ROSWELL: THE U.F.O. COVER-UP
Kamps, John
MIGHTY MORPHIN POWER RANGERS:
THE MOVIE
Kane, Bob
BATMAN FOREVER
Katzenbach, John
JUST CAUSE
Kaylon, Kaan
POCAHONTAS
Keane, Glen
POCAHONTAS
Kesselman, Wendy
SISTER MY SISTER
King, Stephen
CHILDREN OF THE CORN III: URBAN
HARVEST
DOLORES CLAIBORNE
MANGLER, THE
King-Smith, Dick
BABE

Kinsella, W.P.
DANCE ME OUTSIDE
Kletter, Richard
ANDROID AFFAIR, THE
Kluger, Jeffrey
APOLLO 13
Knebel, Fletcher
ENEMY WITHIN, THE
Koontz, Dean R.
HIDEAWAY
Kopit, Arthur
ROSWELL: THE U.F.O. COVER-UP
Korder, Howard
SEARCH AND DESTROY
Kurosawa, Todd
POCAHONTAS
Lasseter, John
TOY STORY
Lawton, J.F.
UNDER SIEGE 2: DARK TERRITORY
Lederer, Charles
KISS OF DEATH
Lehman, Ernest
SABRINA
Leonard, Elmore
GET SHORTY
Lesser, Elana
BALTO
Lewis, Jim
KIDS
Li Xiao
SHANGHAI TRIAD
Lidz, Franz
UNSTRUNG HEROES
Lineweaver, Brad
JACK-O
Lipsky, Eleazar
KISS OF DEATH
Litten, Peter
HEAVEN'S A DRAG
Lovell, Jr., James A.
APOLLO 13
Lucas, Craig
RECKLESS
Lynch, Jr., Vernon
VAMPIRE IN BROOKLYN
MacLaverty, Bernard
LAMB
Magon, Jymn
GOOFY MOVIE, A
Majoribanks, Duncan
POCAHONTAS
Malmuth, Bruce
PENTATHLON
Malone, Mark
BULLETPROOF HEART
Mamet, David
WATER ENGINE, THE
Mancilla, Jess
CAGED HEARTS
Margolis, Seth J.
LOSING ISAIAH
Mark, Diane Mei Lin
PICTURE BRIDE
Marker, Chris
TWELVE MONKEYS
Marriott, Michel
NEW JERSEY DRIVE
Martin, Alan
TANK GIRL
Martin, Ann M.
BABY-SITTERS CLUB, THE
Maslak, Paul
RED SUN RISING
Massey, Icel Dobell
MAGIC IN THE WATER

Mattinson, Burny
POCAHONTAS
Mayer, Daisy von Scherler
PARTY GIRL
Maynard, Joyce
TO DIE FOR
McEnvoy, Paul
HEAVEN'S A DRAG
McEwan, Ian
INNOCENT, THE
McMurtry, Larry
BUFFALO GIRLS
Merlet, Agnes
SON OF THE SHARK, THE
Mikhalkov, Nikita
BURNT BY THE SUN
Mirman, Brad
HIGHLANDER: THE FINAL DIMENSION
Monger, Ifor David
ENGLISHMAN WHO WENT UP A HILL
BUT CAME DOWN A MOUNTAIN, THE
Monger, Ivor
ENGLISHMAN WHO WENT UP A HILL
BUT CAME DOWN A MOUNTAIN, THE
Morris, Bruce
POCAHONTAS
Morris, Jim
OPERATION DUMBO DROP
Mosher, Bob
MAJOR PAYNE
Mosley, Walter
DEVIL IN A BLUE DRESS
Moszkiewicz, Helene
WOMAN AT WAR, A
Murphy, Charles
VAMPIRE IN BROOKLYN
Murphy, Eddie
VAMPIRE IN BROOKLYN
Nakazawa, Keiji
BAREFOOT GEN
Nava, Gregory
MY FAMILY: MI FAMILIA
Nicholson, William
FIRST KNIGHT
Norman, Marhsa
GETTING OUT
Norris, Aaron
TOP DOG
O'Brien, John
LEAVING LAS VEGAS
O'Connor, Joseph
AILSA
Okamura, Kenji
CRIMSON WOLF
Olsen, Arne
MIGHTY MORPHIN POWER RANGERS:
THE MOVIE
Oriolo, Joseph
CASPER
Otto, Whitney
HOW TO MAKE AN AMERICAN QUILT
Oxlade, Boyd
DEATH IN BRUNSWICK
Panzer, William N.
HIGHLANDER: THE FINAL DIMENSION
Paoli, Dennis
CASTLE FREAK
Paz, Ocatvio
I, THE WORST OF ALL
Paz, Senel
STRAWBERRY AND CHOCOLATE
Peckinpah, David
MAN OF THE HOUSE
Perilli, Frank Ray
STEAL BIG, STEAL LITTLE
Peters, Lance
GROSS MISCONDUCT

Pierce, Justin
KIDS
Pileggi, Nicholas
CASINO
Prejean, Sister Helen
DEAD MAN WALKING
Prevel, Jacques
MY LIFE AND TIMES WITH ANTONIN
ARTAUD
Price, David
DR. JEKYLL & MS. HYDE
Price, Richard
CLOCKERS
Prochazka, Jan
COW, THE
Radant, Chris
HOME FOR THE HOLIDAYS
Raimi, Sam
DARKMAN 2: THE RETURN OF DURANT
Rampo, Edogawa
MYSTERY OF RAMPO, THE
Randle, Kevin D.
ROSWELL: THE U.F.O. COVER-UP
Ranft, Joe
TOY STORY
Ray, Fred Olen
JACK-O
Raymo, Chet
FRANKIE STARLIGHT
Rayson, Hannie
HOTEL SORRENTO
Reichardt, Kelly
RIVER OF GRASS
Reit, Seymour
CASPER
Revkin, Andrew
BURNING SEASON, THE
Richardson, Doug
MONEY TRAIN
Rilla, Wolf
VILLAGE OF THE DAMNED
Roberts, William
MAJOR PAYNE
Robinson, James
CYBER BANDITS
Ruby, Cliff
BALTO
Rudnick, Paul
JEFFREY
Scarpelli, Furio
POSTMAN, THE
Scarpelli, Giacomo
POSTMAN, THE
Schiffer, Michael
CRIMSON TIDE
Schmidt, Donald R.
ROSWELL: THE U.F.O. COVER-UP
Schwartz, Sherwood
BRADY BUNCH MOVIE, THE
Scott, Rosie
DESPERATE PREY
Serling, Rod
ENEMY WITHIN, THE
Shakespeare, William
OTHELLO
RICHARD III
Shaw, Sandy
EXECUTIONERS
Shepard, Sam
CURSE OF THE STARVING CLASS
Silliphant, Stirling
VILLAGE OF THE DAMNED
Simmons, Richard Alan
MAJOR PAYNE
Simon, Ellen
MOONLIGHT AND VALENTINO

Sims, Greg H.
FEAR, THE
Skarmeta, Antonio
POSTMAN, THE
Skelton, Barbara
BUSINESS AFFAIR, A
Smith, Jack
ROY COHN/JACK SMITH
Sommers, Jay
GORDY
Stadiem, William
BUSINESS AFFAIR, A
PENTATHLON
Stanton, Andrew
TOY STORY
Stevens, David
SUM OF US, THE
Stevenson, Rick
MAGIC IN THE WATER
Stevenson, Robert Louis
DR. JEKYLL & MS. HYDE
Stewart, Gary
AVENGING ANGEL
Stoker, Bram
DRACULA: DEAD AND LOVING IT
Strain, Jim
JUMANJI
Strauss, Johann
OH ... ROSALINDA!!
Streeter, Edward
FATHER OF THE BRIDE PART II
Tagore, Rabindranath
CHARULATA
Takajo, Masahiko
CRIMSON WOLF
Taylor, Greg
JUMANJI
Taylor, Samuel
SABRINA
Tellini, Piero
WALK IN THE CLOUDS, A
Thorp, Roderick
DIE HARD WITH A VENGEANCE
Tornatore, Giuseppe
PURE FORMALITY, A
Tracy, Don
UNDERNEATH, THE
Tremain, Rose
RESTORATION
Tucker-Davies, Teresa
STEAL BIG, STEAL LITTLE
Twain, Mark
TOM AND HUCK
Ueno, Jiro
NEW YORK COP
Unger, Matt
BIKINI BISTRO
Valtos, William
ALMOST DEAD
Van Allsburg, Chris
JUMANJI
von Trier, Lars
KINGDOM, THE
Vonnegut, Kurt
KURT VONNEGUT'S HARRISON
BERGERON
Vorsel, Niels
KINGDOM, THE
Wachowski, Andy
ASSASSINS
Wachowski, Larry
ASSASSINS
Wagner, John
JUDGE DREDD
Walker, Keith A.
FREE WILLY 2: THE ADVENTURE HOME

Waller, Robert James
BRIDGES OF MADISON COUNTY, THE
Walsh, Ned
GLASS SHIELD, THE
Wellman, Andrew
S.F.W.
Widen, Gregory
HIGHLANDER: THE FINAL DIMENSION
Wilcox, John
AMAZING PANDA ADVENTURE, THE
Wilder, Billy
SABRINA
Williams, Barbara
JURY DUTY
Williams, Terry
HARLEM DIARY: NINE VOICES OF
RESILIENCE
Wilson, August
PIANO LESSON, THE
Wilson, Lanford
REDWOOD CURTAIN
Wisher, William
JUDGE DREDD
Wojnarowicz, David
POSTCARDS FROM AMERICA
Wood, William P.
BROKEN TRUST
Wyndham, John
VILLAGE OF THE DAMNED
Xu Baoqi
ERMO
Young, Paul
BORN TO BE WILD
Zavattini, Cesare
WALK IN THE CLOUDS, A
Zondag, Ralph
POCAHONTAS

SPECIAL EFFECTS

3000cc Productions
HEROIC TRIO, THE
Aaris, Jan
GRUMPIER OLD MEN
Abrahamson, Peter
BORN TO BE WILD
Aeschlimann, Lawrence A.
DARK DEALER
Albiez, Peter
BRADY BUNCH MOVIE, THE
SEVEN
Allder, Nick
BRAVEHEART
Alterian Studios
BORN TO BE WILD
Anderson, Max W.
ARIZONA DREAM
Arbogast, Michael Nathan
TOM AND HUCK
Arbogast, Roy
STEAL BIG, STEAL LITTLE
Bai Le
HEROIC TRIO, THE
Balogh, Gabor
KID IN KING ARTHUR'S COURT, A
Balsmeyer, Randall
SENSE AND SENSIBILITY
Bandini, Pierre
SIX DAYS, SIX NIGHTS
Barkett, Steve
ATTACK OF THE 60-FOOT CENTERFOLD
Barron, Craig
CASINO
Baumgartner, Karl
STALINGRAD
Beall, Gary
MUTANT SPECIES

Beck, Mat
BUSHWHACKED
Becker, Martin
HOW TO MAKE AN AMERICAN QUILT
Belardinelli, Charles
BREACH OF CONDUCT
TALES FROM THE CRYPT: DEMON
KNIGHT
Bellisimo, Thomas "Brooklyn"
TALES FROM THE CRYPT: DEMON
KNIGHT
Bellissimo, Thomas
ANGUS
BREACH OF CONDUCT
SEPARATE LIVES
Belyeu, Jon G.
ASSASSINS
FREE WILLY 2: THE ADVENTURE HOME
Benjamin, Al
BULLETPROOF HEART
Bentley, Gary F.
NATIONAL LAMPOON'S ATTACK OF THE
5'2" WOMEN
OUTSIDE THE LAW
Bierend, Gary
GET SHORTY
Bivins, Ray
JOURNEY OF AUGUST KING, THE
Blitstein, David
INDIAN IN THE CUPBOARD, THE
Bonetto, Jean-Baptiste
CITY OF LOST CHILDREN, THE
Boss Film Studios
OUTBREAK
WATERWORLD
Bresin, Marty
ACROSS THE MOON
WATERWORLD
Brevig, Eric
INDIAN IN THE CUPBOARD, THE
Brink, Conrad
BOYS ON THE SIDE
Brink, Conrad F.
DIE HARD WITH A VENGEANCE
Brisdon, Stuart
FEAST OF JULY
Bryan, Mara
GOLDENEYE
Buechler, John Carl
FEAR, THE
SCANNERS: THE SHOWDOWN
Buena Vista Imaging
CRY, THE BELOVED COUNTRY
Buena Vista Visual Effects
GOLD DIGGERS: THE SECRET OF BEAR
MOUNTAIN
MANGLER, THE
MORTAL KOMBAT
OPERATION DUMBO DROP
Burgdorff, Christian
MUTE WITNESS
Burns, Malcolm
ARABIAN KNIGHT
Buttgereit, Jorg
NEKROMANTIK
Caban, Wilfred
NEW YORK COP
Calanchini, Anne
INDIAN IN THE CUPBOARD, THE
Callari, Lionel
SIX DAYS, SIX NIGHTS
Calvert, Robert
FATHER AND SCOUT
Campfen, Jon
NEVER TALK TO STRANGERS
Cangemi, Danny
SEVEN
Carere, Frank
NEVER TALK TO STRANGERS

Carlucci, John
FATHER AND SCOUT
Carlucci, Lou
LORD OF ILLUSIONS
Cassar, Mario
CUTTHROAT ISLAND
Cassinelli, Bill
CREEP
Cauderlier, Patrick
SIX DAYS, SIX NIGHTS
Cavanaugh, Casey
WILD BILL
Cavanaugh, Lawrence J.
JADE
WILD BILL
CBS Animation Group
BUFFALO GIRLS
Ceglia, Frank
JURY DUTY
PENTATHLON
S.F.W.
Cellucci, Camille
HIDEAWAY
Chagger, Shanni
GREAT ELEPHANT ESCAPE, THE
Chamberlayne, Andy
MALICIOUS
Chesney, Peter M.
VAMPIRE IN BROOKLYN
Chiang, Peter
HACKERS
Cinesite
WATERWORLD
Cinesite Europe Ltd.
ENGLISHMAN WHO WENT UP A HILL
BUT CAME DOWN A MOUNTAIN, THE
Class A Special Effects
MORTAL KOMBAT
Clayton, Jr., Guy
WHILE YOU WERE SLEEPING
Colladant, Dominique
LES MISERABLES
Comer, Bob
HUNTED, THE
Computer Film Company, The
DOLORES CLAIBORNE
Considine, Timothy
DEAD FUNNY
Conti, Walt
FREE WILLY 2: THE ADVENTURE HOME
Corbould, Chris
GOLDENEYE
Cory, Phil
DIE HARD WITH A VENGEANCE
MONEY TRAIN
Coulter, Scott
TALES FROM THE CRYPT: DEMON
KNIGHT
Courtley, Steve
MIGHTY MORPHIN POWER RANGERS:
THE MOVIE
Cousson, Jean-Francois
SIX DAYS, SIX NIGHTS
Cox, Brian
OPERATION DUMBO DROP
Coxon, Gordon
LAMB
Craig, Jordan
KURT VONNEGUT'S HARRISON
BERGERON
Craig, Louis
HIGHLANDER: THE FINAL DIMENSION
LOVE AND HUMAN REMAINS
Criag, Louis
DR. JEKYLL & MS. HYDE
Crosman, Peter
TANK GIRL

Cutler, Rory
DOUBLE, DOUBLE, TOIL AND TROUBLE
JOHNNY MNEMONIC
JUMANJI
MAGIC IN THE WATER
D'Amico, Gary
COMPANION, THE
Dalton, Burt
SHOWGIRLS
Davis, Denise
MANGLER, THE
Dellerson, Steve
MIGHTY MORPHIN POWER RANGERS:
THE MOVIE
TALL TALE: THE UNBELIEVABLE
ADVENTURES OF PECOS BILL
DeLollis, Steve
BLUE TIGER
OPERATION INTERCEPT
Demetrau, George
LES MISERABLES
Denevi, Rodolfo
I, THE WORST OF ALL
Di Sarro, Al
QUICK AND THE DEAD, THE
DiGaetano, III, Joey
MAJOR PAYNE
Digital Domain
APOLLO 13
STRANGE DAYS
Digital Magic
GOOD DAY TO DIE, A
Dikov, Vasil
BEFORE THE RAIN
Dion, Dennis
FATHER OF THE BRIDE PART II
SWIMMING WITH SHARKS
DiSarro, Jr., Alfred A.
CRIMSON TIDE
Dodge, Jr., Norman B.
TWO BITS
Domenjoud, Yves
CITY OF LOST CHILDREN, THE
Donen, Peter
QUICK AND THE DEAD, THE
Dornfeld, Mark
CRY, THE BELOVED COUNTRY
Doublin, Anthony
CHILDREN OF THE CORN III: URBAN
HARVEST
Downey, Roy
USUAL SUSPECTS, THE
Dream Quest Images
CRIMSON TIDE
DR. JEKYLL & MS. HYDE
DRACULA: DEAD AND LOVING IT
Drnec, Tim
THINGS TO DO IN DENVER WHEN
YOU'RE DEAD
Drohan, III, Edward
NEW YORK COP
Drzewiecki, David
NET, THE
Dumas, Don
GEORGIA
Dutton, Syd
FATHERLAND
WALK IN THE CLOUDS, A
Dykstra, John
BATMAN FOREVER
Edge Innovations
FREE WILLY 2: THE ADVENTURE HOME
Edlund, Richard
SPECIES
Effects House, NY, The
CASINO
Ellingson, Andre
NOW AND THEN

Elmendorf, Garry
SUDDEN DEATH
Elswit, Helen Ostenberg
OUTBREAK
Enyart, Scott
COSMIC SLOP
Estes, Ken
ARIZONA DREAM
EXPERT, THE
Evans, Chris
BUSHWHACKED
Evans, John
BEYOND RANGOON
FIRST KNIGHT
RICHARD III
Fantasy II
DOUBLE, DOUBLE, TOIL AND TROUBLE
VAMPIRE IN BROOKLYN
Fantasy II Film Effects
JOHNNY MNEMONIC
LORD OF ILLUSIONS
MAGIC IN THE WATER
ROSWELL: THE U.F.O. COVER-UP
Farhat, Jon
DEAD PRESIDENTS
THREE WISHES
Farns, Ricky
SENSE AND SENSIBILITY
Farrar, Scott
CONGO
Field, Tim
HACKERS
Film Engineering Services Ltd.
AWFULLY BIG ADVENTURE, AN
Film Trick
ONLY THE BRAVE
Fioritto, Larry
BLUE TIGER
HALLOWEEN: THE CURSE OF MICHAEL
MYERS
First Effects
ENGLISHMAN WHO WENT UP A HILL
BUT CAME DOWN A MOUNTAIN, THE
Fischer, Denise
FUN
Fisher, Tommy L.
BATMAN FOREVER
Fly, Niels
KINGDOM, THE
Foley, Maurice
AILSA
Fontana, John
BEFORE THE RAIN
Ford, Thomas C.
WAITING TO EXHALE
Fowler, Ray
MURIEL'S WEDDING
Frazee, Terry
HEAT
STRANGE DAYS
TALL TALE: THE UNBELIEVABLE
ADVENTURES OF PECOS BILL
Frazier, John
BRIDGES OF MADISON COUNTY, THE
OUTBREAK
STARS FELL ON HENRIETTA, THE
Fredburg, James
DON JUAN DEMARCO
Freiling, Randy
BUFFALO GIRLS
FX House
MOSAIC PROJECT, THE
Galloway, Stuart
HIGHLANDER: THE FINAL DIMENSION
Gandaras, Enrique
I, THE WORST OF ALL
Garcia, Bertya
FOUR ROOMS

Gareri, Joe
FOUR ROOMS
Gauthier, Dave
BROKEN TRUST
Gibbs, George
FIRST KNIGHT
Gibson, Charles
BABE
Gill, Danny
GET SHORTY
Gleyze, Olivier
CITY OF LOST CHILDREN, THE
Gorman, Ned
CONGO
Gorry, Colin
PERSUASION
Grigg, Gene
FLUKE
Gross, Rochelle
TANK GIRL
Guynes, Morgan
NOW AND THEN
Hairyhoosen, Ray
MIDNIGHT TEASE 2
Hakian, Josh
BABY-SITTERS CLUB, THE
Hall, Allen
CUTTHROAT ISLAND
Hall, Bob
CANADIAN BACON
PYROMANIAC'S LOVE STORY, A
Hall, Kenneth
TALES FROM THE HOOD
Hardigan, Beverly
PANTHER
Harris, Kevin
MIAMI RHAPSODY
Harris, Tom
FUNNY BONES
Harrison, William
LEAVING LAS VEGAS
Hart, Scott
VAMPIRES AND OTHER STEREOTYPES
Hartigan, Beverly
CYBER BANDITS
Hartigan, John
CANDYMAN: FAREWELL TO THE FLESH
GLASS SHIELD, THE
SILENCE OF THE HAMS
WATER ENGINE, THE
Hendrickson, Gregg
NUMBER ONE FAN
Henry, Erik
MIGHTY MORPHIN POWER RANGERS:
THE MOVIE
TALL TALE: THE UNBELIEVABLE
ADVENTURES OF PECOS BILL
Hessey, Russ
AVENGING ANGEL
DECONSTRUCTING SARAH
Hokanson, Christer
NIXON
Hoki, Larry
DESTINY TURNS ON THE RADIO
Hollander, Richard
MIGHTY MORPHIN POWER RANGERS:
THE MOVIE
Houston, Kent
TWELVE MONKEYS
Hudson, Kevin
DOOM GENERATION, THE
Huebner, Jessica L.
VAMPIRE IN BROOKLYN
Hughs, Dave
HEAVEN'S A DRAG
Hull, Greg
EMPIRE RECORDS

Hutchinson, Peter
DEATH MACHINE
RESTORATION
Hynek, Joel
JUDGE DREDD
Illusion Arts
BATMAN FOREVER
FATHERLAND
WALK IN THE CLOUDS, A
Image Engineering
VAMPIRE IN BROOKLYN
Imageffects Studios
VAMPIRES AND OTHER STEREOTYPES
Industrial Light & Magic
AMERICAN PRESIDENT, THE
CASPER
CONGO
IN THE MOUTH OF MADNESS
INDIAN IN THE CUPBOARD, THE
JUMANJI
SABRINA
VILLAGE OF THE DAMNED
Ingram, Steve
MEET THE FEEBLES
Jacana
SIX DAYS, SIX NIGHTS
Jarvis, Jeff
NICK OF TIME
Jim Henson's Creature Shop
BABE
Jiritano, Drew
AMATEUR
LITTLE ODESSA
ME AND THE MOB
Johnson, Brian
HIGHLANDER: THE FINAL DIMENSION
Johnson, Jay Mark
FOUR ROOMS
Johnson, Margaret
BIG GREEN, THE
CURSE OF THE STARVING CLASS
Johnson, Steve
EVOLVER
Jolly, Arthur
NADJA
Jones, Richard Lee
BAD BOYS
Josephson, Rick H.
LAKOTA WOMAN: SIEGE AT WOUNDED
KNEE
K.N.B. EFX Group
SKINNER
Kabadajic, Srba
GORILLA BATHES AT NOON
Karpman, Sandra Ford
CONGO
Kavanagh, Michael
EXOTICA
MOONLIGHT AND VALENTINO
TOMMY BOY
Kelsey, David
LAST OF THE DOGMEN
THREE WISHES
Kenton, Bernice
HIDEAWAY
Kerr, Addison Grant
AMERICA'S DEADLIEST HOME VIDEO
Kimble, Greg
SEVEN
King, Gary
MY ANTONIA
King, Terry W.
BRADY BUNCH MOVIE, THE
Kirshoff, Steve
BASKETBALL DIARIES, THE
CLOCKERS
DEAD PRESIDENTS
JERKY BOYS: THE MOVIE, THE
KISS OF DEATH

NEW JERSEY DRIVE
SAFE PASSAGE
Knott, Robbie
BORN TO BE WILD
Komperda, Linda
POWDER
Krech, Dan
ANDROID AFFAIR, THE
FAR FROM HOME: THE ADVENTURES OF
YELLOW DOG
Krepela, Neil
HEAT
Kuehn, Brad
FAIR GAME
WATERWORLD
Kujawski, Pyzsard
CHRONICLE OF THE WARSAW GHETTO
UPRISING ACCORDING TO MAREK
EDELMAN
Kuran, Peter
NIXON
L'Intrigue
DR. JEKYLL & MS. HYDE
L2 Communications
VIRTUOSITY
Laforet, John
DANCE ME OUTSIDE
Laird McMurray Film Services
ANDROID AFFAIR, THE
TO DIE FOR
Landerer, Greg
ARIZONA DREAM
Landry, Tim
DR. JEKYLL & MS. HYDE
Langevin, Arthur
CANADIAN BACON
PYROMANIAC'S LOVE STORY, A
Lanteri, Michael
INDIAN IN THE CUPBOARD, THE
Lantieri, Michael
CASPER
CONGO
Larson, Rolf
OUT OF ANNIE'S PAST
Legato, Robert
APOLLO 13
Lemon, Lynda
GOLD DIGGERS: THE SECRET OF BEAR
MOUNTAIN
Lessa, Michael
GOLD DIGGERS: THE SECRET OF BEAR
MOUNTAIN
MAN OF THE HOUSE
OPERATION DUMBO DROP
Lima, James
STRANGE DAYS
Lino, Sergio
DIRTY MONEY
Little, Jeff
ONLY THE BRAVE
Livingston, Donnine
CRY, THE BELOVED COUNTRY
Lockwood, Dean
FAR FROM HOME: THE ADVENTURES OF
YELLOW DOG
Loftin, Robert
FRIDAY
Lombardi, Paul
CASINO
Long, Bruce
COSMIC SLOP
GRANNY, THE
Lorenz, Daktari
NEKROMANTIK
Lorimer, Alan E.
LITTLE PRINCESS, A
Loudon, Chris
NIXON

Lowe, Dennis
FIRST KNIGHT
Loynes, Mervyn
ENGLISHMAN WHO WENT UP A HILL
    BUT CAME DOWN A MOUNTAIN, THE
Lozey, Valentin
BEFORE THE RAIN
Mabil, Chris
DOOM GENERATION, THE
Magic Camera Company
CRACKERJACK
Malivoire, Martin
IN THE MOUTH OF MADNESS
PYROMANIAC'S LOVE STORY, A
SCARLET LETTER, THE
Martin, Dale L.
BOYS ON THE SIDE
NET, THE
UNDER SIEGE 2: DARK TERRITORY
Mass. Illusion
DIE HARD WITH A VENGEANCE
JUDGE DREDD
Matte World Digital
CASINO
Mattox, Bruce
BLUE TIGER
OPERATION INTERCEPT
Mattox, W. Bruce
ZOOMAN
Mattox, Wes
OPERATION INTERCEPT
Maximum Effects
MANGLER, THE
McAlister, Michael
FREE WILLY 2: THE ADVENTURE HOME
GET SHORTY
WATERWORLD
McDonald, Andrew
HEAVEN'S A DRAG
McGovern, Tim
HIDEAWAY
MONEY TRAIN
McLeod, John
NINE MONTHS
WALK IN THE CLOUDS, A
McMurry, Gregory L.
SUDDEN DEATH
Meagher, Michael "Tony"
STRANGE DAYS
Measmer, Mike
CASTLE FREAK
Meddings, Derek
GOLDENEYE
Meinardus, Mike
JUST CAUSE
Mercer, Martin
SWIMMING WITH SHARKS
Mercurio, Joseph P.
WILD BILL
Mesa, William
GALAXIS
Mihill, Thomas "T.J."
CREEP
Milinac, John D.
SOMETHING TO TALK ABOUT
Miyashige, Michihisa
MYSTERY OF RAMPO, THE
MMI
FEAR, THE
Montefusco, Vincent
NEXT DOOR
TWELVE MONKEYS
Montgomery, Peter
ACE VENTURA: WHEN NATURE CALLS
MORTAL KOMBAT
Moore, Randy E.
BIG GREEN, THE
CURSE OF THE STARVING CLASS

Murphy, Paul
CURE, THE
MALLRATS
Murray, Chris
DALLAS DOLL
Nefzer, Ulrich
ROB ROY
Neighbour, Trevor
SECRET OF ROAN INISH, THE
Nelson, Christoper
GRANNY, THE
Nelson, John
JOHNNY MNEMONIC
Nelson, Kimberly K.
FREE WILLY 2: THE ADVENTURE HOME
Newkirk, Dale
GIRL IN THE CADILLAC
Nicholson, Bruce
IN THE MOUTH OF MADNESS
VILLAGE OF THE DAMNED
Nigay, Olivier
WINDOW TO PARIS
Obscure Artifacts
JACK-O
Okovity, Victor
WINDOW TO PARIS
Okun, Jeffrey A.
CUTTHROAT ISLAND
Optical Arts
MUTE WITNESS
Orlov, Victor
MUTE WITNESS
Ormos, Ferenc
CITIZEN X
KID IN KING ARTHUR'S COURT, A
Out of the Blue Visual Effects
POWDER
Palamar, Todd
JACK-O
Paller, Dave
CIRCUMSTANCES UNKNOWN
Parks, Stan
JUMANJI
Patino, Steve
SECRETARY, THE
Patton, Scott
TALES FROM THE CRYPT: DEMON
    KNIGHT
Pearlman, Diane
JUDGE DREDD
Peerless Camera Co.
TWELVE MONKEYS
Peitzman, Tom C.
CONGO
Pepiot, Ken
TANK GIRL
VIRTUOSITY
Performance Solutions
WHEN NIGHT IS FALLING
Perpetual Motion Pictures
ALMOST DEAD
Perry, Doug
ABDUCTED 2: THE REUNION
Phillips, Patrick
FOUR ROOMS
Phillips, Sean
WATERWORLD
Pinney, Clay
AMERICAN PRESIDENT, THE
Pirkis, Richard
HEAVEN'S A DRAG
Plaksine, Igor
WINDOW TO PARIS
Poolman, Max
MANGLER, THE
Portal, Christian
SIX DAYS, SIX NIGHTS

Post Group, The
ATTACK OF THE 60-FOOT CENTERFOLD
Powell, Stephanie
POWDER
Powers, Don
BIGFOOT: THE UNFORGETTABLE
    ENCOUNTER
Price, Jamie
WATERWORLD
Price, Stephen L.
JUMANJI
Pride, Tad
MIGHTY MORPHIN POWER RANGERS:
    THE MOVIE
Pritchett, Darrell D.
DANGEROUS MINDS
Purcell, Bill
KINGFISH: A STORY OF HUEY P. LONG
Quinlivan, Joe
NET, THE
R/Greenberg Associates West, Inc.
DEAD PRESIDENTS
MORTAL KOMBAT
THREE WISHES
Rainone, Thomas C.
CHILDREN OF THE CORN III: URBAN
    HARVEST
LORD OF ILLUSIONS
Ralston, Ken
AMERICAN PRESIDENT, THE
JUMANJI
Rappaport, Mark
PREHYSTERIA! 3
Ratliff, Richard
DRACULA: DEAD AND LOVING IT
Ray, Fred Olen
ATTACK OF THE 60-FOOT CENTERFOLD
Real Life Creatures
ARMAGEDDON: THE FINAL CHALLENGE
Reelistic FX
DIRTY MONEY
Rhythm & Hues
BABE
Richardson, John
BUSHWHACKED
Riley, Steve
BRIDGES OF MADISON COUNTY, THE
Ritchie, Lauren Alexandra
THREE WISHES
Roberts, Dave
BABE
Robiner, Steven
CYBER BANDITS
Robinson, Stuart
MORTAL KOMBAT
Rodenkirchen, Franz
NEKROMANTIK
Rogers, Ted
FAR FROM HOME: THE ADVENTURES OF
    YELLOW DOG
Roper, Susi
TWELVE MONKEYS
Ross, Ted
DOLORES CLAIBORNE
IN THE MOUTH OF MADNESS
Rothman, Conrad
ONLY THE BRAVE
Routly, Lee
CONVICT COWBOY
Routly, Maurice
BLACK FOX
Rushton, Scott
KINGFISH: A STORY OF HUEY P. LONG
S.O.T.A. FX
HOWLING: NEW MOON RISING, THE
Sanderhoff, Terry
POWER OF ATTORNEY

Sato, Atsuki
MYSTERY OF RAMPO, THE
Savitch, Alison
MORTAL KOMBAT
Schepler, Frank W.
NET, THE
Schirmacher, Martin
EROTIQUE
Schlegelmilch, Kuno
FARINELLI
Screaming Mad George
CHILDREN OF THE CORN III: URBAN
HARVEST
Segal, Jeffrey Lyle
AMERICA'S DEADLIEST HOME VIDEO
Segura, Jean-Marc
WINDOW TO PARIS
Shea, Mike
DRACULA: DEAD AND LOVING IT
Shelley, Bob
DESPERADO
Shymkiw, Randy
BAD COMPANY
DECOY
MAGIC IN THE WATER
Sica, Hugo
I, THE WORST OF ALL
Simonaitas, Anthony
TWELVE MONKEYS
Sirrs, Janek
DOLORES CLAIBORNE
Skovgaard, Niels
KINGDOM, THE
Sliger, Scott
VAMPIRES AND OTHER STEREOTYPES
Smirnov, Vladimir
WINDOW TO PARIS
Smoke & Mirrors Ltd.
TOM AND HUCK
Snyman, Eugene
ARMAGEDDON: THE FINAL CHALLENGE
Solis, Leo Leoncio
NET, THE
Sonderhoff, Terry
CRACKERJACK
Soper, Carolyn
ACE VENTURA: WHEN NATURE CALLS
MANGLER, THE
Soupa, Emmanuelle
CITY OF LOST CHILDREN, THE
Spadaccini, Jean-Christophe
CITY OF LOST CHILDREN, THE
Special Effects Systems
NATIONAL LAMPOON'S ATTACK OF THE
5'2" WOMEN
Special Effects Unlimited, Inc.
SHOWGIRLS
Steers, Tony
SHALLOW GRAVE
Steinheimer, R. Bruce
COPYCAT
JADE
Stephenson, John
BABE
Stolba, Jaroslav
FATHERLAND
Stone, F. Lee
NIXON
Stromberg, Robert
FATHERLAND
FOUR ROOMS
Stubbs, Peter
DEATH IN BRUNSWICK
ONLY THE BRAVE
Sullivan, John E.
DIE HARD WITH A VENGEANCE

Surkin, Eddie
CROSSING GUARD, THE
DILLINGER
Sweeney, Matt
APOLLO 13
Tarum, Randy Lee
ROSWELL: THE U.F.O. COVER-UP
Taylor, Bill
FATHERLAND
WALK IN THE CLOUDS, A
Terchov, Pavel
MUTE WITNESS
Theisen, Ginger
INDIAN IN THE CUPBOARD, THE
Thomas, John
DIGGER
FAR FROM HOME: THE ADVENTURES OF
YELLOW DOG
Thompson, Tim
SEVEN
Thorne, Rich
EVOLVER
Tidgwell, David
PEBBLE AND THE PENGUIN, THE
Timmers, Aileen
HIDEAWAY
Tippett, Phil
THREE WISHES
Toffolon, Jean-Pierre
WINDOW TO PARIS
Towler, Ray
DALLAS DOLL
Townley, Jon
HIDEAWAY
VIRTUOSITY
Trans Image Special Effects
CANADIAN BACON
Trifunovich, Neil
WINGS OF COURAGE
Trost, Ron
MORTAL KOMBAT
POWDER
Ultimate Effects
BITTER VENGEANCE
CANDYMAN: FAREWELL TO THE FLESH
CYBER BANDITS
GALAXIS
GHOST BRIGADE
GLASS SHIELD, THE
SILENCE OF THE HAMS
Ultimate Special Effects
MY ANTONIA
Vago, Mark
OUTBREAK
van Kline, Jor
PROPHECY, THE
Van Vliet, John T.
TALES FROM THE CRYPT: DEMON
KNIGHT
Van Zeebroeck, Bruno
FAIR GAME
WALK IN THE CLOUDS, A
Vaupel, Rob
EVOLVER
Vazquez, Bob
TWO BITS
Vezina, Mike
ACE VENTURA: WHEN NATURE CALLS
GOLD DIGGERS: THE SECRET OF BEAR
MOUNTAIN
HIDEAWAY
MAN OF THE HOUSE
Vico, Massimo
FRIENDS
Video Image
DR. JEKYLL & MS. HYDE

VIFX
MIGHTY MORPHIN POWER RANGERS:
THE MOVIE
SUDDEN DEATH
Vincent, Michael S.
BULLETPROOF HEART
Vulich, John
CASTLE FREAK
Ward, Tom
DEVIL IN A BLUE DRESS
Warren, Jr., Gene
BRADY BUNCH MOVIE, THE
JOHNNY MNEMONIC
MAGIC IN THE WATER
ROSWELL: THE U.F.O. COVER-UP
VAMPIRE IN BROOKLYN
Watkins, David H.
WALKING DEAD, THE
Wayne, David
DESTINY TURNS ON THE RADIO
Weiss, Craig
BUFFALO GIRLS
Welker, Frank
MORTAL KOMBAT
Whibley, Alan
RETURN OF THE NATIVE, THE
Williams, Joss
JUDGE DREDD
Williams, Jr., David S.
FOUR ROOMS
Wingrove, Ian
DOOMSDAY GUN
RUN OF THE COUNTRY, THE
Wojtinek, Adolf
INNOCENT, THE
Yagher, Kevin
CHILDREN OF THE CORN III: URBAN
HARVEST
Yeatman, Hoyt
CRIMSON TIDE
Yuricich, Richard
UNDER SIEGE 2: DARK TERRITORY
Zeccara, Paolo
FLUKE
Zelkine, Zalman
WINDOW TO PARIS

STUNTS

Adams, Phil
BODY SHOT
Aguilar, George
JEFFREY
Akerstream, Marc
BULLETPROOF HEART
CRACKERJACK
Alvarez, Ignacio
DOOM GENERATION, THE
Amin, Alan
BANDIT QUEEN
Anderson, Coll
KILIAN'S CHRONICLE
Anderson, Greg
BODILY HARM
Apisa, Robert
MALLRATS
Armstrong, Vic
CUTTHROAT ISLAND
JOHNNY MNEMONIC
ROB ROY
Arnett, M. James
CONGO
FLUKE
Arnett, Seth
ROSWELL: THE U.F.O. COVER-UP
Ateah, Scott
BROKEN TRUST

CIRCUMSTANCES UNKNOWN
MALICIOUS
Avery, Rick
EXPERT, THE
Barker, Rich
ACE VENTURA: WHEN NATURE CALLS
Barringer, Daniel W.
CASINO
Bates, Ken
BAD BOYS
Baxley, Paul
AVENGING ANGEL
DECONSTRUCTING SARAH
Beall, Gary
MUTANT SPECIES
Belardinelli, Charles
FOUR ROOMS
Bellissimo, Tom
FOUR ROOMS
Boyle, Marc
JUDGE DREDD
Boyum, Steve
HEAVYWEIGHTS
Bradley, Dan
HOW TO MAKE AN AMERICAN QUILT
JURY DUTY
MY FAMILY: MI FAMILIA
PROPHECY, THE
Branagan, John
THINGS TO DO IN DENVER WHEN
YOU'RE DEAD
Brewer, Charlie
GRUMPIER OLD MEN
Brubaker, Tony
DEVIL IN A BLUE DRESS
Bruce, Robert
ONCE WERE WARRIORS
Bryant, Kurt
SCANNERS: THE SHOWDOWN
WATER ENGINE, THE
Brzezinski, Robert
SHORT FILM ABOUT KILLING, A
SHORT FILM ABOUT LOVE, A
Bucossi, Peter
JERKY BOYS: THE MOVIE, THE
Butler, Dick
ANGUS
Cain, Lisa
THREE WISHES
Caldwell, Helen
PERSUASION
Cardwell, Shane
FIRST DEGREE
PYROMANIAC'S LOVE STORY, A
Cauderlier, Patrick
CITY OF LOST CHILDREN, THE
Cheung, George Kee
NEW YORK COP
Chlebowski, Janusz
SHORT FILM ABOUT KILLING, A
SHORT FILM ABOUT LOVE, A
Coleman, Doug
CASINO
MURDER IN THE FIRST
STRANGE DAYS
Combs, Gary
DRACULA: DEAD AND LOVING IT
SHOWGIRLS
Crane, Simon
BRAVEHEART
FUNNY BONES
GOLDENEYE
Crawford, Jake
FATHER AND SCOUT
WALK IN THE CLOUDS, A
Creach, Everett L.
ARIZONA DREAM

Croughwell, Charlie
BREACH OF CONDUCT
LITTLE PRINCESS, A
Cudney, Cliff
LORD OF ILLUSIONS
NEW YORK COP
Curtis, Clive
SHALLOW GRAVE
Dashaw, Jeff
SCARLET LETTER, THE
Dashnaw, Jeffrey J.
HOUSEGUEST
Davidson, Bret
OUT OF ANNIE'S PAST
Davis, Bud
ACROSS THE MOON
Davis, Gary
DOLORES CLAIBORNE
Davison, Steve M.
DESPERADO
S.F.W.
Davison, Tim A.
COPYCAT
Dixon, Shane
NICK OF TIME
TALES FROM THE CRYPT: DEMON
KNIGHT
Donahue, Sean
MOSAIC PROJECT, THE
Dowdall, Jim
RICHARD III
Doyle, Chris
DANGER OF LOVE
GALAXIS
Drozda, Petr
STALINGRAD
Dunn, Jim
MAGIC IN THE WATER
Dunne, Joe
BORN TO BE WILD
Elam, Greg
MAJOR PAYNE
Eletheriou, Zef
DALLAS DOLL
Enloe, Wade
DARK DEALER
Erickson, Tom
BLACK FOX
Farfel, Roy
LITTLE ODESSA
SEARCH AND DESTROY
Fife, Randy
DARK DEALER
WALKING DEAD, THE
Fioramonti, Glory
INDICTMENT: THE MCMARTIN TRIAL
SAFE PASSAGE
Forsythe, Rick
NEVER TALK TO STRANGERS
Gibson, Jeff
BATMAN FOREVER
Gilbert, Lance
VIRTUOSITY
Gilbert, Mickey
APOLLO 13
FORGET PARIS
Gilbert, Troy
CLASS OF '61
Gill, Jack
MONEY TRAIN
Glass, Tom
GOOD DAY TO DIE, A
Grace, Martin
AWFULLY BIG ADVENTURE, AN
CIRCLE OF FRIENDS
Graf, Allan
WILD BILL

Habberstad, Jeff
STEAL BIG, STEAL LITTLE
Halty, James
APOLLO 13
BYE BYE, LOVE
Hancock, Dick
ASSASSINS
Hanlan, Ted
BILLY MADISON
Hanlon, Ted
EXOTICA
Hartline, Gene
LAKOTA WOMAN: SIEGE AT WOUNDED
KNEE
Hennessy, Mark
ONLY THE BRAVE
Hewit, Jery
HACKERS
SAFE PASSAGE
Hewitt, Jery
EMPIRE RECORDS
Hice, Freddie
GRUMPIER OLD MEN
Hicks, Bob
DESPERATE PREY
Hodder, Kane
FOUR ROOMS
Hooker, Buddy Joe
HUNTED, THE
JADE
Hutchinson, Rawn
WAITING TO EXHALE
Hymes, Gary M.
CASPER
SUDDEN DEATH
Imada, Jeff
FREE WILLY 2: THE ADVENTURE HOME
IN THE MOUTH OF MADNESS
VILLAGE OF THE DAMNED
Inocalla, Shishir
ABDUCTED 2: THE REUNION
Jackson, Ernie
BAD COMPANY
Janikowski, Ryszard
SHORT FILM ABOUT LOVE, A
Jensen, Gary
USUAL SUSPECTS, THE
Jensen, Jeff
KINGFISH: A STORY OF HUEY P. LONG
Johnson, Pat E.
MORTAL KOMBAT
Jolly, Arthur
NADJA
Jones, Al
3 NINJAS KNUCKLE UP
Jones, Jamie
DANCE ME OUTSIDE
Kelven, Max
SPECIES
King, Rob
OUTSIDE THE LAW
Kirton, Mike
SWIMMING WITH SHARKS
Kirzinger, Ken
DOUBLE, DOUBLE, TOIL AND TROUBLE
Kramer, Joel
HEAT
Lahoda, Ladislav
FATHERLAND
Lambert, Steve
NEXT DOOR
Langlois, Yves
LOVE AND HUMAN REMAINS
Ledger, Bernie
NOSTRADAMUS KID, THE
LeFevour, Rick
LOSING ISAIAH
STUART SAVES HIS FAMILY

LeFlore, Julius
FRIDAY
ZOOMAN
Leonard, Terry
QUICK AND THE DEAD, THE
Leonard, Terry J.
DIE HARD WITH A VENGEANCE
Lerner, Fred
HALLOWEEN: THE CURSE OF MICHAEL
MYERS
UNSTRUNG HEROES
Lesco, Ken
WHITE MAN'S BURDEN
Lew, James
BALLISTIC
Lovelett, Jim
LAST GOOD TIME, THE
Lucescu, Steve
DARKMAN 2: THE RETURN OF DURANT
Lykins, Ray
DIRTY MONEY
Makaro, J.J.
ACE VENTURA: WHEN NATURE CALLS
Marcus, Alan
FOUR ROOMS
McClerkins, Jr., Bufort
GLASS SHIELD, THE
McConnell, Jim
ROSWELL: THE U.F.O. COVER-UP
McDonald, Rocky
DALLAS DOLL
MIGHTY MORPHIN POWER RANGERS:
THE MOVIE
MURIEL'S WEDDING
McKeown, Dave
HIGHLANDER: THE FINAL DIMENSION
Meier, John C.
ROOMMATES
VIRTUOSITY
Mey, Gavin
CRY, THE BELOVED COUNTRY
FRIENDS
MANGLER, THE
Minor, Bob
HIGHER LEARNING
O.J. SIMPSON STORY, THE
PANTHER
Moio, John
SEPARATE LIVES
TIE THAT BINDS, THE
Morgan, Gary
SILENCE OF THE HAMS
Mourino, Edgard
BASKETBALL DIARIES, THE
Mumford, Dean
NOW AND THEN
Mustain, Minor
DR. JEKYLL & MS. HYDE
Muzila, Tom
HUNTED, THE
Neilson, Phil
BOYS ON THE SIDE
NEW JERSEY DRIVE
TWELVE MONKEYS
Nielson, Phil
AMATEUR
Norris, Guy
OPERATION DUMBO DROP
Oliney, Alan
VAMPIRE IN BROOKLYN
Ong, William
BEYOND RANGOON
Orsatti, Ernie
BITTER VENGEANCE
TALL TALE: THE UNBELIEVABLE
ADVENTURES OF PECOS BILL
UNSTRUNG HEROES

Palmisano, Conrad
ASSASSINS
Palmisano, Conrad E.
BATMAN FOREVER
FREE WILLY 2: THE ADVENTURE HOME
Paparazzo, Janet
DEAD FUNNY
Parvnov, Parvan
BEFORE THE RAIN
Paul, Victor
DON JUAN DEMARCO
STUART SAVES HIS FAMILY
Picerni, Charles
BABYSITTER, THE
Picerni, Jr., Charles
SEVEN
Picerni, Jr., Chuck
JUST CAUSE
Picerni, Steve
CRIMSON TIDE
Pock, Bernie
DANGEROUS MINDS
Powell, Dinny
FIRST KNIGHT
Powell, Greg
FIRST KNIGHT
Racki, Branko
CANADIAN BACON
TOMMY BOY
Randall, Jr., Glenn
SPECIES
Rodgers, Mic
BRAVEHEART
VIRTUOSITY
Romano, Patrick
BABY-SITTERS CLUB, THE
BRADY BUNCH MOVIE, THE
CLUELESS
Rondell, R.A.
WATERWORLD
Rosenstein, Deborah
MIDNIGHT TEASE 2
Rosenstein, Smiley
MIDNIGHT TEASE 2
Ruehland, Glenn
DEATH IN BRUNSWICK
Rupp, Jacob
DIGGER
HIDEAWAY
Russo, Mike
KISS OF DEATH
Salamon, Franco
MONTH BY THE LAKE, A
Salvatori, Lynn
INDIAN IN THE CUPBOARD, THE
Sanders, David
POWDER
Sargent, Bobby
UNDERNEATH, THE
Scott, Dennis R.
INDIAN IN THE CUPBOARD, THE
Scott, Walter
TANK GIRL
Sebek, Brandon
WAITING TO EXHALE
Sharpe, Dick
DIRTY MONEY
Smith, Lonnie
GETTING OUT
Smrz, Brian
GET SHORTY
St. Paul, Stuart
DEATH MACHINE
Stacey, Eddie
RUN OF THE COUNTRY, THE

Statham, Patrick
CYBER BANDITS
OUTSIDE THE LAW
SPY WITHIN, THE
Stefanski, Jozef
SHORT FILM ABOUT KILLING, A
Stewart, John
EVOLVER
Stoneham, Jr., John
ANDROID AFFAIR, THE
Stubbs, Melissa
POWER OF ATTORNEY
Sykes, Chris
DARK DEALER
Tellez, Keith
OUTBREAK
Thomas, Betty
FAR FROM HOME: THE ADVENTURES OF
YELLOW DOG
GOLD DIGGERS: THE SECRET OF BEAR
MOUNTAIN
JUMANJI
MAN OF THE HOUSE
Tomsa, Jaroslav
STALINGRAD
Towery, Russell
CURSE OF THE STARVING CLASS
LEAVING LAS VEGAS
Unger, Bela
KID IN KING ARTHUR'S COURT, A
Van Horn, Buddy
NET, THE
OUTBREAK
STARS FELL ON HENRIETTA, THE
Verite, Daniel
LES MISERABLES
Vorobiov, Sergei
MUTE WITNESS
Wafford, Shannon
DIRTY MONEY
Ward, Jeff
CLOCKERS
DEAD PRESIDENTS
Wardlow, John
HUNTED, THE
Washington, William
CANDYMAN: FAREWELL TO THE FLESH
Waters, Chuck
CROSSING GUARD, THE
LAST OF THE DOGMEN
Wayton, Gary
FEAR, THE
GIRL IN THE CADILLAC
Weston, Bill
LAMB
Whinery, Webster
DESTINY TURNS ON THE RADIO
Wilder, Glenn R.
NINE MONTHS
Wilkinson, Nick
SENSE AND SENSIBILITY
Winery, Webster
MAD LOVE
Woodruff, Rob
BEFORE THE RAIN
Woolsey, Brent
CONVICT COWBOY
SCARLET LETTER, THE
Wyatt, Jr., Allan
BIGFOOT: THE UNFORGETTABLE
ENCOUNTER
Zaczynski, Andrzej
SHORT FILM ABOUT LOVE, A
Ziker, Dick
UNDER SIEGE 2: DARK TERRITORY

REVIEW ATTRIBUTION

Films reviewed in this volume are listed below by the author of the review

Banerjee, Shampa
CHARULATA
STRANGER, THE

Bartholomew, David
BODILY HARM
DARK DEALER
FIRST DEGREE
GUMBY: THE MOVIE
INNOCENT LIES

Camp, Brian
AI CITY
BAREFOOT GEN
CRIMSON WOLF
DILLINGER AND CAPONE
FIRST KNIGHT
FRANK & JESSE
GOLD DIGGERS: THE SECRET OF
 BEAR MOUNTAIN
GOOFY MOVIE, A
JUDGE DREDD
MIGHTY MORPHIN POWER
 RANGERS: THE MOVIE
MONEY TRAIN
NINJA SCROLL
RED SUN RISING
SPIKE AND MIKE'S FESTIVAL OF
 ANIMATION '95
TOO OUTRAGEOUS ANIMATION
TOWARD THE TERRA
UNDER SIEGE 2: DARK TERRITORY
WICKED CITY
WINGS OF HONNEAMISE: ROYAL
 SPACE FORCE

Cassady Jr., Charles
ACCUMULATOR 1
AILSA
ANDROID AFFAIR, THE
BABE
BALLISTIC
BITTER VENGEANCE
BLACK IS ... BLACK AIN'T
BREACH OF CONDUCT
BREAK, THE
CLASS OF '61
COLORADO COWBOY: THE BRUCE
 FORD STORY
COVER ME
CRAZYSITTER, THE
DANGER OF LOVE
DARK SIDE OF GENIUS, THE
DARKMAN 2: THE RETURN OF
 DURANT
DEADLY MARIA
DOUBLE HAPPINESS
FRANK AND OLLIE
GORDY
JUPITER'S WIFE
LAST GOOD TIME, THE
LITTLE ODESSA
OPERATION INTERCEPT
OUT OF ANNIE'S PAST

PICTURE BRIDE
PREHYSTERIA! 3
RHYTHM THIEF
SON OF THE SHARK, THE
TIE-DIED: ROCK 'N' ROLL'S MOST
 DEADICATED FANS
WORLD AND TIME ENOUGH

Celeste, Reni
BED YOU SLEEP IN, THE
BLUE VILLA, THE
COW, THE
CRUDE OASIS, THE
CURSE OF THE STARVING CLASS
ERMO
HOW TO MAKE AN AMERICAN
 QUILT
LAKOTA WOMAN: SIEGE AT
 WOUNDED KNEE
MAD LOVE
MY FAMILY: MI FAMILIA
NET, THE
PRIEST
REMOTE CONTROL
SCARLET LETTER, THE
SERIOUS ABOUT PLEASURE
SHORT FILM ABOUT KILLING, A
SHORT FILM ABOUT LOVE, A
VALLEY OF ABRAHAM, THE
VILLAGE OF THE DAMNED
WITHOUT ANESTHESIA

Chris, Cynthia
CAGED HEAT 3000
HE'S A WOMAN, SHE'S A MAN
LAST SAMURAI, THE
NAKED KILLER
RETURN OF THE GOD OF
 GAMBLERS
TWENTY SOMETHING
WIZARD OF DARKNESS

Dearman, Jill
GLORY BOYS, THE
MIDNIGHT TEASE 2
REDWOOD CURTAIN
RENT-A-KID

Forstrom, Michael
CITY UNPLUGGED
CRY, THE BELOVED COUNTRY
FACES OF WOMEN
FRAMEUP
FRIENDS
JLG BY JLG
LAMB
MURIEL'S WEDDING
PURE FORMALITY, A
RIVER OF GRASS
VOYAGE EN DOUCE
WHITE MAN'S BURDEN
WILD REEDS
YOUNGER & YOUNGER

French, Kenneth
CENTURY
GREAT ELEPHANT ESCAPE, THE

Gingold, Michael
AMERICA'S DEADLIEST HOME
 VIDEO
ATTACK OF THE 60-FOOT
 CENTERFOLD
BABY-SITTERS CLUB, THE
CANDYMAN: FAREWELL TO THE
 FLESH
CASTLE FREAK
CHILDREN OF THE CORN III:
 URBAN HARVEST
CITY OF LOST CHILDREN, THE
CREEP
DEATH MACHINE
EMBRACE OF THE VAMPIRE
EVOLVER
FEAR, THE
GRANNY, THE
HALLOWEEN: THE CURSE OF
 MICHAEL MYERS
HIDEAWAY
HIGH RISK
HOWLING: NEW MOON RISING,
 THE
IN THE MOUTH OF MADNESS
JACK-O
JERKY BOYS: THE MOVIE, THE
LORD OF ILLUSIONS
MANGLER, THE
NEKROMANTIK
NUMBER ONE FAN
PHANTOM LOVER, THE
PROPHECY, THE
REASON TO BELIEVE, A
SCANNERS: THE SHOWDOWN
SHALLOW GRAVE
SKINNER
SPECIES
TALES FROM THE CRYPT: DEMON
 KNIGHT
VAMPIRE IN BROOKLYN
VAMPIRES AND OTHER
 STEREOTYPES

Grant, Edmond
ASHES OF TIME
BOULEVARD
EXECUTIONERS
HEROIC TRIO, THE
SHAO LIN POPEYE

Greene, Kent
BATMAN FOREVER
BEYOND RANGOON
CARMEN MIRANDA: BANANAS IS
 MY BUSINESS
DIRTY MONEY
DOLORES CLAIBORNE
GLASS SHIELD, THE
INDIAN IN THE CUPBOARD, THE

POWDER
STRANGE DAYS
THREE WISHES
TO DIE FOR
WATERWORLD

Kaufman, Seth
LAST RIDE, THE
POCAHONTAS: THE LEGEND
ZOOMAN

Kelleher, Ed
DESTINY TURNS ON THE RADIO
DR. JEKYLL & MS. HYDE
FORGET PARIS
GREAT DAY IN HARLEM, A
HOTEL SORRENTO
NADJA
THINGS TO DO IN DENVER WHEN
YOU'RE DEAD
UNDERNEATH, THE

Levich, Jacob
BANDIT QUEEN

Levy, Owen
POSTCARDS FROM AMERICA
PROMISE, THE
ROY COHN/JACK SMITH
WHILE YOU WERE SLEEPING

Lovece, Frank
ARABIAN KNIGHT

Lugowski, David
SENSE AND SENSIBILITY

Mandros, Chris
CIRCUMSTANCES UNKNOWN
GOOD GIRLS DON'T
NEA

McDonagh, Maitland
ADDICTION, THE
BALLET
BASKETBALL DIARIES, THE
CASINO
CLOCKERS
CLUELESS
DEAD MAN WALKING
DEVIL IN A BLUE DRESS
EXOTICA
FUN
HACKERS
HIGHER LEARNING
JADE
JOHNNY MNEMONIC
KINGDOM, THE
MEET THE FEEBLES
MURDER IN THE FIRST
MUTE WITNESS
NEW JERSEY DRIVE
NICK OF TIME
PANTHER
PARTY GIRL
SHOW, THE
TALES FROM THE HOOD
TWELVE MONKEYS
WILD BILL
WINGS OF COURAGE

Milenski, Aaron
ANGUS
AUGUSTIN
DALLAS DOLL
GROSS MISCONDUCT
IN THE DEEP WOODS
KURT VONNEGUT'S HARRISON
BERGERON
ME AND THE MOB
NATIONAL LAMPOON'S SENIOR
TRIP
NINA TAKES A LOVER
RUN OF THE COUNTRY, THE
TO CROSS THE RUBICON
TWOGETHER

Monder, Eric
ACE VENTURA: WHEN NATURE
CALLS
ACROSS THE SEA OF TIME: NEW
YORK 3D
AMATEUR
AMERICAN PRESIDENT, THE
BALTO
BEFORE SUNRISE
BETRAYAL
BLESSING
BUSINESS AFFAIR, A
CLEAN, SHAVEN
CONVENT, THE
CRUMB
DANCER, THE
DIE HARD WITH A VENGEANCE
DREAM A LITTLE DREAM 2
DREAMING OF RITA
ECLIPSE
FATHER OF THE BRIDE PART II
FOR GOD AND COUNTRY
FOUR ROOMS
GOLDENEYE
GRUMPIER OLD MEN
HIGHLANDER: THE FINAL
DIMENSION
IT TAKES TWO
JAR, THE
JOURNEY OF AUGUST KING, THE
KICKING AND SCREAMING
KIDS
KILIAN'S CHRONICLE
LAST OF THE DOGMEN
LAST SUMMER IN THE HAMPTONS
LES MISERABLES
LESSONS OF DARKNESS
LITTLE PRINCESS, A
LOSING ISAIAH
MAJOR PAYNE
MAYA LIN: A STRONG CLEAR
VISION
NEVER TALK TO STRANGERS
NO MERCY
NOBODY LOVES ME
OH ... ROSALINDA!!
OLD LADY WHO WALKED IN THE
SEA, THE
1-900
OPERATION DUMBO DROP
OTHELLO
QUICK AND THE DEAD, THE
RICHARD III

ROB ROY
SAFE
SECRET OF ROAN INISH, THE
SHANGHAI TRIAD
STARS FELL ON HENRIETTA, THE
SUDDEN DEATH
THROUGH THE OLIVE TREES
TOM AND HUCK
TOTAL ECLIPSE
TRAPS
WAITING TO EXHALE
WHEN BILLY BROKE HIS HEAD ...
AND OTHER TALES OF WONDER

Nicastro, Nicholas
NIXON

Noh, David
CIRCLE OF FRIENDS
CUTTHROAT ISLAND
DAY THE SUN TURNED COLD, THE
EROTIQUE
FAIR GAME
FARINELLI
HARLEM DIARY: NINE VOICES OF
RESILIENCE
HYENAS
IN THE NAME OF THE EMPEROR
INNOCENT, THE
JEFFREY
LEAVING LAS VEGAS
LIE DOWN WITH DOGS
LIVING IN OBLIVION
MAN OF THE HOUSE
MIAMI RHAPSODY
MONTH BY THE LAKE, A
MORTAL KOMBAT
PROFESSION: NEO-NAZI
SAFE PASSAGE
SEARCH AND DESTROY
SEX, DRUGS AND DEMOCRACY
SIX DAYS, SIX NIGHTS
STRAWBERRY AND CHOCOLATE
VIRTUOSITY

Pardi, Robert
ABDUCTED 2: THE REUNION
ACROSS THE MOON
ADVENTURES OF MATT THE
GOOSEBOY, THE
ALMOST DEAD
AMERICAN COP
AVENGING ANGEL
AWFULLY BIG ADVENTURE, AN
BAD BLOOD
BIGFOOT: THE UNFORGETTABLE
ENCOUNTER
BLACK FOX
BLUE TIGER
BOCA
BODY CHEMISTRY 4: FULL
EXPOSURE
BODY SHOT
BODY STROKES
BROKEN TRUST
BUFFALO GIRLS
BURNING SEASON, THE
COMPANION, THE
CONVICT COWBOY
COPYCAT

COSMIC SLOP
COUNTRY LIFE
COVER STORY
CREATION OF ADAM
CYBER BANDITS
DANCE ME OUTSIDE
DANGEROUS, THE
DEAD FUNNY
DEATH IN BRUNSWICK
DECONSTRUCTING SARAH
DECOY
DIGGER
DILLINGER
DOOMSDAY GUN
DOUBLE, DOUBLE, TOIL AND
    TROUBLE
ENEMY WITHIN, THE
EXPERT, THE
FREE WILLY 2: THE ADVENTURE
    HOME
FUNNY BONES
GALAXIS
GETTING OUT
GHOST BRIGADE
GIRL IN THE CADILLAC
GOOD DAY TO DIE, A
HUNTED, THE
I LIKE TO PLAY GAMES
INDICTMENT: THE MCMARTIN
    TRIAL
JEFFERSON IN PARIS
JUST CAUSE
KID IN KING ARTHUR'S COURT, A
MAGIC IN THE WATER
MALICIOUS
MARTHA & ETHEL
MOONLIGHT AND VALENTINO
MOSAIC PROJECT, THE
MUTANT SPECIES
MY ANTONIA
NATIONAL LAMPOON'S ATTACK OF
    THE 5'2" WOMEN
NEW YORK COP
NOSTRADAMUS KID, THE
NOT ANGELS BUT ANGELS
OUTSIDE THE LAW
PEBBLE AND THE PENGUIN, THE
PENTATHLON
PIANO LESSON, THE
PLAY TIME
POWER OF ATTORNEY
PUSHING HANDS
PYROMANIAC'S LOVE STORY, A
REFLECTIONS IN THE DARK
SEPARATE LIVES
TALL TALE: THE UNBELIEVABLE
    ADVENTURES OF PECOS BILL
3 NINJAS KNUCKLE UP
TOP DOG
TWO BITS
UNDERCOVER
UP TO A CERTAIN POINT
WALK IN THE CLOUDS, A
WALKING DEAD, THE

Perkins, Penny
BIG GREEN, THE
FEAST OF JULY
MACHINE DREAMS

Riley, Phil
ARMAGEDDON: THE FINAL
    CHALLENGE
ASSASSINS
BAD BOYS
BAD COMPANY
BILLY MADISON
BRADY BUNCH MOVIE, THE
BRIDGES OF MADISON COUNTY,
    THE
BROTHERS MCMULLEN, THE
CASPER
COLDBLOODED
CRACKERJACK
CREW, THE
CRIMSON TIDE
CROSSING GUARD, THE
DANGEROUS MINDS
DESPERATE PREY
DRACULA: DEAD AND LOVING IT
EMPIRE RECORDS
ENGLISHMAN WHO WENT UP A
    HILL BUT CAME DOWN A
    MOUNTAIN, THE
FOOL AND HIS MONEY, A
FRANKIE STARLIGHT
FRIDAY
HEAT
HEAVYWEIGHTS
HOME FOR THE HOLIDAYS
HOUSEGUEST
MESSENGER
NIGHTMARE
NINE MONTHS
NOW AND THEN
ONCE WERE WARRIORS
OUT OF SYNC
OUTBREAK
PAYBACK
RECKLESS
SEVEN
S.F.W.
SPITFIRE
STEAL BIG, STEAL LITTLE
STUART SAVES HIS FAMILY
TANK GIRL
UNSTRUNG HEROES

Royce, Brenda Scott
AMAZING PANDA ADVENTURE,
    THE
BEFORE THE RAIN
BETTER OFF DEAD
BORN TO BE WILD
BOYS ON THE SIDE
BYE BYE, LOVE
CURE, THE
FAR FROM HOME: THE
    ADVENTURES OF YELLOW DOG
FATHER AND SCOUT
FRENCH KISS
GROSSE FATIGUE
HOW TO TOP MY WIFE
JUDICIAL CONSENT

NEXT DOOR
PEREZ FAMILY, THE
RADIO INSIDE
RETURN OF THE NATIVE, THE
ROOMMATES
SECRETARY, THE
SILENCE OF THE HAMS
SISTER MY SISTER
SOMETHING TO TALK ABOUT
SUBSTITUTE WIFE, THE
SUM OF US, THE
TERESA'S TATTOO
TOMMY BOY
TOO YOUNG TO DIE?
WATER ENGINE, THE
WOMAN AT WAR, A

Rubenstein, Leonard
BURNT BY THE SUN
CHRONICLE OF THE WARSAW
    GHETTO UPRISING ACCORDING
    TO MAREK EDELMAN
CONGRESS OF PENGUINS, THE
GORILLA BATHES AT NOON
LAMERICA
MARTHA AND I
PROVINCIAL ACTORS
STALINGRAD
WINDOW TO PARIS

Seulowitz, Robert
APOLLO 13
ARIZONA DREAM
BIKINI BISTRO
BLUE IN THE FACE
BRAVEHEART
BULLETPROOF HEART
CAGED HEARTS
CARRINGTON
CONGO
DON JUAN DEMARCO
FLUKE
JUMANJI
MYSTERY OF RAMPO, THE
POSTMAN, THE
RESTORATION
SABRINA
SMOKE
SWIMMING WITH SHARKS
USUAL SUSPECTS, THE
WHEN NIGHT IS FALLING

Stott, Jennifer
ART FOR TEACHERS OF CHILDREN
BALLOT MEASURE 9
BAR GIRLS
DOOM GENERATION, THE
ETERNITY
HEAVEN'S A DRAG
I AM CUBA
I, THE WORST OF ALL
INCREDIBLY TRUE ADVENTURES
    OF TWO GIRLS IN LOVE, THE
LOVE AND HUMAN REMAINS
METAL AND MELANCHOLY
MINA TANNENBAUM

MOVING THE MOUNTAIN
MY LIFE AND TIMES WITH
   ANTONIN ARTAUD
PERSUASION
PIGALLE
RED FIRECRACKER, GREEN
   FIRECRACKER
UNZIPPED
WIGSTOCK: THE MOVIE
WOODEN MAN'S BRIDE, THE

Streible, Dan
   DEAD PRESIDENTS
   SHOWGIRLS

Trenz, Brandon
   CITIZEN X
   DESPERADO
   FATHERLAND
   GET SHORTY
   JURY DUTY

KINGFISH: A STORY OF HUEY P.
   LONG
MALLRATS
ROSWELL: THE U.F.O. COVER-UP
TOY STORY

Westberg, Jenny
   O.J. SIMPSON STORY, THE
   POCAHONTAS
   SPY WITHIN, THE

OUR CONTRIBUTORS

A.M. Aaron Milenski is assistant director of admissions at Oberlin College. In addition to loving obscure and independent film, he is a guitarist and songwriter. His wife, Jill, is an artist.

B.C. Brian Camp is the programming director at CUNY-TV in New York. He has written for *Sightlines, Outré, Film Comment, Film Library Quarterly*, and *Asian Trash Cinema*. He was educated in film production at Hunter College and in cinema studies at New York University.

B.R. Brenda Scott Royce is a freelance entertainment writer and award-winning playwright. She is the author of *Lauren Bacall: A Bio-Bibliography, Hogan's Heroes: A Complete Reference*, and numerous articles.

B.T. Brandon Trenz is a freelance writer based in Detroit, Michigan. He is also the associate editor of the reference series *Contemporary Theatre, Film and Television*, published by Gale Research.

C.C. Charles Cassady Jr. has worked as a columnist and freelance movie reviewer for various publications around the world. He has contributed reviews to *VideoHound's Golden Movie Retriever* and is the movie columnist of *The Morning Journal*, the daily newspaper of Lorain, Ohio.

C.Ch. Cynthia Chris is a critic and artist who lives in New York City. Her writing on media has appeared in *Afterimage, exposure, The Independent*, and *High Performance*.

C.M. Chris Mandros lives in Baltimore, where he studies and writes about film and video.

D.B. David Bartholomew is the Film Specialist for the New York Public Library's Theatre Collection at Lincoln Center. He is also a freelance video consultant, writer, film critic, and editor.

D.L. David M. Lugowski is a PhD candidate in Cinema Studies at New York University. He is also an associate editor at Baseline, an online information service for the entertainment industry. He has written for *Cineaste, The Movie Guide*, and other publications.

D.N. David Noh was born and raised in Hawaii, where a childhood viewing of GONE WITH THE WIND at a Cinerama theater instilled in him a lifelong love of movies. Educated in film on both coasts, he is a writer living in New York.

D.S. Dan Streible is professor of Radio-TV-Film at the University of Wisconsin, Oshkosh. He is the author of a book on prize-fighting and early film, which will be published by the Smithsonian, and is co-editor of a forthcoming Emile de Antonio reader.

E.G. Edmond Grant, a staff writer for *TV Guide*, also writes *for Films in Review* and *Film Journal*. Previously, he served as managing editor of *Movies on TV*. He produces *Media Funhouse*, a weekly public-access television program.

E.K. Ed Kelleher is associate editor of *Film Journal International*. As Edouard Dauphin, he created the "Drive-In Saturday" column in *Creem* Magazine. His screenwriting credits include six produced features, and he has lectured on film at the School of Visual Arts and New York University.

E.M. Eric Monder is the author of *George Sidney: A Bio-Bibliography* and has contributed articles to *The New York Times, Film Comment*, and the *Directors Guild of America Magazine*. He lives in Manhattan with his wife, Kathi Patterson, who is also a writer.

F.L. Frank Lovece has written about movies for *Entertainment Weekly, The Los Angeles Times, Newsday*, and *Penthouse*. His books include*: Hailing Taxi: The Official Book of the Show, The Brady Bunch Book*, and *The X-Files Declassified*.

J.D. Jill Dearman is a playwright and director whose work has been shown at many New York City theaters. Her most recent work, "You're Under Arrest, Sugar!" was produced at Performance Space 122.

J.L. Jacob Levich is editor of *The Motion Picture Guide* and movies editor of *iGuide*, the World Wide Web-based arts and entertainment magazine.

J.S. Jennifer Stott has been a journalist with *Vogue* and *The Bulletin* (incorporating *Newsweek*), and is also the author of several books on film. She is currently director of sales and promotions for Women Make Movies.

K.F. Kenneth French is a librarian in the areas of reference and special collections. He lives in New Jersey with his wife and son.

K.G. Kent Greene is a film reviewer and associate editor of the biographical database at Baseline, an online information service for the entertainment industry. His writing on film has appeared in *The Village Voice, American Film,* and *Cineaste.*

L.R. Leonard Rubenstein is the author of *The Great Spy Films* and co-editor of *The Cineaste Interviews.* He is a contributor to *World Film Directors, The Encyclopedia of Film, Political Companion to American Film,* and other reference books.

M.F. Michael Forstrom is a freelance writer completing his masters in philosophy from the New School for Social Research.

M.G. Michael Gingold is the managing editor of *Fangoria* magazine, for which he has written since 1988. He has contributed reviews to such books as *The Blockbuster Video Guide* and Steven Scheuer's *Movies on TV and Videocassette.*

M.M. Maitland McDonagh is an associate editor at *iGuide*, the World Wide Web-based arts and entertainment magazine, and the author of three books: *Broken Mirrors/Broken Minds, Filmmaking on the Fringe,* and *The 50 Most Erotic Films of All Time.* She has written on film for a variety of publications.

N.N. Nicholas Nicastro is a filmmaker and critic whose work has appeared in *The New York Times, Film Comment, The New York Observer, Publisher's Weekly,* and *Heterodoxy.* He currently lives in upstate New York.

O.L. Owen Levy is a freelance writer who divides his time between New York and Berlin.

P.P. Penny Perkins is a freelance writer and editor living in Albany, New York.

P.R. Phil Riley has a degree in philosophy and has done graduate work in film and television criticism. He lives in Austin, Texas.

R.C. Reni Celeste is a freelance writer working on her PhD. She recently joined the Visual and Cultural Studies program at the University of Rochester, where she will focus on philosophical approaches to film and visual culture.

R.P. Robert Pardi was managing editor and chief film critic of four editions of *Movies on TV.* He has written for *Cinemax, Billboard, Film Journal International* and Baseline, an online information service for the entertainment industry. He is the author of *Movie Blockbusters* and *Who's Who in Cable and TV,* co-wrote *The Complete Guide to Videocassette Movies,* and contributed to *The International Dictionary of Films and Filmmakers.*

R.S. Robert Seulowitz holds an M.Div. from the Union Theological Seminary, an MhD from Universal Life Church, and a CNE from Drake Institute. Currently the Network Administrator for News America Publishing, he has worked in publishing as a production manager and editor.

S.B. Shampa Banerjee is the author of *One Hundred Indian Feature Films: An Annotated Filmography,* several monographs on Indian films and filmmakers, and a number of post-production scripts in English of significant Indian films, including Satyajit Ray's APU Trilogy and Adoor Gopalakrishnan's THE RAT TRAP, FACE TO FACE, and MONOLOGUE.

S.K. Seth Kaufman is the news editor of *TV Guide Online.* He has written for *The New York Times, The New York Post, People,* and *The New York Observer.* He recently co-wrote a song for the film ED'S NEXT MOVE.

J.W. Jenny Westberg, a mother of four, lives in Portland, Oregon.